Competition Law

Ninth Edition

RICHARD WHISH

BA BCL (Oxon), QC (Hon)

Emeritus Professor of Law at King's College London

DAVID BAILEY

LLB (King's College London), LLM (Harv)

Visiting Professor of Law at King's College London

OXFORD
UNIVERSITY PRESS

OXFORD
UNIVERSITY PRESS
Great Clarendon Street, Oxford, OX2 6DP,
United Kingdom

Oxford University Press is a department of the University of Oxford.
It furthers the University's objective of excellence in research, scholarship,
and education by publishing worldwide. Oxford is a registered trade mark of
Oxford University Press in the UK and in certain other countries

Sixth edition 2008
Seventh edition 2012
Eighth edition 2015

Impression: 1

Published in the United States of America by Oxford University Press
198 Madison Avenue, New York, NY 10016, United States of America

British Library Cataloguing in Publication Data
Data available

Library of Congress Control Number: 2018932221

ISBN 978–0–19–877906–3

Printed in Italy by L.E.G.O. S.p.A.

Preface to the ninth edition

It was only three years ago that we wrote the preface to the eighth edition of this book. We commented then on how much had changed since the previous edition and noted that keeping up to date with developments in competition law and policy is 'stimulating and challenging in equal measure'. It remains so. Barely a day goes by without a development of some kind. What we did not anticipate in 2015 was that we would be preparing the ninth edition against the backdrop of Brexit. The referendum in the UK on 23 June 2016 will lead to its departure from the EU on 29 March 2019. Obviously we had to consider how to deal with this momentous turn of events in this edition of the book. Our conclusion was that there was relatively little at this stage that we could do: the book will publish in Summer 2018, and the UK will remain a Member State of the EU until March 2019; it is possible that there will follow a transitional period (though 'nothing is agreed until everything is agreed') that could run until the end of 2020. This being so we have decided to continue on the basis of the existing law, although at some points in the text we have put down markers for the future: for example it seems unlikely that section 60 of the Competition Act 1998, which requires the competition authorities in the UK to maintain consistency with the jurisprudence of the EU Courts, will survive Brexit in its current form. The Brexit Competition Law Working Group (www.bclwg.org), of which Richard was a member, considered that the major challenges for UK competition law and policy raised by Brexit were not in relation to substantive law: the Competition Act 1998 and the Enterprise Act 2002, which will remain after Brexit, are basically 'fit for purpose'. The important issues to be addressed concern transitional arrangements and international cooperation, with the European Commission, the national competition authorities of the Member States, and with other institutions beyond the EU. There may also be consequences for the private enforcement of EU competition law in the UK courts; for example an infringement of Articles 101 and 102 TFEU will no longer be a tortious breach of statutory duty. At the time of writing, nothing has been decided on any of these issues, and we see little point in speculating on them in this book, the purpose of which is to guide the reader through the law of today rather than what it might look like tomorrow. For us, the authors of this book, the challenge will be to decide what a tenth edition will look like, something which we would prefer to postpone to the future when we will have a better idea of what a post-Brexit world will look like.

In the preface to the eighth edition we mentioned that we had rewritten significant parts of chapter 3 on Article 101(1), in particular in the light of the developing jurisprudence on the concept of a single overall agreement and on the distinction between restrictions of competition by object and by effect. For this edition we have made significant changes to the discussion of abuse of dominance, in particular in light of the judgment of the Grand Chamber of the Court of Justice in *Intel v Commission* in which it 'clarified' the rule in *Hoffmann-La Roche v Commission* that presumes that rebates granted by a dominant firm in return for exclusivity are unlawful. Paragraph 138 of the judgment says that a dominant firm may rebut this presumption with evidence that the rebates were not capable of producing a foreclosure effect. This is more than mere clarification, and is clearly in line with the more 'effects-based' system that the Commission and many commentators have argued for over many years. It remains to be seen how the General Court will actually decide the *Intel* case: the Court of Justice has asked it to reconsider the Commission's decision in the light of Intel's criticisms of the Commission's effects analysis in that case. Separately we have attempted to capture some of the current debate about the circumstances in which it is appropriate for a competition authority to prohibit excessively high prices; we discuss recent cases such as *AKKA/LAA* and *Phenytoin* in chapter 18.

A major revision in this edition will be found in chapter 8 which examines the private enforcement of EU and UK competition law. This reflects not only the adoption of the Damages Directive but also the huge increase in private litigation which has occurred anyway. This is a particularly interesting topic at the moment and we could have said a great deal more than we have. However the policy of our publishers—with which we entirely agree!—is that this book should not increase in length. For this reason we have had to omit some fascinating but very technical points, or to relegate them to a footnote with references to further reading.

We have attempted to distil the salient points from numerous other decisions and judgments at both the EU and the domestic level since the eighth edition. Among the topics of current interest are 'atypical cartels', where the question arises of whether competitors are guilty of infringing Article 101 for example by price signalling, manipulating benchmarks, or using algorithms. We deal with this issue in chapter 13. Another topical area is the treatment of vertical restraints in online commerce, and we have endeavoured in chapter 16 to incorporate new insights in the light of the European Commission's sector inquiry and recent jurisprudence (in particular *Coty Germany GmbH v Parfümerie GmbH*) and decisional practice.

The text of the ninth edition is up to date, as of 8 December 2017, although we have been able to include a few developments in the law after that date. The views expressed in *Whish and Bailey* are personal, and should not be taken as representing the views of any organisation for whom Richard or David act in practice.

As always we have received generous assistance from many friends and colleagues. In particular we wish to thank Claudio Calcagno, Warsha Kale, Michael Grenfell, Roland Green, Charles Dhanowa QC (Hon), Max Kadar, Rosamund Browne, Natalie Rouse, and John Kallaugher. None of them bears any responsibility for the text, but we are grateful to each of them for their comments and suggestions. Special thanks are owed to Diego Hernandez De Lamotte, an LLM student at King's College London, who took on the thankless task of converting the 'old-style' references to cases in the General Court and Court of Justice to their modern format. Above all we must thank our superb research assistant Rakhal Zaman, also a former student of King's College London, who was a pleasure to work with and whose contribution to this edition has been immeasurable.

Preparing this edition of the book was enjoyable but also immensely hard work, which as always took its toll on our social and domestic lives. Anil Sinanan was unable to introduce Richard to any particularly great Bollywood movies to divert his attention, but attending a live performance together by Arijit Singh in Kolkata two days after delivering the manuscript to OUP was a wonderful way to re-enter the earth's orbit. David would like to thank Nikki Pitt for her constant support throughout the writing of this edition, and for showing him that there is much more to life than competition law.

Richard Whish
Marshfield, April 2018

David Bailey
London, April 2018

New to this edition

- New discussion of the private enforcement of EU and UK competition law, including the EU Directive on Antitrust Damages Actions and the UK Consumer Rights Act 2015
- New discussion of the treatment of conditional rebates under Article 102, including the judgment of the Court of Justice in *Intel Corp v Commission*
- New discussion of the phenomena of 'price signalling', algorithmic collusion, and other atypical cartel activities
- Covers recent developments on the application of EU and UK competition law to restrictions of online sales of goods and services
- Briefly considers the possible implications of Brexit for UK competition law
- Incorporates extensive new case law and decisional practice at EU and UK level

Contents

Table of treaties and conventions

Table of EU legislation

Directives

Rules

Table of statutes and statutory instruments

Secondary legislation

United States

Table of CMA reports, decisions and publications

Reports

Table of guidelines, guidance and other publications

OECD>

National bodies

Australia

Canada

New Zealand

United Kingdom

United States

Table of cases

Table of European Cases

Commission Decisions

European Court of Justice

Numerical Table of General Court Cases

Alphabetical Table of General Court Cases

Numerical Table of Court of Justice Cases

Alphabetical Table of Court of Justice Cases

European Ombudsman

Opinions of the Court of Justice

International courts and tribunals

European Court of Human Rights

EFTA

National courts and tribunals

Australia

Austria

Bulgaria

Canada

Czech Republic

Denmark

France

Germany

Hungary

Ireland

Italy

Lithunania

Netherlands

Norway

Russia

Serbia

Singapore

Spain

Switzerland

United Kingdom

Competition Appeal Tribunal

OFCOM

OFGEM

OFT

OFTEL

FTC

List of abbreviations

AAC	average avoidable cost
AC	Appeal Cases
AEC	adverse effect on competition
All ER	All England Reports
Am Ec Rev	American Economic Review
ATC	average total cost
AVC	average variable cost
Bell J Ec	Bell Journal of Economics
CAA	Civil Aviation Authority
CAT	UK Competition Appeal Tribunal
CC	UK Competition Commission
CDDA	UK Company Directors Disqualification Act 1986
CDO	Competition Disqualification Order
Cm	Command Papers
CMA	UK Competition and Markets Authority
CML Rev	Common Market Law Review
CMLR	Common Market Law Reports
Comp Law	Competition Law Journal
CPI	Competition Policy International
CRM	Case Review Meeting
CSOH	Scottish Court of Session Outer House
DG COMP	Directorate General for Competition
DoJ	US Department of Justice
DTI	Department of Trade and Industry
ECC	European Commercial Cases
Ec J	Economic Journal
ECHR	European Convention on Human Rights
ECLR	European Competition Law Review
ECOSOC	Economic and Social Committee
ECN	European Competition Network
ECPR	efficient component pricing rule
ECR	European Court Reports
ECSC	European Coal and Steel Community
EEA	European Economic Area
EFTA	European Free Trade Association

EGLR	Estates Gazette Law Reports
EHRR	European Human Rights Reports
EIPR	European Intellectual Property Review
EL Rev	European Law Review
ERRA	UK Enterprise and Regulatory Reform Act 2013
ESA	EFTA Surveillance Authority
Eu LR	European Law Review
EUMR	European Union Merger Regulation
EWCA	England and Wales Court of Appeal
EWHC	England and Wales High Court
EW Misc	English and Welsh Courts—Miscellaneous
FCA	Financial Conduct Authority
FRAND	fair, reasonable and non-discriminatory
FSR	Fleet Street Reports
FTC	US Federal Trade Commission
GEMA	Gas and Electricity Markets Authority
HHI	Herfindahl-Hirschman Index
ICLQ	International and Comparative Law Quarterly
ICN	International Competition Network
ICPAC	International Competition Policy Advisory Committee
IEHC	Irish High Court
IESC	Irish Supreme Court
IPR	intellectual property rights
J Ind Ec	Journal of Industrial Economics
J L & Ec	Journal of Law and Economics
J Pol Ec	Journal of Political Economy
JECLAP	Journal of European Competition Law & Practice
LIEI	Legal Issues of Economic Integration
LQR	Law Quarterly Review
LRAIC	long-run average incremental cost
LRIC	long-run incremental cost
MFN	most favoured nation
MIF	multilateral interchange fee
MLR	Modern Law Review
NAO	UK National Audit Office
NCA	national competition authority
NIAER	Northern Ireland Authority for Energy Regulation
OECD	Organisation for Economic Co-operation and Development
OEM	original equipment manufacturer
OFCOM	Office of Communications

OFGEM	Office of Gas and Electricity Markets
OFT	UK Office of Fair Trading
OFTEL	Office of Telecommunications
OFWAT	Office of Water Services
OJ	Official Journal of the European Union
OJLS	Oxford Journal of Legal Studies
ORR	Office of Rail Regulation
Ox YEL	Oxford Yearbook of European Law
P & CR	Property and Compensation Reports
PACE	UK Police and Criminal Evidence Act 1984
PIIN	public interest intervention notice
PSR	Payment Systems Regulator
QB	Queen's Bench
Qu J Ec	Quebec Journal of Economics
R&D	research and development
RDC	Recueil des Cours
Rev Ec Stud	Review of Economic Studies
RPI	retail price index
SCC	Supreme Court of Canada Reports
SEP	standard-essential patent
SFO	Serious Fraud Office
SI	Statutory Instrument
SIEC	significant impediment to effective competition
SLC	substantial lessening of competition
SME	small and medium-sized enterprise
SPIIN	special public interest intervention
SSNIP	small but significant non-transitory increase in price
SWIFT	Society for Worldwide International Financial Telecommunications
Swiss Rev ICL	Swiss Review of International Competition Law
TEU	Treaty on European Union
TFEU	Treaty on the Functioning of the European Union
UKCLR	UK Competition Law Reports
UKCN	UK Competition Network
UKHL	UK House of Lords
UK	UK Privy Council
UKSC	UK Supreme Court
UNCTAD	United Nations Conference on Trade and Development
WLR	Weekly Law Reports
WSRA	Water Services Regulation Authority

1

Competition policy and economics

1. Introduction

(A) The growth of competition law

Competition law has grown at a phenomenal rate in recent years in response to the enormous changes in political thinking and economic behaviour that have taken place around the world. There are now more than 130 systems of competition law in the world[1]. Some of them have been in place for a considerable time: for example, the Sherman Act in the United States was adopted in 1890. The competition rules of the European Union were contained in the Treaty of Rome of 1957, the year in which the German Act against Unfair Restraints of Competition was passed. Competition law in the UK began with the Monopolies and Restrictive Practices (Inquiry and Control) Act of 1948. Most of the world's competition laws are much more recent than this, however: for example, the Chinese Anti-Monopoly Law was adopted on 30 August 2007, and the Philippines adopted its law on 11 June 2015. Numerous laws were introduced in the 1980s and 1990s. Many new ones have been adopted in the twenty-first century, for example in India, Singapore, Malaysia, Hong Kong, Ecuador, Swaziland, Egypt and Nigeria.

Competition laws will be found in found in all six continents, and in all types of economies: they are by no means limited to the rich, developed countries; many developing states also have competition legislation. The size of a country is not a determinant of whether it might have a competition law: China and India—with more than three billion citizens between them—have competition laws; but so too do Fiji, Mauritius, the Seychelles and Barbados, with somewhat smaller populations! Many of the countries that had socialist regimes for much of the twentieth century now have competition legislation: this is true of Member States of the EU such as Poland, Romania and Bulgaria; but also of former socialist countries outside the EU such as Russia, Georgia, Armenia and Albania. Competition laws will be found throughout the continent of Africa, from Morocco in the north-west to Zimbabwe and Malawi in the south-east. The ten members of the Association of South East Nations—ASEAN—committed to adopt competition laws by 2015, and all but Cambodia have now done so. More than 135 competition authorities from 122 jurisdictions participate in the work of the International Competition Network

[1] A helpful account of the world's competition laws can be found on the OECD's website at www.oecd.org/competition; another useful source is the website of the International Competition Network, www.internationalcompetitionnetwork.org.

('the ICN'), a virtual organisation which facilitates cooperation between competition authorities. The ICN has considerable influence by facilitating discussion of competition policy and promoting procedural and substantive convergence in competition laws and enforcement. Its work is considered in chapter 12[2].

These developments have been dramatic: 30 years ago it would scarcely have been believable that the world of competition law would look as it does today. It is important to try to understand why there has been this proliferation of competition laws. Competition laws give effect to economic policy, and in recent decades economic policy in most countries has tended to favour a free-market economy in which firms compete with one another for customers. Most of the world's socialist economies have now been dismantled. Many legal monopolies have been abolished in recent years. Economies have been liberalised, trade barriers reduced and many protectionist measures removed. Utility sectors such as gas, electricity, telecommunications and post have been opened up to competition, and many international treaties and agreements have favoured open markets and free trade. Of course none of this is without controversy, nor is it irreversible. Recent events, in particular the financial crisis and the cynical manipulation of markets and disregard for the law in the financial services sector, have tarnished the reputation of liberal capitalism, and it cannot be assumed that there will not be a significant backlash against it. However, for the time being the free-market system is in the ascendancy, and the process of competition is a cornerstone of the free market.

(B) **Competition law and economics**

In so far as a country chooses as its instrument of economic policy the free market, there is a strong argument that there ought to be laws in place to ensure that the market functions properly. A central concern of competition law and policy is that a firm or firms can harm competition—and inflict harm on customers and ultimately consumers -where they possess some degree of market power. The concept of market power is an economic one and means the ability to reduce output or capacity, to raise prices, to reduce the quality of products, to limit the choice available to customers or to suppress innovation without fear of a damaging competitive response by other firms. The concern about market power cannot be expressed in a codified table of rules capable of precise application in the way, for example, that laws on taxation or the relationship of landlord and tenant can. The assessment of market power requires careful economic analysis, and lawyers and their business clients often need input from economists in order to reach robust and defensible conclusions. The same is true of the types of behaviour—for example refusals to deal, tying and bundling, predatory pricing, discrimination, mergers—with which competition law is concerned. These are not matters that can simply be analysed in a rule-based way. Competition lawyers must understand economic concepts, and competition economists must understand legal processes. It is common practice today—and much to be welcomed—that competition lawyers attend courses on economics and vice versa. Competition law is about the economic analysis of markets within a legal process; each case will depend on its own circumstances. A (possibly apocryphal) story is that a competition lawyer once remarked at a competition law conference that, in his view, in any competition law case the lawyer should be in the driving seat; and that a competition economist readily agreed, since he always preferred to have a chauffeur. To the extent that this suggests that there is inevitably a conflict between lawyers and economists it is, by now, outdated: it is better to think of

[2] See ch 12, 'ICN', pp 514–515.

the two as co-pilots of an aeroplane, each understanding the contribution to be made by the other.

In the early days of competition law in the EU the role of economics was not particularly strongly emphasised; the same was true in the US in the early years of antitrust law there[3]. Competition law developed in a fairly formalistic manner, and there were many more 'rules' of a legalistic nature than is the case today. The position—from the middle of the 1990s onwards—has changed dramatically, and it is now widely understood that competition law enforcement is usually justified only where there is a plausible case that a particular practice could lead to significant harmful effects to the competitive process; and that the extent of any harm is related to the degree of market power that a firm, or firms, have or will have on the market[4]. An attempt will be made throughout this book to explain the economic rationale for the application of EU and UK competition law.

(C) **Plan of this chapter**

Section 2 of this chapter describes the practices that competition laws attempt to control in order to protect the process of competition. Section 3 examines the theory of competition and gives an introductory account of why the effective enforcement of competition law is thought to be beneficial for consumer welfare. Section 4 considers the functions that a system of competition law might be expected to fulfil. Section 5 introduces two key economic concepts—market definition and, more importantly, market power—that are of fundamental importance to understanding competition law and policy. It is hoped that a prior awareness of these concepts will facilitate a better understanding of what follows. The chapter will conclude with a table of market share figures that have significance in the application of EU and UK competition law, while reminding the reader that market shares are only ever a proxy for market power and can never be determinative of market power in themselves.

2. **Overview of the Practices Controlled by Competition Law**

Systems of competition law are concerned with practices that are harmful to the competitive process. In particular competition law is concerned with:

- **anti-competitive agreements**: agreements that have as their object or effect the restriction of competition are unlawful, unless they have some redeeming virtue such as the enhancement of economic efficiency. An example of an illegal agreement would be a cartel between competitors, for example to fix prices, to share markets or to restrict output—often referred to as a **horizontal** agreement[5]. Agreements of this kind are severely punished, and in some systems of law can even lead to the

[3] For discussion see Kovacic and Shapiro 'Antitrust Policy: A Century of Economic and Legal Thinking' (2000) 14 Journal of Economic Perspectives 43.

[4] On the 'more economic approach' to EU competition law see Basedow and Wurmnest (eds) *Structure and Effects in EU Competition Law* (Kluwer, 2011); Bourgeois and Waelbroeck (eds) *Ten Years of the Effects-Based Approach in EU Competition Law* (Bruylant, 2012) and Wils 'The Judgment of the EU General Court in *Intel* and the So-Called "More Economic Approach" to Abuse of Dominance' (2014) 37 World Competition 405; Colomo 'Beyond the "More Economics-Based Approach": A Legal Perspective on Article 102 TFEU Case Law' (2016) 53 CML Rev 709.

[5] Note that not all horizontal agreements are necessarily bad; there may be circumstances in which competitors cooperate with one another in a way that delivers economic benefits; on such horizontal cooperation agreements see ch 15.

imprisonment of the individuals responsible for them. Agreements between firms at different levels of the market—known as **vertical** agreements—may also be unlawful when they could be harmful to competition: an example would be where a supplier of goods instructs its retailers not to resell them at less than a certain price, a practice often referred to as resale price maintenance. As a general proposition, vertical agreements are much less likely to harm competition than horizontal ones

- **abuse of substantial market power**: abusive behaviour by a firm that has a dominant position on the market is unlawful. For this purpose a firm is dominant when it has substantial market power that enables it to behave independently on the market without regard to competitors, customers and ultimately consumers. Abuses may be 'exclusionary' or 'exploitative'; in some cases an abuse may be harmful to the single market[6]. An example of an exclusionary abuse would be where a dominant firm reduces its prices to less than cost in order to drive a competitor out of the market or to deter a competitor from entering it, a phenomenon known as predatory pricing. An example of an exploitative abuse would be for the dominant firm to charge an excessive price for its products
- **mergers**: most systems of competition law enable a competition authority to investigate mergers between firms that could be harmful to the competitive process: clearly if one competitor were to acquire its main competitor the possibility exists that the market will become less competitive and consumers may have to pay higher prices as a result. Systems of merger control usually provide that mergers qualifying for investigation cannot be completed until the approval of the relevant competition authority (or court) has been obtained
- **public restrictions of competition**: the state is often responsible for restrictions and distortions of competition, for example as a result of legislative measures, regulations, licensing rules or the provision of subsidies. Some systems of competition law give a role to competition authorities to scrutinise 'public' restrictions of competition and to play a 'competition advocacy' role by commenting on, and even recommending the removal of, such restrictions.

3. The Theory of Competition

Competition means a struggle or contention for superiority, and in the commercial world this means a striving for the custom and business of people in the marketplace: competition has been described as 'a process of rivalry between firms … seeking to win customers' business over time'[7]. The ideological struggle between capitalism and communism was a dominant feature of the twentieth century. Many countries had the greatest suspicion of competitive markets and saw, instead, benefits in state planning and management of the economy. However enormous changes took place as the millennium approached, leading to widespread demonopolisation, liberalisation and privatisation. These phenomena, coupled with rapid technological changes and the opening up of international trade, unleashed unprecedentedly powerful economic forces. These changes impact upon individuals and societies in different ways, and sometimes the effects can be uncomfortable. Underlying them, however, is a growing consensus that, on the whole, markets deliver

[6] See further ch 5, 'Exploitative, exclusionary and single market abuses', pp 207–208.

[7] See para 4.1.2 of the UK *Merger Assessment Guidelines*, September 2010, available at www.gov.uk/cma.

better outcomes than state planning; and central to the idea of a market is the process of competition.

The important issue therefore is to determine the effect which competition can have on welfare. To understand this one must first turn to economic theory and consider what would happen in conditions of perfect competition and compare the outcome with what happens under monopoly, recognising as one does so that a theoretical analysis of perfect competition does not adequately explain business behaviour in the 'real' world[8].

(A) **The benefits of competition**

At its simplest—and it is sensible in considering competition law and policy not to lose sight of the simple propositions—the benefits of competition are:

- lower prices
- better products, for example that are of higher quality or are innovative
- wider choice for consumers
- greater efficiency than would be obtained under conditions of monopoly.

According to neo-classical economic theory, social welfare is maximised in conditions of perfect competition[9]. For this purpose 'social welfare' is not a vague generalised concept, but instead has a more specific meaning: that allocative and productive efficiency will be achieved; the combined effect of allocative and productive efficiency is that society's wealth overall is maximised. Consumer welfare, which is specifically concerned with gains to consumers as opposed to society at large, is also maximised in perfect competition[10]. A related benefit of competition is that it may have the dynamic effect of stimulating innovation as competitors strive to produce new and better products for consumers: this is a particularly important feature of high technology markets.

(i) **Allocative efficiency**

Under perfect competition economic resources are allocated between different goods and services in such a way that it is not possible to make anyone better off without making someone else worse off; 'consumer surplus'—the net gain to a consumer when buying a product—and 'total surplus'—a combination of consumer and producer surplus—are at their largest. Goods and services are allocated between consumers according to the price

[8] See eg on the psychology of competition from the business manager's perspective Porter *Competitive Strategy: Techniques for Analyzing Industries and Competitors* (Macmillan, 1998) and Dagnino (ed) *Handbook of Research on Competitive Strategy* (Edward Elgar, 2013).

[9] The conditions necessary for perfect competition are discussed below, 'Questioning the theory of perfect competition', pp 8–10 later in chapter; for further discussion see Scherer and Ross *Industrial Market Structure and Economic Performance* (Houghton Mifflin, 3rd ed, 1990), chs 1 and 2; Lipsey and Chrystal *Economics* (Oxford University Press, 13th ed, 2015), ch 7; on industrial economics and competition generally see Motta *Competition Policy: Theory and Practice* (Cambridge University Press, 2004); Carlton and Perloff *Modern Industrial Organisation* (Addison Wesley, 4th ed, 2005); Van den Bergh and Camesasca *European Competition Law and Economics: A Comparative Perspective* (Sweet & Maxwell, 2nd ed, 2006); Bishop and Walker *The Economics of EC Competition Law* (Sweet & Maxwell, 3rd ed, 2010), ch 2; Niels, Jenkins and Kavanagh *Economics for Competition Lawyers* (Oxford University Press, 2nd ed, 2016); readers may find helpful, in coping with the terminology of the economics of competition law, Black, Hashimzade and Myles (eds) *Oxford Dictionary of Economics* (Oxford University Press, 5th ed, 2017).

[10] See *Bishop and Walker*, paras 2.17–2.19; *Van den Bergh and Camesasca*, pp 62–69; Orbach 'The Antitrust Consumer Welfare Paradox' (2011) 7 Journal of Competition Law and Economics 133; Albæk 'Consumer Welfare in EU Competition Policy' (2013), available at www.ec.europa.eu.

they are prepared to pay, and, in the long run, price equals the marginal cost[11] of production (cost for this purpose including a sufficient profit margin to have encouraged the producer to invest its capital in the industry in the first place, but no more).

The achievement of allocative efficiency, as this phenomenon is known[12], can be shown analytically on the economist's model[13]. Allocative efficiency is achieved under perfect competition because the producer will expand its production for as long as it is privately profitable to do so. This assumes that the producer is acting rationally and has a desire to maximise its profits. As long as the producer can earn more by producing one extra unit of whatever it produces than it costs to make that unit, it will presumably do so. Only when the cost of producing a further unit (the 'marginal cost') exceeds the price it would obtain for that unit (the 'marginal revenue') will it cease to expand production. Where competition is perfect, a reduction in a producer's own output cannot affect the market price and so there is no reason to do so; the producer will therefore increase output to the point at which marginal cost and marginal revenue (the net addition to revenue of selling the last unit) coincide. This means that allocative efficiency is achieved, as consumers can obtain the amounts of goods or services they require at the price they are prepared to pay: resources are allocated precisely according to their wishes. By contrast, the output of a monopolist is lower than would be the case under perfect competition and there is therefore allocative inefficiency in that situation.

(ii) Productive efficiency

Under perfect competition goods and services will be produced at the lowest cost possible, which means that as little of society's wealth is expended in the production process as necessary. One way that firms in a competitive market try to undercut the prices of their competitors is by reducing their cost of production. Monopolists, free from the constraints of competition, may be high-cost producers. Thus competition is said to be conducive to productive efficiency[14]. Under perfect competition productive efficiency is achieved because a producer is unable to sell above cost (if it did so, customers would immediately desert it for other producers who are selling at cost) and it will not of course sell below cost (because then it would make no profit). In particular, if a producer were to charge above cost, other competitors would move into the market in the hope of profitable activity[15]. They would attempt to produce on a more efficient basis so that they could earn a greater profit. In the long run the tendency will be to force producers to incur the lowest cost possible in order to be able to earn any profit at all: an equilibrium will be reached where price and the average cost of producing goods necessarily coincide. This in turn means that price will never rise above cost and that inefficient producers will exit the market. If on the other hand price were to fall below cost, there would be an exit of capital from the industry and, as output would therefore decrease, price would be restored to the competitive level.

(iii) Dynamic efficiency

A further benefit of competition, albeit one that cannot be proved scientifically and is not captured by the theory of perfect competition, is that producers will be more likely

[11] That is to say, the cost of producing an additional unit of output.

[12] Allocative efficiency is also sometimes referred to as 'Pareto efficiency'.

[13] *Scherer and Ross*, pp 19ff; *Lipsey and Chrystal*, pp 153–155.

[14] For discussion see Vickers 'Concepts of Competition' (1995) 47 Oxford Economic Papers 1.

[15] As will be seen, determining what is meant by 'cost' is, in itself, often a complex matter in competition law: see ch 18, 'Cost concepts', pp 733–735.

to innovate and develop new products as part of the continual battle of striving for consumers' business. Thus competition may have the desirable dynamic effect of stimulating important technological research and development. Schumpeter was a champion of the notion that the motivation to innovate was the prospect of monopoly profits and that, even if existing monopolists earned such profits in the short term, outsiders would in due course enter the market and displace them[16]. A 'perennial gale of creative destruction' would be sufficient to protect the public interest, so that short-term monopoly power need not cause concern. In some market-based economies dynamic efficiency may be more important than allocative and productive efficiency.

It is important to acknowledge that in certain industries, particularly where technology is sophisticated and expensive, one firm may, for a period of time, enjoy very high market shares as well as very high profits; however in due course a competitor may be able to enter that market with superior technology and replace the incumbent firm. In cases such as this, high market shares over a period of time may exaggerate the market power of the firm that is currently the market leader, but vulnerable to dynamic entry[17].

(B) **The harmful effects of monopoly**

The theoretical model just outlined suggests that in perfect competition no producer will be able to affect the market price. The producer is a price-taker, with no capacity to affect price by its own unilateral action. The consumer is sovereign. The reason why the producer cannot affect the price is that any change in its own individual output will have only a negligible effect on the aggregate output of the market as a whole, and it is aggregate output that determines price through the 'law' of supply and demand.

Under conditions of monopoly the position is very different[18]. The monopolist is in a position to affect the market price. Since it is responsible for all the output, and since aggregate output determines price through the relationship of supply to demand, the monopolist will be able either to increase price by reducing the volume of its own production or to reduce sales by increasing price: the latter occurs in the case of highly branded products which are sold at a high price, such as luxury perfumes. Furthermore, again assuming a motive to maximise profits, the monopolist will see that it will be able to earn the largest profit if it refrains from expanding its production to the level that would be attained under perfect competition. The result will be that output is lower than would be the case under perfect competition and that therefore some consumers will be deprived of goods and services that they would have been prepared to pay for at the competitive market price. There is therefore allocative inefficiency in this situation: society's resources are not distributed in the most efficient way possible. The extent of this allocative inefficiency is sometimes referred to as the 'deadweight loss' attributable to monopoly; this is a pure loss to society, rather than simply a transfer of resources from consumers to the monopolist.

The objection to monopoly does not stop there. There is also the problem that productive efficiency may be lower because the monopolist is not constrained by competitive forces to reduce costs to the lowest possible level. Instead the firm becomes 'X-inefficient'. This term, first used by Liebenstein[19], refers to a situation in which resources are used to

[16] *Capitalism, Socialism and Democracy* (Taylor & Francis Books, 1976).

[17] This point was recognised by the General Court in Case T-79/12 *Cisco Systems Inc v Commission* EU:T:2013:635, para 69.

[18] See *Scherer and Ross*, ch 2; *Lipsey and Chrystal*, ch 8.

[19] 'Allocative Efficiency vs X-Efficiency' (1966) 56 Am Ec Rev 392–415.

make the right product, but less productively than they might be: management spends too much time on the golf course, outdated industrial processes are maintained and a general slackness pervades the organisation of the firm. Furthermore the monopolist may not feel the need to innovate, because it does not experience the constant pressure to go on attracting custom by offering better, more advanced, products. Thus it has been said that the greatest benefit of being a monopolist is the quiet life it is able to enjoy. However it is important to bear in mind that inefficient managers of a business may be affected by pressures other than those of competition. In particular their position may be undermined by uninvited takeover bids on stock exchanges from investors who consider that more efficient use could be made of the firm's assets[20]. Competition may be felt in capital as well as product markets: this is sometimes referred to as 'the market for corporate control'.

A final objection to the monopolist is that, since it can charge a higher price than in conditions of competition (it is a price-maker), wealth is transferred from the unfortunate consumer to the monopolist. Some economists would argue that this point is irrelevant: social welfare is concerned with allocative and productive efficiency; and for these purposes it is irrelevant whether wealth lies in the monopolist's or the consumer's hands. While it is not the function of competition authorities themselves to determine how society's wealth should be distributed, it is manifestly a legitimate matter for Governments to take an interest in economic equity, and it may be that one of the ways in which policy is expressed on this issue is through competition law[21].

Thus runs the theory of perfect competition and monopoly. It indicates that there is much to be said for the 'invisible hand' of competition which magically and surreptitiously orders society's resources in an optimal way, as opposed to the lumbering inefficiency of monopoly. However, we must now turn from the models used in the economist's laboratory to the more haphazard ways of commercial life before rendering a final verdict on the desirability of competition.

(C) Questioning the theory of perfect competition

(i) The model of perfect competition is based on assumptions unlikely to be observed in practice

The first point which must be made about the theory of perfect competition is that it is only a theory; the conditions necessary for perfect competition are extremely unlikely to be observed in practice. Perfect competition requires that on any particular market:

- there is an infinite number of buyers and sellers
- all producing identical (or 'homogeneous') products
- consumers have perfect information about market conditions
- there are no 'barriers to entry' preventing the emergence of new competition
- there are no 'barriers to exit' that might hinder firms wishing to leave the industry[22]
- there are no transport, search or other switching costs for consumers.

[20] See eg Hall 'Control Type and the Market for Corporate Control in Large US Corporations' (1977) 25 J Ind Ec 259–273; this issue is discussed further in ch 20, 'Management efficiency and the market for corporate control', pp 834–835.

[21] See 'Goals of competition law', pp 18–24 later in chapter, on the various functions of competition law.

[22] See 'Potential competitors', p 45 later in chapter, for further discussion of barriers to entry and exit.

Of course a market structure satisfying all these conditions is unlikely, if not impossible: we are simply at this stage considering theory, and the theory is based upon a number of assumptions.

Between the polar market structures of perfect competition on the one hand and monopoly on the other, there are many intermediate positions. Many firms sell products which are slightly differentiated from those of their rivals or command some degree of consumer loyalty, so that there will not be the homogeneity required for perfect competition. This means that an increase in price will not necessarily result in a substantial loss of business. It is unlikely that a customer will have such complete information of the market that he will immediately know that a lower price is available elsewhere for the desired product, yet the theory of perfect competition depends on perfect information being available to consumers. This is why legislation sometimes requires that adequate information must be made available to consumers about prices, terms and conditions[23]. There are often barriers to entry and exit to and from markets; this is particularly so where a firm that enters a market incurs 'sunk costs', that is to say costs that cannot be recovered when it ceases to operate in the future.

Just as perfect competition is unlikely to be experienced in practice, monopoly in its purest form is also rare. There are few products where one firm is responsible for the entire output: normally this happens only where a state confers a monopoly, for example to deliver letters. Most economic operators have some competitors; and even a true monopolist may hoist prices so high that customers cease to buy: demand is not infinitely inelastic[24]. In practice, most cases involve not a monopolist, in the etymological sense of one firm selling all the products on a particular market. Rather, competition law concerns itself with firms that have substantial market power. The economic concept of market power is key to understanding and applying competition law. When assessing whether a firm, or firms, have market power it is normal to begin by defining the relevant product and geographical markets; then the competitive constraints upon firms both from within and from outside those markets are considered, as well as countervailing buyer power. These issues are considered further in section 5 of this chapter.

(ii) **Other problems with the theory of perfect competition**

Apart from the fact that perfect competition and pure monopoly are inherently unlikely, there are other problems with the theory itself. It depends on the notion that all business people are rational and that they always attempt to maximise profits, but this is not necessarily the case. Directors of a company may not think that earning large profits for their shareholders is the most important consideration they face: they may be more interested to see the size of their business empire grow or to indulge themselves in the quiet life that monopolists may enjoy[25].

A further problem with the theory of perfect competition is that its assertion that costs are kept to an absolute minimum is not necessarily correct. It is true that the private costs of the producer will be kept low, but that says nothing about the social costs or 'externalities' which arise for society at large from, for example, the air pollution that a factory causes, or the severed limbs that must be paid for because cheap machinery is used which does not include satisfactory safeguards against injury. It has been argued that competition law

[23] This is a possible remedy under UK law following a market or merger investigation: see Enterprise Act 2002, Sch 8, paras 15–19; remedies requiring the provision of clearer information to consumers have been imposed on several occasions: see ch 11, 'The Market Investigations Provisions in Practice', pp 488–493.

[24] Demand is inelastic when a 1% change in price leads to a fall in quantity of less than 1%; it is elastic when a 1% change in price leads to a reduction in quantity of a greater percentage.

[25] *Scherer and Ross*, pp 44–46; see also *Bishop and Walker*, p 21, fn 17.

should not concern itself with these social costs[26], and perhaps it is true that this is a matter best left to specific legislation on issues such as conservation, the environment and health and safety at work; also it would be wrong to suppose that monopolists do not themselves produce social costs. However it is reasonable to be at least sceptical of the argument that in perfect competition the costs of society overall will inevitably be kept at a minimal level. Lastly, there is the difficulty with the theory of perfect competition that it is based on a static model of economic behaviour which may fail to account for the dynamic nature of markets and the way in which they operate over a period of time[27]. Firms such as Xerox and IBM, that may have dominated their industries at a particular time in history, nevertheless have found themselves to be engulfed subsequently by competitive forces in the market. Microsoft's leadership in the information technology sector was rapidly undermined as cloud technology diminished the importance of personal computers as a place to store data. In the world of social media MySpace disappeared almost as quickly as it emerged[28]. Schumpeter's perennial gale of creative destruction may affect even the most powerful economic operators. Yesterday's restraint of competition may be overcome by tomorrow's innovation.

There is a further problem which is that, if perfect competition cannot be attained, some alternative model is needed to explain how imperfect markets work or should work. In particular it is necessary to decide how monopolists or dominant firms should be treated, and an adequate theory will be needed to deal with oligopoly, a common industrial phenomenon which exists where a few firms between them supply most of the products within the market without any of them having a clear ascendancy over the others. Some economists would argue that, as the most common market form is oligopoly, competition policy ought to be designed around an analytical model of this phenomenon rather than the theory of perfect competition[29].

(D) **Questioning competition as a goal in itself**

A separate line of inquiry considers whether competition is so obviously beneficial anyway. There are some arguments that suggest that competition may not yield the best outcome for society.

(i) **Economies of scale and scope and natural monopolies**

The first relates to economies of scale, scope and the phenomenon of 'natural monopoly'[30]. In some markets there may be significant economies of scale, meaning that the average cost per unit of output decreases with the increase in the scale of the outputs produced; economies of scope occur where it is cheaper to produce two products together than to produce them separately. In some markets a profit can be made only by a firm supplying at least one-quarter or one-third of total output; it may even be that the 'minimum efficient scale' of operation is achieved only by a firm with a market share exceeding 50%, so that monopoly may be seen to be a natural market condition[31]. Similarly, economies of scope may be

[26] Bork *The Antitrust Paradox* (The Free Press, 1993), pp 114–115.

[27] See eg Evans and Hylton 'The Lawful Acquisition and Exercise of Monopoly Power and Its Implications for the Objectives of Antitrust' (2008) 4 Competition Policy International 203; Sidak and Teece 'Dynamic Competition in Antitrust Law' (2009) Journal of Competition Law and Economics 581; speech by Alex Chisholm of 10 December 2014 'Giants of digital: separating the signal from the noise and the sound from the fury', available at www.gov.uk/cma.

[28] See 'The rise and fall of MySpace' *Financial Times*, 4 September 2009, available at www.ft.com.

[29] On tacit collusion, oligopoly and parallel behaviour see ch 14.

[30] *Lipsey and Chrystal*, pp 291–293; *Scherer and Ross*, pp 97–141.

[31] See Schmalensee *The Control of Natural Monopolies* (Lexington, 1979); Sharkey *The Theory of Natural Monopoly* (Cambridge University Press, 1982).

essential to profitable behaviour. Natural monopoly means a situation in which economies of scale are so great that having two or more competing producers would not be viable and so efficiency dictates that a single firm serves the entire market. Natural monopoly is an economic phenomenon, driven by technological constraints, to be contrasted with statutory monopoly, where the right to exclude rivals from the market is bestowed by the law. Where natural monopoly exists it is inappropriate to attempt to achieve a level of competition, for example by ordaining that there should be a specific (or minimum) number of competitors in the market which would destroy the efficiency that this entails. This problem may be exacerbated where the 'natural monopolist' is also required to perform a 'universal service obligation', such as the daily delivery of letters to all postal addresses at a uniform price; performance of such an obligation may not be profitable in normal market conditions, so that the state may confer a statutory monopoly on the undertaking entrusted with the task in question. The lawfulness under EU and UK competition law of 'special or exclusive rights' conferred by the state is one of the more complex issues to be considered in this book[32].

Where the minimum efficient scale is very large in relation to total output, a separate question arises as to how that industry can be made to operate in a way that is beneficial to society as a whole. Public ownership may be a solution. Alternatively, a system of regulation could be introduced while leaving the producer or producers in the private sector[33]. A further possibility is that firms should be allowed to bid for a franchise to run the industry in question for a set period of time, at the end of which there will be a further round of bidding. In other words there will be periodic competition to run the industry, although no actual competition within it during the period of the franchise[34]: this happens in the UK, for example, when companies bid for rail franchises or to run the national lottery. The 100% share of the market that a firm might have after it has won the bid does not accurately reflect its market power if it was subject to effective competition when making its bid[35].

(ii) **Network effects and two-sided markets**

(a) Network effects

Certain markets are characterised by 'network effects'[36]. A direct network effect arises where the value of a product increases with the number of other customers consuming the same product. A simple example of a direct network effect is a telecommunications network. Suppose that Telcom has 100 subscribers to its network; suppose further that it is impossible for the users of Telcom's network to communicate with subscribers to competing networks. If a new consumer subscribes to the Telcom system the 100 original subscribers can now make contact with an additional person, without having incurred any additional cost themselves: for this reason the benefit to those subscribers is sometimes described as a network externality. In the same way users of a search engine will benefit as more people use the same one: the more consumers use a particular search engine, the more data it will gather about them, and this in turn will lead to improved search results

[32] See ch 6, 'Article 106', pp 229–251 and ch 9, 'Services of general economic interest', p 368.

[33] See ch 23, 'Regulated Industries', pp 1008–1010.

[34] See Demsetz 'Why Regulate Utilities?' (1968) 11 J L Ec 55–66; for criticism of the idea of franchise bidding see Williamson 'Franchise Bidding for Natural Monopolies in General and with respect to CATV' (1976) 7 Bell J Ec 73–104.

[35] For further discussion of so-called 'bidding markets' see 'Market shares', pp 42–43 later in chapter.

[36] See the UK *Merger Assessment Guidelines*, paras 5.2.20, 5.7.16 and 5.8.6, available at www.gov.uk/cma; see further Johnson 'Network Effects, Antitrust, and Falsifiability' (2017) 5 Journal of Antitrust Enforcement 341.

from which consumers themselves benefit. Where this occurs online sellers and content providers will increasingly want their products and information to be ranked highly by the search engine, so that the system becomes even more valuable to the consumers that use it; this is known as an indirect network effect.

(b) Two-sided markets

In the simple example given above of subscribers joining a telecommunications network, the value of the network increased because of the number of consumers joining it. However there are some markets, often referred to as 'two-sided markets'[37], where two or more groups of customers are catered for, and where a network effect arises as more consumers join one or the other side of the market. A simple example is a newspaper. A newspaper publisher sells advertising space; it also supplies newspapers to citizens, sometimes at a cover price and sometimes free of charge. The publisher's ability to sell advertising space increases according to the number of citizens expected to read the newspaper. Exactly the same is true of commercial television broadcasters: advertising slots during the football World Cup final will be hugely expensive because of the opportunity that exists to advertise products to a large number of people. The same phenomenon characterises supply and demand for credit cards: the more merchants that accept a particular card, the more consumers will select and then use that card; and the more that consumers use that card, the more merchants will accept it[38].

(c) Network effects and competition policy

Network effects may have positive effects on competition, since consumers become better off as a product becomes more popular. The increased utility of a telecommunications network is of value both to the operator and to the subscribers. In the case of a successful credit card system, merchants, the card issuer and consumers benefit. However network effects may also have negative effects on competition, in particular where all, or a significant proportion of, the customers in a particular market decide to opt for the product of one firm or for one particular technology with the result that one firm or one technology ends up dominating a market. A few years ago, when high definition optical disc recorders were first introduced to the market, there were two competing technologies, HD DVD and Blu-ray; the market tipped in favour of Blu-ray when all the major film studios opted for that format. In the same way the market can be seen to have tipped in favour of Google's general internet search engine in the EEA[39]. If tipping does take place, or if it is a likely consequence of a merger, a question for competition policy is to determine how the issue should be addressed. Various possibilities exist, including remedies in merger cases[40] and that third parties should be allowed to have access to the product of

[37] For discussion of two-sided markets see the UK Competition Appeal Tribunal in Case 1262/5/7/16 (T) *Agents' Mutual Ltd v Gascoigne Halman Ltd* [2017] CAT 15, paras 136–142; Rochet and Tirole 'Platform Competition in Two-Sided Markets' (2003) 1 Journal of the European Economic Association 990; the series of essays in (2006) 73 Antitrust LJ 571ff and in (2007) 3 Competition Policy International 147ff; *Bishop and Walker*, paras 3.042–3.045; Auer and Petit 'Two-Sided Markets and the Challenge of Turning Economic Theory into Antitrust Policy' (2015) 60 Antitrust Bulletin 426; and OECD Roundtable *Two-sided markets*, 2009, available at www.oecd.org/competition.

[38] See Baxter 'Bank Interchange of Transactional Paper: Legal and Economic Perspectives' (1983) 23 J L Ec 541.

[39] The European Commission refers to the network effects as one of the barriers to entering the general internet search market: *Google Search (Shopping)*, Commission decision of 27 June 2017, paras 292–296.

[40] See eg Case M 8124 *Microsoft/LinkedIn*, decision of 6 December 2016, paras 347–351 of which specifically discuss the detrimental effects of reaching a 'tipping point'; the Commission subsequently cleared the merger subject to remedies aimed at preserving competition between professional social networks.

the successful firm in whose favour the tipping has occurred: however, mandatory access to the successful products of innovative firms risks chilling the investment that created the product in the first place[41].

A specific point about two-sided markets is that pricing practices that, at first sight, appear to be anti-competitive might have an objective justification in their specific context[42]. For example when an email account is offered free of charge the service provider could be seen to be acting in a predatory manner by supplying at below the cost of production, which would be abusive if it was in a dominant position; however in a two-sided market this analysis may be wrong if the 'free' email account is paid for by the sale of advertising on the other side of the market.

(iii) **Particular sectors**

As well as the complexity of introducing competition into markets that might be regarded as natural monopolies, it is possible that social or political value-judgments may lead to the conclusion that competition is inappropriate in particular economic sectors. Agriculture is an obvious example. Legislatures have tended to the view that agriculture possesses special features entitling it to protection from the potentially ruthless effects of the competitive system. An obvious illustration of this is the Common Agricultural Policy of the EU[43]. Similarly it might be thought inappropriate (or politically impossible) to expose the labour market to the full discipline of the competitive process; this point is demonstrated by the judgment of the European Court of Justice in *Albany International BV v Stichting Bedrijfspensioenfonds Textielindustrie*[44] which concluded that collective bargaining between organisations representing employers and employees is outside Article 101 TFEU. Defence industries may be excluded from competition law scrutiny[45]. Separately there has been a tendency to refrain from insisting that the liberal professions should have to sully their hands with anything as offensive as price competition or advertising, although restrictive practices in the professions have come under competition law scrutiny in recent years[46]; the Court of Justice has held that restrictive professional rules that are proportionate and ancillary to a regulatory system that protects a legitimate public interest fall outside Article 101(1) TFEU[47]. Separately, it is clear that some sporting rules might infringe the competition rules: for example, the Commission decided that the rules of the International Skating Union ('ISU') imposing severe penalties on athletes who took part in speed-skating competitions that had not been authorised by the ISU infringed Article 101(1) TFEU[48].

(iv) **Beneficial restrictions of competition**

Another line of argument is that in some circumstances restrictions of competition can have beneficial results. This may manifest itself in various ways. One example is the

[41] See in particular ch 17, 'Refusal to Supply', pp 713–727 on the law of refusal to supply and the so-called 'essential facilities' doctrine.

[42] See eg Evans 'The Antitrust Economics of Free' (2011) 7 Competition Policy International 70.

[43] On the (non-)application of EU competition law to the agricultural sector see ch 23, 'Agriculture', pp 995–998.

[44] Case C-67/96 EU:C:1999:430; see ch 3, 'Employees trades unions and collective labour relations', pp 90–92.

[45] See ch 23, 'Military Equipment', p 995 for the position in EU law.

[46] See ch 13, 'Advertising Restrictions', pp 559–561.

[47] Case C-309/99 *Wouters v Algemene Raad van de Nederlandse Orde van Advocaten* EU:C:2002:98: see ch 3, 'Regulatory ancillarity: the judgment of the Court of Justice in *Wouters*', pp 138–141.

[48] Commission Press Release IP/17/5184, 8 December 2017; see ch 3, 'The application of Article 101(1) to sporting rules', pp 141–142.

suggestion that firms which are forced to pare costs to the minimum because of the pressures of competition will skimp on safety checks. This argument is particularly pertinent in the transport sector, where fears are sometimes expressed that safety considerations may be subordinated to the profit motive: an example would be where airlines compete fiercely on price. It may be that specific safety legislation can be used to overcome this anxiety; and monopolists seeking to enlarge their profits may show the same disregard for safety considerations as competing firms, a charge levelled against Railtrack (since replaced by Network Rail) in the UK following a series of serious rail accidents in the late 1990s and 2000. Safety was an important issue in the debate preceding the part-privatisation of NATS (formerly National Air Traffic Services). A related argument is that higher alcohol prices—and a restriction of price competition between suppliers of alcohol—might save drinkers, and the rest of society, from the harmful effects of excess drinking[49]; Scotland and England and Wales have both enacted legislation to deal with this problem[50].

Another possibly beneficial restriction of competition could arise where two or more firms, by acting in concert and restricting competition between themselves, are able to develop new products or to produce goods or services on a more efficient scale: the benefit to the public at large may be considerable; EU and UK competition law recognise that, in some cases, agreements may be tolerated which, though restrictive of competition, produce beneficial effects[51]. A further example of the same point is that a producer might impose restrictions on its distributors in order to ensure that they promote its products in the most effective way possible; although this might diminish competition in its own goods (intra-brand competition), the net effect may be to enhance the competitive edge of them as against those produced by its competitors (inter-brand competition)[52]. These examples suggest that a blanket prohibition of agreements that restrict competition would deprive the public of substantial advantages.

(v) **Ethical and other objections**

A more fundamental objection to competition might be that it is considered in some sense to be inherently objectionable. The very notion of a process of rivalry whereby firms strive for superiority may be considered ethically unsound. One argument (now largely discredited) is that 'cut-throat' competition means that firms are forced to charge ever lower prices until in the end the vicious cycle leads them to charge below marginal cost in order to keep custom at all; the inevitable effect of this will be insolvency. The prevailing attitude in much of UK industry during the first half of the twentieth century was that competition was 'harmful' and even destructive and it was this entrenched feeling that led to the adoption of a pragmatic and non-doctrinaire system of control in 1948[53]. It was not until the Competition Act 1998—50 years later—that the UK finally adopted legislation that was motivated in particular by a determination to eradicate cartels[54]. Economically the argument that competition is a cut-throat business that leads to insolvency is implausible, but industrialists do use it.

[49] See the UK Competition and Markets Authority's advice to local authorities: *High-strength alcohol schemes: competition law advice*, December 2014, available at www.gov.uk/cma.

[50] In Scotland see the Alcohol (Minimum Pricing) (Scotland) Act 2012; in *Scottish Whisky Association v Lord Advocate* [2017] UKSC 76 the UK Supreme Court declared the Act was compatible with EU law; in England and Wales see the Licensing Act 2003 (Mandatory Conditions) Order 2014, SI 2014/1252.

[51] On horizontal cooperation agreements generally see ch 15.

[52] On vertical agreements generally see ch 16.

[53] See Allen *Monopoly and Restrictive Practices* (George Allen & Unwin, 1968).

[54] On these powers see ch 10, 'Inquiries and Investigations', pp 401–411 and 'Penalties', pp 420–424.

(vi) Industrial policy

Countries have an obvious interest in promoting successful economic entrepreneurs and in providing employment for their citizens; they may also wish to exercise control over the extent to which it is possible for overseas operators to invest in the local economy. One practical objection to promoting competition is that it may be considered to be inimical to the general thrust of such 'industrial policy'. Admittedly the suggestion has been made that, in conditions of perfect competition, firms will innovate in order to keep or attract new custom. However Governments often encourage firms to collaborate where this would lead to economies of scale or to more effective research and development; and they may adopt a policy of promoting 'national champions' which will be effective as competitors in international markets[55]. In 2017 the UK Government proposed to create an 'Industry Strategy Challenge Fund' that would support UK research and innovation in robotics, clean energy and biotechnology[56]. The UK Competition and Markets Authority ('the CMA') subsequently advised the Government that, when deciding how to allocate funds, policymakers should consider how funding is affected by, and has an effect on, competition and competitiveness[57].

There are circumstances in which the innovator, the entrepreneur and the risk-taker may require some immunity from competition if they are to indulge in expensive technological projects. This is recognised in the law of intellectual property rights which provides an incentive to firms to innovate by preventing the appropriation of commercial ideas which they have developed[58]. A patentee in the UK is given the exclusive right for 20 years to exploit the subject-matter of his or her patent[59]. A similar incentive and/or reward is given to the owners of copyright, registered designs and analogous rights[60]. This is a recognition of the fact that in some circumstances competition suppresses innovation and an indication of the vacuity of relentlessly pursuing the ideal of perfect competition. The relationship between competition law and the law of intellectual property is a fascinating one, in particular the tension between the desire to keep markets open and free from monopoly and the need to encourage innovation precisely by granting monopoly rights; in fact, however, this tension is more apparent than real[61]. These issues will be considered in chapter 19.

(vii) The economic crisis and competition policy

The global economic crisis that commenced in the late 2000s led to loud calls in some quarters for a relaxation, or even the abandonment, of competition law enforcement in order to provide relief to firms facing an uncertain financial future. Competition authorities globally resisted such calls, arguing that competition remained as important in harsh economic times as in benign ones[62].

(viii) Competitions are there to be won

The last point that should be made in this brief survey of objections to competition is that the competitive process contains an inevitable paradox. Some competitors win. By being

[55] This can be an important issue in some merger cases: see ch 20, 'National champions', p 834.

[56] Green Paper *Building our Industrial Strategy*, January 2017, available at www.gov.uk.

[57] Response from the CMA to the Government's Green Paper, April 2017, available at www.gov.uk/cma.

[58] See generally Cornish, Llewelyn and Aplin *Intellectual Property Law: Patents, Copyrights, Trademarks & Allied Rights* (Sweet & Maxwell, 8th ed, 2013).

[59] Patents Act 1977, s 25.

[60] Copyright, Designs and Patents Act 1988, ss 12, 13A–15A, 191, 216, 269.

[61] See ch 19, 'Is there an inevitable tension between intellectual property rights and competition law?', pp 787–788.

[62] See eg Lowe 'Competition Policy and the Economic Crisis' (2009) 5 Competition Policy International 3, available at www.competitionpolicyinternational.com; speech by Alex Chisholm of 11 September 2014 'Public interest and competition-based merger control', available at www.gov.uk/cma.

the most innovative, the most responsive to customers' wishes, and by producing goods or services in the most efficient way possible, one firm may succeed in seeing off its rivals in a Darwinian way. It would be strange, and indeed harmful, if that firm could then be condemned for being a monopolist. As Judge Learned Hand opined in *US v Aluminum Co of America*[63]:

> [A] single producer may be the survivor out of a group of active companies, merely by virtue of his superior skill, foresight and industry ... The successful competitor, having been urged to compete, must not be turned upon when he wins.

(E) **Empirical evidence**

A separate issue is whether there is any empirical evidence to support, or indeed to contradict, the case for competition and, if so, what the evidence can tell us. It is notoriously difficult to measure such things as allocative efficiency or the extent to which innovation is attributable to the pressure of competition upon individual firms. At one time economists suggested that there is some direct causal relationship between industrial structure, the conduct of firms on the market and the quality of their economic performance[64]: this is often referred to as the 'structure-conduct-performance paradigm'. A monopoly can be expected to lead to a restriction of output and a loss of economic efficiency: a natural consequence of this view would be that competition law should be watchful for any acts or omissions that could be harmful to the structure of the market, and in particular for conduct that could foreclose access to it and mergers that lead to fewer players. A more recent view is that this schematic presentation is too simplistic. In particular it is said to be unsound because it is uni-directional and fails to indicate the extent to which performance itself can influence structure and conduct[65]. Good performance, for example, may in itself affect structure by attracting new entrants into an industry.

Other economists have attempted to measure the extent to which monopoly results in allocative inefficiency and leads to a deadweight loss to society[66]. There are of course formidable difficulties associated with this type of exercise, and many of the studies that have been published have been criticised for their methodology. Scherer and Ross devote a chapter of their book to this problem[67] and point out that there has been a dramatic expansion in the range and intensity of empirical research into industrial organisation in recent years. Their conclusion is that, despite the theoretical problems of such research, important relationships do exist between market structure and performance, and that the research should continue[68]. Various studies in recent years have examined the positive relationship between competition, productivity and growth[69].

[63] 148 F 2d 416 (2nd Cir 1945).

[64] This schematic model of industrial behaviour was first suggested by Mason 'Price and Production Policies of Large-Scale Enterprise' (1939) 29 Am Ec Rev Supplement 61–74; see *Scherer and Ross*, chs 3 and 4.

[65] Phillips 'Structure, Conduct and Performance—and Performance, Conduct and Structure' in Markham and Papanek (eds) *Industrial Organization and Economic Development* (Houghton Mifflin, 1970); Sutton *Sunk Costs and Market Structure: Price Competition, Advertising and the Evolution of Concentration* (MIT Press, 1991).

[66] Weiss 'Concentration-Profit Relationship' in Goldschmid et al (eds) *Industrial Concentration: The New Learning* (Little, Brown, 1974); Gribbin *Postwar Revival of Competition as Industrial Policy*; Cowling and Mueller 'The Social Costs of Monopoly Power' (1978) 88 Ec J 724–748, criticised by Littlechild at (1981) 91 Ec J 348–363.

[67] *Industrial Market Structure and Economic Performance*, ch 11.

[68] Ibid, p 447; see also *The development of targets for consumer savings arising from competition policy*, OFT 386, June 2002, available at www.nationalarchives.gov.uk.

[69] See eg Syerson 'What Determines Productivity?' (2011) 49 Journal of Economic Literature 326; *Productivity and competition: A summary of the evidence*, CMA45, July 2015, available at www.gov.uk/cma.

(F) Contestable markets

Some economists have advanced a theory of 'contestable markets' upon which competition law might be based[70]. According to this theory, firms will be forced to ensure an optimal allocation of resources provided that the market on which they operate is 'contestable', that is to say provided that it is possible for firms easily to enter the market without incurring sunk costs[71] and to leave it without loss. In a perfectly contestable market, entry into an industry is free and exit is costless. The emphasis on exit is important as firms should be able to leave an industry without incurring a loss if and when opportunities to profit within it disappear. A perfectly *contestable* market need not be perfectly *competitive*: perfect competition requires an infinite number of sellers on a market; in a perfectly contestable market an economically efficient outcome can be achieved even where there are only a few competitors, since there is always the possibility of 'hit and run' entry into the market. Even an industry in which only one or two firms are operating may be perfectly contestable where there are no impediments to entry or exit, so that intervention by the competition authorities is unnecessary[72]. The theory shifts the focus of competition policy, as it is more sanguine about markets on which few firms operate than the 'traditional' model of perfect competition; having said this, it is questionable whether the theory of contestability really adds a great deal to traditional thinking on industrial economics or whether it simply involves a difference of emphasis.

(G) Effective competition

Effective competition connotes the idea that firms are subject to a reasonable degree of competitive constraint, from actual and potential competitors and from customers, and that the role of a competition authority is to see that such constraints are present or remain on the market[73]. It would also mean no special protection for inefficient competitors.

The idea of effective competition does not appear to be the product of any particular theory or model of competition—perfect, workable, contestable or any other. Indeed, given the number of theories and assumptions already discussed in this chapter, and the many others not discussed, the idea of effective competition, free from theoretical baggage, may have much to commend it. The expression 'effective competition' is found in Article 2(3) of the European Union Merger Regulation ('the EUMR'), as part of the test for determining when a merger is incompatible with the internal market: effective competition must not be significantly impeded. The Framework Directive on electronic communications provides that regulatory obligations should only be imposed where there is no 'effective competition'[74]. The EU Courts and the European Commission have also used the term[75]. In the UK the CMA's *Vision, values and strategy*[76] includes encouraging 'effective competition' where markets and business models are evolving. The Gas and

[70] See Baumol, Panzar and Willig *Contestable Markets and the Theory of Industry Structure* (Harcourt Brace Jovanovich, revised ed, 1988); Bailey 'Contestability and the Design of Regulatory and Antitrust Policy' (1981) 71 Am Ec Rev 178–183.

[71] See 'The model of perfect competition is based on assumptions unlikely to be observed in practice', pp 8–9 earlier in chapter.

[72] See eg *CHC Helicopter Corpn/Helicopter Services Group ASA* Cm 4556 (2000).

[73] See further *Bishop and Walker*, ch 2, 'Effective Competition'.

[74] Directive 2002/21/EC, OJ [2002] L 108/33, recital 27.

[75] See eg Case T-168/01 *GlaxoSmithKline Services Unlimited v Commission* EU:T:2006:265, para 109; Case T-321/05 *AstraZeneca AB v Commission* EU:T:2010:266, para 175; the Commission's *Guidelines on Vertical Restraints* OJ [2010] C 130/1, para 107; the Commission's *Guidance on the Commission's Enforcement Priorities in Applying Article [102 TFEU] to abusive exclusionary conduct by dominant undertakings* OJ [2009] C 45/7, paras 5–6 and 19.

[76] CMA13, January 2014, available at www.gov.uk/cma.

Electricity Markets Authority is required to promote effective competition in the gas and electricity sectors[77]. One of the operational objectives of the Financial Conduct Authority is to promote effective competition in the interests of consumers[78]; the needs of different consumers who use or may use those services, ease of access, ease of switching, entry barriers and innovation may all be relevant to the existence of effective competition[79].

(H) **Conclusion**

What can perhaps be concluded at the end of this discussion is that, despite the range of different theories and the difficulties associated with them, competition does possess sufficient properties to lead to a strong policy choice in its favour. Competitive markets seem, on the whole, to deliver better outcomes than monopolistic or non-competitive ones, and there are demonstrable benefits for consumers[80]. The UK Government has said that:

> Vigorous competition between firms is the lifeblood of strong and effective markets. Competition helps consumers get a good deal. It encourages firms to innovate by reducing slack, putting downward pressure on costs and providing incentives for the efficient organisation of production[81].

This is why competition policy has been so widely embraced in recent years; there is probably a greater global consensus on the desirability of competition and free markets today than at any time in the history of human economic behaviour. In particular, monopoly or near-monopoly does seem to lead to a restriction in output and higher prices; there is a greater incentive to achieve productive efficiency in a competitive market; the suggestion that only monopolists can innovate is unsound; and competition provides the consumer with a greater degree of choice. It may be helpful to summarise the benefits that are expected to be derived from effective competition:

- competition promotes allocative and productive efficiency
- competition leads to lower prices for consumers
- competition means that firms will develop new and better products in order to retain or win business
- competition gives consumers a choice as to the products that they buy.

4. The Function of Competition Law

(A) **Goals of competition law**

The next issue that must be considered is the goal, or goals, of competition law[82]. In recent years many competition authorities have stressed the central importance of consumer welfare when interpreting and applying competition law[83]. A clear statement to this effect

[77] Utilities Act 2000, ss 9 and 13, amending the Gas Act 1986 and the Electricity Act 1989 respectively.

[78] Financial Services and Markets Act 2000, s 1E; note that s 1B(4) requires the FCA to discharge its general functions in a way that promotes effective competition in the interests of consumers; see *The FCA's approach to advancing its objectives*, 2015, available at www.fca.org.uk.

[79] Financial Services and Markets Act 2000, s 1E(2).

[80] Section 25(3) of the Enterprise and Regulatory Reform Act 2013 requires the CMA to 'seek to promote competition, both within and outside the United Kingdom, for the benefit of consumers'.

[81] White Paper *Productivity and Enterprise: A World Class Competition Regime* Cm 5233 (2001), para 1.1.

[82] See generally Zimmer (ed) *The Goals of Competition Law* (Edward Elgar, 2012).

[83] For discussion see eg Farrell and Katz 'The Economics of Welfare Standards in Antitrust' (2006) 2 Competition Policy International 15.

can be found in a speech of the former European Commissioner for competition policy, Neelie Kroes, given in 2005:

> Consumer welfare is now well established as the standard the Commission applies when assessing mergers and infringements of the Treaty rules on cartels and monopolies. Our aim is simple: to protect competition in the market as a means of enhancing consumer welfare and ensuring an efficient allocation of resources[84].

This does not mean that EU competition law is applicable only where supra-competitive prices to end consumers can be demonstrated. The Court of Justice has recognised from the earliest days that consumers can also be indirectly affected by action that harms the competitive process: for example in *T-Mobile* the Court said that the competition rules are 'designed to protect not only the immediate interests of individual competitors or consumers but also to protect the structure of the market and thus competition as such'[85]. This is why Article 102 was held to apply to the acquisition by a dominant undertaking of its main competitor, irrespective of whether this led to the charging of excessive prices[86]. Of course competition can have painful consequences: if one competitor is more efficient than another the former will succeed and the latter will exit the market, defeated. As we will see, EU competition law acknowledges this and does not afford protection to less efficient competitors[87].

It would be reasonable to point out that, although the consumer welfare standard is currently in the ascendancy, many different policy objectives have been pursued in the name of competition law over the years; some of these were not rooted in notions of consumer welfare in the technical sense at all, and some were plainly inimical to the pursuit of allocative and productive efficiency. The result has sometimes been inconsistency and contradiction, but it is as well for the reader to be aware of this before coming to the law itself[88]. Historically there has not been one single, unifying, policy underpinning the competition laws of the EU and the UK. In particular, competition policy does not exist in a vacuum: it is an expression of the current values and aims of society and is as susceptible to change as political thinking generally. Because views and insights shift over a period of time, competition law is infused with tension. Different systems of competition law reflect different concerns, an important point when carrying out comparative analysis[89]. As already noted, competition law has now been adopted in more than 130 countries, whose economies and economic development may be very different from one another. It is impossible to suppose that each system will have identical concerns; some countries will be more enthusiastic about the process of competition than others.

(i) **Consumer protection**

Several different objectives other than the maximisation of consumer welfare in the technical sense can be ascribed to competition law. The first is that competition law should protect the interests of consumers, not (or not only) by protecting the competitive process itself, but by taking direct action against offending undertakings, for example by requiring dominant firms to reduce their prices. It is of course correct in principle that competition

[84] SPEECH/05/512, 15 September 2005, available at www.ec.europa.eu/competition/speeches/.

[85] Case C-8/08 *T-Mobile Netherlands BV* EU:C:2009:343, para 38.

[86] See Case 6/72 *Europemballage and Continental Can v Commission* EU:C:1973:22, paras 20–26.

[87] See 'Protecting competitors', pp 21–22 later in chapter and ch 5, 'Protection of competitors or protection of competition?', pp 200–202.

[88] See Odudu 'The Wider Concerns of Competition Law' (2010) 30 OJLS 599.

[89] On the differences between the policies of competition law in the US and the EU see eg Jebsen and Stevens 'Assumptions, Goals and Dominant Undertakings; the Regulation of Competition under Article 86 of the European Union' (1996) 64 Antitrust LJ 443.

law should be regarded as having a 'consumer protection' function: ultimately the process of competition itself is intended to deliver benefits to consumers. However the possibility exists that competition law might be invoked in a more 'populist' manner; this happens periodically when Ministers (with an eye on public opinion) suggest that excessive prices are being charged by both monopolists and non-monopolists. After a thorough investigation the CMA published a report on the wholesale and retail energy markets in the UK in June 2016 and introduced a number of changes in order to make the market work better for consumers[90]; however the Government was not satisfied and proposed the Domestic Gas and Electricity (Tariff Cap) Bill in February 2018. A problem with using competition law to assume direct control over prices is that competition authorities are ill-placed to determine what price a competitive market would set for particular goods or services, and indeed by fixing a price they may further distort the competitive fabric of the market[91]. Populist measures taken to have electoral appeal may ultimately be more harmful than the high prices themselves.

Similarly the consumer may be harmed—or at least consider himself to be harmed—where a producer insists that all its goods should be sold by dealers at maintained prices, or that dealers should provide a combined package of goods plus after-sales service. Here the consumer's choice is restricted by the producer's decision. Competition law may proscribe resale price maintenance or tie-in sales for this reason, although there are those who argue that this intervention is undesirable: the producer is restricting intra-brand competition, but inter-brand competition may be enhanced as a result[92]. The obsession with protecting the consumer can also be considered short-sighted since, in the longer run, the producer might choose to abandon the market altogether rather than comply with an unreasonable competition law; short-term benefits will then be outweighed by long-term harm to consumer welfare[93].

(ii) Redistribution

A second possible objective of competition law might be the dispersal of economic power and the redistribution of wealth: the promotion of economic equity rather than economic efficiency[94]. Aggregations of resources in the hands of monopolists, multinational corporations or conglomerates could be considered a threat to the very notion of democracy, individual freedom of choice and economic opportunity. This argument was influential in the US for many years at a time when there was a fundamental mistrust of big business. President Roosevelt warned Congress in 1938 that:

> The liberty of a democracy is not safe if the people tolerate the growth of a private power to a point where it becomes stronger than the democratic state itself ... Among us today a concentration of private power without equal in history is growing[95].

It was under the US antitrust laws that the world's largest corporation at the time, AT&T, was dismembered. Some critics of the action brought by the Department of Justice against Microsoft were concerned that it amounted to an attack on a spectacularly successful

[90] Energy Market Investigation, 24 June 2016; full details of this investigation can be found at www.gov.uk/cma.

[91] See eg *Supermarkets* Cm 4842 (2000) declining to regulate the pricing of grocery products, available at www.nationalarchives.gov.uk.

[92] For discussion see Wright 'The Antitrust/Consumer Protection Paradox: Two Policies at War with Each Other' (2012) 121 Yale Law Journal 2216. See in particular ch 16 on vertical agreements.

[93] This is one of Bork's most pressing arguments in *The Antitrust Paradox* (The Free Press, 1993).

[94] See Odudu 'The Distributional Consequences of Antitrust' in Marsden (ed) *Handbook of Research in Trans-Atlantic Antitrust* (Edward Elgar, 2007), ch 23.

[95] 83 Cong Rec 5992 (1938).

business[96], while others welcomed the attempt to restrain its undoubted economic muscle[97]. Likewise there are divergent views on whether competition authorities should take action against internet firms such as Google[98]. The European Commission's decision in June 2017 to impose a fine of €2.42 billion on Google for unlawfully favouring its own comparison shopping service in its general search engine results, and its appeal to the General Court, will generate controversy for a long time to come[99]. Growing concerns about inequality of wealth have led to a renewal of interest in the question of whether competition law has a meaningful role to play[100].

(iii) Protecting competitors

Linked to the argument that competition law should be concerned with redistribution is the view that competition law should be applied in such a way as to protect small firms against more powerful rivals: the competition authorities should hold the ring and ensure that the 'small guy' is given a fair chance to succeed. To put the point another way, there are some who consider that competition law should be concerned with competitors as well as the process of competition. This idea has at times had a strong appeal in the US, in particular during the period when Chief Justice Warren led the Supreme Court in the 1960s. However it has to be appreciated that the arrest of the Darwinian struggle, in which the most efficient succeed and the weak disappear, for the purpose of protecting small business can run directly counter to the idea of consumer welfare in the technical economic sense. It may be that competition law is used to preserve the inefficient and to stunt the performance of the efficient. In the US the 'Chicago School' of economists has been particularly scathing of the 'uncritical sentimentality' in favour of the small competitor, and since the 1980s, in particular, US law developed in a noticeably less sentimental way[101]. To the Chicago School, the essential question in an antitrust case should be whether the conduct under investigation could lead to consumers paying higher prices, and whether those prices could be sustained against the forces of competition; antitrust intervention to protect competitors from their more efficient rivals is harmful to social and consumer welfare. Even firms with high market shares are subject to competitive constraints provided that barriers to entry and exit are low, so that intervention on the part of the competition authority is usually uncalled for.

There seems little doubt that EU competition law has, in some cases, been applied with competitors in mind: this is particularly noticeable in some decisions under Article 102,

[96] For a highly critical view of the *Microsoft* case generally see McKenzie *Antitrust on Trial: How the Microsoft Case Is Reframing the Rules of Competition* (Perseus Publishing, 2nd ed, 2001).

[97] See 'Now Bust Microsoft's Trust' *The Economist*, 13 November 1999; 'Bill Rockefeller?' *The Economist*, 29 April 2000.

[98] See eg Manne and Wright 'Google and the Limits of Antitrust: The Case Against the Antitrust Case Against Google' (2011) 34 Harvard Journal of Law and Public Policy 171; Bork and Sidak 'What does the Chicago School Teach about Internet Search and the Antitrust Treatment of Google?' (2012) 8 Journal of Competition Law and Economics 663; Wiethaus 'Google's Favouring of Own Services: Comments from an Economic Perspective' (2015) 6 JECLAP 506.

[99] Commission decision of 27 June 2017, on appeal Case T-612/17 *Google v Commission*, not yet decided.

[100] See eg Leigh and Triggs 'Markets, Monopolies and Moguls: The Relationship between Inequality and Competition' (2016) 49(4) Australian Economic Review 389; Ennis, Gonzaga and Pike 'Inequality: a Hidden Cost of Market Power' (2017), available at www.ssrn.com; Hovenkamp 'Antitrust Policy and Inequality of Wealth' [2017] CPI Antitrust Chronicle 1; Dierx, Ilzkovitz, Pataracchia, Ratto, Thum-Thysen and Varga 'Does EU Competition Policy Support Inclusive Growth?' (2017) 13(2) Journal of Competition Law & Economics 225; Kukovec 'Economic Law, Inequality, and Hidden Hierarchies on the EU Internal Market' (2016) 38 Michigan Journal of International Law 1, 2–13; Gal 'The Social Contract at the Basis of Competition Law' (August 2017), available at www.ssrn.com.

[101] See eg Fox 'What's Harm to Competition? Exclusionary Practices and Anticompetitive Effect' (2002) 70 Antitrust LJ 371.

and some commentators have traced this phenomenon back to the influence of the so-called 'Freiburg School' of ordoliberalism[102]. Scholars of the Freiburg School, which originated in Germany in the 1930s, saw the free market as a necessary ingredient in a liberal economy, but not as sufficient in itself. The economic problems of the Weimar Republic and Nazi Germany were attributable in part to the inability of the legal system to control and, if necessary, to disperse private economic power. An economic constitution was necessary to constrain the economic power of firms, but without giving Government unrestrained control over their behaviour: public power could be just as pernicious as private. Legal rules could be put in place which would achieve both of these aims. It is not surprising that the beneficiaries of such thinking would be small and medium-sized firms, the very opposite of the monopolists and cartels feared by the members of the Freiburg School. There is no doubt that ordoliberal thinking had an influence on the leading figures involved in the establishment of the three European Communities in the 1950s[103]. This may have led to decisions and judgments in which the law was applied to protect competitors rather than the process of competition, although it may be that the role of ordoliberalism in competition law cases has been exaggerated: some commentators assert that economic efficiency was a key goal of competition policy from the outset[104]. However, without questioning the appropriateness of decisions taken in the early years of the EU, it can be questioned whether it is appropriate in the new millennium to maintain this approach: there is much to be said for applying competition rules to achieve economic efficiency rather than economic equity. The two ideas sit awkwardly together: indeed they may flatly contradict one another, since an efficient undertaking will inevitably be able to defeat less efficient competitors, whose position in the market ought not to be underwritten by a competition authority on the basis of political preference or, as Bork might say, sentimentality. In *Intel v Commission*[105], a case under Article 102 TFEU, the Grand Chamber of the Court of Justice said that:

> not every exclusionary effect is necessarily detrimental to competition. Competition on the merits may, by definition, lead to the departure from the market or the marginalisation of competitors that are less efficient and so less attractive to consumers from the point of view of, among other things, price, choice, quality or innovation[106].

This is an issue that will be considered further in later chapters, and in particular in chapters 5, 17 and 18 on abusive practices on the part of dominant firms where, in particular, we will see that the European Commission is clear that Article 102 is an instrument for the protection of competition and not of competitors as such.

(iv) **Unfair competition**

Another issue is whether and to what extent competition law should concern itself with 'fairness' or fair dealing in the marketplace[107]. It is obviously not 'fair' if one firm pretends that its goods were produced by someone else with a better reputation or brand image,

[102] See Gerber *Law and Competition in Twentieth Century Europe: Protecting Prometheus* (Clarendon Press, 1998), ch VII; Eucken 'The Competitive Order and Its Implementation' (2006) 2 Competition Policy International 219; Ahlborn and Grave 'Walter Eucken and Ordoliberalism: An Introduction from a Consumer Welfare Perspective' (2006) 2 Competition Policy International 197; Vanberg 'The Freiburg School: Walter Eucken and Ordoliberalism' (2011), available at www.eucken.de.

[103] See *Gerber*, pp 263–265; ch IX.

[104] See Akman 'Searching for the Long-Lost Soul of Article 82 EC' (2009) 29 OJLS 267.

[105] Case C-413/14 P EU:C:2017:632.

[106] Ibid, para 134 and case law cited.

[107] See eg Bakhoum 'A Dual Language in Modern Competition Law? Efficiency Approach versus Development Approach and Implications for Developing Countries' (2011) 34 World Competition 495; Lamadrid de Pablo 'Competition Law as Fairness' (2017) 8 JECLAP 147.

and gains a competitive advantage. It would also be 'unfair' for firms to indulge in practices intended to denigrate competitors' products and thereby distort competition. The question is whether competition law should or even can strive to produce 'fairness' as an abstract principle. As with redistribution and the protection of competitors, there is a risk that seeking to achieve fairness as between one market participant and another will itself distort the process of competition.

(v) **Other issues**

In some cases, particularly involving mergers, the relevant authorities might find that other issues require attention: whether they can be taken into account will depend on the applicable law[108]. For example, unemployment and regional policy are issues which arise in the analysis of mergers and cooperation agreements; the ability of competition to dampen price-inflation may be considered to be important; merger controls may be used to prevent foreign takeovers of domestic companies; the UK Government permitted a merger between LloydsTSB and HBOS which might otherwise have been prohibited or subject to modification, because of the economic crisis in the banking sector in the late 2000s[109]; and South African law specifically provides that in certain circumstances the position of historically disadvantaged people—that is to say the victims of apartheid—should be taken into account[110].

(vi) **The single market imperative**

Lastly it is important to understand that competition policy in the context of the EU fulfils an additional but quite different function from those just described (although EU law may be applied with them in mind as well). This is that competition law plays a hugely important part in facilitating and defending the single market[111]. As the current Commissioner for competition policy, Margrethe Vestager, has explained:

> The founding fathers of Europe understood that there would be no genuine integration without a Single Market—and no functioning Single Market without a strong competition policy enforced by a central competition authority[112].

The idea of the single market is that internal barriers to trade within the EU should be dismantled and that goods, services, workers and capital should have complete freedom of movement. Firms should be able to outgrow their national markets and operate on a more efficient, transnational scale throughout the EU. Single market integration remains as important today as it ever was[113]. Competition law has both a negative and a positive role to play in the integration of the single market. The negative one is that it can prevent measures which attempt to maintain the isolation of one domestic market from another: national cartels, export bans and market-sharing will be seriously punished[114]. For example a fine of €149 million was imposed on Nintendo for taking

[108] On the relevant tests to be applied to mergers under EU and UK law see respectively ch 21, 'Substantive Analysis', pp 882–907 and ch 22, 'The "Substantial Lessening of Competition" Test', pp 959–968.

[109] See ch 22, 'Public interest cases', pp 987–989.

[110] South African Competition Act 1998, s 2(f).

[111] See further ch 2 'The single market imperative', pp 52–53; see also Ehlermann 'The Contribution of EC Competition Policy to the Single Market' (1992) 29 CML Rev 257; the Commission's XXIXth *Report on Competition Policy* (1999), point 3.

[112] 'The values of competition policy', speech of 13 October 2015, available at www.ec.europa.eu.

[113] On the importance of market integration see the Commission's *Guidelines on Vertical Restraints* OJ [2010] C 130/1, para 7; Monti *A New Strategy for the Single Market: At the Service of Europe's Economy and Society* (2010), both available at www.ec.europa.eu.

[114] See ch 7, 'Chapter VI: penalties', pp 285–293 on the powers of the European Commission to impose fines for infringements of Articles 101 and 102.

action to prevent exports of game consoles and related products from the UK to the Netherlands and Germany[115]. The Commission's sector inquiry on e-commerce was very much motivated by single market considerations and is part of the broader digital single market initiative[116].

The positive role is that competition law can be moulded in such a way as to encourage trade between Member States, partly by 'levelling the playing fields of Europe' as one contemporary catchphrase puts it, and partly by facilitating cross-border transactions and integration. Horizontal collaboration between firms in different Member States may be permitted in some circumstances[117]; and a producer in one Member State can be permitted to appoint an exclusive distributor in another and so penetrate a market which individually it could not have done[118]. EU competition law has been (and will continue to be) strongly influenced by single market integration; this has meant that decisions have sometimes been taken prohibiting behaviour which a competition authority elsewhere, unconcerned with single market considerations, would not have reached. Faced with a conflict between the narrow interests of a particular firm and the wider aim of integrating national markets, the tendency has been to subordinate the former to the latter.

(B) Competition advocacy and public restrictions of competition

A final point about the function of competition law is that competition authorities can usefully be given a different task, which is to scrutinise legislation that will bring about, or is responsible for, a distortion of competition in the economy. The reality is that states and international regulatory authorities are capable of harming the competitive process at least as seriously as private economic operators on the market itself, for example by granting legal monopolies to undertakings, by limiting in other ways the number of competitors in the market or by establishing unduly restrictive rules and regulations. Some competition authorities are specifically mandated to scrutinise legislation that will distort competition[119]. Competition advocacy has a valuable role to play in all types of economies. In the UK the CMA, acting under section 7 of the Enterprise Act 2002, can bring to the attention of Ministers laws or proposed laws that could be harmful to competition[120]. The Organisation for Economic Co-operation and Development ('the OECD') has published a recommendation on 'competition assessment', that is to say, how competition authorities should assess the competitive effects of state measures[121]. A significant part of the work of the ICN is devoted to competition advocacy[122].

[115] OJ [2003] L 255/33; on appeal to the General Court the fine imposed on Nintendo was reduced to €119 million: Case T-13/03 *Nintendo v Commission* EU:T:2009:131.

[116] See the Final report on the E-commerce Sector Inquiry, COM(2017) 229 final, 10 May 2017 and the Commission's mid-term review of its digital single market strategy, both available at www.ec.europa.eu.

[117] See generally ch 15. [118] See generally ch 16.

[119] See eg s 21(1)(k) of the South African Competition Act 1998, which requires the Competition Commission to 'review legislation and public regulations and report to the Minister concerning any provision that permits uncompetitive behaviour'; and s 49(1) of the Indian Competition Act 2002 which provides that the Competition Commission of India can review legislation, but only if a reference is made to it by either the central or the state governments.

[120] See ch 2, 'Functions of the CMA', pp 67–69.

[121] See the OECD *Recommendation on competition assessment*, October 2009, available at www.oecd.org/competition and ICN *Recommended Practices on Competition Assessment*, April 2014.

[122] The mission statement of the ICN Advocacy Working Group and its work product can be accessed at www.internationalcompetitionnetwork.org.

5. Market Definition and Market Power

Before embarking upon a study of the substantive provisions of the law, it is helpful to discuss the issues of market definition and market power, since these ideas crop up regularly in the text that follows. As noted earlier in this chapter, competition law is concerned, above all, with the problems that occur where one or more firms possess, or will possess after a merger, market power. For example the legal concept of 'a dominant position' in Article 102, as it is currently understood and applied, equates to the economic concept of 'substantial market power'[123]. Market power presents undertakings with the possibility of profitably raising prices, or keeping them high, over a period of time; the expression 'raising price' here includes, and is a shorthand for, other ways in which competition can be restricted, for example by limiting output or capacity, suppressing innovation, reducing the variety or quality of goods or services or by depriving consumers of choice, all of which are clearly inimical to consumer welfare[124]. In a perfectly competitive market no firm has market power; in a pure monopoly one firm has absolute control over consumers. There is a continuum between these two extremes, and many degrees of market power lie along it.

It is the issue of market power that lies at the heart of competition law and policy. A variety of legal tests and expressions will be found in EU and UK competition law, but in essence they all express a concern about the misuse of market power:

- firms should not enter into agreements that have the effect of restricting competition (Article 101 TFEU; Chapter I prohibition, Competition Act 1998): however any such restriction must be appreciable, and there is a '*de minimis*' exception where an agreement does not have as its object the restriction of competition and the parties to the agreement lack market power[125]
- block exemption is not available to parties to agreements where the parties' market share exceeds a certain threshold[126]
- firms should not abuse a dominant position (Article 102 TFEU; Chapter II prohibition, Competition Act 1998)
- 'concentrations' can be prohibited under the EUMR that would significantly impede effective competition
- mergers can be prohibited under UK law that would substantially lessen competition (Part 3 of the Enterprise Act 2002)
- 'market investigations' can be conducted by the CMA where features of a market could have an adverse effect on competition (Part 4 of the Enterprise Act 2002)
- other variants can be found: for example in certain electronic communications markets regulatory obligations can be imposed upon firms that have 'significant market power', which has the same meaning for this purpose as 'dominance' under Article 102[127].

Each of these provisions reflects a concern about the abuse or potential abuse of market power. For example dominant firms may be able to harm consumer welfare because their

[123] See eg *Guidance on the Commission's Enforcement Priorities in Applying Article [102 TFEU] to Abusive Exclusionary Conduct by Dominant Undertakings* OJ [2009] C 45/7, para 10.

[124] See Landes and Posner 'Market Power in Antitrust Cases' (1981) 94 Harvard Law Review 937; Vickers 'Market Power in Competition Cases' (2006) 2 European Competition Journal 3; Blanco *Market Power in EU Antitrust* (Hart, 2011).

[125] See eg ch 3, 'The *De Minimis* Doctrine', pp 147–150.

[126] See eg ch 4 'Block exemptions', pp 176–179.

[127] See ch 23, 'Legislation', pp 1011–1013.

market power enables them to restrict output and to raise prices, or to exclude firms from entering the market or make it difficult for existing ones to stay in it. The concern about certain mergers is that, once the merger has taken place, the merged firm will be able to exercise greater market power than existed prior to the merger.

EU and UK competition law adopt a two-stage procedure when determining whether a firm or firms have or would have market power. First, the relevant market is defined in relation to which market power may exist: this requires a definition of both the relevant product and the relevant geographical market. The second stage is to determine whether a firm or firms have market power in the relevant markets. Although market definition is a common feature of competition law analysis[128], it is important to understand that it is only a means to an end: the crucial question is whether a firm or firms have market power.

(A) **Market definition**

If the notion of 'power over the market' is key to analysing many competition issues, it becomes immediately obvious that it is necessary to understand what is meant by 'the market' or, as will be explained below, the 'relevant market' for this purpose. The concept is an economic one, and in many cases it may be necessary for lawyers to engage the services of economists to assist in the proper delineation of the market, as highly sophisticated economic and econometric analysis is sometimes called for.

In the last 25 years the 'science' of market definition has evolved considerably. There are numerous sources of information on how to define markets. A useful document is the ICN's *Recommended Practices for Merger Analysis*, Part II of which discusses market definition issues[129]. One particular comment in the *Recommended Practices* is worth stressing: defining a market with mathematical precision is rarely possible, since the boundaries of relevant markets may not be precise. Some products may be 'in the market' while others may be 'out of the market'; however products that are in the market are not necessarily a perfect substitute for one another and products that lie outside the market can still provide a competitive constraint, and should not be excluded from competition analysis simply because of the market definition[130]. In practice firms may face a series of competitive constraints both from within and outside the relevant market, and it is essential not to lose sight of this important fact. Of particular importance in the EU is the European Commission's *Notice on the Definition of the Relevant Market for the Purposes of [EU] Competition Law*[131], ('*Notice on Market Definition*' or '*Notice*') which adopts the so-called 'hypothetical monopolist' test (also known as the 'SSNIP test') for defining markets. This *Notice* provides a conceptual framework within which to think of market definition, and then explains some of the techniques that may be deployed when defining markets. The *Notice* attempts to capture the Commission's experience of market definition over many

[128] One alternative to market definition that has been proposed is the so-called 'UPP test', which examines the 'upward pricing pressure' due to a merger between firms selling differentiated products: see Farrell and Shapiro 'Antitrust Evaluation of Horizontal Mergers: An Economic Alternative to Market Definition' (2010) 10 The BE Journal of Theoretical Economics Art 9.

[129] Available at www.internationalcompetitionnetwork.org; see also Swedish Competition Authority, *The Pros and Cons of Market Definition* (November 2017), available at www.konkurrensverket.se.

[130] See eg *Servier*, Commission decision of 9 July 2014, para 2417, on appeal Case T-691/14 *Servier v Commission*, not yet decided.

[131] OJ [1997] C 372/5; more specific guidance on market definition can be found in the Commission's *Guidelines on Vertical Restraints* OJ [2010] C 130/1, paras 86–95; *Guidelines on the applicability of Article 101 TFEU to horizontal co-operation agreements* OJ [2011] C 11/1, paras 112–126, 155–156, 197–199, 229 and 261–262; and *Guidelines on the application of Article 101 TFEU to technology transfer agreements* OJ [2014] C 89/3, paras 19–26.

years, and adopts a similar approach to that taken by the antitrust authorities in the US in the analysis of horizontal mergers[132]; the CMA in the UK has adopted a guideline which adopts the same approach to that of the Commission[133]. Other competition authorities also apply the hypothetical monopolist test[134].

Paragraph 2 of the Commission's *Notice* explains why market definition is important:

> Market definition is a tool to identify and define the boundaries of competition between firms. It serves to establish the framework within which competition policy is applied by the Commission. The main purpose of market definition is to identify in a systematic way the competitive constraints that the undertakings involved face. The objective of defining a market in both its product and geographic dimension is to identify those actual competitors of the undertakings involved that are capable of constraining those undertakings' behaviour and of preventing them from behaving independently of effective competitive pressure.

This paragraph contains a number of important points. First, market definition is an analytical tool that assists in determining the competitive constraints upon undertakings: market definition provides a framework within which to assess the critical question of whether a firm or firms possess market power. Secondly, both the product and geographic dimensions of markets must be analysed. Thirdly, market definition enables the competitive constraints only from *actual* competitors to be identified: it tells us nothing about *potential* competitors. However, as paragraph 13 of the *Notice* points out, there are three main sources of competitive constraint upon undertakings:

- **demand substitutability**
- **supply substitutability**
- **potential competition.**

As will be explained later, **demand substitutability** is the essence of market definition. In some, albeit fairly narrow, circumstances **supply substitutability** may also be part of the market definition; however normally supply substitutability lies outside market definition and is an issue of **potential competition**. It is also necessary, when assessing a supplier's market power, to take into account any **countervailing power** on the buyer's side of the market. It is very important to understand that factors such as potential entry and buyer power are relevant, since this means that a particular share of a market cannot, in itself, indicate that a firm has market power; an undertaking with 100% of the widget market may not have market power if there are numerous potential competitors and no barriers to entry into the market. People must not be seduced by numbers when determining whether a firm has market power; market shares, of course, are helpful; indeed there are circumstances in which they are very important: a market share of 50% or more creates a rebuttable presumption of dominance in a case under Article 102[135], and a market share of 30% or more will prevent the application of the block exemption in Regulation 330/2010 on vertical agreements[136]. However, calculating an undertaking's market share is only one step in determining whether it has market power.

[132] See section 4 of the US Department of Justice and Federal Trade Commission *Horizontal Merger Guidelines* (2010), available at www.justice.gov/atr.

[133] See *Market Definition*, OFT 403, December 2004, available at www.gov.uk/cma.

[134] See eg the *Merger Guidelines of the Australian Competition and Consumer Commission*, available at www.accc.gov.au; the *Mergers and Acquisitions Guidelines of the New Zealand Commerce Commission*, available at www.comcom.govt.nz; and the *Merger Enforcement Guidelines of the Canadian Competition Bureau*, available at www.competitionbureau.gc.ca.

[135] See ch 5, 'The *AKZO* presumption of dominance where an undertaking has a market share of 50% or more', p 190.

[136] See ch 16, 'Article 3: the market share cap', pp 674–677.

(B) Circumstances in which it is necessary to define the relevant market

The foregoing discussion may be rendered less abstract by considering the circumstances in EU and UK competition law in which it may be necessary to define the relevant market.

(i) EU competition law

- Under Article 101(1), when considering whether an agreement has the appreciable effect of restricting competition[137]
- under Article 101(1), when considering whether an agreement has an appreciable effect on trade between Member States[138]
- under Article 101(3)(b), when considering whether an agreement would substantially eliminate competition[139]
- under numerous block exemptions containing market share tests, for example Regulation 330/2010 on vertical agreements[140], Regulation 1217/2010 on research and development agreements[141] and Regulation 1218/2010 on specialisation agreements[142]
- under Article 102, when considering whether an undertaking has a dominant position[143]
- under the EUMR when determining whether a merger would significantly impede effective competition[144].

(ii) UK law

- Under the Chapter I prohibition, when considering whether an agreement has the appreciable effect of restricting competition[145]
- under the Chapter II prohibition, when considering whether an undertaking has a dominant position[146]
- when determining the level of a penalty under the Competition Act 1998[147]
- when scrutinising mergers under Part 3 of the Enterprise Act 2002[148]
- when conducting 'market investigations' under Part 4 of the Enterprise Act 2002[149].

Market definition, therefore, plays an important part in much competition law analysis. Table 1.1 at the end of this chapter captures some of the important market share thresholds that may be relevant in competition law cases.

(C) The relevant product market

The Court of Justice, when it heard its first appeal on the application of Article 102 in *Europemballage Corpn and Continental Can Co Inc v Commission*[150], held that when

[137] See eg Case C-234/89 *Delimitis v Henninger Bräu* EU:C:1991:91, para 16; para 27 of the Commission's *Guidelines on the application of Article [101(3)]* OJ [2004] C 101/97.

[138] OJ [2004] C 101/97, para 55.

[139] See ch 4, 'Fourth condition of Article 101(3): no elimination of competition in a substantial part of the market', pp 172–173.

[140] See ch 16, 'Article 3: the market share cap', pp 674–677.

[141] See ch 15, 'Article 4: duration of exemption and the market share threshold and duration of exemption', pp 609–610.

[142] See ch 15, 'Article 3: the market share threshold', p 614.

[143] See ch 5, 'Dominant Position', pp 187–196.

[144] See ch 21, 'Market definition', pp 887–889.

[145] See ch 9, 'Restriction of competition by effect', pp 357–359.

[146] See ch 9, 'Assessing dominance', pp 380–384.

[147] *Guidance as to the Appropriate Amount of a Penalty*, OFT 423, September 2012, para 2.7.

[148] See ch 22, 'Market definition', pp 961–962.

[149] See ch 11, 'The Market Investigation Provisions on Practice', pp 488–493.

[150] Case 6/72 EU:C:1973:22, para 32.

identifying a dominant position the delimitation of the relevant product market was of crucial importance. This has been repeated by the EU Courts on numerous occasions[151]. In *Continental Can Co Inc*[152] it was the Commission's failure to define the relevant product market that caused the Court of Justice to quash its decision. The Commission had held that Continental Can and its subsidiary SLW had a dominant position in three different product markets—cans for meat, cans for fish and metal tops—without giving a satisfactory explanation of why these markets were separate from one another or from the market for cans and containers generally. The Court of Justice insisted that the Commission should define the relevant product market and support its definition in a reasoned decision.

(i) **The legal test**

The judgments of the Court of Justice show that the definition of the market is essentially a matter of interchangeability. Where goods or services can be regarded as interchangeable, they are within the same product market. In *Continental Can* the Court of Justice enjoined the Commission, for the purpose of delimiting the market, to investigate:

> [those] characteristics of the products in question by virtue of which they are particularly apt to satisfy an inelastic need and are only to a limited extent interchangeable with other products[153].

Similarly in *United Brands v Commission*, where the applicant was arguing that bananas were in the same market as other fresh fruit, the Court of Justice said that this depended on whether the banana could be:

> singled out by such special features distinguishing it from other fruits that it is only to a limited extent interchangeable with them and is only exposed to their competition in a way that is hardly perceptible[154].

(ii) **Measuring interchangeability**

Conceptually, the idea that a relevant market consists of goods or services that are interchangeable with one another is simple enough. In practice, however, the measurement of interchangeability can give rise to considerable problems for a variety of reasons: for example there may be no data available on the issue, or the data that exist may be unreliable, incomplete or deficient in some other way. A further problem is that, in many cases, the data will be open to (at least) two interpretations. It is often the case therefore that market definition is extremely difficult; this is why the EU Courts have recognised that the Commission has a 'margin of assessment' in economic matters such as market definition. However, it is the task of the EU Courts to determine whether the evidence put forward by the Commission is factually accurate and capable of substantiating the Commission's conclusions[155].

(iii) **Commission's *Notice on the Definition of the Relevant Market for the Purposes of [EU] Competition Law***

Useful guidance on market definition is provided by the Commission's *Notice on Market Definition*[156]; the *Notice* has received the approval of the EU Courts[157]. The introduction

[151] See eg Case 322/81 *Nederlandsche Banden-Industrie-Michelin v Commission* EU:C:1983:313, para 37 and Case T-321/05 *AstraZeneca AB v Commission* EU:T:2010:266, paras 30–31.

[152] JO [1972] L 7/25.

[153] Case 6/72 EU:C:1973:22, para 32; for a definition of inelastic demand see ch 1 n 24 earlier.

[154] Case 27/76 *United Brands v Commission* EU:C:1978:22, para 22.

[155] See eg Case T-201/04 *Microsoft Corpn v Commission* EU:T:2007:289, paras 87–89 and Case T-321/05 *AstraZeneca AB v Commission* EU:T:2010:266, para 32.

[156] OJ [1997] C 372/5.

[157] See eg Case T-321/05 *AstraZeneca AB v Commission* EU:T:2010:266, para 86; Case T-427/08 *Confédération européenne des associations d'horlogers-réparateurs (CEAHR) v Commission* EU:T:2010:517, paras 68–70.

of the EUMR in 1990 had, as an inevitable consequence, that the Commission was called upon to define markets in a far larger number of situations than previously. Whereas it may have had to deal with complaints under Article 102, say, 20 times a year in the 1980s, by the 1990s it was having to deal with 100 or more notifications under the EUMR each year, and it now receives at least 300 notifications a year[158]. Furthermore, an Article 102 case would often require the definition of just one market—the one in which the dominant firm was alleged to have abused its position; or perhaps two, for example where the abuse produces effects in a neighbouring market[159]. However a case under the EUMR might be quite different, since the merging parties might conduct business in a number of different markets and the impact of the merger will need to be assessed in each of these markets[160]. This necessarily meant that the Commission was called upon to develop more systematic methods for defining the market.

(iv) **Demand-side substitutability**

As mentioned above, the Commission explains at paragraph 13 of the *Notice* that firms are subject to three main competitive constraints: demand substitutability, supply substitutability and potential competition. It continues that, for the purpose of market definition, it is demand substitutability that is of the greatest significance; supply substitutability may be relevant to market definition in certain special circumstances, but normally this is a matter to be examined when determining whether there is market power; potential competition in the market is always a matter of market power rather than market definition.

Paragraph 14 of the *Notice* states that the assessment of demand substitution entails a determination of the range of products which are viewed as substitutes by the consumer. It proposes a test whereby it becomes possible to determine whether particular products are within the same market. The SSNIP test works as follows: suppose that a producer of a product—for example a widget—were to introduce a **S**mall but **S**ignificant **N**on-transitory **I**ncrease in **P**rice. In those circumstances, would enough customers be inclined to switch their purchases to other producers of widgets, or indeed even to blodgets, to make the price rise unprofitable? If the answer is yes, this would suggest that the market is at least as wide as widgets generally and includes blodgets as well[161]. The same test can be applied to the delineation of the geographic market, which is discussed later. If a firm could raise its price by a significant amount and retain its customers, this would mean that the market would be worth monopolising: prices could be raised profitably, since there would be no competitive constraint. For this reason, the SSNIP test is also referred to sometimes as the 'hypothetical monopolist test'. The hypothetical monopolist test is given formal expression in paragraph 17 of the Commission's *Notice*, where it states that:

> The question to be asked is whether the parties' customers would switch to readily available substitutes or to suppliers located elsewhere in response to a hypothetical small (in the range 5 per cent to 10 per cent) but permanent relative price increase in the products and areas being considered. If substitution were enough to make the price increase unprofitable because of the resulting loss of sales, additional substitutes and areas are included in the relevant market.

[158] See www.ec.europa.eu/comm/competition/mergers/statistics.pdf.

[159] See ch 5, 'The dominant position, the abuse and the effects of the abuse may be in different markets', pp 211–213.

[160] Case M 2547 *Bayer Crop Science/Aventis* concerned a merger in which there were no fewer than 130 affected markets.

[161] It should be noted in passing that the possibility exists that consumers might switch from widgets to blodgets, but not the other way: in other words a phenomenon exists of 'one-way substitutability': see Case T-340/03 *France Télécom v Commission* EU:T:2007:22, paras 88–90.

This formulation of the test takes the 'range' of 5% to 10% to indicate 'significance' within the SSNIP test[162].

(v) The 'Cellophane Fallacy'

It is necessary to enter a word of caution on the hypothetical monopolist test when applied to abuse of dominance cases[163]. A monopolist may already be charging a monopoly price: if it were to raise its price further, its customers may cease to buy from it or switch to alternative products. In this situation the monopolist's 'own-price elasticity'—the extent to which consumers switch from its products in response to a price rise—is high. If a SSNIP test is applied in these circumstances between the monopolised product and another one, this might suggest a high degree of substitutability, since consumers are already at the point where they will cease to buy from the monopolist; the test therefore would exaggerate the breadth of the market by the inclusion of false substitutes. This error was committed by the US Supreme Court in *United States v EI du Pont de Nemours and Co*[164] in a case concerning packaging materials, including cellophane, since when it has been known as the 'Cellophane Fallacy'[165].

In the US the SSNIP test was devised in the context of merger cases[166], and is usually applied only in relation to them. In the European Commission's *Notice*, it states in the first paragraph that the test is to be used for cases under Articles 101, 102 and the EUMR; the Cellophane Fallacy is briefly acknowledged at paragraph 19 of the *Notice*, where it says that in cases under Article 102 'the fact that the prevailing price might already have been substantially increased will be taken into account'[167]. DG COMP's *Discussion Paper on the application of [Article 102 TFEU] to exclusionary abuses*[168] discussed the Cellophane Fallacy in greater detail and acknowledged the need to take particular care, and to resort to other tests than the SSNIP test, when dealing with market definition in Article 102 cases. The Commission's *Guidance on the Commission's Enforcement Priorities in Applying Article [102 TFEU] to Abusive Exclusionary Conduct by Dominant Undertakings*[169] is silent on the issue of the Cellophane Fallacy. A helpful discussion of the Cellophane Fallacy, its implications and ways to deal with the problem will be found in an OECD Roundtable on *Market Definition*[170].

In the UK the Guideline on *Market Definition* notes the problem of the Cellophane Fallacy, and states that the possibility that market conditions are distorted by the presence of market power will be accounted for 'when all the evidence on market definition is weighed in the round'[171]. The decisions of the former Office of Fair Trading ('the OFT')

162 In the UK the CMA has said that it will usually postulate a price rise of 5% when applying the hypothetical monopolist test in merger cases: see *Merger Assessment Guidelines*, September 2010, para 5.2.12, available at www.gov.uk/cma.

163 For discussion see Glick, Cameron and Mangum 'Importing the Merger Guidelines Market Test in Section 2 Cases: Potential Benefits and Limitations' (1997) 42 Antitrust Bulletin 121 and Werden 'Market Delineation under the Merger Guidelines: Monopoly Cases and Alternative Approaches' (2000) 16 Review of Industrial Organisation 211.

164 351 US 377 (1956).

165 See Stocking and Mueller 'The Cellophane Case and the New Competition' (1955) 45(1) Am Ec Rev 29.

166 See section 4 of the *Horizontal Merger Guidelines* (2010), available at www.justice.gov/atr.

167 It has been suggested that the Cellophane Fallacy can also occur in merger cases: see Church and Ware *Industrial Organisation: A Strategic Approach* (McGraw-Hill, 2000), section 19.4.1.

168 December 2005, section 3, available at www.ec.europa.eu.

169 OJ [2009] C 45/7.

170 See OECD Roundtable *Market Definition*, June 2012, available at www.oecd.org/competition.

171 *Market Definition*, OFT 403, December 2004, paras 5.4–5.6; see also OFT Economic Discussion Paper 2 (OFT 342) *The Role of Market Definition in Monopoly and Dominance Inquiries*, National Economic Research Associates, July 2001, available at www.nationalarchives.gov.uk.

in *Aberdeen Journals II*[172] and *BSkyB*[173] and of the CMA in *Phenytoin*[174] all acknowledged a possible Cellophane Fallacy in defining the relevant markets in circumstances where a firm may have already exercised market power. In *BSkyB* the OFT looked at the physical characteristics of premium sports pay-TV channels and consumers' underlying preferences. The concern in *Aberdeen Journals II* was that a 'reverse Cellophane Fallacy'[175] might occur if a SSNIP is applied to an unreasonably low (for example a predatory) price; the test would therefore define the market too narrowly. The OFT looked at the conduct and statements of the allegedly dominant firm to address that concern and corroborate its market definition. On appeal the Competition Appeal Tribunal ('the CAT') stated that, in a case concerning an alleged abuse of a dominant position, the market to be taken into consideration means the market that would exist in normal competitive conditions, disregarding any distortive effects that the conduct of the dominant firm has itself created[176]. In *Phenytoin*[177] the CMA decided that the supra-competitive prices charged by Pfizer and Flynn for an anti-epilepsy drug did not lead to the Cellophane Fallacy because clinical advice meant that pharmacists would not generally switch drugs regardless of the price. It is clear, therefore, that the SSNIP test requires the hypothetical price rise to be applied to the competitive price[178].

The CAT rejected arguments that the Cellophane Fallacy had been perpetrated in both *National Grid plc v Gas and Electricity Markets Authority*[179] and *Barclays Bank v Competition Commission*[180].

(vi) **Supply-side substitutability**

In most cases interchangeability will be determined by examining the market from the customer's perspective. However it is helpful in some situations to consider the degree of substitutability on the supply side of the market. Suppose that A is a producer of widgets and that B is a producer of blodgets: if it is a very simple matter for B to change its production process and to produce widgets, this might suggest that widgets and blodgets are part of the same market, even though consumers on the demand side of the market might not regard widgets and blodgets as substitutable. The judgment of the Court of Justice in *Continental Can v Commission*[181] indicates that the supply side of the market should be considered for the purpose of defining the market. Among its criticisms of the decision the Court of Justice said that the Commission should have made clear why it considered that producers of other types of containers would not be able to adapt their production to compete with Continental Can. The Commission has specifically addressed the issue of supply-side substitutability in subsequent decisions[182]. A good example is *Tetra Pak I*

[172] *Aberdeen Journals (remitted case)*, OFT decision of 25 September 2002, paras 94–99, available at www.gov.uk/cma.

[173] *BSkyB investigation*, OFT decision of 30 January 2003, paras 88–97, available at www.gov.uk/cma.

[174] CMA decision of 7 December 2016, para 4.34, on appeal Case 1275/1/12/17 *Flynn Pharma v CMA* and Case 1276/1/12/17 *Pfizer v CMA*, not yet decided.

[175] For discussion of this problem see Aron and Burnstein 'Regulatory Policy and the Reverse Cellophane Fallacy' (2010) 6 Journal of Competition Law and Economics 973.

[176] Case 1009/1/1/02 *Aberdeen Journals Ltd v OFT* [2003] CAT 11, para 276; the CAT also noted the relevance of the Cellophane Fallacy in Cases 1251/1/12/16 etc *GlaxoSmithKline plc v CMA* [2018] CAT 4, para 384.

[177] CMA decision of 7 December 2016, section 4, available at www.gov.uk/cma.

[178] A 'hypothetical competitive price' was used in *Australian Competition and Consumer Commission v Cement Australia Pty Ltd* [2013] FCA 909, paras 1792–1818.

[179] Case 1099/1/2/08 [2009] CAT 14, paras 41–43.

[180] Case 1109/6/8/09 [2009] CAT 27, paras 53–55.

[181] Case 6/72 EU:C:1973:22, paras 32ff.

[182] See eg *Eurofix-Bauco v Hilti* OJ [1988] L 65/19, para 55, upheld on appeal to the General Court Case T-30/89 *Hilti AG v Commission* EU:T:1991:70 and on further appeal to the Court of Justice Case C-53/92 P EU:C:1994:77; see also *Clearstream*, decision of 2 June 2004, para 200, upheld on appeal to the General Court Case T-301/04 *Clearstream AG v Commission* EU:T:2009:317, paras 58–60.

(BTG Licence)[183], where it took into account the fact that producers of milk-packaging machines could not readily adapt their production to make aseptic packaging machines and cartons in arriving at its market definition.

In paragraphs 20 to 23 of the *Notice on Market Definition* the Commission explains the circumstances in which it considers that supply-side substitutability is relevant to market definition. At paragraph 20 the Commission says that where suppliers are able to switch production to other products and to market them 'in the short term' without incurring significant additional costs or risks in response to small and permanent changes in relative prices, then the market may be broadened to include the products that those suppliers are already producing. A footnote to paragraph 20 suggests that the short term means 'such a period that does not entail a significant adjustment of existing tangible and intangible assets'. A practical example is given in paragraph 22 of an undertaking producing a particular grade of paper: if it could change easily to producing other grades of paper, they should all be included in the market definition. However, where supply substitution is more complex than this, it should be regarded as a matter of determining market power rather than establishing the market[184].

While it may seem unimportant whether the issue of supply-side substitution is dealt with at the stage of market definition or of market power, where competition law deploys a market share test, as for example in Article 3 of Regulation 330/2010[185], the possibility of broadening the market definition through the inclusion of supply-side substitutes may have a decisive effect on the outcome of a particular case.

(vii) **Evidence relied on to define relevant markets**

The SSNIP test establishes a conceptual framework within which markets should be defined. In practice, however, the critical issue is to know what evidence can be adduced to determine the scope of the relevant market. If the world were composed of an infinite number of market research organisations devoted to asking SSNIP-like questions of customers and consumers, market definition would be truly scientific. But of course the world is not so composed, and a variety of techniques, some of considerable sophistication, are deployed by economists and econometricians in order to seek solutions. Chapter 3 of the ICN's *Investigative Techniques Handbook for Merger Review* provides helpful guidance on what might be reliable evidence for market definition in merger cases[186].

The Commission's *Notice*, from paragraph 25 onwards[187], considers some of the evidence that may be available, but it quite correctly says that tests that may be suitable in one industry may be wholly inappropriate in another. A moment's reflection shows that this must be so: for example, the demand-substitutability of one alcoholic beverage for another in the ordinary citizen's mind is likely to be tested by different criteria than an airline choosing whether to purchase aeroplanes from Boeing or Airbus. In *Aberdeen Journals v OFT*[188] the CAT said that there is no 'hierarchy' of evidence on issues such as

[183] OJ [1988] L 272/27, upheld on appeal to the General Court Case T-51/89 *Tetra Pak Rausing SA v Commission* EU:T:1990:41.

[184] Recommended Practice F of the ICN's *Recommended Practices for Merger Analysis* recommends that supply-side substitution should be taken into account when firms could produce or sell in the relevant market 'within a short time frame and without incurring significant sunk costs', available at www.internationalcompetitionnetwork.org.

[185] OJ [2010] L 102/1; on market definition under this block exemption see the Commission's *Guidelines on Vertical Restraints* OJ [2010] C 130/1, Section V, paras 86–92.

[186] Available at www.internationalcompetitionnetwork.org.

[187] See also *Bishop and Walker*, chs 9–14 and 16, which considers techniques that may be relevant to market definition.

[188] Case 1009/1/1/02 [2003] CAT 11.

market definition that would require, for example, 'objective' economic evidence to be given greater weight than 'subjective' evidence such as the statements or conduct of the parties[189]. Both DG COMP[190] and the UK CMA[191] have issued best practices on how economic evidence should be submitted.

(viii) **Examples of evidence that may be used in defining the relevant product market**

As far as definition of the product market is concerned the *Notice* suggests that the following evidence may be available.

(a) Evidence of substitution in the recent past

There may recently have been an event—such as a price increase or a 'shock', perhaps a failure of the Brazilian coffee crop due to a late frost—giving rise to direct evidence of the consequences that this had for consumers' consumption (perhaps a large increase in the drinking of tea).

(b) Quantitative tests

Various econometric and statistical tests have been devised which attempt to estimate own-price elasticities and cross-price elasticities for the demand of a product, based on the similarity of price movements over time, the causality between price series and the similarity of price levels and/or their convergence. Own-price elasticities measure the extent to which demand for a product changes in response to a change in its price. Cross-price elasticities measure the extent to which demand for a product changes in response to a change in the price of some other product. Own-price elasticities provide more information about the market power that an undertaking possesses than cross-price elasticities; however cross-price elasticities help more with market definition, since they provide evidence on substitutability. The Commission uses quantitative economic techniques to help it to define the relevant market in some merger cases[192].

(c) Views of customers and competitors

The Commission will contact customers and competitors in a case that involves market definition and will, where appropriate, specifically ask them to answer the SSNIP question. This happens routinely, for example, when it seeks to delineate markets under the EUMR although it should be understood that customers may not fully understand the nature of the SSNIP question, or may give answers according to their interest in a particular case. For this reason, SSNIP analysis should, ideally, be conducted on the basis of actual data rather than stated preferences.

(d) Marketing studies and consumer surveys

The Commission will look at marketing studies as a useful provider of information about the market, although it specifically states in paragraph 41 of the *Notice* that it will scrutinise 'with utmost care' the methodology followed in consumer surveys carried out *ad hoc* by the undertakings involved in merger cases or cases under Articles 101 and 102. Its

[189] Ibid, para 127; see similarly Case T-175/12 *Deutsche Börse AG v Commission* EU:T:2015:148, para 133.

[190] Staff Working Paper *Best Practices for the Submission of Economic Evidence and Data Collection in Cases Concerning the Application of Articles 101 and 102 TFEU and in Merger Cases*, 2010, available at www.ec.europa.eu/competition/antitrust/legislation/legislation.html.

[191] *Suggested Best Practice for the Submission of Technical Economic Analysis from Parties to the Competition Commission*, available at www.gov.uk/cma.

[192] See ch 21, 'Quantitative tests', p 889.

concern is that the selection of questions in the survey may be deliberately made in order to achieve a favourable outcome[193].

(e) Barriers and costs associated with switching demand to potential substitutes

There may be a number of barriers and/or switching costs that result in two apparent demand substitutes not belonging to one single product market[194]. The Commission deals with these in paragraph 42 of the *Notice*, and gives as examples regulatory barriers, other forms of state intervention, constraints occurring in downstream markets, the need to incur capital investment and other factors.

(f) Different categories of customers and price discrimination

At paragraph 43 the Commission states that the extent of the product market might be narrowed where there exist distinct groups of customers for a particular product: the market for one group may be narrower than for the other, if it is possible to identify which group an individual belongs to at the moment of selling the relevant products and there is no possibility of trade between the two categories of customer[195].

(ix) A word of caution on the *Notice*

It is important to point out a few words of caution about the *Notice on Market Definition*. The problem of the Cellophane Fallacy has already been mentioned[196]. There are three other points about the *Notice*.

First, it is 'only' a Commission Notice: it does not have the force of law, and ought not to be treated as a legislative instrument. However the EU Courts have referred to it on various occasions with approval[197].

A second point about the *Notice* is that, no matter how well it explains the SSNIP test and the evidence that may be used when applying it, the fact remains that in some sectors actual price data about substitutability may not be available: the information that can be captured varies hugely from one sector to another, and in some cases one will be thrown back on fairly subjective assessments of the market for want of hard, scientific evidence. In this situation it may be necessary to predict the likely effect of a SSNIP on customers by looking at various factors such as the physical characteristics of the products concerned or their intended use. In some cases it may not be possible to apply the SSNIP test at all[198]. An example is the Commission's decision in *British Interactive Broadcasting*[199]: there the Commission stated that it could not delineate the markets for interactive broadcasting services by applying a SSNIP test since no data were available in relation to a product that had yet to be launched. In several broadcasting cases the fact that public-sector broadcasting is available 'free-to-air' to end users meant that a SSNIP test was inapplicable[200]. Clearly this is always likely to be a problem in relation to products introduced into the 'new' economy[201].

[193] In the UK see *Good Practice in the Design and Presentation of Consumer Survey Evidence in Merger Inquiries*, March 2011, and CMA retail mergers commentary, CMA62, April 2017, which discusses the use of surveys, both available at www.gov.uk/cma.

[194] See also *Switching Costs*, OFT 655, April 2003, available at www.nationalarchives.gov.uk.

[195] See also *Market Definition*, OFT 403, December 2004, paras 3.8–3.10; Hausman, Leonard and Vellturo 'Market Definition Under Price Discrimination' (1996) 64 Antitrust LJ 367.

[196] See 'The "Cellophane Fallacy"', pp 31–32 earlier in chapter.

[197] See ch 1 n 157 earlier.

[198] See Case T-699/14 *Topps Europe Ltd v Commission* EU:T:2017:2, para 82.

[199] OJ [1999] L 312/1.

[200] See eg Case M 553 *RTL/Veronica/Endemol* OJ [1996] L 134/32, upheld on appeal to the General Court Case T-221/95 *Endemol Entertainment Holding BV v Commission* EU:T:1999:85.

[201] On the issue of market definition in cases involving e-commerce see OFT Economic Discussion Paper 1 (OFT 308) *E-commerce and its implications for competition policy* (Frontier Economics Group, August 2000), ch 4.

A third point about the *Notice* is that there are by now very many cases—in particular under the EUMR—in which the Commission has been called upon to define the market. With more than 6,000 mergers having been notified to the Commission under the EUMR by the end of 2017, there are few sectors in which it has not been called upon to analyse relevant markets. As a consequence of this there is a very considerable 'decisional practice' of the Commission in which it has opined—from cars, buses and trucks to pharmaceuticals and agrochemicals, from banking and insurance services to international aviation and deep-sea drilling[202]. Not unnaturally, an undertaking in need of guidance on the Commission's likely response to a matter of market definition will wish to find out what it has had to say in the past in actual decisions; however the caveat should be entered that the General Court has established that the relevant market must always be defined in any particular case by reference to the facts prevailing at the time and not by reference to precedents[203].

(x) Spare parts and the aftermarket

There are numerous sectors in which a consumer of one product—for example a car—will need to purchase at a later date complementary products such as spare parts. The same can be true where a customer has to buy 'consumables', such as cartridges to be used in a laser printer, or maintenance services. In such cases one issue is to determine how the relevant product market should be defined. If there is a separate market for the complementary product, it may be that an undertaking that has no power over the 'primary' market may nevertheless be dominant in the 'secondary' one[204]. An illustration is *Hugin v Commission*[205], where the Court of Justice upheld the Commission's finding that Hugin was dominant in the market for spare parts for its own cash machines. Liptons, a firm which serviced Hugin's machines, could not use spare parts produced by anyone else for this purpose because Hugin would have been able to prevent this by relying on its rights under the UK Design Copyright Act 1968. Therefore, although for other purposes it might be true to say that there is a market for spare parts generally, in this case, given the use to which Liptons intended to put them, the market had to be more narrowly defined. Liptons was 'locked in', as it was dependent on Hugin, and this justified a narrow market definition. This case, and the judgments of the Court of Justice in *AB Volvo v Erik Veng*[206] and *CICRA v Régie Nationale des Usines Renault*[207], establish that spare parts can form a market separate from the products for which they are needed. Likewise consumables, such as nails for use with nail-guns[208] and cartons for use with filling-machines[209], have been held to be a separate market from the product with which they are used.

[202] See ch 21, 'Access to the Commission's decisions', p 852 on how to access the Commission's decisions under the EUMR.

[203] Cases T-125/97 etc *Coca-Cola v Commission* EU:T:2000:84, para 82; a fresh market analysis was conducted in *BSkyB* pursuant to the *Coca-Cola* judgment, OFT decision of 17 December 2002, paras 29ff, available at www.gov.uk/cma; see also *Market Definition*, OFT 403, December 2004, paras 5.7–5.9, available at www.gov.uk/cma.

[204] See *Bishop and Walker*, paras 4.045–4.046 and 6.020–6.046; this issue often arises in cases concerning alleged 'tie-in transactions', as to which see ch 17, 'Tying', pp 705–713.

[205] Case 22/78 EU:C:1979:138; the Commission's decision was quashed in this case as it had failed to establish the necessary effect on inter-state trade.

[206] Case 238/87 EU:C:1988:477. [207] Case 53/87 EU:C:1988:472.

[208] Case T-30/89 *Hilti AG v Commission* EU:T:1990:27, upheld on appeal to the Court of Justice Case C-53/92 P *Hilti AG v Commission* EU:C:1994:77.

[209] *Tetra Pak II* OJ [1992] L 72/1, upheld on appeal to the General Court Case T-83/91 *Tetra Pak International SA v Commission* EU:T:1994:246, and on appeal to the Court of Justice Case C-333/94 P *Tetra Pak International SA v Commission* EU:C:1996:436.

However, as a matter of economics and competition law, it would be wrong to conclude that the primary and secondary markets are necessarily always discrete. It may be that a consumer, when deciding to purchase the primary product, will also take into account the price of the secondary products that will be needed in the future: this is sometimes referred to as 'whole life costing'. Where this occurs high prices in the secondary market may act as a competitive constraint when the purchaser is making his initial decision as to which primary product to purchase. It is an empirical question whether there is a separate aftermarket. The Commission has stated that it regards the issue as one that needs to be examined on a case-by-case basis[210], and that it will look at all important factors such as the price and life-time of the primary product, the transparency of the prices for the secondary product and the proportion of the price of the secondary product to the value of the primary one. In its investigation of *Kyocera/Pelikan*[211] the Commission concluded that Kyocera was not dominant in the market for toner cartridges for printers, since consumers took the price of cartridges into account when deciding which printer to buy. However in *CEAHR v Commission*[212] the General Court disagreed with the Commission's view that the repairing and maintenance of Swiss watches was part of the market generally for prestige and luxury watches[213]. In *EFIM v Commission*[214] the EU Courts affirmed the Commission's conclusions that there was a primary market for printers and a secondary market for ink-jet cartridges, and that the markets were interrelated in such a way that competition on the primary market prevented the exercise of any power over the secondary market[215]. In 2017 the OECD held a Roundtable on *Competition issues in aftermarkets*[216] which sheds further light on how to define the relevant market or markets for primary and secondary products.

(xi) **Procurement markets**

In some cases the business behaviour under scrutiny is that of buyers rather than sellers. For example where supermarkets merge[217], or where their procurement policies are under investigation[218], the market must be defined from the demand rather than the supply side of the market. In the case of vertical agreements Article 3 of Regulation 330/2010, which contains a market share threshold of 30% for the application of that block exemption, requires that the relevant market be defined from the demand as well as the supply side of the market[219].

[210] XXVth *Report on Competition Policy* (1995), point 86; see also the *Notice on Market Definition* (ch 1 n 131 earlier), para 56; the Commission's *Guidelines on Vertical Restraints* (ch 1 n 185 earlier), para 91; DG COMP's *Discussion paper on the application of [Article 102 TFEU] to exclusionary abuses*, December 2005, paras 243–265.

[211] XXVth *Report on Competition Policy* (1995), point 87.

[212] Case T-427/08 EU:T:2010:517.

[213] Ibid, paras 65–121; when the Commission reconsidered the matter it concluded that the primary and secondary markets were distinct and that there were separate markets for each brand of watch: see Case T-712/14 *CEAHR v Commission* EU:T:2017:748.

[214] Commission decision of 20 May 2009, upheld on appeal to the General Court Case T-296/09 *European Federation of Ink and Ink Cartridge Manufacturers v Commission* EU:T:2011:693 and on further appeal to the Court of Justice Case C-56/12 P EU:C:2013:575.

[215] See Case T-296/09 *EFIM v Commission* EU:T:2011:693, paras 58–92, upheld on appeal to the Court of Justice Case C-56/12 P EU:C:2013:575, paras 36–42.

[216] Available at www.oecd.org/competition.

[217] See eg Case M 1221 *Rewe/Meinl* OJ [1999] L 274/1.

[218] In the UK see the market investigation reports on *Supermarkets* Cm 4842 (2000) and *Groceries*, 30 April 2008.

[219] See ch 16, 'The *Vertical guidelines*', pp 676–677.

(xii) Innovation markets

In the US a 'market for innovation'[220], separate from products already on the market, has been found in some cases involving high technology industries[221]. The Commission's decision in *Shell/Montecatini*[222] suggested that it would be prepared to define a market for innovation, although in other cases it has made use of the more conventional idea of 'potential competition' to deal with the situation[223]. The Commission has issued some guidance on this issue[224]. In *Dow/DuPont*[225] the Commission did not define an innovation market, but instead directly assessed whether the merged firm would have the ability and incentive to reduce competition in innovation for pesticides.

(D) The relevant geographic market

It is also necessary, when determining whether a firm or firms have market power, that the relevant geographic market should be defined[226]. The definition of the geographic market may have a decisive impact on the outcome of a case, as in the *Volvo/Scania* decision[227] under the EUMR: the Commission's conclusion that there were national, rather than pan-European, markets for trucks and buses led to an outright prohibition of that merger[228]. Some products can be supplied without difficulty throughout the Union or even the world. In other cases there may be technical, legal, regulatory or practical reasons why a product can be supplied only within a narrower area. The delineation of the geographic market helps to indicate which other firms impose a competitive constraint on the one(s) under investigation. The cost of transporting products is an important factor: some goods are so expensive to transport in relation to their value that it would not be economic to attempt to sell them on distant markets. Another factor might be legal controls which make it impossible for an undertaking in one Member State to export goods or services to another. This problem may be dealt with by the Commission bringing proceedings against the Member State to prevent restrictions on the free movement of goods (under Articles 34 to 36 TFEU) or of services (under Articles 56 to 62 TFEU). Single market integration should mean that there are fewer claims that fiscal, technical and legal barriers to inter-state trade exist.

(i) The legal test

That the relevant geographic market should be identified is clear from the Court of Justice's judgment in *United Brands v Commission*[229]. The Court said that the opportunities for competition under Article 102 must be considered:

[220] See Rapp 'The Misapplication of the Innovative Market Approach to Merger Analysis' (1995) 64 Antitrust LJ 19; Glader *Innovation Markets and Competition Analysis: EU Competition Law and US Antitrust Law* (Edward Elgar, 2006).

[221] See eg *United States v Flow International Corpn* 6 Trade Reg Rep (CCH) 45,094; US Department of Justice and Federal Trade Commission *Antitrust Guidelines for the Licensing of Intellectual Property*, available at www.justice.gov/atr.

[222] OJ [1994] L 332/48.

[223] See Barnard 'Innovation Market Theory and Practice: An Analysis and Proposal for Reform' (2011) 7 Competition Policy International 159; and Kern 'Innovation Markets, Future Markets, or Potential Competition: How Should Competition Authorities Account for Innovation Competition in Merger Reviews?' (2014) 37 World Competition 173.

[224] See *Guidelines on Horizontal Cooperation Agreements* OJ [2011] C 11/1, paras 119–126 and *Guidelines on Technology Transfer Agreements* OJ [2014] C 89/3, para 26.

[225] Case M 7932, decision of 27 March 2017, paras 343–352, which specifically discuss the concepts of innovation markets as well as product and technology markets.

[226] See generally Fletcher and Lyons 'Geographic Market Definition in European Commission Merger Control' (January 2016), available at www.ec.europa.eu.

[227] Case M 1672, OJ [2001] L 143/74.

[228] See ch 21, 'Outright prohibitions', pp 922–928.

[229] Case 27/76 EU:C:1978:22, paras 10–11.

> with reference to a clearly defined geographic area in which [the product] is marketed and where the conditions are sufficiently homogeneous for the effect of the economic power of the undertaking concerned to be able to be evaluated.

In that case the Commission had excluded the UK, France and Italy from the geographic market since in those countries special arrangements existed as to the importing and marketing of bananas. United Brands argued that, even so, the Commission had drawn the geographic market too widely, since competitive conditions varied between the remaining six Member States[230]; the Court of Justice however concluded that the Commission had drawn it correctly. The significance of the geographic market in determining dominance was emphasised by the Court of Justice in *Alsatel v Novasam SA*[231]. There the Court of Justice held that the facts before it failed to establish that a particular region in France rather than France generally constituted the geographic market, so that the claim that Novasam had a dominant position failed in the absence of evidence of power over the wider, national, market.

(ii) The Commission's *Notice on Market Definition*

The Commission provides helpful guidance on the definition of the relevant geographic market in its *Notice on Market Definition*[232]. As noted previously, the Commission applies the 'hypothetical monopolist test' to define the geographic market: if the price of widgets were to be raised in France by a small but significant amount, would a sufficient number of customers switch to suppliers in Germany and render the price increase unprofitable? If the answer is yes, this would suggest that the relevant market is at least as wide as France and Germany. At paragraph 28 the Commission says that its approach can be summarised as follows:

> it will take a preliminary view of the scope of the geographic market on the basis of broad indications as to the distribution of market shares between the parties and their competitors, as well as a preliminary analysis of pricing and price differences at national and [EU] or EEA level. This initial view is used basically as a working hypothesis to focus the Commission's enquiries for the purposes of arriving at a precise geographic market definition.

In the following paragraph the Commission says that it will then explore any particular configuration of prices or market shares in order to test whether they really do say something about the possibility of demand substitution between one market and another: for example it will consider the importance of national or local preferences, current patterns of purchases of customers and product differentiation. This survey is to be conducted within the context of the SSNIP test outlined earlier, the difference being that, in the case of geographic market definition, the question is whether, faced with an increase in price, consumers located in a particular area would switch their purchases to suppliers further away. Further relevant factors are set out in paragraphs 30 and 31 of the *Notice*, and at paragraph 32 the Commission points out that it will take into account the continuing process of market integration in defining the market, the assumption here being that, over time, the single market should become more of a reality, with the result that the geographic market should have a tendency to get wider. There is no reason in principle why

[230] This decision was reached before the accession to the EU of Greece, Spain and Portugal etc.

[231] Case 247/86 EU:C:1988:469; other cases in which the General Court has upheld the Commission's definition of the geographic market include Case T-151/05 *Nederlandse Vakbond Varkenshouders v Commission* EU:T:2009:144, paras 69–78 and Case T-57/01 *Solvay v Commission* EU:T:2009:519, paras 239–260, annulled on appeal to the Court of Justice for procedural reasons Case C-109/10 P EU:C:2011:686.

[232] See ch 1 n 131 earlier.

the relevant geographic market should not extend to the entire world, and there have been decisions in which this has been so[233].

(iii) Examples of evidence that may be used in defining the relevant geographic market

As far as definition of the geographic market is concerned, the Commission suggests that the following evidence may be available.

(a) Past evidence of diversion of orders to other areas

It may be that direct evidence is available of changes in prices between areas and consequent reactions by customers. The Commission points out that care may be needed in comparing prices where there have been exchange rate movements, where taxation levels are different and where there is significant product differentiation between one area and another.

(b) Basic demand characteristics

The scope of the geographic market may be determined by matters such as national preferences or preferences for national brands, language, culture and life style, and the need for a local presence.

(c) Views of customers and competitors

As in the case of defining the product market, the Commission will take the views of customers and competitors into account when determining the scope of the geographic market.

(d) Current geographic pattern of purchases

The Commission will examine where customers currently purchase goods or supplies. If they already purchase across the EU, this would indicate an EU-wide market.

(e) Trade flows/patterns of shipments

Information on trade flows may be helpful in determining the geographic market, provided that the trade statistics are sufficiently detailed for the products in question.

(f) Barriers and switching costs associated with the diversion of orders to companies located in other areas

Barriers that isolate national markets, transport costs and transport restrictions may all contribute to the isolation of national markets.

(E) The temporal market

It may also be necessary to consider the temporal quality of the market[234]. Competitive conditions may vary from season to season, for example because of variations of weather or of consumer habits. A firm may find itself exposed to competition at one point in a year but effectively free from it at another. In this situation it may be that it has market power during one part of the year but not others.

[233] For example the Commission found global markets for top-level internet connectivity in Case M 1069 *WorldCom/MCI* OJ [1999] L 116/1, para 82 and Case M 1741 *MCI WorldCom/Sprint*, decision of 28 June 2000, para 97.

[234] The temporal market is discussed briefly in the UK Guideline on *Market Definition*, OFT 403, December 2004, paras 5.1–5.3, available at www.gov.uk/cma.

The issue arose in *United Brands v Commission*[235]. There was evidence in that case which suggested that the cross-elasticity of demand for bananas fluctuated from season to season. When other fruit was plentiful in summer, demand for bananas dropped: this suggests that the Commission might have considered that there were two seasonal markets, and that United Brands had no market power over the summer months. The Commission however identified just the one temporal market and held that UBC was dominant within it. On appeal the Court of Justice declined to deal with this issue. In *ABG*[236] on the other hand the Commission did define the temporal market for oil more narrowly by limiting it to the period of crisis which followed the decision of OPEC to increase dramatically the price of oil in the early 1970s. The Commission held that during the crisis companies had a special responsibility to supply existing customers on a fair and equitable basis; the Court of Justice quashed the Commission's decision on the issue of abuse, but not on the definition of the market[237]. In *AstraZeneca v Commission*[238] the Court of Justice held that the General Court[239] had correctly examined the competitive interaction between two pharmaceutical products over the entire period of AZ's alleged abusive behaviour; the gradual increase in the use of one drug at the expense of the other was found to be insufficient for them to be regarded as part of the same market[240].

The fact that electricity as a product is not capable of being stored means that there may be different temporal markets in this sector[241].

(F) **Concluding comment on market definition**

It is undoubtedly the case that market definition has played, and continues to play, an important role in EU and UK competition law. The role of the relevant market will arise frequently in this text. However some commentators consider that market definition should be abandoned since, in their view, inferences of market power from market shares in relevant markets are not meaningful[242]. A less extreme view is that less time should be spent on market definition and more time should be devoted to measuring (or simulating) the competitive effects of business behaviour[243]. Whatever the merits of these criticisms, this chapter has stressed that market definition is not an end in itself; it is simply a step in the process of determining whether a firm, or group of firms, possess (or, in the case of mergers, will possess) market power. The ICN Working Group on Mergers has rightly pointed out that 'the exercise of defining markets provides a useful analytical framework in which to organise the analysis of the effects of the merger on competition'[244]; the same point applies to the analysis of the effects of agreements and unilateral conduct. If one keeps in mind the purpose of market definition and its limitations, a properly defined

[235] Case 27/76 EU:C:1978:22. [236] OJ [1977] L 117/1.

[237] Case 77/77 *BP v Commission* EU:C:1978:141. [238] Case C-457/10 P EU:C:2012:770.

[239] Case T-321/05 *AstraZeneca AB v Commission* EU:T:2010:266, paras 61–107.

[240] Case C-457/10 P EU:C:2012:770, paras 36–51.

[241] See eg *Application in the Energy Sector*, OFT 428, January 2005, para 3.13.

[242] See eg Kaplow 'Why (Ever) Define Markets?' (2011) 124 Harvard Law Review 437; cf Werden 'Why (Ever) Define Markets? An Answer to Professor Kaplow' (2012), available at www.ssrn.com; see also Swedish Competition Authority *The Pros and Cons of Market Definition* (November 2017), available at www.konkurrensverket.se.

[243] See eg Salop 'The First Principles Approach to Antitrust, Kodak, and Antitrust at the Millennium' (2000) 68 Antitrust LJ 187; Carlton 'Market Definition: Use and Abuse' (2007) 3 Competition Policy International 3.

[244] See ICN *Merger Guidelines Workbook*, April 2006, Worksheet A, para 4, available at www.internationalcompetitionnetwork.org; see also Evans 'Lightening Up on Market Definition' in Elhauge (ed) *Research Handbook on the Economics of Antitrust Law* (Edward Elgar, 2012), ch 3.

market is often a helpful starting point for the assessment of market power, the issue to which we now turn.

One final point is that successful challenges to the European Commission's definition of the relevant market have been rare, the EU Courts tending to defer to the Commission's margin of appreciation[245].

(G) **Market power**

The really important question in competition law cases is whether a firm or firms have, or will have after a merger, market power. It will be recalled that market power exists where a firm has the ability profitably to raise prices over a period of time, or to behave analogously for example by restricting output or limiting consumer choice[246]. Three issues are relevant to an assessment of market power: these are usefully summarised in paragraph 12 of the Commission's *Guidance on the Commission's Enforcement Priorities in Applying Article [102 TFEU] to Abusive Exclusionary Conduct by Dominant Undertakings* ('*Guidance on Article 102 Enforcement Priorities*')[247]:

- constraints imposed by the existing supplies from, and the position on the market of, actual competitors (**the market position of the dominant undertaking and its competitors**)
- constraints imposed by the credible threat of future expansion by actual competitors or entry by potential competitors (**expansion and entry**)
- constraints imposed by the bargaining strength of the undertaking's customers (**countervailing buyer power**) (emphasis added).

The same issues are identified by the Commission in its *Guidelines on the application of Article [101(3)]*[248] and in its guidance on the application of Article 101 to particular types of agreements[249]. It will require only a moment's reflection to appreciate that market share figures cannot provide any insights into the influence of potential competitors on the market power of existing ones, since a figure cannot be ascribed to someone not already in the market; nor, for the same reason, can market shares provide information about the extent of any countervailing buyer power. This is why market share figures are, at best, simply a proxy for market power, and cannot be determinative in themselves.

(i) **Actual competitors**

(a) Market shares

Market share figures are, of course, relevant to any assessment of market power. As paragraph 13 of the Commission's *Guidance on Article 102 Enforcement Priorities* says, market shares provide a useful first indication of the structure of any particular market and of

[245] A successful challenge was made in Case T-427/08 *CEAHR v Commission* EU:T:2010:517; BT successfully challenged OFCOM's product and geographic market definition in a regulatory case in Case 1260/3/3/16 *BT v OFCOM* [2017] CAT 25. For discussion see Ferro 'Judicial Review: Do European Courts Care About Market Definition?' (2015) 6 JECLAP 400.

[246] See ch 1 n 124 earlier.

[247] OJ [2009] C 45/7; although this document is specifically concerned with market power of sufficient scale to earn the adjective 'substantial' for the purposes of Article 102 TFEU, the three criteria set out in para 12 of the *Guidance* are relevant to any assessment of market power; for further guidance on the assessment of market power see *Assessment of market power*, OFT 415, December 2004, available at www.gov.uk/cma.

[248] OJ [2004] C 101/97.

[249] See eg *Guidelines on Vertical Restraints* OJ [2010] C 130/1, paras 111–117; *Guidelines on the applicability of Article 101 TFEU to horizontal co-operation agreements* OJ [2011] C 11/1, paras 43–47; and *Guidelines on the application of Article 101 TFEU to technology transfer agreements* OJ [2014] C 89/3, paras 16 and 162–166.

the relative importance of the various undertakings active on it[250]. Market shares provide only a useful *first* indication because they say nothing about competitive constraints from outside the market, such as the possibility of potential entrants into the market exercising a competitive constraint upon firms within it. Even *within* the relevant market, market share figures may not be particularly informative, for example where products are differentiated by brand. Product A might be a much greater competitive constraint on product B than product C: market share figures do not capture this point which is why competition authorities sometimes attach significance to the closeness of competition between products.

The Commission says that it will interpret market shares in the light of the relevant market conditions, and in particular of the dynamics of the market and of the extent to which products are differentiated. It will also look at the development of market shares over time in the case of volatile markets or bidding markets, where firms bid *for* the market, often in auctions[251]. The ICN's *Recommended Practices for the assessment of dominance/substantial market power in the context of unilateral conduct laws*[252] stress that determinations of substantial market power should not be based on market shares alone; rather a comprehensive analysis should be undertaken of all factors affecting competitive conditions in the market under investigation.

As noted earlier in this chapter, there are varying degrees of market power—from none, to 'non-appreciable', to 'substantial', to pure monopoly. Clearly market share figures tell us something about where an undertaking is along this continuum. The higher the market share, the more likely it is that a firm will be found to have market power. Table 1.1 showing market share thresholds at the end of this chapter lists a (large) number of thresholds that have some significance in the application of EU and UK competition law, for example by providing a 'safe harbour' for firms below a certain threshold, or by indicating a fairly stormy sea for firms above a different one. Specific market share rules—such as the presumption of dominance where an undertaking has a market share of 50% or more or the application of the block exemption for vertical agreements provided that the parties' market shares are below 30%—are examined in later chapters of this book.

(b) Market concentration and the Herfindahl-Hirschman Index

In some cases market share figures may be used in order to determine how concentrated a market is, or how concentrated it will be following a merger or the entry into force, for example, of a cooperation agreement. Competition concerns may be greater as the market becomes more concentrated. One way of determining the level of concentration in the market is to use the so-called 'Herfindahl-Hirschman Index' ('the HHI'). This sums up the squares of the individual market shares of all the competitors in a market: the higher the total, the more concentrated the market. According to paragraph 16 of the European Commission's *Guidelines on the assessment of horizontal mergers*[253] the concentration level will be low where the total is below 1,000; moderate if between 1,000 and 1,800; and high where it is above 1,800. This is a relatively simple way of calculating market concentration, and its effectiveness is demonstrated by the following three examples:

250 For a critical discussion of the use of market shares in competition analysis see Kaplow 'Market Share Thresholds: On the Conflation of Empirical Assessments and Legal Policy Judgments' (2011) 7 Journal of Competition Law and Economics 243.

251 See Szilági Pál 'Bidding Markets and Competition Law in the European Union and the United Kingdom' (2008) 29 ECLR 16 and (2008) 29 ECLR 89.

252 Available at www.internationalcompetitionnetwork.org.

253 OJ [2004] C 31/5; see also the Commission's *Guidelines on the assessment of non-horizontal mergers* OJ [2008] C 265/6, para 25.

Example 1

In the widget industry there are 15 competitors: 5 of them each has a market share in the region of 10%, and 10 of them each has a market share in the region of 5%

$$\text{HH1} = 5 \times 10^2 + 10 \times 5^2 = 500 + 250 = 750$$

The market concentration is low.

Example 2

In the blodget industry there are 8 competitors: 2 of them each has a market share in the region of 20%, and 6 of them each has a market share in the region of 10%

$$\text{HH1} = 2 \times 20^2 + 6 \times 10^2 = 800 + 600 = 1400$$

The market concentration is moderate.

Example 3

In the sprocket industry there are 4 competitors: 2 of them each has a market share in the region of 30% and the other 2 each has a market share in the region of 20%

$$\text{HH1} = 2 \times 30^2 + 2 \times 20^2 = 1800 + 800 = 2600$$

The market concentration is high.

The same approach can be used to work out the consequences for the concentration of the market of any of the competitors merging or entering into an agreement with one another. For example if, in Example 2, the two firms with 20% were to merge, the HHI after the agreement would be:

$$40^2 + 6 \times 10^2 = 1600 + 600 = 2200$$

The market concentration will have moved from moderate to high. The difference in the pre- and post-merger concentration levels—that is to say the increase of 800 from 1400 to 2200—is referred to as the 'Delta', represented by the symbol Δ.

If however, in Example 2, two of the firms with 10% had entered into an agreement with one another, the HHI after the agreement would be:

$$2 \times 20^2 + 1 \times 20^2 + 4 \times 10^2 = 800 + 400 + 400 = 1600$$

The market concentration will remain moderate, and the Delta would be merely 200.

The HHI provides some insights into the competitive condition of markets; however it is fairly unsophisticated, not least since it adopts a static view of markets based on market share figures, and is unable to reflect dynamism and innovation. Its role, therefore, is fairly limited: it is at its most useful when screening out mergers that do not give rise to competitive concerns[254]; however little if any reliance would be placed on HHIs at the stage of deciding to prohibit an agreement, conduct or a merger, where much more sophisticated analysis would be undertaken. In *Spar Österreichische Warenhandels v Commission*[255] the General Court rejected an argument that the European Commission had unlawfully failed to use the HHI when assessing the effects of a merger[256].

[254] See ch 21, 'Market shares and concentration levels', pp 889–891 and ch 22, 'Measures of concentration', p 962.

[255] Case T-405/08 EU:T:2013:306.

[256] Ibid, paras 64–66.

(ii) Potential competitors

Recommendation 7 of the ICN's Working Group on *Unilateral Conduct Laws* is that 'The assessment of durability of market power, with a focus on barriers to entry or expansion, should be an integral part of the analysis of dominance/substantial market power'[257]. As paragraph 16 of the Commission's *Guidance on Article 102 Enforcement Priorities* points out, competition is a dynamic process and an assessment of competitive constraints cannot be based solely on the existing market situation: potential entry by new firms and expansion by existing ones must also be taken into account. This is why it is necessary to take barriers to entry and barriers to expansion into account. In the Commission's view, an undertaking would be deterred from raising its prices if expansion is 'likely, timely and sufficient'; in particular paragraph 16 says that to be 'sufficient', entry cannot be simply on a small-scale basis, for example into a market niche, but must be of such a magnitude as to be able to deter any attempt by an undertaking already in the market to increase prices.

Paragraph 17 of the *Guidance* provides examples of such barriers:

- legal barriers, such as tariffs or quotas
- advantages specifically enjoyed by dominant undertakings such as economies of scale and scope; privileged access to essential inputs or natural resources; important technologies; or an established distribution and sales network
- costs and other impediments, for example resulting from network effects, faced by customers in switching to a new supplier
- the conduct of a dominant undertaking, such as long-term exclusive contracts that have appreciably foreclosing effects.

Barriers to exit are also relevant when assessing market power, since high 'sunk costs' that cannot be retrieved on exit act as a disincentive to enter. Barriers to entry and expansion will be considered further in specific chapters of this book[258].

(iii) Countervailing buyer power

Paragraph 18 of the Commission's *Guidance on Article 102 Enforcement Priorities* explains that competitive constraints may be exerted not only by actual or potential competitors, but also by customers if they have sufficient bargaining strength to counterbalance the market power of suppliers[259]. However buyer power may not amount to an effective competitive constraint where it ensures only that a particular or limited segment of customers is shielded from the market power of the supplier. Separately, a buyer may itself exercise market power by reducing the price paid for a product below the competitive level and thus limiting a supplier's output.

Countervailing buyer power will be considered later in this book[260].

(iv) Summary

The discussion above has explained the key features involved in the determination of whether a firm or firms have market power. In particular it was explained that:

- **market definition** is an important part of the analysis of market power, but it is not an end in itself and is simply one stage in the overall process of the assessment of market power

[257] Available at www.internationalcompetitionnetwork.org; see also OECD Roundtable *Barriers to Entry*, 2005, available at www.oecd.org/competition.

[258] See eg ch 5, 'Potential competitors', pp 191–194 on Article 102 TFEU and ch 21, 'Entry', pp 896–897 on the EUMR.

[259] See also OECD Roundtable *Monopsony and Buyer Power*, 2008, available at www.oecd.org/competition.

[260] See eg ch 21, 'Countervailing buyer power', p 896 and ch 22, 'Countervailing buyer power', p 968.

- **market shares** can provide important information about the state of existing competition within the market, but they cannot, in themselves, be determinative of the existence of market power, since they tell us nothing about barriers to expansion and entry, nor about buyer power
- **barriers to expansion and entry** are important, since they provide us with information about the existence of potential competition, something which cannot be captured by a market share figure, precisely because the competition is potential only
- **buyer power** is also an important part of the analysis of market power.

(H) A final reflection on market shares

It has been said several times in this chapter that market share does not, in itself, determine whether an undertaking possesses market power; assessing market power is not and cannot be reduced simply to numbers. This having been said, however, it is interesting to consider the large range of situations in which EU and UK competition law require competition lawyers and their clients to consider market share figures for the purpose of deciding how to handle a particular case. This arises partly from numerous pieces of legislation and guidelines which contain a market share threshold; and partly from case law which has attributed significance to particular market share figures. Table 1.1 sets out a series of market share thresholds that should be embedded in the mind of in-house counsel to *DoItAll*, a diversified conglomerate company conducting business in the EU. The list is not exhaustive, and was compiled in a more light-hearted mood than the rest of this chapter: it does nevertheless reveal how influential market share figures can be in analysing competition law cases in the EU and the UK.

Table 1.1 Table of market share thresholds

0%	With a market share of 0% even the most zealous of competition authorities is unlikely to take action against you
	With a market share of less than 5% your agreements are unlikely to have an appreciable effect on trade between Member States provided that certain other criteria are satisfied[1]
5%	At 5% or more your agreements with undertakings that are not actual or potential competitors may significantly contribute to any 'cumulative' foreclosure effect of parallel networks of similar agreements[2]
	Agreements with undertakings that concern imports and exports have been found to have an effect on trade between Member States where your market share is around the 5% level[3]
	When notifying mergers under the EU Merger Regulation you will be required to provide information about competitors that have more than 5% of the relevant geographic market[4]
10%	At 10% or more the effect of your agreements with actual or potential competitors is no longer *de minimis* under the European Commission's *Notice on Agreements of Minor Importance*[5]; note however that agreements which have an anti-competitive object and which have an appreciable effect on trade between Member States constitute, by their nature and irrespective of any concrete effect that they may produce, appreciable restrictions of competition[6]

15%	It is unlikely that your joint purchasing agreements[7] or your commercialisation[8] agreements infringe Article 101(1) where your market share is below 15%
	At 15% or more the effect of your agreements with undertakings that are not actual or potential competitors is no longer *de minimis* under the *Notice on Agreements of Minor Importance*[9]
20%	With more than 20% of the market you are no longer eligible to take advantage of the 'simplified procedure' for certain horizontal mergers under the EU Merger Regulation[10]
	Under the EU Merger Regulation, in the case of horizontal mergers, markets in which your market share exceeds 20% are 'affected markets', necessitating the provision of substantial information on Form CO to DG COMP[11]
	Block exemption ceases to be provided for specialisation agreements under Regulation 1218/2010 where the parties' market share exceeds 20%[12]; some marginal relief is available up to a market share cap of 25%[13]
	Block exemption ceases to be available for technology transfer agreements between competing undertakings where their combined market share exceeds 20%[14]
25%	At 25% or more block exemption ceases to be available for research and development agreements under Regulation 1217/2010[15]; some marginal relief is provided up to a market share cap of 30%[16] and even, exceptionally, beyond 30%[17]
	Under the EU Merger Regulation at 25% you cease to benefit from a presumption that your merger will not significantly impede effective competition[18]
	Under UK law your merger could be referred for a Phase 2 investigation under the merger provisions of the Enterprise Act 2002[19] where you supply or are supplied with 25% or more of the goods or services of a certain description[20]
30%	Block exemption ceases to be available for vertical agreements where one of the parties' market share exceeds 30%[21], although there is some marginal relief up to 35%[22]
	Your liner consortia agreements run into problems under Commission Regulation 906/2009 on shipping consortia, with some marginal relief of up to 10% (that is to say up to a market share of 33%)[23]
	Block exemption ceases to be available for technology transfer agreements between non-competing undertakings where the market share of either party exceeds 30%[24]
	At less than 30% your non-horizontal mergers are unlikely to give rise to any problems under the EU Merger Regulation; and there is no presumption against them where your market share is more than 30%[25]
	Under the EU Merger Regulation, in the case of vertical mergers, markets in which your market share exceeds 30% are affected markets[26]
	Under the EU Merger Regulation you do not benefit from the simplified procedure in the case of vertical mergers where your market share exceeds 30%[27]

(*continued*)

Table 1.1 *(continued)*

40%	You may be dominant under Article 102 with a market share of 40% or more (there has been only one finding by the European Commission of dominance under Article 102 below 40%)[28]; if you are dominant, you have a special responsibility not to harm competition[29] If your market share is below 40% the UK CMA considers it 'unlikely' that you are dominant[30]; the same point is made in the European Commission's *Guidance on Article 102 Enforcement Priorities*[31] There is unlikely to be a cumulative foreclosure effect arising from your single branding agreements where all the companies at the retail level have market shares below 30% and the total tied market share is less than 40%[32]
45%	
50%	There is a rebuttable presumption that a market share of 50% or more of the market is evidence of a dominant position[33]; this presumption applies in the case of collective dominance as well as single-firm dominance[34] Where the market share of the 5 largest suppliers in a market is below 50%, and the market share of the largest supplier is below 30%, there is unlikely to be a single or cumulative anti-competitive effect arising from their agreements[35] There is unlikely to be such an effect where the share of the market covered by selective distribution systems is less than 50%[36]
55%	
60%	
65%	
70%	
75%	
80%	At 80% you may now be approaching a position of 'super-dominance', where your conduct is more likely to have a strong anti-competitive effect and, therefore, is more likely to fall within Article 102[37]
85%	
90%	At 90% you are approaching 'quasi-monopoly'[38] In the European Commission's view it is unlikely that conduct that maintains, creates or strengthens a market position 'approaching that of monopoly' can normally be justified on the ground that it also creates efficiency gains[39]
95%	
100%	At 100% you are a monopolist.

[1] *Guidelines on the effect on trade concept* OJ [2004] C 101/81, para 52.

[2] *Notice on agreements of minor importance* OJ [2014] C 291/1, para 10; see also the Commission's *Guidelines on Vertical Restraints* OJ [2010] C 130/1, paras 134 and 179; in the UK see *Agreements and concerted practices*, OFT 401, December 2004, para 2.16.

[3] *Guidelines on the effect on trade concept* OJ [2004] C 101/81, para 46.

[4] Regulation 802/2004, OJ [2004] L 133/1, section 7.4.

[5] OJ [2014] C 291/1, para 8(a); in the UK see *Agreements and concerted practices*, OFT 401, December 2004, para 2.16.

[6] *Notice on agreements of minor importance* OJ [2014] C 291/1, para 2.

[7] Commission's *Guidelines on Horizontal Cooperation Agreements* OJ [2011] C 11/1, para 208.

[8] Ibid, para 240.

[9] *Notice on agreements of minor importance* OJ [2014] C 291/1, para 8(b); in the UK see *Agreements and concerted practices*, OFT 401, December 2004, para 2.16.

[10] *Notice on simplified procedure* OJ [2013] C 366/5, para 5(c).

[11] Regulation 802/2004, OJ [2004] L 133/1 as amended, section 6.3(a).

[12] Regulation 1218/2010, OJ [2010] L 335/43, Article 3.

[13] Ibid, Article 5.

[14] Regulation 316/2014, OJ [2014] L 93/17, Article 3(1).

[15] Regulation 1217/2010, OJ [2010] L 335/36, Article 4.

[16] Ibid, Article 7(d).

[17] Ibid, Article 7(e).

[18] Regulation 139/2004, OJ [2004] L 24/1, recital 32.

[19] See ch 22, 'The share of supply test', pp 946–947.

[20] Note that the 'share of supply' test for referring a merger for a Phase 2 investigation is not technically a market share test: see ch 22, 'The share of supply test', pp 946–947.

[21] Regulation 330/2010, OJ [2010] L 102/1, Article 3.

[22] Ibid, Article 7(d)–(e).

[23] Regulation 906/2009, OJ [2009] L 256/31, Articles 5(1) and 5(3); Regulation 697/2014, OJ [2014] L 184/3, provides that Regulation 906/2009 shall apply until 25 April 2020.

[24] Regulation 316/2014, OJ [2014] L 93/17, Article 3(2).

[25] *Guidelines on the assessment of non-horizontal mergers* OJ [2008] C 265/6, para 25.

[26] Regulation 802/2004, OJ [2004] L 133/1 as amended, section 6.3(b).

[27] *Notice on simplified procedure* OJ [2013] C 366/5, para 5(c).

[28] See *Virgin/British Airways* OJ [2000] L 30/1: dominance at 39.7% of the market, upheld on appeal Case T-219/99 *British Airways v Commission* EU:T:2003:343.

[29] On the special responsibility of dominant firms see ch 5, 'The "special responsibility" of dominant firms', p 198.

[30] See *Abuse of a dominant position*, OFT 402, December 2004, para 4.18 and *Assessment of market power*, OFT 415, para 2.12, both available at www.gov.uk/cma.

[31] OJ [2009] C 45/7.

[32] Commission's *Guidelines on Vertical Restraints* (ch 1 n 185), para 141.

[33] See Case C-62/86 *AKZO Chemie v Commission* EU:C:1991:286, para 60.

[34] Case T-191/98 *Atlantic Container Line AB v Commission* EU:T:2003:245, paras 931–932.

[35] Commission's *Guidelines on Vertical Restraints* (ch 1 n 185), para 135.

[36] Ibid, para 179.

[37] See ch 5, 'The degree of market power and super-dominance', pp 195–196.

[38] Ibid.

[39] Commission's *Guidance on Article 102 Enforcement Priorities* OJ [2009] C 45/7, para 30.

2

Overview of EU and UK competition law

1. Introduction

This chapter will provide a brief overview of EU and UK competition law and the relevant institutions; it will also explain the relationship between EU competition law and the domestic competition laws of the Member States, in particular in the light of Article 3 of Regulation 1/2003[1]. The rules of the European Economic Area ('the EEA') are briefly referred to, and the trend on the part of Member States to adopt domestic competition rules modelled on those in the EU is noted. Three diagrams at the end of the chapter explain the institutional structure of EU and UK competition law.

2. EU Law

(A) The EU Treaties

The European Union is established by two Treaties: the Treaty on European Union ('TEU') and the Treaty on the Functioning of the European Union ('TFEU') (formerly known as the Rome Treaty[2]). There are currently 28 Member States of the EU[3]. The referendum in the UK on whether to remain a Member State led to a 'no' vote on 23 June 2016; the UK is due to leave the EU on 29 March 2019[4]. On 1 March 2017 the

[1] Council Regulation 1/2003 on the implementation of the rules on competition laid down in Articles [101 and 102 TFEU], OJ [2003] L 1/1, available at www.ec.europa.eu.

[2] The original name 'European Economic Community' of 1957 was replaced by the 'European Community' by the Maastricht Treaty of 1992, which, in turn, was subsumed into the 'European Union' by the Lisbon Treaty of 2009. References are now to EU, not to EC, competition law.

[3] As to the position of territories such as the Isle of Man and Gibraltar under EU law see Murray *The European Union and Member State Territories: A New Legal Framework Under the EU Treaties* (Springer, 2012).

[4] On 'Brexit' see www.gov.uk/government/policies/brexit and www.ec.europa.eu/commission/brexit-negotiations_en.

European Commission adopted a *White Paper on the future of Europe*[5]. The White Paper describes 'five scenarios' for how the EU might evolve, ranging from the status quo, to a multi-speed Europe to 'doing less more efficiently' to 'doing much more together'. The intention is for the remaining 27 Member States and the EU to agree a way forward by June 2019.

Under the Treaties the Member States confer 'competences' on the EU so that it can fulfil its objectives, one of which is a highly competitive social market economy[6]. Much of EU law is concerned with the elimination of obstacles to the free movement of goods, services, persons and capital; the removal of these obstacles promotes competition within the Union[7]. Initiatives such as the establishment of a public procurement regime[8], the creation of the Euro[9], the 'Europe 2020 Strategy'[10], with its emphasis on 'smart, sustainable and inclusive growth' and the 'Digital Single Market Strategy'[11] also contribute substantially to greater competition within the EU. In addition to this 'macro' effect on competition the TFEU contains specific competition rules that apply to undertakings and to the Member States themselves.

(i) The competition chapter in the TFEU

EU competition law is contained in Chapter 1 of Title VII of Part Three of the TFEU and consists of:

- Article 101(1) which prohibits agreements, decisions by associations of undertakings and concerted practices that have as their object or effect the restriction of competition[12], although this prohibition may be declared inapplicable where the conditions in Article 101(3) are satisfied[13]
- Article 102 which prohibits the abuse by an undertaking or undertakings of a dominant position[14]
- Article 106(1) which imposes obligations on Member States in relation to the Treaty generally and the competition rules specifically, while Article 106(2) concerns the application of the competition rules to public undertakings and private undertakings to which a Member State entrusts particular responsibilities[15]
- Articles 107 to 109 which prohibit state aid to undertakings by Member States that might distort competition in the internal market[16].

[5] See www.ec.europa.eu/commission/white-paper-future-europe_en.

[6] Article 3(3) TEU; see also Article 119(1) TFEU.

[7] For comprehensive analysis of EU law in general see Wyatt and Dashwood's *European Union Law* (Hart, 6th ed, 2011); Chalmers, Davies and Monti *European Union Law* (Cambridge University Press, 3rd ed, 2014); Craig and de Búrca *EU Law: Texts, Cases, and Materials* (Oxford University Press, 6th ed, 2015); da Cruz Vilaça *EU Law and Integration: Twenty Years of Judicial Application of EU Law* (Hart, 2016); Barnard and Peers *European Union Law* (Oxford University Press, 2nd ed, 2017).

[8] On public procurement see Arrowsmith *The Law of Public and Utilities Procurement*, Vol 1 (Sweet & Maxwell, 3rd ed, 2014); Bovis *EU Public Procurement* (Oxford University Press, 2nd ed, 2015); Graells *Public Procurement and the EU Competition Rules* (Hart, 2nd ed, 2015); Bovis *Research Handbook on EU Public Procurement Law* (Edward Elgar, 2016).

[9] On the Euro see Swann *The Economics of Europe* (Penguin, 9th ed, 2000), ch 7; Stiglitz *The Euro and its Threat to the Future of Europe* (Penguin, 2017); see further 'Economic and monetary union', p 53 later in chapter.

[10] See *Europe 2020*, COM(2010) 2020 final, available at www.ec.europa.eu/europe2020/index_en.htm.

[11] See *A Digital Single Market Strategy for Europe*, COM/2015/0192 final; see also speech of Commissioner Vestager of 15 September 2016 'Competition and the Digital Single Market', both available at www.ec.europa.eu.

[12] On Article 101(1) see ch 3.

[13] On Article 101(3) see ch 4.

[14] On Article 102 see chs 5, 17, 18 and 19.

[15] On Article 106 see ch 6, 'Article 106', pp 229–251.

[16] Articles 107–109 are briefly discussed in ch 6, 'Articles 107 to 109 TFEU—State Aids', pp 252–254.

An important additional instrument of EU competition law is the EU Merger Regulation ('the EUMR') which applies to concentrations between undertakings that have an EU dimension[17].

It is necessary to read the competition rules in conjunction with the objectives and principles laid down in the TFEU and the TEU. Article 3(3) TEU states that the EU is to establish an internal market, which, in accordance with Protocol 27 on the internal market and competition annexed to the Treaties, is to include a system ensuring that competition is not distorted. The Protocol has the same force as a Treaty provision[18]. The Lisbon Treaty repealed Article 3(1)(g) of the EC Treaty that established as one of the activities of the European Community the achievement of a system of undistorted competition. In *Konkurrensverket v TeliaSonera Sverige*[19] the Court of Justice referred to Article 3(3) TEU and Protocol 27 as though there was no difference from Article 3(1)(g) EC[20]. In *Timab v Commission*[21] the General Court held that Article 3 TEU, read in conjunction with Protocol 27, has changed neither the purpose of Article 101 nor the rules for the imposition of fines.

Article 3(1)(b) TFEU provides that the EU shall have exclusive competence in establishing the competition rules necessary for the functioning of the internal market. Article 119(1) TFEU provides that the activities of the Member States and the EU shall be conducted in accordance with the principle of an open market economy with free competition.

These references to competition in the TEU and the TFEU have a significant effect on the decisions of the European Commission ('the Commission'), and judgments of the General Court and the Court of Justice (together, 'the EU Courts'), which have often interpreted the specific competition rules teleologically from the starting point of what are now Articles 3(3) TEU and Protocol 27. The EU Courts have produced some notable judgments by interpreting the law teleologically[22], such as the judgment of the Court of Justice in *Continental Can v Commission*[23] which established that mergers could in some circumstances be prohibited under Article 102 TFEU.

(ii) The single market imperative

As mentioned in chapter 1[24], it is important to stress that EU competition law is applied by the Commission and the EU Courts very much with the issue of single market integration in mind. The single market has been described by the Commission as one of the 'EU's biggest assets'[25] which it is determined to protect[26]. Agreements and conduct that might have the effect of dividing the territory of one Member State from another will be closely scrutinised and may be severely punished. The existence of 'single market' competition rules

[17] Council Regulation 139/2004 on the control of concentrations between undertakings, OJ [2004] L 24/1; on the EUMR see ch 21.

[18] See Article 51 TEU. [19] Case C-52/09 EU:C:2011:83.

[20] Ibid, paras 20–22; see similarly Cases T-458/09 etc *Slovak Telekom a.s. v Commission* EU:T:2012:145, paras 36–38.

[21] Case T-456/10 EU:T:2015:296, paras 211–212.

[22] See eg Cases C-68/94 etc *France v Commission* EU:C:1998:148, paras 169–178; Case T-102/96 *Gencor v Commission* EU:T:1999:65, paras 148–158; Case C-194/14 P *AC-Treuhand AG v Commission* EU:C:2015:717, para 36.

[23] Case 6/72 *Europemballage Corpn and Continental Can v Commission* EU:C:1973:22, para 25.

[24] See ch 1, 'The single market imperative', pp 23–24.

[25] See the Commission's *Report on Competition Policy* (2009), para 9, available at www.ec.europa.eu.

[26] See eg Commission's *Guidelines on Vertical Restraints* OJ [2010] C 130/1, para 7; on the Commission's approach to vertical agreements see ch 16, 'The methodology for the analysis of vertical agreements in the Commission's *Vertical guidelines*', pp 644–664.

as well as 'conventional' competition rules is a unique feature of EU competition law. There have been a number of significant accessions to the Union in recent years[27] which, together with the possibility of future accessions, for example by some of the Balkan states, means that single market integration will remain a key feature of EU competition law and policy[28]. The Commission acts as guardian of the single market and is determined to prevent any retreat into economic nationalism[29]. The Court of Justice reaffirmed the importance of the single market imperative in its judgments in *GlaxoSmithKline v Commission*[30] and *Football Association Premier League*[31].

(iii) Economic and monetary union

The creation of the Euro has an important influence on competition within the EU[32]. As explained in chapter 1 the competitive process depends, amongst other things, on consumers having adequate information to enable them to make rational choices[33]. Price comparisons are difficult when the same goods and services are sold in different, variable currencies; the problem is compounded by the cost of exchanging money. The Euro brings a transparency to price information that fundamentally transforms the position, and has a considerable impact on the way in which business is conducted. The aim of the 'Single Euro Payments Area' is to harmonise the payments market across the the EEA by using common procedures and standards for payments in Euro[34].

(iv) The modernisation of EU competition law

In the first half of the 1990s the realisation that there was something wrong with the way in which the competition rules were applied in practice began to become widely recognised, including within the European Commission itself. An obvious problem was that Article 101, on restrictive agreements, and Article 102, on the abuse of dominance, were enforced with insufficient attention to economic principles. There followed the reform of the regime on vertical restraints, which involved a major repositioning of the law and economics of the subject and which appears to have worked well in practice[35]. Similar reforms were effected in relation to horizontal cooperation agreements[36] and technology transfer agreements[37]. The Commission also introduced significant changes into the substantive test and procedures for mergers having an EU dimension[38]. Another policy initiative was the adoption of the Commission's enforcement priorities in relation to the exclusionary conduct of dominant firms[39]. Overarching everything has been the adoption of Regulation 1/2003, which abolished the Commission's 'monopoly' over

[27] See www.ec.europa.eu/enlargement/policy/from-6-to-28-members/index_en.htm.

[28] For details of the progress of talks on future enlargement of the Union see www.ec.europa.eu/neighbourhood-enlargement.

[29] See eg Monti *A New Strategy for the Single Market—Report to the European Commission*, 9 May 2010; speech of Commissioner Vestager of 2 October 2015 'The future of competition', both available at www.ec.europa.eu.

[30] Cases C-501/06 P etc EU:C:2009:610, paras 59–61.

[31] Cases C-403/08 etc EU:C:2011:631, paras 135–144.

[32] See eg the Commission's XXVIIth *Report on Competition Policy* (1997), pp 7–8 and XXVIIIth *Report on Competition Policy* (1998), pp 24–25.

[33] See ch 1, 'The model of perfect competition is based on assumptions unlikely to be observed in practice', pp 8–9.

[34] Regulation 260/2012, OJ [2012] L 94/22; see further www.ec.europa.eu/finance/payments/sepa/index_en.htm.

[35] See ch 16 on vertical agreements.

[36] See ch 15 on horizontal cooperation agreements.

[37] See ch 19 on technology transfer agreements.

[38] See ch 21 generally.

[39] See ch 5, 'The Commission's *Guidance on Article 102 Enforcement Priorities*', pp 182–185.

decision-making under Article 101(3) and requires firms to make their own assessment of the compatibility of their conduct with EU law[40].

Today it is widely accepted that EU competition law involves the economic analysis of business practices and transactions within a legal process; that form-based rules are likely to be harmful rather than helpful; that intervention is justified only where there is evidence supporting a 'theory of harm' that a practice restricts or distorts the competitive process, thereby having an adverse effect on consumer welfare[41]; and that whether particular conduct is likely to harm competition is connected with the degree of market power that an undertaking, or undertakings, have or will have on the market(s) on which they operate.

(B) **Institutions**

(i) **Council of the European Union**

The supreme legislative body of the European Union is the Council of the European Union, often referred to as the Council of Ministers[42]. The Council is not involved in competition policy on a regular basis. However, acting under powers conferred by Articles 103 and 352 TFEU, the Council has adopted several major pieces of legislation, including the EUMR[43] and, with the European Parliament, the EU Damages Directive[44]; it has delegated important powers to the Commission through regulations to enforce the competition rules in the TFEU, in particular Regulation 1/2003[45]; and it has given the Commission power to grant block exemptions in respect of certain agreements caught by Article 101(1) but which satisfy the criteria of Article 101(3)[46].

(ii) **European Commission**

The European Commission is at the core of EU competition policy[47] and is responsible for fact-finding, taking action against infringements of Articles 101 and 102, imposing penalties, adopting block exemption regulations, conducting sectoral inquiries, investigating mergers and state aids, and for developing policy and legislative initiatives. The Commission is also involved in the international aspects of competition policy, including cooperation with competition authorities around the world[48]. One of the Commissioners is responsible for competition matters; this is regarded as one of the most important portfolios within the Commission, and confers upon the incumbent a high public profile. Certain decisions can be taken by the Commissioner for Competition rather than by the College of Commissioners. There are two Hearing Officers[49], directly responsible to the Commissioner, who are responsible for safeguarding the exercise of procedural rights during Commission proceedings enforcing EU competition law[50].

[40] These changes are discussed at 'Regulation 1/2003', pp 76–79 later in chapter, and further in ch 4, 'Regulation 1/2003', pp 174–176 and in ch 7 generally.

[41] See Zenger and Walker 'Theories of Harm in European Competition Law: A Progress Report', available at www.ssrn.com.

[42] See Article 16 TEU and Articles 237–243 TFEU.

[43] OJ [2004] L 24/1; on the EUMR see ch 21 generally.

[44] OJ [2014] L 349/1; on the Directive see ch 8, 'The Damages Directive', pp 311–316.

[45] OJ [2003] L 1/1; on the Commission's powers of enforcement see ch 7.

[46] See ch 4, '*Vires* and block exemptions currently in force', pp 177–178.

[47] See Article 17(1) TEU; see also Case C-344/98 *Masterfoods Ltd v HB Ice Cream Ltd* EU:C:2000:689, para 46.

[48] On the international dimension of competition policy see ch 12.

[49] See www.ec.europa.eu/competition/hearing_officers/index_en.html.

[50] Decision 2011/695/EU, OJ [2011] L 275/33; see Wils 'The Role of the Hearing Officer in Competition Proceedings Before the European Commission' (2012) 35 World Competition 431; see further ch 7, 'The conduct of proceedings', pp 294–297.

DG COMP is the Directorate of the Commission specifically responsible for competition policy. DG COMP's website is an invaluable source of material. From the index page it is possible to navigate to a series of policy areas, including antitrust (that is to say Articles 101 and 102, though there is a specific area for cartels), mergers, state aid and international matters[51]. Within each policy area there is a 'What's new' section as well as relevant legislation, draft legislation and details of current and decided cases; there is also useful statistical and practical information. The website also leads to information about specific sectors such as agriculture and food, consumer goods, energy, financial services and information and communication technologies. The website also has a page dedicated to creating an awareness and interest in consumers in competition policy[52]. There is information about the Commissioner for Competition Policy, the composition of DG COMP and the European Competition Network ('the ECN'), which consists of the Commission and the national competition authorities of the Member States ('the NCAs') who are jointly responsible for the enforcement of Articles 101 and 102[53]. The ECN's website contains information on its work and that of its members[54]. Press Releases about competition matters can be accessed through the website, as can speeches of the Commissioner and officials of DG COMP, policy documents, the *Competition Policy Briefs*, the *Competition Merger Briefs* and the *Competition State Aid Briefs*. It is easy to follow the progress of public consultations through the website[55], and forthcoming Commission events of relevance to competition policy are announced there.

DG COMP publishes an *Annual Management Plan* in which it sets out its key objectives for the year ahead[56]. The Commission's *Annual Report on Competition Policy* provides essential information on matters of both policy and enforcement, as well as a statistical review of DG COMP's activities[57]. DG COMP's website also has links to other important sites, including those of the NCAs[58].

DG COMP has a Director General and three Deputy Directors General. There is also a Chief Competition Economist who reports directly to the Director General. DG COMP is divided into nine administrative units[59]. Directorate A is responsible for policy and strategy, including the ECN, international relations, private enforcement and consumer liaison. Directorates B to F are the operational units, each with responsibility for particular sectors, which conduct cases under Articles 101 and 102 and the EUMR, other than cartel cases, from start to finish; they also deal with state aid cases. Directorate G is exclusively concerned with cartels, the detection, punishment and deterrence of which is a priority of the Commission[60]. Directorate H is responsible for general scrutiny and enforcement in relation to state aid. Directorate R is responsible for the registry, finance and information technology. Formal decisions of the Commission must be vetted by the Legal Service of the Commission, with which DG COMP works closely. The Legal Service represents the Commission in proceedings before the EU Courts[61].

51 See www.ec.europa.eu/comm/competition/index_en.html.

52 See www.ec.europa.eu/competition/consumers/index_en.html.

53 See ch 7, 'Case allocation under Regulation 1/2003', p 299.

54 See www.ec.europa.eu/competition/ecn/index_en.html.

55 See www.ec.europa.eu/competition/consultations/open.html.

56 See www.ec.europa.eu/dgs/competition/index_en.htm.

57 This can be found at www.ec.europa.eu/competition/publications/annual_report/index.html.

58 See www.ec.europa.eu/competition/ecn/competition_authorities.html.

59 See www.ec.europa.eu/dgs/competition/directory/organi_en.pdf.

60 Anti-cartel enforcement represents almost 48% of the Commission's enforcement activity: Commission Communication *Ten Years of Antitrust Enforcement under Regulation 1/2003*, COM(2014) 453, para 11; on cartels see ch 13 generally.

61 For details of the Legal Service see www.ec.europa.eu/dgs/legal_service/index_en.htm.

(iii) General Court

The General Court came into being in September 1989[62]. Among its tasks is the hearing of appeals against Commission decisions in competition matters under Articles 101 and 102, the state aid provisions and under the EUMR[63]. The General Court reviews the legality of decisions according to the provisions of the TFEU[64]. The Court of Justice has said that the judicial review provided for by the Treaties involves review by the General Court of both the law and the facts, and means that the General Court has the power to assess the evidence, to annul a decision and to alter the amount of any fine that has been imposed[65].

The website of the General Court (and of the Court of Justice) is an invaluable source of material where, for example, judgments of the Courts, opinions of the Advocates General and information about pending cases can be found along with statistics on judicial activity and an Annual Report on the work of the EU Courts[66]. Regulation 2015/2422[67] provides for a gradual increase in the number of judges of the General Court: there are due to be two judges per Member State from 1 September 2019. In preparation for its enlarged size, the General Court has introduced a new structure, consisting of nine Chambers of five judges[68].

(iv) Court of Justice

The Court of Justice hears appeals from the General Court on points of law only[69]. The Court of Justice has been strict about what is meant by an appeal on a point of law, and it will not get drawn into factual disputes[70]. The Court also deals with points of EU law referred to it by national courts or tribunals under Article 267 TFEU[71]. The Court of Justice is assisted by an Advocate General, drawn from a panel of 11[72], who delivers an opinion on each case that comes before it. Although not binding, this opinion is frequently, though not always, followed by the Court of Justice. Anyone interested in competition law is strongly recommended to read the opinions of the Advocates General in competition cases, which are frequently of very high quality and contain a large amount of invaluable research material.

(v) Advisory Committee on Restrictive Practices and Dominant Positions

The Advisory Committee on Restrictive Practices and Dominant Positions consists of officials from the NCAs[73]. They attend oral hearings, consider draft decisions of the

[62] Council Decision 88/591, OJ [1988] L 319/1.

[63] See the Rules of Procedure of the General Court, OJ [2015] L105/1.

[64] See Article 261 (penalties); Article 263 (actions for annulment); Article 265 (failures to act); see Kerse and Khan *EU Antitrust Procedure* (Sweet & Maxwell, 6th ed, 2012), paras 8-064–8-177.

[65] See eg Case C-386/10 P *Chalkor v Commission* EU:C:2011:815, para 67.

[66] See www.curia.europa.eu. [67] OJ [2015] L 341/14.

[68] General Court of the European Union Press Release 35/16, 4 April 2016.

[69] See Rules of Procedure of the Court of Justice, OJ [2012] L 265/1; Arnull *The European Union and its Court of Justice* (Oxford EC Law Library, 2nd ed, 2006); Beck *The Legal Reasoning of the Court of Justice of the EU* (Hart, 2013); Bobek 'The Court of Justice of the European Union' in Arnull and Chalmers (eds) *The Oxford Handbook of European Union Law* (Oxford University Press, 2015).

[70] See eg Case C-551/03 P *General Motors BV v Commission* EU:C:2006:229, paras 50–51.

[71] On the Article 267 reference procedure see Anderson *References to the European Court* (Sweet & Maxwell, 2nd ed, 2002); Kerse and Khan (ch 2 n 64 earlier), para 1.57; Hartley *The Foundations of European Union Law* (Oxford University Press, 8th ed, 2014), ch 9.

[72] Council Decision 11009/13 of 18 June 2013, increasing the number of Advocates General from eight to nine, with effect from 1 July 2013, and from 9 to 11 with effect from 7 October 2015.

[73] Provision is made for this Committee by Article 14 of Regulation 1/2003; on this Committee see ch 7, 'Article 14: Advisory Committee', p 276.

Commission and comment on them[74]; they also discuss draft legislation and the development of policy generally.

(vi) Advisory Committee on Concentrations

The Advisory Committee on Concentrations consists of officials from the NCAs; they attend oral hearings and must be consulted on draft decisions of the Commission under the EUMR[75].

(vii) National competition authorities

NCAs are obliged by Article 3(1) of Regulation 1/2003 to apply Articles 101 and 102 TFEU when agreements or conduct affects trade between Member States[76]. NCAs account for 85% of public enforcement of the EU competition rules[77]. NCAs work with the Commission within the ECN to allocate cases, exchange information and develop best practices[78]. In 2017 the Commission made a proposal for a Directive to empower the NCAs to be more effective enforcers[79].

(viii) National courts

National courts have 'an essential part to play' in applying the competition rules[80]. Articles 101 and 102 are directly applicable and produce direct effects: they give rise to rights and obligations on the part of individuals and national courts have a duty to safeguard them. The EU Damages Directive[81] sets out certain rules governing actions for damages for infringements of EU and national competition law[82].

The Commission's website has a searchable database of some of the judgments given by national courts on the application of Articles 101 and 102 in the original language arranged in a chronological order[83]. An Association of European Competition Law Judges periodically brings together members of the judiciary of the Member States[84].

(ix) European Parliament

The European Parliament—in particular its Standing Committee on Economic and Monetary Matters—and the Economic and Social Committee ('ECOSOC'), are consulted on matters of competition policy and may be influential, for example, in the legislative process or in persuading the Commission to take action in relation to a particular issue.

(C) European Economic Area

On 21 October 1991 what is now the EU and its Member States and the Member States of the European Free Trade Association ('EFTA') signed an Agreement to establish the

[74] On consulting the Advisory Committee see Case T-66/01 *Imperial Chemical Industries v Commission* EU:T:2010:255, paras 163–171; this is also a ground of annulment in Case T-691/14 *Servier v Commission*, not yet decided.

[75] See EUMR, Article 19(3)–(7); on this Committee see ch 21, 'Close and constant liaison with Member States', p 921.

[76] See 'Obligation to apply Articles 101 and 102', pp 76–77.

[77] See the Commission's *Report on Competition Policy* (2016), p 16; see further Wils 'Ten Years of Regulation 1/2003—A Retrospective' (2013) 4 JECLAP 293, at 296.

[78] On the ECN, see 'European Commission', pp 54–55.

[79] See www.ec.europa.eu/competition/antitrust/nca.html.

[80] See Regulation 1/2003, OJ [2003] L 1/1, recital 7; on the position of national courts see ch 8 generally.

[81] Directive 2014/104, OJ [2014] L 349/1, recital 3.

[82] On the EU Damages Directive see ch 8, 'The Damages Directive', pp 311–316.

[83] See www.ec.europa.eu/competition/elojade/antitrust/nationalcourts/.

[84] The website of the AECLJ is www.aeclj.com.

European Economic Area[85]; it consists of the Member States of the EU, Norway, Iceland and Liechtenstein. The referendum in Switzerland on joining the EEA led to a 'no' vote, so that that signatory country remains outside. The EEA Agreement entered into force in 1994. It includes rules on competition that follow closely the TFEU and the EUMR. Article 101 on anti-competitive agreements appears as Article 53 of the EEA Agreement; Article 102 on the abuse of a dominant position is mirrored in Article 54; the EUMR is reflected in Article 57; and Article 106 on public undertakings and Article 107 on state aids appear as Articles 59 and 61 of the EEA Agreement respectively.

The EEA Agreement and its associated texts establish a 'twin pillar' approach to jurisdiction: there are two authorities responsible for competition policy, the European Commission and the EFTA Surveillance Authority ('the ESA')[86], but any particular case will be investigated by only one of them. Article 108 of the EEA Agreement established the ESA; it mirrors the European Commission and is vested with similar powers. The ESA is subject to review by the EFTA Court of Justice[87], which sits in Luxembourg. Article 55 of the EEA Agreement provides that the European Commission or the ESA shall ensure the application of Articles 53 and 54; Article 56 of the Agreement deals with the attribution of jurisdiction between these two bodies in cases caught by these Articles[88]; Article 57 provides for the division of competence in respect of mergers.

An important principle of the EEA Agreement is that there should be cooperation between the European Commission and the ESA, in order to develop and maintain uniform surveillance throughout the EEA and in order to promote a homogeneous implementation, application and interpretation of the provisions of the Agreement. Article 58 requires the authorities to cooperate, in accordance with specific provisions contained in Protocol 23 (dealing with restrictive practices and the abuse of market power) and Protocol 24 (dealing with mergers). Similarly Article 106 of the EEA Agreement establishes a system for the exchange of information between the two courts with a view to achieving a uniform interpretation of its terms.

(D) Modelling of domestic competition law on Articles 101 and 102

The Member States of the EU and the EEA have systems of competition law modelled upon Articles 101 and 102[89]. The ECN has published a table showing the extent to which Member States have voluntarily aligned domestic laws with the provisions of Regulation

[85] OJ [1994] L 1/1; the EEA agreement entered into force on 1 January 1994; see Arnesen, Fredriksen, Graver, Mestad, Vedder *Agreement on the European Economic Area: A Commentary* (Hart, 2018); Blanco *EU Competition Procedure* (Oxford University Press, 3rd ed, 2013), ch 28; Broberg *Broberg on the European Commission's Jurisdiction to Scrutinise Mergers* (Kluwer, 4th ed, 2013), ch 7; the Commission Staff Working Paper accompanying the Communication on *Ten Years of Antitrust Enforcement under Regulation 1/2003*, SWD(2014) 230/2, paras 253–264.

[86] The website of the ESA is www.eftasurv.int.

[87] The EFTA States signed an *Agreement on the Establishment of a Surveillance Authority and a Court of Justice* on 2 May 1992: it is reproduced in (1992) 15 Commercial Laws of Europe, Part 10; the Court of Justice delivered two Advisory Opinions on these arrangements: Opinion 1/91 EU:C:1991:490; and Opinion 1/92 EU:C:1992:189; the website of the EFTA Court is www.eftacourt.int.

[88] The division of competences between the European Commission and the ESA was considered in Cases T-67/00 etc *JFE Engineering v Commission* EU:T:2004:221, paras 482–493.

[89] See Gerber *Law and Competition in Twentieth Century Europe: Protecting Prometheus* (Clarendon Press, 1998), ch X; Maher 'Alignment of Competition Laws in the European Community' (1996) 16 Oxford Yearbook of European Law 223; Ullrich 'Harmonisation within the European Union' (1996) 17 ECLR 178; Holmes and Davey (eds) *A Practical Guide to National Competition Rules Across Europe* (Kluwer, 2nd ed, 2007).

1/2003[90]. An easy way of accessing the websites, and the national competition laws, of the NCAs is through a hyperlink provided by DG COMP[91].

The EU has entered into agreements with, respectively, the countries of central and eastern Europe (known as 'the Europe Agreements') and the western Balkans (known as 'the Stabilisation and Association Agreements'). These agreements contain competition provisions and form part of the accession process towards full membership of the EU[92]. Separately, the 'Union for the Mediterranean' means that countries on the Mediterranean coast from Algeria to Turkey are parties to Euro-Mediterranean Association Agreements containing provisions based on the EU competition rules[93].

3. UK Law

The promotion of competition is an important part of UK economic policy[94]. This commitment to competition has manifested itself in important changes in the competition law of the UK. The Competition Act 1998 and the Enterprise Act 2002 fundamentally changed both the substantive provisions and the institutional architecture of the domestic competition law of the UK; in the course of this reform a raft of old legislation[95] was swept away. Another key piece of legislation is the Enterprise and Regulatory Reform Act 2013 ('the ERRA'), which created the Competition and Markets Authority ('the CMA') and abolished its predecessors, the Office of Fair Trading ('the OFT') and the Competition Commission ('the CC'); their competition law functions were transferred to the CMA. Further changes were made to domestic competition law by the Consumer Rights Act 2015, which significantly amended the rules on bringing private actions in the Competition Appeal Tribunal ('the CAT').

(A) Competition Act 1998

The Competition Act 1998 received Royal Assent on 9 November 1998; the main provisions entered into force on 1 March 2000. The Act contains two prohibitions. The 'Chapter I prohibition' is modelled on Article 101(1) TFEU, and forbids agreements, decisions by associations of undertakings and concerted practices that have as their object or effect the restriction of competition[96]. The Chapter II prohibition in the Competition Act is

[90] www.ec.europa.eu/comm/competition/nca/documents.

[91] www.ec.europa.eu/comm/competition/nca/index_en.html.

[92] Since the accessions in May 2004 and January 2007 there are no remaining Europe Agreements; it is possible in principle for agreements between the EU and third countries to have direct effect: see Case 104/81 *Hauptzollamt Mainz v Kupferberg* EU:C:1982:362 and Wyatt and Dashwood's *European Union Law* (Hart, 6th ed, 2011), pp 953–955; however there has yet to be a judgment on whether the competition rules in the Europe Agreements themselves have direct effect; on one occasion the Commission required amendments to Chanel's distribution agreements to remove restrictions on exports to countries with which the EU had negotiated 'Free Trade Agreements', but this was done by agreement and without a reasoned decision on the part of the Commission: *Chanel* OJ [1994] C 334/11.

[93] See www.eeas.europa.eu/euromed/index_en.htm; Geradin and Petit 'Competition Policy and the Euro-Mediterranean Partnership' (2003) 8 European Foreign Affairs Review 153; Geradin *Competition Law and Regional Integration: An Analysis of the Southern Mediterranean Countries* (World Bank, 2004).

[94] See the UK Government's *Strategic Steer for the Competition and Markets Authority*, December 2015, available at www.gov.uk/cma.

[95] In particular the competition provisions in the Fair Trading Act 1973, the Restrictive Trade Practices Act 1976, the Resale Prices Act 1976 and the Competition Act 1980; note that s 11 of the Competition Act 1980, which provides for 'efficiency audits' of public-sector bodies, remains in force but has not been used for many years.

[96] See ch 9, 'The Chapter I Prohibition', pp 347–376.

modelled on Article 102 TFEU and forbids the abuse of a dominant position[97]. Section 60 of the Competition Act contains provisions designed, so far as possible, to maintain consistency between the application of EU and domestic competition law[98]. In practice section 60 has worked well, and decision-makers in the UK have been able to draw upon a body of jurisprudence developed in Luxembourg over 50 years. It remains to be seen what will become of section 60 as a result of the withdrawal of the UK from the EU in March 2019.

The Competition Act gives the CMA and the concurrent sectoral regulators wide powers to obtain information, to carry out on-the-spot investigations, to adopt decisions and to impose penalties for infringements of competition law[99].

(B) Enterprise Act 2002

The Enterprise Act 2002 received Royal Assent on 7 November 2002; the main provisions entered into force on 20 June 2003. The Enterprise Act is a major piece of legislation that amended domestic competition law in a number of ways. First, the Act changed the institutional architecture of the domestic system, for example by creating the CAT and by reducing the powers of the Secretary of State to make decisions in competition cases[100]. Some of the institutional changes brought about by the Act, such as the creation of the OFT, have been superseded by reforms introduced by the ERRA.

Secondly, the Act contained new provisions for the investigation of mergers and markets[101]. Thirdly, the Enterprise Act supplemented and reinforced the Competition Act 1998 in various ways, in particular by introducing a criminal 'cartel offence' which, on indictment, can lead to the imprisonment of individuals for up to five years and/or a fine of an unlimited amount[102]; by providing for company director disqualification for directors who knew or ought to have known of competition law infringements committed by their companies[103]; and by facilitating actions for damages[104].

(C) Changes to domestic law as a result of Regulation 1/2003

The Competition Act 1998 and Other Enactments (Amendment) Regulations 2004[105] effected further changes to competition law in the UK. The Amendment Regulations implemented Regulation 1/2003, in particular, by designating the NCAs responsible for applying Articles 101 and 102 TFEU in the UK[106]. The Amendment Regulations also aligned domestic procedures with those in EU law, for example by abolishing the system of notification to the domestic competition authorities of agreements and/or conduct for guidance and/or a decision.

97 See ch 9, 'The Chapter II Prohibition', pp 376–387.

98 See ch 9, '"Governing Principles Clause": Section 60 of the Competition Act 1998', pp 387–392.

99 On the enforcement powers under the Competition Act 1998 and concurrency see ch 10.

100 See further ch 22, '"Public Interest Cases", "Other Special Cases" and Mergers in the Water Industry', pp 986–993.

101 See further ch 22 (merger investigations) and ch 11 (market investigations); these provisions replaced the merger and monopoly provisions formerly contained in the Fair Trading Act 1973.

102 See ch 10, 'Penalties', pp 420–424.

103 See ch 10, 'Grounds for disqualification', p 447.

104 See ch 8, 'Private Actions in the UK Courts', pp 325–335.

105 SI 2004/1261; the Amendment Regulations entered into force on 1 May 2004.

106 See also Designation of the Competition and Markets Authority as a National Competition Authority Regulations 2014, SI 2014/537.

(D) Enterprise and Regulatory Reform Act 2013

The ERRA received Royal Assent on 25 April 2013; the main provisions on competition entered into force on 1 April 2014. The ERRA made further important alterations to the UK regime. First, the ERRA radically reformed the institutional architecture of the UK system: by abolishing the OFT and the CC and by creating a new institution, the Competition and Markets Authority: the CMA has a variety of functions under the Competition Act and the Enterprise Act, including those formerly exercised by the OFT and the CC. Secondly, the ERRA streamlined and strengthened the provisions on mergers and markets, in particular by formalising the system of market studies, by introducing new timescales for investigations and by enhancing the powers of the CMA to obtain information. Thirdly, the ERRA strengthened the concurrency regime. Lastly it amended the criminal cartel offence to make it easier to prosecute the offence and so increase its deterrent effect.

(E) Consumer Rights Act 2015

The Consumer Rights Act 2015 received Royal Assent on 26 March 2015; the competition provisions entered into force on 1 October 2015. The Consumer Rights Act significantly amended the domestic system of private enforcement of competition law. First, it expanded the jurisdiction of the CAT so that it can hear both 'standalone' and 'follow-on' actions for damages: previously the CAT had jurisdiction only in follow-on cases[107]. Secondly, the Consumer Rights Act introduced a procedure for the CAT to allow a representative to bring collective proceedings on behalf of a defined class of claimants, either on an opt-in or an opt-out basis[108]. Thirdly, it enabled the CAT to approve a collective settlement and the CMA or a sectoral regulator to approve voluntary redress schemes[109]. Finally the Act provided power for the adoption of rules for a 'fast-track procedure' for claims made under section 47A of the Competition Act[110].

(F) Brexit

The result of the referendum of 23 June 2016 was that the UK should leave the EU, a phenomenon that is commonly referred to as 'Brexit'. It is obvious that Brexit will have profound legal, political and economic ramifications for the UK and the EU. Specifically it will have a significant effect on future competition law and practice. As at 8 December 2017 it was not clear what form Brexit will take. As a result, it is not intended to discuss what effect Brexit might have on the domestic competition law of the UK. The reports of the Brexit Competition Law Working Group (a private initiative on the part of several specialists in competition law and policy) and the House of Lords Internal Market Sub-Committee provide numerous insights on the possible implications of Brexit for UK competition law and policy[111].

The UK Government announced in November 2017 that it will publish a review of the UK competition law regime by April 2019[112].

[107] See ch 8, 'Damages claims may be brought in the High Court or the Competition Appeal Tribunal', pp 326–328.

[108] See ch 8, 'Collective redress in the UK', pp 330–332.

[109] See *Competition law redress: A guide to taking action for breaches of competition law*, CMA55, May 2016, available at www.gov.uk/cma.

[110] See ch 8, 'CAT proceedings', pp 327–328.

[111] The BCLWG report is available at www.bclwg.org/activity/bclwg-conclusions; the House of Lords Internal Market Sub-Committee report is available at www.parliament.uk.

[112] This is a requirement imposed by s 46 of the ERRA.

(G) Institutions

A notable feature of UK competition law is the number of institutions involved[113]. Competition law in the UK assigns roles to the Secretary of State[114], the Lord Chancellor, the CMA, the Serious Fraud Office (or, in Scotland, the Lord Advocate), the sectoral regulators, the CAT and to the civil and criminal courts. The competition authorities are also subject to scrutiny by the National Audit Office[115], by the Parliamentary and Health Service Ombudsman and by parliamentary bodies, including the Treasury Committee, the Business, Energy and Industrial Strategy Committee and the Public Accounts Committee of the House of Commons and the EU Select Committee of the House of Lords.

(i) Secretary of State and the Department for Business, Energy and Industrial Strategy

The Secretary of State for Business, Energy and Industrial Strategy ('BEIS') has various functions under the Competition Act, the Enterprise Act and the ERRA. In the exercise of these functions he or she is assisted by the Parliamentary Under-Secretary of State for Small Business, Consumers and Corporate Responsibility whose portfolio includes competition policy. Within BEIS there is a Consumer and Competition Policy Directorate[116].

(a) Appointments

The Secretary of State for BEIS makes most of the senior appointments to the competition authorities, for example of the Chairman, Chief Executive and other members of the CMA Board and the CMA Panel[117]; the members of the CAT[118]; the Registrar of the CAT[119]; and the 'appointed members' of the Competition Service within the CAT[120]. The Secretary of State can also designate bodies which represent consumers to make 'super-complaints' under section 11 of the Enterprise Act 2002[121].

(b) Amendment of legislation, the adoption of delegated legislation and the making or approval of guidance

The Secretary of State is given various powers to amend primary legislation, to adopt delegated legislation and to make or approve rules under the Competition Act, the Enterprise Act and the ERRA. For example under the Competition Act the Secretary of State has power to amend (and has amended) Schedules 1 and 3[122]; to adopt block exemptions from the Chapter I prohibition[123]; to make provision for the determination of turnover for the purpose of setting the level of penalties[124]; to approve the guidance of the CMA as to the appropriate amount of a penalty for infringements of the Chapter I and Chapter II prohibitions

113 The institutional structure of UK competition law is set out in diagrammatic form later in chapter: see Figs 2.1, 2.2 and 2.3, pp 80–81.

114 The Scottish Government also has capacity to make market investigation references to the CMA.

115 See most recently *The UK competition regime*, NAO, 3 February 2016, HC 737, available at www.nao.org.uk, on which see Whish 'The National Audit Office's Report on the UK Competition Regime: How Well is the Regime Performing?' [2016] Comp Law 197.

116 The BEIS website is www.gov.uk/beis.

117 ERRA, Sch 4, paras 1(1) and 9(1).

118 Enterprise Act 2002, s 12(2)(c); note that the President and Chairmen of the Tribunal are appointed by the Lord Chancellor upon the recommendation of the Judicial Appointments Commission: ibid, s 12(2)(a) and (b).

119 Ibid, s 12(3).

120 Ibid, Sch 3, para 1(2).

121 Ibid, s 11(5); see further ch 11, 'Super-Complaints', pp 463–465.

122 Competition Act 1998, s 3(2), s 19(2) (Sch 1, dealing with mergers and concentrations) and s 3(3), s 19(3) (Sch 3, dealing with general exclusions): see ch 9, 'The Chapter I prohibition: excluded agreements', pp 364–371 and 'Exclusions', p 387 respectively.

123 Competition Act 1998, ss 6–8: see ch 9, 'Block Exemptions', p 375.

124 Competition Act 1998, s 36(8): see ch 10, 'Maximum amount of a penalty', p 421.

and/or Articles 101 and 102 TFEU[125]; to determine the criteria for conferring limited immunity on 'small agreements' and 'conduct of minor significance'[126]; to make provision for the exclusion of vertical and land agreements from the Chapter I prohibition[127]; to approve the procedural rules of the CMA[128]; to make regulations on the concurrent application of the Competition Act by the CMA and the sectoral regulators[129]; and to amend the list of appealable decisions in section 46 of the Act[130]. The Secretary of State also has power under paragraph 7 of Schedule 3 to the Competition Act to order that the Chapter I and Chapter II prohibitions do not apply to particular agreements or conduct where there are 'exceptional and compelling reasons of public policy' for doing so[131].

Under the Enterprise Act the Secretary of State has power to make rules or to amend primary legislation in relation to a variety of matters: these include the procedural rules of the CAT[132]; the determination of turnover for the purpose of domestic merger control[133]; the maximum penalties that the CMA can impose for procedural infringements[134]; the payment of fees for merger investigations[135]; for the alteration of the 'share of supply' test applicable to merger cases[136]; and for shortening the period within which Phase 2 merger inquiries should be completed[137]. The Act also enables the Secretary of State to extend the 'super-complaint' system to include sectoral regulators[138] and to make such modifications to the Competition Act as are appropriate for the purpose of eliminating or reducing any differences between that Act and EU law as a result of Regulation 1/2003[139].

Under the ERRA the Secretary of State has power to amend the time limits for making merger references[140]; to modify the time limits for making and completing market investigation references[141]; to introduce time limits for investigations under the Competition Act[142]; and to make a 'sectoral regulator order' removing the concurrent powers given to a regulator to enforce the Competition Act 1998 and/or to make a market investigation reference[143]. The ERRA requires the Secretary of State to prepare and publish a report reviewing the operation of Part 1 of the Competition Act by 1 April 2019[144].

[125] Competition Act 1998, s 38(4): see ch 10, 'The Guidance as to the appropriate amount of a penalty', p 421.

[126] Competition Act 1998, s 39 (small agreements) and s 40 (conduct of minor significance): see ch 10, 'Immunity for small agreements and conduct of minor significance', pp 423–424.

[127] Competition Act 1998, s 50: see ch 9, 'Section 50: land agreements', p 371 and ch 16, 'Repeal of the exclusion for vertical agreements', pp 693–694.

[128] Competition Act 1998, s 51: see the Competition Act 1998 (Competition and Markets Authority's Rules) Order 2014, SI 2014/458.

[129] Competition Act 1998, s 54(4)–(5): see the Competition Act 1998 (Concurrency) Regulations 2014, SI 2014/536; see also Enterprise Act 2002, s 204, which creates a power for the Secretary of State to make regulations in relation to concurrency functions as to company director disqualification: for a discussion of the rules on concurrency see ch 10, 'Concurrency', pp 449–452.

[130] See the Competition Act 1998 (Notification of Excluded Agreements and Appealable Decisions) Regulations 2000, SI 2000/263, reg 10.

[131] See ch 9, 'Public policy', pp 369–370.

[132] Enterprise Act 2002, s 15 and Sch 4, Part 2: see the Competition Appeal Tribunal Rules 2015, SI 2015/1648.

[133] Ibid; see ch 22, 'The turnover test', pp 945–946.

[134] Enterprise Act 2002, s 111(4); see ch 22, 'Investigation powers and penalties', pp 978–979.

[135] Enterprise Act 2002, s 121; see ch 22, 'Fees', p 956.

[136] Enterprise Act 2002, s 123; see ch 22, 'The share of supply test', pp 946–947.

[137] Enterprise Act 2002, s 40(8).

[138] Ibid, s 205; on super-complaints, see ch 10.

[139] Enterprise Act 2002, s 209; see further 'Changes to domestic law as a result of Regulation 1/2003', p 60 earlier in chapter.

[140] Enterprise Act 2002, s 34ZC(6).

[141] Ibid, s 131C and s 137(3).

[142] Competition Act 1998, s 31F.

[143] ERRA, s 52; the Secretary of State and the Scottish Ministers acting jointly have power to make a market investigation reference to the CMA: Scotland Act 2016, s 63.

[144] ERRA, s 46.

(c) Receipt of performance report

The Secretary of State receives an annual performance report from the CMA[145].

(d) Involvement in individual cases

The Secretary of State has little involvement in individual competition cases. The provisions of the Enterprise Act confer upon the CMA the final decision-making role in relation to merger and market investigations[146]. The Secretary of State retains powers in relation to such investigations only in strictly limited circumstances[147].

(ii) The Lord Chancellor

The Lord Chancellor is responsible for appointing the President of the CAT and the panel of chairmen, pursuant to a recommendation from the Judicial Appointments Commission[148]. He or she is also given power to make provision for civil courts in the UK to transfer to the CAT for its determination so much of any proceedings before the court as relates to any question relating to whether an infringement of Articles 101 and 102 TFEU and/or the Chapter I and II prohibitions has been or is being committed[149]. There is also provision to make rules for the receipt of cases by the civil courts that are transferred to them by the CAT[150].

(iii) The CMA

(a) Background to the creation of the CMA

For many years the most important functions in UK competition law were carried out by two competition authorities: the OFT and the CC[151]. In 2010 the Government proposed to simplify the institutional design of domestic competition law[152]. Following a consultation in 2011[153], the Government decided in 2012 to create the Competition and Markets Authority. The Government considered that a single authority would eliminate inefficiency, duplication and overlap in the UK regime. In 2013 the Government published a 'Strategic Steer' to the CMA[154]. In 2015 it published a revised Strategic Steer[155], encouraging the CMA to explore markets where competition could deliver greater consumer choice and encourage more innovation and productivity[156]; to enforce the competition rules fairly and effectively; and to assist the Government in removing unnecessary regulatory burdens on businesses.

[145] Ibid, Sch 4, para 14(1); see 'Annual Reports on performance and concurrency', p 67 see later in chapter.

[146] See ch 22, 'Determination of References by the CMA: Phase 2 Investigations', pp 956–959 (merger investigations) and ch 11, 'Market Investigation References', pp 469–481 (market investigations).

[147] Ibid, explaining Enterprise Act 2002, ss 42–68, s 132, ss 139–153 and Sch 7.

[148] Enterprise Act 2002, s 12(2)(a) and (b) and Sch 2, para 1; the Judicial Appointments Commission's website is www.jac.judiciary.gov.uk.

[149] Enterprise Act 2002, s 16(1)–(4); see the Section 16 Enterprise Act 2002 Regulations 2015, SI 2015/1643.

[150] Ibid, s 16(5); see the Competition Appeal Tribunal Rules 2015, r 71.

[151] *Public Bodies Reform—Proposals for Change*, 14 October 2011, available at www.gov.uk.

[152] *A competition regime for growth: a consultation on options for reform*, 16 March 2011, available at www.gov.uk.

[153] *Growth, competition and the competition regime: Government response to consultation*, 15 March 2012, available at www.gov.uk.

[154] Government's *Strategic Steer for the Competition and Markets Authority 2014–17*, October 2013, available at www.gov.uk/cma.

[155] *Competition regime: Government's Response to the Consultation on the Strategic Steer for the Competition and Markets Authority*, December 2015, available at www.gov.uk/cma.

[156] The CMA had already published, in July 2015, a report outlining the theoretical and empirical evidence on the relationship between competition and productivity: *Productivity and competition: A summary of the evidence*, CMA 45, available at www.gov.uk/cma.

(b) Establishment of the CMA and the CMA Board

The CMA was established on 1 October 2013[157]. The ERRA abolished the OFT[158] and the CC[159]; the competition law functions of those authorities were transferred to the CMA with effect from 1 April 2014[160]. The CMA has a statutory duty to promote competition, both within and outside the UK, for the benefit of consumers[161]. The Board of the CMA consists of a (non-executive) Chairman and no fewer than four other members, appointed by the Secretary of State[162]. The Secretary of State must also appoint a Chief Executive of the CMA, who may not be the same person as the Chairman or a member of the CMA Panel[163]. On 8 December 2017 there were 12 members of the Board, of whom four, including the Chief Executive, were executive members and eight non-executive (of whom two are CMA Panel members)[164]. The CMA Board Rules of Procedure are available on its website, and minutes of its meetings will also be found there[165]. The Board is responsible for the strategic direction, priorities, plans and performance of the CMA, including the adoption of the Annual Plan[166]. It also makes the decision whether to publish a market study notice or to refer a market for a Phase 2 investigation[167]; other operational decisions are delegated by the Board to the members of the Board, the staff of the CMA and to Board committees and sub-committees[168].

Management of the CMA is taken forward through the Executive Committee and its sub-committee, the Operations Committee[169]. The Case and Policy Committee is responsible for ensuring that the CMA has appropriate policies and that case and project teams adhere to those policies[170].

(c) The CMA Panel

A feature of the old UK system for investigating mergers and markets was the fact that Phase 2 investigations were conducted by a separate body (the CC) from Phase 1 (the OFT), thereby avoiding a concern associated with one agency acting as investigator, prosecutor, judge and jury. The ERRA seeks to address this concern by retaining the separation of Phase 1 and 2 decision-making in merger and market cases. The Phase 1 decision-maker is the Senior Director of Mergers or another senior member of CMA staff (for mergers) and the CMA Board (for markets); the CMA's functions in Phase 2 merger and market inquiries are performed by members of the CMA Panel[171]. There is a Chair of the CMA Panel, who is also a member of the CMA Board[172], and five Inquiry Chairs[173]. On 8 December 2017 there were 31 members of the CMA Panel[174]. Members are appointed by the Secretary of State, following an open competition, for a single period of up to eight years[175]. They are appointed for their diversity of background, individual experience and ability, not as representatives of particular organisations, interests or political

157 ERRA, s 25(1). 158 Ibid, s 26(2). 159 Ibid, s 26(1). 160 Ibid, s 27(1).

161 Ibid, s 25(3). 162 Ibid, Sch 4, para 1(3). 163 Ibid, Sch 4, para 9(1)–(2).

164 Ibid, Sch 4, para 27; details of the members of the CMA Board are available at www.gov.uk/cma.

165 See www.gov.uk/cma.

166 See 'The CMA's Vision, Annual Plan and Strategic Assessment', p 66, later in chapter.

167 ERRA, Sch 4, paras 28 and 29(2).

168 The Case and Policy Committee also appoints the 'Case Decision Groups' that take formal decisions under the Competition Act 1998: see *Terms of Reference*, July 2014, para 4(a).

169 The Portfolio and Resource Committee and the Remedies, Undertakings and Commitments Committee were disbanded in January 2015: CMA's *Annual Report and Accounts 2014–15*, July 2015, fn 4.

170 ERRA, Sch 4, para 29(1).

171 Its terms of reference are available at www.gov.uk/cma. 172 ERRA, Sch 4, para 1(4).

173 Deputy Chairs are known as 'Inquiry Chairs' when they chair Phase 2 merger and market inquiries.

174 *Authorisation of staff of the CMA and the CMA Panel Chair and Deputy Chairs*, 1 April 2014, available at www.gov.uk/cma.

175 ERRA, Sch 4, para 3(2).

parties. In each Phase 2 merger or market case an 'inquiry group' will be appointed to conduct the investigation[176]. The Panel Chair must appoint a minimum of three members to serve on an inquiry group[177]. The CMA Board has published rules of procedure for groups conducting mergers and markets inquiries[178].

(d) The staff of the CMA

The Chief Executive of the CMA is responsible for the day-to-day running of the organisation. There are three further Executive Directors who sit on the Board of the CMA. There is a Procedural Officer responsible for reviewing decisions by the case team on certain procedural matters, chairing the oral hearing in Competition Act cases and reporting on the fairness of that hearing to the decision-makers[179]. The office of the General Counsel ensures that decision-makers are aware of significant legal risks before taking a decision[180]. The office of the Chief Economic Adviser plays an important part in cases where in-depth economic analysis is called for[181]. The CMA is divided into three Directorates: Enforcement, Markets and Mergers and Corporate Services; each Directorate is headed by an Executive Director. There are also specific enforcement teams for cartel and criminal investigations[182]. The total number of permanent staff of the CMA at 31 March 2017 was 521, including administrators and specialists such as accountants, economists, business advisers and lawyers[183].

(e) The CMA's Vision, Annual Plan and Strategic Assessment

The CMA's *Vision, values and strategy*[184] says that its 'mission' is 'to make markets work well in the interests of consumers, businesses and the economy'. The CMA has five strategic goals: to deliver effective enforcement, extend competition frontiers, refocus consumer protection, develop integrated performance and achieve professional excellence[185].

The CMA is required, following a public consultation, to publish an Annual Plan containing a statement of its objectives and priorities for the year ahead; both the Annual Plan and the consultation document must be laid before Parliament[186]. The most recent annual plan was published in March 2017 explaining the CMA's strategy, including commitments for work in 2017/18, in accordance with its five strategic goals[187].

The CMA has published its *Strategic Assessment*[188] to identify risks to consumers and to the efficient functioning of markets. The *Strategic Assessment* is intended to help the CMA to identify markets or issues, such as the digital economy and regulated sectors[189], that may become a strategic priority for the CMA.

176 Ibid, paras 56–58.

177 Ibid, para 38(1).

178 Ibid, para 51(1): *CMA Rules of Procedure for Merger, Market and Special Reference Groups*, CMA17, March 2014 (corrected in November 2015).

179 The Competition Act 1998 (Competition and Markets Authority's Rules) Order 2014, SI 2014/458, rr 6(5)–(6) and 8; see further www.gov.uk/procedural-officer-raising-procedural-issues-in-cma-cases.

180 See eg *Competition Act 1998: Guidance on the CMA's Investigation procedures in Competition Act 1998 Cases*, CMA8, March 2014, paras 9.6–9.8 and 12.24–12.25.

181 Ibid.

182 An organisation chart of the structure of the CMA is available at www.gov.uk/cma.

183 CMA's *Annual Reports and Accounts 2016/17*, July 2017, p 107, available at www.gov.uk/cma.

184 CMA13, January 2014, available at www.gov.uk/cma.

185 Ibid.

186 ERRA, Sch 4, paras 12–13.

187 *Annual Plan 2017/18*, CMA59, March 2017, available at www.gov.uk/cma.

188 CMA35, November 2014, available at www.gov.uk/cma.

189 The markets identified in the *Strategic Assessment* have 'strategic significance' for the purposes the CMA's *Prioritisation Principles* (Ch 2 n 199 later): ibid, para 5.39.

(f) Performance framework

The CMA has agreed with the Government a performance management framework[190]. This framework provides a degree of external accountability, so that the CMA can demonstrate that it provides value for money to the taxpayers that pay for it, and improves internal management, so that the CMA prioritises its work properly. The CMA has agreed in particular to a performance target of delivering direct financial benefits to consumers worth more than at least ten times its relevant costs to the taxpayer (measured over a rolling three-year period)[191].

The CMA has estimated that the direct financial benefit to consumers arising from its enforcement of competition and consumer law in the period from 2014 to 2017 was £3.7 billion[192]; this ratio 18.6:1 exceeding the performance target of 10:1.

(g) Annual Reports on performance and concurrency

The CMA must make an Annual Report on its activities and performance to the Secretary of State containing an assessment of the extent to which the objectives and priorities set out in its annual plan have been met and a summary of significant decisions, investigations and other activities in the year[193]. The report must be laid before Parliament and published[194].

The CMA is also required to report annually on the use of concurrent powers in the regulated sectors[195]. This Concurrency Report must include information about the activities of the CMA and the sectoral regulators in relation to the exercise of concurrent powers under the Competition Act and the Enterprise Act[196]. In April 2014 the CMA and the sectoral regulators published a 'baseline' report assessing the state of the concurrency arrangements[197]. The most recent annual concurrency report was published in April 2017 describing actions taken by each of the sectoral regulators; the CMA commented that the number of new cases remained below the level that it would like to see[198].

(h) Functions of the CMA

The CMA plays a central role, and has a variety of functions, in relation to competition law and policy in the UK. The CMA's *Prioritisation Principles*[199] are used to decide which discretionary projects and cases the CMA will take on across its areas of responsibility. The general functions, as opposed to the enforcement functions, of the CMA include obtaining, compiling and keeping under review information relating to the exercise of its functions; making the public aware of ways in which competition may benefit consumers and the economy; providing information and advice to Ministers[200]; and making written recommendations to Ministers about the effect of proposed legislation on competition[201].

As far as public enforcement is concerned the CMA has considerable powers under the Competition Act 1998: it plays the principal role in enforcing the Chapter I and Chapter II prohibitions, and has significant powers to obtain information, enter premises to conduct investigations, adopt interim measures and make final decisions and impose penalties[202];

[190] *Performance Management Framework*, January 2014, available at www.gov.uk. [191] Ibid.
[192] *CMA Impact Assessment 2016/17*, CMA69, July 2017. [193] ERRA, Sch 4, para 14(1)–(2).
[194] Ibid, para 14(3). [195] Ibid, para 16(1). [196] Ibid, para 16(3).
[197] *'Baseline' annual report on concurrency—2014*, CMA24, April 2014, available at www.gov.uk/cma.
[198] *Annual report on concurrency 2017*, CMA63, April 2017, available at www.gov.uk/cma.
[199] CMA16, April 2014; see further ch 10, 'Opening a formal investigation', p 402.
[200] Enterprise Act 2002, ss 5–7.
[201] Ibid, s 7 as amended by the Small Business, Enterprise and Employment Act 2015, s 37 with effect from 26 May 2015; the CMA has made recommendations on competition issues raised by, for example, the Energy Bill, the Bus Services Bill and the Higher Education Bill.
[202] See ch 10 generally.

it also has the power to enforce Articles 101 and 102 TFEU[203]. Many of the decisions of the CMA under the Competition Act 1998 can be appealed on the merits to the CAT[204]. CMA decisions that cannot be appealed to the CAT may, nevertheless, be subject to judicial review by the Administrative Court. Separately, the CMA may bring criminal prosecutions of the 'cartel offence' under the Enterprise Act 2002[205]; in practice the CMA cooperates with the Serious Fraud Office in criminal cases[206].

The CMA also conducts market studies, market investigations and merger inquiries under the Enterprise Act 2002[207]. Decisions under the Enterprise Act 2002 in relation to mergers and market investigations are subject to judicial review by the CAT[208]. The CMA has a duty to keep under review undertakings given as a result of investigations conducted under the monopoly and merger provisions of the now-repealed Fair Trading Act 1973[209]. Separately, the CMA can be asked to conduct 'efficiency audits' of public sector bodies under the Competition Act 1980: this provision has not been used for many years[210].

The CMA has specific responsibilities in relation to competition as a result of provisions in the following legislation:

- the Law Reform (Miscellaneous Provisions) (Scotland) Act 1990
- the Financial Services and Markets Act 2000[211]
- the Transport Act 2000
- the Transport (Scotland) Act 2001[212]
- the Legal Services Act 2007
- the Payment Services Regulations 2009[213]
- the Legal Services (Scotland) Act 2010
- the Groceries Code Adjudicator Act 2013
- the Financial Services (Banking Reform) Act 2013
- the Small Business, Enterprise and Employment Act 2015
- the Consumer Rights Act 2015 and
- the Scotland Act 2016.

The CMA also has various regulatory functions in relation to privatised utilities[214]. The Regulatory Enforcement and Sanctions Act 2008 provides for the reduction and removal of regulatory burdens and requires the CMA to keep its regulatory functions under review.

[203] The Designation of the Competition and Markets Authority as a National Competition Authority Regulations 2014, SI 2014/537, reg 2.

[204] See ch 10, 'Appeals', pp 452–460.

[205] On the cartel offence see ch 10, 'The Cartel Offence and Company Director Disqualification', pp 435–449.

[206] See *Memorandum of Understanding between the CMA and the SFO*, April 2014, available at www.gov.uk/cma.

[207] See ch 11 (market studies and market investigations) and ch 22 (merger inquiries).

[208] See ch 11, 'Review of decisions under Part 4 of the Enterprise Act', pp 486–488 and ch 22, 'Review of decisions under Part 3 of the Enterprise Act', pp 979–981.

[209] See further ch 11, 'Orders and Undertakings under the Fair Trading Act 1973', p 493 and ch 22, 'Enforcement functions of the CMA', pp 977–978.

[210] On efficiency audits see *Halsbury's Laws of England*, Vol 18 (LexisNexis, 5th ed reissue, 2009), para 10.

[211] See ch 9, 'Financial Services and Markets Act 2000', pp 366–367.

[212] See Transport (Scotland) Act 2001 (Conditions attached to PSV Operator's Licence and Competition Test for Exercise of Bus Functions) Order 2001, SI 2001/2748.

[213] SI 2009/209, Part 8.

[214] See the Gas Act 1986 and the Gas (Northern Ireland) Order 1996, SI 1992/231; the Electricity Act 1989 and the Electricity (Northern Ireland) Order 1992, SI 1996/275; the Water Industry Act 1991; and the Water Services (Scotland) Act 2005 (Consequential Provisions and Modifications) Order 2005, SI 2005/3172; and the Water and Sewerage Services (Northern Ireland) Order 2006, SI 2006/3336; the Railways Act 1993; and the Transport Act 2000; the Communications Act 2003; the Energy Act 2004; the Postal Services Act 2011; the Civil Aviation Act 2012; and the Digital Economy Act 2017.

It is important to appreciate that the CMA is not only a competition authority, but also has consumer protection responsibilities under the following legislation:

- the Consumer Protection (Distance Selling) Regulations 2000[215]
- Part 8 of the Enterprise Act 2002
- the Consumer Protection Cooperation Regulation[216]
- the Consumer Protection from Unfair Trading Regulations 2008[217]
- the Consumer Rights (Payment Surcharges) Regulations 2012[218]
- Schedule 3 to the Consumer Rights Act 2015.

The CMA has published guidance on how it uses its consumer powers, which are an important complement to its tools under competition law[219]. The CMA has stated that it will prioritise projects where suspected breaches of consumer law involve systemic market problems for consumers, or impede consumers in the exercise of choice, or where enforcement can be expected to achieve wider impact[220]. The CMA has estimated that its consumer work generated direct financial benefits to consumers of £74.1 million per year in the years from 2013 to 2016[221].

The CMA also has a role in international competition policy: its statutory duty is to seek to 'promote competition, both within *and outside the UK*, for the benefit of consumers' (emphasis added)[222]. To that end, the CMA liaises on competition matters with the European Commission and is a member of the European Competition Network that brings together the Commission and the competition authorities of the Member States[223]. A likely effect of Brexit will be the departure of the UK from the ECN and the end of its role in the development of EU competition law and policy. The CMA attends meetings on competition policy on behalf of the UK at the Organisation for Economic Co-operation and Development and the United Nations Conference on Trade and Development; it is also an active participant in the International Competition Network[224].

A significant amount of the CMA's energies goes into raising awareness of competition law on the part of lawyers, small and medium-sized businesses and local authorities; it may do this by sending warning and advisory letters[225] or by asking local lawyers to share the CMA's competition law compliance materials with their clients[226].

(i) Rules

Section 51 of and Schedule 9 to the Competition Act 1998 make provision for the adoption of procedural rules by the CMA, which require the approval of the Secretary of

[215] SI 2000/2334, as amended by SI 2005/689.

[216] Regulation 2006/2004, OJ [2004] 364/1; see also the Enterprise Act 2002 (Amendment) Regulations, SI 2006/3363 and the Enterprise Act 2002 (Part 8 Community Infringements Specified UK Laws) Order 2006, SI 2006/3372.

[217] SI 2008/1277. [218] SI 2013/3110.

[219] CMA58, August 2016, available at www.gov.uk/cma; Annex A summarises the consumer legislation relevant to the CMA.

[220] *CMA Annual Plan 2017/18*, CMA59, March 2017, para 3.11, available at www.gov.uk/cma.

[221] NAO report, *Protecting consumers from scams, unfair trading and unsafe goods*, 15 December 2016, para 3.20, available at www.nao.org.uk.

[222] ERRA, s 25(3); on the CMA's international role see the speech by Lord Currie of 30 June 2014, available at www.gov.uk/cma.

[223] See ch 7, 'Regulation 1/2003 in Practice', pp 298–300.

[224] On the work of these international bodies see ch 12, 'The Internationalisation of Competition Law', pp 514–519.

[225] A register of warning and advisory letters is available at www.gov.uk/cma.

[226] See eg CMA Press Release, South East lawyers asked to help raise competition law awareness, 25 January 2017.

State[227]; the Competition Act 1998 (Competition and Markets Authority's Rules) Order was adopted under this provision in 2014[228].

(j) Publications, information, guidance etc

The CMA is required by sections 6 and 7 of the Enterprise Act 2002 to provide information to the public and to Ministers[229]. The CMA has published a statement setting out its approach to the transparency of its work, and how it deals with requests for information under the Freedom of Information Act 2000[230]. The Competition Act requires the CMA to publish general advice and information as to how it will apply the law in practice[231]. The CMA Board has adopted a number of guidelines that had been published by the OFT and by the CC[232]; the CMA has also published some guidelines of its own. The CMA's website provides information on UK competition law and policy and includes, among other things, details of current and decided cases under the Competition and Enterprise Acts[233], the numerous guidelines on these Acts, Press Releases, the Annual Plan and the Annual Report of the CMA, consultations and speeches[234]. The National Archives' website contains a wide variety of information, for example on cases, that was published by the CMA's predecessors, the OFT and the CC[235].

(iv) **Serious Fraud Office**

Section 188 of the Enterprise Act 2002 establishes the criminal cartel offence for individuals responsible for 'hard-core' cartels[236]. Serious penalties—of up to five years in prison—can be imposed upon those found guilty of this offence. Prosecutions may be brought by or with the consent of the CMA[237], or by the Serious Fraud Office ('the SFO')[238], working in close liaison with the CMA[239]. In Scotland the prosecution of the criminal offence is the responsibility of the Lord Advocate[240]. Quite apart from the cartel offence, there are some rare circumstances in which some cartel agreements might be illegal under the common law criminal offence of conspiracy to defraud; the SFO is the prosecutor for this offence as well[241].

(v) **Sectoral regulators**

Various sectors in the UK are subject to specific regulatory control, in particular utilities such as telecommunications and water. Several of the sector-specific regulators share concurrent powers with the CMA to enforce Articles 101 and 102 TFEU and the Chapter I and II prohibitions; they are also able to receive super-complaints[242] and to conduct

227 Competition Act 1998, s 51(5).

228 SI 2014/458.

229 See *Competition impact assessment: guidelines for policymakers*, CMA50, September 2015.

230 *Transparency and disclosure*, CMA6, January 2014, as clarified by a CMA note on publishing market sensitive announcements, December 2016.

231 Competition Act 1998, s 52.

232 See www.gov.uk/cma.

233 See www.gov.uk/cma-cases; the Public Register of decisions under the Competition Act 1998 is available at www.gov.uk/government/publications/ca98-public-register.

234 See www.gov.uk/cma.

235 See www.nationalarchives.gov.uk.

236 See ch 10, 'The cartel offence', pp 437–446.

237 Enterprise Act 2002, s 190(2)(b).

238 See *Memorandum of Understanding between the CMA and the SFO*, April 2014; the website of the SFO is www.sfo.gov.uk.

239 Enterprise Act 2002, s 190(1); see ch 10, 'Prosecution and penalty', pp 442–443.

240 See *Memorandum of Understanding between the CMA and the Crown Office and Procurator Fiscal Service*, July 2014, available at www.gov.uk/cma.

241 See ch 10, 'Conspiracy to defraud at common law', pp 448–449.

242 See Enterprise Act 2002, s 11; the Enterprise Act 2002 (Super-complaints to Regulators) Order 2003, SI 2003/1368; the Financial Services and Markets Act 2000, s 234C (FCA); and the Financial Services (Banking Reform) Act 2013, s 68 (PSR).

market studies and to make market investigation references to the CMA. The concurrent regulators are:

- the Gas and Electricity Markets Authority (supported by the Office of Gas and Electricity Markets (OFGEM))
- the Office of Communications (OFCOM)
- the Water Services Regulation Authority (OFWAT)
- the Office of Rail and Road (ORR)
- the Northern Ireland Authority for Utility Regulation (NIAUR)
- the Civil Aviation Authority (CAA)
- Monitor (now part of NHS Improvement)
- the Financial Conduct Authority (FCA)
- the Payment Systems Regulator (PSR).

Each of the concurrent regulators, except for Monitor[243], has a duty to promote competition in the interests of consumers; they must also consider whether the use of their competition law powers is more appropriate before taking enforcement action under their sector-specific, regulatory powers[244]. These concurrent regulators and the CMA are members of the UK Competition Network ('the UKCN'); Monitor attends the UKCN with observer status[245]. The 'mission' of the UKCN is to promote competition for the benefit of consumers and to prevent anti-competitive behaviour by using competition law powers and developing pro-competitive regulatory frameworks[246]. Arrangements are in place for coordination of the performance of the concurrent functions under the Act[247]; the UKCN website is a useful source of material[248]. Each of the concurrent regulators has agreed a *Memorandum of Understanding* with the CMA, which records the basis on which the authorities will cooperate and exchange information[249].

Appeals against 'appealable decisions' of the sectoral regulators under the Competition Act lie to the CAT[250]; references in relation to the licensing functions of the sectoral regulators[251] and market investigations may be made to the CMA[252].

The ERRA gives the Secretary of State the power to remove, by order, from a sectoral regulator any of its concurrency functions, if he or she considers that it is appropriate to do so for the purpose of promoting competition for the benefit of consumers[253]. As a separate matter, regulators should consider whether their decisions might be called into question under Article 106 TFEU on the basis that they might result in infringements of Articles 101 and/or 102[254].

243 Health and Social Care Act 2012, s 62(3) imposes a duty to prevent anti-competitive behaviour in the provision of health care services.

244 ERRA, Sch 14.

245 *Regulated Industries: Guidance on concurrent application of competition law to regulated industries*, CMA10, March 2014, para 3.15.

246 Ibid, Annexe B, *Statement of Intent of the UKCN*, 3 December 2013.

247 On concurrency see ch 10, 'Concurrency', pp 449–452.

248 See www.gov.uk/government/groups/uk-competition-network.

249 The *Memoranda* were signed in 2016 and are available at www.gov.uk/cma.

250 On the meaning of appealable decisions see ch 10, 'Appealable decisions', pp 453–455.

251 On licence modification references see ch 23, 'Regulatory systems in the UK for utilities', pp 1009–1010.

252 Enterprise Act 2002, Sch 9, Part 2.

253 ERRA, s 52; the concurrent regulators that may be the subject of a 'sectoral regulator order' are OFCOM, OFGEM, OFWAT, the ORR, the NIAUR and the CAA.

254 See ch 6 generally, and in particular the reference at 'Introduction', p 222 to a decision of the UK National Lottery Commission (now the Gambling Commission) not to authorise Camelot, the operator of the National Lottery, to provide 'ancillary services', available at www.natlotcomm.gov.uk.

(vi) Competition Appeal Tribunal

(a) Establishment of the CAT

The CAT is established by section 12(1) of the Enterprise Act 2002[255]. It consists of a President[256], a panel of Chairmen appointed by the Lord Chancellor following a recommendation from the Judicial Appointments Commission[257] (judges of the High Court of England and Wales, the Court of Session in Scotland and the High Court in Northern Ireland have been appointed to this panel[258]) and a panel of ordinary members appointed by the Secretary of State[259]. Cases are heard by a Tribunal of three persons, chaired by the President or one person from the panel of Chairmen. Various matters can be dealt with either by the President or by one of the Chairmen sitting alone. The CAT has a Registrar, also appointed by the Secretary of State[260]. Schedule 2 to the Enterprise Act contains provisions on such matters as eligibility for appointment as President or Chairman of the Tribunal. Section 14 of the Enterprise Act and Part I of Schedule 4 deal with the constitution of the Tribunal. Section 13 and Schedule 3 establish the Competition Service, the purpose of which is to fund and provide support services to the Tribunal[261]. The CAT's website provides details of decided and pending cases, and all of its judgments will be found there[262]. The CAT may sit outside London[263]. The CAT publishes an Annual Review and Accounts[264]. On 8 December 2017 the CAT had a staff of 17, including the Registrar and three référendaires. The CAT has a User Group which meets from time to time to discuss its practical operation[265].

(b) Functions of the CAT

The CAT, which is an independent judicial body, has four main functions in relation to competition matters[266]; it also has some functions in relation to regulatory matters. The first function is to hear appeals on the merits from 'appealable decisions' of the CMA and the sectoral regulators under the Competition Act 1998 and Articles 101 and 102 TFEU[267]. Appeals on a point of law or as to the amount of a penalty lie from decisions of the CAT with permission to the Court of Appeal in England and Wales, to the Court of Session in Scotland and to the Court of Appeal of Northern Ireland in Northern Ireland[268]. A further appeal may be taken, with permission, to the UK Supreme Court. It is also possible for the CAT to refer a matter of EU law to the Court of Justice[269].

[255] The Competition Act 1998 had established, within the former CC, appeal tribunals which could hear appeals under that Act; these tribunals have been abolished, and the CAT inherited their functions on 1 April 2003: see s 21 of and Sch 5 to the Enterprise Act.

[256] Enterprise Act 2002, s 12(2)(a).

[257] Ibid, s 12(2)(b). [258] Ibid, s 12(2)(aa), (ab) and (ac). [259] Ibid, s 12(2)(c).

[260] Ibid, s 12(3). [261] Ibid, s 13(2). [262] The website of the CAT is www.catribunal.org.uk.

[263] See the Competition Appeal Tribunal Rules 2015, r 18; the CAT has sat in Belfast, in the *BetterCare* case; in Edinburgh in the *Aberdeen Journals* and *Claymore* cases; and in Cardiff in the *Cardiff Bus* case: for details of these cases see the CAT's website.

[264] Available at www.catribunal.org.uk.

[265] The minutes of the last two User Group meetings are available at www.catribunal.org.uk.

[266] See Bailey 'The Early Case Law of the Competition Appeal Tribunal' in Rodger (ed) *Ten Years of UK Competition Law Reform* (Dundee University Press, 2010), ch 2.

[267] On appealable decisions see ch 10, 'Appealable decisions', pp 453–455; it is also possible that an application for judicial review of the CMA and sectoral regulators may be brought before the Administrative Court: ch 10, 'Appeals', pp 452–453.

[268] Competition Act 1998, s 49: see the Competition Appeal Tribunal Rules 2015, rr 107 and 108 and ch 10, 'Appeals from the CAT to the Court of Appeal and from the Court of Appeal to the Supreme Court', p 460.

[269] See the Competition Appeal Tribunal Rules 2015, r 109 and ch 10, 'Which courts or tribunals in the UK can make an Article 267 reference in a case under the Competition Act 1998?', p 461; a reference for a preliminary ruling was made by the CAT in the *Paroxetine* 'pay-for-delay' appeals: Cases 1251/1/12/16 etc *Generics UK Ltd v CMA* [2018] CAT 4.

The second function of the CAT is to hear any claim for damages or other sum of money brought by claimants who have suffered loss as a result of an infringement of UK or EU competition law[270]. The CAT may also hear claims for an injunction in England and Wales or Northern Ireland[271]. Claims may be brought on a 'standalone' basis, where the claimant must prove the infringement, or may 'follow-on' from a decision of the European Commission, the CMA or a sectoral regulator finding an infringement of competition law. The CAT may also authorise 'collective proceedings' brought by a representative on behalf of a defined class of claimants, either on an opt-in or an opt-out basis[272]. To date there have been two applications to the CAT to make a 'collective proceedings order'; both were unsuccessful[273]. The CAT may also approve collective settlements[274]. Separately, the High Court may transfer a case to the CAT for it to determine whether there has been an infringement of Articles 101 and/or 102 TFEU or of the Chapter I and II prohibitions in the Competition Act[275]; it has done so on two occasions[276].

The CAT's third function is to determine applications for review of decisions of the CMA, the Secretary of State or other Minister in relation to mergers[277] and market investigations[278].

The fourth function of the CAT is to hear appeals against penalties imposed by the CMA for failure to comply with notices requiring the attendance of witnesses or the production of documents during a market or merger investigation[279]. Provision is made by section 41 of the ERRA for the CAT to grant warrants under the Competition Act and the Enterprise Act. This provision had not been activated as at 8 December 2017.

The Communications Act 2003 empowers the CAT to determine appeals against certain decisions taken by OFCOM or the Secretary of State (as the case may be)[280]. The CAT has also been given certain functions under the following legislation:

- the Mobile Roaming (European Communities) Regulations 2007[281]
- Schedule 2A to the Electricity Act 1989 and Schedule 18 to the Energy Act 2004 in relation to determinations by OFGEM in respect of property schemes
- the Payment Services Regulations 2009[282]
- the Energy Act 2010[283]
- the Authorisation of Frequency Use for the Provision of Mobile Satellite Services (European Union) Regulations 2010[284]
- the Postal Services Act 2011[285]
- the Civil Aviation Act 2012[286]

270 On the CAT's jurisdiction to hear damages actions see ch 8, 'CAT proceedings', pp 327–328.

271 Competition Act 1998, s 47A(3)(c).

272 Ibid, s 47B and the Competition Appeal Tribunal Rules 2015, rr 77(1), 78 and 79.

273 Case 1257/7/7/16 *Dorothy Gibson v Pride Mobility Products Ltd* [2017] CAT 9 and Case 1266/7/7/16 *Walter Hugh Merricks v MasterCard Inc* [2017] CAT 16, on appeal to the Court of Appeal.

274 Competition Act 1998, s 49A and s 49B.

275 See the Section 16 Enterprise Act 2002 Regulations 2015, SI 2015/1643.

276 *Sainsbury's Supermarkets Ltd v MasterCard Inc* [2015] EWHC 3472 (Ch) and *Agents' Mutual Ltd v Gascoigne Halman Ltd*, order of 5 July 2016.

277 Enterprise Act 2002, s 120: see ch 22, 'Review of decisions under Part 3 of the Enterprise Act', pp 979–981.

278 Enterprise Act 2002, s 179: see ch 11, 'Review of decisions under Part 4 of the Enterprise Act', pp 486–488.

279 See further ch 11, 'Powers of investigation and penalties', pp 485–486 and ch 22, 'Investigation powers and penalties', pp 978–979.

280 See *Guide to Proceedings*, October 2015, paras 2.29–2.38 and 'Reform', p 74 below.

281 SI 2007/1933.

282 SI 2009/209.

283 Energy Act 2010, ss 20–21.

284 SI 2010/672.

285 Postal Services Act 2011, s 57.

286 Civil Aviation Act 2012, Schs 1, 3–5 and 13.

- the Financial Services (Banking Reform) Act 2013[287]
- the Payment Card Interchange Fee Regulations 2015[288].

(c) Rules

Section 15 of the Enterprise Act 2002 and Part 2 of Schedule 4 provide for the Secretary of State to make rules with respect to proceedings before the CAT. The Competition Appeal Tribunal Rules 2015[289] entered into force on 1 October 2015. Following an Introduction in Part 1, Part 2 of the 2015 Rules deals with appeals to the CAT respectively under the Competition and Communications Acts[290]; Part 3 is primarily concerned with applications for a review of decisions in mergers and market investigations[291]. Part 4 of the Rules deals with claims for damages under section 47A of the Competition Act[292], and provides for a 'fast-track' procedure for certain claims, for example where injunctive relief is sought[293]. Part 5 contains the rules on collective proceedings and collective settlements. Part 6 contains provisions on matters such as hearings, confidentiality, decisions of the CAT, appeals to the Court of Appeal and Article 267 references to the Court of Justice[294]. Part 7 deals with the reference of price control matters to the CMA under the Communications Act 2003.

The CAT published a *Guide to Proceedings* on 1 October 2015 which provides guidance for parties and their legal representatives as to its procedures in relation to all cases which it is competent to entertain and which has the status of a Practice Direction under Rule 115(3) of the 2015 Rules. The CAT has also published a Practice Direction relating to the disclosure and inspection of evidence in damages claims, which entered into force on 9 March 2017[295] and is intended to align the practice of the CAT with the provisions of the EU Damages Directive[296].

(d) Reform

In June 2013 the Government published a consultation document, *Streamlining Regulatory and Competition Appeals: Consultation on Options for Reform*[297]. A key proposal was to change the standard of review in competition and regulatory appeals. To date the Government has not published a response to its consultation. However the Digital Economy Act 2017 changed the standard of review for some appeals to the CAT under the Communications Act 2003 with effect from 31 July 2017, which will be heard according to a judicial review standard rather than on the merits[298].

(vii) **Civil courts**

Actions may be brought in the High Court where there are infringements of Articles 101 and 102 TFEU or the Chapter I and II prohibitions[299]; such actions are usually brought

[287] Financial Services (Banking Reform) Act 2013, ss 76 and 78. [288] SI 2015/1911.

[289] SI 2015/1648. [290] On appeals under the Competition Act see ch 10, 'Appeals', pp 452–460.

[291] See ch 22, 'Review of decisions under Part 3 of the Enterprise Act', pp 979–981 (mergers) and ch 11, 'Review of decisions under Part 4 of the Enterprise Act', pp 486–488 (market investigations).

[292] See ch 8, 'CAT proceedings', pp 327–328

[293] See the Competition Appeal Tribunal Rules 2015, r 58, on which see Case 1250/5/7/16 *Breasley Pillows Ltd v Vita Cellular Foams (UK) Ltd* [2016] CAT 8.

[294] On Article 267 references see ch 10, 'Article 267 References', pp 460–461.

[295] Available at www.catribunal.org.uk.

[296] See the Claims in respect of Loss or Damage arising from Competition Infringements (Competition Act 1998 and Other Enactments (Amendment)) Regulations 2017, SI 2017/385.

[297] Available at www.gov.uk. [298] Digital Economy Act 2017, s 87.

[299] On the enforcement of Articles 101 and 102 TFEU and the Competition Act in the civil courts see ch 8 generally.

in the Chancery Division, but sometimes may be dealt with by the Commercial Court[300]; both are part of the 'Business and Property Courts of England and Wales'. Where the CMA or the CAT has already found such an infringement its decisions are binding in proceedings before the High Court[301]. Provision is made both for the transfer of 'infringement issues' from the High Court to the CAT[302] and for the transfer of all or part of competition law claims to and from the CAT[303].

Where a warrant is required to enter premises under section 28, section 28A or section 62A of the Competition Act 1998, this must be obtained from a judge of the High Court[304]. The High Court may also issue warrants to enter premises in relation to investigations under the EU competition rules[305].

(viii) Criminal courts

The Competition Act 1998 and the Enterprise Act 2002 create several criminal offences. Most notably, the Enterprise Act establishes the 'cartel offence', the commission of which could attract a prison sentence of up to five years as well as a fine[306]. The cartel offence is described in detail in chapter 10[307]. Under the Competition Act various criminal offences may be committed where investigations are obstructed, documents are destroyed or falsified or where false or misleading information is provided[308]. It is a criminal offence to obstruct investigations conducted under the EU competition rules[309], and there are also criminal offences under the Enterprise Act.

4. The Relationship Between EU Competition Law and National Competition Laws

(A) Introduction

All the Member States of the EU have systems of competition law, in large part modelled upon Articles 101 and 102. Some Member States require that domestic law should be interpreted consistently with the EU rules, thereby reinforcing the alignment of EU and domestic law[310]. It follows that many cases will have the same outcome whether they are investigated under EU or under domestic law: for example, a horizontal price-fixing agreement would infringe Article 101(1), and would normally also be caught by any domestic system of competition law in the EU unless, for example, it occurred in a sector which was not subject to the domestic rules. Even though there is a high degree of convergence between EU and domestic competition law, the possibility remains that there

[300] *Practice Direction—Competition Law—Claims Relating to the Application of Articles [101 and 102 TFEU] and Chapters I and II of Part I of the Competition Act 1998*, available at www.justice.gov.uk.

[301] Competition Act 1998, s 58A; see similarly EU Damages Directive, OJ [2014] L 349/1, Article 9(1); the ordinary courts are also bound by findings of fact made by the CMA in the course of its investigation, unless the court directs otherwise: Competition Act 1998, s 58.

[302] See the Section 16 Enterprise Act 2002 Regulations 2015, SI 2015/1643; 'infringement issues' are listed in the Enterprise Act 2002, s 16(6).

[303] Competition Appeal Tribunal Rules 2015, rr 71 and 72 and CPR Part 30, Practice Direction, paras 8.1–8.8.

[304] Competition Act 1998, s 28(1) and s 59; in Scotland the relevant court is the Court of Session: ibid.

[305] Ibid, ss 62 and 63.

[306] Enterprise Act 2002, s 190.

[307] See ch 10, 'The cartel offence', pp 437–446.

[308] Competition Act 1998, ss 42–44, ss 65L–65N and s 72: see ch 10, 'Sanctions', pp 409–411.

[309] Competition Act 1998, s 65L, s 65M, s 65N.

[310] Section 60 of the Competition Act 1998 is an example of this in the UK: see ch 9, '"Governing Principles Clause": Section 60 of the Competition Act 1998', pp 387–392.

could be different outcomes depending on which system of law is applied. In some cases domestic law may be more generous than EU law; in others it may be stricter.

EU law takes precedence over national law, so that where a clash occurs it is the former which must be applied[311]: in *Walt Wilhelm v Bundeskartellamt*[312] the Court of Justice held that conflicts between the EU and national rules on cartels must be resolved by applying the principle that EU law takes precedence. However the *Walt Wilhelm* judgment did not provide answers to all the situations that could arise: for example, could a Member State prohibit an agreement that benefited from an EU block exemption[313]? These matters are now dealt with by Article 3 of Regulation 1/2003.

(B) Regulation 1/2003

Under Regulation 1/2003[314] the Commission shares the competence to apply Articles 101 and 102 with NCAs and national courts; of course NCAs and national courts can also apply domestic competition law. Member States are required by Article 35 of the Regulation to designate the authorities responsible for the application of Articles 101 and 102[315]: in the UK the CMA and the sectoral regulators have been designated as NCAs[316]. Recitals 8 and 9 and Article 3 of the Regulation deal with the relationship between Articles 101 and 102 and national competition laws.

(i) Obligation to apply Articles 101 and 102

Recital 8 states that, in order to ensure the effective enforcement of EU competition law, it is necessary to oblige NCAs and national courts, where they apply national competition law to agreements or practices, to also apply Article 101 or 102 where those provisions are applicable. Article 3(1) therefore provides that, where NCAs or national courts apply national competition law to agreements, decisions by associations of undertakings or concerted practices that may affect trade between Member States, they shall also apply Article 101; similarly they must apply Article 102 to any behaviour prohibited by that provision[317]. It is the concept of 'trade between Member States' that triggers the obligation to apply Articles 101 and 102, which is why the Commission published guidance on it in 2004[318].

[311] See Case 6/64 *Costa v ENEL* EU:C:1964:66; Case 106/77 *Amministrazione delle Finanze dello Stato v Simmenthal* EU:C:1978:49; Case C-213/89 *R v Secretary of State for Transport, ex p Factortame Ltd (No 2)* EU:C:1990:257; Case C-221/89 *R v Secretary of State for Transport, ex p Factortame Ltd (No 3)* EU:C:1991:320; note that NCAs must disapply national law that involves an infringement of EU competition law: Case C-198/01 *Consorzio Industrie Fiammiferi* EU:C:2003:430.

[312] Case 14/68 EU:C:1969:4.

[313] The Court of Justice declined to give an answer to this question in Case C-70/93 *Bayerische Motoren Werke v ALD Auto-Leasing* EU:C:1995:344, and Case C-266/93 *Bundeskartellamt v Volkswagen and VAG Leasing* EU:C:1995:345, since the agreements in those cases were not covered by the block exemption for motor car distribution in force at that time.

[314] See ch 2 n 1 earlier. For further discussion of Article 3 of Regulation 1/2003 see Faull and Nikpay (eds) *The EU Law of Competition* (Oxford University Press, 3rd ed, 2014), paras 2.30–2.76; see also *Modernisation*, OFT 442, December 2004, paras 4.1–4.30 (adopted by the CMA Board with effect from 1 April 2014).

[315] Designated national authorities have the right to participate in judicial proceedings against a decision that they have taken under Article 101 or 102: Case C-439/08 *VEBIC* EU:C:2010:739.

[316] See the Competition Act 1998 and Other Enactments (Amendment) Regulations 2004, SI 2004/1261, reg 3 and Designation of the Competition and Markets Authority as a National Competition Authority Regulations 2014, SI 2014/537, reg 2.

[317] On the temporal effect of this provision see Case C-17/10 *Toshiba Corporation v Úřad pro ochranu hospodářské soutěže* EU:C:2012:72.

[318] *Guidelines on the effect on trade concept contained in Articles [101 and 102 TFEU]* OJ [2004] C 101/81; the Guidelines are discussed in ch 3, 'The Effect on Trade between Member States', pp 150–155.

In *Toshiba v Úřad pro ochranu hospodářské soutěže*[319] the Court of Justice held that the combined effect of Articles 3(1) and 11(6) of Regulation 1/2003 is that the initiation by the Commission of proceedings relieves NCAs of their competence to apply Articles 101 and 102 TFEU and national competition laws. The power of the NCAs is restored once the proceeding initiated by the Commission has concluded[320]; thereafter the NCAs may apply national competition law, provided they comply with EU law, in particular Article 3 and Article 16(2) of Regulation 1/2003[321].

The CMA's view is that the prosecution of *individuals* for commission of the cartel offence contained in section 188 of the Enterprise Act 2002 does *not* trigger the obligation to apply Article 101, since Article 101 is aimed at the anti-competitive agreements of *undertakings* rather than individuals[322]. The Court of Appeal concurred with this view, albeit on different grounds. In *IB v The Queen* the Court held that the cartel offence is not a 'national competition law' in the sense of Article 3 of Regulation 1/2003 and rejected the argument that the Crown Court, which is not a designated competition authority for the purposes of that Regulation, did not have jurisdiction to try an indictment alleging the cartel offence[323]. The Court added that, even if the cartel offence were part of national competition law, it is a part of it which is not concerned with directly applying Article 101[324]. The position is not free from doubt, however[325]. In practice the CMA, when proceeding against individuals under the Enterprise Act, would probably also conduct an investigation against the undertakings involved in the cartel under domestic and/or EU law[326]: whether it would be doing so as a result of an obligation arising from Article 3(1) may be an academic question.

In certain circumstances the use by sectoral regulators of their sector-specific regulatory powers might amount to the application of national competition law, with the consequence that the obligation to apply Articles 101 and 102 TFEU would arise in the event that the agreement or conduct affected trade between Member States[327].

In its *Report on the functioning of Regulation 1/2003*[328] the Commission reported that Article 3(1) had led to a very significant increase in the application of Articles 101 and 102[329]. There is no doubt that Article 3(1) has played an important part in making the EU competition rules (in the words of the Commission) the 'law of the land' in the EU[330].

319 Case C-17/10 EU:C:2012:72, paras 74–78.

320 Ibid, paras 79–91.

321 Article 16(2) prohibits NCAs from contradicting a previous decision of the Commission; on Article 16 of Regulation 1/2003 see ch 8, 'Article 16: uniform application of EU competition law', pp 319–320.

322 See *Modernisation*, OFT 442, December 2004, paras 4.21–4.22 (adopted by the CMA Board with effect from 1 April 2014); see also Dekeyser's comments during a roundtable discussion at [2004] Fordham Corporate Law Institute (ed Hawk), pp 734–735.

323 [2009] EWCA Crim 2575, paras 21–37.

324 Ibid, para 38; if a CMA criminal investigation into an alleged cartel offence were considered to be 'acting under Article 101 or Article 102' for the purposes of Article 11(3) of Regulation 1/2003, the European Commission would have power under Article 11(6), by commencing its own proceedings, to relieve the CMA of the power to proceed.

325 See eg Wils *Principles of European Antitrust Enforcement* (Hart, 2005), paras 153–157 and Wils 'Is Criminalization of EC Competition Law the Answer?' (2005) 28 World Competition 117, at 130–133.

326 *Modernisation*, OFT 442, December 2004, paras 4.23–4.27.

327 Ibid, paras 4.28–4.30.

328 COM(2009) 206 final; see also the Commission Staff Working Paper accompanying the *Report on the functioning of Regulation 1/2003*, SEC(2009) 574 final, paras 139–181 which contains detailed analysis of the operation of Article 3 between 2004 and 2009; both documents are available at www.ec.europa.eu/competition/antitrust/legislation.html.

329 SEC(2009) 574 final, para 25.

330 See Commission Communication *Ten Years of Antitrust Enforcement under Regulation 1/2003: Achievements and Future Perspectives*, COM(2014) 453, para 23.

(ii) **Conflicts: Article 101**

Recital 8 of Regulation 1/2003 states that it is necessary to create a 'level playing field' for agreements within the internal market. What this means is that, if an agreement is not prohibited under EU competition law, it should not be possible for an NCA or national court to apply stricter national competition law to it; this may be termed a 'convergence rule'[331]. Article 3(2) therefore provides that the application of national competition law may not lead to the prohibition of agreements, decisions by associations of undertakings or concerted practices which may affect trade between Member States but which do not restrict competition within the meaning of Article 101(1) or which fulfil the conditions of Article 101(3) or which are covered by a block exemption. There do not appear to have been major difficulties with the application of the convergence rule[332]. In terms of UK law it follows that, in so far as agreements affect trade between Member States but do not infringe Article 101(1) or do satisfy the criteria of Article 101(3), it would not be possible to take action against them under the market investigation provisions of the Enterprise Act 2002[333].

(iii) **Conflicts: Article 102**

The position in relation to Article 102 is different, since Regulation 1/2003 does not demand convergence in relation to unilateral behaviour. Recital 8 of the Regulation states that Member States should not be precluded from adopting and applying on their territory stricter national competition laws which prohibit or impose sanctions on unilateral conduct. Article 3(2) therefore makes provision to this effect[334]. An example of a stricter national law on unilateral behaviour would be one that is intended to protect economically dependent undertakings: several Member States have laws to this effect[335]. In terms of UK law it follows from Article 3(2) that it would be possible to take action under the market investigation provisions of the Enterprise Act 2002 against unilateral behaviour, such as refusal to supply or the imposition of unfair prices or other trading conditions, to stricter effect than the position under Article 102[336]. In so far as legislation such as the UK Gas Act 1986, the Electricity Act 1989 or the Communications Act 2003 provides for the imposition of *ex ante* regulatory controls on the unilateral behaviour of regulated undertakings, and in so far as those controls could be regarded as national competition law, Article 3(2) would allow them to be applied to achieve a stricter outcome than under Article 102. If regulation were intended to protect some other legitimate interest than the protection of competition they could be applied by virtue of Article 3(3) (see later).

In its *Report on the functioning of Regulation 1/2003*[337] the Commission noted that the business and legal communities had criticised the divergence of legal standards on unilateral conduct across the Member States. The Commission considered that the exclusion of unilateral conduct from the scope of the convergence rule was a matter which warranted further reflection.

[331] See Commission's *Guidelines on the application of Article [101(3) TFEU]* OJ [2004] C 101/97, para 14.

[332] See the Commission Staff Working Paper accompanying the *Report on the functioning of Regulation 1/2003*, SEC(2009) 574 final, para 159.

[333] See further ch 11, 'Relationship with Regulation 1/2003', pp 475–476.

[334] For comment see Hildebrand 'Article 3(2) in fine: Time for review' Concurrences No 2-2015.

[335] See the Commission Staff Working Paper accompanying the *Report on the functioning of Regulation 1/2003*, SEC(2009) 574 final, paras 162–169 which provides examples of national rules concerning economic dependence and similar situations, available at www.ec.europa.eu.

[336] See further ch 11, 'Relationship with Regulation 1/2003', pp 475–476.

[337] COM(2009) 206 final, para 27; see also the Commission Staff Working Paper accompanying the *Report on the functioning of Regulation 1/2003*, SEC(2009) 574 final, paras 160–179.

(iv) Protection of 'other legitimate interests'

Recital 9 of Regulation 1/2003 states that its provisions should not preclude Member States from applying national legislation that protects legitimate interests other than the protection of competition on the market, provided that such legislation is compatible with the general principles and other provisions of EU law[338]. Article 3(3) therefore provides that the Regulation does not preclude the application of provisions of national law that 'predominantly pursue an objective different from that pursued by Articles [101 and 102 TFEU]'. Recital 9 of the Regulation says that Articles 101 and 102 have as their objective 'the protection of competition on the market', which provides a benchmark against which to measure whether a national provision pursues an objective different from the EU competition rules. The recital specifically says that a Member State could apply legislation intended to combat unfair trading practices, for example a law that prevents the imposition on customers of terms and conditions that are unjustified, disproportionate or without consideration.

There may be situations in which it will be unclear whether a national provision is predominantly concerned with matters other than the protection of competition. Certain regulatory rules—for example requiring the provision of a universal service or the protection of vulnerable consumers—clearly pursue objectives other than the protection of competition and so could be applied by virtue of Article 3(3)[339]. Consumer laws that provide protection against, for example, unfair contract terms, misleading advertising or sharp selling practices would also seem to pursue a predominantly different objective from Articles 101 and 102 TFEU[340]. However a national rule that was dependent, for example, on a prior finding of significant market power would look more like a rule whose concern was the protection of competition[341]. In that case the derogation provided by Article 3(3) would not be applicable, so that the position would be governed by Article 3(2): a stricter national rule in relation to agreements could not be applied, but a stricter rule on unilateral behaviour could be.

In *Days Medical Aids Ltd v Pihsiang*[342] the English High Court suggested that the common law doctrine of restraint of trade could not be said predominantly to pursue an objective different from Articles 101 and 102 TFEU, with the result that it could not be applied to invalidate an agreement that did not infringe Article 101.

[338] See, to similar effect, Article 21(4) of the EUMR, discussed in ch 21, 'Article 21(4): legitimate interest clause', pp 872–875.

[339] See further *Regulated Industries: Guidance on concurrent application of competition law to regulated industries*, CMA10, March 2014, para 4.12, available at www.gov.uk/cma.

[340] See the Commission Staff Working Paper accompanying the *Report on the functioning of Regulation 1/2003*, SEC(2009) 574 final, para 181.

[341] See eg Communications Act 2003, s 45.

[342] [2004] EWHC 44 (Comm), paras 254–266; see also *Jones v Ricoh UK Ltd* [2010] EWHC 1743 (Ch), para 49.

5. The Institutional Structure of EU and UK Competition Law

Figures 2.1, 2.2 and 2.3 below set out the institutional architecture of EU and UK law.

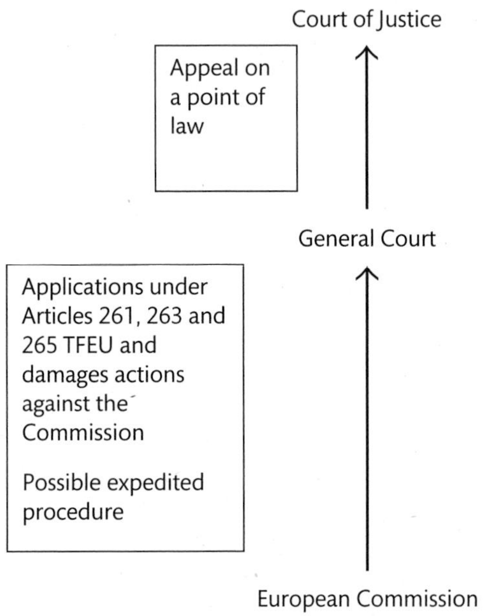

Fig. 2.1 Articles 101 and 102 TFEU; EU Merger Regulation

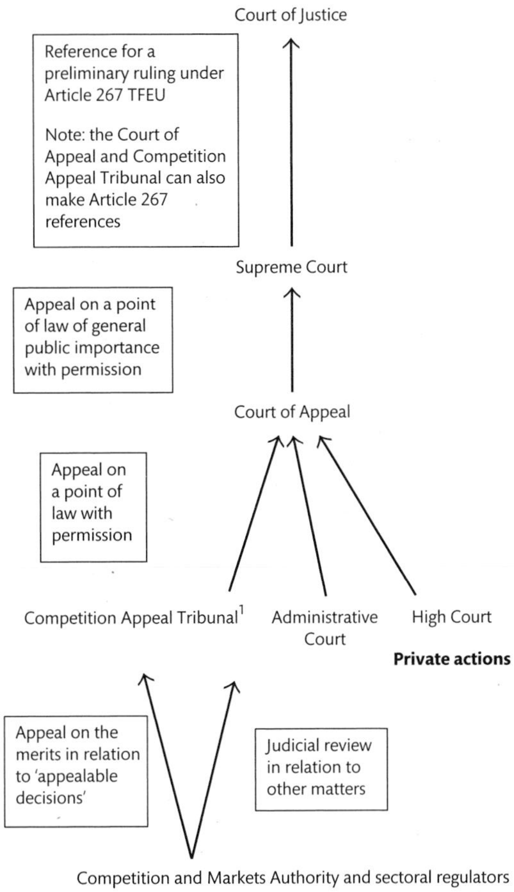

Fig. 2.2 Articles 101 and 102 TFEU; Competition Act 1998, Chapter I and II prohibitions

[1] The Competition Appeal Tribunal also hears actions for damages under sections 47A and 47B of the Competition Act 1998.

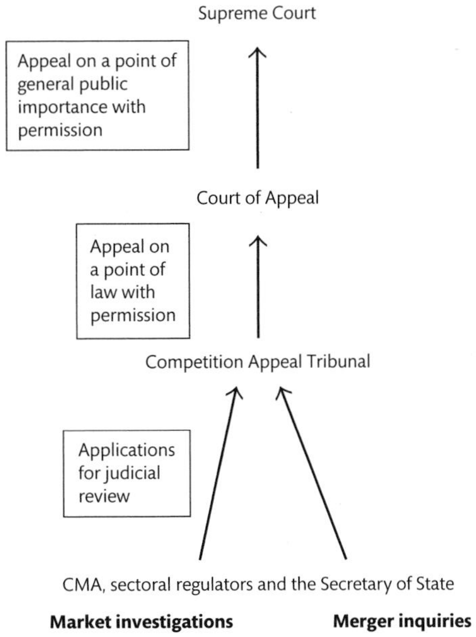

Fig. 2.3 Market investigations and merger inquiries

3

Article 101(1)

1. Introduction

This chapter is concerned with Article 101(1) TFEU which prohibits agreements, decisions by associations of undertakings and concerted practices that are restrictive of competition. Article 101(1) may be declared inapplicable where the criteria set out in Article 101(3) are satisfied: the provisions of Article 101(3) are considered in chapter 4[1]. An agreement which is prohibited by Article 101(1) and which does not satisfy Article 101(3) is stated to be automatically void by virtue of Article 101(2)[2]. The full text of Article 101 is as follows:

1. The following shall be prohibited as incompatible with the internal market: all agreements between undertakings, decisions by associations of undertakings and concerted practices which may affect trade between Member States and which have as their object or effect the prevention, restriction or distortion of competition within the internal market, and in particular those which:
   (a) directly or indirectly fix purchase or selling prices or any other trading conditions;
   (b) limit or control production, markets, technical development, or investment;
   (c) share markets or sources of supply;
   (d) apply dissimilar conditions to equivalent transactions with other trading parties, thereby placing them at a competitive disadvantage;
   (e) make the conclusion of contracts subject to the acceptance by other parties of supplementary obligations which, by their nature or according to commercial usage, have no connection with the subject of such contracts.
2. Any agreements or decisions prohibited pursuant to this Article shall be automatically void.

[1] For further reading on Article 101(1) readers are referred to Rose and Bailey (eds) *Bellamy and Child: European Union Law of Competition* (Oxford University Press, 7th ed, 2013), ch 2; Faull and Nikpay (eds) *The EU Law of Competition* (Oxford University Press, 3rd ed, 2014), ch 3, paras 3.01–3.511.

[2] See ch 8, 'The sanction of voidness', p 336 on the implications of the sanction of voidness in Article 101(2).

3. The provisions of paragraph 1 may, however, be declared inapplicable in the case of:
   - any agreement or category of agreements between undertakings;
   - any decision or category of decisions by associations of undertakings;
   - any concerted practice or category of concerted practices;

   which contributes to improving the production or distribution of goods or to promoting technical or economic progress, while allowing consumers a fair share of the resulting benefit, and which does not:

   (a) impose on the undertakings concerned restrictions which are not indispensable to the attainment of these objectives;

   (b) afford such undertakings the possibility of eliminating competition in respect of a substantial part of the products in question.

Many aspects of the prohibition in Article 101(1) require elaboration. First, the meaning of 'undertakings' and 'associations of undertakings' and then the terms 'agreements', 'decisions' and 'concerted practices' will be explained. The fourth section of this chapter will consider what is meant by agreements, decisions or concerted practices that 'have as their object or effect the prevention, restriction or distortion of competition'. The fifth section deals with the *de minimis* doctrine. Section six explains the requirement of an effect on trade between Member States. The chapter concludes with a checklist of agreements that, for a variety of reasons, normally fall outside Article 101(1).

2. Undertakings and Associations of Undertakings

Five issues must be considered in respect of this term: first, its basic definition for the purpose of Articles 101 and 102[3]; second, the meaning of 'associations of undertakings'; third, whether two or more legal persons form a single economic entity—and therefore comprise one undertaking—and the significance of such a finding; fourth, whether two or more entities may be treated as one undertaking where there is a corporate reorganisation; and fifth which undertaking is liable for an infringement of competition law when one business is sold to another.

The Treaty does not define an 'undertaking'[4]: it has been a task for the EU Courts to clarify its meaning[5]. However it is a critically important term, since only agreements and concerted practices *between undertakings* are caught by Article 101; similarly, Article 102 applies only to abuses committed by dominant *undertakings*. There is no doubt that organs of the Member States (for example public authorities, municipalities, communes, the health service) and entities entrusted by the Member States with regulatory or other functions are capable of distorting competition. The competition law question is whether the distortion of competition is the responsibility of an *undertaking*: if it is, the behaviour in question may infringe Articles 101 and/or 102, subject

[3] The term undertaking has the same meaning under Article 102, and this section discusses cases decided under both Article 101 and Article 102.

[4] For a particularly interesting discussion of this expression see Odudu 'The Meaning of Undertaking within Article 81 EC' in *The Boundaries of EC Competition Law: The Scope of Article 81* (Oxford University Press, 2006), ch 3; note that Article 80 of the former ECSC Treaty and Article 80 of the Euratom Treaty do contain definitions of an undertaking for their respective purposes, as does Article 1 of Protocol 22 of the EEA Agreement.

[5] See Case T-99/04 *AC-Treuhand v Commission* EU:T:2008:256, para 144 (*Organic peroxides*).

to the availability of various defences such as state compulsion[6] or Article 106(2)[7]. However where the behaviour that distorts competition is not that of an undertaking, it will not be subject to competition law scrutiny at all. As will be seen, there have been many cases in which the EU Courts have been asked whether a particular entity, accused of anti-competitive behaviour, qualified as an undertaking for the purpose of the competition rules. The question often arises in the case of so-called 'mixed markets', where a public body and private firms are present on a market and where, typically, the latter complain of anti-competitive conduct on the part of the former. In so far as it is thought that there should be 'competitive neutrality'—more colloquially a level playing field—there would seem to be an attraction in treating all the operators on such markets as undertakings, with the result that their behaviour is subject to competition law scrutiny[8]; however this is not the inevitable outcome, as will be seen in the case law discussed below.

A separate question, considered in chapter 6, is whether Member States themselves may be liable for the anti-competitive behaviour of public undertakings and undertakings that have 'special or exclusive rights'.

(A) **Basic definition**

The Court of Justice held in *Höfner and Elser v Macrotron GmbH*[9] that:

> the concept of an undertaking encompasses every entity engaged in an economic activity regardless of the legal status of the entity and the way in which it is financed.

In *Pavlov*[10] the Court added that:

> It has also been consistently held that any activity consisting in offering goods or services on a given market is an economic activity.

In *Wouters v Algemene Raad van de Nederlandsche Orde van Advocaten*[11] the Court said that the competition rules in the Treaty:

> do not apply to activity which, by its nature, its aim and the rules to which it is subject does not belong to the sphere of economic activity ... or which is connected with the exercise of the powers of a public authority.

These statements are a helpful starting point in understanding the meaning of the term undertaking and will be considered in the text that follows.

(i) **Need to adopt a functional approach**

It is important to understand at the outset that the same legal entity may be acting as an undertaking when it carries on one activity but not when it is carrying on another. A 'functional approach' must be adopted when determining whether an entity, when

[6] See 'State compulsion and highly regulated markets', pp 144–145 later in chapter.

[7] See ch 6, 'Article 106(2)', pp 242–248.

[8] For discussion see *Competition in mixed markets: ensuring competitive neutrality*, OFT 1242, July 2010, available at www.nationalarchives.gov.uk; OECD Roundtables *Competitive Neutrality: Maintaining a Level Playing Field between Public and Private Business* (2012), *Competition Policy and Competitive Neutrality* (2015) and *Inventory of Competitive Neutrality Distortions and Measures* (2015), all available at www.oecd.org/competition; ICN *Training on Demand Series V—State Restraints on Competition*, available at www.internationalcompetitionnetwork.org.

[9] Case C-41/90 EU:C:1991:161, para 21.

[10] Cases C-180/98 etc EU:C:2000:428, para 75.

[11] Case C-309/99 EU:C:2002:98, para 57.

engaged in a particular activity, is doing so as an undertaking for the purpose of the competition rules[12]. As the Court of Justice said in *MOTOE*[13]:

> The classification as an activity falling within the exercise of public powers or as an economic activity must be carried out separately for each activity exercised by a given entity[14].

Thus, for example, a local authority may (a) have powers to adopt bye-laws specifying where cars can and cannot be parked and (b) own land which it operates commercially as a car park. When performing function (a) the authority would, in the language of *Wouters*, be exercising the powers of a public authority and therefore would not be acting as an undertaking; the behaviour in (b), however, would be economic, and therefore that of an undertaking[15]. In *SELEX Sistemi Integrati SpA v Commission*[16] the General Court had to decide whether Eurocontrol, an entity created by Member States of the EU for the purpose of establishing navigational safety in the airspace of Europe, was acting as an undertaking. The Court concluded that some of Eurocontrol's activities—for example setting technical standards, procuring prototypes and managing intellectual property rights—were not economic; however it also concluded that some other activities—for example the provision of technical assistance to national administrations—could be separated from the exercise of its public powers[17] and be characterised as economic[18]. The Court of Justice disagreed and held that the General Court had erred in concluding that the latter activities were economic[19].

(ii) 'Engaged in an economic activity'

The sentence quoted from the *Höfner and Elser* judgment states that every entity engaged in economic activity does so as an undertaking: it is the idea of economic activity, therefore, that needs to be explored.

(a) Offering goods or services on a given market is an economic activity

Economic activity refers to any activity consisting in offering goods or services on a market. It is not the mere possibility that private operators could carry on the activity that is decisive, but the fact that the activity is carried on under market conditions[20]. The Commission held in *Spanish Courier Services*[21] that the Spanish Post Office, in so far as it was providing services on the market, was acting as an undertaking; in *Höfner and Elser* the Court of Justice reached the same conclusion in respect of the employment procurement activities of the German Federal Employment Office[22]. In *Ambulanz Glöckner v Landkreis Südwestpfalz*[23] the Court of Justice held that non-profit-making medical aid organisations, such as the German Red Cross, providing ambulance services for remuneration were acting as undertakings for the purpose of the competition rules[24].

[12] On this point see the Opinion of AG Jacobs in Cases C-67/96 etc *Albany International BV v SBT* EU:C:1999:28, para 207; this Opinion contains an invaluable discussion of the meaning of undertakings in Article 101(1).

[13] Case C-49/07 EU:C:2008:376. [14] Ibid, para 25.

[15] See eg *Eco-Emballages* OJ [2001] L 233/37, para 70: French local authorities were acting as undertakings when entering into contracts in relation to the collection of household waste; see also *Medicall Ambulance v Health Service Executive* [2011] IEHC 76, paras 25–35: Irish State acting as an undertaking when running the public ambulance service.

[16] Case T-155/04 EU:T:2006:387.

[17] Ibid, para 86. [18] Ibid, para 92.

[19] Case C-113/07 P *SELEX Sistemi Integrati SpA v Commission* EU:C:2009:191, paras 77–79.

[20] See AG Opinion in Case C-205/03 P *FENIN v Commission* EU:C:2005:666, para 13.

[21] OJ [1990] L 233/19. [22] Case C-41/90 EU:C:1991:161, para 22.

[23] Case C-475/99 EU:C:2001:577. [24] Ibid, paras 19–22.

A legal entity that acts as a 'facilitator' to a cartel can be an undertaking, even though it does not itself produce the goods or services that are cartelised[24a]. The mere holding of shares in an undertaking does not, in itself, mean that the owner of the shares is itself an undertaking engaged in economic activity; however the position would be different where the shareholder actually exercises control by involving itself in the management of the undertaking[25]. In *Pegler v Commission*[26] the General Court held that a 'dormant' company with no assets, employees or turnover did not offer goods or services on a market and therefore was not acting as an undertaking.

(b) No need for a profit-motive or economic purpose

The fact that an organisation lacks a profit-motive[27] or does not have an economic purpose[28] does not, in itself, mean that an activity is not economic. In *Höfner and Elser* the Federal Employment Office was an undertaking even though it supplied its services free of charge. In *Piau*[29] the General Court held that the practice of football by football clubs is an economic activity[30], and that national associations that group the clubs together are associations of undertakings; the position does not alter because the national associations group amateur clubs alongside professional ones[31]. The General Court also held in this case that FIFA was an association of undertakings[32].

(c) 'Regardless of the legal status of the entity and the way in which it is financed'

An entity is an undertaking whenever it is engaged in economic activity; its legal form is irrelevant. Companies and partnerships of course can qualify as undertakings, but so too can other entities such as agricultural cooperatives[33], P & I clubs[34] and trade associations: it follows that agreements between trade associations may themselves be caught by Article 101(1)[35]. When natural persons engage in economic activity they are undertakings[36], although an individual acting as an employee would

[24a] See Case C-194/14 P *AC-Treuhand v Commission* EU:C:2015:717, paras 33–36 (*Heat stabilisers*); see further ch 13, 'Facilitators', pp 527–528.

[25] Case C-222/04 *Cassa di Risparmio di Firenze* EU:C:2006:8, paras 111–113.

[26] Case T-386/06 EU:T:2011:115, paras 43–49 (*Copper fittings*).

[27] See eg Cases 209/78 etc *Van Landewyck v Commission* EU:C:1980:248, para 88; *P&I Clubs* OJ [1985] L 376/2; *P&I Clubs* OJ [1999] L 125/12; *Distribution of Package Tours During the 1990 World Cup* OJ [1992] L 326/31, para 43; Case C-244/94 *Fédération Française des Sociétés d'Assurance* EU:C:1995:392, para 21; Cases C-67/96 etc *Albany International BV v SBT* EU:C:1999:430, para 85; *UEFA's Broadcasting Regulations* OJ [2001] L 171/12, para 47; for comment on the application of competition law to non-profit-making activities, see Philipson and Posner 'Antitrust and the Not-For-Profit Sector' (2009) 52 Journal of Law and Economics 1.

[28] Case 155/73 *Italy v Sacchi* EU:C:1974:40, paras 13–14; Case C-222/04 *Cassa di Risparmio di Firenze* EU:C:2006:8, para 123.

[29] Case T-193/02 EU:T:2005:22; see also Case C-519/04 P *Meca-Medina v Commission* EU:C:2006:492, para 38: the Commission proceeded on the basis that the International Olympic Committee was an undertaking and an association of undertakings.

[30] Case T-193/02 EU:T:2005:22, para 69. [31] Ibid, para 70. [32] Ibid, para 72.

[33] See eg Case 61/80 *Coöperative Stremsel- en Kleurselfabriek v Commission* EU:C:1981:75; *MELDOC* OJ [1986] L 348/50. [34] *P&I Clubs* OJ [1985] L 376/2; *P&I Clubs* OJ [1999] L 125/12, paras 50–51.

[35] See eg Case 71/74 *FRUBO v Commission* EU:C:1975:61; Case 96/82 *IAZ International Belgium NV v Commission* EU:C:1983:310; *Algemene Schippersvereniging v ANTIB* OJ [1985] L 219/35, upheld on appeal Case 272/85 *ANTIB v Commission* EU:C:1987:235.

[36] See eg *AOIP v Beyrard* OJ [1976] L 6/8 where a patent licence between an individual and a company was held to fall within Article 101(1); *Reuter/BASF* OJ [1976] L 254/40; *RAI v UNITEL* OJ [1978] L 157/39 where opera singers were undertakings; *Vaessen BV v Moris* OJ [1979] L 19/32; Case 35/83 *BAT v Commission* EU:C:1985:32; Case 42/84 *Remia BV and Verenigde Bedrijven Nutricia NV v Commission* EU:C:1985:327; *Breeders' Rights: Roses* OJ [1985] L 369/9; *French Beef* OJ [2003] L 209/12, paras 104–108, upheld on appeal Cases T-217/03 and T-245/03 *FNCBV v Commission* EU:T:2006:391 and on further appeal Cases C-101/07 P etc *FNCBV v Commission* EU:C:2008:741; see also *ONP*, Commission decision of 8 December 2010, paras 587–588 and case law cited, upheld on appeal Case T-90/11 *ONP v Commission* EU:T:2014:1049.

not be[37]; nor would an individual purchasing goods or services as a final consumer, since that behaviour is not economic[38].

In *FENIN*[39] Advocate General Maduro spoke of the Court entering 'dangerous territory' when determining whether a state entity is engaged in economic activity, since the Court must find a balance between the protection of competition and respect for the powers of the state. The case law is clear, however, that the fact that a state entity is carrying out a purely public function in respect of some of its activities does not preclude it from being an undertaking as regards another activity[40]. Public authorities are undertakings when they engage in economic activities, as, for example, the Autonomous Administration of State Monopolies in *Banchero*[41] did when offering goods and services on the market for manufactured tobacco. State-owned corporations may act as undertakings[42], as may bodies entrusted by the state with particular tasks[43] and quasi-governmental bodies which carry on economic activities[44]. Aéroports de Paris, responsible for the planning, administration and development of civil air transport installations in Paris, the Portuguese Airports Authority, ANA and the Finnish Civil Aviation Administration were all found by the Commission to constitute undertakings[45].

In *Aluminium Products*[46] foreign trade organisations in east European countries were regarded as undertakings, even though they had no existence separate from the state under their domestic law: claims of sovereign immunity should be confined to acts which are those of government and not of trade. The same point was made by the Commission in its decision in *Amministrazione Autonoma dei Monopoli di Stato*[47].

(iii) Activities that are not economic

Three activities have been held to be non-economic: those provided on the basis of 'solidarity'; the exercise of public powers; and procurement pursuant to a non-economic activity. Each non-economic activity is discussed in turn below.

(a) Solidarity

There have been several cases in which the question has arisen whether entities providing social protection, for example social security, pensions, health insurance or health care, did so as undertakings[48]. The case law makes a distinction between situations in which such protection is provided in a market context on the one hand, or on the basis of

37 See 'Employees, trades unions and collective labour relations', pp 90–92 later in chapter.

38 On this point see Cases C-180/98 etc *Pavel Pavlov v Stichting Pensioenfonds Medische Specialisten* EU:C:2000:428, paras 78–81.

39 Case C-205/03 P EU:C:2005:666, para 26.

40 Case C-82/01 P *Aéroports de Paris v Commission* EU:C:2002:617, para 81.

41 Case C-387/93 EU:C:1995:439, para 50.

42 See eg Case 155/73 *Sacchi* EU:C:1974:40; Case 41/83 *Italy v Commission* EU:C:1985:120.

43 Such bodies have a limited dispensation from the competition rules by virtue of Article 106(2) TFEU: see ch 6, 'Article 106(2)', pp 242–248.

44 Case 258/78 *Nungesser KG v Commission* EU:C:1982:211.

45 See respectively *Alpha Flight Services/Aéroports de Paris* OJ [1998] L 230/10, paras 49–55, upheld on appeal Case T-128/98 *Aéroports de Paris v Commission* EU:T:2000:290, paras 120–126 and on further appeal Case C-82/01 P EU:C:2002:617, paras 78–82; *Portuguese Airports* OJ [1999] L 69/31, para 12, upheld on appeal Case C-163/99 *Portugal v Commission* EU:C:2001:189; *Ilmailulaitos/Luftfartsverket* OJ [1999] L 69/24, paras 21–23.

46 OJ [1985] L 92/1: see the Commission's XIVth *Report on Competition Policy* (1984), point 57; see similarly *Re Colombian Coffee* OJ [1982] L 360/31.

47 OJ [1998] L 252/47, para 21.

48 See Odudu 'The Meaning of Undertaking within Article [101TFEU]' (2006) 7 Cambridge Yearbook of European Legal Studies 211; Boeger 'Solidarity and EC Competition Law' (2007) 32 EL Rev 319; Odudu 'Economic Activity as a Limit to Community Law' in Barnard and Odudu (eds) *The Outer Limits of EU Law* (Hart, 2009), 225; Szydlo 'Leeway of Member States in Shaping the Notion of an "Undertaking" in Competition Law' (2010) 33 World Competition 549.

'solidarity' on the other. Solidarity was defined by Advocate General Fennelly in *Sodemare v Regione Lombardia*[49] as 'the inherently uncommercial act of involuntary subsidisation of one social group by another'[50]. Social protection that is provided on the basis of solidarity is a non-economic activity. The cases in which this issue has had to be examined are very fact-specific. As Advocate General Jacobs said in *AOK Bundesverband*[51]:

> Schemes come in a wide variety of forms, ranging from State social security schemes at one end of the spectrum to private individual schemes operated by commercial insurers at the other. Classification is thus necessarily a question of degree[52].

In deciding whether the degree of solidarity precludes economic activity, the case law considers the freedom of the scheme to determine the level of contributions and benefits payable. In *Poucet v Assurances Générales de France*[53] the Court of Justice concluded that French regional social security offices administering sickness and maternity insurance schemes to self-employed persons were not acting as undertakings, but it reached the opposite conclusion in relation to a differently-constituted scheme in *Fédération Française des Sociétés d'Assurance*[54]. The difference was that in *Poucet* the benefits payable were identical for all recipients, contributions were proportionate to income, the pension rights were not proportionate to the contributions made and schemes that were in surplus helped to finance those which had financial difficulties; the schemes were based on the principle of solidarity. In *Fédération Française*, on the other hand, the benefits payable depended on the amount of the contributions paid by recipients and the financial results of the investments made by the managing organisation; the manager of the scheme was carrying on an economic activity in competition with life assurance companies. In *Albany International BV v Stichting Bedrijfspensioenfonds Textielindustrie*[55] the Court of Justice held that the pension fund in that case was acting as an undertaking when making investments, the result of which determined the amount of benefits that the fund could pay to its members[56]; as such, this fund was different from the one in *Poucet*.

In *Cisal di Battistello Venanzio & C Sas v INAIL*[57] the Court of Justice held that INAIL, entrusted by law with management of a compulsory scheme providing insurance against accidents at work, was not acting as an undertaking. The INAIL's activities were subject to state supervision and were based on solidarity between healthy workers and those who had suffered an accident at work. In *AOK Bundesverband*[58] the Court of Justice held that German sickness funds were involved in the management of the social security system, fulfilling an exclusively social function founded on the principle of solidarity; it followed that they were not acting as undertakings[59]. In *AG2R Prévoyance v Beaudout Père et Fils SARL*[60] the Court of Justice suggested that AG2R, which operated a scheme

[49] Case C-70/95 EU:C:1997:301. [50] Ibid, para 29.

[51] Cases C-264/01 etc EU:C:2003:304; see also paras 59–68 of the Opinion of AG Mengozzi in Case C-437/09 *AG2R Prévoyance v Beaudout Père et Fils SARL* EU:C:2010:676.

[52] Cases C-264/01 etc EU:C:2003:304, para 36. [53] Cases C-159/91 and 160/91 EU:C:1993:63.

[54] Case C-244/94 EU:C:1995:392.

[55] Cases C-67/96 etc EU:C:1999:430: for commentary on this case see Gyselen (2000) 37 CML Rev 425; see also Cases C-180/98 etc *Pavel Pavlov v Stichting Pensioenfonds Medische Specialisten* EU:C:2000:428, paras 102–119.

[56] Case C-67/96 etc EU:C:1999:430, paras 71–87. [57] Case C-218/00 EU:C:2002:36.

[58] Cases C-264/01 etc EU:C:2004:150; see also, under Article 107 TFEU on state aid, Case C-266/04 *Casino France* EU:C:2005:657, paras 45–55.

[59] The same conclusion was reached in Case C-350/07 *Kattner Stahlbau GmbH v Maschinenbau- und Metal-Berufsgenossenschaft* EU:C:2009:127, paras 33–68.

[60] Case C-437/09 EU:C:2011:112; see also the judgment of the EFTA Court in Case E-5/07 *Private Barnehagers Landsforbund v EFTA Surveillance Authority* [2008] 2 CMLR 818, paras 82–83: Norwegian State not acting as an undertaking when funding municipal kindergartens.

for supplementary reimbursement of healthcare costs that was 'characterised by a high degree of solidarity'[61], might nevertheless be acting as an undertaking where it enjoyed a degree of autonomy, that is to say it was relatively free from state control[62].

(b) Activities connected with the exercise of the powers of a public authority are not economic

Although it is clear that state-owned entities or public authorities are undertakings when engaged in economic activity, the *Wouters* judgment says they are not when their behaviour 'is connected with the exercise of the powers of a public authority'[63]. In *Corinne Bodson v Pompes Funèbres des Régions Libérées SA*[64] a French law entrusted the performance of funeral services to local communes; many of the communes in turn awarded concessions to provide those services to private undertakings. The Court of Justice held that Article 101 did not apply to 'contracts for concessions concluded between communes *acting in their capacity as public authorities* and undertakings entrusted with the provision of a public service' (emphasis added)[65]. An entity exercises 'public powers' where the activity in question is 'a task in the public interest which forms part of the essential functions of the State' and where that activity 'is connected by its nature, its aim and the rules to which it is subject with the exercise of powers ... which are typically those of a public authority'[66]. For the same reason in *SAT Fluggesellschaft v Eurocontrol*[67] the Court of Justice concluded that Eurocontrol was not acting as an undertaking when it created and collected route charges from users of air navigation services on behalf of the states that had created it[68]. In *Calì e Figli*[69] the Court of Justice held that a private company engaged in the public task of anti-pollution surveillance in Genoa harbour would not be acting as an undertaking when discharging that particular responsibility, since this was a task in the public interest, forming part of one of the essential functions of the state in protecting the maritime environment. In *Compass-Datenbank v Republik Österreich*[70] the Austrian State was not acting as an undertaking when the law required it to administer a register of information about companies registered in Austria.

(c) Procurement that is ancillary to a non-economic activity is not economic

In *FENIN v Commission*[71] a complaint was made to the Commission that 26 public bodies in Spain responsible for the operation of the Spanish national health system were abusing their dominant buyer power by delaying unreasonably the payment of invoices. The Commission rejected the complaint on the basis that the public bodies were not acting as undertakings. FENIN, an association representing most undertakings marketing medical goods and equipment used in Spanish hospitals, appealed to the General Court. The General Court dismissed the appeal. Its reasoning was that, when providing health care

[61] Case C-437/09 EU:C:2011:112, para 52. [62] Ibid, paras 53–65.

[63] See to the same effect Case C-138/11 *Compass-Datenbank GmbH v Republik Österreich* EU:C:2012:449, paras 36–38 and the case law cited.

[64] Case 30/87 EU:C:1988:225. [65] Ibid, para 18.

[66] Case C-343/95 *Calì e Figli* EU:C:1997:160, para 23.

[67] Case C-364/92 EU:C:1994:7, para 30; different activities of Eurocontrol were held not to be economic in the *SELEX* case, ch 3 n 19 earlier.

[68] A similar conclusion had earlier been reached by the Commercial Court in London in *Irish Aerospace (Belgium) NV v European Organisation for the Safety of Air Navigation* [1992] 1 Lloyd's Rep 383.

[69] Case C-343/95 EU:C:1997:160. [70] Case C-138/11 EU:C:2012:449, paras 40–51.

[71] Case T-319/99 EU:T:2003:50; it is interesting to compare this judgment with that of the UK Competition Appeal Tribunal in Case 1006/2/1/01 *BetterCare Group Ltd v Director General of Fair Trading* [2002] CAT 7, a judgment which preceded that in *FENIN* and which came to a different view in relation to the procurement activities of the Health Trust in that case: see ch 9, 'Undertakings', pp 348–350.

to citizens, the public bodies did so on the basis of solidarity: that behaviour therefore was not economic. The General Court then held that the activity of purchasing goods should not be dissociated from the purpose to which they would be put. Since the universal provision of health care free of charge was not economic, the ancillary behaviour of procurement for that purpose was not economic either[72]. This judgment was upheld on appeal to the Court of Justice[73]. The position may be different where a health organisation purchasing goods uses them partly for the provision of state-sponsored health care on the basis of solidarity, but also charges certain patients, for example tourists from overseas, according to market principles[74]. The reasoning in *FENIN* was subsequently applied in *SELEX Sistemi Integrati SpA v Commission*[75].

(iv) The professions

Abundant case law has established that members of the professions can be undertakings for the purposes of the competition rules. In *Commission v Italy*[76] the Court of Justice held that customs agents in Italy, who offered for payment services consisting of the carrying out of customs formalities in relation to the import, export and transit of goods, were undertakings; it rejected the Italian Government's argument that the fact that the activity of customs agents is intellectual and requires authorisation and compliance with conditions meant that they were not undertakings. Self-employed medical specialists have been held to be undertakings[77], as have lawyers[78], accountants[79], attestation agents[80] and geologists[81].

(v) Employees, trades unions and collective labour relations

(a) Employees

In *Jean Claude Becu*[82] the Court of Justice held that workers are, for the duration of their employment relationship, incorporated into the undertakings that employ them and thus form part of an economic unit with them; as such they do not constitute undertakings within the meaning of EU competition law[83]. Nor should the dock workers in that case, taken collectively, be regarded as constituting an undertaking[84]. However an ex-employee who carries on an independent business would be[85].

[72] *FENIN*, paras 35–36; on the application of competition law to health care generally see Odudu 'Are State-Owned Health-Care Providers Undertakings Subject to Competition Law?' (2011) 5 ECLR 231.

[73] Case C-205/03 P EU:C:2006:453, paras 25–26; AG Maduro's Opinion in this case contains an extensive review of the law on the issues raised: Case C-205/03 P EU:C:2005:666.

[74] The General Court did not address this point because it had not been raised in the complaint to the Commission: Case T-319/99 EU:T:2003:50, paras 41–44.

[75] See ch 3 n 19 earlier.

[76] Case C-35/96 EU:C:1998:303; see similarly Case T-513/93 *CNSD v Commission* EU:T:2000:91, upholding the Commission's decision in *CNSD* OJ [1993] L 203/27; *Coapi* OJ [1995] L 122/37; *EPI code of conduct* OJ [1999] L 106/14, partially annulled on appeal Case T-144/99 *Institut des Mandataires Agréés v Commission* EU:T:2001:105.

[77] Cases C-180/98 etc *Pavel Pavlov v Stichting Pensioenfonds Medische Specialisten* EU:C:2000:428, para 77.

[78] Case C-309/99 *Wouters v Algemene Raad van de Nederlandsche Orde van Advocaten* EU:C:2002:98, paras 48–49.

[79] Case C-1/12 *Ordem dos Técnicos Oficiais de Contas v Autoridade de Concurrência* EU:C:2013:127, paras 37–38.

[80] Case C-327/12 *Ministero dello Sviluppo economico v SOA Nazionale Costruttori* EU:C:2013:827, paras 27–35.

[81] Case C-136/12 *Consiglio nazionale dei geologi* EU:C:2013:489, para 44.

[82] Case C-22/98 EU:C:1999:419.

[83] Ibid, para 26; see similarly Case C-542/14 *VM Remonts* EU:C:2016:578, para 23.

[84] Case C-22/98 *Becu* EU:C:1999:419, para 27.

[85] See eg *Reuter/BASF* OJ [1976] L 254/40.

In *FNV Kunsten Informatie en Media v Staat der Nederlanden*[86] the Court acknowledged that it is not always easy to determine whether a person is an employee or a self-employed, independent provider of services on a market[87]. It is relevant to consider whether the person has the freedom to choose the time, place and content of his or her work[88]. The classification of a 'self-employed person' under national law does not prevent that person being classified as an employee under EU law if his or her independence is merely notional, thereby disguising an employment relationship.

An employer is liable for any anti-competitive conduct on the part of the employee because the employer and employee are one and the same undertaking[89].

(b) Trades unions

A trade union is not considered to be an undertaking when acting as an agent of its members and is solely an executive organ of an agreement between them[90]; however it will be an undertaking when acting in its own right[91]. In *FNCBV v Commission*[92] the General Court rejected an argument that the application of Article 101 to agreements between associations of farmers to fix prices and to prevent imports of beef into France restricted the freedom of trade union activity[93].

(c) Collective labour relations

In *Albany*[94] the Court of Justice was concerned with a case where organisations representing employers and employees collectively agreed to set up a single pension fund responsible for managing a supplementary pension scheme and requested the public authorities to make affiliation to the fund compulsory. One issue was whether an agreement between such organisations was an agreement between undertakings. The Court of Justice's answer was that it was not. The Treaty's activities include not only the adoption of a competition policy, but also a social policy: this is stated in Article 3(3) TEU and Article 9 TFEU and revealed, for example, in Article 153 TFEU, the purpose of which is to promote close cooperation between Member States in the social field, particularly in matters relating to the right of association and collective bargaining between employers and workers. The Court of Justice's view was that the social objectives pursued by collective agreements would be seriously undermined if they were subject to Article 101 and that therefore they fall outside it[95]. In *Norwegian Federation of Trade Unions v Norwegian Association of Local and Regional Authorities*[96] the EFTA Court applied the *Albany* doctrine to collective labour

[86] Case C-413/13 EU:C:2014:2411.

[87] Ibid, para 32; see also the Irish Competition Act (Amendment) Act 2017, s 2 on identifying 'false self-employed' and 'fully dependent self-employed' workers for the purposes of the application of competition law to collective bargaining.

[88] Case C-413/13 EU:C:2014:2411, paras 36–37.

[89] Case C-542/14 *VM Remonts* EU:C:2016:578, para 24.

[90] Case C-22/98 *Becu* EU:C:1999:419, para 28.

[91] See AG Jacobs in Case C-67/96 *Albany* EU:C:1999:28; see Bradshaw 'Is a Trade Union an Undertaking Under EU Competition Law?' (2016) European Competition Journal 320.

[92] Cases T-217/03 etc EU:T:2006:391, upheld on appeal Cases C-101/07 P etc *FNCBV v Commission* EU:C:2008:741.

[93] Cases T-217/03 etc EU:T:2006:391, paras 97–103.

[94] See ch 3 n 55 earlier; the Court considered its ruling in *Albany* in relation to the standing of a trade union to challenge a state aid decision in Case C-319/07 P *3F v Commission* EU:C:2009:435, paras 47–60.

[95] Ch 3 n 55 earlier, para 59; for critical comment see Van den Bergh and Camesasca 'Irreconcilable Principles? The Court of Justice Exempts Collective Labour Agreements from the Wrath of Antitrust' (2000) 25 EL Rev 492; Boni and Manzini 'National Social Legislation and EC Antitrust Law' (2001) 24 World Competition 239; see also Case C-222/98 *Van der Woude v Stichting Beatrixoord* EU:C:2000:475; Case C-437/09 *AG2R Prévoyance v Beaudout Père et Fils SARL* EU:C:2011:112, paras 28–36.

[96] Case E-8/00 [2002] 5 CMLR 160, paras 33–46.

agreements under Article 53 of the European Economic Area ('EEA') Agreement, but noted that provisions in such agreements which pursue objectives extraneous to that of improving conditions of work and employment may fall within the scope of competition law[97]. In *Holship Norge AS v Norsk Transportarbeiderforbund*[98] the EFTA Court held that the *Albany* exception did not apply to an agreement that went beyond the core object and elements of collective bargaining.

The *Albany* exclusion does not apply in relation to a decision taken by members of the liberal professions, since it is not concluded in the context of collective bargaining between employers and employees[99]. In *FNV Kunsten Informatie en Media v Staat der Nederlanden*[100] the Court of Justice said that the exclusion would not apply to an agreement with an association of self-employed persons unless the reality of the matter was that they were in fact employees, a matter to be determined on a case-by-case basis[101].

(B) **'Associations of undertakings'**

Article 101(1) applies not only to agreements and concerted practices between undertakings; it also applies to the decisions of 'associations of undertakings'. An association does not have to engage in economic activity to be caught by Article 101(1)[102]. It follows that Article 101(1) may be applicable to the *decisions* of an association, even if it does not apply to its *agreements* because the association does not qualify as an undertaking[103]. Where an association is an undertaking, an agreement between it and other undertakings may be caught by Article 101(1)[104]; Article 101(1) also applies to decisions by associations of trade associations[105].

(i) **Basic definition**

An association of undertakings refers to a representative body, usually with members, that typically makes 'decisions' which are followed, whether as a matter of obligation or practice, by its members or those whom it represents[106]. A trade association can be an association of undertakings, as can other entities, such as professional bodies[107]. A trade association does not fall outside Article 101(1) because it is formally approved by a public authority[108] or because its members are appointed by the state[109]. The Court of Justice has specifically stated that the public law status of a national body (for example an association of customs agents) does not preclude the application of Article 101[110].

[97] Ibid, paras 33–46 and 47–59.

[98] Case E-14/15, judgment of 19 April 2016, paras 37–53; when the case returned to the Norwegian Supreme Court it did not reach a conclusion on the applicaton of competition law, although it indicated in its judgment that it doubted that the *Albany* exception applied.

[99] Cases C-180/98 etc *Pavel Pavlov v Stichting Pensioenfonds Medische Specialisten* EU:C:2000:428, paras 67–70.

[100] Case C-413/13 EU:C:2014:2411.

[101] Ibid, paras 31–37.

[102] Cases T-25/95 etc *Cimenteries CBR SA v Commission* EU:T:2000:77, para 1320 (*Cement*), and case law cited.

[103] See the Opinion of AG Slynn in Case 123/83 *BNIC v Clair* EU:C:1984:300.

[104] Cases T-25/95 etc *Cimenteries CBR SA v Commission* EU:T:2000:77, paras 1325 and 2622.

[105] See eg *Cematex* JO [1971] L 227/26; *Milchförderungsfonds* OJ [1985] L 35/35.

[106] See AG Léger's Opinion in Case C-309/99 *Wouters* EU:C:2001:390, para 61.

[107] Case C-309/99 EU:C:2002:98, paras 50–71 (*General Council of the Dutch Bar*); *ONP* Commission decision of 8 December 2010, paras 589–95 (*Association of French pharmacists*); Case C-1/12 *OTOC* [2013] EU:C:2013:127, paras 39–59 (*Association of Portuguese chartered accountants*); Case C-136/12 *Consiglio nazionale dei geologi* EU:C:2013:489, paras 41–45 (*National Council of Italian geologists*).

[108] *AROW v BNIC* OJ [1982] L 379/1; *Coapi* OJ [1995] L 122/37, para 32.

[109] Ibid; see also *Pabst and Richarz KG v BNIA* OJ [1976] L 231/24.

[110] Case C-35/96 *Commission v Italy* EU:C:1998:303, para 40; Cases C-180/98 etc *Pavel Pavlov v Stichting Pensioenfonds Medische Specialisten* EU:C:2000:428, para 85.

In *MasterCard Inc v Commission*[111] it was undisputed that MasterCard had been an association of undertakings when it was owned by a number of banks and operated the MasterCard payment card system on their behalf[112]. However in 2006 MasterCard was floated on the New York Stock Exchange and ceased to be owned by those institutions. The Commission held that it continued to act as an association of undertakings, and that the 'multilateral interchange fees' that it charged infringed Article 101[113]. MasterCard and various of the banks appealed against this finding, arguing that following the flotation MasterCard was a separate entity, answerable to its shareholders and not to its former owners; therefore it ceased to be an association of undertakings. The appeal was rejected by both the General Court[114] and by the Court of Justice[115]. The latter considered that MasterCard, even after the flotation, remained an 'institutionalised form of coordination of the conduct of the banks'; and that the facts that the banks retained some residual decision-making powers in relation to MasterCard's affairs (albeit not the interchange fees) and that there remained 'commonality of interests' between the banks and MasterCard were relevant and sufficient for the purpose of assessing whether it continued to be an association of undertakings[116]. The Court noted that over a period of years MasterCard pursued the same objective of joint regulation of the market, albeit under different forms[117]. The facts of this case were unusual, in particular the flotation of MasterCard during the Commission's administrative procedure, and it would be sensible to understand the Court's judgment in this light.

(ii) Need to adopt a functional approach

A functional approach should be taken when determining whether a body, when engaged in a particular activity, is acting as an association of undertakings[118]. In *Wouters*[119] the Court of Justice held that the General Council of the Dutch Bar was an association of undertakings, and rejected the argument that this was not so in so far as it was exercising its regulatory functions. The Court reached a similar conclusion in *OTOC*[120].

In *API v Ministero delle Infrastrutture e dei Trasporti*[121] the Court held that a body, established by law with responsibilities, among others, for ensuring road safety in Italy, was an association of undertakings in the sense of Article 101 where it was composed principally of representatives of private operators and where no state official had a right of veto over its decisions[122]. The position might be different if a majority of the members of the professional body are appointed by the state, rather than by members of the profession, and if the state specifies the public interest criteria to be applied by the body.

(C) The 'single economic entity' doctrine

Article 101(1) does not apply to agreements between two or more legal persons that form a single economic entity[123]: collectively they comprise a single undertaking, and so there is no agreement *between* undertakings. The most obvious example of this is an agreement between a parent and a subsidiary company, though the relationship between an

[111] Case C-382/12 P EU:C:2014:2201. [112] Ibid, para 64.
[113] Commission decision of 19 December 2007.
[114] Case T-111/08 *MasterCard Inc v Commission* EU:T:2012:260, paras 244–259.
[115] Case C-382/12 P *MasterCard Inc v Commission* EU:C:2014:2201, paras 62–77.
[116] See in particular ibid, para 72 of the judgment. [117] Ibid, para 76.
[118] On this point see the Opinion of AG Jacobs in Cases C-67/96 etc *Albany International BV v SBT* EU:C:1999:28, para 214 and Case C-309/99 *Wouters* EU:C:2002:390, para 64.
[119] Case C-309/99 EU:C:2002:98, paras 50–71. [120] Case C-1/12 EU:C:2013:127, paras 39–59.
[121] Cases C-184/13 etc EU:C:2014:2147. [122] Ibid, paras 32 and 33.
[123] See Odudu and Bailey 'The Single Economic Entity Doctrine in EU Competition Law' (2014) 51 CML Rev 1721.

employer and an employee[124], a principal and agent[125] and between a contractor and sub-contractor[126] is analogous. Numerous important consequences flow from the single economic entity doctrine, as will be seen below: one is that a parent company can be held liable for infringement of the competition rules by a subsidiary[127].

(i) Parent and subsidiary: the basic rule

Firms within the same corporate group can enter into legally enforceable agreements with one another. However such an agreement will not fall within Article 101 if the relationship between them is so close that economically they form a single economic entity, that is to say that they 'consist of a unitary organisation of personal, tangible and intangible elements, which pursue a specific economic aim on a long-term basis, and can contribute to the commission of an infringement of the kind referred to in [Article 101 TFEU]'[128]. Where this is the case the agreement is regarded as the internal allocation of functions within a single undertaking rather than a restrictive agreement between independent undertakings.

(ii) The *Viho* judgment

The proposition that agreements between entities in the same corporate group fall outside Article 101 can be traced back to 1971[129]. The issue was revisited in *Viho v Commission*[130]. Parker Pen had established an integrated distribution system for Germany, France, Belgium, Spain and the Netherlands, where it used subsidiary companies for the distribution of its products. The Commission concluded that Article 101 had no application to this allocation of tasks within the Parker Pen group. This finding was challenged by a third party, Viho, which had been trying to obtain supplies of Parker Pen's products and which considered that the agreements between Parker Pen and its subsidiaries infringed Article 101. The EU Courts upheld the decision of the Commission that Article 101 had no application. The Court of Justice noted that Parker Pen held 100% of the shares in the subsidiary companies, it directed their sales and marketing activities and it controlled sales, targets, gross margins, sales costs, cash flow and stocks:

> Parker and its subsidiaries thus form a single economic unit within which the subsidiaries do not enjoy real autonomy in determining their course of action in the market, but carry out the instructions issued to them by the parent company controlling them[131].

[124] See 'Employees', pp 90–91 earlier in chapter.

[125] See ch 16, 'Commercial Agents', pp 634–637 and, in particular, the Commission's *Guidelines on Vertical Restraints* OJ [2010] C 130/1, paras 12–21.

[126] See ch 16, 'Sub-Contracting Agreements', pp 691–692 and, in particular, the Commission's *Notice on Sub-contracting Agreements* OJ [1979] C 1/2.

[127] See 'Implications of the economic entity doctrine', pp 98–99, later in chapter; note that the same principle means that a principal may be found guilty of participating in a cartel if it was represented at cartel meetings by a commercial agent: see eg *Candle Waxes*, Commission decision of 1 October 2008, paras 399–409.

[128] See Case T-112/05 *Akzo Nobel NV v Commission* EU:T:2007:381, paras 57–58; the Court first adopted this definition as long ago as 1962: see eg Cases 17 and 20/61 *Klockner v High Authority* EU:C:1962:30 and Case 19/61 *Mannesmann v High Authority* EU:C:1962:31.

[129] See Case 22/71 *Béguelin Import v GL Import Export* EU:C:1971:113; Case 15/74 *Centrafarm BV v Sterling Drug Inc* EU:C:1974:114; Case 30/87 *Corinne Bodson v Pompes Funèbres des Régions Libérées SA* EU:C:1988:225, para 19; the Commission reached a similar conclusion in *Re Christiani and Nielsen NV* JO [1969] L 165/12 and in *Re Kodak* JO [1970] L 147/24; see also *TFI/France 2 and France 3*, Commission's XXIXth *Report on Competition Policy* (1999), p 167.

[130] Case T-102/92 EU:T:1995:3, upheld by the Court of Justice in Case C-73/95 P EU:C:1996:405; see also Case T-198/98 *Micro Leader Business v Commission* EU:T:1999:341, para 38 (agreements within the Microsoft group not subject to Article 101); on the similar position in US law see *American Needle, Inc v National Football League* 560 US 183 (2010).

[131] Case C-73/95 P EU:C:1996:405, para 16.

The Court of Justice went on to say that in those circumstances the fact that Parker Pen could divide national markets between its subsidiaries was outside Article 101, although it pointed out that such unilateral conduct could infringe Article 102 where the requirements for its application were satisfied[132]. In its *Guidelines on the applicability of Article 101 of the Treaty on the Functioning of the European Union to horizontal co-operation agreements*[133] the Commission relies on the *Viho* judgment for the proposition that '[w]hen a company exercises decisive influence over another company they form a single economic entity and, hence, are part of the same undertaking'; it adds that the same would be true of 'sister companies, that is to say, companies over which decisive influence is exercised by the same parent company'[134].

(iii) **The test of control**

The test is whether the parent company can, and does in fact, exercise decisive influence over the other with the result that the latter does not enjoy 'real autonomy' in determining its commercial policy on the market. For these purposes it is necessary to examine all the relevant factors relating to the economic, organisational and legal links which tie the subsidiary to the parent company, which will vary from case to case[135]. These factors include the shareholding that a parent company has in its subsidiary, the composition of the board of directors, the extent to which the parent influences the policy of or issues instructions to the subsidiary and similar matters[136].

(a) Parent and wholly-owned subsidiaries

In *Akzo v Commission*[137], one of the appeals in the *Choline Chloride* case, the issue before the Court of Justice was not whether an agreement between a parent and subsidiary infringed Article 101, but whether the Commission could address a decision to a parent company that it was liable for infringing Article 101 where it was a subsidiary company that was actually involved in the cartel. The Court held, referring to earlier judgments such as *Dyestuffs*[138], that where the parent has a 100% shareholding[139] in a subsidiary the parent is in a position to exercise decisive influence over the subsidiary, and there is a rebuttable presumption that the parent does in fact exercise such influence[140]. In those circumstances the Commission may regard the parent as jointly and severally liable for any fine imposed on its subsidiary unless the parent can adduce sufficient evidence that the subsidiary acts independently on the market[141]. The Court added that, where the presumption applies, the Commission is not required to find additional evidence that the parent controlled the subsidiary: the presumption suffices unless rebutted[142]. The evidential burden is on the

[132] Ibid, para 17; as to the possible application of Article 102 see *Interbrew*, Commission's XXVIth *Report on Competition Policy* (1996), pp 139–140.

[133] OJ [2011] C 11/1.

[134] Ibid, para 11.

[135] Case C-440/11 P *Commission v Stichting Administratiekantoor Portielje* EU:C:2013:514, para 66 (*International removal services*).

[136] See eg Case 107/82 *AEG-Telefunken v Commission* EU:C:1983:293, paras 47–53; a useful summary of the case law can be found in Case T-399/09 *HSE v Commission* EU:T:2013:647, paras 11–16 and 29–32 (*Calcium carbide and magnesium based reagents*).

[137] Case C-97/08 P EU:C:2009:536.

[138] Case 48/69 *Imperial Chemical Industries v Commission* EU:C:1972:70.

[139] This includes indirect ownership of 100% of the shares due to the interposition of another company: Case C-508/11 P *Eni Spa v Commission* EU:C:2013:289, para 48 (*Synthetic rubber*).

[140] Case C-97/08 P EU:C:2009:536, para 60; on the rationale for the rebuttable presumption see paras 71–75 of AG Kokott's Opinion in Case C-97/08 P *Akzo v Commission* EU:C:2009:262 and para 89 of AG Mengozzi's Opinion in Cases C-247/11 P etc *Areva SA v Commission* EU:C:2013:579.

[141] Case C-97/08 P EU:C:2009:536, para 61.

[142] Ibid, para 62; there is nothing to prevent the Commission from establishing that a parent controlled a subsidiary by means of other evidence or by a combination of such evidence and the presumption, but, where it does so, it must adopt the same approach to the attribution of liability to other undertakings under investigation in the same case: Cases C-628/10 P etc *Alliance One International v Commission* EU:C:2012:479, para 59 (*Spanish raw tobacco*).

parent to show that the subsidiary acts independently on the market and that any economic, organisational and legal links between the parent and the subsidiary do not mean that they are a single economic entity[143]. In *Akzo* the Court of Justice upheld the General Court's judgment[144] that the parent had failed to rebut the presumption. There have been numerous other cases, before and since *Akzo*, in which a parent company has attempted to rebut the presumption: such attempts usually, though not inevitably, fail[145]. There has been controversy as to whether the presumption is rebuttable in theory, but irrebuttable in practice[146]; the Court of Justice has however rejected this criticism[147]. The presumption has been applied where a parent company owns 'all or almost all' of the shares in the subsidiary. In *Elf Aquitaine v Commission* the General Court applied the presumption to a parent owning 97.55% of the shares in its subsidiary[148].

(b) Majority shareholders

In *Bananas*[149] the Commission did not apply the presumption to an 80% shareholding. Instead it demonstrated that the shareholder, Del Monte, had exercised decisive influence over the subsidiary by virtue of its rights under a partnership agreement and a distribution agreement as well as by issuing instructions to the subsidiary. On appeal the General Court upheld the Commission's decision[150]; the General Court's judgment was affirmed by the Court of Justice[151]. The General Court has declined to apply the *Akzo* presumption to shareholdings of 71.4%[152] and of 60%[153].

(c) Minority shareholders

In *Fuji v Commission*[154] the General Court held that a minority shareholder had exercised decisive influence over a member of the *Gas Insulated Switchgear* cartel, with the consequence that it was liable for the cartel[155]. The crucial issue is whether the minority shareholder exercises decisive influence over the commercial policy of the company, for which purpose the size of the shareholding, the representation on the board of directors of the company, the ability to influence the latter's commercial policy and actual evidence of attempts to do so will all be relevant[156].

Under Article 3(2) of the EU Merger Regulation ('the EUMR') a minority shareholder that would have the 'possibility of exercising decisive influence' over the affairs of an

143 See Case T-541/08 *Sasol v Commission* EU:T:2014:628, paras 145–150 (*Candle waxes*).

144 Case T-112/05 *Akzo Nobel NV v Commission* EU:T:2007:381.

145 See 'Implications of the economic entity doctrine', pp 98–99 later in chapter.

146 See eg Wahl 'Parent Company Liability—A Question of Facts or Presumption?' (2012) 19th St Gallen International Competition Law Forum ICF, available at www.ssrn.com; Leupold 'Effective Enforcement of EU Competition Law Gone Too Far? Recent Case Law on the Presumption of Parental Liability' (2013) 34 ECLR 570.

147 See Case C-289/11 P *Legris v Commission* EU:C:2012:270, para 53 (*Copper fittings*).

148 Cases T-299/08 and T-343/08 EU:T:2011:217, paras 53–56 (*Sodium chlorate*); see also Case C-508/11 P *Eni v Commission* EU:C:2013:289, para 47 (*Butadiere rubber*) (Eni owned 99.97% of Enichem).

149 Commission decision of 15 October 2008, para 404.

150 Case T-587/08 *Fresh Del Monte v Commission* EU:T:2013:129, paras 50–276.

151 Cases C-293/13 P etc *Fresh Del Monte v Commission* EU:C:2015:416, paras 75–99.

152 Case T-45/10 *GEA Group AG v Commission* EU: T: 2015 507, para 168 (*Heat stabilisers*); see similarly Case T-399/09 *HSE v Commission* EU:T:2013:647, paras 11–102 (*Calcium carbide and magnesium based reagents*), in relation to a 74% shareholding.

153 Case T-64/06 *FLS Plast A/S v Commission* EU:T:2012:102, para 36 (*Industrial bags*); see also Case T-392/09 *1. garantovaná a.s. v Commission* EU:T:2012:674, paras 15–57 (*Calcium carbide and magnesium based reagents*).

154 Case T-132/07 *Fuji Electric Co Ltd v Commission* EU:T:2011:344 (*Gas insulated switchgear*).

155 Ibid, para 183.

156 Ibid, para 184; a shareholding of 30%, together with board representation and other links, established that the minority shareholder controlled the subsidiary: ibid, paras 186–203.

undertaking would have sufficient control for there to be a concentration[157]. There are arguments for the adoption of a consistent approach to the notion of control as between the EUMR and Article 101[158]; however the notion of control under the EUMR includes negative control, and has the jurisdictional function of determining which proposed transactions must be scrutinised under that Regulation; the language of the cases under Article 101 suggests that there the requirement is for positive rather than negative control, where the test has substantive, as opposed to jurisdictional, consequences. This was confirmed by the General Court in *Sasol v Commission*[159].

(d) *Parents of a joint venture*

In *Dow Chemical v Commission*[160] the Court of Justice upheld the General Court's judgment[161] that the parents of a joint venture were responsible for the latter's participation in the *Chloroprene Rubber* cartel and could therefore be fined on a joint and several basis. The Court said that where two parent companies have a 50% shareholding in a joint venture that infringes Article 101, and both parents actually exercise decisive influence over the joint venture, the three entities constitute a single undertaking[162]. The Commission must produce evidence of the existence and exercise of decisive influence; there is no presumption to that effect. The Court rejected the argument that, because the joint venture was full-function under the EUMR and autonomous from its parents, the joint venture was an independent undertaking. The autonomy of a full-function joint venture under the EUMR does not prevent its parents from exercising decisive influence over the joint venture for the purposes of Article 101[163].

In *Toshiba v Commission*[164] the Court of Justice upheld the General Court's judgment that Toshiba was jointly and severally liable for the participation of its joint venture in one of the *Cathode ray tubes* cartels, even though it had only a 35.5% shareholding. The evidence showed that Toshiba had in fact exercised decisive influence over the joint venture.

(iv) **Decisions where the single economic entity doctrine did not apply**

In *IJsselcentrale*[165] the Commission rejected the argument that four Dutch electricity generating companies and the joint venture that they controlled formed a single economic entity, and that therefore Article 101 did not apply to agreements between them. The fact that the generators formed part of an indivisible system of public electricity supply did not mean that they were one unit, for they were separate legal persons, not controlled by a single natural or legal person, and were able to determine their own conduct independently. In *Gosmé/Martell-DMP*[166] DMP was a joint subsidiary of Martell and Piper-Heidsieck. Each parent held 50% of the capital of DMP and the voting rights; half of the supervisory board members represented Martell shareholders and half Piper-Heidsieck shareholders; DMP distributed brands not belonging to its parent companies; Martell and Piper-Heidsieck products were invoiced to wholesalers on the same document; DMP

[157] See ch 21, 'The concept of control', pp 854–855; note the more formalistic test of control for the purpose of calculating the turnover of 'undertakings concerned' in Article 5(4) of the EUMR: see ch 21, 'Turnover', pp 863–864.

[158] See Wils 'The Undertaking as Subject of EC Competition Law and the Imputation of Infringements to Natural or Legal Persons' (2000) 25 EL Rev 99, 104–108; cp Jones 'The Boundaries of Undertaking in EU Competition Law' (2012) 8 European Competition Journal 301.

[159] Case T-541/08 EU:T:2014:628, paras 49–50 (*Candle waxes*).

[160] Cases C-179/12 P EU:C:2013:605 (*Chloroprene rubber*); similarly Case C-172/12 P *EI du Pont v Commission* EU:C:2013:601 (*Chloroprene rubber*).

[161] Case T-77/08 *Dow Chemical v Commission* EU:T:2012:47; similarly Case T-76/08 *EI du Pont de Nemours v Commission* EU:T:2012:46.

[162] Cases C-179/12 P *Dow Chemical v Commission* EU:C:2013:605, para 58.

[163] Ibid, paras 64–66.

[164] Case C-623/15 P EU:C:2017:21, paras 45–82.

[165] OJ [1991] L 28/32, paras 22–24.

[166] OJ [1991] L 185/23, para 30.

had its own sales force and it alone concluded the contracts of sale with buying syndicates in France. In these circumstances the Commission concluded that Martell and DMP were independent undertakings, so that an agreement between them to identify and prevent parallel exports infringed Article 101 and attracted fines of €300,000 in the case of Martell and €50,000 in the case of DMP.

If a subsidiary becomes independent of its parent, for example by being sold off, an agreement between the two companies could be caught by Article 101 once the parent–subsidiary relationship ends. In *Austin Rover/Unipart*[167] the relationship between those undertakings following the privatisation of British Leyland and the selling off of Unipart was investigated by the Commission under Article 101, but was found to satisfy the criteria of Article 101(3).

(v) Implications of the economic entity doctrine

Numerous consequences flow from the economic entity doctrine.

First, although an agreement between firms that form a single economic entity does not infringe Article 101(1), the manipulation of a subsidiary by a parent might mean that an infringement arises in other ways; for example a parent might order its subsidiaries to impose export bans on their distributors: the agreements containing such restrictions could themselves infringe Article 101[168].

Secondly, as already noted in *Akzo*, a parent company can be liable for the activities of its subsidiaries[169]. Whereas Article 101 applies to agreements between *undertakings*, Commission decisions must be addressed to *legal entities*, and one undertaking can consist of many entities. Where a parent exercises decisive influence over a subsidiary that has infringed Article 101, the Commission has a discretion whether to penalise the parent company, the subsidiary or both[170]. The Commission regularly addresses infringement decisions to both a parent and its subsidiary, each of which is then jointly and severally liable for the infringement; the parents of a joint venture can also be the addressees of a decision where their joint venture has infringed Article 101[171]. The fact that a subsidiary disobeys the instructions of its parent does not, in itself, rebut the presumption of decisive influence[172].

There have been many appeals in which parents have argued that the presumption that 100% ownership of a subsidiary confers decisive influence has been successfully rebutted: such appeals usually fail. In *Alliance One International v Commission*[173], however, the Court of Justice upheld the General Court's judgment[174] that the presumption had been rebutted by one member of the Standard Group of companies, Trans-Continental Leaf Tobacco Corp, although not by two others, Alliance One International and Standard Commercial Tobacco[175]. In *Gosselin v Commission*[176] the Court of Justice reversed the

[167] OJ [1988] L 45/34. [168] See eg *Re Kodak* JO [1970] L 147/24.

[169] The Commission is not required to determine, as between a parent and subsidiary company (or between other related companies) what their respective liabilities should be for any fine or damages as between themselves: Cases C-231/11 P etc *Commission v Siemens AG Österreich* EU:C:2014:256, paras 58–64.

[170] Case T-541/08 *Sasol v Commission* EU:T:2014:628, para 182 (*Candle waxes*).

[171] See ch 3 n 160 earlier.

[172] Case C-155/14 P *Evonik Degussa GmbH v Commission* EU:C:2016:446, para 41 (*Calcium carbide and magnesium based reagents*).

[173] Cases C-628/10 P etc EU:C:2012:479 (*Spanish raw tobacco*). [174] Case T-24/05 EU:T:2010:453.

[175] Several appeals have succeeded on the basis of inadequate reasoning: eg Case C-90/09 P *General Química v Commission* EU:C:2011:21, paras 75–80 (*Rubber chemicals*); Case C-521/09 P *Elf Aquitaine v Commission* EU:C:2011:620, paras 156–171 (*MCAA*); Case T-185/06 *Air Liquide v Commission* EU:T:2011:275, paras 66–83 (*Hydrogen peroxide*); Case T-234/07 *Koninklijke Grolsch v Commission* EU:T:2011:476, paras 84–92 (*Dutch beer*); Case T-196/06 *Edison v Commission* EU:T:2011:281, paras 56–94, upheld on appeal Case C-446/11 P *Commission v Edison* EU:C:2013:798 (*Bleaching chemicals*); Case T-517/09 *Alstom v Commission* EU:T:2014:999, paras 97–108 (*Power transformers*).

[176] Cases T-208/08 etc EU:T:2011:287, paras 51–59 (*International removal services*).

General Court's conclusion that a parent company had shown that its wholly-owned subsidiary acted independently on the market[177].

Thirdly, where a parent and a subsidiary (or subsidiaries) form a single economic entity, the maximum fine permitted by Article 23(2) of Regulation 1/2003 of 10% of an undertaking's worldwide turnover refers to the entire group's turnover, not just the turnover of the entity that actually committed the infringement: clearly this means that the maximum fine that can be imposed—for example where the subsidiary is part of a large conglomerate group—may be vastly greater than would otherwise be the case[178].

Fourthly, it may be that an action for damages can be brought either against a parent of a subsidiary company, or even against a subsidiary of a parent company; this can have significant implications for jurisdictional issues in civil litigation, potentially increasing the range of countries in which the action may be brought[179].

Fifthly, from a competition authority's point of view, it is desirable to attribute responsibility for infringements of the competition rules to the highest possible entity within a corporate group, not least in the hope that the board of directors of the parent company will take responsibility for eradicating anti-competitive behaviour from the entire organisation.

Sixthly, the economic entity doctrine means that a parent company may bear responsibility for any infringements committed by subsidiaries within the corporate group, and this may lead to the imposition of higher fines because of recidivism[180].

A seventh point is that the Commission and national competition authorities ('NCAs') may carry out a surprise inspection of a legal entity that is part of an economic unit even though the alleged infringement of Articles 101 and 102 was the responsibility of another part of it[181].

A further point is that the logical consequence of the economic entity doctrine is that, when counting the number of undertakings that are party to an agreement for the purpose of applying one of the block exemptions, the entities that form a single undertaking are counted as one[182].

Lastly, the immunity of agreements from Article 101 is in a sense a double-edged weapon: the EU Courts and the Commission have held that EU law can be applied to a parent company not present within the EU because of the conduct of its subsidiaries carried on there[183].

[177] Case C-440/11 P *Commission v Stichting Administratiekantoor Portielje* EU:C:2013:514, paras 80–87 (*International removal services*).

[178] See Case T-112/05 *Akzo Nobel NV v Commission* EU:T:2007:381, paras 90–91 (*Choline chloride*); note however Case C-637/13 P *Laufen Austria AG v Commission* EU:C:2017:51, paras 44–51 (*Bathroom fittings and fixtures*) limiting the maximum fine that could be applied to a subsidiary company *before* it was acquired by another.

[179] See *Provimi Ltd v Aventis Animal Nutrition SA* [2003] EWHC 961 (Comm), paras 31–36; *KME Yorkshire Ltd v Toshiba Carrier UK Ltd* [2012] EWCA Civ 1190, paras 34–39; see further ch 8, 'Private international law', pp 320–323.

[180] On the significance of recidivism to the level of fines see ch 7, 'Adjustments to the basic amount', pp 287–289.

[181] Case T-66/99 *Minoan Lines v Commission* EU:T:2003:337 (*Greek ferries*).

[182] Case 170/83 *Hydrotherm Gerätebau v Andreoli* EU:C:1984:271; this is relevant to the application of the block exemptions on vertical agreements: see ch 16, 'Article 2(4): agreements between competing undertakings', pp 673–674 and on technology transfer agreements: ch 19, 'The exempted agreement must be bilateral', pp 799–800.

[183] See Case 48/69 *ICI v Commission* EU:C:1972:70; Case 6/72 *Europemballage Corpn and Continental Can Co Inc v Commission* EU:C:1973:22; see ch 12 on extraterritoriality generally.

(D) **Corporate reorganisation**

Corporate reorganisations can mean that the entity that controls an undertaking at the time of an infringement decision ('the successor') is different from the entity that committed the infringement. However, such reorganisations do not mean that entities can escape liability for transgressions of EU competition law[184]. For so long as it continues in existence, a legal entity remains liable for its past infringing conduct[185]. In *Compagnie Royale Asturienne des Mines SA and Rheinzink v Commission*[186] the Court of Justice held that:

> a change in the legal form and name of an undertaking does not create a new undertaking free of liability for the anticompetitive behaviour of its predecessor when, from an economic point of view, the two are identical.

The Court applied the reasoning of the *Rheinzink* case in *Autoritá Garante della Concorrenza e del Mercato v Ente tabacchi italiani—ETI*[187]. An Italian court asked it whether the Italian competition authority could impose a fine on ETI, a successor to AAMS, the state-owned tobacco monopoly in Italy, which had originally entered into the cartel under scrutiny but had then transferred the business in question to ETI. The Court of Justice held that ETI could be held liable for the infringement. It made no difference that the activity transferred to ETI occurred not as a result of a private initiative between AAMS and ETI but through the action of the Italian legislature in preparing ETI for privatisation[188].

In order to decide whether a successor may be held liable, the determining factor 'is whether there is a functional and economic continuity between the original infringer and the undertaking into which it was merged'[189]. In *All Weather Sports Benelux v Commission*[190] the General Court held that the Commission must adequately explain its reasoning when it imposes a fine on a successor to the entity that committed the infringement. In *Versalis v Commission*[191] the General Court held that the Commission was entitled to hold a successor liable for the unlawful conduct of its predecessor.

(E) **Liability for competition law infringements when one business is sold to another**

An important question arises where one undertaking commits an infringement of the competition rules, but then sells the business that was responsible for the infringement to

[184] Case T-349/08 *Uralita v Commission* EU:T:2011:622, para 57 (*Sodium chlorate*); for discussion see Dyekjær-Hansen and Hoegh 'Succession for Competition Law Infringements with Special Reference to Due Diligence and Warranty Claims' (2003) 24 ECLR 203; Chandler 'Successor Liability for Competition Law Infringements and How to Avoid It' [2006] Comp Law 63.

[185] See eg Case C-279/89 P *Cascades SA v Commission* EU:C:2000:626, paras 78–80 (*Cartonboard*).

[186] Cases 29 and 30/83 EU:C:1984:130, para 9; see also Case T-134/94 *NMH Stahlwerke GmbH v Commission* EU:T:1999:44, paras 122–141 (*Steel beams*); Case C-297/98 P *SCA Holdings Ltd v Commission* EU:C:2000:633, paras 23–32 (*Cartonboard*); Cases C-204/00 P etc *Aalborg Portland A/S v Commission* EU:C:2004:6, para 59 (*Cement*).

[187] Case C-280/06 EU:C:2007:775.

[188] Ibid, paras 38–52; see also Case C-511/11 P *Versalis v Commission* EU:C:2013:386, paras 56–57 (*Butadiene rubber*).

[189] *PVC* OJ [1989] L 74/1, para 43, upheld on appeal Cases T-305/94 etc *Limburgse Vinyl Maatschappij v Commission* EU:T:1999:80, para 953; see similarly *LdPE* OJ [1989] L 74/21, paras 49–54; other decisions of the Commission dealing with this point are *Peroxygen Products* OJ [1985] L 35/1, *Polypropylene* OJ [1986] L 230/1, and *Welded Steel Mesh* OJ [1989] L 260/1, para 194; OJ [1994] L 239/14, paras 14–43.

[190] Case T-38/92 EU:T:1994:43, paras 26–36.

[191] Case T-103/08 EU:T:2012:868, paras 89–98 (*Chloroprene rubber*), upheld on appeal to the Court of Justice Case C-123/13 P EU:C:2015:150.

a third party. Clearly the purchaser will need to know whether it bears the risk of a future fine in the event that a competition authority finds an infringement. The basic rule of personal responsibility is that, if the undertaking that was responsible for the business is still in existence, it remains liable for the infringement rather than the acquirer[192]. Liability is not removed by the fact that the entity's ownership changes, that it assumes a new name or that it has since ceased to be involved in the economic activity to which the infringement related[193]. For example in *Prestressing steel*[194] the Commission decided that, where an undertaking commits an infringement of Article 101 and then disposes of the assets that were the vehicle of the infringement and withdraws from the market, it will still be held responsible if it is still in existence[195].

There are two exceptions to this basic rule. The first is where the original infringer has ceased to exist, either in law or economically, since a fine imposed on such an entity is likely to have no deterrent effect[196]. In those circumstances, liability may pass to the new operator of the infringing undertaking.

A second exception is where the original infringer still has a legal existence but no longer carries on an economic activity on the relevant market and where there are structural links between the initial entity and the new operator of the undertaking[197]. This exception did not apply in *Hoechst v Commission*[198]. The General Court's finding that the exception did not apply in *Parker ITR Srl v Commission*[199] was set aside by the Court of Justice in *Commission v Parker Hannifin Manufacturing Srl*[200]. The Court sent the case back to the General Court for reconsideration; it upheld the Commission's original decision attributing liability to ITR Rubber under the principle of economic continuity[201].

3. Agreements, Decisions and Concerted Practices

The most obvious target of any system of competition law is agreements between independent firms that are restrictive of competition. Article 101 TFEU prohibits cartel agreements between competitors, for example to fix prices, to share markets or to restrict output: chapter 13 will examine this subject in detail. However it is important to bear in mind that Article 101 can also apply to agreements between firms at different levels of the market, known as vertical agreements: the difficulties in establishing the existence of a vertical agreement are discussed later[202].

The application of Article 101(1) is not limited to formal contracts: this would make evasion of the law simple. Article 101 applies also to cooperation achieved through

[192] Case C-279/98 P *Cascades v Commission* EU:C:2000:626, paras 78–80 (*Cartonboard*). On whether the Commission would enforce a fine imposed on a purchaser of infringing assets see *Bänninger v Commission* [2010] EWHC 1978 (Ch).

[193] Case C-297/98 P *SCA Holdings Ltd v Commission* EU:C:2000:633, paras 25–30 (*Cartonboard*).

[194] Commission decision of 30 June 2010.

[195] Ibid, paras 699, 701–706, upheld on appeal on this point Cases T-426/10 etc *Moreda-Riviere Trefilerías SA v Commission* EU:T:2016:335, paras 317–318 and 353–360 and on further appeal Cases C-457/16 P etc EU:C:2017:819, paras 115–122.

[196] Case C-352/09 P *ThyssenKrupp Nirosta v Commission* EU:C:2011:191, para 144 (*Alloy surcharge*).

[197] Cases C-204/00 P etc *Aalborg Portland A/S v Commission* EU:C:2004:6, para 359 (*Cement*).

[198] Case T-161/05 EU:T:2009:366, paras 50–67 (*MCAA*).

[199] Case T-146/09 EU:T:2013:258, paras 103–130 (*Marine hoses*).

[200] Case C-434/13 P EU:C:2014:2456.

[201] Case T-146/09 RENV *Parker Hannifin Manufacturing Srl v Commission* EU:T:2016:411.

[202] See '"Unilateral" conduct and Article 101(1) in vertical cases', pp 109–114 later in chapter.

informal agreements, decisions of associations of undertakings and concerted practices, irrespective of whether they are legally enforceable and of whether there is any enforcement mechanism. As will be seen, a broad interpretation has been given to each of the terms 'agreement', 'decision' and 'concerted practice'. A difficult issue is whether parallel behaviour by firms in an oligopolistic industry is attributable to an agreement or concerted practice between them, in which case Article 101(1) would be applicable; or whether it is a natural response to the structure of the market, in which case a different competition law solution might be needed[203].

(A) Agreements

In *Bayer v Commission*[204] the General Court reviewed the case law on the meaning of agreement and stated that the concept:

> centres around the existence of a concurrence of wills between at least two parties, the form in which it is manifested being unimportant so long as it constitutes the faithful expression of the parties' intention[205].

In this section examples will be given of fact patterns that have been characterised as agreements for the purposes of Article 101. The possibility that firms might be found to be party to an agreement 'and/or' a concerted practice will then be discussed. Thereafter consideration will be given to the concept of a 'single overall agreement'. The final part of this section will look at the problem of proving that undertakings are party to a vertical agreement. The Court of Justice has stated that the standard of proof for establishing an agreement contrary to Article 101(1) is the same whether the agreement is a horizontal or a vertical one[206]. The fact that one party accepts that it was a party to an agreement does not preclude the other(s) from challenging the existence of the same agreement[207].

(i) Examples of agreements

A legal contract of course qualifies as an agreement, including a compromise of litigation such as a trade mark delimitation agreement[208] or the settlement of a patent action[209].

[203] See ch 14 on the issues of oligopoly, tacit coordination and collective dominance.

[204] Case T-41/96 EU:T:2000:242.

[205] Ibid, para 69; this paragraph was quoted, apparently with approval, by the Court of Justice in the appeal against the General Court's judgment: Cases C-2/01 P etc *Bundesverband der Arzneimittel-Importeure eV v Bayer AG* EU:C:2004:2, para 97.

[206] Case C-260/09 P *Activision Blizzard Germany GmbH v Commission* EU:C:2011:62, para 71 (*Nintendo*).

[207] Case T-18/03 *CD-Contact Data v Commission* EU:T:2009:132, para 51 (*Nintendo*).

[208] See eg *Re Penney's Trade Mark* OJ [1978] L 60/19; *Re Toltecs and Dorcet* OJ [1982] L 379/19, upheld on appeal Case 35/83 *BAT v Commission* EU:C:1985:32; it is not entirely clear what effect embodiment of the compromise in an order of a national court has on the applicability of Article 101(1): see Case 258/78 *LC Nungesser KG v Commission* EU:C:1982:211, paras 80–91, where the Court of Justice was delphic on this issue; the tenor of the judgment in *BAT v Commission* would suggest that the agreement would be caught even where sanctioned by a national court. On trade mark delimitation agreements, see further ch 19, 'Settlements of litigation', pp 812–814.

[209] See eg Case 65/86 *Bayer v Süllhofer* EU:C:1988:448; *Lundbeck*, Commission decision of 19 June 2013, upheld on appeal to the General Court Cases T-472/13 etc *Lundbeck v Commission* EU:T:2016:449, on further appeal to the Court of Justice Case C-591/16 P *Lundbeck v Commission*, not yet decided; *Servier*, Commission decision of 9 July 2014, on appeal Cases T-691/14 etc *Servier v Commission*, not yet decided; see further ch 19, 'Settlements of litigation', pp 812–814.

'Gentleman's agreements'[210] and simple understandings[211] have been held to be agreements, though neither is legally binding; there is no requirement that an agreement should be supported by enforcement procedures[212]. A 'protocol' which reflects a genuine concurrence of will between the parties constitutes an agreement within the meaning of Article 101(1)[213]. Connected agreements may be treated as a single one[214]. An agreement may be oral[215]. The Commission will treat the contractual terms and conditions in a standard-form contract as an agreement within Article 101(1)[216]. An agreement which has expired by effluxion of time but the effects of which continue to be felt can be caught by Article 101(1)[217]. The constitution of a trade association qualifies as an agreement[218]. An agreement entered into by a trade association might be construed as an agreement on the part of its members[219]. An agreement to create a European Economic Interest Grouping, or the bye-laws establishing it, may be caught by Article 101(1)[220]. There may be 'inchoate understandings and conditional or partial agreement' during a bargaining process sufficient to amount to an agreement in the sense of Article 101(1)[221]. Guidelines issued by one person that are adhered to by another can amount to an agreement[222]; and circulars and warnings sent by a manufacturer to its dealers may be treated as part of the general agreement that exists between them, although the Commission lost a case of this kind in *Volkswagen*[223]. The exchange of correspondence can amount to an agreement[224]. There can be an agreement or concerted practice notwithstanding the fact that only one of the participants at a meeting reveals its intentions[225].

[210] See Case 41/69 *ACF Chemiefarma NV v Commission* EU:C:1970:71 (*Quinine*), and Case T-53/03 *BPB plc v Commission* EU:T:2008:254, para 72 (*Plasterboard*).

[211] *Re Stichting Sigarettenindustrie Agreements* OJ [1982] L 232/1 (an 'understanding' between trade associations held to be an agreement); *National Panasonic* OJ [1982] L 354/28, where there was no formal agreement between Panasonic and its dealers, but the Commission still held that there was an agreement as opposed to a concerted practice between them; *Viho/Toshiba* OJ [1991] L 287/39, where the Commission found an understanding between Toshiba's German subsidiary and certain distributors that an export prohibition should apply, even though the standard distribution agreements had been amended to remove an export prohibition clause.

[212] *Soda-ash/Solvay, CFK* OJ [1991] L 152/16, para 11; *PVC* OJ [1994] L 239/14, para 30; *CISAC*, Commission decision of 16 July 2008, para 130.

[213] *HOV SVZ/MCN* OJ [1994] L 104/34, para 46.

[214] *ENI/Montedison* OJ [1987] L 5/13.

[215] Case 28/77 *Tepea v Commission* EU:C:1978:133; Cases T-25/95 etc *Cimenteries CBR SA v Commission* EU:T:2000:77, para 2341 (*Cement*).

[216] *Putz v Kawasaki Motors (UK) Ltd* OJ [1979] 1 16/9; *Sandoz* OJ [1987] L 222/28, upheld on appeal Case 277/87 *Sandoz Prodotti Farmaceutici SpA v Commission* EU:C:1989:363.

[217] Case T-7/89 *SA Hercules (Chemicals) NV v Commission* EU:T:1991:75, para 257 (*Polypropylene*); Case 51/75 *EMI Records Ltd v CBS UK Ltd* EU:C:1976:85, pp 848–849, p 267; Case T-48/98 *Acerinox v Commission* EU:T:2001:289, para 63; *CISAC*, Commission decision of 16 July 2008, para 263, appeal dismissed on this point Case T-401/08 *Teosto v Commission* EU:T:2013:170, para 122; *E.ON/GDF*, Commission decision of 8 July 2009, substantially upheld on appeal Cases T-360/09 *E.ON v Commission* EU:T:2012:332, para 251.

[218] *Re Nuovo CEGAM* OJ [1984] L 99/29.

[219] Cases 209/78 etc *Heintz Van Landewyck v Commission* EU:C:1980:248.

[220] *Orphe*, Commission's XXth *Report on Competition Policy* (1990), point 102; *Tepar* [1991] 4 CMLR 860; *Twinning Programme Engineering Group* OJ [1992] C 148/8.

[221] *Pre-Insulated Pipe Cartel* OJ [1999] L 24/1, para 133, substantially upheld on appeal Cases T-9/99 etc *HFB Holding v Commission* EU:T:2002:70.

[222] *Anheuser-Busch Incorporated/Scottish & Newcastle* OJ [2000] L 49/37, para 26.

[223] See 'Cases following *Bayer*', pp 112–113 later in chapter.

[224] *Nintendo* OJ [2003] L 255/33, para 196, substantially upheld on appeal to the General Court Case T-18/03 *CD-Contact Data v Commission* EU:T:2009:132, paras 52–69 and on appeal to the Court of Justice Case C-260/09 P *Activision Blizzard Germany GmbH v Commission* EU:C:2011:62.

[225] Cases T-202/98 etc *Tate & Lyle v Commission* EU:T:2001:185, para 54.

(ii) Factors that do not affect the existence of an agreement

The following factors do not affect the existence of an agreement within the meaning of Article 101:

- the undertaking was forced into an agreement by other undertakings does not affect the existence of an agreement[226]; this fact may be significant in influencing the Commission to mitigate a fine[227], not to impose a fine[228] or not to institute proceedings at all
- the agreement was never implemented[229]
- the individual who entered into the agreement did not have authority to do so[230]
- formal agreement has not been reached on all matters[231]; it is sufficient that there is a 'concurrence of wills on the principle of a restriction of competition, even if the specific features of the restriction envisaged are still under negotiation'[232].

The fact that one party accepts that it was party to an agreement does not preclude the other(s) from challenging the existence of the same agreement[233].

(iii) Agreement 'and/or' concerted practice

The Commission has stated that agreements and concerted practices are conceptually distinct[234]. However Advocate General Reischl has said that there is little point in defining the exact point at which agreement ends and concerted practice begins[235]. It may be that, in a particular case, linguistically it is more natural to use one term than the other, but legally nothing turns on the distinction: the important distinction is between collusive and non-collusive behaviour[236]. Sometimes the Commission will say that, even if contacts between competitors do not amount to an agreement, they can still be characterised as a concerted practice[237]. In *PVC*[238] the Commission decided that the parties to the cartel had participated in an agreement 'and/or' a concerted practice. On appeal the General Court rejected Enichem's challenge to this 'joint classification' and upheld the Commission[239]. It held that:

> In the context of a complex infringement which involves many producers seeking over a number of years to regulate the market between them the Commission cannot be expected to classify the infringement precisely, for each undertaking and for any given moment, as in any event both those forms of infringement are covered by Article [101] of the Treaty[240].

[226] Case T-83/08 *Denki Kagaku Kogyo Kabushiki Kaisha v Commission* EU:T:2012:48, paras 47 and 61–62 and the case law cited (*Chloroprene rubber*).

[227] *Hasselblad* OJ [1982] L 161/18; *Wood Pulp I* OJ [1985] L 85/1, para 131.

[228] *Burns Tractors Ltd v Sperry New Holland* OJ [1985] L 376/21; *Fisher-Price/Quaker Oats Ltd—Toyco* OJ [1988] L 49/19.

[229] *French Beer*, Commission decision of 29 September 2004, para 64.

[230] Case T-53/03 *BPB plc v Commission* EU:T:2008:254, para 360 (*Plasterboard*); Case C-68/12 *Protimonopolný úrad Slovenskej republiky v Slovenská sporiteľňa a.s.* EU:C:2013:71, para 25.

[231] *Pre-Insulated Pipe Cartel* OJ [1999] L 24/1, para 134.

[232] Case T-240/07 *Heineken Nederland v Commission* EU:T:2011:284, para 45 (*Dutch beer*).

[233] Case T-18/03 *CD-Contact Data v Commission* EU:T:2009:132, para 51 (*Nintendo*).

[234] See *Polypropylene* OJ [1986] L 230/1, para 86.

[235] See Cases 209/78 etc *Van Landewyck v Commission* EU:C:1980:248, p 3310.

[236] Case C-49/92 P *Commission v Anic Partecipazioni* EU:C:1999:356, para 112 (*Polypropylene*).

[237] See eg *Candle waxes*, Commission decision of 1 October 2008, para 239.

[238] OJ [1994] L 239/14, paras 30–31; this decision was taken by the Commission after its earlier decision, OJ [1989] L 74/1, had been annulled by the Court of Justice for infringement of essential procedural requirements: Cases C-137/92 P etc *Commission v BASF* EU:C:1994:247.

[239] Cases T-305/94 etc *NV Limburgse Vinyl Maatschappij v Commission* EU:T:1999:80, paras 695–699; see also Case T-1/89 *Rhône-Poulenc v Commission* EU:T:1991:56, paras 125–127 (*Polypropylene*).

[240] Cases T-305/94 etc *NV Limburgse Vinyl Maatschappij v Commission* EU:T:1999:80, para 696.

The General Court went on to say that joint classification was permissible where the infringement includes elements both of an agreement and of a concerted practice, without the Commission having to prove that there was both an agreement and a concerted practice throughout the period of the infringement[241]. This approach was confirmed by the Court of Justice in *Asnef-Equifax*[242] where, in the case of cooperation between competitors in the form of an indirect exchange of information, it concluded that there was no need to characterise the cooperation specifically as a concerted practice, an agreement or a decision of an association of undertakings.

The Commission has adopted a joint classification approach in many decisions, for example *Cartonboard*[243] and *Pre-Insulated Pipe Cartel*[244] and, more recently, *Rechargeable batteries*[245] and *Trucks*[246]; it has taken this approach in vertical cases as well as horizontal ones[247]. As one former Commission official has put it: the search should not be for an agreement on the one hand or a concerted practice on the other; rather for a 'partnership for unlawful purposes with all the possible disagreements about methods that may occur in such a venture without affecting the cohesion of the shared purpose and design'[248].

(iv) Single overall agreement

(a) The problem of proof

Many cartels are complex and of long duration. Over a period of time some firms may be more active than others in the running of a cartel: some may 'drop out' for a while but subsequently re-enter; others may attend some meetings but not others; there may be few occasions on which all the members of a cartel actually meet or behave precisely in concert with one another. It may not be clear whether firms participated in a single cartel covering, for example, the whole of the EU, or whether there were different cartels, one for France, one for Germany and so on. Similarly it may be difficult to determine what products the cartel applied to: widgets, or widgets and blodgets? Perhaps even widgets, blodgets and sprockets? In some cases a series of practices may be under investigation, and it may not be clear whether a particular undertaking adhered to all or only some of them.

If one were to analyse such situations as consisting of several discrete cartels, involving different firms, areas and practices, a competition authority would have to launch several investigations. This would impose a considerable burden on it; and it might transpire that some of the illegal practices were so far in the past that limitation rules prevent the imposition of fines[249]. If, however, it is possible to show that there has been a single overall agreement only one investigation would be needed and it is less likely that a limitation problem will arise.

[241] See also Case T-655/11 *FSL Holdings v Commission* EU:T:2015:383, paras 419 and 453 (*Exotic fruit*).

[242] Case C-238/05 EU:C:2006:734, para 32 and case law cited.

[243] OJ [1994] L 243/1, para 128.

[244] OJ [1999] L 24/1, paras 131–132.

[245] Commission decision of 12 December 2016, paras 38–40.

[246] Commission decision of 19 July 2016, paras 68–69.

[247] See *Nintendo* OJ [2003] L 255/33, paras 261ff.

[248] Joshua 'Attitudes to Anti-Trust Enforcement in the EU and US: Dodging the Traffic Warden, or Respecting the Law?' [1995] Fordham Corporate Law Institute (ed Hawk), 85.

[249] Under Article 25 of Regulation 1/2003, OJ [2003] L 1/1, the Commission cannot impose fines in relation to an infringement that ended five years or more before it initiated proceedings nor where more than ten years have elapsed since the initiation of proceedings; see Kerse and Khan *EU Antitrust Procedure* (Sweet & Maxwell, 6th ed, 2012), paras 7-265–7-275.

(b) Single overall agreement: terminology

The concept of a 'single overall agreement'[250] for which undertakings bear responsibility, even though they may not be involved in every aspect of its operation on a day-to-day basis, can be traced back to the mid-1980s[251]. A different term that is sometimes used for this phenomenon is a 'single and continuous infringement'. The authors of this book prefer to use the expression 'single overall agreement' which is capable of capturing:

- a series of cartel practices over a period of time and/or
- a series of cartel practices over a broad geographical area and/or
- a series of cartel practices over a range of different products and/or
- a series of distinct cartel practices.

The alternative expression 'single and continuous infringement' is obviously appropriate to capture the first of these ideas, but is less so in the case of the second, third and fourth of them.

(c) Single overall agreement as an objective fact

If the Commission has 'objective reasons' for finding a single overall agreement the General Court has said that it is bound to make such a finding[252]. To put the point another way, the Commission does not have a discretion as to whether to analyse the evidence as a single overall agreement on the one hand or as a series of separate agreements on the other[253]. For example, it cannot artificially conclude that there is a single overall agreement in order to avoid the problem that a cartel ended so long ago that it is out of time to impose a fine; but on the other it could not artificially chop up a single overall agreement in order to impose a number of separate fines, none of which exceeds the 10% worldwide turnover of an undertaking, in circumstances where a fine for a single overall agreement would exceed that cap[254]. In 2015 the Commission found that there were five different cartels in its *Food repackaging* decision[255]; on the other hand in *Optical disc drives* it found that a network of parallel bilateral contacts formed a single overall agreement[256]. The Commission's decision in *Air cargo* was overturned on appeal as it was not clear whether the Commission had found that the airlines were party to a single overall agreement or to

[250] See eg Seifert 'The Single Complex and Continuous Infringement—"Effet" Utilitarianism?' (2008) 29 ECLR 546; Joshua 'Single Continuous Infringement of Article 81 EC: Has the Commission Stretched the Concept Beyond the Limit of Logic?' (2009) 5 European Competition Journal 453; Bailey 'Single, Overall Agreement in EU Competition Law' (2010) 47 CML Rev 473; Riley 'Revisiting the Single and Continuous Infringement of Article 101: The Significance of *ANIC* in a New Era of Cartel Detection and Analysis' (2014) 37 World Competition 293.

[251] See eg *Polypropylene* OJ [1986] L 230/1, upheld on appeal Case T-1/89 *Rhône-Poulenc v Commission* EU:T:1991:56, para 126, and on further appeal Case C-49/92 P *Commission v Anic* EU:C:1999:356, paras 82–83 and 87; Cases T-305/94 etc *NV Limburgse Vinyl Maatschappij v Commission* EU:T:1999:80, para 773 (*PVC II*).

[252] Cases T-373/10 etc *Villeroy & Boch Austria GmbH v Commission* EU:T:2013:455, para 36 (*Bathroom fixtures and fittings*).

[253] The Commission does, however, have a discretion whether to proceed against the entire single overall agreement or only a part of it: Case T-91/11 *Innolux Corp v Commission* EU:T:2014:92, para 137.

[254] See ch 7, 'Article 23: fines', pp 285–286.

[255] Commission decision of 24 June 2015, on appeal Case T-582/15 *Silver Plastics GmbH and Co KG and Johannes Reifenhäuser v Commission*, not yet decided.

[256] Commission decision of 21 October 2015, on appeal Cases T-762/15 etc *Sony v Commission*, not yet decided.

a number of different ones[257]; the Commission subsequently adopted a second decision finding that there was a single overall agreement[258].

The General Court does not have jurisdiction to make its own independent finding as to whether an undertaking participated in a single overall agreement[259].

(d) Conditions for establishing a single overall agreement

In *Team Relocations v Commission*[260] the General Court considered the case law and stated that:

> three conditions must be met in order to establish participation in a single and continuous infringement, namely the existence of an overall plan pursuing a common objective, the intentional contribution of the undertaking to that plan, and its awareness (proved or presumed) of the offending conduct of the other participants[261].

On the first condition, '**an overall plan pursuing a common objective**', the Court of Justice has held that this cannot be determined by a general reference to the distortion of competition[262]. Although the existence of an overall plan is often investigated by considering how the various cartel activities fit together, and whether they are 'complementary', the Court of Justice, disagreeing with the General Court[263], has clarified that complementarity is not a necessary condition for a finding of a single overall agreement[264]. In *BASF v Commission* the General Court annulled the Commission's finding that the global and the European cartels had a common objective; the Commission was therefore time-barred from imposing a fine in respect of the global cartel[265]. In *Villeroy & Boch Austria GmbH v Commission*[266] the Court of Justice held that the fact that the cartel extended over distinct product and geographic markets did not preclude the existence of a single infringement. It follows that an undertaking does not need to be present on the cartelised market for it to participate in a single overall agreement[267].

The second condition, '**the intentional contribution of the undertaking to that plan**', does not require an undertaking to have contributed from the start of the infringement or to have pursued the plan in exactly the same way as other members of the cartel[268]. The fact that some members of the cartel have reservations about whether to participate—or intend to cheat by deviating from the agreed conduct—does not mean that they are not party to an overall agreement[269]. In *Cement*, however, where there were numerous bilateral and multilateral agreements between a large number of undertakings, the General

257 See eg Case T-62/11 *Martinair v Commission* EU:T:2015:984.

258 Commission decision of 17 March 2017, on appeal Cases T-341/17 etc *British Airways v Commission*, not yet decided.

259 Case C-603/13 P *Galp Energia España SA v Commission* EU:C:2016:38 (*Spanish bitumen*).

260 Case T-204/08 EU:T:2011:286 (*International removal services*).

261 Ibid, para 37; this paragraph was quoted with approval by the Court of Justice in the appeal against the General Court's judgment: Case C-444/11 P EU:C:2013:464, paras 51–53.

262 Cases C-239/11 P etc *Siemens v Commission* EU:C:2013:866, para 245 (*Gas insulated switchgear*), affirming a point made by the General Court in its judgment in Cases T-101/05 etc *BASF v Commission* EU:T:2007:380, para 180 (*Choline chloride*).

263 Cases T-101/05 etc *BASF v Commission* EU:T:2007:380, para 181.

264 Cases C-239/11 P etc *Siemens v Commission* EU:C:2013:866, para 248 (*Gas insulated switchgear*); Case C-626/13 P *Villeroy & Boch v Commission* EU:C:2017:54, para 69 (*Bathroom fixtures and fittings*).

265 Cases T-101/05 etc *BASF v Commission* EU:T:2007:380, paras 157–210 (*Choline chloride*).

266 Case C-626/13 P EU:C:2017:54, para 67 (*Bathroom fixtures and fittings*).

267 Case T-29/05 *Deltafina v Commission* EU:T:2010:355, paras 46–51 (*Spanish raw tobacco*); Case T-180/15 *Icap v Commission* EU:T:2017:795, paras 103–104 (*Yen interest rate derivatives*).

268 Case C-444/11 P *Team Relocations v Commission* EU:C:2013:464, para 56 (*International removal services*).

269 Cases C-204/00 P etc *Aalborg Portland A/S v Commission* EU:C:2004:6, para 85 (*Cement*).

Court said that it cannot be *presumed* from this that they form part of a single overall agreement: it is necessary for the Commission to prove that this is the case[270].

As to the third condition, '**awareness ... of the offending conduct** of the other participants', the General Court held in *Soliver v Commission*[271] that the Commission must prove that the undertaking was 'aware of the general scope and the essential characteristics of the cartel as a whole'. The EU Courts have annulled several Commission decisions where it had failed to establish that a particular undertaking knew, or ought to have known, about the offending conduct of the other members of the cartel[272].

(e) Implications of a single overall agreement

The finding of a single overall agreement has important implications. It means, first, that each infringing undertaking is responsible for the overall cartel, even though some did not attend every meeting of the cartel or were not involved in every aspect of its decision-making. Secondly, if the Commission decides that there is a single overall agreement, it is entitled to impose only one fine on the members of the cartel (as opposed to separate fines for different infringements). It is not inconceivable that an undertaking might want to argue that it *did* participate in just one infringement: for example, when the aggregated fines imposed for separate infringements amount to more than the maximum fine permitted for a single infringement[273]. Thirdly, the existence of a single overall agreement may enable the Commission to impose fines in respect of illegal practices that would otherwise be time-barred[274]. Fourthly, a single overall agreement may increase the duration of infringement, and thus result in a larger fine that would otherwise be the case. Fifthly, the different anti-competitive activities of a single overall agreement may lead to higher fines if the Commission considers the overall agreement to be more serious than the sum of its individual parts[275]. Sixthly, it is possible that a single overall agreement may affect the application of the other requirements of Article 101; for example, it may increase the probability that the cartel produces an effect on inter-state trade[276]. Seventhly, undertakings will be jointly and severally liable in damages for the losses caused by the single overall agreement[277]; the precise role of an undertaking may, however, be relevant to contribution[278]. Lastly, the existence of a single overall agreement can affect whether a national court has jurisdiction to hear an action for damages against several undertakings domiciled in different Member States[279].

270 Cases T-25/95 etc *Cimenteries CBR SA v Commission* EU:T:2000:77, paras 4027, 4060, 4109 and 4112 (*Cement*).

271 Case T-68/09 EU:T:2014:867, paras 63–64 (*Car glass*); Case T-758/14 *Infineon Technologies AG v Commission* EU:T:2016:737, para 222 (*Smart card chips*), on appeal Case C-99/17 P, not yet decided.

272 See eg Case T-28/99 *Sigma Tecnologie v Commission* EU:T:2002:76, paras 45–52 (*Pre-insulated pipes*); Case T-59/06 *Low & Bonar v Commission* EU:T:2011:669, paras 58–71 (*Industrial bags*); Case T-385/06 *Aalberts Industries v Commission* EU:T:2011:114, paras 107–120, upheld on appeal Case C-287/11 P EU:C:2013:445, paras 60–67 (*Copper fittings*); Case T-208/06 *Quinn v Commission* EU:T:2011:701, para 150 (*Acrylic glass*); Case T-210/08 *Verhuizingen Coppens v Commission* EU:T:2011:288, paras 28–32, upheld on appeal Case C-441/11 P EU:C:2012:778, paras 66–67 (*International removal services*); Case T-104/13 *Toshiba v Commission* EU:T:2015:610, paras 52–78 (*Cathode ray tubes*); Case T-180/15 *Icap v Commission* EU:T:2017:795, paras 133–145 (*Yen interest rate derivatives*).

273 Case T-68/04 *SGL Carbon v Commission* EU:T:2008:414, paras 122–134; Case T-27/10 *AC-Treuhand v Commission* EU:T:2014:59, paras 222–267 (*Heat stabilisers*), upheld on appeal Case C-194/14 P EU:C:2015:717.

274 *Vitamins* OJ [2003] L 6/1, para 645–649.

275 See to that effect the Opinion of AG Kokott in Case C-441/11 P *Verhuizingen Coppens v Commission* EU:C:2012:317, Opinion of 24 May 2012, para 71 (*International removal services*).

276 Case C-125/07 P *Erste Bank der Österreichischen Sparkassen v Commission* EU:C:2009:576, para 56 (*Austrian banks*); see similarly para 152 of the Opinion of AG Bot in that case.

277 Cases T-373/10 etc *Villeroy & Boch Austria GmbH v Commission* EU:T:2013:445, para 57 and case law cited (*Bathroom fixtures and fittings*).

278 See ch 8, 'Contribution', pp 329–330.

279 Case C-352/13 *Cartel Damage Claims v Akzo Nobel* EU:C:2015:335, paras 15–33.

(f) Partial liability for a single overall agreement

In *Fresh Del Monte v Commission*[280] the Court of Justice upheld the General Court's judgment[281] that the Commission was entitled to find that an undertaking knew about some, but not all, of the elements of the overall cartel; in those circumstances the undertaking is not liable for the elements of the cartel that it did not know about, even though some undertakings may be liable for the whole infringement.

(g) Single and repeated infringement

In some cases the Commission may be unable to prove that an undertaking participated in the entirety of a single overall agreement: there may be no evidence of an undertaking's involvement for a specific period, or it may be that an undertaking leaves and later rejoins the same cartel. In such cases the undertaking can be held responsible for a 'single and repeated infringement'[282]. In *Trelleborg Industrie v Commission*[283] the General Court held that the Commission may impose a fine for the entire duration of a single and repeated infringement, thereby avoiding problems of limitation, except for the period during which the undertaking 'interrupted' its participation in the cartel[284]. The General Court reached a similar conclusion in *FSL Holdings v Commission*[285].

(v) 'Unilateral' conduct and Article 101(1) in vertical cases

The scheme of the EU competition rules is that Article 101 applies to conduct by two or more undertakings which is consensual and that Article 102 applies to unilateral action by a dominant firm. It follows that unilateral conduct by a firm that is not dominant is not caught at all. In a number of vertical cases the Commission has held that conduct which at first sight appeared to be unilateral fell within Article 101(1) as an agreement or a concerted practice; these were cases in which the Commission was concerned either that exports from one Member State to another were being inhibited or that resale prices were being maintained[286]. Several of these decisions were upheld on appeal by the EU Courts; however in a number of cases, beginning with *Bayer AG/Adalat*[287] in 1996, findings of the Commission that there were agreements between a supplier and its distributors have been annulled on appeal[288].

(a) AEG-Telefunken v Commission; Ford v Commission

Two judgments of the Court of Justice in the 1980s provide an important starting point when considering this issue. In *AEG-Telefunken v Commission*[289] the Court of Justice rejected a claim that refusals to supply retail outlets which were objectively suitable to handle AEG's goods were unilateral acts falling outside Article 101(1). The Court of Justice held that the refusals arose out of the contractual relationship between AEG and the established distributors within its selective distribution system and their mutual acceptance, tacit or express, of AEG's intention to exclude from the network distributors who, though qualified technically, were not prepared to adhere to its policy of maintaining a

280 Cases C-293/13 P etc EU:C:2015:416, paras 156–160 (*Bananas*).

281 Case T-587/08 *Fresh Del Monte v Commission* EU:T:2013:129, paras 586–650.

282 See eg Case T-18/05 *IMI v Commission* EU:T:2010:202, paras 96–97 (*Copper plumbing tubes*).

283 Cases T-147/09 EU:T:2013:259 (*Marine hoses*). 284 Ibid, para 88.

285 Case T-655/11 EU:T:2015:383, paras 491–498 (*Exotic fruit*).

286 See Lianos 'Collusion in Vertical Relations under Article 81 EC' (2008) 45 CML Rev 1027; Gippini-Fournier 'The Notion of Agreement in a Vertical Context: Pieces of a Sliding Puzzle' in Bellis and Beneyto (eds) *Rewriting Vertical Restraints in Europe* (Bruylant, 2012).

287 OJ [1996] L 201/1. 288 See 'Cases following *Bayer*', pp 112–113 later in chapter.

289 Case 107/82 EU:C:1983:293.

high level of prices and excluding modern channels of distribution[290]. The frequency of AEG's refusals to supply precluded the possibility that they were isolated acts not forming part of systematic conduct[291]. The *AEG* case suggested that it may be relatively easy to infer an agreement and/or concerted practice between the participants in a selective distribution system who have a strong mutual interest in excluding firms willing to undercut the prevailing retail price[292].

In *Ford v Commission*[293] the Court of Justice held that a refusal by Ford's German subsidiary to supply right-hand drive cars to German distributors was attributable to the contractual relationship between them; at the time right-hand drive cars were sold in Germany to British military forces stationed there: they could then bring them back to the UK, having bought them in Germany at prices considerably below those in the UK. The *Ford* judgment appeared to be a considerable extension of *AEG*. In *AEG* there was an obvious community of interest between participants in the selective distribution system in excluding discounters. In *Ford*, however, the German distributors with whom Ford had entered into contracts did not themselves benefit from the refusal to supply right-hand drive cars: the beneficiaries of this policy were distributors in the UK, who would be shielded from cheaper parallel imports. In *Ford* the 'unilateral' act held to be attributable to the agreements between the supplier and its distributors was not an act for the benefit of those very distributors. However, the main issue in *Ford* was not whether there were agreements between Ford and its German distributors: of course there were. Rather the issue with which the Court of Justice was concerned was whether the agreements, as implemented in practice, satisfied the criteria of Article 101(3), and the Court decided that they did not[294]. This is how the Court distinguished the *Ford* judgment in its judgment in the *Bayer* case[295], and is an important limiting principle.

(b) Subsequent cases prior to Bayer

In a number of decisions after *AEG* and *Ford* the Commission successfully applied Article 101(1) to apparently unilateral conduct[296]. In *Sandoz*[297] it held that, where there was no written record of agreements between a producer and its distributors, unilateral measures, including placing the words 'export prohibited' on all invoices, were attributable to the continuing commercial relationship between the parties and were within Article 101(1). On appeal the Court of Justice upheld the Commission's decision[298]. In *Tipp-Ex*[299] the Commission applied the Court of Justice's judgments in *AEG* and *Ford*, holding that there was an infringement of Article 101 consisting of agreements between Tipp-Ex and its authorised dealers regarding the mutual protection of territories; again the Commission's decision was upheld on appeal[300]. The Commission has said that the fact that a customer is acting contrary to its own best interests in agreeing to its supplier's terms does not mean that it is not party to a prohibited agreement under Article 101(1)[301].

[290] On selective distribution systems see ch 16, 'Selective distribution agreements', pp 654–658.

[291] Case 107/82 EU:C:1983:293, paras 31–39.

[292] On the possibility of a multilateral concerted practice between a supplier and its distributors see ch 9, 'Concerted practices', pp 352–355.

[293] Cases 25/84 and 26/84 EU:C:1985:340.

[294] Ibid, para 12.

[295] See '*Bayer v Commission*', below.

[296] See eg *Konica* OJ [1988] L 78/34; *Bayo-n-ox* OJ [1990] L 21/71; *Bayer Dental* OJ [1990] L 351/46.

[297] OJ [1987] L 222/28.

[298] Case C-277/87 *Sandoz Prodotti Farmaceutici SpA v Commission* EU:C:1989:363; see similarly *Vichy* OJ [1991] L 75/57, upheld on appeal Case T-19/91 *Vichy v Commission* EU:T:1992:28.

[299] OJ [1987] L 222/1.

[300] Case C-279/87 P *Tipp-Ex GmbH v Commission* EU:C:1989:230.

[301] See eg *Gosmé/Martell-DMP* OJ [1991] L 185/23.

In *Volkswagen AG v Commission*[302] the General Court rejected Volkswagen's argument that it had acted unilaterally as opposed to by agreement with its distributors to restrict parallel trade from Italy to Germany and Austria[303].

These cases clearly demonstrate the risks borne by suppliers that attempt to control the resale activities of their distributors; however the *Bayer* case discussed in the next section revealed that the notion of an agreement in Article 101(1) is not infinitely elastic.

(c) Bayer v Commission

In *Bayer AG/Adalat*[304] the Commission adopted a decision that Bayer and its wholesalers were parties to an agreement to restrict parallel trade in a pharmaceutical product, Adalat, from France and Spain to the UK. On this occasion the General Court annulled the decision since the Commission had failed to prove the existence of an agreement[305]; an appeal by the Commission and a parallel importer to the Court of Justice to reverse the General Court's judgment failed[306].

In order to prevent its French and Spanish wholesalers from supplying to parallel exporters to the UK, and thereby to protect its UK pricing strategy, Bayer had reduced the volume of its supplies of Adalat to France and Spain. An important feature of the case was that wholesalers in France and Spain were required to maintain sufficient stocks to enable them to supply local pharmacies with their requirements for drugs: clearly this meant that, if Bayer assessed the level of domestic demand correctly, it could limit the volumes of Adalat supplied to the point where there would be none available for export. Prices for pharmaceuticals in France and Spain were as much as 40% lower than in the UK, so that the market was ripe for parallel trade. The Commission concluded that a tacit agreement existed between Bayer and its wholesalers not to export to the UK that was contrary to Article 101(1): in its view the agreement was evidenced by the fact that the wholesalers had ceased to supply the UK in response to Bayer's tactic of reducing supplies. It has to be said that this would appear to be counter-intuitive, given that the wholesalers had tried every means possible to defy Bayer and to obtain extra supplies for the purpose of exporting to the UK: there was no 'common interest' in this case between Bayer and its wholesalers, whose respective needs were diametrically opposed. To put the point another way, this case was certainly not like *AEG*; if anything it was like *Ford*, where the beneficiary of Ford's restriction of supplies was not the German distributors deprived of supplies, but the UK distributors protected from parallel trade. Bayer did not deny that it had reduced the quantities delivered to France and Spain, but it argued that it had acted unilaterally rather than pursuant to an agreement.

The General Court held that there was no agreement and annulled the Commission's decision. It acknowledged that there could be an agreement where one person tacitly acquiesces in practices and measures adopted by another[307]; however it concluded that the Commission had failed both to demonstrate that Bayer had intended to impose an export ban[308] and to prove that the wholesalers had intended to adhere to a policy on the part of Bayer to reduce parallel imports[309]. The Court was satisfied that earlier judgments,

[302] Case T-62/98 EU:T:2000:180, upheld on appeal to the Court of Justice Case C-338/00 P *Volkswagen AG v Commission* EU:C:2003:473, paras 60–69.

[303] Case T-62/98 EU:T:2000:180, paras 236–239.

[304] OJ [1996] L 201/1; for criticism of the Commission's decision see Lidgard 'Unilateral Refusal to Supply: An Agreement in Disguise?' (1997) 18 ECLR 352; Jakobsen and Broberg 'The Concept of Agreement in Article 81(1) EC: On the Manufacturer's Right to Prevent Parallel Trade within the European Community' (2002) 23 ECLR 127.

[305] Case T-41/96 EU:T:2000:242.

[306] Cases C-2/01 P etc *Bundesverband der Arzneimittel-Importeure eV v Bayer AG* EU:C:2004:2.

[307] Case T-41/96 EU:T:2000:242, para 71.

[308] Ibid, paras 78–110.

[309] Ibid, paras 111–157.

including *Sandoz, Tipp-Ex* and *AEG*, were distinguishable[310]. It also rejected the argument that the wholesalers, by maintaining their commercial relations with Bayer after the reduction of supplies, could thereby be held to have agreed with it to restrain exports[311]. The Court was not prepared to extend the scope of Article 101(1), acknowledging the importance of 'free enterprise' when applying the competition rules[312].

The Commission and a parallel importer appealed to the Court of Justice, which upheld the General Court's judgment[313]. At paragraph 88 of its judgment the Court of Justice held that:

> The mere fact that the unilateral policy of quotas implemented by Bayer, combined with the national requirements on the wholesalers to offer a full product range, produces the same effect as an export ban does not mean either that the manufacturer imposed such a ban or that there was an agreement prohibited by Article [101(1)] of the Treaty.

The Court noted that the Commission's analysis risked confusing the respective roles of Articles 101 and 102[314], and that the *AEG* and *Ford* cases were distinguishable[315].

The importance of the judgments in *Bayer* cannot be overstated. Had the Commission's decision been upheld, the notion that an agreement for the purpose of Article 101(1) requires consensus between the parties would have been virtually eliminated; while this would have given the Commission greater control over restrictions of parallel trade within the EU, it would have done so at the expense of the integrity of the competition rules, which clearly apprehend unilateral behaviour only where a firm has a dominant position in the sense of Article 102.

(d) Cases following Bayer

There have been several cases since *Bayer* in which the Commission's decisions finding vertical agreements have been upheld by the General Court[316]. However a number of findings of the Commission that vertical agreements existed have been annulled on appeal. For example in *JCB* the Commission imposed fines on JCB for various infringements of Article 101, including for entering into agreements with distributors to fix discounts and resale prices[317]. On appeal the General Court annulled the Commission's decision on this point: it was true that JCB had recommended prices to its distributors, and that the prices that it charged to them would influence their own resale prices; however this was not sufficient in itself to show that there was an agreement between JCB and the distributors[318]. In *General Motors Nederland BV v Commission*[319] the General Court heard an appeal against a Commission decision, *Opel Nederland BV*[320], in which it had imposed fines of €43 million on Opel, a subsidiary of General Motors. The General Court annulled one of

310 Ibid, paras 158–171. 311 Ibid, paras 172–182. 312 Ibid, para 180.

313 Cases C-2/01 P and C-3/01 P *Bundesverband der Arzneimittel-Importeure eV v Bayer AG* EU:C:2004:2; *Bayer* was considered and applied by the English Court of Appeal in *Unipart Group Ltd v O2 (UK) Ltd* [2004] EWCA Civ 1034.

314 Cases C-2/01 P and C-3/01 P *Bundesverband der Arzneimittel-Importeure eV v Bayer AG* EU:C:2004:2, para 101.

315 Ibid, paras 107–108.

316 *Glaxo Wellcome* OJ [2001] L 302/1, upheld on this point on appeal Case T-168/01 *GlaxoSmithKline Services v Commission* EU:T:2006:265, paras 65–90; *Nintendo* OJ [2003] L 255/33, upheld on appeal Case T-13/03 *Nintendo v Commission* EU:T:2009:131 and Case T-18/03 *CD-Contact Data v Commission* EU:T:2009:132, paras 46–75: the latter case was also upheld on further appeal Case C-260/09 P *Activision Blizzard Germany v Commission* EU:C:2011:62; *SEP et autres/Peugeot SA*, Commission decision of 5 October 2005, upheld on appeal Case T-450/05 *Peugeot v Commission* EU:T:2009:262.

317 OJ [2002] L 69/1, paras 138–149.

318 Case T-67/01 *JCB Service v Commission* EU:T:2004:3, paras 121–133.

319 Case T-368/00 EU:T:2003:275. 320 OJ [2001] L 59/1.

the Commission's findings: the Commission had argued that Opel's policy was to limit the number of cars that would be supplied to its Dutch dealers in order to prevent exports, and that this policy had been communicated to the dealers and agreed to by them; the General Court held that there was no direct proof in the decision that there had been any such communication, and even less that that measure had entered into the contractual relations between Opel and its dealers[321]. As a consequence the fine was reduced from €43 million to €35 million. A separate finding in this case—that a bonus system that the dealers had undoubtedly agreed to had as its object the restriction of competition—was upheld by the General Court[322].

In a second decision involving *Volkswagen*[323] the Commission fined that company €30.96 million for agreeing to fix prices with its distributors for the VW Passat car. Volkswagen had sent circulars and letters to its distributors urging them not to sell the Passat at discounted prices. In the Commission's view the objectives set out in these circulars or letters became integral parts of the dealership agreement that the distributors had entered into; relying on cases such as *AEG* and others on selective distribution systems[324] the Commission argued that, within a selective distribution system, calls by a supplier such as Volkswagen of the type set out in the circulars and letters became part of the contractual relationship, without the need to prove any acquiescence on the part of the distributors. The General Court rejected the Commission's arguments in *Volkswagen v Commission*[325]: the General Court did not accept the Commission's analysis of the case law on selective distribution, especially given that this would mean that the distributors, who had signed perfectly lawful dealership agreements in the first place, would be taken to have agreed to subsequent calls from Volkswagen that would make the implementation of the agreements illegal. On appeal the Court of Justice set aside the judgment of the General Court[326] in so far as it had suggested that a lawful clause in an agreement could never authorise a call contrary to Article 101[327]; nevertheless the Court of Justice still reached the same substantive conclusion, that the Commission had failed to establish an agreement[328].

(e) Comment

Clearly the judgments in the previous section in which Commission findings of agreements in vertical relationships were annulled mean that it must adduce convincing evidence that there exists 'a concurrence of wills between at least two parties', in the words of the General Court's judgment in *Bayer*. As cases like *Nintendo* show, however, it is dangerous for suppliers, wishing to suppress exports or to maintain resale prices, to suppose that this case law means that this is something that can be achieved without risk. In so far as they can achieve their intended purpose on a purely unilateral basis, *Bayer* shows that Article 101 can be avoided. However it should be stressed that, in that case, if it were not for the stock-holding obligations to supply French and Spanish pharmacies with Adalat, the wholesalers in question could have decided to sell all the Adalat that they acquired to parallel traders: in other words Bayer's unilateral reduction of suppliers was

[321] Case T-368/00 EU:T:2003:275, paras 78–89.
[322] Ibid, paras 97–106, upheld on appeal Case C-551/03 P EU:C:2006:229.
[323] *Volkswagen* OJ [2001] L 262/14, paras 61–69.
[324] See the cases cited in paras 18 and 19 of the General Court's judgment.
[325] Case T-208/01 EU:T:2003:326, paras 30–68.
[326] Case C-74/04 P *Commission v Volkswagen* EU:C:2006:460.
[327] Ibid, paras 43–44.
[328] Ibid, para 54.

not enough, in itself, to staunch the parallel trade. In *General Motors* the Commission lost on the point about Opel's export policy because it had failed to show that the policy had been communicated to its distributors or that they had reacted to a policy known to them: if one reverses the facts—suppose that Opel had communicated the policy and the distributors had changed their behaviour accordingly—there would have been an agreement. As far as *Volkswagen* is concerned, the Commission appears to have argued its case in much too legalistic a manner, basing itself on the terms of the standard-form dealership agreement and the inferences to be drawn from it. Had the Commission argued that the distributors knew of Volkswagen's intentions and altered their pricing practices accordingly, it might have succeeded.

These cases are highly fact-specific, and it would be wrong for suppliers and their distributors to draw too comforting a conclusion from the Commission's succession of defeats. Even less comforting is the possibility that the Commission may find a vertical concerted practice. The Commission accepted commitments under Article 9 of Regulation 1/2003 in a case involving the resale pricing of e-books that resulted in six undertakings abandoning or modifying their vertical relationships[329]. A notable feature of the *e-books* decision is the detailed discussion of the communications that led the Commission to suspect the existence of a concerted practice[330].

(B) **Decisions by associations of undertakings**

Coordination between undertakings may be achieved through the medium of a trade association. A trade association may have a particularly important role where the cartel consists of a large number of firms, in which case compliance with the rules of the cartel needs to be monitored: where only a few firms collude, it is relatively easy for each firm to monitor what the others are doing[331]. The role that trade associations may play in cartels is explicitly recognised in Article 101(1) by the proscription of 'decisions by associations of undertakings' that restrict competition. The term 'decision' is given a wide meaning so as to encompass those acts of an association that serve to coordinate the conduct of its members or those subject to its authority.

The following have been held to be a decision:

- the constitution of a trade association[332]
- regulations governing the operation of an association[333]
- an agreement entered into by an association
- the recommendation of an association if members have tended to comply with recommendations that have been made, and where compliance with the recommendation would have a significant influence on competition[334].

[329] Commission decisions of 12 December 2012 and 25 July 2013.

[330] Commission decision of 12 December 2012, paras 70–81.

[331] See ch 14, 'The theory of oligopolistic interdependence', pp 571–578 on tacit collusion in oligopolistic markets.

[332] See eg *Re ASPA* JO [1970] L 148/9; *National Sulphuric Acid Association* OJ [1980] L 260/24.

[333] *Publishers Association—Net Book Agreements* OJ [1989] L 22/12, upheld on appeal Case T-66/89 *Publishers Association v Commission (No 2)* EU:T:1992:84, partially annulled on appeal to the Court of Justice in Case C-360/92 P *Publishers Association v Commission* EU:C:1995:6; *Sippa* OJ [1991] L 60/19; *Coapi* OJ [1995] L 122/37, para 34; *Nederlandse Federative Vereniging voor de Grootlandel op Elektrotechnisch Gebied and Technische Unie (FEG and TU)* OJ [2000] L 39/1, para 95; *Visa International* OJ [2001] L 293/24, para 53; *Visa International—Multilateral Interchange Fee* OJ [2002] L 318/17, para 55.

[334] Cases 96/82 etc *IAZ International Belgium NV v Commission* EU:C:1983:310.

The application of Article 101(1) is not affected by the fact that a recommendation of an association is not binding upon its members[335] or that it is not unanimously accepted by the members[336].

The application of Article 101(1) to decisions means that the trade association itself may be held liable and be fined[337]; where the Commission intends to impose a fine on the association as well as, or in addition to, its members, this must be made clear in the statement of objections[338]. A decision does not acquire immunity simply because it is subsequently approved and extended in scope by a public authority[339]. In *FNCBV v Commission*[340] the General Court upheld a decision of the Commission in which it had held that, as farm operators, farmers and breeders were engaged in economic activities, they were acting as undertakings; and that it followed that their trade unions and the federations that grouped those unions together were associations of undertakings. The federations, rather than the individual undertakings, were fined in this case[341]: the General Court reduced the fines slightly. Further appeals to the Court of Justice were rejected[342]; the Court confirmed that, in determining the maximum fine that could be imposed on the federations, the Commission was entitled to take into account the members' turnover; even though they had no power to bind their members, they had been engaged in practices directly for the benefit of their members and in cooperation with them[343].

(C) **Concerted practices**

The inclusion of concerted practices within Article 101 means that conduct which is not attributable to an agreement or a decision may nevertheless amount to an infringement[344]. While it can readily be appreciated that loose, informal understandings to limit competition must be prevented as well as agreements, it is difficult both to define the type or degree of coordination within the mischief of the law and to apply that rule to the facts of any given case. In particular there is the problem that parties to a cartel may do all they can to

[335] Case 8/72 *Vereeniging van Cementhandelaren v Commission* EU:C:1972:84; Case 71/74 *FRUBO v Commission* EU:C:1975:61; Cases 209/78 etc *Van Landewyck v Commission* EU:C:1980:248; Case 45/85 *VDS v Commission* EU:C:1987:34, para 32; see also *Distribution of railway tickets by travel agents* OJ [1992] L 366/47, paras 62–69, partially annulled on appeal Case T-14/93 *UIC v Commission* EU:T:1995:96; *Fenex* OJ [1996] L 181/28, paras 32–42; *ONP*, Commission decision of 8 December 2010, paras 597–598 upheld on appeal Case T-90/11 *ONP v Commission* EU:T:2014:1049.

[336] *MasterCard*, Commission decision of 19 December 2007, para 384; the finding that MasterCard remained an association of undertakings was upheld on appeal: see 'Association of undertakings', pp 92–93 earlier in chapter.

[337] See eg *AROW v BNIC* OJ [1982] L 379/1, where BNIC was fined €160,000; *Fenex* OJ [1996] L 181/28, where Fenex was fined €1,000; *Belgian Architects Association* OJ [2005] L 4/10, where the association was fined €100,000; *ONP*, Commission decision of 8 December 2010, where the association was fined €5 million; the Commission's decision was upheld on appeal to the General Court but the fine reduced to €4.75 million, Case T-90/11 *ONP v Commission* EU:T:2014:1049.

[338] Cases T-25/95 etc *Cimenteries CBR SA v Commission* EU:T:2000:77, para 485 (*Cement*).

[339] *AROW v BNIC* OJ [1982] L 379/1; *Coapi* OJ [1995] L 122/37.

[340] Cases T-217/03 and T-245/03 EU:T:2006:391.

[341] Note that the association is obliged to ask for contributions from its members in the event that the association is insolvent: Article 23(4) of Regulation 1/2003; the Commission decided against using this power in *ONP*, Commission decision of 8 December 2011, paras 747–751.

[342] Cases C-101/07 P and C-110/07 P *Coop de France bétail et viande v Commission* EU:C:2008:741.

[343] Ibid, para 97.

[344] For discussion of the notion of a concerted practice see Black *Conceptual Foundations of Antitrust* (Cambridge University Press, 2005), ch 5; Odudu *The Boundaries of EC Competition Law* (Oxford University Press, 2006), pp 71–91; for the treatment of concerted practices under the UK Competition Act 1998 see ch 9, 'Concerted practices', pp 352–355.

destroy incriminating evidence of meetings, emails, faxes and correspondence, making it difficult for the competition authorities to demonstrate that they have been acting illegally. It might be tempting for the competition authority to infer the existence of an agreement or concerted practice from circumstantial evidence such as parallel conduct on the market. This can be dangerous, for it may be that firms act in parallel not because of an agreement or concerted practice, but because their individual appreciation of market conditions tells them that a failure to match a rival's strategy could be damaging or even disastrous. The problem of parallel behaviour in oligopolistic markets will be examined in chapter 14.

It is necessary to consider first the legal meaning of a concerted practice; secondly the question of whether a concerted practice must have been put into effect for Article 101(1) to have been infringed; and, lastly, the burden of proof in such cases.

(i) Meaning of concerted practice

ICI v Commission[345] (usually referred to as the *Dyestuffs* case) was the first important case on concerted practices to come before the Court of Justice. The Commission had fined several producers of dyestuffs which it considered had been guilty of price fixing through concerted practices[346]. The Commission's decision relied upon various pieces of evidence, including the similarity of the rate and timing of price increases and of instructions sent out by parent companies to their subsidiaries and the fact that there had been informal contact between the firms concerned. The Court of Justice upheld the Commission's decision. It said that the object of bringing concerted practices within Article 101 was to prohibit:

> a form of coordination between undertakings which, without having reached the stage where an agreement properly so-called has been concluded, knowingly substitutes practical cooperation between them for the risks of competition[347].

In *Suiker Unie v Commission*[348] (the *Sugar cartel* case) the Court of Justice elaborated upon this test. The Commission had held[349] that various sugar producers had taken part in concerted practices to protect the position of two Dutch producers on their domestic market. The producers denied this as they had not worked out a plan to this effect. The Court of Justice held that it was not necessary to prove that there was an actual plan. Article 101 strictly precluded:

> any direct or indirect contact between such operators, the object or effect whereof is either to influence the conduct on the market of an actual or potential competitor or to disclose to such a competitor the course of conduct which they themselves have decided to adopt or contemplate adopting on the market[350].

These two cases provide the legal test of what constitutes a concerted practice for the purpose of Article 101: there must be a mental consensus whereby practical cooperation is *knowingly* substituted for competition; however the consensus need not be achieved verbally, and can come about by direct or indirect contact between the parties. In *Fresh Del Monte v Commission*[351] the General Court said that it is not necessary to prove a 'meeting of minds' or a 'common course of conduct' in order to establish a concerted practice[352].

[345] Case 48/69 EU:C:1972:70.

[346] *Re Aniline Dyes Cartel* JO [1969] L 195/11.

[347] Case 48/69 EU:C:1972:70, para 64; see similarly Case C-8/08 *T-Mobile Netherlands BV v Raad van bestuur van de Nederlandse Mededingingsautoriteit* EU:C:2009:343, para 26 and the cases cited therein.

[348] Cases 40/73 etc EU:C:1975:174.

[349] *Re European Sugar Cartel* OJ [1973] L 140/17.

[350] Cases 40/73 etc EU:C:1975:174.

[351] Case T-587/08 EU:T:2013:129 (*Bananas*).

[352] Ibid, para 300, upheld on appeal to the Court of Justice Cases C-293/13 P etc EU:C:2015:416; see similarly Case T-83/08 *Denki Kagaku Kogyo Kabushiki Kaisha v Commission* EU:T:2012:48, para 68 (*Chloroprene rubber*).

The European Commission has provided guidance on the meaning of a concerted practice in the section of its *Guidelines on Horizontal Cooperation Agreements* that deals with the exchange of information[353]. It says that the exchange of information between competitors can amount to a concerted practice where it reduces 'strategic uncertainty' in the market, thereby facilitating collusion[354]. In paragraph 62 of those *Guidelines* it refers to the *Cement* case[355], where the General Court found that Lafarge was party to a concerted practice when it received information at a meeting about the future conduct of a competitor: the fact that it merely received such information was not a defence[356]. The Commission then cites the Court of Justice's judgment in *T-Mobile*[357] and says that mere attendance at a meeting where an undertaking discloses its confidential pricing plans to its competitors is likely to be caught by Article 101(1), even in the absence of an explicit agreement to fix prices, adding, in support of this proposition, the presumption in the *Hüls* judgment cited below that contact between competitors leads to common conduct on the market.

(ii) **Must a concerted practice have been put into effect?: the need for a 'causal connection'**

The Court of Justice held in *Hüls*, one of the *Polypropylene* cases, that 'a concerted practice ... is caught by Article [101(1) TFEU], even in the absence of anti-competitive effects on the market'[358]; however, in the *Cement* cases the General Court said that there would be no infringement if the parties can prove to the contrary[359]. In reaching its conclusion in *Hüls* the Court of Justice stated that, as established by its own case law[360], Article 101(1) requires that each undertaking must determine its policy on the market independently. At paragraph 161 the Court acknowledged that the concept of a concerted practice implies that there will be common conduct on the market, but added that there must be a presumption that, by making contact with one another, such conduct will follow.

In *T-Mobile*[361] the Court of Justice held that this presumption of a 'causal connection' between competitor contact and conduct on the market forms an integral part of EU law, in consequence of which a national court[362] applying Article 101 would be bound to apply the same presumption[363]; to put the point a different way, the national court is not permitted to apply stricter national rules of evidence than the EU presumption. The Court also held that the presumption in *T-Mobile* could apply even in the event of a single meeting between competitors[364]. In *Fresh Del Monte v Commission*[365] Del Monte failed to rebut the presumption of a 'causal connection' between its bilateral contacts with two competitors to fix quotation prices for bananas and its market conduct.

353 OJ [2011] C 11/1, paras 60–63. 354 Ibid, para 61.

355 Cases T-25/95 etc *Cimenteries CBR SA v Commission* EU:T:2000:77. 356 Ibid, para 1849.

357 Ch 3 n 347 earlier. 358 Cases C-199/92 P etc *Hüls AG v Commission* EU:C:1999:358, para 163.

359 Cases T-25/95 etc *Cimenteries CBR SA v Commission* EU:T:2000:77, para 1865.

360 Cases 40/73 etc *Suiker Unie v Commission* EU:C:1975:174, para 73; Case 172/80 *Züchner v Bayerische Vereinsbank AG* EU:C:1981:178, para 13; Cases 89/85 etc *Ahlström v Commission* EU:C:1993:120, para 63; Case C-7/95 P *John Deere v Commission* EU:C:1998:256, para 86.

361 See ch 3 n 347 earlier.

362 And also, one can assume, an NCA, though that was not the issue under consideration in *T-Mobile*.

363 Case C-8/08 *T-Mobile Netherlands BV v Raad van bestuur van de Nederlandse Mededingingsautoriteit* EU:C:2009:343, paras 44–53.

364 Ibid, paras 54–62.

365 Commission decision of 15 October 2008, paras 212–240, upheld on appeal Case T-587/08 *Fresh Del Monte v Commission* EU:T:2013:129, paras 563–583 and to the Court of Justice (see ch 3 n 352 earlier).

(iii) The burden of proof

The legal burden of proving the existence of a concerted practice is on the Commission (or the person alleging the infringement of Article 101(1)). The EU Courts have annulled decisions where they were not convinced by the evidence on which the Commission relied[366]. However, the evidential burden of demonstrating that competitor contact did not affect an undertaking's subsequent conduct falls upon the undertaking making such assertion. That is because the presumption discussed in the previous paragraph applies in that situation: it is for the parties to adduce evidence to rebut the presumption. Where the parties are able to produce sufficient evidence to cast doubt on the causal connection between competitor contact and conduct, the overall legal burden remains on the Commission to demonstrate an infringement. For example in *Compagnie Royale Asturienne des Mines SA and Rheinzink GmbH v Commission*[367] the Commission had concluded that the simultaneous cessation of deliveries to a Belgian customer, Schlitz, by CRAM and Rheinzink of Germany was attributable to a concerted practice to protect the German market. The Court of Justice held that there was a possible alternative explanation of the refusal to supply, which was that Schlitz had been failing to settle its accounts on the due date; as the Commission had not dealt with this possible explanation of the conduct in question its decision should be quashed. Similarly, in *CISAC v Commission*[368] the General Court annulled the Commission's finding of a concerted practice because the fight against piracy of copyrighted music was an alternative plausible explanation for the parallel behaviour of collecting societies[369].

(iv) Concluding comment on concerted practices

The EU Courts have deliberately refrained from construing the expression 'concerted practice' in a formalistic or narrow manner. It has been pointed out that 'concerted practices can take many different forms, and the courts have always been careful not to define or limit what may amount to a concerted practice'[370]. Cases on concerted practices will always be highly fact-specific: for example in *'Eturas' UAB v Lietuvos Respublikos konkurencijos taryba*[371] the Court of Justice considered that the use of software, and knowledge of what it could do, could lead to a concerted practice.

It is possible, however, to extrapolate the following propositions from the case law:

- a concerted practice involves a knowing substitution of practical cooperation for the risks of competition[372]
- a concerted practice does not require an actual plan; it strictly precludes contact that could influence conduct on the market or disclose one's future conduct on the market[373]

[366] See eg Cases 40/73 etc *Suiker Unie v Commission* EU:C:1975:174; Cases 29/83 and 30/83 *Compagnie Royale Asturienne des Mines SA and Rheinzink GmbH v Commission* EU:C:1984:130; Cases T-68/89 etc *Società Italiano Vetro v Commission* EU:T:1992:38; Cases C-89/85 etc *Åhlström Osakeyhtiö v Commission* EU:C:1993:120; and Cases T-442/08 etc *CISAC v Commission* EU:T:2013:188, in each of which the EU Courts quashed some or all of the findings of concerted practices.

[367] Cases 29/83 and 30/83 EU:C:1984:130.

[368] Commission decision of 16 July 2008, paras 156–222, annulled on appeal on this point in 21 out of 22 appeals to the General Court, eg Case T-442/08 *CISAC v Commission* EU:T:2013:188, paras 87ff.

[369] Ibid, paras 140–181.

[370] *Argos Ltd v Office of Fair Trading* [2006] EWCA Civ 1318, para 22; similarly *Tesco Stores Ltd v Office of Fair Trading* [2012] CAT 31, para 56 ('concerted practice is a versatile concept').

[371] Case C-74/14 EU:C:2016:42. [372] Case 48/69 *ICI v Commission* EU:C:1972:70, para 64.

[373] Cases 40/73 etc *Suiker Unie v Commission* EU:C:1975:174, paras 173–174.

- there is a presumption that undertakings taking part in concerted action take into account information exchanged between them; and there is no need to prove that the concerted practice produces actual effects on the market[374]
- a concerted practice implies reciprocity, but this is satisfied where one competitor discloses its intentions or conduct on the market to another when the other requests it or, at the very least, accepts it[375]
- the *Hüls* presumption is a substantive rule of law; and a concerted practice can arise from the exchange of information at a single meeting[376].

4. The Object or Effect of Preventing, Restricting Or Distorting Competition

Article 101(1) prohibits agreements that have as their object or effect the prevention, restriction or distortion of competition[377]. It contains an illustrative list of agreements that may be caught such as price fixing and market sharing, but this is insufficient in itself to explain the numerous intricacies involved in understanding how this provision works. Judgments of the General Court and, at the top of the hierarchy, the Court of Justice contain the most authoritative statements of the law, although some of the best analyses will be found in Opinions of the Advocates General; the Commission's decisions, Notices and Guidelines provide important insights into its views on the application of Article 101(1), as do its annual *Report on Competition Policy* and the quarterly Competition Policy Newsletter[378].

The application of Article 101(1) to agreements, in particular by the Commission, was for many years controversial. In essence the complaint of many commentators was that Article 101(1) was applied too broadly, catching many agreements that were not detrimental to competition at all[379]. Agreements that are caught by Article 101(1) are void and unenforceable[380], and may attract a fine, unless they satisfy the criteria set out in Article 101(3). Critics argued that Article 101(1) should be applied to fewer agreements in order to avoid the problems of delay, cost and uncertainty associated with the old

[374] Case C-49/92 P *Commission v Anic Partecipazioni* EU:C:1999:356, para 121.

[375] Cases T-25/95 etc *Cimenteries CBR SA v Commission* EU:T:2000:77, para 1849.

[376] Case C-8/08 *T-Mobile* EU:C:2009:343, paras 58–62.

[377] In the text that follows the term 'restriction' of competition is taken to include the prevention and distortion of competition.

[378] All of these materials are available on DG COMP's website at www.ec.europa.eu/competition.

[379] See eg Bright 'EU Competition Policy: Rules, Objectives and Deregulation' (1996) 16 OJLS 535; there is a considerable amount of academic literature criticising the 'over'-application of Article 101(1): see eg Joliet *The Rule of Reason in Antitrust Law; American, German and Common Market Laws in Comparative Perspective* (1967), pp 77–106, 117 to the end; Korah 'The Rise and Fall of Provisional Validity' (1981) 3 Northwestern Journal of International Law and Business 320; Forrester and Norall 'The Laicization of Community Law: Self-Help and the Rule of Reason' (1984) 21 CML Rev 11; Korah 'EEC Competition Policy—Legal Form or Economic Efficiency' (1986) 39 Current Legal Problems 85; Venit '*Pronuptia*: Ancillary Restraints or Unholy Alliances?' (1986) 11 EL Rev 213; Holley 'EEC Competition Practice: A Thirty-Year Retrospective' [1992] Fordham Corporate Law Institute (ed Hawk), 669, 689; Nazzini 'Article 81 EC Between Time Present and Time Past: A Normative Critique of "Restriction of Competition" in EU Law' (2006) 43 CML Rev 497; Colomo and Lamadrid 'On the Notion of Restriction of Competition: What We Know and What We Don't Know We Know' in Gerard, Merola and Meyring (eds) *The Notion of Restriction of Competition: Revisiting the Foundations of Antitrust Enforcement in Europe* (Bruylant, 2017).

[380] See further ch 8, 'Competition Law as a Defence', pp 336–341.

system of notification of agreements to the Commission for 'negative clearance' under Article 101(1) and/or 'individual exemption' under Article 101(3). These procedural problems no longer exist following the abolition of notification and individual exemption by Regulation 1/2003[381]. Since Regulation 1/2003 the precise sphere of application of Article 101(1) on the one hand and Article 101(3) on the other does not have the significance that it once did[382]; today the real question for undertakings and their professional advisers is whether their agreements infringe Article 101 as a whole.

The EU Courts have repeatedly made clear that, except in those cases where the object of an agreement is anti-competitive, the applicability of Article 101(1) cannot be determined simply by taking into account its formal terms. Rather an agreement must be assessed by taking into consideration the entire factual, legal and economic context in which it operates[383]. It is an undoubted fact that the Commission now adopts a more economically realistic approach to the application of Article 101 than previously[384]. This means that the Commission today takes a much narrower view of what is meant by a restriction of competition for the purpose of Article 101(1); and it also has a narrower approach to the defence provided for in Article 101(3)[385].

(A) **Preliminary comments**

The text that follows will examine the meaning of agreements having as their 'object or effect' the prevention, restriction or distortion of competition. However, a few preliminary comments may be helpful.

First, there are many judgments of the EU Courts that demonstrate that a contractual restriction does not necessarily result in a restriction of competition[386]. It is essential to understand this key point: the concept of a restriction of competition is an economic one, and as a general proposition economic analysis is needed to determine whether an agreement could have an anti-competitive effect. A relatively small class of agreements are considered by law to have as their object the restriction of competition[387]; in the case of all other agreements appreciable anti-competitive effects must be demonstrated for there to be an infringement of Article 101(1)[388].

Secondly, the EU Courts have made clear that the Commission must adequately demonstrate that an agreement is restrictive of competition, and that they will not simply 'rubber-stamp' its analysis: a particularly good example is *European Night Services v Commission*[389], where the General Court exposed the inadequacy of the Commission's reasoning in that case[390].

[381] OJ [2003] L 1/1; see further ch 4, 'Regulation 1/2003', pp 174–176.

[382] Note however that the burden of proof rests with different persons under Article 101(1) and Article 101(3): see ch 4, 'Burden and standard of proof', p 159.

[383] Case 56/65 *Société Technique Minière v Maschinenbau Ulm GmbH* EU:C:1966:38; Case C-234/89 *Delimitis v Henninger Bräu* EU:C:1991:91; Case T-461/07 *Visa Europe Ltd v Commission* EU:T:2011:181, para 67.

[384] See Bourgeois and Waelbroeck (eds) *Ten Years of Effects-Based Approach in EU Competition Law* (Bruylant, 2012).

[385] See ch 4, 'First condition of Article 101(3): an improvement in the production or distribution of goods or in technical or economic progress', pp 162–169 for a discussion of the 'narrow' and the 'broad' interpretations of Article 101(3).

[386] See the cases discussed at 'Commercial ancillarity', pp 135–138 later in chapter.

[387] See 'Agreements that have as their object the prevention, restriction or distortion of competition', pp 122–132.

[388] See 'Agreements that have as their effect the prevention, restriction or distortion of competition', pp 132–144 later in chapter.

[389] Cases T-374/94 etc EU:T:1998:198.

[390] *European Night Services Ltd* OJ [1994] L 259/20.

Thirdly, the EU Courts have said that in a case under Article 101(1) the relevant market does not need to be defined where it is possible, without such a definition, to show that an agreement restricts competition and affects trade between Member States[391]. It follows that market definition is not something that must be undertaken as a preliminary matter in every case, as in the case of Article 102 where it is a necessary precondition to a finding of abuse of a dominant position.

Fourthly, the Court of Justice has stressed that Article 101 aims to protect not only the interests of competitors or of consumers, but also the structure of the market and, in so doing, 'competition as such'[392].

Fifthly, the fact that an anti-competitive agreement may be the most cost-effective or least risky course of action for an undertaking does not preclude the application of Article 101[393]. It is irrelevant whether the anti-competitive agreement is in the parties' commercial interests[394].

(B) Horizontal and vertical agreements

One point is absolutely clear: Article 101 is capable of application both to horizontal agreements (between undertakings at the same level of the market) and to vertical agreements (between undertakings at different levels of the market). It was at one time thought that Article 101 might have no application at all to vertical agreements, but that idea was firmly contradicted by the Court of Justice's judgment in *Consten and Grundig v Commission*[395]; it remains the case that undertakings must carry out a careful assessment of whether their vertical agreements are compliant with the law. In *Allianz Hungária*[396] the Court of Justice said that vertical agreements are often less damaging to competition than horizontal agreements; however they may have an anti-competitive object 'when they have a particularly significant restrictive potential'. The application of Article 101 to vertical agreements will be considered in detail in chapter 16.

(C) The 'object or effect' of preventing, restricting or distorting competition

Article 101(1) prohibits agreements 'which have as their *object or effect* the prevention, restriction or distortion of competition' (emphasis added). It is important to understand the significance of the words 'object or effect' in Article 101(1).

(i) 'Object or effect' to be read disjunctively

It is clear that these are alternative, and not cumulative, requirements for a finding of an infringement of Article 101(1). In *Société Technique Minière v Maschinenbau Ulm*[397] the Court of Justice stated that the words 'object or effect' were to be read disjunctively; this means that where an agreement has as its object the restriction of competition it is

391 Case C-439/11 P *Ziegler SA v Commission* EU:C:2013:513, para 63 and case law cited (*International removal services*).

392 Case C-8/08 *T-Mobile Netherlands* EU:C:2009:343, para 38; Cases C-501/06 P etc *GlaxoSmithKline Services Unlimited v Commission* EU:C:2009:610, para 63; the phrase 'competition as such' is discussed by AG Kokott in *T-Mobile* at para 58 of her Opinion: Case C-8/08 EU:C:2009:110.

393 Case T-472/13 *Lundbeck v Commission* EU:T:2016:449, para 380.

394 Cases C-403/04 P etc *Sumitomo Metal Industries v Commission* EU:C:2007:52, paras 44–45 (*Seamless steel tubes*).

395 Cases 56 and 58/64 EU:C:1966:41.

396 Case C-32/11 *Allianz Hungária Biztosító* EU:C:2013:160, para 43.

397 Case 56/65 EU:C:1966:38.

unnecessary to prove that it will produce anti-competitive effects: only if it is not clear that the object of an agreement is to restrict competition is it necessary to consider whether it might have the effect of doing so. Some commentators have argued that the distinction should be reviewed in light of the general trend away from the formalistic application of competition law to a more 'effects-based' system[398]; however the jurisprudence, based on the clear wording of the TFEU, is clear and unequivocal in supporting and maintaining it: many judgments have repeated it and continue to do so[399].

(ii) The 'object' and 'effect' boxes

The distinction between object and effect restrictions can be depicted pictorially by thinking in terms of two boxes, as in Figure 3.1.

THE OBJECT BOX	THE EFFECTS BOX
Agreements that have as their *object* the restriction of competition	Agreements that have as their *effect* the restriction of competition

Fig. 3.1

The text that follows will explore the still controversial topic of what constitutes a restriction of competition by object, a concept that, after more than 50 years of EU competition law, continues to be hotly debated. After discussing what is meant by a restriction of competition by object an attempt will be made in the text that follows to describe the content of the object box as the law currently stands[400].

(D) Agreements that have as their object the prevention, restriction or distortion of competition

Numerous issues must be considered when trying to understand what is meant by a restriction of competition by object and why the object–effect distinction exists[401].

[398] See eg Gerard 'The Effects-Based Approach under Article 101 TFEU and its Paradoxes: Modernisation at War With Itself? in Bourgeois and Waelbroeck (eds) *Ten Years of Effects-Based Approach in EU Competition Law* (Bruylant, 2012), pp 18–42.

[399] See eg Case C-209/07 *Competition Authority v Beef Industry Development Society Ltd* EU:C:2008:643, paras 15 and 16; Case C-8/08 *T-Mobile Netherlands* EU:C:2009:343, paras 28 and 30; Cases C-501/06 P etc *GlaxoSmithKline Services Unlimited v Commission* EU:C:2009:610, para 55; Case C-32/11 *Allianz Hungária Biztosító Zrt* EU:C:2013:160, paras 33–34; Case C-67/13 P *Groupement des Cartes Bancaires v Commission* EU:C:2014:2204, para 49.

[400] See 'The contents of the object box', pp 128–132 later in chapter, for an attempt to capture the current state of EU competition law.

[401] The following articles capture much of the writing on this subject: Jones 'Left Behind by Modernisation? Restrictions by Object Under Article 101(1)' (2010) European Competition Journal 649; King 'The Object Box: Law, Policy or Myth?' (2011) 7 European Competition Journal 269; Bailey 'Restrictions of Competition by Object under Article 101(1) TFEU' (2012) 49 CML Rev 599; Mahtani 'Thinking Outside the Object Box: An EU and UK Perspective' (2012) 8 European Competition Journal 1; Colomo 'The Divide Between Restrictions by Object and Effect' (2016) 2 Competition Law Review 173; Peeperkorn 'Defining "By Object" Restrictions' Concurrences No 3-2016, 54; Vandenborre and Rupp 'Restrictions by Object or Why No Restriction has Proven More Difficult to Define Than Those That are Obvious' (2016) 9 Global Competition L Rev 25; see also speech of the former Director-General of DG COMP, Alexander Italianer 'The Object of Effects', 10 December 2014, available at www.ec.europa.eu.

(i) Meaning of 'object'

The essential legal criterion for ascertaining whether coordination between undertakings restricts competition by object is the finding 'that such coordination reveals in itself a sufficient degree of harm to competition'[402]. The term 'object' in Article 101 means the objective meaning and purpose of the agreement considered in the economic context in which it is to be applied[403]. It is not necessary to prove that the parties have the subjective intention of restricting competition when entering into the agreement[404]. However, subjective intention may be a relevant factor in assessing whether the object of an agreement is anti-competitive[405]. Where an agreement has an anti-competitive object, it does not cease to be characterised as such because it also has an alternative, lawful, purpose[406]. However the Court of Justice has said that an object restriction may fall outside Article 101(1) where there is an objective justification for it[407], for example the protection of health or safety.

Given that it is not necessary to demonstrate that an agreement that restricts competition by object produces adverse effects, it is obviously important to know what categories of agreement fall within the object box. One answer is that particular agreements restrict by object because the Court of Justice has said that they do: we therefore know, for example, that horizontal price fixing or resale price maintenance do so. This however is an unsatisfying answer to the question, first because it does not explain how those agreements were found to restrict by object in the first place; and secondly because this answer provides no guidance as to how new types of agreement might be added to the box.

(ii) The legal test for identifying restrictions by object

(a) The expansion of the object box

As noted earlier, the essential criterion for identifying an object restriction is whether the coordination of conduct by undertakings reveals in itself a sufficient degree of harm to competition. Cases regularly occur in which the question of whether an agreement restricts by object falls to be determined; recent challenges in the Court of Justice to such a classification failed, for example, in *Beef Industry Development Society*[408], *GlaxoSmithKline v Commission*[409], *T-Mobile*[410], *Pierre Fabre*[411], *Football Association Premier League*[412], *Allianz Hungária Biztosító Zrt*[413] and *ING Pensii*[414]. The judgment in

[402] Case C-67/13 P *Groupement des Cartes Bancaires v Commission* EU:C:2014:2204, para 57.

[403] Cases 29/83 and 30/83 *Compagnie Royale Asturienne des Mines SA and Rheinzinc GmbH v Commission* EU:C:1984:130, paras 25–26.

[404] Ibid; see similarly Case C-277/87 *Sandoz Prodotti Farmaceutici v Commission* EU:C:1989:363; Case T-148/89 *Tréfilunion v Commission* EU:T:1995:68, para 79 (*Polypropylene*); Case C-551/03 P *General Motors BV v Commission* EU:C:2006:229, paras 77–78.

[405] Case C-32/11 *Allianz Hungária Biztosító Zrt* EU:C:2013:160, para 37; Case C-67/13 P *Groupement des Cartes Bancaires* EU:C:2014:2204, para 54; see similarly Case C-8/08 *T-Mobile* EU:C:2009:343, para 27; on the relevance of subjective intention see Odudu 'Interpreting Article 81(1): Object as Subjective Intention' (2001) 26 EL Rev 60 and Odudu 'Interpreting Article 81(1): The Object Requirement Revisited' (2001) 26 EL Rev 379.

[406] Case C-551/03 P *General Motors BV v Commission* EU:C:2006:229, para 64; Case C-209/07 *Competition Authority v Beef Industry Development Society Ltd* EU:C:2008:643, para 21; the same point was made by the General Court in Case T-90/11 *ONP v Commission* EU:T:2014:1049, para 327.

[407] Case C-439/09 *Pierre Fabre Dermo-Cosmétique* EU:C:2011:649, para 39; see also *Guidelines on Vertical Restraints* OJ [2010] C 130/1, para 60.

[408] Case C-209/07 EU:C:2008:643; for comment see Odudu 'Restrictions of Competition by Object—What's the Beef?' [2009] Comp Law 11.

[409] Cases C-501/06 P etc EU:C:2009:610.

[410] Case C-8/08 EU:C:2009:343.

[411] Case C-439/09 EU:C:2011:649.

[412] Cases C-403/08 and C-429/08 *Football Association Premier League Ltd v QC Leisure* EU:C:2011:631.

[413] Case C-32/11 EU:C:2013:160.

[414] Case C-172/14 EU:C:2015:484.

T-Mobile appeared to lay down a very wide test for allocating agreements to the object box: the Court said that, in order to ascribe an anti-competitive object to a concerted practice, 'it is sufficient that it has the potential to have a negative impact on competition', adding that the effects of such a practice are relevant only to the level of any fine or the award of damages to victims of the harm[415]. The Court in *T-Mobile* also said that, in order to find a restriction by object, it is not necessary to demonstrate a direct effect on prices to end users: Article 101 is designed to protect the structure of the market and competition as such[416]. In a subsequent case, *Allianz Hungária Biztosító Zrt*[417], the Court of Justice repeated the formulation in *T-Mobile*[418] and went on to hold that certain bilateral vertical agreements, entered into in a complex factual matrix, restricted competition by object[419].

These judgments, and others, including that of the General Court in *Groupement des Cartes Bancaires*[420], gave the impression that the object box was steadily expanding, to a point where it no longer contained 'obvious restrictions of competition such as price-fixing, market-sharing or the control of outlets', a formulation that had been used by the General Court in *European Night Services v Commission*[421]. The Commission's practice of identifying 'new' object restrictions, for example in the 'pay-for-delay' cases, *Lundbeck* and *Servier*, in conjunction with its *Notice on agreements of minor importance* of 2014[422], in which it states that it regards all 'hard-core' restrictions in block exemptions as restrictions by object[423], added to the impression that the object box was inexorably getting larger.

(b) *Groupement des Cartes Bancaires*

It was against this backdrop that the Court of Justice handed down its judgment in *Groupement des Cartes Bancaires v Commission* in September 2014[424]. The Commission[425] and the General Court[426] had held that a fee structure established by the nine main members of a payment card system, Cartes Bancaires, had the object and effect of restricting competition by preventing the entry by new banks into the sector. The Court of Justice annulled the finding of the General Court that the fee structure restricted competition by object on the basis that it had erred in law and remitted the matter to it to consider whether there was a restriction by effect. The Court of Justice rehearsed well-established law:

- certain types of coordination between undertakings can be regarded, by their very nature, as being harmful to the proper functioning of competition[427]
- some collusive behaviour, such as horizontal price fixing by cartels, is so likely to have negative effects that it is redundant to prove that it has actual effects on the market[428]

[415] Case C-8/08 EU:C:2009:343, para 31; on the scope of this finding see the EFTA Court in Case E-3/16 *Ski Taxi SA v Norwegian Government*, judgment of 22 December 2016, paras 52–55.

[416] Case C-8/08 EU:C:2009:343, paras 36–39. [417] Case C-32/11 EU:C:2013:160. [418] Ibid, para 38.

[419] The case is discussed at '*Allianz Hungária Biztosító*', p 130 later in chapter.

[420] Case T-491/07 EU:T:2012:633. [421] Cases T-374/94 etc EU:T:1998:198.

[422] OJ [2014] C 368/13; a Staff Working Document, SWD(2014) 198 final, accompanying the *De Minimis Notice* gives examples of object restrictions.

[423] OJ [2014] C 368/13, para 13.

[424] Case C-67/13 P EU:C:2014:2204; the Opinion of AG Wahl contains a valuable discussion of the meaning of 'object': EU:C:2014:1958; see also the Opinions of AG Wathelet in Case C-373/14 P *Toshiba v Commission* EU:C:2015:427, paras 40–91 and of AG Saumandsgaard Øe in Case C-179/16 *F Hoffmann-La Roche v AGCM* EU:C:2017:714, paras 145–150.

[425] Commission decision of 17 October 2007. [426] Case T-491/07 EU:T:2012:633.

[427] Case C-67/13 P EU:C:2014:2204, para 50. [428] Ibid, para 51.

- the essential criterion for ascertaining whether coordination between undertakings involves a restriction by object is the finding that such coordination 'reveals in itself a sufficient degree of harm to competition'[429].

Importantly, the Court of Justice added that the General Court had erred in law when concluding that the concept of a restriction of competition by object should not be interpreted restrictively: the Court of Justice's view was that the concept should be limited to coordination which reveals a sufficient degree of harm to competition with the result that there is no need to examine its effects[430].

(c) Comment

The judgment in *Cartes Bancaires* is an important one[431]. For the most part it simply repeats the consistent jurisprudence of the Court of Justice over many years. However the clear statement that the concept of an object restriction should be interpreted restrictively is a very significant one and means, at the very least, that the size of the object box should not be expanded unduly. One way of describing the situation would be to suggest that the very wide test suggested in *T-Mobile* and the outcome in *Allianz Hungária* represent the 'high tide' of expansion of the object box, and that *Cartes Bancaires* marks a return to a more conservative and orthodox approach. In *Ski Taxi SA v Norwegian Government*[432] the EFTA Court said that the presumption of innocence in Article 6(2) of the European Convention on Human Rights means that, in a case of doubt as to whether an agreement restricts competition by object, the 'benefit of the doubt' should be given to the defendants[433]. The EFTA Court also observed that only conduct whose harmful nature is 'easily identifiable', in the light of experience and economics, should be regarded as a restriction of competition by object[434].

(iii) **Allocating cases to the object box**

Irrespective of how large or small the object box might be, there remains a riddle: how much analysis should be undertaken when determining whether a particular agreement belongs to one box or the other? The Court in *Cartes Bancaires*, citing earlier authority, stated that in order to decide this:

> regard must be had to the content of [the agreement's] provisions, its objectives and the economic and legal context of which it forms a part. When determining that context, it is also necessary to take into consideration the nature of the goods or services affected, as well as the real conditions of the functioning and structure of the market or markets in question[435].

Clearly this requires some analysis of the agreement in question to decide whether it falls within the object box; however this gives rise to the possibility that a fairly detailed review of an agreement, in particular of its 'economic context', needs to be carried out in order to allocate it to the object box. This could undermine the very purpose of the object–effect distinction in the first place, which is to eliminate effects analysis in the case of object restrictions: a criticism of the *Allianz Hungária* judgment is that this is what the Court of Justice seemed to require, not least when it stated that it was necessary to take into account the structure of

429 Ibid, para 57. 430 Ibid, para 58.

431 The case was referred back to the General Court which held that the fee structure did have the effect of restricting competition in the market for the issuing of CB payment cards and did not benefit from Article 101(3): Case T-491/07 RENV *CB v Commission* EU:T:2016:379.

432 Case E-3/16, judgment of 22 December 2016. 433 Ibid, para 62. 434 Ibid, para 61.

435 Case C-67/13 P EU:C:2014:2204, para 53.

the market, the existence of alternative distribution channels and the respective importance and market power of the companies concerned[436]. In her Opinion in *T-Mobile* Advocate General Kokott warned against the risk of 'mingling' object and effects analysis[437], a point which was also made by the EFTA Court in *Ski Taxi SA v Norwegian Government*[438].

The authors of this book agree that there is a risk that an extended review of the economic and legal context in an object case might turn into effects analysis, which would undermine the object–effect distinction. It is, perhaps, with this risk in mind that the Court of Justice indicated in *Toshiba v Commission*[439] and in *FSL v Commission*[440] that the analysis of context may be 'limited to what is strictly necessary in order to establish the existence of a restriction of competition by object'. Were it otherwise, with the result that a detailed investigation has to be carried out at the stage of determining whether an agreement restricts by object, there is a risk of the creation of a third box, hovering between the object and effects boxes, for which there is no basis in the Treaty and which would add further complexity to what is already a difficult area.

(iv) Object restrictions and the *de minimis* doctrine

The treatment of object restrictions under the *de minimis* doctrine is dealt with separately later in this chapter[441].

(v) Is it possible to justify object restrictions under Article 101(3)?

As will be explained in chapter 4[442], it is important to understand that it is possible to justify an agreement that restricts competition by object under Article 101(3)[443]. This was stated by the General Court in *Matra Hachette v Commission*[444] and was explicitly recognised by the Court of Justice in *Beef Industry Development Society*[445], *GlaxoSmithKline v Commission*[446] and *Pierre Fabre*[447], although no final decision on the application of Article 101(3) was reached by the Court of Justice in any of those cases. Similarly when *Ski Taxi SA v Norwegian Government*[448] was referred back to the Supreme Court of Norway[449] it noted that it was possible for the taxi companies to defend their 'object restriction' on the basis of efficiencies under the Norwegian equivalent of Article 101(3).

Once it is recognised that object cases can be defended under Article 101(3), the classification of a particular type of agreement as falling within the 'object box' can be seen for what it is: a legal presumption, but a rebuttable one[450]. The presumption shifts the burden

436 Case C-32/11 EU:C:2013:160, para 48.
437 Case C-8/08 EU:C:2009:110, para 45.
438 Case E-3/16, judgment of 22 December 2016, paras 58 and 63.
439 Case C-373/14 P EU:C:2016:26, para 29.
440 Case C-469/15 P EU:C:2017:308, para 107.
441 See 'The *De Minimis* Doctrine', pp 147–150 later in chapter.
442 See ch 4, 'Any type of agreement can be defended under Article 101(3)', pp 159–161.
443 A point emphasised by former Director-General of DG COMP, Alexander Italianer 'Competitor Agreements under EU Competition Law' [2013] Fordham Corporate Law Institute (ed Hawk), ch 2.
444 Case T-17/93 EU:T:1994:89, para 85; see similarly Case C-439/09 *Pierre Fabre Dermo-Cosmétique SA* EU:C:2011:649, paras 49 and 57.
445 Case C-209/07 EU:C:2008:643: the case was remitted to the High Court in Ireland to consider whether the criteria of Article 101(3) were satisfied; however BIDS withdrew its defence before the Court had made a decision on the matter: see Irish Competition Authority Press Release, 25 January 2011, available at www.tca.ie; for comment see Odudu 'Restrictions of Competition by Object—What's the Beef?' [2009] Comp Law 11.
446 Cases C-501/06 P etc EU:C:2009:610.
447 Case C-439/09 *Pierre Fabre Dermo-Cosmétique* EU:C:2011:649; note the Paris Court of Appeal subsequently held that Pierre Fabre's ban on internet sales did not benefit from Article 101(3): judgment of 31 January 2013.
448 Case E-3/16, judgment of 22 December 2016.
449 Judgment of 22 June 2017, para 52.
450 On the use of presumptions see Bailey 'Presumptions in EU Competition Law' (2010) 31 ECLR 20 and Ritter 'Presumptions in EU competition law' (2017), available at www.ssrn.com; see also the OECD Roundtable *Safe harbours and legal presumptions in competition law* (December 2017), available at www.oecd.org.

of proof from the Commission to the parties, and provides a structure within which to analyse agreements. Decisions and/or informal guidance finding that object agreements satisfy the conditions of Article 101(3) might lead to fewer cases in which undertakings challenge the object–effect distinction: this sometimes happens because of the misperception that only restrictions by effect can benefit from Article 101(3)[451].

(vi) Why does Article 101(1) prohibit object restrictions without proof of anti-competitive effects?

Advocate General Kokott's Opinion in *T-Mobile*[452] includes an interesting discussion of why Article 101(1) makes a distinction between object and effect restrictions. First, the classification of certain types of agreement as restrictive by object 'sensibly conserves resources of competition authorities and the justice system'[453]. The fact that a competition authority does not need to demonstrate, for example, that a horizontal price-fixing agreement produces adverse economic effects relieves it of some of the burden that would otherwise rest upon it. Secondly, the Advocate General pointed out that the existence of object restrictions 'creates legal certainty and allows all market participants to adapt their conduct accordingly'[454] adding that, although the concept of restriction by object should not be given an unduly broad interpretation, nor should it be interpreted so narrowly as to deprive it of its practical effectiveness[455]. Thirdly, she pointed out that, just as a law that forbids people from driving cars when under the influence of alcohol does not require, for a conviction, that the driver has caused an accident—that is to say proof of an effect—so, in the same way, Article 101(1) prohibits certain agreements that have the object of restricting competition, irrespective of whether they produce adverse effects on the market in an individual case[456]; such agreements will be permitted, therefore, only where the parties can demonstrate that they will lead to economic efficiencies of the kind set out in Article 101(3), and that a fair share of those efficiencies will be passed on to consumers. The authors of this book agree with this analysis, subject to the caveat that the object box should contain only those agreements that properly belong there.

(vii) Object restrictions and *per se* rules under the Sherman Act

Section 1 of the US Sherman Act 1890 characterises some agreements as *per se* illegal, whereas others are subject to so-called 'rule of reason' analysis[457]. Where there is a *per se* infringement it is not open to the parties to the agreement to argue that it does not restrict competition: it belongs to a category of agreement that has, by law, been found to be restrictive of competition. There is an obvious analogy between an agreement that is *per se* illegal under the Sherman Act and one that is restrictive of competition by object under Article 101(1). However there is an important difference between section 1 of the Sherman Act and Article 101 TFEU in that, even if an agreement has as its object the

[451] Note that the Competition Commission of Singapore, applying a provision that is substantially the same as Article 101, has, on several occasions, concluded that agreements that restricted competition by object produced 'net economic benefits' and were therefore lawful: see eg *United Airlines, Continental Airlines and All Nippon Airways*, 4 July 2011, available at www.ccs.gov.sg; see also the Australian Competition and Consumer Commission's authorisation of minimum retail prices for power tools under the Competition and Consumer Act 2010, 5 December 2014, available at www.accc.gov.au.

[452] Case C-8/08 EU:C:2009:110. [453] Ibid, para 43. [454] Ibid. [455] Ibid, para 44.

[456] Ibid, para 47; see similarly para 136 of AG Geelhoed in Case C-407/04 P *Dalmine v Commission* EU:C:2006:547 (*Seamless steel tubes*).

[457] For discussion of this topic see Werden 'Antitrust's Rule of Reason: Only Competition Matters' (2013) and Hovenkamp 'The Rule of Reason' (2016) University of Pennylsvania Institute for Law & Econ Research Paper No 17-28 and both available at www.ssrn.com.

restriction of competition, that is to say that it infringes Article 101(1) *per se*, the parties can still attempt to justify it under Article 101(3). This possibility does not exist in US law, since there is no equivalent of Article 101(3) in that system. In this sense a judgment such as that of the US Supreme Court in *Leegin*[458], in which it determined that minimum resale price maintenance should be analysed under the rule of reason rather than being *per se* illegal, brings US law into alignment with that of the EU: it has always been possible to argue that resale price maintenance satisfies Article 101(3), even though it is classified as having as its object the restriction of competition for the purpose of Article 101(1)[459].

(viii) **The contents of the object box**

The Court of Justice in *Competition Authority v Beef Industry Development Society Ltd*[460] stated that the notion of restriction of competition by object cannot be reduced to an exhaustive list, and that it should not be limited just to the examples of anti-competitive agreements given in Article 101(1) itself[461]. Ultimately it is for the Court of Justice to determine which agreements should be allocated to the object box. The Commission may decide that a particular type of agreement restricts by object—for example the pay-for-delay agreements in *Lundbeck* and *Servier*—but only the Court can decide that this is the case as a matter of law. The text that follows attempts to state the position as it currently stands, and concludes with a summary of what can currently be found in the object box.

(a) Price fixing and exchanges of information in relation to future prices

Price fixing is specifically cited as an example of an anti-competitive agreement in Article 101(1)(a) of the Treaty, and it is unsurprising that it is characterised as having as its object the restriction of competition, whether horizontal[462] or vertical[463]. The EFTA Court held in *Ski Taxi SA v Norwegian Government*[464] that joint bidding for a contract by actual or potential competitors is capable of restricting competition by object. In *T-Mobile*[465] the Court of Justice said that the exchange of information between competitors 'is tainted with an anti-competitive object if the exchange is capable of removing uncertainties concerning the intended conduct of the participating undertakings'[466]; in that case mobile telephone operators exchanged information about the remuneration that they intended to pay to their dealers for the services that they provided and this was found to restrict by object. In its *Guidelines on Horizontal Cooperation Agreements*[467] the Commission says that it considers the exchange of information between competitors of individualised data regarding intended future prices or quantities to be restrictive of competition by object[468]. In *Bananas*[469] the General Court held that 'pre-pricing communications' in which competitors discussed price-setting factors relevant to the setting of future quotation prices amounted to object restrictions[470]. Other information exchanges require effects analysis[471].

458 *Leegin Creative Leather Products Inc v PSKS Inc* 551 US 877 (2007).

459 See 'Is it possible to justify object restrictions under Article 101(3)?', pp 126–127 earlier in chapter.

460 Case C-209/07 EU:C:2008:643.

461 Ibid, para 23.

462 See ch 13, 'Horizontal Price Fixing', pp 530–541.

463 See ch 16, 'Article 4(a): resale price maintenance', pp 678–679.

464 Case E-3/16, judgment of 22 December 2016.

465 Case C-8/08 EU:C:2009:343.

466 Ibid, para 43.

467 OJ [2011] C 11/1.

468 Ibid, para 74.

469 Case T-587/08 *Fresh Del Monte Produce v Commission* [2013] EU:T:2013:129, paras 293–585, dismissing an appeal against Commission decision of 15 October 2008, paras 263–277; the General Court's judgment was upheld on appeal to the Court of Justice Cases C-293/13 P etc EU:C:2015:416.

470 Case T-587/08 *Fresh Del Monte Produce v Commission* [2013] EU:T:2013:129, paras 293–585 and 263–277.

471 See eg Case C-238/05 *Asnef-Equifax v Asociación de Usuarios de Servcicios Bancarios (Ausbanc)* EU:C:2006:734 and the Commission's *Guidelines on Horizontal Cooperation Agreements* OJ [2011] C 11/1, paras 75–94; information agreements are discussed in ch 13, 'Exchanges of Information', pp 551–559.

(b) Market sharing, quotas, collective exclusive dealing

Market-sharing agreements are specifically mentioned in Article 101(1)(c), and again their treatment as restrictive by object is to be expected, in particular because they are likely to be harmful to the internal market[472]. Agreements to limit output also belong to the object box: they are specifically referred to in Article 101(1)(b). In *Competition Authority v Beef Industry Development Society Ltd*[473] the Court of Justice held that arrangements to enable several undertakings to implement a common policy of encouraging some of them to withdraw from the market in order to reduce overcapacity had the object of restricting competition[474]. The Commission, upheld by the EU Courts, has also characterised collective exclusive dealing as restricting competition by object[475]. It is irrelevant that the victim of a boycott is allegedly operating illegally on the market[476]. In *Lundbeck*[477] and *Servier*[478] the Commission held that 'pay-for-delay' agreements in the pharmaceutical sector restricted competition by object; the decision in *Lundbeck* was upheld on appeal to the General Court[479]. Several recent judgments of the EU Courts held that market-sharing agreements restricted competition by object[480].

(c) Controlling outlets; export bans

The General Court in *European Night Services v Commission* referred to agreements to control outlets as containing obvious restrictions of competition; the control of outlets is not specifically referred to in Article 101(1), but the Court presumably had in mind the imposition on distributors of direct and/or indirect export bans from one Member State to another, which have consistently been found to have as their object the restriction of competition[481]: nothing could be more obviously inimical to the goal of market integration than restrictions of this kind. In *Consten and Grundig v Commission*[482] the Court of Justice held that an agreement conferring absolute territorial protection on a distributor had as its object the restriction of competition and did not satisfy the criteria of Article 101(3). The judgment of the General Court in *GlaxoSmithKline v Commission*[483] somewhat muddied this apparently simple point by suggesting that, in the specific and unusual conditions in which pharmaceutical products are bought and sold, an indirect export ban did not have as its object the restriction of competition[484], although it did restrict competition by effect[485]. However the Court of Justice reversed the judgment of

[472] See ch 13, 'Horizontal Market Sharing', pp 541–544.

[473] Case C-209/07 EU:C:2008:643.

[474] Ibid, paras 33–34.

[475] See eg *Nederlandse Federative Vereniging voor de Grootlandel op Elektrotechnisch Gebied and Technische Unie (FEG and TU)* OJ [2000] L 39/1, para 105, and the further examples given in fn 120 of that decision; the decision was upheld on appeal, Cases T-5/00 and 6/00 EU:T:2003:342 and on further appeal to the Court of Justice EU:C:2006:593.

[476] Case C-68/12 *Protimonopolný úrad Slovenskej republiky v Slovenská sporiteľňa a.s.* EU:C:2013:71, paras 19–21.

[477] Commission decision of 19 June 2013.

[478] Commission decision of 9 July 2014, on appeal to the General Court Cases T-691/14 etc *Servier v Commission*, not yet decided.

[479] Cases T-472/13 etc *Lundbeck A/S v Commission* EU:T:2016:449, on appeal to the Court of Justice Case C-591/16 P *Lundbeck A/S v Commission*, not yet decided.

[480] See eg Case C-172/14 *ING Pensii v Consiliul Concuretnei* EU:C:2015:484; Case C-373/14 *Toshiba Corp v Commission* EU:C:2016:26; Case T-216/13 *Telefónica v Commission* EU:T:2016:369, upheld on appeal to the Court of Justice Case C-487/16 P EU:C:2017:961; for an unusual example of an agreement to 'reduce competitive pressure' of one competing product on another see Case C-179/16 *F Hoffmann-La Roche v AGCM* EU:C:2018:25.

[481] See eg Case 19/77 *Miller International Schallplaten v Commission* EU:C:1978:19, paras 7 and 18; see similarly Case C-551/03 P *General Motors BV v Commission* EU:C:2006:229, paras 64–80; Cases T-175/95 etc *BASF v Commission* EU:T:1999:99, para 133; Case T-176/95 *Accinauto SA v Commission* EU:T:1999:10, para 104.

[482] Cases 56 and 58/64 EU:C:1966:41.

[483] Case T-168/01 *GlaxoSmithKline Services v Commission* EU:T:2006:265.

[484] Ibid, paras 114–147.

[485] Ibid, paras 148–192.

the General Court, repeating that an agreement aimed at prohibiting or limiting parallel trade has as its object the restriction of competition, and that that principle applies to the pharmaceutical sector as it does to any other[486]; the Court of Justice added that, in order to be found to restrict by object, it was not necessary to show that the agreement entailed disadvantages for final consumers[487].

The Court of Justice has also held that the imposition of fixed or minimum resale prices on distributors is restrictive of competition by object[488]. The Court of Justice in *AEG-Telefunken AG v Commission*[489] regarded a selective distribution system as restrictive of competition by object unless it was operated in accordance with the *Metro* doctrine[490]. The Court did not actually use the expression 'by object' in this judgment, but this seems to have been what it meant and was the interpretation that it adopted in its judgment in *Pierre Fabre*[491].

(d) Allianz Hungária Biztosító

In *Allianz Hungária Biztosító*[492] the Court of Justice held that bilateral vertical agreements between car insurance companies and car repair shops concerning the hourly charge for car repairs, which incentivised the repairers to sell more insurance policies on behalf of the insurer contrary to Hungarian consumer law, would restrict by object where, 'following a concrete and individual examination of the wording and aim of those agreements and of the economic and legal context of which they form part, it is apparent that they are, by their very nature, injurious to the proper functioning of normal competition on one of the two markets concerned'. With respect to the Court, it is far from obvious that such agreements are suitable for allocation to the object box, and the analysis suggested by it seems to risk improperly intermingling object and effect analysis. In addition, prior to this judgment the only vertical agreements to be allocated to the object box were export bans, resale price maintenance and selective distribution agreements; the addition of the agreements in *Allianz* increases the range of vertical agreements found to restrict by object and might be regarded as contravening the later pronouncement of the Court of Justice in *Cartes Bancaires* that the concept of an object restriction should be interpreted restrictively.

(e) Benchmark manipulation

There is no doubt that the manipulation of a benchmark such as LIBOR is an egregious offence; particularly given that it is supposed to represent an objective fact, the daily borrowing rate of money. It is however a separate question whether such a manipulation infringes Article 101. In *Yen Interest Rate Derivatives*[493], *Euro Interest Rate Derivatives*[494]

[486] Cases C-501/06 P etc *GlaxoSmithKline Services Unlimited v Commission* EU:C:2009:610, paras 59 and 60.

[487] Ibid, paras 62–64.

[488] Case 161/84 *Pronuptia de Paris GmbH v Schillgalis* EU:C:1986:41, paras 23 and 25.

[489] Case 107/82 EU:C:1983:293, para 34.

[490] On the *Metro* doctrine see ch 16, 'Selective distribution systems', pp 654–658.

[491] Case C-439/09 *Pierre Fabre Dermo-Cosmétique SAS v Président de l'Autorité de la Concurrence and Ministre de l'Économie, de l'Industrie et de l'Emploi* EU:C:2011:649, para 39.

[492] Case C-32/11 EU:C:2013:160; for criticism of this judgment see Harrison 'The Court of Justice's Judgment in *Allianz Hungária* is Wrong and Needs Correcting' [2013] CPI Antitrust Chronicle, May 14 (1); Nagy 'The Distinction between Anti-Competitive Object and Effect after *Allianz*: The End of Coherence in Competition Analysis?' (2013) 36 World Competition 541.

[493] Commission decision of 4 February 2015.

[494] Commission decisions of 4 December 2013 and 7 December 2016; the latter decision is on appeal Cases T-105/17 etc *HSBC Holdings plc v Commission*, not yet decided.

and *Swiss Franc Interest Rate Derivatives*[495] the Commission characterised manipulation of benchmarks as having as its object the restriction of competition because it aimed to distort the normal course of pricing components for interest rate derivatives. In *Icap v Commission*[496] the General Court endorsed the Commission's view that the coordination of the Japanese yen LIBOR panel submissions was intended to influence the extent of the payments due by, or due to, the banks concerned, and therefore had an anti-competitive object.

(ix) The contents of the object box

Following the order of the text earlier, it seems that the contents of the 'object' box can be depicted as shown in Figure 3.2.[497]

Horizontal agreements:

- to fix prices
- to exchange information that reduces uncertainty about future behaviour
- to share markets
- to limit output, including the removal of excess capacity
- to limit sales
- for collective exclusive dealing
- to pay competitors to delay the launch of competing products
- to manipulate a financial benchmark

Vertical agreements:

- to impose fixed or minimum resale prices
- to impose export bans
- selective distribution agreements that do not accord with the *Metro* doctrine
- agreements of the kind under scrutiny in *Allianz Hungária*

Fig. 3.2 The object box

(x) Refinement of the range of agreements within the object box

This presentation of the position somewhat oversimplifies the position in so far as it suggests that the content of the object box is capable of precise definition: it is not. Some

[495] Commission decision of 21 October 2014. [496] Case T-180/15 EU:T:2017:795, para 72.

[497] It will be seen that the contents of the object box correspond to a large extent with the provisions that are blacklisted in Articles 4(a) and 4(b) of Regulation 330/2010 on vertical agreements (ch 16, 'Article 4(a): resale price maintenance', pp 678–679, and ch 16, 'Article 4(b): territorial and customer restrictions', pp 679–682), Article 5 of Regulation 1217/2010 on research and development agreements (ch 15, 'Article 4: duration of exemption and the market share threshold', pp 609–610) and Article 4 of Regulation 1218/2010 on specialisation agreements (ch 15, 'Article 4: hard-core restrictions', pp 614–615).

other agreements may be found to be restrictive by object in light of their particular characteristics or the relevant context[498]; and some that appear to contain object restrictions might be found not to do so[499]. In *Visa International—Multilateral Interchange Fee*[500] and *MasterCard*[501] the Commission concluded that the fixing of the 'multilateral interchange fees' in those card payment systems, which could be seen as a kind of price fixing, restricted competition by effect, but it did not conclude that they did so by object. In *Erauw-Jacquery Sprl v La Hesbignonne Société Coopérative*[502] and *Javico v Yves St Laurent*[503] the Court concluded that export bans, in the specific circumstances of those cases, did not restrict competition by object. This demonstrates that context must be taken into account when determining whether a particular agreement restricts competition by object; however, as suggested earlier, this should be carried out pursuant to a 'quick look' rather than a detailed investigation in order to avoid the mingling of object and effects analysis.

(E) Agreements that have as their effect the prevention, restriction or distortion of competition

(i) Meaning of 'effect'

Where it is not possible to say that the object of an agreement is to restrict competition it is necessary to assess its effect on actual and potential competition before it can be found to infringe Article 101(1)[504]. For an agreement to have the effect of restricting competition the Court of Justice in *MasterCard v Commission*[505] observed that it must be 'liable to have an appreciable adverse impact on the parameters of competition, such as the price, the quantity and quality of the goods or services'. However, nothing in the wording of Article 101(1) requires that, for an agreement to restrict competition by effect, it must harm final consumers. The Commission has explained that an agreement can have such an adverse impact 'by appreciably reducing competition between the parties to the agreement or between any one of them and third parties'[506].

[498] See eg, in the English High Court, *Jones v Ricoh UK Ltd* [2010] EWHC 1743 (Ch), holding that a clause in a confidentiality agreement restricted competition by object in the circumstances of that case; for discussion of the UK case law on this subject see ch 9 'The Object or Effect of Preventing, Restricting or Distorting Competition', pp 355–359.

[499] The process of the US Supreme Court reassigning particular types of agreement from the *per se* standard to rule of reason analysis can be seen in *Continental TV v GTE Sylvania* 433 US 36 (1977), where it overruled an earlier judgment, *US v Arnold Schwinn & Co* 388 US 365 (1967), that had subjected non-price vertical restraints to a *per se* rule; *Broadcast Music Inc v CBS* 441 US 1 (1979), where the rule of reason was applied to the rules of a copyright collecting society: the Supreme Court accepted that the agreement was a price fixing agreement 'in the literal sense', but concluded that it was not a 'naked restraint', but instead enabled copyright owners to market their product more efficiently; *State Oil Co v Khan* 522 US 3 (1997), where the Supreme Court held that maximum resale price maintenance should be tested under the rule of reason and not a *per se* standard; and *Leegin Creative Leather Products, Inc v PSKS, Inc* 551 US 877 (2007) where the Supreme Court decided that agreements on minimum resale prices should be transferred from *per se* to rule of reason analysis.

[500] OJ [2002] L 318/17.

[501] Commission decision of 19 December 2007.

[502] Case 27/87 EU:C:1988:183; see similarly the Commission's decision in *Sicasov* OJ [1999] L 4/27, paras 53–61.

[503] Case C-306/96 EU:C:1998:173.

[504] Case C-382/12 P EU:C:2014:2201, para 93.

[505] Helpful guidance on the Commission's approach to effects analysis can be found in its *Guidelines on the application of Article [101(3)] of the Treaty* OJ [2004] C 101/97, paras 24–27; for discussion of anti-competitive effect see Odudu 'Interpreting Article 81(1): Demonstrating Restrictive Effect' (2001) 26 EL Rev 261.

[506] *Guidelines on Horizontal Cooperation Agreements* OJ [2011] C 11/1, para 27; on restrictive effects generally see paras 26–47.

A restriction by effect can be established by demonstrating effects on competition that have already occurred—actual effects—or effects that are likely to occur in the future[507].

(ii) Extensive analysis of an agreement in its market context is required to determine its effect

In *Brasserie de Haecht v Wilkin*[508] the Court of Justice said that:

> it would be pointless to consider an agreement, decision or practice by reason of its effect if those effects were to be taken distinct from the market in which they are seen to operate, and could only be examined apart from the body of effects, whether convergent or not, surrounding their implementation. Thus in order to examine whether it is caught by Article [101(1)] an agreement cannot be examined in isolation from the earlier context, that is, from the factual or legal circumstances causing it to prevent, restrict or distort competition. The existence of similar contracts may be taken into consideration for this objective to the extent to which the general body of contracts of this type is capable of restricting the freedom of trade[509].

In *Maxima Latvija*[510] the Court of Justice emphasised that an assessment of effects must be based on 'a thorough analysis of the economic and legal context in which the agreements at issue in the main proceedings occur and the specificities of the relevant market'.

A case which demonstrates the depth of analysis that may be required in determining whether an agreement has the effect of restricting competition is *Delimitis v Henninger Bräu AG*[511]. There the Court of Justice considered a provision in an agreement between a brewery and a licensee of a public house owned by the brewery, whereby the licensee was required to purchase a minimum amount of beer each year. The licensee claimed that the agreement was void and unenforceable under Article 101. The Court of Justice said that beer supply agreements of the type under consideration do not have an anti-competitive object[512]. Instead it stressed that the agreement had to be considered in the context in which it occurred[513]. To begin with it was necessary to define the relevant product and geographic markets[514]: these were defined as the sale of beer in licensed premises (as opposed to beer sold in retail outlets) in Germany. Having defined the markets, the Court said that it was necessary to determine whether access to the market was impeded: could a new competitor enter the market, for example by buying an existing brewery together with its network of sales outlets or by opening new public houses[515]? If the answer was that access to the market was impeded, it was necessary to ask whether the agreements entered into by Henninger Bräu contributed to that foreclosure effect, for example because of their number and duration[516]. Only if the answer to both of these questions was yes could it be held that Article 101(1) was infringed. The analysis suggested in this case was specific to

507 Cases C-7/95 P etc *John Deere v Commission* EU:C:1998:256, para 77.

508 Case 23/67 EU:C:1967:54.

509 Ibid; see similarly Cases C-7/95 P etc *John Deere v Commission* EU:C:1998:256, paras 76 and 91 and Cases C-215/96 and C-216/96 *Carlo Bagnsaco v BPN* EU:C:1999:12, para 33; Case C-1/12 *Ordem dos Tecnicos Oficiais de Contas v Autoridade da Concorrencia* EU:C:2013:127, para 70.

510 Case C-345/14 EU:C:2015:784, para 29.

511 Case C-234/89 EU:C:1991:91, para 13; see Korah 'The Judgment in *Delimitis*: A Milestone Towards a Realistic Assessment of the Effects of an Agreement—or a Damp Squib' (1992) 14 EIPR 167; there is a longer version in (1998) 8 Tulane European and Civil Law Forum 17; see similarly Case C-214/99 *Neste Markkinointi Oy v Yötuuli* EU:C:2000:679; Case T-65/98 *Van den Bergh Foods Ltd v Commission* EU:T:2003:281, paras 75–119.

512 Case C-234/89 EU:C:1991:91, para 13.

513 Ibid, para 14.

514 Ibid, paras 16–18; on market definition see ch 1, 'Market definition', pp 26–42.

515 Case C-234/89 EU:C:1991:91, paras 19–23.

516 Ibid, paras 24–27.

the issues raised by beer supply agreements, and is not necessarily the same as would have to be applied, for example, to restrictive covenants taken on the sale of a business or to the rules of a group purchasing association. However the important point about the judgment is its requirement that a full analysis of the agreement in its market context must be carried out before it is possible to determine whether its effect is to restrict competition.

(iii) Allocating cases to the effects box

If an agreement does not have an anti-competitive object, there is no presumption of anti-competitive effects. When deciding whether an agreement falls within the effects box, it is usually necessary to consider five factors[517]:

- the agreement and/or clause in the agreement that is said to constitute a restriction on competition
- the relevant market or markets in which the effects should be assessed[518]
- a theory of harm, that is to say, a theory as to how and why an agreement and/or clause is likely to have negative effects on competition[519]
- the actual context in which competition would occur in the absence of the agreement with the alleged restrictions[520]
- the available evidence on the existence of the alleged effects[521].

The Commission's *Guidelines on the application of Article [101(3)]* describe an important theory of harm as to how an agreement may lead to anti-competitive effects, which is when the parties to an agreement, individually or collectively, have or obtain market power and the agreement contributes to the creation, maintenance or strengthening of that market power or allows the parties to exploit such market power[522]. The degree of market power required for a restriction by effect under Article 101(1) is less than is required for a finding of dominance under Article 102.

(iv) The need to establish a 'counterfactual'

In determining whether an agreement has a restrictive effect on competition it is necessary to consider what the position would have been in the absence of the agreement[523]: by comparing the two situations it should be possible to form a view as to whether the agreement could restrict competition. The need to examine the 'counterfactual' was stressed by the General Court in *O2 (Germany) GmbH & Co, OHG v Commission*[524], where it annulled a Commission decision[525] finding that a roaming agreement in the mobile telephony sector had the effect of restricting competition: the Commission had failed to show what the position would have been in the absence of the agreement, or that the agreement could have restrictive effects on competition[526]. The judgment of the Court of Justice in *MasterCard v Commission*[527] contains a somewhat baffling discussion

[517] Note in some cases it may be possible to show anti-competitive effects by analysing the conduct of the parties to the agreement: *Article 101(3) Guidelines* (ch 3 n 505 earlier), para 27.

[518] Case C-234/89 *Delimitis* EU:C:1991:91, para 13.

[519] On the need to identify a theory of harm see ch 9 'Restriction of competition by effect', pp 357–359.

[520] See 'The need to establish a "counterfactual"', below.

[521] See eg Case T-461/07 *Visa Europe Ltd v Commission* EU:T:2011:181, para 167.

[522] OJ [2004] C 101/97, para 25.

[523] See Case 56/65 *Société Technique Minière v Maschinendau Ulm* EU:C:1966:38; see also the Commission's *Guidelines on Horizontal Cooperation Agreements* OJ [2011] C 11/1, para 29.

[524] Case T-328/03 EU:T:2006:116.

[525] *T-Mobile Deutschland/O2 Germany: Network Sharing Rahmenvertrag* OJ [2004] L 75/32.

[526] Case T-328/03 EU:T:2006:116, paras 65–117.

[527] Case C-382/12 P EU:C:2014:2201.

of counterfactual analysis, apparently concluding that a total prohibition on *ex post* pricing as between issuing and acquiring banks, which had not been contemplated and which MasterCard claimed that it would not have tolerated, could nevertheless amount to a counterfactual hypothesis[528].

(v) Actual and potential competition

In deciding whether Article 101 is infringed the Commission and the EU Courts will not limit their consideration to whether existing competition will be restricted by the agreement; they will also take into account the possibility that an agreement might affect potential competition in a particular market[529]. The Commission will adopt a realistic view of potential competition rather than a theoretical or speculative one[530]. The General Court in *European Night Services v Commission*[531] rejected a finding of the Commission that the establishment of a joint venture, European Night Services, could restrict actual or potential competition between its parents; the Court considered this to be:

> a hypothesis unsupported by any evidence or any analysis of the structure of the relevant market from which it might be concluded that it represented a real, concrete possibility[532].

Potential competition exists when entry is a 'real concrete possibility'. In *Visa Europe Ltd v Commission*[533] the General Court upheld the Commission's decision in *Morgan Stanley/Visa International*[534] that Morgan Stanley was a potential competitor in the acquiring market for payment cards and had been illegally excluded from the Visa payment card system[535].

The 'real concrete possibility' test for potential competition has been considered in several cases. In *Lundbeck v Commission*[536] the General Court upheld the Commission's finding that producers of generic medicines were Lundbeck's potential competitors and that the fact that Lundbeck agreed to pay the generics not to enter the market was 'an important indication' that it perceived them as a competitive threat[537]. The Court of Justice reached the same conclusion in *Toshiba v Commission*[538], since it had attended meetings of the 'Gentlemen's Agreement' over a four-year period, which was regarded as 'a strong indication that a competitive relationship' existed between the various producers. Arguments that undertakings were not potential competitors were also rejected in *Telefónica/Portugal Telecom*[539].

(vi) Commercial ancillarity

A contractual restriction is not the same as a restriction of competition, and the two concepts should not be confused. It may of course be the case that a clause in a contract

[528] Ibid, paras 154–199; several actions for damages against MasterCard in the UK have considered the counterfactual: see ch 9 'Restriction of competition by effect', pp 357–359.

[529] See Case T-504/93 *Tiercé-Ladbroke v Commission* EU:T:1997:84 where a decision was annulled because it failed to take into account a possible restriction of potential competition.

[530] See eg *Konsortium ECR 900* OJ [1990] L 228/31; *Elopak/Metal Box—Odin* OJ [1990] L 209/15; Commission's *Guidelines on Horizontal Cooperation Agreements* OJ [2011] C 11/1, para 10 and fns 3 and 4; see further ch 15, 'Purpose and scope of the Guidelines on Horizontal Cooperation Agreements', pp 601–602.

[531] Cases T-374/94 etc EU:T:1998:198.

[532] Ibid, paras 139–147.

[533] Case T-461/07 EU:T:2011:181.

[534] Commission decision of 3 October 2007.

[535] Case T-461/07 EU:T:2011:181, paras 162–197.

[536] Case T-472/13 *Lundbeck v Commission* EU:T:2016:449, paras 89–330; this case is on further appeal to the Court of Justice, Case C-591/16 P, not yet decided; see also *Fentanyl*, Commission decision of 10 December 2013; *Servier*, Commission decision of 9 July 2014, on appeal Cases T-691/14 etc *Servier v Commission*, not yet decided.

[537] Case T-472/13 *Lundbeck v Commission* EU:T:2016:449, para 205; see also Case T-360/09 *E.ON Ruhrgas and E.ON v Commission* EU:T:2012:332.

[538] Case C-373/14 P EU:C:2016:26, paras 31–33.

[539] Case T-216/13 *Telefónica v Commission* EU:T:2016:369, upheld on appeal Case C-487/16 P EU:C:2017:961.

restricts competition, but equally a restriction of conduct in a contract may be neutral in terms of competitive effects; it may even be pro-competitive. There are plenty of cases, discussed later, in which restrictive clauses were found not to infringe Article 101(1). Reconciling them is not always easy. There appear to be two types of case, although the line between them is sometimes blurred and indistinct. As the UK Competition Appeal Tribunal ('the CAT') has recognised 'competition law is not an area of law in which there is much room for absolute concepts or sharp edges'[540].

(a) Objectively necessary agreements

In some cases the Courts have held that a particular agreement was necessary to enable the parties to achieve a legitimate purpose. In *Société Technique Minière v Maschinenbau Ulm*[541] the Court of Justice held that an exclusive licence granted to a distributor might not infringe Article 101(1) where this seemed to be 'really necessary for the penetration of a new area by an undertaking'[542]. In *LC Nungesser KG v Commission*[543] the Court held that an open exclusive licence of plant breeders' rights would not infringe Article 101(1) where, on the facts of the case, the licensee would not have risked investing in the production of maize seeds at all without some immunity from intra-brand competition[544]. In *Coditel v Ciné Vog Films SA (No 2)*[545] the Court held that an exclusive copyright licence to exhibit a film in a Member State would not necessarily infringe Article 101(1), even where this might prevent transmission of that film by cable broadcasting from a neighbouring Member State, where this was necessary to protect the investment of the licensee. In *Gøttrup-Klim Grovvareforeninger v Dansk Landbrugs Grovvareselskab AmbA*[546] the Court held that a provision in the statutes of a cooperative purchasing association, forbidding its members from participating in other forms of organised cooperation which were in direct competition with it, did not necessarily restrict competition, and may even have beneficial effects on competition[547].

(b) Objectively necessary restrictions

In *Reuter/BASF*[548] the Commission concluded that restrictive covenants imposed on the vendor of a business fall outside Article 101(1) where they are proportionate; this was confirmed by the Court of Justice in *Remia BV and Verenigde Bedrijven and Nutricia v Commission*[549] where it held that, in order to effect the sale of a business together with its associated goodwill, it may be necessary to prevent the vendor from competing with the purchaser; in the absence of such a covenant it may not be possible to sell the business at all[550]. In *Pronuptia de Paris v Schillgalis*[551] the Court of Justice held that many restrictive provisions in franchising agreements designed to protect the intellectual property rights of the franchisor and to maintain the common identity of the franchise system fall outside

[540] Cases 1035/1/1/04 etc *Racecourse Association v OFT* [2005] CAT 29, para 167.

[541] Case 56/65 EU:C:1966:38, p 250.

[542] Cf Cases 56 and 58/64 *Consten and Grundig v Commission* EU:C:1966:41, on which see 'Controlling outlets, export bans', pp 129–130, earlier in chapter; on the single market imperative: see ch 1, The single market imperative', pp 23–24 and ch 2, 'The single market imperative', pp 52–53.

[543] Case 258/78 EU:C:1982:211.

[544] See ch 19, 'Patent licences: territorial exclusivity', pp 791–793.

[545] Case 262/81 EU:C:1982:334.

[546] Case C-250/92 EU:C:1994:413.

[547] Ibid, paras 35–45; the Court of Justice subsequently applied *Gøttrup-Klim* in Case C-399/93 *Luttikhuis v Verenigde Coöperatieve Melkindustrie Coberco BA* EU:C:1995:434, paras 14 and 18; so did the Commission in *P&I Clubs* OJ [1999] L 125/12, paras 66ff.

[548] OJ [1976] L 254/40.

[549] Case 42/84 EU:C:1985:327.

[550] On ancillary restraints under Article 101 see the Commission's *Guidelines on the application of Article [101(3)] of the Treaty* OJ [2004] C 101/97, paras 28–31.

[551] Case 161/84 EU:C:1986:41.

Article 101(1). In *Erauw-Jacquery Sprl v La Hesbignonne Société Coopérative*[552] the Court of Justice held that a provision preventing a licensee from exporting basic seeds protected by plant breeders' rights could fall outside Article 101(1) where it was necessary to protect the right of the licensor to select his licensees. In *Métropole télévision v Commission*[553] the General Court held that what are commonly referred to as 'ancillary restraints' are ones that are 'directly related and necessary to the implementation of a main operation'[554]; the General Court considered that deciding what is ancillary is a 'relatively abstract' matter that does not require a full market analysis[555].

(c) MasterCard v Commission

The judgment of the Court of Justice in *MasterCard v Commission*[556] rejected MasterCard's argument that the 'multilateral interchange fee' ('MIF') charged by an issuing bank to an acquiring bank when making payment to it was objectively necessary to the creation of the payment card system. MasterCard argued that there had to be a default mechanism in place to determine what fee was payable in the absence of agreement between the issuing and acquiring banks; therefore the agreement did not restrict competition at all. The Commission, General Court and Court of Justice all disagreed with MasterCard's argument. The Court of Justice acknowledged the cases discussed earlier, where agreements or clauses in agreements have been held to fall outside Article 101 altogether because of their ancillarity[557]. However the Court's view was that where the agreement in question 'is simply more difficult to implement or even less profitable without the restriction concerned' the test of objective necessity would not be satisfied; in such cases the restriction should be tested under the 'indispensability' criterion in Article 101(3)[558]. It is interesting to compare this judgment with the UK CAT's in *Racecourse Association v OFT*, discussed earlier: they demonstrate the 'blurred and indistinct' lines between different cases; it is not impossible to imagine that the CAT might have been more sympathetic to MasterCard's argument than the EU institutions were. In *Asda v MasterCard*[559] the English High Court held that the MasterCard's MIFs were objectively necessary, since the evidence before the court showed that the MasterCard scheme would not have survived in the counterfactual world.

(d) Comment

The case law discussed in this section established that some agreements will fall outside Article 101(1) because they are objectively necessary to achieve a legitimate purposes; and that in other cases particular restrictions will be found to be ancillary[560]. In these

552 Case 27/87 EU:C:1988:183; see similarly the Commission's decision in *Sicasov* OJ [1999] L 4/27, para 53–61.

553 Case T-112/99 EU:T:2001:215.

554 Ibid, para 104, citing the Commission's *Notice on Ancillary Restraints* OJ [1990] C 203/5, which has since been replaced by the *Notice on restrictions directly related and necessary to concentrations* OJ [2005] C 56/24; ancillary restraints are discussed further in the context of the EU Merger Regulation: see ch 21, 'Contractual restrictions directly related and necessary to a merger: "ancillary restraints"', pp 904–907.

555 Case T-112/99 EU:T:2001:215, para 109; for discussion on whether *Métropole* is out of line with *Remia* and *Gøttrup-Klim* see *Asda Stores Ltd v MasterCard Inc* [2017] EWHC 93 (Comm), paras 164–178 and *Sainsbury's Supermarkets Ltd v Visa Europe Services LLC* [2017] EWHC 3047 (Comm), paras 186–189; both judgments are on appeal to the Court of Appeal.

556 Case C-382/12 P EU:C:2014:2201.

557 Ibid, para 89.

558 Ibid, para 91; note that under Article 101(3) the question is whether the restriction is indispensable to achieve the economic efficiency claimed, that is to say an improvement in the production or distribution of goods or in technical or economics progress.

559 [2017] EWHC 93 (Comm), paras 163–233; cf *Sainsbury's Supermarkets Ltd v Visa Europe Services LLC* [2017] EWHC 3047 (Comm), paras 184–191: Visa's MIFs were not objectively necessary.

560 The ancillary restraints doctrine is an important feature of merger control analysis: see ch 21, 'Contractual restrictions directly related and necessary to a merger: "ancillary restraints"', pp 904–907.

cases the agreement or restriction is ancillary to a commercial purpose: they can be distinguished from the judgment of the Court of Justice in *Wouters*, discussed in the next section, which recognises the idea of 'regulatory ancillarity'.

(vii) Regulatory ancillarity: the judgment of the Court of Justice in *Wouters*

In *Wouters v Algemene Raad van de Nederlandsche Orde van Advocaten*[561] the Court of Justice dealt with a rather different situation. Mr Wouters challenged a rule adopted by the Dutch Bar Council that prohibited lawyers in the Netherlands from entering into partnership with non-lawyers: Wouters wished to practise as a lawyer in a firm of accountants. A number of questions were referred to the Court of Justice as to the compatibility of such a rule with EU competition law. In its judgment the Court, consisting of 13 judges, stated that a prohibition of multi-disciplinary partnerships 'is liable to limit production and technical development within the meaning of Article [101(1)(b)] of the Treaty'[562]; it also considered that the rule had an effect on trade between Member States[563]. However, at paragraph 97 of its judgment the Court stated:

> However, not every agreement between undertakings or any decision of an association of undertakings which restricts the freedom of action of the parties or of one of them necessarily falls within the prohibition laid down in Article [101(1)] of the Treaty. For the purposes of application of that provision to a particular case, account must first of all be taken of the overall context in which the decision of the association of undertakings was taken or produces its effects. More particularly, account must be taken of its objectives, which are here connected with the need to make rules relating to organisation, qualifications, professional ethics, supervision and liability, in order to ensure that the ultimate consumers of legal services and the sound administration of justice are provided with the necessary guarantees in relation to integrity and experience ... It has then to be considered whether the consequential effects restrictive of competition are inherent in the pursuit of those objectives[564].

This is a most interesting, and controversial, judgment. The early part of the judgment reads as though the Court would conclude that Article 101(1) was infringed, whereas from paragraph 97 onwards it explains why Article 101(1) would not be infringed if the rule in question could 'reasonably be considered to be necessary in order to ensure the proper practice of the legal profession, as it is organised in [the Netherlands]'[565]. The judgment means that, in certain cases, it is possible to balance *non-competition* objectives against a restriction of competition, and to conclude that the former outweigh the latter, with the consequence that there is no infringement of Article 101(1). The Court does not make findings of fact in an Article 267 reference; rather it gives a preliminary ruling which the domestic court must apply to the case before it. However, it is clear that the judgment provides a basis on which the Dutch court could decide that the rule in question did not

[561] Case C-309/99 EU:C:2002:98; for comment see Vossestein (2002) 39 CML Rev 841; Monti 'Article 81 EC and Public Policy' (2002) 39 CML Rev 1057; O'Loughlin 'EC Competition Rules and Free Movement Rules: An Examination of the Parallels and their Furtherance by the Court of Justice *Wouters* Decision' (2003) 24 ECLR 62; Loozen 'Professional Ethics and Restraints of Competition' (2006) 31 EL Rev 28; Forrester 'Where Law Meets Competition: Is *Wouters* Like *Cassis de Dijon*' in Ehlermann and Atansiu (eds) *European Competition Law Annual 2004: The Relationship Between Competition Law and the (Liberal) Professions* (Hart, 2006), 271; see also the judgment of the High Court in Ireland that the Medical Council of Ireland was not subject to competition law when making and applying professional rules in *Hemat v The Medical Council* [2006] IEHC 187; the case is noted by Ahern at (2007) 28 ECLR 366.

[562] Case C-309/99 EU:C:2002:98, para 90; see also paras 86 and 94.

[563] Ibid, para 95.

[564] To similar effect see Case T-144/99 *Institut des Mandataires Agréés v Commission* EU:T:2001:105, para 78.

[565] Case C-309/99 EU:C:2002:98, para 107.

infringe Article 101(1). It also would seem from paragraphs 107 and 108 of the *Wouters* judgment that the Court of Justice was disinclined to interfere with the Bar Council's assessment of the need for, and content of, the rules in question; the position should be contrasted with Article 101(3), where the undertaking(s) defending the agreement must provide convincing evidence of economic efficiencies[566].

Numerous questions arise from the judgment in *Wouters*. First, why did the Court of Justice decide that Article 101(1) was not applicable? Secondly, how does this judgment fit with those discussed in section (vi) earlier? Thirdly, how broad is the rule in *Wouters*? Finally, could the Court have decided the case in a different way, but still have come to the conclusion that the rule in question did not infringe Article 101?

(a) Why was Article 101(1) not applicable?

On the first point, the Court of Justice must have felt that it was appropriate to establish that 'reasonable' regulatory rules fall outside Article 101(1). Furthermore, it is possible that the Court was deliberately trying to reach a similar outcome under Article 101 to that which would have been achieved under Article 56 TFEU had the case been argued under the provisions on the free movement of services. It is not inconceivable that the rule in question could have been adopted by the Dutch Government itself, if the regulatory regime for the legal profession in the Netherlands had been different: in that case the rule could not have been challenged under Article 101(1), but might have been under Article 56. Under that provision a Member State may adopt rules which restrict the free movement of services to the extent that they are necessary to achieve a legitimate public interest[567]; the judgment in *Wouters* effectively applies the same reasoning to a case in which the regulatory function was not carried out by a Member State, and so was not susceptible to challenge under Article 56, but by a private body empowered by the state to adopt regulatory rules, subject to control, if at all, under the competition rules[568].

(b) The relationship between the judgment in Wouters *and earlier case law of the EU Courts*

On the second point, the judgment in *Wouters* does have a conceptual similarity to the cases discussed in section (vi) earlier, in that they all are concerned with the idea of ancillarity: restrictions on conduct, even ones that, in a colloquial sense, appear to restrict competition, do not infringe Article 101(1) where they are ancillary to some other legitimate purpose. What is of interest about *Wouters*, however, is that the restriction in that case was not necessary for the execution of a commercial transaction or the achievement of a commercial outcome on the market; instead it was ancillary to a regulatory function 'to ensure that the ultimate consumers of legal services and the sound administration of justice are provided with the necessary guarantees in relation to integrity and experience'[569]. This seems to be a different application of the concept of ancillarity from that in the earlier case law: the *Wouters* case is concerned with what could be described as 'regulatory ancillarity', whereas earlier judgments were concerned with 'commercial

[566] See ch 4, 'Burden and standard of proof, p 159.

[567] See eg Case 33/74 *Van Binsbergen v Bestuur Van de Bedrijfsvereniging voor de Metaalnijverheid* EU:C:1974:131, para 14.

[568] The Court cited Case 107/83 *Klopp* EU:C:1984:270, para 17 and Case C-3/95 *Reisebüro Broede* EU:C:1996:487, para 37, cases on Article 56 TFEU, in para 99 of its judgment in *Wouters*: in these cases it had held that, in the absence of specific EU rules in the field, each Member State is in principle free to regulate the exercise of the legal profession in its territory.

[569] Case C-309/99 *Wouters v Algemene Raad van de Nederlandsche Orde van Advocaten* EU:C:2002:98, para 97.

ancillarity'; perhaps the use of these two terms would be useful in, first, demonstrating a continuity with the earlier case law, through the common use of the idea of ancillarity, while also capturing the difference between the two situations, by distinguishing commercial and regulatory cases.

(c) How broad is the rule in Wouters?

On the third point, that is the breadth of the rule in *Wouters*, there is nothing in the judgment itself that expressly limits its application to so-called 'deontological' (that is to say professional ethical) rules for the regulation of the legal profession, nor to the liberal professions generally. The Court of Justice's judgments in *Meca-Medina v Commission*[570], *OTOC*[571] and *Italian Geologists*[572] confirm that the *Wouters* doctrine can apply to other regulatory rules. In *Meca-Medina* the Court of Justice concluded that the anti-doping rules of the International Swimming Federation had a legitimate objective: to combat drugs in order for competitive sport to be conducted fairly, including the need to safeguard equal chances for athletes, athletes' health, the integrity and objectivity of competitive sport and ethical values in sport[573]; the Court went on to decide that the restrictions of competition inherent in the rules were proportionate[574]. In *OTOC* the Court of Justice held that the training regulations adopted by the Portuguese 'Order of Chartered Accountants' had the legitimate objective of guaranteeing the quality of services provided by accountants[575]. The Court concluded, however, that the regulations went beyond what was necessary to achieve that objective[576]; for example OTOC had the exclusive power to authorise competing training sessions in Portugal, thereby placing OTOC at an obvious advantage over its competitors. The judgment in *OTOC* confirms that only 'reasonable' regulatory rules fall outside Article 101(1)[577]. The same approach can be seen in *API*[578] where the Court of Justice considered that measures that fixed mandatory minimum tariffs for road transport in Italy could not be justified on road safety grounds[579].

In *Wouters* the rules under scrutiny undoubtedly had a public law character: Dutch legislation provided for the regulation of the legal profession, albeit that the rule-making function belonged to a private law association of undertakings. The judgments in *OTOC* and *Italian Geologists* applied the same reasoning to the regulation of chartered accountants and geologists respectively. In *Meca-Medina* the International Olympic Committee ('IOC') was responsible for the regulatory system: the IOC is a creature of public international law, which may explain the Court of Justice's willingness to apply the *Wouters* doctrine in that case. An intriguing question for the future is whether *Wouters* could be extended yet further, to a purely private regulatory system where there is no public component at all. Many sporting organisations have a purely private law character, such as the Football Association in the UK: the Court of Justice may be prepared to extend the *Wouters* case to such bodies. However other cases are less easy to predict: for example, suppose that firms in a particular sector were to adopt rules for the protection of the environment on their own initiative, without any encouragement of the kind cognisable under

570 Case C-519/04 P EU:C:2006:492; see Weatherill 'Anti-Doping Revisited—The Demise of the Rule of "Purely Sporting Interest"?' (2006) 27 ECLR 645; see similarly *UEFA*, Commission Press Release IP/02/942, 27 June 2002.

571 Case C-1/12 *Ordem dos Técnicos Oficiais de Contas* EU:C:2013:127.

572 Case C-136/12 *Consiglio nazionale dei geologi* EU:C:2013:489.

573 Case C-519/04 P EU:C:2006:492, paras 42–45.

574 Ibid, paras 47–56.

575 Case C-1/12 *Ordem dos Técnicos Oficiais de Contas* EU:C:2013:127, paras 94–95.

576 Ibid, paras 96–100; neither Article 101(3) nor Article 106(2) applied to the regulations: paras 101–107.

577 The application of the *Wouters* doctrine was rejected in *ONP*, Commission decision of 8 December 2010, paras 684–691, upheld on appeal on this point Case T-90/11 *ONP v Commission* EU:T:2014:1049.

578 Cases C-184/13 etc EU:C:2014:2147.

579 Ibid, paras 46–57; see also Cases C-427/16 etc *CHEZ Elektro Bulgaria AD* EU:C:2017:890, paras 54–55.

Article 101(3): it remains to be seen whether *Wouters* could be invoked in such a case. In *Slovak Banks*[580] the Court of Justice said that it is for public authorities, and not private undertakings, to ensure compliance with legal requirements. It is not for undertakings to take private initiatives to eliminate competitors that they consider to be acting illegally[581].

(d) *Could the Court of Justice in* Wouters *have reached the same conclusion by a different route?*

On the fourth point, it is interesting to consider whether the Court of Justice could have reached the conclusion that there was no infringement of the competition rules in *Wouters* by some other route than the one it adopted. Perhaps the most obvious alternative solution would have been to hold that the rules did infringe Article 101(1)—as noted, the Court did say that the prohibition on multi-disciplinary partnerships was liable to limit production and technical development within the meaning of Article 101(1)(b)—but that they satisfied the terms of Article 101(3)[582]. However this approach was not available in *Wouters* since, at the relevant time, a decision under Article 101(3) could be made only by the Commission pursuant to a notification under Article 4 of Regulation 17 and no notification had been made. It was not open to the Court of Justice to apply the provisions of Article 106(2) TFEU, since the Bar Council itself was not an entrusted undertaking[583]. The Court could have concluded that there was no effect on trade between Member States, so that Article 101(1) did not apply, thereby in effect referring the matter back to the Netherlands for the application of Dutch competition law; however it expressly held that trade between Member States was affected[584].

(viii) **The application of Article 101(1) to sporting rules**

This discussion of the *Wouters* judgment provides an opportunity for a brief diversion, to discuss the application of Article 101(1) to sporting rules[585]. All sports have rules: footballers, with the exception of goalkeepers, cannot handle the ball; boxers must not hit 'below the belt'; javelin throwers should not throw the javelin at other javelin throwers. These are 'the rules of the game', and self-evidently do not infringe Article 101(1). Similarly, all sports have disciplinary rules: violent conduct can lead to suspension; taking prohibited drugs may lead to bans. Again, football clubs that belong to one league will be prohibited from belonging to another one. A conundrum for EU competition law has been to determine whether, and if so when, sporting rules might infringe Article 101 or 102. It is clear that some rules could have restrictive effects on competition in the market, for example where they go beyond 'the rules of the game' and instead distort competition in neighbouring broadcasting markets[586].

580 Case C-68/12 *Protimonopolný úrad Slovenskej republiky v Slovenská sporiteľňa a.s.* EU:C:2013:71.

581 Ibid, para 20; see similarly, in the context of Article 102, Case T-30/89 *Hilti v Commission* EU:T:1991:70, para 118.

582 On this point see further ch 9, 'Object or effect the prevention, restriction or distortion of competition within the UK', pp 355–359.

583 See ch 6, 'Article 106(2)', pp 242–248 on the derogation from the application of Articles 101 and 102 provided by Article 106(2).

584 Case C-309/99 EU:C:2002:98, para 95.

585 For a general discussion of EU law and sport see Weatherill '"Fair Play Please": Recent Developments in the Application of EC Law to Sport' (2003) 40 CML Rev 51; Van den Bogaert and Vermeersch 'Sport and the EC Treaty: A Tale of Uneasy Bedfellows?' (2006) 31 ECLR 821; Szyszcak 'Competition and Sport' (2007) 32 EL Rev 95; Kienapfel and Stein 'The application of Articles 81 and 82 EC in the sport sector' (2007) 3 Competition Policy Newsletter 6; the Opinion of AG Kokott in Case C-49/07 *MOTOE* EU:C:2008:142; note also the Commission's *Declaration on Sport*, annexed to the final act of the Treaty of Amsterdam, OJ [1997] C 340/136.

586 See eg *London Welsh Rugby Football Club v Rugby Football Union*, decision of 29 June 2012 (rules governing a rugby club's home stadium distorted competition and did not justify refusing London Welsh promotion to the RFU Premiership); on the joint selling of sporting rights see ch 13, 'Joint selling agencies', p 539.

In *Meca-Medina* the General Court had held that a sporting rule that 'has nothing to do with any economic consideration'[587] falls entirely outside Articles 101 and 102. On appeal the Court of Justice held that this was an error of law on the General Court's part and therefore set the judgment aside[588]. The Court of Justice's approach is clearly preferable to that of the General Court: the latter's judgment would mean that sporting rules could not be scrutinised at all under the competition provisions, whereas the Court of Justice's means that they can be tested for anti-competitive effects, albeit that they might be permissible by virtue of the *Wouters* doctrine.

(ix) Have the EU Courts embraced a 'rule of reason'?

As mentioned earlier, critics of Article 101(1) complain that it is applied to too many agreements; they argue for the application of a 'rule of reason', which would result in fewer agreements being caught. The judgments that have just been discussed raise the question of whether the EU Courts have adopted a rule of reason under Article 101(1). Discussion of the rule of reason under Article 101(1) is often very imprecise[589]. It is sometimes used as little more than a slogan by opponents of the judgments of the Courts and, in particular, decisions of the Commission. In so far as the call for a rule of reason is a request for good rather than bad, or reasonable rather than unreasonable, judgments and decisions, no one could disagree with it. However, if proponents of the rule of reason mean that US jurisprudence on the rule of reason under the Sherman Act 1890 should be incorporated into EU competition law, this is misplaced: EU law is different in many ways from US law, not least in that it has the 'bifurcation' of Article 101(1) and Article 101(3), which does not exist in US law, and that it is concerned with the promotion of a single market as well as with 'conventional' competition law concerns[590].

(a) The rule of reason in US law

In US law the rule of reason has a particular meaning. In *Continental TV Inc v GTE Sylvania* the Supreme Court defined the rule of reason as calling for a case-by-case evaluation 'that is, the factfinder weighs all the circumstances of a case in deciding whether a restrictive practice should be prohibited as imposing an unreasonable restraint on competition'[591]. This means that, when determining whether an agreement restrains trade in the sense of section 1 of the Sherman Act, it is necessary to balance the agreement's pro- and anti-competitive effects; where the latter outweigh the former, the agreement will be unlawful. However US and EU competition law are materially different in numerous respects, and terminology should not be imported from US law that could blur this significant fact[592]. The fact that the Court of Justice has handed down reasonable judgments does not mean that it has adopted the rule of reason in the sense in which that expression is used in the US. Various commentators have argued against incorporation into EU law of a rule of reason

[587] Case T-313/02 EU:T:2004:282, para 47.

[588] Case C-519/04 P EU:C:2006:492, paras 33 and 34; the Commission applied *Meca-Medina in International Skating Union's Eligibility Rules*, Commission decision of 8 December 2017, paras 210–266, on appeal Case T-93/18 *ISU v Commission*, not yet decided.

[589] On this point see the Opinion of AG Léger in Case C-309/99 *Wouters* EU:C:2001:390, para 102.

[590] See ch 1, 'The single market imperative', pp 23–24 and ch 2, 'The single market imperative', pp 52–53.

[591] 433 US 36, 49 (1977); see also *National Collegiate Athletic Association v Board of Regents of University of Oklahoma* 468 US 85 (1984); *California Dental Association v Federal Trade Commission* 526 US 756 (1999); *Federal Trade Commission v Actavis* 570 US 756 (2013); for discussion of the rule of reason in US law see Areeda and Hovenkamp *Antitrust Law: An Analysis of Antitrust Principles and Their Application* (Kluwer, 4th ed, 2013), Vol VII, ch 15; Hovenkamp 'The Rule of Reason' (2016) University of Pennylsvania Institute for Law & Econ Research Paper No 17-28, available at www.ssrn.com.

[592] See Whish and Sufrin 'Article 85 and the Rule of Reason' (1987) 7 Ox YEL 1.

modelled upon US experience[593]. The Commission has said that it would 'be paradoxical to cast aside Article [101(3)] when that provision in fact contains all the elements of a "rule of reason"' and that the adoption of the rule of reason under Article 101(1) would 'run the risk of diverting Article [101(3)] from its purpose, which is to provide a legal framework for the economic assessment of restrictive practices and not to allow application of the competition rules to be set aside because of political considerations'[594].

(b) The judgment of the General Court in Métropole

In *Métropole télévision v Commission*[595] the General Court rejected the suggestion that a rule of reason existed under Article 101(1). Six television companies in France had established a joint venture, Télévision par Satellite ('TPS'), to provide digital pay-TV services in French in Europe: TPS would be a competitor to the dominant pay-TV company, Canal+. The parties notified a number of agreements to the Commission. In 1999 the Commission adopted a decision that the creation of TPS was not caught by Article 101(1); however it concluded that a non-competition clause, preventing the parents of TPS from becoming involved in other digital pay-TV satellite companies, did not infringe Article 101(1) for a period of only three years; and that clauses giving TPS rights of pre-emption in relation to certain channels and services offered by its parents and exclusive rights to other channels infringed Article 101(1) but could be permitted under Article 101(3) for three years. Four of the shareholders in TPS appealed the decision to the General Court, arguing that the Commission should have applied a US-style rule of reason[596]; in particular the clauses giving TPS rights of pre-emption and exclusivity would enable TPS to promote competition by entering the market dominated by Canal+[597]. Several well-known judgments of the EU Courts were cited in support of this version of the rule of reason[598]. What is of interest is the explicit way in which the General Court's judgment rejected the applicants' argument:

> According to the applicants, as a consequence of the existence of a rule of reason in [EU] competition law, when Article [101(1)] of the Treaty is applied it is necessary to weigh the pro and anti-competitive effects of an agreement in order to determine whether it is caught by the prohibition laid down in that article. It should, however, be observed, first of all, that contrary to the applicant's assertions the existence of such a rule has not, as such, been confirmed by the [EU] courts. Quite to the contrary, in various judgments the Court of Justice and the [General] Court have been at pains to indicate that the existence of a rule of reason in [EU] competition law is doubtful[599].

The General Court went on to say that the pro- and anti-competitive aspects of an agreement should be considered under Article 101(3)[600]. In the General Court's view:

> Article [101(3)] would lose much of its effectiveness if such an examination had to be carried out already under Article [101(1)] of the Treaty[601].

[593] Whish and Sufrin (1987) 7 Ox YEL 1; Schröter 'Antitrust Analysis and Article 85(1) and (3)' [1987] Fordham Corporate Law Institute (ed Hawk), ch 27; Caspari (formerly Director-General of DG COMP at the Commission) [1987] Fordham Corporate Law Institute (ed Hawk), 361.

[594] *White Paper on Modernisation* OJ [1999] C 132/1, para 57.

[595] Case T-112/99 EU:T:2001:215: for comment on this case see Manzini 'The European Rule of Reason—Crossing the Sea of Doubt' (2002) 23 ECLR 392.

[596] Case T-112/99 EU:T:2001:215, para 68.

[597] Ibid, para 69.

[598] Ibid, paras 68 and 70, referring, *inter alia*, to Case 258/78 *Nungesser and Eisele v Commission* EU:C:1982:211 (*Maize seeds*); Case 262/81 *Coditel v Ciné Vog Films* EU:C:1982:334 and Cases T-374/94 etc *European Night Services v Commission* EU:T:1998:198.

[599] Case T-112/99 EU:T:2001:215, para 72.

[600] Ibid, para 74.

[601] Ibid.

The General Court acknowledged that the EU Courts have been 'more flexible' in their interpretation of Article 101(1), but concluded that this did not mean that they had adopted the 'rule of reason' in the sense argued for by the applicants[602]. Rather, the more flexible judgments of the Courts demonstrate that they are not willing to find a restriction 'wholly abstractly'; instead a full market analysis is required[603]. The General Court came to the same conclusion in *Van den Bergh Foods v Commission*[604] and in *O2 (Germany) v Commission*[605]. The Commission cites *Métropole* in paragraph 11 of its *Guidelines on the application of Article [101(3)]* in support of its proposition that '[t]he balancing of anti-competitive and pro-competitive effects is conducted exclusively within the framework laid down by Article [101(3)]'[606].

(c) Comment

In the authors' view the judgment in *Métropole* was correct to reject the US-style rule of reason in Article 101(1). Of course, the Commission and the EU Courts should be 'reasonable' when applying Article 101(1), but that does not mean that they should import the method of analysis adopted in the quite different context of the Sherman Act. An interesting question is whether the judgment of the Court of Justice in *Wouters* should be read as importing a rule of reason under Article 101(1)[607]. The doctrine of regulatory ancillarity in that case provides for a balancing of restrictions of competition against the reasonableness of regulatory rules adopted for non-competition reasons; as such, it appears to these authors that the *Wouters* judgment does not apply a US-style rule of reason, and it is preferable not to use this expression in order to explain it.

(x) Joint ventures

Article 101(1) does not apply to full-function joint ventures, which are dealt with under the provisions on merger control: this is explained in chapter 21[608].

(F) Article 106(2)

Article 106(2) precludes the application of the competition rules to undertakings in so far as compliance with them would obstruct them in the performance of a task entrusted to them by a Member State. This subject is dealt with in chapter 6[609].

(G) State compulsion and highly regulated markets

The competition rules do not apply to undertakings in so far as they are compelled by law to behave in a particular way: this is sometimes referred to as the 'state compulsion' defence; nor do they apply where a legal framework leaves no possibility for competitive activity on the part of undertakings, that is to say where they operate on highly regulated markets. These two defences have often been invoked, but they are narrowly applied and

[602] Ibid, paras 75–76. [603] Ibid, para 76. [604] Case T-65/98 EU:T:2003:281, para 106.

[605] Case T-328/03 EU:T:2006:116, para 69; for discussion of this case see Marquis '*O2 (Germany) v Commission* and the Exotic Mysteries of Article 81(1) EC' (2007) 32 EL Rev 29.

[606] OJ [2004] C 101/97.

[607] See Korah 'Rule of Reason: Apparent Inconsistency in the Case Law under Article 81' (2002) 1 Competition Law Insight 24.

[608] Ch 21, 'Joint ventures—the concept of full-functionality', pp 857–858.

[609] See ch 6, 'Article 106(2)', pp 242–248.

almost invariably fail[610]. Where undertakings genuinely have no room for autonomous behaviour they would not be liable for infringing Article 101[611]; however the position would alter if a decision to disapply the national legislation has been taken and become definitive[612]. An argument that the Italian sugar market was so highly regulated that there was no scope for competition succeeded in *Suiker Unie v Commission*[613].

The law was summarised by the Court of Justice in *Deutsche Telekom v Commission*[614], where Deutsche Telekom ('DT') argued (in an Article 102 case) that it was not guilty of an illegal margin squeeze because its behaviour was approved by the German regulator of the electronic communications sector. The Court rejected the defence because DT retained the right to adjust its prices for the retail sale of broadband internet access services and thereby bring the margin squeeze to an end: approval by the regulator did not deprive DT of its ability to behave autonomously. The Court of Justice summarised the law at paragraph 80 of its judgment[615]:

> According to the case-law of the Court of Justice, it is only if anti-competitive conduct is required of undertakings by national legislation, or if the latter creates a legal framework which itself eliminates any possibility of competitive activity on their part, that Articles [101 TFEU and 102 TFEU] do not apply. In such a situation, the restriction of competition is not attributable, as those provisions implicitly require, to the autonomous conduct of the undertakings. Articles [101 TFEU and 102 TFEU] may apply, however, if it is found that the national legislation leaves open the possibility of competition which may be prevented, restricted or distorted by the autonomous conduct of undertakings.

The Court's judgment cited several earlier judgments, in particular pointing out that there is no defence where national law merely encourages or makes it easier for undertakings to engage in autonomous anti-competitive conduct[616].

(H) **Commission Notices**

A number of Commission Notices provide guidance on the application of Article 101(1) to various types of agreement; it might be helpful to provide a checklist of these Notices.

[610] The 'state compulsion' defence was rejected in *Wood Pulp I* OJ [1985] L 85/1; *ENI/Montedison* OJ [1987] L 5/13, para 25; *Aluminium Products* OJ [1985] L 92/1; *SSI* OJ [1982] L 232/1, upheld on appeal to the Court of Justice Cases 240/82 etc *SSI v Commission* EU:C:1985:488; *French-West African Shipowners' Committee* OJ [1992] L 134/1, paras 32–38; and in Case T-513/93 *CNSD v Commission* EU:T:2000:91, paras 58–59; see also Cases C-359/95 and 379/95 P *Commission v Ladbroke Racing* EU:C:1997:531, para 33; Case T-228/97 *Irish Sugar v Commission* EU:T:1999:246, para 130; *Airfreight*, Commission decision of 9 November 2010; the 'highly regulated markets' defence was rejected in Cases 209/78 etc *Van Landewyck v Commission* EU:C:1980:248, paras 126–134; Cases 240/82 etc *SSI v Commission* EU:C:1985:488, paras 13–37 and Case 260/82 *NSO v Commission* EU:C:1985:489, paras 18–27; *Greek Ferry Services Cartel* OJ [1999] L 109/24, paras 98–108, upheld on appeal Cases T-56/99 etc *Marlines SA v Commission* EU:T:2003:333; *French-West Africa Shipowners' Committees* OJ [1992] L 134/1; Cases T-202/98 etc *Tate & Lyle plc v Commission* EU:T:2001:185, paras 44–45; *Spanish Raw Tobacco*, Commission decision of 20 October 2004, paras 349–356; *Raw Tobacco Italy*, Commission decision of 20 October 2005, paras 315–324; *Bananas*, Commission decision of 15 October 2008, paras 272, 279, 292, 306, 308, upheld on appeal Cases T-587/08 etc *Fresh Del Monte Produce v Commission* EU:T:2013:129, paras 377–418, and on further appeal Cases C-293/13 and C-294/13 P EU:C:2015:416; *E.ON/GDF Suez*, Commission decision of 8 July 2009, paras 293–297.

[611] See eg Case T-387/94 *Asia Motor France v Commission* EU:T:1996:120, paras 78–100.

[612] See Case C-198/01 *CIF* EU:C:2003:430, paras 54ff.

[613] Cases 40/73 etc EU:C:1975:174; see also Case T-325/01 *Daimler Chrysler v Commission* EU:T:2005:322, para 156.

[614] Case C-280/08 P EU:C:2010:603.

[615] See also para 22 of the Commission's *Guidelines on the applicability of Article 101 TFEU to horizontal co-operation agreements* OJ [2011] C 11/1.

[616] The Court cites Cases 40/73 etc *Suiker Unie v Commission* EU:C:1975:174, paras 36–73 and Case C-198/01 *CIF* EU:C:2003:430 para 56 for this proposition.

(i) Notice on sub-contracting agreements

Article 101(1) does not apply to some sub-contracting agreements[617].

(ii) Notice on the application of the competition rules to cross-border credit transfers

This *Notice* has specific application in the banking sector[618].

(iii) Notice on the application of the competition rules to the postal sector

This *Notice* has specific application in the postal sector[619].

(iv) Notice on the application of the competition rules to access agreements in the telecommunications sector

This *Notice* has specific application in the telecommunications sector[620].

(v) Notice regarding restrictions directly related and necessary to the concentration

Article 101(1) does not apply to ancillary restrictions[621]; this *Notice* is specifically of relevance to the analysis of concentrations under the EUMR, but it provides useful insights into the Commission's thinking more generally[622].

(vi) Notice on agreements of minor importance

This *Notice* is concerned with the *de minimis* doctrine and is examined later[623].

(vii) Guidelines on the effect on trade concept contained in Articles [101 and 102 TFEU]

These are important in determining the jurisdictional scope of Article 101 and are examined later[624].

(viii) Guidelines on the application of Article [101(3) TFEU]

These *Guidelines* are predominantly concerned with the application of Article 101(3); however, paragraphs 13 to 37 discuss the principles under Article 101(1)[625].

(ix) Guidelines on the application of Article 101 TFEU to technology transfer agreements

These *Guidelines* deal at length with the application of Article 101(1) and Article 101(3) to technology transfer agreements and technology pools[626].

(x) Commission Consolidated Jurisdictional Notice

Article 101 does not apply to full-function joint ventures. Paragraphs 91 to 109 examine the concept of full-functionality[627].

617 OJ [1979] C 1/2.
618 OJ [1995] C 251/3.
619 OJ [1998] C 39/2; see ch 23, 'Post', pp 1016–1020.
620 OJ [1998] C 265/2; see ch 23, 'Application of EU competition law', pp 1013–1015.
621 OJ [2005] C 56/244.
622 The *Notice* is discussed in ch 21, 'Jurisdiction', pp 852–875.
623 OJ [2014] C 368/13.
624 OJ [2004] C 101/81.
625 OJ [2004] C 101/97.
626 OJ [2014] C 89/3: see ch 19, 'Technology Transfer Agreements: Regulation 316/2014', pp 798–807.
627 OJ [2008] C 95/1.

(xi) Guidelines on vertical restraints

These *Guidelines* deal with the application of Article 101(1) and Article 101(3) to vertical agreements. Paragraphs 12 to 21 of these *Guidelines* provide specific guidance on the application of Article 101(1) to agreements between principal and agent[628].

(xii) Guidelines on horizontal cooperation agreements

These *Guidelines* deal with the application of Article 101(1) and Article 101(3) to horizontal cooperation agreements[629].

5. The *De Minimis* Doctrine

(A) Introduction

The *de minimis* doctrine was first formulated by the Court of Justice in *Völk v Vervaecke*[630]: agreements that affect competition within the terms of Article 101(1) will nevertheless not be caught where they do not have an appreciable impact either on inter-state trade or on competition[631]. This rule of double appreciability—an appreciable impact both on trade between Member States and on competition—has been repeated by the Court many times since, most recently in *Expedia Inc v Autorité de la Concurrence*[632]. However the *Expedia* judgment introduced an important refinement: the Court held at paragraph 37 that an agreement that restricts competition by object and that has an effect on trade between Member States automatically violates Article 101(1) without any need to demonstrate concrete effects on competition: in other words the Court abandoned the test of double appreciability for object restrictions[633].

The Commission has provided guidance on the issue of appreciability in two documents: its *Guidelines on the effect on trade concept contained in Articles [101 and 102 TFEU]* are discussed in the next section[634]; the Commission published a new *Notice on Agreements of Minor Importance*, revised to give expression to the *Expedia* judgment, in June 2014[635]. The Commission has also published a Staff Working Document[636] on object restrictions for the purposes of the *De Minimis Notice*.

(B) The Commission's *Notice on Agreements of Minor Importance*

(i) Part I of the *Notice*: introductory paragraphs

Part I of the *Notice* contains important statements on the application of the *de minimis* doctrine. Paragraph 1 refers to the case law of the Court of Justice on appreciability. Paragraph 2 states that the *de minimis* doctrine does not apply to object restrictions, citing the *Expedia* judgment. Paragraph 3 explains that the *Notice* uses market share thresholds for determining when a restriction of competition is not appreciable. It points out

[628] OJ [2010] C 130/1; see ch 16, 'Commercial Agents', pp 634–637.

[629] OJ [2011] C 11/1; see ch 15, 'The *Guidelines on Horizontal Cooperation Agreements*', pp 600–604.

[630] Case C-5/69 EU:C:1969:35.

[631] Note that an agreement that does not infringe Article 101 may nevertheless infringe the law of one (or more) of the Member States.

[632] Case C-226/11 EU:C:2012:795, para 16.

[633] For comment see González 'Restrictions by Object and the Appreciability Test: The *Expedia* Case, a Surprising Judgment or a Simple Clarification?' (2013) 34 ECLR 457; King 'How Appreciable is Object? The *De Minimis* Doctrine and Case C-226/11 *Expedia Inc v Autorité de la concurrence*' (2015) 11 European Competition Journal 1.

[634] See 'The effect on trade between Member States', pp 150–155 later in chapter.

[635] OJ [2014] C 291/1.

[636] SWD(2014) 198 final, available at www.ec.europa.eu.

that this 'negative' definition of appreciability (that is to say the explanation of what is *not* an appreciable restriction of competition) does not imply that agreements above the thresholds are caught by Article 101(1): agreements above the thresholds may have only a negligible effect on competition and so not be caught[637]; another way of putting this point is that the *Notice* establishes a 'safe harbour' for agreements below the thresholds, but does not establish a dangerous one for agreements above it. Paragraph 4 makes the important point that the *De Minimis Notice* does *not* deal with the concept of an appreciable effect on trade between Member States: this is dealt with in the Commission's *Guidelines on the effect on trade concept contained in Articles [101 and 102 TFEU]*[638]. Footnote 5 adds, however, that agreements between small and medium-sized enterprises ('SMEs') are unlikely to affect trade between Member States: such undertakings are currently defined as those having fewer than 250 employees and with an annual turnover not exceeding €50 million or an annual balance-sheet total not exceeding €43 million[639].

Paragraph 5 of the *Notice* is important: it states that the Commission will not institute proceedings either upon application or upon its own initiative in respect of agreements covered by the *Notice*; and that, where undertakings assume in good faith that an agreement is covered by the *Notice*, the Commission will not impose fines. Paragraph 5 of the *Notice* adds that, although not binding on them, it is intended to provide guidance to national courts and NCAs, a point confirmed by the Court of Justice in *Expedia*[640]. Paragraph 6 explains that the *Notice* also applies to decisions by associations of undertakings and to concerted practices. Paragraph 7 states that the *Notice* is without prejudice to any interpretation of Article 101 by the EU Courts.

(ii) Part II of the *Notice*: the threshold

The main provision in the *Notice* is contained in Part II, at paragraph 8. It provides as follows:

> The Commission holds the view that agreements between undertakings which affect trade between Member States and which may have as their effect the prevention, restriction or distortion of competition within the internal market, do not appreciably restrict competition within the meaning of Article 101(1):
>
> (a) if the aggregate market share held by the parties to the agreement does not exceed 10% on any of the relevant markets affected by the agreement, where the agreement is made between undertakings[641] which are actual or potential competitors on any of these markets (agreements between competitors); or
>
> (b) if the market share held by each of the parties to the agreement does not exceed 15 % on any of the relevant markets affected by the agreement, where the agreement is made between undertakings which are not actual or potential competitors on any of these markets (agreements between non-competitors).

637 The *Notice* refers to Cases C-215/96 etc *Bagnasco* EU:C:1999:12, paras 34–35 in support of this proposition; the same point will be found in two General Court judgments, Case T-7/93 *Langnese-Iglo GmbH v Commission* EU:T:1995:98, para 98; Cases T-374/94 etc *European Night Services v Commission* EU:T:1998:198, paras 102–103; see also para 9 of the Commission's *Guidelines on Vertical Restraints* OJ [2010] C 130/1.

638 See 'The Effect on Trade between Member States', pp 150–155 later in chapter.

639 See Commission Recommendation 2003/361/EC, OJ [2003] L 124/36 (applicable since 1 January 2005); note also para 11 of the Commission's *Guidelines on Vertical Restraints* OJ [2010] C 130/1 which says that vertical agreements between SMEs would rarely produce an appreciable restriction on competition or on trade between Members States.

640 Case C-226/11 EU:C:2012:795, para 31.

641 Throughout the *Notice* the expression 'undertakings' includes 'connected undertakings' such as parents and subsidiaries: see para 12.

> In cases where it is difficult to classify the agreement as either an agreement between competitors or an agreement between non-competitors the 10% threshold is applicable.

As can be seen the *Notice* treats vertical agreements more generously than horizontal ones, by providing a higher threshold.

A particular problem arises in some sectors where the cumulative effect of many vertical agreements may lead to foreclosure of the market[642]. The *Notice* provides guidance on appreciability in this situation (a) by indicating when a cumulative foreclosure effect is likely and (b) by providing a market share threshold indicating whether particular agreements contribute to that effect. Paragraph 10 provides that a cumulative foreclosure effect is unlikely to exist if less than 30% of the relevant market is covered by parallel agreements having similar effects; where there is a foreclosure effect, individual suppliers or distributors will not be considered to contribute to that effect where their market share does not exceed 5%.

A problem that may arise in application of the *Notice* is that firms may outgrow the market share thresholds established by paragraphs 8 and 9; marginal relief is provided by paragraph 11 where the thresholds (of 10%, 15% and 5% respectively) are exceeded by no more than two percentage points during two successive years.

It is not clear what happens to an agreement when it has outgrown the *Notice*, including the provisions for marginal relief: one possibility is that it becomes retrospectively void; a second is that it becomes unenforceable from the moment that the Notice ceases to apply. The second suggestion appears to be consistent with the scheme of Article 101 TFEU. In the UK the Court of Appeal held in *Passmore v Morland*[643] that an agreement can infringe Article 101(1) at some times and at other times not do so, depending on the surrounding facts: in other words it can drift into and out of voidness.

Paragraph 12 of the *Notice* notes that guidance on market definition is provided by the Commission's *Notice on the Definition of Relevant Market for the Purpose of [EU] Competition Law*[644] and adds that market shares are to be calculated on the basis of sales value data or, where appropriate, purchase value data; where value data are not available, other criteria, including volume data, may be used.

A different point introduced in paragraph 44 of the Commission's *Guidelines on Horizontal Cooperation Agreements*[645] is the suggestion that, where the parties to a horizontal cooperation agreement have a high combined market share, but one of them has only an insignificant one and does not possess important resources, the agreement would be considered unlikely to have a restrictive effect on competition in the market.

(iii) Part II of the *Notice*: the treatment of object restrictions

The judgment of the Court of Justice in *Völk v Vervaecke*[646], that Article 101 applies only where competition is appreciably restricted, concerned an object restriction: the distributor was granted absolute territorial protection. In *Expedia*[647], however, the Court said that a restriction by object affecting trade between Member States 'constitutes, by its nature and independently of any concrete effects that it may have, an appreciable restriction of competition'[648]. The Commission specifically states in paragraph 13 of the Notice that the

[642] See ch 16, 'Factors to be considered in determining whether single branding agreements infringe Article 101(1)', pp 651–653.

[643] [1999] EWCA Civ 696; see to similar effect para 44 of the Commission's *Guidelines on the application of Article [101(3) TFEU]* OJ [2004] C 101/97.

[644] OJ [1997] C 372/5; see ch 1, 'Market definition', pp 26ff.

[645] OJ [2011] C 11/1; see ch 15, 'The *Guidelines on Horizontal Cooperation Agreements*', pp 600–604.

[646] See ch 3 n 630 earlier.

[647] Case C-226/11 EU:C:2012:795.

[648] Ibid, para 37.

safe harbour provided by paragraph 8 does not apply to object restrictions, such as horizontal agreements to fix prices, limit output or sales and to allocate markets or customers. It goes on to say that it will not apply the safe harbour to agreements containing any of the restrictions that are listed as hard-core restrictions in any current or future Commission block exemption regulation[649]; it will be for the Court of Justice to determine in due course whether such hard-core restrictions are, in fact, object restrictions. Paragraph 14 of the *Notice* makes clear that excluded, as opposed to hard-core, restrictions in block exemptions (for example non-compete clauses under Article 5 of Regulation 330/2010) do benefit from the safe harbour in paragraph 8.

(C) **Other examples of non-appreciability**

The *de minimis* doctrine described in the preceding sections stems from the judgment in *Völk v Vervaecke*[650], which referred to the 'weak position' that the persons had on the market in question; this is why the Commission's *Notice* giving expression to the doctrine does so in terms of market share thresholds, which are used as a proxy for undertakings' market power, or rather lack of market power. It should be noted however that appreciability may be relevant to the application of Article 101(1) in a different way: cases can be found in which it was concluded that a restriction of competition was not appreciable, not because the parties to an agreement lacked market power, but because the restriction itself was insignificant in a qualitative sense. For example in *Pavel Pavlov v Stichting Pensioenfonds Medische Specialisten*[651] the Court of Justice concluded that a decision by medical specialists to set up a pension fund entrusted with the management of a supplementary pension scheme did not appreciably affect competition within the internal market: the cost of the scheme had only a marginal and indirect influence on the final cost of the services that they offered. This finding was not linked in any way to the market power of the specialists[652].

6. The Effect on Trade Between Member States

The application of Article 101 is limited to agreements, decisions or concerted practices *which may affect trade between Member States*. The scope of Article 102 is similarly limited. The inter-Member State trade clause is very important in EU competition law, since it defines 'the boundary between the areas respectively covered by [EU] law and the law of the Member States'[653].

Historically both the Commission and the EU Courts have adopted a liberal interpretation of the inter-state trade clause, thereby enlarging the scope of Articles 101 and 102[654]. This was of particular significance at a time when many Member States had no competition

[649] On the list of hard-core restrictions contained in vertical agreements see ch 16, 'Article 4: hard-core restrictions', pp 677–684; on this point note *Volkswagen* OJ [2001] L 262/14, para 79 (resale price maintenance could infringe Article 101(1) even where the parties' market share was below the *de minimis* threshold); see also para 10 of the Commission's *Guidelines on Vertical Restraints* OJ [2010] C 130/1 and the cases referred to in fn 4 of the *Guidelines*.

[650] See ch 3 n 630 earlier.

[651] Cases C-180/98 etc EU:C:2000:428, paras 90–97.

[652] Similar conclusions, where the non-appreciability of restrictions was not related to the parties' market power, can be found in *Irish Banks' Standing Committee* OJ [1986] L 295/28, para 16; *Visa International* OJ [2001] L 293/24, para 54–58 and 63–65; *UEFA's broadcasting regulations* OJ [2001] L 171/12, paras 49–58; and *Identrus* OJ [2001] L 249/12, paras 54–55.

[653] Case 22/78 *Hugin Kassaregister AB v Commission* EU:C:1979:138.

[654] Cf the position in the US where the inter-state commerce clause has been construed flexibly: see eg *Manderville Island Farms v American Crystal Sugar Co* 334 US 219, 237 (1948) and *United States v Morrison* 529 US 598, 610 (2000).

laws of their own, or competition laws that were weak in terms of powers of investigation and sanctions. This point does not have the same significance today, since all the Member States have effective competition laws, and for the most part these are modelled upon Articles 101 and 102[655]. It follows that a cartel and/or abusive behaviour by a dominant firm will be illegal either under domestic or EU law, and to this extent it matters little whether the infringement occurs under one system or the other (or both). However the concept of inter-state trade is of central importance since the entry into force of Regulation 1/2003[656], and the creation of the European Competition Network. Determining whether an agreement or practice has an effect on trade between Member States is important for a series of reasons[657]:

- where there is an effect on trade between Member States, national courts and NCAs that apply national competition law to agreements or practices have an *obligation* to also apply Articles 101 and 102[658]
- where there is an effect on trade between Member States, national courts and NCAs cannot apply stricter national competition law to agreements, although they can apply stricter national law to unilateral conduct[659]
- NCAs that apply Articles 101 and 102 have an obligation to inform the Commission of the fact no later than 30 days before the adoption of the decision[660]. Clearly an NCA could avoid this obligation by reaching the conclusion that there is no effect on trade between Member States
- when the Commission is informed that an NCA intends to adopt a decision on the basis of EU competition law, the Commission has the power to initiate its own proceedings and thereby to terminate the proceedings of the NCA[661]. When the Commission has finished its investigation, the NCA's power to apply EU and domestic competition law revives, subject to its obligation not to adopt a decision that runs counter to the Commission's decision[662]
- the Commission and the NCAs have the right to exchange information for the purpose of applying Articles 101 and 102[663]
- there are cooperation provisions in place that facilitate the enforcement of Articles 101 and 102 by national courts, as well as an obligation for Member States to inform the Commission of court cases deciding on the application of those provisions[664]
- NCAs and national courts that apply Articles 101 and 102 must not take decisions that conflict with decisions adopted by the Commission[665].

Clearly these rules mean that it remains important to know whether an agreement or practice has an effect on trade between Member States. This is why the Commission has published *Guidelines on the effect on trade concept contained in Articles [101 and 102 TFEU]* ('the *Guidelines on inter-state trade*')[666]. They draw substantially on the case law of the EU Courts, going back to *Consten and Grundig v Commission* in 1966[667]. In the account of the *Guidelines on inter-state trade* that follows this case law will not be cited, but the reader should be aware that references to the relevant cases will be found in the footnotes of the *Guidelines*.

655 See ch 2, 'Modelling of domestic competition law on Articles 101 and 102', pp 58–59.
656 OJ [2003] L 1/1.
657 For discussion of Regulation 1/2003 see ch 2, 'The modernisation of EU competition law', pp 53–54 and ch 7 generally.
658 Regulation 1/2003, Article 3(1). 659 Ibid, Article 3(2).
660 Ibid, Article 11(4). 661 Ibid, Article 11(6).
662 Case C-17/10 *Toshiba* EU:C:2012:72, paras 74–91 and, in particular, para 85.
663 Regulation 1/2003, Article 12. 664 Ibid, Article 15. 665 Ibid, Article 16.
666 OJ [2004] C 101/81. 667 Cases 56/64 and 58/64 EU:C:1966:41.

Part 1 of the *Guidelines on inter-state trade* contain a brief introduction explaining, in particular, that they deal with the issue of what is meant by an appreciable effect on inter-state trade, but not with the separate question of what is meant by an appreciable restriction of competition[668]. Part 2 of the *Guidelines* explains the effect on trade criterion, and is divided into four parts: general principles; the concept of 'trade between Member States'; the notion 'may affect'; and the concept of appreciability. Part 3 considers the application of the effect on trade criterion to particular examples of agreements and practices.

(A) **The effect on trade criterion**

(i) **General principles**

Articles 101 and 102 are applicable only where any effect on trade between Member States is appreciable[669]. In the case of Article 101 the question is whether the agreement as a whole affects trade: it is not necessary that each part of the agreement does so[670]; and if the agreement affects trade between Member States it is irrelevant that a particular undertaking that is party to the agreement does not itself produce such an effect[671]. In the case of Article 102 the abuse must have an effect on trade between Member States, but this does not mean that each element of the behaviour must be assessed in isolation to determine its effect: the conduct must be assessed in terms of its overall impact[672].

(ii) **The concept of 'trade between Member States'**

The concept of 'trade' is not limited to traditional exchanges of goods and services across borders: it is a wider concept and covers all cross-border activity, including the establishment by undertakings of agencies, branches or subsidiaries in other Member States[673]. The concept of trade also covers situations where the competitive structure of the market is affected by agreements and/or conduct[674]. There can be an effect on trade between Member States where parts only of those states are affected: the effect does not need to extend to their entire territories[675]. The question of whether trade between Member States is affected is separate from the issue of the relevant geographical market: trade could be affected even though the geographical market is national or even smaller than national[676].

(iii) **The notion 'may affect'**

The Court of Justice has often said that the notion that an agreement or practice 'may affect' trade between Member States means that it must be possible to foresee, with a sufficient degree of probability on the basis of a set of objective factors of law or fact, that the agreement or practice may have an influence, direct or indirect, actual or potential, on the pattern of trade between Member States[677]. Subjective intent to affect trade is not required[678]; and it is sufficient that the agreement or practice is capable of having an effect: it is not necessary to prove that it actually will do so[679]. In determining whether the pattern of trade is influenced it is not necessary to show that trade is or would be restricted or reduced: an increase in trade also means that it has been influenced[680]; the effect on trade criterion is simply jurisdictional, determining whether an examination of an agreement or conduct under the EU competition rules is warranted[681].

[668] *Guidelines on inter-state trade*, para 4. [669] Ibid, para 13. [670] Ibid, para 14.

[671] Ibid, para 15; on this point see the Commission's *amicus curiae* observations of 13 October 2011 in *Orange Caraïbes v l'Autorité de la concurrence*, available at www.ec.europa.eu.

[672] *Guidelines on inter-state trade*, para 17. [673] Ibid, paras 19 and 30. [674] Ibid, para 20.

[675] Ibid, para 21. [676] Ibid, para 22. [677] Ibid, para 23, citing relevant case law.

[678] Ibid, para 25. [679] Ibid, para 26. [680] Ibid, para 34. [681] Ibid, para 35.

The fact that the influence on trade may be 'direct *or indirect*, actual *or potential*' clearly means that the jurisdictional reach of Articles 101 and 102 can be extensive[682]. However, in the case of indirect and potential influence the analysis must not be based on remote or hypothetical effects: a person claiming that trade is affected in this way must be able to explain how and why this is the case[683].

(iv) The concept of appreciability

Any effect on trade must be appreciable. The stronger the market position of the undertakings concerned, the likelier it is that any effect will be appreciable[684]. An undertaking's market share, and the value of its turnover in the products concerned, are relevant to the appreciability of any effect[685]. An assessment of appreciability must be considered in the legal and economic context of any agreement or practice including, in the case of vertical agreements, the cumulative effect of parallel networks[686].

The *Guidelines on inter-state trade* do not provide general quantitative rules on when trade is appreciably affected; however they do provide two examples of situations where trade is normally *not* capable of being appreciably affected.

(a) Small and medium-sized businesses

The *Guidelines* state that agreements between SMEs, as defined in Commission Recommendation 2003/361/EC[687], would not normally affect trade between Member States; however they might do so where they engage in cross-border activity[688]. The point is repeated in paragraph 11 of the Commission's *Guidelines on Vertical Restraints*[689].

(b) A negative rebuttable presumption of non-appreciability

The *Guidelines* also set out a negative rebuttable presumption of non-appreciability. This arises where:

- the aggregate market share of the parties on any relevant market within the EU affected by the agreements does not exceed 5% and
- the parties' turnover is below €40 million: turnover is calculated differently according to whether the agreement is horizontal or vertical[690].

The presumption continues to apply where the turnover threshold is exceeded during two successive calendar years by no more than 10% and the market share threshold by no more than 2%.

(c) A positive rebuttable presumption of appreciability

The *Guidelines* also set out a positive rebuttable presumption of appreciability in the case of agreements that 'by their very nature' are capable of affecting trade between Member States, such as agreements on imports and exports. This arises where:

- the turnover thresholds set out earlier are exceeded and
- the parties' market shares exceed 5%.

This positive presumption does not apply where the agreement covers part only of a Member State[691].

[682] See ibid, paras 36–42. [683] Ibid, para 43 [684] Ibid, para 45. [685] Ibid, paras 46–47.
[686] Ibid, para 49.
[687] OJ [2003] L 124/36: see 'Part I of the *Notice*: introductory paragraphs', pp 147–148 earlier in chapter for the definition of SMEs in the Recommendation.
[688] *Guidelines on inter-state trade*, para 50. [689] OJ [2010] C 130/1.
[690] Ibid, para 52. [691] Ibid, para 53.

A different point is that an object restriction infringes Article 101(1) only if it has an *appreciable* effect on trade between Member States: some quantitative analysis may therefore be required before determining that Article 101(1) is infringed. Because of the need to prove appreciability it is sometimes necessary for the Commission to define the relevant market even in a case involving an object restriction[692].

(B) The application of the effect on trade criterion to particular agreements and conduct

The *Guidelines on inter-state trade* proceed to examine how the effect on trade criterion applies in relation to particular types of agreement and conduct. They do so by reference to three categories: first, agreements and abuse covering or implemented in several Member States[693]; secondly, cases covering a single, or only part of a, Member State[694]; and thirdly, cases involving undertakings located in third countries[695]. It is important to understand that Articles 101 and 102 are capable of application irrespective of where the undertakings concerned are located, provided that the agreement or practice is implemented or has effects within the EU[696]. It is also possible that an export ban imposed by an EU supplier on a distributor in a third country, which prevents the latter from re-importing into the EU, could have an effect on trade between Member States in certain circumstances, for example where there is a significant differential between prices in the different territories, where that differential would not be eroded by customs duties and transport costs, and where significant volumes of a product could be exported from the third country to the EU[697].

There have been some judgments of the EU Courts since the *Guidelines* were published. The General Court held in *Raiffeisen Zentralbank Österreich v Commission*[698] that a banking cartel in Austria had an effect on trade between Member States. In that case there was a series of regional committees within Austria; the Court held that it was not necessary to consider whether each individual committee had an effect on trade: rather it was necessary to look at the cumulative effect of all the committees[699]. The overall cartel in Austria affected the entire country, and the Court said that this raised a strong presumption that trade between Member States was affected[700]. The Court noted that there had been cases in which this presumption had been rebutted[701], but held that it was not rebutted on the facts of this case[702]. In *Ziegler v Commission*[703] the Court of Justice upheld the General Court's judgment[704] rejecting an argument that the Commission had failed to demonstrate an appreciable effect on trade between Member States; the Court held that the positive presumption of appreciability applied to the *International Removal Services* cartel[705].

In *Emanuela Sbarigia v Azienda*[706] the Court of Justice held that it was 'quite obvious' that the legislation that limited the opening hours of pharmacies in Italy could not affect

692 See Case C-439/11 P *Ziegler SA v Commission* EU:C:2013:513, para 63 (*International removal services*).

693 *Guidelines on inter-state trade*, paras 61–76.

694 Ibid, paras 77–99.

695 Ibid, paras 100–109.

696 See further ch 12, 'The Extraterritorial Application of EU Competition Law', pp 502–508.

697 *Guidelines on inter-state trade*, paras 108–109.

698 Cases T-259/02 EU:T:2006:396.

699 Ibid, para 177.

700 Ibid, para 181.

701 See eg Cases C-215/96 and C-216/96 *Bagnasco and others* EU:C:1999:12; *Netherlands Bank II* OJ [1999] L 271/28.

702 Case T-259/02 EU:T:2006:396, paras 182–186; the appeal to the Court of Justice in this case was dismissed, Case C-125/07 P *Erste Bank der Österreichischen Sparkassen AG v Commission* EU:C:2009:576, paras 36–70.

703 Case C-439/11 P EU:C:2013:513.

704 Case T-199/08 EU:T:2011:285, paras 51–74.

705 Case C-439/11 P EU:C:2013:513, paras 99–100.

706 Case C-393/08 EU:C:2010:388.

trade between Member States[707]. It is noticeable in this case that the referring court had itself expressed dissatisfaction with the relevant legislation, as had the Italian competition authority[708]; however the lack of an effect on inter-state trade meant that this matter could not be addressed under the TFEU.

7. Checklist of Agreements that Fall Outside Article 101(1)

At the end of this chapter it may be helpful to set out a checklist of the circumstances in which an agreement might be found not to infringe Article 101(1): the list follows the order of the text of this chapter:

- Article 101(1) does not apply to an agreement that is not between undertakings[709]
- Article 101(1) does not apply to collective agreements between employers and workers[710]
- Article 101(1) does not apply to an agreement between two or more persons that form a single economic entity[711]
- Article 101(1) normally does not apply to agreements between a principal and agent[712]
- Article 101(1) normally does not apply to an agreement between a contractor and a sub-contractor[713]
- Article 101(1) does not apply to unilateral conduct that is not attributable to collusion between two or more undertakings[714]
- Article 101(1) does not apply to an agreement that has neither the object nor the effect of preventing, restricting or distorting competition[715]
- Article 101(1) does not apply to contractual restrictions that enable undertakings to achieve a legitimate purpose and which are proportionate[716]
- Article 101 does not apply to full-function joint ventures[717]
- Article 101(1) does not apply to agreements that have only a theoretical or speculative effect on actual or potential competition[718]
- Article 101(1) does not apply to an agreement if this would obstruct an undertaking or undertakings in the performance of a task of general economic interest entrusted to them by a Member State[719]

707 Ibid, paras 29–33. 708 Ibid, paras 13–15.

709 See 'Undertakings and associations of undertakings', pp 83–101 earlier in chapter.

710 See 'Employees, trades unions and collective labour relations', pp 90–92 earlier in chapter.

711 See 'The "single economic entity" doctrine', pp 93–99 earlier in chapter.

712 See 'The "single economic entity" doctrine' pp 93–99 earlier in chapter and ch 16, 'Commercial Agents', pp 634–637.

713 See 'The single economic entity doctrine', pp 93–99 earlier in chapter and ch 16, 'Sub-Contracting Agreements', pp 691–692.

714 See '"Unilateral" conduct and Article 101(1) in vertical cases', pp 109–114 earlier in chapter.

715 See 'The Object or Effect of Preventing, Restricting or Distorting Competition', pp 119–147 earlier in chapter.

716 See 'Regulatory ancillarity: the judgment of the Court of Justice in *Wouters*', pp 138–141 earlier in chapter.

717 See ch 21, 'Joint ventures—the concept of full-functionality', pp 857–858.

718 This assumes that the agreement does not restrict by object; see 'Actual and potential competition', p 135 earlier in chapter.

719 See 'Article 106(2)', p 144 earlier in chapter and ch 6, 'Article 106(2)', pp 242–248.

- Article 101(1) does not apply to an agreement which undertakings were compelled to enter into by law[720]
- Article 101(1) does not apply to an agreement in a market that is so highly regulated that there is no latitude left for competition[721]
- Article 101(1) does not apply to an agreement that does not have the object of restricting competition and has no appreciable effect on competition[722]
- Article 101(1) does not apply to an agreement that does not have an appreciable effect on trade between Member States[723]
- Article 101(1) does not apply to an agreement that satisfies the criteria of Article 101(3)[724].

[720] See 'State compulsion and highly regulated markets', pp 144–145 earlier in chapter.
[721] See 'State compulsion and highly regulated markets', pp 144–145 earlier in chapter.
[722] See 'The *De Minimis* Doctrine', pp 147–150 earlier in chapter.
[723] See 'The Effect on Trade between Member States', pp 150–155 earlier in chapter.
[724] See ch 4.

4

Article 101(3)

1. Introduction

An agreement that falls within Article 101(1) TFEU is not necessarily unlawful. Article 101(3) provides a 'legal exception' to the prohibition in Article 101(1) by providing that it may be declared inapplicable in respect of agreements, decisions or concerted practices[1], or of categories[2] of agreements, decisions or concerted practices, that satisfy four conditions, the first two positive and the last two negative. To satisfy Article 101(3) an agreement:

- must contribute to improving the production or distribution of goods or to promoting technical or economic progress
- while allowing consumers a fair share of the resulting benefit.

Furthermore the agreement[3]:

- must not impose on the undertakings concerned restrictions which are not indispensable to the attainment of these objectives nor
- afford such undertakings the possibility of eliminating competition in a substantial part of the products in question[4].

[1] For further reading on Article 101(3) readers are referred to Rose and Bailey (eds) *Bellamy and Child: European Union Law of Competition* (Oxford University Press, 7th ed, 2013), ch 3; Faull and Nikpay (eds) *The EU Law of Competition* (Oxford University Press, 3rd ed, 2014), ch 3, paras 3.445–3.511. The reference to decisions is useful since it means eg that the rules of a trade association may satisfy Article 101(3); it will only be rarely that Article 101(3) is applied to a concerted practice, but this can happen: see eg *Re International Energy Agency* OJ [1983] L 376/30; renewed in 1994, OJ [1994] L 68/35; in *CISAC*, Commission decision of 16 July 2008, the Commission concluded that Article 101(3) was not applicable to a concerted practice between 24 copyright collecting societies which amounted to a systematic delineation of the market between them along territorial lines; the decision was annulled on other grounds, eg Case T-442/08 *CISAC v Commission* EU:T:2013:188; the General Court confirmed the Commission's conclusion that Article 101(3) was not applicable in Case T-451/08 *Stim v Commission* EU:T:2013:189, paras 98–108.

[2] The inclusion of 'categories' of agreements is important since it paves the way for block exemptions: see 'Block Exemptions', pp 176–179 later in chapter.

[3] The term 'agreement' should be taken to include decisions and concerted practices in the rest of this chapter.

[4] Note that the UK Competition Act 1998 contains a similar provision in s 9(1): see ch 9, 'The Chapter I prohibition: exemptions', pp 372–376.

Under Regulation 17 of 1962[5] the Commission had the exclusive right to grant so-called 'individual exemption' under Article 101(3) to agreements notified to it[6]. Council Regulation 1/2003[7] abolished the system of notification of agreements to the Commission for 'individual exemption' and instead established the principle that undertakings must decide for themselves whether their agreements are compatible with Article 101 as a whole. Regulation 1/2003 renders the criteria in Article 101(3) directly applicable without prior decision of the Commission with effect from 1 May 2004[8]; since then the Commission shares the competence to apply Article 101(3) with the national competition authorities ('the NCAs')[9] and national courts[10]. There is no such thing as an 'individual exemption': agreements either do, or do not, satisfy Article 101(3).

The Commission has published *Guidelines on the application of Article [101(3)] of the Treaty* ('the *Article 101(3) Guidelines*' or 'the *Guidelines*')[11], which provide guidance to national courts and NCAs, as well as to undertakings and their professional advisers. The *Guidelines* should be applied 'reasonably and flexibly' rather than in a mechanical manner[12]. The Commission has cited the *Guidelines* in several of its decisions[13]. National courts and NCAs have also relied on the principles set out in the *Guidelines*[14]. Additional guidance on the application of Article 101(1) and (3) to agreements is provided by the Commission's guidelines on vertical restraints[15], on horizontal cooperation agreements[16] and on technology transfer agreements[17].

An alternative way of satisfying Article 101(3) is to draft an agreement to satisfy one of the so-called 'block exemptions' issued by the Council of the European Union ('the Council') or by the Commission under powers conferred on it by the Council. Agreements within the terms of a block exemption are valid without the need to consider whether they infringe Article 101(1) in the first place[18].

After discussing the burden and standard of proof under Article 101(3) and the application of that provision to agreements, including restrictions of competition by object, section 2 of this chapter will discuss the criteria in Article 101(3). It will then consider the implications of Regulation 1/2003 for undertakings and their professional advisers, and in particular their need to 'self-assess' the application of Article 101(3) to agreements. The final section in this chapter describes the system of block exemptions.

[5] JO [1962] 204/62, OJ Sp Ed [1962] p 87. [6] Ibid, Article 9(1).

[7] OJ [2003] L 1/1; see 'Regulation 1/2003', pp 174–176 later in chapter for discussion of the implications of Regulation 1/2003.

[8] Regulation 1/2003, Article 1(1) and (2).

[9] Ibid, Article 5. [10] Ibid, Article 6. [11] OJ [2004] C 101/97. [12] Ibid, para 6.

[13] See eg *MasterCard*, Commission decision of 19 December 2007, paras 670–672 and 734; *Morgan Stanley/Visa*, Commission decision of 3 October 2007, paras 311, 313 and 322–324; *ONP*, Commission decision of 8 December 2010, para 707; *Telefónica/Portugal Telecom*, Commission decision of 23 January 2013, paras 436–446; *Lundbeck*, Commission decision of 19 June 2013, paras 1212–1231; *Servier*, Commission decision of 9 July 2014, paras 2062–2122.

[14] See eg *Paroxetine*, CMA decision of 12 February 2016, paras 10.56–10.59, on appeal dismissed on the issue of exemption in Case 1252/1/12/16 *GlaxoSmithKline v CMA* [2018] CAT 4, paras 367-375: the CAT made an Article 267 reference on whether the agreements in *Paroxetine* restricted competition on 27 March 2018; *Asda Stores Ltd v MasterCard Inc* [2017] EWHC 93 (Comm) and *Sainsbury's Supermarkets Ltd v Visa Europe Services LLC* [2018] EWHC 355 (Comm), both citing the *Guidelines* on multiple occasions; B4-71/10 *Decision by head association of German banking industry (Due diligence in the special conditions for online-banking)*, Bundeskartellamt decision of 29 June 2016, paras 343, 416, 427; B7-46/13 *NGA cooperation for roll-out of broadband connections*, Bundeskartellamt decision of 4 April 2014, paras 73, 90–102.

[15] *Guidelines on Vertical Restraints* OJ [2010] C 130/1.

[16] *Guidelines on the applicability of Article 101 [TFEU] to horizontal co-operation agreements* OJ [2011] C 11/1.

[17] *Guidelines on the application of Article 101 [TFEU] to technology transfer agreements* OJ [2014] C 89/3.

[18] See Case C-260/07 *Pedro IV Servicios SL v Total España SA* EU:C:2009:215, para 36; *Guidelines on Vertical Restraints* OJ [2010] C 130/1, para 110(1)–(2).

(A) Burden and standard of proof

Article 2 of Regulation 1/2003 provides that the burden of proving an infringement of Article 101(1) is on the Commission, the NCAs or the person opposing an agreement in a national court, and that the burden of showing that Article 101(3) is satisfied is on the person making that claim[19]. Undertakings relying on Article 101(3) must put forward 'convincing arguments and evidence' that the conditions of that provision are satisfied[20]. The Commission must then examine those arguments and evidence; if it is unable to refute them the undertakings will be taken to have discharged the burden of proof upon them[21]. The Commission does not have to deal with all the justifications for a particular agreement that could conceivably be, but have not been, raised by the parties[22].National rules on the standard of proof apply in Article 101(3) cases before the NCAs and national courts[23].

(B) The conditions of Article 101(3) are cumulative

All four conditions must be satisfied if an agreement is to benefit from Article 101(3): the Court of Justice has stressed this on a number of occasions[24], and paragraph 42 of the *Article 101(3) Guidelines* contains a statement to the same effect. For example the General Court annulled a Commission decision that an agreement satisfied Article 101(3) in *Métropole télévision v Commission*[25] because the Commission had failed to demonstrate that restrictions in the agreement were indispensable[26]. Parties to an agreement covered by a block exemption do not have to show that each of the conditions of Article 101(3) is satisfied: there is a rebuttable presumption that agreements falling within the scope of a block exemption satisfy all four conditions[27].

Paragraph 44 of the *Article 101(3) Guidelines* explains that Article 101(3) applies only for as long as the four conditions contained in it are satisfied; however when applying this rule due consideration must be given to the time that it will take, and the restrictions that may be needed, when firms make sunk investments to realise economic efficiencies.

(C) Any type of agreement can be defended under Article 101(3)

A very important point about Article 101(3) TFEU is that *any* type of agreement that restricts competition may benefit from the exception conferred by that provision. The

19 See similarly Cases 43/82 and 63/82 *VBVB and VBBB v Commission* EU:C:1984:9, para 61.

20 Case C-68/12 *Slovenská sporitel'ňa* EU:C:2013:71, para 32 and case law cited; see generally Castillo de la Torre and Gippini Fournier *Evidence, Proof and Judicial Review in EU Competition Law* (Edward Elgar, 2017), ch 2.

21 Cases 56/64 and 58/64 *Consten and Grundig v Commission* EU:C:1966:41; Cases C-204/00 P etc *Aalborg Portland v Commission* EU:C:2004:6, para 55; Cases C-501/06 P etc *GlaxoSmithKline Services Unlimited v Commission* EU:C:2009:610, paras 82–83.

22 Cases T-357/06 *Koninklijke Wegenbouw Stevin BV v Commission* EU:T:2012:488, para 122 and case law cited.

23 Regulation 1/2003, recital 5; in the UK see *Asda Stores Ltd v MasterCard Inc* [2017] EWHC 93 (Comm), para 305: the standard of proof is the 'balance of probabilities'.

24 See eg Cases 43/82 and 63/82 *VBVB and VVVB v Commission* EU:C:1984:9, para 61; Case C-238/05 *Asnef-Equifax v Asociación de Usuarios de Servicios Bancarios (Ausbanc)* EU:C:2006:734, para 65; Case C-68/12 *Slovenská sporite'ňa* EU:C:2013:71, para 36.

25 Cases T-528/93 etc EU:T:1996:99, para 93.

26 The General Court did so again in Case T-185/00 *M6 v Commission* EU:T:2002:242, para 86, where it considered that the Commission had incorrectly concluded that an agreement would not substantially eliminate competition.

27 *Article 101(3) Guidelines*, para 35.

General Court clearly established this point in *Matra Hachette v Commission*[28]. The Court of Justice has affirmed the position; for example in *Pierre Fabre*[29] it stated that:

> an undertaking has the option, *in all circumstances*, to assert, on an individual basis, the applicability of the exception provided for in Article 101(3) TFEU[30] (emphasis added).

(i) Restrictions of competition by object and Article 101(3)

There appears to be an assumption on the part of some people—both in private practice and in competition authorities—that an agreement that restricts competition by object is incapable of being defended under Article 101(3), but this is simply wrong in law[31]. Even an agreement that has as its *object* the restriction of competition in the sense of Article 101(1) is capable, in principle, of satisfying the conditions of Article 101(3)[32]: in this sense EU law differs from US law, since there are no agreements that are irredeemably, or '*per se*', illegal in the EU system[33]. Of course it will be very difficult to run efficiency arguments in favour of a secret, long-running price-fixing cartel: but that is because it is hard to conceive any such arguments, not because it is impossible in law to do so. An example of a case in which an agreement restrictive of competition by object satisfied the terms of Article 101(3) can be found in *Air France/Alitalia*[34] where the Commission authorised an extensive strategic alliance between those two airlines. It would require convincing evidence to prove that restrictions of competition by object such as horizontal price fixing satisfy Article 101(3)[35], but in exceptional circumstances even this may be possible[36].

In *Beef Industry Development Society* ('BIDS')[37] the Court of Justice held that an agreement between beef processors in Ireland to reduce capacity for beef processing there (some firms would stay in the market, and would pay other firms to exit and to agree not to re-enter for several years) had the object of restricting competition. The Court stressed that any justification for the agreement would have to be made out under Article 101(3)[38]. BIDS subsequently withdrew its claim under Article 101(3), with the result that the national court was not required to reach a conclusion on the matter.

The possibility of an Article 101(3) defence for an object restriction was also considered by the Court of Justice in *GlaxoSmithKline v Commission*[39]. The Court held that a term in a vertical agreement, whereby Spanish wholesale purchasers of pharmaceutical products from Glaxo were charged a higher price if the products were exported from Spain to

[28] Case T-17/93 EU:T:1994:89, para 85; see also Case T-168/01 *GlaxoSmithKline Services Unlimited v Commission* EU:T:2006:265, para 233, upheld on appeal Cases C-501/06 P etc EU:C:2009:610, para 82; Case T-111/08 *MasterCard v Commission* EU:T:2012:260, para 199.

[29] Case C-439/09 *Pierre Fabre Dermo-Cosmétique SAS* EU:C:2011:649.

[30] Ibid, para 57: see also para 49; see similarly Case T-469/13 *Generics (UK) Ltd v Commission* EU:T:2016:454, para 152.

[31] See the *Article 101(3) Guidelines*, para 46.

[32] See Johannes Laitenberger, Director-General of DG COMP, 'The many dividends of keeping markets open, fair and contestable', speech of 27 April 2017, available at www.ec.europa.eu/competition/speeches.

[33] On this point see Case T-460/13 *Ranbaxy v Commission* EU:T:2016:453, para 228; see further ch 3, 'Have the EU Courts embraced the "rule of reason"?', pp 142–144.

[34] OJ [2004] L 362/17. See also *Continental/United/Lufthansa/Air Canada*, Commission decision of 23 May 2013, paras 55–79; this was an Article 9 commitment decision and did not reach a final conclusion on the application of Article 101: however the preliminary analysis of an object restriction under Article 101(3) is nevertheless of interest.

[35] See the *Article 101(3) Guidelines*, para 46.

[36] See eg the former block exemption for horizontal price fixing in the case of containerised cargo carried by international liner conferences, OJ [1986] L 378/1; the exemption was repealed by Article 1 of Regulation 1419/2006, OJ [2006] L 269/1 in October 2008: see ch 23, 'Legislative regime', p 1002.

[37] Case C-209/07 EU:C:2008:643.

[38] Ibid, paras 21 and 39.

[39] Cases C-501/06 P etc EU:C:2009:610.

higher-priced countries such as the UK, restricted competition by object. The Court was not satisfied, however, that the Commission was correct to dismiss Glaxo's arguments in support of the agreement under Article 101(3). GSK subsequently withdrew its request for an individual exemption under Article 101(3) and the Commission concluded that there were insufficient grounds for conducting a further investigation into the alleged infringement[40].

(ii) **Fixing prices and Article 101(3)**

There have been decisions in which the Commission was satisfied that the fixing of prices satisfied the requirements of Article 101(3). These were far from being classic cartel cases: rather they concerned network industries in which prices were 'fixed' between participants in a network that supplied services to one another (the price fixing was business to business, or 'B to B'), whereas 'hard-core' price fixing involves the fixing of prices to customers (business to customer, or 'B to C'). In these decisions the Commission considered that the agreements restricted competition *by effect* rather than *by object*. In *REIMS II*[41] the Commission considered that an agreement between the public postal operators in Europe as to the amount that one operator would pay to another for the onward delivery of letters in the latter's territory satisfied the terms of Article 101(3). The agreement did entail the 'fixing' of prices, in that participants in the scheme were committed to its principles; but this was price fixing of an 'unusual' nature[42], and the Commission identified several efficiencies that would follow from it[43]. Similarly in *Visa International—Multilateral Interchange Fee*[44] the Commission stated that an agreement concerning prices is not always to be classified as a cartel and therefore as inherently incapable of satisfying Article 101(3)[45]: in that decision, adopted under the old procedure in Regulation 17, the Commission granted individual exemption to a 'multilateral interchange fee' agreed upon between 'acquiring' and 'issuing' banks within the Visa system[46].

(D) **Under-application of Article 101(3)**

Since the adoption of Regulation 1/2003 there has not been one Commission decision in which an agreement was found to satisfy Article 101(3). The authors consider that the Commission should do more to identify agreements to which Article 101(3) applies. This would correct the misguided notion that it is legally or evidentially impossible for parties to satisfy the criteria of that provision[47]. This issue will be discussed further below[48].

[40] Commission decision of 27 May 2014, on appeal Case T-574/14 *EAEPC v Commission*, not yet decided.

[41] OJ [1999] L 275/17. [42] Ibid, para 65.

[43] Ibid, paras 69–76; this was a decision where the Commission granted individual exemption under the old procedure in Regulation 17 of 1962: the exemption was renewed in 2003 and expired on 31 December 2006, OJ [2004] L 56/76.

[44] OJ [2002] L 318/17; see similarly *Asda Stores Ltd v MasterCard Inc* [2017] EWHC 93 (Comm), paras 261–421: all but one of the MIFs set by MasterCard satisfied Article 101(3).

[45] Ibid, para 79; the Commission's suggestion in this paragraph that some agreements are inherently incapable of satisfying Article 101(3) is clearly wrong given the judgment of the General Court in the *Matra Hachette* case, ch 4 n 28 earlier.

[46] The individual exemption expired on 31 December 2008; subsequently the Commission accepted commitments from Visa Europe under Article 9 of Regulation 1/2003 that involved a significant reduction of the interchange fees for debit cards and credit cards: see Commission decisions of 8 December 2010 and of 26 February 2014; Regulation 2015/751, OJ [2015] L 123/1 caps the level of interchange fees for debit and credit cards in the EEA with effect from 9 December 2015, on which see issue 3 of the Competition Policy Brief 'The Interchange Fees Regulation' (2015), available at www.ec.europa.eu/competition/publications/cpn.

[47] See Bailey 'Reinvigorating the Role of Article 101(3) under Regulation 1/2003' (2016) 81 Antitrust LJ 111.

[48] The ways in which the Commission might develop precedents under Article 101(3) is discussed in section 3D below.

2. The Article 101(3) Criteria

Each of the four requirements of Article 101(3) will now be examined. It is essential to consider them in conjunction with the *Article 101(3) Guidelines*. The text that follows will emulate the *Guidelines* by reversing the treatment of the second and third conditions set out in Article 101(3) (a fair share to consumers and indispensability): the Commission's view is that consideration of whether consumers would obtain a fair share of any resulting benefit does not arise in the event that any restrictions fail the indispensability test, so that it is logical to consider the latter first[49].

(A) First condition of Article 101(3): an improvement in the production or distribution of goods or in technical or economic progress

The 'improvement' produced by an agreement must be something of objective value to the EU as a whole, not a private benefit to the parties themselves[50]; cost savings that arise simply from the exercise of market power cannot be taken into account[51]. The improvement must 'display appreciable objective advantages of such a character as to compensate for the disadvantages which that agreement entails for competition'[52]; the Commission has declined to accept that an agreement produces an improvement if, in practice, its effect is a disproportionate distortion of competition in the market in question[53].

An agreement must be examined in the light of all the factual arguments and evidence put forward by the parties in support of their argument that Article 101(3) is satisfied[54]. Where an agreement produces effects in more than one market—for example on both sides of a two-sided market such as a payment card system—objective benefits in each of the markets can be taken into account[55]. In *MasterCard v Commission*[56] the General Court rejected the argument that the Commission had applied an excessive standard of proof when it required MasterCard to support its argument that Article 101(3) applied with 'a detailed, robust and compelling analysis that relies in its assumptions and deductions on empirical data and facts'[57]. In *Cartes Bancaires v Commission*[58] the General Court upheld the Commission's conclusions that the restrictive fees for membership of the CB payment card system had the effect of restricting competition, but did not lead to technical or economic progress; in particular there was no evidence that the CB system would collapse in the absence of such fees[59].

The benefits that may be claimed are specified in Article 101(3): the restrictions in the agreement must either contribute to an improvement in the production or distribution

[49] *Article 101(3) Guidelines*, para 39.

[50] Case C-382/12 P *MasterCard v Commission* EU:C:2014:2201, para 234; see also *Asda Stores Ltd v MasterCard Inc* [2017] EWHC 93 (Comm), para 276.

[51] See Cases C-501/06 P etc *GlaxoSmithKline Services Unlimited v Commission* EU:C:2009:610, paras 89–96 and para 49 of the *Article 101(3) Guidelines*.

[52] Cases 56/64 and 58/64 *Consten and Grundig v Commission* EU:C:1966:41; Case T-65/98 *Van den Bergh Foods Ltd v Commission* EU:T:2003:281, para 139, upheld on appeal Case C-552/03 P *Unilever Bestfoods (Ireland) Ltd v Commission* EU:C:2006:607, paras 102–106.

[53] *Screensport/EBU* OJ [1991] L 63/32, para 71.

[54] Cases C-501/06 P etc *GlaxoSmithKline Services Unlimited* EU:C:2009:610, paras 102–104.

[55] Case C-382/12 P *MasterCard v Commission* EU:C:2014:2201, para 237.

[56] Case T-111/08 *MasterCard v Commission* EU:T:2012:260.

[57] Ibid, paras 194–237 (dismissing an appeal against Commission decision of 19 December 2007; the quotation is taken from para 690; see also paras 694–701); see, to the same effect, *Asda Stores Ltd v MasterCard Inc* [2017] EWHC 93 (Comm), para 305 and *Sainsbury's Supermarkets Ltd v Visa Europe Services LLC* [2018] EWHC 355 (Comm), paras 22-25.

[58] Case T-491/07 RENV EU:T:2016:379.

[59] Ibid, paras 361–465 (dismissing an appeal against Commission decision of 17 October 2007, paras 375–503).

of goods[60] or promote technical or economic progress. These concepts overlap, and in the days of individual exemption the Commission sometimes considered that more than one—or even that all—the heads were satisfied[61]. In other cases a particular type of benefit may be obviously appropriate for the agreement in question: for example vertical agreements between suppliers and distributors naturally come under the head of improvements in distribution[62]. The Commission has recognised network externalities as contributing to technical and economic progress from which consumers derive a benefit[63].

An important question is to determine how broad the criteria in the first condition of Article 101(3) are: in what circumstances can a 'benefit' under Article 101(3) justify a restriction of competition under Article 101(1), with the result that an agreement that would have been prohibited under Article 101(1) is in fact permitted as a result of the legal exception provided by Article 101(3)?

The issue of the breadth of Article 101(3) has attracted considerable attention[64] for various reasons. First, the abolition of the Commission's 'monopoly' over decision-making in individual cases under Article 101(3) as a result of the adoption of Regulation 1/2003 means that Article 101(3) decisions are made by NCAs and national courts as well as the Commission: concern was expressed when Regulation 1/2003 was in gestation that the issues raised under Article 101(3) were so broad that they were not appropriate to be decided upon by NCAs and national courts; and that there was a risk that Article 101(3) would be applied inconsistently from one Member State to another. The Commission specifically noted that this risk had not materialised in its quinquennial report on the functioning of Regulation 1/2003[65].

A second point is that Governments often find that social policies that they would like to pursue—for example encouraging undertakings in the drinks industry to restrict the sale of 'cheap' alcohol to young people, or supermarkets to impose a charge for providing environmentally unfriendly plastic bags—may infringe competition law, in particular if a 'narrow' rather than a 'broad' view of Article 101(3) is taken. A third point is that when an economy or industry declines, it might be argued that a broader application of Article 101(3) would permit undertakings to enter into restrictive agreements to enable them to survive[66]. These factors have led to lively debate about the precise role of Article 101(3).

(i) A narrow view of Article 101(3)

A narrow view of Article 101(3) is that it permits only agreements that would bring about improvements in economic efficiency: the very wording of Article 101(3), which speaks of improvements to production and distribution and to technical and economic progress, is clearly suggestive of an efficiency standard. Article 101(3), therefore, simply allows a balancing of the restrictive effects of an agreement under Article 101(1) against the enhancement of efficiency under Article 101(3); in striving to achieve the right balance the other criteria

[60] Note that services are not explicitly referred to here; however para 48 of the *Article 101(3) Guidelines* states that Article 101(3) applies, by analogy, to services; in the UK s 9(1) of the Competition Act 1998 specifically includes improvements in the production or distribution of goods or services.

[61] See eg *Re United Reprocessors GmbH* OJ [1976] L 51/7, where the Commission considered that all four heads were satisfied.

[62] On vertical agreements see ch 16 generally.

[63] *Visa International—Multilateral Interchange Fee* OJ [2002] L 318/17, para 83; on network effects see ch 1, 'Network effects and two-sided markets', pp 11–13; see similarly, under UK law, *LINK Interchange Network Ltd*, OFT decision of 16 October 2001, available at www.nationalarchives.gov.uk.

[64] The following books are illustrative of the literature on this subject: Odudu *The Boundaries of EC Competition Law: The Scope of Article 81* (Oxford University Press, 2006); Townley *Article 81 EC and Public Policy* (Hart, 2009); Geradin, Layne-Farrar and Petit *EU Competition Law and Economics* (Oxford University Press, 2012), paras 3.224–3.237; Van Rompuy *Economic Efficiency: The Sole Concern of Modern Antitrust Policy? Non-Efficiency Considerations under Article 101 TFEU* (Kluwer, 2012); Heide-Jorgensen et al *Aims and Values in Competition Law* (DJØF Publishing, 2013); Witt *The More Economic Approach to EU Antitrust Law* (Hart, 2016).

[65] COM(2009) 206 final, 29 April 2009, para 12.

[66] See OECD Policy Roundtable, *Crisis Cartels* (2011), available at www.oecd.org/competition.

of Article 101(3)—a fair share to consumers, no dispensable restrictions and no substantial elimination of competition—are there to ensure that a reasonable outcome in terms of consumer welfare is achieved. The Commission's *White Paper on Modernisation*[67], which began the process that culminated in the adoption of Regulation 1/2003, explained Article 101(1) and (3) in precisely this way[68]; and the *Article 101(3) Guidelines* are drafted explicitly in terms of economic efficiency[69]. The Commission and the EU Courts have adopted a 'narrow' or economic approach to Article 101(3) in a number of cases under Regulation 1/2003[70]. In *Servier*[71] the Commission examined various alleged efficiencies of five patent settlement agreements under Article 101(3); it did not consider the wider public interest in promoting settlements of litigation. In *International Skating Union*[71a] the Commission applied an efficiency standard, and rejected arguments that the ISU eligibility rules could be justified by the need for a well-organised skating calendar. An attractive way of thinking of Article 101 as a whole is that Article 101(1) is concerned to establish whether an agreement could lead to allocative inefficiency, and that Article 101(3) permits such an agreement where there would be a compensating enhancement of productive efficiency[72].

(ii) A broader approach to Article 101(3)

There are proponents of the view that Article 101(3) should admit broad, non-competition considerations[73]. A broader view of Article 101(3) would allow policies other than efficiency to be taken into account when deciding whether to allow agreements that are restrictive of competition. There are many important policies in the Union, for example on industry[74], the environment[75], employment[76], the regions[77] and culture[78], that go beyond

[67] OJ [1999] C 132/1. [68] Ibid, para 57.

[69] See 'The Commission's approach in the *Article 101(3) Guidelines*', pp 167–169 later in chapter.

[70] See eg *MasterCard*, Commission decision of 19 December 2007, upheld on appeal Case T-111/08 *MasterCard v Commission* EU:T:2012:260, and on further appeal Case C-382/12 P *MasterCard v Commission* EU:C:2014:2201; *Lundbeck*, Commission decision of 19 June 2013, upheld on appeal Cases T-472/13 etc *Lundbeck v Commission* EU:T:2016:449, paras 706–720, on appeal Cases C-591/16 P etc *Lundbeck v Commission*, not yet decided.

[71] Commission decision of 9 July 2014, paras 2062–2122, on appeal Case T-691/14 *Servier v Commission*, not yet decided.

[71a] Commission decision of 8 December 2017, paras 293–301, on appeal Case T-93/18 *ISU v Commission*, not yet decided.

[72] See Odudu *The Boundaries of EC Competition Law: The Scope of Article 81* (Oxford University Press, 2006), in particular ch 6; Odudu 'The Wider Concerns of Competition Law' (2010) 30 OJLS 1.

[73] See eg Ehlermann 'The Modernization of EC Antitrust Policy: A Legal and Cultural Revolution' (2000) 37 CML Rev 537; Wesseling 'The Draft Regulation Modernising the Competition Rules: The Commission is Married to One Idea' (2001) 26 EL Rev 357; Monti 'Article 101 EC and Public Policy' (2002) 39 CML Rev 1057; Lugard and Hancher 'Honey, I Shrunk the Article! A Critical Assessment of the Commission's Notice on Article 81(3)' (2004) 25 ECLR 410; Townley *Article 81 and Public Policy* (Hart, 2009); for discussion of the issues see Sufrin 'The Evolution of Article 81(3) of the EC Treaty' (2006) 51 Antitrust Bulletin 915, 952–967; Townley 'Which Goals Count in Article 101 TFEU? Public Policy and its Discontents: The OFT's Roundtable Discussion on Article 101(3) of [TFEU]' (2011) 32 ECLR 441; Townley 'Is There (Still) Room for Non-Economic Arguments in Article 101 TFEU Cases?' in Heide-Jorgensen et al *Aims and Values in Competition Law* (DJØF Publishing, 2013), ch 5; Baarsma and Rosenboom 'A Veritable Tower of Babel: On the Confusion Between the Legal and Economic Interpretations of Article 101(3) of the Treaty on the Functioning of the European Union' (2015) 11 European Competition Journal 402.

[74] On industry under the TFEU see Article 173 (ex Article 157 EC).

[75] On environmental protection under the TFEU see Article 11 (ex Article 6 EC) and Articles 191–193 (ex Articles 174–176 EC); on the application of competition law to environmental agreements see OECD Roundtable on Competition Policy, *Horizontal Agreements in the Environmental Context* (2012), available at www.oecd.org/competition; Kingston *Greening EU Competition Law and Policy* (Cambridge University Press, 2011), ch 8.

[76] On employment under the TFEU see Articles 145–159 (ex Articles 125–130 EC).

[77] On economic and social cohesion under the TFEU note Articles 174–178 (ex Articles 158–162 EC).

[78] On culture under the TFEU see Article 167 (ex Article 151 EC); see Cases T-451/08 *Stim v Commission* EU:T:2013:189, paras 98–108.

the enhancement of economic efficiency. According to the broader view of Article 101(3) a benefit in terms of any of these policies may be able to justify a restriction of competition under Article 101(1)[79]; another way of putting the point is that it is legitimate to take into account *non*-economic considerations under Article 101(3) as well as economic ones[80].

There were cases before Regulation 1/2003 entered into force when non-economic issues seem to have been taken into account under Article 101(3)[81]. For example industrial policy may be detected in some competition law developments[82]: Amato suggests that the block exemption for specialisation agreements, with its acceptance that rationalisation in production can benefit from Article 101(3), reflects industrial policy rather than economic thinking[83]. In *Metro v Commission*[84] the Court of Justice considered that employment was a relevant factor under the first condition in Article 101(3), saying that the agreement under consideration was 'a stabilising factor with regard to the provision of employment which, since it improves the general conditions of production, especially when market conditions are unfavourable, comes within the framework of the objectives to which reference may be had pursuant to Article [101(3)]'. When considering whether an exemption might be given to a joint venture to produce a 'multi-purpose vehicle' in Portugal in *Ford/Volkswagen*[85] the Commission 'took note' of 'exceptional circumstances' in that it would bring a large number of jobs and substantial foreign investment to one of the poorest regions of the EU, promoting harmonious development, reducing regional disparities and furthering European market integration[86]. The Commission emphasised, however, that this would not be enough in itself to apply Article 101(3) unless the other conditions of that provision were fulfilled[87]. The General Court held that, since the Commission would have applied Article 101(3) to the agreement anyway, its decision could not be impugned for having taken into account improper criteria[88].

In *UEFA* the Commission took note of the financial solidarity that supports the development of European football when applying Article 101(3) to the sale of the media rights to the UEFA Champions League[89]. In *Laurent Piau v Commission*[90] the General Court seems to have accepted that rules of FIFA, the body that controls football worldwide,

[79] For powerful argument as to why these broader issues should not affect the application of competition law see Odudu *The Boundaries of EC Competition Law: The Scope of Article 81* (Oxford University Press, 2006), ch 7; see also Kjølbye 'The New Commission Guidelines on the Application of Article 81(3): An Economic Approach to Article 81' (2004) 25 ECLR 566.

[80] For an interesting review of the issues see the OFT's discussion note 'Article 101(3)—A discussion of narrow versus broad definition of benefits' and the notes of the roundtable discussion held at the OFT on 12 May 2010, available at www.nationalarchives.gov.uk.

[81] For discussion of the policies under consideration in this section see Monti *EC Competition Law* (Cambridge University Press, 2007), ch 4; Schweitzer 'Competition Law and Public Policy: Reconsidering an Uneasy Relationship—The Example of Article 81' in Drexl, Idot and Monéger (eds) *Economic Theory and Competition Law* (Edward Elgar, 2009), ch 9; Jones and Sufrin *EU Competition Law: Text, Cases, and Materials* (Oxford University Press, 6th ed, 2016), pp 242–247.

[82] Note however that Article 173 TFEU provides that the Union's industrial policy is to be conducted 'in accordance with a system of open and competitive markets'; see further OECD Roundtable on Competition Policy, *Industrial Policy and National Champions* (2009), available at www.oecd.org/competition.

[83] Amato *Antitrust and the Bounds of Power* (Hart, 1997), pp 63–64; the relevant block exemption is now Regulation 1218/2010, OJ [2010] L 335/43.

[84] Case 26/76 EU:C:1977:167, para 43; see similarly Case 42/84 *Remia BV and Verenigde Bedrijven Nutricia NV v Commission* EU:C:1985:327, para 42.

[85] OJ [1993] L 20/14.

[86] Ibid, paras 23, 28 and 36; see also the Commission Press Release IP/92/1083, 23 December 1992.

[87] OJ [1993] L 20/14, para 36.

[88] Case T-17/93 EU:T:1994:89, para 139; on this case generally see Swaak (1995) 32 CML Rev 1271.

[89] *Joint selling of the commercial rights of the UEFA Champions League* OJ [2003] L 291/25, para 164 citing the judgments in *Metro* and *Remia*.

[90] Case T-193/02 EU:T:2005:22, upheld on appeal Case C-171/05 P *Piau v Commission* EU:C:2006:149.

that required football players' agents to comply with a mandatory licensing system, could contribute to economic progress by raising professional and ethical standards for players' agents in order to protect football players who have a short playing career[91]. In *Stichting Baksteen*[92] the Commission considered that the restructuring of the Dutch brick industry, involving coordinated closures 'carried out in acceptable social conditions, including the redeployment of employees', promoted technical and economic progress[93]. In *CECED*[94] the Commission authorised under Article 101(3) an agreement between manufacturers of domestic appliances (washing machines etc) which would lead to energy efficiencies, and in doing so noted not only individual economic benefits to consumers from lower energy bills but also the 'collective environmental benefits' that would flow from the agreement[95], referring specifically to the Union's environmental policy in its decision. The Commission reached a similar conclusion when it informally settled cases relating to 'environmental' agreements for water heaters and dishwashers[96].

It is clear, therefore, that a number of factors appear to have been influential in decisions under Article 101(3), not all of which were 'narrow' improvements in economic efficiency. It is important to note, however, that these decisions were all taken during the years when the Commission enjoyed a monopoly over decision-making under Article 101(3). The Commission is well placed to take into account public and private interests and the requirements of different EU policies under Article 101(3)[97]. In *Métropole télévision v Commission*[98] the General Court said that 'in the context of an overall assessment, the Commission is entitled to base itself on considerations *connected with the pursuit of the public interest* in order to grant exemption under Article [101(3)]' (emphasis added)[99].

It is also worth mentioning in passing that 'public interest' criteria can be relevant when deciding whether Article 101(1) is infringed, as the Court of Justice's judgments in *Wouters*[100], and other cases[101], have demonstrated: indeed the suppression of non-economic considerations under Article 101(3) might result in their re-emergence under the *Wouters* case law. Public interest issues are also relevant when deciding whether Article 106(2) permits a derogation from the application of Article 101(1)[102].

(iii) **Comment**

This discussion shows that, over a number of years, there has been uncertainty—even confusion—as to what, exactly, Article 101(3) is intended to achieve. As long as the Commission enjoyed a monopoly over decision-making under Regulation 17 this may not have been too serious a problem: the Commission enjoyed a 'margin of appreciation' when applying Article 101(3)[103] and it would hardly be surprising if, when making

[91] Case T-193/02 EU:T:2005:22, paras 100–106. [92] OJ [1994] L 131/15.

[93] Ibid, paras 27–28. [94] OJ [2000] L 187/47.

[95] Ibid, paras 55–57; see similarly paras 268–271 of the Commission's decision in *ARA, ARGEV*, Commission decision of 17 October 2003, upheld on appeal Case T-419/03 *Altstoff Recycling Austria AG v Commission* EU:T:2011:102.

[96] Commission Press Release IP/01/1659, 26 November 2001; see also the Commission's (2002) 1 Competition Policy Newsletter 50.

[97] The Dutch Competition Authority has published a position paper and an online 'knowledge bank' on the compatibility with competition law of agreements that promote 'sustainable development': available at www.acm.nl/en.

[98] Cases T-528/93 etc EU:T:1996:99; see similarly Case T-168/01 *GlaxoSmithKline Services Unlimited v Commission* EU:T:2006:265, para 244.

[99] Cases T-528/93 etc EU:T:1996:99, para 118.

[100] Case C-309/99 EU:C:2002:98; this case law is discussed in ch 3, 'Regulatory ancillarity: the judgment of the Court of Justice in *Wouters*', pp 138–141.

[101] See eg Case C-1/12 *OTOC* EU:C:2013:127. [102] See ch 6, 'Article 106(2)', pp 242–248.

[103] See Cases 56/64 and 58/64 *Consten and Grundig v Commission* EU:C:1966:41.

decisions in individual cases from 1962 to 2004, it was influenced, at least sometimes, by issues other than economic efficiency. However Regulation 1/2003 makes it necessary to decide on the true content of Article 101(3) because decisions since 1 May 2004 can be made by NCAs and national courts as well as by the Commission itself.

In the authors' view, Article 101(3) should be interpreted in a narrow rather than a broad manner, according to clear legal standards. This would be consistent with both the wording of Article 101(3) and the recitals to the various block exemptions which explain the reasons for permitting certain agreements under Article 101(3) purely in terms of economic efficiency. NCAs and national courts, and the undertakings that enter into agreements that might be challenged under Article 101, need to know the limits of what can be justified under Article 101(3). These institutions, unlike the Commission, seem ill-placed to balance a restriction of competition under Article 101(1) against a broad range of EU policies under Article 101(3). NCAs and national courts do not appear to have had difficulty in considering only economic efficiencies under Article 101(3). In 2009 the Commission reported that 'neither the case practice of the Commission and the national enforcers, nor the experience reported by the business and legal community, indicate major difficulties with the direct application of Article [101(3)] which has been widely welcomed by stakeholders'[104].

(iv) The Commission's approach in the *Article 101(3) Guidelines*

It is clear from the Commission's *Article 101(3) Guidelines* that its view is that Article 101(3) should be applied according to the narrow approach based on economic efficiency[105]. Paragraph 11 of the *Guidelines* states that Article 101(3) allows 'pro-competitive benefits' to be taken into account under Article 101(3), and that these may outweigh any 'anti-competitive effects' under Article 101(1). Paragraph 32 of the *Guidelines* speaks of the 'positive economic effects' of agreements that can be taken into consideration under Article 101(3). Paragraph 33 refers to the achievement of 'pro-competitive effects by way of efficiency gains', explaining that efficiencies may create additional value by lowering the cost of producing an output, improving the quality of the product or creating a new product. Significantly paragraph 42 of the *Guidelines* explicitly states that '[g]oals pursued by other Treaty provisions can be taken into account only to the extent that they can be subsumed under the four conditions of Article 101(3)'. When the *Guidelines*, at paragraphs 48 to 72, reach the point of discussing the first condition of Article 101(3)—an improvement in production or distribution or in technical or economic progress—they do so specifically under the heading of 'efficiency gains', thereby removing any lingering doubt that might still remain that the Commission considers that other, non-economic, considerations could be relevant to the assessment. Similarly paragraph 20 of the Commission's *Guidelines on Horizontal Cooperation Agreements*[106] says that Article 101(3) asks whether any pro-competitive effects of an agreement outweigh its restrictive effects on competition.

It appears that NCAs and national courts are happy to take a lead from the *Article 101(3) Guidelines*[107], although it is obviously open to undertakings to argue that they

[104] *Report on the functioning of Regulation 1/2003*, COM(2009) 206 final, para 12.

[105] It is also noticeable that the approach taken in the *Guidelines* is consistent with the Commission's *Guidelines on the assessment of horizontal mergers* OJ [2004] C 31/5, paras 76–90 and its *Guidance on the Commission's enforcement priorities in applying Article [102 TFEU] to abusive exclusionary conduct by dominant undertakings* OJ [2009] C 45/7, paras 28–31, 46, 62, 74 and 89–90.

[106] OJ [2011] C 11/1; see also *Guidelines on Vertical Restraints* OJ [2010] C 130/1, para 122.

[107] See eg *Asda Stores Ltd v MasterCard Inc* [2017] EWHC 93 (Comm), para 261 citing para 33 of the *Article 101(3) Guidelines* on the economic rationale of Article 101(3) TFEU.

do not fully reflect the jurisprudence of the EU Courts. There may be litigation in the future in which the EU Courts will have to reconsider some of the statements in cases such as *Metro*[108] and *Remia and Nutricia*[109] and decide whether to insist on the narrower, and more justiciable, approach suggested by the Commission. In *GlaxoSmithKline v Commission* the EU Courts addressed GSK's arguments that it had satisfied the first condition of Article 101(3) under the heading 'Evidence of a gain in efficiency', suggesting that they were comfortable with a narrow approach to that provision[110]. In *MasterCard*[111], *Cartes Bancaires*[112] and *Lundbeck*[113] the EU Courts were content to focus solely on efficiencies under Article 101(3).

Paragraph 51 of the *Article 101(3) Guidelines* stresses that all efficiency claims must be substantiated in order to verify:

- the *nature* of the claimed efficiencies, so that it is possible for the decision-maker to verify that they are objective in nature[114]
- the *link* between the agreement and the efficiencies which, as a general proposition, should be direct rather than indirect[115]
- the *likelihood* and *magnitude* of each claimed efficiency and
- *how* and *when* each claimed efficiency would be achieved.

The decision-maker must be able to verify the value of the claimed efficiencies in order to be able to balance them against the anti-competitive effects of the agreement[116]. The Commission's requirement that undertakings must substantiate their claims is an important feature of the *Article 101(3) Guidelines* and its decisional practice since May 2004. Mere speculation or conjecture will be insufficient: there must be 'convincing arguments and evidence'[117] that the agreement will lead to the efficiencies claimed, the burden being on the parties seeking to defend it. In *Lundbeck*[118] the General Court rejected the parties' arguments that their patent settlement agreements had led to efficiencies as it considered that they failed to produce adequate evidence.

The Commission identifies two broad categories of efficiencies in the *Guidelines*, while acknowledging that it is not appropriate to draw clear and firm distinctions between them[119].

(a) *Cost efficiencies*

Paragraphs 64 to 68 consider cost efficiencies which may result, for example, from the development of new production technologies and methods[120], synergies arising from the

108 Case 26/76 EU:C:1977:167. 109 Case 42/84 EU:C:1985:327.

110 Case T-168/01 EU:T:2006:265, paras 247–308; the General Court's judgment in relation to Article 101(3) was upheld on appeal to the Court of Justice, Cases C-501/06 P etc *GlaxoSmithKline Services Unlimited v Commission* EU:C:2009:610, paras 68–168.

111 Case T-111/08 *MasterCard v Commission* EU:T:2012:260, paras 194–237, upheld on appeal to the Court of Justice, Case C-382/12 P *MasterCard v Commission* EU:C:2014:2201.

112 Case T-491/07 RENV *Cartes Bancaires v Commission* EU:T:2016:379, paras 361–465.

113 Case T-469/13 *Generics (UK) v Commission* EU:T:2016:454, paras 344–366.

114 *Article 101(3) Guidelines*, para 52.

115 Ibid, paras 53 and 54; the link between the agreement and the efficiencies was emphasised in *Asda Stores Ltd v MasterCard Inc* [2017] EWHC 93 (Comm), paras 264–265, 272 and 277.

116 *Article 101(3) Guidelines*, paras 55–58.

117 See Case T-168/01 *GlaxoSmithKline Services Unlimited v Commission* EU:T:2006:265, para 235, upheld on appeal Cases C-501/06 P etc *GlaxoSmithKline Services Unlimited v Commission* EU:C:2009:610, para 82; see also the Opinion of AG Mengozzi in Case C-382/12 P *MasterCard v Commission* EU:C:2009:409, para 141 and case law cited.

118 Commission decision of 19 June 2013, para 1218, upheld on appeal on this ground Case T-469/13 *Generics (UK) v Commission* EU:T:2016:454, paras 344–366, on appeal Case C-588/16 P, not yet decided.

119 *Article 101(3) Guidelines*, para 59. 120 Ibid, para 64.

integration of existing assets[121], from economies of scale[122], economies of scope[123] and from better planning of production[124].

(b) *Qualitative efficiencies*

Paragraphs 69 to 72 consider qualitative efficiencies as opposed to cost reductions: research and development agreements are particularly cited in this respect[125], as are licensing agreements and agreements for the joint production of new or improved goods or services[126]; there is also a reference to the possibility of distribution agreements delivering qualitative efficiencies[127].

(B) Third condition of Article 101(3): indispensability of the restrictions

The *Article 101(3) Guidelines* deal with the indispensability of restrictions before the question of a fair share for consumers, since the latter issue would not arise if the restrictions are not indispensable[128]. Paragraph 73 states that the indispensability condition implies a two-fold test: first, whether the restrictive agreement itself is reasonably necessary to achieve the efficiencies; and secondly whether the individual restrictions of competition flowing from the agreement are reasonably necessary for the attainment of the efficiencies. In *MasterCard*[129] the Court of Justice held that the requirement of indispensability in Article 101(3) is conceptually distinct from the ancillary restraints doctrine; the *Guidelines* explain that Article 101(3) involves a balancing of pro- and anti-competitive effects, which is not the case when determining whether a restraint is ancillary[130].

(i) The efficiencies must be specific to the agreement

Paragraphs 75 to 77 consider the first part of the two-fold test: the requirement that the efficiencies are specific to the agreement or, to put the point another way, that there are no other economically practicable and less restrictive means of achieving them[131]. The parties should explain, for example, why they could not have achieved the same efficiencies acting alone[132]. In *OTOC*[133] a system of compulsory training for chartered accountants in Portugal did not satisfy the terms of Article 101(3) because it was not considered to be 'essential' for guaranteeing the quality of accountancy services.

(ii) The indispensability of individual restrictions

Paragraphs 78 to 82 consider whether any individual restrictions of competition flowing from the agreement are indispensable. The parties must demonstrate both that the nature of any restriction and that its 'intensity' are reasonably necessary to produce the claimed efficiencies[134]. A restriction is indispensable if its absence would eliminate or significantly reduce the efficiencies that follow from the agreement or make it significantly less likely

[121] Ibid, para 65. [122] Ibid, para 66. [123] Ibid, para 67. [124] Ibid, para 68.

[125] Ibid, para 70. [126] Ibid, para 71.

[127] Ibid, para 72; accepting payment cards was a qualitative 'benefit' to merchants since it made them more attractive to consumers in *Asda Stores Ltd v MasterCard Inc* [2017] EWHC 93 (Comm), paras 316–328.

[128] Ibid, para 39. [129] Case C-382/12 P *MasterCard v Commission* EU:C:2014:2201, paras 92–93.

[130] *Article 101(3) Guidelines*, para 30.

[131] Ibid, para 75; note that under para 85 of the Commission's *Guidelines on the assessment of horizontal mergers* OJ [2004] C 31/5 efficiencies are recognised in the assessment of mergers only where they can be shown to be merger-specific: see further ch 21, 'Efficiencies', pp 897–898.

[132] *Article 101(3) Guidelines*, para 76.

[133] Case C-1/12 *Ordem dos Técnicos Oficiais de Contas* EU:C:2013:127, para 103.

[134] *Article 101(3) Guidelines*, para 78; the Commission will only intervene where it is reasonably clear that there are realistic and attainable alternatives.

that they will materialise[135]. A restriction may be indispensable only for a certain period; once that time has expired, it will cease to be so[136].

'Hard-core' restrictions in any of the block exemptions—for example horizontal price fixing and the imposition of export bans in vertical agreements—are unlikely to be indispensable[137]. In *Lundbeck*[138] the patent settlements contained restrictions on potential competitors' behaviour that were not indispensable to avoid litigation costs as an alternative, less restrictive settlement was possible. An agreement between undertakings aimed at forcing a third party to comply with the law does not contain indispensable restrictions where it is possible for them to lodge a complaint with competent public authorities to deal with the problem[139].

(C) Second condition of Article 101(3): fair share for consumers

The undertakings concerned must show that a fair share of the benefit that results from an agreement will accrue to consumers if Article 101(3) is to apply: it is helpful to think of this as the 'pass-on' requirement. Paragraph 84 of the *Article 101(3) Guidelines* states that the concept of consumers in Article 101(3) encompasses all direct or indirect users of the products covered by the agreement, including producers that use the products as an input, wholesalers, retailers and final consumers; 'undertakings', in the competition law sense of the term[140], can be consumers for this purpose just as much as a natural person who purchases as a consumer in the lay sense. It is the overall effect on all consumers in the relevant markets that must be taken into consideration under this part of Article 101(3), not the effect on each member of that category of consumers[141].

Where an agreement affects two groups of consumers the parties must show that it yields a fair share to both groups[142]. Negative effects on consumers in one geographic or product market cannot normally be balanced against and compensated by positive effects for consumers in unrelated markets, although this may be possible where markets are related provided that the consumers affected by the restriction and benefiting from the efficiency gains are substantially the same[143].

In *Star Alliance*[144] the Commission slightly relaxed the test set out in the *Guidelines* by taking into account 'out of market efficiencies' where there was 'considerable commonality' between consumers on different markets[145]. If an agreement would leave consumers

[135] Ibid, para 79. [136] Ibid, para 81.

[137] Ibid, para 79; for 'blacklisted' clauses in block exemptions see ch 15, 'Article 4: hard-core restrictions', pp 614–615 (specialisation agreements) and 'Article 5: hard-core restrictions', pp 610–611 (research and development agreements); ch 16, 'Article 4: hard-core restrictions', pp 677–684 (vertical agreements); and ch 19, 'Article 4: hard-core restrictions', pp 802–806 (technology transfer agreements).

[138] Case T-472/13 *Lundbeck v Commission* EU:T:2016:449, para 719.

[139] Case C-68/12 *Protimonopolný úad Slovenskej republky v Slovenská sporiteľňa a.s.* EU:C:2013:71, paras 29–36.

[140] See ch 3, 'Undertakings and Associations of Undertakings', pp 83–101.

[141] Case C-238/05 *Asnef-Equifax v Asociación de Usuarios de Servicios Bancarios (Ausbanc)* EU:C:2006:734, para 70; Case C-382/12 P *MasterCard v Commission* EU:C:2014:2201, para 236; *Asda Stores Ltd v MasterCard Inc* [2017] EWHC 93 (Comm), para 288.

[142] Case T-111/08 *MasterCard v Commission* EU:T:2012:260, para 228; this specific point was not discussed in the Court of Justice's judgment upholding the General Court's judgment, Case C-382/12 P *MasterCard v Commission* EU:C:2014:2201, para 248.

[143] *Article 101(3) Guidelines*, para 43. [144] Commission decision of 23 May 2013.

[145] Ibid, paras 55–80, in particular paras 57–58; Commission Press Release IP/13/456, 23 May 2013; see also speech by Alexander Italianer, former Director-General of DG COMP, 'Competitor agreements under EU competition law', 26 September 2013, available at www.ec.europa.eu/competition/speeches; see also Ducci 'Out-of-Market Efficiencies, Two-Sided Platforms, and Consumer Welfare: A Legal and Economic Analysis' (2016) 12 Journal of Competition Law and Economics 591.

worse off than they would otherwise have been the pass-on condition of Article 101(3) will not have been satisfied[146]; consumers must obtain greater benefits from the agreement than the anti-competitive disadvantage it imposes on them. However, consumers do not have to gain from each and every efficiency achieved, provided that they receive a fair share of the overall benefits[147].

It may be that the pass-on condition is not met if a group of consumers were to bear an unfair proportion of the cost compared with others on whom a restriction of competition conferred relevant benefits[148]. It could be the case that an agreement, for example to produce a new product more quickly than if the parties had proceeded alone, might also lead to greater market power and therefore higher prices; the Commission does not rule out that early access to the new products might amount to a 'fair share' of the benefit for consumers, notwithstanding the higher prices[149]. In *MasterCard* the Commission said that if an agreement is likely to lead to higher prices, consumers must be compensated through increased quality or other benefits[150].

The greater the restriction of competition under Article 101(1), the greater must be the efficiency and the pass-on under Article 101(3)[151]; and where an agreement has substantial anti-competitive and substantial pro-competitive effects paragraph 92 of the *Guidelines* states that the decision-maker should consider that competition is an important long-term driver of efficiency and innovation. The *Guidelines* proceed to discuss the pass-on requirement in relation to cost efficiencies and qualitative efficiencies respectively.

(i) Cost efficiencies

Paragraphs 95 to 101 consider pass-on and the balancing of cost efficiencies. Paragraph 96 notes that cost efficiencies may lead to increased output and lower prices for consumers: in assessing whether this is likely the following factors should be taken into account:

- the characteristics and structure of the market
- the nature and magnitude of the efficiency gains
- the elasticity of demand and
- the magnitude of the restriction of competition.

Paragraph 98 points out that consumers are more likely to benefit from a reduction in the parties' variable costs than in their fixed costs, since pricing and output decisions are determined predominantly by variable costs and demand conditions. Paragraph 99 explains that the actual rate of any pass-on to consumers will depend on the extent to which consumers will expand their demand in response to a lowering of price; this will depend, among other things, on the extent to which sellers are able to discriminate in price between different categories of customers. Paragraph 101 cautions that any reduction in costs, and therefore any prospect of lower prices for consumers, must be balanced against the fact that an agreement being considered under Article 101(3) must necessarily involve a restriction of competition under Article 101(1), which in itself is likely to mean that the parties have the ability to raise their prices as a result of their increased market power: these 'opposing forces' must be balanced against one another.

[146] Commission decision of 23 May 2013, para 85. [147] *Article 101(3) Guidelines*, para 86.

[148] *Asda Stores Ltd v MasterCard Inc* [2017] EWHC 93 (Comm), paras 282 and 286 (rejecting, *obiter*, a 'global approach' assessing all benefits of an agreement against all its detriments).

[149] *Article 101(3) Guidelines*, para 89.

[150] Commission decision of 19 December 2007, para 734, upheld on appeal Case T-111/08 *MasterCard v Commission* EU:T:2012:260, and on further appeal Case C-382/12 P EU:C:2014:2201, para 234.

[151] *Article 101(3) Guidelines*, para 90.

(ii) Qualitative efficiencies

Paragraphs 102 to 104 consider pass-on and the balancing of other types of efficiencies: for example the emergence of a new and improved product might compensate for the fact that an agreement leads to higher prices. Paragraph 103 concedes that this involves a value judgment and that it is difficult to assign precise values to a balancing exercise of this nature. Paragraph 104 acknowledges that new and improved products are an important source of consumer welfare; it continues that, where prices will be higher as a result of the restrictive effect of the agreement on competition, it is necessary to consider whether the claimed efficiencies will create 'real value' for consumers that will compensate for this.

(D) Fourth condition of Article 101(3): no elimination of competition in a substantial part of the market

Paragraph 105 of the *Article 101(3) Guidelines* states that ultimately the protection of the competitive process is given priority over pro-competitive efficiency gains that result from restrictive agreements.

(i) The relationship between Article 101(3) and Article 102

Paragraph 106 of the *Guidelines* explains that the concept of elimination of competition in a substantial part of the market is an autonomous EU concept specific to Article 101(3). Paragraph 106 then considers the relationship between Article 101(3) and Article 102. It refers to case law that establishes that Article 101(3) cannot prevent the application of Article 102[152] and that Article 101(3) cannot apply to agreements that constitute an abuse of a dominant position[153]. Paragraph 106 goes on to explain, however, that not all restrictive agreements concluded by a dominant undertaking necessarily constitute an abuse of a dominant position. The Court of Justice has confirmed that efficiencies are firmly part of Article 102 analysis; the criteria on efficiencies under Article 102 are closely modelled upon the conditions of Article 101(3)[154]. The fact that most block exemptions contain market share caps means that dominant firms will rarely be in a position to rely on them[155].

(ii) Determining whether competition will be substantially eliminated

Paragraphs 107 to 116 explain how to assess whether an agreement will substantially eliminate competition. Paragraph 107 states that it is necessary to evaluate the extent to which competition will be reduced as a result of the agreement: the more that competition is already weakened in the market before the agreement, and the more that the agreement will reduce competition in the market, the more likely it is that the agreement will be considered to eliminate competition substantially. Both actual and potential competition should be taken into account when making the assessment[156]. The degree of actual competition in the market should not be assessed on the basis of

[152] See Cases C-395/96 P etc *Compagnie Maritime Belge Transports SA v Commission* EU:C:2000:132, para 130.

[153] Case T-51/89 *Tetra Pak Rausing SA v Commission* EU:T:1990:41, para 28, and Cases T-191/98 etc *Atlantic Container Line v Commission* EU:T:2003:245, para 1456; in *Decca Navigator System* OJ [1989] L 43/27, para 122, the Commission refused to apply Article 101(3) to an agreement that involved an abuse of a dominant position.

[154] Case C-209/10 *Post Danmark A/S v Konkurrencerådet* EU:C:2012:172, paras 41–42.

[155] See 'The format of block exemptions', pp 178–179 later in this chapter.

[156] *Article 101(3) Guidelines*, paras 108 and 114.

market shares alone, but should be based on more extensive qualitative and quantitative analysis[157]. The *Article 101(3) Guidelines* set out a series of factors that should be taken into account when assessing entry barriers and the possibility of entry into the market on a significant scale, including, for example, the cost of entry including sunk costs, the minimum efficient scale within the industry and the competitive strengths of potential entrants[158].

(E) Judicial review by the General Court

The Commission's decisions on the application of Article 101(3) are subject to judicial review by the General Court and (on a point of law) by the Court of Justice[159]. In *Consten and Grundig v Commission*[160] the Court of Justice indicated that it would not adopt an interventionist stance on applications for annulment. The EU Courts have maintained this approach, emphasising the extent of the margin of appreciation available to the Commission when applying Article 101(3) and (by implication) their unwillingness to interfere with the exercise of this appreciation[161].

Despite their recognition of the margin of appreciation enjoyed by the Commission, the EU Courts have intervened on some occasions. For example in *European Night Services v Commission*[162] the General Court annulled the Commission's decision applying Article 101(3) to a joint venture established by five rail operators to provide overnight services through the Channel Tunnel as it had failed to explain how the agreement infringed Article 101(1) in the first place[163]. The General Court will also annul a Commission decision where it has misapprehended the facts of a particular case[164]. For example in *GlaxoSmithKline v Commission*[165] the General Court annulled the Commission's decision that GSK's standard conditions of sale, which were intended to prevent parallel trade from the low-priced Spanish pharmaceutical market to the higher-priced UK one, did not satisfy the criteria of Article 101(3): GSK argued that the restriction of trade was necessary to promote investment into research and development in the sector. The General Court held that the Commission had failed to carry out a proper examination of the factual arguments and evidence put forward by GSK or to refute its arguments[166]. On appeal the Court of Justice held that the General Court had stated the position accurately and dismissed the Commission's argument that it had misapplied the case law on the burden and standard of proof under Article 101(3)[167].

Other cases in which the Commission's findings under Article 101(3) have been overturned include the Court of Justice's judgment in *Publishers Association v Commission*[168] and the judgments of the General Court in *Métropole télévision v Commission*[169] and *Métropole télévision (M6) v Commission*[170].

[157] Ibid, para 109. [158] Ibid, para 115.

[159] See generally Bailey 'Scope of Judicial Review under Article 81 EC' (2004) 41 CML Rev 1327.

[160] Cases 56/64 and 58/64 EU:C:1966:41.

[161] See eg Case 26/76 *Metro SB-Grossmärkte GmbH v Commission* EU:C:1977:167, paras 45 and 50; Case T-7/93 *Langnese-Iglo GmbH v Commission* EU:T:1995:98, para 178.

[162] Cases T-374/94 etc *European Night Services v Commission* EU:T:1998:198, paras 205–221; see also Case C-360/92 P *Publishers Association v Commission* EU:C:1995:6.

[163] Article 296 TFEU provides that legal acts, such as decisions by the Commission, shall state the reasons on which they are based.

[164] Cases T-79/95 and 80/95 *SNCF and British Railways v Commission* EU:T:1996:155.

[165] Case T-168/01 EU:T:2006:265. [166] Ibid, paras 247–308.

[167] Cases C-501/06 P etc *GlaxoSmithKline Services Unlimited v Commission* EU:C:2009:610, paras 78–88.

[168] Case C-360/92 P EU:C:1995:6. [169] Cases T-528/93 etc EU:T:1996:99.

[170] Cases T-185/00 etc EU:T:2002:242.

3. Regulation 1/2003

(A) The Commission's former monopoly over the grant of individual exemptions

Under Regulation 17 of 1962 the Commission had sole power (subject to review by the EU Courts) to grant 'individual exemptions' to agreements that met the criteria in Article 101(3)[171]. This monopoly over the grant of individual exemptions meant that the Commission had the opportunity to develop its policy towards various types of agreement over a period of time, and in some cases to give expression to this policy in its block exemption regulations. However the monopoly had many drawbacks: the Commission never had sufficient staff to deal with the enormous volume of agreements that were notified to it: the result was that severe delays were experienced; considerable business time was spent collecting the data and preparing the so-called 'Form A/B' on which notifications had to be submitted; substantial expense was incurred, not least on legal and other professional fees; and businesses faced a long period of uncertainty as to the lawfulness of their agreements. The Commission was overburdened with notifications, many of which concerned agreements that had no seriously anti-competitive effect, with the consequence that it was distracted from other tasks, such as the pursuit of cartels and abusive behaviour, which are of much greater significance for the public interest: as recital 3 of Regulation 1/2003 says, 'the system of notification ... prevents the Commission from concentrating its resources on curbing the most serious infringements. It also imposes considerable costs on undertakings'. The problem of the monopoly over the grant of individual exemptions was a real one, and this led the Commission, in the *White Paper on Modernisation* of 1999, to propose abolition of the process of notification altogether; this policy was carried into effect by Regulation 1/2003.

(B) The end of the system of notification for individual exemption

Regulation 1/2003 ended the system of notification for individual exemption with effect from 1 May 2004. Previous editions of this book explained in detail how the system of individual exemptions operated[172].

(C) Self-assessment

The fact that undertakings and their lawyers can no longer notify agreements to the Commission and await an administrative 'stamp of approval' certifying that the criteria of Article 101(3) are satisfied means that they must now be self-reliant and conduct their own 'self-assessment' of the application of that provision. This caused consternation in the business and legal communities at the time that Regulation 1/2003 was being debated; however in practice self-assessment seems to have worked well. This was the conclusion reached by the Commission in its *Report on the functioning of Regulation 1/2003*[173]. A useful Report, *Practical methods to assess efficiency gains in the context of Article [101(3) of the TFEU]*[174], provides a structured framework on how to conduct a self-assessment

[171] Regulation 17, JO [1962] 204/62, Article 9(1).

[172] See the fourth edition, ch 4, pp 136–141; see also Roth and Rose (eds) *Bellamy and Child: European Community Law of Competition* (Sweet & Maxwell, 6th ed, 2008), paras 13-004–13-016.

[173] COM(2009) 206 final, para 12; see further the accompanying Staff Working Paper, SEC(2009) 574 final, para 11; both documents are available at www.ec.europa.eu.

[174] Available at www.bookshop.europa.eu; note that this Report was commissioned by DG Enterprise and Industry rather than DG COMP.

of efficiency claims under Article 101(3); and DG COMP has published best practices concerning the generation as well as the presentation of relevant economic and empirical evidence that may be taken into account in the assessment of competition cases[175]. The judgments of the Competition Appeal Tribunal and High Court in *MasterCard*[176] and of the High Court in *Visa*[177] also provide helpful insights into how Article 101(3) is applied in practice.

(D) **Decision-making under Article 101(3)**

Regulation 1/2003 provides three ways in which the Commission may indicate that an agreement that infringes Article 101 is lawful because it satisfies Article 101(3):

- the acceptance of legally-binding commitments under Article 9
- a finding of inapplicability under Article 10 and
- the provision of informal guidance.

Each of these possibilities is discussed in chapter 7. A few observations may be made here about these provisions. The first is that there have been several Article 9 decisions in cases concerning the possible application of Article 101(3)[178]. A notable example is *British Airways, American Airlines and Iberia*[179] where the Commission accepted commitments, in particular to make landing and take-off slots available at Heathrow, Gatwick and JFK-New York airports, in order to facilitate entry and/or expansion by competitors on various aviation routes from and to the US. Article 9 decisions lead to the Commission closing the case, without any finding of infringement, and as such are conceptually different from individual exemption decisions of the kind that used to be adopted under Regulation 17: under that Regulation the Commission would find that Article 101(1) was inapplicable because Article 101(3) was satisfied. Nevertheless there is a certain resemblance between an Article 9 decision, where the parties formally commit to change their behaviour and could be punished if they were to deviate from that commitment, and an individual exemption under the old system granted subject to conditions and obligations[180].

A second point is that Article 10 and the informal guidance procedure have yet to be used[181]. It is the authors' opinion that judicious use of these procedures by the Commission would be helpful. Since the abolition of individual exemption the Commission has often concluded that Article 101(3) did not apply to an agreement, but it has never adopted an Article 10 decision positively applying that provision. It is understandable that the

175 DG COMP's *Best Practices for the Submission of Economic Evidence and Data Collection in Cases Concerning the Application of Articles 101 and 102 TFEU and in Merger Cases*, available at www.ec.europa.eu/competition.

176 Case 1241/5/7/15 (T) *Sainsbury's Supermarkets Ltd v MasterCard Inc* [2016] CAT 11, paras 280–289; *Asda Stores Ltd v MasterCard Inc* [2017] EWHC 93 (Comm), paras 261–421.

177 *Sainsbury's Supermarkets Ltd v Visa Europe Services LLC* [2018] EWHC 355 (Comm).

178 On commitment decisions see ch 7, 'Article 9: commitments', pp 264–269; Article 9 decisions considering Article 101(3) include: *Visa Europe*, Commission decision of 8 December 2010, on which see (2011) 1 Competition Policy Newsletter 13; *Siemens/Areva*, Commission decision of 18 June 2012; *Continental/United/Lufthansa/Air Canada*, Commission decision of 23 May 2013; *Cross-border access to pay-TV*, Commission decision of 26 July 2016, on appeal Case T-873/16 *Groupe Canal+ v Commission*, not yet decided.

179 Commission decision of 14 July 2010.

180 On commitment decisions see ch 7, 'Article 9: commitments', pp 264–269.

181 See ch 7, 'Article 10: finding of inapplicability' and 'Informal guidance', pp 269–270; in the UK the OFT (now the CMA) issued one Opinion and one short-form Opinion on the domestic equivalent of Article 101(3): see ch 10, 'Opinions and Informal Advice', pp 412–413.

Commission does not want the Article 10 procedure to become a surrogate for the old system of individual exemption for agreements. However the absence of any positive applications of Article 101(3) contributes to a sense, which seems to be quite widely held, that it is simply too difficult to satisfy the criteria of Article 101(3); and perhaps impossible in the case of an object restriction. This means that the lawfulness of an agreement is argued predominantly by reference to the question of what is a restriction of competition for the purposes of Article 101(1). A finding of a restriction of competition would be less problematic if it could be seen—by reference to decided cases as well as to Commission guidance—that Article 101(3) remains available for efficiency-enhancing agreements. The Commission's *Final Report on the E-commerce Sector Inquiry* is helpful in that it identifies various restrictions of competition to which Article 101(3) might be applicable in an individual case[182]. Furthermore it was reported in June 2017 that the Commissioner for Competition had told the European Parliament's Committee on Agricultural and Rural Development that informal guidance or an Article 10 decision might be provided for cooperation between Spanish producers of olive oil[183].

(E) **Notification and individual exemptions under domestic law**

Regulation 1/2003 does not *require* Member States to abolish systems of notification for exemption under *domestic* law; however it would seem in principle to be undesirable to maintain a domestic system of notification[184]. As at 8 December 2017 only Denmark, Italy and Latvia retained a system of notification.

4. Block Exemptions

(A) **Role of block exemptions**

Article 101(3) foreshadowed the advent of block exemptions by providing that the prohibition in Article 101(1) could be declared inapplicable both in relation to agreements and to *categories* of agreements[185]; in other words the Treaty envisages the generic authorisation of agreements as well as pursuant to individual assessment. Most block exemptions are adopted by the Commission, acting under powers conferred upon it by regulations of the Council[186].

Agreements within the terms of a block exemption are valid without specific authorisation. There is much to be said for drafting, for example, a vertical agreement or a transfer technology agreement so that it satisfies the terms of the relevant block exemption as this provides a 'safe harbour' for it; if an agreement satisfies a block exemption, there may be little point in determining whether it infringes Article 101(1) in the first place[187].

[182] Final Report and Staff Working Document, both of 10 May 2017, available at www.ec.europa.eu/competition.

[183] A report to this effect can be found on MLex on 22 June 2017.

[184] See ch 4 n 173 earlier.

[185] The terms 'bloc' and 'group' exemptions are also used: the expression 'block exemption' is used here as it is the most common one, and the one normally used by the Commission.

[186] See '*Vires* and block exemptions currently in force', pp 177–178 later in chapter. There have been two exceptions to this, where the Council itself granted the block exemption: the block exemption for certain agreements in the road and inland waterway sectors was originally provided by Article 4 of Council Regulation 1017/68, OJ [1968] L 175/1, and is now to be found in Article 3 of Council Regulation 169/2009, OJ 2009 L 61/1; and the block exemption for various agreements in the containerised shipping segment of the maritime transport sector was granted by Articles 3 to 6 of Council Regulation 4056/86, OJ [1986] L 378/1: this block exemption was repealed with effect from October 2008 by Council Regulation 1419/2006, OJ [2006] L 269/1.

[187] See Case C-260/07 *Pedro IV Servicios SL v Total España SA* EU:C:2009:215, para 36.

As paragraph 2 of the Commission's *Article 101(3) Guidelines* points out, the system of block exemptions remains in effect, notwithstanding the abolition of individual exemptions as a result of Regulation 1/2003. Paragraph 2 of the *Guidelines* also says that an agreement that is covered by a block exemption cannot be declared invalid by a national court. Article 29 of that Regulation provides the Commission and NCAs, in certain circumstances, with a power to withdraw the benefit of a block exemption in an individual case[188]. A national court cannot withdraw the benefit of a block exemption[189].

(B) ***Vires* and block exemptions currently in force**

The Commission requires authority from the Council to issue block exemptions[190]. The Council has published a number of empowering Regulations; these are listed, along with the Commission Regulations currently in force (if any) under each Council Regulation:

(i) Council Regulation 19/65

Regulation 19/65[191], as amended by Regulation 1215/99[192], authorises the Commission to grant block exemption to vertical agreements and to bilateral licences of intellectual property rights. The following Commission Regulations are in force under Council Regulation 19/65:

- Regulation 330/2010 on vertical agreements[193]; Regulation 330/2010 is discussed in chapter 16[194]
- Regulation 461/2010[195] on vertical agreements relating to the motor vehicle aftermarket; Regulation 461/2010 is discussed in chapter 16[196]
- Regulation 316/2014 on technology transfer agreements[197]; Regulation 316/2014 is discussed in chapter 19[198].

(ii) Council Regulation 2821/71

Regulation 2821/71[199] authorises the Commission to grant block exemption in respect of standardisation agreements, research and development agreements and specialisation agreements. The following Commission Regulations are in force under Council Regulation 2821/71:

- Regulation 1217/2010[200] on research and development agreements; Regulation 1217/2010 is discussed in chapter 15[201]
- Regulation 1218/2010[202] on specialisation agreements; Regulation 1218/2010 is discussed in chapter 15[203].

[188] See 'The format of block exemptions', pp 178–179 later in chapter.
[189] See *Article 101(3) Guidelines*, para 31.
[190] The Council has power to confer such *vires* by virtue of Article 103(2)(b) TFEU.
[191] OJ [1965] p 533, OJ [1965–66] p 35. [192] OJ [1999] L 148/1.
[193] OJ [2010] L 102/1; this Regulation replaced Regulation 2790/99, OJ [1999] L 336/21.
[194] See ch 16, 'Vertical Agreements: Regulation 330/2010', pp 664–687.
[195] OJ [2010] L 129/52; Regulation 461/2010 replaced Regulation 1400/2002, OJ [2002] L 203/30.
[196] See ch 16, 'Regulation 461/2010 on Motor Vehicle Distribution', pp 689–691.
[197] OJ [2014] L 193/17; this Regulation replaced Regulation 772/2004, OJ [2004] L 123/11.
[198] See ch 19, 'Technology Transfer Agreements: Regulation 316/2014', pp 798–807.
[199] OJ [1971] L 285/46, OJ [1971] p 1032.
[200] OJ [2010] L 335/36; this Regulation replaced Regulation 2659/2000, OJ [2000] L 304/7.
[201] See ch 15, 'The block exemption for research and development agreements: Regulation 1217/2010', pp 607–611.
[202] OJ [2010] L 335/43; this Regulation replaced Regulation 2658/2000, OJ [2000] L 304/3.
[203] See ch 15, 'The block exemption for specialisation agreements: Regulation 1218/2010', pp 613–615.

(iii) Council Regulation 1534/91

Regulation 1534/91[204] authorises the Commission to grant block exemption in the insurance sector. There are no Commission Regulations granting block exemption under Regulation 1534/91[205].

(iv) Council Regulation 169/2009

Council Regulation 169/2009[206] itself provides block exemption for certain agreements between small and medium-sized undertakings in the road and inland waterway sectors[207]. There are no Commission Regulations granting block exemption under Regulation 169/2009.

(v) Council Regulation 246/2009

Council Regulation 246/2009[208] authorises the Commission to provide block exemption to consortia between liner shipping companies. The Commission adopted Regulation 906/2009[209] under the powers conferred upon it by Regulation 246/2009; it has been extended in force until 25 April 2020[210].

(vi) Council Regulation 487/2009

Regulation 487/2009[211] authorises the Commission to grant block exemptions for certain agreements in the air transport sector. There are no Commission regulations currently in force under Regulation 487/2009[212].

(C) The format of block exemptions

The typical format of block exemptions is that they begin with a series of recitals which explain the policy of the Commission in adopting the regulation in question; these recitals may be referred to for the purpose of construing the substantive provisions of the regulation where there are problems of interpretation[213]. Each regulation will then confer block exemption upon a particular category of agreements: for example Article 2 of Regulation 330/2010 block exempts vertical agreements, as defined in Article 1(1)(a) thereof. The block exemptions set out so-called 'hard-core restrictions' that must not be included if an agreement is to enjoy block exemption.

Most block exemptions have market share thresholds. For example Article 3 of Regulation 330/2010 provides that an agreement will qualify for block exemption where the supplier's and the buyer's market share does not exceed 30%; where either party's market share exceeds this threshold, their agreement requires individual analysis. Article 4 of the Regulation for research and development agreements has one of 25% and Article 3 of the Regulation for specialisation agreements one of 20%. Article 3 of the Regulation for technology transfer agreements has a 20% cap for agreements between competitors and a 30% cap for those between non-competitors.

[204] OJ [1991] L 143/1.

[205] Regulation 267/2010, OJ [2010] L 83/1 expired on 31 March 2017; see ch 15, 'Insurance sector', pp 625–626.

[206] OJ [2009] L 61/1; this Regulation replaced Council Regulation 1017/68, OJ [1968] L 175/1.

[207] See Article 3.

[208] OJ [2009] L 79/1; this Regulation replaced Regulation 479/92, OJ [1992] L 55/3.

[209] OJ [2009] L 256/31; this Regulation replaced Regulation 823/2000, OJ [2000] L 100/24; on Regulation 906/2009 see Prisker 'Commission adopts new block exemption regulation for liner shipping consortia' (2010) 1 Competition Policy Newsletter 8.

[210] Regulation 697/2014, OJ [2014] L 184/3.

[211] OJ [2009] L 148/1; this Regulation replaced Regulation 3976/87, OJ [1987] L 374/9.

[212] See ch 23, 'Air transport', pp 1005–1008.

[213] On the use of recitals as an aid to interpretation of EU legislation see eg Case C-429/07 *X BV* EU:C:2009:359, para 31.

Article 29(1) of Regulation 1/2003 confers power on the Commission to withdraw the benefit of a block exemption where it finds that a particular agreement covered by a block exemption regulation has effects that are incompatible with Article 101(3). Block exemption has been withdrawn from an agreement on only one occasion, in *Langnese-Iglo*[214]; the Commission's decision to do so was upheld on appeal by the General Court[215].

Article 29(2) of Regulation 1/2003 gives to each NCA a power to withdraw the benefit of a block exemption from agreements which have effects incompatible with the conditions of Article 101(3) within its territory or a part thereof, where that territory has all the characteristics of a distinct geographical market. In such a situation the Member State must demonstrate both that the agreement infringes Article 101(1) and that it does not fulfil the conditions of Article 101(3)[216]. Withdrawal of the benefit of a block exemption applies only from the date of the decision.

Article 6 of Regulation 330/2010 gives power to the Commission, by regulation, to withdraw the benefit of the block exemption from an entire sector, where parallel networks of similar vertical restraints cover more than 50% of a relevant market; Article 7 of Regulation 316/2014 contains a similar provision. These provisions have yet to be used.

(D) **Expiry of block exemptions**

Each block exemption regulation contains an expiry date. For example, Regulation 330/2010 will expire on 31 May 2022. This means that a vertical agreement that will endure beyond that date cannot be said, with certainty, to be exempt from 1 June 2022 onwards. The Commission is well aware of the need for legal certainty and so, if it subsequently adopts a new regulation, it will include transitional provisions for agreements already in force. It is necessary to examine the provisions of each particular regulation to find out what the position is on transition. If an agreement does not satisfy the terms of a new block exemption that replaces an old one, it may nevertheless either fall outside Article 101(1) or satisfy Article 101(3) on an individual basis.

The Commission reviews and consults on the functioning of a block exemption that is about to expire. When so doing it will consider whether a block exemption is necessary and, if so, on what terms it should be renewed. There is no presumption in favour of renewing a block exemption. The Commission will consider alternatives to renewal, including the publication of guidelines; the provision of informal guidance[217]; and/or the adoption of Commission decisions under Article 9[218] or Article 10[219] of Regulation 1/2003.

(E) **Future of block exemptions**

Given that Regulation 1/2003 ended the individual exemption of agreements by the Commission and replaced that system with the 'self-assessment', it can be argued that the idea of block exemptions should also be scrapped. In recent years the range and scope of block exemptions has decreased, as the Commission decided not to renew regulations for certain agreements in the insurance, maritime, air transport and motor vehicle sectors. However the Commission recognises the benefits of legal certainty, and important block exemptions remain in place, such as those for vertical agreements and technology transfer agreements. Furthermore there are numerous guidelines in place on the application of Article 101 to various types of agreement which, though lacking the formality of a block exemption, provide considerable guidance to businesses and their professional advisers.

[214] OJ [1993] L 183/19. [215] Case T-7/93 *Langnese-Iglo GmbH v Commission* EU:T:1995:98.

[216] *Article 101(3) Guidelines*, para 36. [217] See ch 7, 'Informal guidance', pp 269–270.

[218] See ch 7, 'Article 9: commitments', pp 264–269.

[219] See ch 7, 'Article 10: finding of inapplicability', p 269.

5

Article 102

1. Introduction

Article 102 TFEU is an important companion of Article 101[1]. Whereas Article 101 is concerned with agreements, decisions and concerted practices which are harmful to competition, Article 102 is directed towards the unilateral conduct of dominant firms which act in an abusive manner. Article 102 provides as follows:

> Any abuse by one or more undertakings of a dominant position within the internal market or in a substantial part of it shall be prohibited as incompatible with the internal market in so far as it may affect trade between Member States. Such abuse may, in particular, consist in:
>
> (a) directly or indirectly imposing unfair purchase or selling prices or unfair trading conditions;
>
> (b) limiting production, markets or technical development to the prejudice of consumers;

[1] For further reading on Article 102 readers are referred to Ehlermann and Atanasiu (eds) *European Competition Law Annual 2003: What is an Abuse of a Dominant Position?* (Hart, 2006); Ezrachi (ed) *Article 82 EC: Reflections on Its Recent Evolution* (Hart, 2009); Rousseva *Rethinking Exclusionary Abuses in EU Competition Law* (Hart, 2010); Gormsen *A Principled Approach to Abuse of Dominance in European Competition Law* (Cambridge University Press, 2010); Nazzini *The Foundations of European Union Competition Law: Objectives and Principles of Article 102* (Oxford University Press, 2011); Akman *The Concept of Abuse in EU Competition Law: Law and Economic Approaches* (Hart, 2012); Rose and Bailey (eds) *Bellamy and Child: European Union Law of Competition* (Oxford University Press, 7th ed, 2013), ch 10; O'Donoghue and Padilla *The Law and Economics of Article 102 TFEU* (Hart, 2nd ed, 2013); Faull and Nikpay (eds) *The EU Law of Competition* (Oxford University Press, 3rd ed, 2014), ch 4: Niels, Jenkins and Kavanagh *Economics for Competition Lawyers* (Oxford University Press, 2nd ed, 2016), ch 4; Parcu, Monti and Botta *Abuse of Dominance in EU Competition Law: Emerging Trends* (Edward Elgar, 2017); Ibáñez-Colomo 'Beyond the "More Economics-Based Approach": A Legal Perspective on Article 102 TFEU Case Law' (2016) 53 CML Rev 709; see also Reineker and Little (eds) *Dominance 2017* (Law Business Research, 13th ed, 2017).

(c) applying dissimilar conditions to equivalent transactions with other trading parties, thereby placing them at a competitive disadvantage;

(d) making the conclusion of contracts subject to acceptance by the other parties of supplementary obligations which, by their nature or according to commercial usage, have no connection with the subject of such contracts.

The purpose of this chapter is to describe the main features of Article 102. Section 2 contains an overview of the law and practice of Article 102. Section 3 introduces the Commission's *Guidance on the Commission's enforcement priorities in applying Article [102 TFEU] to abusive exclusionary conduct by dominant undertakings* ('the *Guidance on Article 102 Enforcement Priorities*' or 'the *Guidance*')[2], an important document that will be referred to at several points in the text that follows and in later chapters of this book. Section 4 discusses the meaning of undertaking and section 5 examines the requirement of an effect on trade between Member States: concepts that have already been discussed in the context of Article 101[3]. Section 6 considers what is meant by a dominant position under Article 102. Section 7 looks at the requirement that any dominant position must be held in a substantial part of the internal market. Section 8 looks at the central—and most complex—issue in this chapter, the meaning of abuse: more detailed analysis of individual abusive practices will be found in chapters 17, 18 and 19, which examine, respectively, non-pricing abuses, pricing abuses and abuses that can arise in relation to the exercise, or sometimes the non-exercise, of intellectual property rights. Section 9 considers defences to allegations of abuse, and section 10 briefly considers the consequences of infringing Article 102.

2. **Overview of the Law and Practice of Article 102**

Many of the most controversial decisions of the Commission have been taken under Article 102. One was the finding in 2004 of two abuses on the part of Microsoft, a refusal to supply interoperability information to competitors and the tying of a media player with its operating software, for which Microsoft was fined €497.2 million[4]. Another controversial decision was the fine of €1.06 billion imposed on Intel for exclusionary practices including the offering of exclusivity rebates to customers who purchased all or most of their microprocessor chips from that undertaking[5]. Intel lost its appeal against this decision in 2014[6]; on further appeal to the Court of Justice the case was referred back to the General Court for a reassessment of whether the rebates in question could exclude competitors as efficient as Intel from the market[7]. A further controversial decision was *Google*, fined €2.42 billion in June 2017 for abusing its dominant position in general internet

[2] OJ [2009] C 45/7.

[3] On the meaning of undertaking see ch 3, 'Undertakings and Associations of Undertakings', pp 83–101 and on the meaning of effect on trade see ch 3, 'The Effect on Trade Between Member States', pp 150–155.

[4] *Microsoft*, Commission decision of 24 March 2004, upheld on appeal to the General Court Case T-201/04 *Microsoft Corp v Commission* EU:T:2007:289; the *Microsoft* decision is discussed at various places in this book: see in particular ch 17, 'Microsoft', pp 709–710 on the tying abuse and ch 19, 'The *Microsoft* case', pp 818–820 on the refusal to provide interoperability information; for further reading on the *Microsoft* case see Beckner and Gustafson *Trial and Error: United States v. Microsoft* (Citizens for a Sound Economy Foundation, 2nd ed, 2002); McKenzie *Trust on Trial: How the Microsoft Case is Reframing the Rules of Competition* (Perseus Publishing, 2000); Luca Rubini (ed) *Microsoft on Trial: Legal and Economic Analysis of a Transatlantic Antitrust Case* (Edward Elgar, 2010).

[5] *Intel*, Commission decision of 13 May 2009.

[6] Case T-286/09 *Intel v Commission* EU:T:2014:547.

[7] Case C-413/14 P *Intel v Commission* EU:C:2017:632; the judgment is discussed at various points in the text that follows.

search in order to promote its own comparison shopping service[8]. The fact that these very large fines were imposed by the European Commission on US firms highly successful in the ICT sector where EU firms are noticeable by their absence adds a certain frisson to the controversy in this area of law[9].

A complaint on the part of some critics has been that the Commission and EU Courts tend, when applying Article 102 in cases such as *Microsoft*, *Intel* and *Google*, not to concern themselves with the maintenance of the competitive process but, instead, with the protection of competitors, a quite different matter. To put the point another way, in any competition, whether economic, sporting or of some other kind, the most efficient or the fittest person will win: this is an inevitable part of the competitive process. This would suggest that, if a firm ends up as a monopolist simply by virtue of its superior efficiency, this should be applauded, or at least not be condemned. A more specific criticism of the Commission and of the EU Courts has been that they adopt a formalistic (as opposed to an economics-based) approach to the application of Article 102 and that as a consequence business practices of dominant firms have been condemned that did not have, or could not have, any harmful effect on consumer welfare; and which, indeed, may have been pro-competitive. Clearly it would be a strange paradox if it were to transpire that the application of Article 102 resulted in the condemnation of competitive behaviour that benefits consumers. However a number of cases in recent times, culminating in the judgment of the Grand Chamber of the Court of Justice in *Intel* in September 2017, have clearly established that it is not the role of Article 102 to protect less efficient competitors. Paragraph 133 of the *Intel* judgment could hardly be clearer:

> In that respect, it must be borne in mind that it is in no way the purpose of Article 102 TFEU to prevent an undertaking from acquiring, on its own merits, the dominant position on a market. Nor does that provision seek to ensure that competitors less efficient than the undertaking with the dominant position should remain on the market.

The challenge in this area of the law is to devise administrable rules that capture those types of conduct that could exclude from the market firms as efficient, or more efficient, than the dominant undertaking; to avoid rules that could inhibit pro-competitive behaviour; and to achieve a balance between these two desirable outcomes that gives a reasonable degree of certainty to businesses, their professional advisers, competition authorities and to courts.

3. The Commission's *Guidance on Article 102 Enforcement Priorities*

In 2004 the Commission launched a review of the law and practice of Article 102 as it applied to exclusionary (as opposed to exploitative) abuses (this distinction is discussed later in this chapter[10]). In December 2005 a staff working paper was published

[8] Commission decision of 27 June 2017, on appeal to the General Court Case T-612/17 *Google v Commission*, not yet decided.

[9] See eg Sokol 'Troubled Waters Between U.S. and European Antitrust' (2017) 115 Mich L Rev 955, 963–969; see also US Department of the Treasury 'White Paper: The European Commission's recent State Aid investigations of Transfer Pricing Rules, (24 August 2016), available at www.treasury.gov/resource-center/tax-policy/treaties/Documents/White-Paper-State-Aid.pdf; Fox 'We Protect Competition, You Protect Competitors' (2003) 26 World Competition 149.

[10] See 'Exploitative, exclusionary and single market abuses', pp 207–208 later in chapter.

by DG COMP[11] and there followed a feverish debate as to the proper application of Article 102. The outcome of this process was the adoption by the Commission in February 2009 of its *Guidance on Article 102 Enforcement Priorities*. The clear intention of the *Guidance* was that the Commission would, in future, select for investigation allegations of abusive exclusionary conduct only where it seemed plausible that significant harmful effects to consumer welfare were likely to occur. The Commission would not proceed on the basis of form-based rules, but economic effects; and would not intervene to assist less efficient competitors. Paragraph 20 of the *Guidance* set out a series of factors that the Commission would take into account when selecting a case for investigation[12], and also provided specific guidance as to how the Commission would deal with cases on exclusive dealing, tying and bundling, predation and refusal to deal and margin squeeze.

It is important to understand that the *Guidance* is **not** a set of guidelines on the law of Article 102; the document is what it says it is: guidance on the **Commission's enforcement priorities**. The law of exclusionary abuse under Article 102 is contained in the jurisprudence of the EU Courts. In *Post Danmark II* the Court of Justice, in response to a specific question from the Danish Maritime and Commercial Court, said explicitly that the *Guidance*:

> merely sets out the Commission's approach as to the choice of cases that it intends to pursue as a matter of priority; accordingly, the administrative practice followed by the Commission is not binding on national competition authorities and courts[13].

The fact that national courts and national competition authorities ('NCAs') are not bound by the Commission's *Guidance* does not mean, however, that it is not influential; for example in the UK the former Office of Fair Trading and, now, the Competition and Markets Authority, have referred several times to the *Guidance* when investigating allegations of abuse of dominance[14].

The *Guidance* is not binding on the EU Courts: indeed paragraph 3 specifically says that it is not intended to constitute a statement of the law and is without prejudice to the EU Courts' jurisprudence. There have been occasions on which the Court of Justice has applied Article 102 more strictly than the approach that the Commission suggests that it would adopt: one example is *Konkurrensverket v TeliaSonera Sverige AB*[15], where its approach to the abuse of margin squeeze is clearly stricter than the *Guidance*[16]; another is *Tomra*[17] where the Court's application of Article 102 to exclusivity rebates was stricter than the Commission's *Guidance* suggests.

Some commentators consider that this apparent dissonance between the case law of the EU Courts and the Commission's *Guidance* gives rise to legal uncertainty and that the Commission should therefore withdraw it[18]; a less extreme view is that the *Guidance* fails

[11] *Discussion Paper on the application of Article [102] of the Treaty to exclusionary abuses*, available at www.ec.europa.eu/competition/antitrust/art82/index.html.

[12] They are set out below: see 'How is effects analysis conducted in practice?', pp 214–216 later in chapter.

[13] See Case C-23/14 *Post Danmark A/S v Konkurrencerdet* EU:C:2015:651, para 52.

[14] See eg *Flybe*, OFT decision of 5 November 2010; *Idexx*, OFT decision of 17 November 2011; *Unilever*, CMA decision of 10 August 2017; these were all 'no grounds for action' decisions.

[15] Case C-52/09 EU:C:2011:83.

[16] OJ [2009] C 45/9, para 80; for discussion on the issue of margin squeeze see ch 18, 'The Commission's decisional practice', p 775.

[17] Case T-155/06 *Tomra Systems v Commission* EU:T:2010:370 (General Court), upheld on appeal Case C-549/10 P *Tomra Systems v Commission* EU:C:2012:221 (Court of Justice).

[18] See eg Gormsen 'Why the European Commission's Enforcement Priorities on Article 82 EC Should Be Withdrawn' (2010) 31 ECLR 45.

to establish priorities, and may leave undertakings more confused about the law in this area than they were before[19]. To the authors of this book these criticisms are unconvincing. To repeat: the *Guidance* is not a set of guidelines that describe the existing law. Rather it explains why the Commission, with its finite resources, would have a greater interest in investigating some cases than others; in particular it explains that it is the likelihood that particular conduct could cause anti-competitive foreclosure, thereby, ultimately, causing harm to consumers, that legitimates intervention by the Commission[20].

Although the *Guidance* does not bind the EU and national courts, this is not to say that it will not have an influence on the future application of Article 102 to exclusionary behaviour. In *TeliaSonera*[21] Advocate General Mazák said that the *Guidance* does not bind the Court, but that it did provide a 'useful point of reference'[22]. It is noticeable that several judgments of the Court of Justice since the *Guidance* was published have emphasised that the function of Article 102 is not to protect less efficient competitors, culminating in the paragraph from *Intel* set out in the previous section; this is entirely consistent with the Commission's *Guidance*.

Whatever the merits of the criticisms of Article 102 over the years, it is clear that a dominant firm (or one that fears that it might be found to be dominant) must behave with great caution. A transgression of Article 102 may have serious consequences. The Commission (or an NCA) may impose a large fine, as in *Microsoft*, *Intel* and *Google*; and an injured third party may bring an action for an injunction and/or damages in a national court[23]. Furthermore the Commission has explicit power to impose structural remedies, albeit subject to limitations, pursuant to Article 7 of Regulation 1/2003; it did so for the first time in *ARA Foreclosure*[24], and several cases have been closed as a result

[19] See Akman 'The European Commission's Guidance on Article 102 TFEU: From Inferno to Paradiso?' (2010) 73 MLR 605; for further commentary on the debate leading to the *Guidance* and the *Guidance* itself see Ehlermann and Marquis (eds) *European Competition Law Annual 2007: A Reformed Approach to Article 82 EC* (Hart, 2008); Ezrachi 'The European Commission Guidance on Article 82 EC—The Way in Which Institutional Realities Limit the Potential for Reform' [2009] Oxford Legal Research Paper Series (No 27/2009), available at www.ssrn.com; Petit 'From Formalism to Effects?—The Commission's Communication on Enforcement Priorities in Applying Article 82 EC' (2009) 32 World Competition 485; Kellerbauer 'The Commission's New Enforcement Priorities in Applying Article 82 EC to Dominant Companies' Exclusionary Conduct: A Shift Towards a More Economic Approach?' (2010) 31 ECLR 175 (the author is a member of the Commission's Legal Service); Monti 'Article 82 EC: What Future for the Effects-Based Approach?' (2010) 1 JECLAP 2; Geradin 'Is the Guidance Paper on the Commission's Enforcement Priorities in Applying Article 102 TFEU to Abusive Exclusionary Conduct Useful?', available at www.ssrn.com; Pace (ed) *European Competition Law: The Impact of the Commission's Guidance on Article 102* (Edward Elgar, 2011); Padilla 'Whither Article 102 TFEU: A Comment on Akman and Crane' (2016) 81 Antitrust LJ 223.

[20] An interesting question is what the legal position would be if the Commission were to refuse to consider a complaint about conduct that clearly infringes Article 102 according to the jurisprudence of the EU Courts on the basis that it does not comply with the *Guidance on Article 102 Enforcement Priorities*: see Wils 'Discretion and Prioritisation in Public Antitrust Enforcement' (2011) 34 World Competition 353; Petit 'Rebates and Article 102 TFEU: The European Commission's Duty to Apply the Guidance Paper' (November 26, 2015), available at www.ssrn.com.

[21] Case C-52/09 EU:C:2010:483.

[22] Ibid, fn 21; see similarly the UK CAT in Case 1238/3/3/15 *British Telecommunications Plc v OFCOM* [2016] CAT 3, para 91.

[23] It was reported in the media that out-of-court settlements were reached between Microsoft and various of the complainants against it for the payment of damages: a report in the *Financial Times* of October 2005 suggested that Microsoft had paid a total of $3.73 billion; it was similarly reported that Intel had agreed to pay damages to AMD, the complainant in that case, amounting to $1.25 billion: see *Financial Times*, 13 November 2009; numerous damages actions are pending against Google in the courts of several Member States.

[24] Commission decision of 20 September 2016, paras 132–148: note that ARA had offered to make the divestiture required by the decision.

of undertakings offering commitments to divest assets under Article 9 of Regulation 1/2003[25].

4. Undertakings

The term 'undertaking' has the same meaning in Article 102 as in Article 101, and has been discussed in chapter 3[26]. Several of the cases on the meaning of an undertaking have arisen in the context of Article 102, for example where complaints were made to the Commission about the monopsonistic power of the Spanish Health Service[27] or the standard-setting power of Eurocontrol[28]: it was held that neither of those entities was acting as an undertaking, with the consequence that the competition rules did not apply to them. Similarly litigation in Austria turned on whether the Companies Registry in that country, responsible by law for storing data about companies registered there, was acting as an undertaking: the Court of Justice considered that this did not amount to economic activity, so that a refusal to supply data to third parties did not infringe Article 102[29].

The application of the competition rules to public undertakings or to undertakings entrusted with exclusive or special rights will be discussed in chapter 6[30]; four points about Article 102 and the public sector should, however, be noted here. First, the fact that an undertaking has a legal monopoly does not, in itself, remove it from the ambit of Article 102[31]. Secondly, Member States have a duty under Article 4(3) TEU not to do anything 'which could jeopardise the attainment of the Union's objectives', one of which is the internal market which includes a system ensuring that competition is not distorted[32]. This means that a Member State cannot confer immunity on undertakings from Article 102, except to the limited extent provided for in Article 106(2)[33]. Thirdly, the derogation from the competition rules in Article 106(2) has consistently been interpreted narrowly[34]. Lastly, Article 37 TFEU prevents Member States from discriminating in favour of their own state monopolies of a commercial character: this provides the Commission with an alternative weapon for dealing with some monopolies in the public sector[35].

[25] See ch 7, 'Article 9: commitments', pp 264–269.

[26] See ch 3, 'Undertakings and Associations of Undertakings', pp 83–101.

[27] Case T-319/99 *FENIN v Commission* EU:T:2003:50, upheld on appeal to the Court of Justice Case C-205/03 P *FENIN v Commission* EU:C:2006:453.

[28] Case T-155/04 *SELEX Sistemi Integrati v Commission* EU:T:2006:387, upheld on appeal to the Court of Justice Case C-113/07 P *SELEX Sistemi Integrati v Commission* EU:C:2009:191.

[29] Case C-138/11 *Compass-Datenbank* EU:C:2012:449.

[30] See ch 6, 'Article 106 TFEU—compliance with the Treaties', pp 229–251.

[31] Case 311/84 *Centre belge d'études de marché—Télémarketing v CLT* EU:C:1985:394, para 16; see also Case 26/75 *General Motors v Commission* EU:C:1975:150; Case 41/83 *Italy v Commission* EU:C:1985:120; Case 226/84 *British Leyland v Commission* EU:C:1986:421; Case C-41/90 *Höfner v Macrotron* EU:C:1991:161, para 28; Case C-18/93 *Corsica Ferries* EU:C:1994:195, para 43; Case C-242/95 *GT-Link v De Danske Statsbaner (DSB)* EU:C:1997:376, para 35; see also the Commission's decision in *French-West African Shipowners' Committees* OJ [1992] L 134/1, para 64; Case C-351/12 *OSA* EU:C:2014:110, para 81.

[32] Protocol 27 to the Treaties; see eg Case C-260/89 *Elliniki Radiophonia Tiléorassi-Anonimi Etairia (ERT) v Dimotiki Etairia Pliroforissis (DEP)* EU:C:1991:254, para 27; note also that, under Article 119(1) TFEU, Member States (and the EU) are required to observe the principle of an 'open market economy with free competition'.

[33] Case 13/77 *INNO v ATAB* EU:C:1977:185; see ch 6, 'Article 4(3) TEU—duty of sincere cooperation', pp 223–229.

[34] See ch 6, 'Article 106(2)', pp 242–248.

[35] See ch 6, 'Article 37 TFEU—state monopolies of a commercial character', pp 251–252.

5. The Effect on Inter-State Trade

The meaning of this phrase was analysed in chapter 3[36]. For the purpose of Article 102 particular attention should be paid to the Court of Justice's judgment in *Commercial Solvents v Commission*[37] in which it held that the requirement of an effect on trade between Member States would be satisfied where conduct brought about an alteration in the structure of competition in the internal market[38]. This test is of particular importance in Article 102 cases: Article 102 can be applied only where there is already a dominant position and it is unsurprising that the Commission will be concerned with the structure of the market in such cases[39]. In the *Soda-ash* decisions under Article 102[40] the Commission held that rebates offered by ICI and Solvay in their respective markets had the effect of reinforcing the structural rigidity of the EU market as a whole and its division along national lines. In these decisions it was US exporters who were excluded from the EU, but the Commission still held that there was an effect on inter-state trade: imports would have helped to undermine the dominant positions of ICI and Solvay in their respective markets.

The Commission's *Guidelines on the effect on trade concept contained in Articles [101] and [102] of the Treaty*[41] give specific consideration to the circumstances in which abusive behaviour—for example exploitative abuses that harm downstream trading partners and exclusionary abuses that harm competitors—might have an effect on trade between Member States[42].

Under Regulation 1/2003[43] national courts and NCAs must apply Article 102 where an abuse of a dominant position has an effect on trade between Member States[44]. However this does not preclude them from adopting or applying on their own territories stricter national laws controlling unilateral conduct engaged in by undertakings[45]; and the obligation is without prejudice to the application of national laws that predominantly pursue an objective different from those pursued by Articles 101 and 102[46].

[36] See ch 3, 'The Effect on Trade between Member States', pp 150–155.

[37] Cases 6/73 and 7/73 EU:C:1974:18, para 33; see also Cases T-24/93 etc *Compagnie Maritime Belge v Commission* EU:T:1996:139, para 203; Case C-177/16 *AKKA/LAA* EU:C:2017:689, para 26.

[38] The Commission refers to the 'competitive structure' test at para 20 of its *Guidelines on the effect on trade concept contained in Articles [101] and [102] of the Treaty* OJ [2004] C 101/81.

[39] See eg Case 27/76 *United Brands v Commission* EU:C:1978:22; *Tetra Pak I (BTG Licence)* OJ [1988] L 272/27, para 48; *Napier Brown—British Sugar* OJ [1988] L 284/41, paras 77–80; *London European—Sabena* OJ [1988] L 317/47, para 33; *Telekomunikacja Polska*, Commission decision of 22 June 2011, para 887, upheld in Case T-486/11 *Orange Polska SA v Commission* EU:T:2015:1002, on further appeal to the Court of Justice Case C-123/16 P, not yet decided.

[40] *Soda-ash/Solvay* OJ [1991] L 152/21 and *Soda-ash/ICI* OJ [1991] L 152/1; these decisions were annulled on procedural grounds by the General Court: Cases T-30/91 etc *Solvay SA v Commission* EU:T:1995:115; the Commission's appeal to the Court of Justice failed, Cases C-286/95 P etc EU:C:2000:188; the Commission readopted the decisions in December 2000: OJ [2003] L 10/1, which were substantially upheld in Case T-57/01 *Solvay SA v Commission* EU:T:2009:519, and Case T-66/01 *Imperial Chemical Industries Ltd v Commission* EU:T:2010:255; the second *Solvay* judgment was quashed on appeal to the Court of Justice Case C-109/10 P *Solvay SA v Commission* EU:C:2011:686 as Solvay's rights of defence had been infringed as a result of the Commission's failure to grant proper access to the file.

[41] OJ [2004] C 101/81.

[42] Ibid, paras 73–76 (dealing with abuses covering several Member States); paras 93–96 (abuses covering a single Member State); paras 97–99 (abuses covering part only of a Member State); and paras 106–109 (abuses involving undertakings located in third countries).

[43] OJ [2003] L 1/1.

[44] Regulation 1/2003, Article 3(1); see ch 2, 'Obligation to apply Articles 101 and 102', pp 76–77.

[45] Regulation 1/2003, Article 3(2).

[46] Ibid, Article 3(3); on the objective of Articles 101 and 102 TFEU see recital 9 of Regulation 1/2003.

6. Dominant Position

Article 102 applies only where one undertaking has a 'dominant position' or where two or more undertakings are 'collectively dominant'[47]. The expression 'dominant position' is not one that will be found in the economics literature; rather it is a term of art that determines the point at which the unilateral behaviour of an undertaking becomes subject to scrutiny under Article 102.

The Court of Justice in *United Brands v Commission*[48] laid down the following test of what is meant by a dominant position:

> The dominant position thus referred to by Article [102] relates to a position of economic strength enjoyed by an undertaking which enables it to prevent effective competition being maintained on the relevant market by affording it the power to behave to an appreciable extent independently of its competitors, customers and ultimately of its consumers[49].

Paragraph 65 of the Court's judgment in *United Brands* can be understood to equate dominance with the economist's concept of substantial market power; the Commission does so in paragraph 10 of its *Guidance on Article 102 Enforcement Priorities* where it says that the notion of independence referred to by the Court is related to the degree of competitive constraint exerted on the undertaking under investigation. Where competitive constraints are ineffective, the undertaking in question enjoys 'substantial market power over a period of time'; the *Guidance* says that an undertaking has substantial market power if it is 'capable of profitably increasing prices above the competitive level for a significant period of time'[50]. The same definition of dominance is used in the International Competition Network's ('the ICN') *Unilateral Conduct Workbook*[51].

As noted in chapter 1[52], there are degrees of market power: at one end of the spectrum would be a firm with no or only imperceptible market power; at the other end a firm which is a true monopolist. Between these two extremes could be found firms with 'some', or 'appreciable', or 'significant', or 'substantial' market power. It is important to note that the legal expression 'dominant position' is a binary term: either an undertaking is dominant and subject to Article 102; or it is not, in which case its unilateral behaviour is not subject to EU competition law. This is why a finding of dominance is so important; and

[47] The issue of whether any dominance is collective is discussed in ch 14 of this book, which considers in general terms the issues of oligopoly and tacit coordination between independent undertakings.

[48] Case 27/76 EU:C:1978:22, para 65; it has used the same formulation on several other occasions, eg in Case 85/76 *Hoffmann-La Roche v Commission* EU:C:1979:36, para 38.

[49] This definition does not adequately reflect (what is undoubtedly true) that Article 102 also applies to market power on the buying as well as the selling side of the market, since that was not in issue in *United Brands*; a powerful purchaser may be able to behave independently of its sellers who are not 'customers' in the normal sense of that word; for action taken against undertakings with buyer power see *Re Eurofima* [1973] CMLR D217; *Re GEMA* OJ [1971] L 134/15; Case 298/83 *CICCE v Commission* EU:C:1985:150; *UK Small Mines* Commission's XXIst *Report on Competition Policy* (1991), point 107; *Virgin/British Airways* OJ [2000] L 30/1, upheld on appeal to the General Court Case T-219/99 *British Airways plc v Commission* EU:T:2003:343: the Court stated specifically at para 101 of its judgment that Article 102 can apply to undertakings with a dominant position on either side of the market; see also ch 1, 'Procurement markets', p 37.

[50] OJ [2009] C 45/9, para 11; the Commission goes on in this paragraph to explain that 'increase in prices' is a shorthand term which includes other ways of influencing competition to the advantage of the dominant undertaking, eg by decreasing output, innovation, variety or quality of goods or services; on the same point see ch 1, 'Market Definition and Market Power', pp 25–49.

[51] Chapter 3 of the *Workbook* on the 'assessment of dominance' is available on the ICN website at www.internationalcompetitionnetwork.org.

[52] See ch 1, 'Market Definition and Market Power', pp 25–49.

why some commentators would like there to be a fairly generous 'safe harbour' for market shares below a certain percentage[53].

A finding of dominance involves a two-stage assessment. The Court of Justice held in *Continental Can v Commission*[54] that a proper definition of the relevant market is a necessary precondition for any application of Article 102. Market definition has been discussed in detail in chapter 1, in particular the 'hypothetical monopolist' or 'SSNIP' test; the problem of the 'Cellophane Fallacy' in Article 102 cases which might lead to the inclusion of false substitutes in the market definition; and the types of evidence that may be of assistance when defining relevant product, geographical and temporal markets[55].

Having defined the relevant market, it is necessary in an Article 102 case to determine whether an undertaking has a dominant position in that market. This cannot be determined purely by reference to an undertaking's market share. A finding of a dominant position derives from a combination of several factors which, taken separately, are not necessarily determinative[56]; it is necessary to examine (at least) three issues, as set out in paragraph 12 of the *Guidance*:

- constraints imposed by the existing supplies from, and the position on the market of, **actual competitors (the market position of the dominant undertaking and its competitors)**
- constraints imposed by the credible threat of future expansion by actual competitors or entry by **potential competitors (expansion and entry)**
- constraints imposed by the bargaining strength of the undertaking's customers (**countervailing buyer power**) (emphasis added).

Each of these three criteria has been discussed in chapter 1[57]. Some additional commentary will be provided here based on the judgments of the EU Courts and the decisional practice of the Commission in Article 102 cases.

(A) **Actual competitors**

True monopoly is rare, except where conferred by the state. The majority of cases are therefore concerned with the problem of deciding at what point an undertaking, though not a true monopolist, has sufficient power over the market to be dominant.

(i) **Statutory monopolies**

Various cases have concerned undertakings with a statutory monopoly in the provision of goods or services[58]. The Court of Justice has rejected the argument that, because a monopoly is conferred by statute, this immunises the undertaking from Article 102[59]; where an undertaking has a statutory monopoly it must comply with Article 102, its only special privilege being that conferred by Article 106(2)[60].

[53] See 'Findings of dominance below the 50% threshold', pp 190–191 later in chapter.

[54] Case 6/72 EU:C:1973:22, para 32; subsequent judgments have regularly repeated this point: see eg Case T-321/05 *AstraZeneca AB v Commission* EU:T:2010:266, para 30.

[55] See further ch 1, 'Market definition' and following sections, pp 25–42.

[56] *Guidance on Article 102 Enforcement Priorities*, para 11 and case law cited.

[57] See ch 1, 'Market power', pp 42–46.

[58] See eg Case T-229/94 *Deutsche Bahn AG v Commission* EU:T:1997:155, para 57; Case C-351/12 *OSA* EU:C:2014:110, para 86.

[59] See the cases cited at ch 5 n 31 earlier.

[60] See ch 6, 'Article 106(2)', pp 242–248.

(ii) **The relevance of market shares**

In *Hoffmann-La Roche* the Court of Justice pointed out that:

> A substantial market share as evidence of the existence of a dominant position is not a constant factor and its importance varies from market to market according to the structure of these markets, especially as far as production, supply and demand are concerned[61].

The Commission's *Guidance on Article 102 Enforcement Priorities* says that market shares provide a 'useful first indication' of the market structure and of the relative importance of the undertakings active on it[62]. The *Guidance* goes on to explain that an assessment of market power requires that market conditions generally be taken into account, including the dynamics of the market, the extent to which products are differentiated and the trend or development of market shares over time[63].

As far as Article 102 is concerned, it is obvious that the larger the market share, the more likely a finding of dominance. A market share of 100% is rare in the absence of statutory privileges, although not unheard of[64]. However some firms have been found to have very large market shares. For example in *Tetra Pak I (BTG Licence)*[65] Tetra Pak's market share in the market for machines capable of filling cartons by an aseptic process was 91.8%; and in *BPB Industries plc*[66] BPB was found to have a market share in plasterboard of 96%, although the Commission had excluded wet plastering from the market definition. In *Microsoft*[67] Microsoft had over 90% of the market for personal computer operating software systems and at least 60% of the market for work group server operating systems[68]. In *Google*[69] the Commission found that Google was dominant in each national market for general internet search throughout the 31 countries of the European Economic Area and that its market shares exceeded 90% in most.

(a) The Court of Justice's judgment in Hoffmann-La Roche v Commission

In *Hoffmann-La Roche v Commission*[70] the Court of Justice said:

> 41... Furthermore although the importance of the market shares may vary from one market to another the view may legitimately be taken that very large shares are in themselves, and save in exceptional circumstances, evidence of the existence of a dominant position. An undertaking which has a very large market share and holds it for some time ... is by virtue of that share in a position of strength ...

[61] Case 85/76 *Hoffmann-La Roche v Commission* EU:C:1979:36, para 40.

[62] OJ [2009] C 45/9, para 13; see similarly *Servier*, Commission decision of 9 July 2014, para 2561.

[63] OJ [2009] C 45/9, para 13.

[64] In *GVL* OJ [1981] L 370/49 that body had a 100% market share in the market in Germany for the management of performing artists' rights of secondary exploitation; see also *Amministrazione Autonoma dei Monopoli di Stato (AAMS)* OJ [1998] L 252/47, para 31, where the Commission found AAMS held a *de facto* monopoly of the Italian market for the wholesale distribution of cigarettes, upheld on appeal to the General Court Case T-139/98 *AAMS v Commission* EU:T:2001:272, para 52; *Telefónica*, Commission decision of 4 July 2007, para 233, where the Commission found Telefónica had a *de facto* monopoly of the regional market for wholesale broadband access, upheld on appeal to the General Court, Case T-336/07 *Telefónica SA v Commission* EU:T:2012:172, paras 151–167; *Motorola—Enforcement of GPRS standard essential patents*, Commission decision of 29 April 2014, para 225.

[65] OJ [1988] L 272/27, para 44, upheld on appeal to the General Court Case T-51/89 *Tetra Pak Rausing SA v Commission* EU:T:1990:41.

[66] OJ [1989] L 10/50, upheld on appeal to the General Court Case T-65/89 *BPB Industries Plc and British Gypsum Ltd v Commission* EU:T:1993:31 and to the Court of Justice Case C-310/93 P *BPB Industries Plc and British Gypsum Ltd v Commission* EU:C:1995:101.

[67] *Microsoft*, Commission decision of 24 March 2004.

[68] Ibid, paras 430–435 and 473–499.

[69] Commission decision of 27 June 2017, on appeal Case T-612/17 *Google v Commission*, not yet decided.

[70] Case 85/76 EU:C:1979:36; the Commission specifically referred to this paragraph in *Van den Bergh Foods Ltd* OJ [1998] L 246/1, para 258.

(b) The AKZO *presumption of dominance where an undertaking has a market share of 50% or more*

In *AKZO v Commission*[71] the Court of Justice referred to the passage from *Hoffmann-La Roche* quoted above and continued that a market share of 50% could be considered to be very large so that, in the absence of exceptional circumstances pointing the other way, an undertaking with such a market share will be presumed dominant; that undertaking bears the evidential burden of establishing that it is not dominant. Clearly this is an important presumption, which means that firms are at risk of being found to be dominant where they fall considerably short of being monopolists in the strict sense of that term. Some critics of Article 102, who believe that it is applied in too intrusive a manner, would like to see the 50% threshold in *AKZO* raised[72]: perhaps to 75%; the binary effect of Article 102, whereby conduct that is legal when practised by a non-dominant firm becomes illegal when the firm is dominant, would be less pronounced if the presumption of dominance was set at a higher market share threshold. However the EU Courts have frequently affirmed the *AKZO* presumption[73]; indeed in *AstraZeneca* the General Court went so far as to say that the Commission could not disregard the importance to be attached to AZ's very large market share throughout the relevant period of alleged abuse[74].

The Commission does not refer to the *AKZO* presumption in its *Guidance on Article 102 Enforcement Priorities*[75], perhaps suggesting that it is not keen on a presumption that attaches such weight to a market share figure. Instead it notes at paragraph 15 that the higher the market share, and the longer the period of time over which it is held, the more likely it is that it constitutes an important preliminary indication of the existence of a dominant position; however the Commission also says that it would come to a final conclusion on dominance only after examining all the relevant factors that may be relevant to constraining the behaviour of the undertaking under investigation.

(c) Findings of dominance below a market share of 50%

The Court of Justice held in *United Brands* that that firm, with a market share in the range of 40% to 45%, was dominant. In that case other factors were considered to be significant: the market share alone would not have been sufficient to sustain a finding of dominance; however the case shows that a firm supplying less than 50% of the market may be found to hold a dominant position. In *United Brands* the Court said that, even though there was lively competition on the market at certain periods of the year, United Brands could still be held to be dominant for the purposes of Article 102[76]; a dominant position does not therefore imply the absence of any competitive constraint[77].

The decision in *Virgin/British Airways*[78] marked the first (and only) occasion on which an undertaking with a market share of less than 40% has been found by the Commission

[71] Case C-62/86 EU:C:1991:286, para 60.

[72] See O'Donoghue and Padilla *The Law and Economics of Article 102 TFEU* (Hart, 2nd ed, 2013), stating that many commentators consider that the threshold for establishing dominance under Article 102 TFEU is too low.

[73] See eg Case T-30/89 *Hilti v Commission* EU:T:1991:70, para 92; Case T-340/03 *France Télécom v Commission* EU:T:2007:22, paras 99–101; Case T-57/01 *Solvay v Commission* EU:T:2009:519, paras 275–305; Case T-321/05 *AstraZeneca AB v Commission* EU:T:2010:266, paras 242–254, upheld on appeal Case C-457/10 P EU:C:2012:770, paras 176–177.

[74] Case T-321/05 *AstraZeneca AB v Commission* EU:T:2010:266, para 245.

[75] The *Guidance* refers, in fn 8, to *AKZO* as part of the case law on very large market shares.

[76] See eg *Telefónica*, Commission decision of 4 July 2007, para 236 and *BEH Electricity*, Commission commitment decision of 10 December 2015, para 40.

[77] See eg *Servier*, Commission decision of 9 July 2014, para 2552, citing *United Brands*; similarly see *Guidance on Article 102 Enforcement Priorities*, para 10.

[78] OJ [2000] L 30/1.

to be in a dominant position under Article 102. BA was held to be dominant in the UK market for the procurement of air travel agency services with a market share of 39.7%. On appeal the General Court agreed that BA was dominant, noting that its market share was considerably larger than that of any other individual competitor or of the next five competitors combined; its position was reinforced by the world rank held by BA in terms of international scheduled passenger-kilometres flown, the extent of the range of its transport services and its hub network; the Court also considered that BA was an obligatory business partner for travel agents[79]. The General Court stated specifically that the fact that BA's market share was in decline could not, in itself, demonstrate that it was not dominant[80].

Some commentators would like there to be a 'safe harbour' below which a firm could not be found to be dominant. However the case law of the EU Courts does not provide one, and the Commission is not in a position to create one in the absence of jurisprudence enabling it to do so. In paragraph 14 of its *Guidance on Article 102 Enforcement Priorities* the Commission says that dominance is 'not likely' if the undertaking's market share is below 40%; however it goes on to say that there could be some cases below that figure that may deserve its attention. Clearly this falls short of a safe harbour.

(B) **Potential competitors**

As was stressed in chapter 1 and earlier in this chapter, market shares do not in themselves determine whether a firm has a dominant position; in particular they cannot indicate the competitive pressure exerted by firms not yet operating on the market but with the capacity to enter it in a timely manner. The Commission's *Guidance on Article 102 Enforcement Priorities* explains the importance of the impact of expansion by existing competitors and entry by potential ones to any assessment of dominance[81]. In particular paragraph 17 provides examples of various barriers, such as legal barriers; economic advantages enjoyed by the dominant undertaking; costs and network effects that impede customers from switching from one supplier to another; and the dominant firm's own conduct and performance.

(i) **Legal barriers**

Intellectual property rights may constitute barriers to entry, depending on their strength and duration[82], although they do not, in themselves, confer dominance[83]. In *Tetra Pak I (BTG Licence)*[84] the acquisition by Tetra Pak of a company that had the benefit of an exclusive patent and know-how licence was regarded as a factor indicating dominance, as it made entry to the market more difficult for other firms that would be unable to gain access to the licensed technology. In *Servier*[85] the Commission found that the range of patents owned by Servier and its willingness to enforce them were barriers to entry contributing

[79] Case T-219/99 *British Airways plc v Commission* EU:T:2003:343, paras 189–225, upheld on appeal to the Court of Justice Case C-95/04 P *British Airways plc v Commission* EU:C:2007:166.

[80] Case T-219/99 *British Airways plc v Commission* EU:T:2003:343, para 224.

[81] See also Case T-321/05 *AstraZeneca AB v Commission* EU:T:2010:266, para 270.

[82] See eg *Eurofix-Bauco v Hilti* OJ [1988] L 65/19, para 66; *Magill TV Guide/ITP, BBC and RTE* OJ [1989] L 78/43, para 22 (copyright protection of TV listings relevant to finding of dominance), upheld on appeal to the General Court Cases T-69/89 etc *RTE v Commission* EU:T:1991:39, and further on appeal to the Court of Justice Cases C-241 and C-242/91 P EU:C:1995:98.

[83] See eg Case T-321/05 *AstraZeneca AB v Commission* EU:T:2010:266, para 270; similarly see the AG Opinion in Case C-170/13 *Huawei Technologies Co Ltd v ZTE Corp* EU:C:2014:2391, para 57.

[84] OJ [1988] L 272/27, para 44, upheld on appeal Case T-51/89 *Tetra Pak Rausing SA v Commission* EU:T:1990:41: see similarly Case 22/78 *Hugin v Commission* EU:C:1979:138, p 1885.

[85] *Servier*, Commission decision of 9 July 2014, paras 2571–2574.

to its dominant position. Other obvious legal barriers to entry are Government licensing requirements and planning regulations, governmental control of frequencies for the transmission of radio signals[86], statutory monopoly power[87] and tariffs and non-tariff barriers.

(ii) Economic advantages

Various economic advantages have been considered to be barriers to entry or expansion:

- the Court of Justice considered economies of scale to be a relevant factor in *United Brands*[88], and the Commission referred to this matter specifically in *BPB Industries plc*[89] and in *Amazon*[90]; economies of scope would no doubt be treated in the same way[91]
- the control of an essential facility could confer an economic advantage on an incumbent undertaking[92], as could preferential access to natural resources, innovation or R&D; this factor was emphasised by the Commission and the General Court in *Telefónica*[93]
- the Court of Justice treated an undertaking's superior technology as an indicator of dominance in *United Brands*[94], *Hoffmann-La Roche*[95] and *Michelin*[96]
- in *Continental Can*[97] the Commission regarded that firm's access to the international capital market as significant, and this factor was stressed in *United Brands*[98]
- in *United Brands*[99] the Court of Justice described the extent to which UBC's activities were integrated—it owned banana plantations and transport boats and it marketed its bananas itself—and said that this provided that firm with commercial stability which was a significant advantage over its competitors
- in *Hoffmann-La Roche*[100] the Court of Justice pointed to Roche's highly developed sales network as a relevant factor conferring upon it commercial advantages over its rivals. The Commission has treated both vertical integration and the benefit of well-established distribution systems as a barrier to entry in several other decisions[101], since this could impede access for a would-be entrant to the market

[86] *Decca Navigator System* OJ [1989] L 43/27.

[87] Case 311/84 *Centre belge d'études de marché—Télémarketing v CLT* EU:C:1985:394; see Marenco 'Legal Monopolies in the Case Law of the Court of Justice of the European Communities' [1991] Fordham Corporate Law Institute (ed Hawk), 197–222.

[88] Case 27/76 EU:C:1978:22.

[89] See ch 5 n 66 earlier, para 116.

[90] Commission commitment decision of 4 May 2017, para 65(3).

[91] Economies of scale and scope are discussed in ch 1, 'Economies of scale and scope and natural monopolies', pp 10–11.

[92] On essential facilities see ch 17, 'Is the product to which access is sought indispensable to someone wishing to compete in the downstream market?', pp 717–723.

[93] *Telefónica*, Commission decision of 4 July 2007, paras 224–226, upheld on appeal Case T-336/07 *Telefónica SA v Commission* EU:T:2012:172, paras 151–167.

[94] Case 27/76 EU:C:1978:22, paras 82–84.

[95] Case 85/76 EU:C:1979:36, para 48.

[96] Case 322/81 EU:C:1983:313; see also *Eurofix-Bauco v Hilti* (ch 5 n 82 earlier), para 69 and *Tetra Pak I (BTG Licence)* (ch 5, n 84 earlier), para 44; *Michelin* OJ [2002] L 143/1, paras 182–183.

[97] JO [1972] L 7/25.

[98] Case 27/76 EU:C:1978:22, para 122.

[99] Ibid, paras 69–81, 85–90.

[100] Case 85/76 EU:C:1979:36, para 48; see similarly Case 322/81 *Michelin v Commission* EU:C:1983:313, para 58.

[101] See eg *Eurofix-Bauco v Hilti* OJ [1988] L 65/19, para 69; *Napier Brown—British Sugar* OJ [1988] L 284/41, para 56; *PO-Michelin* OJ [2002] L 143/1, paras 191–195.

- in *United Brands*[102] the Court of Justice considered that United Brand's advertising campaigns and brand image were significant factors indicating dominance: United Brands had spent considerable resources establishing the Chiquita brand name which was well protected by trade marks. In its second *Michelin* decision the Commission relied upon the 'indisputable' quality and reputation of the Michelin tyre brand in its finding of dominance[103]. The Commission has noted (in cases under the EU Merger Regulation) that advertising expenditure could make entry difficult into the market for fast-moving consumer goods such as soft drinks[104], sanitary protection[105], and toilet tissue[106]
- in *France Télécom*[107] the General Court held that Wanadoo's 'link-up' with France Télécom conferred on it such advantages over its competitors as to contribute to its dominance
- in *AstraZeneca*[108] the General Court and the Commission considered AZ's 'first-mover' status to be a factor indicating dominance.

(iii) **Costs and network effects**

Costs, and other impediments faced by customers in switching to a new supplier, may be a barrier to expansion or entry[109]. Such costs may result from network effects[110]: this was a relevant consideration in *Microsoft*[111]. The Commission said that the ubiquity of Microsoft in the personal computer operating systems market meant that nearly all commercial applications software was written first and foremost to be compatible with the Microsoft platform. This gave rise to a self-reinforcing dynamic: the more users there were of the Microsoft platform, the more software was written for it, and vice versa[112]. The Commission again referred to network effects in *Google*[113].

The switching costs in *Motorola*[114] were of a different kind from *Microsoft* and *Google*: the widespread adoption of the 2G standard for smartphones meant that mobile phone manufacturers were 'locked-in' to using Motorola's patented technology, and could not switch to other suppliers[115].

(iv) **Conduct**

The Court of Justice in *United Brands v Commission*[116] agreed with the idea that the conduct of a firm could be taken into account in deciding whether it is dominant. This means, for example, that it might be legitimate to take into account the fact that a firm has offered discriminatory rebates to certain customers in deciding whether it is dominant: the rebates may themselves prevent competitors entering the market and so constitute a barrier to entry. In *Michelin v Commission*[117] the Commission had relied on Michelin's

[102] Case 27/76 EU:C:1978:22, paras 91–94. [103] *Michelin* OJ [2002] L 143/1, para 184.

[104] See eg Case M 190 *Nestlé/Perrier* OJ [1992] L 356/1.

[105] See eg Case M 430 *Procter & Gamble/VP Schickendanz* OJ [1994] L 354/32.

[106] See eg Case M 623 *Kimberly-Clark/Scott Paper* OJ [1996] L 183/1.

[107] Case T-340/03 EU:T:2007:22, paras 112–118.

[108] Case T-321/05 EU:T:2010:266, paras 276–283; see also *Telefónica*, Commission decision of 4 July 2007, paras 226–228. [109] *Guidance on Article 102 Enforcement Priorities*, para 17.

[110] On network effects see ch 1, 'Network effects and two-sided markets', pp 11–13.

[111] Commission decision of 24 March 2004.

[112] Ibid, paras 448–459, referring to an 'applications barrier to entry'.

[113] Commission decision of 27 June 2017, paras 292–296, on appeal Case T-612/17 *Google v Commission*, not yet decided.

[114] Commission decision of 29 April 2014, paras 227–236.

[115] See similarly *Unwired Planet v Huawei* [2017] EWHC 711 (Pat), paras 630–680 (SEPs for 2G, 3G and 4G).

[116] Case 27/76 EU:C:1978:22, paras 67–68. [117] Case 322/81 EU:C:1983:313.

price discrimination as an indicator of dominance. Michelin argued before the Court of Justice that this approach was circular: the Commission was saying that because it had offered discriminatory prices, it was dominant, and because it was dominant its discriminatory prices were an abuse. The Court of Justice did not explicitly deal with this issue in its judgment, but in affirming the Commission's decision there is tacit approval of considering conduct as a factor indicating dominance[118]. The Commission also took conduct into account in determining dominance in *Eurofix-Bauco v Hilti*[119], *AKZO*[120] and in *Michelin II*[121].

(v) Performance

The economic performance of an undertaking may be a factor indicating dominance. The fact that a firm had idle capacity was regarded as significant in *Hoffmann-La Roche v Commission*[122]. In *Servier*[123] the Commission found that the persistent and substantial 'economic rents' of Servier were direct evidence of its dominance[124].

(C) Countervailing buyer power

As explained in chapter 1, a further issue of significance is whether a supplier or suppliers are confronted with buyer power[125]. In *Motorola*[126] the Commission emphasised that one of the key elements of countervailing buyer power is a buyer's ability (or credible threat) to switch to competing suppliers, which Apple lacked in that case.

(D) Previous findings of dominance

In *Coca-Cola Co v Commission*[127] the General Court held that, whenever the Commission adopts a decision applying Article 102 (or the EU Merger Regulation), it must define the relevant market and make a fresh analysis of the conditions of competition within it on the basis of the available evidence at the appropriate time; this may lead to a determination of the market which is different from a previous finding[128]. Furthermore a national court (or an NCA) would not be bound in a later case by a previous finding of dominance by the Commission in a different case[129]. However the actual decision in an Article 102 case may serve as a basis for an action for damages brought by a third party before a national court in relation to the same facts, even where the Commission's decision did not impose a fine[130];

[118] See further on the idea that conduct can deter entry Ordover and Salonen 'Predation, Monopolisation and Antitrust' in Schmalensee and Willig (eds) *The Handbook of Industrial Organisation* (North-Holland, 1989); OFT Research Paper 2 *Barriers to Entry and Exit in UK Competition Policy* (London Economics, 1994) and *Assessment of Market Power*, OFT 415, December 2004, paras 5.23–5.28, available at www.gov.uk/cma.

[119] OJ [1988] L 65/19, para 71.

[120] *ECS/AKZO* OJ [1985] L 374/1, para 56, upheld on appeal Case C-62/86 *AKZO Chemie BV v Commission* EU:C:1991:286, para 61.

[121] *PO-Michelin* OJ [2002] L 143/1, paras 197–199.

[122] Case 85/76 EU:C:1979:36, para 48.

[123] Commission decision of 9 July 2014, paras 2579–2585 and 2594–2600, on appeal Case T-691/14 *Servier SAS v Commission*, not yet decided.

[124] See also *Napier Brown—British Sugar* OJ [1988] L 284/41, para 55.

[125] See ch 1, 'Countervailing buyer power', p 45.

[126] Commission decision of 29 April 2014, paras 237–268.

[127] Cases T-125/97 etc EU:T:2000:84; the Commission defined the relevant product and geographic market afresh in its second *Michelin* decision: OJ [2002] L 143/1, paras 109–171.

[128] Cases T-125/87 etc EU:T:2000:84, para 82.

[129] Ibid, para 85.

[130] Ibid, para 86; see also Case C-344/98 *Masterfoods Ltd v HB Ice Cream Ltd* EU:C:2000:689 and Article 16(1) of Regulation 1/2003, discussed in ch 8, 'Article 16: uniform application of EU competition law', pp 319–320 and ch 8, 'Section 58A Competition Act', pp 328–329.

and the Commission is entitled to take into account past assessments of the market in a current investigation when there is nothing to suggest that the conditions of competition on the relevant market have substantially changed compared with earlier decisions[131].

(E) **The degree of market power and super-dominance**

The outcome of several Article 102 cases seems to have turned on the degree of market power that the dominant undertaking enjoyed. For example Tetra Pak's market share in the market for aseptic cartons and carton-filling machines was in the region of 90 to 95%, and it was found to have abused a dominant position where its conduct did not take place in the market in which it was dominant, and was not intended to benefit its position in that market[132]. In *Compagnie Maritime Belge* the shipping conference's market share was 90% or more[133], and it was found to be guilty of an abuse by selectively cutting its prices to some customers, but not to below cost in the sense of the law on predatory pricing[134], whilst charging higher prices to others. In *IMS Health*[135] the Commission, when ordering IMS to grant a licence of its copyright to third parties on the market on a non-discriminatory basis, noted that IMS was in a 'quasi-monopoly situation'[136]. In *Microsoft*[137] the Commission said that Microsoft, with a market share above 90%, had an 'overwhelmingly' dominant position'[138]. The Commissioner for Competition said after the General Court's judgment upholding the Commission's decision that the Court's judgment 'sends a clear signal that super-dominant companies cannot abuse their position to hurt consumers and dampen innovation by excluding competition in related markets'[139].

The Court of Justice in *TeliaSonera*[140] said that, as a general rule, the degree of market strength of a dominant firm is relevant to the assessment of the effects of that firm's conduct rather than to the question of whether an abuse as such exists[141]. The Court stated the same thing in *Tomra*[142], and in *Intel* it said that the Commission should look at the extent of an undertaking's dominant position on the relevant market when considering the likely effects of conditional rebates[143]. The conduct of a firm with a particularly strong market position is more likely to have a correspondingly strong effect on the market and, therefore, is more likely to fall within the mischief of Article 102. A different way of expressing this point is to identify a concept over and above dominance, that we might call 'super-dominance', where the risks of being found to be acting abusively are higher due to the effects of a super-dominant firm's conduct on the market.

The Commission does not use the expression 'super-dominance' in its *Guidance on its Article 102 Enforcement Priorities*. However, one of the factors that the Commission takes into account when deciding whether to intervene is the market strength of the dominant firm. The Commission says that the stronger the dominant position of the undertaking

[131] Case T-699/14 *Topps Europe Ltd v Commission* EU:T:2017:2, para 93.

[132] See 'The dominant position, the abuse and the effects of the abuse may be in different markets', pp 211–213 later in chapter.

[133] See similarly, on the responsibility of a monopolist, Case 7/82 *GVL v Commission* EU:C:1983:52, para 56; this was cited by the Commission in *1998 Football World Cup* OJ [2000] L 5/55, para 85.

[134] See ch 18, 'Selective price cutting but not below cost', pp 764–768.

[135] *NDC Health/IMS Health: Interim Measures* OJ [2002] L 59/18; see also *Deutsche Post AG—Interception of cross-border mail* OJ [2001] L 331/40, paras 103 and 124.

[136] OJ [2002] L 59/18, para 58; this decision was subsequently withdrawn by the Commission: see Commission Press Release IP/03/1159, 13 August 2003.

[137] Commission decision of 24 March 2004.

[138] Ibid, para 435.

[139] See SPEECH/07/539, 17 September 2007.

[140] Case C-52/09 EU:C:2011:83.

[141] Ibid, paras 78–82.

[142] Case C-549/10 P EU:C:2012:221, para 39.

[143] Case C-413/14 P *Intel v Commission* EU:C:2017:632, para 139.

under investigation, the higher the likelihood that conduct protecting that position would have an anti-competitive foreclosure effect on the market. This approach accords with the judgments in *TeliaSonera* and *Tomra*.

7. A Substantial Part of the Internal Market

Once it has been established that a firm has a dominant position on the market, one further jurisdictional question must be answered: is that dominant position held in the whole or a substantial part of the internal market? If not Article 102, by its own terms, does not apply; however the domestic equivalent of Article 102, a variant of which will be found in all the Member States of the EU, may apply.

Obviously there is no problem with the issue of substantiality where an undertaking is dominant throughout the EU. The position may be less obvious where dominance is more localised than this. Suppose that a firm is dominant in just one Member State, or even in a part of one Member State: when will that area be considered to constitute a substantial part of the EU? Four points should be noted.

The first is that the requirement that dominance should exist over a substantial part of the internal market is not the same as the definition of the relevant geographic market: that concept is part of the substantive assessment as to whether an undertaking has a dominant position.

A second point arises from the judgment of the Court of Justice in *Suiker Unie v Commission*[144]. The Court said that for this purpose:

> the pattern and volume of the production and consumption of the said product as well as the habits and economic opportunities of vendors and purchasers must be considered[145].

This indicates that substantiality is not simply a question of relating the *physical* size of the geographic market to the EU as a whole. In *Suiker Unie* the Court considered the ratio of the volume of Belgian and South German production of sugar to EU production overall and concluded on this basis that each of those markets could be considered to be substantial.

The third point is that it is likely that each Member State would be considered to be a substantial part of the internal market, in particular where an undertaking enjoys a statutory monopoly[146], and *Suiker Unie* further established that parts of a Member State can be[147].

The fourth point is that neither the EU Courts nor the Commission have laid down that any particular percentage of the internal market as a whole is critical in determining what is substantial. In *BP v Commission*[148] Advocate General Warner took the view that sole reliance should not be placed on percentages in such cases and was of the opinion that the Dutch market for petrol, which represented only about 4.6% of the EU market as a whole, could be considered substantial. The Court of Justice did not comment on this issue, as it quashed the Commission's finding of abuse on other grounds.

There are numerous examples of the test of substantiality having been satisfied in relation to a single facility: in each of *Merci Convenzionali Porto di Genova v Siderurgica*

[144] Cases 40/73 etc EU:C:1975:174. [145] Ibid, para 371.

[146] Case 127/73 *BRT v SABAM* EU:C:1974:25, para 5; Case T-229/94 *Deutsche Bahn AG v Commission* EU:T:1997:155; Case T-228/97 *Irish Sugar v Commission* EU:T:1999:246, para 99.

[147] It is important to remember however that the abuse must also have an effect on trade between Member States to fall within Article 102: see 'The Effect on Inter-State Trade', p 186 earlier.

[148] Case 77/77 EU:C:1978:107.

Gabriella[149], *Sealink/B&I—Holyhead: Interim Measures*[150], *Sea Containers v Stena Sealink—Interim Measures*[151], *Flughafen Frankfurt/Main*[152], *Corsica Ferries*[153], *Portuguese Airports*[154], *Ilmailulaitos/Luftfartsverket*[155] and *Spanish Airports*[156] ports or airports have been found to be sufficiently substantial. Furthermore the Court of Justice has held that, where national law confers a contiguous series of monopolies within a Member State which, taken together, cover the entire territory of that state, that law creates a dominant position in a substantial part of the internal market[157].

8. Abuse

(A) Introduction

It is not controversial to say that Article 102 is controversial. In the case of Article 101 undertakings are liable only when they enter into agreements or concerted practices that restrict competition; a great deal of the Commission's (and of the NCAs') attention is focused on the deliberate and secret cartelisation of markets, and there are few apologists today for this kind of behaviour[158]. Article 102, on the other hand, bears upon the individual behaviour of dominant firms[159]; by its nature the application of Article 102 involves a competition authority or a court having to decide whether that behaviour deviates from 'normal' or 'fair' or 'undistorted' competition, or from 'competition on the merits', none of which expressions is free from difficulty. It should be added that the controversy surrounding Article 102 is not unique to the EU: all systems of competition law contain provisions on the unilateral conduct of firms with substantial market power, and competition authorities and courts worldwide have had to grapple with the issues under consideration in this chapter. Significant work has been undertaken under the auspices of the ICN on this topic: in particular the Unilateral Conduct Working Group, established in 2006, has adopted *Recommended Practices on Predatory Pricing Analysis Pursuant to Unilateral Conduct Laws*; it is also preparing a 'workbook' on the analysis of unilateral conduct, and has so far produced draft chapters on *Objectives of Unilateral Conduct Laws, Assessment of Dominance/Substantial Market Power, Predatory Pricing Analysis and Exclusive Dealing/Single Branding* and *Tying and Bundling*[160].

The text that follows will examine the meaning of abuse by reference to the underlying purpose of Article 102 as well as the jurisprudence of the EU Courts; it will then consider three categories of cases under Article 102, namely exploitative, exclusionary and single market abuses. However, a few preliminary points may be helpful.

149 Case C-179/90 EU:C:1991:464, para 15. 150 [1992] 5 CMLR 255, para 40.
151 OJ [1994] L 15/8. 152 OJ [1998] L 72/30. 153 Case C-18/93 EU:C:1994:195.
154 OJ [1999] L 69/31, upheld on appeal Case C-163/99 *Portugal v Commission* EU:C:2001:189.
155 OJ [1999] L 69/24. 156 OJ [2000] L 208/36.
157 Case C-323/93 *La Crespelle* EU:C:1994:368, para 17; this reasoning was applied by the Commission in, eg, *Portuguese Airports* OJ [1999] L 69/31, paras 21–22.
158 See ch 13 generally on cartels.
159 Article 102 can also apply to the abuse of collective dominance, although this is not a concept that has been explored in much detail in the case law: see ch 14, 'Abuse of collective dominance under Article 102', pp 591–594.
160 Available at www.internationalcompetitionnetwork.org; many other interesting work products on unilateral conduct laws will be found on this site, along with the current and long-term work plans of the ICN in this area; see also the OECD Roundtable, *Competition on the Merits* (2005), available at www.oecd.org.

(B) Four preliminary points

(i) The 'special responsibility' of dominant firms

It is not unlawful for a firm to have a dominant position; what is prohibited is the abuse of a dominant position. However the Court of Justice in *Michelin v Commission*[161] stated that a firm in a dominant position has a 'special responsibility not to allow its conduct to impair undistorted competition' on the internal market[162]. This statement is routinely repeated in the judgments of the EU Courts and the decisions of the Commission on Article 102[163]. In a sense it is a statement of the obvious: it is clear that Article 102 imposes obligations on dominant firms that non-dominant firms do not bear. Unilateral behaviour is not controlled under Article 101, which applies only to collusive conduct; unilateral acts however can amount to an infringement of Article 102[164]. However the conundrum for anyone interested in Article 102 is to determine what, precisely, is meant by an abuse of a dominant position.

(ii) Article 102 does not contain an exhaustive list of what amounts to abusive behaviour

Article 102 gives examples of conduct that is abusive—charging unfair prices, limiting production and discrimination that places certain trading parties at a competitive disadvantage—but this list is not exhaustive[165]; the Commission and the EU Courts have applied Article 102 to numerous practices not specifically mentioned in it. An example of this is the Court of Justice's judgment in *AstraZeneca AB v Commission*[166] in which it held that a pattern of making misleading misrepresentations to patent offices in various Member States that led to the extension of patent protection for pharmaceutical products to which AZ was not, in fact, entitled amounted to an abuse of a dominant position; the same was true of AZ's requests to public authorities to deregister market authorisations for particular drugs, thereby impeding entry to the market by generic manufacturers. A reading of the list of examples of abusive behaviour in Article 102 would not prepare any but the most imaginative reader to suppose that these practices were abusive; but the EU Courts appear to have had no hesitation in finding them to be illegal. Examples of practices found to be abusive will be given later in this chapter and will be considered in depth in chapter 17 (non-pricing abuses) and chapter 18 (pricing abuses).

(iii) False positives and false negatives

A difficulty with Article 102 is that the line between pro- and anti-competitive conduct is not always an easy one to draw, and there is an obvious danger that, if Article 102 is applied too aggressively, firms might refrain from conduct that is in fact pro-competitive. Clearly it would be the ultimate paradox if a law designed to promote competition in fact

[161] Case 322/81 EU:C:1983:313. [162] Ibid, para 57.

[163] For recent statements to this effect see Case C-457/10 P *AstraZeneca AB v Commission* EU:C:2012:770, para 134; Case C-209/10 *Post Danmark I* EU:C:2012:172, para 23; Case C-413/14 P *Intel v Commission* EU:C:2017:632, para 135.

[164] The respective roles of Articles 101 and 102 are spelt out particularly clearly in the judgment of the General Court in Case T-41/96 *Bayer v Commission* EU:T:2000:242, paras 175–176.

[165] Case 6/72 *Continental Can v Commission* EU:C:1973:22, para 26; Cases C-395/96 P etc *Compagnie Maritime Belge Transports SA v Commission* EU:C:2000:132, para 112; Case C-280/08 P *Deutsche Telekom AG v Commission* EU:C:2010:603, para 173.

[166] Case C-457/10 P EU:C:2012:770, upholding the judgment of the General Court, Case T-321/05 *AstraZeneca AB v Commission* EU:T:2010:266.

were to have the effect of diminishing it[167]. However it is equally clear that unduly lenient treatment on the part of competition authorities and courts could lead to the exclusion from the market of efficient competitors, with adverse consequences for the competitive process and consumer welfare.

A more stylised way of presenting this problem is to consider the difference between what are sometimes referred to as 'false positives' and 'false negatives'[168].

A **false positive** occurs where a competition authority incorrectly concludes that pro-competitive behaviour is abusive: a harm to the firm(s) found guilty, and also to consumers, since the pro-competitive behaviour will be prohibited. The problem here is that the law is over-inclusive.

A **false negative** occurs where a competition authority incorrectly concludes that anti-competitive behaviour is not illegal and therefore permits it: a harm to consumers. Here the law is under-inclusive.

Given the inherent difficulty of determining which unilateral acts are anti-competitive and which are pro-competitive, it is inevitable that competition authorities will sometimes make errors; a policy question when framing rules on unilateral behaviour is to decide which of the two errors is preferable. There is an undoubted perception that the enforcement authorities and the courts in the US are more concerned about false positives than false negatives: that is to say that they err on the side of non-intervention under section 2 of the Sherman Act 1890, which forbids the monopolisation of markets[169], whereas the Commission and the EU Courts perhaps tend the other way[170]. In *Verizon Communications Inc v Law Offices of Curtis Trinko*[171] the US Supreme Court, in a refusal to supply case, was explicit about its fear of false positives:

> Against the slight benefits of antitrust intervention here, we must weigh a realistic assessment of its costs . . . Mistaken inferences and the resulting false condemnations are 'especially costly, because they chill the very conduct the antitrust laws are designed to protect' . . . The cost of false positives counsels against an undue expansion of s. 2 liability[172].

The same attitude helps to explain the conclusion of the Supreme Court in *Pacific Bell v linkLine*[173], where it held that a margin squeeze is not an independent infringement of section 2 of the Sherman Act[174]. In contrast one might note that on many occasions when

[167] A series of essays on the question of whether (mis)application of laws dealing with unilateral conduct has a chilling effect on competition, by Bourgeois, Fingleton and Nikpay, Lewis and Lugard respectively, will be found in chs 15–18 of [2008] Fordham Corporate Law Institute (ed Hawk).

[168] Economics literature sometimes uses the expressions 'Type I errors' and 'Type II errors', but the tendency to confuse which error is of which type (sometimes referred to jocularly as a 'Type III' error) argues in favour of the language of false positives and false negatives.

[169] For discussion of section 2 of the Sherman Act see Sullivan and Harrison *Understanding Antitrust and Its Economic Implications* (LexisNexis, 4th ed, 2003), ch 6; Sullivan and Hovenkamp *Antitrust Law, Policy and Procedure: Cases, Materials, Problems* (LexisNexis, 5th ed, 2004), ch 6; Fox, Sullivan and Peritz *Cases and Materials on US Antitrust in Global Context* (Thomson/West, 2nd ed, 2004), ch 3; Hovenkamp *Federal Antitrust Policy: The Law of Competition and Its Practice* (Thomson/West, 3rd ed, 2005), chs 6–10; Kovacic 'The Intellectual DNA of Modern US Competition Law for Dominant Firm Conduct: The Chicago/Harvard Double Helix' (2007) Columbia Business Law Review 1; for a critique of the 'vacuous standards and conclusory labels that provide no meaningful guidance about which conduct will be condemned as exclusionary' under section 2 of the Sherman Act see Elhauge 'Defining Better Monopolization Standards' (2003) 56 Stanford Law Review 253.

[170] For an interesting discussion of the differences in approach in the US and the EU, suggesting that the position in the US can lead to anti-competitive behaviour escaping sanction, see Fox 'A Tale of Two Jurisdictions and an Orphan Case: Antitrust, Intellectual Property, and Refusals to Deal' (2005) 28 Fordham International Law Journal 952.

[171] 540 US 398 (2004). [172] Ibid. [173] 555 US 438 (2009).

[174] See ch 18, 'The economic phenomenon', pp 771–772.

the EU Courts have been invited to expand Article 102 liability they have done so: for example when establishing that Article 102 could apply to mergers[175]; when deciding that there did not need to be any causation between the market power held by a dominant firm and its abusive behaviour[176]; when accepting that the dominance, abuse and effects of the abuse can be in different markets[177]; when extending the application of Article 102 to collective, as well as to individual, dominance[178]; and when acknowledging the possibility of an individual abuse of a collective dominant position[179]. This record does not suggest the same reticence as that of the US Supreme Court in *Verizon*.

(iv) Single and continuous abuse

Just as it is possible under Article 101 for there to be a 'single overall agreement' that violates that provision[180], so too it is possible for there to be a 'single overall abuse' (or a 'single and continuous abuse') under Article 102. For example in *AstraZeneca v Commission*[181] the General Court confirmed the finding of the Commission that AstraZeneca was guilty of a 'single and continuous' abuse consisting of a deliberate strategy of misleading national patent offices[182]. In *Intel v Commission*[183] the Court of Justice concluded that, for the purposes of establishing jurisdiction on the basis of qualified effects, it was appropriate to look at Intel's 'overall strategy', rather than looking at each separate act on its part, which 'would lead to an artificial fragmentation of comprehensive anticompetitive conduct'[184]. The Commission found a single overall abuse in *Telekomunikacja Polska*[185], in *Romanian Power Exchange: OPCOM*[186] and in *Servier*[187].

(C) What is the purpose of Article 102?

Before considering the jurisprudence of the EU Courts and the practice of the Commission on the meaning of abuse, it is necessary to give some consideration to the underlying purpose of Article 102. The various possible objectives of competition law have been discussed in chapter 1 of this book[188]. There it was pointed out that competition authorities today stress the central importance of consumer welfare when applying competition law, but that other matters such as the redistribution of wealth and the protection of small firms against more powerful rivals have also been influential at various points in time.

(i) Protection of competitors or protection of competition?

A specific criticism of Article 102 is that it is used to protect competitors, including inefficient ones, rather than the process of competition, which is a quite different matter. According to this view Article 102, in effect, subjects dominant firms to a handicap:

175 See '*Continental Can v Commission*', p 209 later in chapter.

176 See 'Causation', pp 209–210 later in chapter.

177 See 'The dominant position, the abuse and the effects of the abuse may be in different markets', pp 211–213 later in chapter.

178 See ch 14, 'Article 102 and Collective Dominance', pp 583–594.

179 See ch 14, 'Abuse of collective dominance under Article 102', pp 591–594.

180 See ch 3, 'Single overall agreement', pp 105–109.

181 Case T-321/05 EU:T:2010:266.

182 Ibid, paras 890–899; this issue was not discussed on appeal to the Court of Justice.

183 Case C-413/14 P EU:C:2017:632.

184 Ibid, paras 54–58; on the qualified effects doctrine as a basis of jurisdiction see ch 12, 'The qualified effects doctrine', pp 504–505.

185 Commission decision of 22 June 2011: see Art 1 of the operative part of that decision.

186 Commission decision of 5 March 2014: see para 320 and Art 1 of the operative part.

187 Commission decision of 9 July 2014: see paras 2961–2963.

188 See ch 1, 'Goals of competition law', pp 18–24.

competitive acts, such as price reductions or the bundling of different products, that are perfectly legal for non-dominant firms, become illegal when a firm is dominant. The complaint is that this means that firms that possess superior efficiency are restrained in order to provide a place in the competitive arena for less efficient ones. This characteristic of Article 102 would be exacerbated if it is, indeed, the case that institutions in the EU have a tendency to be more concerned about false negatives than false positives.

The criticism that Article 102 protects competitors rather than competition brings to mind Robert Bork's attack on the antitrust rules as they were applied in the US in the 1960s and 1970s, and in particular what he regarded as the 'uncritical sentimentality in favour of the small guy' of the enforcement authorities and the courts there at that time[189]. The most high-level accusation of the EU's supposed predilection for protecting competitors rather than competition came from the Assistant Attorney General for Antitrust at the US Department of Justice in response to the judgment of the General Court of the EU in September 2007 upholding the European Commission's decision that Microsoft had abused its dominant position[190]. After expressing 'concern' about the standard applied to unilateral conduct in Europe, the Assistant Attorney General said that:

> In the United States, the antitrust laws are enforced to protect consumers by protecting competition, not competitors[191].

Without saying more, his meaning could hardly have been clearer: that in the EU the prime concern is not with the protection of consumers through competition, but with the protection of competitors.

Some commentators lay the blame for what they see as an unduly interventionist application of Article 102 at the door of the school of ordoliberalism which, through its concern to protect economic freedom, including the right of access to markets unconstrained by barriers such as exclusive agreements or rebating and discounting practices having analogous effects, led to the adoption of formalistic rules capable of having perverse consequences[192].

However, in the opinion of the authors of this book the assertion that the fingerprints of the ordoliberal school are to be found on the case law of Article 102, and that this has led to a systematic bias in favour of competitors and against efficient dominant firms, is at best a misdescription of the true position and at worst little more than a slogan by protagonists of minimalist intervention. One commentator has examined the *travaux préparatoires* of Article 102 and suggested that its drafters were mainly concerned with increasing economic efficiency; their intention was not to protect competitors, but their customers[193]. This explains why the language of Article 102 is predominantly focused on exploitative behaviour, such as the imposition of unfair selling prices, unfair trading conditions and the limitation of markets to the prejudice of consumers, rather than

189 Bork *The Antitrust Paradox* (The Free Press, 1993).

190 Case T-201/04 *Microsoft Corpn v Commission* EU:T:2007:289.

191 See Press Release of 17 September 2007, available at www.justice.gov/atr.

192 For a discussion of ordoliberalism see ch 1, 'Protecting competitors', pp 21–22; for an example of criticism of the impact of ordoliberalism see eg Kallaugher and Sher 'Rebates Revisited: Anti-Competition Effects and Exclusionary Abuse Under Article 82' (2004) 25 ECLR 263; Venit 'Article 82: The Last Frontier—Fighting Fire with Fire' (2005) 28 Fordham International Law Journal 1157; Ahlborn and Padilla 'From Fairness to Welfare: Implications for the Assessment of Unilateral Conduct under EC Competition Law' in Ehlermann and Marquis (eds) *European Competition Law Annual 2007: A Reformed Approach to Article 82 EC* (Hart, 2008).

193 See Akman 'Searching for the Long-Lost Soul of Article 82 EC' (2009) 29 OJLS 267; for a response see Behrens 'The ordoliberal concept of "abuse": of a dominant position and its impact on Article 102 TFEU', available at www.ssrn.com.

exclusionary abuses[194]. It also tends to refute the widely-held belief in the English-language literature that Article 102 is based on ordoliberal foundations.

(ii) Article 102 protects competition; and competition is for the benefit of consumers

Numerous statements to the effect that Article 102 is concerned with the protection of competition rather than the protection of competitors can be found. Many of these come from the Commission (or from Commission officials), but they can also be found in judgments of the EU Courts, particularly in recent years in judgments such as *Deutsche Telekom, TeliaSonera, Post Danmark I, Post Danmark II* and *Intel*.

A clear statement to this effect was made by Neelie Kroes, the former Commissioner for Competition, when discussing the Commission's review of exclusionary abuses at the annual conference at Fordham in September 2005[195]:

> My own philosophy on this is fairly simple. First, it is competition, and not competitors, that is to be protected. Second, ultimately the aim is to avoid consumers harm.
>
> I like aggressive competition—including by dominant companies—and I don't care if it may hurt competitors—as long as it ultimately benefits consumers. That is because the main and ultimate objective of Article 102 is to protect consumers, and this does, of course, require the protection of an undistorted competitive process on the market.

The same idea is stated at several points in the Commission's *Guidance on Article 102 Enforcement Priorities*[196]. A few examples illustrate the point. In paragraph 5 the Commission says that:

> The Commission . . . will direct its enforcement to ensuring that markets function properly and that consumers benefit from the efficiency and productivity which result from effective competition between undertakings.

In paragraph 6 it says that:

> [T]he Commission is mindful that what really matters is protecting an effective competitive process and not simply protecting competitors. *This may well mean that competitors who deliver less to consumers in terms of price, choice, quality and innovation will leave the market* (emphasis added).

The Commission adds, in paragraph 23, that:

> [T]he Commission will normally only intervene where the conduct concerned has already been or is capable of hampering competition from competitors *which are considered to be as efficient* as the dominant undertaking (emphasis added).

Judgments of the Court of Justice themselves stress the importance of protecting the process of competition for the benefit of consumers[197]. Even before the judgment of the Court of Justice in *Intel*, it seemed to go out of its way to stress that Article 102 protects only

[194] See 'Exploitative, exclusionary and single market abuses', pp 207–208 later in chapter on the distinction between exploitative and exclusionary abuses.

[195] SPEECH/05/537, 23 September 2005; numerous statements to the same effect can be found: see eg speech by Lowe 'Innovation and Regulation of Dominant Firms', 23 September 2008 and speech by Commissioner Alumnia 'Converging paths in unilateral conduct', 3 December 2010, available at www.ec.europa.eu.

[196] OJ [2009] C 45/7.

[197] See eg (in a case on Article 101 rather than Article 102) the Court of Justice in Cases C-501/06 P etc *GlaxoSmithKline Services Unlimited v Commission* EU:C:2009:610, para 63; see also the General Court in Case T-340/03 *France Télécom v Commission* EU:T:2007:22, para 266 and Case T-321/05 *AstraZeneca AB v Commission* EU:T:2010:266, para 353.

'as-efficient' competitors, and not inefficient ones. At paragraph 177 of its judgment in *Deutsche Telekom* the Court said that:

> Article [102 TFEU] prohibits a dominant undertaking from, inter alia, adopting pricing practices which have an exclusionary effect *on its equally efficient actual or potential competitors* (emphasis added)[198].

The same language occurs repeatedly throughout the judgment[199]; the same is true of the judgments in *TeliaSonera*[200], *Post Danmark I*[201] and *Intel*[202].

Collectively this reveals a consistent tendency on the part of the Court of Justice and the Commission, at least in recent times, to stress competition, efficiency and consumer welfare as the key objectives of Article 102. It is difficult, therefore, to sustain the argument that the EU institutions today have an active policy of protecting competitors rather than the process of competition.

(D) **Jurisprudence on the meaning of abuse**

Article 102 does not contain an exhaustive list of all the practices that can amount to an abuse. Nor is there one particular judgment of the Court of Justice or the General Court that provides an all-encompassing definition of what is meant by abuse. This is understandable: cases on abuse of dominance turn on their own particular facts—a point stressed on numerous occasions[203]—and the EU Courts have refrained from broad theoretical statements, preferring instead to decide each case on its merits (albeit taking into account earlier judgments). As Philip Lowe, at the time the Director-General of DG COMP, said in his remarks on unilateral conduct in Washington in September 2006:

> [J]ust as physicists strive to find the theory that unifies Newtonian physics and quantum mechanics, so economists strive to find the theory that unifies the various aspects of anti-competitive unilateral conduct. And the economists, just as the physicists, have not yet found it[204].

(i) Hoffmann-La Roche v Commission

One paragraph that is regularly cited on the meaning of abuse will be found in *Hoffmann-La Roche v Commission*[205]. At paragraph 91 the Court of Justice said that abuse is:

> An objective concept relating to the behaviour of an undertaking in a dominant position which is such as to influence the structure of a market where, as a result of the very presence of the undertaking in question the degree of competition is weakened and which, through recourse to methods different from those which condition normal competition in products or services on the basis of the transaction of commercial operators, has the effect of hindering the maintenance of the degree of competition still existing in the market or the growth of that competition.

198 Case C-280/08 P EU:C:2010:603, para 177.

199 Ibid, paras 203, 234, 236, 240, 252–255 and 259.

200 Case C-52/09 *Konkurrensverket v TeliaSonera Sverige AB* EU:C:2011:83, paras 31–33, 39–40, 43, 63–64, 67, 70 and 73.

201 Case C-209/10 *Post Danmark v Konkurrencerådet* EU:C:2012:172, paras 21, 22, 25 and 38.

202 Case C-413/14 P *Intel v Commission* EU:C:2017:632, paras 133, 134, 136, 139, 140.

203 See eg Case C-95/04 P *British Airways plc v Commission* EU:C:2007:166, para 64; see also para 68 of the Opinion of AG Jacobs in Case C-53/03 *Syfait* EU:C:2004:673.

204 See speech of 11 September 2006, available at www.ec.europa.eu.

205 Case 85/76 EU:C:1979:36; for a more recent statement to the same effect see eg Case C-280/08 P *Deutsche Telekom AG v Commission* EU:C:2010:603, para 174 and the case law cited therein.

This is an important paragraph, but it does not provide an overarching definition of abuse. For example it does not capture the idea of exploitative, as opposed to exclusionary, practices of a dominant firm, such as charging customers excessively high prices: such conduct cannot be said to *hinder* competition, and yet it can undoubtedly amount to an abuse of a dominant position, as Article 102 explicitly states. However the Court's judgment in *Hoffmann-La Roche* does introduce the idea that dominant undertakings must refrain from 'methods different from those which condition normal competition'. Of course this begs the question: what is 'normal' competition, a vague and indeterminate word[206]. However the idea of 'normal' competition comes more clearly into focus if slightly different language is used: namely that dominant firms should 'compete on the merits', and that competition that is not on the merits is 'abnormal' competition.

(ii) Competition on the merits

The EU Courts use the language of competition on the merits, noticeably so in some recent judgments. For example in *Deutsche Telekom v Commission*[207] the Court of Justice said, after quoting from paragraph 91 of *Hoffmann-La Roche*, that a dominant firm must not strengthen its dominant position:

> By using methods other than those which come within the scope of competition on the merits[208].

In *AstraZeneca v Commission*[209] the Court of Justice commenced its discussion of abuse by stating that a dominant firm must not eliminate a competitor other than by methods that come within the scope of competition on the merits[210]. In *Post Danmark I*[211], after noting that not every exclusionary effect is necessarily detrimental to competition, the Court of Justice said that:

> Competition on the merits may, by definition, lead to the departure from the market or the marginalization of competitors that are less efficient and so less attractive to consumers from the point of view of, among other things, price, choice, quality or innovation[212].

The Court of Justice repeated this statement in *Intel*[213]. The Commission has given examples of what it considers to be competition on the merits in paragraph 5 of its *Guidance on Article 102 Enforcement Priorities*: offering lower prices, better quality and a wider choice of new and improved goods and services. When compared to business behaviour of this kind, it is not difficult to see that other acts—such as the misleading of patent authorities leading to the award of additional patent protection from generic producers of pharmaceutical products and payments for delaying the launch of a competing product—do not amount to competition on the merits, and are therefore abusive.

(E) Are there or should there be any *per se* rules under Article 102?

The discussion so far suggests that Article 102, as applied today, is concerned to protect consumer welfare; it does not protect competitors as such; and that dominant firms

[206] In *National Grid Plc v Gas & Electricity Markets Authority* [2010] EWCA Civ 114, the English Court of Appeal said that 'normal' competition is not 'a sufficiently hard-edged concept that it can be determined as a matter of law'; it is a 'question of expert appreciation': ibid, para 41.

[207] Case C-280/08 P EU:C:2010:603.

[208] Ibid, para 177; see similarly Case T-201/04 *Microsoft Corp v Commission* EU:T:2007:289, para 1070; Case C-52/09 *TeliaSonera* EU:C:2011:83, para 43.

[209] Case C-457/10 P EU:C:2012:770.

[210] Ibid, para 75. [211] Case C-209/10 EU:C:2012:172. [212] Ibid, para 22.

[213] Case C-413/14 P *Intel v Commission* EU:C:2017:632, para 134.

should compete on the merits and refrain from 'abnormal' competition. However, even if this is the case, there remains a problem: can these ideas be expressed in administrable rules capable of being applied by competition authorities, courts, professional advisers and dominant undertakings themselves? More specifically, is it possible to avoid the problem of false positives and false negatives, both of which are undesirable in principle?

One of the most common complaints about Article 102 is that the Commission and the EU Courts apply it in too formalistic a manner. This criticism can be articulated in various ways. One is the argument that some practices appear to be unlawful *per se*, but that *per se* rules are inappropriate for behaviour such as price cutting and refusals to deal which may, depending on the facts of a particular case, be pro-competitive, anti-competitive, or neutral. Another way of voicing the same criticism is to argue that the Commission and the EU Courts often fail to demonstrate how a particular practice could have significant effects on the market: some critics argue that they fail to articulate a convincing theory of harm and/or to produce evidence that adverse effects would follow from the practice under investigation.

(i) **Are there any *per se* rules under Article 102?**

Historically there was a tendency on the part of both the EU Courts and the Commission to apply *per se* rules, at least to some abuses. This was particularly true of the law on loyalty rebates. The Court of Justice in *Hoffmann-La Roche v Commission* had formulated a rule on exclusive dealing and loyalty rebates by a dominant undertaking in *per se* terms[214]. In paragraph 89 of its judgment, after saying that it would be unlawful for a dominant firm to enter into exclusive dealing agreements with customers, it continued that the same would be true where that firm:

> [a]pplies, either under the terms of agreements concluded with these purchasers or unilaterally, a system of loyalty rebates, that is to say, discounts conditional on the customer's obtaining all or most of its requirements—whether the quantity of its purchases be large or small—from the undertaking in a dominant position.

This approach was followed in several cases on rebates[215].

In *Intel v Commission*[216] the General Court continued to adopt a strict approach to rebates granted in return for exclusivity, which it said were illegal unless the dominant firm could show an objective justification for granting them[217]. However there was an increasing intellectual consensus against the application of *per se* rules to unilateral behaviour, and the judgment of the General Court in *Intel* attracted particular hostility because of its 'formalistic' approach to exclusivity rebates. On appeal the Court of Justice in *Intel v Commission*[218] appears to have recognised this criticism and has, in effect, put an end to *per se* analysis under Article 102, as explained in the following section.

(ii) **Recent case law and decisions do require effects analysis**

The Commission in its *Guidance on Article 102 Enforcement Priorities* said that it would concentrate its enforcement activity on practices likely to have seriously anti-competitive

[214] Case 85/76 EU:C:1979:36.

[215] See eg Case T-203/01 *Michelin v Commission* EU:T:2003:250, para 56; Case T-219/99 *British Airways plc v Commission* EU:T:2003:343, para 244, upheld on appeal to the Court of Justice, Case C-95/04 P EU:C:2007:166; Case T-57/01 *Solvay v Commission* EU:T:2009:519, para 316, annulled on procedural grounds on appeal to the Court of Justice, Case C-109/10 P EU:C:2011:686.

[216] Case T-286/09 EU:T:2014:547.

[217] Ibid, para 81; see also para 94 which refers both to the possibility of objective justification and to an efficiency 'defence'; on defences see 'Defences', pp 217–220 below.

[218] Case C-413/14 P EU:C:2017:632.

effects on the market. In various Article 102 decisions the Commission has sought to produce evidence of anti-competitive effects, even where it considered that it was not legally obliged to do so: this was true, for example, of the decisions in *Microsoft*[219], *Intel*[220], *Servier*[221] and *Google*[222].

Several judgments of the Court of Justice have stressed the need for a demonstration of actual or likely anti-competitive effects. For example in *Deutsche Telekom v Commission*[223] the Court of Justice stated that potential anti-competitive effects must be demonstrated before a margin squeeze is condemned as unlawful[224]. In *TeliaSonera*[225] it said that:

> in order to establish whether [a margin squeeze] is abusive, that practice must have an anti-competitive effect on the market[226].

In *Post Danmark I* the Court of Justice said that when determining whether a pricing practice could be abusive it was necessary to take into account 'all the circumstances' which would include the likely effects of the practice in question[227], a formulation repeated in *Post Danmark II*[228]. In *Intel v Commission* the General Court seemed to be swimming against this tide by saying that a rebate given in return for exclusivity was presumptively unlawful unless it could be objectively justified[229]. On appeal the Court of Justice, at paragraph 137 of its judgment, cited paragraph 89 of the judgment in *Hoffmann-La Roche*, set out in the previous section, that appeared to apply a *per se* rule to loyalty rebates; however in paragraph 138 the Court added an important qualification:

> However, that case-law must be further clarified in the case where the undertaking concerned submits, during the administrative procedure, on the basis of supporting evidence, that its conduct was not capable of restricting competition and, in particular, of producing the alleged foreclosure effects.

This 'clarification' of the law means that if a dominant firm, in response to an allegation of abuse, argues that the practice in question could not have a foreclosure effect, the Commission is obliged to address that argument. It is hard to imagine that a dominant firm that is convinced that its behaviour is not anti-competitive would not submit such evidence. It follows that the Court's qualification would seem, *de facto*, to mean that conduct can be abusive only where it can be shown to be capable of having anti-competitive effects on as-efficient competitors. To put the point another way, there is no *per se* illegality under Article 102.

In passing it should be noted that the specific question in *Intel* was whether exclusivity rebates offered by Intel to its customers were abusive. The Court of Justice concluded that the General Court had failed to examine arguments raised by Intel as to the way in which the Commission conducted its assessment of its rebates: for this reason the General Court's judgment was set aside and the matter was referred back to it for further

[219] Commission decision of 24 March 2004, paras 835–954, upheld on appeal to the General Court Case T-201/04 *Microsoft Corp v Commission* EU:T:2007:289, paras 1031–1090.

[220] Commission decision of 13 May 2009, paras 1597–1616; in Case T-286/09 RENV *Intel v Commission* the General Court has been required by the Court of Justice to conduct a judicial review of the Commission's 'as-efficient competitor' analysis in paras 1002–1576 of its decision.

[221] Commission decision of 9 July 2014, paras 2939–2957, on appeal Case T-691/14 *Servier v Commission*, not yet decided.

[222] Commission decision of 27 June 2017, on appeal Case T-612/17 *Google v Commission*, not yet decided.

[223] Case C-280/08 P *Deutsche Telekom AG v Commission* EU:C:2010:603.

[224] Ibid, paras 250–261; Case C-52/09 *Konkurrensverket v TeliaSonera Sverige AB* EU:C:2011:83, paras 60–77.

[225] Case C-52/09 *Konkurrensverket v TeliaSonera Sverige AB* EU:C:2011:83.

[226] Ibid, para 64.

[227] Case C-209/10 EU:C:2012:172, para 26.

[228] Case C-23/14 EU:C:2015:651, para 29.

[229] Case T-286/09 EU:T:2014:547, paras 81, 94.

examination. It remains to be decided, therefore, whether the rebates in this particular case were abusive[230].

(iii) *De minimis* doctrine under Article 102?

An interesting question related to effects analysis is whether the conduct of a dominant firm could fall outside Article 102 because its effect is *de minimis*. In *Intel v Commission*[231] the General Court held that in a case of abuse of dominance there is no *de minimis* doctrine: since dominance means that the structure of competition on the market is already weakened, it follows that any further weakening of competition may be abusive. This was based on a sentence in paragraph 123 of the Court of Justice's judgment in *Hoffmann-La Roche v Commission*[232]. In *Post Danmark II*[233] a Danish court specifically asked the Court of Justice whether there was an 'appreciability' requirement under Article 102 and it received a very clear answer. After citing paragraph 123 of *Hoffmann-La Roche* the Court of Justice said:

> It follows that fixing an appreciability (*de minimis*) threshold for the purposes of determining whether there is an abuse of a dominant position is not justified. That anticompetitive practice is, by its very nature, liable to give rise to not insignificant restrictions of competition, or even of eliminating competition on the market on which the undertaking concerned operates.

What is unclear is whether the judgment of the Court of Justice in *Intel* by implication overrules *Post Danmark II*. As noted, paragraph 138 of *Intel* states that a dominant firm may respond to an accusation of abuse by submitting evidence that the conduct in question could have no foreclosure effect; if *Post Danmark II* remains good law, this must mean that the dominant firm must prove that there would be no foreclosure effect **whatsoever**, rather than that any foreclosure would be *de minimis*.

The authors of this book consider that there should be a *de minimis* threshold in Article 102 cases. The law ought not to concern itself with trivial or insignificant effects on competition. To require the person alleging an infringement of Article 102 to show an appreciable effect on the market would be consistent with the Court's judgments in *TeliaSonera* and *Intel*, both of which indicate that the degree of dominance is relevant to effects analysis[234].

(F) Exploitative, exclusionary and single market abuses

When reviewing the decisional practice of the Commission and the jurisprudence of the EU Courts, it is possible to identify at least two, and perhaps three, types of abuse. The first consists of **exploitative abuses**. The most obvious objection to a monopolist is that it is in a position to reduce output and increase the price of its products above the competitive level, thereby exploiting customers[235]. However in the absence of barriers to entry a monopolist earning monopoly profits would be expected to attract new entrants to the

[230] For further discussion of rebates generally and the *Intel* case in particular see ch 18, 'Conditional Rebates', pp 746–754.

[231] Case T-286/09 EU:T:2014:547, para 116.

[232] Case 85/76 EU:C:1979:36.

[233] Case C-23/14 EU:C:2015:651, paras 72–73.

[234] Note that in *Streetmap.EU Ltd v Google Inc* [2016] EWHC 253 (Ch), paras 95–98, the English High Court distinguished *Post Danmark II* and held that, where the effect of an abuse is on a separate market from the one in which an undertaking is dominant, it was necessary to show that the effect is an appreciable one: for discussion see Whish 'Article 102 and De Minimis' [2016] Comp Law 53; see also Ibáñez-Colomo 'Appreciability and *De Minimis* in Article 102 TFEU' (2016) 7 JECLAP 651.

[235] See the analysis of price theory in ch 1, 'The Theory of Competition', pp 4–8.

market: in other words exploitation of a monopoly position may in itself increase competition over time.

Of greater long-term significance is behaviour by a dominant firm designed to, or which might have the effect of, preventing the development of competition, and much of the case law of the EU Courts and the decisional practice of the Commission has been concerned with **exclusionary abuses** of this kind. The Commission's *Guidance on Article 102 Enforcement Priorities* recognises the distinction between exploitative and exclusionary abuses, and paragraph 7 explicitly states that it is limited to exclusionary conduct.

In order to illustrate the kind of behaviour which falls within the mischief of Article 102 it is therefore helpful to consider exploitative and exclusionary abuses separately, although this is not to suggest that there is a rigid demarcation between these two categories: the same behaviour may exhibit both characteristics. For example a dominant firm that refuses to supply may have an exploitative purpose (for example where it is threatened or effected in order to make a customer pay a higher price) and/or an exclusionary one (where it is intended to remove a competitor from the market).

A possible third category of cases under Article 102 is concerned with **single market abuses**. For example excessive pricing, as well as being exploitative, may be a ploy to impede parallel imports and to limit intra-brand competition, as in the case of *British Leyland v Commission*[236].

Abusive practices will be considered in greater detail in later chapters of this book, and in particular in chapters 6, 17, 18 and 19. At this stage it is intended to provide an overview of the type of practices that might be found to be abusive.

(G) Exploitative abuses

It is clear from its very wording that Article 102 is capable of application to exploitative behaviour: Article 102(2)(a) gives as an example of an abuse the imposition of **unfair purchase or selling prices or other unfair trading conditions**. Exploitative pricing practices are considered further in chapter 18[237]. There have also been cases on the activities of collecting societies in which their rules have been scrutinised in order to ensure that they do not act in a way that unfairly exploits the owner of the copyright or the would-be licensee of it; collecting societies are considered in chapter 19[238]. Unfair trading conditions were condemned by the Commission in *AAMS*[239] and in *1998 Football World Cup*[240], where it considered that the arrangements for the sale of tickets were unfair to consumers resident outside France.

In its colloquial sense, exploitation suggests the earning of monopoly profits at the expense of the customer. However one of the other 'benefits' of the monopolist is the 'quiet life' and the freedom from the need to innovate and improve efficiency in order to keep up with or ahead of competitors[241]. This raises the question whether inefficiency or inertia on the part of a dominant firm could be an abuse under Article 102. Article 102(2)(b) gives as an example of abuse the limitation of production, markets or technical development to the prejudice of the consumer, and in *British Telecommunications*[242] the

[236] Case 226/84 EU:C:1986:421; see 'Abuses that are harmful to the single market', p 216 later in chapter and ch 18, 'Pricing Practices That are Harmful to the Single Market', pp 782–783.

[237] See ch 18, 'Excessive Pricing', pp 735–746.

[238] See ch 19, 'Collecting societies', pp 820–821.

[239] OJ [1998] L 252/47, paras 33–46, upheld on appeal to the General Court Case T-139/98 *Amministrazione Autonoma dei Monopoli di Stato v Commission* EU:T:2001:272, paras 73–80.

[240] OJ [2000] L 5/55, para 91; see also paras 99–100.

[241] See ch 1, 'The harmful effects of monopoly', pp 7–8.

[242] OJ [1982] L 360/36, upheld on appeal Case 41/83 *Italy v Commission* EU:C:1985:120.

Commission objected to behaviour on BT's part which, among other things, meant that the possible use of new technology was impeded. This is dealt with in chapter 6[243].

(H) **Exclusionary abuses**

Article 102 has most frequently been applied to exclusionary behaviour.

(i) ***Continental Can v Commission***

The Court of Justice established in *Continental Can v Commission*[244] that Article 102 was capable of application to exclusionary abuses as well as exploitative ones. The specific question before the Court was whether mergers could be prohibited under Article 102. One argument against this was that Article 102 was concerned only with the direct exploitation of consumers and not with the more indirect adverse effects that might be produced by harming the competitive process[245]; according to this argument structural changes in the market could not be caught. The Court of Justice rejected this. It was not appropriate to draw a distinction between direct and indirect effects on the competitive process; instead it was necessary to interpret Article 102 in the light of the spirit of the Treaty generally. Article 3(3) TEU provides that the EU shall establish an internal market which, as explained in Protocol 27 to the Treaties, includes 'a system ensuring that competition is not distorted'[246]. Articles 101 and 102 had to be interpreted with this aim in mind: it would be futile to prevent agreements which distort competition under Article 101 but then to allow mergers which resulted in the elimination of competition. The enactment of the EU Merger Regulation means that Article 102 is now largely redundant in respect of mergers[247]; however *Continental Can* remains important to the law on Article 102, since it confirmed that it could be applied to exclusionary as well as to exploitative abuses.

(ii) **Causation**

One of the arguments raised by Continental Can was that, even if mergers were caught by Article 102, it had not **used** its market power to effect the merger; there was a break in the chain of causation between its position on the market and the behaviour alleged to be abusive. It had not, for example, threatened to drive the target firm out of the market by predatory price cutting if it refused to merge. The Court of Justice rejected this argument as well. It was possible to abuse a dominant position without actually exercising or relying on market power[248]. It was an abuse simply for a dominant firm to strengthen its position and substantially to eliminate competition by taking over a rival. Abuse is an objective concept, and the conduct of an undertaking may be regarded as abusive in the absence of any fault and irrespective of the intention of the dominant undertaking. The scope of Article 102 would obviously be reduced if the Commission could apply it only to practices

[243] Ch 6, 'Manifest inability to meet demand', p 239.

[244] Case 6/72 *Europemballage Corpn and Continental Can Co Inc Commission* EU:C:1973:22; the impact of the judgment is discussed in Vogelenzang 'Abuse of a Dominant Position in Article 86: The Problem of Causality and Some Applications' (1976) 13 CML Rev 61.

[245] See eg Joliet *Monopolisation and Abuse of Dominance* (Martinus Nijhoff, 1970); it was also argued in *Continental Can* that mergers were not caught by Article 102 as Article 66(1) of the former ECSC Treaty dealt with them explicitly so that, by inference, the EC Treaty (now TFEU), which was silent on the issue, could not apply to them; and that anyway behaviour could not be abusive unless it was attributable to and caused by the use of the position of dominance (see 'Causation', later in chapter).

[246] This objective was previously contained in Article 3(1)(g) of the EC Treaty and, at the time of the *Continental Can* judgment, in Article 3(f) of the EEC Treaty: see ch 2, 'The competition chapter in the TFEU', pp 51–52.

[247] See 'The benefits of one-stop merger control', pp 864–866.

[248] On this issue see O'Donoghue and Padilla *The Law and Economics of Article 102 TFEU* (Hart, 2nd ed, 2013), pp 262–267.

which were attributable to the exercise of market power that a dominant undertaking enjoys[249]. In *Hoffmann-La Roche* the Court of Justice said that:

> The interpretation suggested by the applicant that an abuse implies that the use of the economic power bestowed by a dominant position is the means whereby the abuse has been brought about cannot be accepted[250].

In *Tetra Pak II*[251] the Court of Justice stated at paragraph 27 of its judgment that 'application of Article [102] presupposes a link between the dominant position and the alleged abusive conduct'. This may appear to contradict the 'no causation' point in *Continental Can*. However, the issue in *Tetra Pak* was whether it is possible for the abuse to take place in a market different from the one in which an undertaking is dominant[252]; the Court was not concerned with the issue of whether the market power had to have been used in order to bring about the abuse.

It is interesting to note that some systems of law—for example Australia and New Zealand—do require a causal connection between the position of dominance and the abusive behaviour: the majority judgment of the UK Privy Council in *Carter Holt Harvey Building Products Group Ltd v The Commerce Commission*[253] contains an interesting discussion of the case law in those two countries. Clearly such an approach will result in fewer findings of abuse; however the *Continental Can* judgment is clear that causation is not required under Article 102. The General Court relied on the judgments of the Court of Justice in *Continental Can* and *Hoffmann-La Roche* in *AstraZeneca AB v Commission*[254], where it said that 'an abuse of a dominant position does not necessarily have to consist in the use of the economic power conferred by the dominant position'[255].

(iii) Horizontal and vertical foreclosure

If a competitor is foreclosed by the superior efficiency of a dominant firm, the foreclosure would not be anti-competitive or abusive[256]. The concern about exclusionary abuses is that a dominant firm is able to behave in a way that leads to anti-competitive foreclosure, and thereby to prevent potential competitors from entering the market. The foreclosure might occur 'upstream' or 'downstream' in the market. Suppose that a firm is vertically integrated: it extracts a raw material, widgets, from its widget mines and processes widgets into widget dioxide: the upstream market is raw widgets, the downstream one is widget dioxide. Harm to competition could occur at either level of the market:

- **horizontal foreclosure**[257] arises where the dominant firm takes action to exclude a competitor that supplies widgets (see Figure 5.1)
- **vertical foreclosure** arises where the dominant firm takes action to exclude a competitor in the downstream market for widget dioxide (see Figure 5.2).

[249] See Vogelenzang 'Abuse of a Dominant Position in Article 86: The Problem of Causality and Some Applications' (1976) 13 CML Rev 61; the Commission relied specifically on this aspect of the *Continental Can* judgment in para 46 of its decision in *Tetra Pak I (BTG Licence)* OJ [1988] L 272/27.

[250] Case 85/76 EU:C:1979:36, at para 91; note the suggestion by AG Reischl at para 7c of his Opinion in *Hoffmann-La Roche* that causation might be treated differently according to the nature of the abuse in question.

[251] Case C-333/94 P *Tetra Pak International v Commission* EU:C:1996:436.

[252] See 'Horizontal and vertical foreclosure', below.

[253] [2004] UKPC 37.

[254] Case T-321/05 EU:T:2010:266.

[255] Ibid, para 354.

[256] See eg Case C-209/10 *Post Danmark A/S v Konkurrencerådet* EU:C:2012:172, para 22; Case C-413/14 P *Intel v Commission* EU:C:2017:632, para 134.

[257] The language of 'horizontal' and 'vertical' foreclosure is taken from paras 69–73 of DG COMP's *Discussion paper on the application of Article [102] of the Treaty to exclusionary abuses*, December 2005; the Commission's *Guidance on Article 102 Enforcement Priorities* does not use the same language, while the Commission's *Guidelines on the assessment of non-horizontal mergers* OJ [2008] C 265/6, paras 30–59, distinguish between 'customer' and 'input' foreclosure, which are synonymous for horizontal and vertical foreclosure respectively.

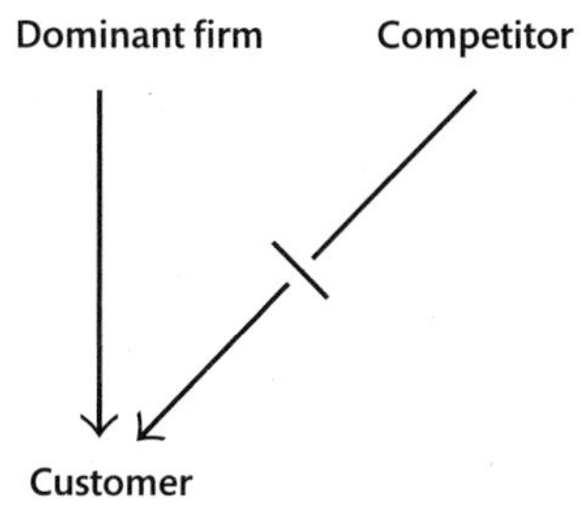

Fig. 5.1 Horizontal foreclosure

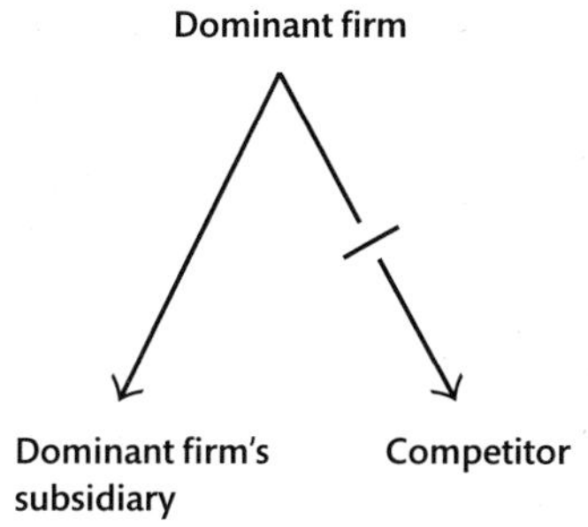

Fig. 5.2 Vertical foreclosure

Many exclusionary abuses are concerned with horizontal foreclosure: for example exclusive purchasing agreements, rebates and predatory pricing. Others however, for example refusal to supply and margin squeezing, are predominantly[258] concerned about harm to competition in the downstream market.

(iv) The dominant position, the abuse and the effects of the abuse may be in different markets

It is not necessary for the dominance, the abuse and the effects of the abuse all to be in the same market. In a simple case, X may be dominant in the market for widgets and charge high prices to exploit its customers or drop its prices in order to eliminate competitors from the widget market: clearly Article 102 can apply to this behaviour. However more complex situations may occur. X might be present on both the widget market and the downstream widget dioxide market, and may act on one of those markets in order to derive a benefit in the other: as we have just seen, there may be a horizontal or a vertical foreclosure of the market.

Some examples will illustrate the range of possibilities.

(a) Michelin v Commission

Michelin was dominant in the market for replacement tyres and committed various abuses in order to protect its position in that market[259].

[258] A refusal to supply may sometimes have a horizontal effect: see ch 17, 'Horizontal foreclosure', p 725.

[259] Case 322/81 EU:C:1983:313.

(b) Commercial Solvents

Commercial Solvents supplied a raw material in which it was dominant to a customer which used it to make an anti-tuberculosis drug[260]. The raw material was the upstream product; the drug was the downstream product. Commercial Solvents decided to produce the drug itself and ceased to supply the customer. Commercial Solvents was found to have abused its dominant position: it refused to supply the raw material in relation to which it was dominant, but this was done to benefit its position in the drug market, where it was not yet present at all.

(c) De Poste-La Poste

The Belgian Post Office, dominant in the market for the delivery of 'normal' letters, abused its dominant position in that market in order to eliminate a competitor in the neighbouring market for business-to-business mail services[261].

(d) Télémarketing

The dominant undertaking, a broadcasting authority with a statutory monopoly, decided to enter the downstream telemarketing sector[262]. It ceased to supply broadcasting services to the only other telemarketer, thereby eliminating it from the market and effectively reserving the telemarketing business to itself.

(e) Sealink/B&I—Holyhead: Interim Measures

Sealink, which owned and operated the port at Holyhead, was considered to have committed an abuse on the market for the provision of port facilities for passenger and ferry services, in which it was dominant, by structuring the sailing schedules there to the advantage of its own downstream ferry operations and to the disadvantage of its competitor at that level of the market, B&I[263]. The same point arose in *Sea Containers v Stena Sealink—Interim Measures*[264].

(f) British Gypsum v Commission

British Gypsum was dominant in the plasterboard market, but not dominant in the neighbouring plaster market (these markets were horizontally, rather than vertically, related)[265]. Among its abuses, British Gypsum gave priority treatment to customers for plaster who remained loyal to it in relation to plasterboard. This differs from the earlier examples, since in *British Gypsum* the abuse was committed in the non-dominated market in order to protect British Gypsum's position in its dominated market.

(g) Tetra Pak II

The Court of Justice concluded that Tetra Pak had infringed Article 102 by tying practices and predatory pricing in the market for non-aseptic liquid repackaging machinery and non-aseptic cartons[266]. It was not dominant in this market, but the abusive conduct was intended to benefit its position in that market. Tetra Pak was dominant in the (horizontally) associated market for aseptic machinery and cartons. The Court of Justice, after citing *Commercial Solvents*, *Télémarketing* and *British Gypsum*, held that 'in special circumstances'[267], there could be an abuse of a dominant position 'where conduct on a

[260] Cases 6/73 etc EU:C:1974:18. [261] OJ [2002] L 61/32, paras 36–51.

[262] Case 311/84 *Centre belge d'études de marché—Télémarketing v CTL* EU:C:1985:394.

[263] [1992] 5 CMLR 255. [264] OJ [1994] L 15/8. [265] Case C-310/93 P EU:C:1995:101.

[266] Case C-333/94 P EU:C:1996:436; the Court of Justice's approach to the issue of abuse was different from that of the Commission's in its decision.

[267] Case C-333/94 P EU:C:1996:436, paras 25–31.

Table 5.1 Dominance, abuse and neighbouring markets

Case	**Market A**	**Market B**
Michelin v Commission	Dominance Abuse Benefit	
Commercial Solvents *Télémarketing* *De Poste-La Poste* *Sealink decisions*	Dominance Abuse	Benefit
British Gypsum	Dominance Benefit	Abuse
Tetra Pak v Commission	Dominance	Abuse Benefit

market distinct from the dominated market produces effects on that distinct market'[268]. The Court of Justice went on to describe the 'close associative links' between the aseptic and non-aseptic markets which amounted to sufficiently special circumstances to engage Article 102: for example Tetra Pak had or could have customers in both markets, it could rely on having a favoured status in the non-dominated market because of its position in the dominated one, and it could concentrate its efforts on the non-aseptic market independently of other economic operators because of its position in relation to the aseptic market. This case extends the scope of application of Article 102 beyond, even, *British Gypsum*. The Commission relied specifically on this aspect of *Tetra Pak II* in its decision in *Microsoft*[269]. Table 5.1 may help to explain the propositions set out in this paragraph.

Many of the Commission's decisions under Article 102 in recent years have involved two markets rather than one[270]. Obvious examples are *Deutsche Telekom v Commission*[271], *Microsoft v Commission*[272] and *TeliaSonera*[273]; in the latter judgment the Court said that Article 102 gives no explicit guidance as to the market in which the abuse takes place: each case must be decided in the light of its specific circumstances[274]. The Commission's decision in *Google*[275] was that Google abused its dominant position in general internet search in order to exclude competitors in the online comparison shopping services markets.

Footnote 39 of the Commission's *Guidance on Article 102 Enforcement Priorities* says that the Commission may pursue predatory practices by dominant firms on markets on which they are not yet dominant. The Commission could presumably apply the reasoning described in this section in the context of neighbouring **product** markets to dominance, abuse and benefits in neighbouring **geographical** markets[276].

268 Ibid, para 27. 269 Commission decision of 24 March 2004, paras 526–540.

270 Case T-219/99 *British Airways plc v Commission* EU:T:2003:343, paras 127–135.

271 Case C-280/08 P EU:C:2010:603. 272 Case T-201/04 EU:T:2007:289.

273 Case C-52/09 EU:C:2011:83. 274 Ibid, paras 84–89.

275 Commission decision of 27 June 2017, paras 341 ff, on appeal to the General Court Case T-612/17 *Google v Commission*, not yet decided.

276 The UK Competition Appeal Tribunal considered that the reasoning in *Tetra Pak II* could be transposed to geographic markets: see Case 1044/2/1/04 *JJ Burgess & Sons v OFT* [2005] CAT 25, paras 379–385; see also *Interbrew* in the Commission's XXVIth *Report on Competition Policy* (1996), point 53, where Interbrew was considered to have acted in non-dominated geographical markets to protect its dominant position in Belgium.

(v) How is effects analysis conducted in practice?

As noted earlier, the Commission has accepted in recent decisions that, where unilateral behaviour of a dominant firm is in issue, effects analysis is needed to show that it is abusive[277]. Judgments such as *Deutsche Telekom* and *TeliaSonera* endorse this approach, and the *Intel* judgment of September 2017 has confirmed irreversibly the move towards a more effects-based approach to the application of Article 102. This section considers how effects analysis is conducted in practice.

(a) Selecting the right cases

The Commission's *Guidance on Article 102 Enforcement Priorities* explains, at paragraph 19, that the aim of its enforcement activity in relation to exclusionary abuses is to ensure that dominant undertakings do not impair effective competition by foreclosing their competitors in an anti-competitive way: the concern is that such behaviour would have an adverse effect on consumer welfare, for example by raising prices, by limiting the quality of goods or services or by reducing consumer choice. 'Anti-competitive foreclosure' differs from 'mere foreclosure', which occurs where the dominant undertaking wins business on the merits as a result of its superior efficiency; this is an important distinction, with which the Court of Justice agrees[278]. Paragraph 20 of the *Guidance* sets out a series of factors which the Commission will take into account when deciding whether to intervene in relation to an alleged exclusionary abuse under Article 102: these factors will enable it to determine whether the conduct in question is likely to lead to an anti-competitive foreclosure of the market. The Commission adds that it would want there to be cogent and compelling evidence before it would intervene. The factors include:

- **the position of the dominant undertaking**: in general, the stronger the dominant position, the higher the likelihood that conduct protecting that position leads to anti-competitive foreclosure
- **the conditions on the relevant market**: these include the conditions of entry and expansion, such as the existence of economies of scale and/or scope and network effects
- **the position of the dominant undertaking's competitors**: even a fairly small competitor may play a significant competitive role where it is the closest competitor to the dominant undertaking, is particularly innovative or has the reputation of systematically cutting prices
- **the position of the customers or input suppliers**: this may include the possible selectivity of the conduct in question, for example where the dominant undertaking applies the practice only to selected customers or input suppliers who may be of particular importance for the entry or expansion of competitors, thereby enhancing the likelihood of anti-competitive foreclosure
- **the extent of the allegedly abusive conduct**: in general, the higher the percentage of total sales in the relevant market affected by the conduct, the longer its duration, and the more regularly it has been applied, the greater is the likely anti-competitive foreclosure effect
- **possible evidence of actual foreclosure**: where the conduct in question has already been taking place, there may be actual evidence of the dominant undertaking's market share having increased, or of competitors having exited the market

[277] See 'Recent case law and decisions do require effects analysis', pp 205–207 earlier.

[278] Case C-209/10 *Post Danmark I* EU:C:2012:172, para 22.

- **direct evidence of any exclusionary strategy**: there may be direct evidence—for example internal documents—of a strategy to exclude competitors, and this may be helpful in interpreting the dominant undertaking's conduct[279].

Paragraph 21 of the *Guidance* explains that, when pursuing a case, the Commission will develop its analysis, that is to say whether particular conduct is likely to have an anti-competitive foreclosure effect, using the general factors set out in paragraph 20, and the specific factors set out in later sections of the *Guidance*. This is an important point to note. Later paragraphs of the *Guidance* discuss particular issues that are relevant to the assessment of anti-competitive foreclosure arising from specific practices. These paragraphs should always be understood within the broader context of the general factors discussed in paragraph 20 of the *Guidance*: they are a complement to, and not a substitute for, that paragraph.

(b) What standard of proof?

It is necessary to determine the standard of proof that the person alleging an exclusionary abuse should satisfy. If every case were to require the demonstration of anti-competitive foreclosure effects beyond reasonable doubt, the enforcement of Article 102 might become all but impossible, which would bring one back to the problem of false negatives and false positives[280]. The Court of Justice has not been consistent on this issue. In *Post Danmark II* the Court of Justice said that the anti-competitive effect of a rebate 'must be probable'[281], the standard applied by the *Guidance*[282] and required by the case law in merger cases[283]. In some cases the EU Courts have required the Commission to show that a practice would merely be 'capable' of restricting competition[284]. In *Post Danmark II*[285] the Court of Justice seems to have used the terms 'capable' and 'likely' interchangeably to denote the standard of proof.

(c) What evidence?

The evidence of effects in an Article 102 case may come from a number of sources, including the economic and market context, contemporaneous documents, witness evidence and/or economic analysis. Paragraph 19 of the *Guidance* says that, when identifying likely consumer harm, the Commission may rely on qualitative and, where appropriate, quantitative evidence[286]. In *Post Danmark II*[287] the Court of Justice recognised that the

[279] On the relevance of intention in abuse of dominance cases see Case C-549/10 P *Tomra Systems v Commission* EU:C:2012:221, paras 17–21; Case T-402/13 *Orange v Commission* EU:T:2014:991, paras 60–63; O'Grady 'The Role of Exclusionary Intent in the Enforcement of Article 102 TFEU' (2014) 37 World Competition 459.

[280] See 'False positives and false negatives', pp 198–199 earlier in chapter above.

[281] Case C-23/14 EU:C:2015:651, para 74; see also para 69.

[282] *Guidance on Article 102 Enforcement Priorities*, paras 19–20.

[283] See eg Case C-12/03 P *Commission v Tetra Laval* EU:C:2005:87, para 42; Cases C-413/06 P *Bertelsmann v Impala* EU:C:2008:392, para 52.

[284] See eg Case T-219/99 *British Airways plc v Commission* EU:T:2003:343, para 293; Case C-549/10 P *Tomra v Commission* EU:C:2012:221, para 68.

[285] Case C-23/14 EU:C:2015:651, paras 31, 35, 38, 50, 68 (capable) and paras 49, 67, 69 (likely); similarly see Case T-201/04 *Microsoft v Commission* EU:T:2007:289, para 561 (no difference between 'risk of elimination of competition' and 'likely to eliminate competition').

[286] On the content and presentation of economic evidence see DG COMP's *Best Practices for the submission of economic evidence and data collection in cases concerning the application of Articles 101 and 102 TFEU and in merger cases*, available at www.ec.europa.eu.

[287] Case C-23/14 EU:C:2015:651, paras 31, 35, 38, 50, 68 ('capable') and paras 49, 67, 69 ('likely'); similarly see Case T-201/04 *Microsoft v Commission* EU:T:2007:289, para 561.

Commission may have recourse to the as-efficient competitor test in rebate cases, which it did in the *Intel* case[288]. This does not mean that effects analysis **must** be based on the as-efficient-competitor test[289]; rather, that test is 'one tool amongst others' for assessing whether there is an exclusionary abuse[290].

Paragraph 22 of the *Guidance* envisages that the anti-competitive effects may be inferred without a detailed analysis where it is clear that 'the conduct can only raise obstacles to competition and that it creates no efficiencies'; Intel's payments to customers to delay or cancel the marketing of its competitor's product (so-called 'naked restrictions') are an example of such conduct[291].

(vi) Examples of exclusionary abuses

The Commission and the EU Courts have condemned many practices that could have anti-competitive foreclosure effects. These will be examined in detail in chapters 17 to 19, which will consider in turn the following abuses:

- exclusive dealing agreements[292]
- tying[293]
- refusals to supply[294]
- miscellaneous other non-pricing abuses[295]
- exclusivity rebates and other practices having effects similar to exclusive dealing agreements[296]
- bundling[297]
- predatory pricing[298]
- margin squeezing[299]
- price discrimination[300]
- refusals to license intellectual property rights or to provide interoperability information[301].

(I) Abuses that are harmful to the single market

As one would expect, Article 102 has been applied to behaviour that is harmful to the single market[302]. Examples will be found later in this book of non-pricing[303] and pricing[304] abuses in which this was an obvious concern.

[288] Commission decision of 13 May 2009, paras 1002–1576, on appeal Case T-286/09 RENV *Intel v Commission*, not yet decided (following the judgment in Case C-413/14 P *Intel v Commission* EU:C:2017:632).

[289] Case C-23/14 EU:C:2015:651, para 57.

[290] Ibid, para 61; similarly see *Guidance on Article 102 Enforcement Priorities*, para 24.

[291] Commission decision of 13 May 2009, paras 1641–1681, upheld on appeal Case T-286/09 *Intel v Commission* EU:T:2014:547, paras 198–220 (this practice was not discussed on further appeal to the Court of Justice).

[292] Ch 17, 'Exclusive Dealing Agreements', pp 698–705.

[293] Ch 17, 'Tying', pp 705–713.

[294] Ch 17, 'Refusal to Supply', pp 713–728.

[295] Ch 17, 'Miscellaneous Other Non-Pricing Abuses', pp 728–731.

[296] Ch 18, 'Conditional Rebates', pp 746–754.

[297] Ch 18, 'Bundling', pp 754–756.

[298] Ch 18, 'Predatory Pricing', pp 756–771.

[299] Ch 18, 'Margin Squeeze', pp 771–777.

[300] Ch 18, 'Price Discrimination', pp 777–782.

[301] Ch 19, 'Article 102 and Intellectual Property Rights', pp 814–827.

[302] See ch 1, 'The single market imperative', pp 23–24 and ch 2, 'The single market imperative', pp 52–53.

[303] See ch 17, 'Non-Pricing Abuses That are Harmful to the Internal Market', pp 727–728.

[304] See ch 18, 'Pricing Practices that are Harmful to the Single Market', pp 782–783.

9. Defences

The term 'abuse' bears great intellectual strain, particularly as there is no equivalent in Article 102 to Article 101(3) whereby an agreement that restricts competition can nevertheless be permitted because it produces economic efficiencies. It would be perverse if the significance of efficiencies were to be recognised under Article 101 but not Article 102. Over a number of years the Commission and the EU Courts came to recognise that there was some conduct which, although presumptively abusive, in fact did not amount to a violation of Article 102 because it had an 'objective justification'[305]. For example in *Sot. Lélos*[306] the Court of Justice stated that the fact that an undertaking is in a dominant position cannot deprive it of its entitlement to protect its own commercial interests when they are attacked; however the Court added that such behaviour cannot be allowed if its purpose is to strengthen the dominant position and thereby abuse it. In *Post Danmark I*[307] the Court was emphatic that a dominant firm may seek to justify behaviour that would otherwise be caught by Article 102, in particular by arguing that it is objectively necessary or that any exclusionary effect on the market is counterbalanced, or outweighed, by advantages in terms of efficiency that also benefit consumers[308]. This is consistent with the Commission's *Guidance on Article 102 Enforcement Priorities* in which, from paragraphs 28 to 31, it says the same thing.

This section will examine what is meant by objective justification; it will briefly consider the question of whether a defence can be based on the principle of non-interference with property rights; and will conclude with a discussion of the burden of proving a defence.

(A) Objective justification

The language of objective justification[309] can be found in many judgments and decisions, coupled with the proposition that, to be objectively justified, the conduct in question must be proportionate. For example in *Centre belge d'études de marché— Télémarketing v CLT*[310] the Court of Justice held that an undertaking in a dominant position in television broadcasting which entrusted 'telemarketing' to its own subsidiary, thereby excluding other firms from entering this market, would be guilty of an abuse where there was no objective necessity for such behaviour[311]. The principles of objective justification and proportionality have been invoked on other occasions[312] and are firmly part of Article 102 analysis.

[305] For an interesting discussion of the concept of objective justification see the Opinion of AG Jacobs in Case C-53/03 *Syfait* EU:C:2004:673, paras 71–72.

[306] Cases C-468/06 etc *Sot. Lélos kai Sia EE v GlaxoSmithKline AEVE Farmakeftikon Proionton* EU:C:2008:504, para 50.

[307] Case C-209/10 EU:C:2012:172. [308] Ibid, paras 40–41.

[309] For discussion see Loewenthal 'The Defence of "Objective Justification" in the Application of Article 82 EC' (2005) 28 World Competition 455; Albors-Llorens 'The Role of Objective Justification and Efficiencies in the Application of Article 82 EC' (2007) 44 CML Rev 1727; Rousseva 'Objective Justification and Article 82 EC in the Era of Modernisation' in Amato and Ehlermann (eds) *EC Competition Law: A Critical Assessment* (Hart, 2007); van der Vijver 'Objective Justification under Article 102 TFEU' (2012) 35 World Competition 55; van der Vijver 'Benighted We Stand: Justifications of Prima Facie Dominance Abuses in EU Member States' (2013) 9 European Competition Journal 465.

[310] Case 311/84 EU:C:1985:394.

[311] Ibid, para 26; see also Case C-95/04 P *British Airways plc v Commission* EU:C:2007:166, para 69.

[312] See eg *BBI/Boosey and Hawkes* OJ [1987] L 286/36; *BPB Industries plc* OJ [1989] L 10/50, para 132, upheld on appeal Case T-65/89 *BPB Industries plc and British Gypsum v Commission* EU:T:1993:31 and further on appeal to the Court of Justice Case C-310/93 P *BPB Industries plc and British Gypsum v Commission* EU:C:1995:101; *Napier Brown—British Sugar* OJ [1988] L 284/41, paras 64 and 70; *NDC Health/IMS Health: Interim Measures* OJ [2002] L 59/18, paras 167–174; *Portuguese Airports* OJ [1999] L 69/31, para 29; *Prokent-Tomra*, Commission decision of 29 March 2006, paras 347–390.

At paragraph 29 of the *Guidance on Article 102 Enforcement Priorities* the Commission says that a claim to objective necessity would have to be based on factors external to the dominant undertaking: for example, where a particular type of conduct is needed in order to guarantee health or safety considerations. The Commission points out that it is normally the task of the public authorities to set and enforce public health and safety standards: this is based on judgments of the General Court in *Hilti*[313] and *Tetra Pak II*[314]. In *Romanian Power Exchange/OPCOM*[315] the Commission rejected OPCOM's argument that its abusive behaviour was objectively justified in order to avoid the risk of criminal charges if it failed to collect VAT[316], and because of the need to avoid a mismatch of cash flow in the Romanian market for the spot-trading of electricity[317].

In *Streetmap.EU Ltd v Google Inc* the English High Court held that Google had an objective justification for displaying its own thumbnail map at or near the top of its search results in response to geographic queries, since there was no other viable or effective way of showing an online map[318].

(B) **Efficiencies**

Conduct that apparently forecloses competitors can be defended on efficiency grounds[319]. At paragraph 30 of the *Guidance* the Commission explains that four cumulative conditions would have to be fulfilled for an efficiency 'defence' to succeed:

- the efficiencies would have to be realised, or be likely to be realised, as a result of the conduct in question
- the conduct would have to be indispensable to the realisation of those efficiencies
- the efficiencies would have to outweigh any negative effects on competition and consumer welfare in the affected markets and
- the conduct must not eliminate all effective competition[320].

The authors of this book are not aware of any case in which an efficiency defence has succeeded under Article 102. The General Court in *Intel v Commission*[321] noted that, in its appeal, Intel had not provided any evidence to show that its exclusivity rebates would lead to increased efficiency. On appeal the Court of Justice acknowledged that a dominant firm could plead efficiencies as a defence to a rebate found capable of foreclosing competition, but did not opine on the application of such a case on the facts of the particular case[322].

[313] Case T-30/89 *Hilti AG v Commission* EU:T:1991:70, paras 102–119.

[314] Case T-83/91 *Tetra Pak International SA v Commission* EU:T:1994:246, paras 136–140, upheld on appeal to the Court of Justice Case C-333/94 P *Tetra Pak International SA v Commission* EU:C:1996:436, para 37.

[315] Commission decision of 5 March 2014.

[316] Ibid, paras 193–195.

[317] Ibid, paras 196–227.

[318] [2016] EWHC 253 (Ch), paras 142–176.

[319] Case C-209/10 *Post Danmark I* EU:C:2012:172, para 42; for discussion see Friederiszick and Gratz 'Hidden Efficiencies: On the Relevance of Business Justifications in Abuse of Dominance Cases' (2015) 11(3) Journal of Competition Law and Economics 671.

[320] Paragraph 30 of the *Guidance* says that the exclusionary conduct of a super-dominant firm is unlikely to satisfy the conditions for an efficiency defence.

[321] Case T-286/09 *Intel v Commission* EU:T:2014:547, paras 94 and 173.

[322] Case C-413/14 P *Intel v Commission* EU:C:2017:632, para 140.

(C) **Abuse of dominance and property rights**

In a number of cases under Article 102 a particular issue has been the extent to which a dominant undertaking could be held to have acted abusively in relation to the way in which it chose to use, or not to use, its own property. Article 345 TFEU provides that:

> The Treaties shall in no way prejudice the rules in Member States governing the system of property ownership.

If it is possible for the Commission, under Article 102, to order the owner, for example, of an essential facility to provide access to it to a third party[323], this clearly affects that undertaking's property rights; but has it affected them to the point where the rules on property ownership in Member States have been prejudiced? The issue arose in relation to *Frankfurt Airport*[324] where the Commission required FAG, the owner and operator of that airport, to allow competition in the market for ground-handling services there. The Commission rejected the argument that this would interfere with the property rights of FAG. The Commission noted that the Court of Justice in *Hauer v Land Rheinland-Pfalz*[325] had acknowledged the existence of a fundamental right to property in the EU legal order; however it had also noted that the constitutions of the Member States recognised that the exercise of property rights may be restricted in the public interest. In the *Frankfurt Airport* decision the Commission said that it followed from the *Hauer* judgment that the competition rules in the Treaty may be considered to constitute restrictions on the right of property which correspond to objectives of general interest pursued by the EU[326]. In the Commission's view, allowing the provision of ground-handling services within the airport would not constitute an excessive or intolerable interference with FAG's rights as owner of the airport; it would not interfere with FAG's own ability to provide these services, and FAG could charge a reasonable fee to third parties for their right to do so.

In his Opinion in *Masterfoods Ltd v HB Ice Cream Ltd*[327] Advocate General Cosmas had no doubt that:

> it is perfectly comprehensible for restrictions to be placed on the right to property ownership pursuant to Articles [101 and 102 TFEU], to the degree to which they might be necessary to protect competition[328].

In *Van den Bergh Foods Ltd v Commission*[329] the General Court rejected an argument that the Commission's decision in *Van den Bergh Foods Ltd*[330], requiring that space be made available in Van den Bergh's freezer cabinets for the ice-cream of competitors, amounted to a disproportionate interference with its property rights[331]. In *Microsoft v Commission* the General Court rejected the argument that Microsoft was entitled to refuse to supply interoperability information to competitors because it was protected by intellectual property rights: this would be inconsistent with the rule, derived from the *Magill* and *IMS Health* cases, that, in exceptional circumstances, there can be an obligation to grant licences to third parties[332].

323 See ch 17, 'Refusal to Supply', pp 713–727.
324 *Flughafen Frankfurt* OJ [1998] L 72/30.
325 Case 44/79 EU:C:1979:290, para 17.
326 OJ [1998] L 72/30, para 90.
327 Case C-344/98 EU:C:2000:689; see also Case C-163/99 *Portugal v Commission* EU:C:2001:189, paras 58–59.
328 Case C-344/98 EU:C:2000:249, para 105.
329 Case T-65/98 EU:T:2003:281.
330 OJ [1998] L 246/1.
331 Case T-65/98 EU:T:2003:281, paras 170–171.
332 Case T-201/04 EU:T:2007:289, paras 690–691; see ch 19, 'The *Microsoft* case', pp 818–820.

When determining the conditions under which an injunction may be sought by a dominant firm to enforce its standard-essential patents in *Huawei Technologies Co Ltd v ZTE Corp*[333], the Court of Justice said that a balance has to be struck between maintaining free competition, on the one hand, and safeguarding the right of an owner of intellectual property to bring an action for infringement, on the other[334].

(D) Burden of proof

In *Microsoft v Commission*[335] the General Court stated that:

> it is for the dominant undertaking concerned, and not for the Commission, before the end of the administrative procedure, to raise any plea of objective justification and to support it with arguments and evidence. It then falls to the Commission, where it proposes to make a finding of an abuse of a dominant position, to show that the arguments and evidence relied on by the undertaking cannot prevail and, accordingly, that the justification cannot be accepted[336].

The General Court went on to state that it was not sufficient for the dominant undertaking to put forward 'vague, general and theoretical arguments' in support of an objective justification[337]. Paragraph 31 of the Commission's *Guidance on Article 102 Enforcement Priorities* adopts the same approach to the burden of proof.

The factors relied upon by the dominant undertaking as the basis for contending that its conduct was objectively justified must normally be ones that the firm took into account at the time of that conduct[338]. It is not sufficient to put forward a justification that did not form any basis for the dominant undertaking's conduct at the time[339].

10. The Consequences of Infringing Article 102

(A) Public enforcement

Where the Commission finds an abuse of a dominant position it has power, pursuant to Article 23 of Regulation 1/2003, to impose a fine[340], and to order the dominant undertaking to cease and desist from the unlawful conduct in question[341]; where necessary, it may also order a dominant undertaking to adopt positive measures in order to bring an infringement to an end[342]. It is even possible for the Commission to order the divestiture of an undertaking's assets, or to break an undertaking up, under the powers conferred by Article 7 of the Regulation 1/2003[343], provided it is proportionate and necessary to

[333] Case C-170/13 EU:C:2015:477, para 42.

[334] See ch 19, 'Seeking an injunction to enforce standard-essential patents', pp 822–823.

[335] Case T-201/04 EU:T:2007:289.

[336] Ibid, para 688; the General Court adopted the same approach in Case T-301/04 *Clearstream Banking AG v Commission* EU:T:2009:317, para 185.

[337] Case T-201/04 EU:T:2007:289, para 698; for discussion of proof generally in Article 102 cases see Paulis 'The Burden of Proof in Article 82 Cases' [2006] Fordham Corporate Law Institute (ed Hawk), ch 20; Nazzini 'The Wood Began to Move: An Essay on Consumer Welfare, Evidence and Burden of Proof in Article 82 EC Cases' (2006) 31 EL Rev 518.

[338] See eg *Clearstream*, Commission decision of 2 June 2004, paras 326–327; see also *Purple Parking Ltd v Heathrow Airport Ltd* [2011] EWHC 987 (Ch), paras 179 and 180–3.

[339] See eg *Napp Pharmaceutical Holdings Ltd v Director General of Fair Trading* [2002] CAT 1, paras 251–254.

[340] See ch 7, 'Article 23: Fines', pp 285–286.

[341] See ch 7, 'Behavioural remedies', pp 261–262.

[342] See ch 7, 'Behavioural remedies', pp 261–262.

[343] OJ [2003] L 1/1; see ch 7, 'Structural remedies', p 262.

bring the infringement to an end and provided that there is no equally effective behavioural remedy or that such a remedy would be more burdensome[344]. This happened in *ARA Foreclosure*[345]: the Commission imposed a structural remedy (in that case with ARA's consent) to make sure that the infringement could not be repeated.

(B) Private enforcement

The civil law consequences of infringing Article 102 are discussed in chapter 8[346].

344 See ch 7, 'Past infringements', pp 262–263.
345 Commission decision of 20 September 2016, paras 132–148.
346 See ch 8, 'Article 102', p 240.

6

The obligations of Member States under the EU competition rules

1. Introduction

This chapter will examine the obligations of Member States in relation to EU competition law. Specifically it will consider the obligations that Article 4(3) TEU and Articles 37 and 106 TFEU place upon Member States; Articles 107 to 109 TFEU on state aid will be briefly mentioned at the end of the chapter. The expression 'Member State' for these purposes includes all organs of the state, including a national competition authority[1] and an economic regulator[2]. Article 4(3) imposes a duty of 'sincere cooperation' on Member States and the EU; Article 37 deals specifically with state monopolies of a commercial character; and Article 106 is concerned with measures that are contrary to the Treaty. In *France v Commission*[3] Advocate General Tesauro spoke of the 'obscure clarity' of Article 37 as opposed to the 'clear obscurity' of Article 106. These provisions are complex and the case law reveals that the encroachment of EU law on national monopolies and state activity is inevitably political and contentious.

Article 3(3) TEU provides that the EU shall establish an internal market which, as explained in Protocol 27 to the Treaties, includes 'a system ensuring that competition is not distorted'[4]. Article 3(3) also provides that one of the EU's objectives is a highly competitive social market economy. Article 119 TFEU provides that the activities of the Member States and the EU shall be conducted in accordance with the principle of an open market economy with free competition[5]. State involvement in economic activities

[1] See eg Case C-198/01 *Consorzio Industrie Fiammiferi (CIF) v Autorità Garante della Concorrenza e del Mercato* EU:C:2003:430, discussed at *'Consorzio Industrie Fiammiferi'*, p 227 later in chapter.

[2] For example in March 2011 the National Lottery Commission (now the Gambling Commission) refused consent to Camelot UK Lotteries Ltd, the operator of the UK Lottery, to provide commercial services such as over-the-counter cash bill payment and mobile phone top-up through its National Lottery terminals as this gave rise to 'serious concerns' about a possible infringement of Article 106 in conjunction with Articles 101 and/or 102.

[3] Case C-202/88 EU:C:1991:120, at para 11 of his Opinion.

[4] This objective was previously contained in Article 3(1)(g) of the EC Treaty: see ch 2, 'The competition chapter in the TFEU', pp 51–52.

[5] The Court of Justice stressed the importance of Article 119 TFEU in Case C-198/01 *Consorzio Industrie Fiammiferi (CIF)* EU:C:2003:430, para 47.

may work against this goal[6]; however Member States may take offence at too much interference at an EU level in domestic economic and social policy. Articles 101 and 102 are essentially private law provisions, conferring rights and imposing obligations on undertakings; many other Articles in the TFEU are primarily of a public law nature, imposing obligations on Member States. The extent to which Member States and undertakings which enjoy special or exclusive rights are subject to Articles 101 and 102 is an issue that is still being explored by the Commission and the EU Courts.

EU law is neutral on the issue of public ownership of industry in itself. Article 345 TFEU provides that the Treaties 'shall in no way prejudice the rules in Member States governing the system of property ownership'. This means that Member States may confer legal monopolies on organs of the state or on undertakings that are not publicly owned, and in cases under Article 106(1)[7] the Court of Justice has held that the conferment of special or exclusive rights on an undertaking is not, in itself, an infringement of EU law. However there is a tension between this principle and the obligation imposed on Member States by Article 106(1) not to enact nor to maintain in force measures contrary to the competition rules, with the result that property rights are not as inviolable as the wording of Article 345 suggests[8]. Indeed some of the judgments of the Court of Justice on the relationship of Article 102 with Article 106(1) have come close to challenging the very existence of those rights[9].

2. **Article 4(3) TEU—Duty of Sincere Cooperation**

Article 4(3) TEU provides that the EU and the Member States shall assist each other in carrying out tasks which flow from the Treaties. Article 4(3) also imposes positive and negative duties on Member States: it requires them to take all appropriate measures to ensure fulfilment of the obligations arising out of the Treaties or resulting from the acts of the EU institutions and to refrain from any measure which could jeopardise the attainment of the EU's objectives. Whether and when Article 4(3) TEU requires a Member State to take or to desist from taking measures depends on the particular circumstances of the case; it is for the Member State to choose the most appropriate course of action to take[10].

There have been many cases in which individuals and undertakings have invoked Article 4(3) in proceedings in the criminal and civil courts of Member States, both as claimant and defendant, to claim that a particular law of a Member State is unenforceable because of its incompatibility with the competition rules in the Treaty; many of these cases have led to references to the Court of Justice under Article 267 TFEU, and will be discussed in this section of the chapter. The Court has established that the obligation of Member States to disapply national legislation that contravenes EU competition law attaches not only to national courts but also to administrative bodies, including national competition authorities[11]. Where a Member State is in breach of its obligations under Article 4(3) it would also be possible for the Commission to take action against it,

[6] Note that Article 119 TFEU does not, by itself, impose obligations on Member States: Case C-181/06 *Deutsche Lufthansa* EU:C:2007:412, para 31.

[7] See eg Case 155/73 *Sacchi* EU:C:1974:40, para 14; Case C-260/89 *ERT v Dimotiki* EU:C:1991:254, para 16; Case C-41/90 *Höfner & Elser v Macrotron GmbH* EU:C:1991:161, para 29.

[8] See further 'Making sense of the case law on Article 102 in conjunction with Article 106(1)', pp 237–242 later in chapter.

[9] See 'Article 106(1)', pp 230–242 later in chapter.

[10] *Ryanair Holdings plc v Competition Commission* [2012] EWCA Civ 1632, para 55.

[11] See Case C-198/01 *Consorzio Industrie Fiammiferi (CIF)* EU:C:2003:430, paras 49–50.

either by initiating an infringement procedure under Article 258 TFEU, as in the case of *Commission v Italy*[12], or, where there is an infringement of Article 106(1), by using its powers under Article 106(3)[13].

(A) The relationship between Article 4(3) TEU and Articles 101 and 102 TFEU

The case law on Article 4(3) is complex, for reasons that are not difficult to understand[14]. It is obvious that measures adopted by Member States may distort competition: they might do so for example by imposing minimum or maximum prices for goods or services; by adopting discriminatory measures of taxation; by imposing regulatory rules that make it difficult for undertakings to enter markets; or by operating restrictive licensing regimes for particular economic activities. Each of these measures might have serious implications for the competitiveness of markets. However the issue that arises in relation to Article 4(3), when read in conjunction with Articles 101 and/or 102, is the extent to which those measures can be challenged, and be found to be unlawful, under EU competition law.

Article 4(3) is addressed to Member States; Articles 101 and 102 are directed to undertakings. The conundrum is to decide when a Member State can be held liable for behaviour of undertakings that infringes the competition rules. On the one hand Member States are naturally jealous of their sovereignty, and do not welcome the use of Article 4(3) to undermine national laws, delegated legislation, regulatory regimes and other measures because they happen to distort competition; a broad use of Article 4(3) would be particularly objectionable given that there are clear legal bases for proceeding against Member States under other Treaty provisions dealing, for example, with the free movement of goods and services. On the other hand the full effectiveness of Articles 101 and 102 could be seriously undermined if Member States could facilitate anti-competitive behaviour by adopting measures that have the same effect on the market as the undertakings would have achieved themselves[15]. The case law of the Court of Justice has sought to achieve a balance and to identify those infringements of Articles 101 and 102 for which Member States must bear responsibility.

(B) The case law predominantly concerns Article 4(3) TEU in conjunction with Article 101 TFEU

It is noticeable that state measures that raise issues in relation to abusive behaviour under Article 102 usually arise in the context of Article 106(1), which imposes a duty on Member States not to enact nor to maintain in force measures in the case of 'public undertakings and undertakings to which Member States grant special or exclusive rights' which

[12] Case C-35/96 EU:C:1998:303; see 'Article 106(3)', pp 248–251 later in chapter.

[13] See further 'Article 106(3)', pp 248–251 later in chapter.

[14] For interesting discussions of the issues involved see Bacon 'State Regulation of the Market and EC Competition Rules: Articles 85 and 86 Compared' (1997) 18 ECLR 283; Ehle 'State Regulation under the US Antitrust State Action Doctrine and under EC Competition Law: A Comparative Analysis' (1998) 19 ECLR 380; Neergaard *Competition Competences: The Tensions between European Competition Law and Anti-Competitive Measures by the Member States* (DJØF Publishing, 1998); Schepel 'Delegation of Regulatory Powers to Private Powers under EC Competition Law: Towards a Procedural Public Interest' (2002) 39 CML Rev 31; Castillo de la Torre 'State Action Defence in EC Antitrust Law' (2005) 28 World Competition 407; OECD Best Practices Roundtable, *The Application of Antitrust Law to State-Owned Enterprises* (2009), available at www.oecd.org/competition; on the position in the US see *North Carolina State Board of Dental Examiners v Federal Trade Commission* 135 S Ct 1101 (2015).

[15] See eg Case C-347/16 *BEB v KEVR* EU:C:2017:816, para 52.

infringe the Treaty and, specifically, the competition rules[16]. The case law on Article 4(3) therefore has been predominantly concerned with the liability of Member States for infringements of Article 101[17]. Before considering the cases themselves it may be helpful to illustrate the type of problem that arises. Suppose the following:

- in Member State A all lawyers belong to a privately-established bar association and agree to comply with the fees that it recommends for legal services
- in Member State B the state itself fixes legal fees
- in Member State C the bar association is established by law but the association is free to decide whether to recommend fees and, if so, to determine the level of those fees
- in Member State D the state requires the bar association to fix fees but leaves it to set the fees
- in Member State E a Government Minister has the power, by order, to decree that all lawyers must comply with a draft tariff of fees prepared by the bar association.

In each of these cases the likely outcome will be that there is little competition in relation to legal fees: the effect is that of a horizontal cartel. However in EU competition law the important question is which, if any, of these situations is unlawful; and, specifically in the case of Article 4(3), whether there is a Member State measure that violates EU law with the consequence that the state must take all appropriate measures to enable EU law to be fully applied[18]. These questions will be considered after the case law has been analysed.

(C) **The case law on Article 4(3) and the competition rules**

(i) **The *INNO* doctrine**

In *INNO v ATAB*[19] the Court of Justice, dealing with the taxation of tobacco in Belgium, held that the combined effect of Article 4(3) TEU and Articles 101 and 102 TFEU[20] meant that a Member State could infringe EU law by maintaining in force legislation which could deprive the competition rules of their effectiveness. Subsequent cases have had to search out the implications of this judgment[21].

(ii) **Unsuccessful application of the *INNO* doctrine**

There have been several judgments in which the Court of Justice has concluded that the *INNO* doctrine did not apply to state involvement in the conduct of undertakings. A challenge to French legislation requiring retailers of books to comply with minimum resale prices imposed by publishers failed since the Court of Justice was not certain that this practice was unlawful under Article 101 anyway[22]; a challenge to fixed minimum prices for petrol also failed, since this was a pure state measure unrelated to any agreement between undertakings[23]. In *Ministère Public v Asjes*[24] Asjes was prosecuted

[16] See 'The obligations on Member States under Article 106(1)', pp 234–242 later in chapter.

[17] See 'The case law on Article 4(3) and the competition rules', pp 225–228 later in chapter.

[18] The utility of this case law has been questioned by Faull and Nikpay (eds) *The EU Law of Competition* (Oxford University Press, 3rd ed, 2014), paras 6.06–6.07.

[19] Case 13/77 EU:C:1977:185.

[20] The Court also referred to Article 3(1)(g) EC but this provision was repealed by the Lisbon Treaty with effect from 1 December 2009; on Article 3(1)(g) and Protocol 27 to the Treaties see ch 2, 'The competition chapter in the TFEU', pp 51–52.

[21] The Opinion of AG Maduro in Case C-94/04 *Cipolla* EU:C:2006:76, paras 31–40 contains a useful review of the case law.

[22] See Case 229/83 *Association des Centres Distributeurs Edouard Leclerc v Au Ble Vert* EU:C:1985:1; Case 254/87 *Syndicat des Libraires de Normandie v L'Aigle Distribution SA* EU:C:1988:413.

[23] Case 231/83 *Cullet v Centre Leclerc, Toulouse* EU:C:1985:29.

[24] Cases 209/84 etc EU:C:1986:188.

for undercutting the air fares approved by the Minister for Civil Aviation and made binding upon all traders by French law. Asjes challenged the compatibility of this law with EU law. The action failed since, at the time, there was no implementing regulation for the application of the competition rules to the air transport sector; this meant that there was no mechanism in place for determining whether any agreements infringed the competition rules[25].

(iii) Successful application of the *INNO* doctrine

(a) BNIC v Yves Aubert

The *INNO* doctrine was successfully applied in *BNIC v Yves Aubert*[26]. BNIC, a French trade association representing wine-growers and dealers in France, established production quotas for the wine-growers. A ministerial decree was then made making these quotas binding on the entire industry and providing for fines to be imposed on anyone who exceeded them. The Court of Justice held that the decree was itself unlawful since it had the effect of strengthening the impact of the prior agreement made within the membership of BNIC; as such it was a breach of France's obligations under the Treaty. It followed that an action brought against Yves Aubert by BNIC for infringement of the extension order failed[27].

(b) Vlaamse Reisbureaus v Sociale Dienst

In *Vlaamse Reisbureaus v Sociale Dienst*[28] a tour operator in Belgium brought an action against an association of travel agents which was passing on to its customers the commission it received from tour operators. By Belgian law the tour operator was permitted in these circumstances to bring an action for unfair competition against the price-cutter. The defendant raised the incompatibility of this law with Article 101(1). The Court of Justice held that there was a constellation of agreements in the industry between tour operators and agents intended to dampen price competition and which infringed Article 101(1); the Belgian legislation buttressed this anti-competitive system by giving it permanent effect, extending it to non-participating undertakings, and by providing penalties for firms which passed on their commission. Therefore the legislation infringed Article 101(1) TFEU and Article 4(3) TEU and the tour operator's action would fail.

(c) Ahmed Saeed

In *Ahmed Saeed Flugreisen v Zentrale zur Bekämpfung Unlauteren Wettbewerbs*[29] the Court of Justice held that the approval by aeronautical authorities of air tariffs fixed by agreement by airlines involved a breach by Member States of their obligations under Article 4(3) TEU and Articles 101 and 102 TFEU. The material distinction between this case and *Ministère Public v Asjes*[30] was that by the time of the litigation in *Ahmed Saeed* the implementing regulation in the air transport sector had come into effect[31], so that there was no longer the problem that existed at the time of the earlier case[32].

[25] Ibid, paras 46–69; however the Court continued that, if an adverse finding had been made under Article 104 or 105(2) TFEU, it would have been contrary to Article 4(3) TEU for France to have reinforced the effects of an unlawful agreement: ibid, paras 70–77; on the application of the competition rules to air transport: see ch 23, 'Air Transport', pp 1005–1008.

[26] Case 136/86 EU:C:1987:524.

[27] In an earlier judgment, Case 123/83 *BNIC v Clair* EU:C:1985:33, the Court of Justice had held that the rules of BNIC infringed Article 101 and that the involvement of the Minister did not prevent the application of Article 101 to them; this confirmed the findings of the Commission in two earlier decisions, *BNIA* OJ [1976] L 231/24 and *BNIC* OJ [1982] L 379/1.

[28] Case 311/85 EU:C:1987:418.

[29] Case 66/86 EU:C:1989:140.

[30] Cases 209/84 etc EU:C:1986:188.

[31] See ch 6 n 25 earlier.

[32] See 'The *INNO* doctrine', p 225 earlier in chapter.

(d) Consorzio Industrie Fiammiferi

In *Consorzio Industrie Fiammiferi*[33] the Court of Justice held that the Italian competition authority was required by Article 4(3) TEU to disapply an Italian law of 1923 which regulated the manufacture and sale of matches in Italy in so far as that law required or facilitated price fixing and market sharing contrary to Article 101; it added that penalties could be imposed on the undertakings involved in the unlawful period, except to the extent that the behaviour in question was required as opposed to merely being permitted by the legislation.

(e) Synthesis

In *Van Eycke v ASPA*[34] the Court of Justice synthesised the case law which, in its view, showed that a Member State would be in breach of Article 4(3) TEU in conjunction with Article 101 TFEU if it were:

> to require or favour the adoption of agreements, decisions or concerted practices contrary to Article [101] or to reinforce their effects, or to deprive its own legislation of its official character by delegating to private traders responsibility for taking decisions affecting the economic sphere[35].

This is a formulation that the Court of Justice has repeated on subsequent occasions[36]. A particularly clear application of the doctrine is to be found in *Commission v Italy*[37], an action brought by the Commission under Article 258 TFEU, challenging—successfully—Italian legislation which required the National Council of Customs Agents to set compulsory tariffs for customs agents. The Court of Justice concluded that the National Council had infringed Article 101(1) by adopting the tariff[38]. However it held further that Italy had also infringed EU law by requiring the Council to compile a compulsory, uniform tariff[39]: by wholly relinquishing to private economic operators the powers of the public authorities to set tariffs[40]; by prohibiting, in the primary legislation, any derogation from the tariff[41]; and by adopting a Decree having the appearance of approving the tariff by public regulation[42]. In *Anonima Petroli Italiana SpA v Ministero delle Infrastrutture e dei Trasporti*[43] the Court of Justice held that Italian legislation providing that the price of road haulage services could not be lower than minimum operating costs, which were themselves fixed by a body composed mainly of private economic operators rather than public officials, violated Article 4(3) TEU and Article 101 TFEU; more specifically the Court did not consider that the fixing of minimum costs satisfied the *Wouters* doctrine[44].

[33] Case C-198/01 EU:C:2003:430; for comment see Nebbia (2004) 41 CML Rev 839; Kaczorowska 'The Power of a National Competition Authority to Disapply National Law Incompatible with EC Law—and its Practical Consequences' (2004) 25 ECLR 591; for discussion of the *CIF* judgment in the UK see Case 1027/2/3/04 *VIP Communications Ltd (in administration) v OFCOM* [2009] CAT 28, paras 20–27.

[34] Case 267/86 EU:C:1988:427. [35] Ibid, para 16.

[36] See eg Case C-185/91 *Reiff* EU:C:1993:886, para 14; Case C-153/93 *Delta Schiffahrts- und Speditionsgesellschaft* EU:C:1994:240, para 14; Case C-38/97 *Autotrasporti Librandi v Cuttica Spedizioni e Servizi Internazionali* EU:C:1998:454, para 26; Case C-338/09 *Yellow Cab Verkehrsbetriebs GmbH v Landeshauptmann von Wien* EU:C:2010:814, para 26; Cases C-184/13 etc *Anonima Petroli Italiana SpA v Ministero delle Infrastrutture e dei Trasporti* EU:C:2014:2147, para 29.

[37] Case C-35/96 EU:C:1998:303; the Commission's decision finding that the National Council itself had infringed Article 101(1), OJ [1993] L 203/27, was upheld on appeal by the General Court in Case T-513/93 *CNSD v Commission* EU:T:2000:91.

[38] Case C-35/96 EU:C:1998:303, para 51. [39] Ibid, para 56. [40] Ibid, para 57.

[41] Ibid, para 58. [42] Ibid, para 59. [43] Cases C-184/13 etc EU:C:2014:2147, para 29.

[44] Ibid, paras 47–57; on the possible application of *Wouters* to minimum legal fees see Case C-427/16 etc *CHEZ Elecktron Bulgaria AD* EU:C:2017:890, paras 40–58. On the *Wouters* doctrine generally see ch 3, 'Regulatory ancillarity: the judgment of the Court of Justice in *Wouters*', pp 138–141.

(iv) *INNO* doctrine applies only where there is an infringement of Article 101

Article 4(3) TEU cannot be used simply because a state measure produces effects similar to those of a cartel. The *INNO* doctrine can be used only to challenge state measures if the requirements for the application of Article 101 TFEU, such as the concepts of undertaking[45] and effect on trade between Member States[46], are met. Furthermore the *INNO* doctrine applies only where any agreement that is entered into is one that infringes Article 101. This was not the case in *AG2R Prévoyance v Beaudout*[47]: there the agreement was the result of collective bargaining between employers' and employees' organisations within the French traditional bakery and pastry-making sector, a type of agreement that the Court of Justice has held to fall outside Article 101[48].

The requirement that there must be an agreement contrary to Article 101 before a Member State can be found to have infringed Article 4(3) places an obvious limit on the scope of the *INNO* doctrine. Several challenges to national legislation have failed where the final determination of prices remained with a Member State: Article 4(3) TEU in conjunction with Article 101 is infringed only where a Member State requires, favours or reinforces an anti-competitive agreement or abandons its own price-setting powers and delegates them to private operators. Thus in *Meng*[49] the Court of Justice declined to strike down a German regulation which prohibited insurance companies from passing on commissions to their customers: unlike the position in *Vlaamse*, where Belgium had acted to reinforce prior agreements between travel agents, there was no agreement in *Meng*[50]; similar conclusions were reached in *Ohra*[51], *Reiff*[52] and in a number of later judgments[53]. In *Arduino*[54] the Court of Justice held that the involvement of the Italian National Bar Council in the production of a draft tariff for legal fees did not divest the tariff adopted by the Minister of the character of legislation[55]; and in *Ministero dello Sviluppo economico v SOA Nazionale Costruttori*[56] the Court of Justice held that Italian legislation on minimum tariffs for the provision of attestation services in the construction sector did not violate Article 4(3) TEU and Article 101(1) TFEU as it did not give effect to an unlawful agreement, nor did it delegate price-fixing powers to private operators.

[45] See Case C-350/07 *Kattner Stahlbau GmbH v Maschinenbau- und Metall- Berufsgenossenschaft* EU:C:2009:127, para 70.

[46] See Case C-393/08 *Emanuela Sbarigia v Azienda USL RM/A* EU:C:2010:388, paras 32–33.

[47] Case C-437/09 EU:C:2011:112, paras 37–39.

[48] See ch 3, 'Collective labour relations', pp 91–92 on the *Albany* judgment.

[49] Case C-2/91 EU:C:1993:885; note that *Meng* was decided at about the same time as Case C-267/91 *Keck and Mithouard* [1993] EU:C:1993:905, in which the Court of Justice declined to apply Article 34 TFEU to national marketing rules forbidding the use of loss-leaders (selling below cost) in retail outlets: see Reich 'The "November Revolution" of the European Court of Justice: *Keck*, *Meng* and *Audi* Revisited' (1994) 31 CML Rev 459.

[50] Case C-2/91 EU:C:1993:885, para 14.

[51] Case C-245/91 EU:C:1993:887.

[52] Case C-185/91 EU:C:1993:886.

[53] See eg Case C-153/93 *Delta Schiffahrts- und Speditionsgesellschaft* EU:C:1994:240; Case C-412/93 *Société d'Importation Edouard Leclerc-Siplec v TFI and M6* EU:C:1995:26; Case C-96/94 *Centro Servizi Spediporto v Spedizioni Marittima del Golfo* EU:C:1995:308; Cases C-140/94 etc *DIP SpA v Commune di Bassano del Grappa* EU:C:1995:330; Case C-38/97 *Autotrasporti Librandi v Cuttica Spedizioni e Servizi Internazionali* EU:C:1998:454; Case C-266/96 *Corsica Ferries* EU:C:1998:306; Case C-446/05 *Ioannis Doulamis* EU:C:2008:157.

[54] Case C-35/99 EU:C:2002:97; for discussion of this case see Thunstrom, Carle and Lindeborg 'State Liability Under the EC Treaty Arising from Anti-Competitive State Measures' (2002) 25 World Competition 515.

[55] Case C-35/99 EU:C:2002:97, paras 40–44; see to similar effect Case C-250/03 *Mauri* EU:C:2005:96, paras 31–38; Cases C-94/04 etc *Cipolla* EU:C:2006:758, paras 48–54; Case C-386/07 *Hospital Consulting Srl v Estate SpA*, EU:C:2008:256; Opinion of AG Mengozzi in Case C-437/09 *AG2R Prévoyance* EU:C:2010:676, paras 36–47.

[56] Case C-327/12 EU:C:2013:827, paras 36–39; see similarly Case C-121/16 *Salumificio Murru SpA v Autotrasporti di Marongiu Remigio* EU:C:2016:543.

(D) Application of the case law to lawyers' fees

Having analysed the case law under the *INNO* doctrine we should return briefly to the alternative situations set out earlier in relation to legal fees[57]:

- in Member State A lawyers agreed to comply with the recommendations of a privately-established bar association: this is an infringement by object of Article 101(1) TFEU, assuming an appreciable effect on inter-state trade; however there is no involvement on the part of the state, so the application of Article 4(3) TEU does not arise[58]
- in the second situation Member State B itself fixed the fees: however in this case there is no suggestion of an agreement, and so there can be no infringement of Article 101(1); this situation may be suitable for 'competition advocacy' by the competition authority of Member State B[59]
- Member State C established a regulatory mechanism, but left it to the bar association to decide whether to recommend fees and, if so, to determine what their level should be: the association in doing so would be infringing Article 101(1), but it is not clear whether Member State C has acted unlawfully; it has given freedom to the bar association to decide how to act, rather than requiring or encouraging the bar association to act anti-competitively
- Member State D, however, delegated its regulatory role to the bar association and required it to fix fees, so that it would be held responsible for the price fixing that ensues[60]
- Member State E could be considered to be strengthening the effect of an agreement contrary to Article 101 by issuing a decree compelling compliance with the bar association's recommendations. However the Court of Justice has held that if the Minister is free to vary the tariff, acting on the advice of other public bodies, there would be no infringement; the decree retains the character of legislation rather than amounting to the encouragement or reinforcement of an agreement[61].

3. Article 106 TFEU—Compliance with the Treaties

Article 106[62] provides that:

1. In the case of public undertakings and undertakings to which Member States grant special or exclusive rights, Member States shall neither enact nor maintain in force any measure contrary to the rules contained in the Treaties, in particular to those rules provided for in Article 18 and Articles 101 to 109.

[57] See 'The case law predominantly concerns Article 4(3) TEU in conjunction with Article 101 TFEU', pp 224–225 earlier in chapter.

[58] On the application of the competition rules to the professions see ch 3, 'The professions', p 90.

[59] On competition advocacy see ch 1, 'Competition advocacy and public restrictions of competition', p 24.

[60] Cases C-427/16 etc *CHEZ Elecktron Bulgaria AD* EU:C:2017:890.

[61] Case C-35/99 *Arduino* EU:C:2002:97; Cases C-94/04 etc *Cipolla* EU:C:2006:758.

[62] For further reading on Article 106 see Buendia Sierra *Exclusive Rights and State Monopolies under EC Law* (Oxford University Press, 1999): this book contains an extensive bibliography of literature on Article 106 at pp 431–451; Rose and Bailey (eds) *Bellamy and Child: European Union Law of Competition* (Oxford University Press, 7th ed, 2013), paras 11.029–11.035; Faull and Nikpay (eds) *The EU Law of Competition* (Oxford University Press, 3rd ed, 2014), paras 6.04–6.08; Buendia Sierra 'Enforcement of Article 106(1) TFEU by the European Commission and the EU Courts' in Lowe and Marquis (eds) *European Competition Law Annual 2013: Effective and Legitimate Enforcement of Competition Law* (Hart, 2016).

2. Undertakings entrusted with the operation of services of general economic interest or having the character of a revenue-producing monopoly shall be subject to the rules contained in the Treaties, in particular to the rules on competition, in so far as the application of such rules does not obstruct the performance, in law or in fact, of the particular tasks assigned to them. The development of trade must not be affected to such an extent as would be contrary to the interests of the Union.
3. The Commission shall ensure the application of the provisions of this Article and shall, where necessary, address appropriate directives or decisions to Member States.

Article 106(1) is a prohibition addressed to Member States themselves; Article 106(2) provides a limited exception for certain undertakings from the application of the competition rules; Article 106(3) provides the Commission with important powers to ensure compliance with Article 106. The case law under Article 106 is complex and still developing. After a long period when it was little used it has proved to be a formidable provision in the process of liberalising numerous markets in Europe, in particular in 'utility' sectors such as telecommunications, energy and post and related services. The Court of Justice has said in *Spain v Commission* that:

> [P]aragraph 2 of Article [106 TFEU], read with paragraph (1) thereof, seeks to reconcile the Member States' interest in using certain undertakings, in particular in the public sector, as an instrument of economic or social policy with the [EU's] interest in ensuring compliance with the rules on competition and the preservation of the unity of the [internal] market[63].

(A) **Article 106(1)**

Article 106(1) is closely related to Article 4(3) TEU: each seeks to ensure effective adherence to the Treaty on the part of Member States. However Article 106 goes beyond Article 4(3) in that it has its own sphere of application and is not limited to compliance with general principles of law. Article 106(1) imposes an obligation on Member States not to enact nor to maintain in force measures '*contrary to those rules contained in the Treaties, in particular to those rules provided for in Article 18 and Articles 101 to 109*'. Two important features of Article 106(1) should be noted at the outset. The first is that Article 106(1) is a 'renvoi' provision or a 'reference rule', that is to say it does not have an independent application but applies only in conjunction with another Article or other Articles of the Treaties. The second point is that Article 106(1) is not limited in its scope only to infringements of the competition rules; although the competition rules (and the rule of non-discrimination in Article 18) are specifically mentioned, measures that infringe, for example, Article 34 on the free movement of goods[64], Article 45 on the free movement of workers[65], Article 49 on the freedom of establishment[66], Articles 56 and 57 on the free movement of services[67] and Articles 63 to 66 on free movement of capital, could all result in an infringement of Article 106(1). It follows that Article 106(1) did not need to have been placed in the chapter of the Treaty on competition law; however the fact that it is there indicates that the Treaty's authors were aware of the potential for Member States to distort competition through the legislative and other measures that they adopt. The importance of Article 106(1) in relation to the competition rules is that, in certain circumstances, a Member State can be liable for the abuses that have been, or would be, carried out by undertakings.

[63] Case C-463/00 EU:C:2003:272, para 82.
[64] See eg Case C-18/88 *RTT* EU:C:1991:474.
[65] See eg Case C-179/90 *Merci* EU:C:1991:464.
[66] See eg *Greek Insurance* OJ [1985] L 152/25.
[67] See eg Case C-260/89 *ERT v Dimotiki* EU:C:1991:254.

(i) Undertakings

Article 106(1) applies to measures concerning 'public undertakings and undertakings to which Member States grant special or exclusive rights'. The term 'undertaking' has been considered in the context of Articles 101 and 102 in earlier chapters[68]. In particular it should be noted that state-owned bodies can be acting as undertakings, but that organs of the state that are not involved in any economic activity fall outside the definition[69].

(ii) Public undertakings

The term 'public undertaking'[70] appears only in Article 106(1) TFEU, and is not defined. There is no uniform notion of this expression among the Member States, and state intervention in and control of economic behaviour takes many different forms. For this reason Advocate General Reischl has stated that the term is a concept of EU law which should be given a uniform interpretation for all Member States[71]. In Article 2(1)(b) of the Transparency Directive[72] the Commission said that a public undertaking means:

> any undertaking over which the public authorities may exercise, directly or indirectly, a dominant influence by virtue of their ownership of it, their financial participation therein, or the rules which govern it.

On appeal the Court of Justice upheld the legality of the Directive and approved this definition, without elaborating further[73]. The crucial question in each case should be whether the state does have such influence, not the legal form of the undertaking in question.

(iii) Undertakings with 'special or exclusive rights'

Article 106(1) applies to measures in the case both of public undertakings and of undertakings having 'special or exclusive rights': sometimes the latter are referred to as 'privileged undertakings' to distinguish them from public undertakings. It is important to understand what each of the expressions 'special' and 'exclusive' means. The Treaty does not define them, but definitions can be found in Article 2(f) and (g) of the Transparency Directive[74]. In *Ambulanz Glöckner*[75] Advocate General Jacobs suggested that 'special or exclusive rights' are rights granted by a Member State to one or a limited number of undertakings that substantially affect the ability of other undertakings to exercise an economic activity in the same geographical area under substantially equivalent conditions. Often special or exclusive rights will have been given to a public undertaking, in which case it is unnecessary to give separate consideration to this head of Article 106(1); however many undertakings may have exclusive or special rights without being 'public'. In *FIFA v Commission*[76] FIFA failed to persuade the General Court that the Secretary of State for Culture, Media and Sport had conferred exclusive or special rights on the BBC and ITV, two free-to-air television stations, by placing World Cup football matches on a list that they would then be able to broadcast on a non-exclusive basis. FIFA's complaint was that this led to a distortion of competition in

[68] See ch 3, 'Undertaking and Associations of Undertakings', pp 83–101 and ch 5, 'Undertakings', p 185.

[69] See in particular ch 3, 'Regardless of the legal status of the entity and the way in which it is financed', pp 86–87.

[70] For detailed discussion of this concept see *Buendia Sierra* (ch 6 n 62 earlier), paras 1.113–1.139.

[71] Cases 188/80 etc *France v Commission* EU:C:1982:134.

[72] Commission Directive 80/723/EEC, OJ [1980] L 195/35; this has now been repealed and replaced by Commission Directive 2006/111/EC, OJ [2006] L 318/17.

[73] Cases 188/80 etc *France v Commission* EU:C:1982:257, para 25.

[74] See ch 6 n 72 earlier; 'exclusive rights' and 'special rights' are defined in respectively Articles 1(5) and 1(6) of Commission Directive 2002/77/EC on competition in the markets for electronic communications networks and services, OJ [2002] L 249/21.

[75] Cases C-475/99 EU:C:2001:284, para 89 of his Opinion.

[76] Case T-68/08 EU:T:2011:44, upheld on appeal Case C-205/11 P *FIFA v Commission* EU:C:2013:478.

which pay-TV companies could not bid for the very valuable right to show such games on an exclusive basis. The Court observed that the pay-TV companies could still broadcast on a non-exclusive basis[77]. In *Ministero dello Sviluppo economico v SOA Nazionale Costruttori*[78] the Court of Justice held that 'attestation organisations' providing certification services in the construction sector in Italy had not been granted special or exclusive rights: no competitive advantage had been given in favour of any particular organisation(s) and entry was possible for anyone that satisfied specified criteria.

(a) Exclusive rights

The following are examples of bodies considered to have been granted exclusive rights:

- a company established by insurance undertakings to perform a specific statutory task[79]
- an agricultural marketing board[80]
- an entity granted a monopoly over the provision of recruitment services[81]
- a dock-work undertaking entrusted with the exclusive right to organise dock work for third parties[82]
- a limited partnership between a Member State, a district authority and eight industrial undertakings responsible for waste management[83]
- a state-owned post office granted a monopoly over postal services which do not form part of a universal service obligation[84].

It would appear that an 'exclusive' right can be granted to more than one undertaking: in *Entreprenørforeningens Affalds v Københavns Kommune*[85] the Court of Justice held that three undertakings authorised to receive building waste in Copenhagen had been granted an exclusive right, but it did not explain why these rights were exclusive rather than special, which would have been a more natural finding[86].

A functional rather than a formalistic approach should be taken to the meaning of 'exclusive rights'. Rights may be exclusive in substance, even though they are not described as such (or as monopolies) in the measure in question. For example in *La Crespelle*[87] the Court of Justice concluded that a scheme for the artificial insemination of cattle in France involved exclusive rights because of the way the national legislation was operated in practice[88]. Furthermore the exclusive rights may derive from a series of different legislative and administrative measures rather than just one[89].

The Court has held that the mere fact that a body exercises powers conferred upon it by the state and that it has a dominant position in the market is not sufficient in itself to establish that it has exclusive rights[90]. This is consistent with an early Commission

[77] Case T-68/08 EU:T:2011:44, paras 174–180. [78] Case C-327/12 EU:C:2013:827, paras 40–43.
[79] Case 90/76 *Van Ameyde v UCI* EU:C:1977:101.
[80] Case 83/78 *Pigs Marketing Board v Redmond* EU:C:1978:214.
[81] Case C-41/90 *Höfner & Elser v Macrotron GmbH* EU:C:1991:161, para 34.
[82] Case C-179/90 *Merci* EU:C:1991:464. [83] Case C-203/96 *Dusseldorp* EU:C:1998:316, para 58.
[84] Case C-340/99 *TNT Traco SpA v Poste Italiane SpA* EU:C:2001:28.
[85] Case C-209/98 EU:C:2000:279.
[86] Cf para 50 of the Opinion of AG Jacobs in Cases C-271/90 etc *Spain v Commission* EU:C:1992:226.
[87] Case C-323/93 EU:C:1994:368.
[88] Although the Court of Justice did not address the point directly, the Opinion of AG Gulmann indicates that the parties agreed that exclusive rights existed: Case C-323/93 EU:C:1994:185.
[89] See *Exclusive Rights to Broadcast Television Advertising in Flanders* OJ [1997] L 244/18, paras 1 and 2, upheld on appeal Case T-266/97 *Vlaamse Televisie Maatschappij NV v Commission* EU:T:1999:144.
[90] Case C-387/93 *Banchero* EU:C:1995:439, paras 47–53.

decision that a copyright collecting society that could derive benefits from national copyright legislation did not have exclusive rights where there was no impediment to other such societies claiming the same benefit[91]; nevertheless the Commission did conclude that the society in question had a dominant position for the purpose of Article 102. The concepts of 'exclusive rights' and 'dominant position' are independent of one another.

(b) *Special rights*

The Court of Justice's judgment in *France v Commission*[92] indicates that there is a distinction between exclusive and special rights. The Court held that the provisions in the Commission's Directive on Telecommunications Equipment[93] were void in so far as they required Member States to remove special rights from national telecommunications services providers, since it had failed to specify which rights were special or why they were incompatible with the Treaty. In the subsequent Directive on Telecommunications Liberalisation[94] the Commission stated at Article 1(4) that, in the telecommunications sector, special rights include:

> rights that are granted by a Member State to a limited number of undertakings, through any legislative, regulatory or administrative instrument which, within a given geographical area, limits to two or more the number of undertakings, otherwise than according to objective, proportional and non-discriminatory criteria[95].

This definition can presumably be carried over to other sectors of the economy, unless there is specific legislation containing a different one. In *Second Operator of GSM Radiotelephony Services in Italy*[96] the Commission decided that the grant to Telecom Italia of the right to operate a GSM radiotelephony network qualified as a special right, since the operator had been designated otherwise than according to objective and non-discriminatory criteria. In *French savings accounts* the Commission concluded that the grant to three banks of the right to distribute tax-free savings products was a special right[97]. In *MOTOE* the power of the Greek Motorcycling Federation, ELPA, to authorise motorcycling events was held to be a special right within the meaning of Article 106(1)[98].

(iv) 'Measures'

For a Member State to be in breach of Article 106(1) it must have adopted a 'measure'. This expression has been given a wide meaning by the Commission, and its approach has been endorsed by the Court of Justice. In an early Directive under Article 34 TFEU[99] the Commission said that measures in that Article included 'laws, regulations,

[91] *GEMA* OJ [1971] L 134/15.

[92] Case C-202/88 EU:C:1991:120, paras 31–47; see similarly Cases C-271/90 etc *Spain v Commission* EU:C:1992:440, paras 32 and 34.

[93] Commission Directive 88/301/EEC, OJ [1988] L 131/73.

[94] Commission Directive 2008/63/EC, OJ [2008] L 162/20; for discussion of this definition see the Opinion of AG Jacobs in Case C-475/99 *Ambulanz Glöckner v Landkreis Südwestpfalz* EU:C:2001:284, paras 83–89.

[95] See similarly Article 2(g) of the Commission's Transparency Directive, ch 6 n 72 earlier.

[96] OJ [1995] L 280/49, para 6; see similarly *Second Operator of GSM Radio Telephony Services in Spain* OJ [1997] L 76/19, para 10.

[97] Commission decision of 10 May 2007.

[98] Case C-49/07 *Motosykletistiki Omospondia Ellados NPID (MOTOE) v Elliniko Dimosio* EU:C:2008:376, para 43.

[99] Commission Directive 70/50/EEC based on the provisions of Article 33(7) on the abolition of measures which have an effect equivalent to quantitative restrictions on imports and are not covered by other provisions adopted in pursuance of the EEC Treaty, JO [1970] L 13/29.

administrative provisions, administrative practices, and all instruments issued from a public authority, including recommendations'; there is no reason to suppose that the expression should have a different meaning under Article 106(1). In another case under Article 34, *Commission v Ireland*[100], the Court of Justice said that a measure did not have to be legally binding, provided that it might be capable of exerting an influence and of frustrating the aims of the Union[101]. The measure does not have to have been adopted by central government or by a national Parliament: a measure of any body that is a manifestation of the state could fall within Article 106(1), such as the local communes in *Corinne Bodson v Pompes Funèbres*[102].

It is clear that the expression 'measures' has a wide meaning under Article 106(1); for example:

- the grant of a second mobile licence subject to a substantial licence fee which had not been levied on the incumbent operator amounted to a measure[103]
- the refusal to grant a ferry company access to a state-run port was a measure[104]
- systems of stepped landing fee discounts at various airports were measures[105].

In each of the above cases the Member State had adopted specific measures which affected the conduct of the public undertaking or the undertaking given special or exclusive rights. In some cases a public authority enters into an agreement with an undertaking granting the latter an exclusive right to perform a particular task: for example to provide funeral services[106]. The question here is whether this amounts to a measure granting exclusive rights, in which case Article 106(1) may apply, or an agreement between undertakings that restricts competition, in which case Article 101(1) may apply. In *Bodson* the Court of Justice considered that Article 101(1) would not be applicable where a local authority was acting pursuant to its public law powers, since it would not be acting as an undertaking[107].

(v) The obligations on Member States under Article 106(1)

Article 106(1) requires Member States to refrain from enacting or maintaining in force any measure contrary to the Treaties, and in particular one which would contravene Article 18, Article 101 or Article 102. The relationship of Article 106(1) with Articles 101 and 102 is complex. Articles 101 and 102 are addressed to undertakings, but Article 106 to Member States: as in the case of Article 4(3)[108] the conceptual issue is to determine how, and in what circumstances, these provisions can operate in such a way as to lead to an infringement of the Treaties by a Member State. For many years this issue was barely addressed at all; however the position began to change as a result of a remarkable series of cases in 1991 in which the Court of Justice delivered four judgments on the relationship between Article 106(1) and other Treaty Articles, including in particular Article 102. A further landmark judgment, in the *Corbeau* case, followed in 1993[109].

[100] Case 249/81 EU:C:1982:402 (the '*Buy Irish*' case). [101] Ibid, para 28.

[102] Case 30/87 EU:C:1988:225.

[103] See eg *Second Operator of GSM Radiotelephony in Italy* OJ [1995] L 280/49; *Second Operator of GSM Radiotelephony in Spain* OJ [1997] L 76/19.

[104] *Port of Rødby* OJ [1994] L 55/52.

[105] See eg *Brussels National Airport (Zaventem)* OJ [1995] L 216/8; *Portuguese Airports* OJ [1999] L 69/31, upheld on appeal Case C-163/99 *Portugal v Commission* EU:C:2001:189; *Spanish Airports* OJ [2000] L 208/36.

[106] Case 30/87 *Corinne Bodson v Pompes Funèbres* EU:C:1988:225.

[107] See ch 3, 'Activities connected with the exercise of the powers of a public authority are not economic', p 89.

[108] See 'Article 4(3) TEU—Duty of Sincere Cooperation', pp 223–229 earlier in chapter.

[109] Case C-320/91 EU:C:1993:198.

(vi) The judgments of 1991

(a) Höfner & Elser v Macrotron

In April 1991 the Court of Justice held in *Höfner & Elser v Macrotron GmbH*[110] that a Member State which had conferred exclusive rights on a public employment agency could be in breach of Article 106(1) where the exercise by that agency of its rights would inevitably involve an infringement of Article 102. In Germany the Federal Employment Office ('the FEO') had a legal monopoly as an intermediary in the employment market, though in practice it was unable to satisfy demand and tolerated 'head-hunting' agencies which, strictly, were acting illegally. An agency seeking payment of its fee for having successfully recruited on behalf of a client was met with the defence that, as the agency was acting unlawfully, it could not enforce the contract; thus the alleged infringement by Germany of EU law was raised as a defence to a contract action between two private undertakings. The matter was referred to the Court of Justice. The Court held that the fact that Germany had granted a legal monopoly to the FEO did not in itself entail a breach of Articles 102 and 106(1)[111]; however there would be a breach if the mere exercise of its right would inevitably lead to an abuse under Article 102. This could be the case if the undertaking was manifestly unable to satisfy demand, as was the case here by the admission of the FEO, and if the legal monopoly prevented a competitor from trying to satisfy that demand[112].

(b) ERT v Dimotiki

In June 1991 the Court of Justice considered in *ERT v Dimotiki*[113] the compatibility with the Treaty of the Greek television and radio station's monopoly over broadcasting. The Court held that the existence of the monopoly in itself was not contrary to the Treaty, but that the manner in which it was exercised could be[114]. Specifically on Article 102 the Court of Justice held that, if a Member State which had granted the exclusive right to transmit television broadcasts then granted the same undertaking the right to retransmit broadcasts, it would infringe Article 106(1) if this created a situation in which the broadcaster would be led to infringe Article 102 by virtue of a discriminatory policy which favours its own broadcasts. In contrast to *Höfner* there do not appear to have been any national rules that obliged ERT to pursue a discriminatory broadcasting policy; it was sufficient that the exclusive rights bestowed on ERT placed it in a position where it might practise discrimination.

(c) Merci Convenzionali Porto di Genova v Siderurgica Gabrielli

In December 1991 the Court of Justice gave its judgment in *Merci Convenzionali Porto di Genova v Siderurgica Gabrielli*[115]. Merci was a private undertaking given an exclusive concession for the handling of loading operations in the harbour of Genoa. As a result of a strike at Merci, Siderurgica was unable to unload goods imported in a ship from Germany. Siderurgica sued for damages. The Court stated that the simple fact of creating a dominant position by granting exclusive rights is not as such incompatible with Article 106(1)[116]; however the Court repeated the ideas in *Höfner* and *ERT* that there could be an infringement by a Member State if the undertaking in question, merely by exercising the exclusive rights granted to it, cannot avoid abusing its dominant position (*Höfner*), or when such rights are liable to create a situation in which that undertaking is induced to commit such abuses (*ERT*)[117]. In this case the Court observed that Merci appeared to have

[110] Case C-41/90 EU:C:1991:161. [111] Ibid, para 29. [112] Ibid, paras 30–31.
[113] Case C-260/89 EU:C:1991:254. [114] Ibid, paras 12 and 32.
[115] Case C-179/90 EU:C:1991:464; see Gyselen (1992) 29 CML Rev 1229.
[116] Case C-179/90 EU:C:1991:464, para 16. [117] Ibid, para 17.

been induced to demand payment for services which had not been requested, to charge disproportionate prices, to refuse to have recourse to modern technology and to treat customers in a discriminatory manner: matters which are specifically mentioned as possible abuses in Article 102(2)(a), (b) and (c)[118].

(d) RTT v GB-Inno-BM

The Court of Justice delivered a further judgment in December 1991, three days after the judgment in *Merci*, in *RTT v GB-Inno-BM*[119]. RTT had exclusive rights in Belgium for the operation of telephone services and for the approval of telecommunications terminal equipment such as telephones; it was also a supplier of telephones itself. GB-Inno sold telephones in Belgium which had been imported from the Far East. RTT asked for an injunction to prevent such sales, since this encouraged people to connect equipment which had not been approved according to Belgian law. The Court referred to earlier case law, that an abuse is committed where an undertaking holding a dominant position on a particular market reserves to itself an ancillary activity which might be carried out by another undertaking as part of its activities on a neighbouring but separate market, with the possibility of eliminating all competition from such an undertaking[120]. The Court went on to say that, where a state measure brings about such a reservation of an ancillary activity, the measure in question infringes Article 106(1)[121]. RTT argued that there would be an infringement of Article 106(1) only where the Member State favoured an abuse, for example by acting in a discriminatory manner[122], but the Court rejected this, stating that the extension of RTT's monopoly was itself a state measure contrary to Article 106(1)[123]. The establishment of a regulatory system which gave RTT the power to determine at will which telephone equipment could be connected to the public telephone network, thereby placing itself at an obvious advantage over its competitors, was unlawful[124].

(vii) The *Corbeau* judgment

A further judgment of great significance was *Corbeau* in 1993[125]. Criminal proceedings had been brought against Corbeau, a businessman from Liège, for infringing the Belgian legal monopoly for postal services. Corbeau was operating a door-to-door express delivery service in the Liège area: he was not conducting the service of delivering letters on a daily-delivery basis. The Court of Justice, after referring to the requirement in Article 106(1) not to enact nor to maintain in force measures contrary to the competition rules[126], considered, under Article 106(2), whether the breadth of the monopoly given to the Belgian Post Office was greater than was necessary to enable it to carry out the task of general economic interest entrusted to it[127]. The significance of the judgment for Article 106(1) was that the Court of Justice, in effect, was ruling that the breadth of the monopoly granted to the Belgian Post Office was, to the extent that it could not be justified under Article 106(2), unlawful under the Treaty. In other words the Court was challenging the exclusive rights themselves, despite its numerous statements that the creation of dominance is not in itself incompatible with the Treaty.

118 Ibid, paras 18 and 19.
119 Case C-18/88 EU:C:1991:474; see Gyselen, ch 6 n 115 earlier.
120 Ibid, para 18, referring to Case 311/84 *CBEM* EU:C:1985:394 (the *Télémarketing* judgment).
121 Case C-18/88 EU:C:1991:474, para 21.
122 Ibid, para 22.
123 Ibid, para 23.
124 In reaching this finding the Court of Justice relied on another of its judgments in 1991, the *Telecommunications Directive* case, ch 6 n 92 earlier, at para 51.
125 Case C-320/91 EU:C:1993:198; see Hancher (1994) 31 CML Rev 105.
126 Case C-320/91 EU:C:1993:198, para 12.
127 For discussion of Article 106(2), and of the *Corbeau* judgment on this issue, see 'Article 106(2)', pp 242–248 later in chapter.

(viii) Making sense of the case law on Article 102 in conjunction with Article 106(1)

The difficulty with these cases, and with the Court of Justice's subsequent judgments[128], is to determine the circumstances in which a Member State can be liable under Article 106(1) for an infringement of Article 102. Three points can be made at the outset. First, as Advocate General Jacobs explained at paragraph 388 of his Opinion in *Albany*[129], a Member State cannot be held responsible for independent anti-competitive behaviour on the part of an undertaking simply because it takes place within its jurisdiction. Article 106(1) can be infringed 'only where there is a causal link between a Member State's legislative or administrative intervention on the one hand and anti-competitive behaviour of undertakings on the other hand'. Secondly, the mere creation of a dominant position by the grant of exclusive rights does not infringe Article 106(1); this has been stressed by the Court of Justice on many occasions[130]: the point is exemplified by the judgment in *Crespelle*[131], where the Court concluded that French legislation conferring legal monopolies on insemination centres for the provision of certain services to cattle breeders did not lead to an abuse for which France was responsible. A third point is that an infringement of Article 106(1) does not require an abuse of a dominant position to have occurred: it is sufficient that there is a risk of an abuse[132].

Helpful though these three points are, they do not shed any light on the circumstances in which a Member State will be found to have infringed Article 106(1) as a result of an abuse that infringes Article 102. Furthermore, the frequently-repeated statement that the mere creation (or reinforcement) of dominance does not in itself infringe Article 106(1) does not sit easily with judgments such as *ERT*, *RTT* and *Corbeau* which do seem, in effect, to have concluded that the monopoly rights in question were incompatible with the Treaty. The judgments of the Court of Justice on the necessary causal link between the measure under Article 106(1) and the abuse under Article 102 are neither clear nor consistent: in *Höfner* the Court considered that a measure would be unlawful where it led to an 'inevitable' abuse; in *ERT* if it would induce an infringement; in *Banchero*[133] the Court of Justice considered that there would be an infringement only if the Member State created a situation in which the undertaking in question 'cannot avoid abusing its dominant position'[134]. In *Dusseldorp*[135] the Court

[128] There have been many subsequent judgments on the relationship between Article 102 and Article 106(1): see in particular Case C-393/92 *Almelo* EU:C:1994:171; Case C-18/93 *Corsica Ferries Italia srl v Corpo del Piloti del Porto de Genoa* EU:C:1994:195; Case C-323/93 *Centre d'Insémination de la Crespelle v Coopérative de la Mayenne* EU:C:1994:368; Case C-111/94 *Job Centre (I)* EU:C:1995:340; Case C-242/95 *GT-Link A/S v De Danske Statsbaner* EU:C:1997:376; Case C-387/93 *Banchero* EU:C:1995:439; Case C-55/96 *Job Centre (II)* EU:C:1997:603; Case C-70/95 *Sodemare v Regione Lombardia* EU:C:1997:301; Case C-163/96 *Silvano Raso* EU:C:1998:54; Case C-266/96 *Corsica Ferries France SA v Gruppo Antichi Ormeggiatori del Porto di Genova* EU:C:1998:306; Case C-203/96 *Dusseldorp* EU:C:1998:316; Cases C-67/96 etc *Albany International BV v SBT* EU:C:1999:430; Cases C-147/97 etc *Deutsche Post AG v GZS* EU:C:2000:74; Case C-258/98 *Giovanni Carra* EU:C:2000:301; Case C-209/98 *Entreprenørforeningens Affalds/Miljøsektion v Københavns Kommune* EU:C:2000:279, on which see van Calster 'Exclusive Rights Ruling No Safe Harbour for Export Restrictions' (2001) 26 CML Rev 502; Case C-340/99 *TNT Traco SpA v Poste Italiane SpA* EU:C:2001:28; Case C-475/99 *Ambulanz Glöckner v Landkreis Südwestpfalz* EU:C:2001:577; Case C-49/07 *Motosykletistiki Omospondia Ellados NPID (MOTOE) v Elliniko Dimosio* EU:C:2008:376.

[129] Cases C-67/96 etc *Albany International BV v SBT* EU:C:1999:28.

[130] Specific paras in which the Court has said this were cited earlier in relation to the 1991 judgments in *Höfner*, *ERT* and *Merci*: see 'The judgments of 1991', pp 235–236 earlier in chapter.

[131] Case C-323/93 *Centre d'Insémination de la Crespelle v Coopérative de la Mayenne* EU:C:1994:368; see also Cases C-180/98 etc *Pavel Pavlov v Stichting Pensioenfonds Medische Specialisten* EU:C:2000:428, para 127.

[132] See Case C-553/12 P *Commission v Dimosia Epicheirisi Ilektrismou AE (DEI)* EU:C:2014:2083, paras 41 and 42 and the case law cited there.

[133] Case C-387/93 EU:C:1995:439.

[134] Ibid, para 51.

[135] Case C-203/96 EU:C:1998:316.

was much less guarded: a Member State infringes Article 106(1) in conjunction with Article 102 'if it adopts any law, regulation or administrative provision which enables an undertaking on which it has conferred rights to abuse its dominant position'[136]. In *Commission v DEI*[137] the General Court went further. A measure in Greece conferred on DEI, a generator of electricity, extensive rights to lignite, the primary natural fuel available in Greece for such generation. The Commission considered this to violate Article 106(1) in conjunction with Article 102. On appeal the General Court annulled the Commission's decision because it considered that the measure, in itself, did not lead to an abuse[138]. However the Commission's appeal to the Court of Justice was successful[139]: the Court noted that undistorted competition, as required by the Treaty, can be guaranteed only if equality of opportunity is secured as between various economic operators[140]. It followed that:

> if inequality of opportunity between economic operators, and thus distorted competition, is the result of a State measure, such a measure constitutes an infringement of Article [106(1)] read together with Article [102][141].

There is therefore a difference between the application of Article 102 to conduct that constitutes an abuse, on the one hand, and the application of Article 102 in conjunction with Article 106(1) to a state measure granting preferential rights that creates inequality of opportunity, and enables a dominant undertaking to distort competition by the mere exercise of those rights[142].

Some formulations of the necessary causal link impose quite a high threshold before a Member State will be found liable; others, such as the one in *DEI*, suggest a lower threshold. What seems clear is that the causal link must be stronger in some kinds of cases than others, depending on how likely it is that abusive behaviour will follow from the measure in question.

Many attempts have been made to make sense of the cases, in particular by identifying specific categories[143]; this is a natural response to the case law, but it is noticeable that different commentators have devised different categories, or have assigned the cases differently. This is not surprising: the cases can be explained in different, and sometimes in overlapping, ways, and the jurisprudence is still evolving. As Advocate General Fennelly stated in his Opinion in *Silvano Raso*[144]:

> I do not think that any general test can be enunciated for determining in advance the existence of such a [causal] link. Instead, in each individual case, it will be necessary to assess the impact of impugned national rules in the economic and factual circumstances in which they operate[145].

[136] Ibid, para 61, citing the *RTT* judgment (see ch 6 n 119 earlier).

[137] Case C-553/12 P EU:C:2014:2083.

[138] Case T-169/08 *DEI v Commission* EU:T:2012:448.

[139] The matter was remitted to the General Court, which upheld the Commission's original decision: Case T-169/08 RENV *DEI v Commission* EU:T:2016:733.

[140] Case C-553/12 P *Commission v DEI* EU:C:2014:2083, para 43.

[141] Ibid, para 44.

[142] See the AG's Opinion in Case C-553/12 P *Commission v DEI* EU:C:2013:807, paras 35–65, and in particular para 58.

[143] See eg *Buendia Sierra* (ch 6 n 62 earlier), paras 5.68–5.109; see also Buendia Sierra in Faull and Nikpay (eds) *The EU Law of Competition* (Oxford University Press, 3rd ed, 2014), paras 5.54–5.92; Edward and Hoskins 'Article 90: Deregulation and EC Law: Reflections arising from the XVI FIDE Conference' (1995) 32 CML Rev 157; AG Jacobs in his Opinion in *Albany* (ch 6 n 129 earlier), paras 396–440; Ritter, Braun and Rawlinson *European Competition Law: A Practitioner's Guide* (Kluwer Law International, 3rd ed, 2005), pp 764–767; see also, on the issue of causation, the Opinion of AG Fennelly in Case C-163/96 *Silvano Raso* EU:C:1997:477, paras 57–66.

[144] Case C-163/96 EU:C:1997:477.

[145] Ibid, para 65.

The text that follows attempts a categorisation, but must be read subject to the caveat that it is simply one way, among several others, of trying to make sense of the jurisprudence of the Court of Justice and the decisional practice of the Commission.

(a) Manifest inability to meet demand

In *Höfner & Elser v Macrotron GmbH*[146] the Court of Justice held that there would be an infringement of Article 106(1) where Germany had created a situation in which the FEO was 'manifestly not in a position to satisfy demand' for recruitment services, and its legal monopoly prevented a competitor from satisfying that demand. The idea that inability to meet demand can be abusive can be traced back to Article 102(2)(b), which gives as an example of abuse 'limiting production, markets or technical development to the prejudice of consumers'. On similar facts to *Höfner*, in *Job Centre (II)*[147] the Court concluded that the enforcement of an employment procurement monopoly enforced in Italy through criminal proceedings was a measure contrary to Article 106(1). In *Albany*[148] the Court seems to have considered that the exclusive right given to the operator of a sectoral pension fund amounted to a limitation of demand[149], although it went on to decide that this could be justified under Article 106(2)[150]. The judgment in *Merci*[151] can be explained, in part, on the basis that the entrusted undertaking had refused to have recourse to modern technology, which resulted in a failure to satisfy the demand of customers. In *Dusseldorp*[152] a requirement that waste for recovery could be supplied only to the entrusted undertaking, and could not be exported to a third undertaking, was held to restrict outlets and to contravene Article 106(1) in conjunction with Article 102[153]. However in *Ambulanz Glöckner v Landkreis Südwestpfalz*[154] Advocate General Jacobs suggested that a Member State would be liable under Article 106(1) only where there is a systemic failure to meet demand and not where there is a failure merely due to inefficient management[155]. The Commission's decisions on courier services[156], on licences for mobile telephony operators[157] and on *Slovakian postal legislation relating to hybrid mail services*[158] can be included, in part, in this category of cases[159].

(b) Conflict of interest

In *ERT v Dimotiki*[160] the Court of Justice held that there would be an infringement of Article 106(1) where Greece had created a situation in which the broadcaster ERT would be led to infringe Article 102 by virtue of a discriminatory policy in favour of its own broadcasts. A notable feature of this case was that it was not necessary for ERT to have actually abused its dominant position in the manner suggested: the granting of the exclusive right made this sufficiently likely that the measure in question infringed Article 106(1).

146 Case C-41/90 EU:C:1991:161.

147 Case C-55/96 EU:C:1997:603; see also Case C-258/98 *Giovanni Carra* EU:C:2000:301.

148 Cases C-67/96 etc EU:C:1999:430.

149 Ibid, para 97.

150 See 'Article 106(2)', pp 242–248 later in chapter.

151 Case C-179/90 EU:C:1991:464.

152 Case C-203/96 EU:C:1998:316.

153 Ibid, para 63.

154 Case C-475/99 EU:C:2001:284.

155 Ibid, para 148 of his Opinion; the Court of Justice did not deal with this point explicitly in Case C-475/99 EU:C:2001:577, though the tone of its comments at paras 62–65 appear to be consistent with the views of the Advocate General.

156 See *Dutch Express Delivery Services* OJ [1990] L 10/47 quashed on appeal Cases C-48/90 etc *Netherlands and Koninklijke PTT Nederland v Commission* EU:C:1992:63; *Spanish International Courier Services* OJ [1990] L 233/19, para 11.

157 See *Second Operator of GSM Radiotelephony Services in Italy* OJ [1995] L 280/49, para 17(ii); *Second Operator of GSM Radiotelephony Services in Spain* OJ [1997] L 76/19, para 21(ii).

158 Decision of 7 October 2008, paras 149–155, upheld on appeal Case T-556/08 *Slovenská pošta a.s. v Commission* EU:T:2015:189 and on further appeal to the Court of Justice Case C-293/15 P EU:C:2016:511.

159 The same decisions can also be included in the 'reservation of an ancillary activity' category: see later in chapter.

160 Case C-260/89 EU:C:1991:254.

The Court seems to have considered it to be inevitable that an undertaking in the position of ERT, because of its conflict of interest, would act abusively. The same idea was presumably present in *RTT v GB-Inno-BM*[161], since the regulatory function of RTT inevitably gave rise to a conflict of interest, although the Court specifically relied there on the extension of monopoly rights to neighbouring markets[162]. In *Silvano Raso*[163], a dock-work scheme granted an undertaking the exclusive right to supply temporary labour to terminal concessionaires, but also enabled it to compete with them on the market for the provision of dock services. The Court explained that the scheme caused a conflict of interest that was a threat for the competitive process: merely by exercising its monopoly rights the entrusted undertaking would be able to distort competition in its favour, for example by imposing on its competitors unduly high costs or by supplying them with labour less suited to the work to be done[164]. A further example of a conflict of interest case is *MOTOE*[165] in which a provision of the Greek Road Traffic Code infringed Articles 102 and 106(1) by granting ELPA, a body which organised motorcycling events, the exclusive and unfettered power to authorise competing motorcycling events in Greece, thereby placing ELPA at an obvious advantage over its competitors. The Court would be less likely to find an infringement of Article 106(1) where provision exists for judicial review of the decisions made by an apparently conflicted undertaking[166].

(c) Reservation of an ancillary activity

In *RTT v GB-Inno-BM*[167] the Court of Justice held that a measure that resulted in the extension of RTT's monopoly to an ancillary activity on a neighbouring but separate market infringed Article 106(1). As noted in the preceding paragraph, the Court of Justice could have reached the same conclusion on the basis of a conflict of interest, but it decided the case specifically on the basis of its earlier judgment in *Télémarketing*[168]. In *Ambulanz Glöckner v Landkreis Südwestpfalz*[169] the Court of Justice held that a law adopted by Länder in Germany concerning the provision of ambulance services infringed Article 106(1) because medical aid organisations that had an exclusive right to provide emergency ambulance services were enabled to also offer non-emergency patient transport services, which could have been carried out by independent operators[170]. The Commission considered that there were abuses under this head in *Dutch Express Delivery Services*[171] and *Spanish International Courier Services*[172]. In each of *Second Operator of GSM Radiotelephony Services in Italy*[173] and *Second Operator of GSM Radiotelephony Services in Spain*[174] the Commission decided that, in requiring a second mobile operator to make a substantial payment for a mobile telephony licence that had not been paid by the incumbent telecommunications companies, there had been state measures capable of extending the monopoly rights of the latter. The judgment of the Court of Justice in *Connect Austria Gesellschaft für Telekommunikations GmbH v Telekom-Control-Kommission*[175], points to the same conclusion. The Commission

[161] Case C-18/88 EU:C:1991:474, para 26. [162] See ch 6, 'Reservation of an ancillary activity', pp 240–241.

[163] Case C-163/96 EU:C:1998:54; the Commission condemned various aspects of the same dock-work legislation in *Provisions of Italian Ports Legislation Relating to Employment* OJ [1997] L 301/17; it noted the conflict of interest created by the legislation at para 30(b) and (c) of its decision, referring to this as 'inherently an abuse'.

[164] Case C-163/96 EU:C:1998:54, paras 28–31. [165] Case C-49/07 EU:C:2008:376.

[166] Case C-67/96 *Albany International BV v SBT* EU:C:1999:430, paras 116–121.

[167] Case C-18/88 EU:C:1991:474.

[168] Case 311/84 EU:C:1985:394; see also Cases C-271/90 etc *Spain v Commission* EU:C:1992:440, para 36.

[169] Case C-475/99 EU:C:2001:577. [170] Ibid, para 43.

[171] OJ [1990] L 10/47, annulled on appeal Cases C-48/90 etc *Netherlands and Koninklijke PTT Nederland v Commission* EU:C:1992:63. [172] OJ [1990] L 233/19, para 10.

[173] OJ [1995] L 280/49, para 17(i). [174] OJ [1997] L 76/19, para 21(i).

[175] Case C-462/99 EU:C:2003:297.

also considered that there was an abuse under this head in *Port of Rødby*[176] where the refusal by a port operator, DSD, to allow Euro-Port A/S access to the port of Rødby eliminated competition in the downstream market for ferry services from Rødby to Puttgarden, in which it was collectively dominant with Deutsche Bahn. Similarly, the Commission objected to Italy[177] and Slovakia[178] respectively extending the statutory monopoly of the incumbent postal operators to the delivery of hybrid mail services, which had previously been open to competition. In *Commission v DEI*[179] Advocate General Wathelet referred to these cases as examples of a theory of 'extension of a dominant position', by which he meant state measures that cause the extension of a dominant position in one market to a related market and have effects similar to those produced by an abuse of that dominant position.

(d) Corbeau

In *Corbeau*[180] the Court of Justice did not discuss Article 106(1) in any detail, but instead considered the extent to which the postal monopoly of the Belgian Post Office could be justified under Article 106(2)[181]. However the interest of the case under Article 106(1) is that, to the extent that the monopoly was not justifiable under Article 106(2), the Court of Justice seems to have considered that it would amount to a measure contrary to Article 106(1). This could be seen as an example of the unlawful extension of a monopoly right to an ancillary activity, as in the cases just discussed. More radically, however, the case seems to suggest that it is possible to strike down monopolies that are too broad: in *RTT*, for example, that company would be able to use its monopoly right to extend its activities into the neighbouring market; in *Corbeau* the Court seems simply to have regarded the monopoly of the Belgian Post Office as too broad in itself. To the extent that this is a correct interpretation of *Corbeau* the judgment is very radical, and seems to go beyond the often-repeated assertion that the grant of an exclusive right is not, in itself, unlawful. Since *Corbeau* a specific Directive has been adopted in the postal sector determining the permitted extent of the 'reserved area' (that is to say the monopoly) in the postal sector[182]. As for the judgment itself, it is possible that this was the 'high tide' of intervention under Article 106(1), and that the Court of Justice has since taken a more cautious approach, as the judgments in *Crespelle*[183] and *Banchero*[184] seem to suggest[185].

(e) Discrimination

In *Merci*[186] the Court of Justice referred to the discriminatory treatment of customers as an abuse for which a Member State could be responsible under Article 106(1). In *GT-Link A/S v De Danske Statsbaner*[187] the Court stated that, where a public undertaking which owns and operates a commercial port waives the port duties on its own ferry services and some of its trading partners whilst charging the full duties to other customers, there could be an infringement of Article 102(2)(c), which refers to the application of dissimilar conditions

[176] OJ [1994] L 55/52. [177] *New Postal Services in Italy* OJ [2001] L 63/59.

[178] *Slovakian postal legislation relating to hybrid mail services*, Commission decision of 7 October 2008, paras 116–148, upheld on appeal Case T-556/08 *Slovenská pošta a.s. v Commission* EU:T:2015:189 and on further appeal to the Court of Justice Case C-293/15 P EU:C:2016:511.

[179] Case C-553/12 P EU:C:2013:807, para 42; the Opinion contains a useful discussion of the cases: ibid, paras 35–65.

[180] Case C-320/91 EU:C:1993:198.

[181] See 'Successful claims based on Article 106(2)', pp 247–248 later in chapter.

[182] See ch 23, 'Legislation', pp 1016–1017.

[183] Case C-323/93 *Centre d'Insémination de la Crespelle v Coopérative de la Mayenne* EU:C:1994:368.

[184] Case C-387/93 EU:C:1995:439.

[185] On these two judgments see *Buendia Sierra* (ch 6 n 62 earlier), paras 5.110–5.128.

[186] Case C-179/90 EU:C:1991:464. [187] Case C-242/95 EU:C:1997:376.

to equivalent transactions placing other trading parties at a competitive disadvantage[188]. Appropriately transparent accounting would be needed to show that this was not the case[189]. In a series of decisions in relation to charges levied for the use both of airports[190] and ports[191] the Commission has expressly condemned price discrimination contrary to Article 102(2)(c), and found the Member State in question to have adopted a measure contrary to Article 106(1). In these cases the airport or port was a natural monopoly[192]; and it may be necessary, under the so-called 'essential facilities doctrine'[193], for the owner of such infrastructure to grant access to third parties on non-discriminatory terms[194].

(f) Excessive pricing

In *OSA*[195] the Court of Justice held that legislation could be contrary to Articles 102 and 106(1) where a monopoly granted to a copyright collecting society enabled it to charge excessive fees for its services.

(ix) **Remedies and direct effect**

Article 106(1) has direct effect when applied in conjunction with another directly applicable provision of EU law, with the consequence that individuals can bring an action in a national court against a Member State which has infringed it[196]. Furthermore, the direct effect of Article 106(1) means that, as in the case of *Höfner*[197], one undertaking may be able to invoke it against another before a national court. An interesting question is whether an individual or a third party can bring an action for damages against a Member State which has acted in breach of Article 106(1). After the *Factortame* litigation in 1996[198], in which the Court of Justice held that in certain circumstances a Member State may have to compensate individuals who suffer loss or damage as a result of infringing EU law, this must at least be arguable.

(B) **Article 106(2)**

Article 106(2) is a somewhat awkwardly drafted provision[199]. It is in three parts. The first part states that undertakings entrusted with the operation of services of general economic interest or having the character of a revenue-producing monopoly shall be subject to the rules in the Treaty, and in particular to the competition rules. The second part states, however, that this subjection to the rules applies only 'in so far as the application

[188] Ibid, para 41; on Article 102(2)(c) generally, see ch 18, 'Price Discrimination', pp 777–782.

[189] Case C-242/95 EU:C:1997:376, para 42.

[190] See *Brussels National Airport (Zaventem)* OJ [1995] L 216/8, paras 12–18; *Portuguese Airports* OJ [1999] L 69/31, paras 24–40; *Spanish Airports* OJ [2000] L 208/36, paras 45–56.

[191] See *Tariffs for Piloting in the Port of Genoa* OJ [1997] L 301/27, paras 11–21.

[192] For discussion of the meaning of natural monopoly see ch 1, 'Economies of scale and scope and natural monopolies', pp 10–11.

[193] See ch 17, 'Refusal to Supply', pp 713–727.

[194] See eg *Port of Rødby* OJ [1994] L 55/52, where the Commission decided that a refusal to allow access to the port was an unlawful extension of the monopoly right enjoyed by the port operator: see 'Reservation of an ancillary activity', pp 240–241 earlier in chapter.

[195] Case C-351/12 *OSA v Léčebné lázně Mariánské Lázně a.s.* EU:C:2014:110, para 89.

[196] See eg Case 155/73 *Sacchi* EU:C:1974:40, para 18; Case C-179/90 *Merci Convenzionale Porto di Genova SpA v Siderurgica Gabrielli SpA* EU:C:1991:464, para 23; Case C-258/98 *Giovanni Carra* EU:C:2000:301, para 11.

[197] See ch 6 n 110 earlier.

[198] Cases C-46/93 etc *Brasserie du Pêcheur SA and Factortame* EU:C:1996:79, paras 31 and 51.

[199] For detailed discussion of Article 106(2) see *Buendia Sierra* (ch 6 n 62 earlier), paras 8.01–8.324; see also Buendia Sierra in *Faull and Nikpay* (ch 6 n 143 earlier), paras 6.136–6.227; Burke *A Critical Account of Article 106(2) TFEU* (Hart, 2018).

of such rules does not obstruct the performance, in law or in fact, of the particular tasks assigned to them'. A useful way to think of Article 106(2) is to ask whether it provides a way of justifying what would otherwise amount to an infringement of the competition rules[200]. Since Article 106(2) results in the non-application of Articles 101 and 102, it must be interpreted strictly[201]. Article 106(2) requires that any restriction of competition should satisfy the principle of proportionality[202]. The burden of proof is on the undertaking seeking to rely on this provision[203]. However to succeed under Article 106(2) it is not necessary to show that an undertaking's survival would be threatened if it were to be subjected to the competition rules[204]; nor to prove that there is no other conceivable measure that could secure that the task in question could be performed[205]. The third part of Article 106(2) adds that the development of trade must not be affected to such an extent as would be contrary to the interests of the EU; the burden is on the Commission to prove this[206].

The effect of Article 106(2) is that some undertakings can successfully claim that Articles 101 and 102 do not apply where their application would prevent them from carrying on the tasks assigned to them by a Member State; however a Member State's interest in doing this must be balanced against the EU's interest in ensuring free competition and an internal market. A good example of circumstances in which Article 106(2) may be applicable is afforded by postal services: all Member States must ensure that users enjoy the right to a universal service involving the permanent provision of a postal service of specified quality at all points in their territory at affordable prices for all users[207]. The postal operator will charge the same price for the delivery of letters to all parts of the country. In effect this means that the inhabitants of urban areas subsidise the postal services of those living in rural ones: delivering a letter from one part of Paris to another is cheaper than from the south-west to the north-east of France. In a sense, therefore, the uniform tariff is discriminatory and could be attacked as such under Article 102. However, in so far as the uniform tariff provides an income to the postal operator that enables it to maintain the universal service, Article 106(2) is applicable and the undertaking is not subject to the competition rules.

A number of points require consideration.

(i) Services of general economic interest

An undertaking can claim to be excluded from the rules in the Treaties only if it has been entrusted with services of general economic interest or if it has the character of a revenue-producing monopoly. It is not enough in itself that the undertaking performs that service; it must have been entrusted with that performance, which will mean that it is under certain obligations[208]. The Court of Justice has ruled that a copyright collecting society to which the state has not assigned any task and which manages private interests on behalf of its members is not an undertaking entrusted with the operation of services of general economic interest[209]. It is not necessary that the undertaking has been entrusted with the performance of the service by a legislative measure; this could have come about, for example, as a result of the terms and conditions of a concession agreement[210]. The fact

[200] See Case C-475/99 *Ambulanz Glöckner v Landkreis Südwestpfalz* EU:C:2001:577.

[201] See Cases C-157/94 etc *Commission v Netherlands* EU:C:1997:499, para 37; see also *REIMS II* OJ [1999] L 275/17, para 92.

[202] See *Buendia Sierra* (ch 6 n 62 earlier), paras 8.115–8.261; also Buendia Sierra in *Faull and Nikpay* (ch 6 n 143 earlier), paras 6.168–6.215.

[203] See Cases C-157/94 etc *Commission v Netherlands* EU:C:1997:499, para 51.

[204] Ibid, para 43.

[205] Ibid, para 58.

[206] See 'Adverse development of trade', p 248 later in chapter.

[207] See Article 3 of Directive 97/67/EC, OJ [1998] L 15/14, as amended by Directive 2008/6/EC, OJ [2008] L 52/3.

[208] See the Opinion of AG Jacobs in Case C-203/96 *Dusseldorp* EU:C:1997:508, para 103.

[209] Case C-351/12 *OSA v Léčebné lázně Mariánské Lázně a.s.* EU:C:2014:110, para 81.

[210] Case 30/87 *Corinne Bodson v Pompes Funèbres* EU:C:1988:225.

that an undertaking is entrusted at its own request does not mean that Article 106(2) is inapplicable as long as its position derives from an act of public authority[211].

The expression 'services of general economic interest' is not defined in the TFEU. The Commission has said that services of general economic interest are 'economic activities which deliver outcomes in the overall public good that would not be supplied (or would be supplied under different conditions in terms of objective quality, safety, affordability, equal treatment or universal access) by the market without public intervention'[212]. Examples of such services are:

- the operation of a universal postal service[213]
- the provision of services, for example in the transport sector, which are not economically viable in their own right[214]
- pension schemes that fulfil a social function[215]
- ambulance services[216]
- the treatment of waste material[217]
- the provision of private medical insurance[218].

The General Court has held that Member States enjoy a wide discretion to define what they regard as services of general economic interest[219]. The protection afforded to services of general economic interest is a sensitive political issue and was addressed at the 1997 Inter-Governmental Conference. Proposals to amend Article 106(2) itself were rejected in favour of the insertion of Article 16 EC by the Treaty of Amsterdam (now Article 14 TFEU). This expressly preserves the application of Article 106 because of:

> the place occupied by services of general economic interest in the shared values of the Union as well as their role in promoting social and territorial cohesion[220].

Article 14 TFEU reinforces the commitment of the EU and Member States to support undertakings required to provide services of general economic interest; however it does

[211] Case T-17/02 *Fred Olsen SA v Commission* EU:T:2005:218, paras 187–190.

[212] Commission Communication *A Quality Framework for Services of General Interest in Europe*, COM(2011) 900 final; see also the AG Opinion in Case C-265/08 *Federutility v Autorità per l'energia elettrica e il gas* EU:C:2009:640, paras 54–55.

[213] Case C-320/91 *Corbeau* EU:C:1993:198, para 15: 'it cannot be disputed that Régie des Postes is entrusted with a service of general economic interest consisting in its obligation to collect, carry and distribute mail on behalf of all users throughout the territory of the Member State concerned, at uniform tariffs …'.

[214] See eg Case 66/86 *Ahmed Saeed* EU:C:1989:140, para 55.

[215] Cases C-67/96 etc *Albany International BV v Stichting Bedrijfspensioenfonds Textielindustrie* EU:C:1999:430, para 105.

[216] Case C-475/99 *Ambulanz Glöckner v Landkreis Südwestpfalz* EU:C:2001:577.

[217] Case C-203/96 *Dusseldorp* EU:C:1998:316, para 67; Case C-209/98 *Entreprenørforeningens Affalds/Miljøsektion v Københavns Kommune* EU:C:2000:279, para 75.

[218] Case T-289/03 *BUPA v Commission* EU:T:2008:29; further examples are contained in the Opinion of AG Colomer in Case C-265/08 *Federutility v Autorità per l'energia elettrica e il gas* EU:C:2009:640, para 53.

[219] See Case T-106/95 *FFSA v Commission* EU:T:1997:23, para 99 and Case T-17/02 *Fred Olsen SA v Commission* EU:T:2005:218, paras 215–228; Case T-295/12 *Germany v Commission* EU:T:2014:675, paras 45–46, pointing out that a Member State's discretion is not unfettered and must not be exercised arbitrarily.

[220] See further the Commission's XXVIIth *Report on Competition Policy* (1997), points 96–98; Ross 'Article 16 EC and Services of General Economic Interest: From Derogation to Obligation' (2000) 25 EL Rev 22; Szyszczak 'Public Services in Competition Markets' in Eeckhout and Tridimas (eds) *Yearbook of European Law* (Oxford University Press, 2001), ch 2; Ross 'Promoting Solidarity: From Public Services to a European Model of Competition?' (2007) 44 CML Rev 1057; Boeger 'Solidarity and EC Competition Law' (2007) EL Rev 319; Szyszczak *The Regulation of the State in Competitive Markets in the EU* (Hart, 2007).

not provide a legal basis for the EU to adopt acts setting out what constitutes a service of general economic interest[221]. The Commission has issued numerous publications clarifying the importance of services of general interest, services of general economic interest and social services of general interest[222]. In December 2009 the Lisbon Treaty entered into force: this reformulated Article 16 EC as Article 14 TFEU and annexed Protocol 26 on services of general interest to the Treaties[223]. Protocol 26 emphasises 'the essential role and the wide discretion of national, regional and local authorities' in the provision of services of general economic interest[224] and confirms that EU law does not affect the competence of Member States to control the provision of non-economic services of general interest.

(ii) Undertakings having the character of a revenue-producing monopoly

This expression is not defined in the TFEU. It would apply to a monopoly created in order to raise revenue for the state; usually this monopoly would be conferred upon a public undertaking which would contribute its profits to the state, but it could also be conferred upon a private undertaking in exchange for revenue. Undertakings that have the character of a revenue-earning monopoly may also be subject to Article 37, and the Court of Justice has established that Article 106(2) may be invoked as a defence in an action under that provision[225].

(iii) Scope of the exception: obstruction of the performance of the tasks assigned

In a number of cases undertakings have argued that they were shielded from the competition rules by virtue of Article 106(2); in *BRT v SABAM*[226] the Court of Justice ruled that, as Article 106(2) involves a derogation from the application of the competition rules, it should be construed narrowly, and the Commission and the EU Courts have consistently done so, thereby maximising the application of Articles 101 and 102. In particular they have been sceptical of the assertion that anti-competitive behaviour is *necessary* to enable undertakings to carry out the tasks assigned to them.

(a) Unsuccessful claims based on Article 106(2)

Claims based on Article 106(2) have often been rejected[227]. For example, in *ANSEAU-NAVEWA*[228] the Commission held that an agreement requiring purchasers in Belgium to

[221] Case T-44/14 *Constantini v Commission* EU:T:2016:223, paras 23–27.

[222] Available at www.ec.europa.eu/services_general_interest/index_en.htm; see *Guide to the application of the European Union rules on state aid, public procurement and the internal market to services of general economic interest, and in particular to social services of general interest*, SWD(2013) 53 final.

[223] Protocols to the Treaties form an integral part thereof: Article 51 TEU.

[224] This point is reiterated by Article 36 of the Charter of Fundamental Rights of the European Union, OJ 2012 C 326/391, which, in accordance with Article 6(1) TEU, has the same legal value as the other Treaties.

[225] See 'Article 37 TFEU—state monopolies of a commercial character', pp 251–252 later in chapter.

[226] Case 127/73 EU:C:1974:25.

[227] As well as the cases mentioned in the text see Case 172/80 *Züchner v Bayerische Vereinsbank* EU:C:1981:178 and *Uniform Eurocheques* OJ [1985] L 35/43, paras 29 and 30 (both cases on banking); *Decca Navigator System* OJ [1989] L 43/27, para 128; *Magill TV Guide/ITP, BBC and RTE* OJ [1989] L 78/43, para 25; *Dutch Express Delivery Services* OJ [1990] L 10/47, paras 16–18; *Spanish International Courier Services* OJ [1990] L 233/19, paras 13–14; Case C-179/90 *Merci Convenzionale Porto di Genova v Siderurgica Gabrielli* EU:C:1991:464, paras 25–28; Case C-18/88 *RTT v GB-Inno-BM* EU:C:1991:474, paras 14–28; *IJsselcentrale* OJ [1991] L 28/32, paras 39–42; Case C-242/95 *GT-Link A/S v De Danske Statsbaner* EU:C:1997:376, paras 47–55; Case C-393/92 *Almelo* EU:C:1994:171, paras 46–51; when this case returned to the Dutch court the claim based on Article 106(2) was unsuccessful: see Hancher (1997) 34 CML Rev 1509; Case T-271/03 *Deutsche Telekom v Commission* EU:T:2008:101, para 314; *CISAC*, Commission decision of 16 July 2008, paras 256–259; the finding of a concerted practice in this case was annulled in a number of appeals, eg Case T-411/08 *Artisjus Magyar Szerzõi Jogvédõ Iroda Egyesület v Commission* EU:T:2013:172.

[228] OJ [1982] L 167/39 as amended at L 325/20; upheld on appeal Cases 96/82 etc *NV IAZ International Belgium v Commission* EU:C:1983:310.

acquire 'conformity labels' before washing machines and dishwashers could be plumbed in infringed Article 101(1) because it had the effect of discriminating against imports from other Member States. The association of Belgian water authorities involved in running the scheme claimed the benefit of Article 106(2). The Commission accepted that they qualified as a body to whom services of a general economic interest had been entrusted, but went on to hold that the scheme in question was much more restrictive than necessary, saying that:

> a possible limitation of the application of the rules on competition can only be envisaged in the event that the undertaking concerned has no other technically and economically feasible means of performing its particular task[229].

Similarly in *British Telecommunications*[230] the Commission rejected BT's defence based on Article 106(2); when the Italian Government challenged this decision before the Court of Justice the Commission's decision was upheld[231]. The Court held that Italy had failed to show that the Commission's censure of BT, for prohibiting private message-forwarding agencies from using its network to forward messages from other Member States, put the performance of its tasks in jeopardy. Article 106(2) also failed in *Air Inter v Commission*[232], where the General Court rejected TAT's appeal against a Commission decision requiring the termination of exclusive rights on French air routes. The General Court accepted that the airline was entrusted with a public task of maintaining unprofitable domestic air routes. However it held that subjection to the competition rules would merely hinder or make more difficult the performance of this task; for Article 106(2) to apply it was necessary to show that this would obstruct it, in fact or in law[233]. The General Court reached a similar conclusion in respect of a recycling scheme in *Duales System Deutschland v Commission*[234].

A particularly important judgment on Article 106(2) is *Corbeau*[235]. As we have seen, the case concerned the operation of an express delivery service in Liège, in contravention of the Belgian Post Office's postal monopoly[236]. The core of the Court of Justice's judgment dealt with the extent to which the postal monopoly could be justified under Article 106(2)[237]. The Court acknowledged that the Post Office was entrusted with a service of general economic interest[238], and that it might be necessary for it to benefit from a restriction of competition in order to be able to offset less profitable activities against profitable ones[239]: put more colloquially, it may be legitimate to prevent an entrant into the market from 'cream-skimming' or 'cherry-picking', leaving the incumbent postal operator to carry out unprofitable services pursuant to its universal service obligation. However the Court continued that:

> the exclusion of competition is not justified as regards specific services dissociable from the service of general interest which meet special needs of economic operators and which call for certain additional services not offered by the traditional postal service, such as collection from the senders' address, greater speed or reliability of distribution or the possibility of changing the destination in the course of transit, in so far as such services, by their nature and the conditions in which they are offered, such as the geographical area in which they are provided, do not compromise the economic equilibrium of the service of general economic interest performed by the holder of the exclusive right[240].

229 OJ [1982] L 167/39, para 66. 230 OJ [1982] L 360/36.
231 Case 41/83 *Italy v Commission* EU:C:1985:120. 232 Case T-260/94 EU:T:1997:89.
233 Ibid, paras 134–141. 234 Case T-151/01 EU:T:2007:154, paras 207–210.
235 Case C-320/91 EU:C:1993:198. 236 See 'The *Corbeau* judgment', p 236 earlier in chapter.
237 Case C-320/91 EU:C:1993:198, paras 13–21. 238 Ibid, para 15. 239 Ibid, paras 17–18.
240 Ibid, para 19.

Since this was a reference under Article 267 TFEU, the Court then stated that it would be for the national court to make a decision under Article 106(2) on the particular facts of the case[241], but it is clear that it was giving a strong indication that it should not be possible to maintain a monopoly over express courier services in order to sustain the basic service of the daily delivery of letters[242].

(b) Successful claims based on Article 106(2)

It would be wrong to suppose from the foregoing that claims based on Article 106(2) are always unsuccessful. This point can be demonstrated by reference to a number of judgments of the Court of Justice. In *Corsica Ferries France SA v Gruppo Antichi Ormeggiatori del Porto di Genova*[243] the Court was concerned with Italian legislation requiring ships from other Member States using the ports of Genoa and La Spezia in Italy to use the services of local mooring companies. It considered that mooring operations were of general economic interest: mooring groups are obliged to provide at any time and to any user a universal mooring service, for reasons of safety in port waters[244]. As a result it was not incompatible with Article 106(1) in conjunction with Article 102 to include in the price of the service a component designed to cover the cost of maintaining the universal mooring service, and Article 106(2) was applicable[245].

In *Albany*[246] the Court of Justice held that the exclusive right of a pension fund to manage supplementary pensions in a particular sector could be justified under Article 106(2), since otherwise 'young employees in good health engaged in non-dangerous activities' would leave the scheme, leaving behind members who would be bad insurance risks, thereby undermining the success of the system[247]. In *Deutsche Post AG v Gesellschaft für Zahlungssysteme mbH and Citicorp Kartenservice GmbH*[248] the Court considered that Article 106(2) justified the grant by a Member State to its postal operators of a statutory right to charge internal postage on items of so-called 'remail'[249]. Environmental considerations led to the successful application of Article 106(2) in *Entreprenørforeningens Affalds/Miljøsektion v Københavns Kommune*[250]. In *Ambulanz Glöckner v Landkreis Südwestpfalz*[251] the Court considered that a national law which protected the providers of emergency ambulance services against competition from independent operators, even on a related non-emergency transport market, could be justified under Article 106(2) if this was necessary for them to perform their tasks in economically acceptable conditions[252]. In *AG2R Prévoyance v Beaudout Père et Fils SARL*[253] the Court considered that Article 106(2) could apply to an exclusive right granted to a provident society to manage a scheme for the supplementary reimbursement of healthcare costs[254].

Although Article 106(2) is drafted in terms of the position of undertakings, it has become clear that Member States themselves can rely on it. For example in *Dusseldorp*[255] the Court of Justice held that the Netherlands could rely on Article 106(2) in relation to its 'Long Term Plan' relating to waste disposal[256]. The Court of Justice has also held that

[241] Ibid, para 20.

[242] See to similar effect Case C-220/06 *Asociación Profesional de Empresas de Reparto y Manipulado de Correspondencia v Administración del Estado* EU:C:2007:815, paras 79–83, a case concerned with the Postal Services Directive; similarly Case C-162/06 *International Mail Spain* EU:C:2007:681, para 38.

[243] Case C-266/96 EU:C:1998:306. [244] Ibid, para 45. [245] Ibid, paras 46–47.

[246] Cases C-67/96 etc *Albany International BV v SBT* EU:C:1999:430. [247] Ibid, paras 98–111.

[248] Cases C-147/97 etc EU:C:2000:74. [249] Ibid, paras 41–54.

[250] Case C-209/98 EU:C:2000:279, paras 74–83. [251] Case C-475/99 EU:C:2001:577.

[252] Ibid, paras 51–65. [253] Case C-437/09 EU:C:2011:112. [254] Ibid, paras 66–81.

[255] Case C-203/96 EU:C:1998:316, para 67.

[256] See also Cases C-157/94 etc *Commission v Netherlands* EU:C:1997:499, paras 51–64.

Article 106(2) may be invoked by a Member State in defence of state aid that might otherwise be incompatible with the internal market[257].

(iv) Adverse development of trade

It is not possible to rely on Article 106(2) if the development of trade would be affected to such an extent as would be contrary to the interest of the EU. This must mean something more than an effect on inter-state trade in the sense of Articles 101 and 102, since without such an effect the EU competition rules would not be applicable anyway. In *Commission v Netherlands* the Court of Justice held that the Commission must prove whether the exclusive right has affected and continued to affect the development of intra-EU trade 'to an extent which is contrary to the interests of the [EU]'[258]. An application will be dismissed where it fails to do so[259]. If the matter were to arise in domestic litigation, not involving the Commission, the claimant would need to demonstrate an adverse effect on the development of trade.

(v) Direct effect

In *Belgische Radio en Televisie (BRT) v SABAM*[260] the Court of Justice held that Articles 101(1) and 102 are directly applicable to the undertakings described in Article 106(2) so that an action may be brought against them in national courts, whether the Commission has acted under Article 106(3) or not. A national court should determine whether the undertaking falls within Article 106(2); if it does not, the court may proceed to apply the competition rules[261]. In cases of doubt the national court can stay the action whilst the opinion of the Commission is sought[262]. It remains uncertain whether the final sentence of Article 106(2), which requires that trade must not be affected contrary to the interests of the EU, has direct effect. It is arguable that only the Commission should carry out the task of assessing the interests of the EU.

(C) Article 106(3)

Article 106(3) provides that the Commission shall ensure the application of Article 106(1) and (2) and that, where necessary, it shall address appropriate decisions or directives to Member States[263]. The Commission began to employ it in the 1980s, most notably in the telecommunications sector[264], and it is an important part of its armoury. The advantage of Article 106(3) from the Commission's perspective is that it can adopt a decision or directive itself; in doing so, it is not subject to any particular procedural framework, although it must of course comply with the general principles of EU law, and must provide adequate reasons for its action, in accordance with Article 296 TFEU[265]. The Commission liaises with other interested parties, including the Parliament, when exercising its powers under

[257] See eg Case T-289/03 *BUPA v Commission* EU:T:2008:29.

[258] Case C-157/94 EU:C:1997:499, paras 65–68; AG Cosmas considered that there should be evidence that the measure has in fact had a substantial effect on intra-EU trade: Cases C-157/94 EU:C:1996:449, para 126; see similarly the Opinion of AG Léger in Case C-309/99 *Wouters* EU:C:2001:390, para 166.

[259] See Case C-159/94 *Commission v France* EU:C:1997:501, paras 109–116.

[260] Case 127/73 EU:C:1974:25.

[261] Case 155/73 *Italy v Sacchi* EU:C:1974:40.

[262] Case C-260/89 *ERT v Dimotiki* EU:C:1991:254, para 34 and Case C-393/92 *Almelo* EU:C:1994:171, para 50.

[263] On Article 106(3) generally, see *Buendia Sierra* (ch 6 n 62 earlier), paras 10.01–10.184 and Buendia Sierra in *Faull and Nikpay* (ch 6 n 143 earlier) paras 6.228–6.271.

[264] See 'Directives', pp 250–251 later in chapter.

[265] The Commission's decision in *Dutch Express Delivery Services* was quashed for various procedural improprieties: see ch 6 n 270 later.

Article 106(3), and particularly when adopting a directive[266]. If the Commission did not have its Article 106(3) powers, it would be able to proceed against measures that offend Article 106(1) only by taking proceedings before the Court of Justice under Article 258 TFEU or by persuading the Council to adopt the measures it favours.

Article 106(3) enables the Commission to adopt both decisions and directives: a decision can be adopted establishing that a Member State is in breach of an EU obligation; but a directive can go further and legislate for the elimination of existing violations of the Treaty and the prevention of future ones.

(i) Decisions

In *Greek Public Property Insurance*[267] the Commission required Greece, by decision under Article 106(3), to alter its domestic legislation requiring that all public property in Greece be insured by Greek public-sector insurance companies and that staff of Greek state-owned banks recommend to their customers insurance with companies affiliated to the public banking sector and controlled by it. When Greece failed to take the necessary measures to do this within the prescribed period the Commission brought an action under Article 258 TFEU for failure to fulfil its Treaty obligations. The Court of Justice held[268] that a decision by the Commission under Article 106(3) is 'binding in its entirety' on the person to whom it is addressed so that the addressee must comply with it until it obtains from the Court a suspension of its operation or a declaration that it is void. In *Spanish Transport Fares*[269] the Commission addressed a decision to Spain condemning its discriminatory fares for passengers from mainland Spain to the Balearic and Canary Islands.

The Commission also adopted decisions under Article 106(3) in:

- *Dutch Express Delivery Services*[270]
- *Spanish International Courier Services*[271]
- *Port of Rødby*[272]
- *Second Operator of GSM Radiotelephony Services in Italy*[273]
- *Second Operator of GSM Radiotelephony Services in Spain*[274]
- *Brussels National Airport (Zaventem)*[275]
- *Exclusive Right to Broadcast Television Advertising in Flanders*[276]
- *Italian Ports Legislation Relating to Employment*[277]
- *Tariffs for Piloting in the Port of Genoa*[278]
- *Portuguese Airports*[279]
- *Spanish Airports*[280]
- *New Postal Services in Italy*[281]

[266] See XXVth *Report on Competition Policy* (1995), point 100.
[267] OJ [1985] L 152/25. [268] Case 226/87 *Commission v Greece* EU:C:1988:354.
[269] OJ [1987] L 194/28.
[270] OJ [1990] L 10/47, annulled on appeal Cases C-48/90 etc *Netherlands and Koninklijke PTT Nederland v Commission* EU:C:1992:63 as the Commission had failed to give the Dutch Government a fair hearing.
[271] OJ [1990] L 233/19. [272] OJ [1994] L 55/52.
[273] OJ [1995] L 280/49. [274] OJ [1997] L 76/19.
[275] OJ [1995] L 216/8.
[276] OJ [1997] L 244/18, upheld on appeal Case T-266/97 *Vlaamse Televisie Maatschappij NV v Commission* EU:T:1999:144.
[277] OJ [1997] L 301/17. [278] OJ [1997] L 301/27.
[279] OJ [1999] L 69/31, upheld on appeal Case C-163/99 *Portugal v Commission* EU:C:2001:189.
[280] OJ [2000] L 208/36. [281] OJ [2001] L 63/59.

- *La Poste*[282]
- *German postal legislation*[283]
- *French savings accounts*[284]
- *Greek lignite*[285]
- *Slovakian postal legislation*[286].

(ii) Directives

The competence of the Commission to adopt directives under Article 106(3) has been considered by the Court of Justice on three occasions. The Transparency Directive[287] was challenged in *France v Commission*[288] on the basis that, since it concerned the surveillance of state aids, it should have been adopted under Article 109 rather than Article 106(3). The Court ruled that the fact that the Commission could have proceeded under Article 109 did not mean that it could not also do so under Article 106(3). Towards the end of the 1980s the Commission's concern about the fragmented nature of the telecommunications market in the EU and the consequent lack of competition led to the adoption of two directives, the first on the telecommunications terminal equipment market[289] and the second on telecommunications themselves[290]. Opposition from Member States to these Directives was considerable and both were challenged before the Court of Justice. In each case the Court upheld the competence of the Commission to have proceeded under Article 106(3)[291]. In *France v Commission*[292] three Member States complained that the Commission should have proceeded under Article 258 rather than Article 106(3). The Court held that there had been no misuse of powers: the Commission may use the powers conferred upon it by Article 106(3) to specify in general terms the obligations that arise under Article 106(1); however the Commission may not use a directive under Article 106(3) to rule upon specific infringements of the TFEU, for which the Article 258 procedure must be used[293]. The Court also held that the fact that the Council had competence to adopt legislation relating to telecommunications did not mean that the Commission had no competence[294]. The Court annulled Articles 2, 7 and 9 of the Directive on terminal equipment since the Commission had failed to explain which rights were 'special' and why they were contrary to EU law[295]. It is not possible to use Article 106(3) for the purpose

[282] OJ [2002] L 120/19. [283] Commission decision of 20 October 2004.

[284] Commission decision of 10 May 2007.

[285] Commission decision of 5 March 2008, annulled on appeal to the General Court Case T-169/08 *DEI v Commission* EU:T:2012:448; however the Court of Justice set aside the General Court's judgment in Case C-553/12 P EU:C:2014:2083 and referred the case back to it for reconsideration: in Case T-169/08 RENV *DEI v Commission* EU:T:2016:733 the General Court upheld the Commission's original decision.

[286] Commission decision of 7 October 2008, upheld on appeal Case T-556/08 *Slovenská pošta a.s. v Commission* EU:T:2015:189 and on further appeal to the Court of Justice Case C-293/15 P EU:C:2016:511.

[287] Commission Directive 80/723/EEC, OJ [1980] L 195/35, repealed and replaced by Commission Directive 2006/111/EC, OJ [2006] L 318/17.

[288] Cases 188/80 etc EU:C:1982:257; for a later challenge related to this Directive see Case C-325/91 *France v Commission* EU:C:1993:245.

[289] Commission Directive 88/301/EEC, OJ [1988] L 131/73; this Directive was replaced by Commission Directive 2008/63/EC, OJ [2008] L 162/20.

[290] Commission Directive 90/388/EEC, OJ [1990] L 192/10; this Directive was replaced by Commission Directive 2002/77/EC, OJ [2002] L 249/21.

[291] See Case C-202/88 *France v Commission* EU:C:1991:120 (terminal equipment); Cases C-271/90 etc *Spain, Belgium and Italy v Commission* EU:C:1992:440 (telecommunications).

[292] See ch 6 n 288 earlier. [293] Case C-202/88 EU:C:1991:120, paras 16–18.

[294] Ibid, paras 19–27; see similarly Cases 188/80 etc *France v Commission* EU:C:1982:257, para 14.

[295] Case C-202/88 EU:C:1991:120, paras 45–47 and 53–58.

of achieving harmonisation, the legislative base for which is provided by Articles 114 and 115 TFEU: this explains why in the telecommunications sector there are Article 106(3) Directives, dealing with the conditions of competition, and a raft of separate measures under Articles 114 and 115 on harmonisation[296].

(iii) Judicial review of the Commission's powers under Article 106(3)

The Commission enjoys a wide discretion under Articles 106(1) and 106(3)[297]. The Court will not annul a decision or directive unless it is reasonably likely that an error on the part of the Commission may have affected it in a material respect. Third parties cannot, except in an exceptional situation, bring an action against a Commission decision not to use its powers under Article 106(3)[298].

4. Article 37 TFEU—State Monopolies of a Commercial Character

Article 37(1) TFEU provides that[299]:

> Member States shall adjust any State monopolies of a commercial character so as to ensure that no discrimination regarding the conditions under which goods are procured and marketed exists between nationals of Member States[300].

Article 37(1) goes on to state that it applies to any body through which a Member State supervises, determines or appreciably influences imports or exports between Member States, and also that it applies to monopolies delegated by the state to others. Article 37(2) obliges Member States not to introduce any new measure contrary to the principles in Article 37(1) or which restricts the scope of the Treaty Articles dealing with the prohibition of customs duties and quantitative restrictions between Member States. However Article 37 does not require the abolition of existing monopolies; only that they should be adjusted to prevent discrimination.

Article 37 is designed to prevent state monopolies of a commercial character discriminating against nationals of other Member States. One way of ensuring that Member States do not discriminate in this way is to alter their public procurement policies, in which area the Council has been active[301]. The Commission continues to monitor the conduct of Member States under Article 37. In *Commission v Greece*[302] the Court of Justice held that Greece was obliged to terminate exclusive rights to import and sell petroleum derivatives since those rights discriminated against exporters of such products in other Member

[296] See ch 23, 'Legislation', pp 1011–1013.

[297] Case C-107/95 P *Bundesverband der Bilanzbuchhalter v Commission* EU:C:1997:71, para 27; see also Case T-266/97 *Vlaamse Televisie Maatschappij NV v Commission* EU:T:1999:144, para 75 and Case T-52/00 *Coe Clerici Logistics SpA v Commission* EU:T:2003:168, paras 106–189.

[298] Case C-107/95 P *Bundesverband der Bilanzbuchhalter v Commission* EU:C:1997:71, para 28; see also Case C-141/02 P *Commission v T-Mobile Austria GmbH, formerly max.mobil Telecommunications service GmbH* EU:C:2005:98, paras 69–73 where the Court of Justice annulled a judgment of the General Court which had suggested greater rights for third parties to challenge the Commission's decision not to act; for comment see Hocepied 'The *Max.mobil* Judgment: the Court of Justice clarifies the role of complainants in Article 86 procedures' (2005) 2 Competition Policy Newsletter 53.

[299] See generally Buendia Sierra *Exclusive Rights and State Monopolies under EC Law* (Oxford University Press, 1999), paras 3.01–3.201; also Buendia Sierra in *Faull and Nikpay* (ch 6 n 143 earlier), paras 6.110–6.125.

[300] Note that Article 37 TFEU is not identical to the original Article 37 EEC, which contained transitional rules that had become redundant.

[301] See ch 2 n 8 earlier. [302] Case C-347/88 EU:C:1990:470.

States and since they upset the normal conditions of competition between Member States. Where the Commission suspects infringement of Article 37 it may take proceedings against the Member State under Article 258 or it may use the powers available to it under Article 106(3)[303]. Where the Commission brings Article 258 proceedings it must prove that a Member State has failed to fulfil its obligations and it must place before the Court of Justice the information needed to enable it to decide whether this is the case[304]. An injured undertaking could bring an action in a national court, as Article 37 is directly effective[305].

In *Commission v Netherlands* the Court of Justice found that import and export monopolies for gas and electricity in the Netherlands, Italy and France amounted to an infringement of Article 37(1)[306]. However the Court considered that Article 106(2) could be invoked by Member States in proceedings brought under Article 37 to justify such monopolies. Justification was possible, provided that the maintenance of monopoly rights was necessary to enable the undertaking in question to perform the tasks of general economic interest entrusted to it under economically acceptable conditions; it was not necessary to demonstrate that the survival of the undertaking itself would be threatened in the absence of such a monopoly. On the facts the Commission failed to satisfy the Court that the monopolies could not be justified under Article 106(2). In *Hanner*[307] the Court of Justice held that Article 37(1) precluded a sales regime that conferred a legal monopoly at the retail level of trade in medicinal preparations on Apoteket, an entity in which the Swedish state had a majority shareholding and the management of which was predominantly in the hands of politicians and civil servants. The Court's concern was that Apoteket's procurement arrangements were liable to discriminate against medicinal preparations from outside Sweden[308]. In an Article 267 reference from Finland, *Visnapuu*,[309] the Court of Justice considered the compatibility of a legal monopoly on the retail sale of alcoholic beverages with Article 37 and held that:

> Article 37 TFEU requires that the organisation and operation of the monopoly be arranged so as to exclude any discrimination between nationals of Member States as regards the conditions under which goods are procured and marketed, so that trade in goods from other Member States is not put at a disadvantage, in law or in fact, in relation to that in domestic goods and that competition between the economies of the Member States is not distorted[310].

5. Articles 107 to 109 TFEU—State Aids

The Treaty provides the Commission with power under Articles 107 to 109 TFEU to deal with state aids that could distort competition in the internal market. A considerable amount of DG COMP's energies go into this issue, but lack of space prevents a detailed discussion of the topic here[311]. DG COMP's website provides information about state aid

[303] See 'Article 106(3)', pp 248–251 earlier in chapter.

[304] See eg Case C-157/94 *Commission v Netherlands* EU:C:1997:499, para 59.

[305] Case 91/78 *Hansen v Hauptzollamt Flensberg* EU:C:1979:65.

[306] Case C-157/94 EU:C:1997:499: the nature of the monopolies varied from state to state.

[307] Case C-438/02 EU:C:2005:332.

[308] Ibid, paras 32–49.

[309] Case C-198/14 EU:C:2015:751, paras 86–96.

[310] Ibid, para 95.

[311] For further reading on state aids see Hancher, Ottervanger and Slot *EU State Aids* (Sweet & Maxwell, 5th ed, 2016); Rose and Bailey (eds) *Bellamy and Child: European Union Law of Competition* (Oxford University Press, 7th ed, 2013), ch 17; Bacon *European Union Law of State Aid* (Oxford University Press, 3rd ed, 2017); Faull and Nikpay (eds) *The EU Law of Competition* (Oxford University Press, 3rd ed, 2014), ch 17; Quigley *European State Aid and Policy* (Hart, 3rd ed, 2015); the Commission's Annual *Reports on Competition Policy* contain a detailed account of its activities under the state aids provisions.

policy, including details of current developments, a register of cases and reports on state aid matters[312].

Article 107(1) provides that:

> Save as otherwise provided in the Treaties, any aid granted by a Member State or through State resources in any form whatsoever which distorts or threatens to distort competition by favouring certain undertakings or the production of certain goods shall, in so far as it affects trade between Member States, be incompatible with the internal market.

Article 107(2) provides that aids having a social character granted to individual consumers, aids to make good the damage caused by national disasters or exceptional occurrences and aids granted to the economy of certain areas of Germany affected by the division of that country after the Second World War[313] shall be compatible with the internal market. Article 107(3) gives the Commission discretion to permit other aids, for example to promote the economic development of areas where the standard of living is abnormally low or where there is serious unemployment, or to promote the execution of an important project of common European interest or to remedy a serious disturbance in the economy of a Member State.

The Commission has published detailed guidance on the application of Article 107 to public funding granted to companies that provide services of general economic interest, including on when 'public service compensation' is compatible with Article 106(2) and exempt from notification to the Commission under Article 108(3)[314].

Article 108 deals with procedure. The Commission may, by Article 108(2)(i), adopt a decision that a state aid which is incompatible with the internal market shall be abolished or altered. If the Member State does not comply with this decision within the stated time, the Commission or another Member State may take the matter to the Court of Justice under Article 108(2)(ii) without having to resort to the procedure under Articles 258 and 259 TFEU[315]. The Commission is required to recover illegal aid[316]. Article 108(3) requires plans to grant or alter aids to be notified to the Commission in sufficient time to enable it to submit its comments. The procedural powers of the Commission in relation to state aids are set out in Council Regulation 2015/1589[317] and Commission Regulation 794/2004[318]. The aid may not be implemented until the Commission has reached a decision. Article 108(3) is directly effective[319] and an individual may seek relief in a domestic court where aid is granted without notification under Article 108(3) or put into effect before the Commission's decision[320].

It can be difficult to tell, in the absence of relevant information, whether competition is being distorted where a Member State controls part of the economy directly or grants financial aids to certain firms. To overcome this problem the Commission issued a Directive in 1980 to increase the transparency of the relationship between Member States and public undertakings[321], which was unsuccessfully challenged in *France v Commission*[322]; the Directive has been amended a number of times and

[312] See eg www.ec.europa.eu/competition/state_aid/newsletter/index.html.

[313] Article 107(2) provides that the Council, acting on a proposal from the Commission, may adopt a decision repealing this point after 1 December 2014.

[314] See www.ec.europa.eu/competition/state_aid/legislation/sgei.html.

[315] It cannot proceed under Article 108(2)(ii) in respect of a later state aid which was not within the scope of an earlier decision: Case C-294/90 *British Aerospace plc v Commission* EU:C:1992:55.

[316] Regulation 2015/1589, OJ [2015] L248/9, Article 16; recovery is required unless it would be contrary to a general principle of EU law.

[317] OJ [2015] L 248/9.

[318] OJ [2004] L 140/1 (as amended).

[319] Case 120/73 *Lorenz v Germany* EU:C:1973:152.

[320] See eg *R v A-G, ex p ICI* [1987] 1 CMLR 72, CA.

[321] OJ [1980] L 195/35.

[322] See ch 6 n 71 earlier.

was codified in 2006[323]. The Commission uses the data that it receives through this Directive to monitor the compatibility of state aids with Article 107.

Article 109 TFEU authorises the Council to adopt regulations on state aid, in particular exempting aid from notification. The Council has adopted Regulation 2015/1588[324] which confers powers on the Commission to adopt 'group exemptions' for certain categories of horizontal state aid, and to adopt a regulation on *de minimis* aids[325].

The State Aid Action Plan in 2005 and the State Aid Modernisation in 2012 have led to substantial changes[326]: a Best Practices Code; the Simplified Procedure Notice; a new framework for analysing various aid measures; a General Block Exemption Regulation[327] and the various *Notices* in support of this modernisation process[328]. These developments have led to changes both in the substantive analysis of state aid, with an increased emphasis on economics, and in legal procedure.

323 Commission Directive 2006/111/EC, OJ [2006] L 318/17.

324 Council Regulation 2015/1588, OJ [2015] L 248/1.

325 The block exemptions are available at www.ec.europa.eu/competition/state_aid/legislation/legislation.html.

326 See www.ec.europa.eu/competition/state_aid/modernisation/index_en.html.

327 Commission Regulation 651/2014, OJ [2014] L 187/1.

328 The block exemptions are available at www.ec.europa.eu/competition/state_aid/legislation/legislation.html.

7

Articles 101 and 102: public enforcement by the European Commission and national competition authorities under Regulation 1/2003

Infringement of Articles 101 and 102 has serious consequences for guilty undertakings. Such is the importance of competition law that undertakings are well advised to put in place effective compliance programmes to ensure that the competition rules are not infringed and that employees understand what types of behaviour must be avoided; the Commission and the EU Courts are unimpressed by arguments sometimes put forward by undertakings that they intended to comply with competition law, but that their employees disobeyed instructions and wrongly entered into price-fixing or similar agreements. In *SIA 'VM Remonts' v Konkurences padome*[1] the Court of Justice said that any anti-competitive conduct on the part of an employee is attributable to the undertaking to which he or she belongs and that the undertaking is, as a matter of principle, liable for that conduct[2].

In 2012 the European Commission published *Compliance Matters: What companies can do better to respect EU competition rules*[3] as a guide to companies to develop a proactive compliance strategy; in this document the Commission draws attention to the case law of the EU Courts which establishes that the existence of a compliance programme is not a mitigating factor when it comes to the determination of fines in cartel cases[4]. Some competition authorities take a more generous approach: for example the Competition and Markets Authority ('the CMA') in the UK has sometimes allowed a reduction of a fine in return for a firm agreeing to implement a competition law compliance programme[5].

[1] Case C-542/14 EU:C:2016:578. [2] Ibid, para 24. [3] Available at www.ec.europa.eu.

[4] See Case T-138/07 *Schindler Holding Ltd v Commission* EU:T:2011:362, para 282, upheld on appeal Case C-501/11 P EU:C:2013:522, para 144.

[5] See ch 10, 'The CMA's six-step approach', pp 421–423; the CAT endorsed this approach in Case 1140/1/1/09 *Eden Brown Ltd v OFT* [2011] CAT 8, para 127; see also the International Chamber of Commerce *Antitrust Compliance Toolkit*, launched in April 2013, available at www.iccwbo.org; Wils 'Antitrust Compliance Programmes & Optimal Antitrust Enforcement' (2013) 1 Journal of Antitrust Enforcement 52; Riley and Sokol 'Rethinking Compliance' (2015) 3 Journal of Antitrust Enforcement 31.

The powers of the Commission to enforce Articles 101 and 102 were originally contained in Regulation 17 of 1962[6]. Major changes in the enforcement of Articles 101 and 102 were effected by Regulation 1/2003[7], which became applicable on 1 May 2004. This chapter will explain the main features of the public enforcement system: there are numerous practitioners' books that provide a more detailed analysis of the position[8]. The chapter will begin with a brief overview of Regulation 1/2003. Section 2 provides a detailed examination of the Commission's enforcement powers; it also describes the procedure introduced by the Commission in 2008 whereby it sometimes settles cartel cases. Section 3 discusses the operation of Regulation 1/2003 in practice, with particular reference to the European Competition Network ('the ECN') that brings together the Commission and the national competition authorities of the Member States ('the NCAs'). The final section of the chapter will provide a brief account of judicial review of the Commission's decisions. Articles 101 and 102 are directly applicable and may be invoked in proceedings in the domestic courts of the Member States: the private enforcement of the competition rules will be considered in chapter 8.

In understanding the extent of—or rather the limits to—the Commission's powers, it is important to have reference to the general principles of EU law some of which, such as respect for the rights of the defence and the principles of proportionality, equal treatment, the protection of legitimate interests, legal certainty and non-retroactivity, have obvious significance for the enforcement of the competition rules[9]. Two further important issues are the relationship between the Commission's procedures and the standards required by the European Convention on Human Rights ('ECHR')[10] and by the Charter of Fundamental Rights of the European Union ('the Charter')[11]; recital 37 of Regulation 1/2003 states that it should be interpreted in accordance with the rights and principles recognised in the Charter, and Article 6(1) TEU provides that the Charter has the same force as the other Treaties[12]. The European Commission publishes an annual report on the application of the Charter by the EU institutions[13], including by

[6] JO 204/62, OJ (Special Edition 1959–62), p 57.

[7] OJ [2003] L 1/1, as amended by Regulation 411/2004, OJ [2004] L 68/1 and Regulation 1419/2006, OJ [2006] L 269/1.

[8] See in particular Kerse and Khan *EU Antitrust Procedure* (Sweet & Maxwell, 6th ed, 2012); Ortiz Blanco *EU Competition Procedure* (Oxford University Press, 3rd ed, 2013); Rose and Bailey (eds) *Bellamy and Child: European Union Law of Competition* (Oxford University Press, 7th ed, 2013), ch 13; Faull and Nikpay (eds) *The EU Law of Competition* (Oxford University Press, 3rd ed, 2014), ch 2; Castillo de la Torre and Gippini Fournier *Evidence, Proof and Judicial Review in EU Competition Law* (Edward Elgar, 2017); for a series of seminal essays on all aspects of public enforcement see Wils *The Optimal Enforcement of EC Antitrust Law* (Kluwer Law International, 2002); Wils *Principles of European Antitrust Enforcement* (Hart, 2005); Wils *Efficiency and Justice in European Antitrust Enforcement* (Hart, 2008): these essays are also available at www.ssrn.com.

[9] On general principles of EU law see the books cited in ch 7 n 8 earlier and *Wyatt and Dashwood's European Union Law* (Hart, 6th ed, 2011), ch 10; Hartley *The Foundations of European Union Law* (Oxford University Press, 8th ed, 2014), ch 5; Tridimas *The General Principles of EU Law* (Oxford University Press, 3rd ed, 2018).

[10] Available at www.echr.coe.int; note that Article 6(2) TEU provides that the EU 'shall accede to the ECHR', but the Court of Justice delivered a negative opinion on the compatibility with EU law of the draft accession agreement: *Opinion 2/13* EU:C:2014:2454.

[11] OJ [2010] C 83/389.

[12] For full discussion of this topic see Wils 'EU Antitrust Enforcement Powers and Procedural Rights and Guarantees: The Interplay between EU Law, National Law, the Charter of Fundamental Rights of the EU and the European Convention on Human Rights' (2011) 34 World Competition 189.

[13] See eg *2016 Report on the application of the EU Charter of Fundamental Rights*, COM(2017) 239, 14 May 2017, available at www.eur-lex.europa.eu.

the EU Courts[14]. Member States must have regard to the Charter when they apply provisions of EU law, including Articles 101 and 102 TFEU[15].

However whilst it is important to ensure that the rights of the defence are properly respected, it is also important to avoid them being so elevated that it becomes disproportionately difficult for the Commission to enforce the law: a balance has to be struck between the private interest of undertakings not to be found guilty of behaviour of which they are innocent and the public interest of punishing serious infringements of the law. A question that has attracted comment[16] is whether the system of enforcement established by Regulation 1/2003, whereby the European Commission acts as 'investigator, prosecutor, judge and jury', is compatible with the right to a fair hearing by an independent tribunal[17]. That question has now been answered in the affirmative by the European Court of Human Rights[18] and by the Court of Justice[19]. However it is important that the General Court exercises a 'full review' of Commission decisions in order to satisfy the requirements of the Charter; in *Groupement des Cartes Bancaires v Commission*[20] the Court of Justice held that the General Court had failed to observe the requisite standard of review[21]; a similar reprimand was made in *Intel v Commission*[22].

1. Overview of Regulation 1/2003

Regulation 1/2003 abolished the notification of agreements to the Commission for individual exemption and the Commission's exclusive power to make decisions on the application of Article 101(3) in individual cases: that provision is now directly applicable in the same way that Articles 101(1), 101(2) and 102 have always been[23]. However Regulation 1/2003 did not only abolish notifications: the opportunity was taken to overhaul comprehensively the enforcement powers of the Commission generally, and the Regulation adopted a number of new provisions including, for example, the possibility of the Commission adopting decisions on the basis of legally binding commitments as to undertakings' future behaviour (Article 9) and the power to conduct inspections at people's homes (Article 21). In 2014 the Commission published a Communication, *Ten Years of Antitrust Enforcement under Regulation 1/2003: Achievements and Future Perspectives*[24] that reviewed the first decade of Regulation 1/2003 in operation[25].

[14] See eg Case C-510/11 P *Kone Oyj v Commission* EU:C:2013:696, paras 20–33 and Case T-9/11 *Air Canada v European Commission* EU:T:2015:994 on the principle of effective judicial protection; Case C-580/12 P *Guardian Industries Corp v Commission* EU:C:2014:2363 on the principle of equal treatment.

[15] Article 51 of the Charter.

[16] See eg Forrester 'Due Process in EC Competition Cases' (2009) 34 EL Rev 817; Wils 'The Increased Level of EU Antitrust Fines, Judicial Review, and the European Convention on Human Rights' (2010) 33 World Competition 5; Editorial 'Towards a More Judicial Approach? EU Antitrust Fines Under the Scrutiny of Fundamental Rights' (2011) 48 CML Rev 1405.

[17] See Article 47(1) of the Charter and Article 6(1) of the ECHR.

[18] *Menarini Diagnostics v Italy*, no 43509/08, judgment of 27 September 2011.

[19] See eg Case C-386/10 P *Chalkor v Commission* EU:C:2011:815, paras 45–82; Case C-199/11 P *Europese Gemeenschap v Otis* EU:C:2012:684, paras 38–64; Cases T-56/09 etc *Saint-Gobain Glass France SA v Commission* EU:T:2014:160, paras 75–87.

[20] Case C-67/13 P EU:C:2014:2204.

[21] Ibid, paras 89–92.

[22] Case C-413/14 P EU:C:2017:632, paras 141–146.

[23] See ch 4, 'Regulation 1/2003', pp 174–176.

[24] COM(2014) 453.

[25] See also the Commission Staff Working Documents *Ten Years of Antitrust Enforcement under Regulation 1/2003*, SWD (2014) 230 and *Enhancing Competition Enforcement by the Member States' Competition Authorities*, SWD (2014) 231; see further 'Ten years of Regulation 1/2003 and possible reform', p 300 later in chapter.

(A) **The content of Regulation 1/2003**

Regulation 1/2003 consists of 11 chapters:

- Chapter I is entitled 'Principles': Article 1 provides for the direct applicability of Articles 101 and 102, Article 2 explains who bears the burden of proof in cases under Articles 101 and 102 and Article 3 deals with the relationship between those provisions and national competition law[26]
- Chapter II of the Regulation sets out the powers of the Commission, the NCAs and national courts
- Chapter III provides for various types of Commission decision: findings of infringement, interim measures, the acceptance of commitments and findings of inapplicability
- Chapter IV is concerned with cooperation between the Commission, NCAs and national courts
- Chapter V deals with the Commission's powers of investigation
- Chapter VI deals with penalties
- Chapter VII is concerned with limitation periods for the imposition and enforcement of penalties
- Chapter VIII deals with hearings and professional secrecy
- Chapter IX provides for the withdrawal of the benefit of block exemption regulations in certain circumstances
- Chapter X contains general provisions
- Chapter XI contains transitional, amending and final provisions.

(B) **Supporting measures**

The Commission has adopted a number of supporting measures necessary for the successful application of Regulation 1/2003. These measures consist of one Commission Regulation and a number of Notices, as follows:

- Commission Regulation 773/2004 relating to the conduct of proceedings under Articles 101 and 102, the 'Implementing Regulation'[27]
- *Notice on cooperation within the network of competition authorities*[28]
- *Notice on the cooperation between the Commission and courts of the EU Member States in the application of Articles [101 and 102 TFEU]*[29]
- *Notice on the handling of complaints by the Commission under Articles [101 and 102 TFEU]*[30]
- *Notice on informal guidance relating to novel questions concerning Articles [101 and 102 TFEU] that arise in individual cases (Guidance letters)*[31]
- *Notice on the effect on trade concept contained in Articles [101 and 102 TFEU]*[32]

[26] The relationship between EU and domestic competition law is discussed in ch 2, 'The Relationship Between EU Competition Law and National Competition Laws', pp 75–79.

[27] OJ [2004] L 123/18, as amended by Regulation 622/2008, OJ [2008] L 171/3 and by Regulation 2015/1348, OJ [2015] L 208/3.

[28] OJ [2004] C 101/43. [29] OJ [2004] C 101/54. [30] OJ [2004] C 101/65.

[31] OJ [2004] C 101/78. [32] OJ [2004] C 101/81.

- *Guidelines on the application of Article [101(3) TFEU]*[33]
- *Notice on the conduct of settlement procedures in view of the adoption of Decisions pursuant to Article 7 and Article 23 of Council Regulation No 1/2003 in cartel cases*[34]
- *Notice on best practices on the conduct of proceedings concerning Articles 101 and 102 TFEU ('Best Practices')*[35].

The following documents provide further details of the Commission's procedure in competition cases[36]:

- *Best Practices for the submission of economic evidence and data collection in cases concerning the application of Articles 101 and 102 TFEU and in merger cases*
- *Decision of the President of the Commission on the function and terms of reference of the hearing officer in certain competition proceedings*
- *Best Practices on the disclosure of information in data rooms*[37].

In 2012 DG COMP published its *Antitrust Manual of Procedures: Internal DG Competition working documents on procedures for the application of Articles 101 and 102 TFEU*[38] (the 'Manual of Procedures') which provides invaluable guidance on all aspects of the Commission's procedure. Practical information relating to issues such as confidentiality and inspections is also available on DG COMP's website[39].

2. **The Commission's Enforcement Powers under Regulation 1/2003**

(A) **Burden and standard of proof**

Article 2 of Regulation 1/2003 provides that the burden of proving an infringement of Article 101(1) or Article 102 is on the person or competition authority alleging the infringement and that the burden of showing that Article 101(3) is satisfied is on the person making that claim. There may be circumstances where the party bearing the burden of proof produces evidence that requires the other party to provide an explanation or justification, failing which it is permissible to conclude that the burden of proof has been satisfied[40]. The Commission's *Guidelines on the application of Article [101(3) TFEU]*[41] explain the kind of evidence that undertakings should provide when defending an agreement under Article 101(3).

The Regulation does not discuss the burden of proof where an undertaking raises objective justification or efficiency as a defence under Article 102. The position is that the evidential burden in such a situation rests with the undertaking asserting the justification[42], and that it is then incumbent on the Commission to show why that justification is inapplicable[43]. Similarly it would seem that an undertaking that asserts that a contractual

[33] OJ [2004] C 101/97.
[34] OJ [2008] C 167/1 as amended by a Communication from the Commission OJ [2015] C 256/2.
[35] OJ [2011] C 308/6. [36] Ibid.
[37] All these documents are available at www.ec.europa.eu/competition.
[38] Available at www.ec.europa.eu.
[39] www.ec.europa.eu/competition/antitrust/information_en.html.
[40] Cases C-501/06 P etc *GlaxoSmithKline Services Unlimited v Commission* EU:C:2009:610, para 83 and case law cited. [41] OJ [2004] C 101/97.
[42] See Case C-209/10 *Post Danmark A/S v Konkurrencerådet* EU:C:2012:172, paras 40–42, citing earlier case law.
[43] See eg Case T-201/04 *Microsoft Corpn v Commission* EU:T:2007:289, para 688.

restriction is ancillary bears the evidential burden of showing that this is so, and that the Commission should then have to show why this is not so[44].

Recital 5 states that Regulation 1/2003 does not affect national rules on the standard of proof.

(B) Chapter II: powers

Articles 4 to 6 deal with the powers of the Commission, the NCAs and national courts respectively.

(i) Article 4: powers of the Commission

Article 4 states that the Commission shall have the powers provided for by Regulation 1/2003: of particular importance are the decision-making powers in Chapter III; the powers of investigation contained in Chapter V; and the powers to impose penalties provided by Chapter VI; these are described below.

(ii) Article 5: powers of the NCAs

Recital 6 of the Regulation states that, to ensure the effective application of the competition rules, NCAs should be associated more closely with their application. Article 5 therefore provides that NCAs shall have the power to apply Articles 101 and 102 in individual cases. For this purpose the NCAs may make decisions requiring the termination of an infringement, ordering interim measures, accepting commitments and imposing fines and periodic penalty payments; they may also decide that there are no grounds for action on their part, but not that the EU competition rules are not infringed[45]; only the European Commission is entitled to adopt a non-infringement decision[46]. In *Bundeswettbewerbsbehörde v Schenker*[47] the Court of Justice held that, in order to ensure that Article 101 is effectively applied in the general interest ('*effet utile*'), an NCA could only exceptionally not impose a fine where an infringement is established[48]: an example would be where an undertaking was a whistleblower whose contribution was decisive in enabling the authority to detect and suppress a cartel[49].

Article 35 of the Regulation requires Member States to designate the competition authority or authorities responsible for the application of Articles 101 and 102 in such a way that its provisions are effectively complied with; the designated authorities can include courts. Designated national authorities must have the right to participate, as a defendant or respondent, in judicial proceedings against a decision that the authority has taken in relation to Articles 101 and/or 102[50]. The Commission works closely with the NCAs through the medium of the ECN, the work of which is discussed in section 3 below.

[44] On this point see a case under the UK Competition Act 1998, Cases 1035/1/1/04 etc *Racecourse Association v OFT* [2005] CAT 29, paras 130–134.

[45] Case C-375/09 *Prezes Urzędu Ochrony Konkurencji I Konsumentów v Tele2 Polska sp. Z o.o., now Netia SA* EU:C:2011:270, paras 19–30; this was a case under Article 102 but there is no reason in principle to suppose that it would have reached a different conclusion in the case of Article 101; see also Case T-402/13 *Orange v Commission* EU:T:2014:991, paras 30–31.

[46] On 'finding of inapplicability' see p 269 later in chapter.

[47] Case C-681/11 EU:C:2013:404.

[48] Note that, since an NCA cannot decide that there has been no infringement of EU competition law, it cannot create a legitimate expectation that an undertaking will not be fined for infringing it: ibid, para 42.

[49] Ibid, paras 44–50.

[50] Case C-439/08 *Vlaamse federatie van verenigingen van Brood- en Banketbakkers, Ijsbereiders en Chocoladebewerkers (VEBIC) VZW* EU:C:2010:739.

In March 2017 the Commission adopted a proposal for a directive[51] designed to empower the NCAs to be more effective enforcers of competition law: in particular the directive would ensure their independence; that they have adequate resources; and that they possess the necessary enforcement and fining powers to prevent distortions of competition in the internal market. This initiative is known as the ECN+, or ECN plus, proposal. As at 8 December 2017, the expectation was that the Directive will be adopted by the end of the mandate of the current Commission in October 2019.

(iii) Article 6: powers of the national courts

Article 6 provides that national courts shall have the power to apply Article 101, in its entirety, and Article 102: the role of national courts is discussed in chapter 8.

(C) Chapter III: Commission decisions

Articles 7 to 10 deal with Commission decisions. The Commission has also issued a *Notice on informal guidance relating to novel questions concerning Articles [101 and 102 TFEU] that arise in individual cases (Guidance letters)*[52] explaining the (rare) circumstances in which it might be prepared to give undertakings informal guidance on the application of the competition rules. In 2008 the Commission introduced a system whereby some cartel cases can be settled. Informal guidance and settlements will be discussed after the powers conferred by Articles 7 to 10 have been described.

(i) Article 7: finding and termination of an infringement

Article 7(1) provides that where the Commission, acting on a complaint or on its own initiative, finds an infringement of Article 101 or 102, it may by decision require an end to it[53]. Article 7(1) continues by stating that the Commission may impose on undertakings behavioural or structural remedies which are proportionate to the infringement and necessary to bring the infringement effectively to an end[54].

(a) Behavioural remedies

A behavioural remedy may be negative, for example to stop a certain kind of conduct, or positive, to order an undertaking to do something. In a typical cartel case the Commission will require the participants in the cartel to stop the illegal behaviour, in so far as they have not already done so, and to refrain from any act or conduct having the same or a similar object or effect in the future[55].

The ability of the Commission to make a positive order under Regulation 17 was confirmed by the Court of Justice in *Commercial Solvents Co v Commission*[56]; there is no reason to suppose that its powers would be any different under Regulation 1/2003. In *Commercial Solvents* that firm was found guilty of an unlawful refusal to supply contrary to Article 102 and was ordered to resume supplies to a former customer.

[51] Proposal for a Directive of the European Parliament and of the Council to empower the competition authorities of the Member States to be more effective enforcers and to ensure the proper functioning of the internal market, 22 March 2017, COM (2017) 142 final; for discussion see Wils 'Competition authorities: Towards more independence and prioritization?', available at www.ssrn.com.

[52] OJ [2004] C 101/78.

[53] See ch 15 of DG COMP's *Manual of Procedures* on the adoption of prohibition decisions.

[54] See Ritter 'Remedies for breaches of EU antitrust law', available at www.ssrn.com.

[55] See eg Article 3 of the Commission's decision in *Gas insulated switchgear* of 24 January 2007; see however Case T-395/94 *Atlantic Container Line AB v Commission* EU:T:2002:49, paras 410–420.

[56] Cases 6/73 and 7/73 EU:C:1974:18.

In *Microsoft*[57] the General Court upheld the Commission's infringement decision, but held that the Commission did not have the right to appoint an independent monitoring trustee to enforce the remedy: this went 'far beyond' retaining an expert to advise it on implementation of the remedies[58].

Whereas an undertaking can be ordered to supply a distributor or customer where it has infringed Article 102, this cannot be done following an infringement of Article 101[59]. Articles 101 and 102 have a different logic: Article 101 prohibits agreements, and the Commission may make an order to terminate them; Article 102 prohibits abuse, and again the Commission can make an order to terminate an abuse. However a refusal to supply cannot in itself be unlawful under Article 101. The Commission could order an undertaking to terminate an agreement not to supply, but it does not follow that it can also make an order to supply. Any further civil law consequences of an infringement of Article 101 should be determined in the national courts[60].

(b) Structural remedies

Regulation 17 did not specifically provide for a structural remedy, and the explicit inclusion of this possibility in Regulation 1/2003 was controversial. Article 7(1) states that structural remedies can be imposed only where there is no equally effective behavioural remedy or where a behavioural remedy would be more burdensome for the undertaking concerned than the structural remedy. Recital 12 adds that changes to the structure of an undertaking as it existed before the infringement was committed would be proportionate only where there is a substantial risk of a lasting or repeated infringement that derives from the very structure of the undertaking. A possible example of this could arise where a vertically-integrated undertaking consistently denies access to an essential facility or discriminates against downstream competitors in relation to a vital input; another example could be where an undertaking repeatedly indulges in a margin squeeze[61]. In *ARA Foreclosure*[62] the Commission adopted an Article 7 decision requiring ARA to divest itself of its interest in infrastructure that was an essential facility: ARA had itself offered this divestiture, and its fine was reduced by 30% to reflect its cooperative approach. In several cases, particularly in the energy sector, structural commitments were offered to, and accepted by, the Commission under Article 9 of the Regulation[63].

(c) Past infringements

Article 7(1) of Regulation 1/2003 ends by providing that the Commission, where it has a legitimate interest in doing so, may adopt a decision that an infringement has been committed in the past[64]. There might be an interest in doing so, for example, in order to clarify an important point of principle or as a way of facilitating a follow-on action for

[57] Commission decision of 24 March 2004, substantially upheld on appeal Case T-201/04 *Microsoft Corpn v Commission* EU:T:2007:289.

[58] Ibid, paras 1251–1279.

[59] Case T-24/90 *Automec v Commission (No 2)* EU:T:1992:97.

[60] Ibid, para 50; see also Cases C-377/05 and C-376/05 *A Brünsteiner GmbH v Bayerische Motorenwerke AG* EU:C:2006:753, paras 48–51.

[61] See ch 17, 'Refusal to Supply', pp 713–727 and ch 18, 'Margin Squeeze', pp 771–777 on these practices.

[62] Commission decision of 20 September 2016, paras 132–148.

[63] See 'Article 9: commitments', pp 264–269 later in chapter.

[64] This was possible under Regulation 17: see Case 7/82 *GVL v Commission* EU:C:1983:52; *Bloemenveilingen Aalsmeer* OJ [1988] L 262/27, paras 164–168; *Distribution of Package Tours During the 1990 World Cup* OJ [1992] L 326/31; *Zera/Montedison* OJ [1993] L 272/28, para 132; *Europe Asia Trades Agreement* OJ [1999] L 193/23, paras 182–185.

damages[65]. However the Commission must explain why there is an EU interest in the adoption of a decision relating to past behaviour, and a failure to do so could lead to the decision being annulled on appeal[66]; an example of such an explanation can be found in *Morgan Stanley/Visa International and Visa Europe* where the Commission gave, among its reasons, that Visa continued to deny that its behaviour was contrary to Article 101 and that it (the Commission) wished to impose a fine[67].

(d) Complainants

Article 7(2) of the Regulation provides that those entitled to lodge a complaint for the purpose of Article 7(1) are natural or legal persons who can show a legitimate interest and Member States. The position of complainants is considered later[68].

(ii) **Article 8: interim measures**

Article 8(1) of the Regulation provides that, in cases of urgency due to the risk of serious and irreparable damage to competition, the Commission, acting on its own initiative[69], may, on the basis of a *prima facie* finding of infringement, order interim measures[70]. Article 8(2) states that an order shall be for a specified period of time, and may be renewed in so far as this is necessary and appropriate. Regulation 17 was silent on the issue of interim measures, but the Court of Justice established in *Camera Care v Commission*[71] that the Commission did have power under Article 3 of that Regulation to grant interim relief. Recital 11 of Regulation 1/2003 says that explicit provision should be made for interim measures. In practice the Commission did not often adopt interim measures under the *Camera Care* judgment: it preferred third parties to seek interim relief in their domestic courts[72] or from NCAs[73]. The Commission has yet to impose interim measures under Article 8[74]: the requirement to establish 'serious and irreparable damage to competition' is not easy to satisfy[75]. On a few occasions the Commission has negotiated an interim settlement with undertakings without formally adopting an interim decision.

65 See ch 8, 'Article 16: uniform application of EU competition law', pp 319–320.

66 See Joined Cases T-22/02 etc *Sumitomo Chemical Co Ltd v Commission* EU:T:2005:349, paras 129–140.

67 Commission decision of 3 October 2007, upheld on appeal Case T-461/07 *Visa Europe v Commission* EU:T:2011:181; see similarly Cases T-23/10 etc *Arkema France v Commission* EU:T:2014:62, paras 109–120.

68 See 'The position of complainants', pp 296–297 later in chapter.

69 Note that interim measures are adopted, if at all, at the initiative of the Commission and not pursuant to any 'right' of complainants to ask the Commission to act: see Nordsjo 'Regulation 1/2003: Power of the Commission to Adopt Interim Measures' (2006) 27 ECLR 299.

70 See ch 17 of DG COMP's *Manual of Procedures* on interim measures.

71 Case 792/79 R EU:C:1980:18.

72 On applications for interim measures in the UK courts see ch 8, 'Interim relief', p 333.

73 On the powers of the CMA in the UK to adopt interim measures see ch 10, 'Interim measures', pp 416–417.

74 The decisions that the Commission adopted prior to Regulation 1/2003 will be relevant if and when it makes any decisions under Article 8: see eg *Ford Werke AG-Interim Measure* OJ [1982] L 256/20: this decision was annulled on appeal to the Court of Justice Cases 228/82 and 229/82 *Ford Werke AG v Commission* EU:C:1984:80; *ECS/AKZO* OJ [1983] L 252/13; *BBI/Boosey and Hawkes: Interim Measures* OJ [1987] L 286/36; *Ecosystem SA v Peugeot SA* [1990] 4 CMLR 449, upheld on appeal Case T-23/90 *Peugeot v Commission* EU:T:1991:45; *Langnese-Iglo/Mars*, unreported decision of 25 March 1992; see XXIInd *Report on Competition Policy* (1992), point 195: this decision was suspended in part in Cases T-24/92 and 28/92 R *Langnese-Iglo GmbH v Commission* EU:T:1992:71; *Sealink/B&I—Holyhead: Interim Measures* [1992] 5 CMLR 255; *Sea Containers v Stena Sealink—Interim Measures* OJ [1994] L 15/8; *Irish Continental Group v CCI Morlaix* [1995] 5 CMLR 177; and *NDC Health/IMS Health: Interim Measures* OJ [2002] L 59/18: this decision was subsequently withdrawn: Commission Press Release 1P/03/1159, 13 August 2003.

75 Commissioner Vestager has questioned whether the test is too strict: see speech of 15 March 2017, available at www.ec.europa.eu.

This happened for example in *Hilti*[76]; the terms of the undertaking were subsequently broken and the Commission took this into account in its final decision.

(iii) Article 9: commitments

Article 9 provides for the adoption of decisions by the Commission whereby undertakings under investigation make legally-binding commitments to meet the concerns expressed to them by the Commission; the Commission then closes its file without making a finding as to whether there has been or continues to be an infringement of Articles 101 and/or 102[77]. Commitments may be behavioural or structural; structural commitments have been accepted in several cases in the energy and transport sectors[78]. The commitments procedure is a more consensual one than infringement proceedings under Article 7. As the Court of Justice explained in *Commission v Alrosa*[79] the Article 9 procedure enables the rapid solution of appropriate cases and is based on considerations of procedural economy. Not every case needs to end with an infringement decision. A competition authority must decide how to make the best use of the limited resources available to it, and in some cases 'efficiency reasons justify that the Commission limits itself to making the commitments binding, and does not issue a formal prohibition decision'[80]. For example commitments may be appropriate where they lead to the termination of conduct that appears to be anti-competitive. Commitment decisions may also educate the broader business and legal communities about practices that may give rise to competition concerns.

There were no provisions in Regulation 17 whereby a case could be settled on the basis of legally-binding commitments; despite this there were several cases in which the Commission did close its file on the basis of informal commitments for which there was no enforcement mechanism[81]. Article 9 of Regulation 1/2003 for the first time provided a legal basis for commitments; it has generated a lot of literature[82]. Commitments have been accepted in 38 cases since Article 9 came into force on 1 May 2004. A table of all the commitments accepted by the Commission to date will be found on the Online Resources that accompany this book[83]. Cases in which commitments were accepted since 6 February 2015, the cut-off date of the eighth edition of this book, are listed in Table 7.1[84].

[76] The undertakings given by Hilti were attached as an Annex to the Commission's final decision: *Eurofix-Bauco v Hilti* OJ [1988] L 65/19; other examples of interim undertakings include *Ford Motor Co*, XVth *Report on Competition Policy* (1985), point 49; *British Sugar/Napier Brown* XVIth *Report on Competition Policy* (1986), point 74; *Irish Distillers Group v GC & C Brands Ltd* [1988] 4 CMLR 840.

[77] See ch 15 of DG COMP's *Manual of Procedures* on commitment decisions.

[78] See 'Comment', pp 268–269 later in chapter.

[79] Case C-441/07 P EU:C:2010:377, para 35; see also Case T-76/14 *Morningstar Inc v Commission* EU:T:2016:481, para 39.

[80] Commission MEMO/04/217 of 17 September 2004.

[81] Significant cases that were settled informally include *IBM*, the Commission's XIVth *Report on Competition Policy* (1984), pp 77–79; *Microsoft (licensing agreements)*, XXIVth *Report on Competition Policy* (1994), pp 364–365; *Interbrew*, XXVIth *Report on Competition Policy* (1996), pp 139–140; *IRI/Nielsen*, ibid, pp 144–148; *Digital*, XXVIIth *Report on Competition Policy* (1997), pp 153–154.

[82] See eg Wils 'Settlements of EU Antitrust Investigations: Commitment Decisions under Article 9 of Regulation 1/2003' (2006) 29 World Competition 345; Whish 'Commitment Decisions under Article 9 of the EC Modernisation Regulation: Some Unanswered Questions' in *Liber Amicorum in Honour of Sven Norberg* (Bruylant, 2006), pp 555–572; Wagner-von Papp 'Best and Even Better Practices in Commitments Procedures After *Alrosa*: The Dangers of Abandoning the "Struggle for Competition Law"' (2012) 49 CML Rev 929; Hjelmeng 'Competition Law Remedies: Striving for Coherence or Finding New Ways?' (2013) 50 CML Rev 1007; Dunne 'Commitment Decisions in EU Competition Law' (2014) 10 Journal of Competition Law and Economics 399.

[83] See www.oup.com/uk/whish9e/.

[84] 'Table of Article 9 commitment decisions', p 265.

Table 7.1 Table of Article 9 commitment decisions

Case name	Article alleged to have been infringed	Date when commitments made legally binding	Date until which commitments to remain in force
Air France/KLM Alitalia and Delta (SkyTeam Alliance)	Article 101: horizontal agreement	12.04.15	12.04.25
		NB: quasi-structural remedy	
BEH Electricity—Bulgarian Energy Holding	Article 102	10.12.15	09.12.20
Container liner shipping	Article 101: horizontal agreement	07.07.16	06.12.20
Credit default swaps/ ISDA/ Markit	Article 101: horizontal agreement	20.07.16	10.07.25
Cross-border access to pay-TV—NBC Universal/ Paramount Pictures C[1]	Article 101: vertical agreement	26.07.16	25.07.21
E-book MFNs and related matters—Amazon EU Sarl	Article 102: vertical agreement	04.05.17	03.05.22

[1] This decision has been appealed to the General Court in Case T-873/16 *Groupe Canal + v Commission*, not yet decided.

(a) Article 9: substantive rules

Article 9(1) of Regulation 1/2003 provides that, where the Commission intends to adopt a decision requiring that an infringement of Articles 101 and/or 102 be brought to an end and the undertakings concerned offer commitments to meet the concerns expressed in its preliminary assessment, the Commission may adopt a decision that makes those commitments legally binding. The final sentence of Article 9(1) provides that the decision may be for a specified period (though this is not a requirement[85]) and shall conclude that there are no longer grounds for action by the Commission. Article 9(2) provides that the Commission may reopen the proceedings in certain specified circumstances, for example where the undertakings concerned act contrary to their commitments.

Recital 13 of the Regulation states that the Article 9 procedure is not appropriate in cases where the Commission intends to impose a fine: commitment decisions are

[85] See Case T-170/06 *Alrosa Company Ltd v Commission* EU:T:2007:220, para 91.

therefore excluded in the case of hard-core cartels. The Commission is never obliged to accept commitments under Article 9 rather than proceeding under Article 7 to a finding of infringement[86]. The Commission enjoys a wide discretion in relation to the acceptance of commitments[87]; the EU Courts, when conducting a judicial review of commitments, will not substitute their economic assessment for that of the Commission[88].

A decision under Article 9 is conceptually distinct from an infringement decision under Article 7: the purpose of Article 7 is to bring an infringement to an end, whereas a decision under Article 9 is intended to address any concerns that the Commission might have following its preliminary assessment[89]. It follows that the Commission is not obliged, when agreeing to accept a commitment under Article 9, to equate the remedy offered with a measure that it could have imposed under Article 7[90]; an undertaking might offer a change of behaviour under Article 9 that the Commission could not have demanded under Article 7[91].

Article 23(2)(c) of Regulation 1/2003 provides that fines can be imposed on an undertaking that fails to comply with a commitment of up to 10% of its total turnover in the preceding business year. Article 24(1)(c) provides for the imposition of periodic penalty payments of up to 5% of average daily turnover in the previous business year for a continuing infringement of a commitment decision. In 2013 the Commission imposed a fine of €561 million on Microsoft for its failure to comply with its commitment to offer users of Windows an unbiased choice of different web browsers by means of a 'Choice Screen' in its operating systems[92]. The size of this fine will presumably impress on firms that give commitments under Article 9 the importance of complying with them[93]. In *CEEES v Commission*[94] the General Court upheld the Commission's decision to reject a complaint about alleged non-compliance with commitments that had been given by Repsol.

(b) Article 9: procedure

The Article 9 procedure is a formal one and entails the initiation of proceedings by the Commission[95]. The Commission does not have to issue a statement of objections: it suffices that it sends the undertakings concerned a 'preliminary assessment' of its case which may be shorter and less formal than a statement of objections. The preliminary assessment may be contained in a letter or may be sent as an independent document. The preliminary assessment or statement of objections gives the undertakings concerned a period of time within which to respond to the Commission's concerns and to offer draft commitments. The Commission has said that proposed commitments must be unambiguous and self-executing[96].

The Court of Justice has held that a third party is not a 'party concerned' in the sense of Article 27(2) of Regulation 1/2003[97] which means that it does not have a right

86 Ibid, para 130. 87 Case C-441/07 P *Commission v Alrosa* EU:C:2010:377, para 94.

88 Ibid, para 67; see also Case T-76/14 *Morningstar Inc v Commission* EU:T:2016:481, para 41.

89 Case C-441/07 P *Commission v Alrosa* EU:C:2010:377, para 46. 90 Ibid, para 47.

91 Ibid, paras 48–50; on the same point see also Case T-76/14 *Morningstar Inc v Commission* EU:T:2016:481, paras 43–45.

92 *Microsoft—Tying*, Commission decision of 6 March 2013.

93 Former Vice-President Almunia emphasised this point at the time of the decision: see Commission Press Release IP/13/196, 6 March 2013.

94 Case T-342/11 *Confederación Española de Empresarios de Estaciones de Servicio v Commission* EU:T:2014:60.

95 See generally *Best Practices*, paras 115–133. 96 Ibid, para 128.

97 Case C-441/07 P *Commission v Alrosa* EU:C:2010:377, para 90, annulling the judgment of the General Court in Case T-170/06 *Alrosa Company Ltd v Commission* EU:T:2007:220, paras 197–204.

of access to the Commission's file in a case being conducted under the commitments procedure[98].

Article 27(4) of the Implementing Regulation provides that, where the Commission intends to adopt an Article 9 decision, it must publish a concise summary of the case and the main content of the commitments; third parties are then given an opportunity to comment within a fixed time limit of not less than one month. The Commission publishes the full text of the draft commitments in their original language on the internet. The process of 'market testing' the draft commitments may reveal weaknesses in them that could lead the Commission to renegotiate them or abandon the Article 9 procedure and revert to the possibility of proceeding to an infringement decision under Article 7: this happened in the case of *CISAC*[99]. In the case of *Google* there was so much hostility to the various commitments offered by that undertaking that the Commission decided not to accept them but to continue with its investigation[100]; this led to the adoption of an infringement decision against Google in June 2017 imposing a fine on it of €2.42 billion[101]. Article 30 of Regulation 1/2003 provides that the Commission must publish its Article 9 decisions.

(c) Article 9: practical considerations

Various practical points should be noted about Article 9 commitments. First, recital 13 of Regulation 1/2003 says that commitment decisions will not conclude whether or not there has been or still is an infringement of the competition rules, and adds that commitment decisions are without prejudice to the powers of NCAs and national courts to decide upon the case, a point repeated in the final sentence of recital 22 and confirmed by the General Court[102]. This has important implications for the parties concerned. There is a possibility that, not least because of the publicity of the commitments procedure itself and the statements that may have been made by the Commission in the course of it, the parties will remain vulnerable to the possibility of a national court finding, for example, that an agreement that has been modified by commitments nonetheless infringes Article 101(1), does not satisfy Article 101(3) and is therefore void pursuant to Article 101(2)[103].

Where undertakings give commitments to the Commission as to their future behaviour the question arises of whether NCAs and/or third parties could challenge conduct that is consistent with the commitments as being unlawful under Articles 101 and/or 102. Article 9 of the Regulation simply states that the Commission's decision 'shall conclude that there are no longer grounds for action by the Commission'. However this does not in itself mean that the Commission has concluded that there is no longer an infringement: it could mean that it has decided, having been offered suitable commitments, that the case is no longer one of its enforcement priorities. It would presumably be unlikely that an NCA would proceed against undertakings that have given commitments to the Commission in relation to future conduct unless, perhaps, it wished to take action against unilateral behaviour that is subject to stricter rules under national law, as permitted by Article 3(2)

98 See also the decision of the Ombudsman in Complaint 2953/2008/FOR against the European Commission, 27 July 2010, rejecting third party access to the Commission's preliminary assessment in E.ON; the decision is available at www.ombudsman.europa.eu/home.faces.

99 See Table 7.1 earlier in chapter.

100 See the Statement by Commissioner Vestager at the European Parliament, 11 November 2014.

101 Commission decision of 27 June 2017, on appeal Case T-612/17 *Google v Commission*, not yet decided.

102 See Case T-342/11 *Confederación Española de Empresarios de Estaciones de Servicio v Commission* EU:T:2014:60, para 67.

103 Case C-547/16 *Gasorba SL v Repsol Comercial de Productos Petrolíferos SA* EU:C:2017:891, para 30.

of Regulation 1/2003. However it is clear that an Article 9 commitment decision does nothing to immunise the parties that offer commitments from the possibility of damages actions in national courts for their future behaviour.

Given that the Article 9 procedure is voluntary on the part of the parties that offer commitments it is unlikely that they would appeal against the substance of an Article 9 decision, and this has never happened; however they may wish to challenge aspects of the Commission's procedure, such as their right of access to the file. Undertakings that offer commitments could appeal against the Commission's refusal to accept them; however, the General Court having said that the Commission is never obliged to accept commitments, it seems unlikely that such appeals will succeed[104]. Third parties may wish to bring Article 9 cases to the General Court. This might happen where they have complained to the Commission of anti-competitive behaviour, but where they believe that a commitment has been accepted which is inadequate to bring an end to the infringement: this happened, unsuccessfully, in the case of *Morningstar v Commission*[105], an appeal against the Commission's decision in *Thomson Reuters*. A third party might also challenge the acceptance of commitments if the Commission's legal basis for proceeding might seem to impugn the conduct of the third party[106].

(d) Comment

A few observations may be made about the Article 9 decisions adopted since Regulation 1/2003 entered into force. The first is that there have been more Article 9 decisions than was anticipated when the Regulation was adopted. A second point is that a significant number of the Article 9 decisions arose from investigations concerning possible infringements of Article 102 rather than Article 101. This is not surprising: as noted, the Article 9 procedure is not used in the case of hard-core cartels, and the Commission adopts several cartel decisions each year under Article 7. Article 102 cases tend to be more complex than cartels, and a negotiated outcome that involves a rapid change of behaviour to the satisfaction of the Commission but no finding of an infringement on the part of the undertaking concerned clearly has benefits for both parties[107].

A third point is that a significant number of the Article 9 decisions—eleven in total—involved gas or electricity markets: the Commission's sectoral investigation of these markets had identified a series of concerns[108], many of which have been allayed as a result of these decisions. A fourth point to note is that in seven out of eleven of the energy cases the Commission accepted structural or quasi-structural rather than, or in addition to, behavioural commitments: an obvious example being ENI's commitment to divest itself of its interests in three cross-border gas pipelines, thereby terminating the conflict of interest that arose from its vertical integration as both a supplier and

[104] This issue was raised, but not decided, in Case T-421/08 *Performing Right Society v Commission* and Case T-433/08 *Società Italiana degli Autori ed Editori v Commission*: as the Court annulled the Commission's finding of a concerted practice in *CISAC* it was not necessary to address the refusal of the Commission to accept commitments under Article 9.

[105] Case T-76/14 EU:T:2016:481.

[106] See Case T-873/16 *Groupe Canal + v Commission*, not yet decided.

[107] For discussion of the Commission's position see 'To commit or not to commit? Deciding between prohibition and commitments' (2014) 3 Competition Policy Brief available at www.ec.europa.eu/competition/publications.

[108] See 'Article 17: investigations into sectors of the economy and into types of agreements', p 277 later in chapter.

transporter of gas[109]. The Commission has imposed a structural remedy in only one case under Article 7, and that was an unusual one in that the remedy was offered as part of a 'settlement'. The structural commitments that the Commission received in these energy cases are not dissimilar to those required in some merger cases including, on some occasions, the appointment of monitoring trustees and the requirement for the Commission to approve the buyer of the assets to be divested.

In *Samsung* the Commission accepted commitments whereby Samsung promised to implement a licensing framework for the determination of FRAND (fair, reasonable and non-discriminatory) royalties for the use of standard-essential patents: for a period of five years it would not seek injunctions in relation to such patents[110]. On the same day as the *Samsung* commitment decision the Commission adopted an infringement decision in *Motorola* establishing that, in certain circumstances, an undertaking can abuse its dominant position by seeking injunctions under standard-essential patents[111]; the Commission did not impose a fine since the issue was a novel one and one on which different results might have arisen in different Member States. This combination of an Article 7 decision in one case with an Article 9 decision in the other helped to clarify the law and to provide guidance as to how such issues might be dealt with in future cases.

The Commission may release undertakings from commitments that are no longer necessary, for example because of an improvement in the competitive structure of the market[112].

(iv) Article 10: finding of inapplicability

Article 10 provides that, where the EU public interest requires, the Commission may adopt a 'finding of inapplicability' that Article 101 and/or Article 102 do not apply to an agreement or practice[113]. Firms do not have a right to ask for such a decision, but the Commission might decide to adopt one (in 'exceptional cases', as recital 14 says) where this would clarify the law and ensure its consistent application throughout the EU; the same recital adds that this might be particularly useful where new types of agreements or practices occur in relation to which there is no case law or administrative practice. The Commission had not adopted any Article 10 decisions by 8 December 2017[114]. It is the opinion of the authors that judicious use of Article 10 of Regulation 1/2003 (or informal guidance, discussed below) on the part of the Commission would be valuable as a way of developing 'precedents', and would serve 'the public interest of the Union', the words used in recital 14.

(v) Informal guidance

The need for undertakings to have legal certainty in order to promote innovation and investment is acknowledged in recital 38 of Regulation 1/2003: it says that where there is genuine uncertainty because of novel or unresolved questions of competition law

[109] Structural commitments (the divestiture of airport slots) were also accepted by the Commission in *British Airways, American Airlines and Iberia*, decision of 14 July 2010; in *Air Canada, Continental Airlines/Deutsche Lufthansa AG/United Air Lines Inc*, decision of 23 May 2013; and in *Air France/KLM/Alitalia/Delta*, Commission decision of 12 May 2015.

[110] *Samsung—enforcement of UMTS standard essential patents*, Commission decision of 29 April 2014.

[111] *Motorola—enforcement of GPRS standard essential patents*, Commission decision of 29 April 2014.

[112] See eg the early termination of Deutsche Bahn's commitments, Commission Press Release 1IP/16/1322, 8 April 2016 and of E.ON's commitments, Commission Press Release IP/16/2646, 26 July 2016.

[113] See ch 18 of DG COMP's *Manual of Procedures* on Article 10 decisions.

[114] See Commission Staff Working Paper accompanying the *Report on the functioning of Regulation 1/2003*, SEC(2009) 574 final, para 114, available at www.ec.europa.eu.

undertakings may seek informal guidance from the Commission[115]. Both Article 10 and recital 38 address the anxieties of those who were concerned that the procedure of notifying agreements for individual exemptions under Article 101(3) was to be abolished. The Commission has issued a *Notice on informal guidance relating to novel questions arising under Articles [101 and 102 TFEU] (Guidance letters)*[116]. The *Notice* points out that undertakings have access to a substantial body of case law, decisional practice, block exemptions, guidelines and notices enabling them to undertake a self-assessment of the legality of their commercial plans[117]; however it also notes that there might be cases in which a guidance letter would be appropriate[118]. The Commission says that issuing a guidance letter would be considered only where the following cumulative criteria are satisfied:

- there is no current case law, guidance or precedent in relation to a particular type of agreement or practice
- guidance would be useful taking into account the economic importance from the point of view of the consumer of the goods or services to which the agreement or practice relates and/or
- the extent to which the agreement or practice corresponds to more widely spread economic usage in the marketplace and/or
- the scope of the investments linked to the transaction in relation to the size of the undertakings concerned and the extent to which the transaction relates to a structural operation such as the creation of a non-full-function joint venture
- guidance can be given on the basis of information already provided to the Commission and no further fact-finding is required[119].

The Commission will not issue guidance letters in relation to purely hypothetical questions[120]. A memorandum should be submitted with a request for a guidance letter containing information specified by the Commission[121]. A guidance letter will set out a summary of the facts on which it is based and the principle legal reasoning underlying the Commission's understanding of the novel questions raised by the request[122]. Guidance letters will be published on the Commission's website, subject to the deletion of business secrets[123]. Guidance letters are not Commission decisions and do not bind NCAs or national courts[124]. No such letters had been issued by 8 December 2017.

(vi) **Settlements of cartel cases**

(a) Introduction

The Commission's procedure in cartel cases is often long and complicated. The Commission's resources are finite, and there is a limit to the number of investigations that it can conduct; a further strain on the Commission's resources is the defence of cases taken on appeal to the EU Courts. This is the context in which the Commission introduced a system for settling cartel cases in 2008[125], which was accompanied by a *Settlements Notice*[126]. The *Notice* does not apply to non-cartel cases under Article 101 nor to abuse cases under Article 102; however the Commission did settle an abuse case in *ARA*, where that undertaking's fine was reduced by 30% to €6 million in recognition of

[115] See ch 22 of DG COMP's *Manual of Procedures* on informal guidance. [116] OJ [2004] C 101/78.
[117] Ibid, para 3. [118] Ibid, para 5. [119] Ibid, para 8. [120] Ibid, para 10.
[121] Ibid, para 14. [122] Ibid, para 19. [123] Ibid, para 21. [124] Ibid, para 25.
[125] Regulation 622/2008, OJ [2008] L 171/3, amending Regulation 773/2004, OJ [2004] L 123/18.
[126] *Notice on the conduct of settlement procedures in view of the adoption of Decisions pursuant to Article 7 and Article 23 of Council Regulation No 1/2003 in cartel cases* OJ [2008] C 167/1 as amended by a Communication from the Commission OJ [2015] C 256/2.

its cooperation in bringing the case to a conclusion sooner than would have occurred in a fully contested procedure[127].

The essence of the settlement procedure is that at a certain point in a cartel investigation the parties, having seen the evidence in the Commission's file, acknowledge their involvement in the cartel and their liability for it; in return for this the Commission reduces the fine that it would otherwise have imposed on them by 10%[128]. The reduction of a fine is a reward for cooperation: settlements are *not* a negotiation between the Commission and the cartelists as to the existence of the infringement or the level of the penalty[129].

Reduced fines under the settlements procedure are conceptually distinct from reductions granted for voluntarily providing information under the Commission's *Leniency Notice*[130]: it follows that an undertaking may be able to obtain cumulative reductions, and this often happens.

(b) Benefits of a system of settlements

A number of benefits follow from the settlements procedure. The advantages to the Commission are that cases can be concluded more quickly and that appeals are unlikely, though not impossible (see the following section): this means that more cartel decisions can be adopted using the same amount of resources. The advantages to the parties, apart from the reduced fine, are that less time and money are spent on the investigation and appeals; that the reputational harm of prolonged exposure in the media as a cartel case continues would be reduced; and that settlement decisions contain much less factual analysis than 'normal' decisions, which makes them less useful for victims of the cartel in follow-on actions for damages.

(c) Settlements procedure

The settlements procedure is described in Part 2 of the Commission's *Settlements Notice*[131]: an overview of the procedure will be found at the end of the *Notice*. Paragraph 5 makes clear that the Commission retains a broad discretion to determine which cases may be suitable for settlement; the Commission cannot impose a settlement on the parties[132], but nor do the parties have a right to settle[133]. The Commission has the right at any time during the procedure to discontinue settlement discussions, in relation to a case generally or to one or more of the parties involved, where it considers that procedural efficiencies are unlikely to be achieved[134].

Where undertakings indicate a willingness to participate in settlement discussions, the Commission may decide to pursue the settlement procedure on the basis of bilateral contacts[135]; it will control their order and sequence[136]. Article 10a(2) of the Implementing Regulation provides that the parties to settlement discussions may be informed by the Commission of:

- its objections to their behaviour
- the evidence used to determine those objections

[127] Commission decision of 20 September 2016; see in particular para 19 of the decision and note that ARA agreed to divest itself of its stake in the infrastructure (for the collection of repackaging waste) that was the 'essential facility' in this case.

[128] *Settlements Notice*, para 32.

[129] Ibid, para 2.

[130] See 'The Commission's *Leniency Notice*', pp 289–292 later in chapter.

[131] OJ [2008] C 167/1.

[132] *Settlements Notice*, para 4; see also recital 4 of Regulation 622/2008.

[133] *Settlements Notice*, para 6; the Commission's broad discretion was confirmed in Case T-267/12 *Deutsche Bahn AG v Commission* EU:T:2016:110, paras 417–419.

[134] Article 10a(4) of Regulation 773/2004; the Commission abandoned settlement discussions in the case of the *Smart card chips cartel*: see Commission Press Release IP/14/960, 3 September 2014.

[135] *Settlements Notice*, para 14.

[136] Ibid, para 15.

- non-confidential versions of relevant documents and
- the range of potential fines.

Article 15(1a) of the Implementing Regulation provides that, once proceedings have been initiated, the Commission will disclose that information to the parties: the idea of this 'early disclosure' is that it should enable the parties to make an informed decision on whether or not to settle[137]. Undertakings can call upon the Hearing Officer at any point during the procedure, whose duty is to ensure that the effective exercise of the rights of defence is respected[138].

Parties opting for the settlement procedure must make a formal request in the form of a settlement submission[139]. The Commission will set a time limit of at least 15 working days for an undertaking to produce a 'settlement submission'[140]. After receipt of a settlement submission the Commission will send the parties a streamlined statement of objections (much shorter than in a fully contentious case); this takes into account the views of the parties, as contained in their submission[141]. The Commission expects the parties to reply, within a period of not less than two weeks, simply confirming that the statement of objections corresponds to their submissions and that they remain committed to the settlement procedure[142]. The Commission may decide not to accept the parties' settlement submission, in which case it could issue a statement of objections in accordance with the standard procedure[143]. If the parties fail to produce a settlement submission the case will continue under the standard investigative procedure[144].

Assuming that the case does proceed to a settlement, the parties will not seek an oral hearing; nor will they request access to the file after receiving the statement of objections: these are examples of the procedural efficiencies that lead to quicker decisions[145]. As already noted, paragraph 32 of the *Settlements Notice* states that the fine imposed by the Commission will be reduced by 10% from what it would otherwise have been; the 10% reduction will be made to the amount of the fine after the 10% cap on the maximum fine payable has been applied[146], and any increase for deterrence will not exceed a multiplication of two[147].

Paragraphs 35 to 40 of the *Settlements Notice* deal with the disclosure of settlement submissions to other parties to the alleged cartel, complainants, NCAs and national courts, and adopt a predominantly cautious approach[148]. Paragraph 41 of the *Settlement Notice* acknowledges the fact that all final decisions taken by the Commission under Regulation 1/2003 can be appealed to the General Court and, on a point of law, to the Court of Justice. The settlement decision in *Paper envelopes* was annulled by the General Court, because the Commission failed to explain the basis on which it had determined the level of the fine

137 Ibid, para 16. 138 Ibid, para 18.

139 See para 20 of the *Settlements Notice* which specifies the content of a settlement submission; note that Article 6(6) of the Damages Directive, OJ [2014] L 349/1, provides that Member States must ensure that, for the purpose of actions for damages, national courts cannot at any time order disclosure of a settlement submission.

140 Article 10a(2), final subparagraph, of Regulation 773/2004 and para 17 of the *Settlements Notice*.

141 *Settlements Notice*, para 25.

142 Article 10a(3) of Regulation 773/2004 and para 26 of the *Settlements Notice*.

143 *Settlements Notice*, para 27.

144 Ibid, para 19; on the standard procedure see 'A typical case', p 296 later in chapter.

145 Settlements Notice, para 28. 146 On this cap see 'Article 23: fines', pp 285–286 later in chapter.

147 On the uplift of fines for deterrence see 'Basic amount of the fine', p 287 later in chapter.

148 See also Article 6(1) of Regulation 773/2004 which provides that a complainant does not have a right to receive a non-confidential version of the statement of objections in a settlement case, but only written information about the nature and subject-matter of the procedure.

on Printeos[149]; there was no criticism of the settlement procedure itself in this case. The Commission subsequently re-adopted its decision against Printeos[150].

(d) Settlement procedure in practice

The settlement procedure is now well established. The first decision, *DRAM*, was adopted in 2010[151]. In the years that followed the number of settlement decisions increased; in 2014 eight of the Commission's ten decisions in cartel cases were settlements. By 8 December 2017 there had been 25 settlement decisions; about 50% of cartel cases are settled.

In most of the settlement decisions the Commission settled with all the participants in the cartel, a 'total' settlement; however in six cases the settlements were 'hybrid' in that some parties did not settle. In *Animal Feed Phosphates* the Commission adopted a settlement decision and a contentious decision on the same day, a 'parallel hybrid' case[152]. In a few decisions, for example *Steel abrasives*[153] and *Canned mushrooms*[154], the settlements were 'staggered hybrid' ones, in that the contentious decision was adopted a considerable time after the settlement decision. The same occurred in *Euro interest rate derivatives*[155] and in *Yen interest rate derivatives*[156]. In *Yen interest rate derivatives* several banks settled with the Commission in December 2013 but Icap, a broker, declined to do so and a contentious decision was taken against it in February 2015[157]. Icap appealed to the General Court, which held that there had been a breach of the principle of the presumption of innocence in the case of Icap, and that in the future the Commission might avoid this problem by adopting decisions on the same date in hybrid cases, as it did in *Animal Feed Phosphates*[158].

An unusual feature of the settlement decision in *Trucks* was that the settlement took place *after* the Commission had sent a statement of objections, the only occasion on which this has happened[159]; such cases are expected to be rare, given that the system was intended to conserve the Commission's resources, including the production of an extensive statement of objections.

(D) **Chapter IV: cooperation**

Recital 15 of Regulation 1/2003 states that the Commission and the NCAs should form a 'network of public authorities'[160]. The network is known as the European Competition Network; its composition and operation in practice are described in section 3 later[161].

[149] Case T-95/15 *Printeos v Commission* EU:T:2016:722; the appeal in Case T-98/14 *Société Générale v Commission* was withdrawn when the Commission reduced the fine imposed by the *EURIBOR* settlement decision of 4 December 2013 from €445 million to €227 million after Société Générale had corrected its value of sales figures.

[150] Commission decision of 16 June 2017, on appeal Case T-466/17 Printeos SA v Commission, not yet decided.

[151] Commission decision of 19 May 2010.

[152] Commission decisions of 20 July 2010; Timab, the non-settling undertaking, unsuccessfully appealed against its decision in Case T-456/10 *Timab Industries and CFPR v Commission* EU:T:2015:296, upheld on appeal to the Court of Justice Case C-411/15 P *Timab Industries v Commission* EU:C:2017:11.

[153] Commission decision of 2 April 2014, on appeal Case T-433/16 *Pometon v Commission*, not yet decided.

[154] Commission decision of 25 June 2014.

[155] Commission decisions of 4 December 2013 and 7 December 2016; the latter decision was addressed to three banks that refused to settle and is on appeal Cases T-105/17 etc *HSBC Holdings plc v Commission*, not yet decided.

[156] Commission decision of 4 December 2013.

[157] Commission decision of 4 February 2015.

[158] Case T-180/15 *Icap plc v Commission* EU:T:2017:795, para 268.

[159] Commission decision of 19 July 2016 imposing fines of €2.93 billion; one undertaking, Scania, did not settle this case and the Commission imposed a fine on it of €880 million on 27 September 2017; Scania has appealed to the General Court in Case T-799/17 *Scania AB v Commission*, not yet decided.

[160] See ch 3 of DG COMP's *Manual of Procedures* on cooperation with the NCAs and on the exchange of information within the ECN.

[161] See 'Case allocation under Regulation 1/2003', p 299 later in chapter.

The members of the ECN are linked by a secure Intranet. Recital 21 adds that cooperation between the Commission and the national courts is also necessary, and recital 22 stresses the need for uniform application of the competition rules on the part of the Commission, NCAs and national courts. Articles 11 to 16 of the Regulation contain provisions to promote cooperation between the Commission, NCAs and national courts. The Commission has issued two important notices on cooperation, the *Notice on cooperation within the network of competition authorities* ('the *Notice on NCA cooperation*')[162] and the *Notice on the co-operation between the Commission and courts of the EU Member States in the application of Articles [101 and 102 TFEU]*[163].

(i) Article 11: cooperation between the Commission and the NCAs

Article 11(1) of the Regulation provides that the Commission and the NCAs are to apply the competition rules in close cooperation[164]. Article 11(2) requires the Commission to transmit to NCAs the most important documents it has collected with a view to the adoption of decisions under Articles 7 to 10 (see earlier) or Article 29(1) (see later). Article 11(3) requires NCAs to inform the Commission in writing before or without delay after commencing proceedings under Article 101 or Article 102; this information may also be made available to the NCAs via the intranet. The *Notice on NCA cooperation* explains that the purpose of Article 11(2) and (3) is to ensure that cases can be allocated to a 'well placed' authority[165]. The *Notice* sets out the principles by reference to which a well-placed authority is to be identified[166]. The NCA of the Member State where competition is substantially affected by a possible infringement will be well placed in most cases[167]. The Commission is particularly well placed where conduct has effects in more than three Member States[168].

Article 11(4) and Article 11(6) are of particular importance. Article 11(4) provides that, not later than 30 days before adopting an infringement decision, accepting commitments or withdrawing the benefit of a block exemption, NCAs must inform the Commission: guidance on the application of Article 11(4) will be found in the *Notice on NCA cooperation*[169]. Article 11(6) provides that the initiation by the Commission of proceedings shall relieve NCAs of their competence to apply Articles 101 and 102[170]; the *Notice* provides guidance on how this provision is to be applied in practice[171]. Article 11(4) and (6) are central to the functioning of Regulation 1/2003 and mean that the Commission can halt the proceedings of an NCA and take a case over itself. The *Notice on NCA cooperation* explains the limited range of circumstances in which the Commission is likely to make

[162] OJ [2004] C 101/43; note that this *Notice* is subject to periodic review by the Commission and the NCAs: ibid, para 70.

[163] OJ [2004] C 101/54; this *Notice* is discussed in ch 8, 'The relationship between the Commission and domestic courts', pp 316–320.

[164] See Wils 'The EU Network of Competition Authorities, the European Convention on Human Rights and the Charter of Fundamental Rights of the EU' in Ehlermann and Atanasiu (eds) *European Competition Law Annual 2002: Constructing the EU Network of Competition Authorities* (Hart, 2003), pp 433–464; Brammer 'Concurrent Jurisdiction under Regulation 1/2003 and the Issue of Case Allocation' (2005) 42 CML Rev 1383; Andreangeli 'The Impact of the Modernisation Regulation on the Guarantees of Due Process in Competition Proceedings' (2006) 31 EL Rev 342; Brammer *Co-operation Between National Competition Agencies in the Enforcement of EC Competition Law* (Hart, 2009).

[165] OJ [2004] C 101/43, paras 16 and 17. [166] Ibid, paras 5–15. [167] Ibid, para 9.

[168] Ibid, para 14. [169] Ibid, paras 43–49.

[170] Article 11(6) of the Regulation requires that, if an NCA is already acting on a case, the Commission shall initiate proceedings only following consultation.

[171] OJ [2004] C 101/43, paras 50–57.

use of Article 11(6)[172]. The power to terminate the proceedings of an NCA had not been exercised in any case as at 8 December 2017[173].

Article 11(5) provides that NCAs may consult with the Commission on any case involving the application of EU competition law.

(ii) **Article 12: exchange of information**

(a) Free movement of information

Article 12 of the Regulation provides for the exchange of information between the Commission and NCAs. It must be read in conjunction with Article 28 which contains provisions restricting the use or disclosure of information covered by an obligation of professional secrecy[174]. The Commission's view is that Article 12 is a key element in the proper functioning of the ECN and a precondition to the efficient and effective allocation of cases[175]. Article 12(1) provides that the Commission and NCAs have the power to provide one another with and use in evidence any matter of fact or law, including confidential information: the exchange of information can take place both between the Commission and the NCAs and also between NCAs[176]. Article 12(2), however, states that information exchanged can be used only for the purpose of applying Articles 101 and 102 and in respect of the subject-matter for which it was collected; an exception to this is that an NCA can use information received in order to apply its domestic law, where the same case involves the parallel application of Article 101 or Article 102 and the outcome would be the same under both systems of law[177]. Article 12 does not apply to information sent to the Commission by national authorities other than NCAs[178].

(b) Restrictions on the use of information

In some Member States natural persons can be the subject of fines, or even terms of imprisonment: this is true, for example, where the 'cartel offence' is committed under the Enterprise Act 2002 in the UK[179]. There are restrictions on the use of information exchanged between competition authorities in these circumstances[180]. The first indent of Article 12(3) provides that information exchanged pursuant to Article 12(1) can be used in evidence to impose sanctions on natural persons only where the law of the transmitting authority foresees sanctions of a similar kind in relation to an infringement of Article 101 or Article 102; this means, for example, that if the law of both the transmitting and the receiving authority were to provide for terms of imprisonment to be imposed, the information exchanged could be used as evidence in a criminal case leading to imprisonment. The second indent of Article 12(3) provides that, where it is not the case that the law of the transmitting authority foresees sanctions of the same kind as the law of the receiving authority, the information can be used by the latter only where it has been collected by the former in a way which respects the same level of protection of the rights of defence of natural persons as provided for under the national rules of the receiving authority; however in this case the information cannot be used to impose custodial sentences at all, but only for other sanctions such as fines.

172 Ibid, para 54.

173 See Commission Staff Working Document *Ten Years of Antitrust Enforcement under Regulation 1/2003*, SWD (2014) 230, para 242.

174 See 'Article 28: professional secrecy', p 297 later in chapter.

175 *Notice on NCA cooperation*, para 26.

176 Ibid, para 27.

177 Note that it follows from this wording that information could not be exchanged for the purpose of applying stricter national law on unilateral behaviour, as to which see ch 2, 'Conflicts: Article 102', p 78.

178 Case C-469/15 P *FSL Holdings v Commission* EU:C:2017:308, para 35.

179 See ch 10, 'The cartel offence', pp 437–446.

180 See the *Notice on NCA cooperation*, para 28(c).

(c) *The exchange of information with third countries*

Article 12 does not discuss the issue of information exchange between the European Commission and institutions outside the EU. To some extent this is dealt with in cooperation agreements entered into, for example, with the US, Canada, Japan and Switzerland[181]. An attempt by AMD, a claimant in proceedings brought in the US, to obtain an order from a court there against Intel requiring it to produce information about alleged violations of EU competition law being investigated by the European Commission failed in *AMD Inc v Intel Corporation*[182]; the Commission indicated in an *amicus curiae* brief to the US court that it did not want it to make such an order.

(iii) **Article 13: suspension or termination of proceedings**

Article 13 contains provisions to avoid the duplication of investigations; the *Notice on NCA cooperation* provides additional guidance[183]. Article 13(1) provides that, where an NCA is dealing with a case, this is a sufficient ground for another NCA or the Commission to suspend proceedings or to reject a complaint; however there is no obligation to do so[184], thereby leaving the NCAs with some discretion as to whether to proceed or not[185]. In *Si.mobil telekomunikacijske storitve d.d. v Commission*[186] the General Court held that the Commission was entitled by Article 13(1) to refuse to deal with a complaint by Si.mobil that it was the victim of abusive behaviour contrary to Article 102 on the basis that the Slovenian NCA was dealing with the case. Article 13(2) states that an NCA or the Commission may reject a complaint that has already been dealt with by another competition authority. In *easyJet Airline Co Ltd v Commission*[187] the General Court upheld the right of the Commission to reject a complaint that, in its view, had already been dealt with by the Dutch NCA. The General Court reached the same conclusion in *VIMC v Commission*[188] in relation to a decision of the Commission that had rejected a complaint on the basis that it was being dealt with by the Austrian NCA. Recital 18 of the Regulation adds that the provisions of Article 13 are without prejudice to the right of the Commission to reject a complaint due to lack of EU interest[189].

(iv) **Article 14: Advisory Committee**

Article 14(1) of the Regulation requires the Commission to consult with the Advisory Committee on Restrictive Practices and Dominant Positions when taking key decisions, such as findings of an infringement or the imposition of a fine[190]. Article 14(2) deals with the constitution of the Advisory Committee. Article 14(3) and (4) explain the consultation procedure, which may take place at a meeting or in writing. Article 14(5) requires the Commission to take the 'utmost account' of the Advisory Committee's opinion. Article 14(7) provides that cases being decided by an NCA may be discussed at the Advisory Committee, and that an NCA may request that the Advisory Committee should be consulted when the Commission is contemplating the initiation of proceedings under Article 11(6).

[181] See ch 12, 'The EU's dedicated cooperation agreements on competition policy', pp 517–519.

[182] Order of 4 October 2004: see also the earlier judgment of the US Supreme Court in *Intel Corporation v Advanced Micro Devices* 542 US 241 (2004); an attempt to obtain the confidential version of the Commission decision of 8 December 2010 in *LCD* failed, *In re Cathode Ray Tube Antitrust Litigation*, judgment of 20 November 2014.

[183] OJ [2004] C 101/43, paras 20–25.

[184] See Case C-17/10 *Toshiba Corp v Úřad pro ochranu hospodářské soutěže* EU:C:2012:72.

[185] OJ [2004] C 101/43, para 22.

[186] Case T-201/11 EU:T:2014:1096.

[187] Case T-355/13 EU:T:2015:36.

[188] Case T-431/16 EU:T:2017:755.

[189] See 'The position of complainants', pp 296–297 later in chapter.

[190] See *Notice on NCA cooperation*, paras 58–68.

(v) Article 15: cooperation with national courts

Article 15 deals with cooperation with national courts: this is discussed in chapter 8[191].

(vi) Article 16: uniform application of EU competition law

Article 16 of the Regulation deals with the effect of Commission decisions on national courts (Article 16(1)) and NCAs (Article 16(2)). The position of national courts is discussed in chapter 8[192]. Article 16(2) provides that NCAs cannot take decisions which would run counter to a decision adopted by the Commission.

(E) Chapter V: powers of investigation

Chapter V of the Regulation gives the Commission various powers of investigation: of particular importance are Article 18, which enables it to request information, and Articles 20 and 21, which enable it to conduct inspections, even of an individual's home.

(i) Article 17: investigations into sectors of the economy and into types of agreements

Article 17(1) enables the Commission to conduct an investigation into a sector of the economy or a type of agreement where it appears that there may be a restriction or distortion of competition, for example because of the lack of new entrants into a market or the rigidity of prices[193]. Article 17(2) gives the Commission the power to request information and to conduct inspections of business (not residential) premises for the purpose of conducting a sectoral investigation. The third indent of Article 17(1) states that the Commission may publish a report on the results of its inquiry and invite comments from interested parties. The Commission does not have any remedial powers following such a sectoral investigation[194]. The European Commission conducts a sectoral investigation under Article 17 in order to obtain a better understanding of the competition conditions within a sector, and decides at the end of the process what should happen next.

The most recent investigation under Article 17 was into *E-commerce*[195]; the inquiry lasted two years. Full information about market investigations, including the reports themselves, can be obtained from DG COMP's website[196].

(ii) Article 18: requests for information

(a) The Commission's powers

Article 18 of Regulation 1/2003 enables the Commission, in order to carry out its duties under the Regulation, to require 'all necessary information'[197]; Article 18(1) of Regulation

[191] See ch 8, 'The relationship between the Commission and domestic courts', pp 316–320. [192] Ibid.

[193] A similar power had existed in Article 12 of Regulation 17, although it was not used on many occasions; the last investigation under Article 12 was *Sports content over third generation mobile networks*, Commission Report of 21 September 2005, available at www.ec.europa.eu.

[194] In this respect sectoral inquiries are like a CMA market study in the UK, on which see ch 11, 'Market Studies', pp 465–469; but not like a market investigation reference under the Enterprise Act 2002, where the CMA does have remedial powers: on market investigations see ch 11, 'Market Investigation References', pp 469–481.

[195] *Final report on the E-commerce sector*, 10 May 2017, COM(2017) 229 final, available at www.ec.europa.eu.

[196] See www.ec.europa.eu/comm/competition/antitrust/sector_inquiries.html.

[197] Information for this purpose includes documents: Case 374/87 *Orkem v Commission* EU:C:1989:387, paras 13–14; Case 27/88 *Solvay & Cie v Commission* EU:C:1989:388, paras 13–14; on the meaning of 'necessary information' see Case C-36/92 P *SEP v Commission* EU:C:1994:205; see also Case T-46/92 *Scottish Football Association v Commission* EU:T:1994:267.

1/2003 provides that the Commission may simply request information, or may require it by decision[198].

Article 18(2) deals with simple requests: the Commission must state the legal basis and the purpose of the request, specify what information is required and fix the time limit within which it is to be provided; it must also explain the penalties in Article 23 of the Regulation for supplying incorrect or misleading information[199]. There is no obligation to comply with a simple request. However, undertakings must respond to a Commission decision requiring information that it considers to be 'necessary' for the detection of a possible infringement of the competition rules[200]: Article 18(3) says that, where the Commission requires information by decision, it must also explain that a penalty can be imposed under Article 23 for not supplying the information at all, and that the undertaking required to provide the information may seek a judicial review of the decision by the General Court. The fact that an undertaking considers that the Commission has no grounds for action under Article 101 does not entitle it to resist a request for information[201]. In *Slovak Telekom v Commission*[202] the General Court held that Article 18(3) entitled the Commission to request information that predated the Slovak Republic's accession to the EU where it might be relevant to an infringement committed after accession[203]. However the Commission would not be entitled to request information for a purpose other than the enforcement of the competition rules, and in exercising its discretion under Article 18 it must have regard to the principle of proportionality[204]. In March 2016 the Court of Justice annulled decisions of the Commission requesting information from a number of undertakings in the cement sector[205]; in particular the Court considered that the Commission's statement of reasons for the decisions were brief, vague and generic and did not make it possible to determine with sufficient precision either the products to which the investigation related or the suspicions of infringement justifying the adoption of the decisions.

Article 18(4) explains who should provide the information: authorised lawyers can supply information on behalf of a client, although the client remains responsible for incomplete, incorrect or misleading information. Article 18(5) requires the Commission to inform NCAs in the relevant Member State of information required of undertakings by decision, and Article 18(6) provides that the Commission can request information from governments and NCAs.

Quite often the Commission will request information under Article 18 *after* it has carried out an on-the-spot investigation under Article 20 or 21[206], for example because it needs to check particular points that have arisen out of the inspection or to pursue certain matters further.

The issue arises under Article 18 (and also where the Commission conducts an inspection under Article 20 or Article 21) of whether it is possible to resist answering questions or providing information on the basis that this would be self-incriminating, or that the

198 See ch 6 of DG COMP's *Manual of Procedures* on requests for information.

199 Penalties were imposed on a number of occasions for the provision of misleading information under Article 11 of Regulation 17: see eg *Telos* OJ [1982] L 58/19; *National Panasonic (Belgium) NV* OJ [1982] L 113/18; *National Panasonic (France) SA* OJ [1982] L 211/32; *Comptoir Commercial d'Importation* OJ [1982] L 27/31; *Peugeot* OJ [1986] L 295/19; *Anheuser-Busch Incorporated/Scottish & Newcastle* OJ [2000] L 49/37.

200 See recital 23 of Regulation 1/2003.

201 See eg *Fire Insurance* OJ [1982] L 80/36 and *Deutsche Castrol* OJ [1983] L 114/26.

202 Cases T-458/09 etc EU:T:2012:145.

203 Ibid, paras 45–52.

204 Case C-36/92 P *SEP v Commission* EU:C:1994:205.

205 See eg Case C-247/14 P *HeidelbergCement AG v Commission* EU:C:2016:149; the Court of Justice published a helpful Press Release 20/76 of 10 March 2016, summarising the other judgments in this case.

206 See 'Article 21: the Commission's powers of inspection', pp 281–284 later in chapter.

information sought is protected by legal professional privilege. Recital 23 of Regulation 1/2003 (in acknowledgement of the case law discussed later) states that undertakings, when complying with a decision requesting information, cannot be forced to admit that they have committed an infringement; however it adds that they are obliged to answer factual questions and to provide documents, even if this information may be used to establish an infringement against them or another undertaking. The Regulation is silent on the issue of legal professional privilege. There was case law of the EU Courts on both types of privilege under Regulation 17, and it will continue to apply under Regulation 1/2003.

(b) Privilege against self-incrimination

In the *Orkem* and *Solvay* cases[207] the Court of Justice considered whether undertakings could refuse to answer certain questions in a Commission request for information on the basis that to do so would be self-incriminating. The Court of Justice's conclusion was that there is a limited privilege against self-incrimination in EU law, which entitles undertakings to refuse to answer questions that would require them to admit to the very infringement the Commission is seeking to establish; however this privilege does not entitle them to refuse to hand over documents to the Commission which might serve to establish an infringement by the undertaking concerned or by another one. It is presumably the case that the same doctrine applies in the case of inspections under Articles 20 and 21. The Court of Justice has held that privilege against self-incrimination can be claimed only where the Commission requires information under compulsion, that is to say in an Article 18(3) case; privilege does not attach to information provided in response to a mere request under Article 18(2)[208].

In *Mannesmann-Röhrenwerke AG v Commission*[209] the General Court held that there is no absolute right to silence in competition proceedings[210], except in so far as a compulsion to provide answers would involve an admission of the existence of an infringement[211]; in the Court's view certain questions asked by the Commission did go beyond what it was entitled to ask[212]. Judgments of the European Court of Human Rights[213] have recognised a right to remain silent in criminal cases involving natural persons, but it seems after the *Mannesmann* judgment that EU law will not extend privilege this far in relation to cases under Articles 101 and 102.

In *Commission v SGL Carbon AG*[214] the Court of Justice held that undertakings are required to produce documents in their possession, even if those documents can be used to establish the existence of an infringement: privilege against self-incrimination applies only where the Commission requires answers to questions addressed to undertakings under investigation[215].

207 Case 374/87 *Orkem v Commission* EU:C:1989:387; Case 27/88 *Solvay & Cie v Commission* EU:C:1989:388; Case T-34/93 *Société Générale v Commission* EU:T:1995:46, paras 72–74; as to privilege against self-incrimination in domestic courts see Case C-60/92 *Otto v Postbank* EU:C:1993:876; on self-incrimination generally see Wils 'Self-Incrimination in EC Antitrust Enforcement: A Legal and Economic Analysis' (2003) 26 World Competition 566; Vesterdorf 'Legal Professional Privilege and the Privilege against Self-Incrimination in EC Law: Recent Developments and Current Issues' in [2004] Fordham Corporate Law Institute (ed Hawk), 701; MacCulloch 'The Privilege Against Self-Incrimination in Competition Investigations: Theoretical Foundations and Practical Implications' (2006) 26 Legal Studies 211.

208 Case C-407/04 P *Dalmine v Commission* EU:C:2007:53, paras 33–36.

209 Case T-112/98 EU:T:2001:61. 210 Ibid, para 66. 211 Ibid, para 67.

212 Ibid, paras 69–74.

213 See eg *Funke v France* [1993] 1 CMLR 897; *Saunders v United Kingdom* (1996) 23 EHRR 313; *O'Halloran v United Kingdom* (2008) 46 EHRR 397.

214 Case C-301/04 P EU:C:2006:432. 215 Ibid, paras 33–51.

(c) Legal professional privilege

That some documents are covered by legal professional privilege under EU law was established by the Court of Justice in *AM & S Europe Ltd v Commission*[216], where certain papers had been withheld from Commission officials during an inspection; the same principle must surely apply to a request for information under Article 18[217]. The *AM & S* case dealt with two issues: first, whether there is a doctrine of privilege in EU law; secondly, if there is one, what mechanism should be adopted to ascertain whether any particular document is privileged. On the first question the Court held that some, but not all, correspondence between a client and an independent lawyer based in the EU (and now the European Economic Area ('the EEA')) was privileged, but that dealings with an in-house lawyer or with a lawyer in a third country were not. The limitation of privilege to correspondence with EU and EEA lawyers is overtly discriminatory; at one point the Commission intended to try to persuade the Council to rectify this[218], but it is understood that it subsequently dropped the idea. Privilege mainly extends to correspondence relating to the defence of a client after the initiation of proceedings by the Commission, although it also applies to correspondence before the initiation of proceedings though intimately linked with their subject-matter. The privilege belongs to the client, not the lawyer. Correspondence between an undertaking's external lawyer and a lawyer acting for a third party does not enjoy privilege[219].

The Court of Justice limited privilege to dealings with independent lawyers because in many Member States employed lawyers are not subject to professional codes of discipline. In some Member States, for example the UK, Ireland and the Netherlands, in-house lawyers may remain subject to the rules of the Bar Council or the Law Society, so that it is arguable that this reason for excluding privilege ought not to apply; however the Court of Justice's judgment in *AM & S* was quite clear that there was no privilege in these circumstances[220]. In *John Deere*[221] the Commission relied on written advice by an in-house lawyer to show that an undertaking knew that it was infringing Article 101. However the position was slightly relaxed in *Hilti v Commission*[222], where the General Court held that privilege does extend to an internal memorandum prepared by an in-house lawyer which simply reports what an independent lawyer has said.

The issue of legal professional privilege for advice given by in-house lawyers was litigated again in a case involving Akzo Nobel Chemicals and its subsidiary, Akcros Chemicals, which were under investigation for participation in an alleged cartel in heat stabilisers[223]. In *Akzo Nobel Chemicals Ltd v Commission*[224] the General Court was invited to reconsider the Court of Justice's ruling in *AM & S*, but it very clearly declined to do so[225]. Akzo appealed against the General Court's judgment to the Court of Justice, in particular on the basis that the in-house lawyer in the *Akzo* case was subject to the legal professional rules of the Dutch Bar Council; however the Court still considered that, as an employee

[216] Case 155/79 EU:C:1982:157.

[217] For further reading on this topic see Gippini-Fournier 'Legal Professional Privilege in Competition Proceedings Before the European Commission: Beyond the Cursory Glance' (2005) 28 Fordham International Law Journal 967 and González-Díaz and Stuart 'Legal professional privilege under EU law: current issues' (2017) 3 *Competition Law & Policy Debate* 56.

[218] See the XIIIth *Report on Competition Policy* (1983), point 78.

[219] *Perindopril (Servier)*, Commission Article 20(4) decision of 23 July 2010.

[220] See however the strong argument of AG Slynn to the contrary in the *AM & S* case; note that under s 30 UK Competition Act 1998 communications with in-house lawyers do enjoy privilege: see ch 10, 'Legal professional privilege', pp 407–408.

[221] OJ [1985] L 35/58; see similarly *London European-Sabena* OJ [1988] L 317/47; privilege was unsuccessfully claimed in *VW* OJ [1998] L 124/60, para 199.

[222] Case T-30/89 EU:T:1991:70.

[223] The Commission adopted an infringement decision in relation to this cartel on 11 November 2009.

[224] Cases T-125/03 etc EU:T:2007:287.

[225] Ibid, paras 165–179.

of Akzo, the lawyer lacked independence from his employer and therefore saw no reason to depart from the position that it had taken in the *AM & S* case[226]. The Court rejected a number of other arguments for departing from *AM & S*, including that the status of privilege in the laws of the Member States had evolved to a point that the law should be revised[227].

On the question of how claims to privilege should be adjudicated the Court of Justice in *AM & S* held, in effect, that it (or, now, the General Court) should fulfil this task. This seems cumbersome, but is better than allowing the Commission itself to see the documents: even if a Commission official were to accept that they were privileged, an undertaking would be bound to suspect that he or she had been influenced by what had been seen. It follows that, as a matter of law, what has to happen in the case of a dispute as to privilege is that the Commission must make a formal decision, requiring the documents in question; this decision may then be appealed to the General Court, which will resolve the issue: indeed this is what happened in the *Akzo* case. The Hearing Officers may resolve disputes as to privilege[228].

(iii) Article 19: power to take statements

Regulation 1/2003 confers power on the Commission by Article 19 to interview natural or legal persons, with their consent, for the purpose of collecting information relating to the subject-matter of an investigation[229]. Article 3 of the Implementing Regulation sets out the procedure for conducting voluntary interviews. The Court of Justice has held that the Commission must record in full any interview it holds[230]. NCAs must be informed of interviews within their territory, and have a right to be present. There are no penalties for providing incorrect or misleading information at an interview[231]. The Commission has used the Article 19 procedure regularly in recent years.

(iv) Article 20: the Commission's powers of inspection

An important part of a competition authority's armoury is the ability to conduct a 'dawn raid'—better described as a 'surprise inspection'—on undertakings: those responsible for hard-core cartels, for example, are perfectly aware that what they are doing is illegal, and they may go to great lengths to suppress evidence of their activities. Article 20 of Regulation 1/2003 enables the Commission to conduct inspections of business premises, either by agreement or by surprise; Article 21 allows an inspection of 'other premises', including an individual's home: this had no counterpart in Regulation 17.

Article 20(1) enables the Commission, in order to be able to carry out its duties under the Regulation, to conduct 'all necessary inspections'. Article 20(2) empowers those conducting the inspection:

- to enter premises
- to examine books and other records, including data stored in electronic form, for example on a hard disk, a CD-ROM or a memory stick
- to take or obtain copies or extracts from them: it is sensible to make photocopying facilities available to the inspectors and to make a duplicate set of all items copied for retention by the undertaking that is being investigated

226 Case C-550/07 P *Akzo Nobel Chemicals Ltd v Commission* EU:C:2010:512, paras 40–51.

227 Ibid, paras 69–77.

228 OJ [2011] L 275/29, Article 4(2)(a).

229 See ch 8 of DG COMP's *Manual of Procedures* on the power to conduct voluntary interviews.

230 Case C-413/14 P *Intel v Commission* EU:C:2017:632, paras 90–91.

231 See the Commission Staff Working Paper accompanying the *Report on the functioning of Regulation 1/2003*, SEC(2009) 574 final, para 84.

- to seal premises, books or records to the extent necessary for the inspection: this can be important, for example, where an inspection will go into a second day (or longer, as sometimes happens) and the inspectors wish to ensure that evidence will not be interfered with overnight[232]. The EU Courts upheld the Commission's decision to impose a fine of €38 million on E.ON Energie AG for breaching a seal that had been affixed to premises during an inspection in 2006[233]
- to ask for explanations of facts or documents and to record the answers.

The rules on self-incrimination and legal professional privilege, discussed earlier, apply to inspections. Undertakings may submit to an inspection voluntarily; however they must submit to an inspection ordered by decision under Article 20(4), which may be conducted without prior announcement: the so-called 'dawn raid'. The Commission does not have an obligation to attempt a voluntary inspection prior to a dawn raid[234].

(a) Voluntary investigations

In the case of a voluntary investigation Article 20(3) requires the Commission's officials and other accompanying persons authorised by the Commission (for example a forensic IT specialist, whose function is to search computer records, emails and other electronic media) to produce an authorisation in writing; it must specify the subject-matter and purpose of the investigation and the penalties which may be imposed for incomplete production of the required books and business records or the provision of incorrect or misleading information. NCAs must be informed of inspections in their territory. The Commission held (in decisions under Regulation 17) that a firm being investigated is under a positive duty to assist the Commission's officials in finding the information they want: it is not sufficient simply to grant them unlimited access to all the filing cabinets or the IT system[235]; this has been confirmed in the case law of the EU Courts[236].

(b) Mandatory investigations

The Commission may adopt a decision under Article 20(4) requiring an undertaking to submit to an inspection[237]. The Court of Justice held in *Dow Chemical Ibérica v Commission*[238] that the Commission does not require prior judicial authorisation in order to conduct an inspection. In 2015 the Court of Justice in *Deutsche Bahn AG v Commission*[239] held that this remains the case, notwithstanding Article 7 of the Charter of Fundamental Rights and Article 8 of the ECHR which enshrine the inviolability of

[232] Recital 25 of Regulation 1/2003 states that seals should not normally be affixed for more than 72 hours.

[233] Commission decision of 30 January 2008, upheld on appeal Case T-141/08 *E.ON Energie v Commission* EU:T:2010:516 and on further appeal Case C-89/11 P EU:C:2012:738; in 2011 a fine of €8 million was imposed for the same reason on Suez Environnement: see Commission Press Release IP/11/632, 24 May 2011; see also the Dutch NCA decision of 20 October 2008 imposing a fine of €269,000 on Sara Lee for breaching seals affixed to a door during an inspection, available at www.acm.nl/en.

[234] Case 136/79 *National Panasonic (UK) Ltd v Commission* EU:C:1980:169, paras 8–16.

[235] See *Fabbrica Pisana* OJ [1980] L 75/30 and *Pietro Sciarra* OJ [1980] L 75/35; the same would be true of an investigation under Article 20(4).

[236] See eg Case C-301/04 P *Commission v SGL Carbon* EU:C:2006:432, para 40.

[237] See *Explanatory note to an authorisation to conduct an inspection in execution of a Commission decision under Article 20(4) of Council Regulation No 1/2003*, as well as a sample *Authorisation to conduct an inspection*, both available at www.ec.europa.eu/competition; note that the *Explanatory note* was revised on 11 September 2015.

[238] Cases 97/87 etc EU:C:1989:380; the case was concerned with Article 14(3) of Regulation 17, the predecessor of Article 20(4) of Regulation 1/2003.

[239] Case C-583/13 P EU:C:2015:404, paras 18–37.

private premises and the development of the case law of the European Court of Human Rights on this topic[240].

The Commission's decision must indicate the subject-matter and purpose of the inspection so that the undertaking to be inspected understands the scope of its duty to cooperate[241]; it may search only for documents within the scope of that decision[242]. The inspection decision can be reviewed by the General Court[243]; however the Commission cannot be expected to define precisely the relevant market or the alleged infringement: an inspection takes place at the beginning of an investigation when the Commission is still gathering evidence to determine whether there has been an infringement[244]. Similarly, the Commission cannot be expected to determine whether the suspected conduct should be categorised as acts of undertakings or of associations of undertakings[245]. The Commission must consult with the relevant NCA before carrying out such an inspection in its territory, but this can be done in an informal manner, by telephone if necessary[246]. The General Court has confirmed that there is no right to the presence of an external lawyer at an inspection[247]. The Commission has said that it will allow the undertaking to consult a lawyer; however it will accept only a short delay for consultation with the lawyer before beginning the inspection[248]. The Commission's decision must explain the penalties for non-compliance with the decision ordering the inspection, and that the decision can be reviewed by the General Court[249]. The Commission imposed fines on several occasions for non-compliance under Regulation 17[250], and it did so under Regulation 1/2003 in *EPH*[251]. Surprise inspections may take place in a number of jurisdictions—not just within the EU—as a result of coordination between different competition authorities[252].

Quite apart from these penalties the Commission has sometimes regarded a lack of cooperation during an inspection as an aggravating factor when it comes to determining the level of the fine for the substantive infringement of Article 101 and/or 102. In *Dutch bitumen*[253] the fine on KWS was increased by 10% because it refused to allow the Commission officials access to the premises and in *Professional videotapes* the fine on

[240] The European Court of Human Rights has held that a dawn raid conducted by the French competition authority did not violate the ECHR: *Janssen Cilag SAS v France*, no 33931/12, judgment of 13 April 2017; the Irish Supreme Court found there to be a violation of Article 8 of the ECHR in *CHR plc v Competition and Consumer Protection Commission* [2017] IESC 34.

[241] Case C-37/13 P *Nexans SA v Commission* EU:C:2014:2030, para 34.

[242] Case C-583/13 P *Deutsche Bahn AG v Commission* EU:C:2015:404, paras 54–69.

[243] As at 8 December 2017, several inspections decisions were on appeal to the General Court: eg Case T-621/16 *České dráhy v Commission*, not yet decided and Case T-249/17 *Casino, Guichard-Perrachon and EMC Distribution v Commission*, not yet decided; see also Case T-54/14 Goldfish BV v Commission EU:T:2016:455.

[244] Case C-37/13 P *Nexans SA v Commission* EU:C:2014:2030, paras 36–37; see also Case C-402/13 *Orange v Commission* EU:C:2014:991, paras 81–84.

[245] Case T-23/09 *CNOP v Commission* EU:T:2010:452, para 41.

[246] Case 5/85 *AKZO Chemie BV v Commission* EU:C:1986:328, para 24.

[247] Case T-357/06 *Koninklijke Wegenbouw Stevin v Commission* EU:T:2012:488, paras 232–233.

[248] *Explanatory note*, para 6.

[249] Such an appeal was dismissed in Case T-23/09 *CNOP and CCG v Commission* EU:T:2010:452.

[250] See eg *CSM NV* (€3,000); *Ukwal* OJ [1992] L 121/45 (€5,000); *Mewac* OJ [1993] L 20/6 (€4,000); *AKZO* OJ [1994] L 294/31 (€5,000).

[251] Commission decision of 28 March 2012 (refusal to submit to an inspection by failing to block an email account and diverting incoming emails), upheld on appeal Case T-272/12 *Energetický a průmyslový and EP Investment Advisors v Commission* EU:T:2014:995.

[252] See Commission MEMO/03/33, 13 February 2003, noting simultaneous inspections in the EU, US, Japan and Canada in relation to the *Heat Stabilisers* cartel.

[253] Commission decision of 13 September 2006, paras 340–341, upheld on appeal Cases T-357/06 etc *Koninklijke Wegenbouw Stevin v Commission* EU:T:2012:488, paras 209–256.

Sony was increased by 30% because one of its employees refused to answer questions during an inspection and another shredded documents during it[254].

(c) The involvement of Member States

Article 20(5) of Regulation 1/2003 provides that officials of NCAs shall, at the request of the Commission, actively assist its officials with their inspections[255]. Where an undertaking refuses to submit to an inspection, Article 20(6) requires the Member State concerned to afford the Commission the necessary assistance to enable the inspection to take place: this may require the involvement of the police or an equivalent enforcement authority. The Commission itself is not entitled to use force to enter premises[256]. Article 20(7) states that, if judicial authorisation is required, for example to obtain entry to premises, this must be applied for. Article 20(8), which gives expression to the judgment of the Court of Justice in *Roquette Frères SA v Commission*[257], sets out the role of the judicial authority in circumstances where it is asked, for example, to issue a warrant ordering entry into premises. The court should ensure that the Commission's decision is authentic and that the coercive measures sought are neither arbitrary nor excessive; for this purpose the court may address questions to the Commission. However the court may not call into question the necessity for the inspection, nor demand that it be provided with all the information in the Commission's file.

(v) Article 21: inspection of other premises

Recital 26 of Regulation 1/2003 states that experience has shown that there are cases where business records are kept in people's homes, and that therefore it should be possible, subject to judicial authorisation, to conduct inspections there. The *SAS/Maersk Air*[258] decision provides an example of this, where important documents relating to a market-sharing agreement were kept in individuals' homes. Article 21 therefore confers a power on the Commission to inspect 'other premises', which can include homes; Article 21(3) requires prior authorisation by a court. This power has been exercised rarely, but in principle it seems correct that the Commission should be able to conduct such inspections where it has reason to believe that the individuals responsible for cartels (or, less likely, abusive practices) are keeping relevant information at home[259].

(vi) Article 22: investigations by NCAs

Article 22(1) of Regulation 1/2003 enables an NCA to conduct an inspection in its territory on behalf of an NCA in another Member State[260]. Article 22(2) provides that NCAs shall carry out inspections which the Commission considers to be necessary under Article 20(1) or Article 20(4)[261]. This power had been used in two cases by 8 December 2017[262].

254 Commission Press Release IP/07/1724, 20 November 2007.

255 On the position in the UK see ch 10, 'EU investigations', p 411.

256 See para 82 of AG Kokott's Opinion in Case C-550/07 P *Akzo Nobel Chemicals and Akcros Chemicals v Commission* EU:C:2010:229.

257 Case C-94/00 EU:C:2002:603.

258 OJ [2001] L 265/15, paras 7, 89 and 123.

259 See Commission Staff Working Paper accompanying the *Report on the functioning of Regulation 1/2003*, SEC(2009) 574 final, para 75; Commission Staff Working Document, *Ten Years of Antitrust Enforcement under Regulation 1/2003*, SWD (2014) 230, para 204.

260 A striking example of this occurred when the UK competition authority conducted an inspection in the UK on behalf of the French competition authority investigating a complaint about behaviour in Réunion in the Indian Ocean.

261 On the position in the UK see ch 10, 'EU investigations', p 411.

262 See Commission Staff Working Document, *Ten Years of Antitrust Enforcement under Regulation 1/2003*, SWD (2014) 230, para 206.

(F) Chapter VI: penalties

Articles 23 and 24 provide for fines and periodic penalty payments. The Commission cannot impose fines on individuals, except in so far as an individual acts as an undertaking[263], nor can it sentence them to terms of imprisonment. Some Member States, including the UK, do have powers to impose sanctions on individuals[264].

(i) Article 23: fines

Article 23 enables fines to be imposed on undertakings both for procedural and for substantive infringements[265]. The General Court has confirmed that Article 23 provides a 'proper legal basis' for the imposition of penalties in accordance with Article 49 of the Charter of Fundamental Rights[266]. Procedural fines can be imposed under Article 23(1) on undertakings that commit offences in relation to requests for information or inspections under Article 17, 18 or 20 of the Regulation (fines cannot be imposed on individuals whose homes are inspected under Article 21). A typical infringement would be the supply of incorrect or misleading information, or the refusal by an undertaking to submit to an inspection.

Article 23(2) provides for very substantial fines to be imposed where undertakings infringe Articles 101 and 102 TFEU, where they contravene an interim measures decision made under Article 8 of the Regulation, or where they fail to comply with a commitment made binding by a decision under Article 9. In these cases the maximum fine that can be imposed is 10% of an undertaking's worldwide turnover in the preceding business year[267]: clearly this can be an enormous amount, in particular since it is not limited to turnover in the market affected by the infringement, nor to turnover within the EU. Decisions can be found where the Commission has had to limit fines because the 10% worldwide turnover limit had been attained[268]; Figure 1.11 of the Commission's Cartel Statistics shows that from 2011 to 2017 the fines on 24 of the 401 undertakings punished for infringing Article 101 represented 9 to 10% of their worldwide turnover[269].

In fixing the level of a fine, the Commission is required by Article 23(3) to have regard to the gravity and to the duration of the infringement. Where a fine is imposed on a trade association Article 23(4) provides that, if the association is insolvent, the association must call for contributions from its members to cover the fine; in case of default the

[263] See ch 3, 'Regardless of the legal status of the entity and the way in which it is financed', pp 86–87; the Commission has never imposed a fine on an individual, although in *French beef* it imposed fines on trade unions representing individual farmers: OJ [2003] L 209/12, upheld on appeal Cases T-217/03 etc *FNCBV v Commission* EU:T:2006:391 and on further appeal, Cases C-101/07 P and C-110/07 P *Coop de France bétail and viande v Commission* EU:C:2008:741.

[264] See ch 10, 'The cartel offence', pp 437–446.

[265] The periodical literature includes Wils 'The European Commission's 2006 Guidelines on Antitrust Fines: A Legal and Economic Analysis' (2007) 30 World Competition 197; Motta 'On Cartel Deterrence and Fines in the European Union' (2008) 29 ECLR 209; Vesterdorf 'The Court of Justice and Unlimited Jurisdiction: What Does It Mean in Practice?' (2009) 6(2) CPI Antitrust Chronicle, Spring 2009; Wils 'The Increased Level of EU Antitrust Fines, Judicial Review, and the ECHR' (2010) 33 World Competition 5; Castillo de la Torre 'The 2006 *Guidelines on Fines*: Reflections on the Commission's Practice' (2010) 33 World Competition 359; and the annual articles on fines by Barbier de La Serre and Lagathu: eg (2015) 6 JECLAP 530, (2016) 7 JECLAP 336 and (2017) 8 JECLAP 409.

[266] See eg Case T-386/10 *Aloys F Dornbracht GmbH & Co KG v Commission* EU:T:2013:450, paras 59–65.

[267] Where an undertaking had no turnover in the preceding year an earlier year can be used: Case C-76/06 *Britannia Alloys v Commission* EU:C:2007:326, paras 10–33.

[268] See eg Case T-71/03 *Tokai Carbon v Commission* EU:T:2005:220, paras 388–390; *Car glass*, Commission decision of 12 November 2008, partially annulled on appeal Case T-68/09 *Soliver NV v Commission* EU:T:2014:867; *Window mountings*, decision of 28 March 2012.

[269] Available at www.ec.europa.eu/competition/cartels/statistics/statistics.pdf.

Commission can impose the fine on the members themselves. A detailed study of the 'science' of setting the right level of a fine is beyond the scope of this book: the practitioners' works cited earlier contain extensive commentary on the subject[270].

It is noticeable that the cartel cases in recent years that have been appealed to the General Court contain at least as much, if not more, analysis of the level of fines than on the finding of the substantive infringement. The General Court has an unlimited jurisdiction on appeal to determine the level of fines; this includes the power to increase as well as to decrease the fines imposed by the Commission[271].

In 2006 the Commission adopted two important Notices (replacing earlier ones) on its fining policy. The first concerned its method of calculating the level of a fine and the second its policy of allowing leniency towards whistleblowers.

(ii) The Commission's guidelines on the method of setting fines

The Commission enjoys a wide margin of appreciation when determining the level of fines[272]. However, in the interests of transparency and impartiality, it decided in 1998 to publish guidelines on its methodology when setting fines[273]; they were replaced in 2006 by new guidelines building on the Commission's subsequent experience[274]. The *Fining Guidelines* respond to the criticism that, even if the Commission has a wide margin of appreciation, it is not an unfettered one[275]; in the US, for example, there are sentencing guidelines that enable the level of a fine (and the duration of a prison sentence) to be predicted with a fairly high degree of accuracy[276]. The Commission points out in the *Guidelines* that fines should have a sufficiently deterrent effect both on the undertakings involved in a particular infringement of the competition rules ('specific deterrence') and also on other undertakings that might be inclined to act unlawfully ('general deterrence')[277]. The Court of Justice has repeatedly held that the need to deter infringements of the competition rules is one of the factors to be taken into account when determining the level of fines[278] and has established that the Commission is entitled to change its methodology for the setting of fines, including introducing higher fines, where this is necessary for the effective enforcement of the competition rules[279]. The Court of Justice has held that an undertaking cannot deduct fines when assessing its taxable profits[280].

The *Fining Guidelines* propose a two-step methodology when setting fines.

270 See ch 7 n 8 earlier. 271 See 'Article 261: penalties', pp 303–304 later in chapter.

272 See eg Cases C-189/02 P etc *Dansk Rørindustri A/S v Commission* EU:C:2005:408, para 172.

273 *Guidelines on the method of setting fines imposed pursuant to Article 15(2) of Regulation No 17 and Article 65(3) of the ECSC Treaty* OJ [1998] C 9/3.

274 *Guidelines on the method of setting fines imposed pursuant to Article 23(2)(a) of Regulation 1/2003* OJ [2006] C 210/2, available at www.ec.europa.eu/competition.

275 The General Court has rejected the argument that the *Fining Guidelines* are unlawful because they give the Commission too much discretion: Case T-386/10 *Aloys F Dornbracht GmbH & Co KG v Commission* EU:T:2013:450, paras 68–78.

276 See the Sentencing Reform Act 1984 and the US Sentencing Commission *Guidelines Manual*, available at www.ussc.gov.

277 *Fining Guidelines*, para 4.

278 See eg Cases 100/80 etc *Musique Diffusion Française SA v Commission* EU:C:1983:158, paras 105–106; Case C-289/04 P *Showa Denko KK v Commission* EU:C:2006:431, para 16.

279 See eg Cases C-189/02 P etc *Dansk Rørindustri Als v Commission* EU:C:2005:408, paras 227–228; Case C-397/03 P *Archer Daniels Midland Co v Commission* EU:C:2006:328, paras 21–22; Cases T-389/10 etc *SLM and Ori Martin v Commission* EU:T:2015:513, paras 83–112, upheld on appeal Case C-490/15 P EU:C:2016:678.

280 Case C-429/07 *Inspecteur van de Belastingdienst v X BV* EU:C:2009:359, para 39.

(a) Basic amount of the fine

The Commission begins by setting a 'basic amount' for the fine, which is determined by reference to the value of the sales of the goods or services to which the infringement relates[281]. It is not necessary for the Commission to conduct a full definition of the relevant market for these purposes[282]. The basic amount will be related to a proportion of the value of such sales, depending on the degree of gravity of the infringement, multiplied by the number of years of infringement[283]. The gravity of the infringement is determined on a case-by-case basis[284]; as a general rule it will be set at a level of up to 30% of the value of sales[285]. Hard-core cartel infringements are likely to be at the top end of the scale[286]. The amount determined as a result of the rules just mentioned will then be multiplied by the number of years of participation in the cartel[287]. Furthermore an amount of between 15 and 25% of the basic amount will be imposed as a sanction for participating in the infringement in the first place, a so-called 'entry fee' intended to act as an additional deterrent[288]. Clearly these rules can lead to enormous fines, in particular where a cartel has lasted for a long time: the *Organic peroxides* cartel lasted for 29 years, which led to a very significant 'multiplier'[289]. However it should be recalled that Article 23(2) of the Regulation provides that a fine cannot exceed 10% of an undertaking's worldwide turnover.

(b) Adjustments to the basic amount

Having determined the basic amount of the fine, the Commission then takes into account various aggravating and mitigating circumstances[290]. Aggravating circumstances are set out in paragraph 28 of the *Guidelines* and include:

- the fact that an undertaking is a recidivist: the basic amount will be increased by up to 100% for each past finding of an infringement of Article 101 or 102, whether by the Commission or an NCA[291]
- refusal to cooperate with or obstruction of the Commission in its investigation[292]
- acting as leader or instigator of the infringement[293].

281 *Fining Guidelines*, paras 12–26; the Court of Justice has said that 'internal' sales within a vertically-integrated undertaking should be taken into account as well as external sales: Case C-580/12 P *Guardian Industries Group v Commission* EU:C:2014:2363, para 59 and Case C-231/14 P *Innolux v Commission* EU:C:2015:451, paras 44–77; Cases C-588/15 P etc *LG v Commission* EU:C:2017:679, paras 65–81.

282 Case T-48/02 *Brouwerij Haacht NV v Commission* EU:T:2005:436, para 59.

283 *Fining Guidelines*, para 19.

284 Ibid, para 20.

285 Ibid, para 21; the Commission adds that the particularities of a given case might mean that it would depart from the methodology in the *Guidelines*, including the 30% figure: ibid, para 37.

286 Ibid, para 23.

287 Ibid, para 24.

288 Ibid, para 25; see also para 7.

289 Commission Press Release IP/03/1700, 10 December 2003.

290 *Fining Guidelines*, paras 27–29.

291 The largest uplifts for recidivism to date for one previous infringement have been in *Power transformers*, Commission decision of 7 October 2009: uplift on ABB of 50%; in *Heat stabilisers*, Commission decision of 11 November 2009, the uplift on Arkema for three previous infringements was 90%, upheld on appeal in Case T-343/08 *Arkema France v Commission* EU:T:2011:218; in *Calcium Carbide*, Commission decision of 22 July 2009, the uplift on Akzo for four previous infringements was 100%, although it qualified for immunity and so did not pay a fine.

292 See the *Dutch bitumen* and *Professional videotapes* decisions discussed at 'Mandatory investigations', pp 282–283 earlier in chapter.

293 See eg *Candle waxes*, Commission decision of 1 October 2008, paras 681–686, where the fine on Sasol was increased by 50% as it was the leader of the cartel; this aspect of the decision was upheld on appeal to the General Court, Case T-541/08 *Sasol v Commission* EU:T:2014:628, paras 353–423; see also Case T-343/06 *Shell Petroleum NV v Commission* EU:T:2012:478 on Shell's role as instigator and leader in the *Dutch bitumen* cartel: the General Court sets out the general principles on instigation at paras 152–158 and on leadership at paras 196–204 of its judgment.

Increases for recidivism have become common. The Court of Justice confirmed in *Groupe Danone v Commission*[294] that the Commission is entitled to treat recidivism as an aggravating circumstance where past infringers need to be induced to change their behaviour[295]. There is no limitation period for considering past infringements[296]: the test is whether an undertaking shows a tendency to infringe the competition rules and not to draw appropriate conclusions from a finding of infringement on the part of the Commission[297]. An uplift can be applied for recidivism even if no fine was imposed on a previous occasion[298]; it would appear to be the case that the fine could be increased for a past infringement even where a firm had blown the whistle on that occasion. The previous infringements do not have to have been in the same product market[299], and may have been committed by different legal entities within the same economic unit[300]. However a previous violation of Article 101 would not provide a pretext for a recidivist uplift of a fine in a subsequent finding of an infringement of Article 102[301]. Several appeals against uplifts for recidivism have been unsuccessful[302]; some have succeeded, for example where the Commission did not articulate its case clearly in the statement of objections[303].

Mitigating circumstances are set out in paragraph 29 and include:

- early termination of infringing behaviour as soon as the Commission began its investigation (this does not apply to secret agreements or concerted practices, in particular cartels[304])
- negligent, as opposed to intentional, infringements
- having a limited role in the infringement
- cooperating with the Commission outside the scope of the *Leniency Notice*[305]
- authorisation or encouragement of the infringement by public authorities or by legislation.

In exceptional cases the inability of an undertaking to pay a fine, to the point that its economic viability would be jeopardised, may be taken into account by the Commission[306]. In assessing whether a fine may result in a firm going into liquidation

294 Case C-3/06 P EU:C:2007:88.

295 Ibid, paras 26–29.

296 Ibid, para 38; see also Case C-413/08 P *Lafarge SA v Commission* EU:C:2010:346, para 72 (*Plasterboard*); Cases T-101/05 and T-111/05 *BASF AG v Commission* EU:T:2007:380, para 67 (*Choline chloride*).

297 Case C-413/08 P *Lafarge SA v Commission* EU:C:2010:346, paras 69–71; the test includes previous cartel infringements committed under the European Coal and Steel Community Treaty: Case T-20/05 *Outokumpu Oyj v Commission* EU:T:2010:204, para 63 (*Copper plumbing tubes*).

298 Case C-3/06 P *Groupe Danone v Commission* EU:C:2007:88, para 41.

299 Cases T-101/05 and T-111/05 *BASF AG v Commission* EU:T:2007:380, para 64.

300 See *Candle waxes*, Commission decision of 1 October 2008, paras 672–678, annulled on appeal to the General Court on procedural grounds Case T-558/08 *Eni SpA v Commission* EU:T:2014:1080, paras 273–307.

301 Case T-57/01 *Solvay v Commission* EU:T:2009:519, paras 506–511 and Case T-66/01 *ICI v Commission* EU:T:2010:255, paras 376–387.

302 See eg the cases in footnotes 291–299 above; Case T-53/07 *UPM-Kymmene Oyj v Commission* EU:T:2012:101, paras 126–141 (*Butadiene rubber*); Case T-343/06 *Shell Petroleum NV v Commission* EU:T:2012:478, paras 244–266 (*Dutch bitumen*).

303 See eg Cases T-56/09 etc *Saint-Gobain Glass France SA v Commission* EU:T:2014:160 (fine reduced from €880 million to €715 million); see also Case T-39/07 *Eni SpA v Commission* EU:T:2011:356 (*Butadiene rubber*); Case T-144/07 *Thyssenkrupp Liften v Commission* EU:T:2011:5129 (*Elevators and escalators*); Case T-558/08 *Eni SpA v Commission* EU:T:2014:1080 (*Paraffin waxes*); Cases C-93/13 P and C-123/13 P *Commission v Versalis SpA and Eni SpA* EU:C:2015:150 (*Chloroprene rubber*).

304 See eg Case T-329/01 *Archer Daniels Midland Co v Commission* EU:T:2006:268, paras 272–287 (*Sodium gluconate*) in which the General Court upheld the Commission's refusal to recognise termination of participation in a secret cartel as an attenuating circumstance.

305 See eg *Power transformers*, Commission decision of 7 October 2009, paras 262–274.

306 *Fining Guidelines*, para 35; see eg *Window mountings*, Commission decision of 28 March 2012.

and exiting the market the Commission will typically consider a firm's financial statements, its liquidity, solvency and other financial ratios and its relations with banks and shareholders[307].

The fact that an undertaking adopts a competition law compliance programme is not a factor that the Commission is obliged to take into account as an attenuating factor[308], nor that it has taken disciplinary action against employees involved in the infringement[309]. The Commission is not required to reduce a fine on the basis that a defendant has paid damages to the victims of its anti-competitive behaviour[310].

The principle of *ne bis in idem* prevents the same person from being fined more than once for the same unlawful conduct. The principle is subject to three cumulative conditions: the facts must be identical; the offender must be the same undertaking; and the legal interest protected must be the same[311]. It follows that the principle does not apply where a fine has been imposed, for example, in the US, since it does not relate to the same interest as that protected by EU law[312]. Furthermore the Commission is permitted to cure a procedural irregularity—for example by reopening a case against a defendant whose rights of the defence have been violated[313]—without infringing the principle of *ne bis in idem*[314]. By readopting decisions in this way the Commission seeks to make the point that, although it may be possible to win procedural points on appeal to the EU Courts, ultimately this will be to no avail if it is possible to cure the procedural deficiency by reopening the case.

(iii) The Commission's *Leniency Notice*

Undertakings that participate in cartels are usually fully aware that their behaviour is unlawful and go to great lengths to maintain secrecy and to avoid detection[315]. Competition authorities therefore face considerable difficulties in detecting cartels. A crucial tool in practice is to incentivise participants in cartels to 'blow the whistle' to the relevant competition authority or authorities[316]. The encouragement of whistleblowing has proved to be immensely successful in the US in prosecuting cartels; the US policy can

307 See Commission MEMO/10/290, 30 June 2010; an application form and a standard-form questionnaire for dealing with claims of inability to pay are available on DG COMP's website: www.ec.europa.eu/competition.

308 See ch 7 n 4 earlier.

309 *Choline chloride*, Commission decision of 9 December 2004, para 217.

310 Case T-59/02 *Archer Daniels Midland Co v Commission* EU:T:2006:272, para 354 (*Citric acid*); Case T-13/03 *Nintendo v Commission* EU:T:2009:131, para 74.

311 Cases C-204/00 P etc *Aalborg Portland A/S v Commission* EU:C:2004:6, para 338 (*Cement*); see generally Wils 'The Principle of "*Ne Bis in Idem*" in EC Antitrust Enforcement: A Legal and Economic Analysis' (2003) 26 World Competition 131.

312 See eg Case C-308/04 P *SGL Carbon AG v Commission* EU:C:2006:433, paras 26–39 (*Graphite electrodes*); Case C-289/04 P *Showa Denko KK v Commission* EU:C:2006:431, paras 50–63 (*Graphite electrodes*); Case T-329/01 *Archer Daniels Midland Co v Commission* EU:T:2006:268 (*Sodium gluconate*), paras 290–295; Case T-59/02 *Archer Daniels Midland Co v Commission* EU:T:2006:272 (*Citric acid*), paras 61–73.

313 See eg *Carbonless paper*, Commission decision of 23 June 2010 reimposing a fine of €21 million on Bolloré following annulment of its earlier decision in Case C-322/07 P *Papierfabrik August Koehler v Commission* EU:C:2009:500; the Commission's second decision was upheld on appeal Case T-372/10 *Bolloré v Commission* EU:T:2012:325 and on further appeal Case C-414/12 P EU:C:2014:301.

314 Case T-24/07 *ThyssenKrupp Stainless AG v Commission* EU:T:2009:236, paras 178–192 (*Alloy surcharge*).

315 See ch 9 of DG COMP's *Manual of Procedures* on dealing with leniency applicants.

316 See Wils 'Leniency in Antitrust Enforcement: Theory and Practice' (2007) 30 World Competition 25; for a global review see Obersteiner 'International Antitrust Litigation: How to Manage Multijurisdictional Leniency Applications' (2013) 4 JECLAP 16; Lachnit 'Apply at Your Own Risk: The Difficulties with Multi-Jurisdictional Leniency Applications' (2016) 23 Maastricht Journal of European and Comparative Law 725; Campbell (ed) *Cartel Regulation* (Global Competition Review, 17th ed, 2017); see also Colino 'The Perks of Being a Whistleblower: Designing Efficient Leniency Programs in New Antitrust Jurisdictions' (2017) 50 Vanderbilt Journal of Transnational Law 535.

be accessed on the home page of the Department of Justice[317]. The Commission's policy is to allow total immunity—a fine of zero—to the first undertaking in a cartel to blow the whistle, and to impose lower fines than would otherwise be the case on undertakings that provide it with further evidence that enables it to proceed more effectively with the investigation of a case. However it should be noted that some major cases are brought on the Commission's own initiative: it is not dependent on whistleblowers[318]; for example the Commission's decision in *Car glass* originated in a 'tip-off' from an anonymous source[319]. The Commission has developed an 'Anonymous Whistleblower Tool' for individuals who are willing to provide information about a cartel on the condition of anonymity: contact is made with the Commission through the encryption tool of an external intermediary[320]. As a general proposition whistleblowing does not affect the liability of a whistleblower to pay damages to victims of a cartel as a matter of civil law[321], except that Article 11(4) of the Damages Directive[322] limits to some extent the joint and several liability of immunity recipients.

The Commission first adopted a *Notice on leniency* in 1996[323] that was replaced in 2002[324]. A new *Notice* was published in 2006 setting out the Commission's current policy; the 2006 *Notice* is intended to provide greater transparency as to what is expected of undertakings when they apply for leniency; it also introduced some procedural innovations[325]. The *Notice* is in line with the principles of the ECN's *Model Leniency Programme*[326]. After some introductory comments, Section II of the *Leniency Notice* explains the circumstances in which an undertaking may qualify for immunity from fines; Section III deals with the possibility of reduced fines; Section IV discusses ways of making 'corporate statements', including the possibility of doing so orally in order to avoid problems that might arise in civil litigation. It should be noted that there is no 'one-stop shop' for leniency applications, either within the EU or internationally: it follows that a potential leniency applicant may have to blow the whistle in a number of different jurisdictions in order fully to protect its position[327]. However, within the EU, there has been fairly substantial convergence of national systems of leniency[328].

(a) Section I: introduction

The *Notice* sets out the framework for the Commission to reward undertakings that are or have been members of secret cartels that cooperate with it in its investigation[329]. The *Notice* recognises two types of leniency: immunity from fines and a reduction of fines. It

[317] See www.justice.gov/atr/public/guidelines.

[318] See eg *Flat glass*, Commission decision of 28 November 2007, para 80, discussed at 'Case allocation under Regulation 1/2003', p 299 later in chapter; *Professional Videotapes*, Commission decision of 20 November 2007, para 44; *Elevators and escalators*, Commission decision of 21 February 2007, para 91.

[319] See *Car glass*, Commission decision of 12 November 2008, para 38; see similarly *Envelopes*, Commission decision of 10 December 2014, para 16.

[320] See Commission Press Release IP/17/591, 16 March 2017; further details are available at www.ec.europa.eu/competition.

[321] See Commission's *Leniency Notice* OJ [2006] C 298/17, para 39.

[322] OJ [2014] L 349/1; see ch 8, 'Article 11: joint and several liability', p 316.

[323] OJ [1996] C 207/4.

[324] OJ [2002] C 45/3.

[325] *Notice on Immunity from fines and reduction of fines in cartel cases* OJ [2006] C 298/17, available at www.ec.europa.eu/competition.

[326] See 'Leniency', p 300 later in chapter.

[327] See eg Case C-428/14 *DHL Express (Italy) srl v Autoritá Garante della Concurrenza e del Mercato* EU:C:2016:274, paras 45–67.

[328] See www.ec.europa.eu/competition/ecn/documents.html.

[329] Note that the *Notice* does not apply to cooperation in relation to vertical agreements, eg involving resale price maintenance; however para 29 of the *Fining Guidelines* (ch 7 n 274 earlier) provides for reductions in fines for cooperation with the Commission 'outside the scope of the *Leniency Notice*'.

states that immunity from fines may be justified where an undertaking makes a decisive contribution to the opening of an investigation or to the finding of an infringement[330]; a reduction of a fine may be justified where an undertaking provides the Commission with evidence that adds 'significant value' to that already in its possession[331]. The Court of Justice has held that a reduction under the leniency programme can be justified only where the conduct of the undertaking concerned demonstrates a genuine spirit of cooperation on its part[332]. The Commission acknowledges in the *Leniency Notice* that the making of corporate statements ought not to expose undertakings to risks in civil litigation not experienced by undertakings that do not cooperate with it[333]. Evidence obtained from a leniency applicant must be supported by corroborative evidence; the Court of Justice has ruled that there is no reason in law why one leniency statement cannot corroborate another[334].

(b) Section II: immunity from fines

Immunity from a fine will be granted to the first undertaking[335] in a cartel to submit information to the Commission that will enable it to carry out an inspection or to find an infringement of Article 101 in connection with the cartel[336]; immunity will not be granted if the Commission already had sufficient evidence to proceed to an inspection or to a final decision[337]. The whistleblower must make a corporate statement to the Commission containing specified information such as a description of the cartel, the names, positions, office locations and, where necessary, home addresses of the individuals involved in the cartel and details of any other competition authorities that have been contacted as well as any other relevant evidence in the whistleblower's possession[338]. The whistleblower must comply with a series of conditions in order to qualify for immunity:

- genuine, continuous and expeditious cooperation[339]
- termination of any involvement in the cartel, unless the Commission considers that continuing involvement might be useful for the preparation of inspections: if the whistleblower were to be absent from cartel meetings, for example, the other participants might guess what has happened and realise that inspections are imminent
- it must not have destroyed, falsified or concealed any relevant evidence when contemplating its application for immunity[340].

The *Leniency Notice* explains the procedure for making an application for immunity[341], including the so-called 'marker system' whereby an undertaking can contact the

[330] *Leniency Notice* OJ [2006] C 298/17, para 4.

[331] Ibid, para 5; 'possession' means physical, not cognitive, possession: Case C-617/13 P *Repsol Lubricantes y Especialidades SA v Commission* EU:C:2016:416, paras 58–75 (*Spanish bitumen*).

[332] Case C-301/04 P *Commission v SGL Carbon AG* EU:C:2006:432, paras 66–70 (*Graphite electrodes*).

[333] *Leniency Notice*, para 6.

[334] Case C-613/13 P *Commission v Keramag Keramische Werke GmbH* EU:C:2017:49 (*Bathroom fittings and fixtures*).

[335] The parents of a joint venture and the joint venture may make a joint immunity application: *Optical disc drives*, Commission decision of 21 October 2015.

[336] *Leniency Notice*, para 8.

[337] Ibid, paras 10 and 11; on the evidence required to qualify for immunity see Case T-521/09 *Alstom Grid SAS v Commission* EU:T:2014:1000, paras 44–89.

[338] *Leniency Notice*, para 9.

[339] For a case in which the Commission denied an undertaking immunity on the ground that it had failed in its duty of cooperation see *Italian raw tobacco*, Commission decision of 20 October 2005, paras 430–485, upheld on appeal to the General Court Case T-12/06 *Deltafina SpA v Commission* EU:T:2011:441, paras 102–182 and on appeal to the Court of Justice Case C-578/11 P *Deltafina SpA v Commission* EU:C:2014:1742.

[340] *Leniency Notice*, para 12.

[341] Ibid, paras 14–22.

Commission and agree with it a date by when it will provide the evidence needed to pass the threshold for leniency. If the undertaking 'perfects' the marker by the agreed date its application will be deemed to have been made at the time of the original approach to the Commission, and will therefore rank higher in the queue of leniency applicants than an undertaking that made an application before the marker was perfected[342].

(c) Section III: reduction of fines

An undertaking that does not qualify for immunity, for example because it was not the first to blow the whistle, may nevertheless qualify for a reduced fine where it provides evidence to the Commission 'which represents significant added value'[343]. Reductions in the range of 20 to 50% are available for such an undertaking[344]. The *Leniency Notice* explains the procedure for such cases[345].

(d) Section IV: corporate statements

The *Leniency Notice* discusses how corporate statements may be made[346], and makes specific provision for such statements to be oral rather than written[347]. The reason for this is the fear that, if an undertaking were to prepare a written corporate statement, this might be discoverable in the event of a treble damages action in the US: this might deter the undertaking from blowing the whistle at all, in which case the cartel might go undetected. An oral statement is rendered into writing by the Commission. As it is not a document of the whistleblower it cannot be discovered from it; and any attempt by a US court to demand that the Commission should hand its own document over would probably fail on public interest grounds[348]. It should be noted, however, that the Commission is entitled to publish non-confidential information provided by a leniency applicant in the public version of its decision[349]. Article 6(6) of the Damages Directive prevents a national court from ordering disclosure of leniency statements[350].

(e) Appeals by leniency applicants

In *Masco v Commission*[351] Masco blew the whistle on a cartel in the bathroom fixtures and fittings sector. As a whistleblower it was not fined by the Commission, but the Commission's decision found Masco to be in a single overall agreement of broader scope than Masco considered to be correct. It therefore appealed, unsuccessfully, against the Commission's decision: Masco's concern was that the decision exposed it to an action for damages for a larger cartel than it considered itself to have participated in.

342 Ibid, para 15. 343 Ibid, paras 24 and 25. 344 Ibid, para 26.

345 Ibid, paras 27–30. 346 Ibid, paras 31–35.

347 Ibid, para 32; Article 2(15) and (16) of the Damages Directive define the terms 'leniency programme' and 'leniency statement' respectively.

348 See *In re Rubber Chemicals Antitrust Litigation* 486 F Supp 2d 1078 (ND Cal 2007) in which the District Court refused a discovery request for certain communications between an EU leniency applicant and the Commission; see further 'The exchange of information with third countries', p 276 earlier in chapter.

349 See Case C-162/15 P *Evonik Degussa GmbH v Commission* EU:C:2017:205 upholding a decision of the Commission to publish a more detailed non-confidential version of the *Hydrogen peroxide* decision of 3 May 2006, including leniency information.

350 See ch 8, 'Article 6: disclosure of evidence in the file of a competition authority', pp 314–315.

351 Case T-378/10 EU:T:2013:469, upheld on appeal to the Court of Justice Case C-614/13 P *Masco Corp v Commission* EU:C:2017:63; for similar appeals see Case T-46/11 *Deutsche Lufthansa AG v Commission* EU:T:2015:987 (annulling *Air cargo*, Commission decision of 9 November 2010 annulled, but the Commission subsequently adopted a second decision on 17 March 2017 which is itself on appeal in Cases T-342/17 etc, not yet decided) and Case T-445/14 *ABB v Commission*, not yet decided (*Power cables*).

(iv) Article 24: periodic penalty payments

Article 24 provides for the imposition of periodic penalty payments on undertakings, for example where they persist in an infringement of Article 101 or Article 102 even after a decision requiring it to end, or where they continue to fail to supply complete and accurate information in response to a Commission request[352]. The fines are up to 5% of an undertaking's average daily turnover in the preceding business year. In July 2006 the Commission held that Microsoft had failed to comply with its obligation to supply full interoperability information in accordance with its decision of March 2004 and imposed a fine of €280.5 million, €1.5 million per day from 16 December 2005 to 20 June 2006[353]. This was followed by a second fine, of €899 million, in February 2008 for charging unreasonable prices for access to interface documentation[354]; that fine was reduced to €860 million on appeal[355].

(G) Chapter VII: limitation periods

(i) Article 25: limitation periods for the imposition of penalties

Article 25 of Regulation 1/2003, which replaces the rules formerly contained in Regulation 2988/74[356], establishes limitation periods for action on the part of the Commission against competition law infringements: the period is three years in the case of provisions concerning requests for information or the conduct of inspections, and five years in the case of all other infringements; provision is made for the interruption of the limitation period in the event of certain action taken by the Commission or an NCA[357]. In *Arkema France v Commission*[358] the General Court rejected the argument that the Commission was time-barred from fining Arkema as it had correctly established the duration of Arkema's participation in the *Heat stabilisers* cartel[359]. The burden of proving the duration of an infringement of the competition rules—and therefore of demonstrating that the limitation period has not expired—rests with the Commission[360]. A finding by the Commission that there has been a single continuous agreement or abuse may mean that the Commission is able to impose fines, provided that it brings proceedings within three or five years of when the infringement ceases[361]; if the correct analysis were to be that there had been a series of separate agreements or abuses, it might transpire that some of them had ended so long ago that a fine could no longer be imposed[362].

In *Trelleborg Industrie SAS v Commission*[363] the General Court held that the Commission had erred in finding that Trelleborg had participated in a 'single and continuous infringement'[364]; rather it had participated in a 'repeated infringement'[365]. However this error did not affect the application of the limitation period[366] or the level of the fine imposed on Trelleborg[367].

The Commission sometimes addresses a decision to an undertaking stating that it has been in a cartel, but does not impose a fine because of the limitation rule. The

352 See ch 20 of DG COMP's *Manual of Procedures* on periodic penalty payments.

353 Commission decision of 12 July 2006.

354 Commission decision of 27 February 2008.

355 Case T-167/08 *Microsoft Corp v Commission* EU:T:2012:323.

356 OJ [1974] L 319/1.

357 Regulation 1/2003, Article 25(3)–(6); for discussion of the rules on interruption under Regulation 2988/74 see Case T-276/04 *Compagnie Maritime Belge SA v Commission* EU:T:2008:237, paras 22–38.

358 Cases T-23/10 and T-24/10 EU:T:2014:62.

359 Ibid, paras 38–108.

360 Case T-120/04 *Peróxidos Orgánicos SA v Commission* EU:T:2006:350, para 52; Case T-58/01 *Solvay SA v Commission* EU:T:2009:520, paras 294–295.

361 Regulation 1/2003, Article 25(1).

362 See ch 3, 'Implications of a single overall agreement', p 108 under Article 101.

363 Cases T-147/09 and T-148/09 EU:T:2013:259.

364 Ibid, paras 50–70.

365 Ibid, paras 72–92; on the concept of repeated infringements see ch 3 'Single and repeated infringement', p 109.

366 *Trelleborg Industrie* (ch 7 n 363 earlier), para 95.

367 Ibid, paras 115–118.

Commission's interest in doing so includes that the undertaking might be sued for damages on a follow-on basis in the courts of a Member State. However the Commission must explain its reason for addressing the decision to the undertaking[368].

(ii) Article 26: limitation period for the enforcement of penalties

Article 26 provides that the limitation period for enforcing fines and periodic penalty payments is five years[369].

(H) Chapter VIII: hearings and professional secrecy

Articles 26 and 27 deal respectively with hearings and with professional secrecy.

(i) Article 27: hearing of the parties, complainants and others

(a) The provisions of Article 27

Article 27(1) provides that, before decisions are taken under Articles 7 and 8 (infringement and interim measures decisions) or under Articles 23 and 24 (fines and periodic penalty payments), the undertakings that are the subject of the proceedings have a right to be heard. The Commission may base its decisions only on objections on which the parties have had an opportunity to comment. Complainants 'shall be closely associated with the proceedings'.

Article 27(2) provides that the rights of the defence shall be fully respected during the Commission's proceedings, including the right to have access to the Commission's file. Article 27(2) of the Regulation makes clear that there is no right of access to confidential information, nor to internal documents of the Commission and the NCAs and correspondence within the ECN. Article 27(3) provides that the Commission may hear third parties with a sufficient interest, and Article 27(4) provides that, where the Commission intends to adopt a decision under Article 9 or 10, it must publish the fact of its intention and allow third parties an opportunity to be heard.

(b) The conduct of proceedings

Commission Regulation 773/2004[370] ('the Implementing Regulation') explains how and when the Commission may initiate proceedings, and how the right to be heard is exercised, in competition cases[371]. Specifically it sets out the rules in relation to the statement of objections that must be sent to the parties and the right to be heard, and confers upon the parties a right to an oral hearing. Failure to hold a hearing is an infringement of an essential procedural requirement which will result in the annulment of the Commission's decision, regardless of whether the error on its part influenced its decision[372]. Third parties with a sufficient interest may also be heard[373]. The Regulation sets out the rules for the

[368] See 'Past infringements', pp 262–263 earlier in chapter.

[369] For litigation under the predecessor of Article 26 in Regulation 2988/74 see Case T-153/04 *Ferrière Nord SpA v Commission* EU:T:2006:277, reversed on appeal to the Court of Justice, Case C-516/06 P *Commission v Ferrière Nord SpA* EU:C:2007:763, paras 27–34; this case traces back to the Commission's decision in *Welded steel mesh*, OJ [1989] L 260/1.

[370] OJ [2004] L 123/18; note that the Implementing Regulation has been amended by Regulation 1792/2006, OJ [2006] L 362/1; Regulation 622/2008, OJ [2008] L 171/3; Regulation 519/2013, OJ [2013] L 158/74 and Regulation 2015/1348, OJ [2015] L 208/3; a consolidated version is available at www.ec.europa.eu.

[371] See ch 10 of DG COMP's *Manual of Procedures* on the opening of proceedings, ch 11 on drafting the statement of objections, ch 12 on access to the file and ch 13 on the right to be heard.

[372] Case C-88/15 P *Ferriere Nord SpA v Commission* EU:C:2017:716, paras 53–55; on the oral hearing see Wils 'The Oral Hearing in Competition Proceedings before the European Commission' (2012) 35 World Competition 397.

[373] They are also entitled to receive a non-confidential version of the statement of objections: Cases T-213/01 and T-214/01 *Österreichische Postsparkasse AG v Commission* EU:T:2006:151.

oral hearing, which is conducted by a Hearing Officer. A Commission decision of October 2011 sets out the terms of reference of the Hearing Officers in competition cases[374]; also of significance is the Commission's *Best practices for the conduct of proceedings concerning Articles 101 and 102 TFEU*[375]. Regulation 1/2003 explains how confidential information is to be dealt with during proceedings, and how disputes should be resolved.

The Commission's *Notice on the rules for access to the Commission's file*[376] explains its current policy on access to the file in the context of the relevant legislation, including Regulation 1/2003 and the Implementing Regulation and the jurisprudence of the EU Courts. Access to the file for competition law purposes is subject to different criteria and exceptions from the right of access to EU documents under Regulation 1049/2001[377]. The *Notice on access to the file* explains who is entitled to access to the file; which documents can be accessed; and when access may be granted. Complaints about denial of access may be taken to the Hearing Officer; another possibility, if the approach to the Hearing Officer does not provide a satisfactory outcome, would be to approach the European Ombudsman[378].

Where the Commission is in possession of documents that might provide exculpatory evidence for a defendant undertaking it must make them available, although a failure to do so would lead to the annulment of the Commission's decision only if their availability would have led to a different outcome[379]. In *Salzgitter v Commission*[380] the Court of Justice confirmed that the Commission may attach probative value to evidence provided by a source that insists on anonymity.

The Court of Justice has established that undertakings are entitled to expect that competition law proceedings will be concluded within a reasonable period[381].

(c) European Ombudsman

Apart from recourse to the Hearing Officer, in recent years a practice has arisen, in some cases, of complaints about maladministration on the part of the Commission being taken to the European Ombudsman[382]. This occurred with some success in the case of *Intel*[383], *Ryanair*[384], *Infineon*[385] and *Crédit Agricole*[386], though was unsuccessful in the case of *X, E.ON*[387]. A complaint may be made to the Ombudsman only after appropriate approaches

374 Decision 2011/695/EU, OJ [2011] L 275/29: the scope of the Hearing Officer's powers under this Decision is discussed in Case C-162/15 P *Evonik Degussa GmbH v Commission* EU:C:2017:205 (*Hydrogen peroxide*) and in Case C-517/15 P *AGC Glass Europe SA v Commission* EU:C:2017:598 (*Car glass*); Wils 'The Role of the Hearing Officer in Competition Proceedings before the European Commission' (2012) 35 World Competition 431.

375 Available at www.ec.europa.eu; see also ch 2 of DG COMP's *Manual of Procedures* on relations with the Hearing Officers.

376 OJ [2005] C 325/7; this *Notice* replaces an earlier one, OJ [1997] C 27/3.

377 OJ [2001] L 145/43; see the *Notice on access to the file*, para 2; for an example of a partially successful request for information under Regulation 1049/2001, OJ [2001] L 145/43, see Case T-181/10 *Reagans SpA v Commission* EU:T:2014:139.

378 See 'European Ombudsman' later.

379 See eg Case T-314/01 *Coöperatieve Verkoop- en Productievereniging van Aardappelmeel en Derivaten Avebe BA v Commission* EU:T:2006:266, paras 66–67 and the case law cited therein.

380 Case C-411/04 P EU:C:2007:54, paras 40–50.

381 See 'Judicial Review', pp 300–305 later in chapter.

382 For further information about the Ombudsman see www.ombudsman.europa.eu; for discussion see Amory and Desmedt 'The European Ombudsman's First Scrutiny of the EC Commission in Antitrust matters' (2009) 30 ECLR 205.

383 Decision of the European Ombudsman of 14 July 2009.

384 Decision of the European Ombudsman of 27 April 2009.

385 Decision of the European Ombudsman of 13 November 2014.

386 Decision of the European Ombudsman of 11 November 2015.

387 Decision of the European Ombudsman of 27 July 2010.

have been made to the institutions concerned; and the Ombudsman's decisions are not binding.

(d) A typical case

In a typical cartel case[388] the Commission's procedure would be as follows[389]:

- a whistleblower applies to the Commission for immunity from fines, or the Commission decides to start an investigation on its own initiative
- the Commission conducts surprise inspections
- the Commission considers the evidence it has obtained and sends requests for or requires further information
- the Commission issues statements of objections to the undertakings it considers to be in the cartel
- the undertakings submit written replies to the statements of objections
- an oral hearing is held[390]
- DG COMP prepares a draft decision
- the draft decision goes to the Commissioner for Competition
- the Advisory Committee is consulted on the draft decision[391]
- the draft decision is seen by the College of Commissioners
- the College adopts the final decision.

(e) The position of complainants

Various provisions in Regulation 1/2003, including Article 27(3), acknowledge that third parties with a sufficient interest have a right to participate in proceedings, although these rights are less than those of the undertakings accused of an infringement. Chapter IV of the Implementing Regulation[392] also deals with the handling of complaints, and the Commission has published a *Notice on the handling of complaints by the Commission under Articles [101 and 102 TFEU]*[393]. Part II of the *Notice on Complaints* discusses the complementary roles of public and private enforcement of the competition rules, pointing out the benefits for complainants, in some circumstances, of going to a court rather than a competition authority: for example only a court can award damages or determine the effect on a contract of the voidness provided for by Article 101(2)[394]. It also explains the provisions on case allocation within the ECN, which should assist a complainant in deciding which public authority it would be sensible to approach if that is preferred to private litigation[395]. Part III of the *Notice on Complaints* explains in detail how the Commission

[388] An Article 102 case would be very similar but, for obvious reasons, would not involve a whistleblower; where the parties decide to settle a cartel case, and the Commission considers this to be an appropriate way to proceed, the procedure may be shorter than the one outlined in the text: see 'Settlements of cartel cases', pp 270–273 earlier in chapter.

[389] A useful flowchart setting out the Commission's procedure in Article 101 and 102 cases will be found in Annex 1 of its *Notice on best practices for the conduct of proceedings under Articles 101 and 102 TFEU* OJ [2011] C 308/6.

[390] In some cases undertakings waive their right to an oral hearing.

[391] See ch 14 of DG COMP's *Manual of Procedures* on the Advisory Committee; one of the grounds for annulment in Case T-691/14 *Servier SAS v Commission*, not yet decided, is that the Commission infringed essential procedural requirements by not convening the Advisory Committee in good time.

[392] OJ [2004] L 123/18.

[393] OJ [2004] C 101/65; see also ch 21 of DG COMP's *Manual of Procedures* on the handling of complaints.

[394] *Notice on Complaints*, para 16. [395] Ibid, paras 19–25.

goes about handling complaints, and specifies the information that must be supplied on Form C, the form that must be used when making a complaint[396]. The *Notice* discusses the well-established case law recognising the Commission's right to prioritise its enforcement efforts and to concentrate on cases that have an 'EU interest'[397]. It is also well settled that complainants do not have a right to a final decision as to the existence or non-existence of an infringement of Articles 101 and/or 102[398]. The final part of the *Notice* explains the Commission's procedure when dealing with complaints, including the procedural rights of complainants[399]. The judgments of the General Court in two third party appeals concerning De Beers' arrangements for the supply of diamonds provide a useful summary of the obligations owed by the Commission when deciding whether to reject a complaint[400].

The Commission is entitled to make use of evidence provided by third parties on condition of their anonymity being maintained, although such evidence would not be sufficient in itself to sustain a finding of infringement but would have to be part of a body of evidence[401].

(ii) Article 28: professional secrecy

Article 28 contains two provisions: first, information collected under the Regulation may be used only for the purpose for which it was acquired; secondly, the Commission and the NCAs must not disclose information acquired or exchanged by them under the Regulation if that information is covered by an obligation of professional secrecy[402]. Paragraph 28(a) of the Commission's *Notice on NCA cooperation* provides guidance on the practical application of Article 28.

(I) Chapter IX: block exemption regulations

Article 29 of Regulation 1/2003 provides power for the Commission and the NCAs to withdraw the benefit of block exemptions in individual cases[403].

(J) Chapter X: general provisions

(i) Article 30: publication of decisions

Article 30(1) requires the Commission to publish its decisions under Articles 7 to 10, 23 and 24, having regard to the legitimate interests of the parties in the protection of their business secrets[404].

(ii) Article 31: review by the EU Courts

Article 31 provides that the EU Courts have unlimited jurisdiction to review decisions in which the Commission has imposed a fine or a periodic penalty payment.

396 Ibid, paras 29–32.

397 Ibid, paras 41–45; see Wils 'Discretion and Prioritisation in Public Antitrust Enforcement' (2011) 34 World Competition 353.

398 See Case C-119/97 P *Ufex v Commission* EU:C:1999:116, para 87; see also Case T-201/11 *Si.mobil telekomunikacijske stortive d.d. v Commission* EU:T:2014:1096, paras 79–108.

399 *Notice on complaints*, paras 53–81.

400 Cases T-104/07 etc *Belgische Vereniging van handelaars in- en uitvoerders geslepen diamant v Commission* EU:T:2013:366 and Cases T-108/07 etc *Spira v Commission* EU:T:2013:367.

401 Case C-411/04 P *Salzgitter Mannesmann GmbH v Commission* EU:C:2007:54, paras 47 and 50.

402 See more generally Article 339 TFEU.

403 For discussion of the possibility of withdrawing the benefit of Regulation 330/2010 from vertical agreements see ch 16, 'Withdrawal of the block exemption by the Commission or by a Member State', p 685–686.

404 On the Commission's obligations under Article 30(1) see Case C-162/15 P *Evonik Degussa GmbH v Commission* EU:T:2017:205, paras 77–102 (*Hydrogen peroxide*).

(K) **Chapter XI: transitional, amending and final provisions**

Articles 35 to 42 contain transitional and final provisions.

(i) **Article 34: transitional provisions**

Article 34(1) provides that all existing notifications for an 'individual exemption' to the Commission lapsed on 1 May 2004[405].

(ii) **Article 35: designation of competition authorities of Member States**

Article 35 requires Member States to designate the competition authority or authorities responsible for the application of Articles 101 and 102[406].

(iii) **Articles 36–42: miscellaneous amendments**

The provisions on the transport Regulations in Articles 36, 38, 39 and 41 have been overtaken by subsequent events[407]. Article 37 repealed Regulation 2988/74 on limitation periods, which are now dealt with by Articles 25 and 26. Article 40 repeals the powers in earlier Regulations to enable the withdrawal of the benefit of block exemptions; since the power to do this is now conferred by Article 29[408], Article 42 is no longer significant.

(iv) **Article 43: repeal of Regulations 17 and 141**

Article 43(1) repealed Regulation 17, except in relation to conditions and obligations attached to individual exemptions already granted by the Commission[409]. Article 43(2) repeals Regulation 141, which had exempted the transport sector from Regulation 17[410].

(v) **Article 44: *Report on the functioning of Regulation 1/2003***

Article 44 required the Commission to report to the Parliament and the Council in 2009 on the functioning of Regulation 1/2003. In its *Report on the functioning of Regulation 1/2003*[411] the Commission reported that the Regulation had worked well in practice, significantly improving its enforcement of Articles 101 and 102 and bringing about coherence in their application throughout the EU. However the Commission also noted certain issues—for example the fact that different Member States have different procedures for the enforcement of Articles 101 and 102 and the divergence of national laws in the area of unilateral conduct—where further evaluation is called for, but left open the question of whether amendments to existing rules or practice are required.

3. **Regulation 1/2003 in Practice**

Since 2004 the European Commission shares the task of enforcing the competition rules in the TFEU with the NCAs of the Member States and with the national courts. The Commission and the NCAs together operate within the framework of the ECN, a manifestation of the duty of sincere cooperation required by Article 4(3) TEU. Articles 101 and 102 are now applied with far greater frequency by the NCAs than by the Commission.

[405] 'Individual exemptions' granted under Regulation 17 continued in force: see ch 4, 'Regulation 1/2003', pp 174–176.

[406] See 'Article 5: powers of the NCAs', pp 260–261 earlier in chapter.

[407] See ch 23, 'Transport', pp 998–1008.

[408] See 'Chapter IX: exemption regulations', p 297 earlier in chapter.

[409] See ch 4, 'Regulation 1/2003', pp 174–176.

[410] See ch 23, 'Transport', pp 999–1008.

[411] *Report on the functioning of Regulation1/2003*, COM(2009) 206 final: see also the Commission's Staff Working Paper accompanying the *Report on the functioning of Regulation 1/2003*, SEC(2009) 574 final; both documents are available at www.ec.europa.eu/competition.

(A) The European Competition Network

The ECN does not have legal identity nor is it an international organisation as such[412]. Rather it provides a framework within which the Commission and the NCAs discuss the sharing of work: for example which authority is best placed to handle a particular investigation. Information is exchanged between competition authorities within the framework of the ECN, as is experience gathered both in relation to actual cases and the development of policy. Members of the ECN are linked by a secure Intranet. The Commission takes the lead role in ensuring coherence in the application of the competition rules, in particular as a result of its examination of draft decisions of the NCAs in conjunction with its power to initiate its own proceedings, and thereby to suspend those of an NCA[413]. Information about the work of the ECN is obtainable from the website of DG COMP including, for example, the number of investigations under Articles 101 and 102 reported to the ECN and the proportion of them that had been started by an NCA on the one hand or the Commission on the other[414]. The Directors General of the NCAs meet once a year to discuss major policy issues within the ECN. The so-called 'ECN Plenary' consisting of officials in the NCAs and the Commission meets four times a year. It has a number of working groups, for example on issues of cooperation, leniency and sanctions, and it also has a number of sectoral sub-groups, for example on the liberal professions, energy and financial services. The Commission publishes a periodical *ECN Brief* which contains information about the activities of the ECN and its members[415].

(B) Case allocation under Regulation 1/2003

The *Notice on NCA cooperation*[416] sets out the jurisdictional principles according to which cases should be allocated within the ECN[417]. An example of a case being reallocated from an NCA to the Commission is *iTunes*, where the UK considered that the Commission was in a better position to consider a complaint that Apple's iTunes service discriminated on price according to the user's country of residence, in particular since this affected the single market[418]. In *Flat glass* several NCAs cooperated with the Commission within the ECN, leading to the imposition by the Commission of fines totalling €488 million[419]. The fact that an NCA has started to investigate a matter does not mean that the Commission cannot carry out a surprise inspection in relation to the same behaviour[420].

(C) 'Soft' convergence

An interesting by-product of Regulation 1/2003 and the establishment of the ECN has been the considerable amount of soft convergence that has taken place in relation to national competition laws and procedures. Although the Regulation did not explicitly require there to be convergence, the reality is that in many respects—for example the abolition of national systems of notification, the alignment of investigative procedures, the introduction of leniency programmes and of commitments procedures similar to

[412] See ch 3 of DG COMP's *Manual of Procedures* on cooperation between the Commission and the NCAs and on the exchange of information within the ECN.

[413] Article 11(6) of Regulation 1/2003, on which see 'Article 11: cooperation between the Commission and the NCAs', pp 274–275 earlier in chapter.

[414] See www.ec.europa.eu/competition/ecn/index_en.html.

[415] Available at www.ec.europa.eu/competition/ecn/index_en.html.

[416] OJ [2004] C 101/43.

[417] *Notice on NCA cooperation*, paras 5–15.

[418] OFT Press Release, 3 December 2004, available at www.nationalarchives.gov.uk; Commission Press Release IP/08/22, 9 January 2008; see also Commission Press Release IP/10/1175, 25 September 2010.

[419] Commission decision of 28 November 2007; see Commission Press Release IP/07/1781, 28 November 2007.

[420] Case T-339/04 *France Télécom v Commission* EU:T:2007:80, para 80.

those in Article 9—national laws have been brought into alignment with those of the EU. Information about the reform of the competition laws of the Member States since Regulation 1/2003 came into force is available on the website of the ECN[421]. The ECN has published several Recommendations on powers of investigation, decision-making and remedies, which are intended to assist Member States in establishing a legal framework that is conducive to the effective enforcement of EU competition law[422].

(D) Leniency

The work of the ECN in the area of leniency has been of particular importance. Under its aegis, 27 of the 28 NCAs now have a leniency programme[423], and the ECN has produced a *Model Leniency Programme* aimed at achieving soft harmonisation through convergence. The *Model Leniency Programme* has been endorsed by the heads of all the NCAs and is available on the ECN's website[424]. Most Member States have aligned their leniency programmes with the key features of the *Model Leniency Programme*[425]; however it is not binding on NCAs[426].

(E) Ten years of Regulation 1/2003 and possible reform

The Commission published a Communication on 9 July 2014, *Ten Years of Antitrust Enforcement under Regulation 1/2003: Achievements and Future Perspectives*[427], in which it reported the increased enforcement of the competition rules over that period. However the Commission noted the need for further action to ensure effective enforcement on the part of the NCAs, in particular to ensure that NCAs are independent, well-resourced and equipped with adequate powers of investigation and enforcement. This, together with the ECN's recommendations on investigative and decision-making powers, led to the Commission's proposal for an 'ECN+' Directive[428].

4. Judicial Review

It is possible to bring an action before the General Court (and ultimately the Court of Justice on points of law) in respect of Commission decisions on competition matters; Article 265 TFEU deals with failures to act, Article 263 with actions for annulment and Article 261 with penalties[429]. The EU Courts have exclusive competence to

[421] See www.ec.europa.eu/comm/competition/ecn/index_en.html.

[422] See www.ec.europa.eu/competition/ecn/documents.html.

[423] The only Member State not to do so is Malta.

[424] See www.ec.europa.eu/comm/competition/ecn/index_en.html.

[425] See MEMO/09/456, 15 October 2009.

[426] Case C-428/14 *DHL Express (Italy) srl v Autoritá Garante della Concorrenza e del Mercato* EU:C:2016:274, paras 29–44.

[427] COM(2014) 453, see also Commission Staff Working Document *Ten Years of Antitrust Enforcement under Regulation 1/2003*, SWD (2014) 230/2.

[428] See Commission Staff Working Document 'Impact Assessment' accompanying the proposed ECN+ Directive, SWD(2017) 114; see also 'Article 5: powers of the NCAs', pp 260–261 earlier in chapter.

[429] See Kerse and Khan *EU Antitrust Procedure* (Sweet & Maxwell, 6th ed, 2012), ch 8; Craig *EU Administrative Law* (Oxford University Press, 2nd ed, 2012), Part II; Bailey 'Scope of Judicial Review Under Article 81 EC' (2004) 41 CML Rev 1328; Forrester 'A Bush in Need of Pruning: The Luxuriant Growth of Light Judicial Review' in Ehlermann and Marquis (eds) *European Competition Law Annual 2009: Evaluation of Evidence and its Judicial Review in Competition Cases* (Hart, 2010); Jaeger 'The Standard of Review in Competition Cases Involving Complex Economic Assessments: Towards the Marginalisation of the Marginal Review?' (2011) 2 JECLAP 295; Castillo de la Torre and Gippini Fournier *Evidence, Proof and Judicial Review in EU Competition Law* (Edward Elgar, 2017).

consider whether acts of the Commission are lawful or not[430]. Proceedings before the General Court must be completed within a reasonable time; reasonableness is tested by reference to the importance of the case for the person concerned, its complexity and the conduct of the parties. In *Groupe Gascogne SA v Commission*[431] the Court of Justice held that the appropriate remedy where an undertaking has been deprived of a fair and impartial hearing within a reasonable time is an action for damages[432]; such an action must be brought in the General Court: where that Court was the institution responsible for the delay, the action can be brought before a different Chamber of the General Court than the one responsible[433]. Damages have been awarded by the General Court in several cases: the largest award as at 8 December 2017 is of €654,523 in *Guardian Europe Sàrl v European Union*[434].

(A) Article 265: failure to act

Under Article 265 it is possible to bring an action against the Commission where, in infringement of the Treaty, it has failed to act. The Commission must have been under a specific duty to carry out the act in question. An action may be brought only where the Commission has been required to act and has failed to do so within two months; the action itself must be brought within the following two months[435]. Article 265 is sometimes invoked by complainants wishing to force the Commission to investigate complaints against undertakings suspected of infringing the competition rules[436].

Where the Commission is guilty of a failure to act, an undertaking that suffers damage in consequence may bring an action against the Commission for compensation under Articles 268 and 340 TFEU[437].

(B) Article 263: action for annulment

Under Article 263 it is possible to bring an action to have various 'acts' of the Commission annulled. Proceedings must be commenced within two months of the applicant hearing of the act in question[438]. Where an action succeeds in part only Article 264 enables the unlawful parts of a decision to be severed and annulled, leaving the remainder intact. Four issues in particular need consideration: who may sue; what 'acts' may be challenged; on what grounds an action may be brought; and whether damages are available once a decision has been annulled.

[430] See Case C-344/98 *Masterfoods* EU:C:2000:689; the EU Courts have no jurisdiction to review decisions by NCAs or judgments of national courts: see Case T-386/09 *Grúas Abril Asistencia, SL v Commission* EU:T:2010:331.

[431] Case C-580/12 P EU:C:2013:770; in an earlier case, Case C-185/95 P *Baustahlgewebe GmbH v Commission* EU:C:1998:608, the Court of Justice had reduced a fine by €50,000 because of the delay in the proceedings.

[432] Case C/580/12 P *Groupe Gascogne* EU:C:2013:770, paras 72–97.

[433] Case C-616/13 P *Productos Asfálticos (PROAS) SA v Commission* EU:C:2016:415, para 82 and case law cited.

[434] Case T-673/15 EU:T:2017:377, on appeal Case C-447/17 P *European Union v Guardian Industries*, not yet decided; see also Case T-479/14 *Kendrion NV v Commission* EU:T:2017:14 (€588,769) and Case T-577/14 *Gascogne Sack Deutschland v Commission* EU:T:2017:1 (€57,000).

[435] Article 265(2); time limits are applied strictly by the General Court: see eg Case T-12/90 *Bayer v Commission* EU:T:1991:25 paras 14, 16 and 46.

[436] See 'The position of complainants', pp 296–297 earlier in chapter.

[437] To date such actions in the context of the competition rules have failed: see eg Case T-64/89 *Automec Srl v Commission* EU:T:1990:42; Case T-28/90 *Asia Motor France v Commission* EU:T:1992:98, paras 48–51.

[438] Article 263(5); see ch 7 n 435 earlier on the General Court's approach to time limits.

(i) **Standing**

Apart from Member States and the EU institutions, Article 263(4) provides that any undertaking may challenge a decision addressed to it or to another person if it is of 'direct and individual concern' to it. This entitles third parties in some situations to sue. In *Metro v Commission*[439] the Court of Justice confirmed that a complainant under Article 3(2) of Regulation 17 (Article 7(2) of Regulation 1/2003) could appeal under Article 263[440]; if one applicant has standing, it is not necessary for other applicants concerned in the same application do so[441]. In some cases the applicant's interest may be altogether too vague to give standing[442]. The recipients of adverse decisions may themselves bring an action under Article 263, and their right to do so is not limited to cases in which fines have been imposed[443].

(ii) **Acts**

It is not only decisions, but other 'acts' which may be challenged under Article 263. Formal decisions of the Commission applying Articles 101 and 102 of course can be challenged. In *Coca-Cola Co v Commission*[444] the General Court held that it is settled law that any measure which produces binding legal effects such as to affect the interest of an applicant by bringing about a distinct change in its legal position is an act or decision which may be the subject of an action under Article 263[445]. In *IBM v Commission*[446] the Court of Justice held that a statement of objections could not normally be challenged, because it was simply a preliminary step in the formal procedure[447]. In *BAT v Commission*[448] the Court of Justice held that letters from the Commission to two complainants, finally rejecting their complaints, were acts capable of challenge under Article 263[449]. Mere silence on the part of an EU institution cannot produce binding legal effects unless express provision to this effect is made for it in EU law[450]. A decision of the Hearing Officer on confidentiality and the publication of a Commission decision is an 'act' that may be reviewed under Article 263[451].

[439] Case 26/76 EU:C:1977:167.

[440] See also Case 43/85 *ANCIDES v Commission* EU:C:1987:347; a third party successfully challenged the grant of an individual exemption in Cases T-528/93 etc *Métropole v Commission* EU:T:1996:99.

[441] Case T-306/05 *Scippacercola v Commission* EU:T:2008:9, para 71.

[442] See eg Case 246/81 *Bethell v Commission* EU:C:1982:224; Case C-70/97 P *Kruidvat BVBA v Commission* EU:C:1998:545.

[443] See eg Case C-652/11 P *Mindo Srl v Commission* EU:C:2013:229.

[444] Cases T-125/97 and T-127/97 EU:T:2000:84.

[445] The General Court cited for this proposition the judgments in Case 60/81 *IBM v Commission* EU:C:1981:264, para 9; Cases C-68/94 and C-30/95 *France v Commission* EU:C:1998:148, para 62; and Case T-87/96 *Assicuriazioni Generali v Commission* EU:T:1999:37, para 37.

[446] Case 60/81 EU:C:1981:264.

[447] See similarly Cases T-10/92 etc *SA Cimenteries CBR v Commission* EU:T:1992:123; Cases T-377/00 etc *Philip Morris International Inc v Commission* [2003] 1 CMLR 676; see also Case C-516/06 P *Commission v Ferriere Nord SpA* EU:C:2007:763 and Case T-274/15 *Alcogroup v Commission* EU:T:2018:179: no Commission act capable of judicial review; Case T-457/08 R *Intel Corp v Commission* EU:T:2009:18: decisions of the Commissioner and of the Hearing Officer in that case not capable of judicial review; cf Case C-517/15 P *AGC Glass Europe v Commission* EU:C:2017:598, paras 56–59, in which a decision of the Hearing Officer on confidential treatment of the *Car glass* decision was held to be amenable to judicial review.

[448] Cases 142 and 156/84 EU:C:1987:490; see also Case 210/81 *Demo-Studio Schmidt v Commission* EU:C:1983:277.

[449] See also Cases T-113/89 etc *Nefarma v Commission* EU:T:1990:82 where a letter from the Commissioner for Competition to a Member State was factual in nature and did not produce legal effects.

[450] Cases T-189/95 etc *Service pour le Groupement d'Acquisitions v Commission* EU:T:1999:317, paras 26–29.

[451] See eg Case C-162/15 P *Evonik Degussa GmbH v Commission* EU:C:2017:205.

(iii) **Grounds of review**

The EU Courts must assess the legality of the Commission's decision according to the grounds of review specified in Article 263(2). The Commission may be challenged on grounds of:

> lack of competence, infringement of an essential procedural requirement, infringement of the Treaties or of any rule of law relating to their application, or misuse of powers.

To some extent these grounds overlap. Of particular significance will be a failure by the Commission to give a fair hearing[452]; a failure to articulate properly the reasoning behind its decision[453]; and a failure to base a decision on adequate evidence[454]. The Commission is not required to set out in its decision exhaustively all the evidence available; it is sufficient if it refers to the conclusive evidence[455].

The General Court generally undertakes a 'full review' of decisions applying Article 101 or 102 on the basis of the evidence adduced by an applicant in support of its appeal[456]. While the General Court cannot use the Commission's 'margin of discretion' as a basis for dispensing with a full review of the law and of the facts[457], it is not entitled to substitute its own reasoning for that of the Commission[458]. The General Court has been prepared to exercise its power of review of the substance and procedural propriety of Commission decisions in an exacting manner[459], although the Court of Justice criticised the inadequacy of the General Court's review in *Groupement des Cartes Bancaires v Commission*[460] and in *Intel v Commission*[461].

(iv) **Actions for damages**

Article 340 TFEU provides for an action for damages to be brought by any person for losses caused by a sufficiently serious breach of EU law. An action for damages does not require that person to bring a successful application for annulment, but, of course, annulment may provide a basis for seeking damages. In *Commission v Schneider Electric*[462] the Court of Justice awarded damages of €50,000 for losses caused by the Commission's erroneous decision to prohibit the *Schneider Electric/Legrand* merger[463].

(C) **Article 261: penalties**

Under Article 261 the General Court has unlimited jurisdiction in respect of penalties imposed by the Commission. Article 31 of Regulation 1/2003 provides that the EU Courts

[452] See eg Case 17/74 *Transocean Marine Paint Association v Commission* EU:C:1974:106 where the members of the association were not given an opportunity to be heard on the conditions which the Commission intended to attach to an individual exemption.

[453] See eg Case 73/74 *Groupement des Fabricants des Papiers Peints de Belgique v Commission* EU:C:1975:160 where the Commission failed to explain the mechanism whereby the agreement in question could affect inter-state trade.

[454] See eg Case 41/69 *ACF Chemiefarma v Commission* EU:C:1970:71 where the Commission's decision was partially annulled for lack of evidence.

[455] Case T-2/89 *Petrofina SA v Commission* EU:T:1991:57.

[456] See eg Case C-386/10 P *Chalkor v Commission* EU:C:2011:815, paras 54 and 62; the General Court must establish of its own motion that the Commission has stated reasons for its decision: ibid, para 61.

[457] Ibid, para 62.

[458] Case C-603/13 P *Galp Energía España v Commission* EU:C:2016:38, para 73.

[459] See eg Cases T-374/94 etc *European Night Services v Commission* EU:T:1998:198 and Case T-328/03 *O2 (Germany) GmbH & Co, OHG v Commission* EU:T:2006:116.

[460] Case C-67/13 P EU:C:2014:2204, paras 89–92.

[461] Case C-413/14 P EU:C:2017:632, paras 141–146.

[462] Case C-440/07 P *Commission v Schneider Electric SA* EU:C:2009:459 and EU:C:2010:324; see also Case T-212/03 *MyTravel v Commission* EU:T:2008:315 these cases are discussed in ch 21, 'Damages claims against the Commission', pp 920–921.

[463] Schneider originally claimed damages of €1.66 billion.

may cancel, reduce or increase fines or periodic penalties imposed. In the exercise of its unlimited jurisdiction the General Court is required to carry out a 'full and unrestricted review' of a penalty decision in its entirety—on factual as well as legal grounds[464]—and the Court is entitled to substitute its own assessment of the amount of the fine for that of the Commission[465]. When the General Court finds that there is a factual error in the Commission's assessment it will not hesitate to adjust the fine. This can occur, for example, where the General Court considers that the Commission has exaggerated the duration of an undertaking's participation in a cartel[466] or has wrongly attributed to an undertaking the role of instigator or ringleader of a cartel[467]. The General Court will also make adjustments to fines where it feels that an undertaking has been the victim of unequal treatment compared with other members of the same cartel[468]. Separately it is important to understand that the General Court has the power to increase, as well as to decrease the level of a fine, and that it has on a few occasions done so[469].

(D) **Expedited procedure**

The General Court can hear some cases under an 'expedited procedure'[470], which, as the name implies, enables the Court to expedite the hearing and determination of appeals[471]. However this procedure has not been used in recent times.

(E) **Interim measures**

It is possible to apply to the General Court for interim measures suspending the operation of a Commission decision pending an appeal. Three conditions must be fulfilled in order for interim relief to be granted: first, the applicant must establish a *prima facie* case that the Commission's assessment is unlawful; secondly, it must demonstrate the urgency of interim measures to prevent it from suffering serious and irreparable damage; and thirdly it must explain why the balance of interests favours the adoption of such measures[472]. In

[464] See Case C-386/10 P *Chalkor v Commission* EU:C:2011:815, paras 62 and 82.

[465] Case C-603/13 P *Galp Energía España v Commission* EU:C:2016:38, para 75.

[466] See eg Cases T-44/00 etc *Mannesmannröhren-Werke AG v Commission* EU:T:2004:218; Case T-58/01 *Solvay SA v Commission* EU:T:2009:520, paras 292–306; Case T-18/05 *IMI plc v Commission* EU:T:2010:202, paras 79–97.

[467] Case T-15/02 *BASF v Commission* EU:T:2006:74, paras 280–464; Case T-29/05 *Deltafina SpA v Commission* EU:T:2010:355, paras 319–336.

[468] See eg Cases T-109/02 etc *Bolloré SA v Commission* EU:T:2007:115, where the fine on Arjo Wiggins Appleton was reduced by €33 million as a result of unequal treatment; Case T-13/03 *Nintendo Co Ltd v Commission* EU:T:2009:131, paras 169–189, where Nintendo's fine was reduced from €149 million to €119 million because the Court considered that Nintendo should have received the same reduction of its fine for cooperation as had been awarded to John Menzies; Case T-18/03 *CD-Contact Data GmbH v Commission* EU:T:2009:132, paras 91–121, where CD-Contact Data's fine was reduced as its passive role in the infringement had not been taken into account as an attenuating circumstance in determining the fine, whereas another undertaking, Concentra, had benefited from a reduction on this basis; Case T-18/05 *IMI v Commission* EU:T:2010:202, paras 152–174.

[469] See eg Cases T-101/05 and T-111/05 *BASF AG v Commission* EU:T:2007:380, paras 212–223 where the fine on BASF was marginally increased.

[470] OJ [2015] L 105/1, Article 151; see further ch 21, 'Examples of third party appeals', pp 918–920.

[471] The procedure has been used in several cases: eg Case T-310/01 *Schneider Electric v Commission* EU:T:2002:254 and Case T-5/02 *Tetra Laval v Commission* EU:T:2002:264.

[472] Examples of cases in which interim measures have been granted are Cases 76/89 R etc *Radio Telefis Eireann v Commission* EU:C:1989:192; Case T-395/94 R *Atlantic Container Line AB v Commission* EU:T:1995:48; Case T-41/96 R *Bayer AG v Commission* EU:T:1996:68; Case T-65/98 R *Van den Bergh Foods Ltd v Commission* EU:T:1998:155.

cases where there is an imminent risk of severe and lasting harm to one or more of the parties, the General Court may suspend the operation of a Commission decision *ex parte*, pending the outcome of the proceedings for interim relief[473]. The General Court granted interim measures that suspended the obligation to provide a bank guarantee in lieu of payment of a fine in two cartel cases[474]. An application for interim measures to suspend a Commission request for information under Article 18 of Regulation 1/2003 failed in *Qualcomm v Commission*[475].

[473] See eg *NDC Health/IMS Health: Interim Measures*, Commission decision of 3 July 2001, suspended on appeal to the General Court Case T-184/01 R *IMS Health v Commission* EU:T:2001:200, upheld on appeal to the Court of Justice Case C-481/01 P(R) EU:C:2002:223.

[474] Case T-393/10 R *Westfälische Drahtindustrie GmbH v Commission* EU:T:2011:178 (*Prestressing steel*); Case T-522/15 R *CCPL v Commission* EU:T:2015:1012 (*Retail food packaging cartel*).

[475] Case T-371/17 R EU:T:2017:485.

8

Articles 101 and 102: private enforcement in the courts of Member States

1. Introduction

Chapter 7 was concerned with the public enforcement of Articles 101 and 102 by the European Commission and the national competition authorities ('NCAs'). This chapter discusses the private enforcement of the competition rules, that is to say the situation where litigants take their disputes to a domestic court or, quite often, to arbitration[1].

Historically the enforcement of competition law was very much the preserve of the European Commission and the NCAs. However competition authorities have limited resources and they are unable to investigate every alleged infringement of the competition rules; private enforcement can therefore be an important complement to their activities. The Commission for a long time was eager that Articles 101 and 102 should be applied more frequently in national courts, thereby relieving it of some of the burden of enforcement[2]. One of the driving forces behind Regulation 1/2003 was the Commission's desire that national courts and NCAs should share with it the task of enforcing the competition rules, thereby enabling the Commission to concentrate its resources on pursuing

[1] See generally Rose and Bailey (eds) *Bellamy and Child: European Union Law of Competition* (Oxford University Press, 7th ed, 2013), ch 16; Rodger (ed) *Competition Law Private Enforcement and Collective Redress Across the EU* (Wolters Kluwer, 2014); Davis and Lianos *Damages Claims for the Infringement of Competition Law* (Oxford University Press, 2015); Marquis and Cisotta (eds) *Litigation and Arbitration in EU Competition Law* (Edward Elgar, 2015); Wilman *Private Enforcement of EU Law before National Courts: The EU Legislative Framework* (Edward Elgar, 2015) ch 6; Mobley (ed) *Private Antitrust Litigation* (Global Competition Review, 2017); Ashton *Competition Damages Actions in the EU* (Edward Elgar, 2nd ed, 2018); OECD Roundtable, *Private remedies* (2008), available at www.oecd.org/competition.

[2] See further Ehlermann and Atanasiu (eds) *European Competition Law Annual 2001: Effective Private Enforcement of EC Antitrust Law* (Hart, 2003); for a contrary view, arguing that 'public antitrust enforcement is inherently superior to private enforcement', see Wils 'Should Private Antitrust Enforcement Be Encouraged in Europe?' (2003) 26 World Competition 473; Wils 'Should Private Antitrust Enforcement be Encouraged' in ch 4 of his book *Principles of European Antitrust Enforcement* (Hart, 2005); Wils 'The Relationship between Public Antitrust Enforcement and Private Actions for Damages' (2009) 31 World Competition 3; Wils 'Private Enforcement of EU Antitrust Law and its Relationship with Public Enforcement: Past, Present and Future' (2017) 40 World Competition 3.

the most serious infringements of the law: the relationship between the Commission and domestic courts is discussed below[3].

The private enforcement of competition law has changed dramatically in recent years. Public enforcement remains extremely important. However, for a variety of reasons, there is now much more private enforcement than used to be the case. It has become normal for the victims of cartels to bring 'follow-on' actions for damages after the Commission or an NCA has adopted a decision finding an infringement of Article 101 or its domestic equivalent; decisions establishing an abuse of dominance may also lead to follow-on actions[4]. Claimants may also choose to have recourse to the courts to vindicate their rights on a 'standalone' basis where they feel that they may obtain a remedy from a court more quickly than from a public authority, or where the public authority decides as a matter of prosecutorial discretion not to investigate a particular complaint. It should be added that only a court can award damages for infringements of competition law: this power is not available to public authorities[5]. Follow-on actions often include a standalone claim, for example where the claimant is of the opinion that the unlawful behaviour was more extensive than established in the competition authority's decision. The private enforcement of competition law has increased, in part, because law firms that specialise in assisting claimants, as opposed to defendants, have established themselves in the marketplace. Furthermore, as we will see, funding arrangements are available that may mitigate the financial risk involved in bringing a claim before a court[6].

The move towards greater private enforcement of competition law was given added impetus by the adoption of the EU Damages Directive in November 2014[7], which entered into force on 27 December 2016. Apart from the Directive, three other instruments of the European Commission are of importance when considering the private enforcement of EU competition law. In 2013 it adopted a Communication that provides guidance on the complex question of how to quantify harm in competition cases[8]. In due course the Commission will publish guidance on the passing on of overcharges[9]. The Commission has also adopted a Recommendation to Member States on common principles for collective redress to the victims of anti-competitive behaviour[10]. Each of these instruments will be discussed in the text that follows.

Section 2 of this chapter will deal with the private enforcement of Articles 101 and/or 102 as a matter of EU law, with particular emphasis on the Damages Directive. Section 3 deals with private actions in the UK courts. Section 4 considers the use of competition

[3] See 'The relationship between the Commission and domestic courts', pp 316–320 later chapter.

[4] See eg in the UK Case 1166/5/7/10 *Albion Water v Dŵr Cymru* [2013] CAT 6; Case 1178/5/7/11 *2 Travel Group plc (in liquidation) v Cardiff City Transport Services Ltd* [2012] CAT 19.

[5] On some occasions competition authorities may reduce the level of a fine in recognition of an undertaking agreeing to pay compensation to the victim of anti-competitive behaviour: see eg *Pre-insulated pipes*, Commission decision of 21 October 1998, para 172; *Nintendo*, Commission decision of 30 October 2002, paras 440–441; *Independent Schools*, OFT decision of 20 November 2006, para 1427.

[6] See 'Funding litigation', p 324 later in chapter.

[7] Directive 2014/14/EU of the European Parliament and of the Council on certain rules governing actions for damages under national law for infringements of the competition law provisions of the Member States and of the European Union, OJ [2014] L 349/1.

[8] *Communication from the Commission on quantifying harm in actions for damages based on breaches of Article 101 or 102 of the Treaty on the Functioning of the European Union* OJ [2013] C 167/19; see also a study by OXERA 'Quantifying antitrust damages: towards non-binding guidance for courts', 2009, available at www.ec.europa.eu; see further 'Quantum', p 312 later in chapter.

[9] See 'Passing on', pp 313–314 later in chapter.

[10] *Commission Recommendation of 11 June 2013 on common principles for injunctive and compensatory collective redress mechanisms in the Member States concerning violations of rights granted under Union law* OJ [2013] L 201/60; see 'Collective redress in the EU', pp 330–332 later in chapter.

law not as a 'sword', where the claimant's cause of action is based on an infringement of competition law, but rather as a 'shield', that is to say as a defence, for example to an action for breach of contract or infringement of an intellectual property right. Section 5 contains a brief discussion of issues that can arise where competition law disputes are referred to arbitration rather than to a court for resolution.

2. EU Law: Actions for Damages

This section will begin with a discussion of the private enforcement of Articles 101 and 102 prior to the Damages Directive; it will then describe briefly the initiative that led to the Directive's adoption. The main focus will be on the Directive itself, the central principle of which is that any natural or legal person who has suffered harm caused by an infringement of competition law shall be able to claim and to obtain full compensation for that harm. The Directive contains important rules on matters such as the disclosure of evidence, the effect of decisions of NCAs and limitation periods designed to ensure that this principle is observed in practice. Section 2 will conclude with a discussion of five matters not dealt with by the Directive: the relationship between the Commission and the domestic courts of the EU; private international law; collective redress; the funding of litigation; and actions for injunctions or other types of relief.

(A) Private enforcement prior to the Directive

Articles 101 and 102 are directly applicable and produce direct effects: they give rise to rights and obligations which national courts have a duty to safeguard and enforce[11]. Until 2001 there had not been a judgment of the Court of Justice dealing specifically with the question of whether Member States have an obligation, as a matter of EU law, to provide a remedy in damages where harm has been inflicted as a result of an infringement of the competition rules[12], although the courts in the UK had assumed, in several cases, that such an action was available[13]. However in 2001 the Court of Justice's judgment in *Courage Ltd v Crehan*[14] clarified the position, emphatically establishing a right to damages. Subsequent case law has been equally, if not more, emphatic[15].

(i) *Courage Ltd v Crehan*

In *Courage Ltd v Crehan* the Court of Justice held that:

> The full effectiveness of Article [101 TFEU] and, in particular, the practical effect of the prohibition laid down in Article [101(1)] would be put at risk if it were not open to any individual to claim damages for loss caused to him by a contract or by conduct liable to restrict or distort competition.
>
> Indeed the existence of such a right strengthens the working of the [EU] competition rules and discourages agreements or practices, which are frequently covert, which

[11] Case 127/73 *BRT v SABAM* EU:C:1974:25, para 16; Case C-453/99 *Courage Ltd v Crehan* EU:C:2001:465, para 23. A court in Iceland has asked the EFTA Court whether compensation should be available for breach of the EEA competition rules in Case E-6/17 *Fjarskipti hf. v Síminn hf.*, not yet decided.

[12] Despite the lack of jurisprudence explicitly recognising a right to damages, the principles of non-discrimination and full effectiveness ('*effet utile*'), the judgment of the Court of Justice in Cases C-6/90 and 9/90 *Francovich v Italy* EU:C:1991:428, and the opinion of AG Van Gerven in Case C-128/92 *HJ Banks v British Coal Corpn* EU:C:1993:860, all pointed towards the possibility of an action for damages.

[13] See 'The availability of damages in the UK courts', p 325 later in chapter.

[14] Case C-453/99 EU:C:2001:465.

[15] See 'Subsequent cases', p 310 later in chapter.

> are liable to restrict or distort competition. From that point of view, actions for damages before the national courts can make a significant contribution to the maintenance of effective competition in the [EU][16].

The judgment in *Courage Ltd v Crehan* was a landmark in the private enforcement of Articles 101 and 102. It was a particularly striking case in that the claimant, Crehan, was not, for example, a customer of a cartel seeking damages for harm inflicted by a horizontal agreement the object of which was to restrict competition. Rather Crehan was himself party to a vertical agreement for the supply of beer by a brewer to him. At most the agreement was one that restricted competition by effect rather than by object, and, as a co-contractor, it was arguable that Crehan should not be able to recover damages as a result of losses caused by an unlawful agreement for which he was himself partly responsible. In English law there is a rule that one party to an agreement cannot recover damages from another party if they are both equally responsible for it ('*in pari delicto*')[17]. The Court of Justice's view was that there should not be an absolute bar to a person in the position of Crehan bringing an action[18]: the national court should take into account matters such as the economic and legal context in which the parties find themselves and the respective bargaining power and conduct of the two parties to the contract[19]. Of particular importance would be whether a person in the position of Crehan found himself in a markedly weaker position than a brewer such as Courage, so as seriously to compromise or even eliminate his freedom to negotiate the terms of the contract and his capacity to avoid the loss or reduce its extent[20]. A further point was that, in a situation such as that in *Crehan*, the restrictive effect of Courage's agreement with Crehan arose from the fact that it was one of many similar agreements having a cumulative effect on competition[21]: in those circumstances Crehan could not be considered to bear significant responsibility for the infringement of the competition rules[22].

(ii) ***Manfredi***

In *Manfredi*[23] the Court of Justice repeated what it had said in *Crehan*. The full effectiveness of Article 101(1) required that:

> any individual can claim compensation for the harm suffered where there is a causal relationship between that harm and an agreement or practice prohibited under Article [101 TFEU][24].

In *Manfredi* there were some specific points about Italian procedural law that seemed to complicate the claimants' actions: for example there were rules that allocated jurisdiction

[16] Case C-453/99 EU:C:2001:465, paras 26–27.

[17] See Monti 'Anticompetitive Agreements: The Innocent Party's Right to Damages' (2002) 27 EL Rev 282 (critical of the judgment); Odudu and Edelman, ibid, 327; on the position in the US see *Perma Life Mufflers Inc v International Parts Corpn* 392 US 134 (1968).

[18] Case C-453/99 EU:C:2001:465, para 28.

[19] Ibid, para 32.

[20] Ibid, para 33; see 'Private enforcement of competition law in practice in the UK', pp 332–335 later in chapter, for a discussion of the outcome of this litigation.

[21] On this point see ch 16, 'Factors to be considered in determining whether single branding agreements infringe Article 101(1)', pp 651–653.

[22] Case C-453/99 EU:C:2001:465, para 34; in Case 1241/5/7/15 T *Sainsbury's Supermarkets Ltd v MasterCard Inc* [2016] CAT 11, paras 405–418 the CAT concluded that Sainsbury's Bank did not bear significant responsibility for the MasterCard multilateral interchange fee; it is interesting to speculate as to what would happen if a third party were to sue an undertaking in the position of Crehan or Sainsbury's for harm suffered as a result of the agreement: the Court of Justice's reasoning would suggest that only Courage or MasterCard should be liable.

[23] Cases C-295/04 etc *Vincenzo Manfredi v Lloyd Adriatico Assicurazioni SpA* EU:C:2006:461.

[24] Ibid, para 61.

in actions for damages based on competition law to a different court from the one that would deal with 'normal' damages claims, thereby increasing the cost and length of the litigation; there were limitation periods that could be harmful to their cause; and there were rules that might prevent them from recovering the full amount of their losses. The Article 267 reference asked the Court of Justice whether these domestic rules were compatible with EU law. The Court of Justice's answer, in essence, was that these were matters of domestic law, provided that they did not offend the EU principles of equivalence and effectiveness. What the *Manfredi* judgment did was to reveal that, despite the Court of Justice's enthusiasm for damages actions, there remained the 'problem' that Member States retain autonomy in relation to the procedural rules of their domestic judicial systems, as well as the substantive rules of recovery in tort, delict, restitutionary and other actions, and that these rules might inhibit successful damages claims[25]. This is precisely why the Damages Directive requires Member States to adjust their laws in order to address some of these problems.

(iii) **Subsequent cases**

The importance of the availability of damages was repeated by the Court of Justice in two cases arising out of cartels in the *Elevators and Escalators* sector. The first was *Europese Gemeenschap v Otis NV*[26], where the EU itself brought a follow-on action for damages pursuant to the Commission's infringement decision: the Court held that the EU was just as entitled to bring an action for damages as anyone else harmed by an infringement of the competition rules[27]. In *Kone AG v ÖBB-Infrastruktur*[28] the Court of Justice held that members of an *Elevators and Escalators* cartel could be liable for damage caused by companies which were *not* members of the cartel but which were able to charge higher prices than they would otherwise have done as a result of increased prices charged by the cartel (so-called 'umbrella pricing'). The importance of the action for damages was also referred to by the Court of Justice in *Pfleiderer*[29].

(B) **The movement towards reform**

A study published in August 2004, usually referred to as the *Ashurst Report*[30], was carried out for the Commission to identify and analyse the obstacles to successful damages actions in the Member States based on infringements of competition law. The Report concluded that the picture was one of 'astonishing diversity and total underdevelopment' and highlighted numerous obstacles to private enforcement of the EU competition rules. This led the Commission to publish a Green Paper in December 2005, *Damages actions for breach of the EC antitrust rules*[31], the purpose of which was to identify the main obstacles to a more efficient system of damages claims and to set out different options to promote more such claims. The Commission received a large number of responses to the Green Paper[32] and subsequently published a White Paper, *Damages actions for breach of the EC Antitrust Rules*[33] in April 2008 together with a Staff Working Paper[34] and an

[25] When the case returned to Italy Mr Manfredi was awarded €889.10 in damages and €500 for legal costs by the small claims court: see Nebbia 'So What Happened to Mr Manfredi? The Italian Decision Following the Ruling of the European Court of Justice' (2007) 28 ECLR 591.

[26] Case C-199/11 EU:C:2012:684, paras 40–43. [27] Ibid, para 44.

[28] Case C-557/12 EU:C:2014:1317. [29] Case C-360/09 EU:C:2011:389.

[30] *Study on the conditions of claims for damages in case of infringement of EC competition rules*, August 2004, available at www.ec.europa.eu/comm/competition.

[31] COM(2005) 672 final, 19 December 2005, available at www.ec.europa.eu/comm/competition; see also the accompanying Staff Working Paper which contains a rich source of research material.

[32] Available at www.ec.europa.eu. [33] COM(2008) 154 final, 2 April 2008. [34] SEC(2008) 404.

Impact Assessment[35]. The *Impact Assessment* suggested that the victims of competition law infringements may be foregoing anything between €5.7 to €23.3 billion in damages per annum as a result of obstacles to private enforcement.

(C) The Damages Directive

The Damages Directive was adopted on 26 November 2014 and was supposed to be implemented by 26 December 2016. Most Member States failed to implement by that date. The position as at 8 December 2017 was that 25 Member States had fully implemented the Directive; Bulgaria, Greece and Portugal had failed to do so[36]. Article 20 requires the Commission to conduct a review of the Directive and to submit a report to the Parliament and Council by 27 December 2020.

(i) A right to full compensation

Chapter I of the Directive deals with its subject-matter, scope and definitions. Article 1 explains that the Directive contains rules to ensure that anyone who has suffered harm caused by an infringement of competition law[37] can effectively exercise the right to claim full compensation for that harm. Article 2 provides definitions of the terms used in the Directive. The key principles of the Directive, which give expression to the prior case law of the Court of Justice in judgments such as *Crehan*, are contained in Articles 3 and 4 of the Directive.

Article 3 reads as follows:

Article 3
Right to full compensation

1. Member States shall ensure that any natural or legal person who has suffered harm caused by an infringement of competition law is able to claim and to obtain full compensation for that harm.
2. Full compensation shall place a person who has suffered harm in the position in which that person would have been had the infringement of competition law not been committed. It shall therefore cover the right to compensation for actual loss and for loss of profit, plus the payment of interest.
3. Full compensation under this Directive shall not lead to overcompensation, whether by means of punitive, multiple or other types of damages.

Article 4 of the Directive gives effect to the well-established jurisprudence of the Court of Justice that Member States must respect the principles of effectiveness and equivalence in the enforcement of Articles 101 and 102[38].

The principle in Article 3 of the Directive is delightfully simple: the victims of anti-competitive behaviour should be compensated, but not over-compensated. In practice, however, establishing the correct amount of compensation—'quantum'—is far from simple. The position is complicated by the fact that a purchaser from a cartel may have 'passed on' at least some of the cartelised price to its own customers. We will deal with each of these topics in turn.

[35] Ibid. [36] www.ec.europa.eu.

[37] Article 2(1) of the Directive provides that an infringement of competition law means an infringement of Article 101 or 102 or of national competition law.

[38] For discussion of these terms see Cases C-295/04 etc *Vincenzo Manfredi v Lloyd Adriatico Assicurazioni SpA* EU:C:2006:461, para 62.

(ii) Quantum

Article 3(2) of the Directive should be read in conjunction with recital 12. Full compensation should put a person who has suffered harm in the position that that person would have been in had the infringement of competition law not taken place. To put the point another way, the claimant must establish the 'counterfactual': how much would it have paid, or what profit would it have made, but for the infringement? The claimant will be awarded the difference between the counterfactual and the position that it finds itself in in 'the real world'. Article 3(2) goes on to specify that a claimant should be able to recover the full value of actual loss suffered—known in Roman law as '*damnum emergens*'—as a result of an infringement of competition law; it should also be able to claim compensation for loss of profit—'*lucrum cessans*'—as well as interest from the time the damage was incurred. Recital 12 emphasises that interest is an essential component of compensation since a considerable amount of time may have passed between the infringement and the award of damages[39]. As noted earlier, the Court of Justice has established that a claimant may also recover umbrella damages[40].

The Commission has issued a *Communication on quantifying harm in damages cases*[41] together with a *Practical Guide* on the same topic[42]. The *Practical Guide* is purely informative and does not bind national courts or parties[43]. It is 68 pages in length and provides extensive analysis of methods and techniques that can be applied to damages claims before discussing the quantification of harm caused, first, by price increases and, secondly, by exclusionary practices.

Recital 45 of the Directive points out that establishing quantum in competition law cases is very fact-intensive and may require the application of complex economic models. This can be costly for claimants who may have difficulties in obtaining the data they require. Article 17(1) of the Directive, which should be read in conjunction with recitals 46 and 47, requires Member States to ensure that courts are empowered to **estimate** the amount of harm suffered by a claimant if it is practically impossible or excessively difficult **precisely** to quantify the harm suffered on the basis of the evidence available. Article 17(2) establishes a rebuttable presumption that cartel infringements cause harm. Article 17(3) requires Member States to ensure that NCAs, if so requested, can assist national courts with respect to the determination of quantum where an NCA considers such assistance to be appropriate.

In practice it has been relatively rare for courts to award damages in competition law cases. This is not because there is a lack of cases: rather what usually happens is that the parties reach a settlement, the terms of which will be kept strictly confidential[44]. This having been said there have been some awards of damages in recent years[45].

[39] On the award of damages see paras 509–547 of the judgment of the UK Competition Appeal Tribunal in Case 1241/5/7/15 (T) *Sainsbury's Supermarkets Ltd v MasterCard Inc* [2016] CAT 11.

[40] Case C-557/112 *Kone* EU:C:2014:1317, paras 28–34.

[41] See ch 8 n 8 earlier.

[42] SWD(2013) 205; the High Court in England and Wales referred to the *Practical Guide* in *Asda Stores v MasterCard Inc* [2017] EWHC 93 (Comm), para 306(3), as did the CAT in Case 1248/5/7/15 *Peugeot SA v NSK Ltd* [2017] CAT 2, para 14.

[43] *Communication*, para 12.

[44] For discussion of settlements see Rodger 'Why Not Court? A Study of Follow-On Actions in the UK' (2013) 1 Journal of Antitrust Enforcement 104; Rodger 'Private Enforcement of Competition Law, The Hidden Story: Competition Litigation Settlements in the UK 2000–2005' (2008) ECLR 96; Rodger 'Private Enforcement of Competition Law, The Hidden Story: Part II—Competition Litigation Settlements in the UK, 2008–2012' (2015) 8 Global Competition Litigation Review 89; F Marcos 'Why There Might Not Be Many Damages Claims Arising from the Spanish Property Insurance Cartel' (2010) Working Paper IE Law School WPLS10-09.

[45] For examples in the UK see 'Private enforcement of competition law in practice in the UK', pp 332–335 later in chapter; for an award of damages in the Netherlands see *TenneT v ABB* District Court of Gelderland, 29 March 2017, NL:RBGEL:2017:1724.

(iii) Passing on

Chapter IV of the Directive deals with 'The passing-on of overcharges'. Put simply, where the customers of a cartel are overcharged, they may pass on some or all of that overcharge to their customers. In these circumstances (at least) two questions arise. First, when a purchaser from the cartel claims damages but has passed the overcharge on to an indirect purchaser, can the defendant raise a 'passing-on defence'? If the answer to this question is no, the immediate purchaser would be over-compensated, as it would be able to recover for harm that it has not actually suffered. The second question is whether, if there has been a pass-on to an indirect purchaser, that indirect purchaser has a right of action against the members of the cartel? If the answer to this question is no, the indirect purchaser would be under-compensated[46]. The Directive provides answers to each of these questions.

Article 12(1) of the Directive provides that anyone who has suffered harm should be able to claim compensation, whether they are a direct or indirect purchaser. Article 12(2) acknowledges the risk of over-compensation of claimants, and therefore requires that Member States shall lay down procedural rules to avoid this risk. Article 13 deals with the passing-on defence. It requires Member States to ensure that defendants can invoke passing-on as a defence; the burden of proof that there has been a pass-on must be placed on the defendant, who may reasonably require disclosure from the claimant or from third parties. Article 14 discusses the position of indirect purchasers. Article 14(1) provides that Member States must ensure that the burden of proof is on indirect purchasers to show that higher prices have been passed on to them; however Article 14(2) provides a presumption in the indirect purchaser's favour where it has been overcharged for products that were the subject of an infringement of competition law, or products derived from such products. Article 15 requires Member States to take measures to ensure that national courts have sufficient information to enable them to understand whether damages actions have been brought by claimants from different levels of the supply chain. Article 16 provides that the Commission will issue guidelines for national courts on how to estimate the share of any overcharge that has been passed on to an indirect purchaser. A report was prepared for the Commission on the *Passing on of Overcharges*[47]. This will lead to Guidelines in due course.

In *Sainsbury's Supermarkets Ltd v MasterCard*[48] Sainsbury's sued MasterCard, which it claimed had charged an excessive 'multilateral interchange fee' ('MIF') contrary to Article 101. The UK Competition Appeal Tribunal (the 'CAT') agreed that the MIF was unlawful. It held that indirect purchasers can bring a claim when they are overcharged: indeed Sainsbury's itself was an indirect purchaser[49]. MasterCard raised a passing-on defence, arguing that Sainsbury's had passed on the overcharge to its customers. The CAT discussed the passing-on defence in paragraphs 479 to 485 of its judgment. Although the Damages Directive had yet to be transposed into UK law, the CAT found it useful

[46] In the US the Supreme Court rejected the passing-on defence in *Hanover Shoe Inc v United Shoe Machinery Corp* 392 US 481 (1968); as a natural corollary the Supreme Court held that sub-purchasers could not sue in *Illinois Brick Co v Illinois* 431 US 720 (1977). Several individual states in the US do allow sub-purchasers to sue: see *California v ARC America Corp* 490 US 93 at 105–106 (1989); the US Antitrust Modernization Commission recommended legislative action to improve the federal law on indirect purchasers: see Chapter III.BIIIB of the Report, available at govinfo.library.unt.edu/amc; these recommendations had not been implemented as at 8 December 2017; see also the US contribution to the OECD Roundtable, *Private Remedies* (2008), available at www.oecd.org/competition.

[47] The report was prepared by Cuatrecasas, Gonçalves Pereira and RBB Economics and is available at www.ec.europa.eu/competition/publications.

[48] Case 1241/5/7/15 (T) [2016] CAT 11, on appeal to the Court of Appeal, not yet decided.

[49] The unlawful MIF was charged by the 'issuing' bank to the 'acquiring' bank in a four-party payment card system, and the acquiring bank then passed on some or all of the overcharge to the merchant (in this case Sainsbury's).

to outline the provisions of Articles 13 to 15. In paragraph 484(2) it acknowledged the existence of the pass-on 'defence' in UK law, although it noted at paragraph 484(3) that it is in reality not a defence at all: rather it simply reflects the need to ensure that a claimant is compensated, but not over-compensated. The CAT went on to hold in paragraph 484(5) that, in law, the pass-on defence should succeed only where, on the balance of probabilities, the defendant shows that there is another class of claimants, downstream of the claimant(s), to whom the overcharge has been passed on. On the facts of the case the CAT rejected MasterCard's defence.

(iv) Disclosure of evidence

Recitals 14 to 29 and Chapter II of the Directive deal with the disclosure of evidence in competition cases. The recitals explain that claimants need information to be able to pursue their claims, but that information may be in the possession of the defendant or third parties (including public authorities). National courts should be able to order disclosure in favour of a claimant, but this process should be under the courts' control, especially as regards the necessity and proportionality of disclosure measures; it is important that business secrets and confidential information should be protected. Information in the possession of a competition authority may be of importance to a claimant; however there should be limits to the documents that can be handed to a claimant, in particular where this might jeopardise a competition investigation. More specifically it is important that nothing is done that could undermine the efficacy of leniency regimes.

The detailed rules on disclosure are contained in Articles 5 to 8 of the Directive.

(a) Article 5: disclosure of evidence

Article 5 requires that Member States shall ensure that national courts are able to order the defendant or a third party to disclose evidence that lies in their control, subject to the provisions of the Directive. Article 5(3) limits disclosure to what is proportionate, and Article 5(4) provides that the order for disclosure can extend to confidential information, subject to there being effective measures in place to protect its confidentiality.

(b) Article 6: disclosure of evidence in the file of a competition authority

Article 6 is concerned specifically with the disclosure of information in the file of a competition authority[50]. Article 6(2) provides that Article 6 is without prejudice to the rules on public access to Parliament, Council and Commission documents under Regulation 1049/2001[51]. Third parties frequently invoke Regulation 1049/2001 in order to try to obtain access to the Commission's file as in *CDC Hydrogene Peroxide v Commission*[52], where the General Court annulled the Commission's decision refusing to disclose an index of the case file in the *Hydrogen peroxide* cartel. Article 6(3) of the Directive provides that Article 6 is without prejudice to EU or national rules that prevent access to the internal documents of competition authorities or of correspondence between them. As a separate matter, there are frequent disputes between claimants and the Commission as to how much information should be redacted from the public version of a cartel decision published by the Commission: the claimant will want the public version to contain as much detail about

[50] Note that the right of access to the Commission's file in EU competition law is available only to undertakings to which it has sent a statement of objections, and not to third parties such as claimants for damages: see Article 27(1) and (2) of Regulation 1/2003, OJ [2003] L 1/1 and Article 15(1) of Regulation 773/2004, OJ [2004] L 123/18.

[51] OJ [2001] L 145/43.

[52] Case T-437/08 EU:T:2011:752; see also Case C-365/12 P *Commission v EnBW Energie Baden-Württemberg* EU:C:2014:112.

the cartel as possible whereas the Commission might err on the side of generous redactions in the defendant's favour[53]. It is also unfortunate that sometimes years can elapse before a public version of the Commission's decision becomes available at all[54].

Article 6(5) provides that certain information can be disclosed only after the competition authority has closed its proceedings. Article 6(6) is of particular importance. It provides that national courts must not at any time order disclosure of leniency statements or settlement submissions. Recital 26 explains the anxiety that disclosure might discourage undertakings that wish to cooperate with competition authorities from doing so for fear that they will be treated more harshly than other firms that are not cooperative[55].

A claimant in a damages action in the US might seek discovery of documents in the European Commission's possession, including leniency applications; such claims have been denied on several occasions where the US court considered it appropriate in order to maintain the confidentiality of the materials sought[56].

(c) Articles 7 and 8: limits on the use of evidence and penalties

Article 7 of the Directive imposes restrictions on the use of evidence acquired through access to the file of a competition authority; Article 8 requires there to be penalties for failing to comply with the disclosure requirements imposed by the Directive.

(v) **Effect of national decisions, limitation periods and joint and several liability**

Chapter III of the Directive deals with the effect in private litigation of national decisions by NCAs, with limitation periods and with joint and several liability.

(a) Article 9: effect of national decisions

Recital 34 of the Directive explains that consistent and effective enforcement of the competition rules requires that final decisions of an NCA or review court should not be relitigated in subsequent actions for damages. Article 9(1) therefore provides that decisions by the public authorities of a Member State that there has been an infringement of competition law shall be binding on the courts of that country in a claim for damages. Article 9(2) adds that decisions in another Member State will constitute *prima facie* evidence that an infringement of competition law has occurred.

(b) Article 10: limitation rules

Article 10 of the Directive requires that Member States must establish clear limitation rules. Limitation periods must not begin before the infringement of competition law

[53] See eg Case C-162/15 P *Evonik Degussa GmbH v Commission* EU:C:2017:205; Case C-517/15 P *AGC Glass Europe SA v Commission* EU:C:2017:598.

[54] This was a particular problem in the case of the Commission's decision in *Airfreight*, decision of 9 November 2010: see Case T-534/11 *Schenker AG v Commission* EU:T:2014:854 and the comments of Peter Smith J in *Emerald Supplies Ltd v British Airways plc* [2014] EWHC 3513 (Ch).

[55] In Case C-360/09 *Pfleiderer AG v Bundeskartellamt* EU:C:2011:389, prior to the adoption of the Directive, the Court of Justice had held that it should be left to national courts to decide on a case-by-case basis, according to national law, whether to order disclosure of leniency material, taking into account all the relevant factors in the case; see also Case C-536/11 *Bundeswettbewehrbehörde v Donau Chemie AG* EU:C:2013:366. The *Pfleiderer* judgment caused consternation on the part of the Commission and the NCAs which adopted a Resolution on 23 May 2012 on *Protection of leniency material in the context of civil damages actions* in which they concluded that domestic courts should, as far as possible, protect leniency materials against disclosure to ensure the effectiveness of leniency programmes.

[56] See eg *In re Rubber Chemicals Antitrust Litigation* 486 F Supp 2d 1078 (ND Cal 2007) (refusing to order disclosure of EU leniency documents) and *In re Cathode Ray Tube Antitrust Litigation*, order of 26 March 2014 (refusing to order disclosure of the confidential Commission decision of 5 December 2012 in *TV and computer monitor tubes*).

ceased; and they cannot start before the claimant knew or reasonably could be expected to know that it had a claim against the infringer. The limitation period must not be less than five years.

(c) *Article 11: joint and several liability*

Article 11(1) provides that undertakings that act jointly to infringe competition law shall be subject to joint and several liability for the harm caused. However Article 11 goes on to establish limitations to the joint and several liability of small and medium-sized undertakings and of leniency applicants. The reason for the latter is to avoid disincentivising whistleblowers from approaching the competition authorities[57].

(D) **The relationship between the Commission and domestic courts**

Articles 6, 15 and 16 of Regulation 1/2003 contain important provisions dealing respectively with the powers of national courts, cooperation between national courts and the Commission and the uniform application of EU competition law. These Articles should be read in conjunction with the Commission's *Notice on the co-operation between the Commission and the courts of the EU Member States in the application of Articles [101 and 102 TFEU]*[58] ('the *Co-operation Notice*'); this *Notice* was amended in 2015 in order to align it with the rules on disclosure of leniency statements and settlement submissions in Article 6 of the Damages Directive[59]. There is a consolidated version of the *Notice* available on the Commission's website[60].

Regulation 1/2003 and the *Co-operation Notice* are silent on the subject of arbitration[61].

(i) **Article 6: powers of the national courts**

Recital 7 of Regulation 1/2003 states that national courts have an 'essential part' to play in applying the competition rules. Article 6 of the Regulation states simply that:

> National courts shall have the power to apply Articles [101 and 102 TFEU].

An important issue, not discussed in Regulation 1/2003, is whether a national court has a duty, of its own motion, to raise issues of competition law irrespective of whether one or more of the litigants do so. This matter was considered by the Court of Justice in *van Schijndel*[62] and is summarised in paragraph 3 of the Commission's *Co-operation Notice*. Where domestic law requires a national court to raise points of law based on binding domestic rules which have not been raised by the parties the same obligation exists where binding EU rules, such as those on competition, exist; the same is the case where the national court has a discretion to raise such points of law. However EU law does not require national courts to raise a point of EU law where this would require them to abandon the passive role assigned to them by going beyond the ambit of the dispute defined by the parties.

[57] In the US, section 213 of the Antitrust Criminal Penalty Enforcement and Reform Act 2004 provides that a whistleblower is subject to single, not treble, damages; this provision is in force until 21 June 2020 (Pub L No 111–190, s 211(a), 124 Stat 1275, codified as at 15 USC s 1).

[58] OJ [2004] C 101/43.

[59] OJ [2015] C 256/5; on Article 6 see 'Article 6: disclosure of evidence in the file of a competition authority', pp 314–315 earlier in chapter.

[60] www.ec.europa.eu. [61] On arbitration see 'Arbitration', pp 341–342 later in chapter.

[62] Cases C-430/93 etc EU:C:1995:441; on this case see Prechal 'Community Law in National Courts: The Lessons from *Van Schijndel*' (1998) 35 CML Rev 681.

(ii) Article 15: cooperation with national courts

Recital 21 of Regulation 1/2003 refers to the importance of consistency in the application of the competition rules across the EU, and to the consequent need to establish arrangements for cooperation between the Commission and national courts, whether those courts are dealing with litigation between private parties, are acting as enforcers of the law or are sitting as courts of appeal or judicial review. Article 15 provides for various types of cooperation with national courts, as set out below. The cooperation envisaged under Article 15 is between the Commission and the national courts, not between the Commission and the litigants themselves: when asked to assist a national court the Commission will not have any direct dealings with the parties to the litigation and, if approached by them, it will inform the national court of the fact[63].

Regulation 1/2003 does not provide for a 'network of national courts' in the way that it establishes a 'network of national competition authorities'[64]. However an 'Association of European Competition Law Judges' was established in 2002 in order to bring together judges of the national courts to discuss and debate points of common interest. Its main aim is to promote knowledge and understanding of competition policy and issues throughout the respective judiciaries of the Member States. Various events are listed on its website, including details of its Annual Conference[65]. The European Commission also provides financial support for the training of national judges in the law and economics of competition.

(a) Requests by national courts for information or an opinion

Article 15(1) of Regulation 1/2003 provides that a national court may request the Commission to transmit to it information in the Commission's possession or to provide it with an opinion concerning the procedural or substantive application of the EU competition rules.

The Commission will endeavour to reply to a request for information within one month[66]. Article 339 TFEU provides that the Commission is not allowed to transmit information covered by the obligation of professional secrecy, which may be both confidential information and business secrets: the Commission will not provide such information to a national court unless the latter can guarantee that it will protect it[67]. The Commission will not transmit to a national court information that would jeopardise the enforcement of competition law[68]. More specifically it will not at any time transmit leniency corporate statements or settlement submissions[69]; and it will not transmit other information in its files until it has either adopted a final decision in a case or otherwise closed its administrative procedure[70].

The Commission will endeavour to reply to a request for an opinion within four months[71]. When giving its opinion the Commission will limit itself to providing the national court with the factual information or the economic or legal clarification asked for without considering the merits of the case[72]. Details of cases where the competent national court has given permission to publish opinions given by DG COMP can be found on its website: there are details of three opinions in 2015, but there was no information

[63] *Co-operation Notice*, para 19.

[64] See ch 7, 'Case allocation under Regulation 1/2003', p 299.

[65] The website of the AECLJ is www.aeclj.com.

[66] *Co-operation Notice*, para 22.

[67] Ibid, paras 23–25.

[68] Ibid, para 26.

[69] Ibid, para 26a; this paragraph is based on Article 6(6) of the Damages Directive.

[70] Ibid, para 26b; this paragraph is based in Article 6(5) of the Damages Directive.

[71] Ibid, para 28.

[72] Ibid, para 29.

available for 2016 or 2017 as at 8 December 2017[73]. Of course a national court requiring advice on a point of law could also, should it prefer to do so, make a preliminary reference under Article 267 TFEU to the Court of Justice[74].

A national court wishing to approach the Commission for assistance in an antitrust case may send an email to a bespoke address: comp-amicus@ec.europa.eu[75].

(b) Submission of judgments to the Commission

Article 15(2) of Regulation 1/2003 requires Member States to submit any written judgment deciding on the application of Articles 101 and 102 to the Commission, without delay after the full written judgment is notified to the parties. The Commission has created a database for such judgments which is accessible on its website[76]. Unfortunately it has not been maintained adequately and very few national judgments are recorded there.

(c) Observations by national competition authorities and the Commission

Article 15(3) of Regulation 1/2003 makes provision for NCAs and the Commission to make observations to national courts[77], sometimes referred to as *amicus curiae* submissions. Each may make written observations acting on their own initiative; oral observations may be made with the permission of the court. In order to enable them to make such observations NCAs and the Commission may request the relevant court to transmit or ensure the transmission to them of documents necessary for an assessment of the case. This provision is similar to the practice in some Member States that enables an NCA to intervene in cases before the national courts; in France, for example, the French Competition Authority may give expert testimony in civil proceedings[78]. Regulation 1/2003 does not provide a procedural framework for the submission of observations; this is therefore a matter for the rules and practices of the court of the Member State to which they are made[79]. Article 6(11) of the Damages Directive requires that NCAs should be able, acting on their own initiative, to submit observations to national courts as to the proportionality of requests by claimants in damages actions for disclosure of evidence in their files; and Article 17(3) provides that Member States must ensure that NCAs are able to provide assistance to national courts hearing competition cases as to the quantum of damages.

The Commission has provided opinions on several occasions: details will be found on DG COMP's website[80]. In the UK the European Commission has made *amicus curiae* submissions in three cases[81].

(d) Wider national powers

Article 15(1) to (3) of Regulation 1/2003 establishes EU rules on cooperation; Article 15(4) states that the rules therein are without prejudice to any wider powers that might exist under national law in a particular Member State allowing competition authorities to make observations.

[73] The website is www.ec.europa.eu/competition.

[74] On Article 267 references see ch 10, 'Which courts or tribunals in the UK can make an Article 267 reference in a case under the Competition Act 1998?', p 461.

[75] The address to use in state aid cases is comp-amicus-state-aid@ec.europa.eu.

[76] See www.ec.europa.eu/competition/elojade/antitrust/nationalcourts.

[77] The sole condition for the Commission to submit observations under Article 15(3) is that the coherent application of Articles 101 and 102 so requires: see Case C-429/07 *Inspecteur van de Belastingdienst v X BV* EU:C:2009:359, para 30.

[78] Commission's *White Paper on modernisation of the rules implementing [Articles 101 and 102 TFEU]* OJ [1999] C 132/1, para 107.

[79] *Co-operation Notice*, paras 34–35.

[80] www.ec.europa.eu/competition.

[81] *National Grid Electricity Transmission Plc v ABB Ltd* [2012] EWHC 869 (Ch); *Deutsche Bahn AG v Morgan Advanced Materials plc* [2014] UKSC 24; and Sainsbury's Supermarkets Ltd v MasterCard Inc, pending before the Court of Appeal.

(iii) Article 16: uniform application of EU competition law

Article 16(1) of Regulation 1/2003, which is concerned with the uniform application of EU competition law, explains the effect of Commission decisions on national courts. Recital 22 of the Regulation points out that it is important that the competition rules should be applied uniformly throughout the EU and that conflicting decisions should be avoided. The Regulation therefore clarifies, in accordance with the case law of the Court of Justice[82], the effect of Commission decisions on national courts (and NCAs). The Regulation also addresses the position of a national court dealing with a case which the Commission is investigating at the same time, without having yet reached a decision.

(a) The effect of Commission decisions

The first sentence of Article 16(1) gives expression to Article 288 TFEU and the Court of Justice's judgment in *Masterfoods*[83]. It states that, where national courts rule on a matter which has already been the subject of a Commission decision under Article 101 or Article 102, they cannot reach conclusions running counter to that of the Commission. The Regulation does not state specifically that an appellate court in a Member State would be bound by a Commission decision even where a lower court had reached a contrary conclusion prior to the Commission's decision; however this point was established by the Court of Justice in *Masterfoods*[84]. If the Commission's decision is on appeal to the General Court or the Court of Justice the national court should stay its proceedings pending a definitive decision on the matter by the EU Courts[85]. If a national court considers that a Commission decision is wrong, and if it has not been the subject of an appeal to the EU Courts, the only option available to the national court would be to make an Article 267 reference to the Court of Justice[86].

The Commission cannot state in the narrative of a decision that an undertaking has committed an infringement of the competition rules unless it also reaches a conclusion to that effect in the operative part of its decision capable of being challenged on appeal: the undertaking therefore has a right to have such a statement redacted from the narrative so that it will not be exposed to the risk, for example, of a damages claim in relation to assertions of fact which it has no ability to challenge[87].

(b) Parallel proceedings

The second sentence of Article 16(1) states that, where a national court is hearing an action, it must avoid giving a decision that would conflict with a decision contemplated by the Commission in proceedings that it has initiated. Article 16(1) adds that the national court in this situation should consider whether to stay its proceedings; if it were to do so, it is likely that the Commission would expedite its own proceedings in order to enable the outcome of the civil dispute to be decided. The national court could order interim measures to protect the interests of the parties while awaiting the Commission's decision[88].

[82] Of particular importance is the judgment of the Court of Justice in Case C-344/98 *Masterfoods Ltd v HB Ice Cream Ltd* EU:C:2000:689; see generally Nazzini *Concurrent Proceedings in Competition Law* (Oxford University Press, 2nd ed, 2016), esp ch 6; Komninos 'Effect of Commission Decisions on Private Antitrust Litigation: Setting the Story Straight' (2007) 44 CML Rev 1387; Wils 'The Relationship between Public Antitrust Enforcement and Private Actions for Damages' (2009) 32 World Competition 3; Rat 'Commitment Decisions and Private Enforcement of EU Competition Law: Friend or Foe?' (2015) 38 World Competition 527.

[83] See ch 8 n 82 earlier.

[84] *Masterfoods*, para 60.

[85] Ibid, paras 52 and 57; *Co-operation Notice*, para 13.

[86] Ibid, para 13.

[87] Case T-474/04 *Pergan Hilfsstoffe für Industrielle Prozesse GmbH v Commission* EU:T:2007:306; in the UK Court of Appeal 'Pergan protection' was given to certain defendants in *Emerald Supplies Ltd v British Airways plc* [2015] EWCA Civ 1024 and this has become standard procedure.

[88] *Masterfoods*, para 58; *Co-operation Notice*, para 14.

Where a national court has reason to believe that the Commission is conducting a parallel investigation of a possible infringement of Article 101 or 102 it could seek information from the Commission under the provisions of Article 15 of Regulation 1/2003 discussed earlier about any proceedings it may have in motion, what it is likely to decide in that case and when. The Commission has a duty under Article 4(3) TEU to cooperate with the courts in Member States in these matters[89].

An excellent judgment of the English High Court setting out the relevant principles in cases of this kind will be found in *Infederation Ltd v Google Inc*[90].

(E) Private international law

Claims for damages for infringements of Articles 101 and 102 must be brought in the domestic courts of the Member States. The Regulation on Jurisdiction and the Recognition and Enforcement of Judgments in Civil and Commercial Matters ('the Brussels Regulation')[91] determines which court (or courts) have jurisdiction to hear a case. The Regulation on the Law Applicable to Non-contractual Obligations ('Rome II')[92] determines which substantive law should be applied to the claim in question.

(i) The Brussels Regulation

Many cartels are international in scope and harm customers and ultimately consumers in more than one country. Claimants seeking damages may have a choice of where to bring their actions. The basic rule under Article 4[93] of the Brussels Regulation is that a defendant domiciled in a Member State should be sued in the courts of that Member State. However there are various exceptions to this rule: for example under Article 7(2)[94] it is also possible to bring an action in relation to a tort, delict or quasi-delict in the courts of the place where the harmful act occurred or may occur: this includes both the place where the damage occurred and the place of the event giving rise to it[95]. Article 8[96] provides

[89] See Case C-234/89 *Delimitis v Henninger Bräu* EU:C:1991:91, para 53; see also Cases C-319/93 etc *Hendrik Evert Dijkstra v Friesland (FRICO Domo) Coöperatie BA* EU:C:1995:433, para 34; on the Commission's duty of sincere cooperation see the order of the Court of Justice in Case C-2/88 R *Zwartveld* EU:C:1990:440, para 18 and Case C-275/00 *Commission v First NV and Franex NV* EU:C:2002:711, para 49.

[90] [2013] EWHC 2295 (Ch), para 25; see also *Secretary of State for Health v Servier Laboratories Ltd* [2012] EWHC 2761 (Ch); *Wm Morrison Supermarkets Plc v MasterCard Inc* [2013] EWHC 1071 (Comm) and [2013] EWHC 3082 (Comm).

[91] Regulation 1215/2012, OJ [2012] L 351/1, which applies to legal proceedings instituted on or after 10 January 2015, replacing the previous regulation, Regulation 44/2001, OJ 2001 L 12/1; the Court of Justice confirmed that an action for damages for infringement of competition law qualified as a 'civil and commercial matter' for the purposes of Regulation 44/2001: Case C-302/13 *flyLAL-Lithuanian Airlines AS, in liquidation v Starptautiskā lidosta Rīga VAS* EU:C:2014:2319, paras 23–38; see also Article 1(1) and recital 10 of Regulation 1215/2012, OJ [2012] L 351/1.

[92] Regulation 864/2007, OJ [2007] L 199/40, which entered into force from 11 January 2009 in all Member States except Denmark: claims arising before that date are governed by s 11 of the Private International Law (Miscellaneous Provisions) Act 1995; for discussion of Rome II see Segan 'Applicable Law "Shopping"? Rome II and Private Antitrust Enforcement in the EU' [2008] Comp Law 251; Holzmueller and von Koeckritz 'Private Enforcement of Competition Law Under the Rome II Regulation' (2010) 3 Global Competition Litigation Review 91; Danov *Jurisdiction and Judgments in Relation to EU Competition Law Claims* (Hart, 2011) ch 5; Ashton *Competition Damages Actions in the EU: Law and Practice* (Edward Elgar, 2nd ed, 2018), ch 7.

[93] Article 4 of Regulation 1215/2012 was Article 2 of Regulation 44/2001.

[94] Article 7(2) of Regulation 1215/2012 was Article 5(3) of Regulation 44/2001; for discussion of the latter see Case C-352/13 *Cartel Damage Claims (CDC) Hydrogen Peroxide SA v Akzo Nobel NV* EU:C:2015:335, paras 34–56 and Case C-27/17 *AB 'flyLAL-Lithuanian Airlines', in liquidation, v Starptautiskā lidosta 'Rīga' VAS, 'Air Baltic Corporation A/S'*, not yet decided; Four Seasons Holdings Inc v Brownlie [2017] UKSC 80, paras 29–31.

[95] Article 7(2) of Regulation 1215/2012.

[96] Article 8 of Regulation 1215/2012 was Article 6 of Regulation 44/2001.

that a defendant domiciled in a Member State can also be sued in the courts of another Member State when it is one of several defendants and the claims are so closely connected that it is expedient to hear them together to avoid the risk of irreconcilable judgments arising from separate proceedings. Article 25[97] provides that the parties to a dispute can agree to subject their dispute to the courts of a particular Member State, and that they may agree that such jurisdiction is to be exclusive; such a clause can extend to liability incurred as a result of an infringement of competition law[98].

There are numerous explanations as to why a particular claimant might choose to bring an action in the courts of Member State A rather than those of B: for example the quality of the lawyers and judges; the rules on the disclosure of evidence; the expense of litigation and the rules on costs; the speed of the procedure and the time within which a judgment might be handed down; the robustness of the appeal system; and the preferences of any firms contributing to the funding of the case. In recent years the majority of damages claims in competition law cases have been brought in the courts of the UK (more precisely of England and Wales), Germany and the Netherlands[99]. A possible effect of the Damages Directive may be that more actions will be brought in other jurisdictions in which legislative changes implementing the Directive improve the environment for private enforcement.

(a) *Anchor defendants*

As noted above, a claimant may have a choice of Member State in which to sue. If a cartel exists of X, domiciled in France, Y in Germany and Z in Italy, the claimant could commence proceedings against X in France, and then suggest to the French court that it should order that Y and Z should be joined to the proceedings on the basis that it would be expedient to hear the claims together. In these circumstances the expression 'anchor defendant' is used to describe the position of X, the defendant that 'anchors' the litigation in France and provides a basis for the French court to join in Y and Z. In *Cartel Damage Claims (CDC) Hydrogen Peroxide SA v Akzo Nobel NV*[100] the claimant commenced proceedings in Germany against Degussa, the only one of six defendants domiciled there. It then sought to join the five other cartelists, each of which was domiciled in another Member State; moreover the claimant reached a settlement with the anchor defendant Degussa and withdrew the action against it. The Court of Justice held that Article 6 of Regulation 44/2001, the forerunner of Article 8 of Regulation 1215/2012, did not preclude the German court from taking jurisdiction on the basis of that provision as long as there was no evidence that the agreement between CDC and Degussa amounted to artificial collusion to make Article 6 applicable: the mere holding of negotiations to reach an out-of-court settlement did not prove such collusion[101].

In *Provimi Ltd v Roche Products Ltd*[102] the claimant sought damages as a result of harm caused by the *Vitamins* cartels which had been condemned by the Commission[103]. Proceedings were commenced in England and Wales against the anchor defendant, Roche Products Ltd ('Roche UK'), on the basis that it was domiciled there. Provimi persuaded

[97] Article 25 of Regulation 1215/2012 was Article 17 of Regulation 44/2001.

[98] Case C-352/13 *Cartel Damage Claims (CDC) Hydrogen Peroxide SA v Akzo Nobel NV* EU:C:2015:335 paras 57–72; see also *Ryanair Ltd v Esso Italiana Srl* [2013] EWCA Civ 1450 and, for a ruling reaching a similar conclusion in relation to an arbitration clause in a supply agreement, *Microsoft Mobile Oy Ltd v Sony Europe Ltd* [2017] EWHC 374 (Ch).

[99] Jones 'Private Enforcement of EU Competition Law: A Comparison with, and Lessons from, the US' in Bergström, Iacovides and Strand (eds) *Harmonising EU Competition Litigation: The New Directive and Beyond* (Hart, 2016).

[100] Case C-352/13 EU:C:2015:335.

[101] Ibid, paras 31 and 32.

[102] [2003] EWHC 961 (Comm).

[103] OJ [2003] L 6/1.

the High Court that it had 'an arguable case' that Roche UK had infringed Article 101(1) by (even unknowingly) implementing the cartels entered into by its Swiss parent company, Roche Vitamine Europa AG. The High Court also acceded to Provimi's request to join the Swiss company on the basis of what is now Article 8 of the Brussels Regulation. The judgment in *Provimi* was criticised[104], and in *Cooper Tire & Rubber Company v Shell Chemicals UK Ltd*[105] the Court of Appeal cast doubt on its correctness; however it did not actually overrule it since the point was not germane to the actual appeal in that case[106]. The correctness of *Provimi* remains an open question[107].

In *Deutsche Bahn AG v Morgan Advanced Materials plc*[108] the UK Supreme Court (disagreeing with the Court of Appeal[109]) held that an action brought against Morgan in the CAT was out of time, which meant that the claimants were unable to treat Morgan as the 'anchor defendant' for their claims against the non-UK defendants.

(b) *Article 29:* lis pendens *and the 'Italian torpedo'*

Article 29[110] of the Brussels Regulation provides that, if litigation between two or more parties is commenced in one Member State, the courts of the other Member States are required to refrain from taking jurisdiction in relation to the same matter. This means that an undertaking, wishing to prevent litigation in one jurisdiction, might start an action elsewhere in order to prevent this happening; this is known as the 'Italian torpedo' tactic: the initiation of an action in, for example, Italy 'torpedoes' the chance of litigation taking place elsewhere. In *National Grid Electricity Transmission plc v ABB Ltd*[111] the claimant commenced proceedings in the High Court in England and Wales in order to pre-empt the possibility of any of the other litigants initiating proceedings in another jurisdiction. In *Cooper Tire & Rubber Company Europe Ltd v Dow Deutschland Inc*[112] the High Court held that Article 29 did not apply where the litigation in Italy involved different parties from those litigating in London. The High Court[113], with which the Court of Appeal agreed[114], also declined to stay the proceedings on a discretionary basis, as permitted by Article 30[115] of the Regulation, having regard to the length of time it would take to conclude the proceedings in Italy.

(ii) **Rome II**

The issue of which substantive law should be applied in a case of non-contractual obligations arising out of a restriction of competition is determined by reference to Article 6(3) of Rome II: the basic rule is that the law of the place where the market is affected or likely

[104] See Bulst 'The *Provimi* Decision of the High Court: Beginnings of Private Antitrust Litigation in Europe' (2003) European Business Organization Law Review 623 and Kennelly 'Antitrust Forum-Shopping in England: Is *Provimi Ltd v Aventis* Correct?' [2010] CPI Antitrust Chronicle, May 10 (2), available at www.competitionpolicyinternational.com.

[105] [2010] EWCA Civ 864, paras 45–47.

[106] In *KME Yorkshire Ltd v Toshiba Carrier UK Ltd* [2012] EWCA Civ 1190 the *Provimi* case had been applied at first instance, but by the time the matter reached the Court of Appeal the point was no longer relevant as the claimant had amended its pleadings to sue the UK subsidiary on a standalone basis for having itself infringed Article 101.

[107] See further *DSG Retail Ltd v MasterCard Inc* [2015] EWHC 3673 (Ch), para 66.

[108] [2014] UKSC 24; note that the CAT allowed the UK claimants to proceed against the non-UK defendants under what is now Article 7(3) (formerly Article 5(3)) of the Brussels Regulation): Case 1173/5/7/10 [2013] CAT 18.

[109] [2012] EWCA Civ 1055.

[110] Article 29 of Regulation 1215/2012 was Article 27 of Regulation 44/2001.

[111] [2009] EWHC 1326 (Ch).

[112] [2009] EWHC 2609 (Comm), paras 66–91; the judgment was not appealed on this point.

[113] Ibid, paras 96–118.

[114] [2010] EWCA Civ 864, paras 48–57.

[115] Article 30 of Regulation 1215/2012 was Article 28 of Regulation 44/2001.

to be affected should be applied. Article 15 explains which matters fall within the scope of the applicable law: Article 15(h) specifies that they include the rules on limitation[116].

(F) Collective redress in the EU

Infringement of Articles 101 and 102 may cause economic harm to a large number of (natural and legal) persons, in particular where higher prices are passed on to many indirect purchasers. The harm to any one person may be small, and insufficient to merit the risk and cost of bringing an action for damages. In these circumstances the right to damages may be more theoretical than real in the absence of a possibility for collective redress, a procedural mechanism enabling many single claims to be bundled into a single court action[117].

The availability of collective redress varies considerably from one Member State to another. The Commission's view is that there should be a coherent approach to collective redress across the EU, not only in competition law but in other areas such as consumer and environmental protection. Rather than proposing a directive, in 2013 the Commission published a Recommendation[118] that sets out a series of common, non-binding principles for collective redress mechanisms in Member States intended to improve access to justice while avoiding the risk of abusive litigation of the kind that is perceived to occur in the US. The Commission's declared intention was that Member States should put in place appropriate measures within two years of the Recommendation (that is to say by 26 July 2015) and that it would review the state of play two years thereafter[119]. The possibilities for collective redress presented by the UK Consumer Rights Act 2015 are discussed later in this chapter[120].

The Recommendation invites Member States to have collective redress systems, and recommends that they should respect the following principles:

- collective redress systems should provide injunctive and compensatory relief where a large number of persons are harmed by the same illegal practice
- collective redress procedures should be fair, equitable, timely and not prohibitively expensive
- as a general rule, collective redress should be available on an 'opt-in' basis: that is to say claimants should expressly consent to inclusion in an action
- provisions should be put in place to ensure that there are no incentives to abuse collective redress litigation (for example contingency fees should not be allowed and the representatives of claimants should act on a not-for-profit basis)
- the central role in collective litigation should be given to the judge.

[116] On the application of the Foreign Limitation Periods Act 1984 to limitation rules in claims governed by foreign law before Rome II entered into force on 11 January 2009 see Case 1240/5/7/15 *Deutsche Bahn v MasterCard* [2016] CAT 13 and Case 1244/5/7/15 *Peugeot Citroën Automobiles UK Ltd v Pilkington Group Ltd* [2016] CAT 14.

[117] For discussion of the issues see Van den Bergh 'Private Enforcement of European Competition Law and the Persisting Collective Action Problem' (2013) 20(1) Maastricht Journal of European and Comparative Law 12; Andreangeli *Private Enforcement of Antitrust through Collective Claims in the EU and US* (Edward Elgar, 2014); Rodger *Competition Law: Comparative Private Enforcement and Collective Redress Across the EU* (Kluwer Law International, 2014).

[118] Commission Recommendation of 11 June 2013 on common principles for injunctive and compensatory collective redress mechanisms in the Member States concerning violations of rights granted under Union law, OJ [2013] L 201/60; before this the Commission had published a consultation document on this topic, *Towards a Coherent European Approach on Collective Redress*, SEC(2011) 173, 4 February 2011, available at www.ec.europa.eu/competition/index_en.html.

[119] See Commission Press Release IP/13/524, 11 June 2013.

[120] See 'Collective redress in the UK', pp 330–332 later in chapter.

In April 2018 the Commission announced a 'New Deal for Consumers', which includes a proposal for consumer bodies to seek redress on behalf of a group of consumers; the proposals are not specifically concerned with competition law but more generally with consumer law[120a].

(G) Funding litigation

The cost of litigation—which can last years—may discourage small and medium-sized enterprises ('SMEs') and consumers from bringing actions for damages. The issue of funding was noted in a Staff Working Paper accompanying the Commission's White Paper on *Damages actions*[121], but the Damages Directive is silent on the issue. As a result, arrangements for funding vary among the Member States. Funding may be provided by the litigants themselves, by professional funders or by the claimant's lawyers working under a so-called 'no win, no fee' agreement. In the UK the funding of claims by third parties in return for a share of the proceeds used to be unlawful under the torts of maintenance and champerty[122]; in 2005, however, the Court of Appeal outlined circumstances in which the professional funding of litigation is acceptable. An important point is that the claimant, and not the funder, should be the person in control of the conduct of the litigation and the person with the primary interest in the outcome[123].

A different approach to litigation funding is taken by Cartel Damage Claims, a company that purchases competition law claims for damages and then pursues the aggregated actions in and out of court. CDC's website explains its business model and its track record in pursuing claims in competition law cases[124].

(H) Actions for injunctions and other types of relief

Crehan and *Manfredi* establish that there is a right to damages for harm caused by an infringement of the competition rules. Quite often a claimant is as interested in obtaining an injunction to bring anti-competitive behaviour to an end as in receiving damages; more specifically the claimant may seek interim relief pending the outcome of a competition investigation by a competition authority.

The Commission has power under Article 8 of Regulation 1/2003 to adopt interim measures[125]; NCAs have similar powers[126]. However the competition authorities, acting in the public interest, are sparing in their adoption of interim measures; a claimant in need of interim relief may find that an application to a national court is a more effective way to proceed, the function of the court being to achieve justice between the parties. In his Opinion in *AOK Bundesverband*[127] Advocate General Jacobs considered that the *Crehan* principle that damages should be available to protect the *effet utile* of Article 101 applied equally to applications for interim relief[128]. Applications for interim relief in the UK courts, which have sometimes been successful, are discussed later[129].

[120a] See Commission Press Release IP/18/304, 11 April 2018.

[121] COM(2008) 165 final, paras 273–276, available at www.ec.europa.eu.

[122] See *Sibthorpe v Southwark Borough Council* [2011] EWCA Civ 25.

[123] *Arkin v Borchard Lines Ltd* [2005] EWCA Civ 655, paras 39–43; note there is a Code of Conduct for Litigation Funders, available at www.associationoflitigationfunders.com.

[124] CDC's website is www.carteldamageclaims.com.

[125] See ch 7, 'Article 8: interim measures', pp 263–264.

[126] On the CMA's powers under UK law to adopt interim measures see ch 10, 'Interim measures', pp 416–417.

[127] Case C-264/01 EU:C:2004:304.

[128] See para 104 of the Opinion.

[129] See 'Interim relief', p 333 later in chapter.

3. Private Actions in the UK Courts

(A) The availability of damages in the UK courts

The UK courts established more than 30 years ago (long before *Crehan*) that damages are available for harm caused by infringements of Articles 101 and 102[130]. The Competition Act 1998 as originally drafted did not explicitly confer a right to damages where the Chapter I and Chapter II prohibitions are infringed. However there is no doubt that damages are available for competition law infringements: this follows from the debate in Parliament on the Competition Bill[131]; from the *Crehan* and *Manfredi* judgments, read in conjunction with section 60(2) of the Act, requiring consistency with the jurisprudence of the EU Courts[132]; from sections 47A and 47B of the Act; and from the Damages Directive, discussed below.

(B) Implementation of the Damages Directive in the UK

The Damages Directive was implemented in the UK by the Claims in Respect of Loss or Damage Arising from Competition Infringements (Competition Act 1998 and Other Enactments (Amendment)) Regulations 2017[133] (the 'Damages Directive Regulations'). They entered into force on 9 March 2017 and apply only to loss or damage suffered on or after that date[134]. The Regulations should be read in conjunction with Practice Directions issued under the Civil Procedure Rules[135], the Competition Appeal Tribunal's Rules and the CAT's *Guide to Proceedings*[136].

(C) The cause of action

The claimant's cause of action in competition cases is normally based on the tort of breach of statutory duty, the statute in question being the European Communities Act 1972[137] or the Competition Act 1998. However in *Courage Ltd v Crehan*[138] the Court of Appeal noted that Crehan would not have been able to recover damages according to the rules of that tort, since the harm he had suffered was not of the kind that Article 101 intended to prevent. However the Court recognised that Crehan should be able to recover damages because of the direction to that effect from the Court of Justice: the EU principle of *effet utile* overrode the position at common law[139].

In *WH Newson Ltd v IMI plc*[140] victims of a cartel pleaded both breach of statutory duty and the tort of conspiracy by unlawful means: the latter tort might lead to a higher award of damages than the former. The Court of Appeal upheld the judgment of the High Court, that section 47A of the Competition Act is 'neutral' as to the cause of action: a case

[130] See eg *Garden Cottage Foods v Milk Marketing Board* [1984] AC 130; *An Bord Bainne Co-operative Ltd v Milk Marketing Board* [1984] 1 CMLR 519, upheld on appeal [1984] 2 CMLR 584; *Bourgoin SA v Minister of Agriculture Fisheries and Food* [1985] 1 CMLR 528, on appeal [1986] 1 CMLR 267.

[131] See eg Lord Simon, HL 2R, 30 October 1997, col 1148; Margaret Beckett, HC 2R, 11 May 1998, col 35; see also DTI Press Release P/98/552, 9 July 1998.

[132] See ch 9, '"Governing Principles Clause": Section 60 of the Competition Act 1998', pp 387–392.

[133] SI 2017/385.

[134] Ibid, Rule 42(1).

[135] See Practice Direction 31C, Disclosure and inspection in relation to competition claims, available at www.justice.gov.uk.

[136] Both available at www.catribunal.org.uk.

[137] This was the approach taken by the House of Lords (now the Supreme Court) as regards the European Communities Act 1972 in *Garden Cottage Foods v Milk Marketing Board* [1984] AC 130 and in most cases since.

[138] [2004] EWCA Civ 637.

[139] Ibid, paras 154–168.

[140] [2013] EWCA Civ 1377.

therefore could be brought in conspiracy provided that the relevant decision disclosed that the constituent requirements for the commission of that tort were satisfied[141].

In *Devenish Nutrition Ltd v Sanofi-Aventis SA*[142] the Court of Appeal held that it is not possible to make a restitutionary award in competition cases; an 'account of profits' was precluded in particular where compensatory damages are an adequate remedy[143].

(D) Burden and standard of proof

The burden of proof in a damages case is on the claimant and it is incumbent on it to prove its allegations on the balance of probabilities[144]. The seriousness of what is alleged is taken into account when considering the probabilities of an infringement having occurred; the more unlikely the allegation, the stronger the evidence must be to establish it[145]. A claimant is allowed some latitude to state its claim in a competition law case[146]; however a claim will be struck out where it does not adequately plead the facts and matters relied on to establish an alleged infringement to the requisite standard[147].

The evidential burden of proving that a restriction in an agreement is an ancillary restraint, and the legal burden of proving that the agreement satisfies the terms of Article 101(3), is on the party arguing this to be the case[148].

(E) Damages claims may be brought in the High Court or the Competition Appeal Tribunal

A claimant seeking a remedy for an infringement of EU or UK competition law can bring an action either in the High Court or in the Competition Appeal Tribunal ('the CAT'). An action may be standalone[149], where the claimant must convince the court that an infringement has been committed; or follow-on, where the European Commission, the Competition and Markets Authority ('the CMA') or a sectoral regulator has already decided that competition law has been infringed, in which case that decision is binding on the court hearing the case.

[141] In the *Newson* case the Court of Appeal held, on the facts of that case, that the Commission's decision in *Copper plumbing tubes* did not show that the defendants had an intent to injure the claimants, a necessary ingredient of the tort of conspiracy; see also *Emerald Supplies Ltd v British Airways plc* [2015] EWCA Civ 1024 where the Court of Appeal struck out claims based on the torts of conspiracy and unlawful interference in a follow-on action based on the Commission's decision in *Air cargo*.

[142] [2008] EWCA Civ 1086, paras 104–111 (per Arden LJ) and 142–149 (per Longmore LJ); for discussion see Bailey and Brown '*Devenish Nutrition Ltd v Sanofi-Aventis SA (France)*: A Case Note' [2009] Comp Law 271.

[143] [2008] EWCA Civ 1086, para 108.

[144] *Shearson Lehman Hutton Inc v Watson Co Ltd* [1989] 3 CMLR 429 at 570; see also *Application by Anley Maritime Agencies Ltd for Judicial Review* [1999] Eu LR 97; *Arkin v Borchard Lines Ltd* [2001] Eu LR 232 and [2003] EWHC 687 (Comm); *Chester City Council v Arriva plc* [2007] EWHC 1373 (Ch), para 10.

[145] See *Ineos Vinyls Ltd v Huntsman Petrochemicals (UK) Ltd* [2006] EWHC 1241 (Ch), para 211; *Chester City Council v Arriva plc* [2007] EWHC 1373 (Ch), para 10.

[146] See eg *Nokia Corp v AU Optronics Corp* [2012] EWHC 731 (Ch), paras 53–57.

[147] See eg *Sel-Imperial Ltd v British Standards Institution* [2010] EWHC 854 (Ch), paras 17–18; *Humber Oil Terminals Trustee Ltd v Associated British Ports* [2011] EWHC 352 (Ch), paras 34 and 45, upheld on appeal [2012] EWCA Civ 36.

[148] *Asda Stores Ltd v MasterCard* [2017] EWHC 93 (Comm), paras 45 and 51 and Sainsbury's Supermarkets Ltd v Visa Europe Services LLC [2018] EWHC 355 (Comm), paras 22–25.

[149] Until 30 September 2015 the CAT could hear only follow-on cases; however s 81 of and Sch 8 to the Consumer Rights Act 2015, amending s 47A of the Competition Act 1998, enabled the CAT also to hear standalone cases with effect from 1 October 2015.

(i) High Court proceedings

Proceedings in the High Court are conducted in accordance with the Civil Procedure Rules. Actions are usually brought in the Chancery Division[150]. The High Court suggested in *Ineos Vinyls Ltd v Huntsman Petrochemicals (UK) Ltd* that a claimant before the court has a duty to inform it of any contact that it may have had with the CMA (or presumably the European Commission)[151]. An overview of damages claims in the High Court will be given later in this chapter[152].

(ii) CAT proceedings

The Competition Act enables the CAT to hear two types of claim. First, section 47A provides for individual claims. A claimant may bring a follow-on action for damages, for any other claim for a sum of money or for an injunction[153] in respect of an infringement decision of the CMA[154], the CAT itself or the European Commission. The claimant can also, since 1 October 2015, bring a standalone action based on an alleged infringement of UK or EU competition law. The second type of action is provided for by section 47B of the Act, which makes provision for collective proceedings, combining two or more claims to which section 47A applies[155].

Proceedings in the CAT are conducted in accordance with the Competition Appeal Tribunal Rules 2015[156]. The CAT has published the Competition Appeal Tribunal *Guide to Proceedings 2015*[157]. Section 49 of the Act provides for an appeal on a point of law, with permission, to the Court of Appeal from a decision of the CAT in a damages claim[158]. Details of claims brought on the basis of sections 47A and 47B can be found on the website of the CAT[159].

Provision is made in the CAT's rules for certain cases to be heard under a 'fast-track procedure'[160], in which case the substantive hearing will be held within a maximum of six months of the order to use the procedure. Various factors are relevant to the decision to make proceedings subject to the fast-track procedure, including whether one or more of the parties is an individual or an SME, whether the substantive hearing is likely to take three days or less and whether the case raises complex or novel issues. Follow-on actions

[150] Civil Procedure Rules, r 30.8(1) and (3); in some cases proceedings may be commenced in the Commercial Court of the Queen's Bench Division: r 30.8(4); see also the CPR *Practice Direction—Competition Law—Claims relating to the application of Articles [101 and 102 TFEU] and Chapters I and II of Part I of the Competition Act 1998*, which deals, among other matters, with Articles 15 and 16 of Regulation 1/2003; it is available at www.justice.gov.uk. In Case 3CL10014 *Martin Retail Group Ltd v Crawley Borough Council*, judgment of 24 December 2013, the Central London County Court held that a restrictive covenant in a commercial lease infringed the Chapter I prohibition; there appears to have been no discussion of whether the case should have been transferred to the High Court.

[151] [2006] EWCA Civ 1241, paras 262–265.

[152] See 'Private enforcement of competition law in practice in the UK', pp 332–335 later in chapter.

[153] Except in Scotland: Competition Act, s 47A(3)(c).

[154] References to the CMA for these purposes includes all sectoral regulators with concurrent power to enforce competition law.

[155] See 'Collective redress in the UK', pp 330–332 later in chapter.

[156] SI 2015/1648; cases commenced before 1 October 2015 were conducted under the Competition Appeal Tribunal Rules 2003 (SI 2003/1372) as amended by the Competition Appeal Tribunal (Amendment and Communications Act Appeals) Rules 2004 (SI 2004/2068).

[157] Available at www.catribunal.org.uk; there is an older *Guide for proceedings* commenced prior to 1 October 2015.

[158] On the scope of s 49 of the Competition Act see *English Welsh & Scottish Railway Ltd v Enron Coal Services Ltd* [2009] EWCA Civ 647, paras 22–24 and *Walter Hugh Merricks CBE v MasterCard Inc* [2017] CAT 21. A case can be appealed further to the Supreme Court where a point of law of general public importance arises, as in *Deutsche Bahn AG v Morgan Advanced Materials plc* [2014] UKSC 24.

[159] www.catribunal.org.uk.

[160] SI 2015/1648, Rule 58; see also paras 5.139–5.149 of the CAT's *Guide to Proceedings*.

for damages are unlikely to be heard on a fast-track basis[161]. An example of the fast-track procedure is *Socrates Training Ltd v The Law Society of England and Wales*[162], where the CAT found that the Law Society had infringed both the Chapter I and Chapter II prohibitions in the Competition Act 1998.

An overview of damages claims in the CAT will be given later in this chapter[163].

(iii) Which forum to choose?

A claimant seeking damages in the UK has two options: the High Court and the CAT, each of which has pros and cons. Some claimants prefer to litigate in the High Court because they are more in control of the pace and conduct of the proceedings; for example, unlike in the CAT, claimants do not need permission to withdraw a claim[164]. Another advantage of the High Court's jurisdiction is the fact that competition claims can be combined with other claims, such as a breach of contract or patent infringement. The High Court also has an impressive track record of dealing with highly complex cases[165].

A reason for selecting the CAT rather than the High Court is that it is a specialist competition body that sits in a panel of three members who collectively have expertise in competition law and policy. The CAT has relatively flexible procedures; the fast-track procedure is useful for certain claims; and the CAT's power to cap the amount of recoverable costs is attractive to some litigants. The CAT is able to offer a 'faster and less expensive route to justice' in some cases[166].

The High Court is able to transfer competition claims to the CAT[167], which it did in *Sainsbury's v MasterCard*[168] and in *Agents' Mutual v Gascoigne Halman*[169], but declined to do in *Unwired Planet v Huawei*[170].

(F) Decisions of the European Commission, the CMA and other NCAs

(i) Section 58A Competition Act

Section 58A of the Competition Act provides that infringement decisions of the European Commission, the CMA and the CAT are binding on the High Court and the CAT once the decision becomes final, that is to say after all appeal routes have been exhausted. In so far as a decision of the Commission becomes binding, section 58A gives expression to Article 16(1) of Regulation 1/2003[171].

In the *Crehan* litigation the Commission concluded, in relation to beer supply agreements entered into by Whitbread[172], Bass[173] and Scottish & Newcastle[174], that access to the

[161] Case 1250/5/7/16 *Breasley Pillows Ltd v Vita Cellular Foams (UK) Ltd* [2016] CAT 8.

[162] Case 1249/5/7/16 [2017] CAT 10; for comment see Armitage 'The (Fast-Track) Trial of Socrates' [2017] Comp Law 145.

[163] See 'Private enforcement of competition law in practice in the UK', pp 332–335 later in chapter.

[164] Competition Appeal Tribunal Rules 2015, r 44.

[165] See eg *Asda Stores Ltd v MasterCard Inc* [2017] EWHC 93 (Comm) (a standalone case under Article 101 and the Chapter I prohibition).

[166] See Hansard (HC Debates), 1 May 2002, cols 415 to 416 on the rationale for introducing the original version of s 47A of the Competition Act 1998.

[167] Enterprise Act 2002, s 16 and Section 16 Enterprise Act 2002 Regulations 2015, SI 2015/1643.

[168] [2015] EWHC 3472 (Ch); the final judgment is [2016] CAT 11.

[169] Order of the High Court of 5 July 2016, available at www.catribunal.org.uk.

[170] [2016] EWHC 958 (Pat); the final judgment is [2017] EWHC 711 (Pat).

[171] See 'Article 16: uniform application of EU competition law', pp 319–320 earlier in chapter.

[172] OJ [1999] L 88/26, upheld on appeal in Case T-131/99 *Shaw v Commission* EU:C:2002:83.

[173] OJ [1999] L 186/1, upheld on appeal in Case T-231/99 *Joynson v Commission* EU:C:2002:84.

[174] OJ [1999] L 186/28.

retail level of the beer market in the UK market was foreclosed. Crehan's agreement was not with any of those brewers but with Courage, and the Commission had not made any findings in relation to Courage's agreements. Park J[175] and the House of Lords on appeal[176] (disagreeing with the Court of Appeal[177]) held that, since those decisions did not deal with the same facts and the same parties, they were not binding on the court, although they were admissible as evidence[178]. Park J conducted his own assessment of the market and reached the conclusion that there was no foreclosure of the UK beer market, and that therefore the agreements in question did not infringe Article 101(1); the House of Lords (now the Supreme Court) upheld this finding.

(ii) Decisions of NCAs

Rule 35 of the Damages Directive Regulations gives effect to Article 9 of the Directive: a final decision of an NCA or a review court in another Member State finding an infringement of Article 101 or 102 is *prima facie* evidence of the infringement; however the decision is not binding. It will be recalled that the Regulations apply only to loss or damage suffered on or after 9 March 2017.

(iii) Section 58: findings of fact by the CMA

Section 58(1) of the Competition Act provides that, unless the court directs otherwise, findings of fact by the CMA in proceedings based on UK or EU competition law are binding on the parties in proceedings before the High Court and before the CAT[179], provided that the time for appeal against the finding has expired, or that the CMA's findings are confirmed on appeal. This means that parties that initiate such proceedings will not have to go through the process of producing all the evidence once again, but can proceed on the 'coat-tail' of the CMA's findings. The wording of the CMA's decision is obviously very important for the purposes of section 58. There is a significant distinction between a statement that 'A and B agreed to fix prices' and one that says 'it appears to the CMA that A and B may have fixed prices': only the former involves a finding of fact. The Court of Appeal has emphasised that section 58(1) applies only to a clearly identifiable finding of fact, and not to passages in a decision from which a finding of fact might arguably be inferred[180].

Section 58(3) of the Act enables rules of court to be made for the CMA to provide assistance to the court in private actions; no such rules have been made[181].

(G) Contribution

A defendant that is sued for damages as a result of an infringement of competition law may seek a contribution from other undertakings guilty of the same infringement: section 1

175 [2003] EWHC 1510 (Ch).

176 [2007] 1 AC 333; for comment see Beal '*Crehan* and Post-Modern Malaise' [2007] Comp Law 17; Hanley (2007) 44 CML Rev 817.

177 [2004] EWCA Civ 637.

178 On this point see *Iberian UK Ltd v BPB Industries and British Gypsum* [1996] 2 CMLR 601 (per Laddie J).

179 On the application of s 58 to s 47A proceedings before the CAT see *Enron Coal Services Ltd (in liquidation) v English Welsh & Scottish Railway Ltd* [2011] EWCA Civ 2, paras 33–56.

180 Ibid, paras 56 and 148.

181 Note however rr 4.1–4.8 of the Practice Direction on claims relating to the application of Articles [101 and 102 TFEU] and Chapters I and II of Part 1 of the Competition Act 1998; the ORR made use of these provisions in *English Welsh & Scottish Railway Ltd v E.ON plc* [2007] EWHC 599 (Comm).

of the Civil Liability (Contribution) Act 1978 makes provision for this. This is a complex matter of tort, rather than competition, law[182].

(H) Collective redress in the UK

As noted earlier in this chapter, the European Commission published a Recommendation in 2013 encouraging Member States to adopt collective redress mechanisms[183]. In the UK there is some scope for collective redress in the High Court, while specific provision is made for collective proceedings in competition cases in the CAT.

(i) High Court: group litigation orders and representative actions

Actions for damages in the High Court may be facilitated by a 'group litigation order'[184], 'representative actions'[185], consolidation[186] or a single trial of multiple claims[187] under the English civil procedure rules. Group litigation orders provide for the case management of claims that give rise to common or related issues of fact or law[188]. Representative actions may provide a convenient means by which to avoid a large number of substantially similar actions. In *Emerald Supplies Ltd v British Airways plc*[189] the Court of Appeal, upholding the decision of the High Court[190], concluded that the procedure could not be used in that case where the claimants wished to represent both direct and indirect purchasers from undertakings in the *Air cargo* cartel[191]. The Court held that these two groups did not have the same interest as required by the relevant rule: an indirect purchaser would presumably agree with the defendant(s) that there is a passing-on defence, so that it (the indirect purchaser) can recover rather than the direct purchaser.

(ii) CAT: collective proceedings

Section 47B of the Competition Act 1998 makes provision for collective proceedings to be brought in the CAT[192].

(a) Opt-in and opt-out collective proceedings

Until 1 October 2015 collective proceedings could be brought only on an 'opt-in' basis, whereby consumers had to make a positive choice to join in the action. Only one representative action was brought, *The Consumers' Association v JJB Sports*[193], and the case demonstrated the weakness of the opt-in model. Millions of consumers had purchased football shirts, but only 130 opted to join in the action. The case was settled by agreement early in

[182] On contribution in English tort law see Jones, Dugdale and Simpson (eds) *Clerk & Lindsell on Torts* (Sweet & Maxwell, 22nd ed, 2017), paras 4-13–4-28; Matthiesson 'Bringing Contribution Proceedings in Cartel Damages Actions in the English Courts' [2016] Comp Law 65; examples of claims for contribution are *WH Newson Holding Ltd v IMI plc* [2013] EWHC 3788 (Ch), upheld on appeal [2016] EWCA Civ 773 and *Emerald Supplies Ltd v British Airways plc* [2014] EWHC 3514 (Ch).

[183] See 'Collective redress in the EU', pp 323–324 earlier in chapter.

[184] Civil Procedure Rules, rr 19.10–19.15; a register of group litigation orders is available at www.gov.uk.

[185] Civil Procedure Rules, r 19.6. [186] Ibid, r 3.1(2)(g).

[187] As occurred in *Asda Stores Ltd v MasterCard Inc* [2017] EWHC 93 (Comm).

[188] The group litigation order procedure has been used in a competition case: *Prentice Ltd v DaimlerChrysler UK Ltd*; the case was settled before trial.

[189] [2010] EWCA Civ 1284.

[190] [2009] EWHC 741 (Ch); for comment see Mulheron '*Emerald Supplies Ltd v British Airways plc*; A Century Later, the Ghost of *Markt* Lives on' [2009] Comp Law 159.

[191] [2010] EWCA Civ 1284, para 62.

[192] See Part 5 of the Competition Appeal Tribunal Rules 2015 and Section 6 of the Competition Appeal Tribunal *Guide to Proceedings 2015*.

[193] Case 1078/7/9/07.

2008 and the action was withdrawn[194]. The Consumers' Association expressed its dissatisfaction with this case. This led in due course to the adoption of the Consumer Rights Act 2015[195] which made significant changes to section 47B, in particular by making provision for 'opt-out' collective actions: in opt-out cases the person appointed to be a class representative brings the claim on behalf of everyone harmed by the competition law infringement except for those who make a positive choice to opt out. It is obvious that, from a class representative point of view, the opt-out model is much more attractive than the opt-in one; however, as we shall see, the first two attempts to bring opt-out actions proved unsuccessful[196].

(b) Collective proceedings orders

Collective proceedings are possible only where the CAT makes a collective proceedings order ('CPO')[197]: the CAT plays a crucial role as a 'gatekeeper' of the system. Claims are eligible for inclusion in collective proceedings only if the CAT considers that they raise the same, similar or related issues of fact or law and are suitable to be brought in collective proceedings[198]. A CPO must authorise the person who brought the proceedings to act as the class representative; describe the class of persons whose claims are eligible for inclusion; and specify whether the proceedings are opt-in or opt-out[199].

(c) Damages in collective proceedings

Section 47C of the Competition Act deals with damages in collective proceedings[200]. The CAT can order that damages be paid to the class representative or to such other person as it thinks fit. In the event that some represented persons do not claim the amount to which they are entitled, section 47C(5) and (6) provide that that amount can be paid to a charity[201] prescribed by an order of the Lord Chancellor or be used to pay all or part of the representative's costs, a term that can include the costs of a funder[202].

(d) Settlements and redress schemes

Sections 49A and 49B of the Competition Act make provision for the CAT to approve the collective settlement of claims in collective proceedings. Section 49C enables the CMA to approve a voluntary redress scheme submitted by businesses. The Competition Act 1998 (Redress Schemes) Regulations 2015[203] govern the approval process and operation of voluntary redress schemes and the CMA has published *Approval of voluntary redress schemes for infringements of competition law*[204] and accompanying application forms. Provision is made by section 49D of the Act for the CMA to require a person seeking approval of a redress scheme to pay some or all of its costs relating to the application. Section 49E gives enforcement powers in respect of such schemes to the intended beneficiaries and to the CMA.

194 Ibid, order of the CAT of 14 January 2008.

195 On the background to the Consumer Rights Act 2015 see the Government's *Private actions in competition law: a consultation on options for reform*, 24 April 2012 and the *Government response to consultation on options for reform*, 29 January 2013, both available at www.gov.uk.

196 See 'Collective proceedings in practice', p 332 later in chapter.

197 Competition Act 1998, s 47B(4); see also the CAT Rules, r 77(1).

198 Competition Act 1998, s 47B(6): see also the CAT Rules, r 79.

199 Competition Act 1998, s 47B(7); see also CAT Rules, r 78.

200 Provision is made in s 47D of the Competition Act 1998 for injunctions to be granted in collective proceedings.

201 The charity currently prescribed is the Access to Justice Foundation: Legal Services Act (Prescribed Charity) Order 2008, SI 2008/2680.

202 Case 1266/7/7/16 *Walter Hugh Merricks CBE v MasterCard Inc* [2017] CAT 16, paras 109–127.

203 SI 2015/1587.

204 CMA40, 2015 available at www.gov.uk/cma; the FCA, Payment Systems Regulator ('the PSR') and OFGEM have published similar guidance.

(e) Collective proceedings in practice

As noted above *The Consumers' Association v JJB Sports*[205] was somewhat unsuccessful from the Consumers' Association's perspective. Two applications have been made to the CAT for an opt-out collective proceedings order since the Consumer Rights Act 2015 entered into force: *Dorothy Gibson v Pride Mobility Products Ltd*[206] and *Walter Hugh Merricks CBE v MasterCard Inc*[207]; they were both unsuccessful. The *Gibson* case related to an Office of Fair Trading ('OFT') decision finding that vertical agreements for the distribution of mobility scooters restricted price competition. A judgment was handed down by the CAT on 31 March 2017 exposing weaknesses in Gibson's application; the CAT adjourned the proceedings and granted permission to the applicant to serve an amended claim form[208]. The application was subsequently withdrawn by consent on 25 May 2017, the applicant having decided that the claim was unlikely to be worthwhile pursuing financially. The *Merricks* case related to the European Commission's decision that MasterCard's intra-EEA MIFs were unlawful. The CAT dismissed the application[209].

(I) Limitation rules

The limitation period for bringing actions in the High Court and the CAT[210] is generally six years from the date on which the loss was suffered[211]. It is also necessary to take into account Part 5 of the Damages Directive Regulations[212] that implement the Damages Directive and apply only to loss or damage suffered on or after 9 March 2017. The limitation period is postponed if material facts are deliberately concealed by the defendant[213], as in the case of secret cartels; time starts to run from when the claimant knew or ought to have known of those facts, which will often be when a competition authority publishes an infringement decision. In *Arcadia Group Brands Ltd v Visa Inc*[214] the High Court agreed with Visa that the facts relevant to the claimants' cause of action were known or reasonably discoverable given the decisions and public pronouncements of the European Commission and the former OFT in relation to the lawfulness of so-called 'multilateral interchange fees'. The impact of the judgment was significant as it meant that the claims against Visa could date back only to 2007, not 1977. The judgment was upheld on appeal to the Court of Appeal[215].

(J) Mediation

The courts may use their powers to encourage parties to mediate and settle their disputes otherwise than by trial. In some cases the High Court and the CAT encourage the parties to consider the possibility of mediation of their dispute, and this process has led to several settlements out of court[216].

(K) Private enforcement of competition law in practice in the UK

Many actions based on competition law have been commenced in the High Court or the CAT. In some cases the claimant's interest is in obtaining interim relief, in others damages

[205] See ch 8 n 193 earlier.

[206] Case 1257/7/7/16; for comment see Noble, Bell and Shah 'Class Actions: The Mobility Scooters Case' [2017] Comp Law 221.

[207] Ch 8 n 202 earlier.

[208] [2017] CAT 9.

[209] [2017] CAT 16; the CAT refused permission to appeal, [2017] CAT 21 but the Court of Appeal granted permission on 19 January 2018; details of the proceedings are available at www.mastercardconsumerclaim.co.uk.

[210] See s 47E of the Competition Act; previously there were different limitation rules for proceedings in the CAT: see the 8th edition of this book, pp 337–338.

[211] Limitation Act 1980, s 2; see generally McGee *Limitation Periods* (Sweet & Maxwell, 7th ed, 2017) and Brealey and Green (eds) *Competition Litigation: UK Practice and Procedure* (Oxford University Press, 2010), ch 4.

[212] SI 2017/385.

[213] Limitation Act 1980, s 32(1)(b).

[214] [2014] EWHC 3561 (Comm).

[215] *Arcadia Group Brands Ltd v Visa Inc* [2015] EWCA Civ 883.

[216] See eg in the CAT Case 1088/3/7/07 *ME Burgess v W Austin & Sons Ltd*, transcript of case management conference of 20 November 2007, available at www.catribunal.org.uk.

or some other remedy. This section provides a brief overview of the cases, including some that were unsuccessful.

(i) Interim relief

In the commercial world the victim of allegedly anti-competitive behaviour sometimes seeks a remedy as a matter of urgency. This could be the case, for example, where a supplier threatens to discontinue supplies; another example would be where a dominant firm reduces its prices to a predatory level, thereby jeopardising a competitor's ability to remain on the market. Applications to the European Commission or the CMA for interim measures, though theoretically possible, are highly unlikely to be successful[217]. For this reason a more promising course of action would be to seek interim relief from the High Court or the CAT.

The test for the grant of interim relief in competition cases is to decide which course (that is to say the grant or the refusal of the injunction) would involve less risk of injustice if it turns out to be wrong[218]. Applications for interim relief have sometimes been rejected on the ground that an award of damages at the trial of the action would be an adequate remedy[219]. However some applications have been successful, particularly where individuals' livelihoods were at stake[220], but also sometimes between more substantial litigants[221]. Interim relief was granted in *Jobserve Ltd v Network Multimedia Television*[222], *Adidas-Salomon AG v Roger Draper and Paul Howorth*[223], *Software Cellular Network Ltd v T-Mobile (UK) Ltd*[224], *Dahabshiil Transfer Services Ltd v Barclays Bank plc*[225] and in *Packet Media Ltd v Telefónica UK Ltd*[226]. Claims were rejected in *Claritas (UK) Ltd v Post Office*[227] and in *AAH Pharmaceuticals Ltd v Pfizer Ltd*[228] where the claimants were considered to have unduly delayed their application to the court, having earlier sought (and failed to obtain) interim measures from the OFT (now the CMA).

(ii) Damages

The High Court has yet to award damages in a competition law case, although it is known that several actions commenced there resulted in settlements[229]. By 8 December 2017 the

[217] See ch 7, 'Article 8: interim measures', pp 263–264 (EU law) and ch 10, 'Interim measures', pp 416–417 (UK law).

[218] See *AAH Pharmaceuticals Ltd v Pfizer Ltd* [2007] EWHC 565 (Ch), paras 49–57; see to similar effect an earlier judgment of the Court of Appeal in *Zockoll Group Ltd v Mercury Communications Ltd* [1997] EWCA Civ 2317.

[219] See eg *Garden Cottage Foods v Milk Marketing Board* [1984] AC 130; *Argyll Group plc v Distillers Co plc* [1986] 1 CMLR 764; *Plessey Co plc v General Electric Co* [1990] ECC 384; *Megaphone v British Telecom*, 28 February 1989, unreported, QBD; *Macarthy v UniChem* [1991] ECC 41.

[220] *Cutsforth v Mansfield Inns* [1986] 1 CMLR 1; *Holleran and Evans v Thwaites plc* [1989] 2 CMLR 917.

[221] Eg ECS succeeded in obtaining an interim injunction against AKZO in the High Court as well as persuading the Commission to proceed under Article 102 in *ECS/AKZO* OJ [1983] L 252/13; see also *Sockel GmbH v Body Shop International plc* [1999] Eu LR 276.

[222] [2001] UKCLR 814, upheld on appeal [2002] UKCLR 184.

[223] [2006] EWHC 1318 (Ch).

[224] [2007] EWHC 1790 (Ch).

[225] [2013] EWHC 3379 (Ch).

[226] [2015] EWHC 2235 (Ch); the injunction was subsequently discharged, [2015] EWHC 3873 (Ch).

[227] [2001] UKCLR 2.

[228] [2007] EWHC 565 (Ch); further examples of unsuccessful applications are *Arriva Scotland West Ltd v Glasgow Airport Ltd* [2011] CSOH 69; *Chemistree Homecare Ltd v Abbvie Ltd* [2013] EWCA Civ 1338; *Bruce v The British Boxing Board of Control* [2014] EWHC 2074 (QB).

[229] Eg some damages claims have been settled between pharmaceutical producers and the Department of Health: see eg Scottish Government Press Release, 13 May 2014, announcing settlement of claims brought by the Devolved NHS against Reckitt Benckiser plc, available at news.gov.scot. In a different case British Airways and Virgin Atlantic made £73.5 million available to settle cases in the UK arising out of the air fuel surcharge cartel: see *Financial Times*, 11 June 2010. See further Rodger 'Private Enforcement of Competition Law, the Hidden Story: Competition Litigation Settlements in the United Kingdom, 2000–2005' (2008) 29 ECLR 96.

CAT had awarded damages in four cases. An award of interim damages of £2 million was made in *Healthcare at Home v Genzyme Ltd*[230], the first (and only) time that this has happened in a competition law case in the UK; this was a follow-on action pursuant to the OFT's decision that Genzyme was guilty of an unlawful margin squeeze[231].

Damages, including interest, were awarded in two more follow-on cases[232]. In *2 Travel v Cardiff City Transport Services Ltd*[233] the CAT awarded both compensatory and exemplary[234] damages amounting to £93,818 against Cardiff City Transport for abusing its dominant position in the provision of local bus services; this followed the OFT's decision in *Cardiff Bus*[235]. In *Albion Water v Dŵr Cymru Cyfyngedig*[236] it awarded compensatory damages but not exemplary ones of £1.85 million against Dŵr Cymru for abusive pricing for the carriage of water; in this case it was the CAT itself that had found there to be abusive behaviour[237].

In *Sainsbury's Supermarkets Ltd v MasterCard Inc*[238] the CAT awarded Sainsbury's damages of £68 million plus interest for harm caused to it by MasterCard's unlawful UK MIFs; this was a standalone case. Interestingly in *Asda Stores Ltd v MasterCard Inc* the High Court reached the conclusion that the same interchange fees did not violate Article 101 and therefore did not award damages[239]. A damages action against Visa also failed as there was found to be no violation of Article 101[240].

(iii) **Declarations and other relief**

A partially successful action was *Hendry v World Professional Billiards and Snooker Association*[241] in which Lloyd J held that, for the most part, the rules of the association did not infringe competition law; however one rule, which restricted the tournaments in which players could participate in certain circumstances, was found to infringe both the Chapter I and Chapter II prohibitions[242], as well, probably, as Articles 101 and 102 TFEU[243]. In *Purple Parking v Heathrow Airport*[244] Mann J found Heathrow Airport guilty of discrimination under Article 102(2)(c) in relation to the provision of valet parking services. In *Arriva The Shires v London Luton Airport*

[230] Case 1060/5/7/06 [2006] CAT 29; note that the CAT held that the claimant could claim damages not only for the period that the OFT and the CAT itself had held that the Chapter II prohibition had been infringed, but also for the subsequent period in which the infringement continued: ibid, para 59; cp Case 1236/5/7/15 *DSG Retail Ltd v MasterCard Inc* [2015] CAT 7, paras 25–37.

[231] OFT decision of 27 March 2003.

[232] As to the date at which damages are to be calculated see the Court of Appeal's judgment in *Courage Ltd v Crehan* [2004] EWCA Civ 637, paras 173–180.

[233] Case 1178/5/7/11 [2012] CAT 19.

[234] Note that, pursuant to Article 3(3) of the Damages Directive, Reg 36 of the Damages Directive Regulations provides that exemplary damages cannot be awarded in relation to loss or damage suffered on or after 9 March 2017.

[235] OFT decision of 18 November 2008.

[236] Case 1166/5/7/10 [2013] CAT 6.

[237] Case 1046/2/4/04 *Albion Water Ltd v Water Services Regulation Authority* [2006] CAT 36, upheld on appeal to the Court of Appeal [2008] EWCA Civ 536 (margin squeeze) and [2008] CAT 31 (excessive pricing).

[238] Case 1241/5/7/15 (T) [2016] CAT 11, on appeal to the Court of Appeal.

[239] [2017] EWHC 93 (Comm), on appeal to the Court of Appeal.

[240] *Sainsbury's Supermarkets Ltd v Visa Europe Services LLC* [2017] EWHC 3047 (Comm), on appeal to the Court of Appeal, not yet decided.

[241] [2002] UKCLR 5; for (critical) comment see Harris 'Abusive Sports Governing Bodies: *Hendry v WPBSA*' [2002] Comp Law 101; on the market definition in this case see Veljanovski 'Markets in Professional Sports: *Hendry v WPSBA* and the Importance of Functional Markets' (2002) 23 ECLR 273.

[242] [2002] UKCLR 5, para 112.

[243] Ibid, para 113.

[244] [2011] EWHC 987 (Ch); the claim was subsequently settled out of court.

Operations[245] Rose J held that it was abusive for Luton Airport to grant National Express the exclusive right to run a coach service between the airport and central London. Both the *Purple Parking* and *Arriva* cases proceeded on the assumption that the airport in question held a dominant position.

(iv) Unsuccessful claims

In *Attheraces v British Horse Racing Board*[246] the High Court concluded that the British Horseracing Board had abused its dominant position under Article 102 by charging excessive and/or discriminatory prices for the supply of information to Attheraces about horseracing events conducted under its auspices; however this judgment was reversed on appeal[247]. An action for a declaration, injunction and damages under the Chapter II prohibition failed in *Chester City Council v Arriva plc*[248] where the court held that the claimant had failed to adduce any evidence demonstrating that Arriva held a dominant position. In *Bookmakers' Afternoon Greyhound Services Ltd v Amalgamated Racing Ltd*[249] the High Court dismissed a claim that arrangements between a number of British racecourses for distributing their rights to broadcast horseracing infringed Article 101 and the Chapter I prohibition; the judgment was affirmed by the Court of Appeal[250]. Several other attempts to invoke the Competition Act in litigation have failed[251]. In *Streetmap.EU v Google Inc*[252] the High Court rejected a claim that Google had abused its dominant position by including a Google map in the results of Google searches, thereby eliminating Streetmap from the online mapping market.

A claimant must be able to demonstrate that the anti-competitive behaviour of which it complains caused the loss it suffered[253]. In *Enron Coal Services Ltd v English Welsh & Scottish Railway Ltd*[254] the Court of Appeal agreed with the CAT[255] that there was insufficient evidence that Enron would have won a contract but for the infringement by EW&S. The fact that the Office of Rail Regulation (now Office of Rail and Road) had found that EW&S had put Enron at a competitive disadvantage did not mean that Enron would have been awarded the contract; a competition authority does not necessarily make findings about causation in an infringement decision[256].

[245] [2014] EWHC 64 (Ch); the claim was subsequently settled out of court: for comment see Smith and Mourkas 'High Court decision in *Arriva v Luton Airport*' [2015] Comp Law 79.

[246] [2005] EWHC 3015 (Ch).

[247] [2007] EWCA Civ 38; for further discussion of this case see ch 18, 'Private litigation and excessive pricing', pp 745–746.

[248] [2007] EWHC 1373 (Ch).

[249] [2010] EWHC 1743 (Ch); the High Court also dismissed, by a separate judgment, counterclaims alleging unlawful collusion between the bookmakers [2008] EWHC 2688 (Ch).

[250] [2009] EWCA Civ 750; for comment see Vajda and Woolfe 'The Chapter I Prohibition: Is It a Safe Bet?' [2010] Comp Law 198.

[251] *Synstar Computer Services (UK) Ltd v ICL (Sorbus) Ltd* [2001] UKCLR 585; *Land Rover Group Ltd v UPF (UK) Ltd (in receivership)* [2002] All ER (D) 323; *Getmapping plc v Ordnance Survey* [2002] EWHC 1089 (Ch); *Intel Corpn v VIA Technologies* [2002] EWHC 1159 (Ch), reversed on appeal [2002] EWCA Civ 1905; *Suretrack Rail Services Ltd v Infraco JNP Ltd* [2002] EWHC 1316 (Ch); *Sel-Imperial Ltd v British Standards Institution* [2010] EWHC 854 (Ch) (striking out two parts of a claim alleging an infringement of Article 101); *Humber Oil Terminals Trustee Ltd v Associated British Ports* [2011] EWHC 352 (Ch), upheld on appeal to the Court of Appeal [2012] EWCA Civ 36.

[252] [2016] EWHC 253 (Ch); for comment see Whish 'Article 102 and *de minimis*' [2016] Comp Law 53.

[253] See eg the judgment of the Queen's Bench Division of the High Court in *Arkin v Bochard Lines Ltd* [2003] EWHC 687 (QB), paras 489–570, where the court found that there was no causation between the conduct complained of and the harm suffered by the claimant.

[254] [2011] EWCA Civ 2. [255] [2009] CAT 36. [256] Ibid, para 150.

4. Competition Law as a Defence

(A) Article 101(2)

(i) The sanction of voidness

Many systems of competition law deploy an important sanction, in addition to the imposition of fines and damages actions, in order to persuade undertakings to obey the law: the sanction of voidness. Article 101(2) TFEU and section 2(4) of the Competition Act 1998 provide that an agreement that restricts competition in the sense of Article 101(1) and that does not satisfy the terms of Article 101(3) is void. In some cases the sanction of voidness may not be a very real one: the members of a price-fixing or a market-sharing cartel would not normally think of trying to enforce their agreement in a court. Their main concern will be to conceal the cartel from the competition authorities, although the latter have considerable powers to unearth this type of practice[257] and to penalise the recalcitrant firms[258]. In other cases, however, the sanction of voidness may be much more significant. If a patentee grants a licence of a patent it will calculate carefully what rate of royalties the licensee should pay and protracted negotiations may take place to settle the other terms of the bargain, for example on the quantities to be produced, the areas in which the products are to be sold and the treatment and ownership of any improvements made by the licensee. For its part the licensee will often have been granted an exclusive territory in which to manufacture and sell. If it transpires that certain aspects of the licence are void and unenforceable this will undermine the deal struck between the parties. The same would be true of an exclusive purchasing term imposed by a supplier on a distributor, as typically occurs in agreements for the sale and purchase of beer and petrol; and of non-competition covenants imposed, for example, when a vendor sells a business as a going concern to a purchaser. In these cases the threat that competition law poses is not that the Commission or some other competition authority will impose a fine, but that a key term of a contract will be unenforceable in commercial litigation. It will be noted from this that the sanction of voidness, as a general proposition, impacts not on serious infringements of the competition rules, such as the operation of cartels, but on more innocuous agreements where the harm to competition is much less obvious; this is a powerful reason for urging competition authorities to adopt a 'realistic' approach to the application of Article 101(1) and its progeny in the Member States to agreements[259].

(ii) *Eco Swiss China Time Ltd v Benetton*

Judges tend to be hostile by instinct to what may be seen as technical—even scurrilous—attempts to avoid contractual obligations by invoking points of competition law. However the Court of Justice's judgment in *Eco Swiss China Time Ltd v Benetton*[260] confirmed how significant the sanction of voidness is in the legal system of the EU: where an agreement infringes Article 101(1), voidness is an important consequence. At the risk of over-simplification, the Court of Justice was asked by the Dutch Supreme Court to determine whether the EU competition rules could be considered to be rules of public policy: on this question

[257] For the Commission's powers of investigation see ch 7, 'Chapter V: powers of investigation', pp 277–284.

[258] See ch 7, 'Chapter VI: penalties', pp 285–293.

[259] See ch 3, 'The Object or Effect of Preventing, Restricting or Distorting Competition', pp 119–147, in particular on what is meant by an agreement having as its 'effect' the restriction of competition.

[260] Case C-126/97 EU:C:1999:269; see also Case C-453/99 *Courage Ltd v Crehan* EU:C:2001:465, paras 20–22.

turned the possibility of an appeal being brought against an arbitral award. The Court of Justice was quite clear[261]:

> Article [101 TFEU] constitutes a fundamental provision which is essential for the accomplishment of the tasks entrusted to the [EU] and, in particular, for the functioning of the internal market. The importance of such a provision led the framers of the Treaty to provide expressly, in Article [101(2) TFEU], that any agreements or decisions prohibited pursuant to that Article are to be automatically void. It follows that where its domestic rules of procedure require a national court to grant an application for annulment of an arbitration award where such an application is founded on failure to observe national rules of public policy, it must also grant such an application where it is founded on failure to comply with the prohibition laid down in Article [101(1) TFEU].

(B) **The 'problem' of Article 101(3) and the Commission's former role in relation to individual exemptions**

Previous editions of this book, at this point, dealt at length with the fact that only the Commission could apply Article 101(3) to individual agreements, and that this threw up numerous problems as to the enforceability of agreements between the parties; these problems concerned the rules on notification, the retrospectivity of individual exemptions, the concept of provisional validity and parallel Commission and national court proceedings. However the entry into force of Regulation 1/2003 on 1 May 2004 abolished the process of notifying agreements to the Commission for an individual exemption[262], and the Regulation itself contains several provisions on the role of national courts in the new regime[263]. For this reason the text on the 'problem' of applying Article 101(3) has been dropped from more recent editions of this book.

(C) **The classic 'Euro-defence'**

As suggested earlier there seems little doubt that the judicial mind is unsympathetic to an Article 101(2) defence where one party to an agreement freely entered into attempts to walk away from it on the ground that it is void under competition law. The maxim '*pacta sunt servanda*'—contracts should be honoured—has a powerful influence where an undertaking purports, on the basis of a 'technicality' of competition law, to avoid a contractual obligation. There are many cases in which Euro-defences have failed, including the *George Michael* case where the singer was attempting to extricate himself from a recording contract that he had entered into with Sony[264]; *Society of Lloyd's v Clementson*[265] and *Higgins v Marchant & Eliot Underwriting Ltd*[266] which concerned the plight of individuals—known as 'names'—called upon by Lloyds of London to contribute substantial sums of money as a result of insurance losses; *Oakdale (Richmond) Ltd v National Westminster Bank plc*[267] concerning the restrictive terms of an all-moneys debenture arrangement; and *Leeds City Council v Watkins*[268] where the judge was highly critical

[261] Case C-126/97 EU:C:1999:269, paras 36–37; this case is discussed further at 'Arbitration', pp 341–342 later in chapter.

[262] See in particular ch 4, 'Regulation 1/2003', pp 176–178.

[263] See 'Private enforcement and Regulation 1/2003', pp 332–335 earlier in chapter.

[264] *Panayiotou v Sony Music Entertainment (UK) Ltd* [1994] ECC 395.

[265] [1995] 1 CMLR 693. [266] [1996] 1 Lloyd's Rep 313.

[267] [1997] ECC 130, upheld on appeal [1997] 3 CMLR 815.

[268] [2003] EWHC 598 (Ch).

of both parties' economics experts[269]. In *Deutsche Bank v Unitech Global Ltd*[270] Teare J rejected the argument that credit and swap agreements involving large sums of money were void and unenforceable simply because they were 'connected' to alleged agreements between banks fixing LIBOR.

However, the fact that many Euro-defences have failed does not mean that the invocation of Article 101(2) is always doomed to failure. Two cases demonstrate how powerful the provision can be. In *Calor Gas Ltd v Express Fuels (Scotland) Ltd*[271] the Scottish Court of Session held that an exclusive dealing agreement was unenforceable by the supplier, Calor Gas, as it infringed Article 101(1); and in *Jones v Ricoh UK Ltd*[272] the High Court held that a clause in a confidentiality agreement infringed Article 101(1) and was unenforceable because it went much further than could reasonably be required to protect the information of the claimant.

(D) **Severance**

Where Article 101(1) is successfully invoked in litigation a problem can arise over the effect of the voidness upon the remainder of the agreement. The Court of Justice has held that, provided that it is possible to sever the offending provisions of the contract from the rest of its terms, the latter remain valid and enforceable[273]. However the Court did not lay down an EU-wide principle of severance, so that the mechanism whereby this is to be effected is a matter to be decided according to the domestic law of each Member State[274]. This in turn gives rise to issues under the Brussels Regulation[275] and Rome II[276]; the former determines where litigation may take place in civil and commercial cases, while the latter determines the law that should be applied in contractual disputes. Assuming that severability is regarded as a matter of substance rather than procedure the Brussels Regulation ought not to affect the outcome of litigation, since in principle Rome II should lead to the same finding of the applicable law, wherever the litigation takes place; however the determination of the applicable law may be crucial to the outcome of the litigation, since different Member States have different methods of severing unlawful restrictions from contracts.

As a matter of English contract law severance is possible in certain circumstances, although the rules on this subject are complex[277]. The Court of Appeal was called upon to examine severability in a competition law context in *Chemidus Wavin Ltd v Société*

[269] Ibid, paras 88–117; Euro-defences also failed in *LauritzenCool AB v Lady Navigation Inc* [2004] EWHC 2607 (Comm); *Days Medical Aids Ltd v Pihsiang Machinery Manufacturing Co Ltd* [2004] ECC 297; *The Qualifying Insurers Subscribing to the ARP v Ross* [2006] ECC 33; *Pirtek (UK) Ltd v Joinplace Ltd* [2010] EWHC 1641 (Ch); *A Nelson & Co Ltd v Guna SpA* [2011] EWHC 1202 (Comm); and *Carewatch Care Services Ltd v Focus Caring Services Ltd* [2014] EWHC 2313 (Ch).

[270] [2013] EWHC 2793 (Comm), paras 16–33.

[271] [2007] CSOH 170.

[272] [2010] EWHC 1743 (Ch).

[273] Case 56/65 *Société Technique Minière v Maschinenbau Ulm* EU:C:1966:38; Case 319/82 *Société de Vente de Ciments et Bétons de l'Est v Kerpen and Kerpen GmbH* EU:C:1983:374.

[274] Case 319/82 *Ciments et Bétons* (ch 8 n 273 earlier); Case 10/86 *VAG France SA v Etablissements Magne SA* EU:C:1986:502.

[275] Regulation 1215/2012 of the European Parliament and of the Council on jurisdiction and the recognition and enforcement of judgments in civil and commercial matters, OJ [2012] L 351/1.

[276] Regulation 864/2007 of the European Parliament and of the Council on the law applicable to non-contractual obligations, OJ [2007] L 199/40.

[277] See *Chitty on Contracts* (Sweet & Maxwell, 32nd ed, 2017), ch 16, paras 16-211–16-220; for discussion of the obligations of a national court to comply with EU law when determining whether to sever clauses in an agreement that infringes Article 101(1) see also *Re The Nullity of a Beer Agreement* [2002] ECC 26 (Austrian Supreme Court).

pour la Transformation[278]. A patentee was suing for royalties payable under an agreement that arguably infringed Article 101(1). The court held that the minimum royalties provision was enforceable, irrespective of whether other parts of the agreement might infringe Article 101(1). Buckley LJ said:

> It seems to me that, in applying Article [101] to an English contract, one may well have to consider whether, after the excisions required by the Article of the Treaty have been made from the contract, the contract could be said to fail for lack of consideration or on any other ground, or whether the contract would be so changed in its character as not to be the sort of contract that the parties intended to enter into at all.

The test in *Chemidus Wavin* has been applied in several subsequent cases[279]. If the effect of severing certain clauses from an agreement would be that its scope and intention would be entirely altered, bringing about a fundamental change in the bargain between the parties, the entire agreement would become unenforceable[280]. This was the conclusion in *English Welsh & Scottish Railway Ltd v E.ON UK plc*[281] where Field J held that the directions of the ORR, that various terms of a coal carriage agreement between the parties were unlawful under the Chapter II prohibition and Article 102 and should be removed or modified, altered the contract so fundamentally that it became void and unenforceable in its entirety.

(E) Void or illegal?

Agreements that infringe Article 101(1) are stated by Article 101(2) to be void; however an important question is whether they are 'merely' void or whether they are also illegal. On this classification turn the important issues of whether any money paid under the contract by one party to the other would be irrecoverable, applying the principle *in pari delicto potior est conditio defendentis* (which roughly translates as 'where both parties are to blame the defendant's position is more powerful')[282], and whether one party to the agreement could bring an action against the other for damages for harm suffered as a result of the operation of the agreement. This issue was discussed earlier in relation to the judgment in *Courage Ltd v Crehan*[283].

(F) Transient voidness

One issue to have come before the Court of Appeal is whether the sanction of voidness in Article 101(2) may be 'turned on and off' depending on the surrounding facts[284]. In *Passmore v Morland plc*[285] the Court of Appeal upheld the Chancery Division's judgment

[278] [1977] FSR 181.

[279] *Inntrepreneur Estates Ltd v Mason* [1994] 68 P & CR 53; *Inntrepreneur Estates (GL) Ltd v Boyes* [1995] ECC 16; *Trent Taverns Ltd v Sykes* [1998] Eu LR 571, upheld on appeal [1999] Eu LR 492.

[280] See *Richard Cound Ltd v BMW (GB) Ltd* [1997] Eu LR 277; *Benford Ltd v Cameron Equipment Ltd* [1997] Eu LR 334 (Mercantile Court); *Clover Leaf Cars Ltd v BMW (GB) Ltd* [1997] Eu LR 535; *First County Garages Ltd v Fiat Auto (UK) Ltd* [1997] Eu LR 712; *Fulton Motors Ltd v Toyota (GB) Ltd* [1998] Eu LR 327.

[281] [2007] EWHC 599 (Comm).

[282] See Goff and Jones *The Law of Restitution* (Sweet & Maxwell, 9th ed, 2016), ch 25.

[283] See '*Courage Ltd v Crehan*', pp 308–309 earlier in chapter.

[284] See the Commission's *Guidelines on the application of Article [101(3) TFEU]* OJ [2004] C 101/97, para 44; see also the judgment of the Court of Justice in Case C-279/06 *CEPSA Estaciones de Servicio SA v LV Tobar e Hijos SL* EU:C:2008:485, para 75.

[285] [1998] 4 All ER 468; aff'd [1999] Eu LR 501.

that an agreement could move from voidness to validity (and back again) according to the effect that it might be having on the market at any particular point in time.

(G) **Article 102**

It may be that a contractual term infringes Article 102, because it amounts to an abuse of a dominant position, as well as infringing Article 101. For example an agreement to purchase one's entire requirements of a particular product from a dominant firm is quite likely to infringe both Article 101 and Article 102[286], because it might foreclose access to the market on the part of competitors; it is irrelevant for this purpose whether the undertaking that accepts the obligation is willing or unwilling to accept it[287]. Similarly a system of loyalty rebates, which falls short of a contractual requirement not to buy from competitors but which may have the same effect, may amount to an abuse[288]. In this situation it has been assumed that the prohibition of Article 102 means that the offending provisions are void, although there is nothing on the face of Article 102, as there is in the case of Article 101(2), to say so. It would follow that a customer tied by an exclusive purchasing commitment which infringes Article 102 could safely ignore it and purchase supplies elsewhere. The impact of any such invalidity on the remainder of the agreement would raise the same question of severability discussed earlier[289]. In *English Welsh & Scottish Railway Ltd v E.ON UK plc*[290] the High Court concluded that abusive terms in coal carriage agreements rendered them void and unenforceable[291].

(H) **Third party as defendant**

The discussion so far has concerned contractual actions where a defendant raises UK or EU competition law as a defence. However on some occasions the competition rules (usually Article 102) are raised as a defence by a third party. In several cases the owner of an intellectual property right such as a patent, registered design or copyright has brought an action against a defendant for infringement; the defendant has then claimed that it has a defence under Article 102 on the basis that the claimant is guilty of abusing its dominant position. In particular, the defendant may claim that, by refusing to grant a licence of the intellectual property right in question, it (the claimant) is guilty of an abuse under Article 102. Whether or not a refusal to license can be abusive is itself a controversial question; it is considered in chapter 19[292]. However even if the claimant is abusing its dominant position, this will not in itself confer on the defendant a valid defence. The courts have established that there must be a sufficient nexus between the claimant's abusive behaviour and the defendant to entitle it to rely on Article 102. In *Chiron Corpn v Organon Teknika Ltd*[293] Aldous J said that:

> The fact that a person is abusing a dominant position does not mean that all wrongdoers have a defence in respect of all actions brought by that person. It is only in those cases where the exercise or existence of that right creates or buttresses the abuse will the court refuse to give effect to the exercise of the right[294].

[286] See eg Case 85/76 *Hoffmann-La Roche v Commission* EU:C:1979:36.
[287] On agreements of this kind see ch 17, 'Tying', pp 705–713.
[288] On practices of this kind see ch 18, 'Conditional Rebates', pp 746–754.
[289] See 'Severance', pp 338–339 earlier in chapter. See also Case 66/86 Ahmed Saeed EU:C:1989:140, para 45.
[290] [2007] EWHC 599 (Comm).
[291] See 'Void or illegal?', p 339 earlier in chapter.
[292] See ch 19, 'Article 102 and Intellectual Property Rights', pp 840–850.
[293] [1993] FSR 324, upheld on appeal [1993] FSR 567.
[294] [1993] FSR 324, para 44.

In several cases the necessary nexus has been lacking[295] and the defence therefore struck out. Where there is a sufficient nexus between the parties, for example where the dominant undertaking is abusing its market power specifically in order to harm the defendant, a defence based on Articles 101 and/or 102 may be pleaded[296].

5. Arbitration

Commercial agreements very often provide for the arbitration of disputes, and it is not uncommon for competition law issues—for example the enforceability of a non-compete clause or of an exclusive purchasing obligation—to be referred to arbitration. A contractual clause referring 'Any disputes related to this Agreement' to arbitration can extend to tortious or delictual claims to damages for harm caused by cartel behaviour as well as 'pure' contractual claims[297].

The subject is complex; there is a growing body of literature on it[298]. The European Commission is conscious of the amount of arbitration (and of other forms of alternative dispute resolution) that takes place; indeed in its own remedies it quite often provides mechanisms for the settlement of disputes[299]. The Commission has been known

[295] See eg *ICI v Berk Pharmaceuticals* [1981] 2 CMLR 91; *British Leyland Motor Corpn v Armstrong Patents Co Ltd* [1984] 3 CMLR 102 (this decision was overturned in the House of Lords (now Supreme Court) on the issue of copyright protection for functional objects: [1986] AC 577); *Ransburg-GEMA AG v Electrostatic Plant Systems* [1989] 2 CMLR 712; *Philips Electronics v Ingman Ltd* [1998] Eu LR 666, ChD; *Sandvik Aktiebolag v KR Pfiffner (UK) Ltd* [1999] Eu LR 755; *HMSO v Automobile Association Ltd* [2001] Eu LR 80; *P&S Amusements Ltd v Valley House Leisure Ltd* [2006] EWHC 99 (Ch).

[296] See eg *British Leyland v TI Silencers* [1981] 2 CMLR 75; *Lansing Bagnall v Buccaneer Lift Parts* [1984] 1 CMLR 224; *Pitney Bowes Inc v Francotyp-Postalia GmbH* [1990] 3 CMLR 466; *Intel Corpn v Via Technologies* [2002] EWCA Civ 1905: see Curley 'Eurodefences and Chips: "A Somewhat Indigestible Dish"' (2003) 25 EIPR 282; *Intergraph Corpn v Solid Systems* [1998] Eu LR 221; see also *Sportswear SpA v Stonestyle Ltd* [2006] EWCA Civ 380; *Oracle America Inc v M-Tech Data Ltd* [2010] EWCA Civ 997, paras 36–39, reversed on appeal [2012] UKSC 27 (both cases under Article 101 rather than Article 102).

[297] *Microsoft Mobile OY (Ltd) v Sony Europe Ltd* [2017] EWHC 374 (Ch).

[298] See *Competition and Arbitration Law* (International Chamber of Commerce, 1993); Atwood 'The Arbitration of International Antitrust Disputes: A Status Report and Suggestions' [1994] Fordham Corporate Law Institute (ed Hawk), ch 15; von Mehren 'Some Reflections on the International Arbitration of Antitrust Issues' ibid, ch 16; Atwood, von Mehren and Temple Lang 'International Arbitration' ibid, ch 17; Schmitthoff 'The Enforcement of EC Competition Law in Arbitral Proceedings' [1996] LIEI 101; Lugard 'EC Competition Law and Arbitration: Opposing Principles?' (1998) 19 ECLR 295 (written prior to the judgment in *Eco Swiss*); Komninos 'Arbitration and the Modernisation of European Competition Law Enforcement' (2001) 24 World Competition 211; Baudenbacher and Higgins 'Decentralization of EC Competition Law Enforcement and Arbitration' [2002] Columbia Journal of Community Law 1; Baudenbacher 'Enforcement of EC and EEA Competition Rules by Arbitration Tribunals Inside and Outside the EU' in Ehlermann and Atansiu (eds) *European Competition Law Annual 2001: Effective Enforcement of EC Antitrust Law* (Hart, 2003); Dolmans and Grierson 'Arbitration and the Modernisation of EC Antitrust Law: New Opportunities and New Responsibilities' (2003) 14 ICC International Court of Arbitration Bulletin, p 37; Blessing *Arbitrating Antitrust and Merger Control Issues* (Helbing & Lichtenhahn, 2003); Nazzini 'International Arbitration and Public Enforcement of Competition Law' (2004) 25 ECLR 153; Nazzini *Concurrent Proceedings in Competition Law: Procedure, Evidence and Remedies* (Oxford University Press, 2004), chs 10 and 11; Bowsher 'Arbitration and Competition' in Ward and Smith (eds) *Competition Litigation in the UK* (Sweet & Maxwell, 2005), ch 11; Landolt *Modernised EC Competition Law in International Arbitration* (Kluwer Law International, 2006); Stylopoulos 'Powers and Duties of Arbitrators in the Application of Competition Law: An EC Approach in the Light of Recent Developments' (2009) 30 ECLR 118; Blanke and Landolt *EU and US Antitrust Arbitration* (Kluwer Law International, 2011); on arbitration and the antitrust rules in the US see *Mitsubishi Motors v Soler Chrysler-Plymouth Inc* 473 US 614 (1985) and *In re Cotton Yarn Antitrust Litigation* 505 F 3d 274 (4th Cir 2007).

[299] See *Bowsher*, ch 8 n 298 earlier, paras 11-036–11-042.

to investigate cases *after* parties have settled a dispute in arbitration proceedings[300]. In *Eco Swiss China Time Ltd v Benetton International NV*[301] the Court of Justice was asked to consider the impact of the competition rules on arbitration proceedings. Benetton had granted a trade mark licence to Eco Swiss to market watches under the Benetton name. Benetton subsequently terminated the licence and Eco Swiss referred the matter to an arbitrator, under Dutch law, in accordance with the agreement. The arbitrator awarded Eco Swiss substantial damages. No competition law point was taken by the parties, and the arbitrator did not raise one. In fact the trade mark licence infringed Article 101(1) and was ineligible for block exemption under Regulation 240/96 on technology transfer agreements[302]. Benetton subsequently decided to argue that the award of damages to Eco Swiss amounted to enforcing an agreement that was contrary to EU competition law. Under Dutch law an arbitration award can be challenged before the courts, in the absence of agreement between the parties, only on grounds of public policy. The Dutch Supreme Court held that the enforcement of competition rules did not amount to public policy in Dutch law, so that if the matter were purely domestic Benetton would be unsuccessful. However, since Benetton's case rested on the EU competition rules, the matter was referred to the Court of Justice under Article 267.

As noted earlier the Court of Justice stressed the fundamental importance of the competition rules in the Treaty, and the importance of the sanction of voidness in ensuring compliance with them[303]. A consequence of this was that, if domestic law allowed an appeal against an arbitration award on grounds of public policy, the possibility that there might be a breach of the EU competition rules should be investigated. On a separate point the Court of Justice recognised that domestic procedural rules which prescribe time limits for the challenging of arbitral awards could have the effect of preventing an appeal based on the competition rules; provided that the time limits were not so fierce as to infringe the requirement of effective application of the competition rules they would themselves be valid.

The Court of Justice did not say anything specifically about the obligations of arbitrators themselves, but the case is of obvious importance to their role. Arbitration is intended to enable parties to disputes to reach a reasonably rapid and cheap settlement of disputes. If an arbitrator ignores points of competition law, but these can subsequently be raised on appeal as, subject to the time limit point, in *Eco Swiss*, the speedy and cheap conclusion of cases would be undermined. It seems sensible therefore that the arbitrator should apply his or her mind to the issue; however the Court of Justice's judgment in *Van Schijndel*[304] established that there is no obligation upon a national court (nor therefore upon an arbitral panel) proactively to root out infringements of the competition rules[305].

It would appear to be the case that an arbitrator could not refer an issue of competition law to the Court of Justice under Article 267; the establishment of an arbitration panel is a consensual process, with the result that it is not a 'court or tribunal of a Member State'[306].

300 See eg the discussion of the *Marathon* case in (2004) (Summer) Competition Policy Newsletter 41–43.

301 Case C-126/97 EU:C:1999:269; see Komninos (2000) 37 CML Rev 459.

302 This Regulation has since been replaced by Regulation 316/2014, OJ [2014] L 93/17; it is discussed in ch 19, 'Technology Transfer Agreements: Regulation 316/2014', pp 798–807.

303 See 'The sanction of voidness', p 336 earlier in chapter.

304 Cases C-430/93 etc EU:C:1995:441: see 'Article 6: powers of the national courts', p 316 earlier in chapter on the point in the text see *Thalès Air Defense v Euromissile*, judgment of the Paris Court of Appeal of 18 November 2004 [2006] ECC 6, where an appeal against an award of damages by an arbitral panel was dismissed since the Article 101 point had not been raised during the course of the arbitration but was only raised after the event.

305 An interesting question is whether an arbitrator in a non-EU country would apply the competition rules, as a matter of public policy, where an agreement infringes Article 101 (or Article 102); on this point see *Bowsher*, ch 8 n 298 earlier, paras 11-063–11-069.

306 Case 102/81 *Nordsee Deutsche Hochseefischerei GmbH v Reederei Mond* EU:C:1982:107; see further the Opinion of AG Colomer in Case C-17/00 *de Coster v Collège des bourgmestres* EU:C:2001:366.

9

Competition Act 1998: substantive provisions

1. Introduction

The purpose of this and the following two chapters is to describe the main provisions of the domestic competition law of the UK. The focus of attention in this chapter is the Competition Act 1998, which prohibits anti-competitive agreements and the abuse of a dominant position[1]. The domestic prohibitions are closely modelled upon Articles 101 and 102, although they are by no means identical in every respect. Infringements of these provisions can attract significant fines, and damages can be awarded to the victims of anti-competitive behaviour. Chapter 10 discusses matters of enforcement and procedure, including the criminal cartel offence for individuals involved in 'hard-core' cartels and the concurrent powers given to the Competition and Markets Authority ('the CMA') and the sectoral regulators to enforce the competition rules. The powers of investigation and enforcement are similar to those in the EU, but there are some differences; for example compulsory interviews are possible in the UK but do not exist under EU law. Chapter 11 considers the system of market studies and market investigations under the Enterprise Act 2002, which deal with market imperfections that are not adequately addressed by the Competition Act.

This chapter is structured as follows. Section 2 provides an overview of the Competition Act. Sections 3 and 4 consider in turn the decisional practice and case law under the so-called Chapter I and Chapter II prohibitions. Section 5 discusses the relationship between EU and domestic competition law, including the important 'governing principles' clause in section 60 of the Competition Act, which is intended to achieve consistency with EU law. Section 6 contains a table of decisions under the Competition Act and Articles 101 and 102 TFEU published on the website of the CMA since completion of the eighth

[1] On the background to the modern domestic competition law of the UK see the fifth edition of this book, pp 306–308; Wilks 'The Prolonged Reform of UK Competition Policy' in Doern and Wilks (eds) *Comparative Competition Policy* (Clarendon Press, 1996); Wilks *In the Public Interest* (Manchester University Press, 1999), pp 296–305; Whish 'The Competition Act 1998 and the Prior Debate on Reform' in Rodger and MacCulloch (eds) *The Competition Act: A New Era for UK Competition Law* (Hart, 2000).

edition of this book in 2015 along with a discussion of the Competition Act in practice. Many decisions of the UK competition authorities will be discussed further in the contextual chapters in the second half of this book[2].

All readers of this book will be aware of the decision of the British electorate in a referendum held in June 2016 to withdraw from the EU. When Brexit happens, this will clearly have a significant effect on competition law and policy in the UK. The manuscript of this edition of the book was handed to the publishers on 8 December 2017, at which time it was not at all clear what the terms will be of any post-Brexit agreement between the UK and the EU. In the final section of this chapter we will describe briefly some of the likely implications for UK competition law and policy of a future Brexit[3].

2. The Competition Act 1998—Overview

(A) Outline of the Act

The Competition Act 1998 received Royal Assent on 9 November 1998; the main provisions entered into force on 1 March 2000. The Act has been amended by the Enterprise Act 2002 and by The Competition Act 1998 and Other (Amendment) Regulations 2004[4] and the Enterprise and Regulatory Reform Act 2013. The Competition Act is divided into four parts, consisting of 76 sections and 14 schedules.

(i) Part I: the Chapter I and Chapter II prohibitions

The most important provisions are found in Part I of the Act, which is divided into five chapters. It contains the prohibitions modelled upon Article 101 TFEU ('the Chapter I prohibition') and Article 102 TFEU ('the Chapter II prohibition'). Part 1 also confers substantial powers of investigation and enforcement on the CMA and the sectoral regulators[5]. The Competition Appeal Tribunal ('the CAT') hears appeals against certain decisions under the Competition Act; it also has other functions under the Enterprise Act. The Secretary of State is required to review the operation of Part 1 of the Competition Act and report to Parliament no later than 2019[6].

(ii) Part II: European investigations

Part II of the Competition Act is concerned with investigations in relation to Articles 101 and 102, giving specific powers to the High Court and the CAT (as the case may be) to issue a warrant authorising the CMA to enter premises in connection with an investigation ordered or requested by the European Commission[7]. Part IIA of the Act is concerned with investigations conducted by the CMA on behalf of a competition authority of another EU Member State pursuant to Article 22 of Regulation 1/2003[8]. Post-Brexit, Regulation 1/2003 will cease to apply in the UK, and it will be necessary to determine how, if at all, the UK competition authorities will cooperate with the European Commission and national competition authorities of the Member States of the EU ('the NCAs').

[2] See eg ch 13, 'UK Law', pp 564–569 on cartels cases and see chs 17 and 18 generally.

[3] On this issue generally see Whish 'Brexit and EU Competition Policy' (2016) 7 JECLAP 297; the papers available on the websites of the Brexit Competition Law Working Group, www.bclwg.org and the Commercial Bar Association, www.combar.com; and the report of the House of Lords EU Internal Market Sub-Committee *Brexit: competition and State aid*, 2 February 2018, available at www.parliament.uk.

[4] SI 2004/1261.

[5] See ch 10, 'Concurrency', pp 449–452 on the concurrent powers of the CMA and the sectoral regulators.

[6] ERRA 2013, s 45. [7] See ch 10, 'EU investigations', p 411. [8] Ibid.

(iii) Part III: amendments to the Fair Trading Act 1973

Part III of the Act amended the Fair Trading Act 1973; these provisions have been repealed and replaced by the Enterprise Act: they are described in chapter 11.

(iv) Part IV: miscellaneous amendments

Part IV of the Competition Act contains supplemental and transitional provisions, including the repeal of sections 44 and 45 of the Patents Act 1977, and provisions on Crown application.

(B) CMA guidelines

Section 52 of the Competition Act requires the CMA to publish general advice and information as to how it will apply the law in practice. The CMA Board has adopted a number of guidelines that had been published by the Office of Fair Trading ('the OFT'), one of its predecessors[9]; the CMA has also published some guidelines of its own. The sectoral regulators have also published guidance in relation to the application of competition law to their respective sectors. On 8 December 2017 the following guidelines, listed in chronological order, had been published under the Competition Act[10]:

- *The application of the Competition Act in the telecommunications sector*[11]
- *Application to the Northern Ireland energy sectors*[12]
- *Agreements and concerted practices*[13]
- *Abuse of a dominant position*[14]
- *Market definition*[15]
- *Powers of investigation*[16]
- *Enforcement*[17]
- *Trade associations, professional and self-regulatory bodies*[18]
- *Assessment of market power*[19]
- *Vertical agreements*[20]
- *Services of general economic interest*[21]
- *Modernisation*[22]
- *Application in the energy sector*[23]
- *Application to services relating to railways*[24]
- *Competing fairly and the application of competition law*[25]
- *The application of the Competition Act in the water and sewerage sectors*[26]
- *Land agreements and competition law*[27]
- *Public bodies and competition law*[28]

[9] A helpful table of the existing guidelines adopted by the CMA can be found in Annexe A to the *Guidance on the CMA's investigation procedures in Competition Act 1998 cases*, CMA8, April 2014, available at www.gov.uk/cma.

[10] The guidelines are available at www.gov.uk/cma. [11] OFT 417, February 2000.

[12] OFT 437, July 2001. [13] OFT 401, December 2004. [14] OFT 402, December 2004.

[15] OFT 403, December 2004. [16] OFT 404, December 2004. [17] OFT 407, December 2004.

[18] OFT 408, December 2004. [19] OFT 415, December 2004. [20] OFT 419, December 2004.

[21] OFT 421, December 2004. [22] OFT 442, December 2004. [23] OFT 428, January 2005.

[24] OFT 430, October 2005. [25] OFT 447, March 2005. [26] OFT 422, March 2010.

[27] OFT 1317, March 2011. [28] OFT 1389, December 2011.

- *Guidance as to the appropriate amount of a penalty*[29]
- *Applications for leniency and no-action in cartel cases*[30], which deals with leniency applications under both the Competition Act 1998 and the Enterprise Act 2002
- *Transparency and disclosure: Statement of the CMA's policy and approach*[31]
- *Guidance on concurrent application of competition law to regulated industries*[32]
- *Guidance on the CMA's investigation procedures in Competition Act 1998 cases*[33]
- *CMA's approach to short-form opinions*[34]
- *The public transport ticketing schemes block exemption: CMA guidance*[35].

(C) Other information about the Competition Act

The CMA's website[36] contains a large amount of information about the Competition Act 1998, and includes, among other things, the guidelines listed above, decisions under the Competition Act, information on current investigations under the Act, Press Releases, consultations, numerous '60-second' summaries to promote compliance with competition law and a form for reporting anti-competitive or market issues[37]. The CMA also publishes a 'blog' to raise awareness and encourage debate about its work[38].

(D) Delegated legislation under the Competition Act

The Secretary of State has made various Orders, Rules and Regulations pursuant to his powers under the Competition Act 1998, including in particular:

- The Competition Act 1998 (Small Agreements and Conduct of Minor Significance) Regulations[39]
- The Competition Act 1998 (Determination of Turnover for Penalties) Order[40]
- The Competition Act 1998 (Concurrency) Regulations 2014[41]
- The Competition Act 1998 (Appealable Decisions and Revocation of Notification of Excluded Agreements) Regulations 2004[42]
- The Competition Act 1998 (Land Agreements Exclusion and Revocation) Order 2004[43]
- The Competition Act 1998 and Other Enactments (Amendment) Regulations 2004[44]
- The Competition Act 1998 (Land Agreements Exclusion Revocation) Order 2010[45]
- The Competition and Markets Authority (Competition Act 1998 Rules) 2014[46]
- The Competition and Markets Authority (Penalties) Order 2014[47]
- The Competition Act 1998 (Public Transport Ticketing Schemes Block Exemption) (Amendment) Order 2016[48].

[29] OFT 423, September 2012.

[30] OFT 1495, July 2013; note that this Guideline is subject to the guidance given in *Cartel Offence: Prosecution Guidance*, CMA9, April 2014.

[31] CMA6, January 2014. [32] CMA10, April 2014. [33] CMA8, April 2014.

[34] CMA27, April 2014. [35] CMA53, September 2016. [36] www.gov.uk/cma.

[37] www.gov.uk/guidance/tell-the-cma-about-a-competition-or-market-problem.

[38] www.competitionandmarkets.blog.gov.uk. [39] SI 2000/262.

[40] SI 2000/309, as amended by SI 2004/1259. [41] SI 2014/536. [42] SI 2004/1078.

[43] SI 2004/1260. [44] SI 2004/1261. [45] SI 2010/1709. [46] SI 2014/458.

[47] SI 2014/559. [48] SI 2016/126.

(E) Literature

A large number of books and articles have been written on the Competition Act[49].

3. The Chapter I Prohibition

The 'Chapter I prohibition', closely modelled upon Article 101(1) TFEU, prohibits agreements that have as their object or effect the prevention, restriction or distortion of competition. It must be interpreted consistently with the analogous provisions of EU law, having regard to any relevant differences between the provisions concerned[50]. In practice the Chapter I prohibition and Article 101 have developed in close harmony, and decision-makers in the UK have been able to draw upon a sophisticated body of EU jurisprudence developed over a period of more than 60 years.

Section 2 contains the Chapter I prohibition itself. Section 3 provides for excluded agreements. Sections 6 and 8 to 10 deal with exemptions.

(A) Section 2(1): the Chapter I prohibition

Section 2(1) provides that:

> Subject to section 3, agreements between undertakings, decisions by associations of undertakings or concerted practices which—
>
> (a) may affect trade within the UK, and
>
> (b) have as their object or effect the prevention, restriction or distortion of competition within the UK,
>
> are prohibited unless they are exempt in accordance with the provisions of this Part.

Section 2(2) provides examples of the kinds of agreements that might be caught by section 2(1)[51]. It may be helpful to consider the terms used in section 2 and to point out various similarities and differences between the Chapter I prohibition and Article 101 TFEU.

(i) 'Subject to section 3'

Section 3 excludes certain agreements from the Chapter I prohibition, some of which do not exist under EU law. These exclusions are considered later[52].

(ii) Agreements between undertakings, decisions by associations of undertakings or concerted practices

These words are identical to those in Article 101(1)[53]. These expressions are ones that have been considered in numerous judgments of the EU Courts which, as a general proposition,

[49] Many of the books published in the immediate aftermath of the passage of the Act are now of little more than historical interest: a full list of them can be found on p 327 of the 6th edition of this book; of current interest see O'Neill and Sanders *UK Competition Procedure* (Oxford University Press, 2007); Green and Brealey (eds) *Competition Litigation: UK Practice and Procedure* (Oxford University Press, 2010); Rodger (ed) *Ten Years of UK Competition Law Reform* (Dundee University Press, 2010); the series of essays in [2010] Comp Law 141–294; Kellaway, Thompson and Brown (eds) *UK Competition Law: The New Framework* (Oxford University Press, 2015).

[50] Competition Act 1998, s 60(2).

[51] See 'Section 2(2): illustrative list', pp 361–362 later in chapter.

[52] See 'The Chapter I prohibition: excluded agreements', pp 364–371 later in chapter.

[53] With the minor exception that the word 'or' in s 2(1) replaces 'and' in Article 101(1).

the CMA and sectoral regulators and courts in the UK are obliged to follow as a result of section 60(2)[54].

(iii) 'Undertakings'

(a) Basic definition

As in the case of EU law[55], the term 'undertaking' refers to any entity engaged in economic activity. The converse is also true: an entity that carries on non-economic activities, such as the exercise of public law powers, is not an undertaking[56].

(b) Need to adopt a functional approach

In *UKRS Training v NSAR*[57] the CAT held that a 'functional approach' is appropriate: where a body carries out several activities it is necessary to consider whether the activity in question can properly be regarded as a discrete function. In that case it held that NSAR was acting as an undertaking when it accredited and audited providers of railway safety training, since a commercial profit-making organisation could perform this function[58].

(c) Economic activity

Economic activity consists in offering goods or services on a market[59]. In *BetterCare Group v Director General of Fair Trading*[60] the OFT (now CMA) rejected a complaint from BetterCare that the North & West Belfast Health and Social Services Trust had abused a dominant position on the basis that the Trust was not an undertaking when it purchased social care from private providers[61]. The Trust had a statutory duty to provide nursing and residential care to elderly people: it had nursing homes of its own, but also 'contracted out' to the private sector. On appeal, after a thorough review of the case law of the EU Courts, the CAT held that the contracting-out activities of the Trust were an economic activity[62]: the fact that it was a purchaser rather than a supplier did not affect the analysis[63]; and the Trust was active on the market for the supply of residential and nursing care services in Northern Ireland[64]. Furthermore the Trust did not provide its services gratuitously, but sought to recover as much as it could of the cost of providing care[65].

The subsequent judgments of the EU Courts in *FENIN v Commission*[66] cast doubt on the correctness of the judgment in *BetterCare*, in that the EU Courts took a robust view

[54] For discussion of s 60 see '"Governing Principles Clause": Section 60 of the Competition Act 1998', pp 387–392 later in chapter.

[55] On the meaning of undertakings in EU law see ch 3, 'Undertakings and Associations of Undertakings', pp 83–101 and ch 5, 'Undertakings', p 185.

[56] See *Agreements and concerted practices*, OFT 401, para 2.5.

[57] Case 1258/5/7/16 [2017] CAT 14, para 67(1); para 67 contains a helpful summary of the relevant case law.

[58] Ibid, paras 68–80.

[59] Ibid, para 59 and case law cited.

[60] Case 1006/2/1/01 [2002] CAT 7; for comment see Skilbeck '*BetterCare*; The Conflict Between Social Policy and Economic Efficiency' [2002] Comp Law 260; Odudu 'Are State-Owned Health-Care Providers Undertakings Subject to Competition Law?' (2011) 32 ECLR 231.

[61] *North & West Belfast Health and Social Services Trust*, case closure decision of 30 April 2002; the OFT's arguments as to why the Trust was not an undertaking are set out at Case 1006/2/1/01 [2002] CAT 7, paras 221–276.

[62] Case 1006/2/1/01 *BetterCare Group Ltd v Director General of Fair Trading* [2002] CAT 7, paras 191–192; the CAT remitted the matter for further consideration and the OFT decided that the Trust was not guilty of abuse and did not need to decide whether it was acting as an undertaking: decision of 18 December 2003, available at www.gov.uk/cma.

[63] Ibid, paras 193–194.

[64] Ibid, paras 195–200.

[65] Ibid, para 201.

[66] Case T-319/99 *FENIN v Commission* EU:T:2003:50, upheld on appeal Case C-205/03 P EU:C:2006:453: see ch 3, 'Procurement that is ancillary to a non-economic activity is not economic', pp 89–90 for discussion of this case, and the comments on it in relation to the *BetterCare* judgment.

that, where a public body purchases goods or services in order to provide a social service, it does not do so as an undertaking. There are factual differences between the two cases: in particular the Trust had a role as a supplier as well as a purchaser of services and charged for its services, albeit not at a full market rate; this was not the case in *FENIN*. At a policy level, however, there was an unwillingness in the *FENIN* judgments to extend the application of the competition rules to the procurement activities of the Spanish Health Service[67], but less of an unwillingness on the CAT's part in *BetterCare* in relation to the Trust. The competition authorities in the UK have not refrained from considering the application of the competition rules to other public-sector entities[68].

In *Institute of Independent Insurance Brokers v Director General of Fair Trading*[69] the CAT considered that the General Insurance Standards Council (GISC), established upon the private initiative of its members rather than pursuant to a statutory requirement, was probably an undertaking[70]. The CAT went further in *UKRS Training v NSAR*[71] and held that a self-regulatory body of the railway industry was an undertaking in so far as it provided services to providers of railway safety training.

(d) Non-economic activity

A body will not be an undertaking where it carries on an activity that is 'of its nature a core function of the State', for example air navigation control and anti-pollution control[72]. It is relevant to consider whether the power exercised by the body derives directly from legislation or is exercised on behalf of the state and, if applicable, whether any charges levied by the body are determined not by it but by a public authority. The guidance on *Public bodies and competition law*[73] considers when state-owned entities or public authorities do not qualify as undertakings.

(e) Undertaking as a single economic entity

An undertaking refers to an 'economic entity', even if in law that entity consists of several natural or legal persons. Treatment of more than one person as a single undertaking may be significant in at least three situations: the Chapter I prohibition does not apply to agreements between two or more persons that constitute a single undertaking[74]; when imputing to a parent company the guilt of a subsidiary[75]; and when asserting jurisdiction over a foreign parent by proceeding against a subsidiary established within the UK[76]. In each instance the test is whether the parent company can, and does in fact, exercise decisive influence over a subsidiary company. Similarly, the relationship between a principal

[67] See also Case T-155/04 *SELEX Sistemi Integrati SpA v Commission* EU:T:2006:387, paras 59–69 and on appeal Case C-113/07 P EU:C:2009:191, paras 65–123.

[68] See eg *Companies House*, OFT decision of 25 October 2002 (commercial provision of information about companies); *Cardiff Bus*, OFT decision of 18 November 2008, ch 7 (offer of commercial bus services).

[69] Case 1002/2/1/01 [2001] CAT 4.

[70] Ibid, paras 252–258 (although this conclusion was not necessary for the judgment).

[71] Case 1258/5/7/16 [2017] CAT 14.

[72] Ibid, paras 63–66, citing the judgments of the Court of Justice in Case C-364/92 *SAT Fluggesellschaft v Eurocontrol* EU:C:1994:7; Case C-113/07P *SELEX Sistemi Integrati v Commission* EU:C:2009:191; and Case C-343/95 *Diego Cali & Figli v SEPG* EU:C:1997:160.

[73] *Public bodies and competition law*, OFT 1389, December 2011.

[74] *Anaesthetists' groups*, OFT decision of 14 April 2003.

[75] OFT decision of 21 September 2009, paras III.13–III.24, upheld on appeal Case 1121/1/1/09 *Durkan Holdings Ltd v OFT* [2011] CAT 6, paras 13–92; see similarly *Construction Recruitment Forum*, OFT decision of 29 September 2009, paras 2.2–2.11.

[76] The relevant case law was discussed in *Sainsbury's Supermarkets Ltd v MasterCard Inc* [2016] CAT 11, para 363(9)–(16).

and agent or between an employer and employee may be so close that they are also treated as a single economic entity[77].

(f) *Undertakings, not persons*

The Chapter I prohibition applies to agreements 'between undertakings', but certain provisions of the Act refer to 'persons' rather than undertakings. The reason for this is that in some contexts the word 'person' is a more appropriate expression; however, in order to prevent undertakings arguing to the contrary, section 59 provides that the expression 'persons' includes 'undertakings'[78]. An unusual finding in *Independent schools*[79] was that the Secretary of State for Defence, in his capacity as the person responsible for the governance of the Royal Hospital School, was acting as an undertaking but that, as he constituted the Crown for this purpose, no penalty could be imposed as a result of section 73(1)(b) of the Act[80]. Other schools involved in this case were undertakings, their charitable status notwithstanding[81].

(iv) **'Agreements'**

As in the case of EU law, the concept of an agreement refers to a concurrence of wills between at least two parties[82]; an agreement may be written or spoken[83] and does not need to be legally binding[84]. The Chapter I prohibition is capable of applying both to agreements between undertakings operating at the same level of trade (horizontal agreements) and to agreements between undertakings at different levels (vertical agreements). Circulars and warnings sent by a manufacturer to its distributors can amount to an agreement[85]. A reluctant participant in an agreement can still be liable, although such reluctance may be relevant to the level of any penalty[86]. It is not legally necessary to distinguish between agreements and concerted practices[87]. In cases involving a supplier's standard terms, the CMA has tended to identify a small number of 'representative' agreements and/or concerted practices as violations of competition law rather than taking action against hundreds or even thousands of similar agreements[88].

(v) **'Decisions by associations of undertakings'**

An association of undertakings refers to 'a self-standing entity with ongoing existence'[89] that typically represents the interests of its members. Trade associations, agricultural cooperatives and associations of sporting bodies are typical examples of associations of

[77] See *ET Plus SA v Welter* [2005] EWHC 2115 (Comm), para 84; Case 1122/1/1/09 *AH Willis v OFT* [2011] CAT 13, paras 27–37; limited liability partnerships of consultant eye surgeons were treated as undertakings in *Conduct in the ophthalmology sector*, CMA decision of 20 August 2015, paras 4.6–4.10.

[78] See HL Report Stage, 23 February 1998, cols 511–512.

[79] OFT decision of 20 November 2006.

[80] Ibid, para 174.

[81] Ibid, paras 1311–1320.

[82] *Argos Ltd v OFT* [2006] EWCA Civ 1318, para 23; on EU law see ch 3, 'Agreements', pp 102–114.

[83] *Online resale price maintenance in the light fittings sector*, CMA decision of 3 May 2017, paras 4.15, 4.27 and 4.59.

[84] *Agreements and concerted practices*, OFT 401, para 2.7, and see *Arriva/First Group*, OFT decision of 5 February 2002, paras 29–33.

[85] *Online resale price maintenance in the commercial refrigeration sector*, CMA decision of 24 May 2016, paras 6.14–6.15 (legal principles) and 6.23–6.25 (on the facts of the case).

[86] *Online resale price maintenance in the bathroom fittings sector*, CMA decision of 10 May 2016, para A.24; *Agreements and concerted practices*, OFT 401, para 2.8.

[87] Cases 1021/1/1/03 etc *JJB Sports plc v OFT* [2004] CAT 17, para 644.

[88] See eg *Online resale price maintenance in the light fittings sector*, CMA decision of 3 May 2017, paras 4.13–4.108 (one reseller); *Online resale price maintenance in the commercial refrigeration sector*, CMA decision of 24 May 2016, paras 6.20–6.38 (three resellers).

[89] *Sel-Imperial Ltd v The British Standards Institution* [2010] EWHC 854 (Ch), paras 36–46.

undertakings[90]. The fact that the association does not carry on an economic activity of its own[91] or that it is only a 'loose knit association' does not prevent it from being an association of undertakings[92].

The term 'decision' has a broad meaning, including the rules of trade associations, recommendations, resolutions of the management committee and rulings of the chief executive; the crucial issue is whether the object or effect of the decision is to influence the conduct or coordinate the activity of the members[93]. The Guideline on *Trade associations, professions and self-regulating bodies*[94] provides additional guidance on the meaning of decisions[95]; it also discusses the extent to which activities of a trade association, such as the promulgation of codes of conduct, can infringe Article 101 TFEU and the Chapter I prohibition[96]. This *Guideline* also has a specific section on the position of the professions[97] and of self-regulating bodies[98].

In *Northern Ireland Livestock and Auctioneers' Association*[99] a non-binding recommendation by the Association as to the commission that its members should charge for the purchase of livestock in Northern Ireland cattle marts was held to be a decision[100]. The Standard Conditions of the Film Distributors' Association were found to be a decision of an association of undertakings; the offending clauses that limited the ability of cinemas to determine their own prices and promotional activities were dropped[101]. In *Rural Broadband Wayleaves*[102] a recommendation by the National Farmers' Union as to the rate to be charged by landowners for the grant of wayleaves for the provision of broadband services in rural areas was a decision of an association of undertakings. In *Conduct in the ophthalmology sector*[103] the Consultant Eye Surgeons Partnership admitted that it had taken a series of decisions as an association of undertakings that coordinated the commercial conduct of limited liability partnerships of consultants vis-à-vis private medical insurers. In *Conduct in the modelling sector*[104] the CMA decided that the Association of Model Agents was an association of undertakings that had participated in agreements and/or concerted practices between agents to fix prices for modelling services.

Standard conditions drawn up by a trade association will be less likely to have an appreciable effect on competition where its members have the freedom to adopt different conditions if they so wish[105].

[90] See ch 3, 'Decisions by associations of undertakings', pp 114–115.

[91] See *GISC*, ch 9 n 69 earlier, paras 248–250.

[92] *Northern Ireland Livestock and Auctioneers' Association*, OFT decision of 3 February 2003, para 35.

[93] *Agreements and concerted practices*, OFT 401, para 2.9.

[94] OFT 408, December 2004. [95] Ibid, paras 2.1–2.5.

[96] Ibid, paras 3.1–3.20; OFGEM investigated whether two trade associations had used a code of practice to restrict third parties from engaging in face-to-face marketing of energy supply: the case file was closed on administrative priority grounds, OFGEM case closure decision, 28 August 2013.

[97] *Trade associations, professions and self-regulating bodies*, paras 6.1–6.7.

[98] Ibid, paras 7.1–7.3. [99] OFT decision of 3 February 2003. [100] Ibid, paras 37–49.

[101] *Notification by the Film Distributors' Association of its Standard Conditions for Licensing the Commercial Exhibition of Films*, OFT decision of 1 February 2002, paras 43–45; see similarly the *Showmen's Guild of Great Britain*, CMA Press Release of 21 December 2016, alleging that some of the Guild's current rules constitute a decision of an association of undertakings that protect existing Guild showmen from competition by new entrants: the CMA accepted commitments from the Guild in this case on 26 October 2017.

[102] Short-form Opinion of 23 August 2012, paras 7.3 and 7.7. [103] CMA decision of 20 August 2015.

[104] CMA decision of 16 December 2016; in this case the CMA liaised with the French and the Italian NCAs that carried out parallel investigations in the modelling services sector.

[105] *Trade associations, professionals and self-regulating bodies*, OFT 408, para 3.18: see OFT Press Release PN 02/03, 9 January 2003, for details of amendment to three trade associations' rules to provide such freedom; see also *Royal Institute of British Architects*, Competition case closure summaries (2003), pp 5–6, available at www.nationalarchives.gov.uk.

The effect that a decision of an association might have on the UK market will depend to a certain extent on the size of the membership of the association concerned: the broader the membership of an association, the greater the influence of the association is likely to be[106].

(vi) 'Concerted practices'

(a) Basic definition

A concerted practice is a form of coordination that knowingly substitutes practical cooperation between undertakings for the risks inherent in competition[107]. The Guideline on *Agreements and concerted practices* discusses the factors that are relevant to determining whether a concerted practice exists, such as whether behaviour in the market is influenced as a result of contact between undertakings[108]. In *Tesco v OFT*[109] the CAT described a concerted practice as a 'versatile concept': it can take many different forms, and the courts have always been careful not to limit what may amount to a concerted practice.

(b) Direct contact between competitors

In *Apex v OFT*[110] fines were imposed on undertakings for participating in collusive tendering in relation to roofing contracts in the West Midlands[111]. On appeal the CAT distilled a number of principles from the case law of the EU Courts[112], including that a concerted practice can arise where there are reciprocal contacts between undertakings which remove or reduce uncertainty as to their future conduct. The CAT continued that:

> reciprocal contacts are established where one competitor discloses its future intentions or conduct on the market to another when the latter requests it or, at the very least, accepts it.

The CAT upheld the finding of an infringement in this case[113]. These principles have been applied in many subsequent decisions on collusive tendering[114]. In one decision, *Bid rigging in the construction industry in England*[115], the OFT imposed fines totalling £129.2 million on 103 undertakings for collusive tendering. On appeal the CAT annulled the decision in relation to four undertakings due to errors of fact[116].

In *Galvanised Steel Tanks*[117] the CMA adopted two decisions, one condemning a price-fixing and market-sharing cartel and the other finding that three members of the cartel had exchanged their current and future pricing intentions with another company, Balmoral Tanks, at a single meeting. An unusual feature of the case was that the meeting was recorded, so there was no doubt about what was said at the meeting. The CMA applied

[106] *Trade associations, professions and self-regulating bodies*, OFT 408, para 5.3.

[107] See ch 3, 'Meaning of concerted practice', pp 116–117.

[108] OFT 401, para 2.13.

[109] Case 1188/1/1/11 *Tesco Stores Ltd v OFT* [2012] CAT 31, paras 55–56, citing the Court of Appeal's judgment in *Argos Ltd v OFT* [2006] EWCA Civ 1318, para 22.

[110] Case 1032/1/1/04 [2005] CAT 4.

[111] OFT decision of 17 March 2004.

[112] Case 1032/1/1/04 [2005] CAT 4, paras 195–206.

[113] For further discussion of this case see ch 13, 'Collusive Tendering', pp 547–549 and Kar and Bailey 'The Apex Judgment: When does a Practice become Concerted?' [2005] Comp Law 17; on concerted practices see also Case 1061/1/1/06 *Makers UK Ltd v OFT* [2007] CAT 11, paras 99–110.

[114] See ch 13, 'Collusive Tendering', pp 547–549.

[115] OFT decision of 21 September 2009.

[116] Case 1118/1/1/09 *GMI Construction Holdings plc v OFT* [2011] CAT 12; Case 1121/1/1/09 *Durkan Holdings Ltd v OFT* [2011] CAT 6, paras 93–125; Case 1122/1/1/09 *AH Willis & Sons Ltd v OFT* [2011] CAT 3; Case 1124/1/1/09 *North Midland Construction plc v OFT* [2011] CAT 14, paras 14–34; the CAT dismissed two appeals on the question of liability: see Case 1126/1/1/09 *ISG Pearce Ltd v OFT* [2011] CAT 10, paras 24–36; Case 1120/1/1/09 *Quarmby Construction Co Ltd v OFT* [2011] CAT 11, paras 8–140.

[117] *Galvanised steel tanks for water storage main cartel infringement*, CMA decision of 19 December 2016 and *Galvanised steel tanks for water storage information exchange infringement*, CMA decision of 19 December 2016.

the EU precedent of *T-Mobile*[118] that a concerted practice can exist where information is exchanged on one occasion. The CMA's decision was upheld on appeal to the CAT[119].

When there is direct contact between two competing undertakings involving the disclosure of future pricing information it is relatively easy to establish a concerted practice[120]. In *Loan Pricing*[121] Royal Bank of Scotland agreed to pay a penalty of £28.59 million in a case where it had provided information about pricing to Barclays Bank, though Barclays did not reciprocate: in other words there was no *exchange* of information in this case. Nevertheless the OFT concluded that there was a concerted practice, since there is a presumption that the recipient of information will take it into account when making its decisions[122]. Barclays was not fined in this case as it had blown the whistle. In *Fuel Surcharges*[123] British Airways and Virgin Atlantic were found to have coordinated their pricing through the exchange of commercially sensitive information: BA agreed to pay a reduced penalty of £58.5 million after admitting the infringement; Virgin blew the whistle and therefore was not fined. In *Supply of products to the furniture industry*[124] fines were imposed on members of two distinct bilateral cartels that involved the allocation of customers, bid-rigging and the exchange of confidential and commercially important information.

(c) Indirect contact between competitors

The Court of Appeal has pointed out that 'even indirect and isolated instances of contact between competitors may be sufficient to infringe Article 101, if their object is to promote artificial conditions of competition in the market'[125]. Three cases, best referred to as *Football Shirts, Toys and Games* and *Dairy Products*, shed light on when indirect contact between undertakings gives rise to a concerted practice. In each case the OFT found a concerted practice as to the retail prices at which these consumer goods were sold to consumers[126]. The interesting feature of these cases is that the OFT decided that the concerted practices had come about not, or not only, from direct contact between the retailers but also through the role played by the supplier in each case.

This is presented in diagrammatic form in Figure 9.1.

In *Football Shirts* and *Toys and Games* the OFT found bilateral agreements between B and A and between B and C. In all three cases the OFT found that there were concerted practices between A, B and C which, as between A and C, were horizontal rather than vertical. At no time was there any direct communication between A and C. These horizontal concerted practices had come about as a result of indirect contact between A and C through the medium of B. This phenomenon is sometimes referred to as one of 'hub and spoke', where B represents the 'hub' and each of A and C is on the end of a 'spoke'.

118 Case C-8/08 *T-Mobile Netherlands* EU:C:2009:343, paras 58–59.

119 Case 1277/1/12/17 *Balmoral Tanks v CMA* [2017] CAT 23.

120 Case 1061/1/1/06 *Makers UK Ltd v OFT* [2007] CAT 11, paras 99–100, distinguishing such a situation from the ones in *Football Shirts* and *Toys and Games*.

121 OFT decision of 20 January 2011.

122 See ch 3, 'Must a concerted practice have been put into effect?', pp 117–118.

123 *Airline passenger fuel surcharges for long-haul passenger flights*, OFT decision of 19 April 2012.

124 *Supply of products to the furniture industry (drawer fronts)*, CMA decision of 27 March 2017 and *Supply of products to the furniture industry (drawer wraps)*, CMA decision of 27 March 2017; Thomas Armstrong (Timber) Ltd was a member of both cartels.

125 *KME Yorkshire Ltd v Toshiba Carrier UK Ltd* [2012] EWCA Civ 1190, para 19.

126 *Football Kit price-fixing*, OFT decision of 1 August 2003; *Hasbro UK Ltd/Argos Ltd/Littlewoods Ltd*, OFT decision of 2 December 2003; *Dairy retail price initiatives*, OFT decision of 10 August 2011; note that, in the case of *Football Shirts*, the Consumers' Association, trading as Which?, brought a follow-on action for damages in the CAT on behalf of consumers that were overcharged: see ch 8, 'CAT collective proceedings', pp 330–332.

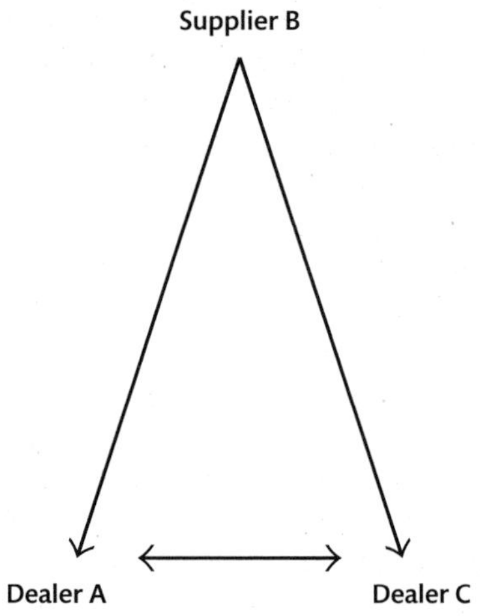

Fig. 9.1

Applying the judgment of the Court of Appeal in *Football Shirts* and *Toys and Games*[127] in *Dairy Products* the CAT held that a concerted practice between A, B and C exists if five conditions are met[128]:

- retailer A discloses to supplier B its future pricing intentions
- A may be taken to intend that B will make use of that information to influence market conditions by passing that information to other retailers (of whom C is, or may be, one)
- B passes that information to C
- C may be taken to know the circumstances in which the information was disclosed by A to B and
- C uses the information in determining its own future pricing intentions.

The CAT explained that it is necessary to prove each retailer's 'state of mind' to establish that discussions between a supplier and a retailer have gone beyond normal commercial dealings, for example as to the retailer's profit margin or the terms of trade, and have instead given rise to an unlawful, albeit indirect, 'horizontal element'[129]. The absence of any legitimate commercial reason for a disclosure by retailer A of its future pricing intentions to supplier B may indicate the requisite state of mind[130]. The CAT left open whether a lesser state of mind, such as recklessness as to transmission or receipt of A's pricing intentions, would be sufficient[131]. In *VM Remonts*, however, the Court of Justice held that liability could be established when A could reasonably have foreseen that B would disclose confidential information about A's intentions to C and A was prepared to accept the risk that this entailed[132].

These cases mean that an undertaking in the position of B must take care to ensure that it does not, consciously or unconsciously, act as the facilitator of horizontal collusion between A and C. Whilst bilateral discussions between a supplier and a dealer of a purely vertical nature about matters such as likely retail prices, profit margins and wholesale

[127] [2006] EWCA Civ 1318, para 141.

[128] Case 1188/1/1/11 [2012] CAT 31, para 57.

[129] See paras 65–66 of the CAT judgment; see also para 106 of the Court of Appeal's judgment.

[130] [2012] CAT 31, para 72.

[131] Ibid, paras 73 and 350–354.

[132] Case C-542/14 *VM Remonts* EU:C:2016:578, para 33; cf the English Court of Appeal's view that the criterion of reasonable foreseeability 'may have gone too far': [2006] EWCA Civ 1318, paras 91 and 140.

prices are permissible, suppliers must be cautious about how they seek to influence the pricing behaviour of their retailers. Retailers, for their part, must be careful about telling suppliers about their intention to maintain or increase retail prices: an authority may consider that A anticipated that B would disclose that information to C, opening up the possibility of a hub and spoke infringement.

(vii) 'Single overall agreement'

In a number of cases the UK competition authorities have found a 'single overall agreement' for which all undertakings bear responsibility, irrespective of their precise involvement from day to day[133]. To find a single overall agreement the CMA must prove the existence of an overall plan pursuing a common objective, the intentional contribution of an undertaking to that plan and its awareness of the conduct of the other participants[134]. The fact that an undertaking does not comply with the plan is irrelevant[135]. Nor is it necessary for the undertaking itself to produce the goods or services that are cartelised[136].

In *Mercedes-Benz commercial vehicles*[137] the OFT dealt, in one investigation, with five cartels in relation to the distribution of Mercedes-Benz trucks and vans; however the OFT declined to find a single overall agreement because the cartels involved different firms, areas and practices over different periods. Similarly, the OFT sometimes found that bid-rigging gave rise to a series of discrete infringements rather than to a single overall agreement[138].

In *Supply of products to the furniture industry (drawer fronts)*[139] the CMA found that two undertakings had engaged in cartel activity from 2006 to 2008 and again in 2011; it was unable to prove that the cartel continued between 2008 and 2011 and so found a 'single and repeated infringement' rather than a single overall agreement.

(viii) 'Object or effect the prevention, restriction or distortion of competition within the UK'

(a) General comments

This concept is understood and applied in the same way as Article 101(1)[140]. Where an agreement has the object of restricting competition, it is unnecessary to prove that it has an anti-competitive effect in order to find an infringement of the Chapter I prohibition. This simple rule has been repeatedly affirmed in the CMA's decisions[141] and the CAT's

[133] See eg *Construction Recruitment Forum*, OFT decision of 29 September 2009, paras 4.332–4.343; *Airline passenger fuel surcharges for long-haul passenger flights*, OFT decision of 19 April 2012, paras 382–388; *Conduct in the modelling sector*, CMA decision of 16 December 2016, paras 4.61–4.68; *Supply of products to the furniture industry (drawer wraps)*, CMA decision of 27 March 2017, paras 5.49–5.52; see further ch 3, 'Single overall agreement', pp 105–109.

[134] *Conduct in the modelling sector*, CMA decision of 16 December 2016, para 4.59; see also *Collusive tendering in the supply and installation of certain access control and alarm systems to retirement properties*, OFT decision of 6 December 2013, paras 3.32–3.34 and 6.9–6.10.

[135] *Access to car parking facilities at East Midlands International Airport*, CAA decision of 17 January 2017, para 110.

[136] *Restrictive arrangements preventing estate and lettings agents from advertising their fees in a local newspaper*, CMA decision of 8 May 2015, para A.49.

[137] *Distribution of Mercedes-Benz commercial vehicles investigation*, OFT decision of 27 March 2013.

[138] See eg *West Midland Roofing Contractors*, decision of 17 March 2004, upheld on appeal in Cases 1032/1/1/04 etc *Apex Asphalt & Paving Co Ltd v OFT* [2005] CAT 4; *Bid rigging in the construction industry in England*, OFT decision of 21 September 2009, paras VI.14–VI.20 (pp 1631–1632); see ch 13, 'Collusive Tendering', pp 547–549 for discussion of the OFT's decisions on bid-rigging.

[139] CMA decision of 27 March 2017, paras 5.49–5.55.

[140] See ch 3, 'The "object or effect" of preventing, restricting or distorting competition', pp 119–147.

[141] See eg *Online sales of posters and frames*, CMA decision of 12 August 2016, para 5.33; *Independent Schools*, OFT decision of 20 November 2006, paras 1348–1358.

jurisprudence[142]. In *Sainsbury's v MasterCard*[143] the CAT emphasised that restrictions by object 'should not be used as a means of avoiding a difficult investigation of anti-competitive effects'; rather, the harmful nature of such restrictions should be 'clear-cut and pronounced without an examination of the effects'. This is consistent with the Court of Justice's view that the concept of an object restriction should be interpreted restrictively[144].

(b) Restriction of competition by object

As in the case of EU law, the 'essential legal criterion' for establishing a restriction of competition by object is whether the coordination between undertakings reveals a sufficient degree of harm to competition[145]. It is not enough for the agreement to be merely capable of resulting in the prevention, restriction or distortion of competition[146]. The CAT's approach in *Agents' Mutual v Gascoigne Halman*[147] was to examine whether the agreement, by its very nature, having regard to the economic and legal context, 'clearly and unambiguously revealed a sufficient degree of harm to competition to make any examination of its effects unnecessary'[148]. In determining that issue, the CAT looked at the content of the agreement, its objectives and its economic and legal context. The parties' intentions may also be relevant, although they are not a determinative factor[149].

The case law establishes that there are some types of agreement and/or concerted practice, such as those which fix prices[150], share markets[151], establish collusive tendering[152] or impose export bans[153], that have the object of restricting competition. However, the category of object restrictions is capable of both growing and shrinking over time. In *Cityhook v OFT*[154] the High Court considered that classifying an alleged collective boycott by purchasers of a supplier offering a new technology as a restriction of competition by object had 'the attraction of simplicity'[155], but recognised that the contrary view was not unreasonable[156]: existing case law established only that a boycott of a purchaser by suppliers was restrictive by object. The judge in *Cityhook* was reluctant to add a 'new' restriction by object to the existing category of such cases. The discovery of 'new' restrictions by object cannot be ruled out, but it is reasonable to suppose that this will be a relatively rare occurrence[157].

[142] See eg Case 1003/2/1/01 *Institute of Independent Insurance Brokers v Director General of Fair Trading* [2001] CAT 4, paras 169–170; Case 1241/5/7/15 (T) *Sainsbury's Supermarkets Ltd v MasterCard Inc* [2016] CAT 11, paras 100–101; Case 1262/5/7/16 (T) *Agents' Mutual v Gascoigne Halman* [2017] CAT 15, paras 148–149.

[143] Case 1241/5/7/15 (T) *Sainsbury's Supermarkets Ltd v MasterCard Inc* [2016] CAT 11, para 101(2).

[144] Case C-67/13 P *Groupement des Cartes Bancaires v Commission* EU:C:2014:2204, para 58.

[145] Case 1241/5/7/15 (T) *Sainsbury's Supermarkets Ltd v MasterCard Inc* [2016] CAT 11, para 101.

[146] Case 1262/5/7/16 (T) *Agents' Mutual v Gascoigne Halman* [2017] CAT 15, para 149(1).

[147] Ibid. [148] Ibid, para 150.

[149] Ibid, para 149(2); see also *Online sales of posters and frames*, CMA decision of 12 August 2016, paras 5.51–5.57; *Memorandum of Understanding on the Supply of Oil Fuels in an Emergency*, OFT decision of 25 October 2001, paras 39–40.

[150] See eg *Stock Check Pads*, OFT decision of 31 March 2006; *Aluminium Space Bars*, OFT decision of 28 June 2006.

[151] See eg *Arriva/First Group*, OFT decision of 5 February 2002; *Care Home Medicine*, OFT decision of 12 December 2013.

[152] See eg *Bid rigging in the construction industry in England*, OFT decision of 21 September 2009, paras III.97–III.114 (cover bidding) and III.143–III.154 (compensation payments).

[153] See eg *Roma-branded mobility scooters: prohibitions on online sales and online price advertising*, OFT decision of 5 August 2013.

[154] *R (Cityhook Ltd) v OFT* [2009] EWHC 57 (Admin). [155] Ibid, para 131.

[156] Ibid, paras 132–135.

[157] See eg *Jones v Ricoh (UK) Ltd* [2010] EWHC 1743 (Ch), para 42 where it was held that a confidentiality agreement restricted competition by object because it went much further than could reasonably be required to protect the information of the claimant; see further ch 3, 'Refinement of the range of agreements within the object box', pp 131–132.

In *Tobacco*[158] the OFT concluded that two tobacco manufacturers and ten retailers had entered into a number of bilateral, vertical agreements whereby the prices of various tobacco brands were linked to those of competitors' brands; the OFT did not find any multilateral or horizontal agreements. The OFT concluded that these 'price-matching' arrangements restricted each retailer's ability independently to set resale prices for cigarettes and considered that they restricted competition by object[159]. On appeal the CAT did not decide the substantive matters in dispute between the parties; it set aside the decision because the OFT had abandoned its defence of the decision[160]. In *Paroxetine*[161] the CMA decided that the settlements of patent disputes between GlaxoSmithKline and two generic producers had the object of restricting competition because Glaxo had paid its potential competitors to stay out of the market. On appeal the CAT considered that the question whether the agreements had the object of restricting competition was of wide importance and that the law was not free from doubt, and therefore referred the matter to the Court of Justice under Article 267 TFEU.[162].

In several cases the parties have successfully argued that an agreement that appeared to be restrictive did not have the object of restricting competition. In *Bookmakers' Afternoon Greyhound Services v Amalgamated Racing* ('*BAGS*')[163] the Court of Appeal endorsed the judge's conclusion that the collective negotiation and exclusive licensing of horseracing media rights was to introduce competition into a previously monopsonistic market and that any increase in price was the consequence of that increase in competition[164]. It followed that the arrangements did not have as their object the restriction of competition[165]. In *Sainsbury's v MasterCard*[166] the CAT was not persuaded that the multilateral interchange fee ('MIF') agreed upon between banks within the MasterCard system pursued the object of restricting competition since its competitive impact was 'very much at large', even after hearing voluminous factual and expert evidence; the CAT subsequently held that the MIF had the effect of restricting competition. In *Agents' Mutual v Gascoigne Halman*[167] the CAT held that none of the contested rules of a new online property portal, OnTheMarket, revealed a sufficient degree of harm to competition; on the contrary, they had the pro-competitive purpose of facilitating entry onto a market.

One final point is that even an agreement that restricts competition by object may be defended under section 9(1) of the Act and (where Article 101(1) applies) Article 101(3) TFEU. The OFT issued two favourable Opinions stating that object restrictions may be legal where they satisfy the criteria of section 9(1)[168].

(c) Restriction of competition by effect

Where an agreement does not have the object of restricting competition there remains the possibility that its actual or potential effect, considered within its legal and economic

[158] OFT decision of 15 April 2010. [159] Ibid, section 6.

[160] Cases 1160–1165/1/1/10 *Imperial Tobacco Group plc v OFT* [2011] CAT 41.

[161] CMA decision of 12 February 2016.

[162] Cases 1252/1/12/16 etc *GlaxoSmithKline plc v CMA* [2018] CAT 4, paras 160-326; the reference for a preliminary ruling was made by order of 27 March 2018.

[163] [2008] EWHC 1978 (Ch), upheld on appeal, [2009] EWCA Civ 750.

[164] [2009] EWCA Civ 750, paras 73–94; the court also pointed out that, in the absence of the racecourses' collaboration, there was only one buyer for the media rights and consequently no competition to be restricted: ibid, para 92.

[165] Ibid, para 94; in reaching its conclusion the Court of Appeal referred to the Court of Justice's judgment in Case C-209/07 *Competition Authority v Beef Industry Development Society Ltd* EU:C:2008:643: see ch 3, 'Market sharing, quotas, collective exclusive dealing', p 129.

[166] Case 1241/5/7/15 (T) *Sainsbury's Supermarkets Ltd v MasterCard Inc* [2016] CAT 11.

[167] Case 1262/5/7/16 (T) *Agents' Mutual v Gascoigne Halman* [2017] CAT 15.

[168] *Newspapers and magazine distribution*, Opinion of 22 October 2008; *Rural Broadband Wayleave Rates*, Short-form Opinion of 23 August 2012.

context, might be to do so[169]. In *Agents' Mutual v Gascoigne Halman*[170] the CAT held that it is necessary to conduct an 'extensive analysis' of the effect of an agreement or provision in its market context, which involves the following steps:

- identifying the relevant agreement or provision said to constitute a restriction of competition
- identifying the market, or markets, in which the effect of that agreement or provision is to be assessed
- presenting a 'theory of harm' that guides the assessment
- testing the theory of harm and the effects that are alleged to occur against the evidence and
- comparing the state of competition with the agreement in place with the position in the 'counterfactual' world in which the agreement had never been made.

In *Paroxetine*[171] the CMA found that settlement agreements between GlaxoSmithKline and two generic producers unjustifiably delayed the latter's efforts to enter the market independently of Glaxo, and had the effect (as well as the object) of restricting competition. On appeal the CAT referred a question to the Court of Justice as to whether a 'real possibility' that the generics would have succeeded against GSK in patent litigation is sufficient to establish a restriction by effect[172].

In *Racecourse Association v OFT*[173] the CAT held that the OFT had relied upon an unconvincing 'shifting, hypothetical counterfactual situation'[174] and that therefore the OFT had failed to demonstrate that the collective selling of broadcasting rights to horseracing events by racecourse owners had anti-competitive effects. In *Sainsbury's v MasterCard*[175] the CAT held that the MasterCard MIF had as its effect the restriction of competition when compared with the counterfactual of voluntary bilateral agreements between 'issuing banks' (which issue MasterCard cards to consumers) and 'acquiring banks' (which act for merchants) for each transaction with a MasterCard card[176]. However Popplewell J reached a different conclusion in *Asda v MasterCard*[177] because he did not consider that the counterfactual of voluntary bilateral interchange fees was realistic. Instead he held that the correct counterfactual was MasterCard's MIFs being set at zero. In Popplewell J's view in this case the MasterCard scheme would have collapsed, as issuing banks would have switched to issuing Visa cards in order to receive higher fees. On this basis, Popplewell J reached the conclusion that MasterCard's MIFs did not have the effect of restricting competition, the opposite conclusion from that of the CAT.

In *Sainsbury's v Visa*[178] Phillips J held that Visa's UK MIF did not have the effect of restricting competition in the acquiring market by comparison with a counterfactual payment scheme in which rules provide for settlement of card transactions at par, that is to say, a zero MIF. This was because there would be no difference in the competitive process between the real and counterfactual worlds. Phillips J therefore disagreed with both the CAT and Popplewell J about what would have happened in the absence of a positive MIF[179]. The Court

[169] OFT 401, para 7.2; see also Case 1003/2/1/01 *Institute of Independent Insurance Brokers v Director General of Fair Trading* [2001] CAT 4, para 170.

[170] Case 1262/5/7/16 (T) *Agents' Mutual v Gascoigne Halman* [2017] CAT 15, para 151; see similarly Case 1241/5/7/15 (T) *Sainsbury's Supermarkets Ltd v MasterCard Inc* [2016] CAT 11, para 127.

[171] CMA decision of 12 February 2016.

[172] Cases 1252/1/12/16 etc *GlaxoSmithKline plc v CMA* [2018] CAT 4, paras 327–349.

[173] [2005] CAT 29, paras 177–202.

[174] Ibid, para 202.

[175] [2016] CAT 11, paras 126–267, on appeal to the Court of Appeal.

[176] Ibid, para 266 contains the CAT's conclusions on effects.

[177] [2017] EWHC 93 (Comm), on appeal to the Court of Appeal.

[178] [2017] EWHC 3047 (Comm), on appeal to the Court of Appeal.

[179] Ibid, paras 162–170.

of Appeal has granted permission to appeal against the orders of the CAT, Popplewell J and Phillips J and it is hoped that the Court of Appeal will clarify whether and, if so, in what way, a MIF restricts or distorts competition.

In *BAGS*[180] the High Court and the Court of Appeal held that the racecourses' collaboration, which meant that they could not sell their rights to licensed betting offices individually, did not have an anti-competitive effect because this arose in the context of a desire by them to create a second distributor of media rights in a market in which there had previously been only one undertaking, which was itself owned by the bookmakers.

A similar conclusion was reached by the CAT in *Agents' Mutual v Gascoigne Halman*[181]. Agents Mutual operated an online property portal and was a new entrant into the market. It required that agents using its services would not advertise through more than one other portal. The CAT concluded that this rule did not have the effect of restricting competition, noting that 'the notion that the entry of a new competitor onto a market should be anticompetitive is an inherently unusual suggestion'[182].

(d) *Ancillary restraints*

In several cases restrictions in agreements fell outside the Chapter I prohibition because they were 'objectively necessary' to facilitate a legitimate commercial activity[183]. In *BAGS*[184] the Court of Appeal accepted that the restrictions on the racecourses were ancillary restraints as they were objectively necessary to enable the creation of a second distributor in the market. In *Asda v MasterCard*[185] the High Court held that MasterCard's MIFs were ancillary restraints to the MasterCard scheme. The court concluded that it must take account of competition facing the MasterCard scheme when considering whether the MIF was objectively necessary, and that the judgment of the General Court in *Métropole*[186] suggesting a 'relatively abstract analysis' was out of line with the Court of Justice's jurisprudence[187]. In *Sainsbury's v Visa* Phillips J considered that *Métropole* remains good law and, if he had found Visa's MIFs had restricted competition, he did not consider the MIFs were objectively necessary for the operation of the Visa scheme[188]. In *Agents' Mutual v Gascoigne Halman*[189] the CAT was satisfied that a provision obliging estate agents to delist from some portals was objectively necessary to achieve the beneficial purpose of a new property portal to enter the market. In each case the court was satisfied that the commercial operation would have been impossible (not merely difficult or less profitable) to carry on without the restriction in question[190].

(ix) **Appreciability**

The Chapter I prohibition applies only where an agreement brings about an *appreciable* restriction of competition[191].

180 [2008] EWHC 1978 (Ch), paras 177–202, upheld on appeal [2009] EWCA Civ 750, paras 95–110.

181 [2017] CAT 15.

182 Ibid, para 197.

183 In addition to the cases discussed in the text see *Pirtek (UK) Ltd v Joinplace Ltd* [2010] EWHC 1641 (Ch), paras 45–59; *Carewatch Care Services Ltd v Focus Caring Services Ltd* [2014] EWHC 2313 (Ch), paras 146–167.

184 [2009] EWCA Civ 750, paras 111–123; see also the High Court's judgment [2008] EWHC 1978 (Ch), paras 469–474 and 496.

185 [2017] EWHC 93 (Comm), paras 118–233.

186 Case T-112/99 *Métropole television v Commission* EU:T:2001:215, para 109.

187 [2017] EWHC 93 (Comm), paras 164–181, relying on Case 42/84 *Remia v Commission* EU:C:1985:327, paras 17–20 and Case C-250/92 *Gøttrup-Klim* EU:C:1994:413, paras 28–35.

188 [2017] EWHC 3047 (Comm), paras 174–191.

189 [2017] CAT 15, paras 241–248, although this was not a necessary finding for the judgment: ibid, para 241.

190 Ibid, paras 152–154 for a helpful summary of the relevant law.

191 See eg Case 1124/1/1/09 *North Midland Construction v OFT* [2011] CAT 14, paras 35–63.

(a) Object restrictions

In EU law[192], an object restriction that has an appreciable effect on trade between Member States is an appreciable restriction of competition. The High Court[193] and the CMA[194] have interpreted the Chapter I prohibition in the same way, holding that an object restriction that has an appreciable effect on trade within the UK constitutes an appreciable effect on competition. In *Mobility Scooters*[195] the OFT decided that a prohibition of internet sales and online price advertising had as its object the restriction of competition and therefore was an appreciable restriction of competition; the decision did not address the condition precedent in EU law, that the agreement should have an effect on trade between Member States: indeed the OFT did not apply Article 101 in *Mobility Scooters* because it was not satisfied that there was any cross-border effect[196]. In *Cleanroom laundry services* and products the CMA concluded, on the basis that section 60(2) Competition Act imports the reasoning in *Expedia*, that an agreement that affects trade *within* the UK and that has an anti-competitive object by its nature has an appreciable effect on competition[197].

(b) Effect restrictions

In determining whether a restriction of competition by effect is appreciable the CMA[198] will have regard to the European Commission's *Notice on Agreements of Minor Importance*[199]. The CMA would not impose fines on undertakings that have relied in good faith on the Commission's *De Minimis Notice*[200]. The fact that an agreement does not comply with the *De Minimis Notice* does not mean, in itself, that any restriction of competition is appreciable: such a finding would require further analysis, in particular to determine how much market power the parties to the agreement possess[201]. In *P&S Amusements Ltd v Valley House Leisure Ltd*[202] the High Court concluded that there was no prospect of it being found that a beer tie in a lease of a public house in Blackpool would be found to have as its effect an appreciable restriction of competition[203]. In *Sainsbury's v MasterCard*[204] the CAT had 'no doubt' that the MasterCard MIFs had an appreciable effect on competition when compared with the more competitive counterfactual world that would have existed in the absence of the MIFs.

[192] Case C-226/11 *Expedia* EU:C:2012:795, para 37; see also the Commission's *Notice on Agreements of Minor Importance*, OJ [2014] C 291/1, which says, in para 2, that it does not apply to object restrictions as a result of the *Expedia* judgment; for discussion of *Expedia* see ch 3, 'Part II of the Notice: the treatment of object restrictions', pp 149–150.

[193] *Carewatch Care Services Ltd v Focus Caring Services Ltd* [2014] EWHC 2313 (Ch), paras 149–150.

[194] *Online resale price maintenance in the light fittings sector*, CMA decision of 3 May 2017, paras 4.156–4.157 and 4.166.

[195] *Roma-branded mobility scooters: prohibitions on online sales and online price advertising*, OFT decision of 5 August 2013, para 3.199.

[196] Ibid, paras 3.152–3.155.

[197] CMA decision of 14 December 2017, para 5.167.

[198] *Agreements and concerted practices*, OFT 401, para 2.18.

[199] OJ [2014] C 291/1; on the market share thresholds used to determine whether a restriction of competition is not appreciable see ch 3, 'The Commission's *Notice on Agreements of Minor Importance*', pp 147–150.

[200] *Agreements and concerted practices*, OFT 401, para 2.19.

[201] Ibid, para 2.20.

[202] [2006] EWHC 1510 (Ch); see also *Independent Media Support Ltd/BBC Broadcast*, OFCOM decision of 30 May 2007, paras 8.1–8.25, upheld on appeal [2008] CAT 13; permission to appeal to the Court of Appeal was refused [2008] EWCA Civ 1402.

[203] Ibid, paras 23–26.

[204] [2016] CAT 11, paras 267–269.

(x) Applicable law and territorial scope

Where the CMA intends to take action in relation to an agreement that it considers may be anti-competitive it must decide whether to do so on the basis of the Chapter I prohibition alone or whether it should also proceed under Article 101 TFEU. Where an agreement affects trade between Member States Article 3(1) of Regulation 1/2003 requires the CMA to apply Article 101[205]. The CMA has regard to the European Commission's *Guidelines on the Effect on Trade Concept contained in Articles [101 and 102 TFEU]*[206] when considering whether an agreement might infringe Article 101 TFEU. Post-Brexit, Regulation 1/2003 will cease to apply in the UK, including the provisions of Article 3.

The Chapter I prohibition applies only where trade *within the UK* is affected. The CMA has said that its focus will be on whether an agreement appreciably restricts competition within the UK since, if it does so, it will also affect trade there[207]. The CAT has held that the 'effect on trade within the UK' does not need to be appreciable[208]. Its reasoning was that in EU law the requirement of an appreciable effect on trade was a jurisdictional rule to demarcate the scope of EU and domestic competition law, and that there was no need to transcribe that reasoning to a purely domestic context. However the High Court has doubted whether the CAT was correct on this point in two cases[209].

(B) Section 2(2): illustrative list

Section 2(2) provides that:

> Subsection (1) applies, in particular, to agreements, decisions or practices which—
>
> (a) directly or indirectly fix purchase or selling prices or any other trading conditions;
>
> (b) limit or control production, markets, technical development or investment;
>
> (c) share markets or sources of supply;
>
> (d) apply dissimilar conditions to equivalent transactions with other trading parties, thereby placing them at a competitive disadvantage;
>
> (e) make the conclusion of contracts subject to acceptance by the other parties of supplementary obligations which, by their nature or according to commercial usage, have no connection with the subject of such contracts.

This list, which exemplifies the sorts of agreement which would infringe section 2(1), is identical to the list in Article 101(1) TFEU. However it is important to stress that, like Article 101(1), the Chapter I prohibition has been applied to agreements that are *not* explicitly mentioned in the list. For example, the exchange of confidential information between competitors about future prices falls within the Chapter I prohibition[210], although there is no specific reference to such agreements in the Act[211]. This is because the list is merely

[205] See ch 2, 'Obligation to apply Articles 101 and 102', pp 76–77.

[206] *Agreements and concerted practices*, OFT 401, para 2.23.

[207] Ibid, para 2.25.

[208] Case 1009/1/1/02 *Aberdeen Journals Ltd v OFT* [2003] CAT 11, paras 459–462; this was a case on the Chapter II prohibition, but in Case 1124/1/1/09 *North Midland Construction plc v OFT* [2011] CAT 14, para 49 the CAT held that its reasoning applies equally to the Chapter I prohibition and that it would be 'irrational' to distinguish between the two; for comment on this issue see Bailey '(Appreciable) Effect on Trade Within the United Kingdom' (2009) 30 ECLR 353.

[209] *P&S Amusements Ltd v Valley House Leisure Ltd* [2006] EWHC 1510 (Ch), paras 21, 22 and 34 and *Pirtek (UK) Ltd v Joinplace Ltd* [2010] EWHC 1641 (Ch), paras 61–67, in particular at para 62.

[210] *Galvanised steel tanks for water storage information exchange infringement*, CMA decision of 19 December 2016, paras 4.41–4.44 and case law cited; this decision was upheld on appeal to the CAT, Case 1277/1/12/17 *Balmoral Tanks v CMA* [2017] CAT 23.

[211] Another example would be restrictions imposed on advertising: see *Lladró Comercial*, OFT decision of 31 March 2003, paras 68–71.

illustrative and in each case the critical issue is whether the agreement has as its object or effect the restriction of competition[212].

Section 2(2)(d) and (e) suggest that agreements to discriminate and tie-ins may amount to infringements of Article 101 or the Chapter I prohibition. It is fair to point out, however, that there have been few cases under Article 101(1)(d) and (e). Discrimination and tie-ins usually give rise to concern in competition law only where there is significant market power on the part of the party which is practising discrimination or which is imposing the tie. For this reason these phenomena are usually investigated, if at all, under Article 102 rather than under Article 101[213].

(C) Section 2(3): extraterritorial application

The extraterritorial scope of the Act is considered in chapter 12[214].

(D) Section 2(4): voidness

Section 2(4) provides that:

> Any agreement or decision which is prohibited by subsection (1) is void.

This mirrors Article 101(2) TFEU. For many firms it is the possibility that their agreements may turn out to be unenforceable that has as much, and in many cases more, significance than the possibility of being fined for infringing the Chapter I prohibition. A considerable compliance effort has to be maintained in order to ensure that important commercial transactions will not be undermined by one or more parties to an agreement subsequently reneging on it and claiming it to be unenforceable. These issues are considered in chapter 8[215]. A few points are worthy of mention here.

(i) Severance

Section 2(4) provides that 'any agreement' which violates section 2(1) is void[216]. Despite the clear wording of both section 2(4) and Article 101(2) TFEU that the agreement is void, it has been established by the Court of Justice that it may be possible to sever the offending clauses, leaving the remainder of the agreement enforceable[217]. The intention is that the courts in the UK should interpret section 2(4) in the same way as the Court of Justice has interpreted Article 101(2)[218], pursuant to section 60(2) of the Act.

English contract law provides that severance is possible in certain circumstances, although the rules on this subject are complex[219]. It is a matter for the applicable law of the contract, rather than the *lex fori* of the court in which the action is brought, to determine whether, and, if so, by what criteria, severance is to be effected[220]. Severability is possible in English law where it would not fundamentally change the character, purpose, scope,

[212] Further examples can be found in *Agreements and concerted practices*, OFT 401, December 2004, paras 3.3–3.27; see further ch 13, 'UK Law', pp 564–569.

[213] See ch 18, 'Price Discrimination', pp 777–782 and ch 17, 'Tying', pp 705–713.

[214] See ch 12, 'Competition Act 1998', pp 509–510.

[215] See also Whish 'The Enforceability of Agreements under EC and UK Competition Law' in Rose (ed) *Lex Mercatoria: Essays on International Commercial Law in Honour of Francis Reynolds* (LLP, 2000).

[216] See generally ch 8, 'Severance', pp 338–339.

[217] Ibid.

[218] HL Report Stage, 9 February 1998, col 890.

[219] See Beale (ed) *Chitty on Contracts* (Sweet & Maxwell, 32nd ed, 2015), paras 16.211–16.220.

[220] See Regulation 593/2008 of the European Parliament and of the Council on the law applicable to contractual obligations, OJ [2008] L 177/6; *Dicey, Morris & Collins on the Conflict of Laws* (Sweet & Maxwell, 15th ed, 2014), chs 32 and 33.

substance or intention of the agreement[221]. In *Agents' Mutual v Gascoigne Halman*[222] the CAT held that the rule by which an estate agent member may list its properties on no more than one other online property portal was not severable from the other membership rules, although this was not a necessary finding for the judgment[223].

(ii) Void or illegal?

In *Gibbs Mew v Gemmell*[224] the Court of Appeal concluded that an agreement that infringes Article 101(1) is not only void and unenforceable, but is also illegal. This has serious consequences: for example a party who has paid money to another under an illegal agreement cannot recover that money unless it can be shown that the parties were not *in pari delicto*[225]. In *Crehan v Courage*[226], a case concerning Article 101 TFEU, the Court of Justice held that it would be contrary to the effective application of Article 101 for national law to impose an absolute bar on an action by one party to an agreement that restricts competition against another party to it[227]; however, EU law does not prevent national law from denying a party who has significant responsibility for the restriction of competition the right to obtain damages from the other contracting party[228]. In *Sainsbury's v MasterCard*[229] the CAT considered that Sainsbury's Bank did not bear significant responsibility for MasterCard's infringement, and that therefore Sainsbury's was entitled to claim damages from MasterCard.

(iii) Transient voidness

In *Passmore v Morland*[230] the Court of Appeal held that an agreement may, in its lifetime, drift into and out of unlawfulness under Article 101(1), and therefore be void and unenforceable at some times but not at others. The same, presumably, is true of section 2(4).

(E) Sections 2(5) and 2(6): interpretation

These provisions explain that, except where the context otherwise requires, any reference in the Act to an agreement includes a reference to a concerted practice and a decision by an association of undertakings.

(F) Section 2(7): the UK

Section 2(7) provides that '"the UK" means, in relation to an agreement which operates or is intended to operate only in a part of the UK, that part'[231]. The UK for this purpose includes England, Wales, Scotland plus the subsidiary islands (excluding the Isle of Man and the Channel Islands) and Northern Ireland.

(G) Section 2(8): the 'Chapter I prohibition'

Section 2(8) provides that:

> The prohibition imposed by subsection (1) is referred to in this Act as 'the Chapter I prohibition'.

The expression 'the Chapter I prohibition' is therefore a legislative one.

[221] *Jones v IOS (RUK) Ltd* [2012] EWHC 348 (Ch), para 43. [222] [2017] CAT 15.
[223] Ibid, paras 276–281. [224] [1998] Eu LR 588; see also *Trent Taverns Ltd v Sykes* [1999] Eu LR 492.
[225] See Goff and Jones *The Law of Unjust Enrichment* (Sweet & Maxwell, 9th ed, 2016), ch 25.
[226] Case C-453/99 EU:C:2001:465; for discussion of *Crehan* see ch 8, '*Courage Ltd v Crehan*', pp 308–309.
[227] Case C-453/99 EU:C:2001:465, para 28. [228] Ibid, paras 31–33.
[229] [2016] CAT 11, paras 405–418, although this was not a necessary finding for the judgment.
[230] [1999] 3 All ER 1005; see ch 8, 'Transient voidness', pp 339–340.
[231] See eg *Arriva/First Group*, OFT decision of 5 February 2002, paras 44–45.

(H) The Chapter I prohibition: excluded agreements

Section 3 provides for exclusions from the Chapter I prohibition. Some, but not all, of these exclusions apply also in the case of the Chapter II prohibition[232]. Section 50 provides for the possibility of vertical and land agreements to be excluded. Vertical agreements were excluded from the Chapter I prohibition from 1 March 2000 to 1 May 2005; land agreements were excluded from 1 March 2000 to 6 April 2011. Vertical and land agreements must now be assessed under the Chapter I prohibition in the same way as any other agreement[233].

Section 3(1) provides that the Chapter I prohibition does not apply in any of the cases in which it is excluded by or as a result of Schedule 1 on mergers and concentrations; Schedule 2 on competition scrutiny under other enactments; and Schedule 3 on planning obligations and other general exclusions[234]. The regulatory rules of the legal profession are subject to competition scrutiny under sections 57 to 61 of the Legal Services Act 2007. Section 3(2) to (5) of the Competition Act makes provision for the Secretary of State to amend Schedules 1 and 3 in certain circumstances, whether by adding additional exclusions or by amending or removing existing ones[235]. Section 3(6) notes that Schedule 3 itself enables the Secretary of State in certain circumstances to exclude agreements from the Chapter I prohibition[236].

Section 59(2) provides that if the effect of one or more exclusions is that the Chapter I prohibition is inapplicable to one or more provisions of an agreement, those provisions do not have to be disregarded when considering whether the agreement itself infringes the prohibition for other reasons. In other words, the effect of the agreement as a whole can be considered.

(i) Schedule 1: mergers and concentrations

Schedule 1 to the Competition Act provides that the Chapter I and Chapter II prohibitions will not apply to mergers under the Enterprise Act nor to concentrations in respect of which the European Commission has exclusive jurisdiction under the EU Merger Regulation ('the EUMR'). The exclusion in Schedule 1 does not require an application to the CMA.

(a) Relationship of the Chapter I and Chapter II prohibitions with UK merger control

Schedule 1, paragraph 1(1) provides that the Chapter I prohibition does not apply to an agreement or combination of agreements which results or would result in any two enterprises 'ceasing to be distinct enterprises' for the purposes of Part 3 of the Enterprise Act[237]. The exclusion applies to any transaction whereby enterprises cease to be distinct, irrespective of whether there is a 'relevant merger situation' capable of being investigated

[232] See 'Exclusions', p 387 later in chapter.

[233] See 'Section 50: vertical agreements' (p 371) and 'Section 50: land agreements', p 371 later in chapter and ch 16, 'Vertical agreements under the Competition Act 1998', pp 693–695.

[234] Sch 4 on professional rules was repealed by Enterprise Act 2002, s 207.

[235] This order-making power is subject to s 71 of the Act, which requires an affirmative resolution of each House of Parliament.

[236] See 'Public policy', pp 369–370 later in chapter on Sch 3, para 7.

[237] See *Guidance on the CMA's jurisdiction and procedure*, CMA2, April 2014, paras 6.68–6.70; for the meaning of 'ceasing to be distinct' see s 26 of the Enterprise Act 2002 and ch 22, 'Enterprises ceasing to be distinct', pp 942–945; the UK exclusion is wider than the disapplication of Article 101 to concentrations in the EU, effected by Article 21(1) of the EUMR, since 'ceasing to be distinct' is a broader concept than that of a concentration under Article 3(2) of the EUMR; see also HL Third Reading, 5 March 1998, col 1365 (Lord Simon of Highbury).

under the Enterprise Act[238]. If this were otherwise the Competition Act would have revolutionised the control of mergers in the UK by bringing all those transactions that are not subject to the Enterprise Act, because they fall below the relevant thresholds, within the scope of the 1998 Act, which would be an absurdity.

Schedule 1, paragraph 1(2) provides in addition that the exclusion of the Chapter I prohibition extends to 'any provision directly related and necessary to the implementation of the merger provisions': this means that 'ancillary restrictions' also fall outside the Chapter I prohibition. To be ancillary the restriction must be both 'directly related [to]' and 'necessary to the implementation of' the merger provisions. The CMA has said that it will generally follow the European Commission's approach as set out in the *Notice on restrictions directly related and necessary to concentrations*[239]. Ancillary restrictions include, for example, appropriately limited non-compete clauses, licences of intellectual property rights and know-how and purchase and supply agreements. The CMA will not normally state in a clearance decision which restrictions are ancillary[240]: it will provide guidance only in the case of novel or unresolved questions giving rise to genuine uncertainty[241].

(b) Newspaper mergers

The exclusion from the Chapter I prohibition for certain newspaper mergers[242] has been repealed[243].

(c) Clawback

Schedule 1, paragraph 4 provides for the possibility of 'withdrawal of the paragraph 1 exclusion' by the CMA. The 'clawback' provision applies only to the Chapter I prohibition[244]; it does not apply to the Chapter II prohibition. Paragraph 4(5) provides that the CMA may, by a direction in writing[245], remove the benefit of the exclusion where it considers that (a) an agreement would, if not excluded, infringe the Chapter I prohibition and (b) the agreement is not a protected agreement[246]. These provisions will be exercised only rarely.

(d) Protected agreements

The CMA cannot exercise the right of clawback in relation to a 'protected agreement'. The Act defines four categories of protected agreement. First, an agreement in relation to which the CMA or Secretary of State, as the case may be, has published its or his decision not to refer a merger for an in-depth 'Phase 2' investigation; the CMA cannot override the decision not to refer a merger under the Enterprise Act by seeking to apply the Competition Act 1998. Secondly, an agreement in relation to which the CMA has found there to be a relevant merger situation. Thirdly, an agreement that would result in enterprises ceasing to be distinct in the sense of section 26 of the Enterprise Act, other than as a result of subsections (3) and (4)(b) of that section[247]. Fourthly, an agreement which the CMA has found gives rise to a merger under section 32 of the Water Industry Act 1991.

[238] See ch 22, 'Relevant merger situations', pp 942–947.

[239] OJ [2005] C 56/24; see ch 21, 'Contractual restrictions directly related and necessary to a merger: "ancillary restraints"', pp 904–907.

[240] *Guidance on the CMA's jurisdiction and procedure*, CMA2, April 2014, para 6.69.

[241] Ibid, para 6.70.

[242] Competition Act 1998, Sch 1, para 3.

[243] Communications Act 2003, s 57; see ch 22, 'Public interest cases', pp 987–989.

[244] See the statement of Lord Simon before the HL Committee, 13 November 1997, col 328.

[245] Competition Act 1998, Sch 3, para 4(7)(a); the direction cannot be retrospective: see para 4(7)(b).

[246] Ibid, Sch 3, para 5; on protected agreements see the following section.

[247] See 'Relationship of the Chapter I and II prohibitions with UK merger control', pp 364–365 earlier in chapter.

(e) Relationship of the Chapter I and Chapter II prohibitions with EU merger control

Paragraph 6 of Schedule 1 provides that the Chapter I prohibition does not apply to concentrations which have a European Union dimension[248]. This provision is necessary in order to comply with Article 21(3) of the EUMR[249]; it provides that no Member State may apply its national legislation on competition to any concentration that has an EU dimension, since the European Commission has exclusive jurisdiction in such cases; the so-called 'one-stop-shop'. Paragraph 6 does not mention ancillary restraints specifically, but since they are deemed to be cleared by a Commission decision permitting a concentration it presumably follows that Member States cannot take action in relation to them[250].

A consequence of Brexit, in the absence of some new arrangement between the UK and the EU, will be the loss of the principle of the one-stop-shop in the UK. It will follow that a merger notified to the European Commission under the EUMR could also be reviewed under the provisions of domestic merger control if the jurisdictional criteria of the Enterprise Act 2002 are satisfied.

(f) No clawback

Since Schedule 1, paragraph 6 deals with matters that are within the exclusive jurisdiction of the European Commission, it follows that the CMA does not in this situation enjoy a right of clawback as it does under paragraph 4 in relation to mergers that are subject to the Enterprise Act 2002.

(ii) **Schedule 2: competition scrutiny under other enactments**

Schedule 2 excludes agreements which are subject to 'competition scrutiny' under another Act[251]: the Government explained during the passage of the Competition Bill that, in so far as particular agreements are subject to competition scrutiny under regimes constructed to deal with the circumstances of specific sectors, it is inappropriate to subject them to the Chapter I prohibition as well, as 'that would just create an unwelcome and unjustified double jeopardy'[252].

(a) Communications Act 2003

Section 293 of the Communications Act 2003 requires the Office of Communications ('OFCOM') periodically to review the 'networking arrangements' between Independent Television Ltd and the 13 regional Channel 3 licensees, including an assessment of their effect on competition. OFCOM conducts annual reviews of these arrangements[253].

(b) Financial Services and Markets Act 2000

The Financial Services Act 2012[254] established the Financial Conduct Authority ('the FCA') with the strategic objective of ensuring that financial markets function well and

[248] See *Merger Assessment Guidelines*, CC2 (Revised) OFT 1254, September 2010, paras 1.13–1.18; on the EUMR generally see ch 21.

[249] For an interpretation of Article 21(3) of the EUMR see the judgments of the Court of Appeal in *Ryanair Holdings plc v OFT* [2012] EWCA Civ 643 and *Ryanair Holdings plc v Competition Commission* [2012] EWCA Civ 1632; see further ch 21, 'The benefits of one-stop merger control', pp 864–867.

[250] See ch 21, 'Contractual restrictions directly related and necessary to a merger: "ancillary restraints"', pp 904–907.

[251] Note that the provisions in the Competition Act, as originally enacted, excluding the supervision and qualification of auditors (Sch 2, paras 2 and 3) and of certain environmental matters (Sch 2, para 6) from the Chapter I prohibition, were repealed by the Competition Act 1998 and Other Enactments (Amendment) Regulations 2004, SI 2004/1261.

[252] HL Committee, 13 November 1997, col 342.

[253] The reviews can be found at www.ofcom.org.uk.

[254] Note s 34 of this Act repealed the exclusion from the Chapter I and II prohibitions for regulatory provisions made by the former Financial Services Authority.

with the operational objectives of securing consumer protection; protecting the integrity of the UK financial system; and promoting effective competition in the interests of consumers[255]. The Financial Services (Banking Reform) Act 2013 established the Payment Systems Regulator ('the PSR') as an independent subsidiary of the FCA; the PSR has the objectives of promoting competition, innovation and the interests of users in the operation of payment systems[256].

The Financial Services Act 2012 amended the Financial Services and Markets Act 2000 in order to enhance the competition scrutiny of regulating provisions or practices adopted by the FCA, PSR and/or the Prudential Regulation Authority[257]. The CMA may give advice to one of these regulators that one or more regulating provisions or practices may cause or contribute to the prevention, restriction or distortion of competition in the supply or acquisition of goods and services in the UK[258]. The relevant regulator is then required to state, with reasons, how it proposes to deal with the advice and publish a response within 90 days[259]. Where the CMA's advice is adverse and, following the regulator's response, the CMA remains of the opinion that the provisions or practices have an anti-competitive effect, the Treasury is given power to give directions to the regulator to remedy the situation, although it is not bound to do so[260]. The CMA has agreed a *Memorandum of Understanding* with the FCA and with the PSR which records the basis on which they will cooperate[261].

(c) Legal Services Act 2007

Sections 57 to 61 of this legislation make provision for competition scrutiny of the regulatory rules of the legal profession by the CMA[262].

(d) No power to amend Schedule 2

There is no power to amend Schedule 2. Section 3 of the Competition Act provides the power to amend only in relation to Schedule 1 and Schedule 3.

(iii) **Schedule 3: general exclusions**

(a) Planning obligations

Paragraph 1 of Schedule 3 provides that the Chapter I prohibition does not apply to agreements involving planning obligations, for example where planning permission is given subject to the developer agreeing to provide certain services or access to facilities[263].

(b) Section 21(2) Restrictive Trade Practices Act 1976

Paragraph 2 of Schedule 3 provided that agreements that were the subject of directions under section 21(2) of the Restrictive Trade Practices Act 1976 were excluded from the Chapter I prohibition. This provision was repealed with effect from 1 May 2007[264].

[255] Financial Services and Markets Act 2000, ss 1B–1E.

[256] Financial Services (Banking Reform) Act 2013, ss 40 and 49–53.

[257] Ibid, ss 140A–140H. [258] Ibid, s 140B. [259] Ibid, s 140G.

[260] Ibid, s 140H.

[261] Available at www.gov.uk/cma.

[262] See *Legal services market study*, Final Report of 15 December 2016.

[263] Town and Country Planning Act 1990, s 106.

[264] Competition Act and Other Enactments (Amendment) Regulations 2004, SI 2004/1261, reg 4, Sch 1, para 50a; for a discussion of s 21(2) of the Restrictive Trade Practices Act 1976 see Vol 47 of *Halsbury's Laws of England*, para 269.

(c) EEA regulated markets

Paragraph 3 of Schedule 3 provides that the Chapter I prohibition does not apply to various matters concerning 'EEA regulated [financial services] markets'. This expression is defined in paragraph 3(5) as meaning a market which is listed by another EEA State[265] and which does not require a dealer on the market to have a presence where trading facilities are provided or on any other trading floor of that market. This exclusion may be repealed after the UK leaves the EU in March 2019.

(d) Services of general economic interest

Paragraph 4 of Schedule 3 provides that neither the Chapter I nor the Chapter II prohibition shall apply to an undertaking:

> entrusted with the operation of services of general economic interest or having the character of a revenue-earning monopoly in so far as the prohibition would obstruct the performance, in law or in fact, of the particular tasks assigned to it.

This provision is modelled upon Article 106(2) TFEU[266], although the language of the Schedule is somewhat less tortuous than that to be found in the Treaty. The Guidelines on *Services of general economic interest exclusion*[267] and *Public bodies and competition law*[268] contain important guidance on this provision. The CMA will interpret the exclusion strictly[269]. The guidance notes that, as various public-sector activities become exposed to competition or economic regulation, it is possible that certain functions that once might have been considered to be administrative or social become regarded as economic; this can have the result that an entity engaged in those activities might come to be regarded as an undertaking, and therefore fall within the purview of competition law[270]. The guidance discusses what is meant by the notion of 'entrusting' an undertaking with the performance of services[271]; it also considers the meaning both of 'services'[272] and of 'general economic interest'[273]. In *Pool Reinsurance* the OFT was not satisfied that the scheme of terrorism reinsurance for commercial property related to services of general economic interest[274].

The CMA's guidance notes that in a number of EU cases Article 106(2) has been held to be applicable where an undertaking was subject to a universal service obligation and needed to be protected from 'cream-skimming' or 'cherry-picking'[275]. However it also notes that in the UK the combined effect of privatisation, liberalisation and EU initiatives has been that the number of exclusive rights held by undertakings has been significantly reduced[276]. The CMA's view is that, in general, effective competition will best serve the interests of consumers over time, which is why it will interpret the exclusion narrowly. The CMA's guidance concludes by saying that it is unlikely that there are any 'revenue-earning monopolies' of the kind referred to in Schedule 3, paragraph 4 in the UK[277].

There is specific guidance on the exclusion of services of general economic interest within the energy, railway and water sectors[278].

[265] Pursuant to Article 47 of Directive 2004/39/EC of the European Parliament and of the Council on markets in financial instruments, OJ [2004] L 145/1.

[266] See ch 6, 'Article 106(2)', pp 242–248.

[267] OFT 421, December 2004.

[268] OFT 1389, December 2011.

[269] *Public bodies and competition law*, OFT 421, December 2004, para 1.9.

[270] Ibid, para 2.7.

[271] Ibid, paras 2.9–2.15.

[272] Ibid, paras 2.16–2.18.

[273] Ibid, paras 2.19–2.22.

[274] OFT decision of 15 April 2004, paras 71–74.

[275] *Services of general economic interest*, OFT 421, para 3.4.

[276] Ibid, para 3.5.

[277] Ibid, paras 4.1–4.4.

[278] *Application in the energy sector*, OFT 428, January 2005, paras 3.34–3.38 and *Application to services relating to railways*, OFT 430, October 2005, paras 3.18–3.21; *Guidance on Ofwat's approach to the application of the Competition Act 1998 in the water and wastewater sector in England and Wales*, March 2017, p 33.

(e) Compliance with legal requirements

Paragraph 5 of Schedule 3 provides that neither the Chapter I nor the Chapter II prohibition applies to an agreement or to conduct that is required to comply with a legal requirement. For this purpose a legal requirement is one imposed by or under any enactment in force in the UK and, prior to Brexit, by or under the TFEU or the EEA Agreement and having legal effect in the UK without further enactment, or under the law in force in another Member State having legal effect in the UK. The CMA's guidance indicates that this exclusion will apply in 'a very limited number of circumstances'[279]. An example of the operation of this exclusion occurred in the case of *Vodafone*[280], in which OFCOM accepted that Vodafone could not be found guilty of infringing the Chapter I prohibition by printing prices on its 'pre-pay mobile phone vouchers' since this was done in order to comply with a licence condition[281]. OFCOM subsequently removed the price publication requirement from Vodafone's licence, so that the exclusion no longer applied.

The exclusion in paragraph 5 of Schedule 3 applies only where the regulated undertaking is *required* to act in a certain way; it does not apply to the discretionary behaviour of that undertaking. In *VIP Communications*[282] OFCOM considered that T-Mobile could rely on Schedule 3, paragraph 5 in refusing to supply certain services to VIP Communications in circumstances where it knew that VIP would use those services in order to act unlawfully in violation of the Wireless Telegraphy Act 1949: OFCOM considered that T-Mobile was required by law to desist from conduct that would result in illegal behaviour[283].

In *Albion Water* the CAT disagreed with OFWAT's view[284] that the provisions of the Water Industry Act 1991 constituted a legal requirement for the purposes of Schedule 3, paragraph 5(3)[285].

(f) Avoidance of conflict with international obligations

Paragraph 6(1) of Schedule 3 enables the Secretary of State to make an order to exclude the application of the Chapter I prohibition from an agreement or a category of agreements where this would be appropriate in order to avoid a conflict between the provisions of the Competition Act and an international obligation of the UK. The order can provide that the exclusion shall apply only in specified circumstances[286] and may be retrospective[287]. Similar provisions are contained in Schedule 3, paragraph 6(4) and (5) for exclusion from the Chapter II prohibition. Schedule 3 paragraph 6(6) extends the meaning of the term 'international obligation' to include inter-governmental arrangements relating to civil aviation: the reason for this is that such arrangements, permitting flights between the UK and other countries, are often not made as treaties[288] and so do not give rise to international 'obligations' as such.

(g) Public policy

Paragraph 7 of Schedule 3 gives power to the Secretary of State to make an order to exclude the application of the Chapter I prohibition from an agreement or a category of agreements where there are 'exceptional and compelling reasons of public policy' for doing so. The order can provide that the exclusion shall apply only in specified

[279] *Public bodies and competition law*, OFT 1389, December 2011, para 3.4.

[280] OFTEL decision of 5 April 2002.

[281] Ibid, para 47.

[282] OFCOM decision of 28 June 2005, appeal rejected in Case 1027/2/3/04 *VIP Communications Ltd (in administration) v OFCOM* [2009] CAT 28.

[283] Ibid, para 205.

[284] OFWAT decision of 26 May 2004, paras 23–24.

[285] Case 1046/2/4/04 *Albion Water Ltd v Water Services Regulation Authority* [2006] CAT 23, paras 931 and 978.

[286] Competition Act, Sch 3, para 6(2).

[287] Ibid, Sch 3, para 6(3).

[288] HL Deb, 9 February 1998, cols 972–973.

circumstances[289], and may be retrospective[290]. Similar provisions are contained in paragraph 7(4) and (5) of Schedule 3 for exclusion from the Chapter II prohibition. Four orders have been made under paragraph 7: three in relation to the defence industry[291], one of which has been repealed[292]; the fourth concerns arrangements for the supply of oil and petroleum products in the event of significant disruption, or threat of significant disruption, to normal supply[293].

(h) Coal and steel

Paragraph 8 of Schedule 3 provides that the Chapter I and Chapter II prohibitions do not apply to agreements and conduct within the exclusive jurisdiction of the European Commission under the former European Coal and Steel Treaty; this provision is now otiose[294].

(i) Agricultural products

Paragraph 9 of Schedule 3 excludes from the Chapter I prohibition agreements that fall outside Article 101 TFEU by virtue of Regulation 1184/2006[295]. If the European Commission decides that an agreement is not excluded from Article 101 by Regulation 1184/2006, the exclusion from paragraph 9 of Schedule 3 ceases on the same date[296]. Provision is made for clawback[297].

(iv) **Professional rules**

Paragraph 1(1) of Schedule 4 provided that the Chapter I prohibition did not apply to designated professional rules. This provision was repealed with effect from 1 April 2003[298]. The application of the Chapter I prohibition to professional rules must be considered in the light of the judgment of the Court of Justice in *Wouters*[299], where it held that certain restrictions of competition might fall outside Article 101 TFEU in so far as they are reasonably necessary for the proper practice of a profession. The CMA has reviewed various markets for professional services; its work has led to the removal of restrictions imposed on the providers of professional services[300].

289 Competition Act, Sch 3, para 7(2).

290 Ibid, Sch 3, para 7(3).

291 Article 346 TFEU provides an exclusion from the EU competition rules for certain matters related to defence; there are no specific exclusions for this area from the Competition Act 1998.

292 Competition Act 1998 (Public Policy Exclusion) Order 2006, SI 2006/605 (maintenance and repair of warships); Competition Act 1998 (Public Policy Exclusion) Order 2007, SI 2007/1896 (strategic and tactical weapons and their supporting technology), repealed with effect from 30 December 2011 by Competition Act 1998 (Public Policy Exclusion) (Revocation) Order 2011, SI 2011/2886; Competition Act 1998 (Public Policy Exclusion) Order 2008, SI 2008/1820 (design, construction, maintenance and disposal of nuclear submarines).

293 The Competition Act 1998 (Public Policy Exclusion) Order 2012, SI 2012/710; this Order follows the expiry of the 'individual exemption' granted in *Memorandum of Understanding on the supply of oil fuels in an emergency*, OFT decision of 25 October 2011.

294 These exclusions ceased to have effect when the ECSC Treaty expired on 23 July 2002; see ch 23, 'Coal and Steel', p 999.

295 OJ [2006] L 214/7, as amended by Regulation 1234/2007, OJ [2007] L 299/1; Regulation 361/2008, OJ [2008] L 121/1 and Regulation 491/2009, OJ [2009] OJ L 154/1; see ch 23, 'Agriculture', pp 995–998.

296 Competition Act, Sch 3, para 9(2).

297 Ibid, para 9(6) and (7).

298 Enterprise Act 2002, s 207.

299 Case C-309/99 *Wouters v Algemene Raad van de Nederlandsche Orde van Advocaten* EU:C:2002:98; on this judgment see further ch 3, 'Regulatory ancillarity: the judgment of the Court of Justice in *Wouters*', pp 138–142.

300 See eg *Legal services market study*, Final Report of 15 December 2016, available at www.gov.uk/cma; see also *Restrictions on business structures and direct access in the Scottish legal profession*, OFT 946, July 2007 and three OFT reports on the likely competition effects of modifications to codes of conduct and other professional rules under the Courts and Legal Services Act 1990, all of which are available at www.nationalarchives.gov.uk.

(v) Section 50: vertical agreements

Section 50 of the Act makes provision for the exclusion or exemption of vertical agreements from the Chapter I, but not the Chapter II, prohibition[301]. This was effected, except in relation to vertical price fixing, by the Competition Act 1998 (Land and Vertical Agreements Exclusion) Order 2000[302]. Following the adoption of Regulation 1/2003 the exclusion of vertical agreements from the Chapter I prohibition was repealed[303] in order to align the treatment of vertical agreements in domestic and EU law[304].

(vi) Section 50: land agreements

Certain agreements relating to land were excluded from the Chapter I, though not the Chapter II[305], prohibition from 1 March 2000 to 5 April 2011[306]; the exclusion was revoked by the Competition Act 1998 (Land Agreements Exclusion Revocation) Order 2010[307] with effect from 6 April 2011. The reason for the exclusion was that commercial leases often contain restrictive covenants and conditions imposed with the legitimate aim of good estate management[308]. The exclusion avoided uncertainty as to whether such covenants and conditions might be rendered void and unenforceable as a result of section 2(4) of the Act.

In order to provide assistance to undertakings and their professional advisers following the revocation of the exclusion for land agreements guidance has been published on the application of the Chapter I and II prohibitions to them[309]. The guidance says that only a minority of land agreements will be caught by the Chapter I prohibition[310]. It also indicates that land agreements are unlikely to be an enforcement priority where none of the parties has a market share of more than 30% in the market for which the land is being used[311]. In a surprising judgment of the London County Court, *Martin Retail Group v Crawley Borough Council*[312], the parties agreed, although it is not clear why, that a clause in a lease limiting the use of premises within a 'shopping parade' restricted competition; the court held that, since the clause did not satisfy the criteria of section 9 of the Act, it was void and unenforceable[313]. In future one would expect the UK courts to follow the Court of Justice's judgment in *Maxima Latvija*[314] and conduct a 'thorough analysis' of the effects of a lease on the market before finding an infringement.

301 On vertical agreements generally see ch 16.

302 SI 2000/310; the CAT held that the Exclusion Order did not apply in Cases 1252/1/12/16 *GlaxoSmithKline plc v CMA* [2018] CAT 4, paras 350-364.

303 This was effected by the Competition Act 1998 (Land Agreements Exclusion and Revocation) Order 2004, SI 2004/1260, which repealed SI 2000/310 that had created the exclusion for vertical agreements in the first place.

304 See further ch 16, 'Repeal of the exclusion for vertical agreements', pp 693–694.

305 On the application of the Chapter II prohibition and Article 102 TFEU to land agreements see *Land agreements and competition law*, OFT 1317, March 2011, paras 6.1–6.15.

306 Competition Act 1998 (Land and Vertical Agreements Exclusion) Order 2000, SI 2000/310, as extended by Competition Act 1998 (Land Agreements Exclusion and Revocation) Order 2004, SI 2004/1260.

307 SI 2010/1709.

308 The registrability of restrictive covenants in commercial leases under the Restrictive Trade Practices Act 1976 was the subject of a test case in *Re Ravenseft Property Ltd's Application* [1978] QB 52.

309 *Land agreements and competition law*, OFT 1317, March 2011; see also the 6th edition of this book, pp 348–350.

310 *Land agreements and competition law*, para 1.5; see also para 4.2.

311 Ibid, para 8.6.

312 [2013] EW Misc 32 (CC); this case appears to have overlooked rule 30.8 of the Civil Procedure Rules which provides that in any county court proceedings raising an issue relating to, among other provisions, the Chapter I prohibition, the county court must transfer the proceedings to the Chancery Division of the High Court.

313 For comment see Armitage 'Competition Law, Land Agreements and the Decision in *Martin Retail Group Ltd v Crawley Borough Council*: An Opportunity Missed?' [2014] Comp Law 267.

314 Case C-345/14 *Maxima Latvija v Konkurences padome* EU:C:2015:784, paras 25–31; on 'Agreements that have as their effect the prevention, restriction or distortion of competition' see ch 3, pp 132–144.

(I) The Chapter I prohibition: exemptions

(i) Introduction

As in the case of EU law undertakings must conduct a self-assessment of whether an agreement that infringes the Chapter I prohibition is legal because it satisfies the criteria of section 9(1) of the Competition Act[315]. Sections 6 and 8 of the Act make provision for the adoption of domestic block exemptions, while section 10 provides for so-called 'parallel exemption' where an agreement satisfies one of the EU block exemptions, or would do if it were to affect trade between Member States[316]. Section 11 of the Act, which provided 'exemptions for other agreements', is now obsolete[317].

The operation of these provisions will be explained further, after a consideration of the criteria of section 9(1).

(ii) Exemption criteria

Section 9(1) provides that an agreement is exempt from the Chapter I prohibition if it:

(a) contributes to—

(i) improving production or distribution, or

(ii) promoting technical or economic progress, while allowing consumers a fair share of the resulting benefit; but

(b) does not—

(i) impose on the undertakings concerned restrictions which are not indispensable to the attainment of those objectives; or

(ii) afford the undertakings concerned the possibility of eliminating competition in respect of a substantial part of the products in question.

The wording of section 9 is very similar to, but not quite identical with, Article 101(3) TFEU. The latter refers to 'improving the production or distribution *of goods*' (emphasis added), but the domestic provision is not so limited, and can therefore be applied to services as well. In applying section 9(1) the CMA has said[318] that it will have regard to the European Commission's *Guidelines on the application of Article [101(3) TFEU]*[319]. The Guideline on *Agreements and concerted practices* does not provide a commentary on section 9(1)[320], presumably since this would duplicate what is said in the *Article 101(3) Guidelines*.

(a) Burden of proof

Section 9(2) provides that undertakings claiming the benefit of section 9(1) bear the burden of proving that its agreement satisfies the criteria of that provision[321]. There is no agreement that cannot be defended under section 9(1). Specifically this means that even

[315] The original process of notification of agreements to the OFT for 'negative clearance' and/or 'individual exemption', pursuant to ss 4–5 of the Competition Act, was repealed by reg 4 of SI 2004/1261 with effect from 1 May 2004; on self-assessment under Article 101(3) TFEU see ch 4, 'Self-assessment', pp 174–175.

[316] On the EU block exemptions see ch 4, 'Block exemptions', pp 176–179.

[317] See ch 23, 'Air transport', pp 1005–1008.

[318] *Agreements and concerted practices*, OFT 401, December 2004, para 5.5.

[319] OJ [2004] C 101/97; these *Guidelines* are discussed in ch 4, 'The Commission's approach in the *Article 101(3) Guidelines*', pp 167–169.

[320] On the application of the criteria in s 9 to land agreements see *The application of competition law following the revocation of the Land Agreements Exclusion Order*, OFT 1317, March 2011, ch 5.

[321] This mirrors Article 2 of Regulation 1/2003, OJ [2003] L 1/1: see ch 4, 'Burden and standard of proof', p 159; on the burden of proof in the context of a claim for damages see *Asda Stores Ltd v MasterCard Inc* [2017] EWHC 93 (Comm), paras 294–302 and *Sainsbury's Supermarkets Ltd v Visa Europe Services LLC* [2018] EWHC 355 (Comm), paras 13-21, both cases are on appeal to the Court of Appeal.

an agreement that restricts competition by object may be legal, provided it satisfies the criteria of that provision.

(b) Scope of section 9(1)

During the parliamentary debates on section 9 the Minister responsible for the Competition Bill stated twice in the House of Lords that he expected the criteria in section 9 to be interpreted in the same broad way as Article 101(3) TFEU. The decision in *Lucite International UK Ltd and BASF plc*[322] gave an indication of the breadth of section 9(1) by referring to the beneficial environmental effects of the agreement under consideration. In May 2010 the OFT (now CMA) published a discussion paper, *Article 101(3)—A Discussion of a Narrow Versus Broad Definition of Benefits*, which noted the debate about whether Article 101(3), and as a corollary section 9(1), should be interpreted in a broad manner having regard to non-economic benefits or more narrowly according to an economic efficiency standard. The European Commission considers that, since Article 101(3) is directly applicable[323], it should be applied according to the narrower approach, and the CMA's duty is to have regard to the Commission's position[324]. The breadth of the criteria in Article 101(3) is discussed in chapter 4, to which reference should be made[325].

(c) The application of section 9(1) to restrictions by object

In *Memorandum of Understanding on the supply of oil fuels in an emergency*[326] the OFT applied section 9(1) to an agreement that was found to restrict competition both by object and effect; the OFT considered that the agreement would improve distribution by enabling the Government to direct supplies of fuel to 'essential users' such as providers of emergency services in the event of a fuel shortage[327].

In *Newspapers and magazine distribution* the OFT published an Opinion on the application of the Chapter I prohibition and section 9(1) to agreements between newspaper and magazine publishers and their respective wholesalers[328]. An interesting feature of the Opinion is that it explains the OFT's thinking on the treatment of sub-national exclusive agreements which confer absolute territorial protection, an object restriction, upon the wholesaler; the OFT indicated that such agreements could satisfy the criteria of section 9(1) if evidence could be adduced to demonstrate that they would lead to economic efficiency[329].

The OFT also countenanced the possibility of an object restriction qualifying for exemption under section 9(1) in the case of *Rural Broadband Wayleave Rates*[330]. The OFT considered that a recommendation to landowners to charge a particular rate for granting wayleaves for granting access to private land could be beneficial by facilitating the roll-out of broadband services in rural areas.

(d) The application of section 9(1) to restrictions by effect

In *LINK Interchange Network Ltd*[331] the OFT applied section 9(1) to arrangements that provided for a centrally-set multilateral interchange fee for the operation of the LINK

322 OFT decision of 29 November 2002, paras 39–41.

323 Regulation 1/2003, OJ [2003] L 1/1, Article 1(2).

324 Competition Act 1998, s 60(3).

325 See ch 4, 'First condition of Article 101(3): an improvement in the production or distribution of goods or in technical or economic progress', pp 162–169.

326 OFT decision of 25 October 2001.

327 Ibid, paras 62–63; the exemption expired on 29 September 2010; the arrangements are now covered by the Competition Act 1998 (Public Policy Exclusion) Order 2012, SI 2012/710.

328 OFT 1025, October 2008.

329 Ibid, paras 4.29–4.144.

330 Short-form Opinion of 23 August 2012.

331 OFT decision of 16 October 2001.

network of automated teller machines, in which the major banks and building societies in the UK participate. The OFT recognised that charging such a fee could lead to an improvement in distribution by preventing one bank from taking a free ride on the investment of others[332]. The OFT considered whether the level of the multilateral interchange fee exceeded the cost of operating the network of cash machines but found that it did not[333]. The OFT granted an individual exemption to the arrangements in question until 16 October 2006; today the parties to such an agreement would have to self-assess the application of section 9(1).

In *Lucite International UK Ltd and BASF plc*[334] the OFT concluded that the restrictions inherent in a long-term agreement for the supply of hydrogen cyanide were indispensable because they helped solve the 'hold-up problem' that may occur when one party is required to invest in client-specific investment[335]. In *Pool Reinsurance*[336] the OFT concluded that rules designed to provide reinsurance against acts of terrorism in the UK restricted competition but satisfied the conditions of section 9. In *Association of British Insurers' General Terms of Agreement*[337] the OFT considered that, if certain provisions of the General Terms of Agreement were amended, it might satisfy section 9(1). The decision was set aside on appeal to the CAT[338]. The OFT subsequently decided to close the file since the case did not constitute an administrative priority[339].

In *Pirtek (UK) Ltd v Joinplace Ltd*[340] the High Court held that, in the event that it was wrong that a franchise agreement did not restrict competition, the agreement plainly contributed to improving the production or distribution of replacement hydraulic hoses due, in particular, to the provision of know-how and assistance to franchisees; it also concluded that the restrictive covenant at issue satisfied the other criteria in section 9(1)[341].

In *MasterCard*[342] the OFT concluded that the domestic interchange fee agreed between the banks participating in the MasterCard scheme did not satisfy the requirement in section 9(1) and Article 101(3) of indispensability since it extended to services that were not within the scope of the payment system[343]. The CAT reached the same conclusion in a standalone action for damages in *Sainsbury's v MasterCard*[344]. In *Asda v MasterCard*[345], however, the High Court held that certain levels of MIFs would qualify for exemption under Article 101(3) and section 9(1). The court held that, in principle, the 'benefit' produced by an agreement is not limited to consumers on the relevant market but includes wider benefits to others, such as technical or economic progress[346]. However, any benefit must also be causally linked to the restrictions in the agreement[347]; be objective, so that profits made by the parties do not count[348]; and must be passed on so that consumers directly or likely to be affected by the agreement are not worse off[349]. In *Sainsbury's v Visa*[350] Phillips J held that if, contrary to his primary

[332] Ibid, paras 42–45. [333] Ibid, paras 47–49.

[334] OFT decision of 29 November 2002, paras 45–46; see ch 16.

[335] See ch 16, 'The hold-up problem', p 641.

[336] OFT decision of 15 April 2004. [337] OFT decision of 22 April 2004.

[338] Case 1036/1/1/04 *Association of British Insurers v OFT*, order of 30 July 2004.

[339] Case closure notice of 29 January 2007. [340] [2010] EWHC 1641 (Ch).

[341] Ibid, paras 68–71.

[342] OFT decision of 6 September 2005, set aside on appeal Cases 1054/1/1/05 etc *MasterCard UK Members Forum Ltd v OFT* [2006] CAT 14; for discussion see Vickers 'Public Policy and the Invisible Price: Competition Law, Regulation and the Interchange Fee' [2005] Comp Law 5.

[343] OFT decision of 6 September 2005, para 519 and paras 533–649.

[344] Case 1241/5/7/15 (T) *Sainsbury's Supermarkets Ltd v MasterCard Inc* [2016] CAT 11, para 288, on appeal to the Court of Appeal.

[345] [2017] EWHC 93 (Comm), paras 261–421; para 292 summarises 'the Article 101(3) exercise', on appeal to the Court of Appeal.

[346] Ibid, paras 266–278. [347] Ibid, paras 264–265. [348] Ibid, paras 273–276.

[349] Ibid, paras 280–282. [350] [2018] EWHC 355 (Comm), on appeal to the Court of Appeal.

conclusion[351], Visa's MIFs did restrict competition within the meaning of Article 101(1), they were not exempt under Article 101(3) and would not have been exempt at any level. The judge concluded that Visa had not demonstrated that its MIFs contributed to net efficiencies[352]. The judge considered that the parties' expert evidence on efficiencies was extensive, but that it often required 'in the end little more than putting a finger in the air'; such an open-textured assessment did not satisfy the rigorous approach to the proof of efficiencies set out in the Commission's *Article 101(3) Guidelines*[353].

In *Agents' Mutual v Gascoigne Halman*[354] the CAT held that a rule of an online property portal by which an estate agent may list its properties on no more than one other portal did not restrict competition; if it had been restrictive, however, the CAT observed that there was no evidence of consumers receiving a 'fair share' of the putative benefits of the rule[355].

(iii) Block exemptions

Section 6 of the Competition Act allows the Secretary of State, acting upon a recommendation from the CMA, to adopt block exemptions. A block exemption may contain conditions and obligations and may be of limited duration, by virtue of sections 6(5) and 6(7) respectively. The procedure for adopting block exemptions is set out in section 8. There are a number of EU block exemptions, and these are applicable to agreements caught by the Chapter I prohibition by virtue of the parallel exemption provisions in section 10[356].

One block exemption has been adopted under the Competition Act, for public transport ticketing schemes that allow passengers to purchase tickets that can be used on the services of the participating travel operators. The block exemption entered into force on 1 March 2001[357] and will expire on 28 February 2026[358]. The CMA has published a guideline on the block exemption[359]; Appendix E contains flowcharts on the application of the block exemption and the Chapter I prohibition.

(iv) Parallel exemptions

Section 10 of the Competition Act makes provision for 'parallel exemptions'. Many agreements are block exempted by an EU block exemption[360]; there are others that would be exempt but for the fact that they do not produce an effect on trade between Member States: since such agreements would not infringe Article 101(1) they would not require or benefit from block exemption under Article 101(3). Section 10(1) and (2) of the Act provides that any agreement that benefits from a block exemption under EU law, or that would do if it were to affect trade between Member States, will also be exempted from the Chapter I prohibition. A consequence of the availability of parallel exemption is that the parties to such agreements do not need a block exemption under domestic law. Section 10(4) ensures that the duration of any parallel exemption is in line with the position in

351 [2017] EWHC 3047 (Comm), on appeal to the Court of Appeal.

352 [2018] EWHC 355 (Comm), paras 26–50; on the burden and standard of proof see paras 13–25.

353 Ibid, para 51. 354 [2017] CAT 15.

355 Ibid, para 275; the CAT specifically noted that its task under s 9 was made more difficult by the 'absence of a full market assessment by a competent competition authority'.

356 See 'Parallel exemptions' above.

357 Competition Act 1998 (Public Transport Ticketing Schemes Block Exemption) Order 2001, SI 2001/319, as amended by three statutory instruments: SI 2005/3347, SI 2011/227 and SI 2016/126.

358 Competition Act 1998 (Public Transport Ticketing Schemes Block Exemption) (Amendment) Order 2011, SI 2016/126.

359 *The public transport ticketing schemes block exemption*, CMA53, September 2016.

360 For discussion of the EU block exemptions see ch 4, 'Block Exemptions', pp 176–179.

EU law. The most important effect of section 10 is that vertical agreements may benefit from Regulation 330/2010[361] and that technology transfer agreements may benefit from Regulation 316/2014[362]. Research and development agreements and specialisation agreements could benefit from Regulation 1217/2010[363] and Regulation 1218/2010[364] respectively.

Section 10(5) makes provision for the CMA, in accordance with rules made under section 51 of the Act, to impose, vary or remove conditions and obligations subject to which a parallel exemption is to have effect, or even to cancel a parallel exemption. Section 10(6) enables this cancellation to be retrospective from before the date of the CMA's notice. However Article 3(2) of Regulation 1/2003 makes clear that, as a matter of EU law, it is not open to the CMA to impose stricter standards upon an agreement that benefits from Article 101(3) TFEU[365]. A different point is that Article 29(2) of Regulation 1/2003[366] specifically authorises a Member State to withdraw the benefit of an EU block exemption in certain, specified, circumstances.

4. The Chapter II Prohibition

The Chapter II prohibition is contained in section 18(1) of the Competition Act 1998. The Guidelines *Abuse of a dominant position*[367], *Assessment of market power*[368] and *Modernisation*[369] provide a useful overview of the Chapter II prohibition. The UK competition authorities and courts also have regard to the European Commission's *Guidance on the Commission's enforcement priorities in applying Article [102 TFEU] to abusive exclusionary conduct by dominant undertakings*[370]. There would appear to be considerable alignment between the European Commission's position set out in the *Guidance* and the application of the Chapter II prohibition in the UK in practice. Whilst the *Guidance* does not purport to state the law of exclusionary abuse under Article 102[371], it does appear to have had an influence on the interpretation and application of the Chapter II prohibition and Article 102 to exclusionary behaviour of dominant undertakings in the UK[372].

[361] See ch 16, 'Vertical Agreements: Regulation 330/2010', pp 664–687.

[362] See ch 19, 'Technology Transfer Agreements: Regulation 316/2014', pp 798–807.

[363] See ch 15, 'The block exemption for research and development agreements: Regulation 1217/2010', pp 607–611.

[364] See ch 15, 'The block exemption for specialisation agreements: Regulation 1218/2010', pp 613–615.

[365] See ch 2, 'Conflicts: Article 102', p 78; the CMA would presumably be under no constraint in a s 10(2) case, where there is, *ex hypothesi*, no EU jurisdiction.

[366] Regulation 1/2003, OJ [2003] L 1/1; see also the European Commission's *Guidelines on Vertical Restraints* OJ [2010] C 130/1, paras 74–78, on which see ch 16, 'Article 29(1) of Regulation 1/2003: withdrawal by the Commission', p 686.

[367] OFT 402, December 2004. [368] OFT 415, December 2004. [369] OFT 442, December 2004.

[370] OJ [2009] C 45/7; for a general discussion see ch 5, 'The Commission's *Guidance on Article 102 Enforcement Priorities*', pp 182–185.

[371] See para 3 of the *Guidance*.

[372] The *Guidance* has been referred to by the CAT in Case 1238/3/3/15 *BT v OFCOM* [2016] CAT 3, paras 90–91 (an appeal under the Communications Act 2003) and Case 1249/5/7/16 *Socrates Training Ltd v Law Society of England and Wales* [2017] CAT 10, fn 15 and para 166; by the CMA in *Paroxetine*, decision of 12 February 2016, fns 1298 and 1300 and *Unfair pricing in respect of the supply of phenytoin sodium capsules in the UK*, decision of 7 December 2016, fns 559 and 1228; by the ORR in its decision in *DB Schenker Rail (UK) Ltd*, decision of 2 August 2010, para 82; by the OFT in *Flybe Ltd*, decision of 5 November 2010, paras 6.36–6.39; *Reckitt Benckiser plc*, decision of 12 April 2011, paras 3.48 and 3.50; *Idexx*, OFT decision of 17 November 2011; *Unilever*, CMA decision of 10 August 2017; and by OFCOM in *Complaint from THUS plc and Gamma Telecom Ltd against BT about alleged margin squeeze in Wholesale Calls pricing*, decision of 20 June 2013, paras 2.36, 6.30 and 6.71.

The competition authorities in the UK have found infringements of the Chapter II prohibition in nine cases. The OFT imposed fines in four cases: it imposed a penalty of £3.21 million for abusive pricing in *Napp*[373], reduced to £2.2 million on appeal[374]; in *Aberdeen Journals*[375] it imposed a fine of £1.32 million for predatory pricing, reduced to £1 million on appeal[376]; in *Genzyme*[377] it fined Genzyme £6.8 million for engaging in various exclusionary practices, reduced to £3 million on appeal[378]; and in *Reckitt Benckiser* that undertaking agreed to pay a fine of £10.2 million for withdrawing and delisting a drug from the NHS prescription channel[379]. The Office of Rail Regulation imposed a fine of £4.1 million in the case of *English Welsh & Scottish Railway Ltd*[380], and the Gas and Electricity Markets Authority imposed a fine of £41.6 million in *National Grid*[381], reduced to £15 million on appeal[382]. In *Cardiff Bus*[383] the OFT concluded that Cardiff Bus had abused its dominant position by engaging in predatory conduct aimed at eliminating a competitor; no fine could be imposed in that case since Cardiff Bus's turnover was below £50 million[384]. In *Paroxetine*[385] the CMA found that GlaxoSmithKline had abused its dominant position by making cash payments and other value transfers to induce three potential competitors to delay their entry into to the UK paroxetine market. Glaxo's conduct did not constitute 'competition on the merits' and it was fined £37.6 million. In *Phenytoin*[386] the CMA imposed fines of £84.2 million on Pfizer and £5.2 million on Flynn Pharma for abusing their respective dominant positions by imposing excessive and unfair prices for an anti-epilepsy drug in the UK.

On two occasions the CAT has found an abuse of a dominant position in circumstances where the competition authority had decided that there was not one[387]. It may be the case that, whereas the competition authorities are keen to avoid false positives (findings of infringement where, in fact, no infringement has taken place), the CAT is keener to avoid false negatives (findings of non-infringement where, in fact, there has been an infringement)[388].

The High Court has found infringements of the Chapter II prohibition in two private actions for damages involving airport facilities[389]. In *Socrates v Law Society*[390] the CAT

[373] OFT decision of 30 March 2001.

[374] Case 1001/1/1/01 *Napp Pharmaceutical Holdings Ltd v Director General of Fair Trading* [2002] CAT 1.

[375] *Aberdeen Journals Ltd—remitted case*, OFT decision of 16 September 2002.

[376] Case 1009/1/1/02 *Aberdeen Journals Ltd v OFT* [2003] CAT 11.

[377] OFT decision of 27 March 2003.

[378] Case 1016/1/1/03 *Genzyme Ltd v OFT* [2004] CAT 4; interim relief was granted against the directions imposed by the OFT: Case 1013/1/03 (IR) *Genzyme Ltd v OFT* [2003] CAT 8.

[379] OFT decision of 13 April 2011.

[380] ORR decision of 17 November 2006.

[381] GEMA decision of 21 February 2008.

[382] Case 1099/1/2/08 *National Grid plc v Gas and Electricity Markets Authority* [2009] CAT 14, upheld on appeal [2010] EWCA Civ 114; the UK Supreme Court refused permission to appeal by order of 5 August 2010.

[383] OFT decision of 18 November 2008.

[384] See ch 10, 'Immunity for small agreements and conduct of minor significance', pp 423–424.

[385] CMA decision of 12 February 2016, on appeal Case 1252/1/12/16 *GlaxoSmithKline v CMA* [2018] CAT 4; the CAT referred the case to the Court of Justice under Article 267 TFEU: see the order of 27 March 2018.

[386] CMA decision of 7 December 2016, on appeal Cases 1275/1/12/17 etc *Flynn Pharma Ltd v CMA*, not yet decided.

[387] Case 1044/2/1/04 *ME Burgess, JJ Burgess and SJ Burgess v OFT* [2005] CAT 25 and Case 1046/2/4/04 *Albion Water Ltd v Water Services Regulation Authority* [2006] CAT 36 and [2008] CAT 31.

[388] On the possible implications of an over- or under-inclusive application of the law on abuse of dominance see *The cost of inappropriate interventions/non interventions under Article [102]*, OFT 864, September 2006, available at www.nationalarchives.gov.uk.

[389] *Purple Parking Ltd v Heathrow Airport Ltd* [2011] EWHC 987 (Ch); *Arriva The Shires Ltd v London Luton Airport Operations Ltd* [2014] EWHC 64 (Ch).

[390] Case 1249/5/7/16 [2017] CAT 10.

held that the Law Society of England and Wales had abused its dominant position on the market for the supply of conveyancing quality scheme ('CQS') accreditation to law firms by obliging accredited firms to obtain their training in mortgage fraud and anti-money laundering exclusively from the Law Society.

(A) The prohibition

(i) Section 18

The prohibition of the abuse of a dominant position is contained in section 18(1) of the Competition Act. Section 18 draws heavily on the text of Article 102[391]:

(1) Subject to section 19, any conduct on the part of one or more undertakings which amounts to the abuse of a dominant position in a market is prohibited if it may affect trade within the UK.

(2) Conduct may, in particular, constitute such an abuse if it consists in—

(a) directly or indirectly imposing unfair purchase or selling prices or other unfair trading conditions;

(b) limiting production, markets or technical development to the prejudice of consumers;

(c) applying dissimilar conditions to equivalent transactions with other trading parties, thereby placing them at a competitive disadvantage; (d) making the conclusion of contracts subject to acceptance by the other parties of supplementary obligations which, by their nature or according to commercial usage, have no connection with the subject of the contracts.

(3) In this section—

'dominant position' means a dominant position within the UK; and 'the UK' means the UK or any part of it.

(4) The prohibition imposed by subsection (1) is referred to in this Act as 'the Chapter II prohibition'.

(ii) 'The Chapter II prohibition'

Section 18(4) of the Act establishes the term 'the Chapter II prohibition' to refer to the prohibition set out in section 18.

(iii) 'Undertakings'

This term has the same meaning as in the Chapter I prohibition and in Articles 101 and 102 TFEU[392]. In *BetterCare*[393] and *NSAR*[394] the CAT ruled that a Northern Ireland healthcare trust and the National Skills Academy for Rail, respectively, were undertakings for the purpose of the Chapter II prohibition[395].

(iv) Affecting trade within the UK

As with the Chapter I prohibition there is a requirement that trade within the UK be affected. Most conduct that is an abuse of a dominant position within the UK will also affect trade there. The CAT has held that there is no need to show an *appreciable* effect on

[391] For detailed discussion of EU and UK law on the abuse of a dominant position see chs 5, 17 and 18.

[392] See 'Undertakings', pp 348–350 earlier in chapter.

[393] Case 1006/2/1/01 *BetterCare Group Ltd v Director General of Fair Trading* [2002] CAT 7.

[394] Case 1258/5/7/16 *UKRS Training Ltd v NSAR Ltd* [2017] CAT 14.

[395] The case is discussed at 'Basic definition', pp 352–355 earlier in chapter.

trade within the UK[396], although the High Court has questioned the correctness of this ruling[397]. The requirement of an effect on trade within the UK could exclude from the scope of the prohibition an abuse of a dominant position within the UK that has its effects entirely outside the UK[398].

(v) Voidness

The Competition Act does not refer explicitly to voidness in the case of the Chapter II prohibition. However in *English Welsh & Scottish Railway v E.ON UK*[399] the High Court held that coal carriage agreements that infringed the Chapter II prohibition (and Article 102 TFEU) were void and unenforceable.

(vi) Market size

Section 18(3) provides that a dominant position means a dominant position in the UK, and that the UK means the UK 'or any part of it'. Unlike Article 102[400], which refers to a dominant position '... within the internal market *or in a substantial part of it*', there is no need for the dominant position to be in the whole or a 'substantial' part of the UK. Thus, a relatively small part of the UK could constitute a 'market' within the meaning of section 18(1). Firms that have market power which is on only a local scale and which therefore run little risk of infringing Article 102 for lack of any appreciable effect on inter-state trade, or are dominant only in an insubstantial part of the internal market, might find that they are infringing the Chapter II prohibition. Local dominance can be expected to be found in some sectors, such as the operation of bus services[401]: there were numerous investigations of bus services under the old Competition Act 1980[402], and a market investigation of local bus services under the Enterprise Act 2002 led to recommendations to open up local bus markets, many of which the Government accepted and implemented[403]. In *First Edinburgh*[404] the OFT concluded that that company had not infringed the Chapter II prohibition by charging predatory prices or by increasing the frequency of bus services in order to foreclose access to the market to a rival bus operator, Lothian Buses plc. In November 2008 Cardiff Bus was found guilty of predatory conduct by running a 'no-frills' service to eliminate 2 Travel, its only competitor, from the market[405]. In *Burgess v OFT*[406] the CAT concluded that Austin, a funeral director, had abused a dominant position by refusing to provide access to a competitor, Burgess, to its local crematorium.

396 Case 1009/1/1/02 *Aberdeen Journals Ltd v OFT* [2003] CAT 11, paras 459–462.

397 See 'Applicable law and territorial scope', p 361 earlier in chapter.

398 See ch 12, 'Chapter II prohibition', pp 509–510.

399 [2007] EWHC 599 (Comm).

400 See ch 5, 'A substantial part of the internal market', pp 196–197.

401 See generally House of Commons Transport Committee: *Competition in the local bus market*, Third Report of Session 2012–13, 4 September 2012; on the application of the competition rules to the bus industry see OFT information leaflets *Frequently asked questions on competition law and the bus industry*, OFT 448, updated July 2006, and *A brief guide to the role of the OFT in the bus industry* and *The OFT and the bus industry*, OFT 397, February 2003.

402 See eg *Thamesway Ltd*, OFT, August 1993; *Fife Scottish Omnibuses Ltd*, OFT, March 1994; *United Automobile Services Ltd*, OFT, March 1995.

403 See *Local bus services market investigation*, Final Report of 20 December 2011 and *Government responses to the Competition Commission's report 'Local Bus Services Market Investigation'*, 29 March 2012; see ch 11, 'The Market Investigation Provisions in Practice', pp 488–493; there were several inquiries under the now-repealed monopoly provisions of the Fair Trading Act 1973: see eg *The supply of bus services in the north-east of England* Cm 2933 (1995).

404 OFT decision of 29 April 2004.

405 OFT decision of 18 November 2008; three individuals and the liquidator of 2 Travel Group, a bus company, brought follow-on actions for damages following the *Cardiff Bus* decision: see ch 8, 'Damages', pp 333–334.

406 Case 1044/2/1/04 [2005] CAT 25.

(vii) The relevant market

As in the case of EU law a finding of dominance must begin with the definition of the relevant market. Market definition has been discussed in detail in chapter 1[407]; as noted there, the relevant market must be analysed from two perspectives: the product market and the geographic market. In *CH Jones*[408] the OFT said that market definition is 'a key process for identifying relevant competitive constraints acting on a supplier of a given product or service'[409]. In *Socrates v Law Society*[410] the CAT emphasised that market definition is a means to an end for determining whether, at any period, an undertaking has substantial market power amounting to dominance[411]; it can also be relevant for assessing the competitive effects of the conduct complained about[412].

Guidance on market definition can be found in several judgments of the CAT[413] and the High Court[414] as well as in the CMA's guideline on *Market Definition*[415]. In general the case law and decisional practice follows the approach of the European Commission's *Notice on the definition of the relevant market for the purposes of [EU] competition law*[416]. In *Paroxetine*[417] the CAT held that the relevant market should reflect relevance to the issue under consideration. It recognised that this approach to market definition was 'novel' and therefore referred a question to the Court of Justice on this issue.

Where the CMA concludes that an allegation of abusive behaviour cannot be substantiated, it may refrain from reaching a conclusion as to the relevant product and geographic markets[418]. However in *Freeserve* the CAT emphasised that it will often be appropriate, for clarity of analysis, for the competition authority to indicate which markets seem to be potentially relevant in a particular case[419].

(viii) Assessing dominance

The Guideline *Assessment of market power*[420] points out that the concept of market power is not a term of art; however market power is a useful tool in assessing potentially anti-competitive behaviour. The *Guideline* states that market power arises where an undertaking does not face effective competitive pressure[421] and can be thought of as the ability profitably to sustain prices above competitive levels or to restrict output or quality below competitive levels[422]. The *Guideline* quotes the well-known definition of a dominant

[407] See ch 1, 'Market definition', pp 26–42.

[408] *Decision on an alleged abuse of a dominant position by CH Jones Limited*, OFT decision of 21 November 2013.

[409] Ibid, para 3.9. [410] Case 1249/5/7/16 [2017] CAT 10. [411] Ibid, para 106.

[412] Ibid, para 114; see also Case 1016/1/1/03 *Genzyme v OFT* [2004] CAT 4, para 318.

[413] Case 1005/1/1/01 *Aberdeen Journals Ltd v Director General of Fair Trading* [2002] CAT 4; Cases 1046/2/4/04 and 1032/2/4/04 (IR) *Albion Water Ltd v Water Services Regulation Authority* [2006] CAT 36, paras 90–117; Case 1099/1/2/08 *National Grid plc v Gas and Electricity Markets Authority* [2009] CAT 14, paras 34–46; Case 1249/5/7/16 *Socrates Training Ltd v Law Society of England and Wales* [2017] CAT 10, paras 102–104.

[414] See eg *Chester City Council v Arriva Plc* [2007] EWHC 1373 (Ch), paras 151–193; *Dahabshiil Transfer Services Ltd v Barclays Bank Plc* [2013] EWHC 3379 (Ch), paras 50–72; *Chemistree Homecare Ltd v Abbvie Ltd* [2013] EWCA Civ 1338, paras 34–48.

[415] OFT 403, December 2004; the Guideline *Abuse of a dominant position*, OFT 402, December 2004, contains a briefer discussion of market definition at paras 4.4–4.9.

[416] OJ [1997] C 372/5. [417] Case 1252/1/12/16 *GlaxoSmithKline v CMA* [2018] CAT 4, paras 397–409, and in particular paras 402–404.

[418] See eg *Association of British Travel Agents and British Airways plc*, decision of 11 December 2002, paras 10–19.

[419] Case 1007/2/3/02 *Freeserve.com plc v Director General of Telecommunications* [2003] CAT 5, para 131.

[420] OFT 415, December 2004, para 1.2; the Guideline *Abuse of a dominant position*, OFT 402, December 2004, contains a briefer discussion of assessing dominance at paras 4.10–4.22.

[421] *Assessment of market power*, para 1.3. [422] Ibid, para 1.4.

position from *United Brands v Commission*[423], the ability to 'prevent effective competition being maintained on the relevant market'[424]. In *Napp Pharmaceutical Holdings v Director General of Fair Trading* (and in subsequent cases) the CAT has adopted the same definition[425]. In *Cardiff Bus* the OFT noted that market power is a question of degree and that it is not necessary for a finding of dominance that an undertaking has eliminated all opportunity for competition in the market[426]. The CAT said the same thing in *Socrates v Law Society*[427]. In *Albion Water v Water Services Regulation Authority*[428] the CAT, perhaps concerned at the lack of findings of infringement of the Chapter II prohibition by the domestic competition authorities, said that:

> when assessing dominance under the Competition Act, it is unnecessary for the competition authority to investigate distant or theoretical possibilities with a view to dotting every 'i' or crossing every 't' that could conceivably be imagined. While a sensible analysis is required, there is no need to make the issue of dominance more complicated than it really is[429].

The Guideline *Assessment of market power* says that an undertaking will not be dominant unless it enjoys 'substantial market power'[430]: the European Commission's *Guidance on Article 102 Enforcement Priorities*[431] makes the same point[432]. The *Guideline* adds that assessing market power requires an examination of the competitive constraints that an undertaking faces, and it proceeds to discuss market shares (Part 4), entry barriers (Part 5) and other factors relevant to an assessment of market power (Part 6). In *Phenytoin*[433] the CMA considered each of these factors when it found that Pfizer and Flynn held dominant positions in their respective markets for manufacturing and distributing Pfizer-manufactured phenytoin sodium capsules.

(a) Market shares

Paragraph 2.11 of the *Guideline* makes the point that there is no fixed market share threshold for the determination of market power: market power depends on a variety of factors of which market share is one; paragraph 2.12 notes that there is a presumption in EU law of dominance at 50% or above[434], and adds that the CMA considers it unlikely that an undertaking would be dominant with a market share below 40%[435]. However in *NCNN 500* OFCOM concluded that BT, with a market share below 31%, was dominant as there were sufficient additional factors indicating dominance[436].

Paragraph 3.3 points out that one of the competitive constraints upon an undertaking comes from existing competitors within the relevant market, and market shares help[437]

[423] Case 27/76 EU:C:1978:22. [424] See ch 5, 'Dominant Position', pp 187–196.

[425] Case 1001/1/1/01 [2002] CAT 1, para 164.

[426] OFT decision of 18 November 2008, paras 5.6–5.7.

[427] Case 1249/5/7/16 [2017] CAT 10, para 134.

[428] Cases 1046/2/4/04 and 1032/2/4/04 (IR) [2006] CAT 36. [429] Ibid, para 185.

[430] *Assessment of market power*, para 2.9.

[431] See ch 5, 'The Commission's *Guidance on Article 102 Enforcement Priorities*', pp 182–185.

[432] OJ [2009] C 45/7, para 10.

[433] CMA decision of 7 December 2016, section 4, on appeal on this issue Cases 1275/1/12/17 etc *Flynn Pharma Ltd v CMA*, not yet decided.

[434] See ch 5, 'The *AKZO* presumption of dominance where an undertaking has a market share of 50% or more', p 190.

[435] The European Commission makes the same point in its *Guidance on Article 102 Enforcement Priorities*, para 14.

[436] OFCOM decision of 1 August 2008, paras 5.1–5.166.

[437] Market share figures do not yield any information about the competitive constraint that arises from the ability of existing firms within the market to expand.

to assess the extent of this constraint. Part 4 of the *Guideline* discusses market shares in more detail. Market power is more likely to exist where an undertaking has a persistently high market share[438]. It is the development of market shares over a period of time that is important, not their calculation at a single point in time[439]. The *Guideline* explains various reasons why market shares might not be a reliable guide to market power, for example because barriers to entry are low or because the market is a 'bidding market'[440]. In the circumstances of the recently liberalised market for the provision of domestic gas meters in *National Grid* the CAT treated market shares as high as 89% as one indicator of market power but as not raising a presumption of dominance[441]. Similarly, in *Socrates v Law Society*[442] the CAT said that the fact that an undertaking holds 100% of a relevant market is 'obviously relevant but does not automatically mean that it has significant market power'[443]. In that case the CAT considered that the Law Society held a dominant position only after its conveyancing quality scheme became an essential or 'must-have' product for most conveyancing solicitors' firms[444].

Paragraphs 4.6 to 4.8 of the *Guideline* provide insights into methods of calculating market shares.

(b) Entry barriers

Paragraph 3.3 of the *Guideline* points out that one of the competitive constraints upon an undertaking comes from potential competition, and entry barriers are relevant to this issue. Part 5 of the *Guideline* discusses barriers to entry; paragraph 5.1 explains that existing firms may experience barriers to expansion, and that such barriers can be analysed in the same way as barriers to entry. Entry barriers are important to the assessment of potential competition: the lower they are, the more likely it is that potential competition will prevent undertakings already in the market from exercising market power[445].

The *Guideline* acknowledges that there are various ways of classifying barriers to entry; it examines the issue under six heads[446]:

- **sunk costs**: that is to say costs that must be incurred to enter a market, but which are not recoverable on exiting the market; such costs give incumbent firms an advantage over potential entrants[447]
- **poor access to key inputs and distribution outlets**: there can be a barrier to entry where an incumbent has privileged access to a scarce input or distribution outlet, for example to essential facilities or intellectual property rights[448]
- **regulation**: for example a limitation on the number of undertakings licensed to operate on a market, or standards that an incumbent is able to satisfy but that new entrants find it difficult to, can amount to a barrier to entry[449]

438 *Assessment of market power*, para 4.2.

439 Ibid, para 4.2.

440 See ch 1, 'Market shares', pp 42–43.

441 Case 1099/1/2/08 [2009] CAT 14, para 51.

442 Case 1249/5/7/16 [2017] CAT 10; see also *Investigation into BT's residential broadband pricing*, OFCOM decision of 2 November 2010, para 3.61.

443 Case 1249/5/7/16 [2017] CAT 10, para 120.

444 Ibid, paras 122–137.

445 *Assessment of market power*, para 5.2.

446 Ibid, para 5.6.

447 Ibid, paras 5.8–5.11; see eg *Unfair pricing in respect of the supply of phenytoin sodium capsules in the UK*, CMA decision of 7 December 2016, paras 4.263–4.267, where the costs of developing a medicinal product and obtaining a marketing authorisation were sunk costs.

448 *Assessment of market power*, paras 5.12–5.15.

449 Ibid, paras 5.16–5.17; see eg *Reckitt Benckiser plc*, OFT decision of 12 April 2011, paras 5.45–5.47, where regulatory restrictions on the prescription of certain pharmaceutical products were found to be a barrier to entry.

- **economies of scale**: the fact that an undertaking may need to enter the market on a large scale can constitute a barrier to entry[450]
- **network effects**: as in the case of economies of scale, network effects can make it hard for a new firm to enter the market where the minimum viable scale of the network is large in relation to the size of the market[451]
- **exclusionary behaviour**: behaviour such as predation, margin squeezing and refusals to supply may act as barriers to entry[452].

The *Guideline* discusses ways of assessing the effects of barriers to entry and the type of evidence that a firm should adduce where it wishes to argue that potential competition (that is to say an absence of barriers to entry) amounts to an effective competition constraint upon its behaviour[453].

(c) Other factors in the assessment of market power

Part 6 of the Guideline *Assessment of market power* considers other matters that are relevant to an assessment of market power. These include:

- **buyer power**: buyer power may act as a constraint on an undertaking's market power; however that buyer power does not come from size alone: the buyer must have a choice of supplier[454], a point emphasised by the CAT in the *Genzyme*[455] and *National Grid*[456] cases
- **behaviour and performance**: the behaviour and performance of the undertaking under investigation may provide evidence of market power[457]; in *Phenytoin*[458] the CMA found that Pfizer and Flynn Pharma were both able consistently to set prices significantly above appropriate measures of cost plus a reasonable rate of return and had both persistently earned an excessive rate of profit
- **economic regulation**: economic regulation may prevent an undertaking from raising prices above a competitive level, although this does not in itself mean that that undertaking does not have market power[459]. In *Napp*[460] the CAT rejected the argument that the Pharmaceutical Price Regulation Scheme, which limits the rate of return on a company's total sales of all its branded prescription medicines to the National Health Service, meant that Napp did not enjoy a dominant position[461]. In *Phenytoin*[462] the CMA rejected the argument that the Secretary of State for Health and Social Care had the power to impose a statutory cap on the price of phenytoin sodium capsules; it also considered that the Department of Health did not have sufficient countervailing power to bring about a reduction in the price of that drug.

450 *Assessment of market power*, paras 5.18–5.20.

451 Ibid, paras 5.21–5.22.

452 Ibid, paras 5.23–5.28.

453 Ibid, paras 5.29–5.36.

454 Ibid, paras 6.1–6.4.

455 Case 1016/1/1/03 *Genzyme Ltd v OFT* [2004] CAT 4, paras 241–289.

456 Case 1099/1/2/08 *National Grid plc v Gas and Electricity Markets Authority* [2009] CAT 14, paras 60–78.

457 Ibid, paras 6.5–6.6.

458 *Unfair pricing in respect of the supply of phenytoin sodium capsules in the UK*, CMA decision of 7 December 2016, paras 4.222–4.225, on appeal Cases 1275/1/12/17 etc *Flynn Pharma Ltd v CMA*, not yet decided.

459 Ibid, para 6.7.

460 Case 1001/1/1/01 *Napp Pharmaceutical Holdings Ltd v Director General of Fair Trading* [2002] CAT 1.

461 Ibid, paras 161–168; see similarly *Paroxetine*, CMA decision of 12 February 2016, para 4.125.

462 *Unfair pricing in respect of the supply of phenytoin sodium capsules in the UK*, CMA decision of 7 December 2016, paras 4.282–4.314, on appeal Cases 1275/1/12/17 etc *Flynn Pharma Ltd v CMA*, not yet decided.

In *ATG Media*[463] the CMA regarded internal documents of ATG as relevant to its preliminary view that ATG held a dominant position for the supply of live online bidding auction platform services to auction houses.

(d) Super-dominance

In *Napp*[464] the CAT recognised that certain firms may be 'super-dominant', with the result that the 'special responsibility' not to impair undistorted competition that they bear may be particularly onerous[465]. In *BT Broadband*[466] BT had a market share in the relevant market of 65–70%, but was not found to enjoy a super-dominant position[467]. In *English Welsh & Scottish Railway*[468] the ORR noted that EW&S had a 'very high degree of market power' which should be considered when determining the scope of its 'special responsibility'.

(ix) **Abuse**

(a) Assessing abuse

Section 18(2) sets out a non-exhaustive list of abuses, in identical terms to those in Article 102 TFEU. Unlike Article 102, sections 18(1) and 18(2) refer to 'conduct' which amounts to an abuse, rather than merely an abuse. It is hard to see how the use of the term 'conduct' improves on the EU version, and indeed it is not entirely apt: there is no doubt, for example, that a refusal to supply could, in certain circumstances, amount to an abuse of a dominant position; semantically it is somewhat strange to characterise inaction as conduct.

The CAT has pointed out that the primary interest to be protected under the Chapter II prohibition is the process of competition, and ultimately the interest of the consumer, rather than the private interest of a particular competitor; but that in some cases protecting the competitive process necessarily involves having regard to the situation of competitors[469].

In *National Grid v Gas and Electricity Markets Authority*[470] the Court of Appeal held that, in an abuse case, it is not necessary to ask, in isolation, whether a dominant undertaking has departed from 'normal competition' or 'competition on the merits': these are not sufficiently hard-edged concepts that they can be determined as a matter of law; rather it is necessary to look at conduct 'in the round' and to decide whether it is abusive as a matter of expert appreciation. The court added that, although there are benchmarks against which to consider whether particular conduct (for example predatory pricing or a refusal to supply) amounts to an abuse, it does not follow that there must be a benchmark for all allegations of abuse, let alone a benchmark that can tell one precisely where the line between lawful and unlawful conduct is to be drawn. Abuse cases are 'highly fact sensitive and dependent upon an evaluation of a wide range of factors'[471]. In *Purple Parking v Heathrow Airport*[472] Mann J said that it is not necessary to bring abuse of dominance cases within any particular 'pigeon-hole' of established cases of abuse[473].

[463] *Decision to accept binding commitments offered by ATG Media in relation to live online bidding auction platform services*, CMA decision of 29 June 2017, para 3.11.

[464] Case 1001/1/1/01 *Napp Pharmaceutical Holdings Ltd v Director General of Fair Trading* [2002] CAT 1, para 219.

[465] Ibid, para 219; see further ch 5, 'The degree of market power and super-dominance', pp 195–196.

[466] OFCOM decision of 11 July 2003.

[467] Ibid, para 2.23.

[468] ORR decision of 17 November 2006.

[469] Case 1046/2/4/04 *Albion Water Ltd v Director General of Water Services* [2005] CAT 40, [2006] CompAR 269, para 262.

[470] [2010] EWCA Civ 114.

[471] Ibid, para 54; see, to similar effect, para 102 of Mann J's judgment in *Purple Parking Ltd v Heathrow Airport Ltd* [2011] EWHC 987 (Ch).

[472] [2011] EWHC 987 (Ch).

[473] Ibid, paras 75–108.

In *Streetmap v Google*[474] Roth J held that a dominant undertaking may commit an abuse where the anti-competitive effect is not on the market where it is dominant but on a separate, associated market[475]. The judge also said that, in principle, the preferential promotion by a dominant firm, by means of its power on the market where it is dominant, of its separate product on a distinct market where it is not dominant, may constitute an abuse if that has the effect of strengthening its position on that other market and is not objectively justified[476]. The judge further held that the test to be applied when considering the question of effect, is whether the conduct is reasonably likely to harm the competitive structure of the market[476a].

The Guideline on *Abuse of a dominant position*[477] contains a brief discussion of the meaning of abuse, but does little more than to repeat what is contained in Article 102 TFEU and section 18. The UK competition authorities will have regard to the European Commission's *Guidance on Article 102 Enforcement Priorities* when considering exclusionary behaviour and have referred to it on several occasions. The guidelines for particular sectors such as energy and railways discuss the concept of abuse in the circumstances of those markets[478]. The CMA will also apply the *Prioritisation principles for the CMA*[479] when selecting cases for investigation.

The jurisprudence of the EU Courts on the meaning of abuse is highly influential in the application of the Chapter II prohibition, not least because of the duty under section 60(2) of the Act[480]: as a result the reader is referred to chapter 5 for a general discussion of the meaning of abuse under Article 102[481]. Abusive practices themselves are considered in detail in chapter 17, which deals with non-pricing abuses, and chapter 18, which deals with pricing abuses. In each chapter specific attention is given to the application of the Chapter II prohibition[482].

(b) Objective justification

A dominant undertaking can defend itself against an accusation of abuse by demonstrating that it had an objective justification for its behaviour[483]. However in *Dahabshiil Transfer Services v Barclays Bank*[484] Henderson J said that the defence of objective justification is not available 'if there are alternative, non-abusive solutions to the problem'[485].

A dominant undertaking must put forward the arguments and evidence necessary to show that its conduct is objectively justified. In *Cardiff Bus* the OFT was not convinced by Cardiff Bus's explanation for launching its new bus services as it was not able to produce any contemporaneous evidence to show that the services were introduced to test market demand for 'no frills' services rather than merely to weaken its principal competitor[486]. In *Purple Parking v Heathrow Airport* Mann J held that a refusal to provide access to Heathrow Airport facilities was not objectively justified by congestion, safety, security or environmental considerations[487]. In *Paroxetine*[488] the CMA did not accept that

474 [2016] EWHC 253 (Ch). 475 Ibid, para 59. 476 Ibid, para 60.

476a Ibid, para 88; see also Case 1252/1/12/16 *GlaxoSmithKline plc v CMA* [2018] CAT 4, para 425.

477 OFT Guideline 402, December 2004.

478 These guidelines are listed at 'CMA guidelines', pp 344–345 earlier in chapter.

479 CMA 16, April 2014: see ch 10, 'Inquiries and Investigations', pp 401–411.

480 See 'Questions arising ... in relation to competition', p 390 later in chapter.

481 See ch 5, 'Abuse', pp 197–216. 482 See chs 17 and 18 generally.

483 Case 1016/1/1/03 *Genzyme Ltd v OFT* [2004] CAT 4, paras 577–578; see ch 5, 'Objective justification', pp 217–218.

484 [2013] EWHC 3379 (Ch). 485 Ibid, para 74.

486 OFT decision of 18 November 2008, paras 1.13 and 7.27.

487 [2011] EWHC 987 (Ch), paras 179–238; the defence of objective justification was also rejected in *Arriva The Shires Ltd v London Luton Airport Operations Ltd* [2014] EWHC 64 (Ch), paras 131–165.

488 CMA decision of 12 February 2016, paras 8.60–8.68, on appeal, Case 1252/1/12/16 *GlaxoSmithKline plc v CMA* [2018] CAT 4, the CAT decided to ask the Court of Justice whether GSK had abused its dominant position by entering into three patent settlement agreements.

Glaxo's conduct was objectively justified since paying potential competitors to delay their efforts to enter the market did not constitute a legitimate defence of Glaxo's patent rights. The defence of objective justification has been accepted in several cases. In *Floe Telecom v OFCOM*[489] the CAT held that OFCOM should have conducted a much more extensive inquiry before concluding that Vodafone's refusal to supply was objectively justified[490]. When OFCOM re-examined the matter, in the light of the CAT's observations, it continued to believe that Vodafone's behaviour was objectively justified[491]. In *VIP Communications*[492] OFCOM considered that T-Mobile's refusal to supply VIP was objectively justified for the same reason that applied in *Floe*[493]. The ORR accepted a defence of objective justification in *Complaint from NTM Sales and Marketing Ltd against Portec Rail Products (UK) Ltd*[494]. In *Flybe*[495] the OFT said that it would have been prepared to decide that Flybe had an objective justification for incurring losses on an aviation route that it had newly entered, and therefore that it had not abused a dominant position[496]; however the OFT decided for other reasons that there were no grounds for action. In *Streetmap v Google*[497] the High Court held that Google's discriminatory conduct was not reasonably likely to give rise to anti-competitive foreclosure and, even if it did have such an effect, it was objectively justified[498]. None of the alternatives put forward by Streetmap could have achieved the legitimate objective of presenting a thumbnail map on Google's search engine without undue delay or increased cost[499].

(c) Efficiencies

A dominant undertaking may justify exclusionary conduct on efficiency grounds. The CMA will have regard to the European Commission's *Article 102 Enforcement Priorities Guidance*[500], which explains that four conditions—modelled upon Article 101(3)—must be fulfilled before an 'efficiency defence' can succeed[501]; this is a reasonable approach and one with which the Court of Justice agrees[502]. The burden of proving the availability of an efficiency defence lies on the dominant firm.

In *BT Wholesale Calls Pricing*[503] OFCOM rejected complaints that BT had imposed a margin squeeze in part because there was an efficiency rationale for its conduct[504] and in part because there was insufficient evidence of anti-competitive effects. In *Paroxetine*[505] the CMA rejected Glaxo's claim that its patent settlements had created efficiencies, in terms of new entry resulting in reduced prices for the NHS, since there was no meaningful impact on the prices charged to pharmacies. The fact that prices had fallen was due to sector-specific regulation and not to Glaxo's conduct.

[489] Case 1024/2/3/04 [2004] CAT 18. [490] Ibid, paras 334–339.

[491] Decision of 28 June 2005, paras 246–312, upheld on appeal to the CAT Case 1024/2/3/04 [2006] CAT 17 and on appeal to the Court of Appeal *Office of Communications v Floe Telecom Ltd* [2009] EWCA Civ 47.

[492] OFCOM decision of 28 June 2005; an appeal to the CAT was rejected in Case 1027/2/3/04 *VIP Communications Ltd (in administration) v OFCOM* [2009] CAT 29.

[493] Ibid, paras 239–254. [494] ORR decision of 19 August 2005, paras 168–185.

[495] OFT decision of 5 November 2010. [496] Ibid, paras 6.97–6.108.

[497] [2016] EWHC 293 (Ch). [498] Ibid, paras 142–176.

[499] Ibid, paras 142–176; the principle of proportionality does not require adoption of an alternative that is much less efficient in terms of greatly increased cost or which imposes an unreasonable burden: ibid, para 149.

[500] OJ [2009] C 45/7, para 30. [501] Ibid.

[502] Case C-209/10 *Post Danmark A/S v Konkurrencerådet* EU:C:2012:172, para 42.

[503] OFCOM decision of 20 June 2013.

[504] Ibid, paras 1.5 and 7.248–7.249 (avoidance of an economically inefficient investment under one of BT's contracts for the wholesale supply of end-to-end voice calls to retailers).

[505] CMA decision of 12 February 2016, paras 8.69–8.74.

(d) Conduct of minor significance

Conduct of minor significance cannot be the subject of a financial penalty[506]: this was the reason that Cardiff Bus was not fined, even though the OFT found it guilty of abuse[507]; this does not apply to transgressions of Article 102 TFEU.

(e) Article 3(2) Regulation 1/2003

Unilateral conduct that is not abusive may, nevertheless, be subject to stricter national rules[508].

(B) **Exclusions**

(i) **Exclusions for mergers subject to UK or EU merger control**

The Chapter II prohibition does not apply to conduct resulting in a relevant merger situation[509] or in a concentration having an EU dimension[510]. This exclusion is closely related to the exclusion of mergers from the Chapter I prohibition, which was described earlier[511].

(ii) **Financial Services and Markets Act 2000**

The exclusion from the Chapter II prohibition for conduct pursuant to the regulatory provisions of the Financial Services and Markets Act 2000 has been repealed[512].

(iii) **Other exclusions**

Section 19(1) provides that the Chapter II prohibition does not apply to cases excluded by Schedule 3[513]. Some of the exclusions in Schedule 3 apply only to the Chapter I prohibition; however paragraph 4 of Schedule 3 (services of general economic interest), paragraph 5 (compliance with legal requirements), paragraph 6 (avoidance of conflict with international obligations) and paragraph 7 (exceptional and compelling reasons of public policy) also exclude the application of the Chapter II prohibition.

5. 'Governing Principles Clause': Section 60 of the Competition Act 1998

This section of this chapter examines the 'governing principles clause' found in section 60 of the Competition Act, which requires that there should be consistency, where possible, in the application of domestic and EU competition law. Section 60 sets out the governing principles to be applied in determining questions which arise in relation to competition within the UK. Essentially the principle is that there should be close conformity between the Act and EU law; section 60 is also applicable in relation to questions arising under the provisions for the disqualification of company directors[514]. Section 60 enables the UK

506 See ch 10, 'Immunity for small agreements and conduct of minor significance', pp 423–424.

507 See 'The Chapter II Prohibition', pp 376–378 earlier in chapter.

508 See ch 2, 'Conflicts: Article 102', p 78.

509 CA 1998, s 19 and Sch 1, para 2 ('normal' mergers).

510 Ibid, s 19 and Sch 1, para 6.

511 See 'Schedule 1: mergers and concentrations', pp 364–366 earlier in chapter.

512 Financial Services Act 2012, Sch 19, para 1; see 'Financial Services and Markets Act 2000', pp 366–367 earlier in chapter.

513 For a discussion of Sch 3 see 'Schedule 3: general exclusions', pp 367–370 earlier in chapter.

514 See s 9A(11) of the Company Directors Disqualification Act 1986, inserted by s 204 of the Enterprise Act 2002.

competition authorities and courts to apply EU competition law when making decisions under the Act.

Once the detailed arrangements for Brexit and any associated agreement between the UK and the EU are known, consideration will need to be given to whether it is appropriate to repeal, or perhaps modify, the duties imposed by section 60[515].

(A) Section 60(1)

Section 60(1) sets out the purpose of the governing principles clause: the duties to which it gives rise are imposed by section 60(2) and (3). Section 60(1) provides that:

> The purpose of this section is to ensure that so far as is possible (having regard to any relevant differences between the provisions concerned), questions arising under this Part in relation to competition within the UK are dealt with in a manner which is consistent with the treatment of corresponding questions arising in [EU] law in relation to competition within the [EU].

The objective of consistency is not absolute: consistency is envisaged only 'so far as is possible', having regard to 'relevant differences' and is required as to 'corresponding questions' that arise 'in relation to competition'. This means that EU jurisprudence is to be followed unless the competition authority or court is driven to a different interpretation by some provision in that part of the Act[516]. Where the factual circumstances of the case law of the EU Courts differ from those in a UK case, the CAT in *BetterCare* observed that its duty under section 60 was to approach an issue of competition law 'in the manner in which we think the European Court would approach it, as regards the principles and reasoning likely to be followed by that Court'[517]. In *UKRS Training v NSAR*[518] the CAT said that section 60 establishes a 'consistency principle' between domestic and EU competition law.

(i) 'So far as is possible'

The purpose of section 60 is to achieve consistency 'so far as is possible'. Clearly this is not possible where the provisions of the Act explicitly differ from EU law: examples of this are given in the next section. Where there is some doubt in a particular case, these words indicate that there is a policy preference towards maintaining consistency with EU law.

(ii) 'Having regard to any relevant differences'

A critical issue is the identification of any 'relevant differences' between EU law and the Act. Some examples appear on the face of the legislation itself: for example it contains some exclusions which are not available under EU law[519]; the Act protects legal professional privilege for communications with in-house lawyers, which does not exist under EU law[520]; the exclusion under the Competition Act for mergers is wider than that provided

[515] For the arguments for and against retention of s 60 see the Reports of the Brexit Competition Law Working Group, available at www.bclwg.org, and of the Commercial Bar Association, available at www.combar.com.

[516] See HL Consideration of Commons' Amendments, 20 October 1998, col 1383 (Lord Simon of Highbury).

[517] Case 1006/2/1/01 *BetterCare Group v Director General of Fair Trading* [2002] CAT 7, para 32.

[518] Case 1258/5/7/16 [2017] CAT 14, para 55; see similarly *Streetmap v Google* [2016] EWHC 293 (Ch), para 38.

[519] On the exclusions from the Chapter I and Chapter II prohibitions see 'The Chapter I prohibition: excluded agreements', pp 364–371 and 'Exclusions', p 387 earlier in chapter.

[520] See ch 10, 'Legal professional privilege', pp 407–408.

for under EU law; and the Act makes specific provision for particular agreements to be excluded, although this is of limited significance since the exclusion of vertical and land agreements from the Chapter I prohibition has been discontinued[521].

Secondly, the procedural and enforcement rules under the Competition Act differ from those in EU law. For example there is an appeal 'on the merits' to the CAT against certain decisions of the CMA and the sectoral regulators and the CAT has a power to remit a case to the competition authorities[522]; in the EU, applications for annulment may provide a less extensive remedy. Another procedural difference is that the provisions on leniency in the UK are different from those in the EU[523]. The same is true of the limitation period for imposing and the method of calculating the level of a fine; the CAT has said that there is a relevant difference between domestic and EU law and practice on the setting of penalties[524].

A further example of a relevant difference, but one that is not apparent on the face of the Act, is that EU competition law is applied, in part, with the objective of single market integration in mind. The Competition Act, presumably, does not have to be applied for this purpose, since the goal of market integration is 'relevantly different' from one arising in relation to competition within the UK: this could lead to some divergence in the way in which the Chapter I and Chapter II prohibitions and Articles 101 and 102 are applied. In *Newspapers and magazine distribution* the OFT's opinion was that a court would be unlikely to import the issue of single market integration into domestic competition analysis[525].

Relevant differences might arise in particular cases; for example the specific features of the telecommunications sector may mean that a different measure of cost should be used to assess alleged predatory pricing[526] from the one suggested by the Court of Justice in *AKZO*[527].

In *Aberdeen Journals v OFT*[528] the CAT concluded that there was no need to import a rule of 'appreciability' into the expression 'affect trade' in the Chapter II prohibition, and that this was a 'relevant difference' from the test of 'effect on trade' in Article 102[529].

(iii) 'Corresponding questions'

In *MasterCard*[530] the OFT considered that the questions under consideration in that case did not 'correspond with' those in the European Commission's decision in *Visa*

[521] See 'Section 50: vertical agreements', p 371 and 'Section 50: land agreements', p 371 earlier in chapter on s 50 of the Competition Act 1998; in Case 1006/2/1/01 *BetterCare Group v Director General of Fair Trading* [2002] CAT 7, para 288, the CAT left open the question of whether para 5 of Sch 3 was relevantly different from EU law.

[522] See eg Case 1005/1/1/01 *Aberdeen Journals v Director General of Fair Trading* [2002] CAT 4, para 190; similarly the CAT has held that its power to adopt its own decision on appeal is a relevant difference: see Case 1027/2/3/04 *VIP Communications v OFCOM* [2007] CAT 3, para 51.

[523] See ch 10, 'Leniency', pp 424–429.

[524] See eg Case 1120/1/1/09 *Quarmby Construction Co Ltd v OFT* [2011] CAT 11, paras 43–48 (on the limitation period), as applied in *Paroxetine*, CMA decision of 12 February 2016, paras K.14-K.17; Cases 1117/1/1/09 etc *GF Tomlinson Building Ltd v OFT* [2011] CAT 7, paras 100–102 (on the method for setting fines).

[525] OFT 1025, October 2008, para 4.13.

[526] OFT 417, February 2000, paras 7.6–7.19 where instead of the EU assessment of predation using average variable costs and average total costs, the OFT (now CMA) and OFCOM will consider long-run incremental cost; see also Case 1007/2/3/02 *Freeserve.com plc v Director General of Telecommunications* [2003] CAT 5, paras 212–225.

[527] See also *Guidance on the Application of the Competition Act 1998 in the Water and Sewerage Sectors*, OFT 422, March 2010, paras 4.39–4.40; on Case C-62/86 *AKZO v Commission* EU:C:1991:286, see ch 18, 'The rule in *AKZO v Commission* and subsequent cases', pp 758–760.

[528] Case 1009/1/1/02 [2003] CAT 11.

[529] Ibid, paras 459–460.

[530] OFT decision of 6 September 2005.

International—Multilateral Interchange Fee[531] since the latter was concerned with a cross-border payment system whereas the UK case involved a purely domestic payment system[532]. The CAT and the High Court adopted an analogous approach in relation to the Commission's decision in *MasterCard*[533] in subsequent actions for damages against MasterCard[534] and against Visa[535].

(iv) 'Questions arising ... in relation to competition'

The duty to maintain consistency arises only where there are 'questions arising in relation to competition'. Clearly this duty applies to substantive issues arising under the Chapter I and II prohibitions. It is less clear whether the duty also applies to the procedures for enforcing the prohibitions. It could reasonably be argued that the procedural rules for public and private enforcement do not themselves raise questions 'in relation to competition'. Indeed it might be undesirable for the CMA or a court to follow the same detailed procedures as exist under EU law. However it was accepted in the House of Lords by the responsible Minister that section 60 does import the general principles of EU law as well as the specific jurisprudence on Articles 101 and 102 themselves, save where there is a relevant difference[536]. Examples of these general principles are equality, legal certainty, legitimate expectation, proportionality and privilege against self-incrimination: each of these is well established in EU law[537]. Other general principles of EU law are the duty to state reasons for a decision with sufficient precision[538], the principle of good administration[539], the right of access to the file[540] and equality of arms[541].

The CAT referred extensively to the jurisprudence of the EU Courts in *Apex v OFT*[542] when considering whether there were procedural defects in a statement of objections issued by the OFT[543]. In *Pernod-Ricard v OFT*[544] the CAT considered that the rights of a third party complainant in competition proceedings raised a question which indirectly arose 'in relation to competition' for the purposes of section 60(2)[545]. However the CAT distinguished *Pernod* in *Dorothy Gibson v Pride Mobility Products*[546], an application to bring collective proceedings for damages, as the various procedural rules that apply to private actions were not questions 'in relation to competition'.

531 OJ [2002] L 318/17. 532 Ibid, paras 97–106.

533 Commission decision of 19 December 2007.

534 Case 1241/5/7/15 (T) *Sainsbury's Supermarkets Ltd v MasterCard Inc* [2016] CAT 11, para 26 and *Asda Stores Ltd v MasterCard Inc* [2017] EWHC 93 (Comm), paras 80–82.

535 *Sainsbury's Supermarkets Ltd v Visa Europe Services LLC* [2017] EWHC 3047 (Comm), paras 138–139.

536 HL Committee, 25 November 1997, cols 960–963.

537 See Dashwood, Dougan, Rodger, Spaventa and Wyatt (eds) *Wyatt and Dashwood's European Union Law* (Hart, 6th ed, 2011), ch 7.

538 Case T-241/97 *Stork Amsterdam BV v Commission* EU:T:2000:41, para 74; the duty to give reasons is also contained in Article 296 TFEU.

539 Case T-127/98 *UPS Europe SA v Commission* EU:T:1999:167, para 37.

540 Cases T-25/95 etc *Cimenteries CBR SA v Commission* EU:T:2000:77, para 142.

541 Ibid, para 143; see *Involving third parties in Competition Act investigations*, OFT 451, April 2006, which substantially brought domestic practice into alignment with EU law and has been adopted by the CMA Board.

542 Case 1032/1/1/04 [2005] CAT 4. 543 Ibid, paras 92–100.

544 Case 1017/2/1/03 [2004] CAT 10.

545 Ibid, paras 228–234; note *Asda Stores Ltd v MasterCard Inc* [2017] EWHC 93 (Comm), para 58(3) referring to the effect of s 60 being to apply the *substantive* principles of EU competition law to the Ch I prohibition.

546 Case 1257/7/7/16 [2017] CAT 9, paras 66–67; see also Case 1120/1/1/09 *Quarmby Construction Co Ltd v OFT* [2011] CAT 11, para 43, distinguishing *Pernod* in relation to limitation periods.

(B) **Section 60(2) and (3)**

Section 60(2) and (3) provide that:

(2) At any time when the court[547] determines a question arising under this Part, it must act (so far as is compatible with the provisions of this Part[548] and whether or not it would otherwise be required to do so) with a view to securing that there is no inconsistency[549] between—

(a) the principles applied, and decision reached, by the court in determining that question; and

(b) the principles laid down by the Treaty[550] and the European Court[551], and any relevant decision of that Court, as applicable at that time in determining any corresponding question arising in [EU] law.

(3) The court must, in addition, have regard to any relevant decision or statement of the Commission.

(i) **The duty of consistency**

Consistency must be maintained between the principles applied and the decision reached by the domestic authority or court and the principles laid down by the Treaty and the EU Courts and any decisions of those Courts in determining corresponding questions that may be applicable at that time. As already noted, general principles of EU law such as equality and proportionality will be imported by virtue of section 60(2).

(ii) **Having regard to decisions or statements of the Commission**

The competition authorities and courts under section 60(3) must 'have regard to' any relevant decision[552] or statement of the Commission; this is a lesser obligation than the obligation to ensure that there is no inconsistency under section 60(2). Decisions and statements of other bodies such as the Council of Ministers[553] or the European Parliament are not included. The Act itself does not explain what is meant by Commission statements. However the CMA's view is that the statements must carry the authority of the Commission as a whole such as, for example, decisions in individual cases under Articles 101 and/or 102, Commission Notices and clear statements about its policy approach as published in its annual *Report on Competition Policy*[554]. In *Albion Water*[555] the Court of Appeal held that the CAT was correct to direct itself by reference to the test of margin

[547] 'Court' in this context, rather unusually, includes the CMA and the sectoral regulators: Competition Act 1998, s 60(5).

[548] 'This Part' of the Act deals with all matters to do with the prohibitions and the enforcement of them, but not investigations under the Enterprise Act 2002.

[549] Section 60(1) puts the objective positively and is preferable to this double negative.

[550] 'Treaty' in this context refers to the Treaty on the Functioning of the European Union: Competition Act 1998, s 59(1); it would not apply to jurisprudence or decisions under the former ECSC Treaty, nor under the EEA Agreement.

[551] 'European Court' refers to both the Court of Justice and the General Court: ibid; it does not refer to the opinions of the Advocates General, as to which see Buxton LJ in *Napp Pharmaceutical Holdings Ltd v Director General of Fair Trading* [2002] EWCA Civ 796, who nevertheless characterised such opinions as 'important and authoritative'; nor to the EFTA Court.

[552] On the meaning of decision see Competition Act 1998, s 60(6).

[553] Documents such as the Minutes of the Council's deliberations about the EUMR or Regulation 1/2003 would therefore not need to be considered, although they could be relevant in a particular case.

[554] *Modernisation*, OFT 442, para 4.11.

[555] *Dŵr Cymru Cyfyngedig v Albion Water Ltd* [2008] EWCA Civ 536.

squeeze as formulated in the relevant European Commission Notice[556] and the case law[557].

In *MasterCard*[558] the OFT said that the duty to 'have regard' to Commission decisions and statements did not mean that it was bound to comply with them, but only to give serious consideration to them[559]. In *Asda v MasterCard*[560] the High Court said that it would give weight to the Commission's *Article 101(3) Guidelines*[561], although it was mindful that they are only guidelines, requiring flexible rather than mechanical application.

(iii) **References to the Court of Justice**

The CAT, the Court of Appeal of England and Wales, the Court of Session in Scotland, the Court of Appeal in Northern Ireland and the UK Supreme Court can make references to the Court of Justice for a preliminary ruling under Article 267 TFEU. This is considered further in chapter 10[562].

(C) **Regulation 1/2003**

Regulation 1/2003 requires that, where an NCA or a court apply domestic competition law they must, in so far as an agreement or conduct has an effect on trade between Member States, also apply Articles 101 and/or 102 TFEU[563]. The relationship between EU and national competition law, and in particular the scope for applying stricter rules than those of the EU, was considered in the final section of chapter 2[564]. There has been no difficulty in applying the EU and domestic competition rules in a harmonious fashion since the adoption of Regulation 1/2003[565], although the European Commission has indicated that the apparent divergence of standards regarding unilateral conduct is an area which merits further evaluation[566].

When Brexit occurs, Regulation 1/2003 will no longer be directly applicable in the UK, save where its provisions are either preserved pursuant to new or transitional arrangements with the EU or explicitly incorporated into domestic legislation.

6. The Competition Act 1998 in Practice

The CMA maintains a register of decisions adopted by itself and the sectoral regulators under the Competition Act. A table of all decisions adopted by the UK competition authorities, including adjustments on appeal, will be found on the Online Resources that accompany this book. Table 9.1 sets out the decisions that have been adopted since the eighth edition of this book was published in February 2015: the cut-off date for the table is 8 December 2017.

556 *Notice on the application of the competition rules to access agreements in the telecommunications sector* OJ [1988] C 265/2.

557 *Dŵr Cymru Cyfyngedig v Albion Water Ltd* [2008] EWCA Civ 536, para 105, referring in particular to the judgment of the General Court in Case T-271/03 *Deutsche Telekom v Commission* EU:T:2008:101, upheld on appeal Case C-280/08 P *Deutsche Telekom v Commission* EU:C:2010:603.

558 OFT decision of 6 September 2005.

559 Ibid, paras 107–116.

560 [2017] EWHC 93 (Comm), para 83.

561 OJ [2004] C 101/97; see ch 4, 'The Commission's approach in the Article 101(3) Guidelines', pp 167–169.

562 See ch 10, 'Article 267 References', pp 460–461.

563 See Art 3 of Regulation 1/2003, OJ [2003] L 1/1.

564 See ch 2, 'The Relationship Between EU Competition Law and National Competition Laws', pp 75–79.

565 See *Communication from the Commission to the European Parliament and the Council: Report on the functioning of Regulation 1/2003*, COM(2009) 206 final, paras 12, 28 and 39.

566 Ibid, para 27.

Table 9.1 Table of published decisions of the CMA and sectoral regulators and appeals under the Competition Act 1998 and/or Articles 101 and 102 TFEU between 6 February 2015 and 8 December 2017

Case name	Date of decision	Outcome	On appeal to the CAT
Worldpay	27.03.15	Decision not to adopt interim measures in relation to a complaint by Worldpay against Visa's interchange fees	
Property sales and letting organisations	08.05.15	Infringement of the Chapter I prohibition **Fines of £735,000**	
Private ophthalmology	20.08.15	Infringement of the Chapter I prohibition and Article 101 TFEU **NB: settlement. Fines of £382,500**	
Paroxetine	12.02.16	Infringement of the Chapter I and II prohibitions and Article 101 TFEU **Fines of £43 million**	Appeals lodged with the CAT on 18.04.16: Cases 1252/1/12/16 etc *GlaxoSmithKline plc v CMA* [2018] CAT 4; on 27.3.18 the CAT made a reference for a preliminary ruling
Online resale price maintenance in the bathroom fittings sector	10.05.16	Infringement of the Chapter I prohibition and/or Article 101 TFEU **NB: settlement. Fines of £786,668**	
Online resale price maintenance in the commercial refrigeration sector	24.05.16	Infringement of Chapter I prohibition and Article 101 TFEU **NB: settlement. Fines of £2.3 million**	
Online sales of posters and frames	12.08.16	Infringement of Chapter 1 prohibition: horizontal price fixing **NB: settlement. Fines of £163,371.** **NB: company disqualification undertaking, 01.12.16: the first disqualification under the Enterprise Act 2002**	

(continued)

Table 9.1 *(continued)*

Case name	Date of decision	Outcome	On appeal to the CAT
SSE **NB: OFGEM**	03.11.16	Acceptance of commitments to address concerns about anti-competitive effects in the electricity connections market	
Pfizer and Flynn Pharma: phenytoin sodium capsules	07.12.16	Two infringements of Chapter II prohibition and Article 102 TFEU **Fine on Pfizer of £84.2 million and on Flynn Pharma of £5.2 million.** **NB also penalty notice to Pfizer Ltd, 12.04.16: penalty of £10,000**	Case 1274/1/12/16 (IR): Flynn application for interim relief, 23.12.16; refused 19.01.17 [2017] CAT 1. The substantive case is on appeal, Case 1276/1/12/17 *Pfizer Inc v CMA* and Case 1275/1/12/17 *Flynn Pharma Ltd v CMA*
Model agencies	16.12.16	Infringement of Chapter I prohibition and Article 101 TFEU horizontal price fixing **Fines of £1.53 million**	
Galvanised steel tanks	19.12.16	Infringement of the Chapter I prohibition and Article 101 TFEU **NB: settlement (price fixing). Fines of £2.6 million.** **Two decisions issued; one for price fixing, the other for the exchange of information by Balmoral Tanks Ltd**	Appeal dismissed in relation to decision on information exchanges: Case 1277/1/12/17 *Balmoral Tanks Ltd v CMA* [2017] CAT 23.
East Midlands International Airport/Prestige Parking Ltd **NB: CAA**	20.12.16	Infringement of Chapter I prohibition **NB: No fines imposed as EMIA qualified for full leniency and PP was no longer trading**	
Supply of products to the furniture industry	27.03.17	Infringement of Chapter I prohibition and Article 101 TFEU **Fines of £2.8 million. NB: settlement.** **Two decisions issued: one for drawer wraps; one for drawer fronts**	

Case name	Date of decision	Outcome	On appeal to the CAT
Online resale price maintenance in the light fittings sector	03.05.17	Infringement of Chapter I prohibition and/or Article 101 **NB: settlement. Fine of £2.7 million for online retail price maintenance**	
Residential estate agent services	31.05.17	Infringement of Chapter I prohibition **Fines of £370,000. NB: hybrid settlement. Note also two company director disqualifications**	
Auction services: ATG Media	29.06.17	Acceptance of commitments to address concerns about exclusionary practices in the market for live online bidding platforms	
Sports equipment sector	24.08.17	Infringement of Chapter I prohibition and Article 101 TFEU **Fines of £1.45 million**	Case 1279/1/12/17 *Ping Europe Ltd v CMA*; interim relief granted by consent on 25.10.17
Showmen's Guild	26.10.17	Acceptance of commitments to address concerns about coordinated exclusionary practices arising from the rules of a funfair association	

A number of points can be made about the public enforcement of the Competition Act since 1 March 2000.

(A) **Total number of infringement decisions**

The OFT found infringements of the Chapter I prohibition and Article 101 TFEU on 34 occasions; one of these decisions, *Attheraces*, was set aside entirely on appeal to the CAT (see below). Since 1 April 2014 the CMA has found 16 infringements of the Chapter I prohibition and/or Article 101 TFEU.

The OFT found infringements of the Chapter II prohibition on five occasions; the ORR, OFGEM and CAA have all found one infringement of the Chapter II prohibition. The CMA has found abuses of a dominant position in two cases.

The fines imposed by the OFT, CMA and sectoral regulators, after allowing for reductions as a result of leniency, settlement and appeals, amount to £1,003 billion.

(B) Findings of infringement by the CAT

The CAT has made its own finding of an infringement of the Chapter II prohibition on two occasions; this happened in appeals from non-infringement decisions of the OFT and Water Services Regulation Authority respectively. In *Burgess v OFT*[567] the CAT concluded that W Austin & Sons had abused a dominant position by refusing to grant access to Burgess, a competing firm of funeral directors, to its crematorium facilities. In *Albion Water*[568] the CAT concluded that Dŵr Cymru had abused its dominant position by applying a margin squeeze to Albion Water, thereby preventing the latter from supplying water to a paper factory in Wales[569].

(C) Appeals against infringement decisions

Several infringement decisions have been appealed to the CAT. Most of them were upheld on substance. Some of the findings of infringements were set aside for want of evidence in *Football Shirts*[570], in *Genzyme*[571] and in the *Construction bid rigging* appeals[572]. The only infringement decision to have been overturned in its entirety was *Attheraces*[573]. The OFT had concluded that the collective selling by the Racecourse Association of the non-licensed betting office ('non-LBO') media rights to horseracing at 59 racecourses in Great Britain infringed the Chapter I prohibition; and that it did not satisfy the criteria of section 9(1) of the Competition Act, which provides a defence for restrictive agreements that produce economic efficiencies. The Racecourse Association (and the British Horseracing Board) appealed to the CAT, which disagreed with the OFT's analysis[574]. The CAT held that the OFT had failed to define the relevant market correctly. The OFT had defined a market for non-LBO media rights, but the CAT considered that this was too narrow: the CAT concluded that this was a sufficient reason in itself to set the decision aside[575]. However the CAT went on to consider whether, assuming that the OFT had correctly defined the relevant market, the collective selling amounted to an infringement of the Chapter I prohibition[576]. The CAT took a robust, 'commonsense' approach to the question of whether competition was restricted on the facts of the case. The CAT concluded that the collective selling was objectively necessary, since there were no other economically practicable means of selling the media rights in question[577].

An infringement decision of the OFT that raised issues of great complexity and controversy was *Tobacco*[578], which involved vertical agreements relating to the competing retail prices of tobacco products. The OFT's view was that the agreements in question had as their object the restriction of competition and were not justifiable under section 9(1) of the Competition Act. Imperial Tobacco and five retailers appealed to the CAT. The CAT did not address any of the substantive issues raised by the appeals because it

567 Case 1044/2/1/04 [2005] CAT 25. 568 Case 1046/2/4/04 [2006] CAT 36.

569 *Dŵr Cymru Cyfyngedig v Albion Water Ltd* [2008] EWCA Civ 536; note that Albion brought a follow-on action for damages in the CAT, which ordered Dŵr Cymru to pay £1,854,493 to Albion for losses resulting from its unlawful behaviour: see ch 8, 'Damages', pp 333–334.

570 Cases 1021/1/1/03 etc *JJB Sports plc v OFT* [2004] CAT 17.

571 Case 1016/1/1/03 *Genzyme v Office of Fair Trading* [2004] CAT 4.

572 Case 1118/1/1/09 *GMI Construction Holdings plc v OFT* [2011] CAT 12; Case 1121/1/1/09 *Durkan Holdings Ltd v OFT* [2011] CAT 6, paras 93–125; Case 1122/1/1/09 *AH Willis & Sons Ltd v OFT* [2011] CAT 3; Case 1124/1/1/09 *North Midland Construction plc v OFT* [2011] CAT 14, paras 14–34.

573 OFT decision of 10 May 2004.

574 Cases 1035/1/1/04 etc *Racecourse Association v OFT* [2005] CAT 29.

575 Ibid, paras 135–150. 576 Ibid, paras 160–176. 577 Ibid, para 171.

578 OFT decision of 15 April 2010.

concluded that the OFT had abandoned its defence of the decision during the main hearing[579]. The CAT therefore allowed the appeals and quashed the decision in relation to each of the appellants. The OFT did not choose, nor was it required, to reach a conclusion as to whether, on second look, the Chapter I prohibition was infringed. Subsequently the Court of Appeal held that two other addressees of the *Tobacco* decision, which had settled with the OFT and agreed to pay fines for infringing the Chapter I prohibition, were not permitted to appeal out of time[580]. In separate claims for judicial review the Court of Appeal held that the two companies should be repaid a sum equal to the fines they had paid in order to rectify the OFT's breach of the principle of equal treatment[581].

In *Paroxetine*[582] the CMA imposed fines of £44.99 million on GlaxoSmithKline and two generic producers for entering into settlements of patent litigation that amounted to the 'buying off' of competition. The CMA found that GSK had made substantial value transfers to the generic producers[583], which bought off their challenges to Glaxo's patent rights in a manner that did not reflect the uncertainty on all sides as to whether those patent rights were valid and infringed, and secured the agreement of the generic companies not to enter the market independently. The CMA considered that the object and effect of the settlement agreements was to restrict competition since they removed the prospect of any meaningful competition between the generics and Glaxo in the supply of paroxetine. The CMA also found that Glaxo's conduct was an abuse of its dominant position. On appeal the CAT decided to refer questions on the issues of potential competition, object, effect, market definition and abuse to the Court of Justice for a preliminary ruling.[584].

In *Phenytoin*[585] the CMA imposed fines of £84.2 million on Pfizer and £5.2 million on Flynn Pharma for charging excessive and unfair prices for an 80-year-old drug. The CMA found that both companies had reaped trading benefits that would not have been available if they had faced effective competition, and that this had an adverse effect on the NHS. The CMA also took into account the fact that the parties' prices were significantly higher than those charged by Pfizer before it sold the marketing authorisation for the drug to Flynn.

(D) Total number of non-infringement decisions

The domestic competition authorities have adopted 63 non-infringement decisions under the Chapter I and Chapter II prohibitions and/or Articles 101 and 102 TFEU. Four decisions were based on the defence provided for in section 9(1), one of which was suspended on appeal.

(E) Appeals against non-infringement and case-closure decisions

The first decision of the OFT under the Competition Act, *General Insurance Standards Council*[586], was a finding of non-infringement of the Chapter I prohibition, and was

[579] Cases 1160/1/1/10 etc *Imperial Tobacco Group plc v OFT* [2011] CAT 41.

[580] *OFT v Somerfield Stores Ltd* [2014] EWCA Civ 400, reversing the order of the CAT extending time for appealing in Cases 1200/1/1/12 etc *Gallaher Group Ltd v OFT* [2013] CAT 5.

[581] *Gallaher Group Ltd and Somerfield Stores Ltd v CMA* [2016] EWCA Civ 719, on appeal to the Supreme Court.

[582] CMA decision of 12 February 2016.

[583] The value transfers in question were payments of cash and the transfer of a restricted volume of product and associated profit margins under distribution agreements.

[584] Cases 1252/1/12/16 etc *GlaxoSmithKline plc v CMA* [2018] CAT 4; the reference was made by order of 27 March 2018.

[585] CMA decision of 7 December 2016, on appeal Cases 1275/1/12/17 etc *Flynn Pharma Ltd v CMA*, not yet decided.

[586] OFT decision of 26 January 2001.

annulled on appeal to the CAT[587]. On several occasions third party complainants have challenged decisions by one of the UK competition authorities to close the file before the CAT. The CAT has sometimes held that the authority had decided that the Chapter I or II prohibition had not been infringed and had made an implicit non-infringement decision; in several cases the CAT found that the authority had closed its file on administrative grounds, without expressing a view on the substance and therefore its 'decision' could not be appealed to the CAT. These cases are discussed in chapter 10[588].

(F) Decisions of sectoral regulators

There have been only three findings of an infringement by a sectoral regulator. In *English Welsh & Scottish Railway*[589] that company admitted exclusionary and discriminatory abuses of a dominant position and agreed to pay a fine of £4.1 million. In *National Grid* OFGEM found that that company had abused its dominant position by entering into long-term exclusionary contracts with gas suppliers[590]. In *Access to car parking facilities at East Midlands International Airport*[591] the CAA found that the owner of East Midlands Airport and Prestige Parking had unlawfully agreed to fix prices of car parking services.

There have been six cases in which a regulator adopted decisions making commitments binding on the undertakings under investigation[592].

In 2011 the Government consulted on whether to retain the regulators' concurrent powers to enforce competition law within their respective spheres of activity. In 2012 the Government decided to retain the concurrency provisions, and to improve the way in which they operate in practice. These changes were introduced by the Enterprise and Regulatory Reform Act 2013 and are described in chapter 10[593]. The CMA has entered into a '*Memorandum of Understanding*' with each of the sectoral regulators in relation to concurrent competition powers[594]. The CMA has published three annual reports on the operation of the concurrency arrangements[595]; in each report the CMA summarises the case work of the regulators and identifies possible future work. In its third report the CMA specifically commented that, while progress had been made on the delivery of cases, the number of new cases remains below the level that the CMA would like to see[596]. If concurrency operates in an unsatisfactory manner, the Secretary of State may make an order removing the competition powers from a sectoral regulator.

[587] Cases 1002–1004/2/1/01 *Institute of Independent Insurance Brokers v Director General of Fair Trading* [2001] CAT 4; on the *GISC* case see earlier in chapter 'General comments', pp 355–356.

[588] See ch 10, 'Successful appeals against implicit non-infringement decisions', pp 454–455.

[589] ORR decision of 17 November 2006.

[590] GEMA decision of 21 February 2008; the infringement decision was upheld on appeal to the CAT and the Court of Appeal but the penalty was reduced: Case 1099/1/2/08 *National Grid plc v Gas and Electricity Markets Authority* [2009] CAT 14, on appeal [2010] EWCA Civ 114; permission to appeal to the UK Supreme Court was refused by order of 5 August 2010.

[591] CAA decision of 17 January 2017.

[592] *SP Manweb*, OFGEM Press Release R/42, 27 October 2005; *Electricity North West Ltd*, OFGEM decision of 24 May 2012; *Severn Trent Plc*, OFWAT decision of 17 January 2013; *Bristol Water plc*, OFWAT decision of 21 March 2015; *Provision of Deep Sea Container rail transport services between ports and key inland destinations in Great Britain*, ORR decision of 18 December 2015; and *SEE plc*, OFGEM decision of 3 November 2016.

[593] Enterprise and Regulatory Reform Act 2013, s 51 and Sch 14; see further Ch 10, 'Concurrency', pp 449–452.

[594] The *Memoranda of Understanding* are available at www.gov.uk/cma.

[595] Enterprise and Regulatory Reform Act 2013, Sch 4, Part 1, para 16; the reports, together with a 'baseline' annual report, are available at www.gov.uk/cma.

[596] Annual report on concurrency 2017, CMA63, April 2017, p 3.

7. Brexit and the Future of UK Competition Law

When the UK leaves the EU Articles 101 and 102 TFEU will cease to have direct effect there and the EUMR will cease to apply. However UK competition law will continue to apply, and in substantive terms this means that there will be relatively little change, as the Chapter I and II prohibitions are very similar to Articles 101 and 102, and the Enterprise Act 2002 provides a mechanism whereby mergers can be vetted for their impact on competition[597]. A Report by the Brexit Competition Law Working Group identified certain issues that would require careful consideration as a result of Brexit, in particular of a transitional nature and concerning cooperation mechanisms between the EU and the UK[598]. As at 8 December 2017, when the manuscript of this book was delivered to the publisher, no firm decisions has been taken about future arrangements consequent upon Brexit. The authors of this book will provide updates on the situation on the Online Resources that accompany this book[599].

[597] On UK merger control generally see ch 22.

[598] Available at www.bclwg.org.uk.

[599] www.oup.com/uk/whish9e/.

10

Competition Act 1998 and the cartel offence: public enforcement and procedure

1. Introduction

Firms that participate in covert anti-competitive behaviour are usually fully aware of the unlawfulness of their conduct. They know, therefore, that they should avoid the creation of incriminating documents that would be discovered by a competition authority when conducting surprise inspections. They may use code-names and resort to other practices to avoid detection. It follows that competition authorities may find it difficult to gather evidence that will satisfy a court to the required standard of proof that there has been illegal behaviour. For this reason, the Competition Act 1998 gives wide powers of investigation to the Competition and Markets Authority ('the CMA') and to the sectoral regulators[1] to enable them to track down evidence of sufficient quality to satisfy the standard of proof set by the law. The Act confers powers to request information, to conduct unannounced 'dawn raids', including, where appropriate, of people's homes, and to require individuals to answer questions as part of an investigation. In March 2017 the CMA launched a campaign called 'Cracking down on Cartels' which offered up to £100,000 to informants that provide it with intelligence about cartels[2].

In understanding the extent of—or rather the limits of—the competition authorities' powers of investigation and enforcement, it is important to have reference to the Human Rights Act 1998, which received Royal Assent on the same day as the Competition Act 1998

[1] In the text of this chapter references to the powers of the CMA include those of the sectoral regulators.

[2] See www.stopcartels.campaign.gov.uk; the CMA also operates a 'Cartels Hotline', which was used in *Supply of solid fuel products*, CMA decision of 29 March 2018.

(9 November 1998) and which entered into force on 2 October 2000[3]. Section 6(1) of the Human Rights Act requires the CMA and sectoral regulators to carry out their functions in a way that is compatible with so-called 'Convention rights', which include the right to a fair trial[4].

This chapter will begin with a consideration of the way in which inquiries and investigations are carried out under the Competition Act. Section 3 will briefly consider the position of complainants to the CMA, while section 4 examines the extent to which it may be possible to receive guidance from the CMA on the application of the Act. Section 5 deals with enforcement of the Competition Act and section 6 with the cartel offence and company director disqualification. Section 7 considers the issue of concurrency. Section 8 contains a discussion of the appeal mechanism under the Competition Act, section 9 examines the possibility of Article 267 references to the Court of Justice and section 10 discusses the reports of the National Audit Office ('the NAO') on the UK competition regime. The private enforcement of the competition rules in the UK was discussed in chapter 8 of this book[5].

2. Inquiries and Investigations

The purpose of the Competition Act is to eradicate anti-competitive agreements and abusive behaviour and it provides the CMA and the sectoral regulators with wide powers to conduct inquiries and investigations. These powers are set out in sections 25 to 29 of the Act; they were amended by the Competition Act 1998 and Other Enactments (Amendment) Regulations 2004 (the 'Amendment Regulations') to bring domestic law into alignment with the principles of Regulation 1/2003[6]. They were amended again by the Enterprise and Regulatory Reform Act 2013 ('the ERRA'); for example, the ERRA gave the CMA the power to require individuals to answer questions as part of an investigation. The CMA's powers are explained in some detail in the Guideline on *Powers of investigation*[7], which, like all the other guidance documents referred to in this chapter, is available on the CMA's website[8].

In 2011 the Government expressed concern with what it considered to be the paucity of decisions and the slowness of the administrative procedures of the UK competition authorities. In 2012 the Government decided to introduce reforms that were intended to speed up investigations and improve the robustness of decision-making: this led to the adoption of the ERRA. The CMA's *Guidance on the CMA's investigation procedures in Competition Act 1998 cases*[9] contains detailed guidance on various aspects of the law and practice on investigations under the Competition Act[10].

[3] On the Human Rights Act 1998 see 'Human Rights Act 1998 and Police and Criminal Evidence Act 1984', p 409 later in chapter and, more generally, Lester, Pannick and Herberg *Human Rights Law and Practice* (LexisNexis, 3rd ed, 2009); for further discussion of procedural issues in the UK see Ward and Smith (eds) *Competition Litigation in the UK* (Sweet & Maxwell, 2003); O'Neill and Sanders *UK Competition Procedure* (Oxford University Press, 2007); Green and Brealey (eds) *Competition Litigation: UK Practice and Procedure* (Oxford University Press, 2010).

[4] Case 1188/1/1/11 *Tesco Stores Ltd v OFT* [2012] CAT 6, para 10.

[5] See ch 8, 'Private Actions in the UK Courts', pp 325–335.

[6] SI 2004/1261.

[7] OFT 404, December 2004, available at www.gov.uk/cma.

[8] www.gov.uk/cma.

[9] CMA8, March 2014, available at www.gov.uk/cma; the *Guidance on the CMA's investigation procedures in Competition Act 1998 cases* should be read alongside the Guidelines listed in Annexe A, which were first published by the OFT and have been adopted by the Board of the CMA.

[10] The *Guidance on the CMA's investigation procedures in Competition Act 1998 cases* does not apply to investigations undertaken by sectoral regulators: ibid, para 1.6.

The ERRA has given the Secretary of State the power to introduce statutory time limits for investigations under the Competition Act[11]. This power might be invoked if a future Government were not satisfied about the amount of time taken by the authorities to investigate and decide cases[12].

(A) Opening a formal investigation

Section 25 of the Competition Act provides that the CMA may conduct an investigation if there are 'reasonable grounds for suspecting' that either of the prohibitions in the Competition Act or that Article 101 or 102 TFEU have been infringed[13]; this is often referred to as the 'section 25 threshold'[14], and requires less evidence than an infringement decision[15]. Section 25 gives the CMA a discretion whether to conduct an investigation: it is not under a duty to conduct one. The CMA had said that it will publish a 'notice of investigation' on its website, providing details of the case and a timetable for the investigation[16].

The manner in which the CMA conducts investigations, and the priority it gives to different phases of an investigation, are matters that fall within its discretion[17]. In *R (Cityhook Ltd) v OFT*[18] the Administrative Court held that the scope of the discretion conferred by section 25 does not become more circumscribed once a decision to investigate has been taken and an investigation commenced[19]. The Administrative Court also confirmed that the domestic competition authorities are entitled to prioritise their enforcement efforts. For example they are entitled to take into account consumer interests and the nature of an alleged infringement when selecting cases for investigation[20]. The CMA's *Prioritisation Principles*[21] explain the principles that the CMA takes into account when selecting a new project or case for investigation.

The Act gives the CMA power to make written inquiries (section 26), to ask questions (section 26A) and to enter business and domestic premises (sections 27 to 29)[22]. These powers are also available to enable the CMA to decide whether to apply for a company director disqualification order[23].

(B) Power to require documents and information

(i) Written inquiries

Where the section 25 threshold has been reached, a written request for information may be made by a notice under section 26 requiring a person to produce to the CMA a specified

[11] ERRA 2013, s 45.

[12] *Growth, Competition and the Competition Regime*, March 2012, para 6.26 (describing the power as a 'necessary backstop').

[13] *Guidance on the CMA's investigation procedures in Competition Act 1998 cases*, ch 5; for guidance on the meaning of 'reasonable grounds for suspecting' see *O'Hara v Chief Constable of the Royal Ulster Constabulary* [1997] AC 286 at 293C–E.

[14] On the circumstances in which the CMA's powers can be used see *Powers of investigation*, para 2; the CMA's powers are equally available to the sectoral regulators listed in s 54 of the Competition Act and it should be assumed throughout this chapter that anything that applies to the CMA applies equally to them unless otherwise stated.

[15] On the s 25 threshold see further 'Written inquiries', pp 402–403 later in chapter; on the sources of the CMA's investigations see *Guidance on the CMA's investigation procedures in Competition Act 1998 cases*, ch 3.

[16] Competition Act 1998, s 25A; *Guidance on the CMA's investigation procedures in Competition Act 1998 cases*, para 5.7.

[17] *Crest Nicholson Plc v OFT* [2009] EWHC 1875 (Admin), paras 45 and 77.

[18] [2009] EWHC 57 (Admin).

[19] Ibid, para 97.

[20] Ibid, paras 102–107 and 110–112.

[21] CMA16, April 2014 available at www.gov.uk/cma.

[22] Note that ss 61–64 of the Competition Act deal with investigations under Articles 101 and 102 TFEU.

[23] Company Directors Disqualification Act 1986, s 9C.

document[24] or specified information which the CMA considers relevant to the investigation[25]. Where it is practical and appropriate to do so, the CMA will send the notice to the proposed addressee in draft[26]. The notice must indicate the subject-matter and purpose of the investigation[27] and the offences involved in the event of non-compliance[28]. Specification can be by reference to a particular item or by category and the notice may state when and where the document or information is to be provided as well as how and in what form[29]. The CMA has the further power to take copies or extracts from a document produced in response to the notice and to ask for an explanation of it, or, if the document is not produced, to ask where it is believed to be[30]. Notices can be addressed to any person, which is defined to include an undertaking[31]; they may be sent not only to the undertakings suspected of infringement, but also to third parties such as complainants, suppliers, customers, competitors, liquidators or administrators of companies[32]. For example, in *Phenytoin* the CMA issued section 26 notices to numerous third parties, including the Chief Pharmaceutical Officer, the Department of Health and numerous pharmacies[33]. It should be noted that while section 26 applies equally to documents and to information, the Guideline on *Powers of investigation* makes clear that the power to obtain information means that the CMA can require a person to create a document incorporating that information: for example a person may be asked to provide market share information or to describe a particular market on the basis of their knowledge or experience or that of their staff[34]. Some section 26 notices are sent after on-site investigations in order to seek clarification of documents obtained[35].

(ii) **Power to ask questions**

The CAT has said that a competition authority should ask itself whether there are witnesses who might be willing to attend a voluntary interview and answer questions on matters relevant to its investigation[36]. There is no duty to attend such an interview, but section 44 provides criminal sanctions for making false or misleading replies[37].

The CMA may, instead of carrying out an interview by agreement, proceed straight to a compulsory one under section 26A of the Act if this is appropriate. The CMA may give written notice to an individual who has a connection with a 'relevant undertaking' (that is to say an undertaking under investigation) requiring him or her to answer relevant questions at a time and place specified in the notice[38]. An individual has a 'connection with' an undertaking if he or she is or was concerned in the management or control of

24 Documents include 'information recorded in any form': eg records held on computers, mobile phones, mobile email and other electronic devices: Competition Act 1998, s 59(1); see *Powers of investigation*, para 3.6.

25 Competition Act 1998, s 26(1), (2); see further *Powers of investigation*, para 3.

26 *Guidance on the CMA's investigation procedures in Competition Act 1998 cases*, para 6.8.

27 Competition Act 1998, s 26(3)(a).

28 Ibid, s 26(3)(b).

29 Ibid, s 26(4) and (5); s 59(3) provides that, if information is not in legible form, the CMA may require a copy in legible form.

30 Ibid, s 26(6); see 'Self-incrimination', p 408 later in chapter for discussion of the scope of the power to request explanations and the law on self-incrimination.

31 Ibid, s 59 which refers to the Interpretation Act 1978 ('person' includes a body of persons corporate or unincorporate).

32 *Powers of investigation*, para 3.4.

33 *Unfair pricing in respect of the supply of phenytoin sodium capsules in the UK*, CMA decision of 7 December 2016, para 2.47.

34 *Powers of investigation*, para 3.7.

35 Ibid, para 3.2.

36 See Case 1188/1/1/11 *Tesco Stores Ltd v OFT* [2012] CAT 31, paras 118–120.

37 See 'Offences', pp 410–411 later in chapter.

38 Competition Act 1998, s 26A(1); this power is similar to the one conferred by s 193(1) of the Enterprise Act 2002 in relation to the cartel offence, see 'Powers to require information and documents', pp 440–441 later in chapter.

the undertaking, or employed by, or otherwise working for, the undertaking[39]. Eligible individuals include current or former directors[40]; partners; temporary or permanent employees; consultants; volunteers or contract staff; and professional advisers[41]. Section 26A notices must indicate the subject-matter and purpose of the investigation and the offences involved in the event of non-compliance[42]. Where a section 26A notice is served on an individual it must also be served on the relevant undertaking[43]. Section 26A interviews will generally be recorded[44] and individuals are entitled to the presence of a lawyer[45]. The CMA has said that it will generally be inappropriate for a lawyer acting only for the undertaking under investigation to attend section 26A interviews[46]. A statement by an individual in response to a requirement under section 26A may be used only in certain circumstances, notably on a prosecution for an offence under section 44[47].

The CMA exercised its power under section 26A to interview former and current employees of the parties under investigation in *Paroxetine*[48].

(C) Power to enter premises without a warrant

Section 27(1) provides that any officer of the CMA who is authorised in writing by the CMA to do so ('an investigating officer') may enter any business premises[49] in connection with an investigation under section 25[50].

The operation of the power of entry varies depending on whether the premises are occupied by a 'third party', that is to say someone who is not suspected of an offence, or by a party under investigation for a possible infringement. In the case of a third party at least two working days' notice of the inspection must be given, together with a document explaining the subject-matter and the purpose of the investigation[51]. If, however, the officer has taken all reasonable steps to give notice but has been unable to do so he may dispense with the notice requirement[52]. In the case of a party under investigation there is no requirement to give prior warning or notice[53], but the subject-matter and purpose of the investigation must be explained. It is not necessary for the CMA first to have attempted to obtain information under the powers conferred by section 26[54].

When entering the premises the officer may:

- take with him or her any necessary equipment; this could be a laptop computer or tape-recording equipment[55]

39 Competition Act 1998, s 26A(7).

40 The CMA considers that the term 'director', for this purpose, includes a *de facto* director and a shadow director: *Guidance on the CMA's investigation procedures in Competition Act 1998 cases*, fn 63.

41 *Guidance on the CMA's investigation procedures in Competition Act 1998 cases*, fn 63; see also the Explanatory Notes to the ERRA, para 317.

42 Competition Act 1998, s 26A(5).

43 Ibid, s 26A(2) and (4).

44 *Guidance on the CMA's investigation procedures in Competition Act 1998 cases*, para 6.26.

45 Ibid, para 6.27.

46 Ibid; for critical comment see Kar and Ford 'In Defence of Rights of Defence: The Corporate's Right to Counsel in UK Competition Act Investigations' [2014] Comp Law 344.

47 Competition Act 1998, s 30A, see 'Self-incrimination', p 408 later in chapter.

48 *Paroxetine*, CMA decision of 12 February 2016, paras 2.14 and 2.22.

49 Competition Act 1998, s 27(6); premises includes any land or means of transport: ibid, s 59(1). See generally *Powers of investigation*, para 4.

50 As to investigations under s 27 on Crown land see the Competition Act 1998, s 73(4)(a) and the Competition Act 1998 (Definition of Appropriate Person) Regulations 1999, SI 1999/2282; the Secretary of State may certify in the interests of national security that specified Crown premises may not be entered under this section (see s 73(8)).

51 Competition Act 1998, s 27(2).

52 Ibid, s 27(3)(b).

53 Ibid, s 27(3)(a).

54 *Powers of investigation*, para 3.2.

55 Ibid, para 4.6.

- require 'any person'[56] to produce any documents which the officer considers relevant, to say where a document may be found, and, in relation to any document produced, may require an explanation of it take copies of or extracts from any document produced (but not the originals)
- require the production in visible, legible and portable form of any relevant information that is held on computer
- take any steps necessary to preserve or prevent interference with any document relevant to the investigation[57].

The procedure when conducting an inspection without a warrant is explained in the Guideline on *Powers of investigation*[58].

Section 27 does not entitle the CMA to use force to enter or once on the premises; it follows that permitted equipment would not include crowbars or other tools. Section 27 entry may therefore be described as a 'right of peaceful entry'. Where force might be required to gain entry, as would be the case for example when the premises are unoccupied, the powers in section 28 must be used. Section 27 does not give a power of search: again this is available only under section 28.

(D) **Power to enter premises with a warrant**

The CMA may apply for a warrant giving power to enter and search business[59] or domestic premises[60] to named officers of the CMA[61] and to non-employees, such as IT experts, who may be able to assist with the investigation[62]. Where the CMA wishes to enter domestic premises, the owner or occupier could invoke his or her right to respect for private and family life, the home and correspondence, which is protected by the Human Rights Act[63]. A section 28 investigation cannot be conducted on Crown land[64].

A warrant may be issued in specified circumstances by the High Court in England and Wales[65] or by the Court of Session in Scotland[66]; in such cases reasonable force may be used to obtain entry[67]. The circumstances are that[68]:

- there are reasonable grounds for suspecting that a document sought by written notice, or by an investigation without a warrant, but not produced, is on the premises

[56] In this instance this term presumably (although not necessarily) refers to an individual rather than to an undertaking, but there is no restriction as to who the person needs to be; it could include secretaries, IT personnel and messengers as well as directors; see HL Committee, 17 November 1997, col 391 (Lord Simon of Highbury).

[57] Competition Act 1998, s 27(5); see also s 59(3).

[58] *Powers of investigation*, paras 4.7–4.11; see also *Guidance on the CMA's investigation procedures in Competition Act 1998 cases*, paras 6.31–6.34.

[59] Competition Act 1998, s 28; see generally *Powers of investigation*, para 5; see also Peretz 'Warrants under Section 28 of the CA 1998: *OFT v D*' [2003] Comp Law 129.

[60] Competition Act 1998, s 28A; the CMA conducted an investigation at an individual's home in the case of *Online sales of posters and frames*, CMA decision of 12 August 2016.

[61] Ibid, s 28(2) (business premises) and s 28A(2) (domestic premises).

[62] Ibid, s 28(3A) (business premises) and s 28A(4) (domestic premises).

[63] Human Rights Act, Sch 1, Art 8; case law of the EU Courts and the ECHR is discussed in the opening section of ch 7, p 256.

[64] Competition Act 1998, s 73(4)(b).

[65] See *Practice Direction: Application for a Warrant under The Competition Act 1998*.

[66] ERRA s 48 makes provision for the CAT to be given the power to issue warrants: Draft Competition Appeal Tribunal (Warrants) (Amendment) Rules were published in September 2013 but no final rules had been adopted as at 8 December 2017.

[67] Competition Act 1998, s 28(2)(a) (business premises) and s 28A(2)(a) (domestic premises).

[68] Ibid, s 28(1) (business premises) and s 28A(1) (domestic premises).

- there are reasonable grounds for suspecting that a document that the CMA could obtain by written notice or by peaceful entry is on the premises but would be interfered with if it were required to be produced
- (in the case of business premises) entry without a warrant for the purpose of investigation has been impossible and there are reasonable grounds for suspecting that documents are on the premises that could have been required if entry had been obtained.

The section 28 powers therefore confer a 'right of forcible entry'.

Investigation by warrant is a serious matter and the investigator's powers are more extensive than under section 26 or 27. The subject-matter and purpose of the investigation, and the offences for non-compliance, must be indicated in the warrant itself[69]. It follows that the party being investigated should inspect this document carefully.

The investigators may use reasonable force to gain entry, but must lock the premises up in as secure a manner as they found them before leaving[70]. They may take 'equipment' to exercise such force but may not use force against any person[71]. As with investigations without a warrant the authorised officer may require documents to be produced, but the scope of this power depends on the situation in which the warrant was issued. The warrant will accordingly specify documents of 'the relevant kind'[72], that is to say those subject to a specific request under section 26 or 27, or those of the kind that could have been required on investigation under section 27 but were not provided. In addition to all the powers investigators would have on entry without a warrant, including the power to require information to be accessed from computers[73], they can also take away *originals* of documents and retain them for three months if copying them on the premises is not practicable or if taking them away appears necessary to prevent their disappearance[74]. Where appropriate the CMA may return duplicate or irrelevant information that it has gathered during an investigation; such information will not be part of the case file[75].

When acting under section 28, but not section 28A, investigating officers have the additional powers contained in section 50 of the Criminal Justice and Police Act 2001[76]. The investigators can also take any other necessary steps to preserve the existence of documents[77]. The procedure when conducting an inspection with a warrant is explained in the Guideline *Powers of investigation*[78]. The first challenge to a warrant was made in the case of *CMA v Concordia International RX (UK) Ltd*[79], in which Marcus Smith J held that the CMA could not rely on material protected by public interest immunity at a hearing to vary a warrant under section 28[79a].

(E) **Powers of surveillance**

The CMA also has powers of directed surveillance and to make use of covert human intelligence sources in order to investigate infringements of the Competition Act[80].

69 Ibid, s 29(1). 70 Ibid, s 28(5) (business premises) and s 28A(6) (domestic premises).
71 *Powers of investigation*, para 5.5.
72 Competition Act 1998, s 28(2)(b) (business premises) and s 28A(2)(b) (domestic premises).
73 Ibid, s 28(3). 74 Ibid, s 28(2)(c), (7) (business premises) and s 28A(2)(c), (8) (domestic premises).
75 *Guidance on the CMA's investigation procedures in Competition Act 1998 cases*, para 6.47.
76 See 'Power to enter premises with a warrant', 405–406.
77 Competition Act 1998, s 28(2)(d) (business premises) and s 28A(2)(d) (domestic premises).
78 *Powers of investigation*, paras 5.10–5.14; *Guidance on the CMA's investigation procedures in Competition Act 1998 cases*, paras 6.35–6.46. 79 [2017] EWHC 2911 (Ch), on appeal to the Court of Appeal.
79a Cf *R (Haralambous) v Crown Court at St Albans* [2018] UKSC 1, in which the UK Supreme Court held that a magistrates' court warrant granted under s 8 of the Police and Criminal Evidence Act 1984 may rely on information that is not disclosed to an interested party, even if that information is vital to explain how and why the court made its order. 80 See 'Powers of surveillance', pp 441–442 later in chapter.

(F) Access to lawyers

There is no statutory right to obtain outside legal help in the case of a section 26A interview or an investigation with or without a warrant[81]. However the CMA's Rules provide expressly for this right 'if the officer considers it reasonable in the circumstances to do so and if he is satisfied that such conditions as he considers ... appropriate ... will be complied with'[82]. The Guideline *Powers of investigation* provides further guidance on this issue[83]. The investigating officer will not wait for an external lawyer to arrive if the firm being investigated has an internal legal adviser[84], apparently irrespective of whether he or she is specialised in competition law.

(G) Limitation on the use of the powers of investigation

(i) Legal professional privilege

Legal professional privilege enables a client to obtain legal advice in confidence[85]. The CMA's power to obtain information, whether by written notice, interview or during an inspection, does not extend to privileged communications[86]. Privileged communications are defined as communications either between a professional legal adviser and his client or those made in connection with, or in contemplation of, legal proceedings and which, for the purposes of those proceedings, would be protected from disclosure in High Court proceedings[87]. 'Professional legal adviser' includes professionally qualified lawyers employed by firms (in-house counsel) as well as those practising in their own right, and in this respect privilege under the 1998 Act is more extensive than under EU competition law[88]. Not only does EU law not extend to correspondence with 'in-house' lawyers; nor does it apply to dealings with independent professional lawyers not qualified in a Member State, which, following Brexit, may include lawyers qualified in the UK[89]. It follows that some communications can legitimately be withheld where the inspection is one that the CMA conducts on its own behalf but not where it is assisting the European Commission's own inspections under Articles 20 and 21 of Regulation 1/2003. The more generous domestic rules on privilege do apply where the CMA conducts an inspection on behalf of the European Commission[90] or on behalf of a competition authority of another Member State[91].

In the case of a dispute as to privilege during an inspection the communication(s) in question may be sealed in an envelope[92]. If the CMA decides to require the disclosure of the communication(s), this decision is subject to judicial review by the Administrative Court.

[81] During the passage of the Competition Bill through Parliament Lord Simon of Highbury stated that the OFT (now CMA) would follow European Commission practice in this regard by giving a firm without internal legal assistance a reasonable period to obtain external help: HL Committee, 17 November 1997, col 404.

[82] SI 2014/458, r 4(1).

[83] *Powers of investigation*, paras 4.10–4.11; see also *Guidance on the CMA's investigation procedures in Competition Act 1998 cases*, paras 6.27 (s 26A interviews) and 6.43–6.44 (inspections).

[84] *Guidance on the CMA's investigation procedures in Competition Act 1998 cases*, para 6.43.

[85] *Three Rivers District Council v Bank of England* [2005] 1 AC 610, paras 23–34; see also *Brennan v United Kingdom* (2002) 34 EHRR 18, para 58.

[86] Competition Act 1998, s 30; see also *Powers of investigation*, para 4.11.

[87] On the English law of litigation privilege see Hollander *Documentary Evidence* (Sweet & Maxwell, 13th ed, 2018); *Halsbury's Laws of England* (5th ed, 2015), vol 12(2), ch 17; in Scotland the privilege is known as 'confidentiality of communications'.

[88] See *Powers of investigation*, paras 6.1–6.2, 9.7–9.9 and 10.5.

[89] For a discussion of privilege in EU competition law see ch 7, 'Legal professional privilege', pp 280–281.

[90] Competition Act 1998, s 65A. [91] Ibid, s 65J.

[92] *Guidance on the CMA's investigation procedures in Competition Act 1998 cases*, para 7.3.

(ii) Self-incrimination

The privilege against self-incrimination means that the CMA may not ask for explanations that might involve admissions of an infringement and will instead seek explanations of matters of fact, such as whether a particular employee was at a particular meeting[93]; however the distinction between these two will not always be clear-cut[94]. A statement made by a person in response to a requirement arising from sections 26 to 28A cannot be used against him or her for the purposes of a prosecution under the cartel offence unless he or she makes statements inconsistent with it and adduces evidence in relation to it[95]. Similar provision is made for statements made during section 26A interviews[96].

Apart from section 26A interviews[97], the CMA's power to demand an 'explanation' of a document is expressly linked to and limited to documents that are produced[98]. In the case of investigations with a warrant, an explanation can be sought in relation to 'any document appearing to be of the relevant kind'[99] without any specific reference to the document having been produced: this is because, in the case of a search, documents may be found as well as produced. The investigator could in theory require explanation of a document that appears to exist but which he or she has been unable to find, but the CMA's guidance does not indicate any intention to act in this way.

(iii) Confidentiality

There are detailed provisions in Part 9 of the Enterprise Act 2002 about restrictions on the disclosure of information obtained during the course of an investigation (and as a result of the operation of Part I of the Competition Act generally)[100]. Parties subject to an investigation or to a request for information must identify any confidential information that is supplied to the CMA in order to support any subsequent claim that it should not be published or disclosed to anyone else; indeed the CMA will usually ask them to do this, particularly where significant amounts of information or numbers of documents are sought. There is no right to withhold information from the CMA's investigators on grounds of confidentiality[101]. The CMA's guidelines explain its procedures for handling confidential information, including the use of practices such as 'confidentiality rings' and 'data rooms', as well as the CMA's powers and obligations as regards publication[102].

93 *Powers of investigation*, para 6.6.

94 The power of the CMA to obtain documents already in existence does not offend the privilege against self-incrimination: see Case C-301/04 P *Commission v SGL Carbon AG* EU:C:2006:432, paras 33–51; this judgment of the Court of Justice will apply to the CMA's actions by virtue of s 60(2) of the Competition Act, on which see ch 9, '"Governing Principles Clause": Section 60 of the Competition Act 1998', pp 387–392.

95 Competition Act 1998, s 30A(1).

96 Ibid, s 30A(2)–(3); s 30A(4) makes similar provision for the an undertaking with which the individual who gave the s 26A statement has a connection on a prosecution under s 44.

97 See 'Power to ask questions', pp 403–404 earlier in chapter.

98 Competition Act 1998, ss 26(6)(a)(ii), 27(5)(b)(ii).

99 Ibid, s 28(2)(e) (business premises) and s 28A(2)(b) (domestic premises).

100 See generally *Transparency and disclosure: Statement of the CMA's policy and approach*, CMA6, January 2014, as amended in December 2016.

101 See r 7 of the CMA's Rules in relation to confidential information provided to the CMA; confidential information is defined in r 1(1).

102 *Powers of investigation*, paras 6.8–6.13 and *Guidance on the CMA's investigation procedures in Competition Act 1998 cases*, paras 7.6–7.17; see also speech by Charles Hollander QC and 'Summary: CMA roundtable on the use of confidentiality rings and disclosure rooms', both dated 7 November 2016 and both available at www.gov.uk/cma.

(iv) Human Rights Act 1998 and Police and Criminal Evidence Act 1984 ('PACE')

The CAT has held that penalty decisions under the Competition Act are 'criminal' for the purpose of Article 6 of the European Convention on Human Rights, which is given effect in domestic law by the Human Rights Act 1998[103]. It follows from this that the undertaking concerned is entitled, amongst other things, to a fair and public hearing by an independent and impartial tribunal and to be presumed innocent: it is for the CMA to prove the infringements alleged[104]. However the CAT also concluded that this did not mean that they should be subject to the same rules of evidence or procedures as ordinary criminal proceedings[105]. In particular the CAT held that the Human Rights Act does not require that the criminal standard of proof 'beyond all reasonable doubt' should be applied; instead it concluded that the civil standard 'balance of probabilities' was the appropriate standard although, where a fine is imposed, this would require a competition authority to provide 'strong and compelling evidence'[106]. In subsequent judgments the CAT has stressed that the standard of proof is the balance of probabilities, laying less emphasis on the requirement that evidence should be 'strong and compelling'[107]. The CMA may rely on presumptions, for example that a firm with a very high market share is dominant; such presumptions do not reverse the burden of proof or set aside the presumption of innocence[108]. The High Court adopts the same approach to the burden and standard of proof as the CAT[109].

On a separate point, in *Toys and Games*[110] the OFT rejected an argument that it should, when conducting voluntary interviews with employees of Hasbro as to the possibility of an infringement of the Chapter I prohibition, have complied with the procedures required by PACE[111]. It would appear that PACE does not apply to interviews pursuant to section 26A[112]. In *Galvanised steel tanks* the CMA carried out interviews with individuals suspected of the criminal cartel offence in accordance with PACE[113].

(H) Sanctions

Both civil penalties and criminal sanctions may be imposed for non-compliance with the powers of investigation[114]. These sanctions must be indicated in section 26 and 26A notices and in warrants issued under sections 28 and 28A and must also be mentioned at the outset of voluntary interviews.

103 Case 1001/1/1/01 *Napp Pharmaceutical Holdings Ltd v Director General of Fair Trading* [2002] CAT 1, paras 93 and 98; see also the interim judgment in this case, Case 1001/1/1/01 [2001] CAT 3, paras 69–70; the European Court of Human Rights reached the same conclusion in *Menarini Diagnostics Srl v Italy*, no 43509/08, judgment of 27 September 2011, paras 38–44.

104 Case 1001/1/1/01 [2002] CAT 1, para 99; see also Case 1188/1/1/11 *Tesco Stores Ltd v OFT* [2012] CAT 31, para 88.

105 Case 1001/1/1/01 [2002] CAT 1, para 101.

106 Ibid, paras 105 and 109.

107 See eg Cases 1021 and 1022/1/1/03 *JJB Sports plc and Allsports Ltd v OFT* [2004] CAT 17, paras 195–208; Case 1061/1/1/06 *Makers UK Ltd v OFT* [2007] CAT 11, paras 45–52.

108 Case 1001/1/1/01 [2002] CAT 1, paras 110–111.

109 See eg *Chester City Council v Arriva* [2007] EWHC 1373 (Ch), para 10; *Bookmakers' Afternoon Greyhound Services Ltd v Amalgamated Racing Ltd* [2008] EWHC 1978 (Ch), para 392; *Asda Stores Ltd v MasterCard Inc* [2017] EWHC 93 (Comm), para 56.

110 *Hasbro UK Ltd, Argos Ltd and Littlewoods Ltd*, OFT decision of 19 February 2003.

111 Ibid, para 186.

112 The *Guidance on the CMA's investigation procedures in Competition Act 1998 cases* does not refer to PACE in connection with s 26A interviews.

113 *Galvanised steel tanks for water storage main cartel infringement*, CMA decision of 19 December 2016, para 2.106.

114 *Powers of investigation*, para 7.

As already described the powers of investigation, and the civil and criminal sanctions, are applicable to 'persons', which can include an undertaking[115]. In addition, under section 72, officers of bodies corporate are liable to punishment if they consent to or connive at an offence or if it is due to neglect on their part[116]. Officer means a director, manager, secretary or other similar officer, or anyone purporting to act as such[117]. There are similar provisions applicable to companies managed by their members (who can be liable) and, in Scotland, to partners and partnerships[118]. The fact that individuals themselves can be personally liable under these provisions of the Competition Act, and that there is even a possibility of imprisonment, no doubt concentrates the minds of those responsible for ensuring compliance with the Act[119].

(i) Penalties: failure to comply with requirements

Sections 40A to 40B of the Competition Act provide for financial penalties on a person who, without reasonable excuse, fails to comply with a requirement imposed under section 26, 26A, 27, 28 or 28A. The maximum amounts that the CMA may impose as a penalty under section 40A are specified in the Competition and Markets Authority (Penalties) Order 2014[120]. Section 40B sets out the main procedural requirements which the CMA must observe when imposing a monetary penalty; the factors which it will have regard to when determining the amount of a penalty are set out in the CMA's statement of policy on penalties[121]. There is a right of appeal to the CAT against decisions of the CMA to impose penalties[122]. In *Phenytoin*[123] a section 40A penalty of £10,000 was imposed on Pfizer for failure to provide information in response to a section 26 notice by the stated deadline.

(ii) Offences

Individuals as well as legal persons may commit offences; the sanctions in some cases include imprisonment[124]. The offences are set out in sections 42 to 44 of the Competition Act and fall into four main categories:

- intentionally obstructing an officer investigating without a warrant[125]
- intentionally obstructing an officer investigating with a warrant[126]
- intentionally or recklessly destroying, disposing of, falsifying or concealing documents, or causing or permitting those things to happen[127]
- knowingly or recklessly supplying information which is false or misleading in a material particular either directly to the CMA, or to anyone else, knowing it is for the purpose of providing information to the CMA[128].

There are no statutory defences to these penal provisions. The penalties can be substantial and depend on whether the offence is tried summarily or is serious enough to be taken

115 Competition Act 1998, s 59(1); see *Powers of investigation*, para 4.3.

116 Competition Act 1998, s 72(2); see *Powers of investigation*, para 7.4.

117 Competition Act 1998, s 72(3).

118 Ibid, s 72(4)–(6).

119 This point is even more significant given the existence of the criminal cartel offence ('The cartel offence', pp 437–446) and company director disqualification ('Company director disqualification', pp 446–448).

120 SI 2014/559.

121 *Administrative Penalties: Statement of Policy on the CMA's approach*, CMA4, January 2014, available at www.gov.uk/cma.

122 Competition Act 1998, s 40A(9) and Enterprise Act 2002, s 114.

123 *Penalty notice under section 40A of the Competition Act 1998—addressed to Pfizer Ltd*, CMA decision of 12 April 2016.

124 See ch 10, n 130 later.

125 Competition Act 1998, s 42(5).

126 Ibid, s 42(7).

127 Ibid, s 43(1).

128 Ibid, s 44(1), (2).

on indictment to the Crown Court[129]. The penalties are financial but in the case of any obstruction of investigators with a warrant, destruction of documents or provision of false or misleading information imprisonment for up to two years is also possible[130].

(l) **EU investigations**

The European Commission has power, under Articles 20 and 21 of Regulation 1/2003, to conduct on-site investigations in relation to suspected infringements of Articles 101 and 102 TFEU, and may seek the assistance of an NCA when doing so. Article 22(1) of the Regulation enables the Commission to ask an NCA to conduct an investigation on its behalf, and Article 22(2) gives the same power to the competition authorities of the other Member States of the EU[131]. Sections 61 to 65 of the Competition Act 1998 set out, in considerable detail, the rules that govern inspections by the CMA under Regulation 1/2003, and the CMA has provided guidance on their application in practice[132].

After the UK leaves the EU, the CMA will no longer be obliged by Articles 20, 21 and 22(2) of Regulation 1/2003 to provide assistance or conduct an investigation on its behalf. However, cooperation between the competition authorities in the UK and the EU is likely to remain a fact of daily life, and there is therefore a respectable argument that sections 61 to 65 of the Competition Act should be retained in some form.

3. **Complaints**

Complaints are an important source of information about possible infringements[133]. Complaints led to the CMA's decisions in, for example, *Online resale price maintenance in the light fittings sector*[134] and *Online resale price maintenance in the bathroom fittings sector*[135]. The Competition Act does not establish a procedure for complaining to the CMA; instead provision is made in the *Guidance on the CMA's investigation procedures in Competition Act 1998 cases*[136] for a 'pre-complaint discussion' as to whether a matter would be likely to be investigated if a formal complaint were to be made.

The *Guidance on the CMA's investigation procedures in Competition Act 1998 cases*[137] states that the CMA will grant 'Formal Complainant' status[138] to any person who has submitted a written, reasoned complaint to the CMA, who requests Formal Complainant status, and whose interests are, or are likely to be, materially affected by the subject matter of the complaint[139]. A Formal Complainant enjoys defined rights in relation to file closures[140], statements of objections[141] and interim measures applications[142].

[129] *Powers of investigation*, para 7.5; the offence would be tried in the High Court of Justiciary in Scotland; note that the financial caps on the fines that can be imposed were removed with effect from 12 March 2015 as a result of the Legal Aid, Sentencing and Punishment of Offenders Act 2012 (Fines an Summary Conviction Regulations) 2015, SI 2015/664.

[130] Competition Act 1998, ss 42(6), (7), 43(2), 44(3); *Powers of investigation*, para 7.7 describes the penalties in detail.

[131] The OFT (now CMA) conducted an investigation on behalf of the French Competition Authority in a case that resulted in fines for four oil companies that distorted competition in a tender process organised by Air France: see Press Release, 4 December 2008, available at www.autoritedelaconcurrence.fr.

[132] *Powers of investigation*, paras 9 and 10.

[133] The separate procedure for nominated bodies to make so-called 'super-complaints' is described in ch 11 'Super-complaints', pp 463–465.

[134] CMA decision of 3 May 2017, para 2.3.

[135] CMA decision of 10 May 2016, para E.1.

[136] CMA8, March 2014, paras 3.16–3.21; see also *Prioritisation principles for the CMA*, CMA 16, April 2014.

[137] CMA8, March 2014.

[138] Ibid, paras 5.12–5.15.

[139] Ibid, para 5.12.

[140] Ibid, paras 10.3–10.4.

[141] Ibid, para 12.7.

[142] Ibid, para 8.11.

What happens to a complaint depends on whether the CMA considers that it reveals a possible breach of the prohibition[143]. If it does, the complaint may trigger an investigation in accordance with the CMA's *Prioritisation Principles*[144]. If no possible breach is indicated, the CMA will inform the complainant as soon as possible that it intends to take no further action. The right of a complainant to challenge a rejection of a complaint is considered in section 8 of this chapter[145].

Complaints may raise difficult questions of confidentiality. Where a complainant provides confidential information to the CMA[146] the CMA requires a non-confidential version of such information that can be disclosed to the complainee[147]. Some complainants wish to remain anonymous and this can make it difficult for the CMA to pursue the complaint. The complainant should explain to the CMA why its identity should not be disclosed; if the CMA is satisfied that this is the case it will seek to maintain the anonymity 'to the extent that this is consistent with the CMA's statutory obligations'[148]; this may not be sustainable once the CMA proposes to adopt an infringement decision[149]. Part 9 of the Enterprise Act 2002 contains rules against the disclosure of certain information about individuals or undertakings unless disclosure is permitted by one of the so-called 'gateways' set out in sections 239 to 242 of the Act. These provisions are explained in the CMA's guidelines[150]. The CMA's Procedural Officer may resolve disputes as to confidentiality[151].

4. **Opinions and Informal Advice**

The Competition Act as originally enacted provided a system of notification to the competition authorities for guidance or a decision as to whether the Chapter I and/or Chapter II prohibitions were being infringed[152]. The Amendment Regulations repealed the provisions on notification with effect from 1 May 2004 to bring domestic law into alignment with EU law[153]. Undertakings must decide for themselves whether their practices are compatible with the competition rules. In certain circumstances, however, the CMA might provide an Opinion[154] or give informal advice in relation to novel or unanswered questions[155].

(A) **Opinions**

The CMA will consider a request for an Opinion only where the following three conditions are fulfilled:

- there is no sufficient precedent in EU or UK case law

143 *Guidance on the CMA's investigation procedures in Competition Act 1998 cases*, paras 4.1–4.6.

144 CMA16, April 2014. 145 See 'Appeals', pp 452–460 later in chapter.

146 Confidential information for this purpose is defined in r 1(1) of the CMA's Rules, SI 2014/458.

147 *Guidance on the CMA's investigation procedures in Competition Act 1998 cases*, paras 8.21, 10.5 and 12.7.

148 The *Guidance on the CMA's investigation procedures in Competition Act 1998 cases*, para 3.20 says that the CMA aims to keep the identity of the complainant confidential while it decides whether to pursue the complaint.

149 *Guidance on the CMA's investigation procedures in Competition Act 1998 cases*, para 3.21.

150 OFT 442, December 2004, para 9 and *Guidance on the CMA's investigation procedures in Competition Act 1998 cases*, paras 7.6–7.17.

151 *Guidance on the CMA's investigation procedures in Competition Act 1998 cases*, para 7.13; on the Procedural Officer see 'Procedure', p 414 later in chapter.

152 The relevant provisions were the Competition Act, ss 12–16 and Schs 5 and 6; they are described at pp 371–376 of the fifth edition of this book.

153 See ch 4, 'Regulation 1/2003', pp 174–176.

154 *Modernisation*, OFT 442, December 2004, paras 7.5–7.19. 155 Ibid, para 7.20.

- there is a need for a published Opinion, for example because of the economic importance for consumers of the goods or services affected by the agreement or conduct in question or because of the scope of the investment related to the agreement or conduct
- it is possible to provide an Opinion without the need for substantial further fact-finding[156].

Undertakings that request an Opinion may withdraw their request[157]. One Opinion had been issued by 8 December 2017: in 2008 the OFT provided guidance to facilitate 'self-assessment' of agreements for the distribution of newspapers and magazines under the Competition Act[158]. The CMA's *Guidance on the CMA's approach to short-form opinions*[159] explains that the CMA is prepared (on a trial basis) to give a 'short-form opinion' on how Article 101 TFEU and/or the Chapter I prohibition apply to proposed agreements that raise novel or unresolved questions and have a material link to the UK[160]. Short-form opinions are also subject to the CMA's *Prioritisation Principles*[161]. The CMA expects to issue short-form opinions in a 'limited number of cases' each year[162]. No short-form opinions had been issued by the CMA by 8 December 2017[163].

(B) **Informal advice**

The CMA may provide confidential informal advice to undertakings on the application of competition law on an *ad hoc* basis, but such advice is not binding[164], and would not be given in a case that does not satisfy the CMA's *Prioritisation Principles*.

5. Enforcement

This section will explain the various possibilities that exist where the CMA or a sectoral regulator intends to take enforcement action under the Competition Act.

(A) Procedure

Where the CMA has 'reasonable grounds for suspecting' an infringement of the Act or of Article 101 or 102 TFEU it will first carry out an investigation pursuant to section 25. Provision is made for the CMA to adopt interim measures during an investigation: this is discussed in section C below.

(i) Statement of objections

If, as a result of its investigation, the CMA proposes to adopt a decision that there is or has been an infringement of the Chapter I and/or Chapter II prohibition or of Articles 101 and/or 102 TFEU section 31 of the Act requires it to give 'written notice'—better known as a 'statement of objections'—to the person or persons 'likely to be affected'[165]

156 Ibid, para 7.5. 157 Ibid, para 7.14.

158 OFT 1025, October 2008; see Muysert and Dobson 'Split Opinion: The Office of Fair Trading Opinion on Newspaper and Magazine Distribution' [2010] Comp Law 262. 159 CMA27, April 2014.

160 Ibid, para 4.4. 161 Ibid, para 1.4. 162 Ibid.

163 The OFT issued two 'short-form opinions': the first concerned a joint purchasing agreement, *P&H/Makro joint purchasing agreement*, Short-form Opinion of 27 April 2010; the second related to recommendations by the National Farmers' Union and the Country Landowners' Association to landowners as to the charges to be levied for the grant of wayleaves to facilitate the roll-out of rural broadband services, *Rural Broadband Wayleave Rates agreement*, Short-form Opinion of 23 August 2012.

164 *Modernisation*, para 7.20. 165 Competition Act 1998, s 31(1)(a).

and to give that person (or persons) an opportunity to make representations[166]. The form of the statement of objections is set out in rules 5 and 6 of the CMA's Rules[167]; rule 6 also deals with access to the file[168] and the right to make written and oral representations[169]. The CAT summarised the principles applicable to the statement of objections in *Apex v OFT*[170]. Where the CMA considers that an agreement infringes the Chapter I prohibition and/or Article 101(1) it may address the statement of objections to fewer than all the persons who are or were party to that agreement[171]. The CMA has exercised this power in several cases[172], which helps it to deliver cases more quickly. Chapter 11 of the *Guidance on the CMA's investigation procedures in Competition Act 1998 cases* explains the CMA's approach to issuing a statement of objections.

(ii) Procedural Officer

The CMA has appointed a Procedural Officer whose function is to preside over hearings and to ensure that the rights of the defence are respected[173]. The parties are entitled to ask the Procedural Officer to review decisions by the case team on procedural matters[174]. Decisions of the Procedural Officer are available on the CMA's website[175].

(iii) Subsequent procedure

Having gone through the procedure just described, the CMA will appoint a three-person 'Case Decision Group' to decide its next steps[176]. The Case Decision Group ('CDG') may include any senior member of staff of the CMA, a member of the Board of the CMA or a member of the CMA Panel[177]. The CDG acts as the decision-maker on behalf of the CMA[178]; this is an attempt to address the criticism that the same case-handlers work on a particular case during both the investigation and the decision-making phases, unlike, for example, the position in the US, where the Department of Justice must take a case to a court[179].

Various possibilities exist following the issue of a statement of objections. One is that the CMA might decide not to proceed with the case or to state that it has no grounds for action[180]. Alternatively, the CMA may close a case, without a finding of

[166] Ibid, s 31(1)(b). [167] SI 2014/458.

[168] Ibid, r 6(2). [169] Ibid, r 6(3)–(4). [170] Case 1032/1/1/04 [2005] CAT 4, para 100.

[171] SI 2014/458, r 5(3); an equivalent power exists for adopting an infringement decision in relation to fewer than all the parties to an agreement: ibid, r 10(2).

[172] See eg *Online resale price maintenance in the bathroom fittings sector*, CMA decision of 10 May 2016, paras 1.2 and E.18–E.19; *Online resale price maintenance in the commercial refrigeration sector*, CMA decision of 24 May 2016, paras 1.2 and C.15–C.16; *Online resale price maintenance in the light fittings sector*, CMA decision of 3 May 2017, paras 1.3 and 4.4.

[173] See r 6(5)–(6) and r 8 of the CMA's Rules, SI 2014/458.

[174] *Guidance on the CMA's investigation procedures in Competition Act 1998 cases*, ch 15.

[175] www.gov.uk/guidance/procedural-officer-raising-procedural-issues-in-cma-cases.

[176] *Guidance on the CMA's investigation procedures in Competition Act 1998 cases*, paras 11.30–11.34; none of the officials involved in the issue of the statement of objections will be appointed to the Case Decision Group.

[177] On the CMA Board and the CMA Panel see ch 2, 'Establishment of the CMA and the CMA Board', pp 65–66.

[178] *Guidance on the CMA's investigation procedures in Competition Act 1998 cases*, para 9.11.

[179] The Government considered, but ultimately rejected, the introduction of a prosecutorial system, such as that deployed in the US, in the UK: *Growth, Competition and the Competition Regime*, March 2012, paras 6.17–6.19.

[180] On challenges to such decisions before the CAT see 'Successful appeals against implicit non-infringement decisions', pp 454–455 later in this chapter.

infringement, by accepting legally binding 'commitments' that the undertaking(s) will modify their behaviour in order to resolve the competition problems that led to the initiation of the investigation (see section B later). A further possibility is that the CDG considers that further fact-finding must be done, in which case the CMA may issue a supplementary statement of objections or a so-called 'letter of facts'[181]. Where the CMA finds an infringement it may give directions to bring the infringement to an end (section D) and may require an infringing undertaking to pay a penalty (section E). Undertakings that 'blow the whistle' on infringements of the Chapter I prohibition or Article 101 TFEU may be able to claim immunity or reductions from penalties that might otherwise have been imposed (section F). Some infringement decisions are adopted following a settlement between the CMA and the undertakings concerned (section G). Section H will consider how the provisions on penalties have been applied in practice.

(B) **Commitments**

Sections 31A to 31E of the Competition Act enable the CMA and sectoral regulators to adopt a decision whereby undertakings under investigation make legally-binding commitments as to their future behaviour in order to address its competition concerns. The CAT has said that commitment decisions 'are an important and useful contribution to overall competition enforcement'[182]. The CMA has adopted existing guidance on the commitments procedure in Part 4 of *Enforcement*[183].

It is for the undertakings concerned to approach the CMA to discuss the possibility of commitments. Commitments may be both structural and behavioural[184]. The CMA has said that it is likely to consider accepting commitments only in limited cases where the competition concerns are readily identifiable and are fully addressed by the commitments offered and where the commitments are capable of being implemented effectively and, if necessary, within a short period of time[185]. The CMA will not, other than in exceptional cases, accept commitments in respect of hard-core cartels or serious abuses of dominance[186]; however such cases might culminate in a settlement whereby the undertakings concerned are fined a lesser sum than they would have been in return for enabling the CMA to reach an infringement decision more quickly than would otherwise have been the case[187].

Section 31(2) enables the CMA to accept commitments from undertakings to take such action or to refrain from taking such action as the CMA considers appropriate; provision is made for the variation[188], substitution[189] and release[190] of commitments. Schedule 6A to the Act sets out the procedural requirements that are to be followed in commitments cases. Where the CMA accepts commitments it will discontinue its investigation and it cannot make a decision finding an infringement under section 31 or issue a direction

[181] *Guidance on the CMA's investigation procedures in Competition Act 1998 cases*, paras 12.27–12.28.

[182] Case 1226/2/12/14 *Skyscanner Ltd v CMA* [2014] CAT 16, para 120.

[183] *Enforcement*, OFT 407, December 2004; on the advantages of the commitments regime over accepting voluntary assurances see the judgments of the CAT in Case 1017/2/1/03 *Pernod-Ricard SA v OFT* [2005] CAT 9, para 7 and Case 1026/2/3/04 *Wanadoo (UK) Plc v OFCOM* [2004] CAT 20, para 124.

[184] *Enforcement*, para 4.6.

[185] Ibid, para 4.3.

[186] Ibid, para 4.4; see eg *Independent Schools*, OFT decision of 23 November 2006; paras 31–32; for an example of an exceptional case in which structural commitments were accepted to deal with predatory pricing see *Severn Trent Plc*, OFWAT decision of 17 January 2013, paras 9.5–9.6.

[187] See 'Settlements', pp 429–430 later in chapter.

[188] Competition Act 1998, s 31A(3)(a).

[189] Ibid, s 31A(3)(b).

[190] Ibid, s 31A(4).

under section 35[191]. Where an undertaking fails to adhere to its commitments the CMA may apply to the court for an order to enforce compliance[192].

There is a consultation process under the commitments procedure in which third parties are given an opportunity to comment[193]. If accepted the CMA will publish the full text of the commitments on its website. Decisions by the CMA not to release commitments when requested by the parties that offered them to do so can be appealed to the CAT[194], as can decisions where there are no longer grounds for competition concerns[195]. Third parties can appeal to the CAT against decisions to accept or release commitments or to accept a material variation[196]. In *Skyscanner v CMA*[197] the CAT held that the OFT had failed properly to take into account Skyscanner's objections to the proposed commitments intended to address competition concerns relating to hotel online bookings.

Table 10.1 provides details of cases in which the UK competition authorities had accepted commitments by 8 December 2017.

(C) **Interim measures**

If the CMA has begun an investigation under section 25 and has not completed it, it may adopt interim measures if this is necessary as a matter of urgency to prevent significant damage to a particular person or category of persons or to protect the public interest[198]; however it cannot adopt interim measures if undertakings are able to show on the balance of probabilities that the criteria in section 9(1) of the Competition Act or Article 101(3) TFEU are satisfied[199].

The domestic competition authorities have not been noticeably keen to use their interim powers[200]. The only occasion on which the OFT adopted interim measures was *London Metal Exchange*[201] where it was concerned that the LME might have been about to abuse its dominant position by extending the hours of trading on its electronic trading platform, LME Select[202]. In order to facilitate the use of interim measures, the ERRA enables the CMA to act because of 'significant damage' (rather than the old test of 'serious, irreparable damage') to a particular person or category of persons. Damage will be significant where a person is or may be restricted in their ability to compete effectively, such that this may significantly damage their commercial position[203]; it does not require

[191] Ibid, s 31B(2); the CMA may continue its investigation only if the circumstances specified in s 31B(4) apply.

[192] Ibid, s 31E; 'court' for this purpose is defined in s 59 of the Act.

[193] Ibid, Sch 6A and *Enforcement*, paras 4.21–4.22.

[194] Competition Act 1998, s 46(3)(g).

[195] Ibid, s 46(3)(h).

[196] Ibid, s 47(1)(c).

[197] Case 1226/2/12/14 [2014] CAT 16; on 16 September 2015 the CMA decided to close the case file and instead monitor developments in the hotel online booking sector.

[198] Competition Act 1998, s 35(1) and (2); the Guideline on *Enforcement*, OFT 407, December 2004 and ch 8 of the *Guidance on the CMA's investigation procedures in Competition Act 1998 cases* explain the CMA's approach to the interim measures procedure.

[199] Competition Act 1998, s 35(8) and (9); see also *Guidance on the CMA's investigation procedures in Competition Act 1998 cases*, para 8.18.

[200] See eg OFCOM decision of 31 July 2013, rejecting BT's request for interim measures in relation to the wholesale supply by BSkyB of Sky Sports 1 and 2; see also CMA decision of 19 December 2014, rejecting Worldpay's request for interim measures in relation to Visa's interchange fees; OFCOM decision of 4 February 2015, rejecting Virgin Media's request for interim measures in relation to the sale of media rights to Premier League matches.

[201] OFT decision of 27 February 2006.

[202] The LME appealed to the CAT against this decision; subsequently the OFT, having received new evidence, withdrew the decision: see Case 1062/1/1/06 *London Metal Exchange v OFT* [2006] CAT 19 (dealing with costs).

[203] *Guidance on the CMA's investigation procedures in Competition Act 1998 cases*, para 8.14; the CAT considered an identical requirement of 'significant damage' for granting interim relief under r 24 of the CAT Rules in Case 1274/1/12/16 (IR) *Flynn Pharma Ltd v CMA* [2017] CAT 1.

Table 10.1 Table of section 31A commitment decisions

Case name	Date of publication of proposed commitments	Date upon which commitments were made legally binding	Date until which commitments will remain in force
Bristol Water (OFWAT)	22.05.14	23.03.15	Remain in force until OFWAT and Bristol Water agree otherwise
Freightliner (ORR)	03.09.15; revised commitments were published on 19.11.15	18.12.15	31.03.19
SEE (OFGEM)	22.06.16	03.11.16	Subject to a review by 08.05.21
ATG Media (CMA)	30.05.17	29.06.17	29.06.22
Showmen's Guild (CMA)	22.08.17	26.10.17	Remain in force until CMA agrees otherwise

a person to leave the market[204]. In *ATG Media*[205] the CMA gave 'serious consideration' to an application for interim measures; however it was not necessary to make a decision as it accepted commitments from ATG to address concerns arising from its 'no less favourable terms' clauses for online auctions of art and antiques.

The CMA must give notice to the affected persons before giving directions, thus giving them an opportunity to make representations[206]. Such notice must indicate the nature of the proposed direction and the CMA's reasons[207]. The CMA has indicated that it may be willing, in some cases, to accept informal interim assurances in lieu of adopting formal interim measures decisions[208]; the OFT accepted informal assurances on a few occasions[209]. Decisions by the CMA to grant or refuse interim measures can be appealed to the CAT[210].

(D) **Directions**

Section 32(1) of the Competition Act provides that, when the CMA has made a decision that an agreement infringes the Chapter I prohibition or Article 101 TFEU, it may give to such person or persons as it considers appropriate directions to bring the infringement to an end. Section 32(3) expands on the content of these directions which may require the parties to an agreement to modify it or require them to terminate it. There are corresponding provisions in section 33 for directions in the case of infringements of the Chapter II prohibition or Article 102 TFEU; in this case section 33(3) provides that the direction may

[204] Ibid, para 8.15.

[205] *Decision to accept binding commitments offered by ATG Media in relation to live online bidding auction platform services*, CMA decision of 29 June 2017, para 2.5.

[206] Competition Act 1998, s 35(3); see also the CMA's Rules, r 13.

[207] Competition Act 1998, s 35(4).

[208] *Enforcement*, paras 3.17–3.20.

[209] See eg *Robert Wiseman Dairies*, OFT Press Release PN 39/01, 14 September 2001; *Oakley (UK) Ltd*, case closure of February 2007; *Nationwide Independent Bodyshop Suppliers Ltd*, case closure of February 2009.

[210] Competition Act 1998, ss 46(3) and 47(1)(d)–(e).

require the person concerned to modify the conduct in question, or require him to cease that conduct. In either case directions may also include other provisions such as positive action and reporting obligations[211]. Recipients of directions must be informed in writing of the facts on which the directions are based and the reasons for them[212]; directions under sections 32 and 33 must be published[213].

(i) Can directions be structural?

It is not clear whether the power to give directions includes the right to impose structural remedies such as the right to require the divestiture of assets or the break-up of an undertaking; Article 7 of Regulation 1/2003 explicitly provides that the European Commission can impose structural and behavioural remedies[214]. Where an infringement of the Chapter I or II prohibitions or of Article 101 or 102 is itself the consequence of a structural change in the market it would seem, in principle, that a structural remedy to bring the infringement to an end would be justified: for example if undertakings were to establish, contrary to the Chapter I prohibition or Article 101, a joint venture company to act as a joint sales agency the most effective remedy would probably be a structural one, requiring the dissolution of the company. It is less obvious, however, that it is possible to impose a structural remedy, for example, to break up a dominant firm guilty of serial abusive behaviour; such a situation would appear to be more suitable for a market investigation reference under the Enterprise Act 2002, under which legislation a structural remedy is, explicitly, available[215]. It is interesting to note that OFWAT accepted structural commitments in one case[216]: commitments are offered voluntarily, so it is not possible to infer from this decision that OFWAT could have imposed a structural remedy in this case.

(ii) The directions provisions in practice

In some cases the CMA may refrain from giving directions if the infringement has ended by the time of its decision[217]. However directions have been issued in several cases[218]. For example in *Napp*[219] that company was ordered to amend its prices for certain morphine medicines to bring its abusive pricing to an end, while in *Lladró Comercial* the OFT required the porcelain producer to modify its distribution agreements to make clear that the practice of resale price maintenance would not continue[220]. Similarly in *Genzyme*[221] the OFT obliged that company to charge separately for Cerezyme, a drug that it produced, and for the various homecare services it provided; and to offer Cerezyme to competing homecare operators at a price no higher than that charged to the National Health Service[222]. There were protracted proceedings in the CAT as to the correct price to be charged by Genzyme[223], during which the CAT stated that the primary responsibility for bringing the abuse to an end in that case rested with Genzyme, rather than with the OFT or the CAT[224].

211 See *Enforcement*, para 2.3.
212 CMA Rules, SI 2014/458, r 12(1).
213 Ibid, r 12(3).
214 See ch 7, 'Structural remedies', p 262.
215 See ch 11, 'Final powers', p 484.
216 *Severn Trent Plc*, OFWAT decision of 17 January 2013.
217 See eg *Online resale price maintenance in the light fittings sector*, CMA decision of 3 May 2017, para 5.4.
218 See eg *Conduct in the modelling sector*, CMA decision of 16 December 2016, paras 5.3–5.5.
219 *Directions given by the Director General of Fair Trading under section 33 of the Competition Act 1998 to Napp Pharmaceutical Holdings Ltd and its subsidiaries*, 4 May 2001, upheld on appeal Case 1001/1/1/01 *Napp Pharmaceutical Holdings Ltd v Director General of Fair Trading* [2002] CAT 1, paras 553–562.
220 OFT decision of 31 March 2003, paras 117–118.
221 OFT decision of 27 March 2003, substantially upheld on appeal Case 1016/1/1/03 *Genzyme Ltd v OFT* [2004] CAT 4.
222 Case 1016/1/1/03 *Genzyme Ltd v OFT* [2005] CAT 32.
223 Case 1013/1/1/03 (IR) *Genzyme Ltd v OFT* [2003] CAT 8.
224 See the transcript of the hearing of 13 October 2004, available at www.catribunal.org.uk.

In *English Welsh & Scottish Railway*[225] the Office of Rail Regulation (now the Office of Rail and Road) ('the ORR') found that EW&S was guilty of abusing a dominant position in the market for the carriage by rail of industrial coal to power stations; it gave directions to EW&S requiring it to remove or modify various terms in the coal carriage agreements it had entered into with some of its customers, including the power company E.ON[226]. The High Court subsequently agreed with EW&S that the directions of the ORR meant that the offending clauses had been void from their inception and that, since they could not be severed, the entire coal carriage agreement was void and unenforceable[227].

In *National Grid v Gas and Electricity Markets Authority*[228] the CAT did not accept the criticism that the regulator's direction that National Grid 'refrain from engaging in conduct having the same or equivalent exclusionary effect' to its abusive contracts was unacceptably vague or inappropriate[229].

In *Phenytoin*[230] the CMA found that each of Pfizer and Flynn had abused a dominant position by imposing unfairly high prices in the UK for phenytoin sodium capsules manufactured by Pfizer. The CMA directed Pfizer and Flynn to reduce their respective prices, but declined to specify the extent of the reduction[231]; the undertakings would have to make their own assessment of the compatibility of their revised prices with competition law. The CAT dismissed an application by Flynn to suspend the directions pending an appeal against the infringement decision[232].

(iii) Persons who may be the subject of directions

Directions may be given to 'appropriate' persons, who will not necessarily be the parties to the agreement or perpetrators of the unlawful conduct. The purpose of this is to enable the CMA to give directions to parent companies, affiliates or private individuals with the ability to influence or procure actions by the infringing persons[233]. Section 34 of the Act allows the court to order an undertaking or its officers to obey a direction relating to the management of that undertaking if the person subject to the direction has failed to comply.

(iv) Enforcement of compliance with directions

If a person subject to directions (whether interim or final) fails to comply without reasonable excuse the CMA may apply to the court[234] for an order requiring compliance within a specified time or, if the direction concerns the management of an undertaking, ordering another officer to carry it out[235]. Breach of such an order would be contempt of court, punishable by fines or imprisonment, at the court's discretion[236]. There is nothing in section 34 that limits the court's order-making powers to persons within the UK[237].

225 ORR decision of 17 November 2006.

226 Ibid, paras D2–D5.

227 [2007] EWHC 599 (Comm); E.ON's appeal against these directions to the CAT, arguing that they were excessive in scope and too uncertain to be valid, was withdrawn, Case 1076/2/5/07 *E.ON UK plc v ORR*, order of 7 January 2008; on the doctrine of severance in the English law of contract see *Chitty on Contracts* (Sweet & Maxwell, 32nd ed, 2015), paras 16-211–16-220.

228 Case 1099/1/2/08 [2009] CAT 14.

229 Ibid, para 222: however the CAT accepted that the time limit set for compliance with the directions was unrealistic: ibid, para 226; see also Case 1046/2/4/04 *Albion Water Ltd v Water Services Regulation Authority* (remedy) [2009] CAT 12, paras 37–39.

230 *Unfair pricing in respect of the supply of phenytoin sodium capsules in the UK*, CMA decision of 7 December 2016.

231 Ibid, paras 7.1–7.5 and Annex B.

232 Case 1274/1/12/16 (IR) *Flynn Pharma Ltd v CMA* [2017] CAT 1.

233 See *Enforcement*, para 2.2.

234 'Court' for this purpose is defined in Competition Act 1998, s 59(1).

235 Ibid, s 34.

236 *Enforcement*, para 2.9.

237 On the territorial scope of the Act see ch 12, 'The Extraterritorial Application of UK Competition Law', pp 508–512.

(E) Penalties

Section 36(1) of the Competition Act provides that a penalty may be imposed for an infringement of the Chapter I prohibition or Article 101 TFEU; section 36(2) provides correspondingly for an infringement of the Chapter II prohibition or Article 102 TFEU. Where more than one infringement has occurred, it is possible to impose one penalty for each infringement[238]. As a prerequisite for the imposition of a penalty section 36(3) requires that the CMA must be satisfied that the infringement has been committed intentionally or negligently[239]; it is sufficient to decide that the infringement was *either* intentional *or* negligent, without deciding which[240], and the distinction between intention and negligence goes, at most, to mitigation of the fine[241]. Intention may be deduced from internal documents or from deliberate concealment of the agreement or conduct in question[242]. The fact that a practice has not previously been found to infringe the competition rules does not mean that the infringement cannot be committed intentionally or negligently[243].

In fixing the level of a fine, the CMA is required by section 36(7A) to have regard to the seriousness of the infringement and the desirability of deterring both the infringing undertaking and others from infringing the Chapter I and II prohibitions and Articles 101 and 102 TFEU[244]. Other than in matters of legal principle there is limited precedent value in other penalty decisions; each case turns on its own facts[245].

The Competition Act does not specify a limitation period for the imposition or recovery of penalties. The CAT has held that neither the limitation period in Article 25 of Regulation 1/2003[246] nor the Limitation Act 1980[247] applies to the imposition of penalties under the Competition Act[248]. Penalties received by the CMA are paid into the Consolidated Fund[249]: that is to say they go to the Government and not, for example, to the victims of the anti-competitive behaviour. The latter may be able to obtain compensation through recourse to the courts[250]. Where a penalty has not been paid by the date required by the CMA it may be recovered through the courts as a civil debt[251]. An appeal to the CAT postpones the obligation to pay any penalty until the appeal is determined[252]; however the CAT normally adds interest to any penalty upheld[253].

[238] Case 1117/1/1/09 *GF Tomlinson v OFT* [2011] CAT 7, para 122.

[239] See *Enforcement*, paras 5.4–5.13.

[240] Case 1001/1/1/01 *Napp Pharmaceutical Holdings Ltd v Director General of Fair Trading* [2002] CAT 1, para 453; on the meaning of 'intentional' and 'negligent' see paras 456 and 457 of that judgment.

[241] Case 1009/1/1/02 *Aberdeen Journals Ltd v OFT* [2003] CAT 11, para 484.

[242] *Enforcement*, para 5.11.

[243] *Paroxetine*, CMA decision of 12 February 2016, para 11.8.

[244] Added by ERRA 2013, s 44, with effect from 1 April 2014.

[245] *Kier Group plc v OFT* [2011] CAT 3, para 116; see similarly *Eden Brown Ltd v OFT* [2011] CAT 8, paras 78 and 97.

[246] Case 1120/1/1/09 *Quarmby Construction Co Ltd v OFT* [2011] CAT 11, paras 43–48 (finding that there is a 'relevant difference' for the purposes of s 60 of the Competition Act), on which see ch 9, '"Governing Principles Clause": Section 60 of the Competition Act 1998', pp 387–392.

[247] Case 1120/1/1/09 *Quarmby Construction Co Ltd v OFT* [2011] CAT 11, paras 54–56.

[248] Note however that the Limitation Act 1980 does apply to the recovery of penalties as a civil debt under s 37 of the Competition Act.

[249] Competition Act 1998, s 36(9).

[250] See ch 8, 'EU Law: Actions for Damages', pp 308–324.

[251] Competition Act 1998, s 37.

[252] Ibid, s 46(4); there is no provision for the CMA to ask for security for the penalty (or for the costs of the appeal): it follows that, if an undertaking goes out of business in the meantime, the penalty may be irrecoverable.

[253] See the Competition Appeal Tribunal Rules 2015, SI 2015/1648, r 105(1); see eg Case 1001/1/1/01 *Napp Pharmaceutical Holdings Ltd v Director General of Fair Trading* [2002] CAT 1, paras 542–543; Case 1099/1/2/08 *National Grid Plc v Gas and Electricity Markets Authority* [2009] CAT 14, para 229(c); Cases 1114/1/1/09 etc *Kier Group plc v OFT* [2011] CAT 3, para 343.

(i) Maximum amount of a penalty

Section 36(8) provides that penalties may not exceed 10% of an undertaking's worldwide turnover in the business year preceding the CMA's decision[254]. The CMA imposed the maximum fine that could be imposed on Flynn Pharma in *Phenytoin*[255].

(ii) The *Guidance as to the appropriate amount of a penalty*

Guidance as to the appropriate amount of a penalty[256] ('the *Guidance on penalties*') has been published pursuant to section 38 of the Competition Act; the *Guidance* has been approved by the Secretary of State, as required by that provision[257]. Paragraph 1.4 of the *Guidance* sets out the CMA's policy objectives in setting the level of penalties: to reflect the seriousness of the infringement and to deter the infringing undertakings ('specific deterrence') and to deter other undertakings from engaging or continuing to engage in anti-competitive practices ('general deterrence').

The CAT must have regard to the *Guidance on penalties*[258] when setting the amount of a penalty. While neither the CMA nor the CAT is bound to follow the *Guidance* in all respects in every case, reasons must be given for any significant departure from it[259]. In *Kier v OFT* the CAT held that it will consider whether the final penalty is reasonable and proportionate having regard to those policy objectives[260].

Paragraph 1.17 explains that undertakings found to have infringed both UK and EU competition law will not be fined twice for the same anti-competitive effects[261].

(iii) The CMA's six-step approach

In determining the level of the penalty the CMA adopts a six-step approach[262]; the CMA must give reasons for its decision, including setting out the methodology whereby it reaches its conclusion[263]:

- **Step 1—starting point**[264]: the starting point is to apply a percentage of the 'relevant turnover' of the undertaking to be fined according to the seriousness of the infringement[265]; this reflects not only the seriousness of the infringement but also, by applying the percentage to turnover, the scale of the undertaking in the relevant market. The starting point is determined on a case-by-case basis but cannot exceed 30% of an undertaking's relevant turnover[266]. The starting point must reflect adequately the seriousness of the infringement and must secure specific and general

[254] See the Competition Act 1998 (Determination of Turnover for Penalties) Order 2000, SI 2000/309, as amended with effect from 1 May 2004 by SI 2004/1259.

[255] *Unfair pricing in respect of the supply of phenytoin sodium capsules in the UK*, CMA decision of 7 December 2016, para 7.145, on appeal Case 1275/1/12/17 *Flynn Pharma v CMA*, not yet decided.

[256] OFT 423, September 2012; earlier *Guidance* was published in March 2000 and in December 2004.

[257] *Guidance on penalties*, para 1.8.

[258] Competition Act 1998, s 38(8); the CAT considered its role in penalty appeals in Cases 1114/1/1/09 etc *Kier Group plc v OFT* [2011] CAT 3, paras 74–77 and in Case 1277/1/12/17 *Balmoral Tanks Ltd v CMA* [2017] CAT 23, para 134.

[259] *Argos Ltd and Littlewoods Ltd v OFT* and *JJB Sports plc v OFT* [2006] EWCA Civ 1318, para 161; the OFT gave reasons for departing from its *Guidance on penalties* in *Independent fee-paying schools*, OFT decision of 20 November 2006, paras 1424–1432.

[260] See Cases 1114/1/1/09 etc *Kier Group plc v OFT* [2011] CAT 3, para 175.

[261] For possible exceptions to this principle see *Guidance on penalties*, para 1.18.

[262] Ibid, para 2.1.

[263] Case 1061/1/1/06 *Makers UK Ltd v OFT* [2007] CAT 11, para 134.

[264] *Guidance on penalties*, paras 2.3–2.11.

[265] Ibid, para 2.3.

[266] Ibid, paras 2.5 and 2.11; relevant turnover for this purpose means the turnover in the relevant product and geographic markets affected by the infringement in the undertaking's last business year prior to the infringement: ibid, para 2.7; this gives effect to the judgment in Cases 1114/1/1/09 etc *Kier Group plc v OFT* [2011] CAT 3, paras 130–139 (a case dealing with the 2004 *Guidance*).

deterrence[267]. Hard-core cartel infringements and serious abuses of dominance are likely to be at the upper end of the range[268]. In determining the seriousness of an infringement the CMA will take a number of factors into consideration including the nature of the infringement and the effect of the anti-competitive behaviour on competitors, third parties and, most importantly, consumers[269]. In cases based on Articles 101 and/or 102 TFEU, effects in another Member State may be taken into account if that Member State expressly gives its consent[270]

- **Step 2—adjustment for duration**[271]: having established the starting point the CMA, at Step 2, may increase or, exceptionally, decrease[272] the penalty to take into account the duration of the infringement. Where the infringement lasts longer than one year the penalty may be increased by not more than the number of years of the infringement; the CMA may treat part of a year as a whole year, although in some cases a smaller multiplier has been applied[273]
- **Step 3—adjustment for aggravating and mitigating factors**[274]: at Step 3 the CMA will consider whether there are any aggravating and mitigating factors
- Aggravating factors include[275]:
  - persistent and repeated unreasonable behaviour that delays the CMA's enforcement action
  - an undertaking was a leader in, or the instigator of, the infringement
  - directors or senior managers were involved in the infringement
  - retaliatory or coercive action was taken against other undertakings in order to continue the infringement
  - the infringement was continued after the commencement of an investigation
  - repeated infringements by the same undertaking or undertakings in the same group (recidivism)
  - intentional rather than negligent infringement
  - retaliation against a leniency applicant
- Mitigating factors include[276]:
  - an undertaking acted under severe duress or pressure
  - genuine uncertainty on the part of an undertaking as to whether its agreement or conduct constituted an infringement
  - adequate steps having been taken with a view to ensuring compliance with competition law[277]

[267] *Guidance on penalties*, paras 2.5 and 2.11.

[268] Ibid, para 2.5; the CMA chose a starting point of 30% in *Unfair pricing in respect of the supply of phenytoin sodium capsules in the UK*, CMA decision of 7 December 2016, para 7.75, on appeal Case 1275/1/12/17 *Flynn Pharma v CMA*, not yet decided.

[269] Ibid, paras 2.4 and 2.6. [270] Ibid, para 2.10. [271] Ibid, para 2.12.

[272] Note Case 1032/1/1/04 *Apex Asphalt Paving Co Ltd v OFT* [2005] CAT 4, para 278: in the case of collusive tendering, the fact that a particular tendering process might take place over a short period does not necessarily mean that there should be a reduction of the penalty.

[273] See eg *Hasbro UK Ltd, Argos Ltd and Littlewoods Ltd*, OFT decision of 19 February 2003, para 323, where the OFT applied a multiplier of 1.2, as opposed to 2, where the duration of the infringement was in the region of 14½ months.

[274] *Guidance on penalties*, paras 2.13–2.15. [275] Ibid, para 2.14. [276] Ibid, para 2.15.

[277] See eg *Bathroom fittings sector: Ultra Finishing*, CMA decision of decision of 10 May 2016 (5%); *Online resale price maintenance in the commercial refrigeration sector: ITW Ltd*, CMA decision of 24 May 2016, paras 7.40–7.44 (reduction of 10%).

  - termination of the infringement as soon as the CMA intervenes
  - cooperation which enables the CMA's enforcement process to be concluded more effectively and/or speedily

- **Step 4—adjustment for specific deterrence and proportionality**[278]: at Step 4 the CMA will consider whether any adjustments should be made for specific deterrence (concerned with dissuading the undertaking on which the penalty is imposed from infringing competition law in the future) and proportionality. Increases for specific deterrence will generally be limited to cases in which an undertaking generates a significant proportion of its turnover outside the relevant market or where an undertaking has made gains from its behaviour that exceed the proposed penalty[279]. The CMA will also assess whether the proposed penalty is 'appropriate in the round'; a penalty may be decreased to ensure that it is not disproportionate[280]
- **Step 5—adjustment to prevent the maximum penalty being exceeded and to avoid double jeopardy**[281]: at Step 5 the CMA will adjust the penalty to ensure that the statutory maximum penalty of 10% of worldwide turnover is not exceeded[282]. If a fine has been imposed by the European Commission or by a court or competition authority in another Member State this must also be taken into account at Step 5 in order to avoid double jeopardy[283]
- **Step 6—application of reductions under the CMA's leniency programme and for settlement agreements**[284]: at Step 6 the CMA will reduce a penalty when it grants leniency and/or settlement applications. In exceptional circumstances, the CMA may also reduce a penalty for financial hardship[285]. The fact that a company is no longer trading and is either in administration or liquidation at the time of the decision does not, in itself, constitute financial hardship[286].

(iv) Immunity for small agreements and conduct of minor significance

Section 39, in conjunction with section 36(4), of the Competition Act confers immunity from penalties for infringing the Chapter I prohibition in the case of 'small agreements', other than price-fixing agreements[287], where the CMA is satisfied that an undertaking acted on the reasonable assumption that section 39 gave it immunity. A 'small agreement' is one where the combined turnover of the parties in the preceding calendar year was

278 *Guidance on penalties*, paras 2.16–2.20.

279 Ibid, para 2.17; see eg *Unfair pricing in respect of the supply of phenytoin sodium capsules in the UK*, CMA decision of 7 December 2016, paras 7.102–7.123 (increase of 400% for specific deterrence of Pfizer), on appeal Case 1276/1/12/17 *Pfizer v CMA*, not yet decided.

280 *Guidance on penalties*, para 2.20; the CMA decreased Ping's fine at Step 4 to reflect Ping's size and financial position and the limited impact of its infringement: CMA decision of 24 August 2017, paras 5.89–5.90, on appeal Case 1279/1/12/17 *Ping Europe Ltd v CMA*, not yet decided.

281 *Guidance on penalties*, paras 2.21–2.24.

282 See 'Maximum amount of a penalty', p 421 earlier in chapter; note that, prior to 1 May 2004, the maximum penalty under s 36(8) was calculated by reference to UK turnover rather than worldwide turnover, and that this may, in some cases, require a further adjustment of the penalty: see *Guidance on penalties*, para 2.22 and *Bid-rigging in the construction industry in England*, OFT decision of 21 September 2009, para VI.370 (p 1711).

283 *Guidance on penalties*, para 2.24. 284 Ibid, paras 2.25–2.27. 285 Ibid, para 2.27.

286 See eg *Online sales of posters and frames*, CMA decision of 12 August 2016, para 6.45 and *Conduct in the modelling sector*, CMA decision of 16 December 2016, para 5.99.

287 A price-fixing agreement for this purpose is defined in s 39(9) of the Act; see *Conduct in the ophthalmology sector*, CMA decision of 20 August 2015, para 5.16 ('price-fixing' includes minimum, non-binding recommended prices).

£20 million or less[288]. The *Mobility Scooters* cases[289] involved 'small agreements' and the parties therefore benefited from immunity under section 39. Provision is made by section 39(3)–(8) for the CMA to withdraw this immunity, subject to the observation of some basic procedures[290]. In August 2017 the CMA announced that it had withdrawn immunity from TGA Holdings Ltd, which it considered was likely to have infringed competition law by preventing retailers from freely advertising their prices[291]; the CMA subsequently announced that it would not be taking the case forward as TGA had taken several steps to address its concerns[292]. There is no immunity from penalties for agreements that infringe Article 101 TFEU, which is why section 39 refers only to 'partial' immunity in its heading.

Section 40 provides similar partial immunity for 'conduct of minor significance'. Conduct is of minor significance where the perpetrator's worldwide turnover in the preceding calendar year was £50 million or less[293]. Section 40(3)–(8) provides power for withdrawal of the immunity. There is no immunity from penalties for infringements of Article 102 TFEU[294].

Immunity provided by sections 39 and 40 does not prevent the CMA from taking other enforcement action, and the immunity does not prevent third parties from bringing damages actions[295]. This point is nicely illustrated by the case of *Burgess v OFT*[296]. The CAT found that Austin had abused a dominant position by refusing one of its competitors, Burgess, access to its crematorium. The CAT noted that Austin would not be subject to a penalty since its conduct was of minor significance under section 40 of the Act[297]. Burgess subsequently brought a 'follow-on' action for damages that was settled out of court[298]. Similarly in *Cardiff Bus* Cardiff Bus was found guilty of abusive conduct but, due to its turnover, it benefited from immunity under section 40[299]; subsequently, however, the CAT ordered Cardiff Bus to pay damages of £93,818 to 2 Travel for losses suffered as a result of the abuse[300].

(F) **Leniency**

A crucial tool in the detection of covert cartels has proved to be the policy of encouraging whistleblowers to approach the competition authorities with information about a cartel. Subject to a series of conditions, a 'whistleblower' can obtain immunity from civil and criminal penalties that might otherwise have been imposed. Furthermore, with effect from 9 March 2017, an immunity recipient is not jointly and severally liable in damages for the harm caused by a cartel[301]; it will normally be obliged to compensate only

[288] See the Competition Act 1998 (Small Agreements and Conduct of Minor Significance) Regulations 2000, SI 2000/262, reg 3.

[289] See *Roma-branded mobility scooters: prohibitions on online sales and online price advertising*, OFT decision of 5 August 2013, paras 4.5–4.6 and *Mobility scooters supplied by Pride Mobility Products Limited: prohibition on online advertising of prices below Pride's RRP price advertising*, OFT decision of 27 March 2014, paras 4.5–4.6.

[290] The CMA must give the parties or persons in respect of which the immunity is withdrawn written notice of its decision and must specify a date which gives them time to adjust: Competition Act 1998, ss 39(5), (8), 40(5), (8).

[291] CMA Press Release, 23 August 2017.

[292] CMA case closure statement, 19 October 2017.

[293] See the Competition Act 1998 (Small Agreements and Conduct of Minor Significance) Regulations 2000, SI 2000/262, reg 4.

[294] See eg *Unfair pricing in respect of the supply of phenytoin sodium capsules in the UK*, CMA decision of 7 December 2016, paras 7.48–7.50.

[295] *Enforcement*, para 5.20.

[296] Case 1044/2/1/04 *JJ Burgess & Sons v OFT* [2005] CAT 25.

[297] Ibid, paras 117–118.

[298] Case 1088/5/7/07, order of 18 February 2008.

[299] *Abuse of a dominant position by Cardiff Bus*, OFT decision of 18 November 2008.

[300] Case 1178/5/7/11 *2 Travel Group plc (in liquidation) v Cardiff City Transport Services Ltd* [2012] CAT 19 (awarding £33,818.79 in compensatory damages, plus interest, and £60,000 in exemplary damages).

[301] Unless the victim is unable to obtain full compensation from other cartelists.

its own customers[302]. A parent company may make a leniency application on behalf of a subsidiary[303].

There are two sets of guidance on the CMA's leniency policy: the *Guidance as to the appropriate amount of a penalty*[304] deals with civil cases under the Competition Act 1998 and *Applications for leniency and no-action in cartel cases* ('*Leniency and no-action guidance*')[305] deals with both civil and criminal cases. The *Leniency and no-action guidance* supplements, but does not replace, the earlier guidance; it provides a comprehensive view of the current position and is the suggested starting point for anyone needing guidance on the subject. A pro-forma corporate leniency agreement and pro-forma no-action letters as well as a checklist for conducting internal inquiries before making a leniency application are included in the Annexes to the *Leniency and no-action guidance*. The CMA has published an information note on the handling of leniency applications within the regulated sectors: the essential rule is that in the first instance contact should be made with the CMA[306].

(i) Terminology

The *Leniency and no-action guidance*[307] sets out the terminology of the subject, including the following:

- 'leniency': this is a 'catch all' term that refers to all the types of immunity and reduced fines that are available under the *Guidance*
- 'corporate immunity': this refers to immunity granted to undertakings from penalties for infringing the Chapter I prohibition or Article 101 TFEU
- 'criminal immunity': this refers to immunity granted to individuals from prosecution for the cartel offence
- 'blanket criminal immunity': this refers to immunity granted to *all* current and former employees and directors of an undertaking from prosecution for the cartel offence
- 'individual immunity': this refers to criminal immunity granted to one or more individuals but not as part of blanket criminal immunity
- 'Type A immunity': this refers to a situation where an undertaking is granted *guaranteed* corporate immunity and all of its current and former employees and directors who cooperate with the CMA are granted 'blanket' criminal immunity for cartel activity; Type A immunity is available where the undertaking was the first to apply and there was no pre-existing civil and/or criminal investigation into such activity
- 'Type B immunity': this refers to a situation where the type of immunity available under Type A is granted on a *discretionary* rather than an automatic basis. Type B immunity is available where the undertaking was the first to apply but there was already a pre-existing civil and/or criminal investigation into the cartel activity

302 Competition Act 1998, Sch 8A, para 15, inserted by the Claims in respect of Loss or Damage arising from Competition Infringements (Competition Act 1998 and Other Enactments (Amendment)) Regulations 2017, SI 2017/385, Sch 1, paras 14–16.

303 *Collusive tendering for mastic asphalt flat-roofing contracts in Scotland*, decision of 15 March 2005, para 396.

304 OFT 423, September 2012.

305 OFT 1495, July 2013.

306 Arrangements for the handling of leniency applications in the regulated sectors, CMA Information Note of 3 November 2017, available at www.gov.uk/cma.

307 See Table A and the Glossary of Terms of the *Leniency and no-action guidance*.

- 'Type B leniency': this refers to a situation where an undertaking is granted any level of reduction of, but not immunity from, a penalty in a cartel case. As in the case of Type B immunity, Type B leniency arises where the undertaking was the first to apply but there was already an investigation under way into the cartel in question
- 'Type C leniency': this refers to a situation in which a reduction in the penalty of up to 50% is granted where the undertaking was not the first to apply whether or not there was already a pre-existing civil and/or criminal investigation into the cartel.

(ii) Key features of the UK leniency system

Paragraph 1.8 sets out the key features of the UK leniency system, including:

- informal guidance: the CMA will provide confidential guidance on a no-names basis about 'hypothetical' cases when asked
- a 'marker system': markers will be available while the scope of leniency is agreed, thereby enabling an undertaking to preserve its position in a queue of leniency applicants
- guarantees of criminal immunity: criminal immunity is available for all cooperating current and former employees and directors in Type A immunity cases
- availability of immunity or a reduced penalty where a leniency applicant is the first to approach the CMA but there is a pre-existing investigation: this refers to Type B immunity or Type B leniency cases
- availability of reduced sanctions where a leniency applicant is not the first to apply: this refers to Type C leniency for undertakings and the possibility of individual immunity for cooperating current and former employees and directors
- a commitment not to apply for a 'Competition Disqualification Order'[308]: no disqualification order will be sought against any director who benefits from leniency in respect of the activities to which the grant of leniency relates
- oral applications: applications do not always have to be in writing
- applications may be made by undertakings or individuals
- a 'high threshold for coercion': the CMA imposes a high bar, both as to the circumstances and standard of proof, in which an undertaking will be found to be a coercer and therefore ineligible for corporate and/or criminal immunity.

Another notable feature of the UK leniency system is that it applies to resale price maintenance as well as horizontal cartel activity[309]. The *Leniency and no-action guidance* adds that leniency might be available where vertical behaviour might be said to facilitate horizontal cartel activity[310].

(iii) Eligibility for leniency

The *Leniency and no-action guidance* explains that five conditions must be satisfied for an applicant to obtain leniency:

- **Admission:** the applicant must admit that it infringed the competition law prohibitions in the Competition Act and/or TFEU (in the case of undertakings) or is guilty of the cartel offence (in the case of individuals)
- **Information:** the applicant must provide the CMA with all non-legally privileged information, documents and evidence available to it regarding the cartel

[308] See 'Company director disqualification', pp 446–448 later in chapter.

[309] *Leniency and no-action guidance*, paras 4.44–4.48.

[310] Ibid, para 2.3.

- **Cooperation:** the applicant must maintain continuous and complete cooperation throughout the CMA's investigation and during any subsequent criminal or civil proceedings
- **Termination:** the applicant must refrain from participating any further in the cartel once it has blown the whistle unless the CMA directs otherwise[311]
- **Absence of coercion:** the immunity applicant must not have 'coerced' another undertaking to participate in the cartel; this condition does not apply to Type C leniency.

The CMA will not accept applications for leniency after it has issued a statement of objections in relation to a cartel[312].

(a) Type A immunity

To qualify for Type A immunity, the applicant must be the first to provide the CMA with evidence of cartel activity and there was no pre-existing civil and/or criminal investigation into such activity; immunity will not be available if the CMA already has sufficient evidence to prove the cartel[313]. The CMA must also be satisfied that the five conditions for the grant of leniency are, and continue to be, met[314].

(b) Type B immunity/leniency

Type B cases often arise as a result of the CMA conducting an inspection at an undertaking's premises. Type B applicants must be the first to provide evidence of the cartel and thereby add 'significant value' to the CMA's investigation[315]; they must also satisfy the conditions set out earlier on eligibility for leniency[316]. The grant of immunity or a reduced penalty in Type B cases is discretionary: it depends on the CMA's assessment of where the public interest lies in a particular case[317]. The CMA has insufficient experience in granting Type B leniency to give guidance about the percentage reductions that might be available, but it could be as much as 100%[318]; the CMA reduced the fine imposed on the Type B leniency applicant in *Supply of products to the furniture industry (drawer wraps)*[319] by 100%.

(c) Type C leniency

Type C leniency is available where another undertaking has already blown the whistle, or where an undertaking has coerced another to participate in cartel activity; the other four leniency conditions must also be satisfied[320]. Discounts in Type C cases are typically in the range of 25 to 50%[321]. In determining the amount of any discount the applicant's position in a queue of leniency is not decisive[322]. Instead the CMA will carry out a balancing exercise, weighing up the benefit of receiving additional evidence against the disbenefit of granting leniency to multiple parties in a single investigation, taking into account the evidence the CMA already has, the probative value of the evidence provided and the overall level of cooperation[323]. In *Galvanised steel tanks*[324] the CMA reduced the fine imposed

311 Ibid, paras 4.44–4.48.

312 Ibid, para 2.41; nor will the CMA accept immunity applications from an individual after he or she has been charged with a cartel offence.

313 Ibid, para 2.9. 314 Ibid, para 2.11. 315 Ibid, para 2.15. 316 Ibid, para 2.17.

317 Ibid, para 2.18; see also para 2.23. 318 Ibid, para 6.9.

319 CMA decision of 27 March 2017, paras 2.38 and 6.7.

320 *Leniency and no-action guidance*, paras 2.24 and 2.26. 321 Ibid, para 6.9.

322 Ibid, para 6.10. 323 Ibid, paras 2.27 and 6.8.

324 *Galvanised steel tanks for water storage main cartel infringement*, CMA decision of 19 December 2016, paras 5.59–5.60.

on a Type C applicant by 30% because it had provided 'significant added value' to the civil and criminal investigations, in particular by limiting its internal investigations, providing its employees with separate legal representation and support and by making its witnesses available for interview.

(d) The coercer test

Type A and Type B immunity are not available to an undertaking that has coerced another firm or firms into taking part in cartel activity. The *Leniency and no-action guidance* does not provide a definition of coercion, but indicates that there must be evidence of 'clear, positive and ultimately successful steps' from an undertaking to force another to join the cartel. Physical violence or threats of physical violence and strong economic pressure such as the organisation of a collective trade boycott of a small firm that might cause it to exit the market might be examples of coercion[325]. The *Guidance* notes that neither corporate immunity nor criminal immunity has been refused because of coercion[326].

(iv) **Actions before applying for leniency**

The *Guidance* sets out the considerations that firms, individuals and their advisers should consider before applying for leniency: for example seeking confidential guidance from the CMA[327]; how to conduct internal investigations prior to an approach to the CMA for leniency[328]; and maintaining confidentiality and securing evidence[329].

(v) **Checking the availability of leniency and initial application**

The *Guidance* explains that individuals or undertakings may approach the CMA to ascertain the availability of Type A immunity[330]. It also describes the 'marker system'[331] and the 'application package' of information to be submitted by leniency applicants[332].

(vi) **Cooperation throughout investigation**

A leniency applicant is expected to maintain continuous and complete cooperation throughout the CMA's investigation. This duty implies that an applicant must adopt a 'constructive approach' and genuinely assist the CMA[333] and not, for example, seek to deny involvement in the cartel[334]. Leniency applicants are required to disclose any information which is capable of having some reasonable bearing on the CMA's investigation[335]. The *Guidance* also explains the investigative steps that the CMA may wish to carry out with the cooperation of the leniency applicant such as interviewing witnesses and conducting physical searches of relevant premises[336].

(vii) **Leniency and no-action agreements**

Chapter 6 of the *Guidance* describes the timing and process for signing leniency and no-action agreements[337].

[325] *Leniency and no-action guidance*, para 2.52.
[326] Ibid, paras 2.51 and 2.59.
[327] Ibid, paras 3.3–3.7.
[328] Ibid, paras 3.8–3.14.
[329] Ibid, paras 3.24–3.28.
[330] Ibid, paras 4.2–4.6.
[331] Ibid, paras 4.7–4.14.
[332] Ibid, paras 4.15–4.21.
[333] Ibid, para 5.4.
[334] Ibid, paras 5.9–5.11; the CMA does not exclude the making of certain limited representations commenting on specific elements of its case.
[335] Ibid, paras 5.12–5.19.
[336] Ibid, paras 5.25–5.29.
[337] Standard form leniency and no-action agreements are annexed to the *Leniency and no-action guidance*.

(viii) **Disclosure and information**

Chapter 7 of the *Guidance* deals with the disclosure of leniency information. Such information may be disclosed in a statement of objections under the Competition Act or during a prosecution of a cartel offence. Neither a court nor the CAT may make a disclosure order in respect of a 'cartel leniency statement'[338], whether or not it has been withdrawn[339]; such statements are not admissible in evidence in private actions[340].

(ix) **Other issues relating to criminal proceedings**

Chapter 8 of the *Guidance* will be discussed later in the context of the cartel offence under the Enterprise Act 2002[341].

(x) **Other procedural issues: leniency plus/penalties**

Chapter 9 of the *Guidance* describes both the CMA's 'leniency plus' policy and the CMA's method of calculating penalties for leniency applicants. If a firm is already cooperating with an investigation in respect of one cartel, and comes forward with information that entitles it to total immunity in relation to a second cartel, it may receive 'leniency plus' in the form of an additional reduction in the penalty to be applied in relation to the first cartel[342]. The *Leniency and no-action guidance* indicates that reductions under this policy are not likely to be high and will depend on factors such as the amount of effort by the applicant to uncover the second cartel and whether the CMA would have been likely to discover the second cartel in any event[343].

As far as penalties are concerned, the CMA will not calculate penalties for Type A or Type B immunity applicants[344]. Where a Type B or Type C applicant has provided evidence of previously unknown facts relevant to the infringement, the CMA will not take account of that evidence when calculating the penalty[345].

(xi) **Bad faith/withdrawal of leniency/revocation of no-action letters**

Chapter 10 explains the circumstances in which a leniency application might fail due to a failure to cooperate with the CMA. Paragraphs 10.1 to 10.5 discuss the idea of bad faith, whereby an applicant taking positive steps to hinder an investigation going beyond non-cooperation—which can even lead to prosecution of individuals under sections 43 and 44 of the Competition Act and section 201 of the Enterprise Act. The *Guidance* also explains the CMA's approach to withdrawing a leniency marker and revoking a leniency agreement or no-action letter.

(G) **Settlements**

The CMA operates a system of settlements[346] which is designed to achieve efficiencies through the adoption of a streamlined administrative procedure, resulting in the early

338 Defined by Competition Act 1998, Sch 8A, para 4(4).

339 Competition Act 1998, Sch 8A, para 28(b); see also *Leniency and no-action guidance*, para 7.14.

340 Competition Act 1998, Sch 8A, para 32(2).

341 See 'The cartel offence', pp 437–446 later in chapter.

342 See *Guidance on penalties*, OFT 423, September 2012, paras 3.21–3.22; leniency plus was awarded in *Collusive tendering for mastic asphalt flat-roofing contracts in Scotland*, OFT decision of 15 March 2005, para 410, in *Tobacco*, OFT decision of 15 April 2010, para 2.93 and in *Galvanised steel tanks for water storage: main cartel infringement*, CMA decision of 19 December 2016, para 5.61.

343 *Leniency and no-action guidance*, para 9.3. 344 Ibid, para 9.5. 345 Ibid, para 9.6.

346 The Competition Act 1998 (Competition and Markets Authority's Rules) 2014, SI 2014/458, r 9; *Guidance on penalties*, OFT 423, September 2012, paras 2.1 and 2.26; for comment see also Lawrence and Sansom 'The Increasing Use of Administrative Settlement Procedures in UK and EC Competition Investigations' [2007] Comp Law 163 and Burrows and Gilbert 'OFT Competition Act Enforcement: Key Developments over the First Decade' [2010] Comp Law 178.

adoption of infringement decisions and/or resource savings. Once the CMA considers that the evidential standard for issuing a statement of objections is met, it *may* enter into discussions with the defendants about the possibility of a settlement[347]. To be eligible for settlement a defendant must[348]:

- make a 'clear and unequivocal' admission of the infringement
- terminate its involvement in the infringement
- confirm that it will pay a penalty set at a maximum amount, including a discount for settlement and
- agree to procedural cooperation with the CMA.

If the CMA is satisfied that these conditions are met, and that the case is suitable for settlement[349], the CMA will agree that the settling parties should pay a lower penalty than would otherwise have been imposed. The 'settlement discount' is capped at 20% if settlement occurs before the CMA has issued a statement of objections and 10% thereafter[350]. This process should be distinguished from applications for leniency whereby full immunity or a reduced penalty are allowed in return for the provision of information to the CMA that enables it to investigate a case[351]. The *Guidance on the CMA's investigation procedures in Competition Act 1998 cases* describes the procedure for settling cases[352].

Table 10.2 provides details of cases in which the competition authorities have settled cases under the Competition Act between 6 February 2015, the cut-off date for the eighth edition of this book, and 8 December 2017.

(H) The penalty provisions in practice

By 8 December 2017 penalties had been imposed in 47 cases under the Chapter I and Chapter II prohibitions and Articles 101 and 102 TFEU.

(i) Statistical analysis

The total amount of the penalties imposed under the Competition Act (and Articles 101 and 102) by 8 December 2017 was £1.239 billion before reductions for leniency and £1.226 billion after leniency. On appeal to the CAT (and the Court of Appeal) some of the penalties were reduced. There have been some high-profile cases where considerable fines were imposed[353]. The *Airline Passenger Fuel Surcharges* case is of interest as BA ultimately agreed to pay a fine of £58.5 million, which is the largest fine imposed in the UK for a single infringement of the Chapter I prohibition and Article 101(1) TFEU[354]. In *Phenytoin* a fine of £84.2 million was imposed on Pfizer for excessive pricing, which is the highest fine imposed for a breach of the Chapter II prohibition[355].

347 *Guidance on the CMA's investigation procedures in Competition Act 1998 cases*, paras 14.4 and 14.6.

348 Ibid, paras 14.7–14.8. 349 Ibid, paras 14.5–14.6. 350 Ibid, para 14.27.

351 See 'Leniency', pp 424–429 earlier in chapter.

352 *Guidance on the CMA's investigation procedures in Competition Act 1998 cases*, paras 14.10–14.23.

353 See eg *Tobacco*, decision of 15 April 2010: fines of £225 million were imposed but most of the decision was annulled on appeal: see ch 10 n 610 later in chapter.

354 OFT decision of 19 April 2012; BA originally agreed to pay a fine of £121.5 million in 2007, but the fine was re-calculated following earlier abortive criminal proceedings and subsequent CAT decisions on penalties.

355 CMA decision of 7 December 2016, on appeal Case 1276/1/12/17 *Pfizer v CMA*, not yet decided.

Table 10.2 Table of settlements

Case name	Date of decision	Amount of the penalty and type of Infringement	Amount of penalty (before and after settlement)
Property sales and letting organisations	08.05.15	Infringement of the Chapter I prohibition	£852,500 (before) £735,000 (after)
Private ophthalmology	20.08.15	Infringement of the Chapter I prohibition and Article 101 TFEU	£450,000 (before) £382,500 (after)
Online resale price maintenance in the bathroom fittings sector	10.05.16	Infringement of the Chapter I prohibition and/or Article 101 TFEU	£983,335 (before) £786,668 (after)
Online resale price maintenance in the commercial refrigeration sector	24.05.16	Infringement of Chapter I prohibition and Article 101 TFEU	£2.87 million (before) £2.3 million (after)
Online sales of posters and frames	12.08.16	Infringement of Chapter 1 prohibition Note: company disqualification undertaking, 01.12.16	£ 204,214 (before) £163,371 (after)
Galvanised steel tanks: main cartel	19.12.16	Infringement of the Chapter I prohibition and Article 101 TFEU	£3.36 million (before) £2.6 million (after)
Supply of products to the furniture industry (drawer wraps)	27.03.17	Infringement of Chapter I prohibition and Article 101 TFEU	£1.88 million (before) £1.5 million (after)
Supply of products to the furniture industry (drawer fronts)	27.03.17	Infringement of Chapter I prohibition and Article 101 TFEU	£1.64 million (before) £1.3 million (after)
Online resale price maintenance in the light fittings sector	03.05.17	Infringement of Chapter I prohibition and/or Article 101 TFEU	3.45 million (before) £2.7 million (after)
Residential estate agent services	31.05.17	Infringement of Chapter I prohibition **Note: hybrid settlement**	£457,541 (before) £370,084 (after)

Table 10.3 Table of penalties

Decision	Date of the decision	Amount of the penalty and type of infringement	Amount of the penalty after appeal to the CAT
Restrictive arrangements preventing estate and letting agents from advertising their fees in a local newspaper	08.05.15	**£735,000** Infringement of Chapter I prohibition and Article 101 TFEU	No appeal
Conduct in the ophthalmology sector	20.08.15	**£382,500** Infringement of Chapter I prohibition and Article 101 TFEU	No appeal
Paroxetine	12.02.16	**£44.99 million** Infringement of the Chapter I and II prohibitions and Article 101 TFEU	Article 267 reference to the Court of Justice[1]
Online resale price maintenance in the commercial refrigeration sector	24.05.16	**£2.2 million** Infringement of Chapter 1 prohibition and Article 101 TFEU **Note: settlement**	No appeal
Online sales of posters and frames	12.08.16	**£163,371** Infringement of Chapter 1 prohibition **Note: settlement** **Note: company director disqualification undertaking, 01.12.16**	No appeal
Phenytoin	07.12.16	**Fine on Pfizer of £84.2 million and on Flynn of £5.2 million** **Note: penalty notice to Pfizer Ltd, 12.04.16: £10,000** Two infringements of Chapter II prohibition and Article 102 TFEU	On appeal[2]
Conduct in the modelling sector	16.12.16	**£1.53 million** Infringement of Chapter I prohibition and Article 101 TFEU	No appeal

(*Continued*)

Table 10.3 *Continued*

Decision	Date of the decision	Amount of the penalty and type of infringement	Amount of the penalty after appeal to the CAT
Galvanised steel tanks: main cartel	19.12.16	**£2.6 million** Infringement of the Chapter I prohibition and Article 101 TFEU **Note: settlement**	No appeal
Galvanised steel tanks: information exchange	19.12.16	**£130,000** Infringement of the Chapter I prohibition and Article 101 TFEU	Upheld on appeal[3]
East Midlands International Airport/ Prestige Parking Ltd (CAA)	17.01.17	**£12.5 million** (before leniency) **£0** (after leniency) Infringement of Chapter I prohibition	No appeal
Supply of products to the furniture industry (drawer wraps)	27.03.17	**£1.5 million** Infringement of Chapter I prohibition and Article 101 TFEU **Note: settlement**	No appeal
Supply of products to the furniture industry (drawer fronts)	27.03.17	**£1.3 million** Infringement of Chapter I prohibition and Article 101 TFEU **Note: settlement**	No appeal
Online resale price maintenance in the light fittings sector	03.05.17	**£2.7 million** Infringement of Chapter I prohibition and Article 101 TFEU **Note: settlement**	No appeal
Residential estate agent services	31.05.17	**£370,084** Infringement of Chapter I prohibition and Article 101 TFEU **Note: hybrid settlement** **Note: company director disqualification undertaking, 10.4.18**	No appeal

[1] Cases 1252/1/12/16 etc *GlaxoSmithKline plc v CMA* [2018] CAT 4; see also the order of 27 March 2018.
[2] Case 1276/1/12/17 *Pfizer Inc v CMA* and Case No 1275/1/12/17 *Flynn Pharma Ltd v CMA*, not yet decided.
[3] Case 1277/1/12/17 *Balmoral Tanks Ltd v CMA* [2017] CAT 23.

(ii) Appeals against decisions imposing penalties

There have been numerous appeals to the CAT in relation to the penalties imposed by the OFT for infringements of the Competition Act. Clearly, when fines are imposed of the magnitude of those handed down in *Phenytoin* there is every incentive to appeal to the CAT in the hope of a reduction. On appeal the CAT may impose a fine or revoke or vary the fines imposed by the CMA[356]. The CAT's practice has been to review the OFT's application of the *Guidance on penalties* and then to make its own assessment of the level of the penalty on the basis of a 'broad brush' approach, taking the case as a whole[357]. The CAT has emphasised that the policy objectives of the Competition Act will not be achieved unless the Tribunal is prepared to uphold severe penalties for serious infringements[358]. In some cases the CAT decided not to interfere with the OFT's determination[359]; however the CAT has amended the OFT's decisions on penalties on several occasions, usually downwards[360] but on one occasion upwards[361]. The CAT's approach can be seen, for example, in *Construction*[362] in which the penalty of £129.2 million imposed by the OFT was reduced by the CAT to £63.9 million. The CAT held that the penalties imposed by the OFT for 'simple' cover pricing were excessive given, in particular, the nature of the infringement and the harm it was likely to cause, and the general mitigation resulting from the perceptions of legitimacy in the construction industry[363].

In *National Grid* the CAT reduced the penalty from £41.6 million to £30 million to reflect the fact that the Gas and Electricity Markets Authority had been closely involved in discussions with National Grid that had led to the infringing agreements[364]; the Court of Appeal further reduced the fine to £15 million for the same reason[365]. In *Interclass v OFT*[366] the Court of Appeal said that penalty appeals to it are unlikely to be successful unless the CAT erred in principle or the penalty was clearly disproportionate or discriminatory[367].

(iii) Aggravating factors

In *Genzyme* the OFT considered that the fact that Genzyme had committed a further infringement after the OFT had begun its investigation into Genzyme's pricing practices was an aggravating factor[368]. In the first *Hasbro* case[369] the OFT increased Hasbro's fine by 10% at Step 4 because senior management were aware of the infringement and because the resale price maintenance took place on Hasbro's initiative[370].

[356] Competition Act 1998, Sch 8, para 3(2)(b).

[357] The English Court of Appeal has endorsed this approach: *Argos Ltd v OFT* [2006] EWCA Civ 1318, para 163.

[358] Case 1001/1/1/01 *Napp Pharmaceutical Holdings Ltd v Director General of Fair Trading* [2002] CAT 1, para 502.

[359] See eg Cases 1032 and 1033/1/1/04 *Apex Asphalt and Paving Co Ltd v OFT* [2005] CAT 4 and Case 1067/1/1/06 *Achilles Paper Group Ltd v OFT* [2006] CAT 24.

[360] Case 1001/1/1/01 *Napp Pharmaceutical Holdings Ltd v Director General of Fair Trading* [2002] CAT 1, paras 533–534; Case 1009/1/1/02 *Aberdeen Journals Ltd v OFT* [2003] CAT 11, paras 491–499; Case 1016/1/1/03 *Genzyme Ltd v OFT* [2005] CAT 32, paras 700–708; Cases 1014 and 1015/1/1/03 *Argos Ltd v OFT* [2005] CAT 13; Cases 1019–1022/1/1/03 *JJB Sports Plc v OFT* [2005] CAT 22.

[361] See 'The CAT can increase penalties', p 435 later in chapter.

[362] Cases 1114/1/1/09 etc *Kier Group plc v OFT* [2011] CAT 3.

[363] Ibid, paras 92–118.

[364] Case 1099/1/2/08 *National Grid plc v Gas and Electricity Markets Authority* [2009] CAT 14, paras 201–220.

[365] *National Grid plc v Gas and Electricity Markets Authority* [2010] EWCA Civ 114, paras 90–115.

[366] [2012] EWCA Civ 1056.

[367] Ibid, para 59.

[368] OFT decision of 27 March 2003, para 436.

[369] OFT decision of 28 November 2002.

[370] Ibid, paras 89–92; the OFT increased the fine imposed on Royal Bank of Scotland by 10% for instigating the infringement in *Loan Pricing*: see OFT decision of 20 January 2011, paras 385–388.

In several cases[371] the fines were increased by between 5 and 20% on undertakings whose senior management had been involved in the infringements. In *Construction* the OFT increased a fine by 15% because the company had paid an individual to engage in cover pricing[372].

(iv) The CAT can increase penalties

The CAT has power to increase as well as to decrease a penalty[373]. In *Football Shirts* the CAT increased the penalty on one of the appellants, Allsports, by £170,000 because Allsports had been less cooperative than the OFT had thought[374].

(v) Infringement decisions in which no penalty was imposed

There have been occasions when the OFT (now CMA) found an infringement but decided not to impose a penalty. In *Northern Ireland Livestock and Auctioneers' Association*[375] the OFT decided not to impose a penalty on the Association which had recommended to its members a standard commission that should be paid by purchasers of livestock at Northern Ireland cattle marts, since the recommendation was publicised, there was no attempt to conceal it and since the beef industry in Northern Ireland had been badly hit by the unfortunate combination of 'mad cow' disease and foot and mouth disease[376]. In *Lladró Comercial*[377] no penalty was imposed on Lladró, despite a finding that it had fixed the retail selling price of its merchandise, since the European Commission had sent a comfort letter to Lladró which it could reasonably have interpreted as suggesting that its agreements did not infringe the Competition Act[378].

6. The Cartel Offence and Company Director Disqualification

The UK Government stated in a White Paper in 2001[379] that UK policy towards cartels should be made tougher, including by provision for the punishment of individuals. The Enterprise Act 2002 introduced two provisions designed to encourage individuals to ensure compliance with competition law[380]. First, Part 6 of the Act established the 'cartel offence', the commission of which can lead, on indictment, to a term of imprisonment of up to five years and/or an unlimited fine[381]. Secondly, the Act introduced the possibility of company directors being disbarred from office for a period of up to 15 years where they

[371] *Construction Bid-rigging*, OFT decision of 21 September 2009, paras VI.301–VI.314 (pp 1696–1698) (increase of 5–10%); *Construction Recruitment Forum*, OFT decision of 29 September 2009, paras 5.311–5.334 (increase of 5–15%); *Airline Passenger Fuel Surcharges*, OFT decision of 19 April 2012, para 447 (increase of 20%); *Online resale price maintenance in the bathroom fittings sector*, CMA decision of 10 May 2016, paras 7.34–7.37 (increase of 10%); *Supply of products to the furniture industry (drawer wraps)*, CMA decision of 27 March 2017, para 6.27 (increase of 15%).

[372] OFT decision of 21 September 2009, paras VI.295–VI.299 (p 1695); see similarly para IV.4424 (p 1197).

[373] Competition Act 1998, Sch 8, para 3(2)(b).

[374] Cases 1019–1022/1/1/03 *JJB Sports Plc & Allsports Ltd v OFT* [2005] CAT 22, paras 208–235.

[375] OFT decision of 3 February 2003.

[376] Ibid, para 72; see similarly Case T-86/95 *Compagnie Générale Maritime v Commission* EU:T:2002:50, para 481, where the General Court decided that no fine should be imposed on a cartel, among other reasons, because it was not secret but was widely known to exist.

[377] OFT decision of 31 March 2003. [378] Ibid, para 124.

[379] *Productivity and Enterprise—A World Class Competition Regime* Cm 5233 (2001), available at www.nationalarchives.gov.uk.

[380] Some types of cartel activity might also infringe s 4 of the Fraud Act 2006: see Corker and Smith, arguing against the application of the Fraud Act to price fixing, in 'Cartels: Who's Liable?' (2007) 157 New Law Journal 1593.

[381] Enterprise Act 2002, s 190(1).

knew, or ought to have known, that their company was guilty of an infringement of EU or UK competition law[382]. These important provisions attempt to address the problem that the imposition of fines—even very substantial ones—on undertakings may not have a sufficiently deterrent effect, especially where the cost of the fines is simply transferred to customers through higher prices; and that if a fine is so large that it results in the insolvency and liquidation of an undertaking, this will result in the loss of a competitor from the market, a somewhat perverse achievement for a system of competition law[383]. The criminal sanction is an important feature of US law on cartels: there have been many high-profile cases in recent years in which senior executives of major companies have had to serve terms of imprisonment[384]. Other countries have also introduced or strengthened criminal sanctions against individuals for cartel activity[385].

The Government's consultation on *Options for reforming the UK competition regime* of 2011[386] found that the deterrent effect of the cartel offence had been weaker than intended. The Government considered that the need to prove dishonesty[387], a key feature of the original cartel offence, may be making it unduly difficult to prosecute cases successfully. It therefore recommended that the requirement to prove dishonesty should be removed; and that the offence should not apply to agreements made openly. These proposals were contentious[388]: some commentators objected to them because they considered dishonesty conveyed the seriousness of the cartel offence; others felt that dishonesty is an established concept of criminal law that is understood by juries. The Government listened to these arguments but rejected them. Its proposals were effected by the ERRA, which introduced three important changes to the cartel offence. First, it removed the requirement that

382 Ibid, s 204.

383 For discussion of criminalisation, both generally and as a matter of UK law, see Hammond and Penrose 'Proposed criminalisation of cartels in the UK', OFT 365, November 2001; OECD *Cartel Sanctions against Individuals* (2003); MacCulloch 'Honesty, Morality and the Cartel Offence' (2007) 28 ECLR 355; Whelan 'A Principled Argument for Personal Criminal Sanctions as Punishment under EC Cartel Law' (2007) 4 Competition Law Review 7; Stephan 'The UK Cartel Offence: Lame Duck or Black Mamba', Centre for Competition Policy Working Paper No 08-19 (November 2008); Kane *The Law of Criminal Cartels: Practice and Procedure* (Oxford University Press, 2009); Rodger (ed) *Ten Years of UK Competition Law Reform* (Dundee University Press, 2010), chs 10–11; Beaton-Wells and Ezrachi (eds) *Criminalising Cartels* (Hart, 2011); Whelan 'Legal Certainty and Cartel Criminalisation within the EU Member States' (2012) 71 Cambridge Law Journal 677; Whelan 'Improving Criminal Cartel Enforcement in the UK: The Case for the Adoption of BIS's "Option 4"' (2012) European Competition Journal 589; Furse *The Criminal Law of Competition in the UK and in the US* (Edward Elgar, 2012); Wardhaugh *Cartels, Markets and Crime* (Cambridge University Press, 2014); Whelan *The Criminalization of European Cartel Enforcement* (Oxford University Press, 2014); Jones and Williams 'The UK Response to the Global Effort Against Cartels: Is Criminalization Really the Solution?' (2014) 2 Journal of Antitrust Enforcement 100; Galloway 'Securing the Legitimacy of Individual Sanctions in UK Competition Law' (2017) 40 World Competition 121.

384 See ch 13, 'Recent action against cartels around the world', pp 523–524.

385 See eg the Trade Practices Amendment (Cartel Conduct and Other Measures) Act 2009 in Australia; the Competition Amendment Act 2009 in South Africa; the Federal Law of Economic Competition in 2011 in Mexico; and the Competition (Amendment) Act 2012 in Ireland; Austria, Germany, Hungary, Poland and Italy apply criminal penalties to bid-rigging offences.

386 *A Competition Regime for Growth: A Consultation on Options for Reform*, March 2011.

387 The test for determining dishonesty was set out by the Court of Appeal in *R v Ghosh* [1982] QB 1053; the Supreme Court held in 2017 that part of the test set out in *Ghosh* is wrong in law and should no longer be applied: *Ivey v Genting Casinos (UK) Ltd t/a Crockfords* [2017] UKSC 67, paras 52–75.

388 See eg Stephan 'How Dishonesty Killed the Cartel Offence' [2011] Criminal Law Review 446; Bailin 'Doing Away With Dishonesty' [2011] Comp Law 169; Wardhaugh 'Closing the Deterrence Gap: Individual Liability, the Cartel Offence and the BIS Consultation' [2011] Comp Law 175; the series of essays on the cartel offence in issue 8(3) of the European Competition Journal in 2012; Summers 'What Should the Dishonesty Element of the UK Cartel Offence be Replaced With?' [2012] Comp Law 53; Patel 'The Removal of Dishonesty from the Cartel Offence and the Publication Defence: A Panacea?' [2012] CPI Antitrust Chronicle, May 12(1); Stephan 'Is there public support for cartel criminalisation?' Concurrences No 2-2016, Art N 78515, p 40.

the defendant must have acted dishonestly[389]; the sections that follow will describe the offence in its current form; the seventh edition of this book described the law on dishonesty[390]. Secondly, the ERRA reduced the scope of the cartel offence by specifying certain circumstances in which it is not committed[391]. Thirdly, it created three defences to the cartel offence[392]. These provisions entered into force on 1 April 2014.

(A) The cartel offence

(i) Definition of the cartel offence

Section 188 of the Enterprise Act 2002 establishes the 'cartel offence'. This offence is quite distinct from Article 101 TFEU and the Chapter I prohibition in the Competition Act: this means that where a price-fixing agreement is detected the possibility exists that the undertakings involved may be the subject of a civil investigation, leading to the imposition of fines, and that the individuals responsible for setting up the agreement may be prosecuted criminally under the cartel offence. An example of this occurred in the *Marine hoses* case, where the European Commission imposed fines of €131 million on various undertakings engaged in allocating tenders, market sharing and price fixing[393], while three individuals were imprisoned in the UK for infringing section 188[394]. The criminal prosecution of individuals is likely to precede the proceedings against the undertakings, as happened in the *Galvanised steel tanks* case[395], to ensure that the more rigorous evidential standards in criminal cases affecting individuals whose personal liberty is at stake are observed.

In *IB v The Queen* the Court of Appeal held that the original cartel offence was not a 'national competition law' in the sense of Article 3 of Regulation 1/2003; had it decided to the contrary it was arguable that the Crown Court, which is not a designated competition authority for the purposes of that Regulation, would have had no jurisdiction to impose a penalty under section 188 of the Enterprise Act[396]. The Government's view is that the current cartel offence is also not a 'national competition law' for the purposes of Regulation 1/2003[397].

Section 188 of the Enterprise Act provides (in formalistic, indeed tortuous, terms) that an individual is guilty of an offence if he or she agrees with one or more other persons that undertakings[398] will engage in one or more of the following cartel activities:

- direct and indirect price fixing[399]
- limitation of supply[400] or production[401]

[389] ERRA 2013, s 47(8).

[390] Whish and Bailey *Competition Law* (Oxford University Press, 7th ed, 2012), pp 426–427.

[391] Enterprise Act 2002, s 188A; see 'Circumstances in which cartel offence is not committed', p 439 later in chapter.

[392] Enterprise Act 2002, s 188B; see 'Defences', p 440 later in chapter.

[393] Commission decision of 28 January 2009.

[394] See 'The cartel offence in practice', pp 445–446 later in chapter.

[395] See *Galvanised steel tank for water storage: main cartel infringement*, CMA decision of 19 December 2016, paras 2.103–2.108 and para 2.114.

[396] [2009] EWCA Crim 2575, paras 21–39.

[397] *Growth, Competition and the Competition Regime*, March 2012, para 7.30.

[398] The term 'undertaking' has the same meaning for this purpose as it has in the Competition Act 1998: Enterprise Act 2002, s 188(7).

[399] Enterprise Act 2002, s 188(2)(a); indirect price fixing would include, eg, agreements about relative price levels or price ranges, rebates and discounts: see the DTI's *Enterprise Bill: Explanatory Notes*, para 391.

[400] Enterprise Act 2002, s 188(2)(b).

[401] Ibid, s 188(2)(c).

- market sharing[402] or
- bid-rigging[403].

The Act specifically provides that, in relation to price fixing and the limitation of supply or production, the parties must have entered into a reciprocal agreement[404]; this is not specified in relation to market sharing and bid-rigging, since these actions are, by their nature, reciprocal. The *Cartel Offence Prosecution Guidance* ('the *Prosecution guidance*')[405] provides an illustrative list of arrangements between undertakings that do not give rise to an offence on the part of the individuals, such as unilateral or non-reciprocal restrictions[406].

The cartel offence applies only in respect of horizontal agreements[407]: vertical agreements, including resale price maintenance, are not covered by the cartel offence. The cartel offence will have been committed irrespective of whether the agreement reached between the individuals is implemented by the undertakings, and irrespective of whether or not they have authority to act on behalf of the undertaking at the time of the agreement. Individuals could also be prosecuted for the inchoate offences of attempting to commit the offence[408] and conspiracy to do so[409]. If an agreement is entered into outside the UK, proceedings may be brought only where it has been implemented in whole or in part in the UK[410].

(ii) Prosecution guidance

The Enterprise Act requires the CMA to publish guidance on the principles to be applied in determining whether it will prosecute the cartel offence[411]. The CMA's *Prosecution guidance*[412] explains that the CMA will apply the test in the Code for Crown Prosecutors which has two cumulative stages: an 'evidential stage' and a 'public interest stage'. These will be examined in turn. A decision not to prosecute the cartel offence does not preclude the CMA from taking action under the Competition Act or applying for disqualification of a company director[413]; this occurred in *Supply of products to the furniture industry*[414].

(a) Evidential stage

At this stage the CMA considers whether it has sufficient evidence to provide a 'realistic prospect' of conviction of the individuals under investigation[415]. The CMA must consider the statutory exclusions and defences and decide whether they affect the prospects of conviction[416].

(b) Public interest stage

If the CMA decides that a case satisfies the evidential stage, it will usually bring criminal charges against the individual or individuals concerned[417]. Prosecution is not

[402] Ibid, s 188(2)(d) and (e).

[403] Ibid, s 188(2)(f): a definition of bid-rigging is provided by s 188(5) of the Act; there is no offence where the person requesting the bids is aware of the bid-rigging arrangements: ibid, s 188(1)(b).

[404] Ibid, s 188(3).

[405] CMA9, March 2014, available at www.gov.uk/cma.

[406] *Prosecution guidance*, para 4.9.

[407] Enterprise Act 2002, ss 188(4) and 189.

[408] Criminal Attempts Act 1981, s 1.

[409] Criminal Law Act 1977, s 1.

[410] Enterprise Act 2002, s 190(3).

[411] Ibid, s 190A(1).

[412] CMA9, March 2014, available at www.gov.uk/cma.

[413] *Prosecution guidance*, para 3.4.

[414] See *Supply of products to the furniture industry (drawer wraps)*, CMA decision of 27 March 2017, paras 2.22–2.23.

[415] *Prosecution guidance*, para 4.1.

[416] Ibid, paras 4.1–4.2.

[417] Ibid, para 4.26.

automatic however; the CMA may refrain from prosecution if that would be in the public interest[418]. In making its assessment of the public interest the CMA will consider four questions:

- How serious is the offence committed? 'Hard-core cartels' are generally regarded as serious and individuals involved in them are likely to be prosecuted[419]. In determining the seriousness of the offence the CMA will consider the harm inflicted by the cartel, especially to customers[420]
- What is the level of culpability of the accused? The culpability of an individual is determined by reference to his or her level of involvement in the making or enforcing of the cartel. Instigating or being the ringleader of a cartel[421], using the cartel to preserve or increase the profits of an individual or undertakings[422] and taking steps to conceal the cartel[423] are relevant to the assessment of culpability
- What is the impact on the community? The CMA will consider the wider effects of the cartel on the community and markets, such as a diminution of public funds or the stifling of innovation
- Is prosecution a proportionate response to the behaviour in question?

These questions are not exhaustive and not every question will be relevant in every case; rather the CMA will make an overall assessment of the public interest in each case[424].

(iii) Circumstances in which the cartel offence is not committed

Section 188A sets out the circumstances in which the cartel offence is not committed. An individual does not commit an offence if 'relevant information' about the arrangements is disclosed to customers[425] or published in any of the *London Gazette, Edinburgh Gazette* or *Belfast Gazette*[426] before the arrangements are implemented[427]. Relevant information for this purpose includes the names of the relevant undertakings; a description of the nature of the arrangements that shows why they are or might otherwise fall within section 188(1); and a description of the relevant products or services[428]. These provisions are intended to give firms a practical way of preventing innocuous agreements from inadvertently being caught by the cartel offence.

Section 188A(3) provides that an individual does not commit the cartel offence when the agreement is made in order to comply with a legal requirement. For this purpose a legal requirement is one imposed by or under any enactment in force in the UK; by or under the TFEU or the EEA Agreement and having legal effect in the UK without further enactment; or by a law in force in another Member State having legal effect in the UK[429].

418 Ibid. 419 Ibid, para 4.32; see para 2.2 for a definition of 'hard-core cartel'.
420 Ibid, para 4.33. 421 Ibid, para 4.35. 422 Ibid, para 4.36.
423 Ibid, para 4.37. 424 Ibid, para 4.28.
425 Enterprise Act 2002, s 188A(1)(a); s 188A(1)(b) adapts the notification requirement in cases of bid-rigging.
426 The Enterprise Act 2002 (Publishing of Relevant Information under section 188A) Order 2014, SI 2014/535.
427 Enterprise Act 2002, s 188A(1)(c).
428 Ibid, s 188A(2); the Secretary of State may, by order, specify further information to be provided: s 188A(2)(d).
429 This mirrors the wording of the exclusion from the Chapter I and II prohibitions for compliance with legal requirements conferred by Competition Act 1998, Sch 3, para 5.

(iv) Defences

Section 188B provides three defences to the commission of the cartel offence. An individual will have a defence where he or she can show that:

- at the time of making the agreement he or she had no intention to conceal the nature of the arrangements from customers[430]
- at the time of making the agreement he or she had no intention to conceal the nature of the arrangements from the CMA[431]. Individuals are not required to notify arrangements to the CMA, but the CMA will consider arrangements brought to its attention[432]
- before the making of the agreement he or she took reasonable steps to ensure that the nature of the arrangements would be disclosed to professional legal advisers for the purposes of obtaining legal advice about them before entering into or implementing those arrangements[433].

The CMA's *Prosecution guidance* provides that the CMA will assess the credibility and strength of the evidence that a defence applies[434]; the standard of proof for the defences is the balance of probabilities[435]. The CMA says that 'professional legal adviser' includes external and in-house lawyers qualified in the UK and in other jurisdictions[436]. The CMA expects individuals to make a genuine attempt to seek legal advice about the proposed arrangement; the defence is unlikely to be available to individuals who give only incomplete or false information to a lawyer[437].

(v) Powers of investigation and search

The CMA may conduct an investigation if there are reasonable grounds for suspecting that the cartel offence has been committed[438], and the Enterprise Act gives it powers to require information and documents[439] and to enter and search premises under a warrant[440]. There are criminal sanctions for non-compliance with the powers of investigation: for example the intentional destruction of documents could lead to a maximum prison sentence of five years[441].

(a) Powers to require information and documents

The CMA can, by written notice, require a person to answer questions, provide information or produce documents for the purposes of a criminal investigation[442]; the term 'document' includes information recorded in any form and includes information that may be held electronically[443]. The CMA can exercise this power against any person it has reason to believe has relevant information[444], who must provide the information or documents required other than communications protected by legal professional privilege[445] or confidential information between a bank and its client[446]. The CMA can also require, in writing, a person to attend a 'compulsory interview' to answer questions on any matter relevant to the investigation. Section 197 of the Act imposes restrictions on the use of statements (but not of documents) obtained under section 193 (and section 194, dealt with later)[447]

430 Enterprise Act 2002, s 188B(1). 431 Ibid, s 188B(2). 432 *Prosecution guidance*, para 4.23.
433 Enterprise Act 2002, s 188B(3). 434 *Prosecution guidance*, para 4.22. 435 Ibid, para 4.18.
436 Ibid, para 4.24.
437 Note that, as a matter of EU law, reliance upon legal advice is not a defence under Articles 101 and 102 TFEU: Case C-681/11 *Bundeswettbewerbsbehorde v Schenker* EU:C:2013:404, para 43.
438 Enterprise Act 2002, s 192(1).
439 Ibid, s 192(2). 440 Ibid, s 194. 441 Ibid, s 201. 442 Ibid, s 193. 443 Ibid, s 202.
444 Ibid, s 193(1). 445 Ibid, s 196(1). 446 Ibid, s 196(2). 447 Ibid, s 197.

in order to protect against self-incrimination. There are also restrictions on the disclosure of confidential information[448].

(b) Power to enter premises under a warrant

The CMA may apply to the High Court (or in Scotland the procurator fiscal may apply to the sheriff) for a warrant authorising a named officer of the CMA, or any other authorised person such as a forensic IT expert, to enter premises[449]. This power permits forcible entry into and a search of the premises[450]; explanations of documents can be required[451] and the CMA can require that information stored in an electronic form can be taken away in a visible and legible form[452]. The CMA's officers may take away original documents[453]. Privileged information cannot be insisted upon[454]. A warrant may be issued, first, if there are reasonable grounds for believing that there are documents on any premises that the CMA could require by written notice[455] and, secondly, if a person has failed to comply with a written notice[456]; or if it is not practicable to serve such a notice[457]; or if the service of such a notice might seriously prejudice the investigation[458].

The CMA may exercise seize and sift powers that enable its officers pre-emptively to seize material when it is not reasonably practicable to determine on the premises whether the material is seizeable or not[459]. It is an offence to obstruct a search[460]. The CMA exercised these powers in *Galvanised steel tanks water storage: main cartel infringement*[461], when it seized and sifted images of desktop and laptop hard drives, server folders and mobile phones.

The exercise of these powers is subject to strict safeguards such as a requirement to give a written notice of what material has been seized[462] and an obligation to return any material which is subject to legal privilege[463].

(vi) **Powers of surveillance**

(a) Enterprise Act: intrusive surveillance and property interference

The Enterprise Act gives powers of 'intrusive surveillance' and 'property interference' to the CMA for the purpose of investigating the commission of the cartel offence: these powers are not available for investigations under the Competition Act[464]. In certain circumstances the Chairman of the CMA, with prior approval from the Investigatory Powers Commissioner's Office ('the IPCO')[465], may issue an authorisation for the presence of an individual or the planting of surveillance devices in residential premises, including hotels, and in private vehicles in order to hear or see what is happening there ('intrusive surveillance'). The criteria for the grant of an authorisation are contained in section 32(3) of the Regulation of Investigatory Powers Act 2000 and include situations in which the use of intrusive surveillance is necessary for the prevention or detection of a serious crime, such as the cartel offence, and where it is necessary to act in the interests of the economic well-being of the UK. The CMA could use these powers, for example, to obtain a

[448] Ibid, ss 237–246. [449] Ibid, ss 194 and 195. [450] Ibid, s 194(2)(a) and (b).
[451] Ibid, s 194(2)(c). [452] Ibid, s 194(2)(d). [453] Ibid, s 194(2)(b)(i).
[454] Ibid, s 196. [455] Ibid, s 194(1)(a). [456] Ibid, s 194(1)(b)(i).
[457] Ibid, s 194(1)(b)(ii). [458] Ibid, s 194(1)(b)(iii).
[459] Ibid, s 194(5) incorporating the statutory powers of seizure under the Criminal Justice and Police Act 2001, s 50.
[460] Enterprise Act 2002, s 201(6). [461] CMA decision of 19 December 2016, para 2.105.
[462] Criminal Justice and Police Act 2001, s 52. [463] Ibid, s 55.
[464] Enterprise Act 2002, s 199 amending Regulation of Investigatory Powers Act 2000, ss 32ff and Enterprise Act 2002, s 200 amending Police Act 1997, ss 93–94.
[465] The IPCO has a website, www.ipco.org.uk.

recording of a meeting of cartel members in a hotel room following a 'tip-off' from one of their employees or a disaffected member of the cartel. An authorisation by the Chairman of the CMA under section 93 of the Police Act 1997, as amended by section 200 of the Enterprise Act, allows for the covert installation of a surveillance device: if it were not for this section the installation would involve some element of trespass.

(b) Further powers: directed surveillance, covert human intelligence sources and access to communications data

The CMA also has powers that are regulated by the Regulation of Investigatory Powers Act 2000. The Regulation of Investigatory Powers (Directed Surveillance and Covert Human Intelligence Sources) Order 2010[466] lists the CMA as one of the public authorities that are able to authorise 'directed surveillance': this would allow it, for example, to carry out covert surveillance of a person's office[467]; the CMA may also use 'covert human intelligence sources', for example by asking informants to attend cartel meetings and to report back to it[468]. The Regulation of Investigatory Powers (Communications Data) Order 2010[469] provides that the CMA may be given access to communications data such as the times, duration and recipients of telephone calls, though not their content. The first two of these powers are available in both civil and criminal investigations: the last only for a criminal case.

(c) Codes of Practice

The CMA exercises the powers described in the preceding paragraph in accordance with the Codes of Practice issued by the Home Office in December 2014[470].

(vii) ***Prosecution and penalty***

The cartel offence is triable on indictment before a jury in the Crown Court, where a term of imprisonment of up to five years may be imposed[471] or an unlimited fine[472], or in a magistrates' court, where the maximum prison sentence would be six months and where a fine may also be imposed[473]. Four criminal prosecutions of the cartel offence in its original form were brought before Southwark Crown Court in London[474]. Prosecutions may be brought by the Serious Fraud Office ('the SFO') or the CMA[475]; the CMA will generally undertake this function[476]. If the SFO agrees to accept a case it may carry out additional inquiries using its powers under section 2 of the Criminal Justice Act 1987, which are broadly the same as the powers of the CMA under the Enterprise Act[477]. The SFO is bound by the Code for Crown Prosecutors[478]. Prosecutions in Scotland are brought by the Lord

466 Regulation of Investigatory Powers (Covert Human Intelligence Sources: Matters Subject to Legal Privilege) Order 2010, SI 2010/521.

467 See Regulation of Investigatory Powers Act 2000, s 28.

468 Ibid, s 29.

469 SI 2010/480, specifying the CMA as a relevant public authority for the purpose of Regulation of Investigatory Powers Act 2000, s 25.

470 www.gov.uk/government/publications/covert-surveillance-and-covert-human-intelligence-sources-codes-of-practice.

471 A custodial sentence can be imposed only where the court is of the opinion that the offence is so serious that only such a sentence can be justified: Powers of Criminal Courts (Sentencing) Act 2000, s 79.

472 Enterprise Act 2002, s 190(1)(a).

473 Ibid, s 190(1)(b); the maximum fine in the magistrates' court would be £5,000: Magistrates Courts' Act 1980, s 32(9).

474 See 'The cartel offence in practice', pp 445–446 later in chapter.

475 Enterprise Act 2002, s 190(2)(a).

476 *Prosecution guidance*, para 1.4.

477 Ibid, paras 3.20–3.23.

478 Available on the website of the Crown Prosecution Service: www.cps.gov.uk.

Advocate[479]. Third parties are able to bring prosecutions with the consent of the CMA[480], although this will presumably be extremely rare, if they happen at all.

The CMA has agreed a *Memorandum of Understanding* with the SFO which records the basis on which they will cooperate to investigate and/or prosecute individuals in respect of the cartel offence where 'serious or complex fraud' is suspected; the CMA has agreed a similar *Memorandum* with the National Casework Division of the Crown Office in Scotland: both *Memoranda* are available on the CMA's website[481]. Initial inquiries into possible cartel activity will be undertaken by the CMA; if it considers that the SFO's 'acceptance' criteria are satisfied—that is to say that serious or complex fraud may be involved[482]—the CMA will refer the matter to the SFO, the Director of which will endeavour to decide whether to accept the case, or to require the CMA to make further inquiries, within 28 days[483]. Where the SFO accepts a CMA referral the SFO can request the CMA to provide staff to assist with the investigation, under the direction of an SFO case controller[484].

Both the CMA and the SFO are bound by the disclosure provisions of the Criminal Procedure and Investigations Act 1996 which require them to disclose to the defendant any prosecution material which, in the prosecutor's opinion, might undermine the case for the prosecution against the accused.

The CMA is responsible for the grant of leniency and the issue of no-action letters, but where this could affect the outcome of an SFO investigation the CMA will consult with it[485]. The SFO would not prosecute a cartel as a conspiracy to defraud or under the Fraud Act 2006 where the CMA has granted immunity under the Enterprise Act[486]. There is no system in the UK of 'plea bargaining' of the kind that operates under the criminal provisions in US law[487].

(viii) *Parallel CMA criminal and civil investigations*

When the CMA first receives information about alleged cartel activity it may not immediately be clear whether the case will involve a criminal prosecution of individuals, or whether it will 'merely' lead to an administrative procedure against the undertakings concerned under the Competition Act. In order not to compromise any criminal prosecution the CMA will, where appropriate, follow the procedures required by PACE and its associated Codes of Practice from the outset; this will include giving individuals the standard criminal caution before being questioned, and allowing the presence of a legal adviser.

Where the CMA is conducting an investigation under the Competition Act and the SFO is simultaneously investigating a criminal case, the two investigating teams will maintain an 'ongoing dialogue' in order to ensure that the administrative procedure does not prejudice the parallel criminal investigation[488]. If the CMA conducts both the

[479] In Scotland the Lord Advocate exercises the same powers as the SFO under the Criminal Law (Consolidation) (Scotland) Act 1995.

[480] Enterprise Act 2002, s 190(2)(b); the Explanatory Notes to the Act state that the CMA's consent is required to prevent vexatious private prosecutions against recipients of leniency.

[481] www.gov.uk/cma.

[482] The SFO regards the cartel offence as potentially involving serious or complex fraud: see the Background note to the *CMA and SFO Memorandum of Understanding*.

[483] *CMA and SFO Memorandum of Understanding*, paras 5.2 and 5.3.

[484] Ibid, para 6.1.

[485] Ibid, para 13; leniency and no-action letters are discussed later.

[486] Ibid, para 10.4; see similarly *Leniency and no-action guidance*, para 8.2.

[487] For discussion of the possible benefits of introducing plea bargaining for criminal cartel cases in the UK see Lawrence, O'Kane, Rab and Nakhwal 'Hardcore Bargains: What Could Plea Bargaining Offer in UK Criminal Cartel Cases?' [2008] Comp Law 17.

[488] *CMA and SFO Memorandum of Understanding*, para 9.1.

criminal and administrative proceedings, different case teams are established for each investigation. Statements obtained under the Competition Act will usually not be available for the purposes of a criminal prosecution if they have not been obtained according to criminal law standards; it may therefore be necessary to conduct a further interview in accordance with PACE procedures.

There are restrictions on the use of statements made under compulsion in response to powers exercised under sections 193 and 194 to protect against self-incrimination[489]. Documents produced during a criminal investigation may be used in a parallel civil investigation. In *Galvanised steel tanks*[490] the CMA's civil investigation team used materials, such as interview transcripts and an audio-visual recording of a meeting, that had been gathered for the purposes of an earlier criminal investigation.

It is possible that a civil claim for damages might be stayed until a criminal trial has been held[491].

(ix) **No-action letters**

Section 190(4) of the Enterprise Act provides for the issue by the CMA of so-called 'no-action letters' whereby individuals who provide information about cartels to the CMA are granted immunity from prosecution. This is a further example of encouraging whistle-blowers to provide information about cartels in return for leniency[492]. The CMA has published guidance on the issue of no-action letters in its *Leniency and no-action guidance*[493]. A pro-forma no-action letter for individuals is set out at Annex B of that document. The CMA cannot offer leniency from prosecution in Scotland since that is a matter for the Lord Advocate; however the Lord Advocate will accord serious weight to any recommendation from the CMA as to leniency in a case falling to be prosecuted in Scotland when deciding whether to prosecute[494].

The CMA will not reach a final decision on whether an individual will be required to admit participation in the criminal offence until the investigation is at or near its conclusion and until specialist criminal counsel has had the opportunity to advise the CMA on this issue[495]. If the CMA decides that it is appropriate that an individual who qualifies for criminal immunity should make an admission of participation in it, that individual will be offered immunity only on condition that such an admission is made[496]; if such an admission is deemed not to be appropriate, the individual will be offered a 'comfort letter' stating that the CMA does not consider that there is sufficient evidence for it to prosecute[497]. If an individual works for an undertaking that is not itself a coercer[498], the individual will not be refused criminal immunity unless he or she enjoyed a position of power independent of their position within the undertaking and used that power for the purpose of coercion[499].

[489] Enterprise Act 2002, s 197; statements may be used in court against the person who made them only in a prosecution for making false or misleading statements under s 201(2) or for making an inconsistent statement in respect of a prosecution for another offence.

[490] See *Galvanised steel tanks for water storage main cartel infringement*, CMA decision of 19 December 2016, paras 2.107 and 2.109.

[491] *Secretary of State for Health v Norton Healthcare Ltd* [2004] Eu LR 12, para 40.

[492] On leniency for undertakings see 'Leniency', pp 424–429 earlier in chapter.

[493] OFT 1496, July 2013, Part 7.

[494] See paras 13–16 of the *Memorandum of Understanding between the [CMA] and the National Casework Division, Crown Office, Scotland*, OFT 546, June 2009.

[495] *Leniency and no-action guidance*, para 8.14. [496] Ibid, para 8.15. [497] Ibid.

[498] See 'The coercer test', p 428 earlier on the position of undertakings that are coercers seeking immunity.

[499] *Leniency and no-action guidance*, para 2.57.

Where an undertaking is granted Type A immunity[500] all current and former employees and directors will gain 'blanket' criminal immunity[501]; the same is true where Type B immunity is granted[502]. Blanket criminal immunity is not available in Type B leniency and Type C leniency cases: in those cases the CMA will consider granting individual immunity[503]. Immunity may also be granted to individuals on their own account, that is to say irrespective of any approach to the CMA by an undertaking[504]. There will be automatic criminal immunity where an individual tells the CMA about cartel activity before any other individual or undertaking and where there is no pre-existing criminal or civil investigation[505]. In other cases criminal immunity may be available on a discretionary basis[506]. Guidance is provided on the process of interviewing individuals who apply for criminal immunity[507]. The *Leniency and no-action guidance* also examines the relationship between the cartel offence and immunity or leniency applications to the European Commission[508], in particular in light of the concern that exposure to criminal proceedings in the UK might deter undertakings from applying for leniency to the Commission. One way of addressing this is to allow an undertaking that applies to the Commission also to put down a 'marker' for Type A blanket immunity on a no-names basis with the CMA[509].

(x) Extradition

The Extradition Act 2003 makes provision for the extradition of individuals who commit the cartel offence or who conspire to or attempt to commit it. This means that, in so far as another country, such as the US, has a criminal offence that corresponds with the cartel offence, it can apply to the UK for the extradition of an individual or individuals and vice versa. This provision, of course, is not retrospective, so that there is no possibility of anyone being extradited under the Extradition Act in respect of conduct occurring before section 188 of the Enterprise Act entered into force on 20 June 2003.

(xi) Relationship between the cartel offence and proceedings against cartels under EU competition law

Where a European Commission cartel investigation involves a potential criminal cartel offence under the Enterprise Act the CMA will cooperate with the Commission to coordinate the progress of the two investigations[510].

(xii) The cartel offence in practice

There have been four criminal prosecutions of the cartel offence. The first case under the original cartel offence, that is to say with the requirement of dishonesty, arose from a cartel in the supply of marine hoses, and resulted in terms of imprisonment on three individuals between two and a half and three years[511], reduced slightly on appeal to the Court of Appeal[512]; it declined, because of the circumstances of that case[513], to lay down any general guidance as to the terms of imprisonment to be imposed in other cases. The OFT's criminal investigation in the *Marine hoses* case was closely coordinated with those of the competition authorities in other jurisdictions, including the European Commission, which imposed fines of €131 million on the undertakings involved in this case[514],

500 See 'Terminology', pp 425–426 earlier in chapter on the terminology used in this section.
501 *Leniency and no-action guidance*, para 2.10; see also para 2.38.
502 Ibid, paras 2.16 and 2.38–2.40. 503 Ibid, para 2.34. 504 Ibid, para 2.34.
505 Ibid, para 2.35. 506 Ibid, para 2.36. 507 Ibid, paras 5.30–5.34.
508 Ibid, paras 8.1–8.13. 509 Ibid, paras 4.41–4.43 and 8.7.
510 *CMA and SFO Memorandum of Understanding*, para 9.2.
511 See OFT Press Release 72/08, 11 June 2008.
512 See *R v Whittle* [2008] EWCA Crim 2560. 513 See ch 10 n 515 later. 514 See ch 10 n 393 earlier.

and the US Department of Justice, where the same individuals pleaded guilty to illegal price fixing and agreed to terms of imprisonment there[515].

In 2008 the OFT charged four employees of British Airways in connection with a cartel in fuel surcharges for long-haul passenger flights; each of them pleaded not guilty[516]. At their trial in the spring of 2010 at Southwark Crown Court the OFT decided to withdraw the proceedings, and the defendants were formally acquitted. This was because, at a very late stage in the proceedings, after the commencement of the trial, a substantial volume of electronic material was discovered which neither the OFT nor the defence had been able to review; the OFT's opinion was that it would not have been fair to seek an adjournment of the trial while the fresh evidence was analysed[517]. Three non-executive directors of the OFT conducted a review of what had occurred in this case, and made a number of recommendations as to steps to be taken to ensure that appropriate lessons were learned from the experience[518].

The third case arose from a cartel in the supply of galvanised steel tanks for water storage. In 2014 the CMA charged three individuals; one pleaded guilty and the other two pleaded not guilty[519]. At their trial in June 2015, the defendants argued that they had not acted dishonestly; rather they had sought to protect jobs in response to cut-throat competition[520]. *Galvanised steel tanks* was the first criminal case to be tried by a jury, who acquitted the defendants[521]. In September 2015 the individual who pleaded guilty to the charges was sentenced to six months' imprisonment, suspended for 12 months, and ordered to do 120 hours' community service within 12 months[522]. The CMA subsequently adopted two infringement decisions under the Competition Act[523].

In March 2016 an individual pleaded guilty to the cartel offence in relation to the *Supply of precast concrete draining products*[524]; he was given a two-year prison sentence, suspended for two years, made the subject of a six-month curfew order and disqualified from acting as a company director for seven years[525]. The CMA subsequently decided that there was insufficient evidence to charge anyone else.

(B) Company director disqualification

The Enterprise Act 2002 introduced a second provision designed to encourage individuals to ensure compliance with competition law: under section 204, which inserted new

[515] See the US Department of Justice Press Release of 12 December 2007, available at www.justice.gov; as part of the US plea agreement in this case the defendants had agreed not to seek from the UK court a shorter term of imprisonment than the one agreed to in the US proceedings: the Court of Appeal expressed its 'doubts' as to the propriety of the US prosecutor seeking to inhibit the way in which the proceedings in the UK could be conducted: *R v Whittle* [2008] EWCA Crim 2560, para 28.

[516] OFT Press Release 93/08, 7 August 2008; British Airways agreed to pay a penalty of £121.5 million, subsequently reduced to £58.5 million, for its admitted participation in this cartel: see 'Statistical analysis', p 430 earlier in chapter.

[517] OFT Press Release 47/10, 10 May 2010; for critical comment see Purnell, Bellamy, Kar, Piccinin and Sahathevan 'Criminal Cartel Enforcement—More Turbulence Ahead? The Implications of the *BA/Virgin Case*' [2010] Comp Law 313.

[518] See the 'Project Condor Board Review', available at www.nationalarchives.gov.uk.

[519] See *Supply of galvanised steel tanks for water storage: criminal investigation*, available at www.gov.uk/cma.

[520] 'Water-tank cartel case hinges on whether defendants acted 'dishonestly' UK judge tells jury', MLex report, 24 June 2015.

[521] CMA Statement following completion of criminal cartel prosecution, 24 June 2015; see speech by Stephen Blake 'The UK steel tanks criminal cartel trial: implications for criminalisation and leniency', 13 November 2015, available at www.gov.uk/cma.

[522] CMA Press Release, 14 September 2015.

[523] *Galvanised steel tanks for water storage main cartel infringement* and *Galvanised steel tanks for water storage information exchange infringement*, CMA decisions of 19 December 2016.

[524] See *Supply of precast concrete drainage products: criminal investigation*, available at www.gov.uk/cma.

[525] CMA announcement, 15 September 2017.

sections into the Company Directors Disqualification Act 1986 ('the CDDA 1986'), company directors can be disqualified for up to 15 years where their companies are guilty of a competition law infringement: disqualification of individuals is *not* limited to circumstances in which the cartel offence has been committed, but applies to any infringement of Articles 101 and 102 TFEU and of the Chapter I and Chapter II prohibitions[526]. It is for the High Court (or the Court of Session in Scotland) to make a competition disqualification order ('a CDO'), not the CMA or the sectoral regulators[527]: their function is to determine whether to seek such an order, which the CDDA 1986 gives them power to do[528], and whether to accept an undertaking in lieu of an order, for which provision is also made[529]. The current guidance on these powers was published in June 2010[530].

Three company directors were disqualified for periods of between five and seven years as a result of their participation in the *Marine hoses* cartel[531]; these disqualifications were based on the fact that they had committed the criminal cartel offence, and were disqualified under section 2, rather than section 9A, of the CDDA 1986: the court did not need to invoke the additional power conferred by section 204 of the Enterprise Act. The same was true in the case of *Precast concrete draining products*[532].

The power conferred by section 204 of the Enterprise Act was used for the first time in December 2016, when a director of Trod Ltd, which had been fined for horizontal price fixing, gave a disqualification undertaking not to act as a director of any UK company for five years[533]. In April 2018 two directors of Frost Estate Agents Ltd in Burnham-on-Sea gave disqualification undertakings not to act as a director of any UK company for, respectively, three and three-and-a-half years; both directors had been actively involved in the *Residential estate agency services* cartel[533a].

(i) Grounds for disqualification

Under section 9A of the CDDA 1986 the court must make a CDO against a person if a company of which he is a director commits an infringement of EU and/or UK competition law[534] and the court considers that his conduct as a director makes him unfit to be concerned in the management of a company[535]; the *Guidance* states that the term 'director', for this purpose, includes a *de facto* director[536]. In deciding whether the conduct of a director makes him unfit, the court must have regard to whether his conduct contributed to the breach of competition law; or, where this is not the case, whether he had reasonable grounds to suspect a breach and took no steps to prevent it; or, if he did not know of the breach, he ought to have done[537]. Furthermore the court may have regard to his conduct as a director of a company in connection with any other breach of competition law[538]. The maximum period of disqualification is 15 years[539], and during that time it is a criminal offence to be a director of a company, to act as a receiver of a company's property, to promote, form or manage a company or to act as an insolvency practitioner[540]. Any person involved in the management of a company in contravention of a CDO is personally liable for the debts of the company[541] and may be placed on a public register maintained by the Secretary of State for Business, Energy and Industrial Strategy[542].

[526] CDDA 1986, s 9A(4). [527] Ibid, s 9E(3).

[528] Ibid, s 9A(10): s 9D provides that the Secretary of State may make regulations as to the concurrent functions of the CMA and the sectoral regulators in relation to CDOs; in the text that follows the term CMA is used to include the powers of the sectoral regulators. [529] CDDA 1986, s 9B.

[530] *Director disqualification orders in competition cases*, OFT 510, June 2010; see also *Company directors and competition law*, OFT 1340, June 2011. [531] OFT Press Release 72/08, 11 June 2008.

[532] CMA announcement, 15 September 2017. [533] CMA Press Release, 1 December 2016.

[533a] See CMA Press Release, 10 April 2018. [534] CDDA 1986, s 9A(2). [535] Ibid, s 9A(3).

[536] *Director disqualification orders*, para 2.3; see also para 4.5. [537] CDDA 1986, s 9A(5)(a) and (6).

[538] Ibid, s 9A(5)(b). [539] Ibid, s 9A(9). [540] Ibid, ss 1(1) and 13.

[541] Ibid, s 15(1)(a). [542] Ibid, s 18.

(ii) Procedure

The CMA has power to make inquiries and investigations under sections 26 to 29 of the Competition Act for the purpose of deciding whether to apply for a disqualification order[543]. The CMA may accept undertakings in lieu of seeking a CDO[544]. When deciding whether to apply for an order the CMA will take into account the factors set out in its guidance[545]. It will follow a five-step process in which it will consider:

- whether there has been a breach of competition law
- the nature of the breach and whether a financial penalty has been imposed
- whether the company in question benefited from leniency
- the extent of the director's responsibility for the breach of competition law and
- whether there are any aggravating and mitigating factors[546].

The *Guidance* explains each of these five factors. The CMA will not seek a CDO in respect of any current director whose company has benefited from leniency in relation to the activities to which the leniency relates[547]; this largesse would not extend to a director who has been removed as a director as a result of his or her role in the breach of competition law or for opposing the relevant application for leniency, nor to a director who fails to cooperate with the leniency process[548]. The extent of the director's responsibility for the breach of competition law will be relevant to the decision whether to apply to the court. In particular the CMA will ask whether the director's conduct contributed to the breach[549]; whether he had reasonable grounds to suspect breach but took no steps to prevent it[550]; and whether he ought to have known of the breach[551]. The *Guidance* sets out various aggravating and mitigating factors[552]. The CMA would not seek a CDO if an individual is being prosecuted under the cartel offence, since the court dealing with that matter would have the right to make a CDO anyway[553]; nor would it proceed against anyone who is the beneficiary of a no-action letter[554]. The CMA must send a notice to anyone in relation to whom it applies for a CDO: the information that will be contained in this notice is set out in the *Guidance*[555].

(C) Conspiracy to defraud at common law

It is possible that cartel agreements might amount to conspiracy to defraud, a criminal offence at common law[556]. In *Norris v Government of the United States of America*[557] the US Government sought extradition of Mr Norris under the Extradition Act 2003. The conduct complained of by the US authorities was price fixing contrary to section 1 of the Sherman Act 1890. Under the Extradition Act the US had to demonstrate 'double criminality', that is to say that price fixing was illegal under US law and that the same conduct, if it had occurred in the UK, would have been punishable there by a term of

543 Ibid, s 9C, inserted by Enterprise Act 2002, s 204.

544 CDDA 1986, s 9B; *Director disqualification orders*, paras 3.1–3.5.

545 Ibid, paras 4.1–4.29.

546 Ibid, para 4.2.

547 Ibid, para 4.13.

548 Ibid, para 4.14.

549 Ibid, paras 4.19–4.20.

550 Ibid, para 4.21.

551 Ibid, paras 4.22–4.23.

552 Ibid, paras 4.25–4.26.

553 Ibid, paras 4.27–4.28.

554 Ibid, para 4.29; on no-action letters see 'No-action letters', pp 444–445 earlier in chapter.

555 *Director disqualification orders*, paras 5.1–5.2.

556 See Lever and Pike 'Cartel Agreements, Criminal Conspiracy and the Statutory "Cartel Offence"' (2005) 26 ECLR 90 and (2005) 26 ECLR 164; Lester 'Prosecuting Cartels for Conspiracy to Defraud' [2008] Comp Law 134.

557 [2008] 1 AC 920, reversing the judgment of the High Court on this point in *Ian Norris v The Government of the USA* [2007] EWHC 71 (Admin).

imprisonment of at least 12 months. At the relevant time the cartel offence under the Enterprise Act 2002 did not exist. The Administrative Court held that price fixing could amount to conspiracy to defraud, a criminal offence at common law pre-dating the Enterprise Act, where there is an agreement 'between two or more persons dishonestly to prejudice or to risk prejudicing another's right, knowing that they have no right to do so'[558]. On appeal, however, the House of Lords held that 'mere' price fixing did not amount to conspiracy to defraud: it followed that there was no double criminality and that Norris could not be extradited on this ground[559]. A price-fixing agreement could be conspiracy to defraud only where there were aggravating features: fraud, misrepresentation, violence and intimidation were referred to as examples[560]. *Norris* was subsequently followed by the Court of Final Appeal in Hong Kong[561].

7. Concurrency

An important feature of the Competition Act is that concurrent powers are given to the CMA and the sectoral regulators to enforce the Chapter I and Chapter II prohibitions and Articles 101 and 102 TFEU. In their respective spheres of activity the Office of Communications, the Gas and Electricity Markets Authority, the Water Services Regulation Authority, the Civil Aviation Authority, the Office for the Regulation of Gas and Electricity (Northern Ireland), the Office of Rail and Road, NHS Improvement[562], the Payment Systems Regulator and the Financial Conduct Authority enjoy concurrent powers. The ERRA introduced the 'primacy duty'—the requirement that the sectoral regulators (apart from NHS Improvement) should consider whether the use of their competition powers would be more appropriate than their sector-specific powers when deciding what action to take in a particular case[563]. A decision by a regulator to use its sector-specific regulatory powers does not prevent the CMA from investigating the same matter under the Competition Act[564]. One of the CMA's strategic goals is to 'extend the frontiers of competition', in particular within regulated sectors[565].

(A) The Concurrency Regulations and the *Concurrency Guidance*

The Competition Act (Concurrency) Regulations 2014[566] and the *Guidance on concurrent application of competition law to regulated industries* ('the *Concurrency*

558 Ibid, para 56.

559 Mr Norris was subsequently extradited to the US on the different ground of perverting the course of justice; he was convicted and sentenced to 18 months' imprisonment: see US Department of Justice Press Release, 10 December 2010, available at www.justice.gov/atr.

560 [2008] 1 AC 920, para 17; see also *R v GG plc* [2008] UKHL 17, a case arising out of the SFO's prosecution of a number of pharmaceutical companies for price fixing prior to the entry into force of the cartel offence in the Enterprise Act 2002: the SFO subsequently sought leave to amend the indictment in this case, but this was refused: see *R v GG plc (No 2)* [2008] EWCA Crim 3061.

561 *HKSAP v Yip* FACC No 4 of 2010, judgment of 13 December 2010.

562 NHS Improvement is the operational name for the organisation that brings together several NHS bodies, including Monitor, which has concurrent powers under the Health and Social Care Act 2012; see *Application of the Competition Act 1998 in the healthcare sector: guidance for providers*, September 2014, available at www.gov.uk.

563 ERRA 2013, Sch 14.

564 *Guidance on concurrent application of competition law to regulated industries*, CMA10, March 2014, para 4.7.

565 See *Competition and Markets Authority Annual Plan 2014/15*, CMA8, April 2014, paras 4.2 and 4.7.

566 SI 2014/536 adopted pursuant to Competition Act 1998, s 54; these Regulations replaced earlier ones (SI 2004/1077) with effect from 1 April 2014.

guidance')[567] seek to ensure that concurrency operates in a satisfactory manner. The *Concurrency guidance* provides the best picture of the operation of the concurrency provisions. It explains that the regulators have the same powers as the CMA[568], save that only the latter can issue guidance on penalties and make and amend the CMA's Rules[569]. Additional information about the concurrency regime will be found in the memoranda of understanding that the CMA has entered into with the various sectoral regulators; guidance is also available as to how applications for leniency should be made; there is also an annual report on concurrency[570].

Complaints may be made to the CMA or the relevant regulator[571]; the same is true for applications for interim measures[572]. The *Concurrency guidance* explains that cases will be allocated between the CMA and the regulators (save for NHS Improvement) according to which of them is 'better or best placed' to act[573]. The *Guidance* sets out the principles by reference to which a 'better or best-placed' authority is to be identified[574]. In the event of a dispute on jurisdiction the CMA will decide which authority shall handle the case[575].

Once a case has been allocated the Concurrency Regulations make provision for the CMA to direct a regulator to transfer a case to it where the CMA is satisfied that its enforcement of the prohibitions in the Competition Act and/or Articles 101 and 102 TFEU, rather than the regulator, would promote competition, within any market or markets in the UK, for the benefit of consumers[576]. The CMA expects that it will exercise this power sparingly[577].

The *Guidance* also discusses the relationship between the regulators' powers under competition law and their sector-specific powers[578] and explains the law on confidentiality and disclosure of information[579]. A key feature of the concurrency arrangements is the requirement to share information about current cases, including drafts of statements of objections, commitment decisions and infringement decisions.

567 CMA10, March 2014; note that all of the concurrent regulators have published guidelines on the application of competition law to their respective sectors, which are available at www.gov.uk/government/collections/uk-competition-network-ukcn-documents.

568 *Concurrency guidance*, paras 2.2–2.3.

569 Ibid, para 2.4; the CMA must consult with the regulators when issuing guidance on penalties, commitments and amending the CMA's Rules; note also that only the CMA can proceed under Part 6 of the Enterprise Act in relation to the cartel offence.

570 Available at www.gov.uk.

571 *Concurrency guidance*, para 3.37; the authorities will strive to allocate the case within two months of the first authority to receive the complaint: ibid, para 3.24.

572 Ibid, para 3.40.

573 Ibid, para 3.22; see paras 3.21–3.25 generally on case allocation; reg 5(5) of the Concurrency Regulations provides that NHS Improvement will normally be responsible for cases principally concerned with the provision of healthcare services for the purposes of the NHS in England.

574 Ibid. The principles of case allocation set out in the European Commission's *Network Notice*, OJ 2004 C 101/43, will be taken into account where Article 101 or 102 apply: ibid, para 3.38.

575 The Competition Act (Concurrency) Regulations 2014, SI 2014/536, reg 5(1)–(4); see also *Concurrency guidance*, para 3.23.

576 The Competition Act (Concurrency) Regulations 2014, SI 2014/536, reg 8; on the circumstances in which the CMA may exercise jurisdiction where a case has already been allocated to a regulator see *Concurrency guidance*, paras 3.26–3.29.

577 *Concurrency guidance*, para 3.28.

578 Ibid, paras 4.2–4.7 (Competition Act and sector-specific regulation) and paras 4.8–4.12 (EU competition law and sector-specific regulation).

579 Ibid, paras 5.1–5.7.

(B) UK Competition Network

The UK Competition Network ('UKCN') brings together the CMA and all the regulators, except NHS Improvement which has observer status[580]. The mission of the UKCN is to promote competition and deter anti-competitive behaviour in the regulated sectors[581]. The *Concurrency guidance* describes the work and procedure of the UKCN[582]; meetings of the UKCN are chaired by a representative of the CMA[583]. The UKCN will focus on six 'priority areas': strategic dialogue; cooperation in the enforcement of competition law; enhancing capabilities; sharing best practice; advocacy; and the preparation of the CMA's 'concurrency report'[584].

(C) The concurrency arrangements in practice

The only infringement decisions to have been adopted by a sectoral regulator by 8 December 2017 were taken by the ORR in *English Welsh & Scottish Railway*[585]; by OFGEM in *National Grid*[586] and by the CAA in *Access to car parking facilities at East Midlands International Airport*[587]. Some commentators have criticised the under-enforcement of the competition provisions by the regulators[588]. There are various possible explanations for the small number of infringement decisions by sectoral regulators. One is that the sectoral regulators have an option whether to apply competition law to anti-competitive conduct or to use their sector-specific regulatory powers. It is not unusual to see, for example, that OFCOM or OFGEM have required regulated undertakings' licence conditions to be amended to address problems of market failure[589]: in practical terms this may be a simpler and quicker way to proceed, with a knock-on effect on the number of infringement decisions, although the duty of primacy introduced by the ERRA may alter the situation[590]. Another explanation for the relative lack of findings of infringement might be that the sectoral regulators consider that they are unable to satisfy the standard of proof under the Competition Act[591]. A third explanation might be that the demonopolisation and liberalisation of regulated sectors began in the UK a considerable time ago, in the 1980s, with the result that such markets are reasonably competitive[592].

In some cases a sectoral regulator may assist with the CMA's investigation; for example NHS Improvement assisted the CMA in *Conduct in the ophthalmology sector*[593]. The

580 Ibid, para 3.1; the UKCN's website is www.gov.uk/government/collections/uk-competition-network-ukcn-documents.

581 See UKCN Statement of Intent in *Concurrency guidance*, Annexe B.

582 *Concurrency guidance*, paras 3.15–3.20. 583 Ibid, para 3.15. 584 Ibid, paras 3.1–3.6.

585 ORR decision of 16 November 2006.

586 GEMA decision of 21 February 2008, on appeal Case 1099/1/2/08 *National Grid Plc v Gas and Electricity Markets Authority* [2009] CAT 14, and on appeal to the Court of Appeal [2010] EWCA Civ 114.

587 CAA decision of 17 January 2017.

588 See eg Bloom 'The Competition Act at 10 Years Old: Enforcement by the OFT and the Sector Regulators' [2010] Comp Law 141 and Pimlott 'Concurrency and the Role of the Competition Appeal Tribunal as Supervisor of the Sectoral Regulators' [2010] Comp Law 162; for a discussion of the possible explanations for the small number of infringement decisions by the regulators see Whish 'National Competition Law Goals and the Commission's Guidance on Article 82 EC: The UK Experience' in Pace (ed) *European Competition Law: The Impact of the Commission's Guidance on Article 102* (Edward Elgar, 2011), ch 7.

589 See eg OFGEM's *Energy Supply Probe*, 2008, available at www.ofgem.gov.uk.

590 See ch 10, n 563 earlier.

591 A point noted by the CAT in Case 1021/1/1/03 *JJB Sports plc v OFT* [2004] CAT 17, para 205.

592 See ch 23 'Demonopolisation, liberalisation and privatisation', pp 1008–1009.

593 CMA decision of 20 August 2015; see *Annual report on concurrency*, CMA63, 28 April 2017, fn 10.

sectoral regulators have also adopted several commitment decisions[594] and a number of non-infringement decisions[595]. Some of the non-infringement decisions were successfully appealed to the CAT[596]; in *Albion Water* the CAT set aside OFWAT's non-infringement decision and substituted its own finding of an infringement[597].

(D) **Annual concurrency reports**

The CMA is required, after consultation with the regulators, to publish an annual report on the operation of the concurrency arrangements and on decisions on the use of the concurrent competition powers by the CMA and sector regulators[598].

The Secretary of State has the power to remove the concurrent powers of any sector regulator except NHS Improvement[599]. This section enables him or her to make a 'sectoral regulator order' only if it is appropriate to do so for the purpose of promoting competition, within any market in the UK, for the benefit of consumers. There is a symbolic significance in this: the Government is committed to the idea that competition law should be applied in the regulated sectors to a greater extent than has been the case to date.

8. **Appeals**

The Competition Act deals with appeals in sections 46 to 49 and in Schedule 8, as amended by the Enterprise Act 2002. The powers available to the CMA and the sectoral regulators under the Act are considerable. To balance this, and to ensure compliance with the Human Rights Act 1998 which requires that decisions should be made by an independent and impartial tribunal, it was felt that an appeal on the merits—not merely the possibility of judicial review—should be available; furthermore that the appellate body should be one with appropriate expertise in matters of competition law. For this reason appeals are taken to the CAT[600]. The Supreme Court and the Court of Appeal have both emphasised that appellate courts should exercise caution before overturning the economic judgments of an expert tribunal[601].

Decisions that cannot be appealed to the CAT may be challenged by way of judicial review before the Administrative Court[602]. There are four well-established grounds of challenge in judicial review: illegality, irrationality, procedural irregularity and the principle of proportionality[603]. It may be that permission to apply for judicial review would be

594 See the 'Table of commitments decisions', p 417.

595 See the 'Table of published decisions' available on the Online Resources at www.oup.com/uk/whish9e/.

596 See, in particular, the history of the litigation of the *Freeserve*, *Floe I* and *Albion Water* cases the 'Table of published decisions' available on the Online Resources at www.oup.com/uk/whish9e/.

597 Case 1046/2/4/04 *Albion Water Ltd v Water Services Regulation Authority* [2006] CAT 36, upheld on appeal [2008] EWCA Civ 536.

598 ERRA 2013, Sch 4, para 16; the annual concurrency reports are available at www.gov.uk.

599 ERRA 2013, s 52.

600 The establishment and the functions of the CAT are described in ch 2, 'Functions of the CAT', pp 72–74; proceedings before the CAT are governed by the Competition Appeal Tribunal Rules 2015, SI 2015/1648.

601 *Société Cooperative De Production Seafrance SA v CMA* [2015] UKSC 75, para 44; *Napp Pharmaceutical Holdings Ltd v Director General of Fair Trading* [2002] EWCA Civ 796, paras 31 and 34 and *National Grid Plc v Gas and Electricity Markets Authority* [2010] EWCA Civ 114, paras 24–26; *Interclass Holdings Ltd v OFT* [2012] EWCA Civ 1056, para 59.

602 On the judicial review procedure, see Part 54 of the Civil Procedure Rules 1998, available at www.justice.gov.uk.

603 For a helpful summary of the relevant principles of judicial review see Case 1226/2/12/14 *Skyscanner Ltd v CMA* [2014] CAT 16, paras 32–33 and 106–107 (irrationality), 47–49 (procedural impropriety) and 104 (illegality).

refused if the Administrative Court were to consider that a particular decision could be appealed to the CAT[604].

(A) 'Appealable decisions'

Section 46[605] of the Competition Act sets out a list of 'appealable decisions' and states that the recipients of such decisions may appeal them to the CAT; appealable decisions include, for example, decisions as to whether the Chapter I and Chapter II prohibitions or Articles 101 and 102 TFEU have been infringed[606], interim measures decisions and decisions as to the imposition of, or the amount of, a penalty[607]. As can be seen from the Table of Competition Act decisions in chapter 9 many of the OFT's infringement decisions have been appealed to the CAT[608], both as to substance and as to the level of the penalty. For the most part the OFT's infringement decisions were upheld by the CAT. However the OFT withdrew its decision in *MasterCard*[609]; and was held to have abandoned its defence of the decision in *Tobacco*[610]. Only two infringement decisions have been annulled in their entirety on substantive grounds[611]. The penalties imposed by the OFT have been reduced in some cases, as shown in the Table of penalties earlier in this chapter[612].

Section 47 of the Competition Act gives third parties with a sufficient interest a right to appeal to the CAT in relation to appealable decisions. The CAT has said that there is no difference in principle between its treatment of an appeal against an infringement decision and an appeal by a third party against a non-infringement decision[613]. In practice, however, the CAT's role in third party appeals has been to control the adequacy of the authority's reasons and their correctness in law. There have been several appeals to the CAT by third parties disappointed that a competition authority had failed to find an infringement. In some cases the authority had explicitly decided that there was no infringement, so that there was no doubt that an appealable decision had been adopted; in some other cases, however, the authority closed the file without explicitly or consciously deciding that there was no infringement: in these cases the CAT has had to decide whether, at least implicitly, a finding of non-infringement had been reached, in which case an appealable decision could be brought before the CAT. If a decision is not appealable to the CAT, a third party can seek a judicial review in the Administrative Court[614].

(i) Successful appeals against explicit non-infringement decisions

There have been several successful appeals[615] by third parties against explicit non-infringement decisions of the OFT or a sectoral regulator. The first decision of the OFT under the

604 See *R (Sivasubramaniam) v Wandsworth County Court* [2002] EWCA Civ 1738, paras 46–47 and the case law there cited; on judicial review where an appeal system is in place see Craig *Administrative Law* (Sweet & Maxwell, 8th ed, 2016), paras 9-017–9-029.

605 As amended by art 10 of the Competition Act 1998 (Notification of Excluded Agreements and Appealable Decisions) Order 2000, SI 2000/263.

606 Competition Act 1998, s 46(3)(a) and (b).

607 Ibid, s 46(3)(i).

608 See ch 9, 'The Competition Act 1998 in Practice', pp 392–395.

609 Cases 1054–1056/1/1/05 *MasterCard UK Members Forum Ltd v OFT* [2006] CAT 15.

610 Cases 1160/1/1/10 etc *Imperial Tobacco plc v OFT* [2011] CAT 41.

611 Cases 1035/1/1/04 etc *Racecourse Association v OFT* [2005] CAT 29; Case 1122/1/1/09 *AH Willis & Sons Ltd v OFT* [2011] CAT 13.

612 See 'Table of penalties', pp 432–433 earlier in chapter.

613 Case 1046/2/4/04 *Albion Water Ltd v Director General of Water Services* [2005] CAT 40, para 243, citing earlier judgments in Case 1007/2/3/02 *Freeserve.com plc v Director General of Telecommunications* [2003] CAT 5 and Case 1044/2/1/04 *JJ Burgess & Sons v OFT* [2005] CAT 25.

614 In Case 1071/2/1/06 *Cityhook v OFT* Cityhook not only appealed to the CAT but also sought judicial review in the Administrative Court: [2009] EWHC 57 (Admin).

615 For an example of an unsuccessful appeal against an explicit non-infringement decision see Case 1073/2/1/06 *Terry Brannigan v OFT* [2007] CAT 23.

Competition Act, *General Insurance Standards Council*[616], was taken on appeal by third parties to the CAT[617]. The CAT disagreed with the OFT's finding that the rules of GISC, which prevented its insurer members from dealing with insurance intermediaries unless they were themselves members of GISC, did not infringe the Chapter I prohibition and remitted the case to the OFT for further consideration. As the rule to which the appellants had taken objection was then dropped the OFT was able to adopt a second non-infringement decision[618].

An appeal was brought by a third party against a decision by the OFT that there had been no infringement of the Chapter II prohibition in *Refusal to supply JJ Burgess Ltd with access to Harwood Park Crematorium*[619]. The case concerned a refusal on the part of Austin, a funeral director, to provide access to a crematorium to a competitor, JJ Burgess. In *Burgess v OFT*[620] the CAT set aside the OFT's non-infringement decision and substituted its own finding of infringement. The CAT was frustrated at the amount of time that the administrative proceedings had taken, and was concerned that a small operator such as JJ Burgess had failed to get redress from the OFT. It is of interest to note that the Consumers' Association (now known as Which?) intervened in support of JJ Burgess, and that the CAT welcomed the intervention.

In *Floe Telecom v Director General of Telecommunications*[621] the CAT annulled a non-infringement decision of OFTEL (now OFCOM)[622]. OFCOM subsequently adopted a second non-infringement decision that was upheld on appeal to the CAT, albeit on different grounds from those given by OFCOM[623]. On further appeal the Court of Appeal set aside the CAT's judgment and reinstated OFCOM's decision[624]. In *Albion Water/Thames Water*[625] the CAT set aside OFWAT's non-infringement decision for lack of reasoning. In *Albion Water/Dŵr Cymru*[626] the CAT annulled OFWAT's finding of non-infringement and substituted its own decision that Dŵr Cymru had abused its dominant position by imposing a margin squeeze on Albion Water[627] and by charging unfairly high prices[628].

(ii) Successful appeals against implicit non-infringement decisions

The CAT has handed down a number of judgments in which it held that the OFT or one of the sectoral regulators had adopted an appealable decision that the Competition Act or that Article 101 or 102 TFEU had not been infringed, despite their protestations that they had simply closed their file on administrative grounds[629]. In *Claymore v OFT* the CAT

616 OFT decision of 26 January 2001.

617 Cases 1002–1004/2/1/01 *Institute of Independent Insurance Brokers v Director General of Fair Trading* [2001] CAT 4.

618 *General Insurance Standards Council*, OFT decision of 13 November 2002.

619 OFT decision of 12 August 2004; there had been an earlier decision to the same effect in *Harwood Park Crematorium*, OFT decision of 6 August 2002; this decision was withdrawn by the OFT by decision of 9 April 2003 pursuant to s 47(5) of the Competition Act.

620 Case 1044/2/1/04 [2005] CAT 25.

621 Case 1024/2/3/04 [2004] CAT 18.

622 *Disconnection of Floe Telecom Ltd's Services by Vodafone Ltd*, OFTEL decision of 3 November 2003.

623 OFCOM decision of 28 June 2005, upheld on appeal Case 1024/2/3/04 *Floe Telecom Ltd v OFCOM* [2006] CAT 17.

624 *OFCOM v Floe Telecom Ltd* [2009] EWCA Civ 47.

625 Case 1042/2/4/04 [2006] CAT 7.

626 OFWAT decision of 26 May 2004.

627 Case 1046/2/4/04 *Albion Water Ltd v Water Services Regulation Authority* [2006] CAT 23 and [2006] CAT 36, upheld on appeal to the Court of Appeal [2008] EWCA Civ 536.

628 Case 1046/2/4/04 [2008] CAT 31.

629 See Case 1006/2/1/01 *BetterCare Group v Director General of Fair Trading* [2002] CAT 6; Case 1008/2/1/02 *Freeserve.com plc v Director General of Telecommunications* [2003] CAT 3; Case 1007/2/3/02 *Claymore Dairies Ltd and Express Dairies plc v Director General of Fair Trading* [2002] CAT 8; Case 1017/2/1/03 *Pernod-Ricard SA v OFT* [2004] CAT 10; for comment on the issue of appealable decisions see Bailey 'When are Decisions Appealable Under the Competition Act 1998?' [2003] Comp Law 41; Alese 'The Office Burden: Making a Decision Without Making a Decision for a Third Party' (2003) 24 ECLR 616; Rayment 'What is an Appealable Decision under the Competition Act 1998?' [2004] Comp Law 132.

summarised the law on the meaning of an appealable decision as follows[630]. First, the question of whether an appealable decision has been taken is primarily a question of fact, to be decided in accordance with the particular circumstances of the case. Secondly, whether such a decision has been taken is a question of substance, not form, to be determined objectively: the test to be applied is whether a decision has been taken on an appealable matter, 'either expressly or by necessary implication'. Thirdly, there is a distinction between the exercise of an administrative discretion not to proceed to the adoption of a decision, and the adoption of an appealable decision. If the CMA were to close a case file because it concluded that, as a matter of priority, other cases have a higher importance, that would not amount to an appealable decision[631]. Similarly, the CMA is unlikely to adopt an appealable decision where it closes the file because the matter complained of is the subject of private litigation[632].

The case law requires the UK competition authorities to be clear about their selection of cases for investigation and, as a consequence, of their rejection of others on the ground that they are not an administrative priority. As a result the authorities have published guidance on the prioritisation of their work[633].

(iii) **Unsuccessful appeals by third party complainants**

In five cases, *Aquavitae v OFWAT*[634], *Independent Water v OFWAT*[635], *Casting Book v OFT*[636], *Cityhook v OFT*[637] and *Independent Media v OFCOM*[638], the CAT held that the OFT or the sectoral regulator had not adopted a decision that could be appealed to the CAT. In the cases of *Aquavitae* and *Independent Water* the CAT accepted that the regulator had chosen to deal with the problems in question using its sector-specific regulatory powers and therefore had not adopted an appealable decision that the Chapter II prohibition had not been infringed. In *Casting Book* and *Cityhook* the CAT was satisfied that the OFT had closed its investigation into alleged anti-competitive behaviour for reasons genuinely independent of the merits of the case and without having reached any conclusion on those merits. In *Independent Media* the CAT was satisfied that, when OFCOM decided to close its file, it had 'genuinely abstained from expressing a firm view, one way or the other, on the question of infringement'[639]; however it considered that the position of the complainant was therefore an unsatisfactory one, but one that could be remedied only by legislation[640].

The jurisdictional skirmishes just described could be avoided if the CAT were to be given jurisdiction to hear all cases arising under the Competition Act[641].

(B) **The Competition Appeal Tribunal Rules 2015**

The CAT's rules of procedure are contained in the Competition Appeal Tribunal Rules 2015[642]. The CAT has published *A Guide to Proceedings*[643], which describes the Tribunal's

[630] [2003] CAT 3, para 122.

[631] Ibid, para 125; on this point the CAT specifically referred to the judgment of the General Court in Case T-24/90 *Automec v Commission (No 2)* EU:T:1992:97; see also Case 1071/2/1/06 *Cityhook v OFT* [2007] CAT 18, paras 145 ff.

[632] Note that this was a reason for the European Commission's closure of the file in the *Automec* case, ch 10 n 631 earlier.

[633] See ch 10 n 21 earlier.

[634] Case 1012/2/3/03 [2003] CAT 17.

[635] Case 1058/2/4/06 [2007] CAT 6.

[636] Case 1068/2/1/06 [2006] CAT 35.

[637] Case 1071/2/1/06 [2007] CAT 18.

[638] Case 1087/2/3/07 [2007] CAT 29.

[639] Ibid, para 42.

[640] Ibid, para 56; see similarly the President's statement in the CAT's *Annual Review and Accounts 2006/2007*, p 4, available at www.catribunal.org.uk.

[641] The Government raised this possibility in its public consultation, *Streamlining Regulatory and Competition Appeals—Consultation on Options for Reform*, 19 June 2013, para 5.44.

[642] SI 2015/1648.

[643] October 2015, available at www.catribunal.org.uk; the *Guide* is a Practice Direction within the meaning of r 115(3) of the Competition Appeal Tribunal Rules 2015.

functions and its procedures relating to appeals, applications for review and private actions for damages and injunctions. The CAT has also created a User Group to discuss points relating to the practical operation of the Tribunal; the minutes of the meetings are available on its website[644]. The CAT has pointed out that, when a case reaches it, the matter ceases to be an administrative procedure, as it is when the competition authority acts as investigator, prosecutor and decision-maker, and becomes, instead, a judicial proceeding[645].

When interpreting and applying its Rules the CAT must ensure that each case is dealt with justly and at proportionate cost[646]. The CAT must also actively manage cases and ensure that each case proceeds in the quickest and most efficient manner possible[647]. Four features of the CAT's procedure should be noted[648]:

- each party's case must be fully set out in writing as early as possible, together with the evidence relied on
- the CAT will generally indicate a target date for the main hearing, with straightforward cases to be completed within six to nine months
- the CAT will establish effective fact-finding procedures
- the CAT will plan the structure of the main hearing, with a defined time limit.

Once an appeal has been lodged with the CAT it can be withdrawn only with the Tribunal's permission unless the authority withdraws the decision under challenge; the CAT has said that improper pressure should not be applied by one litigant upon another to withdraw an appeal.

(C) Procedure before the CAT

The rules of the CAT give the CAT broad case-management powers[649]; a brief perusal of the CAT's website reveals a substantial number of rulings on procedural issues[650]. The procedure before the CAT is predominantly written; submissions should be kept as short as possible. Where an expert is asked to produce a report, that expert's duty is to assist the Tribunal, and this overrides his or her obligation to the person from whom the instructions were received and from whom payment was received[651]. In appeals where facts are in dispute between the competition authority and the appellants, such as *Toys and Games*[652], *Football Shirts*[653] and *Dairy Products*[654], the CAT's ability to probe the evidence and to provide for the cross-examination of witnesses has been an important feature of the procedure. *Tobacco*[655] illustrates the way that evidence can be tested before the CAT: in that case the witness evidence did not support the OFT's decision. In *Paroxetine*[656] and

644 See www.catribunal.org.uk/5300/User-Group.html.

645 Case 1001/1/1/01 *Napp Pharmaceutical Holdings Ltd v Director General of Fair Trading* [2002] CAT 1, para 117.

646 Competition Appeal Tribunal Rules 2015, r 4(1); see also r 2(2).

647 Ibid, r 4(4)–(5); *Guide to Proceedings*, para 3.3.

648 *Guide to Proceedings*, para 3.5.

649 Competition Appeal Tribunal Rules 2015, rr 19–24 (appeals) and rr 53–57 (claims for damages).

650 www.catribunal.org.uk.

651 *Guide to Proceedings*, October 2015, para 7.67 and CPR 35.3(1); see Case 1009/1/1/02 *Aberdeen Journals Ltd v OFT* [2003] CAT 11, para 288; see also Case 1000/1/1/01 *Napp Pharmaceutical Holdings Ltd v Director General of Fair Trading* [2002] CAT 1, para 254; see also (in proceedings in the High Court) *Leeds City Council v Watkins* [2003] UKCLR 467, para 88.

652 Cases 1014 and 1015/1/1/03 *Argos Ltd and Littlewoods Ltd v OFT* [2004] CAT 24.

653 Cases 1021 and 1022/1/1/03 *JJB Sports plc and Allsports Ltd v OFT* [2004] CAT 17.

654 Case 1188/1/1/11 *Tesco Stores Ltd v OFT* [2012] CAT 31.

655 Cases 1160/1/1/10 etc *Imperial Tobacco plc v OFT* [2011] CAT 41.

656 Cases 1252/1/12/16 etc *GlaxoSmithKline plc v CMA* [2018] CAT 4.

Socrates v Law Society[657] the CAT used a so-called 'hot tub' for the joint presentation and scrutiny of the experts' oral evidence, which shortened the time required for economic evidence at trial.

An appellant is not limited to placing before the CAT the evidence it has placed before the CMA[658], although the CAT has power to rule that evidence should not be admitted[659]. The fact an appellant did not put forward a positive case to the CMA may cast doubt on the veracity of the evidence put forward during an appeal[660]. The CMA is normally expected to defend its decision on the basis of the material before it when it took its decision, although it may be permitted to adduce new evidence to ensure the fairness of the appeal process[661]. The CAT has held that the strict rules of evidence do not apply in proceedings before it, and has held that it will be guided by overall considerations of fairness, rather than technical rules[662]. As a result the CAT tends to be more concerned with the weight to be attached to disclosed documents rather than their admissibility[663].

Where third parties appeal against a decision of one of the competition authorities the CAT considers that the appellant must show why the decision should be set aside on the basis of the material before the authority.

The CAT may expedite any proceedings before it. There is also a 'fast-track procedure' for less complex claims to be decided quickly with limited risk as to costs[664]. The policy behind the fast-track procedure is to help individuals and small and medium-sized enterprises ('SMEs') to obtain access to justice, in particular injunctive relief, in an appropriate case[665]. The CAT has held that follow-on actions for damages in cartel cases are generally not suitable for the fast-track procedure[666].

(D) **Appeal on the merits**

The Competition Act provides for an appeal 'on the merits' and the powers of the CAT are extensive: considerably wider than those of a court exercising judicial review[667]. The CAT has held that an appeal on the merits requires it to consider whether a decision was the right one rather than whether a decision was within the range of reasonable responses[668]. The appeals process does not envisage a re-run of the administrative procedure; rather the CAT reviews a decision through the prism of the specific errors that are alleged by an appellant[669]. The CAT has demonstrated that it is willing to exercise a robust form of

657 Case 1249/5/7/16 *Socrates Training Ltd v Law Society* [2017] CAT 10, para 13.

658 See Case 1001/1/1/01 *Napp Pharmaceutical Holdings Ltd v Director General of Fair Trading* [2001] CAT 3, para 76; see also the Court of Appeal judgment in *British Telecommunications Plc v Office of Communications* [2011] EWCA Civ 245, paras 62–63 per Toulson LJ.

659 Competition Appeal Tribunal Rules 2015, r 21; *Guide to Proceedings*, paras 7.71–7.78; see also Case 1188/1/1/11 *Tesco Stores Ltd v OFT* [2012] CAT 31, para 124 and Case 1279/1/12/17 *Ping Europe Ltd v CMA* [2018] CAT 8.

660 See Case 1061/1/1/06 *Makers UK Ltd v OFT* [2007] CAT 11, paras 42 and 79.

661 See Case 1188/1/1/11 *Tesco Stores Ltd v OFT* [2012] CAT 31, para 124 and case law cited; Case 1252/1/12/16 *GlaxoSmithKline plc v CMA* [2016] CAT 24.

662 Cases 1014 and 1015/1/1/03 *Argos Ltd and Littlewoods Ltd v OFT* [2003] CAT 16, para 105.

663 Case 1262/5/7/16 (T) *Agents' Mutual Ltd v Gascoigne Halman Ltd* [2017] CAT 5, para 9.

664 Competition Appeal Tribunal Rules 2015, r 58; *Guide to Proceedings*, paras 5.139–5.149.

665 Case 1249/5/7/16 *Socrates Training Ltd v Law Society* [2016] CAT 10, para 3.

666 Case 1250/5/7/16 *Breasley Pillows Ltd v Vita Cellular (Foams) Ltd* [2016] CAT 8, paras 28–31.

667 Case 1007/2/3/02 *Freeserve.com plc v Director General of Telecommunications* [2003] CAT 5, para 106.

668 Case 1083/3/3/07 *Hutchison 3G UK Ltd v OFCOM* [2008] CAT 11, para 164.

669 Case 1151/3/3/10 *British Telecommunications Plc v OFCOM* [2010] CAT 17, para 78, upheld on appeal to the Court of Appeal [2011] EWCA Civ 245.

merits review in appeals under the Act: in several cases the CAT has set aside findings of infringement for want of evidence[670].

(E) **The powers of the CAT**

The CAT's powers are set out in paragraph 3 of Schedule 8 to the Competition Act, and include the power to adopt interim measures[671], to confirm or set aside the decision that is the subject of the appeal, to remit the matter to the CMA or sectoral regulator, to impose or revoke or vary the amount of a penalty[672], to give directions, for example to bring an end to an abuse of a dominant position[673] or to make a decision, for example finding an infringement of the Chapter I or II prohibitions[674].

As one might expect, the way in which the CAT exercises its jurisdiction will depend on the particular circumstances of the case. In *Aberdeen Journals*[675] the CAT was dissatisfied with the OFT's treatment of product market definition in a Chapter II case but remitted the matter to the OFT for further consideration rather than substituting its finding which, as a matter of law, it was at liberty to do. Similarly in *Freeserve*[676] the CAT remitted the issue of whether BT was guilty of abusive pricing practices to OFCOM. In each of these cases the CAT was mindful of the need to avoid the risk of converting itself from an appellate tribunal into a court of first instance. However there have been some occasions when the CAT has made its own decisions on substance, as in the *Burgess v OFT* and the *Albion Water v OFWAT* cases that were discussed earlier[677]. The CAT has on a number of occasions substituted its own finding on the level of penalties[678].

(F) **Costs**

The Competition Appeal Tribunal Rules 2015[679] enable the CAT to make such order as it thinks fit in relation to costs[680]. The Court of Appeal has confirmed that the CAT rules do not apply the conventional rule in civil litigation that 'costs follow the event': the CAT has a wide discretion in relation to costs and has repeatedly said that 'the only rule is that there are no rules'[681]. However the Rules set out several factors that the Tribunal may take into account in making a costs order, such as the conduct of the parties.

[670] See eg Case 1118/1/1/09 *GMI Construction Holdings plc v OFT* [2011] CAT 12; Case 1121/1/1/09 *Durkan Holdings Ltd v OFT* [2011] CAT 6, paras 93–125; Case 1122/1/1/09 *AH Willis & Sons Ltd v OFT* [2011] CAT 3; Case 1124/1/1/09 *North Midland Construction plc v OFT* [2011] CAT 14, paras 14–34; Case 1188/1/1/11 *Tesco Stores Ltd v OFT* [2012] CAT 31, paras 486–488.

[671] Competition Act 1998, Sch 8, para 3(2)(d) and Competition Appeal Tribunal Rules 2015, r 24; see Case 1274/1/12/16 (IR) *Flynn Pharma v CMA* [2017] CAT 1, paras 29–33 and case law cited.

[672] The penalty is automatically suspended pending the appeal (Competition Act 1998, s 46(4)), but the CAT may order that interest is payable (ibid, Sch 8, para 10 and SI 2015/1648, r 105): see Case 1099/1/2/08 *National Grid Plc v Gas and Electricity Markets Authority* [2009] CAT 14, para 229(c).

[673] See eg Case 1016/1/1/03 *Genzyme Ltd v OFT* [2005] CAT 32 and Cases 1034/2/4/04 (IR) and 1046/2/4/04 *Albion Water Ltd v Water Services Regulation Authority* [2009] CAT 12.

[674] The Court of Appeal confirmed that the CAT had such jurisdiction in *Dŵr Cymru Cyfyngedig v Albion Water Ltd* [2008] EWCA Civ 536, paras 112–128.

[675] Case 1005/1/1/01 *Aberdeen Journals Ltd v Director General of Fair Trading* [2002] CAT 4.

[676] Case 1007/2/3/02 *Freeserve.com plc v Director General of Telecommunications* [2003] CAT 5; OFCOM subsequently adopted a second non-infringement decision on 2 November 2010 and the appeal was subsequently withdrawn.

[677] See 'Successful appeals against explicit non-infringement decisions', pp 453–454 earlier in chapter.

[678] See 'Table of penalties' at pp 432–433 earlier in chapter.

[679] SI 2015/1648; on costs generally see *Guide to Proceedings*, October 2015, paras 8.1–8.10.

[680] Competition Appeal Tribunal Rules 2015, r 104(2); even if the parties reach an agreement on costs, the CAT considers it has the power to make an alternative costs order: see Cases 1014 and 1015/1/1/03 *Argos Ltd v OFT* [2005] CAT 15, paras 4–5.

[681] *Quarmby Construction Co Ltd v OFT* [2012] EWCA Civ 1552, para 23.

In the *Merger Action Group* case (dealing with a merger under the Enterprise Act rather than an enforcement decision under the Competition Act) the CAT gave the following guidance on its approach to costs (expenses in Scotland):

- the CAT must always exercise its discretion so as to deal with a case justly[682]
- the factors relevant to the award of costs are too many and too varied to be identified exhaustively, but the CAT will normally consider:
  - the success or failure overall or on particular issues
  - the parties' conduct in relation to the proceedings
  - nature, purpose and subject-matter of the proceedings[683]
- the CAT considers that there is no inconsistency between the CAT's discretion, and an approach to its exercise which adopts a specific starting point[684]; for example the starting point in appeals under the Competition Act is that a successful party would normally (but not always) obtain a costs award in its favour[685].

In addition to this general guidance some more specific trends can be discerned.

First, the CAT has not wanted to deter small or medium-sized firms from appealing against cartel decisions for fear of having to pay the authority's costs if unsuccessful: this can be seen in *Apex v OFT*[686], although the CAT also noted other factors in that case that contributed to its decision to make no order for costs against the unsuccessful appellant[687]. The CAT rejected the argument that there should be no costs award against an authority where it has taken a decision conscientiously and in good faith[688]. However in *Sepia Logistics v OFT*[689] the CAT awarded costs to the OFT in a case where the unsuccessful appellant was not a substantial undertaking, but where the appeal lacked merit and did not involve novel points of law. Similarly in *National Grid* the CAT decided that the regulator 'should not have to pick up the tab' for the costs of rebutting points, in particular on market definition, which the CAT considered were 'bound to fail'[690].

A second point is that the CAT does not have the same anxiety in the case of more substantial firms. In *Aberdeen Journals v OFT*[691] the CAT expressed concern at the significant costs to the public purse involved in competition law appeals, a point repeated in *Genzyme v OFT*[692] and in *Football Shirts*[693]. In *National Grid* the CAT specifically pointed out that the appellant was a large and well-resourced company and that an award of costs against it would be unlikely to dissuade such a company from bringing an appeal[694].

Thirdly, it is clear that the CAT has, on some occasions, felt disquiet at the level of the fees charged by City law firms for their advice; and in particular at the number of hours

682 Case 1107/4/10/08 *Merger Action Group v Secretary of State for Business, Enterprise and Regulatory Reform* [2009] CAT 19, para 16.

683 Ibid, para 19. 684 Ibid, para 21.

685 See eg Cases 1035/1/1/04 etc *Racecourse Association v OFT* [2006] CAT 1, para 8; Cases 1140/1/1/09 etc *Eden Brown Ltd v OFT* [2011] CAT 29, para 18.

686 Case 1032/1/1/04 *Apex Asphalt and Paving Co Ltd v OFT* [2005] CAT 11; see similarly in the context of a follow-on action for damages Case 1028/5/7/04 *BCL Old Co Ltd v Aventis SA* [2005] CAT 2.

687 Ibid, para 26. 688 Cases 1140/1/1/09 etc *Eden Brown Ltd v OFT* [2011] CAT 29, paras 8–18.

689 Case 1072/1/1/06 [2007] CAT 14.

690 Case 1099/1/2/08 *National Grid Plc v Gas and Electricity Markets Authority* [2009] CAT 14.

691 Case 1009/1/1/02 [2002] CAT 21.

692 Case 1013/1/1/03 (IR) and Case 1016/1/1/03 consent order of 14 November 2005 and Case 1016/1/1/03 consent order of 29 November 2005.

693 Cases 1019/1/1/03 etc *Umbro Holdings Ltd v OFT* [2005] CAT 26.

694 Case 1099/1/2/08 [2009] CAT 24, para 16.

charged by partners as opposed to associates[695]. The CAT capped the amount of costs that could be recovered in *Socrates v Law Society*[696], a case that had been allocated to the fast-track procedure. Fourthly, the Tribunal's 'general position' is that interveners should not expect to recover their costs[697].

(G) Appeals from the CAT to the Court of Appeal and from the Court of Appeal to the Supreme Court

Appeals on points of law lie, with permission, from the CAT to the Court of Appeal[698]. The CAT has said that permission to appeal should be granted sparingly[699]; permission will be granted where there is a real prospect of success or there is some other compelling reason why the appeal should be heard[700]. The Court of Appeal has recognised that the CAT is a specialised body with whose assessment it should hesitate to interfere[701]. However the Court of Appeal can and will intervene where the CAT has misdirected itself in law[702].

Appeals on points of law of general public importance lie, with permission, from the Court of Appeal, to the Supreme Court. The Supreme Court has emphasised that appellate courts should approach appeals challenging the economic judgments of expert tribunals with an appropriate degree of caution[703].

9. Article 267 References

The preliminary ruling procedure of Article 267 TFEU enables the Court of Justice to rule on questions of EU law referred by national courts or tribunals[704]. Two questions arise: first, can an Article 267 reference be made by a court or tribunal when applying the Competition Act, as opposed to Articles 101 and/or 102 TFEU; and second, which courts or tribunals in the UK are able to make an Article 267 reference.

(A) Can an Article 267 reference be made where a court or tribunal is applying the Competition Act 1998?

The jurisprudence of the Court of Justice strongly suggests that references under Article 267 will be possible in cases where only the Competition Act is applicable, but where

[695] See eg Cases 1035/1/1/04 etc *Racecourse Association v OFT* [2006] CAT 1, paras 30–35; Case 1049/4/1/05 *UniChem Ltd v OFT* [2005] CAT 31, paras 27–31; and Case 1104/6/8/08 *Tesco plc v Competition Commission* [2009] CAT 26, paras 42–46.

[696] See eg Case 1249/5/7/16 *Socrates Training Ltd v Law Society* [2017] CAT 12; the CAT imposed a costs management order in a case transferred from the High Court: Case 1262/5/7/16 (T) *Agents' Mutual Ltd v Gascoigne Halman Ltd* [2016] CAT 15.

[697] Case 1239/4/12/15 *Ryanair Holdings plc v CMA* [2015] CAT 15, para 3; for an example of an intervener being awarded its costs see Cases 1005/1/1/01 etc *Aberdeen Journals Ltd v Office of Fair Trading* [2003] CAT 21, paras 22–23.

[698] Competition Act 1998, s 49.

[699] Case 1151/3/3/10 *British Telecommunications Plc v OFCOM* [2010] CAT 22, para 7(c).

[700] See eg Case 1023/4/1/03 *IBA Health Ltd v OFT* [2003] CAT 28, paras 4–5.

[701] See eg *OFT v Somerfield Stores Ltd* [2014] EWCA Civ 400, para 24 and case law cited.

[702] See eg *OFCOM v Floe Telecom Ltd* [2006] EWCA Civ 768 (on jurisdiction of the CAT); *OFCOM v Floe Telecom Ltd* and *T-Mobile Ltd v Floe Telecom Ltd* [2009] EWCA Civ 47 (disagreeing with the CAT's reasons for dismissing appeal); *National Grid plc v Gas and Electricity Markets Authority* [2010] EWCA Civ 114, paras 90–115 (disagreeing with the CAT's assessment of the penalty); *OFT v Somerfield Stores Ltd* [2014] EWCA Civ 400 (finding that the CAT had erred in law when it extended time to appeal).

[703] *Société Cooperative De Production Seafrance SA v CMA* [2015] UKSC 75, para 44 and case law cited.

[704] See generally Green and Brealey (eds) *Competition Litigation: UK Practice and Procedure* (Oxford University Press, 2010), ch 21; it is for the referring court or tribunal to determine the content of the questions to be put to the Court of Justice, which will not opine on questions raised by the parties to the litigation unless the referring court asks it to: Cases C-376/05 etc *A Brünsteiner GmbH v Bayerische Motorenwerke AG* EU:C:2006:753, paras 25–29.

guidance on Articles 101 and/or 102 would be helpful[705]. This approach helpfully avoids national laws based upon the EU rules being interpreted in a substantially different way from the meaning given to them by EU institutions.

(B) Which courts or tribunals in the UK can make an Article 267 reference in a case under the Competition Act 1998?

It is clear that the Supreme Court, the Court of Appeal, the High Court and the CAT can make Article 267 references. In March 2018 the CAT referred ten questions to the Court of Justice for a preliminary ruling in *Paroxetine*; this was the first time it had made an Article 267 reference. What is less clear is whether the CMA or the sectoral regulators could make a reference. It is a matter of EU law to determine who qualifies as courts or tribunals[706]. Lord Simon, in the House of Lords debate on the Competition Bill, thought that it would be possible for the authorities to make a reference[707], although he subsequently resiled from this position[708]. It may be that the point will not arise, since the authorities may determine of their own volition not to attempt to make such a reference. In *Syfait* the Court of Justice held that the Greek Competition Authority was neither a court nor tribunal for the purposes of Article 267[709].

The courts and tribunals in the UK will presumably lose the ability to refer questions to the Court of Justice after the UK leaves the EU, though this will depend on the outcome of the Brexit negotiations.

10. NAO Reports on the UK Competition Regime

The NAO has published three reports on the UK competition regime: in 2005[710], 2009[711] and 2016[712]. These reports are a significant part of the structure of accountability for the competition authorities. In its 2016 Report the NAO found that the CMA had taken significant steps to tackle the failings identified in previous reports, and that action had been taken to improve the detection of anti-competitive behaviour, to build a pipeline of cases and to improve the robustness of its work. At the time of its Report, the NAO said that there had yet to be a substantial flow of new decisions; it also noted that awareness of competition law, especially among SMEs, was low. In its Annual Plans for 2016/17 and for 2017/18 the CMA committed to step up the pace, scale and impact of its enforcement and to support businesses in understanding and complying with competition law[713].

The Secretary of State is due to report to Parliament on the operation of Part 1 of the Competition Act by 31 March 2019[714].

[705] See eg Case C-542/14 *SIA 'VM Remonts' v Konkurences padome* EU:C:2016:578, para 17 and the case law cited.

[706] See eg Case C-54/96 *Dorsch Consult Ingenieurgesellschaft mbH v Bundesbaugesellschaft Berlin mbH* EU:C:1997:413; Case C-178/99 *Salzman* EU:C:2001:331; on this point see Brown and Jacobs *The Court of Justice of the European Communities* (Sweet & Maxwell, 5th ed, 2000), pp 223–227; Dashwood, Dougan, Rodger, Spaventa and Wyatt (eds) *European Union Law* (Hart, 6th ed, 2011), pp 214–216.

[707] HL Committee, 25 November 1997, col 963.

[708] Ibid, col 975.

[709] Case C-53/03 *Synetairismos Farmakopoion Aitolias & Akarnanias and Others v GlaxoSmithKline Plc* EU:C:2005:333, paras 29–38.

[710] *The Office of Fair Trading: Enforcing competition in markets*, HC 593, 2005–6, 17 November 2005.

[711] *The Office of Fair Trading: Progress report on maintaining competition in markets*, HC 127, 2008–9, 5 March 2009.

[712] *UK competition authorities: the UK competition regime*, HC 737, 2015–16, 5 February 2016; for comment see Whish 'The National Audit Office's Report on the UK Competition Regime: How Well is the Regime Performing?' [2016] Comp Law 191.

[713] Available at www.gov.uk/cma.

[714] ERRA 2013, s 46.

11

Enterprise Act 2002: market studies and market investigations

1. Introduction

When the UK Competition and Markets Authority[1] ('the CMA') discovers markets that appear not to be working well for consumers, and when it seems unlikely that any problems that exist will be corrected by normal competitive forces, it will consider whether there is a sufficiently strong case to enforce the prohibition of anti-competitive agreements or the abuse of a dominant position. However in some cases direct enforcement action may not be the most effective way of dealing with a problematic market. A question then arises as to whether the CMA has other tools available to address any market failure, and as to remedies that might be appropriate to address that failure.

In UK competition law there are two other ways in which a problem of market failure may be tackled in circumstances where the Chapter I and Chapter II prohibitions are inapplicable for want of evidence of an agreement or abuse. First, the CMA may conduct a 'market study'[2] in order to understand as well as possible how markets are working and whether the needs of consumers are being met. Secondly, the CMA may make a 'market investigation reference' under Part 4 of the Enterprise Act 2002 in order to discover whether any features of a market prevent, restrict or distort competition; if so the CMA group conducting the market reference must consider how those adverse effects and any detriment to customers could be remedied. Each of these tools will be described in this chapter.

Section 2 of this chapter describes the CMA's 'general function' of gathering information about markets and section 3 explains what is meant by a 'super-complaint'. Section 4

[1] See ch 2, 'The CMA', pp 64–70.

[2] The OECD reports that 58 jurisdictions that participated in a 2015 survey use market studies in some form in their work: see OECD Background Paper *Methodologies for Market Studies* (June 2017) p 5, available at www.oecd.org/competition.

discusses the purpose, procedure and outcomes of market studies. Market studies sometimes lead to market investigation references, though, as explained later, there are several other possible outcomes of a market study. Section 5 describes the making and determination of market investigation references under Part 4 of the Enterprise Act 2002. The Enterprise Act was amended by the Enterprise and Regulatory Reform Act 2013 ('the ERRA'), and the text that follows incorporates those amendments. 'Public interest cases' are briefly referred to in section 6, while sections 7 and 8 deal with the issue of enforcement and other supplementary matters. Section 9 of the chapter considers how the market investigation provisions work in practice. The final section of the chapter briefly refers to the enforcement and review of undertakings and orders still in force under the monopoly provisions in the former Fair Trading Act 1973.

2. Gathering Information About Markets

Section 5 of the Enterprise Act 2002 provides that one of the general functions of the CMA is to obtain, compile and keep under review information about matters relating to the carrying out of its functions. One of the ways in which the CMA carries out this general function is by conducting 'market studies' of markets that appear not to be working well for consumers[3]. The CMA also gathers information by carrying out desktop research and engaging with market participants and other interested persons prior to conducting a market study[4]. The CMA has published 'calls for information' to enable it to understand as well as possible how markets are working[5]. The CMA has also published reports on significant matters without designating them as market studies; these tended to be investigations that involved information gathering without any expectation that one of the outcomes usually expected of a market study would follow[6].

3. Super-Complaints

Section 11 of the Enterprise Act 2002 provides for so-called 'super-complaints' to be made to the CMA[7]. Section 205 of the Enterprise Act enables the Secretary of State to extend the system so that super-complaints can be made to the sectoral regulators[8]; this was effected by statutory instrument[9]. The coordination of super-complaint concurrent duties is based on policies agreed and applied through the UK Competition Network[10].

[3] See 'Market Studies', pp 465–469 later in chapter.

[4] See *Market Studies and Market Investigations: Supplemental guidance on the CMA's approach*, CMA3, January 2014, revised July 2017, para 1.8, available at www.gov.uk/cma; see also para 299 of the *Explanatory Notes* to the ERRA.

[5] See eg *Call for information: commercial use of consumer data*, CMA38con, January 2015, which led to a report: CMA38, June 2015, available at www.gov.uk/cma.

[6] See eg *Online reviews and endorsements*, CMA41, June 2015 and *Online search: Consumer and firm behaviour*, April 2017, available at www.gov.uk/cma.

[7] There is a separate system of super-complaints in relation to markets for financial services and payment systems: Financial Services Act 2012, s 234C (to the FCA) and Financial Services (Banking Reform) Act 2013, s 68 (to the PSR).

[8] Note that NHS Improvement does not have power to deal with super-complaints: see *Regulated Industries: Guidance on concurrent application of competition law to regulated industries*, CMA10, March 2014, fn 112.

[9] The Enterprise Act 2002 (Super-complaints to Regulators) Order 2003, SI 2003/1368, as amended by SI 2006/522.

[10] The UKCN's website is www.gov.uk/government/groups/uk-competition-network.

(A) Purpose of super-complaints

The idea of a super-complaint is that a designated consumer body can make a complaint to the CMA about features of a market for goods or services in the UK that appear to be significantly harming the interests of consumers[11]. This is a way of making the consumer's voice more powerful: individual consumers often lack the knowledge, motivation or experience to complain effectively, but a designated consumer body should have the resources and ability to do so.

(B) Super-complainants

Consumer bodies are designated by the Secretary of State[12]. There is *Guidance for bodies seeking designation as super-complainants* on the designation criteria and on how to apply for designated status[13]. As of 8 December 2017 the Secretary of State had designated the following bodies as super-complainants:

- The Campaign for Real Ale
- The Consumer Council for Water
- Which?
- The General Consumer Council for Northern Ireland
- Citizens Advice
- The National Consumer Council
- The Scottish Association of Citizens Advice Bureaux[14].

The Secretary of State rejected an application by What Car? to become a super-complainant because it did not satisfy the criteria in the *Guidance*[15].

(C) Guidance

The *Super-complaints: Guidance for designated consumer bodies*[16] is intended to assist those wishing to make a super-complaint: it describes the information that should be contained in a super-complaint, how cases will be handled and possible outcomes.

(D) Procedure

When making a super-complaint, a super-complainant must set out the reasons why, in its view, a market in the UK for goods or services has a feature, or combination of features, that is or appears to be significantly harming the interests of consumers and should therefore be investigated. The CMA must respond to a super-complaint by publishing a 'fast-track' report on what action, if any, it intends to take within 90 days[17]; the Secretary of State has power to amend the 90-day period[18]. The CMA, when dealing with a super-complaint, can request information under section 5(1) of the Enterprise Act 2002;

[11] Enterprise Act 2002, s 11(1).

[12] Ibid, s 11(5) and (6); see also the Electricity Act 2002 (Part 8 Designated Enforcers: Criteria for Designation, Designation of Public Bodies as Designated Enforcers and Transitional Provisions) Order 2003, SI 2003/1399, as amended by SI 2006/522.

[13] The *Guidance* is available at www.nationalarchives.gov.uk.

[14] See the Enterprise Act 2002 (Bodies Designated to make Super-complaints) (Amendment) Order 2009, SI 2009/2079, which came into force on 1 October 2009.

[15] See www.nationalarchives.gov.uk.

[16] OFT 514, July 2003, available at www.gov.uk/cma.

[17] Enterprise Act 2002, s 11(2).

[18] Ibid, s 11(4).

however it has formal powers to demand information under section 174 of the Act only where it has published a 'market study notice' or believes that it has power to make a market investigation reference.

In practice the requirement to investigate and report within 90 days imposes a considerable burden on the CMA to gather evidence, synthesise it and form a view, which in turn results in a corresponding burden on the parties that are the subject of the super-complaint; the 90-day period leaves little time for the CMA and the parties concerned to consider possible remedies to any problems identified.

(E) **Outcomes of super-complaints**

A super-complaint can lead to a number of responses, including, though not limited to, competition or consumer law enforcement, referral to a sectoral regulator, the launch of a market study by the CMA or a market investigation reference[19].

It is quite often the case that a super-complaint will lead to a market study or even to a market investigation reference: in other words a super-complaint may lead to a lengthy period of scrutiny of the market, and the firms that operate on the market, to which the complaint relates. The super-complaint on *Payment protection insurance* of September 2005 led to a lengthy market study that was followed by a market investigation reference in February 2007. The Competition Commission published its final report in January 2009; there was then a judicial review which resulted in the Commission having to reconsider one of its proposed remedies. The final order did not enter into force until April 2012.

Several super-complaints have led to recommendations that firms' behaviour, regulation, guidance and/or legislation should be changed. For example the CMA responded to the super-complaint on *Pricing practices in the groceries market* by making recommendations to the Government that led to the Chartered Trading Standards Institute publishing guidance on pricing practices[20]. The Office of Rail and Road ('the ORR') recommended a national campaign to increase passenger awareness about the right to claim compensation in response to the super-complaint on *Rail delay refunds*[21].

Table 11.1 gives details of two super-complaints made since the publication of the eighth edition of this book and completed by 8 December 2017. A table of all the super-complaints made to date will be found on the Online Resources that accompany this book[22].

4. **Market Studies**

The CMA conducts 'market studies' of markets that appear not to be working well for consumers but where enforcement action under competition or consumer law does not, at first sight, appear to be the most appropriate response. The sectoral regulators also conduct market studies in the sectors for which they are responsible[23]. There is an obvious similarity between market studies in the UK and the sectoral investigations that the

[19] *Super-complaints: Guidance for designated consumer bodies*, para 2.25.

[20] *Pricing Practices in the Groceries Market*, 16 July 2015.

[21] *ORR super-complaint response report: Which? Super-complaint—compensation arrangements in the market for passenger rail services*, 18 March 2016, available at www.orr.gov.uk.

[22] www.oup.com/uk/whish9e/.

[23] See eg OFGEM's *Energy Supply Probe* (February 2008), available at www.ofgem.gov.uk; OFCOM's review, *Pay TV* (March 2010), available at www.ofcom.org.uk; and FCA's *Asset Management Market Study* (June 2017), available at www.fca.org.uk.

Table 11.1 Table of super-complaints

Title	Date of super-complaint	Super-complainant	Date of announcement of result	Outcome
Misleading and opaque pricing in the grocery sector	21.04.15	Which?	16.07.16	CMA identified potentially misleading practices. The Government tabled legislative proposals to improve unit pricing; and ASDA formally committed to implement changes to promotional practices. On 06.07.17 the CMA found that ASDA had complied with its commitment and formally closed the case
Rail compensation super-complaint (ORR)	21.12.15	Which?	18.03.16	ORR issued recommendations to train operators to improve consumer awareness of compensation claims for delays. ORR will continue to monitor matters

European Commission conducts under Article 17 of Regulation 1/2003[24]. The CMA welcomes reasoned suggestions of UK markets to be considered for market studies, and has produced a notification form which can be accessed on its website[25].

(A) **Guidance**

The CMA Board has adopted the OFT's guideline, *Market Studies: Guidance on the OFT approach*[26], subject to certain changes effected by the ERRA which are described in the CMA's own guideline, *Market Studies and Market Investigations: Supplemental guidance on the CMA's approach*[27] ('*Supplemental guidance*') and incorporated in the text that follows. These guidance documents explain why the CMA conducts market studies; how it

[24] On sectoral inquiries see ch 7, 'Article 17: investigations into sectors of the economy and into types of agreements', p 277.

[25] www.gov.uk/cma.

[26] OFT 519, June 2010, available at www.gov.uk/cma.

[27] CMA3, January 2014, revised July 2017.

chooses and manages them; what their possible outcomes might be; and its evaluation of previous studies.

(B) Purpose of market studies

Market studies are intended to enable the CMA to understand as well as possible how markets are working and whether the needs of consumers are being met[28]. A market study is not limited to a relevant market in an economic sense; and it may deal with practices across a range of goods and services[29]. An important feature of market studies is that they are a way of scrutinising the extent to which governmental behaviour and legislation might have a harmful effect on the way in which markets work[30]. The market studies into, for example, *Pharmacies, Taxi services, Public procurement, European State Aid Control* and *Public subsidies* were all concerned with what might be termed 'public' as opposed to private distortions of competition[31]: several market studies ended with advice being given to the Government, as Table 11.2 on market studies later shows. The Government has indicated that it will respond to reports on public restrictions of competition within 90 days[32].

Market studies are distinct from market investigations, although it is possible that a market study might lead to a market investigation reference. This occurred, for example, in the cases of *Store card credit services, Local buses* and *Payday lending*: the possibility that a market study might be followed by a market investigation can lead to a somewhat prolonged scrutiny of some markets.

(C) Procedure

The general function contained in section 5 of the Enterprise Act 2002 is the only legal basis for market studies. That Act leaves open when, and the manner in which, the CMA should conduct a market study. The CMA applies its *Prioritisation Principles*[33] when deciding whether to conduct a market study. The actual decision to launch a market study is taken by the Board of the CMA[34].

(i) Identifying markets to study

Market studies may be triggered in various ways: for example the CMA might commence one on its own initiative, sometimes after a less formal preliminary assessment of a market[35]; trading standards officers might bring problems to the CMA's attention; or a market study might be prompted by a super-complaint from a designated consumer body or a request by any other interested stakeholders.

(ii) Market study notice

Section 130A of the Enterprise Act requires the CMA to publish a market study notice on commencement of a market study under section 5 of that Act. A market study notice must specify the timetable within which the CMA must complete the study, the scope of the market study and the period during which representations may be made to the CMA

[28] CMA's *Supplemental guidance*, para 2.1.

[29] *Market studies: Guidance on the OFT approach*, OFT 519, June 2010, para 2.3.

[30] Ibid, paras 2.8–2.10.

[31] See the UK Contribution to the OECD Best Practices Roundtable *Market Studies* (2008), available at www.oecd.org/competition.

[32] See the Government's White Paper *Productivity and Enterprise—A World Class Competition Regime* Cm 5233 (2001), paras 4.15 and 6.37.

[33] CMA16, April 2014.

[34] CMA's *Supplemental guidance*, para 2.7.

[35] See 'Gathering information about markets', p 463 earlier in chapter.

in relation to the market[36]. The CMA may exercise its powers to require information only once it has published a market study notice[37].

(iii) Stages of a market study

Chapter 4 of the *Market Studies Guidance* explains how the CMA goes about market studies. The major stages of a study include selection of a market; pre-launch work; the decision to launch a market study; gathering and analysis of evidence[38]; and consultation on the CMA's findings.

If the CMA proposes to make a market investigation reference, it must consult on that proposal within six months of the publication of the market study notice[39]. The CMA will also carry out preparatory work on the proposed reference, such as identifying the information that it will need to obtain from interested parties[40]. If the CMA decides not to make a reference, it must publicise that decision within the same six-month period[41]. A study concludes with the publication of a market study report.

(iv) Market study report

Where the CMA has published a market study notice, section 131B of the Enterprise Act requires the CMA to publish a 'market study report' setting out its findings and actions (if any) that will be taken as a result of the study; this must be done within 12 months of publication of the market study notice[42]. Strict time limits are imposed on the conduct of market studies in order to disturb the operation of the market as little as possible.

If the CMA proposes to make a market investigation reference, the market study report must contain the decision of the CMA whether to make a reference (or accept undertakings in lieu of a reference), its reasons for that decision and such information as the CMA considers appropriate for facilitating a proper understanding of its reasons for that decision[43]. If the CMA decides to make a reference, it will be made at the same time as the market study report is published[44].

(D) Outcomes of market studies

Various outcomes may follow a market study by the CMA, including:

- a clean bill of health for the market in question
- consumer-focused action, for example to raise consumers' awareness in such a way that they make better purchasing decisions
- making recommendations to business to change its behaviour[45], for example on matters such as information about after-sales services, standard terms and conditions and improving consumer redress
- making recommendations to Government to amend legislation or take some other action to remove 'public' restrictions of competition

[36] Enterprise Act 2002, s 130A(3).

[37] Ibid, s 174(1)(a); on the CMA's investigative powers see the CMA's *Supplemental guidance*, paras 2.11–2.16.

[38] Enterprise Act 2002, s 5(3) provides a statutory basis for the CMA to outsource the market study or part of it to an external consultancy; see *Market Studies: Guidance on the OFT approach*, para 4.16.

[39] Enterprise Act 2002, s 131B(1).

[40] *Supplemental guidance*, paras 3.37–3.38.

[41] Enterprise Act 2002, s 131B(3).

[42] Ibid, s 131B(4), although a tighter time limit than this could be imposed: ibid, s 131C.

[43] Ibid, s 131B(5).

[44] Ibid, s 131B(6), that is to say, within 12 months of publication of the market study notice.

[45] See eg *Legal Services Market Study*, December 2016, paras 7.24–7.125.

- investigation or enforcement action under competition or consumer law
- a market investigation reference or undertakings in lieu of such a reference[46].

The CMA estimated that consumer savings as a result of its market studies and reviews from 2014 to 2017 amounted to £887 million each year[47].

(E) **Examples of market studies**

The CMA's website provides details of completed and current market studies[48]. Table 11.2 lists the market studies carried out by the CMA since the publication of the eighth edition of this book and completed by 8 December 2017[49].

5. Market Investigation References

(A) **Overview of the system of market investigations**

Part 4 of the Enterprise Act 2002 establishes the system of market investigation references. Chapter 1 of Part 4 of the Act is entitled 'Market investigation references': it deals both with the making of references and their determination. Chapter 2 of Part 4 of the Act deals with 'public interest cases', which are rare in practice and are described in section 6 later in brief outline. Chapter 3 contains rules on enforcement that set out the various undertakings that can be accepted by the CMA in the course of market investigations and the orders that may be made to remedy any adverse effects on competition and detrimental effects on consumers. Chapter 4 deals with supplementary matters such as investigatory powers and applications for review by the Competition Appeal Tribunal ('the CAT').

The market investigation regime is an important feature of the UK system of competition law, and recognises that not every market failure can be cured through the application of Articles 101 and 102 TFEU and the Chapter I and Chapter II prohibitions in the Competition Act 1998[50]. The market investigation regime focuses on understanding how markets work and on how consumers engage in markets, rather than simply on the behaviour of individual firms[51]. A market investigation enables the CMA to investigate whether features of the market have an adverse effect on competition and provides a wide range of remedies to eliminate, as far as possible, such adverse effects and any detrimental effects on customers that the CMA identifies. However the market investigation system does not provide for any sanctions for past behaviour or for the award of compensation for loss caused by a market failure.

46 *Market Studies: guidance on the OFT approach*, paras 5.1–5.13.

47 See the CMA's *Annual Report and Accounts 2016/17*, HC 24, p 73, available at www.gov.uk/cma.

48 See www.gov.uk/cma.

49 A complete list of all market studies can be found on the Online Resources that accompany this book.

50 See eg Geroski 'The UK Market Inquiry Regime' [2004] Fordham Corporate Law Institute (ed Hawk), 1; Freeman 'Market Investigations in the United Kingdom: The Story So Far' in Monti et al (eds) *Economic Law and Justice in Times of Globalisation* (Nomos, 2007); Ahlborn and Piccinin 'Between Scylla and Charybdis: Market Investigations and the Consumer Interest' in Rodger (ed) *Ten Years of UK Competition Law Reform* (Dundee University Press, 2010); speech by Alex Chisholm 'CMA: how we intend to use market investigations to extend the frontiers of competition', 9 December 2014, available at www.gov.uk/cma.

51 See *Guidelines for market investigations: Their role, procedures, assessment and remedies*, CC3 (revised), April 2013, para 18.

Table 11.2 Table of market studies

Completed market studies	Date of report	Outcome of study
Retirement income market study **(FCA)**	March 2015	The FCA found that competition was not working well for savers. In particular there was a lack of switching between providers, thereby reducing competitive constraints against incumbents and raising entry barriers in the market. The FCA introduced various measures that require providers to enable comparison of annuities and to improve the quality of information given to savers reaching retirement
Prepayment review: understanding supplier charging practices and barriers to switching **(OFGEM)**	June 2015	OFGEM reviewed prepayment tariffs in the retail gas market. It found low rates of switching by existing prepayment customers to cheaper prepayment tariffs or to other payment method tariffs. This meant that customers were losing out on substantial savings. OFGEM also observed restricted competition and a limited prepayment tariff choice which, according to suppliers, was due to commercial, technical and regulatory barriers. OFGEM requested the CMA to assess competition in this market segment in more detail. OFGEM also intended to verify to what extent regulatory obligations exacerbate the concerns of suppliers. OFGEM noted that the introduction of smart metering was likely to reduce the relative costs of prepayment and to increase choice of prepayment tariffs
Review of the non-domestic gas metering market **(OFGEM)**	March 2016	Despite a liberalisation of the non-domestic gas metering market over ten years ago, OFGEM noted that the market was not working well because gas suppliers were faced with substantial costs when switching to competing meter providers. In particular, market entrants were generally unable to adopt meter assets *in situ* and were thus required to replace the existing meter. This cost barrier meant that the market position of the incumbent meter provider (National Grid) was entrenched.OFGEM made recommendations to market participants, encouraging National Grid to sell or lease meter assets *in situ* to incoming meter providers. Gas suppliers were recommended to tender the appointment of meter providers to reduce costs. OFGEM continues to monitor any improvements in the effectiveness of competition and will take further action if necessary

Completed market studies	Date of report	Outcome of study
Credit card market study **(FCA)**	July 2016	The FCA concluded that for the most part competition is effective. However it raised concerns about the scale of credit card debt borne by consumers. In particular the FCA seeks voluntary industry commitments and will introduce rules to increase the incentives of retail banks to support consumers in addressing persistent credit card debt
Investment and corporate banking market study **(FCA)**	October 2016	The FCA concluded that there was effective competition between investment banks and that the market worked well for large corporate clients. However there was concern about contractual clauses that restricted clients' choice of providers for future services; also about league tables that adversely affect clients in pitches and about conflict of interests in initial public offering ('IPO') allocations. The FCA has introduced measures to ban trade restraint clauses and has been working with the industry and other regulators to remedy the other concerns
Legal services	December 2016	The market for legal services lacked transparency to the detriment of individual consumers and small businesses. The CMA suggested measures that would increase transparency on price and quality by developing comparison tools and review platforms. While legal services regulation was not a major barrier to effective competition, the CMA recommended that the Ministry of Justice adapt the regulatory framework to enable greater consumer protection
Asset management market study **(FCA)**	June 2017	The FCA found that there was weak price competition and high profit margins despite a large number of market participants. Investors also lacked clear information about the aims of funds and there was insufficient transparency and benchmarks for fund performance. The FCA made various proposals to remedy the identified competition problems and to render the UK asset management market more attractive to investors. Specific measures include higher fiduciary duties of asset managers, cost transparency, reporting requirements and the increase of countervailing bargaining power of investors. In September 2017 the FCA decided to make a market investigation reference to the CMA on investment consultancy and fiduciary management services

(*continued*)

Table 11.2 (*continued*)

Completed market studies	Date of report	Outcome of study
Digital comparison tools	September 2017	The CMA found that digital comparison tools ('DCTs') are overall useful for consumers by assisting them to make informed comparisons about and purchases of products and services. However the CMA opened a follow-up competition investigation against a home insurance comparison website for its use of 'most favoured nation' clauses ('MFNs') that limit the insurers' ability to offer cheaper rates on competing DCTs. The CMA will also keep under review other practices such as non brand-bidding, negative matching and non-resolicitation agreements, because they might limit competition between DCTs. The CMA recommended DCTs to review their contracts in the light of these suspect practices. Other recommendations include greater information transparency from DCTs and stronger cooperation amongst sectoral regulators to ensure effective competition between DCTs for important products like financial services, energy and insurance
Care homes	November 2017	The CMA examined the care homes market (including nursing homes) for the elderly with a particular focus on whether residents are treated fairly with reference to contract terms and practices of care homes. The CMA decided not to make a market investigation reference but identified problems over choice, consumer protection and funding and made a series of recommendations to Government, local authorities, sectoral regulators and the care home industry

(B) Guidelines and other relevant publications

Various guidelines, rules and other publications seek to explain the operation of the UK system of market investigations. The CMA Board has adopted a number of guidelines that had been published by its predecessors, the OFT and the Competition Commission; the CMA has also published a guideline of its own. By 8 December 2017 the following guidelines had been published under the Enterprise Act[52]:

- *Market investigation references: Guidance about the making of references under Part 4 of the Enterprise Act* ('*Guidance on making references*')[53]

[52] The guidelines are available at www.gov.uk/cma.

[53] OFT 511, March 2006.

- *Guidelines for market investigations: Their role, procedures, assessment and remedies* (*'Market investigation guidelines'*)[54]
- *Suggested best practice for submissions of technical economic analysis from parties to the Competition Commission*[55]
- The CMA's *Supplemental guidance*[56].

The CMA Board has adopted the guidance published by the Chairman of the former Competition Commission on *Disclosure of Information in Merger and Market Inquiries*[57]. Acting under Schedule 4 to the ERRA, the CMA has adopted the *CMA Rules of Procedure for Merger, Market and Special Reference Groups 2014*[58].

(C) The making of references

Section 131 of the Enterprise Act provides for two types of market investigation references: 'ordinary references' and 'cross-market references'[59].

(i) Power to make ordinary references

The CMA (concurrently with the sectoral regulators)[60] may make an ordinary reference when it has 'reasonable grounds for suspecting'[61] that one or more 'features' of a market prevent, restrict or distort competition in the supply or acquisition of goods or services in the UK or in a part thereof[62]. Features of a market include:

- the structure of the market concerned or any aspect thereof[63]
- the conduct of persons supplying or acquiring goods or services who operate on that market, whether that conduct occurs in the same market or not[64] and
- conduct relating to the market concerned of customers of any person who supplies or acquires goods or services[65].

Conduct for these purposes includes a failure to act and need not be intentional[66]. The CMA, when making a reference, is not required to specify whether particular features of a market are a matter of structure on the one hand or of conduct on the other[67]. A decision to make a market investigation reference is made by the CMA Board[68]; the Board cannot delegate the exercise of this power.

Part II of the *Guidance on making references* contains a helpful discussion of the CMA's interpretation of the reference test set out in section 131 of the Enterprise Act. In chapter 4 it discusses the meaning of 'prevention, restriction or distortion of competition'. In chapter 5 it considers structural features of markets, including:

- the concentration level within a market
- vertical integration

[54] CC3 (revised), April 2013. [55] CC2com3, 24 February 2009.

[56] CMA3, January 2014, revised July 2017. [57] CC7, July 2003, revised July 2017.

[58] CMA17, March 2014, available at www.gov.uk/cma.

[59] These are legislative expressions: Enterprise Act 2002, s 131(6).

[60] On the powers of the sectoral regulators in relation to market investigation references see the Enterprise Act 2002, Sch 9, Part 2.

[61] The 'reasonable grounds for suspecting' test does not impose a particularly high threshold: Case 1054/6/1/05 *Association of Convenience Stores v OFT* [2005] CAT 36, para 7.

[62] Enterprise Act 2002, s 131(1). [63] Ibid, s 131(2)(a). [64] Ibid, s 131(2)(b).

[65] Ibid, s 131(2)(c). [66] Ibid, s 131(3). [67] *Guidance on making references*, para 1.9.

[68] See the CMA's *Supplemental guidance*, para 1.23.

- conditions of entry, exit and expansion
- regulations and government policies
- informational asymmetries
- switching costs and
- countervailing power.

Chapter 6 deals with firms' conduct, in particular the conduct of oligopolies, facilitating practices, custom and practice and networks of vertical agreements. Chapter 7 considers the conduct of customers, which section 131(2)(c) of the Act considers to be a feature of a market, and specifically addresses the issue of search costs, that is to say the cost that customers may have to incur in order to make an informed choice.

(ii) **Power to make cross-market references**

The CMA (concurrently with the sectoral regulators) may make a 'cross-market reference' where it has reasonable grounds for suspecting that one or more features of more than one market prevent, restrict or distort competition in the supply or acquisition of goods or services in all or part of the UK[69]. It should be noted that cross-market references can be made only in relation to features of a market relating to conduct[70]. The subjection of the same practices across markets to the market investigation regime is useful since it enables the CMA to scrutinise practices that are not confined to one market, such as collective licensing of performance copyright[71]. As at 8 December 2017 no references of this type had been made.

(iii) **Ministerial power to make references**

Section 132 of the Enterprise Act allows the Secretary of State (or the Scottish Ministers and the Secretary of State acting jointly[72]) to make a reference when he or she is not satisfied with a decision of the CMA not to make an ordinary or cross-market reference under section 131, or when he considers that the CMA will not make such a reference within a reasonable period.

Section 132 sits a little oddly with Parliament's intention that the Secretary of State should be removed from cases except where exceptional public issues arise, for which special provision is made[73]. The section 132 power had not been exercised by 8 December 2017[74].

(iv) **The discretion of the CMA whether to make a reference**

The CMA has a discretion to make a market investigation reference once the reference test is met. Paragraph 2.1 of the *Guidance on making references* says that the CMA will make an ordinary market investigation reference only when the following criteria, in addition to the statutory ones, are met:

- it would not be more appropriate to deal with any competition issues under the Competition Act 1998 or by other means, for example by using the powers of the sectoral regulators

[69] Enterprise Act 2002, s 131(1) and (2A). [70] Ibid.

[71] CMA's *Supplemental guidance*, para 2.36; see also the *Government Response to Consultation, 'Growth, Competition and the Competition Regime'*, 15 March 2012, para 4.6, available at www.gov.uk.

[72] Enterprise Act 2002, s 132(5)(c), inserted by the Scotland Act 2016, s 64.

[73] See 'Public Interest Cases', pp 481–482 later in chapter.

[74] The House of Commons Business and Enterprise Committee asked the Secretary of State to refer the UK retail market for beer, but he declined to do so: see *Pub Companies*, HC 26-1, 21 April 2009, available at www.parliament.uk.

- it would not be more appropriate to accept undertakings in lieu of a reference[75]
- the scale of the suspected problem, in terms of the adverse effect on competition, is such that a reference would be appropriate
- there is a reasonable chance that appropriate remedies will be available.

The *Guidance on making references* provides further insights into each of these criteria.

(a) Relationship between the Competition Act and market investigations

The CMA's policy is to consider first whether a suspected problem can be addressed under the Competition Act 1998; it would consider a market investigation reference only where it has reasonable grounds to believe that market features restrict competition, but do not establish a breach of the Chapter I and/or Chapter II prohibitions (or of Articles 101 and/or 102 TFEU), or when action under the Competition Act has been or is likely to be ineffective for dealing with any adverse effect on competition identified[76]. The *Guidance on making references* explains that a market investigation reference might be appropriate for dealing with parallel behaviour in oligopolistic markets[77] or with problems arising from parallel networks of similar vertical agreements[78]. It adds that the majority of references are likely to involve industry-wide market features or multi-firm conduct, of which tacit coordination and parallel vertical agreements are examples[79]. The CMA will review these criteria in the light of emerging case law on the Chapter II prohibition should it appear that it is inadequate to deal with conduct by a single dominant firm which has an adverse effect on competition[80]; also it may make a reference where there has been an infringement of the Chapter II prohibition and it seems that a structural remedy going beyond what could be imposed under the Competition Act is necessary[81].

(b) Relationship with Regulation 1/2003

The *Guidance on making references* discusses the relationship between Regulation 1/2003 and the market investigation provisions[82]. Article 3(1) of Regulation 1/2003 requires national competition authorities to apply Articles 101 and 102 where they apply 'national competition law' to agreements or abusive conduct that affect trade between Member States[83]. Market investigations are likely to be regarded as a 'national competition law' for the purpose of Article 3 of Regulation 1/2003. Indeed, the *Market investigation guidelines* explain that the 'market investigation regime sits within the broad spectrum of competition law, operating alongside other regulatory mechanisms, including prohibitions, by allowing the competition authorities the opportunity to assess whether competition in a market is working effectively'[84].

Article 3(2) of Regulation 1/2003 provides that it is not possible to apply stricter national competition law than Article 101 to agreements that affect inter-state trade, but this is possible in the case of unilateral conduct that infringes Article 102. The *Guidance on making references* points out that Article 3(2) does not prevent investigations of agreements and conduct that infringe Articles 101 and 102, but that it does affect the remedies

[75] See 'Undertakings in lieu of a reference', pp 483–484 later in chapter.

[76] *Guidance on making references*, para 2.3.

[77] Ibid, para 2.5; on this point see *Local bus services*, OFT 1158, January 2010, para 5.28.

[78] Ibid, para 2.6. [79] Ibid, para 2.7. [80] Ibid, para 2.8, second indent.

[81] Ibid, para 2.8, third indent; on structural remedies under the Competition Act, see ch 10, 'Can directions be structural?', p 418.

[82] *Guidance on making references*, paras 2.9–2.18.

[83] See generally ch 2, 'The Relationship Between EU Competition Law and National Competition Laws', pp 75–79.

[84] *Market investigation guidelines*, para 18.

that can be imposed[85]. The decision to make a reference, the publication of provisional findings and of a provisional decision on remedies do not engage Article 3 of Regulation 1/2003 because they are preparatory acts.

Where Article 101 is applicable to an agreement or agreements, it is unlikely that the CMA Board would make a reference in the first place[86]. If a reference has been made, the CMA group could recommend that the benefit of any block exemption be withdrawn[87]. The *Guidance* also notes that the CMA could impose remedies in relation to behaviour that amounted to an infringement of Article 102, in which case the CMA would take those remedies into account if it were subsequently to investigate an infringement of that provision[88]. In *Store card credit services* the Competition Commission was satisfied that its proposed remedies were not in conflict with EU law[89]. In *Payment protection insurance* the Competition Commission rejected an argument that its remedies package infringed the EU freedom of establishment[90]. In *Energy* the CMA was satisfied that its proposed remedies were compatible with the provisions of the EU Energy Directives[91].

(c) Scale of the problem

The *Guidance on making references* discusses the proposition that a reference would be made only where the scale of a suspected problem, in terms of its effect on competition, is such that a reference would be an appropriate response. The CMA will consider whether the adverse effects on competition of features of a market are likely to have a significant detrimental effect on customers through higher prices, lower quality, less choice or less innovation; where the effect is insignificant the CMA would consider that the burden on business and the cost of a reference would be disproportionate[92]. The limited evidence of consumer detriment was an important factor in the decision not to refer *Isle of Wight ferry services*[93].

The *Guidance on making references* also says that, generally speaking, the CMA would not refer a very small market; a market only a small proportion of which is affected by the features having an adverse effect on competition; or a market where the adverse effects are expected to be short-lived[94]. In *Newspaper and magazine distribution* the OFT decided not to make a reference where any adverse effect on competition appeared to be offset by customer benefits in the form of lower prices and wider circulation[95].

(d) Availability of remedies

The CMA would not refer a market if it appeared that there were unlikely to be any available remedies to deal with an adverse effect on competition, for example where a market is global and a remedy under UK law would be unlikely to have any discernible effect[96]. The CMA decided not to refer the markets for *Legal services*[97] or for *Digital comparison tools*[98] because any consumer detriment could be adequately addressed by making recommendations to industry and regulators.

[85] *Guidance on making references*, para 2.12.

[86] Ibid, para 2.14; this point was noted in its decision not to make a reference of the UK beer and pub market: *CAMRA's super-complaint*, OFT 1279, October 2010, para 9.41 and fn 227.

[87] *Guidance on making references*, paras 2.17–2.18.

[88] Ibid, para 2.15.

[89] Final Report of 7 March 2006, para 10.9.

[90] Final Report of 29 January 2009, para 10.66.

[91] Final Report of 24 June 2016, para 15.98.

[92] *Guidance on making references*, para 2.27, on whether the cost of making a reference would be disproportionate; see *CAMRA super-complaint*, OFT 1279, October 2010, para 9.37.

[93] OFT 1135, October 2009, paras 7.24 and 7.33.

[94] *Guidance on making references*, para 2.28.

[95] OFT 1121, September 2009, paras 5.16–5.25; see also *Guidance on making references*, para 2.29.

[96] *Guidance on making references*, paras 2.30–2.32.

[97] Final Report of 15 December 2016, para 1.10.

[98] Final Report of 26 September 2017, para 2.7.

(v) Consultation before making a reference

Section 169 of the Enterprise Act requires the CMA to consult before making a reference and section 172 requires it to give reasons for its decision; these may be given after the date of the reference[99]. The Act leaves open the form and extent of the consultation process: the consultation may be a public one, though not necessarily so. An example of the consultation provisions operating in practice is afforded by the reference of *Personal current accounts* and *SME banking*: following two market studies, the CMA published its proposal to make a reference on 18 July 2014, and called for comments by 17 September 2014; the reference was made on 6 November 2014 and the final report was published on 9 August 2016.

(vi) Content and variation of references

Section 133 specifies what the CMA must include in an ordinary or cross-market market investigation reference; in particular it must provide a description of the goods or services to which the feature or combination of features that are restrictive of competition relate[100]. A reference may be framed so as to require the CMA to confine its investigation to goods or services supplied or acquired in a particular place or to or from particular persons[101]. Provision is made for the variation of references[102]. This occurred, for example, in the case of *Store card credit services* so that network cards and insurance services such as payment protection insurance could be included in the investigation[103]. In *Classified directory advertising services* a notice clarifying the scope of the reference was issued, although the reference itself was not varied.

The CMA's *Supplemental guidance* provides that the CMA Board may append to a reference an 'advisory steer' setting out the scope of the market investigation and the issues that could be the focus of the investigation[104]. The CMA market investigation reference group is expected to take the advisory steer into account, but ultimately must make its statutory decisions independently of the CMA Board[105].

(vii) Restrictions on the ability to make a reference

The CMA cannot make a reference if it has accepted undertakings in lieu of a reference within the preceding 12 months[106]. This limitation does not apply where an undertaking has been breached[107]; nor where it was accepted on the basis of false or misleading information[108].

(viii) Market investigation references in practice

By 8 December 2017 18 references had been made under the market investigation provisions of the Enterprise Act. Most references were made by the OFT or the CMA, but the ORR, OFCOM, OFGEM and the FCA had each made one: the most recent investigations are set out in Table 11.3 on market investigation references towards the end of this chapter with some accompanying commentary[109]. A list of all the market investigation references to date will be found on the Online Resources that accompany this book[110].

99 Enterprise Act 2002, s 172(6).

100 Ibid, s 133(1)(c) (ordinary references) and s 133(1)(d) (cross-market references).

101 Ibid, s 133(2) and (3); this power was exercised in the case of *BAA airports*.

102 Ibid, s 135; see also *Market investigation guidelines*, para 27.

103 See OFT Press Release 41/05, 3 March 2005; a variation was also made in the case of *Domestic bulk liquefied petroleum gas*, OFT Press Release, 20 October 2004.

104 CMA's *Supplemental guidance*, para 3.39.

105 Ibid.

106 Enterprise Act 2002, s 156(A1) (cross-market references) and s 156(1) (ordinary references); on undertakings in lieu see 'Undertakings in lieu of a reference', pp 502–503 later in chapter.

107 Enterprise Act 2002, s 156(2)(a).

108 Ibid, s 156(2)(b).

109 See 'Table of market investigation references', pp 483–484 later in chapter.

110 www.oup.com/uk/whish9e/.

(D) The determination of references

(i) The CMA Panel and market reference groups

Once a market investigation reference has been made, the Chair of the CMA Panel[111] will appoint a 'group' to conduct the investigation. The Chair must appoint at least three members of the CMA Panel to serve on a market reference group[112]. Members appointed to a group play no role in the decision to refer a market for investigation; they are responsible for the determination of the reference. To describe the system in a different way, following a preliminary 'Phase 1' investigation, the CMA Board decides whether to make a reference; if a market is referred, a group of CMA Panel members carries out an in-depth 'Phase 2' investigation of that market and takes the final decision[113]. These arrangements imitate the old division of functions between the OFT and the Competition Commission; they are an attempt to address the concern that the same institution can choose which markets to investigate, decide to make a reference, carry out an in-depth investigation and, if it finds an adverse effect on competition, take remedial action. The CMA group gathers and analyses the evidence with a 'fresh pair of eyes' and may conclude that there are no adverse effects[114].

(ii) Questions to be decided

(a) Ordinary references

Once a reference has been made the CMA must decide whether any feature, or combination of features, prevents, restricts or distorts competition in the referred market(s)[115]. If the CMA considers that there is an adverse effect on competition, it must decide three additional questions:

- first, whether it should take action to remedy, mitigate or prevent the adverse effect on competition or any detrimental effect on customers it has identified[116]: detrimental effects are defined as higher prices, lower quality, less choice of goods or services and less innovation[117]
- secondly, whether it should recommend that anyone else should take remedial action[118]
- thirdly, if remedial action should be taken, what that action should be[119].

The CAT has stated that it is likely to be a relatively rare case in which the CMA, having identified an adverse effect on competition and detrimental effects, will exercise its discretion to take no remedial action under the Act[120]. When considering remedial action, the CMA must have regard to the need to achieve as comprehensive a solution as is reasonable and practical to the adverse effect on competition and any detrimental effects on customers[121], and may in particular have regard to the effect of any action on any relevant

[111] The membership and role of the CMA Panel is described in ch 2, 'The CMA', pp 64–70.

[112] ERRA, Sch 4, para 38.

[113] For reasons of operational efficiency some of the CMA staff that work on Phase 1 will also work on Phase 2: the CMA's *Supplemental guidance*, para 1.22.

[114] See *Market investigation guidelines*, paras 22 and 156.

[115] Enterprise Act 2002, s 134(1)–(3).

[116] Ibid, s 134(4)(a); the phrase 'remedy, mitigate or prevent' in ss 134 and 138 of the Act recognises that there may be cases where an adverse effect on competition cannot, because of the constraints of reasonableness or practicability, be fully remedied or prevented, but only mitigated.

[117] Enterprise Act 2002, s 134.

[118] Ibid, s 134(4)(b).

[119] Ibid, s 134(4)(c).

[120] Case 1104/6/8/08 *Tesco plc v Competition Commission* [2009] CAT 6, para 57; for an example of the CMA deciding to take no remedial action to remedy an adverse effect on competition see *Private motor insurance*, Final Report of 24 September 2014, paras 38–39, 10.5 and 10.152.

[121] Enterprise Act 2002, s 134(6).

customer benefits[122]. If the CMA finds that there is no anti-competitive outcome, the question of remedial action does not arise.

(b) Cross-market references

In the case of cross-market references the CMA must decide, in relation to each feature or combination of features, whether the feature or combination of features prevents, restricts or distorts competition in the referred market(s)[123]; if the CMA finds an 'adverse effect on competition'[124], it must decide on suitable remedies[125], bearing in mind the same considerations as it would for ordinary references.

(iii) **Procedure**

The procedures of the CMA during market investigation references are set out in the *CMA Rules of Procedure for Merger, Market and Special Reference Groups 2014*[126]. There are also several guidance documents describing the CMA's approach to, and procedures for, market investigations[127]. The major stages of an investigation include:

- the publication of an administrative timetable
- gathering and verification of evidence
- providing a statement of issues
- hearings
- notifying a provisional decision[128]
- publication of the final report and implementing any remedies[129].

In July 2017 the CMA revised its *Supplemental guidance* to streamline its procedures. In particular, the CMA will consider possible remedies at the same time as assessing potential problems in order to help it reach the right outcome at the end of the inquiry[130].

Each investigation has its own home page on the CMA's website, and it is a simple matter to follow the progress of an investigation by referring to it. This accords with the CMA's commitment to be open and transparent in its working[131]. The home page sets out the core documents of an inquiry; contains the CMA's announcements, for example on its provisional findings and final report; and makes available the submissions and the evidence provided to the CMA. The home page may also contain surveys and working papers of relevance to the investigation and an account of roundtable discussions, for example with academic economists, held on particular topics: for example in *Groceries* economic roundtables were held on local competition and on buyer power; in *Local buses* researchers were appointed for a study on distinguishing exclusionary conduct, tacit coordination and competition; and in *Payday lending* a market research agency was instructed to carry out a customer survey[132].

(iv) **Investigations and reports**

Section 136(1) of the Act requires the CMA to prepare and publish a report within the period permitted by section 137. Section 137(1) requires the CMA to do so within

[122] Ibid, s 134(7); on the meaning of relevant customer benefits, see s 134(8). [123] Ibid, s 134(1A).

[124] Ibid, s 134(2A). [125] Ibid, s 141(2A).

[126] CMA17, March 2014; subject to these rules, each market investigation group can determine its own procedure: ERRA, Sch 4, para 51(5).

[127] See 'Guidelines and other relevant publications', pp 472–473 earlier in chapter.

[128] CMA's *Supplemental guidance*, paras 3.57–3.58. [129] Ibid, p 28. [130] Ibid, para 3.46.

[131] See *Transparency and Disclosure: Statement of CMA's policy and approach*, CMA6, January 2014, and CMA6 clarification note, 2 December 2016, available at www.gov.uk/cma.

[132] Final Report of 24 February 2015.

18 months of the date of the reference[133]. The 18-month period may be extended by no more than six months where there are 'special reasons' for doing so[134]. The CMA has stated that it may extend the inquiry period in complex cases, where for example there are multiple parties, issues or markets[135]. The time limits in section 137 may however be reduced by the Secretary of State[136].

The CMA's report must contain its decisions on the questions to be decided under section 134, its reasons for those decisions and such information as the CMA considers appropriate for facilitating a proper understanding of those questions and the reasons for its decisions[137]. The final report on *Retail banking* sets out, for example, a summary of the CMA's findings, the industry background and regulatory framework, market definition, the features of the markets that prevent, restrict or distort competition, the detrimental effects on customers, the need for remedial action and the decisions on remedies[138].

(v) Duty to remedy adverse effects

When the CMA has prepared and published a report under section 136 and concluded that there is an adverse effect on competition, section 138(2) requires it to take such action as it considers to be reasonable and practicable to remedy, mitigate or prevent the adverse effect on competition and any detrimental effects on customers that have resulted from, or may result from, the adverse effect on competition[139]. The CMA would, where it is possible to do so, prefer to address the root cause of the problem—that is to say the adverse effect on competition—than the consequences of it[140]. When deciding what action to take the CMA must be consistent with the decisions in its report on the questions it is required to answer, unless there has been a material change of circumstances since the preparation of the report or the CMA has a special reason for deciding differently[141]. In making its decision under section 138(2) the CMA shall have regard to the need to achieve as comprehensive a solution as is reasonable and practicable to any adverse effects on competition or detrimental effects on customers[142], having regard to any relevant customer benefits of the market features concerned[143].

Experience of the first few years of the market investigation regime revealed that the 'remedies phase' could be quite protracted. Prior to the ERRA the remedies phase fell outside the statutory period within which the investigation must be conducted. It is probably correct to suggest that many parties under investigation were not in a great hurry to facilitate a quicker adoption of remedies. The ERRA introduced time limits for the implementation of remedies[144]. Section 138A of the Enterprise Act provides that the CMA must discharge its duty under section 138(2), that is to say, implement its chosen remedies, within six months of the date of the publication of its report under section 136. The six-month period may be extended by no more than four months where there are 'special reasons' for doing so[145]. The CMA has said that it may extend the remedies timetable

[133] ERRA, Sch 12, para 2 reduced the original time limit of two years to 18 months with effect from 1 April 2014.

[134] Enterprise Act 2002, s 137(2A); only one such extension is possible: ibid, s 137(2C).

[135] See the CMA's *Supplemental guidance*, para 3.7.

[136] Enterprise Act 2002, s 137(3).

[137] Ibid, s 136(2).

[138] Final Report of 9 August 2016.

[139] Enterprise Act 2002, s 138(2).

[140] *Market investigation guidelines*, para 330.

[141] Enterprise Act, s 138(3); see eg *BAA airports*, Final Report of 19 July 2011 concluding that there were no material changes in circumstances that would justify amending its original decision in *BAA airports*; that decision was upheld on appeal to the CAT in Case 1185/6/8/11 *BAA Ltd v Competition Commission* [2012] CAT 3, and on further appeal to the Court of Appeal [2012] EWCA Civ 1077.

[142] Enterprise Act 2002, s 138(4).

[143] Ibid, s 138(5).

[144] ERRA, Sch 12, para 5.

[145] Enterprise Act 2002, s 138A(2); only one such extension is possible: s 138B(2).

where, for example, it does 'consumer testing' of the implementation of its remedies or it has to grapple with complex practical issues[146]. The CMA may use its investigatory powers for the purpose of implementing its remedies[147]; it may 'stop the clock' if a person fails to comply with a requirement of a notice under section 174 and that failure prevents the CMA from properly discharging its duty under section 138(2)[148].

(vi) **Market investigation guidelines**

The *Market investigation guidelines*[149] provide an overview of the market investigation regime, describe how the CMA conducts a market investigation and then deal in turn with issues of market characteristics and outcomes, market definition, the assessment of competition and remedial action. The *Guidelines* contain an extremely useful guide to the competitive process and various factors that adversely affect competition.

6. Public Interest Cases

Chapter 2 of Part 4 of the Enterprise Act provides for 'public interest cases'[150]. These provisions enable the Secretary of State to intervene in market investigation references that raise 'public interest considerations'. The Enterprise Act specifies national security as a public interest consideration[151]; the Secretary of State can add a new public interest consideration by statutory instrument, but this would require the approval of Parliament[152]. The CMA has a function of informing the Secretary of State of cases that might raise public interest considerations[153], and the CMA must bring to his attention any representations about the exercise of the powers as to what constitutes a public interest consideration[154].

There are two types of public interest cases: 'restricted public interest references' and 'full public interest references'. By 8 December 2017 there had been no interventions by the Secretary of State; such cases will be rare and are discussed here only briefly[155].

(A) **Issuing intervention notices**

The Secretary of State may give an 'intervention notice' to the CMA if he or she believes that one or more public interest considerations are relevant to a market investigation[156]; this must be done during a fixed period beginning with the publication of a market study notice, or, where there is no such notice, the start of the CMA's consultation on making a reference, but in each case before a reference is made[157]. Section 140(1) specifies the information that an intervention notice must contain.

(B) **Restricted public interest references**

In restricted public interest references the CMA investigates whether features of the market have an adverse effect on competition and, if so, considers the question of remedies;

146 See the CMA's *Supplemental guidance*, para 4.7.
147 Ibid, para 4.8; see Enterprise Act 2002, s 174(1)(b).
148 *Supplemental guidance*, para 4.8; see Enterprise Act 2002, s 138A(3).
149 CC3 (Revised), April 2013, available at www.gov.uk/cma.
150 See generally *Supplemental guidance*, paras 2.18–2.30.
151 Enterprise Act 2002, s 153(1).
152 Ibid, s 143(3) and (4).
153 Ibid, s 152(1).
154 Ibid, s 152(3).
155 The procedure in public interest cases is described in the CMA's *Supplemental guidance*, paras 3.15–3.19.
156 Enterprise Act 2002, s 139(1).
157 Ibid, s 139(1A)–(1B); see also *Supplemental guidance*, para 2.23.

it must prepare one set of remedies on the basis that the Secretary of State might decide the case, and a separate set of remedies in case the matter reverts to it[158]. The CMA must report to the Secretary of State within 18 months of the reference[159]. The Secretary of State must then decide, within 90 days of receipt of the report, whether any public interest considerations raised by the intervention notice are relevant to the remedial action proposed by the CMA[160]; if so the Secretary of State may take such action as he considers to be reasonable and practicable to remedy the adverse effects on competition identified by the CMA in the light of the relevant public interest considerations[161]. If the Secretary of State does not make and publish his decision within 90 days of receipt of the report, the matter reverts to the CMA which will proceed on the basis of the remedies that it proposed in the eventuality of the matter reverting to it[162].

(C) **Full public interest references**

In full public interest references the CMA must report on any competition issues and on the admissible public interest considerations, as well as possible remedies[163]. The Secretary of State may appoint one or more 'public interest experts' to advise the CMA[164]; the CMA must have regard to the views of any such expert on admissible public interest considerations and possible remedies[165]. The CMA's report must be given to the Secretary of State within 18 months of the reference[166], and must contain its decisions on the questions it is required to answer together with the reasons for those decisions[167]. The Secretary of State must decide whether to make an 'adverse public interest finding' within 90 days of receipt of the report from the CMA[168]. The Secretary of State is not entitled to diverge from the finding of the CMA on the competition issues[169]. Enforcement powers are conferred upon the Secretary of State to accept undertakings or to make orders to remedy, mitigate or prevent any of the effects adverse to the public interest[170]. Provision is made for cases to revert to the CMA where the Secretary of State decides to make no finding at all in the matter or where he fails to make and publish the decision within the 90-day period[171].

7. Enforcement

Chapter 3 of Part 4 of the Enterprise Act deals with the powers of the CMA to accept undertakings or to impose orders to ensure compliance with the Act and to monitor and enforce them. It begins with the powers to accept undertakings in lieu of a reference; it then sets out the interim and final powers of the CMA. Undertakings and orders are legally binding and enforceable in the courts[172]. The CMA is required to maintain a register of undertakings and orders made under the market investigation provisions in the Enterprise Act; it is accessible on the CMA's website[173].

158 Enterprise Act 2002, s 141.

159 Ibid, s 144(1); the CMA may extend the 18-month period by no more than six months if it has special reasons for doing so: s 144(1B).

160 Ibid, s 146. 161 Ibid, s 147. 162 Ibid, s 148.

163 Ibid, s 141A(2)–(6). 164 Ibid, s 141B.

165 Ibid, s 141A(7); the CMA's report must also include a summary of the expert's views: ibid, s 142(2)(d).

166 Ibid, s 144(1). 167 Ibid, s 143A. 168 Ibid, s 146A.

169 Ibid, s 146A(5). 170 Ibid, s 147A. 171 Ibid, s 148A.

172 Ibid, s 167; as to whether a person injured by breach of an undertaking or order could bring an action for damages, see *MidKent Holdings v General Utilities plc* [1996] 3 All ER 132, brought under s 93 of the (now repealed) Fair Trading Act 1973.

173 Enterprise Act 2002, s 166; the CMA's website is www.gov.uk/cma.

(A) Undertakings and orders

(i) Undertakings in lieu of a reference

Section 154(2) of the Act gives power to the CMA to accept an undertaking in lieu of a reference[174]. It can do this only where it considers that it has the power to make a reference and otherwise intends to make such a reference[175]. In proceeding under section 154(2) the CMA must have regard to the need to achieve as comprehensive a solution as is reasonable and practicable to the adverse effect on competition concerned and any detrimental effects on customers[176], taking into account any relevant customer benefits[177]. The CMA has said that it considers that undertakings in lieu are unlikely to be common[178]; following a preliminary investigation the CMA may not be in possession of sufficient information to know whether undertakings in lieu would be adequate to remedy any perceived detriments to competition. This having been said, it may be that, as the system develops, more use will be made of them: some firms may decide that it would be preferable to offer undertakings in lieu than to bear the intrusion and cost of an 18-month investigation; others, however, may prefer a fairly prolonged delay before potentially having to abandon the behaviour in question. If firms were to offer undertakings in lieu but the CMA were to proceed nevertheless to make a market investigation reference, they could apply to the CAT for a review of the decision. It is likely that the CMA (or a sectoral regulator) will find it easier to make use of the undertaking in lieu provisions when there are only a few firms involved (or even just one) than when a large number of firms are under investigation.

Before accepting undertakings in lieu the CMA is obliged to publish details of the proposed undertakings, to allow a period of consultation and to consider any representations received[179]; a further period of consultation is required should the CMA intend to modify the undertakings[180]. If an undertaking in lieu has been accepted it is not possible to make a market investigation reference within the following 12 months[181], unless there is a breach of the undertaking or unless it was accepted on the basis of false or misleading information[182].

Undertakings in lieu of a reference had been accepted in three cases by 8 December 2017, *Postal franking machines*[183], *BT*[184], a case involving OFCOM, and *Extended warranties on domestic electrical goods*[185].

In *Postal franking machines* the OFT accepted undertakings from the two leading suppliers of franking machines, Pitney Bowes and Neopost, together with Royal Mail; the undertakings were intended to facilitate greater customer choice and more competition in the market, for example by making better price information available and encouraging the provision of third party maintenance services. This market had been the subject of an investigation under the now-repealed Fair Trading Act 1973 in 1988; the OFT decided to review the market since the undertakings given in 1988 appeared not to have been effective.

In *BT* OFCOM accepted more than 230 separate undertakings in lieu of a reference from BT in order to achieve operational separation between 'Openreach', which owned and operated the monopoly part of BT's business, and those parts of its business where it is subject to competition. OFCOM remained concerned, however, that BT still had the

[174] See generally *Guidance on making references*, paras 2.20–2.26.
[175] Enterprise Act 2002, s 154(1). [176] Ibid, s 154(3). [177] Ibid, s 154(4).
[178] *Guidance on making references*, paras 2.21 and 2.25. [179] Enterprise Act 2002, s 155(1)–(3).
[180] Ibid, s 155(4)–(5). [181] Ibid, s 156(1). [182] Ibid, s 156(2).
[183] OFT decision of 17 June 2005. [184] OFCOM decision of 22 September 2005.
[185] OFT decision of 27 June 2012.

ability and incentive to favour its own retail business when making strategic decisions about Openreach[186]. BT sought to address this concern by establishing Openreach as a distinct company with its own staff, management and strategy. In July 2017, OFCOM accepted BT's proposal and agreed to release BT from its undertakings in lieu[187]. The intention is that Openreach will serve all of its customers equally and BT will no longer be able to favour its own vertically-integrated business units.

In *Extended warranties* the OFT accepted undertakings from Dixons, Comet and Argos; the undertakings provided for the creation of a comparison website for extended warranties that would help consumers to shop around and make more informed decisions. The CAT rejected an application by John Lewis for a review of an OFT decision implementing the undertakings as it was out of time[188].

(ii) Interim undertakings and orders

The CMA, after a report has been published, can accept interim undertakings or make interim orders to prevent[189] or reverse[190] 'pre-emption action', that is to say, action which might impede the taking of any remedial action by the CMA. The Secretary of State may exercise these powers in public interest cases[191].

(iii) Final powers

Sections 159 to 161 of the Enterprise Act deal with the final undertakings and orders that are available to the CMA after it has completed its investigation and reached its conclusion on the questions contained in section 134. Section 159 provides for the acceptance of undertakings and section 160 for the making of an order where an undertaking is not being fulfilled or where false or misleading information was given to the CMA prior to the acceptance of the undertaking. Section 161 empowers the CMA to make a final order. The orders that can be made are set out in Schedule 8 to the Act; they include orders to restrict certain conduct on the part of firms, and also to prohibit acquisitions or even to provide for the division of a business[192]. The provisions that may be contained in an undertaking are not limited to those permitted by Schedule 8 in the case of orders[193]. The CMA has a choice of whether to seek undertakings or to make an order, and will proceed on the basis of practicality such as the number of parties concerned and their willingness to negotiate and agree undertakings in the light of the CMA's report[194].

The first order to be made under these powers was the *Store Cards Market Investigation Order* of 27 July 2006. It made provision for full information to be made available to consumers on store card statements[195]. In *Classified directory advertising services* final undertakings were accepted from Yell, the publisher of *Yellow Pages*[196]. Final orders had been made in 13 cases by 8 December 2017.

[186] Details of OFCOM's review can be found at www.ofcom.org.uk.

[187] OFCOM Statement of 13 July 2017.

[188] Case 1203/6/1/12 *John Lewis plc v OFT* [2013] CAT 7.

[189] Enterprise Act 2002, ss 157 and 158.

[190] Ibid, ss 157(2B) and 158(2B), inserted by s 35 of the ERRA.

[191] Enterprise Act 2002, s 157(6)(a).

[192] On structural remedies under the Act and its predecessors see speech of Peter Freeman of 7 October 2010, available at www.nationalarchives.gov.uk.

[193] Enterprise Act 2002, s 164(1).

[194] *Market investigation guidelines*, para 92.

[195] Available at www.nationalarchives.gov.uk; the Order was slightly amended in 2011 in order to take into account the entry into force of Directive 2008/48/EC on credit agreements for consumers, OJ [2008] L 133/66.

[196] Available at www.nationalarchives.gov.uk; on 15 March 2013 Yell (now known as hibu) was released from the undertakings following a change in circumstances.

(B) Review of enforcement undertakings and orders

Section 162 of the Act requires the CMA to keep enforcement undertakings and enforcement orders under review[197] and to ensure that they are complied with[198]; it is also required to consider whether, by reason of a change of circumstances, there is a case for release, variation, supersession or revocation[199]. Section 167 provides that there is a duty to comply with orders and undertakings; this duty is owed to anyone who may be affected by a breach of that duty[200]. Any breach of the duty is actionable if such a person sustains loss or damage[201], unless the subject of the undertaking or order took all reasonable steps and exercised all due diligence to avoid a breach of the order or undertaking[202]. Compliance with an order or undertaking is also enforceable by civil proceedings brought by the CMA[203] for an injunction.

8. Supplementary Provisions

Chapter 4 of Part 4 of the Enterprise Act contains a number of supplementary provisions.

(A) Regulated markets

Section 168 provides that, where the CMA or the Secretary of State considers remedies in relation to regulated markets such as telecommunications, gas and electricity they should take into account the various sector-specific regulatory objectives that the sectoral regulators have. These may go beyond preventing adverse effects on competition: for example there is a legal obligation to ensure the maintenance of a universal postal service.

(B) Consultation, information and publicity

Sections 169 to 172 of the Enterprise Act impose various consultation, information and publication obligations on the CMA and the Secretary of State.

(C) Powers of investigation and penalties

Section 174 gives the CMA powers to require information for the purpose of market studies[204] and market investigation references[205]. The CMA can impose a penalty on a person who, without reasonable excuse, fails to comply with a notice given under section 174[206] or who intentionally obstructs or delays a person who is trying to copy documents required to be produced[207]. The maximum amounts that the CMA may impose as a penalty under section 174(1) and (3) are specified in the Competition and Markets

[197] Enterprise Act 2002, s 162(1).

[198] Ibid, s 162(2)(a); the CMA took action against Barclays, Santander and Lloyds Banking Group for breaching the final order in *Payment protection insurance*; details are available at www.gov.uk/cma.

[199] Ibid, s 162(2)(b)–(c); see eg CMA *Notice of revocation of the Northern Ireland PCA banking market investigation Order 2008* (as amended in 2011), 14 October 2016, available at www.gov.uk/cma.

[200] Enterprise Act 2002, s 167(2)–(3).

[201] Ibid, s 167(4); as to whether such a person could bring an action for damages, see ch 11 n 172 earlier.

[202] Ibid, s 167(5).

[203] Ibid, s 167(6).

[204] These powers may be exercised only after the CMA has published a market study notice: ibid, s 174(1)(a).

[205] These powers may be exercised during the investigation and for the purpose of implementing any remedies.

[206] Enterprise Act 2002, s 174A(1).

[207] Ibid, s 174A(3).

Authority (Penalties) Order 2014[208]. It is a criminal offence for a person intentionally to alter, suppress or destroy any document that he or she has been required to produce under section 174[209]: a person guilty of this offence could be fined or imprisoned for a maximum of two years[210].

Sections 174B to 174E set out the main procedural requirements that the CMA must observe when imposing a penalty; the factors which it will have regard to when determining the amount of a penalty are set out in the *Administrative penalties: Statement of policy on the CMA's approach*[211]. There is a right of appeal to the CAT against decisions of the CMA to impose monetary penalties: the CAT may quash the penalty or substitute a different amount or different dates of payment[212].

(D) **Reports**

Section 177 of the Act makes provision for excisions of inappropriate matter from reports made under the provisions on public interest cases[213], and section 178 allows a dissenting member of a CMA group to publish his or her reasons for disagreeing with the majority. Dissenting opinions had occurred on four occasions by 8 December 2017: in *Rolling stock leasing*, where one member dissented on the comprehensiveness of the remedies package[214]; in *Groceries*, where there was a split decision in relation to the competition test to be inserted in the planning regime[215]; in *Energy*, where one member dissented because he considered the remedies did not go far enough[216]; and in the remittal in *Private healthcare*, where there was a split decision as to whether the divestment remedy was proportionate[217].

(E) **Review of decisions under Part 4 of the Enterprise Act**

Section 179 of the Act makes provision for review of decisions under Part 4 of the Act[218]. Section 179(1) provides that any person aggrieved by a decision of the CMA or the Secretary of State may apply to the CAT for review of that decision: the aggrieved person could be a third party with sufficient interest. The application must be made within two months of the date on which the applicant was notified of the disputed decision or of its date of publication, whichever is earlier[219]. When dealing with applications under section 179(1) the CAT must apply the same principles as would be applied by a court on an application for judicial review[220]. The fact that the CAT is a specialist tribunal does not mean that it should apply judicial review principles in a different way to the ordinary courts[221]; the CAT's task is to review the lawfulness of the decision[222]. The CAT may dismiss the

[208] SI 2014/559. [209] Enterprise Act 2002, s 174A(4). [210] Ibid, s 174A(6).

[211] CMA4, January 2014, para 4.11, available at www.gov.uk/cma.

[212] Enterprise Act 2002, s 174D(10) and s 114.

[213] See 'Public Interest Cases', pp 481–482 earlier in chapter on public interest cases.

[214] Final Report of 7 April 2009, para 9.272 and Note of dissent accompanying the report.

[215] Final Report of 30 April 2008, paras 11.100–11.104.

[216] Final Report of 24 June 2016, statement of dissent of Professor Martin Cave.

[217] Final Report of 5 September 2016, paras 12.320–12.321.

[218] Part 3 of the Competition Appeal Tribunal Rules 2015, SI 2015/1648, makes provision for applications under s 179.

[219] Competition Appeal Tribunal Rules 2015, SI 2015/1648, r 25(2). [220] Enterprise Act 2002, s 179(4).

[221] *British Sky Broadcasting Group plc v Competition Commission* [2010] EWCA Civ 2, paras 28–41, dealing with merger control, but which would apply in the same way to market investigations.

[222] Case 1109/6/8/09 *Barclays Bank plc v Competition Commission* [2007] CAT 27, para 22; the CAT provided a helpful summary of the relevant judicial review principles in Case 1185/6/8/11 *BAA Ltd v Competition Commission* [2012] CAT 3, para 20.

application or quash the whole or part of the decision to which it relates[223]; and, in the latter situation, it may refer the matter back to the original decision-maker for further consideration[224]. An appeal may be brought before the Court of Appeal, with permission, against the CAT's decision on a point of law[225].

It is possible to make some generalised comments about the applications for review that have been made under the market investigation provisions. First, it is noticeable that several applications challenged the decisions to impose certain remedies; this happened in five investigations—*Groceries, Payment protection insurance, BAA airports, Private healthcare* and *Aggregates*[226]. Aspects of the remedies imposed in two investigations—*Groceries* and *Payment protection insurance*—were successfully challenged before the CAT. In *Tesco v Competition Commission*[227] and *Barclays v Competition Commission*[228] the CAT was critical of the Competition Commission's approach to evaluating the likely costs and benefits of its remedies. On reconsideration of the matters referred back to the Commission, it adopted essentially the same remedies. Two appeals brought by BAA against the Commission's decision that it should divest itself of three UK airports were ultimately unsuccessful[229]. In *Private healthcare* the appeal by HCA International led to the CMA's decision in relation to insurance patients and the related divestment remedy being quashed and remitted to the CMA[230]. The CMA subsequently confirmed its finding of an adverse effect on competition ('AEC'), but concluded that divestment was no longer proportionate.

A second point to note is that three applications to the CAT challenged a decision *not* to make a market investigation reference: one case was successful[231], one was unsuccessful[232] and one did not proceed to judgment[233].

A third point is that the CMA must act fairly; where there is a defect in this respect the CAT will be prepared to quash the decision in question. In *BMI Healthcare v Competition Commission*[234] a party successfully persuaded the CAT that the Competition Commission's decision to use a 'disclosure room' during the *Private healthcare* investigation should be annulled due to procedural irregularities on the Commission's part. In a subsequent appeal in relation to the same investigation, *HCA International v CMA*[235], the CMA accepted that it had erred in its final report in *Private healthcare* and that fairness required that the parties be given an opportunity to comment on its revised 'insured prices analysis'[236]. The CAT quashed the CMA's decisions that there was an AEC in relation to insured patients and that HCA should divest itself of two hospitals in central London and

[223] Enterprise Act 2002, s 179(5)(a).

[224] Ibid, s 179(5)(b); on which see the ruling on relief in Case 1104/6/8/08 *Tesco plc v Competition Commission* [2009] CAT 9.

[225] Enterprise Act 2002, s 179(6) and (7).

[226] See 'The Market Investigation Provisions in Practice', pp 488–493 later in chapter.

[227] Case 1104/6/8/09 [2009] CAT 6.

[228] Case 1109/6/8/09 [2009] CAT 27.

[229] Case 1110/6/8/09 *BAA Ltd v Competition Commission* [2009] CAT 35, reversed on appeal by the Court of Appeal [2010] EWCA Civ 1097: the UK Supreme Court refused to grant BAA permission to appeal; the Competition Commission's decision of 19 July 2011 that there was no material change of circumstances justifying different remedies was upheld on appeal to the CAT: Case 1185/6/8/11 [2012] CAT 3 and on further appeal to the Court of Appeal [2012] EWCA Civ 1077.

[230] Case 1229/6/12/14 *HCA International Ltd v CMA* [2014] CAT 23.

[231] Case 1052/6/1/05 *Association of Convenience Stores v OFT* [2005] CAT 36.

[232] Case 1191/6/1/12 *Association of Convenience Stores v OFT* [2012] CAT 27.

[233] Case 1148/6/1/09 *CAMRA v OFT*, order of 7 February 2011.

[234] Case 1218/6/8/13 [2013] CAT 24.

[235] Case 1229/6/12/14 *HCA International Ltd v CMA* [2014] CAT 23.

[236] Ibid, para 13; at para 55 the CAT said that the CMA's concession and decision to look at the matter afresh was 'the responsible thing for it to do in the circumstances'.

referred the matter back to the CMA[237]. The CMA subsequently reaffirmed its AEC decision on insured patients, but considered that divestment was no longer proportionate[238].

A fourth point is that a couple of appeals have challenged the CMA's decision *not* to find an AEC. In *AXA PPA Healthcare Ltd v CMA*[239] the CAT held that the CMA had rationally concluded that the formation of anaesthetist groups did not give rise to an AEC in *Private healthcare*; there was insufficient evidence to support the theory of harm that anaesthetist groups have market power arising from the joint setting of prices. In *Federation of Independent Practitioner Organisations v CMA*[240] the Court of Appeal unanimously upheld the CMA's decision that there was no AEC resulting from insurers' buyer power in relation to consultants and the restrictions placed on consultants' fees.

9. The Market Investigation Provisions in Practice

By 8 December 2017 a total of 18 market investigation references had been made, 15 of which had been completed; one was pending, into investment consultants, launched on 14 September 2017[241]. The three investigations completed since the publication of the 8th edition of this book are set out in Table 11.3 below.

A number of points can be made about the market investigations that have so far been completed.

(A) Meaning of 'adverse effect on competition'

Analysis must begin with the meaning of the terms 'features of the market' and 'adverse effect on competition' which appear in sections 131 and 134 of the Enterprise Act 2002. The CMA uses economic thinking to facilitate its analysis of competition in the market under investigation. The CMA has not laid down a definitive test of what constitutes an AEC, but its guidelines and reports indicate that it sees the issue in terms of a realistic comparison between 'a well-functioning market' and the competitive conditions observed in practice[242]. The text that follows will briefly examine the approach that has been taken to identifying an AEC.

(i) Market definition

In its reports the CMA defines the relevant market and, in doing so, identifies those products or services that currently constrain the prices of those under investigation[243]. Market definition provides a helpful framework for evidence gathering and economic analysis. The goods or services specified in the reference may or may not correspond to the relevant market. The Competition Commission undertook considerable econometric analysis and modelling to inform its market definition in *Groceries*[244]. In *Private healthcare* the CMA took into account the results of its patient survey as a useful source of information about

[237] www.competitionandmarkets.blog.gov.uk

[238] Final Remittal Report of 5 September 2016.

[239] Case 1228/6/12/14 [2015] CAT 5.

[240] [2016] EWCA Civ 777, dismissing an appeal against a majority CAT decision: Case 1230/6/12/14 [2015] CAT 8.

[241] A table of all the investigations from 20 June 2003 to date will be found at www.oup.com/uk/whish9e/.

[242] See eg the market investigations in *Home credit*, Final Report of 30 November 2006, para 8.4; *Groceries*, Final Report of 30 April 2008, para 10.7; and *Rolling stock leasing*, Final Report of 7 April 2009, paras 8.4–8.6 and 8.20; *Private motor insurance*, Final Report of 24 September 2014, paras 6.4, 6.22, 6.56 and 6.108–6.109; see also *Market investigation guidelines*, paras 30 and 320.

[243] This is consistent with the *Market investigation guidelines*, part 3, section 2.

[244] See the Final Report of 30 April 2008, paras 4.13–4.14.

Table 11.3 Table of market investigation references

Title of report	Date of reference	Date of report	Outcome
Payday lending	27.06.13	24.02.15	Adverse effect on competition in relation to payday lending. Various measures proposed to increase price competition between payday lenders and to help borrowers to get a better deal
Energy (Note: reference by OFGEM)	26.06.14	24.06.16	Adverse effect on competition at the retail level of energy supply, but not at the wholesale level. A core concern was that many individual customers and microbusinesses were still on default tariffs. Various measures proposed to enable consumers to switch to cheaper energy suppliers. The CMA also suggested a transitional price cap for customers on prepayment meters until the introduction of smart meters enables them to access better supply offers. These measures will be implemented by a combination of CMA Orders and recommendations to OFGEM
Retail banking	06.11.14	09.08.16	Adverse effect on competition in retail banking. In particular established banks do not compete hard enough for individual customers and smaller market entrants face expansion barriers. Consumers pay supra-competitive prices for retail banking services without benefitting from new technology The CMA is implementing various measures and reforms to ensure that customers have greater access to new technological advances and that expansion barriers for new entrants are reduced. Further remedies will be introduced to facilitate the switching of banks and thereby to generate savings for overdraft users These measures will be implemented in liaison with other public bodies, such as the FCA and HM Treasury

the relevant market[245]. The CMA also used a customer survey to help it to determine the degree of substitutability between payday loans and other credit products in *Payday lending*[246].

(ii) **Counterfactual**

The CMA will normally try to identify the appropriate 'counterfactual' against which to determine whether any feature or features of the market lead to an AEC[247]. The CMA sometimes refers to a 'well-functioning market'; this does not require perfect competition[248], but is likely to be a market in which competition is as effective as possible given the nature of the product[249].

(iii) **Theories of harm**

The CMA use economics to frame their analysis of a particular market and consider various 'theories of harm' which may arise from one or more 'features' of the market. A theory of harm is a hypothesis of how harmful effects might arise in a market and adversely affect customers[250]. The *Market investigation guidelines* explain that competitive harm can flow from five main sources[251]:

- unilateral market power
- barriers to entry and expansion
- coordinated conduct
- vertical relationships
- weak customer response.

This list is not exhaustive. The *Market investigation guidelines* provide guidance on each source of competitive harm as well as the CMA's assessment of competition, and include consideration of issues such as switching costs and barriers to entry; and market imperfections, such as informational asymmetries. In *Federation of Independent Practitioner Organisations v CMA*[252] the Court of Appeal said that the existence or absence of detrimental effects on customers is 'plainly a material indication' of whether there is an AEC.

In practice, as one would expect, different theories of harm have been examined in different market investigations. In *Northern Ireland personal banking*[253] the features of the market harming competition were that banks had unduly complex charging structures and practices; that they did not fully or sufficiently explain them; and that customers generally did not actively search for alternative suppliers[254]. In *BAA airports*[255] the theory of harm was different: it was that BAA's common ownership of many airports in the UK meant that there was a lack of competition between them, resulting in problems such as a lack of responsiveness to the interests of airlines and passengers. This feature of the airports market could have an AEC in more than one market: for example if there were

[245] Final Report of 2 April 2014, paras 5.13–5.14 and fn 187.

[246] Final Report of 24 February 2015, paras 5.20–5.24.

[247] See eg *Aggregates*, Final Report of 14 January 2014, paras 5.78, 8.4–8.6, 8.40–8.41, 8.56, 8.228, 8.417, 8.484 and 8.494.

[248] See *Market investigations guidelines*, para 330, citing *Payment protection insurance*, Final Report of 29 January 2009, para 104; see also *Rolling stock leasing*, Final Report of 7 April 2009, para 4.28.

[249] See eg *Groceries*, Final Report of 30 April 2008, para 10.7; *Statutory audit services*, Final Report of 15 October 2013, para 8.7; *Retail banking*, Final Report of 9 August 2016, paras 5.125, 5.136, 5.154 and 5.184.

[250] See *Market investigations guidelines*, para 163.

[251] Ibid, para 170.

[252] [2016] EWCA Civ 777, para 39.

[253] Final Report of 15 May 2007.

[254] Ibid, para 5.9.

[255] Final Report of 19 March 2009, para 8.2.

inadequate investment at an airport caused by lack of competition between airports, that lack of investment may adversely affect competition between airlines[256]. In *Local buses*[257] the combination of high levels of concentration in the relevant market, the presence of barriers to entry and expansion and customer conduct led to an AEC. In *Energy*[258] and *Retail banking*[259] a weak customer response to differences in price and quality gave suppliers a position of unilateral market power over their existing customers, which led to AECs.

(iv) Performance and prices

In some cases the level of prices and profitability have been considered as factors indicating the lack of competitive pressure in a market[260]. In *Home credit*[261] the Competition Commission concluded that the fact that excessive profits were being earned was not in itself an AEC, although it was indicative of features of the market, such as an incumbency advantage and a lack of customer switching, that did produce an AEC. In *Payday lending*[262] the CMA found that the largest lenders had earned profits significantly above their cost of capital from 2008 to 2013, which was consistent with a lack of effective price competition. On other occasions a number of conceptual and practical difficulties have constrained the ability to conduct informative profitability analysis[263].

(B) Findings of adverse effects on competition

In all but one of its reports the Competition Commission or the CMA has found one or more AECs[264]; no adverse finding was made in *Movies on pay TV* owing to the emergence of new 'video on demand' services[265]. A few comments may be helpful about the adverse findings to date.

First, a number of references have involved oligopolistic markets where competition between suppliers was weak[266]. For example in *Aggregates*[267] a combination of structural and conduct features of the cement markets in Great Britain were found to give rise to an overarching feature: coordination among the three largest cement producers Cemex, Hanson and Lafarge. In *Energy*[268] the CMA found that each of the six large energy suppliers had unilateral market power over its customer base and was able to charge standard variable tariffs materially above any level justified by the costs of an efficient domestic retail supply.

Secondly, a recurrent theme has been problems for consumers who did not have access to clear and effective information about the products or services on offer, and where there

[256] Ibid, para 8.2. [257] Final Report of 20 December 2011, para 11.28.

[258] Final Report of 24 June 2016, section 9. [259] Final Report of 9 August 2016, section 11.

[260] See eg *Store card credit services*, Final Report of 7 March 2006, paras 8.11 and 8.82; *Groceries*, Final Report of 30 April 2008, para 6.76; *Classified directory advertising services*, Final Report of 21 December 2006, section 7.

[261] Final Report of 30 November 2006, paras 3.61–3.143.

[262] Final Report of 24 February 2015, para 6.8.

[263] See eg the Final Reports in *Liquefied petroleum gas*, para 5.16 (profitability analysis was inconclusive) and *Rolling stock leasing*, para 8.18 (profitability analysis was not practicable).

[264] Note that ERRA 2013, Sch 4, paras 55 and 57 provide that a finding of an AEC requires at least a two-thirds majority of the CMA group; on this point see *Private healthcare*, Final Report of 2 April 2014, paras 10.4–10.6.

[265] Final Report of 2 August 2012.

[266] See eg *Northern Ireland personal banking*, Final Report of 15 May 2007, paras 4.306–4.307; *Groceries*, Final Report of 30 April 2008, para 8.40; *Statutory audit services*, Final Report of 15 October 2013, paras 12.1–12.3; and *Local buses*, Final Report of 20 December 2011, paras 8.242–8.243.

[267] Final Report of 14 January 2014, paras 12.3–12.6. [268] Final Report of 24 June 2016, para 9.283.

appeared to be impediments to switching on their part, whether for reasons of inertia or because of technical and practical difficulties[269]. This was an important issue in both *Energy*[270] and *Retail banking*[271] and several other market investigations[272].

A third point is that the impact of government policy and economic regulation has been a concern in several investigations, including *Classified directory advertising services*[273]; *Rolling stock leasing*[274] and *BAA airports*[275]. In *Energy*[276] the CMA found that some of OFGEM's regulatory measures were restricting the behaviour of suppliers and constraining the choices of consumers in ways that reduced consumer welfare[277].

(C) **Remedies**

If the CMA concludes that there is an AEC, it must remedy the position as fully and effectively as possible[278]. The *Market investigation guidelines* discuss different types of remedies and the principles relevant to selecting and implementing them[279].

In *Private motor insurance*, unusually, the Competition Commission was unable to remedy the inefficiencies arising from the fact that the insurer liable for a non-fault driver's claim is often not the party controlling the costs: it concluded that none of the available remedies provided an effective and proportionate solution[280]. Separately, in two investigations—*BAA airports*[281] and *Aggregates*[282]—compulsory divestiture was ordered to remedy competition problems resulting from structural features of the relevant markets[283].

In *Private healthcare*[284] the CMA originally ordered the divestiture of two hospitals to remedy the AECs for the provision of insured and self-pay private healthcare services in central London. Following a successful appeal by HCA[285], the owner of the two hospitals, the CMA reinvestigated and decided, by a majority, that divestment was no longer proportionate, since there was insufficient certainty that the benefits of a structural remedy would outweigh its costs[286]. In *Energy*[287] and *Retail banking*[288] the CMA chose a

[269] See eg *Private healthcare*, Final Report of 2 April 2014, paras 10.8–10.9.

[270] Final Report of 24 June 2016, section 9 and paras 20.5–20.11.

[271] Final Report of 9 August 2016, paras 11.3–11.6 (personal current accounts), 11.9–11.11 (business current accounts) and 11.14–11.16 (SME lending).

[272] See eg *Store card credit services*, Final Report of 7 March 2006, paras 8.159 and 8.165; *Home credit*, Final Report of 30 November 2006, paras 7.14–7.15; *Northern Ireland personal banking*, Final Report of 15 May 2007, paras 4.222–4.228; and *Payment protection insurance*, Final Report of 29 January 2009, para 9.2.

[273] Final Report of 21 December 2006, paras 8.25–8.26; Yell's successor was released from the undertakings in light of the effects on classified directories of internet usage by consumers and advertisers: Final Decision of 15 March 2013.

[274] Final Report of 7 April 2009, paras 6.212–6.226.

[275] Final Report of 19 March 2009, paras 6.60–6.88.

[276] Final Report of 24 June 2016, paras 9.478–9.513.

[277] Ibid, paras 9.478–9.513.

[278] On the CAT's case law see 'Review of decisions under Part 4 of the Enterprise Act', pp 486–488 earlier in chapter.

[279] *Market investigation guidelines*, paras 322–393; see also *CMA's Supplemental guidance*, para 4.14.

[280] Final Report of 24 September 2014, paras 26–40 (summary).

[281] Final Report of 19 March 2009, section 10; the CMA evaluated the remedies in *BAA airports*: see the Report of 16 May 2016.

[282] Final Report of 14 January 2014, paras 13.7–13.138.

[283] The requirements for the design and implementation of divestiture remedies are set out in paras 3–30 of Annex B to the *Market investigation guidelines*.

[284] Final Report of 2 April 2014, paras 11.9–11.244.

[285] Case 1228/6/12/14 *HCA International Ltd v CMA* [2014] CAT 23.

[286] Final Remittal Report of 5 September 2016, paras 12.314–12.321.

[287] Final Report of 24 June 2016, paras 20.22–20.31.

[288] Final Report of 9 August 2016, section 19.

'package' of measures to remedy the AECs and their respective detrimental effects on customers[289].

(D) **Evaluation of the system**

The CMA is committed to evaluating the effectiveness of market studies and market investigations[290]. Action taken following market studies and market investigations was estimated to have saved consumers an average of £887 million every year between 2014 and 2017[291].

10. Orders and Undertakings Under the Fair Trading Act 1973

The monopoly provisions in the Fair Trading Act 1973 were superseded by the market investigation provisions in the Enterprise Act 2002. Over the years the CMA's predecessors published a large number of reports dealing with many sectors of the economy and numerous practices. Many of these reports led to the Secretary of State accepting undertakings or, in some cases, making orders designed to remedy any competition problems identified. Despite the repeal of the substantive provisions of the Fair Trading Act some of these undertakings and orders remain in force[292].

The CMA maintains a *Register of orders and undertakings* containing details of orders and undertakings made under the Fair Trading Act and the Enterprise Act[293]. The CMA has a continuing obligation to keep these orders and undertakings under review and may give advice to the Secretary of State as to whether their release, revocation, variation or termination is appropriate[294]. The CMA has published guidance on its approach to the variation and termination of merger, monopoly and market undertakings and orders[295].

289 See generally *Market investigation guidelines*, para 328.

290 See eg CMA's *Annual Plan 2017/18*, CMA59, March 2017, para 5.17.

291 See CMA's *Annual Report and Accounts 2016/17*, HC 24, p 73.

292 Enterprise Act 2002, Sch 24, paras 14–18.

293 The *Register* is accessible at www.gov.uk/government/collections/markets-orders-and-undertakings-register; the contents of the register are available to the public between 10.00 am and 4.00 pm on working days: see the CMA Registers of Undertakings and Orders (Available Hours) Order 2014, SI 2014/558.

294 Enterprise Act 2002, s 162(3).

295 *Guidance on the CMA's approach to the variation and termination of merger, monopoly and market undertakings and orders*, CMA11, January 2014, as amended August 2015.

12

The international dimension of competition law

1. Introduction

This book so far has described the main provisions, other than those dealing with mergers[1], of EU and UK competition law, and the way in which those provisions are enforced. This chapter is concerned with the international dimension of competition law.

Dramatic changes have taken place in the world's economies in a remarkably short period. State-controlled economies have been exposed to the principles of the market; legal monopolies have been reduced or eliminated; domestic markets have been increasingly opened up to foreign trade and investment; and there are a great number of multinational companies operating around the world. These changes have led to an enormous growth of international trade, a development that is promoted by the World Trade Organization ('the WTO'). These developments present significant challenges for systems of competition law. The adverse effects of cartels and anti-competitive behaviour on the part of dominant firms and of mergers are not constrained by national boundaries. It is possible for a few producers to operate a cartel that has significant effects throughout the world: the OPEC oil cartel is an obvious example of this, although there are both legal and political constraints that prevent competition authorities from tackling this particular organisation[2]. In recent years several cartels have come to light that had a genuinely global reach: the *Air cargo* and *Car parts* cartels being good examples of this[3]; non-US citizens responsible for unlawful cartels face the possibility of extradition to the US, imprisonment[4]

[1] On mergers see chs 20–22.

[2] To the extent that the actors in this cartel are sovereign States as opposed to undertakings, the doctrine of sovereign immunity prevents the application of the EU competition rules: see ch 3, 'Undertakings and associations of undertakings', pp 83–101 on the meaning of 'undertakings' in Articles 101 and 102; on sovereign immunity in US law see the Foreign Sovereign Immunity Act 1976, 28 USC §§ 1602–1611 and the joint Department of Justice and Federal Trade Commission *Antitrust Guidelines for International Enforcement and Cooperation* (January 2017), para 4.2.1, available at www.justice.gov/atr; note also the position in the US on foreign sovereign compulsion, ibid, para 4.2.2, and the Act of State doctrine, ibid, para 3.33.

[3] See ch 13, 'EU Policy Towards Cartels', pp 524–530.

[4] See ch 13, 'Recent action against cartels around the world', pp 523–524.

and individual liability to fines. Undertakings such as Google provide services, such as its search engine, that are truly global: Google has been the subject of competition law investigations in several jurisdictions, including the US, the EU and India. International mergers, for example between car manufacturers, aluminium producers or telecommunications companies, may produce effects in a multitude of countries, and may be subject to notification to a large number of different competition authorities[5].

These developments raise an obvious but important point: transnational conduct and mergers necessitate an international response, whereas for the most part systems of competition law are purely national in scope. The rules of the EU are an important exception, since they apply throughout the 28 Member States and three Contracting States of the European Economic Area ('the EEA'). Formal and informal cooperation between competition authorities is needed to address transnational behaviour. Indeed, it is now common practice for competition authorities to cooperate closely with one another when they are conducting investigations that have an international dimension[6].

Sections 2 to 6 of this chapter are concerned with the question of whether one country can apply its competition rules extraterritorially against an undertaking or undertakings in another country, where the latter behave in an anti-competitive manner having adverse effects in the territory of the former; and whether there should be laws (so-called 'blocking statutes') to prevent the 'excessive' assertion of extraterritorial jurisdiction. However the international dimension of competition law has undoubtedly evolved beyond these somewhat parochial concerns: section 7 describes the work of international organisations, such as the International Competition Network ('the ICN'), that encourage cooperation between competition authorities and promote convergence between competition policies, procedures and substantive analysis.

2. Extraterritoriality: Theory

The limits upon a State's jurisdictional competence—and therefore upon its ability to apply its competition laws to overseas undertakings—are matters of public international law[7]. There are two elements to a State's jurisdictional competence:

- **subject-matter jurisdiction**: a State has jurisdiction to make laws, that is to say to 'lay down general or individual rules through its legislative, executive or judicial bodies'[8]
- **enforcement jurisdiction**: a State has jurisdiction to enforce its laws, that is 'the power of a State to give effect to a general rule or an individual decision by means of substantive implementing measures which may include even coercion by the authorities'[9].

[5] See ch 20, 'The Proliferation of Systems of Merger Control', pp 832–833.

[6] On international cooperation see 'The Internationalisation of Competition Law', pp 514–519 later in chapter.

[7] For a general account of the relevant principles of public international law see Crawford *Brownlie's Principles of Public International Law* (Oxford University Press, 8th ed, 2012), ch 20–22; Harris and Sivakumaran *Cases and Materials on International Law* (Sweet & Maxwell, 8th ed, 2015), ch 6; Shaw *International Law* (Cambridge University Press, 8th ed, 2017), ch 12; see also International Bar Association *Report of the Task Force on Extraterritorial Jurisdiction* (2009), available at www.ibanet.org; Mills 'Rethinking Jurisdiction in International Law'; (2014) 84 British Yearbook of International Law 187; Evans *International Law* (Oxford University Press, 4th ed, 2014), ch 11; Dixon and McCorquodale *Cases and Materials on International Law* (Oxford University Press, 6th ed, 2016), ch 8.

[8] This is also known as a State's 'legislative' or 'prescriptive' jurisdiction; see the Opinion of AG Darmon in Cases C-89/85 etc *A Ahlström Osakeyhtiö v Commission* EU:C:1988:258 (*Wood Pulp I*).

[9] Ibid.

It is not necessarily the case that the limits of subject-matter and enforcement jurisdiction should be the same: they do not have to be coextensive. An assertion of subject-matter jurisdiction by one State over natural or legal persons in another may not lead to a conflict at all, provided that the former does not seek to enforce its law in the territory of another State. However when a State goes further and seeks enforcement—for example by serving a claim for damages on a person located in another State or demanding the production of evidence there—the possibility of conflict is obvious. Most of the controversial conflicts between States in these matters have concerned enforcement rather than subject-matter jurisdiction, and it is essentially against enforcement measures that States have adopted blocking statutes[10]. An issue that has arisen in the US is whether it is possible to apply its competition law extraterritorially as a way of gaining access to foreign markets[11].

(A) **Subject-matter jurisdiction**

As far as subject-matter jurisdiction is concerned, it is generally accepted in public international law that a State has power to make laws affecting conduct within its territory (the 'territoriality principle') and to regulate the behaviour of its citizens abroad, citizens for this purpose including companies incorporated under its law (the 'nationality principle'). The territoriality principle has been extended in a logical way so that a State is recognised as having jurisdiction not only where acts originate in its territory (known as 'subjective territoriality'), but also where the objectionable conduct originates abroad but is completed within its territory ('objective territoriality'). The classic textbook illustration is of a shot being fired across a national boundary: although part of the conduct happened outside the State, it will have jurisdiction as the harmful event occurred within it. A consequence of this is that more than one State may assert jurisdiction in the same matter where the conduct in question straddles national borders. What is controversial is whether, in the area of economic law, it is legitimate to apply the idea of objective territoriality to the *effects* of an agreement entered into, or an anti-competitive act committed in, another State.

For the purpose of subject-matter jurisdiction the territoriality and nationality principles are sufficient to comprehend a great number of infringements of competition law, either because the overseas undertaking will have committed some act—for example acquiring a competitor or charging predatory prices—within the territory of the State concerned to apply its law, or because an agreement will have been made between a foreign undertaking and a firm domiciled within the State in question. Alternatively it may be that an act has been committed within that State by a subsidiary company of an overseas parent. In this case the question arises whether it is legitimate to treat the two companies as being a single economic entity, so that the parent can be held responsible for the unlawful conduct of the subsidiary. If so the territoriality principle will suffice to establish jurisdiction over the parent company. The single economic entity doctrine is a significant and well-established feature of EU law[12].

However even the objective territoriality principle and the economic entity theory may not be sufficient to account for all cases in which a State may wish to assume jurisdiction over foreign undertakings. For example if all the producers of widgets in Japan were to agree not to export widgets to the UK, their agreement could obviously produce

[10] See 'Resistance to Extraterritorial Application of Competition Law', pp 512–514 later in chapter.

[11] See 'The extraterritorial application of US antitrust law to gain access to foreign markets', pp 501–502 later in chapter.

[12] See ch 3, 'The "single economic entity" doctrine', pp 93–99 and 'The economic entity doctrine', pp 502–503 later in chapter.

commercial effects in the UK; however it is hard to see how it can be meaningfully said that there is any conduct there.

The controversial public international law question is whether a State may assert subject-matter jurisdiction simply on the basis that foreign undertakings produce commercial effects within its territory, even though they are not present there and have not committed any act there. The traditional principles of public international law are inadequate to deal with these issues, since they were developed with physical rather than economic conduct in mind. As a matter of logic, it does not seem absurd to suggest that harmful economic effects as well as physical ones emanating from another State ought in some cases to establish jurisdiction: it is not difficult to see the analogy between a shot being fired across the border of one State into a neighbouring one and a conspiracy by firms in one State to charge fixed and excessive prices or to boycott customers in another one. The EU Court of Justice has recognised the notion of jurisdiction under public international law based on 'qualified effects', that is to say, the criteria of 'immediate, substantial and immediate effects'[13]. However the 'effects doctrine' is not without its critics, and the UK Government historically was hostile to the idea[14]. It is not clear what the position of the UK Government is today. The Brexit Competition Law Working Group in its *Conclusions and Recommendations* of July 2017 recommended that the UK Competition Act 1998 should be amended post-Brexit specifically to embrace the qualified effects doctrine[15].

(B) **Enforcement jurisdiction**

Enforcement jurisdiction tends to give rise to the most acute conflicts between States[16]. It is generally recognised that even if subject-matter jurisdiction exists in relation to the conduct of someone in another State, it is improper to attempt to enforce the law in question within that State's territory without its permission. For these purposes enforcement does not mean only the exaction of penalties and the making of final orders such as perpetual injunctions, but refers to all authoritative acts such as the service of a summons, a demand for information or carrying out an investigation. Gathering information can be a particular problem for competition authorities: as business often transcends national borders, a national authority may need to seek evidence located outside its jurisdiction. A problem is that jurisdictional rules developed in the nineteenth century are not particularly well suited to the business context or the information technology of the twenty-first century.

The Hague Convention on the Taking of Evidence Abroad in Civil or Commercial Matters[17] provides for one State to assist another in the gathering of evidence: this Convention is given effect in UK law by the Evidence (Proceedings in Other Jurisdictions) Act 1975. Since 1 January 2004 EU Regulation 1206/2001[18] has governed cooperation between the courts of the Member States (except Denmark) in the taking of evidence in

[13] See Case C-413/14 P *Intel v Commission* EU:C:2017:632, paras 41–46 and 49.

[14] See Jennings 'Extraterritorial Jurisdiction and the United States Antitrust Laws' (1957) 33 British Yearbook of International Law 146; Higgins 'The Legal Bases of Jurisdiction' in Olmstead (ed) *Extraterritorial Application of Laws and Responses Thereto* (1984); Lowe *Extraterritorial Jurisdiction* (Grotius, 1983), pp 138–186; on the UK's position, see further 'The Extraterritorial Application of UK Competition Law', pp 508–512 later in chapter.

[15] See para 2.4 of the Report, available at www.bclwg.org.

[16] See *Brownlie*, pp 310–312.

[17] Cmnd 3991 (1968); as of 8 December 2017 there were 59 States that had acceded to the Hague Evidence Convention: www.hcch.net/en/home.

[18] OJ [2001] L 174/1.

civil or commercial matters[19]. The recognition and enforcement of foreign judgments is an important part of private international law: most foreign judgments can be enforced in the UK[20], though not where they are penal[21]. However cooperation on evidence and the enforcement of judgments is often not provided by one State to another where the former takes exception to an attempt by the latter to assert its law extraterritorially, and most legal systems contain restrictions on the divulging by competition authorities of confidential information.

The UK and the US agreed to relax these rules in so far as this might assist the pursuit of criminal cartels, which are now covered by the UK/US Mutual Assistance Treaty[22]; requests for mutual assistance in criminal matters are the responsibility of the Home Office[23]. The International Antitrust Enforcement Assistance Act 1994[24] helps the US agencies to obtain evidence located abroad by providing for reciprocal agreements to be entered into between the US and other countries to facilitate the exchange of information, including confidential information. The US has entered into dedicated cooperation agreements with the Australia, Brazil, Canada, Chile, Colombia, the EU, Israel, Japan, Mexico and Peru[25]. It has also entered into *Memoranda of Understanding on Antitrust Cooperation* with China, India, Russia and South Korea[26].

Part 9 of the Enterprise Act 2002 consolidates and codifies the powers of the UK Competition and Markets Authority ('the CMA') to disclose information to overseas public authorities for the purpose (among other matters) of civil and criminal competition law investigations. Section 237 of the Enterprise Act imposes a general restriction on the disclosure of information; however section 243 sets out circumstances in which, subject to conditions[27], information can be disclosed to an overseas competition authority. Information gathered by the CMA during a merger or market investigation cannot be disclosed[28], and the Secretary of State has power in certain circumstances to direct that information should not be disclosed[29].

3. The Extraterritorial Application of US Antitrust Law

(A) The *Alcoa*, *Hartford Fire Insurance* and *Empagran* cases

US law permits jurisdiction to be taken on the basis of effects alone[30]. In *United States v Aluminum Co of America*[31] (*Alcoa*) Judge Learned Hand said that:

[19] The Hague Convention and Regulation 1206/2001 were considered in an action for damages under Article 101 TFEU: see *Secretary of State for Health v Servier Laboratories Ltd* [2013] EWCA Civ 1234.

[20] See Cheshire, North and Fawcett *Private International Law* (Oxford University Press, 15th ed, 2017), ch 15; Dicey, Morris and Collins *The Conflict of Laws* (Sweet & Maxwell, 15th ed with 3rd supp, 2016), ch 15.

[21] Treble damage awards in the US are probably penal: *British Airways Board v Laker Airways Ltd* [1984] QB 142 at 163 and, in the Court of Appeal, at 201; see also the Protection of Trading Interests Act 1980, s 5, which introduced a statutory prohibition on the enforcement of awards of multiple damages: 'Resistance to Extraterritorial Application of Competition Law', pp 512–514 later in chapter.

[22] Accessible at www.gov.uk/guidance/mutual-legal-assistance-mla-requests; see also the Cooperation Agreement between the UK, Australia and New Zealand in respect of competition and consumer enforcement (October 2003), available at www.accc.gov.au.

[23] For further information see the *Requests for Mutual Legal Assistance in Criminal Matters: Guidelines for Foreign Authorities* (2015), available at www.gov.uk/guidance/mutual-legal-assistance-mla-requests.

[24] 15 USC §§ 6201–6212.

[25] See the DoJ/FTC *International Guidelines*, ch 5.

[26] See www.justice.gov/atr/public/international/int-arrangements.html.

[27] See in particular ss 243(6) and 244 of the Enterprise Act 2002.

[28] Ibid, s 243(3)(d).

[29] Ibid, s 243(4).

[30] See Waller *Competition Policy in the Global Economy* (Institute for Consumer Antitrust Studies: Online Case Book, 2007), ch 1, available at www.luc.edu/law/centers/antitrust/publications/online_casebook.html.

[31] 148 F 2d 416 (2nd Cir 1945); for comment see Winerman and Kovacic 'Learned Hand, Alcoa and the Reluctant Application of the Sherman Act' (2013) 79 Antitrust LJ 295.

> it is settled law . . . that any State may impose liabilities, even upon persons not within its allegiance, for conduct outside its borders which has consequences within its borders which the State reprehends; and these liabilities other States will ordinarily recognise[32].

The US courts had not always accepted this view[33]; the statement may not have been necessary to the case[34]; and as formulated the doctrine was extremely wide. However *Alcoa* was of seminal importance and triggered off much controversy between the US and other countries. There was some disagreement between US lower courts as to whether the effects on US commerce had to be substantial[35]; this was resolved by the Foreign Trade Antitrust Improvements Act 1982 ('FTAIA'), which provides that the Sherman Act 1890[36] does not apply to conduct involving trade or commerce with foreign nations unless such conduct has a 'direct, substantial and foreseeable effect' on trade or commerce in the US[37].

In *Hartford Fire Insurance Co v California*[38] the Supreme Court repeated that jurisdiction could be taken over 'foreign conduct that was meant to produce and did in fact produce some substantial effect in the United States'[39]. The joint Department of Justice/Federal Trade Commission *Antitrust Guidelines for International Enforcement and Cooperation* ('the DoJ/FTC *International Guidelines*') of 2017[40] explain, by reference to a series of illustrative examples, how those enforcement agencies interpret the jurisdictional scope of US antitrust law in the light of these, and other, judgments.

A controversial issue is whether a foreign plaintiff can sue for damages in a US court, even though the harm it claims to have suffered occurred outside the US. For plaintiffs this is an attractive prospect, given that damages actions are well established in the US, where damages can be trebled, cases can be funded by contingency fees and unsuccessful plaintiffs do not have to pay the costs of successful defendants[41]. The question of access to US courts reached the Supreme Court in a case arising from the *Vitamins* cartels,

[32] *Alcoa* (ch 12 n 31), 444.

[33] See eg *American Banana Co v United Fruit Co* 213 US 347 (1909) in which the Supreme Court held that the Sherman Act did not apply to activities outside the US.

[34] It is arguable that there was conduct within the US since one of the firms involved in the alleged conspiracy, Aluminum Ltd of Canada, had its effective business headquarters in New York and was in the same group as the Aluminum Company of America.

[35] See eg *Industrie Siciliana Asfalti, Bitumi, SpA v Exxon Research & Engineering Co* 1977-1 Trade Case (CCH) (SDNY 1977) (no substantial effect required) and *Todhunter-Mitchell & Co Ltd v Anheuser-Busch* 383 F Supp 586 (ED Pa 1974) (requiring proof of a substantial effect).

[36] 15 USC §§ 1–7.

[37] 15 USC § 6a.

[38] 509 US 764 (1993); for comment on this case see Roth 'Jurisdiction, British Public Policy and the US Supreme Court' (1994) 110 LQR 194; Dam 'Extraterritoriality in an Age of Globalization: The *Hartford Fire* Case' (1993) Sup Ct Rev 289; Trenor 'Jurisdiction and the Extraterritorial Application of Antitrust Laws after *Hartford Fire*' (1995) 62 University of Chicago Law Review 1582; Waller 'From the Ashes of *Hartford Fire*: The Unanswered Questions of Comity' [1998] Fordham Corporate Law Institute (ed Hawk), ch 3; see also *United States v Nippon Paper* 109 F 3d 1 (1st Cir 1997), for comment on which see Reynolds, Sicilian and Wellman 'The Extraterritorial Application of the US Antitrust Laws to Criminal Conspiracies' (1998) 19 ECLR 151.

[39] For an overview of the development of the extraterritorial application of US law see Desautels-Stein 'Extraterritoriality, Antitrust, and the Pragmatist Style' (2008) 22 Emory International Law Review 499.

[40] See ch 12 n 2 earlier.

[41] On private enforcement of US antitrust law see Hovenkamp *Antitrust Enterprise: Principle and Execution* (Harvard University Press, 2006), ch 4; on private enforcement of EU and UK competition law see ch 8 of this book.

Hoffmann-La Roche Ltd v Empagran SA[42]. The Court had to consider the application of the FTAIA, and concluded that, if the plaintiffs had suffered harm not in the US but in Ukraine, Panama, Australia and Ecuador, they could not sue in the US; the Court of Appeals for the District of Columbia subsequently concluded that the foreign plaintiffs could not recover damages in the US[43]. The Court was sensitive to the argument that over-exposure to treble damages claims in the US on the part of non-US plaintiffs might amount to a serious deterrent to members of cartels, for example in Europe or East Asia, making a whistleblowing application to local competition authorities: the UK, Germany, Canada and the US enforcement authorities had all submitted *amicus curiae* briefs pointing out this danger to the Court. However the Supreme Court judgment in *Empagran* left open the question of whether foreign plaintiffs could sue in the US if the foreign injury that they had suffered was inseparable from the domestic harm caused by the cartel to customers in the US[44].

In *Motorola Mobility LLC v AU Optronics Corp*[45] Motorola claimed damages in respect of purchases that it had made of mobile phones containing LCD panels; 99% of the phones used LCD panels that had been purchased in Asia. Motorola argued that its foreign injury was inseparable from the higher prices for phones in the US caused by an LCD cartel in Asia. Posner J, giving the judgment of the Court, rejected the claim, since the immediate victims of the cartel were Motorola's Asian subsidiaries and any foreign injury was not inseparable from any effects of the cartel in the US[46].

(B) **Comity**

Some US courts, drawing on the principle of judicial comity, have attempted to apply the effects doctrine in a relatively restrictive way, requiring not only that there should be a direct and substantial effect within the US, but also that the respective interests of the US in asserting jurisdiction and of other States which might be offended by such assertion should be weighed against one another[47]. The origins of this approach can be traced back to Brewster's *Antitrust and American Business Abroad* in 1958 in which he called for a 'jurisdictional rule of reason'. The DoJ/FTC *International Guidelines* of 2017 set out various factors relevant to comity analysis, including the relative significance to the alleged violation of conduct within the US, as compared to conduct abroad; the nationality of the persons involved or affected by the conduct; the presence or absence of an intention to affect US consumers, markets or exporters; and the relative significance

[42] 544 US 155 (2004); for comment see Wurmnest 'Foreign Private Plaintiffs, Global Conspiracies, and the Extraterritorial Application of US Antitrust Law' (2005) 28(2) Hastings International and Comparative Law Reveview 205; Connor and Bush 'How to Block Cartel Formation and Price Fixing: Using Extraterritorial Application of the Antitrust Laws as a Deterrence Mechanism' (2008) 112 Penn State Law Review 813.

[43] *Empagran SA v Hoffmann-La Roche Ltd* 417 F 3d 1267 (DC Cir 2005); see similarly *In re Monosodium Glutamate Antitrust Litigation* 477 F 3d 535 (8th Cir 2007) and *In re Dynamic Random Access Memory (DRAM) Antitrust Litigation* 546 F 3d 981 (9th Cir 2008).

[44] See further Sowell 'New Decisions Highlight Old Misgivings: A Reassessment of the Foreign Trade Antitrust Improvements Act Following *Minn-Chem*' (2014) 66 Florida Law Review 511.

[45] 775 F 3d 816 (2015).

[46] Note the Antitrust Modernization Commission made a recommendation in 2007 that foreign purchases should not give rise to a claim under the FTAIA 1982, but the recommendation has not been enacted; the Report is available at www.govinfo.library.unt.edu/amc/.

[47] See *Timberlane Lumber Co v Bank of America* 549 F 2d 597 (9th Cir 1976) and *Mannington Mills v Congoleum Corp* 595 F 2d 1287 (3rd Cir 1979); for an account of this development see Fox 'Reasonableness and Extraterritoriality' [1986] Fordham Corporate Law Institute (ed Hawk), p 49.

and foreseeability of the effects on the US compared to the effects abroad[48]. Dealing with the problem of conflicts of jurisdiction by resort to the criterion of reasonableness has its critics, not least because a court hardly seems an appropriate forum in which to carry out such a delicate balancing process[49]. The principle of comity, however, is an important one; the Supreme Court has warned that rampant extraterritorial application of US law 'creates a serious risk of interference with a foreign nation's ability independently to regulate its own commercial affairs'[50]. Similarly, in *Motorola Mobility*[51] Posner J declined to apply US law in a manner that would 'enormously increase the global reach of the Sherman Act, creating friction with many foreign countries and resentment at the apparent effort of the United States to act as the world's competition police officer'.

(C) **The extraterritorial application of US antitrust law to gain access to foreign markets**

US antitrust law may be applied where US companies are obstructed by anti-competitive behaviour in their attempts to gain access to foreign markets. The 'Structural Impediments Initiative'[52] in the US identified the lax enforcement of the Japanese Anti-Monopoly Act against Japanese undertakings as a contributing factor to the difficulties of US firms in expanding into Japanese markets; the Japanese Large Scale Retail Stores Act was considered to be an additional obstacle to would-be importers. The DoJ threatened to apply the US antitrust rules against Japanese restrictive practices having the effect of excluding US exporters from Japanese markets[53]. Subsequently the Japanese Government substantially increased the penalties that can be imposed for infringement of the Japanese legislation[54]. The first case in which the US challenged conduct abroad that denied foreign access was *US v Pilkington*[55]: the case was settled through a consent decree whereby

[48] See the DoJ/FTC *International Guidelines*, para 3.2. See also Note 'Comity And Extraterritoriality In Antitrust Enforcement' (2011) Harvard Law Review 1269.

[49] See Judge Wilkey in *Laker Airways Ltd v Sabena* 731 F 2d 909 at 945–952 (DC Cir 1984), [1984] ECC 485; Rosenthal and Knighton *National Laws and International Commerce: The Problem of Extraterritoriality* (Routledge & Kegan Paul 1982); Mann 'The Doctrine of International Jurisdiction Revisited After Twenty Years' (1984) 186 RDC 19.

[50] 544 US 155 at 165 (2004). [51] See ch 12 n 45 earlier.

[52] See Lipsky 'Current Developments in Japanese Competition Law: Antimonopoly Act Enforcement Guidelines Resulting from the Structural Impediments Initiative' (1991) 60 Antitrust LJ 279 and Anwar 'The Impact of the Structural Impediments Initiative on US–Japan Trade' (1992–93) 16 World Competition 53; see also the dispute between Eastman-Kodak and Fuji, which ended up as a complaint by the US to the disputes settlement body of the WTO, noted by Furse 'Competition Law and the WTO Report: "*Japan—Measures Affecting Consumer Photographic Film and Paper*"' (1999) 20 ECLR 9.

[53] See the DoJ's *Antitrust Enforcement Policy Regarding Anticompetitive Conduct that Restricts US Exports*, 3 April 1992; see also Rill 'International Antitrust Policy—A Justice Department Perspective' [1991] Fordham Corporate Law Institute (ed Hawk), pp 29–43; Coppel 'A Question of Keiretsu: Extending the Long Arm of US Antitrust' (1992) 13 ECLR 192; Ohara 'The New US Policy on the Extraterritorial Application of Antitrust Laws, and Japan's Response' (1993–94) 17 World Competition 49; Davidow 'Application of US Antitrust Laws to Keiretsu Practices' (1994–95) 18 World Competition 5; Yamane and Seryo 'Restrictive Practices and Market Access in Japan—Has the JFTC been Effective in Eliminating Barriers in Distribution?' (1999) 22 World Competition 1.

[54] See Yamada 'Recent Developments of Competition Law and Policy in Japan' [1997] Fordham Corporate Law Institute (ed Hawk), ch 5; also by the same author 'Japanese Antitrust Law; Recent Developments and an Agenda for the Years Ahead' (2011) 2 JECLAP 165.

[55] (1994–2) Trade Cases (CCH) para 70,482 (1994); for comment see Byowitz 'The Unilateral Use of US Antitrust Laws to Achieve Foreign Market Access: A Pragmatic Assessment' [1996] Fordham Corporate Law Institute (ed Hawk), ch 3.

Pilkington agreed not to enforce certain provisions in technology licences against US firms. The DoJ may also take action against foreign cartels that have no effect within the US, but that raise prices in relation to transactions where the US Government contributes more than half the funding[56].

4. The Extraterritorial Application of EU Competition Law

This section will deal with subject-matter and enforcement jurisdiction under Articles 101 and 102 TFEU, and will then discuss the position under the EU Merger Regulation ('the EUMR').

(A) Articles 101 and 102: subject-matter jurisdiction

Articles 101 and 102 apply only to the extent that an agreement or abuse has an appreciable effect upon trade between Member States; the meaning of this phrase was analysed in chapter 3, to which reference should be made[57]. There is no reason in principle why, for example, an East Asian cartel or the unilateral conduct of a US firm might not satisfy this test, particularly given the liberal way in which it has been applied. In *Javico v Yves St Laurent*[58] the Court of Justice held that it was possible that an export ban imposed upon distributors in the Ukraine and Russia could have an appreciable effect on competition and trade between Member States and therefore infringe Article 101(1). There are three (independently sufficient) ways in which jurisdiction may be asserted over non-EU undertakings:

- the 'single economic entity' doctrine
- the 'implementation doctrine' and
- the 'qualified effects' doctrine.

Each basis for jurisdiction will be discussed in turn below.

(i) The single economic entity doctrine

In the *Dyestuffs* case[59] the Court of Justice established the single economic entity doctrine. The Court held that Geigy, Sandoz and ICI, three non-EU undertakings, had participated in illegal price fixing within the EU through the medium of subsidiary companies located in the EU but under the control of non-EU parents. The Court looked beyond the legal façade of the separate legal personalities of the parent and subsidiary companies, and held that each non-EU parent and EU subsidiary formed a single economic entity. This approach has been criticised, not only because of the refusal to respect the independent legal personalities of the companies concerned, but also because the Court seemed prepared to hold that a parent controlled its subsidiary on limited evidence[60]; however the EU Courts and the Commission have relied on the single economic entity doctrine on numerous occasions, both in the subject-matter and enforcement

[56] See the DoJ's Press Release, 18 August 2000, in relation to a construction cartel in Egypt.

[57] See ch 3, 'The Effect on Trade between Member States', pp 150–155.

[58] Case C-306/96 EU:C:1998:173.

[59] Cases 48/69 etc *ICI v Commission* EU:C:1972:70.

[60] On *Dyestuffs* see Mann 'The *Dyestuffs* Case in the Court of Justice of the European Communities' (1973) 22 ICLQ 35; Acevedo 'The EC *Dyestuffs* Case: Territorial Jurisdiction' (1973) 36 MLR 317.

jurisdiction contexts[61]. The crucial issue is whether the parent could and in fact did exercise decisive influence over its subsidiary. The fact that a parent owns all the shares in the subsidiary means that it could exert decisive influence and also creates a rebuttable presumption that such influence was actually exercised[62]. The exercise of decisive influence can be indirect and may be established even if the parent does not interfere in the day-to-day business of the subsidiary. The economic, organisational and legal links that tie the subsidiary to the parent company are all relevant to this issue[63]. A possible consequence of the single economic entity doctrine is that a claimant can sue for damages in the English courts against a UK subsidiary of a foreign parent that participated in an agreement contrary to Article 101 TFEU, provided the UK subsidiary at least knowingly implemented that agreement[64].

(ii) **The implementation doctrine**

In *Wood Pulp I*[65] the Commission, in finding that there was a concerted practice between undertakings in several non-EU countries, held that jurisdiction could be based on the effects of the concerted practice in the EU. On appeal the Court of Justice held[66] that, on the facts of the case, jurisdiction could be justified by reference to the universally recognised territoriality principle of public international law. The Court held that the cartel had been *implemented* within the EU; it was immaterial for this purpose whether this implementation was effected by subsidiaries, agents, sub-agents or branches within the EU. Since the agreement was implemented within the EU, it was unnecessary to have recourse to the effects doctrine. The Commission expressly cited the *Wood Pulp I* judgment in *Amino Acids*, where it imposed fines on a cartel including US, Japanese and Korean companies[67].

The Court of Justice in *Wood Pulp I* did not comment on what the position would have been if the agreement had been formed *and implemented* outside the EU, but had produced economic effects within it; an example would be a collective boycott by members of a non-EU cartel, whereby they refuse to supply customers within the EU: could one argue in such circumstances that this agreement is 'implemented' within the EU by the refusal to supply there? Linguistically this seems hard to sustain; however there is no doubt in this situation that the *effects* of the agreement would be felt within the EU. This is the issue to which we now turn.

[61] The doctrine may be used to overcome any perceived difficulty in sending a decision to a company in a non-EU State by serving it instead on the EU subsidiary.

[62] See eg Cases C-628/10 P etc *Alliance One International v Commission* EU:C:2012:479, paras 46–47; see generally ch 3, 'Parent and wholly-owned subsidiaries', pp 95–96.

[63] *Alliance One International*, para 45 and the case law cited.

[64] See *Provimi Ltd v Aventis Animal Nutrition SA* [2003] EWHC 961 (Comm), para 31; cf *Cooper Tire & Rubber Company Europe Ltd v Dow Deutschland Inc* [2010] EWCA Civ 864, paras 45–47; this point is discussed in ch 8, 'Private international law', pp 320–323.

[65] OJ [1985] L 85/1.

[66] Cases C-89/85 etc *A Ahlström Osakeyhtiö v Commission* EU:C:1988:447, paras 11–23; for comment see Ferry 'Towards Completing the Charm: The *Wood Pulp* Judgment' (1989) 11 EIPR 19; Mann 'The Public International Law of Restrictive Trade Practices in the European Court of Justice' (1989) 38 ICLQ 375; Lowe 'International Law and the Effects Doctrine in the European Court of Justice' (1989) 48 Cambridge Law Journal 9; Christoforou and Rockwell 'EC Law: The Territorial Scope of Application of EC Antitrust Law—the *Wood Pulp* Judgment' (1989) 30 Harvard International Law Journal 195; Lange and Sandage 'The *Wood Pulp* Decision and its Implications for the Scope of EC Competition Law' (1989) 26 CML Rev 137; Van Gerven 'EC Jurisdiction in Antitrust Matters: The *Wood Pulp* Judgment' [1989] Fordham Corporate Law Institute (ed Hawk), ch 21.

[67] OJ [2001] L 152/24, para 182.

(iii) The qualified effects doctrine

The Commission has quite often asserted that EU law recognises the effects doctrine[68], and several Advocates General have appeared to support this view[69]. However there was no definitive statement from the Court of Justice on this issue until its judgment in *Intel v Commission*[70].

The Commission had fined Intel because of practices that abusively excluded AMD from the market for chipsets and related products[71]. These practices included conditional rebates offered by Intel of the US to Lenovo in China. The Commission asserted that Intel's conduct overall (not the Lenovo rebates in isolation) was implemented in the EU and produced effects there. The General Court upheld the Commission on both grounds[72]. The Court of Justice unequivocally endorsed the qualified effects doctrine as a basis for jurisdiction. Just as the implementation doctrine was necessary in order to prevent undertakings from evading Articles 101 and 102 (for example by forming their agreements outside the EU)[73], so too the qualified effects doctrine pursues the same objective, namely preventing conduct outside the EU that could have anti-competitive effects within it: Intel's argument that EU law does not recognise a qualified effects test must therefore be rejected as unfounded[74]. To apply, the effects must be foreseeable, immediate and substantial[75]. The foreseeability criterion can be satisfied on the basis of the 'probable' effects of the conduct[76]. When considering whether any effects could be substantial, the Commission was entitled to take into account Intel's overall strategy towards AMD, and not the effect of the Lenovo rebates in isolation: otherwise it would be possible to fragment artificially a course of conduct in order to evade jurisdiction[77].

The Court of Justice in *Intel* concluded that the qualified effects doctrine can be used by the Commission to establish an infringement of EU competition law. An interesting question is whether the same principles apply to private actions for damages under Article 101 TFEU. Two actions in the UK, *iiyama v Schott*[78] and *iiyama v Samsung*[79], considered this question. Both actions were brought on the basis that the claimants had suffered loss within the EU when they purchased finished goods there incorporating components that were the subject of an unlawful cartel outside the EU (in this case in East Asia). The Court of Appeal held that the claimants had a real prospect of success in claiming that Article 101 had been infringed, and that they had suffered losses as a result of the intra-group importation of products into the EU that contained components sold at an alleged overcharge in Asia[80]. The Court considered that *Intel* provided substantial

[68] See eg the Commission's XIth *Report on Competition Policy* (1981), points 34–42; the Commission's decisions in *Wood Pulp* OJ [1985] L 85/1 and *Aluminum Products* OJ [1985] L 92/1 were explicitly adopted on the basis of the effects doctrine; see also the *Guidelines on the effect on trade concept contained in Articles [101 and 102 TFEU]* OJ [2004] C 101/81, para 100.

[69] See eg AG Mayras in Cases 48/69 etc *ICI v Commission* EU:C:1972:32, para 693; AG Roemer in Case 6/72 *Continental Can v Commission* EU:C:1972:101; AG Warner in Cases 6 and 7/73 *Commercial Solvents v Commission* EU:C:1974:18; AG Darmon in Cases C-89/85 etc *A Ahlström Osakeyhtiö v Commission* EU:C:1988:258; AG Wathelet in Case C-231/14 P *Innolux v Commission* EU:C:2015:292, paras 49–53; and AG Wahl in Case C-413/14 P *Intel v Commission* EU:C:2016:788, paras 296–304.

[70] Case C-413/14 P *Intel v Commission* EU:C:2017:632.

[71] Commission decision of 13 May 2009.

[72] Case T-286/09 *Intel v Commission* EU:T:2014:547.

[73] Case C-413/14 P *Intel v Commission* EU:C:2017:632, para 44.

[74] Ibid, paras 45–47.

[75] Ibid, para 49.

[76] Ibid, para 51.

[77] Ibid, paras 54–57.

[78] [2016] EWHC 1207 (Ch); for comment see Coulson, Blacklock and Gwilliam 'The Territorial Limits of Article 101 TFEU: To What Extent Can Claims Relating to Global Cartels be Brought in the English Courts?' [2017] Comp Law 83.

[79] [2016] EWHC 1980 (Ch).

[80] [2018] EWCA Civ 220; the defendants in both actions have applied to the UK Supreme Court for permission to appeal.

support for the claimants' argument that a worldwide cartel that was intended to produce substantial indirect effects in the EU may satisfy the qualified effects test[81]. The question whether there were qualified effects would require a full examination of the facts and the operation of the cartels as a whole, and on this basis the court held that both actions should go forward to trial.

(B) Articles 101 and 102: enforcement jurisdiction

(i) Initiating proceedings

Where proceedings are started by the Commission under Article 101 or 102, Article 2(2) of Regulation 773/2004[82] requires that the undertakings concerned must be informed. If the undertaking cannot be served within the EU, the question arises whether a statement of objections may be sent to it abroad. As suggested earlier this could be considered to contravene public international law, since it amounts to an enforcement of one State's law in the territory of another[83]. However the Court of Justice has rejected the notion that service without the consent of the foreign State is invalid and vitiates the proceedings. Provided that the non-EU undertaking has received the statement of objections in circumstances which enabled it to take cognisance of the case against it, the service is valid. In *Geigy v Commission*[84] the Commission sent its statement of objections to Geigy's Swiss offices. Geigy returned it, acting on instructions from the Swiss authorities, claiming that the service was unlawful both under internal and public international law. The Court of Justice rejected this. It is sufficient for EU law purposes, therefore, for the Commission to send a registered letter to the non-EU undertaking concerned.

(ii) Information and investigations

The Court of Justice has not been called upon to consider the extent to which the Commission may require information from or conduct investigations of undertakings domiciled outside the EU under Articles 18 and 20 respectively of Regulation 1/2003[85]. There would seem to be little objection to the Commission simply asking for information under Article 18(2), there being no compulsion to comply with such a request; in practice the Commission does send Article 18(2) requests to non-EU undertakings. It is less certain whether the Commission can make a demand for information under Article 18(3) of the Regulation, and the better view is that this is not possible[86]. If, however, the non-EU parent owns subsidiaries within the EU, the Commission may require the subsidiaries to provide information that may be held by a non-EU parent. This might be possible if the parent and the subsidiary form a single economic entity and the subsidiary is able to obtain the information from a non-EU parent located outside the EU[87].

[81] [2018] EWCA Civ 220, para 95.

[82] OJ [2004] L 123/18.

[83] The initiation of proceedings is unlikely to be an issue of enforcement, as it is not in itself a coercive act.

[84] See Case 52/69 EU:C:1972:73 (one of the *Dyestuffs* cases).

[85] OJ [2003] L 1/1: on the conduct of Commission investigations see ch 7, 'Chapter V: powers of investigation', pp 277–285; in Case 27/76 *United Brands Continentaal BV v Commission* EU:C:1978:22 the Court of Justice suggested at one point that the Commission might have obtained some information which it needed from United Brands; however United Brands had subsidiaries within the EU, so that it cannot be deduced from this remark that the Court was advocating extraterritorial requests for information under Article 11(3) of Regulation 17, the predecessor of Regulation 1/2003.

[86] See eg *Liquid Crystal Displays*, Commission decision of 8 December 2010, where the Commission took an Article 18(3) decision of this kind.

[87] See the EU contribution to the OECD's *Roundtable Cartel Jurisdiction Issues, including the Effects Doctrine* (2008), para 15, available at www.ec.europa.eu/competition/international/multilateral/oecd_submissions.html.

It is inconceivable that Article 20 entitles the Commission to carry out an investigation abroad unless it has the authorisation of the State concerned. However the fact that the Commission intends to investigate a trade association within the EU which represents non-EU undertakings does not entitle that association to refuse to submit to the investigation[88]; and if the Commission carries out an investigation in a new Member State of the EU and discovers information relating to infringements carried out by undertakings prior to that State's accession to the EU, the Commission is entitled to take that information into account[89]. In *Slovak Telekom v Commission*[90] the General Court held that the Commission was entitled to require Slovak Telekom to furnish it with information relating to conduct that took place prior to the accession of the Slovak Republic to the EU[91]. The Commission will not be sympathetic to the argument that a non-EU parent of an EU subsidiary is unable to provide it with information because of some constraint imposed upon it by its domestic law[92].

(iii) Final decisions

Two problems arise in relation to final decisions addressed to non-EU undertakings. First, there is the problem of serving a final decision on a non-EU undertaking. A finding of infringement is more an act of enforcement than merely serving a statement of objections, and so is more open to objection in terms of public international law. For this reason the Commission will often look to address its decision to a subsidiary within the EU, as it did in the *Dyestuffs* case, or seek the assistance of the foreign State concerned[93]. However the Court of Justice has held that service direct upon the non-EU undertaking is valid provided that, as in the case of a statement of objections, it reaches the undertaking and enables it to take cognisance of it; it is no defence that the undertaking received the decision and sent it back without reading it[94].

The second problem is whether it is possible for the final decision to include orders against and impose penalties upon a non-EU undertaking. While the Court of Justice does not object to orders being made against foreign undertakings[95], it would not be possible to enforce the order in the territory of a foreign State. It would, however, be possible to seize any assets that were present within the EU.

(C) EU Merger Regulation

(i) The jurisdictional criteria in the EUMR

Under Article 1(2) of the EUMR[96] concentrations that have a Union dimension must be pre-notified to the European Commission. Concentrations have a Union dimension

[88] *Ukwal* OJ [1992] L 121/45.

[89] Cases 97/87 etc *Dow Chemical Ibérica SA v Commission* EU:C:1989:380, paras 61–65.

[90] Cases T-458/09 etc EU:T:2012:145.

[91] Ibid, para 45; see also Case T-293/11 *Holcim (Deutschland) v Commission* EU:T:2014:127, para 134.

[92] See *Centraal Stikstof Verkoopkantoor (CSV)* OJ [1976] L 192/27; *Secretary of State for Health v Servier Laboratories Ltd* [2013] EWCA Civ 1234.

[93] In *Dyestuffs* the Commission tried in the first place to serve the final decision on the non-EU undertakings by using diplomatic channels; only when this failed did it serve the EU subsidiaries.

[94] See Case 6/72 *Europemballage and Continental Can v Commission* EU:C:1973:22.

[95] See eg Cases 6 and 7/73 *Istituto Chemioterapico Italiano Spa and Commercial Solvents Corp v Commission* EU:C:1974:18, para 45, where the Court of Justice upheld the Commission's order that supplies to Zoja be resumed; this would clearly affect CSC in the US; see also *Warner-Lambert/Gillette* OJ [1993] L 116/21, where the Commission ordered Gillette, a US company, to reassign trade marks in third countries to Eemland Holdings NV in order to remove distortions of competition within the EU; the decision was not appealed.

[96] OJ [2004] L 24/1, see ch 21 for a general discussion of the EUMR.

where the combined turnover of the undertakings involved exceeds €5,000 million worldwide, provided that at least two of the undertakings have a turnover within the EU of at least €250 million and that two-thirds of their business is not within one and the same Member State[97]; Article 1(3) of the EUMR contains an alternative set of jurisdictional criteria to address the problem of multiple notification to Member States. Articles 4(4) and (5), 9 and 22 of the EUMR provide for the referral of cases between the Commission and the national competition authorities of the Member States.

The jurisdictional criteria in the EUMR clearly mean that concentrations involving undertakings which conduct a substantial proportion of their business outside the EU, or which involve transactions far removed physically from the EU, may, nevertheless, have a Union dimension. Countless numbers of concentrations that have little or no effect within the EU must be notified because of the way in which the thresholds in the EUMR operate. For example a joint venture between two substantial undertakings that brings about a merger of their widget businesses in Thailand could be notifiable under the EUMR, even though the joint venture will have no presence or effect on the EU market, if the parents exceed the turnover thresholds in Article 1. Cases such as this may, however, benefit from the simplified procedure used for the speedy disposal of some notifications under the EUMR[98].

(ii) *Gencor v Commission*

In *Gencor/Lonrho*[99] the Commission prohibited a merger between two South African undertakings on the basis that it would have created a dominant duopoly (collective dominance) in the platinum and rhodium markets, as a result of which effective competition would be significantly impeded in the internal market. Gencor appealed to the General Court, *inter alia*, on the ground that the Commission did not have jurisdiction under the EUMR to prohibit activities in South Africa which, furthermore, the Government there had approved. In *Gencor v Commission*[100] the General Court upheld the Commission's decision, and reviewed at some length the jurisdictional position[101]. As to the territorial scope of the EUMR the General Court noted that the parties to the merger exceeded the turnover thresholds in Article 1(2) of the EUMR[102]. It acknowledged that recital 11 of the EUMR required that the parties should have substantial operations in the EU, but stated that these operations could as well consist of sales as production. The Court added that the implementation doctrine, espoused by the Court of Justice in *Wood Pulp I*, did not contradict the recognition of jurisdiction in this case: the requirement in Article 1(2) of the EUMR, that at least two of the parties should have turnover in excess of €250 million within the EU, was consistent with the judgment in *Wood Pulp I*, since it meant that they must have acted in some way on the EU market.

On the compatibility of the Commission's decision with public international law[103], the General Court said that application of the EUMR is justified under public international law where it is foreseeable that a proposed concentration will have an immediate and substantial effect in the EU[104]. This is, of course, the qualified effects

[97] The thresholds are considered in detail in ch 21, 'Article 1: concentrations having a Union dimension', pp 859–864.

[98] See the Commission's *Notice on a simplified procedure for treatment of certain concentrations under Council Regulation (EC) No 139/2004* OJ [2013] C 366/5; this procedure is explained briefly in ch 21, 'Short Form CO', pp 877–878.

[99] OJ [1997] L 11/30.

[100] Case T-102/96 EU:T:1999:65; for comment see Fox 'The Merger Regulation and Its Territorial Reach: *Gencor Ltd v Commission*' (1999) 20 ECLR 334.

[101] Case T-102/96 EU:T:1999:65, paras 48–111.

[102] Ibid, paras 78–88.

[103] Ibid, paras 89–111.

[104] Ibid, para 90.

test that was endorsed by the Court of Justice in *Intel v Commission*[105]. The General Court's view in *Gencor* was that these criteria were satisfied, but went on to consider whether the exercise of jurisdiction in this case 'violated a principle of non-interference or the principle of proportionality'[106]: in other words it acknowledged that comity analysis should be undertaken when applying the EUMR. The Court's view was that neither principle was violated, so that there was no jurisdictional objection to the Commission's decision.

Clearly this judgment is of considerable significance. It confirmed the Commission's subject-matter jurisdiction in relation to the harmful effects of a merger between two non-EU companies in the EU. In practice, of course, the Commission could have great problems in enforcing a prohibition decision against non-EU undertakings which are unwilling to cooperate and which are protected by their national Governments. However the Commission works closely with the competition authorities in other jurisdictions, and in particular with the DoJ and the FTC in the US, in order to try to prevent serious conflicts breaking out[107].

5. The Extraterritorial Application of UK Competition Law

The view has always been taken in the UK that jurisdiction cannot be based simply upon commercial effects, but should be based only on the territoriality and nationality principles. This is clearly stated in the Aide-Memoire which the UK Government submitted to the Court of Justice following the Commission's decision in *Dyestuffs*[108], and is further illustrated by the Protection of Trading Interests Act 1980 which is considered later in this chapter. The submissions of the UK Government in the *Wood Pulp I* case vehemently resisted the adoption of the effects doctrine as a matter of EU law[109]. It is not clear whether Brexit will cause the UK Government to maintain its traditional hostility to the effects doctrine. As noted earlier, the Brexit Competition Law Working Group suggested that it would be appropriate, post-Brexit, to adopt the qualified effects doctrine.

The domestic competition statutes do not always deal explicitly with jurisdictional issues, but, even where they do not do so, in practice they are not applied extraterritorially on the basis of effects. However it should be noted that the Enterprise and Regulatory Reform Act 2013 ('ERRA'), which created the CMA[110], imposes a duty on it to promote competition, within *and outside the UK*, for the benefit of consumers[111]. In February 2017 the CEO of the CMA said that it was firmly committed to being an active 'contributor to the development of competition and consumer law internationally'[112].

105 See 'The qualified effects doctrine', pp 504–505 earlier in chapter.

106 Case T-102/96 EU:T:1999:65, para 102.

107 See further 'The EU's dedicated cooperation agreements on competition enforcement', pp 517–519 earlier in chapter.

108 Cases 48/69 etc *ICI Ltd v Commission* EU:C:1972:70. The Aide-Memoire is produced in full in *Lowe*, pp 144–147; details are given there of various diplomatic exchanges between the US and UK Governments on jurisdictional conflicts and other expressions of the UK's views at pp 147–186; see also the UK Government's *Amicus Curiae* brief in *Washington Public Power Supply System v Western Nuclear Inc* [1983] ECC 261.

109 On 'The qualified effects doctrine' see pp 504–505 earlier in chapter.

110 ERRA 2013, s 25(1); on the CMA see ch 2, 'The CMA', pp 64–70.

111 ERRA 2013, s 25(3).

112 See speech of 4 February 2017 by Andrea Coscelli 'CMA's role as the UK exits the European Union', available at www.gov.uk/cma.

(A) Competition Act 1998

(i) Chapter I prohibition

The Chapter I prohibition in the Competition Act 1998 has been discussed in chapter 9[113]. On the issue of jurisdiction section 2(1), which contains the Chapter I prohibition, provides that an agreement will be caught only where it may affect trade and competition within the UK. This in itself does not answer the jurisdictional issue of whether the Act is applicable to undertakings that are located outside the UK. The answer to this question is given by section 2(3), which provides that:

> Subsection (1) applies only if the agreement, decision or practice is, or is intended to be, implemented in the UK.

Section 2(3) is specifically intended to give legislative effect in the UK to the 'implementation doctrine' established by the Court of Justice in *Wood Pulp I*[114]. It follows that agreements implemented in the UK by non-UK undertakings would be caught by the Chapter I prohibition, provided that they meet all the other requirements of that prohibition. Conversely, an agreement that is not implemented in the UK falls outside the Chapter I prohibition, even though it produces effects there; an example might be a collective boycott of a UK customer by several non-UK undertakings.

In *Intel v Commission*[115] the Court of Justice held that the jurisdictional reach of EU competition law can be justified on the basis of 'qualified effects' in the EU. This raises the question whether the Chapter I prohibition can be applied on the same basis. Section 60(2) of the Competition Act could be taken to suggest that the answer is yes, since it imposes a duty to interpret the Chapter I prohibition in the same way as the Court of Justice has interpreted Article 101. However the explicit wording of section 2(3) is likely to mean that there is a 'relevant difference'[116] between the Competition Act and the case law of the EU Courts, with the consequence that the UK competition authorities and courts are not required to adopt the qualified effects doctrine. The position might be different if the CMA were to investigate a case in which Article 101 (or Article 102) is involved, and where the implementation doctrine could not establish jurisdiction: presumably (prior to Brexit) it would be required to apply EU law, including the qualified effects doctrine.

The guidelines on the Competition Act are silent on the issue of extraterritoriality, which perhaps is itself indicative of the delicate and complex nature of this issue.

(ii) Chapter II prohibition

The Chapter II prohibition has also been discussed in chapter 9[117]. There is no mention of extraterritorial application in section 18, which sets out the Chapter II prohibition. In particular there is no equivalent of section 2(3) limiting the ambit of the Chapter II prohibition to conduct that is implemented in the UK. Section 18(3) does require that the dominant position must be within the UK. In the debate during the passage of the Competition Bill Lord Simon explained that this would not be the case if the market in which the dominant position is held was entirely outside the UK; however there could be a case in which the dominant position extends beyond the UK, provided that it includes some part of the UK territory[118].

113 See ch 9, 'The Chapter I Prohibition', pp 347–376.
114 HL Committee, 13 November 1997, col 261 (Lord Simon of Highbury).
115 Case C-413/14 P EU:C:2017:632, paras 41–46.
116 See ch 9, '"Governing Principles Clause": Section 60 of the Competition Act 1998', pp 387–392.
117 See ch 9, 'The Chapter II Prohibition', pp 376–387.
118 HL Third Reading, 5 March 1998, col 1336 (Lord Simon of Highbury).

An interesting question is whether the Chapter II prohibition would apply in a case where the dominant position is (wholly or partly) within the UK but the abuse occurs in a related market outside the UK. The Court of Justice's judgment in *Intel* suggests that Chapter II might apply, provided that it is foreseeable that the conduct will have an immediate and substantial effect in the UK. Further, and in any event, the conduct must affect trade within the UK[119]. In practice, the UK competition authorities might encounter difficulties in enforcing a decision in respect of foreign undertakings, especially if the foreign Government is unwilling to cooperate with the UK's proposed action.

(B) Enterprise Act 2002

(i) Market studies and market investigations

As far as subject-matter jurisdiction is concerned, the CMA[120] must publish a 'market study notice' where it proposes to carry out its functions under section 5 of the Enterprise Act to consider the extent to which a matter in relation to the acquisition or supply of goods or services of one or more than one description in the UK has or may have effects adverse to the interests of consumers and to assess possible remedial action[121].

The CMA may also make a market investigation reference where it has reasonable grounds for suspecting that one or more features of a market in the UK for goods or services prevent, restrict or distort competition there or in a part of it[122]. For these purposes section 131(6) of the Enterprise Act provides that a 'market in the United Kingdom' includes a market which operates there and in another country or territory or in a part of another country or territory ('supra-national markets')[123] and any market which operates only in a part of the UK ('sub-national markets')[124]. Where the geographical market is wider than the UK, a market investigation would be concerned only with the UK part of it[125]. In determining whether to exercise its discretion to make a reference, the CMA will consider whether an effective remedy might be available to cure any competition problems: where the relevant market is global, or at least much wider than the UK, it may be that a remedy that applied only to the UK would have little discernible impact on the competition problem there, in which case a reference would not be made[126].

As far as enforcement jurisdiction is concerned, the CMA has power to obtain information under section 174 of the Enterprise Act 2002[127]. The Act is silent on the territorial scope of these provisions, as is the guidance on market studies and market investigations[128]. It is thought to be unlikely that the CMA would seek to exercise these powers against persons or undertakings with no presence in the UK. As far as remedies are concerned, sections 154 to 161 set out a number of possibilities, ranging from the acceptance

[119] On this requirement see ch 9, 'Applicable law and territorial scope', p 361.

[120] References to the powers of the CMA include those of the concurrent sectoral regulators; on s 5 of the Enterprise Act see ch 11, 'Gathering Information About Markets', p 463.

[121] Enterprise Act 2002, s 130A; the market study provisions are described in ch 11, 'Market Studies', pp 465–469.

[122] Enterprise Act 2002, s 131(1); note that the CMA may also make a reference in relation to practices across markets under s 131(2A); the system of market investigations is described in ch 11, 'Market Investigation References', pp 469–481.

[123] Enterprise Act 2002, s 131(6)(a). [124] Ibid, s 131(6)(b).

[125] *Market investigation references: Guidance about the making of references under Part 4 of the Enterprise Act*, OFT 511, March 2006, para 4.11; this *Guidance* was adopted by the CMA Board with effect from 1 April 2014.

[126] Ibid, para 2.30. [127] See ch 11, 'Powers of investigation and penalties', pp 485–486.

[128] *Market investigation references: Guidance about the making of references under Part 4 of the Enterprise Act*, OFT 511, March 2006; *Guidelines for market investigations: Their role, procedures, assessment and remedies*, CC 3 (Revised), April 2013.

of voluntary undertakings in lieu of a reference to the making of final orders, using the powers provided by Schedule 8 to the Act. Again, the Act is silent as to the territorial scope of these powers, but it is assumed that they are not available extraterritorially[129].

(ii) Mergers

As far as subject-matter jurisdiction is concerned, sections 22(1) and 33(1) of the Enterprise Act provide that merger references may be made where a relevant merger situation has been or would be created, and where that situation has resulted or would result in 'a substantial lessening of competition within any market or markets in the United Kingdom for goods or services'[130]. Section 22(6) provides that a 'market in the United Kingdom' includes supra-national[131] and sub-national markets[132]. Further jurisdictional requirements for the application of domestic merger control are that:

- the value of the turnover of the enterprise being acquired amounts to more than £70 million in the UK[133] or
- the 25% 'share of supply' test is satisfied in the UK or in a substantial part of it[134].

The CMA's *Jurisdictional and procedural guidance* states that these requirements apply equally to non-UK companies that sell to (or acquire from) UK customers or suppliers[135].

As far as enforcement jurisdiction is concerned, section 109 of the Enterprise Act gives the CMA the power to obtain information in relation to anticipated and completed mergers. The Act is silent on the extraterritorial application of these provisions; it is thought that they would not be used against persons or undertakings with no presence in the UK. The remedies available in merger cases are set out in sections 71 to 95 of the Act. Section 86(1) of the Act provides that an enforcement order may extend to a person's conduct outside the UK if (and only if) he is a UK national, a body incorporated under UK law or a person carrying on business within the UK[136]. In *Akzo Nobel/Metal Holding*[137] the Competition Commission (now CMA) prohibited the acquisition by Akzo Nobel, a Dutch company, of 51% of the shares of Metlac Holding. On appeal the Competition Appeal Tribunal upheld the Commission's decision to make an enforcement order against Akzo because it carried on business in the UK[138]. The CAT's judgment was affirmed by the Court of Appeal: the fact that Akzo conducted strategic and operational management of its subsidiaries carrying on business in the UK was sufficient for it to carry on business there[139]. The Court of Appeal said that if all a parent company did was to exercise its rights as a shareholder of a UK subsidiary, leaving the management of that to its directors, the parent would not be carrying on business in the UK[140].

(iii) The cartel offence

The cartel offence in section 188 of the Enterprise Act 2002 is committed only where the agreement is implemented in whole or in part in the UK[141]. Subject to that, individuals

[129] OFT 511, March 2006, para 2.30, seems to make this assumption.

[130] The merger provisions of the Enterprise Act 2002 are described in ch 22.

[131] Enterprise Act 2002, s 22(6)(a). [132] Ibid, s 22(6)(b). [133] Ibid, s 23(1).

[134] Ibid, s 23(2)–(4). [135] CMA2, January 2014, fn 63.

[136] A similar limitation is found in relation to restrictions on share dealings: Enterprise Act 2002, ss 77(7) and 78(5).

[137] Final Report of 21 December 2012, available at www.nationalarchives.gov.uk.

[138] Case 1204/4/8/13 *Akzo Nobel NV v Competition Commission* [2013] CAT 13, paras 69–116.

[139] *Akzo Nobel NV v Competition Commission* [2014] EWCA Civ 482, paras 34–36; see also *Ryanair Holdings v CMA* [2014] CAT 3, paras 222–239: Ryanair held to be carrying on business in the UK.

[140] [2014] EWCA Civ 482, para 37.

[141] Enterprise Act 2002, s 190(3); see ch 10, 'The cartel offence', pp 437–446.

guilty of the cartel offence would be liable to a fine and/or imprisonment, irrespective of their domicile or place of residence. An important additional point is that the Extradition Act 2003 makes provision for the possibility of extradition from or to the UK[142].

6. Resistance to Extraterritorial Application of Competition Law

(A) Introduction

The *Alcoa*[143] case triggered off a number of battles between the US and other States which objected to the extraterritorial application of US antitrust laws[144]. Apart from diplomatic protests, several countries have passed 'blocking statutes' or 'executive orders'[145], whereby they attempt to thwart excessive assumptions of jurisdiction[146]. There are no provisions in EU law which have this effect: instead this is essentially a matter for individual Member States. The UK has taken a consistently hostile view of the extraterritorial application of US law, which culminated in the Protection of Trading Interests Act 1980[147].

The earliest attempt by the UK Government to prevent the extraterritorial application of US law came in 1952[148]; thereafter it secured the passage of the Shipping Contracts and Commercial Documents Act 1964, the provisions of which were used on several occasions to prevent disclosure of information to US authorities[149]. The courts in the UK have also objected to US practice. In *British Nylon Spinners v ICI*[150] the Court of Appeal ordered ICI not to comply with a court order in the US, requiring it to reassign certain patents to Du Pont; the US court considered that the parties were dividing the market horizontally. In *Rio Tinto Zinc v Westinghouse Electric*[151] the House of Lords (now the UK Supreme Court) declined to assist in the process of discovery in a US court, investigating an alleged uranium cartel, where it considered that the information acquired would subsequently be used for an improper assertion of extraterritorial jurisdiction. The UK courts are obliged by the Evidence (Proceedings in Other Jurisdictions) Act 1975 to assist in requests for discovery by foreign courts[152]. However the Act provides exceptions to this obligation, and the House of Lords considered that this case fell within these exceptions for two reasons: first, because the request for information was in reality a 'fishing expedition' without

[142] See ch 10, 'Extradition', p 445; note that in *Norris v Government of the USA* [2008] 1 AC 920, the House of Lords concluded that 'mere' price fixing did not amount to criminal conspiracy to defraud at common law, with the result that he could not be extradited on that basis (his alleged infringement predated the entry into force of the provisions of the Enterprise Act); however Mr Norris was extradited for a different reason—that he had obstructed the course of justice—and for this he was sentenced in the US to a term of 18 months in jail: see DoJ Press Release, 10 December 2010, available at www.justice.gov/atr/.

[143] See 'The *Alcoa, Hartford Fire Insurance* and *Empagran* cases', pp 498–500 earlier in chapter.

[144] See Griffin 'Foreign Governmental Reactions to US Assertions of Extraterritorial Jurisdiction' (1998) 19 ECLR 64, and the references in fn 1 thereof.

[145] See Morris 'Iron Curtain at the Border: Gazprom and the Russian Blocking Order to Prevent the Extraterritoriality of EU Competition Law' (2014) 35 ECLR 601.

[146] The English Court of Appeal held that a French blocking statute did not prevent disclosure in an action for damages under Article 101 in *Secretary of State for Health v Servier Laboratories Ltd* [2013] EWCA Civ 1234.

[147] For similar statutes in Australia and Canada see respectively the Foreign Antitrust Judgment (Restriction of Enforcement) Act 1979 and the Foreign Extraterritorial Measures Act 1985.

[148] See *Lowe*, pp 138–139. [149] Ibid, pp 139–143.

[150] [1955] Ch 37 and [1953] Ch 19. [151] [1978] AC 547.

[152] The 1975 Act implements the Hague Convention in the UK, on which see 'Enforcement jurisdiction', pp 497–498 earlier in chapter.

merit; and, secondly, because Rio Tinto might incriminate itself under EU competition law by divulging the documents sought.

The 1975 Act did not allow a court to resist a request for information simply because the foreign court was making a claim to extraterritorial jurisdiction; this is now dealt with by section 4 of the Protection of Trading Interests Act 1980 (discussed later). At common law a UK court has discretion to order a litigant to restrain foreign proceedings which are oppressive: in *Midland Bank plc v Laker Airways plc*[153] the Court of Appeal ordered Laker to discontinue proceedings against Midland Bank in the US which would have involved the extraterritorial application of US antitrust law. In *British Airways Board v Laker Airlines Ltd*[154], however, the House of Lords refused British Airways' application for a stay; in this case there was no doubt that BA was carrying on business in the US, so that it was subject to US law on conventional jurisdictional principles. If Laker were deprived of the opportunity to litigate in the US, it would have been unable to sue in the UK since it had no cause of action under English law. In those circumstances the House of Lords allowed the US litigation to go ahead.

(B) **Protection of Trading Interests Act 1980**

The Protection of Trading Interests Act 1980 contains wide-ranging provisions[155]. It is not limited to blocking US enforcement of antitrust laws, but may be invoked in any case in which US law is being applied in a way which could harm the commercial interests of the UK[156]. Section 1 enables the Secretary of State to make orders requiring UK firms to notify him of, and forbidding them to comply with, measures taken under the law of a foreign country affecting international trade and which threaten to damage the trading interests of the UK. This power has been exercised on a few occasions[157]. One of the orders was concerned with competition law[158], but not with the specific issue of extraterritoriality; the objection was to an alleged breach by the US of Treaty obligations concerning air travel between the US and the UK[159]. Section 2 of the Act gives the Secretary of State power to prohibit compliance with a requirement by an overseas authority to submit commercial information to it which is not within its territorial jurisdiction. Section 3 provides for the imposition of penalties upon anyone who fails to comply with orders under the foregoing provisions, but, consistently with the UK approach to these issues, these may be imposed only in accordance with the UK's conventional interpretation of the international law principles of territoriality and nationality. Section 4 provides that a UK

[153] [1986] QB 689. [154] [1985] AC 58.

[155] See generally on this Act Huntley 'The Protection of Trading Interests Act—Some Jurisdictional Aspects of Enforcement of Antitrust Laws' (1981) 30 ICLQ 213; Lowe 'Blocking Extraterritorial Jurisdiction—The British Protection of Trading Interests Act 1980' (1981) 75 American Journal of International Law 257; Jones 'Protection of Trading Interests Act 1980' (1981) 40 Cambridge Law Journal 41; Collins 'Blocking and Clawback Statutes: The UK Approach' [1986] Journal of Business Law 372 and 452.

[156] The Shipping Contracts and Commercial Documents Act 1964 could be invoked only where there was an infringement of UK jurisdiction; the 1980 Act is wider, as it applies where there is harm to UK commercial interests, whether there is an infringement of jurisdiction or not.

[157] See eg the Protection of Trading Interests (US Cuban Assets Control Regulations) Order 1992, SI 1992/2449; Extraterritorial US Legislation (Sanctions against Cuba, Iran and Libya) (Protection of Trading Interests) Order 1996, SI 1996/3171.

[158] Protection of Trading Interests (US Antitrust Measures) Order 1983, SI 1983/900.

[159] The *vires* of the Order in this case were challenged, unsuccessfully, by the plaintiff in the US antitrust action: see *British Airways Board v Laker Airways Ltd* [1984] QB 142; on appeal [1985] AC 58; the House of Lords also reversed the Court of Appeal's decision that Laker should discontinue its US action against British Airways as this would mean there was no forum in which it could sue: see ch 12 n 154 earlier.

court should not comply with a foreign tribunal's request for assistance in the discovery process where this would infringe UK sovereignty. This is statutory reinforcement of the judgment in *Rio Tinto Zinc v Westinghouse Electric Corpn*[160].

Section 5 provides that foreign multiple damages awards shall not be enforceable in the UK. This means that a claimant in the UK could not enforce a treble damages award obtained in the US[161]. In *Service Temps Inc v MacLeod*[162] the Scottish Court of Session held that section 5 prohibited the enforcement of an order of a US court that the directors and shareholders of a Scottish company pay treble damages for a breach of US state antitrust law[163]. Section 6 provides that, where a UK defendant has paid US multiple damages, an action may be brought in the UK to 'claw back' the excess of such damages over the amount actually required to compensate the claimant. This provision symbolises the degree of antipathy in the UK towards certain aspects of US antitrust practice.

7. The Internationalisation of Competition Law

It is clearly unsatisfactory that there should be acrimonious disputes between States over the extraterritorial application of competition law[164]. Principles of public international law do not provide an adequate answer to the problems that arise when genuine conflicts occur between competition authorities, and yet the scope for such conflicts could increase as more States adopt their own codes of competition law and as business becomes increasingly international. Transnational mergers pose a particular problem where several competition authorities investigate the same transaction and have different perceptions of whether it should be permitted or not. A different, and more positive, point is that many competition authorities have taken steps towards international cooperation in order to deal with cartels, anti-competitive conduct and mergers that transcend national boundaries. Cooperation between the competition authorities in the EU and the US, for example, is now a fact of daily life: if anything the degree of cooperation is probably greater than could have been imagined in the early 1990s, when the first US/EU Cooperation Agreement was entered into.

(A) **ICN**

The International Competition Network ('the ICN') is a virtual network that plays a key role in facilitating international cooperation between competition authorities. The ICN's 'mission statement' is to advocate the adoption of superior standards and procedures in competition policy around the world, formulate proposals for procedural and substantive convergence, and to seek to facilitate effective international cooperation to

160 [1978] AC 547; see 'Introduction', pp 494–495 earlier in chapter.

161 At common law foreign judgments can normally be enforced in the UK but 'penal' judgments cannot be; note that under s 5 of the Act the whole sum is unenforceable, not just the penal element; one order has been made under s 5, the Protection of Trading Interests Act (Australian Trade Practices) Order 1988, SI 1988/569 (concerning a provision of Australian merger control).

162 [2013] CSOH 162; s 5 of the Act was also considered by the English Court of Appeal in *Lewis v Eliades* [2003] EWCA Civ 1758, paras 40–53; permission to appeal was refused [2004] 1 WLR 1393.

163 [2013] CSOH 162, paras 31–38.

164 See Dabbah *The Internationalisation of Antitrust Policy* (Cambridge University Press, 2003); Gerber *Global Competition: Law, Markets and Globalization* (Oxford University Press, 2010); Papadopoulos *The International Dimension of EU Competition Law and Policy* (Cambridge University Press, 2010); Ezrachi (ed) *Research Handbook on International Competition Law* (Edward Elgar, 2012); Lewis (ed) *Building New Competition Law Regimes* (Edward Elgar, 2013).

the benefit of member agencies, consumers and economies worldwide[165]. The ICN was established in October 2001 following the so-called 'ICPAC Report'[166]. Membership is open to national and multinational organisations responsible for the enforcement of competition law; by 8 December 2017 135 competition authorities from 122 jurisdictions were members of the ICN. The ICN also seeks advice and contributions from the private sector and from non-governmental organisations involved in the application of competition law.

The ICN has established various working groups over the years of its existence: there are currently five, on mergers, cartels, unilateral conduct, advocacy and agency effectiveness. The work plans of these groups and their output can be accessed on the ICN's website. These working groups have published a series of recommended practices, toolkits, workbooks and various other working documents, all of which provide an essential source of learning and guidance. An example of their output is the ICN *Merger Guidelines Workbook*, which provides guidance for countries that are new to or in the early years of merger control; it is commended to anyone interested in the subject. The ICN's *Anti-Cartel Enforcement Manual* has also been influential in strengthening and aligning anti-cartel enforcement around the world.

The ICN has also made a number of recommendations that have led to 'soft harmonisation' of jurisdictional criteria, substantive analysis, procedural rules and enforcement techniques in numerous jurisdictions[167].

The ICN's website[168] is an invaluable source of material, including the working documents mentioned above, links to the sites of its members and e-learning for agency officials on competition law and policy.

(B) **OECD**

The Organisation for Economic Co-operation and Development ('the OECD') is active in matters of competition policy. It has published a number of 'best practice roundtables' on various aspects of competition policy, details of which can be found on its website[169]. In particular the OECD has been at the forefront of policy in relation to cartels. In 1998 it published a *Recommendation of the Council concerning Effective Action Against Hard Core Cartels*[170] in which it called upon its member countries to ensure that their laws 'effectively halt and deter hard-core cartels', and invited non-member countries to associate themselves with the *Recommendation* and to implement it[171]. Separately, in 2014, the OECD published a *Recommendation concerning International Co-operation on Competition Investigations and Proceedings*[172], the title of which sufficiently reveals its contents. In 2017 the OECD held a Roundtable on the *Extraterritorial reach of competition remedies*[173], which discussed how authorities approach enforcement in cross-border competition cases.

165 See ICN Operational Framework of 13 February 2012, available at www.internationalcompetitionnetwork.org.

166 The ICN was established following the *Final Report of the International Competition Policy Advisory Committee to the US Attorney General and Assistant Attorney General for Antitrust*, February 2000; see also Janow and Lewis 'International Antitrust and the Global Economy' (2001) 24 World Competition 3.

167 For a summary of the soft harmonisation see ICN *Statement of Achievements 2001–2013*, April 2013, available on its website.

168 www.internationalcompetitionnetwork.org.

169 Available at www.oecd.org/competition.

170 OECD C(98)35/final, 25 March 1998.

171 The OECD has also published several other documents on the issue of anti-cartel enforcement, available at www.oecd.org/competition.

172 OECD C(2014)108, 16 September 2014.

173 Available at www.oecd.org.competition.

(C) WTO

Chapter 5 of the post-war Havana Charter for an International Trade Organization contained an antitrust code[174]; however this was not incorporated into the General Agreement on Tariffs and Trade of 1947, the organisation from which the WTO developed. The WTO was established on 1 January 1995, and is predominantly concerned with issues of trade, rather than with competition policy[175]. The rules of the WTO do not impose obligations on undertakings in relation to competition. In 2004 the WTO decided that the interaction between trade and competition policy would no longer form part of its work during the 'Doha Round'[176].

(D) UNCTAD

The United Nations Conference on Trade and Development ('UNCTAD') has taken an interest in the development of competition policy for many years[177]. In 1980 the General Assembly of the UN adopted a voluntary, non-binding code, *The Set of Multilaterally Agreed Equitable Principles and Rules for the Control of Restrictive Business Practices*[178], setting out suggested core principles to be adopted in systems of competition law. UNCTAD fulfils an important role in providing technical assistance to developing countries[179].

(E) International cooperation agreements

International cooperation between competition authorities has been advanced by the adoption of many bilateral and multilateral agreements[180]. For example the US has negotiated agreements in relation to competition law enforcement with Germany, Australia, Canada and Russia[181]. The Closer Economic Relations Agreement, which entered into force between Australia and New Zealand on 1 January 1983[182], provides for close cooperation between those two countries, even allowing for one country to apply the other's law where it is appropriate to do so. Denmark, Iceland, Norway and Sweden entered into an agreement on cooperation in competition law matters in April 2003[183]. Regional agreements have an important role to play in developing a cooperative approach to competition issues; the EU itself is an example of regional cooperation, and Chapter 15 of the North American Free Trade Agreement contains provisions for consultation, cooperation and coordination between the US, Canada and Mexico in matters of competition policy.

174 The Charter is set out in Wilcox *A Charter for World Trade* (The Macmillan Company, 1949), pp 231–327.

175 On the relationship between trade and competition policy see the series of essays in the Journal of International Economic Law for 1999; a series of essays on this topic will also be found in [1998] Fordham Corporate Law Institute (ed Hawk), chs 13–19; see also Iacobucci 'The Interdependence of Trade and Competition Policies' (1997–98) 21 World Competition 5 and Davidow and Shapiro 'The Feasibility and Worth of a WTO Competition Agreement' (2003) 37 Journal of World Trade 49.

176 Further information can be found on the WTO's website, www.wto.org.

177 See Brusick 'UNCTAD's Role in Promoting Multilateral Cooperation on Competition Law and Policy' (2001) 24 World Competition 23; Lianos 'The Contribution of the United Nations to the Emergence of Global Antitrust Law' (2007) 15 Tulane Journal of International and Comparative Law 145.

178 Resolution 35/63 of 5 December 1980; the UN reaffirmed the code by resolution of 4 October 2000.

179 See eg UNCTAD *Model Law on Competition* (2004), available at www.unctad.org.

180 See eg Zanetti *Cooperation Between Antitrust Agencies at the International Level* (Hart, 2002).

181 Antitrust Cooperation Agreements are available at www.justice.gov/atr.

182 See Brunt 'Australian and New Zealand Competition Law and Policy' [1992] Fordham Corporate Law Institute (ed Hawk), ch 7.

183 Available at www.konkurrensverket.se.

(F) The EU's dedicated cooperation agreements on competition enforcement

The EU has entered into dedicated cooperation agreements with the US, Canada, Japan, South Korea and Switzerland[184]; each of these agreements is broadly modelled on the one with the US. The text that follows will first examine the agreements with the US; it will then discuss cooperation in practice; and finally will note DG COMP's efforts to cooperate with other jurisdictions.

(i) The EU/US Cooperation Agreement of 23 September 1991

The first EU/US Cooperation Agreement was entered into on 23 September 1991[185]. The French Government successfully challenged the legal basis on which the Commission had proceeded, since the Council of Ministers should have been involved in the adoption of the Agreement[186]. The position was rectified by the adoption of a joint decision of the Council and the Commission of 10 April 1995[187].

The Agreement sets out detailed rules for cooperation on various aspects of the enforcement of EU and US competition law. Article II requires the competent authorities in each jurisdiction to notify each other whenever they become aware that their enforcement activities may affect important interests of the other party. Article II(3) contains special provisions on the timing of notifications in the case of mergers. Article III deals with the exchange of information between the authorities in each jurisdiction, and provides for regular meetings between officials of the EU and the US to discuss matters of mutual interest. Article IV deals with cooperation and coordination in enforcement activities, in relation to which each agency will assist the other. Article V is a novel provision going beyond Article IV, as it embodies the idea of 'positive comity': one agency may ask the other to take action in order to remedy anti-competitive behaviour in the *former's* territory[188]. The idea of positive comity is taken further in the second Cooperation Agreement, discussed later.

Article VI requires the parties to avoid conflicts in enforcement activities, and lays down criteria that should be taken into account when an agency is deciding whether to proceed. These criteria reflect the principle of (negative) comity discussed in the context of the US 'jurisdictional rule of reason'[189]. Article VII of the Agreement requires the parties to consult with one another in relation to the matters dealt with by it. Article VIII provides that neither party to the Agreement can be required to provide information to the other where this is prohibited by the law of the party possessing it or where to do so would be incompatible with important interests of the party possessing it; furthermore each party agrees to keep the information it receives from the other confidential to the fullest extent possible. Article IX provides that neither party can be required to do anything under the Agreement that would be inconsistent with existing laws. The Agreement is terminable on 60 days' notice by either party.

184 Available at www.ec.europa.eu/competition/international/bilateral; see generally Papadopoulos *The International Dimension of EU Competition Law and Policy* (Cambridge University Press, 2010).

185 [1991] 4 CMLR 823.

186 Case C-327/91 *France v Commission* EU:C:1994:305; for comment see Riley 'Nailing the Jellyfish: The Illegality of the EC/US Government Competition Agreement' (1992) 13 ECLR 101 and again in (1995) 16 ECLR 185.

187 OJ [1995] L 95/45, corrected by OJ [1995] L 131/38; for comment see Ham 'International Cooperation in the Antitrust Field and in particular the Agreement between the United States and the Commission of the European Communities' (1993) 30 CML Rev 571; Torremans 'Extraterritorial Application of EC and US Competition Law' (1996) 21 EL Rev 280.

188 See Atwood 'Positive Comity—Is It a Positive Step?' [1992] Fordham Corporate Law Institute (ed Hawk), ch 4.

189 See 'Comity', pp 500–501 earlier in chapter.

(ii) The Positive Comity Agreement of 4 June 1998

A second EU/US Cooperation Agreement was entered into on 4 June 1998, and develops the principle of positive comity in Article V of the first Agreement. The Council and the Commission gave their approval to the Positive Comity Agreement in a joint Decision of 29 May 1998[190]. Article I provides that the Agreement is to apply where one party can demonstrate to the other that anti-competitive activities are occurring within the latter's territory which are adversely affecting the interests of the former. Article II contains definitions; it is important to note that mergers do not fall within the scope of this Agreement as a result of the definition of 'competition law(s)' in Article II(4). Article III contains the principle of positive comity: the competition authorities of a 'Requesting Party' may request the authorities in the Requested Party to investigate and, if warranted, to remedy anti-competitive activities in accordance with the latter's competition laws. Article IV provides that the Requesting Party may defer or suspend the application of its law while the Requested Party is applying its. Article V deals with confidentiality and the use of information. Article VI provides that the Positive Comity Agreement shall be interpreted consistently with the 1991 Agreement. The Positive Comity Agreement is terminable on 60 days' notice by either party.

(iii) The cooperation agreements in practice

The cooperation agreements have been highly successful in practice[191]. Cooperation between the Commission and the competition authorities in the US, Canada, Japan, South Korea and Switzerland is now a fact of daily life: if anything the degree of cooperation has been greater than could have been imagined in the early 1990s. The Commission's annual *Report on Competition Policy* (and the Staff Working Paper that accompanies it) describe specific cases in which the authorities worked together[192]: obvious examples include *E-books*[193], where the US DoJ and European Commission cooperated closely throughout their respective investigations, and *Smiths Group/Morpho Protection*[194], where DG COMP worked closely with the DoJ in the US on the timing of its Phase I investigation and the remedies phase. An EU–US merger working group has published guidelines on 'best practices' to be followed where the same transaction is being investigated on both sides of the Atlantic[195].

A great deal of attention, including press coverage, is given to the few cases where there is friction between the EU and the US, as in the cases of *Boeing/McDonnell Douglas*[196] and

[190] OJ [1998] L 173/26; the first case to be initiated on the basis of positive comity was *Sabre*: see the Commission's XXXth *Report on Competition Policy* (2000), point 453.

[191] The OCED has compiled an inventory of 142 cooperation agreements, including their purpose and provisions on eg information exchanges, confidentiality, coordination of investigations and regular meetings; accessible at www.oecd.org/competition.

[192] See eg *Report on Competition Policy for 2005*, SEC(2006)761 final, pp 187–191.

[193] See Commission Press Release IP/12/1367, 13 December 2012 (on the Commission's commitments decision) and speech by acting Assistant Attorney General Sharis Pozen of 11 April 2012, referring to this case as 'a shining example of how far we have come in our cooperation efforts', available at www.justice.gov/atr.

[194] See Case M 8087, Commission decision of 18 January 2017, on which see Dumont et al 'Smiths/Morpho Detection: maintaining security through innovation' Competition Merger Brief 2/2017, available at www.ec.europa.eu/competition/publications.

[195] Available at www.ec.europa.eu/competition/international/legislation/agreements.html.

[196] Case M 877, OJ [1997] L 336/16; for comment see Bavasso '*Boeing/McDonnell Douglas*: Did the Commission Fly Too High?' (1998) 19 ECLR 243; Banks 'The Development of the Concept of Extraterritoriality under European Merger Law Following the *Boeing/McDonnell Douglas* Decision' (1998) 19 ECLR 306; Fiebig 'International Law Limits on the Extraterritorial Application of the European Merger Control Regulation and Suggestions for Reform' (1998) 19 ECLR 323.

GE/Honeywell[197]. In the *Boeing* case the FTC in the US reached a majority decision not to oppose the merger, while the European Commission seemed likely, at one point, to prohibit it in its entirety; in the event commitments to modify the transaction were offered to the Commission with the result that it was given conditional clearance. No such solution was found in the case of *GE/Honeywell*, where a genuine conflict occurred between the DoJ in the US, which cleared the merger, and the Commission, which prohibited it. However these exceptional cases ought not to obscure the fact that a large number of cases, particularly mergers, are successfully completed without any friction between the two jurisdictions. No matter how sophisticated the machinery for cooperation between the EU and the US, or between any constellation of other competition authorities, there will always be some cases in which there is disagreement as to the appropriate outcome[198]. The success of the Cooperation Agreements should be assessed on the basis of how rare these cases are, and on this basis they have been very successful.

(iv) *Memoranda of Understanding on Cooperation*

DG COMP signed a *Memorandum of Understanding on Cooperation* with the Brazilian competition authorities in October 2009[199]. It agreed similar *Memoranda* with the Russian Anti-Monopoly Service in March 2011[200]; with the agencies in China with responsibility for its competition law in September 2012[201]; with the Competition Commission of India in November 2013[202]; and with the South African Competition Commission in June 2016[203].

[197] Case M 2220, Commission decision of 3 July 2001, upheld on appeal Case T-210/01 *General Electric v Commission* EU:T:2005:456; for a review of EU/US procedures and cooperation since this case see Vandergrift and Lucas 'The *GE/Honeywell* Saga? Ehh, What's Up Doc? A Comparative Approach between US and EU Merger Control Proceedings Almost 15 Years Later' (2014) 35 ECLR 172.

[198] See eg Case M 6166 *Deutsche Börse/NYSE Euronext*, Commission decision of 1 February 2012, upheld on appeal Case T-175/12 *Deutsche Börse v Commission* EU:T:2015:148, where the merger was cleared in the US but prohibited in the EU owing to serious competition problems in the markets for EU financial derivatives.

[199] See Commission Press Release IP/09/1500, 9 October 2009.

[200] See Commission Press Release IP/11/278, 10 March 2011.

[201] See the *Memorandum of Understanding*, 20 September 2012; see further *Practical Guidance for Cooperation on Reviewing Mergers*, 15 October 2015.

[202] See Commission Press Release IP/13/1143, 21 November 2013.

[203] Available at www.ec.europa.eu/competition.

13

Horizontal agreements (1): cartels

1. Introduction

This chapter is concerned with the prohibition of cartels, also referred to as 'hard-core' horizontal agreements. Cartels are the most obviously harmful anti-competitive practice known to competition law, and are a prime target of competition authorities. The mysteries of some aspects of competition policy should not be allowed to obscure the simple fact that competitors are meant to compete with one another for the business of their customers, and not to collude with one another to distort the process of competition. Horizontal agreements between independent undertakings to fix prices, divide markets, to restrict output and to fix the outcome of supposedly competitive tenders are among the most serious restrictions of competition[1]. Not surprisingly, virtually all systems of competition law are united in condemning 'hard-core cartels', even if they may differ in the ways in which such cartels may be prosecuted and punished[2].

Writing in 1776 Adam Smith famously remarked in *The Wealth of Nations* that:

> People of the same trade seldom meet together, even for merriment and diversion, but the conversation ends in a conspiracy against the public, or in some contrivance to raise prices.

[1] In the remainder of the chapter, unless the context indicates otherwise, it will be assumed that there is an agreement and/or concerted practice; the question of what constitutes an agreement and/or concerted practice is dealt with in chapter 3.

[2] For detailed texts on cartels and competition law see Sakkers and Ysewyn *European Cartel Digest* (Kluwer, 2009); Harding and Joshua *Regulating Cartels in Europe* (Oxford University Press, 2nd ed, 2010); Jephcott and Lübigg *Law of Cartels* (Jordans, 2nd ed, 2011); Gerard et al 'Cartels and Collusive Behaviour', vol III of Siragusa and Rizza (eds) *EU Competition Law* (Claeys and Casteels, 2012); Utton *Cartels and Economic Collusion* (Edward Elgar, 2013); Kaplow *Competition Policy and Price Fixing* (Princeton University Press, 2013); Rose and Bailey (eds) *Bellamy and Child: European Union Law of Competition* (Oxford University Press, 7th ed, 2013), ch 5; Wardhaugh *Cartels, Markets and Crime* (Cambridge University Press, 2014); Arbaut and Sakkers in Faull and Nikpay (eds) *The EU Law of Competition* (Oxford University Press, 3rd ed, 2014), ch 8.

Evidence suggests that the tendency of competitors to meet in smoke-filled rooms—or perhaps now in smoke-free internet chat rooms—is just as strong today as it was in the eighteenth century: cartels appear to be alive and kicking throughout the world. The phenomenon described by Smith was not a new discovery in 1776: cartels were recognised—and prohibited—in the days of the Eastern Roman Empire (Byzantium)[3]. The Constitution of Zeno of AD 483 punished price fixing in relation to clothes, fishes, sea urchins and other goods with perpetual exile, usually to Britain[4]. Adam Smith's comment was prescient: cartels have thrived through the subsequent centuries, often with implicit or even explicit support from Governments. Even the adoption of competition laws with tough sanctions (including the imprisonment of individuals) has not been sufficient to suppress competitors' mutual self-interest in attempting to control the market[5]. Sometimes a consultancy firm might act as a 'facilitator' of a cartel: the facilitator itself may be held to have violated Article 101[6].

The scheme of this chapter is as follows. Section 2 discusses the widespread consensus among competition authorities worldwide that cartels should be condemned, and gives examples of recent enforcement that led to the imposition of significant fines and sentences of imprisonment. Section 3 looks at the European Commission's anti-cartel enforcement and judicial practice in the EU. The chapter then considers the application of Article 101 to particular types of cartels: horizontal price fixing, market sharing, production quotas and other 'hard-core' cartel practices. The final section of this chapter looks at anti-cartel enforcement and judicial practice in the UK.

2. Widespread Consensus that Cartels Should be Prohibited

(A) The global agenda

There is a very real sense today among the world's competition authorities that, if competition law is about one thing above all, it is the determination to root out and terminate hard-core cartels. In the European Union Mario Monti, the former Commissioner for Competition, once described cartels as 'cancers on the open market economy'[7], and the Supreme Court in the US has referred to cartels as 'the supreme evil of antitrust'[8]. Officials of the US Department of Justice have written that 'cartels have no legitimate purpose and serve only to rob consumers of the tangible blessings of competition'[9]. At both a moral and a practical level there is not a great deal of difference between price fixing and theft. US law has for many decades treated hard-core cartels as *per se* illegal and as

[3] Price fixing was also a punishable offence according to IV.2.18 of Kautilya's *Arthashastra* which predated the Justinian code (see next footnote).

[4] See Codex Iustinianus, c 4, 59, 2, p 186 (Weidmann, 1954): exile to Rome for commission of the UK criminal cartel offence under the Enterprise Act 2002 is thought unlikely to have a sufficiently deterrent effect and is therefore not an available option; see generally Green 'From Rome to Rome: The Evolution of Competition Law into a Twenty-First Century Religion' [2010] Comp Law 7.

[5] See Connor and Lande 'Cartels as Rational Business Strategy: Crime Pays' (2012) 34 Cardozo Law Review 427, concluding that the overall level of anti-cartel sanctions is 'far too low'; see also section 2.6 of the OECD's *Business and Finance Outlook* (2017), suggesting that the total value of sales affected by cartel behaviour from 1990 to 2015 was approximately $7.5 trillion: available at www.oecd.org.

[6] See 'Facilitators', pp 527–528 later in chapter.

[7] See speech by Monti 'Fighting Cartels Why and How? Why should we be concerned with cartels and collusive behaviour', 11 September 2000, available at www.ec.europa.eu.

[8] *Verizon Communications v Law Offices of Curtis v Trinko* 540 US 398 (2004).

[9] Werden, Hammond and Barnett 'Deterrence and Detection of Sanctions: Using all the Tools and Sanctions' (2011) 56 Antitrust Bulletin 207, 208.

criminal offences, punishable not only by fines but also by the imprisonment of individuals. Other countries have introduced criminal sanctions, including in some cases terms of imprisonment, to be imposed on individuals for participation in hard-core cartels[10].

(B) The OECD and the fight against cartels

The Organisation for Economic Co-operation and Development ('the OECD') has been at the forefront of policy in relation to cartels. This in itself reflects an obvious but important point, that cartels are often an international phenomenon, whereas for the most part systems of competition law are purely national in scope. The rules of the EU are an important exception, since they apply throughout the Member States and Contracting States of the European Economic Area ('the EEA'). Cartels with a global reach, such as those in *LIBOR* and *Car parts*, necessitate an international response, and the OECD is in an important position to give a lead in this respect.

In 1998 the OECD adopted a *Recommendation of the Council concerning Effective Action Against Hard Core Cartels* in which it called upon its member countries to ensure that their laws 'effectively halt and deter hard-core cartels', and invited non-member countries to associate themselves with the *Recommendation* and to implement it. The *Recommendation* urges countries to provide for effective sanctions of a kind and at a level to deter firms and individuals from participating in hard-core cartels as well as effective enforcement procedures to detect and remedy the harm inflicted by such cartels. The *Recommendation* defined a hard-core cartel as:

> an anti-competitive agreement, anti-competitive concerted practice, or anti-competitive arrangement by competitors to fix prices, make rigged bids (collusive tenders), establish output restrictions or quotas, or share or divide markets by allocating customers, suppliers, territories, or lines of commerce.

Subsequently the OECD has published a number of further documents which are of particular interest to the issue of cartel enforcement[11]. The OECD has examined the harm that arises from cartels: whilst acknowledging how difficult it is to quantify such harm, it found that it amounted to billions of dollars worldwide each year. The OECD has also discussed the need to penetrate the cloak of secrecy that surrounds hard-core cartels, and the contribution that the encouragement of whistleblowers can make to this need. Whistleblowing and leniency applications were discussed in chapters 7 and 10 of this book, and are an important feature of competition authorities' pursuit of cartels[12]. Strong sanctions against firms and individuals increase the effectiveness of leniency programmes. The OECD has advocated the imposition of larger penalties in cartel cases; in its view sanctions have yet to reach the optimal level for deterrence. In 2017 the OECD held a roundtable discussion on *Algorithms and collusion*, addressing among other topics the questions of whether the traditional antitrust concepts of agreement and tacit collusion are 'fit for purpose' in a digital age of algorithms, price-tracking software and artificial intelligence, and whether antitrust liability can be imposed on the algorithms' creators and users.

The OECD has stressed the need for greater international cooperation in combating cartels which, as noted earlier, often transcend national boundaries. The cooperation between competition authorities is discussed in chapter 12 of this book[13].

[10] See 'Recent action against cartels around the world', pp 523–524 later in chapter.

[11] The OECD documents referred to in this section can all be found at www.oecd.org/competition.

[12] See ch 7, 'The Commission's *Leniency Notice*', pp 289–292 and ch 10, 'Leniency', pp 424–429.

[13] See ch 12, 'The Internationalisation of Competition Law', pp 514–519.

(C) The ICN and the fight against cartels

The International Competition Network ('the ICN') also provides an important contribution to the global 'fight against cartels'. The ICN has a cartels working group: it is composed of two sub-groups, one of which looks at the legal framework and the other at enforcement techniques. The work plan and publications of the cartels working group are available on the ICN's website[14]. The ICN has produced a helpful series of *Anti-Cartel Enforcement Templates* which summarise anti-cartel laws in over 45 jurisdictions. The ICN has published an *Anti-Cartel Enforcement Manual*, each chapter of which discusses enforcement techniques and identifies approaches that have proven effective and successful. It has also compiled a set of educational materials prepared by competition authorities in order to raise public awareness about the effects of cartels and the importance of combating them. It organises webinars on current topics and holds an annual Cartel Workshop.

(D) Recent action against cartels around the world

The commitment of competition authorities around the world to the detection and prohibition of cartels is demonstrated by the number of cases that have been decided in recent years, both in 'mature' systems of competition law and in new jurisdictions, and in all types of economy. A few examples of major cartel cases in recent years illustrate how active competition authorities throughout the world have been:

- in the US the total fines imposed amounted to $3.6 billion in 2015, the largest figure in the history of US antitrust[15]; the fines are paid into a public fund designed to help victims of crime. In 2016 22 individuals were sentenced to imprisonment. There is an ongoing investigation by the DoJ into wide-ranging cartel activity in the automotive parts sector. The investigation started in 2010 and, by December 2016, the DoJ had indicted 65 individuals[16], charged 47 companies[17] and imposed a total of over €2.7 billion in criminal fines
- in India the Competition Commission of India imposed fines in June 2012 of approximately €800 million on 11 manufacturers of cement for cartelising the industry[18]; on appeal the decision was set aside by the Competition Appellate Tribunal and remitted to the Commission which adopted a second decision in August 2016 imposing fines of almost €950 million on ten manufacturers[19]
- in South Korea the Korean Fair Trade Commission imposed fines in 2014 of approximately €91 million on 21 construction companies for collusive tendering in relation to work on subway stations[20]
- in China the National Development and Reform Commission imposed fines of approximately €51.9 million on eight shipping lines for price fixing[21]

[14] www.internationalcompetitionnetwork.org.

[15] See Criminal Enforcement Trend Charts, available at www.justice.gov/atr.

[16] The US focuses increasingly on holding corporate executives accountable for antitrust infringements: see eg speech of former Deputy Attorney General Yates of 9 September 2015, available at www.justice.gov/atr.

[17] See Press Release of 8 November 2016, available at www.justice.gov/atr.

[18] See Press Release of 20 June 2012, available at www.cci.gov.in; the decision has been appealed to the Competition Appellate Tribunal.

[19] See Press Release of 31 August 2016, available at www.cci.gov.in.

[20] See KFTC's Press Release of 2 January 2014, available at www.ftc.go.kr/eng/index.do.

[21] Details of the case are available at www.en.ndrc.gov.cn.

- in 2017 an Australian court imposed a fine of $25 million on Nippon for unlawfully coordinating prices with other shipping lines for the transportation of motor vehicles[22].

A number of countries—for example Australia, Brazil, Canada, France, Germany (for collusive tendering), Iceland, Ireland, Indonesia, Israel, Japan, Korea, Mexico, Norway, the Slovak Republic, Russia, Thailand, UK and Zambia—provide for criminal sanctions in cartel cases.

3. EU Policy Towards Cartels

The Commission attaches a high priority to cartels. There is a Cartel Directorate within DG COMP that has responsibility for prosecuting cartel cases and, in conjunction with the Directorate for Policy and Strategy, for developing policy and engaging with the OECD and ICN. The Commission's commitment to a tougher policy in cartels is demonstrated in various ways. First, the *Leniency Notice* encourages participants in cartels to provide evidence to the Commission of their unlawful behaviour in return for immunity or a reduction in fines[23]. Whistleblowing has been very successful in bringing cartels to light, as can be seen from the statistics discussed later. Secondly, the Commission's *Fining Guidelines* provide for the imposition of substantial penalties imposed on firms that participate in cartels[24]. Thirdly, the introduction of a settlement system in 2008 has led to the adoption of speedier decisions than had previously been possible[25]: by 8 December 2017 the Commission had settled 25 cartel cases. Fourthly, the Commission has promoted greater cooperation between national competition authorities ('NCAs') and itself, and each other, in combating cartels[26]. Fifthly, actual evidence of the Commission's keenness to punish and eradicate cartels is the number of cases that have been decided in recent years[27].

Bearing in mind that undertakings that cartelise markets can also be sued for damages[28], and that individuals in some Member States face the possibility of imprisonment[29], it is hard to believe that the deterrent effect of the law on cartels in the EU is insubstantial[30]; and yet the Commission (and the NCAs) continue to discover them in significant numbers and in all kinds of markets[31]. In numerous cases the Commission increases the fine that would otherwise have been paid because an undertaking is a recidivist, that is to say a repeat offender[32]; and it often discovers a series of cartels in the same industry[33]. Some

[22] Details of the case are available at www.accc.gov.au/media.

[23] See ch 7, 'The Commission's *Leniency Notice*', pp 289–292.

[24] See ch 7, 'The Commission's guidelines on the method of setting fines', pp 286–289.

[25] See ch 7, 'Settlements of cartel cases', pp 270–273.

[26] See ch 7, 'Chapter IV: cooperation', pp 273–277.

[27] See 'Recent decisions against cartels' pp 529 below.

[28] See ch 8 generally.

[29] See eg ch 10, 'The cartel offence', pp 437–446 on the position in the UK.

[30] On the issue of deterrence and cartels generally see Wils *The Optimal Enforcement of EC Antitrust Law Essays in Law and Economics* (Kluwer, 2002), ch 2 and Wils *Efficiency and Justice in European Antitrust Enforcement* (Hart, 2008), ch 3.

[31] DG COMP's website, www.ec.europa.eu/competition/index_en.html, includes a drop-down menu on cartels; the 'What's new?' section provides details of new cases in which inspections have been carried out, proceedings initiated, a statement of objections sent or a decision adopted.

[32] See eg *Nitrine butadiene rubber*, Commission decision of 23 January 2008, where Bayer's fine was increased by 50% for recidivism; see further ch 7, 'Adjustments to the basic amount', pp 287–289.

[33] See eg *Nitrine butadiene rubber*, Commission decision of 23 January 2008: this was the fourth decision in the synthetic rubber industry in just over three years.

of these cartels were of very long duration: for example 35 years in the case of *Animal feed phosphates*[34] and 29 years in each of the cartels in *Sorbates*[35] and *Organic peroxides*[36]. Some of these cartels were notable for cartelising several products at the same time, as for example in *Calcium and magnesium reagents*[37]. It is also noticeable in the Commission's decisions how often cartel meetings were held during or just after trade association meetings, as for example in the cases of *Industrial bags*[38], *Copper fittings*[39] and *Polyurethane foam*[40].

(A) **Statistics**

From 1990 to 2017 the Commission imposed fines totalling €27.6 billion on 835 companies for cartel activities[41]. In the years from 2013 to 2017 the fines amounted to €9.3 billion; in the case of the *Trucks* cartel alone the fines amounted to €3.8 billion[42]. The Commission's statistics on its enforcement activity in relation to cartels are available on its website and are regularly updated. These statistics speak eloquently of the Commission's continuing determination to search for and eradicate cartels. In the calendar year 2016 the Commission adopted six decisions in which the fines totalled €3.726 billion, the largest amount to have been imposed in a single year. The fines are paid into the EU budget: to that extent they benefit the treasuries of the Member States, whose contributions are proportionally reduced. In other words, ultimately European taxpayers directly benefit from the penalties imposed upon members of cartels. A separate point is that the Commission has estimated that it saved consumers €6.8–10.2 billion in 2016 as a result of its anti-cartel enforcement[43].

This picture of rigorous enforcement is clear. Some commentators have expressed concerns about the high level of fines imposed by the Commission and, in particular, about the combination of powers vested in it and the lack of a 'fresh pair of eyes' within the system[44]. However the judgments of the European Court of Human Rights in *Menarini Diagnostics v Italy*[45] and of the Court of Justice in *Chalkor v Commission*[46] make clear that administrative decision-making, which is subject to full judicial control, satisfies

[34] Commission decision of 20 July 2010; not all of the producers were involved for the entire period.

[35] Commission decision of 1 October 2003, substantially upheld on appeal Case T-410/03 *Hoechst v Commission* EU:T:2008:211.

[36] Commission decision of 10 December 2003, upheld on appeal Case T-99/04 *AC-Treuhand v Commission* EU:T:2008:256.

[37] Commission decision of 22 July 2009, upheld on appeal Cases T-384/09 etc *SKW Stahl-Metallurgie Holding v Commission* EU:T:2014:27, and on further appeal Cases C-154/14 P etc *SKW Stahl-Metallurgie v Commission* EU:C:2016:445.

[38] Commission decision of 30 November 2005.

[39] Commission decision of 20 September 2006, substantially upheld on appeal Cases T-375/06 etc *Viega v Commission* EU:T:2011:106, and on further appeal Case C-276/11 P EU:C:2013:163.

[40] Commission decision of 29 January 2014.

[41] www.ec.europa.eu/competition/cartels/statistics/statistics.pdf; after adjustments caused by appeal judgments the figure reduces to €25.2 billion.

[42] Commission decisions of 19 July 2016 and of 27 September 2017; the latter decision is on appeal Case T-799/17 *Scania v Commission*, not yet decided.

[43] *EU Competition Policy in Action* (2017), available at www.ec.europa.eu.

[44] See eg Forrester 'Due Process in EC Competition Cases: A Distinguished Institution with Flawed Procedures' (2009) 6 EL Rev 817 and the essays in Ehlermann and Marquis (eds) *Evaluation of Evidence and its Judicial Review in Competition Cases* (Hart, 2010); Editorial comments 'Towards a More Judicial Approach? EU Antitrust Fines Under the Scrutiny of Fundamental Rights' (2011) 48 CML Rev 1405.

[45] Application no 43509/08, judgment of 27 September 2011, paras 57–67.

[46] Case C-386/10 P EU:C:2011:815, paras 45–54 (*Copper plumbing tubes*); see also Case C-501/11 P *Schindler Holding v Commission* EU:C:2013:522, paras 30–38 (*Elevators and escalators*); Cases T-56/09 etc *Saint-Gobain Glass France v Commission* EU:T:2014:160, paras 75–87, and in particular para 80 (*Car glass*).

the requirements of the European Convention on Human Rights and the EU Charter of Fundamental Rights[47]. The EFTA Court reached the same conclusion in *Posten Norge*[48].

The Commission remains committed to an extremely tough stance on cartels. However it is receptive to claims that too high a fine may mean that an offending firm is put out of business[49]: not an attractive proposition for a competition authority, since this would mean that there would be fewer competitors on the market than there were before. The Commission reduced some of the fines in *Prestressing steel*[50], *Bathroom fittings and fixtures*[51] and *Animal feed phosphates*[52] for this reason.

(B) Concealment of cartels

Firms that participate in cartels are usually fully aware of the unlawfulness of their conduct. They often go to great lengths to suppress evidence of their illegal activity: for example in *Gas insulated switchgear*[53] the participants in the cartel used codes to conceal their companies' names and encryption software to protect the secrecy of emails and telephone conversations; made use of free email providers and the anonymous mailboxes made available by them; sent messages as password-protected documents: the passwords were regularly changed; systematically destroyed emails; downloaded attachments onto memory sticks rather than onto their computers; and made use of mobile telephones provided by a member of the cartel that contained encryption options[54]. Similar practices were used in *Cathode ray tubes*[55]. In *High power voltage cables*[56] the Commission used forensic information technology to recover several thousand documents that had been deleted by an employee of one of the offending firms.

(C) Proof of participation in a cartel

It follows from the previous section that competition authorities may find it difficult to gather evidence that will satisfy a court to the required standard of proof that there has been a secret cartel. In *Aalborg Portland v Commission*[57] the Court of Justice recognised that 'if the Commission discovers evidence explicitly showing unlawful contact between traders, such as the minutes of a meeting, it will normally be only fragmentary and sparse, so that it is often necessary to reconstitute certain details by deduction'[58].

[47] For discussion see Wils 'The Increased Level of EU Antitrust Fines, Judicial Review, and the European Convention on Human Rights' (2010) 33 World Competition 5; Merola and Derenne (eds) *The Role of the Court of Justice of the European Union in Competition Law Cases* (Bruylant, 2012).

[48] Case E-15/10 *Posten Norge AS v EFTA Surveillance Authority* [2012] EFTA Ct Rep 246, paras 91 and 100.

[49] *Guidelines on the method of setting fines* OJ [2006] C 210/2, para 35; the General Court has rejected the argument that para 35 gives the Commission too much discretion: Case T-386/10 *Dornbracht v Commission* EU:T:2013:450, paras 76–77; see Kienapfel and Wils 'Inability to Pay—First cases and practical experiences' (2010) 3 Competition Policy Newsletter 3.

[50] Commission decision of 30 June 2010.

[51] Commission decision of 23 June 2010, upheld on this point in Case T-376/10 *Mamoli Robinetteria v Commission* EU:T:2013:442, paras 180–183, and on further appeal on this point in Case C-619/13 P EU:C:2017:50, paras 113–114.

[52] Commission decision of 20 July 2010, paras 224–240.

[53] Commission decision of 24 January 2007.

[54] Ibid.

[55] Commission decision of 5 December 2012; see similarly *LCD*, Commission decision of 8 December 2010, para 302, and *Freight forwarding*, Commission decision of 28 March 2012 (using code names based on the names of vegetables when fixing prices).

[56] Commission Press Release IP/14/358, 2 April 2014.

[57] Cases C-204/00 P etc EU:C:2004:6 (*Cement*).

[58] Ibid, para 55.

The Court said that in most cases the existence of an anti-competitive practice or agreement must be inferred from coincidences and indicia which, taken together, may, in the absence of another plausible explanation, constitute evidence of an infringement[59]. For example, in *Total Marketing Services SA v Commission* the Court held that attendance by an undertaking at meetings involving anti-competitive activities 'creates a presumption of the illegality of its participation, which that undertaking must rebut through evidence of public distancing, which must be perceived as such by the other parties to the cartel'[60]. The reason for the presumption is that, having participated in the cartel without publicly distancing itself from what was discussed, the undertaking has given the other participants to believe that it subscribed to what was decided there and that it would comply with it[61]. Presumptions are one way that EU law supports the effectiveness and administrability of anti-cartel enforcement[62].

(D) **Facilitators**

In *Organic peroxides*[63] the members of the cartel used the services of a third party, AC-Treuhand, to organise cartel meetings. The Commission concluded that AC-Treuhand itself was a party to the unlawful agreement and fined it a nominal amount of €1,000; on appeal the Commission's decision was upheld[64]. In *Heat stabilisers*[65] AC-Treuhand was again fined, on this occasion €348,000 for facilitating two separate cartels. The Commission's decision was again upheld on appeal[66]; the Court of Justice held that a facilitator could be liable provided that it:

> intended to contribute by its own conduct to the common objectives pursued by all the participants and that it was aware of the actual conduct planned or put into effect by other undertakings in pursuit of the same objectives or that it could reasonably have foreseen it and that it was prepared to take the risk[67].

In *Icap v Commission*[68] the General Court upheld a finding of the Commission that Icap, a broker, had facilitated the manipulation of benchmarks used in the trading of Yen interest rate derivatives[69]. In *Eturas*[70] the Court of Justice gave a preliminary ruling on the circumstances in which the administrator of an online booking system could be liable for facilitating a horizontal concerted practice to restrict discounts offered by travel agents;

59 Ibid, para 57. 60 Case C-634/13 P EU:C:2015:614, para 21 (*Candle waxes*).

61 Case C-403/04 P *Sumitomo Metal Industries Ltd v Commission* EU:C:2007:52, para 48 (*Seamless steel tubes*).

62 See OECD Roundtable *Safe harbours and legal presumptions in competition law* (2017), available at www.oecd.org/competition.

63 Commission decision of 10 December 2003; the Commission had found a facilitator of cartel practices liable for infringing Article 101 as long ago as 1980 in its decision in *Italian cast glass*, Commission decision of 17 December 1980.

64 Case T-99/04 *AC-Treuhand v Commission* EU:T:2008:256, paras 112–138; for comment see Harding 'Capturing the Cartel's Friends: Cartel Facilitation and the Idea of Joint Criminal Enterprise' (2009) 34 EL Rev 298.

65 Commission decision of 11 November 2009.

66 Case T-27/10 *AC-Treuhand v Commission* EU:T:2014:59, paras 43–47, upheld on appeal Case C-194/14 P EU:C:2015:717.

67 Case C-194/14 P *AC-Treuhand v Commission* EU:C:2015:717, para 30.

68 Case T-180/15 EU:T:2017:795, on appeal Case C-39/18 P *Commission v Icap*, not yet decided.

69 Commission decision of 4 February 2015; in an earlier settlement decision another broker, RP Martin, had agreed to pay a fine of €247,000 for facilitating the manipulation of the Yen benchmark: Commission decision of 4 December 2013.

70 Case C-74/14 EU:C:2016:42.

the Lithuanian Supreme Court subsequently held the administrator to have facilitated the concerted practice[71].

(E) **Single overall agreement**

The EU Courts have also developed the idea that a number of firms can have been party to a single overall cartel agreement that has lasted for many years, and for which they all bear responsibility[72]. This can be important in practice. It may be that there has been cartelisation of a particular product market for many years, but that the participants in the cartel have fluctuated over time; the geographical extent of it may have changed; and the types of cartel behaviour may have altered. If such a situation can be regarded as a single overall agreement it means that only one investigation will be needed and it is much less likely that some of the illegal practices are so far in the past that rules of limitation prevent the imposition of fines. This subject is dealt with in chapter 3.

(F) **Public distancing from a cartel**

In *Tréfileurope v Commission*[73] the General Court held that the fact that an undertaking does not abide by the outcome of meetings which have a manifestly anti-competitive purpose does not relieve it of full responsibility for its participation in the cartel, if it has not publicly distanced itself from what was agreed or discussed[74]. This has been repeated on numerous occasions[75]. In *Westfalen v Commission*[76] the General Court said that the notion of 'public distancing' as a means of excluding liability must be interpreted narrowly[77].

An act of 'public distancing' must be expressed firmly and unambiguously[78], since the understanding of the other members of the cartel is of 'critical importance' when determining whether an undertaking has distanced itself[79]. The General Court has suggested, for example, that an undertaking should write to the other members of the cartel to say that it did not wish to be considered to be a member of the cartel nor to participate in anti-competitive behaviour[80]. In *Comap v Commission*[81] the Court of Justice noted that an undertaking could either distance itself publicly from anti-competitive activities or denounce those activities to a competition authority[82]. Public distancing from a cartel does not **require** an undertaking to blow the whistle to an authority.

In *Total Marketing Services SA v Commission*[83] the Court of Justice clarified that public distancing is required in order to rebut the presumption that an undertaking that

[71] Case No A-97–858/2016, judgment of 2 May 2016 of the Lithuanian Supreme Court, available (in Lithuanian) at www.lvat.lt.

[72] See ch 3, 'Single overall agreement', pp 105–109.

[73] Case T-141/89 EU:T:1995:62, para 85 (*Welded steel mesh*).

[74] See Bailey 'Publicly Distancing Oneself from a Cartel' (2008) 32 World Competition 177.

[75] See eg Cases T-25/95 etc *Cimenteries CBR SA v Commission* EU:T:2000:77, paras 1353, 1389 and 3199, upheld on appeal Cases C-204/00 P etc EU:C:2004:6, para 81 (*Cement*); Case C-290/11 P *Comap v Commission* EU:C:2012:271, para 74 (*Copper fittings*).

[76] Case T-303/02 EU:T:2006:374 (*Industrial and medical gases*).

[77] Ibid, para 103.

[78] Case T-377/06 *Comap v Commission* EU:T:2011:108, para 76 (*Copper fittings*); similarly see Case T-110/07 *Siemens v Commission* EU:T:2011:68, para 55 (*Gas insulated switchgear*).

[79] Case T-540/08 *Esso Société anonyme française v Commission* EU:T:2014:630, para 40 (*Candle waxes*).

[80] Case T-61/99 *Adriatica di Navigazione v Commission* EU:T:2003:335, para 138 (*Greek ferries*); Case T-302/02 *Westfalen v Commission* EU:T:2006:374, para 103 (*Industrial and medical gases*).

[81] Case C-290/11 P EU:C:2012:271 (*Copper fittings*).

[82] Ibid, para 75.

[83] Case C-634/13 P EU:C:2015:614 (*Candle waxes*).

participated in anti-competitive meetings is liable; however public distancing is not the only way of showing the end of an undertaking's participation in a cartel[84]. Nevertheless the Court held that the absence of public distancing can be a fact used to prove that an undertaking's anti-competitive conduct has continued[85].

(G) Recent decisions against cartels

The Commission's determination to combat cartels is demonstrated by its decisional practice in recent years. In 2008 fines of €1.383 billion were imposed in *Car glass*[86]; the fine imposed on Saint-Gobain, of €896 million, was, at the time, the largest ever to have been imposed on one undertaking in an Article 101 decision. In 2010 fines of €799 million were imposed on 11 air cargo carriers for fixing fuel and security surcharges[87]; the Commission's decision was annulled on appeal to the General Court[88], but the Commission subsequently readopted its decision, which is itself on appeal[89]. In 2012 the Commission imposed fines on seven undertakings totalling €1.47 billion for operating two cartels of *Cathode ray tubes*[90]. The Commission used the settlement procedure in 2013 to adopt two decisions imposing fines totalling €1.49 billion for manipulating *EURIBOR* and *Yen LIBOR*[91]. UBS would have been fined €2.5 billion for its involvement in cartelising *Yen LIBOR*, but received immunity for revealing the existence of the cartels.

In *Trucks* the Commission adopted two decisions: first, a settlement decision[92] imposing fines of €2.93 billion on five producers for infringements of Article 101, including agreeing on gross list prices and on the timing and cost of the introduction of new emission technologies; and, secondly, a standard decision imposing a fine of €880 million on Scania, which had declined to settle the case[93].

(H) Judicial review

Undertakings found to have infringed Article 101 have a right to apply to the General Court for annulment of the decision. The EU Courts must review decisions by carrying out an 'in-depth review' of the law and of the facts[94]. Where the Commission is guilty of factual errors the General Court will, of course, either annul the decision or reduce the level of fines. Where the Commission has made a procedural error and lost an appeal before the EU Courts, it has often reopened its administrative procedure in order to

84 Ibid, paras 22–24. 85 Ibid, para 28.

86 Commission decision of 12 November 2008, substantially upheld on appeal but some reduction of fines Cases T-56/09 etc *Saint-Gobain Glass France v Commission* EU:T:2014:160.

87 Commission decision of 9 November 2010.

88 See eg Case T-67/11 *Martinair v Commission* EU:T:2015:984 and 12 other judgments handed down on the same day; in the case of British Airways, the Commission's decision was annulled only partly, to the extent to which BA had petitioned the Court: Case T-48/11 *British Airways v Commission* EU:T:2015:988, upheld on appeal to the Court of Justice Case C-122/16 *British Airways v Commission* EU:C:2017:406.

89 Commission decision of 17 March 2017, on appeal Cases T-338/17 etc *Air France v Commission*, not yet decided.

90 Commission decision of 5 December 2012, upheld on appeal Cases T-92/13 etc *Philips v Commission* EU:T:2015:605.

91 Commission decision of 4 December 2013; see also Commission MEMO/13/1090, 4 December 2013.

92 Commission decision of 19 July 2016.

93 Commission decision of 27 September 2017, on appeal Case T-799/17 *Scania v Commission*, not yet decided.

94 Case C-501/11 P *Schindler Holding v Commission* EU:C:2013:522, para 37 (*Elevators and escalators*).

correct the error[95]. The readopted decisions are often appealed and were mostly affirmed in the cases of *PVC*[96], *Alloy surcharges*[97] and *Steel beams*[98].

The General Court has unlimited jurisdiction in relation to the level of fines[99]; this includes the right to increase as well as to decrease them, which may act as a disincentive to appeal in some cases[100]. However the Court is fairly reluctant to interfere with the Commission's margin of appreciation in relation to the level of fines, and, as already noted, the Commission's statistics show that, overall, the level of reductions by the Court is not great.

4. **Horizontal Price Fixing**

Horizontal price fixing would be regarded by most people as the most blatant and undesirable of restrictive trade practices[101]. However price fixing has not always attracted the opprobrium that it does today. In the UK, for example, it was characteristic of most industries during the first half of the twentieth century that prices were set at an agreed level; this was thought to provide stability, to protect firms against cyclical recession and overseas competition, and to facilitate orderly and rational marketing from which purchasers too would benefit[102]. The introduction of power to inhibit price fixing in the Monopolies and Restrictive Practices (Inquiry and Control) Act 1948 was resented and even now resistance to price competition remains deep-rooted in some parts of the economy.

It might be assumed that in the absence of competition laws—or at any rate in the absence of any realistic prospect of being detected and punished for breaking competition laws—all competitors would find the urge to cartelise and to maximise their joint profits an irresistible one. Participation in a cartel itself has its 'price' and membership will be more profitable to some firms than others[103]. Costs will be incurred in negotiating to fix the price at which the product is to be sold and these costs will inevitably increase as more firms are brought into the cartel and the range of products to be cartelised is extended. Firms may find it difficult both to agree a common price and to remain faithful

[95] *PVC* OJ [1994] L 239/14; *Alloy Surcharge*, Commission Press Release IP/06/1851, 20 December 2006; *Steel beams*, Commission Press Release IP/06/1527, 8 November 2006; *Italian concrete reinforcing bars*, Commission Press Release IP/09/1389, 30 September 2009; *Carbonless paper*, Commission Press Release IP/10/788, 23 June 2010; *Gas insulated switchgear*, Commission Press Release IP/12/705, 27 June 2012.

[96] Case T-305/94 *Limburgse Vinyl Maatschappij v Commission* EU:T:1999:80, upheld on further appeal Cases C-238/99 P etc EU:C:2002:582.

[97] Case T-24/07 *ThyssenKrupp Stainless v Commission* EU:T:2009:236, upheld on further appeal Case C-352/09 P EU:C:2011:191.

[98] Cases T-405/06 etc *ArcelorMittal Luxembourg v Commission* EU:T:2009:90, upheld on further appeal Cases C-201/09 P etc EU:C:2011:190.

[99] Article 261 TFEU; see ch 7, 'Judicial Review', pp 300–305 on appeals to the General Court.

[100] See Case T-91/11 *Innolux v Commission* EU:T:2014:92, paras 168–169, upheld on further appeal Case C-231/14 P EU:C:2015:717. The General Court increased the fine in Cases T-101/05 etc *BASF v Commission* EU:T:2007:380, para 222; and it refused to reduce the fines even though the Commission had erred in its assessment in Case T-364/10 *Duravit v Commission* EU:T:2013:477, para 386 (*Bathroom fittings and fixtures*), upheld on further appeal Case C-609/13 P EU:C:2017:46.

[101] For a critical discussion of the law and policy on price fixing see Kaplow *Competition Policy and Price Fixing* (Princeton University Press, 2013).

[102] See eg Allen *Monopoly and Restrictive Practices* (George Allen & Unwin, 1968), ch 14.

[103] See Scherer and Ross *Industrial Market Structure and Economic Performance* (Houghton Mifflin, 3rd ed, 1990), chs 7 and 8; Bishop and Walker *The Economics of EC Competition Law* (Sweet & Maxwell, 3rd ed, 2010), paras 5-007–5-033; Niels, Jenkins and Kavanagh *Economics for Competition Lawyers* (Oxford University Press, 2nd ed, 2016), ch 5.

to the level set. It will be to the advantage of more efficient firms to fix a lower price, since output (and so their revenue) will then be greater; the producer of strongly differentiated goods will want a higher price, which will cover the cost of promoting its brand image. Having fixed prices, further expense will have to be incurred in monitoring the agreement. Meetings or discussions will be necessary to reappraise matters from time to time, resources will need to be expended in policing it to ensure that individual firms are not cheating by cutting prices secretly, offering discounts and bonuses or altering the quality of the product[104]. To prevent cheating, the cartel may fix quotas and provide for reprisals on firms that exceed them. Further resources may have to be devoted to arrangements such as collective boycotts, patent pooling and the offer of aggregated rebates in order to prevent new entrants coming on to the market with a view to sharing in any supra-competitive profits that are being earned. A system of collective resale price maintenance may have to be established to buttress the stability of the cartel. A trade association or 'cartel consultancy' may be used to reinforce the cartel[105].

The problems inherent in the cartelisation process itself explain why in some industries price fixing has a tendency to break down in the long term and why the parties may attempt to limit competition in other ways than by directly fixing prices. For example, it may be easier to prevent 'cheating' where each firm is given an exclusive geographical market or a particular class of customers with which to deal. Furthermore the fact that price fixing becomes more difficult as the number of cartelists increases may be considered to signify that competition authorities ought to monitor those markets where collusion is most likely to be profitable because of the high level of concentration that exists or the homogeneity of the products sold[106].

It should not be assumed from the foregoing comments that price fixing is rare. Even the existence of competition laws backed up by severe penalties has not dissuaded some firms from cooperating in an attempt to control the market. Experience shows that some industries are particularly prone to cartelisation: any review of enforcement activity in this area will quickly reveal, for example, that this is true of the cement, chemical and construction sectors. It is also important to appreciate that prices can be fixed in numerous different ways, and that a fully effective competition law must be able to comprehend not only the most blatant forms of the practice but also a whole range of more subtle collusive behaviour whose object is to limit price competition. For example, where firms agree to restrict credit to customers, to abstain from offering discounts and rebates, to refrain from advertising prices, to notify one another of the prices they charge to customers or intend to recommend their distributors to charge, or to adopt identical cost accounting methods, the object or effect of the agreement may be to diminish or prevent price competition. Indeed, agreements to divide markets or fix production quotas can in a sense be seen as covert price-fixing agreements, in that they limit the extent to which firms can compete with one another on price. These and other similar agreements will be dealt with separately later in this chapter.

(A) **Article 101(1)**

Article 101(1)(a) provides that agreements, decisions and concerted practices which 'directly or indirectly fix purchase or selling prices or any other trading conditions' may

[104] It is not uncommon for a cartel to break down, or to run the risk of doing so, because of the extent of cheating indulged in by members: see eg *Zinc Producer Group* OJ [1984] L 220/27, paras 23–63; *Prestressing steel*, Commission decision of 30 June 2010, paras 604, 863, 952 and 1018; the appeals against this decision are mentioned at ch 13, n 240 later.

[105] See 'Facilitators', pp 527–528 earlier in chapter.

[106] See Posner *Antitrust Law* (University of Chicago Press, 2nd ed, 2002), ch 4.

be caught. Many aspects of Article 101(1) have been discussed earlier in this book. The expressions 'agreement' and 'concerted practice' are given a wide meaning[107]: specifically, the Commission may find a 'single overall agreement'[108], may adopt a dual classification of an agreement 'and/or' a concerted practice[109]; and attendance at meetings at which prices are discussed between competitors is highly incriminating[110]. A key principle of Article 101(1) is that competing undertakings must determine their conduct and pricing independently. Price-fixing agreements have been held on numerous occasions to have as their *object* the restriction of competition for the purposes of Article 101(1), so that there is no need also to show that they have the effect of doing so[111]. Parties cannot argue that their price-fixing agreement does not appreciably restrict competition: the case law has decided that it does, provided that the agreement has an appreciable effect on trade between Member States, a conceptually different point[112]. The Commission is not obliged to engage in market definition in cartel cases if it can show that the cartel appreciably affects trade between Member States by other means[113]. Furthermore Article 101(1) is capable of being applied extraterritorially to cartels entered into outside but implemented or producing qualified effects within the EU[114]. This section examines more closely the application of Article 101(1) to price-fixing agreements.

(i) Price fixing in any form is caught

It is clear from the decisions of the Commission and the judgments of the EU Courts that it is not just blatant price fixing that is caught, but that Article 101(1) will catch any agreement that directly or indirectly distorts price competition. In *IFTRA Rules on Glass Containers*[115] the Commission condemned rules of a glass manufacturers' association which might reduce price competition by including an obligation not to offer discounts, an open information scheme, the adoption of a common accounting procedure and a term providing for the charging of uniform delivered prices. In this decision the Commission pointed out that in the particular product market the potential for non-price competition was weak, the corollary being that maintenance of price competition was particularly important. An agreement not to discount off published prices was held to infringe Article 101(1) in *FETTCSA*[116], even though the parties had not expressly agreed on the level of their published prices. In *Vimpoltu*[117] an agreement to observe maximum discounts and to offer the same credit terms was caught.

Many other decisions have condemned agreements which might directly or indirectly facilitate level pricing. The medium through which price fixing is achieved does not affect

107 See ch 3, 'Agreements, Decisions and Concerted Practices', pp 101–119.

108 See ch 3, 'Single overall agreement', pp 105–109.

109 Ch 3, 'Agreement "and/or" concerted practice', pp 104–105.

110 Ch 3, 'Meaning of concerted practice', pp 116–117.

111 Ch 3, 'Price fixing and exchanges of information in relation to future prices', p 128; note that there are some exceptional circumstances in which price fixing has been found not to restrict competition by object, but to do so by effect: ch 3, 'Refinement of the range of agreements within the object box', pp 131–132.

112 Case C-226/11 *Expedia* EU:C:2012:795, para 37; see ch 3, 'The *De Minimis* Doctrine', pp 147–150.

113 Case C-439/11 P *Ziegler v Commission* EU:C:2013:513, para 63 (*International removal services*); see also Case T-82/08 *Guardian v Commission* EU:T:2012:494, paras 90 (*Flat glass*); see ch 3, 'The Effect on Trade Between Member States', pp 150–155.

114 See ch 12, 'The Extraterritorial Application of EU Competition Law', pp 502–508.

115 OJ [1974] L 160/1; see similarly *IFTRA Rules for Producers of Aluminium Containers* OJ [1975] L 228/10.

116 OJ [2000] L 268/1, paras 132–139 (citing *IFTRA Rules on Glass Containers* and *IFTRA Rules for Producers of Aluminium Containers*), upheld on appeal Case T-213/00 *CMA CGM v Commission* EU:T:2003:76, para 184.

117 OJ [1983] L 200/44; see similarly *Italian Flat Glass* OJ [1989] L 33/44 (offer of identical discounts), annulled on appeal Cases T-68/89 etc *Società Italiano Vetro SpA v Commission* EU:T:1992:38.

the applicability of Article 101(1). Prior consultation on price lists, with a commitment not to submit quotations before such consultation, is prohibited[118]. A substantial body of material on information agreements now exists[119], restrictions upon advertising may be caught[120], as are agreements on terms and conditions which limit price competition[121], agreements on recommended prices[122], maximum pricing[123], surcharges[124] and collective resale price maintenance[125]. Objection has been taken to a scheme whereby members of a cartel at times refused to sell and at others themselves purchased zinc on the London Metal Exchange in order to maintain its price[126]. Where an industry considers that cooperation is necessary because of the depressed state of the market, this is a matter that should be weighed at the stage of considering whether the terms of Article 101(3) are met.

Price fixing as part of a strategy to isolate national markets is caught[127], and agreements between distributors are caught as well as between producers[128]. An agreement the effect of which is to maintain a traditional price differential between two geographical markets will infringe Article 101(1)[129]. Fixing the price of imports into the EU has been caught[130], as has manipulating the price of exports within the EU[131].

In *British sugar*[132] the Commission did not find that the prices for sugar had actually been fixed, but that the parties could rely on the other participants to pursue a collaborative strategy of higher pricing in 'an atmosphere of mutual certainty'[133]. In *Fenex*[134] the Commission considered that the regular and consistent practice of drawing up and circulating recommended tariffs to members of a trade association infringed Article 101(1)[135]. In *Dole v Commission*[136] the Court of Justice upheld the General Court's judgment confirming the Commission's finding that three producers of bananas had infringed Article 101(1)

[118] *Re Cast Iron Steel Rolls* OJ [1983] L 317/1: the parties here had established an 'alarm system' in the event that competition authorities should become aware of their cartel; the decision was upheld on appeal, Cases 29 and 30/83 *Compagnie Royale Asturienne des Mines SA and Rheinzink GmbH v Commission* EU:C:1984:130.

[119] See 'Exchanges of Information', pp 551–559 later in chapter.

[120] See 'Advertising Restrictions', pp 559–561 later in chapter.

[121] See 'Agreements Relating to Terms and Conditions', pp 549–551 later in chapter.

[122] Case 8/72 *Cementhandelaren v Commission* EU:C:1972:84; see also *Ferry Operators Currency Surcharges* OJ [1996] L 26/23.

[123] *European Glass Manufacturers* OJ [1974] L 160/1.

[124] *Air cargo*, Commission decision of 9 November 2010, annulled on appeal Cases T-9/11 etc *Air Canada v Commission* EU:T:2015:994: the Commission adopted a second decision on 17 March 2017, which is itself now on appeal in Cases T-338/17 etc *Air France v Commission*, not yet decided; *Freight forwarding*, Commission decision of 28 March 2012, upheld on appeal Cases T-265/12 etc *Schenker v Commission* EU:T:2016:111, and on further appeal Cases C-263/16 P etc EU:C:2018:58; *Steel abrasives*, Commission decision of 2 April 2014.

[125] Cases 43 and 63/82 *VBVB & VBBB v Commission* EU:C:1984:9.

[126] *Zinc Producer Group* OJ [1984] L 220/27.

[127] Case 41/69 *ACF Chemiefarma NV v Commission* EU:C:1970:71.

[128] Cases 100/80 etc *Musique Diffusion Française SA v Commission* EU:C:1983:158.

[129] *Scottish Salmon Board* OJ [1992] L 246/37.

[130] *Re Franco-Japanese Ballbearings Agreement* OJ [1974] L 343/19; *Re French and Taiwanese Mushroom Packers* OJ [1975] L 29/26; *Wood Pulp I* OJ [1985] L 85/1; *Aluminum Imports* OJ [1985] L 92/1.

[131] *Milchförderungsfonds* OJ [1985] L 35/35.

[132] OJ [1999] L 76/1, substantially upheld on appeal Cases T-202/98 etc *Tate & Lyle v Commission* EU:T:2001:185.

[133] See the Commission's XXVIIIth *Report on Competition Policy* (1998), pp 138–140.

[134] OJ [1996] L 181/28. [135] Ibid, paras 45–74.

[136] Case C-286/13 P EU:C:2015:184, dismissing an appeal against Case T-588/08 *Dole v Commission* EU:T:2013:130, dismissing an appeal against *Bananas*, Commission decision of 15 October 2008; a separate appeal was also unsuccessful in Case T-587/08 *Fresh Del Monte Produce v Commission* EU:T:2013:129, but the fine was reduced on further appeal Cases C-293/13 P etc EU:C:2015:416.

by holding weekly bilateral phone calls to discuss or disclose their pricing intentions[137]. The Court held that these discussions reduced uncertainty as to the quotation prices set by the producers and concerned the fixing of prices[138]. Where undertakings agree to increase prices, and announce to their customers what those increases will be, it is irrelevant to a finding of infringement of Article 101 that prices are subsequently negotiated with individual customers that differ from what was agreed: the General Court has stated that price announcements always have an impact on the final outcome even if the final price is negotiated with the customer[139].

(ii) **Price fixing in any context is caught**

The Commission has applied Article 101 to price-fixing cartels of industrial products such as cement, construction and chemicals as well as of services, such as insurance[140], banking[141], transport[142] and the professions[143]. The Commission has also been prepared to examine carefully markets in which price competition is already limited by extraneous factors, in order to ensure that firms do nothing further to limit competition[144]. The application of Article 101 will not be affected by the fact that the state itself sanctioned or extended the effect of a price-fixing agreement[145].

In a number of cases[146] the Commission has characterised financial benchmarks as a component of the price of interest rate derivatives products and the manipulation of financial benchmarks as price fixing[147]. The anti-competitive objective of the manipulation is said to be 'reducing in advance uncertainty that would have otherwise prevailed in the market about the future conduct of competitors'[148]. In *Icap v Commission*[149] the

[137] Note the Commission also found that the banana importers exchanged quotation prices which enabled them to monitor prices: decision of 15 October 2008, paras 273–277.

[138] Case C-286/13 P EU:C:2015:184, para 134.

[139] See eg Cases T-109/02 etc *Bolloré v Commission* EU:T:2007:115, paras 450–453 (*Carbonless paper*).

[140] See eg *Re Nuovo CEGAM* OJ [1984] L 99/29 (common tariff system infringed Article 101(1)); *Re Fire Insurance* OJ [1985] L 35/20, upheld on appeal Case 45/85 *VdS v Commission* EU:C:1987:34 (recommendations on tariffs infringed Article 101(1)).

[141] See eg *Austrian banks—'Lombard Club'*, Commission decision of 11 June 2002, substantially upheld on appeal Cases T-259/02 etc *Raiffeisen Zentralbank Österreich AG v Commission* EU:T:2006:396, and on further appeal Cases C-125/07 P etc *Erste Bank der Österreichische Sparkassen AG v Commission* EU:C:2009:576.

[142] *Greek ferries* OJ [1999] L 109/24, upheld on appeal Cases T-56/99 etc *Marlines v Commission* EU:T:2003:333; *Freight forwarding*, Commission decision of 28 March 2012, upheld on appeal Cases T-265/12 etc *Schenker v Commission* EU:T:2016:111, and on further appeal Cases C-263/16 P etc EU:C:2018:58.

[143] *Belgian architects*, Commission decision of 24 June 2004; *ONP*, Commission decision of 8 December 2010, substantially upheld on appeal Case T-90/11 *ONP v Commission* EU:T:2014:1049.

[144] Cases 209/78 etc *Van Landewyck v Commission* EU:C:1980:248; similarly see Case 85/76 *Hoffmann-La Roche v Commission* EU:C:1979:36, para 123; *British Sugar plc* OJ [1999] L 76/1, para 87, upheld on appeal Case T-202/98 *Tate & Lyle v Commission* EU:T:2001:185.

[145] *AROW v BNIC* OJ [1982] L 379/1; *Zinc Producer Group* OJ [1984] L 220/27; *Benelux Flat Glass* OJ [1984] L 212/13 (where competition was also limited by the similar costs faced by glass producers and the structure of the market); see ch 3, 'State compulsion in highly regulated markets', pp 144–145 and ch 6 generally on the relationship of the competition rules with state regulation of economic activity.

[146] See eg *Yen interest rate derivatives*, Commission settlement decision of 4 December 2013 and standard decision of 4 February 2015 (the appeal at ch 13 n 149 below was successful as to Icap's liability for one cartel the fine imposed on Icap); *Euro interest rate derivatives*, Commission settlement decision of 4 December 2013 and standard decision of 7 December 2016; the latter decision has been appealed to the General Court Cases T-105/17 etc *HSBC Holdings v Commission*, not yet decided; *Swiss franc interest rate derivatives (CHF LIBOR)*, Commission decision of 21 October 2014; *Swiss franc interest rate derivatives (Bid-ask spread infringement)*, Commission decision of 21 October 2014.

[147] See Piccinin 'Oil price-rigging' (2013) Competition Law Insight 7; Pascall 'Tail Wagging the Dog: The Manipulation of Benchmark Rates—A Competitive Bone of Contention' (2016) 39 World Competition 161.

[148] *Euro interest rate derivatives*, Commission settlement decision of 4 December 2013, para 57.

[149] Case T-180/15 EU:T:2017:795, para 72.

General Court held that the coordination of the Japanese Yen LIBOR panel submissions was intended to influence the extent of the payments due from, or due to, the participating banks, and so clearly had an anti-competitive object.

(iii) **Price signalling**

An interesting question, to which there is no clear answer in the decisional practice of the Commission or the jurisprudence of the EU Courts, is whether price 'signalling' can infringe Article 101[150]. This refers to a situation in which there is no direct agreement or concerted practice between undertakings to fix prices, nor a systematic exchange of information between them. Rather the firms send signals to one another about their future commercial intentions, for example through interviews conducted with the media, speeches at conferences or discussions with customers that are relayed back to competitors. It is not hard to see the theory of harm in such circumstances: signals about future pricing intentions may facilitate parallel behaviour; and it seems reasonable to suggest that if undertakings consciously resort to price signalling practices they could be taken, depending on the evidence, to have 'knowingly substituted practical cooperation for the risks inherent in competition', the definition of a concerted practice established in the *Dyestuffs* judgment[151]. Paragraph 63 of the Commission's *Guidelines on Horizontal Cooperation Agreements* acknowledges the possibility that, depending on the facts of the case, price signalling could violate Article 101. In *Wood Pulp*[152] the Commission did condemn price announcements, but that finding was overturned on appeal to the Court of Justice which was not satisfied that the Commission had demonstrated a concerted practice to fix prices[153]. The Commission accused several operators in the container shipping sector of price signalling, but the case was closed when the liner shipping companies gave commitments under Article 9 of Regulation 1/2003 to desist from signalling practices in future. To put the point another way, this investigation did not lead to a finding that price signalling infringed Article 101, although the Commission's intervention did lead to a change in commercial behaviour[154].

Price signalling has been considered in several other jurisdictions. The Dutch Competition Authority accepted commitments to abandon certain signalling practices[155]. In the US price signalling theoretically could be a conspiracy that restrains trade, contrary to section 1 of the Sherman Act 1890, but a more promising way of challenging the practice might be as an unfair commercial practice contrary to section 5 of the Federal Trade Commission Act 1914[156]. In the UK the Competition and Markets Authority ('the CMA') used the domestic market investigation system to terminate price signalling in relation to cement, rather than bringing a case under Article 101[157].

[150] There is a discussion of price signalling in the OECD's Roundtable *Unilateral Disclosure of Information with Anticompetitive Effects* (2012), available at www.oecd.org/competition.

[151] See ch 3, 'Concerted practices', pp 115–119.

[152] OJ [1985] L 85/1.

[153] Cases C–89/85 etc *A Ahlström Osakeyhtiö v Commission* EU:C:1993:120.

[154] Commission decision of 7 July 2016, available at www.ec.europa.eu; for comment see Camesasca and Grelier '"Close Your Eyes"? Navigating the Tortuous Waters of Conscious Parallelism and Signalling in the European Union' (2016) 7 JECLAP 599; see also Rabinovici 'Public Exchange of Information after Container Shipping' (2017) 8 JECLAP 149 and Motta et al 'Recent Developments at DG Competition: 2015/2016' (2016) Review of Industrial Organization 585, two articles by DG COMP officials involved in the case.

[155] Decision of 7 January 2014, available at www.acm.nl.

[156] On section 5 FTC Act see the *U-Haul* case, details available at www.ftc.gov; see generally on the position in the US Page 'Signaling and Agreement in Antitrust', available at www.ssrn.com.

[157] *Aggregates, cement and ready-mixed concrete*, Final Report of 14 January 2014.

(iv) Algorithmic collusion

In the digital age algorithms and price-tracking software are a fact of daily life. The traditional cartel came about as a result of human actors meeting in smoke-filled rooms, or more recently in internet chat rooms; today it is possible that parallel prices are achieved by software rather than by direct human interaction. Software is available that monitors prices: most of us will have used a digital comparison tool of some kind, for example when looking for flights, holidays or car insurance. The transparency afforded by the digital world affords enormous benefits to consumers. At the same time, however, there are obvious dangers where undertakings use software that systematically searches for the prices of their competitors; and perhaps automatically adjusts prices in order to come into alignment with those prices. This may lead to the textbook model of perfect competition, promoted by perfect information: marginal cost and marginal revenue coincide and allocative efficiency is maximized. In this case the digital world may finally deliver the theoretical model that the bricks and mortar one never quite achieved. However, a less happy possibility—from a consumer welfare perspective—is that the software may actually be a way of policing, or even achieving, a collusive outcome. At this point interesting competition law questions arise.

- If an undertaking uses pricing software to enforce a cartel, is that unlawful?
- What if an undertaking writes software with the intention that the software will facilitate collusion?
- What if the software has 'artificial intelligence' such that it achieves a collusive outcome not intended by the user (or even the author) of the software?

These are questions that are now being considered, as a matter of urgency, by competition authorities. There is little decisional practice addressing these questions to date. There is however a growing academic literature on the topic[158], and in June 2017 the OECD held a Roundtable on *Algorithms and Collusion*[159].

In principle it is not difficult to see that, just as an undertaking is responsible for its employees[160], so too it must take personal responsibility for its price-tracking software. However it will be recalled from the discussion in chapter 3 that where one undertaking adapts intelligently to the behaviour of another this is not in itself a violation of Article 101(1); it presumably follows that the same is true of price-tracking software that aligns 'intelligently' with competitors' prices. On the other hand, price-tracking software may be deployed as a way of policing and enforcing a prior price-fixing agreement. This is a simple case: the exchange of information to support a cartel is unlawful[161], and the use of price-tracking software to achieve the same end is no different. In the UK case of *Trod Ltd: posters and frames*[162] Trod was fined £163,371 for price fixing that had been reinforced by price-tracking software. A director of Trod was disqualified from acting as a company director for five years. In the US the Department of Justice took action against David

[158] See eg Ezrachi and Stucke *Virtual Competition: The Promise and Perils of the Algorithm-Driven Economy* (Harvard University Press, 2016); Heinemann and Gebicka 'Can Computers Form Cartels? About the Need for European Institutions to Revise the Concertation Doctrine in the Information Age' (2016) 7 JECLAP 431; Mehra 'Antitrust and the Robo-Seller: Competition in the Time of Algorithms' (2016) 100 Minnesota Law Review 1323; Mehra '*US v Topkins*: Can Price Fixing be Based on Algorithms?' (2016) 7 JECLAP 470.

[159] Available at www.oecd.org/competition.

[160] Case C-542/14 *SIA 'VM Remonts' v Konkurences padome* EU:C:2016:578, paras 23–24.

[161] See 'Information exchange in support of a cartel', pp 552–553 later in chapter.

[162] CMA decision of 21 July 2016, available at www.gov.uk/cma.

Topkins who subsequently agreed to pay a fine of $20,000 for adopting pricing algorithms to implement an agreement illegally fixing the prices of posters and writing computer code to bring this about.

What is of greater interest is whether the use of software could, in itself, give rise to an unlawful agreement and/or concerted practice. In *'Eturas' UAB v Lietuvos Respublikos konkurencijos taryba*[163] the Court of Justice received an Article 267 reference from the Lithuanian Supreme Administrative Court. Eturas had developed software which it supplied to many travel agents in Lithuania; the software was used by customers booking holidays online. Eturas had suggested to the travel agents, in messages sent to the mailboxes, that it would be possible to set the software in such a way that travel agents would not pass on more than 3% of their commission to their customers; it would be possible to override this 'default' position, but otherwise travel agents would align on this policy. The Lithuanian Competition Authority decided that there was a concerted practice on prices between the travel agents, and that Eturas was a facilitator of that concerted practice. The Court of Justice provided guidance to the Supreme Court on the circumstances in which a concerted practice might be held to arise and, when the case returned to the Supreme Court, it confirmed that 29 travel agencies were guilty of collusion and that Eturas was a facilitator; the appeals of several other agencies were successful[164].

Cases on concerted practices are highly fact-specific: in a case such as *Eturas* what is important is to know whether the travel agents had read the messages in their mailboxes and how much prior discussion there had been about the software before it was made available. The Lithuanian Supreme Court's judgment is available only in Lithuanian, but it appears to have examined the evidence in great detail, and to have categorised the travel agents according to their state of knowledge. The importance of the case is that it was the use of software, and knowledge of what it could do, that led to the finding of a concerted practice. The wise course for the travel agents would have been to 'publicly distance' themselves from any possible collusion by telling Eturas that they did not wish to participate in coordination of discounts and by asking Eturas to refrain from sending further messages about commissions[165].

(v) Horizontal price fixing in conjunction with other infringements of Article 101(1)

In many cases undertakings have been found guilty of price fixing in conjunction with other types of horizontal collusion. In *Polypropylene*[166] the Commission found price fixing and market sharing; in *Belgian roofing felt*[167] the parties were found guilty of price fixing, establishing production quotas and taking collective action to prevent imports into Belgium; in *Italian flat glass*[168] the Commission condemned firms for the apportionment of quotas and agreements to exchange products as well as for fixing prices. In *Pre-insulated pipes*[169] the Commission identified infringements of virtually every kind, including market sharing, systematic price fixing, collective tendering, exchanging sensitive sales information and attempts to eliminate the only substantial non-member of the

[163] Case C-74/14 EU:C:2016:42. [164] Available at www.lvat.lt.

[165] Note however that the Court of Justice did *not* require that any public distancing should be from the other travel agents, but only from Eturas: Case C-74/14 EU:C:2016:42, paras 47 and 48; see further 'Public distancing from a cartel', pp 528–529 earlier in chapter.

[166] OJ [1986] L 230/1.

[167] OJ [1986] L 232/15, upheld on appeal Case 246/86 *Belasco v Commission* EU:C:1989:301.

[168] OJ [1989] L 33/44.

[169] OJ [1999] L 24/1, substantially upheld on appeal Cases T-9/99 etc *HFB Holding v Commission* EU:T:2002:70.

cartel. As Karel Van Miert, a former Commissioner for Competition, said: 'it is difficult to imagine a worse cartel'[170]. In *Plasterboard*[171] the Commission found market sharing combined with the exchange of information on future prices and sales volumes; the decision on this point was affirmed by the General Court[172]. In *Industrial bags*[173] the Commission imposed fines of €290.71 million on 16 firms for agreeing on prices and sales quotas by geographical area, sharing the orders of large customers, organised collusive bidding and the exchange of information on sales volumes. In *Candle waxes* the Commission condemned the division of markets and exchange of information by certain firms to support the fixing of prices in that industry[174]. In *Cathode ray tubes*[175] the Commission found the parties guilty of price fixing; of dividing markets; of allocating customers; and of exchanging commercially sensitive information.

(vi) **Buyers' cartels**

Buyers' cartels may be caught by Article 101(1). In *Spanish raw tobacco*[176] and *Italian raw tobacco*[177] the Commission found that tobacco processors had colluded on the prices and other trading conditions that they would offer to tobacco growers and other intermediaries; on the allocation of suppliers and quantities; on the exchange of information in order to coordinate their purchasing behaviour; and on the coordination of bids for public auctions. The Commission considered that the buyers' cartels had an anti-competitive object[178], even though an agreement to pay *lower* prices than might have been paid in the absence of the agreement might have been expected to lead to lower prices for consumers. It is not necessary that consumers be deprived of price competition for there to be an infringement by object[179]. In the Commission's view an agreement on purchasing eliminates the autonomy of strategic decision-making and competitive conduct, preventing the undertakings concerned from competing on the merits and enhancing their position vis-à-vis less efficient firms[180]. In some cases sellers and buyers are both found guilty of cartel activity[181].

In *Scrap lead-acid batteries*[182] the Commission imposed fines of €68 million on recycling companies that purchased automotive batteries for recycling from scrap dealers. The recycling companies were guilty of agreeing the *maximum* prices that they would

[170] Commission Press Release IP/98/917, 21 October 1998. [171] OJ [2005] L 166/8.

[172] Case T-53/03 *BPB v Commission* EU:T:2008:254.

[173] Commission decision of 30 November 2005.

[174] Commission decision of 1 October 2008, paras 2, 276 and 328(2), substantially upheld on appeal Cases T-540/08 etc *Esso ea v Commission* EU:T:2014:630.

[175] Commission decision of 5 December 2012, substantially upheld on appeal Cases T-104/13 etc *Toshiba Corp v Commission* EU:T:2015:610, upheld on further appeal Cases C-623/15 P etc EU:C:2017:21.

[176] OJ [2007] L 102/14, substantially upheld on appeal Case T-24/05 *Alliance One International v Commission* EU:T:2010:453 and on further appeal Case C-628/10 P EU:C:2012:479; Case T-29/05 *Deltafina v Commission* EU:T:2010:355, upheld on further appeal Cases C-537/10 P etc EU:C:2011:475; Case T-37/05 *World Wide Tobacco España v Commission* EU:T:2011:76, upheld on further appeal Case C-2401/11 P EU:C:2012:269.

[177] OJ [2006] L 353/45, upheld on appeal Case T-12/06 *Deltafina v Commission* EU:T:2011:441, and on further appeal Case C-578/11 P EU:C:2014:1742.

[178] See ch 3, 'The "object or effect" of preventing, restricting or distorting competition', pp 119ff on the 'object or effect' distinction in Article 101(1).

[179] Case C-8/08 *T-Mobile* EU:C:2009:343, para 39. [180] See *Italian raw tobacco*, para 285.

[181] See eg *Dutch Bitumen*, Commission decision of 13 September 2006 upheld on appeal Case T-357/06 *Koninklijke Wegenbouw Stevin v Commission* EU:T:2012:488, paras 110–115, and on further appeal Case C-586/12 P EU:C:2013:863.

[182] Commission decision of 8 February 2017, on appeal Case T-222/17 *Recyclex v Commission*, not yet decided.

pay for scrap batteries, exchanging price information and for agreeing on the volumes that they would buy. In her statement at the time of the decision Commissioner Vestager said that the cartel meant that prices were set by collusion with the result that there was no competition on the merits[183].

(vii) Joint selling agencies

The Commission considers that joint selling is likely to have the object of restricting competition since it coordinates the pricing policy of competitors[184]. There have been several examples of the Commission finding that joint selling agencies infringed Article 101(1)[185]. Joint selling by sporting associations such as UEFA (a European association of national football associations) may infringe Article 101(1): the Commission will consider both the horizontal effects of joint selling, for example in so far as it prevents the individual sale of broadcasting rights by particular football clubs, as well as any vertical foreclosure effects[186]. In some cases, however, the Commission found the conditions of Article 101(3) were fulfilled[187].

(B) Article 101(3)

The Commission has stated that price-fixing agreements are unlikely to satisfy Article 101(3)[188]. This attitude is manifested in Regulation 1217/2010[189] on research and development agreements and Regulation 1218/2010[190] on specialisation agreements: neither block exemption is available to agreements containing obvious restrictions of competition, such as the fixing of prices, the limitation of output or the allocation of markets or customers. It should be recalled, however, that, as a matter of law, it is always open to the parties to an agreement to argue that the criteria of Article 101(3) are satisfied[191]. On a few occasions the Commission has permitted arrangements that could limit price competition. For example in *Uniform eurocheques*[192] the Commission considered that Article 101(3)

[183] Statement/17/247 of 8 February 2017; note that the Commission calculated the fine by reference to the cartelists' purchases of scrap batteries, but added 10% since that turnover was reduced by the cartel behaviour.

[184] Commission's *Guidelines on Horizontal Cooperation Agreements* OJ [2011] C 11/1, para 234; note, in the specific context of agricultural products to which special rules apply, the Commission's *Guidelines on the application of the specific rules set out in Articles 169, 170 and 171 of the CMO Regulation for the olive oil, beef and veal and arable crops sectors* OJ [2015] C 431/1.

[185] See eg *Astra* OJ [1993] L 20/23; *HOV SVZ/MCN* OJ [1994] L 104/34, upheld on appeal Case T-229/94 *Deutsche Bahn AG v Commission* EU:T:1997:155, and on further appeal Case C-436/97 P EU:C:1999:205; see also the Commission's *Guidelines on Horizontal Cooperation Agreements* OJ [2011] C 11/1, paras 234–235 and 246.

[186] *Joint selling of the media rights of the UEFA Champions League on an exclusive basis* OJ [2002] C 196/3; see also Commission Press Release IP/03/1105, 24 July 2003 on the application of Article 101(3) to UEFA's sale of the media rights to the Champions League.

[187] See eg *Floral* OJ [1980] L 39/51; *UIP* OJ [1989] L 226/25; *Cekanan* OJ [1990] L 299/64; *Ansac* OJ [1991] L 152/54; on horizontal cooperation agreements generally see ch 15.

[188] See eg Commission's *Guidelines on the application of Article [101(3)]* OJ [2004] C 101/97, paras 46 and 79 and *Guidelines on Horizontal Cooperation Agreements* OJ [2011] C 11/1, para 246.

[189] OJ [2010] L 335/36; on this Regulation see ch 15, 'The block exemption for research and development agreements: Regulation 1217/2010', pp 607–611.

[190] OJ [2010] L 335/43; on this Regulation see ch 15, 'The block exemption for specialisation agreements: Regulation 1218/2010', pp 613–615.

[191] Case T-17/93 *Matra Hachette v Commission* EU:T:1994:89, para 85; see ch 4, 'Any type of agreement can be defended under Article 101(3)', pp 159–161.

[192] OJ [1985] L 35/43.

applied to an agreement whereby commissions for the cashing of Eurocheques were fixed: this meant that consumers using such cheques knew that they would be charged a common amount throughout the EU. In *Insurance intermediaries*[193] the Commission indicated its intention to authorise agreements between non-life insurers to fix maximum discounts[194].

The Commission's decision in *REIMS II*[195], which authorised an agreement fixing the level of cross-border mail charges between 17 postal operators, was discussed in chapter 4[196]. In *Visa International—Multilateral Interchange Fee*[197] the Commission stated that it is not the case that an agreement concerning prices is always to be classified as a restriction by object or incapable of satisfying Article 101(3)[198]: in that decision it authorised the multilateral interchange fee ('MIF') agreed upon between 'acquiring' and 'issuing' banks within the Visa system until the end of 2007. The Commission accepted commitments from Visa Europe under Article 9 of Regulation 1/2003[199] in respect of the MIFs for its debit cards[200] and credit cards[201]. In *MasterCard*[202] the Commission decided that the intra-EEA MIFs imposed in that card system had the appreciable effect of restricting competition in the acquiring market because, in the absence of that MIF, the merchant fees set by acquiring banks would have been lower. The Commission also found that MasterCard had failed to show any objective advantages that counterbalanced the disadvantages of the MIF for merchants and their customers, with the result that Article 101(3) did not apply. The Commission's decision was upheld on appeal[203], although two English courts reached different conclusions to the Commission in relation to domestic (as opposed to cross-border) MIFs for MasterCard and Visa cards, albeit on the basis of different arguments and evidence[204]. Since 9 December 2015 a Regulation has capped the level of cross-border and domestic MIFs for debit and credit cards[205].

In *AuA/LH*[206] the Commission found that a 'lasting alliance' between Austrian Airlines and Lufthansa which entailed joint pricing and market sharing[207] satisfied the criteria of Article 101(3) as the alliance would result in 'important synergistic effects and attractive connections for consumers': the Commission could foresee cost savings, improved network connection, better planning of frequencies, a higher load factor, improved organisation of sales systems and ground-handling services, potential for new sales channels such as e-ticketing and access, on Austrian Airlines's part, to a superior airmiles scheme[208]. In *Star alliance*[209] the Commission considered that a joint venture between United,

[193] OJ [1987] C 120/5.

[194] See also *Nuovo CEGAM* OJ [1984] L 99/29; *P&I Clubs* OJ [1985] L 376/2; *Associazione Bancaria Italiana* OJ [1987] L 43/51; *Tariff Structures in the Combined Transport of Goods* OJ [1993] L 73/38.

[195] OJ [1999] L 275/17; the Commission extended the application of Article 101(3) to this agreement until 2006: OJ [2004] L 56/76.

[196] See ch 4, 'Any type of agreement can be defended under Article 101(3)', pp 159–160.

[197] OJ [2002] L 318/17. [198] Ibid, para 79.

[199] See ch 7, 'Article 9: commitments', pp 264–269 on Article 9 of Regulation 1/2003.

[200] Commission decision of 8 December 2010. [201] Commission decision of 26 February 2014.

[202] Commission decision of 19 December 2007.

[203] Case T-111/08 *MasterCard v Commission* EU:T:2012:260, upheld on further appeal Case C-382/12 P *MasterCard v Commission* EU:C:2014:2201.

[204] See *Asda Stores Ltd v MasterCard Inc* [2017] EWHC 93 (Comm) and *Sainsbury's Supermarkets Ltd v Visa Europe Services LLC* [2017] EWHC 3047 (Comm); the orders in both cases are on appeal to the Court of Appeal, not yet decided.

[205] Regulation 2015/751 on interchange fees for card-based payment transactions, OJ [2015] L 123/1.

[206] OJ [2002] L 242/25; for legal and regulatory reasons these undertakings were unable to merge in the sense of the EUMR which is why this case was conducted under Article 101.

[207] OJ [2002] L 242/25, para 76. [208] Ibid, paras 87–88.

[209] Commission decision of 23 May 2013.

Lufthansa and Air Canada would have the object and effect of restricting competition on the Frankfurt–New York route for premium passengers. The Commission specifically noted, however, that the airlines' cooperation created some efficiencies on several related routes[210]. The case was ultimately closed on the airlines giving commitments under Article 9 of Regulation 1/2003[211].

In *IFPI 'Simulcasting'*[212] the Commission concluded that an agreement that facilitated the grant of international licences of copyright to 'simulcast' music on the internet involved price restrictions[213] but that it benefited from Article 101(3) because it created efficiencies in the field of collective management of copyright and neighbouring rights[214].

(C) **Collective dominance**

The possible application of Article 102 to parallel pricing is considered in chapter 14[215].

5. Horizontal Market Sharing

Competition may be eliminated between independent undertakings in other ways than through direct or indirect price fixing. One way of doing so is for firms to agree to apportion particular markets between themselves. For example, three firms in the UK might agree that each will have exclusivity in a particular geographical area and that none will poach on the others' territories; a similar device is division of the market according to classes of customers, for example that one firm will supply trade customers only, another retailers and another public institutions. Geographical market-sharing agreements may be easier and more effective than price fixing from the cartel's point of view, because the expense and difficulties of fixing common prices are avoided: the agreement means that there will be no price competition anyway. Policing the agreement is also relatively simple, because the mere presence of a competitor's goods on one's own 'patch' reveals cheating. Geographical market sharing is particularly restrictive from the consumer's point of view since it diminishes choice: at least where the parties fix prices a choice of product remains and it is possible that the restriction of price competition will force the parties to compete in other ways. Market-sharing agreements in the EU context may be viewed particularly seriously because, apart from the obviously anti-competitive effects already described, they partition geographical markets and retard the process of single market integration which is a prime aim of the EU.

It is not inconceivable that in some cases market sharing might be beneficial: in other words that restrictions accepted might enhance efficiency, in particular by enabling firms to compete more effectively with large undertakings. For example, several small retailers may decide to combine to promote their own 'house-label' in order to try to match other multiple chains[216]. Individually they may be weak and unable to afford the enormous costs involved in advertising and promotion, but in combination they may be able to do so. It could be argued that each retailer should be able to claim an exclusive sales territory so that it will be encouraged to take its full part in the marketing campaign in the knowledge that it will reap the benefit in its area. The corollary is that without this incentive it will not promote the brand label so actively and enthusiastically. The argument is similar

[210] Ibid, paras 55–80.

[211] On commitment decisions under Article 9 see ch 7, 'Article 9: commitments', pp 264–269.

[212] OJ [2003] L 107/58. [213] Ibid, paras 61–80. [214] Ibid, paras 84–123.

[215] See ch 14, 'Abuse of collective dominance under Article 102', pp 591–594.

[216] See eg Commission's *Guidelines on Horizontal Cooperation Agreements* OJ [2011] C 11/1, para 252.

to that applicable to many vertical restraints[217]. The conclusion ought therefore to be that in some exceptional cases horizontal market sharing should be permitted.

(A) **Article 101(1)**

Market sharing is specifically mentioned in Article 101(1)(c), and the EU Courts consider that agreements to share markets have as their object the restriction of competition[218]. There are two obvious reasons for this. First, geographical market sharing can be achieved relatively easily in the EU context, since there are many ways of segregating national markets from one another. Until a single market is established, the factual, legal and economic disparities between national markets will continue to act as an obstacle to inter-state trade. Secondly, one of the priorities of the Commission is to take action to prevent any collusive behaviour which might inhibit the process of single market integration. It can be anticipated that horizontal market sharing will be punished severely.

(i) **Market sharing in any form is caught**

The Commission has uncovered and condemned written market-sharing agreements. In *Luxembourg Brewers*[219] there was a written agreement between five brewers, which sought to defend the Luxembourg market against imports from other Member States. The Commission considered that the agreement had as its object the restriction of competition. In *Needles*[220] the Commission imposed fines of €60 million in relation to a written product and geographic market-sharing agreement between Coats and Prym; on appeal the fines were reduced slightly since the Commission had erred in some of its assessment[221]. A market-sharing agreement may also be oral: in *Power transformers* fines totalling €67.6 million were imposed on seven producers which operated a 'gentlemen's agreement' to share the Japanese and European markets[222]. In *Gas insulated switchgear*[223] the Court of Justice upheld the General Court's judgment confirming the Commission's finding[224] that there had been, amongst other things, a 'common understanding' that Japanese undertakings would not compete for contracts for switchgear apparatus in Europe and vice versa[225]. The Court said that market sharing is a 'simple concept which may be implemented easily' and, in principle, without interaction between the participating undertakings[226].

The number of firms dividing up markets can be as few as two, as in *Soda-ash—Solvay/ICI*[227] and *EPEX Spot/Nord Pool Spot*[228], or as many as an entire industry.

[217] See ch 16, 'Vertical agreements: possible benefits to competition', pp 640–642.

[218] See Cases C-239/11 P etc *Siemens v Commission* EU:C:2013:866, para 218; see further ch 3, 'Market sharing, quotas, collective exclusive dealing', p 129.

[219] OJ [2002] L 253/21, upheld on appeal Cases T-49/02 etc *Brasserie nationale v Commission* EU:T:2005:298.

[220] Commission decision of 26 October 2004.

[221] Cases T-30/05 etc EU:T:2007:267.

[222] Commission decision of 7 October 2009, upheld on appeal Case T-519/09 *Toshiba v Commission* EU:T:2014:263 and on further appeal Case C-373/14 P EU:C:2016:26.

[223] Case C-239/11 P EU:C:2013:866, upholding the General Court's judgment in Cases T-110/07 etc *Siemens v Commission* EU:T:2011:68.

[224] Commission decision of 24 January 2007.

[225] Cases T-133/07 etc *Mitsubishi v Commission* EU:T:2011:345; see similarly *High voltage power cables*, Commission decision of 2 April 2014, on appeal Cases T-419/14 etc *The Goldman Sachs Group v Commission*, not yet decided.

[226] Cases T-133/07 etc *Mitsubishi v Commission* EU:T:2011:345, para 186.

[227] OJ [1991] L 152/1, annulled on appeal Cases T-30/91 etc *Solvay v Commission* EU:T:1995:115, upheld on further appeal Cases C-286/95 P *Commission v ICI* EU:C:2000:188. The Commission readopted its decision: OJ [2003] L 10/1, upheld on appeal Case T-58/01 *Solvay v Commission* EU:T:2009:520, annulled on further appeal for procedural reasons in Case C-110/10 P *Solvay v Commission* EU:C:2011:687.

[228] Commission decision of 5 March 2014.

In *Cement*[229] the Commission found that cement producers had agreed on the 'non-transhipment of cement to home markets', which prohibited any export of cement within Europe which could threaten neighbouring markets.

In some cases there have been elements both of vertical and horizontal market division; distributors must refrain from market division as well as producers[230].

(ii) **Market sharing in any context is caught**

The market sharing between E.ON and GDF in *Gas*[231] ostensibly arose in the legitimate context of the operation of a jointly-owned pipeline. The Commission found, however, that E.ON and GDF had agreed to refrain from selling gas transported from Russia over the pipeline into each other's home markets; each firm was fined €533 million. On appeal the General Court rejected the argument that the market-sharing agreements were 'ancillary restraints' to the proper functioning of the pipeline. The Court also held, however, that the Commission's assessment of potential competition from GDF in Germany had been incorrect; E.ON had held a lawful national monopoly from 1980 to 1998 and it had been practically impossible for GDF to enter the market during that period. The fines imposed on each firm were reduced to €320 million. In *Telefónica/Portugal Telecom*[232] the Commission imposed fines of €79 million on two undertakings for agreeing not to compete with one another in Spain and Portugal following the exit by Portugal Telecom from a Brazilian joint venture with Telefónica. The context was very different in *ING Pensii*[233], but the conclusion was the same: the Court of Justice held that agreements between 14 Romanian private pension funds to share clients had an anti-competitive object; the number of clients affected by such an agreement was irrelevant to the existence of the object restriction[234].

In *Lundbeck v Commission*[235] the General Court upheld the Commission's conclusion that a 'pay for delay' agreement 'constitutes an extreme form of market sharing'[236], since an incumbent firm pays a potential competitor in order to induce that competitor to discontinue its efforts to enter the market. That conclusion was unaffected by the context of a settlement of a patent dispute in that case.

(iii) **Market sharing in conjunction with other infringements of Article 101(1)**

Market sharing is often combined with other infringements of Article 101(1). In *Quinine*[237] the Court of Justice upheld the Commission's decision[238] to fine the members of the quinine cartel who had indulged in price fixing, the allocation of quotas and market division, and there have been many other similar cases since. The infringements in the

[229] OJ [1994] L 343/1, para 45; see similarly *Seamless Steel Tubes* OJ [2003] L 14/1, on appeal Cases T-67/00 etc *JFE Engineering v Commission* EU:T:2004:221, on further appeal Cases C-403 and 405/04 P *Sumitomo Metal Industries v Commission* EU:C:2007:52.

[230] See eg Cases 100–103/80 *Musique Diffusion Française SA v Commission* EU:C:1983:158 in which the Court of Justice upheld the Commission's decision (OJ [1980] L 60/21) that distributors had engaged in concerted practices *amongst themselves* to isolate the French market.

[231] Commission decision of 8 July 2009, substantially upheld on appeal Cases T-360/09 etc *E.ON Ruhrgas v Commission* EU:T:2012:332.

[232] Commission decision of 23 January 2013, upheld on appeal Cases T-216/13 etc *Telefónica v Commission* EU:T:2016:369, and on further appeal Case C-487/16 P *Telefónica v Commission* EU:C:2017:961.

[233] Case C-174/14 EU:C:2015:484, para 56.

[234] Ibid, para 56.

[235] Cases T-472/13 etc EU:T:2016:449, on further appeal Cases C-591/16 P etc *Lundbeck v Commission*, not yet decided.

[236] Cases T-472/13 etc EU:T:2016:449, para 435.

[237] Case 41/69 *ACF Chemiefarma NV v Commission* EU:C:1970:71.

[238] JO [1969] L 192/5.

Pre-insulated pipes[239] decision were wide-ranging. The Commission accused the parties of dividing national markets and, ultimately, the whole European market amongst themselves; of price fixing; and of taking measures to hinder the one substantial competitor outside the cartel and to drive it out of the market. The fines amounted to €92 million. In *Prestressing steel*[240] the Commission found evidence of more than 550 cartel meetings over a period of 18 years, during which 17 prestressing steel producers had operated price-fixing and market-sharing agreements.

Article 101(1) has also been applied to horizontal agreements involving customer restrictions[241].

(B) **Article 101(3)**

A horizontal geographical market-sharing agreement is unlikely to satisfy the criteria of Article 101(3), in view of the single market imperative. In exceptional circumstances, however, Article 101(3) may be applicable to market sharing that is indispensable for improvements in efficiency[242].

6. **Quotas and Other Restrictions on Production**

A further way in which a cartel might be able to earn supra-competitive profits is by agreeing to restrict its members' output. If output is reduced, price will rise; the oil cartel operated by OPEC does not fix prices as such, but instead determines how much oil each member country will export. Horizontal agreements to limit production need to be carefully monitored, because over-production by some members of the cartel would result in the market price falling, unless the scheme is run in conjunction with a price-fixing system, as often happens. In the absence of price fixing, the cartel members will often agree on a quota system whereby they will each supply a specified proportion of the entire industry output within any given period. As in the case of price fixing there will be costs involved in negotiating these quotas, because some firms will be larger or more efficient or expanding more rapidly than others so that there may have to be hard and protracted bargaining. The quotas having been fixed, the cartel will need a mechanism to prevent cheating. This may be done, for example, by requiring detailed information about production and sales to be supplied to a trade association or 'cartel consultancy'. The cartel may use a system whereby those that exceed their allocated quotas have to make compensating payments to those who, as a necessary corollary, fail to dispose of theirs. Complicated rules may have to be settled on how such payments are to be made. A firm which 'over-produces' will have to sell its products on the market at a higher price than it

[239] OJ [1999] L 24/1, substantially upheld on appeal Cases T-9/99 etc *HFB Holding v Commission* EU:T:2002:70.

[240] Commission decision of 30 June 2010; there have been innumerable appeals in this case: they were unsuccessful but for Case T-389/10 *SLM v Commission* EU:T:2015:513 (reduction in the fine) and Case T-418/10 *voestalpine Austria Draht v Commission* EU:T:2015:516 (reduced participation in the cartel); the General Court's judgments were upheld on further appeal in Cases C-490/15 P etc *Ori Martin SA v Commission* EU:C:2016:678.

[241] See eg *Re William Prym-Werke and Beka Agreement* OJ [1973] L 296/24 where the Commission required the deletion of a customer restriction clause; *Atka Al S v BP Kemi A/S* OJ [1979] L 286/32 where BP was to supply customers with consumption of at least 100,000 gallons; *Belgian roofing felt* OJ [1986] L 232/15.

[242] See eg *Transocean Marine Paint Association* JO [1967] L 163/10.

would wish if it is to make a profit and make a payment to the other cartel members; the loss to consumers of such schemes is clear.

Some agreements which involve restrictions of production may be beneficial: specialisation agreements, joint production, research and development agreements, restructuring cartels and standardisation agreements may in some circumstances be considered desirable. This chapter is concerned with restrictions on production which limit output without producing any compensating benefits; agreements involving restrictions of production which may be objectively necessary for some legitimate objective will be discussed in chapter 15.

(A) **Article 101(1)**

Article 101(1)(b) specifically applies to agreements to 'limit or control production, markets, technical development, or investment' and has been applied to agreements to limit production on many occasions. Straightforward quota systems have often been condemned[243].

In *Peroxygen products*[244] the Commission found that, as well as sharing markets geographically, members of the cartel had entered into a series of detailed national agreements dividing markets in agreed percentages. In *MELDOC*[245] a quota and compensation scheme in the dairy sector in the Netherlands was held to infringe Article 101, and the Commission imposed fines totalling €6,565,000. An exacerbating fact in this decision was the fact that the Dutch milk producers also agreed to a coordinated response to the threat posed to their market position by imports from other Member States. An agreement not to expand production without the approval of rival firms infringes Article 101(1)[246] and the Commission will not easily be persuaded that a quota scheme will bring about beneficial specialisation[247]. It is not permissible to establish a joint venture to apportion orders between competitors[248], nor will the Commission allow joint production that simply limits competition without producing any compensating benefits[249]. Not infrequently quota agreements confer on particular undertakings exclusive or priority rights in supplying their own domestic markets: they will certainly not be tolerated[250].

An interesting example of a quota scheme condemned by the Commission is *Associated Lead Manufacturers Ltd (White Lead)*[251]. Firms producing white lead in the UK, Germany and the Netherlands agreed that each would supply one-third of the white lead to be exported to non-EU countries. A central office was established which gathered information from them on their deliveries of white lead. The producers supplied this office with details of *all* deliveries, including exports to other EU countries. The Commission held that in practice the quota scheme related to all exports, that is to say to intra-EU as well as extra-EU trade, and that it clearly amounted to an attempt to limit and control markets within the terms of Article 101(1)(b). Furthermore the Commission held that it was

243 See eg *Zinc Producer Group* OJ [1984] L 220/27; *Benelux Flat Glass* OJ [1984] L 212/13; also the various cement cases decided by the Commission involving quota arrangements: see *Re Cementregeling voor Nederland* JO [1972] L 303/7; *Re Cimbel* JO [1972] L 303/24; *Re Nederlandse Cement-Handelmaatshappij NV* JO [1972] L 22/16; see also *Belgian roofing felt* OJ [1986] L 232/15; *Welded Steel Mesh* OJ [1989] L 260/1; *Italian flat glass* OJ [1989] L 33/44, annulled on appeal for lack of evidence Cases T-68/89 etc *Società Italiana Vetro SpA v Commission* EU:T:1992:38.

244 OJ [1985] L 35/1.

245 OJ [1986] L 348/50.

246 *Re Cimbel* JO [1972] L 303/24.

247 *Re Italian cast glass* OJ [1980] L 383/19.

248 *Air Forge* Commission's XIIth *Report on Competition Policy* (1982), point 85.

249 *Re WANO Schwarzpulver GmbH* OJ [1978] L 322/26.

250 Case 41/69 *ACF Chemiefarma NV v Commission* EU:C:1970:71.

251 OJ [1979] L 21/16.

irrelevant that the quotas were not always meticulously observed: an agreement did not cease to be anti-competitive because it was temporarily or even repeatedly circumvented by one of the parties to it[252].

In *Compagnie Royale Asturienne des Mines SA and Rheinzink GmbH v Commission*[253] the Court of Justice held that it was an infringement of Article 101(1) for competitors to supply products to each other on a continuing basis. Whereas this might be acceptable to deal with certain emergencies, it was not permissible for competitors to enter into agreements of indeterminate length and for considerable quantities. The effect of doing so was to institutionalise mutual aid in lieu of competition, producing conditions on the market analogous to those brought about by quota arrangements. In *Soda-ash—Solvay/CFK*[254] the Commission condemned an agreement whereby Solvay agreed to allow CFK a guaranteed minimum sales tonnage and to purchase from it any shortfall in order to compensate it. The first fine for a substantive infringement of Article 101 in the maritime transport sector was imposed in *French-West African shipowners' committees*[255] upon shipowners which had agreed to a cargo-sharing system in respect of traffic between France and various West African countries.

An elaborate 'price before tonnage scheme' was found to be anti-competitive by the Commission in *Cartonboard*[256] which involved the 'freezing' of market shares, the constant monitoring and analysis of them, and the coordination of 'machine downtime' in an effort to sustain prices and control supply. In *Europe Asia trades agreement*[257] the Commission concluded that an agreement for 'capacity non-utilisation' coupled with the exchange of information in relation to maritime transport infringed Article 101(1); in its view the agreement artificially limited liner shipping capacity, thereby reducing price competition[258].

Quotas are a feature of numerous cartels[259]. In *Zinc phosphate*[260] the Commission considered that the 'cornerstone' of the cartel was the allocation of sales quotas, although it also found that there was an agreement on the fixing of 'bottom' or recommended prices and some allocation of customers[261]. In *Gas insulated switchgear*[262] the Commission found that not only were the members of the cartel dividing the global market along geographical lines, but that they had also agreed worldwide quotas; and that the agreed European quota had itself been divided between the European undertakings in the cartel[263]. In *Heat stabilisers* the Commission found agreements to establish quotas, to fix prices and to exchange information that had been supervised by a consultancy firm[264]. In *Prestressing steel*[265] the Commission found that the producers

[252] Similarly see *Re Cast Iron and Steel Rolls* OJ [1983] L 317/1 where the Commission fined various French undertakings which operated a quota scheme in respect of deliveries to the Saarland in Germany.

[253] Cases 29 and 30/83 EU:C:1984:130. [254] OJ [1991] L 152/16. [255] OJ [1992] L 134/1.

[256] OJ [1994] L 243/1, paras 129–132, on appeal Cases T-311/94 etc *BPB de Eendracht v Commission* EU:T:1998:93.

[257] OJ [1999] L 193/23. [258] Ibid, paras 148–156.

[259] In addition to the cases mentioned in the text, see eg *Spanish bitumen*, Commission decision of 4 October 2007, para 373, substantially upheld on appeal Cases T-462/07 *Galp Energia España v Commission* EU:T:2013:459, on further appeal Case C-603/13 P EU:C:2016:38; *Animal Feed Phosphates*, Commission decision of 20 July 2010, paras 154–155.

[260] OJ [2003] L 153/1. [261] Ibid, paras 64–72.

[262] Commission decision of 24 January 2007, substantially upheld on appeal Case T-117/07 *Areva v Commission* EU:T:2011:69, partially annulled on further appeal Case C-247/11 P EU:C:2014:257.

[263] Commission decision of 24 January 2007, paras 116–120.

[264] Commission decision of 11 November 2009, paras 380–387, upheld on appeal Case T-46/10 *Faci SpA v Commission* EU:T:2014:138, and on further appeal Case C-291/14 P EU:C:2015:398.

[265] Commission decision of 30 June 2010.

had pursued the object of restricting competition through a coordination of their pricing policy, quotas and allocation of customers. The Commission stated that legislation imposing production quotas for wire rod, a raw material, did not justify privately agreed quotas for prestressing steel[266].

(B) **Article 101(3)**

It is unlikely that quotas and other restrictions on production would satisfy Article 101(3), although agreements on capacity and production volume may be permitted when indispensable to efficiencies brought about by a specialisation agreement[267].

7. Collusive Tendering

Collusive tendering between actual or potential competitors[268] is a practice whereby firms agree amongst themselves to collaborate over their response to invitations to tender. It is particularly likely to be encountered in the engineering and construction industries where firms compete for very large contracts; often the tenderee will have a powerful bargaining position and the contractors feel the need to concert their bargaining power. From a contractor's point of view collusion over tendering has other benefits apart from the fact that it can lead to higher prices: it may mean that fewer contractors actually bother to price any particular deal (tendering itself can be a costly business) so that overheads are kept lower; it may mean that a contractor can make a tender which it knows will not be accepted (because it has been agreed that another firm will tender at a lower price) and yet which indicates that it is still interested in doing business, so that it will not be crossed off the tenderee's list; and it may mean that a contractor can retain the business of its established, favoured customers without worrying that they will be poached by its competitors.

The OECD has held a number of Roundtables on issues related to collusive tendering and public procurement, and on the related issue of corruption. Its key findings are contained in a book on *Competition and Procurement*[269].

(A) **Collusive tendering takes many forms**

At its simplest, the firms invited to tender agree to quote identical prices, the hope being that in the end each will receive its fair share of orders. Level tendering, however, is extremely suspicious and is likely to attract the attention of the competition authorities, so that more subtle arrangements are normally made. The more complicated these are, the greater will be the cost to the tenderers themselves. One system is to notify intended quotes to each other, or more likely to a central secretariat, which will then cost the order and eliminate those quotes that it considers would result in a loss to some or all of the association's members. Another system is to rotate orders, in which case the firm whose turn it is to receive an order will ensure that its quote is lower than everyone else's. Again it may be that orders are allocated by a trade association that will advise each member how it should proceed.

[266] Ibid, para 1032.

[267] See the Commission's *Guidelines on Horizontal Cooperation Agreements* OJ [2011] C 11/1, paras 183–186; on specialisation agreements, see ch 15, 'The block exemption for specialisation agreements: Regulation 1218/2010', pp 613–615.

[268] See ch 3, 'Actual and potential competition', p 135.

[269] OECD, 2011, available at www.oecd.org.

(B) **Article 101(1)**

There is no doubt that collusive tendering is caught by Article 101(1)[270]. The Commission condemned the practice in *Sugar*[271]. In *Building and construction industry in the Netherlands*[272] the Commission imposed a fine of €22.5 million on the SPO, an association of trade associations, for operating a system whereby construction firms pre-selected the undertaking 'entitled' to win a particular contract. The fact that the Dutch Government approved of the system did not provide a defence under Article 101(1): rather it led to the Commission threatening proceedings against the Netherlands under Article 258 TFEU for having encouraged this anti-competitive behaviour. In *Pre-insulated pipes*[273] the Commission concluded that the allocation of contracts on the basis of 'respect for existing "traditional" customer relationships', as well as various measures to support the bid-rigging, infringed Article 101(1)[274].

Collusive tendering has been a noticeable feature of cartel cases in recent years. Firms may go to great lengths to rig every aspect of the competitive process. For example in *Elevators and escalators*[275] the Commission imposed fines of €992 million on a series of undertakings for bid-rigging, price fixing, allocation of projects, market sharing and the exchange of information in relation to the installation and maintenance of lifts and escalators in Belgium, Germany, Luxembourg and the Netherlands[276]. The Commission said that the undertakings concerned informed each other of calls for tender and coordinated their bids according to pre-agreed cartel quotas. In *Car glass*[277] the Commission imposed fines of €1.3 billion—at the time the largest set of fines for one decision in the history of Article 101. The Commission objected to, amongst other illicit practices, cover pricing: that is to say bids that gave the pretence of competition, but that were deliberately set at a higher price than that of the member of the cartel whose turn it was to be awarded a contract[278]. The EU Courts have been equally opposed to such practices. In *International removal services*[279] the Court of Justice held that agreements on cover quotes had as their object the restriction of competition[280] and that they were among the most serious restrictions of competition[281]. The Commission condemned several practices designed to rig tenders in *High voltage power cables*[282], and imposed a substantial fine. Several of the Commission's infringement decisions in relation to car parts featured collusive tendering[283].

[270] Note that in some countries there is a specific law against collusive tendering, eg section 298 of the Criminal Code in Germany and section 168b of the Criminal Code in Austria; in the UK collusive tendering may be illegal under the criminal cartel offence; see ch 10, 'The cartel offence', pp 437–446.

[271] OJ [1973] L 140/17.

[272] OJ [1992] L 92/1, upheld on appeal Case T-29/92 *SPO v Commission* EU:T:1995:34.

[273] OJ [1999] L 24/1, substantially upheld on appeal Cases T-9/99 etc *HFB Holding v Commission* EU:T:2002:70.

[274] OJ [1999] L 24/1, para 147.

[275] Commission decision of 21 February 2007, substantially upheld on appeal Cases T-141/07 etc *General Technic-Otis v Commission* EU:T:2011:363, upheld on further appeal Cases C-493/11 P etc EU:C:2012:355.

[276] Note that fines of €75.4 million have also been imposed by the Austrian Competition Authority in this sector: the press release can be found at www.bwb.gv.at.

[277] Commission decision of 12 November 2008, substantially upheld on appeal but some reduction of fines Cases T-56/09 etc *Saint-Gobain Glass France v Commission* EU:T:2014:160.

[278] Commission decision of 12 November 2008, para 103.

[279] Commission decision of 11 March 2008, as amended by decision of 24 July 2009, para 366.

[280] Case C-440/11 P *Commission v Stichting Administratiekantoor Portielje* EU:C:2013:514, para 95.

[281] Ibid, para 111.

[282] Commission decision of 2 April 2014 on appeal Cases T-419/14 etc *Goldman Sachs Group v Commission*, not yet decided.

[283] *Wire harnesses*, Commission decision of 10 July 2013; *Parking heaters*, Commission decision of 17 June 2015; *Alternators and starters*, Commission decision of 27 January 2016.

In *SIA 'VM Remonts' v Konkurences padome*[284] the Court of Justice established that an undertaking, X, could be liable for collusive tendering where a third party service provider, Y, brought about the infringement by exchanging commercially sensitive information with competitors of X if X could reasonably have foreseen that Y would share the information and if X was prepared to accept the risk that this entailed[285].

In *Ski Taxi SA v Staten v/Konkurransetilsynet*[286] the Norwegian Competition Authority fined two taxi companies for submitting a joint bid in response to an invitation to tender for the provision of taxi services from a hospital in Oslo[287]. The Authority considered that the taxi companies were actual or at least potential competitors[288], and that the joint bid had the object of restricting competition. On appeal the Supreme Court of Norway asked the EFTA Court for an 'advisory opinion' on the application of the EEA equivalent to Article 101 TFEU to joint bidding. Specifically the Norwegian Court wished to know whether joint bidding could be restrictive of competition by object. The EFTA Court held that in principle joint bidding could be restrictive by object[289], and added that the fact that the joint character of the bid was known to the hospital did not prevent it from being restrictive by object[290]. When the case returned to the Norwegian Supreme Court it held on the facts of the case that the joint bid did indeed restrict by object with the result that the Norwegian Competition Authority's decision was correct[291]. The Supreme Court said that if the parties wished to argue that joint bidding could lead to efficiency gains, they should do so under the EEA equivalent of Article 101(3) TFEU[292]; the Court rejected the argument that joint bidding was an ancillary restraint[293]. The case demonstrates that parties to joint bidding should proceed with caution[294].

(C) **Article 101(3)**

In *Building and construction industry in the Netherlands* the Commission rejected arguments in favour of the application of Article 101(3) to collusive tendering[295].

8. **Agreements Relating to Terms and Conditions**

We have seen earlier that apart from agreements directly fixing prices, supra-competitive profits can also be earned in other ways, for example by limiting production, fixing quotas and dividing markets geographically. Similarly restrictive agreements which limit competition in the terms and conditions offered to customers can have this effect. An agreement not to offer discounts is in effect a price restriction, as would be an agreement not to offer credit; it may well exist to buttress a price-fixing agreement. In some market conditions it might be that non-price competition is particularly significant because of

[284] Case C-542/14 EU:C:2016:578. [285] Ibid, para 31.

[286] Case E-3/16, judgment of 22 December 2016, available at www.eftacourt.int.

[287] Decision of 4 July 2011.

[288] It was disputed during the course of the proceedings whether the taxi companies were actual or potential competitors, but by the time of the request to the EFTA Court it had been established that they were.

[289] Case E-3/16, paras 88–102. [290] Ibid, paras 105–108.

[291] Case no 2015/203, judgment of 22 June 2017, available (in English) at www.domstol.no.

[292] Ibid, para 52. [293] Ibid, para 56–58.

[294] See eg Thomas 'Two Bids or not to Bid? An Exploration of the Legality of Joint Bidding and Subcontracting Under EU Competition Law' (2015) 6 JECLAP 629 and Ritter 'Joint Tendering under EU Competition Law' (2017), available at www.ssrn.com.

[295] OJ [1992] L 92/1, paras 115–131.

the limited opportunities that exist for price cutting; for example, in an oligopolistic market one oligopolist might be able to attract custom because it can offer a better after-sales service or guarantees or a free delivery service[296].

Although competition in terms and conditions is an important part of the competitive process, it is also true to say that in some circumstances standardisation of terms and conditions can be beneficial. This might have the effect of enhancing price transparency: that is to say a customer might be able more easily to compare the 'real' cost of goods or services on offer if he or she does not have to make some (possibly intuitive) allowances for the disparity in two sets of terms and conditions on offer. Again a trade association may have the knowledge and expertise (and legal resources) to draft appropriate standard form contracts which suit the needs of individual members whereas, acting individually, they would be unable to negotiate and conclude a set of terms and conditions suitable for their purpose. This standard-setting function is usually tolerated under competition law, provided it does not become a medium for the restriction of competition. Industry-based codes of practice may fall within the ambit of competition legislation, although they may be desirable and may be encouraged or even required by consumer legislation[297].

(A) **Article 101(1)**

Article 101 is capable of catching agreements which limit competition on terms and conditions, and to the extent that this is effected through the medium of trade associations the application of that Article to 'decisions by associations of undertakings' is apposite. The Commission has condemned agreements only to supply on prescribed general conditions of sale[298] and it has also objected to them where they formed part of wider reciprocal exclusive dealing arrangements[299]. In *Vimpoltu*[300] the Commission condemned an agreement on terms and conditions that limited important 'secondary aspects of competition'. In *Publishers Association: Net Book Agreements*[301] agreements to impose on resellers standard conditions of sale and measures taken to implement this were condemned, as they deprived retailers of the ability to deviate from fixed retail prices. In *TACA*[302] the Commission concluded that an agreement that prohibited members of a liner conference from entering into individual service contracts at rates negotiated between a shipper and an individual line infringed Article 101(1); under the agreement members were permitted to offer standard service contracts only on the terms negotiated by the TACA secretariat, which constituted a serious fetter on their ability to compete with one another. In *Marine hoses*[303] the parties agreed sales conditions as part of a plan to control rival bids for marine hoses tenders. In *Freight forwarders*[304] the Commission took objection to 14 undertakings fixing both the prices and trading conditions of international air freight forwarding.

[296] On oligopoly generally see ch 14, 'The theory of oligopolistic interdependence', pp 571–578.

[297] See eg s 8 of the Enterprise Act 2002.

[298] See *European Glass Manufacturers* OJ [1974] L 160/1; see similarly *FEDETAB* OJ [1978] L 224/29.

[299] See eg *Donck v Central Bureau voor de Rijwielhandel* OJ [1978] L 20/18.

[300] OJ [1983] L 200/44.

[301] OJ [1989] L 22/12.

[302] OJ [1999] L 95/1, paras 379–380, upheld on this point on appeal Cases T-191/98 etc *Atlantic Container Line AB v Commission* EU:T:2003:245; the Commission subsequently adopted a revised version of *TACA* OJ [2003] L 26/53.

[303] Commission decision of 28 November 2009, decision annulled in part and fines reduced on appeal Cases T-146/09 etc *Parker ITR and Parker Hannifin v Commission* EU:T:2013:258, judgment set aside, on further appeal Case C-434/13 P EU:C:2014:2456; the case was referred back to the General Court for reassessment, which subsequently upheld the decision but reduced the fines, Case T-146/09 RENV EU:T:2016:411.

[304] Commission decision of 28 March 2012, upheld on appeal Cases T-251/12 etc *EGL v Commission* EU:T:2016:114 and on further appeal Cases C-263/16 P etc *Schenker v Commission* EU:C:2018:58.

(B) Article 101(3)

The Commission has recognised the advantages of accessible and non-binding standard terms and conditions for the sale of consumer goods or services and has indicated that their use will not infringe Article 101(1) unless their application in practice seriously limits customer choice[305]. Also the Commission applied Article 101(3) in the fire insurance sector to an agreement whereby insurance companies would be likely (though not obliged) to adopt the standard terms and conditions of a trade association[306].

9. Exchanges of Information

(A) Introduction

An important competition law issue is whether undertakings run the risk of infringing Article 101 when they exchange information with one another[307]. This is an issue that the Commission has given consideration to over many years, from as early as 1968 in its *Notice on Cooperation Agreements*[308] and in numerous decisions from the 1970s onwards. In 2010 the Commission published helpful guidance on exchanges of information in its *Guidelines on the applicability of Article 101 [TFEU] to horizontal co-operation agreements* (*'Guidelines on Horizontal Cooperation Agreements'* or 'the *Guidelines*')[309]. The *Guidelines* draw substantially on the case law of the EU Courts[310], in particular *John Deere v Commission*[311], *Asnef-Equifax*[312] and *T-Mobile*[313]. Reference will be made to the *Guidelines on Horizontal Cooperation Agreements* later, although the reader is reminded that this document is not legally binding; however it explains in a helpful way the Commission's thinking on how Article 101 should apply to exchanges of information. The *Guidelines* do not apply to the extent that sector-specific rules, for example on agreements in the insurance sector, are in place[314]. The *Horizontal Cooperation Guidelines* begin by describing the arguments in favour of and against exchanges of information; they then explain the different types of exchange of information; thereafter the concept of a concerted practice and exchanges of information that have as their object or effect the restriction of competition are dealt with. This is followed by a short discussion of the criteria in Article 101(3). This sequence will broadly be retained in the text that follows.

[305] See the Commission's *Guidelines on Horizontal Cooperation Agreements* OJ [2011] C 11/1, paras 302–305.

[306] *Concordato Incendio* OJ [1990] L 15/25.

[307] See generally *The Pros and Cons of Information Sharing* (Swedish Competition Authority, 2006) for a series of essays on the law and economics of information sharing; see also Capobianco 'Information Exchange under EC Competition Law' (2004) 41 CML Rev 1247 and Bennett and Collins 'The Law and Economics of Information Sharing: The Good, the Bad and the Ugly' (2010) 6 European Competition Journal 311; OECD Roundtable *Information Exchanges Between Competitors under Competition Law* (2010), available at www.oecd.org/competition.

[308] JO [1968] C 75/3; this *Notice* was repealed by the Commission's *Guidelines on the applicability of Article [101] to Horizontal Cooperation Agreements* OJ [2001] C 3/2, which in turn have been replaced by the Commission's *Guidelines on Horizontal Cooperation Agreements* OJ [2011] C 11/1, para 18.

[309] OJ [2011] C 11/1; for comment see the series of essays in Antitrust Chronicle, February 2011 (1), available at www.competitionpolicyinternational.com.

[310] A judgment which the *Guidelines* do not mention but is relevant to this issue is that of the Court of Justice in *Steel Beams*, Case C-194/99 P *Thyssen Stahl v Commission* EU:C:2003:527.

[311] Cases C-7/95 and C-8/95 P EU:C:1998:256 and EU:C:1998:257.

[312] Case C-238/05 EU:C:2006:734.

[313] Case C-8/08 EU:C:2009:343.

[314] *Guidelines on Horizontal Cooperation Agreements*, para 18; see ch 15, 'Insurance sector', pp 625–626.

(B) Arguments for and against exchanges of information

It is important to understand that information—including, therefore, the exchange of information—may be highly beneficial, to competitors, consumers and to the competitive process. The *Guidelines on Horizontal Cooperation Agreements* acknowledge that exchanging information is a common feature of many competitive markets[315]. Competitors cannot compete in a statistical vacuum: the more information they have about market conditions, the volume of demand, the level of capacity that exists in an industry and the investment plans of rivals, the easier it is for them to make rational and effective decisions on their production and marketing strategies. Competitors may benefit, without harming their customers, by exchanging information on matters such as methods of accounting, stock control, book-keeping or the draftsmanship of standard-form contracts.

However there are, of course, dangers to the competitive process if certain types of information are exchanged in certain market conditions. In most cases the question is whether the exchange of information is likely to have significant anti-competitive effects, although some types of information exchange may have the object of restricting competition. The *Guidelines on Horizontal Cooperation Agreements* identify two main competition concerns arising from the exchange of information between competitors: first, it may enable undertakings to predict each other's future behaviour and to coordinate their behaviour on the market; and secondly, it may result in anti-competitive foreclosure of the market in which the exchange of information takes place or of a related market. The Commission says that it does not claim that these concerns are exclusive or exhaustive[316].

The problem for competition law is to distinguish those exchanges of information that have a neutral or beneficial effect upon efficiency from those which seriously threaten the competitive process by facilitating collusive behaviour.

(C) Types of exchange of information

Information is exchanged in various contexts. It is therefore necessary to characterise the exchange of information in order to ascertain whether competition is likely to be harmed. Two situations should be noted.

(i) Information exchange in support of a horizontal cooperation agreement

Where an exchange of information forms part of a horizontal cooperation agreement its assessment should be carried out in combination with the assessment of that agreement; an obvious example would be the parties to a production agreement sharing information about costs. Exchanges of information that are necessary for the implementation of research and development or specialisation agreements may benefit from the block exemption for those agreements[317].

(ii) Information exchange in support of a cartel

There have been many cases in which the Commission has held that the exchange of information was unlawful where it was part of a mechanism for monitoring and/or enforcing compliance with an unlawful cartel agreement. The exchange of information enables members of a cartel to be sure that each of them is complying with the agreed rules. Information exchange can take various forms: data can be directly shared between

[315] *Guidelines on Horizontal Cooperation Agreements*, para 57. [316] Ibid, section 2.2.1, fn 1.

[317] See *Guidelines on Horizontal Cooperation Agreements*, para 88, fn 1; see generally ch 15 on block exemption Regulations 1217/2010 and 1218/2010.

competitors or indirectly exchanged through a trade association or a third party, such as a common supplier or cartel consultancy.

In *Gas insulated switchgear*[318] the Commission imposed fines of €750.7 million on a cartel involving European and Japanese firms that divided the market geographically and allocated quotas. A feature of this case was that cartel secretaries were appointed in Europe and Japan whose function was to receive and disseminate among the members information about forthcoming projects in the sector; this led to discussions about who was interested in winning the contract, whether some members of the cartel would make cover bids to give the (false) impression of competition, and to a final report as to who had actually won the contest[319]. The illegality of information exchanges of this kind is established by virtue of the fact that it is a mechanism for supporting behaviour that is illegal anyway[320]. Just as ancillary restrictions supportive of a legitimate agreement are legal[321], the exchange of information pursuant to an illegal cartel agreement is itself illegal.

(D) **Agreement and/or concerted practice to exchange information**

To infringe Article 101(1) there must be an agreement and/or concerted practice between undertakings to exchange information or a decision by an association of undertakings to the same effect. In *Asnef-Equifax v Ausbanc*[322] the Court of Justice held that, where credit institutions participated in the creation of a register of information about the solvency of customers, it was not important to decide whether this happened as a result of an agreement, a concerted practice or a decision of an association of undertakings[323]. Paragraphs 60 to 63 of the *Guidelines on Horizontal Cooperation Agreements* provide guidance on the concept of concerted practice in the context of exchange of information. The case law on this concept is discussed in chapter 3 of this book[324]. The *Guidelines* say that Article 101(1) applies to sharing between competitors of 'strategic data', that is to say data that reduces strategic uncertainty in the market[325]. The *Guidelines* also explain that a unilateral disclosure of strategic information can give rise to a concerted practice[326]; there is a presumption that, by receiving such information from a competitor, a firm accepts it and adapts its future conduct on the market[327]. The General Court said the same thing in *Bathroom fittings and fixtures*[328].

The possibility that 'price signalling' might be treated as a concerted practice was discussed earlier in this chapter[329]. Where a firm makes a unilateral announcement that is genuinely public, for example in the press, a concerted practice is unlikely[330]. In *Wood*

[318] Commission decision of 24 January 2007, substantially upheld on appeal Cases T-117/07 etc *Areva v Commission* EU:T:2011:69, partially annulled on further appeal Cases C-247/11 P etc EU:C:2014:257.

[319] Commission decision of 24 January 2007, paras 121–123.

[320] *Guidelines on Horizontal Cooperation Agreements*, para 59.

[321] See ch 3, 'Commercial ancillarity', pp 135–138.

[322] Case C-238/05 EU:C:2006:734.

[323] Ibid, paras 30–32.

[324] See ch 3, 'Concerted practices', pp 115–119.

[325] *Guidelines on Horizontal Cooperation Agreements*, para 86, which explains that 'strategic data' includes information relating to prices, customer lists, production costs, quantities, turnovers, sales, capacities, qualities, marketing plans, risks, investments, technologies, research and development programmes and their results.

[326] *Guidelines on Horizontal Cooperation Agreements*, para 62.

[327] Ibid, para 62; for discussion of the case law establishing this presumption see ch 3, 'Concerted practices', pp 115–119.

[328] Case T-368/10 *Rubinetteria Cisal v Commission* EU:T:2013:460, para 42.

[329] See 'Price signalling', p 535 earlier in chapter.

[330] *Guidelines on Horizontal Cooperation Agreements*, para 63; the possibility cannot be entirely ruled out in cases where competitors make public announcements to signal future strategic behaviour to one another.

Pulp II[331] the Court of Justice ruled that the fact that pulp producers publicly announced price rises to users before those rises came into effect was not, in itself, sufficient to constitute an infringement of Article 101(1)[332].

(E) **Assessment under Article 101(1)**

This section will consider the application of Article 101(1) to exchanges of information[333], and in particular the types of information exchanges that have as their object or effect the restriction of competition.

(i) **Restriction of competition by object**

The case law of the EU Courts has established that any discussion among competitors about their prices is likely to be regarded as giving rise to an anti-competitive price-fixing agreement. Paragraph 74 of the *Guidelines* suggests that the exchange of information between competitors that identify the future intended prices or quantities of individual firms has as its object the restriction of competition and is unlikely to satisfy the criteria of Article 101(3). The *Guidelines* do not say, but it is the case, that there does not need to be a direct effect on prices paid by end consumers[334]. Nor is it necessary for A and B, members of a cartel, to have explicitly *agreed* that they will increase their prices: the mere fact of providing information to one another about future pricing behaviour—or even for one to provide such information to the other—is likely to be sufficient for a finding of an agreement on prices. Furthermore, the fact that A discloses its prices to B after having disclosed its prices to A's customers does not mean that A and B are not party to an unlawful price-fixing agreement[335]. Where, however, A and B compete on some, but not all, of the cartelised product markets, it cannot be presumed that the exchange of information relating to a market on which they do not compete is anti-competitive: it is necessary for the Commission to prove that this is the case[336].

In *Dole v Commission*[337] the Court of Justice upheld the General Court's judgment[338] confirming the Commission's decision that three producers of bananas were party to a concerted practice that restricted competition by object where they regularly communicated with one another, before setting the prices that they quoted to their customers on a weekly basis, as to the factors that they considered were relevant for setting quotation prices for the week ahead, including their views on prices trends. These pre-pricing communications made it possible to reduce uncertainty for each of the producers as to the foreseeable conduct of competitors, and therefore had 'the object of creating conditions of competition that do not correspond to the normal conditions on the market'[339].

In two settlement cases, *EURIBOR* and *Yen LIBOR*, several banks admitted that they had infringed Article 101(1) by informing each other of their strategies and submissions for the calculation of benchmark interest rates, matters that would normally be regarded

[331] Cases C-89/85 etc *A Ahlström Osakeyhtiö v Commission* EU:C:1993:120. [332] Ibid, paras 59–65.

[333] See *Guidelines on Horizontal Cooperation Agreements*, paras 105–110 for helpful examples of the Commission's thinking on a number of hypothetical situations.

[334] See eg Case C-8/08 *T-Mobile Netherlands BV v Raad van Bestuur van de Nederlandse Mededingingsautoriteit* EU:C:2009:343, paras 36–39.

[335] Case T-368/10 *Rubinetteria Cisal v Commission* EU:T:2013:460, para 45 (*Bathroom fittings and fixtures*).

[336] Case T-380/10 *Wabco Europe v Commission* EU:T:2013:129, para 79 (*Bathroom fittings and fixtures*).

[337] Case C-286/13 P EU:C:2015:184.

[338] Case T-588/08 *Dole v Commission* EU:T:2013:130, paras 553 and 583–585.

[339] Case C-286/13 P EU:C:2015:184, para 134.

as confidential[340]. The Commission imposed fines totalling €1.49 billion[341]. This was followed by the Commission imposing fines of €485 million on three other banks that had also participated in the *EURIBOR* cartel[342]; those banks chose not to settle with the Commission. Another contested case that involved the exchange of information that pursued the object of restricting competition was *Smart card chips*[343]: the Commission imposed fines totalling €138 million on four undertakings that had bilaterally discussed pricing, customers, contract negotiations, production capacity and utilisation and future market conduct.

It is not a defence for an undertaking to argue that it attended a meeting at which prices were discussed, but that it maintained silence throughout the meeting, and gave no indication of its own intentions. Attendance is sufficient to implicate the undertaking in the price fixing unless it left the meeting and took positive action to 'publicly distance' itself from the unlawful behaviour[344]. In *T-Mobile*[345] the Court of Justice confirmed that an exchange of price information between competitors at a single meeting could give rise to a concerted practice that has as its object the restriction of competition[346]. The message could hardly be clearer: do not remain at a meeting at which competitors discuss future prices or quantities.

(ii) Restrictions of competition by effect

Exchanges of information that do not support an agreement that is itself anti-competitive, and that do not concern future prices or quantities, do not restrict competition by object; however they may do so by effect. This requires a full analysis of the market. The point is made clearly in the Court of Justice's judgment in *Asnef-Equifax*[347]:

> [t]he compatibility of an information exchange system . . . with the [EU] competition rules cannot be assessed in the abstract. It depends on the economic conditions on the relevant markets and on the specific characteristics of the system concerned, such as, in particular, its purpose and the conditions of access to it and participation in it, as well as the type of information exchanged—be that, for example, public or confidential, aggregated or detailed, historical or current—the periodicity of such information and its importance for the fixing of prices, volumes or conditions of service[348].

In *T-Mobile* the Court of Justice explained that the purpose of this analysis is to determine whether the exchange could 'reduce or remove' uncertainty between undertakings so that competition is restricted[349], a point it reiterated in *Dole v Commission*[350]. The Commission's *Guidelines on Horizontal Cooperation Agreements* explain how it approaches 'pure' exchanges of information; the crucial question always is whether the

[340] Commission decisions of 4 December 2013; on the settlement procedure see ch 7 'Settlements of cartel cases', pp 270–273.

[341] The fines were imposed by two decisions: one for manipulating EURIBOR and the other for manipulating Yen LIBOR.

[342] Commission decision of 7 December 2016, on appeal Cases T-105/17 etc *HSBC Holdings v Commission*, not yet decided.

[343] Commission decision of 3 September 2014, upheld on appeal Cases T-762/14 etc *Koninklijke Philips NV v Commission* EU:T:2016:738, on further appeal Case C-98/17 P, not yet decided.

[344] See eg Case T-83/08 *Denki Kagaku Kogyo v Commission* EU:T:2012:48, para 53 (*Chloroprene rubber*); see further 'Public distancing from a cartel', pp 528–529 earlier in chapter.

[345] Case C-8/08 EU:C:2009:343. [346] Ibid, paras 58–61.

[347] Case C-238/05 EU:C:2006:734. [348] Ibid, para 54.

[349] Case C-8/08 *T-Mobile Netherlands BV v Raad van Bestuur van de Nederlandse Mededingingsautoriteit* EU:C:2009:343, para 35.

[350] Case C-286/13 P EU:C:2015:184, para 121 (*Bananas*).

exchange could enable competing undertakings to achieve and/or sustain coordination. The *Guidelines* examine two issues, each of which accords with economic theory: the economic conditions on the relevant markets and the characteristics of information exchanged.

(iii) The economic conditions on the relevant markets

In the first place it is important to consider the characteristics of the market. Paragraph 76 of the *Guidelines* explains that exchanges of information are more likely to have anti-competitive effects in markets where conditions for coordination are propitious. The *Guidelines* say that coordination is more likely on markets which are sufficiently transparent, concentrated, non-complex, stable and symmetric. Each of these factors is explored further in succeeding paragraphs of the *Guidelines*. They point out that exchanges of information are not likely to be anti-competitive in very fragmented markets, unless the information exchanged increases transparency or changes the market situation in another way that is conducive for coordination[351]. This illustrates a more general point made by the *Guidelines*: whether an exchange of information facilitates collusive behaviour depends on not only the initial market conditions but also how the exchange of information may change those conditions. In deciding whether coordination will be sustainable the Commission will consider whether there is a credible threat of retaliation to prevent other firms from cheating[352].

The economic conditions of the market have been influential in the assessment of information exchange in Commission decisions under Article 101(1)[353]. In *UK Agricultural Tractor Registration Exchange*[354] the Commission condemned an information-exchange system, placing considerable emphasis on the fact that the UK tractor market was oligopolistic: in particular it took into account that four firms on the UK market had a combined market share of approximately 80% and that in some geographical areas the concentration was higher; that barriers to entry were high, especially as extensive distribution and servicing networks were necessary; that the market was stagnant or in decline and there was considerable brand loyalty; and that there was an absence of significant imports[355]. The Commission published a Press Release after this decision in which it said that the same result would not necessarily arise in the car market, which is much more competitive[356]. In *Eudim*[357] the Commission was more relaxed about the exchange of information between wholesalers of plumbing, heating and sanitary materials since the affected markets were sufficiently competitive.

In *Asnef-Equifax*[358] the question arose of whether agreements between credit institutions in Spain for the exchange of information about the creditworthiness of borrowers were restrictive of competition. The Court said that agreements of the type under consideration do not have as their object the restriction of competition[359]. Instead it stressed that the agreements had to be considered in the context in which they occurred[360]. The Court specifically noted that the market in question was a fragmented one: that is to say

[351] *Guidelines on Horizontal Cooperation Agreements*, para 79; on this point see the judgment of the Court of Justice in *Steel beams*, Case C-194/99 P *Thyssen Stahl AG v Commission* EU:C:2003:527, para 86.

[352] *Guidelines on Horizontal Cooperation Agreements*, para 85.

[353] See eg *International Energy Program* OJ [1983] L 376/30; see also *Non-ferrous Semi-manufacturers* Commission's Vth *Report on Competition Policy* (1975), point 39.

[354] OJ [1992] L 68/19.

[355] Ibid, para 35; see similarly *Wirtschaftsvereinigung Stahl* OJ [1998] L 1/10, paras 39 and 44–46; this decision was annulled on appeal Case T-16/98 *Wirtschaftsvereinigung Stahl v Commission* EU:T:2001:117.

[356] Commission Press Release IP/92/148, 4 March 1992.

[357] OJ [1996] C 111/8.

[358] Case C-238/05 EU:C:2006:734.

[359] Ibid, para 48.

[360] Ibid, para 49.

that it was not concentrated, which would have been a factor conducive to coordinated behaviour[361]. It seems fairly clear that the Court considered that the exchange in question did not infringe Article 101(1).

(iv) **Characteristics of the information exchanged**

An important consideration is the type or quality of information that is exchanged. The Commission's *Guidelines on Horizontal Cooperation Agreements* explain that the exchange between competitors of strategic data is more likely to infringe Article 101(1)[362]. The *Guidelines* point out that information on prices and quantities is the most strategic in nature, followed by information about costs and demand[363]. The exchange of investment plans may also be strategic[364]. The *Guidelines* explain that the strategic usefulness of data also depends on its market coverage, aggregation, age and frequency of exchange. The exchange must affect a sufficiently large part of the relevant market in order for it to be capable of having a restrictive effect on competition[365]. The exchange of individual data about particular undertakings is more problematic than aggregated data[366]. The age of the data is relevant[367]: the question is whether the information facilitates collusive behaviour, so that historic data are less significant than future ones[368]. The Commission tends to regard information that is more than one year old as historic[369]. The frequency of exchange is also a relevant factor[370].

The *Guidelines* point out that the exchange of 'genuinely public information' is unlikely to infringe Article 101(1)[371]; information is genuinely public in nature if the costs of obtaining it are the same for all competitors and customers. If the information exchanged is in the public domain, but is not equally accessible to competitors and customers, the Commission considers that Article 101(1) may apply as it would do to any other agreement. The General Court made the same point in *Bananas*[372]. A further consideration is whether the information exchanged is shared with customers or not: the Commission states in the *Guidelines on Horizontal Cooperation Agreements* that the more the information is shared with customers, the less likely it is to be problematic[373].

For obvious reasons the Commission has always been concerned about price information, but other concerns can be seen. In *Re Cimbel*[374] it condemned the obligation upon members of a trade association that they should inform each other of projected increases in industrial capacity: such an obligation could prevent one firm from gaining an advantage over competitors by expanding in time to meet an increase in demand. In *Steel beams*[375] the Commission found an information exchange on orders and deliveries of beams by individual companies in each Member State to go 'beyond what is admissible'[376], since the figures exchanged showed the deliveries and orders received by each individual company for delivery to their respective markets; this information was updated every

361 Ibid, para 58; as this was an Article 267 TFEU reference the Court did not make a finding on the facts of the case.

362 OJ [2011] C 11/1, para 86. 363 Ibid. 364 See eg *Zinc Producer Group* OJ [1984] L 220/27.

365 *Guidelines on Horizontal Cooperation Agreements*, paras 87–88. 366 Ibid, para 89.

367 Ibid, para 90. 368 Ibid, para 90. 369 Ibid, para 90, fn 2. 370 Ibid, para 91.

371 Ibid, para 92. 372 Case T-587/08 *Fresh Del Monte v Commission* EU:T:2013:129, para 323.

373 *Guidelines on Horizontal Cooperation Agreements*, para 94; see similarly *UK Agricultural Tractor Registration Exchange* OJ [1992] L 68/19; *Re VNP and COBELPA* OJ [1977] L 242/10; *Genuine Vegetable Parchment Association* OJ [1978] L 70/54.

374 OJ [1972] L 303/24.

375 OJ [1994] L 116/1, paras 263–272, upheld on appeal to the General Court Cases T-141/94 etc *Thyssen Stahl v Commission* EU:T:1999:48, paras 385–412 and further upheld on appeal to the Court of Justice Case C-194/99 P EU:C:2003:527.

376 OJ [1994] L 116/1, para 267.

week and circulated rapidly among the participants. The Commission added that the exchange was not limited to figures 'of a merely historical value with no possible impact on competition'[377]. The General Court confirmed the Commission's assessment, since the exchange of confidential information undermined the principle that every undertaking must determine its market strategy independently. In *Wirtschaftsvereinigung Stahl* the Commission decided that an exchange of information on deliveries and market shares in relation to various steel products infringed Article 65(1) ECSC; on appeal the General Court annulled this decision because the Commission had erred in its findings of fact[378].

(F) **Assessment under Article 101(3)**

An information agreement may satisfy the criteria of Article 101(3) because of its beneficial effects. The Commission discusses the application of Article 101(3) to exchanges of information in paragraphs 95 to 104 of its *Guidelines*. They should be read in conjunction with the Commission's *Article 101(3) Guidelines*[379]. The Commission explains in paragraph 95 that benchmarking, whereby undertakings measure their performance against 'best practice' in their industry, may enable them to improve their efficiency[380]. In certain situations information may be exchanged to ensure an optimal allocation of resources, thereby reducing any mismatch between supply and demand. By spreading technological know-how, information agreements can help to increase the number of firms capable of operating on the market[381]. The exchange of consumer data in markets characterised by asymmetric information about consumers may bring about efficiencies; an example would be the exchange of information between credit institutions about the solvency and default record of their customers[382].

Consumers too can benefit from an increase in public information: the more they know about the products available and their prices, the easier it will be for them to make satisfactory choices. Indeed perfect competition is dependent on consumers having perfect information about the market[383]: market transparency is, in general, to be encouraged. Quite often the reason why a market does not work well for consumers is that the information available to them is too sparse or confusing; in some markets there may actually be too much information for consumers to be able to digest. The Commission says that consumers are less likely to benefit from exchanges of future pricing intentions than exchanges of present and past data[384]. Further, the parties must show that the subject-matter, aggregation, age, confidentiality, frequency and coverage of their exchange of information carries the lowest risks of facilitating collusion indispensable for creating efficiencies[385]. The Commission rejected arguments that the exchange of information in *UK Agricultural Tractor Registration Exchange*[386] would generate efficiencies in terse terms.

[377] Ibid, para 268.

[378] OJ [1998] L 1/10, annulled on appeal Case T-16/98 *Wirtschaftsvereinigung Stahl v Commission* EU:T:2001:117.

[379] OJ [2004] C 101/97; see ch 4, 'The Commission's approach in the *Article 101(3) Guidelines*', pp 167–169.

[380] *Guidelines on Horizontal Cooperation Agreements*, para 95; see Henry 'Benchmarking and Antitrust' (1993) 62 Antitrust LJ 483; on benchmarking and EU law see Carle and Johnsson 'Benchmarking and EC Competition Law' (1998) 19 ECLR 74; Boulter 'Competition Risks in Benchmarking' (1999) 20 ECLR 434.

[381] See Teece 'Information Sharing, Innovation and Antitrust' (1993) 62 Antitrust LJ 465.

[382] In *Asnef-Equifax*, ch 13 n 312 earlier, the Court of Justice suggested that such an exchange of information might satisfy the criteria of Article 101(3).

[383] See ch 1, 'The model of perfect competition is based on assumptions unlikely to be observed in practice', pp 8–9.

[384] *Guidelines on Horizontal Cooperation Agreements*, paras 99–100.

[385] Ibid, para 101.

[386] OJ [1992] L 68/19.

Some exchanges of information in the insurance sector were given block exemption by Articles 2(a) and 3 of Regulation 267/2010 until 31 March 2017[387].

(G) **Fines**

The Commission's decisions imposing fines of €60 million in *Bananas* and €1.49 billion in *Euro and Yen interest rate derivatives* make it clear that it will not hesitate to punish competing undertakings that contact one another in respect of sensitive business matters; it is important not artificially to increase the transparency of the market[388].

10. **Advertising Restrictions**

The function of advertising in competition policy raises important and controversial issues that can be dealt with only briefly here[389]. Advertising is an essential part of the competitive process. Unless the consumer knows what goods and services are on offer and what their price is he or she will be unable to choose what to buy and competition between suppliers will be diminished.

Competition is about attracting business and a vital part of the process is to advertise one's products. Therefore competition policy should ensure that advertising is not restricted[390]. Indeed it may be thought appropriate to impose upon businesses a duty to advertise prices, terms and conditions or details of quality in order to provide the consumer with the information needed to enable him or her to make a rational choice; however it should be noted that a perverse consequence of forcing undertakings to publicise their prices could be to facilitate tacit collusion between them. A separate point is that the significance of advertising means that steps should be taken to ensure the truth of advertisements and, perhaps, to prevent the appropriation of innovative advertising ideas by competitive rivals; comparative advertising, whereby a competitor's products are unfavourably compared with one's own, might also be objected to[391].

In some circumstances collaboration between undertakings in their advertising activities may not be harmful. For example, a group of small producers may decide to sell a product under a common label and agree on the specifications and publicity of the product in question; they will all contribute to the advertising costs of this product. By doing this they may be able to present a strong brand image that will enhance their ability to compete with other firms on the market. Such schemes may be pro-competitive, although it will be necessary to ensure that nothing in the agreement limits competition unnecessarily, such as direct price fixing or market sharing. Also there may be a case for collaboration on advertising—for example by agreeing to limit the number of industrial

[387] OJ [2010] 83/1; the Commission decided not to renew the block exemption and, therefore, from 1 April 2017 insurance firms must self-assess their exchanges of information under Article 101.

[388] See also *Fatty acids* OJ [1985] L 3/17, in which a fine of €50,000 was imposed.

[389] See eg Cowling *Advertising and Economic Behaviour* (Macmillan, 1975); Telser 'Advertising and Competition' (1964) 72 J Pol Ec 536; Benham 'Effect of Advertising on the Price of Eyeglasses (1972) 15 J L & Ec 337; Scherer and Ross *Industrial Market Structure and Economic Performance* (Houghton Mifflin, 3rd ed, 1990), pp 436ff; Barigozzi and Peitz 'Comparative Advertising and Competition Policy' (2005), available at www.ssrn.com; Kobayashi and Muris 'I Can See Clearly Now: Lee Benham, Eyeglasses, and Empirical Analysis of Advertising and the Effects of Professional Regulation' (2013) 9 Competition Policy International 156.

[390] Restrictions on advertising in the US are regarded as an indirect form of price fixing and are accordingly *per se* illegal; cf *California Dental Association v Federal Trade Commission* 526 US 756 (1999).

[391] Note Directive 2006/114/EC concerning misleading and comparative advertising, OJ [2006] L 376/21.

exhibitions visited in a year—if this will have the effect of rationalising advertising efforts and reducing advertising costs.

A quite different point is that advertising costs are a serious barrier to entry to new firms wishing to enter a market as well as being a wasteful use of resources[392]. In some markets, such as lager, detergents and breakfast cereals, enormous amounts of money are spent in building up a brand image and it is argued that new entrants would be unable to expend the money on advertising necessary to match this. The problem, it is said, is accentuated by the fact that established firms have the accumulated advantage of past advertising and also that they have the capacity to indulge in 'predatory' advertising, that is short-term expensive campaigns designed to prevent the new entrant establishing a toe-hold in the market. Opinion on the barrier-raising effect of advertising is divided. Bork and other commentators have argued forcefully that it should not be treated as a barrier and there is empirical evidence which sheds doubt on the argument[393].

A separate objection to advertising comes from a quite different quarter, namely the liberal professions. They sometimes argue that advertising is inimical to their ethical standards and that consumer protection in their spheres of activity is best served by maintaining professional standards through self-regulation, codes of practice and professional ethics.

(A) **Article 101(1)**

Article 101(1) applies to agreements to restrict advertising that have anti-competitive effects. In several decisions the Commission has stated that it considers that such restrictions limit an important aspect of competitive behaviour[394]. In *Consumer detergents*[395] the Commission found that three producers of washing powder had unlawfully agreed to restrict their promotional activity as well as fix prices. In the case of trade fairs, the Commission has held that the rules for participation may infringe Article 101(1), in particular when participants are required not to take part in other fairs, thus limiting their competitive opportunities. In 1988 the Commission, for the first time in a trade fair case, imposed a fine of €100,000 on the *British Dental Trade Association*[396] for anti-competitive exclusion of would-be exhibitors.

In several decisions[397] the Commission has revealed a benevolence towards advertising restrictions which might promote a particular brand image without seriously impairing competition in other ways. In *Belgian Roofing Felt*[398], however, the Commission condemned joint advertising of roofing felt under the Belasco trade mark where this led to the uniform image of products in a sector in which individual advertising may facilitate differentiation and therefore competition. The Commission's *Guidelines on Horizontal Cooperation Agreements* provide guidance on the application of Article 101 to so-called 'commercialisation agreements'[399], which may involve joint advertising. The *Guidelines* state that joint advertising might lead to anti-competitive effects if it entails a significant commonality of costs which might increase the risk of collusive behaviour[400].

392 See eg Turner 'Conglomerate Mergers and s 7 of the Clayton Act' (1965) 78 Harvard Law Review 1313.

393 See eg Bork *The Antitrust Paradox* (The Free Press, 1993), pp 314–320.

394 See eg *Re Vimpoltu* OJ [1983] L 200/44; *Austrian Banks* OJ [2004] L 56/1, para 79.

395 Commission decision of 13 April 2011, para 25.

396 OJ [1988] L 233/15; the Commission decided that, for a period of ten years, Article 101(3) applied to the Association's rules as modified to satisfy the Commission.

397 *Re VVVF* OJ [1969] L 168/22; *Re Association pour la Promotion du Tube d'Acier Soude Electriquement* JO [1970] L 153/14; *Re Industrieverband Solnhofener Natursteinplatten* OJ [1980] L 318/32.

398 OJ [1986] L 232/15, upheld on appeal Case 246/86 *Belasco v Commission* EU:C:1989:301.

399 OJ [2011] C 11/1, paras 225–256.

400 Ibid, para 243; see ch 15, 'Commercialisation Agreements', pp 617–619.

Restrictions on comparative advertising by patent agents practising at the European Patent Office were held to infringe Article 101(1) in *EPI Code of Conduct*[401] but to benefit from Article 101(3) for a short period whilst new rules were adopted[402].

(B) Article 101(3)

The Commission has accepted that it can sometimes be advantageous to rationalise and coordinate advertising efforts. For example, the Commission has permitted trade fair rules requiring participants to limit the number of occasions on which they exhibit elsewhere and restricting the extent to which they are allowed to advertise in other ways[403]. The Commission has often applied conditions to such authorisations. For example in *UNIDI*[404] the Commission required the introduction of an arbitration procedure to deal with complaints by exhibitors excluded from an exhibition. In *VIFKA*[405] it required the removal of a provision requiring exhibitors of office equipment not to exhibit elsewhere for a period of two years, as this was too long.

11. Anti-Competitive Horizontal Restraints

The agreements so far considered have been concerned with cartels limiting competition and raising prices to earn supra-competitive profits. It is likely however that, in the absence of barriers to entry, this in itself will attract new entrants into the market. It is because of this that the members of a cartel will frequently take further action designed to fend off the possibility of new competition in just the same way that a monopolist might. For example, a collective reciprocal exclusive dealing arrangement might be negotiated whereby a group of suppliers agree with a group of dealers to deal only with one another. The effect may be to exclude other producers from the market if they cannot find retail outlets for their products. This is not an inevitable result however: to have an anti-competitive foreclosing effect there would have to be a lack of alternative retail outlets, for example due to barriers to entry at the retail level. A common pricing system may be supported by an aggregated rebates cartel, whereby purchasers are offered rebates calculated according to their purchases from all the members of the cartel; the disincentive to buy elsewhere is obvious[406]. Again it may be decided to boycott any dealer who handles the products of producers outside the cartel. As one would expect, exclusionary devices such as these that can cause serious harm to the competitive process are *per se* illegal in the US[407], although the US Supreme Court has said that 'the category of restraints classed

[401] OJ [1999] L 106/14, paras 39–45, partially annulled on appeal Case T-144/99 *Institut des Mandataires Agréés v Commission* EU:T:2001:105; see the Commission's XXIXth *Report on Competition Policy* (1999), pp 53 and 159–160.

[402] OJ [1999] L 106/14, paras 46–48.

[403] *Re CECIMO* OJ [1969] L 69/13, renewed OJ [1979] L 11/16 and again OJ [1989] L 37/11; *Re BPICA* OJ [1977] L 299/18, renewed OJ [1982] L 156/16; *Re Cematex* JO [1971] L 227/26, renewed OJ [1983] L 140/27; *Re UNIDI* OJ [1975] L 228/14, renewed OJ [1984] L 322/10; *Re Society of Motor Manufacturers and Traders Ltd* OJ [1983] L 376/1; *VIFKA* OJ [1986] L 291/46; *Internationale Dentalscbau* OJ [1987] L 293/58; *Sippa* OJ [1991] L 60/19.

[404] OJ [1984] L 322/10, upheld on appeal Case 43/85 *ANCIDES v Commission* EU:C:1987:347.

[405] OJ [1986] L 291/46.

[406] Aggregated rebates cartels are unlikely where prices are *not* fixed, because they would discriminate against those offering lower prices.

[407] See eg *Klor's Inc v Broadway-Hale Stores Inc* 359 US 207, 212 (1959): for a review of US case law see Glazer 'Concerted Refusals to Deal under Section 1 of the Sherman Act' (2002) 70 Antitrust LJ 1; see also the UK Competition Appeal Tribunal in Case 1003/2/1/01 *Institute of Independent Insurance Brokers v Director General of Fair Trading* [2001] CAT 4, para 189.

as group boycotts is not to be expanded indiscriminately'[408]. The pejorative label given to group boycotts conceals the fact that in some cases independent firms will inevitably decide to refuse to deal with certain people, for example by refusing inadequately trained people entrance to a profession or inefficient dealers access to a branded product. A distinction should be made between naked restraints that are clearly intended to be exclusionary on the one hand and agreements which promote efficiency and which therefore may be permitted.

The Commission and the EU Courts have often condemned collective exclusive dealing arrangements and other potentially exclusionary practices. Often such agreements are entered into by a national association that is keen to keep imports out of the domestic market. A more obvious target for the Commission it is hard to imagine and the EU Courts have usually upheld its findings. A scheme designed to keep washing machines out of the Belgian market was found by the Court of Justice to infringe Article 101(1)[409], as was a marketing system that could prevent imports of fruit into the Netherlands[410]. The Court agreed with the Commission that an exclusive purchasing agreement that obliged members of an association to acquire rennet solely from a Dutch cooperative was unlawful[411]. The Court also held that practices designed to buttress the collective resale price maintenance of Dutch and Belgian books infringed Article 101[412].

The Court of Justice upheld the Commission's decision to condemn rigid collective exclusive dealing systems in two cigarette cases, affecting the Belgian and Dutch markets respectively[413]. The Commission has dealt with many other similar situations, always striking such agreements down[414]. In *Hudson's Bay—Dansk Pelsdyravlerforening*[415] the Commission imposed a fine of €500,000 on a Danish trade association for imposing an obligation on its members that they should sell their entire production to a subsidiary of the association, thereby preventing them from selling their products to other Member States. In *Dutch mobile cranes*[416] the Commission imposed fines on a trade association found to have operated a price-fixing system whereby its members were obliged to charge 'recommended' rates for the hiring of mobile cranes; it also condemned the rules of a second association that effectively prohibited members from hiring cranes from firms not affiliated to it.

In *Dutch electrotechnical equipment*[417] the Commission imposed fines of €4.4 million on FEG and €2.15 million on TU for entering into collective exclusive dealing arrangements intended to prevent supplies to non-members of the associations by directly and

[408] *Federal Trade Commission v Indiana Federation of Dentists* 476 US 447, 458 (1986); see also Bork *The Antitrust Paradox* (The Free Press, 1993), ch 17.

[409] Cases 96/82 etc *NV IAZ International Belgium v Commission* EU:C:1983:310; note the additional fine subsequently imposed by the Commission in this case: *Re IPTC Belgium SA* OJ [1983] L 376/7.

[410] Case 71/74 *FRUBO v Commission* EU:C:1975:61; see similarly *Irish Timber Importers Association*, XXth *Report on Competition Policy* (1990), point 98.

[411] Case 61/80 *Cooperatieve Stremsel- en Kleurselfabriek v Commission* EU:C:1981:75.

[412] Cases 43 and 63/82 *VBVB & VBBB v Commission* EU:C:1984:9.

[413] Cases 209/78 etc *Van Landewyck v Commission* EU:C:1980:248; Cases 240/82 etc *SSI v Commission* EU:C:1985:488 and Case 260/82 *NSO v Commission* EU:C:1985:489.

[414] *Re Gas Water-Heaters* OJ [1973] L 217/34; *Re Stoves and Heaters* OJ [1975] L 159/22; *Re Bomée Stichting* OJ [1975] L 329/30; *Groupement d'Exportation du Leon v Société d'investissements et de Cooperation Agricoles (Cauliflowers)* OJ [1978] L 21/23; *Donck v Centraal Bureau voor de Rijwielhandel* OJ [1978] L 20/18; *Re IMA Rules* OJ [1980] L 318/1; *Re Italian Flat Glass* OJ [1981] L 326/32.

[415] OJ [1988] L 316/43, upheld on appeal Case T-61/89 *Dansk Pelsdyravlerforening v Commission* EU:T:1992:79.

[416] OJ [1995] L 312/79, upheld on appeal Cases T-213/95 etc *SCK and FNK v Commission* EU:T:1997:157.

[417] OJ [2000] L 39/1, upheld on appeal Cases T-5/00 etc *NAVEG v Commission* EU:T:2003:342, on further appeal Cases C-105/04 P etc EU:C:2006:592; see also the Commission's XXIXth *Report on Competition Policy* (1999), p 135.

indirectly restricting the freedom of members to determine their selling prices independently. The facts of this case resemble many of the decisions of the Commission on collective exclusive dealing from the 1970s and 1980s[418]: the fact that there are still arrangements like this in existence is perhaps a vindication of the Commission's desire to focus its resources on the elimination of practices that one might have assumed had long since been discontinued.

In *Dutch bitumen*[419] the Commission imposed fines of €266.71 million for price fixing on the part of eight suppliers and six purchasers of road bitumen in the Netherlands. An interesting feature of the case is that the large construction companies that were in the cartel were not particularly concerned that the suppliers were fixing prices: road building in the Netherlands is paid for, ultimately, by the taxpayer. The large construction companies were simply concerned to win as many orders as possible, and there were price rebates on offer from the suppliers that discriminated in favour of them, and against smaller competitors: in other words the pricing system in this case operated to exclude third parties from the market. On appeal the General Court upheld the Commission's decision, and specifically noted that the system was intended to restrict competition[420].

In *Visa Europe/Morgan Stanley*[421] the Commission imposed a fine of €10.2 million on Visa for refusing to admit Morgan Stanley to the Visa system without objective justification. This is an example of an anti-competitive horizontal restraint in that Visa consists of a number of undertakings that determine who may become a Visa member. There was a rule that said that membership was not available to a bank that issued a card that would compete with the Visa card. The rule did not restrict competition by object, but the way the rule had been applied in relation to Morgan Stanley had an appreciable anti-competitive effect. That was because Morgan Stanley did not issue a card that competed with Visa *within the EU*: Morgan Stanley's Discover Card had a presence only in the US. Furthermore Visa had, in practice, allowed other banks to join that did have cards in Europe, so that the rule had been applied in a discriminatory manner. Visa appealed to the General Court, which upheld the Commission's decision[422]. In particular, the General Court rejected Visa's complaint that the Commission had not conducted an analysis comparing the situation on the acquiring market if Morgan Stanley had joined the Visa scheme with the situation with Morgan Stanley remaining outside the scheme[423].

In *Groupement des cartes bancaires*[424] the Commission decided that the way in which certain rules of the 'Cartes Bancaires' payment card system were applied in France had the object and effect of restricting competition. The rules imposing pricing measures operated in favour of the major banks in France and to the detriment, for example, of banks established by retailers such as Carrefour and Auchan and internet banks. On appeal the General Court upheld the Commission's finding of an infringement by object[425]. However, on further appeal, the Court of Justice held that the General Court had been incorrect to have characterised the pricing measures as having as their object the restriction of competition. The case was remitted to the General Court for further

418 See ch 13 n 414 earlier.

419 Commission decision of 13 September 2006, substantially upheld on appeal Cases T-361/06 etc *Ballast Nedam v Commission* EU:T:2012:491, annulled on further appeal to the Court of Justice Case C-612/12 P *Ballast Nedam v Commission* EU:C:2014:193; other appeals were unsuccessful eg Case C-586/12 P *KWS v Commission* EU:C:2013:863.

420 Cases T-354/06 *BAM NBM v Commission* EU:T:2012:485, paras 70–72.

421 Commission decision of 3 October 2007.

422 Case T-461/07 *Visa Europe v Commission* EU:T:2011:181.

423 Ibid, paras 162–191.

424 Commission decision of 17 October 2007.

425 Case T-491/07 *CB v Commission* EU:T:2012:633.

consideration[426], which subsequently held that the pricing measures had an appreciable effect of restricting competition in the market for issuing payment cards[427].

12. **UK Law**

The UK competition authorities share the European Commission's determination to eliminate cartels[428]. The Competition Act 1998 gives to the CMA and sectoral regulators substantial powers of investigation and enforcement[429], resembling those of the Commission, to enforce Article 101 TFEU and the Chapter I prohibition. Some introductory points can be made in respect of the CMA's approach to cartels in the UK. First, there are a number of Guidelines on the Competition Act[430]; paragraphs 3.3 to 3.27 of the Guideline on *Agreements and Concerted Practices*[431] provide examples of agreements that might infringe Article 101(1) and/or the Chapter I prohibition. A second introductory point is that a booklet has been published to enable purchasers to identify cartel activity and to encourage them to bring their suspicions to the CMA's attention[432]. Thirdly, the CMA has a dedicated cartels and criminal enforcement group[433]. Fourthly, the CMA has a policy of encouraging whistleblowers to approach it with information about cartels[434]. Finally, the Enterprise Act 2002 establishes a criminal 'cartel offence' which can result in the fining or imprisonment of individuals involved in cartel activity[435].

Anti-cartel enforcement was somewhat limited in the early years of the Competition Act 1998. The position began to change from 2004 onwards through a series of decisions imposing fines for collusive tendering in the construction sector[436]. In 2009, the *Construction bid-rigging*[437] decision imposed fines of £129.2 million on 103 undertakings involved in unlawful cover pricing and other bid-rigging activities. The decision followed the largest investigation ever undertaken under the Competition Act. It also made use of a novel 'fast-track offer', whereby fines for undertakings implicated in bid-rigging (that had not already applied for leniency) were reduced in return for cooperation. On appeal, however, the Competition Appeal Tribunal ('the CAT') reduced the fines, which, in its view, were excessive and insufficiently tailored to the circumstances of individual firms[438].

In the 2010s, the competition authorities continued to uncover and punish cartel agreements. For example in *Airline passenger fuel surcharges*[439] British Airways admitted colluding with Virgin Atlantic over the price of long-haul passenger fuel surcharges between August 2004 and January 2006; BA agreed to pay a fine of £58.5 million. There was no fine on Virgin as it had blown the whistle. In *Dairy Products*[440] fines of £49.51 million were imposed on supermarkets and suppliers of dairy products for unlawful exchanges of future retail pricing intentions. Seven parties admitted the infringement and agreed

[426] Case C-67/13 P EU:C:2014:2204. [427] Case T-491/07 RENV EU:T:2016:379.

[428] See generally chs 9 and 10 on the substantive and procedural rules of the Competition Act 1998.

[429] See ch 10, 'Inquiries and Investigations', pp 401–411 and 'Enforcement', pp 413–435.

[430] See ch 9, 'CMA guidelines', pp 345–346.

[431] OFT 401, December 2004; see also *Trade Associations, professions and self-regulating bodies*, OFT 408, December 2004.

[432] *Cartels and the Competition Act 1998: a Guide for Purchasers*, available at www.gov.uk/cma.

[433] See ch 2, 'The staff of the CMA', p 66. [434] See ch 10, 'Leniency', pp 424–429.

[435] See ch 10, 'The cartel offence', pp 437–446.

[436] See 'Collusive Tendering', pp 567–568 later in chapter. [437] Decision of 21 September 2009.

[438] Cases 1114/1/1/09 etc *Kier Group v OFT* [2011] CAT 3; Cases 1117/1/1/10 etc *Tomlinson v OFT* [2011] CAT 7; Cases 1125/1/1/09 etc *Barrett Estate Services v OFT* [2011] CAT 9; the Court of Appeal further reduced the fine in one case: *Interclass Holdings v OFT* [2012] EWCA Civ 1056.

[439] OFT decision of 19 April 2012. [440] OFT decision of 10 August 2011.

to pay a reduced penalty. Tesco declined to settle and appealed to the CAT. The CAT quashed a number of findings of infringement against Tesco for lack of evidence[441], but upheld the decision that Tesco had participated in three unlawful concerted practices[442]. In 2013, the Office of Fair Trading ('the OFT') adopted five decisions imposing fines of £2.8 million for arrangements to share markets, coordinate prices and exchange information in relation to Mercedes-Benz commercial vehicles[443]. Mercedes-Benz was found to have acted as a 'facilitator' to one of its dealers' infringements. The CMA has adopted a series of decisions condemning cartels in markets ranging from the modelling sector to local estate agents to furniture products; these cases are mentioned in the sections below.

(A) **Horizontal price fixing**

The *Airline passenger fuel surcharges* and *Dairy Products* cases have already been referred to. The decisions to date in relation to collusive tendering are discussed further in section E below. The decisions in *Football Shirts* and *Toys and Games*, which involved horizontal and vertical price fixing, were discussed in detail in chapter 9[444].

In some cases allegations of price fixing have been settled informally, in particular in the early years of the Competition Act[445]. In recent years, however, the competition authorities have been committed to the pursuit, unveiling and elimination of price-fixing agreements. In *Northern Ireland Livestock and Auctioneers' Association*[446] a recommendation by the Association as to the commission that its members should charge for the purchase of livestock in Northern Ireland cattle marts infringed the Chapter I prohibition; no fine was imposed, not least because the infringement occurred at a time when the beef sector was suffering as a result of so-called 'mad cow' disease[447]. In *Stock Check Pads*[448] fines of £168,318 were imposed in the case of price fixing and market sharing of stock check pads, used by staff in cafes and restaurants to record customers' orders. In *Aluminium Spacer Bars*[449] four companies had to pay fines of £898,470 for price fixing, customer allocation and market sharing for aluminium spacer bars used in double glazing. In *Construction Recruitment Forum*[450] fines of £39.27 million were imposed for price fixing in conjunction with a collective boycott. On appeal the CAT reduced the fines due to errors in the OFT's calculation of the fines[451].

In 2016 the CMA adopted two decisions imposing fines totalling £2.73 million for price fixing or the exchange of information in *Cylindrical galvanized steel tanks*[452]; the finding that Balmoral Tanks was guilty of an illegal exchange of information that took place at a single meeting was upheld on appeal to the CAT[453]. In *Conduct in the modelling sector*[454] the CMA imposed fines totalling £1.53 million on five model

441 Case 1188/1/1/11 *Tesco v OFT* [2012] CAT 31, paras 487–488.

442 Ibid, para 487(a)–(c).

443 CMA decisions of 27 March 2013.

444 See ch 9, 'Agreements', p 350.

445 See eg *Royal Institute of British Architects* Weekly Gazette of the OFT, Competition case closure summaries, 17–23 May 2003; see similarly the case closures in *The Notaries Society*, 30 April 2004 and *British Chemical Distributors and Traders Association*, 11 May 2004; *Nationwide Independent Bodyshop Suppliers Limited*, February 2009; *UK Asbestos Training Association*, 26 March 2013, all available at www.nationalarchives.gov.uk.

446 OFT decision of 3 February 2003.

447 Ibid, paras 37–49.

448 OFT decision of 4 April 2006, upheld on appeal in Case 1067/1/1/06 *Achilles Group Ltd v OFT* [2006] CAT 24.

449 OFT decision of 29 June 2006, upheld on appeal in Case 1072/1/1/06 *Sepia Logistics Ltd v OFT* [2007] CAT 13.

450 OFT decision of 29 September 2009.

451 Cases 1140/1/1/09 etc *Eden Brown v OFT* [2011] CAT 8.

452 *Galvanised steel tanks for water storage main cartel decision*, decision of 19 December 2016 and *Galvanised steel tanks for water storage information exchange decision*, decision of 19 December 2016.

453 Case 1277/1/12/17 *Balmoral Tanks Ltd v CMA* [2017] CAT 23.

454 CMA decision of 16 December 2016.

agencies and a trade association for agreeing to fix minimum prices and a common approach to pricing. In *Access to car parking facilities at East Midlands International Airport*[455] the Civil Aviation Authority found that East Midlands International Airport and Prestige had unlawfully agreed that Prestige should not sell its car parking services at the airport at below a minimum price, which was linked to the price of the airport's own car parking services. Neither party was fined, however, since the airport had blown the whistle and Prestige was no longer trading.

In *Residential estate agency services*[456] the CMA decided that six Somerset estate agents had participated in a price-fixing cartel in relation to estate agency services. One estate agent was not fined because it had blown the whistle; the CMA imposed fines totalling £370,084 on the other five estate agents, four of whom admitted the infringement, while the fifth denied that it was guilty of an infringement, but did not appeal to the CAT[457].

In *LINK Interchange Network*[458] the multilateral interchange fee collectively agreed between banks whose customers withdraw cash from cash points was held to satisfy the criteria of section 9(1) of the Competition Act. A subsequent decision that MasterCard's MIFs infringed the Chapter I prohibition was withdrawn and the investigation was subsequently closed[459]; the High Court has concluded that MasterCard's MIFs and Visa's MIFs do not restrict competition at all, albeit for different reasons[460].

(B) **Agreements relating to terms and conditions**

Agreements on terms and conditions and codes of practice may be caught by the Chapter I prohibition.

(C) **Horizontal market sharing**

The first fine to be imposed under the Competition Act in a cartel case occurred in *Market Sharing by Arriva and FirstGroup*[461], where those two companies were found to have shared bus routes in the Leeds area. The *Stock Check Pads*[462] and *Aluminium Spacer Bars*[463] decisions both included findings of market sharing. In *Supply of care home medicines* a fine of £370,226 was imposed on Hamsard for agreeing with Lloyds Pharmacy to share the market for prescription medicines supplied to care homes in England[464]. Fines of £1.71 million were imposed for market sharing in *Specialist laundry services*[465].

(D) **Quotas and other restriction on production**

As would be expected the CMA has stated that an agreement seeking to limit or control production will almost invariably infringe Article 101 and/or the Chapter I prohibition[466]. In exceptional circumstances section 9 may be applicable. For example, the *Memorandum*

455 Civil Aviation Authority decision of 20 December 2016.
456 CMA decision of 31 May 2017.
457 *Residential estate agency services*, CMA decision of 31 May 2017; on 10 April 2018 the CMA announced that two individuals had been disqualified from acting as company directors as a result of this infringement of the Competition Act 1998.
458 CAT decision of 16 October 2001.
459 See the page on CMA cases at www.gov.uk/cma.
460 See n 204 earlier.
461 OFT decision of 30 January 2002.
462 OFT decision of 4 April 2006, upheld on appeal in Case 1067/1/1/06 *Achilles Group Ltd v OFT* [2006] CAT 24.
463 OFT decision of 29 June 2006, upheld on appeal in Case 1072/1/1/06 *Sepia Logistics Ltd v OFT* [2007] CAT 13.
464 OFT decision of 20 March 2014.
465 CMA decision of 14 December 2017.
466 *Agreements and Concerted Practices*, OFR 401, December 2004, paras 3.12-3.13.

of Understanding on the supply of oil fuels in an emergency[467] enabled the Government to direct supplies of fuel to 'essential users' such as providers of emergency services in the event of a fuel shortage and was held to benefit from section 9 of the Competition Act for a period of ten years[468].

(E) Collusive tendering

Beginning with *West Midland Roofing Contractors* in 2004 there have been a number of decisions condemning collusive tendering. The fines imposed in these cases were as follows:

- *West Midland Roofing Contractors*[469]: £971,186, reduced to £297,625 after leniency and to £288,625 after appeal[470]
- *Mastic Asphalt Flat-roofing Contracts in Scotland*[471]: £231,445, reduced to £87,353 after leniency
- *Felt and Single Ply Roofing Contracts in Western-Central Scotland*[472]: £238,576, reduced to £138,515 after leniency
- *Flat Roof and Car Park Surfacing Contracts in England and Scotland*[473]: £1.852 million, reduced to £1.557 million after leniency
- *Bid rigging in the construction industry in England*[474]: £194.1 million, reduced to £129.2 million after leniency and the 'fast-track offer' and to £63.992 million after appeals
- *Access control and alarm systems*[475]: £53,410, including a reduction of 20% after settlement with one of the parties.

The judgment of the CAT in *Apex Asphalt and Paving Co Ltd v OFT*[476] is particularly useful on the legal analysis of collusive tendering. Various roofing contractors, including Apex, had been found guilty of colluding in relation to the making of tender bids for flat roofing contracts in the West Midlands. Having set out the principles of relevance to determining whether undertakings are party to a concerted practice[477], the CAT proceeded to apply them to a tendering process in which some of the participating undertakings make 'cover bids', that is to say that they submit a price for a contract that is not intended to win the contract (the reason for doing this is that it maintains the appearance of competition, and indicates that the person offering the cover bid wishes to continue participating in future invitations to tender). In the CAT's view:

- a tendering process is designed to produce competition in a very structured way
- bidders are sometimes required to certify that they have not had contact with competitors in the preparation of their bids

[467] OFT decision of 25 October 2001.

[468] Ibid, paras 62–63; see now the Competition Act 1998 (Public Policy Exclusion) Order 2012, SI 2012/710.

[469] OFT decision of 17 March 2004.

[470] Case 1032/1/1/04 *Apex Asphalt and Paving Co Ltd v OFT* [2005] CAT 4 and Case 1033/1/1/04 *Richard W Price Ltd v OFT* [2005] CAT 5.

[471] OFT decision of 7 April 2005.

[472] OFT decision of 11 July 2005.

[473] OFT decision of 23 February 2006.

[474] OFT decision of 21 September 2009.

[475] OFT decision of 6 December 2013.

[476] Case 1032/1/1/04 [2005] CAT 4.

[477] Ibid, para 206.

- where the tendering is selective rather than open to all potential bidders the loss of independence through knowledge of the intentions of other selected bidders is particularly likely to distort competition[478].

The CAT was satisfied on the facts of the case that Apex was party to a concerted practice. The CAT applied the same reasoning in *Makers UK Ltd v OFT*[479], an unsuccessful appeal against the OFT's decision in *Flat Roof and Car Park Surfacing Contracts in England and Scotland*. The OFT's decision in *Construction bid-rigging* was discussed earlier. A report in June 2010 found that there had been significant improvements in awareness of competition law and changes in behaviour since the *Construction bid-rigging* decision[480]. On appeal the CAT upheld the decision in four cases[481], partially annulled the decision in four cases[482], and reduced the fines in 20 cases[483].

Two decisions in relation to the supply of furniture parts resulted in fines of £2.8 million for bid-rigging and the illegal exchange of sensitive information[484].

(F) **Exchanges of information**

In *Exchange of Information on Future Fees by Certain Independent Fee-Paying Schools*[485] the participant schools submitted details of their current fee levels, proposed fee increases (expressed as a percentage) and the resulting intended fee levels to the bursar of one of the schools, who then circulated the information to all the other participants in a tabular form. The OFT concluded that this agreement restricted competition by object; it made no finding as to the effect of the agreement[486]. Each school agreed to pay a nominal fine of £10,000, and they agreed to make *ex gratia* payments of £3 million into a trust fund to benefit pupils who attended the schools during the period of the information exchange[487]. In *Loan pricing*[488] the OFT found that Royal Bank of Scotland had unlawfully disclosed generic and specific confidential future pricing information for loan products to Barclays; RBS admitted the infringement and agreed to pay a fine of £28.59 million. There was no fine on Barclays as it had blown the whistle. As noted earlier, the CAT upheld the CMA's decision to fine Balmoral Tanks for the unlawful exchange of pricing information that took place at a single meeting in July 2012[489].

[478] Ibid, paras 208–212; the UK has issued guidance to public-sector procurers on achieving value through competitive tenders *Making competition work for you*, available at www.nationalarchives.gov.uk; see also OECD *Guidelines for Fighting Bid-Rigging in Public Procurement* (2009), available at www.oecd.org.

[479] Case 1061/1/1/06 [2007] CAT 11, paras 103–110.

[480] *Evaluation of the impact of the OFT's investigation into bid rigging in the construction industry*, OFT 1240, see also OFT Press Release 60/10, 4 June 2010.

[481] Case 1121/1/1/09 *Durkan Holdings Ltd v OFT* [2011] CAT 6, paras 13–92; Case 1126/1/1/09 *ISG Pearce Ltd v OFT* [2011] CAT 10, paras 11–36; Case 1120/1/1/09 *Quarmby Construction Co Ltd v OFT* [2011] CAT 11, paras 8–140; Case 1124/1/1/09 *North Midland Construction plc v OFT* [2011] CAT 14, paras 35–63.

[482] Case 1121/1/1/09 *Durkan Holdings Ltd v OFT* [2011] CAT 6, paras 93–125; Case 1118/1/1/09 *GMI Construction Holdings plc v OFT* [2011] CAT 12; Case 1122/1/1/09 *AH Willis & Sons Ltd v OFT* [2011] CAT 13; Case 1124/1/1/09 *North Midland Construction plc v OFT* [2011] CAT 14, paras 14–34.

[483] See Cases 1114/1/1/09 etc *Kier Group plc v OFT* [2011] CAT 3; Cases 1117/1/1/09 etc *GF Tomlinson Building Ltd v OFT* [2011] CAT 7; Cases 1125/1/1/09 etc *Barrett Estate Services Ltd v OFT* [2011] CAT 9; Case 1121/1/1/09 *Durkan Holdings Ltd v OFT* [2011] CAT 6, paras 126–180; Case 1124/1/1/09 *North Midland Construction plc v OFT* [2011] CAT 14, paras 64–111.

[484] *Supply of products to the furniture industry (drawer wraps)* and *Supply of products to the furniture industry (drawer fronts)*, CMA decisions of 27 March 2017.

[485] OFT decision of 20 November 2006. [486] Ibid, paras 1348–1358.

[487] OFT Press Releases 165/06, 22 November 2006 and 182/06, 21 December 2006.

[488] OFT decision of 20 January 2011.

[489] Case 1277/1/12/17 *Balmoral Tanks Ltd v CMA* [2017] CAT 23.

In *Motor Car Insurers*[490] the OFT accepted commitments from private motor insurers, whereby pricing information would be exchanged through an IT product only if it was at least six months old, anonymised, aggregated across at least five insurers and already 'live' in the insurance policies sold by brokers.

(G) Advertising restrictions

The CMA accepts that the restriction of advertising may diminish competition; however, attempts to curb misleading advertising, or to ensure that advertising is legal, truthful and decent, are unlikely to have an appreciable effect on competition[491]. In *Property sales and lettings*[492] the CMA imposed fines totalling £735,000 on an association of estate agents in Hampshire, three of its members and a newspaper publisher for agreeing to prevent estate agents from advertising their fees or discounts in the local property newspaper. The CMA found that the trade association had been used by its members 'as a vehicle to facilitate the contractual arrangements on behalf of each of its members'[493].

(H) Anti-competitive horizontal restraints

Other anti-competitive agreements may also be subject to the Chapter I prohibition. A rule of the *General Insurance Standards Council* that meant that intermediaries could not sell the general insurance products of GISC's members unless they (the intermediaries) were also members of GISC was held to be a collective boycott and therefore a restriction of competition contrary to the Chapter I prohibition[494]. Such a practice could be upheld, if at all, only by recourse to the criteria in section 9(1) of the Competition Act[495]. In *Construction Recruitment Forum*[496] the CAT held that a collective boycott of a new entrant was among the most serious kind of infringement[497]. The file has been closed on several other cases concerning allegedly exclusionary rules of sports and professional associations, often following amendments to ensure open, non-discriminatory access to those associations[498]. However, in *Showmen's Guild of Great Britain*[499] the CMA accepted legally-binding commitments from the Guild that would open up the market for non-member showmen to participate in fairs and reduce restrictions on rival fairs opening close to the Guild's fares.

490 OFT decision of 2 December 2011.

491 See also *Trade Associations, professions and self-regulating bodies*, OFT 408, December 2004, para 3.14.

492 CMA decision of 8 May 2015. 493 Ibid, para 5.57.3.

494 Case 1003/2/1/01 *Institute of Independent Insurance Brokers v Director General of Fair Trading* [2001] CAT 4, quashing the non-infringement decision of 26 January 2001 and remitting the matter to the OFT; a second non-infringement decision was adopted on 22 November 2002 after the offending rule was dropped.

495 Ibid, para 261. 496 OFT decision of 29 September 2009.

497 Cases 1140/1/1/09 etc *Eden Brown Ltd v OFT* [2011] CAT 8, para 75.

498 *English Rugby Ltd*, case closure of 6 August 2003; *Glasgow Solicitors Property Centre*, OFT Press Release 154/03, 1 December 2003; *Bar Council of Northern Ireland*, OFT Press Release 02/11, 5 January 2011.

499 CMA decision of 26 October 2017.

14

Horizontal agreements (2): oligopoly, tacit collusion and collective dominance

1. Introduction

This chapter is concerned with the related topics of oligopoly, tacit collusion and collective dominance. Oligopoly exists where a few firms between them supply all or most of the goods or services on a market without any of them having a clear ascendancy over the others. Oligopolies can lead to a well-known problem for competition law and policy: oligopolists are able, by virtue of the characteristics of the market, to behave in a parallel manner and to derive benefits from their collective market power without, or without necessarily, entering into an agreement or concerted practice of the kind generally prohibited by competition law. This phenomenon is known in economics as 'tacit collusion'[1] and is the result of each firm's individual and rational response to market conditions. The problem of tacit collusion presents a challenge for competition authorities. Where the evidence is insufficient to establish an infringement of Article 101 or 102 the question arises whether there are other ways to address oligopolistic market failure, and, if so, what remedies might be appropriate to address that failure.

This chapter will begin with a discussion of the theory of oligopolistic interdependence and of possible ways of dealing with the 'oligopoly problem'. Sections 3 and 4 will consider the extent to which Articles 101 and 102 can be used to address it. Section 5 of the chapter discusses UK law and, in particular, the use of market investigations to address market failure in oligopolies. The extent to which the problem of parallel behaviour can be addressed by EU and UK law on the control of mergers is discussed in, respectively, chapters 21 and 22.

[1] See 'Terminology: "tacit collusion"; "conscious parallelism"; "tacit coordination"; "coordinated effects",' p 573 later in chapter.

2. The Theory of Oligopolistic Interdependence

(A) Outline of the theory

The basic objection to monopoly is that a profit-maximising monopolist is able to restrict output and thereby increase the price of its goods or services. As a result it earns supra-competitive profits and society is deprived of the output it has suppressed. In perfect competition no firm has sufficient power over the market to affect prices by an alteration in its output; each firm 'takes' the price from the market and a perfectly competitive market will produce an optimum level of output at the lowest possible price[2]. In reality few markets are perfectly competitive or monopolistic; many are oligopolistic. As we shall see, economic analysis is not conclusive when predicting the outcome of oligopolistic market structures: it may reveal that parallel conduct is 'innocent' where oligopolists simply react to one another's conduct; alternatively it may suggest that there must have been explicit collusion.

(i) The meaning of oligopoly and a warning about the term

Oligopoly is a phenomenon that exists somewhere on the continuum that begins at monopoly and ends at perfect competition, or 'polypoly', where 'mono' means one, 'oligo' a few and the first 'poly' in polypoly means many.

There is a vast literature on the 'problem' of oligopoly[3]. The expression oligopoly is not entirely helpful in describing the situation of concern for competition law and policy, since there are many markets in which there are only a few sellers and yet which are highly competitive; and there are others in which there may be many firms and yet a failure of the competitive process. Economic models of oligopolists competing on price or output are supportive of this point[4]: some oligopolies lead to the same results as perfect competition; others might lead to uncompetitive outcomes. For this reason the problem of 'oligopoly' is not the fact of 'fewness', in itself, but the ability and incentive of oligopolists to exercise 'market power' and thereby suppress output and profitably raise price to the detriment of consumers. It is true

[2] See ch 1, 'The benefits of perfect competition', pp 5–7.

[3] See eg Turner 'The Definition of Agreement under the Sherman Act: Conscious Parallelism and Refusals to Deal' (1962) 75 Harvard Law Review 655; Posner 'Oligopoly and the Antitrust Laws: A Suggested Approach' (1969) 21 Stanford Law Review 1562; Tirole *The Theory of Industrial Organisation* (MIT Press, 1988), ch 6; Scherer and Ross *Industrial Market Structure and Economic Performance* (Houghton Mifflin, 3rd ed, 1990), chs 6–8; Monti 'Oligopoly: Conspiracy? Joint Monopoly? Or Enforceable Competition?' (1996) 19 World Competition 59; Lopatka 'Solving the Oligopoly Problem: Turner's Try' (1996) 41 Antitrust Bulletin 843; Neven 'Oligopolies and Competition Law' [2008] Fordham Competition Law Institute (ed Hawk), p 749; Bishop and Walker *The Economics of EC Competition Law* (Sweet & Maxwell, 3rd ed, 2010), paras 7-049–7-075; Ivaldi, Jullien, Rey, Seabright and Tirole 'The Economics of Tacit Collusion' Final Report for DG Competition, March 2003; Stroux *US and EC Oligopoly Control* (Kluwer, 2004); Werden 'Economic Evidence on the Existence of Collusion: Reconciling Antitrust Law with Oligopoly' (2004) 71 Antitrust LJ 719; Brock 'Antitrust Policy and the Oligopoly Problem' (2006) 51 Antitrust Bulletin 227; Engel 'How Much Collusion? A Meta-Analysis of Oligopoly Experiments' (2007) 3 Journal of Competition Law and Economics 491; O'Donoghue and Padilla *The Law and Economics of Article 102 TFEU* (Hart, 2nd ed, 2013), pp 185–200; Petit 'The Oligopoly Problem in EU Competition Law' in Lianos and Geradin (eds) *Research Handbook in European Competition Law* (Edward Elgar, 2013); Lipsey and Chrystal *Principles of Economics* (Oxford University Press, 13th ed, 2015), pp 175–190; see also some of the earlier economics literature, eg Hall and Hitch 'Price Theory and Business Behaviour' (1939) 2 Oxford Economic Papers 12; Sweezy 'Demand under Conditions of Oligopoly' (1937) 47 J Pol Ec 568; Stigler 'The Kinky Oligopoly Demand Curve' (1947) 55 J Pol Ec 431.

[4] For a general discussion of these models see Church and Ware *Industrial Organisation: A Strategic Approach* (McGraw-Hill/Irwin, 2000), ch 8; Bishop and Walker *The Economics of EC Competition Law* (Sweet & Maxwell, 3rd ed, 2010), paras 2-020–2-033; Carlton and Perloff *Modern Industrial Organisation* (Pearson, 4th ed, 2015), ch 6; Niels, Jenkins and Kavanagh *Economics for Competition Lawyers* (Oxford University Press, 2nd ed, 2016), paras 7.95–7.101.

that the fewer the number of players in a market, the more likely it is that market power will exist; however, the identification of market power is not simply a matter of counting heads. There is, nevertheless, a certain catchiness in talking of 'the oligopoly problem', and there is no harm in using the expression provided that the caveat just entered is kept in mind.

(ii) **The oligopoly problem**

The main argument against oligopoly is that the characteristics of the market in which oligopolists operate are such that they will not compete with one another on price and will have little incentive to compete in other ways; furthermore they will be able to earn supra-competitive profits without entering into an agreement or concerted practice of the kind generally prohibited by systems of competition law.

The problem can be identified by comparing the position in an oligopoly with a perfectly competitive market. Thus the theory runs that in an oligopolistic market rivals are interdependent: they are acutely aware of each other's presence and are bound to match one another's marketing strategy; the result is a stable, non-competitive market and price competition is minimal or non-existent. The literature on so-called 'game theory' and 'the Prisoner's Dilemma', which recognises that firms take into account the likely actions (and reactions) of competitors when deciding how to behave, is supportive of this explanation of oligopoly[5].

The argument can be taken further. Oligopolists recognise their interdependence as well as their own self-interest in maximising profits. By matching each other's conduct they will be able to charge a higher, profit-maximising price, without communicating with one another. There does not need to be any communication: the structure of the market is such that, through interdependence and mutual self-awareness, oligopoly can produce quasi-monopoly prices. A separate objection is that the non-competitive environment in which oligopolists function may enable them to act in an inefficient manner. These theoretical arguments have been buttressed by empirical research which purports to show that there is a direct correlation between industrial structure and profit levels, which are said to increase in line with the concentration ratio of the industry in question[6], although the soundness of much of this evidence has been challenged[7]. The distinction between firms' behaviour in perfect competition and in oligopolistic markets can be depicted pictorially as follows:

PERFECT COMPETITION	OLIGOPOLY
A firm that cuts reduces its price will have an imperceptible effect on its competitors, who have no need to respond. A firm cannot increase its price because consumers would switch to alternative suppliers.	An oligopolist that reduces its price will have a significant effect on its main rivals, who are likely to respond. An oligopolist cannot increase its price unilaterally because it would be likely to be deserted by its customers if it were to do so.

[5] See *Tirole*, pp 205–208; *Scherer and Ross*, pp 208–215; *Bishop and Walker*, paras 2-28–2-30; *Lipsey and Chrystal*, pp 188–192; Franzosi 'Oligopoly and the Prisoner's Dilemma: Concerted Practices and "As If" Behaviour' (1988) 9 ECLR 385; *Carlton and Perloff*, ch 6; *Church and Ware*, chs 3 and 4; Cabral *Introduction to Industrial Organization* (MIT Press, 2000); Van den Bergh and Camesasca *European Competition Law and Economics: A Comparative Perspective* (Sweet & Maxwell, 2nd ed, 2006), pp 156–159; Motta *Competition Policy: Theory and Practice* (Cambridge University Press, 2004), ch 8; see generally Phlips *Competition Policy: A Game Theoretic Perspective* (Cambridge University Press, 1995).

[6] See eg Bain 'Relation of Profit Rate to Industry Concentration' (1951) 65 Qu J Ec 293–324.

[7] See eg Weiss 'The Concentration and Profits Issue' in *Industrial Concentration: The New Learning* (Little, Brown, 1974); Brozen 'The Concentration-Collusion Doctrine' (1977) 46 Antitrust LJ 826.

The logical conclusion of the case against oligopoly is that, since it is the market structure itself which produces the problem, structural measures should be taken to remedy it by deconcentrating the market. Unless this is done, there will be an area of consciously parallel behaviour in pricing strategies which is beyond the reach of competition laws and yet which harms both competition and consumers.

(iii) Terminology: 'tacit collusion'; 'conscious parallelism'; 'tacit coordination'; 'coordinated effects'

There is little doubt that there are markets in which it is possible for firms to coordinate their behaviour without entering into an agreement or being party to a concerted practice in the sense of Article 101(1) TFEU; such behaviour will be to their own self-advantage and to the disadvantage of consumers. This situation is often described by economists as 'tacit collusion': enjoying the benefits of a particular market structure without actually entering into an agreement to do so. If the firms in question had achieved the same end through explicit collusion, economists would have the same objection—that prices are higher than they would be without coordination. Economists have no particular interest in whether collusion is 'tacit' or 'explicit': it is the effects of the collusion that matter.

Lawyers, however, are considerably less comfortable with the expression 'tacit collusion'. They associate the notion of collusion with actively conspiratorial behaviour of the kind captured by the expressions 'agreement' and 'concerted practice' in Article 101, whereas tacit collusion may occur without the need for an agreement or concerted practice[8]. For many lawyers, to ask whether tacit collusion could alternatively be caught by the concept of collective dominance under Article 102 is bizarre, since any behaviour that could be called collusive in a legal sense would be caught by Article 101 anyway. If behaviour is not collusive under Article 101, lawyers not unnaturally feel uncomfortable at characterising the same behaviour as tacitly collusive and abusive under Article 102. An alternative expression for the conduct in question, 'conscious parallelism', may cause lawyers slightly less discomfort, the opprobrious word 'collusive' being avoided; but even 'consciousness' seems to move the inquiry back to a search for a conspiracy that should really be investigated, if at all, under Article 101.

In the interests of finding terminology that is meaningful and tolerable both to economists and to lawyers when considering the application of Article 102 it might be better to use the expression 'tacit coordination', since this at least eliminates the pejorative word 'collusion' whilst retaining the notion of parallel behaviour which is beneficial to the oligopolists and disadvantageous to consumers. In the context of merger control, competition authorities routinely examine whether a merger would lead to 'coordinated effects' on the market, which again has the benefit of avoiding reference to the idea of collusion.

(iv) 'Non-collusive oligopoly'

An additional complication is the recognition that certain mergers might give rise to competition problems where they would result in 'non-collusive oligopoly', that is to say a situation in which one or more members of an oligopoly, without being individually dominant, would be able to derive benefits from their enhanced market power after a

[8] The notion of collusiveness is also inherent in the ideas of 'contract' and 'conspiracy' prohibited by s 1 Sherman Act; for the treatment of parallel behaviour under US law see *Re High Fructose Corn Syrup Antitrust Litigation* 295 F 3d 651 (7th Cir 2002); see further Kovacic et al 'Plus Factors and Agreement in Antitrust Law' (2011) 110 Michigan Law Review 393.

merger without being dependent on the coordinated response of the other oligopolists. This chapter is concerned with the 'conventional' theory of oligopoly in which firms act in a coordinated manner rather than with non-collusive oligopoly: that phenomenon can be addressed under the EU Merger Regulation ('the EUMR') and is discussed in chapter 21[9].

(v) The conditions needed for the successful exercise of collective market power

For tacit coordination to occur it is necessary for firms to indulge in a common form of behaviour[10]. Typically this would involve the charging of similar prices; however it might also involve parallel decisions to reduce production or not to expand capacity: such decisions would, through the suppression of output, in themselves have an impact on prices in the industry in question. There are three conditions for tacit coordination:

- **transparency**: each firm must be able to monitor quickly and easily how the others are behaving on the market: successful parallel behaviour requires that no one should deviate from the common conduct; a sufficient degree of transparency is therefore vital to each economic operator to enable it to know what the others are doing, both in terms of their prices and their output
- **sustainability**: tacit coordination will be sustainable only if a firm's incentive to 'cheat' on the coordination is negated by rivals' ability to nullify the benefits of cheating. There must be what economists refer to as a 'deterrent mechanism'. The most obvious deterrent would be a sharp price war which would be harmful to everyone, and would send a severe warning that abandonment of tacit coordination will be to everyone's disadvantage
- **absence of effective competitive constraints**: the reactions of competitors, customers and consumers should not be such as to jeopardise the results expected from the tacit coordination[11].

(B) Criticisms of the theory

The theory of oligopolistic interdependence has attracted criticism[12]. This section will examine five particular issues.

(i) How interdependent are oligopolists?

The first is that the theory tends to overstate the interdependence of oligopolists. Even in a symmetrical three-firm oligopoly one firm might be able to steal a march on its rivals by cutting its price if, for example, there would be a delay before the others discovered what it had done: in the meantime the price-cutter may make sufficient profit to offset the cost of any subsequent retaliation. It may also be that the rivals will be unable to expand their capacity to meet the increased demand that could be expected to follow a price cut. Anyway, an expansion in output may simply mean that the price-cutter attracts new customers, not that existing ones switch from its rivals.

[9] See ch 21, 'The non-collusive oligopoly gap', pp 883–885.

[10] The indicia of tacit coordination have been particularly well explained in the Commission's *Guidelines on the assessment of horizontal mergers* OJ [2004] C 31/5; they are discussed in ch 21, 'Coordinated effects', pp 893–895.

[11] As will be seen, the Court of Justice's judgment in *Impala* (see ch 14 n 138 later) defines collective dominance under the EUMR consistently with the conditions set out in this paragraph: see 'The judgment of the Court of Justice in *Compagnie Maritime Belge Transports v Commission*', pp 589–591 later in chapter.

[12] See eg Bork *The Antitrust Paradox* (Free Press, 1993), ch 8.

(ii) Does the theory of oligopolistic interdependence reflect markets in the real world?

A second problem is that the theory of oligopolistic interdependence oversimplifies how markets operate in real life. In a symmetrical, stable oligopoly where producers produce identical goods at the same costs interdependence may be strong, but in reality market conditions are usually more complex. The oligopolists will almost inevitably have different cost levels; they may be producing differentiated goods and will usually benefit from at least some consumer loyalty; and their market shares will often not be equal. Furthermore there may be a fringe of smaller sellers that may exert a competitive constraint on the oligopolists and, depending on barriers to entry, other firms not operating on the market may enter in response to oligopolists earning supra-competitive profits. Many other factors affect the competitive environment in which oligopolists operate. The concentration of the market on the buying side is also important: the more concentrated it is, the less the oligopolists might compete with one another since it will be relatively easy to detect attempts to attract the custom of particular customers. The transparency of price information is significant: the easier it is to conceal the price of goods or services from competitors, the less will be the interdependence or mutual awareness of the oligopolists. Similarly oligopolists may be able, through secret rebates, to charge prices lower than those in their published price lists. These, and many other, factors mean that oligopolistic markets differ considerably from one another and this in turn makes it difficult to provide a convincing theoretical explanation of how all oligopolies function and how they should be dealt with.

(iii) Why are some oligopolistic markets competitive?

A third problem with the theory of interdependence is that it fails to explain why competition is intense in some oligopolistic markets. Firms quite clearly do compete with one another in some oligopolies. Such competition may take various forms. Open price competition may be limited, although price wars do break out periodically in some oligopolistic markets, for example between supermarkets or petrol companies. Where open price competition is restricted, this does not mean that secret price cutting does not occur. Non-price competition may be particularly strong in oligopolistic markets. This may manifest itself in various ways: offering better quality products and after-sales service; striving for a lead in innovation and research and development (sometimes described as the 'grass-roots' of competition in oligopoly); by introducing loyalty schemes of the kinds offered by airlines and supermarkets; and by making large investments in advertising to promote brand image[13]. Whilst expenditure on advertising has been objected to because it is wasteful of resources and amounts to a barrier to entry to new entrants, it is a form of non-price competition that is inconsistent with the suggestion that oligopolists do not compete with one another[14].

(iv) How do oligopolists achieve a supra-competitive price?

A fourth objection to the theory of oligopolistic interdependence is that it does not explain satisfactorily its central proposition, which is that oligopolists can earn supra-competitive profits without explicitly colluding. The interdependence theory says they cannot increase price unilaterally because they will lose custom to their rivals and yet, to earn supra-competitive profits, prices must have been increased from time to time: how could

[13] This is a particular feature of certain retail markets such as breakfast cereals, household detergents and alcoholic drinks such as lagers.

[14] See *Scherer and Ross*, pp 592–610.

this have been achieved without explicit collusion? A possible answer to this is that a pattern of price leadership develops whereby one firm raises its price and this acts as a signal to the others to follow suit. Prices therefore remain parallel without overt communication between the oligopolists, although this is not particularly convincing[15]. Economists have suggested that price leadership may take three forms[16]. Dominant price leadership exists where a dominant firm raises its price and other firms in the industry follow suit because it is in their best interests to do so. This is not what happens in an oligopoly, where no firm is dominant. Secondly, barometric price leadership occurs where one firm raises its price because increased costs (for example, in wages or raw materials) force it to do so: other firms faced with the same increase in costs then follow suit. It would be unreasonable to condemn parallel increases in price if they are explicable on an objective basis in this way. The third type of price leadership is termed collusive: here there is an understanding that firms in an industry will follow the signal emitted from time to time by the price leader. However in this case it would seem to be perfectly reasonable to brand their action as an agreement or a concerted practice under competition law.

(v) Why is a market oligopolistic in the first place?

A fifth criticism of the theory of interdependence is that it concentrates solely on the tendency to non-collusive price fixing without asking why a market is oligopolistic in the first place: this might be because of the superior efficiency associated with economies of scale. In this case, it is necessary to consider at what point the advantages arising from these economies are offset by the adverse effects of a loss of competition. A separate, but related, point is to ask why a market continues to be oligopolistic over time: if oligopolists earn supra-competitive profits over a short period, that would ordinarily attract new entrants to the market and increase competition in the long run.

(C) Possible ways of dealing with the oligopoly problem

Having considered this theoretical debate, the pertinent question is what, if anything, should be done about oligopoly in competition law, assuming that a problem exists. There would appear to be at least four approaches.

(i) A structural approach

If economic theory were to demonstrate convincingly that oligopoly inevitably leads to uncompetitive outcomes, and also that there are no redeeming features of oligopolistic markets, this would suggest that the problem should be seen as a structural one and dealt with as such. In this case it would be necessary to establish legal rules preventing the structure of the market from becoming conducive to tacit coordination in the first place. As will be seen in chapters 20 to 22, this is an important function of merger control. An important question however is whether further structural powers are needed to deconcentrate industries that become oligopolistic other than through the process of mergers: should systems of competition law include powers to dismantle oligopolistic markets, or at least to inject competitiveness into a sleepy, uncompetitive, market? Where an infringement of Article 101 or 102 TFEU is the consequence of the structural conditions of the market and there is no effective behavioural remedy, Article 7 of Regulation

[15] See Posner *Antitrust Law* (University of Chicago Press, 1976), p 59.

[16] See Markham 'The Nature and Significance of Price Leadership' (1951) 41 Am Ec Rev 891–905; the classification suggested there was adopted in the former Monopolies and Mergers Commission's report *Parallel Pricing* Cmnd 5330 (1973).

1/2003 provides for the possibility of structural remedies to bring that infringement to an end[17]. UK law does not explicitly provide such a power under the Competition Act 1998. However a structural solution to the problem of oligopolistic markets is possible under the market investigation provisions of the Enterprise Act 2002[18]. It goes without saying that it would require an exceptional case for these draconian remedies to be used, but it is important to be aware that the possibility exists.

(ii) A behavioural approach

An alternative approach is to see the problem as essentially behavioural in nature, in which case control is necessary to prevent oligopolists behaving in a way that is uncompetitive. Some would favour making any parallelism in price between oligopolists illegal[19]. This however would be quite inappropriate: it would be absurd to forbid firms from behaving in a parallel manner if this is a rational response to the structure of the market. To put the point another way, it would be strange indeed if competition law were to mandate that firms should behave irrationally, by not acting in parallel, in order to avoid being found to have infringed competition law.

Where oligopolists explicitly collude, for example to fix prices or to share markets, there is no reason why they—like firms in less concentrated markets—should not be subject to Article 101 and its domestic equivalents. The term 'concerted practice' catches any form of coordination between undertakings which 'knowingly substitutes practical cooperation between them for the risks of competition'[20]. However when the concept of a concerted practice is applied to the behaviour of oligopolists a different problem arises: it can be difficult to distinguish conduct which is collusive in the sense of Article 101 from parallel conduct which is attributable to the oligopolistic structure of a market. This problem is compounded by the fact that in many cases there is little or no evidence of unlawful contact between firms, such as the minutes of a meeting: firms that rig the market are wise enough usually to destroy incriminating evidence. The danger is that a competition authority or court will too readily reach the conclusion that parallel conduct means that there is collusion; this can be avoided only by considering the alternative plausible explanations for such conduct, including an economic analysis of the market in question. An understanding of the economics of oligopoly is vital when trying to decide whether parallel conduct is the result of collusion (in the legal sense) or not[21].

As a separate matter, it may be appropriate in oligopolistic markets to prohibit 'facilitating practices' that lead to parallel behaviour: an obvious example is the exchange of information between oligopolists that makes it easier for them to behave in the same way. As we have seen, the structure of the market is one of the factors taken into account when analysing information exchanges under Article 101[22]. The possibility that an agreement might facilitate parallel behaviour may also be considered when applying the criteria of Article 101(3)[23].

[17] See ch 7, 'Structural remedies', p 262.

[18] See 'Market studies and market investigations under the Enterprise Act 2002', pp 594–596 later in chapter and ch 11, 'Final powers', p 484.

[19] See eg Posner 'Oligopoly and the Antitrust Laws: A Suggested Approach' (1969) 21 Stanford Law Review 1562.

[20] Cases 48/69 etc *ICI v Commission* EU:C:1972:70, para 64.

[21] See further the discussion in ch 3, 'Concerted practices', pp 115–119.

[22] See ch 13, 'Exchanges of Information', pp 551–559 and 'Article 101(1), the exchange of information and other facilitating practices', pp 581–582 later in chapter.

[23] See 'Article 101(3)', p 583 later in chapter.

Finally, it may be sensible to prohibit the behaviour of firms that hold a collective dominant position if it has the effect of foreclosing access to the market for competitors of the oligopolists; as will be seen, there have been a few cases in which Article 102 has been used to deal with behaviour of this sort.

(iii) A regulatory approach

A different possibility would be to regulate oligopolists' prices[24]. This, however, would be a counsel of despair. As a matter of policy economic regulation should be a remedy of last resort. Competition authorities should not be price regulators; they should be the guardians of the competitive process. Where markets are oligopolistic and entry is limited, competition authorities should be concerned with the question of whether there are barriers to entry and whether the state itself, for example through restrictive licensing rules, regulation or legislation, is responsible for a lack of effective competition.

(iv) A market investigation approach

The problem of price parallelism and the possibility that oligopolists are charging supra-competitive prices without actually conspiring to do so may be tackled by conducting a market investigation; this may enable a competition authority to understand better why an oligopolistic market exists and why it is not functioning well, and to determine what can be done to improve the situation. The provisions on 'sectoral inquiries' in the EU[25] and on 'market studies' and 'market investigations' in the UK[26] are examples of this approach.

3. Article 101

(A) Does parallel behaviour amount to a concerted practice under Article 101?

Both the Commission and the EU Courts appreciate that price competition in an oligopoly may be muted and that oligopolists react to one another's conduct, so that parallel behaviour does not, in itself, amount to a concerted practice under Article 101(1)[27]. In *Dyestuffs*[28] the Court of Justice said at paragraphs 65 and 66 that:

> By its very nature, then, the concerted practice does not have all the elements of a contract but may *inter alia* arise out of coordination which becomes apparent from the behaviour of the participants. *Although parallel behaviour may not itself be identified with a concerted practice,* it may however amount to strong evidence of such a practice if it leads to conditions of competition which do not respond to the normal conditions of the market, having regard to the nature of the products, the size and number of the undertakings, and the volume of the said market. Such is the case especially where the parallel behaviour is such as to permit the parties to seek price equilibrium at a different level from that which would have resulted from competition, and to crystallise the status quo to the detriment of effective freedom of movement of the products in the [internal] market and free choice by consumers of their suppliers (emphasis added).

[24] See eg BEREC Report on Oligopoly Analysis and Regulation, December 2015, available at www.berec.europa.eu.

[25] On sectoral inquiries see ch 7, 'Article 17: investigations into sectors of the economy and into types of agreements', p 277.

[26] On market studies and market investigations see ch 11, 'Market Studies', pp 465–469 and ch 11, 'Market Investigation References', pp 469–481.

[27] On concerted practices generally see ch 3, 'Concerted practices', pp 115–119.

[28] Cases 48/69 etc EU:C:1972:70.

The Court added at paragraph 68 that the existence of a concerted practice could be appraised correctly only:

> if the evidence upon which the contested decision is based is considered, not in isolation, but as a whole, account being taken of the specific features of the products in question.

In *Dyestuffs* the Commission had fined ten producers of dyestuffs which it considered were guilty of price fixing through concerted practices. The Court of Justice upheld the Commission's decision. It rejected the parties' argument that they had acted in a similar manner only because of the oligopolistic market structure. The dyestuffs market was not a pure oligopoly: rather it was one in which firms could realistically be expected to adopt their own pricing strategies, particularly in view of the compartmentalisation of the markets along national boundaries. The Court recognised that there might be situations in which a firm must take into account a rival's likely responses, but said that this did not entitle them actually to coordinate their behaviour: Although every producer is free to change its prices, taking into account in so doing the present or foreseeable conduct of its competitors, nevertheless it is contrary to Article 101 for a producer to cooperate with its competitors, in any way whatsoever, in order to determine a coordinated course of action relating to a price increase and to ensure its success by prior elimination of uncertainty as to each other's conduct regarding the essential elements of that action, such as the amount, subject-matter, date and place of the increases[29].

In *Züchner v Bayerische Vereinsbank*[30] the Court of Justice repeated that intelligent responses to a competitor's behaviour would not bring firms within the scope of Article 101(1). In *Zinc Producer Group*[31] the Commission said that it did not intend to condemn parallel action between 1977 and 1979 which might be explicable in terms of 'barometric price leadership'[32], saying that in such circumstances 'parallel pricing behaviour in an oligopoly producing homogeneous goods will not in itself be sufficient evidence of a concerted practice'[33]. In *Peroxygen Products*[34], however, the Commission rejected an argument that an agreement between oligopolists fell outside Article 101(1) since, even without the agreement, the structure of the market would have meant that they would have behaved in the same way. In the Commission's view the very fact that the firms had entered into an agreement at all indicated that the risks of competition might have led to different market behaviour.

In *Wood Pulp*[35] the Commission held that 40 producers of wood pulp and three of their trade associations were guilty of a concerted practice to fix prices in the EU. There had been parallel conduct on the market from 1975 until 1981, but there was no evidence of explicit agreements to fix prices. However the Commission concluded that there was a concerted practice, basing its finding on two factors. The first was that there had been a quarterly announcement of prices that had created an artificial transparency on the market so that producers could rapidly discover their competitors' prices. The second was that, in the Commission's view, an economic analysis of the market demonstrated that it was not a narrow oligopoly in which parallel pricing might be expected. On appeal the Court of Justice substantially annulled the Commission's findings[36]. The fact that pulp producers announced price rises to users in advance on

[29] Ibid, para 118. [30] Case 172/80 EU:C:1981:178, para 14. [31] OJ [1984] L 220/27.
[32] See 'Criticisms of the theory', pp 574–576 earlier in chapter. [33] OJ [1984] L 220/27, paras 75–76.
[34] OJ [1985] L 35/1, para 50. [35] OJ [1985] L 85/1.
[36] Cases C-89/85 etc *A Ahlström Osakeyhtiö v Commission* EU:C:1993:120; for comment see Jones '*Wood Pulp*: Concerted Practice and/or Conscious Parallelism?' (1993) 14 ECLR 273; Van Gerven and Varano 'The *Wood Pulp* Case and the Future of Concerted Practices' (1994) 31 CML Rev 575.

a quarterly basis did not in itself involve an infringement of Article 101(1): making information available to third parties did not eliminate the producers' uncertainty as to what each other would do[37]. Furthermore the system of price announcements, and the simultaneity and parallelism of prices, could be explained other than by the existence of a concerted practice. The system of price announcements had developed as a compromise between customers' desire to know input prices in advance and producers' desires to maximise profits in the event of a strengthening of the market[38]. The simultaneity of price announcements could be explained by the high degree of market transparency: information was widely available on the market as buyers informed each other of the prices available, some agents acted for several producers and so were well informed about prices and the trade press was dynamic[39]. As to the parallelism of announced prices, the evidence of experts appointed by the Court was that the market was more oligopolistic (on both sides of the market) than the Commission had supposed, and that economic problems had discouraged producers from engaging in price cutting which their competitors would inevitably follow. The experts also considered that there was evidence to suggest that there could not have been concertation: for example, market shares had varied from time to time, which would be unlikely if there had been a concerted practice; and the alleged cartel members had not tried to establish production quotas, which they could be expected to have done if they wished to control the market[40].

In *British Sugar*[41] British Sugar deployed the argument that the oligopolistic nature of the market meant that price competition was limited, and that its price leadership should not be regarded as evidence of a concerted practice. The Commission's reply to this was that, where competition in a market is already restricted, it should be particularly vigilant to ensure that the competition which does exist is not restricted[42]; the General Court upheld this finding on appeal[43]. This is consistent with the judgments in *Steel Beams*[44].

In *CISAC*[45] the Commission found that 24 collecting societies had taken part in a concerted practice that limited their ability to offer services outside their domestic territory. The Commission considered that the only explanation for the societies' parallel conduct was collusion between them[46]. On appeal, however, the General Court held that the Commission had failed to prove that there had been a concerted practice to the 'requisite legal standard'[47]. The Court considered that the Commission's assessment of the documentary evidence was flawed[48]. The General Court acknowledged, however, that parallel behaviour could be evidence of a concerted practice where there is no plausible alternative explanation[49]. The Court held that there was an explanation of parallelism in this case other than collusion, which was the fight against the unauthorised use of musical works[50]. The Commission had failed to show that this alternative explanation was implausible and, therefore, this aspect of its decision was annulled[51].

[37] Cases C-89/85 etc *A Ahlström Osakeyhtiö v Commission* EU:C:1993:120, paras 59–65.
[38] Ibid, paras 71–79. [39] Ibid, paras 80–88. [40] Ibid, paras 89–125.
[41] OJ [1999] L 76/1; see also *Cartonboard* OJ [1994] L 243/1, para 73. [42] OJ [1999] L 76/1, para 87.
[43] Cases T-202/98 etc *Tate & Lyle v Commission* EU:T:2001:185, para 46.
[44] Case T-141/94 *Thyssen Stahl AG v Commission* EU:T:1999:48, para 302, upheld on appeal Case C-194/99 P EU:C:2003:527.
[45] Commission decision of 16 July 2008. [46] Ibid, paras 156–223.
[47] Cases T-442/08 etc *CISAC v Commission* EU:T:2013:188. [48] Ibid, paras 106–132.
[49] Ibid, paras 96–102 and 137. [50] Ibid, paras 134–139. [51] Ibid, paras 140–181.

The case law establishes that the Commission must prove the existence of a concerted practice and that, when it relies solely on firms' parallel behaviour as proof of a concerted practice, it must address any alternative explanations advanced by the parties of that behaviour and demonstrate why they are not convincing[52].

(B) Article 101(1), the exchange of information and other facilitating practices

The previous section has discussed the difficulties in proving that parallel behaviour is attributable to collusion between firms as opposed to the oligopolistic structure of the market. Parallel behaviour does not provide evidence of a concerted practice if there is an alternative plausible explanation of that behaviour. However this is not to say that Article 101(1) cannot be deployed in other ways to deal with the problem of parallel behaviour: in particular it can be applied to what are often referred to as 'facilitating practices', that is to say practices that make it easier for firms to achieve the benefits of tacit coordination. An obvious facilitating practice is an exchange of information that artificially increases the transparency of the market and so makes parallel behaviour easier. It is for this reason that the application of Article 101(1) to exchanges of information focuses, amongst other things, on the structure of the market[53]. It was the oligopolistic structure of the market in *UK Agricultural Tractor Registration Exchange*[54] that led the Commission to conclude that Article 101(1) had been infringed; and the more competitive nature of the cars' market that led it to the opposite conclusion in relation to it[55]. In *Thyssen Stahl v Commission*[56] the General Court held that, where the structure of a market is oligopolistic, it is all the more important to ensure the decision-making independence of undertakings and residual competition, and that therefore the exchange of recent data on market shares could infringe Article 101(1)[57]. The Court of Justice confirmed the Commission's application of this principle in *Bananas* when condemning three banana importers for disclosing price trends or indications of quotation prices for the forthcoming week[58].

The Commission will look for other practices that facilitate non-competitive conduct on the part of oligopolists. For example at paragraph 20 of its *Guidelines on Vertical Restraints*[59] it says that it will examine agency agreements, even where the principal bears

[52] The Commission considered that there was no alternative plausible explanation than the existence of a concerted practice for the anti-competitive parallel conduct of Apple and four publishers in *E-books*, Commission decision of 12 December 2012, paras 70–81, a commitment decision under Article 9(1) of Regulation 1/2003; note however that a commitment decision does not involve a formal finding of infringement of competition law: see ch 7, 'Article 9: commitments', pp 264–269.

[53] See ch 13, 'Exchanges of Information', pp 551–559.

[54] OJ [1992] L 68/19, para 16, upheld on appeal to the General Court in Cases T-34/92 etc *Fiatagri UK Ltd v Commission* EU:T:1994:258 and on appeal to the Court of Justice in Cases C-7/95 P etc *John Deere v Commission* EU:C:1998:256.

[55] See ch 13, 'The economic conditions on the relevant markets', pp 556–557; para 79 of the Commission's *Guidelines on Horizontal Cooperation Agreements* is specifically concerned with information agreements in oligopolistic markets.

[56] See ch 14 n 44 earlier.

[57] Cases C-7/95 P etc *John Deere v Commission* EU:C:1998:256, paras 393–412; see similarly Case T-53/03 *BPB v Commission* EU:T:2008:254, paras 108–109.

[58] Commission decision of 15 October 2008, para 280, upheld on appeal Case T-588/08 *Dole Food v Commission* EU:T:2013:130, paras 51–585, upheld on further appeal Case C-286/13 P *Dole Food v Commission* EU:C:2015:184, paras 129–134; note that the decision was substantially upheld in a related appeal Case T-587/08 *Fresh Del Monte v Commission* EU:T:2013:129, substantially upheld on further appeal Cases C-293/13 P etc EU:C:2015:416.

[59] OJ [2010] C 130/1.

all the financial and commercial risks, if they could facilitate collusion[60]. This could happen, in the Commission's view, if a number of principals use the same agents whilst collectively preventing others from doing so, or where they use agents to collude on marketing strategy or to exchange sensitive information between themselves. Similar concerns are expressed throughout the *Guidelines* as to the possibility of vertical agreements facilitating collusion[61].

The Commission's *Guidelines on Horizontal Cooperation Agreements*[62] state that, in assessing horizontal cooperation agreements other than 'hard-core' cartels of the kind that almost always fall within Article 101(1)[63], the characteristics of the market will be taken into account[64]: some agreements may be found not to be anti-competitive where the market is reasonably competitive, but to be problematic where it is oligopolistic. The application of these *Guidelines* is considered in some detail in chapter 15[65].

The Commission has applied the *de minimis* doctrine narrowly in the case of an oligopoly[66] and has more readily found an appreciable effect on inter-state trade of an agreement where the market was oligopolistic[67].

(C) **Price signalling**

A phenomenon that has generated controversy in recent years is 'price signalling', by which is meant the unilateral, public disclosure of information to third parties that may lead to coordination between competitors. The OECD has noted that greater transparency, including of price, is generally efficiency-enhancing[68], although concerns may arise where announcements of future prices provide a focal point around which competitors can align their behaviour. The Commission's *Guidelines on Horizontal Cooperation Agreements*[69] say that price announcements can amount to a concerted practice if they reduce 'strategic uncertainty'. There has yet to be a decision of the Commission or of a national competition authority that has found price signalling to be an infringement of competition law and that has been confirmed on appeal[70].

The Commission objected to the system of price announcements in *Wood Pulp*[71], but its decision was annulled on appeal. In *Container Shipping*[72] the Commission was

[60] As a general principle agency agreements fall outside Article 101(1): see ch 16, 'Commercial Agents', pp 634–637.

[61] See eg the following paragraphs in the *Guidelines on Vertical Restraints* OJ [2010] C 130/1, all of which refer to the possibility of the facilitation of collusion: paras 100(b)–(c), 101, 115, 121, 130, 134, 151, 154, 157, 166 (specifically on exclusive dealerships in an oligopolistic market), 168, 175, 178, 181, 182, 206, 211, 212, 224 and 227.

[62] OJ [2011] C 11/1.

[63] That is to say those agreements that have as their object the restriction of competition: see ch 3, 'Agreements that have as their object the prevention, restriction or distortion of competition', pp 122–132 and ch 13 generally.

[64] OJ [2011] C 11/1, paras 39–47.

[65] See ch 15 generally.

[66] *Floral* OJ [1980] L 39/51, on the *de minimis* doctrine see ch 3, 'The *De Minimis* Doctrine', pp 147–150.

[67] *Cast Iron and Steel Rolls* OJ [1983] L 317/1, upheld on appeal Cases 29/83 etc *Compagnie Royale Asturienne des Mines SA and Rheinzink GmbH v Commission* EU:C:1984:130.

[68] OECD Policy Roundtable *Unilateral Disclosure of Information with Anticompetitive Effects* (2012), available at www.oecd.org/competition.

[69] OJ [2011] C 11/1, para 63.

[70] In addition to the cases mentioned in the text see *KPN/T-Mobile/Vodafone*, Dutch NCA commitment decision of 7 January 2014; *U-Haul International Inc*, FTC settlement order of 20 July 2010.

[71] Cases C-89/85 etc *A Ahlström Osakeyhtiö v Commission* EU:C:1993:120.

[72] Commission commitment decision of 7 July 2016.

concerned that announcements of future price increases for liner shipping services could be a way for liner companies to 'test' whether competitors were likely to follow price rises, thereby reducing strategic uncertainty and diminishing incentives to compete; the announcements, and the responses to them, might enable the liner companies to align their prices at higher levels[73]. The Commission's preliminary conclusion was that these price announcements constituted a concerted practice that had as its object the restriction of competition[74]. In the end the Commission did not decide whether there had been an infringement and instead accepted commitments from the liner companies aimed at increasing price transparency for customers while decreasing the likelihood of coordination of prices[75].

Given the uncertainty of the law in this area—not least as to the application of the concept of a concerted practice—some would take the view that the Commission should have adopted an infringement decision in *Container Shipping*, perhaps with no fine. Of course this would expose the Commission to the risk that the decision might then be overturned on appeal, but law is made through the adoption of infringement decisions in uncertain areas, which then have to pass scrutiny by the EU Courts.

(D) **Article 101(3)**

The structure of the market will be relevant to the analysis of agreements under Article 101(3), in particular since that provision requires that there should be no elimination of competition[76]. The fact that the Commission's block exemptions are subject to market share caps means that firms in an oligopoly will often not be able to avail themselves of these legal instruments[77]. In *P&O Stena Line*[78] the Commission decided that the criteria of Article 101(3) were satisfied in the case of a joint venture for cross-channel ferry services for a limited period of three years; the decision considered at length whether there was a risk that the joint venture would create a duopoly on the 'short sea tourist market', but concluded that the joint venture and Eurotunnel, the operator of the Channel Tunnel, could be expected to compete with each other rather than to act in parallel to raise prices[79].

An agreement might be found to satisfy Article 101(3) where it would have the effect of introducing more competition into an oligopolistic market[80].

4. **Article 102 and Collective Dominance**

An issue that has generated controversy in EU competition law has been the application—or non-application—of Article 102 TFEU (and the EUMR) to so-called 'collective dominance'[81]. Discussion of this question in relation to Article 102 can be traced back at

[73] Ibid, paras 37–39. [74] Ibid, paras 47–55.

[75] For comment see Camesasca and Grelier '"Close Your Eyes"? Navigating the Tortuous Waters of Conscious Parallelism and Signalling in the European Union' (2016) 7 JECLAP 599; Rabinovici 'Public Exchange of Information after Container Shipping' (2017) 8 JECLAP 149; Motta et al, 'Recent Developments at DG Competition: 2015/2016' (2016) Review of Industrial Organization 585.

[76] See ch 4, 'Determining whether competition will be substantially eliminated', pp 172–173.

[77] On the market share caps in the block exemptions see ch 4, 'The format of block exemptions', pp 178–179.

[78] OJ [1999] L 163/61. [79] Ibid, para 127. [80] See eg *Carlsberg* OJ [1984] L 207/26.

[81] At various times the expressions 'collective dominance', 'joint dominance' and 'oligopolistic dominance' have been used interchangeably.

least to the early 1970s[82]; an enormous body of literature has developed[83]. This section[84] will consider in particular the development of the law and decisional practice on collective dominance under Article 102; it would appear to be the case that the expression 'collective dominance' has the same meaning under Article 102 as 'coordinated effects' has under the EUMR[85].

(A) **The linguistic background**

There is a linguistic background to the issue of collective dominance. Article 102 applies to '[a]ny abuse *by one or more undertakings* of a dominant position within the internal market' (emphasis added). The same wording has been adopted in numerous domestic systems of competition law[86]. The fact that Article 102 is capable of application to dominance held on the part of more than one undertaking clearly envisages the possibility, though not the inevitability, of 'collective' dominance being enjoyed by legally and economically separate undertakings; a narrow reading would be that the reference to more than one undertaking refers to different legal entities within the same corporate group[87]. In contradistinction to Article 102, Article 2(3) of the EUMR as it was originally drafted in 1989[88] provided that a concentration that creates or strengthens a dominant position as a result of which competition would be significantly impeded in the common market or a substantial part of it may be declared incompatible with the common market; however this provision does not refer

[82] See ch 14 n 93 later.

[83] See eg Whish and Sufrin 'Oligopolistic Markets and EC Competition Law' (1992) 12 Oxford Yearbook of European Law 59; Winkler and Hansen 'Collective Dominance under the EC Merger Control Regulation' (1993) 30 CML Rev 787; Ridyard 'Economic Analysis of Single Firm and Oligopolistic Dominance under the European Merger Regulation' (1994) 15 ECLR 255; Rodger 'Oligopolistic Market Failure: Collective Dominance versus Complex Monopoly' (1995) 16 ECLR 21; Briones 'Oligopolistic Dominance: Is There a Common Approach in Different Jurisdictions?' (1995) 16 ECLR 334; Soames 'An Analysis of the Principles of Concerted Practice and Collective Dominance: A Distinction without a Difference' (1996) 17 ECLR 24; Morgan 'The Treatment of Oligopoly under the European Merger Control Regulation' (1996) 41 Antitrust Bulletin 203; Tillotson and MacCulloch 'EC Competition Rules, Collective Dominance and Maritime Transport' (1997) 21 World Competition 51; Venit 'Two Steps Forward and No Steps Back: Economic Analysis and Oligopolistic Dominance after *Kali* und *Salz*' (1998) 35 CML Rev 1101; Elliott 'The Gencor Judgment: Collective Dominance, Remedies and Extraterritoriality under the Merger Regulation' (1999) 24 EL Rev 638; Korah '*Gencor v Commission*: Collective Dominance' (1999) 20 ECLR 337; Stroux 'Is EC Oligopoly Control Outgrowing Its Infancy?' (2000) 23 World Competition 3; Fernandez 'Increasing Powers and Increasing Uncertainty: Collective Dominance and Pricing Abuses' (2000) 25 EL Rev 645; Stroux, commenting on *CMBT v Commission* (2000) 37 CML Rev 1249; Etter 'The Assessment of Mergers in the EC under the Concept of Collective Dominance' (2000) 23 World Competition 103; Kloosterhuis 'Joint Dominance and the Interaction Between Firms' (2000) ECLR 79; Monti 'The Scope of Collective Dominance under Article 82' (2001) 38 CML Rev 131; Niels 'Collective Dominance—More than Just Oligopolistic Interdependence' (2001) 22 ECLR 168; Temple Lang 'Oligopolies and Joint Dominance in Community Antitrust Law' [2002] Fordham Corporate Law Institute (ed Hawk), ch 12.

[84] Part of the text that follows is based on 'Collective Dominance' in the Liber Amicorum in Honour of Lord Slynn of Hadley, O'Keeffe and Bavasso (eds) *Judicial Review in European Union Law* (Kluwer Law International, 2000), ch 37.

[85] See ch 21, 'Coordinated effects', pp 893–895; the concept of collective dominance is also discussed in the Commission's *Guidelines on market analysis and the assessment of significant market power under the [EU] regulatory framework for electronic communications networks and services*, OJ [2002] C 156/6, paras 86–106; on 14 February 2018 the Commission published drafts of revised Guidelines and an accompanying Explanatory Note: see www.ec.europa.eu.

[86] See eg s 18(1) of the UK Competition Act 1998.

[87] See 'One or more undertakings: the narrow view of Article 102', p 585 later in chapter.

[88] Note that Article 2(3) of the current EUMR, Regulation 139/2004, OJ [2004] L 24/1, places emphasis on the question of whether a merger would significantly impede effective competition in the internal market, 'in particular as a result of the creation or strengthening of a dominant position'.

specifically to a dominant position *enjoyed by one or more undertakings*. Linguistically, therefore, it could be argued—as indeed it was by France (among others) in the *Kali und Salz* case[89]—that the EUMR applies only to single firm dominance, even if Article 102 is capable of application to collective dominance. It took many years for the EU Courts to determine the proper scope of Article 102 and the EUMR: in each case in favour of the application of the law in question to collective dominance.

(B) The definition of collective dominance under Article 102

(i) 'One or more undertakings': the narrow view of Article 102

Article 102 prohibits the abuse of a dominant position 'by one or more undertakings'. The 'narrow' view of the reference to more than one undertaking was that it meant that the market power and behaviour of undertakings within the same corporate group could be aggregated and dealt with under Article 102. In several of the cases on Article 102 a dominant position was found to exist among the members of a group forming a single economic entity. For example in *Continental Can*[90] three different companies in the same group were involved in the Commission's analysis: Continental Can (a US company), SLW (its German subsidiary) which held a dominant position in Germany and Europemballage (also its subsidiary) which acquired a competitor, TDV. It was the overall effect of these companies' position and behaviour which led to a finding of abuse of dominance. Similarly in *Commercial Solvents*[91] there were two legal entities within the same corporate group, the US parent, Commercial Solvents, and its Italian subsidiary, ICI. It is easy enough to see that the reference in Article 102 to an abuse *by one or more undertakings* might be thought to refer to an abuse that could be attributed to separate legal entities within the same corporate group; it should be added, however, that if those entities are to be regarded as *one* undertaking—as they should be—the approach set out above fails to explain what is meant by an abuse by more than one undertaking[92].

(ii) 'One or more undertakings': the wide view of Article 102

An alternative approach to the reference in Article 102 to one or more undertakings is that it has a wider meaning, so that legally and economically independent firms might be considered to hold a 'collective dominant position'. It would follow that abusive market behaviour on the part of collectively dominant firms could be controlled under Article 102 (and, after the adoption of the EUMR, that the Commission would have control over a larger number of concentrations if the same approach could be taken in relation to that legal instrument). The Commission dabbled with the idea of collective dominance under Article 102 in the early 1970s[93], but the Court of Justice appeared to have rejected it in

[89] Cases C-68/94 etc *France v Commission* EU:C:1998:148, annulling the Commission's conditional clearance decision in Case M 308 *Kali+Salz/MdK/Treuhand* OJ [1994] L 186/38.

[90] JO [1972] L 7/25, the decision was annulled on appeal due to the Commission's failure to define the relevant product market in Case 6/72 *Europemballage Corpn and Continental Can Co Inc v Commission* EU:C:1973:22.

[91] JO [1972] L 299/51, upheld on appeal Cases 6/73 etc EU:C:1974:18.

[92] See ch 3, 'The "single economic entity" doctrine', pp 93–99.

[93] See eg the *Report on the Behaviour of the Oil Companies during the period from October 1973 to March 1974*, COM(75) 675, 10 December 1975; *Sugar Cartel* OJ [1973] L 140/17 where the Commission held that two Dutch producers held a collective dominant position: the Court of Justice said nothing about this because it considered there was no abuse by the companies anyway, Cases 40/73 etc *Suiker Unie v Commission* EU:C:1975:174.

Hoffmann-La Roche v Commission[94]. There the Court seemed to suggest that problems of tacit coordination could not be controlled under Article 102:

> A dominant position must also be distinguished from parallel courses of conduct which are peculiar to oligopolies in that in an oligopoly the courses of conduct interact, whilst in the case of an undertaking occupying a dominant position the conduct of the undertaking which derives profits from that position is to a great extent determined unilaterally[95].

This apparent rejection of Article 102 as a tool for controlling oligopolistic behaviour was understandable. Oligopolists that participate in agreements or concerted practices would be caught by Article 101(1) anyway. The Court of Justice appears to have taken the view that where oligopolists behave in an identical fashion because of the structure of the market on which they operate, rather than because of participation in an agreement or concerted practice, they should not be condemned for abusing their position if their conduct is rational—even inevitable—behaviour. An approach to the 'oligopoly problem' which is based on the concept of abuse in Article 102 seemed inappropriate: or to put it another way, where there was no collusion in the sense of Article 101, the Court was not prepared to characterise the economist's notion of tacit coordination as abusive under Article 102. After *Hoffmann-La Roche* a period of relative inactivity followed. For example in *Alcatel v NOVASAM*[96] the Commission invited the Court of Justice to adopt a theory of collective dominance in an Article 267 reference, but the Court declined to comment on the point in its judgment. In *Magill*[97] the Commission took objection to the refusal of three television companies to grant licences of copyright in their TV schedules to a third party wishing to produce a TV listings magazine. The Commission could have tried a collective dominance approach to the case, holding that the companies had collectively abused a collective dominant position in the TV schedules market; instead it found three individual dominant positions on the part of each company, and three individual abuses.

(iii) Confirmation of the wide view

Any suggestion that the concept of collective dominance had been laid to rest was subsequently shown to be wrong. In *Italian Flat Glass*[98] the Commission held that three Italian producers of flat glass had a collective dominant position and that they had abused it. As participants in a tight oligopolistic market they enjoyed a degree of independence from competitive pressures that enabled them to impede the maintenance of effective competition, notably by not having to take into account the behaviour of other market participants. The conduct held to fall within Article 102 had already been condemned earlier in the decision as a concerted practice under Article 101. However the decision opened up the possibility that in other situations the conduct of oligopolists, *though not within Article 101*, might be attacked under Article 102. On appeal the General Court overturned the Commission's decision on collective dominance on the ground that the Commission had simply 'recycled' the facts relied on as constituting an infringement of Article 101, instead of properly defining the relevant product and

[94] Case 85/76 EU:C:1979:36.

[95] Ibid, para 39; similarly see Case 172/80 *Gerhard Züchner v Bayerische Vereinsbank* EU:C:1981:178, para 10.

[96] Case 247/86 EU:C:1988:469.

[97] *Magill TV Guide* OJ [1989] L 78/43, upheld on appeal to the General Court in Cases T-69/89 etc *RTE v Commission* EU:T:1991:39 and on appeal to the Court of Justice in Case C-241/91 P EU:C:1995:98.

[98] OJ [1989] L 33/44.

geographic markets in order to weigh up the undertakings' market power, as is necessary in Article 102 cases.

Nevertheless, the General Court confirmed the principle of collective dominance at paragraph 358 of its judgment:

> There is nothing, in principle, to prevent two or more independent economic entities from being, on a specific market, united by such economic links that, by virtue of that fact, together they hold a dominant position vis-à-vis the other operators on the same market. This could be the case, for example, where two or more independent undertakings jointly have, through agreements or licences, a technological lead affording them the power to behave to an appreciable extent independently of their competitors, their customers and ultimately of their consumers[99].

The judgment in *Italian Flat Glass* was exciting and frustrating in equal measure. Collective dominance on the part of 'two or more independent entities' could exist under Article 102, although the Commission had failed to demonstrate that it existed in this particular case. Clearly, the General Court considered that infringements of Articles 101 and 102 were conceptually independent of one another: this is why the Commission was not permitted simply to 'recycle the facts' used to find an infringement of Article 101 in order to determine an abuse of collective dominance[100]. Each Article must be applied according to its own terms. Behaviour that amounts to a concerted practice is not automatically also abusive; and vice versa[101]. However, what is frustrating about the judgment is that it did not advance our understanding of what collective dominance or abuse of collective dominance consists of. Given that we now have the benefit of the judgments in *Compagnie Maritime Belge Transports v Commission* under Article 102 and *France v Commission*[102], *Gencor v Commission*[103], *Airtours v Commission*[104] and *Bertelsmann v Impala*[105] under the EUMR it is not necessary to spend time in trying to understand what was meant by paragraph 358 of *Italian Flat Glass*. It is sufficient to say that an important landmark had been reached in this judgment, but that later case law has clarified the meaning of the concept of collective dominance.

(iv) Further judgments and decisions on collective dominance under Article 102

In the years after *Italian Flat Glass* there were several more judgments and decisions in which collective dominance was referred to, but not until *France v Commission* and *Gencor v Commission* under the EUMR and *Compagnie Maritime Belge Transports v Commission* under Article 102 did a true picture begin to emerge of what was meant by the concept. In *Almelo*[106] the Court of Justice said that:

> 42 However, in order for such a collective dominant position to exist, the undertakings in the group must be linked in such a way that they adopt the same conduct on the market.

[99] Cases T-68/89 etc *Società Italiano Vetro SpA v Commission* EU:T:1992:38; note that the reference to *Hoffmann-La Roche* in this paragraph is a reference to the meaning of market power as defined in that judgment, not to the meaning of collective dominance which, as mentioned earlier, the Court appeared to reject.

[100] The differences between Articles 101 and 102 are very clearly stated in the judgment of the General Court in Case T-41/96 *Bayer v Commission* EU:T:2000:242, paras 174–180 and by the Court of Justice in the appeal to it from that judgment, Cases C-2/01 P etc *Commission v Bayer* EU:C:2004:2, para 70.

[101] This point is specifically confirmed at paras 43 and 44 of the Court of Justice's judgment in Cases C-395/96 P etc *Compagnie Maritime Belge Transports v Commission* EU:C:2000:132: see 'The judgment of the Court of Justice in *Compagnie Maritime Belge Transports v Commission*', pp 589–590 later in chapter.

[102] Cases C-68/94 etc EU:C:1998:148.

[103] Case T-102/96 EU:T:1999:65.

[104] Case T-342/99 EU:T:2002:416.

[105] Case C-413/06 P EU:C:2008:392.

[106] Case C-393/92 *Almelo v NV Energiebedrijf IJsselmij* EU:C:1994:171.

> 43 It is for the national court to consider whether there exist between the regional electricity distributors in the Netherlands links which are sufficiently strong for there to be a collective dominant position in a substantial part of the [internal] market.

This formulation suggested that the Court of Justice was looking at what economists would look at: the adoption of the same conduct on the market or, in other words, tacit coordination. This was an improvement on *Italian Flat Glass*, in that it provided an economic rationale for collective dominance, but it still failed to explain what could amount to collective dominance. In *Spediporto*[107], *DIP*[108] and *Sodemare*[109] the Court of Justice repeated the *Almelo* formulation, but did not advance its notion of collective dominance. In the *Bosman case*[110] Advocate General Lenz assumed that football clubs in a professional football league could be 'united by such economic links' as to be regarded as collectively dominant; the Court did not address the issue. In the meantime the Commission made findings of collective dominance in a number of decisions, both under Article 102 and under the EUMR. The decisions under Article 102 did not greatly add to the notion of collective dominance, since they involved undertakings which unmistakably were linked in some way. For example in three decisions in the maritime transport sector the undertakings were members of liner conferences. In *French-West African Shipowners' Committees*[111] the Commission concluded that members of the shipowners' committees had abused a collective dominant position by taking action designed to prevent other shipping lines establishing themselves as competitors on routes between France and 11 west African states[112]. This decision was adopted after the General Court's judgment in *Italian Flat Glass*, and the Commission specifically imposed a fine for the infringement of Article 102 as well as the agreements that were caught by Article 101. In *Cewal*[113] the Commission found collective dominance between shipping lines that were members of a liner conference. The Commission's finding of collective dominance was upheld on appeal to the General Court[114] and to the Court of Justice[115]: the latter judgment is of major importance as it synthesised the earlier judgments on collective dominance under Article 102 and laid down a much clearer concept of what is meant by collective dominance[116].

In *TACA*[117] the Commission imposed fines totalling €273 million on the members of a liner conference for abuses of collective dominance. On appeal General Court upheld the Commission's finding of collective dominance[118]; the Court stated specifically that, although competition between undertakings in a collectively dominant position was necessarily restricted, this did not imply that competition between them should be entirely eliminated[119]. The Commission's finding that members of TACA had abused their collective dominant position by inducing competitors to join their shipping conference, thereby harming the competitive structure of the market, was annulled, as were the fines[120].

[107] Case C-96/94 *Centro Servizi Spediporto Sri v Spedizioni Marittima del Golfo Srl* EU:C:1995:308, para 33.

[108] Cases C-140/94 etc *DIP SpA v Commune di Bassano del Grappa* EU:C:1995:330, para 26.

[109] Case C-70/95 *Sodemare SA, Anni Azzurri Holding SpA and Anni Azzurri Rezzato Sri v Regione Lombardia* EU:C:1997:301, para 46.

[110] Case C-415/93 *Union royale belge des sociétés de football association v Bosman* EU:C:1995:293.

[111] OJ [1992] L 134/1. [112] Ibid, paras 52–69. [113] OJ [1993] L 34/20.

[114] Cases T-24/93 etc *Compagnie Maritime Belge Transports v Commission* EU:T:1996:139.

[115] Cases C-395/96 P etc *Compagnie Maritime Belge Transports v Commission* EU:C:2000:132.

[116] See 'The judgment of the Court of Justice in *Compagnie Maritime Belge Transports v Commission*', pp 589–590 later in chapter.

[117] OJ [1999] L 95/1.

[118] Cases T-191/98 etc *Atlantic Container Line v Commission* EU:T:2003:245, paras 649–657.

[119] Ibid, paras 653–655. [120] Ibid, paras 1192–1369 and 1597–1634.

The Commission also reached a finding of collective dominance in *Port of Rødby*[121], where it considered that two ferry undertakings that fixed common rates, coordinated timetables and marketed their services jointly were collectively dominant. In *Irish Sugar*[122] the Commission found 'vertical' collective dominance between Irish Sugar and a distributor of sugar, Sugar Distributors Ltd ('SDL'). Without finding legal or *de facto* control of SDL, the Commission concluded that the combination of Irish Sugar's equity holding, the structure of policy-making of the two companies and the communication process established to facilitate it, led to direct economic ties between them which created a clear parallelism of interest which amounted to collective dominance of the markets for industrial and retail sugar in Ireland[123]. On appeal the General Court upheld this finding of vertical collective dominance, without shedding any particular light on what this concept consists of[124].

These judgments and decisions under Article 102 after the General Court's judgment in *Italian Flat Glass* see the concept of collective dominance being quite regularly applied, and thereby becoming more familiar to officials, courts and practitioners. However, they did relatively little to answer any of the questions raised by that judgment, other than to affirm the idea of the adoption of common conduct on the market as a significant feature of collective dominance[125].

(v) The judgment of the Court of Justice in *Compagnie Maritime Belge Transports v Commission*

Important light was shed on the meaning of collective dominance by the judgment of the Court of Justice in *Compagnie Maritime Belge Transports v Commission*[126], an appeal from the General Court's judgment[127] upholding the Commission's decision in *Cewal*[128] that there had been an infringement of Article 102. The Court deals with collective dominance at paragraphs 28 to 59 of its judgment. At paragraph 36 it states that collective dominance implies that a dominant position may be held by two or more economic entities legally independent of each other provided that from an economic point of view 'they present themselves or act together on a particular market as a collective entity'. The Court says that this is how the expression 'collective dominant position' should be understood in the judgment. It will be noted that this definition of collective dominance focuses on the notion of a collective entity, and not on the links between the undertakings in question. The Court then states that, in order to establish collective dominance, it is necessary to examine 'the economic links or factors which give rise to a connection between the undertakings concerned'[129], citing its earlier judgments in *Almelo*[130] under Article 102 and *France v Commission*[131] under the EUMR: the Court does not appear to consider that collective dominance has a different meaning under these two provisions. It continues that 'in particular' it must be asked whether economic links exist which enable them to act independently of their competitors[132]. However it then says that the fact that

[121] OJ [1994] L 55/52. [122] OJ [1997] L 258/1.

[123] Ibid, paras 111–113.

[124] Case T-228/97 EU:T:1999:246, paras 61–64, upheld on appeal Case C-497/99 P EU:C:2001:393; the Commission applied the General Court's judgment in *Coca-Cola*, decision of 22 June 2005, paras 23–25, a decision under Article 9 of Regulation 1/2003, on which see ch 7, 'Acts', p 302.

[125] See however *Notice on Access Agreements in the Telecommunications Sector* OJ [1998] C 265/2, para 79.

[126] Cases C-395/96 P etc EU:C:2000:132; for commentary on this judgment, see Stroux (2000) 37 CML Rev 1249.

[127] Case T-24/93 EU:T:1996:139. [128] OJ [1993] L 34/20. [129] Ibid, para 41.

[130] Case C-393/92 P EU:C:1994:171. [131] Cases C-68/94 etc EU:C:1998:148.

[132] Cases C-395/96 P etc EU:C:2000:132, para 42.

undertakings have entered into agreements does not in itself mean that they are collectively dominant[133]; but they might be if it caused them to appear as a collective entity[134]. Importantly, the Court of Justice then says that:

> the existence of an agreement or of other links in law is not indispensable to a finding of a collective dominant position; such a finding may be based on other connecting factors and would depend on an economic assessment and, in particular, on an assessment of the structure of the market in question[135].

This passage is consistent with the Court of Justice's judgment in *France v Commission* on collective dominance under the EUMR, where it had placed emphasis on 'connecting factors' rather than on economic links in determining whether there was collective dominance[136], and it is explicit that the existence of an agreement or concerted practice is not a pre-requisite to a finding of collective dominance. On the actual facts of the case the Court was satisfied that the members of the liner conference in question were collectively dominant[137].

This is clearly an important judgment on collective dominance under Article 102: specifically, it would appear that the Court of Justice considers that the test of collective dominance is the same under Article 102 and the EUMR; and the Court specifically states that there is no legal requirement of an agreement or other links in law for there to be a finding of collective dominance. It is therefore possible that undertakings could be held to be collectively dominant where the oligopolistic nature of the market is such that they behave in a parallel manner, thereby appearing to the market as a collective entity. The judgment of the Court of Justice in *Bertelsmann v Impala*[138] is consistent with this interpretation: the essence of collective dominance is parallel behaviour within an oligopoly, that is to say tacit coordination. The General Court's judgment in *Piau v Commission*[139] states that legally independent economic entities may be collectively dominant where 'they present themselves or act together on a particular market as a collective entity'[140]. The General Court went on to say that there were three cumulative conditions for a finding of collective dominance:

- each member of the dominant oligopoly must have the ability to know how the other members are behaving in order to monitor whether or not they are adopting the common policy
- the situation of tacit coordination must be sustainable over time, meaning that there must be an incentive not to depart from the common policy on the market
- the foreseeable reaction of current and future competitors, as well as of consumers, must not jeopardise the results expected from the common policy[141].

In *Piau* the General Court concluded that FIFA, national football associations and the football clubs forming them were collectively dominant on the market for the provision of players' agents' services, but that there was no abusive behaviour on their part[142]. In *EFIM v Commission*[143] the General Court rejected the applicant's arguments that four

133 Ibid, para 43. 134 Ibid, para 44. 135 Ibid, para 45.

136 Cases C-68/94 etc EU:C:1998:148. 137 Cases C-395/96 P etc EU:C:2000:132.

138 Case C-413/06 P *Bertelsmann v Impala* EU:C:2008:392; see similarly Case T-342/99 *Airtours v Commission* EU:T:2002:146.

139 Case T-193/02 EU:T:2005:22; note that paras 43–50 of the DG COMP's *Discussion Paper on the application of Article [102 TFEU] to exclusionary abuses* summarises the concept of collective dominance in the same terms, available at www.ec.europa.eu.

140 Case T-193/02 EU:T:2005:22, para 110.

141 Ibid, para 111. 142 Ibid, paras 117–121.

143 Case T-296/09 *European Federation of Ink and Ink Cartridge Manufacturers v Commission* EU:T:2011:693, upheld on appeal to the Court of Justice in Case C-56/12 P EU:C:2013:575.

ink-jet cartridge manufacturers held a collective dominant position. The Court repeated the three conditions for a finding of collective dominance[144] and concluded that the structure of the market for ink-jet printers was not sufficiently conducive to tacit coordination as the market shares of the main original equipment manufacturers had been fluctuating and Kodak had been able to enter the market[145].

One final point is that the Court of Justice has said that, where a market is highly heterogeneous and characterised by a high degree of internal competition, such as the market for legal services in the Netherlands, collective dominance would not be found in the absence of structural links[146].

(C) Abuse of collective dominance under Article 102

Having established that Article 102 is applicable to collective as well as single firm dominance, it is necessary to consider what kind of conduct would constitute an abuse of a collective dominant position under that provision: it is important to recall that it is not unlawful, in itself, under Article 102 to have a dominant position (whether individual or collective); for there to be an infringement of Article 102 there must be conduct which amounts to an abuse[147]. What qualifies as an abuse of collective dominance is underdeveloped in the case law of the EU Courts[148], although a few competition authorities in and outside the EU have made findings of an abuse of a collective dominant position[149]. The economic theory around which the doctrine of collective dominance has developed under the EUMR is that in certain market conditions firms may be able to derive benefits from tacit coordination; and the very reason why the Commission might prohibit under the EUMR a concentration that would create or strengthen a collective dominant position is that it would make it easier for firms to benefit from this phenomenon[150]. Does it follow from this that tacit coordination, when actually practised, should be condemned as an abuse of a collective dominant position under Article 102[151]? Is price parallelism in itself an abuse? To put the point another way, does symmetry require that, since predicted tacit coordination can be prevented through the prohibition of a concentration under the EUMR, actual coordination should be condemned under Article 102? If the answer to this question is no, what types of behaviour ought to be condemned under Article 102?

144 Ibid, para 71. 145 Ibid, paras 72–76.

146 Case C-309/99 *Wouters v Algemene Raad van de Nederlandsche Orde van Advocaten* EU:C:2002:98.

147 See ch 5, 'The "special responsibility" of dominant firms', p 198; the point is made specifically in relation to collective dominance by the Court of Justice in its judgment in *CMBT v Commission* at paras 37–38.

148 Paragraphs 74–76 of the DG COMP's *Discussion Paper on the application of Article [102 TFEU] to exclusionary abuses* had virtually nothing to say about the idea of the abuse of a collective dominant position, and para 4 of the Commission's subsequent *Guidance on the Commission's Enforcement Priorities in Applying Article [102 TFEU] to Abusive Exclusionary Conduct by Dominant Undertakings* OJ [2009] C45/7 is explicitly limited to single dominant firms; both documents are available at www.ec.europa.eu.

149 See eg *Evrotur SAT TV v Musicauthor*, Bulgarian NCA decision of 28 December 2006; *Telefónica, Vodafone and Orange*, Spanish NCA decision of 19 December 2012; *EKI Transfers*, Serbian NCA decision of 12 January 2010, upheld on appeal *EKI Transfers v Serbian Competition Authority*, judgment of the Serbian Supreme Court of 20 September 2013; *Gazprom Neft, Lukoil, Rosneft and TNK-BP*, Russian NCA statement of 27 June 2016 describing enforcement action and appeals between 2007 and 2012.

150 See ch 21, 'Coordinated effects', pp 893–895.

151 For discussion see Mezzanotte 'Using Abuse of Collective Dominance in Article 102 TFEU to Fight Tacit Collusion: the Problem of Proof and Inferential Error' (2010) 33 World Competition 77; Petit 'Re-Pricing Through Disruption in Oligopolies with Tacit Collusion: A Framework for Abuse of Collective Dominance' (2016) 39 World Competition 119.

(i) Exploitative abuse of a collective dominant position

Commentators on Article 102 habitually make a distinction between those abuses that are 'exploitative' and those that are 'exclusionary', whilst recognising that this is not a watertight distinction[152]. It could be argued that tacit coordination by collectively dominant undertakings is exploitative, since prices are charged which are higher than they would be in a competitive market, albeit without the need to enter into an explicit agreement. However the Commission has not attempted to condemn tacit coordination itself under Article 102, and it is submitted that, as a matter of law and policy, it should not be able to do so for two reasons. First, as we have seen, the case law has come to associate the economic concept of tacit coordination with the legal concept of collective dominance, and it is not an offence for a firm or group of firms to have a dominant position; what is offensive is to abuse a dominant position. Secondly, tacit coordination comes about in certain market conditions because the collectively dominant firms react rationally according to the conditions of the market on which they operate. To condemn their parallel behaviour as abusive in itself would be a nonsense: if Article 102 were to mandate that firms must behave *irrationally* in order to comply with the law, it would be a very odd provision. This explains the position taken by the Court of Justice as long ago as *Hoffmann-La Roche*: parallel behaviour should be condemned where it is attributable to an agreement or concerted practice contrary to Article 101(1); it is not, in itself, abusive under Article 102[153]. It might seem that this shows an inconsistency between the law under Article 102 and the EUMR: how can it be that the prospect of tacit coordination can be avoided under the Merger Regulation and yet the actuality of the same behaviour cannot be condemned under Article 102? The truth is that the difference makes perfect sense: it is precisely because of the difficulty that competition law has in addressing the problem of tacit coordination when it does occur that systems of merger control seek to prevent a market structure that will be conducive to this phenomenon from arising in the first place.

A distinct issue is whether collectively dominant firms may abuse their position by charging *excessively high* prices: here the abuse would lie not in the *parallelism* of the prices, but in their level. Article 102(2)(a) explicitly condemns unfairly high prices, and collectively dominant firms may be in a position to restrict output and thereby charge supra-competitive prices just as much as an individually dominant firm. In principle, therefore, it would seem that action could be taken against excessive pricing in an oligopoly[154]. Such actions are likely to be rare, however, since the Commission understandably does not want to act as a price regulator. There have been very few investigations of unfairly high prices under Article 102, and those that have been conducted were often motivated by different considerations, for example that the excessive prices were a ploy to impede parallel imports[155]. The Commission contemplated a finding of an exploitative abuse of a collective dominant position of a different nature in its *P&I* decision[156]. The P & I clubs were members of the International Group, and were found to be collectively

[152] See ch 5, 'Exploitative, exclusionary and single market abuses', pp 207–208; the Commission itself made this distinction in its decision on *P&I Clubs* OJ [1999] L 125/12, paras 127–136.

[153] See 'The definition of collective dominance under Article 102', pp 585–591 earlier in chapter.

[154] See eg *Telefónica, Vodafone and Orange*, Spanish NCA decision of 19 December 2012, condemning excessive pricing of wholesale text message termination services by three mobile phone operators that held a collective dominant position.

[155] See ch 18, 'Excessive Pricing' pp 735–746 and 'Pricing Practices That are Harmful to the Single Market', pp 782–784.

[156] OJ [1999] L 125/12.

dominant. They had limited the level of insurance cover available to customers: this was considered by the Commission to be contrary to Article 102(2)(b), since it 'left a very substantial share of the demand unsatisfied' however an alteration in the rules of the Group meant that the Commission did not reach a formal finding to this effect[157].

(ii) Exclusionary abuse of a collective dominant position

Article 102 has been applied by the Commission to exclusionary abuses of collective dominance on several occasions. Exclusionary abuses are considered in chapters 17 and 18. It seems reasonable in principle that Article 102 should be applicable to the exclusionary behaviour not only of individually but also of collectively dominant undertakings. Given that tacit coordination is likely to arise where a few firms, without explicit collusion, are able to set prices above the competitive level, the 'subversive' effect of new entrants into markets conducive to this phenomenon is likely to be welcomed by competition authorities: their entry may make tacit coordination less easy to achieve. In *Cewal*[158] the Commission held that Article 102 had been infringed where collectively-dominant members of a liner conference were found to have engaged in various practices with the intention of eliminating competitors from the market, such as selective price cutting and the grant of loyalty rebates. The findings of abuse were upheld on appeal to the General Court[159] and the Court of Justice[160], although the fines were annulled by the Court of Justice since the Commission had not referred to the possibility that they might be imposed in the statements of objections sent to the individual members of the conference[161]. The Commission's findings of abuse in *TACA*[162]—refusal by members of a liner conference to offer individual service contracts to customers and the abusive alteration of the competitive structure of the market by acting to eliminate potential competition—were annulled on appeal to the General Court for lack of evidence[163].

In *BASF*[164] the Commission rejected a complaint that 13 producers and distributors of plant protection products had, *inter alia*, abused a collective dominant position by filing false complaints to Polish and Austrian authorities and engaging in lobbying of government officials aimed at eliminating the complainant from the market. On appeal the General Court upheld the Commission's decision and specifically pointed out that it was not clear that the conduct at issue could fall within the concept of abuse[165].

The Commission may wish to investigate allegations of exclusionary behaviour by collectively dominant firms where the alleged victims of that behaviour are actual or potential competitors which might be able to subvert tacit coordination on the market.

(iii) Individual abuse of a collective dominant position

A further question under Article 102 is whether a collective dominant position can be abused only by all of the undertakings which hold that position, or whether it is possible

157 Ibid, paras 128–132.

158 OJ [1993] L 34/2; exclusionary abuse was also found in the earlier *French-West African Shipowners' Committees* decision: OJ [1992] L 134/1; see also *P&I Clubs* (ch 14 n 152 earlier) paras 134–136.

159 Cases T-24/93 etc *Compagnie Maritime Belge Transports SA v Commission* EU:T:1996:139.

160 See ch 14 n 126 earlier.

161 See Cases C-395/96 P etc EU:C:2000:132, paras 140–150; the Commission subsequently readopted its infringement decision: OJ [2005] L 171/28, upheld on appeal in Case T-276/04 *Compagnie Maritime Belge SA v Commission* EU:T:2008:237.

162 OJ [1999] L 95/1.

163 Cases T-191/98 etc *Atlantic Container Line v Commission* EU:T:2003:245.

164 Commission decision of 19 June 2015.

165 Case T-480/15 *Agria Polska v Commission* EU:T:2017:339, para 72, on appeal to the Court of Justice Case C-373/17 P, not yet decided.

for one or some of them to commit an abuse. To put the matter another way, must there be 'collective' abuse of collective dominance; or can there also be 'individual' abuse? This has been clearly answered by the General Court in *Irish Sugar v Commission*[166]:

> undertakings occupying a joint dominant position may engage in joint or individual abusive conduct.

It should be noted that *Irish Sugar* was a case on vertical, as opposed to horizontal, collective dominance. It would have been helpful if the judgment had explained in more detail how the Court arrived at its conclusion: it does not fit well with the idea that collectively dominant undertakings should present themselves to the market as a single entity, which implies that they are bound to behave collectively rather than individually. However, if one of several collectively dominant undertakings resorts to exclusionary behaviour in order to foreclose access to the market for competitors, it could be argued that this is done to protect the dominant oligopoly, and not just that one firm; perhaps this could explain why, at least in some cases, it may be possible for there to be an individual abuse of a collective dominant position.

5. UK Law

(A) Competition Act 1998

The Chapter I and Chapter II prohibitions in the Competition Act 1998 are modelled on Articles 101 and 102 TFEU, and section 60 of that Act requires that consistency should be maintained with the jurisprudence of the EU Courts and that account should be taken of the decisional practice of the Commission[167]. It follows that the discussion in the earlier part of this chapter of the application of Articles 101 and 102 to behaviour in oligopolistic markets is directly relevant under the Competition Act. However two additional points should be made about the domestic law of the UK in relation to this issue. First, the market investigation provisions of the Enterprise Act 2002 provide an alternative mechanism to address market failure that may arise in oligopolies[168]. Secondly, the domestic system of merger control provides a way of preventing the emergence of market structures that are conducive to tacit coordination. The following section briefly examines the extent to which the provisions on market studies and market investigations may be deployed to deal with the problem of tacit coordination; the UK system of merger control is described in chapter 22.

(B) Market studies and market investigations under the Enterprise Act 2002

The provisions of the Enterprise Act 2002 on market studies and market investigations have been described in chapter 11. The Competition and Markets Authority's ('the CMA') policy is to consider first whether a suspected problem of market failure can be addressed under Article 101 or 102 TFEU or under the Competition Act 1998[169]. However, as the

[166] Case T-228/97 EU:T:1999:246, para 66.

[167] On s 60 of the Act see ch 9, '"Governing Principles Clause": Section 60 of the Competition Act 1998', pp 387–392.

[168] A market study, which may or may not lead to a market investigation reference, may also fulfil this function: see ch 11, 'Market Studies', pp 465–469.

[169] *Market investigation references*, OFT 511, March 2006, para 2.1, available at www.gov.uk/cma; this guidance was adopted by the CMA Board with effect from 1 April 2014.

discussion in the early part of this chapter has shown, the 'problem' of oligopoly is a complex one, and the tools provided by Articles 101 and 102 and their domestic analogues are not always suitable for this purpose. The possibility of a market study or a market investigation, as a 'safety net' for those situations in which there is a failure of the competitive market mechanism that cannot be dealt with under the prohibition provisions, is in principle desirable; this is not to deny, however, that there are some people in business and legal circles who view these powers with a certain scepticism, since market studies and market investigations can be time-consuming, expensive and intrusive. The Enterprise and Regulatory Reform Act 2013 sought to address these criticisms by introducing time limits for the completion of market studies and shortening the period in which a Phase 2 market investigation must be completed[170].

(i) Market studies

The CMA may launch a market study of an oligopolistic market that appears not to be working well but where enforcement action under EU and/or UK competition law does not, at first sight, appear to be the most appropriate response. Market studies are intended to enable the CMA to understand as well as possible how markets are working and whether the needs of consumers are being met. There may be some circumstances in which the CMA might find that the lack of competition in an oligopolistic market may be attributable to a 'public' restriction of competition—for example legislation or regulatory rules—in which case it could play an advocacy role in trying to remove the problem[171]. Several market studies have been carried out to see whether market conditions were conducive to parallel behaviour[172].

(ii) Market investigations

The CMA (concurrently with the sectoral regulators) will consider making a market investigation reference where it has reasonable grounds to believe that features of a market restrict competition, but not to establish a breach of EU or UK competition law, or when action under the latter provisions has been or is likely to be ineffective for dealing with any adverse effect on competition identified. The CMA's *Guidance on making market investigation references* states that a reference might be appropriate for dealing with tacit coordination in oligopolistic markets[173]. There could be problems associated with oligopolistic markets that are not capable of being addressed under the Competition Act, not least because of the uncertainty as to what constitutes an abuse of a collective dominant position[174]. The possibility exists, therefore, of market investigation references, in particular where problems arise that are industry-wide or that involve multi-firm conduct[175].

The *Guidance on making market investigation references* refers to the possibility that firms in an oligopoly may be able to coordinate their behaviour for mutual advantage or, at least, lack an incentive to compete, and sets out various factors of a market, such as high barriers to entry, the homogeneity of products and the symmetry of firms' market shares that might be conducive to parallel behaviour[176]. It says that many of the markets that the CMA is likely to be interested in will be oligopolistic[177]; in such markets, price

[170] On the applicable time limits see *Market studies and market investigations: Supplemental guidance on the CMA's approach*, CM3, January 2014 (revised July 2017), available at www.gov.uk/cma; see also ch 11, 'Procedure', pp 467–468.

[171] See ch 11, 'Market Studies', pp 465–469.

[172] See ch 11, 'Examples of market studies', p 469.

[173] *Market investigation references*, para 2.5; see ch 11, 'Market Investigation References', pp 469-481.

[174] Ibid, para 2.5.

[175] Ibid, para 2.7.

[176] Ibid, paras 5.5–5.7; see also *Guidelines for market investigations: Their role, procedures, assessment and remedies*, CC3 Revised, April 2013, paras 237–261, available at www.gov.uk/cma.

[177] *Market investigation references*, para 6.4.

competition may be limited, and firms instead may compete through advertising, loyalty-inducing schemes and similar practices: though these practices may be pro-competitive, they could also be harmful to competition where they raise barriers to entry to new competitors[178]. The CMA also notes that tacit coordination can have a severe effect on competition[179]. In such a case the CMA would look at the pattern of price changes over time, price inertia and the oligopolists' rates of return compared to returns in comparable markets or to the cost of capital[180]. Switching costs and informational inadequacies may be relevant to the state of competition in a market[181], and the CMA will consider whether there are any facilitating practices that make it easier for firms to act in a coordinated manner[182].

The operation of the market investigation provisions in practice was discussed in chapter 11; several investigations were concerned with switching costs and imperfect information for consumers in concentrated markets[183]. In *Aggregates, cement and ready-mix concrete*[184] the Competition Commission (now CMA) concluded that a combination of structural and conduct features of British cement markets gave rise to coordination among the three largest producers[185]. The Commission opted for a package of remedies that would undermine and thereby address the coordination; in particular the Commission required Lafarge Tarmac to divest a cement plant to a new producer[186]. The Commission also adopted two remedies that would reduce the transparency of the market and thus make it more difficult for the producers to coordinate their behaviour: limits on the publication of cement market data[187] and a prohibition on suppliers sending generic price announcement letters to their customers[188].

In *Energy*[189] the CMA found that some characteristics of the supply of gas and electricity to domestic customers may be conducive to tacit coordination, but concluded that there was insufficient evidence of suppliers using price announcements to signal their future pricing intentions[190]. Similarly, the CMA found no evidence of coordinated behaviour in the concentrated markets examined in *Retail Banking*[191].

178 Ibid, para 6.5. 179 Ibid, para 6.6. 180 Ibid, para 6.7.

181 Ibid, para 6.8; on switching costs see OFT Economic Discussion Paper 5 (OFT 655) *Switching Costs* (National Economic Research Associates, April 2003), available at www.nationalarchives.gov.uk.

182 OFT 511, paras 6.9–6.11.

183 See ch 11, 'Findings of adverse effects on competition', pp 491–492.

184 Final Report of 14 January 2014, available at www.nationalarchives.gov.uk.

185 Ibid, paras 8.429–8.434; see also paras 12.3–12.7.

186 Ibid, paras 13.7–13.138; see Case M 7550 *Holcim Lafarge Divestment Business*, decision of 24 April 2015.

187 Ibid, paras 13.139–13.175; see the Cement Market Data Order 2016, 13 April 2016, available at www.gov.uk/cma.

188 Ibid, paras 13.176–13.209; see the Price Announcement Order 2016, 22 January 2016, available at www.gov.uk/cma.

189 Final Report of 24 June 2016, available at www.gov.uk/cma.

190 Ibid, paras 9.353–9.374.

191 Final Report of 9 August 2016, para 10.16, available at www.gov.uk/cma; see similarly *Northern Irish Personal Banking*, Final Report of 15 May 2007, paras 4.288–4.307, available at www.nationalarchives.gov.uk.

15

Horizontal agreements (3): cooperation agreements

1. Introduction

The previous two chapters have considered the law on hard-core cartels and the phenomenon of tacit coordination in oligopolistic markets. However it is important to appreciate that not all contact between competitors is undesirable. Some horizontal agreements may be beneficial, such as an agreement between pharmaceutical companies to combine their research and development ('R&D') efforts to develop new and better drugs, or between two small businesses to produce products on a joint basis, thereby achieving economies of scale. The Commission's *Guidelines on the Applicability of Article 101 of the Treaty on the Functioning of the European Union to Horizontal Cooperation Agreements*[1] ('the *Guidelines on Horizontal Cooperation Agreements*' or 'the *Guidelines*') recognise that horizontal cooperation 'can be a means to share risk, save costs, increase investments, pool know-how, enhance product quality and variety, and launch innovation faster'. It follows that competition law cannot simply prohibit all horizontal agreements: efficiency gains may follow from cooperation that are sufficient to outweigh any restriction of competition that it might entail.[2] This chapter is concerned with horizontal cooperation agreements which the competition authorities in the EU and the UK may be prepared to countenance.[3]

[1] OJ [2011] C 11/1.

[2] See generally OECD Roundtable *Competition Issues in Joint Ventures* (2000), available at www.oecd.org/competition.

[3] For discussion of the position in the US see the Department of Justice and Federal Trade Commission *Antitrust Guidelines for Collaborations Among Competitors*, April 2000, available at www.justice.gov/atr; see also Brodley 'Joint Ventures and Antitrust Policy' (1982) 95 Harvard Law Review 1523; McFalls 'The Role and Assessment of Classical Market Power in Joint Venture Analysis' (1997–98) 66 Antitrust LJ 651; Werden 'Antitrust Analysis of Joint Ventures: An Overview' ibid, 701; Correia 'Joint Ventures: Issues in Enforcement Policy' ibid, 737.

2. Full-Function Joint Ventures

Where firms decide to cooperate, the medium for their collaboration can vary widely from one case to another. For example firms that cooperate in R&D may simply meet on a periodic basis to discuss matters of common interest; they may share out research work and pool the results; they may establish a committee to oversee the R&D programme; or they may go further and establish a joint venture company to conduct their R&D, while maintaining their independence as producers and suppliers to the market. The same range of possibilities exists in relation to other types of cooperation, for example on production and commercialisation. As a matter of competition law the medium chosen for the horizontal cooperation will not normally affect the legal analysis of an agreement, with one very important exception: where the parties to an agreement establish a joint venture to carry out their objectives, this may amount to a concentration (to use the language of the EU Merger Regulation ('the EUMR')) or a relevant merger situation (the term used in the UK Enterprise Act 2002); if so, the joint venture will be considered not under Article 101 or the Chapter I prohibition of the Competition Act 1998, but under the EUMR or the domestic merger control provisions of the Member States[4]. It follows that it is necessary in any particular case to begin by considering whether parties intend to create a full-function joint venture amounting to a concentration or a merger: the meaning of a concentration under the EUMR is dealt with in chapter 21[5]; and chapter 22 considers what is meant by a merger in UK law[6]. It may even be the case that contractual integration, without the establishment of a joint venture company, will amount to a full-function joint venture under the EUMR[7]. If the joint venture does not constitute a concentration or merger then it will be relevant to consider the possible application of Article 101 TFEU and the Chapter I prohibition[8]. Paragraph 21 of the *Guidelines on Horizontal Cooperation Agreements* notes that cooperation that falls to be analysed under Article 101 may have similar effects to those of a horizontal merger, suggesting, without saying so, that a similar approach ought to be taken to both phenomena.

3. The Application of Article 101 to Horizontal Cooperation Agreements and the Commission's *Guidelines on Horizontal Cooperation Agreements*

(A) Introduction

The general principles involved in the application of Article 101(1) and Article 101(3) have been described in chapters 3 and 4 of this book; this chapter assumes a knowledge of those principles and focuses specifically on the jurisprudence of the EU Courts and the decisional practice and the *Guidelines* of the Commission in relation to horizontal cooperation agreements under Article 101[9].

[4] See *Guidelines on Horizontal Cooperation Agreements*, para 2.

[5] See ch 21, 'Article 3: meaning of a concentration', pp 853–859.

[6] See ch 22, 'Enterprises ceasing to be distinct', pp 942–946.

[7] See ch 21, 'Joint ventures—the concept of full-functionality', pp 857–858.

[8] See further Faull and Nikpay (eds) *The EU Law of Competition* (Oxford University Press, 3rd ed, 2014), paras 7.29–7.142.

[9] For a helpful analysis of the Commission's approach to the application of Article 101 to horizontal cooperation agreements see Morais *Joint Ventures in Competition Law* (Hart, 2013) and Faull and Nikpay (eds) *The EU Law of Competition* (Oxford University Press, 3rd ed, 2014), ch 7.

(B) The case law and decisions on horizontal cooperation agreements

There is very little case law of the EU Courts specifically on the application of Article 101 to horizontal cooperation agreements[10]. A few cases have reached the Court of Justice from national courts under the procedure in Article 267 TFEU[11], such as *Gøttrup-Klim Grovvareforeninger v Dansk Landbrugs Grovvareselskab*[12]. As for Commission decisions, since the entry into force of Regulation 1/2003 in May 2004 the Commission could decide that a particular agreement satisfies the criteria of Article 101(3) only by adopting a declaration of inapplicability under Article 10 of that Regulation, something which, to date, it has declined to do[13]; nor has it provided informal guidance on any such agreement[14]. Prior to Regulation 1/2003 the Commission could grant a so-called 'individual exemption' stating that Article 101(3) applied to a horizontal cooperation agreement[15]; where it did so there was usually little incentive for the parties to challenge the finding that the agreement infringed Article 101(1) in the first place. An exception to this was the judgment of the General Court in *European Night Services v Commission*[16] where an appeal was successfully brought against the Commission's decision, in which it had attached conditions and obligations to an individual exemption which the parties considered to be unduly onerous. The Court concluded that the Commission had failed to demonstrate that a joint venture to run overnight passenger services between the UK and continental Europe would appreciably restrict competition. Another exception to the proposition that undertakings authorised by the Commission to go ahead with a horizontal cooperation agreement under Article 101(3) would be unlikely to appeal was *O2 (Germany) v Commission*[17], where O2 was successful in persuading the General Court that national roaming agreements in the German mobile telephony sector did not restrict competition in the sense of Article 101(1), and therefore did not need to rely on Article 101(3)[18].

There have been some other cases in which a third party has challenged the Commission's decision that Article 101(3) was satisfied, but these have usually been unsuccessful[19]. Significant exceptions to this include *Métropole télévision v Commission*[20] and *M6 v Commission*[21], where the General Court upheld two consecutive appeals by a third party that the Commission had erred in law in concluding that the rules of the European Broadcasting Union satisfied Article 101(3)[22].

[10] See the helpful summary of the case law in the judgment of the UK Competition Appeal Tribunal in Case 1262/5/7/16 (T) *Agents' Mutual Ltd v Gascoigne Halman Ltd* [2017] CAT 15, paras 183–184.

[11] See ch 2, 'Court of Justice', p 56 on the Article 267 procedure.

[12] Case 250/92 EU:C:1994:413; see also Case 61/80 *Coöperatieve Stremsel- en Kleurselfabriek v Commission* EU:C:1981:75; Cases C-399/93 etc *HG Oude Luttikhuis v Coberco* EU:C:1995:434;.

[13] See ch 7, 'Article 10: finding of inapplicability', p 269.

[14] See ch 4, 'Self-assessment', pp 174–175 on informal guidance.

[15] See ch 4, 'The Commission's former monopoly over the grant of individual exemptions', p 174.

[16] Cases T-374/94 etc EU:T:1998:198: see ch 3, 'Actual and potential competition', p 135; see similarly Cases T-79/95 and 80/95 *SNCF v Commission* EU:T:1996:155; the recipients of an individual exemption in *TPS* OJ [1999] L 90/6 appealed unsuccessfully to the General Court in Case T-112/99 *Métropole v Commission* EU:T:2001:215.

[17] Case T-328/03 EU:T:2006:116.

[18] The case is discussed in ch 3, 'The need to establish a "counterfactual"', pp 134–135.

[19] See eg Case 43/85 *ANCIDES v Commission* EU:C:1987:347; Case T-17/93 *Matra Hachette SA v Commission* EU:T:1994:89.

[20] Cases T-528/93 etc EU:T:1996:99.

[21] Cases T-185/00 etc EU:T:2002:242.

[22] See ch 4, 'Judicial review by the General Court', p 173.

(C) The *Guidelines on Horizontal Cooperation Agreements*

The Commission published its *Guidelines on Horizontal Cooperation Agreements* in 2011[23]. The *Guidelines* consist of seven chapters. In the first, the Commission explains the purpose and scope of the *Guidelines* and sets out basic principles for the assessment of horizontal cooperation agreements under Article 101. Chapters then follow on agreements relating to each of the following matters: information exchange; R&D; production; purchasing; commercialisation; and standardisation[24]. This chapter will follow the structure of the *Guidelines*, with the exception that the exchange of information, which in some circumstances may be tantamount to a cartel, has already been discussed in chapter 13[25]; the chapter will conclude with a discussion of various other types of agreement that are not discussed in the *Guidelines* but which may be permissible and with a brief review of the position under UK law.

Paragraph 19 of the *Guidelines* says that they should be read in conjunction with the Commission's *Guidelines on the application of Article [101(3)] of the Treaty*[26] which provide important insights into its approach generally to the application of both Article 101(1) and Article 101(3) and, in particular, to the evidence needed to mount a successful argument based on the latter provision[27].

(i) Actual and potential competitors

Undertakings are actual competitors if they are active on the same market[28]; potential competitors are those that, in response to a small but significant non-transitory increase in price ('SSNIP')[29], would undertake the necessary investments to enter the market 'within a short period of time'[30]. What constitutes a short period depends on the particular facts of any case[31]; in *Visa Europe v Commission*[32] the General Court said that the essential factor is the need for entry to take place with sufficient speed to exert a competitive constraint on market participants[33].

One of the criticisms of the Commission by the General Court in *European Night Services v Commission*[34] was that it had failed convincingly to demonstrate that the agreement restricted potential competition. In *Lundbeck v Commission*[35] the General Court

[23] For a helpful discussion of the Commission's intentions when adopting the new *Guidelines* see the speech of the former Director-General of DG COMP, Alexander Italianer, 'Doing Business in Europe: the Review of the Rules on Co-operation Agreements Between Competitors', 1 March 2011, available at www.ec.europa.eu; see also a series of articles in the February 2011 edition of Competition Policy International, available at www.competitionpolicyinternational.com; the 2011 *Guidelines* replaced earlier ones adopted in 2001: OJ [2001] C 3/2.

[24] Note that, whereas the 2001 *Guidelines* contained a separate chapter on environmental agreements, this is not true of the 2011 *Guidelines*; however agreements setting out standards on environmental performance are covered by ch 7: see 'Standardisation Agreements', pp 619–623 later in chapter.

[25] See ch 13, 'Exchanges of Information', pp 551–559.

[26] OJ [2004] C 101/97.

[27] The *Article [101(3)] Guidelines* are discussed in ch 4, 'The Article 101(3) Criteria', pp 162–173.

[28] *Guidelines on Horizontal Cooperation Agreements*, para 10.

[29] See ch 1, 'Demand-side substitutability', pp 30–31.

[30] *Guidelines on Horizontal Cooperation Agreements*, para 10.

[31] The Commission says in fn 3 to para 10 that a longer period might be considered to be 'short' in the case of a party to the agreement than when asking whether a third party might be a competitive constraint on the parties to the agreement; on the timing of potential competition see also Case T-472/13 *Lundbeck v Commission* EU:T:2016:449, paras 163 and 203.

[32] Case T-461/07 EU:T:2011:181.

[33] Ibid, paras 189–190.

[34] Cases T-374/94 etc EU:T:1998:198, paras 135–146.

[35] Commission decision of 19 June 2013, upheld on appeal Cases T-472/13 etc *Lundbeck v Commission* EU:T:2016:449, on appeal Cases C-591/16 P etc, not yet decided; see also *Servier*, Commission decision of 9 July 2014, paras 1156–1183, on appeal Cases T-691/14 etc *Servier v Commission*, not yet decided.

held that producers of generic medicines were potential competitors of Lundbeck because they had taken steps and made investments in order to enter the market at the time of their agreement with Lundbeck; the fact that Lundbeck owned patents relating to a particular production process did not preclude potential competition[36]. The perception of the undertaking present on the market is a relevant factor in assessing whether other undertakings were potential competitors[37].

The assessment of potential competition must be based on realistic grounds, and a theoretical possibility is not sufficient[38]. In this formulation of potential competition the Commission refers to a policy statement that it made at point 55 of its XIIIth *Report on Competition Policy* in 1983[39], and to its decision in *Elopak/Metal Box-Odin*[40], where it concluded that a joint venture between those two undertakings to design a new kind of carton did not infringe Article 101(1) since they were not actual or potential competitors[41]. It is not necessary to show that a new entrant would have successfully entered the market but for the agreement in question[42].

(ii) Purpose and scope of the *Guidelines on Horizontal Cooperation Agreements*

Paragraph 1 of the *Guidelines* explains that they are concerned with cooperation agreements between actual or potential competitors. The *Guidelines* also apply to agreements between undertakings that are active in the same product market but in different geographic markets but without being potential competitors. The *Guidelines* are a complement to the block exemptions for R&D agreements[43] and for specialisation agreements[44]. The *Guidelines* do not apply to 'pure' vertical agreements, which are the subject of the *Guidelines on Vertical Restraints* and which may benefit from Regulation 330/2010 on vertical agreements[45]; however the *Guidelines on Horizontal Cooperation Agreements* do apply to vertical agreements entered into between competitors to the extent that they are not eligible for block exemption under Regulation 330/2010[46].

As mentioned, the *Guidelines* apply to six types of agreements: information exchange, R&D, production, purchasing, commercialisation and standardisation. In any particular case it is necessary to characterise the agreement in order to be able to determine whether it falls into any of these six categories and, if so, which one. Agreements in commercial practice do not divide themselves neatly in this way: for example undertakings that agree to conduct R&D together will often decide to produce and commercialise the product if the R&D is successful, while the parties to a joint production agreement might agree

36 Case T-472/13 *Lundbeck v Commission* EU:T:2016:449, paras 120–124 and 166.

37 Ibid, paras 104 and 302 and the case law cited.

38 *Guidelines on Horizontal Cooperation Agreements*, para 10; see ch 3, 'Actual and potential competition', p 135.

39 See also Faull 'Joint Ventures under the EEC Competition Rules' (1984) 9 EL Rev 358.

40 OJ [1990] L 209/15.

41 Other decisions in which the Commission reached a similar conclusion include *Optical Fibres* OJ [1986] L 236/30; *Mitchell Cotts/Sofiltra* OJ [1987] L 41/31; *Konsortium ECR 900* OJ [1990] L 228/31; *Iridium* OJ [1997] L
16/87; *Cégétel+4* OJ [1999] L 218/14; see also a related decision, *Télécom Développement* OJ [1999] L 218/24; *P&I Clubs* OJ [1999] L 125/12; *Société Air France/Alitalia Linee Aeree Italiane SpA* OJ [2004] L 362/17, paras 110–126.

42 Case T-472/13 *Lundbeck v Commission* EU:T:2016:449, paras 159, 233 and 471.

43 See 'The block exemption for research and development agreements: Regulation 1217/2010', pp 607–611 later in chapter.

44 See 'The block exemption for specialisation agreements: Regulation 1218/2010', pp 613–615 later in chapter.

45 See ch 16, 'Vertical Agreements: Regulation 330/2010', pp 664–687.

46 *Guidelines on Horizontal Cooperation Agreements*, para 12 and fn 11.

to some joint R&D as a by-product of their cooperation. Paragraphs 13 and 14 of the *Guidelines* attempt to provide a basis for allocating agreements to the appropriate category by introducing the notion of an agreement's 'centre of gravity'.

When determining the centre of gravity of an agreement account should be taken of two factors: the first is the starting point of the cooperation and the second is the degree of integration of the different functions that are being combined[47]. Two examples are given. In the first, the parties enter into an R&D agreement and envisage the possibility of proceeding, if successful, to joint production: here, the cooperation originates as an R&D agreement and is characterised as such. In the second, the parties agree to integrate their production facilities, but only partially to integrate their R&D: here, the agreement is essentially concerned with production and should be analysed as such.

Paragraph 18 of the *Guidelines* says that they do not apply to the extent that sector-specific rules apply, as in the case of certain agreements in the agriculture[48] and transport[49] sectors.

(iii) Basic principles for the assessment of horizontal cooperation agreements under Article 101

Chapter 1.2 of the *Guidelines* begins, at paragraph 20, by explaining that agreements are analysed under Article 101 in two stages:

- first, determine whether the agreement has as its object or effect the restriction of competition, contrary to Article 101(1); if so
- secondly, analyse any pro-competitive effects in the framework of Article 101(3)[50].

Paragraph 20 also points out that, in the event that any pro-competitive effects do not outweigh any restriction of competition, Article 101(2) stipulates that the agreement is automatically void.

(a) Article 101(1)

Paragraphs 23 to 31 discuss agreements that restrict competition by object and those that may restrict by effect: these ideas were explored in detail in chapter 3 of this book[51]. In relation to anti-competitive effects, paragraph 28 says that they are likely to occur where it can be expected that, due to the agreement, the parties would be able to profitably raise prices or reduce output, product quality, product variety or innovation; and that this depends on various factors such as the nature and content of the agreement, the parties' individual or joint market power and the extent to which the agreement contributes to the creation, maintenance, strengthening or exploitation of that market power. Without using the term, paragraph 29 says that, when determining whether an agreement has or could have anti-competitive effects, it is necessary to consider the 'counterfactual', that is to say the competitive position in the absence of the agreement[52].

The *Guidelines* then discuss, in turn, the *nature and content of the agreement* and *market power and other market characteristics*. In essence, what the *Guidelines* purport to do is to set out various theories of harm—the expression actually used in paragraph 32 is 'types of possible competition concerns'—in the section on the nature and content of the agreement, and to explain aspects of market power in the following section.

[47] *Guidelines*, para 14.
[48] See ch 23, 'Agriculture', pp 995–998.
[49] See ch 23, 'Transport', pp 999–1008.
[50] See ch 4, 'The Article 101(3) Criteria', pp 162–173, for discussion of the nature and scope of the provisions of Article 101(3).
[51] See ch 3, 'The object or effect of preventing, restricting or distorting competition', pp 119ff.
[52] For discussion of the counterfactual see ch 3, 'The need to establish a "counterfactual"', pp 134–135.

Paragraph 32 says that the *nature and content of the agreement* relate to factors such as the area and objective of the cooperation, the competitive relationship between the parties and the extent to which they combine their activities. These determine the types of competition concerns that can arise from horizontal cooperation agreements. Paragraph 33 notes that such agreements may result in exclusivity, because the parties cease to compete with one another or with third parties; or in reduced independence of decision-making, because the parties contribute assets to the cooperation or alter their financial interests as a result of it. The following paragraphs set out competition concerns that may follow as a result:

- **higher prices**: paragraph 34 discusses the possibility that the loss of competition between the parties may lead to them—and potentially to their competitors—raising prices: in the parlance of the *Horizontal Merger Guidelines*, the concern is about 'non-coordinated effects'[53]
- **coordination**: paragraphs 35 to 37 discuss the possibility that horizontal cooperation agreements may facilitate coordination between the parties, within or outside the field of cooperation, for example as a result of the disclosure of strategic information to each other or the achievement of a significant commonality of costs (for example where they jointly produce an input that represents a high proportion of the value of a product that they sell in competition with one another): in the parlance of the *Horizontal Merger Guidelines*, the concern is about 'coordinated effects'[54]
- **foreclosure**: agreements such as production and standardisation agreements might give rise to concerns about anti-competitive foreclosure of access to the market.

Paragraphs 39 to 47 discuss market power, a topic that has been considered in chapter 1 of this book[55]. Paragraph 43 says that the starting point for the analysis of market power is the position of the parties on the markets affected by the cooperation. It refers to the need to define the relevant market(s) by using the methodology in the Commission's *Notice on Market Definition*[56]; the *Guidelines* provide additional guidance on purchasing and technology markets. Paragraph 44 makes the obvious point that, where the parties have a low combined market share, their agreement is unlikely to give rise to anti-competitive effects. It adds that what amounts to a 'low' market share is sometimes discussed in specific chapters of the *Guidelines* which sometimes provide 'safe harbour' thresholds[57]; and that the Commission's *De Minimis Notice* also provides guidance on this[58]. Paragraph 44 adds an important point, that if one of just two parties has only an insignificant market share and if it does not possess important resources, even a high combined market share normally cannot be seen as indicating a likely restrictive effect on competition.

(b) Article 101(3)

Paragraph 48 of the *Guidelines* refers to Article 2 of Regulation 1/2003, which provides that the burden of proving that an agreement satisfies the conditions of Article 101(3) rests on the undertaking(s) seeking to defend the agreement[59]. Paragraph 50 explains that, just as the block exemptions for R&D and specialisation agreements are premised upon the

[53] See ch 21, 'Non-coordinated effects', pp 891–893. [54] See ch 21, 'Coordinated effects', pp 893–895.

[55] See ch 1, 'Market power', pp 42–46. [56] OJ [1997] C 372/5; see ch 1 'Market definition', pp 26–42.

[57] See eg *Guidelines*, para 208 which provides a safe harbour for joint purchasing agreements where the parties have a market share not exceeding 15% of their purchasing or selling markets: see 'Restrictions by effect', p 616 later in chapter.

[58] See ch 3, 'The *De Minimis* Doctrine', pp 147–150.

[59] See on this point ch 4, 'Burden and standard of proof', p 159.

idea that the combination of complementary skills can be a source of substantial efficiencies, so too the analysis of agreements on an individual basis under Article 101(3) will to a large extent focus on identifying complementary skills and assets. Paragraph 52 says that agreements that do not involve the combination of complementary skills are less likely to lead to efficiency gains that benefit consumers[60].

4. Information Exchange

Chapter 4 of the *Guidelines on Horizontal Cooperation Agreements* discusses the exchange of information. Paragraph 57 points out that information exchange may generate efficiency gains; whereas paragraph 58 notes that it can also lead to restrictions of competition. The subject is complex, and careful analysis is required. We have chosen to deal with this subject in the chapter on cartels[61], but this is not intended to suggest that the exchange of information is by its nature cartel-like behaviour. There is a long and complicated continuum: at one end can be found exchanges of information which are, in truth, cartels, or mechanisms for monitoring and enforcing cartels; at the other are exchanges that make markets more efficient[62]. We do not wish to pretend that a clear line can be drawn that separates 'bad' from 'good' exchanges of information, by allocating some to the chapter on cartels and others to this chapter; this is why they are dealt with in one place only.

5. Research and Development Agreements

One of the forms in which competition may manifest itself is in the research and development aspects of an undertaking's activities. Sometimes an undertaking may wish to collaborate with its competitors in order to undertake the R&D. Chapter 3 of the *Guidelines on Horizontal Cooperation Agreements* deals with agreements that have as their centre of gravity R&D[63]. Chapter 3.2 deals with market definition in R&D cases, first in relation to existing product and technology markets and then in relation to markets for innovation, also referred to as 'R&D efforts'; chapter 3.3 considers the assessment of R&D agreements under Article 101(1) and chapter 3.4 discusses the application of Article 101(3). Chapter 3.5 provides five examples of how Article 101 would apply to various types of agreement. Regulation 1217/2010 confers block exemption on some R&D agreements[64].

(A) Market definition

The key to defining markets in R&D cases is to identify those products, technologies or R&D efforts that act as a competitive constraint on the parties to the agreement[65]. In some

[60] *Guidelines on Horizontal Cooperation Agreements*, para 53 refers the reader to the *Guidelines on the application of [Article 101(3)]* OJ [2004] C 101/97.

[61] See ch 13, 'Exchanges of information', pp 551–559.

[62] See generally OECD *Information exchanges between competitors under competition law* (2010), available at www.oecd.org/competition.

[63] For a useful discussion of research and development agreements see *Faull and Nikpay*, paras 7.143–7.234.

[64] OJ [2010] L 335/36; see 'The block exemption for research and development agreements: Regulation 1217/2010', pp 607–611 later in chapter.

[65] *Guidelines*, para 112.

cases innovation leads to the creation of a new product which is merely a slight improvement on an existing one; at the other end of the spectrum an entirely new product may be created that forms a new market. Some innovation falls between these two extremes.

(i) Existing product and technology markets

Where an agreement concerns improvements to existing products, they and their close substitutes form the relevant market[66]. Where R&D is aimed at a significant change of existing products, or even the creation of a new one to replace them, the old and the potentially new products do not belong to the same market; however in this situation the possibility exists that cooperation in the new market could lead to coordination in the old one[67]. Where the R&D concerns an important component in a final product the market for the component may be relevant to the competition assessment, but the existing market for the final product may also be relevant if the component is technically or economically a key element in the final product and if the parties have market power with respect to that product[68]. In some cases the market may be one for technology rather than products[69], and paragraphs 116 to 118 explain how the market should be defined and market share calculated in those circumstances; the Commission's *Technology Transfer Guidelines* also discuss this topic[70].

(ii) Competition in innovation (R&D efforts)

Where the parties conduct R&D in relation to innovation and the creation of entirely new products the position is more complex, and the *Guidelines* say at paragraph 119 that it may not be sufficient in such cases to look only at existing product and/or technology markets[71]. Paragraph 120 says that it may be possible to identify competing 'poles' of R&D, in which case it is necessary to consider whether, if two competing undertakings were to enter into an R&D agreement, there would be a 'sufficient number of remaining R&D poles'. The remaining poles must be 'credible': the credibility of an R&D pole is assessed according to the nature, scope and size of other R&D efforts, their access to financial and human resources, know-how, patents and other specialised assets and their capability to exploit the results. Where it is not possible to identify R&D poles, the Commission would limit its assessment to related product and/or technology markets[72].

(iii) Market shares

Paragraphs 123 to 126 of the *Guidelines* discuss how market shares should be calculated in the case of R&D agreements, and in particular the different approaches to be taken when dealing with innovation and entirely new products as opposed to the improvement of existing ones. Since market shares are particularly important when considering the application of the R&D block exemption, this issue will be discussed in section D later on Regulation 1217/2010[73].

[66] Ibid, para 113. [67] Ibid, para 114. [68] Ibid, para 115.

[69] See eg *Servier*, decision of 9 July 2014, paras 2616–2667 (defining relevant product and technology markets), on appeal Case T-691/14 *Servier v Commission*, not yet decided.

[70] OJ [2014] C 89/3, paras 19–26; see further ch 19, 'Technology markets', p 801.

[71] For discussion on competition in innovation see *Innovation and Competition Policy* (OFT 377, 2002), available at www.nationalarchives.gov.uk; Gilbert 'Competition and Innovation' in Collins (ed) *Issues in Competition Law and Policy* (ABA, 2006); speech by the Director-General of DG COMP, Johannes Laitenberger, 'Competition and Innovation', 9 December 2015, available at www.ec.europa.eu.

[72] *Guidelines*, para 122.

[73] See 'The block exemption for research and development agreements: Regulation 1217/2010', pp 607–611 later in chapter.

(B) The application of Article 101(1) to R&D agreements

(i) R&D agreements that normally fall outside Article 101(1)

The following R&D agreements are unlikely to have anti-competitive effects and would normally not be caught by Article 101(1):

- R&D agreements that relate to cooperation 'at an early stage, far removed from the exploitation of possible results'[74]
- R&D agreements between non-competitors[75], unless there is a possibility of a foreclosure effect and one of the parties has significant market power with respect to key technology[76]
- the outsourcing of R&D to research institutes and academic bodies which are not active in the exploitation of the results[77]
- 'pure' R&D agreements that do not extend to joint exploitation of the results; such agreements would fall within Article 101(1) only where they appreciably reduce effective competition in innovation[78].

(ii) Main competition concerns

Paragraphs 127 to 140 of the *Guidelines* discuss the assessment of R&D agreements under Article 101(1). Three possible anti-competitive effects are noted:

- a reduction or slowing down of innovation
- a restriction of competition or the facilitation of coordination between the parties in markets outside the scope of the agreement
- foreclosure of access to the market, although this would be a problem only if at least one of the parties to the agreement has significant market power (though not necessarily dominance)[79].

(iii) Restrictions by object

Paragraph 128 says that an R&D agreement would restrict competition by object if it is in reality a tool to engage in a disguised cartel; however it adds that an R&D agreement which includes the joint exploitation of future results is not necessarily restrictive of competition[80].

(iv) Restrictions by effect

Paragraphs 129 to 140 consider when R&D agreements might infringe Article 101(1) because of their anti-competitive effects. Paragraph 133 states that an R&D agreement is likely to infringe Article 101(1) only where the parties have market power on the existing markets or where competition with respect to innovation is appreciably reduced; no market share figure is given for the application of Article 101(1) to R&D agreements[81], although the Commission points out that a safe haven is provided by Article 4 of Regulation 1217/2010, the block exemption for R&D agreements, where the parties' market share is below 25%[82]. The *Guidelines* say that where the parties have a market share of more than 25% it does not necessarily follow that Article 101(1) is infringed, but

[74] *Guidelines*, para 129. [75] Ibid, para 130. [76] Ibid, fn 1 to para 130.
[77] Ibid, para 131. [78] Ibid, para 132. [79] Ibid, para 127. [80] Ibid, para 128.
[81] Ibid, para 133. [82] Ibid, para 134; on the block exemption see section D later in chapter.

they continue by saying that an infringement becomes more likely as the parties' position on the market becomes stronger[83]. Paragraph 137 explains that an R&D agreement that extends to joint production and/or marketing would need to be scrutinised for competition concerns more carefully than one that relates purely to R&D. The *Guidelines* then provide guidance on R&D agreements in relation to entirely new products or technologies[84] and on agreements that lie between the improvement of existing products or technologies and the development of entirely new ones[85].

(C) The application of Article 101(3) to R&D agreements

Paragraphs 141 to 146 discuss the assessment of R&D agreements under Article 101(3)[86]. Paragraph 142 states that the hard-core restrictions that are listed in Article 5 of Regulation 1217/2010, and which prevent the application of the block exemption, would be unlikely to be regarded as indispensable in the case of the individual assessment of an agreement under Article 101(3). Paragraphs 145 and 146 deal with the date for assessing the application of Article 101(3): they explain that it is necessary to take into account any sunk costs that the parties incur when investing in the R&D project and the time that they may need to be able to recoup their investment[87]; and also that different aspects of an agreement may need to be assessed at different times: for example the effects of cooperation in R&D should be considered at the date of the original agreement, but joint production may give rise to issues at a later date, if and when the agreement leads to the development of successful products[88].

(D) The block exemption for R&D agreements: Regulation 1217/2010

Acting under powers conferred upon it by Council Regulation 2821/71[89] the Commission adopted a block exemption for R&D agreements on 14 December 2010[90]. Regulation 1217/2010 entered into force on 1 January 2011 and will expire on 31 December 2022[91].

The Regulation consists of 22 recitals and 9 Articles. Recital 2 refers specifically to Article 179(2) TFEU, which calls upon the EU to encourage undertakings, including small and medium-sized ones, in their R&D activities and to support efforts on their part to cooperate with one another. Article 1 defines key terms such as 'research and development agreement', 'exploitation of the results', 'actual competitor' and 'potential competitor'. Article 2 confers block exemption on R&D agreements subject to the provisions of the Regulation. Article 3 sets out conditions for application of the block exemption. Article 4 imposes a market share cap and deals with the duration of the exemption. Article 5 sets out a list of 'hard-core' restrictions the inclusion of which prevents an agreement from benefiting from block exemption. Article 6 provides that certain 'excluded restrictions' do not benefit from block exemption, although their inclusion in an agreement does not prevent application of the Regulation to the rest of it. Article 7 contains provisions on the application of the market share threshold. Withdrawal of the block exemption by the Commission or by the national competition authorities of a Member State ('NCAs') is possible by virtue of Article 29 of Regulation 1/2003.

[83] *Guidelines*, para 135. [84] Ibid, para 138. [85] Ibid, para 139.

[86] For examples of R&D agreements that were found to satisfy the criteria of Article 101(3) see *Asahi/St Gobain* OJ [1994] L 354/87; *Philips/Osram* OJ [1994] L 378/34.

[87] *Guidelines*, para 145. [88] Ibid, para 146. [89] OJ [1971] L 285/46.

[90] Regulation 1217/2010, OJ [2010] L 335/36. [91] Ibid, Article 9; note also recital 22.

(i) Article 1: definitions

Article 1 contains definitions of expressions used in Regulation 1217/2010. Of particular importance is Article 1(1)(a) which defines an R&D[92] agreement as one between two or more parties relating to the conditions under which they pursue:

(a) joint research and development of contract products or contract technologies and joint exploitation of the results of that research and development;

(b) joint exploitation of the results of research and development of contract products or contract technologies jointly carried out pursuant to a prior agreement between the same parties; or

(c) joint research and development of contract products or contract technologies.

Article 1(1) also includes within the definition of an R&D agreement those where one party merely finances the R&D activities of another party[93]. Recital 9 of the Regulation states that joint exploitation can be considered as the natural consequence of joint R&D: exploitation is defined in Article 1(1)(g) to include:

> the production or distribution of the contract products or the application of the contract technologies or the assignment or licensing of intellectual property rights or the communication of know-how required for such manufacture or application.

R&D and exploitation are 'joint' where the work is carried out by a joint team, organisation or undertaking, is jointly entrusted to a third party or is allocated between the parties by way of specialisation in research and development or exploitation[94].

(ii) Article 2: exemption

Article 2(1) confers block exemption on R&D agreements, subject to the provisions of the Regulation. Article 2(2) provides that the block exemption also applies to provisions in R&D agreements which relate to the assignment or licensing of intellectual property rights:

> provided that those provisions do not constitute the primary object of such agreements, but are directly related to and necessary for their implementation.

(iii) Article 3: conditions for exemption

Article 3(1) provides that block exemption is available subject to the conditions set out in paragraphs 2 to 5 thereof; Article 3 should be read in conjunction with recitals 11 and 12. It should be stressed that these conditions are applicable only where an agreement infringes Article 101(1) so that the parties wish to avail themselves of the block exemption; if an agreement is not restrictive in the sense of Article 101(1), there is no need to comply with Article 3 of the Regulation.

Article 3(2) provides that all the parties must have full access to the final results of the joint R&D for the purposes of further research or exploitation; however if they limit their rights of exploitation in accordance with the Regulation, for example by agreeing to specialise in the context of exploitation, access to the rights may be limited accordingly. The third sentence of Article 3(2) specifically provides that research institutes, academic bodies or undertakings which supply R&D as a commercial service but are not normally active in exploitation of the results may agree to confine their use of the results to conducting further research. This means, for example, that a pharmaceutical company that

[92] The term R&D itself is defined in Article 1(1)(c) of the Regulation.

[93] Regulation 1217/2010, recital 8 and Article 1(1)(a)(iv)–(vi).

[94] Ibid, Article 1(1)(m).

enters into an R&D agreement with a research institute or a university can require its partner not to exploit the results commercially but to limit itself only to further research; if this restriction were not possible, the pharmaceutical company might refrain from beneficial joint R&D with the undertaking in question for fear that it would extend its activities beyond research into commercialisation.

Article 3(3) provides that, subject to Article 3(2), where an agreement provides only for joint R&D, each party must be granted access to pre-existing know-how of the other parties if it is indispensable for the purposes of its exploitation of the results; the agreement can provide for compensation to be paid for such access, but the rate must not be so high as to impede such access.

Article 3(4) provides that joint exploitation is permissible only where it relates to results of cooperation in R&D which are protected by intellectual property rights or constitute know-how and which are indispensable for the manufacture of the contract products or the application of the contract technologies. The reason for this condition is that cooperation at the level of exploitation should be limited to those cases in which joint R&D has led to economic benefits; where this is not the case, the rationale for granting block exemption to joint exploitation is not satisfied.

Article 3(5) provides that undertakings charged with manufacture by way of specialisation in production must be required to fulfil orders for supplies from all the parties, except where the R&D also provides for joint distribution or where the parties have agreed that only the party manufacturing the contract products may distribute them. The explanation for this is that where, for example, one party agrees to produce widgets and the other blodgets, each should have access to the products produced by the other and be able to compete in the relevant market; this is not necessary, however, where the parties carry out their distribution jointly.

(iv) Article 4: duration of exemption and the market share threshold

Article 4 deals with the duration of the exemption and the market share threshold; Article 4 should be read in conjunction with recitals 13 to 16. A distinction is made between the treatment of agreements between non-competing undertakings and agreements between competing ones. Paragraphs 123 and 124 of the *Guidelines on Horizontal Cooperation Agreements* explain that, where existing products or technologies are being improved or replaced, market shares can be based on the existing ones; paragraph 125 specifically discusses the calculation of market shares for technology markets. Paragraph 126 says that, where the agreement relates to innovation, market shares cannot be calculated, in which case the agreement is treated as one between non-competing undertakings and Articles 4(1) and 4(3) of the Regulation apply.

Article 4(1) provides that the exemption shall apply to agreements between non-competing undertakings[95] for the duration of their R&D; where the results are jointly exploited the exemption shall continue to apply for seven years from the time the contract products or contract technologies are first put on the market within the internal market. These rules apply irrespective of the parties' market share; if it were necessary to take action in relation to an agreement between non-competing undertakings, this would be done by withdrawal of the block exemption[96]. Article 4(3) provides that, at the end of the

[95] For the definition of this term see Regulation 1217/2010, Article 1(1)(r)–(t); note in particular that a 'competing undertaking' under the block exemption includes one that might enter within three years in response to a SSNIP (as to which see ch 1, 'Demand-side substitutability', pp 30–31), rather than a period of one year that is the usual test when determining whether a potential competitor for the purpose of Article 101(1).

[96] Regulation 1217/2010, recital 18; on withdrawal of the block exemption see 'Withdrawal of the block exemption p 611 later in chapter.

seven-year period, the exemption will continue as long as the parties' combined market share does not exceed 25%.

Article 4(2) deals with the position where the parties are competing undertakings. In that case the block exemption applies only if, at the time the parties entered into the agreement, their share of the market for the contract products or contract technologies did not exceed 25%; in the case of paid-for R&D the financing party's market share is also to be taken into account for the purposes of this rule[97]. Article 7 contains rules on how to apply the market share threshold; it contains specific rules to deal with the situation where the undertakings outgrow the market share cap[98].

(v) Article 5: hard-core restrictions

Article 5(1), which is shorter and less restrictive than its predecessor, prevents the block exemption from applying where agreements contain 'severe restrictions of competition'[99] which 'directly or indirectly, in isolation or in combination with other factors under the control of the parties, have as their object' any of the following:

- a restriction of the freedom of the parties to carry out R&D in a field unconnected to the agreement
- a limitation on output or sales. There are exceptions to this: the setting of production or sales targets in the event of joint exploitation or joint distribution; specialisation in the context of exploitation[100]; and a non-competition clause during the period of joint exploitation. Recital 15 to Regulation 1217/2010 also states that field-of-use restrictions will not be regarded as constituting limitations of output or sales (nor as restrictions on territories or customers)
- the fixing of prices when selling the contract products or licensing the contract technologies to third parties, with the exception of fixing the prices or royalties charged to immediate customers in the event of joint exploitation or distribution
- a restriction of the territories to which or the customers to whom the parties may passively sell the contract products or license the contract technologies, with the exception of the requirement exclusively to license the results to another party
- a requirement not to make any, or to limit, active sales in territories or to customers which have not been exclusively allocated to one of the parties by way of specialisation in the context of exploitation
- a requirement to refuse to meet demand from customers in the parties' respective territories or from customers otherwise allocated between the parties by way of specialisation in the context of exploitation, who would market them in other territories within the internal market
- a requirement to make it difficult for users or resellers to obtain the contract products from other resellers within the internal market.

The inclusion of any of these provisions excludes the entire agreement, not just the offensive provisions, from the block exemption. Where such provisions fall within Article 101(1), which is likely to be the case[101], paragraph 142 of the *Guidelines* states that they are less likely to satisfy the terms of Article 101(3) on an individual basis, but continues that

[97] Regulation 1217/2010, Article 4(2)(b). [98] Ibid, Article 7(d)–(f). [99] Ibid, recital 15.

[100] Note that Regulation 2659/2000 did not apply to specialisation in exploitation.

[101] Note that even hard-core restrictions might, as a matter of law, fall outside Article 101(1) where they could not have an appreciable effect on inter-state trade: see ch 3, 'The concept of appreciability', pp 153–154.

undertakings may be able to demonstrate that such restrictions are indispensable to an R&D agreement.

(vi) Article 6: excluded restrictions

Article 6 lists two 'excluded restrictions' which are not block exempted, but the inclusion of which does not prevent the application of the Regulation to the remaining parts of the agreement if they are severable from the excluded restrictions; both obligations were regarded as 'hard-core' under the previous block exemption Regulation. The first is an obligation not to challenge the validity of intellectual property rights relevant to, or arising from, the R&D, without prejudice to the right to terminate the agreement in the event of such a challenge. The second excluded restriction is an obligation not to grant licences to third parties to manufacture the contract products or to apply the contract technologies unless the agreement provides for exploitation of the results of the R&D by at least one of the parties to the agreement.

(vii) Article 7: application of the market share threshold

Article 7 was referred to earlier in the context of the market share cap in Article 4.

(viii) Article 8: transitional period

Transitional provisions are contained in Article 8[102].

(ix) Article 9: period of validity

The Regulation entered into force on 1 January 2011 and will expire on 31 December 2022.

(x) Withdrawal of the block exemption

As explained in chapter 4 of this book, Article 29 of Regulation 1/2003 enables the Commission and the NCAs to withdraw the benefit of a block exemption from agreements which have effects which are incompatible with Article 101(3). As noted earlier, recital 18 of Regulation 1217/2010 says that this might be done in the exceptional circumstance that an agreement between non-competing undertakings is harmful to competition. Recital 21 gives some further examples of when this might happen, for example where the R&D agreement substantially restricts the scope for third parties to carry out R&D or where the contract products or technologies do not face effective competition in the internal market.

6. Production Agreements

Chapter 4 of the *Guidelines on Horizontal Cooperation Agreements* deals with production agreements[103]. Paragraph 150 notes that such agreements vary in form and scope, from production carried out by a jointly-controlled company to sub-contracting agreements. The *Guidelines* apply to all forms of joint production agreements, including horizontal sub-contracting agreements, that is to say agreements between undertakings operating in the same market irrespective of whether they are actual or potential competitors[104]. Vertical sub-contracting agreements between undertakings operating at different levels

[102] Agreements that were exempt under the previous block exemption, Regulation 2659/2000, but not under Regulation 1217/2010, remained exempt until 31 December 2012.

[103] See further *Faull and Nikpay*, paras 7.235–7.322.

[104] *Guidelines on Horizontal Cooperation Agreements*, para 151.

of the market are not covered by the *Guidelines on Horizontal Cooperation Agreements*; however they may be covered by the Commission's *Guidelines on Vertical Restraints*, by the block exemption for vertical agreements, Regulation 330/2010, or by the Commission's *Notice on Sub-contracting Agreements*[105].

In determining whether Article 101(1) applies to production agreements, the relevant product and geographic markets must be defined; it may also be necessary to consider the possibility that there may be a 'spillover effect' in an upstream, downstream or neighbouring market[106].

(A) The application of Article 101(1) to production agreements

(i) Main competition concerns

The Commission expresses three main concerns about production agreements. First, they may lead to a direct restriction of competition between the parties, even if they market the products independently[107]. Secondly, they may lead to a coordination of the parties' competitive behaviour, in particular when the production agreement leads to a high commonality of their variable costs[108]. The Commission's third concern is that production agreements may lead to third parties being foreclosed from a related market; however it notes that a foreclosure effect is likely only if at least one of the parties has a 'strong market position' in the market where the risks of foreclosure are assessed[109].

(ii) Restrictions by object

Paragraph 160 states that horizontal agreements to fix prices, limit output or to share markets or customers have as their object the restriction of competition. However it goes on to explain that in two situations restrictions concerning output and prices in the context of joint production would not amount to restrictions by object. The first is where the parties agree on the level of output that is the subject-matter of the production agreement; the second is an agreement on the prices at which the jointly-produced products (and only those products) will be sold, provided that this is necessary for joint production.

(iii) Restrictions by effect

Paragraphs 162 to 182 deal with production agreements that may have the effect of restricting competition. Paragraph 163 explains that it is necessary to consider what the situation would have been in the absence of the agreement—that is to say to identify the 'counterfactual'; if the production agreement enables the parties to enter a market that they would otherwise have been unable to, the agreement will not be found to have as its effect the restriction of competition. Paragraph 165 says that none of the competition concerns discussed in paragraphs 157 to 159 would arise where the parties to a production agreement lack market power. Market power is discussed in paragraphs 168 to 173: the *Guidelines* do not provide a 'safe harbour' for agreements below a specific threshold[110], although the

[105] OJ 1979 C 1/2; on which see *Guidelines*, para 154; see further ch 16, 'Sub-Contracting Agreements', pp 691–692.

[106] *Guidelines on Horizontal Cooperation Agreements*, para 156; note that spillover effects must also be considered in the case of a joint venture that amounts to a concentration under the EUMR: see ch 21, 'Articles 2(4) and 2(5) of the EUMR: full-function joint ventures and "spillover effects"', pp 902–904.

[107] *Guidelines on Horizontal Cooperation Agreements*, para 157; see also para 174.

[108] Ibid, para 158; see also paras 175–182.

[109] Ibid, para 159.

[110] Note the Commission's *De Minimis Notice* provides a safe harbour for agreements between competitors that do not contain object restrictions where the parties' combined market share is below 10%: see ch 3, 'The *De Minimis* Doctrine', pp 147–150.

Commission draws attention to the 20% threshold below which agreements may benefit from the block exemption for specialisation agreements[111]. Even where the parties have high market shares, a production agreement may not have the appreciable effect of restricting competition where the market is dynamic, that is to say it is one in which entry occurs and market positions change frequently[112]. The *Guidelines* make the point that a production agreement is more likely to restrict competition by effect where it extends to commercialisation of the products rather than being limited purely to production: the nearer the parties' agreement brings them to the consumer, the higher the risk to competition[113].

(B) The application of Article 101(3) to production agreements

Paragraphs 183 to 186 discuss the possible application of Article 101(3) to production agreements[114].

(C) The block exemption for specialisation agreements: Regulation 1218/2010

Acting under powers conferred upon it by Council Regulation 2821/71[115] the Commission adopted a new block exemption for specialisation agreements on 14 December 2010[116]. The Regulation entered into force on 1 January 2011 and will expire on 31 December 2022[117].

The Regulation consists of 16 recitals and 7 Articles. Recitals 6 and 7 rehearse the arguments in favour of specialisation agreements, such as enabling the parties to operate more efficiently and supply products more cheaply. However recital 12 warns of the need to prevent agreements that would result in a substantial elimination of competition. Article 1 contains definitions. Article 2 confers block exemption on specialisation agreements subject to the provisions of the Regulation. Article 3 imposes a market share cap of 20%. Article 4 sets out a list of 'hard-core' restrictions the inclusion of which prevents an agreement from benefiting from block exemption. Article 5 contains provisions on the application of the market share threshold.

(i) Article 1: definitions

Article 1 of Regulation 1218/2010 contains definitions of expressions used in the Regulation. Article 1(2)(a) defines 'specialisation agreement'[118]: this term covers unilateral specialisation agreements, reciprocal specialisation agreements and joint production agreements. Each of these terms is then defined.

A unilateral specialisation agreement means an agreement between two parties:

> which are active on the same product market by virtue of which one party agrees to fully or partly[119] cease production of certain products or to refrain from producing those products and to purchase them from the other party, who agrees to produce and supply those products[120].

[111] See 'Article 3: the market share threshold', p 614 later in chapter; the Commission also provides a 'safe harbour' for horizontal sub-contracting agreements with a view to expanding production, where the parties' market share is below 20%: *Guidelines on Horizontal Cooperation Agreements*, para 169.

[112] *Guidelines on Horizontal Cooperation Agreements*, para 171.

[113] Ibid, para 167.

[114] For examples of production agreements authorised by the Commission under Article 101(3) see eg *Fiat/Hitachi* OJ [1993] L 20/10; *Ford/Volkswagen* OJ [1993] L 20/14; *Exxon/Mobil* OJ [1994] L 144/20: see Commission's XXIVth *Report on Competition Policy* (1994), pp 169–171; *Fujitsu/AMD* OJ [1994] L 341/66.

[115] OJ [1971] L 285/46.

[116] OJ [2010] L 335/43.

[117] Regulation 1218/2010, Article 7.

[118] See also ibid, recitals 7 and 8.

[119] Regulation 1218/2010 applies to partial cessation of production; its predecessor applied only in the case of a total cessation.

[120] Ibid, Article 1(1)(b).

A reciprocal specialisation agreement means an agreement between two or more parties:

> which are active on the same product market, by virtue of which two or more parties on a reciprocal basis agree fully or partly[121] to cease or refrain from producing certain but different products and to purchase these products from the other parties, who agree to produce and supply them[122].

A joint production agreement means an agreement between two or more parties:

> by virtue of which two or more parties agree to produce certain products jointly[123].

(ii) Article 2: exemption

Article 2(1) of Regulation 1218/2010 confers block exemption on specialisation agreements as defined in Article 1. Article 2 adds that block exemption extends to specialisation agreements:

> containing provisions which relate to the assignment or licensing of intellectual property rights to one or more of the parties, provided that those provisions do not constitute the primary object of such agreements, but are directly related to and necessary for their implementation.

Article 2(3) provides that the exemption also applies to specialisation agreements whereby the parties accept an exclusive purchase or supply obligation, each of which expression is defined in Article 1; and to agreements whereby the parties jointly distribute the products that are the subject of the agreement, rather than selling them independently. Recital 9 of the Regulation explains that, in order to ensure that the benefits of specialisation materialise without one party leaving the market downstream of production entirely, unilateral and reciprocal specialisation agreements must provide for supply and purchase obligations between the parties or for joint distribution; the supply and purchase obligations do not have to be exclusive, but if they are, they are block exempted by virtue of Article 2(3).

(iii) Article 3: the market share threshold

Article 3 is important, its primary concern being to ensure that the parties to a specialisation agreement do not possess significant market power. Article 3 provides that the block exemption applies on condition that the combined market share of the participating undertakings does not exceed 20%. The expression 'parties' includes 'connected undertakings', as defined in Article 2(2). Article 5 contains rules on how to apply the market share threshold; it contains specific rules to deal with the situation where the undertakings outgrow the market share cap[124]. Recital 10 of the Regulation says that, where the 20% market share threshold is exceeded, there is no presumption that an agreement infringes Article 101(1) or that it fails to satisfy Article 101(3): rather an individual assessment of the agreement would have to be conducted.

(iv) Article 4: hard-core restrictions

Article 4(1) prevents the block exemption from applying where agreements contain 'hard-core restrictions'[125], that is to say agreements which:

> directly or indirectly, in isolation or in combination with other factors under the control of the parties, have as their object any of the following:
>
> (a) the fixing of prices when selling the products to third parties with the exception of the fixing of prices charged to immediate customers in the context of joint distribution;

[121] See ch 15 n 119 earlier.
[122] Regulation 1218/2010, Article 1(1)(c).
[123] Ibid, Article 1(1)(d).
[124] Ibid, Article 5(d) and (e).
[125] See also ibid, recital 11.

(b) the limitation of output or sales with the exception of:

(i) provisions on the agreed amount of products in the context of unilateral or reciprocal specialisation agreements or the setting of the capacity and production volume in the context of a joint production agreement; and

(ii) the setting of sales targets in the context of joint distribution;

(c) the allocation of markets or customers.

The inclusion of any of these provisions excludes the entire agreement, not just the offensive provisions, from the block exemption[126].

(v) Article 5: application of the market share threshold

Article 5 was referred to earlier in the context of the market share cap in Article 4[127].

(vi) Article 6: transitional period

Transitional provisions are contained in Article 6.

(vii) Article 7: period of validity

The Regulation entered into force on 1 January 2011 and will expire on 31 December 2022.

(viii) Withdrawal of the block exemption

Article 29 of Regulation 1/2003 enables the Commission and the NCAs to withdraw the benefit of a block exemption from agreements which have effects which are incompatible with Article 101(3)[128]. Recital 15 of Regulation 1218/2010 says that this might happen, for example, where the relevant market is very concentrated and competition is already weak, in particular because of the individual market positions of other market participants or links between other market participants created by parallel specialisation agreements.

7. Purchasing Agreements

Chapter 5 of the *Guidelines on Horizontal Cooperation Agreements* deals with joint purchasing agreements[129]. Surprisingly the *Guidelines* do not refer to the judgment of the Court of Justice on joint purchasing organisations in *Gøttrup-Klim Grovvareforeninger v Dansk Landbrugs Grovvareselskab*[130]. The Court of Justice held that a provision in the statute of a cooperative purchasing association, forbidding its members from participating in other forms of cooperation that were in direct competition with it, did not necessarily restrict competition and may even have beneficial effects on competition[131]. The *Guidelines* point out that joint purchasing usually aims at the creation of buyer power: for example an alliance of retailers who group together to negotiate lower prices with their suppliers; it may be that this enables them in turn to offer lower prices to consumers[132]. The

[126] *Guidelines*, para 37. [127] See the previous section.

[128] See ch 4, 'The format of block exemptions', pp 178–179.

[129] See further *Faull and Nikpay*, paras 7.362–7.406; see also *The competitive effect of buyer groups* (OFT 863, January 2007), available at www.nationalarchives.gov.uk.

[130] Case C-250/92 EU:C:1994:413; see also Case 61/80 *Cooperatieve Stremsel- en Kleurselfabriek v Commission* EU:C:1981:75 and Cases C-399/93 etc *HG Oude Luttikhuis v Coberco* EU:C:1995:434; on the position in the US see eg *US v Topco Associates Inc* 405 US 596 (1972) and the *Antitrust Guidelines for Collaborations Among Competitors*, April 2000, available at www.ftc.gov.

[131] Case C-250/92 EU:C:1994:413, para 34.

[132] *Guidelines on Horizontal Cooperation Agreements*, paras 194 and 196.

Guidelines consider the horizontal relationship between the members of the group purchasing organisation; the vertical relationships, between it and its suppliers and between it and its members, fall to be considered under the rules on vertical agreements[133].

Joint purchasing must be considered in the context of the relevant procurement market[134]; in some cases it may also be necessary to look at the selling market, if the parties to the joint purchasing agreement also actively compete in that market[135].

(A) Application of Article 101(1) to joint purchasing agreements

(i) Main competition concerns

The *Guidelines* set out three possible concerns raised by joint purchasing agreements. The first arises in the purchasers' *selling* market: if they have a significant degree of market power (not necessarily amounting to dominance) in that market, it may be that they will have no incentive to pass on to consumers any lower prices that they extract from their suppliers[136]; the possibility of a collusive outcome in the selling market is discussed further in paragraphs 213 to 216 of the *Guidelines*. The second concern is that, if the parties have significant market power in their *purchasing* market, they may force their suppliers to reduce the range or quality of the products they produce[137]. The third concern is that purchasers with buyer power may be able to foreclose competing purchasers by limiting their access to efficient suppliers[138].

(ii) Restrictions by object

Joint purchasing agreements restrict competition by object if they serve as a disguised cartel[139]; however where the parties agree the price to be paid for the products that are the subject of the joint purchasing agreement, this would not amount to a restriction by object: rather an effects analysis would have to be conducted to determine whether any of the concerns expressed above might arise[140].

(iii) Restrictions by effect

In determining whether joint purchasing could have the effect of restricting competition it is necessary to look both at the purchasing and the selling markets[141]. The extent of the parties' market power is obviously relevant to any assessment of possible restrictive effects. There is no threshold *above* which such effects can be presumed; however 'in most cases it is unlikely' that Article 101(1) would be infringed where the market shares in both the purchasing and selling markets are below 15%, and anyway the conditions of Article 101(3) would be likely to be fulfilled[142]. Where these market share thresholds are exceeded a detailed assessment of the effects of an agreement would be required involving, but not limited to, factors such as market concentration and any possible countervailing power of strong suppliers[143].

The application of Article 101 to 'B2B' joint purchasing, that is to say joint procurement through an electronic marketplace, was considered by the Commission in *Covisint*, leading to the closure of the file[144].

[133] Ibid, para 194; see ch 16, 'Article 2(2): associations of retailers', p 670, on the application of Article 2(2) of Regulation 330/2010, the block exemption for vertical agreements, to agreements between associations of retailers and their suppliers and their members.

[134] *Guidelines on Horizontal Cooperation Agreements*, para 198; see also ch 1, 'Procurement markets', p 37.

[135] *Guidelines*, para 199. [136] Ibid, para 201. [137] Ibid, para 202. [138] Ibid, para 203.

[139] Ibid, para 205. [140] Ibid, para 206. [141] Ibid, para 207. [142] Ibid, para 208.

[143] Ibid, para 209.

[144] Commission Press Release IP/01/1155, 31 July 2001; see further Vollebregt 'E-Hubs, Syndication and Competition Concerns' (2000) 10 ECLR 437; Commission's XXXIst *Report on Competition Policy* (2001), pp 58–60.

(B) Application of Article 101(3) to joint purchasing agreements

Paragraphs 217 to 220 of the *Guidelines* discuss Article 101(3) and joint purchasing agreements[145]. Paragraph 217 notes that joint purchasing can give rise to significant efficiency gains, leading to lower prices, reduced transaction, transportation and storage costs, and innovation on the part of suppliers. Paragraph 218 notes that an obligation to purchase exclusively through the joint purchasing organisation may be regarded as indispensable to achieve the necessary volume for the realisation of economies of scale, but says that this must be assessed in the context of each case. In *Rennet*[146] the Commission considered that an exclusive purchasing requirement that members of a cooperative should purchase all their rennet from the cooperative was a restriction of competition and that it did not satisfy the criteria of Article 101(3).

Paragraph 219 stresses that, for Article 101(3) to apply to a joint purchasing agreement, a fair share of the benefit must be passed on to consumers: efficiencies that benefit only the parties to the agreement are not relevant; a critical issue is whether the parties to the joint purchasing agreement have market power in their selling market(s).

8. Commercialisation Agreements

Chapter 6 of the *Guidelines on Horizontal Cooperation Agreements* deals with commercialisation agreements, that is to say cooperation between competitors in the selling, distribution or promotion of their products[147]. Distribution agreements generally are covered by the regime for vertical agreements, including some non-reciprocal agreements entered into between competitors[148]. Where competitors agree on a reciprocal basis to distribute one another's products, horizontal issues arise as well, and they should be analysed in accordance with the *Guidelines*; the same may be true of non-reciprocal agreements[149]. Where joint commercialisation is agreed upon pursuant to some other cooperation, for example on R&D or joint production, the agreement should be analysed under the corresponding chapter of the *Guidelines*[150].

(A) The application of Article 101(1) to commercialisation agreements

(i) Main competition concerns

The main competition concern about commercialisation agreements is that they may lead to cartel behaviour: price fixing[151], output limitation[152], market division[153] and/or parallel behaviour through the exchange of strategic information[154]. Further concerns about collusive outcomes are expressed in paragraphs 242 to 245 of the *Guidelines*.

[145] For examples of joint purchasing agreements that the Commission authorised under Article 101(3) see *National Sulphuric Acid Association* OJ [1980] L 260/24; *National Sulphuric Acid Association (No 2)* OJ [1989] L 190/22; *ARD/MGM* OJ [1989] L 284/36; *European Broadcasting Union* OJ [1993] L 179/23, annulled on appeal Cases T-528/93 etc *Métropole télévision SA v Commission* EU:T:1996:99 and readopted as *Eurovision* OJ [2000] L 151/18, annulled on appeal Cases T-185/00 etc *Métropole télévision SA v Commission* EU:T:2002:242; the Commission decided that Article 101(3) did not apply in the case of *Rennet* OJ [1980] L 51/19, upheld on appeal Case 61/80 *Coöperatieve Stremsel- en Kleurselfabriek v Commission* EU:C:1981:75, and *Screensport/EBU Members* OJ [1991] L 63/32.

[146] See ch 15 n 145 earlier. [147] *Guidelines on Horizontal Cooperation Agreements*, para 225.

[148] Ibid, para 226; see ch 16, 'Article 2(4): agreements between competing undertakings', pp 673–674 on Article 2(4) of Regulation 330/2010.

[149] *Guidelines*, para 227. [150] Ibid, para 228. [151] Ibid, para 230.

[152] Ibid, para 231. [153] Ibid, para 232. [154] Ibid, para 233.

(ii) Restrictions by object

The commercialisation agreements most likely to give rise to concern under Article 101(1) are those that give rise to horizontal price fixing. The *Guidelines* say that joint selling is likely to have as its object the restriction of competition, since it eliminates price competition between the parties on substitute products and may also restrict the total volume of products to be delivered by the parties within the framework of a system for allocating orders[155]. There have been several examples of the Commission finding that joint sales agencies infringed Article 101(1)[156]; in some of these cases the Commission found the conditions of Article 101(3) were fulfilled[157].

The *Guidelines* also express the concern that reciprocal distribution agreements between undertakings that are active in different geographical markets may be an instrument for market partitioning if they do so in order to eliminate competition between them: such agreements restrict competition by object; while it would be necessary to consider whether a non-reciprocal agreement constitutes the basis for a mutual understanding to avoid entering each other's territory[158].

(iii) Restrictions by effect

Paragraph 237 of the *Guidelines* says that a commercialisation agreement would not normally restrict competition if it is objectively necessary to allow one party to enter a market it could not have entered individually; it gives an example of consortia projects in which a number of parties participate, where no one firm could compete for the project individually[159]. Paragraph 240 provides a safe harbour for commercialisation agreements where the parties' market share is below 15%; above that figure an individual assessment would be required.

(B) The application of Article 101(3) to commercialisation agreements

Paragraphs 246 to 251 discuss Article 101(3). Paragraph 246 says that commercialisation agreements can give rise to significant efficiencies; however price fixing can generally not be justified 'unless it is indispensable for the integration of other marketing functions, and this integration will generate substantial efficiencies'. Any efficiencies must result from the integration of economic activities[160], and must be clearly demonstrated[161]. Paragraph 250 stresses the need to show that any efficiencies will be passed on to consumers, and says that the greater the parties' market power, the less likely this is to be the case; the paragraph suggests that a pass-on is likely where the parties' market share is less than 15% (although it is questionable in that case whether the agreement would infringe Article 101(1) in the first place).

The Commission has, on a few occasions, concluded that joint selling arrangements satisfied the criteria of Article 101(3). In *Cekanan*[162] the Commission authorised a joint venture that would enable the parties, based in Sweden and Germany, to enter new markets in the EU with new types of packaging. In the case of *UIP*[163] the Commission

155 Ibid, paras 234–235; on joint selling see *Faull and Nikpay*, paras 7.323–7.361.

156 See eg *Floral* OJ [1980] L 39/51; *UIP* OJ [1989] L 226/25; *Cekanan* OJ [1990] L 299/64; *Ansac* OJ [1991] L 152/54.

157 See 'The application of Article 101(3) to commercialisation agreements', pp 618–619.

158 *Guidelines on Horizontal Cooperation Agreements*, para 236.

159 See similarly ibid, para 30.

160 Ibid, para 247.

161 Ibid, para 248.

162 OJ [1990] L 299/64.

163 OJ [1989] L 226/25, renewed by comfort letter OJ [1999] C 205/6; see the Commission's XXIXth *Report on Competition Policy* (1999), pp 148–149.

decided that a joint venture for the distribution and licensing of the films of Paramount, Universal Studios and MGM satisfied Article 101(3). An issue of particular interest in recent years has been the collective selling of broadcasting rights to sporting events[164]. The Commission authorised the rules of UEFA for selling such rights[165]; and it accepted commitments under Article 9 of Regulation 1/2003 in relation to joint selling by the German Bundesliga and the English Premier League[166].

The Commission has published Guidelines on joint selling of olive oil, beef and veal, and arable crops, which describe the derogations from the competition rules that allow producers of those products to sell jointly through producer organisations[167].

9. Standardisation Agreements

Chapter 7 of the *Guidelines on Horizontal Cooperation Agreements* deals with standardisation agreements and standard terms. Standardisation agreements have as their primary objective the definition of technical or quality requirements with which current or future products, production processes or methods may comply[168], including agreements setting out standards on environmental performance[169]. Standard terms are covered by the *Guidelines* to the extent that they establish standard conditions of sale or purchase between competitors and consumers for competing products[170]. The *Guidelines* do not apply to standards set as part of the exercise of public powers[171]; nor to professional rules[172]. The *Guidelines* take into account the Commission's practice and case law since the earlier guidelines of 2001[173], in particular as regards the use of intellectual property rights in standardisation[174]. They also incorporate insights from

[164] See eg Brinckman and Vollebregt 'The Marketing of Sport and its Relation to EC Competition Law' (1998) 19 ECLR 281; Fleming 'Exclusive Rights to Broadcast Sporting Events in Europe' (1999) 20 ECLR 143; Bishop and Oldale 'Sports Rights: The UK Premier League Football Case' (2000) 21 ECLR 185; Nitsche 'Collective Marketing of Broadcasting by Sports Associations in Europe' (2000) 21 ECLR 208; Commission's XXXIst *Report on Competition Policy* (2001), point 166.

[165] OJ [2003] L 291/25.

[166] See ch 7, 'Article 9: commitments', pp 264–269 discussing the Article 9 commitments procedure and providing details of these two cases; for NCA decisions on joint selling see ECN Brief 02/2012 and ECN Brief 02/2014.

[167] OJ [2015] C 431/1.

[168] *Guidelines on Horizontal Cooperation Agreements*, para 257.

[169] For discussion of agreements specifically concerned with environmental matters see the Commission's XXVIIIth *Report on Competition Policy* (1998), points 129–134 and pp 150–153 on *EUCAR, ACEA, EACEM and Valpak*; XXIXth *Report on Competition Policy* (1999), p 160 on *JAMA; CECED* OJ [2000] L 187/47; *CEMEP*, Commission Press Release IP/00/58, 23 May 2000; *Dishwashers and Water Heaters*, Commission Press Release IP/01/1659, 26 November 2001; *DSD* OJ [2001] L 319/1, upheld on appeal by the General Court in Case T-289/01 *Duales System Deutschland v Commission* EU:T:2007:155; *Eco-Emballages* OJ [2001] L 233/37; *ARA, ARGEV, ARO* OJ [2004] L 75/59, upheld on appeal Case T-419/03 *Altstoff Recycling Austria v Commission* EU:T:2011:102.

[170] Note that the sector-specific block exemption for cooperation on standards terms in the insurance sector has expired; the *Guidelines* provide guidance on standard terms in all industries.

[171] *Guidelines on Horizontal Cooperation Agreements*, para 258; on this subject see Case C-113/07 P *SELEX Sistemi Integrati v Commission* EU:C:2009:191, para 92.

[172] *Guidelines on Horizontal Cooperation Agreements*, para 258; on this subject see *Belgian Architects Association* OJ [2005] L 4/10, paras 39–44.

[173] See eg *Ship Classification*, Commission commitment decision of 14 October 2009; Case T-432/05 *EMC Development v Commission* EU:T:2010:189, upheld on appeal Case C-367/10 P EU:C:2011:203.

[174] See eg *Rambus*, Commission commitment decision of 9 December 2009; *Qualcomm*, Commission MEMO/09/516, 24 November 2009; *Standards for future mobile phone services*, Commission Press Release IP/13/208, 7 March 2013.

the best practice of standard-setting organisations and the body of literature that has developed[175]. This section will consider the application of Articles 101(1) and 101(3) to standardisation agreements; it will then briefly discuss the position in relation to standard terms.

(A) The application of Article 101(1) to standardisation agreements

(i) Main competition concerns

Standardisation agreements may have effects in four markets:

- in the market for the product itself
- in the technology market where the standard involves the selection of technology
- in the service market for the setting of standards
- in the market for testing and certification[176].

Paragraph 263 of the *Guidelines* acknowledges that standardisation agreements 'usually produce significant positive economic effects'[177], in particular by promoting innovation and ensuring interoperability[178]. However paragraph 264 notes that standard-setting may harm competition in three ways: a reduction in price competition following anti-competitive discussions; foreclosure of innovative technologies; and the prevention of effective access to the standard. Standards that involve intellectual property rights may in particular lead to foreclosure effects[179]. Each of these negative effects is discussed in the subsequent paragraphs of the *Guidelines*[180].

(ii) Restrictions by object

Agreements that use a standard as part of a broader restrictive agreement aimed at excluding actual or potential competitors restrict competition by object[181]. The Commission gives as an example of this its decision in *Pre-insulated pipe cartel*[182], where part of the infringement of Article 101(1) was the use of norms and standards to prevent or delay the introduction of new technology to the market that would have led to price reductions. Agreements to reduce competition by using the disclosure of most restrictive licensing terms prior to the adoption of a standard as a cover for jointly fixing prices are also treated

[175] See eg Shapiro 'Setting Compatibility Standards: Cooperation or Collusion?' in Dreyfuss, Zimmerman and First (eds) *Expanding the Boundaries of Intellectual Property* (Oxford University Press, 2001); Farrell, Hayes, Shapiro and Sullivan 'Standard Setting, Patents, and Hold-Up' (2007) 74 Antitrust LJ 603; Madero and Banasevic 'Standards and Market Power' [2008] CPI Antitrust Chronicle, May 12 (1) available at www.competitionpolicyinternational.com; OECD *Standard Setting* (2010), available at www.oecd.org/competition; Mariniello 'Fair, Reasonable and Non-Discriminatory (FRAND) Terms: A Challenge for Competition Authorities' (2011) 7 Journal of Competition Law and Economics 523; DG ENTR *Patents and Standards* (2014), available at www.ec.europa.eu; Layne-Farrr 'The Economics of FRAND' in Blair and Sokol (eds) *Antitrust Intellectual Property and High Tech Handbook* (Cambridge University Press, 2017); Nazzini 'Level Discrimination and FRAND Commitments Under EU Competition Law' (2017) 40 World Competition 213.

[176] *Guidelines on Horizontal Cooperation Agreements*, para 261.

[177] Ibid, paras 263 and 308.

[178] See ibid, paras 325–332 for examples of the Commission's approach to the application of Article 101 to standardisation agreements; see further *Faull and Nikpay*, paras 7.498–7.537.

[179] *Guidelines*, paras 267–269; see also *European Telecommunications Standards Institute* OJ [1995] C 76/6; Commission's XXVth *Report on Competition Policy* (1995), pp 131–132 and the cases cited in ch 15 n 174 earlier.

[180] *Guidelines on Horizontal Cooperation Agreements*, paras 265–268.

[181] Ibid, para 273.

[182] OJ [1999] L 24/1, para 147.

as restrictions by object[183]. Agreements requiring members of a standard-setting organisation to sell products only that comply with a standard may, in certain circumstances, restrict competition by object[184]: this is consistent with the Commission's past practice[185].

(iii) **A (fairly) safe harbour**

Paragraphs 277 to 291 of the *Guidelines* are headed 'Agreements normally not restrictive of competition': in other words they produce a safe harbour, although the use of the word 'normally' means that this harbour is fairly safe rather than entirely so. To begin with the *Guidelines* say that standardisation agreements may have the effect of restricting competition only where the parties have market power[186]: however they do not provide a market share threshold for this purpose. The *Guidelines* say that there is no presumption that an undertaking holding or exercising intellectual property rights essential to a standard has market power[187]. Where there is effective competition between several voluntary standards, standardisation agreements do not restrict competition[188].

Paragraphs 280 to 286 of the *Guidelines* set out four principles, and state that standard-setting agreements that comply with them normally fall outside Article 101(1). The principles are that[189]:

- participation in the standard-setting is unrestricted
- the procedure for adopting the standard is transparent
- there is no obligation to comply with the standard
- there is effective access to the standard on fair, reasonable and non-discriminatory ('FRAND') terms.

These four principles are consistent with the General Court's judgment in *EMC v Commission*[190] where it held that the adoption of a non-binding standard following an open, non-discriminatory and transparent procedure does not restrict competition[191]. In cases involving intellectual property rights, effective access to the standard involves good faith disclosure of rights that might be essential for its implementation and a commitment to license on FRAND terms[192].

The *Guidelines* provide guidance on methods to assess the level of FRAND in the event of a dispute[193]. In a case involving patents that had been held to be valid, essential and to have been infringed by an 'implementer' of telecommunications standards used by mobile phones, the English High Court held that there is only one set of FRAND terms for a given set of circumstances[194]; what is FRAND can be determined by considering what

[183] *Guidelines on Horizontal Cooperation Agreements*, para 274; note that this does not prevent *ex ante* unilateral disclosure of most restrictive licensing terms, as described in para 299 of the *Guidelines*; nor does it prevent the creation of patent pools that comply with the principles in the Commission's *Technology Transfer Guidelines* OJ [2014] C 89/3; for discussion of patent pools see ch 19, 'Technology pools', pp 808–811.

[184] *Guidelines on Horizontal Cooperation Agreements*, para 293.

[185] See eg *Video Cassette Recorders* OJ [1977] L 47/42, para 23.

[186] *Guidelines on Horizontal Cooperation Agreements*, para 277.

[187] Ibid, para 277. [188] Ibid, para 277. [189] Ibid, paras 280–283.

[190] Case T-432/05 *EMC Development v Commission* EU:T:2010:189, upheld on appeal to the Court of Justice Case C-367/10 P EU:C:2011:203.

[191] Ibid, paras 79–104 and 113–130.

[192] *Guidelines on Horizontal Cooperation Agreements*, paras 284–286; see also Commission MEMO/09/549, 10 December 2009 on IPCom agreeing to take over Robert Bosch GmbH's commitment to grant irrevocable patent licences on FRAND terms following its acquisition of Bosch's mobile telephony patent portfolio.

[193] *Guidelines on Horizontal Cooperation Agreements*, para 299.

[194] *Unwired Planet v Huawei* [2017] EWHC 711 (Pat), para 164, on appeal to the Court of Appeal, not yet decided.

a willing licensor and a willing licensee acting without holding out or holding up would agree upon[195].

(iv) Restrictions by effect

Paragraph 279 of the *Guidelines* says that there is no presumption that, where the four principles are not satisfied, an agreement infringes Article 101(1) or that it will fail to satisfy Article 101(3). Rather an effects-based assessment will be required, as set out in paragraphs 292 to 299. A standardisation agreement that departs from the principles may be caught by Article 101(1) where the members of a standard-setting organisation are not free to develop alternative standards or products[196], or where access to a standard or to the standard-setting process is limited[197]. In *Ship Classification*[198] the Commission was concerned that the rules of the International Association of Classification Societies foreclosed third parties; the case was closed on the parties giving commitments under Article 9 of Regulation 1/2003[199] that ensured access to a standard-setting body and its information.

The market shares of the goods or services based on the standard are also relevant to the application of Article 101(1), although the *Guidelines* acknowledge that a high market share will not necessarily signify a competition problem[200]. A standard-setting agreement that clearly discriminates against any of the participating or potential members could lead to a restriction of competition[201].

(B) The application of Article 101(3) to standardisation agreements

The *Guidelines* state that standardisation agreements frequently give rise to significant efficiency gains[202]. Different standards have different beneficial effects: EU-wide standards facilitate market integration; compatibility standards promote technical interoperability between complementary products; while standards on quality, safety and environmental aspects of a product facilitate customer choice. Standards may also reduce transaction costs and promote innovation. For the benefits of standardisation agreements to be realised, the necessary information to apply the standard must be available to those wishing to enter the market[203]. All competitors in the markets affected should have the possibility of being involved in discussions on the standards, unless it can be shown that this would give rise to significant inefficiencies or unless there are recognised procedures for the collective representation of interests, as happens in the case of standards bodies[204]. Standards that are binding on an industry are in principle not indispensable[205]. Standards that facilitate interoperability or encourage competition between new and existing products are presumed to benefit consumers[206]. Where the result of a standardisation agreement is the establishment of a *de facto* industry standard, anti-competitive foreclosure must be avoided[207].

195 Ibid, para 170; the court also had regard to the terms of comparable licences: ibid, para 171.

196 Ibid, para 293.

197 Ibid, paras 294 and 295; see also Commission MEMO/13/553, 13 June 2013 on the European Payments Council ceasing to develop standards for e-payments that could exclude new entrants.

198 Commission decision of 14 October 2009; see Dohms and Rieder 'Commitment Decision in the *Ship Classification* Case: Paving the way for more competition' (2010) 1 Competition Policy Newsletter 41.

199 On commitment decisions under Article 9 see ch 7, 'Article 9: commitments', pp 264–269.

200 *Guidelines on Horizontal Cooperation Agreements*, para 296.

201 Ibid, para 297.

202 Ibid, para 308.

203 Ibid, para 309.

204 Ibid, para 316.

205 Ibid, para 318.

206 Ibid, para 321; see eg *X/Open Group* OJ [1987] L 35/36 (establishing industry-wide standards for computer software).

207 Ibid, para 324; see eg *Canon/Kodak*, Commission's XXVIIIth *Report on Competition Policy* (1998), p 147.

(C) The application of Article 101(1) to standard terms

Standard terms may have three negative effects on the downstream market where the undertakings using the terms compete by selling their products to consumers[208]: first, a limitation of choice and innovation in cases where the standard terms define the scope of the product sold; secondly, a distortion in the conditions of sale; and, thirdly, market foreclosure where standard terms become industry practice[209].

(i) Restrictions by object

Standard terms may have the object of restricting competition where they are really a disguised cartel or contain provisions that directly affect price[210].

(ii) Restrictions by effect

Effectively accessible and non-binding standard terms for the sale of consumer goods or services generally do not restrict competition[211]. Paragraphs 303 to 305 of the *Guidelines* describe two situations in which a more detailed assessment of such terms is required. The first is where the widespread use of standard terms that define the scope of the product limits product variety and innovation. The second is where the standard terms are a decisive part of the transaction with the customer. Individual assessment is most likely to be necessary where the standard terms are binding[212]. Paragraphs 333 to 335 of the *Guidelines* provide examples of the Commission's approach to the application of Article 101 to standard terms.

(D) The application of Article 101(3) to standard terms

Possible improvements in efficiency attributable to standard terms are considered at paragraphs 312 to 313: in particular standard terms can facilitate switching by making it easier to compare products. However, the use of binding standard terms is unlikely to be indispensable[213]. Paragraphs 322 to 323 consider the extent to which standard terms yield a fair share of any benefits to consumers.

(E) Article 102 and standards

In two cases—*Motorola Mobility* and *Samsung*—the Commission considered that, where an undertaking commits, during a standard-setting procedure, to license any standard-essential patents on FRAND terms to a licensee wishing to produce products to the standard, it could be an infringement of Article 102 TFEU for the owner of the patent to seek an injunction from a court in the event of a failure by the parties to reach a FRAND agreement. In *Motorola—Enforcement of GPRS standard essential patents*[214] the Commission found that Motorola was guilty of abusing a dominant position because the would-be licensee in that case, Apple, had agreed to submit the FRAND dispute to the binding resolution of a national court. The outcome in *Samsung—Enforcement of UMTS standard essential patents*[215] was different as the Commission accepted legally-binding

[208] *Guidelines*, para 262.

[209] Ibid, paras 270–272; see further *Faull and Nikpay*, paras 7.538–7.551.

[210] *Guidelines*, paras 275–276; for examples of agreements relating to terms and conditions condemned by the European Commission under Article 101(1) see ch 13, 'Agreements Relating to Terms and Conditions', pp 549–551.

[211] *Guidelines on Horizontal Cooperation Agreements*, paras 301–302.

[212] Ibid, para 306.

[213] Ibid, para 320.

[214] Commission infringement decision of 29 April 2014, on which see 'Standard essential patents' (2014) 8 Competition Policy Brief, available at www.ec.europa.eu.

[215] Commission commitment decision of 29 April 2014.

commitments from Samsung under Article 9 of Regulation 1/2003. The commitments provide for a mechanism for resolving FRAND disputes in relation to Samsung's standard-essential patents. There have been several cases in which courts have considered what would constitute a FRAND royalty[216]. The Commission may also proceed under Article 102 where it believes that a dominant firm may be guilty of abusing a standard-setting procedure, for example through 'patent ambushing'[217].

10. **Other Cases of Permissible Horizontal Cooperation**

As the General Court stated in *Matra Hachette v Commission*[218], there is no type of agreement which is incapable of satisfying the criteria of Article 101(3). For example in *REIMS II*[219] the Commission considered that Article 101(3) was applicable to a price-fixing agreement 'with unusual characteristics' in the postal services sector. The fact that a horizontal cooperation agreement does not fit into one of the categories discussed in the *Guidelines* does not mean that it falls within Article 101(1) or cannot satisfy the terms of Article 101(3). In each case, the question is whether the parties can demonstrate either that there is no restriction of competition or that the agreement will bring about efficiencies of the type envisaged in Article 101(3).

(A) **Restructuring agreements**

There may be circumstances in which an industry faces severe problems—perhaps because of recession or because of over-capacity within it—where the competition authorities may be prepared to countenance some degree of cooperation to overcome this. As a general proposition, each undertaking on the market should make its own independent decision as to what and how much to produce. However making rational decisions about how to 'slim down' production in some economic sectors, perhaps where capital investment is high or where there is extensive vertical integration, may be difficult in the absence of an intelligent understanding of what competitors are going to do. There is a danger that each competitor may slim down so much that the market goes from a position of over-capacity to under-capacity; it may be difficult to put the process into reverse. A different consideration is that the restructuring of industry has a social cost involving loss of employment and harm to the fabric of local communities; there is therefore a political component as well as an economic one to this issue[220].

Restructuring agreements, whereby undertakings agree on their respective levels of output, are likely to infringe Article 101(1): output limitation has as its object the restriction of competition[221]. In *Beef Industry Development Society*[222] the Court of Justice had no doubt that an agreement between processors of beef in Ireland to reduce their beef-processing capacity there—those that would remain in the market would pay those that

[216] See eg in the UK *Unwired Planet v Huawei* [2017] EWHC 711 (Pat); in Germany *Saint Lawrence v Vodafone*, judgment of 31 May 2016; in the US *Microsoft v Motorola* 795 F 3d 1024 (9th Cir 2015) (considering what would be a 'RAND' rate).

[217] See ch 19, 'Vexatious behaviour and abuse of process', pp 825–827.

[218] Case T-17/93 EU:T:1994:89, para 85.

[219] OJ [1999] L 275/17; the Commission extended the application of Article 101(3) to this agreement until 2006: OJ [2003] C 94/3.

[220] See ch 4, 'The Article 101(3) Criteria', pp 162–173 for a discussion of the issues which can legitimately be taken into account under Article 101(3).

[221] See ch 3, 'Market sharing, quotas, collective exclusive dealing', p 129.

[222] Case C-209/07 EU:C:2008:643.

would leave the market to do so—had as its object the restriction of competition: any arguments that the agreement would lead to economic efficiencies were required to be raised under Article 101(3)[223]. The matter was referred back to the Irish High Court, but no decision was reached on the application of Article 101(3) as the BIDS withdrew its defence[224]; the Commission wrote an *amicus curiae* brief in this case explaining how Article 101(3) might apply to agreements that seek to remove excess capacity[225].

The fact that an industry faces a crisis does not mean that undertakings can enter into agreements that restrict competition and claim immunity from Article 101(1), although the crisis may help to mitigate the level of a fine[226]. However where a restructuring agreement is entered into pursuant to state aid authorised by the Commission, it may not infringe Article 101(1) where it is so indissolubly linked to the purpose of the aid that it cannot be separately evaluated[227].

In the 1980s the Commission did allow restructuring agreements under Article 101(3) on a few occasions[228] and in *Stichting Baksteen*[229] the Commission allowed plans for restructuring the Dutch brick industry, which involved agreed action to close plants and to cut capacity under Article 101(3).

(B) **Insurance sector**

In the insurance sector the Commission has authorised a number of horizontal cooperation agreements[230], for example in *Nuovo CEGAM*[231], *Concordato Incendio*[232], *Teko*[233], *P&I Clubs*[234], *Assurpool*[235] and again in *P&I Clubs*[236].

Council Regulation 1534/91 authorises the Commission to grant block exemptions in the insurance sector[237]. There are no Commission Regulations granting block exemption under Regulation 1534/91. Following a detailed review of Regulation 267/2010[238], the Commission allowed the block exemption to lapse on 31 March 2017, and decided not to adopt a new one[239]. The Commission concluded that a block exemption is no longer warranted since its *Guidelines on Horizontal Cooperation Agreements*[240] provide guidance on the assessment of joint compilations, tables and studies under Article 101. The principle

[223] Ibid, paras 39–40.
[224] See Press Release by the Irish Competition Authority of 25 January 2011, available at www.ccpc.ie.
[225] The brief is available on DG COMP's website: www.ec.europa.eu.
[226] See eg Case T-145/89 *Baustahlgewebe v Commission* EU:T:1995:66, para 122.
[227] Case T-197/97 *Weyl Beef Products v Commission* EU:T:2001:28, para 83.
[228] See eg the Commission's XIIth *Report on Competition Policy* (1982), points 38–41; XIIIth *Report on Competition Policy* (1983), points 56–61; see also XXIIIrd *Report on Competition Policy* (1993), points 82–89; *Synthetic Fibres* OJ [1984] L 207/17; *BPCL/ICI* OJ [1984] L 212/1; *ENI/Montedison* OJ [1987] L 5/13; *Enichem/ICI* OJ [1988] L 50/18; *Bayer/BP Chemicals* OJ [1988] L 150/35; *Shell/AKZO* Commission's XIVth *Report on Competition Policy* (1984), point 85; *EMC/DSM (LVM)* OJ [1988] C 18/3.
[229] OJ [1994] L 131/15; see XXIVth *Report on Competition Policy* (1994), pp 178–180.
[230] See further Rose and Bailey (eds) *Bellamy and Child: European Union Law of Competition* (Oxford University Press, 7th ed, 2013), paras 12.121–12.134; *Faull and Nikpay*, paras 11.178–11.219.
[231] OJ [1984] L 99/29. [232] OJ [1990] L 15/25. [233] OJ [1990] L 13/34.
[234] OJ [1985] L 376/2. [235] OJ [1992] L 37/16.
[236] OJ [1999] L 125/12; some other cases have been settled informally: see eg Commission's XXVIth *Report on Competition Policy* (1996), pp 131–132; XXVIIIth *Report on Competition Policy* (1998), points 111–115.
[237] OJ [1991] L 143/1.
[238] OJ [2010] L 83/1; see the Commission Report on the functioning of Regulation 267/2010, COM(2016) 153 final, 17 March 2016 and accompanying staff working document; see also two studies on issues relating to the insurance production process, available at 'Financial Services' page of DG COMP's website.
[239] Commission MEX/16/4369, 13 December 2016.
[240] See 'The *Guidelines on Horizontal Cooperation Agreements*', pp 600–604 earlier in chapter.

of 'self-assessment' of agreements under Article 101(1) and (3) now applies in the insurance sector.

(C) **Banking sector**

The Commission has dealt with many horizontal cooperation agreements in the banking sector[241]. Such agreements might be found not to affect trade between Member States, as the Court of Justice concluded in *Bagnasco*[242] and the Commission in *Dutch Banks*[243]. The Commission has published a *Notice on Cross-border Credit Transfers*[244] on the extent to which cooperation between banks is permissible under the competition rules in order to improve cross-border credit transfers. In its decision in *Uniform Eurocheques*[245] the Commission permitted an agreement which fixed standard terms and conditions in relation to the cashing of Eurocheques. The Commission also permitted a second agreement relating to the production and finishing of the actual Eurocheques and cheque cards[246]. A cooperation agreement was authorised for ten years in *Banque Nationale de Paris/Dresdner Bank*[247] between two major banks operating in neighbouring Member States.

In *Cartes Bancaires*[248] the Commission decided that certain fees imposed by the CB system hindered the issuing of cards by new members, and were restrictive of competition by object and effect[249]. The Commission also found that the fees were not justified under Article 101(3) by the need to prevent free-riding in the CB system[250]. On appeal the General Court agreed with the Commission that there was a restriction by object which could not be defended under Article 101(3)[251]. However the Court of Justice reversed the judgment of the General Court: the Court held that the General Court failed to apply the 'essential legal criterion' for identifying restrictions by object—whether an agreement reveals a sufficient degree of harm to competition[252]—and failed to interpret the concept of 'object' restrictively[253]. The matter was referred back to the General Court, which upheld the Commission's alternative finding that there was a restriction by effect and rejected CB's arguments under Article 101(3)[254].

The Commission decided in *Visa International—Multilateral Interchange Fee* that Visa International's 'multilateral interchange fee' ('MIF') agreed upon between banks participating within the Visa system satisfied the criteria of Article 101(3)[255]; subsequently the Commission accepted commitments from Visa under Article 9(1) of Regulation 1/2003 as to the future level of the MIF for its debit cards[256] and for its credit cards[257]. In *MasterCard*[258] the Commission concluded that the MasterCard's intra-EEA MIF had

[241] Commission Press Release IP/08/596, 17 April 2008; see *Faull and Nikpay*, paras 11.16–11.102.

[242] Cases C-215/96 etc EU:C:1999:12.

[243] OJ [1999] L 271/28.

[244] OJ [1995] C 251/3; see Commission's XXVth *Report on Competition Policy* (1995), points 45–48; XXVIth *Report on Competition Policy* (1996), point 109 and pp 128–130.

[245] OJ [1985] L 35/43.

[246] OJ [1989] L 36/16; most of this agreement was cleared under Article 101(1) rather than exempted under Article 101(3); for other exemptions on banking see *Belgian Banks* OJ [1986] L 7/27; *Associazione Bancaria Italiana* OJ [1986] L 43/51.

[247] OJ [1996] L 188/37; Commission's XXVIth *Report on Competition Policy* (1996), point 108.

[248] Commission decision of 17 October 2007.

[249] Ibid, paras 193–251 (object) and 252–370 (effect).

[250] Ibid, paras 375–503.

[251] Case T-491/07 EU:T:2012:633.

[252] Case C-67/13 P EU:C:2014:2204, para 57.

[253] Ibid, para 58.

[254] Case T-491/07 RENV EU:T:2016:379, paras 65–360 (effect) and 361–465 (Article 101(3)).

[255] OJ [2002] L 318/17.

[256] Commission decision of 8 December 2010; on commitments decisions under Article 9 see ch 7, 'Article 9: Commitments', pp 264–269.

[257] Commission decision of 26 February 2014.

[258] Commission decision of 19 December 2007.

the effect of appreciably restricting competition, contrary to Article 101(1), and did not satisfy Article 101(3): that decision was upheld on appeal to the General Court[259] and to the Court of Justice[260]. The Commission has sent statements of objections to MasterCard and to Visa in respect of their inter-regional interchange fees[261]. In December 2015 the Regulation on interchange fees for card-based payment transactions capped MIFs for payments made with debit and credit cards[262].

The banking and payments subgroup of the European Competition Network ('the ECN') has published an information paper on competition enforcement in the payments sector[263].

(D) Transport

Several horizontal cooperation agreements have been allowed in the transport sector. The Commission has closed a few investigations into airline alliances by accepting commitments given by the parties under Article 9(1) of Regulation 1/2003[264].

11. The Application of the Chapter I Prohibition in the UK Competition Act 1998 to Horizontal Cooperation Agreements

(A) Introduction

The general principles involved in the application of the Chapter I prohibition in the Competition Act 1998 have been described in chapter 9[265]; the procedural aspects of Chapter I were dealt with in chapter 10[266]. Agreements that benefit from block exemption under EU law, or that would do so if they were to affect trade between Member States, enjoy parallel exemption under UK law; it follows, for example, that research and development agreements, horizontal technology transfer agreements, and specialisation agreements might benefit from this facility[267]. In April 2018 the CMA published a short guide, 'Joint ventures and competition law: dos and don'ts', which provides a checklist of issues to bear in mind when creating and managing joint ventures.

(B) Decisions and judgments under the Competition Act

The domestic competition authorities have examined—and in some cases permitted—horizontal cooperation agreements in a few cases[268], such as *LINK Interchange Network*[269], *Memorandum of Understanding on the Supply of Oil Fuels in an Emergency*[270] and *Pool Reinsurance Company*[271]. They have already been discussed in chapter 9[272]. The Office of Fair Trading ('the OFT') issued a 'Short-form Opinion' in *Makro-Self Service/Palmer & Harvey* on a joint purchasing agreement indicating that, following some modifications

[259] Case T-111/08 *MasterCard Inc v Commission* EU:T:2012:260.

[260] Case C-382/12 P *MasterCard Inc v Commission* EU:C:2014:2201.

[261] *MasterCard II* Commission Press Release IP/15/5323, 9 July 2015 and *Visa* Commission Daily News MEX/17/2341, 3 August 2017.

[262] OJ [2015] L 123/1; see 'The Interchange Fees Regulation' (2015) 3 Competition Policy Brief.

[263] Available at www.ec.europa.eu.

[264] See ch 23, 'Transport', pp 999–1008; see ch 7, 'Article 9: commitments', pp 264–269 on the Article 9 procedure.

[265] See ch 9, 'The Chapter I Prohibition', pp 347–376.

[266] See ch 10 generally.

[267] Competition Act 1998, s 10; on parallel exemptions see ch 9, 'Parallel exemptions', pp 375–376.

[268] See also OFT Press Release 130/11, 6 December 2011 (accepting voluntary assurances from five Public Sector Buying Organisations), available at www.nationalarchives.gov.uk.

[269] Decision of 16 October 2001.

[270] Decision of 25 October 2001.

[271] Decision of 15 April 2004.

[272] See ch 9, 'Exemption criteria', pp 372–375.

to prevent inappropriate exchanges of information, the agreement would be unlikely to raise competition concerns[273]. The OFT also issued a favourable 'Short-form Opinion' in relation to collaboration between competing landowners that was designed to facilitate the roll-out of broadband in rural areas[274].

In *Sainsbury's Supermarkets v MasterCard*[275] the Competition Appeal Tribunal ('the CAT') concluded that the effect of the MasterCard UK MIF was to restrict competition that would otherwise have existed through bilateral interchange fees in the acquiring market[276] and did not satisfy Article 101(3). The CAT awarded Sainsbury's damages of £69.3 million in respect of the overcharge in relation to debit and credit cards, plus interest. However the High Court reached a different conclusion in *Asda Stores v MasterCard*[277]: Popplewell J held that the MIFs were objectively necessary and not restrictive of competition as the MasterCard scheme would not have survived in their absence[278]. Further, and in any event, the MIFs set by MasterCard were below the lawful 'exemptible' level under Article 101(3)[279]. The different outcomes appear to be the result of the CAT and the High Court disagreeing as to the appropriate counterfactual, that is to say, what would have happened in the absence of the MIFs. In *Sainsbury's Supermarkets v Visa Europe Services*[280] the High Court held that Visa's MIFs did not restrict competition in the acquiring market because they did not result in less competition that would be obtrained in the absence of the MIFs[281].

In *Agents' Mutual v Gascoigne Halman*[282] the CAT held that a rule of a mutual association of estate agents, forbidding agents from listing properties on more than one other online property portal, did not have the object[283] or effect[284] of restricting competition, and was likely to be pro-competitive since it was an essential part of the association's strategy to enter the online property portal market.[285] The CAT's judgment in this case is a most interesting one, in which it takes a realistic approach to the question of whether competition was restricted on the facts of the case. In the absence of the 'one other portal rule', the CAT considered there would have been no entry and no competition to be restricted[286]. Further, the CAT held that the apparently restrictive one other portal rule was objectively necessary for the pro-competitive launch of a new property portal.[287]

(C) **Block exemption for ticketing agreements**

The Secretary of State has adopted a block exemption for public transport ticketing schemes: it is discussed in chapter 9[288].

[273] Opinion of 27 April 2010, available at www.nationalarchives.gov.uk.
[274] Opinion of 23 August 2012, available at www.nationalarchives.gov.uk.
[275] Case 1241/5/7/15 (T) [2016] CAT 11, on appeal to the Court of Appeal, not yet decided.
[276] Ibid, paras 266–267.
[277] [2017] EWHC 93 (Comm), on appeal to the Court of Appeal, not yet decided.
[278] Ibid, para 253. [279] Ibid, para 255. [280] Ibid.
[281] [2017] EWHC 3047 (Comm), paras 88–173, on appeal to the Court of Appeal, not yet decided.
[282] [2017] CAT 15. [283] Ibid, paras 178–195, and in particular para 184.
[284] Ibid, paras 196–239, and in particular para 196.
[285] Ibid, paras 161–175, 184(5), 197, 238, 240 and 242.
[286] Ibid, para 233. [287] Ibid, paras 241–248.
[288] See ch 9, 'Block exemptions', p 375.

16

Vertical agreements

1. Introduction

The previous three chapters have been concerned with horizontal relationships between undertakings. This chapter deals with the application of Article 101 TFEU and the Chapter I prohibition in the UK Competition Act 1998 to vertical agreements, and assumes a knowledge of the contents of chapters 3, 4 and 9[1]. The chapter begins with a brief description of the distribution chain, and then contains sections on how the law applies to vertical integration and to agency agreements. Section 5 discusses the competition policy considerations raised by vertical agreements, including the challenges presented by the emergence of online commerce. Section 6 explains the application of Article 101 to various vertical agreements in the light of the case law of the EU Courts and the position of the Commission in its *Guidelines on Vertical Restraints*[2] ('the *Vertical guidelines*' or 'the *Guidelines*'). This will be followed by a section on the provisions of Regulation 330/2010, the block exemption for vertical agreements. Section 8 deals with the application of Article 101(3) to vertical agreements. The chapter then contains sections on Regulation 461/2010 on motor vehicle distribution and on sub-contracting agreements. Section 11 will look at the position in UK law. To the extent that vertical agreements might result in the abuse of a dominant position, contrary to Article 102 TFEU and the Chapter II prohibition in the Competition Act 1998, they are dealt with in chapters 17 and 18.

[1] For further reading on Article 101 and vertical agreements see Goyder *EU Distribution Law* (Hart, 5th ed, 2011); Rose and Bailey (eds) *Bellamy and Child: European Union Law of Competition* (Oxford University Press, 7th ed, 2013), ch 6; Faull and Nikpay (eds) *The EU Law of Competition* (Oxford University Press, 3rd ed, 2014), ch 9; Wijckmans and Tuytschaever *Vertical Agreements in EU Competition Law* (Oxford University Press, 3rd ed, 2018).

[2] OJ [2010] C 130/1, replacing earlier guidelines of 2000, OJ [2000] C 291/1; the *Guidelines* are without prejudice to the case law of the EU Courts: ibid, para 4.

2. **The Distribution Chain**

A producer of goods or a supplier of services will either require them for its own consumption or will want to supply them to the market. A firm wishing to sell its products must decide how to do so. There are various possibilities: it may carry out both the production and the sales and distribution functions itself: this is often referred to as vertical integration; it may use the services of a commercial agent to find customers; or it may supply its products to an independent distributor whose function is to resell them to other persons, who may or may not be the final consumer.

For many products it is possible to depict a fairly simple distribution chain: for example a producer may sell goods to a retailer, who deals with the final consumer (see Figure 16.1):

Fig. 16.1

In other markets a wholesaler may carry out an important intermediate function, standing between the producer and the retailer (see Figure 16.2):

Fig. 16.2

A vertically-integrated producer might deal directly with the consumer, for example by mail order, by establishing its own retail outlets or by selling through the internet. An example of vertical integration is Apple supplying music from its 'iTunes' music website direct to the consumer[3] (see Figure 16.3):

[3] See 'Vertical Integration', pp 632–633 later in chapter.

Fig. 16.3

There can, of course, be many other configurations, in which quite different relationships are involved in the delivery of goods or services to their final consumer. For example a brand owner in the food industry might sub-contract manufacture to a sub-contractor; the brand owner may then negotiate sales directly with supermarkets, and engage a transport company to arrange for the physical distribution of the products from the sub-contractor to the supermarket, in which case the diagram would look quite different (see Figure 16.4):

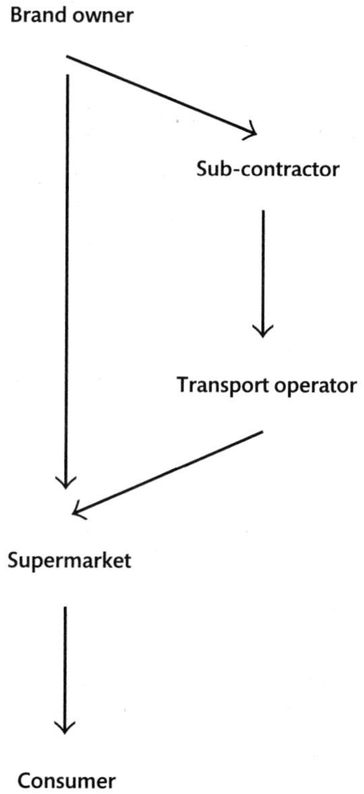

Fig. 16.4

The advent of e-commerce increases the range of distribution possibilities, because the internet enables us to search for the goods and services that we want online. For example a manufacturer might:

- sell its products direct to consumers through its own website
- sell to retailers, who sell from both brick and mortar stores and through their own websites

- sell to retailers who also sell through third party platforms
- allow their products to be shown on price comparison websites.

From the consumer's point of view the product in question is visible in many different ways (see Figure 16.5):

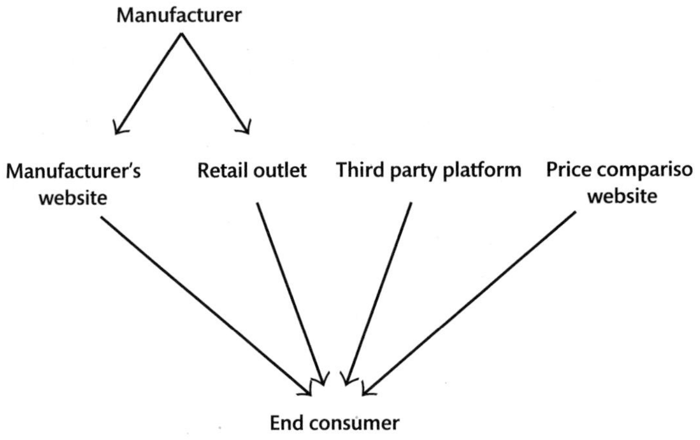

Fig. 16.5

The text that follows will use the term 'wholesaler' to mean a firm whose business is to resell goods, but not to the final consumer; the term 'retailer' will be used to describe firms whose function is to sell goods to consumers; and the term 'buyer' will be used to refer to both wholesalers and retailers. This chapter will provide some guidance on how competition law impacts upon vertical relationships.

3. Vertical Integration

One option available for firms is vertical integration. This can be achieved internally by setting up retail outlets or by establishing subsidiary companies to which the task of distribution is entrusted. Some firms may be able to sell their products through the internet, thereby eliminating the need to appoint distributors: this process is known as disintermediation. Alternatively vertical integration may be achieved through external growth, by taking over distribution networks downstream in the market.

(A) Arguments for and against vertical integration

Various considerations will influence a producer in its decision whether to integrate vertically[4]. On the one hand it may be costly to set up or take over one's own distribution

[4] See Coase 'The Nature of the Firm' (1937) 4 Economica 386; Williamson 'The Vertical Integration of Production; Market Failure Considerations' (1971) 61 Am Ec Rev 112; Lever and Neubauer 'Vertical Restraints, Their Motivation and Justification' (2000) 21 ECLR 7.

channels; also it may be more efficient to appoint another undertaking with knowledge of and expertise in the distributive trade than to attempt to break into this area oneself. On the other hand vertical integration may mean that a high degree of efficiency and coordination can be achieved in a way that would not occur where products are distributed by third parties.

(B) Non-application of Article 101 to agreements within a single economic entity

Article 101(1) does not apply to agreements between firms that form a single economic entity. The most obvious example of this is an agreement between a parent company and its wholly-owned subsidiary. The Court of Justice considered such an intra-group agreement in *Viho v Commission*[5] and held that Article 101(1) does not apply to provisions forbidding a subsidiary from exporting or selling below a minimum price[6]. Vertical integration which is achieved through internal growth may not be the most efficient use of resources in terms of allocative efficiency and yet it may be the logical defensive response of firms fearful of transgressing Article 101[7].

Agreements entered into between members of the group and third parties are subject to Article 101 in the same way as any other.

(C) Application of Article 102 to firms within a single economic entity

Vertical integration may be relevant when deciding whether an undertaking holds a dominant position within the meaning of Article 102[8], and the group may be guilty of an abuse of a dominant position in the way in which it behaves on the market[9].

(D) Application of the EU Merger Regulation to vertical integration

Vertical mergers are notifiable to the Commission under the EU Merger Regulation where they are a concentration that has an EU dimension[10]. As a general proposition vertical integration is likely to increase economic efficiency, a fact that is explicitly recognised in the Commission's *Guidelines on the assessment of non-horizontal mergers*[11]. However there have been occasions on which the Commission has required modifications to, or even the abandonment of, mergers that are likely to produce harmful vertical effects[12]. An obvious example of this is *Deutsche Börse/London Stock Exchange*[13], which was prohibited by the Commission because the merged firm would have the ability and incentive to foreclose competitors on certain markets for settlement and custody services.

[5] Case C-73/95 P EU:C:1996:405, paras 15–17.

[6] See ch 3, 'The "single economic entity" doctrine', pp 93–99.

[7] AG Warner's Opinion warned of this danger in Case 30/78 *Distillers v Commission* EU:C:1980:74.

[8] See ch 5, 'Economic advantages', pp 192–193.

[9] See *Interbrew* Commission's XXVIth *Report on Competition Policy* (1996), point 53 and pp 139–140 and *GVG/FS*, Commission decision of 27 August 2003, paras 72–81.

[10] See ch 21, 'Article 1: concentrations having a Union dimension', pp 859–864 on these turnover thresholds.

[11] See ch 21, 'Non-horizontal mergers', pp 899–902.

[12] See ch 21, 'Recent cases on non-horizontal mergers', p 902.

[13] Case M 7995, Commission decision of 29 March 2017, para 678.

4. Commercial Agents

Some producers choose to sell through commercial agents. The function of a sales agent is to negotiate business and to enter into contracts on the producer's behalf[14]. In this case the agent may be paid a commission for the business it transacts or it may be paid a salary. Commercial agency is a more common feature of distribution in continental Europe than in the UK. There is a Directive on the treatment of commercial agents[15], which provides them with protection against wrongful dismissal and with compensation where this occurs.

(A) Non-application of Article 101 to agency agreements

Where an agent simply negotiates or transacts on behalf of a principal it is treated by EU competition law as forming part of the same economic entity of the principal. In *voestalpine AG v Commission*[16] the General Court held that:

> two factors have been taken to be the main parameters for determining whether there is a single economic unit: first, whether the intermediary takes on any economic risk and, second, whether the services provided by the intermediary are exclusive.

If the agent does not bear any risk itself, no property passes to it under the agreement, it does not directly share in the profits (or losses) of its principal's business and it conducts business predominantly for the principal; restrictions imposed upon the principal or agent will normally fall outside Article 101(1)[17].

(B) The Commission's *Vertical guidelines*

As early as 1962 the Commission published a *Notice on agency agreements*[18] stating that they were not subject to Article 101(1). The 1962 *Notice* has been superseded by paragraphs 12 to 21 of the Commission's *Vertical guidelines*[19]. The *Guidelines* draw on the decisional practice of the Commission and the jurisprudence of the EU Courts, in particular *DaimlerChrysler v Commission*[20] and *Confederación Española de Empresarios de Estaciones de Servicio v Compañía de Petróleos*[21].

Paragraph 12 of the *Vertical guidelines* defines agency agreements as those that cover a situation where one person negotiates and/or concludes contracts on behalf of another for the purchase or sale of goods or services, by or from the principal[22]. Paragraph 13 provides that the determining factor in assessing whether Article 101(1) is applicable is

[14] Agents are sometimes appointed simply to canvass potential customers or to introduce them to the producer rather than to negotiate contracts.

[15] Council Directive on the Coordination of the Laws of Member States relating to Self-Employed Commercial Agents 86/653, OJ [1986] L 382/17.

[16] Case T-418/10 *voestalpine AG v Commission* EU:T:2015:516, para 139; see generally paras 132–163, dismissing an appeal in *Prestressing Steel*, Commission decision of 30 June 2010, paras 773–779.

[17] See eg Cases 40/73 etc *Suiker Unie v Commission* EU:C:1975:174, para 480.

[18] *Notice on exclusive dealing contracts with commercial agents* OJ [1962] 139/2921.

[19] OJ [2010] C 130/1.

[20] Case T-325/01 EU:T:2005:322; the General Court upheld a finding of agency in Case T-66/99 *Minoan Lines v Commission* EU:T:2003:337, paras 121–130.

[21] Case C-217/05 EU:C:2006:784; a judgment that the *Vertical guidelines* do not mention, but which is relevant to this issue, is that of the Court of Justice in Case C-266/93 *Bundeskartellamt v Volkswagen* EU:C:1995:345.

[22] The *Vertical guidelines* do not use the language of 'genuine agency agreements' and 'non genuine agent agreements' which had been used in their predecessor: see OJ [2000] C 291/1, para 13.

'the financial or commercial risk borne by the agent in relation to the activities for which it has been appointed as an agent by the principal'[23]; paragraph 13 states that it is immaterial whether the agent acts for one or several principals, a view that is difficult to reconcile with the judgment of the Court of Justice in *Vlaamse Reisbureaus*[24]; the parties' views and the position under domestic law are similarly irrelevant. Paragraphs 14 to 17 examine the meaning of risk for this purpose. Paragraphs 18 to 21 consider the application of Article 101(1) to agency agreements.

(i) **The criterion of risk**

(a) Paragraphs 14 to 17 of the Vertical guidelines

Paragraph 14 states that there are three types of financial or commercial risk that are material to the definition of an agency agreement:

- 'contract-specific risks' that are directly related to the contracts concluded and/or negotiated by the agent on behalf of the principal, such as the financing of stocks
- those risks that are related to 'market-specific investments', meaning risks that the agent undertakes in order to be appointed
- those risks that are related to other activities that the principal requires the agent to perform on the same product market, such as risks relating to after-sales or repair services[25].

Paragraph 15 states that, where the agent bears no or only insignificant risks in relation to these matters, the agency agreement falls outside Article 101(1): in such a case the selling or purchasing function forms an integral part of the principal's activities, despite the fact that the agent is a separate legal entity. Paragraph 15 states that it is immaterial whether the agent bears risks that are related to the activity of providing agency services in general, such as the risk of the agent's income being dependent upon its success as an agent.

Paragraph 16 provides that an agency agreement exists and Article 101(1) would not normally be applicable where the title to the goods does not vest in the agent; nor where the agent does not supply services itself and where the agent does not:

- contribute to the costs relating to the supply/purchase of the contract goods or services, including the cost of transport
- maintain at its own cost or risk stocks of the contracts goods
- undertake responsibility towards third parties for damage caused by the products sold
- take responsibility for customers' non-performance of the contract
- have to invest in sales promotion
- make market-specific investments in equipment, premises or training of personnel
- undertake other activities within the same product market required by the principal, unless these activities are fully reimbursed by the principal.

Paragraph 17 provides that the list in paragraph 16 is not exhaustive and that, where the agent does incur one or more of the costs or risks listed, Article 101(1) may apply as it

23 For critical comment on the use of the criterion of risk see Zhang 'Toward an Economic Approach to Agency Agreements' (2013) 9 Journal of Competition Law and Economics 553.

24 Case 311/85 *Vereniging van Vlaamse Reisbureaus v Sociale Dienst van de Plaatselijke en Gewestelijke Overheidsdiensten* EU:C:1987:418.

25 See eg Case T-325/01 *DaimlerChrysler v Commission* EU:T:2005:322, paras 110–111; Case T-418/10 *voestalpine AG v Commission* EU:T:2015:516, paras 142–148.

would do to any other vertical agreement. Paragraph 17 states that the question of risk must be assessed on a case-by-case basis and with regard to economic reality rather than legal form. The Commission explains that, for practical reasons, the analysis may start with the assessment of the contract-specific risks since, if they are incurred by the agent, it will be sufficient to conclude that the agent is an independent undertaking.

(ii) Non-application of Article 101(1) to agency agreements

Paragraph 18 of the *Vertical guidelines* provides that, where an agency agreement does not fall within Article 101(1), all obligations on the agent will fall outside that provision, including limitations on the territory in which or the customers to which the agent may sell the goods or services and the prices and conditions at which the goods or services will be sold or purchased.

(iii) Application of Article 101(1) to agency agreements

Paragraphs 19 and 20 of the *Vertical guidelines* indicate two situations in which there could be an infringement of Article 101(1) in the case of an agency agreement.

The first situation is where there are exclusivity provisions: either that the principal will not appoint other agents or that the agent will not act for other principals. The Commission says that the former are unlikely to infringe Article 101(1), but that single branding provisions and post-term non-compete provisions, which concern inter-brand competition[26], could infringe Article 101(1) if they lead to foreclosure of the market: the Commission refers to paragraphs 129 to 150 of the *Guidelines* on this. The idea that non-compete provisions in an agency agreement could infringe Article 101(1) was noted with approval by the Court of Justice in *CEPSA*[27], although they may be block exempted where they satisfy the terms of Regulation 330/2010; and otherwise they may satisfy Article 101(3) on an individual basis. In *Repsol*[28] the Commission identified a possible foreclosure effect arising from a long-term exclusive supply agreement, which was addressed by accepting commitments offered by Repsol under Article 9 of Regulation 1/2003[29].

Paragraph 20 deals with the second situation in which Article 101(1) might be infringed, which is where the agency agreement facilitates collusion: this could occur where a number of principals use the same agents whilst collectively excluding others from using these agents; or where they use agents for collusion on marketing strategy or to exchange sensitive market information between the principals. In *E-books*[30] the Commission was concerned that five publishers had entered into identical agency agreements with Apple as part of a common global plan to increase retail prices of e-books; the case was closed on the parties giving commitments under Article 9 of Regulation 1/2003[31] that terminated the agency agreements and preserved competition in prices between retailers.

Paragraph 21 of the *Guidelines* states that, where the agent bears one or more of the risks described in paragraph 16, the agreement between agent and principal does not

[26] This expression is explained at 'Inter-brand and intra-brand competition', pp 637–639 later in chapter.

[27] Case C-217/05 *Confederación Española de Empresarios de Staciones de Servicio v Compañía de Petróleos SA* EU:C:2006:784, para 62.

[28] Commission decision of 12 April 2006, paras 20–24; the General Court dismissed an appeal alleging non-compliance with those commitments in Case T-342/11 *CEEES v Commission* EU:T:2014:60.

[29] Note the Court of Justice gave a preliminary ruling on the legal effect of this commitment decision in Case C-547/16 *Gasorba SL v Repsol Comercial de Productos Petrolíferos SA* EU:C:2017:891; on 8 February 2018 the Spanish Supreme Court held that Repsol's supply agreements were excessively long: the judgment is available (in Spanish) at www.poderjudicial.es.

[30] Commission decisions of 13 December 2012 and 25 July 2013.

[31] On commitments decisions under Article 9 see ch 7, 'Article 9: commitments', pp 264–269.

constitute an agency agreement. Instead the agent will be treated as an independent undertaking, and the agreement with it is capable of infringing Article 101(1)[32].

(C) Application of Article 102 to agency agreements

Even if a producer distributes products through an agent, so that Article 101(1) is inapplicable, the practices of the firms concerned might constitute an abuse of Article 102 where one or both of them have a dominant position[33].

5. Vertical Agreements: Competition Policy Considerations

(A) Introduction

In this section the competition policy considerations raised by vertical agreements will be examined. It is the task of competition policy, first, to decide which restraints in vertical relationships give rise to a restriction of competition and, secondly, to distinguish harmless or beneficial restrictions from those which should be prohibited.

(B) Vertical agreements: possible detriments to competition

(i) Inter-brand and intra-brand competition

The application of Article 101 to vertical agreements has long been controversial[34]. It is fairly obvious that horizontal agreements, for example to fix prices or to limit output, should be prohibited: in this situation firms combine their market power to their own advantage[35]; vertical agreements do not involve a *combination* of market power[36]. As the Court of Justice stated in *Allianz Hungária*[37], vertical agreements are 'often less damaging to competition than horizontal agreements'[38]. Apart from vertical agreements that have the object of restricting competition[39], vertical agreements are likely to raise competition concerns only where there is a degree of market power at the level of the supplier or the buyer or at both levels. Where this is the case competition with other firms' products—'inter-brand competition'—may be limited; as a result it may be desirable to ensure that there is competition between distributors and retailers in relation to the products of the firm with market power—so-called 'intra-brand competition'[40].

Suppose that A is the brand owner of Wonder Widgets and B is the brand owner of Beautiful Blodgets. A requires its retailers to purchase Wonder Widgets only from it and not to buy the competing products of M, N and O—a so-called 'single branding agreement' also known as an exclusive purchasing agreement[41]. The diagonal line means that the retailers and M, N and O have no access to each other (see Figure 16.6).

[32] See eg *Souris/Topps*, Commission decision of 26 May 2004, paras 97–104.

[33] Abusive practices are considered in detail in chs 17 and 18.

[34] For further discussion of the arguments in favour of and against vertical agreements see Motta *Competition Policy: Theory and Practice* (Cambridge University Press, 2004), Part VI; Van den Bergh and Camesasca *European Competition Law and Economics: A Comparative Perspective* (Sweet & Maxwell, 2nd ed, 2006), ch 6; Bishop and Walker *The Economics of EC Competition Law* (Sweet & Maxwell, 3rd ed, 2010), paras 5-034–5-054.

[35] *Vertical guidelines*, para 98. [36] Ibid, para 98. [37] Case C-32/11 EU:C:2013:160.

[38] Ibid, para 43; see similarly Case C-345/14 *Maxima Latvija* EU:C:2015:784, para 21.

[39] See ch 3, 'Agreements that have as their object the prevention, restriction or distortion of competition', pp 122–132.

[40] *Vertical guidelines*, para 102. [41] See 'Single branding agreements', pp 651–653 later in chapter.

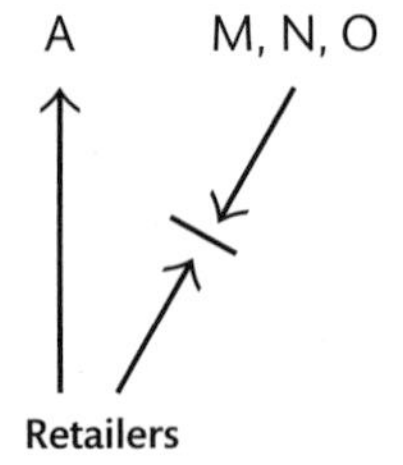

Fig. 16.6

The question in this case would be whether the single branding agreement has an effect on inter-brand competition, that is to say on competition between the brands of A and those of its competitors, M, N and O; this will depend on how much market power A has.

Suppose now that B requires its retailers X, Y and Z not to sell Beautiful Blodgets at less than the recommended price of €100, and not to sell to customers who live in an area allotted to one of the other retailers (see Figure 16.7).

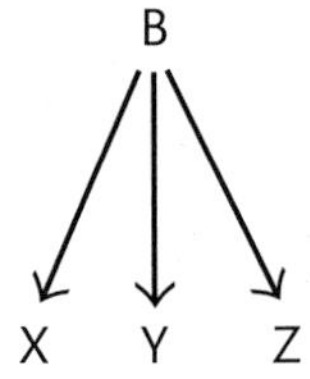

Fig. 16.7

The question in this case is whether the agreements have a significant effect on intra-brand competition between the three retailers X, Y and Z. They do not restrict competition between B and its competitors; however the extent of inter-brand competition in the relevant market will affect the extent to which a restriction of intra-brand competition is a cause for concern.

(ii) *Consten and Grundig v Commission*

In *Consten and Grundig v Commission*[42] Grundig of Germany had appointed Consten as its exclusive distributor for France for its electronic goods. Consten wanted as much protection as possible from intra-brand competition. Grundig was willing to give this protection, and required its distributors in other Member States not to export to France, and assigned its trade mark to Consten in France so that it could bring an action for trade mark infringement against any parallel importer. The result of this was that Consten enjoyed 'absolute territorial protection' against parallel imports into France from the other Member States. It was argued that Article 101(1) should not apply to vertical agreements at all, leaving it to Article 102 to deal with vertical restraints where a firm had substantial market power. The Court of Justice rejected this argument[43] and concluded that the exclusive agreement in that case which conferred upon the distributor absolute

[42] Cases 56 and 58/64 EU:C:1966:41.

[43] Ibid; see further ch 3, 'Horizontal and vertical agreements', p 121.

territorial protection against parallel imports of the producer's goods was caught by Article 101(1) and did not satisfy the criteria of Article 101(3)[44].

(iii) The single market imperative and intra-brand competition

As a general proposition competition law has less concern with restrictions of intra-brand competition than with restrictions of inter-brand competition: a restriction of intra-brand competition is likely to raise concerns only where inter-brand competition is weak. However to this must be added a further concern of EU competition law, which has been mentioned several times in this book already: the integrity of the single market. The EU Courts and the Commission have, from the earliest days, been concerned about vertical agreements that segregate one national market from another, even where the restrictions relate to intra-brand rather than to inter-brand competition. The strict treatment of export bans, the determination to maintain parallel imports and the reluctance to allow distributors to enjoy absolute territorial protection are all issues affecting intra-brand rather than inter-brand competition. The law on vertical agreements in the EU therefore has a component—single market integration—that will not be found in other (domestic) systems of competition law[45]. The thought that the single market will at some point be completed, so that this consideration will disappear, is manifestly wrong: the judgments in *Football Association Premier League*[46] and *Pierre Fabre*[47] demonstrate that the single market imperative remains in place.

(iv) The commentary in the *Vertical guidelines* on the negative effects of vertical restraints

In determining whether a vertical agreement has a restrictive effect on competition, it is necessary to consider what the market situation would have been in the absence of the vertical restraints in the agreement[48]. Useful guidance on analysing the anti-competitive effects of an agreement can be found in the Commission's *Guidelines on the application of Article [101(3)] of the Treaty* ('the *Article 101(3) Guidelines*')[49]. Those guidelines make clear that negative effects are likely to occur when at least one of the parties has or obtains some degree of market power and the agreement contributes to the creation, maintenance or strengthening of that market power or allows the parties to exploit it, a point repeated in paragraph 97 of the *Vertical guidelines*. Paragraph 100 of the Commission's *Vertical guidelines* notes four possible negative effects arising from vertical restraints which EU competition law aims at preventing:

- anti-competitive foreclosure of other suppliers or buyers by raising barriers to entry
- softening of competition between the supplier and its competitors and/or facilitation of both explicit and tacit collusion, often referred to as a reduction of inter-brand competition[50]

[44] Absolute territorial protection may be permitted in exceptional circumstances, as in Case 262/81 *Coditel II* EU:C:1982:334: see ch 3, 'Objectively necessary agreements', p 136.

[45] See the *Vertical guidelines*, para 7.

[46] Cases C-403/08 and C-429/08 *Football Association Premier League Ltd v QC Leisure* EU:C:2011:631.

[47] Case C-439/09 *Pierre Fabre Dermo-Cosmétique SAS v Président de l'Autorité de la Concurrence* EU:C:2011:649.

[48] *Vertical guidelines*, para 97.

[49] OJ [2004] C 101/97, paras 24–27; on agreements that have as their effect the restriction of competition see ch 3, 'Agreements that have as their effect the prevention, restriction or distortion of competition', pp 132–144.

[50] On practices, including vertical agreements, that may facilitate tacit collusion see ch 14, 'Article 101(1), the exchange of information and other facilitating practices', pp 581–582.

- softening of competition between the buyer and its competitors and/or facilitation of collusion, commonly referred to as a reduction of intra-brand competition between distributors of the same brand
- the creation of obstacles to market integration.

Paragraph 101 of the *Guidelines* explains that foreclosure, softening of competition and collusion in the upstream or downstream market may harm consumers in particular by raising wholesale prices, depriving consumers of choice, lowering quality or reducing the level of innovation. Paragraphs 103 to 105 consider the circumstances in which vertical restraints are more likely to have negative effects; for example:

- exclusive arrangements are generally more anti-competitive than non-exclusive arrangements since they result in one firm sourcing all or practically all of its demand from another
- a combination of vertical restraints will usually increase their individual negative effects; however certain combinations may have the reverse effect: for example a maximum resale price used to prevent an exclusive distributor from raising price beyond a certain level
- the negative effects arising from vertical restraints are reinforced when several suppliers and their respective buyers organise their trade in a similar way, leading to so-called 'cumulative effects' within the market leading to a restriction of competition.

(C) Vertical agreements: possible benefits to competition

Having set out the Commission's views as to the possible detriments to competition arising from vertical agreements, it is important to stress that there are also significant arguments in their favour. Some theorists argue that vertical restraints are not a suitable target for competition authorities at all[51]; a more realistic view is that they should be investigated only where at least one of the parties has market power[52]. Paragraph 106 of the *Vertical guidelines* states that vertical restraints often have positive effects, in particular by promoting non-price competition and improved quality of service. Paragraph 107 sets out nine situations in which vertical restraints may help to realise efficiencies and the development of new markets; the Commission says that it does not claim that the list is complete or exhaustive[53].

(i) The free-rider problem

One retailer may take a free ride on the investment of another. For example a retailer may invest in a particular brand and create a demand for it: a retailer may not be prepared to make this investment if it fears that a 'free-rider' could acquire the goods in questions from an alternative source and sell them without having contributed towards the creation of that demand. The Commission states that free-riding between buyers can occur only on pre-sales services and not on after-sales services; it adds that free-riding is usually

[51] See eg Bork *The Antitrust Paradox* (The Free Press, 1993), chs 14 and 15.

[52] See eg Easterbrook 'Vertical Arrangements and the Rule of Reason' (1984) 53 Antitrust LJ 135; Bock 'An Economist Appraises Vertical Restraints' (1985) 30 Antitrust Bulletin 117; for criticism of the permissive view of vertical restraints adopted by many commentators see Comanor 'Vertical Price Fixing, Vertical Market Restrictions and the New Antitrust Policy' (1985) 98 Harvard Law Review 983 and Pitofsky 'Can Vertical Arrangements Injure Consumer Welfare?' in Pitofsky (ed) *How the Chicago School Has Overshot the Mark* (Oxford University Press, 2008).

[53] See further *Vertical guidelines*, paras 108–109.

a problem only where the product is relatively new or complex and of reasonably high value. A free-rider problem can arise where a supplier invests in promotion at a retailer's premises which a competing supplier takes advantage of: a non-compete provision may be justified to prevent this type of free-riding.

Exclusive distribution agreements may be used to prevent the problem of free-riding: for example if A appoints B as the exclusive distributor for France, this will provide some degree of immunity from intra-brand competition. Absolute territorial protection will not usually be countenanced in vertical agreements, because of the EU objective of creating a single internal market. However a term conferring exclusivity (but not absolute territorial protection) on a distributor might not infringe Article 101(1) at all, in particular where third parties from outside the territory may sell into it[54]: in this case the exclusivity may provide a distributor with the incentive to promote a product effectively, thereby increasing the degree of inter-brand competition.

(ii) Opening up and entering new markets

A 'special case of the free-rider problem' is where a manufacturer wants to enter a new geographic market and this requires its distributor to make 'first time investments'. It may be necessary to protect the distributor from competition so that it can recoup its investment by temporarily charging a higher price; this may mean that distributors in other markets should be restrained for a limited period from selling in the new market.

(iii) The certification free-rider issue

In some sectors certain retailers have a reputation for stocking only 'quality' products. In such a case a manufacturer must limit its sales to such retailers, since otherwise its products may be delisted. Exclusive or selective distribution may be justified for a period of time in these circumstances.

(iv) The hold-up problem

This refers to a situation in which a supplier or buyer needs to make client-specific investments, and will not commit to these until supply agreements have been concluded. It may be that an undertaking making an investment will require a long-term supply agreement, so that it knows that it will recoup its costs. Where the supplier makes the investment, it may wish the buyer to agree to a non-compete, or to an analogous, provision; a buyer may seek the benefit of an exclusive distribution, customer allocation or exclusive supply provision[55].

(v) The hold-up problem where know-how is transferred

Where know-how is supplied by one firm to another it may be necessary to impose a non-compete provision on the recipient of the know-how to ensure that it is not used by competitors of the owner of it.

(vi) The 'vertical externality issue'

Vertical restraints can be used to align the incentives of the parties so that one party does not act in a way that would harm the interests of the other. There may be situations where

[54] See further 'The single market imperative and intra-brand competition', p 639 earlier, and 'Article 4(b): territorial and customer restrictions', pp 679–682 later in chapter.

[55] For an example of the 'hold-up problem' under UK law see *Lucite International (UK) Ltd and BASF plc*, decision of 29 November 2002, paras 44–46, available at www.nationalarchives.gov.uk.

the manufacturer needs the retailer to improve sales levels or not to price too high in order to obtain benefits. The negative externality of too high pricing by a retailer can be avoided by imposing a maximum resale price on the retailer[56].

(vii) **Economies of scale in distribution**

Economies of scale in distribution may lead to lower retail prices[57]. Various vertical agreements might contribute to this, including exclusive distribution and exclusive purchasing.

(viii) **Capital market imperfections**

In some cases banks or equity markets may be unwilling to provide sufficient capital for the needs of the business of a supplier or a buyer. In such cases the supplier may lend to the buyer or vice versa. An obvious example is a brewer which makes a loan available to the operator of a public house or a café. A supplier in such a case may wish to impose a non-compete, or an analogous, provision; and a buyer may insist, for example, on exclusive supply.

(ix) **Uniformity and quality standardisation**

Vertical restraints may help to promote the brand image of a product and increase its attractiveness to consumers by bringing about uniformity and quality standardisation. This is typical of selective distribution and franchising systems.

6. **Vertical Agreements: Article 101(1)**

(A) **Introduction**

This section will consider the application of Article 101(1) to vertical agreements[58]. Given the breadth of the block exemption for vertical agreements, in many cases it is not necessary, in practical terms, to decide whether an agreement infringes Article 101(1) in the first place: if an agreement is within the 'safe haven' of Regulation 330/2010 and therefore satisfies the criteria of Article 101(3) the parties may have little interest in arguing, or even knowing, that the agreement did not infringe Article 101(1) in the first place. Paragraph 110 of the Commission's *Vertical guidelines* suggests, at indents (1) and (2), that there is no need to consider the application of Article 101(1) to agreements that are within the safe haven of the block exemption. This is a sensible and pragmatic point, and one with which the Court of Justice agrees[59]. However it would be incorrect to conclude that, *because* an agreement benefits from block exemption, it *therefore* infringes Article 101(1); and in some cases an agreement may not benefit from the block exemption, for example because the market share of one of the parties exceeds 30 per cent, in which case the parties may wish to argue that Article 101(1) is not infringed. This is exemplified by the Commission's finding that Interbrew's agreements, which imposed a single branding provision on cafés and bars in Belgium, did not infringe Article 101(1), once they had been modified to its satisfaction[60].

[56] This is sometimes known as the 'double marginalisation problem'; see *Vertical guidelines*, para 107(f).

[57] On economies of scale see ch 1, 'Economies of scale and scope and natural monopolies', pp 10–11.

[58] For further discussion of this topic readers are referred to Faull and Nikpay (eds) *The EU Law of Competition* (Oxford University Press, 3rd ed, 2014), ch 9.

[59] See Case C-260/07 *Pedro IV Servicios SL v Total España SA* EU:C:2009:215, para 36.

[60] Commission Press Release IP/03/545, 15 April 2003.

(B) The *de minimis* doctrine

Paragraphs 8 to 11 of the *Vertical guidelines* point out that agreements of minor importance usually fall outside Article 101(1) altogether. These paragraphs refer to the Commission's 2001 *Notice on Agreements of Minor Importance*[61]. That *Notice* is no longer in force, having been replaced by the 2014 *De Minimis Notice*, which is described in chapter 3[62]. Vertical agreements entered into by non-competing undertakings whose individual market share does not exceed 15 per cent are usually *de minimis*, although an object restriction, such as an export ban, that has an appreciable effect on inter-state trade will be presumed to have an appreciable effect on competition[63].

(C) The combined effect of the *de minimis* doctrine and the block exemption

The combined effect of the *De Minimis Notice* and the block exemption is that the Commission considers that most vertical agreements where the market share of each of the parties is below 15% fall outside Article 101(1) altogether; and that most vertical agreements, even if they are caught by Article 101(1), will be block exempted under Regulation 330/2010, provided that the supplier's and the buyer's market share is below 30% and that the agreement does not contain any of the 'hard-core' restrictions in Article 4 of that Regulation[64]. As a consequence a very large number of vertical agreements will enjoy the benefit of one of these two 'safe havens'. Individual examination of vertical agreements will be necessary only where none of the safe havens is available, for example because the supplier's market share exceeds 30% or because the parties wish to include a 'hard-core restriction' in their agreement. Agreements containing hard-core restrictions are unlikely to satisfy the criteria of Article 101(3), since there are often less restrictive means of achieving efficiencies. Where the market share of one of the parties exceeds 30% it may be that it has a dominant position, in which case restrictions in its vertical agreements may amount to an abuse of a dominant position contrary to Article 102 TFEU: firms have been found to be dominant where they had a market share in the region of 40%, and they are presumed to be dominant at 50%[65]. Table 16.1 sets out the market share figures that are relevant for the assessment of vertical agreements.

It follows that the need to examine a vertical agreement under Article 101(1) and Article 101(3) in an individual case is likely to be relatively rare: it is most likely to be necessary where the supplier or the buyer has a market share in excess of 30% but does not have a dominant position in the sense of Article 102.

(D) The case law of the EU Courts on vertical agreements

The Court of Justice and the General Court have repeatedly made clear that, except in those cases where the *object*[66] of an agreement is anti-competitive, for example because of

[61] OJ [2001] C 368/13. [62] See ch 3, 'The *De Minimis* Doctrine', pp 147–150.

[63] *Vertical guidelines*, para 10 states that the applicable case law of the EU Courts is relevant in this respect, referring in particular to Case 5/69 *Völk v Vervaecke* EU:C:1969:35; to this must be added the judgment in Case C-226/11 *Expedia* EU:C:2012:795, para 37; see further ch 3, 'Part II of the *Notice*: the threshold', pp 148–149.

[64] See 'Article 4: hard-core restrictions', pp 677–684 later in chapter.

[65] See ch 5, 'The *AKZO* presumption of dominance where an undertaking has a market share of 50% or more', p 190.

[66] See ch 3, 'Agreements that have as their object the prevention, restriction or distortion of competition', pp 122–132.

Table 16.1 Market shares and vertical agreements

50%	An undertaking with a market share of more than 50% is presumed to be dominant; that undertaking will bear the evidential burden of establishing that it is not dominant
40%	An undertaking with a market share of more than 40% may be dominant
30%	If an agreement is caught by Article 101(1) it will benefit from block exemption if the supplier's and the buyer's market share is below 30% and the agreement does not contain hard-core restrictions. A vertical agreement will not benefit from the block exemption where one or more parties has a market share of more than 30%
15%	An agreement between non-competitors will benefit from the *De Minimis* Notice where the market share of each of the parties is below 15% and the agreement does not contain any restrictions by object

the imposition of an export ban, the application of Article 101(1) to an agreement cannot be ascertained simply by taking into account its formal terms; rather it has to be assessed in its economic context in order to determine whether it could have an effect on competition in the relevant market[67]. This case law is discussed in chapter 3 of this book[68]. Of particular importance in the context of vertical agreements are the judgments in *Société Technique Minière v Maschinenbau Ulm*[69], *Brasserie de Haecht v Wilkin*[70], *Pronuptia de Paris v Schillgalis*[71], *Delimitis v Henninger Bräu*[72] and *Maxima Latvija*[73], each of which makes clear that, in 'effect' rather than 'object' cases under Article 101(1), a thorough analysis of all the relevant facts is required before a conclusion can be reached as to whether competition is restricted by a vertical agreement.

Notwithstanding these important judgments there was a tendency on the part of the Commission over many years to adopt a formalistic approach to the application of Article 101(1) to vertical agreements, and a reluctance to follow the lead suggested by the EU Courts; the result was that large numbers of vertical agreements needed to satisfy the conditions of Article 101(3) and, in particular, the rules in the block exemptions adopted by the Commission. The Commission responded to the criticism that it applied Article 101(1) too extensively: its *Vertical guidelines* of 2000 adopted a less formalistic and more economics-based approach to the application of Article 101(1); their successor of 2010 maintains this approach. As a result Article 101(1) is now interpreted in a way that fewer vertical agreements fall within its scope than was once the case.

(E) The methodology for the analysis of vertical agreements in the Commission's *Vertical guidelines*

Paragraphs 110 to 127 of the *Guidelines* establish the methodology of analysis for determining whether vertical agreements infringe Article 101.

(i) The four steps involved in assessing vertical agreements under Article 101

Paragraph 110 of the *Vertical guidelines* suggests that four steps should be taken when assessing vertical agreements under Article 101:

[67] See the Opinion of AG Wahl in Case C-230/16 *Coty* EU:C:2017:603, para 48.

[68] See ch 3, 'The "object or effect" of preventing, restricting or distorting competition', pp 121–122.

[69] Case 56/65 EU:C:1966:38. [70] Case 23/67 EU:C:1967:54. [71] Case 161/84 EU:C:1986:41.

[72] Case C-234/89 EU:C:1991:91. [73] Case C-345/14 EU:C:2015:784.

- first, the relevant market should be defined in order to determine the supplier's and the buyer's market share
- secondly, where the market share of each of the parties is below 30% the block exemption will usually be applicable, provided that there are no hard-core restrictions contrary to Article 4 of Regulation 330/2010[74]
- the third step is that, where either party's market share exceeds 30%, it will be necessary to consider whether the agreement falls within Article 101(1)
- lastly, where Article 101(1) is infringed, it will be necessary to consider whether the agreement benefits from the exception conferred by Article 101(3).

(ii) Relevant factors for the assessment under Article 101(1)

Paragraphs 111 to 121 set out the factors that the Commission considers to be relevant to the analysis of agreements under Article 101(1). Paragraph 111 mentions nine factors that are relevant to this assessment:

- the nature of the agreement
- the market position of the parties
- the market position of competitors
- the position of the buyers of the contract products
- entry barriers
- the maturity of the market
- the level of trade affected by the agreement
- the nature of the product
- 'other factors'.

Each of these factors is expanded upon in the succeeding paragraphs. Paragraph 117 discusses entry barriers and emphasises the significance of sunk costs in determining how high the entry barriers are in a particular industry[75]. Paragraph 121 deals with 'other factors' that may be relevant: these include whether there is a 'cumulative effect' within the market of similar vertical agreements leading to a restriction of competition, the regulatory environment and behaviour that may indicate or facilitate horizontal collusion.

(iii) Relevant factors for the assessment under Article 101(3)

Paragraphs 122 to 127 discuss the application of Article 101(3) to vertical agreements. They should be read in conjunction with the Commission's *Article 101(3) Guidelines*[76]. Paragraph 123 states that it is necessary to take into account the investments made by any of the parties and the time needed and the restraints required to commit and recoup an efficiency-enhancing investment. Paragraphs 124 to 127 rehearse the conditions of Article 101(3). Paragraph 127 states that, in the absence of rivalry between undertakings, a dominant undertaking will lack adequate incentives to continue to create and pass on efficiency gains to consumers: in other words an anti-competitive agreement on the part of a dominant undertaking is unlikely to satisfy Article 101(3)[77].

[74] See 'Article 4: hard-core restrictions', pp 677–684 later in chapter.

[75] On barriers to entry see ch 1, 'Potential Competitors', p 45.

[76] OJ [2004] C 101/97; for discussion of the *Article 101(3) Guidelines* see ch 4, 'The Article 101(3) Criteria', pp 162ff.

[77] Note that a dominant firm has the right to raise efficiencies as a defence to abusive behaviour: Case C-413/14 P *Intel v Commission* EU:C:2017:632, para 140.

(iv) Application of the methodology to particular types of agreement

This chapter will now consider the approach of the EU Courts and the Commission to different types of vertical agreement. The Commission's *Guidelines* contain helpful references to the case law of the Courts: due to constraints of space not all of these judgments are mentioned in the text that follows, but the reader should be aware of this useful reference point. The *Guidelines* must be read subject to the case law of the EU Courts rather than the other way round.

(F) Direct and indirect export bans

As a general proposition direct and indirect export bans imposed on distributors will violate Article 101(1) as they are inimical to the single market. The *Guidelines* do not contain a specific section dealing with the application of Article 101(1) to export bans, other than the commentary on Article 4(b) of the block exemption[78]. There is however a wealth of precedent on this subject and single market integration is an important feature of EU competition law. Parallel trade should always be possible within the EU. This section will consider the approach of the EU Courts and the Commission to direct and indirect export bans.

(i) Direct export bans

A producer may agree with a distributor that it will sell only to that distributor in a particular territory and that it will impose a term on its other distributors banning them from selling into the allotted territory. Such export bans will normally infringe Article 101(1), and will not be permitted under Article 101(3) except in exceptional circumstances. Export bans are blacklisted by Article 4(b) of Regulation 330/2010, and their inclusion prevents the application of the block exemption to the agreement in question[79].

Export bans have as their object the restriction of competition; anti-competitive effects do not need to be demonstrated for there to be an infringement of Article 101(1). In *General Motors v Commission*[80] the Court of Justice held that this was so even if an agreement does not have the restriction of competition as its sole aim but also pursues other legitimate objectives[81], adding that the same was true if the restriction of exports happened as a result of indirect rather than direct measures[82]. In *GlaxoSmithKline v Commission*[83] the General Court rejected the Commission's view that Glaxo's dual pricing system involved an indirect export ban that had as its object the restriction of competition. On appeal the Court of Justice reaffirmed its case law that agreements aimed at prohibiting or limiting parallel trade have as their object the restriction of competition; that this applies to the pharmaceutical sector as to any other; that, for an agreement to restrict competition by object, it was not necessary that final consumers be deprived of advantages; and that Article 101 protects 'competition as such'[84]. However the Court of Justice agreed with the General Court that the Commission had failed to deal appropriately with Glaxo's arguments and evidence under Article 101(3)[85]. The Court of Justice's judgments in *Football Association Premier League*[86] and *Pierre Fabre*[87] are also emphatic

[78] See 'Article 4(b): territorial and customer restrictions', pp 679–682 later in chapter.
[79] Ibid. [80] Case C-551/03 P EU:C:2006:229. [81] Ibid, para 64.
[82] Ibid, para 68. [83] Case T-168/01 EU:T:2006:265, paras 114–147.
[84] Cases C-501/06 P etc *GlaxoSmithKline Services Unlimited v Commission* EU:C:2009:610, paras 54–67.
[85] Case T-168/01 *GlaxoSmithKline Services Unlimited v Commission* EU:T:2006:265, paras 214–316, upheld on appeal Cases C-501/06 P etc EU:C:2009:610, paras 68–118.
[86] Cases C-403/08 etc EU:C:2011:631, paras 134–146. [87] Case C-439/09 EU:C:2011:649, paras 37–47.

that agreements that impede single market integration are prohibited unless there are exceptional circumstances.

Examples of export bans condemned by the Commission and the EU Courts are legion[88], and the national competition authorities of the Member States ('the NCAs') have been equally opposed to them[89]. In *Colgate-Palmolive v Swiss Competition Commission*[90] the Swiss Supreme Court held that a restriction on passive sales from Austria into Switzerland was a restriction of competition contrary to Swiss competition law, irrespective of any quantitative assessment, and that a fine could be imposed. It is highly likely that the Commission or an NCA will impose a fine where it discovers an export ban, although reluctant distributors which accepted the ban under duress may not themselves be fined[91]; alternatively it may be that the fine on unwilling participants will be reduced[92]. In a serious case the fine for imposing export bans could be substantial. In *VW I*[93] the Commission found that VW had brought pressure to bear on dealers in Italy not to supply VW cars to purchasers who might ship them to higher-priced countries. VW was fined €102 million for what were considered by the Commission to be egregious infringements of Article 101; the fine was reduced to €90 million on appeal[94]. When determining the level of fines, and in particular ensuring that they have a deterrent effect, the Commission is entitled to take into account the central position within a distribution system of the manufacturer, which must display special vigilance and ensure that it observes the competition rules when concluding distribution agreements[95].

(ii) **Indirect export bans**

Indirect measures that have the same effect as an export ban will be found to have the object of restricting competition, contrary to Article 101(1), and are unlikely to satisfy Article 101(3). Indirect export bans are blacklisted by Article 4(b) of Regulation 330/2010, and their inclusion in an agreement would prevent the application of the block exemption[96].

The Commission will take a wide view of the term 'agreement' for the purpose of establishing whether an export ban infringes Article 101(1) and, in particular, that conduct that may appear to be unilateral may be characterised as sufficiently consensual to be caught by that provision[97]. In some cases it may also be possible to establish a concerted practice between a supplier and its distributors to divide up the internal market[98]. As pointed out in chapter 3, however, the Commission's findings of a vertical agreement have been overturned on appeal in several cases[99]. A different point is that in *Activision Blizzard*[100], an

[88] See ch 16 n 120 later for examples of such cases since 2000; for a list of cases in the preceding 20 years or so see p 623 n 102 of the sixth edition of this book.

[89] See eg *Witt Hvidevarer*, decision of the Danish NCA of 24 November 2010, available at www.kfst.dk; *SUPN*, decision of the Czech NCA of 15 September 2010 (imposing a fine of CZK 17,283,000 for export bans on lignite fuels), available at www.uohs.cz; *Hyundai Motor Vehicles*, decision of the Bulgarian NCA of 6 November 2012 (imposing total fines of €8 million for retail price maintenance ('RPM'); and Case 26 Kt 11/16m *Makita Werkzeug Gesellschaft mbH*, judgment of Austrian Cartel Court of 7 December 2016 (imposing a fine of €1.5 million for RPM and exports bans).

[90] Case no 2C_180/2014, judgment of 28 June 2016.

[91] See eg *Kawasaki* OJ [1979] L 16/9; *Johnson and Johnson* OJ [1980] L 377/16; *John Deere* OJ [1985] L 35/58.

[92] See eg *BMW Belgium* OJ [1978] L 46/33; *Hasselblad* OJ [1982] L 161/18.

[93] OJ [1998] L 124/60.

[94] Case T-62/98 *Volkswagen AG v Commission* EU:T:2000:180, upheld on appeal to the Court of Justice Case C-338/00 P *Volkswagen AG v Commission* EU:C:2003:473.

[95] Case T-13/03 *Nintendo Co Ltd v Commission* EU:T:2009:131, paras 79–80.

[96] See 'Article 4(b): territorial and customer restrictions', pp 679–682 later in chapter.

[97] See ch 3, '"Unilateral" conduct and Article 101(1) in vertical cases', pp 109–114.

[98] See in particular Cases 100–103/80 *Musique Diffusion Française SA v Commission* EU:C:1983:158.

[99] See ch 3, 'Cases following *Bayer*', pp 112–113.

[100] Case C-260/09 P *Activision Blizzard Germany GmbH v Commission* EU:C:2011:62.

appeal in the *Nintendo* case, the Court of Justice held that the standard of proof for demonstrating the existence of a vertical agreement is the same as in the case of a horizontal agreement[101].

An example of an indirect export ban would arise if a producer provides that its guarantees are available to consumers in a particular Member State only if they buy the product from a distributor in that State; this obviously acts as a strong disincentive to purchase elsewhere. In *Zanussi*[102] the Commission condemned such an arrangement, and it has taken similar action on several occasions since[103]. As a general proposition customer guarantees should be available for products no matter where they are marketed in the single market. The Commission's approach was endorsed by the Court of Justice in *ETA Fabriques d'Ebauches v DK Investments SA*[104], in which it held that the partitioning of national markets by denying the benefit of guarantees to imported goods infringed Article 101(1). However it may be legitimate to provide that the guarantee should extend only to services that a local representative is bound to provide in accordance with local safety and technical standards[105], and it is permissible to withhold the guarantee from products sold by a dealer who is not an authorised member of a selective distribution system[106]. A requirement that a distributor that exports goods into the territory of another distributor should pay a service fee to the latter as compensation for the after-sales service that it is required to provide may be treated as an export ban where the fee does not relate to the value of the service to be provided; so may the provision to distributors of financial support conditional on products supplied being used only within a distributor's allotted territory[107].

Exports may be impeded in numerous other ways that are contrary to Article 101(1), including:

- the use of monitoring clauses in contracts to prevent or control parallel importing, whereby a producer requires information as to the destination of its products, and by the imposition on products of serial numbers which enable their movement from one territory to another to be traced[108]
- price discrimination devised to prevent exports[109]

[101] Ibid, paras 71–72. [102] OJ [1978] L 322/26.

[103] See *Matsushita Electrical Trading Company*, Commission's XIIth *Report on Competition Policy* (1982), point 77; *Ford Garantie Deutschland*, XIIIth *Report on Competition Policy* (1983), points 104–106; *Fiat*, XIVth *Report on Competition Policy* (1984), point 70; XVIth *Report on Competition Policy* (1986), point 56; *Sony*, XVIIth *Report on Competition Policy* (1987), point 67; Mathiak 'The Commission persuades Saeco to implement an international guarantee for its products and closes the complaint file' (October 2000) Competition Policy Newsletter 48.

[104] Case 31/85 EU:C:1985:494. [105] See *Zanussi* (ch 16 n 102 earlier), para 14.

[106] Case C-376/92 *Metro v Cartier* EU:C:1994:5, paras 32–34.

[107] *JCB* OJ [2002] L 69/1, paras 155–167; on appeal the General Court confirmed the Commission's approach on this point but annulled its finding of infringement for lack of evidence: Case T-67/01 *JCB Service v Commission* EU:T:2004:3, paras 136–145.

[108] See eg *Victor Hasselblad AB* OJ [1982] L 161/18: its cameras had serial numbers on them and the Commission considered that this afforded an opportunity to Hasselblad to discover whether there had been any parallel importing; *Sperry New Holland* OJ [1985] L 376/21; *Newitt/Dunlop Slazenger International* OJ [1992] L 131/32, paras 59–60.

[109] See eg *Pittsburgh Corning Europe* JO [1972] L 272/35; *Kodak* JO [1970] L 147/24; Case 30/78 *Distillers v Commission* EU:C:1980:186; the Commission considered that Glaxo had failed to demonstrate that its dual pricing policy satisfied the requirements of Article 101(3) in *GlaxoSmithKline* OJ [2001] L 302/1: the Commission's decision was annulled on this point in Case T-168/01 *GlaxoSmithKline Services v Commission* EU:T:2006:265, paras 233–317, and that aspect of the General Court's judgment was upheld on appeal to the Court of Justice in Cases C-501/06 P etc EU:C:2009:610, paras 68–168; see ch 4 'Judicial review by the General Court', p 173.

- withdrawal of discounts previously granted to a dealer in so far as it exported the products in question to another Member State[110]
- a policy of buying up supplies of its product imported from one Member State into another in order to protect distributors in the second Member State from cheap imports: this does not prevent parallel imports in itself, but it does deprive consumers in the second Member State of cheaper imports[111]
- restrictions on cross-supplies between distributors to prevent parallel imports between Member States[112]
- a requirement that a product be resold only in a particular form[113] or not resold in a repackaged form[114] might be found to affect exports
- reducing supplies to a distributor in a particular territory so that there are none available for export, where this is done by agreement or concerted practice[115]
- the supply of a product for a customer's own use[116] and
- a requirement that only foreign customers pay a 15% deposit for a new vehicle unjustifiably hindered cross-border car sales[117].

(iii) Recent enforcement activity

What has been noticeable since 2000 is that all of the Commission decisions[118] in vertical cases, with the exception of *VW II*[119] which concerned resale price maintenance, involved direct or indirect export bans[120]. For example in *Nintendo*[121] the Commission condemned the prevention of parallel trade in video games and their consoles and

[110] *Gosmé/Martell* OJ [1991] L 185/23; see similarly *Newitt/Dunlop Slazenger International* OJ [1992] L 131/32, paras 54–57; *Ford Agricultural* OJ [1993] L 20/1, paras 13–14 (discounts dependent on non-export and penalties for exporting infringed Article 101(1)).

[111] *Konica* OJ [1988] L 78/34; see similarly *Newitt/Dunlop Slazenger International* OJ [1992] L 131/32, para 58.

[112] *German Spectacle Frames* [1985] 1 CMLR 574; *JCB* OJ [2002] L 69/1, paras 174–178.

[113] *Colombian Coffee* OJ [1982] L 360/31 (coffee beans had to be resold only in a roasted form); see similarly the 'green banana' clause in Case 27/76 *United Brands Co v Commission* EU:C:1978:22.

[114] *Bayer Dental* OJ [1990] L 351/46.

[115] *Sandoz* OJ [1987] L 222/28, para 30, upheld on appeal Case C-277/87 *Sandoz Prodotti Farmaceutici SpA v Commission* EU:C:1989:363; see also *Chanelle Veterinary Ltd v Pfizer Ltd (No 2)* [1999] Eu LR 723 (Irish Supreme Court): delisting not attributable to an agreement; see further 'The definition of a vertical agreement', p 667 later in chapter.

[116] *Bayo-n-ox* OJ [1990] L 21/71, upheld on appeal Case T-12/90 EU:T:1991:25, and on further appeal Case C-195/91 P *Bayer v Commission* EU:C:1994:412.

[117] *DaimlerChrysler* OJ [2002] L 257/1, paras 173–175, upheld in part on appeal Case T-325/01 *DaimlerChrysler AG v Commission* EU:T:2005:322.

[118] The Commission also settled some vertical cases informally: see eg *OMV/Gazprom*, Commission Press Release IP/05/195, 17 February 2005.

[119] OJ [2001] L 262/14, annulled on appeal in Case T-208/01 *Volkswagen v Commission* EU:T:2003:326; on further appeal the Court of Justice agreed that the Commission's decision should be annulled, but on different grounds from those of the General Court: Case C-74/04 P *Commission v Volkswagen* EU:C:2006:460.

[120] See *Nathan-Bricolux* OJ [2001] L 54/1; *Opel* OJ [2001] L 59/1, substantially upheld on appeal to the General Court Case T-368/00 *General Motors Nederland BV v Commission* EU:T:2003:460 and on appeal to the Court of Justice Case C-551/03 P *General Motors BV v Commission* EU:C:2006:229; *JCB* OJ [2002] L 69/1, upheld in part on appeal to the General Court Case T-67/01 *JCB Service v Commission* EU:T:2004:3 and on appeal to the Court of Justice Case C-167/04 P *JCB Service v Commission* EU:C:2006:594; *GlaxoSmithKline* OJ [2001] L 302/1: see ch 16 n 109 earlier; *DaimlerChrysler* OJ [2002] L 257/1, partially annulled on appeal Case T-325/01 *DaimlerChrysler AG v Commission* EU:T:2005:322; *Yamaha*, Commission decision of 16 July 2003 (fine of €2.56 million); *Souris/Topps*, Commission decision of 26 May 2004 (fine of €1.59 million).

[121] OJ [2003] L 255/33.

imposed a fine of €167.8 million on the manufacturer and its distributors; this was the largest fine ever to have been imposed by the Commission for an unlawful vertical agreement under Article 101; the General Court slightly reduced two of the fines on appeal[122], but the finding of infringement was upheld. After a period of inactivity in the 2000s, in 2017 the Commission opened investigations into the distribution practices of several manufacturers, specifically to determine whether they were restricting their retailers' ability to sell licensed merchandise outside their contractual territory and online[123].

(iv) Export bans falling outside Article 101(1) or satisfying Article 101(3)

There have been some occasions on which the Court of Justice has concluded that an export ban, in the context of a specific type of agreement, did not have as its object the restriction of competition and could fall outside Article 101[124]. An example is *Javico v Yves St Laurent*[125], where an export ban was imposed on distributors *outside*, rather than within, the EU: obviously such cases do not trigger the same concerns about single market integration in the way that export bans imposed upon EU distributors do[126].

Paragraphs 60 to 64 of the *Vertical guidelines* state that there may be circumstances in which hard-core sales restrictions do not infringe Article 101(1) at all or may in an individual case satisfy Article 101(3):

- a prohibition on resale may fall outside Article 101(1) where there is an objective justification, for example, on grounds of health or safety[127]
- where a distributor makes substantial investments to enter a new market, restrictions of passive sales into its territory by other distributors during the first two years of it operating on the market do not infringe Article 101(1)[128]
- where a new product is genuinely being tested in a limited territory, restrictions of active sales outside that test area will not be caught by Article 101(1) for the period of the testing or introduction of the product[129]
- wholesalers within a selective distribution system may be prevented from actively selling to retailers in other territories, where this is necessary to protect the investment of wholesalers obliged to invest in particular promotional activities within their territories[130]
- a dual pricing policy, under which products intended for export are priced at a premium to equivalent products intended for the domestic market, may satisfy Article 101(3), in particular where higher prices correspond to substantially higher costs for the manufacturer[131].

[122] See Case T-13/03 *Nintendo Co Ltd v Commission* EU:T:2009:131 and Case T-18/03 *CD-Contact Data GmbH v Commission* EU:T:2009:132, upheld on appeal Case C-260/09 P *Activision Blizzard Germany GmbH (formerly CD-Contact Data GmbH) v Commission* EU:C:2011:62 see also Case T-12/03 *Itochu Corp v Commission* EU:T:2009:130, where the appeal was dismissed in its entirety.

[123] See eg Commission Press Release IP/17/1646, 14 June 2017.

[124] See eg Case 27/87 *Erauw-Jacquery Sprl v La Hesbignonne Société Coopérative* EU:C:1988:183.

[125] Case C-306/96 EU:C:1998:173; on *Javico* see ch 3, 'Refinement of the range of agreements within the object box', pp 131–132.

[126] The Commission specifically refers to *Javico* in fn 5 of its *Vertical guidelines*.

[127] *Vertical guidelines*, para 60; see eg *Kathon/Biocide* OJ [1984] C 59/6.

[128] *Vertical guidelines*, para 61. [129] Ibid, para 62. [130] Ibid, para 63.

[131] Ibid, para 64; in such cases the Commission would investigate the extent to which such a pricing policy is likely to limit sales and hinder the distributor in reaching more and different customers.

These paragraphs demonstrate the extent to which the Commission has moved away from a prescriptive, formalistic approach to the application of Article 101 and towards a more economics-oriented approach.

(G) **Application of Article 101(1) to assessment of other types of vertical agreements**

Paragraphs 128 to 229 of the *Guidelines* provide guidance on the application of Article 101 and Regulation 330/2010 to ten types of vertical agreements: single branding, exclusive distribution, exclusive customer allocation, selective distribution, franchising, exclusive supply, up-front access payments, category management agreements, tying and resale price restrictions. Each of these categories will be examined in this section, followed by a brief discussion of parity provisions, also referred to as 'most favoured nation' clauses, that competition authorities have been looking at in recent years.

(i) **Single branding agreements**

Single branding agreements[132] have as their main element that the buyer is obliged or induced to concentrate its orders for a particular product on one supplier[133]. Exclusive purchasing and non-compete obligations are obvious examples of single branding agreements.

(a) Possible detriments to inter-brand competition

The Commission considers that single branding agreements may restrict inter-brand competition; this could happen by foreclosing access on the part of other suppliers to the market, by softening competition, by facilitating collusion and by limiting in-store inter-brand competition[134].

(b) Application of the block exemption to single branding agreements

Regulation 330/2010 applies to single branding agreements, provided that the market share of each of the parties is less than 30%[135] and provided that the duration of the non-compete obligation is five years or less[136]. Where the block exemption applies, it will not be necessary to consider further whether Article 101(1) is infringed or whether Article 101(3) applies on an individual basis; however the *Guidelines* provide guidance for those cases in which 'self-assessment' of agreements is necessary because the block exemption is not applicable[137].

(c) Factors to be considered in determining whether single branding agreements infringe Article 101(1)

Paragraphs 132 to 143 of the *Vertical guidelines* set out the factors that are to be considered in determining whether single branding agreements infringe Article 101(1). The approach taken by the Commission is an economic one, and is consistent with the many judgments of the EU Courts (not referred to in the *Guidelines*) which have held that such agreements must be assessed in their economic context in order to determine whether they have an anti-competitive effect: single branding agreements do not have the *object*

[132] Ibid, paras 129–150. [133] Ibid, para 129. [134] Ibid, para 130.

[135] See 'Article 3: the market share cap', pp 674–677 later in chapter.

[136] See 'Article 5(1)(a): non-compete obligations', pp 684–685 later in chapter on Article 5(1)(a) of Regulation 330/2010; as will be explained there, in certain, limited, circumstances a period of more than five years may be permitted.

[137] *Vertical guidelines*, para 139.

of restricting competition[138]. Judgments of particular note on this issue include *Brasserie de Haecht v Wilkin*[139], *Delimitis v Henninger Bräu*[140], *BPB Industries v Commission*[141] and *Neste Markkinointi v Yötuuli*[142]. The Court of Justice referred to its judgment in *Delimitis* in *Maxima Latvija v Konkurences padome*[143], in which a lease gave the 'anchor tenant' of a commercial development the right to prevent the lessor from renting commercial premises to third parties. The Court held that the clause did not restrict competition by object[144]; rather it was necessary to carry out a 'thorough analysis' of the economic and legal context in which the agreement operates and the specificities of the relevant market to determine whether it could contribute appreciably to foreclosure of access to the market[145].

The *Guidelines* explain that single branding agreements with one supplier may result in anti-competitive foreclosure where they prevent an important competitive constraint from being exercised by existing and future competitors; this may be the case in particular where the supplier is an unavoidable trading partner, for example because its brand is a 'must stock item'. It follows that the market position of the supplier is particularly important for the analysis of single branding agreements under Article 101(1)[146]. The duration of a single branding agreement will also be relevant[147]. The higher the market share and the longer the duration, the more likely it is that there will be a significant foreclosure of the market[148]. Paragraph 133 of the *Vertical guidelines* states that agreements on the part of non-dominant undertakings of less than a year are unlikely to infringe Article 101(1)[149]; between one and five years they may do; and agreements of more than five years would normally be caught. Single branding agreements are more likely to result in anti-competitive foreclosure when entered into by dominant undertakings[150].

Where there are parallel networks of single branding agreements, their cumulative effect may be to foreclose access to the market[151]; this would be unlikely where the largest supplier in the market has a market share of less than 30% and the market share of the five largest suppliers is below 50%[152]. In *Langnese/Schöller*[153] the Commission found that exclusive purchasing agreements concluded by those two suppliers with retailers in respect of 'single-item' ice-cream infringed Article 101(1) and did not satisfy Article 101(3).

138 See eg Case T-65/98 *Van den Bergh Foods Ltd v Commission* EU:T:2003:281, para 80.

139 Case 23/67 EU:C:1967:54.

140 Case C-234/89 EU:C:1991:91; see Lasok 'Assessing the Economic Consequences of Restrictive Agreements: A Comment on the *Delimitis* Case' (1991) 12 ECLR 194; Korah 'The Judgment in *Delimitis*—A Milestone Towards a Realistic Assessment of the Effects of an Agreement—or a Damp Squib' (1993) 8 Tulane European and Civil Law Forum 17.

141 Case T-65/89 EU:T:1993:31, para 66.

142 Case C-214/99 EU:C:2000:679.

143 Case C-345/14 EU:C:2015:784.

144 Ibid, paras 21–23.

145 Ibid, paras 26–31.

146 *Vertical guidelines*, para 132; see similarly *Spices* OJ [1978] L 53/20; *DSD* OJ [2001] L 319/1, paras 121–140, upheld on appeal Case T-289/01 *Duales System Deutschland GmbH v Commission* EU:T:2007:155.

147 *Vertical guidelines*, para 133.

148 Ibid.

149 See Case C-214/99 *Neste Markkinointi Oy v Yötuuli* EU:C:2000:679, where the Court of Justice concluded that exclusive purchasing agreements for petrol of not more than one year's duration did not infringe Article 101(1); see also Case E-7/01 *Hegelstad Eiendomsselskap Arvid B Hegelstad v Hydro Texaco AS* [2003] 4 CMLR 236.

150 See ch 17, 'Is the tie capable of having an anti-competitive effect?', pp 711–712.

151 *Vertical guidelines*, para 134.

152 Ibid, para 135.

153 OJ [1993] L 183/19, substantially upheld on appeal Cases T-7/93 and T-9/93 *Langnese-Iglo GmbH etc v Commission* EU:T:1995:98, and EU:T:1995:99 and on further appeal Case C-279/95 P EU:C:1998:447; see also the Commission's decision on Article 101 in *Van den Bergh Foods Ltd* OJ [1998] L 246/1, upheld on appeal Case T-65/98 *Van den Bergh Foods Ltd v Commission* EU:T:2003:281: the same dispute was the subject of an Article 267 reference in Case C-344/98 *Masterfoods Ltd v HB Ice Cream Ltd* EU:C:2000:689.

Other relevant factors to the application of Article 101(1) are the level of entry barriers[154], countervailing power[155] and the level of trade affected[156].

(d) The application of Article 101(3)

Article 101(3) issues are discussed in paragraphs 144 to 148 of the *Vertical guidelines*: this is considered later[157].

(ii) **Exclusive distribution agreements**

A supplier may grant exclusive distribution rights[158] to a distributor for a particular territory: for example it might appoint X as the exclusive distributor for France and Y as the exclusive distributor for Germany. The supplier may also agree that it will not sell its products directly into the territories granted to X and Y.

(a) Possible detriments to intra-brand competition and to market integration

The Commission's main concern in relation to exclusive distribution agreements is that intra-brand competition will be reduced and that the market will be partitioned[159]. A separate concern arises when most or all suppliers in a particular market adopt exclusive distribution agreements since this may soften competition and facilitate collusion, both at the suppliers' and the distributors' level of the market; this would entail harm to inter-brand competition. The Commission also notes that exclusive distribution may lead to foreclosure of other distributors and thereby reduce competition at that level.

(b) Application of the block exemption to exclusive distribution agreements

Regulation 330/2010 applies to exclusive distribution agreements, provided that the market share of the supplier and the buyer is less than 30% and that there are no 'hard-core' restrictions[160]. In particular there should be no restrictions on passive sales (sales in response to unsolicited orders)[161] to other territories; where there is a combination of exclusive distribution and selective distribution, there must be no restrictions even of active sales by retailers to end users[162], and there must be no restrictions on sales between authorised distributors[163]. The *Guidelines* provide guidance for those cases in which individual assessment of agreements is necessary because the block exemption is not applicable[164].

(c) Factors to be considered in determining whether exclusive distribution agreements infringe Article 101(1)

The Commission sets out the factors that are to be considered in determining whether Article 101(1) is infringed in paragraphs 153 to 160 of the *Vertical guidelines*. There is no reference to the judgment of the Court of Justice in *Société Technique Minière v Maschinenbau Ulm*[165], where the Court held that an exclusive distribution agreement does not have as its object the restriction of competition, but must be considered in its market context to determine whether it has this effect. The reason that the Court of Justice took a stricter line in *Consten and Grundig v Commission*[166] was that in that case the distributor was given absolute territorial protection against parallel imports[167]: because

154 *Langnese/Schöller* (ch 16 n 153), para 136.
155 Ibid, para 137.
156 Ibid, paras 138–141.
157 See 'Vertical Agreements: Individual Application of Article 101(3)', pp 687–688 later in chapter.
158 *Vertical guidelines*, paras 151–167.
159 Ibid, para 151.
160 On Article 4 of Regulation 330/10 see 'Article 4: hard-core restrictions', pp 677–684 later in chapter.
161 Regulation 330/2010, Article 4(b).
162 Ibid, Article 4(c); see also *Vertical guidelines*, para 152.
163 Regulation 330/2010, Article 4(d).
164 *Vertical guidelines*, para 152.
165 Case 56/65 EU:C:1966:38.
166 Cases 56 and 58/64 EU:C:1966:41.
167 See '*Consten and Grundig v Commission*', pp 638–639 earlier in this chapter.

of the single market imperative in EU competition law, absolute territorial protection almost always infringes Article 101(1) and only rarely benefits from Article 101(3)[168]. It is important however to bear in mind that an exclusive distribution agreement may not infringe Article 101(1) at all where there is not the additional element of absolute territorial protection and where it provides a distributor with an incentive to promote a product effectively.

As far as Article 101(1) is concerned the Commission states that the market position of the supplier and its competitors is of 'major importance', since the loss of intra-brand competition is problematic only if inter-brand competition is limited[169]. The stronger the position of the supplier, the more serious is the loss of intra-brand competition[170]. In *Audible/Apple*[171] the supplier, a subsidiary of Amazon and the world's largest producer of downloadable audiobooks and other spoken-word content, had agreed to distribute its audiobooks exclusively through Apple's iTunes[172]. The Commission and the Bundeskartellamt investigated the agreement, but the case was closed after the parties agreed to terminate the exclusivity provisions. Where there are strong competitors, the restriction of intra-brand competition will generally be outweighed by inter-brand competition[173], although there may be a risk of collusion and/or softening of competition where the number of competitors is 'rather small'[174]. The *Guidelines* also discuss the possibility of exclusive distribution agreements having a foreclosure effect, which is considered unlikely unless the exclusive distributor has buyer power in the downstream market[175]; the *Guidelines* also discuss the relevance of the maturity of the market[176] and of the level of trade affected[177].

(d) The application of Article 101(3)

Article 101(3) issues are discussed in paragraphs 161 to 164 of the *Vertical guidelines*; this is considered later[178].

(iii) **Exclusive customer allocation agreements**

Exclusive customer allocation[179] refers to the situation in which a supplier agrees to sell its products to a distributor who will resell only to a particular class of customers. Exclusive customer allocation is discussed in paragraphs 168 to 173 of the *Vertical guidelines*, and is treated in much the same way as exclusive distribution, although the Commission makes a few specific comments on exclusivity as to customers[180]; in particular it says that the allocation of final consumers is unlikely to satisfy the criteria of Article 101(3)[181].

(iv) **Selective distribution agreements**

Selective distribution agreements[182] are often deployed by producers of branded products. The producer establishes a system in which the products can be bought and resold only by authorised distributors and retailers. Non-authorised dealers will not be able to

[168] See 'Export bans falling outside Article 101(1) or satisfying Article 101(3)', pp 650–651 earlier in chapter.

[169] *Vertical guidelines*, para 153. [170] Ibid, para 153.

[171] Commission Press Release IP/17/97, 19 January 2017.

[172] Apple had also agreed to source audiobooks exclusively from Audible; this provision was also dropped.

[173] *Vertical guidelines*, para 154. [174] Ibid, para 154. [175] Ibid, paras 155 and 156.

[176] Ibid, para 158. [177] Ibid, paras 159 and 160.

[178] See 'Vertical Agreements: Individual Application of Article 101(3)', pp 687–688 later in chapter.

[179] *Vertical guidelines*, paras 168–173. [180] Ibid, paras 169–172. [181] Ibid, para 172.

[182] Ibid, paras 174–188; see generally Monti 'Restraints on Selective Distribution Agreements' (2013) 36 World Competition 489.

obtain the products, and the authorised dealers will be told that they can resell only to other members of the system or to the final consumer[183]. The *Vertical guidelines* state that selective distribution systems may restrict intra-brand competition, may foreclose access to the market, and may soften competition and/or facilitate collusion between suppliers or buyers[184]. In determining the application of Article 101 to selective distribution agreements, a distinction must be made between a 'purely qualitative' system and a 'quantitative' system; a purely qualitative selective distribution system will not infringe Article 101(1) at all even though, by its very nature, it may involve the restrictions just mentioned.

(a) Purely qualitative selective distribution systems

In *Metro SB-Großmärkte GmbH v Commission*[185] and in *NV L'Oréal v PVBA De Nieuwe AMCK*[186] the Court of Justice established three criteria that must be satisfied for a selective distribution system to be treated as purely qualitative and therefore outside Article 101(1); these criteria are cumulative:

- the product must be of a type that justifies a producer restricting the type of outlets by which they may be resold
- the criteria by which a supplier selects retail outlets through which its products are resold must be purely qualitative in nature, laid down uniformly for all potential retailers and applied in a non-discriminatory manner and
- any restrictions that are imposed on authorised distributors must go no further than is objectively necessary to protect the quality of the product in question.

The EU Courts have frequently reaffirmed the position[187]. Each criterion will be considered in turn.

First, **the product must justify selective distribution**, which suppresses price competition in favour of non-price competition. For example, products that are technically complex may necessitate specialist sales staff and a suitable after-sales service. Examples of such products are cars[188], cameras[189], electronic equipment such as hi-fis[190], consumer durables[191], clocks and watches[192] and computers[193]. It is possible that a product that originally benefited from the *Metro* doctrine may cease to do so where it becomes sufficiently well understood that selective distribution is no longer justifiable. Selective distribution may also be appropriate where it enables a producer to protect the brand image of its products and thereby strengthen inter-brand competition. In this category may be placed

183 *Vertical guidelines*, para 174. 184 Ibid, para 175. 185 Case 26/76 EU:C:1977:167, para 20.

186 Case 31/80 *L'Oréal NV v de Nieuwe AMCK* EU:C:1980:289, para 16.

187 See eg Case 99/79 *Lancôme SA v Etos BV* EU:C:1980:193, paras 20–26; Case 126/80 *Maria Salonia v Giorgio Poidomani* EU:C:1981:136; Case 210/81 *Demo-Studio Schmidt v Commission* EU:C:1983:277; Case 107/82 *AEG-Telefunken v Commission* EU:C:1983:293; Case 75/84 *Metro v Commission (No 2)* EU:C:1986:399; Case C-439/09 *Pierre Fabre Dermo-Cosmétique SAS* EU:C:2011:649, paras 40–41; Case C-230/16 *Coty* EU:C:2017:941, para 24.

188 *BMW* OJ [1975] L 29/1; note that there is a specific block exemption for agreements relating to motor vehicle aftermarkets: see 'Regulation 461/2010 on Motor Vehicle Distribution', pp 689–691 later in chapter.

189 *Kodak* JO [1970] L 147/24. 190 *Grundig* OJ [1985] L 223/1 and again OJ [1994] L 20/15.

191 Case 107/82 *AEG-Telefunken v Commission* EU:C:1983:293; it was only when AEG's system was applied in a discriminatory way that it came within Article 101(1).

192 *Omega Watches* JO [1970] L 242/22; *Junghans* OJ [1977] L 30/10; note however that the Court of Justice in Case 31/85 *ETA Fabriques d'Ebauches SA v DK Investment SA* EU:C:1985:494, doubted that mass-produced Swatch watches would qualify for selective distribution under the *Metro* doctrine: ibid, para 16.

193 *IBM Personal Computers* OJ [1984] L 118/24.

perfumes and luxury cosmetic products[194], ceramic tableware[195] and gold and silver jewellery[196]. In *Coty*[197] the Court of Justice confirmed that the 'allure of luxury' is a feature of a product that can justify selective distribution[198]. Separately, newspapers, the special characteristic of which is their extremely short shelf-life, may necessitate careful, and thus selective, distribution[199]. The Commission has doubted whether plumbing fittings qualify for such treatment[200].

The second requirement for a system to fall outside Article 101(1) is that **qualitative criteria are applied in a uniform and non-discriminatory manner to all potential distributors**. Where this is the case, any dealer that satisfies the qualitative criteria should be able to join the system and distribute the product in question: there is no quantitative restriction on the number of dealers in the system. It may be helpful to identify examples of qualitative criteria[201]:

- a requirement that a producer's goods be sold only to retail outlets which employ suitably trained staff
- a requirement for resellers to have suitable premises in an appropriate area
- use of a suitable shop name consistent with the status of the brand
- an obligation to provide a proper after-sales service
- a restriction on sales to non-authorised distributors and retailers
- a restriction not to advertise products at 'cash-and-carry prices'.

A problem is that it is not always obvious whether a particular requirement is 'qualitative' or not. Criteria that do not relate to the technical proficiency of outlets[202] but extend to such matters as the holding of minimum stocks, stocking the complete range of products, the achievement of a minimum turnover or a minimum percentage of turnover[203] in the products in question and the promotion of products have sometimes been treated as quantitative, although they have often been found to satisfy the criteria of Article 101(3)[204].

The third requirement to fall outside Article 101(1) is **proportionality**: any restrictions that are imposed on appointed distributors must go no further than is objectively necessary to protect the quality of the product in question[205]. In *Hasselblad*[206] objection was taken by the Commission to provisions that enabled the producer to exercise supervision of the

[194] Case 99/79 *Lancôme SA etc v Etos BV* EU:C:1980:193; Case T-19/92 *Groupement d'Achat Édouard Leclerc v Commission* EU:T:1996:190, paras 113–123; Case T-88/92 *Groupement d'Achat Édouard Leclerc v Commission* EU:T:1996:192, paras 105–117.

[195] *Villeroy & Boch* OJ [1985] L 376/15.

[196] *Murat* OJ [1983] L 348/20.

[197] Case C-230/16 EU:C:2017:941.

[198] Ibid, para 25.

[199] See eg Case 126/80 *Maria Salonia v Giorgio Poidomani* EU:C:1981:136; Case 243/83 *Binon v Agence et Messageries de la Presse* EU:C:1985:284; Commission's Notice *Agence et Messageries de la Presse* OJ [1987] C 164/2; Commission's XXIXth *Report on Competition Policy* (1999), pp 161–162.

[200] *Grohe* OJ [1985] L 19/17; *Ideal Standard* OJ [1985] L 20/38.

[201] See eg *Villeroy & Boch* OJ [1985] L 376/15; cf *Grundig* OJ [1985] L 233/1.

[202] *Vichy* OJ [1991] L 75/57, upheld on appeal Case T-19/91 EU:T:1992:28 (restriction on the sale of Vichy products except to officially appointed pharmacists was quantitative).

[203] *Yves St Laurent* OJ [1992] L 12/24, mostly upheld on appeal Case T-19/92 *Groupement d'Achat Édouard Leclerc v Commission* EU:T:1996:190, paras 148–155; Case T-88/92 *Groupement d'Achat Édouard Leclerc v Commission* EU:T:1996:192, paras 141–148.

[204] See eg *Parfums Givenchy* OJ [1992] L 236/11; *Grundig* OJ [1994] L 20/15; *Sony Pan-European Dealer Agreement (PEDA)*, Commission's XXVth *Report on Competition Policy* (1995), pp 135–136.

[205] In the UK the CMA carried out a detailed analysis of the proportionality of a ban on internet sales within a selective distribution system for golf clubs: *Ping*, CMA decision of 24 August 2017, on appeal Case 1279/1/12/17 *Ping Europe Ltd v CMA*, not yet decided.

[206] OJ [1982] L 161/18; see also *Grohe* OJ [1985] L 19/17; *Ideal Standard* OJ [1985] L 20/38.

advertising of its distributors and retailers, as this would mean that control could be exercised over advertisements indicating cuts in prices. In *AEG-Telefunken v Commission*[207] the Court of Justice made clear that restrictions would not be permitted simply in order to guarantee dealers a minimum profit margin.

In relation to e-commerce, the Court of Justice held in *Pierre Fabre*[208] that a restriction on distributors that prevented them entirely from selling non-prescription cosmetic products online could not be justified by the need to provide individual advice to the customer or by the protection of brand image. However in *Coty*[209] the distributors were allowed to sell online through their own websites, but they were restricted from selling through third party marketplaces such as Amazon and eBay. The Court held that such a restriction would fall outside Article 101(1) provided that it was a proportionate way of preserving the luxury image of the products in question[210].

(b) Selective distribution systems that are not purely qualitative

Where a selective distribution system is not purely qualitative in the sense of the *Metro* doctrine it may be caught by Article 101(1). In *AEG-Telefunken v Commission*[211] the Court of Justice said that a selective distribution system is restrictive of competition by object unless it operates in accordance with the *Metro* doctrine[212]. The Court did not actually use the term 'object' in *AEG*, but this was the interpretation that it adopted in its judgment in *Pierre Fabre*[213].

In determining whether a selective distribution system that is not purely qualitative infringes Article 101(1) the Commission will look at the market position of the supplier and its competitors, since the loss of intra-brand competition is problematic only where inter-brand competition is weak[214]. A further issue is whether, in a particular market, there is a number of selective distribution systems in operation: where this is the case the Commission is anxious that there may be a lack of intra-brand competition, a foreclosure of certain types of distributors and retailers (for example those that sell only online) and that collusion may be facilitated[215]. In *Metro v Commission (No 2)*[216] the Court of Justice held that where, in a particular market, the existence of a number of selective distribution systems leaves no room for other methods of distribution or results in a rigidity in price structure which is not balanced by other types of competition, Article 101(1) may apply after all[217].

(c) Application of the block exemption to selective distribution systems

Selective distribution agreements may benefit from the block exemption conferred by Regulation 330/2010. To do so the market share held by each of the parties must be below 30%[218], and the requirements of Articles 4(a), 4(c), 4(d) and 5(c)[219] must be respected. Where a selective distribution system benefits from the block exemption, but there are minimal efficiency-enhancing effects, for example because the product is not suitable for this form of distribution, the block exemption could be withdrawn where appreciable

[207] Case 107/82 EU:C:1983:293, para 42. [208] Case C-439/09 EU:C:2011:649, paras 42–46.

[209] Case C-230/16 EU:C:2017:941. [210] Ibid, para 58. [211] Case 107/82 EU:C:1983:293, para 34.

[212] On the *Metro* doctrine see 'Purely qualitative selective distribution systems', pp 655–657 earlier in chapter.

[213] Case C-439/09 EU:C:2011:649, para 39. [214] *Vertical guidelines*, para 177.

[215] Ibid, para 178. [216] Case 75/84 EU:C:1986:399.

[217] Ibid, paras 41 and 42; a similar argument was considered, but rejected, in Case T-19/92 *Groupement d'Achat Édouard Leclerc v Commission* EU:T:1996:190, paras 178–192 and in Case T-88/92 *Groupement d'Achat Édouard Leclerc v Commission* EU:T:1996:192, paras 170–184.

[218] See 'Article 3: the market share cap', pp 674–677 later in chapter.

[219] See *Vertical guidelines*, para 182; these provisions are explained at 'Article 4: hard-core restrictions', pp 677–684 later in chapter.

anti-competitive effects occur[220]. The Commission has indicated that the benefit of the block exemption may be withdrawn from selective distribution systems where there is a 'cumulative effect' problem; however it says that such a problem is unlikely to arise when the share of the market covered by selective distribution is below 50%, or where this figure is exceeded but the aggregate market share of the five largest suppliers is below 50%[221]. An individual supplier with a market share of less than 5% is unlikely to be considered as making a contribution to the cumulative effect[222].

In *Yamaha*[223] the Commission imposed a fine of €2.56 million on Yamaha for operating a selective distribution system in a way that led to the partitioning of the single market and to the fixing of resale prices[224]. Yamaha's selective distribution system failed to benefit from the block exemption partly because in several markets its market share exceeded 30%[225] and partly because there were violations of Article 4(a), (b) and (d)[226]. In *Pierre Fabre*[227] the Court of Justice held that a clause that *de facto* entirely prohibited internet selling by distributors in a selective distribution agreement causes the agreement to lose the benefit of the block exemption under Article 4(c)[228]. However in *Coty*[229] the Court of Justice concluded that a clause preventing a retailer from selling online via a third party platform, while leaving it free to sell through its own website, did not violate Article 4(b) or 4(c) of Regulation 330/2010[230].

In some systems of domestic law a selective distribution system is binding on unauthorised third parties, who can be sued for unfair competition if they obtain and attempt to sell the products; in German law there is a requirement on the producer which uses such a system to ensure that it is 'impervious', that is to say that its products are kept within the system; however the imperviousness ('Lückenlosigkeit') of the system is not a requirement for its validity under EU competition law[231].

(d) The application of Article 101(3)

Selective distribution agreements may satisfy Article 101(3) on an individual basis[232]. In several cases the Commission has found various aspects of selective distribution not to infringe Article 101(1), but applied Article 101(3) to other aspects[233]. In other cases the Commission has permitted quantitative restrictions of outlets under Article 101(3) where it considered that this improved distribution of goods[234].

(v) Franchising agreements

A franchise agreement[235] enables a franchisee to operate as an independent business whilst using the name and know-how of the franchisor. The transfer of intellectual

220 *Vertical guidelines*, para 176.

221 Ibid, paras 75 and 179.

222 Ibid, para 179, final sentence; see also the Commission's *Notice on Agreements of Minor Importance* OJ [2014] C 291/1, para 10.

223 Commission decision of 16 July 2003.

224 Ibid, paras 88–147.

225 Ibid, para 168.

226 Ibid, paras 169–174.

227 Case C-439/09 EU:C:2011:649.

228 Ibid, paras 57–59.

229 Cases C-230/16 EU:C:2017:941.

230 Ibid, para 69; for comment see 'EU competition rules and marketplace bans: Where do we stand after the Coty judgment?' Competition Policy Brief 1/2018, available at www.ec.europa.eu.

231 Case C-376/92 *Metro-SB-Großmärkte GmbH v Cartier* EU:C:1994:5, para 28; see also Case C-41/96 *VAG-Händlerbeirat eV v SYD-Consult* EU:C:1997:283.

232 *Vertical guidelines*, paras 185–186; see further 'Vertical Agreements: Individual Application of Article 101(3)', pp 687–688 later in chapter.

233 See eg *Kodak* JO [1970] L 147/24; *Omega* JO [1970] L 242/22; *SABA* OJ [1976] L 28/19, upheld on appeal Case 26/76 *Metro v Commission (No 1)* EU:C:1977:167.

234 See eg *Yves Saint Laurent* OJ [1992] L 12/24; *Parfums Givenchy* OJ [1992] L 236/11, appeal held to be inadmissible in Case T-87/92 *Kruidvat v Commission* EU:T:1996:191, upheld on further appeal Case C-70/97 P EU:C:1998:545.

235 *Vertical guidelines*, paras 189–191.

property rights from the franchisor to the franchisee is the feature of franchises that distinguishes them from other distribution systems. In a franchise, the franchisee pays a fee to the franchisor for the right to use the know-how, trade marks, designs, logos and other intellectual property rights ('IPRs') of the franchisor. The franchisee also accepts obligations to preserve the integrity of its business format.

(a) *Pronuptia v Schillgalis*

The application to franchising agreements of Article 101 was explored by the Court of Justice in *Pronuptia de Paris v Schillgalis*[236]. Mrs Schillgalis, the franchisee for Hamburg, Oldenburg and Hanover, was in dispute with Pronuptia, the franchisor, over her royalty payments and in the course of litigation pleaded that the agreement was void as it contravened Article 101. The Court of Justice held that certain restrictions in a franchise agreement do not infringe Article 101(1):

- restrictions intended to maintain a common business format, since it is important that all franchised outlets should achieve the same standard
- restrictions to protect the franchisor's intellectual property
- the recommendation of resale prices
- territorial exclusivity granted to a franchisee where the trade mark is not well-known and without absolute territorial protection.

The Court concluded that restrictions that divided the market territorially or that imposed minimum resale price maintenance fell within Article 101(1), although they might satisfy Article 101(3) in certain circumstances[237].

(b) *Application of the block exemption to franchising*

Regulation 330/2010 will apply to franchising agreements, provided that the market share of each of the parties is below 30% and that there are no Article 4 hard-core restrictions. Paragraph 190 of the *Vertical guidelines* refers to paragraphs 24 to 46, which deal specifically with the meaning of vertical agreements in the block exemption and the extent to which the licensing of IPRs, including franchise agreements, are covered by it[238].

(vi) **Exclusive supply agreements**

Exclusive supply agreements[239] have as their main element that the supplier is obliged or induced to sell the contract products only to one buyer, in general or for a particular use[240]. Exclusive supply agreements may benefit from the block exemption, provided that the supplier's and the buyer's market shares satisfy the 30% cap[241]. Paragraphs 194 to 199 discuss the application of Article 101(1) to exclusive supply agreements that are not covered by the block exemption; paragraphs 200 to 201 consider the application of Article 101(3)[242]. In considering whether Article 101(1) applies to such agreements the buyer's market share in its downstream market will be of particular importance: the greater its

[236] Case 161/84 EU:C:1986:41; see Venit '*Pronuptia*: Ancillary Restraints or Unholy Alliances' (1986) 11 EL Rev 213.

[237] See *Vertical guidelines*, para 47.

[238] On Article 2(3) of Regulation 330/2010 see 'Article 2(3) is applicable only where there is a vertical agreement', pp 671–673 later in chapter.

[239] *Vertical guidelines*, paras 192–202.

[240] Ibid, para 192; see *Audible/Apple*, Commission Press Release IP/17/97, 19 January 2017.

[241] *Vertical guidelines*, para 193.

[242] See 'Vertical Agreements: Individual Application of Article 101(3)', pp 687–688 later in chapter.

market share there, the more likely there is to be an anti-competitive effect[243]; the duration of the supply obligation will also be of relevance[244]. Other matters, such as entry barriers[245], the countervailing power of suppliers[246] and the level of trade affected[247], are also discussed.

(vii) Up-front access payments

Up-front access payments[248] are fees paid by a supplier to a buyer to remunerate the latter for services supplied: for example 'slotting allowances' may be paid to a supermarket in return for access to shelf space, and pay-to-stay fees may be paid to ensure the continued presence of a product on the shelf for a longer period. Paragraph 203 of the *Guidelines* explains that, where the supplier's and buyer's market shares do not exceed 30%, up-front access payments are block exempted. The *Guidelines* then explain the extent to which such payments might infringe Article 101(1), either by foreclosure of the downstream[249] or the upstream[250] market or by the facilitation of collusion[251]; the possibility that up-front access payments might lead to efficiencies is discussed in paragraphs 207 and 208, for example by improving the use of shelf space or by ensuring that the supplier shares the risk that the introduction of a new product might fail.

(viii) Category management agreements

A category management agreement[252] is an agreement between a supplier and a distributor whereby the latter entrusts the supplier with the marketing of a category of products, not only the marketing of the supplier's own products: for example a supplier might be appointed the 'category captain' for breakfast cereals or for non-alcoholic beverages within a chain of supermarkets. Paragraph 209 states that such agreements will benefit from the block exemption where both parties' market shares do not exceed 30%. Paragraph 210 acknowledges that in most cases category management agreements do not raise competition concerns; however the possibility that they might have a foreclosure effect upstream in the market is noted in that paragraph[253], and the Commission suggests that any analysis should be conducted as it would be in the case of single branding agreements[254]. The possibility that category management might facilitate collusion between distributors or between suppliers is discussed in paragraphs 211 and 212 respectively, and their scope for improving efficiency in paragraph 213.

(ix) Tying agreements

A tying agreement[255] arises where a supplier makes the supply of one product (the 'tying product') conditional upon the buyer also buying a separate product (the 'tied product'). Tying may constitute an abuse of a dominant position contrary to Article 102[256]; however, a vertical agreement imposing a tie may also infringe Article 101(1) where it has a 'single branding' effect in relation to the tied product[257]. Tying agreements benefit from the block

[243] *Vertical guidelines*, para 194.

[244] Ibid, para 195; the Commission considers that exclusive supply agreements of more than five years are unlikely to fulfil the criteria of Article 101(3).

[245] Ibid, para 197. [246] Ibid, para 198. [247] Ibid, para 199. [248] Ibid, paras 203–208.

[249] Ibid, para 204. [250] Ibid, para 205. [251] Ibid, para 206. [252] Ibid, paras 209–213.

[253] A Dutch court cited para 210 of the *Guidelines* in *Nestlé v Mars*, judgment of 7 August 2013, finding that a category management agreement between Mars and petrol stations restricted competition, available at www.rechtspraak.nl.

[254] *Vertical guidelines*, paras 132 to 141; see 'Single branding agreements', pp 651–653 earlier in chapter.

[255] *Vertical guidelines*, paras 214–222. [256] See ch 17, 'Tying', pp 705–713.

[257] *Vertical guidelines*, para 214.

exemption when the market share of the supplier, on the markets both for the tying and for the tied products, and the market share of the buyer on the relevant upstream markets are below the 30% cap[258]. Where the market share threshold is exceeded paragraphs 219 to 221 discuss the application of Article 101(1) to tying agreements: the market position of the supplier is the most important issue[259]; the position of its competitors and the entry barriers to the market for the tying product must also be considered[260]. Tying is less likely to be problematic where customers possess significant buyer power[261]. Paragraph 222 considers the possibility of tying practices benefiting from the exception conferred by Article 101(3)[262].

(x) **Pricing restrictions**

(a) Minimum and fixed resale prices infringe Article 101(1)

The imposition upon distributors and retailers of minimum or fixed resale prices[263] will be held to infringe Article 101(1): such agreements are considered to have as their object the restriction of competition[264]. The Commission has condemned resale price maintenance on various occasions[265], as have various NCAs[266]. Competition authorities are also committed to enforcement in relation to pricing restrictions in online commerce[267]. Horizontal agreements to impose resale price maintenance will also be caught[268]. Furthermore this practice amounts to a hard-core restriction contrary to Article 4(a) of the block exemption[269]; paragraph 48 of the *Guidelines* considers a range of practices that might be considered as having as their 'direct or indirect object', to use the words of Article 4, the imposition of minimum or fixed resale prices[270].

258 Ibid, para 218. 259 Ibid, para 219. 260 Ibid, para 220. 261 Ibid, para 221.

262 See 'Vertical Agreements: Individual Application of Article 101(3)', pp 687–688 later in chapter.

263 *Vertical guidelines*, paras 223–229.

264 See ch 3, 'Price fixing and exchanges of information in relation to future prices', p 128; in the US the maintenance of minimum resale prices was for many years illegal *per se* as a result of the Supreme Court decision in *Dr Miles Medical Co v John D Park & Sons Co* 220 US 373 (1911); however in *Leegin Creative Leather Products, Inc v PSKS, Inc* 551 US 877 (2007) the Supreme Court explicitly overruled *Dr Miles*, holding that resale price maintenance should be subject to a rule of reason standard henceforth; for comment see Klein 'Competitive Resale Price Maintenance in the Absence of Free Riding' (2009) 76 Antitrust LJ 431 and Brunell 'Overruling *Dr Miles*: The Supreme Trade Commission In Action' (2007) 52 Antitrust Bulletin 475.

265 See eg *Deutsche Phillips* OJ [1973] L 293/40; *Gerofabriek* OJ [1977] L 16/8; *Hennessey/Henkel* OJ [1980] L 383/11 where the Commission rejected the argument that setting resale prices was justified for the protection of the product's brand image; *Novalliance/Systemform* OJ [1997] L 47/11; *Nathan-Bricolux* OJ [2001] L 54/1, paras 86–90; *Volkswagen II* OJ [2001] L 262/14, annulled on appeal for lack of evidence of an agreement between Volkswagen and its dealers in Case T-208/01 *Volkswagen v Commission* EU:T:2003:326, upheld on appeal, but on different grounds: Case C-74/04 P *Commission v Volkswagen AG* EU:C:2006:460; for discussion see ch 3, 'Cases following *Bayer*', pp 112–113; *JCB* OJ [2002] L 69/1, paras 168–173; *CD prices*, Commission Press Release IP/01/1212, 17 August 2001; *Yamaha*, Commission decision of 16 July 2003.

266 See eg Case 24 Kt 33/15 *Samsung Electronics Austria GmbH*, judgment of Austrian Cartel Court of 9 September 2015; *Lego*, German NCA decision of 12 January 2016; *AB InBev*, German NCA decision of 18 December 2016; *ITW Ltd*, UK NCA decision of 24 May 2016.

267 See eg Commission Press Release IP/17/201, 2 February 2017: the Commission has commenced an investigation into whether any of Asus, Denon & Marantz, Philips and Pioneer restricted the ability of online retailers to set their own prices; on the position in the UK see 'Pricing restrictions', pp 694–695 later in chapter.

268 See eg Cases 43/82 *VBBB and VBVB v Commission* EU:C:1984:9.

269 See 'Article 4(a): resale price maintenance', pp 678–679 later in chapter; see generally Gippini-Fournier 'Resale Price Maintenance in the EU: in *statu quo ante bellum*?' [2009] Fordham Corporate Law Institute (ed Hawk), pp 515–549.

270 See 'Article 4(a): resale price maintenance', pp 678–679 later in chapter on para 47 of the *Vertical guidelines*.

(b) Minimum and fixed prices under Article 101(3)

Paragraph 225 of the *Vertical guidelines* acknowledges that resale price maintenance might lead to efficiencies in the sense of Article 101(3)[271]. Paragraph 225 gives, as a 'most notable' example, resale price maintenance imposed by a manufacturer that introduces a new product to the market, where this induces the distributor to increase its sales efforts for the new product, thereby expanding overall demand and making the launch a success, itself a benefit to consumers[272]. On one occasion the Commission appeared to be sympathetic to the idea that a newspaper publisher should be allowed to impose a cover price on newspapers[273]. It should be recalled that an agreement that restricts competition by object may be legal, provided that it satisfies the criteria of Article 101(3)[274], and that the Commission has set out, in its *Article 101(3) Guidelines*[275], the type of evidence that is required to apply that provision.

(c) Recommended and maximum resale prices

Paragraphs 226 to 229 of the *Vertical guidelines* consider the extent to which it is lawful to recommend a resale price to a distributor or retailer or to impose a *maximum* rather than a minimum price[276]. Article 4(a) of the block exemption provides that these practices are not 'hard-core' restrictions, 'provided that they do not amount to a fixed or minimum sale price as a result of pressure from, or incentives offered by, any of the parties'[277]. The Court of Justice has said that a maximum resale price will amount to a fixed or minimum price if it is not 'genuinely possible for the reseller to lower that sale price'[278]. Agreements containing recommendations or maximum prices would therefore be block exempted, provided that the market share of each of the parties does not exceed the cap of 30%[279]. Where the block exemption is not applicable the *Guidelines* state that the Commission will consider whether recommended or maximum prices might work 'as a focal point for the resellers and might be followed by most or all of them'[280]; it will also examine whether these practices could soften competition or facilitate collusion between suppliers[281].

271 On the possible efficiencies of RPM see Peeperkorn 'Resale Price Maintenance and Its Alleged Efficiencies' (2008) European Competition Journal 201; Jones 'Resale Price Maintenance: A Debate About Competition Policy in Europe' (2009) European Competition Journal 425; Gyselen 'Resale Price Maintenance: Growing Convergence between the US and the EC in Sight?' in Bulterman et al (eds) *Views of European Law from the Mountain* (Kluwer, 2009); the series of essays in [2010] CPI Antitrust Chronicle, available at www.competitionpolicyinternational.com; Lao 'Free Riding: An Overstated, and Unconvincing, Explanation for Resale Price Maintenance' in Pitofsky (ed) *How the Chicago School Overshot the Mark* (Oxford University Press, 2008), pp 196–232.

272 Note the Australian Competition and Consumer Commission decision of 5 December 2014 allowing Tooltechnic Systems to impose minimum retail prices for power tools in order to address concerns about free-riding, available at www.accc.gov.au.

273 See the Commission's XXIXth *Report on Competition Policy* (1999), pp 161–162 (although the Commission never revealed publicly what conclusion it reached on the matter); the Commission's Notice in *Agence et Messageries de la Presse* OJ [1987] C 164/2 had suggested that it might countenance resale price maintenance for newspapers and periodicals; see also Case 243/85 *Binon & Cie v SA Agence et Messageries de la Presse* EU:C:1985:284, para 46.

274 See ch 4, 'Any type of agreement can be defended under Article 101(3)', pp 159–161.

275 OJ [2004] C 101/97.

276 In *Albrecht v Herald Co* 390 US 145 (1968) the US Supreme Court condemned *per se* the imposition of maximum resale prices; however it overruled itself in *State Oil v Khan*, substituting a rule of reason approach to this particular phenomenon: 522 US 3 (1997); see the series of articles in (1997–98) 66 Antitrust LJ 531, 537 and 567.

277 See also recital 10 of Regulation 330/2010.

278 Case C-279/06 *CEPSA Estaciones de Servicio SA v LV Tobar e Hijos SL* EU:C:2008:485, para 71; the Court of Justice considered the application of Article 4(a) of the old block exemption, Regulation 2790/99, which is in the same terms as its successor.

279 *Vertical guidelines*, para 226.

280 Ibid, para 227.

281 Ibid, para 227.

The market power of the supplier is an important factor to be taken into consideration[282]; the stronger its power over the market, the greater the risk that a maximum or recommended price will lead to uniform pricing[283]. Paragraph 229 considers the possible application of Article 101(3) to maximum or recommended prices. In *Repsol* the Commission accepted commitments from Repsol to modify its long-term exclusive supply agreements with service stations selling its fuel, but which explicitly allowed it to impose maximum or recommended prices[284].

(xi) Parity provisions

In recent years competition authorities have taken an increasing interest in 'parity provisions', also referred to as 'most favoured nation' clauses or, as a shorthand, 'MFNs'. As the words suggest, the idea of a nation being given favourable treatment is one that is used in the world of international trade, where nation A agrees that it will treat the goods of nation B as, or more, favourably than those of other nations. The same language has often been used in commercial relationships between undertakings, where company A agrees with company B that it will offer terms as favourable, or no less favourable, than those offered to company C. However it is slightly odd to equate company B with a nation, and for this reason the expression 'parity provision' is a more appropriate one in the private sphere, and it is the one that is increasingly used.

Parity provisions usually relate to prices, for example where A requests B not to supply products to C at prices lower than those agreed with B; an alternative price parity provision would require A to offer to B any lower prices offered to C. Non-price parity provisions are also possible, for example where A requests B not to agree to a business model with C that it different from the one that has been agreed with B; another example of a non-price parity provision would be an agreement not to offer better service terms to C.

(a) Possible detriments to competition

MFNs, or parity provisions, have been known to competition authorities for a long time. However it has been the rise of online marketplaces, or 'platforms', such as Amazon and Booking.com that has led to an increasing interest in them in recent years. Various theories of harm have been identified.

One is that parity provisions may lead to a reduction of intra-brand competition at retail level where a platform A demands that supplier B agrees that A will be given parity with retailers C, D and E[285]: this will cause there to be less competition in the selling of B's products. An example would be where the use of a price parity provision makes resale price maintenance more effective or transforms a recommended or maximum resale price into a minimum resale price[286]. A different theory of harm is that parity provisions may reduce inter-brand competition between platform A and other online retailers, X, Y and Z, for whom the parity provision may make entry or expansion more difficult[287]. Another theory of harm is that the use of parity provisions may facilitate collusion not at

[282] Ibid, para 228.

[283] Ibid; on this point see Opinion of AG Mengozzi in Case C-279/06 *CEPSA Estaciones de Servicio SA v LV Tobar e Hijos SL* EU:C:2008:163, para 91 (citing the equivalent para of the previous *Guidelines*, OJ [2000] C 290/1, para 227).

[284] Commission decision of 12 April 2006.

[285] Commission Staff Working Document accompanying the *Final Report on the E-commerce Sector Inquiry*, SWD(2017) 154 final, 10 May 2017, para 622; see further Lear 'Can "Fair" Prices Be Unfair? A Review of Price Relationship Agreements', OFT 1438, September 2012.

[286] *Vertical guidelines*, para 48; see also Fletcher and Hviid 'Retail Price MFNs: Are they RPM "at its worst"?', available at www.competitionpolicy.ac.uk.

[287] *Vertical guidelines*, para 48.

the retail level of the market, but between suppliers to the platform: this was the concern in the Commission's *Apple/e-books* case.

(b) Possible benefits to competition

Parity provisions may lead to efficiencies[288]. For example they may enable an online marketplace to recoup investments and to avoid free-riding. They may also be used by new entrants using a business model based on having the best available resale prices.

(c) Recent enforcement activity

Over the years the Commission closed its files in several cases concerning parity provisions after the offending provisions were abandoned[289]. More recently, in *Apple/e-books* the Commission investigated agency agreements between Apple and five publishers of e-books that contained a price parity provision; it accepted Article 9 commitments from Apple and the publishers in which they agreed to terminate the agency agreements and promised not to enter into such agreements for five years[290]. In *Amazon/e-books* the Commission investigated price and non-price parity provisions in agreements between Amazon and publishers of e-books. The Commission suspected that the parity provisions made it harder for other retailers of e-books to compete with Amazon by developing new and innovative products. Amazon entered into legally-binding commitments to bring the parity provisions to an end[291].

Parity provisions used by online travel agents ('OTAs') in their agreements with hotels have been the subject of extensive investigation by several NCAs. A 'wide parity clause' is one that requires a hotel (or hotel chain) not to sell rooms at lower prices through other online sellers, nor on its own website, than through the OTA; a 'narrow parity clause' requires the hotel not to sell at lower prices on its own website. In France, Italy and Sweden Booking.com gave commitments to the NCAs to abandon wide parity clauses and only to apply narrow parity clauses. The NCAs considered that a narrow parity clause was justifiable to prevent the hotel taking a 'free ride' on the investment of Booking.com in establishing its platform: otherwise members of the public might use Booking.com to find a hotel that suits their needs, but then book it at a lower price on the hotel's own website. In Germany, however, the NCA decided to adopt a stricter approach and prohibited Booking.com's narrow price parity clause as well. Since then the legislatures in France, Austria and Italy have enacted laws banning wide and narrow price parity provisions in the hotel sector. The result is a patchwork of different enforcement and legislative solutions in different Member States. The Commission and the NCAs will have to work out a solution over the years ahead[292].

7. Vertical Agreements: Regulation 330/2010

(A) Introduction

It was explained earlier that the Commission over many years tended to adopt a formalistic (insufficiently economics-oriented) approach to the application of Article 101(1); as

288 Staff Working Document (ch 16, n 285), para 623.

289 Commission Press Release IP/04/1314, 26 October 2004 (Hollywood Studios and Pay-TV broadcasters); Commission Press Release IP/05/710, 10 June 2005 (E.ON and Gazprom); Commission Press Release IP/11/257, 4 March 2011 (Hollywood Studios and producers of cinema digital equipment).

290 Commission decisions of 12 December 2012 and of 25 July 2013; see also *US v Apple Inc* 791 F 3d 290 (2nd Cir 2015).

291 Commission decision of 4 May 2017; note this was a case under Article 102.

292 See the Report on the monitoring exercise carried out in the online hotel booking sector by EU competition authorities in 2016, available at www.ec.europa.eu.

a result it was necessary for many agreements to be brought within the 'safe haven' of one of the Commission's block exemptions[293]. It originally adopted Regulation 67/67[294], and subsequently Regulation 1983/83 for exclusive distribution agreements[295], Regulation 1984/83 for exclusive purchasing agreements[296] and Regulation 4087/88 for franchise agreements[297]. However dissatisfaction with the over-application of Article 101(1) and the formalistic nature of the block exemptions became widespread, and led to the publication in 1997 of the Commission's *Green Paper on Vertical Restraints in [EU] Competition Policy*[298] suggesting a range of possible options for reform. This document paved the way for the adoption in 1999 of Commission Regulation 2790/99[299]. The new block exemption was radical in various ways[300]: it was much broader in scope than its predecessors, applying to virtually all vertical agreements in both the goods and services sector; it was more economics-based, in particular by including a market share cap for determining which agreements would benefit from the block exemption; and it was less prescriptive than its predecessors, containing a relatively limited list of 'hard-core' restrictions that could not be included in an agreement. Regulation 2790/99 was a considerable improvement on the system it replaced and entered into force on 1 June 2000. The Regulation was accompanied by extensive *Guidelines on Vertical Restraints* and appears to have worked well in practice[301].

Regulation 330/2010 replaced Regulation 2790/99. With the exception of the application of the market share cap to the buyer in all cases, Regulation 330/2010 represented a mild evolution of the law, as opposed to the revolution of Regulation 2790/99.

(B) **Brief description of the provisions of the block exemption**

The Commission adopted Regulation 330/2010 on 20 April 2010[302]. It entered into force on 1 June 2010 and will expire on 31 May 2022[303]. Article 1 defines certain key terms such as 'vertical agreements', 'vertical restraints', 'competing undertakings' and 'non-compete obligation'. Article 2 is the provision that actually confers block exemption upon certain vertical agreements pursuant to Article 101(3) TFEU; Article 3 imposes a market share cap of 30% on both the supplier and the buyer. Article 4 sets out a list of hard-core restrictions that will prevent the block exemption from applying to the entire agreement. Article 5 sets out a list of 'excluded restrictions' that do not benefit from the block exemption. Subsequent provisions deal with matters such as the withdrawal of the block exemption, calculation of market share and turnover thresholds and transitional arrangements.

[293] Part of the text that follows is based on the authors' article 'Regulation 330/2010: The Commission's New Block Exemption for Vertical Agreements' (2010) 47 CML Rev 1757; on Regulation 330/2010 see also Wijckmans and Tuytschaever *Vertical Agreements in EU Competition Law* (Oxford University Press, 3rd ed, 2018), Part II.

[294] 10 JO Comm Eur 849 [1967]. [295] OJ [1983] L 173/1.

[296] OJ [1983] L 173/5. [297] OJ [1988] L 359/46.

[298] COM(96) 721 final; see the Commission's XXVIth *Report on Competition Policy* (1996), points 46–50. There was a *Follow-up to the Green Paper on Vertical Restraints* OJ [1998] C 365/3; see the Commission's XXVIIIth *Report on Competition Policy* (1998), points 34–53.

[299] Regulation 2790/99, OJ [1999] L 336/21; see the Commission's XXIXth *Report on Competition Policy* (1999), points 8–19.

[300] For a detailed description of the provisions of Regulation 2790/99 see the sixth edition of this book, pp 640–662.

[301] See De Boer and Posthuma 'Ten Years On: Vertical Agreements under Article 81' (2009) 30 ECLR 424.

[302] OJ [2010] L 102/1. [303] Regulation 330/2010, Article 10.

The Regulation is without prejudice to the application of Article 102[304]. The Regulation should be read in conjunction with the accompanying *Vertical guidelines*[305].

(C) Article 1: definitions

Article 1 contains important definitions. These will be explained later, in the specific context in which they are used in the Regulation. Of particular importance is Article 1(1)(a) which defines a 'vertical agreement' as:

> an agreement or concerted practice entered into between two or more undertakings each of which operates, for the purposes of the agreement or the concerted practice, at a different level of the production or distribution chain, and relating to the conditions under which the parties may purchase, sell or resell certain goods or services.

The Regulation applies to vertical agreements to the extent that they contain 'vertical restraints'. Article 1(1)(b) provides that 'vertical restraint' means a restriction of competition in a vertical agreement falling within Article 101(1). These key expressions will be discussed in the context of Article 2 later.

Article 1(2) of Regulation 330/2010 contains rules extending the expressions 'undertaking', 'supplier' and 'buyer' to include connected undertakings.

(D) Article 2: scope of the block exemption

(i) Article 2(1): block exemption for vertical agreements

Article 2(1) confers block exemption on vertical agreements to the extent that they contain vertical restraints pursuant to Article 101(3)[306]. Several points should be noted about Article 2(1).

(ii) Many vertical agreements do not infringe Article 101(1)

It is worth repeating that many vertical agreements do not infringe Article 101(1)[307]; where an agreement does not infringe Article 101(1) it follows that, no matter how generous and flexible the Regulation is, it will not be necessary to bring the agreement in question within its terms. Despite this, however, many undertakings endeavour to satisfy the block exemption, which provides a 'safe haven' for many vertical agreements: as explained earlier, most firms will have no interest in knowing whether their agreement infringes Article 101(1) if they know that it benefits from block exemption under Article 101(3) anyway[308]. Recital 9 of the Regulation states that there is no presumption that agreements infringe Article 101(1) or that it will fail to satisfy Article 101(3) where either of the parties' market shares exceeds the prescribed threshold in Article 3, a point repeated in paragraphs 23 and 96 of the *Guidelines*. Where the thresholds are exceeded an agreement requires individual analysis[309]. An example of a vertical agreement not

[304] On the relationship between Article 101(3) and Article 102 see ch 4, 'Fourth condition of Article 101(3): no elimination of competition in a substantial part of the market', pp 172–173.

[305] OJ [2010] C 130/1. [306] *Vertical guidelines*, paras 23–25.

[307] See 'Vertical Agreements: Article 101(1)', pp 642–664 earlier in chapter.

[308] See 'Introduction', p 629 earlier in chapter.

[309] On the burden of proof in this situation see Article 2 of Regulation 1/2003, OJ [2003] L 1/1 and ch 4, 'Burden and standard of proof', p 159.

infringing Article 101(1) would be a purely qualitative selective distribution system[310]; only to the extent that it is not purely qualitative—for example because the product is not of the type that necessitates selective distribution[311] or because quantitative as well as qualitative criteria are applied[312]—is it necessary to have resort to the block exemption. Similarly, many single branding agreements fall outside Article 101(1): only those agreements that significantly contribute to foreclosure of the market are caught[313]. Again, the application of the Regulation, and specifically the application of Article 5(1) to a non-compete obligation, would be relevant only in the case of those agreements that infringe Article 101(1).

(iii) If it is not forbidden, it is permitted

A second point to stress about the Regulation is that, in relation to a vertical agreement as defined in Article 1(1)(a), if the Regulation does not prohibit something, it is permitted. This is the consequence of not stating what must be included in a vertical agreement, but only stating the hard-core restrictions which must not be in it, and is an essential feature of the Regulation. Block exemption is available under Regulation 330/2010 to all vertical agreements, as defined, subject to Articles 2(2), 2(4) and 2(5) on agreements made by associations of retailers, agreements between competing undertakings and agreements subject to other block exemptions, Article 3 on market share, and to Articles 4 and 5 which deal with particular vertical restraints that the Commission has concerns about.

(iv) The definition of a vertical agreement

Paragraph 25 of the *Vertical guidelines* discusses the meaning of 'vertical agreement'[314]. Indent (a) of that paragraph explains the distinction between an agreement and/or concerted practice on the one hand and unilateral conduct, which is not caught by Article 101 but could be by Article 102, on the other. The Commission sets out the circumstances in which an apparently unilateral act on the part of one party might, in fact, be characterised as an agreement and/or concerted practice due to the explicit or tacit acquiescence of the other[315].

(v) The exempted agreement may be multilateral

Article 2(1) confers block exemption on agreements between two *or more* undertakings[316]. However the Regulation applies only where each of the undertakings operates, for the purposes of the agreement, at a different level of the market[317]. Some illustrations may help (see Figures 16.8 and 16.9).

[310] See 'Selective distribution agreements', pp 654–658 earlier in chapter.

[311] See eg *Grohe* OJ [1985] L 19/17; note that, where it *is* necessary to apply the Regulation to a selective distribution system, the definition of this term in Article 1(1)(e) does not bring into account the nature of the product; this consideration is relevant only to the *Metro* doctrine and the question of whether the system falls outside Article 101(1) altogether.

[312] See 'Purely qualitative selective distribution systems', pp 655–657 earlier in chapter.

[313] See eg Case C-234/89 *Delimitis v Henninger Bräu* EU:C:1991:91.

[314] The definition of a vertical agreement is identical to that in Council Regulation 1215/99, OJ [1999] L 148/1.

[315] On the meaning of agreements and concerted practices see ch 3, 'Agreements, Decisions and Concerted Practices', pp 101–119.

[316] Pursuant to the power conferred on the Commission by Article 1(a) of Council Regulation 19/65, OJ [1965] L 36/533, as amended by Council Regulation 1215/99, OJ [1999] L 148/1.

[317] *Vertical guidelines*, para 25(c).

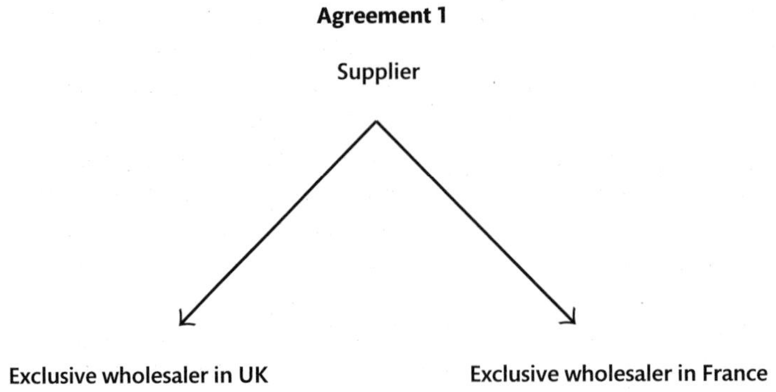

Fig. 16.8

(a) The agreement is trilateral
(b) The supplier supplies goods to each wholesaler
(c) It is agreed that neither wholesaler will sell into the other's territory.

The agreement in Figure 16.8 is not vertical since there are two parties, the wholesalers, at the same level of the production and distribution chain.

Fig. 16.9

(a) The agreement is trilateral
(b) The agreement sets out the mutual rights and obligations of each party.

The agreement in Figure 16.9 is vertical since each party operates at a different level of the production and distribution chain.

Where the agreement is in the form of Agreement 2, Article 3(2) provides that the market shares of the supplier and the wholesaler on their respective downstream markets and the market share of the wholesaler and the retailer on their respective purchase markets would have to be considered for the purpose of the market share cap in Article 3(1)[318].

(vi) 'For the purposes of the agreement'

The definition of a vertical agreement in Article 1(1)(a) refers to undertakings which operate, '*for the purposes of the agreement or concerted practice*, at a different level of the production or distribution chain' (emphasis added). It follows that the fact that two firms that are both manufacturers enter into an agreement does not in itself mean that the agreement is horizontal rather than vertical. If a manufacturer of a chemical were to supply the

[318] Ibid, para 90.

chemical to another chemical manufacturer, the relationship would still be vertical since, for the purposes of that agreement, each undertaking would be operating at a different level of the market. The expression 'for the purposes of the agreement' is essential to this analysis since, without it, it would not be possible to say that the two chemical companies operate 'at a different level of the production or distribution chain'. However Article 2(4) of the Regulation guards against the risk that vertical agreements as defined could be used as a cloak for horizontal restrictions by denying block exemption to certain agreements between competing undertakings[319].

(vii) Agreements with final consumers would not be vertical agreements

Agreements entered into with final consumers would not be vertical agreements, since they would not be entered into 'between two or more undertakings': a final consumer in the sense of a member of the public buying goods or services is not engaged in economic activity and therefore not an undertaking[320]. For the same reason, however, such agreements would not infringe Article 101(1) in the first place, and therefore would not need to be block exempted.

(viii) 'Relating to the conditions under which the parties may purchase, sell or resell certain goods or services'

To qualify as a vertical agreement it must relate to the conditions under which the parties may purchase, sell or resell certain goods or services. It appears, therefore, that rental and leasing agreements would not be covered[321]; nor would bartering agreements. Provisions in vertical agreements which do not themselves relate to purchase, sale or resale would not be covered: an example would be a covenant not to compete in research and development[322].

(ix) Interconnection agreements

In many industries undertakings require access to an infrastructure owned by someone else in order to be able to operate on the market: for example in the electronic communications sector access to, and interconnection of, all forms of communications networks may be crucial; in electricity access will be needed to the national grid. Where access is provided there will be an 'interconnection agreement' between the owner of the infrastructure and the service provider. It would seem that such an agreement would be vertical in the sense of Article 2(1), since it would relate to the 'conditions under which the parties may purchase, sell or resell ... services'[323]. However in many such cases the owner of the infrastructure would have a market share in excess of 30%, so that Article 3(1) would prevent the application of the block exemption[324].

(x) Agency

Many agency agreements fall outside Article 101(1); paragraphs 12 to 21 of the *Vertical guidelines* deal with this[325]. However those paragraphs suggest that some agency agreements could fall within Article 101(1), if they could foreclose access to the market or if

[319] See 'Article 2(4): agreements between competing undertakings', pp 673–674 later in chapter.

[320] *Vertical guidelines*, para 25(b): on the meaning of the term 'undertaking' see ch 3, 'Basic definition', pp 84–92; however the supplier would be an undertaking, and could infringe Article 102 if the terms of that provision were satisfied: on Article 102 generally see ch 5.

[321] *Vertical guidelines*, para 26. [322] Ibid, para 26.

[323] Note however that the agreement would not be vertical in so far as it is a rental or leasing arrangement: see the previous section.

[324] Where the infrastructure is indispensable for a firm to operate on a downstream market Article 102 may be applicable: see ch 17, 'Is the product to which access is sought indispensable to someone wishing to compete in the downstream market?', pp 717–723.

[325] See 'The Commission's *Vertical guidelines*', pp 634–637 earlier in chapter.

they might facilitate collusion. It is necessary to consider whether an agency agreement that does fall within Article 101(1) would be eligible for block exemption. In such a situation the agent is operating at a different level of the market from the principal in the sense of Article 1(1)(a) of the Regulation. Therefore, to the extent that the agreement relates to the conditions under which the principal or the agent may purchase, sell or resell goods or services, the Regulation could apply: a point specifically noted in paragraph 19 of the *Vertical guidelines*. In such cases it will be necessary to avoid the inclusion of hard-core restrictions listed in Article 4[326]; paragraph 49 of the *Guidelines* states that an obligation on an agent preventing it from sharing its commission with its customers would be a 'hard-core' restriction under Article 4(a). Also it will be necessary to avoid Article 5 non-compete obligations that are not block exempted[327].

(xi) **Article 2(2): associations of retailers**

A common business phenomenon is that small retailers establish an association for the purchase of goods, which they then resell to final consumers[328]. This is necessary to enable the retailers to achieve some bargaining power in their dealings with large manufacturers and/or intermediaries. Consumers will benefit if the retailers are enabled to obtain lower prices which are transmitted on to them.

Article 2(2)[329] provides that *vertical* agreements entered into between such an association and (a) its suppliers or (b) its members can benefit from block exemption, provided that all its members are retailers of goods and provided that no individual member of the association, together with its connected undertakings[330], has a total annual turnover in excess of €50 million[331].

The Regulation does not define the term retailer, but paragraph 29 of the *Vertical guidelines* says that '[r]etailers are distributors reselling goods to final consumers'[332]. The concluding words of Article 2(2) provide that the block exemption for such vertical agreements is without prejudice to the application of Article 101 to the horizontal agreement between the members of the association or decisions of the association itself[333]. Paragraph 30 of the *Guidelines* explains that the lawfulness of a vertical agreement entered into by an association of retailers under Article 2(2) can be determined only after it has been concluded that any underlying horizontal agreement between the members of the association is itself lawful.

(xii) **Article 2(3): ancillary provisions in relation to intellectual property rights**

Article 2(3) deals with the important question of the extent to which vertical agreements which contain provisions on intellectual property rights can benefit from

326 On Article 4 generally see 'Article 4: hard-core restrictions', pp 677–684 later in chapter.

327 On Article 5 generally see 'Article 5: obligations in vertical agreements that are not exempt', pp 684–685 later in chapter.

328 See ch 15, 'Purchasing Agreements', pp 615–617.

329 *Vertical guidelines*, paras 28 and 29.

330 Articles 1(2) and 8 of Regulation 330/2010 deal respectively with connected undertakings and the calculation of turnover.

331 The final sentence of para 29 of the *Guidelines* states that where only a limited number of the members of the association have a turnover exceeding €50 million and where those members together represent less than 15% of the aggregate turnover of all the members, 'the assessment under Article 101 will normally not be affected'; this presumably refers to the *individual* assessment under Article 101. The meaning of this is opaque: if this is intended to mean that the block exemption would still be applicable, it does not provide any legal justification for this view.

332 It presumably follows that if the association purchases for its own use, Article 2(2) would not be applicable since the group does not purchase in order to *sell* to final consumers.

333 On such agreements see ch 15, 'Purchasing Agreements', pp 615–617.

Regulation 330/2010[334]. The first sentence of Article 2(3) provides that the exemption shall apply to vertical agreements:

> containing provisions which relate to the assignment to the buyer or use by the buyer of intellectual property rights[335], provided that those provisions do not constitute the primary object of such agreements and are directly related to the use, sale or resale of goods or services by the buyer or its customers.

Essentially the policy is that Regulation 330/2010 will apply where any provisions relating to intellectual property rights are ancillary to the main purpose of the vertical agreement[336]; although the Regulation itself does not use the term, it is helpful to call such provisions 'IPR provisions'. The policy of Article 2(3) is simple to state; however the actual application of Article 2(3) is not without its difficulties. A number of points should be noted: the five headings (xiii–xvii) used below are based upon paragraph 31 of the Commission's *Guidelines*.

(xiii) **Article 2(3) is applicable only where there is a vertical agreement**

For Article 2(3) to apply to the IPR provisions—that is to say if they are to benefit from block exemption—there must be a vertical agreement; Article 1(1)(a) defines this as an agreement relating to the conditions under which the parties may purchase, sell or resell goods or services. It follows that 'pure' licences—for example of know-how or of a trade mark—would not be covered, since they would not relate to the conditions under which the parties purchase, sell or resell goods or services: rather, they would authorise the use of the know-how or of the trade mark. A different point is that Article 2(3) should be understood in conjunction with Article 2(5) (see later), which prevents the application of Regulation 330/2010 where another block exemption is applicable: a pure know-how licence, for example, may qualify for block exemption under Regulation 316/2014[337] on technology transfer agreements[338]. Paragraph 33 of the *Guidelines* gives five examples of agreements that would not benefit from block exemption under Regulation 330/2010:

- the provision of a recipe for the production of a drink under licence
- the production and distribution of copies from a mould or master copy
- a pure licence of a trade mark or sign for the purposes of merchandising
- sponsorship contracts[339]
- copyright licensing such as broadcasting contracts concerning the right to record and/or the right to broadcast an event[340].

[334] *Vertical guidelines*, paras 31–45.

[335] Intellectual property rights are defined in Article 1(1)(f) to include 'industrial property rights, know-how, copyright and neighbouring rights'; know-how is defined in Article 1(1)(g) as 'a package of non-patented practical information, resulting from experience and testing by the supplier, which is secret, substantial and identified'.

[336] Although the term 'ancillary' does not feature in Article 2(3) itself, recital 3 states that the Regulation 'includes vertical agreements containing ancillary provisions on the assignment or use of intellectual property rights'.

[337] OJ [2014] L 93/17.

[338] See ch 19, 'Technology Transfer Agreements: Regulation 316/2014', pp 798–807.

[339] On sponsorship contracts see *Danish Tennis Federation Commission* OJ [1996] C 138/6, Commission's XXVIIIth *Report on Competition Policy* (1998), p 160 (comfort letter issued).

[340] See *Telenor/Canal+/Canal Digital*, Commission decision of 29 December 2003, a case concerning the licensing of premium content channels, protected by copyright, to a pay-TV platform, where the Commission decided that Regulation 2790/99 was not applicable: ibid, para 196.

(xiv) The IPR provisions must be for the use of the buyer

Article 2(3) applies only where the supplier transfers IPRs to the buyer; it does not apply where the buyer transfers IPRs to the supplier. It follows that a sub-contracting agreement, whereby one undertaking asks another to manufacture goods on its behalf, often with the use of its IPRs, would not be covered by the block exemption[341], since the IPRs are supplied by the buyer to the supplier, rather than the other way around. However many sub-contracting agreements do not infringe Article 101(1) at all, so that block exemption is unnecessary[342]; and the *Vertical guidelines* state that, where the buyer simply provides specifications to the supplier as to the goods or services to be supplied, the block exemption remains applicable[343]: in that case there are no IPR provisions, and Article 2(3) is irrelevant.

(xv) The IPR provisions must not be the object of the agreement

For Article 2(3) to apply the IPR provisions must not be the 'primary' object of the agreement: in the language of the *Guidelines*, '[t]he primary object must be the purchase, sale or resale of goods or services and the IPR provisions must serve the implementation of the vertical agreement'[344].

(xvi) The IPR provisions must be directly related to the use, sale or resale of goods or services by the buyer or its customers

A trade mark licence to a distributor is generally necessary for and ancillary to the distribution of goods or services, so that an exclusive licence would benefit from the block exemption, provided that it satisfies the other rules in the Regulation[345]. A sale of hard copies of software, where the reseller does not acquire a licence to any rights over the software, is regarded as an agreement for the supply of goods for resale[346]. Paragraphs 43 to 45 of the *Vertical guidelines* examine the application of the block exemption to franchise agreements. The Commission's view is that Regulation 330/2010 is capable in principle of application to franchise agreements, other than industrial franchise agreements: the latter would be subject, if at all, to Regulation 316/2014 on technology transfer agreements[347]. Paragraph 44 of the *Guidelines* states that most franchise agreements would be covered by Article 2(3), since the IPR provisions in them are directly related to the use, sale or resale of goods or services by the franchisee. It adds that, where a franchise agreement 'only or primarily concerns licensing of IPRs', it would not be covered by the block exemption; however the Commission will normally analyse such an agreement by analogy to the principles contained in the Regulation and *Guidelines*.

Where the franchisor franchises a business method, the franchisor must calculate its market share on the market where the business method is to be exploited for the purpose of the market share cap in Article 3 (see section 7(E) later)[348].

Paragraph 45 of the *Vertical guidelines* sets out a series of typical IPR-related obligations that are found in franchise agreements and which, if restrictive of competition,

341 *Vertical guidelines*, para 34.

342 Ibid, para 22 and the Commission's *Notice on Sub-contracting Agreements* OJ [1979] C 1/2, discussed at 'Sub-Contracting Agreements', pp 691–692 later in chapter.

343 *Vertical guidelines*, para 34.

344 Ibid, para 35.

345 Ibid, para 39.

346 Ibid, para 41; this would cover the sale of software subject to a 'shrink-wrap' licence, the conditions in which the end user is deemed to accept by opening the package.

347 The Commission notes the difference between industrial franchise and non-industrial franchise agreements at para 43 of the *Vertical guidelines*; see ch 19, 'Technology Transfer Agreements: Regulation 316/2014', pp 798–807.

348 *Vertical guidelines*, para 92.

would be regarded as ancillary and therefore would benefit from block exemption. These are obligations on the franchisee:

- not to engage, directly or indirectly, in any similar business
- not to acquire financial interests in competing undertakings
- not to disclose secret know-how to third parties
- to grant a non-exclusive licence to the franchisor of know-how obtained from exploitation of the franchise
- to assist the franchisor in action to protect the IPRs
- only to use the franchisor's know-how for the purpose of the franchise
- not to assign the rights and obligations under the franchise agreement without the consent of the franchisor.

(xvii) The IPR provisions must not have an illegitimate object or effect

Article 2(3) provides that the IPR provisions will be exempt only in so far as they 'do not contain restrictions of competition having the same object or effect as vertical restraints which are not exempted under this Regulation'[349]. Thus it is not possible to avoid the provisions of Articles 4 and 5 of the Regulation (see sections 7(F) and (G) later) by attaching the vertical restraints which they seek to prevent to the IPR provisions rather than to the vertical agreement itself.

Article 2(3) should also be understood in conjunction with Article 2(5), which prevents the application of the Regulation where another block exemption is applicable (see section 7(D)(xix) later).

(xviii) Article 2(4): agreements between competing undertakings

Article 2(4) provides that the block exemption does not apply to vertical agreements entered into between competing undertakings as defined in Article 1(1)(c) of the Regulation; this applies to agreements at any level of the market: for example the undertakings may be competing as manufacturers, wholesalers or as retailers[350]. Article 1(1)(c) provides that undertakings compete where they are active on the same relevant market (actual competitors) and where, in the absence of the vertical agreement, they would realistically be able to enter and compete on the market 'within a short period of time' in response to a small but permanent increase in relative prices[351] (potential competitors). Paragraph 27 of the *Vertical guidelines* says that this assessment must be 'realistic', not 'theoretical'. It also says that a 'short time' would normally not be longer than a year. Separately, the *Guidelines* state that, where a distributor provides specifications to a manufacturer to produce particular goods under the distributor's brand name, it is not to be considered a manufacturer of such own-brand goods.

Article 2(4) provides that the block exemption is applicable to a non-reciprocal vertical agreement between competing undertakings where:

- the supplier is a manufacturer and a distributor of goods, whilst the buyer is a distributor not manufacturing goods competing with the contract goods[352]. In this case the manufacturer conducts its own distribution, but also appoints other distributors

[349] Ibid, para 37. [350] Ibid, paras 27–28.

[351] The *Guidelines* do not state that the potential suppliers' response must have been triggered by a price rise by 'competing undertakings', but presumably this is what the spirit of Article 1(1)(c) is envisaging.

[352] At para 27 of the *Vertical guidelines* the Commission states that an 'own-brand' retailer would not be treated as a manufacturer for this purpose.

which are, according to the definition in Article 1(1)(c), 'competing undertakings'. Paragraph 28 of the *Guidelines* describes this phenomenon as 'dual distribution' or

- the supplier is a provider of services at several levels of trade, whilst the buyer does not provide competing services at the level of trade where it purchases the contract services. This is the analogue of the previous situation, adjusted for the purposes of an agreement in the services sector.

Where a vertical agreement between competitors falls outside Article 2(4), it should be considered under the Commission's *Guidelines on Horizontal Cooperation Agreements*[353].

(xix) Article 2(5): agreements within the scope of another block exemption

Article 2(5) of the Regulation provides that 'This Regulation shall not apply to vertical agreements *the subject matter of which* falls within the scope of any other block exemption regulation, unless otherwise provided for in such a regulation' (emphasis added)[354]. The italicised words are important: Article 2(5) does not say that the Regulation shall not apply to an agreement that is exempt under another regulation; rather, it says that it does not apply to agreements which, generically, are of a kind covered by another regulation. It follows that vertical agreements covered by the block exemptions for technology transfer agreements[355], the distribution of motor vehicles[356], R&D agreements[357] and specialisation agreements[358] would not be covered by Regulation 330/2010 except to the extent provided for in those specific Regulations. If an agreement fails to satisfy the criteria for exemption in any of these Regulations, Article 2(5) prevents the agreement from being exempted by Regulation 330/2010. Article 2(5) would also prevent Regulation 330/2010 from applying to any agreement within the scope of any future block exemption[359].

(E) Article 3: the market share cap

(i) Why a market share test?

One of the key features of Regulation 330/2010 is the inclusion of a market share cap for determining which agreements would benefit from block exemption[360]. It is a manifestation of the 'economics-oriented approach' that characterises the Regulation.

Market power is at the heart of economic analysis of such agreements (whether under Article 101(1) or 101(3)), and the market share cap is a useful proxy for the non-existence of market power. Where the parties' market shares do not exceed 30%, recital 8 states that it can be presumed that vertical agreements that do not contain hard-core restrictions improve production or distribution from which consumers will derive a fair share of the benefit. In other words the market share cap is a filter for identifying agreements that satisfy Article 101(3).

[353] See para 12 of its *Guidelines on Horizontal Cooperation Agreements* OJ [2011] C 11/1; see ch 15, 'Purpose and scope of the *Guidelines on Horizontal Cooperation Agreements*', pp 601–602.

[354] *Vertical guidelines*, para 45.

[355] Regulation 316/2014, OJ [2014] L 93/17; see ch 19, 'Technology Transfer Agreements: Regulation 316/2014', pp 798–807.

[356] Regulation 461/2010, OJ [2010] L 129/52; see 'Regulation 461/2010 on Motor Vehicle Distribution', pp 689–691 later in chapter.

[357] Regulation 1217/2010, OJ [2010] L 335/36: see ch 15, 'The block exemption for R&D agreements: Regulation 1217/2020', pp 607–611.

[358] Regulation 1218/2010, OJ [2010] L 335/43; see ch 15, 'The block exemption for specialisation agreements: Regulation 1218/2010', pp 613–615.

[359] The Commission specifically says this in para 46 of the *Vertical guidelines*.

[360] Section V of the *Vertical guidelines* deals with market definition and market share calculation issues; see generally ch 1, 'Market Definition and Market Power', pp 25–46.

Recital 9 makes two different, and important, points: first, that no such presumption can be made where either of the parties' market shares exceed 30%; but, secondly, that there is no presumption that, where the thresholds are exceeded, an agreement infringes Article 101(1) or that it cannot benefit from Article 101(3)[361]. Where the thresholds are exceeded an agreement requires individual analysis.

(ii) What market share?

Of course it is possible to argue about what the market share cap should be. The predecessor to Regulation 330/2010 set the fairly generous market share threshold of 30%[362]: thousands, if not hundreds of thousands, of agreements will have benefited from the safe harbour provided by this figure. A higher market share cap of, say, 40% would come close to saying that only vertical restraints, other than the hard-core restrictions set out in Article 4, imposed by dominant undertakings are problematic: perhaps it is not surprising that the Commission has been unwilling to diminish the role of Article 101 to this extent.

In *JCB* the Commission held that block exemption was unavailable to JCB's distribution agreements since its market share was in the region of 40 to 45%[363]. The 30% cap prevented the application of the block exemption in *Telenor/Canal+/Canal Digital*[364].

In the case of Interbrew's single branding agreements for bars and cafés in Belgium the Commission concluded that, notwithstanding Interbrew's market share of around 56%, the agreements did not appreciably restrict competition once the extent of the exclusivity had been limited only to pils lager[365].

(iii) Whose market share?

Article 3(1) of Regulation 330/2010 requires that the market share of each of the parties must not exceed 30%. Article 3(1) provides that the block exemption shall apply:

> on condition that the market share held by the supplier does not exceed 30% of the relevant market on which it sells the contract goods or services and the market share held by the buyer does not exceed 30% of the relevant market on which it purchases the contract goods or services.

Regulation 2790/99, the predecessor to Regulation 330/2010, applied only to vertical agreements that did not exceed a supplier's market share cap; apart from the case of an exclusive supply obligation[366], the buyer's market share was irrelevant under the old regime. When it was proposed in 2009, the extension of the market share cap to that of the buyer in all cases was controversial. Concerns were expressed at the complexity that might be involved in its application[367], in particular because of the inherent difficulty in assessing how the relevant market should be defined. However, a buyer's market share cap was included in Regulation 330/2010 for two reasons in particular. First, the Commission took into account the increase in large distributors' market power since the adoption of

[361] See similarly paras 23 and 96 of the *Guidelines*.

[362] See Article 3 of Regulation 2790/99, OJ [1999] L 336/21.

[363] OJ [2002] L 69/1, para 198; the Commission also considered that block exemption was unavailable as a result of the presence of hard-core restrictions in the agreements: ibid, para 199; on hard-core restrictions see 'Article 4: hard-core restrictions', pp 677–684 later in chapter.

[364] Commission decision of 29 December 2003, para 196.

[365] Commission Press Release IP/03/545, 15 April 2003.

[366] See Article 3(2) of Regulation 2790/99 in conjunction with Article 1(c).

[367] See eg RBB Economics 'Comments on Proposed Changes to EC Commission Guidelines on Vertical Restraints', 2009, available at www.ec.europa.eu.

Regulation 2790/99[368]. Secondly, applying the cap to the buyer's market share recognises that vertical restraints are not necessarily imposed by a supplier on a buyer: it is also possible that the restraint is 'buyer-led'[369]; the inclusion in the *Guidelines* of sections on up-front access payments and category management agreements can also be attributed to this fact.

Article 3(1) states that the relevant market share is that of the buyer on the market 'on which it purchases the contract goods or services'; block exemption does not depend on the (potentially) much larger number of market(s) in which a distributor sells or resells products[370]. The market on which a buyer buys will usually be wider than the market(s) on which it sells: for example it may procure internationally but sell nationally; or purchase nationally and sell regionally or locally[371]. However there is likely to be some relationship between the buyer's power in the purchasing and the selling markets. Article 3(1) may be seen as a compromise between the avoidance of undue complexity on the one hand and the desire of the Commission not to ignore the power of buyers on the other. In the event that a vertical agreement causes problems in the retail market, there is the possibility of withdrawing the benefit of the block exemption[372].

The application of the market share cap to include that of the buyer in all cases gives rise to compliance issues for the parties to vertical agreements. The supplier will need to ask each buyer for information about, and assurances as to, its market share in its purchasing markets; obviously these may fluctuate over time; their veracity will need to be checked; the market share figure may be exceeded in the case of some buyers but not others; and different agreements may need to be used in the case of those that exceed the market share from those of others. Furthermore the supplier will need to negotiate with each of its buyers individually in order to avoid any possibility of being accused of participating in a 'hub and spoke' conspiracy of the kind that various competition authorities have been looking at in recent years[373].

Article 3(2) of Regulation 330/2010 deals with the position where there is a multipartite agreement. Article 3(2) provides that, where an undertaking that is party to an agreement both buys and sells the contract goods or services, it must respect both the seller's and the buyer's market share threshold. Paragraph 90 of the *Guidelines* gives the obvious example of an agreement between a manufacturer, a wholesaler and a retailer, where the wholesaler would have to have a market share of 30% or less both in its buying and selling markets.

(iv) The *Vertical guidelines*

Paragraph 23 of the *Guidelines* explains that competition concerns will arise for most vertical restraints only if there is market power at the level of the supplier or the buyer or at both levels. It then rehearses the terms of Article 3(1). Paragraphs 72 and 73 of the *Guidelines* deal with the situation where a supplier uses the same distribution agreement

[368] See speech by former Commissioner Almunia, SPEECH/10/172, 20 April 2010; for further reading on the anti-competitive effects of buyer power see the OECD's Roundtable *Monopsony and Buyer Power* (2008), available at www.oecd.org/competition and *The competitive effects of buyer groups* (OFT 863, January 2007) and the literature there cited.

[369] On these vertical restraints see 'Up-front access payments' and 'Category management agreements', p 660 earlier in chapter.

[370] The position would have been much more complex if the Commission had maintained the position it had adopted in its draft Regulation of 28 July 2009, which did depend on the buyer's market share in the market(s) in which it sold or resold the products acquired under the agreement.

[371] *Vertical guidelines*, para 89.

[372] See 'Withdrawal of the block exemption by the Commission or by a Member State', pp 685–686.

[373] See eg, in the UK, *Argos Ltd v OFT* [2006] EWCA Civ 1318.

to distribute a portfolio of goods and/or services, and has a market share of more than 30% for some of those products and less than 30% for others: the Commission states that the block exemption will not apply in the former case but would in the latter.

Section V of the *Guidelines* (paragraphs 86 to 95) discusses various issues concerning market definition and market share calculation. Paragraph 89 examines questions concerning the relevant product market; the Commission states that in most cases the relevant market will be defined by examining the market from the buyer's perspective. Paragraph 90 deals with the position where there are more than two parties to the agreement[374]. Paragraph 91 discusses the position of original equipment manufacturer suppliers; and paragraph 92 deals with market shares in the context of franchising agreements. Paragraphs 93 to 95 deal specifically with the calculation of market shares under the Regulation.

(v) Article 6

Article 6 provides that the Commission may disapply the block exemption where 50% of a relevant market is covered by a network of similar vertical agreements. This market share test is dealt with later[375], and will have only rare application.

(F) Article 4: hard-core restrictions

Recital 10 of the Regulation states that vertical agreements 'containing certain types of severe restrictions of competition such as minimum and fixed resale-prices, as well as certain types of territorial protection, should be excluded from the benefit of the block exemption established by this Regulation irrespective of the market share of the undertakings concerned'[376]. Article 4 contains the list of 'hard-core' restrictions which lead to the exclusion of the entire vertical agreement—not just the provision in question—from the block exemption[377]. Article 4 is to be contrasted with Article 5, which denies block exemption to certain specific obligations, but which does not deprive the rest of the agreement of the benefit of the block exemption[378]. Paragraph 70 of the *Guidelines* states that there is no severability for hard-core restrictions.

Each of the hard-core restrictions in Article 4 relates to a restriction of intra-brand competition[379], although the Commission's view is that in some cases restrictions of intra-brand competition can affect inter-brand competition by softening competition and/or facilitating horizontal collusion[380]. Paragraph 47 of the *Guidelines* states that an agreement that contains a hard-core restriction of the kind listed in Article 4 'is presumed to fall within Article 101(1)'. This is a reference to agreements that, in the terms of Article 101 TFEU, have the 'object' of restricting competition: paragraphs 23 and 96 of the *Guidelines* specifically refer to hard-core restrictions as restrictions of competition by object. A restriction of competition by object (and thus a hard-core restriction) that

[374] See 'The exempted agreement may be multilateral', pp 667–668 earlier in chapter.

[375] See 'Article 6: disapplication of the block exemption by Commission Regulation', pp 686–687 later in chapter.

[376] See *Vertical guidelines*, paras 47–59.

[377] Ibid, para 47.

[378] See 'Article 5: obligations in vertical agreements that are not exempt', pp 684–685 later in chapter.

[379] Restrictions of inter-brand competition, or situations in which inter-brand competition is weak, are specifically dealt with in other parts of the Regulation, eg Article 2(4); Article 3; Article 5; and the provisions for withdrawal of the block exemption, as to which see 'Withdrawal of the block exemption by the Commission or by a Member State', pp 685–686 later in chapter.

[380] For an example of a situation where the Commission was concerned that 'most-favoured nation' clauses might be causing price parallelism see its investigations of Hollywood studios, Commission Press Release IP/04/1314, 26 October 2004 and Commission Press Release IP/11/257, 4 March 2011; on MFNs generally see 'Parity provisions', pp 663-664 earlier in chapter.

appreciably affects trade between Member States constitutes an appreciable restriction of competition, such that the *de minimis* doctrine does not apply[381]. However a hard-core restriction may fall outside Article 101(1) where it does not have an appreciable effect on inter-state trade[382]. Separately, paragraphs 60 to 64 of the *Vertical guidelines* acknowledge that there are situations in which hard-core restrictions may be objectively necessary for an agreement of a particular type and therefore fall outside Article 101(1) altogether, or fulfil the conditions of Article 101(3)[383]. Paragraph 47 of the *Guidelines* states that it is presumed that agreements containing hard-core restrictions are unlikely to satisfy Article 101(3), but continues that undertakings may be able to demonstrate that Article 101(3) applies in a particular case, and refers to paragraphs 106 to 109 of the *Guidelines* which discuss possible efficiencies related to vertical restraints generally and to Section VI.2.10 (paragraphs 223 to 229) which consider arguments against, but also possible justifications for, resale price maintenance specifically.

Article 4 provides that block exemption will not be available to agreements which 'directly or indirectly, in isolation or in combination with other factors under the control of the parties, have as their object' the matters dealt with below, such as resale price maintenance and excessive territorial protection. Article 4 applies only according to the object, and *not* the effect, of an agreement. The word 'object' in Article 4 of the Regulation, and in Article 101(1) TFEU, does not refer to the subjective intention of the parties; rather to the purpose of the agreement judged by objective standards[384]. The scope of the exclusion of the block exemption is nonetheless quite extensive as it will prevent the block exemption from applying where the agreement 'directly or indirectly, in isolation or in combination with other factors' has one of the forbidden objects.

(i) **Article 4(a): resale price maintenance**

Article 4(a) provides that the block exemption will not be available where the object of the agreement is:

> the restriction of the buyer's ability to determine its sale price, without prejudice to the possibility of the supplier imposing a maximum sale price or recommending a sale price, provided that they do not amount to a fixed or minimum sale price as a result of pressure from, or incentives offered by, any of the parties[385].

This formulation explicitly recognises that the imposition of maximum[386] resale prices and the recommendation[387] of prices is permitted; this, however, is subject to the proviso that follows, which itself must be read in conjunction with the words 'directly or indirectly' in the opening part of Article 4. Paragraph 48 of the *Vertical guidelines* picks up on the idea that the agreement may have the direct *or indirect* object of resale price maintenance. A contractual restriction establishing a minimum price would be a simple

[381] Case C-226/11 EU:C:2012:795, para 37; see further ch 3, 'The *De Minimis* Doctrine', pp 147–150.

[382] Case 5/69 *Völk v Vervaecke* EU:C:1969:35; Case C-306/96 *Javico v Yves Saint Laurent* EU:C:1998:173.

[383] See 'Export bans falling outside Article 101(1) or satisfying Article 101(3)', pp 650–651 earlier in chapter.

[384] See ch 3, 'Agreements that have as their object the prevention, restriction or distortion of competition', pp 122–132.

[385] See *Guidelines*, paras 48 and 49 and 'Recommended and maximum resale prices', pp 662–663 earlier in chapter.

[386] The Commission said in *Nathan-Bricolux* OJ [2001] L 54/1 that the imposition of maximum resale prices does not, in itself, infringe Article 101(1): see para 87; the Court of Justice has never ruled on the imposition of maximum prices.

[387] The Court of Justice held in Case 161/84 *Pronuptia de Paris v Pronuptia de Paris Irmgard Schillgalis* EU:C:1986:41 that the recommendation of prices would not, in itself, infringe Article 101(1): see para 25.

example of an agreement the *direct* object of which is to fix prices. Paragraph 48 gives examples of price maintenance through indirect means:

> fixing the distribution margin, fixing the maximum level of discount the distributor can grant from a prescribed price level, making the grant of rebates or reimbursement of promotional costs by the supplier subject to the observance of a given price level, linking the prescribed resale price to the resale prices of competitors, threats, intimidation, warnings, penalties, delay or suspension of deliveries or contract terminations in relation to the observance of a given price level[388].

Measures taken to identify price-cutting distributors might also amount to 'indirect pressure' to fix prices; paragraph 48 suggests that printing a recommended resale price or an obligation to apply a most favoured customer clause would reduce the incentive to cut price and so could be within the mischief of Article 4. The paragraph acknowledges that the use of a particular 'supportive' measure or the recommendation of prices is not, in itself, a hard-core restriction. In the case of domestic litigation, it is for the national court to determine, on the basis of the evidence before it, whether a resale price is recommended, fixed or a minimum one[389].

In the case of agency agreements Article 101(1) would normally not be applicable[390]. However where such an agreement falls within Article 101(1), paragraph 49 of the *Guidelines* states that a restriction on the agent preventing or restricting the sharing of commission with its customers, whether fixed or variable, would amount to a hard-core restriction. The agent should be left free to lower the effective price paid by the customer without reducing the income for the principal[391].

(ii) **Article 4(b): territorial and customer restrictions**

The opening words of Article 4(b) provide that the block exemption will not be available where the object of the agreement is:

> the restriction of the territory into which, or of the customers to whom, a buyer party to the agreement, without prejudice to a restriction on its place of establishment, may sell the contract goods or services.

This important provision deals with the extent to which it is possible to grant territorial or customer exclusivity[392].

(a) Article 4(b): the hard-core restriction

Article 4(b) is concerned only with restrictions on the *buyer's* right to sell, and not to restrictions on the supplier's sales, which are not to be treated as hard-core. The expression 'without prejudice to a restriction on its place of establishment' in Article 4(b) means that the benefit of the block exemption will not be lost if it is agreed that the buyer will restrict its distribution outlet(s) and warehouse(s) to a particular address, place or territory[393]. The same expression recurs in Article 4(c) in the context of selective distribution (see later). Paragraph 50 of the *Guidelines* refers to the 'direct/indirect object' dichotomy in the opening words of Article 4. Indirect measures to restrict the buyer could include:

[388] The Court of Justice used a similar formulation in Case C-506/07 *Lubricarga v Petrogal Española* EU:C:2009:504, para 53, referring to 'threats, intimidation, warnings, penalties or incentives'.

[389] See Case C-260/07 *Pedro IV Servicios SL v Total España SA* EU:C:2009:215, paras 79 and 80, citing Case C-279/06 *CEPSA Estaciones de Servicio SA v LV Tobar e Hijos SL* EU:C:2008:485, paras 67, 70 and 71.

[390] See 'Commercial Agents', pp 634–637 earlier in chapter.

[391] See Case 311/85 *Vereniging van Vlaamse Reisbureaus v Sociale Dienst van de Plaatselijke en Gewestelijke Overheidsdiensten* EU:C:1987:418, para 24.

[392] *Vertical guidelines*, paras 49–52. [393] Ibid, para 50.

> refusal or reduction of bonuses or discounts, termination of supply, reduction of supplied volumes or limitation of supplied volumes to the demand within the allocated territory or customer group, threat of contract termination, requiring a higher price for products to be exported, limiting the proportion of sales that can be exported or profit pass-over obligations.

The withholding of a guarantee service could also amount to indirect means[394]. These practices would be more likely to be considered indirect measures to restrict the buyer's freedom when operated in conjunction with a monitoring system for detecting parallel trade. Clearly this paragraph of the *Vertical guidelines* is based on the Commission's decisional practice, upheld by the EU Courts, over many years[395].

Paragraph 50 of the Guidelines specifically points out that an obligation on the reseller relating to the display of the supplier's brand names is not regarded as hard-core under Article 4(b)[396].

(b) Article 4(b): exceptions

Article 4(b) provides four exceptions to the prohibition on territorial and customer restrictions; the first is particularly important, since it deals with the distinction between active and passive sales.

Exception 1: it is permissible to have a restriction:

> of active sales into the exclusive territory or to an exclusive customer group reserved to the supplier or allocated by the supplier to another buyer, where such a restriction does not limit sales by the customers of the buyer.

Several points should be noted about Article 4(b)(i). The first is that a restriction of active sales to other territories or customers is permitted, provided that there are no restrictions on passive sales by the buyer. This is not stated specifically in Article 4(b); it is stated explicitly, however, in paragraph 51 of the *Vertical guidelines*. Secondly, the restriction must be on active sales into the territory or customer group 'reserved to the supplier or allocated by the supplier to another buyer'. Paragraph 51 explains that this means that the buyer must be protected against sales by all other buyers of the supplier within the EU, 'irrespective of sales by the supplier'. It follows that protection against active selling will not be lost because a vertical agreement does not impose a restriction on the supplier, but only on its buyers; to put the point another way, *sole* distributorships (which leave the supplier free to supply in the distributor's territory) can benefit from block exemption as well as *exclusive* distributorships, where the supplier agrees that it will not supply to customers in the latter's territory. It is apparently not possible to restrict active sales into an area reserved to a licensee of know-how or of a patent, although no explanation is given of why this should be so. Thirdly, exclusive distribution may be combined with exclusive customer allocation under Article 4(b)(i), provided that passive selling is not restricted.

Paragraph 51 of the *Guidelines* deals with the distinction between active and passive sales, which can be depicted as follows:

ACTIVE SALES	PASSIVE SALES
Actively approaching individual customers to sell goods or services	Responding to unsolicited requests from individual customers, including delivery of goods or services to such customers

[394] Ibid, para 50 and case law cited. [395] See 'Direct and indirect export bans', pp 646–651 earlier in chapter.

[396] This is presumably based on the judgment of the Court of Justice in Case 161/84 *Pronuptia de Paris v Pronuptia de Paris Irmgard Schillgalis* EU:C:1986:41.

Paragraph 51 of the *Guidelines* gives examples of active selling: establishing a warehouse or distribution outlet in another's exclusive territory, approaching individual customers by sending unsolicited emails, and advertising to a specific customer group or customers in a particular territory through advertisements on the internet. It adds that advertisement or promotion that is attractive for the buyer only if it reaches a specific group of customers or customers in a specific territory is active selling.

Paragraph 51 also gives an example of passive selling: 'general advertising or promotion'; advertising that reaches customers in other territories or customer groups will be regarded as general if it would make sense for the buyer to invest in that advertising or promotion even if it would only reach customers in its own territory or customer group.

Paragraphs 52 to 54 of the *Guidelines* explain the Commission's thinking in relation to online sales on the internet. Paragraph 52 states that, in principle, every distributor must be allowed to use the internet to sell products, and that, in general, the use of a website to sell products amounts to passive selling[397]. It follows that, if a customer visits the website of a distributor and if such contact leads to a sale, that is treated as a passive sale. Paragraph 52 adds that offering different language options on the website does not, of itself, change the passive character of such selling. The Commission then gives four examples of hard-core restrictions of passive selling:

- an agreement that a distributor in one territory will prevent customers in another distributor's territory from viewing its website or will automatically re-route customers to other distributors' websites: however it is permissible for a website to have links to those of other distributors and/or the supplier
- an agreement that a distributor will terminate customers' transactions over the internet if their credit card data reveal an address that is not within the distributor's territory
- an agreement that a distributor will limit its proportion of overall sales made over the internet. However it is permitted to require that the distributor will sell at least a certain absolute amount (in value or volume) offline so as to ensure an efficient operation of its 'brick and mortar' shop, that is to say, its physical point of sale: the absolute amount may be the same for all distributors, or may be determined individually for each buyer on the basis of objective criteria
- an agreement that the distributor will pay a higher price for products intended to be resold by the distributor online rather than offline[398]. However paragraph 64 of the *Guidelines* acknowledges that there may be circumstances in which dual pricing, though treated as hard-core under Article 4(b), may satisfy Article 101(3) on an individual basis. Such circumstances may be present where sales online lead to substantially higher costs for the supplier than offline sales.

Paragraph 53 of the *Guidelines* discusses the circumstances in which internet sales might be regarded as active rather than passive, with the result that it would be permissible under the block exemption to restrict them. Advertising specifically addressed to certain customers would be considered to be active, as would paying a search engine or online advertisement provider to have advertisements displayed specifically to users in a particular territory. Paragraph 54 explains that the supplier may impose quality standards

[397] See *Roma-branded mobility scooters*, OFT decision of 5 August 2013, para 3.232, finding agreements that prevented online sales and online price advertising of mobility scooters were hard-core restrictions within the meaning of Article 4(b), available at www.gov.uk/cma.

[398] See *CIBA/Alcon*, Hungarian NCA decision of 6 August 2015, condemning a supplier's rebate system requiring online resellers to pay higher prices for contact lenses than offline distributors.

for the use of the internet site to resell its goods, just as the supplier may do for selling in shops or by catalogue. In particular the supplier may require that its distributors have one or more brick and mortar shops or showrooms as a condition for becoming a member of the distribution system.

In *Yamaha*[399] the Commission considered that a restriction on internet selling infringed Article 101(1)[400] and was not covered by the block exemption[401]. In *Pierre Fabre Dermo-Cosmétique*[402] the Court of Justice held that a general and absolute prohibition of online selling imposed on members of a selective distribution system is a 'hard-core' restriction under Article 4(c)[403]. A restriction on the use of third party platforms for internet sales was considered not to infringe Article 4(b) in *Coty*[404]. Several NCAs have taken action against restrictions on selling or advertising via the internet[405]. Following the Commission's *E-commerce* sector inquiry[406] it is investigating whether several manufacturers have restricted retailers from selling cross-border to consumers within the EU[407].

Exception 2: it is permissible to have a restriction of sales—both active and passive—to end users by a buyer operating at the wholesale level of trade. Paragraph 55 of the *Guidelines* explains that this means that the supplier can keep the wholesale and retail levels of the market separate, with the result that buyers of its goods can specialise in their particular level of activity in the market; it adds that the supplier may, if it wishes, permit wholesalers to sell to some end users, for example large customers, though not to others.

Exception 3: it is permissible to have a restriction on sales—both active and passive—by members of a selective distribution system to unauthorised distributors in any territory where the system is currently operated or where the supplier does not yet sell the contract products[408]. A selective distribution system is defined in Article 1(1)(e) to mean a system where the supplier agrees to supply the contract goods or services only to distributors selected on the basis of specified criteria and those distributors agree not to sell to unauthorised distributors. It should be noted that this definition of a selective distribution system in the Regulation is not limited by reference to the nature of the goods or services in question; nor does it specify that the criteria should be qualitative rather than quantitative[409].

Exception 4: it is possible to restrict the buyer of components for use from selling them—both actively and passively—to a customer who would use them to manufacture goods that would compete with those of the supplier. Paragraph 55 of the *Guidelines* explains that the term 'component' includes any intermediate goods and the term 'incorporation' refers to the use of any input to produce the goods.

399 Commission decision of 16 July 2003. 400 Ibid, paras 107–110. 401 Ibid, para 171.

402 Case C-439/09 *Pierre Fabre* EU:C:2011:649. 403 Ibid, paras 54–59.

404 Case C-230/16 EU:C:2017:941, para 69.

405 See eg *Roma-branded mobility scooters*, OFT decision of 5 August 2013; *Ultra Finishing Ltd*, CMA decision of 10 May 2016; *Bang & Olufsen*, French NCA decision of 12 December 2012; *Pioneer*, Austrian Cartel Court decisions of March–June 2014; see also OECD's Roundtable *Vertical Restraints for On-line Sales* (2013), available at www.oecd.org/competition.

406 Final Report of 10 May 2017, available at www.ec.europa.eu.

407 See eg Commission Press Release IP/17/1549, 6 June 2017 (Guess) and Commission Press Release IP/17/1646, 14 June 2017 (Nike, Sanrio and Universal Studios).

408 This is the way para 55 of the *Vertical guidelines* interprets the phrase 'within the territory reserved by the supplier to operate that system' in Article 4(b)(iii) of the Regulation.

409 *Vertical guidelines*, para 176. 410 Ibid, paras 56–57.

(iii) Article 4(c): the restriction of active or passive sales to end users by members of a selective distribution system operating at the retail level of trade

Article 4(c) prevents the application of the block exception when there are restrictions on active or passive sales by selected distributors at the retail level of trade to end users[410]. Paragraph 56 of the *Vertical guidelines* says that the end users may be a professional buyer or a final consumer. However there is a proviso to Article 4(c), which is that the distributor may be prohibited from operating out of an unauthorised place of establishment: without this proviso the distributor would not be complying with the 'specified criteria' that make the system selective, and would effectively be operating as an unauthorised distributor[411]. The Court of Justice has said that the internet cannot be understood as a 'virtual' place of business in this context; the internet is a method of selling and marketing goods[412].

Paragraph 56 of the *Guidelines* also explains that it is permitted to impose a restriction 'to protect an exclusive distribution system operated elsewhere', referring back to paragraph 51; paragraph 51 addresses Article 4(b)(i) of the Regulation, which permits restrictions on active, but not on passive sales. It presumably follows, therefore, that members of a selective distribution system can be prevented from actively selling to users in a territory or customer group allocated exclusively to another distributor, but cannot be prevented from passive selling. Paragraph 56 goes on to say that dealers within a selective distribution system should be free to sell to all end users, including with the help of the internet. The Court of Justice agrees with this point[413]. Paragraph 56 of the *Guidelines* explains that obligations which dissuade dealers from using the internet to reach a greater number and variety of consumers by imposing criteria for online sales which are not overall equivalent to the criteria imposed for sales from the brick and mortar shop will be regarded as hard-core. This does not mean that the same criteria must be applied to online and offline sales, but that any differences in those criteria 'should pursue the same objectives and achieve comparable results and that the difference between the criteria must be justified by the different nature of these two distribution modes'.

Paragraph 57 of the *Guidelines* explains that, within the territory in which a selective distribution system is operated, there cannot be exclusive distribution, since this would violate the rule in Article 4(c) that there must be the possibility of both active and passive sales to end users. In other words, selective distribution may be combined with exclusive distribution under the block exemption if active and passive selling is not restricted[414].

A restriction on the use of third party platforms for internet sales was considered not to infringe Article 4(c) in *Coty*[415].

(iv) Article 4(d): restrictions on cross-supplies within a selective distribution system

Article 4(d) prevents the application of the block exemption where there is a restriction of cross-supplies between distributors within a selective distribution system, including distributors at different level of trade[416]. In *Yamaha*[417] the Commission objected to obligations on official distributors to sell only to final customers, since this amounted to a restriction on cross-supplies within the network. It is not possible to require an authorised distributor to purchase solely from one source: it must be able to buy from any approved distributor[418].

411 On this point see ibid, para 57.
412 Case C-439/09 *Pierre Fabre* EU:C:2011:649, paras 56–58.
413 Ibid, para 59.
414 This is the way the point is expressed in para 152 of the *Vertical guidelines*.
415 Case C-230/16 EU:C:2017:941, para 69.
416 *Vertical guidelines*, para 58.
417 Commission decision of 16 July 2003.
418 *Vertical guidelines*, para 58.

(v) Article 4(e): restrictions on the supplier's ability to supply components to third parties

Article 4(e) designates as hard-core a restriction on the ability of a supplier of components to sell them as spare parts to end users or to repairers or service providers not entrusted by the buyer with the repair or servicing of its goods[419]. End users and independent service providers should be free to obtain spare parts; but the buyer can insist that repairers and service providers within its system should buy the spare parts only from itself[420].

(G) Article 5: obligations in vertical agreements that are not exempt

Recital 11 of the Regulation states that certain conditions are attached to the block exemption in order to ensure 'access to or to prevent collusion on the relevant market'[421]. Where an agreement contains an obligation of the kind set out in Article 5, that obligation does not benefit from block exemption: this is true whether the parties' market shares are above or below the market share cap. The block exemption continues to apply however to the remaining parts of the vertical agreement if they are 'severable' from the non-exempted obligation[422]. Neither the Regulation nor the *Guidelines* discuss the notion of 'severability' for the purpose of Article 5; whether a contractual obligation is 'severable' for the purpose of Article 101(2) is a matter for the applicable law of the contract[423].

Article 5 contains three exclusions.

(i) Article 5(1)(a): non-compete obligations

Article 5(1)(a) excludes from the block exemption:

> any direct or indirect non-compete obligation, the duration of which is indefinite or exceeds five years[424].

Article 1(1)(d) provides that 'non-compete obligation' means an obligation not to manufacture, purchase, sell or resell goods or services which compete with the contract goods or services: this is what most people would understand by this expression. However Article 1(1)(d) goes on to provide that the term also includes any obligation on the buyer to purchase from the supplier or from an undertaking designated by the supplier more than 80%[425] of the buyer's total purchases of the contract goods or services and their substitutes on the relevant market, calculated on the basis of the value or, where such is standard industry practice, the volume of its purchases in the preceding calendar year. The Commission's concern is not just that a 100% requirements contract could foreclose access to the market, but that lesser commitments of 'more than 80%' also might do so.

An agreement that is 'tacitly renewable' is treated as having an indefinite duration. Paragraph 66 of the *Vertical guidelines* states that non-compete obligations are block exempted where their duration is limited to five years or less and no obstacles exist that hinder the buyer from effectively terminating at the end of five years should it so wish. Article 5(2) contains a derogation from the rule contained in Article 5(1)(a): longer periods are block exempted when the contract goods or services are sold from land and premises owned by the supplier or leased from third parties. The Court of Justice has held that the terms 'premises' and 'land' refer to a part of a building and a parcel of land, not the

[419] Ibid, para 59. [420] Ibid, para 59. [421] Ibid, paras 65–69. [422] Ibid, paras 65 and 71.

[423] See ch 8, 'Severance', pp 338–339. [424] *Vertical guidelines*, paras 66–67.

[425] A literal interpretation would mean that an obligation to purchase 80% of the buyer's total purchases would not amount to a non-compete obligation, but that an obligation to purchase 81% would, since only the latter applies to 'more than 80%'.

entire territory allocated to a distributor[426]. Paragraph 67 of the *Guidelines* states that 'artificial ownership constructions' to take advantage of this derogation will not be permitted. These 'longer periods' mean that beer and petrol agreements in 'tied' houses and garages will be permissible for more than five years[427].

There have been many cases in the English courts in which the validity of beer ties has been considered[428].

(ii) Article 5(1)(b): post-term non-compete obligations

Article 5(1)(b) excludes from the block exemption:

> any direct or indirect obligation causing the buyer, after termination of the agreement, not to manufacture, purchase, sell or resell goods or services[429].

Article 5(3) contains a derogation from Article 5(1)(b) for a post-term ban of not more than one year on sales of competing goods or services from the point of sale at which the buyer operated during the contract period where this is indispensable to protect know-how transferred from the supplier to the buyer. Article 5(3) also provides that Article 5(1)(b) is without prejudice to the possibility of imposing a restriction which is unlimited in time on the use and disclosure of know-how which has not entered the public domain. Know-how for this purpose is defined in Article 1(1)(g) of the Regulation, and must be 'substantial', that is to say significant and useful to the buyer for the use, sale or resale of the contract goods or services[430].

(iii) Article 5(1)(c): competing products in a selective distribution system

Article 5(1)(c) excludes from the block exemption an obligation causing the members of a selective distribution system not to sell the brands of particular competing suppliers[431]. It is permissible, subject to Article 5(1)(a), to require a selective distributor not to handle competing brands in general[432]; however Article 5(1)(c) prevents the exemption from applying where there is a boycott of particular competing suppliers. Paragraph 69 of the *Guidelines* explains that this is to prevent the exclusion of 'a specific competitor or certain specific competitors'.

(H) Withdrawal of the block exemption by the Commission or by a Member State

Regulation 330/2010 does not confer power on the Commission or Member States to withdraw the benefit of the block exemption for vertical agreements in an individual case, since this power is conferred by Article 29(1) and (2) of Regulation 1/2003[433]; it is

[426] Case C-117/12 *La Retoucherie de Manuela v La Retoucherie de Burgos* EU:C:2013:72, para 29.

[427] See eg *Whitbread* OJ [1999] L 88/26, upheld on appeal Case T-131/99 *Shaw v Commission* EU:T:2002:83; *Bass* OJ [1999] L 186/1, upheld on appeal Case T-231/99 *Joynson v Commission* EU:T:2002:84; Case T-25/99 *Roberts v Commission* EU:T:2001:177.

[428] See eg *Holleran v Thwaites* [1989] 2 CMLR 917; *Inntrepreneur Estates (GL) Ltd v Boyes* [1993] 2 EGLR 112; *Little v Courage Ltd* (1994) 70 P & CR 469; *Star Rider Ltd v Inntrepreneur Bub Co* [1998] 1 EGLR 53; *Greenall Management Ltd v Canavan (No 2)* [1998] Eu LR 507; *Gibbs Mew plc v Gemmell* [1998] Eu LR 588; *Trent Taverns Ltd v Sykes* [1998] Eu LR 492; *Passmore v Morland* [1999] Eu LR 501; *Crehan v Courage* [1999] Eu LR 409; the *Crehan* case was referred to the Court of Justice under Article 267 TFEU in Case C-453/99 EU:C:2001:465, as to which see ch 8, '*Courage Ltd v Crehan*', pp 308–309.

[429] *Vertical guidelines*, para 68.

[430] It is not necessary for the know-how to be 'indispensable' as had been required by Article 1(f) of the old block exemption Regulation 2790/99.

[431] *Vertical guidelines*, para 69. [432] Ibid.

[433] See recitals 13 and 14 of Regulation 330/2010 and recital 10 of Regulation 1/2003; on withdrawal see generally the *Vertical guidelines*, paras 74–78.

worth noting in passing that this power has never been used[434]. Recital 15 of Regulation 330/2010 refers to Article 29 of Regulation 1/2003 and states that, in determining whether the benefit of block exemption should be withdrawn pursuant to that provision, the anti-competitive effects that may derive from parallel networks of vertical agreements having similar effects and which significantly restrict access to a relevant market or competition therein are of particular importance: the recital says that selective distribution and non-compete obligations are examples of provisions that might lead to such cumulative effects. The power in Article 29 of Regulation 1/2003 is different from the power in Article 6 of Regulation 330/2010 (see section 7(I) later), where the block exemption may be disapplied from all vertical agreements in a particular relevant market; under Article 29 the block exemption is withdrawn 'in a particular case'[435].

(i) Article 29(1) of Regulation 1/2003: withdrawal by the Commission

Article 29(1) provides that the Commission may withdraw the benefit of the block exemption in an individual case where an agreement has effects that are incompatible with Article 101(3). As noted earlier this could be so where there is a 'cumulative effect' within the market of similar vertical agreements leading to an unjustified restriction of competition[436]. Paragraphs 74 to 78 of the *Guidelines* discuss the withdrawal procedure. Paragraph 77 states that the Commission would have the burden of proving that Article 101(1) is infringed and that the agreement does not fulfil the conditions of Article 101(3). Paragraph 77 also states that a withdrawal decision can only have *ex nunc* effect, so that block exemption will persist until the time of the withdrawal.

(ii) Article 29(2) of Regulation 1/2003: withdrawal by a Member State

Article 29(2) confers power on the competition authorities of Member States to withdraw the benefit of the block exemption where agreements to which the Regulation applies have effects incompatible with Article 101(3) 'in the territory of a Member State, or in a part thereof, which has all the characteristics of a distinct geographic market'. Paragraph 78 of the *Guidelines* states that, where the geographic market is wider than a Member State, the Commission has the sole power to withdraw the block exemption. In other cases the power is concurrent.

(I) Article 6: disapplication of the block exemption by Commission Regulation

Recital 16 of the Regulation introduces the idea of the Commission disapplying the block exemption from agreements in a given market[437]. Article 6 provides that the Commission may by regulation declare that, where parallel networks of similar vertical restraints cover more than 50% of a relevant market, the block exemption shall not apply to vertical agreements containing specific restraints in that market. Article 1a of Council Regulation 19/65 provides that such a regulation shall not become applicable earlier than six months following its adoption: as paragraph 84 of the *Vertical guidelines* says, time may be needed for the undertakings concerned to adapt their agreements.

The Commission discusses the 'disapplication' of Regulation 330/2010 in paragraphs 79 to 85 of Part IV of the *Guidelines*. As it explains in paragraph 80, a regulation under

[434] The Commission withdrew the benefit of an old block exemption, Regulation 1984/83, from exclusive purchasing agreements in the German market for impulse ice-cream in *Langnese* OJ [1993] L 183/19; the Commission's decision was upheld on appeal in Case T-7/93 *Langnese-Iglo v Commission* EU:T:1995:98.

[435] See recital 13 of Regulation 330/2010.

[436] Ibid, recital 15 and *Vertical guidelines*, paras 75–76.

[437] *Vertical guidelines*, paras 79–85.

Article 8 removes the benefit of the block exemption and restores the full application of Article 101(1) and (3). The Commission would have to decide how to proceed in relation to any individual agreements, and might take a decision in an individual case in order to provide guidance to undertakings in the market generally. The Commission may in some cases have a choice of whether it wishes to proceed under Article 29(1) of Regulation 1/2003 (against a particular undertaking or particular agreements) or under Article 6 of Regulation 330/2010: paragraph 82 of the *Guidelines* says that, in making this choice, the Commission would consider the number of competing undertakings contributing to the cumulative effect or the number of geographic markets within the EU that are affected. Paragraph 85 of the *Guidelines* states that a regulation under Article 8 would not affect the exempted status of the agreements in question prior to its entry into force.

(J) **Articles 7 and 8: market share and turnover**

Article 7 deals with the calculation of market share[438]. Article 7(a) provides that market share shall be calculated by reference to market sales value; where market sales value data are not available, estimates based on other reliable market information, including sales volumes, may be used. Article 7(b) provides that the market share data should be calculated by reference to the preceding calendar year. Article 7(d) to (g) provide some marginal relief for up to two years where the market share rises above 30% but not beyond 35%.

Article 8 explains how turnover is to be calculated for the purpose of the rules in Article 2(2).

(K) **Articles 9 and 10: transitional provisions and entry into force**

The Regulation entered into force on 1 June 2010. Transitional relief until 1 June 2011 was provided for agreements already block exempted under Regulation 2790/99. The new Regulation will expire on 31 May 2022.

8. Vertical Agreements: Individual Application of Article 101(3)

Vertical agreements that infringe Article 101(1) and that are ineligible for block exemption under Regulation 330/2010 may nevertheless satisfy the terms of Article 101(3) on an individual basis.

Section VI of the *Vertical guidelines* provides guidance on the application of Article 101(3) to vertical agreements where this is needed in individual cases because Article 101(1) is infringed and the block exemption is inapplicable. The positive effects of vertical restraints are described in paragraph 107[439], and some general comments on the application of Article 101(3) will be found at paragraphs 122 to 127[440]. There is a presumption that hard-core restrictions of the kind listed in Article 4 of the block exemption are unlikely to satisfy Article 101(3)[441], although undertakings may be

[438] See generally ibid, paras 93–95.
[439] See 'Vertical agreements: possible benefits to competition', pp 640–642 earlier in chapter.
[440] See 'Relevant factors for the assessment under Article 101(3)', p 645 earlier in chapter.
[441] *Vertical guidelines*, para 47.

able to demonstrate that Article 101(3) applies in an individual case[442]; as the General Court stated in *Matra Hachette v Commission*[443] the parties to any kind of agreement—including, therefore, an agreement containing hard-core restrictions—are entitled to defend it under Article 101(3). Individual assessment of agreements is most likely to be necessary where either of the parties' market shares exceed the 30% market share cap. What is unclear is whether the Commission will ever adopt a decision saying that it considers that an agreement satisfies Article 101(3): it could do this only by adopting a 'declaration of inapplicability' under Article 10 of Regulation 1/2003, something it has never done; of by providing informal guidance, again which has never occurred[444].

Specific guidance is given on the application of Article 101(3) to single branding agreements at paragraphs 144 to 148. Where a 'client-specific investment' is made, a non-compete obligation of more than five years may be allowed under Article 101(3)[445]: this is consistent with the Commission's past practice where, for example, 15-year exclusive purchase agreements have been allowed where an investment is made in the building of new power stations[446]. Where a non-compete clause is included in an exclusive distribution agreement this may be permitted for the duration of the agreement, even where this is for longer than the five years permitted by the block exemption[447]. In *DSD*[448] the Commission considered that the criteria of Article 101(3) were satisfied in relation to an agreement whereby DSD, an undertaking in Germany which operated a nationwide system for the collection and recovery of sales packaging, agreed to purchase collection and sorting services exclusively from one collector in each designated district: the exclusivity made it possible for the parties to plan the provision of services on a long-term basis and to organise it reliably, and this gave practical effect to a scheme intended to provide a high level of environmental protection[449].

The possible application of Article 101(3) to exclusive distribution agreements is considered at paragraphs 161 to 164 of the *Vertical guidelines*. The Commission states that, in the absence of a foreclosure effect, a non-compete obligation of more than five years may be allowed when it is part of an exclusive distribution agreement[450]. The Commission specifically notes that exclusive distribution is most likely to have efficiency-enhancing effects where the products involved are new, complex or have qualities that are difficult to assess prior to consumption[451]. Paragraph 172 of the *Guidelines* considers the possible improvements in efficiency attributable to exclusive customer allocation. Article 101(3) and selective distribution agreements are considered at paragraphs 185 and 186; exclusive supply is dealt with at paragraphs 200 to 201; up-front access payments at paragraphs 207 and 208; category management at paragraph 213; and tying at paragraph 222. The circumstances in which, in an individual case, resale price maintenance might lead to efficiencies are discussed in paragraph 225[452].

[442] See the discussion in 'Recommended and maximum resale prices', pp 662–663 earlier in chapter.

[443] Case T-17/93 EU:T:1994:89, para 85; see also para 46 of the Commission's *Guidelines on the application of Article [101(3)]* OJ [2004] C 101/97.

[444] See ch 7, 'Article 10: finding of inapplicability', p 269.

[445] *Vertical guidelines*, para 146.

[446] See eg *Isab Energy* [1996] 4 CMLR 889, Commission's XXVIth *Report on Competition Policy* (1996), pp 133–134; *REN/Turbogás* [1996] 4 CMLR 881, XXVIth *Report on Competition Policy* (1996), pp 134–135.

[447] *Vertical guidelines*, para 161.

[448] OJ [2001] L 319/1, upheld on appeal Case T-289/01 *Duales System Deutschland GmbH v Commission* EU:T:2007:155.

[449] OJ [2001] L 319/1, paras 141–163.

[450] *Vertical guidelines*, para 161.

[451] Ibid, para 164.

[452] See 'Minimum and fixed prices under Article 101(3)', p 662 earlier in chapter.

9. Vertical Agreements: Enforcement

In the 1980s and 1990s the Commission frequently investigated vertical agreements and often imposed fines on firms that it considered to be acting contrary to the single market imperative. In the 2000s what has been noticeable is the dearth of cases brought by the Commission in relation to vertical agreements: indeed there has not been a Commission decision finding an infringement of Article 101 in the case of a vertical agreement since *Peugeot* in October 2005[453]. The Commission's enforcement activities in recent years have been overwhelmingly focused on detecting and penalising hard-core cartels and the enforcement of Article 102.

The lack of action on the Commission's part in relation to vertical agreements under Article 101 ought not, however, to be interpreted as a downgrading, on its part, of the importance of the internal market, nor of an increased tolerance of restrictions of parallel trade[454]. One explanation for the reduced enforcement action on the part of the Commission against vertical restraints under Article 101 is that there have been numerous cases at national level, both on the part of the NCAs and in the national courts[455]. This is hardly surprising: while the Commission grapples with large, often EU-wide (or even global), cartels and major cases of abuse of dominance, problems in relation to distribution systems, which are often arranged along national lines, are resolved at the level of the Member States. A further explanation for the lack of enforcement action on the part of the Commission—which cannot be proven empirically, but which is plausible—is that the EU regime for vertical agreements is well understood by undertakings and their legal advisers and that it works well in practice.

The rise of e-commerce has led to the Commission becoming active again in relation to vertical restraints. For example it is investigating whether agreements between major US film studios and European pay-TV broadcasters prevent the provision of pay-TV services between Member States[456]. The Commission has launched a number of cases following its *E-commerce* sector inquiry, because of the need to clarify the application of Article 101 to possible restrictions of online commerce. The Commission has issued three Press Releases. In the first it said that it had launched investigations in relation to the online pricing of consumer electronics, the geo-blocking of videogames and hotel price discrimination[457].

In the second it announced that it was investigating the online distribution practices of a clothing company, Guess[458]. The third investigation is of the licensing and distribution practices of Nike, Sanrio and Universal Studios[459].

10. Regulation 461/2010 on Motor Vehicle Distribution

The single market in the sale and after-sale servicing of motor vehicles has been slow to develop: differing tax regimes and methods of distribution, fluctuating exchange

[453] Commission decision of 5 October 2005, upheld as to substance on appeal Case T-450/05 *Peugeot v Commission* EU:T:2009:262.

[454] On the 'single market imperative' see *Vertical guidelines*, para 7; see also Chapter 1 'The single market imperative', pp 23–24 and ch 2, 'The single market imperative', pp 52–53.

[455] For examples of cases brought by NCAs see ch 16 n 89 and n 266 earlier in chapter.

[456] Commission Press Release IP/14/15, 13 January 2014; see also *Paramount* Commission commitment decision of 26 July 2016, on appeal Case T-873/16 *Groupe Canal + v Commission*, not yet decided.

[457] Commission Press Release IP/17/201, 2 February 2017.

[458] Commission Press Release IP/17/1549, 6 June 2017.

[459] Commission Press Release IP/17/1646, 14 June 2017.

rates and the fact that certain Member States drive on the 'wrong' side of the road, have meant that this market remains much less integrated than others. The Commission has, for years, monitored price differentials between Member States[460]. Over the years the Commission has condemned a number of anti-competitive practices in the market for motor cars, in particular the partitioning of national markets to prevent sales of vehicles from low- to high-priced Member States, and has adopted numerous decisions finding infringements both of Article 101(1)[461] and, on a few occasions, of Article 102[462]. The Commission also closed its file on the basis of informal assurances in several cases[463] and accepted commitments under Article 9 of Regulation 1/2003 in four cases[464].

As far as the system of block exemptions is concerned the distribution of motor vehicles has, since 1985, been subject to a legislative regime separate from that for vertical agreements generally[465]. There have been many cases brought before the EU Courts relating to the special regime for cars[466]. The Commission has published several reports on the distribution of motor vehicles, noting the market for new car sales is highly competitive, although competition was more limited in the markets for repair and maintenance and spare parts due to their brand-specific nature[467].

[460] See eg Commission Press Release IP/10/913, 9 July 2010; DG COMP's website contains useful material on car distribution: www.ec.europa.eu.

[461] See eg *BMW Belgium* OJ [1978] L 46/33, upheld on appeal Case 32/78 *BMW v Commission* EU:C:1979:191; *Ford Werke* OJ [1983] L 327/31, upheld on appeal Cases 25 and 26/84 *Ford Werke AG v Commission* EU:C:1985:340; *Fiat*, XIVth *Report on Competition Policy* (1984), point 70; *Alfa Romeo* ibid, point 71; *Peugeot* OJ [1986] L 295/19; *Citroen*, Commission Press Release IP(88)778; *Peugeot* OJ [1992] L 66/1, upheld on appeal Case T-9/92 *Peugeot v Commission* EU:T:1993:38 and on appeal to the Court of Justice Case C-322/93 P EU:C:1994:257; *Volkswagen* OJ [1998] L 124/60, substantially upheld on appeal Case T-62/98 *Volkswagen AG v Commission* EU:T:2000:180 and on appeal to the Court of Justice Case C-338/00 P *Volkswagen AG v Commission* EU:C:2003:473; *Opel* OJ [2001] L 59/1, substantially upheld on appeal Case T-368/00 *General Motors Nederland BV v Commission* EU:T:2003:275 and on appeal to the Court of Justice Case C-551/03 P *General Motors BV v Commission* EU:C:2006:229; *Peugeot*, Commission decision of 5 October 2005, substantially upheld on appeal to the General Court Case T-450/05 *Automobiles Peugeot v Commission* EU:T:2009:262; the Commission's decision in *Volkswagen II* [2001] L 262/14 was annulled on appeal Case T-208/01 *Volkswagen AG v Commission* EU:T:2003:326 and on appeal to the Court of Justice Case C-74/04 P *Commission v Volkswagen AG* EU:C:2006:460; and the Commission's decision in *DaimlerChrysler* OJ [2002] L 257/1 was partially annulled on appeal Case T-325/01 *DaimlerChrysler v Commission* EU:T:2005:322.

[462] See eg Case 226/84 *BL v Commission* EU:C:1986:421; Case 26/75 *General Motors Continental NV v Commission* EU:C:1975:150.

[463] See eg *Audi*, Commission Press Release IP/03/80, 20 January 2003; *General Motors*, Commission Press Release IP/06/302, 13 March 2006; *BMW*, Commission Press Release IP/06/303, 13 March 2006.

[464] *DaimlerChrysler* OJ [2007] L 317/76; *Fiat* OJ [2007] L 332/77; *Opel* OJ [2007] L 330/44; *Toyota Motor Europe* OJ [2007] L 329/52.

[465] The old block exemptions were Regulation 123/85, OJ [1985] L 15/16, which was replaced by Regulation 1475/95, OJ [1995] L 145/25, which in turn was replaced by Regulation 1400/2002, OJ [2002] L 203/30.

[466] In addition to the cases in n 461 earlier, see Case 10/86 *VAG France v Magne* EU:C:1986:502; Case C-70/93 *BMW v ALD* EU:C:1995:344; Case C-266/93 *Bundeskartellamt v Volkswagen AG* EU:C:1995:345; Case C-226/94 *Grand Garage Albigeois* EU:C:1996:55; Case C-309/94 *Nissan France* EU:C:1996:57; Case C-128/95 *Fontaine* EU:C:1997:72; Case C-41/96 *VAG-Handlerbeirat eV v SYD-Consult* EU:C:1997:283; Case C-230/96 *Cabour SA v Automobiles Peugeot SA* EU:C:1998:181; Case C-125/05 *VW-Audi Forhandlerforeningen v Skaninavisk Motor Co A/S* EU:C:2006:531; Cases C-376/05 and C-377/05 *A Brünsteiner GmbH v BMW* EU:C:2006:753; Case C-421/05 *City Motors Groep NV v Citroën Belux NV* EU:C:2007:38; cf also in the EFTA Court Case E-3/97 *Jan and Kristian Jæger AS v Opel Norge AS* [1999] 4 CMLR 147 and, in the English courts, *Cound v BMW* [1997] Eu LR 277 and *Clover Leaf Cars v BMW* [1997] Eu LR 535.

[467] *Evaluation Report on the operation of Commission Regulation (EC) No 1400/2002*, SEC(2008) 1946, 28 May 2008; see also *The Future Competition Law Framework applicable to the Motor Vehicle Sector*, COM(2009) 388 final, 22 July 2009.

Since 1 June 2013 vertical agreements relating to the purchase, sale or resale of new motor vehicles fall within the regime set out in Regulation 330/2010. Article 3 of Regulation 461/2010[468] provides a separate block exemption for vertical agreements relating to purchase, sale or resale of spare parts for motor vehicles or repair and maintenance services for motor vehicles, provided they satisfy the requirements of Regulation 330/2010 and do not contain any of the specified additional hard-core restrictions in Article 5 of Regulation 461/2010. In particular a supplier must be free to sell spare parts to authorised distributors or independent repairers[469]; this is intended to ensure effective competition on the repair and maintenance markets[470]. Article 29 of Regulation 1/2003 enables the Commission or a Member State to withdraw the benefit of the block exemption in certain circumstances[471]. Article 6 of Regulation 461/2010 gives the power to the Commission by regulation to disapply the block exemption to vertical agreements containing specific restraints in a relevant market more than 50% of which is covered by parallel networks of similar vertical restraints. The Commission is required to monitor the operation of Regulation 461/2010 and will prepare a report on its application by 31 May 2021. Agreements relating to motor vehicle aftermarkets are subject to Regulation 461/2010 until 31 May 2023.

The Commission has published *Supplementary guidelines* which deal not only with the interpretation of the block exemption itself, but also, in Section IV, with the application of Article 101(1) to single branding and selective distribution in the motor vehicle sector[472].

11. **Sub-Contracting Agreements**

Sub-contracting agreements are a common feature of the commercial world. A contractor often entrusts another undertaking—the sub-contractor—to manufacture goods, supply services or to perform work under the contractor's instructions. Where the sub-contractor simply supplies goods or services to the contractor, the agreement would be a vertical one and the agreement would be governed by the Commission's *Vertical guidelines* and by the block exemption for vertical agreements[473]. Where a sub-contracting agreement is entered into between competing undertakings it falls to be considered under the Commission's *Guidelines on Horizontal Cooperation Agreements*[474]. However in some cases the contractor transfers know-how to the sub-contractor in order for it to be able to perform the tasks entrusted to it. The Commission has adopted a *Notice on Sub-contracting Agreements* to explain the application of Article 101(1) to this situation[475].

[468] OJ [2010] L 129/52; for commentary see Clark and Simon 'The New Legal Framework for Motor Vehicle Distribution: A Toolkit to Deal with Real Competition Breakdowns' (2010) 1 JECLAP 491.

[469] See Article 5(b) of Regulation 461/2010, on which see *Supplementary guidelines on vertical restraints in agreements for the sale and repair of motor vehicles and for the distribution of spare parts for motor vehicles* OJ [2010] C 138/16, para 23.

[470] See recital 17 of Regulation 461/2010.

[471] See ibid, recitals 20 and 23; on the powers to withdraw the benefit of the block exemption see 'Withdrawal of the block exemption by the Commission or by a Member State', pp 685–686 earlier in chapter.

[472] OJ [2010] C 138/16.

[473] See the Commission's *Guidelines on Horizontal Cooperation Agreements* OJ [2011] C 11/1, para 154.

[474] Ibid, paras 150–153; on these *Guidelines* generally see ch 15, 'Production Agreements', pp 611–615.

[475] OJ [1979] C 1/2; see also *Vertical guidelines*, para 22; for further discussion of sub-contracting see Rose and Bailey (eds) *Bellamy and Child: European Union Law of Competition* (Oxford University Press, 7th ed, 2013), paras 7.192–7.200; note also that in some cases an agreement might amount to a technology transfer agreement that benefits from block exemption under Regulation 316/2014: see ch 19, 'Technology Transfer Agreements: Regulation 316/2014', pp 798–807.

The Commission's view is that sub-contracting agreements of the kind just described do not infringe Article 101(1). Subject to the proviso explained later, clauses in such agreements which stipulate that any technology or equipment provided by the contractor to the sub-contractor may not be used except for the purpose of the agreement generally fall outside Article 101(1); so too are restrictions on making that technology or equipment available to third parties and a requirement that goods, services or work arising from the use of the technology or equipment will be supplied only to the contractor. The proviso referred to is that the technology or equipment must be necessary to enable the sub-contractor to manufacture the goods, supply the services or carry out the work: where this is the case, the sub-contractor is not regarded as an independent supplier in the market. This proviso is satisfied where the sub-contractor makes use of intellectual property rights or know-how belonging to the contractor. However it would not be satisfied if the sub-contractor could have obtained access to the technology or equipment in question acting on its own.

The *Sub-contracting Notice* sets out other permissible clauses. In particular the contractor can require the sub-contractor to pass on to it on a non-exclusive basis any technical improvements made during the agreement; an exclusive licence may be acceptable where any improvements or inventions on the part of the sub-contractor cannot be made without use of the contractor's intellectual property rights. The sub-contractor must be free, however, to dispose of the results of its own research and development.

12. **UK Law**

This section considers the application of UK competition law, in particular the Chapter I prohibition of the Competition Act 1998 and the Enterprise Act 2002, to vertical agreements.

(A) **Vertical integration**

It is possible for vertical integration to be investigated under the market investigation provisions of the Enterprise Act 2002[476]; in its guidance on these provisions[477] the Competition and Markets Authority ('the CMA') specifically notes that vertical integration may foreclose competitors and add to entry barriers within an industry[478]. The CMA's predecessors, the Competition Commission and, before it, the Monopolies and Mergers Commission, conducted several investigations in which it was necessary to consider the effect of vertical integration[479]. Following an inquiry into the *Supply of Beer*[480] the 'Big Six' brewers were not permitted to own more than 2,000 retail outlets each and subsequently had to divest themselves of 21,900 retail outlets[481]. Following the *Energy market investigation*[482] the CMA concluded that vertically-integrated electricity companies were not behaving in ways that harmed the competitive position of non-integrated firms to the detriment of consumers.

[476] See ch 11 for a description of the market investigation provisions in the Enterprise Act 2002.

[477] *Market investigation references*, March 2006, para 5.1, available on the CMA's website at www.gov.uk/cma.

[478] Ibid, para 5.8.

[479] See eg *Gas and British Gas plc*, Cm 2315–2318 (1993); *Foreign Packaged Holidays*, Cm 3813 (1997); *Aggregates, cement and ready-mix concrete market investigation*, Final Report of 14 January 2014.

[480] *The Supply of Beer*, Cm 651 (1989).

[481] These changes were effected by the Supply of Beer (Loan Ties, Licensed Premises and Wholesale Prices) Order 1989, SI 1989/2258 and the Supply of Beer (Tied Estate) Order 1989, SI 1989/2390; these orders were subsequently revoked: the Supply of Beer (Tied Estate) (Revocation) Order 2002, SI 2002/3204 and the Supply of Beer (Loan Ties, Licensed Premises and Wholesale Prices) (Revocation) Order 2003, SI 2003/52.

[482] Final Report of 24 June 2016, section 7.

Vertical mergers can be investigated under the Enterprise Act 2002 where the value of the turnover of the enterprise to be acquired is more than £70 million[483].

(B) Commercial agents

There is no specific guidance on the treatment of agency agreements under the Competition Act 1998. However, as a result of section 60(3) of the Act, the CMA, in its application of the Chapter I prohibition, has regard to paragraphs 12 to 21 of the European Commission's *Vertical guidelines*[484]. In *Vodafone*[485] the agreements entered into between Vodafone and its distributors that fixed the retail prices of pre-pay mobile phone vouchers were not agency agreements[486]; however Vodafone was not guilty of infringing the Chapter I prohibition since it was acting pursuant to a regulatory obligation[487].

(C) Vertical agreements under the Competition Act 1998

(i) The exclusion of vertical agreements from the Chapter I prohibition until 30 April 2005

Section 50(1) of the Competition Act 1998 gives a power to the Secretary of State to exclude vertical agreements from the Chapter I prohibition. The Competition Act 1998 (Land and Vertical Agreements Exclusion) Order 2000[488] excluded all vertical agreements, with the exception of those imposing minimum or fixed resale prices, from the Chapter I prohibition from March 2000 until 30 April 2005.

(ii) Repeal of the exclusion for vertical agreements

The adoption of Regulation 1/2003 meant that there was much to be said for aligning the domestic law on vertical agreements with the position under EU law. It was decided, therefore, that the exclusion from the Chapter I prohibition should be repealed, and that there should be consistency, where possible, in the application of domestic and EU competition law to vertical agreements. The statutory instrument was therefore repealed with effect from 1 May 2005 (allowing a period of one year from the entry into force of Regulation 1/2003 during which undertakings could adapt their agreements)[489], since when there has been no special treatment for vertical agreements under the Competition Act. The position is now that vertical agreements that affect trade between Member States are subject to Article 101 including, when applicable, Regulation 330/2010 or Regulation 461/2010; and that agreements that do not affect trade between Member States are subject to the Chapter I prohibition, which is interpreted consistently with the jurisprudence of the EU Courts according to section 60(2) of the Competition Act[490], and the EU block exemption by virtue of section 10 of the Act which provides for parallel exemption[491]. This means that many agreements are exempt from both EU and UK law, and that there is no need for the UK to adopt a block exemption of its own for vertical agreements.

[483] Enterprise Act 2002, s 23(1)(b); on vertical mergers, see ch 22, 'Non-horizontal mergers', pp 965–966.

[484] See 'Commercial Agents', pp 634–637 earlier in chapter; on s 60 of the Competition Act 1998 see ch 9, ' "Governing Principles Clause": Section 60 of the Competition Act 1998', pp 387–392.

[485] OFTEL decision of 5 April 2002. [486] Ibid, paras 35–37. [487] Ibid, para 47.

[488] SI 2000/310; the CAT considered the Exclusion Order did not apply in Cases 1252/1/12/16 *GlaxoSmithKline plc v CMA* [2018] CAT 4, paras 350–364.

[489] See the Competition Act 1998 (Land Agreements Exclusion and Revocation) Order 2004, SI 2004/1260.

[490] For discussion of s 60 see ch 9, '"Governing Principles Clause": Section 60 of the Competition Act 1998', pp 387–392.

[491] For discussion see ch 9, 'Parallel exemptions', pp 375–376.

The European Union (Withdrawal) Bill will, if enacted, bring an end to the direct effect of EU law in the UK, and it would follow that, as a matter of domestic law, vertical agreements would no longer benefit from Regulation 330/2010. The Brexit Competition Law Working Group recommended that section 10 of the Competition Act should be repealed and replaced by a series of domestic block exemptions[492].

(iii) *Guidance on Vertical agreements*

The *Guidance on Vertical agreements*[493]discusses the application of Articles 101 and 102 TFEU and the Chapter I and Chapter II prohibitions to vertical agreements. The *Guidance* also deals with the (now repealed) Exclusion Order and the possible application of the Enterprise Act to vertical agreements. The *Guidance* concludes with some discussion of the competitive assessment of vertical agreements.

(iv) **Decisional practice under the Competition Act**

A number of vertical agreements have been investigated under the Competition Act 1998.

(a) Pricing restrictions

Vertical agreements involving the imposition of minimum resale prices have been condemned on a number of occasions. In *John Bruce, Fleet Parts and Truck and Trailer Components*[494] vertical price fixing between John Bruce and Fleet Parts was held to be outside the Exclusion Order and so an infringement of the Chapter I prohibition[495]. In *Hasbro*[496] a fine of £4.95 million was imposed on Hasbro for imposing minimum resale prices on its distributors[497]. In *Toys and Games*[498] much larger fines, of £17.28 million on Argos and of £5.37 million on Littlewoods, were imposed for a mixture of horizontal and vertical price fixing[499]; Hasbro was given full immunity because of its cooperation with the Office of Fair Trading ('the OFT')[500]. On appeal the findings of infringement were upheld by the Competition Appeal Tribunal ('the CAT'), although the fines were slightly reduced[501]. In *Lladró Comercial*[502] provisions in *Lladró*'s standard-form documentation imposed minimum resale prices; however no fine was imposed since the European Commission had sent to *Lladró* a comfort letter that could be interpreted to mean that this practice did not infringe competition law[503]. In *Football Shirts* fines totalling £18.6 million were imposed for a mixture of horizontal price fixing and resale price maintenance in relation to replica football kits[504]. Some of the findings of infringement were annulled on appeal to the CAT[505], and the fines were reduced to £14.92 million[506].

The pricing restrictions in *Tobacco*[507] were different: there were a number of bilateral, vertical agreements whereby the prices of various tobacco brands were linked to those of competitors' brands. These 'price-matching' arrangements were found to restrict each retailer's ability independently to set resale prices for cigarettes. On appeal, however, the

[492] Final Report of 26 July 2017, para 2.12, available at www.bclwg.org; on the power to adopt block exemptions see Competition Act 1998, s 6; see ch 9 'Block exemptions', p 375.

[493] OFT 419, December 2004. [494] OFT decision of 17 May 2002. [495] Ibid, paras 35–37.

[496] OFT decision of 28 November 2002. [497] Ibid, para 47. [498] OFT decision of 19 February 2003.

[499] On the finding of a multilateral agreement in this case see ch 9, 'Indirect contact between competitors', pp 353–355.

[500] On leniency under the Competition Act 1998 see ch 10, 'Leniency', pp 424–429.

[501] Cases 1014 and 1015/1/1/03 *Argos Ltd and Littlewoods Ltd v OFT* [2005] CAT 13, upheld on appeal [2006] EWCA Civ 1318.

[502] OFT decision of 31 March 2003. [503] Ibid, paras 120–125. [504] OFT decision of 1 August 2003.

[505] Cases 1021/1/1/03 etc *JJB Sports plc v OFT* [2004] CAT 17, upheld on appeal [2006] EWCA Civ 1318.

[506] Cases 1019/1/1/03 etc *Umbro Holdings Ltd v OFT* [2005] CAT 22, upheld on appeal [2006] EWCA Civ 1318.

[507] OFT decision of 15 April 2010; on arrangements of this kind see *Can Fair Prices be Unfair? A Review of Price Relationship Agreements*, LEAR, April 2011.

CAT set aside the decision on procedural grounds; it did not deal with the substantive matters in dispute[508]. The Court of Appeal held that two companies that did not appeal the Tobacco decision could recover the fines imposed on them, on the grounds that the OFT had breached the requirements of fairness and equal treatment[508a]

There have been several cases of pricing restrictions in online commerce. Two decisions concerned so-called 'mobility scooters', *Roma Medical Aids Ltd*[509] and *Pride Mobility Products Ltd*[510]. In *Roma* that company committed two infringements: first, prohibiting online sales by certain retailers and, second, prohibiting online advertising by certain retailers of any prices. In *Pride* the arrangements between Pride and eight online retailers unlawfully prohibited the latter from advertising prices below the prices recommended by Pride. No fines were imposed in either case, due to the small size of the undertakings[511]. However, a claimant tried to bring an opt-out collective action for damages on behalf of pensioners who may have suffered harm as a result of the price restrictions in the *Pride* case[512]; the action was ultimately withdrawn.

In *Hotel Online Booking*[513] InterContinental Hotels, Booking.com and Expedia offered commitments allowing online travel agents to offer discounts on room-only accommodation, which the OFT (now CMA) accepted under section 31A of the Competition Act. On appeal the CAT quashed the OFT's decision because it had failed to consider the objections of a third party to the proposed commitments[514]. The CMA subsequently closed the file on administrative priority grounds[515].

Several suppliers have admitted an infringement of Article 101(1) TFEU and the Chapter I prohibition by imposing restrictions on their dealers from discounting online prices[516]. The CMA treated these restrictions of discounting as a form of resale price maintenance. The CMA has also written to other suppliers that it suspects of engaging in similar practices in relation to internet sales.

The file has been closed on a few cases concerning alleged resale price maintenance, either following assurances that the offending behaviour would be terminated[517] or because there were no grounds for action[518].

(b) Non-price restrictions

In *DSG Retail Ltd*[519] exclusive distribution agreements between Compaq and Hewlett-Packard, manufacturers of desktop computers, and Dixons were found not to infringe the Chapter I and Chapter II prohibitions[520]. In *Lucite International UK Ltd*[521] a long-term vertical agreement for the supply of hydrogen cyanide by BASF to Lucite International was, at the time, excluded from the Chapter I prohibition[522]; it was not appropriate to withdraw the exclusion as it was possible that the agreement would have been granted an exemption: it conferred individual and collective benefits on users and consumers by lessening environmental pollution[523].

[508] Cases 1160/1/1/10 etc *Imperial Tobacco v OFT* [2011] CAT 41.

[508a] [2016] EWCA Civ 719, on appeal to the UK Supreme Court, not yet decided.

[509] OFT decision of 5 August 2013. [510] OFT decision of 27 March 2014.

[511] See Competition Act 1998, s 39(3), on which see 'Immunity for small agreements and conduct of minor significance', ch 10, 423–424.

[512] See Case 1257/7/7/16 *Dorothy Gibson v Pride Mobility Products Ltd* [2017] CAT 9.

[513] OFT decision of 31 January 2014. [514] Case 1226/2/12/14 *Skyscanner Ltd v CMA* [2014] CAT 16.

[515] CMA case closure decision of 16 September 2015.

[516] See eg *Ultra Finishing Ltd*, CMA decision of 10 May 2016; *ITW Ltd*, CMA decision of 10 June 2016; *Poole Lighting Ltd*, CMA decision of 3 May 2017.

[517] See eg *Swarovski*, OFT Press Release 86/04, 18 May 2004.

[518] See eg *Sports bras*, CMA case closure decision of 13 June 2014.

[519] OFT decision of 18 April 2001. [520] Ibid, paras 97–98 and 111 and 118.

[521] OFT decision of 29 November 2002. [522] Ibid, paras 11–14. [523] Ibid, paras 39–41.

In *Ping*[524] the CMA imposed a fine of £1.45 million on Ping which had infringed Article 101 TFEU and the Chapter I prohibition by preventing two retailers from selling its golf clubs on their websites. The CMA acknowledged that Ping was pursuing a genuine commercial aim of promoting in-store custom fitting, but decided that an internet sales ban was a disproportionate way of achieving that aim.

(D) **Enterprise Act 2002**

Vertical agreements may be investigated under the market investigation provisions in the Enterprise Act 2002: these have been described in chapter 11. They will not be used where use of the Competition Act is more appropriate[525]. A market investigation might be appropriate, for example, where vertical agreements are prevalent in a market and have the cumulative effect of preventing the entry of new competitors[526]. In *Movies on Pay TV*[527] the Competition Commission (now CMA) found that no features of the market for the supply of pay-TV services restricted competition as there was credible competition for the acquisition from major Hollywood studios of the rights to stream movies and as new video-on-demand services had been launched which imposed a competitive constraint on the pay-TV market. In *Private motor insurance*[528] the CMA concluded that price parity provisions in contracts between motor insurance providers and price comparison websites distorted competition; the CMA ordered that the offending clauses be terminated[529]. Following its market study into *Digital comparison tools*[530] the CMA opened an investigation under the Competition Act 1998 into the use of price parity provisions in relation to home insurance sold on Compare The Market, a price comparison website[531].

[524] CMA decision of 24 August 2017, on appeal Case 1279/1/12/17 *Ping Europe Ltd v CMA*, not yet decided.

[525] *Market investigation references* (OFT 511, 2006), para 2.3; note that the former Competition Commission published various reports on vertical agreements under the now-repealed provisions of the Fair Trading Act 1973, including *The Supply of Beer* (earlier); *Carbonated Soft Drinks*, Cm 1625 (1992); *Newspaper and Periodicals*, Cmnd 7214 (1978) and Cm 2422 (1993); *Fine Fragrances*, Cm 2380 (1993); *Electrical Goods*, Cm 3675 and Cm 3676 (1997); *Foreign Packaged Holidays*, Cm 3813 (1997); and *New Cars*, Cm 4660 (2000).

[526] *Market investigation references*, para 2.6; see also paras 5.9 and 6.15–6.18 and *Guidelines for market investigations: Their role, procedures, assessment and remedies* (CC3 (Revised), 2013), paras 262–294.

[527] Final Report of 2 August 2012.

[528] Final Report of 24 September 2014.

[529] Private Motor Insurance Market Investigation Order 2015, 18 March 2015.

[530] Final Report of 24 September 2017.

[531] Details of the case are available at www.gov.uk/cma.

17

Abuse of dominance (1): non-pricing practices

1. Introduction

The previous four chapters have been concerned with the application of EU and UK competition law to horizontal and vertical agreements between undertakings. The focus of attention in this and chapters 18 and 19 turns to a different issue: the extent to which the unilateral acts of dominant firms might infringe Article 102 TFEU and the Chapter II prohibition in the Competition Act 1998[1].

This chapter is concerned with non-pricing practices; abusive pricing practices are considered in chapter 18. There is no legal significance in this division of the material: pricing and non-pricing practices can have the same anti-competitive effect. However analysis of pricing abuses requires an understanding of a number of cost concepts, and these are introduced at the beginning of chapter 18[2]. Abuses that involve the exercise, or non-exercise, of intellectual property rights are considered in chapter 19. This chapter will deal in turn with exclusive dealing agreements; tying; refusals to supply; abusive non-pricing practices that are harmful to the single market; and miscellaneous other non-pricing practices which might infringe Article 102 or the Chapter II prohibition. Reference will be made where appropriate to the Commission's *Guidance on the Commission's Enforcement Priorities in Applying Article [102 TFEU] to Abusive Exclusionary Conduct by Dominant Undertakings* ('*Guidance on Article 102 Enforcement Priorities*')[3]. The reader is reminded that this document does not contain guidelines on the law of Article 102; rather it provides valuable insights as to why the Commission thinks that some practices are more likely than others to be harmful to consumers, and so to be appropriate for enforcement action[4].

Before considering non-pricing practices under Article 102, it may be helpful to recall some of the main principles underlying that provision:

- a dominant firm has a special responsibility not to impair genuine undistorted competition on the market

[1] See ch 5 on Article 102 and ch 9, 'The Chapter II Prohibition', pp 376–387.
[2] See ch 18, 'Cost concepts', pp 733–735.
[3] OJ [2009] C 45/7.
[4] For a general discussion see ch 5, 'The Commission's *Guidance on Article 102 Enforcement Priorities*', pp 182–185.

- care must be taken in the application of Article 102 not to prevent dominant firms from being able to compete 'on the merits'[5]
- Article 102 has been applied to exploitative abuses, to exclusionary practices and to actions that harm the single market[6]
- Article 102 may be applied to firms that are dominant in one market and that commit abuses to protect their position in neighbouring markets, which may be horizontally contiguous to or, often, vertically upstream or downstream of the dominated market[7]
- a distinction should be drawn between horizontal and vertical foreclosure of the market[8] and
- defences based on objective justification and/or economic efficiency are available to dominant undertakings accused of abusing a dominant position[9].

2. Exclusive Dealing Agreements

(A) EU law

The application of Article 101 to vertical agreements was considered in chapter 16[10]. Regulation 330/2010 on vertical agreements confers block exemption on vertical agreements where the supplier and the buyer each has a market share of 30% or less[11], provided that the agreement contains no hard-core restrictions contrary to Article 4[12]. As a general proposition Article 5 of the block exemption limits the permissible duration of a non-compete clause to five years[13]. Where either party's market share exceeds 30%, an individual assessment of a vertical agreement is necessary to determine whether it infringes Article 101(1)[14] and whether it satisfies the terms of Article 101(3)[15]. Article 101(3) does not provide a defence to an agreement that amounts to an abuse of a dominant position[16]; and the Commission has said that it is unlikely that a dominant undertaking can defend an agreement under Article 101(3), even if it is not abusive, where it maintains, creates or strengthens a market position approaching monopoly[17].

5 See ch 5, 'Introduction', pp 180–181.

6 See ch 5, 'Exploitative, exclusionary and single market abuses', pp 207–208.

7 See ch 5, 'The dominant position, the abuse and the effects of the abuse may be in different markets', pp 211–213.

8 See ch 5, 'Horizontal and vertical foreclosure', pp 210–211.

9 See ch 5, 'Defences', pp 217–220.

10 For further reading on exclusive dealing see Motta *Competition Policy: Theory and Practice* (Cambridge University Press, 2004), pp 363–372; O'Donoghue and Padilla *The Law and Economics of Article 102 TFEU* (Hart, 2nd ed, 2013), pp 423–460; section 7 of DG COMP's *Discussion paper on the application of Article [102] of the Treaty to exclusionary abuses*, available at www.ec.europa.eu; Melamed 'Exclusive Dealing Agreements and Other Exclusionary Conduct—Are There Unifying Principles?' (2006) 73 Antitrust LJ 375; Klein and Murphy 'Exclusive Dealing Intensifies Competition for Distribution' (2008) 75 Antitrust LJ 433; Zenger 'When Does Exclusive Dealing Intensify Competition for Distribution? Comment on Klein and Murphy' (2010) 77 Antitrust LJ 205.

11 Regulation 330/2010, OJ [2010] L 102/1, Article 3: see ch 16, 'Article 3: the market share cap', pp 674–677.

12 See ch 16, 'Article 4: hard-core restrictions', pp 677–684.

13 See ch 16, 'Article 5: obligations in vertical agreements that are not exempt', pp 684–685.

14 See ch 16, 'Vertical Agreements: Article 101(1)', pp 642–664.

15 See ch 16, 'Vertical Agreements: Individual Application of Article 101(3)', pp 687–688.

16 See the Commission's *Guidelines on Vertical Restraints* OJ [2010] C 130/1, para 127 and case law cited and para 106 of its *Guidelines on the application of Article [101(3)] of the Treaty* OJ [2004] C 101/97.

17 See para 127 of the Commission's *Guidelines on Vertical Restraints* OJ [2010] C 130/1.

A difference between the application of Article 101 and Article 102 to such agreements is that, where an agreement infringes Article 101, both (or all) of the parties to the agreement will have committed an infringement and will be liable accordingly. In the case of Article 102, however, it is the dominant firm that infringes the competition rules, since Article 102 applies to a dominant firm's *unilateral* behaviour; the conclusion of an anti-competitive agreement can be an abusive unilateral act, so that the dominant firm can be fined and sued for damages, as well as being unable to enforce the offending provisions in the agreement[18].

(i) The application of Article 102 to exclusive purchasing agreements

The most obvious vertical agreement that could infringe Article 102 is one whereby a customer is required to purchase all or most of a particular type of goods or services only from a dominant supplier. Various terminology can be used to describe such agreements—'exclusive purchasing', 'single branding', 'requirements contracts' and 'non-compete obligations'. Each of these terms connotes the same idea: that the purchaser is prevented from purchasing competing products from anyone other than the dominant firm. The Commission's *Guidance on Article 102 Enforcement Priorities* uses the term exclusive purchasing agreements, and this is the one that will be used in the text that follows. The treatment of pricing practices such as the grant of rebates that have the same effect as exclusive purchasing agreements is considered in chapter 18[19].

(a) Meaning of exclusivity

The term 'exclusive dealing agreement' can apply both to an exclusive supply obligation, whereby a supplier is restricted from supplying to anyone other than a specific downstream customer; and to an exclusive purchasing obligation, whereby a downstream customer is forbidden to acquire products except from a specific supplier. In practice the cases are predominantly concerned with exclusive purchasing obligations.

It is important to note that the concern is not just that a 100% exclusive purchasing obligation could foreclose access to the market, but that lesser commitments might do so. As we will see, the Court of Justice in *Hoffmann-La Roche v Commission* held that it may be abusive for a dominant firm to enter into an agreement requiring a customer to buy 'most of its requirements' from that firm[20]. The Commission treats an agreement to purchase 80% or more of a buyer's requirements of a particular product as analogous to an exclusive purchasing commitment[21].

(b) Judgments of the EU Courts

There is not a great deal of judicial precedent on the application of Article 102 to exclusive purchasing agreements. There is however a strong possibility that Article 102 will be applied to such agreements when entered into by a dominant firm. Once the Court of Justice had held in *Suiker Unie v Commission*[22] that it was contrary to Article 102 for a dominant firm to foreclose competition by offering loyalty rebates to customers that purchase only from it, it was inevitable that the same condemnation would apply

[18] On the final point see ch 8, 'Article 102', p 340.

[19] See ch 18, 'Conditional rebates', pp 746–754.

[20] See 'Judgments of the EU Courts', later in chapter.

[21] *Guidelines on Vertical Restraints* OJ [2010] C 130/1, para 29; similarly see Case T-286/09 *Intel Corp v Commission* EU:T:2014:546, para 135; the General Court's judgment was set aside on other grounds on appeal to the Court of Justice, Case C-413/14 P EU:C:2017:632.

[22] Cases 40/73 etc EU:C:1975:174.

to an exclusive purchasing commitment. This was confirmed in *Hoffmann-La Roche v Commission*[23]. The Court of Justice held that:

> An undertaking which is in a dominant position on a market and ties purchasers—even if it does so at their request—by an obligation or promise on their part to obtain all or most of their requirements exclusively from the said undertaking abuses its dominant position within the meaning of Article [102] of the Treaty, whether the obligation in question is stipulated without further qualification or whether it is undertaken in consideration of the grant of a rebate[24].

This language suggested a *per se* approach on the part of the Court of Justice: that any exclusive purchasing agreement on the part of a dominant undertaking is abusive, irrespective of the actual or likely effect of the agreement on competition. However this is not the case. A dominant firm can always try to argue that its conduct has an objective justification or that it is economically efficient[25]. Furthermore the position should now be considered in the aftermath of the Court of Justice's judgment in *Intel v Commission*[26]. Intel was a case on loyalty rebates, but its reasoning would seem to apply with equal force to exclusive purchasing. The Court of Justice considered the passage in *Hoffmann-La Roche* cited above but then went on to say:

> However, that case-law must be further clarified in the case where the undertaking concerned submits, during the administrative procedure, on the basis of supporting evidence, that its conduct was not capable of restricting competition and, in particular, of producing the alleged foreclosure effects[27].

This 'clarification' of the law means that if, as seems very likely, a dominant firm submits evidence that its exclusive purchasing agreement could not have a foreclosure effect, the Commission must assess whether it is capable of having such an effect. In particular, the Commission must analyse the extent of the firm's dominant position; the market coverage of the agreement; the terms of the agreement and its duration; and the possible existence of a strategy aiming to exclude competitors that are at least as efficient as the dominant undertaking from the market[28]. It would seem to follow that an exclusive purchasing agreement can be abusive only where it can be shown to be capable of having a foreclosure effect on as-efficient competitors and has no objective justification[29]. To put the point another way, exclusive purchasing is not *per se* illegal under Article 102[30].

In passing it should be noted that it is no defence that the customer willingly entered into the agreement, or even that it requested exclusivity: the issue in these cases is not whether the agreement is oppressive to the customer, but whether it could horizontally foreclose competitors as efficient (or more efficient) than the dominant firm in the relevant market[31]. In *Almelo*[32] the Court of Justice considered that an exclusive purchasing clause in a supply contract for electricity could infringe Article 102 if entered into by a dominant firm, even where the clause was requested by local distributors.

(c) The Commission's approach to exclusive purchasing agreements

The Commission discusses exclusive purchasing agreements at paragraphs 129 to 150 of its *Guidelines on Vertical Restraints*[33]: those *Guidelines* are predominantly concerned

[23] Case 85/76 EU:C:1979:36; see also Case T-65/89 *BPB Industries plc and British Gypsum v Commission* EU:T:1993:31, paras 65–77, upheld on appeal Case C-310/93 P EU:C:1995:101.

[24] Case 85/76 EU:C:1979:36, para 89.

[25] See ch 5, 'Defences', pp 217–220.

[26] Case C-413/14 P *Intel Corp v Commission* EU:C:2017:632.

[27] Ibid, para 138.

[28] Ibid, para 139.

[29] On the possibility of objective justification see Case T-155/06 *Tomra Systems ASA v Commission* EU:T:2010:370, para 224, upheld on appeal Case C-541/10 P EU:C:2012:221.

[30] See ch 5, 'Are there or should there be any *per se* rules under Article 102?', p 205.

[31] Case 85/76 EU:C:1979:36, para 120.

[32] Case C-393/92 EU:C:1994:171.

[33] OJ [2010] C 130/1: see ch 16, Single branding agreements', pp 651–653.

with the treatment of such agreements under Articles 101(1) and 101(3). The Commission provides some insights into its thinking on the application of Article 102 in paragraphs 33 to 36 and in paragraph 46 of its *Guidance on Article 102 Enforcement Priorities* (paragraphs 37 to 46 deal with the analogous case of conditional rebates[34]). The Commission acknowledges that a customer of a dominant undertaking may have no objection to an exclusive purchasing obligation, in particular if it is compensated in some way for accepting it; however this does not, in itself, mean that such obligations should be tolerated: the Commission will focus its attention on whether they are likely to be harmful for consumers as a whole, which may be the case where they have the effect of preventing the entry or expansion of competing undertakings[35].

Paragraph 35 of the *Guidance* refers back to paragraph 20, which sets out a range of factors that the Commission will take into account when deciding whether to initiate enforcement proceedings in relation to a possibly anti-competitive foreclosure of the market[36]. Paragraph 36 discusses some additional factors that the Commission will look at in the case of exclusive purchasing obligations. In particular it will ask whether the dominant undertaking's competitors are unable to compete for an individual customer's entire demand. If a customer is bound to purchase a certain amount of its needs from the dominant undertaking—for example because a particular brand is a 'must-stock item' or because other suppliers lack the capacity to satisfy the whole of the customer's needs—a risk arises that competitors will be excluded from the market altogether. Because of this the Commission considers that in such a situation even an exclusive purchasing obligation of short duration can lead to anti-competitive foreclosure. Where, however, suppliers can compete for the customer's entire demand, the Commission says that exclusive purchasing is unlikely to hamper effective competition unless the dominant undertaking imposes a very long period of exclusivity: the longer the duration, the greater the likely foreclosure effect.

The Commission has taken action in relation to exclusive purchasing agreements in several cases[37]. For example in *Soda-ash*[38] the Commission fined Solvay €20 million and ICI €10 million for requiring customers to enter into long-term indefinite requirements contracts and granting fidelity and top slice rebates designed to exclude competitors from the market. The Commission condemned exclusivity terms and retroactive rebates in *Prokent-Tomra*[39].

There have been other interventions. In *Istituto/IMC and Angus*[40] the Commission took action in a case where the dominant supplier of a raw material was refusing to supply a customer except on terms which would have foreclosed its competitors; the Commission persuaded IMC and Angus to offer supply contracts that would last two years with automatic renewal for one year unless terminated by six months' notice. The Commission brought an end to exclusive contracts entered into by AC Nielsen for the procurement of data in relation to fast-moving consumer goods in 1997[41]. The Commission proceeded

[34] See ch 18, '*Intel* and the Commission's *Guidance on Article 102 Enforcement Priorities*', pp 751–752.

[35] See the Commission's *Guidance on Article 102 Enforcement Priorities*, para 34.

[36] See ch 5, 'How is effects analysis conducted in practice?', pp 214–216.

[37] In addition to the cases mentioned in the text see eg *BPB Industries plc* OJ [1989] L10/50, upheld on appeal Case T-65/89 *BPB Industries plc v Commission* EU:T:1993:31, paras 65–77, upheld on appeal Case C-310/93 P EU:C:1995:101.

[38] *Soda-ash/Solvay* OJ [1991] L 152/21 and *Soda-ash/ICI* [1991] L 152/40, annulled on procedural grounds Cases T-37/91 etc *ICI v Commission* EU:T:1995:119, upheld on appeal Cases C-286/95 P EU:C:2000:188; the Commission readopted the decisions: OJ [2003] L 10/1, upheld on appeal Case T-57/01 *Solvay v Commission* EU:T:2009:519, paras 365–383, set aside on appeal for procedural reasons Case C-101/10 P EU:C:2011:462.

[39] Commission decision of 29 March 2006, upheld on appeal Case T-155/06 EU:T:2010:370, upheld on appeal Case C-549/10 P EU:C:2012:221.

[40] Commission's XVIth *Report on Competition Policy* (1986), point 76.

[41] Commission's XXVIIth *Report on Competition Policy* (1997), pp 144–148.

against Nordiron in respect of exclusive, long-term supply clauses for Molybdenum99, a base product for radiopharmaceuticals used in nuclear medicine; following the receipt of a statement of objections Nordiron dropped the clauses[42]. The Commission required Frankfurt Airport to abandon long-term contracts covering periods from three to ten years which it had entered into with airlines for the provision of ramp-handling services[43]; the Commission had required the termination of Frankfurt Airport's monopoly of such services and, not surprisingly, was unwilling to see this replaced by long-term exclusive terms that would have the same effect in practice of excluding third parties. Agreement was reached with the Commission that the contracts would be for a period of one year only, automatically renewable but terminable on six months' notice[44].

The Commission has accepted commitments under Article 9 of Regulation 1/2003[45] in several cases that resulted in allegedly dominant undertakings abandoning or modifying exclusive purchasing obligations. The Coca-Cola Company agreed that it would refrain from entering into exclusive purchasing commitments with customers in 2004; the company also agreed not to require customers to purchase a specified minimum percentage of their requirements from it[46]. In *Distrigaz* the Commission accepted commitments from Distrigaz to limit the duration of future agreements for the supply of gas to industrial customers and electricity generators to five years, and to gas resellers to two years; that it would reduce the volume of gas subject to long-term supply commitments; and that its supply contracts would not contain restrictions on resale and use[47]. A similar outcome was achieved in *EDF: Long-term contracts in France*[48].

The Commission has been investigating whether Google is guilty of unlawfully requiring third parties not to source online search advertisements from Google's competitors[49].

(ii) Article 102 applies to *de facto* as well as to contractual exclusivity

In *Van den Bergh Foods*[50] the Commission concluded that it was an abuse of a dominant position for Van den Bergh to provide freezer cabinets free of charge to retail outlets on condition that they were to be used exclusively for the storage of its ice cream products[51]. The consequence of this practice was that, *de facto*, Van den Bergh achieved outlet exclusivity, since retailers were unlikely to, and in practice did not, maintain a second freezer in their shops; in effect, therefore, the retailers would purchase ice cream exclusively from Van den Bergh. This decision, which was upheld on appeal to the General Court[52] and to the Court of Justice[53], demonstrates that Article 102 can be applied to *de facto* as well as to contractual exclusivity[54]. The Commission notes in paragraph 33 of its *Guidance on Article 102 Enforcement Priorities* that 'stocking requirements', of which *Van den Bergh* is an example, may in practice lead to the same effect as exclusive purchasing agreements.

42 Commission's XXVIIIth *Report on Competition Policy* (1998), pp 169–170.

43 *Frankfurt Airport* OJ [1998] L 72/30.

44 Commission Press Release IP/98/794, 8 September 1998.

45 See ch 7, 'Article 9: commitments', pp 264–269 on Article 9 of Regulation 1/2003.

46 Commission decision of 22 June 2005. 47 Commission decision of 11 October 2007.

48 Commission decision of 17 March 2010; see also *Gas Natural/Endesa*, Commission Press Release IP/00/297, 27 March 2000, where Gas Natural agreed to settle the case informally by reducing the length of its supply agreement to 12 years and to allow its customer, Endesa, to purchase a proportion of its requirements elsewhere.

49 Commission Press Release IP/16/2532, 14 July 2016. 50 OJ [1998] L 246/1.

51 Ibid, para 265. 52 Case T-65/98 *Van den Bergh Foods Ltd v Commission* EU:T:2003:281.

53 Case C-552/03 P *Unilever Bestfoods (Ireland) v Commission* EU:C:2006:607.

54 See para 94 of the Opinion of AG Cosmas in Case C-344/98 *Masterfoods Ltd v HB Ice Cream Ltd* EU:C:2000:249.

In *De Beers*[55] the Commission considered that long-term exclusive supply terms for rough diamonds agreed between Alrosa and De Beers could infringe Article 102. Alrosa and De Beers were competitors in the relevant market, and the Commission's concern was that the supply arrangement led to De Beers, *de facto*, acting as an exclusive distributor. De Beers entered into legally-binding commitments to bring the arrangements to an end[56].

(iii) Is there an objective justification for a long-term supply agreement?

Where a supplier has to make a client-specific investment in order to be able to supply a product, the efficiency gains likely to result from a long-term supply agreement may counteract any likely negative effects on competition[57]. It is open to a dominant undertaking to show that 'the exclusionary effect produced may be counterbalanced, outweighed even, by advantages in terms of efficiency that also benefit consumers'[58].

The Commission says at paragraph 46 of its *Guidance on Article 102 Enforcement Priorities* that it will consider evidence demonstrating that exclusive purchasing agreements result in advantages to particular customers if they are necessary for the dominant undertaking to make certain relationship-specific investments in order to be able to supply those customers[59].

(B) UK law

(i) The UK courts' approach to exclusive purchasing agreements

In *Claymore Dairies Ltd v OFT*[60] the Competition Appeal Tribunal ('the CAT') was critical of the Office of Fair Trading's ('the OFT') investigation into whether Robert Wiseman Dairies had entered into agreements with two customers in Scotland that, *de facto*, resulted in an exclusive purchasing arrangement[61] and therefore set the decision on this point aside[62].

In *National Grid*[63] the Gas and Electricity Markets Authority ('OFGEM') concluded that National Grid had abused its dominant position by entering into long-term contracts with gas suppliers that rent gas meters from National Grid; its view was that the payment structure had the effect of preventing gas suppliers from acquiring less expensive and/or more technologically advanced meters from competitors. National Grid was fined £41.6 million; on appeal to the CAT[64] and the Court of Appeal[65] OFGEM's decision on substance was upheld, though the fine was reduced to £15 million. A consequence of the finding of infringement was that National Grid's customers were able to renegotiate their agreements with National Grid, since the existing ones would be void and unenforceable[66].

55 Commission decision of 22 February 2006.

56 The Commission's commitment decision was annulled by the General Court in Case T-170/06 *Alrosa Co Ltd v Commission* EU:T:2007:220, but reinstated by the Court of Justice in Case C-441/07 P *Commission v Alrosa Co Ltd* EU:C:2010:377.

57 See the Commission's *Guidelines on Vertical Restraints*, paras 107(d) and 146.

58 Case C-413/14 P *Intel v Commission* EU:C:2017:632, para 140 and case law cited.

59 See recital 37 of the Commission's decision and the final two paras of the Commission's MEMO/07/407, 11 October 2007.

60 Case 1008/2/1/02 [2005] CAT 30. 61 Ibid, paras 287–313. 62 Ibid, para 318.

63 OFGEM decision of 21 February 2008.

64 Case 1099/1/2/08 *National Grid plc v Gas and Electricity Markets Authority* [2009] CAT 14.

65 [2010] EWCA Civ 114; the Supreme Court refused National Grid permission to appeal: order of 28 July 2010.

66 A further consequence was that two 'follow-on' actions for damages were brought against National Grid, but were settled: Case 1199/5/7/12 *Capital Meters Ltd v National Grid plc* and Case 1198/5/7/12 *Siemens plc v National Grid plc*.

In *Arriva The Shires Ltd v London Luton Airport Operations Ltd*[67] the High Court concluded that the award of an exclusive right[68] to operate coach services from Luton Airport to central London for a period of seven years amounted to abusive behaviour. Unlike the cases discussed earlier, in which a customer purchased exclusively from a dominant firm, in this case Luton Airport had limited its ability to supply its airport facilities to competitors of its downstream customer[69]. The parties subsequently reached a settlement, the details of which are not in the public domain.

(ii) The UK competition authorities' approach to exclusive purchasing agreements

The guideline on *Vertical agreements*[70] sets out the thinking of the Competition and Markets Authority ('the CMA') on the assessment of vertical restraints, including efficiencies that may be associated with them[71]. Guidelines have also been published on the application of, among other provisions, Article 102 and the Chapter II prohibition, in the telecommunications[72], water and sewerage[73], energy[74] and rail[75] sectors. Apart from the one on water and sewerage, these guidelines predate the Commission's *Guidelines on Vertical Restraints* and *Guidance on Article 102 Enforcement Priorities*.

The UK competition authorities have intervened on a few occasions in relation to exclusive agreements, but closed the case because the exclusivity was modified[76] or there was insufficient evidence of an infringement[77]. In *English Welsh & Scottish Railway Ltd*[78], however, the Office of Rail Regulation (now the Office of Rail and Road ('the ORR')) found that EW&S had abused its dominant position in various ways, including by entering into exclusive agreements for the carriage of coal to power stations: a fine of £4.1 million was imposed. The ORR adopted a commitment decision in the case of *Freightliner* whereby that undertaking promised not to enter into exclusivity arrangements for the transport of deep sea containers until 31 March 2019[79].

The CMA has accepted legally-binding commitments under section 31A of the Competition Act in three cases. In *Certas*[80] commitments were given to replace five-year exclusive purchasing agreements in relation to road fuels purchased by filling stations in the Western Isles and to put more flexible arrangements in place. In *epyx*[81] that company agreed to relax exclusivity provisions in relation to the supply of vehicle service, maintenance and repair platforms in the UK. In *ATG Media*[82] the CMA accepted

67 [2014] EWHC 64 (Ch); for comment see Smith and Mourkas 'High Court Decision in *Arriva v Luton Airport*' [2015] Comp Law 79.

68 easyBus was permitted to operate from the airport using smaller vehicles, a matter which itself was held to give rise to abusive discrimination: [2014] EWHC 64 (Ch), paras 124–130.

69 Ibid, para 8; note that the judgment did not determine whether Luton Airport had a dominant position as the issue of abuse was tried as a preliminary issue: ibid, paras 6 and 167.

70 OFT 419, December 2004.

71 Ibid, paras 7.1–7.29.

72 *The application of the Competition Act in the telecommunications sector*, OFT 417, February 2000.

73 *The application of the Competition Act in the water and sewerage sectors*, OFT 422, March 2010.

74 *Application in the energy sector*, OFT 428, January 2005.

75 *Application to services relating to railways*, OFT 430, October 2005.

76 See eg *Bacardi* OFT decision of 30 January 2003, set aside on appeal Case 1017/2/1/03 *Pernod Ricard SA and Campbell Distillers v OFT* [2004] CAT 10 and [2005] CAT 9; *Calor Gas Northern Ireland*, OFT case closure of 30 June 2003, reducing five-year exclusivity to two years, available at www.nationalarchives.gov.uk.

77 See eg *Bunker Fuel Cards*, OFT decision of 6 November 2013, finding no grounds for action due to insufficient evidence of dominance, available at www.nationalarchives.gov.uk.

78 ORR decision of 17 November 2006; the abusive agreements were held to be void and unenforceable: *English Welsh & Scottish Railway Ltd v E.ON UK plc* [2007] EWHC 599 (Comm).

79 ORR decision of 18 December 2015.

80 CMA decision of 24 June 2014.

81 CMA decision of 9 September 2014.

82 CMA decision of 29 June 2017.

commitments from ATG that it would no longer insist on being the exclusive supplier of live online bidding auction platform services to auction houses for five years.

3. Tying

This section considers the extent to which tying may infringe Article 102 TFEU and/or the Chapter II prohibition in the Competition Act 1998[83].

(A) Terminology and illustrations of tying

Tying is the practice of a supplier of one product, the tying product, requiring a buyer also to buy a second product, the tied product. Tying may take various forms[84]:

- **contractual tying**: the tie may be the consequence of a specific contractual stipulation: for example in *Hilti* the dominant firm required users of its nail guns and nail cartridges to purchase nails exclusively from it[85]
- **refusal to supply**: the effect of a tie may be achieved where a dominant undertaking refuses to supply the tying product unless the customer purchases the tied product
- **withdrawal or withholding of a guarantee**: a dominant supplier may achieve the effect of a tie by withdrawing or withholding the benefit of a guarantee unless a customer uses a supplier's components as opposed to those of a third party[86]
- **technical tying**: this occurs where the tied product is physically integrated into the tying product, so that it is impossible to take one product without the other: this is what happened in *Microsoft*, discussed later[87]
- **bundling**: this is closely related to the idea of tying. It refers to a situation in which two products are sold as a single package at a single price. Two types of bundling should be noted:
  - pure bundling: this occurs where it is only possible to purchase the two products together
  - mixed bundling: this occurs where the two products are sold separately; however, when they are sold together they are available at a discount to the price that would be charged if they were purchased separately.

The extent to which bundling might lead to an infringement of Article 102 is discussed in chapter 18 on pricing abuses, since it may be necessary to analyse the price of the bundle to determine whether this is the case[88].

[83] For further reading on tying and bundling see Nalebuff *Bundling, Tying, and Portfolio Effects* (DTI Economics Paper No 1, 2003), available at www.gov.uk; Motta *Competition Policy: Theory and Practice* (Cambridge University Press, 2004), pp 460–483; O'Donoghue and Padilla *The Law and Economics of Article 102 TFEU* (Hart, 2nd ed, 2013), ch 11; Van den Bergh and Camesasca *European Competition Law and Economics: A Comparative Perspective* (Sweet & Maxwell, 2nd ed, 2006), pp 264–276; section 8 of DG COMP's *Discussion paper on the application of Article [102 TFEU] to exclusionary abuses*; Bishop and Walker *The Economics of EC Competition Law* (Sweet & Maxwell, 3rd ed, 2010), paras 6-63–6-83.

[84] Some of these are described in para 48 of the Commission's *Guidance on Article 102 Enforcement Priorities*.

[85] See '*Hilti*', p 709 later in chapter.

[86] The Commission required an end to this practice in *Novo Nordisk*: XXVIth *Report on Competition Policy* (1996), pp 142–143.

[87] See '*Microsoft*', pp 709–710 later in chapter.

[88] See ch 18, 'Bundling', pp 754–756.

(B) Policy considerations: arguments for and against tying

The arguments against tying are that it takes away a customer's freedom of choice, as it cannot buy the tied product where it would wish; that tying might foreclose competitors that are deprived of outlets for their brand of the tied product; and that it involves the dominant firm 'leveraging' its position in relation to the tying product to achieve increased sales in the market for the tied product, which results in horizontal foreclosure of the market[89]. Of course the leverage theory assumes that the firm possesses substantial market power. However this theory was subjected to sustained criticism, in particular by 'the Chicago School' of economists[90]: the central thrust of this criticism was that a monopolist can earn its monopoly profit only once, and that if it has monopoly power over product A, it cannot increase its profit by leveraging its position into product B[91]. The insights of the Chicago School were persuasive, and there is now general recognition that *per se* illegality is inappropriate for tying: it is now subjected in the US to a full analysis of the effects of tying[92].

Apart from theoretical scepticism about the leverage theory, it is now generally accepted that tying is a normal feature of commercial life, and not something that should be regarded as inherently suspicious. Tying involves the integration of components into one product and this can lead to significant economic efficiencies, resulting in lower costs of production and distribution and in improvements of quality. Manufacturing activity, by its very nature, involves the bringing together of different components, and it would be perverse to suggest that, when engaged in by a dominant firm, such behaviour should be stigmatised as presumptively unlawful: the presumption should be the other way[93].

A few illustrations of the benefits of tying may assist. Tying may be used to maintain the efficiency of the tying product: for example a piece of equipment may function at its best only if a particular chemical or material is used which is available solely from the manufacturer, because it has a patent or relevant know-how. Another reason for tying may be to enable economies of scale or scope to be achieved: a manufacturer of a photocopying machine which also supplies ink, paper and spare parts will be able to reduce costs if all these items are delivered to customers at the same time; tying these products may lead to lower prices. A third reason for tying is to enable a producer to discriminate between customers: the manufacturer of a photocopying machine may wish to charge high-volume users more than low-volume ones; this it can do by tying photocopying paper: the customer which uses the machine the most will pay the most and the tie operates as a substitute for putting a meter onto the machine[94]. Discrimination of this kind

[89] See ch 5, 'Horizontal and vertical foreclosure', pp 210–211.

[90] On the 'Chicago School' of antitrust analysis see eg Posner 'The Chicago School of Antitrust' (1979) 127 U Penn Law Review 925; Kovacic 'The Intellectual DNA of Modern US Competition Law for Dominant Firm Conduct: The Chicago/Harvard Double Helix' (2007) 1 Columbia Business Law Review 1; Pitofsky (ed) *How the Chicago School Overshot the Mark* (Oxford University Press, 2008); Kobayashi and Muris 'Chicago, Post-Chicago, and Beyond: Time to Let Go of the 20th Century' (2012) 78 Antitrust LJ 147; Bougette, Deschamps and Marty 'When Economics Met Antitrust: The Second Chicago School and the Economization of Antitrust Law' (2015) 16 Enterprise & Society 313.

[91] See eg Bork *The Antitrust Paradox* (Basic Books, 1978), ch 19; Bowman 'Tying Arrangements and the Leverage Problem' (1957) 67 Yale Law Journal 19; Turner 'The Validity of Tying Arrangements under the Antitrust Laws' (1958) 72 Harvard Law Review 73; for a review of the different arguments see Scherer and Ross *Industrial Market Structure and Economic Performance* (Houghton Mifflin, 3rd ed, 1990), pp 565–569.

[92] *US v Microsoft* 253 F 3d 34 (DC Cir 2001).

[93] For a discussion of efficiency explanations for the practice of tying and bundling see Nalebuff *Bundling, Tying, and Portfolio Effects* (DTI Economics Paper No 1, 2003), part 4.3, available at www.gov.uk; Evans and Salinger 'Why Do Firms Bundle and Tie? Evidence from Competitive Markets and Implications for Tying Law' (2004) 22 Yale Journal on Regulation 38.

[94] See Bowman 'Tying Arrangements and the Leverage Problem' (1957) 67 Yale Law Journal 19.

is not as obviously undesirable as might at first be thought; charging different customers different prices whose costs are the same does not, of itself, mean that there is foreclosure[95]. A further example of a tying practice that may promote efficiency is where X produces game consoles and computer games that operate only with those consoles: as consumers buy more consoles of a particular type, software writers produce more games that are compatible with it. This, in due course, may lead to higher sales of consoles and, therefore, lower prices overall. In this case the network effect leads to efficiencies to the benefit of consumers[96].

However there may be circumstances in which tying might have an anti-competitive foreclosure effect on the market. Some 'post-Chicago' economists have identified some vitality in the 'leveraging' theory, for example where the firm with dominance over the tying product also has some market power in relation to the tied product and is able to raise barriers to entry in that market[97].

(C) **EU law**

Article 101(1)(e) and Article 102(2)(d) specifically state that tie-in agreements may amount to infringements. Although Article 101 may apply to such agreements[98], most cases have been brought under Article 102, including the landmark decision in *Microsoft*[99]. Article 102(2)(d) gives as an example of abuse:

> making the conclusion of contracts subject to acceptance by the other parties of supplementary obligations which, by their nature or according to commercial usage, have no connection with the nature of such contracts.

The Court of Justice has established that tying practices may also be caught by Article 102 where they do not fall within the precise terms of Article 102(2)(d): in *Tetra Pak v Commission* the Court concluded that there was an unlawful tie even though the products in question were connected by commercial usage, a situation not covered by Article 102(2)(d)[100].

Concerns about tying and bundling have also arisen in cases under the EU Merger Regulation, such as *Tetra Laval/Sidel*[101], *GE/Honeywell*[102] and *Microsoft/LinkedIn*[103]; however the General Court concluded that the Commission had committed manifest errors of assessment in its findings as to leveraging and the strengthening of the merged entity's dominant position in *Tetra Laval v Commission*[104] and in *General Electric v Commission*[105]. The Commission's *Guidelines on the assessment of non-horizontal mergers*[106] explain the circumstances in which it will proceed against a merger on the basis of so-called 'conglomerate effects'[107].

[95] See Case C-209/10 *Post Danmark A/S v Konkurrencerådet* EU:C:2012:172, para 30.

[96] See ch 1, 'Network effects', pp 11–12.

[97] See Whinston 'Tying, Foreclosure and Exclusion' (1980) 80 Am Ec Rev 837; *Bundling, Tying, and Portfolio Effects* (DTI Economics Paper No 1, 2003), para 4.4.2; Elhauge 'Tying, Bundled Discounts, and the Death of the Single Monopoly Profit Theory' (2009) 123 Harvard Law Review 397.

[98] See the Commission's *Guidelines on Vertical Restraints* OJ [2010] C 130/1, paras 214–222.

[99] Commission decision of 24 March 2004, upheld on appeal Case T-201/04 *Microsoft Corpn v Commission* EU:T:2007:289.

[100] Case C-333/94 P EU:C:1996:436, para 37; see also Case T-201/04 *Microsoft Corpn v Commission* EU:T:2007:289, para 861, although the abuse in that case fell fully within Article 102(2)(d) anyway: ibid, para 862.

[101] Case M 2416, decision of 30 October 2001.

[102] Case M 2220, decision of 3 July 2001.

[103] Case M 8124, decision of 6 December 2016, paras 295–352.

[104] Case T-5/02 EU:T:2002:264, upheld on appeal Case C-12/03 P *Commission v Tetra Laval* EU:C:2005:87.

[105] Case T-210/01 *General Electric v Commission* EU:T:2005:456.

[106] OJ [2008] C 265/6.

[107] Ibid, paras 91–121; see ch 21, 'Conglomerate mergers', p 901.

In determining whether there is an infringement of Article 102, five issues must be addressed:

- Does the accused undertaking have a dominant position?
- Has the dominant undertaking tied two distinct products?
- Was the customer coerced to purchase both the tying and the tied products?
- Is the tie capable of having an anti-competitive foreclosure effect?
- Is there an objective justification for the tie?

Each of these requirements will be considered in turn; the Commission's views, set out in its *Guidance on Article 102 Enforcement Priorities*, as to the circumstances in which it might consider it appropriate to take enforcement action in relation to tying practices will be incorporated into the text that follows.

(i) Does the accused undertaking have a dominant position?

Clearly there can be an infringement of Article 102 only if an undertaking has a dominant position, and this would be in the tying market; there is no need for dominance in the tied market. Footnote 34 of the Commission's *Guidance on Article 102 Enforcement Priorities* states that, in the 'special' case of tying in aftermarkets[108], Article 102 could be infringed where an undertaking is dominant in either the tying or the tied market.

(ii) Has the dominant undertaking tied two distinct products?

The notion of tying is, at first sight, simple enough; a customer is forced to purchase two distinct products that could have been bought individually. However a moment's reflection reveals that there is a real difficulty in determining when two or more products should be regarded as distinct so that their sale together should be regarded as a tie[109]. A car is sold with wheels and tyres: clearly this does not involve a tie; there will also be a spare wheel: presumably this is not a tie; the car may be fitted with a radio: this perhaps does amount to a tie; if the purchaser is required to insure the car with an insurance company specified by the manufacturer or dealer, this presumably would be a tie. In the same way a pair of shoes would not be regarded as a tie; nor would the sale of shoes with laces; but a requirement to purchase a particular brand of polish with the shoes presumably would be. It is necessary to determine at what point a case becomes one of tying: the burden of proving that two products are the subject of a tie is on the person alleging the infringement.

According to the formulation in Article 102(2)(d) products are tied when they have no connection either 'by their nature or according to commercial usage'. The Commission says in paragraph 51 of its *Guidance on Article 102 Enforcement Priorities*[110], citing the General Court's judgment in *Microsoft*, that it considers two products to be distinct if, in the absence of tying (or bundling), a substantial number of customers would purchase or would have purchased the tying product without also buying the tied product from the same supplier. It notes that there might be direct evidence that customers, when given a choice, purchase the tying and the tied products separately; or indirect evidence, such as the presence on the market of undertakings that manufacture or sell the tied product without the tying one.

[108] See ch 1, 'Spare parts and the aftermarket', pp 36–37.

[109] For an interesting discussion of this issue in the Irish Supreme Court, concluding that a savings protection scheme was an integral part of the service provided by credit unions so that there was no tie, see *The Competition Authority v O'Regan* [2007] IESC 22; for comment see Gorecki 'The Supreme Court Judgment in the *Irish League of Credit Unions* Case: Setting New Standards or Misapplying Current Case Law?' [2008] 29 ECLR 499.

[110] See to similar effect para 215 of the Commission's *Guidelines on Vertical Restraints*.

The EU Courts have examined the 'distinct products' requirement in three high-profile cases[111].

(a) Hilti

In *Eurofix-Bauco v Hilti*[112] the Commission held that the requirement that users of Hilti's patented nail cartridges should also acquire nails from it was an abuse of a dominant position; a fine of €6 million was imposed for this and other infringements. Hilti appealed[113], challenging the Commission's finding that the nail guns, the cartridge strips and the nails were three distinct product markets rather than forming one indivisible whole, a 'powder actuated fastening system' comprising the nail guns and their consumables. The General Court held that there were three markets, and that independent producers should be free to manufacture consumables intended for use in equipment manufactured by others unless in so doing they would infringe intellectual property rights[114].

(b) Tetra Pak

In *Tetra Pak II*[115] Tetra Pak required customers to whom it supplied liquid packaging machines to purchase cartons from it; it also insisted that only it should provide the services of repair and maintenance. Tetra Pak argued that it supplied an integrated distribution system for liquid and semi-liquid foods intended for human consumption and could not therefore be guilty of an abuse in tying the supply of its filling machines to the supply of its cartons. The Commission stated at paragraph 119 of its decision that it was not customary to tie cartons to machines and concluded that the cartons formed a separate market upon which the dominant firm was trying to eliminate competition. The EU Courts upheld this finding[116].

(c) Microsoft

The question of whether two distinct products were the subject of a tie was a key issue in *Microsoft*. The Commission found that Microsoft had tied its Media Player to its personal computer operating system[117]. On appeal the General Court upheld the Commission's decision[118]. The Court agreed that the operating system and the media player were separate products[119]. The Court noted that the IT and communications industry was in

[111] See also *Rio Tinto Alcan*, Commission decision of 20 December 2012, paras 14–27; *Ryanair/Dublin Airport Authority*, Commission decision of 20 January 2014, para 113.

[112] OJ [1988] L 65/19.

[113] Case T-30/89 *Hilti AG v Commission* EU:T:1991:70, upheld on appeal Case C-53/92 P *Hilti AG v Commission* EU:C:1994:77.

[114] Case T-30/89 *Hilti AG v Commission* EU:T:1991:70, para 68.

[115] OJ [1992] L 72/1.

[116] Case T-83/91 *Tetra Pak International SA v Commission* EU:T:1994:246, paras 60–78, upheld on appeal Case C-333/94 P EU:C:1996:436; for comment see Korah 'The Paucity of Economic Analysis in the EEC Decisions on Competition: *Tetra Pak II*' (1993) 46 Current Legal Problems 148, 156–172.

[117] *Microsoft*, Commission decision of 24 March 2004, upheld on appeal Case T-201/04 *Microsoft Corpn v Commission* EU:T:2007:289; for comment on the finding of a tie in the *Microsoft* decision see Art and McCurdy 'The European Commission's Media Player Remedy in its *Microsoft* Decision: Compulsory Code Removal Despite the Absence of Tying or Foreclosure' (2004) 11 ECLR 694 (the authors of this article were advisers to Microsoft during this case); Banasevic, Huby, Pena Castellot, Sitar and Piffaut 'Commission adopts Decision in the *Microsoft* case' (2004) (Summer) Competition Policy Newsletter 46–47 (the authors of this article were officials at DG COMP at the time of the decision).

[118] Case T-201/04 *Microsoft Corpn v Commission* EU:T:2007:289; for discussion of the case by DG COMP officials see Kramler, Buhr and Wyns 'The judgment of the Court of First Instance in the *Microsoft* case' (2007) 3 Competition Policy Newsletter 39; see also Montagnani 'Remedies to Exclusionary Innovation in the High-Tech Sector: Is there a Lesson from the Microsoft Saga?' (2007) 30 World Competition 623.

[119] Case T-201/04 *Microsoft Corpn v Commission* EU:T:2007:289, paras 912–944.

constant and rapid evolution, so that what appear to be separate products may subsequently be regarded as forming a single one[120]; it then pointed out that its function was to consider whether the operating system and Windows Media Player ('WMP') were separate products *in May 1999* when the conduct complained of was alleged to be harmful, rather than at the time of the judgment (September 2007) when a different answer might be given[121]. The Court said that the distinctness of the products had to be determined by reference to consumer demand[122]. In its view there was a functional difference between system software (the operating system itself) and applications software (word processing, media players etc)[123]; there were operators on the market that supplied the tied product (a media player) without the tying product (an operating system): the Court pointed out that case law had established that this was 'serious evidence' of there being separate products[124]; Microsoft supplied WMP as a separate product to work with its competitors' operating systems[125]; it was possible to download Microsoft's media player independently from its website[126]; Microsoft promoted WMP as a standalone product[127]; it had a separate licence agreement for WMP[128]; and customers did acquire media players from Microsoft's competitors[129].

In *Microsoft (tying)*[130] the Commission's preliminary assessment was that Microsoft had tied Internet Explorer to its dominant Windows operating system. In the end the Commission accepted commitments from Microsoft to bring an end to the Article 102 proceedings against it: Microsoft agreed that it would offer users of Windows a choice among different web browsers. In 2013 the Commission imposed a fine of €561 million on Microsoft for failing to comply with these commitments for 14 months[131], the first time this has happened in EU competition law.

(iii) Was the customer coerced to purchase both the tying and the tied products?

The language of Article 102(2)(d) suggests that a component of the abuse of tying is that the customer is coerced into acquiring the tied product: '*making* the conclusion of contracts subject to acceptance by the other parties of supplementary obligations' (emphasis added). A contractual stipulation obviously satisfies this test[132]. However in *Microsoft* there was no contractual requirement to take WMP; rather it was included in the operating software, whether customers wanted it or not: in the parlance of the subject, this was 'technical bundling'. The General Court concluded that there was coercion of customers to take WMP because it was impossible to uninstall it from the operating software system[133]; the Court was unimpressed by the fact that there was no extra charge for the inclusion of WMP[134]. The Commission considers that the anti-competitive foreclosure effect of technical tying is likely to be greater than contractual tying or bundling since it may be costly to reverse and may reduce the opportunities for resale of individual components[135].

[120] Ibid, para 913. [121] Ibid, para 914. [122] Ibid, para 917. [123] Ibid, para 926.
[124] Ibid, para 927. [125] Ibid, para 928. [126] Ibid, para 929. [127] Ibid, para 930.
[128] Ibid, para 931. [129] Ibid, para 932.

[130] Commission decision of 16 December 2010; see Buhr, Wenzel Bulst, Foucault and Kramler 'The Commission's Decision in the Microsoft Internet Explorer Cases and Recent Developments in the Area of Interoperability' (2010) 1 Competition Policy Newsletter 28.

[131] Commission decision of 6 March 2013.

[132] The Commission accepted commitments from Rio Tinto Alcan to resolve concerns relating to the contractual tying of its aluminum smelting technology to its smelter equipment in a decision of 20 December 2012.

[133] Case T-201/04 *Microsoft Corpn v Commission* EU:T:2007:289, para 963.

[134] Ibid, para 967–969; cf *Streetmap.EU v Google* [2016] EWHC 253 (Ch), paras 51–53.

[135] See the Commission's *Guidance on Article 102 Enforcement Priorities*, para 53.

(iv) Is the tie capable of having an anti-competitive foreclosure effect?

To amount to an abuse tying must have, or be capable of having, an anti-competitive foreclosure effect. The Commission discusses factors that it would take into account when deciding whether tying might lead to anti-competitive foreclosure in paragraphs 52 to 58 of its *Guidance*. It refers to the general factors set out in paragraph 20[136], and then considers additional ones of significance in tying cases. As noted above, paragraph 53 suggests that technical tying may have a greater anti-competitive foreclosure effect than contractual tying or bundling. Paragraph 55 expresses the concern that tying might result in less competition for customers interested only in buying the tied, but not the tying, product, leading to higher prices for the former. Paragraph 57 notes that, if prices for the tying product are regulated, the dominant undertaking may decide to raise prices in the tied market in order to compensate for the loss of revenue in the tying market. A further concern set out in paragraph 58 is that entry into the tying market alone may be made more difficult if there is a limited number of alternative suppliers of the tied product.

The Commission has applied Article 102 to several tying practices. In *IBM*[137] it brought an end to IBM's practices of 'memory bundling' and 'software bundling', accepting an undertaking that IBM would offer its System/370 central processing units without a main memory or with only sufficient memory as was needed for testing[138]. In *Eurofix-Bauco v Hilti*[139] the EU Courts upheld the Commission's decision that the requirement of Hilti that users of its patented nail cartridges should also acquire nails from it exploited customers and harmed competition and was an abuse of a dominant position. In *London European-Sabena*[140] the Commission concluded that an attempt by Sabena to stipulate that access to its computer reservation system on the part of London European should be conditional upon the latter using Sabena's ground-handling services was an abuse. In *De Post/La Poste*[141] the Commission objected to the Belgian postal operator giving a more favourable tariff for its general letter mail service to customers who also purchased its new business-to-business mail service.

In *Centre belge d'études de marché—Télémarketing v CLT*[142] the Court of Justice held that it was an abuse for the Luxembourg radio and television station, which had a statutory monopoly, to insist that advertisers should channel their advertising through its advertising manager or an agency appointed by it. This amounted to an extension of its monopoly power from one market into a neighbouring one, a kind of 'tie-in' that prevented other advertising agencies from competing with it and which limited the commercial freedom of users. In *Napier Brown-British Sugar*[143] the Commission applied this principle when condemning British Sugar's refusal to allow customers to collect sugar at ex-factory prices, thereby reserving to itself the distribution function in respect of this product.

In *Microsoft* the General Court agreed with the Commission's finding that the tie led to a foreclosure of the market[144]. It considered that the inclusion of WMP had appreciably

136 See ch 5, 'How is effects analysis conducted in practice?', pp 214–215.

137 Commission's XIVth *Report on Competition Policy* (1984), points 94–95; see further on this matter XVIth *Report on Competition Policy* (1986), point 75 and XVIIth *Report on Competition Policy* (1987), point 85; for comment see Vickers 'A Tale of Two EC Cases: *IBM* and *Microsoft*' (2008) 4(1) Competition Policy International 3.

138 Note that the Commission closed the file on complaints that IBM had tied its mainframe hardware to its mainframe operating system: Commission Press Release IP/11/1044, 20 September 2011.

139 OJ [1988] L 65/19, upheld on appeal Case T-30/89 *Hilti AG v Commission* EU:T:1991:70, and on appeal Case C-53/92 P *Hilti AG v Commission* EU:C:1994:77.

140 OJ [1988] L 317/47.

141 OJ [2002] L 61/32.

142 Case C-311/84 EU:C:1985:394.

143 OJ [1988] L 284/41.

144 Case T-201/04 *Microsoft Corpn v Commission* EU:T:2007:289, paras 1031–1090.

altered the balance of competition in favour of Microsoft to the detriment of competitors[145]. The Court referred to the ubiquity of the Windows operating system which, in 2002, enjoyed a market share of more than 90%[146]. It also said that users who find that WMP is pre-installed on their operating system would be less likely to make use of an alternative media player[147]. The Court considered that the inclusion of WMP created disincentives for manufacturers of computers to include the media player of a competitor in their computers[148]. The General Court also agreed with the Commission that the ubiquity of Windows was likely to have a strong influence upon content providers and software designers[149] and noted market surveys that demonstrated a trend towards the use of WMP to the detriment of other media players[150].

In *Google Android*[151] the Commission is investigating whether Google has abused its dominant position in general internet search services by insisting that manufacturers pre-install Google's search engine and internet browser on mobile devices using the Android mobile operating system.

(v) **Is there an objective justification for the tie?**

A dominant undertaking is entitled to demonstrate that tying is objectively justified or enhances efficiency: the burden of proof is on the dominant firm[152]. Paragraph 62 of the Commission's *Guidance on Article 102 Enforcement Priorities* says that it will consider claims that tying (and bundling) may lead to savings in production or distribution that would benefit consumers.

In *Hilti* the Commission's concern was that the practice of tying would prevent producers of nails from supplying users of Hilti nail guns. Hilti argued that its behaviour was objectively justifiable as it was necessary to maintain safety standards, so that operators would not be injured by nail guns. The Commission rejected this argument, concluding that Hilti's primary concern was the protection of its commercial position rather than a disinterested wish to protect users of its products. The General Court upheld this finding, pointing out that in the UK, where the competitors were selling their nails, there were laws about product safety and authorities that enforced them. In those circumstances it was not the task of Hilti to take steps on its own initiative to eliminate products which, rightly or wrongly, it regarded as dangerous or inferior to its own[153]. The scope for mischief, were a dominant undertaking permitted to take such steps, is obvious.

The General Court concluded in *Microsoft* that Microsoft had failed to show any objective justification for tying WMP with its operating software[154].

(D) **UK law**

As in the case of Article 102(2)(d), section 18(2)(d) of the Competition Act 1998 specifically states that a tie-in agreement may constitute an abuse.

In *Pricing of BT Analyst*[155] the Office of Communications ('OFCOM') received a complaint that BT had tied a billing analysis product, BT Analyst, to the provision of business telephony services. OFCOM's conclusion was that the billing product was part of the telephony service, and that therefore there was no tie[156]. On two earlier occasions the

145 Ibid, para 1034. 146 Ibid, para 1038. 147 Ibid, para 1041. 148 Ibid, para 1043.

149 Ibid, para 1060. 150 Ibid, para 1078.

151 See Commission Press Release IP/16/1492 and MEMO/16/1484, both of 20 April 2016.

152 See ch 5, 'Defences', pp 217–220.

153 See further para 29 of the Commission's *Guidance on Article 102 Enforcement Priorities* which refers specifically to the proposition in *Hilti* discussed in the text.

154 Case T-201/04 *Microsoft Corpn v Commission* EU:T:2007:289, paras 1144–1167.

155 OFCOM decision of 27 October 2004.

156 Ibid, paras 46–53. 157 *Swan Solutions Ltd/Avaya Ltd*, OFCOM decision of 6 April 2001.

Office of Telecommunications[157] (now OFCOM) and the OFT[158] were asked to investigate allegations of tie-in practices, but in each case they concluded that there was one single market over which there was no dominance, rather than a dominated primary market and a separate, secondary, market[159].

In *Genzyme* the OFT imposed a fine of £6.8 million on that company for abusing its dominant position in two ways, one of which was to engage in the abusive bundling of a drug and homecare services for patients suffering from Gaucher's disease[160]. On appeal the CAT held that the OFT had not proved that the bundling had sufficiently adverse effects for it to be abusive[161].

In *Streetmap.EU v Google*[162] the High Court was unimpressed with the claimant's argument that displaying a thumbnail map only from Google Maps on Google's search engine results pages constituted tying or bundling. Roth J noted that internet users were under no obligation to click on Google Maps and remained free, without penalty, to use any other online mapping provider or none at all.

In *Socrates v Law Society*[162a] the CAT held that the Law Society had abused its dominant position by tying its training in anti-money laundering and mortgage fraud to its accreditation scheme for conveyancing law firms.

4. Refusal to Supply

There are circumstances in which a refusal on the part of a dominant firm to supply goods or services can amount to an abuse of a dominant position. Refusal to supply is a controversial topic in competition law[163]; some introductory comments may be helpful before considering some specific cases.

(A) Preliminary comments

First, as a general proposition, most legal systems allow firms to contract with whomsoever they wish. At paragraph 56 of his Opinion in *Oscar Bronner*[164] Advocate General Jacobs pointed out that:

> the right to choose one's trading partners and freely to dispose of one's property are generally recognised principles in the laws of the Member States

and that:

> incursions on those rights require careful justification.

The Commission begins the section on refusal to supply in its *Guidance on Article 102 Enforcement Priorities* by repeating these same points.

A second consideration is that forcing a dominant undertaking to supply may not be beneficial for competition if it means that 'free-riders' can take advantage of investments that have been made by other firms in the market. At paragraph 57 of his Opinion in *Oscar Bronner*[165] Advocate General Jacobs pointed out that allowing competitors to

[158] *ICL/Synstar*, OFT decision of 26 July 2001.

[159] On this point see ch 1, 'Spare parts and the aftermarket', pp 36–37.

[160] OFT decision of 27 March 2003.

[161] Case 1016/1/1/03 *Genzyme Ltd v OFT* [2004] CAT 4, paras 527–548.

[162] [2016] EWHC 253 (Ch), paras 51–53. [162a] [2017] CAT 10, paras 138–177.

[163] For further reading on refusals to supply see Motta *Competition Policy: Theory and Practice* (Cambridge University Press, 2004), pp 66–68; O'Donoghue and Padilla *The Law and Economics of Article 102 TFEU* (Hart, 2nd ed, 2013), ch 10; section 9 of DG COMP's *Discussion paper on the application of Article [102] of the Treaty to exclusionary abuses*; Bishop and Walker *The Economics of EC Competition Law* (Sweet & Maxwell, 3rd ed, 2010), paras 6-119–6-135.

[164] Case C-7/97 EU:C:1998:264. [165] Ibid.

demand access to the 'essential facilities'[166] of dominant firms, which might seem to be pro-competitive by enabling claimants to enter the market in the short term, might ultimately be anti-competitive, if the consequence would be to discourage the necessary investment for the creation of the facility in the first place. At paragraph 58 the Advocate General stressed the importance of the fact that the primary purpose of Article 102 is to prevent distortions of competition, and not to protect the position of particular competitors[167]. While accepting that the case law did, in certain circumstances, impose a duty on dominant firms to supply, the Advocate General advised that the duty should be appropriately confined and should be invoked only where a clear detriment to competition would follow from a refusal.

The Commission notes in paragraph 75 of its *Guidance* that the existence of an obligation to supply—even for a fair remuneration—may undermine undertakings' incentive to invest and innovate, which could be detrimental to consumers; and that, where a competitor can take a 'free ride' on the investment of the dominant firm, it is unlikely itself to invest and innovate, again to the detriment of consumers. However it also notes, in paragraph 82, that these considerations would not apply where an obligation to supply has already been imposed by regulation compatible with EU law, in which case a public authority will already have undertaken a balance of the parties' incentives; or where the upstream market position of the dominant undertaking has been developed under the protection of special or exclusive rights financed by state resources[168]. In these circumstances the Commission would simply be concerned to identify whether a refusal to supply could result in anti-competitive foreclosure, without applying the stringent rules discussed later that would otherwise be applicable.

A third point is that when considering the law of refusal to supply it is helpful to keep in mind the distinction between horizontal and vertical foreclosure[169]. Most cases on refusal to supply involve harm to the downstream market, that is to say vertical foreclosure: this section will be primarily concerned with cases of this kind. However there have been some cases that were concerned with horizontal foreclosure, and these are noted towards the end of this section[170], as are cases where the refusal was motivated by discrimination on grounds of nationality[171] and where the withholding of sales was a way of preventing parallel exports to a higher-priced Member State[172].

A fourth point is that a dominant firm may refuse to supply for reasons other than the exclusion of a competitor: for example that a customer is a bad debtor, that there is a shortage of stocks or that production has been disrupted[173]. In *United Brands*[174] the Court of Justice invoked the principle of 'proportionality' and said that a dominant firm, like any other, is entitled to take measures to protect its legitimate commercial interests but those measures must be proportionate to the threat it faces.

[166] See 'Is the product to which access is sought indispensable to someone wishing to compete in the downstream market?', pp 717–723 later for discussion of this, and related, expressions.

[167] See also President of the General Court in Case T-184/01 R *IMS Health Inc v Commission* EU:T:2005:95, para 145, cf the view of the President of the Court of Justice in Case C-481/01 P (R) EU:C:2002:223, para 84.

[168] See eg Case 7/82 *GVL v Commission* EU:C:1983:52; see also DG COMP's *Discussion paper on the application of Article [102] of the Treaty to exclusionary abuses*, para 236; on the meaning of special or exclusive rights see ch 6, 'Undertakings with "special or exclusive rights"', pp 231–233.

[169] See ch 5, 'Horizontal and vertical foreclosure', pp 210–215.

[170] See 'Horizontal foreclosure', p 725 later in chapter.

[171] See 'Refusal to supply on the basis of nationality', p 725 later in chapter.

[172] See 'Refusal to supply to prevent parallel imports', p 726 later in chapter.

[173] See Opinion of AG Jacobs in Case C-53/03 *Syfait* EU:C:2004:673, para 67.

[174] Case 27/76 EU:C:1978:22, para 189.

(B) EU law

(i) Vertical foreclosure: competitive harm in a downstream market

Most refusal to supply cases concern a vertically-integrated undertaking that is dominant in an upstream market and which refuses to supply an existing or a new customer in a downstream market on which it is also present. Paragraph 76 of the Commission's *Guidance on Article 102 Enforcement Priorities* explains that the section in that document that deals specifically with refusal to supply is concerned only with cases of this kind[175]. Paragraph 84 of the *Guidance* suggests that a refusal to supply a new customer is capable of infringing Article 102 as well as the disruption of an existing relationship: case law supports this proposition[176]. However the Commission adds that it is more likely that termination of an existing relationship will be found to be abusive than a *de novo* refusal to supply: for example if a customer has made specific investment to use an input supplied by the dominant supplier, this might lead to the conclusion that the input has become indispensable[177]. A different reason might be because the existence of a prior relationship indicates that supplying the input does not imply a risk that the owner of the input will receive inadequate compensation for its investment.

In *Commercial Solvents v Commission*[178] the Court of Justice held that a refusal to supply a downstream customer could amount to an abuse of a dominant position. Zoja was an Italian producer of a drug used in the treatment of tuberculosis; it was dependent upon supplies of a raw material, amino-butanol, the dominant supplier of which was Commercial Solvents. When the latter refused to make amino-butanol available to Zoja the Commission found that it had abused its dominant position and ordered it to resume supplies. The Commission's decision was upheld on appeal to the Court of Justice. Commercial Solvents was not only a dominant supplier of amino-butanol in the upstream market for the raw material; its refusal to supply Zoja coincided with the emergence of Commercial Solvent's own subsidiary, ICI, onto the downstream market for the anti-TB drug on which Zoja was operating: the refusal to supply would eliminate Zoja from the downstream market. The Court of Justice said that:

> [a]n undertaking which has a dominant position in the market in raw materials and which, with the object of reserving such raw material for manufacturing its own derivatives, refuses to supply a customer, which is itself a manufacturer of these derivatives, and therefore risks eliminating all competition on the part of this customer, is abusing its dominant position[179].

There have been many cases on refusal to supply of this kind since *Commercial Solvents*; *Magill*, *Oscar Bronner* and *Microsoft* are of particular note and will be discussed later and/or in chapter 19[180]. The quest for the Commission and the EU Courts has been to find the correct balance between upholding the right of undertakings, whether dominant or not,

[175] Note that the Commission has given specific guidance on the application of Article 102, including on refusal to supply, in the electronic communications and postal services sectors: see ch 23, 'Application of EU competition law', pp 1013–1015 and 'Application of EU competition law', pp 1017–1020.

[176] Eg the successful complainant in the *Magill* case was a new, rather than an existing, customer; see similarly Case T-301/04 *Clearstream v Commission* EU:T:2009:317 and *Telekomunikacja Polska*, Commission decision of 22 June 2011, upheld on appeal Case T-486/11 *Telekomunikacja Polska v Commission* EU:T:2015:1002, on appeal Case C-123/16 P *Orange Polska v Commission*, not yet decided; in a case on margin squeeze the Court of Justice stated that it should make no difference to a finding of abuse whether a customer is an existing or a new one: see Case C-52/09 *TeliaSonera Sverige AB* EU:C:2011:83, paras 90–95.

[177] This could provide an explanation for the outcome in *Commercial Solvents*, discussed later.

[178] Cases 6 and 7/73 EU:C:1974:18.

[179] Ibid, para 25.

[180] See ch 19, 'Compulsory licences', pp 815–820.

to choose their trading partners freely on the one hand and ensuring that vertically-integrated dominant undertakings do not exclude competitors from downstream markets to the detriment of consumers on the other.

The case law appears to establish that, in determining whether a refusal to supply a customer in a downstream market amounts to an abuse of a dominant position, five issues must be addressed[181]:

- Is there a refusal to supply?
- Does the accused undertaking have a dominant position in an upstream market?
- Is the product to which access is sought indispensable to someone wishing to compete in the downstream market?
- Would a refusal to grant access lead to the elimination of effective competition in the downstream market?
- Is there an objective justification for the refusal to supply?

Each of these issues will be examined in turn, followed by a comment on possible remedial action.

(a) Is there a refusal to supply?

The Commission's *Guidance on Article 102 Enforcement Priorities*[182] points out that both a refusal to supply outright and a 'constructive refusal' can be a concern. Two cases, *Telekomunikacja Polska*[183] and *Slovak Telekom*[184], make clear that an offer of supplies on terms that are unreasonable—'making an offer you cannot accept'—will be treated as a constructive refusal to supply.

(b) Does the accused undertaking have a dominant position in an upstream market?

It is a statement of the obvious that, for there to be an infringement of Article 102, the accused must hold a dominant position; and in cases of the kind under consideration in this section the dominant position will be in an upstream market. Three points about this merit consideration.

The first is that the way in which the upstream market is defined will inevitably be influenced by the definition of the downstream market. For example in *Sealink/B&I—Holyhead*[185] a ferry operator, B&I, wished to have access to the port of Holyhead in north Wales in order to operate ferry services to and from Ireland. The port at Holyhead was owned by Sealink, which was also present on the downstream market for ferry services. The Commission noted that there were three 'corridors' for short-sea routes between Great Britain and Ireland: the northern corridor, served, for example, by Stranraer in Scotland; the central corridor, served predominantly by Holyhead; and the southern corridor, served by Fishguard, Pembroke and Swansea in south and west Wales. The Commission defined the upstream market as

[181] But note that the Commission would not apply such strict standards where an undertaking is already subject to a regulatory duty to deal or where its upstream market position has been derived from state resources: see 'Preliminary comments', pp 713–714 earlier in chapter.

[182] OJ [2009] C 45/7, para 79, giving examples of what might amount to a 'constructive' refusal to supply.

[183] Commission decision of 22 June 2011, upheld on appeal Case T-486/11 EU:T:2015:1002, on appeal Case C-123/16 P, not yet decided.

[184] Commission decision of 15 October 2014, on appeal to the General Court Case T-851/14 *Slovak Telekom v Commission*, not yet decided.

[185] [1992] 5 CMLR 255; note that this highly-influential case was an interim measures decision of the Commission that was not appealed to the EU Courts.

the provision of port facilities for passenger and ferry services on the central corridor route; however, had it considered that the downstream market was all short-sea crossings between Great Britain and Ireland, it could not have defined the upstream market so narrowly; in this case, Holyhead Harbour (or more precisely the services available there) would not have been indispensable for B&I to be able to compete in the downstream market.

A second point about market definition in refusal to supply cases is that the dominant firm may not be operating on an upstream market at all; it may not supply the input to which access is sought to anyone. This does not mean that, in competition law terms, it cannot have market power over the input in question: the Court of Justice has said that it is sufficient that there is a potential, or even a hypothetical, market[186]. The Commission notes this point in paragraph 79 of its *Guidance on Article 102 Enforcement Priorities*.

A quite different point is that many Member States have laws that impose obligations on undertakings, *whether dominant or not*, to supply customers which are in a position of 'economic dependency': examples are article L420-2, paragraph 2 of the French Commercial Code and section 20 of the German Act against Unfair Restraints of Competition of 1957[187]. It should be recalled that Article 3(2) of Regulation 1/2003 permits the application of national legal provisions that are stricter than Article 102 to unilateral behaviour[188]. The fact that domestic laws consider such conduct to be reprehensible even, in some cases, where the supplier is not dominant might make it easier to conclude that the same conduct amounts to an abuse where the supplier is dominant. However competition policy in the EU today is predominantly concerned with consumer welfare, and the protection of economically dependent firms is not necessarily consistent with this aim[189]. As we shall see, it is well established that a duty to deal does not arise under Article 102 from 'mere' dominance; rather it turns on the *indispensability* of access to an upstream product or service for someone to be able to compete in a downstream market. The criterion of indispensability limits the scope of Article 102, and is a conscious attempt to link findings of abuse to anti-competitive foreclosure from downstream markets to the detriment of consumers.

(c) Is the product to which access is sought indispensable to someone wishing to compete in the downstream market?

Case law has established that a vertically-integrated undertaking is not required to deal with customers with which it competes in a downstream market simply because it is dominant in relation to an upstream market. It is necessary that the product or service to which a customer seeks access is 'indispensable' if it is to be able to compete in the downstream market. The word indispensable is the one that the EU Courts have tended to use; alternative expressions for the input to which access is sought are 'essential facilities' and 'objectively necessary'. The former expression has its antecedents in US antitrust, and there is a vast amount of periodical literature on the essential facilities

[186] See Case C-418/01 *IMS Health GmbH & Co v NDC Health GmbH & Co* EU:C:2004:257, para 44; this point is helpfully discussed in Pitofsky, Patterson and Hooks 'The Essential Facilities Doctrine under US Antitrust Law' (2002) 70 Antitrust LJ 443, 458–461; see also DG COMP's *Discussion paper*, para 227.

[187] A useful guide to such laws will be found in Bocker, Reinker and Little (eds) *Dominance* (Global Competition Review, 13th ed, 2017), which specifically addresses the question, in relation to each jurisdiction, whether there are any rules applicable to the unilateral conduct of non-dominant firms.

[188] See ch 2, 'Conflicts: Article 102', p 78.

[189] For discussion of the aims of competition policy see ch 1, 'Goals of competition law', pp 18–24.

doctrine[190]; as we shall see, the Supreme Court has significantly limited the scope of the doctrine in recent years[191]. The term essential facilities is particularly apt where an undertaking seeks access to a physical infrastructure such as a port, airport, railway network or pipeline: it is a fairly natural use of language to regard such infrastructures as 'facilities', and 'essential' carries the same meaning as 'indispensable'. However the case law has demonstrated that there can also be an obligation, for example, to license intellectual property rights or to provide proprietary information to a third party[192], where the expression 'essential facility' is a less natural one. Perhaps because of this the Commission refers to inputs that are 'objectively necessary' in paragraphs 83 and 84 of its *Guidance on Article 102 Enforcement Priorities*. The text that follows will use the term indispensability in deference to the case law, but it would seem that all three expressions can be used interchangeably.

The requirement for indispensability became clear in *Oscar Bronner GmbH*[193]. Bronner was an Austrian publisher of a daily newspaper, *Der Standard*, and wished to have access to the highly developed home-delivery distribution system of its much larger competitor, Mediaprint; Bronner complained that a refusal to allow such access amounted to an infringement of the Austrian equivalent of Article 102. The Austrian court asked the Court whether such a refusal would infringe Article 102. The entire tone of the judgment is sceptical towards Bronner's case. The Court of Justice stated that the first task for the national court would be to determine whether there was a separate market for the home-delivery of newspapers in Austria, and whether there was insufficient substitutability between Mediaprint's nationwide system and other, regional, schemes. If the market was the nationwide delivery of newspapers to homes, the national court would be bound to conclude that Mediaprint had a monopoly, and, since this extended to the entire territory of Austria, that this monopoly would be held in a substantial part of the internal market[194].

The Court of Justice then moved on to the question of abuse. It pointed out that in *Commercial Solvents* the effect of the refusal to supply the raw material by the dominant firm was likely to eliminate all competition in the downstream market between its own subsidiary and anyone else[195]. The Court of Justice then referred to the *Magill* case[196], saying that the refusal by the owner of an intellectual property right to license it to a third party could, in exceptional circumstances, involve an abuse[197]; in the Court's view *Magill* was an exceptional case for four reasons. First, the information sought by Magill was *indispensable* to the publication of a comprehensive listings guide: without it Magill could not publish a magazine at all; secondly, there was a demonstrable potential consumer

[190] The following articles capture much of the writing on this subject: Areeda 'Essential Facilities: An Epithet in Need of Limiting Principles' (1990) 58 Antitrust LJ 841; Temple Lang 'Defining Legitimate Competition: Companies' Duties to Supply Competitors and Access to Essential Facilities' (1994) 18 Fordham International Law Journal 439; Ridyard 'Essential Facilities and the Obligation to Supply Competitors under UK and EC Competition Law' (1996) 17 ECLR 438; Lipsky and Sidak 'Essential Facilities' (1999) 51 Stanford Law Review 1187; Korah 'Access to Essential Facilities under the Commerce Act in the Light of Experience in Australia, the European Union and the United States' (2000) 31 Victoria University of Wellington Law Review 231; Capobianco 'The Essential Facility Doctrine: Similarities and Differences between the American and European Approaches' (2001) 26 EL Rev 548; Doherty 'Just What are Essential Facilities?' (2001) 38 CML Rev 397; Pitofsky, Patterson and Hooks 'The Essential Facilities Doctrine under US Antitrust Law' (2002) 70 Antitrust LJ 443.

[191] See later in this section.

[192] See ch 19, 'Compulsory licences', pp 815–820 on the *Magill* and *Microsoft* cases.

[193] Case C-7/97 EU:C:1998:569. [194] Ibid, paras 32–36. [195] Ibid, para 38.

[196] Cases C-241/91 P etc *RTE and ITP v Commission* EU:C:1995:98; for an analysis of this case see ch 19, 'The *Magill* case', pp 816–817.

[197] Case C-7/97 EU:C:1998:569, para 39.

demand for the would-be product; thirdly, there were no objective justifications for the refusal to supply; and fourthly, the refusal would eliminate all competition in the secondary market for TV guides[198]. The Court of Justice said, therefore, that, for there to be an abuse, it would have to be shown that refusal to grant access to the home-delivery service would be likely to eliminate all competition in the daily newspaper market (the downstream market) on the part of the person requesting the service and that the home-delivery service was indispensable to carrying on business in the newspaper market[199]. In the Court of Justice's view, use of Mediaprint's home-delivery service was not indispensable, since there were other means of distributing daily newspapers, for example through shops, kiosks and by post[200]; furthermore there were no technical, legal or economic obstacles that made it impossible for other publishers of daily newspapers to establish home-delivery systems of their own[201]. On the question of whether access to the distribution system should be considered indispensable the Court of Justice said that:

> 45. It should be emphasised in that respect that, in order to demonstrate that the creation of such a system is not a realistic potential alternative and that access to the existing system is therefore indispensable, it is not enough to argue that it is not economically viable by reason of the small circulation of the daily newspaper or newspapers to be distributed.
> 46. For such access to be capable of being regarded as indispensable, it would be necessary at the very least to establish, as the Advocate General has pointed out at point 68 of his Opinion, that it is not economically viable to create a second home-delivery scheme for the distribution of daily newspapers with a circulation comparable to that of the daily newspapers distributed by the existing scheme.

In the Court of Justice's view, the behaviour of Mediaprint did not amount to an abuse of a dominant position.

The Court of Justice's judgment in *Oscar Bronner* established that the key to the law on refusal to supply a competitor in a downstream market is indispensability. The input to which access is sought must be something that is incapable of being duplicated, or which could be duplicated only with great difficulty. An input will be indispensable if duplication is:

- **physically impossible**: for example there may be only one point on the coastline of a country where a deep-sea port can be established; and planning or environmental reasons may make it impossible to build a competing airport, a nationwide system of gas transportation or a second rail network
- **legally impossible**: for example where an undertaking owns intellectual property rights, such as the copyright in *Magill*
- **not economically viable**, although the Court of Justice was careful to point out in *Bronner* that it is not sufficient for a small firm to argue that, because of its smallness, it should be entitled to use its larger competitor's infrastructure; rather economic non-duplicability asks whether the market is sufficiently large to sustain a second facility such as the dominant firm's system[202]; this presages the idea of the 'as efficient competitor' test in relation to non-pricing abuses[203].

The requirement of indispensability means that it is not sufficient that it would be *convenient* or *useful* to have access: access must be *essential*. In *Tiercé Ladbroke v Commission*[204] the

[198] Ibid, para 40. [199] Ibid, para 41.
[200] Ibid, para 42. [201] Ibid, para 44.
[202] See also Case C-418/01 *IMS Health GmbH & Co v NDC Health GmbH & Co* EU:C:2004:257, paras 28–30.
[203] On the 'as-efficient competitor test' see ch 5, 'Article 102 protects competition; and competition is for benefit of consumers', pp 202–203.
[204] Case T-504/93 EU:T:1997:84; for comment see Korah 'The Ladbroke Saga' (1998) 19 ECLR 169.

General Court rejected arguments that the supply of sound and television pictures of horse races was indispensable for the downstream betting market, a service which the defendants did not provide. In *European Night Services v Commission*[205] the General Court was not convinced that the supply of train paths, locomotives and train crews were indispensable services.

The Commission discusses the requirement of indispensability—or in its parlance 'objective necessity'—in paragraph 83 of its *Guidance on Article 102 Enforcement Priorities*. In paragraph 83 it refers to *Magill*, *Bronner* and *Microsoft* and says that, in determining whether an input is indispensable, it will normally make an assessment of whether it could be duplicated by competitors in the foreseeable future; duplication is taken to mean the creation of an alternative source of efficient supply capable of allowing competitors to exert a competitive constraint on the dominant undertaking in the downstream market.

Facilities that have been held to be indispensable and to which access has been mandated under Article 102 include:

- **ports**: the *Sealink/B&I—Holyhead* decision has been noted earlier; another example of access being mandated to a port is *Port of Rødby*[206]
- **airports**: in *Frankfurt Airport*[207] the Commission required that the airport authority should terminate its monopoly over ground-handling services and grant access to third parties wishing to supply such services there[208]
- **rail networks**: in *GVG/FS*[209] the Commission concluded that Ferrovie dello Stato, the Italian state-owned railway company, had abused its dominant position by preventing a German railway operator from providing rail transport from Germany to Milan. The abuses consisted of refusal to grant access to the Italian railway infrastructure[210]; a refusal to supply traction (a locomotive, driver and ancillary services)[211]; and a refusal to enter into an international grouping of the kind necessary for cross-border rail passenger services[212]
- **gas pipelines**: the Commission has taken action in relation to access to gas pipelines in a number of cases[213]. In each of *Gaz de France*[214], *E.ON*[215] and *ENI*[216], the Commission accepted commitments, under Article 9 of Regulation 1/2003, some of which were structural, to address concerns about possibly abusive refusals to deal[217]

205 Cases T-374/94 etc EU:T:1998:198.

206 OJ [1994] L 55/52; note that the Commission's interim measures decision in the case of *Irish Continental Group v CCI Morlaix*, reported in the Commission's XXVth *Report on Competition Policy* (1995), pp 120–121 and at [1995] 5 CMLR 177, was different from the *Sealink* case in that the port operator in the *Irish Continental* case was not active on the downstream ferry market; see also *Tariffs for Piloting in the Port of Genoa* OJ [1997] L 301/27.

207 OJ [1998] L 72/30; note that Council Directive 96/67/EC, OJ [1997] L 272/36 liberalises ground-handling at airports and prevents discriminatory fees.

208 See 'The Commission's approach to exclusive purchasing agreements', pp 700–702 earlier in chapter on the termination of long-term supply contracts.

209 OJ [2004] L 11/17. 210 Ibid, paras 119–131. 211 Ibid, paras 132–146.

212 Ibid, paras 147–152.

213 See eg *Gaz de France and Ruhrgas*, Commission Press Release IP/04/573, 30 April 2004, where those two gas companies agreed to grant the Norwegian subsidiary of US gas producer Marathon access to their gas networks: a comment on the case will be found by Fernández Salas, Klotz and Moonen (2004) (Summer) Competition Policy Newsletter 41.

214 Commission decision of 3 December 2009.

215 Commission decision of 4 May 2010; note that the Commission released E.ON from its commitments because they were no longer necessary to ensure sufficient gas transport capacity for E.ON's competitors: Commission Press Release IP/16/2646, 26 July 2016.

216 Commission decision of 29 September 2010.

217 See ch 7, 'Article 9 commitments', pp 264–269; and on Commission interventions in gas markets see ch 23, 'Energy', pp 1020–1023.

- **oil storage**: in *Disma* the Commission required access to equipment for storing jet fuel and transferring it to supply points at Milan's Malpensa Airport; this case was brought under Article 101 rather than Article 102, since a number of undertakings owned the infrastructure in question[218]
- **telecommunications wires and cables**: the essential facilities doctrine is capable of application to telecommunications networks[219]. Recent cases of refusal, or constructive refusal, to grant access to such a network are *Telekomunikacja Polska*[220] and *Slovak Telekom*[221]
- **set-top boxes**: it may be possible to invoke the essential facilities doctrine to obtain access to set-top boxes which are necessary, for example, for the provision of interactive television services[222]
- **computerised airline reservation system**: the Commission has ordered that access be made available to a computerised reservation in the air transport sector[223]
- **interlining**: in *British Midland/Aer Lingus* the Commission required Aer Lingus to provide 'interlining facilities' to a competing airline, so that passengers of the latter would be able, in certain circumstances, to fly on the aeroplanes of the former[224]
- **cross-border payment systems**: the Commission may insist that access be granted to a cross-border payment system[225]. In *Society for Worldwide International Financial Telecommunications* SWIFT controlled the only international network for transferring payment messages; it also operated the only network capable of supplying connections for banking establishments anywhere in the world. The Commission considered that the network constituted a 'basic infrastructure in its own right, since to refuse any entity access to such a network is tantamount to a *de facto* exclusion from the market for international transfers'[226]. The Commission's view was that it was a manifest abuse of a dominant position to lay down unjustified admission criteria and to apply them in a discriminatory manner[227]. SWIFT agreed to grant access to any entity meeting the criteria laid down by the European Monetary Institute for admission to domestic payment systems[228]

[218] *Disma*, Commission's XXIIIrd *Report on Competition Policy* (1993), pp 141–143.

[219] Commission *Notice on the Application of the Competition Rules to Access Agreements in the Telecommunications Sector* OJ [1998] C 265/2, paras 49–53 and 87–98.

[220] Commission decision of 22 June 2011, upheld on appeal Case T-486/11 EU:T:2015:1002, on further appeal to the Court of Justice Case C-123/16 P, not yet decided.

[221] Commission decision of 15 October 2014, on appeal to the General Court Case T-851/14, not yet decided; see Commission Press Release IP/14/1140 and Commission MEMO/14/590 of the same date.

[222] See eg Case JV.37 *BSkyB/KirchPayTV* (under the EU Merger Regulation), Commission Press Release IP/00/279, 21 March 2000; *British Interactive Broadcasting* OJ [1999] L 312/1, paras 173–181 (a case under Article 101).

[223] *London European-Sabena* OJ [1988] L 317/47; see also *Lufthansa*, Commission Press Release IP/99/542, 20 July 1999, where the Commission imposed a fine of €10,000 under Council Regulation 2299/89 on a code of conduct for computerised reservation systems.

[224] OJ [1992] L 96/34.

[225] Commission *Notice on the Application of the Competition Rules to Cross-border Credit Transfers* OJ [1995] C 251/3; see also the Commission's XXVIth *Report on Competition Policy* (1996), point 109, on the ECU Banking Association.

[226] Commission's XXVIIth *Report on Competition Policy* (1997), point 68. [227] Ibid.

[228] For details of the settlement see the Commission's XXVIIth *Report on Competition Policy* (1997), pp 143–145; note that Article 35(1) of Directive 2015/2366 on payment services in the internal market, OJ [2015] L 337/35, requires Member States to ensure that rules on access to payment systems shall be objective, non-discriminatory and proportionate, and that they do not inhibit access more than is necessary to safeguard against specific risks such as settlement risk, operational risk and business risk and to protect the financial and operational stability of the payment system.

- **cross-border securities clearing and settlement services**: in *Clearstream (Clearing and Settlement)*[229] the Commission found that Clearstream had abused its dominant position in relation to clearing and settlement services for registered services by refusing to deal with Euroclear Bank; the Commission's decision was upheld on appeal to the General Court[230]
- **postal networks**: the Commission's view is that there can be an obligation to provide access to postal networks[231]
- **premium TV content**: the Commission has regarded premium TV content as an essential input for pay-TV operators[232]
- **intellectual property rights and or proprietary information**: it may be that access to intellectual property rights and/or proprietary information is regarded as indispensable[233]
- **spare parts**: it may be that spare parts necessary for the repair of a particular product could be regarded as indispensable[234], depending on how the relevant market is defined[235]
- **waste collection infrastructure**: the Commission has regarded household collection infrastructure as indispensable for waste collectors[236].

It may be helpful to reflect on why there have been so many cases of this kind in the EU and why the Supreme Court in the US has retreated from the essential facilities doctrine in recent years. As far as the EU is concerned, from the 1980s onwards the Commission (and many Member States) developed a policy that favoured the demonopolisation and liberalisation of sectors that for much of the twentieth century were regarded as natural monopolies, or inappropriate for the market mechanism; often these sectors were under state control or in state ownership. Exposing sectors such as telecommunications, energy and transport to competition was considered desirable. However competition would be slow to emerge where service providers could compete only if they had access to important infrastructures such as telecommunication wires and cables, the electricity grid, gas and oil pipelines, ports, airports and railway lines owned and operated by vertically-integrated dominant undertakings. In many Member States this problem was overcome by the establishment of regulatory regimes that mandate access to such infrastructures on reasonable, non-discriminatory terms[237]; and in some systems of competition law there are specific rules requiring undertakings in particular sectors to supply[238]. It may be

[229] Commission decision of 2 June 2004; see Martínez and Bufton 'The *Clearstream* decision: the application of Article 82 to securities clearing and settlement' (2004) (Summer) Competition Policy Newsletter 49.

[230] Case T-301/04 *Clearstream v Commission* EU:T:2009:317.

[231] Commission *Notice on the Application of the Competition Rules to the Postal Sector* OJ [1998] C 39/9, paras 2.8–2.9.

[232] For a summary of the Commission's decisional practice see Géradin 'Access to Content by New Media Platforms: A Review of the Competition Law Problems' (2005) 30 EL Rev 68.

[233] See ch 19, 'Compulsory licences', pp 815–820 on the *Magill* and *Microsoft* cases.

[234] See Case 22/78 *Hugin Kassaregister v Commission* EU:C:1979:138; the Commission's decision in this case finding an abusive refusal to supply was annulled by the Court of Justice as it had failed to demonstrate an effect on trade between Member States: see ch 3, 'The Effect on Trade between Member States', pp 150–155.

[235] Market definition in the case of 'aftermarkets' is discussed in ch 1, 'Spare parts and the aftermarket', pp 36–37.

[236] *ARA Foreclosure*, Commission decision of 20 September 2016, paras 78–100.

[237] See ch 23, 'Regulated Industries', pp 1008–1010.

[238] See para 53 of the Opinion of AG Jacobs in Case C-7/97 *Oscar Bronner* EU:C:1998:264; see also Part IIIA of the Australian Trade Practices Act 1974, inserted by the Competition Policy Reform Act 1995, and s 8(b) of the South African Competition Act 1998; on the provisions in Australian law see Kench and Pengilley 'Part IIIA: Unleashing a Monster?' in Hanks and Williams (eds) *Trade Practices Act: A Twenty-Five Year Stocktake* (Federation Press, 2001).

sensible in principle that situations of natural or persistent monopoly should be dealt with by a system of *ex ante* regulation rather than by competition law: a competition authority is likely to be ill-equipped to deal with the persistent disputes in relation to access, and the appropriate price for access, that arise in relation to essential facilities. However EU competition law has proved to be an important adjunct to *ex ante* regulation, as the cases in this section have demonstrated[239].

In the US the first case on the 'essential facilities doctrine' is considered to have been *United States v Terminal Railroad Association of St Louis*[240], although the term was not used in that case. However, in *Verizon Communications Inc v Law Offices of Curtis Trinko*[241], the Supreme Court adopted a notably unenthusiastic approach to the essential facilities doctrine. A case was brought under section 2 of the Sherman Act asserting the right of third parties to have access to Verizon's local telecommunications network. The New York and federal telecommunications regulators had conducted investigations and concluded them; the plaintiff was not satisfied with the outcome, and therefore brought a claim based on competition law. The Supreme Court dismissed the claim, stating that mandatory supply 'may lessen the incentive for the monopolist, the rival, or both to invest in those economically beneficial facilities'[242]. There is little doubt that the Supreme Court was reluctant to allow the plaintiff in *Trinko* to obtain, through private antitrust litigation, what it had failed to achieve by complaining to the public institutions with sector-specific responsibility for telecommunications. The US Federal Trade Commission has said that the *Trinko* judgment ought not to apply to the *public* enforcement of the antitrust rules in regulated sectors, since the incentives of private litigants to sue are different from those of a competition authority[243].

(d) Would a refusal to grant access lead to the elimination of effective competition in the downstream market?

In *Commercial Solvents* the Court of Justice spoke of the risk of the refusal to supply 'eliminating *all* competition' on the downstream market (emphasis added); but in an earlier part of the judgment it had noted that the refusal to supply Zoja would result in the elimination of *one* of the principal manufacturers of the downstream product—in other words it was not correct to say that the removal of Zoja from the market would eliminate *all* competition. To limit the application of Article 102 to refusals to supply that eliminate *all* competition downstream would restrict it considerably. In *Microsoft v Commission*[244] the General Court said, at paragraph 563, that it was not necessary for the Commission to demonstrate that 'all' competition on the market would be eliminated; it was sufficient to show that the refusal to supply is liable, or likely, to eliminate all *effective* competition[245]. The General Court reaffirmed this proposition in *CEAHR v Commission*[246].

[239] See also ch 6, 'Making sense of the case law on Article 102 in conjunction with Article 106(1)', pp 237–242 on the role of Article 102 in circumstances where a Member State is responsible for anti-competitive behaviour on the part of public undertakings and undertakings entrusted with exclusive or special rights and ch 18, 'Margin Squeeze', pp 771–777 on the phenomenon of a 'margin squeeze' on the part of vertically-integrated dominant undertakings which is closely related to refusals to supply.

[240] 224 US 383 (1912); see also *Aspen Skiing Co v Aspen Highlands Skiing Corp* 472 US 585 (1985).

[241] 540 US 398 (2004); for comment see Géradin 'Limiting the Scope of Article 82 EC: What Can the EU Learn from the US Supreme Court's Judgment in *Trinko* in the Wake of *Microsoft*, *IMS*, and *Deutsche Telekom?*' (2004) 41 CML Rev 1519.

[242] 540 US 398, 408 (2004).

[243] 'Is There Life After *Trinko* and *Credit Suisse*? The Role of Antitrust in Regulated Industries', FTC statement of 15 June 2010, available at www.ftc.gov.

[244] Case T-201/04 EU:T:2007:289.

[245] See similarly the Commission's *Guidance on Article 102 Enforcement Priorities*, para 85.

[246] Case T-712/14 EU:T:2017:748, para 91.

In the Commission's view, harm to competition in the downstream market is likely to be greater where the dominant undertaking has a higher rather than a lower market share in the downstream market. The Commission also discusses, in paragraphs 86 to 88 of the *Guidance*, whether any refusal to supply would be likely to have an adverse effect on consumer welfare. In paragraph 87 it specifically says that it would look to see whether the refusal would result in innovative products not being brought to the market or follow-on innovation being stifled. On this point it specifically refers to the General Court's judgment in *Microsoft*, where this was considered to be a relevant factor in the finding of abuse, and *IMS Health*; it might also have referred to *Magill*, where this was clearly an influential matter—Magill wished to produce a composite TV listings magazine which at the time did not exist. In paragraph 88 the Commission says that it also would be concerned about harm to consumer welfare where an upstream input price is regulated, the downstream price is not regulated, and the refusal to supply might lead to the extraction of more profits in the downstream market.

(e) Is there an objective justification for the refusal to supply?

A refusal to supply a downstream customer would not be unlawful where there is an objective justification for it[247]. The dominant firm is required to show that its refusal is objectively necessary in the sense that it pursues a legitimate interest other than its own commercial advantage, and that it has behaved in a proportionate way. Possible justifications are that:

- the customer is a bad debtor, has become a credit risk or has failed to observe its contractual obligations
- the customer will use the input for an illegal purpose[248]
- the dominant firm has capacity constraints that make it impossible for access to be provided[249]
- the dominant firm needs to realise an adequate return on investments required to develop its input business[250]
- granting access might affect negatively both the dominant firm's incentive to innovate and that of downstream competitors[251].

The existence of an objective justification is ultimately a question of fact to be determined in the particular circumstances of each case. Vague, general and theoretical arguments are insufficient[252].

(f) Remedies

If a competition authority determines that a dominant undertaking is abusively refusing to supply an input, it will have to decide what remedial action should be taken: it can impose a fine for past abuse, but what directions should it issue as to future behaviour? An obvious possibility is the application of an obligation to grant access on 'reasonable and non-discriminatory' terms. In *Microsoft* it took three years and two decisions imposing periodic penalty payments[253] before Microsoft began to comply with its obligation to supply interoperability information on reasonable terms.

[247] See ch 5, 'Objective justification', pp 217–218.

[248] See 'UK case law', pp 726–727 later in chapter.

[249] The Commission rejected the airport authority's arguments on capacity constraints in *Frankfurt Airports* OJ [1998] L 72/30, paras 74–88.

[250] See the Commission's *Guidance on Article 102 Enforcement Priorities*, para 89.

[251] Ibid, para 90.

[252] Case T-201/04 *Microsoft Corpn v Commission* EU:T:2007:289, paras 697–698.

[253] Commission decision of 12 July 2006 and Commission decision of 27 February 2008; the latter decision was substantially upheld on appeal Case T-167/08 *Microsoft Corpn v Commission* EU:T:2012:323.

In *ARA Foreclosure*[254] the dominant firm agreed to a structural solution to its abusive refusal to give access to essential household waste collection infrastructure: ARA simply sold the part of the infrastructure that it owned. In return for ARA's cooperation the Commission imposed a fine of €6 million, which was 30% lower than it otherwise would have been.

(ii) Horizontal foreclosure

(a) Refusal to supply a distributor as a disciplining measure

A refusal to supply may be abusive where a dominant firm does so as a disciplinary measure against a distributor who handles competitors' products: this would be an example of horizontal foreclosure, whereby the dominant supplier takes steps to exclude a competitor in the upstream market in which it is dominant. This happened in *United Brands v Commission*[255], where United Brands was trying to prevent its distributor, which was not subject to an exclusive purchasing obligation, from taking part in a competitor's advertising campaign. The Court of Justice held that it was abusive to stop supplying a long-standing customer which abides by normal commercial practice, and that orders should be met which were in no way out of the ordinary. United Brand's objective was to prevent the distributor from selling competitors' products; this was not a case in which United Brands was seeking to eliminate a competitor in a downstream market.

(b) Refusal to supply a potential competitor in the supplier's market

It may be an abuse to refuse supplies as an exclusionary tactic against a customer trying to enter an upstream market in competition with the supplier. In *BBI Boosey & Hawkes: Interim Measures*[256] the Commission found that Boosey & Hawkes had abused a dominant position by refusing to supply brass band instruments to a distributor which was intending to commence the manufacture of such instruments in competition with it. The Commission said that the dominant firm was entitled to take reasonable steps to protect its commercial interest, but that such measures must be fair and proportional to the threat[257]; in its view it was not reasonable 'to withdraw all supplies immediately or to take reprisals against that customer'[258].

(c) Refusal to supply an existing competitor in the supplier's market

In *British Midland v Aer Lingus*[259] the Commission found that Aer Lingus had abused its dominant position on the London–Dublin route by refusing 'to interline' with British Midland for two years following the latter's entry to that route. Interlining, under which airlines agree to accept each other's tickets, was an accepted industry practice, and Aer Lingus's refusal to intervene was a 'highly unusual step' that created an artificial barrier to new entry.

(iii) Refusal to supply on the basis of nationality

Discrimination on grounds of nationality is contrary to Article 18 TFEU. In *GVL v Commission*[260] the Court of Justice held that it was abusive for a national copyright collecting society to refuse to admit to membership nationals of other Member States. The Commission's decision condemning the ticketing arrangements in *Football World Cup 1998*[261] was based on the fact that they discriminated in favour of French residents.

[254] Commission decision of 20 September 2016.
[255] Case 27/76 EU:C:1978:22.
[256] OJ [1987] L 286/36.
[257] Ibid, para 19.
[258] Ibid.
[259] [1992] OJ L 96/34.
[260] Case 7/82 EU:C:1983:52.
[261] OJ [2000] L 5/55; see Weatherill 'Fining the Organisers of the 1998 World Cup' (2000) 21 ECLR 275.

(iv) Refusal to supply to prevent parallel imports and exports

Refusals to supply that are harmful to the internal market are discussed below[262].

(C) UK case law

In *JJ Burgess & Sons v OFT*[263] the CAT concluded that W Austin & Sons had abused a dominant position by refusing to grant access to Harwood Park Crematorium for the purpose of conducting cremations; in doing so the CAT annulled a decision of the OFT[264] that there had been no abuse. The CAT's judgment surveyed the case law on refusal to supply[265] and formulated three propositions that were sufficient to reach a finding on the facts of that case, while noting that these were not intended to contain an exhaustive statement of the law on refusal to supply[266]:

- an abuse may occur where a dominant undertaking, without objective justification, refuses supplies to an established existing customer who abides by regular commercial practice, at least where the refusal to supply is disproportionate and operates to the detriment of consumers (*United Brands*)
- such an abuse may occur if the potential result of the refusal to supply is to eliminate a competitor in a downstream market where the dominant undertaking is itself in competition with the undertaking potentially eliminated, at least if the goods or services in question are indispensable for the activities of the latter undertaking, and there is a potential adverse effect on consumers (*Commercial Solvents*)
- it is not an abuse to refuse access to facilities that have been developed for the exclusive use of the undertaking that has developed them, at least in the absence of strong evidence that the facilities are indispensable to the service provided, and there is no realistic possibility of creating a potential alternative[267] (*Oscar Bronner*).

Problems of refusal to supply have sometimes been settled informally following investigation[268].

In *Disconnection of Floe Telecom Ltd's Services by Vodafone Ltd*[269] Floe complained to OFCOM that Vodafone was abusively refusing to supply it with certain services necessary for it to operate in the market for mobile telephony. OFCOM decided that Vodafone had an objective justification for the refusal, since Floe would have been acting unlawfully on the market. Floe appealed to the CAT which quashed the decision[270]. OFCOM was asked to reconsider the matter but, in a second decision[271], maintained its position that there had not been an unlawful refusal to supply. Floe's appeal against the second decision was unsuccessful[272].

There have been a number of cases before the courts concerning refusals to supply by dominant firms that allegedly infringed the Chapter II prohibition; most of these were

[262] See 'Non-Pricing Abuses That are Harmful to the Internal Market', pp 727–728 later in chapter.

[263] Case 1044/2/1/04 [2005] CAT 25. [264] OFT decision of 12 August 2004.

[265] Case 1044/2/1/04 [2005] CAT 25, paras 291–313. [266] Ibid, para 312. [267] Ibid, para 311.

[268] See eg the 2000 *Annual Report of the Director General of Fair Trading*, p 46 (assurances by cement producers to supply bulk cement for resale); note each of the guidelines cited in ch 17 nn 72–75 earlier discuss the circumstances in which a refusal to supply might amount to an abuse.

[269] OFCOM decision of 3 November 2003; see also *Disconnection of VIP Communications Ltd's Services by T-Mobile Ltd*, OFCOM decision of 31 December 2003.

[270] Case 1024/2/3/04 *Floe Telecom Ltd v OFCOM* [2004] CAT 18.

[271] OFCOM decision of 28 June 2005; see also *Re-investigation of VIP Communications*, OFCOM decision of 28 June 2005.

[272] Case 1024/2/3/04 *Floe Telecom Ltd v OFCOM* [2006] CAT 17, reversed on appeal, *OFCOM v Floe Telecom Ltd* [2009] EWCA Civ 47.

unsuccessful[273]. Other applications have been more successful. Interim relief was successfully obtained in a refusal to supply case in *Software Cellular Network Ltd v T-Mobile (UK) Ltd*[274]. In *Purple Parking Ltd v Heathrow Airport Ltd*[275] Purple Parking complained that it had been abusively excluded from operating a 'meet and greet' service for passengers at Heathrow Airport. The High Court was sceptical that Purple Parking would be able to demonstrate that the forecourts to various terminals at Heathrow Airport were 'essential' for the claimant that operated a 'meet and greet' service for passengers arriving there[276]; however the court did consider that the airport was guilty of abusive discrimination and therefore provided Purple Parking with declaratory relief. In *Dahabshiil Transfer Services Ltd v Barclays Bank plc* an interim injunction was granted to Dahabshiil requiring Barclays to continue providing certain services to the claimants pending the trial of the action[277]; the case was subsequently settled.

In *SEE plc*[278] OFGEM accepted commitments under section 31A of the Competition Act, requiring SEE to ensure that essential connection services are provided to independent operators on a non-discriminatory basis.

5. Non-Pricing Abuses that are Harmful to the Internal Market

Non-pricing practices that are harmful to the internal market will be held to infringe Article 102[279]. In *BL v Commission*[280] the Court of Justice upheld the decision of the Commission that BL had abused a dominant position by refusing to supply type-approval certificates for Metro cars imported from the continent; this practice was part of a strategy of British Leyland aimed at discouraging parallel imports into the UK. In *United Brands v Commission*[281] one of the abuses committed by United Brands was to impose a restriction on its distributors against exporting green, unripened bananas: in practice this amounted to an export ban, since it would not be possible to export bananas that were already ripe. In *Amministrazione Autonoma dei Monopoli dello Stato v Commission*[282] the General Court held that AAMS had abused its dominant position on the Italian market for the wholesale distribution of cigarettes by imposing distribution agreements on foreign producers which contained terms limiting the access of foreign cigarettes to the Italian market; a fine of €6 million was imposed. In *Romanian Power Exchange/OPCOM*[283] the Commission imposed a fine of €1.03 million on OPCOM, the operator of the only power exchange in Romania, for discriminating on the basis of nationality

[273] See eg *Claritas (UK) Ltd v Post Office and Postal Preference Ltd* [2001] UKCLR 2; *Land Rover Group Ltd v UPF (UK) Ltd* [2002] All ER (D) 323; *Getmapping plc v Ordnance Survey* [2002] UKCLR 410; *Intel Corpn v VIA Technologies* [2002] UKCLR 576, reversed on appeal [2002] EWCA Civ 1905; *AAH Pharmaceuticals Ltd v Pfizer Ltd* [2007] EWHC 565 (Ch); *Attheraces Ltd v British Horseracing Board Ltd* [2007] EWCA Civ 38; *Humber Oil Terminals Trustee Ltd v Associated British Ports* [2011] EWHC 352 (Ch), upheld on appeal [2012] EWCA Civ 36; *Chemistree Homecare Ltd v Abbvie Ltd* [2013] EWHC 264 (Ch), upheld on appeal [2013] EWCA Civ 1338; an interim injunction was initially granted in *Packet Media Ltd v Telefónica UK Ltd* [2015] EWHC 2235 (Ch), but subsequently discharged for lack of evidence of dominance: [2015] EWHC 3873 (Ch).

[274] [2007] EWHC 1790 (Ch). [275] [2011] EWHC 987 (Ch). [276] Ibid, paras 143 and 144.

[277] [2013] EWHC 3379 (Ch). [278] OFGEM decision of 3 November 2016.

[279] See ch 5, 'Abuses that are harmful to the single market', p 216; see also the Commission's XXVIIth *Report on Competition Policy* (1997), point 63.

[280] Case 226/84 EU:C:1986:421; see also Commission Press Release IP (87) 390 *Re Volvo Italia* [1988] 4 CMLR 423.

[281] Case 27/76 EU:C:1978:22.

[282] OJ [1998] L 252/47, upheld on appeal Case T-139/98 *Amministrazione Autonoma dei Monopoli dello Stato v Commission* EU:T:2001:272.

[283] Commission decision of 5 March 2014.

and place of establishment on the market for services facilitating short-term trading in electricity in Romania.

The suppression of parallel trade in the pharmaceutical sector may be treated differently. In *Sot. Lélos kai Sia EE and others v GlaxoSmithKline*[284] the Court of Justice was asked by the Athens Court of Appeal whether it could be an abuse of a dominant position for Glaxo to have ceased to supply wholesalers in Greece in order to prevent exports of pharmaceutical products from Greece to higher-priced Member States. The Court of Justice held that Article 102 must be interpreted as meaning that an undertaking occupying a dominant position on the relevant market for medicinal products which, in order to put a stop to parallel exports carried out by certain wholesalers from one Member State to other Member States, refuses to meet 'ordinary' orders from those wholesalers, is abusing its dominant position. However it went on to say that it is for the national court to ascertain whether the orders are ordinary in the light of both the size of those orders in relation to the requirements of the market in the first Member State and the previous business relations between that undertaking and the wholesalers concerned. Without actually saying so, this judgment would appear to mean that Glaxo was not under any obligation to supply more of the products in question than were needed to meet domestic demand in Greece: in other words that, in the context of the pharmaceutical sector, it was legitimate to limit supplies in such a way that parallel trade would be restricted.

The Commission has also taken action against non-pricing practices that would have harmed the internal market for energy and transport. In *BEH Electricity*[285] the Commission was concerned that BEH's contracts for the wholesale supply of electricity contained territorial restrictions on the resale of electricity. BEH gave commitments to the Commission to abandon the destination clauses and to set up a new power exchange in Bulgaria and supply minimum volumes of electricity to the exchange for five years. In *Gazprom*[286] the Commission consulted in March 2017 on proposed commitments to remove restrictions on the resale of gas in Central and East European gas markets and to ensure gas prices reflect competitive price benchmarks. In *Lithuanian Railways*[287] the Commission imposed a fine of €27.8 million for dismantling 19 kilometres of rail track connecting Lithuania and Latvia, thereby preventing a customer from using a rival's services. The rail operator has since agreed to rebuild the track.

6. Miscellaneous Other Non-Pricing Abuses

Article 102 has been applied to non-pricing practices that do not fit under any of the headings so far deployed in this chapter[288]. Some are concerned with the exercise (or non-exercise) of intellectual property rights, and are discussed in chapter 19[289]. Some other cases are discussed below.

[284] Cases C-468/06 and C-478/06 *Sot. Lélos kai Sia EE v GlaxoSmithKline* EU:C:2008:504; note a previous Article 267 reference on the same facts was held to be inadmissible: Case C-53/03 *Syfait* EU:C:2005:333; the Opinion of AG Jacobs in *Syfait* contains invaluable insights on the law on refusal to supply: EU:C:2004:673, paras 53–104.

[285] Commission decision of 10 December 2015.

[286] Commission Press Release IP/17/555, 13 March 2017.

[287] Commission decision of 2 October 2017, on appeal Case T-814/17 *Lietuvos geležinkeliai v Commission*, not yet decided.

[288] For further reading see O'Donoghue and Padilla *The Law and Economics of Article 102 TFEU* (Hart, 2nd ed, 2013), ch 12.

[289] See ch 19, 'Compulsory licences', pp 815–820.

(A) Harming the competitive structure of the market

In *Continental Can v Commission*[290] the Court of Justice held that Article 102 may be applied to mergers in certain circumstances[291]. However the inadequacy of Article 102 as a tool for controlling EU mergers lay behind the Commission's eagerness for a specific regulation, which finally emerged in 1989 after a gestation period of 16 years[292]. The application of Article 102 to mergers after the EU Merger Regulation is dealt with in chapter 21.

Even though mergers with an EU dimension are now dealt with under the EU Merger Regulation, the *Continental Can* judgment also establishes that it can be an abuse to alter the competitive structure of a market where competition on that market is already weakened as a result of the presence of the dominant undertaking on it. This is demonstrated by *Tetra Pak I (BTG Licence)*[293], where the Commission objected to the acquisition, by merger, of an exclusive licence of patents and know-how which would prevent competitors from entering Tetra Pak's market. In *Servier*[294] the Commission found that Servier had abused its dominant position for a cardiovascular medicine by acquiring scarce technologies as a 'defence mechanism' against potential competition.

A different example of harming the structure of the market occurred in *Irish Sugar v Commission*[295], where the General Court held that it was an abuse of a dominant position for Irish Sugar, the dominant undertaking in the Irish sugar market, to purchase a competitor's sugar from a wholesaler and a retailer and to replace it with its own, a so-called 'product swap'[296]. *Irish Sugar* was applied by the General Court to the so-called 'naked restrictions' in *Intel v Commission*[297], whereby Intel paid manufacturers to delay the marketing of devices containing chips produced by its main competitor, AMD[298].

The Commission held in *Decca Navigator System*[299] that it is an abuse for an undertaking in a dominant position to enter into an agreement with an actual or potential competitor with the intention of sharing markets or stunting the efforts of competitors.

(B) Vexatious litigation

In *ITT Promedia v Commission*[300] the General Court held that bringing legal proceedings, which is the expression of the fundamental right of access to a judge[301], may constitute an abuse of a dominant position, but only in exceptional circumstances. The Commission stated that entering into litigation could be abusive if a dominant firm brings an action:

> (i) which cannot reasonably be considered as an attempt to establish its rights and can therefore only serve to harass the opposite party, and (ii) which is conceived in the framework of a plan whose goal is to eliminate competition.

290 Case 6/72 EU:C:1973:22, paras 20–26.

291 See also *Warner-Lambert/Gillette* OJ [1993] L 116/21.

292 Council Regulation 4064/89/EEC, OJ [1990] L 257/13; that Regulation has since been replaced by Council Regulation 139/2004, OJ [2004] L 24/1.

293 OJ [1988] L 272/27, upheld on appeal Case T-51/89 *Tetra Pak Rausing SA v Commission* EU:T:1990:41; see also *Trans-Atlantic Conference Agreement* OJ [1999] L 95/1, annulled on appeal for lack of evidence Cases T-191/98 etc *Atlantic Container Line AB v Commission* EU:T:2003:245.

294 Commission decision of 9 July 2014, on appeal Cases T-691/14 etc *Les Laboratoires Servier v Commission*, not yet decided.

295 Case T-228/97 EU:C:1999:246.

296 Ibid, paras 226–235.

297 Case T-286/09 EU:T:2014:547; Intel did not appeal against this part of the General Court's judgment.

298 Ibid, paras 198–220.

299 OJ [1989] L 43/27.

300 Case T-111/96 *ITT Promedia v Commission* EU:T:1998:183, para 60.

301 Article 47 of the Charter of Fundamental Rights, on which see Case C-170/13 *Huawei Technologies v ZTE Corp* EU:C:2015:477, paras 42, 57 and 59.

The parties agreed that vexatious litigation could amount to an abuse in the circumstances envisaged by the Commission[302]. On this basis the General Court upheld the decision of the Commission not to proceed against Belgacom following a complaint from Promedia[303]. The General Court has since held that the two conditions identified above must be interpreted and applied restrictively in a manner that does not frustrate access to the courts[304]. The General Court also stated in *ITT Promedia* that a claim for the performance of a contractual obligation could amount to an abuse where the claim 'exceeds what the parties could reasonably expect under the contract or if the circumstances applicable at the time of the conclusion of the contract have changed in the meantime'[305].

In *Compagnie Maritime Belge Transports SA v Commission*[306] Cewal, a liner conference, had concluded an agreement with the Zairean Maritime Freight Management Office (the so-called 'Ogefrem agreement') granting Cewal exclusive rights to the freight trade between Zaire (now Democratic Republic of the Congo) and northern Europe. When Ogefrem allowed a third party, Grimaldi and Cobelfret, a small amount of the trade in question, Cewal repeatedly insisted that Ogefrem should strictly comply with the terms of the agreement. The Court of Justice upheld the Commission's finding that it was abusive of Cewal to insist on its exclusive rights under the Ogefrem agreement in circumstances where the insistence was intended to remove its only competitor from the market and where Cewal had a discretion under the contract whether to insist on its performance or not[307].

(C) **Preferential treatment**

The extent to which a dominant firm is entitled to favour its own non-dominant products is controversial[308]. In the Commission's view, an abuse may involve the preferential promotion by a dominant firm of a separate product on a closely related market where it is not dominant, if that has the effect of strengthening its position on the non-dominated market and is not objectively justified.

In *Google Search (Shopping)*[309] the Commission imposed a fine of €2.42 billion, the highest fine ever, on Google for abusing its dominant position in general online search by systematically giving prominent placement in its search engine results to its own comparison shopping service, while demoting competing comparison shopping services. The Commission gathered a large amount of evidence showing that Google's conduct increased Google Shopping's traffic and revenues and decreased competitors' traffic and revenues. On this basis the Commission concluded that Google had stifled competition on the merits for comparison shopping markets and protected its

[302] Case T-111/96 *ITT Promedia v Commission* EU:T:1998:183, paras 57–58; for discussion of vexatious litigation as an abuse see Lianos and Regibeau '"Vexatious"/"Sham" Litigation in EU and US Antitrust Law: A Mechanism Design Approach', 2017, available at www.ucl.ac.uk.

[303] Ibid, paras 59 and 68–82; the General Court reaffirmed these conditions in Case T-321/05 *AstraZeneca v Commission* EU:T:2010:266, para 311; Case T-480/15 *Agria Polska v Commission* EU:T:2017:339, paras 65–72.

[304] Case T-119/09 *Protégé International v Commission* EU:T:2012:421, para 49.

[305] Case T-111/96 EU:T:1998:183, para 140.

[306] Cases C-395/96 P etc EU:C:2000:132.

[307] Ibid, paras 84–88.

[308] See eg Vesterdorf 'Theories of Self-Preferencing and Duty to Deal—Two Sides of the Same Coin?' (2015) 1 Competition Law & Policy Debate 4; Petit 'Theories of self-preferencing under Article 102: a Reply to Bo Vesterdorf', available at www.i-comp.org; Temple Lang 'Comparing *Microsoft* and *Google*: The Concept of Exclusionary Abuse' (2016) 39 World Competition 5.

[309] Commission decision of 27 June 2017; for a helpful summary of the Commission's case see Commission Press Release IP/17/1784 and MEMO/17/1785, both of 27 June 2017.

dominant position in general search. Google has appealed to the General Court, arguing, among other things, that the Commission erred by failing to take account of the competitive constraint exercised by merchant platforms, such as Amazon, and by treating quality improvements as abusive[310].

(D) **Other cases**

The General Court upheld the Commission's rejection of a complaint that lobbying for the imposition of anti-dumping duties constituted an abuse of a dominant position in *Industrie des poudres sphériques v Commission*[311].

The judgments in *AstraZeneca v Commission*[312] will be discussed in chapter 19 in the context of intellectual property rights; however it should be noted that it establishes that misuse of regulatory procedures can amount to an abuse of a dominant position[313]. The same chapter discusses the Court of Justice's judgment in *Huawei v ZTE*[314], where the Court concluded that in certain circumstances it can amount to an abuse of a dominant position to seek an injunction enforcing standard essential patents[315].

In *Amazon*[316] the Commission examined clauses in Amazon's contracts that required e-book publishers to offer Amazon the same price, distribution terms or promotion offered to other retailers. The Commission's preliminary assessment was that these 'parity provisions' could make it more difficult for other e-book platforms to compete with Amazon by reducing publishers' and competitors' ability and incentives to develop new e-books and alternative distribution services. The Commission announced in May 2017 that it had accepted commitments from Amazon to abandon the parity provisions and not to include them in new contracts for five years. It is important to stress that there was no finding of infringement by the Commission: Amazon did not concede on dominance or abuse.

In *Agria Polska v Commission*[317] the General Court upheld the Commission's rejection of a complaint that manufacturers and distributors of plant protection products had waged a campaign of filing false notices to Polish and Austrian authorities and lobbied government officials to eliminate the complainants from the market. The General Court held that it was 'not obvious' that the defendants' behaviour amounted to a cartel or an abuse of a collective dominant position[318].

310 Case T-612/17 *Google v Commission*, not yet decided.

311 Case T-5/97 EU:T:2000:278.

312 Case T-321/05 EU:T:2010:266, upheld on appeal Case C-457/10 P EU:C:2012:770.

313 See ch 19, 'Vexatious behaviour and abuse of process', pp 825–827.

314 Case C-170/13 EU:C:2015:477.

315 See ch 19, 'Seeking an injunction to enforce standard essential patents', pp 822–824.

316 OJ [1989] L 43/27.

317 Commission decision of 19 June 2015, upheld on appeal Case T-480/15 EU:T:2017:339, on appeal Case C-373/17 P, not yet decided.

318 Case T-480/15 EU:T:2017:339, para 53.

18

Abuse of dominance (2): pricing practices

1. Introduction

This chapter will consider abusive pricing practices under Article 102 TFEU and the Chapter II prohibition in the Competition Act 1998. The chapter will first discuss various cost concepts used in determining whether a price is abusive. It will then deal in turn with excessive pricing; conditional rebates; bundling; predatory pricing; margin squeeze; price discrimination; and practices that are harmful to the single market. This taxonomy is over-schematic, in that the categories overlap with one another: for example price discrimination may be both exploitative and exclusionary, and an excessively high price may in reality be a way of preventing parallel imports or of excluding a competitor from the market; nevertheless this division may provide helpful insights into the way in which the law is applied in practice. In each section the application of Article 102 by the European Commission and by the EU Courts will be considered first, followed by cases in the UK. Reference will be made where appropriate to the Commission's *Guidance on the Commission's Enforcement Priorities in Applying Article [102 TFEU] to Abusive Exclusionary Conduct by Dominant Undertakings* ('the *Guidance on Article 102 Enforcement Priorities*' or 'the *Guidance*')[1]. The *Guidance* says that, as a general proposition, the Commission will intervene only where a pricing practice has been, or is capable of, hindering competition from undertakings that are 'as efficient' as the dominant undertaking[2]. Similarly in *Intel v Commission*[3] the Court of Justice stressed that Article 102 does not seek to ensure that competitors less efficient than the undertaking with the dominant position should remain on the market.

The law on abusive pricing practices is complex. Dominant firms may infringe Article 102 where they raise their prices to unacceptably high levels; they may also be found to have abused their dominant position where they cut their prices, if such cuts can be

[1] OJ [2009] C 45/7; for a general discussion see ch 5, 'The Commission's *Guidance on Article 102 Enforcement Priorities*', pp 182–185.

[2] Ibid, paras 23 and 27.

[3] Case C-413/14 P EU:C:2017:632, para 133.

characterised not as normal, competitive responses on the merits, but as strategic behaviour intended to eliminate competitors. Not unnaturally a dominant firm, or one that is anxious that it might be found to be dominant, may feel itself to be on the horns of a dilemma where both a price rise and a price cut might be considered to be abusive; the dilemma might become a trilemma if leaving prices where they are might be considered to be evidence of a concerted practice with the other undertakings on the market, and if the word trilemma were to exist.

2. Cost Concepts

Analysis of whether a dominant undertaking's pricing practices are abusive typically requires consideration of its costs: this is acknowledged in paragraph 25 of the Commission's *Guidance on Article 102 Enforcement Priorities*. A price may infringe Article 102 where the difference between the price charged and the costs incurred is excessive; discrimination may be abusive where it lacks a cost justification; and a price may be unlawful where the price charged is below cost. However it is important to understand at the outset that the apparently simple term 'cost' may be quite complicated in practice; it may be helpful therefore to begin this chapter by outlining some of the cost concepts that are deployed in competition analysis[4].

(A) Fixed costs and sunk costs

Fixed costs are costs that do not vary with the amount of goods or services that a firm produces; for example a manufacturing firm must buy or rent land on which to build a factory, and will probably incur property taxes as well: these costs are fixed, as they must be paid irrespective of the firm's output.

Sunk costs are a particular type of fixed cost: a sunk cost is one that a firm has already incurred and which cannot be recovered, for example if it were to exit the market. The reason that costs may be sunk is that certain assets cannot be used for more than one purpose, and so have no or very little second-hand value. A typical sunk cost is advertising expenditure (the 'asset' being the advertising campaign) incurred in promoting a new product: if the product fails, the expense involved cannot be recovered. Another example of a sunk cost would be expenditure incurred in designing and/or producing a product for a specific customer, for which no one else would have any use.

(B) Marginal cost

Marginal cost is the cost incurred by a firm when producing an additional unit of output; it does not include any element of a firm's fixed costs, since fixed costs do not vary with output. Marginal cost usually decreases as the scale of a firm's output expands, but increases as a firm's output reaches total capacity. Marginal cost is a theoretical measure of cost: it is not used in practice[5]. More useful are the concepts of variable costs and avoidable costs, described below.

[4] Further definitions of various cost concepts can be found in Black *Oxford Dictionary of Economics* (Oxford University Press, 5th ed, 2017); the Commission's *Guidance on Article 102 Enforcement Priorities* OJ [2009] C 45/7, fn 18; Niels, Jenkins and Kavanagh *Economics for Competition Lawyers* (Oxford University Press, 2nd ed, 2016), pp 163–171; the ICN's *Unilateral Conduct Workbook*, ch 4: 'Predatory Pricing Analysis', paras 43–68.

[5] Marginal cost determines the level of output a firm will produce under conditions of perfect competition; on perfect competition see ch 1, 'The benefits of perfect competition', pp 5–7.

(C) Variable costs

Variable costs are costs that vary with the amount of products (rather than each additional unit of output) that a firm produces: for example a firm's expenditure on items such as raw materials, fuel and maintenance will vary according to the amount of its output; variable costs do not include any element of a firm's fixed costs.

(D) Avoidable costs

Avoidable costs refer to those costs which a firm would avoid incurring (or to put the matter another way, the savings it would make) by ceasing a particular activity over a specified period of time; for example where a firm is accused of predatory pricing over an 18-month period, it may be relevant to ask what costs it would have avoided if it had not produced the units that were the subject of the predation over those 18 months. Avoidable costs include some **fixed**, depending on the period of time in question, and **variable** costs, but omit **common costs**, that is to say costs that arise where two or more products are produced together even though they could be produced separately.

(E) Average variable cost ('AVC')

A firm's **average variable cost** is calculated by dividing all its variable costs by the total of its actual output. This calculation indicates the average cost of each extra unit of output.

(F) Average avoidable cost ('AAC')

A firm's **average avoidable cost** is calculated by dividing all its avoidable costs by its output. AAC and AVC are the same when only variable costs can be avoided. However AAC will be higher than a firm's AVC when it includes some fixed costs.

(G) Long-run incremental cost ('LRIC')

Long-run incremental cost refers to the fixed and variable costs that a firm incurs when deciding to produce a particular product or increment of output.

(H) Long-run average incremental cost ('LRAIC')

Long-run average incremental cost is calculated by dividing all its long-run incremental costs by its output. LRAIC is the same as the **average total cost** of a firm producing a single product. It will be lower than the average total cost of a firm producing multiple products that benefits from economies of scope[6], since LRAIC excludes costs that are common to several products.

(I) Average total cost ('ATC')

A firm's **average total cost** is calculated by dividing both its variable costs and its fixed costs by the total of its output. It will, of course, be higher than its average variable cost.

[6] Economies of scope occur where it is cheaper to produce two products together than to produce them separately; see ch 1, 'Economies of scale and scope and natural monopolies', pp 10–11.

(J) Stand alone cost

The **stand alone cost** of a firm refers to the cost that it would incur if it were to produce just a single product, so that there would be no common costs as a result of its other activities.

3. Excessive Pricing

Excessive pricing raises interesting questions for competition law[7]. Economic theory tells us that a monopolist can restrict output and charge prices that exceed the competitive level: this is why competition is viewed favourably, because in competitive conditions it is the market that establishes the correct price for goods and services through the 'law' of supply and demand[8]. It might seem obvious therefore that competition authorities should take direct steps to control prices that greatly exceed the competitive level. There is no doubt that 'unfair prices' can be unlawful under Article 102: paragraph (a) of that provision specifically says so, as does section 18(2)(a) of the Competition Act 1998. However some systems of competition law do not prohibit excessively high prices, most noticeably US antitrust law[9]. In systems such as the EU, including that of the UK, excessively high prices can be abusive and therefore unlawful, but the competition authorities bring cases only rarely: this is a matter of prosecutorial discretion rather than law.

As we shall see there are persuasive arguments against competition authorities taking direct control over excessive prices under competition law, although one should 'never say never'. We need to understand three issues. First, what are the arguments against the direct control of prices? Secondly, why, despite the need for restraint on the part of competition authorities, might there sometimes be a case for intervention against excessive prices? Thirdly, where intervention is appropriate, how can we determine whether a price is so excessive as to be abusive? Finally we will examine some actual cases, noting that there have been rather more than usual in recent years, albeit in markets where the conditions of competition were imperfect.

(A) Arguments against direct control

The most obvious case against the application of competition law to excessive prices is that, if normal market forces have their way, the fact that a monopolist is able to earn

[7] For further reading on exploitative pricing see Abbott 'Excessive Pharmaceutical Prices and Competition Law: Doctrinal Development to Protect Public Health' (June 2017), available at www.ssrn.com; Niels, Jenkins and Kavanagh *Economics for Competition Lawyers* (Oxford University Press, 2nd ed, 2016), pp 222–232; Evans and Padilla 'Excessive Prices: Using Economics to Define Administrable Legal Rules' (2005) 1 Journal of Competition Law and Economics 97; *The Pros and Cons of High Prices* (Swedish Competition Authority, 2007); Fletcher and Jardine 'Towards an Appropriate Policy for Excessive Pricing' in Ehlermann and Marquis (eds) *European Competition Law Annual 2007: A Reformed Approach to Article 82 EC* (Hart Publishing, 2008); Bishop and Walker *The Economics of EC Competition Law* (Sweet & Maxwell, 3rd ed, 2010), paras 6-14–6-19; Akman and Garrod 'When are Excessive Prices Unfair?' (2011) 7 Journal of Competition Law and Economics 403; Liyang 'Excessive Prices within EU Competition Law' (2011) 7 European Competition Journal 47; OECD Roundtable *Excessive Prices* (2011), available at www.oecd.org/competition; O'Donoghue and Padilla *The Law and Economics of Article 102 TFEU* (Hart, 2nd ed, 2013), ch 14.

[8] See ch 1, 'The harmful effects of monopoly', pp 7–8.

[9] Section 2 of the Sherman Act 1890 applies to monopolisation and attempts to monopolise, but not to exploitation: see Gal 'Monopoly Pricing as an Antitrust Offense in the US and the EC: Two Systems of Belief about Monopoly' (2004) 49 Antitrust Bulletin 343; the provisions on abuse of a dominant position in, eg, Singapore and Hong Kong do not specify unfair or excessive prices to be examples of abusive behaviour, although that is not to say that such practices necessarily fall outside those provisions.

supra-competitive profits should, in the absence of barriers to expansion and entry, attract new entrants to the market. In the meantime the fact a monopolist is able to earn supra-competitive profits may provide it with the necessary incentive to carry out expensive and risky research and development[10]. In *Verizon Communications Inc v Law Offices of Curtis Trinko* the US Supreme Court said that[11]:

> The opportunity to charge monopoly prices—at least for a short period—is what attracts 'business acumen' in the first place; it induces risk taking that produces innovation and economic growth.

If one accepts this view of the way that markets work, the extraction of monopoly profits will ultimately be self-defeating and will act as an important signal to other firms to enter the market. In this case one should accept with equanimity periods during which a firm earns a monopoly profit: the market will in due course correct itself, and direct control of high prices will have the effect of undesirably distorting this process. Advocate General Wahl made this point in his Opinion in *Autortiesību un komunicēšanās konsultāciju aģentūra—Latvijas Autoru apvienība v Konkurences padome* ('*AKKA/LAA*')[12].

However markets may fail to function in the manner just described for various reasons, not least where the state creates legal barriers to entry or expansion or grants a legal monopoly to a particular undertaking[13]. It is a statement of the obvious that if a dominant undertaking has a legal monopoly or is protected by legal barriers the capacity of the market to 'auto-correct' does not exist: in such circumstances there may be a case for intervention against excessive prices. This helps to explain a case such as *AKKA/LAA*[14], where the Latvian Competition Council condemned under Article 102(2)(a) and the equivalent provision of Latvian law the prices of a collective management organisation (also known as a collecting society) that had the benefit of a legal monopoly to issue copyright licences in Latvia for the public performance of musical works[15].

Apart from the question of whether it is sound policy for competition authorities to control excessive prices, there are more pragmatic considerations.

- By what standard should the 'excessiveness' of a price be determined?
- Can this standard be expressed in an administrable rule?
- What is the appropriate remedy where a competition authority determines that a price is excessive?
- Should a competition authority try to be a price regulator?

As a general proposition the 'regulator' of price should be the market, which is the expression of the aggregated interests of consumers. Some consumers might be prepared to buy goods and services at the market price, others might not: that is their choice. If this price-setting function cannot be performed by the market it may be that sector-specific regulation, overseen by a bespoke regulator, is needed to act as a surrogate for competition[16]. Competition authorities should be cautious about adopting such a role.

This discussion can be summed up quite simply: as a general proposition competition authorities are reluctant to investigate allegations of excessive pricing; however an

[10] See eg Schumpeter *Capitalism, Socialism and Democracy* (1942) and see ch 1, 'Dynamic efficiency', pp 6–7.

[11] 540 US 398 (2004).

[12] Case C-177/16 EU:C:2017:286, para 3.

[13] Ibid, para 4 of AG Wahl's Opinion.

[14] Case C-177/16 EU:C:2017:689.

[15] Several of the cases on excessive prices under Article 102 concern copyright collecting societies: see eg Case 395/85 *Tournier* EU:C:1989:319; Case 110/88 *Lucazeau* EU:C:1989:326; Case C-52/07 *Kanal 5 and TV 4* EU:C:2008:703; Case C-351/12 *OSA* EU:C:2014:110.

[16] See ch 23 'Regulatory systems in the UK for utilities', pp 1009–1010

important competition law motto is 'never say never', and there may be markets in which intervention is justifiable.

(B) When might it be legitimate for a competition authority to investigate excessive prices?

Most competition authorities have a prosecutorial discretion that enables them to select which cases to investigate. It is noticeable that, although Article 102 and its national analogues in the Member States of the EU are capable of applying to the excessive prices of a dominant undertaking, there are very few actual cases. This is because competition authorities, as a general proposition, choose not to investigate allegedly high prices[17]. A competition authority concerned about high prices in a particular sector would normally ask how and why it is possible for such prices to be charged: the high prices should act as a signal for existing and potential competitors to expand output or to enter the market and to attract customers by offering lower prices. If this is possible it will be difficult for the firm charging high prices to maintain them at a persistently higher level than would be expected in a competitive market. However if a dominant firm is indulging in exclusionary behaviour in order to maintain excessively high prices, the logical response for a competition authority would not be to cap its prices: that would act as a disincentive to other firms to attempt to enter the market; the better response would be to take action against the exclusionary abuse. Alternatively, it may be that the authority should carry out a market study to determine whether market imperfections (as opposed to abusive behaviour) are responsible for the high prices, for example inappropriate regulation, planning controls and/or licensing restrictions imposed by the state. Another possibility is that the high prices are sustainable because the market is one in which there will never be effective competition, in which case sector-specific regulation might be the sensible solution.

(i) Imperfect markets

Notwithstanding the prosecutorial discretion of competition authorities that causes them to be reticent about investigating high prices under competition law, there may be some circumstances in which it is sensible for them to do so. As noted, the market may not be able to 'auto-correct' to cure the problem of excessive prices. We are wise enough to know that markets will rarely be 'perfect' in the sense of economic theory[18]; however we also know that markets may be decidedly imperfect, for example where the state confers a legal monopoly. This is why in some cases a competition authority might decide to proceed directly against the excessively high prices of a dominant firm: this might particularly be so where alternative solutions such as a market study or competition advocacy seem unlikely to be effective. Article 102 in these circumstances can be seen to provide a 'safety net', providing the competition authority with a legal basis for intervention if this is considered necessary and appropriate.

As noted earlier, several of the cases on excessive prices involved copyright collecting societies, which often operate on a market where there is a *de facto* or even a *de jure* monopoly: this can clearly be seen to be an imperfect market where competition law intervention is justifiable. Several cases have been brought in the pharmaceutical sector

[17] A national court cannot choose the cases it hears: it must deal with any case brought before it; several of the cases discussed in this section arose in private litigation and resulted in Article 267 references to the Court of Justice.

[18] See ch 1, 'Questioning the theory of perfect competition', pp 8–10.

where, for a variety of reasons, the market may not provide a solution to the problem of high prices[19].

(ii) Excessive prices that are exclusionary or harmful to the single market

The previous section suggested that competition law intervention might be appropriate in the case of imperfect markets, because competitive entry will not provide a solution to the problem. A quite different reason for taking action might be that the excessive prices are not attributable to a monopolist 'gouging' its customers by taking advantage of its dominant position; rather the excessive prices might be an exclusionary abuse or a device for harming the internal market. An example of the former would be a dominant firm charging a price for access to an essential facility that is, in reality, a (constructive) refusal to supply: the price is so high that no customer is willing to pay it. The exclusionary abuse of refusal to supply is discussed in chapter 17; other examples of non-pricing practices that harm the internal market are also given[20]. Excessive pricing that is harmful to the internal market is discussed in chapter 18[21].

(C) When is an excessive price abusive?

The discussion so far suggests that competition authorities are wise, as a general proposition, not to get drawn into cases on excessively high prices, but that sometimes they may need to do so. National courts do not have a prosecutorial discretion and so they are obliged to confront the issue if litigants raise it, whether they wish to or not. It follows that competition law has to provide guidance as to the circumstances in which a price can be so high as to be considered to be abusive.

(i) The price must be excessive and unfair

There is no doubt, as a matter of law, that excessive prices may violate Article 102. Article 102(2)(a) gives as an illustration of abuse:

> directly or indirectly imposing **unfair purchase**[22] **or selling prices** or other unfair trading conditions[23] (emphasis added).

It is important to note that, according to Article 102, it is not simply that the price is **excessive** that makes it unlawful; Article 102(2)(a) says that the price must be **unfair**. This means that unfairness is something beyond excessiveness, and that both have to be proven in a case on abusively high prices[24].

The starting point for any discussion of the subject of excessive pricing is the Court of Justice's judgment in *United Brands v Commission*[25]. It is worth citing paragraphs 248

[19] See 'EU cases on excessive pricing', pp 741–743 and 'UK cases on excessive pricing', pp 743–746 later in chapter.

[20] See ch 17, 'Refusal to Supply', pp 713–727 and ch 17, 'Non-pricing Abuses that are Harmful to the Internal Market', pp 727–728.

[21] See 'Pricing Practices that are Harmful to the Single Market', pp 782–784 later in chapter.

[22] For cases in which complaints about unfairly low prices demanded by buyers were rejected see Case 298/83 *CICCE v Commission* EU:C:1985:150 where the Court of Justice rejected an appeal against a Commission decision rejecting such an allegation; *The Association of British Travel Agents and British Airways*, OFT decision of 11 December 2002 rejecting a complaint that BA was paying unfairly low commission to travel agents.

[23] For examples of the imposition of unfair trading conditions, as opposed to unfair prices, see *1998 Football World Cup* OJ [2000] L 5/55; *Amministrazione Autonoma dei Monopoli di Stato* OJ [1998] L 252/47, paras 33–46, upheld on appeal Case T-139/98 *AAMS v Commission* EU:T:2001:272, paras 73–80.

[24] This was stated by the Court of Justice in Case 27/76 *United Brands v Commission* EU:C:1978:22 and repeated by it in Case C-177/16 *AKKA/LAA* EU:C:2017:689, para 36.

[25] Case 27/76 EU:C:1978:22; note that abusive prices had been discussed by the Court of Justice prior to *United Brands*: see Case 78/70 *Deutsche Grammophon GmbH v Metro-SB-Grossmärkte GmbH* EU:C:1971:59; Case 40/70 *Sirena v Eda* EU:C:1971:18; Case 26/75 *General Motors v Commission* EU:C:1975:150.

to 252 of the Court's judgment in full, with an explanation of the emphasised passages to follow:

> 248. The imposition by an undertaking in a dominant position directly or indirectly of unfair purchase or selling prices is an abuse to which exception can be taken under Article [102] of the Treaty.
>
> 249. It is advisable therefore to ascertain whether the dominant undertaking has made use of the opportunities arising out of its dominant position in such a way as **to reap trading benefits which it would not have reaped if there had been normal and sufficiently effective competition.**
>
> 250. In this case charging **a price which is excessive because it has no reasonable relation to the economic value of the product supplied** would be such an abuse.
>
> 251. **This excess could, inter alia, be determined** objectively if it were possible for it to be calculated by making a comparison between the selling price of the product in question and its cost of production, which would disclose the amount of the profit margin; however the Commission has not done this since it has not analysed [United Brands'] costs structure.
>
> 252. The questions therefore to be determined are **whether the difference between the costs actually incurred and the price actually charged is excessive, and, if the answer to this question is in the affirmative, whether a price has been imposed which is either unfair in itself or when compared to competing products.**

The basic test is therefore whether the price exceeds what the dominant undertaking would have obtained in the counterfactual world of **normal and sufficiently effective competition**. The question to ask is whether the price **bears no reasonable relation to the economic value of the product or service supplied.**

The Court considers how to calculate excess in paragraph 251, where it suggests that this may, among other methods, be determined by comparing the price charged for a product with the cost of its production. The Court then says in paragraph 252 that two more specific questions need to be addressed:

- **is the difference between the costs actually incurred and the price actually charged excessive?** and
- if so, **is the price that has been imposed either unfair in itself or when compared to competing products?**

(ii) Is the price excessive?

One way of determining whether a price is excessive is to ask whether its price is too great in relation to its cost: as Advocate General Wahl remarked in *AKKA/LAA* this question asks, in effect, whether the dominant firm is taking too large a margin or making too much profit[26]. However the words 'inter alia' in paragraph 251 are important. The Court did **not** say that a determination that prices are excessive always requires an examination of the price charged and the cost of production; only that this is one way **among others—'inter alia'**—of answering the question. In a case like *United Brands* cost/price analysis could have been and, in the Court's view, should have been conducted. However the Commission did not conduct an analysis of the disputed prices and cost of bananas, and the Court annulled the Commission's finding of excessive pricing because of its failure to do so[27].

[26] Case C-177/16 EU:C:2017:286, para 18.

[27] Case 27/76 EU:C:1978:22, paras 254–268.

However in some cases a price/cost analysis may not be feasible. For example, it may be that there are no reliable cost data available, as was the case when the Commission investigated the prices that Deutsche Post was charging for the onward transmission of cross-border mail[28]. Price/cost comparison also makes little sense in the case of intangible goods such as copyrighted musical works: what is the 'cost' of an enchanting melody that entered a person's mind on the top of an Alpine mountain or when walking along an empty beach? Excessiveness in such cases may be have to be assessed, for example, by comparing the disputed price with those in other markets rather than on the basis of profitability. It is because price/cost analysis cannot always produce an answer to the question of whether a price is excessive that the Court of Justice said in *United Brands*[29], and again in *AKKA/LAA*[30], that there might be other ways of determining whether this is the case. Competition authorities have 'a certain margin of manoeuvre' with respect to the methodology to be followed when determining whether a price is excessive[31], and it may be sensible to combine different methods[32]. In particular, depending on the circumstances of the case, it may be appropriate to proceed on the basis of a comparison of the dominant undertaking's prices with an appropriate comparator, for example the prices of non-dominant firms, or the dominant firm at a different point of time, or the dominant firm in different geographical markets[33]. Any chosen comparator must be selected in accordance with 'objective, appropriate and verifiable criteria', and the comparison must be made on a consistent basis[34].

Whichever methods of comparison are adopted, there must be a 'significant and persistent' difference between the disputed price and the price that would be expected in a competitive market[35]. Ultimately, the competition authority should have a 'sufficiently complete and reliable set of elements which point in one and the same direction'[36].

(iii) Is the excessive price unfair?

Having established that a price is excessive, it will be abusive only if it is also 'unfair': according to paragraph 252 of the judgment in *United Brands* the price has to either be 'unfair in itself', or when compared to competing products. *United Brands* does not elaborate on these ideas, although they both imply a somewhat subjective assessment for the identification of an abusively high price[37].

As to whether an excessive price is **unfair in itself**, it is necessary to determine whether the excessive price bears no reasonable relation to the 'economic value' of the product. The economic value of a product in the hands of a purchaser does not always or necessarily correspond to its cost of production plus a reasonable rate of return[38]. For example television companies usually pay a price for the right to broadcast football matches that far outstrips the costs of filming the match. They are willing to pay such high prices because the economic value of the broadcasting rights is enhanced by the potential to attract subscribers to the television channel and to increase advertising revenue through high audience figures.

[28] *Deutsche Post AG—Interception of cross-border mail* OJ [2001] L 331/40.

[29] Case 27/76 EU:C:1978:22, para 253.

[30] Case C-177/16 EU:C:2017:689, para 37; see also Case 1001/1/1/01 *Napp Pharmaceutical Holdings Ltd v Director General of Fair Trading* [2002] CAT 1, para 392.

[31] Case C-177/16 *AKKA/LAA* EU:C:2017:689, para 49.

[32] See the AG's Opinion in Case C-177/16 *AKKA/LAA* EU:C:2017:286, paras 43–45.

[33] Ibid, para 19. [34] Case C-177/16 EU:C:2017:689, paras 38, 41, 44 and 51.

[35] Ibid, para 55. [36] See the AG's Opinion in Case C-177/16 EU:C:2017:286, para 54.

[37] See Case 1046/2/4/04 *Albion Water Ltd v Water Services Regulation Authority* [2008] CAT 31, para 216 (referring to a 'considerable margin of appreciation').

[38] *Scandlines*, Commission decision of 23 July 2004, paras 226–227 and 232.

In *AKKA/LAA* Advocate General Wahl suggested that an excessive price could be unfair in itself where a dominant firm has charged for a service that a customer neither requested nor received[39] or where it charges an excessive price to impede cross-border trade[40].

The suggestion that a price may be determined as **unfair when compared to competing products** is somewhat awkward, indeed circular in a case where comparators have been used in the first place to determine whether a price is excessive. Any comparator used for the assessment of whether an excessive price is unfair must be sufficiently similar to the product concerned in order for the comparison to be meaningful[41]. For example it might be possible to compare the dominant firm's price with the prices charged in:

- a neighbouring market for the same product[42]
- a discrete segment of the relevant market[43]
- another Member State[44]
- an international benchmark[45].

It may be useful to carry out several comparisons in order to gather sufficiently reliable evidence that the disputed price is significantly and persistently above the normal competitive price and is therefore unfair.

(iv) EU cases on excessive pricing

(a) Commission cases

The Commission has only rarely taken action against excessive pricing. Its decision in *United Brands*[46] that the price of bananas in Germany was too high was annulled by the Court of Justice on the ground that the Commission had failed to conduct a price/cost analysis. Its cases against *BL* and *General Motors* were motivated by single market considerations: on appeal the case against BL was upheld but the GM decision was annulled[47]. In *Scandlines Sverige AB v Port of Helsingborg*[48] the Commission rejected a complaint that port charges at the port of Helsingborg were excessively high[49]. The Commission carried out an extensive investigation of the costs incurred by the port. However a simple 'cost-plus' approach was insufficient to establish that the prices were unfair, since it was necessary also to look at the economic value of the services provided. The Commission noted that ferry operators benefited from the location of the port, a fact that was relevant to the economic value of the port services. The Commission also looked to see if the port charges were unfair when compared with prices charged for other services provided in the same port, and with prices charged to ferry operators in

39 See eg Case C-179/90 *Merci Convenzionali Porto di Genova* EU:C:1991:464, para 19; Case C-385/07 P *Der Grüne Punkt—Duales System Deutschland v Commission* EU:C:2009:456, paras 141–147.

40 See 'Pricing Practices that are Harmful to the Single Market', pp 782–784 later in chapter.

41 *Scandlines*, Commission decision of 23 July 2004, para 169; Case C-177/16 *AKKA/LAA* EU:C:2017:689, para 51.

42 See eg Case 30/87 *Corinne Bodson v Pompes Funebres* EU:C:1988:225.

43 See eg Case 1001/1/1/01 *Napp Pharmaceutical Holdings Ltd v Director General of Fair Trading* [2002] CAT 1.

44 See eg Case 395/87 *Ministere Public v Tournier* EU:C:1989:319.

45 See eg *Standard & Poor*, Commission decision of 15 November 2011.

46 OJ [1975] L 29/14.

47 See 'Pricing Practices that are Harmful to the Single Market', pp 782–784 later in chapter.

48 Commission decision of 23 July 2004; a second complaint against the port, by Sundbusserne, was also rejected.

49 See similarly *Ryanair/DAA-Aer Lingus*, Commission decision of 17 October 2013, para 83 (rejecting a complaint of excessive airport charges).

other ports[50]. The Commission concluded that, in particular given that the burden of proving an abuse was upon it, there was no infringement of Article 102[51].

In *Deutsche Post AG—Interception of cross-border mail*[52] the Commission considered that Deutsche Post's prices for the onward transmission of cross-border mail were excessive. In doing so the Commission said that, as it could not make a detailed analysis of Deutsche Post's costs, it would have to use an alternative benchmark to determine whether it was guilty of abuse[53]; this it did by comparing Deutsche Post's prices for cross-border mail with its domestic tariff[54], and it decided that there was indeed an abuse. It should perhaps be added that, although cost analysis may be difficult, it is certainly not impossible; some competition authorities have carried out complex cost analyses[55]. In *Standard & Poor*[56] the Commission considered that the fees charged by S&P to financial institutions for using international securities identification numbers were unfair on the basis of a standard set by an international standard-setting body as a benchmark. The Commission accepted commitments under Article 9 of Regulation 1/2003 that changed S&P's pricing policy[57]. The Commission is investigating Gazprom's prices for gas in several Central and East European Member States of the EU, and it is possible that commitments will be given by Gazprom to introduce a new formula for establishing its prices[58]. The Commission has opened an investigation into whether Aspen Pharma has been charging excessive prices for five life-saving cancer medicines[59].

(b) *Article 267 references to the Court of Justice*

Several cases on excessive prices have been referred by national courts to the Court of Justice. In *Corinne Bodson v Pompes Funèbres*[60] one question before the Court of Justice was whether Pompes Funèbres, which had been given an exclusive concession to provide 'external services' for funerals in a particular French town, was guilty of charging excessive prices. The Court of Justice said that, given that more than 30,000 communes in France had not granted exclusive concessions such as that enjoyed by Pompes Funèbres, but instead had left the service unregulated or operated it themselves, it must be possible to make a comparison between the prices charged by undertakings with concessions and other undertakings:

> Such a comparison could provide a basis for assessing whether or not the prices charged by the concession holders are fair[61].

[50] Commission decision of 23 July 2004, para 86.

[51] See Lamalle, Lindström-Rossi and Teixeira 'Two important rejection decisions on excessive pricing in the port sector' (2004) (Autumn) Competition Policy Newsletter 40.

[52] OJ [2001] L 331/40. [53] Ibid, para 159. [54] Ibid, paras 160–166.

[55] In the UK see eg the report of the former Competition Commission in *The Supply of Banking Services by Clearing Banks to Small and Medium Sized Enterprises*, Cm 5319 (2002), paras 2.243–2.431 and *Market investigation into payment protection insurance* (2009), paras 6.99–6.138; in South Africa see the judgment of the Competition Tribunal in Case No 011502 *Competition Commission v Sasol Chemical Industries Ltd*, judgment of 5 June 2014.

[56] Commission decision of 15 November 2011.

[57] On Article 9 see ch 7, 'Article 9: commitments', pp 264–269.

[58] Details of this case can be found at www.ec.europa.eu.

[59] Commission Press Release IP/17/1323, 15 May 2017; note the decision of the Italian NCA of 29 September 2016 finding that Aspen Pharma's prices for the same drugs were abusive: AGCM Press Release of 14 October 2016, available at www.agcm.it. The Italian administrative court of first instance dismissed the appeal lodged by Aspen Pharma in its entirety: see Case 12806/2016 *TAR Lazio*, judgment of 13 June 2017.

[60] Case 30/87 EU:C:1988:225. [61] Ibid, para 31.

The idea in *Bodson* of using a comparator to establish whether prices were excessive was repeated in *Lucazeau v SACEM*[62], which concerned the level of royalties charged for the playing of recorded music in discotheques; the Court of Justice again suggested that a comparison should be made with the level of fees charged in other Member States. In *Ministère Public v Tournier*[63], another case concerning the level of royalties charged to discotheques by a French performing rights society, the Court of Justice said that excessive or disproportionate costs should not be taken into account in determining the reasonableness of prices. The society in question had a *de facto* monopoly and the Court of Justice suggested that it was the very lack of competition which had led to high administrative costs: the society had no incentive to keep them down.

In *AKKA/LAA*[64] the Latvian Competition Council had fined AKKA/LAA, a copyright collecting society, for charging excessive fees for the performance of musical works. Several questions were referred to the Court of Justice by the Administrative Division of the Supreme Court of Latvia. The Court of Justice repeated the test of unfairly high pricing in paragraph 252 of *United Brands*[65]. It held that it was valid to determine the lawfulness of AKKA/LAA's prices by comparing them with those charged by collecting societies in other Member States[66] and went on to give guidance as to how a comparative analysis should be conducted in the circumstances of that case. It said that, to be unlawful, the prices would need to be significantly higher, and persistently so, when compared with prices in other Member States[67].

(v) UK cases on excessive pricing

(a) Decisions of competition authorities

There have been three occasions on which cases investigated by competition authorities have led to excessive pricing being found to be abusive in the UK[68].

In *Napp Pharmaceutical Holdings Ltd*[69] Napp was held to have infringed the Chapter II prohibition by operating a discriminatory discount policy, by predatory price cutting and by charging excessive prices. Napp supplied sustained release morphine (referred to by its trade name of MST) to hospitals and to patients in the community. Napp's prices for sales to the community were found to be excessive since:

- prices for sales to the community were more than ten times higher than to hospitals
- the profit margin Napp earned on community sales of MST was excessive since it exceeded the margins it earned on both sales of other products and on the sale of MST to other markets
- the actual prices of MST significantly exceeded what a competitive price for it would be likely to be.

On appeal the Competition Appeal Tribunal ('the CAT') noted the difficulties involved in determining whether a price is excessive, and concluded that the various methods used in the decision were 'among the approaches that may reasonably be used', adding 'there are,

[62] Case 110/88 EU:C:1989:326; see similarly Case C-351/12 *OSA v Léčebné lázně Mariánské Lázně a.s.* EU:C:2014:110, para 87.

[63] Case 395/87 EU:C:1989:319; recent cases on the level of royalties charged by a collecting society include Case C-52/07 *Kanal 5 Ltd v STIM upa* EU:C:2008:703 and Case C-351/12 *OSA v Léčebné lázně Mariánské Lázně a.s.* EU:C:2014:110.

[64] Case C-177/16 EU:C:2017:689. [65] Ibid, para 36. [66] Ibid, para 38. [67] Ibid, para 56.

[68] In addition to the cases mentioned in the text see also *London Stock Exchange issuer fees*, OFT 713, March 2004, which did not make a formal finding of excessive pricing but led to a reduction in issuing fees.

[69] OFT decision of 30 March 2001, paras 203–234.

no doubt, other methods'[70]. The CAT upheld the finding of excessive pricing[71], but considered that there were certain mitigating factors in favour of Napp, not least the uncertainty of the law on this issue, and it therefore reduced the fine that had been imposed from £3.21 million to £2.2 million[72]. Following the decision in *Napp* prices for sales to the community fell significantly[73].

The complexity of determining access prices in the case of essential facilities is vividly illustrated by *Albion Water v Water Services Regulation Authority*. The CAT handed down several judgments in an appeal against a finding by OFWAT[74] that Dŵr Cymru was not guilty of offering an excessive price for the transportation of water through its water pipelines. The CAT's judgment in October 2006 reviewed the position at great length; it included extensive discussion of relevant cost principles[75] and of the 'efficient component pricing rule' ('the ECPR') advocated by some commentators as a methodology for determining the access price to essential facilities: the ECPR deducts from the retail price of a product the cost that an undertaking would avoid if it did not provide an upstream service such as the carriage of water[76]. The CAT decided that the ECPR was not a safe methodology to use in the case before it[77], and concluded that the evidence 'strongly suggested' that the price quoted by Dŵr Cymru was excessive[78]. Following a further investigation of the costs involved by OFWAT the CAT concluded[79] that Dŵr Cymru had offered prices that were so excessive that they were unfair and therefore abusive: the quoted access price to the Ashgrove system materially exceeded the costs reasonably attributable to the distribution of water by Dŵr Cymru; it was exclusionary as well as exploitative. Albion brought a 'follow-on' action for damages against Dŵr Cymru: the CAT awarded compensatory damages of £1.85 million; the claim for 'exemplary' damages was dismissed because it had not been established that Dŵr Cymru intended to charge an unlawfully excessive price or that it was reckless as to whether the price was excessive[80].

In *Unfair pricing in respect of the supply of phenytoin sodium capsules in the UK*[81] the Competition and Markets Authority ('the CMA') imposed fines of nearly £90 million on Pfizer and Flynn Pharma for charging excessive and unfair prices for phenytoin sodium capsules, a drug used for the treatment of epilepsy; Pfizer was the manufacturer of the drug and Flynn the distributor. Until September 2012 Pfizer manufactured and distributed the drug under the brand name 'Epanutin': as long as it was branded it was subject to price regulation. Pfizer sold the UK marketing authorisations for the drug to Flynn which de-branded, or 'genericised', the drug, at which point price regulation ceased to apply[82]. Both Pfizer as manufacturer and Flynn as distributor raised the price of the drug by a considerable amount, so much so that the CMA concluded that they were each guilty of excessive and unfair pricing. The CMA found that the prices were abusively high, because they materially exceeded cost plus a reasonable rate of return, they were several multiples

[70] Case 1001/1/1/01 *Napp Pharmaceutical Holdings Ltd v Director General of Fair Trading* [2002] CAT 1, para 392.

[71] Ibid, paras 389–442. [72] Ibid, paras 497–541.

[73] *Evaluating the impact of the OFT's 2001 abuse of dominance case against Napp Pharmaceuticals*, OFT 1332, June 2011.

[74] OFWAT decision of 26 May 2004.

[75] Case 1046/2/4/04 [2006] CAT 23, in particular paras 448–637.

[76] Ibid, paras 638–836. [77] Ibid, para 835. [78] Ibid, para 637.

[79] Case 1046/2/4/04 [2008] CAT 31; see also [2009] CAT 12, on remedy and costs.

[80] Case 1166/5/7/10 [2013] CAT 6.

[81] CMA decision of 7 December 2016, on appeal Case 1276/1/12/17 *Pfizer Inc v CMA* and Case 1275/1/12/16 *Flynn Pharma Ltd v CMA*, not yet decided.

[82] One of Pfizer and Flynn's grounds of appeal is to determine whether price regulation continued to apply to the generic version of the drug.

of the prices that Pfizer had charged for Epanutin and they had a materially harmful effect on the health service[83]. A four-week appeal against the decision ended on 24 November 2017, and the CAT's judgment is awaited[84]. The CMA is investigating two further cases of suspected excessive prices in the pharmaceutical sector: one against Actavis UK in relation to hydrocortisone tablets[85] and one against Concordia in relation to liothyronine tablets[86].

There have been several unsuccessful complaints to public authorities in the UK about excessive pricing. In *Thames Water Utilities/Bath House and Albion Yard*[87] OFWAT decided that Thames Water had not charged an excessive amount for the carriage of water extracted by Enviro-Logic to the latter's customers. In *SSL International*[88] the Office of Fair Trading ('the OFT') concluded that, although it was possible that the prices of SSL's male condoms were high, a substantial amount of time and expense would be needed to decide whether they were excessive. Moreover, if the outcome of the case had been the imposition of a price cap there was a risk that it might stifle emerging competition.

(b) Private litigation and excessive pricing

A particularly interesting case on excessive pricing arose in *Attheraces v The British Horseracing Board*[89], a 'standalone' action by Attheraces with no involvement on the part of any competition authority. Attheraces, a broadcaster, required so-called 'pre-race data' about British horse races in the possession of the British Horseracing Board ('the BHB'), the administrator and regulator of British horseracing. Attheraces wanted to make these data available to overseas bookmakers. It complained, and the judge at first instance held[90], that BHB had abused a dominant position by threatening to refuse to supply Attheraces, by charging it unfair prices, and by discriminating against it. The Court of Appeal allowed the appeal by BHB. Mummery LJ stated at the outset that the nature of the issues under consideration were ones that might more satisfactorily be solved by arbitration or by a specialist body equipped with appropriate expertise and flexible powers, rather than within the adversarial procedures of an ordinary private action[91]. The Court of Appeal referred to paragraph 250 of the Court of Justice's judgment in *United Brands v Commission* that a price that significantly exceeds the economic value of the product supplied could be abusive, but pointed out that this formulation 'begs a fundamental question: what constitutes economic value?'[92]. The court concluded that it was not possible to conclude that a price was abusive simply on the basis of a 'cost-plus' approach: that is to say that it is not sufficient merely to show that a price exceeds cost by more than a 'reasonable' amount[93]. In so far as the judge had reached his conclusion on the basis of cost plus a reasonable return he had adopted too narrow an approach: in particular he was wrong to reject BHB's contention that, in considering the economic value of the data, the amount that the overseas bookmakers were willing to pay Attheraces was relevant[94]. The Court of Appeal specifically noted that the principal object of Article 102 was to protect consumers—in this case

[83] The decision is available at www.gov.uk/cma; for comment see Bokhari and Lyons 'Pfizer and Flynn: How are "excessive" prices for generic drugs possible and should competition authorities do more about exploitative pricing?', available at www.competitionpolicy.wordpress.com.

[84] An application by Flynn for interim relief to suspend the CMA's direction to reduce its prices was rejected: Case 1275/1/12/16 (IR) *Flynn Pharma Ltd v CMA* [2017] CAT 1.

[85] CMA Press Release of 16 December 2016.

[86] CMA Press Release of 21 November 2017.

[87] OFWAT decision of 31 March 2003.

[88] Case closure of 11 May 2005.

[89] [2007] EWCA Civ 38; the judgment was considered by the High Court in *Humber Oil Terminals Trustee Ltd v Associated British Ports* [2011] EWHC 352 (Ch), paras 17–21 and 33.

[90] *Attheraces Ltd v The British Horseracing Board Ltd* [2005] EWHC 3015 (Ch).

[91] [2007] EWCA Civ 38, para 7.

[92] Ibid, para 204.

[93] Ibid, para 209.

[94] Ibid, para 218.

the ultimate punters who bet on horse races—and not competitors such as Attheraces: it said that there was little, if any, evidence of harm to competition[95].

4. Conditional Rebates

Article 102 does not specifically state that offering rebates to customers is abusive: however consistent case law of the EU Courts has established that in certain circumstances rebates and analogous pricing practices (for example granting discounts and setting target bonuses) may constitute an abuse[96]. The case law on this topic has generated great controversy over the years: many commentators have argued that it is too 'formalistic'; or, to say the same thing in a different way, that it has failed to reflect a more economics, effects-based approach to the enforcement of Article 102[97].

In September 2017 the judgment of the Grand Chamber of the Court of Justice in *Intel v Commission*[98] significantly reoriented the law on conditional rebates, requiring an effects-based analysis in rebate cases. As a result of the *Intel* judgment the authors have jettisoned the discussion on rebates in previous editions of this book. Instead we will discuss the topic in five sections:

- section A will explain why the treatment of conditional rebates under Article 102 has been controversial
- section B will consider how the judgment of the Court of Justice in *Intel* 'reorientates' the law
- section C will examine the compatibility of the Commission's *Guidance on Article 102 Enforcement Priorities* with the judgment in *Intel* and conclude that they are broadly in alignment with one another
- section D will discuss some unanswered questions about the law on rebates after *Intel*
- section E will conclude with a brief review of the treatment of rebates in the UK.

(A) **Why is the law on conditional rebates controversial?**

(i) *Hoffmann-La Roche v Commission*

In *Hoffmann-La Roche v Commission*[99] the Court of Justice held that Hoffmann-La Roche had abused its dominant position both by entering into exclusive purchasing agreements

[95] Ibid, para 215.

[96] For further reading on exclusive dealing agreements and rebates see the OECD Roundtables on *Loyalty and Fidelity Discounts and Rebates* (2002), *Bundled and Loyalty Discounts and Rebates* (2008), and *Fidelity Rebates and Competition* (2016), all available at www.oecd.org/competition; Fumagalli, Motta and Calcagno *Exclusionary Practices—The Economics of Monopolisation and Abuse of Dominance* (Cambridge University Press, 2018), chs 2–3; DG COMP's *Discussion paper on the application of Article [102] of the Treaty to exclusionary abuses* (December 2005), section 7; Bishop and Walker *The Economics of EC Competition Law* (Sweet & Maxwell, 3rd ed, 2010), paras 6-28–6-59; Niels, Jenkins and Kavanagh *Economics for Competition Lawyers* (Oxford University Press, 2nd ed, 2016), pp 189–199; O'Donoghue and Padilla *The Law and Economics of Article 102 TFEU* (Hart, 2nd ed, 2013), chs 8–9; Morell, Glöckner and Towfigh 'Sticky Rebates: Loyalty Rebates Impede Rational Switching of Consumers' (2015) 11 Journal of Competition Law and Economics 431.

[97] See generally ch 5, 'Are there or should there be any *per se* rules under Article 102?', pp 204–207.

[98] Case C-413/14 P EU:C:2017:632.

[99] Case 85/76 EU:C:1979:36; exclusivity rebates had been condemned in an earlier case that was predominantly concerned with cartelisation of the sugar market, Cases 43/73 etc *Suiker Unie v Commission* EU:C:1975:174, paras 517–528: however the *Hoffmann-La Roche* judgment is regarded as the seminal case on the topic.

with some of its customers and by offering others rebates conditional upon 'fidelity'. In relation to the latter the Court said at paragraph 89 of its judgment that it was unlawful for a dominant firm to tie a customer by an exclusive purchasing commitment and that:

> The same applies if the [dominant] undertaking, without tying the purchasers by a formal obligation, applies, either under the terms of the agreements concluded with these purchasers or unilaterally, a system of fidelity rebates, that is to say discounts conditional on the customer's obtaining all or most of its requirements—whether the quantity of its purchases be large or small—from the undertaking in a dominant position[100].

This passage equates the law on fidelity rebates with the prohibition of exclusive purchasing agreements. The EU Courts have frequently reaffirmed the position taken by the Court of Justice towards conditional rebates in *Hoffmann-La Roche*[101]. As we will see, in paragraph 137 of its judgment in *Intel* the Court of Justice repeated paragraph 89 of the judgment in *Hoffmann-La Roche*. Crucially, however, it then went on to 'clarify' the case law: the significance of this clarification will be discussed below.

(ii) Terminology

It may be helpful to make a few initial points about the terminology used in discussion of rebates. The first is that in *Hoffmann-La Roche* the Court did not take exception to rebates in themselves, but to rebates that were conditional upon exclusive purchasing: it is the **conditionality** of the rebate that may trigger the application of Article 102[102]. The second point is that case law and the literature use the terms 'fidelity' rebates and 'loyalty' rebates interchangeably. The General Court in *Intel*[103] preferred to call fidelity and loyalty rebates 'exclusivity' rebates, although this term was not used by the Court of Justice in that case. Thirdly, the Court in *Hoffmann-La Roche* was concerned about rebates conditional upon a customer acquiring 'all or most' of its requirements from the dominant undertaking: in *Intel* the General Court was satisfied that a requirement to purchase 80% or more constituted 'most' of a customer's requirements[104].

(iii) The controversy

Paragraph 89 of *Hoffmann-La Roche* adopted a strict approach: it was abusive for a dominant undertaking to tie a customer by an exclusive purchasing agreement or by offering fidelity rebates. Various objections have been taken to this approach. First, paragraph 89, read literally, suggests a '*per se*' standard, but it is questionable whether any conduct should be *per se* illegal under Article 102[105]. Secondly, the case law seemed to be too unresponsive to the economics of the marketplace in which even dominant firms must have the right to compete. A rebate is a price cut, and as a general proposition competition law should encourage, or at least not discourage, price competition. Thirdly, the approach in *Hoffmann-La Roche* appeared to some to be unduly favourable to competitors, rather than to the process of competition. Fourthly, the judgment in *Hoffmann-La Roche* condemns

[100] Case 85/76 EU:C:1979:36.

[101] See eg Case T-65/89 *BPB Industries plc and British Gypsum v Commission* EU:T:1993:31, para 68; Case T-228/97 *Irish Sugar v Commission* EU:T:1999:246, para 197; Case T-57/01 *Solvay SA v Commission* EU:T:2009:519, paras 314–341; Case T-155/06 *Tomra Systems ASA v Commission* EU:T:2010:370, para 208.

[102] Note that the Commission's *Guidance on Article 102 Enforcement Priorities* discusses this topic under the heading 'Conditional rebates'.

[103] Case T-286/09 *Intel v Commission* EU:T:2014:547, para 76.

[104] Ibid, para 135; this finding was not considered on appeal by the Court of Justice.

[105] See ch 5, 'Are there or should there be any *per se* rules under Article 102?', pp 204–207.

conduct by reference to its form, which sits awkwardly with the move, supported by the Commission, towards a more economics, effects-based application of Article 102. Finally, an effects-based approach to rebates would suggest that they should be condemned only when they are capable of eliminating a competitor 'as efficient' as (or even more efficient than) the dominant firm: in this case it is arguable that price/cost analysis should be deployed to determine whether the rebates result in below-cost selling by the dominant undertaking. There is a huge amount of literature critical of *Hoffmann-La Roche* and its progeny[106]. By the time of *Intel* the criticism had become cacophonous, and the Court of Justice responded.

(B) ***Intel v Commission***

(i) The Commission's decision

In *Intel* the Commission imposed a fine of €1.06 billion for a single and continuous infringement of Article 102, consisting of two practices. The first was the grant of rebates to four manufacturers of computers conditional on their purchasing all or most of their central processing units ('CPUs') from Intel. Specifically, the Commission found that Intel's rebates were capable of anti-competitive foreclosure as an 'as efficient' competitor would have had to price its CPUs below average avoidable cost[107]. The second practice consisted of Intel making payments to customers to delay, cancel or restrict the marketing of a competitor's CPUs, a so-called 'naked restriction'[108].

(ii) The judgment of the General Court

On appeal the General Court upheld the Commission's decision in its entirety[109]. In its judgment the Court made a distinction between three types of rebate:

- '**quantity rebates**': these are simply linked to the volume of sales to a customer, and the General Court considered them to be presumptively lawful[110]
- '**exclusivity rebates**': these are conditional on customers buying only from the dominant undertaking and the General Court considered them to be presumptively unlawful unless objectively justified
- '**third category rebates**': that is to say rebates that are neither quantity nor exclusivity rebates, but which may have a loyalty-inducing effect; these may be unlawful, depending upon an appraisal of all the circumstances of the case[111].

[106] See eg Ridyard 'Exclusionary Pricing and Price Discrimination Abuses Under Article 82—An Economic Analysis' (2002) 19 ECLR 286; Temple Lang and O'Donoghue 'Defining Legitimate Competition: How to Clarify Pricing Abuses under Article 82 EC' (2002) 26 Fordham International Law Journal 83; Kallaugher and Sher 'Rebates Revisited: Anti-Competitive Effects and Exclusionary Abuse Under Article 82' (2004) 21 ECLR 263; Gyselen 'Rebates, Competition on the Merits or Exclusionary Practice?' in Ehlermann and Atanasiu (eds) *European Competition Law Annual 2003: What is an Abuse of a Dominant Position?* (Hart, 2006), p 287.

[107] Commission decision of 13 May 2009, paras 1002–1576.

[108] For comment see Allibert, Bartha, Bösze, Hödlmayr, Kaminski and Scholz 'Commission finds abuse of dominance in the *Intel* case' (2009) 3 Competition Policy Newsletter 31.

[109] Case T-286/09 *Intel v Commission* EU:T:2014:547.

[110] Ibid, para 75; see Case 85/76 *Hoffmann-La Roche v Commission* EU:C:1979:36, para 90; see similarly Case C-95/04 P *British Airways plc v Commission* EU:C:2007:166, para 84.

[111] Rebates of this kind were found to be unlawful in eg Case 322/81 *NV Nederlandse Banden-Industrie Michelin v Commission* EU:C:1983:313; Case C-95/04 P *British Airways plc v Commission* EU:C:2007:166; and Case T-203/01 *Michelin v Commission* EU:T:2003:250.

The General Court's judgment was widely criticised[112], although not universally so[113]. Specific objection was taken to the 'form-based' approach to exclusivity rebates and to the '*per se*' nature of the prohibition. The latter criticism was incorrect, since the General Court held that a dominant undertaking could attempt to defend its exclusivity rebates on the basis that they were objectively justified or economically efficient; it did not say that they were *per se*—in and of themselves—abusive[114].

(iii) The Opinion of Advocate General Wahl

When Intel appealed to the Court of Justice, Advocate General Wahl added his voice to the criticism. He considered that the General Court was wrong to take a form-based approach to exclusivity rebates. More specifically he disagreed with the General Court's identification of three categories of rebate: in his view there are only two categories: quantity rebates which are presumptively lawful; and other rebates which require a full examination of their actual or potential effects.

(iv) The judgment of the Court of Justice

The Court of Justice's judgment contains only four paragraphs on the specific topic of rebates, but they significantly reorientate the law. In paragraph 137 the Court restated paragraph 89 of the judgment in *Hoffmann-La Roche*; the Court voiced no criticism of that presumption, which in formal terms remains good law. However it is the following paragraph that is so important and it is worth quoting in full:

> 138 However that case law must be further clarified where the undertaking concerned submits, during the administrative procedure, on the basis of supporting evidence, that its conduct was not capable of restricting competition and, in particular, of producing the alleged foreclosure effects.

Paragraph 138 does much more than to 'clarify' the law. It allows a dominant undertaking, on the basis of 'supporting evidence', to argue that its rebates were not capable of foreclosing access to the market. When a dominant undertaking produces such evidence, the Commission is required to undertake an economic analysis to determine whether the rebates could have a foreclosure effect. Paragraph 139 of the judgment says that, when doing so, the Commission **must** consider:

- the extent of the dominant firm's position on the market
- the share of the market covered by the challenged practice
- the conditions and arrangements for granting the rebates in question and

[112] See eg Venit (who was counsel to Intel in the case) 'Case T-286/09 *Intel v Commission*—The Judgment of the General Court: All Steps Backward and No Steps Forward' (2014) 10 European Competition Journal 203; Ahlborn and Piccinin 'The *Intel* Judgment and Consumer Welfare—A Response to Wouter Wils' (2015) 1 Competition Law & Policy Debate 60; Peeperkorn 'Conditional pricing: Why the General Court is Wrong in *Intel* and What the Court of Justice can do to Rebalance the Assessment of Rebates' Concurrences No 1-2015, 43; Petit '*Intel*, Leveraging Rebates and the Goals of Article 102 TFEU' (2015) 11 European Competition Journal 269; Geradin 'Loyalty Rebates After Intel: Time to the European Court of Justice to Overrule Hoffmann-la Roche' (2015) 11(3) Journal of Competition Law and Economics 579.

[113] See eg Wils 'The Judgment of the EU General Court in *Intel* and the So-Called "More Economic Approach" to Abuse of Dominance' (2014) 37 World Competition 405; Whish '*Intel v Commission*: Keep Calm and Carry On!' (2015) 6 JECLAP 1 (for a response see Sher 'Keep Calm—Yes; Carry On—No!: A Response to Whish on *Intel*' (2015) 6 JECLAP 219); Wardhaugh '*Intel*, Consequentialist Goals and the Certainty of Rules: the Same Old Song and Dance, My Friend' (2016) 11 Competition Law Review 215.

[114] Case T-286/09 *Intel v Commission* EU:T:2014:547, paras 81 and 173.

- the possible existence of a strategy aiming to exclude as-efficient competitors from the market[115].

Paragraph 140 adds that, where the rebates could eliminate an as efficient competitor from the market, it is still possible for the dominant firm to demonstrate that they are objectively justified or that they lead to efficiencies to the benefit of consumers.

The logic of the *Intel* judgment suggests that the Commission could issue a statement of objections to a dominant undertaking simply accusing it of infringing Article 102 by offering conditional rebates: this would be to apply the *Hoffmann-La Roche* presumption, which the Court restates in paragraph 137. However the dominant firm would then almost inevitably respond with a claim that its evidence shows that the rebates do not have a foreclosure effect, and the Commission would then have to respond with its own economic analysis. Given that this is the case, it is impossible to suppose that the Commission (or a national competition authority) would not conduct an effects analysis in the first place; all the more so given that this is what the Commission says that it will do in its *Guidance on Article 102 Enforcement Priorities*[116]. It follows that the Commission would not proceed simply on the basis of the *Hoffmann-La Roche* presumption alone, and it did not do so in *Intel*.

The Court of Justice does not specifically endorse the General Court's identification of three categories of rebate; nor does it specifically agree with Advocate General Wahl that there are only two categories. However the Court requires an effects-based approach to the treatment of rebates generally, whether of the type covered by the presumption in *Hoffmann-La Roche* or of the 'third category'; this accords with the approach of the Advocate General and by implication disagrees with the General Court.

(v) Remittal to the General Court

In *Intel* the Commission had relied on the presumption in *Hoffmann-La Roche* to accuse Intel of abuse. However the Commission also conducted an extensive economic analysis of Intel's rebates, using the as-efficient competitor test, and concluded that this led to the same conclusion: the rebates were abusive. Intel challenged the Commission's analysis. The General Court held that, since there was no legal obligation on the Commission to conduct an effects analysis (the rebates were illegal by virtue of *Hoffmann-La Roche*), there was no need to review this aspect of the Commission's decision. The Court of Justice ruled that this was an error on the General Court's part, and that it had failed to carry out a proper judicial review; it therefore remitted the case to it for further appraisal[117]. The General Court will now have to resolve disputes between Intel and the Commission on issues such as the size of Intel's captive sales base and the appropriate period to calculate Intel's costs, and decide the case according to the standards set by the Court of Justice[118].

[115] These factors are consistent with those suggested by the Commission in para 20 of its *Article 102 Guidance*: see '*Intel* and the Commission's *Guidance on Article 102 Enforcement Priorities*', pp 751–752 later in chapter.

[116] See further '*Intel* and the Commission's *Guidance on Article 102 Enforcement Priorities*', pp 751–752 later in chapter.

[117] Case C-413/14 P EU:C:2017:632, paras 141–147; for discussion of the Court of Justice's judgment see Venit 'The Judgment of the European Court of Justice in *Intel v Commission*: A Procedural Answer to a Substantive Question?' (2017) 13 European Competition Journal 1; Petit 'The CJEU Judgment in *Intel v Commission*: The Rule of Reason in Abuse of Dominance Cases' available at www.ssrn.com.

[118] Case T-286/09 RENV *Intel v Commission*, not yet decided.

(C) *Intel* and the Commission's *Guidance on Article 102 Enforcement Priorities*

In its *Guidance*[119] the Commission stated its intention to adopt an effects-based approach to the selection of cases under Article 102, and in paragraph 20 set out a series of factors, such as the position of the dominant undertaking, the extent of the allegedly abusive conduct and evidence of a strategy to eliminate competitors, that it would take into account: these factors are consistent with those suggested in paragraph 139 of the Court of Justice's judgment in *Intel*.

In its *Guidance* the Commission discusses additional factors that it will take into account when deciding whether to intervene in relation to conditional rebates. At paragraph 37 of the *Guidance* it draws a distinction between conditional rebates applicable to all sales ('retroactive rebates') as opposed to rebates paid only on incremental sales ('incremental rebates'). The Commission notes that retroactive rebates may foreclose the market significantly as they may make it less attractive for customers to switch even small amounts of demand to competitors[120]. The Commission says that anti-competitive foreclosure is more likely in cases where competitors are not able to compete on equal terms for the entire demand of each individual customer[121]. This may be so when a customer is bound to purchase a certain amount of its needs from a dominant firm, for example because that firm is an unavoidable trading partner whose product is a 'must-stock item'.

In order to assess whether a conditional rebate can lead to anti-competitive foreclosure the Commission says that it intends to investigate the dominant firm's prices, rebates and costs, thereby responding to the criticism that analysis in this area is insufficiently cost-oriented. The Commission will seek to determine the 'effective price' a rival would have to offer a customer as compensation for the loss of a conditional rebate if the latter switched part of its demand from the dominant firm[122]. The Commission considers that:

- where a dominant firm is charging an effective price below AAC, the rebate is generally capable of foreclosing competitors as efficient as the dominant firm
- where a dominant firm is charging an effective price that is between AAC and LRAIC, other relevant factors, such as competitors' counterstrategies, should be taken into account to determine the possibility of anti-competitive foreclosure
- where a dominant firm is selling at an effective price above LRAIC, the rebate is normally not capable of anti-competitive foreclosure.

Paragraphs 27 and 45 of the *Guidance* explain that the cost/price analysis will be integrated into a more general assessment of anti-competitive foreclosure, taking into account other relevant quantitative and qualitative evidence. An important consideration will be whether the rebate system is applied with an individualised or a standardised threshold since the former is more likely to create a loyalty-enhancing effect[123].

In *Intel*[124] the Commission considered that its decision was consistent with its *Article 102 Guidance*[125], concluding that Intel's rebates would have led an 'as-efficient' competitor

[119] See ch 5, 'The Commission's *Guidance on Article 102 Enforcement Priorities*', pp 182–185.

[120] *Guidance on Article 102 Enforcement Priorities*, para 40.

[121] Ibid, para 39.

[122] Ibid, para 41; this is a specific application of the methodology for all exclusionary pricing abuses: ibid, paras 23–27.

[123] Ibid, para 45; on this point see *Coca-Cola*, Commission decision of 22 June 2005 (accepting commitments under Article 9 of Regulation 1/2003 from the Coca-Cola Company to, *inter alia*, refrain from setting target rebates to customers conditional upon them reaching individually-set purchase thresholds during a prescribed reference period); on Article 9 see ch 7, 'Article 9: commitments', pp 264–269.

[124] Commission decision of 13 May 2009.

[125] Ibid, para 916.

to price its CPUs below AAC. As noted earlier, the General Court declined to review this part of its decision, but it has since been requested by the Court of Justice to do so.

It is noticeable that the Court of Justice in *Intel* does not refer to the Commission's *Guidance on Article 102 Enforcement Priorities* at all[126]. However the authors do not see anything in the Court's judgment that is not aligned with the Commission's approach, which is to take an effects-based approach to rebates cases and, where appropriate, to be guided by the as-efficient competitor principle. Indeed, as noted earlier, paragraph 139 of the judgment in *Intel* refers to similar factors to those mentioned in paragraph 20 of the Commission's *Guidance*. On 24 January 2018 the Commission imposed a fine of €997 million on Qualcomm for having made significant payments to Apple on condition that it would purchase smartphone and tablet chipsets exclusively from Qualcomm[127]. The Commission specifically noted in its press release that its assessment had taken into account the factors set out in paragraph 20 of the *Guidance*, and had rejected a price/cost test submitted by Qualcomm, which is consistent with the *Intel* judgment.

(D) Unanswered questions after *Intel*

There is no doubt that the *Intel* judgment has changed the law on conditional rebates. 'The move towards a more effects-based approach to the application of Article 102 is strongly reflected in the judgment of the Court of Justice in the *MEO* case[128] and the Opinion of Advocate General Wathelet in *Orange Polska*[129]. Unsurprisingly, however, there are some questions about the impact of the *Intel* judgment that are not yet clear.

(i) The application of the as-efficient competitor test

The Court of Justice is clear in *Intel* that Article 102 does not seek to ensure that competitors who are less efficient than the dominant firm can remain on the market; competition on the merits may lead to the elimination of less efficient competitors, and that is part of the competitive process[130]. This statement is a helpful guiding principle when considering what is meant by the 'abuse' of a dominant position. However it is helpful to distinguish the general principle that Article 102 protects efficient, but not inefficient, competitors from the as-efficient competitor test ('the AEC test') when used in a technical sense. When the AEC test is used technically, it refers to the process whereby a price cut by a dominant firm is analysed to determine whether it is selling at below some appropriate measure of cost (for example AAC or LRAIC')[131]. When the Court of Justice specifically discussed rebates in *Intel* it did not say that their lawfulness depends on price/cost analysis, that is to say application of the AEC test; rather it said in paragraph 138 that a dominant undertaking can produce 'supporting evidence' that its rebates have no foreclosure effect. In *Tomra v Commission*[132] the Court held that charging 'negative prices' is not a requirement for a finding that rebates are abusive[133]. It made the same point in *Post Danmark II*[134], although it went on to say that there was no reason to exclude, in principle, the use of an AEC test[135]. It follows that there is no legal obligation in a case on rebates to

[126] The General Court had said that the *Guidance* was irrelevant to the Intel investigation as it predated its publication: Case T-286/09 EU:T:2014:547, paras 154–158.

[127] Commission decision of 24 January 2018, on appeal Case T-235/18 *Qualcomm v Commission*, not yet decided.

[128] Case C-525/16 *MEO v Autoridade de Concurrência* EU:C:2018:270.

[129] Case C-123/16 P *Orange Polska SA v Commission* EU:C:2018:87.

[130] Case C-413/14 P EU:C:2017:632, paras 133 and 134.

[131] See 'Cost concepts', pp 733–735 earlier in chapter.

[132] Case C-549/10 P EU:C:2012:221, para 73.

[133] Ibid, para 73.

[134] Case C-23/14 EU:C:2015:651, paras 56–57.

[135] Ibid, para 58; Judge Cruz Vilaça was the Judge Rapporteur in both *Post Danmark II* and *Intel*.

conduct price/cost analysis, but that either side (the Commission or the dominant undertaking) may do so as part of the 'supporting evidence'. Protecting efficient competition is a principle; application of the AEC test is not a legal necessity.

(ii) Could a rebate above cost be unlawful?

If price/cost analysis is conducted, and this shows that the rebate involves the dominant undertaking selling at below cost, an abuse would be established in the absence of a convincing justification. However an intriguing question is whether a rebated price above cost can be unlawful. In *Post Danmark II* the Court of Justice acknowledged that, in some markets, the emergence of an as-efficient competitor is practically impossible: for example where, as in that case, the dominant undertaking was a postal operator with a very large market share in the relevant market that had had a statutory monopoly with all the structural advantages that that entailed[136]. In those circumstances even above-cost rebates could have an anti-competitive foreclosure effect[137].

(iii) *Intel* and the *de minimis* test

It is unclear after *Intel* whether it continues to be the case, as the Court has indicated in *Post Danmark II*[138], that there is no *de minimis* doctrine under Article 102[139]. The factors mentioned in paragraph 139 of the judgment in *Intel*, such as the degree of dominance and the extent of market coverage of the practice in question, would seem to suggest that any anti-competitive foreclosure effect would have to be significant or appreciable.

(E) UK law

In *Napp Pharmaceutical Holdings*[140] Napp was held to have abused its dominant position in the market for sustained release morphine by offering very large discounts to hospitals while charging excessive prices to patients in the community; more particularly Napp had targeted particular competitors, offering larger discounts to hospitals where it faced or anticipated competition and by granting higher discounts for specific products that were under competitive threat[141]. It was considered that Napp's intention was to eliminate competitors; Napp was not simply 'meeting competition': its reaction to its competitors was held to be unreasonable and disproportionate[142]. On appeal the CAT found that Napp's discounts meant that it was selling at less than cost, and that they were therefore abusive[143].

In *English Welsh & Scottish Railway*[144] the Office of Rail Regulation found that EW&S had abused its dominant position in a number of ways, including by offering discounts having an exclusionary effect in relation to the carriage of coal to various power stations: a fine of £4.1 million was imposed.

Several cases concerning discounts and rebates have been closed because significant consumer detriment was unlikely and they were no longer an administrative priority[145].

[136] Ibid, para 59.

[137] When this case returned to the Danish courts Post Danmark withdrew its appeal, and the Danish NCA adopted a decision on 31 May 2017, finding that Post Danmark's rebates violated Article 102 with respect to three customers, available at www.kfst.dk.

[138] Case C-23/14 EU:C:2015:651, paras 72–74.

[139] See ch 5, '*De minimis* doctrine under Article 102?', p 207.

[140] OFT decision of 30 March 2001.

[141] Ibid, paras 144–202.

[142] Ibid, paras 197–202.

[143] Case 1001/1/1/01 *Napp Pharmaceutical Holdings Ltd v Director General of Fair Trading* [2002] CAT 1, paras 217–352.

[144] ORR decision of 17 November 2006; see Part IIA of the decision.

[145] *British Airways*, case closure of 30 April 2007; *Walkers Snacks Ltd*, case closure of 3 May 2007; *Supply of regional print advertising*, case closure of 14 March 2012.

The CMA's 'no grounds for action' decision following its *Investigation relating to supplies of impulse ice cream*[146] contains a clear and concise analysis of the actual and potential effects of Unilever's rebates for single-wrapped impulse ice-cream.

5. **Bundling**

(A) **EU law**

The application of Article 102 to tie-in agreements was considered in chapter 17[147]. It may be possible to achieve the same effect as a tie-in agreement through pricing practices[148].

(i) **Rebates having a tying effect**

In *Eurofix-Bauco v Hilti*[149] the Commission held that it was an abuse of a dominant position to reduce discounts to customers for orders of nail cartridges without nails[150]; the Commission's decision was upheld on appeal[151]. In *Tetra Pak II*[152] the Commission held that Tetra Pak had adopted a pricing policy that was a means of persuading customers to use its maintenance services[153]. In *Michelin II*[154] the Commission found that Michelin had a bonus scheme that enabled it to leverage its position on the market in new tyres to preserve or improve its position on the neighbouring retreads market[155].

(ii) **'Across-the-board' rebates**

In *Hoffmann-La Roche v Commission*[156] the Court of Justice condemned Hoffmann-La Roche's 'across-the-board' rebates, which were offered to customers which acquired the whole range of its vitamins; these rebates meant that customers were dissuaded from acquiring any particular vitamin from other suppliers[157]. The Court of Justice noted specifically that such rebates infringed Article 102(2)(d)[158]. The Commission's *Guidance on Article 102 Enforcement Priorities* says that it will generally compare the incremental price that customers pay for each of the dominant firm's products in a bundle to the dominant firm's LRAIC; an incremental price below LRAIC suggests that an equally efficient competitor may be foreclosed from the market[159]. Given the judgments

[146] CMA decision of 10 August 2017. [147] See ch 17, 'Tying', pp 705–713.

[148] For further reading on tying and bundling see DG COMP's *Discussion paper on the application of Article [102] of the Treaty to exclusionary abuses* (December 2005) section 8; Fumagalli, Motta and Calcagno *Exclusionary Practices—The Economics of Monopolisation and Abuse of Dominance* (Cambridge University Press, 2018), ch 4; Niels, Jenkins and Kavanagh *Economics for Competition Lawyers* (Oxford University Press, 2nd ed, 2016), pp 204–214; Van den Bergh and Camesasca *European Competition Law and Economics: A Comparative Perspective* (Sweet & Maxwell, 2nd ed, 2006), pp 264–276; Bishop and Walker *The Economics of EC Competition Law* (Sweet & Maxwell, 3rd ed, 2010), paras 6-63–6-83; O'Donoghue and Padilla *The Law and Economics of Article 102 TFEU* (Hart, 2nd ed, 2013), ch 11.

[149] OJ [1988] L 65/19. [150] Ibid, para 75.

[151] Case T-30/89 *Hilti AG v Commission* EU:T:1991:70, upheld on appeal Case C-53/92 P *Hilti AG v Commission* EU:C:1994:77.

[152] OJ [1992] L 72/1, upheld on appeal Case T-83/91 *Tetra Pak International SA v Commission* EU:T:1994:246, and on appeal to the Court of Justice Case C-333/94 P *Tetra Pak International SA v Commission* EU:C:1996:436.

[153] OJ [1992] L 72/1, paras 111–114; see also para 139. [154] OJ [2002] L 143/1.

[155] Ibid, paras 300–311. [156] Case 85/76 EU:C:1979:36. [157] Ibid, para 110.

[158] Ibid, para 111; for a similar case under US law see *Le Page's v 3M* 323 F 3d 141 (3rd Cir 2003), which was considered in *ZF Meritor LLC v Eaton Corp* 696 F 3d 254 (3rd Cir 2012).

[159] OJ [2009] C 45/7, paras 59–60; in the case of competing bundles of products the Commission will investigate whether the price of the dominant firm's bundle is predatory: ibid, para 61.

of the Court of Justice in *Tomra v Commission*[160] and in *Post Danmark II*[161] that price/cost analysis is not necessary to find that a rebate scheme is abusive, it is questionable whether below-cost selling needs to be established when across-the-board rebates are under scrutiny. However this does not mean that the Commission cannot take this issue into account when deciding as a matter of its enforcement priorities whether to prosecute a case[162].

(iii) Delivered pricing as a tie-in

In *Napier Brown-British Sugar*[163] the Commission held that British Sugar's delivered pricing system constituted an abuse of a dominant position, although it did not impose a fine in respect of this offence as it was the first decision on this particular practice. Until 1986 British Sugar had refused to allow customers to collect sugar at an ex-factory price. The Commission, relying on the Court of Justice's judgment in *Télémarketing*[164], held that British Sugar had reserved to itself an ancillary market (the delivery of sugar) as part of its activity on a neighbouring but separate market (the sale of sugar). The Commission's view was that there was no objective justification for this conduct on the part of British Sugar.

(iv) Bundling

A firm may sell two or more products together as a bundle and charge more attractive prices for the bundle than for the constituent parts of it. Bundling may have the same effect as a tie-in agreement[165]. In *Digital* the Commission objected to the fact that Digital offered prices which were more attractive when the customer purchased software services in a package with hardware services than when purchasing software services alone[166]. In *De Poste-La Poste*[167] the Commission imposed a fine of €2.5 million on the Belgian Post Office for, in effect, offering lower prices to customers in the market for the delivery of letters if they also made use of a separate 'B2B' ('business-to-business') service that it provided.

(B) UK law

In *BSkyB*[168] the OFT was not satisfied that BSkyB's bundling of sports and film premium channels had produced an anti-competitive effect since competitors had not been foreclosed; it therefore found that the Chapter II prohibition had not been infringed[169]. A similar conclusion was reached in respect of the discounts given by BSkyB on the rates charged to distributors of its premium television channels[170].

In *Genzyme*[171] a penalty of £6.8 million was imposed on that company for two pricing abuses, one of which was to charge a price to the National Health Service for a drug that included the price of home delivery, thereby reserving to itself the ancillary, but separate,

[160] Case C-549/10 P *Tomra Systems ASA v Commission* EU:C:2012:221, para 73.

[161] Case C-23/14 EU:C:2015:651, para 62.

[162] See ch 18 n 159 earlier.

[163] OJ [1988] L 284/41.

[164] Case 311/84 EU:C:1985:394.

[165] For a detailed discussion of this topic see Nalebuff *Bundling, Tying, and Portfolio Effects* (DTI Economics Paper No 1, 2003), available at www.gov.uk/government/publications.

[166] Commission's XXVIIth *Report on Competition Policy* (1997), pp 153–154; see similarly the Commission's action against AC Nielsen to prevent the charging of bundled prices: XXVIth *Report on Competition Policy* (1996), pp 144–148.

[167] OJ [2002] L 61/32.

[168] OFT decision of 17 December 2002.

[169] Ibid, paras 548–600.

[170] Ibid, paras 601–646.

[171] OFT decision of 27 March 2003.

activity of providing home care services[172]. This part of the infringement decision was annulled on appeal to the CAT for want of evidence of anti-competitive effects[173].

In *IDEXX Laboratories*[174] the OFT concluded that it had no grounds for action under Article 102 and the Chapter II prohibition since it was unlikely that IDEXX's bundling of animal diagnostic testing equipment and external laboratory tests would foreclose competitors. The OFT had regard to the European Commission's *Guidance* and concluded that an equally efficient competitor operating in only the external laboratory market could match IDEXX's effective incremental price in that market without making losses[175].

These cases illustrate the point that the behaviour of a dominant firm should be considered abusive only where it actually has an anti-competitive effect or where there is a realistic possibility of such an effect[176].

6. Predatory Pricing

This section considers the extent to which predatory price cutting—selling at a loss—can amount to an infringement of Article 102 or the Chapter II prohibition in the Competition Act; it also considers the rare circumstances in which selective price cutting to retain customers may amount to an abuse even though no loss is incurred[177].

(A) Introduction

The idea of predatory price cutting is simple enough: that a dominant firm deliberately reduces prices to a loss-making level when faced with competition from an existing competitor or

[172] Ibid, paras 294–363; the second practice condemned was a margin squeeze: see 'Findings of unlawful margin squeeze', p 776 later in chapter.

[173] Case 1016/1/1/03 *Genzyme Ltd v OFT* [2004] CAT 4, paras 546–548.

[174] Decision of 17 November 2011.

[175] Ibid, paras 6.18–6.34; because IDEXX's rebates were found to exceed AAC, it was considered unnecessary to conduct a detailed assessment of LRAIC.

[176] An allegation of anti-competitive bundling was rejected for this reason in *Alleged cross-subsidy of BT's discounts*, OFTEL decision of 28 May 2003.

[177] For further reading on predatory pricing see DG COMP's *Discussion paper on the application of Article [102] of the Treaty to exclusionary abuses* (December 2005), section 6; OECD Roundtable on *Predatory Foreclosure* (2004), available at www.oecd.org/competition; Niels, Jenkins and Kavanagh *Economics for Competition Lawyers* (Oxford University Press, 2nd ed, 2016), pp 171–181; Bishop and Walker *The Economics of EC Competition Law* (Sweet & Maxwell, 3rd ed, 2010), paras 6-84–6-118; Motta, Fumagalli and Calcagno *Exclusionary Practices—The Economics of Monopolisation and Abuse of Dominance* (Cambridge University Press, 2018), ch 1; Van den Bergh and Camesasca *European Competition Law and Economics: A Comparative Perspective* (Sweet & Maxwell, 2nd ed, 2006), pp 280–298; O'Donoghue and Padilla *The Law and Economics of Article 102 TFEU* (Hart, 2nd ed, 2013), ch 6; for literature in leading periodicals see eg Areeda and Turner 'Predatory Pricing and Related Practices under Section 2 of the Sherman Act' (1975) 88 Harvard Law Review 697; Scherer 'Predatory Pricing and the Sherman Act: A Comment' (1976) 89 Harvard Law Review 869; Williamson 'Predatory Pricing: A Strategic and Welfare Analysis' (1977) 87 Yale Law Journal 284; Baumol 'Quasi-Permanence of Price Reductions: A Policy for Prevention of Predatory Pricing' (1979) 89 Yale Law Journal 1; Brodley and Hay 'Predatory Pricing: Competing Economic Theories and the Evolution of Legal Standards' (1981) 66 Cornell Law Review 738; Williamson *Antitrust Economics* (Blackwell, 1987), pp 328–338; Mastromanolis 'Predatory Pricing Strategies in the European Union: A Case for Legal Reform' (1998) 19 ECLR 211; Edlin 'Stopping Above-Cost Predatory Pricing' (2002) 111 Yale Law Journal 941; Elhauge 'Why Above-Cost Price Cuts to Drive Out Entrants Are Not Predatory—And the Implications for Defining Costs and Market Power' (2003) 112 Yale Law Journal 681; see also the ICN's Unilateral Working Group *Report on Predatory Pricing* (2008), *Unilateral Conduct Workbook*, ch 4, Predatory Pricing Analysis (2012) and *Recommended Practices for Predatory Pricing Analysis Pursuant to Unilateral Conduct Law*, all available at www.internationalcompetitionnetwork.org.

a new entrant to the market; the existing competitor having been disciplined, or the new entrant having been foreclosed, the dominant firm then raises its prices again, thereby causing consumer harm[178]. Attempts to eliminate an existing competitor may be more expensive and difficult to achieve than deterring a new one from entry, especially where the existing competitor is committed to remaining in the market. Where a dominant undertaking has a reputation for acting in a predatory manner, this in itself may deter new entrants: not only predatory pricing itself but also the reputation for predation may be a barrier to entry[179].

The Court of Justice has acknowledged that competition 'on the merits', including price competition, may lead to the elimination of competitors that are less efficient than a dominant firm[180]. Dominant firms, like any other, have the right to compete on price. The law on predatory price cutting has to tread a fine line between not condemning dominant firms for competitive price cutting on the one hand while not condoning unreasonable exclusionary predation on the other: this takes us back to the debate about 'false positives' and 'false negatives' discussed in chapter 5[181]. It would be perverse if the effect of competition law were to be that dominant firms choose not to compete on price for fear that, by doing so, they would be found guilty of an infringement[182].

Some commentators have questioned whether a monopolist would ever benefit from predatory price cutting. Bork argues that in practice predation is too expensive for the predator; that the predator will not earn monopoly profits until some distant future time when the new firm has disappeared; and that if it is easy to drive firms out, it will be correspondingly easy for new firms to enter when the predator begins to reap a monopoly profit in the future[183]; if one agrees with this view, competition authorities ought not to concern themselves at all with the issue. However that extreme position now has fairly few advocates. Economists today acknowledge that dominant firms are able to act in a predatory manner[184], and game theory can help to demonstrate this[185]. There is no doubt that predatory price cutting can amount to an infringement of Article 102 and the Chapter II prohibition in the Competition Act 1998.

(B) **The Areeda and Turner test**

Many attempts have been made to frame an economic test of when a price is predatory. Areeda and Turner[186] suggested that a price should be deemed predatory under US law where it was below a dominant firm's AVC[187].

178 See, to that effect, *Guidance on Article 102 Enforcement Priorities*, para 63.

179 On this point see para 68 of the Commission's *Guidance on Article 102 Enforcement Priorities*; see also Bolton, Broadley and Riordan 'Predatory Pricing: Strategic Theory and Legal Policy' (2000) 88 Georgetown Law Journal 2239.

180 Case C-209/10 *Post Danmark A/S v Konkurrencerådet* EU:T:2012:172, para 22.

181 See ch 5, 'False positives and false negatives', pp 198–200.

182 See eg the US Supreme Court in *Matsushita v Zenith Radio* 475 US 574, 594 (1986): 'mistaken inferences in cases such as this chill the very conduct that antitrust laws are designed to protect'.

183 See eg Bork *Antitrust Paradox* (Basic Books, 1978), pp 148–155; see also Koller 'The Myth of Predatory Pricing: An Empirical Study' (1971) 4 Antitrust Law and Economics Review 105; Easterbrook 'Predatory Strategies and Counterstrategies' (1981) 48 University of Chicago Law Review 263.

184 For a helpful review of contemporary economic theory and empirical evidence on predatory pricing see Shapiro and Kaplow 'Antitrust' in Polinsky and Shavell (eds) *Handbook of Law and Economics*, vol 2 (Elsevier, 2008), 1073 at 1195–1197.

185 See eg Phlips *Competition Policy: A Game-Theoretic Perspective* (Cambridge University Press, 1995).

186 See Areeda and Turner 'Predatory Pricing and Related Practices under Section 2 of the Sherman Act' (1975) 88 Harvard Law Review 697.

187 See 'Cost Concepts', pp 733–735 earlier in chapter on the meaning of this and various other cost concepts; for case law in the US on the cost standard to be applied to predation in the airline industry see *US v American Airlines Inc* 355 F 3d 1109 (10th Cir 2003) and *Spirit Airlines Inc v Northwest Airlines Inc* 431 F 3d (6th Cir 2005).

The Areeda and Turner test relies exclusively on a cost/price analysis. Some commentators think that the test should be less strict, and that predation should be condemned only where it can also be demonstrated that a predator will be able to recoup any losses it has made through the exercise of its market power in the future: the Supreme Court of the US has required proof of recoupment as a key component of unlawful predation[188]. Others question whether the Areeda and Turner test is strict enough, arguing that pricing above AVC could be exclusionary in some circumstances, especially where there is evidence of an intention to discipline or deter competitors or where in practice it has this effect. However there are difficulties with a legal rule that requires specific proof of a predator's intention. In the ruthless process of competition any competitor that enters a race wishes to win, so that by necessary implication it must also have 'intended' that its competitors should lose; in this sense a requirement of intention is hardly meaningful[189]. In so far as a requirement of intention means that evidence of a 'smoking gun' should be adduced, for example in the form of written memoranda, minutes of meetings and emails documenting a settled policy of eliminating competitors, this may be difficult for a competition authority to find: well-advised companies will be aware that they should not generate incriminating documents of this kind and that they should destroy those that they do. A rule requiring evidence of intention to eliminate would make more sense where it has an objective quality based in economics, for example that a predator's conduct, by departing from short-term profit maximisation, makes commercial sense only as a way of eliminating a competitor; this variant of intention is very different from proving the subjective intention of the predator, but can be difficult to prove as a matter of economic analysis. This discussion demonstrates some of the problems involved in establishing a suitable test for cases on predatory price cutting.

(C) **EU law**

(i) **The rule in *AKZO v Commission* and subsequent cases**

In *ECS/AKZO*[190] the Commission imposed a fine of €10 million on AKZO for predatory price cutting. ECS was a small UK firm producing benzoyl peroxide. Until 1979 it had sold this product to customers requiring it as a bleach in the treatment of flour in the UK and Eire. It then decided also to sell it to users in the polymer industry. AKZO, a Dutch company in a dominant position on the market, informed ECS that unless it withdrew from the polymer market it would reduce its prices, in particular in the flour additives market, in order to harm it. Subsequently AKZO did indeed reduce its prices. In holding that AKZO had abused its dominant position the Commission declined to adopt the Areeda and Turner test of predatory price cutting, according to which pricing above AVC should be presumed lawful[191]. While accepting that cost/price analysis is an element in deciding whether a price is predatory, the Commission considered that it was also

[188] See *Brooke Group Ltd v Brown Williamson Tobacco* 509 US 209 (1993); *Weyerhaeuser Co v Ross-Simmons Hardwood Lumber Co Inc* 549 US 312 (2007); on recoupment in US law see Joskow and Klevorick 'A Framework for Analysing Predatory Pricing Policy' (1979) 89 Yale Law Journal 213; Elzinga and Mills 'Testing for Predation: Is Recoupment Feasible?' (1989) 34 Antitrust Bulletin 869; Edlin (see ch 18 n 177 earlier); on recoupment in a number of jurisdictions see Table 4 of ICN Unilateral Working Group Report on *Predatory Pricing* (2008), available at www.internationalcompetitionnetwork.org; in EU law see 'Is it necessary to show the possibility of recoupment?', pp 760–761 later in chapter.

[189] For judicial scepticism in the US on the role of intent in a case of predation see *Barry Wright Corp v ITT Grinnell Corp* 724 F 2d 227, 232 (1st Cir 1983) and *AA Poultry Farms Inc v Rose Acre Farms Inc* 881 F 2d 1396, 1401–1402 (1989).

[190] OJ [1985] L 374/1.

[191] See 'The Areeda and Turner test', pp 757–758 earlier in chapter.

relevant whether the dominant firm had adopted a strategy of eliminating competition, what the effects of its conduct would be likely to be and what a competitor's likely reaction to the conduct of the dominant firm would be.

On appeal[192] the Court of Justice upheld the Commission's finding of predatory pricing, saying that not all price competition can be considered legitimate[193]. The Court confirmed the Commission's rejection of the Areeda/Turner test. It established two standards to determine whether prices are predatory, which can be depicted as shown in Table 18.1, where the dominant firm's prices range from 0 to 100.

In *Tetra Pak v Commission* the EU Courts[194] upheld the Commission's finding[195] that Tetra Pak had abused its dominant position by predatory pricing in relation to its non-asceptic cartons. Tetra Pak was found to have sold non-asceptic cartons at a loss in seven Member States; it was able to subsidise its losses from its substantial profits on the market for asceptic cartons, where it had virtually no competition[196].

In *Wanadoo*[197] the Commission applied the rule in *AKZO v Commission* and imposed a fine of €10.35 million on the subsidiary of France Télécom for having priced residential broadband internet services at levels that, until August 2001, fell considerably below AVC, and which subsequently were approximately equivalent to variable cost, but were significantly below ATC. The judgments of the General Court and the Court of Justice in *France Télécom v Commission*[198] confirmed the Commission's decision, in particular

Table 18.1

100	Where a dominant firm is charging prices above ATC, it is not guilty of predation under the rule in *AKZO v Commission*
ATC	Where a dominant firm is selling at less than ATC, but above AVC, it is guilty of predation where this is done as part of a plan to eliminate a competitor[1]; such a pricing policy runs the risk of eliminating undertakings that are as efficient as the dominant firm but, due to their smaller financial resources, incapable of withstanding the competition waged against them
AVC	Where a dominant firm is selling at less than AVC, it is (rebuttably) presumed to be acting abusively since every sale would generate a loss for the dominant firm[2]
0	

[1] Case C-62/86 *AKZO v Commission* EU:C:1991:286, para 72.

[2] Ibid, para 71.

[192] Case C-62/86 *AKZO v Commission* EU:C:1991:286. [193] Ibid, para 70.

[194] Case T-83/91 *Tetra Pak International SA v Commission* EU:T:1994:246, upheld on appeal to the Court of Justice Case C-333/94 P *Tetra Pak International SA v Commission* EU:C:1996:436; see Korah 'The Paucity of Economic Analysis in the [EC] Decisions on Competition: *Tetra Pak II*' (1993) 46 Current Legal Problems 148, 172–181.

[195] OJ [1992] L 72/1.

[196] This type of intervention is envisaged by fn 39 of the Commission's *Guidance on Article 102 Enforcement Priorities*.

[197] Commission decision of 16 July 2003.

[198] Case T-340/03 EU:T:2007:22, upheld on appeal Case C-202/07 P EU:C:2009:214; for comment on the General Court's judgment see Gal 'Below-Cost Price Alignment: Meeting or Beating Competition? The *France Télécom* Case' (2007) 28 ECLR 382.

its approach as to costs[199]. The General Court held that the analysis of costs involves a complex economic assessment, and that the Commission 'must be afforded a broad discretion'[200]. The Court noted that, since the case concerned a new product in an expanding market, the Commission had spread the costs over a period of 48 months when determining whether France Télécom was selling at a loss[201]; this did not amount to a manifest error of assessment[202]. The Court also rejected the argument that there were methodological problems with the actual calculations of the Commission[203].

In *Post Danmark I*[204], a case concerning the distribution of unaddressed mail in Denmark, the Court of Justice held that prices above average incremental costs[205] but below ATC were unlikely to be abusive, even if applied selectively to one customer of a particular competitor, when it could not be shown that the dominant firm had deliberately sought to eliminate that competitor. The Court stated that actual or likely exclusionary effects must be demonstrated before such a price cut could be unlawful[206]. The Court explained that generally an as-efficient competitor can compete with a dominant undertaking's prices without suffering unsustainable losses 'to the extent that a dominant undertaking sets its prices at a level covering the bulk of the costs attributable to the supply of the goods or services in question'[207]. It is clear that the Court's view was that the pricing policy in question was unlikely to infringe Article 102[208].

(ii) **Intention to eliminate competition**

Proving intention is sometimes relevant to the EU law on pricing abuses. The Court of Justice in *AKZO v Commission*[209] decided that pricing above AVC but below ATC could be abusive where there was evidence of an intention on the part of the dominant firm to eliminate a competitor[210]. The Commission, in paragraph 66 of its *Guidance on Article 102 Enforcement Priorities*, says that it may rely on documentary evidence of a predatory strategy.

(iii) **Is it necessary to show the possibility of recoupment?**

It was pointed out earlier that US law prohibits predatory price cutting only if it can be shown that the predator has the ability to recoup any losses incurred[211]. Many commentators have argued that a recoupment rule should be adopted under Article 102[212], although some argue to the contrary[213]. It is of interest to note that the Privy Council, a court in the UK that hears appeals from some countries in the British Commonwealth, said in *Carter Holt Harvey Building Products Group Ltd v The Commerce Commission*[214] that:

> It is the ability to recoup losses because its price-cutting has removed competition and allows it to charge supra-competitive prices that harms competitors[215].

[199] Case T-340/03 EU:T:2007:22, paras 122–169; France Télécom's appeal to the Court of Justice on this point was dismissed as inadmissible: Case C-202/07 P EU:C:2009:214, paras 69–73.

[200] Case T-340/03 EU:T:2007:22, para 129. [201] Ibid, para 137. [202] Ibid, para 155.

[203] Ibid, paras 162–169. [204] Case C-209/10 *Post Danmark v Konkurrencerådet* EU:T:2012:172.

[205] This was a measure of cost used by the Danish NCA: ibid, para 31. [206] Ibid, para 44.

[207] Ibid, para 38.

[208] Ibid, paras 36–39; the matter was referred back to the Danish Supreme Court which decided that, according to the criteria laid down by the Court of Justice, there had been no abuse: Case 2/2008, judgment of 15 February 2013, available at www.supremecourt.dk.

[209] Case C-62/86 *AKZO v Commission* EU:C:1991:286. [210] Ibid, para 72.

[211] On the view of the UK competition authorities on this issue see 'The *Aberdeen Journals* case', pp 769–770 later in chapter.

[212] See eg Gal 'Below-Cost Price Alignment: Meeting or Beating Competition? The *France Télécom* Case' (2007) 28 ECLR 382 at 383.

[213] See eg Ritter 'Does the Law of Predatory Pricing and Cross-Subsidisation Need a Radical Rethink?' (2004) 27 World Competition 613.

[214] [2004] UKPC 37. [215] Ibid, para 67.

The EU Courts have not adopted a requirement of recoupment under Article 102. In *AKZO v Commission* the Court of Justice acknowledged the significance of recoupment by noting that a dominant firm has no interest in applying prices below average variable cost:

> except that of eliminating competitors so as to enable it subsequently to raise its prices by taking advantage of its monopolistic position[216].

However it did not expressly incorporate the need to prove the possibility of recoupment as part of the abuse. In *Tetra Pak II* it was argued before the Court of Justice that EU law should require proof of recoupment before condemning price cutting. The Court of Justice, upholding the finding that Tetra Pak was guilty of abusive predatory pricing, remarked that:

> it would not be appropriate, *in the circumstances of the present case,* to require in addition proof that Tetra Pak had a realistic chance of recouping its losses. It must be possible to penalise predatory pricing whenever there is a risk that competitors will be eliminated[217] (emphasis added).

The *Tetra Pak* case was one in which the anti-competitive intention of Tetra Pak, manifested in a series of abusive acts contrary to Article 102, was particularly clear; furthermore its market power was considerable, so that may explain why the Court felt that 'in the circumstances of the present case' it was not necessary to impose a requirement to prove recoupment.

In *France Télécom v Commission*[218] the Court of Justice was invited to introduce a recoupment requirement into the test of predation in a case of pricing below AVC. The Court cited the *AKZO* and *Tetra Pak* cases, and concluded that:

> it does not follow from the case-law of the Court that proof of the possibility of recoupment of losses suffered by the applicant, by an undertaking in a dominant position, of prices lower than a certain level of costs constitutes a necessary precondition to establishing that such a pricing policy is abusive[219].

The Court of Justice pointed out that the Commission is not precluded from finding that the possibility of recoupment is a relevant factor in assessing whether a pricing practice is abusive. This fits well with the approach adopted by the Commission in paragraph 71 of its *Guidance on Article 102 Enforcement Priorities*.

(iv) **Defences**

In *France Télécom v Commission*[220] the Court of Justice said that prices below AVC are 'prima facie abusive'[221], thereby confirming the possibility that such prices would not be unlawful where there is an objective justification. The same is true for prices above AVC but below ATC. It would be wrong to have a *per se* rule that selling at below cost

[216] Case C-62/86 *AKZO v Commission* EU:C:1991:286, para 71.

[217] Case C-333/94 P *Tetra Pak International SA v Commission* EU:C:1996:436, para 44; see also Case C-333/94 P EU:C:1996:256, paras 76–78 of the Opinion of AG Colomer, who considered that proof of recoupment was not necessary; yet in Cases C-395 and 396/96 P *Compagnie Maritime Belge v Commission* EU:C:2000:518 AG Fennelly considered that recoupment should be part of the test for predatory pricing: ibid, para 136; see similarly the Opinion of AG Mazák in Case C-202/07 P *France Télécom v Commission* EU:C:2008:520, paras 68–76.

[218] Case C-202/07 P EU:C:2009:214. [219] Ibid, para 110. [220] Ibid.

[221] Ibid, para 109; AG Mazák made the same point in para 95 of his Opinion in this case; cf Case C-333/94 P *Tetra Pak International SA v Commission* EU:C:1996:436, para 41, where the Court of Justice said that prices below AVC must 'always' be considered abusive.

is always illegal[222]. For example it is arguable that a dominant firm should sometimes be able to sell below cost: sales promotions may involve below-cost selling; and the disposal of old stock at the end of the season at a price below cost would presumably not be unlawful.

Separately, it may be possible for a dominant firm to defend prices that would otherwise amount to an abuse on the basis that it was meeting competition. However the Court of Justice has held that a dominant firm does not have an 'absolute right' to align its prices on those of its competitors where this would mean that it was selling at below cost[223]. Clearly it is necessary to balance the interest of the dominant firm to minimise its losses and the interests of competitors to enter or expand.

(v) Are the standards of AVC and ATC always appropriate?

A complicating factor in applying cost-based rules to determine whether prices are predatory is that it may not always be appropriate to apply the standards of AVC or ATC. In some industries fixed costs are very high but variable costs are low. An obvious example is telecommunications, where it is likely to have been very expensive to establish the original infrastructure of wires and cables; once they have been laid, however, the actual cost of carrying telephone calls is low, and may be as low as zero. The AVC of telephone calls is so low that there would hardly ever be predatory prices if the AVC standard were to be applied; and the ATC standard would require proof of the predator's intention to eliminate competition, following the judgment in *AKZO v Commission*, with the difficulties that this entails.

If the AVC and ATC standards in *AKZO v Commission* are inappropriate to determine whether prices are predatory in industries such as these, an alternative rule is needed. The Commission suggested as long ago as 1998[224] that the *AKZO* standards are not appropriate in a network industry such as telecommunications[225] and that a standard based on LRIC might be preferable[226]. Indeed, even a price above LRIC could be considered predatory, if it does not recover some of the common costs that are incurred where a firm supplies a range of different products: for this reason, a 'combinatorial' approach may be taken towards the assessment of cost, whereby a firm's LRIC is combined with its 'stand alone cost', that is to say the cost that it would incur if it had no other activities at all[227].

The Commission proceeded, for the first time in a formal decision, on the basis of LRIC in *Deutsche Post*[228]. UPS complained that Deutsche Post was using revenue from its profitable letter-post monopoly to finance a strategy of below-cost selling in the commercial parcels market, which was open to competition. The Commission's view was that Deutsche Post, in the period from 1990 to 1995, had received revenue from this business that did not cover the incremental cost of providing it[229]. By remaining

[222] In the UK the CAT considered that the *AKZO* presumption that prices below AVC are abusive should be rebuttable in rare cases: see Case 1009/1/1/02 *Aberdeen Journals Ltd v OFT* [2003] CAT 11, para 357.

[223] Case C-202/07 P *France Télécom v Commission* EU:C:2009:214, paras 41–48 referring to earlier case law and confirming the judgment of the General Court in Case T-340/03 *France Télécom v Commission* EU:T:2007:22.

[224] *Notice on the Application of the Competition Rules to Access Agreements in the Telecommunications Sector* OJ [1998] C 265/2.

[225] Ibid, paras 113–115.

[226] See 'Long-run incremental cost', p 734 earlier in chapter.

[227] See 'Stand alone cost', p 735 earlier and *The Competition Act 1998: The application to the telecommunications sector*, OFT 417, February 2000, para 7.11.

[228] OJ [2001] L 125/27.

[229] Ibid, para 36; the Commission sets out the relevant cost concepts at paras 6 and 7 of the decision.

in the market without any foreseeable improvement in revenue, Deutsche Post was considered to have restricted the activities of competitors which were in a position to provide the service at a price that would cover their costs[230]. The Commission therefore concluded that Deutsche Post was guilty of predatory pricing; however it did not impose a fine for this infringement, since this was the first time that it had applied the LRIC standard[231].

(vi) The Commission's approach to predation in its *Guidance on Article 102 Enforcement Priorities*

The circumstances in which the Commission might consider it appropriate to take action in relation to predatory conduct are discussed in paragraphs 63 to 74 of the *Guidance on Article 102 Enforcement Priorities*. The Commission says that a dominant firm engages in predatory conduct when it deliberately incurs losses or forgoes profits in the short term and causes anti-competitive foreclosure.

The Commission suggests, in paragraphs 26 and 64 of its *Guidance*, that a preferable standard to AVC might be AAC because, over a period of time, a firm might have to incur not just variable costs but additional fixed ones. Suppose that a firm is accused of predating over a period of three years: during that time some of its machinery might have to be replaced, and this would normally be regarded as a fixed cost. The AAC standard includes not only the average of the variable costs incurred over that period, but also adds in any fixed costs. It follows that, in some cases, AVC and AAC might be the same; but that in others—depending on the duration of the conduct under examination—AAC could be higher than AVC due to the inclusion of some fixed costs. The expression 'avoidable cost' is used because it refers to the amount of money that the dominant firm would have saved if it had not been involved in the production of widgets during the period in question. Of course, the Commission is bound by the law as laid down by the EU Courts; on the other hand, the suggestion that AAC, as a matter of economics, is a sounder standard than AVC in a case such as this seems compelling, and this is one of those areas where the EU Courts might, in future, be prepared to defer to the compelling logic of the *Guidance*.

The Commission's view is that pricing below AAC will generally be a clear indication of sacrificing profits, although it may also look at whether a dominant firm incurred a loss that it could have avoided. The Commission adds that only pricing below LRAIC is capable of foreclosing as-efficient competitors from the market. Paragraph 68 of the *Guidance* then refers back to paragraph 20, which sets out a range of factors that the Commission will take into account when deciding whether to intervene; the Commission must be satisfied that below-cost pricing results in anti-competitive foreclosure. It is not necessary for a competitor to have exited the market: disciplining a rival to prevent it competing may suffice[232]. The Commission states that consumer harm warranting intervention may arise if a dominant undertaking can reasonably expect its market power after the predatory conduct to be greater than it otherwise would have been, for example by increasing its prices or by moderating a decline in prices[233].

[230] OJ [2001] L 125/27.

[231] Ibid, para 47; a fine of €24 million was imposed for the separate abuse of offering conditional rebates; on conditional rebates see 'Conditional rebates', pp 746–754 earlier in chapter.

[232] *Deutsche Post*, para 69. [233] Ibid, paras 70–71.

On 8 December 2015 the Commission sent a statement of objections to Qualcomm accusing it of engaging in predatory pricing between 2009 and 2011 by selling certain baseband chipsets below cost with the aim to foreclose a competitor, Icera, from the market. No final decision had been taken as at 8 December 2017[234].

(vii) Predatory price cutting and cross-subsidisation

An undertaking that enjoys a legal monopoly in relation to a service such as the collection, sorting and delivery of post[235] is able to use the profits in its area of monopoly to support low prices in other markets where it faces competition: this was the essence of UPS's complaint in the *Deutsche Post* case[236]. Cross-subsidisation may facilitate abusive pricing practices such as predation and selective price cutting[237]. This raises the interesting question of whether cross-subsidisation is an abuse of a dominant position in itself. There are no decisions of the Commission or judgments of the EU Courts finding that cross-subsidy is, in itself, an abuse of a dominant position, although the Commission in its *Notice on the Application of the Competition Rules to the Postal Sector*[238] suggests that there could be circumstances in which it could be an abuse to subsidise activities open to competition by allocating their costs to those services in relation to which the postal operator enjoys a monopoly[239]. Despite this statement, however, in principle it would appear that the existing rules described in this chapter are sufficient to control the behaviour of dominant firms; the adoption of a rule forbidding cross-subsidy itself is unnecessary. This was the view of the General Court in *UPS Europe v Commission*[240].

Where cross-subsidy is a problem there are other ways of dealing with it. In the case of regulated industries, specific rules are often imposed to prevent the practice[241]. Useful remedies that the Commission can deploy in Article 102 cases include a requirement to establish different legal entities, the maintenance of separate accounts and full financial transparency of dominant firms' pricing practices.

(viii) Selective price cutting but not below cost

A contentious issue under Article 102 is whether it can be unlawful for a dominant firm to cut its prices selectively, but not to below any relevant measure of cost, to customers that might defect to a competitor, while leaving prices to other customers at a higher level. Such a policy might amount to unlawful discrimination contrary to Article 102(2)(c) where it involves the application of dissimilar conditions to equivalent transactions, thereby placing other trading parties at a competitive disadvantage[242]. The specific issue under consideration in this section is whether selective price cutting could be held to be abusive irrespective of whether it infringes Article 102(2)(c) and, more specifically, where

234 Qualcomm has sought the annulment of a request for information sent by the Commission in this case: its application for interim measures was rejected in Case T-371/17 R *Qualcomm Inc v Commission* EU:T:2017:485.

235 On the extent of the permissible monopoly today in postal services under EU law today see ch 23, 'Legislation', pp 1016–107.

236 OJ [2001] L 125/27, para 5.

237 See Hancher and Buendia Sierra 'Cross-subsidisation and EC Law' (1998) 35 CML Rev 901; Abbamonte 'Cross-subsidisation and Community Competition Rules: Efficient Pricing Versus Equity?' (1998) 23 EL Rev 414; on the relationship between these concepts see Case 1007/2/3/02 *Freeserve.com plc v Director General of Telecommunications* [2003] CAT 5, paras 171–225.

238 OJ [1998] C 39/2, para 3.3.

239 See also the Opinion of AG Mengozzi in Case C-209/10 *Post Danmark A/S v Konkurrencerådet* EU:C:2011:342.

240 Case T-175/99 EU:T:2012:172, para 61.

241 See ch 23, 'Regulated Industries', pp 1008–1010.

242 See 'EU law', pp 779–782 later in chapter.

the undertaking harmed is a competitor operating at the same level of the market as the dominant firm rather than a trading party in a downstream market. The position can be depicted as shown in Figure 18.1.

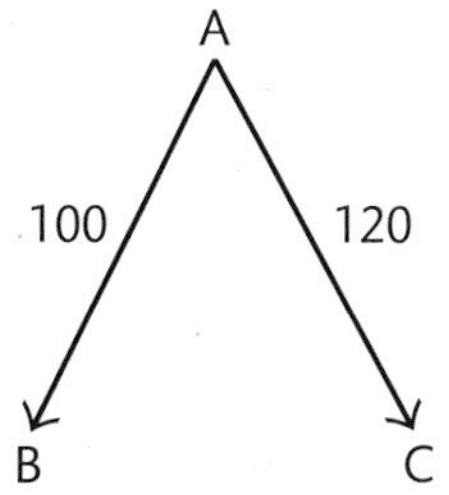

Fig. 18.1 Article 102(2)(c) discrimination

A charges B a price of 100 per widget, but charges C a price of 120; B and C need widgets to manufacture blodgets, a market in which they compete. Clearly the discrimination puts C at a competitive disadvantage in the blodget market as against B. It may be, in a case such as this, that B is a subsidiary of A, or closely associated with it; this may help to explain why A practises discrimination in the first place. The detriment to competition occurs downstream from A's market for widgets: that is to say it amounts to vertical foreclosure, or to secondary-line injury, to be contrasted with the horizontal foreclosure, or primary-line injury, in the example shown in Figure 18.2[243].

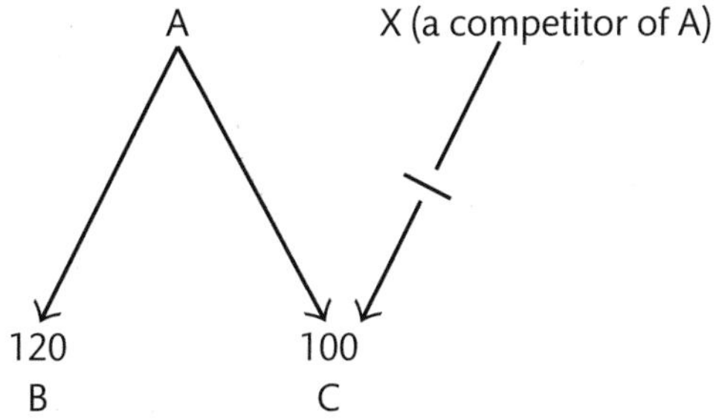

Fig. 18.2 Selective price cutting as an abuse

In this example A charges B 120 and C 100. B requires widgets for blodgets; C requires them for sprockets. Blodgets and sprockets do not compete, so that there is no harm to competition between B and C in the downstream market. The motivation for A's price cut to C is that A fears that it is going to lose C's business to X; X is able to supply a different input to C from which C could just as easily produce sprockets. The purpose of the selective price cut is to eliminate competition at A's level of the market: the case is one of horizontal foreclosure.

The question of whether selective price cutting such as this is abusive is controversial[244]. Provided that the dominant firm is not making a loss, it is not guilty of predatory price

[243] For discussion of this terminology see ch 5, 'Horizontal and vertical foreclosure', pp 210–211.

[244] See eg Elhauge 'Why Above-Cost Price Cuts To Drive Out Entrants Are Not Predatory—and the Implications for Defining Costs and Market Power' (2003) 112 Yale Law Journal 681; some commentators have written in defence of a rule that prohibits above-cost predatory pricing in certain circumstances: see eg Edlin 'Stopping Above-Cost Predatory Pricing' (2002) 111 Yale Law Journal 941; Ritter 'Does the Law of Predatory Pricing and Cross-subsidisation Need a Radical Rethink?' (2004) 27 World Competition 613.

cutting; it has not offered exclusionary rebates; and for the reasons just given it may not be infringing Article 102(2)(c). It would appear that, in making selective price cuts, the dominant firm is competing 'on the merits' with X, and that it has not acted abusively. The Court of Justice appeared to agree with this view in its judgment in *Post Danmark I*[245] (see later). The EU Courts have often stated that dominant firms are allowed to 'meet' competition, which is what A appears to have done[246]; and it is obviously in C's interest, and in the interest of C's customers, that it is the beneficiary of lower prices. Despite this, however, it is possible that selective price cuts of this nature may be held to be abusive, albeit only in narrowly defined circumstances.

(a) *Eurofix-Bauco/Hilti*

In *Eurofix-Bauco/Hilti*[247] the Commission imposed a fine of €6 million on Hilti for abusing its dominant position in a number of ways. Hilti had taken action to prevent customers from purchasing nails from its competitors. Apart from entering into tie-in agreements with some customers[248], Hilti singled out competing firms' main customers and offered them particularly favourable conditions; it removed quantity discounts from long-standing customers who bought from its competitors; and it classified certain customers as 'unsupported', which meant that they qualified for lower quantity discounts than 'supported' firms: it appeared to the Commission that the 'unsupported' firms were ones that had purchased nails and nail cartridges other than from Hilti. Hilti had also given away some products free of charge. The Commission said that the pricing abuses in this case did not hinge on whether the prices were below cost, but on whether Hilti could rely on its dominance to offer discriminatory prices to its competitors' customers with a view to damaging the competitors' business; in other words the Commission did not apply the rule in *AKZO v Commission* nor Article 102(2)(c). The General Court, upholding the decision of the Commission, stated that Hilti's strategy was not a legitimate mode of competition on the part of an undertaking in a dominant position[249].

(b) *Irish Sugar v Commission*

The Commission considered that Irish Sugar had abused its dominant position contrary to Article 102 by offering selective price cuts in *Irish Sugar*[250]. The General Court annulled the finding that Irish Sugar had applied selectively low prices to potential customers of a competitor, ASI, on factual grounds[251]; however it upheld the finding that Irish Sugar had been guilty of granting selective rebates to particular customers[252].

(c) *Compagnie Maritime Belge v Commission*

In *Compagnie Maritime Belge v Commission*[253] the Commission investigated the policy of 'fighting ships', whereby members of a liner conference in the maritime transport sector, Cewal, reduced their charges to the level, or to below the level, of their one competitor, Grimaldi and Cobelfret; they also operated the fighting ships on the same route and at the same time as Grimaldi's. The Commission concluded that the policy was one of selective

[245] Case C-209/10 EU:C:2012:172.

[246] See eg the judgment of the General Court in Case T-228/97 *Irish Sugar v Commission* EU:T:1999:246, para 112 and the judgments referred to in the footnote to that paragraph; for a general discussion of 'meeting' rather than 'beating' competition see Springer '"Meeting Competition": Justification of Price Discrimination under EC and US Antitrust Law' (1997) 18 ECLR 251.

[247] OJ [1988] L 65/19. [248] See ch 17, '*Hilti*', p 709.

[249] Case T-30/89 *Hilti AG v Commission* EU:T:1991:70, para 100. [250] OJ [1997] L 258/1.

[251] Case T-228/97 EU:T:1999:246, paras 117–124. [252] Ibid, paras 215–225.

[253] OJ [1993] L 34/20.

price cutting intended to eliminate the competitor and that Article 102 was infringed. The Commission's decision was upheld by the General Court[254]. The Court of Justice agreed that there was an infringement of Article 102, although the fines were annulled for technical reasons[255]. Advocate General Fennelly, urging that the application of Article 102 to selective price cutting should be approached with reserve, remarked that:

> Price competition is the essence of the free and open competition which it is the objective of [EU] policy to establish on the internal market. It favours more efficient firms and it is for the benefit of consumers both in the short and the long run. Dominant firms not only have the right but should be encouraged to compete on price[256].

In the Advocate General's view, non-discriminatory price cuts by a dominant undertaking which do not entail below-cost sales should not normally be regarded as being anti-competitive:

> In the first place, even if they are only short lived, they benefit consumers and, secondly, if the dominant undertaking's competitors are equally or more efficient, they should be able to compete on the same terms. [EU] competition law should thus not offer less efficient undertakings a safe haven against vigorous competition even from dominant undertakings. Different considerations may, however, apply where an undertaking which enjoys a position of dominance approaching a monopoly, particularly on a market where price cuts can be implemented with relative autonomy from costs, implements a policy of selective price cutting with the demonstrable aim of eliminating all competition. In those circumstances, to accept that all selling above cost was automatically acceptable could enable the undertaking in question to eliminate all competition by pursuing a selective pricing policy which in the long run would permit it to increase prices and deter potential future entrants for fear of receiving the same targeted treatment[257].

In its judgment the Court of Justice followed the Advocate General, holding that the selective price cutting on the facts of this case was abusive[258]. After noting that the scope of the special responsibility of dominant undertakings must be considered in the light of the specific circumstances of each case[259], the Court of Justice noted that the maritime transport market is 'a very specialised sector'[260]; it declined to establish a general rule for selective price cutting on the part of liner conferences, but upheld the Commission's finding of abuse.

The Court made clear that selective price cutting can be abusive in its own right. However it is important to point out a number of features of the *Compagnie Maritime Belge* case that restrict the scope of this precedent and which should therefore limit its application in the future. First, maritime transport is, as the Court of Justice remarked, an unusual sector in which an incumbent dominant firm is able to target its competitors and eliminate them by strategic behaviour with little regard to cost; secondly, the conference had 90% or more of the market: it therefore was 'super-dominant', and subject to particularly close scrutiny under Article 102[261]; thirdly, the conference had only one competitor, Grimaldi and Cobelfret; and fourthly, there was a 'smoking gun', that is to say evidence of an intention on the part of the conference to eliminate Grimaldi from the market: indeed the smoke was seen by the judges of the Court of Justice, where the appellants admitted

254 Cases T-24/93 etc EU:T:1996:139.

255 Cases C-395/95 and 396/95 P *Compagnie Maritime Belge v Commission* EU:C:2000:132; for comment see Preece '*Compagnie Maritime Belge*: Missing the Boat?' (2000) 21 ECLR 388.

256 Cases C-395/95 P etc EU:C:2000:518, para 117.

257 Ibid, para 132.

258 See paras 112–121 of the Court of Justice's judgment.

259 Ibid, para 114.

260 Ibid, para 115.

261 See ch 5, 'The degree of market power and super-dominance', pp 195–196.

that they had this intention[262]. The Court of Justice did not say, but may also have been influenced by the fact, that the liner conference itself was the product of a horizontal agreement amongst its members: there was, in effect, a horizontal collective boycott of Grimaldi, which would be a serious offence under Article 101(1)[263]. The case should be read with these special features in mind; this makes it a less menacing precedent than it might otherwise appear to be, with the consequence that other dominant firms, operating in less unusual circumstances, should be free to respond to competition by price cuts that are not contrary to any of the other pricing abuses under Article 102 described in this chapter.

(d) Post Danmark I

In *Post Danmark I*[264] Post Danmark enjoyed a legal monopoly for certain postal services in Denmark, but faced competition in the 'unaddressed' mail sector, that is to say mail of a promotional nature sent to all postal addresses. The Danish competition authority found that Post Danmark had abused its dominant position by selective price cutting and price discrimination within the meaning of Article 102(2)(c); however it could not establish on the basis of the evidence available that Post Danmark had deliberately sought to eliminate its main competitor[265]. On appeal the Danish Supreme Court sought the opinion of the Court of Justice under Article 267 TFEU whether the policy of selective price cutting[266] could infringe Article 102. The Court of Justice held that:

> the fact that the practice of a dominant undertaking may, like the pricing policy in issue in the main proceedings, be described as 'price discrimination', that is to say, charging different customers or different classes of customers different prices for goods or services whose costs are the same or, conversely, charging a single price to customers for whom supply costs differ, cannot of itself suggest that there exists an exclusionary abuse[267].

The Court of Justice went on to say that selective price cutting which did not involve selling below cost could not be considered to have anti-competitive effects in the absence of evidence of an intention to eliminate competitors[268]. The Court did not refer to its earlier judgment in *Compagnie Maritime Belge v Commission* on this issue[269], perhaps because, as noted earlier, it was a truly exceptional case. When the *Post Danmark* case returned to the Supreme Court in Denmark it concluded that Post Danmark had not abused its dominant position by offering price-cuts to large-scale customers[270]. The Court's judgment is consistent with the Commission's *Guidance on Article 102 Enforcement Priorities* which states that normally only pricing below LRAIC is capable of foreclosing 'as-efficient' competitors[271].

[262] *Compagnie Maritime Belge*, para 119.

[263] See ch 13, 'Anti-Competitive Horizontal Restraints', pp 561–564.

[264] Case C-209/10 EU:C:2012:172; for comment see Rousseva and Marquis 'Hell Freezes Over: A Climate Change for Assessing Exclusionary Conduct under Article 102 TFEU' (2013) 4 JECLAP 32.

[265] Case C-209/10 EU:C:2012:172, para 29.

[266] Note that the issue of whether Post Danmark had infringed Article 102(2)(c) TFEU was not part of the Article 267 reference.

[267] Case C-209/10 EU:C:2012:172, para 30. [268] Ibid, para 36.

[269] Cf the Opinion of AG Mengozzi: EU:C:2011:342, paras 69–78 and 85–96, which discussed the judgment in *Compagnie Maritime Belge* at some length, but which concluded that it was of 'marginal relevance' to the facts of *Post Danmark* (para 94).

[270] Judgment of the Danish Supreme Court, 15 February 2013, available at www.supremecourt.dk.

[271] *Guidance on Article 102 Enforcement Priorities*, para 67.

(D) UK law

There have been four cases in which predatory pricing has been established by competition authorities in the UK: *Napp*, *Aberdeen Journals*, *EW&S* and *Cardiff Bus*; allegations of predation have been rejected on a number of occasions.

(i) *Napp Pharmaceutical*

In *Napp Pharmaceutical Holdings Ltd*[272] Napp was found guilty of charging predatory prices for sustained release morphine by selling some products to hospitals at less than direct cost, which the OFT considered, on the facts of the case, to be a proxy for AVC[273]. Napp's argument that sales below cost to hospitals were objectively justified was rejected since Napp would be able to recover the full price from follow-on sales to patients in the community[274]; indeed the very reason that Napp was able to earn high margins on sales to the community was that it had been successful in stifling competition in relation to sales to hospitals[275]. On appeal the CAT held that Napp, as an undertaking which it considered to be 'super-dominant'[276], had abused its dominant position by charging prices below cost to hospitals in order to ward off a competitor[277]. The CAT held that, as Napp had offered prices below AVC to hospitals, it was not necessary to determine whether it had a plan to eliminate competition[278]; however the CAT found that such a plan existed in any event[279].

(ii) The *Aberdeen Journals* case

In *Aberdeen Journals Ltd*[280] the OFT imposed a penalty of £1,328,040 on Aberdeen Journals for predatory pricing by failing to cover its AVC from 1 March to 29 March 2000. This decision was set aside by the CAT as it was not satisfied by the way in which the OFT had defined the relevant product market[281]. The OFT adopted a second decision, concluding again that Aberdeen Journals was guilty of predatory pricing[282]. On appeal the CAT held that Aberdeen Journals had sold advertising in one of its newspapers at less than AVC contrary to the Chapter II prohibition[283]. The judgment contains several important points on the cost-based rules relating to predatory pricing:

- the rules are not an end in themselves and ought not to be applied mechanistically[284]
- the time period over which costs are to be calculated is important[285] since the longer the timescale, the more likely costs will be assessed as variable rather than fixed, with the result that a failure to cover them will give rise to a presumption of predation[286]
- the longer a dominant firm prices below total costs, the easier it would be to draw an inference of intention to eliminate competition, save in exceptional circumstances[287]

272 OFT decision of 30 March 2001. 273 Ibid, paras 188–196. 274 Ibid, paras 192–195.

275 Ibid, para 195.

276 Case 1001/1/1/01 *Napp Pharmaceutical Holdings Ltd v Director General of Fair Trading* [2002] CAT 1, paras 219 and 343; for comment on the finding of predatory pricing in this case see Ahlborn and Allan 'The *Napp* Case: A Study of Predation' (2004) 26 World Competition 233.

277 Case 1000/1/1/01 [2002] CAT 1, para 352. 278 Ibid, paras 228 and 307.

279 Ibid, paras 310 and 333. 280 OFT decision of 16 July 2001.

281 Case 1005/1/1/01 *Aberdeen Journals Ltd v Director General of Fair Trading* [2002] CAT 4, paras 182–186.

282 *Aberdeen Journals Ltd—remitted case*, OFT decision of 16 September 2002.

283 Case 1009/1/1/02 *Aberdeen Journals Ltd v OFT* [2003] CAT 11. 284 Ibid, paras 380 and 411.

285 Ibid, paras 353–356 and 382–387.

286 See the discussion of variable and fixed costs at 'Cost Concepts', pp 733–735 earlier in chapter.

287 Case 1009/1/1/02 [2003] CAT 11, para 356.

- pricing below cost would not be unlawful where there is an objective justification for it, though this would be particularly difficult when such pricing occurred in response to a new entrant or as part of a strategy to eliminate a competitor[288]
- it was a form of recoupment for a dominant firm to engage in predatory pricing in one market so that it could protect its market share or supra-competitive profits in another market and that, in the circumstances of those cases, further evidence of recoupment was unnecessary[289].

(iii) *EW&S*

In *English Welsh & Scottish Railway*[290] the Office of Rail Regulation found that EW&S had abused its dominant position in several ways, including by predatory pricing[291].

(iv) *Cardiff Bus*

In *Cardiff Bus*[292] that undertaking was held to have engaged in predatory conduct intended to eliminate 2 Travel, a rival bus company, from the market[293]. No fine was imposed due to Cardiff Bus's small turnover[294]. The liquidator of 2 Travel subsequently brought a 'follow-on' action for damages against Cardiff Bus in the CAT: an award of compensatory damages of £33,818 was made; the CAT also awarded exemplary damages of £60,000 to punish Cardiff Bus for its 'outrageous behaviour'[295].

(v) Cases where predatory pricing was not established

There have been several cases in which a complaint of predatory pricing was not upheld[296]. In *The Association of British Travel Agents and British Airways plc*[297] BA reduced the commission it paid to travel agents for the sale of BA tickets; this meant that BA could sell those same tickets at lower prices on its own website. In the OFT's view the sale by BA of lower-priced tickets did not amount to predatory pricing: rather the sale of tickets online was cheaper than through a brick and mortar travel agent and so there was an objective justification for this price differential[298]. In *Complaint against BT's pricing of digital cordless phones*[299] the Office of Communications ('OFCOM') rejected a complaint about BT's pricing of digital cordless telephones because BT was neither dominant[300] nor guilty of predatory pricing[301].

In *Claymore Dairies v OFT*[302] the CAT was critical of an investigation into whether Robert Wiseman Dairies was guilty of predatory pricing in relation to the sale of milk in Scotland: in particular it was not satisfied that the issue whether Wiseman's prices were above ATC had been sufficiently investigated[303], and it therefore quashed the finding on this point[304].

[288] Ibid, paras 357–358 and 371.

[289] Ibid, para 445; see similarly Case 1001/1/1/01 *Napp Pharmaceutical Holdings Ltd v Director General of Fair Trading* [2002] CAT 1, para 261.

[290] ORR decision of 17 November 2006.

[291] See Part IIC of the decision.

[292] OFT decision of 18 November 2008.

[293] See ch 7 of the decision.

[294] Cardiff Bus benefited from immunity under s 40 of the Competition Act 1998, on which see ch 10, 'Immunity for small agreements and conduct of minor significance', pp 423–424.

[295] Case 1178/5/7/11 *2 Travel Group plc (in liquidation) v Cardiff City Transport Services Ltd* [2012] CAT 19.

[296] In addition to the cases mentioned in the text see *First Edinburgh/Lothian*, OFT decision of 9 June 2004; *DB Schenker Rail (UK) Ltd*, ORR decision of 3 August 2010 and the judgment of the High Court in *Chester City Council v Arriva Plc* [2007] EWHC 1373 (Ch).

[297] OFT decision of 11 December 2002.

[298] Ibid, paras 38–45.

[299] OFCOM decision of 1 August 2006.

[300] Ibid, paras 151–429.

[301] Ibid, paras 430–662.

[302] Case 1008/2/1/02 [2005] CAT 30.

[303] Ibid, para 256.

[304] Ibid, para 318.

In *Alleged abuse of a dominant position by Flybe*[305] the OFT concluded that there were no grounds for action against Flybe, which had been accused by Air Southwest of predatory pricing on the air route from Newquay to London Gatwick. The OFT's view was that there was no abuse on that particular route, since Flybe was not in a dominant position on it[306]. The OFT also stated that there was an objective justification for Flybe to expect to and to incur initial losses on entering a new route[307].

In *Severn Trent Laboratories*[308] OFWAT investigated whether that company had priced below cost to win contracts to provide water-analysis services, in particular by subsidising its losses from profits on sales to an affiliated company. Severn Trent offered commitments to divest the affiliated company, which OFWAT accepted under section 31A of the Competition Act. There was no formal finding of an infringement in this case; OFWAT noted that, while commitments are not normally appropriate in cases of predatory pricing, the structural remedy given by Severn Trent removed its ability to leverage its market power in the future.

7. Margin Squeeze

(A) The economic phenomenon

A margin squeeze can occur where a firm is dominant in an upstream market and supplies a key input to undertakings that compete with it in a downstream market[309]. In such a situation the dominant firm may have a discretion as to the price it charges for the input, and this could have an effect on the ability of firms to compete with it in the downstream market. Suppose that A supplies widgets, essential for the manufacture of widget dioxide; that B is a subsidiary of A; and that C is an independent downstream competitor (see Figure 18.3).

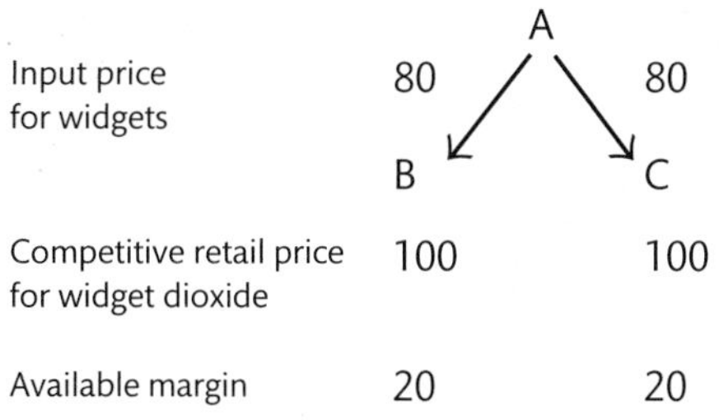

Fig. 18.3 Vertical margin squeeze: example 1

[305] OFT decision of 26 November 2010.

[306] Ibid, paras 5.12–5.20.

[307] Ibid, paras 6.97–6.99; reference was made in fn 67 of the decision to para 28 of the Commission's *Guidance on Article 102 Enforcement Priorities* on objective justification.

[308] OFWAT decision of 17 January 2013; on commitment decisions under s 31A see ch 10, 'Commitments', pp 415–416.

[309] For further reading on margin squeezing see O'Donoghue and Padilla *The Law and Economics of Article 102 TFEU* (Hart, 2nd ed, 2013), ch 7; Gaudin and Mantzari 'Margin Squeeze: An Above-Cost Predatory Pricing Approach' (2016) 12 Journal of Competition Law and Economics 151; Niels, Jenkins and Kavanagh *Economics for Competition Lawyers* (Oxford University Press, 2nd ed, 2016), pp 199–203; Heimler 'Is a Margin Squeeze an Antitrust or a Regulatory Violation?' (2010) 6 Journal of Competition Law and Economics 879; OECD Roundtable *Margin Squeeze* (2009), available at www.oecd.org/competition; Crocioni 'Price Squeeze and Imputation Test—Recent Developments' (2005) 10 ECLR 558; Géradin and O'Donoghue 'The Concurrent Application of Competition Law and Regulation: The Case of Margin Squeeze Abuses in the Telecommunications Sector' (2005) 1 Journal of Competition Law and Economics 355; Colley and Burnside 'Margin Squeeze Abuse' (2006) 2 European Competition Journal 185.

In this example C will be able to compete with B in the downstream market for widget dioxide only if C can transform the widgets into widget dioxide for a price of less than 20: if it cannot do so, it could not charge 100 in the retail market and make a profit. If, on the other hand, A had charged 60 for the widgets, the available margin would be 40, as in Figure 18.4.

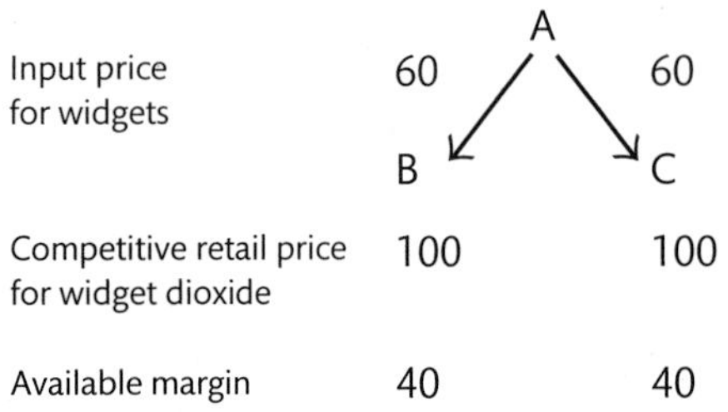

Fig. 18.4 Vertical margin squeeze: example 2

In each situation the total revenue of the integrated undertaking AB amounts to 100, but A has 'squeezed' the margin available to C in example 1 in a way that makes it more difficult for C to remain in the market for widget dioxide than in example 2. However, it is a complex matter to determine when a squeeze becomes abusive. For example if, in example 1, B can transform widgets into widget dioxide for, say, 15, whereas C is less efficient and can perform the same task only for 25, there is no reason why C should be able to demand a lower input price: the fact is that it is not as efficient as B, and so does not merit protection from it. However if B's own cost of transformation is 25, and C's is 15, the input price is being manipulated to protect B from a more efficient competitor, C, and so there is an abusive margin squeeze, subject to any objective justification.

There may be other ways of addressing the pricing practices of the vertically-integrated entity AB. One is to inquire whether the input price charged by A to C is excessive; another is to determine whether the retail price charged by B is predatory. Both of these issues were explored earlier in this chapter. If A were to charge higher prices to C than it charges to B, there might be a case of discrimination contrary to Article 102(2)(c), which is discussed towards the end of this chapter. However the focus of this section is whether A is guilty of manipulating the relationship of its upstream and downstream prices in order to eliminate its downstream competitor by a margin squeeze. This possibility does not exist in US law[310].

(B) **EU law**

The Court of Justice has established that margin squeeze exists as an independent abuse in its own right[311]. In *Konkurrensverket v TeliaSonera Sverige*[312] the Court of Justice said that:

> A margin squeeze, in view of the exclusionary effect which it may create for competitors who are at least as efficient as the dominant undertaking, in the absence of any objective justification, is in itself capable of constituting an abuse within the meaning of Article 102 TFEU[313].

[310] See *Pacific Bell Telephone Co v linkLine Communications Inc* 555 US 438 (2009); for comment see the series of essays in the CPI Antitrust Chronicle April 9 (1), available at www.competitionpolicyinternational.com.

[311] See eg Case C-280/08 P *Deutsche Telekom AG v Commission* EU:C:2010:603, para 183 and subsequent cases discussed later.

[312] Case C-52/09 EU:C:2011:83.

[313] Ibid, para 31.

The case law establishes that, in determining whether a margin squeeze amounts to an abuse of a dominant position, five issues must be addressed.

- Is the accused undertaking operating on an upstream and a downstream market?
- Does the accused undertaking hold a dominant position in the upstream market?
- Do the dominant firm's upstream and downstream prices allow an undertaking as efficient as the dominant firm to compete on the downstream market?
- Is the margin squeeze capable of producing anti-competitive effects?
- Is there an objective justification for the margin squeeze?
- Each of these issues will be discussed in turn; then the Commission's decisional practice in relation to the abuse of margin squeeze will be reviewed.

(i) **Is the accused undertaking operating on an upstream and a downstream market?**

Margin squeeze cases involve vertically-integrated firms that operate both on an upstream market and a downstream market. For example in *Deutsche Telekom*[314] DT had a dominant position in relation to the so-called 'local loop', that is to say the final section of the telecommunications network that connects a customer's premises to the local switching point. DT also provided retail services, making use of the local loop, to its own customers: it was therefore vertically-integrated. Separately, DT made wholesale capacity on its local loop available to operators that would themselves like to provide retail services; however DT supplied that capacity at a price that squeezed the margin of its downstream competitors. The Commission therefore imposed a fine of €12.6 million on DT. The decision was upheld on appeal to the General Court[315] and to the Court of Justice[316].

(ii) **Does the accused undertaking hold a dominant position in the upstream market?**

Article 102 applies only where an undertaking has a dominant position: this would be in the upstream market in margin squeeze cases. It is not necessary to establish a dominant position on the downstream market as well[317].

(iii) **Do the dominant firm's upstream and downstream prices allow an undertaking as efficient as the dominant firm to compete on the downstream market?**

In *Deutsche Telekom v Commission*[318] the Court of Justice stated that a margin squeeze means that the dominant firm leaves an insufficient margin between the prices of its upstream and downstream products; and that it is this difference, rather than the specific level of the wholesale or retail price, that is the essence of the abuse[319]. The General Court and the Court of Justice upheld the Commission's finding that DT was guilty of an abusive margin squeeze in two ways: initially by charging retail prices that were less than DT's wholesale prices; and later by leaving an insufficient margin between its upstream and

314 OJ [2003] L 263/9. 315 Case T-271/03 *Deutsche Telekom AG v Commission* EU:T:2008:101.

316 Case C-280/08 P *Deutsche Telekom AG v Commission* EU:C:2010:603.

317 Case C-52/09 *Konkurrensverket v TeliaSonera Sverige* EU:C:2011:83, para 89; in a reference to the EFTA Court a court in Iceland has specifically asked whether a dominant undertaking accused of a margin squeeze in the telecommunications sector must be shown to be dominant in the downstream relevant retail market: Case E-6/17 *Fjarskipti hf v Síminn hf*, not yet decided.

318 Case C-280/08 P EU:C:2010:603. 319 Ibid, para 183.

downstream products[320]. The Court of Justice held that the approval of DT's wholesale prices by a national regulator did not absolve it of responsibility to comply with Article 102 where it had the scope to adjust its retail prices (by raising them) to end the margin squeeze[321].

In *TeliaSonera*[322] the Swedish competition authority had brought proceedings alleging that TeliaSonera was guilty of a margin squeeze in relation to retail broadband services. The Swedish court sought the opinion of the Court of Justice, under Article 267 TFEU, on the criteria for establishing an abusive margin squeeze. The Court repeated its formulation in *Deutsche Telekom* of the test of when a margin squeeze is an abuse[323]. The Court rejected the argument that a margin squeeze can be an abuse only if it also amounts to an abusive refusal to supply: such an approach would unduly reduce the effectiveness of Article 102[324]. The Court continued by saying that the following factors are generally not relevant when establishing whether a margin squeeze infringes Article 102:

- the absence of any regulatory obligation on the dominant firm to supply the upstream product[325]
- the degree of dominance held[326]
- the absence of a dominant position on the downstream market[327]
- whether the customers to whom the pricing practice is applied are new or existing customers[328]
- the inability to recoup losses[329]
- the fact that the markets involve new as opposed to established technology[330].

(iv) Is the margin squeeze capable of producing anti-competitive effects?

In *Telefónica v Commission*[331] the Court of Justice, referring to its earlier case law[332], stressed that Article 102 applies only to a margin squeeze that has exclusionary effects on competitors which are at least as efficient as the dominant firm[333]. The General Court was satisfied that Telefónica's margin squeezing had produced such effects in the retail market for broadband internet services[334]; Telefónica's appeal to the Court of Justice on this point was dismissed as partly inadmissible and partly unfounded[335].

(v) Is there an objective justification for the margin squeeze?

A margin squeeze will not be abusive if there is an objective justification for it: the burden of proof would be on the dominant firm[336]. The Commission has said that 'meeting

[320] Case T-271/03 EU:T:2008:101, upheld on appeal Case C-280/08 P EU:C:2010:603.

[321] Case C-280/08 P EU:C:2010:603, paras 77–96.

[322] Case C-52/09 EU:C:2011:83; when the case returned to Sweden the Stockholm District Court concluded that TeliaSonera was guilty of a margin squeeze and imposed a fine of SEK 144 million; the finding was upheld on appeal to the Market Court, but the fine was reduced to SEK 35 million: see www.marknadsdomstolen.se.

[323] Case C-52/09 EU:C:2011:83, paras 31–35.

[324] Ibid, paras 54–58; see similarly Case T-336/07 *Telefónica and Telefónica España v Commission* EU:T:2012:172, paras 180–181, upheld on appeal Case C-295/12 P EU:C:2914:2062, paras 75, 95, 118 and 150; this is a stricter approach than the one suggested in para 80 of the Commission's *Guidance on Article 102 Enforcement Priorities*: see 'The Commission's decisional practice', p 775 later in chapter.

[325] Case C-52/09 EU:C:2011:83, paras 47–59.

[326] Ibid, paras 78–82.

[327] Ibid, paras 83–89.

[328] Ibid, paras 90–95.

[329] Ibid, paras 96–103.

[330] Ibid, paras 104–111.

[331] Case C-295/12 P EU:C:2014:2062.

[332] Case C-52/09 *Konkurrensverket v TeliaSonera Sverige* EU:C:2011:83, paras 60–67 and case law cited.

[333] Case C-295/12 P EU:C:2014:2062, para 124.

[334] Case T-336/07 EU:T:2012:172, paras 275–276.

[335] *Telefónica* (ch 18 n 333 earlier), paras 116–125.

[336] See eg *Telefónica*, Commission decision of 4 July 2007, paras 619–664.

competition' does not legitimise a margin squeeze that enables a dominant firm to impose losses on its competitors that it does not incur itself[337].

(vi) The Commission's decisional practice

In its *Guidance on Article 102 Enforcement Priorities* the Commission discusses its approach to margin squeeze within the context of refusal to supply. Since the *Guidance* was issued, however, the Court of Justice has established that these practices are legally distinct: more specifically, as just noted, it has held that a price might amount to an abusive margin squeeze even where the dominant undertaking is not under a duty to deal. To put the point another way: the Court of Justice's view is that the dominant firm could decide not to supply the upstream product at all without violating Article 102; however, if it does choose to supply it, it must not do so at a price that would squeeze the margin of an equally-efficient competitor. The reader is reminded that the *Guidance* is an expression of the Commission's enforcement priorities rather than a set of guidelines on the law of Article 102[338]; it is ultimately for the Court of Justice to determine the substantive rules on margin squeeze.

Paragraph 80 of the Commission's *Guidance* says that it will generally rely on the LRAIC of the dominant firm's downstream operations to determine whether it has squeezed the margin available to an equally-efficient competitor. The Commission may use the LRAIC of a downstream competitor in cases where it is not possible to allocate the costs of a vertically-integrated dominant firm[339]; this is consistent with the approach envisaged in paragraph 45 of the Court of Justice's judgment in *TeliaSonera*.

The Commission has taken action in relation to margin squeezing in *Napier Brown-British Sugar*[340], *Deutsche Telekom*[341], *Telefónica*[342] and *Slovak Telekom*[343]. In *Slovak Telekom* that company was fined €38 million, but its parent, Deutsche Telekom, was fined an additional €31 million as it was a recidivist, having already been fined in the Commission's 2003 decision. In 2013 the Commission accepted commitments under Article 9 of Regulation 1/2003 from Deutsche Bahn that it would apply a new pricing tariff for the supply of traction current to downstream rail operators in Germany, thereby terminating a suspected margin squeeze[344].

[337] Ibid, para 638.

[338] See ch 5, 'The Commission's Article 102 Enforcement Priorities Guidance', pp 182–185.

[339] *Guidance on Article 102 Enforcement Priorities*, fn 55.

[340] *Napier Brown–British Sugar* OJ [1988] L 284/41; see also *National Carbonising* OJ [1976] L 35/6 under Article 66 of the former European Coal and Steel Community Treaty and the Commission's *Notice on the Application of the Competition Rules to Access Agreements in the Telecommunications Sector* OJ [1998] C 265/2, paras 117–119.

[341] OJ [2003] L 263/9, upheld on appeal to the General Court Case T-271/03 *Deutsche Telekom AG v Commission* EU:T:2008:101 and on further appeal to the Court of Justice Case C-280/08 P *Deutsche Telekom AG v Commission* EU:C:2010:603.

[342] Commission decision of 4 July 2007, imposing a fine of €151.8 million; see Le Meur, Gurpegui and Vierti 'Margin Squeeze in the Spanish Broadband Market: A Rational and Profitable Strategy' (2007) 3 Competition Policy Newsletter 22; the decision was upheld on appeal Case T-336/07 *Telefónica and Telefónica España v Commission* EU:T:2012:172, and on further appeal to the Court of Justice Case C-295/12 P EU:C:2014:2062; see also Case T-398/07 *Spain v Commission* EU:T:2012:173, a related appeal in the same case by the Spanish Government.

[343] Commission decision of 15 October 2014, imposing a fine of €69.9 million; see Commission Press Release IP/14/1140 and Commission MEMO/14/590 of the same date; the decision is on appeal to the General Court Case T-851/14 *Slovak Telekom v Commission*, not yet decided.

[344] Commission decision of 18 December 2013: the Commission released Deutsche Bahn from these commitments on 8 April 2016 as it was satisfied that there was now effective competition in the market; on commitment decisions see ch 7, 'Commitments', pp 264–269.

(C) **UK law**

There have been a number of complaints about margin squeezing in the UK, two of which were successful[345].

(i) **Findings of unlawful margin squeeze**

In *Genzyme*[346] a fine of £6.8 million was imposed on that company for abusing its dominant position in two ways, one of which was to have imposed a margin squeeze[347]. The finding of a margin squeeze was upheld on appeal to the CAT[348]. Genzyme was the producer of a drug, Cerezyme, used in the treatment of Gaucher's disease. Genzyme delivered the drug to patients in their homes; a competitor in the downstream market, Healthcare at Home, provided the same service. Genzyme was found guilty of squeezing the margin available to Healthcare at Home. Following protracted but unsuccessful negotiations as to the price that Genzyme should charge for Cerezyme in order to avoid a margin squeeze, the CAT handed down a judgment on remedy[349]. Subsequently Healthcare at Home brought a 'follow-on' action for damages in the CAT[350]. An award of interim damages was made, and the case was settled late in 2006[351]. OFWAT rejected a margin squeeze complaint against Anglian Water Services in December 2015 concluding that, in the case of water services, Independent Water Networks was not the victim of a squeeze and that, in the case of sewerage services, there was a margin squeeze but not one that was likely to have an adverse effect on competition[352].

In *Albion Water/Dŵr Cymru* the Court of Appeal[353] upheld a judgment of the CAT overturning a non-infringement decision by OFWAT[354], and finding that Dŵr Cymru was guilty of abusive margin squeezing[355].

(ii) **Rejections of complaints about margin squeezes**

A complaint about margin squeeze was rejected by the OFT in *Companies House*[356]. In *BSkyB*[357] the OFT investigated complaints that BSkyB was guilty of a margin squeeze by setting its wholesale prices for the provision of premium channels at a level that would mean that distributors with the same efficiency as BSkyB would have to operate at a loss[358]. Following an extensive economic analysis, the conclusion was reached that there were insufficient grounds for believing that there was an abusive margin squeeze.

[345] See also the CAT's discussion of the relevant law on margin squeeze in Case 1238/3/3/15 *British Telecommunications plc v OFCOM* [2016] CAT 3, paras 90–107.

[346] OFT decision of 27 March 2003. [347] Ibid, paras 364–385.

[348] Case 1016/1/1/03 *Genzyme Ltd v OFT* [2004] CAT 4; the CAT reviewed the case law at paras 489–493 of its judgment.

[349] Case 1016/1/1/03 *Genzyme Ltd v OFT* [2005] CAT 32.

[350] Case 1060/5/7/06 *Healthcare at Home v Genzyme Ltd* [2006] CAT 29.

[351] See the Order of the CAT of 11 January 2007.

[352] See *Fairfield Competition Act 1998 investigation decision summary*, available at www.ofwat.gov.uk.

[353] *Dŵr Cymru Cyfyngedig v Water Services Regulation Authority* [2008] EWCA Civ 536.

[354] OFWAT decision of 26 May 2004.

[355] Case 1046/2/4/04 *Albion Water Ltd v Water Services Regulation Authority* [2006] CAT 36, paras 896–919; see also the Interim Judgment of 22 December 2005 [2005] CAT 40, paras 385–419.

[356] OFT decision of 25 October 2002, paras 29–36.

[357] OFT decision of 17 December 2002.

[358] Ibid, paras 341–547.

The Office of Telecommunications, and its successor OFCOM, have investigated a number of cases of margin squeezing, and have always reached the conclusion that there was no abuse or no grounds for action[359]. In each case OFCOM concluded that, even if there was a margin squeeze, there was insufficient evidence of an anti-competitive effect. In *Investigation into BT's residential broadband pricing*[360] OFCOM conducted a detailed analysis of BT's financial performance and concluded that, while certain measures of profitability indicated that BT's margin on residential broadband products was negative during the relevant period, there was insufficient evidence of an abuse. OFCOM concluded that it had no grounds for action in respect of *BT's Wholesale calls pricing*[361] even though BT had earned a negative margin for ten months, since there was insufficient evidence of anti-competitive effects.

In *Electricity North West*[362] OFGEM accepted commitments to address concerns that that company had imposed a margin squeeze when charging for connections to its network.

8. Price Discrimination

This section considers the extent to which price discrimination may infringe Article 102 or the Chapter II prohibition of the Competition Act 1998[363]. The extent to which other types of discrimination, in particular on the grounds of nationality, might lead to an infringement of Article 102 is discussed in chapter 17 on non-pricing abuses[364].

(A) The meaning of price discrimination

Price discrimination may be defined as the sale or purchase of different units of a good or service at prices not directly corresponding to differences in the cost of supplying them. There can be discrimination both where different, non-cost-related prices are charged for the sale or purchase of goods or services of the same description and also where identical prices are charged in circumstances in which a difference in the cost of supplying them would justify their differentiation.

[359] *BT/UK-SPN*, OFTEL decision of 22 May 2003, paras 21–53; *Alleged anti-competitive practices by BT in relation to BTOpenworld's consumer broadband products*, OFCOM decision of 20 November 2003, paras 6.1–6.162; *Investigation against BT about potential anti-competitive behaviour*, OFCOM decision of 12 July 2004, paras 108–128; *BT 0845 and 0870 retail price change*, OFCOM decision of 19 August 2004, paras 3.24–3.100; *Suspected margin squeeze by Vodafone, O2, Orange and T-Mobile*, OFCOM decision of 26 May 2004, paras 148–178; *Complaint from Gamma Telecom against BT about reduced rates for Wholesale Calls from 1 December 2004*, OFCOM decision of 16 June 2005, paras 47–120; *NCCN 5000*, OFCOM decision of 1 August 2008, paras 6.8–6.219; *Complaint from THUS plc and Gamma Telecom Limited against BT about alleged margin squeeze in Wholesale Calls pricing*, OFCOM decision of 20 June 2013, sections 6–7; *Complaint from TalkTalk Telecom Group against BT*, OFCOM decision of 21 October 2014.

[360] OFCOM decision of 2 November 2010, section 4; an appeal to the CAT in Case 1026/2/3/04 *Wanadoo UK plc v OFCOM* which had been adjourned pending the adoption of this decision was subsequently withdrawn: see order of the CAT of 16 December 2010.

[361] OFCOM decision of 20 June 2013, paras 1.30–1.37.

[362] OFGEM decision of 24 May 2012.

[363] For further reading on price discrimination see Motta, Fumagalli and Calcagno *Exclusionary Practices—The Economics of Monopolisation and Abuse of Dominance* (Cambridge University Press, 2018), ch 2; Van den Bergh and Camesasca *European Competition Law and Economics: A Comparative Perspective* (Sweet & Maxwell, 2nd ed, 2006), pp 254–264; Bishop and Walker *The Economics of EC Competition Law* (Sweet & Maxwell, 3rd ed, 2010), paras 6-29–6-36; Niels, Jenkins and Kavanagh *Economics for Competition Lawyers* (Oxford University Press, 2nd ed, 2016), pp 181–189; O'Donoghue and Padilla *The Law and Economics of Article 102 TFEU* (Hart, 2nd ed, 2013), ch 15; Scherer and Ross *Industrial Market Structure and Economic Performance* (Houghton Mifflin, 3rd ed, 1990), ch 13.

[364] See ch 17, 'Non-Pricing Abuses That are Harmful to the Internal Market', pp 727–728.

There are many costs involved in supplying goods or services which may result in the charging of differentiated yet non-discriminatory prices. For example, apart from the cost of transporting goods, a manufacturer may incur heavier costs where it has to handle a series of small orders from a particular customer rather than a single, annual one. Orders for large quantities of goods may mean that a producer can plan long production runs and achieve economies of scale which lead to lower unit costs. The incidence of different contractual terms and conditions, payment of local taxes and duties, the different costs involved in operating distributorship networks from one area to another, may all explain the charging of different prices. However it can be difficult to determine whether differences in the cost of supplying goods or services justify, objectively, the charging of differentiated prices; and even more difficult to calculate the justifiable differentiation.

It is important to appreciate that price discrimination can be positively beneficial in terms of allocative efficiency, since it may result in an *increase* in output[365]: a theatre might be able to sell 80% of its tickets to the public at £40 each, or alternatively 100% of its tickets by charging 70% of its customers £50 and the remaining 30% £10 each (for example to impoverished students). Through such discrimination more theatre tickets will have been sold than would otherwise have been the case: resources have been more efficiently allocated. A specific example of efficient price discrimination is so-called 'Ramsey pricing'. This occurs where a company supplies different products which share common costs[366]. It may be that customers for product A are highly price sensitive, but that customers for product B are not; if customers for product B are charged high prices and customers for product A low ones—that is to say if prices are marked up in inverse proportion to customers' respective price sensitivities—output will be increased and economic efficiency will therefore be maximised. The principle of Ramsey pricing has been accepted by regulators and competition authorities in some sectors[367], although it was rejected in two UK investigations of call-termination charges in the mobile telephony sector[368].

In practice the allocative effects of discrimination will vary from one market situation to another: the question is ultimately an empirical rather than a theoretical one. There is no case for a *per se* prohibition of price discrimination, even on the part of a dominant firm. It may be that preventing discrimination has the effect of redistributing income from poorer consumers to richer ones[369]. This can be illustrated by imagining what might happen if discrimination is prevented. A producer may charge £10 per widget in a prosperous area and £5 per widget in a poorer one. If this discrimination is prevented the producer may sell at a uniform price of, say, £7 in both areas. It is reasonable to assume that as a result fewer people in the poorer area will buy widgets, and that those that do will pay a higher proportion of their income than those in the prosperous one. The net effect therefore is to transfer wealth from poorer consumers with the result that more prosperous ones will be better off.

[365] See eg Schmalensee 'Output and Welfare Implications of Third Degree Price Discrimination' (1981) 71 Am Ec Rev 242; Gifford and Kudrle 'The Law and Economics of Price Discrimination in Modern Economies: Time for Reconciliation?' (2010) 43 University of California Davis Law Review 1235.

[366] On the meaning of common costs see 'Avoidable costs', p 734 earlier in chapter.

[367] See Pflanz 'What Price is Right? Lessons from the UK Calls-to-Mobile Inquiry' (2000) 21 ECLR 147.

[368] Mobile phone charges inquiry Report of 18 February 2003, paras 2.213–2.215, available at www.gov.uk; the report was unsuccessfully challenged in *R v Competition Commission, Director General of Telecommunications, ex p T-Mobile (UK) Ltd, Vodafone Ltd, Orange Personal Communication Services Ltd* [2003] EWHC 1555 (Admin); *British Telecommunications plc v OFCOM*, Final Determination of 9 February 2012, para 2.527: an application for review of the determination was dismissed by the CAT [2012] CAT 11, upheld on appeal to the Court of Appeal [2012] EWCA Civ 154.

[369] See Bishop 'Price Discrimination under Article 86: Political Economy in the European Court' (1981) 44 MLR 282.

(B) EU law

Article 102(2)(c) specifically gives as an example of abuse:

> applying dissimilar conditions to equivalent transactions with other trading parties, thereby placing them at a competitive disadvantage.

Clearly therefore price discrimination may infringe Article 102; so too could other types of discrimination, such as refusals to supply and preferential terms and conditions[370]. However it is important to recognise that price discrimination is not, in and of itself, an exclusionary abuse, as the Court of Justice clearly stated in *Post Danmark I*[371].

Price discrimination may be exploitative of customers, for example where higher prices are charged to 'locked-in' customers unable to switch to alternative suppliers; it can also be harmful to the competitive process, where it leads to a distortion of competition in markets downstream of the dominant undertaking. The case law establishes that, in determining whether there is an infringement of Article 102(2)(c), five issues must be addressed.

- Does the accused undertaking have a dominant position?
- Has the dominant undertaking entered into equivalent transactions with other trading parties?
- Is the dominant undertaking guilty of applying dissimilar conditions to equivalent transactions?
- Could the discrimination place other trading parties at a competitive disadvantage?
- Is there an objective justification for the discrimination?

Each of these requirements will be considered in turn.

(i) Does the accused undertaking have a dominant position?

Clearly there can be an infringement of Article 102 only if an undertaking has a dominant position, and this would be in the upstream market; there is no need for the firm to be present, still less dominant, in the downstream market.

(ii) Has the dominant undertaking entered into equivalent transactions with other trading parties?

Article 102 does not require that all trading partners of a dominant undertaking must have the benefit of the same prices. According to the formulation in Article 102(2)(c) different treatment must be examined only where compared transactions are 'equivalent'. Factors to be considered in determining whether one transaction is equivalent with another include the nature of the product supplied and the costs of supply. In *United Brands v Commission*[372] the Court of Justice recognised that a dominant firm may charge different prices to reflect the different economic and competitive conditions in the different markets on which it operates[373]. In *Irish Sugar*[374] the Commission found that Irish Sugar had infringed Article 102(2)(c) in several ways, in particular by practising discrimination against sugar packers in Ireland. This part of the decision was upheld on appeal[375]: the General Court rejected the argument that Irish Sugar's dealings with sugar packers

[370] See Colomo 'Exclusionary Discrimination under Article 102 TFEU' (2014) 51 CML Rev 141.

[371] Case C-209/10 EU:C:2012:172, para 30.

[372] Case 27/76 EU:C:1978:22.

[373] Ibid, para 227.

[374] OJ [1997] L 258/1.

[375] Case T-228/97 *Irish Sugar plc v Commission* EU:T:1999:246, paras 125–149 (sugar export rebates to industrial customers) and 150–172 (higher prices charged to competing sugar packers).

were not comparable to those with its other customers[376]. In *Clearstream v Commission* the General Court confirmed the Commission's decision that there had been an infringement of Article 102(2)(c)[377]. The General Court considered that Clearstream had provided equivalent primary clearing and settlement services for cross-border transactions to two groups of comparable customers[378].

(iii) Is the dominant undertaking guilty of applying dissimilar conditions to equivalent transactions?

To amount to an abuse of a dominant position the dominant firm must have applied dissimilar conditions. In *Michelin I*[379] the Court of Justice quashed a finding of an infringement of Article 102(2)(c), as it was not satisfied that Michelin had applied dissimilar conditions[380]. In *Virgin/British Airways*[381] the Commission concluded that BA was not only guilty of abuse by offering travel agents loyalty rebates; there was discrimination contrary to Article 102(2)(c), since travel agents in the same circumstances received different levels of remuneration[382]. This finding was upheld on appeal to the General Court[383] and to the Court of Justice[384]. The General Court noted that BA's reward scheme led to different rates of commission being applied to an identical amount of revenue generated by the sale of BA tickets by two travel agents, and that this distorted the level of remuneration received by them[385]. The General Court agreed with the Commission's finding that BA's reward schemes were abusive:

> in that they produced discriminatory effects within the network of travel agents established in the UK, thereby inflicting on some of them a competitive disadvantage within the meaning of subparagraph (c) of the second paragraph of Article [102 TFEU][386].

In *Portuguese Airports*[387] the Commission adopted a decision establishing that Portugal had infringed Article 106 read in conjunction with Article 102 in respect of a system of discounts on landing charges at the airports of Lisbon, Oporto, Faro and the Azores. Discounts were offered to airlines according to the number of flights that landed at Portuguese airports. This discounting structure meant that Portuguese airlines enjoyed the highest discounts on their flights; airlines from beyond the Iberian peninsula received meagre discounts. On appeal the Court of Justice acknowledged that quantity discounts linked solely to the volume of purchases may be permissible, but said that the rules for calculating the discounts must not result in the application of dissimilar conditions to equivalent transactions contrary to Article 102(2)(c)[388]. It went on to say that:

> where, as a result of the thresholds of the various discount bands, and the levels of discount offered, discounts (or additional discounts) are enjoyed by only some trading parties, giving them an economic advantage which is not justified by the volume of business

[376] Ibid, para 164. [377] Case T-301/04 *Clearstream Banking AG v Commission* EU:T:2009:317.
[378] Ibid, paras 169–190. [379] OJ [1981] L 353/33. [380] Case 322/81 EU:C:1983:313, paras 87–91.
[381] OJ [2000] L 30/1. [382] Ibid, paras 108–111.
[383] Case T-219/99 *British Airways plc v Commission* EU:T:2003:343, paras 233–240.
[384] Case C-95/04 P *British Airways plc v Commission* EU:C:2007:166, paras 133–141.
[385] Case T-219/99 *British Airways plc v Commission* EU:T:2003:343, paras 235–236.
[386] Ibid, para 240.
[387] OJ [1999] L 69/31, paras 24–40; Article 102(2)(c) has been applied to discriminatory practices at a number of EU airports: see eg *Alpha Flight Services/Aéroports de Paris* OJ [1998] L 230/10, upheld on appeal Case T-128/98 EU:T:2000:290, and on further appeal to the Court of Justice Case C-82/01 P EU:C:2002:617; *Brussels National Airport (Zaventem)* OJ [1995] L 216/8, paras 12–18; *Ilmailulaitos/Luftfartsverket* OJ [1999] L 69/24, paras 38–56; *Spanish Airports* OJ [2000] L 208/36, paras 45–56.
[388] Case C-163/99 *Portugal v Commission* EU:C:2001:189, para 50.

> they bring or by any economies of scale they allow the supplier to make compared with their competitors, a system of quantity discounts leads to the application of dissimilar conditions to equivalent transactions.
>
> In the absence of any objective justification, having a high threshold in the system which can only be met by a few particularly large partners of the undertaking occupying a dominant position, or the absence of linear progression in the increase of the quantity discounts, may constitute evidence of such discriminatory treatment[389].

The Court of Justice noted that the highest discount rate was enjoyed only by the two Portuguese airlines, that the discount rate was greatest for the highest band and that the airports concerned enjoyed a natural monopoly; it concluded that in these circumstances the discounts were discriminatory[390].

In *Ryanair/DAA-Aer Lingus*[391] the Commission rejected a complaint by Ryanair that Dublin Airport was guilty of discrimination since it had not applied dissimilar conditions[392]; the fact that the services used and charges paid did not 'match perfectly' the needs of each airline did not in itself make the charges abusive[393].

(iv) Could the discrimination place other trading parties at a competitive disadvantage?

The wording of Article 102(2)(c) specifically requires that one component of the abuse is the infliction of 'competitive disadvantage'[394]. In some cases little attention was given to this issue. In *Corsica Ferries*[395] the Court of Justice said that Article 102(2)(c) applied to 'dissimilar conditions to equivalent transactions with trading partners', without mentioning the requirement of competitive disadvantage at all[396]. In the Commission's decisions on EU airports[397] scant attention was given to the need for competitive disadvantage. The same was true in *Deutsche Post AG—Interception of cross-border mail*[398]. It may be that this element of the offence will be applied in a particularly liberal manner where, as in those decisions and as in *Corsica Ferries*, the discrimination is practised on national lines, to the detriment (though not the competitive disadvantage) of undertakings in other Member States.

In *British Airways v Commission*[399] the Court of Justice gave some consideration to the requirement of competitive disadvantage in Article 102(2)(c)[400]. It was explicit that it is necessary in a case under this provision to show that competition is distorted: the distortion may be between the suppliers or between the customers of the dominant undertaking[401]. There must be a finding that the discriminatory behaviour:

> tends to distort that competitive relationship, in other words to hinder the competitive position of some of the business partners of that undertaking in relation to others[402].

The Court held that it is sufficient that the behaviour 'tends' to distort competition; there is no need to show an actual quantifiable deterioration in the competitive position of the business partners taken individually[403]. The Court of Justice concluded that the General Court had sufficiently satisfied itself that the test of Article 102(2)(c) was met[404].

389 Ibid, paras 52–53. 390 Ibid, paras 54–57. 391 Commission decision of 17 October 2013.
392 Ibid, paras 90–110. 393 Ibid, para 108.
394 See Case 85/76 *Hoffmann-La Roche v Commission* EU:C:1979:36 (specifically finding competitive disadvantage).
395 Case C-18/93 *Corsica Ferries Italia Srl v Corporazione dei Piloti del Porto di Genova* EU:C:1994:195.
396 Ibid, para 43. 397 See ch 18 n 387 earlier. 398 OJ [2001] L 331/40, paras 121–134.
399 Case C-95/04 P *British Airways plc v Commission* EU:C:2007:166. 400 Ibid, paras 142–148.
401 Ibid, para 143. 402 Ibid, para 144. 403 Ibid, para 145.
404 Ibid, paras 146–148; see also paras 104–112 of the Opinion of AG Kokott in Case C-109/10 P *Solvay SA v Commission* EU:C:2011:256 which criticised the General Court for failing to analyse the competitive relationships between Solvay's customers; the Court of Justice set aside the General Court's judgment for procedural reasons.

In *Clearstream v Commission*[405] the General Court concluded that the discrimination against a trading partner continuously over a period of five years 'could not fail' to cause that partner a competitive disadvantage[406].

In MEO the Portuguese NCA decided it had no grounds for action against a Portuguese copyright collecting society that charged MEO a different price to another television company for an equivalent service. In an Article 267 reference[407] the Court of Justice held that the mere fact that one company had to pay more than another did not mean that competition is distorted. It is necessary to examine all the relevant circumstances of the case to establish a competitive disadvantage, such that the discriminatory price 'has an effect on the costs, profits or any other relevant interest' of a trading partner compared with its competitors.

(v) Is there an objective justification for the discrimination?

A dominant firm may be able successfully to argue that discrimination is objectively justified or enhances efficiency. As already noted, differential pricing may increase a dominant firm's output and enable customers to obtain a product which they might not otherwise be able to afford. In *Portugal v Commission* Portugal failed to show any objective justification for its discriminatory discounts[408].

(C) UK law

In *BT/BSkyB broadband promotion*[409] OFTEL concluded that any discrimination in relation to the promotion of BT's broadband services did not have a material effect on competition, and in *BT TotalCare*[410] OFTEL rejected an allegation that BT had been guilty of discrimination in relation to the provision of certain broadband services.

In *English Welsh & Scottish Railway*[411] the Office of Rail Regulation ('the ORR') found that EW&S had abused its dominant position in several ways, including by discriminating between customers[412].

In *Purple Parking v Heathrow Airport*[413] the High Court concluded that Heathrow Airport was guilty of abusive discrimination in relation to the provision by it of access to the forecourts of Terminals 1, 3 and 5. In *Arriva The Shires v Luton Airport*[414] the High Court held that the terms of a concession granted by Luton Airport unlawfully discriminated in favour of one coach operator over another.

OFCOM has sent a statement of objections to Royal Mail accusing it of infringing competition law by treating a customer, Whistl UK, in a discriminatory manner contrary to Article 102(2)(c) TFEU and section 18(2)(c) of the Competition Act: as at 8 December 2017 the case was continuing[415].

[405] Case T-301/04 EU:T:2009:317. [406] Ibid, para 194.

[407] Case C-525/16 *MEO v Autoridade da Concorrência* EU:C:2018:270, paras 26, 28 and 37; at para 31 the Court cited *Intel* (ch 18 n 117 earlier) for the circumstances that are relevant for identifying a competitive disadvantage.

[408] Case C-163/99 EU:C:2001:189, paras 67–78. [409] OFTEL decision of 19 May 2003.

[410] OFTEL decision of 10 June 2003. [411] ORR decision of 17 November 2006.

[412] See Part IIB of the decision.

[413] [2011] EWHC 987 (Ch), paras 132–141 (dissimilar conditions to equivalent transactions), 145–167 (competitive disadvantage) and 179–241 (no objective justification).

[414] [2014] EWHC 64 (Ch), paras 124–130.

[415] See OFCOM Update note 28 July 2015, available at www.ofcom.org.uk.

9. Pricing Practices that are Harmful to the Single Market

The Commission and the EU Courts will condemn pricing practices on the part of dominant firms that are harmful to the single market[416]. High prices that are charged in order to prevent parallel imports will infringe Article 102.

(A) Excessive pricing that impedes parallel imports and exports

In *BL*[417] the Commission condemned that firm for charging £150 to any importer of BL cars from the continent requiring a type-approval certificate to enable the cars to be driven in the UK. The purpose of the excessive pricing was not to exploit a monopoly situation by earning excessive profits, but to impede parallel imports into the UK: the Commission's action was motivated by single-market considerations, and not by a desire to establish itself as a price regulator; the circumstances in *General Motors* were the same[418]. The Commission's decision in *BL* was upheld on appeal by the Court of Justice, which accepted that the price charged by BL was disproportionate to the value of the service provided[419]. In *Deutsche Post AG—Interception of cross-border mail*[420] the Commission decided that, by charging an excessive amount for the onward transmission of cross-border mail, Deutsche Post was preventing users of the mail system from taking advantage of the developing single market for postal services.

(B) Geographic price discrimination

In *United Brands v Commission*[421] the Court of Justice held that UBC had abused its dominant position by charging different prices for its bananas according to the Member State of their destination. It sold bananas to distributors/ripeners at Rotterdam and Bremerhaven, and charged the lowest price for bananas destined for Ireland and the highest for those going to West Germany. The different prices were not based on differences in costs: in fact transport to Ireland, for which UBC itself paid, cost more than to other countries so that, if anything, prices should have been higher there. UBC was also condemned for including clauses in contracts with distributors which had the effect of preventing parallel imports from one country to another by prohibiting the export of unripened bananas[422].

The decision is curious[423]. UBC claimed that it was being required to achieve a common market by adopting a uniform pricing policy for all Member States and that this was an unreasonable requirement on the part of the Commission. The Court of Justice retorted that it was permissible for a supplier to charge whatever local conditions of supply and demand dictate, that is to say that there is no obligation to charge a uniform price throughout the EU. However it added that the equation of supply with demand could be taken into account only at the level of the market at which a supplier operates. In *United Brands* this would mean that only a retailer in a given Member State could consider what

[416] See eg Case 7/82 *GVL v Commission* EU:C:1983:52.

[417] OJ [1984] L 207/11.

[418] OJ [1975] L 29/14, annulled on appeal for want of evidence in Case 26/75 *General Motors v Commission* EU:C:1975:150.

[419] Case 226/84 EU:C:1986:421.

[420] OJ [2001] L 331/40.

[421] Case 27/76 EU:C:1978:22.

[422] See ch 17, 'Non-Pricing Abuses That are Harmful to the Internal Market', pp 727–728.

[423] For criticism see Bishop 'Price Discrimination under Article 86: Political Economy in the European Court' (1981) 44 MLR 282; Zanon 'Price Discrimination under Article 86 of the EEC Treaty: the *United Brands* Case' (1982) 31 ICLQ 36.

price the market could bear; UBC could not do so since it did not sell bananas at retail level in Member States: it supplied distributors/ripeners at Rotterdam and Bremerhaven. In the Court of Justice's view, therefore, UBC was entitled to take into account local market conditions only 'to a limited extent'. The reasoning has been questioned: supply and demand at retail level would inevitably exert a backward influence on UBC, and anyway it, rather than retailers, employed the staff who carried out market research and monitored the level of demand throughout the EU. A different criticism of the judgment is that it could have undesirable redistributive effects. The logical response of UBC would be to charge a uniform price higher than that in Ireland but lower than that in Germany; this would benefit the Germans at the expense of the Irish. It is therefore arguable that the discrimination in *United Brands* should not have been condemned; the practice that was rightly found to be abusive was the prohibition on the export of unripened (green) bananas, since this is what had the effect of harming the single market. In the absence of this practice, bananas could have moved from low- to high-priced parts of the EU.

The Commission also condemned geographical price discrimination in *Tetra Pak II*[424]. The Commission concluded that the relevant geographic market was the EU as a whole, and yet Tetra Pak had charged prices that varied considerably from one Member State to another. The Commission said that the price differences could not be explained in economic terms and lacked objective justification. They were possible because of Tetra Pak's policy of market compartmentalisation which it maintained by virtue of its other abusive practices.

(C) Rebates that impede imports and exports

The Commission will condemn rebates and similar practices which have the effect of impeding imports and exports. Pricing practices that were intended to dissuade customers from importing from other Member States were held to be abusive in *Plasterboard*[425] and in *Michelin II*[426]. The Commission's decision in *Irish Sugar*[427] was prompted by single market considerations. Irish Sugar had a share of the Irish sugar market in excess of 90% and was found to have acted abusively by seeking to restrict competition from other Member States. In particular Irish Sugar was found to have offered selectively low prices to customers of an importer of French sugar and to have offered 'border rebates' to customers close to the border with Northern Ireland and who were therefore in a position to purchase cheaper sugar from the UK. On appeal the General Court annulled the former finding[428], but agreed that the border rebates were unlawful[429]. The General Court stressed the importance of the competitive influence on one national market from neighbouring markets, the very essence of an internal market[430].

[424] OJ [1992] L 72/1, paras 154, 155 and 160, upheld on appeal Case T-83/91 *Tetra Pak International SA v Commission* EU:T:1994:246, upheld on further appeal Case C-333/94 P *Tetra Pak International SA v Commission* EU:C:1996:436.

[425] Case T-65/89 *BPB Industries plc and British Gypsum v Commission* EU:T:1993:31, paras 117–122.

[426] OJ [2002] L 143/1, paras 240–247, 271 and 312–314.

[427] OJ [1997] L 258/1.

[428] Case T-228/97 *Irish Sugar v Commission* EU:T:1999:246, paras 117–124.

[429] Ibid, paras 173–193.

[430] Ibid, para 185.

19

The relationship between intellectual property rights and competition law

This chapter considers the relationship between intellectual property rights and competition law. After a brief introduction, section 2 will discuss the application of Article 101 to licences of intellectual property rights; section 3 will examine the provisions of Regulation 316/2014[1], the block exemption for technology transfer agreements. Section 4 will consider the application of Article 101 to various other agreements concerning intellectual property rights such as technology pools and settlements of litigation. This will be followed by a section on the application of Article 102 to the way in which dominant undertakings exercise their intellectual property rights, including an examination of the controversial subject of refusals to license intellectual property rights. Section 6 of this chapter will look at the position in UK law.

1. Introduction

(A) Definitions

It is not possible to deal with the substantive law of intellectual property here in detail[2]. For present purposes the term 'intellectual property' includes patents, registered and

[1] OJ [2014] L 93/17.

[2] For a general account of the law see Cornish, Llewellyn and Aplin *Intellectual Property: Patents, Copyrights, Trademarks and Allied Rights* (Sweet & Maxwell, 8th ed, 2013); Bently and Sherman *Intellectual Property Law* (Oxford University Press, 4th ed, 2014); Jacob, Alexander and Fisher *Guidebook to Intellectual Property* (Hart, 2014); Torremans and Holyoak *Intellectual Property Law* (Oxford University Press, 8th ed, 2016); for specific discussion of the relationship between intellectual property rights and EU competition law see Korah *Intellectual Property Rights and the EC Competition Rules* (Hart, 2006); Ehlermann and Atanasiu (eds) *European Competition Law Annual: The Interaction between Competition Law and Intellectual Property Law* (Hart, 2007); Anderman (ed) *The Interface Between Intellectual Property Rights and Competition Policy* (Cambridge University Press, 2007); Stothers *Parallel Trade in Europe: Intellectual*

unregistered designs, copyrights including computer software, trade marks and analogous rights such as plant breeders' rights. It should also be taken to include know-how, defined for the purpose of the block exemption on technology transfer agreements as 'a package of practical information, resulting from experience and testing': such information must be secret, substantial and identified in a sufficiently comprehensive manner that it is possible to verify that it is secret and substantial[3]; although not strictly speaking an intellectual property right[4], know-how may be extremely valuable and may be sold or 'licensed' for considerable amounts of money.

(B) **Intellectual property rights and the single market**

Generally speaking intellectual property rights are the product of, and are protected by, national systems of law. However, the growth of international commerce has resulted in an increasing measure of international cooperation, such as the Patent Cooperation Treaty[5]. The existence of different national laws on intellectual property presents particular difficulties in the EU in so far as this is detrimental to the goal of single market integration. Much of this chapter is concerned with the problem that intellectual property rights may be used in a way that compartmentalises the internal market. While the Treaties do not affect the existence of intellectual property rights, there are circumstances in which the exercise of such rights may be restricted by EU law[6]. This may be the case whenever the exercise of such rights appears to be the object, the means or the consequence of an agreement[7].

The Court of Justice developed the 'exhaustion of rights' doctrine to prevent an undertaking that has consented to the sale of goods on the market within the EU from using a national intellectual property right to prevent the free movement of those goods around the EU[8]; the doctrine does not apply to goods placed on the market outside the EU[9]. Article 118(1) TFEU provides for the creation of EU intellectual property rights by the European Parliament and the Council. Various harmonisation measures have been adopted to reduce the differences between different national

Property, Competition and Regulatory Law (Hart, 2007); Oliver (ed) *Oliver on Free Movement of Goods in the European Union* (Hart, 5th ed, 2010); Leslie *Antitrust Law and Intellectual Property Rights: Cases and Materials* (Oxford University Press, 2010); Ghidini *Innovation, Competition and Consumer Welfare in Intellectual Property Law* (Edward Elgar, 2010); Anderman and Schmidt *EU Competition Law and Intellectual Property Rights: The Regulation of Innovation* (Oxford University Press, 2nd ed, 2011); Käseberg *Intellectual Property, Antitrust and Cumulative Innovation in the EU and the US* (Hart, 2012); Rose and Bailey (eds) *Bellamy and Child: European Union Law of Competition* (Oxford University Press, 7th ed, 2013), ch 9; Tritton *Intellectual Property in Europe* (Sweet & Maxwell, 4th ed, 2014); Faull and Nikpay (eds) *The EU Law of Competition* (Oxford University Press, 3rd ed, 2014), ch 10; Turner *Intellectual Property and EU Competition Law* (Oxford University Press, 2nd ed, 2015); Hemphill 'Intellectual Property and Competition Law' in Dreyfuss and Pila (eds) *Oxford Handbook of Intellectual Property Law* (Oxford University Press, 2017).

[3] Regulation 316/2014, Article 1(1)(i); the Regulation is considered at 'Technology Transfer Agreements: Regulation 316/2014', pp 798–799 later in chapter.

[4] Know-how is protected by the law of obligations: see generally on confidential information *Cornish, Llewellyn and Aplin*, ch 8.

[5] See www.wipo.int/pct/en; see further *Cornish, Llewellyn and Aplin*, paras 1.30–1.34.

[6] See eg Case 78/70 *Deutsche Grammophon v Metro* EU:C:1971:59, para 11.

[7] Case T-472/13 *Lundbeck v Commission* EU:T:2016:449, para 486 and case law cited.

[8] See Coates, Kyølbye and Peeperkorn in Faull and Nikpay (eds) *The EU Law of Competition* (Oxford University Press, 3rd ed, 2014), paras 10.36–10.58.

[9] Ibid, paras 10.51–10.55.

systems of law[10]. The 'European Union Trade Mark' Regulation[11] enables a single, EU-wide trade mark to be granted; the 'Community Designs' Regulation makes similar provision for designs[12]. There are also two Regulations creating a European patent with 'unitary effect'[13] and an Agreement to set up a Unified Patent Court[14]; these provisions are not yet in effect: if the Agreement is ratified, they will enable a single unitary patent to be enforced in one court throughout most of the EU[15]. The Commission has also made proposals to modernise EU legislation on copyright for online content as part of its Digital Single Market Strategy[16].

(C) Is there an inevitable tension between intellectual property rights and competition law?

The essential characteristic of intellectual property rights is that they confer upon their owners an exclusive right to behave in a particular way. For example the UK Patents Act 1977 grants the owner of a patent the right to prevent others from producing the patented goods or applying the patented process for a period of 20 years; patents may be granted where the invention is novel, involves an 'inventive step' and is capable of industrial application[17]. A patent does not necessarily make the patentee a monopolist in an economic sense: there may be other products that compete with the subject-matter of the patent; however the General Court has pointed out that the possession of an exclusive right 'normally results in keeping competitors away, since public regulations require them to respect that exclusive right'[18].

Because intellectual property rights confer exclusive rights upon their owners on the one hand, whereas competition law strives to keep markets open on the other, it is easy to suppose that there is an inherent tension between these two areas of law and policy[19]. However it is generally accepted that this is simplistic and wrong[20]. As paragraph 7 of the

[10] See eg the Directives on computer software, Directive 2009/24, OJ [2009] L 111/16; on rental rights, Directive 2006/115, OJ [2006] L 376/28; on the duration of copyright, Directive 2006/116, OJ [2006] L 372/12, as amended by Directive 2011/77, [2011] L 265/1; on satellite broadcasting and cable transmissions, Directive 93/83, OJ [1993] L 248/15; on databases, Directive 96/9, OJ [1996] L 77/20; on biotechnology, Directive 98/44, OJ [1998] L 213/3; on designs, Directive 98/71, OJ [1998] L 289/28; on copyright and related rights, Directive 2001/29, OJ [2001] L 167/10; on orphan works, Directive 2012/28, OJ L 299/5.

[11] Regulation 2017/1001, OJ [2017] L 154/1, which entered into force on 1 October 2017.

[12] Regulation 6/2002, OJ [2002] L 3/1.

[13] Regulation 1257/2012, OJ [2012] L 361/1 and Regulation 1260/2012, OJ [2012] L 361/89; on the power to create unitary patent protection see Cases C-274/11 etc *Spain and Italy v Council* EU:C:2013:240.

[14] EU Doc 16351/12; see www.unified-patent-court.org.

[15] See www.ec.europa.eu/growth/industry/intellectual-property/patents/unitary-patent_en.

[16] See www.ec.europa.eu/digital-single-market/en/policies/copyright.

[17] Article 52(1) European Patent Convention; on the law of patents see *Cornish, Llewellyn and Aplin*, chs 3–7.

[18] Case T-321/05 *AstraZeneca AB v Commission* EU:T:2010:266, para 362.

[19] For general discussion of the relationship between intellectual property and competition law and policy see the publications cited in ch 19 n 2 earlier.

[20] See eg Tom and Newberg 'Antitrust and Intellectual Property: From Separate Spheres to Unified Field' (1997–98) 66 Antitrust LJ 167 on the 'marked reduction in antitrust hostility toward intellectual property' in the US in the previous 50 years; see also *Report for the European Commission on Multi-Party Licensing* (Charles River Associates, April 2003), pp 58–59; Kovacic and Reindl 'An Interdisciplinary Approach to Improving Competition Policy and Intellectual Property Policy' (2005) 28 Fordham International Law Journal 1062; Lianos 'Competition Law and Intellectual Property Rights: Is the Property Rights' Approach Right?' in Bell and Kilpatrick (eds) *Cambridge Yearbook of European Legal Studies* (Hart, 2006); Hovenkamp, Janis, Lemley and Leslie *IP and Antitrust: An Analysis of Antitrust Principles Applied to Intellectual Property Law* (Wolters Kluwer, 2nd ed, 2010); Jacob 'Competition Authorities Support Grasshoppers: Competition Law as a Threat to Innovation' (2013) 9 Competition Policy International 15.

European Commission's *Guidelines on the application of Article 101 of the Treaty on the Functioning of the European Union to technology transfer agreements*[21] ('the *Technology Transfer Guidelines*' or 'the *Guidelines*') says:

> Indeed, both bodies of law share the same basic objective of promoting consumer welfare and an efficient allocation of resources. Innovation constitutes an essential and dynamic component of an open and competitive market economy.

Similarly, the US Department of Justice and the Federal Trade Commission have recognised that 'intellectual property and antitrust laws work in tandem to bring new and better technologies, products, and services to consumers at lower prices'[22]. Commissioner Vestager has said that competition law can 'complement intellectual property law in situations where the way that intellectual property law is exercised may fall short of promoting consumer welfare'[23]. It is a difficult and delicate matter to determine at what point, if at all, the exercise of an intellectual property right could be so harmful to consumer welfare that competition law should override the position as it would be on the basis of intellectual property law alone.

2. Licences of Intellectual Property Rights: Article 101

(A) Introduction

A patentee may decide, instead of producing the patented goods or applying the patented process itself, to grant a licence to another firm enabling it to do so. The same may be true of any other intellectual property right. There are many reasons why a firm may choose to grant a licence. A patentee may lack the resources to produce in quantity; it may wish to limit its own production to a particular geographical area and to grant licences for other territories; or it may wish to apply a patented process for one purpose and to allow licensees to use it for others. A patentee may wish to impose various restrictions upon its licensees, for example as to the quantity or quality of goods that may be produced or the price at which they may be sold; these provisions relate to the patentee's own products and so can be restrictive only of 'intra-technology competition'[24].

The argument for controlling restrictions of intra-technology competition in patent licences is weak. Given that a patentee has an exclusive right to produce and sell the patented goods, it is not obvious why it should not be able to impose whatever restrictions it chooses upon its licensees; the ability to do so is a manifestation of the rights conferred by the law. Indeed the grant of a licence can be seen as increasing competition, by introducing a licensee onto the market which, without the licence, would not be there at all[25]; the block exemption on technology transfer agreements[26] and the *Technology Transfer Guidelines* recognise that licences 'will usually improve economic efficiency and be pro-competitive'[27]. Even if the patentee imposes restrictions of intra-technology competition,

[21] OJ [2014] C 89/3.

[22] *Antitrust Enforcement and Intellectual Property Rights: Promoting Innovation and Competition* (April 2007); see also *To Promote Innovation: The Proper Balance of Competition and Patent Law and Policy* (October 2003) and *The Evolving IP Marketplace: Aligning Patent Notice and Remedies with Competition* (March 2011), all available at www.ftc.gov.

[23] See speech by Margrethe Vestager of 11 September 2015, available at www.ec.europa.eu.

[24] For discussion of this expression see the *Technology Transfer Guidelines*, paras 11–12.

[25] The Commission expressed this view in its *Notice on Patent Licensing Agreements* JO [1962] 2922; this *Notice* was withdrawn in 1984, OJ [1984] C 220/14.

[26] Recital 4 of Regulation 316/2014, OJ [2014] L 93/17.

[27] *Technology Transfer Guidelines*, paras 8, 9, 17 and 156ff.

these are likely to be compensated for by the stimulation of competition between undertakings using competing technologies—so-called 'inter-technology competition'.

Article 101(1) has been applied to intra-technology restrictions in patent (and other) licences, in particular where they divide national markets: the 'single market imperative' is as influential in this area of EU competition law as it is elsewhere[28]. The *Guidelines* refer to intra-technology competition as an 'important complement' to inter-technology competition, since it may lead to lower prices for the products incorporating the licensed technology[29]. Some terms in patent licences may affect inter-technology competition: examples are tie-in clauses requiring a licensee to acquire particular technology or products solely from the patentee and non-competition clauses forbidding the licensee to compete or to handle technology or products which compete with the patentee's: provisions such as these may foreclose the opportunities of other producers. Objection might also be taken to terms that seek to extend a patentee's rights beyond the protection afforded to it by the law.

(B) **Typical terms in licences of intellectual property rights**

It will facilitate an understanding of EU law on licensing agreements to have some knowledge of typical clauses that may be found in them. In the absence of legal controls it would be a matter for the parties to the agreement to settle the terms of the licence through the bargaining process. It would be wrong to assume that it is always the patentee that is in the more powerful bargaining position: a patentee may be an individual inventor and his prospective licensee a powerful company, in which case the former's position may be weak.

(i) **Territorial exclusivity**

A licensee may consider that the risk involved in exploitation of a patent is that the high level of capital investment required is so great that it would not be worth taking a licence at all unless it is given immunity from intra-technology competition from the licensor, other licensees and their customers[30]: these issues have been discussed already in relation to vertical agreements[31]. A licensee will often be taking a greater risk than a 'mere' distributor, since it has to invest in production as well as distribution, and so may require more protection against free riders than a distributor needs. The extent of the exclusivity required will be a calculation for the licensee; the amount actually given, apart from any limiting legal constraints, will be a matter for bargaining between the licensor and licensee[32].

The licensor could grant to the licensee an exclusive right to manufacture and sell the goods in a particular territory and agree to refrain from granting similar rights to anyone else there; in this situation the licensor retains the right to produce the goods in the territory itself: this is known as a 'sole' licence. A sole licence may be distinguished from an 'exclusive' licence, where the licensor also agrees not to produce the goods in the licensee's territory itself; this gives the licensee more protection than in the case of a sole licence. The licensee's position may be further reinforced by the licensor agreeing to impose export bans on its other licensees preventing them, or requiring them to prevent their customers, from selling into the licensed territory. Apart from imposing export bans, there are indirect ways of achieving the same end: for example a maximum quantities clause can limit the amount that a licensee can produce to the anticipated level of demand on its domestic market.

[28] See ch 1, 'The single market imperative', pp 23–24 and ch 2, 'The single market imperative', pp 52–53.

[29] *Technology Transfer Guidelines*, para 27.

[30] Ibid, para 8.

[31] See ch 16, 'Vertical agreements: possible benefits to competition', pp 640–642.

[32] See further the *Technology Transfer Guidelines*, paras 189–203.

Territorial exclusivity is important not only in the world of bricks and mortar but also in the digital economy, and may be achieved, for example, by 'geo-blocking' in one Member State the viewing online of films and video games obtained in another one[33]. It would be undesirable for the law to intervene and to ban exclusivity if the result would be to deter firms from accepting licences to exploit new technology. As we shall see, the mere grant of territorial exclusivity in a licence of an intellectual property right does *not* necessarily infringe Article 101(1); this will depend on the effect that this would have on the market. However, given the imperative of single market integration, where a licensor grants a licensee absolute territorial protection against any form of intra-technology competition there will almost certainly be an infringement of Article 101(1) and it is unlikely that the terms of Article 101(3) will be satisfied.

(ii) Royalties

A licensor will usually require the licensee to pay royalties for use of the patent[34]. The parties are generally free to determine the royalty payable and the mode of payment without transgressing Article 101(1). The licensee may be required to make lump-sum payments, and in some situations the parties may agree upon a profit-sharing scheme. The licensor may ask for a payment 'up-front' before production begins. A licensor may stipulate that the licensee must pay a royalty for the use of a technology that is no longer covered by a patent; this is permissible under Article 101(1) provided that the licensee is free to terminate the licence[35].

(iii) Duration

A licensor will specify what the duration of the agreement should be. It may decide to grant only a limited licence which will expire before the patent itself, after which it can reconsider its position. On the other hand the licence may continue after the patent has expired, for example by requiring the licensee to continue to pay royalties or to take licences of newly discovered technology; such provisions may be seen as an unwarranted extension of the rights conferred by the patent.

(iv) Field of use restrictions

A common clause is a 'field of use' restriction whereby a licensor limits the licensee's authority to produce goods to a particular purpose: a chemical protected by a patent may be useful both medicinally and industrially and the licensee could be limited to production for one purpose only[36]. Field of use clauses are normally seen as a reasonable exploitation of the patentee's position, although the restriction may infringe Article 101 where it partitions the single market[37].

(v) Best endeavours and non-competition clauses

To ensure that the licensee exploits the patent (and that the patentee receives adequate royalties) the licensee may be required to produce minimum quantities or to use its best endeavours to do so[38]. A non-competition clause, whereby the licensee is forbidden to

[33] See the European Commission's Final Report on the E-commerce Sector Inquiry, 10 May 2017, SWD(2017) 154 final, available at www.ec.europa.eu.

[34] *Technology Transfer Guidelines*, paras 184–188.

[35] Case C-567/14 *Genentech Inc v Hoechst and Sanofi-Aventis Deutschland* EU:C:2016:526, para 39 and case law cited.

[36] *Technology Transfer Guidelines*, paras 208–215.

[37] See *Windsurfing International* OJ [1983] L 229/1, substantially upheld on appeal Case 193/83 *Windsurfing International Inc v Commission* EU:C:1986:75.

[38] See *Technology Transfer Guidelines*, paras 226–233.

compete by using its own or rival technology, may encourage it to concentrate on producing the patented goods. Article 101(1) may apply to such a clause if it has an anti-competitive foreclosure effect.

(vi) No-challenge clauses

The licensor may insist upon a no-challenge clause whereby the licensee agrees not to challenge the validity of the intellectual property right in question[39]. A licensee with intimate knowledge of, say, a patented process may be in the best position to show that it lacks originality, and a licensor may be unwilling to grant a licence at all if it knows that the licensee might undermine its position by successfully applying for the patent to be revoked[40].

(vii) Improvements

A licensor may be fearful that the licensee will build upon the knowledge that becomes available from using the patent and emerge as a strong competitor; it may therefore require the licensee to grant back to it any know-how or intellectual property rights acquired and not to grant licences to anyone else[41]. Objection may be taken to this practice if the licensor requires the licensee to grant it exclusive access to such know-how, since this deprives the licensee of the opportunity to pass on the technology to third parties.

(viii) Tying and bundling

The licensor may make the licensing of technology conditional upon the licensee taking a licence for another technology or purchasing a product from the licensor or a designated third party; or may bundle two technologies or a technology and a product together[42]. These practices are capable of foreclosing access to the market, but may also lead to economic efficiencies if, for example, it is an indispensable element in quality control.

(ix) Prices, terms and conditions

The licensor may wish to fix the prices at which the licensee sells or the terms and conditions on which it does so. The Commission, however, takes the view that the licensee should be free to determine its own pricing and sales policy when it brings the patented products to the market.

(C) The application of Article 101(1) to licences of intellectual property rights

(i) Patent licences: territorial exclusivity

In a series of decisions from the early 1970s the Commission applied Article 101(1) to various clauses found in patent licences, and in particular to territorial restrictions, although in some cases it decided that the criteria in Article 101(3) were satisfied[43]. The position

[39] Ibid, paras 133–140.

[40] See Case 65/86 *Bayer and Maschinenfabrik Hennecke* EU:C:1988:448, paras 15–19.

[41] *Technology Transfer Guidelines*, paras 129–132. [42] Ibid, paras 221–225.

[43] In chronological order the Commission's decisions on patent licences are *Burroughs AG and Deplanque & Fils Agreement* OJ [1972] L 13/50; *Burroughs AG and Geha-Werke GmbH Contract* OJ [1972] L 13/53; *Davidson Rubber Co Agreements* OJ [1972] L 143/31; *Raymond and Nagoya Rubber Ltd Agreement* OJ [1972] L 143/39; *Kabelmetal/Luchaire* OJ [1975] L 222/34; *Zuid-Nederlandsche Bronbemaling en Grondboringen BV v Heidemaatschappij Beheer NV* OJ [1975] L 249/27; *AOIP v Beyrard* OJ [1976] L 6/8; *Vaessen BV v Moris* OJ [1979] L 19/32; *IMA AG Windsurfing International Inc* OJ [1983] L 229/1, substantially upheld on appeal Case 193/83 *Windsurfing International Inc v Commission* EU:C:1986:75; *Velcro/Aplix* OJ [1985] L 233/22; the Commission has reached decisions on other types of licences in which it has applied similar principles: see eg ch 19 n 64 later.

today is that the mere grant of exclusive territorial rights to a patent licensee does not necessarily infringe Article 101(1)[44]. A relatively benign treatment is taken towards territorial exclusivity, as is demonstrated by the *Technology Transfer Guidelines*[45].

In *Consten and Grundig v Commission* the Court established that the use of intellectual property rights could contribute to an infringement where it enabled a distributor to enjoy absolute territorial protection in its allotted territory. The reason for the strict treatment of the agreement in *Consten and Grundig* was that it went beyond the mere grant of exclusive distribution rights in France by assigning to Consten the GINT trade mark for France and thereby enabling Consten to repel parallel imports from other Member States[46]. The distinction drawn by the Court of Justice in this case—between the existence of an intellectual property right on the one hand and its improper exercise on the other—provided the foundation of much of the law in this area including, in particular, the exhaustion of rights doctrine.

In *Nungesser v Commission*[47] (often referred to as the *Maize Seeds* case) the Court had to consider whether an exclusive licence of plant breeders' rights[48] by its very nature infringed Article 101(1): in other words, whether such agreements had as their object the restriction of competition[49]. The Court distinguished between:

- an 'open exclusive licence', whereby a licensor agrees not to license anyone else in the licensee's territory, and not to compete there itself and
- a 'closed exclusive licence' that eliminates all competition from third parties[50].

As to open exclusive licences, the Court of Justice noted that a licensee of new technology might be deterred from accepting the risk of cultivating and marketing a new product unless it knew that it would not encounter intra-technology competition from other licensees in its territory[51]. It followed that an open licence that does not affect the position of third parties such as parallel importers does not have as its object the restriction of competition; the application of Article 101 to such an agreement requires an assessment of its effects upon competition[52]. Closed exclusive licences confer absolute territorial protection upon a licensee and are therefore likely to be caught by Article 101(1)[53] and unlikely to benefit from Article 101(3)[54].

In various judgments since *Maize Seeds* the Court of Justice has concluded that provisions involving territorial exclusivity did not infringe Article 101(1). In *Coditel v Ciné Vog Films*[55] the Court acknowledged that, in the special circumstances of a performance copyright, a licensee may need absolute territorial protection from retransmissions of

44 *Technology Transfer Guidelines*, paras 10–18 and paras 156ff; on the position in the US see the DoJ/FTC *Antitrust Guidelines for the Licensing of Intellectual Property* of 6 April 1995, available at www.justice.gov/atr; the *Guidelines* state at para 2.0 that there is no presumption that intellectual property creates market power, a point with which the US Supreme Court agreed in *Illinois Tool Works Inc v Independent Ink Inc* 547 US 28 (2006); the *Guidelines* also say that licences of intellectual property rights are generally pro-competitive; the approach in the *Guidelines*, which suggests that terms in licences should be subject to a 'rule of reason' standard, was endorsed by the DoJ/FTC report on *Antitrust Enforcement and Intellectual Property Rights* of April 2007: see in particular chapter 4 of the report.

45 *Technology Transfer Guidelines*, paras 189–203.

46 See ch 3, 'Objectively necessary agreements', p 136.

47 Case 258/78 EU:C:1982:211.

48 Plant breeders' rights are analogous to patents.

49 See ch 3, 'Agreements that have as their object the prevention, restriction or distortion of competition', pp 122–132 for a discussion of agreements that have as their object the restriction of competition.

50 Case 258/78 EU:C:1982:211, para 53.

51 Ibid, para 57. 52 Ibid, para 58. 53 Ibid, paras 60–63.

54 Ibid, paras 68–79. 55 Case 262/81 EU:C:1982:334, para 15.

films from neighbouring Member States. In *Louis Erauw-Jacquery Sprl v La Hesbignonne Société*[56] the Court held that a prohibition on the export of so-called 'basic seeds' did not infringe Article 101(1), but rather was a manifestation of Erauw-Jacquery's plant breeders' rights and necessary for their protection against any improper handling of the seeds[57]. In *Pronuptia de Paris v Schillgalis*[58] the Court suggested that the grant of exclusive territorial rights to a franchisee for a particular territory might not infringe Article 101(1) where the business name or symbol of the franchise was not well known[59]. In *Football Association Premier League v QC Leisure*[60] neither the parties nor the Court doubted the lawfulness of the exclusive licences for the broadcasting of Premier League matches.

Collectively these cases demonstrate that open exclusivity does not necessarily infringe Article 101(1); in particular where a licensee accepts risk and markets a new product the licence may not be caught. Even absolute territorial protection may not infringe Article 101(1) in exceptional circumstances, such as those in *Louis Erauw-Jacquery*.

(ii) Patent licences: non-territorial restrictions

The Commission's decisions have sometimes applied Article 101(1) to non-territorial restrictions in licences of intellectual property rights, as have some judgments of the EU Courts. In *Windsurfing International*[61] the Commission found that many aspects of a patent licence agreement relating to windsurfing boards and rigs infringed Article 101(1); on appeal the Court of Justice substantially upheld the Commission's findings[62]. The treatment of non-territorial restrictions will be considered later in the context of Articles 4 and 5 of Regulation 316/2014[63].

(iii) Know-how licences

The owner of know-how does not have a proprietary right that can be asserted against third parties; it is protected by the law of obligations. The Commission applied the principles that it had developed in its decisions on patent licences to licences of know-how[64]. This culminated in the adoption of Regulation 556/89[65] granting block exemption to know-how licences. An anxiety for the Commission was that spurious claims to exclusivity might be made for agreements that do not in practice improve economic efficiency; this is why successive block exemption regulations have stipulated that know-how must be secret and substantial[66]. In practice the licensing of know-how is as important and as common as patent licensing, so that the application of the block exemption to this category of agreements is important for industry.

56 Case 27/87 EU:C:1988:183, paras 10–11.

57 See 'Licences of plant breeders' rights', pp 796–797 later in chapter.

58 Case 161/84 EU:C:1986:41; the judgment in *Pronuptia* has been applied by the English High Court on two occasions: *Pirtek (UK) Ltd v Joinplace Ltd* [2010] EWHC 1641 (Ch), paras 48–60 and *Carewatch Care Services Ltd v Focus Caring Services Ltd* [2014] EWHC 2313 (Ch), paras 153–167.

59 *Pronuptia*, para 24.

60 Cases C-403/08 etc EU:C:2011:631, para 141.

61 OJ [1983] L 229/1.

62 Case 193/83 *Windsurfing International Inc v Commission* EU:C:1986:75.

63 See 'Article 4: hard-core restrictions', pp 802–806 later in chapter.

64 In chronological order the Commission's decisions on know-how licences are *Boussois/Interpane* OJ [1987] L 50/30; *Mitchell Cotts/Sofiltra* OJ [1987] L 41/31; *Rich Products/Jus-Rol* OJ [1988] L 69/21; *Delta Chemie/DDD Ltd* OJ [1988] L 309/34; see also *ICL/Fujitsu*, XVIth *Report on Competition Policy* (1986), point 72.

65 Corrected version at OJ [1990] L 257/15; this Regulation was replaced by Regulation 240/96, which was replaced by Regulation 772/2004, which in turn has been replaced by Regulation 316/2014: see 'Technology Transfer Agreements: Regulation 316/2014', pp 798–807 later in chapter.

66 See now Regulation 316/2014, Article 1(1)(i).

(iv) Copyright licences

As we have seen, the Court of Justice held that absolute territorial protection was not contrary to Article 101(1) in the specific context of a performance copyright in *Coditel v Ciné Vog Films*[67]. However in *Football Association Premier League v QC Leisure*[68] the Court of Justice concluded that the terms of the English Premier League's licences with foreign broadcasters, which prohibited the import into the UK from Greece of satellite broadcasts of live Premier League football matches, conferred absolute territorial protection contrary to Article 101(1) and did not benefit from Article 101(3)[69].

The Commission has taken action in relation to copyright licences on a few occasions and in doing so it has applied the principles developed in relation to patent and know-how licences. In *Neilson-Hordell/Richmark*[70] the Commission objected to clauses in a licence of technical drawings and the products they represent; it required the abandonment of a no-challenge clause, a royalties clause extending to products not protected by any copyright of the licensor, a non-competition clause which was to continue after the agreement and an exclusive grant-back to the licensor of the improvements. In *Ernest Benn Ltd*[71] the Commission condemned a standard contractual term which prevented the export of books from the UK.

In *Film Purchases by German Television Stations*[72] the Commission investigated exclusive licence agreements entered into between MGM/UA, a major US film production and distribution company, and ARD, an association of public broadcasting organisations in Germany. The agreements granted ARD exclusive television rights to a large number of MGM/UA's feature films in most cases for a period of 15 years. The Commission's view was that the agreements restricted competition, in particular because of the large number of the licensed rights and the duration of the exclusivity[73]. However the Commission decided that the criteria of Article 101(3) were satisfied following modifications to the agreements, for example so that ARD would license the films to third parties at certain periods known as 'windows'.

In *Cross-border access to pay-TV*[74] the Commission sent a statement of objections to six major film studios and to Sky UK, alleging that their film copyright licences prevent cross-border passive sales of pay-TV services and grant absolute territorial exclusivity in relation to the film studios' content. In the Commission's view, the licences had as their object the restriction of competition and could not be justified by the specific subject-matter of the copyright or by economic efficiencies. The Commission accepted commitments from one of the film studios, Paramount, not to apply the offending clauses, but the case against the other five studios was ongoing at 8 December 2017[75].

[67] Case 262/81 EU:C:1982:334; see 'Patent licences: territorial exclusivity', pp 791–793 earlier in chapter.

[68] Cases C-403/08 etc *Football Association Premier League Ltd v QC Leisure* EU:C:2011:631.

[69] Ibid, paras 134–146.

[70] Commission's XIIth *Annual Report on Competition Policy* (1982), points 88–89.

[71] Commission's IXth *Report on Competition Policy* (1979), points 118 and 119; see also *The Old Man and the Sea*, VIth *Report on Competition Policy* (1976), point 164; *STEMRA*, XIth *Report on Competition Policy* (1981), point 98; *Knoll/Hille-Form* Commission's XIIth *Report on Competition Policy* (1983), points 142–146.

[72] OJ [1989] L 284/36; the decision is criticised by Rothnie 'Commission Re-Runs Same Old Bill' (1990) 12 EIPR 72.

[73] OJ [1989] L 284/36, paras 41–46.

[74] Commission Press Release IP/15/5432, 23 July 2015.

[75] Commission commitment decision of 26 July 2016; the Commission's acceptance of these commitments is the subject of an appeal to the General Court on the ground that there was no legal basis for accepting them given that the underlying agreements did not infringe Article 101: see Case T-873/16 *Groupe Canal + v Commission*, not yet decided.

There is no specific block exemption for copyright licences, although Regulation 330/2010 on vertical agreements or Regulation 316/2014 on technology transfer agreements may apply where the licensing of copyright is ancillary to an agreement covered by one of those Regulations[76]. The Commission will normally apply the principles set out in Regulation 316/2014 to copyright licences[77], although not necessarily in the case of performance copyright[78].

(v) Software licences

In *Sega and Nintendo*[79] the Commission required the deletion of clauses in licences of computer software with publishers of video games which, in the Commission's view, enabled Sega and Nintendo to control the market for video games[80]. In *Microsoft Internet Explorer*[81] the Commission required Microsoft to remove clauses from its software licences providing for minimum distribution volumes for its Internet Explorer browser technology and imposing a prohibition on advertising competitors' browser technology. A minimum quantities clause is normally considered not to be restrictive of competition at all[82]; the Commission's concern here, however, was that the two clauses in question could foreclose competitors. The Commission closed the file after these amendments had been made; the Commission did not give a ruling on whether Microsoft's behaviour overall might amount to an abuse of a dominant position[83]. Microsoft's refusal to make interoperability information, assumed to be protected by intellectual property rights, available to competitors was found to be an abuse of a dominant position in 2004[84].

There are some typical clauses in software licences that have no analogies in the general law, for example prohibiting decompilation of a computer program and restrictions on copying[85]. Software licences are now covered by Regulation 316/2014[86].

(vi) Trade mark licences

The Commission has applied Article 101(1) to exclusive trade mark licences but decided that, where there was no absolute territorial protection, the criteria of Article 101(3) were satisfied. In *Davide Campari-Milano SpA Agreement*[87] the Commission considered that Article 101(3) applied in the case of a standard form agreement whereby firms were licensed to use the Campari trade mark and were given exclusive rights in their own territory to apply that mark and required not to pursue an active sales policy elsewhere.

In *Moosehead/Whitbread*[88] the Commission investigated an exclusive licence of a trade mark with associated know-how. The licensee wished to manufacture and to promote

[76] See 'Article 1: definitions', pp 798–799 later in chapter.

[77] *Technology Transfer Guidelines*, para 48. [78] Ibid, para 49.

[79] See the Commission's XXVIIth *Report on Competition Policy* (1997), point 80 and pp 148–149; see also, on the similar *Sony* case, the XXVIIIth *Report on Competition Policy* (1998), pp 159–160.

[80] Cm 2781 (1995).

[81] See the Commission's XXIXth *Report on Competition Policy* (1999), points 55 and 56 and p 162: details of Microsoft's notification in this case can be found at OJ [1998] C 175/3; for a separate investigation of Microsoft's licensing terms, following a complaint by Santa Cruz Operation in relation to the UNIX operating system, see the Commission's XXVIIth *Report on Competition Policy* (1997), point 79 and pp 140–141.

[82] *Technology Transfer Guidelines*, para 183(e).

[83] Commission's XXIXth *Report on Competition Policy* (1999), point 56.

[84] See 'The *Microsoft* case', pp 818–820 later in chapter.

[85] It may be arguable that, by analogy from the *Erauw-Jacquery* judgment (ch 19 n 56 earlier) on the propagation of seeds, a restriction on copying software is outside Article 101(1).

[86] See 'Article 1: definitions', pp 798–799 later in chapter.

[87] OJ [1978] L 70/69; see similarly *Goodyear Italiana SpA's Application* OJ [1975] L 38/10.

[88] OJ [1990] L 100/32; see Subiotto '*Moosehead/Whitbread*: Industrial Franchises and No-Challenge Clauses Relating to Licensed Trade Marks in the EEC' (1990) 11 ECLR 226.

the Moosehead brand, a popular Canadian beer, in the UK. The licence prohibited active selling outside the UK[89]. The Commission concluded that the exclusive trade mark and the restriction on active sales infringed Article 101(1), as did a non-competition clause[90]. The know-how was considered by the Commission to be ancillary to the trade mark, so that the block exemption for know-how licensing in force at that time, Regulation 556/89, was not applicable[91]; presumably the same conclusion would be reached under Regulation 316/2014[92]. However the Commission decided that Article 101(3) applied to the agreement as consumers would have the benefit of another beer from which to choose[93]. The agreement contained a no-challenge clause in respect of the trade mark, but the Commission held this to be outside Article 101(1) because the mark was not well known and its non-availability to competitors was not a barrier to entry[94]. The *Technology Transfer Guidelines* state that an agreement of the kind at issue in *Moosehead/Whitbread* would now be eligible for block exemption[95].

Where a trade mark is ancillary to a vertical agreement or to a technology transfer agreement, it may benefit from the block exemption for those agreements[96].

(vii) **Licences of plant breeders' rights**

In *Louis Erauw-Jacquery Sprl v La Hesbignonne Société*[97] the Court of Justice was asked to rule on the application of Article 101(1) to two clauses in a licence for the propagation and sale of certain varieties of cereal seeds. Erauw-Jacquery had licensed La Hesbignonne to propagate 'basic seeds' and to sell seeds reproduced from them ('reproductive seeds'). Clause 2(f) of the licence prohibited the export of basic seeds; clause 2(i) required the licensee not to resell the reproductive seeds below minimum selling prices. The Court held that the export ban in relation to basic seeds did not infringe Article 101(1): a plant breeder is entitled to reserve the propagation of basic seeds to institutions approved by him and an export ban is objectively justifiable to protect this right[98]. Basic seeds are not intended for sale to farmers for sowing, but are intended solely for the purpose of propagation; it follows that an export ban of this kind arises from the existence of the plant breeders' rights and is not an improper exercise of it[99]. The Court concluded that the provision imposing minimum resale prices for reproductive seeds had as its object and effect the restriction of competition[100] but that the national court must decide on the facts whether it had an effect on trade between Member States[101].

In *Sicasov*[102] the Commission applied the Court's judgment in the *Erauw-Jacquery* case to the standard licences of Sicasov, a French cooperative of plant breeders. The Commission explains in more detail than the judgment in *Erauw-Jacquery* the distinction between basic seeds, which are intended only for propagation, and 'certified' seeds, intended for sale to farmers for sowing[103]. The breeder is entitled to control the destination of basic seeds by virtue of its plant breeders' rights[104], but cannot control certified seeds that have been put onto the market with its consent[105]. It followed that

[89] On the meaning of active selling, see ch 16, 'Article 4(b): territorial and customer restrictions', pp 679–682.

[90] OJ [1990] L 100/32, para 15(1).

[91] Ibid, para 16(1); a corrected version of Regulation 556/89 will be found at OJ [1990] L 257/15.

[92] See 'Article 1: definitions', pp 798–799 later in chapter.

[93] OJ [1990] L 100/32, para 15(2).

[94] Ibid, para 15(4).

[95] See the *Technology Transfer Guidelines*, fn 35.

[96] See 'Article 1: definitions', pp 798–799 later in chapter.

[97] Case 27/87 EU:C:1988:183.

[98] Ibid, para 10.

[99] This was the view of AG Mischo in this case, and of the Commission: Case 27/87 EU:C:1987:538, para 9.

[100] Case 27/87 EU:C:1988:183, para 15.

[101] Ibid, para 19.

[102] OJ [1999] L 4/27.

[103] Ibid, paras 21–27.

[104] Ibid, para 50, citing *Erauw-Jacquery*.

[105] Ibid, para 51.

obligations not to entrust basic seeds to a third party, not to export them and related provisions did not infringe Article 101(1)[106]. However a restriction on the export of certified seeds did infringe Article 101(1)[107] but was found to satisfy the terms of Article 101(3)[108].

In *Roses*[109] the Commission condemned two clauses in a standard licence of plant breeders' rights. The first was an exclusive grant-back clause, which effectively removed the sub-licensee from the market for mutations which it discovered. The second was a no-challenge clause: the fact that plant breeders' rights are conferred only after a national authority's involvement does not mean that there might not have been an error of appreciation that could be challenged by a licensee.

(viii) Sub-contracting agreements

Sub-contracting agreements typically involve a licence from the principal to the sub-contractor. Horizontal sub-contracting agreements have been considered in chapter 15 and vertical ones in chapter 16[110].

(D) The application of Article 101(3) to licences of intellectual property rights

Licensing agreements that are not covered by Regulation 316/2014 and that contain provisions which are not ancillary to an agreement covered by that Regulation or by Regulation 330/2010 on vertical agreements[111] may still fulfil the conditions of Article 101(3)[112]. When assessing the validity of their licences under Article 101, firms will derive guidance from the block exemptions. The Commission has said that the restrictions listed as 'hard core' in Article 4 of Regulation 316/2014 would be likely to benefit from the exception conferred by Article 101(3) only in exceptional circumstances[113]; however it also says that there is no presumption that agreements that fall outside the block exemption are caught by Article 101(1) or fail to satisfy the terms of Article 101(3)[114].

In *Telenor/Canal+/Canal Digital*[115] the agreements concerned the licensing of material protected by artistic copyright and fell outside the block exemptions for vertical agreements and technology transfer agreements because the licences were not ancillary to either type of agreement[116]. However, the Commission decided that the criteria of Article 101(3) were satisfied and therefore permitted for five years agreements concerning the distribution of pay-TV premium content channels on the satellite platform of Canal Digital in the Nordic region.

[106] Ibid, paras 53–61. [107] Ibid, paras 62–64.

[108] Ibid, paras 73–77; note that the block exemption Regulation on technology transfer agreements at the time did not apply since the standard licence did not correspond with any of the provisions listed in Article 1(1) thereof: ibid, para 72.

[109] OJ [1985] L 369/9; see Harding 'Commission Decision on Breeders' Rights in Relation to Roses: Hard Line on Breeders' Rights Maintained' (1986) 9 EIPR 284.

[110] See ch 15, 'Production Agreements', pp 611–615 and ch 16, 'Sub-Contracting Agreements', pp 691–692.

[111] On ancillary provisions see 'Article 1: definitions', pp 798–799 later in chapter.

[112] See the *Technology Transfer Guidelines*, paras 18 and 174ff.

[113] Ibid, para 18. [114] Ibid, para 43.

[115] Commission decision of 29 December 2003.

[116] On Article 2(3) of the vertical block exemption see ch 16, 'Article 2(3): ancillary provisions in relation to intellectual property rights', pp 670–671.

3. Technology Transfer Agreements: Regulation 316/2014

Acting under powers conferred on it by Council Regulation 19/65[117] the Commission has adopted Regulation 316/2014[118] conferring block exemption on technology transfer agreements pursuant to Article 101(3) of the Treaty. In view of the 'overall positive experience' with the application of the previous block exemption, Regulation 772/2004[119], the Commission considered it was appropriate to adopt a new block exemption[120].

Regulation 316/2014 entered into force on 1 May 2014 and will expire on 30 April 2026[121]. Regulation 316/2014, the format of which is very similar to its predecessor Regulation 772/2004, consists of 19 recitals and 11 Articles. Article 1 contains a series of definitions. Article 2 confers block exemption on certain technology transfer agreements. Article 3 imposes market share caps, which differ depending on whether an agreement is horizontal or vertical, the former being treated more strictly. Article 4 contains a list of hard-core restrictions, which prevent the block exemption from applying to the entire agreement: the list is stricter for horizontal than for vertical agreements. Article 5 sets out certain restrictions that are excluded from the block exemption, but which do not prevent the application of the Regulation to the rest of the agreement. Subsequent provisions deal with matters such as the withdrawal of the block exemption, calculation of market share thresholds and transitional arrangements. Regulation 316/2014 should be read in conjunction with the Commission's *Technology Transfer Guidelines*.

(A) Article 1: definitions

Article 1 of the Regulation contains a series of definitions. Some of these will be explained in the text that follows, in the specific context in which they are used in the Regulation. Two particular definitions merit a brief explanation at this stage. First, it is worth considering the term 'technology rights': if there are no technology rights, there can be no 'transfer' to which the block exemption could apply[122]. Article 1(1)(b) defines 'technology rights' as know-how[123] and the following rights, or a combination thereof:

- patents
- utility models, designs, topographies of semiconductor products, supplementary protection certificates for medicinal products and plant breeder's rights
- software copyright[124].

The second definition meriting a brief mention is 'technology transfer agreement' in Article 1(1)(c). This term refers to a technology rights licensing agreement between two undertakings for the purpose of production of contract products[125] or an assignment of

[117] JO [1965] 533, OJ Sp Ed [1965–66] 87.

[118] OJ [2014] L 93/17; for comment on Regulation 316/2014 see Barazza 'The Technology Transfer Block Exemption Regulation and Related Guidelines: Competition Law and IP Licensing in the EU' (2014) 9 Journal of Intellectual Property Law and Practice 186 and Rab 'New EU Technology Transfer Block Exemption: A Note of Caution' (2014) 5 JECLAP 436.

[119] OJ [2004] L 123/11.

[120] Recital 2 of Regulation 316/2014.

[121] Regulation 316/2014, Article 11.

[122] See the *Technology Transfer Guidelines*, para 44.

[123] Regulation 316/2014, Article 1(1)(i); see also the *Technology Transfer Guidelines*, para 45.

[124] Note that copyright, other than software copyright, would not be included in this term; see 'Copyright licences', pp 794–795 earlier on the Commission's approach to copyright licences in the *Technology Transfer Guidelines*; see also the Commission's decision in *Telenor/Canal+/Canal Digital* discussed at 'The application of Article 101(3) to licences of intellectual property rights', p 797 earlier in chapter.

[125] On the meaning of 'product' and 'contract products' see Article 1(1)(f) and (g) of the Regulation.

technology rights for the same purpose[126]. Recital 7 of the Regulation explains that it applies only to agreements whereby a licensor permits a licensee (or its sub-contractor) to exploit the licensed technology for the production of goods or services: it therefore does not apply to technology transfer agreements that allow for sub-licensing[127]. Recital 7 also explains that the Regulation does not apply to technology pools[128].

Article 1(2) of the Regulation provides that the terms 'undertaking', 'licensor' and 'licensee' include 'connected undertakings', as defined therein.

(B) **Article 2: block exemption**

Article 2 of the Regulation provides that, subject to the provisions of the Regulation, Article 101(1) shall not apply to technology transfer agreements.

Several points should be noted about Article 2(1).

(i) **Many technology transfer agreements do not infringe Article 101(1)**

It is worth recalling that many technology transfer agreements do not infringe Article 101(1) at all, and therefore do not need to be block exempted. Recital 4 of Regulation 316/2014 acknowledges that such agreements usually improve economic efficiency and are pro-competitive; paragraph 9 of the *Technology Transfer Guidelines* adds that there is no presumption that licence agreements give rise to competition concerns. Indeed paragraph 17 of the *Guidelines* goes so far as to say that licence agreements 'have substantial pro-competitive potential'; it continues that 'the vast majority of those agreements are indeed pro-competitive'. Paragraph 42 specifically says that 'many licence agreements fall outside Article 101(1)'. Recital 13 of the Regulation states that there is no presumption that agreements above the market share thresholds in Article 3 infringe Article 101(1); where the thresholds are exceeded an agreement requires individual analysis[129]. It is almost unthinkable that the Commission would have made such statements in, say, the 1970s and 1980s, and this shows how far the Commission has moved towards an economics-oriented approach to Article 101.

(ii) **If it is not forbidden, it is permitted**

A second point to note about the Regulation is that, in relation to a technology transfer agreement as defined in Article 1(1)(c), if the Regulation does not prohibit something, it is permitted[130]. This is the consequence of not stating what must be included in a technology transfer agreement, but only stating the hard-core restrictions which must not be in it, and is an essential feature of the Regulation. It follows from the maxim that 'if something is not forbidden, it is permitted' that the only way in which the Commission could take action would be either by arguing that the provision is a 'hard-core restriction' under Article 4; an 'excluded restriction' under Article 5; or by withdrawing the benefit of the Regulation under Article 6 (see sections D to F later).

(iii) **The exempted agreement must be bilateral**

An interesting distinction between the block exemption for vertical agreements and the one for technology transfer is that the latter is applicable only in the case of bilateral agreements, whereas the former is capable of application to multilateral ones[131]. Council

126 See the *Technology Transfer Guidelines*, para 66.

127 See further ibid, para 60.

128 On pooling agreements see 'Technology pools', p 808 later in chapter.

129 See the *Technology Transfer Guidelines*, para 43.

130 The same maxim applies under the vertical block exemption: see ch 16, 'If it is not forbidden, it is permitted', p 667.

131 Ch 16, 'The exempted agreement may be multilateral', pp 667–668.

Regulation 19/65 does not provide a legal basis for block exemption of multilateral technology transfer agreements[132]. However the block exemption can apply to an agreement between a licensor and licensee where the licensor makes stipulations for more than one level of trade[133]. For example the licensor may impose obligations on the licensee not only in relation to its own production and sales; it may also require the licensee to impose terms on its own distributors, for example requiring them to maintain a selective distribution system. The agreement between the licensor and licensee is still a bilateral agreement, and so capable of being covered by the block exemption; however the agreement(s) between the licensee and any distributor would not be covered by Regulation 316/2014, but might satisfy the block exemption for vertical agreements[134].

Where a technology transfer agreement is multilateral, but of the same nature as one covered by Regulation 316/2014, the Commission will analyse the agreement by analogy to the principles contained in the Regulation[135].

(iv) Duration

The block exemption will run until 30 April 2026. However Article 2(2) provides that the exemption lasts only as long as the intellectual property right in the licensed technology has not expired, lapsed or been declared invalid; or, in the case of know-how, that the exemption lasts only as long as the know-how remains secret. The block exemption will cease to apply on the date of the last intellectual property right to expire, become invalid or enter the public domain[136].

(v) Ancillary provisions in relation to other intellectual property rights

Article 2(3) provides that Regulation 316/2014 also applies to provisions on intellectual property rights that do not constitute 'technology rights' where those provisions are 'directly related' to the production of the contract products (sometimes referred to as 'ancillary provisions')[137].

(vi) Relationship with other block exemptions

Article 9 provides that Regulation 316/2014 does not apply to licensing arrangements in research and development agreements[138] or specialisation agreements[139] that benefit from the block exemption applicable to those agreements[140].

(C) Article 3: the market share cap

Recital 5 of Regulation 316/2014 states that the likelihood that a technology transfer agreement improves economic efficiency and is pro-competitive depends on the parties' degree of market power. The Regulation applies only to technology transfer agreements that do not exceed a market share cap; the cap provides an indication of the parties' degree of market power[141]. Where the parties' market shares are below the applicable threshold (subject, of course, to compliance with the other terms of the Regulation) it can be

[132] Specific provision for the block exemption of multilateral vertical agreements was made by Council Regulation 1215/99, OJ [1999] L 148/1.

[133] Recital 6 of Regulation 314/2016.

[134] See further the *Technology Transfer Guidelines*, paras 55 and 75–78.

[135] Ibid, para 57.

[136] Ibid, para 67.

[137] Ibid, paras 46–50.

[138] Regulation 1217/2010: see ch 15, 'The block exemption for research and development agreements: Regulation 1217/2010', pp 607–611.

[139] Regulation 1218/2010: see ch 15, 'The block exemption for specialisation agreements: Regulation 1218/2010', pp 613–615.

[140] *Technology Transfer Guidelines*, paras 69–78.

[141] Ibid, para 25.

presumed that the conditions of Article 101(3) are fulfilled[142]. Recital 13 states that there is no presumption that an agreement above the thresholds infringes Article 101(1) or that it is incapable of satisfying the terms of Article 101(3) on an individual basis. Article 3(1) of the Regulation requires that the combined market share of the parties does not exceed 20% of the affected relevant technology and product market for horizontal agreements; Article 3(2) provides that, in the case of vertical agreements, the market share of each of the parties must not exceed 30%.

(i) **Horizontal agreements**

In order to determine whether an agreement is a horizontal agreement it is necessary to ask whether the parties to an agreement are 'competing undertakings' as defined in Article 1(1)(n) of the Regulation[143]. Undertakings may compete on a technology market or on a product market.

(a) Technology markets

Article 1(1)(n)(i) provides that undertakings compete on the relevant technology market where they license out competing technology rights[144]. The relevant technology market includes technologies which are regarded as interchangeable with or substitutable for the licensed technology rights, by reason of the technologies' characteristics, their royalties and their intended use[145]. This definition captures only *actual* competitors in the technology market: it does not apply to potential competitors[146].

(b) Product markets

Article 1(1)(n)(ii) provides that undertakings compete on the relevant product market where, even without a technology transfer agreement, they are both active on the relevant product and geographic markets on which the contract products are sold (actual competitors) and where they might realistically be able to enter and compete on the market within 'a period of one to two years'[147] in response to a small but permanent increase in relative prices (potential competitors). The relevant product market includes products which are regarded as interchangeable with or substitutable for the contract products by reason of the products' characteristics, their prices and their intended use[148].

(ii) **Vertical agreements**

Where an agreement is not horizontal, because it is not between competing undertakings as defined in Article 1(1)(n), it is vertical, and so the higher market share cap of 30% is applicable. An agreement will not be horizontal where one party can use its intellectual property to prevent the other entering the market, or where both parties need the other's technology to operate on the market: these are referred to as 'one-way' and 'two-way' blocking positions, as to which the Commission will require objective evidence, for example court judgments[149]. It can be the case that two undertakings compete in relation to existing products, but that a licence by A to B is not between competitors because A's technology is so innovative that B's technology is now obsolete or uncompetitive: such an

[142] Recitals 10 and 11 of Regulation 316/2014; see similarly *Technology Transfer Guidelines*, para 79.

[143] See further the *Technology Transfer Guidelines*, paras 27–39.

[144] Article 1(1)(j) of Regulation 772/2004 provided that undertakings should compete 'without infringing each others' intellectual property rights'; this qualification was omitted by Regulation 316/2014.

[145] *Technology Transfer Guidelines*, para 22. [146] Ibid, para 83. [147] Ibid, para 34.

[148] Ibid, para 21.

[149] Ibid, paras 29 and 33; this is one of the issues raised in Case T-691/14 *Servier v Commission*, not yet decided.

agreement would be regarded as vertical and therefore subject to the higher market share cap (and the more lenient list of hard-core restrictions)[150].

Where the parties are not competing undertakings at the time of the agreement, but subsequently become so, they will usually continue to be considered to be non-competing: Article 4(3) of the Regulation provides that this means that the less strict list of hard-core restrictions for agreements between non-competitors will continue to apply, unless the agreement is amended in any material respect[151].

(iii) **Technology markets**

Paragraphs 19 to 26 of the *Technology Transfer Guidelines* discuss market definition for the purpose of analysing technology transfer agreements. They explain that such agreements can have an effect on competition both in the upstream technology market and in the downstream product market[152]. Article 8(d) explains that a licensor's share of a technology market is to be calculated by reference to the value of the licensed technology on the relevant product market, which the *Guidelines* call the technology's 'footprint' on the product market[153]; this figure is calculated on the basis of both the licensor's and its licensee's sales[154]. Where a new technology has yet to generate any sales a market share of zero is assigned[155]. In *Servier* the Commission decided that Servier held a dominant position on the relevant market for perindopril technology in the EU[156].

(iv) **Product markets**

A licensee's share of a product market is calculated on the basis of its sales of products incorporating the licensor's technology and competing products, that is to say the total sales of the licensee on the product market in question; sales by other licensees are not taken into account[157].

(v) **Article 8: calculation of market shares and marginal relief**

Article 8(a) of the Regulation deals with the calculation of market shares, which should be done by reference to market sales value data. Where such data are not available, estimates based on other reliable information, including sales volumes, may be used to establish the market share of the undertaking concerned. Article 8(b) provides that market shares should be calculated on the basis of data relating to the preceding calendar year.

Article 8(e) provides some marginal relief for up to two years where the market share caps of 20 or 30% are subsequently exceeded.

(vi) **Examples**

The *Technology Transfer Guidelines* provide examples of how the market share figures operate, both in relation to horizontal and vertical licensing agreements[158].

(D) **Article 4: hard-core restrictions**

Recital 14 of the Regulation states that technology transfer agreements should not enjoy block exemption when they contain 'severely anti-competitive restraints such as the

150 *Technology Transfer Guidelines*, para 37.

151 See 'Article 4: hard-core restrictions', pp 802–806 later in chapter.

152 *Technology Transfer Guidelines*, para 20.

153 Ibid, paras 87–88; see also para 25.

154 Ibid, para 86.

155 Ibid, para 90.

156 Commission decision of 9 July 2014, paras 2061–2667, on appeal, including on the issue of market definition, Case T-691/14 *Servier v Commission*, not yet decided.

157 *Technology Transfer Guidelines*, para 91.

158 Ibid, para 93.

fixing of prices charged to third parties ... irrespective of the market shares of the undertakings concerned'. The *Guidelines* explain that:

> [t]he classification of a restraint as a hardcore restriction of competition is based on the nature of the restriction and experience showing that such restrictions are almost always anti-competitive[159].

The block exemption ceases to apply to the entire agreement, not just to the offending provisions[160]. The Commission considers that the hard-core restrictions are restrictions by object under Article 101(1) and are unlikely to satisfy Article 101(3)[161]. The Regulation contains one set of hard-core restrictions for agreements between competing undertakings in Article 4(1) and a different set for agreements between non-competing undertakings in Article 4(2). As one would expect the provisions are stricter in the case of agreements between competing undertakings than between non-competing undertakings[162]. Article 4(3) provides that, where the parties were non-competing at the time that they entered into an agreement, Article 4(2) applies to their agreement throughout its lifetime unless the agreement is subsequently amended in any material respect[163]; in other words the agreement does not metamorphose into a horizontal one, and so become subject to the stricter standard of Article 4(1), simply because the firms subsequently become competitors.

(i) Agreements between competing undertakings: horizontal agreements

The concern of the Commission is that a technology transfer agreement between competing agreements might be a cloak for, or have the effect of, a cartel[164]. Article 4(1) therefore provides that block exemption is not available for agreements that, directly or indirectly, in isolation or in combination with other factors, have as their object restrictions concerning prices, output, the allocation of markets or customers, and the exploitation by the licensee of its own technology: such restrictions are regarded as hard-core. The provisions on price and output are simple, but those on markets and customers can be complex. In some cases restrictions are treated as hard-core only where an agreement is reciprocal, that is to say where each undertaking grants a licence to the other and where the licences concern competing technologies or can be used for the production of competing products[165]; the same restriction in a non-reciprocal agreement[166] is not regarded as hard-core[167]. Where a non-reciprocal agreement becomes a reciprocal one due to the conclusion of a second licence between the same parties, they may have to revise the first licence in order to avoid the inclusion of a hard-core restriction[168].

(a) Prices

Article 4(1)(a) provides that the block exemption is not applicable to an agreement between competing undertakings that restricts a party's ability to determine its prices to

[159] Ibid, para 94. [160] Ibid, para 95.

[161] Ibid, para 14; however the Commission also states that the undertakings can 'always plead an efficiency defence' in an individual case: para 94.

[162] Ibid, para 27.

[163] Article 4(3) gives the example of entering into a new technology transfer agreement between the parties concerning competing technology rights; see similarly the *Technology Transfer Guidelines*, para 39.

[164] See generally the *Technology Transfer Guidelines*, paras 97–116.

[165] Regulation 316/2014, Article 1(1)(d). [166] Ibid, Article 1(1)(e).

[167] See the *Technology Transfer Guidelines*, para 98.

[168] Ibid; the Commission will take into account the time lapsed between the conclusion of the first and the second licence.

third parties. It is immaterial whether the agreement concerns fixed, minimum, maximum or recommended prices[169]. Where there are cross licences between two undertakings that have no pro-competitive purpose and where the parties agree to pay running royalties to one another the Commission might treat the case as sham and tantamount to a price-fixing agreement[170]. Article 4(1)(a) (and Article 4(1)(d)) may be infringed where royalties are based on the sales of products irrespective of whether the licensed technology was used in the production of those products[171].

(b) Output

Article 4(1)(b) provides that the block exemption is not applicable to an agreement between competing undertakings that has as its object the limitation of output, other than a limitation on the output of contract products imposed on the licensee in a non-reciprocal agreement or imposed on only one of the parties in a reciprocal agreement. Non-reciprocal agreements are treated more favourably than reciprocal ones since they are less likely to lead to a restriction of output and they are more likely to lead to an improvement in economic efficiency[172].

(c) The allocation of markets and customers

Article 4(1)(c) provides that the block exemption does not apply to an agreement between competing undertakings that allocates markets or customers[173]. However there are four exceptions to this[174]:

- an obligation on the licensor and/or the licensee in a non-reciprocal agreement not to produce with the licensed technology rights within the exclusive territory reserved for the other party[175] and/or not to sell actively and/or passively into the exclusive territory or to the exclusive customer group reserved for the other party[176]. The *Guidelines* state that, by implication, a sole licence does not constitute a hard-core restriction; it does not matter whether the sole licence is reciprocal[177]
- the restriction, in a non-reciprocal agreement, of active sales by the licensee into the exclusive territory or to the exclusive customer group allocated by the licensor to another licensee provided the latter was not a competing undertaking of the licensor at the time of the conclusion of its own licence. Such restrictions are likely to encourage the protected licensee to exploit the licensed technology more efficiently[178]
- an obligation on the licensee to produce the contract products only for its own use provided that the licensee is not restricted in selling the contract products actively and passively as spare parts for its own products: these are known as 'captive use restrictions'[179]
- an obligation on the licensee in a non-reciprocal agreement to produce the contract products only for a particular customer where the licence was granted in order to create an alternative source of supply for that customer[180].

169 Ibid, para 99. 170 Ibid, para 100. 171 Ibid, para 101; see also paras 184–188.

172 Ibid, para 103; see also paras 204–207.

173 The terms 'exclusive territory' and 'exclusive customer group' are defined in Article 1(1)(q) and (r) of the Regulation; for further discussion of exclusive licensing and sales restrictions see the *Technology Transfer Guidelines*, paras 189–203.

174 The *Technology Transfer Guidelines* make clear that neither a sole licence (para 109) nor a field of use restriction (paras 113–114) is a hard-core restriction.

175 Ibid, para 107. 176 Ibid, para 108. 177 Ibid, para 109. 178 Ibid, para 110.

179 Ibid, para 111; see also paras 216–220. 180 Ibid, para 112.

(d) Exploitation by the licensee

Article 4(1)(d) provides that the block exemption does not apply to an agreement between competing undertakings that restricts the licensee's ability to exploit its own technology rights or that prevents any of the parties to the agreement from carrying out research and development, unless such a provision is indispensable to prevent the disclosure to a third party of the licensed know-how[181]. Where such a restriction is found in an agreement between non-competing undertakings it is not regarded as hard-core but is excluded from the block exemption under Article 5[182].

(ii) **Agreements between non-competing undertakings: vertical agreements**

Article 4(2) of the Regulation provides that block exemption is not available for agreements between non-competing undertakings that, directly or indirectly, in isolation or in combination with other factors, have as their object restrictions concerning prices, territories and customer groups or sales within a selective distribution system[183].

(a) Prices

Article 4(2)(a) provides that the block exemption does not apply to an agreement between non-competing undertakings that restricts a party's ability to determine its prices when selling products to third parties. However it is permissible to impose a maximum price or to recommend a price provided that this does not amount to a fixed or minimum price as a result of pressure from, or incentives offered by, any of the parties. Paragraph 118 of the *Technology Transfer Guidelines* provides examples of agreements that would be considered to fix prices indirectly, for example fixing a licensee's margin, fixing the maximum level of discounts and making threats or intimidating a licensee as to a particular price level.

(b) Territories and customer groups

Article 4(2)(b) provides that the block exemption does not apply to an agreement between non-competing undertakings that restricts the territory into which, or the customer group to whom, the licensee may passively sell the contract goods[184]. Paragraph 119 of the *Technology Transfer Guidelines* provides examples of indirect methods of preventing passive sales, such as financial incentives, monitoring mechanisms to identify the final destination of the contract products and, in some cases, quantity limitations. Article 4(2)(b) provides five exceptions to the prohibition on restrictions on passive sales by the licensee:

- a restriction of passive sales into an exclusive territory or to an exclusive customer group reserved for the licensor
- an obligation to produce the contract goods only for its own use provided that the licensee is not restricted in selling the contract products actively and passively as spare parts for its own products
- an obligation to produce the contract products only for a particular customer where the licence was granted in order to create an alternative source of supply for that customer
- a restriction of sales to end users by a licensee operating at the wholesale level of trade
- a restriction of sales to unauthorised distributors by the members of a selective distribution system.

[181] Ibid, paras 115–116. [182] See 'Article 5: excluded restrictions', p 806 later in chapter.

[183] See generally the *Technology Transfer Guidelines*, paras 117–127; the term 'selective distribution system' is defined in Article 1(1)(o) of the Regulation.

[184] The terms 'exclusive territory' and 'exclusive customer group' are defined in Article 1(1)(q) and (r) of the Regulation.

Regulation 316/2014 does not provide an exception for a restriction on passive sales by licensees to exclusive territories or customer groups reserved to another licensee during the latter's first two years of selling the contract products. Instead, paragraph 126 of the *Guidelines* states that, where a licensee wishes to enter a new market and substantial investment is necessary, it may be protected from passive sales by other licensees during the first two years of operating on the market *without infringing Article 101(1)*[185].

The *Guidelines* make clear that Article 4(2)(b) does not prohibit sales restrictions on the licensor[186]; nor does it apply to restrictions on active or passive sales by licensees to exclusive territories or customer groups reserved to the licensor[187].

(c) *Restrictions in selective distribution systems*

Article 4(2)(c) provides that the block exemption does not apply where an agreement between non-competing undertakings restricts active or passive sales to end users by a licensee which is a member of a selective distribution system and which operates at the retail level, without prejudice to the possibility of prohibiting a member of the system from operating out of an unauthorised place of establishment.

(E) **Article 5: excluded restrictions**

Recital 15 of the Regulation states that, in order to protect incentives to innovate, certain restrictions should be excluded from the block exemption, in particular exclusive grant-back obligations for the licensee's improvements[188]; however the inclusion of an Article 5 restriction does not prevent the application of the block exemption to the remaining parts of the agreement if they are 'severable' from the excluded restriction[189].

Article 5(1) lists two excluded restrictions:

- exclusive grant-backs[190]: an obligation on the licensee to grant an exclusive licence or to assign rights to the licensor or a third party designated by the licensor in respect of its own improvements[191] to, or its own new applications of, the licensed technology
- no-challenge clauses: an obligation on the licensee not to challenge the validity of intellectual property rights held by the licensor in the Union, without prejudice to the right of the licensor to terminate the licence in the event of such a challenge[192].

Article 5(2) also excludes a restriction, in an agreement between non-competing undertakings, that imposes an obligation limiting the licensee's ability to exploit its own technology or limiting either of the party's ability to carry out research and development, unless the latter restriction is indispensable to prevent the disclosure of the licensed know-how to third parties[193].

185 See similarly the *Guidelines on Vertical Restraints*, OJ [2010] C 130/1, para 61.

186 See the *Technology Transfer Guidelines*, para 120.

187 Ibid, para 121.

188 Ibid, paras 128–143. 189 Ibid, para 128.

190 See generally *Assessment of potential anticompetitive conduct in the field of intellectual property rights and assessment of the interplay between competition policy and IPR protection*, November 2011, section 2f, available at www.ec.europa.eu.

191 Unlike Article 5(1)(a) of Regulation 772/2004, Article 5(1)(a) of Regulation 316/2014 does not distinguish between severable and non-severable improvements.

192 See the *Technology Transfer Guidelines*, paras 133–140.

193 Ibid, paras 141–143.

(F) Article 6: withdrawal in individual cases

Recital 16 of the Regulation states that the provisions of Articles 3 to 5 mean that agreements to which the block exemption applies normally will not eliminate competition in respect of a substantial part of the products in question, with the result that the fourth requirement of Article 101(3) will be satisfied. However, as a safety net, the possibility exists of either the Commission or the national competition authorities ('the NCAs'), in certain circumstances, withdrawing the benefit of the block exemption[194]. The authority doing so bears the burden of proving that an agreement falls within the scope of Article 101(1) and that the terms of Article 101(3) are not satisfied[195]. This power has never been used.

(i) Article 6(1): withdrawal by the Commission in individual cases

Article 6(1) provides that the Commission may withdraw the benefit of the block exemption in an individual case where an agreement has effects that are incompatible with Article 101(3). Recital 17 states that this may happen in particular where incentives to innovate are reduced or where access to markets is hindered, and Article 6(1) gives examples of when this could be so[196].

(ii) Article 6(2): withdrawal by an NCA of a Member State

Article 6(2) provides that an NCA may withdraw the benefit of the block exemption under the same circumstances specified in Article 6(1) where a technology transfer agreement has effects incompatible with Article 101(3) in the territory of a Member State or a part thereof that has all the characteristics of a distinct geographic market.

(G) Article 7: non-application of the Regulation

Article 7(1) of the Regulation provides that the Commission may by regulation declare that the block exemption does not apply to technology transfer agreements containing specific restraints relating to a market where parallel networks of similar technology transfer agreements cover more than 50% of the relevant market[197]. Article 7(2) adds that a regulation adopted pursuant to Article 7(1) will not become applicable earlier than six months following its adoption. Where the Commission exercises the power conferred on it by Article 7 it may make a decision in an individual case to provide guidance on the application of Article 101 to the agreements that will have lost the benefit of the block exemption[198].

(H) Article 8: application of the market share thresholds

This provision was dealt with in the context of Article 3 earlier[199].

(I) Articles 9 to 11: other block exemptions, transitional period and period of validity

Article 9 was discussed in the context of Article 2 earlier[200]. Article 10 granted transitional relief to agreements that satisfied Regulation 772/2014 until 31 March 2015. Article 11 provides that Regulation 316/2014 will expire on 30 April 2026.

[194] See generally ibid, paras 144–148.
[195] Ibid, para 146.
[196] Ibid, para 147.
[197] See generally ibid, paras 149–155.
[198] Ibid, para 150.
[199] See 'Article 8: calculation of market share and marginal relief', p 807 earlier in chapter.
[200] See 'Article 2: relationship with other block exemptions', p 800 earlier in chapter.

4. The Application of Article 101 to Other Agreements Relating to Intellectual Property Rights

The previous two sections of this chapter considered the application of Article 101 to agreements to license intellectual property rights, with particular reference to technology transfer agreements and the block exemption conferred by Regulation 316/2014. In this section the application of Article 101 to other agreements relating to intellectual property rights will be examined.

(A) Technology pools

It is not uncommon for two or more undertakings to 'pool' their technology[201]. The *Technology Transfer Guidelines* define technology pools as arrangements whereby two or more parties assemble a package of technology that is licensed to contributors to the pool and to third parties[202]. A pooling arrangement can be fairly simple and informal; however a pool may have an elaborate structure, for example by entrusting its management to a separate entity. In some cases a technology pool may be linked to an industry standard. Industry standards are sometimes established by law ('*de jure*'); in others they may become a standard as a matter of fact ('*de facto*'). It may be that, in order to comply with a standard, access is needed to intellectual property rights, and these rights might be managed through a technology pool[203]. It follows that, just as agreements to establish standards might sometimes infringe Article 101[204], so too might the creation and operation of a pool where it is the subject of an agreement between undertakings and where it could foreclose access to the market[205].

It may also be the case that, within a particular industry, there may be more than one technology pool, and that the different pools may compete with one another. There may be considerable benefits for a firm or firms which control a standard or a technology pool if the industry 'tips' towards that standard or technology as the industry norm[206]. Obvious industries in which one witnesses this phenomenon are mobile telephony[207] and information and communications technology, where the 'battle of the standards' may be fierce.

(i) Effects of technology pools

Technology pools may have both pro-competitive and anti-competitive effects[208].

[201] See generally the report prepared for the European Commission on *Multi-Party Licensing* (Charles River Associates, April 2003), available at www.ec.europa.eu.

[202] *Technology Transfer Guidelines*, para 244.

[203] Ibid, para 245.

[204] See ch 15, 'Standardisation Agreements', pp 619–624; see generally Telvas *The Interface between Competition Law, Patents and Technical Standards* (Kluwer, 2014) and Torti *Intellectual Property Rights and Competition in Standard Setting: Objectives and Tensions* (Routledge, 2015).

[205] The Commission condemned a patent pooling scheme in *Video Cassette Recorders Agreements* OJ [1978] L 47/42; see also *Comcast-Mannesmann*, Commission's XIth *Report on Competition Policy* (1981), point 93; *IGR Stereo Television* ibid, point 94 and XIVth *Report on Competition Policy* (1984), point 92.

[206] Eg the DVD industry tipping to Sony's Blu-ray technology for the next generation of DVD players rather than Toshiba's HD DVD platform.

[207] See Commission Press Release IP/02/1651, 12 November 2002 dealing with pooling arrangements in relation to third generation ('3G') mobile telephony standards; for discussion see Choumelova 'Competition law analysis of patent licensing arrangements—the particular case of 3G3P' (2003) (Spring) Competition Policy Newsletter 41.

[208] See generally the DoJ/FTC report on *Antitrust Enforcement and Intellectual Property Rights: Promoting Innovation and Competition*, ch 3, available at www.ftc.gov.

(a) Pro-competitive effects

The *Guidelines* recognise that technology pools may be pro-competitive. For example firms that need access to the technology in the pool will get the benefit of a 'one-stop shop', dealing only with the pool, instead of having to negotiate individually with a number of different owners; this can lead to a reduction in costs[209].

(b) Anti-competitive effects

The *Guidelines* also explain that pools may be restrictive of competition in two ways. First, the pooling of technology implies joint selling: if the pooled technologies are substitutes for one another this amounts to a price-fixing cartel[210]. Secondly, technology pools may reduce innovation by foreclosing alternative technologies from obtaining access to the market, in particular when they support an industry standard or establish a *de facto* industry standard[211].

(c) Regulation 316/2014

Recital 7 of Regulation 316/2014 states that it does not apply to 'agreements for the pooling of technologies with the purpose of licensing them to third parties'[212].

(ii) Assessment of the formation and operation of technology pools

The *Guidelines* state that, when determining the likely effects of a technology pool, it is useful to consider the way in which it is formed, organised and operated[213].

(a) Open participation

Technologies are more likely to be chosen on the basis of price and quality when all interested parties may participate in a standard and the creation of a pool, thereby reducing the risk that the pool will harm competition[214].

(b) Selection and nature of the pooled technologies

The Commission makes a distinction between the situation where the pooled technologies are substitutes for one another and where they are complements to each other[215], but acknowledges that the distinction is not clear-cut in all cases[216]. Where the pooled technologies are substitutes for one another the concern is that the royalties payable will be higher than they would otherwise be[217] and that this amounts to bundling and price fixing between competitors. The inclusion of significant substitutable technologies in the pool would violate Article 101(1) and be unlikely to satisfy the criteria of Article 101(3)[218].

Where the pooled technologies are complements the arrangement is likely to reduce transaction costs and to lead to lower overall royalties[219]. The *Guidelines* distinguish between 'essential' and 'non-essential' technologies: a technology is 'essential' if it has no viable substitutes for use with the pooled technologies either to produce a product (or process) or for complying with a standard supported by the pool[220]. Essential technologies are necessarily complementary and, subject to certain conditions, generally fall

[209] Ibid, para 245; see also *MPEG-2* OJ [1998] C 229/6 and the Commission's XXIXth *Report on Competition Policy* (1999), points 55 and 56 and p 162; see similarly *Philips/Matsushita—D2B* OJ [1991] C 220/2; *Philips International—DCC* OJ [1992] C 333/8; *European Telecommunications Standards Institute's Intellectual Property Rights Policy* OJ [1994] C 76/5.

[210] *Technology Transfer Guidelines*, para 246. [211] Ibid, para 246.

[212] See further ibid, para 247. [213] Ibid, para 248. [214] Ibid, para 249.

[215] Ibid, para 251. [216] Ibid, para 254. [217] Ibid, para 253.

[218] Ibid, para 255. [219] Ibid, para 253. [220] Ibid, para 252.

outside Article 101[221]. Where a pool encompasses 'non-essential' technologies, the agreement is likely to be caught by Article 101(1) where the pool has market power[222]. The Commission will be less concerned about pools where, for example, technologies which, over time, become non-essential are excluded from the pool[223]; where licensors remain free to license their technologies independently of the pool, so that a licensee could put together its own technological package; or where it is possible to take a licence of part only of the pooled technology at a lower royalty rate[224].

(c) Selection and function of independent experts

The involvement of independent experts in the creation and operation of the pool may be a helpful factor, for example where they ensure that the pool comprises only essential technologies[225]. The Commission has a preference for there to be dispute-resolution mechanisms that are independent of the pool and its members[226].

(d) Exchange of sensitive information

The Commission is anxious that the operation of a pool does not lead to the exchange of sensitive information that could lead to collusion, particularly in oligopolistic markets, and will examine what safeguards have been put in place to prevent this[227].

(iii) A safe harbour

The Commission considers that the way in which a pool is created and operated generally falls outside Article 101(1)—irrespective of the market position of the parties—if seven conditions are fulfilled[228]:

- the process of creating a pool is open to all interested technology rights owners
- safeguards to ensure that only essential technologies are pooled
- safeguards to ensure that sensitive information is only exchanged to the extent necessary for the creation and operation of the pool
- pooled technologies are non-exclusively licensed into the pool
- pooled technologies are licensed on FRAND (fair, reasonable and non-discriminatory) terms
- freedom to challenge the validity and essentiality of the pooled technologies
- freedom to develop competing products and technology.

(iv) Assessment of individual restraints in agreements between the pool and its licensees

Regulation 316/2014 does not apply to licences granted by the pool to a third party[229], although they may not infringe Article 101(1) at all[230]. In assessing agreements between the pool and its licensees the Commission states that account should be taken of four principles[231]:

- the stronger the market position of the pool, the greater the risk of anti-competitive effects

221 See section (iii) later in chapter.
222 *Technology Transfer Guidelines*, para 262. 223 Ibid, para 263. 224 Ibid, para 264.
225 Ibid, paras 256–257. 226 Ibid, para 258. 227 Ibid, para 259. 228 Ibid, para 230.
229 Recital 7 of Regulation 316/2014; see also *Technology Transfer Guidelines*, para 266.
230 See eg *Philips/Sony CD Licensing program*, Commission Press Release IP/03/1152, 7 August 2003.
231 *Technology Transfer Guidelines*, para 267.

- the stronger the market position of the pool, the more likely it is that a failure to grant a licence to all potential licensees or licensing on discriminatory terms will infringe Article 101
- pools should not unduly foreclose third party technologies or limit the creation of alternative pools
- technology transfer agreements should not contain any of the 'hard-core' restrictions listed in Article 4 of Regulation 316/2014.

The Commission acknowledges that the undertakings creating a technology pool are normally free to fix royalties for the technology package and to determine each technology's share of the royalties[232].

Where a technology pool has a dominant position on the market, the royalties and other licensing terms that it offers should be non-excessive and non-discriminatory and the licences granted should be non-exclusive; this is to ensure that there is no anti-competitive foreclosure effect[233]. However it is permissible to charge different royalty rates for different uses and in different product markets[234].

The Commission is also concerned to ensure that a technology pool does not foreclose third party technologies from the market: licensors and licensees must therefore be free to develop competing products and standards and must be free to grant and obtain licences outside the pool[235]. Any grant-back obligations towards the pool should be non-exclusive and limited to developments that are essential or important to the use of the pooled technology[236]. Non-challenge clauses in an agreement between the pool and third parties are likely to be caught by Article 101(1) because they may 'shield' invalid patents[237].

(B) **Copyright pools**

Closely related to technology pools are copyright pools. In *IFPI 'Simulcasting'*[238] the Commission considered an agreement under the terms of which two collecting societies, acting on behalf of record companies, established a 'one-stop shop' whereby an international licence could be granted to radio and television broadcasters wishing to 'simulcast' programmes to the public both by conventional radio and television and also, at the same time, via the internet. The Commission required the deletion of territorial restrictions[239]. It concluded that the joint fixing by the societies of the simulcasting royalty fee infringed Article 101(1)[240]. However, it considered that the agreement met the requirements of Article 101(3) as it would enable a collecting society to grant a 'one-stop shop' licence for simulcasting across the EU which would give consumers a wider access to audio and video music programmes through the internet[241]. The Commission required the parties to charge for their administrative costs separately from the royalties[242], which were the subject of the horizontal agreement: this meant that broadcasters could exercise a competitive choice on the basis of different societies' costs.

[232] Ibid, para 268; this is subject to any commitment on the part of the owner of the technology to grant a licence on FRAND terms.

[233] Ibid, para 269. [234] Ibid. [235] Ibid, para 270.

[236] Ibid, para 271. [237] Ibid, para 272.

[238] OJ [2003] L 107/58; for comment on this decision see Pereira 'From discothèques to websites, a new approach to music copyright licensing: the *Simulcasting* decision' (2003) (Spring) Competition Policy Newsletter 44.

[239] OJ [2003] L 107/58, para 3 and paras 27–28. [240] Ibid, paras 69–80.

[241] Ibid, paras 86–87. [242] Ibid, paras 99–107.

(C) Settlements of litigation

(i) Settlement agreements

The *Technology Transfer Guidelines* acknowledge that, in principle, settlements are 'a legitimate way to find a mutually acceptable compromise to a bona fide legal disagreement'[243]. Where the parties to a dispute agree, as part of a settlement, to license, or to cross-license, the technology in circumstances where one party had the ability to exclude the other from the market by virtue of that technology, the licence is generally not caught by Article 101(1)[244]. However the individual terms of settlement agreements may be caught by Article 101(1)[245].

(a) 'Pay for delay' agreements

Settlement agreements that do not involve the transfer of technology rights, and are based on a value transfer from one party in return for limiting the entry or expansion by the other, may be caught by Article 101(1)[246]. In several decisions the Commission has applied Article 101 to settlements of patent disputes in the pharmaceutical sector[247].

In *Lundbeck*[248] the Commission found that, irrespective of any patent dispute, Lundbeck had transferred value[249] to four generic companies to induce them to accept restrictions on their efforts to enter the market for the term of the agreements. The Commission concluded that each agreement had as its object the restriction of competition since Lundbeck had paid its potential competitors to stay out of the market; the Commission did not examine the effects of the agreements. On appeal the General Court rejected the argument that the generics were not potential competitors of Lundbeck[250]. It also rejected the contention that the agreements reflected the parties' assessment of the strength of the patents as they could not be explained on any basis that was not anti-competitive. The Court acknowledged that settlements are often intended to avoid the cost and uncertainty of litigation, but held that the agreements at issue had the object of restricting competition 'since they consisted in agreements intended to delay the market entry of generic undertakings, in exchange for significant reverse payments'[251]. According to the Court, they were 'market exclusion agreements'[252]. The total amount of fines of €146 million was also upheld.

The *Lundbeck* case, like many pay for delay cases, is contentious[253]. A criticism of the Commission's intervention has been that undertakings might now be unable to settle

[243] *Technology Transfer Guidelines*, para 235; on the position in the US see the judgment of the US Supreme Court in *Federal Trade Commission v Actavis Inc* 570 US 756 (2013); see also the DoJ/FTC report on *Antitrust Enforcement and Intellectual Property Rights: Promoting Innovation and Competition*, pp 88–91; Shapiro 'Antitrust Limits to Patent Settlements' (2003) Rand Journal of Economics 391; Elhauge and Krueger 'Solving the Patent Settlement Puzzle' (2012) Texas Law Review 283; Hovenkamp, 'Anticompetitive Patent Settlements and the Supreme Court's Actavis Decision' (2014) 15 Minnesota Journal of Law, Science and Technology 3; Gallasch, 'Activating Actavis in Europe—the Proposal of a "Structured Effects Based" Analysis for Pay for Delay Settlements' (2016) 36 Legal Studies 683.

[244] *Technology Transfer Guidelines*, para 236. [245] Ibid, para 237. [246] Ibid, paras 237–238.

[247] These decisions followed the Commission's *Pharmaceutical Sector Inquiry Report* of 8 July 2009, available at www.ec.europa.eu.

[248] Commission decision of 19 June 2013.

[249] The 'value' consisted of substantial cash payments and the transfer of a restricted volume of Lundbeck's product and associated profit margins.

[250] Case T-472/13 *Lundbeck v Commission* EU:T:2016:449, paras 89–330.

[251] Ibid, para 539; see also paras 363, 369, 401, 429, 475, 526, 539, 573, 801.

[252] Case T-460/13 *Ranbaxy v Commission* EU:T:2016:453, paras 221–222.

[253] See eg de Margerie '"Pay-for-Delay" Settlements: In Search of the Right Standard' (2013) 36 World Competition 85; Subiotto and Diaz '*Lundbeck v Commission*: Reverse Payment Patent Settlements as Restrictions of Competition by Object' (2017) 8 JECLAP 27 (the authors represented Lundbeck).

litigation; however the Commission's monitoring of patent settlements in the pharmaceutical sector suggests that this has not been the case[254]. Lundbeck and the generics are nevertheless anxious to test the General Court's assessment of potential competition and the meaning of 'object' in Article 101(1), and have therefore appealed to the Court of Justice[255].

In *Johnson & Johnson/Novartis*[256] the Commission imposed fines of €16.3 million on those firms for entering into a 'co-promotion agreement' that provided one of Novartis's subsidiaries with financial incentives not to launch a generic product. In *Servier*[257] the Commission fined Servier and five generics a total of €427.7 million for entering into settlement agreements that had the object and effect of restricting competition by delaying the entry of competing medicines, contrary to Article 101(1). The settlements contained no-challenge and non-compete clauses that were limited to products that (allegedly) infringed Servier's patents. However, in *Lundbeck v Commission* the General Court held that Article 101(1) may apply to clauses even if they do not exceed the subject-matter, territorial and temporal scope of a patent. It is sufficient for the Commission to show the settlement has the object of restricting competition because it excludes potential competitors from the market in exchange for payment[258]. The Commission also found that Servier had infringed Article 102 by inducing the settlements and by acquiring scarce competing technologies as a 'defence mechanism' against generic entry.

Where a settlement agreement includes a licence of technology rights, and it might result in delayed entry onto the market, the Commission will consider whether it is a hard-core restriction under Articles 4(1)(c) and (d) of Regulation 316/2014[259].

(b) Cross-licensing

The *Technology Transfer Guidelines* discuss cross-licensing as a means of settling disputes. Cross-licences that impose restrictions on the parties' use of their technologies, including restrictions on licensing to third parties, may infringe Article 101, in particular where the parties have significant market power and where the agreement imposes restrictions that clearly go beyond what is required to give access to the disputed technology[260]. The *Guidelines* say that any settlement between the parties does not inhibit their future opportunity to innovate and thereby gain a competitive advantage over each other[261].

(c) No-challenge clauses

No-challenge clauses in a settlement agreement are generally regarded as falling outside Article 101, since this is regarded as an inherent aspect of any such agreement[262]. However in *Servier*[263] the Commission found that no-challenge clauses were anti-competitive because Servier had 'bought off' challenges to its patent rights in a manner that did not

[254] 8th Report on the monitoring of Patent Settlements, 9 March 2018, para 48, available at www.ec.europa.eu.

[255] Cases C-591/16 P etc *Lundbeck v Commission*, not yet decided.

[256] Commission decision of 10 December 2013; there was no settlement of litigation in this case.

[257] Commission decision of 9 July 2014, on appeal Cases T-691/14 etc *Servier v Commission*, not yet decided; see also Commission Press Release IP/14/799, 9 July 2014, for a helpful summary of the case.

[258] Case T-472/13 EU:T:2016:449, paras 486–500.

[259] *Technology Transfer Guidelines*, para 239; the *Guidelines* also discuss cross-licensing in settlement agreements (paras 240–241) and no-challenge clauses (paras 242–243).

[260] Ibid, para 240. [261] Ibid, para 241. [262] Ibid, para 242.

[263] Commission decision of 9 July 2014, paras 1184–1191, on appeal Cases T-691/14 etc *Servier v Commission*, not yet decided.

reflect the uncertainty as to whether those rights were valid and secured the agreement of competitors not to enter the market.

(ii) Trade mark settlements

The Commission will carefully scrutinise trade mark delimitation agreements whereby owners of independent trade marks accept restrictions on the exercise and use of their respective marks[264]. This means that legal advisers must be careful when advising clients as to the terms on which they should settle a trade mark dispute, since it may be that the settlement itself will contravene Article 101(1)[265]. In *BAT v Commission*[266] the Court of Justice established that trade mark delimitation agreements are permissible and fall outside Article 101(1) where they serve to avoid confusion or conflict; however there must be a genuine dispute between the parties and the agreement must be no more restrictive than necessary to overcome the problem of confusion.

In *Chiquita/Fyffes*[267] the Commission took the view that an agreement between Chiquita and Fyffes whereby Fyffes agreed not to use the Fyffes trade mark in continental Europe for a period of 20 years infringed both Articles 101 and 102. The alleged infringement of Article 102 lay in the fact that the inability of Fyffes to use that mark diminished its ability to compete vigorously with Chiquita in Europe. Following the Commission's intervention, Chiquita abandoned the agreement.

(D) Concerted refusal to license intellectual property rights

In *Credit Default Swaps Information Market*[268] the Commission was concerned that the International Swaps and Derivatives Association ('ISDA'), Markit and some of their members had refused to license intellectual property rights and data used by the industry for calculating the price of credit default swaps. The case was closed after ISDA and Markit gave commitments under Article 9 of Regulation 1/2003 that prevented investment banks from influencing their licensing decisions and promised to grant FRAND licences[269].

5. Article 102 and Intellectual Property Rights

The law of intellectual property confers exclusive rights, whereas Article 102 prohibits the abuse of a dominant position. The question arises whether Article 102 can be applied in

[264] See *Sirdar and Phildar Trade Marks* [1975] 1 CMLR D93; *Re Penney's Trade Mark* OJ [1978] L 60/19 (Article 101 inapplicable to a trade mark agreement which was a genuine attempt to settle litigation and not an attempt to partition the market); *Syntex/Syntbelabo* [1990] 4 CMLR 343 (Commission required modification of trade mark agreement that unjustifiably partitioned markets); *Toltecs and Dorcet Trade Marks* OJ [1982] L 379/19 (this decision was the subject of the appeal in *BAT v Commission* later); *Hershey/Herschi*, XXth *Report on Competition Policy* (1990), point 111; *Chiquita/Fyffes plc*, XXIInd *Report on Competition Policy* (1992), points 168–176 (agreement by Fyffes not to use the Fyffes trade mark in continental Europe contrary to Article 101; also an abuse of a dominant position under Article 102); see *Fyffes plc v Chiquita Brands International Inc* [1993] ECC 193 on the litigation in the English High Court in this case.

[265] See generally Singleton 'IP Disputes: Settlement Agreements and Ancillary Licences' (1993) 15 EIPR 48.

[266] Case 35/83 EU:C:1985:32; for comment see Alexander (1985) 22 CML Rev 709.

[267] Commission's XXIInd *Report on Competition Policy* (1992), points 168–176.

[268] Commission commitment decisions of 20 July 2016; see Commission Press Release IP/16/2586, 20 July 2016.

[269] The commitments complement Directive 2014/65/EU on markets in financial instruments (MiFID 2), OJ [2014] L 173/349 and Regulation 600/2014 on markets in financial instruments, OJ [2014] L 173/84, which apply from 1 January 2018.

such a way as to limit the exclusive rights given by intellectual property law[270]. The Court of Justice has made clear that the mere ownership of intellectual property rights cannot be attacked under Article 102[271]; however Article 102 may apply to an improper exercise of such rights[272]. Article 8(2) of the WTO agreement on Trade-Related Aspects of Intellectual Property Rights (the so-called 'TRIPS Agreement') makes the same distinction.

(A) Compulsory licences

A question that has been much debated is the extent to which the owner of an intellectual property right can be compelled to grant a licence of it to a third party under Article 102. As a general proposition the owner of an intellectual property right is entitled to determine how it should be exploited and a compulsory licence should be imposed only in exceptional circumstances.

(i) The *Renault* and *Volvo* judgments

In *Renault*[273] and in *Volvo v Erik Veng*[274] third parties wished to be granted licences of the car manufacturers' intellectual property rights in order to produce spare parts, and claimed that a refusal to grant such licences was an abuse of a dominant position under Article 102. The Court of Justice adopted an orthodox approach to the application of Article 102 to compulsory licensing and held that, in the absence of EU harmonisation of laws on designs and models, it was a matter for national law to determine the nature and extent of protection for such matters. In *Volvo* the Court stated at paragraph 8 that:

> the right of the proprietor of a protected design to prevent third parties from manufacturing and selling or importing, without its consent, products incorporating the design constitutes the very subject-matter of its exclusive rights. It follows that an obligation imposed upon the proprietor of a protected design to grant to third parties, even in return for a reasonable royalty, a licence for the supply of products incorporating the design would lead to the proprietor thereof being deprived of the substance of its exclusive right, and that a refusal to grant such a licence cannot in itself constitute an abuse of a dominant position.

The Court added, however, that a car manufacturer might be guilty of abusing its dominant position where it refused to supply spare parts to independent repairers in an

[270] For further discussion of this subject see Tritton *Intellectual Property in Europe* (Sweet & Maxwell, 4th ed, 2014), ch 11; Anderman and Schmidt *EU Competition Law and Intellectual Property Rights: The Regulation of Innovation* (Oxford University Press, 2nd ed, 2011), chs 3–11; Kjølbye 'Article 82 EC as Remedy to Patent System Imperfections: Fighting Fire with Fire?' (2009) 32 World Competition 163; Vickers 'Competition Policy and Property Rights' (2010) 120 Ec J 375; Temple Lang 'Potential Downstream Markets in European Antitrust Law: A Concept in Need of Limiting Principles' (2011) 7 Competition Policy International 106; Coates, Kyølbye and Peeperkorn in Faull and Nikpay (eds) *The EU Law of Competition* (Oxford University Press, 3rd ed, 2014), paras 10.214–10.261.

[271] Article 345 TFEU provides that the Treaties 'shall in no way prejudice the rules in Member States governing the system of property ownership'.

[272] See Case 24/67 *Parke, Davis & Co v Probel* EU:C:1968:11 where the Court of Justice said that ownership of a patent is not an abuse in itself although 'the utilisation of the patent could degenerate into an improper exploitation of the protection'; the ownership of intellectual property is a factor to be taken into account in assessing whether a firm has a dominant position: see ch 5, 'Legal barriers', pp 191–192.

[273] Case 53/87 *Consorzio italiano della componentistica di ricambio per autoveicoli e Maxicar v Régie national des usines Renault* EU:C:1988:472.

[274] Case 238/87 EU:C:1988:477; see Korah 'No Duty to Licence Independent Repairers to Make Spare Parts: the *Renault*, *Volvo* and *Bayer* Cases' (1988) 12 EIPR 381; Groves 'The Use of Registered Designs to Protect Car Body Panels' (1989) 10 Business Law Review 117.

arbitrary manner, charged unfair prices for spare parts[275] or decided no longer to produce spare parts for models still in circulation.

(ii) The *Magill* case

A less orthodox approach was taken by the Commission in *Magill TV Guide/ITP, BBC and RTE*[276], variously known as the *Magill* case or the *TV Listings* case. Magill wished to publish the listings of three television companies broadcasting in the UK and Ireland in a single weekly publication. At the time there was no publication which contained the details of all three companies' programmes for a week in advance; this information was available only in daily newspapers for the day in question, or on a Saturday for the weekend. There was an obvious public demand for listings magazines, which were widely available in continental countries. Copyright protection was available for TV listings under UK and Irish law, which is why Magill required a licence. The Commission concluded that the three television companies had abused their individual dominant positions in relation to their own TV listings by refusing to make them available to Magill and required that advance information be supplied in order to enable comprehensive weekly TV guides to be published. The Commission's decision was appealed to the General Court and the Court of Justice, each of which upheld it[277]. The Court of Justice stated that the abuse consisted of the refusal to provide basic information by relying on national copyright provisions, thereby preventing the appearance of a new product, a comprehensive guide to television programmes, which the television companies did not offer and for which there was a potential consumer demand[278]; the Court also noted that there was no objective justification for the refusal[279] and that the result of the refusal was to reserve to the television companies the downstream market for television guides[280].

The case was controversial and led to numerous comments and articles, mainly adverse[281]. It appeared to sit oddly with the earlier judgments of the Court of Justice in *Renault* and *Volvo*; it meant that the possibility of compulsory licensing had been introduced under Article 102; and it could be seen to be an application of the so-called 'essential facilities doctrine' to intellectual property rights[282]. In *Oscar Bronner v Mediaprint*[283] the Court of Justice stressed the exceptional circumstances in *Magill*[284]. However a particular anxiety was that the precedent might be applied to intellectual property rights that were the consequence of substantial risk-taking and investment—for example patents and computer software—as opposed to a mere list of television programmes, though this did

[275] In Case T-198/98 *Micro Leader Business v Commission* EU:T:1999:341 the General Court held that the Commission, before rejecting a complaint against Microsoft concerning the exercise of its copyright protection, should have investigated whether its prices were discriminatory contrary to Article 102(2)(c): ibid, paras 49–59.

[276] OJ [1989] L 78/43.

[277] Cases T-69/89 etc *RTE v Commission* EU:T:1991:39, upheld by the Court of Justice Cases C-241/91 P etc *RTE and ITP v Commission* EU:C:1995:98.

[278] Cases C-241/91 P EU:C:1995:98, para 54. [279] Ibid, para 55. [280] Ibid, para 56.

[281] For comment on the Court of Justice's judgment see eg Pombo 'Intellectual Property and Intra-Community Trade' [1996] Fordham Corporate Law Institute (ed Hawk), 491–505; Crowther 'Compulsory Licensing of Intellectual Property Rights' (1995) 20 EL Rev 521; Anderman and Schmidt *EU Competition Law and Intellectual Property Rights: The Regulation of Innovation* (Oxford University Press, 2nd ed, 2011), pp 102–109.

[282] See ch 17, 'Is the product to which access is sought indispensable to someone wishing to compete in the downstream market?', pp 717–723; see generally Cotter 'Intellectual Property and the Essential Facilities Doctrine' (1999) 44 Antitrust Bulletin 211 on the question of whether intellectual property rights can be regarded as essential facilities.

[283] Case C-7/97 EU:C:1998:569. [284] Ibid, para 40.

not happen in practice. There is little doubt that the Commission and the EU Courts were influenced in *Magill* by the fact that information as prosaic as TV listings was entitled to copyright protection: most systems of law in the Member States would not have conferred intellectual property protection at all in such circumstances[285]. However this was not an explicit part of the reasoning in the Commission's decision or the Courts' judgments.

(iii) *IMS Health*

In the next case to deal with this matter, *IMS Health v NDC Health*[286], the Court of Justice repeated the formulation of the Court in *Bronner*. The *IMS* case was an Article 267 reference from a German court[287]. NDC Health was seeking a licence from IMS, the world leader in data collection on pharmaceutical sales and prescriptions, that would give it access to IMS's copyrighted format for processing regional sales data in Germany, the so-called '1,860 brick structure'. After considering whether the brick structure might be an indispensable requirement for NDC, as required by the *Bronner* judgment[288], the Court went on to consider the questions of whether a refusal to license NDC might exclude all competition in a secondary market[289], and whether it might prevent the emergence of a new product[290]. On the latter point the Court agreed with Advocate General Tizzano that, in achieving a balance between the need to protect the economic freedom of the owner of an intellectual property right on the one hand and the protection of competition on the other:

> the latter can prevail *only where refusal to grant a licence prevents the development of the secondary market to the detriment of consumers*[291] (emphasis added).

In seeking some limitation to what might be meant by 'exceptional circumstances', this last statement of the Court of Justice in *IMS* was helpful: even if one acknowledges that there is room for debate as to what is meant by 'the development of the secondary market'—what, for example, is a 'new' product—nevertheless the Court establishes clearly that there is no right to a licence simply to duplicate what the owner of the intellectual property right in question is already doing[292].

285 Directive 96/9 on the legal protection of databases, OJ [1996] L 77/20 adopts criteria for originality which differ from UK and Irish copyright laws at the time of the *Magill* case.

286 Case C-418/01 EU:C:2004:257; for comment see Sufrin 'The *IMS* Case' [2004] Comp Law 18; Brinker 'Essential Facility Doctrine and Intellectual Property Law: Where Does Europe Stand in the Aftermath of the *IMS Health* Case?' [2004] Fordham Corporate Law Institute (ed Hawk), 137; Eilmansberger 'The Essential Facilities Doctrine under Art. 82: What is the State of Affairs after *IMS Health and Microsoft?*' (2005) 16 King's College Law Journal 329; Fox 'A Tale of Two Jurisdictions and an Orphan Case: Antitrust, Intellectual Property, and Refusals to Deal' (2005) 28 Fordham International Law Journal 952; Ahlborn, Evans and Padilla 'The Logic & Limits of the "Exceptional Circumstances Test" in *Magill* and *IMS Health*' (2005) 28 Fordham International Law Journal 1109.

287 Note that the Commission had adopted interim measures against IMS in *NDC Health/IMS: (Interim Measures)* OJ [2002] L 59/18; for comment see Korah 'The Interface between IP and Antitrust: The European Experience' (2001–02) 69 Antitrust LJ 801; Fine '*NDC/IMS*: In Response to Professor Korah' (2002) 70 Antitrust LJ 247; the Presidents of the General Court and the Court of Justice suspended the Commission's decision pending the General Court's final judgment; both noted that there was a serious dispute as to whether the circumstances in *IMS* were exceptional: Case T-184/01 R EU:T:2001:259 (Order of the President of General Court), upheld on appeal Case C-481/01 P (R) EU:C:2002:223 (Order of the President of the Court of Justice); in due course the Commission withdrew the interim measures decision, so that the appeal to the General Court was itself withdrawn: see Commission Press Release IP/03/1159, 13 August 2003.

288 See ch 17, 'Is the product to which access is sought indispensable to someone wishing to compete in the downstream market?', pp 717–723 on the meaning of indispensability in this context.

289 Case C-418/01 EU:C:2004:257, paras 40–47. 290 Ibid, paras 48–50.

291 Ibid, para 48; see similarly paras 53–54 of the Opinion of AG Maduro in Case C-109/03 *KPN Telecom* EU:C:2004:437.

292 Ibid, para 239.

(iv) The *Microsoft* case

The *Magill* and the *IMS* cases established the possibility of a claim to a licence under Article 102 in exceptional circumstances, in particular where the licensee intended to produce a new product for which there was a potential consumer demand. The potential significance of this approach was dramatically revealed in the Commission's decision in the *Microsoft* case of 24 March 2004[293]. The Commission held that Microsoft was dominant in two markets, one for personal computer operating systems and the other for work group server operating systems. The Commission held that Microsoft had abused its dominant position by refusing to supply competitors with interoperability information to enable them to develop and distribute products that would compete with Microsoft's on the market for servers. The Commission also found Microsoft guilty of an abuse by tying its operating system with its Windows Media Player[294]. For the two abuses Microsoft was fined €497 million. The Commission's findings of abuse, and the fine, were upheld on appeal to the General Court in *Microsoft v Commission*[295]. A number of points should be noted about the abusive refusal to supply.

(a) The Commission and the General Court assumed that Microsoft enjoyed intellectual property protection

The first point is that the Commission and the General Court proceeded on the assumption that Microsoft's interoperability information was protected by the law of intellectual property, without actually reaching a conclusion on the point[296]. The Court noted that, in making this assumption, the Commission had imposed upon itself the strictest legal test, that is to say the one most favourable to Microsoft[297].

(b) The General Court's summary of the applicable law

The General Court then proceeded to analyse the relevant case law, referring in particular to *Magill*, *Bronner* and *IMS Health*, from which it drew the following conclusion:

> 331 It follows from the case law cited above that the refusal by an undertaking holding a dominant position to license a third party to use a product covered by an intellectual property right cannot in itself constitute an abuse of a dominant position within the meaning of Article [102 TFEU]. It is only in exceptional circumstances that the exercise of the exclusive right by the owner of the intellectual property right may give rise to such an abuse.

[293] OJ [2007] L 32/23; see Banasevic, Huby, Pena, Castellot, Sitar and Piffaut 'Commission adopts Decision in the *Microsoft* case' (2004) (Summer) Competition Policy Newsletter 44–46; Lévêque 'Innovation, Leveraging and Essential Facilities: Interoperability Licensing in the EU *Microsoft* Case' (2005) 28 World Competition 71; Dolmans, O'Donoghue and Loewenthal 'Are Article 82 and Intellectual Property Interoperable? The State of the Law Pending the Judgment in *Microsoft v Commission*' (2007) 3 Competition Policy International 107; Vesterdorf 'Article 82 EC: Where do we stand after the *Microsoft* judgment?' (2008) 1 ICC Global Antitrust Review 1; O'Donoghue and Padilla *The Law and Economics of Article 102 TFEU* (Hart, 2nd ed, 2013), pp 555–559.

[294] See ch 17, 'Tying', pp 705–713 for discussion of the tying infringement; see also McMahon 'Interoperability: "Indispensability" and "Special Responsibility" in High Technology Markets' (2007) 9 Tulane Journal of Technology and Intellectual Property 123.

[295] Case T-201/04 EU:T:2007:289; for discussion of the case by Commission officials see Kramler, Buhr and Wyns 'The judgment of the Court of First Instance in the *Microsoft* case' (2007) 3 Competition Policy Newsletter 39; see also Howarth and McMahon '"Windows has Performed an Illegal Operation": The Court of First Instance's Judgment in *Microsoft v Commission*' (2008) 29 ECLR 117.

[296] Case T-201/04 EU:T:2007:289, paras 283–290.

[297] Ibid, para 284.

332 It also follows from that case law that the following circumstances, in particular, must be considered to be exceptional:

- in the first place, the refusal relates to a product or service indispensable to the exercise of a particular activity on a neighbouring market;
- in the second place, the refusal is of such a kind as to exclude any effective competition on that neighbouring market;
- in the third place, the refusal prevents the appearance of a new product for which there is potential consumer demand.

333 Once it is established that such circumstances are present, the refusal by the holder of a dominant position to grant a licence may infringe Article [102 TFEU] unless the refusal is objectively justified.

334 The Court notes that the circumstance that the refusal prevents the appearance of a new product for which there is potential demand is found only in the case law on the exercise of an intellectual property right.

(c) The General Court's benign application of the 'new product' requirement

The Court concluded that the requirement of indispensability was satisfied[298] and that all effective competition would be eliminated on a secondary market[299]. A notable feature of the General Court's judgment is its treatment of the 'new product' requirement[300]. The Court began by noting that this consideration was one that should be understood in the context of Article 102(2)(b) which prohibits abusive conduct which consists of 'limiting production, markets or technical development to the prejudice of consumers'[301]. However the Court did not make a finding, nor did it require the Commission to have made a finding, that any specific new product—such as the composite TV listings magazine in *Magill*—would have resulted from the provision of interoperability information; rather the Court said that the new product criterion should be read to include a restriction of technical development[302], and that the Commission's emphasis on this factor was not manifestly incorrect[303]. In the Court's view Microsoft's refusal meant that consumers were increasingly locked into Microsoft's platform at the work group server level[304]; and that competitors were prevented from developing operating systems distinguishable from the Windows systems already on the market[305]. The Court concluded with the rather bizarre statement that Microsoft had 'impaired the effective competitive structure on the work group server operating systems market by acquiring a significant market share on that market'[306]. The General Court rejected Microsoft's claim that its behaviour was objectively justified[307].

The Court seems to have taken a somewhat benign approach to the 'new product' rule in this judgment[308]. It can be anticipated that future cases will have to examine further the scope of the new product rule, both as to the 'newness' of the product and the possibility that a restriction of technical development may suffice[309].

(d) Remedy

An obvious difficulty with a case such as *Microsoft* is to determine an appropriate remedy, and to ensure that there is proper compliance. After the Commission's decision in *Microsoft* in March 2004 there were protracted negotiations between the Commission and Microsoft

[298] Ibid, paras 369–436. [299] Ibid, paras 479–620. [300] Ibid, paras 643–665.
[301] Ibid, para 643. [302] Ibid, para 647. [303] Ibid, para 649. [304] Ibid, paras 650–652.
[305] Ibid, paras 653–659. [306] Ibid, para 664. [307] Ibid, paras 688–712.
[308] See Vickers 'A Tale of Two EC Cases: *IBM* and *Microsoft*' (2008) 4 Competition Policy International 3.
[309] On this point see para 62 of the AG's Opinion in Case C-418/01 *IMS Health GmbH & Co OHG v NDC Health GmbH & Co KG* EU:C:2003:537; see also O'Donoghue and Padilla *The Law and Economics of Article 102 TFEU* (Hart, 2nd ed, 2013), pp 554–563.

as to whether the latter was making the necessary interoperability information available to the market on reasonable and non-discriminatory terms. The Commission appointed a Trustee to provide technical advice on compliance[310], although the General Court subsequently ruled that the Commission lacked the power to have done so[311]. The Commission decided in July 2006 that Microsoft had failed to provide interoperability information, as required by its decision, from 16 December 2005 to 20 June 2006, and therefore imposed a daily periodical payment penalty of €1.5 million on Microsoft which totalled €280.5 million[312]. In February 2008 the Commission imposed a further penalty of €899 million on Microsoft for charging unreasonable prices for the information from 21 June 2006 until 21 October 2007[313]; on appeal the General Court substantially upheld the Commission's findings[314]. In October 2007 the Commission announced that it had finally reached agreement with Microsoft on compliance with its decision[315].

(B) The Commission's *Guidance on Article 102 Enforcement Priorities*

Paragraphs 75 to 90 of its *Guidance on Article 102 Enforcement Priorities* describe the Commission's approach to refusals to license intellectual property or to provide proprietary information[316]. The *Guidance* does not purport to state the law under Article 102; rather it explains the factors that inform the Commission's enforcement. Refusals to supply will be an enforcement priority if the Commission is satisfied that:

- the refusal relates to a product or service that is objectively necessary to be able to compete effectively on a downstream market
- the refusal is likely to lead to the elimination of effective competition on the downstream market[317] and
- the refusal is likely to lead to consumer harm.

It is noticeable that the Commission applies the same factors to a refusal to license intellectual property rights as to other types of refusal to supply, although it may be more difficult to establish them in such cases. In deciding whether a refusal is likely to lead to consumer harm the Commission specifically says that it would look to see whether the refusal would result in innovative products not being brought to the market or follow-on innovation being stifled[318]. The evidential burden is on the dominant firm to demonstrate any negative impact which an obligation to supply is likely to have on its own level of innovation[319].

(C) Collecting societies

Article 102 may be applied to the activities of collecting societies, that is to say organisations that manage copyright on behalf of authors and publishers; in particular they collect royalties from the media, websites and other users on behalf of their members and

[310] See eg Commission Press Release IP/05/1215, 5 October 2005.

[311] Case T-201/04 *Microsoft Corpn v Commission* EU:T:2007:289, paras 1251–1279.

[312] Commission decision of 12 July 2006.

[313] Commission decision of 27 February 2008.

[314] Case T-167/08 *Microsoft Corpn v Commission* EU:T:2012:323.

[315] Commission Press Release IP/07/1567, 22 October 2007; see also Commission MEMO/08/106, 21 February 2008.

[316] OJ [2009] C 45/7; for a general discussion see ch 5, 'The Commission's *Guidance on Article 102 Enforcement Priorities*', pp 182–185.

[317] On this point the *Guidance on Article 102 Enforcement Priorities* does not refer to, but is consistent with, paras 332 and 563 of the General Court's judgment in Case T-201/04 *Microsoft Corpn v Commission* EU:T:2007:289.

[318] *Guidance on Article 102 Enforcement Priorities*, para 87, which specifically cites the judgments of the Court of Justice and General Court in respectively *IMS* and *Microsoft* in support of this approach.

[319] Ibid, para 90.

distribute them in return for a fee. Article 102 has been invoked both by the Commission[320] and before domestic courts, several of which have referred questions to the Court of Justice under Article 267 TFEU[321].

The Court of Justice has indicated that there is nothing intrinsically objectionable about the establishment of collecting societies, which may be necessary in order that individual artists can obtain a reasonable return for their endeavours[322]. However the activities of a society may amount to a breach of Article 102 in various ways. EU law forbids national societies from discriminating against undertakings from other Member States[323]. The royalties charged by a collecting society for licences to broadcast music may be excessive[324]. In *CISAC* the Commission prohibited the International Confederation of Societies of Authors and Composers and 24 collecting societies from restricting competition by limiting their ability to offer services outside the domestic territory of each collecting society[325]. On appeal the General Court annulled the Commission's finding of a concerted practice because the 'fight against piracy' was a plausible alternative explanation for the societies' parallel behaviour[326]. However the General Court upheld the Commission's finding that territorial membership and exclusivity clauses in the societies' agreements infringed Article 101(1)[327].

Other aspects of collecting societies' activities have been condemned, such as clauses in the constitution which unreasonably restrict an author's right to act unilaterally and provisions which are unreasonable vis-à-vis the media or which attempt to extend the protection of copyright to non-copyrighted works[328].

(D) **Miscellaneous cases concerning intellectual property rights**

(i) **Unlawful acquisition of technology**

In *Tetra Pak Rausing v Commission*[329] the General Court upheld the Commission's decision[330] that it was an abuse of Tetra Pak's dominant position in the market for cartons

[320] *GEMA* JO [1971] L 134/15; *Interpar v GVL GmbH* OJ [1981] L 370/49; *GEMA Statutes* OJ [1982] L 94/12; *BIEM-FPI*, XIIIth *Report on Competition Policy* (1983), points 147–150; *GEMA*, XVth *Report on Competition Policy* (1985), point 81; *GVL* OJ [1981] L 370/49, upheld on appeal to the Court of Justice Case 7/82 *GVL v Commission* EU:C:1983:52; the Commission's decision not to proceed with complaints against SACEM, a French collecting society, was unsuccessfully challenged in Case T-114/92 *BEMIM v Commission* EU:T:1995:11 and in Case T-5/93 *Roger Tremblay v Commission* EU:T:1995:12, upheld on appeal to the Court of Justice Case C-91/95 P EU:C:1996:407; for comment see Torremans and Stamatoudi 'Collecting Societies: Sorry, the Community is No Longer Interested!' (1997) 2 EL Rev 352.

[321] Case 127/73 *Belgische Radio en Televisie v SABAM* EU:C:1974:25; Case 22/79 *Greenwich Film Production v SACEM* EU:C:1979:245; Case 402/85 *Basset v SACEM* EU:C:1987:197; Case 395/87 *Ministère Public v Tournier* EU:C:1989:319; Case 110/88 *Lucazeau v SACEM* EU:C:1989:326; Case C-52/07 *Kanal 5 Ltd and TV 4 AB v Föreningen Svenska Tonsättares Internationella Musikbyrå (STIM) upa* EU:C:2008:703; Case C-351/12 *OSA v LIML* EU:C:2014:110; Case C-177/16 *Autortiesību un komunicēšanās konsultāciju aģentūra—Latvijas Autoru apvienība v Konkurences padome (AKKA/LAA)* EU:C:2017:689; Case C-525/16 MEO v Autoridade da Concorrência EU:C:2018:270.

[322] See Case 127/73 *BRT v SABAM* EU:C:1974:25, paras 8–15.

[323] *Re GEMA* JO [1971] L 134/15; Case 7/82 *GVL v Commission* EU:C:1983:52.

[324] See Case C-177/16 *Autortiesību un komunicēšanās konsultāciju aģentūra—Latvijas Autoru apvienība v Konkurences padome (AKKA/LAA)* EU:C:2017:689.

[325] Commission decision of 16 July 2008; the President of the General Court rejected applications for interim measures in Case T-411/08 R *Artisjus Magyar Szerzői Jogvédő Iroda Egyesület v Commission* EU:T:2008:503.

[326] Cases T-442/08 etc *CISAC v Commission* EU:T:2013:188; the finding of a concerted practice was not challenged and thus not annulled in Case T-451/08 *Stim v Commission* EU:T:2013:189.

[327] See Case T-401/08 *Säveltäjäin Tekijänoikeustoimisto Teosto v Commission* EU:T:2013:170, paras 59–75.

[328] The most thorough decision on these issues remains the Commission's decision in *Re GEMA* JO [1971] L 134/15; on the lawfulness of 'supplementary mechanical reproduction fees' see Case 402/85 *Basset v SACEM* EU:C:1987:197.

[329] Case T-51/89 EU:T:1990:41.

[330] *Tetra Pak I (BTG Licence)* OJ [1988] L 272/27.

and machines for packaging milk to acquire Liquipak and thereby obtain the benefit of an exclusive licence relating to technology for a new method of sterilising cartons suitable for long-life milk. This finding was despite the fact that the licence complied with the provisions of the block exemption in force at the time on patent licensing agreements. In *Servier*[331] the Commission concluded that Servier had abused its dominant position by acquiring, but not using, the most advanced competing technologies to produce a drug, Perindopril, thereby making it more difficult for generic competitors to enter the market.

(ii) Demanding excessive royalties

In *Eurofix-Bauco v Hilti*[332] the Commission held that it was an abuse to demand an 'excessive' royalty with the sole object of blocking, or at any rate unreasonably delaying, a licence of right which was available under UK patent law. This was seen as part of Hilti's strategy of preventing competition in respect of its nail cartridges.

In *Duales System Deutschland*[333] the Commission concluded that it was an abuse of a dominant position for DSD, an undertaking that operated a comprehensive system for the collection and recycling of waste in Germany, to contain a provision in its trade mark agreement that its clients would pay a royalty for sales packaging bearing its 'Green Dot' trade mark, irrespective of whether the client actually used the services of DSD. This could dissuade those clients from using the services of competitors. The Commission's decision was upheld on appeal[334].

The Commission closed an investigation of whether Qualcomm had failed to license its 3G mobile technology on FRAND terms, deciding that it was no longer an administrative priority[335].

(iii) Seeking an injunction to enforce standard-essential patents

Undertakings that participate in the setting of a standard may own essential patents ('SEPs'), a licence for which is needed by anyone wishing to comply with the standard. Where an undertaking commits, during a standard-setting procedure, to license any SEPs on FRAND terms to a licensee wishing to produce products that conform to the standard, the question arises whether it could be an abuse of a dominant position for the owner of the SEP to seek an interim injunction from a court in the event of a failure by the parties to reach a FRAND agreement[336].

[331] Commission decision of 9 July 2014, paras 2800ff on appeal Cases T-691/14 etc *Servier v Commission*, not yet decided.

[332] OJ [1988] L 65/19, para 78, upheld on appeal Case T-30/89 *Hilti AG v Commission* EU:T:1991:70, para 99.

[333] OJ [2001] L 166/1, paras 111–113.

[334] Case T-151/01 *Duales System Deutschland GmbH v Commission* EU:T:2007:154, upheld on appeal Case C-385/07 P *Duales System Deutschland GmbH v Commission* EU:C:2009:456.

[335] Commission MEMO/09/516, 24 November 2009.

[336] For further discussion of this subject see Mariniello 'Fair Reasonable and Non-Discriminatory (FRAND) Terms: A Challenge for Competition Authorities' (2011) 7 Journal of Competition Law and Economics 523; Petit 'Injunctions for FRAND-Pledged SEPs: The Quest for an Appropriate Test of Abuse Under Article 102 TFEU' (2013) European Competition Journal 677; O'Donoghue and Padilla *The Law and Economics of Article 102 TFEU* (Hart, 2nd ed, 2013), pp 695–711; Jones 'Standard Essential Patents: FRAND Commitments, Injunctions and the Smartphone Wars' (2014) 9 European Competition Journal 1; Zografos 'The SEP Holder's Guide to the Antitrust Galaxy: FRAND and Injunctions' (2014) 37 World Competition 53; 'Standard-essential patents' (June 2014) Competition Policy Brief available at www.ec.europa.eu; Henningsson 'Injunctions for Standard-Essential Patents under FRAND Commitment: A Balanced, Royalty-Oriented Approach' (2016) 47 International Review of Intellectual Property and Competition Law 438; Communication from the Commission on 'Standard Essential Patents for a European digitized economy', April 2017, available at www.ec.europa.eu.

In the so-called *Orange Book* case[337] the German Federal Court of Justice adopted a narrow approach to the application of Article 102, holding that the SEP owner abuses its dominant position only if the alleged infringer has made a binding, unconditional offer to conclude a FRAND agreement and, where it uses the teachings of the patent, pays royalties into an escrow account.

In *Motorola—Enforcement of GPRS standard essential patents*[338] the Commission took a stricter approach, deciding that Motorola had abused its dominant position by seeking an injunction in circumstances where the would-be licensee in that case, Apple, was willing to submit the FRAND dispute to the binding resolution of a German court. The Commission also considered that it was abusive for Motorola to insist that any settlement eventually reached with Apple should contain a commitment on the latter's part not to challenge Motorola's patents[339]. In *Samsung—Enforcement of UMTS standard essential patents*[340] the Commission accepted commitments from Samsung, whereby FRAND disputes in relation to Samsung's SEPs would be resolved by a model dispute resolution procedure[341].

The issue of FRAND licensing was the subject of an Article 267 reference by the Landgericht in Düsseldorf to the Court of Justice in *Huawei Technologies Co Ltd v ZTE Corp*[342]. The reference was made before the Commission's decisions in *Motorola* and *Samsung* of 29 April 2014. The Landgericht was aware of the Commission's investigations and that its position might differ from the German *Orange Book* standard and so considered that it was appropriate to make an Article 267 reference. The Court of Justice noted that there could be exceptional circumstances in which the exercise of an intellectual property right could amount to an abuse of a dominant position citing, for example, the *Magill TV listings* case[343]; however the Court pointed out that the facts of *Huawei* were unlike any previous case. The Court noted that Huawei had committed to ETSI, the relevant standard-setting organisation, that it would license its SEPs on FRAND terms, and then said that:

> 53 In those circumstances, and having regard to the fact that an undertaking to grant licences on FRAND terms creates legitimate expectations on the part of third parties that the proprietor of the SEP will in fact grant licences on such terms, a refusal by the proprietor of the SEP to grant a licence on those terms may, in principle, constitute an abuse within the meaning of Article 102 TFEU.
>
> 54 It follows that, having regard to the legitimate expectations created, the abusive nature of such a refusal may, in principle, be raised in defence to actions for a prohibitory injunction or for the recall of products.

The Court of Justice went on to say that it follows, in effect, that seeking an injunction to enforce an SEP could itself amount to an abuse of a dominant position. The Court

[337] KZR 39/06, judgment of 6 May 2009, available at www.bundesgerichtshof.de.

[338] Commission decision of 29 April 2014.

[339] Commission decision of 29 April 2014, paras 271–420; the Commission also explained why Motorola's conduct was not objectively justified: ibid, paras 421–491.

[340] Commission commitment decision of 29 April 2014.

[341] Commission decision of 29 April 2014; see also Commission MEMO/09/549, 10 December 2009: following its acquisition of Robert Bosch's mobile telephony patent portfolio and discussions with the Commission, IPCom agreed to take over Bosch's commitment to grant irrevocable patent licences on FRAND terms; this issue has also arisen under the Merger Regulation: see eg Case M 6381 *Google/Motorola Mobility*, decision of 13 February 2012, paras 128–149.

[342] Case C-170/13 EU:C:2015:477; for comment see the essays in the CPI Antitrust Chronicle, October 2015 (2), available at www.competitionpolicyinternational.com; Grasso 'The ECJ Ruling in *Huawei* and the Right to Seek Injunctions Based on FRAND-Encumbered SEPs under EU Competition Law: One Step Forward' (2016) 39 World Competition 213.

[343] Cases C-241/91 P and C-242/91 P *RTE and ITP v Commission* EU:C:1995:98.

acknowledged that the owner of an intellectual property right must not be deprived of the opportunity to have recourse to a court to enforce it; but on the other hand the commitment to license an SEP on FRAND terms does have certain consequences for the owner.

The rest of the Court's judgment sets out the steps that must be taken by the owner of an SEP and the would-be licensee when negotiating a licence:

- the proprietor of an SEP which considers that an SEP is the subject of an infringement cannot, without infringing Article 102 TFEU, bring an action for a prohibitory injunction or for the recall of products against the alleged infringer without notice or prior consultation with the alleged infringer[344]
- the proprietor of the SEP in question must alert the alleged infringer of the infringement complained about by designating that SEP and specifying the way in which it has been infringed[345]
- after the alleged infringer has expressed its willingness to conclude a licence on FRAND terms, the proprietor of the SEP must present to that alleged infringer a specific, written offer for a licence on FRAND terms, in accordance with the undertaking given to the standardisation body, specifying, in particular, the amount of the royalty and the way in which that royalty is to be calculated[346]
- it is for the alleged infringer diligently to respond to that offer, in accordance with recognised commercial practices in the field and in good faith[347]
- should the alleged infringer not accept the offer made to it, the owner of the SEP may rely on the abusive nature of an action for a prohibitory injunction or for the recall of products only if it has submitted to the proprietor of the SEP in question, promptly and in writing, a specific counter-offer that corresponds to FRAND terms[348].

The alleged infringer must provide appropriate security, in accordance with recognised commercial practices in the field, for example by providing a bank guarantee or by placing the amounts necessary on deposit[349]. If no agreement is reached on the details of the FRAND terms following the counter-offer by the alleged infringer, the parties may, by common agreement, request that the amount of the royalty be determined by an independent third party, by decision without delay[350].

On 29 November 2017 the Commission published a communication, *Setting out the EU approach to Standard Essential Patents*[351], which provides guidance on the licensing, valuation and enforcement of SEPs.

(iv) **FRAND licences for standard-essential patents**

In *Unwired Planet v Huawei*[352] the English High Court considered whether various licence terms offered by the owner of SEPs subject to a FRAND undertaking and by a would-be licensee were FRAND[353]. The court held that there is only one set of licence terms and one royalty rate that are FRAND in a given set of circumstances[354]. The court

[344] Case C-170/13 EU:C:2015:477, para 60. [345] Ibid, para 61. [346] Ibid, para 63.
[347] Ibid, para 65. [348] Ibid, para 66. [349] Ibid, para 67. [350] Ibid, para 68.
[351] COM(2017) 712 final, available at www.ec.europa.eu.
[352] [2017] EWHC 711 (Pat); para 806 contains a helpful summary of the court's conclusions. Huawei and Unwired Planet have both appealed to the Court of Appeal.
[353] See generally Nazzini 'Level Discrimination and FRAND Commitments Under EU Competition Law' (2017) 40 World Competition 213; Layne-Farrar and Wong-Ervin 'Methodologies for Calculating FRAND Damages: An Economic and Comparative Analysis of the Case Law from China, the European Union, India, and the United States' (2017), available at www.ssrn.com.
[354] [2017] EWHC 711 (Pat), paras 147–168.

identified three ways to determine a FRAND royalty: first, to determine a benchmark rate that is governed by the value of the patentee's portfolio[355]; secondly, to use comparable licences[356]; and, thirdly, as a cross-check, to calculate the patentee's share of relevant SEPs and apply that share to the total aggregate royalty for a standard[357]. The court used these methods to set the FRAND royalty rate. As for the other terms, an SEP holder may offer to grant only a worldwide licence[358], but cannot insist on a licence that bundles SEPs and non-SEPs[359].

(v) Patent assertion entities

In sectors such as information and communications technology, there are so-called patent assertion entities or 'PAEs' (sometimes known as 'patent trolls') that purchase a large portfolio of patents and make their money by licensing the patents and/or suing alleged infringers[360]. The activities of PAEs may give rise to competition concerns where, for example, they evade the FRAND commitments given by the original patentee and demand excessive royalties: a practice known as 'privateering'[361]. The US Federal Trade Commission has published a study on PAE activities that made recommendations to reduce 'nuisance litigation' initiated by PAEs[362].

(vi) Vexatious behaviour and abuse of process

In *BBI/Boosey and Hawkes: Interim Measures*[363] the Commission seems to have regarded it as an aspect of Boosey and Hawkes' abusive behaviour to have brought vexatious litigation against an undertaking for 'slavish imitation' of its products[364]. On one occasion the Commission intimated that it might be an abuse for a dominant firm to register a trade mark knowing that a competitor already uses that mark[365].

In *AstraZeneca*[366] the Commission imposed a fine of €60 million on AstraZeneca for misuse of regulatory procedures. AstraZeneca had a patent for a highly successful drug, Losec. AstraZeneca was found by the Commission to have abused regulatory procedures in two ways. First, it had succeeded in persuading various patent authorities to grant it 'supplementary protection certificates', extending the period of patent protection, on the basis of misleading information: this had the effect of delaying entry onto the market by generic producers who might have been able to supply the drug at considerably lower prices. Secondly, AstraZeneca held a market authorisation that allowed the drug to be

355 Ibid, para 176.

356 Ibid, paras 157, 179, and 187–196.

357 Ibid, para 178.

358 Ibid, paras 524–572.

359 Ibid, para 787, although it does not follow that making a first offer that bundles SEPs and non-SEPs necessarily infringes Article 102 as 'everything will depend on the circumstances'.

360 See Popofsky and Laufert 'Patent Assertion Entities and Antitrust: Operating Company Patent Transfers' (April 2013) Antitrust Source 1; Boscheck 'Patent Trolls: In Search of Efficient Regulatory Standards' (2016) 39 World Competition 67; speech by a former Director General, Alexander Italianer 'Shaken, not stirred. Competition Law Enforcement and Standard Essential Patents', 21 April 2015, available at www.ec.europa.eu.

361 See *Unwired Planet v Huawei* [2015] EWHC 2097 (Pat), paras 37–48 (Unwired Planet was a PAE).

362 'Patent Assertion Entity Activity: An FTC Study', October 2016, available at www.ftc.gov.

363 OJ [1987] L 286/36, para 19.

364 See further ch 17, 'Vexatious litigation', pp 729–730.

365 *Osram/Airam*, XIth *Report on Competition Policy* (1981), point 97.

366 Commission decision of 15 June 2005; see De Souza 'Competition in Pharmaceuticals: the challenges ahead post *AstraZeneca*' (2007) (Spring) Competition Policy Newsletter 39; Gunther and Breuvart 'Misuse of Patent and Drug Regulatory Approval Systems in the Pharmaceutical Industry: An Analysis of US and EU Converging Approaches' (2005) 26 ECLR 669; Murphy 'Abuse of Regulatory Procedures—The *AstraZeneca* Case: Parts 1, 2 and 3' (2009) 30 ECLR 223, 289 and 314; O'Donoghue and Padilla *The Law and Economics of Article 102 TFEU* (Hart, 2nd ed, 2013), pp 660–670.

sold in a capsule form. AstraZeneca withdrew the capsules from the market, selling them in tablet form instead and brought about the end of the market authorisations; this meant that the generic companies could not market their capsules. On appeal the General Court largely upheld the Commission's decision[367], although some findings of commission of the second abuse were set aside for want of evidence[368].

A fundamental disagreement between AstraZeneca and the Commission concerned the concept of abuse. AstraZeneca argued that an abuse can exist only when a dominant undertaking has wilfully acquired or enforced the patent knowing that it is invalid. The General Court rejected this[369]. In paragraph 355 of its judgment it held that:

> the submission to the public authorities of misleading information liable to lead them into error and therefore to make possible the grant of an exclusive right to which an undertaking is not entitled, or to which it is entitled for a shorter period, constitutes a practice falling outside the scope of competition on the merits which may be particularly restrictive of competition.

The Court stated that a dominant firm has a special responsibility not to impair undistorted competition that requires it, at the very least, to inform the public authorities of any errors in information it provides to them[370]. The General Court rejected a claim by AstraZeneca that it was being made subject to an obligation to protect the interests of generics manufacturers or parallel importers by maintaining the marketing authorisations[371]. On appeal the Court of Justice upheld the General Court's judgment[372], and specifically held that the General Court had not misinterpreted the concept of 'competition on the merits'[373].

In *Rambus* the Commission sent a statement of objections alleging that Rambus had infringed Article 102 by conducting a so-called 'patent ambush'. This refers to the phenomenon of an undertaking participating in the setting of an industry standard, but doing so in a deliberately deceptive manner by not disclosing the existence of patents that would be necessary for anyone making use of the standard. This means that, once the standard is set, the owner of the patents will be able to demand unreasonable royalties from licensees that need access to the technology in question[374]. The Commission subsequently focused on whether Rambus was charging too much for its technology. The Commission closed its investigation when it accepted commitments from Rambus to impose a worldwide cap on its royalty rates for five years[375]. The commitments addressed a symptom of the patent

[367] Case T-321/05 *AstraZeneca AB v Commission* EU:T:2010:266, paras 239–294 (dominance), paras 352–381 (legal analysis of the first abuse), paras 474–613 (proof of the first abuse), paras 666–696 (legal analysis of the second abuse) and paras 757–865 (proof of the second abuse).

[368] Ibid, paras 824–861; the fine on AstraZeneca was reduced to €52.5 million for this reason.

[369] Ibid, paras 355–356: 'proof of the deliberate nature of the conduct and of the bad faith of the undertaking in a dominant position is not required for the purposes of identifying an abuse of a dominant position'; see also paras 493 and 814; the Commission may, nevertheless, take into account evidence of anti-competitive intention: ibid, para 359.

[370] Ibid, para 358. [371] Ibid, paras 815–817.

[372] Case C-457/10 P *AstraZeneca AB v Commission* EU:C:2012:770.

[373] Ibid, paras 76–98, in particular para 98.

[374] See Commission MEMO/07/330, 23 August 2007; the Commission closed an investigation of whether Boehringer, a pharmaceutical company, had infringed Article 102 by exclusionary 'misuse of the patent system': see Commission Press Release IP/11/842, 6 July 2011.

[375] Commission commitment decision of 9 December 2009; for comment see Schellingerhout and Cavicchi 'Patent ambush in standard-setting: the Commission accepts commitments from Rambus to lower memory chip royalty rates' (2010) 1 Competition Policy Newsletter 32.

ambush rather than the alleged ambush itself[376]. Because of the danger of patent ambush, standard-setting organisations often require the firms involved in the setting of standards to declare that they own SEPs and promise to license on FRAND terms.

6. UK Law

(A) Licences of intellectual property rights: the Chapter I prohibition

There are no specific provisions in the Competition Act 1998 on licences of intellectual property rights, and the Competition and Markets Authority ('the CMA') has not published a guideline on the subject[377]. As a general proposition it can be anticipated that the Chapter I prohibition will be applied to agreements in the same way as Article 101 TFEU[378]. The possibility exists that some of the jurisprudence of the EU Courts might not be applied to a purely domestic agreement in so far as that jurisprudence reflects single market considerations that need not be applied within the UK[379].

Any technology transfer agreement that is exempt under Regulation 316/2014, or that would be if the agreement in question were to have an effect on trade between Member States, is also exempt from the Chapter I prohibition[380]. This means that many agreements are currently exempt from both EU and UK law. After the UK leaves the EU in March 2019, it may be necessary for the UK to adopt a block exemption of its own for technology transfer agreements.

(B) Settlements of litigation

In *Paroxetine*[381] the CMA decided that GlaxoSmithKline had settled litigation with two generic companies on terms that infringed the Chapter I and II prohibitions. The CMA found that GSK had 'induced' the generics not to continue their independent efforts to enter the market, by making payments to them and by giving additional value in the form of a distribution agreement. GSK would not derive any benefit from the settlement agreements other than the maintenance of its monopoly position. The CMA concluded that the object and the effect of the agreements was to restrict competition and that there was an abuse of a dominant position on the part of GSK. The CMA imposed fines totalling £44.99 million. On appeal the CAT considered that the questions whether the agreements had the object and/or effect of restricting competition were of wide importance and that the law was not free from doubt, and therefore made an Article 267 reference to the Court of Justice.

[376] In the US the Federal Trade Commission required Rambus to license its technology for computer memory subject to maximum royalty rates: *In the Matter of Rambus Inc*, Final Order of 2 February 2007, reversed on appeal *Rambus Inc v FTC* (DC Cir 2008), *certiorari* denied 129 S Ct 1318; details of these proceedings are available at www.ftc.gov; see also *Broadcom Corp v Qualcomm Inc* 501 F 3d 297 (3rd Cir 2007); for discussion of issues arising from the adoption of standards and intellectual property rights see: Petritsi 'The Case of Unilateral Patent Ambush Under EC Competition Rules' (2005) 28 World Competition 25; Farrell, Hayes, Shapiro and Sullivan 'Standard Setting, Patents and Hold-Up' (2007) 74 Antitrust LJ 603; Royall, Tessar and Vincenzo 'Deterring "Patent Ambush" in Standard Setting: Lessons from Rambus and Qualcomm' (2009) 23 Antitrust 34.

[377] A draft Guideline was published in November 2001, OFT 418, but it was not published in final form.

[378] See 'The application of Article 101(1) to licences of intellectual property rights', p 791 earlier. For a general account of the Chapter I prohibition see ch 9, 'The Chapter I Prohibition', pp 347–376.

[379] See ch 9, '"Governing Principles Clause": Section 60 of the Competition Act 1998', pp 387–392.

[380] See ch 9, 'Parallel exemptions', pp 375–376.

[381] CMA decision of 12 February 2016, on appeal Cases 1252/1/12/16 etc *GlaxoSmithKline v CMA* [2018] CAT 4; the order referring ten questions for a preliminary ruling was made on 27 March 2018 and is available at www.catribunal.org.uk.

(C) **The Chapter II prohibition**

The Chapter II prohibition may apply to an improper exercise of intellectual property rights in the same way as Article 102 TFEU[382]. A firm's conduct is not immune from the Chapter II prohibition purely on the basis that its market power stems from the holding of intellectual property rights[383]. In *Capita Business Services and Bromcom Computers*[384] Capita gave voluntary assurances that it would provide 'interface information' to a third party to enable it to have access to data on Capita's server; the case was therefore closed. In *Reckitt Benckiser*[385] Reckitt admitted committing an abuse by withdrawing and delisting a drug, Gaviscon Original Liquid, from the NHS prescription channel in 2005[386]. In *Paroxetine*[387] the CMA concluded that GSK's conduct did not constitute competition on the merits because it had paid potential entrants to abandon their efforts to enter the market. On appeal the CAT decided that it was necessary to refer questions on market definition and abuse to the Court of Justice for a preliminary ruling.

(D) **Market investigations**

The market investigation provisions of the Enterprise Act 2002 may also be relevant where features of a market have an adverse effect on competition as a result of intellectual property rights[388]. In *Movies on pay TV*[389] no features of the markets relating to the supply and acquisition of the intellectual property rights licensed by the six largest Hollywood studios gave rise to an adverse effect on competition[390].

[382] See 'Article 102 and Intellectual Property Rights', pp 814–827 earlier in chapter.

[383] *BSkyB*, OFT decision of 17 December 2002, paras 331–340.

[384] Weekly Gazette of the OFT, Competition case closure summaries, 26 April–2 May 2003, available at www.gov.uk; see also British Standards Institution agrees to grant online licence, OFT Press Release PN 94/03, 7 July 2003.

[385] OFT decision of 13 April 2011.

[386] A 'follow-on' action for damages against Reckitt Benckiser brought by various bodies in the National Health Service was settled out of court: see ch 8, 'Damages', p 333, n 229.

[387] CMA decision of 12 February 2016, on appeal Cases 1252/1/12/16 etc *GlaxoSmithKline v CMA* [2018] CAT 4, paras 379-409 (on market definition) and 410-432 (on abuse).

[388] These provisions have been described in ch 11.

[389] Final Report of 2 August 2012, available at www.nationalarchives.gov.uk.

[390] Reports under the now-repealed monopoly provisions of the Fair Trading Act 1973 dealing with intellectual property issues include *Exhaust Gas Analysers*, Cm 2386 (1993); *Recorded Music*, Cm 2599 (1994); *Historical On-line Database Services*, Cm 2554 (1994); *Video Games*, Cm 2781 (1995); *Performing Rights*, Cm 3147 (1996).

20

Mergers (1): introduction

1. Introduction

This chapter briefly introduces the subject of merger control. This book so far has been concerned essentially with two issues: anti-competitive agreements and abuse of a dominant position. Merger control is an important third component of most, though not all, systems of competition law. The EU Merger Regulation ('the EUMR') will be described in chapter 21 and the merger provisions in the UK Enterprise Act 2002 in chapter 22. Before doing so it may be useful to make some preliminary observations about the subject of mergers generally and about systems of merger control in particular. The issues introduced in this chapter will be discussed in more depth in the two that follow.

2. Terminology

(A) The meaning of 'merger' and 'concentration'

A true merger involves two separate undertakings merging entirely into a new entity: a high-profile example was the fusion in 1996 of Ciba-Geigy and Sandoz to form the major pharmaceutical and chemical company Novartis[1]; a further example in 2017 was the creation of DowDuPont as a result of the merger of Dow Chemical and DuPont[2]. However it is important to understand that the expression 'merger' as used in competition policy includes a far broader range of corporate transactions than full mergers of this kind[3]. Where A acquires all, or a majority of, the shares in B, this would be described as a merger if it results in A being able to control the strategic business decisions of B; even the acquisition of a minority shareholding may be sufficient, in particular circumstances, to qualify as a merger. Under the EUMR the question is whether A will acquire 'the possibility of exercising decisive influence' over the strategic commercial behaviour of B[4]; under the

[1] Case M 737, decision of 17 July 1996; the Commission's decisions are available on DG COMP's website at www.ec.europa.eu/competition.

[2] Case M 7932, decision of 27 March 2017.

[3] See generally the OECD Roundtable *Definition of Transaction for the Purpose of Merger Control Review* (2013), available at www.oecd.org/competition.

[4] See ch 21, 'The concept of control', pp 854–855.

Enterprise Act the question is whether A would at least have 'material influence' over B[5]. The acquisition of assets—for example a well-known brand name—can amount to a merger[6]. Two or more undertakings which merge part of their businesses into a newly-established joint venture company, 'Newco', may be found to be parties to a merger[7]. In each case the essential question is whether previously independent businesses have come or will come under common control with the consequence that, in the future, the market will function less competitively than it did prior to the merger. For the sake of convenience the term 'merger' will be used in this and the following chapters to encompass all these phenomena unless the context requires a different usage. When discussing the EU system an alternative expression, 'concentration' will also sometimes be used, since that is the word used in the EUMR itself.

(B) The horizontal, vertical and conglomerate effects of mergers

Many systems of competition law provide that certain mergers cannot be completed until the approval of the relevant competition authority has been obtained. Merger control is concerned about the possibility that a merger will lead to the market being less competitive in the future than it currently is, leading to adverse effects for consumers. The main concern of competition authorities when assessing a merger is whether it will have adverse **horizontal** effects; there may also be concerns about **vertical** and **conglomerate** effects, but these concerns are rarer. It is possible that the same case can give rise to horizontal, vertical and conglomerate concerns[8].

(i) Horizontal effects

Horizontal effects occur where a merger takes place between actual or potential competitors in the same product and geographic markets and at the same level of the production or distribution cycle. As a general proposition the horizontal effects of mergers present a much greater danger to competition than vertical (or conglomerate) ones, in the same way that horizontal agreements are treated more strictly than vertical agreements. Horizontal mergers may be scrutinised both for their 'unilateral' or 'non-coordinated' effects and for their 'coordinated' effects[9].

(ii) Vertical effects

Vertical effects may be experienced where a merger occurs between firms that operate at different, but complementary, levels of the market for the same final product: for example A might produce a raw material (an 'upstream' product) for a product produced by B (a 'downstream' product). Often such mergers will enhance, or be neutral, in terms of economic efficiency, but there is a possibility that vertical integration may have a harmful effect on competition, either because it could foreclose access to the market on the

[5] See ch 22, 'Enterprises ceasing to be distinct', pp 942–945.

[6] See eg Case M 890 *Blokker/Toys 'R' Us*, decision of 26 June 1997 (EU law) and *Société Coopérative de Production SeaFrance v CMA* [2015] UKSC 75 (UK law).

[7] See in particular ch 21, 'Joint ventures—the concept of full-functionality', pp 857–858 on the application of the EUMR to so-called 'full-function' joint ventures.

[8] See eg Case M 2220 *General Electric/Honeywell*, decision of 3 July 2001; on appeal to the General Court the Commission's finding on horizontal effects was upheld but the findings of vertical and conglomerate effects were annulled: see Case T-210/01 *General Electric v Commission* EU:T:2005:456.

[9] See further 'Unilateral or non-coordinated effects', pp 838–839 later in chapter; on horizontal effects under the EUMR see ch 21, 'Horizontal mergers', pp 889–899; for their treatment under UK law see ch 22, 'Horizontal mergers', pp 962–965.

part of third parties or because it could lead to collusion between the merged entity and third parties[10].

(iii) Conglomerate effects

There have been a few occasions on which competition authorities have had concerns about mergers not on the basis of horizontal or vertical effects, but because of possible conglomerate effects: for example that a merger between A and B who are neither horizontal competitors, nor functionally related vertically, might enable the merged entity AB to use its market power in two different but related, or even unrelated, markets to foreclose competitors. Whether conglomerate mergers should be controlled at all is a matter of controversy: the Department of Justice and the Federal Trade Commission in the US long ago abandoned any interest in the conglomerate effects of mergers[11]. The European Commission considers that conglomerate mergers will not lead to any competition problems 'in the majority of circumstances'[12], but it has made adverse findings on conglomeracy on a few occasions[13].

3. Merger Activity

In the corporate world there are frequent bouts of 'merger mania' when the level of merger activity is very high[14]; enormous fees are earned by financial and legal (including competition law) advisers during these periods. The cyclical nature of this phenomenon is illustrated by the high degree of merger activity in the second half of the 1980s, and again in the mid-1990s. From 1998 to 2001 there was a period of frenetic merger activity, although this then declined markedly as the global economy slowed. Another upswing commenced in 2005 and continued through to 2007, not least as private equity firms became involved in ever-larger acquisitions of well-established firms. In a speech in June 2007 Commissioner Kroes spoke of a 'tsunami' of mergers which she welcomed since it involved the cross-border restructuring of markets in many sectors from energy to banking and from air transport to telecommunications[15]. The financial crisis that erupted in 2008 led to a sharp decline in merger activity in the following years. DG COMP's Table of Statistics, reproduced in chapter 21[16], shows clearly the peaks and troughs of merger notifications under the EUMR: from 211 in 2003 up to 402 in 2007 and down to 277 in 2013; in 2016 the number was back up to 362.

A notable feature of mergers in recent years has been their increasing complexity, size and geographical reach. Very large mergers have taken place in many sectors

[10] See further 'Vertical effects', pp 839–840 later in chapter; on vertical effects under the EUMR see ch 21, 'Vertical mergers', pp 900–902; for their treatment under UK law see ch 22, 'Non-horizontal mergers', pp 965–966.

[11] See Scherer and Ross *Industrial Market Structure and Economic Performance* (Houghton Mifflin, 3rd ed, 1990), pp 188–190.

[12] *Guidelines on the assessment of non-horizontal mergers* OJ [2008] C 265/6, para 92.

[13] See further 'Conglomerate effects', p 840 later in chapter; on conglomerate effects under the EUMR see ch 21, 'Conglomerate mergers', p 901; for their treatment under UK law see ch 22, 'Non-horizontal mergers', pp 965–966.

[14] See Gort 'An Economic Disturbance Theory of Mergers' (1969) 83 The Quarterly Journal of Economics 624; Scherer and Ross *Industrial Market Structure and Economic Performance* (Houghton Mifflin, 3rd ed, 1990), pp 153–159; Martynova and Renneboog 'A Century of Corporate Takeovers: What Have We Learned and Where Do We Stand?' (2008) 32 Journal of Banking and Finance 2148; Bhagwat, Dam and Harford 'The Real Effects of Uncertainty on Merger Activity' (2016) 29 The Review of Financial Studies 3000.

[15] Speech by Kroes 'European Competition Policy in a changing world and globalised economy: fundamentals, new objectives and challenges ahead', 5 June 2007, available at www.ec.europa.eu/competition.

[16] See ch 21, 'Table of EUMR statistics', pp 923–924.

as companies have sought to restructure and consolidate their place in an increasingly global market. For example in the pharmaceuticals industry Pfizer and Warner-Lambert merged to become the largest pharmaceutical company in the world[17]. Major mergers have taken place in the car industry, for example between Daimler-Benz and Chrysler[18], between Ford and Volvo[19], between Renault and Nissan[20], between Fiat and Chrysler[21] and between Nissan and Mitsubishi[22]. In the oil industry Exxon merged with Mobil to become the largest oil company in the world[23], and BP Amoco merged with Arco[24]. Telecommunications has also seen a high degree of merger activity[25]. As at 8 December 2017 the merger in 1999 of VodafoneAirTouch and Mannesmann[26] was the largest merger by value. It is obvious that the size, complexity and number of mergers that have been occurring places significant burdens on the authorities responsible for merger control.

4. The Proliferation of Systems of Merger Control

A particularly noticeable feature of competition policy in the last 20 years or so has been the proliferation of systems of competition law around the world. More than 130 countries now have competition law, and at least 110 of these laws include merger control. The profusion of systems of merger control has a greater impact on most firms than rules against cartels and abusive behaviour, not because these firms disregard the latter but because their transactions are often subject to mandatory pre-notification under the former. This means that any sizable transaction with an international dimension—of which there are many—may have to be notified to 10, 20 or even more competition authorities. Law firms advising on international transactions must be able to obtain access to all the relevant merger laws and guidelines in order to determine where filings must be made[27]. Many competition lawyers in firms handling such cases will spend a substantial amount of time overseeing and coordinating a number of national filings; the initial enthusiasm of junior competition lawyers for such work often fades when it becomes apparent that the coordination of filings in Australia, Europe and the US entails an 18-hour working day or longer. It is important for lawyers to manage the expectations of clients who may not fully appreciate how long and tortuous the regulatory road may be ahead of them before the transaction is able to proceed.

The problems that multiple notification can cause to the merging firms themselves—for example the cost of multiple filing, the workload involved in generating the data necessary for each filing, the delay involved in obtaining clearances from numerous jurisdictions, the differing procedural and substantive laws from one jurisdiction to another—are obvious. One of the major issues facing the 'world' of competition law—using this term both in its physical sense and to refer to the constituency of interested parties affected by merger control consisting of competition authorities, legal and

[17] Case M 1878, decision of 22 May 2000.

[18] Case M 1204, decision of 22 July 1998.

[19] Case M 1452, decision of 26 March 1999.

[20] Case M 1519, decision of 12 May 1999.

[21] Case M 5518, decision of 24 July 2009.

[22] Case M 8099, decision of 5 October 2016.

[23] Case M 1383, decision of 29 September 1999.

[24] Case M 1532, decision of 29 September 1999.

[25] See Manigrassi et al, 'Recent developments in telecoms mergers' Competition Merger Brief 3/2016, available at www.ec.europa.eu/competition.

[26] Case M 1795, decision of 12 April 2000.

[27] Some helpful sources are Rowley and Baker *Merger Control: International Mergers* (Sweet & Maxwell looseleaf, updated semi-annually); Dabbah and Lasok *Merger Control Worldwide* (Cambridge University Press, 2nd ed, 2012); Clarke *International Merger Policy: Applying Domestic Law to International Markets* (Edward Elgar, 2014); Global Legal Insights *Merger Control 2017*, available at www.globallegalinsights.com; Davies (ed) *Merger Control: The International Regulation of Mergers and Joint Ventures in 71 jurisdictions worldwide* (Global Competition Review, 2018).

business advisers, politicians, economists, the merging firms and their competitors, suppliers and customers—is to devise a sensible mechanism for investigating and adjudicating upon mergers having an international dimension in a way that minimises the administrative burden on businesses and competition authorities while at the same time ensuring that mergers do not escape scrutiny which could have detrimental effects upon competition.

Some systems of merger control use jurisdictional thresholds based on the turnover of the firms involved in the transaction (such as the EU); others use the value of the assets to be acquired (for example this is the case in Japan); others use the likely market share that the parties would have after the merger (which is used in the UK and Germany). Whatever thresholds are used[28], it is important that merger control is designed in a way that only mergers that could produce significant anti-competitive effects within a particular jurisdiction can be investigated in depth by the authority of that jurisdiction.

The issue of multiple notification is given active consideration in various international fora, notably the International Competition Network ('the ICN') which published a *Practical Guide to International Enforcement Cooperation in Mergers* in 2015[29]. International cooperation between competition authorities has been discussed in chapter 12[30], while attempts in the EU to avoid multiple filing in the Member States by introducing the idea of the 'one-stop shop' of notifying the European Commission will be discussed in chapter 21[31].

5. **Why Do Firms Merge?**

There are many reasons why firms merge, most of which are beneficial to, or at least not harmful to, the economy; there are others that are more problematic and might require a more interventionist approach to mergers.

(A) **Economies of scale and scope**

An argument in favour of some mergers is the achievement of economies of scale and scope[32]. A firm will produce goods at the lowest marginal cost where it is able to operate at the minimum efficient scale. If it operates on a smaller scale than this, marginal cost will increase and there will be a consequent loss of allocative efficiency. Economies of scale may be *product-specific*, where they enable a product to be produced more cheaply; *plant-specific*, where they mean that the overall use of a multi-product plant is made more rational; or *firm-specific*, where they result in lower overall costs. It may be that a firm can achieve economies of scale by internal growth; equally, however, it may be that this can most easily be achieved by external growth, that is by merging with other firms. Whereas economies of scale arise from carrying on more of the same activity, economies of scope are the economic benefits generated from carrying on related activities; an obvious example would be lowering overall administrative expenditure through the operation of different lines of production.

[28] See OECD Roundtable *Jurisdictional nexus in merger control regimes* (2016), available at www.oecd.org/competition.

[29] The ICN website is www.internationalcompetitionnetwork.org.

[30] See in particular ch 12, 'The Internationalisation of Competition Law', pp 514–519.

[31] See ch 21, 'Article 21: one-stop merger control', pp 864–866.

[32] These concepts are discussed in ch 1, 'Questioning competition as a goal in itself', pp 10–16.

Whether mergers succeed in delivering the economies of scale and scope expected of them is another matter: some commentators have argued that post-merger performance is not noticeably better than before the transaction[33].

(B) Other efficiencies

A merged firm may be able to operate more efficiently for other reasons. For example it may be cheaper to take over a distributor than to set up a distribution network on a contractual basis; backward integration may guarantee supplies to a firm concerned about the availability of raw materials; a merger might mean that a firm will have improved access to loan and equity capital than it had when operating alone. A merger may result in a firm that is better able to carry out research and development and with access to a greater pool of industrial technology; quite often a merger is motivated by a desire to acquire the patents and know-how of a particular firm. Another possibility is that a merged firm may be able to make better use of the management skills of its constituent parts.

(C) National champions

Firms within one nation state—or within one political grouping such as the European Union—may wish to merge in order to become a 'national champion' (or a 'European champion'). Governments may encourage mergers that will create larger domestic firms more capable of competing on international markets, although 'national champions' free from the disciplining effect of competition on their domestic markets may lack the skills necessary to succeed in the wider world[34].

(D) Management efficiency and the market for corporate control

An explanation for some mergers is that one firm competes to run another. The threat of a successful takeover bid acts as an important influence upon the existing management of a firm to ensure that it functions as efficiently as possible. Where shareholders are satisfied with the current management's performance they will not sell their shares to another bidder, unless it is overbidding: the new regime would not be capable of generating greater profits than the existing one. If shareholders are dissatisfied, they may prefer to sell at the price offered and to reinvest the proceeds elsewhere; the result is likely to be that the old management will be replaced by the bidder. According to this argument rivalry for the control of firms through mergers and acquisitions is itself part of the competitive process, and should not be unduly interfered with[35]. It is particularly attractive if one agrees with

[33] See Scherer and Ross *Industrial Market Structure and Economic Performance* (Houghton Mifflin, 3rd ed, 1990), pp 167–174; Meeks *Disappointing Marriage: A Study of the Gains from Merger* (Cambridge University Press, 1977); see also Röller, Stennek and Verboven 'Efficiency Gains from Mergers', The Research Institute of Industrial Economics, Working Paper 543 (2000), available at www.ec.europa.eu/competition; OECD Roundtable *Dynamic Efficiencies in Merger Analysis* (2007), available at www.oecd.org/competition.

[34] The European Commission is resolutely opposed to the creation by Member States of 'national champions': see ch 21, 'Outright prohibitions', pp 922–928; for interesting discussion of the issue see OECD Roundtable *Competition Policy, Industrial Policy and National Champions* (2009), available at www.oecd.org/competition.

[35] See eg Easterbrook and Fischel 'The Proper Role of a Target's Management in Responding to a Tender Offer' (1981) 94 Harvard Law Review 1161; Coffee 'Regulating the Market for Corporate Control: A Critical Assessment of the Tender Offer's Role in Corporate Governance' (1984) 84 Columbia Law Review 1145; Rock 'Antitrust and the Market for Corporate Control' (1989) 77 California Law Review 1367.

the view that shareholders' influence over directors through the Annual General Meeting has been seriously diminished in listed companies with dispersed share ownership; at least the ability to sell to a bidder exercises some influence on the management of the company's affairs. If the threat of takeovers is considered to have this significant role, this has implications for merger policy: an interventionist approach to mergers on the part of a public authority in itself distorts the market for corporate control and thus weakens its disciplining effect on management.

(E) **Exiting an industry**

Mergers present firms that wish to do so with an opportunity of exiting an industry. In a free market it is important to encourage entrepreneurs to invest their money and skills in setting up new businesses and in entering new markets. Just as it is desirable to prevent the erection of barriers to entry and expansion that prevent new firms from competing on the market, so too it is necessary to avoid barriers to exit that make it difficult to leave the market. The incentive to set up a firm, invest risk capital and develop new products may be diminished if it is not possible to sell the enterprise in question as a valuable going concern. It is quite common, for example, for firms to acquire small undertakings which possess useful know-how or intellectual property rights and, from the perspective of the innovator of such technology, the freedom to sell may be an important element in the reward for the risks taken. A strict approach to mergers could have an undesirable effect if it were to make exit unduly difficult.

(F) **Greed, vanity, fear and drugs**

Having rehearsed some of the arguments in favour of mergers, and therefore against too strict a system of merger control, some opposing views should be mentioned. A sceptical view is that many mergers cannot be explained in the rational economic terms outlined earlier, but that instead they are fuelled by the speculative greed of individuals or companies or the personal vanity of a particularly swashbuckling senior executive; it will not take a great deal of imagination to think of certain high-profile entrepreneurs that might answer this description. Some mergers seem to be motivated by simple fear: if every other undertaking in a particular sector appears to be involved in mergers, it may be considered important not to be left behind in the process of industry consolidation. For some individuals 'deal-making' has the same stimulating effect as mood-changing drugs, altogether more exciting than the mundane task of managing a firm well. Even if one shares these sceptical explanations of why firms merge, however, it does not follow that merger control is the appropriate tool to deal with the 'problem'.

(G) **Increasing market power**

Of course it might be that the real reason why firms wish to merge is that this will eliminate competition between them, increase their market power and give them the ability to restrict output and raise price. It would be very foolish in today's world of vigorous merger control for merging firms to make such a claim for their merger, although it is sometimes surprising what firms do say in press releases, intended to impress shareholders, as to the expected economic benefits of a merger: for example a claim that a merger will 'eliminate wasteful capacity' and return an industry to greater profitability is unlikely to charm a competition authority into submission; even less charming is a press release that announces that 'this merger will create the dominant world player in the market for widgets'[36]. Competition authorities routinely ask for copies of firms' documents (both internal and from external advisers) setting out the business rationale for a particular transaction, and these sometimes contain statements and data that are unhelpful to the prospect of unconditional clearance. The systems of merger control in place in the EU, the UK and elsewhere presumably inhibit the incidence of cases in which firms merge in order to increase their market power, but it is important to bear in mind that, in the absence of a system of merger control, firms would be able to do precisely this.

6. What is the Purpose of Merger Control?

This brings us to the central question: what is the purpose of merger control? There are many reasons why Governments, firms, shareholders, employees and individuals might object to mergers. A Government may object to a merger on a number of grounds: for example it might disapprove of a foreign firm taking over a native one, or of a merger that does not fit with its own industrial policy, or of a transaction that would lead to production facilities being closed down leading to unemployment. A firm might object to being the target of a hostile bid, or to a merger between two rivals that might give them a competitive edge. Shareholders (whether legal or natural persons) might be concerned that corporate transactions will have an adverse effect on the value or effectiveness of their shares. Company law is concerned with issues such as the oppression of minority shareholders, and complex regulatory systems also exist to protect shareholders generally. Reference should be made to standard works[37] on the laws and regulations that deal with these matters; in particular in the UK the City Code on Takeovers and Mergers[38] provides an important system of regulatory protection. An individual might have qualms about foreign ownership of indigenous firms or the possibility that a takeover might lead to redundancy. These are perfectly understandable concerns, but they are not issues with which competition policy is concerned. Competition policy is predominantly concerned with maintaining the process of competition in the marketplace, not as an end in itself, but as a way of maximising consumer welfare[39].

Some systems of merger control do allow broader 'public interest' criteria to be taken into account in the overall assessment of a merger, a matter that will be discussed later. However most competition authorities are concerned with the assessment of the competitive effects of mergers.

(A) Is merger control necessary?

It is reasonable to point out that some systems of competition law do not have specific rules on mergers. US, UK and EU law all began with rules on anti-competitive agreements and monopolisation or abuse of dominance before subsequently introducing merger control at a later stage. For small and developing economies it may be that, if anything, mergers might be helpful for local businesses if this means that they can grow to an efficient scale that will enable them to compete more effectively in international markets. Having said this, merger control is still necessary to control mergers that are harmful to competition

[36] See ch 1, 'Evidence relied on to define relevant markets', pp 33–34 on the probative value of statements made by an undertaking.

[37] See eg Davies and Worthington (eds) *Gower: Principles of Modern Company Law* (Sweet & Maxwell, 10th ed, 2016) ch 28.

[38] For further information see www.thetakeoverpanel.org.uk.

[39] See ch 1, 'Consumer protection', pp 19–20.

in domestic markets. As a general proposition firms that are able to compete at home tend to be better at competing effectively abroad.

A different question is whether merger control is necessary to prevent the creation or strengthening of market power before it occurs, given that there are legal controls—such as Article 102 TFEU—on the abuse of market power. One answer to this question is that merger control is not simply about preventing future abuses: it is also about maintaining competitive markets that lead to better outcomes for consumers[40]. Another is that investigations into the unilateral conduct of dominant firms are lengthy, complex and cumbersome, and that competition authorities lack the resources to police every alleged infringement; exclusive reliance on *ex post* control would be unlikely to be effective. In the UK attempts have been made to evaluate the gains to consumers from merger control in specific cases and they would appear to be significant[41].

(B) **Assessing the competitive effects of mergers**

Assessing the competitive effects of mergers is far from simple. A helpful starting point is the *ICN Merger Guidelines Workbook* produced by a Subgroup of the ICN ('the *Workbook*')[42]. This was produced as a tool for countries that are new to or in the early years of merger control; however it is commended to anyone interested in the subject. In particular the *Workbook* contains a series of eight 'Worksheets' on key matters that are of importance when conducting a substantive assessment of mergers, for example market definition, market structure and concentration, unilateral and coordinated effects, and market entry and expansion; these Worksheets set out the economic principles that are relevant to each subject and provide illustrative case studies. Some of the issues dealt with in the Worksheets, such as market definition and market structure, are relevant to all competition analysis, and have been discussed in chapter 1 of this book. Others, such as unilateral and coordinated effects, are specific to merger control and are considered further later. In 2017 the ICN published revised *Recommended Practices for Merger Analysis*.

A complicated feature of merger control is that it is necessarily forward-looking: a competition authority is called upon to consider whether a merger will lead to harmful effects on competition in the future[43]. Most mergers must be notified to the competition authority and cleared before they are put into effect, in which case the substantive analysis is entirely forward-looking. Even in those few jurisdictions, such as the UK, New Zealand and Australia, where a merger can be implemented prior to approval by the competition authority, because there is no duty to pre-notify[44], the assessment is still about predicting the future effects of the merger on the market. The predictive nature of merger control is different from the assessment of agreements and conduct under Articles 101 and 102 TFEU and the Chapter I and II prohibitions in the Competition Act 1998, where the competition authority will usually be investigating behaviour that has already taken place and

[40] On this point see Case T-102/96 *Gencor v Commission* EU:T:1999:65, para 106.

[41] See ch 22, 'Evaluation of remedial action', p 986; see further Nelson and Sun Su 'Consumer Savings from Merger Enforcement: A Review of the Antitrust Agencies' Estimates' (2002) 69 Antitrust LJ 921 and Balto and Higgins 'Brief Response on Consumer Savings from Merger Enforcement' (2000–01) 15 Antitrust 87.

[42] The *Workbook* is available at www.internationalcompetitionnetwork.org; see also OECD Roundtable *Substantive Criteria used for Assessment of Mergers* (2003), *Standard for merger review* (2009) and *Economic evidence in merger analysis* (2011), all available at www.oecd.org/competition.

[43] See Case C-12/03 P *Commission v Tetra Laval BV* EU:C:2005:87, at para 42.

[44] On the voluntary nature of pre-notification in UK law see ch 22, 'Notifying mergers to the CMA', pp 948–951.

trying to verify, for example, whether and when the members of an alleged cartel met or whether the pricing practices of a dominant firm amounted to a margin squeeze.

The fact that merger control is about predicting future behaviour means, necessarily, that it must be in part theoretical: a competition authority that decides to challenge a merger must have a *theory of competitive harm* as to why the market will work less well for consumers in the future than it does prior to the merger. However it would not be acceptable for the authority to be able to proceed against a merger purely on the basis of theory. There is nothing unlawful about merger activity, and the market for corporate control, in which firms compete for the right to acquire and manage businesses, is an important feature of a free-market economy. Intervention on the part of competition authorities should not be permissible on the basis of mere speculation. It follows that the competition authority should be required to produce *evidence* showing how its theory of competitive harm applies to the merger. Furthermore the competition authority should also have to demonstrate that the market, after the merger has been consummated, will be less competitive than if there had been no merger: in other words the authority will need not only to predict the likely outcome of the merger, but also to consider the *counterfactual*, that is to say the position if the merger were not to occur.

(i) Theories of competitive harm

Most mergers cause no harm to competition. However there are cases where it can be predicted that the merger will change the structure of the market in ways that provide the merged entity with the incentive and the ability to exercise market power. A competition authority concerned about a particular merger will need to articulate its theory as to how competition will be harmed[45]. Various theories of competitive harm have been developed.

(a) Unilateral or non-coordinated effects

Unilateral effects occur where A merges with B and the merged entity, AB, will be able, as a result of the merger, to exercise market power[46]. The most obvious manifestation of the exercise of market power is the ability to increase price, but there are other possibilities: for example a reduction of output, quality, variety or innovation[47]. It is helpful to think of the expression 'price increase' as shorthand which includes all these different manifestations of the exercise of market power. The ability to exercise market power is particularly likely if, prior to the merger, an increase in price on the part of A would have been likely to cause a substantial number of customers to divert their purchases to B: post-merger AB would not lose any profits as a result of such a shift, since AB would benefit from the increased sales of B's products. Economists use 'diversion ratios' between A and B to estimate this effect[48].

It may even be that, after the merger, C, a competitor of AB, will also be able to exercise market power because, if AB were to raise its prices, some customers would divert to C, which in turn could raise its own prices. C may be able to do this without coordinating its behaviour

[45] See Zenger and Walker 'Theories of Harm in European Competition Law: A Progress Report', in Bourgeois and Waelbroeck (eds) *Ten Years of Effects-based Approach in EU Competition Law* (Bruylant, 2012), available at www.ssrn.com.

[46] See the *Workbook*, Worksheet C; unilateral effects are sometimes referred to as non-coordinated effects, in order to differentiate them from the coordinated effects discussed in the next section.

[47] On detriments to innovation see Federico, Langus and Valletti 'Horizontal Mergers and Product Innovation: An Economic Framework', 2017, available at www.ssrn.com.

[48] Niels, Jenkins and Kavanagh *Economics for Competition Lawyers* (Oxford University Press, 2nd ed, 2016), ch 7.4.2.

with that of AB, in which case C's behaviour can itself be characterised as unilateral or non-coordinated. This is the phenomenon sometimes known as 'non-collusive oligopoly'[49].

(b) Coordinated effects

Coordinated effects occur where A merges with B and this results in a situation where AB will be able, or more able than when A and B were independent, to coordinate their competitive behaviour on the market with other firms, for example with C and D, and thereby exercise collective market power[50]. As the *Workbook* suggests, three conditions must be met for coordination to be successful[51]. First it must be possible for AB, C and D to coordinate their behaviour in some way, for example by charging the same prices or, perhaps, by aligning their behaviour on output and capacity expansion. Secondly, it must be costly for those firms to deviate from coordination, for example because 'cheats' will be punished. Third, AB, C and D must be free from competitive constraint from other participants in the market, for example E and F.

(c) Vertical effects

As a general proposition it is unlikely that a merger will produce adverse vertical effects[52]. Indeed a merger between an upstream firm, A, with a downstream firm, B, is likely to be neutral in terms of economic efficiency or even highly beneficial. For example if A and B are independent each will need to earn a margin on its operation—perhaps A as a producer and B as a distributor. The merged AB will need to earn only one margin: the elimination of 'double marginalisation' may lead to lower costs, and therefore to lower prices for the customers of AB. However there may be circumstances in which a vertical merger may harm competition, first, where it forecloses other firms in the industry from entering the market and, secondly, where the vertical integration of AB makes it more likely that there will be coordinated effects on the market.

An example of foreclosure could arise where A, a firm in an upstream market, acquires access through a merger with B, a firm in a downstream market, to an important downstream product, for example a distribution system such as a gas pipeline that is difficult to duplicate. The merged entity AB may have the incentive to deny competitors in the upstream market access to the distribution system, thereby foreclosing them from the downstream market. Similarly where B, a firm in a downstream market, merges with A, a firm that has substantial market power in relation to an important raw material or input in an upstream market, the merged entity AB may have the incentive to deny competitors in the downstream market access to that input. The concern here is that competitors in the downstream market will be unable to obtain supplies of the raw material or input, or that they will be able to do so only on discriminatory terms, with the result that they will be unable to compete effectively. These two examples of foreclosure can be depicted diagrammatically as shown in Figures 20.1 and 20.2, where the diagonal lines represent the foreclosure effect that arises from the merger of A and B:

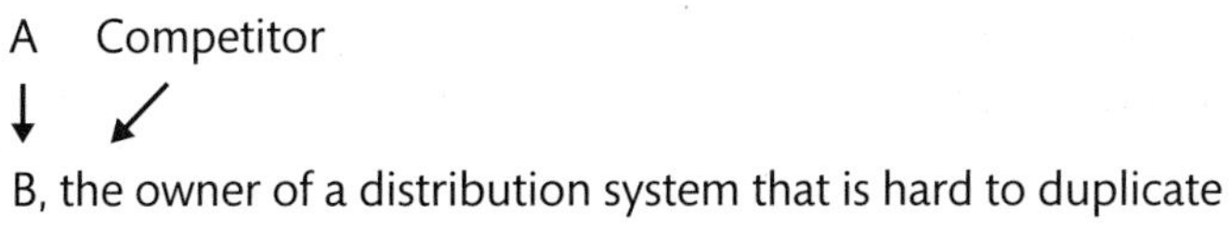

Fig. 20.1 Foreclosure of access to a downstream distribution system

[49] On the treatment of non-collusive oligopoly under the EUMR see ch 21, 'The non-collusive oligopoly gap', pp 883–885 and under UK law see ch 22, 'Unilateral effects', pp 962–964; an example of such a case in the US is *FTC v HJ Heinz Company and Milnot Corpn* 246 F 3d 708 (DC Cir 2001).

[50] See the *Workbook*, Worksheet D. [51] Ibid, para D.6.

[52] Ibid, Worksheet H; see also OECD Roundtable *Vertical mergers* (2007), available at www.oecd.org/competition.

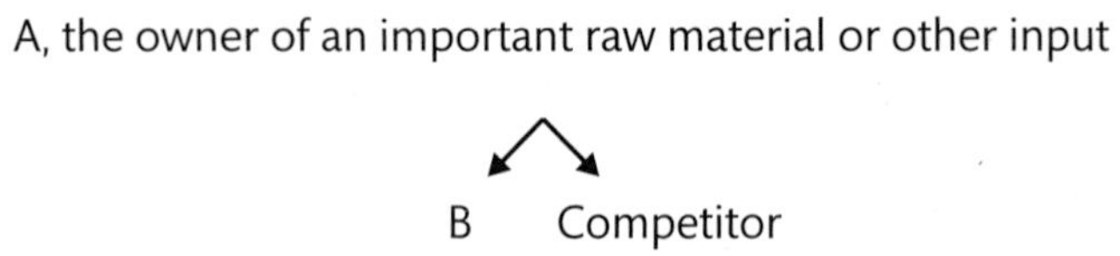

Fig. 20.2 Foreclosure of access to an important input

A merger of vertically-related firms might also increase the possibility of the merged entity, AB, being able to coordinate its behaviour with other competitors if, for example, it will lead to increased price transparency or if it will make it easier to detect firms that deviate from the coordinated behaviour.

In considering whether a merger could give rise to adverse vertical effects a competition authority should not only consider whether the merged entity would have the ability and the incentive to exercise market power; it should also consider carefully whether this would lead to harm to consumers, taking into account in particular the possibility that the merger may give rise to significant economic efficiencies that might be passed on to them in lower prices.

(d) Conglomerate effects

As a general proposition conglomerate mergers are unlikely to give rise to adverse competitive effects[53]. They do not involve the removal of actual or potential competitors from the market as in the case of horizontal mergers; nor do they bring together firms that have a vertical relationship in relation to the same final product, where there may be incentives to foreclose competitors from the upstream or downstream market. Furthermore, as in the case of vertical mergers, conglomerate mergers often result in efficiency gains, for example where the merged entity AB is able to offer complementary products that do not compete with one another to a customer desiring both: if A produces widgets and B blodgets, a 'one-stop shop' may be highly beneficial to a customer that requires both products. The theory of harm in the case of conglomerate effects is particularly speculative—for example that AB might decide to 'tie' the two complementary products together in a way that will foreclose competitors, or to price a bundled package of both of them to similar effect. It is possible that tie-in transactions and bundling practices would violate laws that forbid the abuse of a dominant position although the law on this subject is controversial in itself[54]. It is even more controversial that a merger should be prohibited on this ground. Intervention on conglomerate grounds is a possibility in EU and UK law, but would require convincing evidence in support of the theory of harm[55].

(ii) **Evidence**

Having identified a theory (or theories) of competitive harm, a competition authority must then search for reliable evidence in support of that theory: its case must be based

[53] Ibid, Worksheet H; see also OECD Roundtable *Portfolio Effects in Conglomerate Mergers* (2002), available at www.oecd.org/competition.

[54] See ch 17, 'Tying', pp 705–713 and ch 18, 'Bundling', pp 754–756.

[55] On the position under the EUMR see ch 21, 'Recent cases on non-horizontal mergers', p 902 and under UK law see ch 22, 'Non-horizontal mergers', pp 965–966.

on facts. The ICN produced, in 2005, a helpful *Investigative Techniques Handbook*[56], chapter 3 of which identifies five types of evidence that may be of use in merger reviews: evidence that was produced before the merger was contemplated, such as corporate strategy documents, planning documents and sales reports; documents produced for the purpose of the merger, such as surveys, reports and economic analyses; descriptive evidence from participants in the market, such as customers, suppliers and competitors; written responses to requests for information from the competition authority; and expert and quantitative evidence, for example from industry experts and economists. Chapter 4 of the *Investigative Techniques Handbook* discusses various types of quantitative analyses, such as the measurement of critical loss[57], which may be helpful when predicting whether a merger might lead to anti-competitive effects. The Worksheets already referred to in the ICN's *Merger Guidelines Workbook* also provide summaries of evidence of value when assessing, for example, whether a merger might lead to adverse unilateral[58] or coordinated[59] effects[60]. The OECD's Roundtable on *Economic Evidence in Merger Analysis* is another useful resource on this issue[61].

Competition authorities increasingly use, in unilateral effects cases, a range of quantitative techniques that endeavour to predict the effect that a merger will have on the post-merger level of prices[62]. If such modelling could produce robust and reliable results the traditional analysis of defining the relevant market, assessing market power and then considering unilateral effects could be considerably abbreviated, perhaps with no need for market definition at all. However the science of merger simulation is not yet sufficiently robust for this, and the technique, at most, can form only part of the overall body of evidence in a particular case[63]. Market definition, measuring market shares and merger simulation are complementary, not alternative, tools of merger analysis.

The Court of Justice has made clear that, where a merger is challenged on conglomerate grounds, the evidence on which the Commission relies must be particularly convincing, given that the chains of cause and effect between the merger and the predicted adverse effects 'are dimly discernible, uncertain and difficult to establish'[64].

An important issue in relation to evidence is to decide what standard of proof a competition authority should have to attain before it can take action to block or require the modification of a merger: should it have to prove its case that a merger would be harmful to competition 'on the balance of probabilities', or should it have to go further and show 'beyond reasonable doubt' that the merger would have detrimental effects? If a competition authority can intervene too easily, on the basis of weak evidence, the possibility exists that 'false positives' might arise: that is to say that some innocuous mergers might be blocked; however, if the criteria for intervention are too demanding, or if the standard of proof is set at a very high level, 'false negatives' might occur: some harmful mergers might

56 The *Handbook* is available at www.internationalcompetitionnetwork.org.

57 See also Langenfeld and Li 'Critical loss analysis in evaluating mergers' (2001) 46 Antitrust Bulletin 299.

58 See Worksheet C—Unilateral Effects, para C.10.

59 See Worksheet D—Coordinated Effects, paras D.9–D.16.

60 See also the OECD Roundtable *Managing Complex Mergers* (2008), available at www.oecd.org/competition.

61 Available at www.oecd.org/competition.

62 See OECD Roundtable *Economic Evidence in Merger Analysis* (2011), available at www.oecd.org/competition.

63 On merger simulation see Buettner, Federico and Lorincz 'The Use of Quantitative Economic Techniques in EU Merger Control' (2016) 31 Antitrust Magazine 68 (the authors are members of the DG COMP Chief Competition Economist's Team).

64 Case C-12/03 P *Commission v Tetra Laval BV* EU:C:2005:87, para 44.

be cleared[65]. Being realistic, it is inevitable that some errors of both kinds will be made by competition authorities: it is a matter of public policy to decide which of the two types of error is the more troubling.

(iii) The counterfactual

Merger assessment involves predicting the effect on competition in the market if a particular transaction is consummated. This necessarily involves a comparison between the situation if the merger goes ahead and the position if it did not happen: the competitive situation without the merger is often referred to as the counterfactual[66]. The counterfactual will usually be the prevailing conditions before the merger, although there may be cases in which it is necessary to take into account conditions as they would be in the near future if, for example, it is known that other firms are about to enter or exit the market or to expand capacity; another example would be that one of the merging firms was on the point of failing, so that it would not be present on the market in the future anyway. The UK Competition and Markets Authority ('the CMA') explicitly states the counterfactual in each of its merger inquiry reports.

(C) The substantive test: SLC, dominance, SIEC

Any system of merger control must set a substantive test against which to determine whether a particular merger should be modified or prohibited. When the EUMR was in the process of being reformed in the years leading up to 2004 there was an interesting and important debate as to the most appropriate formulation[67]. Many systems, such as the US and the UK, permit the prohibition of a merger which will 'substantially lessen competition' ('SLC')[68]; the original Merger Regulation of 1989 required intervention where a merger would 'create or strengthen a dominant position as a result of which effective competition would be significantly impeded'[69]. Many Member States of the EU use the same formulation; some, for example France and Greece, have both SLC and dominance tests. The test in the EUMR was changed in 2004: the question is whether the merger would 'significantly impede effective competition' ('SIEC'), in particular (but not exclusively) as a result of the creation or strengthening of a dominant position[70].

(D) Guidelines

There are abundant guidelines on the substantive assessment of mergers. Reference has already been made to the ICN's *Merger Guidelines Workbook* and *Investigative Techniques Handbook*[71]. Many competition authorities have also published guidelines on substantive

[65] These phenomena are also referred to as Type I and Type II errors: see Black, Hashimzade and Myles (eds) *Oxford Dictionary of Economics* (Oxford University Press, 4th ed, 2012), and ch 5, 'False positives and false negatives', pp 203–204; see further OECD Roundtable *Agency decision-making in merger cases: Prohibition and conditional clearances* (2016), available at www.oecd/org/competition.

[66] See the *Workbook*, paras 2.9 and 2.10; see also a series of papers presented at the Swedish Competition Authority's conference on *The Pros and Cons of Counterfactuals*, 2013, available at www.konkurrensverket.se.

[67] See eg OECD Roundtables *Substantive Criteria used for the Assessment of Mergers* (2003) and *Standard of Merger Review* (2010), available at www.oecd.org/competition; the European Commission's *Green Paper on the Review of Council Regulation (EEC) No 4064/89*, COM(2001) 745/6 final, paras 159–169.

[68] See eg s 7 Clayton Act 1914 in the US; s 50 Trade Practices Act 1974 in Australia; s 92 Competition Act 1985 in Canada; s 12A Competition Act 1998 in South Africa.

[69] EUMR, Articles 2(2) and 2(3), on which see ch 21, 'Substantive Analysis', pp 882ff.

[70] For further discussion of this issue see ch 21, 'Adoption of the "significant impediment to effective competition" test', pp 883–887.

[71] The ICN has also published 'Recommended Practices' on matters such as remedies, notifications and merger procedures; these are all available at www.internationalcompetitionnetwork.org.

assessment. Of particular importance are the 2010 *Horizontal Merger Guidelines* in the US[72] and the joint guidelines of the OFT and Competition Commission in the UK which have been adopted by the CMA which has replaced those two bodies[73]. The European Commission has published *Guidelines on the assessment of horizontal mergers*[74] and *Guidelines on the assessment of non-horizontal mergers*[75]. Guidelines must strike an appropriate balance between providing guidance for firms and their advisers as to what might be expected of a system of merger control and avoiding too much speculation, which can lead to a loss of certainty.

A specific issue in systems of merger control is whether a merger which reduces competition but which would lead to gains in efficiency should be permitted: the US Guidelines address this issue specifically in paragraph 4 and do, in very limited circumstances, recognise efficiency arguments[76]. In the UK section 30 of the Enterprise Act 2002 allows the CMA to take into account 'relevant customer benefits' in certain circumstances[77]; while the European Commission's *Horizontal Guidelines* take efficiencies into account within the overall assessment of a merger[78]. Another issue that sometimes arises is whether a merger should be allowed in order to save a 'failing firm', even though there will be less competition in the market after the merger than before[79]. A failing firm defence does exist in US law[80], has been applied under the EUMR[81] and is recognised in an appropriate case under the guidelines in the UK[82].

(E) **Remedies**

It is quite often the case that most aspects of a particular merger give rise to no competition concerns. However it may be, for example, that there are certain parts of the businesses of A and B that overlap horizontally, in which case a competition authority, rather than prohibiting the entire transaction, may look for a remedy whereby its competition concern is assuaged and the rest of the deal is allowed to proceed. The most obvious remedy is the divestiture of one or other of the overlapping businesses so that there will be no accretion of market power. Some cases may require more complex remedies, for example a right of access to an essential facility or the licensing of technology to competitors on reasonable and non-discriminatory terms. Devising and implementing satisfactory remedies is often a complex matter. The OECD made a number of recommendations as to

[72] These are available at www.justice.gov.atr, on which see Shaprio 'The 2010 *Horizontal Merger Guidelines*: From Hedgehog to Fox in Forty Years' (2010) 77 Antitrust LJ 701.

[73] *Merger Assessment Guidelines*, CC2 (revised) and OFT 1254, September 2010, available at www.gov.uk/cma.

[74] OJ [2004] C 31/5. [75] OJ [2008] C 265/6.

[76] The complexity of allowing efficiencies as a defence in a merger case is vividly illustrated by the *Superior Propane* case in Canada: see *The Commissioner of Competition v Superior Propane Inc* [2003] 3 FC 529, judgment of 31 January 2003 (Federal Court of Appeal); see also the European Commission's (2003) (Summer) Competition Policy Newsletter 43–49; Williamson 'Economies as an Antitrust Defense: The Welfare Trade-Off' (1968) 58 Am Ec Rev 158; Gerard 'Merger Control Policy: How to Give Meaningful Consideration to Efficiency Claims?' (2003) 40 CML Rev 1367; Kwoka 'The Changing Nature of Efficiencies in Mergers and in Merger Analysis' (2015) 60 Antitrust Bulletin 231.

[77] See ch 22, 'Efficiencies', pp 966–967; note in particular *Merger Assessment Guidelines*, CC2 (revised) and OFT 1254, September 2010, section 5.7.

[78] See the *Horizontal Guidelines*, paras 76–88; see further ch 21, 'Efficiencies', pp 897–898.

[79] See the OECD Roundtable *Failing Firm Defence* (2009), available at www.oecd.org/competition.

[80] See the *Horizontal Merger Guidelines*, section 11.

[81] See ch 21, 'The "failing firm" defence', pp 898–899 and the Commission's *Horizontal Merger Guidelines*, paras 76–88.

[82] *Merger Assessment Guidelines* (CC2 (revised) and OFT 1254, September 2010), paras 4.3.8–4.3.18 (using the expression 'exiting firm scenario'); see further ch 22, 'The exiting firm scenario', pp 960–961.

best practices following its roundtable on *Merger Remedies*[83]. In 2016 the ICN published a *Merger Remedies Guide*[84] that provides a practical guide as to the key principles and range of tools available in the establishment of suitable remedies. In 2005 the European Commission published a *Merger Remedies Study*[85] in which it reviewed the effectiveness of 96 remedies accepted in 40 cases in the five-year period from 1996 to 2000. This *Study* had an important bearing on the Commission's revised *Notice on remedies acceptable under the EUMR*[86] of 2008. In the UK careful attention is given to remedies and the CMA conducts a rolling programme for the review of the success of past remedies[87].

(F) Evaluation of merger decisions

Competition authorities increasingly evaluate the impact of their decisions to clear or modify mergers. This process of 'self-evaluation' enables authorities to test the accuracy of their predictions about individual mergers and to improve the quality of future decision-making[88].

(G) Merger control and the public interest

As noted at the start of this chapter, numerous arguments may be made against mergers that have nothing to do with the maintenance of competitive markets. It would be possible to devise a system of merger control that allows intervention for non-competition reasons; in so far as it does so the law in question can hardly be called 'competition' law; indeed prohibiting mergers on social grounds or for reasons of industrial policy may be directly antagonistic to the process of competition[89]. Some of the arguments sometimes heard are these[90]:

(i) Loss of efficiency and 'short-termism'

Some commentators would argue that mergers, far from promoting economic efficiency, have a disruptive effect upon the management of one or both of the merged firms and may be detrimental to their long-term prospects. This claim is made in particular of contested

[83] See also the OECD Roundtable *Remedies in Cross-Border Merger Cases* (2013), both available at www.oecd.org/competition.

[84] Available at www.internationalcompetitionnetwork.org.

[85] Available at www.ec.europa.eu/competition/index_en.html.

[86] See ch 21, 'Remedies', pp 907–913.

[87] OJ [2008] C 267/1; see ch 22, 'Undertakings in lieu of a reference', pp 953–955 and '"Final powers" or "remedies"', pp 973–977.

[88] See OECD Roundtable *Impact Evaluation of Merger Decisions* (2011), available at www.oecd.org/competition.

[89] In Germany the head of the Monopoly Commission resigned when the Minister for Economics approved a merger between two supermarkets, Endeka and Kaiser's Tengelemann, that both the Bundeskartellamt and the Monopoly Commission considered to be anti-competitive: Press Release of 17 March 2016, available at www.monopolkommission.de.

[90] For useful discussion of mergers and the public interest see Fairburn and Kay (eds) *Mergers and Mergers Policy* (Oxford University Press, 1989); Jacquemain (ed) *Merger & Competition Policy in the European Community* (Blackwell, 1990); Neven, Nuttall and Seabright *Mergers in Daylight: The Economics and Politics of European Merger Control* (CEPR, 1993); Lewis 'The Political Economy of Antitrust' [2001] Fordham Corporate Law Institute (ed Hawk), pp 617ff; Bishop and Walker *The Economics of EC Competition Law* (Sweet & Maxwell, 3rd ed, 2010), chs 7 and 8; speech by Lewis at the sixth Annual ICN Conference in Moscow, 2006 available at www.internationalcompetitionnetwork.org; OECD Roundtable *Public interest considerations in merger control* (2016), available at www.oecd.org/competition; Reader 'Accommodating "public interest" considerations in domestic merger control', CCP Working Paper 16-3, available at www.ssrn.com.

takeover bids, where it is possible that the management of the target company will either be removed by the new shareholders or will resign rather than stay on in the new conditions. Sceptics of the way in which the market for corporate control functions would argue that it is not inevitable that the decisions of shareholders will produce the best result in the public interest, although it may yield the best financial deal for the shareholders themselves. In particular many would argue that a problem with takeovers is that they are motivated more by short-term profit-taking than by genuine concern for the long-term prospects of companies. This may be particularly true of institutional investors in the market which are in the habit of regularly turning over their investments in pursuit of short-term gains.

(ii) Concentration of wealth

Mergers may be objected to on the ground that they lead to firms of such size and with such power as to be antithetical to a balanced distribution of wealth. This of course is a socio-political argument, but one which has become more widely accepted as aggregate industrial concentration has increased. In the US the merger control provisions laws were strengthened at a time when this problem was a dominant concern[91].

(iii) Unemployment and regional policy

Another objection to mergers is that they may lead to the closure of factories or offices and result in serious unemployment. Mergers that savour of 'asset-stripping' and which appear to have no regard for the social problems that may follow attract particular opprobrium from sceptics of the free market. Opposition to acquisitions by private equity funds in recent years was partly inspired by this concern. Similarly the market operating in its unfettered form may not attach much weight to the desirability of maintaining a balanced distribution of wealth and job opportunities; the market has no reason to be sentimental about such matters. Governments can choose to adopt a regional policy, however, and it is possible to give expression to this issue in mergers policy as well as in laws on tax, planning and state aids.

(iv) Overseas control

Mergers may result in the control of indigenous firms passing to overseas companies, in which case any economic advantages of the merger may be thought to be outweighed by the desirability of maintaining the decision-making process and profits at home. In 2005 the OECD specifically called for merger laws to treat foreign firms no less favourably than domestic firms in like circumstances[92]. Strong opposition was expressed in the US in 2006 when the possibility of sea ports there coming under the control of Dubai Ports became known. Many UK firms have expanded abroad, in particular into the US, and this makes it somewhat difficult to argue that UK firms should themselves be shielded from hostile foreign takeover bids: this did not prevent fierce opposition being expressed to a proposed acquisition of AstraZeneca by Pfizer in 2014, a proposal that was eventually dropped. The case for intervention against foreign takeovers may be more compelling where there is a lack of reciprocity[93] between the laws of the two countries: if the law of country A *prevents* inward investment, whereas country B permits it, there may be a case for blocking a takeover by a firm from A of a firm in B. The European Commission has proposed legislation that would create an EU framework for screening

[91] See eg *Brown Shoe Co v United States* 370 US 294, 344 (1962).

[92] OECD *Recommendation on Merger Review* (2005), available at www.oecd.org/competition.

[93] Or, to put the matter more colloquially, where the 'playing fields' are not even.

foreign takeovers and investments on grounds of security and public policy[94]. The UK Government has also published a Green Paper setting out proposals to strengthen its powers for scrutinising the national security implications of foreign investments[95].

(v) Special sectors

Some sectors of the economy—for example the electronic and print media—are especially sensitive and this may mean that concentration of ownership within them requires special consideration. In the UK, as in several other countries, media mergers are subject to special provisions[96] and mergers in industries such as oil, banking[97] and defence may be particularly closely scrutinised; the UK also has a special regime for mergers in the water industry[98] and the Communications Act 2003 contains special provisions on media mergers[99]. Article 21(4) of the EUMR specifically recognises that Member States may have a 'legitimate interest' in investigating a merger other than on grounds of harm to competition[100].

7. Designing a System of Merger Control

Where a country decides to adopt a system of merger control, a number of issues have to be addressed. In chapters 21 and 22 the EU and UK systems will be described; most cases would probably result in the same outcome, irrespective of which of these two laws is applied: the dominant consideration in each jurisdiction is the impact of a merger on competition, and the analysis will be conducted in much the same way in each of them. Despite this, however, it will be seen that the provisions themselves—for example on jurisdiction, notification, procedure and substantive analysis, remedies—are actually quite different.

The following are some of the issues that must be confronted in designing a system of merger control.

- Which transactions should be characterised as mergers? How should the acquisition of minority shareholdings and of assets be dealt with? Will joint ventures be considered as a matter of merger control or under the legal provisions that prohibit anti-competitive agreements?
- How should the jurisdictional test be framed for determining those mergers that can be investigated? Should the test be based on turnover, the value of assets acquired, market share or some other criterion?
- To what extent should a system of merger control apply to transactions consummated outside a country but which have effects within it?
- Should mergers be subject to a system of mandatory pre-notification, or should it be a matter for the parties to decide whether to notify? In the latter case, in what

[94] Commission Proposal for a Regulation establishing a framework for screening of foreign direct investments into the European Union, COM(2017) 487 final.

[95] *National Security and Infrastructure Review*, 17 October 2017, and the Government's response to its consultation, 15 March 2018, both available at www.gov.uk/beis.

[96] See ch 22, 'Public interest cases', pp 987–989.

[97] See the discussion of the Lloyds TSB/HBOS merger in ch 22, 'The public interest provisions in practice', p 989.

[98] See ch 22, 'Mergers in the water industry', pp 991–993.

[99] Communications Act 2003, ss 351–354.

[100] See ch 21, 'Article 21(4): legitimate interest clause', pp 872–875.

circumstances and for how long after a merger has been completed should a competition authority be allowed to review a case?

- To what extent should the parties be permitted to integrate their operations and discuss their affairs pending the outcome of a merger investigation?
- What should be the time period within which a merger investigation must be completed?
- What should be the substantive test for reviewing mergers? Should it be based solely on competition criteria, or should any or all of the other issues discussed above (for example unemployment, regional policy and overseas control) also be taken into account?
- How should the specific issues of (a) efficiency and (b) failing firms be dealt with?
- What mechanism should be put in place for the negotiation of remedies that would overcome any problems identified by the competition authority?
- Who should make decisions in merger cases? A Commission, in which case who should appoint the Commissioners? A court? A Minister in the Government?
- What checks and balances should there be to guarantee due process within merger control? What system of judicial review or appeals should be put in place to test the findings of the decision-maker in merger cases? How quickly will any judicial review or appeal be completed?

These are just some of the many interesting and important issues that arise in relation to the control of mergers. With these preliminary observations in mind, this book will now describe the systems in force in the EU and UK.

21

Mergers (2): EU law

1. Introduction

The EU system of merger control[1] is contained in the EU Merger Regulation, Regulation 139/2004[2] ('the EUMR'). Section 2 of this chapter provides an overview of EU merger control. The terms 'merger' and 'concentration' are used interchangeably throughout this chapter. Section 3 sets out the jurisdictional rules which determine whether a particular merger should be investigated by the European Commission in Brussels or by the national competition authorities ('the NCAs') of the Member States. Section 4 deals with procedural matters such as the mandatory pre-notification to the Commission of concentrations that have a Union dimension and the procedural timetable within which the Commission must operate. Section 5 discusses the substantive analysis of mergers under the EUMR and section 6 explains the procedure whereby the Commission may authorise a merger on the basis of commitments, often referred to as remedies, offered by the parties to address its competition concerns. The chapter then contains sections on the Commission's powers of investigation and enforcement, on judicial review of Commission decisions by the EU Courts and on cooperation between the Commission

[1] For further reading on the EU Merger Regulation readers are referred to Schwalbe and Zimmer *Law and Economics in European Merger Control* (Oxford University Press, 2009); Rosenthal and Thomas *European Merger Control* (Hart, 2010); Rose and Bailey (eds) *Bellamy and Child: European Union Law of Competition* (Oxford University Press, 7th ed, 2013), ch 8; Lowe and Marquis (eds) *European Competition Law Annual 2010: Merger Control in European and Global Perspective* (Hart, 2013); Faull and Nikpay (eds) *The EU Law of Competition* (Oxford University Press, 3rd ed, 2014), ch 5; Bas *The Substantive Appraisal of Joint Ventures under the EU Merger Control Regime* (Kluwer Law International, 2014); Levy *European Merger Control Law: A Guide to the Merger Regulation* (LexisNexis, 13th ed, 2016); Lindsay and Berridge *The EU Merger Regulation: Substantive Issues* (Sweet & Maxwell, 5th ed, 2017); as to mergers under the EEA Agreement see ch 2, 'European Economic Area', pp 57–58 and Broberg *The European Commission's Jurisdiction to Scrutinise Mergers* (Kluwer International, 4th ed, 2013), ch 7; on international merger control see Elliott and Bellis (eds) *Merger Control* (Sweet & Maxwell, 3rd ed, 2017); Davies (ed) *Merger Control: The International Regulation of Mergers and Joint Ventures in 72 Jurisdictions Worldwide* (GCR, 2017).

[2] OJ [2004] L 24/1.

and other competition authorities, both within and outside the EU. Section 10 considers how the merger control provisions work in practice.

2. Overview of EU Merger Control

(A) Brief description of the EU system of merger control

The Commission first proposed a merger control regulation as early as 1973[3]. The issue was controversial as opinions differed substantially between Member States on the extent to which mergers should be controlled at the EU level as opposed to domestically. It was not until 21 December 1989 that the Council of Ministers adopted Regulation 4064/1989; it entered into force on 21 September 1990. Regulation 4064/1989 was amended quite significantly by Regulation 1310/97[4], and was repealed and replaced by the current EUMR with effect from 1 May 2004[5].

The EU system of merger control requires mergers that have a Union[6] dimension to be pre-notified to the Commission; it is unlawful to consummate a merger without a prior clearance from the Commission (there are some minor exceptions to this proposition). Whether or not a merger has a Union dimension is determined by reference to the turnover of the undertakings concerned in a transaction. Where a merger has a Union dimension the Commission has sole jurisdiction in relation to it: this is the principle of 'one-stop merger control'. However there are some circumstances in which the Commission might allow jurisdiction (wholly or in part) over a merger having a Union dimension to be ceded to one or more Member States; in certain situations it is obliged to do this. There are also some circumstances in which Member States may transfer jurisdiction to the Commission over mergers that do not have a Union dimension. Once the Commission has jurisdiction it is required, within fixed time limits, to determine whether a merger could significantly impede effective competition in the internal market or a substantial part of it; in conducting this assessment the Commission asks, in particular, whether the merger could create or strengthen a dominant position. Most cases are completed within 25 working days of the notification, known as a Phase I investigation. In approximately 3% of cases the Commission finds, at the end of its Phase I investigation, that it has serious doubts as to the compatibility of the merger with the internal market and proceeds to an in-depth Phase II investigation; this may take an additional 90 working days, and there are provisions for this period to be extended for up to an additional 35 working days[7].

The Commission has wide-ranging powers under the EUMR, including the power to prohibit a merger in its entirety. This is rare—there have been only 27 prohibitions in the entire lifetime of EU merger control, five of which were annulled on appeal[8]. However there have been numerous occasions on which the Commission has authorised a merger

[3] Commission Proposal for a Regulation of the Council of Ministers on the Control of Concentrations between Undertakings, OJ [1973] C 92/1; for successive drafts see OJ [1982] C 36/3; OJ [1984] C 51/8; OJ [1986] C 324/5; OJ [1988] C 130/4.

[4] OJ [1997] L 180/1.

[5] For discussion of the changes introduced by Regulation 139/2004 see González Diaz 'The Reform of European Merger Control: *Quid Novi Sub Sole?*' (2004) 27 World Competition 177.

[6] The EUMR uses the expression 'Community dimension'; however the post-Lisbon term 'Union dimension' is more appropriate today and will be used throughout this chapter.

[7] The Phase II period may be even longer in cases where the Commission 'stops the clock' because of the need for additional information for which one of the undertakings is responsible: see 'Phase II investigations', pp 880–881 later in chapter.

[8] See 'Comment', pp 922–931 later in chapter.

only after the parties had offered commitments to remedy its competition concerns: this has happened in roughly 5% of cases. When the parties offer commitments in this way they become legally binding upon them[9]. The Commission works closely both with the NCAs of the Member States, in particular within the EU Merger Working Group, and with competition authorities in other jurisdictions, when exercising its powers under the EUMR[10].

(B) Institutional arrangements

The full College of Commissioners takes the most important decisions under the EUMR, for example to prohibit a merger or to clear it subject to commitments at the end of a Phase II investigation. The fact that the full Commission is sometimes involved in decisions of considerable economic and political importance means that there may be a degree of lobbying of individual Commissioners, not just of the Commissioner for competition[11].

Some powers are delegated by the Commission to the Commissioner for competition. For example decisions at the end of Phase I and unconditional clearances in Phase II can be taken by the Commissioner for competition, who in turn may delegate certain functions to the Director-General of the Directorate General for Competition ('DG COMP'). Within DG COMP there is a Deputy Director General with special responsibility for mergers. Unit 2 of Directorate A of DG COMP deals with mergers case support and policy. Case work is handled by merger units within Directorates B to F, each of which has specific sectoral responsibilities[12]. DG COMP has a Chief Competition Economist who reports directly to the Director General to provide independent economic advice on cases and policy[13]. The Commission also has two Hearing Officers with a range of functions including overseeing the fairness of the Commission's proceedings and arranging and conducting oral hearings[14].

The Advisory Committee on Concentrations[15] provides the Member States with the opportunity of input into the decision-making process. Appeals against decisions of the Commission are taken to the General Court. Appeals to the General Court in merger cases are sometimes handled under the so-called 'expedited procedure'[16].

(C) The Implementing Regulation and the Commission's Notices and Guidelines

In addition to the EUMR anyone interested in EU merger control will require a number of other texts, in particular the Implementing Regulation and a series of Commission Notices

[9] On commitments, or 'remedies' as they are often referred to, see 'Remedies', pp 907–913 later in chapter.

[10] See 'International Cooperation', pp 921–922 later in chapter.

[11] See eg Marsden 'Lobbying for climate change in EU Competition Policy–just don't talk about the weather' Concurrences No 1-2009, 11; McLeod 'Brussels' hamstrung press corp and the dumbing down of news' Concurrences No 1-2009, 18; Mariani and Pieri 'Lobbying Activities and EU Competition Law: What Can be Done and How?' (2014) 5 JECLAP 423.

[12] See ch 2, 'European Commission', pp 54–55.

[13] On the Chief Competition Economist see further www.ec.europa.eu/dgs/competition/economist/role_en.html.

[14] On the Hearing Officers see further www.ec.europa.eu/competition/hearing_officers/index_en.html.

[15] See 'International Cooperation', pp 921–922 later in chapter.

[16] On judicial review under the EUMR and the expedited procedure see 'Judicial Review', pp 915–921 later in chapter.

and Guidelines, including the Guidelines on '*Best Practices*'[17]. The General Court has stated that the Commission is bound by its Notices, provided that the Notices do not depart from the rules in the Treaty or from the EUMR[18]; however the Commission retains 'great freedom of action' where a Notice allows it to choose the types of evidence or the economic approach most appropriate to a particular case[19]. All of the materials set out later can be accessed on DG COMP's website[20]; the Commission has also published a helpful compendium of materials, *EU Competition Law: Merger Legislation*, available on the same website.

(i) The Implementing Regulation

The Implementing Regulation, Regulation 802/2004[21] (which replaced earlier legislation), contains rules on notifications to the Commission, time limits, the right to be heard and hearings, access to the file and the treatment of confidential information and remedies. Regulation 802/2004 has been amended several times, in particular in order to provide the format for Form RM, a form used when undertakings offer commitments to the Commission in order to remedy competition concerns that it may have identified[22], and to simplify the procedure for reviewing 'unproblematic' mergers[23].

(ii) Commission Notices and Guidelines

The Commission has published numerous Notices and Guidelines on procedural and substantive matters, each of which will be referred to where appropriate in the text that follows:

- *Notice on the definition of the relevant market*[24]
- *Guidelines on the assessment of horizontal mergers*[25]
- *Notice on restrictions directly related and necessary to concentrations*[26]
- *Notice on case referral in respect of concentrations*[27]
- *Notice on access to the file*[28]
- *Consolidated Jurisdictional Notice*[29]
- *Guidelines on the assessment of non-horizontal mergers*[30]
- *Notice on remedies acceptable under the EUMR*[31]
- *Notice on a simplified procedure for treatment of certain concentrations*[32].

(iii) Best Practice Guidelines

The Commission has also published Guidelines setting out 'Best Practices' on various aspects of merger control:

- *Best Practices on the conduct of EC merger control proceedings* (January 2004)
- *Best practices for the submission of economic evidence and data collection concerning the application of Articles 101 and 102 TFEU and in merger cases* (October 2011)

17 Readers involved in merger proceedings in the UK may also wish to refer to ch 18 of *Mergers: Guidance on the CMA's jurisdiction and procedure*, CMA2, January 2014, which explains the CMA's role in relation to mergers under the EUMR, available at www.gov.uk/cma.

18 See Case T-282/06 *Sun Chemical Group BV v Commission* EU:T:2007:203, para 55 and the judgments referred to therein.

19 See Case T-210/01 *General Electric v Commission* EU:T:2005:456, para 519.

20 See www.ec.europa.eu/competition/index_en.html.

21 OJ [2004] L 133/1.

22 See 'Remedies', pp 907–913 later in chapter.

23 See 'Short Form CO', pp 877–878 later in chapter.

24 OJ [1997] C 372/5.

25 OJ [2004] C 31/5.

26 OJ [2005] C 56/24.

27 OJ [2005] C 56/2.

28 OJ [2005] C 325/7.

29 OJ [2008] C 95/1.

30 OJ [2008] C 265/6.

31 OJ [2008] C 267/1.

32 OJ [2013] C 366/5.

- *Best Practice Guidelines: the Commission's model texts for divestiture commitments and the trustee mandate* (December 2013)
- *Guidance on the preparation of public versions of Commission decisions adopted under the Merger Regulation* (May 2015)
- *Best Practices on the disclosure of information in data rooms* (June 2015).

(D) Access to the Commission's decisions

DG COMP's website is an important source of material about the operation of the EUMR. As well as the legislation and guidance just referred to, the website provides a large amount of information about completed cases and current investigations; these can be searched for by reference to the case number, a company's name, decision type or by industry sector. The website also contains interesting statistical information, regularly updated, about the EUMR in practice (for example the number of notifications each year and the number of conditional clearances or prohibitions) and useful studies and reports on matters such as unilateral effects, tacit coordination and the impact of vertical and conglomerate mergers on competition[33]. DG COMP also publishes *Competition Merger Briefs* that provide helpful information on matters of both policy and enforcement[34].

Each notification received by the Commission is given a case number, which will be prefixed with an 'M' (as in Case M 4600 *TUI/First Choice*). When a merger is notified a summary of it will appear on DG COMP's website and a provisional deadline for the decision will be given; the website is updated as the investigation progresses.

The Commission's decisions can be accessed in various ways. A press release summarising the Commission's finding in cases other than those for which the simplified procedure applies[35] will usually be published in English, French, German and in the language of the notification. The press release is normally issued on the day of adoption of the decision. It can be obtained on the Rapid database of the Commission's website[36]. Phase I decisions—that is to say cases that do not require 'in-depth' investigation—are not themselves published in the Official Journal, other than a brief statement of the outcome. Phase I decisions are published on DG COMP's website, but only in the language in which the parties notified. Decisions following a Phase II investigation are more widely available. Summaries of Phase II decisions are published in the Official Journal together with the final report of the Hearing Officer and the opinion of the Advisory Committee on Concentrations. The non-confidential version of the full decisions are published on the Commission's website; there may be a lengthy delay between the adoption of a decision and its appearance on the website while agreement is reached between the parties and the Commission as to what confidential information should be omitted from the published version.

3. Jurisdiction

This section will deal with the following matters:

(A) Article 3: meaning of a concentration: the EUMR applies to mergers or, more precisely, to 'concentrations', a term defined in Article 3 and further explained in the case

[33] See www.ec.europa.eu/competition/mergers/studies_reports/studies_reports.html.

[34] See www.ec.europa.eu/competition/publications/cpn.

[35] On this procedure see 'Notification', pp 876–878 later in chapter.

[36] See www.europa.eu/rapid.

law of the EU Courts and in the Commission's *Consolidated Jurisdictional Notice* ('the *Jurisdictional Notice*').

(B) Articles 1 and 5: concentrations having a Union dimension: the EUMR applies to concentrations that have a 'Union dimension'. The meaning of this term is found in Article 1, and is further explained in the *Jurisdictional Notice*. It is determined by reference to the turnover of the 'undertakings concerned', including their affiliated undertakings as set out in Article 5.

(C) One-stop merger control: as a general proposition concentrations that have a Union dimension are investigated by the Commission and not by the Member States; this is the principle of 'one-stop merger control'.

(D) Article 4(4) and Article 9: referral of concentrations having a Union dimension to the competent authorities of the Member States: in certain cases Article 4(4) and Article 9 provide a mechanism whereby concentrations that have a Union dimension can be reviewed by the competent authorities of the Member States, either because the undertakings concerned or a Member State make a request to that effect. The Commission's *Notice on Case Referral in respect of concentrations* ('the *Case Referral Notice*') provides important guidance on this topic.

(E) Article 4(5) and Article 22: referral of concentrations not having a Union dimension by Member States to the Commission: in certain cases Article 4(5) and Article 22 provide a mechanism whereby concentrations that do not have a Union dimension can be investigated by the Commission, either because the undertakings concerned or a Member State make a request to that effect. Again the *Case Referral Notice* provides important guidance.

(F) Article 21(4): legitimate interest clause: Member States are not allowed to apply their domestic competition law to concentrations that have a Union dimension except in the circumstances in which Article 4(4) or Article 9 are applicable. However provision is made by Article 21(4) for Member States to investigate a concentration having a Union dimension where it threatens to harm some 'legitimate interest' of the State other than the maintenance of competition.

(G) Defence: Member States retain jurisdiction to examine the national security aspects of mergers as a result of Article 346 TFEU.

Each of these propositions will be examined in turn.

(A) Article 3: meaning of a concentration

Part B of the *Jurisdictional Notice* deals with the meaning of a concentration. The footnotes in the *Jurisdictional Notice* contain many references to the decisional practice of the Commission and the judgments of the EU Courts, and the reader should be aware of these useful reference points. Article 3(1) of the EUMR provides that:

> A concentration shall be deemed to arise where a change of control on a lasting basis results from:
>
> (a) the merger of two or more previously independent undertakings or parts of undertakings, or
>
> (b) the acquisition, by one or more persons already controlling at least one undertaking, or by one or more undertakings, whether by purchase of securities or assets, by contract or by any other means, of direct or indirect control of the whole or parts of one or more other undertakings.

(i) Article 3(1)(a): mergers

Mergers in the sense of Article 3(1)(a) are dealt with in paragraphs 9 and 10 of the *Jurisdictional Notice*, which provides examples of cases covered by it such as *AstraZeneca/*

Novartis[37] and *Chevron/Texaco*[38]. Paragraph 10 explains that there can be factual ('*de facto*') mergers where, in the absence of a legal merger, activities of previously independent entities are combined with the result that a single economic unit is created under a permanent, single economic management; examples given are *Price Waterhouse/Coopers & Lybrand*[39] and *Ernst & Young/Andersen Germany*[40].

(ii) Article 3(1)(b): acquisition of control

In practice most cases are concerned with the acquisition of control in the sense of Article 3(1)(b) of the EUMR: the *Jurisdictional Notice* deals with this concept from paragraphs 11 to 123. It begins by discussing the concept of control; it then deals in turn with the acquisition of sole control and of joint control.

(a) The concept of control

Article 3(2) of the EUMR defines control for the purpose of determining whether there is a concentration[41]:

> Control shall be constituted by rights, contracts or any other means which, either separately or in combination and having regard to the considerations of fact or law involved, confer the possibility of exercising decisive influence on an undertaking, in particular by:
>
> (a) ownership or the right to use all or part of the assets of an undertaking;
>
> (b) rights or contracts which confer decisive influence on the composition, voting or decisions of the organs of an undertaking.

Clearly this is a very broad concept[42], and control can exist on a legal ('*de jure*') or a factual ('*de facto*') basis[43]. The most common means for the acquisition of control is the acquisition of shares, sometimes in conjunction with a shareholders' agreement, in the case of joint control, or the acquisition of assets[44]. However it is also possible for control

[37] Case M 1806, decision of 26 July 2000.

[38] Case M 2208, decision of 26 January 2001; see also Case M 5747 *Iberia/British Airways*, decision of 14 July 2010.

[39] Case M 1016, decision of 20 May 1998.

[40] Case M 2824, decision of 27 August 2002.

[41] It would seem that the notion of control in Article 3(2) of the EUMR is broader than the one used when applying the single economic entity doctrine under Article 101 TFEU: see ch 3, 'The test of control', pp 95–97.

[42] Note that, under the UK Enterprise Act 2002, the concept of 'material influence' is broader than 'the possibility of exercising decisive influence' under Article 3(2) EUMR with the result that some transactions that might not be caught under EU merger control could be under the UK system: see ch 22, 'Enterprises ceasing to be distinct', pp 942–945, and paras 21, 49 and 64 of the General Court's judgment in Case T-411/07 *Aer Lingus Group plc v Commission* EU:T:2010:281. Note also that it is possible that the acquisition by A of a shareholding in B, although insufficient to provide the possibility of exercising decisive influence in the sense of Article 3(2) of the EUMR, may give rise to the possibility of coordinated behaviour between A and B and so require consideration under Article 101 TFEU: see Cases 142 and 156/84 *BAT v Commission* EU:C:1987:490, in particular paras 37–39; see also *Warner-Lambert/Gillette* OJ [1993] L 116/21, paras 33–39; *BT-MCI* OJ [1994] L 223/36; *BiB* OJ [1999] L 312/1; see further OECD Roundtable *Minority Shareholdings* (2008), available at www.oecd.org/competition; DotEcon Ltd 'Minority interests in competitors' (OFT 1218, March 2010), available at www.dotecon.com and the essays in [2012] CPI Antitrust Chronicle, January; Fotis and Zevgolis *The Competitive Effects of Minority Shareholdings* (Hart, 2016); the possibility that the EUMR might be reformed to give the Commission jurisdiction over the acquisition of some acquisitions of minority shareholdings was floated by the Commission in July 2014, but this initiative appears to have been abandoned: see Commissioner Vestager's speech of 10 March 2016 'Refining the EU merger control system', available at www.ec.europa.eu.

[43] *Jurisdictional Notice*, para 16.

[44] Ibid, para 17; for an example of an acquisition of assets constituting a concentration see Case M 5727 *Microsoft/Yahoo! Search Business*, decision of 18 February 2010, paras 14–19.

to be acquired on a contractual basis[45]. A franchise agreement is not normally sufficient to establish control[46]. In exceptional cases a situation of economic dependence resulting from, for example, long-term supply agreements, could give rise to control[47]. It is important to understand that the concept of control as used in the EUMR may be different from the one used in other EU or national laws on matters such as taxation or the media[48]. It should be added that, when deciding under Article 5(4) whether the turnover of affiliated companies should be included within group turnover, a stricter notion of control is applied than in the case of Article 3.

The acquisition of control of assets—for example the transfer of the client base of a business or of intangible assets such as brands, patents or copyrights—will be considered a concentration only if they amount to a business with a market presence to which a market turnover can be clearly attributed[49]. To amount to a concentration the acquisition of control must be on a lasting basis, resulting in a change in the structure of the market[50]. Where several undertakings acquire a company, with the intention of dividing up the assets at a later stage, the first acquisition may be regarded as purely transitory with the result that it would not amount to a concentration: the subsequent division of the assets in question would however have to be investigated, and could give rise to more than one concentration[51]. The same analysis could be applied where an operation envisages the joint control of a new operation for a start-up period followed by a conversion to sole control: where the joint control does not exceed a year there would not be a concentration during that period[52].

Where an interim buyer, such as a bank, acquires an undertaking on the basis of an agreement in the future to sell it on to an ultimate buyer, the Commission will examine the case as one of acquisition by the ultimate buyer[53]: this is sometimes referred to in practice as a 'warehousing' arrangement. Several transactions may be regarded as a single concentration in the sense of Article 3 where they are unitary in nature, that is to say where they are interdependent in such a way that one transaction would not have been carried out without the other and if they ultimately lead to control by the same undertaking(s)[54]. In *Canon/Toshiba Medical Systems*[55] the Commission has issued a statement of objections in relation to Canon's use of a warehousing arrangement to implement a merger without the prior approval of the Commission.

Article 5(2) of the EUMR establishes a rule that allows the Commission to consider successive transactions occurring within a two-year period to be treated as a single concentration: this is an 'anti-avoidance' rule to ensure that the same persons do not break a transaction down into a series of sales of assets over a period of time with the aim of avoiding the application of the EUMR[56]. The internal restructuring of an undertaking that does not result in a change of control is not covered by the EUMR[57].

(b) Sole control

Sole control may be enjoyed on a legal or a factual basis. Legal control is normally acquired where an undertaking acquires a majority of the voting rights of a company,

[45] *Jurisdictional Notice*, para 18. [46] Ibid, para 19.

[47] Ibid, para 20; for an example of long-term supply and financing agreements giving rise to a concentration see Case M 7839 *Outokumpu/Hernandez Edelstahl*, decision of 16 December 2015, paras 11–14.

[48] *Jurisdictional Notice*, para 23. [49] Ibid, para 24.

[50] Ibid, para 28; see also recital 20 of the EUMR. [51] Ibid, paras 29–33. [52] Ibid, para 34.

[53] Ibid, para 35.

[54] Ibid, paras 36–47; on the existence of a single concentration see Case T-282/02 *Cementbouw Handel & Industrie v Commission* EU:T:2006:64, paras 101–149 and Case T-704/14 *Marine Harvest ASA v Commission* EU:T:2017:753, paras 85–229, on appeal to the Court of Justice Case C-10/18 P, not yet decided.

[55] See Commission Press Release IP/17/1924, 6 July 2017.

[56] *Jurisdictional Notice*, paras 49–50. [57] Ibid, para 51.

but could also occur, for example, where a minority shareholder owns shares that confer special rights to determine the strategic direction of the company to be acquired[58]. Factual control can occur where a minority shareholder is able to veto the strategic decisions of an undertaking: although it cannot impose decisions, the fact that it can block decisions means that it has the possibility of exercising decisive influence in the sense of Article 3(2) of the EUMR. This is often referred to as negative control[59]. Factual control can also exist where a minority shareholder is likely to be able at shareholders' meetings to achieve a majority: the Commission will look at past voting behaviour to try to predict what the position is likely to be in the future[60]. In *Electrabel/Compagnie Nationale du Rhône*[61] the Commission concluded that Electrabel had acquired sole control over CNR, despite being a minority shareholder, on the basis of a number of different considerations, including that it was assured of a *de facto* majority at CNR's General Meeting; as the concentration had not been notified, but sole control had been acquired, Electrabel was fined €20 million for 'gun-jumping'[62]. The Commission's decision, and the fine, were confirmed on appeal to the General Court[63] and to the Court of Justice[64]. Depending on the facts of the case, a shareholding of less than 25% can be found to provide the possibility of exercising decisive influence: for example in *CCIE/GTE*[65] CCIE acquired 19% of the voting rights in EDIL and was found to have acquired control, the remaining shares being held by an independent investment bank whose approval was not needed for important commercial decisions.

An option to purchase or convert shares does not in itself confer control unless the option will be exercised in the near future according to legally binding agreements[66].

(c) Joint control

Joint control occurs where two or more undertakings have the possibility of exercising decisive influence over another undertaking. Joint control typically arises from the fact that the undertakings in question enjoy negative control, that is to say the power to reject strategic decisions, which means that they have to act in common in order to determine the joint venture's commercial policy[67]. Joint control can be established both on a legal and a factual basis[68]. Joint control can arise where:

- there are only two parent companies each with the same number of voting rights[69]
- in the absence of voting equality, parent companies enjoy veto rights, either by virtue of the statute of the joint venture or a shareholders' agreement between the parents[70]. The veto rights must be related to strategic decisions of the joint venture on issues such as the budget, business plan, major investments or the appointment of senior management[71] or

[58] Ibid, paras 56–58. [59] Ibid, para 54. [60] Ibid, para 59.

[61] Case M 4994, decision of 10 June 2009.

[62] See similarly Case M 7184 *Marine Harvest/Morpol*, decision of 23 July 2014, finding a shareholding of 48.5% gave rise to *de facto* sole control, upheld on appeal Case T-704/14 *Marine Harvest ASA v Commission* EU:T:2017:753. On gun-jumping see 'Suspension of concentrations', pp 878–879 later in chapter.

[63] Case T-332/09 *Electrabel v Commission* EU:T:2012:672.

[64] Case C-84/13 P *Electrabel v Commission* EU:C:2014:2040.

[65] Case M 258, decision of 25 September 1992; similarly in Case M 8465 *Vivendi/Telecom Italia*, decision of 30 May 2017, paras 5–9, a shareholding of 23.9% was found sufficient to confer sole control.

[66] *Jurisdictional Notice*, para 60. [67] Ibid, para 62. [68] Ibid, para 63.

[69] Ibid, para 64. [70] Ibid, para 65.

[71] Ibid, paras 67–73; see eg Case M 6141 *China National Agrochemical Corporation/Koor Industries/Makhteshim Agan Industries*, decision of 3 October 2011, where a right to veto the appointment and removal of senior management was sufficient to confer joint control.

- in the absence of veto rights, it is likely, in fact or in law, that the parents will act jointly in the exercise of their voting rights, whether as a result of a legally binding agreement[72] or as a matter of fact, because of 'strong common interests'[73].

(iii) Changes in the quality of control

A concentration can occur where there is a change in the quality of control of an undertaking: there may be a change from sole to joint control[74]; a change in the identity of the parent companies so that there is a change in the nature of the joint control; and a change from joint to sole control[75]. However a change from negative to positive control is not regarded as a concentration[76]. A short-form notification may be made in the case of a change from joint to sole control[77].

(iv) Joint ventures—the concept of full-functionality

Article 3(4) of the EUMR provides that:

> The creation of a joint venture performing on a lasting basis all the functions of an autonomous economic entity shall constitute a concentration within the meaning of Article 3(1)(b).

Concentrations in the sense of Article 3(4) are known as 'full-function joint ventures'. A joint venture will be full-function where it:

- enjoys operational autonomy
- has activities beyond one specific function for the parents
- deals with its parents on an arm's length basis after a start-up period
- is intended to operate on a lasting basis.

Each factor is discussed in turn below, followed by the implications of whether a joint venture is full-function or not.

(a) Operational autonomy

The *Jurisdictional Notice* explains that the requirement of autonomy in Article 3(4) refers to operational autonomy: its parents will be responsible for its strategic decisions, which is precisely why they will be considered to be in joint control in the first place[78]. To be operationally autonomous the joint venture must have sufficient resources to operate independently on a market: this means that it must have a management dedicated to its day-to-day operations and access to sufficient resources including finance, staff and assets to carry on the business activities provided for in the joint-venture agreement[79].

(b) Activities beyond one specific function for the parents

A joint venture will not be full-function where it takes over one specific function of its parents' activities, such as R&D or production; similarly a joint sales company would not be full-function[80]. Partial-function joint ventures must be analysed under Article 101

[72] *Jurisdictional Notice*, para 75. [73] Ibid, paras 76–80.
[74] See eg Case M 5141 *KLM/Martinair*, decision of 17 December 2008.
[75] *Jurisdictional Notice*, paras 83–90. [76] Ibid, para 83.
[77] See Annex II of the Implementing Regulation. [78] *Jurisdictional Notice*, para 93.
[79] Ibid, para 94; see eg Case M 6800 *PRSfM/STIM/GEMA/JV*, decision of 16 June 2015.
[80] *Jurisdictional Notice*, para 95; for an example of a joint venture found not to be full-function see Case M 3003 *Electrabel/Energia Italia/Interpower*, decision of 23 December 2002.

and/or national competition law. The acquisition of joint control of an undertaking that itself is not fully functional does not constitute a concentration under Article 3(4)[81].

(c) Sale/purchase relations between the joint venture and its parents

A joint venture may not be sufficiently autonomous where its parents have a strong presence as suppliers to or purchasers from it; however the Commission recognises that the joint venture might be dependent on sales to or purchases from its parents during its 'start-up' period, which should normally not exceed three years[82]. Where sales are made to the parents on a lasting basis the Commission will consider whether the joint venture is geared to play an active role on the market independently of its parents: the proportion of sales made to the market will be an important consideration, and if the joint venture sells more than 50% of its output to the market it would normally be considered to be full-function[83]. The Commission is more sceptical about long-term purchases from the parents, which might mean that the joint venture is closer to being a sales agency[84]; however it recognises that, where the joint venture operates on a 'trade market', it may be full-function even though it purchases from its parents[85]. A trade market is one where undertakings specialise in the selling and distribution of products without being vertically integrated and where different sources of supply are available for the products in question. In such a case a joint venture could be considered to be full-function provided that it has the necessary facilities and is likely to obtain a substantial proportion of its supplies not only from its parents but also from competing sources.

As a matter of substantive analysis, contractual provisions in agreements between a full-function joint venture and its parents may amount to ancillary restraints; or they may require separate assessment under Article 101 TFEU[86].

(d) Operation on a lasting basis

To be full-function a joint venture must be established on a lasting basis; the fact that the parents provide for dissolution of the joint venture, for example in the event of its failure or fundamental disagreement between them, does not mean that it is not established on a lasting basis[87]. If the joint venture is established for a short, finite period—for example in order to construct a specific project such as a power plant—it would not be considered to be long-lasting[88]. An enlargement of the activities of a full-function joint venture may amount to a new concentration, as will a change from being partial-function to being full-function[89].

(e) Implications of full-functionality

It is important to know whether a joint venture is full-function or not since this determines whether the EUMR is capable of application. A full-function joint venture having a Union dimension is subject to mandatory pre-notification to the Commission. If the joint venture is not full-function, the possibility remains that it might be subject to Article 101 TFEU and/or national competition law[90].

[81] Case C-248/16 *Austria Asphalt GmbH v Bundeskartellanwalt* EU:C:2017:643, para 35.

[82] *Jurisdictional Notice*, para 97. [83] Ibid, para 98. [84] Ibid, para 101. [85] Ibid, para 102.

[86] See further 'Contractual restrictions directly related to and necessary for a merger: "ancillary restraints"', pp 904–907 later in chapter.

[87] *Jurisdictional Notice*, para 103. [88] Ibid, para 104.

[89] Ibid, paras 106–109; for an example of a joint venture changing from partial-function to full-function see Case M 5241 *American Express/Fortis/Alpha Card*, decision of 3 October 2008, paras 13–15.

[90] For an example of a partial-function joint venture investigated under Article 101 TFEU see *BHP Billiton/Rio Tinto*, Commission Press Release IP/10/45, 25 January 2010.

(v) Exceptions

Article 3(5) of the EUMR provides that certain operations will not amount to a concentration: the acquisition of securities by credit or other financial institutions on an investment basis where the voting rights are not exercised other than to protect the investment; the acquisition of control according to the law of a Member State relating to liquidation, winding up and similar matters; and acquisition by financial holding companies in relation to such matters. The *Jurisdictional Notice* explains that these provisions are construed narrowly, and they have rarely been applied in practice[91]. They did apply, however, in *Lagardère/Natexis/VUP*[92]; this finding was upheld on appeal[93].

(B) Article 1: concentrations having a Union dimension

Part C of the Commission's *Jurisdictional Notice* deals with the notion of Union dimension. As a general proposition concentrations having a Union dimension are investigated exclusively by the Commission; concentrations that do not do so are subject to the merger laws of the Member States[94]. Given that 27 of the 28 Member States have a system of merger control[95], and that one transaction might be subject to investigation under a number of them, there may be significant advantages in being subject to EU rather than Member State law: this is discussed further later in the context of one-stop merger control[96].

(i) Thresholds

Turnover is used as a proxy for the economic resources that would be combined as a result of a concentration, and it is allocated geographically in order to reflect the geographical distribution of those resources[97]. Turnover thresholds are used in order to provide a relatively simple and objective mechanism for determining the allocation of jurisdiction; they are not intended in any sense to act as a way of predicting the market power of the undertakings concerned: that is a matter of substantive assessment, to be conducted by the competition authority (or authorities) that have jurisdiction[98]. Article 1 of the EUMR sets out the numerical thresholds to establish Union jurisdiction: it should be noted that the EUMR does not require that the undertakings concerned should be domiciled within the EU, nor that the transaction in question should take place there[99]. The method of calculating turnover is set out in Article 5.

Article 1(1) provides that the EUMR shall apply to all concentrations having a Union dimension as defined in Article 1(2) or Article 1(3). The criteria set out in Articles 1(2) and 1(3) of the EUMR are *alternative* grounds on which a concentration may have a Union dimension.

(a) Article 1(2)

Article 1(2) provides that a concentration has a Union dimension where:

(a) the combined aggregate worldwide turnover of all the undertakings concerned is more than EUR 5,000 million; and

[91] *Jurisdictional Notice*, paras 110–116.

[92] Case M 2978, decision of 7 January 2004.

[93] Case T-279/04 *Éditions Odile Jacob SAS v Commission* EU:T:2010:384, upheld on appeal Case C-551/10 P EU:C:2012:681.

[94] See Case C-170/02 P *Schlüsselverlag JS Moser GmbH v Commission* EU:C:2003:501, at para 34: 'the [EU] legislature intended to lay down a clear division between the activities of the national authorities and those of the [EU] authorities, by avoiding successive definitions of positions by those different authorities on the same transaction ...'.

[95] Luxembourg is the only Member State not to do so.

[96] See 'Article 21: one-stop merger control', pp 864–867 later in chapter.

[97] *Jurisdictional Notice*, para 124.

[98] Ibid, para 127.

[99] On the territorial scope of the EUMR see ch 12, 'The jurisdictional criteria in the EUMR', pp 506–508.

(b) the aggregate [Union]-wide turnover of each of at least two of the undertakings concerned is more than EUR 250 million,

unless each of the undertakings concerned achieves more than two-thirds of its aggregate [Union]-wide turnover within one and the same Member State.

Article 1(2) is intended to reflect the overall size of the undertakings concerned on a worldwide basis; to establish that there is a minimum level of activities within the EU; and to exclude purely domestic transactions. It is not unusual for very substantial transactions to fall outside the EUMR as a result of the two-thirds rule where two undertakings from the same Member State are involved: this is particularly likely to happen in the case, for example, of banks, insurance companies and undertakings in the energy sector that operate predominantly in their domestic market. For example the *Lloyds TSB Group plc/Abbey National plc* case in 2001 was not subject to the EUMR, since at least two-thirds of the turnover of each of those banks arose in the UK; however the merger was prohibited under UK merger control[100]. In 2008 the *Lloyds TSB plc/HBOS plc* merger again fell outside the jurisdiction of the Commission because of the two-thirds rule, but on this occasion the merger was permitted by the UK Government on the ground of 'exceptional public interest' due to the financial crisis, and in particular the perilous state at that time of the banking system[101].

A controversial case arose in 2005 when Gas Natural, a Spanish company active in the energy sector, notified its intention to make a hostile public bid for Endesa, another Spanish company primarily active in the electricity sector, to the Spanish Competition Authority; Gas Natural claimed that the two-thirds rule was applicable with the consequence that the Commission lacked jurisdiction. Endesa lodged a complaint with the Commission, arguing that the two-thirds rule did not apply. The Commission rejected Endesa's argument[102]; its decision was upheld on appeal to the General Court[103].

In June 2009 the Commission published a *Report on the functioning of Regulation No 139/2004* in which it concluded that 'the present form of the two-thirds rule merits further consideration'[104], noting that some mergers that fell outside its jurisdiction because of this rule gave rise to competition concerns and yet were permitted under national law on 'public interest' grounds. The Commission invited the Council to 'take note' of this information[105]; as at 8 December 2017 the Council had not indicated whether it intends to pursue this matter.

(b) Article 1(3)

Article 1(3) provides an alternative basis of jurisdiction to Article 1(2). A concentration that does not meet the Article 1(2) thresholds nevertheless has a Union dimension where:

(a) the combined aggregate worldwide turnover of all the undertakings concerned is more than EUR 2,500 million; and

(b) in each of at least three Member States, the combined aggregate turnover of all the undertakings concerned is more than EUR 100 million;

[100] Cm 5208 (2001). [101] See ch 22, 'Public interest cases', pp 987–989.

[102] See Commission Press Release IP/05/1425, 15 November 2005.

[103] Case T-417/05 *Endesa v Commission* EU:T:2006:219.

[104] *Communication from the Commission to the Council: Report on the functioning of Regulation No 139/2004*, COM(2009) 2101 final; the Report should be read in conjunction with the accompanying Commission Staff Working Paper containing a more detailed review.

[105] On the utility of the two-thirds rule see also Commission Staff Working Document accompanying White Paper, *Towards more effective EU merger control*, SWD(2014) 221 final, fn 83.

(c) in each of the three Member States included for the purpose of (b), the aggregate turnover of each of at least two of the undertakings concerned is more than EUR 25 million; and

(d) the aggregate [Union]-wide turnover of each of at least two of the undertakings concerned is more than EUR 100 million;

unless each of the undertakings concerned achieves more than two-thirds of its aggregate [Union]-wide turnover within one and the same Member State.

The purpose of Article 1(3) is to give jurisdiction to the Commission in cases where a concentration does not have a Union dimension in the sense of Article 1(2), but nevertheless could be expected to have a substantial impact in at least three Member States[106]. In practice there have not been a large number of concentrations filed under Article 1(3), although it is interesting to note that jurisdiction in *Ryanair/Aer Lingus I*, which the Commission prohibited in 2007, was based on Article 1(3)[107]. What is more common in practice is that parties to a concentration that does not have a Union dimension make use of the procedure provided by Article 4(5) of the EUMR to request that their transaction be reviewed by the Commission on a one-stop shop basis[108].

(c) Possible reform

The EU dimension thresholds in Article 1 of the EUMR are an imperfect method of allocating jurisdiction to the appropriate forum; but they at least have the merit of being relatively easy to apply in practice. In the Commission's *Report on the functioning of Regulation No 139/2004* of June 2009 it noted that, despite the addition of Article 1(3) to the EUMR, there continue to be a number of transactions with significant cross-border effects which remain outside its jurisdiction, concluding that 'there is further scope for "one-stop-shop" review'[109]. In July 2014 the Commission proposed a series of possible amendments to the EUMR to capture those transactions; as at 8 December 2017 no further action had been taken in relation to those proposals.

More recently the question has arisen of whether the jurisdictional criteria ought to be amended to deal with cases where one undertaking acquires another for a large amount of money, and yet without the jurisdictional criteria of the EUMR being triggered. Good examples would be the acquisition of a 'start-up' company in the ICT sector with (so far) low turnover, but with a (potentially) large user base and valuable data sets; another would be the purchase of a pharmaceutical company which has developed a new drug with great potential but that does not yet have a marketing authorisation and so no turnover. The policy concern is that firms that have significant market power in sectors such as these are able to smother the future emergence of competition by systematically acquiring promising new entrants to the market which have not yet generated much turnover. Facebook's acquisition of WhatsApp for $19 billion[110] was investigated by the Commission only because it was referred to it by the parties under Article 4(5) of the EUMR: the transaction did not involve sufficient turnover to have an EU dimension under Article 1 of the EUMR. As at 8 December 2017 the Commission had not tabled any proposals on this topic[111].

[106] *Jurisdictional Notice*, para 126.

[107] Case M 4439 *Ryanair/Aer Lingus*, decision of 27 June 2007, upheld on appeal Case T-342/07 *Ryanair v Commission* EU:T:2010:280.

[108] See 'Pre-notification referrals: Article 4(5)', pp 869–870 later in chapter.

[109] *Communication from the Commission to the Council: Report on the functioning of Regulation No 139/2004*, COM(2009) 2101 final, para 13.

[110] Case M 7217 *Facebook/WhatsApp*, decision of 3 October 2014; see in particular paras 9–12.

[111] Thresholds based on transaction value have come into effect in Germany (Act against Restraints of Competition 2013, s 35(1a)) and Austria (Cartel Act 2005, s 9(4)).

(ii) Notion of undertaking concerned

The first step in determining whether a concentration has a Union dimension is to identify the 'undertakings concerned', an expression that is used in Article 1 of the EUMR. Having done so, turnover is calculated in the manner set out in Article 5; Article 5(4) identifies those other entities that form part of the same group as the undertakings concerned and whose turnover should therefore be included in the calculation. Where the concentration is a merger in the sense of Article 3(1)(a) of the EUMR the undertakings concerned are the merging entities[112]. In cases of the acquisition of control under Article 3(1)(b) it can be a complicated matter to determine who are the undertakings concerned.

The *Jurisdictional Notice* gives extensive guidance on this:

- where A acquires sole control of B, the undertakings concerned will be A and B[113]
- however if A acquires part of B, the undertakings concerned will be A and the part of B to be acquired, in accordance with Article 5(2) of the EUMR: after the concentration has been effected the economic strength of the rest of B would be irrelevant to the position of the merged entity[114]
- where A and B jointly control C and A acquires B's interest in C, the undertakings concerned are A and C: as in the previous example, once the transaction has been put into effect the position of B is irrelevant to the economic strength of A and C[115]
- where A and B establish a new entity, C, the undertakings concerned are A and B[116]
- however if A and B acquire joint control of an existing entity, C, each of A, B and C is an undertaking concerned[117].

If a joint venture, C, acquires D, the question arises of whether C, or its parents A and B, should be regarded as the undertakings concerned. The answer to this question may have a decisive effect on jurisdiction: if A and B are undertakings concerned and their group turnover is added into the calculation of turnover, it is more likely that the transaction will be found to have a Union dimension:

- if C is a full-function joint venture and is already operating on the market, it will be regarded as an undertaking concerned, along with D[118]
- if C is a mere vehicle for the acquisition by A and B of D the Commission will consider each of A and B to be undertakings concerned, along with D[119].

In *HeidelbergCement/Schwenk/Cemex Hungary/Cemex Croatia*[120] the Commission decided that HeidelbergCement and Schwenk, rather than their jointly-owned full-function joint venture, DDC, were the undertakings concerned, with the consequence that the proposed transaction did have an EU dimension[121]; the Commission prohibited the transaction. The parents of the joint venture have appealed to the General Court claiming, amongst other things, that the transaction did not have an EU dimension[122].

(iii) Relevant date for establishing jurisdiction

The relevant date for determining whether a concentration has a Union dimension is the date when a final agreement was concluded or a public bid was announced or a controlling interest was acquired, whichever date is earlier[123].

[112] *Jurisdictional Notice*, para 132. [113] Ibid, para 134. [114] Ibid, para 136.
[115] Ibid, para 138. [116] Ibid, para 139. [117] Ibid, para 140. [118] Ibid, para 146.
[119] Ibid, para 147. [120] Case M 7878, decision of 5 April 2017. [121] Ibid, paras 37–44.
[122] Case T-380/17 *HeidelbergCement and Schwenk Cement v Commission*, not yet decided.
[123] *Jurisdictional Notice*, paras 155–156.

(iv) Turnover

Article 5(1) of the EUMR defines turnover as the amounts derived by undertakings in the preceding financial year 'from the sale of products and the provision of services falling within the undertakings' ordinary activities'[124]. Sales rebates, VAT and other taxes directly related to turnover (for example taxes on alcoholic drinks and cigarettes) are deducted from any turnover figure, as is internal turnover within a group of companies. Article 5(5)(a) of the EUMR provides that turnover between a joint venture and its parents should be excluded from the calculation of turnover; but Article 5(5)(b) provides that turnover between a joint venture and third parties should be apportioned equally between its parents.

The *Jurisdictional Notice* explains that the Commission will usually base its findings on turnover on the most recent audited accounts of the undertakings concerned; it will rely on management or other provisional accounts only in exceptional circumstances[125]. Where there are major differences between the EU's accounting standards and those of a non-Member State the Commission may consider it necessary to ask for the accounts to be restated according to EU standards[126]. The *Notice* explains the circumstances in which the Commission will accept an adjustment to the figures in the audited accounts, for example where there has since been a divestiture of part of the business of an undertaking concerned[127].

In determining jurisdiction it is necessary not only to take into account the turnover of the undertakings concerned but also that of other undertakings within the same group. This can be problematic where undertakings such as private equity funds do not have consolidated accounts: care must be taken to ensure that all relevant turnover is brought into the calculation. Article 5(4) of the EUMR provides that the aggregate turnover of an undertaking concerned shall be calculated by adding together the respective turnovers of the following, where (b) refers to subsidiaries, (c) to parents and (d) to affiliates:

(a) the undertaking concerned;

(b) those undertakings in which the undertaking concerned directly or indirectly:

  (i) owns more than half the capital or business assets, or

  (ii) has the power to exercise more than half the voting rights, or

  (iii) has the power to appoint more than half the members of the supervisory board, the administrative board or bodies legally representing the undertakings, or

  (iv) has the right to manage the undertakings' affairs;

(c) those undertakings which have in an undertaking concerned the rights or powers listed in (b);

(d) those undertakings in which an undertaking as referred to in (c) has the rights or powers listed in (b);

(e) those undertakings in which two or more undertakings as referred to in (a) to (d) jointly have the rights or powers listed in (b).

The *Jurisdictional Notice* provides fairly extensive guidance on these provisions[128]. An important point is that the criteria in Article 5(4), such as 'the power to exercise more than half the voting rights' or 'the right to manage the undertakings' affairs', are considerably stricter than the concept of 'control' set out in Article 3(2); Article 5(4) provides

[124] Several points relating to the calculation of turnover are referred to in the General Court's judgment in Case T-417/05 *Endesa SA v Commission* EU:T:2006:219.

[125] *Jurisdictional Notice*, paras 169–170.

[126] Ibid, para 171.

[127] Ibid, paras 172–174.

[128] Ibid, paras 175–194.

'bright-line' criteria for determining which group turnover should be added to that of the individual undertakings concerned in a transaction[129]. The Commission's decision in *SoFFin/Hypo Real Estate* considers the application of the EUMR, and in particular the calculation of group turnover, where a state-owned body (in that case the German Special Fund Financial Market Stabilisation) acquires a distressed financial institution[130]. In *EDF/CGN/NNB* the Commission aggregated the turnover of a Chinese state-owned enterprise with that of the Central Chinese Assets Supervision Administrative Commission as the latter exercised control over it: in consequence the concentration had a Union dimension[131].

(v) Geographic allocation of turnover

It is important to be able to determine where turnover arises, since Article 1(2) and (3) of the EUMR refer to global, Union and Member State turnover. The general rule is that turnover should be attributed to the place where the customer is located[132]; the *Jurisdictional Notice* explains how this principle is applied in practice to the sale of goods[133] and the provision of services[134].

(vi) Conversion of turnover into Euros

For the purposes of the EUMR turnover must be calculated in Euros: for many undertakings this will require conversion from another currency. The annual turnover should be converted at the average European Central Bank rate for the 12 months concerned; and this average can be obtained from DG COMP's website[135].

(vii) Provisions for credit and other financial institutions and insurance undertakings

Article 5(3) of the EUMR provides specific rules for the calculation of turnover of credit and other financial institutions. Their operation is explained in the Commission's *Jurisdictional Notice*[136].

(viii) Illustrations

A few examples may help to illustrate how the jurisdictional rules just outlined operate in practice. See Figure 21.1.

(C) Article 21: one-stop merger control

(i) The benefits of one-stop merger control

As a general proposition it is undesirable, both for businesses and for competition authorities, if a particular concentration has to be investigated under two or more systems of law.

129 Ibid, para 184.

130 Case M 5508, decision of 14 May 2009; see similarly Case M 6113 *DSM/Sinochem/JV*, decision of 19 May 2011, paras 8–16; see also recital 22 of the EUMR.

131 Case M 7850, decision of 10 March 2016, paras 29–50; for comment see Fountoukakos and Puech-Baron 'The EU merger regulation and transactions involving states or state-owned enterprises: Applying rules designed for the EU to the People's Republic of China' Concurrences No 1-2012; see similarly Case M 6801 *Rosneft/TNK-BP*, decision of 8 March 2013.

132 *Jurisdictional Notice*, para 196.

133 Ibid, paras 197–198.

134 Ibid, paras 199–202; for an example of a case in which the geographical allocation of turnover was crucial to jurisdiction see Case M 4439 *Ryanair/Aer Lingus*, decision of 27 June 2007, upheld on appeal Case T-342/07 *Ryanair v Commission* EU:T:2010:280.

135 *Jurisdictional Notice*, para 204; the website is www.ec.europa.eu/competition/mergers/exchange_rates.html.

136 *Jurisdictional Notice*, paras 206–220.

Example 1

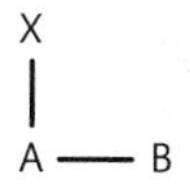

A acquires B: A is the wholly-owned subsidiary of X

Undertakings concerned: A and B (Article 5(1))

Turnover to be taken into account: A and B (undertakings concerned) and X (X's turnover is included as a result of Article 5(4)(c))

Example 2

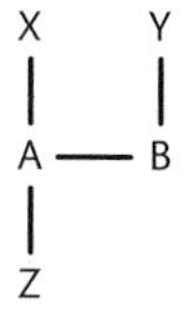

A acquires B, a division of Y; A is a part of X, and A has a wholly-owned subsidiary, Z

Undertakings concerned: A and B (Article 5(1))

Turnover to be taken into account: A and B (undertakings concerned: disregard the turnover of Y, as A is acquiring B only, a part of Y: Article 5(2)); X (Article 5(4)(c)) and Z (Article 5(4)(b))

Example 3

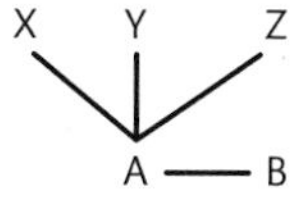

A acquires B. A is jointly controlled by X, Y and Z

Undertakings concerned: A and B

Turnover to be taken into account: A and B (undertakings concerned); X, Y and Z (this is based on the language of Article 5(4)(c) of the EUMR and is supported by paragraph 182 of the Commission's *Consolidated Jurisdictional Notice*)

Example 4

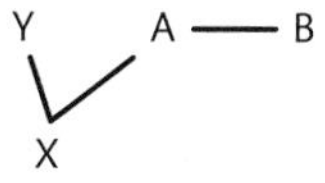

A acquires B; A has joint control of X with Y

Undertakings concerned: A and B

Turnover to be taken into account: A and B (undertakings concerned); but is the turnover of X relevant? The answer to this question could determine whether the concentration has a Union dimension if A and B's combined turnover falls below the Union dimension thresholds. The Commission states at paragraph 187 of its *Consolidated Jurisdictional Notice* that it would allocate a 50% share of X's turnover to A in these circumstances.

Fig. 21.1 Illustrative examples

Multiple investigations lead to administrative inefficiency, duplication, delay, expense, uncertainty and the possibility of conflicting decisions. A central principle of the EUMR is the idea of one-stop merger control: that is to say that concentrations having a Union dimension should be investigated within the EU only by the Commission. This policy is given expression in Article 21 of the EUMR. Article 21(2) provides that, subject to review by the EU Courts, only the Commission may take decisions in respect of concentrations having a Union dimension; Article 21(3) adds that no Member State shall apply its national legislation on competition to such concentrations[137]. However, as explained below, there are some circumstances in which cases can be 'reattributed' from and to the Commission. A different point is that Article 21(4) of the EUMR provides that, in defined circumstances, a Member State may take appropriate measures in relation to a concentration where this is necessary to protect a 'legitimate interest'; this provision is discussed in section F later.

Article 21(1) of the EUMR adds that Regulation 1/2003, the Regulation that gives the Commission the power to enforce Articles 101 and 102 TFEU, shall have no application to concentrations as defined in the EUMR[138]. However Article 21(1) makes clear that the Commission retains the right to use its powers under Regulation 1/2003 in relation to joint ventures that do not have a Union dimension and which have as their object or effect the coordination of the competitive behaviour of undertakings that remain independent.

(ii) **The benefits of more flexible jurisdictional rules**

Notwithstanding the principle of one-stop merger control the EUMR makes provision for 'case referral', that is to say for the reattribution, in defined circumstances, of cases between the Commission and the NCAs. The Commission's *Notice on Case Referral in respect of concentrations* ('the *Case Referral Notice*')[139] provides detailed guidance on the reattribution of jurisdiction under the EUMR, both on the guiding principles[140] and on the mechanics of the system[141]. It also contains helpful flow charts[142]. The case referral rules were 'flexibilised' by the 2004 Regulation to make reattribution easier than under the original Merger Regulation; it was felt that more flexibility was desirable in order to enable the more appropriate competition authority or authorities to conduct the investigation of cases[143]. Further changes were proposed by the Commission in 2014 but no further action has been taken[144].

In certain cases a concentration that has a Union dimension can be referred by the Commission to Member States under the provisions of Article 4(4) and Article 9: this is described in section D below; and a concentration that does not have a Union dimension can be referred under Article 4(5) and Article 22 by Member States to the Commission: this is dealt with in section E later. The idea of reattribution is consistent with the principle of subsidiarity[145]. The case referral procedures in the EUMR are carried out by the Commission in close and constant liaison with the national competition authorities[146]. The merging parties can attempt to precipitate a reallocation of jurisdiction before a formal filing has been made either to the Commission or to the national competition authority or authorities[147]. When considering case referrals the Commission takes into account

[137] It is arguable that a national court could apply Articles 101 and 102 to concentrations having a Union dimension, in so far as those provisions are capable of applying to concentrations, on the basis that they are directly effective, though there is no example of this having happened: for discussion of the point see Cook and Kerse *EC Merger Control* (Sweet & Maxwell, 5th ed, 2009), pp 19–22; Levy *European Merger Control Law: A Guide to the Merger Regulation* (LexisNexis, 2003), ch 21.

[138] Theoretically the Commission may be able to proceed under Articles 101 and 102, in so far as they are capable of application to a concentration, under Article 105 TFEU; at the time of the adoption of the original Merger Regulation the Commission said that it would do so only rarely, and in practice it has never done so; see the Commission's statement entered in the minutes of the Council [1990] 4 CMLR 314; see also the books cited at ch 21 n 137 earlier.

[139] OJ [2005] C 56/2; see also *Joint Statement of the Council and the Commission on the functioning of the network of Competition Authorities* available at www.ec.europa.eu/competition/ecn/documents.html.

[140] *Case Referral Notice*, Section II (paras 8–45).

[141] Ibid, Section III (paras 46–82).

[142] Ibid, pp 20–23.

[143] Ibid, paras 4–7.

[144] See COM(2014) 449 final, available at www.ec.europa.eu.

[145] *Case Referral Notice*, para 8.

[146] Ibid, paras 53–58.

[147] See sections D(i) and E(i) later in chapter.

the need for legal certainty, so that a referral should normally be made only where there is a compelling reason for departing from the 'original jurisdiction'[148].

(D) Article 4(4) and Article 9: referral of concentrations having a Union dimension to the competent authorities of the Member States

The starting point is that concentrations that have a Union dimension benefit from a one-stop shop; the Commission acknowledges that the fragmentation of such cases, that is to say the partial referral of aspects of a concentration having a Union dimension to one or more Member States, is undesirable in principle even though possible as a matter of law[149].

Case referrals of concentrations having a Union dimension may be made following a request from the parties to a concentration prior to a notification having been made ('pre-notification referrals') or following a request from a Member State (or Member States) after a notification ('post-notification referrals'). The Commission's decision to refer a case to a Member State is capable of being challenged by a third party that would prefer the Commission to investigate the case[150]; the reverse may not be true[151].

(i) Pre-notification referrals: Article 4(4)

Article 4(4) allows the parties to a transaction to make a 'reasoned submission' to the Commission that a concentration will significantly affect competition in a market within a Member State which presents all the characteristics of a distinct market and therefore that it should be examined, in whole or in part, by that Member State[152]; the parties do not have to demonstrate that the effect on competition is likely to be adverse[153]. In July 2014 the Commission proposed that the wording of Article 4(4) should be amended to eliminate the sense of 'self-incrimination' of having to claim that a transaction would have a significant effect on competition: the Commission's proposal was that parties simply show that the transaction is likely to have its main impact in the Member State concerned[154]. No further action has been taken on this initiative. A reasoned submission must be made on Form RS, the format of which is set out in Annex III of the Implementing Regulation[155].

Having made a request the Commission will transmit it to all Member States without delay. The Member State referred to in the Form RS must express its agreement or disagreement with the request within 15 working days; if it does not do so it is deemed to have agreed. Unless the Member State disagrees with the request the Commission has a discretion to refer whole or part of the case to the Member State in question for it to be investigated under that State's national competition law; this decision must be made within 25 working days of receipt of the Form RS. If the Commission does not take a decision within this period it is deemed to have referred the case. The Commission is most likely to make a referral where the effects of a concentration are likely to be felt within a national market, or a market that is narrower than national, and where the markets are likely to be within one and the same Member State[156]. Where a concentration might affect competition in a number of national markets the Commission might consider it appropriate to retain jurisdiction: this would avoid the need for coordinated investigations by a number

[148] *Case Referral Notice*, paras 13–14.

[149] Ibid, paras 11–12.

[150] See Case T-119/02 *Royal Philips Electronics v Commission* EU:T:2003:101, paras 252–300; Cases T-346/02 etc *Cableuropa SA v Commission* EU:T:2003:256, paras 100–157.

[151] See Case T-224/10 *Association belge des consommateurs test-achats ASBL v Commission* EU:T:2011:588, paras 74–85.

[152] *Case Referral Notice*, paras 16–23.

[153] Ibid, para 17.

[154] White Paper *Towards more effective EU merger control*, COM(2014) 449 final, para 75.

[155] Regulation 802/2004, OJ [2004] L 133/1; as to Form RS see the *Case Referral Notice*, paras 59–64.

[156] *Case Referral Notice*, para 20.

of competition authorities and the danger of conflicting outcomes. However referral to a number of Member States might occur, especially where competitive conditions vary from one State to another; fragmentation of jurisdiction is less of a concern where the parties themselves have made a request under Article 4(4)[157]. The final paragraph of Article 4(4) provides that, where the whole of the case is referred to a Member State, the duty to notify the case to the Commission ceases to apply.

(ii) Post-notification referrals: Article 9

Article 9 of the EUMR provides a mechanism whereby Member States may make a request that a concentration having a Union dimension should be referred to them[158]. Article 9(2) establishes two situations in which a Member State may make such a request.

(a) Article 9(2)(a)

The first is where a concentration threatens to affect significantly competition in a market within a Member State that presents all the characteristics of a distinct market. Where the Commission considers that these criteria are fulfilled it has a discretion to refer the whole or part of the case to the Member State that made the request[159].

(b) Article 9(2)(b)

The second is where a concentration affects competition within a Member State which presents all the characteristics of a distinct market and which does not constitute a substantial part of the internal market: the latter expression is likely to refer to a geographical market that is narrow in scope and within a single Member State[160]. Where the Commission considers that these criteria are fulfilled it has an obligation to refer the whole or part of the case relating to the distinct market concerned[161]: the Commission would not be able to take action against a concentration that does not impede competition in a substantial part of the internal market anyway[162].

As a general rule the decision to refer must be taken within 35 working days of the working day following receipt of the notification[163]. Once a referral has been made the competent authority of the Member State must decide upon the case 'without undue delay'. Within 45 working days of the referral the Member State must inform the undertakings concerned of the preliminary competition assessment and what further action, if any, it proposes to take[164]; other than this the only time constraints on the Member State are those imposed by national law. Member States may take only the measures strictly necessary to safeguard or restore effective competition on the market concerned[165]. Where the Commission refuses a request a Member State may appeal to the General Court[166].

(iii) Statistics

The statistics on Article 4(4) and Article 9 are of interest[167]. In the years immediately preceding 1 May 2004, when the current EUMR became applicable, Member States were making quite a large number of Article 9 requests—in 2003 the figure was ten. After 2004 the number of Article 9 requests diminished to some extent, although there were seven referrals in 2010. Refusals are rare: out of a total of 112 Article 9 requests to have been made by 8 December 2017 only 14 were refused; interestingly however three of those nine refusals were in 2014. Undertakings have made use of the Article 4(4) procedure on a

[157] Ibid, para 22. [158] Ibid, paras 33–41. [159] EUMR, Article 9(3).
[160] *Case Referral Notice*, para 40. [161] EUMR, Article 9(3), final paragraph.
[162] Ibid, Article 2(3). [163] Ibid, Article 9(4)(a). [164] Ibid, Article 9(6).
[165] Ibid, Article 9(8). [166] Ibid, Article 9(9).
[167] See 'Table of EUMR statistics', pp 923–924 later in chapter for a statistical table of merger notifications.

number of occasions: by 8 December 2017 there had been 149 requests under Article 4(4), and none had been refused. On several occasions the Commission referred part of the case to a Member State under Article 4(4)[168].

(iv) Article 4(4) and Article 9 in practice

Referrals to a Member State can give rise to problems for the undertakings concerned. In *Interbrew/Bass* the European Commission referred part of the case to the UK[169]. The UK authorities recommended that the transaction should be prohibited[170], a particularly unfortunate outcome given that the sale agreement had been entered into without a condition that approval from the UK authorities was required. Following a judicial review the transaction was permitted to go ahead in an amended form[171]. In *Tesco/Carrefour*[172] the concentration was approved by the European Commission in December 2005; however the intended acquisitions in Slovakia were prohibited following an Article 9(2)(b) referral of that part of the transaction[173]. In *Foster Yeoman/Aggregate Industries*[174] the UK requested a referral which led to a decision accepting remedies to resolve the competition concerns[175]. A third party may appeal against a Commission decision to refer a case under Article 9[176].

In its *Report on the functioning of Regulation No 139/2004* of June 2009[177] the Commission stated that Article 9 is generally believed to function effectively and is a useful tool underpinned by the principle of the 'most appropriate authority'[178]. The Commission considered that the pre-notification referral mechanisms had considerably enhanced the efficiency and jurisdictional flexibility of merger control in the EU, although it noted that some stakeholders had expressed concern about the overall timing and cumbersomeness of all the referral procedures[179].

(E) Article 4(5) and Article 22: referral of concentrations not having a Union dimension by Member States to the Commission

The starting point in the case of concentrations not having a Union dimension is that they are subject to the national systems of merger control of the Member States. With the exception of Luxembourg every Member State has provisions on merger control, and it can happen that one transaction may be reviewable in numerous jurisdictions: in its *Report on the functioning of Regulation No 139/2004* of June 2009[180] the Commission noted that in 2007 there were at least 100 transactions that were notifiable in three or more Member States. As noted already multiple filings can be undesirable for businesses and competition authorities. The EUMR makes provision for concentrations not having a Union dimension to be referred to the Commission, in which case they may benefit from the principle of one-stop merger control. As the statistics in the text that follows show these provisions, and in particular Article 4(5), are used quite often.

(i) Pre-notification referrals: Article 4(5)

Article 4(5) allows the parties to a concentration that is capable of being reviewed under the national competition laws of at least three Member States to make a reasoned

[168] See eg Case M 7997 *Steinhoff International/Darty*, decision of 30 May 2016.

[169] Case M 2044, decision of 22 August 2000.

[170] *Interbrew SA/Bass plc*, Cm 5014 (2001).

[171] *Interbrew SA and Interbrew UK Holdings Ltd v Competition Commission and Secretary of State for Trade and Industry* [2001] EWHC Admin 367.

[172] Case M 3905, decision of 22 December 2005.

[173] See decision of 17 January 2007, available at www.antimon.gov.sk.

[174] Case M 4298, decision of 6 September 2006.

[175] OFT decision of 22 December 2006.

[176] See 'Appeals against Article 9 references', p 919 later in chapter.

[177] *Communication from the Commission to the Council*, COM(2009) 2101 final.

[178] Ibid, section 4.2.

[179] Ibid, paras 17–21.

[180] Ibid, para 12.

submission that it should be examined by the Commission[181]. They must do so on Form RS, and the Commission must transmit the submission to the Member States without delay. In 2014 the Commission proposed to simplify Article 4(5) cases by abolishing Form RS and permitting parties to notify eligible transactions directly to the Commission[182]. No further action has been taken on this initiative.

Member States competent to examine the concentration must disagree with the request within 15 working days. If one Member State expresses disagreement, the case will not be referred (in other words the case referral process under Article 4(5) can be vetoed by a single Member State, although this is not the case under Article 22). Only seven of the 337 Article 4(5) requests had been vetoed by a Member State by 8 December 2017. However if there is no disagreement within the stipulated period the concentration is deemed to have a Union dimension[183] and falls to be dealt with under the provisions of the EUMR; Member States can no longer apply their national competition law to the case, which proceeds on the basis of one-stop merger control. The Commission considers the most appropriate cases for referral under Article 4(5) are those where:

- the potential impact on competition will be felt in markets that are wider than national in geographic scope[184]
- the markets affected are national or narrower, but competition concerns arise in a number of Member States; this may lead to a more coherent and consistent outcome[185]
- there are no competition concerns at all, but a referral will avoid the burden of multiple Member State filings[186].

(ii) Post-notification referrals: Article 22

Article 22 of the EUMR provides a mechanism whereby Member States may refer concentrations that do not have a Union dimension to the Commission for it to investigate[187]: the concentration in question must affect trade between Member States[188] and must threaten to affect competition significantly within the territory of the Member State or States making the request[189]. In 2010 the Commission accepted a request from six Member States to investigate the acquisition by Proctor & Gamble of Sara Lee's air-freshener business: the interesting point about this is that the transaction was not notifiable under the merger control provisions of five of the six referring Member States, and yet the Commission still accepted the referral. There is nothing in the wording of the EUMR to prevent a request in such circumstances, and when the original Merger Regulation was introduced in 1989 one of the justifications for the Article 22 procedure was that some Member States did not have a system of merger control: it seemed sensible in those circumstances to allow references to the Commission of mergers that could be harmful to competition and that would

181 *Case Referral Notice*, paras 24–32.

182 White Paper *Towards more effective EU merger control*, COM(2014) 449 final, paras 65–66.

183 Note that under Article 22 the Commission has a discretion whether to accept a request, whereas under Article 4(5), in the absence of a veto by a Member State, the Commission must accept jurisdiction.

184 *Case Referral Notice*, para 28. 185 Ibid, para 29. 186 Ibid, para 32.

187 Ibid, paras 42–45; see De Stefano, Motta and Zuehlke 'Merger Referrals in Practice—Analysis of the Cases under Article 22 of the Merger Regulation' [2011] JECLAP 542.

188 The Commission's *Notice on the notion of effect on trade concept contained in Articles [101] and [102] of the Treaty* OJ [2004] C 101/81, may, by analogy, provide helpful guidance on the application of this expression; see the *Case Referral Notice*, fn 36.

189 EUMR, Article 22(1).

have an effect on trade between Member States[190]. However the interesting point about the *Sara Lee* case is that the referring Member States *did* have systems of merger control, but the transaction in question was below the national jurisdictional thresholds[191].

The Commission may invite Member States to make a request under Article 22[192]. When the Commission receives an Article 22 request it must inform the competent authorities of the Member States without delay; other Member States may join the request within 15 working days of being informed of the initial request, and national time limits as to merger control are suspended until the jurisdictional question has been decided[193]. Silence on the part of a Member State does not mean that it is deemed to have joined the request. If a Member State decides not to join the request its national time limits revive[194]. That Member State can then apply its own law, even if the Commission accepts the request from other Member States: to put the point another way, the principle of one-stop merger control does not necessarily apply in an Article 22 case, since Member States retain the right to disagree with a request and to apply their own law[195]. The Commission must decide, within a further ten working days from the end of the period given to Member States to decide whether to join the request, whether to examine the concentration[196]. If the Commission does not take a decision it is deemed to have accepted the request[197]. If the Commission does decide to examine the case it may request the parties to make a formal notification[198]. Once the Commission has taken jurisdiction the case proceeds in accordance with the provisions of the EUMR[199]. The Commission was contemplating an extension of Article 22 that would give it EEA-wide jurisdiction in cases referred under that provision[200]. No further action has been taken on this initiative.

(iii) **Statistics**

The statistics on Article 4(5) and Article 22 are of interest, and demonstrate in particular that undertakings have found the Article 4(5) procedure to be a useful provision[201]. In the early years of EU merger control Article 22 requests were rare; three were made by Member States that had no system of merger control at all at the relevant time, and each of them led to an outright prohibition by the Commission[202]. By 8 December 2017

[190] Three prohibitions under the EUMR were of mergers referred by Member States that had no merger control provisions: see Case M 553 *RTL/Veronica/Endemol*, decision of 17 July 1996, upheld on appeal Case T-221/95 *Endemol Entertainment Holding BV v Commission* EU:T:1999:85; Case M 784 *Kesko/Tuko*, decision of 20 November 1996, OJ [1997] L 110/53, upheld on appeal Case T-22/97 *Kesko Oy v Commission* EU:T:1999:327; Case M 890 *Blokker/Toys 'R' Us*, decision of 26 June 1997, OJ [1998] L 316/1.

[191] This point was discussed in the Staff Working Paper, SEC (2009) 808 final/2, accompanying the Commission's *Report on the functioning of Regulation No 139/2004*, para 144.

[192] EUMR, Article 22(5). [193] Ibid, Article 22(5). [194] Ibid.

[195] See eg Case M 7054 *Cemex/Holcim Assets* where Spain made an Article 22 referral but the Czech Republic retained jurisdiction; Case M 5828 *Procter & Gamble/Sara Lee Air Care*, decision of 31 March 2010, where the Commission reviewed the merger in Belgium, Portugal, Spain and the UK pursuant to Article 22; the merger was also reviewed under national law in Austria, Bulgaria, Cyprus, Hungary, Italy, Poland and Slovak Republic.

[196] For examples of decisions not to examine a concentration following an Article 22 request see Case M 3986 *Gas Natural/Endesa*, Commission Press Release IP/05/1356, 27 October 2005 and Case M 6502 *London Stock Exchange Group plc/LCH Clearance Group Ltd*, decision of 6 July 2012.

[197] EUMR, Article 22(3).

[198] Ibid; the parties in an Article 22 case will already have made a notification to the NCA(s), and it is possible that the Commission will be able to glean the information it requires from those notifications.

[199] EUMR, Article 22(4).

[200] White Paper *Towards more effective EU merger control*, COM(2014) 449 final, para 69.

[201] See 'Table of EUMR statistics', p 923–924 later in chapter for a statistical table of merger notifications.

[202] See ch 21 n 190 earlier.

Member States had made 33 Article 22 requests, four of which were refused; 337 Article 4(5) requests had been received, seven of which were refused.

(iv) Article 4(5) and Article 22 in practice

As already noted, three early Article 22 requests led to outright prohibitions of the concentrations in question. More recently Article 4(5) and Article 22 requests have continued to lead to problems for the undertakings concerned. For example an Article 4(5) request in the case of *Metso/Aker Kvaerner* led to a Phase II investigation and was cleared only subject to commitments[203]. Commitments have been required following Article 22 requests in a number of cases[204]. Three Article 22 cases, *Glatfelter/Crompton Assets*[205], *Aegean/Olympic II*[206] and *Cemex/Holcim Assets*[207], were cleared unconditionally following a Phase II investigation. In June 2009 the Commission reported that Articles 4(5) and 22 have worked well in practice, albeit that they are sometimes perceived to be slow and cumbersome[208]. No further action has been taken in response to the Commission's 2014 proposals to overcome this problem.

(F) Article 21(4): legitimate interest clause

The principle of one-stop merger control means that a Member State cannot apply its competition law to a concentration having a Union dimension except where Article 4(4) or Article 9 apply. However there may be circumstances in which a Member State wishes to investigate and perhaps to prohibit a concentration for some other reason: for example because it objects to a domestic undertaking being acquired by a foreign one; because the concentration might lead to unemployment and social disruption; or because the sector in question is a sensitive one in which the Member State wishes to maintain a strong influence which might be undermined by wider participation. Some interventions by a Member State to prevent a concentration involving an undertaking from another Member State might infringe the Treaty, for example Article 49 TFEU on the right of establishment or Article 63 TFEU on the free movement of capital; in such a situation the Commission may proceed against the Member State in question by bringing proceedings before the Court of Justice under Article 258 TFEU. In other cases the Commission might bring proceedings against a Member State that tries to block a concentration having a Union dimension on the basis that this involves a violation of the EUMR itself since Article 21 confers exclusive competence on the Commission in relation to concentrations having a Union dimension (see section (ii) later). The Commission made a declaration to the European Parliament in March 2006 stressing its determination to use these legal provisions to ensure that the principles of the single market are upheld[209]. The Commission has consistently expressed its opposition to national protectionist

203 Case M 4187, decision of 12 December 2006; see similarly Case M 4209 *Thule/Schneeketten*, subsequently abandoned by the parties; for an example of a conditional Phase I clearance following an Article 4(5) request see Case M 6857 *Crane Co/MEI Group*, decision of 19 July 2013.

204 Case M 2698 *Promatech/Sulzer Textil*, decision of 24 July 2002; Case M 3136 *GE/AGFA NDT*, decision of 5 December 2005; Case M 3099 *AREVA/Urenco/ETC*, decision of 6 October 2004; Case M 3796 *Omya/J.M. Huber*, decision of 19 July 2006, OJ [2007] L 72/24; Case M 4980 *ABF/GBI Business*, decision of 23 September 2008; Case M 5675 *Syngenta/Monsanto*, decision of 17 November 2010.

205 Case M 4215, decision of 20 December 2006, OJ [2007] L 151/41.

206 Case M 6796, decision of 9 October 2013.

207 Case M 7054, decision of 9 September 2014.

208 *Communication from the Commission to the Council*, COM(2009) 2101 final, paras 17–21.

209 Commission Declaration of 15 March 2006, available at www.europarl.europa.eu.

measures[210]. The Commission does not believe that the creation of 'national champions' justifies non-compliance with, or exemption from, competition law[211].

Article 21(4) of the EUMR provides that Member States may take appropriate measures to protect legitimate interests other than those taken into consideration by the EUMR that are compatible with the general principles and other provisions of EU law. Public security, plurality of the media and prudential rules—that is to say rules designed to ensure the stability and financial adequacy of banks, insurance companies and similar undertakings—are regarded as legitimate interests for this purpose. Any other legitimate interest must be communicated to the Commission, which must inform the Member State in question of its decision within 25 working days of the communication.

(i) Authorised applications of Article 21(4)

Decisions to allow a Member State to proceed on the basis of Article 21(4) are rare: by 8 December 2017 only eight had been granted[212]. Article 21(4) is applied strictly since it is a derogation from the principle of the EUMR that concentrations having a Union dimension should be subject to a one-stop shop[213].

In *Lyonnaise des Eaux SA/Northumbrian Water Group*[214] the Commission accepted that the UK was entitled to investigate the regulatory aspects of a transaction whereby Lyonnaise des Eaux acquired a UK water undertaking, while the Commission considered the competition issues. The UK also investigated the *Independent Newspaper* case under the (now-repealed) newspaper merger provisions of the Fair Trading Act 1973[215]. In *Sun Alliance/Royal Insurance*[216] the Commission acknowledged that the UK could consider whether the merger would be in accordance with the Insurance Companies Act 1982, but said that this would be done in close liaison with it. In *Electricité de France/London Electricity*[217] the UK requested a referral under Article 9 of the EUMR and claimed a legitimate interest under Article 21(4); the Commission did not accept either request: the concerns of the UK energy regulator were not with the concentration itself but with the conduct of the merged undertakings after it would have taken place, to which the regulatory authority could apply national regulatory provisions. In *Thomson-CSF/Racal* the UK investigated the public security aspects of the proposed transaction under the domestic merger provisions[218]. In *MBDA/SNPE/JV* the European Commission cleared

[210] See eg speeches by former Commissioner Kroes 'European competition policy facing a renaissance of protectionism—which strategy for the future?', 11 May 2007 and by former Vice-President Almunia 'Some highlights from EU competition enforcement', 19 September 2014, both available at www.ec.europa.eu/competition/speeches; see further Nourry and Jung 'EU State Measures against Foreign Takeovers: "Economic Patriotism in All But Name"' (2006) 2 Competition Policy International 99; Nourry and Jung 'Protectionism in the Age of Austerity—A Further Unlevelling of the Playing Field?' (2012) 8 Competition Policy International 1; Jones and Davies 'Merger Control and the Public Interest: Balancing EU and National Law in the Protectionist Debate' (2014) 10 European Competition Journal 453.

[211] See the Commission's contribution to the OECD Roundtable *Competition Policy, Industrial Policy and National Champions* (2009), pp 145–147, available at www.oecd.org/competition.

[212] See 'Table of EUMR statistics', pp 923–924 later in chapter for a statistical table of merger notifications.

[213] See the Commission's contribution to the OECD Roundtable *Public Interest Considerations in Merger Control* (2016), available at www.oecd.org/competition.

[214] Case M 567, decision of 21 December 1995, OJ [1995] C 11/3; the Monopolies and Mergers Commission, as it was then called, subsequently published a report *Lyonnaise des Eaux SA and Northumbrian Water Group plc*, Cm 2936 (1995) identifying possible public interest detriments: see *1999 Annual Report of the Director General of Fair Trading*, p 35.

[215] Case M 423, decision of 14 March 1994, OJ [1994] C 85/6.

[216] Case M 759, decision of 18 June 1996, OJ [1996] C 225/12.

[217] See the Commission's XXIXth *Report on Competition Policy* (1999), paras 193 and 197–198.

[218] Commission Press Release IP/00/628, 16 June 2000.

the concentration under the EUMR, and the UK accepted behavioural remedies to alleviate public security concerns[219]. In *News Corp/BSkyB*[220] and *Fox/Sky*[221] the Commission cleared the merger, but acknowledged the right of the UK to consider its potential effects on the plurality of the media in the UK[222].

(ii) Prohibited applications of Article 21(4)

In *Banco Santander Central Hispano/A Champalimaud*[223] a concentration in the financial services sector having a Union dimension was notified to the Commission. The Portuguese Minister of Finance opposed the concentration, claiming to have anxieties about the prudential supervision of Mundial Confiança, an insurance undertaking, and also because he considered that the concentration would interfere with Portuguese national interests; further it would prejudice an integral sector of the Portuguese economy and financial system. The concerns of the Minister were increased by the parties' procedural impropriety in failing to notify the Minister of Finance. The Commission rejected these arguments and required the Minister to suspend his opposition to the transaction[224].

The Commission took a similar view in *Secil/Holderbank/Cimpor*. The Portuguese Minister of Finance objected to the proposed acquisition of a Portuguese cement company, Cimpor, which the Portuguese Government was in the process of privatising. The proposed acquisition had a Union dimension and therefore fell within the Commission's exclusive jurisdiction[225]. The Commission adopted a decision requiring Portugal to withdraw the decisions it had taken opposing the acquisition on the ground that Portugal had failed to show that it had a legitimate interest in the sense of Article 21(4) of the EUMR[226]. The Government of Portugal challenged the Commission's decision, but in *Portugal v Commission*[227] the Court of Justice held that the Commission can conclude that a decision of a Member State on the public interest is incompatible with EU law even where that interest has not been communicated to it by the Government asserting it; and that the Commission is entitled to require by an Article 21 decision that the state measure in question should be withdrawn.

In *UniCredito/HVB*[228] the Commission cleared the proposed acquisition by UniCredito of Italy of HVB. However Poland required UniCredito to divest itself of shares in a Polish bank, BPH, which was indirectly controlled by HVB; it decided that the retention by UniCredito of these shares would breach an earlier contract, whereby UniCredito had purchased another bank, Pekao, as part of the process of bank privatisation in Poland.

219 See DTI Press Release P/2002/754, 27 November 2002 and DTI Press Release P/2002/802, 17 December 2002.

220 Case M 5932, decision of 21 December 2010; Case M 8788 *Apple/Shazam* was referred to the Commission by six Member States under Article 22 EUMR.

221 Case M 8354, decision of 7 April 2017.

222 See ch 22, 'European mergers', pp 990–991.

223 Case M 1616, decision of 3 August 1999, OJ [1999] C 306/37; see Mohamed 'National Interests Limiting EU Cross-Border Mergers' (2000) 21 ECLR 248.

224 Commission decisions of 20 July 1999 and 20 October 2000: see the Commission's XXIXth *Report on Competition Policy* (1999), paras 194–196.

225 The notification in this case was withdrawn by the parties before the Commission had reached a decision: Case M 2054.

226 See Commission Press Release IP/00/1338, 22 November 2000; in Case C-367/98 *Commission v Portugal* EU:C:2002:326 the Court of Justice ruled that the law under which the Portuguese Government had proceeded was itself in violation of Article 63 TFEU.

227 Case C-42/01 EU:C:2004:379; see Mäkel 'The Court of Justice rules for the first time on Article 21(3) of the merger regulation in Case C-42/01 *Portuguese Republic v Commission*' (2005) 1 Competition Policy Newsletter 19.

228 Case M 3894, decision of 18 October 2005; see Busa and Cuadrado 'Application of Article 21 of the Merger Regulation in the *E.ON/Endesa case*' (2008) 2 Competition Policy Newsletter 1.

The Commission considered that the measures adopted by the Polish Government violated both Article 21 of the EUMR[229] and Articles 49 and 63 TFEU[230]; however these cases were subsequently closed.

In *E.ON/Endesa*[231] the Commission approved the proposed acquisition by E.ON of Germany of a Spanish undertaking in the energy sector, Endesa. Spain took steps to impede the acquisition leading to two decisions of the Commission finding violations of Article 21 of the EUMR[232]. In March 2007 the Commission made a formal request to Spain to comply with these decisions[233]. Spain failed to satisfy the Commission with the result that the Commission referred the matter to the Court of Justice. The Court held that Spain had breached its obligations under EU law[234].

The Commission also came to a preliminary conclusion that Italy was in breach of Article 21 of the EUMR in *Abertis/Autostrade*[235], a transaction that the Commission cleared[236] but which Italy objected to on the basis that it was concerned that Abertis, of Spain, would not be able to carry out the investment required to maintain and improve the motorway network in Italy. The case was eventually closed after Italy withdrew the obstacles to the merger[237].

(G) **Defence**

Article 346(1)(b) TFEU provides that a Member State 'may take such measures as it considers necessary' in matters of security connected with its defence industry; such measures must not adversely affect the conditions of competition in the internal market regarding products which are not intended for specifically military purposes. A Member State may investigate the military aspects of a concentration and the Commission the civilian aspects; this distinction in itself inevitably raises the problem of how to deal with products that have a 'dual-use', that is to say that can be used both for military and for civilian purposes. The UK Government successfully invoked Article 346(1)(b) in relation to the proposed takeover of VSEL by British Aerospace[238], where both companies produced military equipment for the British defence forces; it required British Aerospace not to notify the military element of the takeover to the Commission. Subsequent to this the UK has invoked Article 346 in a few cases[239]. However, several mergers involving the defence industry in Europe have been notified to the Commission[240], which might suggest that the Commission is taking a stricter view in relation to the application of Article 346.

[229] Commission Press Release IP/06/277, 8 March 2006.

[230] Commission Press Release IP/06/276, 8 March 2006; Articles 49 and 63 TFEU protect the right of establishment and the free movement of capital respectively.

[231] Case M 4110, decision of 25 April 2006.

[232] See Commission Press Release IP/06/1265, 26 September 2006 and Commission Press Release IP/06/1853, 20 December 2006.

[233] Commission Press Release IP/07/296, 7 March 2007.

[234] Case C-196/07 *Commission v Kingdom of Spain* EU:C:2008:146; see similarly the Commission's decision in Case M 4685 *Enel/Acciona/Endesa*: Spain appealed against this decision in Case T-65/08 *Spain v Commission*, but withdrew its appeal in June 2010.

[235] See Commission Press Release IP/06/1418, 18 October 2006 and Commission Press Release IP/07/117, 31 January 2007.

[236] Case M 4249, decision of 22 September 2006.

[237] See Commission Press Release IP/08/1521, 16 October 2008.

[238] DTI Press Notice P/94/623, 19 October 1994: see Case M 528, Commission decision of 24 November 1994; see also Case M 529 *VSEL/GEC*, decision of 7 December 1994.

[239] See eg Case M 724 *GEC/Thomson-CSF(II)*, decision of 15 May 1996; Case M 820 *British Aerospace/Lagardère*, decision of 23 September 1996; Case M 1438 *British Aerospace/GEC Marconi*, decision of 25 June 1999.

[240] These cases can be accessed at http://ec.europa.eu/competition/elojade/isef/index.cfm?clear=1&policy_area_id=2.

4. Notification, Suspension of Concentrations, Procedural Timetable and Powers of Decision

This section will deal with the following matters:

(A) Notification: concentrations that have a Union dimension are required by Article 4 to be notified on Form CO to the Commission.

(B) Suspension of concentrations: Article 7 provides that concentrations that have a Union dimension are automatically suspended until they are declared compatible with the internal market; this period may be waived in appropriate cases.

(C) Procedural timetables and powers of decision of the Commission: strict time limits are imposed on the Commission's decision-making in order to disturb the operation of the market as little as possible: the EU Courts have stressed the importance of speedy procedures under the EUMR on several occasions[241]. The Commission can make a range of decisions when reviewing concentrations.

(A) Notification

Article 4(1) of the EUMR provides that concentrations with a Union dimension must be notified to the Commission following the conclusion of the agreement, the announcement of the public bid, or the acquisition of a controlling interest but prior to their implementation. Notification may also be made where undertakings demonstrate to the Commission a good faith intention to conclude an agreement or to make a public bid: this means that they can begin the investigative procedure, with the benefit of the fixed time limits, before the formal legalities of the transaction have been completed. The Commission publishes a notice of concentrations having a Union dimension in the Official Journal. Articles 4(4) and 4(5) provide that the parties may make reasoned submissions for the reallocation of cases to or from the Commission[242]. Fines can be imposed for providing incorrect or misleading information in a notification or in response to a Commission request for information and for implementing a concentration without prior approval[243].

The Commission may declare a notification to be incomplete—for example because it omits information that ought to have been included—in which case the time limits for reaching a decision will not have begun to run. Rejection of a notification may have serious consequences for the undertakings concerned which may wish to conclude the transaction by a certain date. DG COMP has published *Best Practices on the conduct of EC merger control proceedings*[244] which clarifies the day-to-day conduct of proceedings under the EUMR. The *Best Practices Guideline* suggests that, even in the simplest of cases, there should be pre-notification contact with DG COMP: the discussions should be commenced at least two weeks prior to notification and will be held in strict confidence[245]. Pre-notification discussions can cover a range of matters from jurisdictional questions and waivers of informational requirements to substantive analysis and possible remedies. The Commission prefers there to be business representatives present at meetings who have knowledge of the relevant markets as well as legal advisers[246]. The *Guideline* says that a 'Case team allocation

[241] See eg Case C-170/02 P *Schülsselverlag JS Moser v Commission* EU:C:2003:501, paras 33 and 34; Case C-42/01 *Portuguese Republic v Commission* EU:C:2004:379, paras 51 and 53.

[242] See 'Pre-notification referrals: Article 4(4)', pp 867–868 and 'Pre-notification referrals: Article 4(5)', pp 869–870 earlier in chapter.

[243] See 'Powers of Investigation and Enforcement', pp 913–915 later in chapter.

[244] Available at www.ec.europa.eu/competition/mergers/legislation/legislation.html.

[245] *Best Practices Guideline*, paras 5–8.

[246] Ibid, para 9.

request' should be submitted to DG COMP to facilitate its initial contact with the parties, followed by more detailed submissions or a draft Form CO[247]. The *Guideline* explains that there may be 'state-of-play' meetings between the notifying parties and officials from DG COMP at key stages of the investigation; DG COMP may also meet with interested third parties, and it may even hold 'triangular meetings' if it would be helpful to hear everyone concerned in a single forum[248]. The *Guideline* also discusses access to the Commission's file following the issuance of a statement of objections in a Phase II investigation[249], the review of 'key documents' and issues of confidentiality[250]. Officials from DG COMP meet on Mondays to allocate new cases to a particular case team.

Regulation 802/2004[251] sets out the format in which a notification (or a reasoned submission) is to be made.

(i) **Form CO**

Notifications are made in the format known as Form CO. An original, signed version of the Form CO, on paper, must be submitted to the Commission together with a further three paper copies with annexes and two copies of the notification in CD- or DVD-ROM format[252]; the notification is sent to a registry (known as the Greffe) which registers its time of arrival, at which point the merger review timetable begins to run. Form CO requires the notifying firms to provide substantial information: Annex I of Regulation 802/2004 explains the information that must be provided. The pre-notification meetings required by DG COMP's *Best Practices Guideline* provide an opportunity for the parties, their advisers and the officials from DG COMP dealing with the case to satisfy themselves that the Form CO, when it is eventually submitted, contains all the information needed for the Commission to commence its investigation[253].

(ii) **Short Form CO**

In certain circumstances a 'Short Form CO' may be submitted, relieving the parties from some of the informational burden that they would otherwise bear. The procedure is set out in the Commission's *Notice on a simplified procedure for treatment of certain concentrations*[254]. The procedure is available for:

- joint ventures that have no, or negligible, activities in the EEA: turnover thresholds are used to indicate when this is the case
- concentrations where the parties are not engaged in business activities in the same product and geographical markets or in markets that are vertically related to one another
- transactions where the parties' combined market shares are below 20% in the case of a horizontal concentration or, in the case of a vertical concentration, where the parties do not have an individual or combined market share in excess of 30% at any level of the market
- cases where a party is to acquire sole control of an undertaking over which it already has joint control

[247] Ibid, paras 10–23. [248] Ibid, paras 30–39.

[249] See also the Commission's *Notice on access to the file* OJ [2005] C 325/7.

[250] *Best Practices Guideline*, paras 42–47.

[251] OJ [2004] L 133/1, as subsequently amended; this Regulation replaces the earlier Regulation 447/98, OJ [1998] L 61/1.

[252] See the Commission's *Communication pursuant to Regulation 802/2004 on the format in which notifications should be delivered to the Commission* OJ [2014] C 25/4.

[253] It remains possible that, notwithstanding pre-notification discussions, it becomes apparent to the Commission post-notification that a Form CO is, in fact, incomplete.

[254] OJ [2013] C 366/5.

- mergers where the combined market share of the parties to a transaction is less than 50% and the increment resulting from the transaction is less than 150 under the Herfindahl-Hirschman Index ('HHI')[255].

The Commission is less likely to apply the simplified procedure if any of the 'special circumstances' mentioned in paragraph 20 of its *Guidelines on the assessment of horizontal mergers*[256] are present[257].

When a Short Form CO is permitted the Commission will usually adopt a short-form clearance decision within 25 working days from the date of notification[258]. A significant proportion of cases are dealt with under the simplified procedure. For example in 2016 there were 362 merger notifications and 247 cases in which a merger was cleared under the simplified procedure[259]. The Commission hopes that the revised simplified procedure will result in an increase of 10% in the number of cases benefitting from the simplified procedure[260]. Cases dealt with under the simplified procedure are still subject to the standstill obligation in Article 7 of the EUMR, but the parties may apply for a derogation under Article 7(3)[261].

(iii) **Reasoned submissions**

Annex III of Regulation 802/2004 sets out the requirements for a Form RS where the parties seek a reallocation of jurisdiction to or from the Commission.

(B) **Suspension of concentrations**

Article 7(1) of the EUMR requires automatic suspension of a concentration that the Commission has jurisdiction to investigate before notification and before it has been declared compatible with the internal market: this provision has been described by the General Court as one of the 'founding principles' of the EUMR[262]. Article 7(2) provides that, in the case of a public bid, the bid may be implemented provided that the concentration is notified to the Commission without delay and that the acquirer does not exercise the voting rights attached to the shares in question[263]. Article 14 provides penalties for 'gun-jumping'—that is to say implementing the transaction before receiving the Commission's approval—in breach of Article 7(1): infringement of Article 7 could lead to a fine of as much as 10% of the worldwide turnover of the undertakings concerned. There have been four fines imposed for gun-jumping[264]. In 2017 the Commission issued two statements of objections in relation to alleged infringements of Article 7(1); in April 2018 the Commission decided one of those cases by imposing a fine of €125 million on Altice for 'gun-jumping'[265].

[255] On the HHI see 'Market shares and concentration levels', pp 889–891 later in chapter.

[256] OJ [2004] C 31/5; on the *Horizontal merger guidelines* see pp 889–899 later in chapter.

[257] OJ [2013] C 366/5, para 11.

[258] On the procedure see the Commission's *Notice on simplified procedure* OJ [2013] C 366/5.

[259] See 'Table of EUMR statistics', pp 923–924 later in chapter for a statistical table of merger notifications.

[260] See Commission Press Release IP/13/1214, 5 December 2013.

[261] See 'Suspension of concentrations', pp 878–879 later in chapter.

[262] Case T-411/07 *Aer Lingus Group v Commission* EU:T:2010:281, para 80; Article 7(1) of the EUMR is the subject of an Article 267 reference to the Court of Justice in Case C-633/16 *Ernst & Young P/S v Konkurrencerådet*, not yet decided.

[263] See Case M 2283 *Schneider/Legrand*, decision of 10 October 2001, OJ [2004] L 101/1 and Case M 2416 *Tetra Laval/Sidel*, decision of 30 October 2001, OJ [2004] L 43/13 where unconditional bids for shares on the Paris Stock Exchange had been made.

[264] See 'Powers of Investigation and Enforcement', pp 913–915 later in chapter.

[265] Case M 7993 *Altice/PT Portugal*, Commission Press Releases IP/17/1368, 18 May 2017 (SO) and IP/18/3522, 24 April 2018 (decision); and Case M 8179 *Canon/Toshiba Medical Systems*, Commission Press Release IP/17/1924, 6 July 2017; for discussion of what constitutes gun-jumping see the Opinion of AG Wahl in Case C-633/16 *Ernst & Young P/S v Koncurrencerådet* EU:C:2018:23.

Article 7(3) provides that the Commission may grant a derogation from the provisions on suspension, subject to conditions where appropriate. A request for derogation from the automatic suspension must be reasoned, and the Commission will take into account the effects of the suspension on the undertakings concerned by a concentration or on a third party, and the threat to competition that the concentration poses. A few Article 7(3) derogations are allowed each year, as the Table of EUMR Statistics demonstrates[266].

(C) Procedural timetable and powers of decision of the Commission

(i) Phase I investigations

(a) Possible decisions at the end of Phase I

The Commission is required by Article 6 to examine a concentration that has been notified by the parties in accordance with the EUMR as soon as the notification is received. It must then make a decision either that the concentration:

- is outside the EUMR (Article 6(1)(a))[267] or
- is compatible with the internal market (Article 6(1)(b)): this finding extends to any restrictions directly related and necessary to the concentration ('ancillary restraints')[268] or
- as modified by the parties no longer raises serious doubts and so may be declared compatible with the internal market: such a decision will be subject to conditions and obligations ('commitments')[269] (Article 6(1)(b) in conjunction with Article 6(2)) or
- raises serious doubts as to its compatibility with the internal market (Article 6(1)(c)); in this situation the Commission must initiate a Phase II investigation[270].

A decision under Article 6(1)(a) or (b) can be revoked where it is based on incorrect information for which one of the undertakings is responsible or where it has been obtained by deceit[271], where there has been a breach of an obligation attached to a decision[272], or where the decision is illegal in accordance with general principles of EU law[273].

(b) Timetable

Phase I decisions must generally be made within 25 working days of the day following notification[274]. If the notification is incomplete the period begins on the day following

[266] See 'Table of EUMR statistics', pp 923–924 later in chapter; see eg Case M 8553 *Banco Santander/Banco Popular Group*, decision of 7 June 2017.

[267] Article 6(1)(a) decisions are rare; for an example see Case M 7940 *Netto/Grocery Store at Armitage Avenue Little Hutton*, decision of 30 January 2016.

[268] On ancillary restraints see 'Contractual restrictions directly related and necessary to a merger: "ancillary restraints"', pp 904–907 later in chapter.

[269] See 'Remedies', pp 907–913 later in chapter.

[270] An Article 6(1)(c) decision cannot be challenged before the EU Courts: Case T-48/03 *Schneider Electric v Commission* EU:T:2006:34, upheld on appeal Case C-188/06 P EU:C:2007:158; see similarly Case T-902/16 *HeidelbergCement v Commission* EU:T:2017:846.

[271] EUMR, Article 6(3)(a): see Case M 1397 *Sanofi/Synthélabo*, Commission Press Release IP(99)255, 23 April 1999, where the Commission revoked its decision as the notifying parties had failed to produce information about activities in a particular market; the Commission reopened its examination of the case, but allowed a partial derogation from the Article 7(3) suspension that would otherwise have automatically occurred, since the parties were preparing to offer suitable undertakings to overcome any competition concerns and because of the significant prejudice that a delay could have caused to the parties and their shareholders.

[272] Article 6(3)(b): see Case M 1069 *World Com/MCI*, decision of 8 July 1998, OJ [1999] L 116/1.

[273] Case T-251/00 *Lagardère SCA and Canal SA v Commission* EU:T:2002:278, paras 130 and 138–141.

[274] EUMR, Article 10(1).

receipt of complete information. The Phase I time limit may be extended to 35 working days where a Member State makes a request for a reference under Article 9, or where the undertakings concerned offer commitments pursuant to Article 6(2)[275].

The Phase I timetable of 25, sometimes extended to 35, working days can place great strain on all the relevant parties—the business people, the professional advisers and the staff at DG COMP—which is why pre-notification contacts are so important. The overwhelming majority of cases are dealt with within the Phase I time limit, a not inconsiderable achievement given the complexity and size of many of the transactions notified.

(ii) Phase II investigations

(a) Possible decisions at the end of Phase II

Where a concentration raises serious doubts about compatibility with the internal market the Commission will commence proceedings in accordance with Article 6(1)(c) of the EUMR. An Article 6(1)(c) decision inaugurates an in-depth Phase II investigation.

The decisions the Commission may make at the end of Phase II are set out in Article 8. It may decide that the concentration:

- is compatible with the internal market, having regard to the provisions of Article 2(2) and, in some cases, Articles 2(4) and 2(5)[276] (Article 8(1)): this finding extends to any ancillary restraints or
- is compatible with the internal market, subject to commitments to ensure compliance with modifications proposed by the parties (Article 8(2)): again this extends to any ancillary restraints or
- is incompatible with the internal market (Article 8(3)) or
- in so far as it has already been implemented, or implemented in breach of a condition attached to an Article 8(2) decision, must be reversed, or modified in an appropriate way (Article 8(4))[277].

Further the Commission may order such interim measures as may be appropriate (Article 8(5)) or revoke a decision taken under Article 8(2) where the Commission based its decision of compatibility on incorrect information or where the undertakings concerned have acted in breach of an obligation attached to the Commission's decision (Article 8(6)).

(b) Timetable

Article 10 lays down the timetable within which the Commission must reach any of the decisions provided for in Article 8. Decisions under Articles 8(1) to 8(3) must be taken within 90 working days of the date on which proceedings were initiated[278]. The Phase II time limit may be extended to 105 working days where the undertakings concerned offer commitments pursuant to Article 8(2) between working days 55 and 65 of a Phase II investigation[279]. The Phase II time limit may be further extended, at the request of the parties, for a period of up to 20 more working days.

Article 10(4) provides that the Phase II time limits may exceptionally be suspended where the Commission has had to obtain additional information owing to

[275] Ibid, second indent.

[276] See 'Articles 2(4) and 2(5) of the EUMR: full-function joint ventures and "spillover effects"', pp 902–904 later in chapter.

[277] Article 8(4) cannot be used to order the divestiture of shares in a company that do not confer control within the meaning of the EUMR: Case T-411/07 *Aer Lingus Group plc v Commission* EU:T:2010:281, para 66.

[278] EUMR, Article 10(3). [279] Ibid, second sentence.

circumstances for which one of the undertakings involved is responsible. This provision is sometimes invoked; in *Oracle/PeopleSoft*[280] the Commission did 'stop the clock' pursuant to this provision in circumstances where it may have suited all the parties concerned, given that it meant that the decision under the EUMR could be taken after the proceedings instituted by the US Department of Justice had been concluded[281]. In *Omya/J.M. Huber*[282] the Commission stopped the clock because the parties had failed to provide the information it had requested; the Commission's decision was upheld on appeal[283].

Where the Commission fails to reach a decision within the prescribed time scale, whether in Phase I or Phase II, the concentration is deemed to be compatible with the internal market[284].

(c) Phase II procedure

A Phase II investigation is usually an exhausting and exhaustive exercise for all concerned. The timetables are tight, given that the investigation is 'in depth'. During the 90 working day period there will normally[285] be:

- a detailed market investigation by the Commission, including the sending of questionnaires to the parties, competitors and customers
- a peer review panel within DG COMP, to test the strength of the case
- a statement of objections sent by the Commission to the undertakings concerned
- a period for the parties to reply to the statement of objections
- access for the parties to the case file of the Commission[286]
- an oral hearing which may last for one or two days
- a meeting (or meetings) of the Advisory Committee on Concentrations
- a period within which commitments can be discussed and an opportunity for interested third parties to comment on any such commitments[287]
- consultation of other Directorates General
- the preparation of a draft decision for discussion and adoption by the Commission of the final decision.

Achieving all these steps within the Phase II time limits can be extremely difficult, especially since many of the cases that come to the Commission are immensely complex. The

[280] Case M 3216, decision of 26 October 2004, OJ [2005] L 218/6.

[281] *US and Plaintiff States v Oracle Corporation*, available at www.justice.gov/atr.

[282] Case M 3796, decision of 19 July 2006, OJ [2007] L 72/24.

[283] Case T-145/06 *Omya v Commission* EU:T:2009:27; for more recent examples of the clock being stopped see Case M 7000 *Liberty Global/Ziggo*, decision of 10 October 2014; Case M 7612 *Hutchison 3G UK/Telefónica UK*, decision of 11 May 2016.

[284] EUMR, Article 10(6).

[285] It is not inevitable that the full procedure will be followed: eg it may be that the parties offer suitable commitments during the beginning of the Phase II procedure, thereby obviating the need for a statement of objections and/or the completion of the in-depth investigation; sometimes the parties choose not to have an oral hearing, not least because this can provide an occasion for third parties that object to the transaction to address their concerns orally to the Commission and the NCAs that attend the hearing: on the latter point see Wils 'The Oral Hearing in Competition Proceedings Before the European Commission' (2012) 35 World Competition 397.

[286] On access to the file see Case T-221/95 *Endemol Entertainment Holding BV v Commission* EU:T:1999:85, para 68 and Wils 'The Role of the Hearing Officer in Competition Proceedings Before the European Commission' (2012) 35 World Competition 431.

[287] See 'Remedies', pp 907–913 later in chapter.

Chief Competition Economist and his team may play an important part in Phase II cases where in-depth economic analysis is called for[288].

(iii) 'Phase III'

Even when a final decision, whether under Phase I or II, has been made there may be a further period of uncertainty and delay for the undertakings concerned. Where the parties have offered commitments as a condition of clearance it may take a considerable period of time to implement them: practitioners sometimes use the expression 'Phase III' to describe this phase of some merger cases[289]. Further delay may occur where there are appeals to the EU Courts, either by the undertakings concerned, or by third parties dissatisfied with the decision of the Commission[290].

5. Substantive Analysis

Once the Commission has jurisdiction in relation to a concentration its task is to determine whether it is 'compatible with the internal market' or not.

Article 2(1) sets out certain criteria that the Commission must take into account when making its appraisal[291]. Article 2(2) provides that:

> A concentration which would not significantly impede effective competition in the [internal] market or in a substantial part of it, in particular as a result of the creation or strengthening of a dominant position, shall be declared compatible with the [internal] market.

Article 2(3) provides that:

> A concentration which would significantly impede effective competition, in the [internal] market or in a substantial part of it, in particular as a result of the creation or strengthening of a dominant position, shall be declared incompatible with the [internal] market.

The burden of proof is on the Commission to produce convincing evidence that a merger is incompatible with the internal market[292]. The Court of Justice has held that there is no presumption that a merger is compatible with, or incompatible with, the internal market[293]; rather the Commission must adopt a decision 'in accordance with its assessment of the economic outcome attributable to the merger which is most likely to ensue'[294]. To put the point another way, intervention should be possible only where a merger would be likely to enable firms, individually or collectively, to exercise market power and thereby significantly impede effective competition.

[288] On the role of the Chief Economist see www.ec.europa.eu/dgs/competition/economist/role_en.html.

[289] On commitments see 'Remedies', pp 907–913 later in chapter.

[290] On judicial review of Commission decisions see 'Judicial Review', pp 915–921 later in chapter.

[291] See 'Article 2(1): the appraisal criteria', p 887 later in chapter.

[292] See eg Case C-12/03 P *Commission v Tetra Laval BV* EU:C:2005:87, paras 37–51; Case T-210/01 *General Electric v Commission* EU:T:2005:456, paras 60–64.

[293] Case C-413/06 P *Bertelsmann and Sony Corporation of America v Impala* EU:C:2008:392, para 48; see similarly Case T-210/01 *General Electric v Commission* EU:T:2005:456, para 61.

[294] Case C-413/06 P *Bertelsmann and Sony Corporation of America v Impala* EU:C:2008:392, para 52; see also Case T-79/12 *Cisco Systems v Commission* EU:T:2013:635, para 47, rejecting the contention that the Commission should prove beyond any reasonable doubt that a merger does not lead to competition concerns.

(A) Adoption of the 'significant impediment to effective competition' test

The Commission will declare a merger to be incompatible with the internal market where it would significantly impede effective competition, in particular as a result of the creation or strengthening of a dominant position. This formulation is subtly different from the test in the original Merger Regulation of 1989, which asked whether the merger would create or strengthen a dominant position as a result of which effective competition would be significantly impeded. The change in the substantive test was made in 2004 following a protracted debate which focused, in particular, on the respective merits of a test based on dominance, on the one hand, and on a substantial lessening of competition ('SLC'), on the other; and on the specific question of whether the dominance test left a 'gap' which meant that some mergers that could be harmful to competition could not be challenged under the EUMR. The compromise that emerged from this debate was the significant impediment to effective competition ('SIEC') test.

(i) The dominance/SLC debate

By the time that the original Merger Regulation was adopted there was a reasonable amount of jurisprudence on the meaning of dominance under Article 102, in particular in cases such as *Continental Can v Commission*[295] and *United Brands v Commission*[296]; it was obviously attractive to deploy that jurisprudence for the purpose of merger control. In the years that followed the adoption of the Merger Regulation the Commission was able to adapt the dominance test and to apply it successfully to cases on single-firm dominance[297] and to collective dominance[298]; it also prohibited some vertical mergers under the dominance test[299]. For the most part the EU system of merger control developed very successfully, with one exception: the possibility that it could not be used to deal with problems of 'non-collusive oligopoly'.

(ii) The non-collusive oligopoly gap

The perception that there could be a 'gap'[300] in the coverage of the Merger Regulation arose as a result of the *Airtours/First Choice* decision[301]. Airtours' proposed acquisition of First Choice would reduce the number of major tour operators in the UK from four to three. No firm would be individually dominant after the merger. The Commission prohibited the transaction on the basis that it would create a collective dominant position: however the language it used, in particular in paragraph 54 of its decision, suggested that each firm remaining on the market would be able *unilaterally* to exercise market power, without any need to act in a *coordinated* manner. On appeal the General Court annulled

[295] Case 6/72 *Europemballage and Continental Can v Commission* EU:C:1973:22.

[296] Case 27/76 *United Brands Co v Commission* EU:C:1978:22.

[297] See eg Case M 53 *Aerospatiale-Alenia/de Havilland*, decision of 2 October 1991, OJ [1991] L 334/42: this was the first prohibition decision under the Merger Regulation.

[298] See eg Case M 308 *Kali und Salz* OJ [1994] L 186/38, on appeal Cases C-68/94 and C-30/95 *France v Commission* EU:C:1998:148; Case M 619 *Gencor/Lonrho*, decision of 24 April 1996, OJ [1997] L 11/30, upheld on appeal Case T-102/96 *Gencor v Commission* EU:T:1999:65: this was the first prohibition decision based on collective dominance.

[299] See eg Case M 490 *Nordic Satellite Distribution*, decision of 19 July 1995, OJ [1996] L 53/20.

[300] See generally Kokkoris *Merger Control in Europe: The Gap in the ECMR and National Merger Legislations* (Routledge, 2011).

[301] Case M 1524, decision of 22 September 1999, OJ [2000] L 93/1.

the Commission's decision and equated collective dominance with coordinated effects[302]. It followed that, if the Commission did think that the problem in *Airtours/First Choice* was one of unilateral as opposed to coordinated effects, there was a gap in the Merger Regulation's coverage; if such a gap did exist it was because of the word 'dominance' which did not cover all unilateral effects.

A few examples (Figures 21.2, 21.3 and 21.4) may shed some light on the conundrum. In the following examples we assume that A, B and C produce high-quality products that are differentiated from one another; in other words the market is not one that is particularly conducive to coordinated behaviour[303]. In each case the proposal is that A will merge with B.

Example 1

Before the merger

A	B	C
50	30	20

After the merger

AB	C
80	20

Fig. 21.2

After the merger AB will probably be individually dominant. The merger can be challenged under the dominance test.

Example 2

Before the merger

A	B	C
20	25	55

After the merger

AB	C
45	55

Fig. 21.3

302 Case T-342/99 *Airtours plc v Commission* EU:T:2002:146: see 'Coordinated effects', pp 893–895 later in chapter; for comment on the *Airtours* case see eg O'Donoghue and Feddersen (2002) 39 CML Rev 1171; Stroux 'Collective Dominance under the Merger Regulation: A Serious Evidentiary Reprimand for the Commission' (2002) 27 EL Rev 736; Overd 'After the *Airtours* Appeal' (2002) 23 ECLR 375; Haupt 'Collective Dominance under Article 82 EC and EC Merger Control in the Light of the *Airtours* Judgment' (2002) 23 ECLR 434; Nikpay and Houwen 'Tour de Force or a Little Local Turbulence? A Heretical View on the *Airtours* Judgment' (2003) 24 ECLR 193.

303 See 'Coordinated effects', pp 893–895 later in chapter.

After the merger AB will certainly not be individually dominant since its market share will be less than C's; if the market is not conducive to coordination AB and C will not be collectively dominant either. The merger cannot be challenged under the dominance test.

Example 3

Before the merger

A	B	C
35	20	45

After the merger

AB	C
55	45

Fig. 21.4

After the merger AB will be larger than C, but it is unlikely that, with these market shares, it would be found to be individually dominant; as in Example 2 if the market is not conducive to coordination AB and C will not be collectively dominant either. The merger cannot be challenged under the dominance test.

The key question is whether, in Examples 2 and 3, AB and C might be more able, on an individual basis, to exercise market power after the merger than they were before it; if so there is clearly a case for intervention, but intervention is not possible on the basis of individual or collective dominance, as those terms are currently understood and applied.

(iii) The solution: 'SIEC'

Given the uncertainty raised by *Airtours*, some commentators queried whether dominance was an appropriate test: an alternative would be to ask whether a merger would 'substantially lessen competition' ('SLC')[304]: this is the test in the UK and US[305]. However other commentators were far from convinced that a move to a SLC test was necessary or desirable: the dominance test was firmly established, had worked well in practice, and it was unclear that there really was a non-collusive oligopoly gap or that dominance could not be adapted to deal with it[306].

The solution adopted by the Council in the EUMR of 2004 was disarmingly simple: it retains the vocabulary of Article 2 of the old Merger Regulation but rearranges it in a way that retains the existing law of dominance while at the same time closing the gap.

[304] See eg Whish 'Substantive analysis under the EC Merger Regulation: should the dominance test be replaced by "substantial lessening of competition"?' in *EC Competition Law & Policy Developments & Priorities* (Hellenic Competition Commission, 2002), pp 45–62; speech by Vickers 'How to reform the EC merger test?', 8 November 2002, available at www.nationalarchives.gov.uk; Fingleton 'Does Collective Dominance Provide Suitable Housing for All Anti-Competitive Oligopolistic Mergers' [2002] Fordham Corporate Law Institute (ed Hawk), 181–199.

[305] See ch 22, 'The "Substantial Lessening of Competition" Test', pp 959–968.

[306] See eg Böge and Muller 'From the Market Dominance Test to the SLC Test: Are There Any Reasons for a Change?' (2002) 23 ECLR 495; Levy 'Dominance vs SLC: A Subtle Distinction', 8 November 2002, available at www.ibanet.org.

The wording within each of Articles 2(2) and 2(3) was simply reversed. The test is now whether a merger would lead to an SIEC, in particular by creating or strengthening a dominant position[307]. The revised formulation envisages that most cases will be dealt with under the dominance standard as a result of the inclusion of the words '*in particular*': this responds to the concern that a repeal of the dominance test would lead to uncertainty and 'undo' years of know-how and decisional practice of the Commission: recital 26 of the EUMR specifically refers to the desirability of preserving the existing jurisprudence and decisional practice under the old Regulation[308]. However the SIEC test does not make dominance the exclusive test, and enables the Commission to prohibit or require the modification of a merger that would not create or strengthen a dominant position but would 'significantly impede effective competition'. Recital 25 makes clear that this formulation is intended to provide jurisdiction to deal with the 'gap', that is to say the problem of non-collusive oligopoly. The application of the substantive test to cases of non-collusive oligopoly since 2004 will be considered later[309].

(iv) The need for a causal link between the concentration and the SIEC

In *France v Commission*[310] the Court of Justice held that there must be a causal link between the concentration and the deterioration of the competitive structure of the market for the EUMR to apply. In that case the Court of Justice was considering whether a 'failing firm' defence existed under the EUMR[311]. It held that a concentration should not be blocked where the target would have failed anyway and its market share would have accrued to the acquirer, since the concentration did not cause the harm to competition. In *De Beers/LVMH*[312] the Commission's clearance was specifically based on the absence of any causal link between the creation of the joint venture and the strengthening of De Beer's dominant position in the market for rough diamonds.

(v) The 'counterfactual'

The application of the SIEC test involves a comparison of the prospects for competition with the merger against the situation without the merger: the 'counterfactual'[313]. In many cases the conditions of competition at the time of the merger will be the counterfactual; however the Commission may take into account future changes to the market that can reasonably be predicted[314].

[307] See Röller and de la Mano 'The Impact of the New Substantive Test in European Merger Control' (2006) 2 European Competition Journal 8; Maier-Rigaud and Parplies 'Five Years After The Introduction of the SIEC Test: What Explains the Drop in Enforcement Activity?' (2009) ECLR 565; Levy 'The SIEC Test Five Years On: Has it Made a Difference?' (2010) 6 European Competition Journal 211; Calviño 'When Do Mergers Raise Concerns? An Analysis of the Assessment Carried Out by the European Commission under the New Merger Regulation' (2011) 2 JECLAP 521.

[308] The Commission's *Guidelines on the assessment of horizontal mergers* OJ [2004] C 31/5 make the same point at para 4.

[309] See 'Non-coordinated effects', pp 891–893 later in chapter.

[310] Cases C-68/94 and C-30/95 EU:C:1998:148; this case was decided under the original Merger Regulation: there is no reason to suppose that the requirement of a causal link would not apply in the case of the reformulated substantive test.

[311] See 'The "failing firm" defence', pp 898–899 later in chapter.

[312] Case M 2333, decision of 25 July 2001, paras 112–114; see similarly Case M 2816 *Ernst & Young France/Andersen France*, decision of 5 September 2002, paras 75 and 90; Case M 4381 *JCI/VB/FIAMM*, decision of 5 October 2007, paras 708ff.

[313] *Guidelines on the assessment of horizontal mergers* OJ [2004] C 31/5, para 9; on the counterfactual see further ch 20 'The counterfactual' p 842.

[314] *Guidelines on the assessment of horizontal mergers*, para 9.

(vi) Article 2(1): the appraisal criteria

Article 2(1) of the EUMR sets out a list of 'appraisal criteria' which the Commission must take into account when investigating concentrations. It provides that:

> In making this appraisal, the Commission shall take into account:
>
> (a) the need to maintain and develop effective competition within the [internal] market in view of, among other things, the structure of all the markets concerned and the actual or potential competition from undertakings located either within or outwith the [Union];
>
> (b) the market position of the undertakings concerned and their economic and financial power, the alternatives available to suppliers and users, their access to supplies or markets, any legal or other barriers to entry, supply and demand trends for the relevant goods and services, the interests of the intermediate and ultimate consumers, and the development of technical and economic progress provided that it is to consumers' advantage and does not form an obstacle to competition.

The information required in relation to affected markets by Form CO reflects the appraisal criteria set out in Article 2(1). The list of factors in Article 2(1) is not exhaustive: the Commission must consider all matters relevant to the assessment of a merger. Article 2(1) does not establish a hierarchy, giving greater weight to one assessment factor than another; the impact that the different appraisal criteria have on the Commission's determination will vary from case to case.

(B) Publication of merger guidelines

The Commission has published three texts of particular importance to the substantive assessment of mergers, the *Notice on Market Definition*[315], the *Guidelines on the assessment of horizontal mergers*[316] and the *Guidelines on the assessment of non-horizontal mergers*[317]. Their content can be divided into four main categories: market definition, horizontal mergers, vertical mergers and conglomerate mergers. The remainder of this section will proceed on this basis.

(C) Market definition

The substantive assessment of mergers under the EUMR begins with a definition of the relevant product and geographic markets, the main purpose of which is to identify the competitive constraints upon the undertakings concerned[318]. Some commentators believe that too much emphasis is placed on market definition in EU merger control, not least because there are econometric techniques that make it possible to predict whether a particular merger would lead to an increase in prices without a formal determination of the relevant market or of market power[319]. Whatever the merits of this opinion may be, current practice assigns an important role to market definition: notifying parties are required to identify any 'affected markets' in their Form CO (see the following section). In *France v Commission*[320] the Court of Justice held that a proper definition of the relevant market is a precondition for any assessment of the effect of a concentration on competition under the EUMR[321].

[315] OJ [1997] C 372/5. [316] OJ [2004] C 31/5. [317] OJ [2008] C 265/6.

[318] *Notice on Market Definition* OJ [1997] C 372/5, para 2.

[319] See 'Quantitative tests' p 889 later in chapter.

[320] Cases C-68/94 etc EU:C:1998:148.

[321] Ibid, para 143; subsequent judgments have regularly repeated this point: see eg Case T-151/05 *Nederlandse Vakbond Varkenshouders v Commission* EU:T:2009:144, para 51.

Market definition, including the Commission's *Notice on Market Definition*, has been discussed in detail in chapter 1 to which the reader is referred[322]; also of interest is a report prepared for the Commission on geographical market definition in merger cases which contains some suggestions for change in current practice[323]. A few specific points about market definition under the EUMR follow.

(i) Form CO: 'affected markets'

Sections 6 to 8 of Form CO require the notifying parties to provide information in relation to 'affected markets'. Affected markets are defined to mean, in the case of horizontal relationships, relevant markets where two or more parties to a concentration have a combined market share of 20% or more; and, in the case of vertical relationships, where their individual or combined market share is more than 30% at one or more levels of the market. The information required in relation to these affected markets is substantial, including an estimate of the total size of the market, the parties' market shares for each of the last three financial years, the HHI before and after the merger, the structure of supply and demand, details of barriers to entry and analyses, reports, surveys and comparable documents from the last two years relevant to a competitive assessment of the affected markets. The *quid pro quo* for the supply of such extensive information is that the Commission should be able to make an assessment of the case within the time limits of the EUMR. As noted earlier the information contained in Form CO must be accurate and complete[324]; if it is not the notification may be declared incomplete, in which case the time within which a decision must be made will not have begun to run. This is why extensive preparation in advance of notification, including contact with DG COMP, is so crucial[325]. It is important to understand that one merger might involve a number of affected markets: multi-product firms may have many overlapping products. For example in the case of *Bayer/Aventis Crop Science*[326] the Commission considered that there were in the region of 130 affected markets for crop protection, professional pest control and animal health products.

(ii) Commission decisions

In the period up to 8 December 2017 the Commission had adopted more than 6,000 decisions under the EUMR, and these contain many useful insights into its likely definition of the relevant market. Practitioners refer to the decisional practice of the Commission for guidance when defining the relevant market. However in many clearance decisions the Commission does not reach a conclusion on market definition, since it is clear that to do so would not materially affect its assessment; the Commission will say that, however the market is defined, it is satisfied that the concentration would not be incompatible with the internal market.

(iii) Effect of decisions on market definition

In *Coca-Cola Co v Commission*[327] the General Court stated clearly that a market definition in an earlier decision of the Commission could not be binding in the case of a subsequent

[322] See ch 1, 'Market definition', pp 25–42.

[323] See Fletcher and Lyons, *Geographic Market Definition in European Commission Merger Control*, January 2016, available at www.ec.europa.eu.

[324] See 'Notification' pp 876–878 earlier in chapter. [325] Ibid.

[326] Case M 2547, decision of 17 April 2002, OJ [2004] L 107/1; see similarly Case M 3465 *Syngenta CP/Advanta*, decision of 17 August 2004.

[327] Cases T-125/97 and T-127/97 EU:T:2000:84; it follows that notifying parties should not expect that the Commission will define a relevant market in the way it did in a previous decision: see Case T-151/05 *NVV v Commission* EU:T:2009:144, paras 136–140.

investigation, either by the Commission itself or a national court or competition authority: each case must turn on the particular facts and circumstances prevailing at the time[328]. However the Commission is entitled to take into account its previous decisions where there are no indications that the conditions of competition have since changed[329].

(iv) Quantitative tests

The Commission increasingly uses quantitative techniques and statistical tests to help it to define the relevant market and to assess the likely effects of a merger[330]. In *Unilever/Sara Lee*[331] the Commission used a merger simulation model to predict that a hypothetical monopolist of male deodorants would be able to increase prices by 5% profitably, which indicated that male deodorants were in a separate market from female or unisex deodorants.

(D) Horizontal mergers

The Commission's *Guidelines on the assessment of horizontal mergers*[332] ('the *Horizontal merger guidelines*' or 'the *Guidelines*') provide guidance as to how the Commission assesses concentrations when the undertakings concerned are actual or potential competitors on the same relevant market[333]. The *Guidelines* deal in turn with:

- market shares and concentration thresholds
- the likelihood that a merger would have anti-competitive effects
- countervailing buyer power
- the possibility of entry into the market as a competitive constraint
- efficiencies
- failing firms.

This sequence will be retained in the text that follows. Paragraph 13 stresses that the *Guidelines* are not to be applied in a mechanical manner in each and every case; rather the competitive analysis in a particular case will be based on an overall assessment of the foreseeable impact of the merger in the light of the relevant factors and conditions. In *Sun Chemical Group v Commission*[334] the General Court held that the Commission enjoys a discretion enabling it to take into account or not to take into account particular factors[335].

(i) Market shares and concentration levels

The *Horizontal merger guidelines* note that market shares and concentration levels provide useful first indications of the market structure and of the competitive importance

[328] On this issue see Bokobza, Kadar and Ringborg '*Viking Steel*: The SSAB/Rautaruukki merger' Competition Merger Brief 1/2014, available at www.ec.europa.eu/competition/publications/cpn.

[329] Case T-699/14 *Topps Europe Ltd v Commission* EU:T:2017:2, para 93.

[330] See Buettner, Federico and Lorincz 'The Use of Quantitative Economic Techniques in EU Merger Control' (2016) available at www.ec.europa.eu; Oldale and Padilla 'EU Merger Assessment of Upward Pricing Pressure: Making Sense of UPP, GUPPI, and the Like' (2013) 4 JECLAP 375; see further ch 20, 'Evidence', pp 840–842, on merger simulation.

[331] Case M 5658 *Unilever/Sara Lee*, decision of 17 November 2010, paras 92–94.

[332] OJ [2004] C 31/5; note that prior to the adoption of the *Horizontal merger guidelines* the Commission had published two reports on the topic, *The Economics of Unilateral Effects* and *The Economics of Tacit Collusion*, each prepared by Ivaldi, Julien, Seabright and Tirole: the reports can be accessed on DG COMP's website; for discussion of the *Guidelines* see Voigt and Schmidt 'The Commission's Guidelines on Horizontal Mergers: Improvement or Deterioration?' (2004) 41 CML Rev 1583.

[333] *Horizontal merger guidelines*, para 5.

[334] Case T-282/06 EU:T:2007:203.

[335] Ibid, para 57.

of the merging parties and their competitors[336]. The reference to 'useful first indications' is important: market shares and concentration levels are simply a device for conducting a first screening of a merger: they would not normally be determinative in themselves of the outcome of a case[337].

(a) Market shares

The Commission usually looks at current market shares, although it may adjust them if it is certain that changes are about to occur because of exit, entry or expansion[338]; and in some industries, for example where there are 'large, lumpy' orders—such as irregular purchases of major capital equipment—it may be necessary to look at historical data[339]. Market shares of 50% or more may in themselves be evidence of the existence of a dominant position, although they are not normally conclusive[340]; and the Commission may find a dominant position in the case of market shares between 40 and 50%, and even sometimes of less than 40%, depending on the other factors relevant to the case[341]. In *Ryanair Holdings plc v Commission*[342] the General Court rejected Ryanair's argument that the Commission had placed 'excessive weight' on the market shares that the merged entity would have had on some air routes[343]. The *Horizontal merger guidelines* state that a merger may be presumed to be compatible with the internal market where the market share of the undertakings concerned does not exceed 25%[344].

(b) Concentration levels

The *Horizontal merger guidelines* state that the overall concentration level in a market may provide useful information about the competitive situation, and that it may use the HHI in order to measure it[345]. The Commission is unlikely to be concerned about a market with a post-merger HHI of less than 1,000[346]. The Commission is also unlikely to be concerned where there would be a post-merger HHI between 1,000 and 2,000 and a delta[347] below 250, or a post-merger HHI above 2,000 and a delta below 150, unless there were special circumstances such as:

- the merger involves a potential entrant or a recent entrant with a small market share
- one or more of the parties are important innovators in ways not reflected in market shares

336 *Horizontal merger guidelines*, para 14.

337 On this point see eg Case M 6458 *Universal Music Group/EMI Music*, decision of 21 September 2012, paras 300–303.

338 *Horizontal merger guidelines*, para 15; a point not made in the *Horizontal merger guidelines* is that sometimes the Commission will, when investigating one merger, take into account the fact that a subsequent notification has been received in relation to a different merger in the same sector that will have an impact on the future competitive structure of the market: see eg Case M 938 *Price Waterhouse/Coopers & Lybrand*, decision of 15 October 1997, OJ [1997] L 50/27, paras 108–111; Case M 2389 *Shell/DEA*, decision of 20 December 2001, para 21; Case M 4600 *TUI/First Choice*, decision of 4 June 2007, paras 66–68 and Case M 6214 *Seagate/HDD Business of Samsung*, decision of 19 October 2011, paras 10–18 (discussing the 'priority principle' for the assessment of parallel transactions).

339 *Horizontal merger guidelines*, para 15.

340 On this point see Case T-342/07 *Ryanair Holdings plc v Commission* EU:T:2010:280, para 41 and the judgments cited therein.

341 *Horizontal merger guidelines*, para 17.

342 Case T-342/07 EU:T:2010:280.

343 Ibid, paras 41–60.

344 *Horizontal merger guidelines*, para 18, referring to recital 32 of the EUMR; note however that this 'safe harbour' does not exist in the case of a collective dominant position involving the undertakings concerned and other third parties.

345 *Horizontal merger guidelines*, para 16; the HHI is explained in ch 1, 'Market concentration and the Herfindahl-Hirschman Index', pp 43–44.

346 *Horizontal merger guidelines*, para 19.

347 The delta refers to the change in the HHI as a result of the merger.

- there are significant cross-shareholdings among the market participants
- one of the merging firms is a maverick firm with a high likelihood of disrupting coordinated conduct
- indications of past or ongoing coordination or facilitating practices are present
- one or more of the merging parties had a pre-merger market share of 50% or more[348].

The *Horizontal merger guidelines* say that HHIs below the thresholds set out earlier may be used as an indicator of the absence of competition concerns, but that they do not give rise to a presumption either of the existence or the absence of such concerns[349]. In *Sun Chemical Group BV v Commission*[350] the General Court held, however, that 'the greater the margin by which those thresholds are exceeded, the more the HHI values will be indicative of competition concerns'[351]. In *Spar Österreichische Warenhandels v Commission*[352] the General Court rejected an argument that the Commission had unlawfully failed to use the HHI when assessing the effects of a horizontal merger[353].

In *Cisco Systems v Commission*[354] the General Court agreed with the Commission's assessment of *Microsoft/Skype*[355], and in particular that very high market shares and a high degree of concentration on the narrowest possible market for consumer communications were not in themselves indicative of a degree of market power that would significantly impede effective competition.

(ii) **Possible anti-competitive effects of horizontal mergers**

The *Horizontal merger guidelines* discuss the possible anti-competitive effects of horizontal mergers from paragraphs 22 to 63, dealing in turn with non-coordinated effects[356] and coordinated effects; there is also a brief discussion of mergers with potential competitors. The footnotes in the *Guidelines* contain many references to the case law of the EU Courts and the decisional practice of the Commission: due to constraints of space these judgments and decisions are not reproduced in the text that follows, but the reader should be aware of this useful reference point.

(a) Non-coordinated effects

Paragraph 24 of the *Horizontal merger guidelines* explains that a horizontal merger may remove important competitive constraints on one or more firms in the market, thereby enhancing their market power and leading to significant price increases. Paragraph 25 notes that generally this will happen as a result of the creation or strengthening of a dominant position on the part of one firm whose market share, after the merger, will be appreciably larger than its next competitor. However the same paragraph also refers to the possibility of non-collusive oligopoly, that is to say a situation in which the firms remaining in the market after the merger will be able to exercise market power, and therefore increase prices, even though there is little likelihood of coordination among them and even though they are not individually dominant.

Paragraph 26 explains that a number of factors are relevant to a determination of whether non-coordinated effects might occur, but explains that not all of them must

348 *Horizontal merger guidelines*, para 20. 349 Ibid, para 21.

350 Case T-282/06 EU:T:2007:203. 351 Ibid, para 138.

352 Case T-405/08 EU:T:2013:306; the merger in question was Case M 5047 *Rewe/ADEG*, decision of 23 June 2008.

353 Case T-405/08 *Spar Österreichische Warenhandels* EU:T:2013:306, paras 64–66; in any event the post-merger HHI values did not provide any clear indication of the existence of competition problems: paras 69–70.

354 Case T-79/12 EU:T:2013:635. 355 Case M 6281, decision of 7 October 2011.

356 Note that the expression 'unilateral' effects is sometimes used as an alternative for non-coordinated effects: see fn 27 of the *Horizontal merger guidelines*.

be present in a particular case and that the factors set out in the *Guidelines* are not an exhaustive list. The following factors are listed:

- **the merging firms will have large market shares**: the larger the addition of market share, the more likely it is that the merger will produce an SIEC[357]
- **the merging firms are close competitors**: the higher the degree of substitutability between the merging firms' products, the more likely it is that the merger will produce an SIEC[358]
- **customers of the merging parties will have limited possibilities of switching to other suppliers**[359]
- **competitors are unlikely to increase supply if prices increase**: in this case the merging parties will have an incentive to reduce output to less than the levels prior to the merger, thereby increasing price[360]
- **the merging firms will be able to hinder expansion by competitors**: for example they may control patents or other types of intellectual property that would make expansion or entry by rivals more difficult[361]
- **the merger would remove an important competitive force**: for example the removal of a particularly innovative firm as a competitor[362], or a merger between two particularly innovative firms, may change the competitive dynamics of the market considerably[363].

The most common ground for intervention on the part of the Commission is the possibility of non-coordinated effects arising from horizontal mergers. Recent prohibition decisions such as *Ryanair/Aer Lingus III*[364], *UPS/TNT Express*[365], *Hutchison 3G UK/Telefónica UK*[366], *HeidelbergCement/Schwenk/Cemex Hungary/Cemex Croatia*[367], and *Deutsche Börse/London Stock Exchange*[368] were adopted for this reason. In each of these cases the merged firm would have held a very high market share and been protected by high barriers to entry and expansion; the Commission prohibited the mergers to prevent firms from acquiring the *unilateral* ability to raise prices in a way that would be privately profitable to themselves and harmful to consumers.

The Commission has accepted remedies because of non-coordinated effects in several Phase II cases in recent years[369]. In *T-Mobile/tele.ring*[370] the Commission required a

[357] Ibid, para 27.

[358] Ibid, paras 28–30; para 29 discusses various methods of evaluating cross-substitutability eg through customer preference surveys, estimating cross-price elasticities and diversion ratios; see eg Case M 7758 *Hutchison 3G Italy/WIND/JV*, decision of 1 September 2016, paras 772–813.

[359] *Horizontal merger guidelines*, para 31. [360] Ibid, paras 32–35. [361] Ibid, para 36.

[362] Ibid, para 37; see eg Case M 5650 *T-Mobile/Orange*, decision of 1 March 2010, where the Commission's concerns included the possible elimination of the mobile operator H3G (Three) from the market.

[363] *Horizontal merger guidelines*, para 38; see eg Case M 5675 *Syngenta/Monsanto sunflower seed business*, decision of 17 November 2010, where the Commission's concerns included the elimination of one of the most important innovators in the market for sunflower seeds.

[364] Case M 6663, decision of 27 February 2013.

[365] Case M 6570, decision of 30 January 2013, annulled on appeal for procedural reasons Case T-194/13 *United Parcel Service v Commission* EU:T:2017:144; the Commission has appealed to the Court of Justice Case C-265/17 P *Commission v UPS*, not yet decided.

[366] Case M 7612, decision of 11 May 2016, on appeal Case T-399/16 *CK Telecoms Investments v Commission*, not yet decided.

[367] Case M 7878, decision of 5 April 2017, on appeal Case T-380/17 *HeidelbergCement and Schwenk Cement v Commission*, not yet decided.

[368] Case M 7995, decision of 29 March 2017.

[369] See 'Clearances subject to commitments', pp 929–931 later in chapter.

[370] Case M 3916, decision of 26 April 2006; see Lübking '*T-Mobile Austria/tele.ring*: Remedying the loss of a maverick' (2006) 2 Competition Policy Newsletter 46.

remedy as a result of non-coordinated effects in an oligopolistic market where the number of mobile telephony operators in Austria would be reduced from five to four, and the merging parties would not become the market leader: in other words this was a case of non-collusive oligopoly that the adoption of the SIEC test was designed to address[371]. Similar findings of non-collusive oligopoly in the mobile telephony sector were found in *Hutchison 3G Austria/Orange Austria*[372], *Hutchison 3G UK/Telefónica Ireland*[373], *Telefónica Deutschland/E-Plus*[374] and *Hutchison 3G UK/Telefónica UK*[375]. A further case is *BASF/CIBA*[376] where the Commission accepted commitments within a Phase I investigation.

In *Microsoft/LinkedIn*[377] the Commission found that the merger might foreclose competing professional social networks from offering greater privacy protection and thereby restrict consumer choice; the merger was cleared subject to commitments. In *Dow/Du Pont*[378] one of the Commission's theories of harm was that the merger would have reduced innovation in the pesticide sector; the parties agreed to divest almost the entirety of Du Pont's global R&D organisation[379].

(b) Coordinated effects

Paragraph 39 of the *Horizontal merger guidelines* explains that in some markets the structure may be such that firms will consider it possible, economically rational, and hence preferable, to adopt on a sustainable basis a course of action aimed at selling at increased prices. Some mergers might lead to an SIEC by increasing the likelihood that firms will be able to behave in a coordinated manner without entering into an agreement or resorting to a concerted practice contrary to Article 101 TFEU. Such coordination might concern prices, but it could also occur in relation to levels of production, the expansion of capacity, the allocation of markets or contracts in bidding markets[380].

Paragraph 41 says that coordination is more likely to occur where it is fairly simple to reach a common understanding on the terms of coordination. It adds that three further conditions must be satisfied for coordination to be sustainable: these are taken from paragraph 62 of the General Court's judgment in *Airtours v Commission*[381]. First it must be possible for the coordinating firms to monitor whether the terms of coordination are being adhered to; secondly, there must be some credible deterrent mechanism to maintain the discipline of the coordinating firms and to keep it internally stable; and thirdly there must be no constraint from outsiders that could jeopardise the results expected from coordination and make it externally unstable. In *Bertelsmann v Impala*[382] the Court of Justice has said that these three conditions should not be applied in a mechanical way: they should be looked at taking into account 'the overall economic mechanism of

[371] See 'The non-collusive oligopoly gap', pp 883–885 earlier in chapter; another example of non-collusive oligopoly is Case M 3687 *Johnson & Johnson/Guidant*, decision of 25 August 2005, paras 312–325 in relation to endovascular stents.

[372] Case M 6497, decision of 12 December 2012.

[373] Case M 6992, decision of 28 May 2014.

[374] Case M 7018, decision of 2 July 2014.

[375] Case M 7612, decision of 11 May 2016, on appeal Case T-399/16 *CK Telecoms UK Investments v Commission*, not yet decided.

[376] Case M 5355, decision of 12 March 2009.

[377] Case M 8124, decision of 6 December 2016, on which see the *Competition Merger Brief* 1/2017, available at www.ec.europa.eu; see similarly Case M 7217 *Facebook/WhatsApp*, decision of 3 October 2014.

[378] Case M 7932, decision of 27 March 2017, on which see the *Competition Merger Brief* 2/2017, available at www.ec.europa.eu.

[379] See also Case M 7278 *GE/Alstom*, decision of 8 September 2015, paras 944–1077; see generally 'EU merger control and innovation' *Competition Policy Brief* 1/2016, available at www.ec.europa.eu.

[380] *Horizontal merger guidelines*, para 40.

[381] Case T-342/99 EU:T:2002:146.

[382] Case C-413/06 P EU:C:2008:392, para 125.

a hypothetical tacit coordination'. The conditions for coordination are then explored in succeeding paragraphs of the *Guidelines*. They point out that a reduction in the number of firms in the market may be a factor that facilitates coordination; but also that other factors, such as the removal of a 'maverick' firm likely to disrupt an oligopoly, need to be examined[383]. In deciding whether coordination is likely to result from the merger the Commission will look at evidence of past coordination or evidence of coordination in similar markets[384]. In *Impala v Commission*[385] the General Court observed that the close alignment of prices over a significant period of time might, together with other factors, be sufficient to prove evidence of past coordination.

The *Guidelines* discuss the following factors:

- **reaching terms of coordination**: this is more likely to occur if it is easy to arrive at a common perception as to how the coordination should occur[386]. A number of matters are relevant when determining whether coordination would be easy, though these should not be applied in a mechanistic way[387]:
  - is the economic environment simple and stable?
  - are there a few, rather than many, firms in the market?
  - are the products homogeneous rather than complex?
  - are price and demand conditions stable rather than constantly changing?
  - is the market one in which there is little innovation?
  - in the case of coordination by way of market division would it be easy to allocate customers, for example on the basis of geography?
  - do other factors in the market increase transparency and so make it easier to coordinate prices?
  - are the firms symmetric in terms of cost structures, market shares, capacity levels and levels of vertical integration?
- **monitoring deviations**: coordination will work only if the coordinating firms are able to monitor one another to ensure that no one is cheating, for example by lowering price, expanding output or improving quality. Markets must be sufficiently transparent to prevent this happening[388]. Paragraphs 50 and 51 of the *Guidelines* discuss factors relevant to a determination of transparency: for example transparency is higher where transactions take place on a public exchange than where they are negotiated privately on a bilateral basis
- **deterrent mechanisms**: coordination will work only if there is a sufficient threat that there will be retaliation against a firm that deviates[389]. Paragraphs 53 to 55 of the *Guidelines* discuss the credibility of deterrent mechanisms: the coordinating firms must have an economic incentive to retaliate against any firms that deviate; and the deviation does not necessarily have to be in the same market as the coordination
- **reactions of outsiders**: coordination will work only if there is no effective competitive constraint from non-coordinating actual or potential competitors[390].

In *Sony/Bertelsmann*[391] the Commission originally had concerns that the merger might lead to coordinated effects, but, during its Phase II investigation, reached the conclusion

[383] *Horizontal merger guidelines*, para 42. [384] Ibid, para 43.
[385] Case T-464/04 EU:T:2006:216, paras 252–254, upheld on appeal Case C-413/06 P EU:C:2008:392, paras 124–128.
[386] *Horizontal merger guidelines*, para 44. [387] Ibid, paras 45–48. [388] Ibid, para 49.
[389] Ibid, para 52. [390] Ibid, paras 56–57. [391] Case M 3333, decision of 19 July 2004.

that the merger should be cleared unconditionally. In *Impala v Commission*[392] a third party successfully challenged the Commission's clearance decision; the General Court considered that the market was a transparent one in which coordination was plausible[393]. However the merging parties successfully appealed to the Court of Justice[394]; it considered that the General Court had committed a number of errors of law and that, specifically in relation to tacit coordination, it had failed to consider the transparency of the recorded music market 'by reference to a postulated monitoring mechanism forming part of a plausible theory of tacit co-ordination'[395]. The Court therefore set aside the judgment of the General Court and referred the matter back to it; however it was not necessary to adjudicate on the appeal due to a subsequent alteration in the market[396].

The Commission has been concerned about coordinated effects in several cases. In *Areva/Urenco/ETC*[397] various commitments, including a cessation of the flow of commercially sensitive information between a joint venture and its parents, were required as a condition of clearance. Commitments were also required as a condition of clearance in *Linde/BOC*[398], including the divestment of various wholesale supply contracts for helium and the termination of structural links, through a series of Asian joint ventures, between the merged entity and a competitor, Air Liquide. In *Travelport/Worldspan*[399] the Commission concluded, following a Phase II investigation, that a 'four to three' merger in the market for global distribution services would not give rise to coordinated effects since the complexity of the pricing structure and product offerings in that case limited the transparency of the market and therefore the possibility of successfully monitoring coordinated behaviour. In *ABF/GBI Business*[400] remedies were required to address the reduction from three to two competitors on the Spanish and Portuguese markets for yeast. In two Phase II cases in the cement sector[401] the Commission noted that the sector is prone to coordination, but cleared both mergers unconditionally since they were unlikely to make possible coordination easier, more stable or more effective. The Commission also identified the possibility of coordinated effects in *TeliaSonera/Telenor/JV*[402], *Hutchison 3G Italy/Wind/JV*[403] and in *AB InBev/SABMiller*[404].

[392] Case T-464/04 EU:T:2006:216; for comment see Völcker and O'Daly 'The Court of First Instance's *Impala* Judgment: A Judicial Counter-Reformation in EC Merger Control?' (2006) 27 ECLR 589; Brandenburger and Janssens 'The *Impala* Judgment: Does EC Merger Control Need to be Fixed or Fine-Tuned?' (2007) 3 Competition Policy International 301.

[393] Case T-464/04 EU:T:2006:216, paras 288–294.

[394] Case C-413/06 P *Bertelsmann AG and Sony Corporation of America v Impala* EU:C:2008:392; for comment see Golding 'The *Impala* Case: A Quiet Conclusion but a Lasting Legacy' (2010) 31 ECLR 261 and Luebking and Ohrlander 'The Joint Venture Sony/BMG: final ruling by the European Court of Justice' (2009) 2 Competition Policy Newsletter 68.

[395] Case C-413/06 P EU:C:2008:392, paras 117–134.

[396] Case T-464/04 *Impala v Commission* EU:T:2009:225; note that, while the litigation in the EU Courts was proceeding, the Commission adopted a second decision clearing the Sony/Bertelsmann merger, Case M 3333, decision of 3 October 2007: see Lübking, Kijewski, Dupont, Jehanno and Eberl (2007) 3 Competition Policy Newsletter 85.

[397] Case M 3099, decision of 6 October 2004.

[398] Case M 4141, decision of 6 June 2006.

[399] Case M 4523, decision of 21 August 2007.

[400] Case M 4980, decision of 23 September 2008; for comment see Amelio, de la Mano, Maximiano and Porubsky 'ABF/GBI Business: coordinated effects baked again' (2009) 1 Competition Policy Newsletter 91.

[401] See Case M 7009 *Holcim/Cemex West*, decision of 5 June 2014, paras 126–290 and Case M 7054 *Cemex/Holcim assets*, decision of 9 September 2014.

[402] Case M 7419; the parties withdrew the notification before the Commission had adopted a decision.

[403] Case M 7758, decision of 1 September 2016, paras 954–1211.

[404] Case M 7881, decision of 24 May 2016, paras 52–106.

(c) Mergers with a potential competitor

Paragraphs 58 to 60 of the *Horizontal merger guidelines* discuss mergers with potential competitors. Such a merger could lead to non-coordinated, or coordinated, effects where the potential competitor significantly constrains the behaviour of the firms active on the market. This is the case if the potential competitor possesses assets that could easily be used to enter the market without incurring significant sunk costs. Paragraph 60 states that for a merger with a potential competitor to give rise to significant anti-competitive effects two conditions must be satisfied: first, the potential competitors must already exert a significant constraining influence; and second, there must be a lack of other potential competitors which could maintain competitive pressure after the merger.

(d) Mergers creating or strengthening buyer power

Paragraphs 61 to 63 of the *Horizontal merger guidelines* explain that mergers that create or strengthen the market power of a buyer may lead to an SIEC where the merged entity is likely to use its buyer power vis-à-vis its suppliers in order to foreclose competitors. However the Commission recognises that buyer power may be beneficial for competition, in particular if it leads to lower costs that are passed on to consumers. Paragraph 63 states that the Commission will analyse the competitive conditions in upstream markets and evaluate the positive and negative effects of increased buyer power, which is what it did in *AB InBev/SABMiller*[405].

(iii) Countervailing buyer power

Paragraph 64 of the *Horizontal merger guidelines* explains that the competitive pressure on a supplier can come not only from competitors but also from a customer if it has countervailing buyer power, that is to say bargaining strength vis-à-vis a seller due to its size, commercial significance and its ability to switch to alternative suppliers. The Commission will consider to what extent a buyer could immediately switch to other suppliers, credibly threaten to integrate vertically (and therefore self-supply) or sponsor upstream expansion or entry; it is more likely that large and sophisticated customers will have this kind of countervailing buyer power than smaller firms in a fragmented industry[406]. In *Sun Chemical Group v Commission*[407] the General Court rejected an argument by a third party objecting to the clearance of a merger that the Commission had failed to apply the *Guidelines* on countervailing power correctly[408].

(iv) Entry

Paragraph 68 of the *Horizontal merger guidelines* explains that if entry into a market is sufficiently easy a merger is unlikely to lead to an SIEC: for entry to amount to a sufficient competitive constraint it must be shown to be likely, timely and sufficient:

- **likelihood of entry**: entry must be sufficiently profitable taking into account the price effects of injecting additional output into the market and the potential responses of the incumbents on the market; the amount of sunk costs will be relevant to the analysis[409]. Barriers to entry include:

[405] Ibid, paras 318–329.

[406] *Horizontal merger guidelines*, para 65; for comment see Inderst and Mazzarotto 'Can the SIEC Test be Used to Assess Effects From Buyer Power?' (2017) 8 JECLAP 185.

[407] Case T-282/06 EU:T:2007:203.

[408] Ibid, paras 209–217; the merger in question was Case M 4071 *Apollo/Akzo Nobel IAR*, decision of 29 May 2006.

[409] *Horizontal merger guidelines*, para 69.

- legal advantages such as regulatory rules limiting the number of market participants or tariff and non-tariff trade barriers
- technical advantages such as access to essential facilities, natural resources, R&D and intellectual property rights
- incumbency advantages such as brand loyalty, established relationships with customers and other reputational advantages[410]

- **timeliness**: entry will be regarded as a competitive constraint only where it would be sufficiently swift and sustained to deter or defeat the exercise of market power; what constitutes an appropriate time period for entry will depend on the characteristics and dynamics of the market, but it should normally occur within two years[411]
- **sufficiency**: entry must be of sufficient scope and magnitude to deter or defeat the anti-competitive effects of the merger[412].

(v) Efficiencies

Recital 29 of the EUMR says that, when determining the impact of a merger on competition, it is appropriate to take account of any substantiated and likely efficiencies put forward by the undertakings concerned; the recital adds that the Commission should publish guidance on the conditions under which it may take efficiencies into account[413]. This it has done in paragraphs 76 to 88 of the *Horizontal merger guidelines*. In *Ryanair Holdings plc v Commission*[414] Ryanair argued that the Commission had made a manifest error in assessing Ryanair's claim that the concentration would lead to efficiencies; the General Court rejected the argument, and was content to cite the Commission's *Horizontal merger guidelines* and to determine whether it had applied them correctly[415]. The Commission explains in paragraph 76 that efficiencies brought about by a merger may counteract the effects on competition and the potential harm to consumers that would otherwise have occurred. In making its appraisal of a merger the Commission takes all relevant factors into account including the development of technical and economic progress, as set out in the appraisal criteria in Article 2(1) of the EUMR. It is important to understand that this approach means that there is no 'efficiency defence'—if the merger will lead to an SIEC it cannot be saved on efficiency grounds: rather the Commission will factor any possible efficiencies into its overall assessment of whether the merger will lead to an SIEC.

Paragraph 78 explains that, for efficiencies to be taken into account, they must produce a benefit to consumers, be merger-specific and be verifiable; these conditions are cumulative:

- **benefit to consumers**: efficiencies should be substantial and timely and should benefit consumers in the relevant markets where it is likely that competition problems might occur[416]. The efficiency gain might be lower prices, though cost reductions

[410] Ibid, para 71. [411] Ibid, para 74. [412] Ibid, para 75.

[413] Compare the *Horizontal merger guidelines* on efficiencies with the Commission's *Guidelines on the application of Article [101(3)] of the Treaty* OJ [2004] C 101/97, paras 48–72, which are clearly motivated by similar considerations; the *Article 101(3) Guidelines* are discussed in ch 4, 'The Commission's approach in the *Article 101(3) Guidelines*', pp 167–169; see further Gerard 'Merger Control Policy: How to Give Meaningful Consideration to Efficiency Claims?' (2003) 40 CML Rev 1367; Colley 'From "Defence" to "Attack"? Quantifying Efficiency Arguments in Mergers' (2004) 25 ECLR 342; 'Efficiencies' in ICN *Merger Guidelines Project* (April 2004), ch 6, available at www.internationalcompetitionnetwork.org; Ilzkovitz and Meiklejohn (eds) *European Merger Control: Do We Need an Efficiency Defence?* (Edward Elgar, 2006); see also OECD Roundtable *Competition Policy Dynamic Efficiencies in Merger Analysis* (2008), including a European Commission contribution discussing different types of efficiencies, available at www.oecd.org/competition.

[414] Case T-342/07 EU:T:2010:280. [415] Ibid, paras 386–443.

[416] *Horizontal merger guidelines*, para 79.

that simply follow from a reduction in output would not qualify[417]; new or improved products or services could also amount to an efficiency gain[418]. Efficiency gains may enable a firm in an oligopolistic market to increase output and reduce prices, thereby reducing the incentive to act in a coordinated manner[419]. There must be an incentive to pass efficiency gains on to consumers, and the Commission will be more sceptical where the merger will lead to a monopoly or a very high degree of market power[420]

- **merger specificity**: the efficiencies must be a direct result of the notified merger and must not be capable of being achieved by less anti-competitive alternatives; the burden of proof is on the notifying parties[421]
- **verifiability**: the efficiencies must be verifiable such that the Commission can be reasonably certain that they are likely to materialise, and it is incumbent on the parties to produce the relevant information in due time to demonstrate that the efficiencies are merger-specific and likely to be realised[422].

In *Inco/Falconbridge*[423] the Commission considered, but rejected, arguments that the merger would generate efficiencies; the parties were more successful in advancing efficiency arguments in *Korsnäs/Assidomän Cartonboard*[424], albeit in a case which it seems the Commission would have cleared unconditionally anyway. Efficiencies were given extensive consideration in *Deutsche Börse/NYSE Euronext*,[425] in *UPS/TNT Express*[426] and in *Hutchison 3G UK/Telefónica UK*[427], but the Commission prohibited all three mergers. In *Nynas/Shell/Harburg Refinery*[428] the Commission accepted that the acquisition by Nynas of Shell's refinery at Harburg would lead to efficiencies, but the merger was allowed anyway as, without the acquisition, the refinery would have been closed. In *GE/Alstom*[429] the Commission agreed with the parties that gas product and gas services savings would benefit consumers, were merger-specific and were verifiable, but concluded that the efficiencies were insufficient to counteract the potential harm to consumers.

(vi) The 'failing firm' defence

Paragraph 89 of the *Horizontal merger guidelines* explains that the Commission may decide that an otherwise problematic merger is nevertheless capable of being found compatible with the internal market where one of the parties is a failing firm[430]. Three cumulative criteria are relevant:

- the allegedly failing firm would in the near future be forced out of the market because of financial difficulties if not taken over by another firm

417 Ibid, para 80. 418 Ibid, para 81. 419 Ibid, para 82.

420 Ibid, para 84. 421 Ibid, para 85.

422 Ibid, paras 86–88; on this point see Case T-175/12 *Deutsche Börse v Commission* EU:T:2015:148, para 362.

423 Case M 4000, decision of 4 July 2006, paras 529–550.

424 Case M 4057, decision of 12 May 2006: see paras 57–64; see also Case M 4854 *TomTom/Tele Atlas*, decision of 14 May 2008, paras 238–250.

425 Case M 6166, decision of 1 February 2012, paras 1133–1342, upheld on appeal Case T-175/12 EU:T:2015:148.

426 Case M 6570, decision of 30 January 2013; the Commission's decision was annulled on appeal to the General Court for procedural reasons in Case T-194/13 *United Parcel Service v Commission* EU:T:2017:144: the Commission has appealed to the Court of Justice Case C-265/17 P *Commission v UPS*, not yet decided.

427 Case M 7612, decision of 11 May 2016, paras 2337–2608, on appeal Case T-399/16 *CK Telecoms UK Investments v Commission*, not yet decided.

428 Case M 6360, decision of 2 September 2013, paras 443–474.

429 Case M 7278 *GE/Alstom*, decision of 8 September 2015, paras 1362–1363.

430 See Cases C-68/94 and C-30/95 *France v Commission* EU:C:1998:148; for further discussion see the EU contribution to the OECD Roundtable *Failing Firm Defence* (2009), available at www.oecd.org/competition.

- there is no less anti-competitive alternative than the notified merger
- in the absence of the merger the assets of the failing firm would inevitably exit the market[431].

It is for the notifying parties to provide in due time the relevant information to support a failing firm defence[432]. The Commission rejected a failing firm defence in *JCI/VB/FIAMM*[433]. However the defence was invoked successfully twice in 2013, in *Nynas/Shell/Harburg Refinery*[434], where it was a division of Shell, rather than Shell itself, that was failing; and in *Aegean/Olympic II*[435], where Olympic was in a much worse state than at the time of the previous proposed merger between Aegean and Olympic[436].

(E) **Non-horizontal mergers**

The Commission's *Guidelines on the assessment of non-horizontal mergers*[437] ('the *Non-horizontal guidelines*' or 'the *Guidelines*') provide valuable guidance as to how the Commission assesses concentrations where the undertakings concerned are active on different relevant markets. The *Guidelines* deal in turn with vertical mergers and with conglomerate mergers[438]. The *Guidelines* draw on the decisional practice of the Commission and the jurisprudence of the EU Courts since the EUMR entered into force in 1990. The text below does not cite this case law, but the reader should be aware that the *Guidelines* contain many useful references to relevant precedents. The *Guidelines* begin with an overview; they then discuss the significance of market shares and concentration levels; thereafter the specific issues arising in relation to vertical and conglomerate mergers are dealt with in turn. This sequence will be retained in the text that follows.

(i) **Overview**

The *Guidelines* acknowledge that non-horizontal mergers are less likely to significantly impede effective competition than horizontal ones for two reasons[439]:

- they do not entail the loss of direct competition between the merging firms in the same relevant market[440]
- they provide substantial scope for efficiencies, for example by integrating complementary activities which may lead to lower prices and higher output[441] or by enabling a broader portfolio of products to be offered to customers, thereby giving them the benefit of 'one-stop-shopping'[442].

The *Guidelines* also point out however that non-horizontal mergers may lead to an SIEC where they would alter the ability and incentive of the merged entity and its competitors in a way that could be harmful to consumers[443]. The Commission considers that (as in the case of horizontal mergers) non-horizontal mergers should be scrutinised for

431 *Horizontal merger guidelines*, para 90. 432 Ibid, para 91.

433 Case M 4381, decision of 5 October 2007.

434 Case M 6360, decision of 2 September 2013, paras 312–362.

435 Case M 6796, decision of 9 October 2013.

436 Case M 5830, decision of 26 January 2011; for comment see Komninos and Jeram 'Changing Mind in Changed Circumstances: *Aegean/Olympic II* and the Failing Firm Defence' (2011) 5 JECLAP 605.

437 OJ [2008] C 265/6; see also Church *Impact of Vertical and Conglomerate Mergers* (2004) and EAGCP *Non-Horizontal Mergers Guidelines: Ten Principles* (2006), both available at available at www.ec.europa.eu.

438 For a discussion of the differences see ch 20, 'The horizontal, vertical and conglomerate effects of mergers', pp 830–831.

439 *Non-horizontal guidelines*, para 12. 440 Ibid, para 12. 441 Ibid, para 13.

442 Ibid, para 14. 443 Ibid, para 15.

possible non-coordinated and possible coordinated effects[444]. Non-coordinated effects could accrue where a merger could lead to foreclosure of competitors[445]; coordinated effects if the merger would make it possible, or make it easier, for firms to act in a coordinated manner[446]. The Commission considers possible efficiencies that would arise from a merger as part of its assessment[447].

(ii) Market shares and concentration levels

The *Guidelines* state that the Commission is unlikely to have competition concerns where the market share of the new entity after the merger would be below 30% and where the post-merger HHI would be below 2,000[448]. However there may be some cases where 'special circumstances' might lead the Commission to investigate a merger below these thresholds, for example where a merger involves a company that is likely to expand significantly in the near future, for example because of a recent innovation: in this case its market share would not reflect its likely competitive impact on the market in the future; or where there are factors at play that suggest that the merger could facilitate coordination, for example the removal of a firm 'with a high likelihood of disrupting coordinated conduct' (often referred to as a 'maverick')[449]. There is no presumption *against* a non-horizontal merger above the 30% and 2,000 thresholds[450].

(iii) Vertical mergers

(a) Non-coordinated effects: foreclosure

The *Guidelines* distinguish two types of foreclosure: **input foreclosure** and **customer foreclosure**[451].

Input foreclosure occurs where the merged entity would be likely to restrict access to products or services by competitors in a downstream market, thereby raising their costs and making it harder for them to compete in that market. The *Guidelines* say that it is not necessary to show that any competitor would be forced to leave the market, only that the higher input cost would lead to higher prices for consumers[452]. The assessment requires an analysis of whether the merged entity would have:

- the **ability to foreclose** access to inputs, which requires a 'significant degree of market power'[453]
- an **incentive to foreclose**, which requires an analysis of whether the foreclosure would be profitable[454]
- an **overall likely impact on effective competition**, because it would lead to increased prices in the downstream market, for example by raising rivals' costs or raising barriers to entry[455].

Likely efficiencies will be taken into account as part of the assessment[456].

Customer foreclosure occurs where a supplier integrates with an important customer in a downstream market: this may mean that potential rivals in the upstream market no longer have access to a sufficient customer base downstream[457]. As in the case of input foreclosure, the *Guidelines* require an analysis of:

- the **ability to foreclose** access to downstream markets[458]

444 Ibid, para 17. 445 Ibid, para 18. 446 Ibid, para 19. 447 Ibid, para 21.
448 Ibid, para 25. 449 Ibid, para 26. 450 Ibid, para 27.
451 See the EU contribution to OECD Roundtable *Vertical Mergers* (2007), available at www.oecd.org/competition.
452 *Non-horizontal guidelines*, para 31. 453 Ibid, paras 33–39. 454 Ibid, paras 40–46.
455 Ibid, paras 47–51. 456 Ibid, paras 52–57. 457 Ibid, para 58. 458 Ibid, paras 60–67.

- whether there is an **incentive to foreclose** access to downstream markets[459]
- whether there is an **overall likely impact on competition**[460].

(b) Other non-coordinated effects

The *Guidelines* briefly suggest other possible non-coordinated effects that might be problematic, for example obtaining access to commercially sensitive information about the activities of rivals in upstream or downstream markets leading to less aggressive pricing in the downstream market[461].

(c) Coordinated effects

The *Guidelines* discuss the possibility that a non-horizontal merger might lead to a situation in which coordination becomes possible, or more possible, than it previously was: as in the case of horizontal mergers, discussed earlier, the *Guidelines* explain that it is necessary to consider four issues:

- **reaching terms of coordination**
- **monitoring deviations**
- **deterrent mechanisms**
- **reactions of outsiders**[462].

(iv) Conglomerate mergers

The *Non-horizontal guidelines* also discuss the possibility that a conglomerate merger could lead to an SIEC[463], although they note that usually there will be no problem[464]; as in the case of vertical mergers they consider first non-coordinated effects and then coordinated effects.

(a) Non-coordinated effects

The *Guidelines* explain that the primary concern is that a conglomerate merger could lead to a foreclosure effect, for example by enabling the merged entity to indulge in tying, bundling or other exclusionary practices[465]. As in the case of vertical mergers, the *Guidelines* explain that it is necessary to consider:

- the **ability to foreclose**[466]
- the **incentive to foreclose**[467]
- the **overall likely impact** on prices and choice[468].

(b) Coordinated effects

The *Guidelines* also explain that the possibility exists of coordinated effects arising from conglomerate mergers, for example by reducing the number of effective competitors[469].

[459] Ibid, paras 68–71. [460] Ibid, paras 72–77.

[461] Ibid, para 78. [462] Ibid, paras 79–90.

[463] For further reading see Völcker 'Leveraging as a Theory of Competition Harm in EC Merger Control' (2003) 40 CML Rev 581; OECD Roundtable *Portfolio Effects in Conglomerate Mergers* (2002), available at www.oecd.org/competition; Neven 'The Analysis of Conglomerate Effects in EU Merger Control', available at www.ec.europa.eu; Proctor 'Conglomerate Mergers: Lessons from Vertical Foreclosure' (2015) 38 World Competition 571.

[464] *Non-horizontal guidelines*, para 92.

[465] Ibid, para 93; on tying and bundling see ch 17, 'Tying', pp 705–713 and ch 18, 'Bundling', pp 754–756.

[466] *Non-horizontal guidelines*, paras 95–104. [467] Ibid, paras 105–110.

[468] Ibid, paras 111–118. [469] Ibid, paras 119–121.

(v) Recent cases on non-horizontal mergers

The Commission has conducted Phase II investigations because of vertical concerns in a number of a cases[470]. In *Google/DoubleClick*[471] the Commission considered that the existence of strong competitors, such as Microsoft, meant that the merged firm would have neither the ability nor incentive to foreclose them and therefore concluded that the transaction did not give rise to vertical concerns. In *Tom-Tom/Tele-Atlas*[472] and *Navteq/Nokia*[473] the Commission concluded that foreclosure of the input market for navigable digital maps would not be profitable for the merged firms; both mergers were cleared without conditions. Remedies were required to address vertical concerns in *Thomson/Reuters*[474], *UTC/Goodrich*[475], *Arm/Giesecke and Devrient/Gemalto/JV*[476] and *Liberty Global/De Vijver Media*[477].

In *Pepsico/The Pepsico Bottling Group*[478] the Commission rejected concerns about conglomeracy, concluding that the merged entity would not have the ability to foreclose competitors by bundling its soft drinks with its savoury snacks[479]. Conglomerate concerns were also rejected in *Proctor & Gamble/Gillette*[480], *Pernod Ricard/Allied Domecq*[481] and *News Corp/BSkyB*[482]. However the Commission did have concerns about conglomerate effects in *Intel/McAfee* which led to Phase I commitments[483]; the same happened in the case of *Microsoft/LinkedIn*[484] and in *Broadcom/Brocade*[485]. In *Microsoft/Skype*[486] the Commission considered that the merger would not have conglomerate effects: this finding was upheld on appeal[487].

In 2017, the Commission blocked the *Deutsche Börse/London Stock Exchange Group*[488] merger partly because of vertical concerns; in the Commission's view, the merged firm would have the ability and incentive partially to foreclose post-trade service providers and in particular its closest competitor. Later that year the General Court in *KPN v Commission*[489] accepted a claim by a third party objecting to the Commission's clearance of the *Liberty Global/Ziggo*[490] transaction that the Commission had failed to analyse the vertical effects of the merger on the markets for premium pay-TV sports channels.

(F) Articles 2(4) and 2(5) of the EUMR: full-function joint ventures and 'spillover effects'

Where a full-function joint venture has a Union dimension it falls to be analysed within the procedural framework of the EUMR. In so far as it would bring about a change in the

[470] In addition to the cases mentioned in the text see eg Case M 4403 *Thales/Finmeccanica/AAS/Telespazio*, decision of 4 April 2007; Case M 4504 *SFR/Télé 2*, decision of 18 July 2007.

[471] Case M 4731, decision of 11 March 2008; see Brockhoff, Jehano, Pozzato, Buhr, Eberl and Papandropoulos '*Google/DoubleClick*: The first test for the Commission's non-horizontal merger guidelines' (2008) 2 Competition Policy Newsletter 53.

[472] Case M 4854, decision of 14 May 2008.

[473] Case M 4942, decision of 2 July 2008; on the *TomTom* and *Navteq* decisions see Esteva Mosso, Mottl, De Coninck and Dupont 'Digital maps go vertical: *TomTom/Tele Atlas and Nokia/NAVTEQ*' (2008) 3 Competition Policy Newsletter 70; De Coninck 'Economic analysis in vertical mergers' (2008) 3 Competition Policy Newsletter 48.

[474] Case M 4726, decision of 19 February 2008.

[475] Case M 6410, decision of 26 July 2012.

[476] Case M 6564, decision of 6 November 2012.

[477] Case M 7194, decision of 24 February 2015.

[478] Case M 5633, decision of 26 October 2009.

[479] Ibid, paras 29–40.

[480] Case M 3732, decision of 15 July 2005.

[481] Case M 3779, decision of 24 June 2005.

[482] Case M 5932, decision of 21 December 2010.

[483] Case M 5984, decision of 26 January 2011.

[484] Case M 8124, decision of 6 December 2016.

[485] Case M 8314, decision of 12 May 2017.

[486] Case M 6281, decision of 7 October 2011.

[487] Case T-79/12 *Cisco Systems Inc v Commission* EU:T:2013:635.

[488] Case M 7995, decision of 29 March 2017, paras 544–709, for discussion see Competition Merger Brief 2/2017, available at www.ec.europa.eu.

[489] Case T-394/15 EU:T:2017:756.

[490] Case M 7000 *Liberty Global/Ziggo*, decision of 10 October 2014.

structure of the market it will be investigated in accordance with the provisions of Article 2(1) to (3) that have just been discussed. However there is a further possibility that needs to be considered in relation to full-function joint ventures, which is whether the creation of the joint venture could lead to a coordination of the behaviour of undertakings that remain independent of one another: this is sometimes referred to as a 'spillover effect'. This is tested according to the provisions of Articles 2(4) and 2(5) of the EUMR which are based upon Article 101 TFEU and the decisional practice of the Commission.

Article 2(4) provides that:

> To the extent that the creation of a joint venture constituting a concentration pursuant to Article 3 has as its object or effect the coordination of the competitive behaviour of undertakings that remain independent, such coordination shall be appraised in accordance with the criteria of [Article 101(1) and (3)] of the Treaty, with a view to establishing whether or not the operation is compatible with the [internal] market.

Article 2(5) provides that:

> In making this appraisal, the Commission shall take into account in particular:
>
> - whether two or more parent companies retain, to a significant extent, activities in the same market as the joint venture or in a market which is downstream or upstream from that of the joint venture or in a neighbouring market closely related to this market,
> - whether the coordination which is the direct consequence of the creation of the joint venture affords the undertakings concerned the possibility of eliminating competition in respect of a substantial part of the products or services in question.

(i) A practical example

The operation of these provisions is best understood with the benefit of an example (see Figure 21.5).

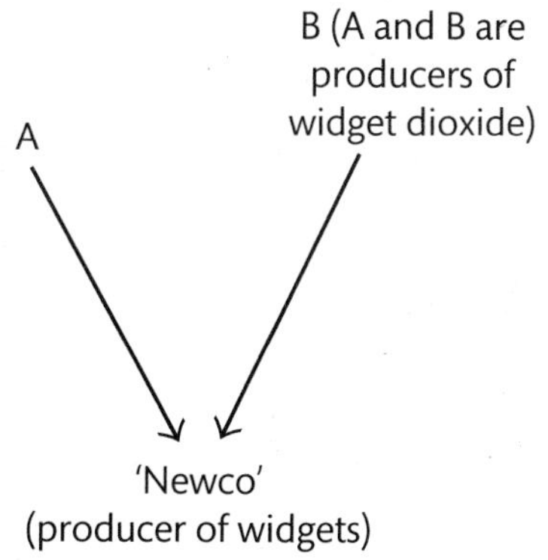

Fig. 21.5 Example of a full-function joint venture

Suppose that two producers of widgets, A and B, decide to merge their widget production into a joint venture, 'Newco'. Suppose further that both A and B will continue to produce widget dioxide, a raw material essential for the production of widgets, and that they will supply this raw material to Newco. In this case A and B will retain a presence in the 'upstream' market for widget dioxide[491].

[491] It is equally possible that the spillover effects might occur in a downstream or a horizontally neighbouring market.

The merger of the two widget businesses will be tested according to the criteria in Article 2(1) to (3) of the EUMR and the *Horizontal merger guidelines*.

- What will Newco's market share and market power be?
- Will there be countervailing buyer power?
- Would the merger lead to merger-specific efficiency gains?

However the additional question that has to be asked of this joint venture is whether the participation of A and B in the affairs of Newco will lead to them acting in a coordinated manner in the upstream market, for example because they will get to know about one another's pricing policy or capacity-expansion plans in relation to widget dioxide. This is the question that will be appraised in accordance with the criteria of Articles 2(4) and 2(5) of the EUMR.

(ii) Articles 2(4) and 2(5) in practice

In practice Articles 2(4) and 2(5) have not given rise to many difficult cases. The first Phase II investigation where possible spillover effects were considered was in the case of a joint venture between the telecommunications operators BT and AT&T[492]. The Commission identified certain 'candidate markets' in which coordination was a possibility and then considered, first, whether that coordination would happen as a result of the joint venture and, secondly, whether any restriction of competition would be appreciable. The joint venture was approved subject to commitments to eliminate the risk of parental coordination, including a divestiture of ACC, a wholly-owned subsidiary of AT&T[493]. In another Phase II investigation, *Areva/Urenco/ETC JV*[494], the Commission was concerned that a joint venture would lead to coordination between Areva and Urenco as a result of the increased scope for the exchange of information through the joint venture in relation to uranium enrichment. Commitments were given to reinforce firewalls between the parties and the joint venture and between the parties themselves[495]. The Commission examined possible spillover effects in *Sony/Bertelsmann*[496] and in *Telefónica UK/Vodafone UK/EE/JV*[497] but decided that they were not a concern.

(G) Contractual restrictions directly related and necessary to a merger: 'ancillary restraints'

(i) Introduction

Recital 21 and Articles 6(1)(b), 8(1) and 8(2) of the EUMR recognise that certain contractual restrictions may be directly related to and necessary for the successful implementation of a merger; a decision that clears a merger is deemed also to clear such restrictions. An obvious example would be where two undertakings merge their widget businesses into a joint venture 'Newco' and agree not to compete with the widget business of Newco, since to do so would undermine the very purpose of the transaction. The question is whether clauses of this kind, often referred to for the sake of simplicity as

[492] Case JV 15 *BT/AT&T*, decision of 30 March 1999; a Phase II investigation into spillover effects was ended when the concentration in Case JV 27 *Microsoft/Liberty Media/Telewest* was abandoned; the first decision in a Phase I case was Case JV 1 *Schibsted Multimedia AS/Telenor AS/Telia AB*, decision of 27 May 1996; commitments have been accepted in some Phase I cases, eg Case M 1327 *NC/Canal+/CDPQ/Bank America*, decision of 3 December 1998; Case JV 37 *BSkyB/KirchPay TV*, decision of 21 March 2000.

[493] See the Commission's XXIXth *Report on Competition Policy* (1999), para 185.

[494] Case M 3099, decision of 6 October 2004.

[495] Ibid, paras 222–225 and 231–232.

[496] Case M 3333, decision of 19 July 2004, paras 176–182.

[497] Case M 6314, decision of 4 September 2012, para 585.

'ancillary restraints', are cleared at the same time as the merger. The Commission has published a series of notices on this subject, the most recent of which is the 2005 *Notice on restrictions directly related and necessary to concentrations* (the '*Notice on ancillary restraints*')[498]. Also of relevance is the Commission's decision in *Telefónica SA/Portugal Telecom SGPS SA*[499] imposing fines of €79 million for the inclusion in an agreement whereby Telefónica acquired sole control of a joint venture supplying mobile telephony services in Brazil of a non-compete clause that meant that the parties would not compete with one another in Portugal and Spain respectively[500]. Although the EUMR provides that a clearance decision will clear any ancillary restraints, it is for the undertakings concerned to conduct a self-assessment of which restrictions are ancillary (as in the case of Article 101 TFEU generally since the adoption of Regulation 1/2003). The Commission will not state in a clearance decision which restraints are ancillary: it will provide guidance only in the case of specific novel or unresolved issues giving rise to genuine uncertainty, other disputes having to be resolved before national courts[501]. Where a restriction is not ancillary this is not in itself prejudicial to it: rather it is then subject to independent examination under Articles 101 and 102 TFEU and national competition law[502]. In *Siemens/Areva*[503], a case under Article 9 of Regulation 1/2003[504], the Commission accepted legally-binding commitments from those undertakings to restrict the length and scope of non-compete and confidentiality provisions that it considered to be excessive and therefore non-ancillary to an earlier concentration having a Union dimension.

(ii) General principles

Paragraph 11 of the *Notice* explains that the criteria of direct relation and necessity are objective in nature: it is not sufficient simply that the parties regard them as such. A restriction will be 'necessary' only where, without it, the merger could not be implemented or could be implemented only under considerably more uncertain conditions, at substantially higher cost, over an appreciably longer period or with considerably greater difficulty[505]. Examples given are restrictions necessary to protect the value of the business transferred, to maintain the continuity of supply after the break-up of a former economic entity or enabling the start-up of a new entity, regard being had to the duration, subject-matter and geographical field of application of the restriction in question[506].

(iii) Principles applicable in cases of the acquisition of an undertaking

Paragraph 17 of the *Notice on ancillary restraints* explains that, as a general proposition, it is the acquirer that may need protection, for example to ensure that it acquires the full value of the business it has paid for; greater scepticism is shown to restrictions providing

[498] OJ [2005] C 56/24, replacing the previous *Notice*, OJ [2001] C 188/5.

[499] Commission decision of 23 January 2013, upheld on appeal Case T-208/13 *Portugal Telecom v Commission* EU:T:2016:368 and Case T-216/13 *Telefónica SA v Commission* EU:T:2016:369, upheld on further appeal Case C-487/16 P EU:C:2017:961.

[500] See in particular paras 367–433 of the *Telefónica/Portugal Telecom* decision discussing the ancillary restraints doctrine.

[501] *Notice on ancillary restraints*, paras 2–6; in practice disputes as to whether a restriction is ancillary are quite often dealt with in arbitration proceedings: on the arbitration of competition law see ch 8, 'Arbitration', pp 341–342.

[502] *Notice on ancillary restraints*, para 7.

[503] See Commission Press Release IP/12/618, 18 June 2012.

[504] On commitments see ch 7, 'Article 9: commitments', pp 264–269.

[505] *Notice on ancillary restraints*, para 13.

[506] Ibid.

protection to the vendor. The *Notice* examines three types of restriction, non-compete clauses, licence agreements and purchase and supply obligations:

- **non-compete clauses**: these may be necessary to guarantee the transfer to the acquirer of the full value of the assets transferred including both the physical assets and the intangible ones such as goodwill and know-how[507]. Their duration, geographical field of application and subject-matter and personal scope must be limited to what is needed to implement the concentration[508]. As a general proposition a period of up to three years is justifiable where goodwill and know-how are transferred, and two years where only goodwill is included[509]. The geographical scope of the clause should be limited to the area in which the vendor has offered the relevant products or services prior to the transfer[510], and the clause should similarly be limited to the products or services forming the economic activity of the undertaking transferred[511]. Non-solicitation and confidentiality clauses have a comparable effect and are therefore evaluated in the same way[512]
- **licence agreements**: it may be that the vendor retains intellectual property rights in order to exploit them for activities other than those transferred to the acquirer, but licenses them to the acquirer for its purposes. Such licences—for example of patents or know-how—can be ancillary, but territorial limitations on the buyer as to the place of manufacture will not be; nor will restrictions protecting the licensor rather than the licensee[513]
- **purchase and supply agreements**: these may be needed in order to avoid the disruption of traditional lines of purchase and supply within the business transferred, in favour of both the acquirer and the purchaser, for up to five years; however exclusivity provisions and similar clauses would not be regarded as ancillary[514].

(iv) Principles applicable in cases of full-function joint ventures

Paragraphs 36 to 44 examine the same types of restriction in the case of full-function joint ventures:

- **non-compete obligations**: in the case of joint ventures an obligation not to compete with the joint venture is necessary to ensure good faith during negotiations, to fully utilize the joint venture's assets and to enable the joint venture to assimilate the know-how and goodwill transferred to it; obligations of this kind can be regarded as ancillary for the entire lifetime of the joint venture, not just for the period of two or three years envisaged in the case of the acquisition of a business from another undertaking[515]. Non-solicitation and confidentiality clauses are evaluated in the same way[516]
- **licence agreements**: the principles are the same as for the acquisition of an undertaking[517]

[507] Ibid, para 18. [508] Ibid, para 19.

[509] Ibid, para 20; longer periods may exceptionally be permitted: see fn 21 of the *Notice*.

[510] Ibid, para 22. [511] Ibid, para 23. [512] Ibid, para 26.

[513] Ibid, paras 27–31; note however that licences that go beyond ancillarity in the terms of the *Notice* may be block exempted under Regulation 316/2014 on technology transfer agreements: see ch 19, 'Technology Transfer Agreements: Regulation 316/2014', pp 798–807.

[514] *Notice on ancillary restraints*, paras 32–35; note however that vertical agreements that go beyond ancillarity in terms of the *Notice* might be block exempted under Regulation 330/2010 on vertical agreements: see ch 16, 'Vertical Agreements: Regulation 330/2010', pp 664–687.

[515] *Notice on ancillary restraints*, para 36. [516] Ibid, para 41. [517] Ibid, paras 42–43.

- **purchase and supply obligations**: again the same principles apply as in the case of the acquisition of an undertaking[518].

6. Remedies

In practice, the majority of mergers are cleared unconditionally, within Phase I. At the other end of the spectrum, outright prohibitions are rare. Between the unconditional clearance and the outright prohibition of concentrations there is another important group of cases: those where the Commission grants clearance, but subject to 'commitments' by the parties to modify their proposed transaction in order to remedy the competition problems identified by the Commission. The negotiation of such commitments is an important feature of many merger cases. By 8 December 2017 the Commission had accepted commitments in 290 Phase I cases and 122 Phase II cases. This means that something in the region of 6% of notifications of mergers having a Union dimension required modification before approval was forthcoming from the Commission[519].

The Commission has published two texts that are relevant to its consideration of remedies: the *Notice on remedies*[520] and *Best Practice Guidelines: the Commission's model texts for divestiture commitments and the trustee mandate*[521].

(A) The legal basis for commitments

The legal basis for commitments as a way of settling merger cases is provided by Article 6(2) of the EUMR for Phase I investigations and Article 8(2) for Phase II investigations. Each of Articles 6 and 8 provides that the Commission may attach conditions and obligations to a decision to clear a merger; such conditions and obligations are intended to ensure that the undertakings concerned comply with the commitments that they make to the Commission to modify their transaction. Recital 30 of the EUMR states that Phase I commitments are appropriate where the competition problem is easily identifiable and can easily be remedied: it adds that transparency and effective consultation of Member States and interested third parties should be ensured throughout the procedure[522]. Recital 31 explains the various consequences of failure to comply with conditions and obligations. These include:

- the possibility of the Commission ordering that a merger that has already been carried into effect, but in breach of a condition given in Phase I (Article 6(3)) or Phase II (Article 8(4)), should be dissolved
- the power to take interim measures to restore or maintain conditions of effective competition in the event of a breach of a Phase I or Phase II condition (Article 8(5))
- the power to revoke a decision where undertakings commit a breach of an obligation attached to a decision (Article 8(6)).

Article 14(2) of the EUMR provides for fines of up to 10% of the aggregate turnover of the undertakings concerned to be imposed in the event of failure to comply with a condition

[518] Ibid, para 44.

[519] The statistics in this paragraph can be accessed at www.ec.europa.eu/competition/mergers/statistics.pdf.

[520] OJ [2008] C 267/1, replacing the previous *Notice*, OJ [2001] C 68/3.

[521] Available at www.ec.europa.eu/competition/mergers/legislation/best_practice.html.

[522] See also para 81 of the *Notice on remedies*.

or obligation attached to a decision; Article 15(1)(c) provides for periodic penalty payments to be imposed in the event of a failure to comply with an obligation.

(B) The Commission's *Notice on remedies*

The Commission published its revised *Notice on remedies* in October 2008. The Commission also adopted Regulation 1033/2008[523] which amended the Implementing Regulation in order to provide the format for a new form, Form RM, which undertakings must submit to the Commission when offering remedies; Regulation 1033/2008 also clarifies that an independent trustee or trustees may be appointed to assist the Commission in overseeing the parties' compliance with the commitments that they give. The revised *Notice* reflects the insights resulting from DG COMP's 2005 *Merger Remedies Study*[524] in which it looked at the design, implementation and effectiveness of 96 remedies that it had accepted in 40 cases under the EUMR from 1996 to 2000. The study concluded that care is needed to define the right scope of a divested business; to ensure its interim preservation until divestiture; to approve adequate purchasers; and to ensure effective monitoring of the implementation of the remedies.

(i) General principles

Section II of the *Notice on remedies* discusses the general principles relevant to remedies. Most of the discussion is about the need for remedies to address the possibility that a merger might significantly impede effective competition in the sense of Article 2(3) of the EUMR, but paragraph 4 states that the *Notice* is also relevant to remedies required to address possible spillover effects under Article 2(4). Paragraph 6 of the *Notice* acknowledges that the Commission is not in a position to impose unilaterally conditions on the clearance of a merger: it can do so only pursuant to commitments offered by the parties[525]. Paragraph 7 explains the Commission's need to introduce Form RM. Only the parties to a transaction have the relevant information necessary to demonstrate that a remedy would address the Commission's competition concerns: they therefore must provide that information to the Commission so that it can conduct an assessment. However paragraph 8 of the *Notice* notes that the Commission retains the burden of proving that a merger, as modified by the commitments proposed, would nevertheless significantly impede effective competition[526].

The amended Implementing Regulation established a new Annex, Annex IV, which sets out the information that must be contained in Form RM. It requires the notifying parties to submit detailed information concerning the commitments offered and, in particular, to provide specific information if the commitments offered consist of the divestiture of a business. The Commission may waive the provision of certain information if it considers that it is not necessary in a particular case. Form RM is divided into five sections dealing respectively with:

- a description of the commitment
- its suitability to remove competition concerns

[523] OJ [2008] L 279/3.

[524] Available at www.ec.europa.eu/competition/mergers/studies_reports/studies_reports.html; see also Davies and Lyons *Mergers and Merger Remedies in the EU* (Edward Elgar, 2008); Hoeg *European Merger Remedies: Law and Policy* (Hart, 2014); and OECD Best Practices Roundtable, *Remedies in Merger Cases* (2011), available at www.oecd.org/competition.

[525] See Case T-210/01 *General Electric v Commission* EU:T:2005:456, para 52; Case T-87/05 *EDP v Commission* EU:T:2005:333, para 105.

[526] See Case T-87/05 *EDP v Commission* EU:T:2005:333, paras 62ff.

- an explanation of any deviation from the Commission's Model Texts for divestiture commitments and the trustee mandate
- a summary of the commitments
- information on any business to be divested.

The last of these five sections requires a considerable amount of information about the nature of the business to be divested including:

- the assets (including intellectual property rights and brands) to be transferred
- an organisational chart identifying the personnel currently working for the business concerned
- the customers of the business
- financial data including turnover for the last two years of the business involved and a prediction for the next two years
- an explanation of why the business will be acquired by a suitable purchaser within the time-frame proposed in the commitments offered.

The collection and presentation of this information will sometimes be a complex task and yet it will have to be supplied to the Commission within the tight timetables of the EUMR, whether the case is a Phase I or a Phase II one. The parties and their professional advisers will therefore need to begin the process of designing possible remedies and preparing a draft Form RM at quite an early stage of the investigation, very probably at a time when they are still arguing that the case is not one that gives rise to a significant impediment to effective competition or a spillover effect.

The *Notice* places considerable emphasis on the need for commitments to be effectively implemented and monitored. Paragraph 14 states that where the parties submit remedies that are extensive and complex it is unlikely that they will be acceptable, citing the cases of *ENI/EDP/GDP*[527] and *Volvo/Scania*[528] as examples. The Commission has a wide discretion as to the form that the commitments in question may take[529]. Paragraphs 15 to 17 make clear that there is a strong preference for structural remedies, such as divestitures and granting access to key infrastructure, over behavioural ones, although the use of the latter cannot automatically be ruled out[530]. There are various disadvantages to behavioural remedies: pre-merger competition is preferable to post-merger regulation; remedies may increase transparency in the market, making tacit coordination easier; and they require continual monitoring and enforcement. The Commission considers that a commitment as to future behaviour would be acceptable 'only exceptionally in very specific circumstances'[531].

(ii) Different types of remedies

Section III of the *Notice* discusses different types of remedies. Paragraphs 22 to 57 deal with divestiture of a business to a suitable purchaser; paragraphs 58 to 60 discuss the

[527] Case M 3440, decision of 9 December 2004, OJ [2005] L 302/69, upheld on appeal Case T-87/05 *EDP v Commission* EU:T:2005:333, para 102.

[528] Case M 1672, decision of 15 March 2000, OJ [2001] L 143/74.

[529] Case T-177/04 *easyJet v Commission* EU:T:2006:187, para 197 and the cases cited therein.

[530] The possibility of behavioural remedies has been confirmed by the EU Courts in a number of judgments, eg Case C-12/03 P *Commission v Tetra Laval* EU:C:2005:87, paras 85–89; for further discussion see Ezrachi 'Behavioural Remedies in EC Merger Control—Scope and Limitations' (2006) 29 World Competition 459.

[531] For an example of a Phase I merger cleared on the basis of behavioural remedies see Case M 6564 *ARM/Giesecke & Devrient/Gemalto/JV*, decision of 6 November 2012, paras 214–237.

removal of links with competitors; and paragraphs 61 to 69 consider 'other remedies'. The final part of Section III is concerned with review clauses.

(a) Divestiture of a business to a suitable purchaser

Paragraph 23 of the *Notice* explains that divested activities must consist of a viable business that, if operated by a suitable purchaser, can compete effectively with the merged entity on a lasting basis; the business should be divested as a going concern. Paragraphs 25 to 31 discuss the importance of determining the correct scope of the business to be divested. Paragraph 30 states that the business to be divested must be viable as such. The resources of a possible purchaser will not be taken into account at the stage of assessing the remedy: this will require a separate approval decision when a candidate purchaser is presented. An exception to this is discussed at paragraphs 56 and 57 of the *Notice*: where a specific purchaser is identified during the investigation itself and the parties enter into a legally-binding agreement to sell, the Commission will decide in its final decision whether the purchaser is suitable and there will be no need for a subsequent approval. The Commission welcomes 'fix it first' remedies of this kind, in particular where the identity of the purchaser is crucial for the effectiveness of the proposed remedy[532].

Paragraphs 32 and 33 of the *Notice* say that the Commission has a clear preference for the divestiture of an existing business that can operate on a standalone basis, that is to say independently of inputs from or cooperation with the merged entity. Paragraphs 35 and 36 discuss the situation where it is necessary to 'carve-out' a business from the merged entity's other businesses, that is to say to put a set of assets together capable of being divested that did not previously exist as a separate entity[533]; the Commission is not in favour of carve-outs, although it recognises that it would be disproportionate to rule them out altogether and in practice they are quite common. The Commission would be more sympathetic to the sale of a standalone business with a 'reverse carve-out' of any business to be retained by the merged entity. Paragraph 37 expresses scepticism about the divestiture of assets such as brands that have not been a uniform and viable business in the past. Paragraph 43 states that, when the parties commit to a divestiture, they would normally be expected to agree not to reacquire influence over the divested business for a period of ten years.

Paragraphs 47 to 57 contain a detailed discussion of the need to transfer the business to a suitable purchaser, that is to say a purchaser who is independent of the parties, who has the financial resources, expertise, incentive and ability to maintain and develop the divested business, and who will be in a position to acquire the business without regulatory problems. The *Notice* deals in turn with cases where the Commission requires the business to be divested within a fixed time limit after the conditional decision (paragraph 52), or requires the identification of an 'up-front' buyer before the transaction can be completed (paragraphs 53 to 55)[534], or accepts a 'fix-it-first' solution (see earlier). Paragraphs 44 to 46 explain that in some cases it may be possible to offer alternative commitments consisting of a preferred option but also a second one in case the first is not achieved.

[532] See eg Case M 7881 *AB InBev/SABMiller*, decision of 24 May 2016 where the proposed commitments identified Asahi as the prospective purchaser; see similarly Case M 7917 *Boehringer Ingelheim/Sanofi Animal Health*, decision of 9 November 2016.

[533] On carve-out remedies see DG COMP's 2005 *Merger Remedies Study*, pp 74–80.

[534] For examples of the requirement of up-front buyers to be approved by the Commission see Case M 7567 *Ball/Rexam*, decision of 15 January 2016 and Case M 7637 *Liberty Global/BASE Belgium*, decision of 4 February 2016; the Commission rejected the up-front buyer proposed in Case M 6663 *Ryanair/Aer Lingus III*, decision of 27 February 2013.

Sometimes this is referred to as a 'Crown Jewel' commitment: examples can be found in *Nestlé/Ralston Purina*[535] and *Johnson & Johnson/Guidant*[536].

(b) *Removal of links with competitors*

The removal of links with competitors—for example by divesting a minority shareholding in a joint venture or by terminating a distribution agreement—is discussed in paragraphs 58 to 60. Paragraph 59 explains that, in exceptional cases, it may be sufficient to agree to waive voting rights attached to shares rather than actually to sell them. In *Glencore/Xstrata*[537] Glencore agreed to divest its minority shareholding in Nystar as a condition of the Commission's approval.

(c) *Other remedies*

Paragraphs 61 to 69 deal with other remedies, in particular commitments to grant access to key infrastructure, networks and key technology such as patents. Remedies of this kind have been accepted in many cases, which are helpfully cited in footnotes to the main text. Considerable emphasis is placed, in paragraph 66, on the need for there to be effective monitoring of remedies of this kind; this may include separation of accounting so that the cost of operating a key infrastructure can be ascertained and a fast-track dispute resolution mechanism to determine disputes about access. Paragraph 69 repeats the point made earlier that the Commission considers that behavioural remedies as to future behaviour will be acceptable only in exceptional circumstances. Paragraph 70 states that there may be cases in which a non-divestiture remedy is acceptable for a limited period of time.

(d) *Review clauses*

Commitments should normally contain a review clause that allows the Commission to grant an extension of time or to waive, modify or substitute the commitments. This issue is discussed in paragraphs 71 to 76.

(iii) **Procedural issues**

Section IV of the *Notice* is concerned with procedure, dealing in turn with Phase I and Phase II commitments. Article 19(1) of the Implementing Regulation requires that Phase I commitments be submitted within 20 working days of the date of receipt of the notification; Article 10(1), second sub-paragraph of the EUMR provides that the deadline for the Commission to make a Phase I decision is extended from 25 to 35 working days where commitments are offered. Paragraph 82 emphasises the need for Phase I commitments to be offered in a timely manner, given the tight timetables involved. Article 19(2) of the Implementing Regulation requires that Phase II commitments be submitted within 50 working days of the date on which the Commission decided to conduct a Phase II investigation; this deadline can be extended by a further 15 working days where commitments are submitted between day 55 and 65 of a Phase II investigation. Paragraphs 88 to 94 discuss timing issues, including the 'exceptional circumstances' in which it may be possible to offer commitments after the deadline has expired.

(iv) **Implementation of commitments**

Section V of the *Notice* discusses in turn the divestiture process, the approval of purchasers, the obligations of the parties during the interim period, the role of the monitoring and divestiture trustees, and the obligations of the parties following implementation of

[535] Case M 2337, decision of 27 July 2001. [536] Case M 3687, decision of 25 August 2005.
[537] Case M 6541, decision of 22 November 2012.

the divestiture. Paragraph 97 explains that the divestiture process can be divided into two periods. In the 'first divestiture period' the parties look for a suitable purchaser. If they are unsuccessful there follows the 'trustee divestiture period' when a divestiture trustee is appointed to sell the business. Paragraph 98 states that the Commission's experience is that short divestiture periods contribute to the success of the divestiture, and that it would normally expect the first divestiture period to last around six months and the trustee divestiture period around three months. A further period of three months is foreseen for closing the transaction.

As paragraphs 101 to 106 explain, the Commission will require to be satisfied that the purchaser is a suitable one, and if it thinks that this is not the case it will adopt a decision to that effect: such a decision could be challenged before the General Court, for example by a potential purchaser rejected by the Commission[538]. In *Éditions Odile Jacob SAS v Commission* a monitoring trustee had approved a prospective purchaser, Wendel Investissement, for various publishing assets owned by Editis: the sale was a condition of the clearance of the *Lagardère/Natexis/VUP* transaction[539]; a competing purchaser of the assets, Éditions Odile, successfully challenged the approval of Wendel as the purchaser since the trustee that reported on Wendel's suitability as a purchaser was insufficiently independent of the publishing assets[540]. Éditions Odile also challenged the Commission's decision to re-approve Wendel as the purchaser, but was not successful second time round[541].

It is not unknown for the sale to a purchaser itself to amount to a merger having a Union dimension, with the result that it has to be notified to the Commission under the EUMR[542]. A good example of this is the *Asahi/AB InBev CEE Divestment Business*[543], a divestment pursuant to the remedies required by the Commission in *AB InBev/SABMiller*[544].

Paragraphs 107 to 116 discuss the obligations of the parties pending the divestiture of the business, dealing in turn with three points: safeguards for the interim preservation of the viability of the business; the necessary steps for a carve-out process if relevant; and the necessary steps to prepare the divestiture of the business. The parties will be required to hold the business separate from any retained business and a 'hold separate manager' will normally be required to be appointed.

Paragraphs 117 to 127 contain a helpful discussion of the respective roles of the monitoring and divestiture trustees[545]. Five main tasks of the monitoring trustee are:

- to ensure that the business to be divested is not degraded during the interim period
- in carve-out cases to monitor the splitting of assets and the allocation of personnel between the divested and retained businesses
- to oversee the parties' efforts to find a potential purchaser and to transfer the business
- to act as a contact point for any requests by third parties
- to report on these issues to the Commission in periodic compliance reports.

[538] See the (unsuccessful) appeal by a potential purchaser in Case T-342/00 *Petrolessence v Commission* EU:T:2003:97; cf, under UK law, Case 1081/4/1/07 *Co-operative Group Ltd v OFT* [2007] CAT 24: see ch 22, 'Undertakings in lieu of a reference', pp 953–955.

[539] Case M 2978, decision of 7 January 2004.

[540] Case T-452/04 EU:T:2010:385, upheld on appeal Cases C-553/10 P etc EU:C:2012:682.

[541] Case T-471/11 *Éditions Odile Jacob SAS v Commission* EU:T:2014:739, upheld on appeal Case C-514/14 P *Éditions Odile Jacob SAS v Commission* EU:C:2016:55.

[542] See para 104 of the *Notice* and the example given in fn 2 thereof.

[543] Case M 8357, decision of 1 March 2017.

[544] Case M 7881, decision of 24 May 2016.

[545] See also the Commission's *Best Practice Guidelines: The Commission's Model Texts for Divestiture Commitments and the Trustee Mandate under the EC Merger Regulation*, 5 December 2013.

The divestiture trustee—described in paragraph 118 of the *Notice* as the 'eyes and ears' of the Commission—will be given an irrevocable and exclusive mandate to dispose of the business within a specific deadline to a suitable purchaser; a minimum price will not be specified. The monitoring and divestiture trustees may be, but do not have to be, the same person or institution. In the Commission's experience auditing firms and other consulting firms may be particularly well placed to act as a monitoring trustee; investment banks seem to be particularly suitable for the role of divestiture trustee.

Paragraph 128 states that the Commission will wish to be able to monitor compliance with commitments for a period of ten years after the adoption of its decision and will reserve the right to request information from the parties for that period.

(v) Review of commitments

Commitments normally include a review clause allowing the Commission, upon request by the parties, to grant an extension of deadlines or, in exceptional circumstances, to waive, modify or substitute the commitments. In *Lufthansa/Swiss*[546] the Commission rejected Lufthansa's request for a partial waiver of commitments that had been given to secure approval at Phase I[547].

(C) Remedies in practice

Remedy-setting sometimes involves extensive cooperation with competition authorities in other jurisdictions such as the US[548]. In several cases third parties have appealed to the General Court in relation to cases in which (in their opinion) the Commission had been too generous to the parties to a merger in accepting commitments[549]. Some cases in which the Commission has accepted commitments in recent Phase II cases are discussed in the final section of this chapter[550].

7. Powers of Investigation and Enforcement

The Commission is given wide powers of investigation and the ability to impose fines for transgression of the EUMR; these powers are broadly in alignment with the rules contained in Regulation 1/2003[551], although there is no power to conduct a 'dawn raid' on the homes of natural persons under the EUMR. To enable the Commission to carry out its functions the EUMR gives it powers to request information (Article 11), to carry out on-the-spot investigations (Article 13)[552] and to impose fines and periodic penalties (Articles 14 and 15) for breach of the Regulation's provisions. Article 11 requests for information are a standard feature of almost all investigations, and may be sent both to the notifying parties and to other undertakings—for example competitors, suppliers and customers—which might be able to supply DG COMP with relevant information. Fines for providing incorrect or misleading information or for breaking seals affixed to premises, books or records during an inspection can be up to 1% of the aggregate group worldwide turnover of the undertakings concerned in

[546] Case M 3770 *Lufthansa/Swiss*, decision of 25 July 2016, on appeal Case T-712/16 *Lufthansa v Commission*, not yet decided.

[547] Case M 3770, decision of 4 July 2005.

[548] See ch 12, 'The cooperation agreements in practice', pp 518–519.

[549] See 'Appeals against conditional clearances', pp 919–920 later in chapter.

[550] See 'The EUMR in Practice', pp 922–931 later in chapter.

[551] OJ [2003] L 1/1.

[552] See Case M 1157 *Skanska/Scancem*, decision of 19 December 1997, para 11; the Commission's MEMO/07/573, 13 December 2007; Case M 6106 *Caterpillar/MWM*, decision of 19 October 2011, para 14.

the preceding financial year[553]. Fines for implementing a merger without notifying it and without the Commission's authority pursuant to Article 7 of the EUMR, for implementing a merger in breach of an Article 8 decision or for failing to comply with a condition or obligation attached to a decision can be as much as 10% of the aggregate group worldwide turnover in the preceding financial year[554]. In determining the amount of a fine the Commission is required by Article 14(3) to bear in mind the nature and gravity of the infringement. Article 15 provides the Commission with the power to impose periodic penalty payments of up to 5% of average daily turnover where firms continue, for example, to fail to supply correct information or to submit to an inspection. Clearly the possibility of a heavy fine, in association with the power under Article 8(4) to require the reversal of a concentration already effected, means that it is highly unwise to proceed without complying with the requirements of the EUMR. The EU Courts are given unlimited jurisdiction by Article 16 to review decisions imposing fines or periodic penalty payments.

The first fine (of €33,000), for failure to notify and for carrying out an operation without the prior approval of the Commission, was imposed in 1998 in *Samsung*[555]; this phenomenon is often referred to as 'gun-jumping'[556]. In *AP Møller*[557] a larger fine, of €219,000, was imposed for failure to notify and for putting into effect three concentrations which were discovered in the course of an investigation of a notified concentration. In setting the level of the fine the Commission noted that the failure to notify was not intentional but that there had been 'qualified negligence'. AP Møller was a large European undertaking that could be expected to have a good knowledge of the EUMR, and the concentrations had been operated for a considerable time before they were brought to the Commission's attention. A mitigating factor was that there had been no damage to the competitive process. A much larger fine of €20 million was imposed in *Electrabel/Compagnie Nationale du Rhône*[558] in 2009: the Commission concluded that Electrabel had acquired *de facto* control of CNR several years earlier, in December 2003, without having received prior approval from the Commission. The Commission also imposed a fine of €20 million in the case of *Marine Harvest* where Marine Harvest, by acquiring a stake of 48.5% in Morpol, had acquired *de facto* control of it[559]; the Commission's decision was upheld on appeal to the General Court[560]. The merger itself was cleared at the end of Phase I, subject to conditions[561]. On 24 April 2018 the Commission imposed a fine of €125 million on Altice for 'gun-jumping'[562]; it is investigating the same issue in *Canon/Toshiba Medical*[563].

[553] EUMR, Article 14(1). [554] Ibid, Article 14(2).

[555] Case M 920, decision of 18 February 1998, OJ [1999] L 225/12.

[556] On gun-jumping see Modrall and Ciullo 'Gun-Jumping and EU Merger Control' (2003) 24 ECLR 424; Alomar, Moonen, Navea and Redondo '*Electrabel/CNR*: the importance of the standstill obligation in merger proceedings' (2009) 3 Competition Policy Newsletter 58; Modrall 'The EU Gets Tough on Gun-Jumping' (2017) 21(8) The M&A Lawyer 12.

[557] Case M 969, decision of 10 February 1999, OJ [1999] L 183/29.

[558] Case M 4994, decision of 10 June 2009; upheld on appeal to the General Court Case T-332/09 *Electrabel v Commission* EU:T:2012:672, and on appeal to the Court of Justice Case C-84/13 P EU:C:2014:2040.

[559] Commission decision of 23 July 2014; for comment see Kadar and Mauger 'Harvesting salmon, jumping guns: the *Marine Harvest* early implementation case' *Competition Merger Brief* 1/2014, available at www.ec.europa.eu/competition/publications/cpn.

[560] Case T-704/14 *Marine Harvest ASA v Commission* EU:T:2017:753, on appeal to the Court of Justice Case C-10/18 P, not yet decided.

[561] Case M 6850, decision of 30 September 2013.

[562] Commission Press Release IP/18/3522, 24 April 2018.

[563] Commission Press Release IP/17/1924, 6 July 2017.

Small fines were imposed for the provision of incorrect information in 1999 in *Sanofi/ Synthélabo, KLM/Martinair* and *Deutsche Post*[564]; in *BP/Erdölchemie* in 2002[565]; and in *Tetra Laval/Sidel*[566] in 2004. The case of *Facebook* was dramatically different: there the Commission fined Facebook €110 million for providing misleading information during the Commission's investigation of its acquisition of WhatsApp. Facebook had told the Commission in 2014 both in its Form CO and in a reply to a request for information that it would not be able to establish reliable automated matching between Facebook users' accounts and WhatsApp users' accounts; however in 2016 Facebook announced updates to its terms of service and privacy policy, including the possibility of linking WhatsApp users' phone numbers with Facebook users' identities[567].

In *Ahlström/Kvaerner*[568] the Commission imposed fines of €950,000 on Mitsubishi, a third party, rather than the parties to the concentration, as Mitsubishi had failed to provide information in response to requests from the Commission under Article 11 of the EUMR.

8. Judicial Review

Decisions of the Commission under the EUMR are subject to judicial review by the EU Courts on the grounds set out in Article 263 TFEU, that is to say lack of competence, infringement of an essential procedural requirement, infringement of the Treaty or of any rule of law or misuse of powers[569]. Fines and periodic penalty payments are also subject to review, by virtue of Article 261 TFEU and Article 16 of the EUMR. In the early days of EU merger control appeals were relatively few, although there were some landmark judgments, for example on the meaning of collective dominance[570]. However in the second half of the 1990s widespread public disquiet was being expressed about the position of the Commission in relation to mergers and, in particular, about the combination of powers vested in it and the lack of a 'fresh pair of eyes' within the system; or, to put the matter another way, that there was insufficient judicial control of the Commission by the EU Courts. It was during this period that prohibition decisions under the EUMR began to increase in number, culminating in a record number of five prohibitions in 2001[571]. As if in response to this criticism there followed a dramatic series of annulments by the General Court of Commission prohibition decisions in 2002: *Airtours v Commission*[572], *Schneider Electric v Commission*[573] and *Tetra Laval v Commission*[574]. In these judgments the General Court, while acknowledging that the Commission enjoys a margin of appreciation when

[564] See the Commission's XXIXth *Report on Competition Policy* (1999), Box 9, pp 73–74; the *Deutsche Post* decision will be found at OJ [2001] L 97/1.

[565] Case M 2624, decision of 19 June 2002: €35,000.

[566] Case M 3255, decision of 7 July 2004: €90,000.

[567] Commission Press Release IP/17/1369, 18 May 2017.

[568] Case M 1634, decision of 14 July 2000, see the Commission's (2000) 3 Competition Policy Newsletter 62–63.

[569] See generally ch 7, 'Judicial Review', pp 300–305.

[570] See Cases C-68/94 etc *France v Commission* EU:C:1998:148, paras 169–178; Case T-102/96 *Gencor v Commission* EU:T:1999:65, paras 148–158.

[571] See the statistical table of notifications at 'Table of EUMR statistics', pp 923–925 later in chapter.

[572] Case T-342/99 *Airtours v Commission* EU:T:2002:146.

[573] Case T-310/01 *Schneider Electric v Commission* EU:T:2002:254.

[574] Case T-5/02 *Tetra Laval v Commission* EU:T:2002:264, upheld on appeal Case C-12/03 P *Commission v Tetra Laval* EU:C:2005:87; for comment on *Schneider* and *Tetra Laval* see Temple Lang 'Two Important Merger Regulation Judgments: The Implications of *Schneider-Legrand* and *Tetra Laval-Sidel*' (2003) 28 EL Rev 259.

dealing with complex economic matters, nevertheless demonstrated that it was prepared to look quite deeply into both the Commission's findings of facts and into the inferences drawn from them when determining whether its analysis was vitiated by manifest errors of assessment. While each of these three judgments necessarily turned on its own facts, collectively they sent a strong signal to the Commission that it needed to be more rigorous in its investigations, and they succeeded in assuaging some of the concerns about the excessive power of the Commission and weak supervision by the General Court.

A different complaint about judicial review has been that, even if the General Court is prepared to exercise effective judicial control over the Commission, the time taken to obtain a judgment from the General Court is so long that the process is essentially without purpose. This has been addressed, to some extent, by the so-called 'expedited procedure', discussed later. More radical solutions, such as the introduction of a specialist competition court at a lower level than the General Court[575], or even changing the role of the Commission to that of a prosecutor only, the actual decision to be taken by the General Court, seem, for the time being, to be in abeyance.

Appeals against decisions of the Commission have, in recent years, become more common, both on the part of merging parties and on the part of aggrieved third parties. Advisers therefore need to explain to clients not only the time limits under the EUMR, but also that a real possibility exists of protracted litigation in the EU Courts after the Commission has reached its final decision. The *Sony/Bertelsmann* case discussed later is particularly instructive in this respect[576].

(A) Acts

Only acts that produce binding legal effects may be appealed under Article 263 TFEU[577]. In the context of the EUMR the General Court has ruled that a decision under Article 6(1)(c) to initiate a Phase II investigation is not an appealable act[578]; nor was a letter from the Commission expressing an opinion about the nature of commitments offered in an earlier case[579] and a decision not to take proceedings against Italy in relation to the *Abertis/Autostrade* case[580].

(B) Standing

Article 263 TFEU allows any natural or legal person to institute proceedings against a decision which is addressed to it or which is addressed to another person but which is of direct and individual concern to that person.

(i) The parties to the transaction

It is obvious that the parties to the transaction have standing, for example where a merger is prohibited: examples of successful appeals were given earlier; there have also been several unsuccessful appeals against prohibition decisions[581]. An interesting question

[575] See ch 2, 'Court of Justice', p 56.

[576] See 'The approach to evidence', 917–918 later in chapter.

[577] See ch 7, 'Acts', p 302.

[578] Case T-48/03 *Schneider Electric v Commission* EU:T:2006:34, upheld on appeal Case C-188/06 P EU:C:2007:158; see similarly Case T-902/16 *HeidelbergCement v Commission* EU:T:2017:846.

[579] Case T-57/07 *E.ON Ruhrgas International AG v Commission* EU:T:2009:297.

[580] Case T-58/09 *Schemaventotto SpA v Commission* EU:T:2010:342.

[581] See eg Case T-102/96 *Gencor Ltd v Commission* EU:T:1999:65; Case T-87/05 *EDP v Commission* EU:T:2005:333; Case T-210/01 *General Electric v Commission* EU:T:2005:456; Case T-342/07 *Ryanair Holdings plc v Commission* EU:T:2010:280.

is whether parties that offer commitments to the Commission as a condition of being allowed to proceed with a transaction can then appeal to the General Court that the Commission had no right to insist on remedies. On the one hand it can be argued that offering commitments is a voluntary act on the part of the parties, so that they ought not to be able to challenge the Commission[582]; on the other hand the parties can argue that they were effectively 'forced' into offering commitments in order to save what they could from the transaction, not least because the time limits imposed by the EUMR were soon to be reached. The General Court rejected an appeal of this kind in *Cementbouw v Commission*: it acknowledged that Cementbouw had standing to bring the appeal but rejected it on substance[583].

(ii) Third parties

Third parties have the right to challenge merger decisions of the Commission provided that they can demonstrate that the decision is of direct and individual concern to them. Article 18(4) of the EUMR provides that natural or legal persons showing a sufficient interest have a right to be heard during the Commission's administrative procedure, and the General Court has held that such persons have standing to appeal[584]. In some cases third parties that were not involved in the administrative procedure have also been found to have standing to appeal[585]. However a third party that is in liquidation has been held not to have an interest in the final judgment of the court[586]. Many third party appeals have been unsuccessful, but this may be of little comfort to undertakings that have received a clearance from the Commission but then have to undergo a period of further uncertainty while the appeal process plays out. It is arguable that the rules on standing should be somewhat stricter in relation to third parties, at least where the appellant is a competitor of the merging parties whose objection to the transaction has nothing to do with consumer welfare considerations; objections from customers and consumers are likely to be much more meritorious[587]. Further discussion of third party appeals will be found later.

(C) The approach to evidence

In *Commission v Tetra Laval*[588] the Court of Justice held that the Commission has a margin of discretion in relation to economic matters, but the EU Courts must not refrain from reviewing the Commission's interpretation of information of an economic nature[589]. The EU Courts must establish whether the evidence relied on by the Commission is factually

[582] See the Opinion of AG Kokott in Case C-202/06 P *Cementbouw Handel Industrie BV v Commission* EU:C:2007:255, para 69.

[583] Case T-282/02 EU:T:2006:64, paras 293–321, upheld on appeal Case C-202/06 P EU:C:2007:814.

[584] See Case T-2/93 *Air France v Commission* EU:T:1994:55, paras 42–47; the General Court has held that the appellants lacked standing in Case T-350/03 *Wirtschaftskammer Kärnten v Commission* EU:T:2006:257 and in Case T-224/10 *Association belge des consommateurs test-achats ASBL v Commission* EU:T:2011:588, paras 74–85.

[585] Case T-342/00 *Petrolessence SA v Commission* EU:T:2003:97, paras 36–42.

[586] Case T-269/03 *Socratec v Commission* EU:T:2009:211; see similarly Case T-145/03 *Festival Crociere v Commission* EU:T:2006:98.

[587] Third parties in the US have standing only where they can show that they would suffer direct antitrust injury: see *Cargill Inc v Monfort of Colorado Inc* 479 US 104 (1986); in a case on state aids the Court of Justice took a stricter view on the rights of third parties to appeal in Case C-260/05 P *Sniace SA v Commission* EU:C:2007:700, paras 49–61.

[588] Case C-12/03 P *Commission v Tetra Laval* EU:C:2005:87, para 39.

[589] See further Bailey 'Standard of Proof in EC Merger Proceedings: A Common Law Perspective' (2003) 40 CML Rev 845; Castillo de la Torre and Gippini Fournier *Evidence, Proof and Judicial Review in EU Competition Law* (Edward Elgar, 2017), ch 2.

accurate, reliable and consistent; whether that evidence contains all relevant information; and whether the evidence is capable of substantiating the conclusions drawn from it[590]. In *Tetra Laval* the Commission's conclusions were held to be inaccurate as they were based on insufficient, incomplete, insignificant and inconsistent evidence[591].

In *Bertelsmann v Impala*[592] the Court of Justice held that the General Court was wrong to expect the Commission to apply 'particularly demanding requirements' to the notifying parties' evidence and arguments in response to the statement of objections[593].

(D) The expedited procedure

The expedited procedure[594] enables the General Court to deal with cases more quickly than is usual; this is particularly important in the case of a decision prohibiting a merger, since a prolonged appeal may mean that market conditions change so substantially between the Commission's prohibition decision and the General Court's eventual judgment that, even after a successful appeal, it is no longer possible to proceed with the deal. The pleadings in a case under the expedited procedure are simplified and greater emphasis is placed on the oral hearing; this procedure is not suitable for a case involving a substantial number of points of appeal. Requests for an expedited procedure have sometimes been refused[595].

By 8 December 2017 the General Court had given judgments in 12 merger cases in which the expedited procedure had been used[596].

The shortest period between the lodging of an appeal and the judgment in an expedited procedure case was seven months in *EDP v Commission*[597] and the longest was 21 months in *Impala v Commission*[598]. Judgments in cases under the expedited procedure are likely to be shorter than in a 'normal' appeal[599]. In *Impala* the General Court was critical of the fact that Impala, having asked for the expedited procedure to be used, was itself responsible for slowing the progress of the case[600].

(E) Examples of third party appeals

(i) Appeals against the Commission's refusal to take jurisdiction

In *Schlüsselverlag JS Moser GmbH v Commission*[601] a merger was cleared by the relevant competition authority in Austria. Schlüsselverlag complained to the Commission that the merger in question had a Union dimension, and that therefore the Commission should have investigated it, not the domestic authority in Austria. The Court of Justice rejected the Commission's argument that it was not obliged to define its position when asked to do so by the appellant: the Court of Justice considered that it was vital, given that the Commission has sole jurisdiction in relation to concentrations having a Union dimension, that it should be required to take a decision if asked to do so[602]. However

[590] Case C-12/03 P *Commission v Tetra Laval* EU:C:2005:87, para 39; similarly Case T-175/12 *Deutsche Börse v Commission* EU:T:2015:148, para 66.

[591] Case C-12/03 P EU:C:2005:87, para 40.

[592] Case C-413/06 P EU:C:2008:392.

[593] Ibid, paras 87–96.

[594] OJ [2015] L 105/1, Article 151.

[595] An example is Case T-145/06 *Omya AG v Commission* EU:T:2009:27, para 12.

[596] A Table of Expedited Procedure merger cases will be found in the Online Resources that accompany this book, www.oup.com/uk/whish9e/.

[597] Case T-87/05 EU:T:2005:333.

[598] Case T-464/04 EU:T:2006:216.

[599] Case T-87/05 *EDP v Commission* EU:T:2005:333, para 39.

[600] Case T-464/04 EU:T:2006:216, paras 544–554, set aside on other grounds on appeal to the Court of Justice Case C-413/06 P EU:C:2008:392.

[601] Case C-170/02 P EU:C:2003:501.

[602] Ibid, paras 25–30.

the appeal was rejected as the appellant had unduly delayed the making of its complaint to the Commission[603]. In *Endesa v Commission*[604] the General Court rejected Endesa's argument that a hostile bid for it by Gas Natural had a Union dimension and therefore fell within the jurisdiction of the Commission.

(ii) Appeals against Article 9 references

In *Cableuropa v Commission*[605] the General Court held that a third party that objected to the Commission's decision to refer a merger to the Spanish competition authorities under Article 9 of the EUMR had the standing to challenge that decision[606], but upheld the Commission's decision on the merits. However a third party does not have standing to challenge a Commission decision declining to refer a merger under Article 9[607].

(iii) Appeals against unconditional clearances

There have been several unsuccessful appeals by third parties against unconditional clearance decisions of the Commission[608]. However in one particularly striking case, *Impala v Commission*[609], a third party successfully persuaded the General Court that the Commission had wrongly cleared a merger with the result that the clearance decision in *Sony/Bertelsmann* was annulled[610]. This meant that the Commission had to re-investigate the case, leading to a second clearance decision in October 2007, more than three years after the original decision[611].

(iv) Appeals against conditional clearances

There have been several appeals by third parties against conditional clearance decisions, usually unsuccessful[612]. A successful case was *BaByliss v Commission*[613] where the Commission required commitments in relation to certain national markets, for example Germany and Austria, but not in relation to others, for example Spain and Italy, in order to clear a merger[614]. BaByliss appealed to the General Court claiming among other things that the Commission should not have authorised the concentration without commitments in relation to markets with serious competition problems. The General Court accepted the argument and annulled the Commission's decision in so far as it concerned the markets in the countries not covered by the commitments[615]. This led to a second decision

603 Ibid, paras 31–40.

604 Case T-417/05 EU:T:2006:219.

605 Cases T-346/02 and T-347/02 EU:T:2003:256; see similarly Case T-119/02 *Royal Philips Electronics v Commission* EU:T:2003:101, paras 254–300.

606 Ibid, paras 47–82.

607 Case T-224/10 *Association belge des consommateurs test-achats ASBL v Commission* EU:T:2011:588, paras 74–85.

608 See eg Case T-2/93 *Air France v Commission* EU:T:1994:55; Case T-290/94 *Kayserberg v Commission* EU:T:1997:186; Case T-282/06 *Sun Chemical Group BV v Commission* EU:T:2007:203; Case T-151/05 *Nederlandse Vakbond Varkenshouders v Commission* EU:T:2009:144; Case T-79/12 *Cisco Systems Inc v Commission* EU:T:2013:635.

609 Case T-464/04 EU:T:2006:216; note that, on appeal to the Court of Justice, the General Court's judgment was reversed: Case C-413/06 P *Bertelsmann AG v Impala* EU:C:2008:392.

610 Case M 3333 *Sony/Bertelsmann*, decision of 19 July 2004.

611 Case M 3333, decision of 3 October 2007.

612 See eg Case T-119/02 *Royal Philips Electronics BV v Commission* EU:T:2003:101; Case T-158/00 *ARD v Commission* EU:T:2003:246; Case T-177/04 *easyJet v Commission* EU:T:2006:187; Case T-48/04 *Qualcomm Wireless Business Solutions Europe BV v Commission* EU:T:2009:212; Case T-224/10 *Association belge des consommateurs test-achats ASBL v Commission* EU:T:2011:588; Case T-162/10 *Niki Luftfahrt GmbH v Commission* EU:T:2015:283.

613 Case T-114/02 *BaByliss v Commission* EU:T:2003:100.

614 Case M 2621 *SEB/Moulinex*, decision of 8 January 2002.

615 Case T-114/02 *BaByliss v Commission* EU:T:2003:100, paras 308–411.

again clearing the merger subject to conditions[616]. Another successful case was *KPN v Commission*[617] where the General Court annulled the decision in *Liberty Global/Viggo* because the Commission had failed to analyse properly the vertical effects of the merger.

A different point arose in *Petrolessence v Commission*[618] where the Commission required certain assets to be divested as a condition of approving a merger[619]. A potential purchaser of the assets was rejected by the Commission on the basis that it would not be an effective competitor and was therefore an unsuitable purchaser. The General Court held that Petrolessence had standing to appeal[620], but it was unsuccessful on the merits[621].

(v) Appeals seeking access to information

In various cases applicants have successfully appealed to the General Court seeking access to information in the Commission's possession[622].

(F) Damages claims against the Commission

Two (unsuccessful) applications for damages have been made to the General Court for harm suffered as a result of a prohibition decision of the Commission which had been annulled on appeal[623]. In *Commission v Schneider Electric*[624] the Commission's prohibition of the *Schneider/Legrand* merger had been annulled on appeal to the General Court[625]. Schneider sued the Commission for damages, and was successful before the General Court[626]; however the Court of Justice reversed the General Court's judgment since it considered that Schneider's financial loss was not actually caused by the Commission's prohibition decision[627].

In *MyTravel Group plc v Commission*[628] MyTravel, formerly Airtours, sued the Commission for damages arising from its decision in *Airtours/First Choice*[629] which was annulled on appeal by the General Court[630]. The Court held that it cannot be ruled out in principle that manifest and grave defects underlying the Commission's substantive analysis could constitute breaches that are sufficiently serious to give rise to a claim for damages. However, taking into account the complexity of merger control and the Commission's margin of appreciation, the Court concluded that the Commission had not

616 Case M 2621 *SEB/Moulinex II*, decision of 11 November 2003, see the Commission's *Annual Report on Competition* (2003), paras 259–262.

617 Case T-394/15 EU:T:2017:756.

618 Case T-342/00 EU:T:2003:97.

619 Case M 1628 *TotalFina/Elf*, decision of 9 February 2000, OJ [2001] L 143/1.

620 Case T-342/00 EU:T:2003:97, paras 36–42.

621 Ibid, paras 100–123.

622 See Case T-111/07 *Agrofert Holding v Commission* EU:T:2010:285, annulled in part on appeal to the Court of Justice Case C-477/10 P *Commission v Agrofert Holdings* EU:C:2012:394; Case T-237/05 *Éditions Jacob v Commission* EU:T:2010:224, annulled in part on appeal to the Court of Justice Case C-404/10 P *Commission v Éditions Odile SAS* EU:C:2012:393; Case T-403/05 *MyTravel v Commission* EU:T:2008:316, annulled on appeal to the Court of Justice Case C-506/08 P *Sweden v Commission* EU:C:2011:496, paras 72–103 and 109–119.

623 See generally Bailey 'Damages Actions under the EC Merger Regulation' (2007) 44 CML Rev 101.

624 Case C-440/07 P *Commission v Schneider Electric SA* EU:C:2009:459.

625 Case T-310/01 *Schneider Electric SA v Commission* EU:T:2002:254.

626 Case T-351/03 *Schneider Electric SA v Commission* EU:T:2007:212.

627 Case C-440/07 P *Commission v Schneider Electric SA* EU:C:2009:459, paras 205 and 218–223; Schneider was awarded damages for the cost of having to undergo a second investigation of its transaction as a result of the annulment of the first Commission decision.

628 Case T-212/03 EU:T:2008:315.

629 Case M 1524, decision of 22 September 1999, OJ [2000] L 93/1.

630 Case T-342/99 *Airtours v Commission* EU:T:2002:146.

committed a sufficiently serious error in either its assessment of collective dominance or of the remedies offered by MyTravel to justify the award of damages against it.

In *UPS v Commission*[631] UPS is suing the Commission for damages arising from its decision in *UPS/TNT Express*[632], which was annulled on appeal by the General Court for procedural reasons[633].

9. International Cooperation

(A) Close and constant liaison with Member States

Article 4(3) TEU establishes the principle of cooperation between Member States and the institutions of the EU. In the context of the EUMR Article 19 sets out detailed provisions to establish liaison between the Commission and the Member States. Notifications under the EUMR must be transmitted to the competent authorities of Member States, which must be able to express their views on the Commission's treatment of cases; and the Advisory Committee on Concentrations must be consulted before important decisions—for example at the end of Phase II, or imposing fines—are taken. The Advisory Committee's opinion is not binding on the Commission, but considerable importance is attached to it. The General Court in *Kayserberg v Commission*[634] rejected a claim by a third party objecting to the Commission's clearance of the *Procter & Gamble/VP Schickedanz* transaction[635]; the third party was arguing that the Advisory Committee had not been properly consulted.

The Commission also cooperates with the EFTA Surveillance Authority pursuant to the provisions of the EEA Agreement[636]. This cooperation is provided for by Articles 57 and 58 of the EEA Agreement and Protocol 24.

As a separate matter the heads of the national competition authorities of the EU and the Commission have adopted best practices to handle cross-border mergers that do not benefit from the one-stop shop under the EUMR[637].

(B) Relations with non-EU countries

(i) Reciprocity

Article 24 addresses the issue of reciprocity of treatment of mergers by non-EU countries. Some systems of law make it difficult, if not impossible, for foreign firms to take over local ones. Not surprisingly resentment is felt where, for example, a British firm is prevented from taking over a foreign one in circumstances in which, were the roles reversed, there would be no obstacle to the merger under UK law. Article 24(1) of the EUMR requires Member States to inform the Commission of any difficulties encountered by their undertakings in the case of concentrations in non-EU countries. Where it appears that a non-EU country is not affording reciprocal treatment to that granted by a Member State, the Commission may seek a mandate from the Council of Ministers to negotiate comparable treatment.

[631] Case T-834/17 *UPS v Commission*, not yet decided.

[632] Case M 6570, decision of 30 January 2013.

[633] Case T-194/13 *UPS v Commission* EU:T:2017:144, on appeal to the Court of Justice Case C-265/17 P *Commission v UPS*, not yet decided.

[634] Case T-290/94 EU:T:1997:186, paras 57–58.

[635] Case M 430, OJ [1994] L 354/32.

[636] See ch 2, 'European Economic Area', pp 57–58.

[637] Available at www.ec.europa.eu/competition/ecn/mergers.html.

(ii) The international dimension

It is possible that a transaction might fall within the merger control systems of the EU, the US, Canada and many other countries. The problems associated with the international dimension—the burden on companies of multiple filings, the need for cooperation between competition authorities and the desirability of an expeditious and harmonious outcome—are considerable. These have been discussed in chapter 12, including the territorial reach of the EUMR and cooperation agreements between the EU, the US, Canada, Japan, South Korea and Switzerland[638].

10. The EUMR in Practice

(A) Statistics

From 21 September 1990, when the original EUMR entered into force, until 8 December 2017 the number of notifications received and decisions reached by the Commission were as shown in Table 21.1.

(B) Table of Phase II investigations

Table 21.2 contains a list of cases in which a Phase II investigation was completed between the publication of the eighth edition of this book in 2015 and 8 December 2017[639].

(C) Comment

(i) Outright prohibitions

Outright prohibitions are rare: by 8 December 2017 there had been only 27 examples, of which five were annulled on appeal to the General Court[640].

The first concentration to be blocked, in 1991, was *Aerospatiale-Alenia/de Havilland*[641]. Aerospatiale and Alenia intended to purchase the De Havilland division of Boeing. The Commissioner responsible for Industry disagreed violently over the decision with the Competition Commissioner, in particular as industrial policy considerations were not taken on board. However the language of Article 2(3) of the EUMR does not provide for industrial policy to be taken into account, and the decision helped to establish that the test of the compatibility of a concentration with the internal market was its impact on competition[642].

The second concentration to be blocked, in 1994, was *MSG Media Service*[643]. Three companies intended to establish a German pay-TV joint venture, MSG. In the Commission's view the joint venture would give MSG a lasting dominant position on the pay-TV market for administrative and technical services; it would give Bertelsmann and Kirch a dominant position on the German-speaking pay-TV market; and it would protect and strengthen the dominant position of Deutsche Telekom for cable infrastructure. This was

[638] See ch 12, 'EU Merger Regulation', pp 506–508 and 'The EU's dedicated cooperation agreements on competition policy', pp 517–519.

[639] A complete list of all Phase II cases can be found at www.ec.europa.eu/competition/mergers/cases.

[640] See 'Prohibition decisions annulled on appeal', pp 928–929 later in chapter.

[641] Case M 53, decision of 2 October 1991, OJ [1991] L 334/42.

[642] See Fox 'Merger Control in the EEC—Towards a European Merger Jurisprudence' [1991] Fordham Corporate Law Institute (ed Hawk), 738–739.

[643] Case M 469, decision of 9 November 1994, OJ [1994] L 364/1.

Table 21.1 Table of EUMR statistics

21 September 1990 to 30 November 2017

I.) NOTIFICATIONS

	90	91	92	93	94	95	96	97	98	99	00	01	02	03	04	05	06	07	08	09	10	11	12	13	14	15	16	November 17	Total
Number of notified cases	11	64	59	59	95	110	131	168	224	276	330	335	277	211	247	318	356	402	348	259	274	309	283	277	303	337	362	**360**	**6785**
Cases withdrawn - Phase 1	0	0	3	1	6	4	5	9	5	7	8	8	3	0	3	6	7	5	10	6	4	9	4	1	6	6	8	**7**	**141**
Cases withdrawn - Phase 2	0	0	0	1	0	0	1	0	4	5	5	4	1	0	2	3	2	2	3	2	0	1	1	0	0	2	1	**2**	**42**

II.) REFERRALS

	90	91	92	93	94	95	96	97	98	99	00	01	02	03	04	05	06	07	08	09	10	11	12	13	14	15	16	November 17	Total
Art 4(4) request (Form RS)	0	0	0	0	0	0	0	0	0	0	0	0	0	0	2	14	13	5	9	8	6	10	13	11	16	13	16	**13**	**149**
Art 4(4) referral to Member State	0	0	0	0	0	0	0	0	0	0	0	0	0	0	2	11	13	5	9	6	7	10	12	9	14	12	11	**14**	**135**
Art 4(4) partial referral to Member State	0	0	0	0	0	0	0	0	0	0	0	0	0	0	0	0	0	1	0	0	0	1	0	2	0	2	4	**1**	**11**
Art 4(4) refusal of referral	0	0	0	0	0	0	0	0	0	0	0	0	0	0	0	0	0	0	0	0	0	0	0	0	0	0	0	**0**	**0**
Art 4(5) request (Form RS)	0	0	0	0	0	0	0	0	0	0	0	0	0	0	20	28	38	51	23	23	26	18	22	13	19	20	23	**13**	**337**
Art 4(5) referral accepted	0	0	0	0	0	0	0	0	0	0	0	0	0	0	16	24	39	50	22	25	24	17	22	11	19	19	22	**15**	**325**
Art 4(5) refusal of referral	0	0	0	0	0	0	0	0	0	0	0	0	0	0	2	0	0	2	0	0	1	0	1	0	0	1	0	**0**	**7**
Art 22 request	0	0	0	1	0	1	1	1	0	0	0	0	2	1	1	4	4	3	2	1	3	1	3	1	1	1	0	**1**	**33**
Art 22(3) referral (Art 22. 4 taken in conjunction with article 6 or 8 under Reg. 4064\89)	0	0	0	1	0	1	1	1	0	0	0	0	2	1	1	3	3	2	3	1	2	2	2	1	1	1	0	**1**	**30**
Art 22(3) refusal of referral																1	1	0	0	0	1	0	1	0	0	0	0	**0**	**4**
Art 9 request	0	1	1	1	1	0	3	7	4	9	4	9	8	10	4	7	6	3	5	3	11	2	2	2	2	3	3	**1**	**112**
Art 9.3 partial referral to Member State	0	0	1	0	1	0	0	6	3	2	3	6	7	1	1	3	1	1	2	0	3	0	1	0	0	1	1	**0**	**44**
Art 9.3 full referral	0	0	0	1	0	0	3	1	1	3	2	1	4	8	2	3	1	1	2	1	4	2	1	0	0	0	0	**0**	**41**
Art 9.3 refusal of referral	0	1	0	0	0	0	0	0	0	1	0	0	0	1	0	0	0	1	0	1	1	0	0	0	3	3	1	**1**	**14**

III.) FIRST PHASE DECISIONS

	90	91	92	93	94	95	96	97	98	99	00	01	02	03	04	05	06	07	08	09	10	11	12	13	14	15	16	November 17	Total
Art 6.1 (a) out of scope Merger Regulation	2	5	9	4	5	9	6	4	4	1	1	1	1	0	0	0	0	0	0	0	0	0	0	0	1	1	1	**0**	**55**
Art 6.1 (b) compatible	5	47	43	49	78	90	109	118	196	225	278	299	238	203	220	276	323	368	307	225	253	299	254	252	280	297	327	**317**	**5976**
Art 6.1(b) compatible, under simplified procedure (figures included in 6.1(b) compatible above)	0	0	0	0	0	0	0	0	0	0	41	141	103	110	138	169	211	238	190	143	143	191	171	166	207	222	247	**249**	**3080**
Art 6.1 (b) in conjunction with Art 6.2 (compatible w. commitments)	0	3	4	0	2	3	0	2	12	16	26	11	10	11	12	15	13	18	19	13	14	5	9	11	12	13	19	**17**	**290**

(Continued)

Table 21.1 (*Continued*)

IV.) PHASE II PROCEEDINGS INITIATED

																												November	
	90	**91**	**92**	**93**	**94**	**95**	**96**	**97**	**98**	**99**	**00**	**01**	**02**	**03**	**04**	**05**	**06**	**07**	**08**	**09**	**10**	**11**	**12**	**13**	**14**	**15**	**16**	**17**	**Total**
Art 6.1 (c)	0	6	4	4	6	7	6	11	11	20	18	21	7	9	8	10	13	15	10	5	4	8	10	6	8	11	8	**6**	**252**

V.) SECOND PHASE DECISIONS

																												November	
	90	**91**	**92**	**93**	**94**	**95**	**96**	**97**	**98**	**99**	**00**	**01**	**02**	**03**	**04**	**05**	**06**	**07**	**08**	**09**	**10**	**11**	**12**	**13**	**14**	**15**	**16**	**17**	**Total**
Art 8.1 compatible (8.2 under Reg. 4064/89)	0	1	1	1	2	2	1	1	3	0	3	5	2	2	2	2	4	5	9	0	1	4	1	2	2	1	1	**0**	**58**
Art 8.2 compatible with commitments	0	3	3	2	2	3	3	7	4	7	12	9	5	6	4	3	6	4	5	3	2	1	6	2	5	7	6	**2**	**122**
Art 8.3 prohibition	0	1	0	0	1	2	3	1	2	1	2	5	0	0	1	0	0	1	0	0	0	1	1	2	0	0	1	**2**	**27**
Art 8.4 restore effective competition	0	0	0	0	0	0	0	2	0	0	0	0	2	0	0	0	0	0	0	0	0	0	0	0	0	0	0	**0**	**4**

VI.) OTHER DECISIONS

																												November	
	90	**91**	**92**	**93**	**94**	**95**	**96**	**97**	**98**	**99**	**00**	**01**	**02**	**03**	**04**	**05**	**06**	**07**	**08**	**09**	**10**	**11**	**12**	**13**	**14**	**15**	**16**	**17**	**Total**
Art 6.3 decision revoked	0	0	0	0	0	0	0	0	0	1	0	0	0	0	0	0	0	0	0	0	0	0	0	0	0	0	0	**0**	**1**
Art 8.6 decision revoked	0	0	0	0	0	0	0	0	0	0	0	0	0	0	0	0	0	0	0	0	0	0	0	0	0	0	0	**0**	**0**
Art 14 decision imposing fines	0	0	0	0	0	0	0	0	1	4	1	0	1	0	1	0	0	0	0	1	0	0	0	0	1	0	0	**1**	**11**
Art 7.3 derogation from suspension (7.4 under Reg. 4064/89)	1	1	2	3	3	2	4	5	13	7	4	7	14	8	10	6	2	3	6	5	1	3	2	1	1	1	0	**4**	**119**
Art 21	0	0	0	0	0	1	0	1	0	1	1	0	1	0	0	0	2	1	0	0	0	0	0	0	0	0	0	**0**	**8**

Table 21.2 EUMR Table of Phase II investigations

Name of case	Cleared?	Cleared with commitments?	Prohibited?
Case M 7194 *Liberty Global/De Vijver Media*		Yes (24.02.15)	
Case M 7265 *Zimmer Holdings Inc/Biomet Inc*		Yes (03.03.15)	
Case M 7292 *DEMB/Mondelez/Charger Opco*		Yes (05.05.15)	
Case M 7612 *Hutchison 3G UK/Telefónica UK*			Yes (11.05.15)
Case M 7421 *Orange/Jazztel*			
NB: Article 9 request by Spain, rejected on 26 January 2015		Yes (19.05.15)	
Case M 6800 *PRSfM/STIM/GEMA/JV*		Yes (16.06.15)	
NB: Article 4(5) request			
Case M 7429 *Siemens/Dresser-Rand*	Yes (29.06.15)		
Case M 7408 *Cargill/Adm Chocolate Business*		Yes (17.07.15)	
Case M 7278 *General Electric/Alstom*		Yes (08.09.15)	
Case M 7630 *Fedex/TNT Express*	Yes (08.01.16)		
Case M 7567 *Ball/Rexam*		Yes (15.01.16)	
Case M 7555 *Staples/Office Depot*		Yes (10.02.16)	
Case M 7637 *Liberty Global/Base Belgium*		Yes (18.04.16)	
Case M 7724 *Airbus Safran Launchers/Arianespace*		Yes (20.07.16)	
Case M 7758 *Hutchison/VimpelCom*		Yes (01.09.16)	
Case M 7801 *Westinghouse (Wabtec)/Faiveley*		Yes (04.10.16)	
Case M 7932 *Dow/DuPont*		Yes (27.03.17)	
Case M 7995 *Deutsche Börse/London Stock Exchange*			Yes (29.03.17)

(Continued)

Table 21.2 (*Continued*)

Name of case	Cleared?	Cleared with commitments?	Prohibited?
Case M 7878 *HeidelbergCement/Schwenk/Cemex Croatia*			Yes (05.04.17)
NB The substantive decision is on appeal Case T-380/17 as to the substantive decision			
Case M 7962 *Syngenta/ChemChina*		Yes (05.04.17)	
Case M 8222 *Knorr-Bremse/Haldex*			
NB: abandoned by the parties			

the first of several concentrations in the media sector to be prohibited outright: the rapid changes in technology in this sector, and the possibility that concentrations could have serious foreclosure effects on third parties, particularly through vertical integration, help to explain the Commission's cautious approach[644].

Three of the outright prohibitions—*RTL/Veronica/Endemol*[645], *Kesko/Tuko*[646] and *Blokker/Toys 'R' Us*[647]—were requests from Member States under Article 22 of the EUMR. That these requests led to prohibitions is perhaps not surprising: at the time the Member States making the requests (the Netherlands and Finland) had no domestic system of merger control and had obviously concluded that there was a very serious threat to competition, so that the cases were always likely to raise serious doubts.

Of the other outright prohibitions *Gencor/Lonrho*[648] was an important case on the meaning of collective dominance or, to use more modern language, coordinated effects[649]. In *Saint-Gobain/Wacker-Chemie/NOM*[650] the Commission found that the merged entity would enjoy very high market shares in relation to silicon carbide, substantially higher than its competitors, that potential competition and countervailing power were weak and that the case could not be 'saved' by an efficiency or a failing firm defence. In *Volvo/Scania*[651] the Commission prohibited a merger that would lead to high market shares for buses and trucks in a series of national markets, Sweden, Finland, Denmark, Norway and Ireland: the delimitation of national markets, rather than a European-wide one, was a

644 See also Case M 490 *Nordic Satellite Distribution*, decision of 19 July 1995, OJ [1996] L 53/20; Case M 553 *RTL/Veronica/Endemol*, decision of 17 July 1996, OJ [1996] L 134/32 (this concentration was subsequently cleared in an amended form: OJ [1996] L 294/14); Case M 993 *Bertelsmann/Kirch/Premiere*, decision of 27 May 1998, OJ [1999] L 53/1; Case M 1027 *Deutsche Telekom/BetaResearch* OJ [1999] L 53/31.

645 Case M 553 *RTL/Veronica/Endemol*, decision of 17 July 1996, OJ [1996] L 134/32, upheld on appeal Case T-221/95 *Endemol Entertainment Holding BV v Commission* EU:T:1999:85.

646 Case M 784 *Kesko/Tuko*, decision of 20 November 1996, OJ [1997] L 174/47, upheld on appeal Case T-22/97 *Kesko v Commission* EU:T:1999:327.

647 Case M 890 *Blokker/Toys 'R' Us*, decision of 26 June 1997, OJ [1998] L 316/1.

648 Case M 619, decision of 24 April 1996, OJ [1997] L 11/30, upheld on appeal Case T-102/96 *Gencor v Commission* EU:T:1999:65.

649 See 'Coordinated effects', pp 893–895 earlier in chapter.

650 Case M 774, decision of 4 December 1996, OJ [1997] L 247/1.

651 Case M 1672, decision of 15 March 2000, OJ [2001] L 143/74.

crucial feature of this case. In the countries where the Commission identified a problem the evidence showed that Volvo and Scania were each other's closest competitors. The concentration in *SCA/Metsä Tissue*[652] was prohibited as it would have led to very high market shares in hygienic tissue products in Scandinavia and Finland. The Commission blocked the concentration in *CVC/Lenzing*[653] because the merged entity would have market power in the man-made fibre sector and because CVC already controlled Lenzing's main rival.

The prohibition decision in *GE/Honeywell*[654] was particularly controversial. This was an agreed merger between two US undertakings which had been cleared in the US. The Commission prohibited it, predominantly because of its vertical and conglomerate effects, on grounds that were anathema to the US Department of Justice. On appeal to the General Court the Commission's reasoning on both vertical and conglomerate effects was severely criticised; nevertheless GE's appeal was unsuccessful, because the General Court accepted that there were some horizontal effects that justified the prohibition of the merger[655].

In *ENI/EDP/GDP*[656] the Commission prohibited a proposed acquisition by EDP, the incumbent electricity company in Portugal, of GDP, the incumbent gas company. The Commission was concerned both at the horizontal and vertical implications of the transaction, and resisted suggestions that a Portuguese 'national champion' should be created. An expedited appeal was made to the General Court which upheld the Commission's decision[657].

A proposed merger was prohibited in *Ryanair/Aer Lingus*[658], where the Commission was particularly concerned that the merged airline would have accounted for around 80% of intra-European air traffic from and to Dublin airport: an appeal by Ryanair to the General Court was unsuccessful[659]. A further attempt by Ryanair to acquire Aer Lingus was prohibited in 2013[660]. The second Ryanair prohibition is noticeable for the Commission's refusal to approve Flybe, a third airline, as a suitable purchaser of Aer Lingus's operations on 43 routes on which it competed with Ryanair.

In *Olympic Airways/Aegean Airlines*[661] the Commission prohibited the merger that would have led to the parties having very high market shares (and in some cases a monopoly) on various air routes within Greece; however a merger of these two airlines was subsequently cleared unconditionally in 2013 when the Commission accepted that Olympic had become a failing firm[662].

In *Deutsche Börse/NYSE Euronext*[663] the Commission prohibited a merger that would have led to a near-monopoly in the market for financial products bought and sold on traditional exchanges (rather than 'over-the-counter'). The exclusion of over-the-counter sales from the relevant product market was crucial to the outcome in this case. The Commission concluded

[652] Case M 2097, decision of 31 January 2001, OJ [2002] L 57/1.

[653] Case M 2187, decision of 17 October 2001, OJ [2004] L 82/20.

[654] Case M 2220, decision of 3 July 2001.

[655] Case T-210/01 *General Electric v Commission* EU:T:2005:456.

[656] Case M 3440 *ENI/EDP/GDP*, decision of 9 December 2004, OJ [2005] L 302/69.

[657] Case T-87/05 *EDP v Commission* EU:T:2005:333.

[658] Case M 4439, decision of 27 June 2007.

[659] Case T-342/07 *Ryanair v Commission* EU:T:2010:280; Aer Lingus failed in a separate appeal against the Commission's decision not to require Ryanair to divest itself of all its shares in Aer Lingus, Case T-411/07 *Aer Lingus Group v Commission* EU:T:2010:281, see further ch 22, 'Time limits and prior notice', p 947 on this issue.

[660] Case M 6663, decision of 27 February 2013.

[661] Case M 5830, decision of 26 January 2011.

[662] Case M 6796, decision of 9 October 2013.

[663] Case M 6166, decision of 1 February 2012, upheld on appeal Case T-175/12 *Deutsche Börse v Commission* EU:T:2015:148.

that the efficiencies the merger might bring about were insufficient to prevent a finding of an SIEC[664]. The Commission's decision was upheld on appeal to the General Court[665].

In *Hutchison 3G UK/Telefónica UK*[666] the Commission was concerned that a merger in the UK mobile telephony market would have created a market leader able to influence the entire mobile network there; the merger would have been likely to lead to higher prices and less investment in mobile telecommunications networks. In *HeidelbergCement/Schwenk/Cemex Hungary/Cemex Croatia*[667] the Commission prohibited a merger that would have led to an SIEC and consequently increased prices for grey cement in Croatia. In *Deutsche Börse/London Stock Exchange*[668] the Commission blocked the merger because it would have created a *de facto* monopoly in the markets for clearing fixed income instruments.

(ii) Prohibition decisions annulled on appeal

Five prohibition decisions have been annulled on appeal. In *Airtours/First Choice*[669] the Commission had prohibited the proposed hostile acquisition by Airtours of First Choice on the basis of collective dominance[670]. The General Court, in an excoriating judgment, annulled the decision on the basis of manifest error of assessment: it was particularly critical of the Commission's assessment of the evidence and of its reasoning[671]. The mergers in *Schneider Electric/Legrand*[672] and *Tetra Laval/Sidel*[673] were both prohibited by the Commission, but each decision (together with additional decisions requiring the mergers to be reversed) was annulled on appeal to the General Court[674]; an appeal by the Commission in *Tetra Laval/Sidel* was unsuccessful[675]. In *Schneider/Legrand* the General Court subsequently awarded Schneider damages for some of the economic loss it had suffered[676]. The prohibition decision in *MCI WorldCom/Sprint*[677] was annulled by the General Court since the parties had terminated their agreement by the time of the Commission's decision; the mere fact that they were continuing to negotiate an agreement in a modified form did not entitle the Commission to adopt a decision[678].

In *UPS/TNT Express*[679] the Commission prohibited a merger that would have led to non-collusive oligopoly, the only prohibition decision to date for this reason. In some national markets within the EU the merger would have left three competitors, and in others two, in the market for the express delivery of small packages; however the merged

[664] Case M 6166, decision of 1 February 2012, paras 1133–1342.

[665] Case T-175/12 *Deutsche Börse v Commission* EU:T:2015:148.

[666] Case M 7612, decision of 11 May 2016, on appeal Case T-399/16 *CK Telecoms UK Investments v Commission*, not yet decided.

[667] Case M 7878, decision of 5 April 2017, on appeal Case T-380/17 *HeidelbergCement and Schwenk Cement v Commission*, not yet decided.

[668] Case M 7995, decision of 29 March 2017.

[669] Case M 1524 *Airtours/First Choice*, decision of 22 September 1999, OJ [2000] L 93/1.

[670] See 'The non-collusive oligopoly gap', pp 883–885.

[671] Case T-342/99 EU:T:2002:146.

[672] Case M 2283, decision of 10 October 2001.

[673] Case M 2416, decision of 30 October 2001.

[674] Case T-310/01 *Schneider Electric v Commission* EU:T:2002:254 (annulment of prohibition decision); Case T-77/02 *Schneider Electric v Commission* EU:T:2002:255 (annulment of divestiture decision); Case T-5/02 *Tetra Laval v Commission* EU:T:2002:264 (annulment of prohibition decision); Case T-80/02 *Tetra Laval v Commission* EU:T:2002:265 (annulment of divestiture decision).

[675] Case C-12/03 P *Commission v Tetra Laval* EU:C:2005:87 (appeal seeking annulment of the General Court's prohibition decision); Case C-13/03 P *Commission v Tetra Laval* EU:C:2005:88 (appeal seeking annulment of the General Court's divestiture decision).

[676] See 'Damages claims against the Commission', pp 920–921 earlier in chapter.

[677] Case M 1741, decision of 28 June 2000; see the Commission's XXXth *Report on Competition Policy* (2000), point 249 and Box 6.

[678] Case T-310/00 *MCI Inc v Commission* EU:T:2004:275; see further 'Withdrawal of notifications', p 931 later in chapter.

[679] Case M 6570, decision of 30 January 2013.

entity would not be the largest operator in any of these markets. The Commission considered the parties' efficiency claims in detail, but was not convinced that any efficiency benefits from the merger could offset its detriment to competition. This decision was annulled on appeal as the Commission had violated the rights of defence of UPS by failing to disclose changes that it had made to an econometric model that was part of the evidence used to identify a substantial impediment to effective competition[680]. It was not necessary for UPS to show that, but for the procedural irregularity, the Commission's decision would have been different; it was sufficient to show that there was 'even a slight chance' that UPS would have been better able to defend itself[681]. The Commission has appealed to the Court of Justice[682].

(iii) **Unconditional clearances**

It is not inevitable that a case that is taken to a Phase II investigation will lead to a prohibition or require a remedy. A significant proportion of Phase II cases culminate in an unconditional clearance: indeed the merger in *Sony/Bertelsmann* was cleared unconditionally by the Commission twice[683]. This contradicts the view sometimes expressed that, by the time a case reaches Phase II, the Commission has already made up its mind about the outcome; it is possible to demonstrate to the Commission that a merger will not significantly impede effective competition. By 8 December 2017 this had happened in 58 cases out of a total of 211[684].

(iv) **Clearances subject to commitments**

A notable feature of the EUMR is that a majority of Phase II decisions have resulted in clearances subject to commitments. This is shown both in the statistical Table and in the Table of Phase II investigations earlier. The Commission's approach to remedies in merger cases was discussed earlier, and its preference for structural rather than behavioural commitments was noted[685].

There are many recent examples of structural remedies at the end of Phase II. In *Sonoco/Ahlstrom*[686] the parties agreed to divest themselves of a plant in Norway that manufactured paper core to an 'up-front' buyer. In *Inco/Falconbridge*[687] the parties agreed to the divestment of a nickel refinery in Norway to an up-front buyer; interestingly in this case the Commission required that the merged entity should agree to provide important input materials to the buyer on a long-term basis. In *Gaz de France/Suez*[688] the parties agreed to divest various assets in order to address concerns about horizontal overlaps at both the wholesale and retail levels of the gas and electricity markets in France and Belgium; the remedy included a termination of the link between the operator of gas network infrastructure and the supply of gas, effectively an unbundling remedy, as well as an agreement to invest in enhancing the capacity and functioning of the gas network[689]. In *Kronospan Group/Constantia*[690] the Commission was concerned that Kronospan's acquisition of three companies owned by Constantia that produced raw particle board used in the manufacture of furniture would lead to a significant impediment to effective competition;

680 Case T-194/13 *United Parcel Service, Inc v Commission* EU:T:2017:144, paras 198–222.

681 Ibid, para 210. 682 Case C-265/17 P *Commission v United Parcel Service*, not yet decided.

683 See 'Coordinated effects', pp 893–895 earlier in chapter.

684 For comment see Maier-Rigaud and Parplies 'EU Merger Control Five Years After the Introduction of the SIEC Test: What Explains the Drop in Enforcement Activity?' (2009) 11 ECLR 565.

685 See 'Remedies', pp 907–913 earlier in chapter. 686 Case M 3431, decision of 6 October 2004.

687 Case M 4000, decision of 21 July 2006. 688 Case M 4180, decision of 14 November 2006.

689 See Bachour et al '*Gaz de France/Suez*: Keeping energy markets in Belgium and France open and contestable through far-reaching remedies' (2007) 1 Competition Policy Newsletter 83.

690 Case M 4525, decision of 19 September 2007.

the simple remedy in this case was that Kronospan would acquire only two of the three companies: the third one, Fundermax of Austria, would remain with Constantia. In *Lufthansa/SN Holding*[691] and *Lufthansa/Austrian Airlines*[692] the Commission accepted commitments that would lead to take-off and landing slots becoming available at various European airports: this would enable competitors to compete with the merged entities on routes such as Brussels to Vienna; ancillary remedies, on matters such as participation in Lufthansa's Frequent Flyer Programme, were also accepted.

Structural remedies were also given, for example, in *Unilever/Sara Lee Body Care*[693], *Syngenta/Monsanto's sunflower seed business*[694], *Johnson & Johnson/Synthes*[695], *Südzucker/ED&F MAN*[696], *United Technologies/Goodrich*[697], *Outokumpu/Inoxum*[698], *Munksjö/Ahlstrom*[699], *Syniverse/MACH*[700], *INEOS/Solvay*[701], *GE/Alstom*[702], *Ball/Rexam*[703] and three mobile telephony cases, *Hutchison/Telefónica Ireland*[704], *Telefónica Deutschland/E-Plus*[705] and *Hutchison/VimpelCom/JV*[706]. The decision in *Dow/Du Pont*[707] is of interest as the Commission required the parties to divest most of Du Pont's global R&D operations due to the detriment to innovation in the pesticides sector that might be a consequence of the merger.

There have also been some cases in which behavioural commitments have been accepted. For example in *Deutsche Bahn/English Welsh & Scottish Railway Holdings*[708] (a Phase I case) the Commission accepted commitments by Deutsche Bahn to fulfil EW&S's expansion plans for rail freight transport in France by investing in locomotives and personnel and to provide fair and non-discriminatory access to EW&S's driver training schools. In *SFR/Télé 2*[709] a series of remedies was offered to ensure that Vivendi, the owner of valuable television content, would not discriminate against competitors in the downstream pay-TV market; nor that it would weaken competitors in the upstream market for the acquisition of television content. In *PRSfM/STIM/GEMA/JV*[710] the Commission accepted behavioural remedies requiring a joint venture formed by copyright collecting societies to offer copyright administration services on fair, reasonable and non-discriminatory terms. Behavioural remedies were also accepted in *Intel/McAfee*[711] and *Microsoft/LinkedIn*[712] where the concern was with possible conglomerate effects.

It is a notable feature of some cases, particularly in the energy and telecommunications sectors, that the package of remedies may be very complex: obvious examples of this are *E.ON/MOL*[713], a merger impacting on the gas sector in Hungary, where the Commission required a divestment on the part of MOL, a release of gas to the wholesale market and access to storage facilities for customers that succeeded in buying the gas; *Gaz de France/*

[691] Case M 5335, decision of 22 June 2009.

[692] Case M 5440, decision of 28 August 2009 upheld on appeal to the General Court Case T-162/10 *Niki Luftfahrt GmbH v Commission* EU:T:2015:283.

[693] Case M 5658, decision of 17 November 2010.

[694] Case M 5675, decision of 17 November 2010.

[695] Case M 6266, decision of 19 April 2012.

[696] Case M 6286, decision of 16 May 2012.

[697] Case M 6410, decision of 26 July 2012.

[698] Case M 6471, decision of 7 November 2012.

[699] Case M 6576, decision of 24 May 2013.

[700] Case M 6690, decision of 29 May 2013.

[701] Case M 6905, decision of 8 May 2014.

[702] Case M 7278, decision of 8 September 2015.

[703] Case M 7567, decision of 15 January 2016.

[704] Case M 6992, decision of 28 May 2014.

[705] Case M 7018, decision of 2 July 2014.

[706] Case M 7758, decision of 1 September 2016, on appeal Case T-19/17 *Fastweb v Commission*, not yet decided.

[707] Case M 7932, decision of 27 March 2017.

[708] Case M 4746, decision of 7 November 2007.

[709] Case M 4504, decision of 18 July 2007.

[710] Case M 6800, decision of 16 June 2015.

[711] Case M 5984, decision of 26 January 2011.

[712] Case M 8124, decision of 6 December 2017.

[713] Case M 3696, decision of 21 December 2005, OJ [2006] L 253/20.

Suez, referred to earlier; *T-Mobile/tele.ring*, a case that was discussed in the context of non-collusive oligopoly[714]; and *Friesland Foods/Campina*[715] where, apart from structural remedies, a complex set of commitments were accepted to ensure that competitors downstream from the merged entity would have access to raw milk in the Netherlands and that, over a period of time, a competitor to the merged entity might emerge. An interesting feature of the *Universal/EMI*[716] clearance was that it was conditional not only on a divestiture but also on Universal committing not to include a 'Most Favoured Nation' clause in its favour in any new or renegotiated contract with its digital customers in the EEA for ten years.

(v) **Withdrawal of notifications**

There have been many cases in which the parties to a merger subject to a Phase II investigation have chosen to withdraw the notification. Out of 211 cases to have gone to a Phase II investigation by 8 December 2017 42 were then withdrawn. It would be reasonable to assume that at least some of these withdrawals were made because it seemed inevitable that the Commission would otherwise have prohibited the merger. In this sense the total of 27 prohibitions may understate the number of cases that might, but for withdrawal, have led to an outright prohibition.

Article 6(1)(c) of the EUMR provides that the Commission shall conclude a Phase II investigation with a decision, unless it is satisfied that the parties have abandoned the merger. The Commission's *Consolidated Jurisdictional Notice* explains, at paragraphs 117 to 121, the procedure to be followed in such circumstances.

[714] See 'Non-coordinated effects', pp 891–893 earlier in chapter.

[715] Case M 5046, decision of 17 December 2008; see de la Mano et al (2009) 1 Competition Policy Newsletter 84.

[716] Case M 6458, decision of 21 September 2012.

22

Mergers (3): UK law

1. Introduction

UK law on the control of mergers is contained in Part 3 of the Enterprise Act 2002, which entered into force on 20 June 2003; the Enterprise Act was amended by the Enterprise and Regulatory Reform Act 2013 ('the ERRA'), and the text that follows incorporates those amendments[1]. The Enterprise Act 2002 involved a major overhaul of the domestic system of merger control contained in the Fair Trading Act 1973, which it repealed[2]. Specifically the Enterprise Act removed the Secretary of State from decision-making in merger cases other than where exceptional public interest issues arise; the 2002 Act gave the central role of determining whether a merger would 'substantially lessen competition' ('SLC') to the Office of Fair Trading ('the OFT') and the Competition Commission[3]. Since 1 April 2014 the functions of the OFT and Competition Commission have been exercised by the Competition and Markets Authority ('the CMA')[4].

Section 2 of this chapter provides an overview of the domestic system of merger control. Section 3 explains the procedures of the CMA when determining whether a merger should be referred for an in-depth 'Phase 2' investigation and when deciding to accept 'undertakings in lieu' of a reference. Section 4 describes how Phase 2 investigations are conducted and section 5 discusses the way in which the CMA applies the SLC test in practice. Section 6 explains the enforcement powers in the Enterprise Act, as amended by the ERRA, including the remedies that the CMA can impose in merger cases. Various supplementary matters are dealt with in section 7. Section 8 considers how the merger

[1] For more detailed texts on the merger control provisions of the Enterprise Act 2002 readers are referred to Parr, Finbow and Hughes *UK Merger Control: Law and Practice* (Sweet & Maxwell, 3rd ed, 2016); Parker and Majumdar *UK Merger Control* (Hart, 2nd ed, 2016).

[2] Merger control was first introduced in the UK by the Monopolies and Mergers Act 1965.

[3] See the Government's White Paper on *Productivity and Enterprise—a World Class Competition Regime*, Cm 5233, July 2001, available at www.gov.uk; see also the Government's Response of December 2001.

[4] See ch 2, 'The CMA', pp 64–70.

control provisions work in practice and contains a table of the Phase 2 decisions under the Enterprise Act to have been published on the website of the CMA since the last edition of this book, from 2015 to 8 December 2017[5]. Section 9 contains a brief account of the provisions on public interest cases, other special cases and mergers in the water industry. In reading this chapter it should be recalled that, as a general proposition, a 'concentration' that has a 'Union dimension' under the EU Merger Regulation ('the EUMR') cannot be investigated under domestic law[6], although exceptions to this are to be found in Article 4(4)[7], Article 9[8] and in Article 21(4)[9] of the EUMR. Obviously withdrawal by the UK from the EU will change the position considerably, and many mergers that are currently subject to a 'one-stop shop' under the EUMR will also be subject to investigation in the UK as well.

2. Overview of UK Merger Control

(A) Part 3 of the Enterprise Act 2002

Part 3 of the Enterprise Act 2002 consists of five chapters[10]. Chapter 1 of Part 3 of the Act is entitled 'Duty to make references': it deals both with jurisdictional matters, such as the meaning of 'relevant merger situations', and with the substantive assessment of mergers under the SLC test. The overwhelming majority of mergers will be considered under Chapter 1. However Chapter 2 contains provisions on 'public interest' cases and Chapter 3 addresses 'other special cases': these provisions are invoked only rarely; the provisions on public interest and other special cases, and on water mergers, are described briefly in section 9 of this chapter[11]. Chapter 4 of Part 3 of the Enterprise Act contains rules on enforcement, which set out the various undertakings that can be accepted by the CMA in the course of merger investigations and the orders that it may make, as well as certain automatic restrictions on the integration of firms during the currency of an investigation. Chapter 5 deals with numerous supplementary matters such as merger notices, investigatory powers, review by the Competition Appeal Tribunal ('the CAT') and the payment of fees.

The ERRA 2013 strengthened the UK merger regime by amending Part 3 of the Enterprise Act 2002 in several ways[12]: for example it gave the CMA power to gather information during Phase 1 investigations; it introduced new time limits for completing Phase 1 investigations and for implementing Phase 2 remedies; and it strengthened the ability of the CMA to adopt interim measures in order to prevent anything being done that could prejudice the outcome of a merger investigation.

[5] A table of Phase 2 decisions since the 8th edition of this book is available at www.oup.com/uk/whish9e/.

[6] See ch 21, 'Article 21: one-stop merger control', pp 864–866.

[7] See ch 21, 'Pre-notification referrals: Article 4(4)', pp 867–868.

[8] See ch 21, 'Post-notification referrals: Article 9', p 868.

[9] See ch 21, 'Article 21(4): legitimate interest clause', pp 872–875.

[10] The Government's *Explanatory Notes* to the Bill as introduced into Parliament on 26 March 2002 are a helpful adjunct to the Act itself; the Competition Appeal Tribunal has noted that they may be used as an aid to ascertaining the intention of Parliament: see Case 1023/4/1/03 *IBA Health Ltd v OFT* [2003] CAT 27, para 222.

[11] See '"Public Interest Cases", "Other Special Cases" and Mergers in the Water Industry', pp 986–993 later in chapter.

[12] See Todorovic 'The Reform of the UK Merger Regime in the Enterprise and Regulatory Reform Act 2013—Not Much to Shout About?' [2013] Comp Law 338.

(B) Brief description of the system of merger control in the UK

The system of control for 'ordinary' mergers (as opposed to public interest or other special cases) in the Enterprise Act is as follows. The CMA has a duty to refer certain mergers for an in-depth Phase 2 investigation; in some circumstances it has a discretion not to refer, and some mergers cannot be referred at all. There is no obligation on firms to pre-notify mergers to the CMA, although provision is made for doing so on a voluntary basis. In practice many firms choose to have pre-merger discussions with the CMA, not least because power exists to refer a merger for a Phase 2 investigation after it has been consummated and, where appropriate, to require a merger to be reversed: a highly undesirable outcome for the firms concerned. Provision is made for firms to offer, and the CMA to accept, legally-binding undertakings to modify a merger in lieu of a Phase 2 investigation.

In cases where the CMA is concerned that there is a realistic prospect of a merger leading to an SLC and where it is not possible to agree a remedy the merger will be referred for a Phase 2 investigation. Only a small proportion of mergers caught by the Enterprise Act are referred for a Phase 2 investigation. The decision-making authority in a Phase 2 case is an independent group of experts, selected from members of the 'CMA Panel' appointed by the Secretary of State: this 'Inquiry Group', consisting of at least three people, is separate from the team that made the decision at the end of Phase 1[13]. When conducting a Phase 2 investigation, the CMA Inquiry Group must determine:

- whether there is a 'relevant merger situation' that qualifies for investigation and, if so,
- whether the relevant merger situation would lead to an SLC within any market or markets in the UK for goods or services and, if so,
- the appropriate action to remedy, mitigate or prevent the SLC and any adverse effects of it.

The CMA has available to it a number of final powers following its investigation including, where necessary, the power to make an order prohibiting a merger outright, attaching conditions to it or even unscrambling a merger that has already taken place.

(C) Institutional arrangements

The CMA's Markets and Mergers Directorate has a Mergers Unit that has specific responsibility for mergers. There is an Executive Director for Markets and Mergers, a Senior Director of Mergers and a few directors of mergers. The CMA employs administrative, legal, economics and accounting staff to perform its duties. There are also mergers intelligence staff who scan sources of information and who report weekly to a Mergers Intelligence Committee on whether any unnotified mergers may give rise to an SLC[14].

Sectoral regulators do not have concurrent powers in relation to mergers in the way that they do under the Competition Act 1998 and the market investigation provisions in the Enterprise Act[15]; however they are routinely asked to provide input into the deliberations of the CMA where appropriate, and in the case of media and National Health Service mergers OFCOM and NHS Improvement respectively must be involved[16]. Phase 1 and Phase 2 decisions of the CMA are subject to judicial review by the CAT.

[13] See ch 2, 'The CMA', pp 64–70.

[14] *Guidance on the CMA's mergers intelligence function*, CMA56, June 2016.

[15] See ch 10, 'Concurrency', pp 449–452.

[16] *Mergers—Guidance on the CMA's jurisdiction and procedure*, CMA2, January 2014, paras 2.16, 7.13–7.16 and ch 7; on NHS mergers see CMA *Guidance on the review of NHS mergers*, CMA29, 31 July 2014; see also 'The Merger Provisions in Practice', pp 981–986 later in chapter, for discussion of mergers in the healthcare sector.

The Secretary of State is not involved in merger cases, unless there is a public interest consideration: such cases are rare[17].

(D) Guidelines, rules of procedure and other relevant publications

In addition to Part 3 of the Enterprise Act various guidelines, rules and other publications seek to explain the operation of the UK system of merger control. Section 106 of the Act requires the CMA to prepare and publish general advice and information about the making of merger references and about the way in which relevant customer benefits may affect the taking of enforcement action. Section 107 of the Act imposes additional publicity requirements on the CMA and the Secretary of State: for example references, undertakings and orders must all be published.

The CMA Board has adopted a number of guidelines that had been published by the OFT and the Competition Commission on the substantive assessment of mergers; the CMA has also published some guidelines of its own. On 8 December 2017 the following guidelines, listed in chronological order, had been published under the Enterprise Act:

- *Merger Remedies: Competition Commission Guidelines*[18]
- *Suggested best practice for submissions of technical economic analysis from parties to the Competition Commission*[19]
- *Merger Assessment Guidelines*[20]
- *Mergers—Exceptions to the duty to refer and undertakings in lieu of reference guidance*[21]
- *Good practice in the design and presentation of consumer survey evidence in merger inquiries*[22]
- *Chairman's Guidance on Disclosure of Information in Merger Inquiries, Market Investigations and Reviews of Undertakings and Orders accepted or made under the Enterprise Act 2002 and Fair Trading Act 1973*[23]
- *Mergers: Guidance on the CMA's approach to jurisdiction and procedure*[24]
- *Administrative penalties: Statement of policy on the CMA's approach*[25]
- *Transparency and disclosure: Statement of the CMA's policy*[26]
- *Remedies: Guidance on the CMA's approach to the variation and termination of merger, monopoly and market undertakings and orders*[27]
- *A Quick Guide to UK Merger Assessment*[28]
- *Mergers: How to notify the CMA of a merger*[29]
- *Guidance on the review of NHS mergers*[30]
- *Water and sewerage mergers: Guidance on the CMA's procedure and assessment*[31]
- *Guidance on the CMA's mergers intelligence function*[32]

[17] See 'The public interest provisions in practice', p 989 later in chapter.

[18] CC8, November 2008: note that Appendix A of CC8 has been replaced by *Mergers: Guidance on the CMA's jurisdiction and procedure*, CMA2, January 2014.

[19] CC2 com 3, February 2009. [20] OFT 1254/CC2 (Revised), September 2010.

[21] OFT 1122, December 2010, as amended by CMA64, June 2017.

[22] OFT 1230/CC2 com 1, March 2011. [23] CC7 (Revised), April 2013.

[24] CMA2, January 2014. [25] CMA4, January 2014. [26] CMA6, January 2014.

[27] CMA11, January 2014, revised August 2015. [28] CMA18, March 2014.

[29] www.gov.uk/mergers-how-to-notify-the-cma-of-a-merger. [30] CMA29, July 2014.

[31] CMA49, November 2015. [32] CMA56, June 2016, updated 5 September 2017.

- *Retail mergers commentary*[33]
- *Guidance on initial enforcement orders and derogations in merger investigations*[34].

Acting under Schedule 4 to the ERRA the CMA has adopted the *CMA Rules of Procedure for Merger, Market and Special Reference Groups*[35].

The Secretary of State has made numerous orders under the Enterprise Act of relevance to merger investigations: these will be referred to in the text that follows as appropriate.

3. The CMA's Duty to Make References: Phase 1 Investigations

Chapter 1 of Part 3 of the Enterprise Act is entitled 'Duty to make references', and is central to the domestic system of merger control. Chapter 1 contains both jurisdictional rules, explaining what is meant by a merger and which mergers can be investigated under the Act, and substantive rules, setting out the test to be applied by the CMA when investigating mergers. The procedures of the CMA in merger investigations will be explained in the text that follows[36].

Sections 22 to 32 of the Enterprise Act deal with the position of the CMA in relation to mergers that have already been consummated ('completed mergers') and sections 33 to 34 set out the relevant provisions in relation to mergers that have yet to be completed ('anticipated mergers'). As noted previously, there is no duty under UK law to pre-notify mergers to the CMA. There are no penalties under domestic law for consummating a non-notified merger, as under the EUMR. The CMA may however impose a financial penalty on a person who, without a reasonable excuse, fails to comply with interim measures at Phase 1[37] or Phase 2[38]. In practice many firms bring their transactions to the attention of the CMA on a voluntary basis prior to completion; however a number of completed mergers that were not notified have resulted in an order for divestiture of assets already acquired[39].

Sections 35 to 41 of the Act are concerned with the determination of references by the CMA Inquiry Group.

(A) Duty to make references: completed mergers

(i) Duty to refer

Section 22(1) of the Enterprise Act provides that the CMA has a duty to make a Phase 2 reference if it believes that it is or may be the case that a 'relevant merger situation' has been created and that the creation of that situation has resulted, or may be expected to result, in an SLC within any market or markets in the UK, or a part of the UK, for goods or services. The Act therefore imposes a duty, rather than conferring a discretion, on the CMA to refer mergers of the kind set out in section 22(1): this means that it is possible for a firm that is opposed to a particular merger, for example the victim of a hostile bid, a customer or a competitor, to apply to the CAT for a review of the decision of the CMA not to make a reference. The fact that a decision not to refer a merger can be challenged, as well as a decision to refer one, has resource implications for the CMA, which has to take care

[33] CMA62, April 2017. [34] CMA60, September 2017. [35] CMA17, March 2014.

[36] See 'CMA procedure in Phase 1', pp 947–956 and 'Determination of references by the CMA', pp 956–959 later in chapter.

[37] Enterprise Act 2002, s 72. [38] Ibid, ss 80–81.

[39] See 'Completed mergers', p 981 later in chapter.

to ensure that it publishes a decision setting out the primary evidence and the reasoning that led to its decision in a manner which is clear to all interested parties.

(a) The IBA Health *case*

The first application by a third party for a review concerned a proposed acquisition by iSOFT Group plc of Torex plc, two direct competitors in the supply of software applications to hospitals; the merger would result in the merged entity having a significant market share. This case led to an important judgment of the Court of Appeal which examined the nature of the duty to make a Phase 2 reference under the Act. The OFT had decided that it would not refer the iSOFT/Torex merger to Phase 2. IBA Health, a competitor, challenged the decision not to make a reference before the CAT; the CAT concluded that the OFT's decision should be quashed and that the matter should be reconsidered. In reaching this conclusion the CAT considered the scheme of the merger control provisions in the Act and noted that the role of the OFT (now the CMA) in Phase 1 is to act as a 'first screen' in relation to mergers, but not to be a decision-maker: that is the function of the Inquiry Group conducting the Phase 2 investigation. Section 33 imposes a duty on the CMA to refer a merger where it believes that 'it is or *may be*' the case that a merger '*may be* expected to result' in an SLC (emphasis added). In the CAT's view this formulation (and in particular the appearance in section 33(1) of the word 'may' in two places (the so-called 'double may')) meant that if the OFT (now the CMA) did not consider that a merger would result in an SLC, but if it was possible that the Inquiry Group might credibly have that view, the OFT (now the CMA) was obliged to refer:

> If there is room for two views, the statutory duty of the [CMA] is to refer the matter[40].

The CAT considered that, as the OFT (now the CMA) had not asked whether there was a significant prospect that the Competition Commission (now the CMA Phase 2 Inquiry Group) might consider that the merger would give rise to an SLC, it had failed to ask itself the correct question and so had erred in law[41]; the CAT also held that the OFT's decision was defective because it was not based on sufficient evidence and was insufficiently reasoned[42]. The OFT considered that the CAT's formulation of the duty upon it would significantly lower the threshold for referring mergers to Phase 2 and might lead to many more mergers being referred: this raised important policy questions, as a result of which the OFT appealed to the Court of Appeal. The Court of Appeal upheld the decision of the CAT to quash the decision and refer the matter back to the OFT on the facts of the case, but concluded that the CAT's formulation of the duty to refer was incorrect[43]. The Vice-Chancellor considered that the CAT's 'two part' test was wrong and that it would make various provisions in the Act unworkable:

> the relevant belief is that the merger may be expected to result in a substantial lessening of competition, not that the [CMA] may in due course decide that the merger may be expected to result in a substantial lessening of competition.[44].

The Vice-Chancellor explained that the words in section 33 should be applied in accordance with their ordinary meaning.

[40] Case 1023/4/1/03 *IBA Health Ltd v OFT* [2003] CAT 27, para 192. [41] Ibid, para 232.

[42] When the OFT reconsidered the case it found that there could be an SLC in relation to the supply of laboratory information management systems to NHS hospitals, but did not refer the merger to Phase 2 as iSOFT offered undertakings in lieu: see OFT Press Release 56/04, 24 March 2004.

[43] *OFT v IBA Health Ltd* [2004] EWCA Civ 142; for comment see Parr 'Merger Control in the Wake of *IBA Health*' [2007] Comp Law 282.

[44] *OFT v IBA Health Ltd* [2004] EWCA Civ 142, para 38.

(b) Guidance

Part 2 of the *Merger Assessment Guidelines*[45] provides guidance on the CMA's duty to refer in the light of this judgment and of some specific guidance that the Vice-Chancellor provided on the proper application of section 33(1) in paragraphs 44 to 49 of his judgment. The CMA must form a reasonable belief, objectively justified by relevant facts, as to whether a merger will lessen competition substantially. The CMA must make a Phase 2 reference where it believes that a merger is more likely than not to result in an SLC, that is to say, that it believes there is more than a 50% chance that an SLC will occur. The *Guidelines* go on to say that a Phase 2 reference can be made at lower ranges of probability than 50%: if the CMA believes that the degree of likelihood is not fanciful, but has less than a 50% chance of occurring, the CMA has a wide margin within which to exercise its judgement as to whether it may be the case that the merger would result in an SLC[46]. In such cases the CMA will have a duty to refer when it believes there to be a 'realistic prospect' that the merger will result in an SLC.

(c) The UniChem case

In *UniChem v OFT* UniChem objected to the fact that the OFT had not referred a proposed acquisition by Phoenix Healthcare Distribution Ltd of East Anglian Pharmaceuticals Ltd to Phase 2. The CAT considered that much of the OFT's decision was soundly based, but nevertheless quashed it since the OFT had made primary findings of fact about UniChem's position on the market on the basis of information provided by the merging parties but without any reference to UniChem itself. In the CAT's view a 'balanced and fair procedure' would have been for the OFT to have checked these important facts with UniChem[47]. On reconsideration of the matter the OFT again cleared the merger without a Phase 2 reference[48].

(d) The Celesio case

In *Celesio AG v OFT*[49] Celesio unsuccessfully challenged the decision of the CMA not to refer a proposed acquisition by the Boots Group plc of Alliance UniChem plc; the CAT rejected a submission by Celesio that the CMA is always under a duty to refer a merger where the prospect of there being an SLC is greater than fanciful[50].

(e) Gathering information in relation to a possible reference

Section 109 gives the CMA power to require, by notice, the production of documents and the supply of information in relation to a possible reference under section 22 or 33. The CMA may impose monetary penalties where it considers that a person has, without reasonable excuse, failed to comply with a notice[51]. Separately, it is a criminal offence for notifying parties or third parties to provide the CMA with false or misleading information.

[45] CC2 (Revised), OFT 1254, September 2010, paras 2.2–2.7.

[46] Case 1049/4/1/05 *UniChem v OFT* [2005] CAT 8, para 172 (distinguishing the term 'margin of judgment' from the broader concept of discretion).

[47] Ibid, paras 268–269. [48] Available at www.nationalarchives.gov.uk.

[49] Case 1059/4/1/06 [2006] CAT 9.

[50] Ibid, para 74; note also Case 1227/4/12/14 *AC Nielsen Co Ltd v CMA* where Nielsen challenged the decision of the CMA not to refer the acquisition by IRI of Aztec Group to Phase 2: the decision was quashed and the matter remitted to the CMA to make a new decision in the light of newly-available evidence: [2014] CAT 8.

[51] Enterprise Act 2002, s 110; on penalties see 'Investigation powers and penalties', pp 978–979 later in chapter.

(ii) Discretion not to refer

The duty imposed on the CMA by section 22(1) must be read subject to the provisions of section 22(2) and (3), which provide a discretion not to refer certain mergers and which prevent the reference of some others. Section 22(2) provides the CMA with a discretion not to make a reference in two situations.

(a) Markets of insufficient importance

The first is where the CMA believes that the market or markets concerned are not of sufficient importance to justify the making of a Phase 2 reference[52]. The primary purpose of this provision is to avoid references where the costs involved would be disproportionate to the size of the market concerned. The guidance has been revised three times, and the current position is explained in *Mergers—Exceptions to the duty to refer in markets of insufficient importance*[53] (the '*De minimis guidance*'[54]). The *De minimis guidance* says that the CMA will apply the *de minimis* exception by carrying out a 'broad cost–benefit analysis', asking whether the benefits of making a reference in terms of preventing customer harm are likely materially to exceed the public costs (not the costs of the parties) of making a reference[55]. The *De minimis guidance* suggests that the public cost of a Phase 2 reference in June 2017 was around £400,000.

The *De minimis guidance* establishes an upper and a lower threshold:

- where the annual value of the market(s) concerned is, in aggregate, more than £15 million, the CMA will generally consider the case to be of sufficient importance to justify a reference[56]
- where the annual value of the market(s) concerned is, in aggregate, less than £5 million the CMA will generally consider that a reference is not justified; a reference below this threshold would be exceptional[57].

In cases where the annual value of the market(s) concerned is below £15 million the CMA will typically consider three issues:

- whether clear-cut undertakings in lieu of a reference could, in principle, be offered by the parties[58]
- whether the expected customer harm resulting from the merger is materially greater than the cost of a Phase 2 reference to the public purse[59]
- the wider implications of the CMA's decisions for its treatment of future cases[60].

The first occasion on which the CMA exercised its discretion not to refer a merger under the revised *De minimis guidance* occurred in June 2017[61].

[52] Ibid, s 22(2)(a).

[53] CMA64, June 2017; for earlier versions of the guidance on *de minimis* mergers see *Exception to the duty to refer: markets of insufficient importance*, OFT 516b, in force from 2007 to 2010, and *Exceptions to the duty to refer and undertakings in lieu of reference guidance*, OFT 1122, December 2010, in force from 2010 to 2017.

[54] The *De minimis guidance* amends the *Exceptions guidance*, OFT 1122, December 2010, which remains unaltered in relation to other matters.

[55] *De minimis guidance*, paras 8–12. [56] Ibid, para 14. [57] Ibid, para 15.

[58] Ibid, paras 16, discussed further in paras 18–27.

[59] Ibid, para 16, discussed further in paras 28–39.

[60] Ibid, para 16, discussed further in paras 40–44.

[61] *IBA/Mallinckrodt*, CMA decision of 26 June 2017, available at www.gov.uk/cma.

(b) Customer benefits

The second situation in which there is a discretion not to make a reference is where any 'relevant customer benefits' in relation to the creation of the merger concerned outweigh the expected SLC and any adverse effects of it[62]. Section 30 defines relevant customer benefits for this purpose: there must be a benefit for 'relevant customers'[63] in the form of lower prices, higher quality or greater choice of goods or services in any market in the UK (which need not be the market in which the SLC has occurred or would occur) or greater innovation in relation to such goods or services[64]; and the benefit must have accrued, or be expected to accrue within a reasonable period, as a result of the merger, and be unlikely to have accrued without the merger or a similar lessening of competition[65]. The notion of relevant customer benefits occurs elsewhere in the Act, in particular in relation to Phase 2 investigations[66]. However, whereas the CMA is asked by section 22 at the Phase 1 stage to consider whether any relevant customer benefits would outweigh an SLC and any adverse effects of the SLC arising from the merger as a whole[67], the CMA Inquiry Group at Phase 2 is asked to consider the effect that any remedial action it might take would have on any relevant customer benefits[68].

The *Exceptions guidance* cautions that cases in which relevant customer benefits are established are likely to be rare[69]. The parties must adduce detailed and verifiable evidence of 'relevant customer benefits'[70], that they will have the incentive to pass on these benefits to customers and that the merger will leave customers better off than they would otherwise have been[71]. However parties do not need to establish a benefit to consumers generally, which would be a very difficult thing to demonstrate. The CMA would need to exercise its judgment in circumstances where a merger gave rise to relevant customer benefits for some customers but not others[72]. Even where such benefits can be established the CMA has a discretion whether to refer a merger; in exercising its discretion the CMA will have regard to the benefits of a Phase 2 investigation, including the possibility of remedies that could preserve any relevant customer benefits[73].

A separate point is that there may be cases in which predicted customer benefits would increase the rivalry in a market, in which case this fact could be taken into account as part of the SLC test, rather than as a subsequent counterweight to a possible SLC[74].

[62] Enterprise Act 2002, s 22(2)(b).

[63] On the meaning of relevant customers see ibid, s 30(4); the term includes customers in a chain of customers beginning with the immediate customers of the merging parties, and includes future customers.

[64] Ibid, s 30(1)(a); these benefits are not limited to efficiencies affecting rivalry: see *Exceptions guidance*, para 4.3.

[65] Enterprise Act 2002, s 30(2) and (3): note that these subsections set out the test for completed mergers and for anticipated mergers respectively.

[66] See 'Efficiencies', pp 966–967 later in chapter.

[67] *Exceptions guidance*, para 4.4.

[68] The effect of possible remedial action on relevant customer benefits was discussed extensively in *Global Radio Holdings Ltd/GMG Radio Holdings Ltd*, Final Report of 21 May 2013, paras 9.203–9.291, available at www.gov.uk/cma; customer benefits have also been discussed in some cases in the healthcare sector: see 'Healthcare' pp 985–986 later in chapter.

[69] *Exceptions guidance*, para 4.8.

[70] Ibid, para 4.9.

[71] Ibid, para 4.12.

[72] This may be the case where a merger gives rise to relevant customer benefits in one market but causes an SLC in another market: see ibid, paras 4.3 and 4.13.

[73] Ibid, para 4.5.

[74] Ibid, para 4.2 and fn 36; see also section 5.7 of the *Merger Assessment Guidelines*.

(iii) Circumstances in which a reference cannot be made

Section 22(3) sets out various circumstances in which a reference cannot be made, for example:

- where the CMA has failed to reach a decision within the time limit for completing Phase 1 investigations[75]
- where the CMA is considering whether to accept an undertaking in lieu of a Phase 2 reference[76]
- where the merger has been, or is being, considered under the provisions on anticipated mergers[77]
- in certain public interest cases[78]
- where the European Commission is deciding whether it has jurisdiction under Article 4(5) or Article 22 of the EUMR[79].

(B) Duty to make references: anticipated mergers

Most mergers are brought to the attention of the CMA on a voluntary basis prior to their consummation; there is a statutory basis for pre-notification, though its use is not obligatory[80]. Section 33(1) of the Enterprise Act imposes a duty on the CMA to make a reference of anticipated mergers where it believes that it is or may be the case that arrangements are in progress or in contemplation which, if carried into effect, would result in the creation of a relevant merger situation and the creation of that situation may be expected to result in an SLC within any market or markets in the UK for goods or services[81]. The CMA will generally consider that 'arrangements are in progress or in contemplation' where the merger has been publicly announced[82]. A merger may be 'in contemplation' without there being a binding agreement: in *London Stock Exchange plc/Deutsche Börse AG and Euronext NV* the CMA said that there must be 'genuine consideration' on the part of the acquirer to enter into the transaction; its interest in the transaction must be real; there must be an intention to enter into the transaction within a reasonable time; and the acquirer must be capable of bringing the transaction about[83].

As in the case of section 22 for completed mergers the CMA has a duty, rather than a discretion, to refer anticipated mergers, although it has a discretion not to refer markets of insufficient importance or mergers where relevant customer benefits would outweigh the SLC concerned[84]. An additional discretionary ground for non-reference exists for anticipated mergers, where the arrangements are not sufficiently advanced, or are not sufficiently likely to proceed, to justify the making of a Phase 2 reference[85]. Section 33(3) sets out circumstances in which a reference cannot be made, which mirror the provisions of section 22(3)[86].

[75] Enterprise Act 2002, s 22(3)(za): see 'Procedural timetable', pp 952–953 later in chapter.

[76] Enterprise Act 2002, s 22(3)(b): see 'Undertakings in lieu of a reference', pp 953–954 later in chapter.

[77] Enterprise Act 2002, s 22(3)(c): see section B later on anticipated mergers.

[78] Enterprise Act 2002, s 22(3)(d): see 'Public interest cases', pp 987–989 later in chapter.

[79] Enterprise Act 2002, s 22(3)(e) and (f): on the Article 4(5) and Article 22 procedure in the EUMR see ch 21, 'Article 4(5) and Article 22: referral of concentrations not having a Union dimension by Member States to the Commission', pp 869–872.

[80] See 'Notifying mergers to the CMA', pp 948–951 later in chapter.

[81] Enterprise Act 2002, s 33(1).

[82] *Mergers: Guidance on the CMA's jurisdiction and procedure*, para 4.4.

[83] See the Final Report of 1 November 2005, para 3.26, available at www.nationalarchives.gov.uk.

[84] Enterprise Act 2002, s 33(2)(a) and (c).

[85] Ibid, s 33(2)(b); see *Exceptions guidance*, paras 3.1–3.5.

[86] See 'Duty to make references: completed mergers', pp 936–941 earlier in chapter.

Pursuant to section 34, provision has been made for the aggregation of two or more transactions that take place between the same parties within a two-year period[87].

(C) Relevant merger situations

Section 23 of the Enterprise Act defines what is meant by 'relevant merger situations'. For there to be a relevant merger situation:

- two or more enterprises must have ceased to be distinct, and
- the merger must satisfy either
  - the turnover test or
  - the share of supply test.

(i) Enterprises ceasing to be distinct

A merger occurs where two or more 'enterprises' 'have ceased to be distinct'[88].

(a) 'Enterprises'

'Enterprise' means the activities, or part of the activities[89], of a business[90]. The leading case on the meaning of an enterprise is *Société Coopérative de Production SeaFrance v CMA*[91]. SeaFrance had operated a ferry service between Dover and Calais until 16 November 2011, when it went into liquidation in France and its operations ceased. On 2 July 2012 most of SeaFrance's assets were acquired by Groupe Eurotunnel. Eurotunnel had come to an arrangement with Société Coopérative de Production SeaFrance ('SCOP'), a workers' cooperative: the intention was that Eurotunnel would operate the ferry service and that SCOP would operate and crew the ships. The ferry service was resumed on 20 August 2012 using three of the same ships and mostly the same employees who had been involved in the former operations of SeaFrance. The Competition Commission considered that Eurotunnel's acquisition of the assets of SeaFrance constituted a merger qualifying for investigation and that it would lead to an SLC[92]; more specifically Eurotunnel had acquired an enterprise consisting of 'activities', even though the ships had been laid up for many months. On appeal the CAT remitted this issue to the CMA, which by then had replaced the Competition Commission, for further consideration[93]. The CMA reached the same conclusion as the Commission and prohibited the merger for a second time[94]. The CAT upheld the CMA decision[95], but the Court of Appeal allowed an appeal by a majority of two to one[96]. Ultimately the Supreme Court[97] unanimously reversed the Court of Appeal and confirmed the findings of the CMA and the CAT.

[87] The Enterprise Act 2002 (Anticipated Mergers) Order 2003, SI 2003/1595.

[88] Enterprise Act 2002, s 23(1)(a) and (2)(a); see Parker and Pritchard 'Jurisdictional Frontiers in UK Merger Control: "Enterprises Ceasing to be Distinct"' [2010] Comp Law 90.

[89] Part of the activities of a business means that the sale of a division of a company may be investigated, provided that the other requirements of s 23 are satisfied.

[90] Enterprise Act 2002, s 129(1); the Court of Appeal considered s 129 in *Akzo Nobel NV v Competition Commission* [2014] EWCA Civ 482, para 34.

[91] [2015] UKSC 75.

[92] Final Report of 6 June 2013, available at www.nationalarchives.gov.uk.

[93] Cases 1216/4/8/13 etc *Groupe Eurotunnel SA v Competition Commission* [2013] CAT 30.

[94] Final Report of 24 June 2014, available at www.gov.uk/cma.

[95] Cases 1233/3/3/14 etc *Groupe Eurotunnel SA v CMA* [2015] CAT 1.

[96] [2015] EWCA Civ 487. [97] See ch 22 n 91 earlier.

Lord Sumption, delivering the judgment of the Supreme Court, began by saying that what constitutes activities is a question of law[98]. He then said that the merger control provisions in the Enterprise Act are not limited to the acquisition of a business as a 'going concern'; the fact that SeaFrance had discontinued the ferry service in November 2011 did not in itself mean that no activities were acquired in July 2012[99]. There would be a real possibility of avoiding merger control if mere suspension of an activity were to mean that there was no merger qualifying for investigation[100].

As to the test of what constitutes an enterprise, Lord Sumption said that this is a matter of economic substance and not just legal form[101]. He distinguished the acquisition of 'bare assets' from assets amounting to an enterprise, since the Act does not apply to a case in which a purchaser simply buys equipment, hires employees and so on[102]. For the Act to apply the assets must constitute an enterprise and therefore give the acquirer something more than might have been acquired by merely going into the market and buying factors of production:

> the extra must be attributable to the fact that the assets were previously employed in combination in the 'activities' of the target enterprise[103].

On the facts of the case Lord Sumption considered that the finding that the 'embers' of an enterprise has been acquired was 'unimpeachable' and rejected the view of the majority in the Court of Appeal that such a finding was 'irrational'; indeed he pointed out that in cases of complex economic evaluation appellate courts should exercise caution when reviewing the decisions of a competition authority or the CAT[104].

(b) 'Cease to be distinct'

Enterprises cease to be distinct if they are brought under common ownership or control[105]. Control for this purpose is defined broadly in section 26 of the Act: there can be a merger in the sense of the Act without one firm acquiring outright, or even legal, control of another. Three levels of control are identified:

- *de jure* or legal control, which refers to a person controlling two enterprises in company law terms[106]
- *de facto* control, which refers to a person who is able, directly or indirectly, to control the policy of a company in practice
- material influence, which refers to a person who is in a position, directly or indirectly, materially to influence the policy of a company[107].

For this purpose the 'policy' of a company means the management of its business, including its strategic direction and its ability to define and achieve its commercial objectives[108].

[98] *Société Coopérative de Production SeaFrance SA v CMA* [2015] UKSC 75, para 31.

[99] Ibid, paras 32–35.

[100] See further, under similar provisions in the (now repealed) Fair Trading Act 1973, *AAH Holdings plc/Medicopharma NV*, Cm 1950 (1992), paras 6.101–6.102.

[101] [2015] UKSC 75, para 38.

[102] Ibid, para 39; see similarly the CAT in Case 1216/4/8/13 *Groupe Eurotunnel SA v Competition Commission* [2013] CAT 30, para 105.

[103] [2015] UKSC 75, para 39. [104] Ibid, para 44. [105] Enterprise Act 2002, s 26(1).

[106] Ibid, s 26(2) and s 129(1) and (2); see *Mergers: Guidance on the CMA's jurisdiction and procedure*, para 4.30.

[107] Enterprise Act 2002, s 26(3); *Mergers: Guidance on the CMA's jurisdiction and procedure*, paras 4.28–4.29.

[108] *Mergers: Guidance on the CMA's jurisdiction and procedure*, para 4.14.

'*Material influence*' is wider than '*decisive influence*' in Article 3(2) of the EUMR, with the result that some transactions that would not amount to mergers under EU law would do under UK law[109]. Material influence may be based on an acquirer's shareholding, its board representation or other factors[110]. Since a shareholding of 25% or more generally enables a shareholder to block special resolutions of a company the CMA considers that a shareholding of 25% or more is likely to confer the ability materially to influence the policy of the company[111].

There can be material influence even where the shareholding is less than 25%, although there is no presumption to that effect; the CMA will examine any shareholding greater than 15% to determine whether this is the case, and even a shareholding of less than 15% might attract scrutiny in exceptional cases[112]. When doing so the CMA will concentrate on substance rather than form, and will consider, for example, the size of the acquirer's shareholding compared to those of other shareholders; patterns of attendance at recent shareholders' meetings; the existence of any special voting or veto rights attached to the shareholding under consideration; any power to appoint directors or senior management and any other special provisions in a company's constitution conferring an ability materially to influence policy[113]. In *Ryanair/Aer Lingus*[114] the Competition Commission concluded that Ryanair's shareholding of 29.82% in Aer Lingus gave it the ability materially to influence the policy of Aer Lingus, in particular to impede or prevent possible combinations of Aer Lingus with other airlines[115].

In *BSkyB Group plc/ITV plc* BSkyB's holding of 17.9% of the shares in ITV made it the largest shareholder by some margin; the Competition Commission considered that, on the basis of voting behaviour at past general meetings of ITV and BSkyB's industry knowledge and standing, a holding of 17.9% would have enabled BSkyB to block any special resolutions and have material influence over ITV[116]. BSkyB's appeal against this finding to the CAT was unsuccessful[117]. The CAT held that once there is material influence over a company's policy there will be little scope for the exercise of any discretion under section 26(3) to decline to treat that influence as giving rise to common control[118].

It is also possible to acquire material influence over policy through board representation as well as, or in addition to, by a shareholding[119]; and also as a result of other factors, such as the provision of consultancy services to the target company or as a result of financial arrangements[120].

A transition from one level of control to another (for example from material influence to *de facto* control) would itself amount to a merger for the purposes of the Enterprise Act. As a result, if Company A acquires Company B in stages, this could give rise to several different mergers: first when A acquires material influence over B; secondly when A acquires *de facto* control; and finally when it achieves *de jure* (or legal) control[121].

109 On Article 3(2) of the EUMR see ch 21 'Article 3: meaning of a concentration', pp 853–859; for an example of a transaction that was considered to give rise to material influence under the Enterprise Act, though not to decisive influence under the EUMR, see *Centrica plc/Lake Acquisitions Ltd*, OFT decision of 7 August 2009.

110 *Mergers: Guidance on the CMA's jurisdiction and procedure*, paras 4.16–4.17.

111 Ibid, para 4.19. 112 Ibid, para 4.20. 113 Ibid, para 4.21.

114 Final Report of 28 August 2013, available at www.gov.uk/cma.

115 The finding of material influence was not appealed to the CAT.

116 See *BSkyB Group plc/ITV plc*, Final Report of 14 December 2007, paras 3.39–3.62, available at www.nationalarchives.gov.uk.

117 Case 1095/4/8/08 *British Sky Broadcasting Group plc v Competition Commission* [2008] CAT 25, paras 110–145.

118 Ibid, paras 97–105; see also *Mergers: Guidance on the CMA's jurisdiction and procedure*, para 4.22.

119 *Mergers: Guidance on the CMA's jurisdiction and procedure*, paras 4.23–4.25.

120 Ibid, paras 4.26–4.27. 121 Ibid, para 4.32 and the decisions cited in fn 46 of the *Guidance*.

The CMA, in its substantive assessment of a merger, may not treat the acquisition of material influence in the same way that it would treat *de facto* or *de jure* control[122]. Section 29 of the Act provides that, where a person acquires control in stages within a two-year period, those stages can be regarded as having occurred simultaneously on the date when the last of them occurred.

The Act does not define the period of time that a merger should last in order for it to qualify as a relevant merger situation. Paragraphs 4.35 to 4.39 of the *Mergers: Guidance on the CMA's jurisdiction and procedure* provide guidance on temporary merger situations, such as 'break-up bids' and cases where a person incrementally builds up a stake in a target company.

When deciding whether enterprises have come under common control or ownership, 'associated persons' and any companies that they control will be treated as one person; section 127(4) defines associated persons broadly and includes any individual, their partners, trustees and business partners[123]. In *Groupe Eurotunnel v Competition Commission* the CAT held that Eurotunnel and the SCOP were 'associated persons' because they had 'acted together' to acquire SeaFrance's vessels and related assets[124]. Shareholders of a new joint venture are not necessarily treated as 'associated persons'; for this to be the case there must be evidence that they acted together to secure or exercise control of an enterprise[125].

The award of a rail franchise under the provisions of the Railways Act 1993 qualifies as the acquisition of control for the purposes of section 23 of the Enterprise Act[126].

(ii) **The turnover test**

A merger can be investigated under the Enterprise Act only where it satisfies either the turnover test or the share of supply test. Section 23(1)(b) of the Act provides that a relevant merger situation has been created where the value of the turnover in the UK of the enterprise being taken over exceeds £70 million: the requirement that there must be turnover in the UK provides the jurisdictional nexus for the application of the Act. The CMA will keep the turnover threshold under review and advise the Secretary of State from time to time whether it is still appropriate[127]; the Secretary of State has power to amend the figure[128]. Section 28(2) provides that an enterprise's turnover shall be determined in accordance with an order to be made by the Secretary of State: the Enterprise Act 2002 (Merger Fees and Determination of Turnover) Order 2003[129] explains how turnover is to be calculated for the purpose both of the turnover test and the calculation of any merger fees payable[130]. The CMA has published guidance on the application of the turnover test[131]. Turnover is calculated by adding together the turnover of the enterprise being taken over and that of any associated enterprises. The period by reference to which turnover is calculated is the business year preceding the date of completion of a merger or, in the case of anticipated mergers, the date of the decision to make a Phase 2 reference[132]. Annexe B of

[122] See eg paras 63 and 64 of the OFT's *Report to the Secretary of State on Acquisition by British Sky Broadcasting Group plc of a 17.9 per cent stake in ITV plc*, 27 April 2007.

[123] Enterprise Act 2002, s 127(1); see further *Mergers: Guidance on the CMA's jurisdiction and procedure*, paras 4.40–4.41.

[124] Cases 1216/4/8/13 etc [2013] CAT 30, paras 51–57.

[125] *Project Canvas*, OFT decision of 19 May 2010, paras 39–42; *Tramlink Nottingham Consortium*, OFT decision of 12 September 2011, paras 12–14, both available at www.nationalarchives.gov.uk.

[126] See *FirstGroup plc/ScotRail*, Final Report of 28 June 2004, para 3.12, available at www.nationalarchives.gov.uk.

[127] Enterprise Act 2002, s 28(5). [128] Ibid, s 28(6). [129] SI 2003/1370 (as amended).

[130] On merger fees see 'Fees', p 956 later in chapter.

[131] *Mergers: Guidance on the CMA's jurisdiction and procedure*, paras 4.47–4.52.

[132] Ibid, para 4.51.

Mergers: Guidance on the CMA's jurisdiction and procedure provides further guidance on the calculation of turnover.

(iii) **The share of supply test**

Section 23(2)(b) of the Enterprise Act provides that a relevant merger situation has been created where the merged enterprises supply or acquire 25% or more of a particular description of goods[133] or services[134] in the UK[135] or a substantial part of it; the supply of services includes permitting or making arrangements to permit the use of land for various purposes such as caravan sites or car parks[136]. Guidance is available on the share of supply test[137]. The share of supply test requires an *increment* in the share of supply, no matter how small that increment may be[138]. An obvious corollary of this is that the share of supply test does not apply to non-horizontal mergers[139]. The share of supply test enables a merger to be investigated which could give rise to competition problems even though the turnover threshold of £70 million is not achieved: this may be necessary in the case of narrowly-defined product markets or small geographic markets. The CMA has a discretion in determining whether goods or services are of the same description and whether the 25% threshold is achieved[140], in relation to which it can use value, cost, price, quantity, capacity, number of workers or any other criteria considered appropriate[141].

To determine whether the share of supply test is met the CMA will have regard to any reasonable description of a set of goods or services[142]; this will often be a standard recognised by the industry in question, although this will not always be the case. The CMA may also consider different forms of supply, for example the wholesale or resale of goods[143]. When deciding whether the share of supply test is satisfied the CMA is not required to define the relevant product or geographic markets in accordance with the small but significant non-transitory increase in price ('SSNIP') test[144]: the share of supply test is jurisdictional, and does not require a full market analysis. A review of the case lists of merger decisions of the CMA and its predecessors reveals that there are quite a large number of cases in which jurisdiction over a particular merger arises from the parties' share of supply[145].

In determining whether the share of supply test is satisfied in relation to a substantial part of the UK the CMA will be guided by the judgment of the House of Lords (now the Supreme Court) in *South Yorkshire Transport v Monopolies and Mergers Commission*[146] which held (under analogous provisions in the old Fair Trading Act 1973) that the part must be of such size, character and importance as to make it worth consideration for the purpose of merger control. According to the CMA, among the factors to be taken into account in deciding whether the merger is 'worth' consideration and can therefore be

[133] Enterprise Act 2002, s 23(3). [134] Ibid, s 23(4).

[135] On the supply or acquisition of goods or services in the UK see *Mergers: Guidance on the CMA's jurisdiction and procedure*, paras 4.57–4.60.

[136] The Enterprise Act 2002 (Supply of Services) Order 2003, SI 2003/1594.

[137] *Mergers: Guidance on the CMA's jurisdiction and procedure*, paras 4.53–4.62.

[138] Ibid, para 4.54. [139] Ibid, para 4.56, fourth indent.

[140] Enterprise Act 2002, s 23(5). [141] Ibid, s 23(5)–(8).

[142] *Mergers: Guidance on the CMA's jurisdiction and procedure*, para 4.56, second indent.

[143] Enterprise Act 2002, s 23(6) and (7).

[144] *Mergers: Guidance on the CMA's jurisdiction and procedure*, para 4.56, first indent; on the SSNIP test see ch 1, 'Market definition', pp 26–42.

[145] See eg www.gov.uk/cma.

[146] [1993] 1 All ER 289; see also *Stagecoach Holdings v Secretary of State for Trade and Industry* 1997 SLT 940.

referred are the size of the specified area, its population, its social, political, economic, financial and geographic significance, and whether it has any particular characteristics that might render it special or significant[147]. These factors were applied in *Archant/Independent News and Media* in determining that the acquisition of some local newspapers, in different localities that were not contiguous, occurred in a substantial part of the UK[148]. The *South Yorkshire Transport* test has also been applied to find that a single town or borough is a substantial part of the UK[149].

(iv) Time limits and prior notice

A reference of a completed merger cannot be made if the enterprises ceased to be distinct more than four months prior to the Phase 2 reference[150] or, if later, more than four months before notice was given to the CMA of the merger or the fact of the merger was made public[151]. In certain circumstances these time limits can be extended[152]. In January 2011 it was considered that the time limits for reaching a decision on the acquisition by Ryanair of a minority shareholding in Aer Lingus during 2006 did not begin to run until appeals to the General Court against the European Commission's decisions relating to Ryanair's bid for Aer Lingus had been concluded[153]. The CAT[154] and the Court of Appeal[155] dismissed Ryanair's appeal against this finding.

Section 27 deals with the question of when enterprises cease to be distinct, in particular where ownership or control is obtained over a period of time. Section 27(2) provides that mergers are treated as having been completed when all the parties to a transaction became contractually bound to proceed: the existence of options or other conditions are irrelevant until the option is exercised or the condition satisfied[156]. Where ownership or control has been acquired incrementally over a period of time through a series of transactions they can be treated as having occurred on the date of the last transaction, subject to a two-year cut-off period[157]. In *Archant/Independent News and Media* the Competition Commission rejected Archant's argument that the reference had been made outside the four-month statutory period; it also concluded that two successive transactions should be regarded as having occurred on the date of the later of the two[158].

(D) CMA procedure in Phase 1

The principal stages of a CMA merger investigation (covering both Phase 1 and Phase 2) are explained in Figure 22.1.

[147] *Mergers: Guidance on the CMA's jurisdiction and procedure*, paras 4.61–4.62.

[148] See the Final Report of 22 September 2004, Appendix C, paras 23–31, available at www.nationalarchives.gov.uk.

[149] See *Arriva/Sovereign Bus and Coach Company*, Final Report of 7 January 2004, paras 3.10–3.14; *Tesco/Co-Op store acquisition in Slough*, Final Report of 28 November 2007, para 4.6 (Slough); *Cineworld/Hollywood Green Leisure Park*, OFT decision of 24 April 2008, paras 10–12 (London Borough of Haringey); all these decisions are available at www.nationalarchives.gov.uk.

[150] Enterprise Act 2002, s 24(1)(a).

[151] Ibid, s 24(1)(b), (2) and (3); on the issue of when a merger is 'made public' see *Mergers: Guidance on the CMA's jurisdiction and procedure*, para 4.44.

[152] Enterprise Act 2002, ss 25 and 122.

[153] See OFT Press Release 1/11, 4 January 2011.

[154] Case 1174/4/1/11 *Ryanair Holdings plc v OFT* [2011] CAT 23.

[155] *Ryanair Holdings plc v OFT* [2012] EWCA Civ 643.

[156] Enterprise Act 2002, s 27(3).

[157] Ibid, s 27(5) and (6); on this point see *Mergers: Guidance on the CMA's jurisdiction and procedure*, para 4.46 and the decisional practice cited therein.

[158] See the Final Report of 22 September 2004, Appendix C, paras 17–22, available at www.nationalarchives.gov.uk.

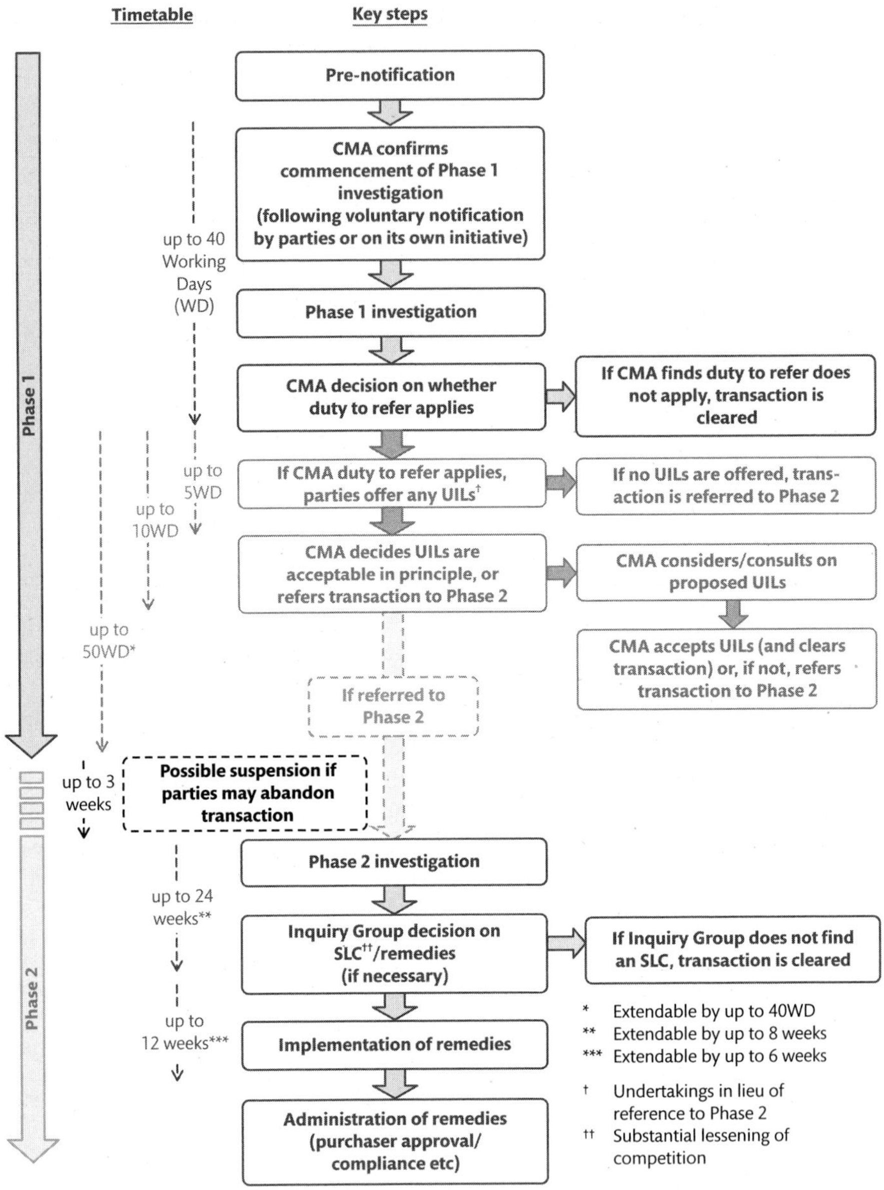

Fig. 22.1 Principal stages of a CMA merger investigation.
Source: *A quick guide to the UK merger assessment*, **CMA18, March 2014, available on the CMA's website, www.gov.uk/cma.**

A fuller diagram outlining the key stages and indicative timing of a typical Phase 1 case are helpfully set out in a table to be found at pages 38 to 41 of the *Mergers: Guidance on the CMA's approach to jurisdiction and procedure*.

(i) Notifying mergers to the CMA

Chapter 6 of *Mergers: Guidance on the CMA's jurisdiction and procedure* discusses the process of notification. There is no duty to pre-notify mergers under UK law, and in that sense the system is a 'voluntary' one as opposed to that in the EUMR where notification is compulsory. The risks of not notifying and/or completing a merger are described in paragraph 6.21 of *Mergers: Guidance on the CMA's jurisdiction and procedure*, and include being required to reverse the merger. In practice the parties to mergers often seek 'informal advice' from the CMA[159], and there is also a legal basis for making a notification using a 'merger notice'[160].

(a) The CMA's market intelligence function

There is no duty to notify mergers to the CMA, and quite often the parties do not do so. The CMA gathers intelligence about merger activity from monitoring the press, liaising with other public bodies and listening to third party complainants[161]. When hearing from third parties the CMA will take particular note of comments from customers, since they would suffer from an anti-competitive merger; a more sceptical view will be taken of complaints from horizontal competitors of the merging parties, who could expect to benefit from less competition in the market[162]. The CMA will not listen to complaints about non-competition issues, unless the case is one in which the Secretary of State has issued a public interest intervention notice[163]: the substantive test is whether the merger might substantially lessen competition, and that is the CMA's concern[164].

If the parties to a transaction go ahead without discussing the matter with the CMA they run the risk that their completed merger might be detected by the CMA and referred to a Phase 2 investigation; this happens quite frequently, and there are several examples of cases where the CMA has required a divestiture of assets that had already been acquired[165]. The CMA does not treat completed mergers more favourably than anticipated ones[166]. In cases where a merger is not notified, but the CMA learns about it by other means, it will send an 'enquiry letter' if there is a reasonable prospect that it is under a duty to make a reference. A copy of a standard enquiry letter is available on the CMA's website[167]. The prohibition decision in *ICE/Trayport* was the first time that a case called in by the CMA's Mergers Intelligence Committee was prohibited[168].

(b) Informal advice

The CMA will provide informal advice on substantive, and where relevant jurisdictional, issues arising from an anticipated merger that is not in the public domain[169]. The CMA will consider a request for informal advice only where the following two conditions are fulfilled:

- the party seeking advice must demonstrate a good faith intention of proceeding with a confidential transaction[170]

159 See 'Informal advice', pp 949–950 later in chapter.

160 Enterprise Act 2002, s 96; see 'Notification using a merger notice', pp 950–951 later in chapter.

161 *Mergers: Guidance on the CMA's jurisdiction and procedure*, paras 6.5–6.8 and *Guidance on the CMA's mergers intelligence function*, CMA56, June 2016, amended in September 2017.

162 *Mergers: Guidance on the CMA's jurisdiction and procedure*, paras 6.12 and 6.13.

163 See '"Public Interest Cases", "Other Special Cases" and Mergers in the Water Industry', pp 986–993 later in chapter.

164 See *Mergers: Guidance on the CMA's jurisdiction and procedure*, para 6.14.

165 See 'Completed mergers', p 981 later in chapter.

166 *Mergers: Guidance on the CMA's jurisdiction and procedure*, para 6.20.

167 www.gov.uk/cma.

168 CMA decision of 17 October 2016, upheld on appeal Case 1271/4/12/16 *Intercontinental Exchange Inc v CMA* [2017] CAT 6.

169 *Mergers: Guidance on the CMA's jurisdiction and procedure*, paras 6.25–6.38.

170 Hypothetical advice will not be given; the CMA will generally expect a good faith intention to proceed with the transaction in question.

- the party must explain why there is a genuine competition issue, that is to say that there is a theory of harm that the CMA might reasonably rely upon as a credible reason for a Phase 2 reference[171]; the CMA cannot be used to endorse the advice of professional advisers that a transaction gives rise to no competition problem.

Paragraph 6.35 of the *Mergers: Guidance on the CMA's jurisdiction and procedure* specifies the contents of applications for informal advice. The CMA will endeavour to indicate whether it will provide informal advice within five working days of receiving an application and, if so, provide that advice within a further five working days. Urgent cases may be handled more quickly. Informal advice will be given only once and generally by a senior member of the Merger Unit. There is no prescribed format for the provision of informal advice: it may be provided by a CMA official at a meeting or over the telephone. In some cases the advice may simply be that the CMA is unable to provide meaningful guidance at that stage as the substantive analysis will depend on the 'market testing' of the proposed transaction. The fact that a party has applied for informal advice and the content of that advice are confidential[172]. Such advice is not binding on the Phase 1 case team or the Phase 2 Inquiry Group.

(c) Pre-notification discussions

The CMA encourages pre-notification discussions, which it considers to be beneficial both to the parties and to the CMA[173]. Among the benefits are that the CMA team can learn about the affected markets and identify the information that will be needed by the CMA. The CMA is required, within fixed time limits, to determine whether it is under a duty to refer and, if so, whether there are any 'undertakings in lieu' that might remedy its competition concerns. That being so, *Mergers: Guidance on the CMA's jurisdiction and procedure* suggests that, in potentially problematic cases, parties may wish to engage in more detailed pre-notification discussions. Pre-notification discussions are held in confidence and may cover a range of matters from jurisdictional questions and the scope of possible information requests to substantive analysis and possible remedies. The *Guidance* says that a 'case team allocation form' should be submitted to the CMA to enable a case team to be constituted and make initial contact with the parties. The case team will endeavour to review submissions, such as a draft merger notice.

(d) Notification using a merger notice

Sections 96 to 101 of the Enterprise Act provide for mergers in the public domain that qualify for investigation under the Act to be pre-notified to the CMA[174]. Merger notices must be made in the prescribed form[175]. Notification may be made where companies demonstrate to the CMA a good faith intention to proceed with the transaction or to make a public bid: this means that the parties can begin the Phase 1 procedure, with the benefit of the fixed time limits, before the formal legalities of the transaction have been completed. However the CMA may declare a merger notice to be incomplete—for example because it omits information that ought to have been included[176]—in which case the time limits for

[171] This is the standard used by the CMA to decide whether a merger should be subject to the Phase 1 'Case Review Meeting procedure', on which see *Mergers: Guidance on the CMA's jurisdiction and procedure*, paras 7.34–7.49.

[172] Informal advice is only for members of the Board, senior executive officers and general counsel of the company making the request: *Mergers: Guidance on the CMA's jurisdiction and procedure*, para 6.37 and fn 108.

[173] Ibid, paras 6.39–6.48.

[174] Ibid, paras 6.49–6.53.

[175] Ibid, paras 6.54–6.55; a copy can be downloaded from the CMA's website, www.gov.uk/cma.

[176] *Mergers: Guidance on the CMA's jurisdiction and procedure*, paras 6.56–6.58.

reaching a Phase 1 decision will not begin to run[177]. The Enterprise Act 2002 (Merger Prenotification) Regulations 2003[178] make further provision in relation to merger notices, and the procedure is explained in Annexe A of *Mergers: Guidance on the CMA's jurisdiction and procedure*. A fee must be paid in advance when using this procedure[179].

(e) Own-initiative investigations

In cases where the parties do not notify the CMA and implement a transaction without the prior approval of the CMA, the CMA may commence an investigation on its own initiative[180]. The Phase 1 timetable will start in such cases on the working day after the CMA confirms that it has sufficient information to enable it to begin its investigation[181]. The CMA can, and often does, seek information by sending an 'enquiry letter' to the parties or by issuing a formal notice under section 109 of the Enterprise Act; the CMA is given the ability to impose fines for non-compliance with notices[182].

(f) Fast-track references

Under a 'fast-track' procedure certain cases can be dealt with by the CMA more quickly than is usual[183]. The CMA may, at the request of the parties, accelerate the making of a Phase 2 reference in cases where it is satisfied that a reference must be made. This has been done in several cases[184].

(ii) **The assessment process**

Chapter 7 of the *Mergers: Guidance on the CMA's jurisdiction and procedure* explains how it goes about its assessment of mergers. The *Guidance* begins by discussing the gathering of supplementary information and the verification of it, which involves consultation with third parties and public bodies[185]. There are financial penalties for both notifying parties and third parties that supply false or misleading information[186]. Paragraphs 7.21 to 7.27 of the *Guidance* explain the CMA's rights and obligations as regards confidentiality. The circumstances in which the CMA may make an interim order to prevent or unwind preemptive action that might prejudice a Phase 2 reference are also explained[187].

The *Mergers: Guidance on the CMA's jurisdiction and procedure*[188] explains that the CMA's approach to Phase 1 decision-making differs depending on whether a merger raises 'no serious competition issues' or raises 'more complex or material competition issues'. In cases that do not raise any competition concerns a director of mergers takes the decision to clear the merger; the case team prepares a Phase 1 clearance decision, which

[177] Enterprise Act 2002, s 100(1). [178] SI 2003/1369.

[179] See *Mergers: Guidance on the CMA's jurisdiction and procedure*, ch 20; see 'Fees', p 956 later in chapter on the payment of fees.

[180] *Mergers: Guidance on the CMA's jurisdiction and procedure*, paras 6.59–6.60.

[181] Ibid, paras 6.19 and 6.51.

[182] See 'Investigation powers and penalties', pp 978–979 later in chapter.

[183] *Mergers: Guidance on the CMA's jurisdiction and procedure*, paras 6.61–6.65.

[184] See eg *Thomas Cook/Cooperative Group/Midlands Cooperative Society*, OFT Press Release 28/11, 2 March 2011: the joint venture was subsequently cleared: Final Report of 16 August 2011, both available at www.nationalarchives.gov.uk; *BT Group plc/EE Ltd*, CMA Press Release, 18 May 2015: the merger was cleared unconditionally on 15 January 2016; *Ladbrokes plc/Gala Coral Group Ltd*, CMA Press Release, 11 January 2016: the merger was cleared subject to divestiture remedies on 26 July 2016; *Tesco plc/Booker Group plc*, CMA decision of 12 July 2017: the merger was cleared subject to divestiture remedies on 20 December 2017.

[185] *Mergers: Guidance on the CMA's jurisdiction and procedure*, paras 7.2–7.13.

[186] Ibid, paras 7.17–7.20.

[187] Ibid, paras 7.28–7.31; on the CMA's enforcement powers see 'Enforcement', pp 969–978 later in chapter.

is reviewed by senior CMA staff[189]. A different procedure is followed in complex or more problematic cases. In such cases there will be a 'state-of-play' meeting between the parties and officials from the CMA; the purpose of these meetings is to inform the parties about the CMA's possible competition concerns and whether the Merger Unit is minded to hold a 'Case Review Meeting' ('CRM')[190]. If the CMA intends to hold a CRM, it will send an 'issues letter' setting out the relevant evidence and the core arguments for a Phase 2 reference; an issues letter is neither a provisional decision nor a statement of objections[191]. The parties are given an opportunity to respond, in writing or at an 'issues meeting', and in practice they usually do both[192]. Issues meetings are normally attended by the case team, the Senior Director of Mergers (or another senior member of the CMA's staff), who will be the Phase 1 decision-maker, a legal officer, a senior economist and an official from outside the Merger Unit appointed to act as a 'devil's advocate' at the CRM.

Thereafter a CRM will take place within the CMA: it is usually chaired by the Director of Mergers, and will be attended by those officials present at the issues meeting, potentially also with a representative from the Office of the Chief Economic Adviser, and, where appropriate, individuals in the Markets and Mergers Directorate. As noted earlier, an official will be charged specifically with acting as a 'devil's advocate' at the CRM, to test the soundness of the case team's assessment and to argue the contrary position. After the CRM there is a separate so-called 'SLC decision meeting', at which the Phase 1 decision-maker hears a report on the discussions at the CRM and the overall recommendation following the CRM. A provisional decision on whether to refer the merger for a Phase 2 investigation is normally taken at this meeting; in a minority of cases that decision may be deferred until after a draft written decision has been prepared or a particular fact has been verified. Once the Phase 1 decision has been drafted, it becomes final when signed by the Phase 1 decision-maker. Notifying parties are contacted one hour before the public announcement of the decision and are informed of the timing and the nature of the decision. The decision is then publicly announced.

If an issues letter has been sent, but the CMA Phase 1 decision-maker decides *not* to make a Phase 2 reference, the Court of Appeal has said that it must be shown that the likelihood of an SLC has been removed and that the material relied on by the CMA can reasonably be regarded as dispelling the uncertainties highlighted by the issues letter[193].

(iii) **Procedural timetable**

Section 34ZA of the Enterprise Act contains time limits within which the CMA must complete Phase 1 investigations[194]. In general Phase 1 decisions must be made within 40 working days from the first working day after a satisfactory merger notice has been filed[195], or, in the absence of a merger notice, the first working day after the CMA has informed the merging parties that it has sufficient information to begin its investigation[196]. The Secretary of State may amend the time limit of 40 working days by order[197].

[188] *Mergers: Guidance on the CMA's jurisdiction and procedure*, paras 7.32–7.59.

[189] Ibid, para 7.33. [190] Ibid, para 7.34. [191] Ibid, para 7.36.

[192] It is not the CMA's practice to provide third parties with an opportunity to comment on the issues letter given time constraints and confidentiality: ibid, para 7.40.

[193] See *OFT v IBA Health Ltd* [2004] EWCA Civ 142, paras 73 and 100.

[194] Note s 103 of the Enterprise Act 2002 requires the CMA to have regard to the need for making a decision as soon as reasonably practicable.

[195] Time begins to run only from when the CMA confirms that it has received a complete merger notice under s 96(2A) of the Enterprise Act 2002.

[196] This time limit does not apply where a case is referred to the CMA by the European Commission under Article 4(4) or 9(2) of the EUMR: Enterprise Act 2002, s 34ZA(5).

Section 34ZB provides that the CMA may extend the initial period of 40 working days if it considers that a relevant person has failed, with or without a reasonable excuse, to comply with its powers of investigation. The CMA may also extend the initial period by no more than 20 working days where an intervention notice is in force[198].

Where the CMA fails to reach a decision within the prescribed time scale, no Phase 2 reference can be made[199]. There are some minor exceptions to this proposition: for example, if the parties provide false or misleading information in a merger notice, this will extend the period within which the CMA can decide whether its duty to refer a merger is met[200].

(iv) Ancillary restraints

Mergers and 'any provision directly related and necessary to the implementation of the merger provisions' are excluded from the Competition Act 1998[201]. The CMA's treatment of ancillary restrictions generally follows the approach of the European Commission under the EUMR[202]. The parties must decide for themselves whether restraints are ancillary; the CMA will not normally deal with this issue in a clearance decision. It will provide guidance only on novel or unresolved questions giving rise to genuine uncertainty.

(v) Undertakings in lieu of a reference

(a) Legal basis

Section 73 of the Act gives power to the CMA to accept an undertaking in lieu of making a Phase 2 reference[203]. The CMA must have regard to the need to achieve as comprehensive a solution as is reasonable and practicable to the SLC and any adverse effects resulting from it[204], taking into account any relevant customer benefits[205].

(b) Guidance on undertakings in lieu

The CMA's *Mergers—Exceptions to the duty to refer and undertakings in lieu of reference guidance* ('the *Exceptions guidance*')[206] contains a number of important insights on the law and practice of undertakings in lieu of a reference. The CMA considers that undertakings in lieu of a Phase 2 reference are appropriate only where 'the competition concerns raised by the merger and the proposed remedies to address them are clear-cut, and those remedies are effective and capable of ready implementation'[207]. In *Co-operative Group (CWS) Ltd v OFT*[208] the CAT held that the OFT (now the CMA) cannot be expected to conduct a detailed investigation when exercising its power to accept undertakings in lieu of a reference[209]. The CMA's starting point is to seek undertakings that restore competition to the level that would have existed without the merger, although there may be cases

197 Enterprise Act 2002, s 34ZC(6).

198 Only one such extension is possible: ibid, s 34ZC(2).

199 Ibid, s 22(3)(za) and s 33(3)(za).

200 Ibid, s 100(1); see also *Mergers: Guidance on the CMA's jurisdiction and procedure*, Annexe A, para A.9.

201 Competition Act 1998, Sch 1; on this exclusion see ch 9, 'Schedule 1: mergers and concentrations', pp 364–366.

202 *Mergers: Guidance on the CMA's jurisdiction and procedure*, paras 6.68–6.70.

203 See *Mergers—Exceptions to the duty to refer and undertakings in lieu of reference guidance*, OFT 1122, December 2010, ch 5, available at www.gov.uk/cma.

204 Enterprise Act 2002, s 73(3).

205 Ibid, s 73(4).

206 OFT 1122, December 2010, adopted by the CMA Board with effect from 1 April 2014 and available at www.gov.uk/cma; the amendments to the *Exceptions guidance* in June 2017 did not relate to undertakings in lieu.

207 *Exceptions guidance*, paras 5.6–5.9 and 8.5; see also *Mergers: Guidance on the CMA's jurisdiction and procedure*, para 8.3.

in which it accepts a different outcome[210]. The *Exceptions guidance* makes clear that the CMA has a strong preference for structural remedies at Phase 1[211], such as divestitures, over behavioural ones; indeed the CMA has said that it is 'highly unlikely' that it would accept behavioural remedies at Phase 1[212]. In some cases the CMA may insist on the parties securing a purchaser who has agreed to acquire the business to be divested before it accepts undertakings in lieu[213]; the CMA has continued the OFT's practice to require 'up-front buyers' in appropriate cases[214]. The CMA will always bear in mind the proportionality of remedies[215].

(c) Procedure

Useful guidance on the CMA's procedures for handling undertakings in lieu of a reference can be found in *Mergers: Guidance on the CMA's jurisdiction and procedure*. There are fixed timetables for considering, accepting and implementing undertakings in lieu of a Phase 2 reference. The tightness of the timetables means that the parties should consider whether, and if so what, remedies might be possible as early as possible in the procedure[216]. The parties may offer undertakings in lieu before or after the Phase 1 decision-maker has decided to refer the merger for a Phase 2 investigation. If parties offer undertakings in lieu before they are notified of the CMA's decision to initiate a Phase 2 investigation, the case team will, so far as possible, provide guidance on the suitability of those remedies[217]. If, however, the parties prefer to wait for the CMA's reasoned decision to refer a merger to Phase 2, then section 73A(1) gives the parties five working days in which to offer undertakings in lieu[218]. Where the parties offer undertakings in lieu, they must do so in writing using the prescribed form[219]. The time limit means that parties should not expect to engage in iterative discussions with the CMA or negotiations over undertakings in lieu.

It should be noted that the CMA has discontinued the 'envelope procedure' that the OFT used to adopt in order to consider multiple offers of undertakings in lieu. In the CMA's view the parties should be well placed to identify and offer a clear-cut solution to the competition problem within the statutory time period. However, as public policy benefits can be achieved through the Phase 1 remedies process, the CMA will, where appropriate, ask the parties to modify their proposed remedies to address adequately the competition concerns identified by the CMA[220]. The Act does not allow the CMA to consider new or revised offers of undertakings in lieu after the statutory deadline.

The CMA must decide whether it has reasonable grounds for believing that the undertakings in lieu (or a modified version thereof) might be accepted by the CMA. It must reach that decision within a period of ten working days from when it notified the parties of its reasons to make a Phase 2 reference[221]. If the CMA informs the parties that undertakings in lieu might be accepted, it then has a further period of 50 working days to decide whether to accept the undertakings in lieu or not[222]. The 50-working-day period may be

[208] Case 1081/4/1/07 [2007] CAT 24.
[209] Ibid, paras 179–180.
[210] *Exceptions guidance*, para 5.11.
[211] Ibid, paras 5.20 and 8.2.
[212] *Mergers: Guidance on the CMA's jurisdiction and procedure*, para 8.4.
[213] *Exceptions guidance*, paras 5.31–5.37.
[214] See eg *Origin UK Operations/Bunn Fertiliser*, CMA decision of 16 October 2017.
[215] *Exceptions guidance*, paras 5.14–5.19.
[216] *Mergers: Guidance on the CMA's jurisdiction and procedure*, para 8.7.
[217] Ibid, paras 8.7–8.9; the parties will formally have an opportunity to offer undertakings in lieu at the end of the issues meeting.
[218] Ibid, paras 8.10–8.11.
[219] Ibid, paras 8.14–8.17.
[220] Ibid, paras 8.20–8.21.
[221] Enterprise Act 2002, s 73A(2); see *Mergers: Guidance on the CMA's jurisdiction and procedure*, paras 8.18–8.19.

extended by no more than 40 working days where there are 'special reasons' for doing so[223]. The CMA would not expect to extend the Phase 1 remedies period unless the case involves an 'up-front buyer', it is necessary for the CMA to consult interested third parties or there is some other exceptional circumstance[224].

Once the undertakings in lieu have been accepted, the CMA oversees their actual implementation[225].

(d) Effect of accepting undertakings in lieu

If an undertaking in lieu has been accepted, it is not possible to make a Phase 2 reference[226], although the position is different if the CMA was not in possession of material facts at the time the undertaking was accepted[227]. Section 75 gives the CMA power to make an order where the undertaking in lieu is not being fulfilled or where false or misleading information was given prior to the acceptance of the undertaking[228].

(e) Examples

Undertakings in lieu of a reference were accepted by the OFT, one of the CMA's predecessors, on a number of occasions. In most cases the undertaking was structural, typically to divest assets[229]. In *Aggregate Industries Ltd/Foster Yeoman Ltd* the OFT accepted undertakings in lieu that were intended to address not only non-coordinated but also coordinated effects, the first case of this kind[230]. The OFT accepted its largest ever remedies package in *Co-operative Group Ltd/Somerfield Ltd*, consisting of divestitures in 133 local areas in which the OFT had identified competition concerns; in 24 cases the OFT required an up-front buyer[231]. There has been one occasion on which a quasi-structural remedy was accepted: in *Tetra Laval Group/Carlisle Process Systems* an undertaking was given to grant an irrevocable EEA-wide licence of a package of intellectual property rights to a third party, approved 'up-front' by the OFT, that would enable it to compete on the market for equipment used in the industrial manufacture of cheddar cheese[232].

The CMA has quite often accepted undertakings in lieu of a Phase 2 reference: of 62 Phase 1 decisions in 2015/16, nine were to accept undertakings in lieu; the equivalent figure for 2016/17 was nine out of 57 decisions[233]. In *Müller/Dairy Crest*[234] the CMA accepted undertakings in lieu that required Müller to enter into a toll processing agreement with Medina Dairy; the agreement contained extensive provisions on pricing, the transfer of know-how, firewalls and sending a compliance statement to the CMA.

(vi) Communication and publication of Phase 1 decisions

The Enterprise Act requires the CMA to provide the parties with the reasons for its Phase 1 decision[235]. All decisions on public merger cases must be published[236]; the decision is placed on the CMA's website as soon as confidential information has been removed[237].

[222] Enterprise Act 2002, s 73A(3); see *Mergers: Guidance on the CMA's jurisdiction and procedure*, paras 8.27–8.39.

[223] Enterprise Act 2002, s 73A(4); only one such extension is possible: ibid, s 73B(2); see further *Mergers: Guidance on the CMA's jurisdiction and procedure*, paras 8.23–8.24.

[224] *Mergers: Guidance on the CMA's jurisdiction and procedure*, para 8.25.

[225] Ibid, paras 8.40–8.49. [226] Enterprise Act 2002, s 74(1). [227] Ibid, s 74(2). [228] Ibid, s 75.

[229] See eg *Boots plc/Alliance UniChem plc*, OFT decision of 7 February 2006, upheld on appeal Case 1059/4/1/06 *Celesio AG v OFT* [2006] CAT 9. [230] OFT decision of 3 January 2007.

[231] OFT decision of 15 January 2009. [232] OFT decision of 20 November 2006.

[233] See the statistics available on the website of the CMA: www.gov.uk/cma.

[234] CMA decision of 19 October 2015. [235] Enterprise Act 2002, s 34ZA(1)(b). [236] Ibid, s 107.

[237] See *Mergers: Guidance on the CMA's jurisdiction and procedure*, paras 9.1–9.2; disagreements about confidentiality between the parties and the case team may be referred to, and resolved by, the Procedural Officer: para 9.3.

(vii) Fees

Pursuant to section 121 of the Enterprise Act provision is made by the Enterprise Act 2002 (Merger Fees and Determination of Turnover) Order 2003 (as amended)[238] for the payment of fees in connection with the exercise of the functions of the CMA (and, exceptionally, the Secretary of State) in relation to mergers. Further guidance on merger fees can be found in chapter 20 of the *Mergers: Guidance on the CMA's jurisdiction and procedure*[239].

4. Determination of References by the CMA: Phase 2 Investigations

(A) The Phase 2 Inquiry Group and case team

Once a Phase 2 reference has been made, the Chair of the CMA Panel[240] will appoint an 'Inquiry Group' to conduct the investigation. The Chair must appoint at least three (and usually no more than five) members of the CMA Panel to serve on a Phase 2 Inquiry Group[241]. The members of the Inquiry Group are collectively the Phase 2 decision-makers[242]; they play no role in Phase 1 decision-making. These arrangements mimic the old division of functions between the OFT and the Competition Commission; they are intended to provide a 'fresh pair of eyes' within UK merger control. Inquiry Groups are supported by a case team, which typically consists of administrative staff from within the Merger Unit, lawyers, economists, business advisers and, where appropriate, other professional experts[243].

(B) Questions to be decided in relation to completed mergers

Section 35(1) of the Enterprise Act requires the CMA, in the form of the Phase 2 Inquiry Group, to decide, first, whether a merger situation has been created[244] and secondly whether, if so, the creation of that situation has resulted, or may be expected to result, in an SLC within any market or markets in the UK for goods or services[245]. The CMA will always try to identify how the market would look if the merger were not to happen: in other words it will attempt to establish the 'counterfactual' in order to determine the extent of any SLC[246]. The CAT has endorsed the use of a 'counterfactual' as an analytical tool used to assist in answering the statutory questions[247]. The way in which the CMA is likely to apply the SLC test is considered in section 5 later[248]. If the CMA considers

238 SI 2003/1370, as amended most recently by SI 2014/534.

239 See also *Merger fees information*, CMA January 2016 and, in relation to mergers between water enterprises, paras 2.17–19 of *Water and sewerage mergers: Guidance on the CMA's procedure and assessment*, CMA40, 13 November 2015.

240 See *Mergers: Guidance on the CMA's jurisdiction and procedure*, para 10.3; the membership and role of the CMA Panel is described in ch 2, 'The CMA Panel', pp 65–66.

241 *Mergers: Guidance on the CMA's jurisdiction and procedure*, para 10.4.

242 See Enterprise Act 2002, s 34C.

243 For reasons of operational efficiency some of the CMA staff who work on Phase 1 will also work on Phase 2: *Mergers: Guidance on the CMA's jurisdiction and procedure*, para 10.8.

244 Enterprise Act 2002, s 35(1)(a).

245 Ibid, s 35(1)(b).

246 See eg *Ticketmaster/Live Nation*, Final Report of 7 May 2010, paras 6.1–6.102, available at www.nationalarchives.gov.uk.

247 Case 1095/4/8/08 *British Sky Broadcasting Group plc v Competition Commission* [2008] CAT 25, para 91, upheld on appeal to the Court of Appeal [2010] EWCA Civ 2, para 55; see similarly Case 1145/4/8/09 *Stagecoach Group plc v Competition Commission* [2010] CAT 14, paras 19–20.

248 See 'The "Substantial Lessening of Competition" Test', pp 959–968 later in chapter.

that there is an 'anti-competitive outcome'[249], it must decide three additional questions: first, whether it should take remedial action[250]; secondly, whether it should recommend that anyone else should take remedial action[251]; and thirdly, if remedial action should be taken, what that action should be[252]. When considering remedial action the CMA must have regard to the need to achieve as comprehensive a solution as is reasonable and practical to the SLC and any adverse effects resulting from it[253], and may in particular have regard to the effect of any action on any relevant customer benefits[254]. If the CMA finds that there is no anti-competitive outcome, no question of considering remedies arises.

(C) Questions to be decided in relation to anticipated mergers

Section 36 requires the CMA to decide similar questions in relation to anticipated mergers, with the necessary linguistic adjustments to address the fact that such mergers are yet to be completed.

(D) Investigations and reports

Section 37 of the Enterprise Act contains provisions for the cancellation and variation of Phase 2 references, for example where a referred merger has been abandoned: as will be seen from the Table of merger references later in this chapter, a significant number of mergers are abandoned following a Phase 2 reference[255]. Section 38(1) of the Act requires the CMA to prepare and publish a report within the period permitted by section 39. Section 39(1) requires the CMA to do so within 24 weeks of the date of the reference, a longer period than the 90 working days available to the European Commission in a Phase II case under the EUMR[256]. The 24-week period may be extended by no more than eight weeks where there are 'special reasons' for doing so[257], or where there has been a failure to comply with a requirement of a notice under section 109[258]. The Competition Commission extended the inquiry period on several occasions[259]; for example it extended the period in the case of two bids for the London Stock Exchange due to the 'exceptional complexity' of the inquiry[260].

The time limits in section 39 may be reduced by the Secretary of State[261]. The report must contain the decisions of the CMA on the questions to be decided under section 35

249 This term is defined in Enterprise Act 2002, s 35(2).

250 Ibid, s 35(3)(a).

251 Ibid, s 35(3)(b).

252 Ibid, s 35(3)(c).

253 Ibid, s 35(4).

254 Ibid, s 35(5); see 'Customer benefits', p 940 earlier in chapter.

255 Note that a Phase 2 investigation can be suspended for up to three weeks if the CMA considers that an anticipated merger will be abandoned and the parties so request: Enterprise Act 2002, s 39(8A).

256 See ch 21, 'Phase II investigations', pp 880–881.

257 Enterprise Act 2002, s 39(3): special reasons might be the illness or incapacity of a member of the group of members investigating the case or an unexpected merger of competitors: *Explanatory Notes*, para 132; only one such extension is possible: ibid, s 40(4).

258 Enterprise Act 2002, s 39(4); the Competition Commission used this power in *Ryanair Holdings plc/Aer Lingus plc* and in *Royal Bournemouth and Christchurch Hospitals NHS Foundation Trust/Poole Hospital NHS Foundational Trust*, both available at www.nationalarchives.gov.uk.

259 See eg *Stericycle Inc/Ecowaste Southwest Ltd*, Final Report of 21 March 2012 (to enable the Commission to assess new evidence and alternative remedies) and *Imerys Minerals Ltd/Goonvean Ltd*, Final Report of 10 October 2013 (to allow time for parties to comment on an addendum to the provisional findings), both available at www.nationalarchives.gov.uk.

260 See the Final Report of 1 November 2005, Appendix A, para 6, available at www.nationalarchives.gov.uk.

261 Enterprise Act 2002, s 40(8).

or 36, its reasons for those decisions and such information as the CMA considers appropriate for facilitating a proper understanding of those questions and its reasons for its decisions[262].

(E) Duty to remedy the anti-competitive effects of mergers

Where the CMA has prepared and published a report under section 38 within the time limits established by section 39 and has concluded that there is an anti-competitive outcome section 41(2) requires it to take such action as it considers to be reasonable and practicable to remedy, mitigate or prevent the SLC and any adverse effects of it[263]. In doing so the CMA must be consistent with the decisions in its report on the questions it is required to answer, unless there has been a material change of circumstances since the preparation of the report or the CC has a special reason for deciding differently[264]. In *Ryanair Holdings v CMA*[265] the CAT upheld a finding of the CMA[266] that there had been no material change in circumstances causing it to change its view that Ryanair should divest itself of its shares in Aer Lingus down to no more than 5%. In making its decision under section 41(2) the CMA must have regard to the need to achieve as comprehensive a solution as is reasonable and practicable to the SLC and any resulting adverse effects[267].

(F) Time limits for the implementation of remedies

The CMA must implement its chosen remedies within 12 weeks of the date of the publication of its final report[268]. The 12-week period may be extended by no more than six weeks where there are 'special reasons' for doing so[269], or where there has been a failure to comply with a requirement of a notice under section 109[270]. These time limits were introduced by the ERRA in order to streamline what had previously been quite a lengthy process of implementation. Chapter 14 of *Mergers: Guidance on the CMA's jurisdiction and procedure* provides guidance on the implementation of remedies following the final report.

(G) CMA procedure in Phase 2

The procedures of the CMA Inquiry Group during Phase 2 investigations are set out in the *CMA Rules of Procedure for Merger, Market and Special Reference Groups* 2014[271]. Rule 7 of the *Rules of Procedure* requires the CMA to draw up an administrative timetable for its investigation. The Phase 2 Inquiry Group has wide-ranging investigatory powers to enable it to carry out its investigation effectively[272], and can impose penalties for non-compliance[273]. *Mergers: Guidance on the CMA's jurisdiction and procedure* contains

[262] Ibid, s 38(2); on the duty to give reasons see Case 1051/4/8/05 *Somerfield plc v Competition Commission* [2006] CAT 4, para 62.

[263] Enterprise Act 2002, s 41(2); this provision does not simply require the CMA to lessen the chances of an SLC occurring: *Ryanair Holdings plc v CMA* [2015] EWCA Civ 83, para 58.

[264] Enterprise Act 2002, s 41(3); for an example of a material change of circumstances see the *Notice* of 15 May 2012 in the case of *Stericycle, Inc/Ecowaste Southwest Ltd.*

[265] [2015] CAT 14.

[266] Final decision on possible material change of circumstances, 11 June 2015.

[267] Enterprise Act 2002, s 41(4).

[268] Ibid, s 41A(1); note that Phase 2 Inquiry Groups are appointed to act until a merger reference is 'finally determined', which includes the acceptance of final undertakings or making of a final order: ibid, s 79(2)(e).

[269] Ibid, s 41A(2); only one such extension is possible: s 41B(2).

[270] Ibid, s 41A(3).

[271] CMA17, March 2014, available at www.gov.uk/cma.

[272] Enterprise Act 2002, s 109.

[273] Ibid, s 110.

a helpful outline of the key stages of a Phase 2 investigation at pages 95 to 98. The major stages of a reference include the gathering and verification of evidence; providing a statement of issues; notifying provisional findings[274]; notifying and considering possible remedies; the publication of the final report; and deciding on remedies[275]. Hearings will be held with third parties and with the main parties to the proceedings; where appropriate there will also be hearings on remedies. Often the CMA visits appropriate facilities of the merging parties in order better to understand the context of the merger. Each investigation has its own home page on the CMA's website[276], which sets out the core documents of the inquiry.

5. The 'Substantial Lessening of Competition' Test

The Enterprise Act subjects mergers to an SLC test. This section considers how the CMA applies the SLC test in practice.

(A) Publication of merger guidelines

Section 106(1) of the Enterprise Act requires the CMA to publish general advice and information about the making and assessment of merger references. In September 2010 the OFT and Competition Commission published joint *Merger Assessment Guidelines*[277] ('the *Assessment Guidelines*'). The CMA Board has adopted the *Assessment Guidelines*, which therefore set out the CMA's approach to the SLC test, including an explanation of the concepts of 'theories of harm' and the 'counterfactual'[278]. The *Guidelines* then deal in turn with:

- market definition
- measures of concentration
- unilateral and coordinated effects of horizontal mergers
- non-horizontal mergers
- efficiencies
- barriers to entry and expansion and
- countervailing buyer power.

This section will follow the same sequence. The CMA says that it will have regard to the *Assessment Guidelines* but will apply them flexibly, departing from them where appropriate.

(B) A substantial lessening of competition

(i) What is an SLC?

The Act does not define an SLC. In *Global Radio Holdings Ltd v Competition Commission*[279] the CAT held that a 'substantial' lessening of competition did not have to be 'large',

[274] It can happen that the assessment of a merger may change between the provisional findings and the final report: see eg *British Salt Ltd/New Cheshire Salt Works*, *Stagecoach/Eastbourne Buses* and *Ticketmaster/Live Nation*, all available at www.nationalarchives.gov.uk.

[275] *Rules of procedure for merger, market and special reference groups*, CMA17, March 2014, rule 7.2.

[276] www.gov.uk/cma.

[277] CC2 Revised, OFT 1254, September 2010, available at www.gov.uk/cma.

[278] Part 3 of the *Guidelines* briefly discuss the concept of a relevant merger situation; however this part must be read in light of *Mergers: Guidance on the CMA's jurisdiction and procedure*, CMA2, January 2014.

[279] Case 1214/4/8/13 [2013] CAT 26.

'considerable' or 'weighty'; a finding that there is a 'significant lessening of competition' is sufficient, regardless of whether that lessening is large in absolute terms[280]. The *Assessment Guidelines* explain that a merger gives rise to an SLC when it has a significant effect on rivalry over time, thereby reducing the competitive pressure on firms to improve their offer to customers or become more efficient or innovative[281]. There are three main reasons why mergers may lead to an SLC: unilateral effects; coordinated effects; and vertical or conglomerate effects: these theories of harm were explained in chapter 20[282]. A merger that gives rise to an SLC will be expected to lead to an adverse effect for customers[283].

(ii) Theories of harm

The CMA devises a theory or theories of harm in order to provide a framework for assessing the effects of a merger[284]. A theory of harm describes possible changes arising from the merger and compares any effect on rivalry and expected harm to customers as compared with the situation likely to arise without the merger[285]. The Phase 2 Inquiry Group's assessment of the effects of a merger is not limited by the Phase 1 decision-maker's conclusions on a theory (or theories) of harm[286].

(iii) The counterfactual

(a) The approach to the counterfactual

The application of the SLC test involves a comparison of the prospects for competition with the merger against the situation without the merger: the 'counterfactual'[287]. The counterfactual is affected by the extent to which events and their consequences are foreseeable, but does not suppose that infringements of competition law will occur. The Phase 1 decision-maker generally adopts the prevailing conditions of competition as the counterfactual, whereas the Phase 2 Inquiry Group selects the most likely future situation in the absence of the merger[288]. The need to examine the counterfactual was emphasised by the CAT in *Stagecoach Group v Competition Commission*[289], where it held that a decision finding that a merger would create a monopoly for local buses in Preston as the choice of counterfactual was not supported by the evidence[290]. Paragraph 4.3.6 of the *Assessment Guidelines* describes three situations in which the CMA may use a counterfactual other than the prevailing conditions of competition; they are 'the exiting firm scenario', commonly referred to as the so-called 'failing firm defence'; 'the loss of potential entrant scenario'; and the situation where there are competing bids and parallel transactions[291].

(b) The exiting firm scenario

If a firm were to exit the market, irrespective of the merger under consideration, that merger would not be the cause of any SLC. Paragraph 4.3.8 of the *Assessment Guidelines* says that three considerations are relevant to an assessment of the exiting firm scenario:

- first, whether the firm would have exited the market either because of financial difficulties or for another reason, such as, for example, a change in the corporate strategy of the selling firm

[280] Ibid, para 24. [281] *Assessment Guidelines*, para 4.1.3.

[282] See ch 20, 'Theories of competitive harm', pp 838–840. [283] *Assessment Guidelines*, para 4.1.3.

[284] Ibid, para 4.2.1. [285] Ibid. [286] Ibid, para 4.2.6.

[287] Ibid, paras 4.3.1–4.3.29; for further discussion see Davis and Cooper 'On the Use of Counterfactuals in Merger Inquiries', 28 April 2010, available at www.nationalarchives.gov.uk.

[288] *Assessment Guidelines*, paras 4.3.5–4.3.6. [289] Case 1145/4/8/09 [2010] CAT 14.

[290] Ibid, paras 37–133.

[291] See further *Assessment Guidelines*, paras 4.3.8–4.3.27; the award of rail franchise awards is a further example: ibid, paras 4.3.28–4.3.29.

- secondly, whether there would have been an alternative purchaser for the firm or its assets and
- thirdly, what would have happened to the sales of the firm in the event of it leaving the market?

The exiting firm scenario has been accepted in a small number of cases[292]; the Phase 1 decision-maker will require compelling evidence that the acquired firm would leave the market and that there is no less anti-competitive purchaser for the firm or its assets[293]. The CMA accepted an exiting firm argument in Phase 1 in *Chemring Group plc/Wallop Defence Systems Ltd*[294].

The Phase 2 Inquiry Group will generally consider the three 'exiting firm' considerations as part of its SLC analysis. The Competition Commission concluded that a merger could be 'saved' by the 'exiting firm scenario' in several cases[295]. In *British Salt/New Cheshire Salt Works*[296] the Commission found that British Salt's acquisition of New Cheshire Salt Works would not result in an SLC since the latter would have closed in the foreseeable future due to large increases in actual and projected energy prices: an interesting point about this case is that the Commission changed its mind between its provisional and its final determination. In *STS/Butlers*[297] the Commission accepted arguments that the merger would not result in an SLC because the vendor would have closed the acquired business in any event for commercial and strategic reasons as opposed to financial difficulties. In *Optimax Clinics/Ultralase*[298] the Commission cleared the merger unconditionally as Ultralase would have exited the market anyway and its market share would have accrued to Optimax.

(C) **Market definition**

The *Assessment Guidelines* explain that market definition, though not an end in itself, provides a framework for the analysis of the competitive effects of the merger[299]. Market definition and the assessment of effects should not be viewed as distinct analyses and may overlap in practice[300]. The *Guidelines* say that in defining markets the Phase 1 decision-maker will usually make an initial assessment but may not reach a conclusion; whereas the Phase 2 Inquiry Group will usually reach a conclusion: this difference reflects their respective roles under the Act[301]. The *Guidelines* explain that the relevant market contains the most significant competitive alternatives available to the customers of the merged firms and includes the sources of competition to the merging firms that are the immediate

[292] See eg the OFT decisions in *First West Yorkshire/Black Prince Buses*, 26 May 2005; *Tesco/Kwik Save stores*, 11 December 2007; *CDMG/Ferryways and Searoad Stevedores*, 24 January 2008; *Home Retail Group plc/Focus DIY stores* (one store only), 15 April 2008; *HMV plc/Zavvi*, 28 April 2009.

[293] *Assessment Guidelines*, para 4.3.10; cf *Boparan/Bernard Matthews*, CMA decision of 12 January 2017, paras 20–27: Bernard Matthews would have exited the market, but other suppliers would have recaptured some of its assets.

[294] CMA decision of 3 May 2016.

[295] In addition to the cases mentioned in the text see *Long Clawson Dairy Ltd/Millway*, Final Report of 14 January 2009, paras 5.28 and 6.1; *Ratcliff Palfinger/Ross & Bonnyman*, Final Report of 10 June 2011, section 4; *Stena AB/DFDS Irish Sea ferry services*, Final Report of 29 June 2011, all available at www.nationalarchives.gov.uk.

[296] Final Report of 8 November 2005, paras 5.28 and 6.1, available at www.nationalarchives.gov.uk.

[297] Final Report of 31 August 2011, paras 5.8–5.45, available at www.nationalarchives.gov.uk.

[298] Final Report of 20 November 2013, section 5, available at www.nationalarchives.gov.uk.

[299] *Assessment Guidelines*, paras 5.2.1–5.2.2.

[300] Ibid, para 5.1.1.

[301] Ibid, para 5.2.4; the term 'definition of the relevant market' should be understood with this difference in mind.

determinants of the effects of the merger[302]. The *Guidelines* explain the methodology for market definition and in particular the 'hypothetical monopolist test'[303]; among the factors that will be considered are the 'closeness' of substitution, that is to say the intensity of competition between products, the variable profit margins of the products and the sensitivity of customers to changes in price.

(D) Measures of concentration

The *Assessment Guidelines* explain that, as part of their assessment of the effects of a merger, the CMA may use measures of concentration in both Phase 1 and Phase 2[304]. There are several ways in which concentration can be measured: market shares; number of firms; concentration ratios; and the Herfindahl-Hirschman Index ('HHI')[305]. When interpreting these measures the CMA may have regard to the extent to which products are differentiated; changes in concentration over time; how widely the market is defined; and the level of variable profit margins[306]. The CMA's Phase 1 decision-maker may have regard to the following market share and concentration thresholds[307]:

- it is unlikely to be concerned about unilateral effects in a market where products are undifferentiated and where the post-merger market share is less than 40%
- it is unlikely to be concerned about mergers that reduce the number of firms from five to four (or above)
- a market with a post-merger HHI of more than 2,000 may be regarded as highly concentrated; however horizontal mergers that result in a change of the concentration level of less than 150 are unlikely to give rise to competition concerns
- a market with a post-merger HHI of more than 1,000 may be regarded as concentrated; horizontal mergers that result in a change of less than 250 are unlikely to be problematic.

The HHI thresholds may be most informative at Phase 1 for mergers in a market where the product is undifferentiated and where firms compete on output; this is based on the insights of an economic model of oligopolistic markets[308]. The Phase 1 decision-maker may also have regard to the thresholds used by the European Commission in its *Guidelines on the assessment of non-horizontal mergers*[309].

(E) Horizontal mergers

(i) Unilateral effects

Many Phase 2 investigations are concerned with the unilateral effects of horizontal mergers. Unilateral effects may arise where a merged firm finds it profitable to increase prices (or reduce output or quality) as a result of the loss of competition between the merged parties[310]. The *Assessment Guidelines* describe four theories of harm giving rise to unilateral

[302] Ibid, para 5.2.1.

[303] Ibid, paras 5.2.9–5.2.20; on the tests for defining the relevant market see ch 1, 'Market definition', pp 26–42.

[304] *Assessment Guidelines*, paras 5.3.1–5.3.6.

[305] Ibid, para 5.3.4; for further discussion see ch 1, 'Market concentration and the Herfindahl-Hirschman Index', pp 43–44.

[306] *Assessment Guidelines*, para 5.3.2. [307] Ibid, para 5.3.5. [308] Ibid, para 5.3.5, third indent.

[309] Ibid, para 5.3.5, first indent; on the Commission's *Non-horizontal guidelines* see ch 21, 'Non-horizontal mergers', pp 899–902.

[310] *Assessment Guidelines*, para 5.4.1.

effects: loss of existing competition; the elimination of potential competition; increased buyer power; and the vertical effects arising from horizontal mergers[311]. Each theory is briefly discussed in turn below.

The first theory of harm concerns the loss of existing competition and varies according to whether the merger involves differentiated or undifferentiated products[312]. This distinction is based on an extensive economic literature[313] and reflects the importance of product differentiation—for example by brand or quality—for the way in which competition concerns may arise[314]. The distinction is one of degree and ought not to be treated too literally. Where products are highly differentiated market shares may be an imperfect proxy for competition concerns; the more important issue is the 'closeness of substitution' between products. The higher the degree of substitutability between the merging firm's products, the closer the competition between them would have been without the merger and the more likely it will be that the merger will give rise to unilateral effects[315]. It may be necessary for the CMA to analyse the change in the pricing incentives of the merged firms resulting from bringing their products under common control[316]. The potential response of other suppliers to any attempt by the merged firm to increase price can also have an effect on pricing incentives. In some cases not only the merging parties, but also their rivals, may be able to share the benefit of greater post-merger profitability: this is a reference to the 'problem' of non-collusive oligopoly referred to in chapter 21[317].

The *Assessment Guidelines* adopt a different approach to mergers involving undifferentiated products and set out a series of factors that make unilateral effects more likely in such cases[318]:

- the market is concentrated
- there are a few firms in the affected market after the merger
- the merged firm has a large market share
- there are weak competitive constraints from rivals
- the merger eliminates a significant competitive force in the market and
- customers have little choice of alternative supplier perhaps as a result of switching costs or network effects.

The second way in which unilateral effects may arise is if a merger eliminates potential competition[319]. In *Akzo Nobel NV/Metlac Holdings Srl*[320] the merged firm had the ability

[311] Ibid, paras 5.4.1–5.4.21; the expression 'non-coordinated effects' is sometimes used as an alternative for unilateral effects.

[312] Ibid, paras 5.4.4–5.4.12.

[313] See eg Chamberlin 'Product Heterogeneity and Public Policy' (1950) Am Ec Rev 86; Farrell and Shapiro 'Horizontal Mergers: An Equilibrium Analysis' (1990) 80 Am Ec Rev 107; Werden 'A Robust Test for Consumer Welfare Enhancing Mergers Among Sellers of Differentiated Products' (1996) 44(4) J Ind Ec 409; Werden and Froeb 'Unilateral Competitive Effects of Horizontal Mergers' in Buccirossi (ed) *Handbook of Antitrust Economics* (MIT Press, 2008) and Shapiro 'The 2010 *Horizontal Merger Guidelines*: From Hedgehog to Fox in Forty Years' (2011) 77 Antitrust LJ 701; Coate 'Unilateral Effects Analysis in Merger Review: Limits and Opportunities' (2014) European Competition Journal 231.

[314] See similarly the US *Horizontal Merger Guidelines* of August 2010, section 6.1, available at www.justice.gov/atr; for further discussion see Bishop and Walker *The Economics of EC Competition Law* (Sweet & Maxwell, 3rd ed, 2010), paras 7-017–7-036.

[315] *Assessment Guidelines*, para 5.4.6.

[316] Ibid, para 5.4.6.

[317] Ibid, para 5.4.11; see further ch 21, 'The non-collusive oligopoly gap', pp 883–885.

[318] *Assessment Guidelines*, paras 5.4.4–5.4.5; the importance of these factors will depend on the particular facts of each case.

[319] Ibid, paras 5.4.13–5.4.18.

[320] Final Report of 21 December 2012, paras 9.116–9.155, available at www.nationalarchives.gov.uk.

to raise prices unilaterally in part because the merger removed a potential competitor from the market for metal packaging coatings for beer and beverage cans.

The *Assessment Guidelines* recognise, thirdly, that a merger may lead to an increase in buyer power and lead to an SLC[321], which occurred in *Stonegate Farmers Ltd/Deans Food Group Ltd*[322]. The *Guidelines* point out, however, that an increase in buyer power is unlikely to give rise to unilateral effects in many cases; indeed greater buyer power may even be pro-competitive in so far as its benefits are passed on to consumers[323].

Finally, a horizontal merger may have vertical effects, which are discussed in section F later in chapter[324].

(ii) **Coordinated effects**

The *Assessment Guidelines* discuss the problem of coordinated effects arising from mergers[325]. They begin by explaining the differences between explicit and tacit coordination, both of which can be germane to the substantive analysis[326]. It is necessary to consider evidence of pre-existing coordination and the characteristics of the market[327]. Paragraph 5.5.9 of the *Assessment Guidelines* says that there are three necessary conditions for coordination to be possible:

- first, firms must be able to reach and monitor the terms of coordination
- secondly, coordination needs to be 'internally sustainable': firms must have the incentive to coordinate and the existence of an effective mechanism to punish and deter cheating and
- thirdly, coordination needs to be 'externally sustainable', implying the absence of effective competitive constraints.

Each of these conditions is explored further in succeeding paragraphs of the *Guidelines*[328]. The CMA will consider the impact of the merger on the likelihood and effectiveness of coordination[329].

There have not been many cases under the Enterprise Act in which coordinated effects have been considered in detail. As already noted, undertakings in lieu of a Phase 2 reference were accepted in *Aggregate Industries Ltd/Foster Yeoman Ltd*, partly because of concerns about coordinated effects[330]. The Competition Commission was primarily concerned with the possibility that the merger in *DS Smith/LINPAC Containers* might lead to coordinated effects but concluded that, even though the conditions for achieving coordination might be present on the market, smaller suppliers would have the incentive to respond to any increase in the price of corrugated cardboard sheet by expanding output through existing and new capacity; the Commission also rejected the suggestion that the acquisition of LINPAC would remove a maverick from the market[331]. In *Napier Brown Foods plc/James Budgett Sugars Ltd* the Commission found that coordinated effects

[321] *Assessment Guidelines*, paras 5.4.19–5.4.21.

[322] Final Report of 20 April 2007, paras 6.93–6.102, available at www.nationalarchives.gov.uk.

[323] *Assessment Guidelines*, para 5.4.19.

[324] Ibid, para 5.4.22–5.4.23. [325] Ibid, paras 5.5.1–5.5.19.

[326] Ibid, para 5.5.3; the problem of tacit coordination in oligopolistic markets was discussed in detail in chapter 14, to which the reader is referred.

[327] Ibid, paras 5.5.5–5.5.9; see *AGC Automotive Europe SA/NordGlass*, CMA decision of 28 September 2015, in which there was evidence of a cartel in the past, but the merger did not substantially increase the risk of coordination in automotive glass.

[328] Ibid, paras 5.5.10–5.5.18. [329] Ibid, para 5.5.19.

[330] OFT decision of 3 January 2007; see similarly *Lloyds Pharmacy Ltd/Independent Pharmacy Care Centres plc*, OFT decision of 8 June 2007, both available at www.nationalarchives.gov.uk.

[331] See the Final Report of 21 October 2004, paras 5.50–5.99, available at www.nationalarchives.gov.uk.

probably were occurring in the market for industrial sugar in Great Britain prior to the merger, but that the merger would not make any coordinated effects more sustainable or effective[332]. In several cases concerns about a merger leading to tacit coordination identified at Phase 1 have been allayed following an in-depth Phase 2 investigation[333]. In *Anglo American/Lafarge*[334] the Competition Commission concluded that the joint venture proposed by those firms would make coordination in the bulk cement market more likely to emerge and would increase the effectiveness and sustainability of any pre-existing coordination[335]. The parties agreed to divest one of Lafarge's cement plants, an associated quarry, rail depots and a portfolio of ready-mix concrete plants to remedy the problem of coordinated effects.

(F) **Non-horizontal mergers**

Section 5.6 of the *Assessment Guidelines* discusses vertical and conglomerate mergers. The *Guidelines* acknowledge that non-horizontal mergers can lead to efficiencies which may result in the merged firm competing more vigorously[336]. They state that it is a 'well-established principle' that most non-horizontal mergers do not raise competition concerns[337], although they may weaken rivalry and result in an SLC under certain conditions.

The theories of how rivalry may be weakened by non-horizontal mergers typically involve the merged firm harming the ability of its competitors to compete[338]. Paragraph 5.6.6 of the *Guidelines* provides that the CMA will typically frame their analysis by asking:

- Would the merged firm have the ability to harm its rivals, for example through raising prices or refusing to supply them?
- Would the merged firm find it profitable to behave in this manner?
- Would the overall effect of the merged firm's behaviour give rise to an SLC?

The analysis of the above questions may overlap in practice as relevant factors may affect the answer to more than one question. The *Guidelines* explain, by way of illustration, how these questions might be answered in relation to a vertical merger where the theory of harm relates to partial input foreclosure[339].

The *Assessment Guidelines* briefly discuss other possible theories of harm arising from total input foreclosure, customer foreclosure, conglomerate mergers, diagonal mergers[340] and coordinated effects. In particular they explain that a conglomerate merger could raise concerns if the merged entity were to sell complementary products at a price that, owing to the discounts that apply across the product range, is lower than the price charged when they are sold separately, thereby foreclosing competitors[341]. As in the case

332 See the Final Report of 15 March 2005, paras 5.44–5.63, available at www.nationalarchives.gov.uk.

333 See eg *Wienerberger Finance Service BV/Baggeridge Brick plc*, Final Report of 10 May 2007, paras 5.44–5.63; *Woolworths Group plc/Bertram Group Ltd*, Final Report of 4 September 2007; *BOC/Ineos*, Final Report of 18 December 2008 (note that this merger was blocked on grounds other than coordinated effects), all available at www.nationalarchives.gov.uk.

334 Final Report of 1 May 2012, available at www.nationalarchives.gov.uk.

335 Ibid, paras 6.102–6.264; note that the Commission also found anti-competitive horizontal unilateral effects: para 6.35.

336 *Assessment Guidelines*, para 5.6.4.

337 Ibid, para 5.6.1.

338 Ibid, para 5.6.5.

339 Ibid, paras 5.6.9–5.6.12.

340 For an explanation of diagonal mergers see ibid, para 5.6.13, fourth indent.

341 Ibid, para 5.6.13, third indent; on the concept of mixed bundling see ch 17, 'Terminology and illustrations of tying', p 705; on the question of whether a merger might lead to behaviour that might be abusive, see 'Relationship with Article 102', p 985 later in chapter.

of vertical mergers, the CMA would consider the merged firm's ability and incentive to foreclose access to a market. In practice conglomeracy does not appear to have been a significant concern in merger cases under the Enterprise Act[342].

The Competition Commission identified possible vertical issues in *Deutsche Börse AG/London Stock Exchange plc*[343] and concluded that the acquisition of LSE by either Deutsche Börse or Euronext may be expected to lead to an SLC in the market for the provision of on-book trading services within the UK because of the ability and incentive to foreclose entry or expansion to other providers of trading services. Vertical problems were identified in *Railway Investments Ltd/Marcroft Holdings Ltd* that were remedied by a divestiture of some of Marcroft's freight wagon maintenance business[344]. In *Ticketmaster/Live Nation* the Commission investigated a merger between Ticketmaster, the largest ticket agent in the UK, and Live Nation, one of the largest promoters of live music events. The Commission provisionally found that the merger would result in the loss of a new entrant, CTS Eventim, as an effective competitor in the ticketing market, but changed its mind in light of new evidence and arguments[345]. Eventim was dissatisfied with the clearance decision and applied to the CAT for a review; however the Commission decided that it would reconsider the matter and asked the CAT to quash the final report and refer the matter back to the Commission[346]. The merger was subsequently cleared unconditionally[347]. In *London Stock Exchange Group/Frank Russell*[348] the CMA considered, but rejected, vertical and conglomerate concerns as it considered the merged firm would not have the ability to foreclose its competitors.

In *BT/EE*[349] the CMA examined various foreclosure theories of harm. It concluded that the merged entity would have neither the ability to foreclose rivals in either wholesale mobile or mobile backhaul, nor the incentive to engage in foreclosure strategies. On that basis, the CMA cleared the merger unconditionally.

In *ICE/Trayport*[350] the CMA investigated a completed merger and required ICE to divest itself of Trayport due to vertical concerns about the transaction; the CMA's decision was upheld on appeal to the CAT[351]. This is understood to be the first occasion on which a divestiture has been required in the case of a completed merger for vertical reasons.

(G) **Efficiencies**

The *Assessment Guidelines* consider efficiencies as part of the assessment of whether a merger gives rise to an SLC[352]. To be relevant efficiencies must increase rivalry among the remaining firms in the market so that the merger does not result in an SLC[353]. The Phase 1

[342] For an example of conglomerate effects being considered see eg *AG BARR/Britvic*, Final Report of 9 July 2013, paras 6.92–6.113, available at www.nationalarchives.gov.uk.

[343] See the Final Report of 1 November 2005, paras 5.136–5.170, available at www.nationalarchives.gov.uk.

[344] See the Final Report of 12 September 2006, paras 7.74–7.133, available at www.nationalarchives.gov.uk.

[345] See the Final Report of 22 December 2009, available at www.nationalarchives.gov.uk.

[346] Case 1150/4/8/10 *CTS Eventim AG v Competition Commission* [2010] CAT 7.

[347] See the Final Report of 7 May 2010, available at www.nationalarchives.gov.uk.

[348] CMA decision of 7 November 2014, available at www.gov.uk/cma.

[349] See the Final Report of 15 January 2016; for comment see the speech of 5 July 2015 by the CEO of the CMA, Andrea Coscelli 'Recent CMA activity in the telecoms, media and technology space': both are available at www.gov.uk/cma.

[350] See the Final Report of 17 October 2016, www.gov.uk/cma; the Final Order requiring divestiture was made on 21 July 2017.

[351] Cases 1271/4/12/16 etc *Intercontinental Exchange Inc v CMA* [2017] CAT 6.

[352] *Assessment Guidelines*, paras 5.7.1–5.7.18.

[353] Ibid, para 5.7.4.

decision-maker will require the parties to prove, on the basis of compelling evidence, that the efficiencies are timely, likely and sufficient to prevent an SLC from arising and are merger-specific[354]. The Phase 2 Inquiry Group will expect the parties to demonstrate that the same criteria are met on the balance of probabilities. The *Guidelines* describe different types of supply-side efficiencies, such as cost savings, and demand-side efficiencies, such as pricing effects which arise when lowering the price of one product increases demand for it and other products that are used with it[355].

In *Global Radio UK Ltd/GCap Media plc*[356] the OFT took into account efficiency arguments in considering a merger between two radio stations and relied, for the first time, on evidence of efficiencies to conclude that there would not be an SLC in London advertising markets[357]. The OFT noted in particular that the evidential burden for demonstrating efficiencies should not be so high that it is impossible to meet, nor be so rigid and immutable as to be incapable of variation according to the context[358]. In *Tradebe Environment Services Ltd/Sita UK Ltd*[359] the Competition Commission found that a completed joint venture between these firms would lead to a reduction from three to two players in the healthcare risk waste sector. However the Commission cleared the merger unconditionally, in particular because it would generate rivalry-enhancing efficiencies that would benefit customers and could not be achieved by less anti-competitive means[360].

Efficiencies may also be relevant to merger analysis in determining whether a merger generates 'relevant customer benefits' for the purpose of section 30 of the Act sufficient to offset any SLC. In *Central Manchester University Hospitals/University Hospital of South Manchester*[361] the CMA decided that it would be disproportionate to prohibit the merger due to the loss of substantial 'relevant customer benefits', including reductions in patient mortality, clinical complications and infection rates.

(H) **Barriers to entry and expansion**

The *Assessment Guidelines* point out that an important part of the analysis of a merger is a consideration of any barriers to entry or expansion faced by competitors[362]. Market power is unlikely to exist where there are low barriers to entry into or expansion in the market[363]. Barriers to entry and expansion include[364]:

- **absolute advantages**: these exist where an incumbent firm owns or has access to important assets or resources which are not accessible to another firm: this could be the case, for example, where a system of regulation limits the number of firms that can operate on a market or where an existing firm has preferential access to essential facilities or owns intellectual property rights

[354] Ibid; see *Sports Universal Process SAS/Prozone Group Ltd*, OFT decision of 26 October 2011, paras 60–61, recognising that efficiencies may arise from the merger, but expressing doubt that they were merger-specific.

[355] For an example of purchasing efficiencies see *Asda Stores Ltd/Netto Foodstores Ltd*, OFT decision of 23 September 2010, paras 65–76, available at www.nationalarchives.gov.uk.

[356] OFT decision of 8 August 2008; for comment see Didierlaurent and Stephanou 'UK Merger Control: Tuning into Efficiencies' [2010] Comp Law 55.

[357] OFT decision of 8 August 2008, paras 139–189; the OFT specifically relied on demand-side efficiencies as it was not satisfied that the cost savings were sufficient.

[358] Ibid, para 145.

[359] See the Final Report of 28 March 2014, available at www.gov.uk/cma.

[360] Ibid, paras 6.65–6.73; the Commission also took into account the strength of the remaining competitor, SRCL, in the sector: ibid, paras 6.133–6.137.

[361] Final Report of 1 August 2017, paras 15.9–15.327, available at www.gov.uk/cma.

[362] *Assessment Guidelines*, para 5.8.1.

[363] See further ch 1, 'Market power', pp 42–46.

[364] *Assessment Guidelines*, para 5.8.5.

- **intrinsic or structural advantages**: these arise from the technology, production or other factors required to establish an effective presence in the market
- **economies of scale**: the fact that a firm may need to enter or expand on a large scale can constitute a barrier to entry; even large-scale entry or expansion will generally be successful only if that firm expands the total market significantly or replaces an existing firm
- **strategic advantages**: these arise from being first into the market and may be a particular problem in markets which exhibit network effects.

In deciding whether entry and/or expansion might prevent a merger leading to an SLC the CMA will consider whether it would be likely, timely and sufficient[365]. The *Guidelines* provide insights into the way in which the CMA will assess the likelihood, timeliness and sufficiency of entry or expansion[366]. The CMA may consider entry or expansion within two years as timely, although they regard this issue as one that must be assessed on a case-by-case basis. In *Zipcar/Streetcar* entry and expansion were found to be sufficiently likely, timely and sufficient to prevent the merged firm from exercising market power and thus prevent an SLC[367].

In April 2017 the CMA published a report on the assessment of entry and expansion in eight merger clearance decisions[368]. It found that 'the propensity and impact of entry and expansion' had been correctly assessed in some cases, but not others; it also recommended that the CMA take greater account of the potential cost of entry, the ability for firms to expand and the impact of local market conditions.

(l) Countervailing buyer power

The *Assessment Guidelines* consider that countervailing buyer power could exist where a customer is able to use its negotiating strength to constrain the ability of a merged firm to increase prices; this is a factor that makes an SLC finding less likely[369]. An SLC is unlikely to arise where all the customers of the merged firm possess countervailing buyer power after the merger. In cases where only some customers have countervailing power, the CMA will look at the extent to which that power can be relied on to protect all customers[370]. The *Guidelines* set out various factors that affect the ability of buyers to constrain the power of a supplier, such as their ability to switch, the existence of alternative suppliers and the ability of buyers to either sponsor new entry or enter the supplier's market itself[371]. Any buyer power must remain effective following the merger[372].

The buyer power of major retailers of carbonated soft drinks was a significant factor in the clearance of the merger in *Cott Beverages Ltd/Macaw (Holdings) Ltd*[373]. However this argument did not succeed in the case of a merger between the UK's two principal suppliers of eggs in *Stonegate Farmers Ltd/Deans Food Group Ltd*[374]; rather, the merger was found to result in an SLC between the merging parties in the procurement of shell eggs[375].

[365] Ibid, para 5.8.3. [366] Ibid, paras 5.8.8–5.8.13.

[367] Final Report of 22 December 2010, paras 7.29–7.57, available at www.nationalarchives.gov.uk.

[368] KPMG Report 'Entry and expansion in UK merger cases: An ex-post evaluation', 6 April 2017, available at www.gov.uk.

[369] *Assessment Guidelines*, para 5.9.1. [370] Ibid, para 5.9.1.

[371] Ibid, paras 5.9.2–5.9.7. [372] Ibid, para 5.9.8.

[373] See the Final Report of 28 April 2006, paras 5.34–5.46, available at www.nationalarchives.gov.uk.

[374] See the Final Report of 20 April 2007, paras 6.64–6.73, available at www.nationalarchives.gov.uk.

[375] Ibid, paras 6.93–6.102.

6. Enforcement

Chapter 4 of Part 3 of the Enterprise Act, as amended by the ERRA, gives the CMA powers of enforcement. To enable the CMA to carry out its merger control functions, the Act provides for the making of 'initial enforcement orders' during Phase 1 and the acceptance of 'undertakings in lieu' of a Phase 2 reference; it then sets out certain interim restrictions on dealings during the course of a merger inquiry, and concludes with the final undertakings and orders that the CMA Phase 2 Inquiry Group may accept or impose. Undertakings and orders are legally binding and enforceable in the courts[376]; section 89 of the Act makes clear that undertakings[377] may contain provisions that go beyond the order-making powers in Schedule 8.

Section 90 of the Act provides that Schedule 10 shall have effect when accepting certain enforcement undertakings or making orders other than initial and interim orders. Schedule 10 establishes the procedural requirements that the CMA must satisfy when it intends to accept, vary or release an undertaking or, as the case may be, make, vary or revoke an order; paragraphs 1 to 5 of the Schedule deal with the acceptance of undertakings and the making of orders; paragraphs 6 to 8 with their termination. The purpose of Schedule 10 is to require the CMA to set out clearly what it is proposing to do and the reasons for it.

The CMA is required to maintain a register of undertakings and orders made under the merger provisions in the Enterprise Act; it is accessible to the public on the CMA's website[378].

(A) Initial enforcement orders: Phase 1 investigations

There is no duty to pre-notify mergers to the CMA under UK law, and quite a large percentage of the cases referred for a Phase 2 investigation is of completed mergers. This gives rise to a concern that the CMA Phase 2 Inquiry Group might investigate a case in which it considers that there is an SLC, only to find that the merging businesses have become so intermingled that it is difficult in practice to reverse the process and to restore conditions of effective competition. For this reason the ERRA strengthened the powers of the CMA to adopt interim measures during both Phase 1 and Phase 2 investigations so that the CMA's final position will not be prejudiced.

The CMA has published guidance on the circumstances in which it will impose an initial enforcement order, the form that an order will typically take and the timing for imposing, varying and revoking orders[379].

(i) Initial orders to prevent pre-emptive action

Under section 72 of the Act the CMA may make an initial enforcement order where it has reasonable grounds for suspecting that two or more enterprises have ceased to be distinct or that arrangements are in progress or in contemplation which, if carried into effect, will result in two or more enterprises ceasing to be distinct and that pre-emptive action is in progress or in contemplation[380]. 'Pre-emptive action' means action that might prejudice

[376] See 'Enforcement functions of the CMA', pp 977–978 later in chapter.

[377] 'Undertakings' includes undertakings in lieu of a reference, interim undertakings and final undertakings.

[378] Enterprise Act 2002, s 91; the CMA's website is www.gov.uk/cma.

[379] CMA60, September 2017, available at www.gov.uk/cma; see also the *Initial enforcement order* and *Derogation request* templates, available at www.gov.uk/cma.

[380] See *Mergers: Guidance on the CMA's jurisdiction and procedure*, paras 7.28–7.31 and para C.1; the CMA made an initial enforcement order in *Heineken/Diageo Assets*, order of 6 November 2015, which was subsequently revoked on 7 December 2015.

a Phase 2 reference or impede the taking of any remedial action[381]. An initial order may prohibit the doing of things that the CMA considers would constitute pre-emptive action; may impose obligations as to the carrying on of any activities or the safeguarding of assets; may appoint a trustee to conduct or supervise matters[382]; and may require the provision of information[383].

(ii) Initial orders to unwind pre-emptive action

Section 72(3B) of the Act, inserted by the ERRA, provides that the CMA may make an initial enforcement order where it has reasonable grounds for suspecting that a merger has occurred and that pre-emptive action has or may have been taken[384].

(iii) The CMA's approach to making initial orders

Annexe C to the *Mergers: Guidance on the CMA's jurisdiction and procedure* explains the CMA's approach to making initial orders. The CMA expects to make initial orders in respect of anticipated mergers at Phase 1 in 'relatively rare' cases[385], such as where the parties have 'jumped the gun' and exchanged commercially sensitive information that is not objectively necessary for commercial due diligence[386]. The risk of pre-emptive action is generally much higher for completed mergers than for anticipated mergers. Given this, the variety of activities that may constitute pre-emptive action and the information asymmetry between the parties and the CMA at the outset of a merger inquiry, the CMA normally expects to make an initial order suspending, and/or preventing further integration of, completed mergers[387]. The CMA may impose an initial order at any time during a Phase 1 inquiry; however such an order is more likely to be effective if it is made as soon as possible after the merger is completed[388]. The CMA has a template initial order for completed mergers[389].

The *Guidance* provides that the CMA may grant a derogation from the provisions of an initial order[390]. A request for derogation must be reasoned and supported by evidence. Derogations have only a prospective effect; they cannot authorise actions that have already occurred in breach of an initial order. Derogations will be published on the CMA's website[391].

(iv) Undertakings in lieu of a Phase 2 reference

The ability of the CMA to accept undertakings in lieu of a Phase 2 reference has already been discussed[392].

(B) Interim restrictions and powers: Phase 2 investigations

(i) Statutory restrictions on dealings

Sections 77 and 78 of the Enterprise Act impose automatic restrictions on certain dealings in relation to completed and anticipated mergers when a Phase 2 reference has been

[381] Enterprise Act 2002, s 72(8).

[382] On monitoring trustees and hold separate managers see *Mergers: Guidance on the CMA's jurisdiction and procedure*, paras C.27–C.36.

[383] Enterprise Act 2002, s 72(2) and para 9 of Sch 18.

[384] See *Mergers: Guidance on the CMA's jurisdiction and procedure*, paras C.37–C.38.

[385] Ibid, paras C.5 and C.7. [386] Ibid, paras C.5 and C.9, first indent. [387] Ibid, para C.11.

[388] Ibid, para C.13; this will either be when the CMA sends an 'enquiry letter' to the parties or soon after a notification: ibid, para C.14.

[389] Ibid, para C.18; the template is available at www.gov.uk/cma.

[390] Ibid, paras C.19–C.23. [391] www.gov.uk/cma.

[392] See 'Undertakings in lieu of a reference', pp 953–955 earlier in chapter.

made; these are imposed in order to prevent any further integration of the businesses concerned[393]. Section 77 provides that, when a reference has been made of a completed merger and no undertaking has been given in relation to it, no one may, without the consent of the CMA, complete any outstanding matters in relation to that merger or transfer the ownership or control of any enterprises to which the reference relates[394]; any consent of the CMA may be general or special, and may be revoked[395]. Section 78 provides that, when a reference is made of an anticipated merger, no one may, without the consent of the CMA, directly or indirectly acquire an interest in shares in a company if any enterprise to which the reference relates is carried on by or under the control of that company[396]; again any consent of the CMA may be general or special, and may be revoked[397]. These provisions are quite technical and section 79 deals with numerous points of interpretation, in particular to make clear what is meant by a share acquisition for the purposes of section 78. The Competition Commission gave consent to Heinz for the disposal of its ethnic foods business during the course of its investigation in *Heinz/HP Foods Group* which otherwise would not have been possible due to the statutory restriction on share dealings and due to the subsequent interim undertakings that had been given to the Commission under the provisions described in the following paragraph[398]. Section 78 does not apply to the transfer of assets; the CMA may put in place interim measures to deal with this issue.

(ii) **Interim undertakings and orders to prevent pre-emptive action**

Any initial orders that have been made during a Phase 1 investigation will continue in force if and when the CMA initiates a Phase 2 investigation. However the CMA will keep any such initial orders under review and may seek additional interim measures to prevent or unwind any integration of the merging parties' businesses[399].

(a) Legal basis

Under section 80(2) of the Act the CMA may accept an interim undertaking from the parties for the purpose of preventing pre-emptive action. Where the CMA has reasonable grounds for suspecting that pre-emptive action has or may have been taken, section 80(2A) provides that the CMA may accept undertakings to restore the position that would have existed but for the pre-emptive action. Provision also exists for the CMA to make interim orders to prevent or unwind pre-emptive action[400]. Pre-emptive action means action that might prejudice the Phase 2 reference or impede the taking of any action that the CMA might consider to be justified as a result of its decision on the reference[401]. Undertakings and orders may be varied[402].

(b) Guidance

The CMA Board has adopted the Competition Commission's *Merger Remedies: Competition Commission Guidelines*[403] ('*Remedies Guidelines*'). Annexe C to the *Mergers: Guidance on the CMA's jurisdiction and procedure* also provides guidance on interim measures during Phase 2 inquiries. The CMA will normally expect to receive interim

393 See *Mergers: Guidance on the CMA's jurisdiction and procedure*, para C.8 and fn 350.

394 Enterprise Act 2002, s 77(2). 395 Ibid, s 77(5). 396 Ibid, s 78(3). 397 Ibid, s 78(3).

398 See the Final Report of 24 March 2006, paras 3.17–3.21, available at www.nationalarchives.gov.uk.

399 See *Mergers: Guidance on the CMA's jurisdiction and procedure*, para 11.9.

400 Enterprise Act 2002, s 81(2) and (2A). 401 Ibid, s 80(10).

402 Ibid, s 80(5)(b) and s 81(5)(b); see eg the consent given to Deans to process liquid egg on behalf of Stonegate in *Stonegate Farmers Ltd/Deans Food Group Ltd*, available at www.nationalarchives.gov.uk.

403 CC8, November 2008, available at www.gov.uk/cma.

undertakings from the acquirer in the case of a completed merger to clarify or supplement the statutory restrictions on dealing[404]; the CMA may also seek to restrict the flow of commercially sensitive information between the parties pending the outcome. The CMA explains that it might find it necessary to appoint a 'hold separate' manager to operate the business separately from that of the acquirer, and that a monitoring trustee might have to be appointed as well[405].

(c) Interim orders in practice

In *Bucher Industries AG/Johnstone Sweepers Ltd* the Competition Commission was concerned that Bucher appeared not to be complying with its interim undertaking to prevent the integration of the Bucher and Johnstone businesses pending the completion of the investigation and required both an apology from Bucher and the appointment of a monitoring trustee to ensure compliance with the undertaking[406]. A monitoring trustee was also appointed in relation to a completed joint venture in the case of *Stagecoach/Scottish Citylink*[407]. In *Tesco/Co-op Store*[408] the Competition Commission gave directions to prevent Tesco from carrying out any further work on a store in Slough that could impede any remedial action. In *Sports Direct/JJB Sports*[409] the Commission made an interim order to ensure both that the stores purchased by Sports Direct remained viable and that it had options for divestment after it had completed its investigation.

In *Stericycle International LLC/Sterile Technologies Group Ltd* Stericycle purchased STG's clinical waste management business at auction without making a notification. The case was referred for a Phase 2 investigation, and the Competition Commission made an interim order to prevent any further integration of the two businesses and issued directions for the appointment of a monitoring trustee; subsequently further directions were issued for the appointment of a hold-separate manager[410]. Stericycle challenged the directions before the CAT[411]; the CAT upheld the interim order, holding that it was 'well within the [Competition Commission's] margin of appreciation to propose the appointment of a [hold separate manager] in this case'[412], and that Stericycle was well aware of the risk it was taking by completing the transaction without approval from the competition authorities[413]. The Competition Commission considered that the fact that substantial integration of the two businesses had already taken place made it more, not less, important to appoint a hold separate manager[414]. The final outcome of this case was that Stericycle was required to sell off part of the business that it had acquired to a suitable purchaser[415].

In *Ryanair/Aer Lingus*[416] the Competition Commission made an interim order to prevent Ryanair from taking any action that might impair the ability or incentive of Aer

[404] *Remedies Guidelines*, para 1.32; on s 77 of the Act see 'Statutory restrictions on dealings', pp 970–971 earlier in chapter.

[405] *Remedies Guidelines*, paras 12–15; the risk factors making the appointment of a hold separate manager more likely are listed in para 14; see also *Mergers: Guidance on the CMA's jurisdiction and procedure*, para C.31.

[406] See the Final Report of 15 September 2005, para 9.3, available at www.nationalarchives.gov.uk.

[407] See the Final Report of 23 October 2006, para 8.56; see similarly *Capita/IBS*, Final Report of 4 June 2009, both available at www.nationalarchives.gov.uk.

[408] See the Final Report of 28 November 2007, paras 3.44–3.49, available at www.nationalarchives.gov.uk.

[409] See the Final Report, para 3.6, available at www.nationalarchives.gov.uk.

[410] The order and directions will be found at www.nationalarchives.gov.uk.

[411] Case 1070/4/8/06 *Stericycle International LLC v Competition Commission* [2006] CAT 21; for comment see Freeman '*Stericycle*: A Lifeline for the UK's Voluntary Merger Control Regime' [2007] Comp Law 298.

[412] Case 1070/4/8/06 [2006] CAT 21, para 140. [413] Ibid, para 137. [414] Ibid, para 158.

[415] For the final undertakings in this case see www.nationalarchives.gov.uk.

[416] For the interim order and undertakings in this case see www.gov.uk/cma.

Lingus to compete independently pending its Phase 2 investigation; Aer Lingus also gave interim undertakings. These interim measures turned out to be important as the Commission found that Ryanair's completed acquisition of a minority interest in Aer Lingus had resulted in an SLC and so required Ryanair to reduce its shareholding in Aer Lingus to 5%[417]. The Commission's final report was upheld on appeal to the CAT[418] and to the Court of Appeal[419].

(iii) Interim undertakings and orders: penalties

Section 94A of the Enterprise Act provides that the CMA may impose a financial penalty on a person who, without reasonable excuse, fails to comply with an initial order at Phase 1 or with interim undertakings or interim orders at Phase 2. The penalty is capped at 5% of the total turnover, both inside and outside the UK, of the enterprises owned or controlled by that person[420]. The Secretary of State may by order reduce the penalty to a level below 5%[421]. Pursuant to the obligation under section 94B, the CMA has published guidance on the use of its power to impose penalties, and the considerations for determining the amount of the penalty imposed under section 94A[422].

(C) 'Final powers' or 'remedies'

Sections 82 to 84 of the Enterprise Act deal with 'final powers', that is to say the remedial action that the CC may take after it has completed its inquiry and reached its conclusion[423]. Section 82 provides for the acceptance of final undertakings and section 83 for the making of an order where an undertaking is not being fulfilled or where false or misleading information was given to the CMA prior to the acceptance of an undertaking. Section 84 gives the power to the CMA to make a final order. As a general rule the CMA prefers to proceed by accepting undertakings rather than by making final orders: only a small number of Phase 2 merger cases have been resolved by way of a final order[424]. The CMA may proceed to the making of a final order in the event of undue delay in obtaining suitable undertakings after the completion of an investigation[425]. Final undertakings may contain provisions that go beyond the order-making powers in the Act[426]. Provision is made for the variation of remedies[427].

[417] See the Final Report of 28 August 2013, available at www.gov.uk/cma.

[418] Case 1219/4/8/13 *Ryanair Holdings plc v CMA* [2014] CAT 3.

[419] *Ryanair Holdings plc v CMA* [2015] EWCA Civ 83.

[420] Enterprise Act 2002, s 94A(2); see also the Enterprise Act 2002 (Mergers) (Interim Measures: Financial Penalties) (Determination of Control and Turnover) Order 2014, SI 2014/533.

[421] Enterprise Act 2002, s 94A(6).

[422] *Administrative penalties: Statement of policy on the CMA's policy*, CMA4, January 2014, available at www.gov.uk/cma.

[423] See *Remedies Guidelines*, CC8, November 2008, which the CMA adopted with effect from 1 April 2014, available at www.gov.uk/cma.

[424] See eg *Tesco/Co-op Store*, Final Report of 28 November 2007 and Final Order of 23 April 2009, available at www.nationalarchives.gov.uk; *Eurotunnel SA/SeaFrance SA*, Final Report of 6 June 2013 and Final Order of 18 September 2014; the order was made following two appeals to the CAT (on which see n 93 and n 95 earlier in chapter), available at www.gov.uk/cma; the CMA made a Final Order in *Ryanair/Aer Lingus* on 11 June 2015, also available at www.gov.uk/cma.

[425] See eg *FirstGroup plc/ScotRail*, Final Report of 28 June 2004, para 14, available at www.nationalarchives.gov.uk.

[426] Enterprise Act 2002, s 89.

[427] Ibid, s 82(2)(b) (variation of final undertakings) and s 83(5)(c) (variation of final orders); for an example of several variations of a remedy see *FirstGroup plc/ScotRail*, Final Report of 28 June 2004, www.nationalarchives.gov.uk.

(i) Schedule 8 to the Enterprise Act

The orders that can be made are set out in Schedule 8 to the Act, and are extensive[428]. They include 'general restrictions on conduct' (paragraphs 2 to 9); 'general obligations to be performed' (paragraphs 10 and 11); 'acquisitions and divisions' (paragraphs 12 to 14); and 'supply and publication of information' (paragraphs 16 to 19); supplementary provisions as to the making of orders are to be found in paragraphs 21 and 22 of Schedule 8. An order may not interfere with conditions in patent licences or licences of registered designs[429]. It is specifically provided that an order may prohibit the performance of an agreement already in existence[430]. An order may provide for the revocation or modification of conditions in the licences of regulated undertakings[431]. Section 87 of the Act allows the person making an order to give directions to an individual or to an office-holder in a company or association to take action or to refrain from action for the purpose of carrying out or ensuring compliance with the order; failure to comply with such directions may lead to court action[432]. Section 88 sets out the minimum contents of any final order or order to replace an undertaking in lieu of a reference.

(ii) General restrictions on conduct

Paragraphs 2 to 9 of Schedule 8 provide for orders to impose restrictions on conduct. An order may prohibit the making or performance of an agreement or require the termination of one (paragraph 2)[433]; and may forbid refusals to supply (paragraph 3), tie-ins (paragraph 4), discrimination (paragraph 5), preferential treatment (paragraph 6) and deviation from published price lists (paragraph 7). Price regulation is also a possibility (paragraph 8). An order may prohibit the exercise of voting rights attached to shares, stocks or securities (paragraph 9).

(iii) General obligations to be performed

Paragraph 10 of Schedule 8 provides that an order may require a person to supply goods or services, and it can be specified that they should be of a particular standard or that they should be applied in a particular manner: for example a bus company could be required to maintain a certain frequency of service[434]. Paragraph 11 of the Schedule enables an order to require that certain activities should be carried on separately from other activities.

(iv) Acquisitions and divisions

Paragraph 12 of Schedule 8 provides that an order may prohibit or restrict the acquisition of the whole or part of an undertaking or the assets of another person's business. Paragraph 13 provides for the division of any business, whether by sale of any part of an undertaking or assets or otherwise; paragraph 13(3) deals with associated issues such as the transfer or creation of property, rights, liabilities and obligations, the adjustment of contracts, share ownership and other matters. Provision is made for the buyer of a business to be approved by the CMA[435], and for the appointment of a trustee to oversee the divestment of a business[436].

[428] On the territorial scope of the CMA's order-making powers see the Enterprise Act 2002, s 86(1), on which see *Akzo Nobel NV v Competition Commission* [2014] EWCA Civ 482.

[429] Enterprise Act 2002, s 86(2).

[430] Ibid, s 86(3).

[431] Ibid, s 86(5) and Sch 9, Part 1.

[432] Ibid, s 87(4)–(8).

[433] Such an order may not deal with terms and conditions in contracts of employment or the physical conditions in which workers work: ibid, Sch 8, para 2(2).

[434] See *Explanatory Notes* to the Enterprise Bill, para 225.

[435] Enterprise Act 2002, Sch 8, para 13(3)(k).

[436] Ibid, Sch 8, para 13(1).

In *Somerfield plc/Wm Morrison* the Competition Commission required Somerfield to divest four grocery stores that it had acquired from Morrison[437]. Somerfield appealed to the CAT arguing that the Commission's remedy was unreasonable, and that it (Somerfield) should be given the option of selling either the stores that it had acquired or the stores that it already owned: since it was the common ownership of the stores that was responsible for the SLC, the situation could be remedied by divesting either the new or the original stores. The CAT dismissed the appeal[438] and held that reversing the acquisition was a simple, direct and easily understandable approach. The onus was therefore on Somerfield to show why divestment of its original stores would be an equally effective remedy[439]. The CAT considered that Somerfield had failed to show that this was the case, in particular because the Commission had been correct to think that Somerfield's existing stores were less attractive to a potential purchaser than the ones that it had acquired from Morrison, meaning that it was less likely that selling the existing stores would be an effective remedy.

In *Ryanair Holdings v Competition Commission*[440] the CAT held that the Commission (now CMA) is entitled to opt for one-off structural remedies, which are more likely to be comprehensive and do not need ongoing monitoring[441]. The CAT further held that the fact that structural remedies may result in a substantial loss for the parties as a result of a forced sale within a set timetable does not mean that they are unreasonable or disproportionate[442].

(v) Supply and publication of information

The ERRA repealed paragraph 15 and amended paragraph 17 of Schedule 8 to enable the CMA to require parties to publish non-pricing information without also having to require parties to publish pricing information. Paragraph 16 allows a prohibition on the practice of recommending prices to dealers. Paragraph 17 enables an order to require a person to publish accounting, pricing and/or non-pricing information. Paragraph 18 provides that orders can specify the manner in which information is to be published. There is a general power in paragraph 19 to require a person to provide the competition authorities with information, and for that information to be published.

(vi) National security, media and financial stability mergers

Paragraphs 20, 20A and 20B make provision for orders to be made in relation to 'public interest cases' under Chapter 2 of Part 3 of the Act[443].

(vii) Monitoring compliance and determination of disputes

Paragraph 20C gives the CMA power to appoint a third party expert to monitor the implementation of remedies, including compliance with orders and to determine disputes.

(viii) The CMA's approach to remedies

The CMA's approach to remedies is described in the *Remedies Guidelines*. Part 1 of the *Remedies Guidelines* explains the objectives of remedial action: the CMA will seek the least costly and intrusive remedies that it considers will be effective to address any SLC and its adverse effects[444]. Part 2 provides an overview of the types of remedies. The CMA generally prefers structural remedies to behavioural ones[445], although the use of the latter

[437] See the Final Report of 2 September 2005, paras 11.9–11.23, available at www.nationalarchives.gov.uk.
[438] Case 1051/4/8/05 *Somerfield plc v Competition Commission* [2006] CAT 4.
[439] Ibid, paras 99–105.
[440] Case 1219/4/8/13 [2014] CAT 3.
[441] Ibid, para 202.
[442] Ibid, paras 209–214.
[443] See 'Public interest cases', pp 987–989 later in chapter.
[444] *Remedies Guidelines*, para 1.8.
[445] Ibid, para 2.14.

cannot be ruled out[446]. Part 3 of the *Remedies Guidelines* explains the principles relevant to divestiture remedies, including the criteria for identifying a suitable purchaser. Part 4 discusses behavioural remedies and emphasises the need for there to be effective and adequately resourced arrangements for monitoring and enforcement. The use of trustees and third party monitors to assist in the monitoring and implementation of undertaking or orders is discussed in Part 5. The implementation of remedies is further discussed in chapter 14 of *Mergers: Guidance on the CMA's jurisdiction and procedure.*

(ix) Examples of Phase 2 remedies

The Competition Commission, one of the CMA's predecessors, opted for structural remedies in the majority of cases that gave rise to an SLC[447]. The CMA has required divestitures in several cases, notably in *Ladbrokes plc/Gala Coral Group Ltd* where it decided that around 350 to 400 betting shops should be sold to one or more suitably qualified up-front buyers[448], the largest ever divestiture in the retail sector[449].

In both *Hamsard 2786 Ltd/Academy Music Holdings Ltd*[450] and *SvitzerWijsmuller A/S/Adsteam Marine Ltd*[451] the Competition Commission was offered behavioural remedies, including price controls, but rejected them in favour of partial divestitures. In rare cases an outright prohibition of an anticipated merger may be preferable, as occurred in *Serviced Dispense Equipment Ltd (SDEL)/Coors Brewers Ltd*[452]. However behavioural remedies are possible: the Competition Commission accepted a retail price cap and other behavioural remedies in *Dräger Medical AG & Co KGaA/Hillenbrand Industries Inc*[453] and undertakings on both fares and the level of service, frequency and configuration of bus routes in Scotland, in particular in the Glasgow and Edinburgh areas, in *FirstGroup plc/ScotRail*[454]. In *Nufarm/AH Marks* the Competition Commission found that, while divestiture would not be disproportionate, a package of behavioural remedies would be more targeted in addressing its competition concerns. The CMA may exceptionally accept behavioural remedies even though it considers divestiture would be more effective, as occurred in *Macquarie UK Broadcast Ventures/National Grid Wireless*[455] given the unique circumstances of the digital switchover process in the broadcasting sector.

In another unusual case, *Imerys Minerals Ltd/Goonvean Ltd*[456], the Competition Commission decided that full divestiture was disproportionate; that partial divestiture was ineffective and that the most effective and proportionate remedy was a price control remedy[457]. In *Breedon Aggregates Ltd/Aggregate Industries UK Ltd*[458] the CMA required

[446] See the three situations described ibid, para 2.16.

[447] See 'The Merger Provisions in Practice', pp 981–986 later in chapter.

[448] An up-front buyer was also required in *Kemira GrowHow Oyj/Terra Industries Inc*, Final Report of 11 July 2007, paras 15.56–15.58, available at www.nationalarchives.gov.uk.

[449] See CMA Press Release, 26 July 2016; for other recent cases of divestitures required at Phase 2 see eg *Iron Mountain Inc./Recall Holdings Ltd*, CMA Press Release, 16 June 2016; *Celesio AG/Sainsbury's Supermarkets Ltd*, CMA Press Release, 29 July 2016; *Diebold Inc/Wincor Nixdorf*, CMA Press Release, 16 March 2017, all available at www.gov.uk/cma.

[450] See the Final Report of 23 January 2007, paras 6.47–6.67, available at www.nationalarchives.gov.uk.

[451] See the Final Report of 9 February 2007, paras 9.13–9.17, available at www.nationalarchives.gov.uk.

[452] See the Final Report of 11 March 2005, paras 6.42–6.48; see also *BOC Ltd/Ineos Chlor Ltd*, Final Report of 18 December 2008, paras 11.14–11.85, both available at www.nationalarchives.gov.uk.

[453] See the Final Report of 19 May 2004, paras 10.26–10.40, available at www.nationalarchives.gov.uk.

[454] See the Final Report of 28 June 2004, paras 6.8–6.36, available at www.nationalarchives.gov.uk.

[455] See the Final Report of 11 March 2008, paras 10.68–10.88, available at www.nationalarchives.gov.uk.

[456] See the Final Report of 10 October 2013, para 9.115, available at www.nationalarchives.gov.uk.

[457] Compare *AkzoNobel NV/Metlac Holdings Srl*, Final Report of 21 December 2012, paras 11.19–11.42, rejecting a price control remedy owing to its complexity, ineffectiveness and need for monitoring, available at www.nationalarchives.gov.uk.

[458] See the Final Report of 9 April 2014, CMA26, para 7.151, available at www.gov.uk/cma.

Breedon to make divestments in two areas, but allowed it to cap the price at which it would sell asphalt from two plants in Inverness as the competition concerns in that area were of a relatively short duration. Price caps were also accepted in two cases involving rail franchises, *Arriva Rail North Ltd/Northern Rail Franchise*[459] and *First Group/MTR South Western Rail Franchise*[460]. In *Reckitt Benckiser/K-Y brand*[461] the CMA insisted on an intellectual property remedy: Reckitt Benckiser had to license the K-Y brand to a competitor for eight years to enable it to develop a rival product.

The CMA will also consider whether it should recommend action by persons other than the merging parties[462]. For example it might suggest to the Government that it should amend legislation or regulations that inhibit entry into a particular market; the Government has given a commitment to give a public response to any such recommendation; this happened in *Dräger Medical AG & Co KGaA/Hillenbrand Industries Inc*[463].

(D) Enforcement functions of the CMA

Section 92(1) of the Act requires the CMA to keep enforcement undertakings and enforcement orders under review and to ensure compliance with sections 77 and 78, which restrict certain dealings. The CMA must consider whether undertakings or orders are being complied with and whether, by reason of a change of circumstances, there is a case for release, variation or supersession[464].

The CMA also has a responsibility to keep under review undertakings and orders arising from merger cases conducted under the now-repealed Fair Trading Act 1973[465]. *Remedies: Guidance on the CMA's approach to the variation and termination of merger, monopoly and market undertakings and orders*[466] sets outs how the CMA will decide on the variation and termination of final undertakings and orders under the merger provisions of the Fair Trading Act and the Enterprise Act. In 2016 the CMA reviewed 71 structural merger remedies that had been put in place before 1 January 2005 and decided 51 of them should be removed. It carried out a similar review of behavioural merger remedies, concluding that all but one should be released[467].

Section 94 of the Enterprise Act provides that orders and undertakings can be enforced through the courts. There is a duty to comply with orders and undertakings, and that duty is owed to anyone who may be affected by a contravention of it[468]; any breach of the duty is actionable if such a person sustains loss or damage[469], though a defence exists if the person in question took all reasonable steps and exercised all due diligence to avoid a

459 See the Final Report of 2 November 2016, available at www.gov.uk/cma.

460 See the CMA's Press Release, 18 August 2017 (undertakings given in lieu of a Phase 2 investigation); cf *Cineworld/City Screen*, Final Report of 8 October 2013 (rejecting price cap proposed by the merging parties, local authorities and third parties; the cinema in question was eventually sold to a third party: CMA Press Release, 16 February 2015).

461 See the CMA Press Release, 28 June 2016.

462 *Remedies Guidelines*, para 2.22.

463 See the Final Report, paras 10.16–10.25, available at www.nationalarchives.gov.uk.

464 Enterprise Act 2002, s 92(2); further information on cases in which undertakings or orders are being reviewed can be found on the CMA's website, www.gov.uk/cma.

465 See ibid, Sch 24 and the Enterprise Act 2002 (Enforcement Undertakings) Order 2006, SI 2006/354 and the Enterprise Act 2002 (Enforcement Undertakings and Orders) Order 2006, SI 2006/355.

466 CMA11, January 2014, revised August 2015, available at www.gov.uk/cma.

467 Details of the CMA's review are available at www.gov.uk/cma.

468 Enterprise Act 2002, s 94(2) and (3).

469 Ibid, s 94(4); as to whether a person injured by breach of an undertaking or order could bring an action for damages, see *MidKent Holdings v General Utilities plc* [1996] 3 All ER 132, brought under s 93 of the (now-repealed) Fair Trading Act 1973.

contravention of the order or undertaking[470]. The CMA maintains a register of undertakings and orders on its website; it is open to physical inspection between 10.00 and 16.00 on working days[471]. Compliance with an order or undertaking is enforceable by civil proceedings brought by the CMA[472] for an injunction (or interdict in Scotland). Similar provisions apply in relation to breaches of the statutory restrictions on certain dealings provided for in sections 77 and 78[473].

7. Supplementary Provisions

Chapter 5 of Part 3 of the Enterprise Act contains a number of supplementary provisions. Some of these, such as the merger notice procedure and the payment of fees, have already been considered[474]. Two issues of particular importance remain to be considered: the information powers of the CMA and its ability to impose penalties, and the review of decisions on mergers by the CAT.

(A) Investigation powers and penalties

Sections 109 to 117 of the Enterprise Act, as amended by the ERRA, deal with the CMA's powers of investigation and with penalties. Section 109(1) provides that the CMA may 'for a permitted purpose' require, by notice, the attendance of witnesses[475], the production of documents[476] and the supply of various information[477]. Among the 'permitted purposes' are using the investigation powers to assist the CMA to carry out any functions, including enforcement functions, in connection with a Phase 1 or Phase 2 merger investigation[478]. It should be noted that the CMA will also be able to use these powers before it begins a Phase 1 investigation if the functions for which it is exercising the powers fall within a permitted purpose[479]. Subject to the time limit contained in section 110A, the CMA can impose a penalty on a person who, without reasonable excuse, fails to comply with a notice given under section 109[480] or who obstructs or delays a person who is trying to copy documents required to be produced[481]. Section 110A provides that no penalty may be imposed if more than four weeks have passed since the 'relevant day' when, essentially, the CMA's powers of investigation ceased to apply[482]. The maximum amounts that the CMA may impose as a penalty under section 110(1) and (3) are specified in the Competition and Markets Authority (Penalties) Order 2014[483]. It is a criminal offence for a person intentionally to alter, suppress or destroy any document that he or she has been required to produce under

470 Enterprise Act 2002, s 94(5).

471 The CMA Registers of Undertakings and Orders (Available Hours) Order 2014, SI 2014/558.

472 Enterprise Act 2002, s 94(6).

473 Ibid, s 95.

474 See 'Notifying mergers to the CMA', pp 948–951 earlier in chapter.

475 Enterprise Act 2002, s 109(1).

476 Ibid, s 109(2).

477 Ibid, s 109(3); a notice given under this section must explain the consequences of non-compliance: s 109(4).

478 Ibid, s 109(A1); 'enforcement functions' are defined in s 109(8A).

479 See *Explanatory Notes* to the ERRA, para 229; the *Notes* give the example of the CMA believing that a merger is about to be completed and using its information-gathering powers to decide if pre-emptive action will occur.

480 Enterprise Act 2002, s 110(1); a penalty of £20,000 was imposed on Hungryhouse Holdings Ltd for failing to comply with a s 109 notice on 24 November 2017, decision available at www.gov.uk/cma.

481 Ibid, s 110(3).

482 The 'relevant day' specified in s 110A depends on the particular purpose for which the CMA has exercised its power under s 109.

483 SI 2014/559.

section 109[484]: a person guilty of this offence could be fined or imprisoned for a maximum of two years[485].

Sections 111 to 116 set out the main procedural requirements that the CMA must observe when imposing a monetary penalty; the factors which it will have regard to when determining the amount of a penalty are set out in the *Administrative penalties: Statement of policy on the CMA's policy*[486]. There is a right of appeal to the CAT against decisions of the CMA to impose monetary penalties: the CAT may quash the penalty or substitute a different amount or different dates for payment[487]. The CMA and its predecessors have used or threatened to use its section 109 powers, both on parties to the transaction under consideration and third parties[488]: these powers can avoid delays in the provision of information and ensure that the information provided is full and accurate.

(B) **Review of decisions under Part 3 of the Enterprise Act**

Section 120(1) of the Enterprise Act provides that any person aggrieved by a decision of the CMA or the Secretary of State may apply to the CAT for a review of that decision. The CAT considered it difficult to conceive of a situation where the merging parties objecting to a final finding of an SLC would not be persons aggrieved by that decision, even if they were prepared to comply with it[489]. An aggrieved person could also be a third party with sufficient interest[490].

Part 3 of the Competition Appeal Tribunal Rules[491] makes provision for proceedings under section 120 of the Act. An application for review must be made within four weeks of the date on which the applicant was notified of the disputed decision or of its date of publication, whichever is earlier[492]; the date of publication is the date when the parties receive the reasons for a Phase 1 decision, rather than an earlier Press Release stating the content of the decision but without its reasoning[493]. The CAT has indicated that, as a general proposition, a main hearing in merger cases should be held within three months of the final decision[494]; the CAT has succeeded in dealing with cases within a short time period, considerably shorter than appeals to the General Court under the EUMR.

When dealing with cases under section 120(1) the CAT must apply the same principles as would be applied by the Administrative Court on an application for judicial review[495]. The fact that the CAT is a specialist competition tribunal does not mean that it should apply different principles[496].

In *SCOP v CMA*[497] the Supreme Court said that an appellate court should exercise caution when reviewing the economic judgments of expert tribunals such as the CMA and CAT, particularly in merger cases where delays caused by appeals may unsettle the market and damage the interests of the businesses involved[498]. Similarly, the CAT has

[484] Enterprise Act 2002, s 110(5). [485] Ibid, s 110(7).

[486] CMA4, January 2014, available at www.gov.uk/cma. [487] Enterprise Act 2002, s 114.

[488] See also *Mergers: Guidance on the CMA's jurisdiction and procedure*, paras 7.3 and 7.17 on when the CMA is likely to use its powers under s 109.

[489] See Case 1145/4/8/09 *Stagecoach Group Plc v Competition Commission* [2010] CAT 1, para 12.

[490] See Case 1107/4/10/08 *Merger Action Group v Secretary of State for Business, Enterprise and Regulatory Reform* [2008] CAT 36, paras 32–48.

[491] SI 2015/1648. [492] Competition Appeal Tribunal Rules 2015, SI 2015/1648, r 25.

[493] See Case 1030/4/1/04 *Federation of Wholesale Distributors v OFT* [2004] CAT 11, paras 22–26.

[494] See Case 1075/4/8/07 *Stericycle International LLC v Competition Commission* [2007] CAT 9, para 7.

[495] Enterprise Act 2002, s 120(4).

[496] *OFT v IBA Health Ltd* [2004] EWCA Civ 142, paras 52 and 88–106; *BSkyB Group plc v Competition Commission* [2010] EWCA Civ 2, paras 28–41.

[497] [2015] UKSC 75. [498] Ibid, para 44.

said that it should show particular restraint in second-guessing the 'educated predictions for the future that have been made by an expert and experienced decision-maker', such as the CMA[499].

The CAT may dismiss the application or quash the whole or part of the decision to which it relates[500]; and, in the latter situation, it may refer the matter back to the original decision-maker for further consideration[501]. An appeal may be brought before the Court of Appeal, with permission, against the CAT's decision on a point of law[502].

It is possible to make some general observations about the applications for review of merger decisions. First, it is noticeable that third parties have brought a number of applications for review[503]. The challenges by third parties to the OFT's decisions not to refer the *iSOFT/Torex, Phoenix Healthcare/East Anglian Pharmaceuticals* and *Boots/Alliance UniChem* mergers have already been discussed in the context of the duty to refer certain mergers for a Phase 2 investigation[504]. A third party successfully appealed against the clearance decision in *Ticketmaster/Live Nation*[505], leading to a reinvestigation and a second clearance decision[506]. In *AC Nielsen v CMA*[507] a third party challenged a decision not to refer a merger, but the CMA decided that it would reconsider the matter in light of new evidence, with the consequence that the CAT quashed the decision not to refer and referred the matter back to the CMA; the CMA subsequently adopted a second clearance decision[508].

A second point to note is that the jurisdiction of UK merger control has been tested in several cases. For example in *Akzo Nobel v Competition Commission*[509] the Court of Appeal upheld the Commission's enforcement jurisdiction to prohibit *Akzo Nobel/Metlac*. A very different aspect of jurisdiction—the meaning of enterprises ceasing to be distinct—was contested in *Groupe Eurotunnel v Competition Commission*[510] and *SCOP v CMA*[511], which was discussed in the section on relevant merger situations earlier in this chapter[512].

A third point is that several merging parties have challenged the substantive analysis of the UK competition authorities. In *Stagecoach v Competition Commission*[513] the CAT held that the Commission's choice of counterfactual was unreasonable and unsupported by the evidence. Other appeals have been unsuccessful: for example, the CAT and the Court of Appeal dismissed appeals by BSkyB against the final decisions in *BSkyB/ITV*[514] and by Ryanair against the final decision in *Ryanair/Aer Lingus*[515]. ICE's appeal against the prohibition of its completed acquisition of Trayport was rejected by the CAT[516].

499 Case 1190/4/8/12 *SRCL v Competition Commission* [2012] CAT 14, para 15.

500 Enterprise Act 2002, s 120(5)(a). 501 Ibid, s 120(5)(b). 502 Ibid, s 120(6) and (7).

503 For comment see Burrows 'Review of Merger Decisions by the CAT: A Question of Evidence' [2006] Comp Law 169.

504 See 'Duty to make references: completed mergers', pp 936–941 earlier in chapter; see also Case 1059/4/1/06 *Celesio AG v OFT* [2006] CAT 9.

505 Case 1150/4/8/10 *CTS Eventim AG v Competition Commission* [2010] CAT 7.

506 Final Report of 7 May 2010, available at www.nationalarchives.gov.uk.

507 Case 1227/4/12/14 [2014] CAT 8. 508 CMA decision of 20 October 2014.

509 [2014] EWCA Civ 482, confirming the CAT's judgment in Case 1204/4/813 *Akzo Nobel NV v Competition Commission* [2013] CAT 13.

510 Cases 1216/4/8/13 etc *Groupe Eurotunnel SA v Competition Commission* [2013] CAT 30.

511 [2015] UKSC 75.

512 See 'Enterprises ceasing to be distinct', pp 941–945 earlier in chapter.

513 Case 1145/4/8/09 *Stagecoach Group plc Competition Commission* [2010] CAT 14.

514 See 'Public interest cases', pp 987–989 later in chapter.

515 Case 1219/4/8/13 *Ryanair Holdings plc v CMA* [2014] CAT 3, upheld on appeal to the Court of Appeal [2015] EWCA Civ 83.

516 *ICE/Trayport*, CMA decision of 17 October 2016, upheld on appeal Cases 1271/4/12/16 etc *Intercontinental Exchange Inc v CMA* [2017] CAT 6.

A fourth point is that several applications unsuccessfully challenged the remedies imposed to prevent or mitigate an SLC; this happened in *Cooperative Group/Fairways Group*[517], *Somerfield/Morrisons*[518] and *Stericycle/Ecowaste Southwest*[519].

8. The Merger Provisions in Practice

The merger provisions of the Enterprise Act entered into force on 20 June 2003. Table 22.1 contains a list of cases in which a Phase 2 investigation was completed between the cut-off date for the eighth edition of this book, 6 February 2015, and 8 December 2017.

A number of interesting points emerge from Phase 2 cases under the Enterprise Act.

(A) Basic statistical analysis

By 8 December 2017 186 mergers had been referred for a Phase 2 investigation under the Act. The largest number of references during a financial year was 18, which occurred in 2004/05; there were 17 in 2005/06; the smallest was five in 2016/17[520].

(B) Abandoned mergers

Quite a few mergers that are referred for a Phase 2 investigation are then abandoned by the parties: the CMA's statistics show that this had happened in 30 cases by 8 December 2017. There are various possible explanations for this. One is that the parties may consider that it is too expensive, in terms of professional fees, to undergo an in-depth investigation by a CMA Phase 2 Inquiry Group, especially where the value of the business acquired is fairly small. The concern that too many 'small' mergers could be referred for a Phase 2 investigation led to the most recent *De minimis guidance*[521]. Another explanation for the abandonment of a merger might be that the parties realise that there is such a strong likelihood that the outcome of the investigation will be substantial remedies, or even an outright prohibition, that it is not worth continuing with the transaction.

A third explanation for some abandonments is that an acquisition agreement may have been conditional on the merger not being referred for a Phase 2 investigation.

(C) Completed mergers

It is noticeable that a significant number of mergers referred for a Phase 2 investigation were completed ones. The UK system does not require pre-notification of mergers, and the parties are perfectly entitled to complete a transaction without prior clearance, although they need to be aware of the risks of doing so. The CMA will take care, in the case of a completed merger, to ensure that there is no further intermingling of assets once the matter has come to their attention and become the subject of an investigation[522].

It is important to note that in several cases of completed mergers the CMA and its predecessor, the Competition Commission, required substantial remedies, including, in some, the total reversal of a transaction.

517 See 'Undertakings in lieu of a reference', pp 953–955 earlier in chapter.
518 See 'Acquisitions and divisions', pp 974–975 earlier in chapter.
519 Case 1190/4/8/12 *SRCL Ltd v Competition Commission* [2012] CAT 14.
520 These figures are based on the statistics available on the CMA's website: www.gov.uk/cma.
521 See 'Markets of insufficient importance', p 939 earlier in chapter.
522 See 'Enforcement', pp 969–978 earlier in chapter.

Table 22.1 Phase 2 merger references under the Enterprise Act 2002

Title	Date of reference	Date of publication	Finding of substantial lessening of competition?	Remedy
Xchanging Holdings Ltd/ Xchanging, Inc	02.12.2014	29.04.15	No	
Pork Farms Caspian Ltd/Kerry Foods **NB: completed merger**	05.01.15	03.06.15	No	
Sonoco Products Co/ Weidenhammer Packaging Group GmbH **NB: completed merger**	27.01.15	03.07.15	No	
Reckitt Benckiser/ Johnson and Johnson	07.01.15	12.08.15	Yes	RB required to license one of its brands to a competitor for eight years
Ashford St Peter's NHS Foundation Trust/Royal Surrey County NHS Foundation Trust	18.02.15	16.09.15	No	
Poundland Group/99 Stores Ltd	17.04.15	18.09.15	No	
SouthWest Water/ Bournemouth Water	08.06.15	05.11.15	No	
BT/EE **NB: fast-track reference to Phase 2**	09.06.16	15.01.16	No	
Linergy Ltd/Ulster Farm By-Products Ltd **NB: completed merger**	28.07.15	06.01.16	No	
Pearson VUE/ learndirect Ltd **NB: abandoned 6 January 2016**	16.12.15			
Celesio/Sainsbury's	29.12.15	29.07.16	Yes	Celesio to sell pharmacies in 12 areas of England and Wales

Title	Date of reference	Date of publication	Finding of substantial lessening of competition?	Remedy
Fenland Laundries Ltd/ Fisher Services Ltd **NB: abandoned 7 January 2016**	04.01.16			
Ladbrokes plc/Coral Group Ltd **NB: fast-track reference to Phase 2**	11.01.16	26.07.16	Yes	Ladbrokes and Coral must sell around 350 to 400 betting shops
Iron Mountain/Recall **NB: undertakings in lieu not accepted**	14.01.16	16.06.16	Yes	Some local divestitures required
ICE/Trayport **NB: completed merger**	03.05.16	17.10.16	Yes	ICE must divest itself of Trayport
Arriva Rail North Ltd/ Northern Rail Franchise	20.05.16	02.11.16	Yes	Unregulated fares capped on three routes
Diebold Inc/Wincor Nixdorf AG **NB: completed merger**	30.08.16	16.03.17	Yes	Divestiture required
VTech Holdings Ltd/ LeapFrog Enterprises Inc **NB: completed merger**	30.08.16	12.01.17	No	
Central Manchester University Hospitals NHS Foundation Trust/ University Hospital of South Manchester NHS Foundation Trust	27.02.17	01.08.17	Yes, but substantial patient benefits so merger cleared	
Cygnet/Cambian Group plc	03.05.17	16.10.17	Yes	Divestiture required
Cardtronics Holdings Limited/DirectCash Payments Inc	15.05.17	22.09.17	No	
Euro Car Parts/Andrew Page	22.05.17	31.10.17	Yes	Divestiture required
Tesco/Booker	12.07.17	20.12.17	No	
Just Eat/Hungryhouse	19.05.17	16.11.17	No	

(i) Full unscrambling

In a few cases, such as *Stericycle/Ecowaste* and *VPS/SitexOrbis*, the acquisition in question had to be fully unscrambled. Divestiture was required on vertical grounds in *ICE/Trayport*[523].

(ii) Substantial unscrambling

In some cases, such as *Ryanair/Aer Lingus, Global Radio/CMG* and *Anglo American/Lafarge*, the Competition Commission required significant unscrambling of the transaction.

(iii) Partial unscrambling

In a few cases partial divestiture was considered to be appropriate: for example in *Breedon Aggregates/Aggregates Industries* the CMA required Breedon to sell an asphalt and a ready-mix concrete plant; interestingly, however, the CMA imposed a price control for the supply of asphalt in the Inverness area where it considered the competition concerns would be of a 'relatively short duration'.

(D) The number of findings of an SLC

An SLC was found in 91 out of the 143 mergers to have been investigated by 8 December 2017.

(E) The number of outright prohibitions

There have been some cases in which a merger was prohibited in its entirety: the CMA's statistics show that this had happened in ten cases by 8 December 2017. The completed mergers in section A have already been referred to. The first occasion on which the CC prohibited an anticipated merger in its entirety was in *Knauf Insulation/Superglass Insulation*; the Competition Commission rejected various remedies suggested by Knauf to address concerns over its ability, after the merger, to raise prices[524]. The second merger to be blocked was *BOC/Ineos Chlor* as it would have led to higher prices and/or lower service levels than would otherwise be the case in the markets for the distribution of packaged chlorine[525]. In *BBC Worldwide/Channel 4/ITV* a joint venture that would lead to an SLC in the supply of UK TV video-on-demand content at both the wholesale and retail levels was blocked[526]. The merger in *SDEL/Coors* was prohibited because it would have led to an SLC in the market for technical services equipment for dispensing draught beer[527]. More recently in *Akzo/Metlac* the Commission blocked the merger as it would have resulted in unilateral effects due to a loss of actual and potential competition[528]. In *Eurotunnel/SeaFrance* the Competition Commission and, following successful appeals to the CAT, the CMA concluded that the only appropriate remedy would be to prohibit Groupe Eurotunnel from operating ferry services

[523] See n 516 earlier in chapter.

[524] See the Final Report of 26 November 2004, paras 9.1–9.21, www.nationalarchives.gov.uk.

[525] See the Final Report of 18 December 2008, paras 10.1 and 11.14–11.16, available at www.nationalarchives.gov.uk.

[526] See the Final Report of 4 February 2009, paras 5.4–5.92, available at www.nationalarchives.gov.uk.

[527] See the Final Report of 11 March 2005, available at www.nationalarchives.gov.uk.

[528] See the Final Report of 21 December 2012, upheld on appeal to the CAT Case 1204/4/8/13 *Akzo Nobel NV v Competition Commission* [2013] CAT 13, upheld on appeal to the Court of Appeal [2014] EWCA Civ 482.

on the Dover–Calais route[529]. In *Royal Bournemouth and Christchurch Hospitals NHS Foundation Trust/Poole Hospital NHS Foundation Trust* the Competition Commission found that the loss of competition caused by the merger would result in less pressure to maintain and improve the quality of services offered to patients[530]. The Commission rejected the parties' arguments that the merger would give rise to 'relevant customer benefits', and decided that the only effective remedy was to prohibit the merger. The CMA required the divestiture of Trayport due to vertical concerns in *ICE/Trayport*[531].

(F) Relationship with Article 102

In *Railway Investments/Marcroft Holdings*[532] the Competition Commission concluded that the deterrent effects of Article 102 TFEU and/or the Chapter II prohibition of the Competition Act 1998 were too uncertain to counteract the incentives of Railway Investments to indulge in the anti-competitive behaviour predicted[533].

(G) Healthcare

The Health and Social Care Act 2012 makes provision for mergers involving NHS foundation trusts[534]. Section 79(1) provides that, for the purposes of Part 3 of the Enterprise Act, when 'the activities of two or more NHS foundation trusts cease to be distinct activities' or 'the activities of one or more NHS foundation trusts and the activities of one or more businesses cease to be distinct activities', they shall be treated as two or more enterprises ceasing to be distinct for the purposes of UK merger control[535]. Where the CMA decides to investigate a merger involving an NHS foundation trust it must notify NHS Improvement[536], the regulator for healthcare services in England. NHS Improvement must then advise the CMA on the effect of the merger on relevant customer benefits for NHS patients[537].

Three mergers involving NHS foundation trusts have been taken to Phase 2. In October 2013 the Competition Commission prohibited a merger of two NHS foundation trusts in Dorset[538]. In the case of *Ashford St Peter's NHS Foundation Trust/Royal Surrey County NHS Foundation Trust*[539] the CMA decided there was no SLC. In August 2017 the CMA identified an SLC in its investigation of *Central Manchester University Hospitals Foundation Trust/University Hospital of South Manchester NHS Foundation Trust*[540]; however the

[529] See the Final Report of 6 June 2013, partially overturned on appeal to the CAT Cases 1216/4/8/13 etc *Groupe Eurotunnel SA v Competition Commission* [2013] CAT 30; following remittal and a re-investigation see Final Decision of 27 June 2014, upheld on appeal to the CAT Cases 1233/3/3/14 etc *Groupe Eurotunnel SA v CMA* [2015] CAT 1, reversed on appeal to the Court of Appeal [2015] EWCA Civ 487, but the CMA's appeal to the Supreme Court was allowed: [2015] UKSC 75.

[530] See the Final Report of 17 October 2013, available at www.nationalarchives.gov.uk.

[531] See n 516 earlier in chapter.

[532] See the Final Report of 12 September 2006, available at www.nationalarchives.gov.uk.

[533] Ibid, paras 7.114–7.126.

[534] See further *CMA Guidance: Review of NHS mergers*, CMA29, July 2014 and *Competition review of NHS mergers: A short guide for managers of NHS providers*, both available at www.gov.uk/cma.

[535] See further *Supporting NHS providers: guidance on transactions for NHS foundation trusts*, August 2014, updated March 2015, available at www.gov.uk.

[536] Health and Social Care Act 2012, s 79(4).

[537] Ibid, s 79(5); see further *Supporting NHS providers: guidance on merger benefits*, August 2014, available at www.gov.uk.

[538] See n 530 earlier in chapter.

[539] See the Final Report of 16 September 2015, available at www.gov.uk.

[540] See the Final Report of 1 August 2017, available at www.gov.uk.

merger was cleared as it would give rise to substantial benefits for the care of patients, including in relation to patient mortality, clinical complications and infection rates. Later in August 2017 the CMA, for the first time, cleared an NHS merger at Phase 1 on the basis of the patient benefits that would be likely to accrue in the case of *Heart of England NHS Foundation Trust/University Hospitals Birmingham NHS Foundation Trust*[541].

(H) **Evaluation of remedial action**

In 2017 the CMA published an analysis of merger remedies in past cases and the lessons that can be learned for future cases[542].

9. 'Public Interest Cases', 'Other Special Cases' and Mergers in the Water Industry

A key feature of the merger provisions in the Enterprise Act is that the Secretary of State should not be involved in individual cases, and that decisions should be taken by the CMA: competition analysis in normal merger cases should be carried out by a specialist competition authority[543]. However there may be situations in which the investigation of a merger may be justifiable on grounds of a wider public interest than its detrimental effect on competition. The essence of the provisions about to be discussed is that, where a merger is referred to the CMA on public interest grounds, it is for the Secretary of State to take the final decision on whether the merger operates or may be expected to operate against the public interest and on any remedies required to prevent this[544]. There are three categories of case: public interest cases, other special cases and European mergers. The provisions are deliberately framed narrowly, given that UK policy is that the predominant concern in merger control should be a transaction's effect on competition. Certain mergers—such as the attempted acquisition in 2014 of AstraZeneca, a British–Swedish company, by Pfizer of the US—led to calls from some commentators to protect indigenous businesses from foreign takeover or to promote industrial policy[545]. In the authors' view, however, there is much to be said for resisting calls for a stricter approach to merger control based on non-competition criteria[546].

In October 2017 the Government published a Green Paper setting out proposals to strengthen its powers for scrutinising the national security implications of foreign investments[547]. In the short-term the Government proposes to amend the turnover and share of supply tests for military and dual-use products and advanced technology. Among

541 CMA Press Release, 30 August 2017; see also Derby Teaching Hospitals/Burton Hospitals, CMA decision of 15 March 2018, paras 134-209.

542 *Understanding past merger remedies*, CMA48, April 2017, available at www.gov.uk/cma.

543 See the Government's White Paper on *Productivity and Enterprise: A World Class Competition Regime*, Cm 5233 (2001), para 5.23.

544 See generally *Mergers: Guidance on the CMA's jurisdiction and procedure*, paras 16.1–16.27 and the *Assessment Guidelines*, Part 6; see further McElwee 'Politics and the UK Merger Control Process: The Public Interest Exceptions and Other Collision Points' [2010] Comp Law 77.

545 A power does exist, under s 13 of the Industry Act 1975, for the Secretary of State to issue an order prohibiting a non-UK person from gaining control of manufacturing undertakings deemed to be of special importance to the UK; the provision has never been used and, in the case of a concentration having an EU dimension, would be subject to the supervision of the European Commission under Article 21(4) of the EUMR, as to which see ch 21 'Article 21(4): legitimate interest clause', pp 872–875.

546 See Alex Chisholm 'Public interest and competition-based merger control', speech of 11 September 2014, available at www.gov.uk/cma.

547 See the Government's *National Security and Infrastructure Review*, 17 October 2017, and its response to the consultation, 15 March 2018, both available at www.gov.uk/beis.

possible longer-term reforms is the introduction of mandatory notification for foreign investment into the provision of 'essential functions' in key parts of the economy, such as civil nuclear, defence, energy, telecommunications and transport.

(A) **Public interest cases**

Chapter 2 of Part 3 of the Enterprise Act, containing sections 42 to 58A, deals with public interest cases. A merger fee is payable in public interest cases in the same way as in conventional competition cases.

(i) **Public interest considerations**

The Secretary of State may give a public interest intervention notice (a 'PIIN') to the CMA if he believes that one or more public interest considerations are relevant to the consideration of a relevant merger situation[548]. As at 8 December 2017 the following public interest considerations were recognised:

- national security (including public security)[549]
- the need for accurate presentation of news and free expression of opinion in newspapers[550]
- the need for a sufficient plurality of views in newspapers in each market for newspapers in the UK[551]
- the need for plurality of media ownership[552]
- the need for a wide range of high-quality broadcasting, appealing to a wide variety of tastes and interests[553]
- the need for media owners to be committed to the objectives set out in section 319 of the Communications Act 2003[554]
- the interest of maintaining the stability of the UK financial system[555].

The Secretary of State may add a new public interest consideration to section 58 of the Enterprise Act by statutory instrument: this requires the approval of Parliament[556].

(ii) **Procedure in public interest cases: Phase 1**

The procedure to be followed in a case where a PIIN is given is explained in paragraphs 16.7 to 16.15 of *Mergers: Guidance on the CMA's jurisdiction and procedure*. In Phase 1 the CMA will publish an invitation to comment seeking third party views on both competition and public interest issues; at the end of its review it will report to the Secretary of State on the jurisdictional and competition issues: these findings are binding upon him[557]. The CMA will report on whether undertakings in lieu might be an appropriate

[548] Enterprise Act 2002, s 42(2).

[549] Ibid, s 58(1) and (2); national security has the same meaning as under Article 21(4) EUMR: ibid s 58(2).

[550] Ibid, s 58(2A), as added by s 375 of the Communications Act 2003; see also the former Department of Trade and Industry's guidance document, *Enterprise Act 2002, Public Interest Intervention in Media Mergers*, available at www.nationalarchives.gov.uk and OFCOM's *Guidance on the public interest test for media mergers*, May 2004, available at www.ofcom.org.uk.

[551] Enterprise Act 2002, s 58(2B). [552] Ibid, s 58(2C)(a).

[553] Ibid, s 58(2C)(b). [554] Ibid, s 58(2C)(c).

[555] Inserted by the Enterprise Act 2002 (Specification of Additional Section 58 Consideration) Order 2008, SI 2008/2645, adopted under s 58(3) and (4) of the Enterprise Act 2002: see *Mergers: Guidance on the CMA's jurisdiction and procedure*, para 16.6.

[556] Enterprise Act 2002, s 58(3) and (4). [557] Ibid, s 46(2).

way of dealing with any competition concerns. The CMA will also pass to the Secretary of State a summary of any representations it has received on public interest matters: at this stage it would not be expected to provide advice on these issues, although such advice will be provided after a Phase 2 investigation by the independent Phase 2 Inquiry Group conducting the case[558].

In a case concerning media issues OFCOM will provide a separate report on any public interest issues[559]. It is then for the Secretary of State to decide whether to make a Phase 2 reference[560]. Among the choices available to him or her are to make a reference, even where the merger gives rise to no competition concerns but where there is a public interest concern that may operate against the public interest; and, conversely, to decide not to make a reference, notwithstanding a competition concern found by the CMA, where he or she considers that this is justified by one or more public interest considerations.

The CMA has a function of advising the Secretary of State on mergers that might raise public interest considerations[561], and the CMA and OFCOM must bring to his or her attention any representations about the exercise of his or her powers as to what constitutes a public interest consideration[562].

If the Secretary of State concludes that there are no public interest concerns the matter proceeds as a 'normal' merger, and the CMA will confine itself to an analysis of any possible competition issues[563].

(iii) Procedure in public interest cases: Phase 2

Where a Phase 2 reference is made, with or without competition grounds, the CMA reports to the Secretary of State who makes the final decision on the public interest test and on the remedial steps required. The CMA, in the form of a Phase 2 Inquiry Group, does make recommendations to the Secretary of State at this stage on the public interest issues. The Secretary of State has 30 days from the receipt of the CMA's report to publish his or her decision[564]: the CMA's findings on competition are binding, but he or she must decide how to proceed in relation to any public interest issues.

Enforcement powers are conferred upon the Secretary of State to accept undertakings or to make orders to remedy, mitigate or prevent any of the effects adverse to the public interest which have resulted from, or may result from, the creation of any relevant merger situation. The powers available are set out in Schedule 7 to the Act[565], and include the ability to order anything permitted by Schedule 8[566]; paragraph 20 of Schedule 8 enables action to be taken in the interests of national security, and paragraphs 20A[567] and 20B[568] enable appropriate action to be taken following investigations of media mergers and mergers affecting the stability of the UK financial system respectively. Provision is made for cases to revert to the CMA where an intervention notice ceases to have effect, either because the Secretary of State decides that a public interest consideration should not be taken into account, or because parliamentary approval for a public interest consideration is not given[569].

558 See section (iii) later in chapter.

559 Enterprise Act 2002, s 44A; on the role of OFCOM see *Guidance on the public interest test for media mergers*, May 2004, December 2010 and *Local Media assessment guidance*, both available at www.ofcom.org.uk.

560 Enterprise Act 2002, s 45. 561 Ibid, s 57(1). 562 Ibid, s 57(2).

563 Ibid, s 56. 564 Ibid, s 54(5). 565 Ibid, s 55(2).

566 See 'Final powers and remedies', pp 973–977, earlier in chapter.

567 Inserted by s 389 of the Communications Act 2003.

568 Inserted by para 4 of the Enterprise Act 2002 (Specification of Additional Section 58 Consideration) Order 2008, SI 2008/2645.

569 Enterprise Act 2002, s 56.

(iv) The public interest provisions in practice

By 8 December 2017 four PIINs had been issued under the public interest provisions (as opposed to the 'special' public interest provisions discussed below), *BSkyB/ITV, LloydsTSB/HBOS, Global Radio Holdings Ltd/GMG Radio Holdings Ltd* and *Hytera Communications Corporation Ltd/Sepura plc*. In the case of the acquisition by BSkyB of 17.9% of the shares of ITV plc the Secretary of State issued an intervention notice on 26 February 2007[570]. A reference was made to the Competition Commission which considered that the acquisition would give rise to an SLC; however it did not consider that the acquisition endangered the plurality of the media[571]. The Secretary of State decided in January 2008 that BSkyB should reduce its shareholding in ITV to below 7.5%[572]. On appeal the CAT dismissed BSkyB's application for review of the Competition Commission's assessment of the acquisition and its finding of an SLC, but upheld Virgin Media's challenge to the Commission's interpretation of the media plurality provisions[573]. The Court of Appeal rejected a further appeal by BSkyB on the competition points, but allowed its appeal, and that of the Commission and the Secretary of State, on the media plurality point[574]. The Court of Appeal's judgment contains invaluable guidance on the media plurality provisions[575]. In February 2010 the Secretary of State accepted final undertakings from BSkyB.

The second case, *LloydsTSB/HBOS*, arose against the background of exceptional instability in global financial markets. The Secretary of State issued an intervention notice in September 2008[576]; he subsequently decided not to refer the merger to the Competition Commission[577]. The CAT dismissed an application for review of the Secretary of State's decision[578].

In *Global Radio Holdings Ltd/GMG Radio Holdings Ltd* it was announced by the Department for Culture, Media and Sport that the merger would not be referred to the CMA on media plurality grounds[579]; the case proceeded on the basis of competition concerns and divestitures were required on this basis[580].

In *Hytera Communications/Sepura* the Secretary of State accepted statutory undertakings from the parties involved in the transaction as a result of which it was not referred to the CMA for further assessment[581]: the concerns in this case were to do with national security, and in particular to provide assurance that sensitive information and technology would be protected in relation to radio devices used by emergency services in the UK.

[570] www.nationalarchives.gov.uk. [571] See www.nationalarchives.gov.uk.

[572] See www.nationalarchives.gov.uk.

[573] Cases 1095/4/8/08 and 1096/4/8/08 *British Sky Broadcasting Group plc v Competition Commission and the Secretary of State for Business, Enterprise and Regulatory Reform* [2008] CAT 25; the CAT also dismissed the appellants' mirror-image challenges to the partial divestiture remedy.

[574] *British Sky Broadcasting Group plc v Competition Commission* [2010] EWCA Civ 2.

[575] Ibid, paras 78–123.

[576] The relevant public interest consideration, the stability of the UK financial system, was created by the Enterprise Act 2002 (Specification of Additional Section 58 Consideration) Order 2008, SI 2008/2645.

[577] See www.nationalarchives.gov.uk; see also the OFT's *Report to the Secretary of State on anticipated acquisition by Lloyds TSB plc of HBOS plc*, 24 October 2008, available at www.nationalarchives.gov.uk.

[578] Case 1107/4/10/08 *Merger Action Group v Secretary of State for Business, Enterprise and Regulatory Reform* [2008] CAT 36.

[579] See the Government announcement of 11 October 2012, available at www.gov.uk.

[580] See 'The Merger Provisions in Practice', pp 981–986 earlier in chapter.

[581] See the Decision Notice of the Secretary of State for Business, Energy and Industrial Strategy of 12 May 2017, available at www.gov.uk.

(B) 'Special public interest cases'

(i) Procedure in special public interest cases

Sections 59 to 66 of the Enterprise Act are concerned with an exceptional category of mergers that may be referred for investigation on public interest grounds, even though they do not meet either the turnover or the share of supply thresholds for reference contained in section 23 of the Act[582]. No merger fee is payable in relation to special public interest cases. The procedure is described in paragraphs 16.23 to 16.27 of *Mergers: Guidance on the CMA's jurisdiction and procedure.*

Two types of merger may be considered under the 'special public interest' provisions. The first is mergers involving certain government contractors or sub-contractors who may hold or receive confidential information or material relating to defence; the second type is certain mergers in the newspaper and broadcasting sectors that do not qualify for investigation under the general merger rules because they fall below the turnover or share of supply tests[583]. Such cases are not scrutinised on competition grounds, but against public interest considerations only. In such cases the Secretary of State serves a special public interest intervention notice (a 'SPIIN')[584]. The CMA will then conduct an initial investigation and give a report to the Secretary of State[585]; in media cases OFCOM will report on the media public interest considerations. The Secretary of State has power to refer to make a Phase 2 reference[586], but must accept the CMA's decision as to whether a special merger situation has been created[587]. The CMA will then conduct a Phase 2 investigation and report to the Secretary of State[588]; he or she has power to take enforcement action[589], but must accept the view of the CMA as to whether a special merger situation has been created or may be expected[590]. The Secretary of State has similar enforcement powers to those in public interest cases[591].

(ii) The special public interest provisions in practice

There have been two cases under these provisions. In the first, *Insys Group Ltd/Lockheed Martin UK Ltd*, the Secretary of State issued a SPIIN in August 2005; he subsequently accepted undertakings in lieu of a reference to the Competition Commission[592]. The Secretary of State also issued, in May 2009, a SPIIN in the case of *Atlas Elektronik UK Ltd/ QinetiQ*; that case was also settled by undertakings in lieu of a reference[593].

(C) European mergers

Where a merger has been completed or is in contemplation which has a Union dimension under the EUMR but which gives rise to a public interest consideration the Secretary of State may give a 'European intervention notice' to the CMA[594], and has power to make an order to provide for the taking of action to remedy, mitigate or prevent effects adverse to the public interest which have resulted from, or may be expected to result from, the creation of the merger[595]. This provides a legal basis to proceed against mergers in relation to which the UK asserts a 'legitimate interest' under Article 21(4) of the EUMR[596]. Further

[582] See 'The turnover test', pp 945–946 earlier and 'The share of supply test', pp 946–947 earlier in chapter.
[583] Communications Act 2003, ss 378–380, amending ss 59 and 61 of the Enterprise Act 2002.
[584] Enterprise Act 2002, s 59. [585] Ibid, s 61. [586] Ibid, s 62.
[587] Ibid, s 62(5). [588] Ibid, ss 63 and 65. [589] Ibid, s 66. [590] Ibid, s 66(4).
[591] Ibid, Sch 7, paras 9 and 11. [592] See www.nationalarchives.gov.uk.
[593] Ibid. [594] Enterprise Act 2002, s 67. [595] Ibid, s 68.
[596] On Article 21(4) of the EUMR, see ch 21, 'Article 21(4): legitimate interest clause', pp 872–875.

provision is made in relation to European merger cases by the Enterprise Act (Protection of Legitimate Interests) Order 2003[597]. The procedure is described in paragraphs 16.16 to 16.22 of *Mergers: Guidance on the CMA's jurisdiction and procedure.* No merger fee is payable in relation to European mergers.

European intervention notices have been issued on six occasions. The first four cases were settled on the basis of undertakings accepted by the Secretary of State to safeguard UK national security[598]. The fifth European intervention notice was issued by the Secretary of State on 4 November 2010 in relation to News Corp's proposed acquisition of the shares in BSkyB that it did not already own[599]; however, following considerable controversy, News Corp abandoned its proposal in July 2011[600]. The sixth such notice was issued on 16 March 2017 in relation to 21st Century Fox's intention to acquire the shares of Sky that it does not already own. On 20 September 2017 the Secretary of State referred the merger for a Phase 2 investigation on the public interest grounds of media plurality and genuine commitment to broadcasting standards. On 23 January 2018, the CMA provisionally found that the merger would not be in the public interest due to media plurality concerns, but not due to a lack of a genuine commitment to meeting broadcasting standards in the UK. The CMA also identified three possible remedies, which were prohibition of the merger, divestment of Sky News or a behavioural remedy.

(D) Mergers in the water industry

The Water Industry Act 1991, as amended by the Enterprise Act 2002 and the Water Act 2014, contains special rules for mergers between water enterprises in England and Wales[601]. The relevant provisions are sections 32 to 35 of the Water Industry Act, as substituted by section 70 of the Enterprise Act 2002 and sections 14 and 15 of the Water Act 2014; these provisions must be read in conjunction with Schedule 4ZA to the 1991 Act, as inserted by Schedule 6 to the Enterprise Act. The purpose behind this special regime is to ensure that mergers do not adversely affect the ability of the Water Services Regulation Authority ('OFWAT') to carry out its regulatory functions effectively by reducing the number of companies whose performances can be compared: OFWAT should be able to make use of 'comparative' or 'yardstick' competition. The CMA is responsible for water mergers, but in certain circumstances it must seek the opinion of OFWAT; the Secretary of State is not involved in the investigation of such mergers.

Under the Water Industry Act, as amended, mergers between water enterprises in England and Wales are subject to a mandatory in-depth investigation by the CMA[602], unless the turnover of one or both of the enterprises is less than £10 million[603]. The CMA

[597] SI 2003/1592, as amended by the Enterprise Act 2002 (Protection of Legitimate Interests) (Amendment) Order 2014, SI 2014/891.

[598] Note that the CMA's website, www.gov.uk/cma, contains details of similar undertakings (and variations of undertakings) given under the now-repealed provisions of the Fair Trading Act 1973: see eg *British Aerospace plc/General Electric Company plc* where the undertakings were varied in 2007.

[599] See www.nationalarchives.gov.uk; on 21 December 2010 the European Commission had cleared the merger unconditionally under the EUMR: Case M 5932, Commission decision of 21 December 2010.

[600] See Competition Commission News Release 41/11, 25 July 2011, available at www.nationalarchives.gov.uk.

[601] See further Weir 'Comparative Competition and the Regulation of Mergers in the Water Industry of England and Wales' (2000) XLV Antitrust Bulletin 811; Barnes 'Holding Back the Flow: Do the UK Water Merger Control Rules Risk Dampening Investment in the Sector?' (2007) 1 European Business Law Journal 205.

[602] Water Industry Act 1991, s 32.

[603] Ibid, s 33(1); s 15 of the Water Act 2014 requires the CMA to advise the Secretary of State from time to time whether this figure remains appropriate.

must determine whether a water merger would prejudice the ability of OFWAT to make comparisons between water enterprises[604]. In certain circumstances the CMA may decide not to conduct an in-depth Phase 2 investigation, for example where the merger would not hamper the ability of OFWAT to make comparisons between water enterprises or where a merger would lead to relevant customer benefits: usually the CMA must seek the opinion of OFWAT before reaching such a conclusion[605]. The first CMA clearance of a water merger under these provisions in Phase 1 occurred in the case of *Severn Trent plc/ Dee Valley plc*[606].

The CMA does not consider that its informal advice procedure is suitable for advising on the mandatory reference procedure[607]. Section 14 of the Water Act 2014 gives the CMA the power to accept undertakings in lieu of a Phase 2 investigation, a power which it previously lacked: OFWAT's opinion must be sought before accepting such undertakings.

Part 3 of the Enterprise Act applies to water mergers, subject to any modifications that the Secretary of State might make by regulation: thus the time limits and powers that the CMA has in relation to mergers generally also apply in the case of water mergers[608]. In November 2015 the CMA published new guidance, *Water and sewerage mergers: Guidance on the CMA's procedure and assessment* that take into account the changes to the law in this sector introduced by the Water Act 2014 with effect from 18 December 2015[609]. Those changes include new exceptions to the CMA's duty to refer and the possibility of accepting undertakings in lieu[610].

There were two Phase 2 references[611] of water mergers under these provisions prior to the creation of the CMA, *Mid-Kent Water/South-East Water* and *South Staffordshire/ Cambridge Water*[612]. In the *Mid-Kent* case the Competition Commission concluded that there was a possibility that OFWAT's ability to carry out comparisons might be prejudiced, but only to a limited degree; and the Commission was satisfied in this case that the merger would generate customer benefits[613]. The Commission required the merging parties to make a one-off price reduction to their customers totalling £4 million. In the *South Staffordshire* case the Commission was satisfied that the merger would not significantly affect OFWAT's task of assessing water companies' performance and setting price controls. The first Phase 2 investigation by the CMA under the special rules in the water sector was *Pennon Group plc/Bournemouth Water Investments Ltd*; it was cleared unconditionally[614].

604 Water Industry Act 1991, Sch 4ZA, as inserted by Enterprise Act 2002, Sch 6.

605 See s 14 of the Water Act 2014, amending s 32 of the Water Industry Act 1991.

606 CMA decision of 22 December 2016.

607 See *Mergers: Guidance on the CMA's jurisdiction and procedure*, paras 6.34 and 17.2.

608 Water Industry Act 1991, Sch 4ZA, paras 1, 2 and 4(3).

609 CMA 49, November 2015; see also the *Statement of intent: An agreement on the working arrangements between the CMA and Ofwat for the special water merger regime*, 13 November 2015, available at www.ofwat.gov.uk.

610 See also Water Mergers (Miscellaneous Amendments) Regulations 2015, SI 2015/1936, introducing time limits for Phase 1 and considering undertakings in lieu of a reference for water mergers.

611 Note that the Competition Commission investigated eight mergers under the Water Industry Act 1991 prior to its amendment by the Enterprise Act 2002, three of which were prohibited outright: see *General Utilities plc/Colne Valley Water Co/Rickmansworth Water Co*, Cm 1929 (1990); *General Utilities plc/Mid Kent Water Co*, Cm 1125 (1990); *Southern Water plc/Mid Sussex Water Co*, Cm 1126 (1990); *Lyonnaise des Eaux SA/Northumbrian Water Group plc*, Cm 2936 (1995); *Wessex Water plc/South West Water*, Cm 3430 (1996) (prohibited outright); *Severn Trent plc/South West Water*, Cm 3429 (1996) (prohibited outright); *Mid Kent Holdings and General Utilities/SAUR Water Services*, Cm 3514 (1997) (prohibited outright); *Vivendi Water UK plc/First Aqua (JVCo) Ltd*, Cm 5681 (2002).

612 See www.nationalarchives.gov.uk.

613 See the Final Report of 1 May 2007, paras 8.108–8.160.

614 See CMA Press Release, 5 November 2015.

Where a merger does not involve one water company acquiring another it will be subject to the general merger rules. In such a case the CMA will look to OFWAT for advice on those aspects of the merger which will impact upon its ability to regulate the water undertakings or which might impact upon its wider ability to regulate other licensed providers of water and sewerage services.

23

Particular sectors

1. Introduction

The final chapter of this book will deal with three issues. First it will examine those sectors of the economy that are wholly or partly excluded from EU competition law, namely nuclear energy, military equipment and agriculture; the special regime for coal and steel products under the former European Coal and Steel Community ('the ECSC') Treaty is briefly referred to. Secondly, it will describe how the EU competition rules apply to the transport sector. Finally, the chapter will consider the specific circumstances of so-called 'regulated industries' such as electronic communications, post and energy and the way in which EU and UK competition law apply to them. Constraints of space mean that these matters can be described only in outline; references to specialised literature on the application of competition law to particular sectors will be provided where appropriate.

2. Nuclear Energy

The Treaty establishing the European Atomic Energy Community ('Euratom') deals with agreements regulating the supply and price of various nuclear materials[1]. Articles 101 and 102 are capable of application to agreements and to the abuse of a dominant position to the extent that the Euratom Treaty is not applicable[2]. In *Siemens/Areva*[3] the Commission

[1] See further Cameron *Competition in Energy Markets* (Oxford University Press, 2nd ed, 2007), ch 9; Rose and Bailey (eds) *Bellamy and Child: European Union Law of Competition* (Oxford University Press, 7th ed, 2013), paras 1.005 and 12.088, Part 3; Cusack 'A Tale of Two Treaties: An Assessment of the Euratom Treaty in Relation to the EC Treaty' (2003) 40 CML Rev 117; Ferro 'Competition Law and the Nuclear Sector: An EU Outlook' (2010) 13 Nuclear Law Bulletin 13.

[2] The Commission has adopted a sympathetic attitude towards cooperation agreements in the nuclear industry under Article 101(3): see eg *United Reprocessors GmbH* OJ [1976] L 51/7; *KEWA* OJ [1976] L 51/15; *GEC/Weir* OJ [1977] L 327/26; *Amersham International and Buchler GmbH Venture* OJ [1982] L 314/34; *Scottish Nuclear, Nuclear Energy Agreement* OJ [1991] L 178/31.

[3] Commission decision of 20 December 2012.

considered that non-compete clauses in agreements between those firms in respect of civil nuclear technology could infringe Article 101; Areva and Siemens offered commitments reducing the scope and duration of the clauses, which the Commission accepted under Article 9(1) of Regulation 1/2003[4].

3. Military Equipment

Article 346(1)(b) TFEU provides that a Member State may take such measures as it thinks necessary for the protection of the essential interests of its security which are connected with the production of or trade in arms, ammunitions and war materials; however these measures must not adversely affect the conditions of competition in the internal market regarding products which are not intended specifically for military purposes[5]. The Council of Ministers has drawn up a list of the products to which Article 346(1) applies, although it has not been published; Article 346(2) provides that the Council may, acting unanimously on a proposal from the Commission, amend this list. There have been some concentrations in which the Commission's jurisdiction to apply the EU Merger Regulation ('the EUMR') was limited by Article 346[6].

4. Agriculture

Articles 38 to 44 TFEU subject agriculture to a special regime with its own philosophy[7]. Article 42 provides that 'the rules on competition shall apply to production of and trade in agricultural products only to the extent determined by the European Parliament and the Council'. The Commission engages in 'competition advocacy' in the agriculture sector, by recommending legislative change and other actions to address 'public' restrictions of competition[8].

(A) Council Regulations 1184/2006 and 1308/2013

Article 1 of Regulation 1184/2006[9] provides that Articles 101 and 102 TFEU shall apply to the production of or trade in the products listed in Annex I to the Treaties except for those covered by Regulation 1308/2013 ('the CMO Regulation')[10], subject to the derogations set out in Article 2. Article 2 provides that Article 101(1) shall *not* apply to agreements that form an integral part of a national market organisation or that are necessary for the attainment of the objectives set out in Article 39 TFEU[11]. These derogations are

[4] On Article 9 of Regulation 1/2003 see ch 7, 'Article 9: commitments', pp 264–269.

[5] See further Rose and Bailey (eds) *Bellamy and Child: European Union Law of Competition* (Oxford University Press, 7th ed, 2013), paras 11.061–11.063; Faull and Nikpay (eds) *The EU Law of Competition* (Oxford University Press, 3rd ed, 2014), paras 3.05–3.15.

[6] See ch 21, 'Defence', p 875.

[7] See further Rose and Bailey (eds) *Bellamy and Child: European Union Law of Competition* (Oxford University Press, 7th ed, 2013), paras 12.148–12.159; on the common agricultural policy 2014–2020 see OECD *Evaluation of Agricultural Policy Reforms in the European Union* (2017), available at www.oecd.org.

[8] Documents on advocacy, enforcement and other initiatives in agriculture are available at www.ec.europa.eu/competition/sectors/agriculture/overview_en.html.

[9] OJ [2006] L 214/7. [10] OJ [2013] L 347/671.

[11] On Article 39 see 'The second derogation: common market organisations', pp 997–998 later in chapter. Article 2 contains a sentence dealing with the activities of farmers' associations; this is not a further exception, but rather an embellishment of the policy expressed in that provision: see *Milchförderungsfonds* OJ [1985] L 35/35, paras 21–22; *Bloemenveilingen Aalsmeer* OJ [1988] L 262/27, paras 150–152.

interpreted strictly, and the Commission must give adequate reasons in the event that it allows such a derogation[12]. The derogations provided for in Article 2 of Regulation 1184/2006 relate only to the application of Article 101. There is an equivalent derogation from the Chapter I prohibition of the UK Competition Act 1998 in relation to agricultural products[13]. There is no derogation from the application of Article 102 and the Chapter II prohibition to the agricultural sector.

The CMO Regulation establishes a common organisation of agricultural markets for a number of sectors included in Annex I to the Treaties; it adopts the same approach as Regulation 1184/2006 to the application of the competition rules in those sectors[14]. The Commission has published guidelines on joint sales by producers of olive oil, beef and veal and arable crops[15]. It contains useful insights into the Commission's approach to the derogations contained in Articles 169 to 171 of the CMO Regulation.

In *Milk Marque Ltd*[16] the Court of Justice was asked to consider the relationship between national competition law and the EU rules on the agricultural sector. The Court concluded that the existence of specific EU rules did not deprive national competition authorities of the Member States ('NCAs') of their right to apply national law to a milk producers' cooperative in a powerful position on the market; however they should refrain from any measure which might undermine or create exceptions to the common organisation of the market in milk or compromise the objectives of the common agricultural policy.

(B) **Annex I products**

If a product is *not* mentioned in Annex I to the Treaties, it cannot benefit from the derogations provided by Article 2 of Regulation 1184/2006 and is fully subject to the competition rules[17]. In *Pabst and Richarz/BNIA*[18] the Commission applied Article 101 to the French trade association responsible for armagnac, pointing out that, as this product did not appear in Annex I, it was to be treated as an industrial product. In *BNIC v Clair*[19] the Court of Justice held, for the same reason, that cognac was an industrial product and rejected an argument that it should be treated in a special way because of its importance to the economic welfare of a particular region of France.

In *BNIC v Yves Aubert*[20] the Court of Justice had to deal with the application of the competition rules to a demand by BNIC for a levy claimed against a wine grower for having exceeded a marketing quota. One issue was whether the competition rules could be applied to brandy. The Court, having observed that brandies are not listed in Annex I and so are industrial rather than agricultural products, added that the fact that some of the proceeds of levies raised by BNIC were intended for measures on wine and must, which do appear in Annex I, did not affect the application of Article 101(1). In *Dansk Pelsdyravlerforening v Commission*[21] the General Court rejected a claim that animal furs should be treated as an agricultural product; in *Gøttrup-Klim Grovvareforeninger v Dansk Landbrugs Grovvareselskab AmbA*[22] the Court of Justice held that fertiliser and

[12] See Case C-265/97 P *VBA and Florimex v Commission* EU:C:2000:170; Case C-266/97 P *VBA and Florimex v Commission* EU:C:2000:171.

[13] Competition Act 1998, Sch 3, para 9.

[14] OJ [2013] L 347/671.

[15] OJ [2015] C 431/1.

[16] Case C-137/00 *R v Monopolies and Mergers Commission and the Secretary of State for Trade and Industry, ex p Milk Marque Ltd* EU:C:2003:429.

[17] See Case 61/80 *Coöperatieve Stremsel- en Kleurselfabriek v Commission* EU:C:1981:75 (rennet was not mentioned in Annex I).

[18] OJ [1976] L 231/24.

[19] Case 123/83 EU:C:1985:33.

[20] Case 136/86 EU:C:1987:524.

[21] Case T-61/89 EU:T:1992:79.

[22] Case C-250/92 EU:C:1994:413, paras 21–27.

plant protection products were not agricultural products. In *Sicasov* the Commission acknowledged that seeds fell within Annex I, but concluded that neither of the derogations in Regulation 26 (now Regulation 1184/2006) was applicable[23].

(C) The first derogation: national market organisations

Article 2 of Regulation 1184/2006 provides that Article 101 shall not apply to agreements that form an integral part of a national market organisation. However the CMO Regulation (and its predecessors) established a common organisation for many agricultural products, so that most national marketing organisations have ceased to exist. The Commission has construed this derogation from the application of Article 101(1) strictly[24]. In *FRUBO v Commission*[25] the Court of Justice upheld the Commission's decision[26] that a Dutch fruit-marketing organisation did not benefit from the immunity contained in Article 2(1) since it was not a national marketing organisation. In *Scottish Salmon Board*[27] the Commission found that, as there was a common organisation of the market in fishery products[28], the Scottish Salmon Board could not rely on the national market organisation defence.

In *New Potatoes*[29] rules were laid down by seven economic committees in France, acting under a French law of 1962, to organise and regulate the production and marketing of new potatoes. The rules were intended to deal with the problem of a slump in the market at a time of over-production. The Commission was asked to declare that Article 101(1) was not applicable: as there was no common organisation of the market in question, the Commission had to decide whether the system constituted a national market organisation. It held that this term must be defined in a way that would be consistent with the objectives of a common organisation under the second exception of Article 2 of Regulation 26: thus the objectives of the common agricultural policy, contained in Article 39 TFEU and referred to below, were read into the first exception of Article 2. The Commission decided that the arrangements of various producer groups formed an integral part of the national market organisation in question and that, therefore, Article 101(1) was not infringed.

(D) The second derogation: common market organisations

Article 2 of Regulation 1184/2006 and Article 209 of the CMO Regulation permit agreements that are necessary for the attainment of the objectives of the common agricultural policy. Article 39 sets out these objectives under five heads:

- to increase agricultural productivity
- to ensure a fair standard of living for the agricultural community
- to stabilise markets
- to ensure the availability of supplies
- to ensure supplies to consumers at reasonable prices.

[23] OJ [1999] L 14/27, paras 65–69.

[24] As well as the decisions mentioned in the text see *Cauliflowers* OJ [1978] L 21/23; *Bloemenveilingen Aalsmeer* OJ [1988] L 262/27; *Sugar Beet* OJ [1990] L 31/32; *Sicasov* OJ [1999] L 14/27; *British Sugar* OJ [1999] L 76/1, paras 185–188.

[25] Case 71/74 EU:C:1975:61.

[26] *Geeves and Zonen v FRUBO* OJ [1974] L 237/16.

[27] OJ [1992] L 246/37, para 22.

[28] See Council Regulation 3796/81, OJ [1981] L 379/1.

[29] OJ [1988] L 59/25.

Article 39(2) provides that, in implementing the common agricultural policy, account shall be taken, among other matters, of:

> the particular nature of agricultural activity, which results from the social structure of agriculture and from structural and natural disparities between the various agricultural regions.

The aims expressed in Article 39 are not necessarily consistent with the normal competitive process. The Court of Justice has held that the aims in Article 39 prevail over the objectives of the competition rules[30].

In *FRUBO v Commission*[31] the Court of Justice rejected a defence based on the second derogation in Article 2. A noticeable feature of the judgment is that, although some of the heads of Article 39 may have been satisfied, not all of them were: to put the matter another way, in order to come within this derogation it is necessary to satisfy all five heads of Article 39[32]. In practice it is likely that the objectives of Article 39 are expressly or impliedly advanced by the provisions of any particular regulation establishing a common organisation of an agricultural sector, with the result that the parties to an agreement cannot argue that their agreement will have this effect[33].

In *Bloemenveilingen Aalsmeer*[34] the Commission rejected an argument that exclusive dealing agreements between auctioneers and flower traders in respect of live plants and floricultural products could advance the objectives of Article 39. It published a decision to this effect, not only as the rules in question were the subject of litigation in the Dutch courts, but also as similar rules were being applied by other auction houses[35]. In *Scottish Salmon Board*[36] the Commission rejected an argument that the Board's conduct was permissible as the industry was in economic difficulties; the Commission said that, if this was so, EU initiatives should be taken to deal with the problem: it was not for the parties themselves to take action which was unlawful under Article 101. In *Sicasov*[37] the Commission held that an agreement for the licensing of seeds was not necessary for the attainment of the objectives in Article 39 TFEU[38]. The Commission rejected defences based on the second derogation in *French beef*[39], *Raw Tobacco Spain*[40], *Raw Tobacco Italy*[41] and *Bananas*[42].

In *Endive Producers Association*[43] the Court of Justice adopted a narrow construction of the derogation for agreements in the agricultural sector; in particular it does not apply to agreements **between** producer organisations, or association of producer organisations or with other types of organization; and even **within** an organization the derogation applies only to the extent that coordination is strictly necessary to carry out the objectives assigned to the relevant organisation[44].

30 See Case C-671/15 *Président de l'Autorité de la concurrence v Association des producteurs vendeurs d'endives* EU:C:2017:860, para 37.

31 Case 71/74 EU:C:1975:61, paras 22–27.

32 See similarly Cases T-70/92 etc *Florimex v Commission* EU:T:1997:69, para 153 and Case T-217/03 *FNCBV v Commission* EU:T:2006:391, para 206.

33 See eg *Cauliflowers* OJ [1978] L 21/23; *Milchförderungsfonds* OJ [1985] L 35/35.

34 OJ [1988] L 262/27.

35 Ibid, para 168.

36 OJ [1992] L 246/37, para 22.

37 OJ [1999] L 14/27.

38 Ibid, para 68.

39 OJ [2003] L 209/12, paras 135–149, upheld on appeal Cases T-217/03 etc *FNCBV v Commission* EU:T:2006:391, paras 197–209.

40 Commission decision of 20 October 2004, paras 337–348, upheld on appeal Case T-33/05 *Compañía española de tabaco en rama, SA v Commission* EU:T:2011:24, paras 153–164.

41 Commission decision of 20 October 2005, paras 306–311.

42 Commission decision of 15 October 2008, paras 344–349.

43 Case C-671/15 *Président de l'Autorité de la concurrence v Association des producteurs vendeurs d'endives* EU:C:2017:860.

44 Ibid, paras 66 and 67.

5. Coal and Steel

Coal and steel were originally dealt with by the Treaty of Paris of 1951 establishing the European Coal and Steel Community (the 'ECSC Treaty'). The ECSC Treaty contained rules on competition that were similar to Articles 101 and 102 TFEU, although there were some material differences. The ECSC Treaty expired on 23 July 2002[45]. The coal and steel sectors are now subject to Articles 101 and 102 TFEU and the EUMR.

6. Transport

The TFEU contains special provisions on transport in Articles 90 to 100[46]. Article 90(1) provides that these provisions are applicable to road, rail and inland waterway transport; Article 90(2) provides that the European Parliament and the Council of Ministers may lay down appropriate provisions for sea and air transport. Thus the Treaty itself recognises a distinction between these two categories, the difficulty being that the latter are subject to numerous international arrangements and are of particular political sensitivity. Articles 101 and 102 do apply to the transport sector (including air transport[47]), but in 1962 Council Regulation 141[48] provided that Regulation 17, which contained the Commission's powers to enforce the competition rules, did not apply to transport. The procedural lacuna left by Regulation 141 was filled in three stages: first, Council Regulation 1017/68[49] adopted specific provisions on the application of the competition rules to transport by road, rail and inland waterway (that is to say inland transport); secondly, Council Regulation 4056/86[50] provided the Commission with powers in the maritime transport sector; last came Council Regulation 3975/87[51] to deal with air transport. Each of these Regulations has since been repealed and replaced; the current provisions are contained in Council Regulation 169/2009 on transport by rail, road and inland waterway[52]; Council Regulation 1419/2006 on maritime transport[53]; and Council Regulations 411/2004[54] and 487/2009[55] on air transport. The procedural rules for the enforcement of Articles 101 and 102 in the transport sector are contained in Regulation 1/2003[56].

(A) Inland transport

(i) Legislative regime

Council Regulation 1017/68 provided that certain technical agreements do not infringe Article 101, and that some cooperation agreements between small and medium-sized undertakings benefit from block exemption. That Regulation was repealed in 2009 by Council Regulation 169/2009[57]. The exception for technical agreements will now be found

[45] *Communication from the Commission concerning certain aspects of the treatment of competition cases resulting from the expiry of the ECSC Treaty* OJ [2002] C 152/5, section 2.

[46] See further Rose and Bailey (eds) *Bellamy and Child: European Union Law of Competition* (Oxford University Press, 7th ed, 2013), paras 12.160–12.199; Faull and Nikpay (eds) *The EU Law of Competition* (Oxford University Press, 3rd ed, 2014), ch 15; Rabinovici 'The Application of EU Competition Rules in the Transport Sector' (2014) 5 JECLAP 227, (2015) 6 JECLAP 287 (with Chirico) and (2016) 7 JECLAP 280.

[47] See Cases 209/84 etc *Ministère Public v Asjes* EU:C:1986:188 and Case 66/86 *Ahmed Saeed Flugreisen v Zentrale zur Bekämpfung Unlauteren Wettbewerbs* EU:C:1989:140.

[48] OJ (Sp ed, 1959–62) 291. [49] OJ [1968] L 175/1. [50] OJ [1986] L 378/4.

[51] OJ [1987] L 374/1. [52] OJ [2009] L 61/1. [53] OJ [2006] L 269/1. [54] OJ [2004] L 68/1.

[55] OJ [2009] L 148/1.

[56] OJ [2003] L 1/1, Articles 36–43, see ch 7, 'Chapter XI: transitional, amending and final provisions', p 298.

[57] OJ [2009] L 61/1.

in Article 2 of Regulation 169/2009, and the block exemption for certain cooperation agreements in Article 3.

Numerous Directives have been adopted with the intention of opening up the railway sector to competition. An important development was Directive 2012/34 establishing a single European railway area[58]. The most recent initiative is the so-called 'fourth railway package' that consists of two pillars: a 'market pillar' that seeks to make it easier for new operators to enter the market and to strengthen the independence and impartiality of rail infrastructure managers to make sure that railway companies have equal access to tracks and stations[59]; and a 'technical pillar' that, among other things, establishes an EU Agency for Railways[60].

The rail sector is subject to a complex regulatory regime under UK law, and the Office of Rail and Road (the 'ORR') enjoys concurrent powers to apply the Competition Act 1998 and market investigation provisions of the Enterprise Act 2002 to this sector[61]. The ORR has published guidance on its approach to the enforcement of the Competition Act 1998 in relation to the supply of services relating to railways and to monitoring and reviewing markets[62].

(ii) Practical application of the competition rules to inland transport

The Commission has adopted several decisions in relation to inland transport. In *EATE Levy*[63] it condemned an agreement between French waterway carriers and French forwarding agents imposing a levy of 10 per cent on freight charges for boat charters to destinations outside France, as it discriminated in favour of French carriers; the Court of Justice upheld the Commission on appeal[64]. In *Tariff Structures in the Combined Transport of Goods*[65] the Commission considered that the criteria in Article 101(3) were satisfied in the case of a tariff structure agreement between the rail companies of the EU on the sale of rail haulage in the international combined transport of goods.

In *European Night Services*[66] the Commission concluded that a joint venture established by five rail operators to provide night sleeper services through the Channel Tunnel between the UK and continental Europe satisfied the criteria of Article 101(3). Under the system of granting individual exemptions then in force[67], the Commission made its decision subject to conditions and obligations to which the parents of the joint venture objected; the Commission limited the exemption to a period of time, eight years, which the parties considered would prevent them from earning an adequate return on what was a major long-term investment. On appeal the General Court held in *European Night*

[58] OJ [2012] L 343/32.

[59] See Regulation 2016/2337 on common rules for the normalisation of the accounts of railway undertakings, OJ [2016] L 352/20; Regulation 2016/2338 concerning the opening of the market for domestic passenger transport services by rail, OJ [2016] L 352/22 and Directive 2016/2370 as regards the opening of the market for domestic passenger transport services by rail and the governance of the railway infrastructure, OJ [2016] L 352/1.

[60] See Regulation 2016/796 on the European Union Agency for Railways, OJ [2016] L 138/1; Directive 2016/797 on the interoperability of the rail system within the European Union, OJ [2016] L 138/44; Directive 2016/798 on railway safety, OJ [2016] L 138/102.

[61] See *CMA/ORR Memorandum of Understanding*, 22 May 2014; on concurrency under the Competition Act 1998 see ch 10, 'Concurrency', pp 449–452 and under the Enterprise Act 2002 see ch 11, 'Super-Complaints', pp 463–465 and 'Power to make ordinary references', pp 473–474.

[62] Both available at www.orr.gov.uk.

[63] OJ [1985] L 219/35.

[64] Case 272/85 *ANTIB v Commission* EU:C:1987:235.

[65] OJ [1993] L 73/38.

[66] OJ [1994] L 259/20.

[67] On the old system of notification and individual exemptions see ch 4, 'The Commission's former monopoly over the grant of individual exemptions', p 174.

Services v Commission[68] that the Commission had failed to demonstrate that the agreement between the rail operators had the effect of restricting competition, with the consequence that its decision should be annulled; the General Court went further, holding that, even if there was an appreciable effect on competition, the Commission had failed to demonstrate that the exemption should be subject to the conditions and obligations imposed or should be granted for such a short period[69]. In another case relating to the Channel Tunnel, *ACI*[70], the Commission authorised, subject to conditions, the creation of a joint venture company to market intermodal rail services through the tunnel[71].

In *HOV SVZ/MCN*[72] the Commission imposed a fine on Deutsche Bahn of €11 million for imposing discriminatory rail transport tariffs for the inland carriage of sea-borne containers to and from Germany, depending on whether they were shipped through German ports on the one hand or Belgian and Dutch ones on the other. The decision was upheld on appeal to the General Court[73]. In *GVG/FS*[74] the Commission concluded that the Italian rail operator, Ferrovie dello Stato, had abused a dominant position by refusing to provide access to the Italian rail infrastructure, to enter into negotiations for the formation of an international grouping and to provide traction. In *Deutsche Bahn*[75] the Commission accepted commitments under Article 9 of Regulation 1/2003 to resolve concerns about its pricing system for traction current in Germany. In *Baltic Rail Transport*[76] the Commission imposed a fine of €27.8 million on the Lithuanian rail operator, AB Lietuvos geležinkeliai, for dismantling 19 kilometres of track connecting Lithuania and Latvia, and thereby preventing one of its major customers from using the rail freight services of a competitor.

In the UK the ORR imposed a fine of £4.1 million on a rail freight operator, EW&S, for abusing its dominant position in the market for the haulage of coal by rail, in particular by acting in a discriminatory and a predatory manner[77]. In *Freightliner* the ORR accepted commitments from Freightliner that removed provisions on exclusive purchasing, minimum volumes and loyalty rebates from its agreements for the provision of deep sea container rail transport services[78]. The ORR has adopted a number of non-infringement decisions in relation to the rail sector[79].

[68] Cases T-374/94 etc EU:T:1998:198; see similarly the Commission's decision in *Eurotunnel* OJ [1994] L 354/66: the Commission had granted exemption to the operating agreement for the Channel Tunnel, but its decision was annulled on appeal by the General Court in Cases T-79/95 etc *SNCF v Commission* EU:T:1996:155 since the Commission had failed to demonstrate that the agreement would be restrictive of competition; for the eventual outcome of this case see the Commission's XXIXth *Report on Competition Policy* (1999), p 163.

[69] For further comment on this case see ch 3, 'Actual and potential competition', p 135.

[70] OJ [1994] L 224/28.

[71] More recently the Commission authorised a 'new Eurostar' joint venture under the EUMR, subject to conditions: Case M 5655, decision of 17 June 2010; subsequently it authorised SNCF's sole acquisition of Eurostar: Case M 7449, decision of 13 May 2015.

[72] OJ [1994] L 104/34.

[73] Case T-229/94 *Deutsche Bahn AG v Commission* EU:T:1997:155; a further appeal to the Court of Justice was held to be inadmissible, Case C-436/97 P EU:C:1999:205.

[74] OJ [2004] L 11/17; for comment see Stehmann 'Applying Essential Facility Reasoning to Passenger Rail Services in the EU—The Commission Decision in the *GVG* Case' (2004) 25 ECLR 390.

[75] Commission decision of 18 December 2013; see ch 7 'Article 9: commitments', pp 264–269 on Article 9 of Regulation 1/2003.

[76] Commission decision of 2 October 2017, on appeal Case T-814/17 *Lietuvos geležinkeliai v Commission*, not yet decided.

[77] ORR decision of 17 November 2007; subsequent private actions against EW&S arising out of this decision are discussed in ch 8, 'Unsuccessful claims', p 335 and 'Severance', pp 338–339.

[78] ORR decision of 18 December 2015.

[79] See 'Table of published decisions' in ch 9, pp 393–395 and in the Online Resources that accompany this book, www.oup.com/uk/whish9e/.

Following a market investigation reference under the Enterprise Act 2002 rolling stock lessors were ordered to provide train companies with information that would enable them to negotiate more effectively with the rolling stock companies[80].

(B) Maritime transport

(i) Legislative regime

For many years maritime transport was subject to a special procedural and substantive regime of its own, set out in Council Regulation 4056/86[81]. The cumulative effect of Regulation 1/2003 and of Council Regulation 1419/2006[82] is that the special regime has been terminated and the sector is now subject to the same procedural and substantive rules as the rest of the economy.

(a) Procedural rules

Regulation 17 of 1962[83], which gave the Commission power to enforce Articles 101 and 102, did not apply to the maritime transport sector. Council Regulation 4056/86[84] provided the Commission with power to enforce Articles 101 and 102 in relation to international maritime transport services from or to one or more EU ports with effect from 1987. Regulation 1/2003[85] repealed these special procedural rules with effect from 1 May 2004; the Commission has had the power to apply Articles 101 and 102 to the entire maritime transport sector since October 2006[86].

(b) Substantive rules

Article 2 of Regulation 4056/86 excluded 'technical agreements' from the scope of Article 101. More controversially, Articles 3 and 4 of Regulation 4056/86 provided block exemption for 'liner conferences', that is to say agreements between carriers concerning the operation of scheduled maritime transport services, allowing them to fix prices and regulate capacity. Regulation 4056/86 was repealed by Regulation 1419/2006[87]; horizontal cooperation agreements in the maritime transport sector are now subject to the Commission's *Guidelines on Horizontal Cooperation Agreements*[88].

(c) Block exemption for shipping consortia

Council Regulation 246/2009[89] authorises the Commission to grant block exemption to some shipping consortia. Under the powers conferred upon it the Commission adopted Regulation 906/2009[90] which confers block exemption on shipping consortia in so far as they provide international liner shipping services from or to one or more EU ports[91]; the block exemption does not apply in the event that the consortium involves certain 'hardcore restrictions' such as price fixing to third parties[92], and there is a 30% market share threshold above which a consortium would not benefit from the block exemption[93].

[80] Rolling Stock Leasing Market Investigation Order 2009, which was found to have been successful following a review by the ORR: public letter of 3 July 2015, available at www.orr.gov.uk; see the discussion in ch 11, 'Market Investigation References in Practice', pp 488–492.

[81] OJ [1986] L 378/4. [82] OJ [2006] L 269/1. [83] JO [1962] 13/204. [84] OJ [1986] L 378/4.

[85] OJ [2003] L 1/1.

[86] 'Cabotage' and 'international tramp vessel services' were excluded from the normal procedural rules in Regulation 1/2003 until October 2006: see Regulation 1419/2006, OJ [2006] L 269/1, Article 2.

[87] Commission Guidelines on the application of Article 101 TFEU to maritime transport services were in force from 2008 to 2013: OJ [2008] C 245/2.

[88] OJ [2011] C 11/1; see ch 15, 'The *Guidelines on Horizontal Cooperation Agreements*', pp 600–604.

[89] OJ [2009] L 79/1; this Regulation replaced Regulation 479/92, OJ [1992] L 55/3.

[90] OJ [2009] L 256/31, which was extended until 25 April 2020 by Regulation 697/2014, OJ [2014] L 184/3.

[91] Regulation 906/2009, Articles 1 and 3. [92] Ibid, Article 4. [93] Ibid, Article 5.

(ii) Practical application of the competition rules to maritime transport

The relationship between the Commission and certain operators in the maritime transport sector has not been particularly harmonious. There have been a number of decisions in which the Commission has found infringements of Articles 101 and 102. The first fine in this sector was imposed in *Secretama*[94], for supplying incorrect information in response to a request for information by the Commission under Article 16(3) of Regulation 4056/86. The Commission also imposed fines of €5,000 on *Ukwal*[95] and €4,000 on *Mewac*[96] for failing to submit to investigations under Article 18 of Regulation 4056/86.

The first decision of the Commission imposing a fine for a substantive infringement of Articles 101 and 102 in the maritime transport sector was *French-West African Shipowners' Committees*[97]. The Commission considered that the Committees had cartelised the entire trade in liner cargo between France and various West African ports; quotas had been established and procedures established to ensure compliance. The infringements arose both under Article 101 and under the concept of collective dominance in Article 102. The result of the practices was to exclude third parties from the trade. Various defences (for example that the agreements were 'technical' under Article 2 of Regulation 4056/86, that the block exemption under Article 3 was applicable and that the Committees were subject to 'state compulsion'[98]), were rejected. In fixing the level of the fines, which exceeded €15 million, the Commission noted that usually when it applies the competition rules in new circumstances it proceeds with moderation; on this occasion however it saw no reason for moderation, since the parties were well aware of the illegality of their conduct and that the block exemption in Regulation 4056/86 was unavailable[99].

In *Cewal*[100] the Commission imposed fines totalling €10.1 million on members of a liner conference, Cewal, for abusing their collective dominant position by taking action designed to eliminate their principal independent competitors, for example by offering lower freight rates and by offering loyalty rebates. The Commission's finding of collective dominance and its condemnation of the abusive practices were upheld by the EU Courts[101]; however the fines on the appellants were annulled by the Court of Justice because the Commission's statement of objections had been addressed directly only to the conference, Cewal, and not to its individual members, who had merely received a copy. The Commission subsequently served a new statement of objections on Compagnie Maritime Belge, one of the members of the conference, informing it that the Commission intended to impose a fine upon it for the infringements that it had found in the original decision and that had been upheld on appeal; this led to the imposition of a fine of €3.4 million on CMB[102]. CMB's appeal to the General Court, which included pleas that the Commission's second decision was unreasonably delayed and infringed the limitation rules, was unsuccessful[103].

In *TAA*[104] and in *FEFC*[105] the Commission prohibited price fixing in relation to the land-leg of combined transport operations; even though Council Regulation 4056/86

[94] OJ [1991] L 35/23. [95] OJ [1992] L 121/45. [96] OJ [1993] L 20/6. [97] OJ [1992] L 134/1.

[98] See ch 3, 'State compulsion and highly regulated markets', pp 144–145.

[99] OJ [1992] L 134/1, para 74(g).

[100] OJ [1993] L 34/20; the treatment of collective dominance in this case is discussed in ch 14, 'The judgment of the Court of Justice in *Compagnie Maritime Belge Transports v Commission*', pp 589–591, and the condemnation of the lower freight rates is discussed in ch 18, '*Compagnie Maritime Belge v Commission*', pp 766–768.

[101] Cases T-24/93 etc *Compagnie Maritime Belge NV v Commission* EU:T:1996:139, upheld on appeal to the Court of Justice Cases C-395/96 and C-396/96 P EU:C:2000:132.

[102] Commission decision of 30 April 2004.

[103] Case T-276/04 *Compagnie Maritime Belge v Commission* EU:T:2008:237. [104] OJ [1994] L 376/1.

[105] OJ [1994] L 378/17.

conferred block exemption on price fixing in relation to the maritime element of the transportation of containers, the Commission did not consider that this should extend to the non-maritime part of a journey; the Commission's approach was upheld by the General Court on appeal[106]. The Commission imposed a fine in *Ferry Operators*[107] on five ferry operators who colluded with one another in order to overcome difficulties experienced in currency fluctuations following the devaluation of the pound sterling in September 1992. In *Europe Asia Trades Agreement*[108] the Commission held that agreements not to use capacity and to exchange information infringed Article 101(1) and failed to satisfy the criteria of Article 101(3). In *Trans-Atlantic Conference Agreement*[109] the Commission imposed fines totalling €273 million for infringement of Article 101 and for abusing a collective dominant position contrary to Article 102 by altering the competitive structure of the market and by placing restrictions on the availability and contents of service contracts. This decision was partially annulled on appeal: in particular the General Court disagreed with most of the findings of abuse contrary to Article 102; the fines in this case were annulled[110]. In *Greek Ferries*[111] the Commission imposed fines of €9.12 million for fixing ferry prices between Italy and Greece. In *Far East Trade and Tariff and Surcharges Agreement* it imposed fines totalling €6.932 million where the parties to the agreement in question had agreed not to discount from their published tariffs; however these fines were quashed on appeal to the General Court on the ground that the Commission had failed to give good reasons for their belated imposition[112]. On a less hostile note, in *P&O Stena Line*[113] the Commission authorised, for three years, a joint venture to provide short cross-channel ferry services between the UK and France and Belgium. In 2001 the Commission renewed this authorisation for a period of six years[114].

In *Container liner shipping*[115] the Commission investigated the phenomenon of 'price signalling', whereby liner shipping companies 'signalled' future prices to one another by making regular public announcements of possible price increases on their websites and via the press. The Commission was concerned that these announcements might make it possible for the companies to coordinate their behaviour and charge higher prices. The Commission accepted commitments under Article 9 of Regulation 1/2003 that terminated the general price increase announcements and required the carriers to provide more information to customers[116].

106 Cases T-395/94 etc *Atlantic Container Line v Commission* EU:T:2002:49 (*TAA*), paras 142–178 and Cases T-86/95 etc *Compagnie Generale Maritime v Commission* EU:T:2002:50 (*FEFC*), paras 230–277; on these judgments see Fitzgerald 'Recent judgments in the liner shipping sector' (2002) (June) Competition Policy Newsletter 41.

107 OJ [1997] L 26/23. 108 OJ [1999] L 193/23.

109 OJ [1999] L 95/1; the Commission subsequently authorised an amended version of the liner conference in *Revised TACA* OJ [2003] L 26/53; see Commission Press Release IP/02/1677, 14 November 2002.

110 Cases T-191/98 etc *Atlantic Container Line v Commission* EU:T:2003:245.

111 OJ [1999] L 109/24, upheld on appeal to the General Court Cases T-56/99 etc *Marlines v Commission* EU:T:2003:333, upheld on further appeal to the Court of Justice Case C-112/04 P *Marlines v Commission* EU:C:2005:554.

112 Case T-213/00 *CMA CGM v Commission* EU:T:2003:76.

113 OJ [1999] L 163/61; see also the Commission's XXVIth *Report on Competition Policy* (1996), points 84–87; and the XXVIIth *Report on Competition Policy* (1997), points 81–84 and pp 134–138.

114 Commission Press Release IP/01/806, 7 June 2001 and XXXIst *Report on Competition Policy* (2001), point 160.

115 Commission decision of 7 July 2016.

116 For comment see eg Camesasca and Grelier '"Close Your Eyes"? Navigating the Tortuous Waters of Conscious Parallelism and Signalling in the European Union' (2016) 7 JECLAP 599.

(C) Air transport

(i) Legislative regime

A number of measures have been adopted in order to liberalise air transport in the EU. In the first liberalisation package of 1987[117] the Council of the EU adopted a Directive on fares for scheduled air services between Member States[118] and a Decision on the sharing of passenger capacity between Member States[119]. The 1987 package was regarded as a first step towards the completion of the internal market in air transport. In 1990 Regulation 2343/90[120] on access for air carriers to scheduled intra-EU routes was adopted. In 1991 the Council adopted Regulation 249/91[121] on air cargo services between Member States and Regulation 295/91 on compensation to passengers denied boarding ('bumped') in air transport; the latter was replaced by Regulation 261/2004[122].

In 1992 a further liberalisation package was adopted in relation to the licensing of air carriers, access of EU carriers to intra-EU routes (cabotage) and the freedom of EU air carriers to set their own fares. These provisions are now contained in Regulation 1008/2008[123].

There have been other liberalising measures. For example Regulation 95/93[124] establishes common rules for the allocation of slots at EU airports in order to ensure that they are made available on a neutral, transparent and non-discriminatory basis. Council Regulation 2299/89 established a *Code of Conduct for Computerised Reservation Systems*[125]. The ground-handling sector was liberalised to allow greater access to the market by Directive 96/67[126].

Despite these liberalisation measures there remain impediments to undistorted competition in air transport markets. The lack of slots at premier airports distorts the market, as do bilateral agreements between individual Member States and third countries governing access to air space and which discriminate in favour of national carriers: some of these agreements were successfully challenged by the Commission before the Court of Justice under Article 43 TFEU in the so-called '*Open Skies*' judgment[127]. Following that judgment, Regulation 847/2004[128] requires Member States to notify the Commission of negotiations with third countries and to ensure that their agreements comply with EU law. An important step forward was the signature of the *Air Transport Agreement* between the US, the EU and the Member States on 30 April 2007[129] which authorises US and EU airlines to fly between any city in the US and any city in the EU; this agreement took effect on 30 March 2008 and was amended in June 2010[130]. In 2015 the Commission

[117] See the Commission's XVIIth *Report on Competition Policy* (1987), points 43–45.

[118] Council Directive 87/601/EEC, OJ [1987] L 374/12.

[119] Council Decision 87/602/EEC, OJ [1987] L 374/19.

[120] OJ [1990] L 217/8, repealed by Regulation 2408/92, OJ [1992] L 240/8, which was recast by Regulation 1008/2008 on common rules for the operation of air services in the [EU], OJ [2008] L 293/3.

[121] OJ [1991] L 36/1; see now Regulation 1008/2008, OJ [2008] L 293/3. [122] OJ [2004] L 46/1.

[123] OJ [2008] L 293/3.

[124] OJ [1993] L 14/1, as amended in particular by Regulation 793/2004, OJ [2004] L 138/50.

[125] OJ [1989] L 220/1, as amended by Council Regulations 3089/93/EEC, OJ [1993] L 278/1 and 323/99/EC, OJ [1999] L 40/1; a fine of €10,000 was imposed under this Regulation in the case of *Lufthansa*, Commission Press Release IP/99/542, 20 July 1999; it has since been repealed and replaced: Regulation 80/2009, OJ [2009] L 35/47.

[126] OJ [1996] L 272/36.

[127] See Cases C-466/98 etc *Commission v United Kingdom* EU:C:2002:624; see *Communication from the Commission on the consequences of the Court judgments of 5 November 2002 for European air transport policy*, COM(2002) 649 final, 19 November 2002.

[128] OJ [2004] L 157/7. [129] OJ [2007] L 134/4.

[130] Commission Press Release IP/10/818, 24 June 2010; Norway and Iceland acceded to the Air Transport Agreement with effect from 21 June 2011.

reported on the successful implementation and progress of the 'Single European Sky' between 2012 and 2014[131].

For many years air transport was subject to a special competition law regime contained in Council Regulation 3975/87[132]. It conferred power on the Commission to enforce the competition rules in the air transport sector to air transport services *between EU airports*; air transport between EU airports and third countries could be investigated only under the procedure provided for in Articles 104 and 105 TFEU[133]. The position is now much simpler: the procedural regime is that of Regulation 1/2003[134], and Council Regulation 411/2004[135] provides that the Commission's powers under that Regulation apply to *all* routes, not only those within the EU.

Council Regulation 3976/87[136], as subsequently amended, gave the Commission power to publish block exemptions in the air transport sector. For many years there were block exemptions for consultations between carriers on passenger tariffs on routes within the EU and for arrangements on slot allocation and airport scheduling: however these have now lapsed. Council Regulation 3976/87 was replaced, in 2009, by Council Regulation 487/2009[137]; however there are currently no block exemptions in the air transport sector.

The UK Civil Aviation Authority ('CAA') enjoys concurrent powers to enforce the Competition Act 1998 to airport operation and air traffic services. The CAA has issued guidance on the application of its competition powers and on its prioritisation principles in consumer protection, competition law and economic regulation[138] and has adopted one infringement decision for fixing the price of car parking at East Midlands International Airport[139].

(ii) Practical application of the competition rules to air transport

The Commission has reviewed several cooperation agreements in the air transport sector under Article 101, for example *Lufthansa/SAS*[140], *Austrian Airlines/Lufthansa*[141], *Société Air France/Alitalia Linee Aeree Italiane SpA*[142] and *Austrian Airlines/SAS*[143]. In cases that arose prior to Regulation 1/2003 the Commission sometimes granted individual exemptions to cooperation agreements, subject to conditions and obligations: that was true of the first three cases cited earlier. Since Regulation 1/2003 the Commission contemplated closing the *Austrian Airlines/SAS* case on the basis of commitments offered by the parties under Article 9[144]; however that case did not reach a final decision. In *British Airways/American Airlines/Iberia*[145] the Commission accepted commitments under Article 9 of Regulation 1/2003 that would lead to the divestment of slots at London Heathrow and Gatwick airports and associated remedies that would facilitate entry and/or expansion on air routes between London and various US cities such as New York, Boston, Dallas and Miami; as a consequence the Commission closed its investigation. The Commission

[131] COM(2015) 663 final, 16 December 2015.

[132] OJ [1987] L 374/1.

[133] For the use of these provisions specifically in relation to air transport prior to the adoption of Regulation 3975/87 see Cases 209/84 etc *Ministère Public v Asjes* EU:C:1986:188; Case 66/86 *Ahmed Saeed Flugreisen v Zentrale zur Bekämpfung Unlauteren Wettbewerbs* EU:C:1989:140; see also *Emerald Supplies Ltd v British Airways plc* [2017] EWHC 2420 (Ch), on appeal to the Court of Appeal, not yet decided.

[134] OJ [2004] L 1/1. [135] OJ [2004] L 68/1. [136] OJ [1988] L 374/9. [137] OJ [2009] L 148/1.

[138] Both available at www.caa.co.uk. [139] CAA announcement of 20 December 2016.

[140] OJ [1996] L 54/28; see Crocioni 'The *Lufthansa/SAS* Case: Did the Commission Get the Economics Right?' (1998) 19 ECLR 116.

[141] OJ [2002] L 242/25. [142] Commission decision of 7 April 2004, OJ [2004] L 362/117.

[143] See the Commission's *Market Test Notice* OJ [2005] C 233/18.

[144] See ch 7, 'Article 9: commitments', pp 264–269 on the Article 9 procedure.

[145] Commission decision of 14 July 2010.

accepted similar commitments from Air Canada/United/Lufthansa[146] to modify the cooperation between those airlines in the Star airline alliance. A similar outcome was achieved in relation to the transatlantic joint venture between Air France–KLM, Alitalia and Delta[147]. In *Brussels Airlines/TAP* the Commission issued a statement of objections in relation to a code-sharing agreement on the Brussels–Lisbon route that granted each airline unlimited rights to sell seats on each other's flights on a route where they had previously competed[148].

In some cases an alliance between two airlines may fall to be considered under the EUMR rather than Article 101. This happened for example in *Alitalia/KLM* where the Commission regarded the alliance as a full-function joint venture, even though the parties did not create a corporate vehicle for the cooperation; the Commission cleared the merger after the parties agreed to modify the transaction to address its competition concerns[149]. The Commission cleared a merger subject to conditions in the case of *Air France/KLM*[150]; the clearance was unsuccessfully challenged in the General Court by a third party, easyJet[151]. The Commission has prohibited the proposed acquisition of Aer Lingus by Ryanair on two occasions[152]; Aer Lingus was subsequently acquired by IAG, subject to conditions[153]. The Commission also blocked the proposed acquisition by Olympic Airlines of Aegean Airlines which would have led to a quasi-monopoly on the Greek air transport market[154]; however a merger of these two airlines was cleared unconditionally in 2013 when the Commission accepted that Olympic had become a failing firm[155]. Mergers were cleared after Phase II investigations in the cases of *Lufthansa/SN Holding (Brussels Airlines)*[156] and *Lufthansa/Austrian Airlines*[157] on the basis of remedies offered to address the concerns about a reduction of competition on various routes: the remedies, centred on the divestment of slots at certain airports, resemble those in the *British Airways/American Airlines/Iberia* and *Air Canada/United/Lufthansa* cases. There have been several other mergers between airlines that have been reviewed, and cleared, by the Commission[158].

Quite apart from the cooperation agreements and mergers in the air transport sector just referred to, the Commission has also proceeded against cartels (or alleged cartels) in this sector. In *SAS/Maersk Air*[159] the Commission imposed fines of €39.4 million on SAS and €13.1 million on Maersk for market sharing, in particular with the consequence that SAS acquired a *de facto* quasi-monopoly on the Stockholm to Copenhagen route. The Commission's decision was upheld on appeal[160]. In *Air cargo* the Commission imposed fines of €799 million on 11 airlines for participation in a cartel in the provision of air cargo services[161]. On appeal the General Court annulled the Commission's decision due

[146] Commission decision of 23 May 2013. [147] Commission decision of 12 May 2015.

[148] Commission Press Release IP/16/3563, 16 October 2016.

[149] Case JV 19, Commission decision of 11 August 1999.

[150] See Case M 3280, Commission decision of 11 February 2004.

[151] Case T-177/04 *easyJet Co Ltd v Commission* EU:T:2006:187.

[152] See Case M 4439 *Ryanair/Aer Lingus I*, Commission decision of 27 June 2007, upheld on appeal Case T-342/07 *Ryanair Holdings plc v Commission* EU:T:2010:280 and Case M 6663 *Ryanair/Aer Lingus III*, Commission decision of 27 February 2013.

[153] Case M 7541, decision of 14 July 2015. [154] Case M 5830, decision of 26 January 2011.

[155] Case M 6796, decision of 9 October 2013. [156] Case M 5335, decision of 22 June 2009.

[157] Case M 5440, decision of 28 August 2009.

[158] See eg Case M 5889 *United/Continental*, decision of 27 July 2010; Case M 6607 *US Airways/American Airlines*, decision of 5 August 2013; Case M 7333 *Alitalia/Etihad*, decision of 14 November 2014.

[159] OJ [2001] L 265/15.

[160] Case T-241/01 *SAS v Commission* EU:T:2005:296.

[161] Commission decision of 9 November 2010.

to a contradiction between the operative part of the decision, which said that there were four separate infringements, and the reasons for the decision, which found a single and continuous infringement[162]. In March 2017 the Commission readopted its infringement decision finding a single overall agreement and imposed fines of €776 million[163]. Numerous follow-on actions for damages against the offending airlines have been commenced in the UK[164] and elsewhere[165]. The courts in the UK do not have jurisdiction to hear an action for damages for breach of Article 101 in relation to air transport routes between the EU and third countries during the period before Regulation 1/2003 entered into force on 1 May 2004[166].

In the UK a market investigation of BAA's ownership of seven UK airports led to an order that BAA should divest itself of three airports, including the London airports at Gatwick and Stansted[167]. In 2016 the Competition and Markets Authority ('the CMA') estimated that the remedies in *BAA airports* will lead to benefits for passengers of around £870 million by 2020[168].

7. Regulated Industries

(A) Demonopolisation, liberalisation and privatisation

One of the most dramatic economic developments in the final two decades of the twentieth century was the demonopolisation and liberalisation of industries that for many years had been the preserve of state-owned monopolies; in many cases this process was coupled with privatisation or partial privatisation of state-owned undertakings[169]. Obvious examples are the so-called 'utilities' such as telecommunications, gas, electricity and water. The problems for competition policy that arise where former monopolists are 'released' into the free market are obvious: in so far as there is no effective competition, which is particularly likely to be the case in the early years, they may be able to charge excessive prices; and they may also be able to adopt tactics intended to foreclose new competitors from entering the market. At the same time it is necessary to ensure that former monopolists provide adequate services of an appropriate standard. A complicating factor is that utilities are often subject to a requirement that they comply with a 'universal service obligation', for example a duty to undertake the daily delivery of letters or to maintain an electricity or water supply to business and residential premises. Undertakings that are subject to a

162 Cases T-9/11 etc *Air Canada v Commission* EU:T:2015:994; British Airways did not obtain the relief it wanted and appealed unsuccessfully to the Court of Justice: Case C-122/16 P EU:C:2017:861.

163 Commission decision of 17 March 2017, on appeal Cases T-326/17 etc *Air Canada v Commission*, not yet decided; the total fines were slightly lower because Martinair's total turnover was lower in 2016 than in 2009.

164 See eg *Air Canada v Emerald Supplies Ltd* [2015] EWCA Civ 1024.

165 See eg www.aircargosettlement2.com in the US and Canada and *East West Debt BV v British Airways Plc* in the Netherlands.

166 *Emerald Supplies Ltd v British Airways Plc* [2017] EWHC 2420 (Ch), on appeal to the Court of Appeal not yet decided.

167 *BAA airports*, Final Report of 19 March 2009, quashed in Case 1110/6/8/09 *BAA v Competition Commission* [2009] CAT 35, reversed on appeal in *Competition Commission v BAA Ltd* [2010] EWCA Civ 1097; BAA unsuccessfully appealed against a further decision finding that there were no material changes in circumstances since the 2009 Report: Case 1185/618/11 [2012] CAT 3, upheld on appeal [2012] EWCA Civ 1077.

168 *Evaluation of the CC's 2009 market investigation remedies*, 16 May 2016.

169 On privatisation see Vickers and Yarrow *Privatisation and Economic Analysis* (MIT Press, 1987); Veljanovski (ed) *Privatisation and Competition: A Market Prospectus* (Hobart Paperback 28, 1988); Graham and Prosser *Privatising Public Enterprises* (Oxford University Press, 1991).

universal service obligation of this kind may need some immunity from competition so that they can make sufficient profits to enable them to perform it, which is why, for example, postal operators historically enjoyed a legal monopoly over the delivery of letters of less than a certain weight and size[170].

(B) **EU law and the liberalisation of markets**

In the EU considerable steps have been taken towards the liberalisation of utilities and the development of a single market, albeit with greater success in some sectors than in others. Directives have been adopted in the case of electronic communications, post and energy markets to open up markets and encourage the emergence of competition. At the same time the European Commission has been adapting the principles of competition law and applying them to these sectors; in particular the so-called 'essential facilities doctrine' may play an important role in enabling third parties to gain access to physical infrastructures where this is objectively necessary for the provision of competitive services[171]. Markets can also be liberalised by the removal of unjustified 'public' restrictions of competition, including regulatory rules. Competition advocacy is an important responsibility of competition authorities in the EU (and elsewhere), that is to say to comment and, where appropriate, to criticise restrictions of competition for which the State is responsible[172].

(C) **Regulatory systems in the UK for utilities**

In the UK detailed regulatory regimes were established for the industries that were privatised in the 1980s and 1990s, namely telecommunications, gas, electricity, water, aviation and rail transport. These regimes provide, among other matters, for price control where persistent market power means that the normal process of competition will not deliver competitive prices to consumers[173]. Many other *ex ante* regulatory obligations are imposed on regulated undertakings, for example not to discriminate unduly, to avoid certain cross-subsidies and to share 'essential facilities'. The sectoral regulators[174] act as a surrogate for competition, at least until effective competition develops, by imposing constraints on what the regulated undertakings can do; the regulators are charged with the responsibility of protecting consumers, promoting competition where possible and controlling prices. In a sense, regulators 'hold the fort' until competition arrives. Regulated undertakings operate subject to licences that impose obligations upon them and that attempt to prevent conduct, among other things, that will be exclusionary, discriminatory or exploitative. The regulators monitor these

170 On the permitted 'reserved area' for letters under EU law see 'Legislation', pp 1016–1017 later in chapter.

171 See ch 17, 'Is the product to which access is sought indispensable to someone wishing to compete in the downstream market?', pp 717–723 on the essential facilities doctrine, noting the need, discussed there, to impose constraints upon it; these constraints are not so important where a facility was developed by a state-owned monopolist as opposed to an undertaking operating in the private sector: see the Opinion of AG Mazák in Case C-52/09 *Konkurrensverket v TeliaSonera AB* EU:C:2010:483, paras 24–28.

172 On competition advocacy, see ch 1, 'Competition advocacy and public restrictions of competition', p 24.

173 See generally Armstrong, Cowan and Vickers *Regulatory Reform: Economic Analysis and British Experience* (MIT Press, 1994); Helm and Jenkinson (eds) *Competition in Regulated Industries* (Oxford University Press, 1998); Baldwin and Cave *Understanding Regulation: Theory, Strategy and Practice* (Oxford University Press, 1999), in particular chs 14–18.

174 See ch 2, 'Sectoral regulators', pp 70–71.

licences and have powers to enforce compliance with them; in the event of disputes with regulated undertakings as to the appropriate terms for inclusion in a licence, the regulators can make a so-called 'modification reference' to the CMA which will decide whether the matters referred operate, or may be expected to operate, against the public interest and, if so, whether the effects adverse to the public interest could be remedied by modifications to the licences[175]. The sectoral regulators also have concurrent powers, with the CMA, to apply Articles 101 and 102 TFEU and the Chapter I and Chapter II prohibitions in the Competition Act 1998 in the sectors for which they are responsible[176].

(D) **Price caps**

A particular problem in the regulated industries is the control of prices. A central proposition of competition policy is that price should be determined by the market, and not by the state or an agency of the state. Competition authorities take action against excessive prices only rarely[177]. However where there is monopoly or near-monopoly, in particular in relation to essential services such as voice telephony, broadband services or the supply of electricity, price control may be necessary; where this is the case, various techniques can be deployed to determine what the price should be. One method of capping prices is to fix an upper limit on the rate of return permissible on the capital invested in an industry: this, however, may encourage regulated bodies to over-invest, in order to expand the base on which profit can be earned; furthermore this technique does nothing to encourage efficiency. In the UK the price control function has therefore been exercised through the 'RPI minus X' formula. The Retail Prices Index or 'RPI' measures average prices for a group of goods and services; inflation is measured by the annual increase in the RPI. RPI minus X means that each year regulated undertakings are allowed to increase their prices only by the increase in the RPI, less a particular percentage as fixed by the relevant regulator[178]. Over a period of time this formula leads to a reduction in prices in real terms, thereby benefiting consumers and forcing the regulated undertakings to increase efficiency in order to continue in profit. The RPI minus X formula encourages firms to become more efficient since, if they can cut their costs, they will make a higher profit. A further benefit of the RPI minus X formula is that it is relatively simple to apply: the regulator sets the figure, after which all that is necessary is to check that the price is not being exceeded. When deciding the value of X for the purpose of RPI minus X, the regulator is asked, in effect, to determine the extent to which added efficiency is possible within the industry in question[179].

In the text that follows relevant provisions of EU and UK law will be briefly discussed, so that the reader has an idea of the regulatory environment of the electronic communications, post, energy and water markets and of the possible application of competition law to them. However the text is intended as a mere introduction to subject-matter that is substantial and complex; references to more detailed literature will be provided where appropriate.

[175] Guidance on regulatory references to the CMA is available on its website, www.gov.uk/cma.

[176] On concurrency under the Competition Act 1998 see ch 10, 'Concurrency', pp 449–452.

[177] See ch 18, 'Excessive Pricing', pp 735–746.

[178] See generally *Incentive Regulation: Reviewing RPI-X and Promoting Competition* (Centre for the Study of Regulated Industries, 1992).

[179] RPI minus X has been replaced by 'Revenue set to deliver strong Incentives, Innovation and Outputs' in the energy sector: *RIIO: A new way to regulate energy networks*, 2010, available at www.ofgem.gov.uk.

8. Electronic Communications

(A) EU law

(i) Legislation

EU law on electronic communications and the internet has evolved in response to changing markets, technologies, business models and greater reliance on the internet[180].

(a) Common regulatory framework

A series of Directives, dating back to 1990, have been adopted under Article 114 TFEU to bring about harmonisation necessary for the establishment of an internal market[181]; by the end of that decade[182] the convergence of the telecommunications, media and information technology sectors meant it was desirable that a single regulatory framework for electronic communications should cover all transmission networks and services. This led to the adoption of a package of five Directives and one Decision in 2002[183]. The package was amended in December 2009 by two further Directives[184]. Under this common regulatory framework national regulatory authorities are required to impose regulatory obligations on undertakings in the electronic communications sector that have significant market power, which for this purpose is given the same meaning as dominance in Article 102, in any relevant markets. The Commission published a Recommendation on *Relevant Product and Service Markets* to be regulated in accordance with the rules set out in the package[185]; a new Recommendation was published in October 2014[186]. The Commission has also published guidelines on *Market Analysis and the Calculation of Significant Market Power*, which are to be applied by national regulatory authorities in reaching their conclusions on those issues[187]. A 'Body of European Regulators for Electronic Communications' has been established to ensure the consistent application of the regulatory package[188].

[180] See further Rose and Bailey (eds) *Bellamy and Child: European Union Law of Competition* (Oxford University Press, 7th ed, 2013), paras 12.135–12.147.

[181] See generally Nihoul and Rodford *EU Electronic Communications Law* (Oxford University Press, 2nd ed, 2011); Rose and Bailey (eds) *Bellamy and Child: European Union Law of Competition* (Oxford University Press, 7th ed, 2013), paras 12.004–12.087; Faull and Nikpay (eds) *The EU Law of Competition* (Oxford University Press, 3rd ed, 2014), ch 13.

[182] Commission Working Document *Proposed New Regulatory Framework for Electronic Communications Networks and Services*, COM(2001) 175 final, 28 March 2001.

[183] See Directive of the European Parliament and of the Council on a common regulatory framework for electronic communications networks and services, OJ [2002] L 108/33 (the 'Framework Directive'); Directive of the European Parliament and of the Council on the authorisation of electronic communications networks and services, OJ [2002] L 108/22 (the 'Authorisation Directive'); Directive of the European Parliament and of the Council on access to, and interconnection of, electronic communications networks and associated facilities, OJ [2002] L 108/7 (the 'Access Directive'); Directive of the European Parliament and of the Council on universal service and users' rights relating to electronic communications networks and services, OJ [2002] L 108/51 (the 'Universal Service Directive'); Directive of the European Parliament and of the Council concerning the processing of personal data and the protection of privacy in the electronic communications sector, OJ [2002] L 201/37 (the 'Data Protection Directive'); and the *Radio Spectrum* decision, OJ [2002] L 108/1.

[184] Directive 2009/136/EC of the European Parliament and of the Council of 25 November 2009 amending the Universal Service Directive and the Data Protection Directive, OJ [2009] L 337/11; Directive 2009/140/EC of the European Parliament and of the Council amending the Framework Directive, the Access Directive and the Authorisation Directive, OJ [2009] L 337/37.

[185] OJ [2003] L 114/45.

[186] The Commission Recommendation of 9 October 2014, together with an explanatory note, is available at www.ec.europa.eu.

[187] OJ [2002] C 165/6.

[188] Regulation 1211/2009/EC, OJ [2009] L 337/1; note the Commission's proposal for a Regulation to establish BEREC as an EU agency: COM(2016) 591 final, 14 September 2016.

In accordance with its Digital Single Market Strategy[189], in 2016 the Commission made a Proposal for a Directive establishing the European Electronic Communications Code, which would incorporate the Framework Directive, Authorisation Directive, Access Directive and Universal Service Directive into a single code[190]. The proposed Directive would also amend the market review procedure, the imposition of access obligations, spectrum management, universal service obligations, end-user protections and governance; these proposals are designed to address the growing need for increased connectivity of the digital single market and incentivising investment in high-speed broadband networks.

(b) Article 106(3) TFEU

The Commission has adopted a series of Directives pursuant to Article 106(3) TFEU[191]. The first of these was the Telecommunications Terminal Equipment Directive of 1988[192], which required Member States to withdraw special or exclusive rights granted to undertakings with respect to the importation, marketing, connection and bringing into service of telecommunications terminal equipment and the maintenance of such equipment. The Commission subsequently adopted the Telecommunications Services Directive of 1990[193], which began the process of opening up telecommunications markets themselves to competition. The Services Directive has been amended several times in order to expand its scope; it was successively extended to apply to the satellite[194], cable[195] and mobile telephony[196] sectors, and ultimately required full competition in telecommunications markets[197]. The Commission has also amended the original Services Directive to require that, where a single operator owns both a telecommunications and a cable network, they must be established as separate legal entities[198]. A consolidating Directive, bringing all these pieces of legislation into a single legal instrument, was adopted in September 2002[199].

(c) Net neutrality

Net neutrality refers to the principle that users should have access to online content and services without any discrimination or interference, such as blocking or slowing down, by internet access providers[200]. Proponents of net neutrality argue that equal treatment of data is integral to an open internet, whereas critics say that internet traffic needs to be managed and not all data is equally valuable. Regulation 2015/2120 on open internet access enshrines the principle of net neutrality into EU law with effect from 30 April 2016[201].

189 COM/2015/0192 final, 6 May 2015.

190 COM(2016) 590 final/2, 12 October 2016.

191 On the Commission's powers to adopt directives under Article 106(3) see ch 6, 'Article 106(3)', pp 248–251.

192 Commission Directive 88/301/EEC, OJ [1988] L 131/73; on the (mostly unsuccessful) challenge to this Directive see Case C-202/88 *France v Commission* EU:C:1991:120, and for comment see Naftel 'The Natural Death of a Natural Monopoly' (1993) 14 ECLR 105; on France's failure to implement the Directive correctly see Case C-91/94 *Tranchant v Telephone Store* EU:C:1995:374; see also Case C-146/00 *Commission v France* EU:C:2001:668.

193 Commission Directive 90/388/EEC, OJ [1990] L 192/10; this Directive was unsuccessfully challenged in Cases C-271/90 etc *Spain v Commission* EU:C:1992:440.

194 Commission Directive 94/46/EC, OJ [1994] L 268/15.

195 Commission Directive 95/51/EC, OJ [1995] L 256/49.

196 Commission Directive 92/1/EC, OJ [1996] L 20/59.

197 Commission Directive 96/19/EC, OJ [1996] L 74/13.

198 Commission Directive 99/64/EC, OJ [1999] L 175/39.

199 Commission Directive 2002/77/EC, OJ [2002] L 249/21.

200 For discussion see Maniadaki *EU Competition Law, Regulation and the Internet: The Case of Net Neutrality* (Kluwer, 2014); Alexiadis 'EU Net Neutrality policy and the mobile sector: The need for competition law standards', Concurrences Review 3-2016.

201 OJ [2015] L 310/1, Article 3(1).

All internet traffic must be treated equally[202]. Internet access providers are able to offer specialised services of higher quality, such as internet TV, provided these services are not supplied at the expense of the quality of the open internet[203].

(ii) **Application of EU competition law**

The Commission has been active in applying the competition rules to the telecommunications sector for many years. In 1991 it published *Guidelines on the Application of EEC Competition Rules in the Telecommunications Sector*[204], and in 1998 it adopted the *Notice on the Application of the Competition Rules to Access Agreements in the Telecommunications Sector*[205]. The latter of these two instruments is of particular interest. Part I is entitled 'Framework', and discusses the relationship between the competition rules and sector-specific regulation. Part II deals with market definition, and Part III provides detailed analysis of the application of the principles of competition law to access agreements; the most extensive discussion is of the 'essential facilities doctrine' under Article 102, but the Notice also contains useful guidance on other types of abuse.

(a) Article 101

The Commission has adopted numerous favourable decisions on strategic alliances in the electronic communications sector, such as *BT/MCI*[206], *Atlas*[207], *Iridium*[208], *Phoenix/GlobalOne*[209], *Uniworld*[210], *Unisource*[211], *Cégétel+4*[212] and *Télécom Développement*[213]. It also approved the *GSM MoU Standard International Roaming Agreement*, which enables GSM mobile telephone users in one country to use the network in another country[214]. In *T-Mobile Deutschland/O2 Germany* the Commission authorised an agreement that would enable the parties to roam on one another's 3G networks[215]. On appeal the General Court was critical of the Commission's finding that the roaming agreement had the effect of restricting competition and partially annulled the decision[216].

In *Telefónica/Portugal Telecom*[217] the Commission imposed fines of €79 million where those two undertakings had included a non-compete clause in an agreement concerning the dissolution of a Brazilian joint venture that provided that they would not compete with one another in Portugal and Spain respectively. The Commission considered that the non-compete obligation unlawfully hindered the integration of the EU telecommunications sector and rejected the argument of the parties that the offending clause was an ancillary restraint.

(b) Article 102

In 1998 the Commission objected to possible excessive or discriminatory prices for calls to mobile telephones[218], which ended in May 1999 following significant price reductions[219].

[202] Ibid, Article 3(3). [203] Ibid, Article 3(5).
[204] OJ [1991] C 233/2. [205] OJ [1998] C 265/2. [206] OJ [1994] L 223/36.
[207] OJ [1996] L 239/29. [208] OJ [1997] L 16/87. [209] OJ [1996] L 239/57.
[210] OJ [1997] L 318/24.
[211] OJ [1997] L 318/1; this decision was subsequently withdrawn due to changes in the market: Commission Press Release IP/01/1, 3 January 2001.
[212] OJ [1999] L 218/14. [213] OJ [1999] L 218/24.
[214] See the Commission's XXVIIth *Report on Competition Policy* (1997), point 75 and pp 139–140.
[215] OJ [2004] L 75/32.
[216] Case T-328/03 *O2 (Germany) GmbH v Commission* EU:T:2006:116.
[217] Commission decision of 23 January 2013, substantially upheld on appeal Case T-208/13 *Portugal Telecom v Commission* EU:T:2016:368 and Case T-216/13 *Telefónica v Commission* EU:T:2016:369; the latter was on further appeal Case C-487/16 P EU:C:2017:961.
[218] See the Commission's XXVIIIth *Report on Competition Policy* (1998), points 79–81.
[219] See Commission Press Release IP/99/298, 4 May 1999 and Commission's XXIXth *Report on Competition Policy* (1999), pp 375–380.

In 1999 the Commission launched a sector inquiry into leased lines, mobile roaming services and the local loop[220]. The leased line investigation ended in December 2002, as a result of substantial price decreases[221]. The problem of excessive prices for international mobile calls was addressed by the Roaming Regulation[222].

The Commission has taken action against incumbent operators for impeding access to the market for the provision of residential broadband internet access: it concluded that Wanadoo of France[223] was guilty of predatory pricing contrary to Article 102; that Deutsche Telekom of Germany[224] and Telefónica of Spain[225] were guilty of margin squeezes; Telekomunikacja Polska of Poland[226] imposed unfair trading conditions; and Slovak Telekom, and its parent company Deutsche Telekom, were fined €38.8 million for refusing to supply access to unbundled local loops in the Slovak Republic and imposing a margin squeeze[227]. Acting under Article 102 in conjunction with Article 106 the Commission took action against Italy and Spain as a result of their discriminatory treatment of the second operators of mobile telephony in those countries[228]; however it declined to take similar action against Austria, which had not discriminated in favour of the incumbent operator[229].

(c) EUMR

The Commission has investigated many concentrations in the electronic communications sector under the EUMR. In *MCI WorldCom/Sprint*[230] the Commission prohibited an agreed merger between two US undertakings which, in its view, would have created a dominant firm in the market for 'top-level' internet interconnectivity. The Commission has granted conditional clearance to a number of concentrations in the fixed line[231] and mobile telephony sectors[232]. However, in *Hutchison 3G UK/Telefónica UK*[233] the Commission prohibited a merger that would have reduced the number of mobile network

[220] See the Commission's XXIXth *Report on Competition Policy* (1999), points 74–76; see further the XXXth *Report* (2000), points 157–160 and XXXIst *Report* (2001), points 125–131.

[221] See Commission Press Release IP/02/1852, 11 December 2002.

[222] Regulation 531/2012, OJ [2012] L 172/10.

[223] Commission decision of 16 July 2003, upheld on appeal Case T-340/03 *France Télécom SA v Commission* EU:T:2007:22, and on further appeal Case C-202/07 P EU:C:2009:214.

[224] OJ [2003] L 263/9, upheld on appeal Case T-271/03 *Deutsche Telekom AG v Commission* EU:T:2008:101, and on further appeal Case C-280/08 P EU:C:2010:603.

[225] Commission decision of 4 July 2007, upheld on appeal Case T-336/07 *Telefónica and Telefónica España v Commission* EU:T:2012:172, and on further appeal Case C-295/12 P EU:C:2014:2062; separately the General Court dismissed an appeal by Spain against the Commission's decision: Case T-398/07 *Spain v Commission* EU:T:2012:173.

[226] Commission decision of 22 June 2011, upheld on appeal Case T-486/11 *Telekomunikacja Polska v Commission* EU:T:2015:1002, on appeal Case C-123/16 P *Orange Polska v Commission*, not yet decided.

[227] Commission decision of 15 October 2014, on appeal Case T-851/14 *Slovak Telekom v Commission*, not yet decided.

[228] See *Second Operator of GSM Radiotelephony Services in Italy* OJ [1995] L 280/49; *Second Operator of GSM Radiotelephony Services in Spain* OJ [1997] L 76/19.

[229] Case T-54/99 *max.mobil Telekommunikation Service GmbH v Commission* EU:T:2002:20, upheld on appeal Case C-141/02 P *Commission v max.mobil* EU:C:2005:98.

[230] Case M 1741, decision of 28 June 2000, annulled on appeal for technical reasons Case T-310/00 *MCI Inc v Commission* EU:T:2004:275.

[231] See eg Case M 1439 *Telia/Telenor* OJ [2001] L 40/1; Case M 2803 *Telia/Sonera* OJ [2002] C 201/19; Case M 1069 *WorldCom/MCI* OJ [1999] L 116/1.

[232] The cases are summarised in *Competition Merger Briefs* 1/2016 and 3/2016, which are available at www.ec.europa.eu/competition/publications/cpn.

[233] Case M 7612, decision of 11 May 2016, on appeal Case T-399/16 *CK Telecoms UK Investments v Commission*, not yet decided.

operators in the UK from four to three, hampered the development of the UK mobile network infrastructure and hindered the ability of mobile virtual operators to compete.

(B) UK law

The Office of Communications ('OFCOM')[234] is responsible for regulating the media and communications industries and has considerable regulatory powers under the Communications Act 2003. OFCOM is required by the common regulatory framework to review certain markets to determine whether they are 'effectively competitive'[235]. If OFCOM determines that a market is not effectively competitive, it must identify undertakings with significant market power on that market and impose on them appropriate specific regulatory obligations or maintain or amend such obligations where they already exist[236].

(i) Competition Act 1998

OFCOM has concurrent powers with the CMA to apply Articles 101 and 102 TFEU and the Chapter I and Chapter II prohibitions[237]. A Guideline has been adopted, *Competition Act 1998: The Application in the Telecommunications Sector*[238], to explain the application of the competition rules in this sector; in particular it discusses the approach that will be taken to determining costs in a network industry such as telecommunications[239].

OFCOM has adopted numerous decisions in which it concluded that there had been no infringement of the competition rules or no grounds for action on its part[240]. In several cases where OFCOM came to the conclusion that there was no infringement of the Chapter II prohibition, it did so explicitly on the basis that it was not satisfied that a competitor as efficient as the firm under investigation would be unable to compete on the market[241]. Many disputes in the electronic communications sector are now being dealt with, not under competition law, but under sector-specific legislation[242]. In practical terms this may be a simpler and quicker way to address problems of market failure, with an obvious knock-on effect on the number of infringement decisions.

(ii) Enterprise Act 2002

OFCOM also has concurrent powers with the CMA in relation to market investigation references under the Enterprise Act 2002[243]. OFCOM accepted extensive 'undertakings in lieu' offered by BT to create Openreach as a digital network business in order to address concerns that arose from its vertical integration as both a wholesaler and retailer of electronic communications services[244]. These undertakings in lieu were released in July 2017

[234] Office of Communications Act 2002, s 1.

[235] In identifying such markets, OFCOM is required to take the utmost account of recommendations and guidelines published by the Commission as to what product and service markets should be analysed: Article 16(1) of the Framework Directive.

[236] Communications Act 2003, s 45. [237] Ibid, s 371. [238] OFT 417 (2000).

[239] Ibid, paras 7.5–7.12.

[240] See ch 9, 'Table of published decisions', pp 393–395.

[241] See eg *Investigation into BT's residential broadband pricing*, OFCOM decision of 2 November 2010; *Complaint from TalkTalk Group against BT about alleged margin squeeze in relation to superfast broadband pricing*, OFCOM decision of 22 October 2014: both decisions are available at www.ofcom.org.uk.

[242] See eg Communications Act 2003, ss 185–191 which contain OFCOM's duties and powers in relation to resolving certain regulatory disputes.

[243] Communications Act 2003, s 370; on market investigations see ch 11, 'Market Investigation References', pp 469–481.

[244] OFCOM Final statements on the Strategic Review of Telecommunications and BT undertakings of 22 September 2005, available at www.ofcom.org.uk.

when OFCOM accepted a legal separation of BT and Openreach[245]. OFCOM made a market investigation reference in *Pay TV movies*[246], but no features of the market relating to the supply and acquisition of subscription pay-TV movie rights were found to have an adverse effect on competition.

9. Post

(A) EU law

(i) Legislation

Development of EU law and policy in the postal sector has come about partly through initiatives of the Council of Ministers and the Commission[247], and partly as a result of the very important judgment of the Court of Justice in the *Corbeau* case[248]. The Commission first began to take an interest in the postal sector, and the possibility of applying the competition rules to it, in the late 1980s. This culminated in the adoption of the Commission's Green Paper on *The Development of the Single Market for Postal Services*[249]. It proposed that all postal services, except ordinary internal letter deliveries, should be liberalised. In 1993 the Commission issued a communication setting out *Guidelines for the Development of [EU] Postal Services*[250]. The Council asked the Commission to draft a proposal for a legislative framework; there are now two legislative instruments, the Directive of the European Parliament and of the Council on *Common Rules for the Development of the Internal Market of [EU] Postal Services and the Improvement of Quality of Service*[251] and the Commission *Notice on the Application of the Competition Rules to the Postal Sector*[252]. The Directive entered into force on 10 February 1998[253]. The *Notice* was adopted by the Commission on 17 December 1997. These two measures should be seen as part of a single package, the Directive intended to liberalise access to certain postal activities in the EU and the *Notice* to ensure that it is understood how the competition rules impact upon the sector.

The Directive establishes common rules throughout the EU on six matters:

- the provision of a universal service
- the extent of the permissible monopoly and the conditions governing the provision of non-monopolised services
- tariff principles and transparency of accounts for universal service provision
- the setting of quality standards for universal service provision
- the harmonisation of technical standards
- the creation of independent national regulatory authorities.

As regards the first two matters the Directive establishes *minimum* standards as to the universal standards and *maximum* limits to the permissible monopoly. Member States

[245] OFCOM Statement of 13 July 2017, available at www.ofcom.org.uk.

[246] OFCOM reference of 4 August 2010, available at www.ofcom.org.uk.

[247] See further Rose and Bailey (eds) *Bellamy and Child: European Union Law of Competition* (Oxford University Press, 7th ed, 2013), paras 12.135–12.147.

[248] Case C-320/91 *Corbeau* EU:C:1993:198: see 'The *Corbeau* case and the universal service obligation', pp 1017–1018 later in chapter.

[249] COM(91) 476, June 1991. [250] COM(93) 247. [251] Directive 97/67/EC, OJ [1998] L 15/14.

[252] OJ [1998] C 39/2.

[253] The Directive was implemented in the UK by the Postal Services Regulations 1999, SI 1999/2107.

are entitled to confer lesser, but not broader, monopoly rights than those set out in the Directive. Article 7(1) provides essentially that the services 'which may be reserved' (that is which may remain a monopoly) shall be 'the clearance, sorting, transport and delivery of items of domestic correspondence, provided they weigh less than 350 grams'. The monopoly was reduced to letters weighing less than 50 grams by Directive 2002/39/EC[254]. The monopoly was abolished by Directive 2008/06/EC in 16 Member States by 31 December 2010; the remaining Member States followed suit two years later[255].

All postal services in the EU are now open to competition. Directive 2008/06 also contains provisions relating to the universal service and the powers and role of independent national regulatory authorities. The Commission and the national regulators together operate within the framework of the European Regulators Group for Postal Services[256].

(ii) **Application of EU competition law**

(a) The Corbeau *case and the universal service obligation*

There is general agreement among Member States that there are societal benefits in the maintenance of a universal postal service, that is to say a right of access to a minimum range of postal services, of a specified quality, which must be provided in all Member States at affordable prices for the benefit of all users, irrespective of their geographical location. People living in remote rural areas should have access to these services on no less favourable terms than those living in major conurbations; there is an obvious benefit, in terms of social cohesion, if all members of society can communicate with one another through the postal system, no matter where they live. A complex policy issue is to determine whether, and if so how extensive, a legal monopoly needs to be granted to the undertaking charged with performing this universal service in order to enable it to perform its duties; this question turns in part on how costly the universal service obligation is to the undertaking that has to perform it. Clearly the maintenance of a universal service is likely to be expensive, and the relevant provider will need to be assured of sufficient profits to pay for it; competitors should not be able to 'pick the cherries' or, depending on taste, 'skim the cream' and earn profits from lucrative services, while leaving the unprofitable services to the undertaking charged with the universal service obligation.

These issues came before the Court of Justice in the *Corbeau case*[257]. Corbeau had been charged with infringing a Belgian criminal law that conferred a monopoly on the Régie des Postes to collect, carry and distribute post in Belgium. Corbeau offered local courier services, but not a basic postal service. The Belgian court sought a preliminary ruling on the compatibility of the monopoly conferred by Belgian law with Articles 102 and 106 TFEU. The task for the Court of Justice was to determine whether Belgium was in breach of Article 106(1) in maintaining in force a measure contrary to Article 102, or whether the rights conferred on Régie des Postes satisfied the terms of Article 106(2). This provision does permit a restriction of competition—or even the elimination of all competition—where this is necessary to enable an undertaking to carry on the task entrusted to it[258]. At paragraph 15 of its judgment the Court noted that it could not be disputed that Régie des Postes was entrusted with a service of general economic interest[259]; the question was

[254] Article 1 of Directive 2002/39/EC, OJ [2002] L 176/21, amending Article 7 of Directive 97/67/EC.

[255] OJ [2008] L 52/3, substantially amending Directive 97/96/EC.

[256] OJ [2010] C 217/7.

[257] See ch 23, n 248 earlier; for comment see Flynn and Rizza 'Postal Services and Competition Law—A Review and Analysis of the EC Case Law' (2002) 25 World Competition 475.

[258] See ch 6, 'Article 106(2)', pp 242–248.

[259] *Corbeau* (ch 23, n 248 earlier), para 15.

the extent to which a restriction of competition was necessary to enable it to carry on that function[260]. The Court continued at paragraph 17:

> The starting point of such an examination must be the premise that the obligation on the part of the undertaking entrusted with that task to perform its services in conditions of economic equilibrium presupposes that it will be possible to offset less profitable sectors against the profitable sectors and hence justifies a restriction of competition from individual undertakings where the economically profitable sectors are concerned.

In the following paragraph the Court of Justice notes that, in the absence of a monopoly, it would be possible for individual undertakings 'to concentrate on the economically profitable operations' (in other words, to 'cherry pick'). But the Court went on, at paragraph 19:

> However, the exclusion of competition is not justified as regards specific services dissociable from the service of general interest which meet special needs of economic operators and which call for certain additional services not offered by the traditional postal service, such as collection from the senders' address, greater speed or reliability of distribution or the possibility of changing the destination in the course of transit in so far as such specific services, by their nature and the conditions in which they are offered, such as the geographical area in which they are provided, do not compromise the economic equilibrium of the service of general economic interest performed by the holder of the exclusive right.

At paragraph 20 the Court said that the application of the foregoing tests would be a task for the national court dealing with the case.

The importance of this carefully crafted judgment is clear: postal monopolies may be consistent with EU competition law, but subject to the important tests set out in paragraph 19[261]. That paragraph makes clear that it is possible, as a matter of law, that a Member State may have conferred a monopoly that is wider than is legitimate for the purpose of maintaining the universal service, and that, where this is the case, the monopoly rights in question may be unenforceable. The Commission's *Notice* explains the circumstances in which a legitimate monopolist might nonetheless be found guilty of infringing the competition rules. The Commission has itself taken action to strike down monopolies that go beyond what is justifiable under the *Corbeau* judgment. The legal monopoly over the delivery of letters came to an end as a result of Directive 2008/06/EC.

(b) The Commission's Notice on competition in the postal sector

This *Notice* explains how the Commission applies the competition rules in the postal sector[262]. It is divided into nine parts. After a preface and a discussion of terminology, the *Notice* considers market definition in the postal sector. Part 3 considers the issue of cross-subsidisation[263]; the position of public undertakings and the freedom to provide services are then looked at, followed by state measures and state aid. Part 8 discusses what are meant by services of general economic interest in Article 106(2) TFEU.

(c) Article 101

In *REIMS II*[264] the Commission decided that the criteria of Article 101(3) were satisfied in the case of an agreement between the postal operators of the EU as to the amount that

260 Ibid, para 16.

261 See also Case C-340/99 *TNT Traco SpA v Poste Italiane SpA* EU:C:2001:281.

262 OJ [1998] C 39/2.

263 See also Case T-175/99 *UPS v Commission* EU:T:2002:78, upholding the Commission's rejection of a complaint that Deutsche Post had abused a dominant position by using income from its reserved letter market to finance the acquisition of a shareholding in DHL.

264 OJ [1999] L 275/17: the Commission renewed the authorisation it had given in this case: OJ [2004] L 56/76; see also Cases C-147/97 and C-148/97 *Deutsche Post v GZS* EU:C:2000:74, dealing with the right of Deutsche Post to impose charges for cross-border mail prior to the agreement on terminal dues.

one operator would pay to another when a letter posted in the former's country had to be delivered in the territory of the latter, so-called 'terminal dues'.

(d) Article 102

In *Spanish International Courier Services*[265] the Commission held that it was unlawful for Spain to reserve to the Spanish Post Office, which already had a monopoly of the basic postal service, the ancillary activity of international courier services. In practice the Spanish Post Office was unable to meet the demand for international courier services (for example it did not cover the whole territory of Spain, nor did it extend to all countries in the world), so that there was a limitation of supply and technical development in the sense of Article 102(2)(b) TFEU[266]. In *Deutsche Post*[267] the Commission imposed a fine of €24 million on the incumbent operator in Germany for offering loyalty rebates to customers of its business parcels service, and it also concluded that it was guilty of predatory pricing[268]. In *New Postal Services with a Guaranteed Day- or Time-Certain Delivery in Italy*[269] the Commission concluded that an Italian Decree excluding competition for a specific type of hybridised electronic mail service was contrary to Article 106(1) in conjunction with Article 102. In *Slovakian postal legislation*[270] the Commission concluded that Slovakia had infringed Article 102 by extending the Slovakian Post Office's monopoly over the basic letter service to hybrid mail services.

In *De Post/La Poste*[271] the Commission imposed a fine of €2.5 million on the Belgian postal operator for giving a more favourable tariff for its general letter mail service to those customers who also used its new business-to-business mail service. In *Post Danmark v Konkurrencerådet*[272] the Court of Justice held that selective price cutting by a dominant postal undertaking in the market for the delivery of so-called 'unaddressed mail' to a level lower than its average total costs but higher than its average incremental costs, did not necessarily infringe Article 102; when the case returned to the Danish Supreme Court it confirmed that this practice was not abusive[273]. In *Post Danmark II*[274] the Court of Justice held that a retroactive rebate scheme for direct advertising mail operated by a dominant postal undertaking in the bulk mail market could have an exclusionary effect[275]; the as-efficient competitor test had no relevance in this case, since the dominant undertaking had a 95% market share and a statutory monopoly on the distribution of letters weighing up to 50 grams[276]. There was no need to show that the rebate scheme in that case was of a serious or appreciable nature[277]. Post Danmark subsequently withdrew its appeal against the infringement decision that gave rise to the Court of Justice's preliminary ruling[278].

(e) EUMR

A number of concentrations in the postal sector have been notified to the Commission under the EUMR. The Commission has granted conditional clearance in several

[265] OJ [1990] L 233/19.

[266] See similarly *Dutch Express Delivery Services* OJ [1990] L 10/47, annulled on appeal for procedural reasons Cases C-48/90 and 66/90 *Netherlands v Commission* EU:C:1992:63.

[267] OJ [2001] L 125/27; see also *Deutsche Post AG II* OJ [2001] L 331/40 imposing a 'symbolic' fine of €1,000 on Deutsche Post for abusing its dominant position in relation to so-called 'A-B-A remail'.

[268] See ch 18, 'Predatory price cutting and cross-subsidisation', p 764.

[269] OJ [2001] L 63/59.

[270] Commission decision of 7 October 2008, upheld on appeal Case T-556/08 *Slovenská pošta v Commission* EU:T:2015:189, and on further appeal Case C-293/15 P EU:C:2016:511.

[271] OJ [2002] L 61/32.

[272] Case C-209/10 EU:C:2012:172.

[273] Judgment of 15 February 2013, available at www.supremecourt.dk.

[274] Case C-23/14 EU:C:2015:651.

[275] Ibid, paras 28–46.

[276] Ibid, paras 53–62.

[277] Ibid, paras 72–74.

[278] MLex report of 4 July 2016, available at www.mlex.com.

cases, including *TNT/Canada Post*[279], *Post Office/TPG/SPPL*[280] and *Posten/Post Danmark*[281]. However in *UPS/TNT Express*[282] the Commission prohibited a merger that would have significantly impeded effective competition in the market for the express delivery of small packages in 15 Member States. On appeal the General Court annulled the prohibition decision, because the Commission failed to disclose to UPS the final version of the price concentration model and thus violated UPS's rights of defence[283].

(B) UK law

The Postal Services Act 2011 establishes the regulatory framework for the postal sector. Under that Act OFCOM is responsible for the regulation of postal services; its primary duty is to secure the provision of an efficient universal postal service. In March 2012 OFCOM decided to remove traditional price control regulation from Royal Mail and to increase its pricing and operational freedom; it also introduced measures to secure the universal postal service and to increase competition[284]. OFCOM has concurrent powers with the CMA to apply Articles 101 and 102 TFEU and the Chapter I and Chapter II prohibitions in the Competition Act 1998. In June 2001 the UK Post Office was held not to have abused its dominant position in the postal services market by refusing to license its Royal Mail trade mark to an operator in the market for consumer lifestyle surveys[285]. In July 2015 OFCOM issued a statement of objections to Royal Mail accusing it of abusing its dominant position by engaging in discriminatory conduct against competing postal operators[286].

10. Energy

(A) EU law

(i) Legislation

Article 194 TFEU provides that EU policy on energy shall aim, in a spirit of solidarity between Member States, to ensure the functioning of the energy market; ensure security of energy supply in the EU; promote energy efficiency; and promote the interconnection of energy networks[287]. However the accomplishment of an internal energy market has been a gradual process. The Council took the initiative in the 1990s by adopting Directives that established a procedure to improve the transparency of prices for gas and electricity in

[279] Case M 102, decision of 2 December 2001; in addition to the cases mentioned in the text see Case M 787 *PTT Post/TNT-GD Net*, decision of 22 July 1996 and Case M 1168 *DHL/Deutsche Post*, decision of 26 June 1998.

[280] Case M 1915, decision of 13 March 2001.

[281] Case M 5152, decision of 21 April 2009.

[282] Case M 6570, decision of 30 January 2013.

[283] Case T-194/13 *United Parcel Service v Commission* EU:T:2017:144, on appeal Case C-265/17 P *Commission v United Parcel Service*, not yet decided; separately, UPS has brought an action for damages against the Commission: Case T-834/17 *UPS v Commission*, not yet decided.

[284] OFCOM publishes an annual report on the postal sector, available at www.ofcom.org.uk.

[285] See *Consignia/Postal Preference Service Ltd*, decision of 15 June 2001, available at www.nationalarchives.gov.uk; see also the interim High Court judgment in *Claritas v Post Office* [2001] UKCLR 2.

[286] See www.ofcom.org.uk.

[287] See further Rose and Bailey (eds) *Bellamy and Child: European Union Law of Competition* (Oxford University Press, 7th ed, 2013), paras 12.088–12.120; Faull and Nikpay (eds) *The EU Law of Competition* (Oxford University Press, 3rd ed, 2014), ch 12.

the EU[288]; which required Member States to take steps to ensure the possibility of transit of gas and electricity between Member States;[289] and which established common rules for the internal market in gas and electricity[290]. This was followed by a second wave of reform in 2003 when the Council adopted Directives establishing a new set of common rules for the internal market in gas and in electricity[291].

In 2007 the Commission conducted a sectoral inquiry under Article 17 of Regulation 1/2003 and concluded that energy markets in the EU were not functioning well: in particular many energy markets were highly concentrated; there is an absence of cross-border integration and cross-border competition; and there is insufficient unbundling of network and supply activities[292]. In 2009 the Council and the European Parliament adopted a third package of legislative measures[293] that have as their objective a single EU energy market. In 2012 the Commission published a Communication on *Making the internal energy market work*[294], which explained the benefits of integrated EU energy markets and called on Member States to implement fully the third package. This was followed, in 2016, by a Communication on *Clean Energy for All Europeans*[295], which proposed legislation on energy efficiency, renewable energy, the design of the electricity market, security of electricity supply and governance rules for the Energy Union. The creation of an 'Energy Union' is one of the Commission's political priorities, which seeks to bring about a fully integrated European energy market and a low-carbon economy[296].

(ii) **Application of EU competition law**

(a) Article 101

The Commission has investigated a number of agreements in the energy sector[297]. The privatisation of the electricity industry in Great Britain led to a decision that the Article 101(3) applied to the *Scottish Nuclear, Nuclear Energy Agreement*[298]. In 1995 the Commission gave its approval to a joint venture established by nine gas companies to construct and operate a gas interconnector between the UK and Belgium[299]. The Commission

[288] Council Directive 90/377/EEC, OJ [1990] L 185/16 (gas) and Council Directive 90/377/EEC, OJ [1990] L 185/16 (electricity).

[289] Council Directive 91/296/EEC, OJ [1991] L 147/37 (gas), as amended by Council Directive 95/49/EC, OJ [1995] L 233/86 and Council Directive 90/547/EEC, OJ [1990] L 313/30 (electricity).

[290] Council Directive 98/30/EC, OJ [1998] L 204/1, as amended by Council Directive 95/49/EC, OJ [1995] L 233/86 (gas) and Council Directive 96/92/EC, OJ [1997] L 27/20 (electricity).

[291] Council Directive 2003/55/EC, OJ [2003] L 176/57 (gas) and Council Directive 2003/54, OJ [2003] L 176/37 (electricity).

[292] COM(2006) 851 final.

[293] Regulation 713/2009 establishing the EU Agency for co-operation of national energy regulators, OJ [2009] L 211/1; Regulation 714/2009 on conditions for access to the network for cross-border exchanges in electricity, OJ [2009] L 211/15; Regulation 715/2009 on conditions for access to the natural gas transmission networks, OJ [2009] L 229/29; Directive 2009/72/EC concerning common rules for the internal market in electricity, OJ [2009] L 211/55 and Directive 2009/73/EC concerning common rules for the internal market in natural gas, OJ [2009] L 211/94.

[294] COM(2012) 663 final, 15 November 2012.

[295] COM(2016) 860 final, 30 November 2016.

[296] See the Reports on the State of the Energy Union, available at www.ec.europa.eu.

[297] See Scholz and Purps 'The Application of EU Competition Law in the Energy Sector' (2015) 6 JECLAP 200, Scholz and Vohwinkel (2016) 7 JECLAP 56 and Scholz and Vohwinkel (2017) 8 JECLAP 190.

[298] OJ [1991] L 178/31; see also the notices in OJ [1990] C 191/9 (dealing with ten notifications) and in OJ [1990] C 245/9 (dealing with eight notifications). A joint venture to develop independent generators of electricity was the subject of a favourable notice in 1992, OJ [1992] C 92/4.

[299] See eg Commission's XXVth *Report on Competition Policy* (1995), point 82.

has also approved a number of long-term agreements for the supply of gas[300] and electricity[301]. However it has taken action (or is taking action) in a number of cases involving territorial restrictions and profit-sharing mechanisms in gas supply agreements[302]. In *IJsselcentrale*[303] the Commission held that an agreement between all the generators of electricity in the Netherlands and a joint subsidiary that only the latter could import and export electricity to and from that country entailed a restriction of competition that infringed Article 101(1).

(b) Article 102

Following the Commission's sectoral inquiry[304], it brought a number of cases under Article 102 in the energy sector. This enforcement action led to a striking number of decisions under Article 9 of Regulation 1/2003, in which structural commitments were offered to, and accepted by, the Commission to address its concerns about exclusionary practices by vertically-integrated undertakings[305]. In *OPCOM*[306] the Commission imposed a fine of just over €1 million on OPCOM, the operator of the only power exchange in Romania, for discriminating on the basis of nationality and place of establishment on the market for services facilitating short-term trading in electricity in Romania. The Commission has opened an investigation into the behaviour of TenneT, a German grid operator, that may have infringed Article 102 by limiting the cross-border flow of electricity between Denmark and Germany: it has been market testing possible commitments[307].

In *Gazprom* the Commission's preliminary assessment was that Gazprom had abused its dominant position by imposing territorial restrictions in supply agreements and pursuing an unfair pricing policy in Bulgaria, Estonia, Latvia, Lithuania and Poland. In 2017 the Commission market tested commitments offered by Gazprom that would abandon the territorial restrictions and ensure that gas prices in Central and Eastern Europe reflect competitive price benchmarks[308].

(c) EUMR

The Commission has investigated several mergers involving undertakings in the energy sector[309]. The Commission prohibited a proposed acquisition by EDP, the incumbent electricity company in Portugal, of GDP, the incumbent gas company[310]; the Commission's decision was upheld on appeal to the General Court[311].

[300] See eg *Transgás/Turbogás*, Commission's XXVIth *Report on Competition Policy* (1996), p 135 and *British Gas Network Code*, XXVIth *Report on Competition Policy* (1996), pp 136–137.

[301] See eg *REN/Turbogás* OJ [1996] C 118/7 and *ISAB Energy* OJ [1996] C 138/3; see also Commission's XXXth *Report on Competition Policy* (2000), pp 154–155.

[302] See Wäktare 'Territorial restrictions and profit sharing mechanisms in the gas sector: the Algerian case' (2007) 3 Competition Policy Newsletter 19.

[303] OJ [1991] L 28/32; the decision was (eventually) partly annulled on appeal in Case T-16/91 *RV Rendo v Commission* EU:T:1996:189.

[304] See 'Legislation', pp 1020–1021 earlier in chapter.

[305] For a table of these and other decisions under Article 9 of Regulation 1/2003 see ch 7, 'Table of Article 9 Commitment Decisions', p 265; see also Faull and Nikpay (eds) *The EU Law of Competition* (Oxford University Press, 3rd ed, 2014), paras 12.140–12.178.

[306] Commission decision of 5 March 2014.

[307] Commission Press Release IP/18/2622, 27 March 2018.

[308] Commission Press Release IP/17/555, 13 March 2017.

[309] See eg Case M 3696 *E.ON/MOL*, decision of 21 December 2005; Case M 4180 *GDF/Suez*, decision of 14 November 2006; Case M 5224 *EdF/British Energy*, decision of 22 December 2008.

[310] Case M 3440 *ENI/EDP/GDP*, decision of 9 December 2004.

[311] Case T-87/05 *EDP v Commission* EU:T:2005:333.

(B) **UK law**

The regulatory regimes for the gas and electricity sectors are respectively contained in the Gas Act 1986 and Electricity Act 1989[312]. Both sectors are regulated by the Gas and Electricity Markets Authority[313], which is assisted by the Office of Gas and Electricity Markets ('OFGEM').

(i) **Competition Act 1998**

OFGEM has concurrent powers with the CMA to apply Articles 101 and 102 TFEU and the Chapter I and Chapter II prohibitions. A *Guideline* has been adopted under the Act, *Competition Act 1998: Application in the Energy Sector*[314], and a *Guideline* on its application to the energy sector in Northern Ireland[315]. OFGEM imposed a fine of £46.1 million on National Grid for abusing its dominant position in the market for the supply of domestic gas meters[316]. On appeal OFGEM's finding of abuse was upheld by the Competition Appeal Tribunal ('the CAT') and by the Court of Appeal, but the fine it had imposed was reduced to £15 million[317]. OFGEM has accepted commitments in two cases to address suspected abusive behaviour[318].

(ii) **Enterprise Act 2002**

In the *Energy market investigation*[319] the CMA did not find any competition problems in the gas wholesale market. However, it identified aspects of the electricity wholesale market rules that give rise to an adverse effect on competition ('AEC'). The CMA concluded that a combination of features of retail energy markets gave rise to an AEC through an overarching feature of weak customer response which, in turn, gave suppliers a position of unilateral market power concerning their inactive customer base which they are able to exploit through their pricing policies or otherwise. The CMA also identified certain regulatory features of the retail market that gave rise to an AEC. The CMA imposed a package of remedies to address the AECs that it had identified, including recommendations to OFGEM and the Government to amend the regulatory framework and a transitional price cap on domestic customers on prepayment meters.

11. **Water**

The Water Industry Act 1991 provides a regulatory regime for water in the UK: the regulator is the Water Services Regulation Authority ('WSRA')[320], assisted by the Office of Water Services ('OFWAT')[321]. The WSRA regulates prices for the provision of water to households. The Water Acts 2003 and 2014 increase the opportunities for competition in the supply of water services to non-household customers in England.

[312] See Harker and Waddams 'Introducing Competition and Deregulating the British Domestic Energy Markets: A Legal and Economic Discussion' [2007] Journal of Business Law 244.

[313] Utilities Act 2000, s 1; the principal objective and general duties of the GEMA are contained in s 4AA of the Gas Act 1986 and s 3A of the Electricity Act 1989, as amended respectively by ss 16 and 17 of the Energy Act 2010.

[314] OFT 428, January 2005.

[315] OFT 437, July 2001.

[316] Decision of 25 February 2008.

[317] Case 1097/1/2/08 *National Grid plc v Gas and Electricity Markets Authority* [2009] CAT 14, on appeal [2010] EWCA Civ 114; National Grid's request for permission to appeal to the Supreme Court was refused.

[318] *SP Manweb*, OFGEM decision of 27 October 2005 and *SEE*, OFGEM decision of 7 November 2016.

[319] Final Report of 24 June 2016.

[320] Water Act 2003, s 34.

[321] OFWAT's website is www.ofwat.gov.uk.

(A) **Competition Act 1998**

The WSRA has concurrent powers with the CMA to apply Articles 101 and 102 TFEU and the Chapter I and Chapter II prohibitions. A Guideline has been adopted under the Act, *Competition Act 1998: Application in the Water and Sewerage Sectors*[322]. There have been several complaints about exclusionary behaviour by incumbents in the water sector, but the WSRA tended to conclude either that there was no infringement[323] or that the complaint was not one that it wished to pursue under competition law[324].

One case is particularly striking, *Albion Water v WSRA*[325], where the WSRA had rejected two complaints against an incumbent water undertaking, Dŵr Cymru. On appeal the CAT concluded that Dŵr Cymru was guilty of abusing its dominant position and annulled the regulator's decision to the contrary[326]. Albion Water subsequently brought a follow-on action for damages in the CAT relying on the CAT's findings of infringement. The CAT ordered Dŵr Cymru to pay Albion Water damages of approximately £1.85 million for the losses it had suffered as a result of Dŵr Cymru's abusive behaviour[327].

The WSRA has accepted commitments in two cases: in *Severn Trent*[328] the commitments were to divest Severn Trent Laboratories in order to allay concerns about predatory pricing to win contracts to supply water analysis services; and in *Bristol Water*[329] the commitments were to bring about a clearer separation of Bristol Water's downstream developer services functions in order to address concerns that Bristol Water was acting in a discriminatory manner against 'self-lay organisations'.

(B) **Enterprise Act 2002**

There are special rules requiring certain mergers between water companies to be referred to the CMA; these have been amended, to bring the system more closely into alignment with the law on 'normal' mergers under Part 3 of the Enterprise Act 2002[330]. These rules were further amended by the Water Act 2014 with effect from 18 December 2015, to introduce certain exceptions to the mandatory reference of water mergers that meet the jurisdictional thresholds for a Phase 2 investigation.

[322] OFT 422, March 2010; see also Bailey 'The Emerging Co-Existence of Regulation and Competition Law in the UK Water Industry' (2002) 25 World Competition 127.

[323] See ch 9, 'Table of published decisions', pp 393–395.

[324] See eg Case 1058/2/4/06 *Independent Water Company Ltd v WSRA* [2007] CAT 6.

[325] Case 1046/2/4/04 [2006] CAT 23 and [2006] CAT 36, upheld on appeal *Dŵr Cymru Cyfyngedig v WSRA* [2008] EWCA Civ 536.

[326] Case 1046/2/4/04 [2006] CAT 23, [2006] CAT 36 and [2008] CAT 31.

[327] Case 1166/5/7/10 *Albion Water Ltd v Dŵr Cymru Cyfyngedig* [2013] CAT 6.

[328] Decision of 23 March 2015.

[329] Decision of 17 January 2013.

[330] See ch 22, 'Mergers in the water industry', pp 991–993.

Bibliography

There is a considerable body of literature on competition law. The following books are particularly recommended.

UK and EU competition law combined

Colino *Competition Law of the UK and EU* (Oxford University Press, 7th ed, 2011)

Graham *EU and UK Competition Law* (Pearson, 2nd ed, 2013)

Middleton, Rodger, MacCulloch and Galloway *Cases and Materials on UK and EC Competition Law* (Oxford University Press, 2nd ed, 2009)

Nazzini *Competition Enforcement and Procedure* (Oxford University Press, 2nd ed, 2016)

Rodger and MacCulloch *Competition Law and Policy in the EC and UK* (Routledge, 5th ed, 2014)

Slot and Farley *An Introduction to Competition Law* (Hart, 2nd ed, 2017)

EU competition law

Akman *The Concept of Abuse in EU Competition Law: Law and Economic Approaches* (Hart, 2012)

Ashton *Competition Damages Actions in the EU* (Edward Elgar, 2nd ed, 2018)

Blanco (ed) *EU Competition Procedure* (Oxford University Press, 3rd ed, 2013)

Buendia Sierra *Exclusive Rights and State Monopolies under EC Law* (Oxford University Press, 1999)

Ezrachi *EU Competition Law: An Analytical Guide to the Leading Cases* (Hart, 5th ed, 2016)

Faull and Nikpay (eds) *The EU Law of Competition* (Oxford University Press, 3rd ed, 2014)

Fox and Gerard *EU Competition Law: Cases, Text and Context* (Edward Elgar, 2017)

Frese *Sanctions in EU Competition Law* (Hart, 2014)

Gormsen *A Principled Approach to Abuse of Dominance in European Competition Law* (Cambridge University Press, 2010)

Goyder *EU Distribution Law* (Hart, 5th ed, 2011)

Goyder and Albors-Llorens *Goyder's EC Competition Law* (Oxford University Press, 5th ed, 2009)

Jones and Sufrin *EU Competition Law: Text, Cases, and Materials* (Oxford University Press, 6th ed, 2016)

Jones and van der Woude *EU Competition Law Handbook* (Sweet & Maxwell, updated annually)

Kerse and Khan *EU Antitrust Procedure* (Sweet & Maxwell, 6th ed, 2012)

Kokkoris (ed) *Competition Cases from the European Union* (Sweet & Maxwell, 2nd ed, 2010)

Korah *An Introductory Guide to EC Competition Law and Practice* (Hart, 9th ed, 2007)

Monti *EC Competition Law* (Cambridge University Press, 2007)

Nazzini *The Foundations of European Union Competition Law* (Oxford University Press, 2011)

O'Donoghue and Padilla *The Law and Economics of Article 102 TFEU* (Hart, 2nd ed, 2013)

Odudu *The Boundaries of EC Competition Law* (Oxford University Press, 2006)

Ritter, Braun and Rawlinson *European Competition Law: A Practitioner's Guide* (Kluwer Law International, 3rd ed, 2005)

Rose and Bailey (eds) *Bellamy and Child: European Union Law of Competition* (Oxford University Press, 7th ed, 2013)

Rousseva *Rethinking Exclusionary Abuses in EU Competition Law* (Hart, 2010)

Sauter *Coherence in EU Competition Law* (Oxford University Press, 2016)
Szyszczak *The Regulation of the State in Competitive Markets in the EU* (Hart, 2007)
Townley *Article 81 EC and Public Policy* (Hart, 2009)
Van Bael and Bellis *Competition Law of the European Community* (Kluwer Law International, 5th ed, 2010)
Wijckmans and Tuytschaever *Vertical Agreements in EU Competition Law* (Oxford University Press, 3rd ed, 2018)
Wils *The Optimal Enforcement of EC Antitrust Law: Essays in Law and Economics* (Kluwer Law International, 2002)
Wils *Principles of European Antitrust Enforcement* (Hart, 2005)
Wils *Efficiency and Justice in European Antitrust Enforcement* (Hart, 2008)

UK competition law

Brealey and Green (eds) *Competition Litigation* (Oxford University Press, 2010)
Kellaway, Thompson and Brown (eds) *UK Competition Law: The New Framework* (Oxford University Press, 2015)
O'Kane *The Law of Criminal Cartels: Practice and Procedure* (Oxford University Press, 2009)
O'Neill and Sanders *UK Competition Procedure: The Modernised Regime* (Oxford University Press, 2007)
Rodger (ed) *Ten Years of UK Competition Law Reform* (Dundee University Press, 2010)

Mergers and concentrations

Broberg *The European Commission's Jurisdiction to Scrutinise Mergers* (Kluwer Law International, 4th ed, 2013)
Cook and Kerse *EC Merger Control* (Sweet & Maxwell, 5th ed, 2009)
Elliott and Bellis (eds) *Merger Control* (Sweet & Maxwell, 3rd ed, 2017)
Hoeg *European Merger Remedies: Law and Policy* (Hart, 2014)
Levy *European Merger Control Law: A Guide to the Merger Regulation* (LexisNexis, updated annually)
Lindsay and Berridge *The EU Merger Regulation: Substantive Issues* (Sweet & Maxwell, 5th ed, 2017)
Lowe and Marquis (eds) *European Competition Law Annual 2010: Merger Control in European and Global Perspective* (Hart, 2013)
Parker and Majumdar *UK Merger Control* (Hart, 2nd ed, 2016)
Parr, Finbow and Matthews *UK Merger Control: Law and Practice* (Sweet & Maxwell, 3rd ed, 2016)

Intellectual property

Anderman and Ezrachi *Intellectual Property and Competition Law: New Frontiers* (Oxford University Press, 2011)
Anderman and Kallaugher *Technology Transfer and the New EU Competition Rules: Intellectual Property Licensing after Modernisation* (Oxford University Press, 2nd ed, 2018)
Anderman and Schmidt *EU Competition Law and Intellectual Property Rights: The Regulation of Innovation* (Oxford University Press, 2nd ed, 2011)
Cornish, Llewelyn and Aplin *Intellectual Property* (Sweet & Maxwell, 8th ed, 2013)
Desai, Lianos and Waller *Brands, Competition Law and IP* (Cambridge University Press, 2015)
Devlin *Antitrust and Patent Law* (Oxford University Press, 2016)
Hovenkamp, Janis, Lemley et al *IP and Antitrust: An Analysis of Antitrust Principles Applied to Intellectual Property Law* (Wolters Kluwer Law & Business, 3rd ed, 2016)

Käseberg *Intellectual Property, Antitrust and Cumulative Innovation in the EU and the US* (Hart, 2012)

Turner *Intellectual Property and EU Competition Law* (Oxford University Press, 2nd ed, 2015)

Economics

Bishop and Walker *The Economics of EC Competition Law: Concepts, Application and Measurement* (Sweet & Maxwell, 3rd ed, 2010)

Black, Hashimzade and Myles (eds) *Oxford Dictionary of Economics* (Oxford University Press, 5th ed, 2017)

Carlton and Perloff *Modern Industrial Organization* (Addison Wesley, 4th ed, 2005)

Fumagalli, Motta and Calcagno *Exclusionary Practices: The Economics of Monopolisation and Abuse of Dominance* (Cambridge University Press, 2018)

Geradin, Layne-Farrar and Petit *EU Competition Law and Economics* (Oxford University Press, 2012)

Hylton *Antitrust Law: Economic Theory and Common Law Evolution* (Cambridge University Press, 2003)

Lipsey and Chrystal *Economics* (Oxford University Press, 13th ed, 2015)

Motta *Competition Policy: Theory and Practice* (Cambridge University Press, 2004)

Niels, Jenkins and Kavanagh *Economics for Competition Lawyers* (Oxford University Press, 2nd ed, 2016)

Sullivan and Harrison *Understanding Antitrust and Its Economic Implications* (LexisNexis, 6th ed, 2014)

Tirole *The Theory of Industrial Organization* (MIT Press, 1988)

Miscellaneous

Amato *Antitrust and the Bounds of Power: The Dilemma of Liberal Democracy in the History of the Market* (Hart, 1997)

Blanco *Market Power in EU Antitrust Law* (Hart, 2011)

Bork *The Antitrust Paradox* (Free Press, 1993)

Castillo de la Torre and Gippini Fournier *Evidence, Proof and Judicial Review in EU Competition Law* (Edward Elgar, 2017)

Coates *Competition Law and Regulation of Technology Markets* (Oxford University Press, 2011)

Elhauge and Geradin *Global Competition Law and Economics* (Hart, 2nd ed, 2011)

Ezrachi and Stucke *Virtual Competition* (Harvard University Press, 2016)

Fatur *EU Competition Law and the Information and Communication Technology Network Industries* (Hart, 2012)

Gal *Competition Policy for Small Market Economies* (Harvard University Press, 2003)

Gerber *Law and Competition in Twentieth-Century Europe* (Oxford University Press, 1998)

Gerber *Global Competition* (Oxford University Press, 2010)

Hovenkamp *The Antitrust Enterprise: Principle and Execution* (Harvard University Press, 2008)

Kaplow *Competition Policy and Price Fixing* (Princeton University Press, 2013)

Posner *Antitrust Law* (University of Chicago Press, 2nd ed, 2001)

Stucke and Grunnes *Big Data and Competition Policy* (Oxford University Press, 2016)

Zimmer (ed) *The Goals of Competition Law* (Edward Elgar, 2012)

Statutes, Treaties, EU regulations etc

Middleton *Blackstone's UK and EU Competition Documents* (Oxford University Press, 8th ed, 2015)

Tolley and Bavasso (eds) *Butterworths Competition Law Handbook* (LexisNexis, 23rd ed, 2017)

Important websites

Competition Appeal Tribunal	www.catribunal.org.uk
Competition and Markets Authority	www.gov.uk/cma
Court of Justice	www.curia.europa.eu
Department for Business, Energy and Industrial Strategy	www.gov.uk/beis
European Commission, DG COMP	www.ec.europa.eu/competition
European Competition Network	www.ec.europa.eu/competition/ecn
EUR-Lex	www.eur-lex.europa.eu
International Competition Network	www.internationalcompetitionnetwork.org
National Archives	www.nationalarchives.gov.uk
Organisation for Economic Co-operation and Development	www.oecd.org/competition
UK case law	www.bailii.org
UK Competition Network	www.gov.uk/government/collections/ uk-competition-network-ukcn-documents
UK legislation	www.legislation.gov.uk
US Department of Justice	www.justice.gov/atr
US Federal Trade Commission	www.ftc.gov

Index